UNITY LIBRARY 8 ARCHIVES
S0-ADX-260

The NIV

Interlinear Hebrew-English Old Testament

The NIV

Interlinear Hebrew-English Old Testament

Volume 3 / 1 Chronicles—Song of Songs

Edited by
John R. Kohlenberger III

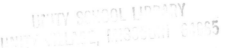

12/02

THE NIV INTERLINEAR HEBREW-ENGLISH OLD TESTAMENT, VOL. 3

Grand Rapids, Michigan

Library of Congress Cataloging in Publication Data (Revised)

Bible. O.T. Hebrew 1979.
The NIV interlinear Hebrew-English Old Testament.
Includes bibliographies.
CONTENTS: v. 1. Genesis–Deuteronomy.— v. 2. Joshua–II Kings.—
v. 3. I Chronicles–Song of Songs.
1. Bible. O.T. Interlinear translations. English. I. Kohlenberger, John R.
II. Bible. O.T. English. New International. 1979. III. Title.
BS715 1979 221.4'4 82-1987
ISBN 0-310-38880-5 (v. 1) AACR2
ISBN 0-310-38890-2 (v. 2)
ISBN 0-310-44200-1 (v. 3)

The Hebrew text used for this translation is the *Biblia Hebraica Stuttgartensia*, commonly known as the Stuttgart Bible.

Printed in the United States of America

83 84 85 86 87 88 — 10 9 8 7 6 5 4 3 2

Gift

CONTENTS

ACKNOWLEDGMENTS

Once again, it is my privilege to give public credit to those individuals whose behind-the-scenes involvement has made this lengthy and tedious project enjoyable.

I wish to thank first the Zondervan Publishing House—especially editors Stan Gundry, Paul Hillman, and Doris Rikkers—for their generous support and cooperation, but especially for their patience with my slow pace in completing this volume.

I wish to thank also the people of SeTyp and Auto-Graphics for their continuing excellence in the exacting work of typesetting the English text. And for their meticulous work of setting the Hebrew text in place, I thank Ralph and Jeanne Kunselman and R. Burwell Davis.

Thanks also to Dr. Ronald Youngblood for his careful and critical reading of the translation and biblical texts. Though not all of his suggestions relating to the translation have been followed, they were nonetheless most valuable. This volume has been improved by his involvement.

Once again, above all I must praise God for His continuing encouragement through my family—not only my wife, Carolyn, and our daughter, Sarah, but also our new son, Joshua, who was born in time to give new insights into the meaning of Psalm 127.

TO MY SON
JOSHUA DAVID

INTRODUCTION

In this, the third volume of the *NIV Interlinear Hebrew-English Old Testament,* only a few matters need special introduction. The reader is referred to volume 1 (pp. ix-xxx) for a discussion of the texts, translation techniques and characteristics, and usage of the volumes of this set and to volume 2 (pp. xi-xii) for its contents and organization.

Textual Format and Reference Tools

Volume 3, following the Greek (and English) canonical order, completes the books of history and contains all of the books of wisdom and poetry. In these latter books, as in the prophets of volume 4, the NIV translation becomes most significant in relation to the analysis of the form of the literature. The interlinear translation, as it is set word by word from margin to margin, does not display the most striking and significant feature of Hebrew poetry—the parallelism of lines. The NIV, on the other hand, is specially indented to show the pairs, triplets, and quatrains of lines so important to be considered together as "sets" in the interpretation of the hymns and proverbs of Scripture. Thus, the NIV helps greatly in interpretation, not only in presenting an excellent idiomatic rendering of the word-for-word translation of the interlinear text but also in showing the interrelation of the lines of poetry.

For special help in understanding the nature of Hebrew poetry, the reader is referred to the fine general introduction in chapter 4 of Ronald Barclay Allen, *Praise! A Matter of Life and Breath* (Nashville: Nelson, 1980), and to the slightly more technical discussion and bibliography in Part Twelve:I of R. K. Harrison, *Introduction to the Old Testament* (Grand Rapids: Eerdmans, 1969). For special help in the translation of the Hebrew proper, the reader is once again referred to the outstanding liberal-critical commentaries of the Anchor Bible (Garden City: Doubleday) and International Critical Commentary (Edinburgh: T & T Clark) series. The latter provides detailed treatment of grammatical and textual difficulties, while the former is most valuable in providing insights from the lexical, literary, and cultural materials of Ugarit and Qumran. I have also profited greatly from Robert Gordis, *Koheleth—the Man and His World* (New York: Schocken, 1951) and Christian D. Ginsburg, *The Song of Songs and Coheleth* (1857; reprint ed. New York: KTAV, 1970).

The Aramaic of Ezra

Unique to this volume and to Daniel in volume 4 are the extended passages in Aramaic in Ezra 4:8–6:18 and 7:12–26. Except for certain matters of spelling and vocalization, biblical Aramaic is very similar to biblical Hebrew. One major difference requires special attention for the purposes of this volume.

Unlike Hebrew, which has two "states" of nominal inflection, Aramaic has three. The *absolute* and *construct* states correspond to their equivalents in Hebrew, and thus they correspond also in the way in which they are translated in this volume. The third, the *emphatic* or *determined* state, corresponds to a Hebrew noun with the definite article prefixed (in fact, some scholars argue that this state should rather be considered a suffixed article), and thus is translated by means of the definite article in English. For example, the absolute state: טְעֵם, *order* (Ezra 4:21); the construct state: טַעַם, *command-of* (6:14); the emphatic or determined state: טַעְמָא, *the-order* (4:21).

For further information on the orthography, inflection, and syntax of biblical Aramaic, I have found Alger F. Johns, *A Short Grammar of Biblical Aramaic* (Berrien Springs, Michigan: Andrews University Press, 1963), more clearly written than the standard beginning grammar of Franz Rosenthal, *A Grammar of Biblical Aramaic* (Wiesbaden: Otto Harrasowitz, 1961). The Aramaic section (pp. 1078–1118) of Brown, Driver and Briggs, *Hebrew and English Lexicon of the Old Testament* (Oxford: Oxford University Press, 1907), is most complete and helpful in its treatment of the inflection and definition of the Aramaic of Ezra, while the Aramaic section (pp. 1045–1138) by Walter Baumgartner in *Lexicon in Veteris Testamenti Libros* (Leiden: Brill and Grand Rapids: Eerdmans, 1953) is more up to date in etymology and bibliography.

אָדָם שֵׁת אֱנוֹשׁ׃ קֵינָן מַהֲלַלְאֵל יָרֶד׃ חֲנוֹךְ מְתוּשֶׁלַח
Methuselah Enoch (3) Jared Mahalalel Kenan (2) Enosh Seth Adam (1:1)

לָמֶךְ׃ נֹחַ שֵׁם חָם וָיָפֶת׃ בְּנֵי יֶפֶת גֹּמֶר וּמָגוֹג
and-Magog Gomer Japheth sons-of (5) and-Japheth Ham Shem Noah (4) Lamech

וּמָדַי וְיָוָן וְתֻבָל וּמֶשֶׁךְ וְתִירָס׃ וּבְנֵי
and-sons-of (6) and-Tiras and-Meshech and-Tubal and-Javan and-Madai

גֹּמֶר אַשְׁכְּנַז* וְדִיפַת וְתוֹגַרְמָה׃ וּבְנֵי יָוָן אֱלִישָׁה
Elishah Javan and-sons-of (7) and-Togarmah and-Diphath Ashkenaz Gomer

וְתַרְשִׁישָׁה כִּתִּים וְרוֹדָנִים׃ בְּנֵי חָם כּוּשׁ וּמִצְרַיִם פּוּט
Put and-Mizraim Cush Ham sons-of (8) and-Rodanim Kittim and-Tarshish

וּכְנָעַן׃ וּבְנֵי כּוּשׁ סְבָא וַחֲוִילָה וְסַבְתָּא וְרַעְמָא
and-Raamah and-Sabta and-Havilah Seba Cush and-sons-of (9) and-Canaan

וְסַבְתְּכָא וּבְנֵי רַעְמָא שְׁבָא וּדְדָן׃ וְכוּשׁ יָלַד
he-fathered and-Cush (10) and-Dedan Sheba Raamah and-sons-of and-Sabteca

אֶת־ נִמְרוֹד הוּא הֵחֵל לִהְיוֹת גִּבּוֹר בָּאָרֶץ׃ וּמִצְרַיִם
and-Mizraim (11) on-the-earth mighty-warrior to-be he-grew he Nimrod ***

יָלַד אֶת־ לוּדִיִּים° וְאֶת־ עֲנָמִים וְאֶת־ לְהָבִים וְאֶת־ נַפְתֻּחִים׃
Naphtuhites and Lehabites and Anamites and Ludites *** he-fathered

וְאֶת־ פַּתְרֻסִים וְאֶת־ כַּסְלֻחִים אֲשֶׁר יָצְאוּ מִשָּׁם
from-there they-came who Casluhites and Pathrusites and (12)

פְּלִשְׁתִּים וְאֶת־ כַּפְתֹּרִים׃ וּכְנַעַן יָלַד אֶת־ צִידוֹן
Sidon *** he-fathered and-Canaan (13) Caphtorites and Philistines

בְּכֹרוֹ וְאֶת־ חֵת׃ וְאֶת־ הַיְבוּסִי וְאֶת־ הָאֱמֹרִי
the-Amorite and the-Jebusite and (14) Heth and firstborn-of-him

וְאֵת הַגִּרְגָּשִׁי׃ וְאֶת־ הַחִוִּי וְאֶת־ הָעַרְקִי וְאֶת־ הַסִּינִי׃
the-Sinite and the-Arkite and the-Hivite and (15) the-Girgashite and

וְאֶת־ הָאַרְוָדִי וְאֶת־ הַצְּמָרִי וְאֶת־ הַחֲמָתִי׃ בְּנֵי
sons-of (17) the-Hamathite and the-Zemarite and the-Arvadite and (16)

שֵׁם עֵילָם וְאַשּׁוּר וְאַרְפַּכְשַׁד וְלוּד וַאֲרָם וְעוּץ
and-Uz and-Aram and-Lud and-Arphaxad and-Asshur Elam Shem

וְחוּל וְגֶתֶר וָמֶשֶׁךְ׃ וְאַרְפַּכְשַׁד יָלַד אֶת־
*** he-fathered and-Arphaxad (18) and-Meshech and-Gether and-Hul

שָׁלַח וְשֶׁלַח יָלַד אֶת־ עֵבֶר׃ וּלְעֵבֶר יֻלַּד
he-was-born and-to-Eber (19) Eber *** he-fathered and-Shelah Shelah

שְׁנֵי בָנִים שֵׁם הָאֶחָד פֶּלֶג כִּי בְיָמָיו
in-days-of-him because Peleg the-one name-of sons two-of

נִפְלְגָה הָאָרֶץ וְשֵׁם אָחִיו יָקְטָן׃
Joktan brother-of-him and-name-of the-earth she-was-divided

Historical Records From Adam to Abraham

To Noah's Sons

1 Adam, Seth, Enosh, [2]Kenan, Mahalalel, Jared,
[3]Enoch, Methuselah, Lamech, Noah.

[4]The sons of Noah:[a]
Shem, Ham and Japheth.

The Japhethites

[5]The sons[b] of Japheth:
Gomer, Magog, Madai, Javan, Tubal, Meshech and Tiras.
[6]The sons of Gomer:
Ashkenaz, Riphath and Togarmah.
[7]The sons of Javan:
Elishah, Tarshish, the Kittim and the Rodanim.

The Hamites

[8]The sons of Ham:
Cush, Mizraim,[c] Put and Canaan.
[9]The sons of Cush:
Seba, Havilah, Sabta, Raamah and Sabteca.
The sons of Raamah:
Sheba and Dedan.
[10]Cush was the father[d] of
Nimrod, who grew to be a mighty warrior on earth.
[11]Mizraim was the father of
the Ludites, Anamites, Lehabites, Naphtuhites,
[12]Pathrusites, Casluhites (from whom the Philistines came) and Caphtorites.
[13]Canaan was the father of
Sidon his firstborn,[e] and of the Hittites,
[14]Jebusites, Amorites, Girgashites,
[15]Hivites, Arkites, Sinites,
[16]Arvadites, Zemarites and Hamathites.

The Semites

[17]The sons of Shem:
Elam, Asshur, Arphaxad, Lud and Aram.
The sons of Aram[f]:
Uz, Hul, Gether and Meshech.
[18]Arphaxad was the father of Shelah,
and Shelah the father of Eber.
[19]Two sons were born to

[a]4 Septuagint; Hebrew does not have *The sons of Noah:*
[b]5 *Sons* may mean *descendants* or *successors* or *nations;* also in verses 6-10, 17 and 20.
[c]8 That is, Egypt; also in verse 11
[d]10 *Father* may mean *ancestor* or *predecessor* or *founder;* also in verses 11, 13, 18 and 20.
[e]13 Or *of the Sidonians, the foremost*
[f]17 One Hebrew manuscript and some Septuagint manuscripts (see also Gen. 10:23); most Hebrew manuscripts do not have this line.

*6 Most mss have *sheva* under the *kaph* (כְּ–).

°11 ק לוּדִים

וְיָקְטָן יָלַד אֶת־אַלְמוֹדָד וְאֶת־שָׁלֶף וְאֶת־חֲצַרְמָוֶת
Hazarmaveth and Sheleph and Almodad *** he-fathered and-Joktan (20)

וְאֶת־יָרַח׃ וְאֶת־הֲדוֹרָם וְאֶת־אוּזָל וְאֶת־דִּקְלָה׃ וְאֶת־עֵיבָל וְאֶת־
and Ebal and (22) Diklah and Uzal and Hadoram and (21) Jerah and

אֲבִימָאֵל וְאֶת־שְׁבָא׃ וְאֶת־אוֹפִיר וְאֶת־חֲוִילָה וְאֶת־יוֹבָב כָּל־אֵלֶּה
these all-of Jobab and Havilah and Ophir and (23) Sheba and Abimael

בְּנֵי יָקְטָן׃ שֵׁם ׀ אַרְפַּכְשַׁד שָׁלַח׃ עֵבֶר פֶּלֶג רְעוּ׃
Reu Peleg Eber (25) Shelah Arphaxad Shem (24) Joktan sons-of

שְׂרוּג נָחוֹר תָּרַח׃ אַבְרָם הוּא אַבְרָהָם׃ בְּנֵי אַבְרָהָם
Abraham sons-of (28) Abraham he Abram (27) Terah Nahor Serug (26)

יִצְחָק וְיִשְׁמָעֵאל׃ אֵלֶּה תֹּלְדוֹתָם בְּכוֹר יִשְׁמָעֵאל
Ishmael firstborn-of descendants-of-them these (29) and-Ishmael Isaac

נְבָיוֹת וְקֵדָר וְאַדְבְּאֵל וּמִבְשָׂם׃ מִשְׁמָע וְדוּמָה
and-Dumah Mishma (30) and-Mibsam and-Adbeel and-Kedar Nebaioth

מַשָּׂא חֲדַד וְתֵימָא׃ יְטוּר נָפִישׁ וָקֵדְמָה אֵלֶּה הֵם
they these and-Kedemah Naphish Jetur (31) and-Tema Hadad Massa

בְּנֵי יִשְׁמָעֵאל׃ וּבְנֵי קְטוּרָה פִּילֶגֶשׁ אַבְרָהָם
Abraham concubine-of Keturah and-sons-of (32) Ishmael sons-of

יָלְדָה אֶת־זִמְרָן וְיָקְשָׁן וּמְדָן וּמִדְיָן וְיִשְׁבָּק
and-Ishbak and-Midian and-Medan and-Jokshan Zimran *** she-bore

וְשׁוּחַ וּבְנֵי יָקְשָׁן שְׁבָא וּדְדָן׃ וּבְנֵי מִדְיָן
Midian and-sons-of (33) and-Dedan Sheba Jokshan and-sons-of and-Shua

עֵיפָה וָעֵפֶר וַחֲנוֹךְ וַאֲבִידָע וְאֶלְדָּעָה כָּל־אֵלֶּה
these all-of and-Eldaah and-Abida and-Hanoch and-Epher Ephah

בְּנֵי קְטוּרָה׃ וַיּוֹלֶד אַבְרָהָם אֶת־יִצְחָק
Isaac *** Abraham and-he-fathered (34) Keturah descendants-of

בְּנֵי יִצְחָק עֵשָׂו וְיִשְׂרָאֵל׃ בְּנֵי עֵשָׂו אֱלִיפַז רְעוּאֵל וִיעוּשׁ
and-Jeush Reuel Eliphaz Esau sons-of (35) and-Israel Esau Isaac sons-of

וְיַעְלָם וְקֹרַח׃ בְּנֵי אֱלִיפַז תֵּימָן וְאוֹמָר צְפִי
Zephi and-Omar Teman Eliphaz sons-of (36) and-Korah and-Jalam

וְגַעְתָּם קְנַז וְתִמְנָע וַעֲמָלֵק׃ בְּנֵי רְעוּאֵל נַחַת
Nahath Reuel sons-of (37) and-Amalek and-Timna Kenaz and-Gatam

זֶרַח שַׁמָּה וּמִזָּה׃ וּבְנֵי שֵׂעִיר לוֹטָן וְשׁוֹבָל
and-Shobal Lotan Seir and-sons-of (38) and-Mizzah Shammah Zerah

וְצִבְעוֹן וַעֲנָה וְדִישׁוֹן וְאֵצֶר וְדִישָׁן׃ וּבְנֵי
and-sons-of (39) and-Dishan and-Ezer and-Dishon and-Anah and-Zibeon

לוֹטָן חֹרִי וְהוֹמָם וַאֲחוֹת לוֹטָן תִּמְנָע׃
Timna Lotan and-sister-of and-Homam Hori Lotan

Eber:
One was named Peleg,[g] because in his time the earth was divided; his brother was named Joktan.
20 Joktan was the father of
Almodad, Sheleph, Hazarmaveth, Jerah,
21 Hadoram, Uzal, Diklah,
22 Obal,[h] Abimael, Sheba,
23 Ophir, Havilah and Jobab. All these were sons of Joktan.

24 Shem, Arphaxad,[i] Shelah,
25 Eber, Peleg, Reu,
26 Serug, Nahor, Terah
27 and Abram (that is, Abraham).

The Family of Abraham

28 The sons of Abraham:
Isaac and Ishmael.

Descendants of Hagar

29 These were their descendants:
Nebaioth the firstborn of Ishmael, Kedar, Adbeel, Mibsam,
30 Mishma, Dumah, Massa, Hadad, Tema,
31 Jetur, Naphish and Kedemah. These were the sons of Ishmael.

Descendants of Keturah

32 The sons born to Keturah, Abraham's concubine:
Zimran, Jokshan, Medan, Midian, Ishbak and Shuah.
The sons of Jokshan:
Sheba and Dedan.
33 The sons of Midian:
Ephah, Epher, Hanoch, Abida and Eldaah.
All these were descendants of Keturah.

Descendants of Sarah

34 Abraham was the father of Isaac.
The sons of Isaac:
Esau and Israel.
35 The sons of Esau:
Eliphaz, Reuel, Jeush, Jalam and Korah.
36 The sons of Eliphaz:
Teman, Omar, Zepho,[j] Gatam and Kenaz;
by Timna: Amalek.[k]
37 The sons of Reuel:
Nahath, Zerah, Shammah and Mizzah.

[g] 19 *Peleg* means *division.*
[h] 22 Some Hebrew manuscripts and Syriac (see also Gen. 10:28); most Hebrew manuscripts *Ebal*
[i] 24 Hebrew; some Septuagint manuscripts *Arphaxad, Cainan* (see also note at Gen. 11:10)
[j] 36 Many Hebrew manuscripts, some Septuagint manuscripts and Syriac (see also Gen. 36:11); most Hebrew manuscripts *Zephi*
[k] 36 Some Septuagint manuscripts (see also Gen. 36:12); Hebrew *Gatam, Kenaz, Timna and Amalek*

בְּנֵי שׁוֹבָל עַלְיָן וּמָנַחַת וְעֵיבָל שְׁפִי וְאוֹנָם
and-Onam Shephi and-Ebal and-Manahath Alian Shobal sons-of (40)

וּבְנֵי צִבְעוֹן אַיָּה וַעֲנָה׃ בְּנֵי עֲנָה דִּישׁוֹן
Dishon Anah sons-of (41) and-Anah Aiah Zibeon and-sons-of

וּבְנֵי דִישׁוֹן חַמְרָן וְאֶשְׁבָּן וְיִתְרָן וּכְרָן׃
and-Keran and-Ithran and-Eshban Hamran Dishon and-sons-of

בְּנֵי־אֵצֶר בִּלְהָן וְזַעֲוָן יַעֲקָן בְּנֵי דִישׁוֹן עוּץ
Uz Dishon sons-of Jaakan and-Zaavan Bilhan Ezer sons-of (42)

וַאֲרָן׃ וְאֵלֶּה הַמְּלָכִים אֲשֶׁר מָלְכוּ בְּאֶרֶץ אֱדוֹם
Edom in-land-of they-reigned who the-kings and-these (43) and-Aran

לִפְנֵי מְלָךְ־מֶלֶךְ לִבְנֵי יִשְׂרָאֵל בֶּלַע בֶּן־בְּעוֹר וְשֵׁם
and-name-of Beor son-of Bela Israel of-sons-of king to-reign before

עִירוֹ דִּנְהָבָה׃ וַיָּמָת בָּלַע וַיִּמְלֹךְ
then-he-became-king Bela when-he-died (44) Dinhabah city-of-him

תַּחְתָּיו יוֹבָב בֶּן־זֶרַח מִבָּצְרָה׃ וַיָּמָת
when-he-died (45) from-Bozrah Zerah son-of Jobab in-place-of-him

יוֹבָב וַיִּמְלֹךְ תַּחְתָּיו חוּשָׁם מֵאֶרֶץ
from-land-of Husham in-place-of-him then-he-became-king Jobab

הַתֵּימָנִי׃ וַיָּמָת חוּשָׁם וַיִּמְלֹךְ
then-he-became-king Husham when-he-died (46) the-Temanite

תַּחְתָּיו הֲדַד בֶּן־בְּדַד הַמַּכֶּה אֶת־מִדְיָן
Midian *** the-one-defeating Bedad son-of Hadad in-place-of-him

בִּשְׂדֵה מוֹאָב וְשֵׁם עִירוֹ עֲוִית׃ וַיָּמָת
when-he-died (47) Avith city-of-him and-name-of Moab in-country-of

הֲדָד וַיִּמְלֹךְ תַּחְתָּיו שַׂמְלָה מִמַּשְׂרֵקָה׃
from-Masrekah Samlah in-place-of-him then-he-became-king Hadad

וַיָּמָת שַׂמְלָה וַיִּמְלֹךְ תַּחְתָּיו שָׁאוּל
Shaul in-place-of-him then-he-became-king Samlah when-he-died (48)

מֵרְחֹבוֹת הַנָּהָר׃ וַיָּמָת שָׁאוּל וַיִּמְלֹךְ
then-he-became-king Shaul when-he-died (49) the-river from-Rehoboth-of

תַּחְתָּיו בַּעַל חָנָן בֶּן־עַכְבּוֹר׃ וַיָּמָת בַּעַל חָנָן
Hanan Baal when-he-died (50) Acbor son-of Hanan Baal in-place-of-him

וַיִּמְלֹךְ תַּחְתָּיו הֲדַד וְשֵׁם עִירוֹ
city-of-him and-name-of Hadad in-place-of-him then-he-became-king

פָּעִי וְשֵׁם אִשְׁתּוֹ מְהֵיטַבְאֵל בַּת־מַטְרֵד
Matred daughter-of Mehetabel wife-of-him and-name-of Pai

בַּת מֵי זָהָב׃ וַיָּמָת הֲדָד וַיִּהְיוּ אַלּוּפֵי
chiefs-of and-they-were Hadad and-he-died (51) Zahab Me daughter-of

The Edomites

The People of Seir

38 The sons of Seir:
Lotan, Shobal, Zibeon, Anah, Dishon, Ezer and Dishan.
39 The sons of Lotan:
Hori and Homam. Timna was Lotan's sister.
40 The sons of Shobal:
Alvan,[l] Manahath, Ebal, Shepho and Onam.
The sons of Zibeon:
Aiah and Anah.
41 The son of Anah:
Dishon.
The sons of Dishon:
Hemdan,[m] Eshban, Ithran and Keran.
42 The sons of Ezer:
Bilhan, Zaavan and Akan.[n]
The sons of Dishan[o]:
Uz and Aran.

The Rulers of Edom

43 These were the kings who reigned in Edom before any Israelite king reigned[p]:
Bela son of Beor, whose city was named Dinhabah.
44 When Bela died, Jobab son of Zerah from Bozrah succeeded him as king.
45 When Jobab died, Husham from the land of the Temanites succeeded him as king.
46 When Husham died, Hadad son of Bedad, who defeated Midian in the country of Moab, succeeded him as king. His city was named Avith.
47 When Hadad died, Samlah from Masrekah succeeded him as king.
48 When Samlah died, Shaul from Rehoboth on the river[q] succeeded him as king.
49 When Shaul died, Baal-Hanan son of Acbor succeeded him as king.
50 When Baal-Hanan died, Hadad succeeded him as king. His city was named Pau,[r] and his wife's name was Mehetabel daughter of Matred, the

[l] 40 Many Hebrew manuscripts and some Septuagint manuscripts (see also Gen. 36:23); most Hebrew manuscripts *Alian*
[m] 41 Many Hebrew manuscripts and some Septuagint manuscripts (see also Gen. 36:26); most Hebrew manuscripts *Hamran*
[n] 42 Many Hebrew and Septuagint manuscripts (see also Gen. 36:27); most Hebrew manuscripts *Zaavan, Jaakan*
[o] 42 Hebrew *Dishon*, a variant of *Dishan*
[p] 43 Or *before an Israelite king reigned over them*
[q] 48 Or *River*
[r] 50 Many Hebrew manuscripts, some Septuagint manuscripts, Vulgate and Syriac (see also Gen. 36:39); most Hebrew manuscripts *Pai*

°46 ק עוית

אֱדוֹם אַלּוּף תִּמְנָע אַלּוּף עַלְיָה אַלּוּף יְתֵת׃ אַלּוּף אָהֳלִיבָמָה
Oholibamah Chief (52) Jetheth Chief Alvah Chief Timna Chief Edom

אַלּוּף אֵלָה אַלּוּף פִּינֹן׃ אַלּוּף קְנַז אַלּוּף תֵּימָן אַלּוּף מִבְצָר׃
Mibzar Chief Teman Chief Kenaz Chief (53) Pinon Chief Elah Chief

אַלּוּף מַגְדִּיאֵל אַלּוּף עִירָם אֵלֶּה אַלּוּפֵי אֱדוֹם׃ אֵלֶּה
these (2:1) Edom chiefs-of these Iram Chief Magdiel Chief (54)

בְּנֵי יִשְׂרָאֵל רְאוּבֵן שִׁמְעוֹן לֵוִי וִיהוּדָה יִשָּׂשכָר* וּזְבֻלוּן׃
and-Zebulun Issachar and-Judah Levi Simeon Reuben Israel sons-of

דָּן יוֹסֵף וּבִנְיָמִן נַפְתָּלִי גָּד וְאָשֵׁר׃ בְּנֵי
sons-of (3) and-Asher Gad Naphtali and-Benjamin Joseph Dan (2)

יְהוּדָה עֵר וְאוֹנָן וְשֵׁלָה שְׁלוֹשָׁה נוֹלַד לוֹ מִבַּת־ שׁוּעַ
Shua by-Bath to-him he-was-born three and-Shelah and-Onan Er Judah

הַכְּנַעֲנִית וַיְהִי עֵר ׀ בְּכוֹר יְהוּדָה רַע בְּעֵינֵי
in-eyes-of wicked Judah firstborn-of Er and-he-was the-Canaanite-woman

יְהוָה וַיְמִיתֵהוּ׃ וְתָמָר כַּלָּתוֹ יָלְדָה
she-bore daughter-in-law-of-him and-Tamar (4) so-he-put-to-death-him Yahweh

לוֹ אֶת־ פֶּרֶץ וְאֶת־ זָרַח כָּל־ בְּנֵי יְהוּדָה חֲמִשָּׁה׃ בְּנֵי־ פֶרֶץ
Perez sons-of (5) five Judah sons-of all-of Zerah and Perez *** to-him

חֶצְרוֹן וְחָמוּל׃ וּבְנֵי זֶרַח זִמְרִי וְאֵיתָן וְהֵימָן
and-Heman and-Ethan Zimri Zerah and-sons-of (6) and-Hamul Hezron

וְכַלְכֹּל וָדָרַע כֻּלָּם חֲמִשָּׁה׃ וּבְנֵי כַּרְמִי עָכָר
Achar Carmi and-sons-of (7) five all-of-them and-Dara and-Calcol

עוֹכֵר יִשְׂרָאֵל אֲשֶׁר מָעַל בַּחֵרֶם׃
against-the-devoted-thing he-violated who Israel one-bringing-disaster-of

וּבְנֵי אֵיתָן עֲזַרְיָה׃ וּבְנֵי חֶצְרוֹן אֲשֶׁר נוֹלַד־
he-was-born who Hezron and-sons-of (9) Azariah Ethan and-sons-of (8)

לוֹ אֶת־ יְרַחְמְאֵל וְאֶת־ רָם וְאֶת־ כְּלוּבָי׃ וְרָם הוֹלִיד אֶת־
*** he-fathered and-Ram (10) Kelubai and Ram and Jerahmeel *** to-him

עַמִּינָדָב וְעַמִּינָדָב הוֹלִיד אֶת־ נַחְשׁוֹן נְשִׂיא בְּנֵי יְהוּדָה׃
Judah people-of leader-of Nahshon *** he-fathered and-Amminadab Amminadab

וְנַחְשׁוֹן הוֹלִיד אֶת־ שַׂלְמָא וְשַׂלְמָא הוֹלִיד אֶת־ בֹּעַז׃
Boaz *** he-fathered and-Salma Salma *** he-fathered and-Nahshon (11)

וּבֹעַז הוֹלִיד אֶת־ עוֹבֵד וְעוֹבֵד הוֹלִיד אֶת־ יִשָׁי׃
Jesse *** he-fathered and-Obed Obed *** he-fathered and-Boaz (12)

וְאִישַׁי הוֹלִיד אֶת־ בְּכֹרוֹ אֶת־ אֱלִיאָב וַאֲבִינָדָב
and-Abinadab Eliab *** firstborn-of-him *** he-fathered and-Jesse (13)

הַשֵּׁנִי וְשִׁמְעָא הַשְּׁלִישִׁי׃ נְתַנְאֵל הָרְבִיעִי רַדַּי הַחֲמִישִׁי׃
the-fifth Raddai the-fourth Nethanel (14) the-third and-Shimea the-second

daughter of Me-Zahab.
51Hadad also died.

The chiefs of Edom were:
Timna, Alvah, Jetheth,
52Oholibamah, Elah, Pinon,
53Kenaz, Teman,
Mibzar, 54Magdiel and
Iram. These were the chiefs of Edom.

Israel's Sons

2 These were the sons of Israel:
Reuben, Simeon, Levi, Judah, Issachar, Zebulun,
2Dan, Joseph, Benjamin, Naphtali, Gad and Asher.

Judah

To Hezron's Sons

3The sons of Judah:
Er, Onan and Shelah. These three were born to him by Bathshua,[t] a Canaanite woman. Er, Judah's firstborn, was wicked in the LORD's sight; so the LORD put him to death.
4Tamar, Judah's daughter-in-law, bore him Perez and Zerah. Judah had five sons in all.

5The sons of Perez:
Hezron and Hamul.
6The sons of Zerah:
Zimri, Ethan, Heman, Calcol and Darda[u]—five in all.
7The son of Carmi:
Achar,[v] who brought disaster on Israel by violating the ban on taking devoted things.[w]
8The son of Ethan:
Azariah.
9The sons born to Hezron were:
Jerahmeel, Ram and Caleb.[x]

From Ram Son of Hezron

10Ram was the father of Amminadab, and Amminadab the father of Nahshon, the leader of the people of Judah.
11Nahshon was the father of Salmon,[y] Salmon the father of Boaz,
12Boaz the father of Obed and Obed the father of Jesse.

[t]3 Or *by the daughter of Shua*
[u]6 Many Hebrew manuscripts, some Septuagint manuscripts and Syriac (see also 1 Kings 4:31); most Hebrew manuscripts *Dara*
[v]7 *Achar* means *disaster; Achar* is called *Achan* in Joshua.
[w]7 The Hebrew term refers to the irrevocable giving over of things or persons to the LORD, often by totally destroying them.
[x]9 Hebrew *Kelubai*, a variant of *Caleb*
[y]11 Septuagint (see also Ruth 4:21); Hebrew *Salma*

**1* Most mss have *dagesh* in the first *sin* (יִשָּׂ).

°*51* ק עלוה

אֹצֶם הַשִּׁשִּׁי דָּוִיד הַשְּׁבִעִי׃ וְאַחְיֹתֵיהֶם°
and-sisters-of-them (16) the-seventh David the-sixth Ozem (15)

צְרוּיָה וַאֲבִיגָיִל וּבְנֵי צְרוּיָה אַבְשַׁי וְיוֹאָב וַעֲשָׂה־אֵל
El and-Asah and-Joab Abishai Zeruiah and-sons-of and-Abigail Zeruiah

שְׁלֹשָׁה׃ וַאֲבִיגַיִל יָלְדָה אֶת־עֲמָשָׂא וַאֲבִי עֲמָשָׂא יֶתֶר
Jether Amasa now-father-of Amasa *** she-bore and-Abigail (17) three

הַיִּשְׁמְעֵאלִי׃ וְכָלֵב בֶּן־חֶצְרוֹן הוֹלִיד אֶת־עֲזוּבָה אִשָּׁה
wife Azubah by he-fathered Hezron son-of and-Caleb (18) the-Ishmaelite

וְאֶת־יְרִיעוֹת וְאֵלֶּה בָנֶיהָ יֵשֶׁר וְשׁוֹבָב וְאַרְדּוֹן׃
and-Ardon and-Shobab Jesher sons-of-her and-these Jerioth and-by

וַתָּמָת עֲזוּבָה וַיִּקַּח־לוֹ כָלֵב אֶת־אֶפְרָת
Ephrath *** Caleb to-him and-he-married Azubah when-she-died (19)

וַתֵּלֶד לוֹ אֶת־חוּר׃ וְחוּר הוֹלִיד אֶת־אוּרִי וְאוּרִי
and-Uri Uri *** he-fathered and-Hur (20) Hur *** to-him and-she-bore

הוֹלִיד אֶת־בְּצַלְאֵל׃ וְאַחַר בָּא חֶצְרוֹן אֶל־בַּת־
daughter-of into Hezron he-went and-later (21) Bezalel *** he-fathered

מָכִיר אֲבִי גִלְעָד וְהוּא לְקָחָהּ וְהוּא בֶּן־שִׁשִּׁים
sixty son-of when-he he-married-her and-he Gilead father-of Makir

שָׁנָה וַתֵּלֶד לוֹ אֶת־שְׂגוּב׃ וּשְׂגוּב הוֹלִיד אֶת־יָאִיר
Jair *** he-fathered and-Segub (22) Segub *** to-him and-she-bore year

וַיְהִי־לוֹ עֶשְׂרִים וְשָׁלוֹשׁ עָרִים בְּאֶרֶץ הַגִּלְעָד׃
the-Gilead in-land-of towns and-three twenty to-him and-he-was

וַיִּקַּח גְּשׁוּר־וַאֲרָם אֶת־חַוֺּת יָאִיר מֵאִתָּם
from-among-them Jair Havvoth *** and-Aram Geshur but-he-captured (23)

אֶת־קְנָת וְאֶת־בְּנֹתֶיהָ שִׁשִּׁים עִיר כָּל־אֵלֶּה בְּנֵי
descendants-of these all-of town sixty settlements-of-her and Kenath ***

מָכִיר אֲבִי־גִלְעָד׃ וְאַחַר מוֹת־חֶצְרוֹן בְּכָלֵב אֶפְרָתָה
Ephrathah in-Caleb Hezron death-of and-after (24) Gilead father-of Makir

וְאֵשֶׁת חֶצְרוֹן אֲבִיָּה וַתֵּלֶד לוֹ אֶת־אַשְׁחוּר אֲבִי
father-of Ashhur *** to-him and-she-bore Abijah Hezron now-wife-of

תְקוֹעַ׃ וַיִּהְיוּ בְנֵי־יְרַחְמְאֵל בְּכוֹר חֶצְרוֹן הַבְּכוֹר ׀
the-firstborn Hezron firstborn-of Jerahmeel sons-of and-they-were (25) Tekoa

רָם וּבוּנָה וָאֹרֶן וָאֹצֶם אֲחִיָּה׃ וַתְּהִי אִשָּׁה אַחֶרֶת
another wife and-she-was (26) and-Ahijah and-Ozem and-Oren and-Bunah Ram

לִירַחְמְאֵל וּשְׁמָהּ עֲטָרָה הִיא אֵם אוֹנָם׃ וַיִּהְיוּ
and-they-were (27) Onam mother-of she Atarah and-name-of-her to-Jerahmeel

בְנֵי־רָם בְּכוֹר יְרַחְמְאֵל מַעַץ וְיָמִין וָעֵקֶר׃
and-Eker and-Jamin Maaz Jerahmeel firstborn-of Ram sons-of

13Jesse was the father of
Eliab his firstborn; the
second son was Abina-
dab, the third Shimea,
14the fourth Nethanel, the
fifth Raddai, 15the sixth
Ozem and the seventh
David. 16Their sisters
were Zeruiah and Abi-
gail. Zeruiah's three sons
were Abishai, Joab and
Asahel. 17Abigail was the
mother of Amasa, whose
father was Jether the
Ishmaelite.

Caleb Son of Hezron

18Caleb son of Hezron had
children by his wife Azu-
bah (and by Jerioth).
These were her sons:
Jesher, Shobab and Ar-
don. 19When Azubah
died, Caleb married
Ephrath, who bore him
Hur. 20Hur was the father
of Uri, and Uri the father
of Bezalel.
21Later, Hezron lay with the
daughter of Makir the fa-
ther of Gilead (he had
married her when he was
sixty years old), and she
bore him Segub. 22Segub
was the father of Jair,
who controlled twenty-
three towns in Gilead.
23(But Geshur and Aram
captured Havvoth Jair,[a]
as well as Kenath with
its surrounding settle-
ments—sixty towns.) All
these were descendants
of Makir the father of Gilead.

24After Hezron died in Caleb
Ephrathah, Abijah the
wife of Hezron bore him
Ashhur the father[b] of
Tekoa.

Jerahmeel Son of Hezron

25The sons of Jerahmeel the
firstborn of Hezron:
Ram his firstborn,
Bunah, Oren, Ozem and[c]
Ahijah. 26Jerahmeel had
another wife, whose
name was Atarah; she
was the mother of Onam.
27The sons of Ram the
firstborn of Jerahmeel:
Maaz, Jamin and Eker.

[a]23 Or *captured the settlements of Jair*
[b]24 *Father* may mean *civic leader* or *military leader;* also in verses 42, 45, 49-52 and possibly elsewhere.
[c]25 Or *Oren and Ozem, by*

°16 ק ואחיותיהם

(28) וַיִּהְיוּ בְנֵי־אוֹנָם שַׁמַּי וְיָדָע וּבְנֵי שַׁמַּי
Shammai and-sons-of and-Jada Shammai Onam sons-of and-they-were (28)

נָדָב וַאֲבִישׁוּר׃ (29) וְשֵׁם אֵשֶׁת אֲבִישׁוּר אֲבִיהָיִל וַתֵּלֶד
and-she-bore Abihail Abishur wife-of and-name-of (29) and-Abishur Nadab

לוֹ אֶת־אַחְבָּן וְאֶת־מוֹלִיד׃ (30) וּבְנֵי נָדָב סֶלֶד וְאַפָּיִם
and-Appaim Seled Nadab and-sons-of (30) Molid and Ahban *** to-him

וַיָּמָת סֶלֶד לֹא בָנִים׃ (31) וּבְנֵי אַפַּיִם יִשְׁעִי וּבְנֵי
and-sons-of Ishi Appaim and-sons-of (31) children no Seled and-he-died

יִשְׁעִי שֵׁשָׁן וּבְנֵי שֵׁשָׁן אַחְלָי׃ (32) וּבְנֵי יָדָע אֲחִי
brother-of Jada and-sons-of (32) Ahlai Sheshan and-sons-of Sheshan Ishi

שַׁמַּי יֶתֶר וְיוֹנָתָן וַיָּמָת יֶתֶר לֹא בָנִים׃
children no Jether and-he-died and-Jonathan Jether Shammai

(33) וּבְנֵי יוֹנָתָן פֶּלֶת וְזָזָא אֵלֶּה הָיוּ בְּנֵי
descendants-of they-were these and-Zaza Peleth Jonathan and-sons-of (33)

יְרַחְמְאֵל׃ (34) וְלֹא־הָיָה לְשֵׁשָׁן בָּנִים כִּי אִם־בָּנוֹת
daughters only but sons to-Sheshan he-was and-not (34) Jerahmeel

וּלְשֵׁשָׁן עֶבֶד מִצְרִי וּשְׁמוֹ יַרְחָע׃ (35) וַיִּתֵּן
and-he-gave (35) Jarha and-name-of-him Egyptian servant and-to-Sheshan

שֵׁשָׁן אֶת־בִּתּוֹ לְיַרְחָע עַבְדּוֹ לְאִשָּׁה וַתֵּלֶד
and-she-bore as-wife servant-of-him to-Jarha daughter-of-him *** Sheshan

לוֹ אֶת־עַתָּי׃ (36) וְעַתַּי הֹלִיד אֶת־נָתָן וְנָתָן
and-Nathan Nathan *** he-fathered and-Attai (36) Attai *** to-him

הוֹלִיד אֶת־זָבָד׃ (37) וְזָבָד הוֹלִיד אֶת־אֶפְלָל וְאֶפְלָל
and-Ephlal Ephlal *** he-fathered and-Zabad (37) Zabad *** he-fathered

הוֹלִיד אֶת־עוֹבֵד׃ (38) וְעוֹבֵד הוֹלִיד אֶת־יֵהוּא וְיֵהוּא
and-Jehu Jehu *** he-fathered and-Obed (38) Obed *** he-fathered

הוֹלִיד אֶת־עֲזַרְיָה׃ (39) וַעֲזַרְיָה הֹלִיד אֶת־חָלֶץ וְחֶלֶץ
and-Helez Helez *** he-fathered and-Azariah (39) Azariah *** he-fathered

הֹלִיד אֶת־אֶלְעָשָׂה׃ (40) וְאֶלְעָשָׂה הֹלִיד אֶת־סִסְמָי וְסִסְמָי
and-Sismai Sismai *** he-fathered and-Eleasah (40) Eleasah *** he-fathered

הֹלִיד אֶת־שַׁלּוּם׃ (41) וְשַׁלּוּם הוֹלִיד אֶת־יְקַמְיָה
Jekamiah *** he-fathered and-Shallum (41) Shallum *** he-fathered

וִיקַמְיָה הֹלִיד אֶת־אֱלִישָׁמָע׃ (42) וּבְנֵי כָלֵב אֲחִי
brother-of Caleb and-sons-of (42) Elishama *** he-fathered and-Jekamiah

יְרַחְמְאֵל מֵישָׁע בְּכֹרוֹ הוּא אֲבִי־זִיף וּבְנֵי מָרֵשָׁה
Mareshah and-sons-of Ziph father-of he firstborn-of-him Mesha Jerahmeel

אֲבִי חֶבְרוֹן׃ (43) וּבְנֵי חֶבְרוֹן קֹרַח וְתַפֻּחַ וָרֶקֶם
and-Rekem and-Tappuah Korah Hebron and-sons-of (43) Hebron father-of

28 The sons of Onam:
Shammai and Jada.
The sons of Shammai:
Nadab and Abishur.
29 Abishur's wife was named
Abihail, who bore him
Ahban and Molid.
30 The sons of Nadab:
Seled and Appaim. Seled
died without children.
31 The son of Appaim:
Ishi, who was the father
of Sheshan.
Sheshan was the father
of Ahlai.
32 The sons of Jada, Shammai's brother:
Jether and Jonathan. Je-
ther died without chil-
dren.
33 The sons of Jonathan:
Peleth and Zaza.
These were the descend-
ants of Jerahmeel.
34 Sheshan had no sons—only
daughters.
He had an Egyptian ser-
vant named Jarha.
35 She-
shan gave his daughter
in marriage to his ser-
vant Jarha, and she bore
him Attai.
36 Attai was the father of Nathan,
Nathan the father of
Zabad,
37 Zabad the father of Ephlal,
Ephlal the father of
Obed,
38 Obed the father of Jehu,
Jehu the father of Aza-
riah,
39 Azariah the father of
Helez,
Helez the father of Elea-
sah,
40 Eleasah the father of Sismai,
Sismai the father of Shallum,
41 Shallum the father of
Jekamiah,
and Jekamiah the father
of Elishama.

The Clans of Caleb

42 The sons of Caleb the
brother of Jerahmeel:
Mesha his firstborn, who
was the father of Ziph,
and his son Mareshah,[d]
who was the father of
Hebron.
43 The sons of Hebron:
Korah, Tappuah, Rekem

[d] 42 The meaning of the Hebrew for this phrase is uncertain.

וְשָׁמַע׃ וְשֶׁמַע הוֹלִיד אֶת־ רַחַם אֲבִי יָרְקְעָם וְרֶקֶם
and-Rekem Jorkeam father-of Raham *** he-fathered and-Shema (44) and-Shema

הוֹלִיד אֶת־ שַׁמָּי׃ וּבֶן־ שַׁמַּי מָעוֹן וּמָעוֹן אֲבִי
father-of and-Maon Maon Shammai and-son-of (45) Shammai *** he-fathered

בֵּית־צוּר׃ וְעֵיפָה פִּילֶגֶשׁ כָּלֵב יָלְדָה אֶת־ חָרָן וְאֶת־מוֹצָא
Moza and Haran *** she-bore Caleb concubine-of and-Ephah (46) Zur Beth

וְאֶת־ גָּזֵז וְחָרָן הֹלִיד אֶת־ גָּזֵז׃ וּבְנֵי יָהְדָּי
Jahdai and-sons-of (47) Gazez *** he-fathered and-Haran Gazez and

רֶגֶם וְיוֹתָם וְגֵישָׁן וָפֶלֶט וְעֵיפָה וָשָׁעַף׃
and-Shaaph and-Ephah and-Pelet and-Geshan and-Jotham Regem

פִּלֶגֶשׁ כָּלֵב מַעֲכָה יָלַד שֶׁבֶר וְאֶת־ תִּרְחֲנָה׃
Tirhanah and Sheber he-bore Maacah Caleb concubine-of (48)

וַתֵּלֶד שַׁעַף אֲבִי מַדְמַנָּה אֶת־ שְׁוָא אֲבִי מַכְבֵּנָה
Macbenah father-of Sheva *** Madmannah father-of Shaaph and-she-bore (49)

וַאֲבִי גִבְעָא וּבַת־ כָּלֵב עַכְסָה׃ אֵלֶּה הָיוּ
they-were these (50) Acsah Caleb and-daughter-of Gibea and-father-of

בְּנֵי כָלֵב בֶּן־ חוּר בְּכוֹר אֶפְרָתָה שׁוֹבָל אֲבִי
father-of Shobal Ephrathah firstborn-of Hur son-of Caleb descendants-of

קִרְיַת יְעָרִים׃ שַׂלְמָא אֲבִי בֵּית־ לָחֶם חָרֵף אֲבִי בֵית־ גָּדֵר׃
Gader Beth father-of Hareph Lehem Beth father-of Salma (51) Jearim Kiriath

וַיִּהְיוּ בָנִים לְשׁוֹבָל אֲבִי קִרְיַת יְעָרִים הָרֹאֶה
Haroeh Jearim Kiriath father-of of-Shobal descendants and-they-were (52)

חֲצִי הַמְּנֻחוֹת׃ וּמִשְׁפְּחוֹת קִרְיַת יְעָרִים הַיִּתְרִי
the-Ithrite Jearim Kiriath and-clans-of (53) the-Manahathites half-of

וְהַפּוּתִי וְהַשֻּׁמָתִי וְהַמִּשְׁרָעִי מֵאֵלֶּה
from-these and-the-Mishraite and-the-Shumathite and-the-Puthite

יָצְאוּ הַצָּרְעָתִי וְהָאֶשְׁתָּאֻלִי׃ בְּנֵי שַׂלְמָא
Salma descendants-of (54) and-the-Eshtaolite the-Zorathite they-descended

בֵּית לֶחֶם וּנְטוֹפָתִי עַטְרוֹת בֵּית יוֹאָב וַחֲצִי הַמָּנַחְתִּי
the-Manahathite and-half-of Joab Beth Atroth and-Netophathite Lehem Beth

הַצָּרְעִי׃ וּמִשְׁפְּחוֹת סֹפְרִים יֹשְׁבֵו יַעְבֵּץ
Jabez ones-living-of ones-being-scribes and-clans-of (55) the-Zorite

תִּרְעָתִים שִׁמְעָתִים שׂוּכָתִים הֵמָּה הַקִּינִים הַבָּאִים
the-ones-coming the-Kenites these Sucathites Shimeathites Tirathites

מֵחַמַּת אֲבִי בֵית־ רֵכָב׃ וְאֵלֶּה הָיוּ בְּנֵי
sons-of they-were and-these (3:1) Recab house-of father-of from-Hammath

דָוִיד* אֲשֶׁר נוֹלַד־ לוֹ בְּחֶבְרוֹן הַבְּכוֹר ׀ אַמְנֹן לַאֲחִינֹעַם
of-Ahinoam Amnon the-firstborn in-Hebron to-him he-was-born who David

and Shema. [44]Shema was the father of Raham, and Raham the father of Jorkeam. Rekem was the father of Shammai. [45]The son of Shammai was Maon, and Maon was the father of Beth Zur.

[46]Caleb's concubine Ephah was the mother of Haran, Moza and Gazez. Haran was the father of Gazez.

[47]The sons of Jahdai:
Regem, Jotham, Geshan, Pelet, Ephah and Shaaph.

[48]Caleb's concubine Maacah was the mother of Sheber and Tirhanah. [49]She also gave birth to Shaaph the father of Madmannah and to Sheva the father of Macbenah and Gibea. Caleb's daughter was Acsah.

[50]These were the descendants of Caleb:
The sons of Hur the firstborn of Ephrathah: Shobal the father of Kiriath Jearim, [51]Salma the father of Bethlehem, and Hareph the father of Beth Gader.

[52]The descendants of Shobal the father of Kiriath Jearim were:
Haroeh, half the Manahathites, [53]and the clans of Kiriath Jearim: the Ithrites, Puthites, Shumathites and Mishraites. From these descended the Zorathites and Eshtaolites.

[54]The descendants of Salma:
Bethlehem, the Netophathites, Atroth Beth Joab, half the Manahathites, the Zorites, [55]and the clans of scribes[e] who lived at Jabez: the Tirathites, Shimeathites and Sucathites. These are the Kenites who came from Hammath, the father of the house of Recab.[f]

The Sons of David

3 These were the sons of David born to him in Hebron:
The firstborn was Amnon the son of Ahinoam of Jezreel;

[e]55 Or *of the Sopherites*
[f]55 Or *father of Beth Recab*

*1 Most mss have the *bireq* under and the *zaqeph* over the *vav* (דָוִיד).

°55 ק ישבי

הַיִּזְרְעֵאלִית שֵׁנִי דָּנִיֵּאל לַאֲבִיגַיִל הַכַּרְמְלִית׃ (2) הַשְּׁלִשִׁי
the-third (2) the-Carmelite of-Abigail Daniel second the-Jezreelite

לְאַבְשָׁלוֹם בֶּן־ מַעֲכָה בַּת־ תַּלְמַי מֶלֶךְ גְּשׁוּר הָרְבִיעִי
the-fourth Geshur king-of Talmai daughter-of Maacah son-of of-Absalom

אֲדֹנִיָּה בֶן־ חַגִּית׃ (3) הַחֲמִישִׁי שְׁפַטְיָה לַאֲבִיטָל הַשִּׁשִּׁי
the-sixth of-Abital Shephatiah the-fifth (3) Haggith son-of Adonijah

יִתְרְעָם לְעֶגְלָה אִשְׁתּוֹ׃ (4) שִׁשָּׁה נוֹלַד־ לוֹ בְחֶבְרוֹן
in-Hebron to-him he-was-born six (4) wife-of-him of-Eglah Ithream

וַיִּמְלָךְ־ שָׁם שֶׁבַע שָׁנִים וְשִׁשָּׁה חֳדָשִׁים וּשְׁלֹשִׁים וְשָׁלוֹשׁ שָׁנָה
year and-three and-thirty months and-six years seven there and-he-reigned

מָלַךְ בִּירוּשָׁלָֽם׃ (5) וְאֵלֶּה נוּלְּדוּ־ לוֹ בִּירוּשָׁלָיִם
in-Jerusalem to-him they-were-born and-these (5) in-Jerusalem he-reigned

שִׁמְעָא[g] וְשׁוֹבָב וְנָתָן וּשְׁלֹמֹה אַרְבָּעָה לְבַת־ שׁוּעַ בַּת־
daughter-of Shua by-Bath four and-Solomon and-Nathan and-Shobab Shimea

עַמִּיאֵל׃ (6) וְיִבְחָר וֶאֱלִישָׁמָע וֶאֱלִיפָֽלֶט׃ (7) וְנֹגַהּ וְנֶפֶג
and-Nepheg and-Nogah (7) and-Eliphelet and-Elishama and-Ibhar (6) Ammiel

וְיָפִֽיעַ׃ (8) וֶאֱלִישָׁמָע וְאֶלְיָדָע וֶאֱלִיפֶלֶט תִּשְׁעָה׃ (9) כֹּל
all (9) nine and-Eliphelet and-Eliada and-Elishama (8) and-Japhia

בְּנֵי דָוִיד מִלְּבַד בְּנֵי־ פִילַגְשִׁים וְתָמָר אֲחוֹתָֽם׃
sister-of-them and-Tamar concubines sons-of besides David sons-of

(10) וּבֶן־ שְׁלֹמֹה רְחַבְעָם אֲבִיָּה בְנוֹ אָסָא בְנוֹ
son-of-him Asa son-of-him Abijah Rehoboam Solomon and-son-of (10)

יְהוֹשָׁפָט בְּנוֹ׃ (11) יוֹרָם בְּנוֹ אֲחַזְיָהוּ בְנוֹ יוֹאָשׁ
Joash son-of-him Ahaziah son-of-him Joram (11) son-of-him Jehoshaphat

בְּנוֹ׃ (12) אֲמַצְיָהוּ בְנוֹ עֲזַרְיָה בְנוֹ יוֹתָם בְּנוֹ׃
son-of-him Jotham son-of-him Azariah son-of-him Amaziah (12) son-of-him

(13) אָחָז בְּנוֹ חִזְקִיָּהוּ בְנוֹ מְנַשֶּׁה בְנוֹ׃ (14) אָמוֹן
Amon (14) son-of-him Manasseh son-of-him Hezekiah son-of-him Ahaz (13)

בְּנוֹ יֹאשִׁיָּהוּ בְנוֹ׃ (15) וּבְנֵי יֹאשִׁיָּהוּ הַבְּכוֹר יוֹחָנָן
Johanan the-firstborn Josiah and-sons-of (15) son-of-him Josiah son-of-him

הַשֵּׁנִי יְהוֹיָקִים הַשְּׁלִשִׁי צִדְקִיָּהוּ הָרְבִיעִי שַׁלּֽוּם׃
Shallum the-fourth Zedekiah the-third Jehoiakim the-second

(16) וּבְנֵי יְהוֹיָקִים יְכָנְיָה בְנוֹ צִדְקִיָּה בְנוֹ׃
son-of-him Zedekiah son-of-him Jeconiah Jehoiakim and-successors-of (16)

(17) וּבְנֵי יְכָנְיָה אַסִּר שְׁאַלְתִּיאֵל בְּנוֹ׃
son-of-him Shealtiel captive Jeconiah and-descendants-of (17)

(18) וּמַלְכִּירָם וּפְדָיָה וְשֶׁנְאַצַּר יְקַמְיָה הוֹשָׁמָע וּנְדַבְיָה׃
and-Nedabiah Hoshama Jekamiah and-Shenazzar and-Pedaiah and-Malkiram (18)

the second, Daniel the
son of Abigail of Carmel;
2the third, Absalom the
son of Maacah daughter
of Talmai king of Geshur;
the fourth, Adonijah the
son of Haggith;
3the fifth, Shephatiah the
son of Abital;
and the sixth, Ithream,
by his wife Eglah.
4These six were born to
David in Hebron, where
he reigned seven years
and six months.
David reigned in Jerusalem
thirty-three years, 5and these
were the children born to him
there:
Shammua,[g] Shobab, Nathan and Solomon. These four were by Bathsheba[h] daughter of Ammiel.
6There were also Ibhar,
Elishua,[i] Eliphelet,
7Nogah, Nepheg, Japhia,
8Elishama, Eliada and
Eliphelet—nine in all.
9All these were the sons
of David, besides his
sons by his concubines.
And Tamar was their sister.

The Kings of Judah

10Solomon's son was Rehoboam,
Abijah his son,
Asa his son,
Jehoshaphat his son,
11Jehoram[j] his son,
Ahaziah his son,
Joash his son,
12Amaziah his son,
Azariah his son,
Jotham his son,
13Ahaz his son,
Hezekiah his son,
Manasseh his son,
14Amon his son,
Josiah his son.
15The sons of Josiah:
Johanan the firstborn,
Jehoiakim the second son,
Zedekiah the third,
Shallum the fourth.
16The successors of Jehoiakim:
Jehoiachin[k] his son,
and Zedekiah.

The Royal Line After the Exile

17The descendants of Jehoiachin the captive:
Shealtiel his son, 18Malkiram, Pedaiah, Shenazzar, Jekamiah, Hoshama

[g]5 Hebrew *Shimea*, a variant of *Shammua*
[h]5 One Hebrew manuscript, Septuagint and Vulgate (see also 2 Samuel 11:3 and elsewhere); most Hebrew manuscripts *Bathshua*
[i]6 Two Hebrew manuscripts and some Septuagint manuscripts (see also 2 Samuel 5:15 and 1 Chron. 14:5); most Hebrew manuscripts *Elishama*
[j]11 Hebrew *Joram*, a variant of *Jehoram*
[k]16 Hebrew *Jeconiah*, a variant of *Jehoiachin*; also in verse 17

וּבְנֵי פְדָיָה זְרֻבָּבֶל וְשִׁמְעִי וּבֶן־ זְרֻבָּבֶל
Zerubbabel and-son-of and-Shimei Zerubbabel Pedaiah and-sons-of (19)

מְשֻׁלָּם וַחֲנַנְיָה וּשְׁלֹמִית אֲחוֹתָם׃ וַחֲשֻׁבָה
and-Hashubah (20) sister-of-them and-Shelomith and-Hananiah Meshullam

וָאֹהֶל וּבֶרֶכְיָה וַחֲסַדְיָה יוּשַׁב חֶסֶד חָמֵשׁ׃ וּבֶן־
and-descendant-of (21) five Hesed Jushab and-Hasadiah and-Berekiah and-Ohel

חֲנַנְיָה פְּלַטְיָה וִישַׁעְיָה בְּנֵי רְפָיָה בְּנֵי אַרְנָן בְּנֵי
sons-of Arnan sons-of Rephaiah sons-of and-Jeshaiah Pelatiah Hananiah

עֹבַדְיָה בְּנֵי שְׁכַנְיָה׃ וּבְנֵי שְׁכַנְיָה שְׁמַעְיָה
Shemaiah Shecaniah and-descendants-of (22) Shecaniah sons-of Obadiah

וּבְנֵי שְׁמַעְיָה חַטּוּשׁ וְיִגְאָל וּבָרִיחַ וּנְעַרְיָה וְשָׁפָט
and-Shaphat and-Neariah and-Bariah and-Igal Hattush Shemaiah and-sons-of

שִׁשָּׁה׃ וּבֶן־ נְעַרְיָה אֶלְיוֹעֵינַי וְחִזְקִיָּה וְעַזְרִיקָם שְׁלֹשָׁה׃
three and-Azrikam and-Hizkiah Elioenai Neariah and-son-of (23) six

וּבְנֵי אֶלְיוֹעֵינַי הֹדַיְוָהוּ וְאֶלְיָשִׁיב וּפְלָיָה וְעַקּוּב
and-Akkub and-Pelaiah and-Eliashib Hodaviah Elioenai and-sons-of (24)

וְיוֹחָנָן וּדְלָיָה וַעֲנָנִי שִׁבְעָה׃ בְּנֵי יְהוּדָה
Judah descendants-of (4:1) seven and-Anani and-Delaiah and-Johanan

פֶּרֶץ חֶצְרוֹן וְכַרְמִי וְחוּר וְשׁוֹבָל׃ וּרְאָיָה בֶן־ שׁוֹבָל
Shobal son-of and-Reaiah (2) and-Shobal and-Hur and-Carmi Hezron Perez

הוֹלִיד אֶת־ יַחַת וְיַחַת הוֹלִיד אֶת־ אֲחוּמַי וְאֶת־ לָהַד אֵלֶּה
these Lahad and Ahumai *** he-fathered and-Jahath Jahath *** he-fathered

מִשְׁפְּחוֹת הַצָּרְעָתִי׃ וְאֵלֶּה אֲבִי עֵיטָם יִזְרְעֶאל וְיִשְׁמָא
and-Ishma Jezreel Etam father-of and-these (3) the-Zorathite clans-of

וְיִדְבָּשׁ וְשֵׁם אֲחוֹתָם הַצְלֶלְפּוֹנִי׃ וּפְנוּאֵל אֲבִי
father-of and-Penuel (4) Hazzelelponi sister-of-them and-name-of and-Idbash

גְדֹר וְעֵזֶר אֲבִי חוּשָׁה אֵלֶּה בְנֵי־ חוּר בְּכוֹר
firstborn-of Hur descendants-of these Hushah father-of and-Ezer Gedor

אֶפְרָתָה אֲבִי בֵּית לָחֶם׃ וּלְאַשְׁחוּר אֲבִי תְקוֹעַ הָיוּ
they-were Tekoa father-of and-to-Ashhur (5) Lehem Beth father-of Ephrathah

שְׁתֵּי נָשִׁים חֶלְאָה וְנַעֲרָה׃ וַתֵּלֶד לוֹ נַעֲרָה אֶת־ אֲחֻזָּם
Ahuzzam *** Naarah to-him and-she-bore (6) and-Naarah Helah wives two-of

וְאֶת־ חֵפֶר וְאֶת־ תֵּימְנִי וְאֶת־ הָאֲחַשְׁתָּרִי אֵלֶּה בְּנֵי נַעֲרָה׃
Naarah descendants-of these Haahashtari and Temeni and Hepher and

וּבְנֵי חֶלְאָה צֶרֶת יִצְחַר וְאֶתְנָן׃ וְקוֹץ הוֹלִיד
he-fathered and-Koz (8) and-Ethnan and-Zohar Zereth Helah and-sons-of (7)

אֶת־ עָנוּב וְאֶת־ הַצֹּבֵבָה וּמִשְׁפְּחוֹת אֲחַרְחֵל בֶּן־ הָרוּם׃
Harum son-of Aharhel and-clans-of Hazzobebah and Anub ***

and Nedabiah.
19The sons of Pedaiah:
Zerubbabel and Shimei.
The sons of Zerubbabel:
Meshullam and Hananiah.
Shelomith was their sister.
20There were also five others:
Hashubah, Ohel, Berekiah, Hasadiah and Jushab-Hesed.
21The descendants of Hananiah:
Pelatiah and Jeshaiah, and the sons of Rephaiah, of Arnan, of Obadiah and of Shecaniah.
22The descendants of Shecaniah:
Shemaiah and his sons:
Hattush, Igal, Bariah, Neariah and Shaphat—six in all.
23The sons of Neariah:
Elioenai, Hizkiah and Azrikam—three in all.
24The sons of Elioenai:
Hodaviah, Eliashib, Pelaiah, Akkub, Johanan, Delaiah and Anani—seven in all.

Other Clans of Judah

4 The descendants of Judah:
Perez, Hezron, Carmi, Hur and Shobal.
2Reaiah son of Shobal was the father of Jahath, and Jahath the father of Ahumai and Lahad. These were the clans of the Zorathites.
3These were the sons[l] of Etam:
Jezreel, Ishma and Idbash. Their sister was named Hazzelelponi.
4Penuel was the father of Gedor, and Ezer the father of Hushah.
These were the descendants of Hur, the firstborn of Ephrathah and father[m] of Bethlehem.
5Ashhur the father of Tekoa had two wives, Helah and Naarah.
6Naarah bore him Ahuzzam, Hepher, Temeni and Haahashtari. These were the descendants of Naarah.
7The sons of Helah:
Zereth, Zohar, Ethnan,
8and Koz, who was the father of Anub and Hazzobebah and of the clans of Aharhel son of Harum.

l3 Some Septuagint manuscripts (see also Vulgate); Hebrew *father*
m4 *Father* may mean *civic leader* or *military leader;* also in verses 12, 14, 17, 18 and possibly elsewhere.

°24 ק הודויהו °7 ק וצחר

וַיְהִי יַעְבֵּץ נִכְבָּד מֵאֶחָיו
more-than-brothers-of-him being-honorable Jabez and-he-was (9)

וְאִמּוֹ קָרְאָה שְׁמוֹ יַעְבֵּץ לֵאמֹר כִּי יָלַדְתִּי
I-gave-birth because to-say Jabez name-of-him she-called and-mother-of-him

בְּעֹצֶב׃ וַיִּקְרָא יַעְבֵּץ לֵאלֹהֵי יִשְׂרָאֵל לֵאמֹר אִם־ בָּרֵךְ
to-bless if to-say Israel to-God-of Jabez and-he-cried-out (10) in-pain

תְּבָרְכֵנִי וְהִרְבִּיתָ אֶת־ גְּבוּלִי וְהָיְתָה
now-let-her-be territory-of-me *** and-you-would-enlarge you-would-bless-me

יָדְךָ עִמִּי וְעָשִׂיתָ מֵּרָעָה לְבִלְתִּי עָצְבִּי
to-have-pain-me not from-harm and-you-keep with-me hand-of-you

וַיָּבֵא אֱלֹהִים אֵת אֲשֶׁר־ שָׁאָל׃ וּכְלוּב אֲחִי־ שׁוּחָה
Shuhah brother-of and-Kelub (11) he-requested what *** God and-he-granted

הוֹלִיד אֶת־ מְחִיר הוּא אֲבִי אֶשְׁתּוֹן׃ וְאֶשְׁתּוֹן הוֹלִיד אֶת־
*** he-fathered and-Eshton (12) Eshton father-of he Mehir *** he-fathered

בֵּית רָפָא וְאֶת־ פָּסֵחַ וְאֶת־ תְּחִנָּה אֲבִי עִיר נָחָשׁ אֵלֶּה אַנְשֵׁי רֵכָה׃
Recah men-of these Nahash Ir father-of Tehinnah and Paseah and Rapha Beth

וּבְנֵי קְנַז עָתְנִיאֵל וּשְׂרָיָה וּבְנֵי עָתְנִיאֵל חֲתַת׃
Hathath Othniel and-sons-of and-Seraiah Othniel Kenaz and-sons-of (13)

וּמְעוֹנֹתַי הוֹלִיד אֶת־ עָפְרָה וּשְׂרָיָה הוֹלִיד אֶת־
*** he-fathered and-Seraiah Ophrah *** he-fathered and-Meonothai (14)

יוֹאָב אֲבִי גֵּיא חֲרָשִׁים כִּי חֲרָשִׁים הָיוּ׃ וּבְנֵי
and-sons-of (15) they-were craftsmen because Harashim Ge father-of Joab

כָּלֵב בֶּן־ יְפֻנֶּה עִירוּ אֵלָה וָנָעַם וּבְנֵי אֵלָה וּקְנַז׃
and-Kenaz Elah and-sons-of and-Naam Elah Iru Jephunneh son-of Caleb

וּבְנֵי יְהַלֶּלְאֵל זִיף וְזִיפָה תִּירְיָא וַאֲשַׂרְאֵל׃
and-Asarel Tiria and-Ziphah Ziph Jehallelel and-sons-of (16)

וּבֶן־ עֶזְרָה יֶתֶר וּמֶרֶד וְעֵפֶר וְיָלוֹן וַתַּהַר
and-she-bore and-Jalon and-Epher and-Mered Jether Ezrah and-son-of (17)

אֶת־ מִרְיָם וְאֶת־ שַׁמַּי וְאֶת־ יִשְׁבָּח אֲבִי אֶשְׁתְּמֹעַ׃
Eshtemoa father-of Ishbah and Shammai and Miriam ***

וְאִשְׁתּוֹ הַיְהֻדִיָּה יָלְדָה אֶת־ יֶרֶד אֲבִי גְדוֹר וְאֶת־
and Gedor father-of Jered *** she-bore the-Judean and-wife-of-him (18)

חֶבֶר אֲבִי שׂוֹכוֹ וְאֶת־ יְקוּתִיאֵל אֲבִי זָנוֹחַ וְאֵלֶּה בְּנֵי
children-of and-these Zanoah father-of Jekuthiel and Soco father-of Heber

בִּתְיָה בַת־ פַּרְעֹה אֲשֶׁר לָקַח מָרֶד׃ וּבְנֵי
and-sons-of (19) Mered he-married whom Pharaoh daughter-of Bithiah

אֵשֶׁת הוֹדִיָּה אֲחוֹת נַחַם אֲבִי קְעִילָה הַגַּרְמִי וְאֶשְׁתְּמֹעַ
and-Eshtemoa the-Garmite Keilah father-of Naham sister-of Hodiah wife-of

9 Jabez was more honorable than his brothers. His mother had named him Jabez,[n] saying, "I gave birth to him in pain." 10 Jabez cried out to the God of Israel, "Oh, that you would bless me and enlarge my territory! Let your hand be with me, and keep me from harm so that I will be free from pain." And God granted his request.

11 Kelub, Shuhah's brother, was the father of Mehir, who was the father of Eshton. 12 Eshton was the father of Beth Rapha, Paseah and Tehinnah the father of Ir Nahash.[o] These were the men of Recah.

13 The sons of Kenaz:
Othniel and Seraiah.
The sons of Othniel:
Hathath and Meonothai.[p] 14 Meonothai was the father of Ophrah.
Seraiah was the father of Joab,
the father of Ge Harashim.[q] It was called this because its people were craftsmen.
15 The sons of Caleb son of Jephunneh:
Iru, Elah and Naam.
The son of Elah:
Kenaz.
16 The sons of Jehallelel:
Ziph, Ziphah, Tiria and Asarel.
17 The sons of Ezrah:
Jether, Mered, Epher and Jalon. One of Mered's wives gave birth to Miriam, Shammai and Ishbah the father of Eshtemoa. 18 (His Judean wife gave birth to Jered the father of Gedor, Heber the father of Soco, and Jekuthiel the father of Zanoah.) These were the children of Pharaoh's daughter Bithiah, whom Mered had married.
19 The sons of Hodiah's wife, the sister of Naham:
the father of Keilah the Garmite, and Eshtemoa the Maacathite.

n9 *Jabez* sounds like the Hebrew for *pain*.
o12 Or *of the city of Nahash*
p13 Some Septuagint manuscripts and Vulgate; Hebrew does not have *and Meonothai*.
q14 *Ge Harashim* means *valley of craftsmen*.

*10 Most mss have no *dagesh* in the *mem* (מֵּ).

הַמַּעֲכָתִי׃ וּבְנֵי שִׁימוֹן אַמְנוֹן וְרִנָּה בֶּן־חָנָן וְתוּלוֹן

and-Tilon Hanan Ben and-Rinnah Amnon Shimon and-sons-of (20) the-Maacathite

וּבְנֵי יִשְׁעִי זוֹחֵת וּבֶן־זוֹחֵת׃ בְּנֵי שֵׁלָה בֶן־

son-of Shelah sons-of (21) Zoheth and-Ben Zoheth Ishi and-descendants-of

יְהוּדָה עֵר אֲבִי לֵכָה וְלַעְדָּה אֲבִי מָרֵשָׁה וּמִשְׁפְּחוֹת

and-clans-of Mareshah father-of and-Laadah Lecah father-of Er Judah

בֵּית־עֲבֹדַת הַבֻּץ לְבֵית אַשְׁבֵּעַ׃ וְיוֹקִים וְאַנְשֵׁי

and-men-of and-Jokim (22) Ashbea at-Beth the-linen worker-of house-of

כֹזֵבָא וְיוֹאָשׁ וְשָׂרָף אֲשֶׁר־בָּעֲלוּ לְמוֹאָב וְיָשֻׁבִי לָחֶם

Lehem and-Jashubi in-Moab they-ruled who and-Saraph and-Joash Cozeba

וְהַדְּבָרִים עַתִּיקִים׃ הֵמָּה הַיּוֹצְרִים וְיֹשְׁבֵי נְטָעִים

Netaim and-ones-living-of the-potters they (23) ancient-ones and-the-records

וּגְדֵרָה עִם־הַמֶּלֶךְ בִּמְלַאכְתּוֹ יָשְׁבוּ שָׁם׃ בְּנֵי

descendants-of (24) there they-stayed in-work-of-him the-king with and-Gederah

שִׁמְעוֹן נְמוּאֵל וְיָמִין יָרִיב זֶרַח שָׁאוּל׃ שַׁלֻּם בְּנוֹ מִבְשָׂם

Mibsam son-of-him Shallum (25) Shaul Zerah Jarib and-Jamin Nemuel Simeon

בְּנוֹ מִשְׁמָע בְּנוֹ׃ וּבְנֵי מִשְׁמָע חַמּוּאֵל

Hammuel Mishma and-descendants-of (26) son-of-him Mishma son-of-him

בְּנוֹ זַכּוּר בְּנוֹ שִׁמְעִי בְנוֹ׃ וּלְשִׁמְעִי בָּנִים

sons and-to-Shimei (27) son-of-him Shimei son-of-him Zaccur son-of-him

שִׁשָּׁה עָשָׂר וּבָנוֹת שֵׁשׁ וּלְאֶחָיו אֵין בָּנִים רַבִּים

many children not but-to-brothers-of-him six and-daughters ten six

וְכֹל מִשְׁפַּחְתָּם לֹא הִרְבּוּ עַד־בְּנֵי יְהוּדָה׃

Judah people-of as they-became-numerous not clan-of-them so-entire-of

וַיֵּשְׁבוּ בִּבְאֵר־שֶׁבַע וּמוֹלָדָה וַחֲצַר שׁוּעָל׃

Shual and-Hazar and-Moladah Sheba in-Beer and-they-lived (28)

וּבְבִלְהָה וּבְעֶצֶם וּבְתוֹלָד׃ וּבִבְתוּאֵל וּבְחָרְמָה

and-in-Hormah and-in-Bethuel (30) and-in-Tolad and-in-Ezem and-in-Bilhah (29)

וּבְצִיקְלָג׃ וּבְבֵית מַרְכָּבוֹת וּבַחֲצַר סוּסִים וּבְבֵית

and-in-Beth Susim and-in-Hazar Marcaboth and-in-Beth (31) and-in-Ziklag

בִּרְאִי וּבְשַׁעֲרָיִם אֵלֶּה עָרֵיהֶם עַד־מְלֹךְ דָּוִיד׃

David to-reign until towns-of-them these and-in-Shaaraim Biri

וְחַצְרֵיהֶם עֵיטָם וָעַיִן רִמּוֹן וְתֹכֶן וְעָשָׁן

and-Ashan and-Token Rimmon and-Ain Etam and-villages-of-them (32)

עָרִים חָמֵשׁ׃ וְכָל־חַצְרֵיהֶם אֲשֶׁר סְבִיבוֹת הֶעָרִים

the-towns ones-around that villages-of-them and-all-of (33) five towns

הָאֵלֶּה עַד־בָּעַל זֹאת מוֹשְׁבֹתָם וְהִתְיַחְשָׂם

and-to-keep-record-them settlements-of-them this Baal as-far-as the-these

°20 ק ותילון

[20]The sons of Shimon:
Amnon, Rinnah, Ben-Hanan and Tilon.
The descendants of Ishi:
Zoheth and Ben-Zoheth.
[21]The sons of Shelah son of Judah:
Er the father of Lecah, Laadah the father of Mareshah and the clans of the linen workers at Beth Ashbea, [22]Jokim, the men of Cozeba, and Joash and Saraph, who ruled in Moab and Jashubi Lehem. (These records are from ancient times.) [23]They were the potters who lived at Netaim and Gederah; they stayed there and worked for the king.

Simeon

[24]The descendants of Simeon:
Nemuel, Jamin, Jarib, Zerah and Shaul;
[25]Shallum was Shaul's son, Mibsam his son and Mishma his son.
[26]The descendants of Mishma:
Hammuel his son, Zaccur his son and Shimei his son.
[27]Shimei had sixteen sons and six daughters, but his brothers did not have many children; so their entire clan did not become as numerous as the people of Judah. [28]They lived in Beersheba, Moladah, Hazar Shual, [29]Bilhah, Ezem, Tolad, [30]Bethuel, Hormah, Ziklag, [31]Beth Marcaboth, Hazar Susim, Beth Biri and Shaaraim. These were their towns until the reign of David. [32]Their surrounding villages were Etam, Ain, Rimmon, Token and Ashan—five towns—[33]and all the villages around these towns as far as Baalath.[r] These were their settlements. And they kept a genealogical record.

[r]33 Some Septuagint manuscripts (see also Joshua 19:8); Hebrew *Baal*

לָהֶם׃ וּמְשׁוֹבָב וְיַמְלֵךְ וְיוֹשָׁה בֶּן־ אֲמַצְיָה׃
Amaziah son-of and-Joshah and-Jamlech and-Meshobab (34) for-them

וְיוֹאֵל וְיֵהוּא בֶּן־ יֽוֹשִׁבְיָה בֶּן־ שְׂרָיָה בֶּן־עֲשִׂיאֵל׃
Asiel son-of Seraiah son-of Joshibiah son-of and-Jehu and-Joel (35)

וְאֶלְיוֹעֵינַי וְיַעֲקֹבָה וִישׁוֹחָיָה וַעֲשָׂיָה וַעֲדִיאֵל
and-Adiel and-Asaiah and-Jeshohaiah and-Jaakobah also-Elioenai (36)

וִישִׂימִאֵל וּבְנָיָה׃ וְזִיזָא בֶּן־ שִׁפְעִי בֶּן־ אַלּוֹן בֶּן־
son-of Allon son-of Shiphi son-of and-Ziza (37) and-Benaiah and-Jesimiel

יְדָיָה בֶּן־ שִׁמְרִי בֶּן־ שְׁמַעְיָה׃ אֵלֶּה הַבָּאִים
the-ones-being-listed these (38) Shemaiah son-of Shimri son-of Jedaiah

בְּשֵׁמוֹת נְשִׂיאִים בְּמִשְׁפְּחוֹתָם וּבֵית אֲבוֹתֵיהֶם
fathers-of-them and-family-of of-clans-of-them leaders by-names

פָּרְצוּ לָרוֹב׃ וַיֵּלְכוּ לִמְבוֹא גְדֹר עַד
at Gedor to-outskirt-of and-they-went (39) to-greatness they-increased

לְמִזְרַח הַגָּיְא לְבַקֵּשׁ מִרְעֶה לְצֹאנָם׃ וַיִּמְצְאוּ
and-they-found (40) for-flock-of-them pasture to-search the-valley to-east-of

מִרְעֶה שָׁמֵן וָטוֹב וְהָאָרֶץ רַחֲבַת יָדַיִם וְשֹׁקֶטֶת
and-being-peaceful measures spacious-of and-the-land and-good rich pasture

וּשְׁלֵוָה כִּי מִן־ חָם הַיֹּשְׁבִים שָׁם לְפָנִים׃ וַיָּבֹאוּ
and-they-came (41) formerly there the-ones-living Ham from now and-quiet

אֵלֶּה הַכְּתוּבִים בְּשֵׁמוֹת בִּימֵי ׀ יְחִזְקִיָּהוּ מֶלֶךְ־ יְהוּדָה
Judah king-of Hezekiah in-days-of by-names the-ones-being-listed these

וַיַּכּוּ אֶת־ אָהֳלֵיהֶם וְאֶת־ הַמְּעִינִים אֲשֶׁר נִמְצְאוּ־
they-were-found who the-Meunites and dwellings-of-them *** and-they-attacked

שָׁמָּה וַיַּחֲרִימֻם עַד־ הַיּוֹם הַזֶּה וַיֵּשְׁבוּ
then-they-settled the-this the-day to and-they-destroyed-them at-there

תַּחְתֵּיהֶם כִּי־ מִרְעֶה לְצֹאנָם שָׁם׃ וּמֵהֶם ׀
and-from-them (42) there for-flock-of-them pasture because in-place-of-them

מִן־ בְּנֵי שִׁמְעוֹן הָלְכוּ לְהַר שֵׂעִיר אֲנָשִׁים חֲמֵשׁ
five-of men Seir into-hill-country-of they-invaded Simeon sons-of from

מֵאוֹת וּפְלַטְיָה וּנְעַרְיָה וּרְפָיָה וְעֻזִּיאֵל בְּנֵי יִשְׁעִי
Ishi sons-of and-Uzziel and-Rephaiah and-Neariah and-Pelatiah hundreds

בְּרֹאשָׁם׃ וַיַּכּוּ אֶת־ שְׁאֵרִית הַפְּלֵטָה לַעֲמָלֵק
of-Amalek the-escapee remainder-of *** and-they-killed (43) at-head-of-them

וַיֵּשְׁבוּ שָׁם עַד הַיּוֹם הַזֶּה׃ וּבְנֵי רְאוּבֵן
Reuben and-sons-of (5:1) the-this the-day to there and-they-lived

בְּכוֹר־ יִשְׂרָאֵל כִּי הוּא הַבְּכוֹר וּבְחַלְּלוֹ יְצוּעֵי
beds-of but-when-to-defile-him the-firstborn he now Israel firstborn-of

34Meshobab, Jamlech, Jo-
shah son of Amaziah,
35Joel, Jehu son of Joshibiah, the son of Seraiah,
the son of Asiel, 36also Elioenai, Jaakobah, Jeshohaiah,
Asaiah, Adiel, Jesimiel, Benaiah, 37and Ziza son of
Shiphi, the son of Allon,
the son of Jedaiah, the son
of Shimri, the son of Shemaiah.

38The men listed above by
name were leaders of their
clans. Their families increased
greatly, 39and they went to the
outskirts of Gedor to the east
of the valley in search of pasture for their flocks. 40They
found rich, good pasture, and
the land was spacious, peaceful and quiet. Some Hamites
had lived there formerly.
41The men whose names
were listed came in the days of
Hezekiah king of Judah. They
attacked the Hamites in their
dwellings and also the Meunites who were there and
completely destroyed[l] them,
as is evident to this day. Then
they settled in their place, because there was pasture for
their flocks. 42And five hundred of these Simeonites, led
by Pelatiah, Neariah, Re-
phaiah and Uzziel, the sons of
Ishi, invaded the hill country
of Seir. 43They killed the remaining Amalekites who had
escaped, and they have lived
there to this day.

Reuben

5 The sons of Reuben the
firstborn of Israel (he was
the firstborn, but when he
defiled his father's marriage

[l]41 The Hebrew term refers to the irrevocable giving over of things or persons to the LORD, often by totally destroying them.

°41 ק המעונים

אָבִיו נִתְּנָה בְּכֹרָתוֹ לִבְנֵי יוֹסֵף בֶּן־
father-of-him she-was-given firstborn-right-of-him to-sons-of Joseph son-of

יִשְׂרָאֵל וְלֹא לְהִתְיַחֵשׂ לַבְּכֹרָה׃ (2) כִּי יְהוּדָה
Israel so-not to-be-listed according-to-the-birthright (2) though Judah

גָּבַר בְּאֶחָיו וּלְנָגִיד מִמֶּנּוּ
he-was-strong among-brothers-of-him and-though-ruler from-him

וְהַבְּכֹרָה לְיוֹסֵף׃ (3) בְּנֵי רְאוּבֵן בְּכוֹר יִשְׂרָאֵל
but-the-firstborn-right to-Joseph (3) sons-of Reuben firstborn-of Israel

חֲנוֹךְ וּפַלּוּא חֶצְרוֹן וְכַרְמִי׃ (4) בְּנֵי יוֹאֵל שְׁמַעְיָה
Hanoch and-Pallu Hezron and-Carmi (4) descendants-of Joel Shemaiah

בְנוֹ גּוֹג בְּנוֹ שִׁמְעִי בְנוֹ׃ (5) מִיכָה בְנוֹ רְאָיָה
son-of-him Gog son-of-him Shimei son-of-him (5) Micah son-of-him Reaiah

בְנוֹ בַּעַל בְּנוֹ׃ (6) בְּאֵרָה בְנוֹ אֲשֶׁר הֶגְלָה תִּלְּגַת
son-of-him Baal son-of-him (6) Beerah son-of-him whom he-exiled Tiglath

פִּלְנְאֶסֶר מֶלֶךְ אַשֻּׁר הוּא נָשִׂיא לָראוּבֵנִי׃ (7) וְאֶחָיו
Pileser king-of Assyria he leader of-the-Reubenite (7) and-relatives-of-him

לְמִשְׁפְּחֹתָיו בְּהִתְיַחֵשׂ לְתֹלְדוֹתָם הָרֹאשׁ יְעִיאֵל
by-clans-of-him when-to-be-listed by-records-of-them the-chief Jeiel

וּזְכַרְיָהוּ׃ (8) וּבֶלַע בֶּן־ עָזָז בֶּן־ שֶׁמַע בֶּן־ יוֹאֵל הוּא
and-Zechariah (8) and-Bela son-of Azaz son-of Shema son-of Joel he

יוֹשֵׁב בַּעֲרֹעֵר וְעַד־ נְבוֹ וּבַעַל מְעוֹן׃ (9) וְלַמִּזְרָח
one-settling in-Aroer and-to Nebo and-Baal Meon (9) and-to-the-east

יָשַׁב עַד־ לְבוֹא מִדְבָּרָה לְמִן־ הַנָּהָר פְּרָת כִּי
he-occupied to to-enter into-desert to-from the-River Euphrates because

מִקְנֵיהֶם רָבוּ בְּאֶרֶץ גִּלְעָד׃ (10) וּבִימֵי שָׁאוּל
livestocks-of-them they-increased in-land-of Gilead (10) and-in-days-of Saul

עָשׂוּ מִלְחָמָה עִם־ הַהַגְרִאִים וַיִּפְּלוּ בְּיָדָם
they-waged war against the-Hagrites and-they-were-defeated at-hand-of-them

וַיֵּשְׁבוּ בְּאָהֳלֵיהֶם עַל־ כָּל־ פְּנֵי מִזְרָח
and-they-occupied in-dwellings-of-them through entire-of regions-of east

לַגִּלְעָד׃ (11) וּבְנֵי־ גָד לְנֶגְדָּם יָשְׁבוּ בְּאֶרֶץ
of-the-Gilead (11) and-sons-of Gad at-next-to-them they-lived in-land-of

הַבָּשָׁן עַד־ סַלְכָה׃ (12) יוֹאֵל הָרֹאשׁ וְשָׁפָם הַמִּשְׁנֶה
the-Bashan as-far-as Salecah (12) Joel the-chief and-Shapham the-second

וְיַעְנַי וְשָׁפָט בַּבָּשָׁן׃ (13) וַאֲחֵיהֶם לְבֵית
then-Janai and-Shaphat in-the-Bashan (13) and-relatives-of-them by-family-of

אֲבוֹתֵיהֶם מִיכָאֵל וּמְשֻׁלָּם וְשֶׁבַע וְיוֹרַי וְיַעְכָּן וְזִיעַ
fathers-of-them Michael and-Meshullam and-Sheba and-Jorai and-Jacan and-Zia

bed, his rights as firstborn
were given to the sons of Joseph son of Israel; so he could
not be listed in the genealogical record in accordance with
his birthright, 2 and though
Judah was the strongest of his
brothers and a ruler came from
him, the rights of the firstborn
belonged to Joseph)— 3 the
sons of Reuben the firstborn
of Israel:
Hanoch, Pallu, Hezron and Carmi.
4 The descendants of Joel:
Shemaiah his son, Gog his son,
Shimei his son, 5 Micah his son,
Reaiah his son, Baal his son,
6 and Beerah his son, whom Tiglath-Pileser[u] king of Assyria took into exile. Beerah was a leader of the Reubenites.
7 Their relatives by clans, listed according to their genealogical records:
Jeiel the chief, Zechariah,
8 and Bela son of Azaz, the son of Shema, the son of Joel. They settled in the area from Aroer to Nebo and Baal Meon.
9 To the east they occupied the land up to the edge of the desert that extends to the Euphrates River, because their livestock had increased in Gilead.
10 During Saul's reign they waged war against the Hagrites, who were defeated at their hands; they occupied the dwellings of the Hagrites throughout the entire region east of Gilead.

Gad

11 The Gadites lived next to them in Bashan, as far as Salecah:
12 Joel was the chief, Shapham the second, then Janai and Shaphat, in Bashan.
13 Their relatives, by families, were:
Michael, Meshullam, Sheba, Jorai, Jacan, Zia

[u]6 Hebrew *Tilgath-Pilneser,* a variant of *Tiglath-Pileser;* also in verse 26

וָעֵבֶר שִׁבְעָה׃ אֵלֶּה ׀ בְּנֵי אֲבִיחַיִל בֶּן־חוּרִי בֶּן־יָרוֹחַ בֶּן־
son-of Jaroah son-of Huri son-of Abihail sons-of these (14) seven and-Eber

גִּלְעָד בֶּן־מִיכָאֵל בֶּן־יְשִׁישַׁי בֶּן־יַחְדּוֹ בֶּן־בּוּז׃ אֲחִי
Ahi (15) Buz son-of Jahdo son-of Jeshishai son-of Michael son-of Gilead

בֶּן־עַבְדִּיאֵל בֶּן־גּוּנִי רֹאשׁ לְבֵית אֲבוֹתָם׃ וַיֵּשְׁבוּ
and-they-lived (16) fathers-of-them of-family-of head Guni son-of Abdiel son-of

בַּגִּלְעָד בַּבָּשָׁן וּבִבְנֹתֶיהָ וּבְכָל־ מִגְרְשֵׁי
pastures-of and-on-all-of and-in-villages-of-her in-the-Bashan in-the-Gilead

שָׁרוֹן עַל־ תּוֹצְאוֹתָם׃ כֻּלָּם הִתְיַחְשׂוּ
they-were-recorded all-of-them (17) extensions-of-them as-far-as Sharon

בִּימֵי יוֹתָם מֶלֶךְ־ יְהוּדָה וּבִימֵי יָרָבְעָם מֶלֶךְ־יִשְׂרָאֵל׃
Israel king-of Jeroboam and-in-days-of Judah king-of Jotham in-days-of

בְּנֵי־ רְאוּבֵן וְגָדִי וַחֲצִי שֵׁבֶט־ מְנַשֶּׁה מִן־ בְּנֵי־
men-of from Manasseh tribe-of and-half-of and-Gadite Reuben sons-of (18)

חַיִל אֲנָשִׁים נֹשְׂאֵי מָגֵן וְחֶרֶב וְדֹרְכֵי קֶשֶׁת
bow and-ones-using-of and-sword shield ones-handling-of men ability

וּלְמוּדֵי מִלְחָמָה אַרְבָּעִים וְאַרְבָּעָה אֶלֶף וּשְׁבַע־
and-seven-of thousand and-four forty battle and-ones-being-trained-of

מֵאוֹת וְשִׁשִּׁים יֹצְאֵי צָבָא׃ וַיַּעֲשׂוּ מִלְחָמָה
war and-they-waged (19) military ones-being-ready-of and-sixty hundreds

עִם־ הַהַגְרִיאִים וִיטוּר וְנָפִישׁ וְנוֹדָב׃ וַיֵּעָזְרוּ
and-they-were-helped (20) and-Nodab and-Naphish and-Jetur the-Hagrites against

עֲלֵיהֶם וַיִּנָּתְנוּ בְיָדָם הַהַגְרִיאִים וְכֹל
and-all-of the-Hagrites into-hand-of-them and-they-were-given against-them

שֶׁעִמָּהֶם כִּי לֵאלֹהִים זָעֲקוּ בַמִּלְחָמָה
during-the-battle they-cried-out to-God because who-with-them

וְנַעְתּוֹר לָהֶם כִּי־ בָטְחוּ בוֹ׃ וַיִּשְׁבּוּ
and-they-seized (21) in-him they-trusted because for-them and-to-answer-prayer

מִקְנֵיהֶם גְּמַלֵּיהֶם חֲמִשִּׁים אֶלֶף וְצֹאן מָאתַיִם
two-hundreds and-sheep thousand fifty camels-of-them livestocks-of-them

וַחֲמִשִּׁים אֶלֶף וַחֲמוֹרִים אַלְפָּיִם וְנֶפֶשׁ אָדָם מֵאָה
hundred human and-living-of two-thousands and-donkeys thousand and-fifty

אָלֶף׃ כִּי־ חֲלָלִים רַבִּים נָפָלוּ כִּי מֵהָאֱלֹהִים
from-the-God because they-fell many ones-slain indeed (22) thousand

הַמִּלְחָמָה וַיֵּשְׁבוּ תַחְתֵּיהֶם עַד־ הַגֹּלָה׃
the-exile until in-place-of-them and-they-occupied the-battle

וּבְנֵי חֲצִי שֵׁבֶט מְנַשֶּׁה יָשְׁבוּ בָּאָרֶץ
in-the-land they-settled Manasseh tribe-of half-of and-people-of (23)

and Eber—seven in all.
[14]These were the sons of
Abihail son of Huri, the
son of Jaroah, the son of
Gilead, the son of Mi-
chael, the son of Jeshi-
shai, the son of Jahdo,
the son of Buz.
[15]Ahi son of Abdiel, the
son of Guni, was head of
their family.
[16]The Gadites lived in Gilead,
in Bashan and its outly-
ing villages, and on all
the pasturelands of Shar-
on as far as they ex-
tended.
[17]All these were entered in
the genealogical records during the reigns of Jotham king
of Judah and Jeroboam king of
Israel.

[18]The Reubenites, the Gadites and the half-tribe of
Manasseh had 44,760 men
ready for military service—
able-bodied men who could
handle shield and sword, who
could use a bow, and who
were trained for battle. [19]They
waged war against the Ha-
grites, Jetur, Naphish and
Nodab. [20]They were helped in
fighting them, and God handed the Hagrites and all their
allies over to them, because
they cried out to him during
the battle. He answered their
prayers, because they trusted
in him. [21]They seized the livestock of the Hagrites—fifty
thousand camels, two hun-
dred fifty thousand sheep and
two thousand donkeys. They
also took one hundred thousand people captive, [22]and
many others fell slain, because
the battle was God's. And they
occupied the land until the exile.

The Half-Tribe of Manasseh

[23]The people of the half-tribe
of Manasseh were numerous;
they settled in the land from

מִבָּשָׁן עַד־בַּעַל חֶרְמוֹן וּשְׂנִיר וְהַר־חֶרְמוֹן הֵמָּה
they Hermon indeed-Mount-of indeed-Senir Hermon Baal to from-Bashan

רָבוּ׃ וְאֵלֶּה רָאשֵׁי בֵית־אֲבוֹתָם
fathers-of-them family-of heads-of and-these (24) they-were-numerous

וְעֵפֶר וְיִשְׁעִי וֶאֱלִיאֵל וְעַזְרִיאֵל וְיִרְמְיָה וְהוֹדַוְיָה
and-Hodaviah and-Jeremiah and-Azriel and-Elial and-Ishi and-Epher

וְיַחְדִּיאֵל אֲנָשִׁים גִּבּוֹרֵי חַיִל אַנְשֵׁי שֵׁמוֹת רָאשִׁים לְבֵית
of-family-of heads names men-of bravery warriors-of men and-Jahdiel

אֲבוֹתָם׃ וַיִּמְעֲלוּ בֵּאלֹהֵי אֲבוֹתֵיהֶם
fathers-of-them to-God-of but-they-were-unfaithful (25) fathers-of-them

וַיִּזְנוּ אַחֲרֵי אֱלֹהֵי עַמֵּי־הָאָרֶץ אֲשֶׁר־הִשְׁמִיד אֱלֹהִים
God he-destroyed whom the-land peoples-of gods-of to and-they-prostituted

מִפְּנֵיהֶם׃ וַיָּעַר אֱלֹהֵי יִשְׂרָאֵל אֶת־רוּחַ ׀ פּוּל
Pul spirit-of *** Israel God-of so-he-stirred-up (26) from-before-them

מֶלֶךְ־אַשּׁוּר וְאֶת־רוּחַ תִּלְגַת פִּלְנֶסֶר מֶלֶךְ אַשּׁוּר
Assyria king-of Pileser Tiglath spirit-of indeed Assyria king-of

וַיַּגְלֵם לָראוּבֵנִי וְלַגָּדִי וְלַחֲצִי
and-of-half-of and-of-the-Gadite of-the-Reubenite and-he-exiled-them

שֵׁבֶט מְנַשֶּׁה וַיְבִיאֵם לַחְלַח וְחָבוֹר וְהָרָא וּנְהַר
and-river-of and-Hara and-Habor to-Halah and-he-took-them Manasseh tribe-of

גּוֹזָן עַד הַיּוֹם הַזֶּה׃ בְּנֵי לֵוִי גֵּרְשׁוֹן קְהָת וּמְרָרִי׃
and-Merari Kohath Gershon Levi sons-of *(27[1]) the-this the-day to Gozan

וּבְנֵי קְהָת עַמְרָם יִצְהָר וְחֶבְרוֹן וְעֻזִּיאֵל׃
and-Uzziel and-Hebron Izhar Amram Kohath and-sons-of (28[2])

וּבְנֵי עַמְרָם אַהֲרֹן וּמֹשֶׁה וּמִרְיָם וּבְנֵי אַהֲרֹן
Aaron and-sons-of and-Miriam and-Moses Aaron Amram and-children-of (29[3])

נָדָב וַאֲבִיהוּא אֶלְעָזָר וְאִיתָמָר׃ אֶלְעָזָר הוֹלִיד אֶת־
*** he-fathered Eleazar (30[4]) and-Ithamar Eleazar and-Abihu Nadab

פִּינְחָס פִּינְחָס הֹלִיד אֶת־אֲבִישׁוּעַ׃ וַאֲבִישׁוּעַ הוֹלִיד
he-fathered and-Abishua (31[5]) Abishua *** he-fathered Phinehas Phinehas

אֶת־בֻּקִּי וּבֻקִּי הוֹלִיד אֶת־עֻזִּי׃ וְעֻזִּי הוֹלִיד אֶת־
*** he-fathered and-Uzzi (32[6]) Uzzi *** he-fathered and-Bukki Bukki ***

זְרַחְיָה וּזְרַחְיָה הוֹלִיד אֶת־מְרָיוֹת׃ מְרָיוֹת הוֹלִיד
he-fathered Meraioth (33[7]) Meraioth *** he-fathered and-Zerahiah Zerahiah

אֶת־אֲמַרְיָה וַאֲמַרְיָה הוֹלִיד אֶת־אֲחִיטוּב׃ וַאֲחִיטוּב
and-Ahitub (34[8]) Ahitub *** he-fathered and-Amariah Amariah ***

הוֹלִיד אֶת־צָדוֹק וְצָדוֹק הוֹלִיד אֶת־אֲחִימַעַץ׃ וַאֲחִימַעַץ
and-Ahimaaz (35[9]) Ahimaaz *** he-fathered and-Zadok Zadok *** he-fathered

Bashan to Baal Hermon, that is, to Senir (Mount Hermon).
[24]These were the heads of their families: Epher, Ishi, Eliel, Azriel, Jeremiah, Hodaviah and Jahdiel. They were brave warriors, famous men, and heads of their families.
[25]But they were unfaithful to the God of their fathers and prostituted themselves to the gods of the peoples of the land, whom God had destroyed before them.
[26]So the God of Israel stirred up the spirit of Pul king of Assyria (that is, Tiglath-Pileser king of Assyria), who took the Reubenites, the Gadites and the half-tribe of Manasseh into exile. He took them to Halah, Habor, Hara and the river of Gozan, where they are to this day.

Levi

6 The sons of Levi:
Gershon, Kohath and Merari.
[2]The sons of Kohath:
Amram, Izhar, Hebron and Uzziel.
[3]The children of Amram:
Aaron, Moses and Miriam.
The sons of Aaron:
Nadab, Abihu, Eleazar and Ithamar.
[4]Eleazar was the father of Phinehas,
Phinehas the father of Abishua,
[5]Abishua the father of Bukki,
Bukki the father of Uzzi,
[6]Uzzi the father of Zerahiah,
Zerahiah the father of Meraioth,
[7]Meraioth the father of Amariah,
Amariah the father of Ahitub,
[8]Ahitub the father of Zadok,
Zadok the father of Ahimaaz,
[9]Ahimaaz the father of

*27 The Hebrew numeration of chapter 6 begins with verse 16 in English. The number in brackets indicates the English numeration.

הוֹלִיד אֶת־עֲזַרְיָה וַעֲזַרְיָה הוֹלִיד אֶת־יוֹחָנָן׃ וְיוֹחָנָן
and-Johanan (36[10]) Johanan *** he-fathered and-Azariah Azariah *** he-fathered

הוֹלִיד אֶת־עֲזַרְיָה הוּא אֲשֶׁר כִּהֵן בַּבַּיִת אֲשֶׁר־
that in-the-temple he-served-as-priest who he Azariah *** he-fathered

בָּנָה שְׁלֹמֹה בִּירוּשָׁלִָם׃ וַיּוֹלֶד עֲזַרְיָה אֶת־אֲמַרְיָה
Amariah *** Azariah and-he-fathered (37[11]) in-Jerusalem Solomon he-built

וַאֲמַרְיָה הוֹלִיד אֶת־אֲחִיטוּב׃ וַאֲחִיטוּב הוֹלִיד אֶת־
*** he-fathered and-Ahitub (38[12]) Ahitub *** he-fathered and-Amariah

צָדוֹק וְצָדוֹק הוֹלִיד אֶת־שַׁלּוּם׃ וְשַׁלּוּם הוֹלִיד
he-fathered and-Shallum (39[13]) Shallum *** he-fathered and-Zadok Zadok

אֶת־חִלְקִיָּה וְחִלְקִיָּה הוֹלִיד אֶת־עֲזַרְיָה׃ וַעֲזַרְיָה
and-Azariah (40[14]) Azariah *** he-fathered and-Hilkiah Hilkiah ***

הוֹלִיד אֶת־שְׂרָיָה וּשְׂרָיָה הוֹלִיד אֶת־יְהוֹצָדָק׃
Jehozadak *** he-fathered and-Seraiah Seraiah *** he-fathered

וִיהוֹצָדָק הָלַךְ בְּהַגְלוֹת יְהוָה אֶת־יְהוּדָה וִירוּשָׁלִָם
and-Jerusalem Judah *** Yahweh when-to-exile he-left and-Jehozadak (41[15])

בְּיַד נְבֻכַדְנֶאצַּר׃ בְּנֵי לֵוִי גֵּרְשֹׁם קְהָת וּמְרָרִי׃
and-Merari Kohath Gershom Levi sons-of (1[16]) Nebuchadnezzar by-hand-of

וְאֵלֶּה שְׁמוֹת בְּנֵי־גֵרְשׁוֹם לִבְנִי וְשִׁמְעִי׃
and-Shimei Libni Gershom sons-of names-of and-these (2[17])

וּבְנֵי קְהָת עַמְרָם וְיִצְהָר וְחֶבְרוֹן וְעֻזִּיאֵל׃
and-Uzziel and-Hebron and-Izhar Amram Kohath and-sons-of (3[18])

בְּנֵי מְרָרִי מַחְלִי וּמֻשִׁי וְאֵלֶּה מִשְׁפְּחוֹת הַלֵּוִי
the-Levite clans-of and-these and-Mushi Mahli Merari sons-of (4[19])

לַאֲבוֹתֵיהֶם׃ לְגֵרְשׁוֹם לִבְנִי בְנוֹ יַחַת בְּנוֹ
son-of-him Jehath son-of-him Libni of-Gershom (5[20]) by-fathers-of-them

זִמָּה בְנוֹ׃ יוֹאָח בְּנוֹ עִדּוֹ בְנוֹ זֶרַח בְּנוֹ
son-of-him Zerah son-of-him Iddo son-of-him Joah (6[21]) son-of-him Zimmah

יְאָתְרַי בְּנוֹ׃ בְּנֵי קְהָת עַמִּינָדָב בְּנוֹ
son-of-him Amminadab Kohath descendants-of (7[22]) son-of-him Jeatherai

קֹרַח בְּנוֹ אַסִּיר בְּנוֹ׃ אֶלְקָנָה בְנוֹ וְאֶבְיָסָף
and-Ebiasaph son-of-him Elkanah (8[23]) son-of-him Assir son-of-him Korah

בְּנוֹ וְאַסִּיר בְּנוֹ׃ תַּחַת בְּנוֹ אוּרִיאֵל בְּנוֹ
son-of-him Uriel son-of-him Tahath (9[24]) son-of-him and-Assir son-of-him

עֻזִּיָּה בְנוֹ וְשָׁאוּל בְּנוֹ׃ וּבְנֵי אֶלְקָנָה
Elkanah and-descendants-of (10[25]) son-of-him and-Shaul son-of-him Uzziah

עֲמָשַׂי וַאֲחִימוֹת׃ אֶלְקָנָה בְּנֵו אֶלְקָנָה צוֹפַי בְּנוֹ
son-of-him Zophai Elkanah sons-of Elkanah (11[26]) and-Ahimoth Amasai

Azariah,
Azariah the father of Johanan,
[10]Johanan the father of Azariah (it was he who served as priest in the temple Solomon built in Jerusalem),
[11]Azariah the father of Amariah,
Amariah the father of Ahitub,
[12]Ahitub the father of Zadok,
Zadok the father of Shallum,
[13]Shallum the father of Hilkiah,
Hilkiah the father of Azariah,
[14]Azariah the father of Seraiah,
and Seraiah the father of Jehozadak.
[15]Jehozadak was deported when the LORD sent Judah and Jerusalem into exile by the hand of Nebuchadnezzar.

[16]The sons of Levi:
Gershon,[v] Kohath and Merari.
[17]These are the names of the sons of Gershon:
Libni and Shimei.
[18]The sons of Kohath:
Amram, Izhar, Hebron and Uzziel.
[19]The sons of Merari:
Mahli and Mushi.
These are the clans of the Levites listed according to their fathers:
[20]Of Gershon:
Libni his son, Jehath his son,
Zimmah his son, [21]Joah his son,
Iddo his son, Zerah his son
and Jeatherai his son.
[22]The descendants of Kohath:
Amminadab his son,
Korah his son,
Assir his son, [23]Elkanah his son,
Ebiasaph his son, Assir his son,
[24]Tahath his son, Uriel his son,
Uzziah his son and Shaul his son.
[25]The descendants of Elkanah:
Amasai, Ahimoth,
[26]Elkanah his son,[w] Zophai his son,

[v]16 Hebrew *Gershom*, a variant of *Gershon*; also in verses 17, 20, 43, 62 and 71
[w]26 Some Hebrew manuscripts, Septuagint and Syriac; most Hebrew manuscripts *Ahimoth* [26]*and Elkanah. The sons of Elkanah:*

*See the note on page 15.

°11 ק בני

וְנַחַת בְּנוֹ׃ אֱלִיאָב בְּנוֹ יְרֹחָם בְּנוֹ אֶלְקָנָה
Elkanah son-of-him Jeroham son-of-him Eliab (12[27]) son-of-him and-Nahath

בְּנוֹ׃ וּבְנֵי שְׁמוּאֵל הַבְּכֹר וְשֵׁנִי וַאֲבִיָּה׃
and-Abijah and-second the-firstborn Samuel and-sons-of (13[28]) son-of-him

בְּנֵי מְרָרִי מַחְלִי לִבְנִי בְנוֹ שִׁמְעִי בְנוֹ
son-of-him Shimei son-of-him Libni Mahli Merari descendants-of (14[29])

עֻזָּה בְנוֹ׃ שִׁמְעָא בְנוֹ חַגִּיָּה בְנוֹ עֲשָׂיָה
Asaiah son-of-him Haggiah son-of-him Shimea (15[30]) son-of-him Uzzah

בְּנוֹ׃ וְאֵלֶּה אֲשֶׁר הֶעֱמִיד דָּוִיד עַל־ יְדֵי־
ones-over-of at David he-put-in-charge whom and-these (16[31]) son-of-him

שִׁיר בֵּית יְהוָה מִמְּנוֹחַ הָאָרוֹן׃ וַיִּהְיוּ
and-they-were (17[32]) the-ark after-resting-of Yahweh house-of music-of

מְשָׁרְתִים לִפְנֵי מִשְׁכַּן אֹהֶל־ מוֹעֵד בַּשִּׁיר עַד־
until with-the-music Meeting Tent-of tabernacle before ones-ministering

בְּנוֹת שְׁלֹמֹה אֶת־ בֵּית יְהוָה בִּירוּשָׁלִָם וַיַּעַמְדוּ
and-they-performed in-Jerusalem Yahweh temple-of *** Solomon to-build

כְּמִשְׁפָּטָם עַל־ עֲבוֹדָתָם׃ וְאֵלֶּה
and-these (18[33]) duty-of-them for according-to-regulation-of-them

הָעֹמְדִים וּבְנֵיהֶם מִבְּנֵי הַקְּהָתִי הֵימָן
Heman the-Kohathite from-sons-of and-sons-of-them the-ones-serving

הַמְשׁוֹרֵר בֶּן־ יוֹאֵל בֶּן־ שְׁמוּאֵל׃ בֶּן־ אֶלְקָנָה
Elkanah son-of (19[34]) Samuel son-of Joel son-of the-one-making-music

בֶּן־ יְרֹחָם בֶּן־ אֱלִיאֵל בֶּן־ תּוֹחַ׃ בֶּן־ צִיף° בֶּן־ אֶלְקָנָה
Elkanah son-of Zuph son-of (20[35]) Toah son-of Eliel son-of Jeroham son-of

בֶּן־ מַחַת בֶּן־ עֲמָשָׂי׃ בֶּן־ אֶלְקָנָה בֶּן־ יוֹאֵל בֶּן־
son-of Joel son-of Elkanah son-of (21[36]) Amasai son-of Mahath son-of

עֲזַרְיָה בֶּן־ צְפַנְיָה׃ בֶּן־ תַּחַת בֶּן־ אַסִּיר בֶּן־ אֶבְיָסָף
Ebiasaph son-of Assir son-of Tahath son-of (22[37]) Zephaniah son-of Azariah

בֶּן־ קֹרַח׃ בֶּן־ יִצְהָר בֶּן־ קְהָת בֶּן־ לֵוִי בֶּן־ יִשְׂרָאֵל׃
Israel son-of Levi son-of Kohath son-of Izhar son-of (23[38]) Korah son-of

וְאָחִיו אָסָף הָעֹמֵד עַל־ יְמִינוֹ
right-hand-of-him at the-one-serving Asaph and-associate-of-him (24[39])

אָסָף בֶּן־ בֶּרֶכְיָהוּ בֶּן־ שִׁמְעָא׃ בֶּן־ מִיכָאֵל בֶּן־ בַּעֲשֵׂיָה
Baaseiah son-of Michael son-of (25[40]) Shimea son-of Berekiah son-of Asaph

בֶּן־ מַלְכִּיָּה׃ בֶּן־ אֶתְנִי בֶּן־ זֶרַח בֶּן־ עֲדָיָה׃
Adaiah son-of Zerah son-of Ethni son-of (26[41]) Malkijah son-of

בֶּן־ אֵיתָן בֶּן־ זִמָּה בֶּן־ שִׁמְעִי׃ בֶּן־ יַחַת
Jahath son-of (28[43]) Shimei son-of Zimmah son-of Ethan son-of (27[42])

Nahath his son, [27]Eliab his son,
Jeroham his son, Elkanah his son
and Samuel his son.[x]
[28]The sons of Samuel:
Joel[y] the firstborn
and Abijah the second son.
[29]The descendants of Merari:
Mahli, Libni his son,
Shimei his son, Uzzah his son,
[30]Shimea his son, Haggiah his son
and Asaiah his son.

The Temple Musicians

[31]These are the men David put in charge of the music in the house of the LORD after the ark came to rest there.
[32]They ministered with music before the tabernacle—the Tent of Meeting—until Solomon built the temple of the LORD in Jerusalem. They performed their duties according to the regulations laid down for them.
[33]Here are the men who served, together with their sons:
From the Kohathites:
Heman, the musician,
the son of Joel, the son of Samuel,
[34]the son of Elkanah, the son of Jeroham,
the son of Eliel, the son of Toah,
[35]the son of Zuph, the son of Elkanah,
the son of Mahath, the son of Amasai,
[36]the son of Elkanah, the son of Joel,
the son of Azariah, the son of Zephaniah,
[37]the son of Tahath, the son of Assir,
the son of Ebiasaph, the son of Korah,
[38]the son of Izhar, the son of Kohath,
the son of Levi, the son of Israel;
[39]and Heman's associate Asaph, who served at his right hand:
Asaph son of Berekiah, the son of Shimea,
[40]the son of Michael, the son of Baaseiah,[z]
the son of Malkijah, [41]the son of Ethni,
the son of Zerah, the son

x27 Some Septuagint manuscripts (see also 1 Samuel 1:19,20 and 1 Chron. 6:33,34); Hebrew does not have *and Samuel his son.*
y28 Some Septuagint manuscripts and Syriac (see also 1 Samuel 8:2 and 1 Chron. 6:33); Hebrew does not have *Joel.*
z40 Most Hebrew manuscripts; some Hebrew manuscripts, one Septuagint manuscript and Syriac *Maaseiah*

*See the note on page 15.

°20 ק צוף

בֶּן־ גֵּרְשֹׁם בֶּן־ לֵוִי׃ (29[44]) וּבְנֵי מְרָרִי אֲחֵיהֶם
son-of Gershom son-of Levi (29[44]) and-sons-of Merari associates-of-them

עַל־ הַשְּׂמֹאול אֵיתָן בֶּן־ קִישִׁי בֶּן־ עַבְדִּי בֶּן־ מַלּוּךְ׃
at the-left-hand Ethan son-of Kishi son-of Abdi son-of Malluch

(30[45]) בֶּן־ חֲשַׁבְיָה בֶּן־ אֲמַצְיָה בֶּן־ חִלְקִיָּה׃ (31[46]) בֶּן־
(30[45]) son-of Hashabiah son-of Amaziah son-of Hilkiah (31[46]) son-of

אַמְצִי בֶּן־ בָּנִי בֶּן־ שָׁמֶר׃ (32[47]) בֶּן־ מַחְלִי בֶּן־ מוּשִׁי בֶּן־
Amzi son-of Bani son-of Shemer (32[47]) son-of Mahli son-of Mushi son-of

מְרָרִי בֶּן־ לֵוִי׃ (33[48]) וַאֲחֵיהֶם הַלְוִיִּם
Merari son-of Levi (33[48]) and-fellows-of-them the-Levites

נְתוּנִים לְכָל־ עֲבוֹדַת מִשְׁכַּן בֵּית הָאֱלֹהִים׃
ones-being-assigned to-all-of duty-of tabernacle house-of the-God

(34[49]) וְאַהֲרֹן וּבָנָיו מַקְטִירִים עַל־ מִזְבַּח
(34[49]) but-Aaron and-descendants-of-him ones-offering on altar-of

הָעוֹלָה וְעַל־ מִזְבַּח הַקְּטֹרֶת לְכֹל מְלֶאכֶת
the-burnt-offering and-on altar-of the-incense for-all-of work-of

קֹדֶשׁ הַקֳּדָשִׁים וּלְכַפֵּר עַל־ יִשְׂרָאֵל כְּכֹל אֲשֶׁר
Most-Holy-of the-Holy-Places and-to-atone for Israel as-all that

צִוָּה מֹשֶׁה עֶבֶד הָאֱלֹהִים׃ (35[50]) וְאֵלֶּה בְּנֵי
he-commanded Moses servant-of the-God (35[50]) and-these descendants-of

אַהֲרֹן אֶלְעָזָר בְּנוֹ פִּינְחָס בְּנוֹ אֲבִישׁוּעַ בְּנוֹ׃
Aaron Eleazar son-of-him Phinehas son-of-him Abishua son-of-him

(36[51]) בֻּקִּי בְנוֹ עֻזִּי בְנוֹ זְרַחְיָה בְנוֹ׃
(36[51]) Bukki son-of-him Uzzi son-of-him Zerahiah son-of-him

(37[52]) מְרָיוֹת בְּנוֹ אֲמַרְיָה בְנוֹ אֲחִיטוּב בְּנוֹ׃
(37[52]) Meraioth son-of-him Amariah son-of-him Ahitub son-of-him

(38[53]) צָדוֹק בְּנוֹ אֲחִימַעַץ בְּנוֹ׃ (39[54]) וְאֵלֶּה
(38[53]) Zadok son-of-him Ahimaaz son-of-him (39[54]) and-these

מוֹשְׁבוֹתָם לְטִירוֹתָם בִּגְבוּלָם לִבְנֵי
settlements-of-them by-locations-of-them in-territory-of-them to-descendants-of

אַהֲרֹן לְמִשְׁפַּחַת† הַקְּהָתִי כִּי לָהֶם הָיָה הַגּוֹרָל׃
Aaron of-clan-of the-Kohathite because for-them he-was the-lot

(40[55]) וַיִּתְּנוּ לָהֶם אֶת־ חֶבְרוֹן בְּאֶרֶץ יְהוּדָה וְאֶת־
(40[55]) and-they-gave to-them *** Hebron in-land-of Judah with

מִגְרָשֶׁיהָ סְבִיבֹתֶיהָ׃ (41[56]) וְאֶת־ שְׂדֵה הָעִיר וְאֶת־
pasturelands-of-her ones-around-her (41[56]) but field-of the-city and

חֲצֵרֶיהָ נָתְנוּ לְכָלֵב בֶּן־ יְפֻנֶּה׃ (42[57]) וְלִבְנֵי
villages-of-her they-gave to-Caleb son-of Jephunneh (42[57]) so-to-sons-of

of Adaiah,
42the son of Ethan, the son
of Zimmah,
the son of Shimei, 43the
son of Jahath,
the son of Gershon, the
son of Levi;
44and from their associates,
the Merarites, at his left
hand:
Ethan son of Kishi, the
son of Abdi,
the son of Malluch, 45the
son of Hashabiah,
the son of Amaziah, the
son of Hilkiah,
46the son of Amzi, the son
of Bani,
the son of Shemer, 47the
son of Mahli,
the son of Mushi, the son
of Merari,
the son of Levi.

48Their fellow Levites were
assigned to all the other duties
of the tabernacle, the house of
God. 49But Aaron and his descendants were the ones who
presented offerings on the altar of burnt offering and on
the altar of incense in connec-
tion with all that was done in
the Most Holy Place, making
atonement for Israel, in accordance with all that Moses
the servant of God had commanded.

50These were the descend-
ants of Aaron:
Eleazar his son, Phinehas
his son,
Abishua his son, 51Bukki
his son,
Uzzi his son, Zerahiah
his son,
52Meraioth his son, Ama-
riah his son,
Ahitub his son, 53Zadok
his son
and Ahimaaz his son.

54These were the locations of
their settlements allotted as
their territory (they were assigned to the descendants of
Aaron who were from the Kohathite clan, because the first
lot was for them):
55They were given He-
bron in Judah with its surrounding pasturelands.
56But the fields and villages
around the city were given
to Caleb son of Jephunneh.
57So the descendants of

*See the note on page 15.

†39 Most mss have the accent under the *pe* (פַּחַת־).

אַהֲרֹן נָתְנוּ אֶת־ עָרֵי הַמִּקְלָט אֶת־ חֶבְרוֹן וְאֶת־ לִבְנָה וְאֶת־
and Libnah and Hebron *** the-refuge cities-of *** they-gave Aaron

מִגְרָשֶׁהָ וְאֶת־ יַתִּר וְאֶת־ אֶשְׁתְּמֹעַ וְאֶת־ מִגְרָשֶׁהָ׃ וְאֶת־
and (43[58]) pastures-of-her and Eshtemoa and Jattir and pastures-of-her

חִילֵז וְאֶת־ מִגְרָשֶׁהָ אֶת־ דְּבִיר וְאֶת־ מִגְרָשֶׁהָ׃ וְאֶת־
and (44[59]) pastures-of-her and Debir *** pastures-of-her and Hilen

עָשָׁן וְאֶת־ מִגְרָשֶׁהָ וְאֶת־ בֵּית שֶׁמֶשׁ וְאֶת־ מִגְרָשֶׁהָ׃
pastures-of-her and Shemesh Beth and pastures-of-her and Ashan

וּמִמַּטֵּה בִנְיָמִן אֶת־ גֶּבַע וְאֶת־ מִגְרָשֶׁהָ וְאֶת־ עָלֶמֶת
Alemeth and pastures-of-her and Geba *** Benjamin and-from-tribe-of (45[60])

וְאֶת־ מִגְרָשֶׁהָ וְאֶת־ עֲנָתוֹת וְאֶת־ מִגְרָשֶׁהָ כָּל־ עָרֵיהֶם
towns-of-them all-of pastures-of-her and Anathoth and pastures-of-her and

שְׁלֹשׁ־ עֶשְׂרֵה עִיר בְּמִשְׁפְּחוֹתֵיהֶם׃ וְלִבְנֵי קְהָת
Kohath and-to-descendants-of (46[61]) among-clans-of-them town ten three-of

הַנּוֹתָרִים מִמִּשְׁפַּחַת הַמַּטֶּה מִמַּחֲצִית מַטֵּה חֲצִי
half-of tribe-of from-half-of the-tribe from-clan-of the-ones-being-left

מְנַשֶּׁה בַּגּוֹרָל עָרִים עֶשֶׂר׃ וְלִבְנֵי גֵרְשׁוֹם
Gershom and-to-descendants-of (47[62]) ten towns by-the-lot Manasseh

לְמִשְׁפְּחוֹתָם מִמַּטֵּה יִשָּׂשכָר וּמִמַּטֵּה אָשֵׁר
Asher and-from-tribe-of Issachar from-tribe-of by-clans-of-them

וּמִמַּטֵּה נַפְתָּלִי וּמִמַּטֵּה מְנַשֶּׁה בַּבָּשָׁן עָרִים
towns in-the-Bashan Manasseh and-from-tribe-of Naphtali and-from-tribe-of

שְׁלֹשׁ עֶשְׂרֵה׃ לִבְנֵי מְרָרִי לְמִשְׁפְּחוֹתָם מִמַּטֵּה
from-tribe-of by-clans-of-them Merari to-descendants-of (48[63]) ten three-of

רְאוּבֵן וּמִמַּטֵּה־ גָד וּמִמַּטֵּה זְבוּלֻן בַּגּוֹרָל עָרִים
towns by-the-lot Zebulun and-from-tribe-of Gad and-from-tribe-of Reuben

שְׁתֵּים עֶשְׂרֵה׃ וַיִּתְּנוּ בְנֵי־ יִשְׂרָאֵל לַלְוִיִּם אֶת־ הֶעָרִים
the-towns *** to-the-Levites Israel sons-of so-they-gave (49[64]) ten two

וְאֶת־ מִגְרְשֵׁיהֶם׃ וַיִּתְּנוּ בַגּוֹרָל מִמַּטֵּה בְנֵי־
sons-of from-tribe-of by-the-lot and-they-gave (50[65]) pastures-of-them and

יְהוּדָה וּמִמַּטֵּה בְנֵי־ שִׁמְעוֹן וּמִמַּטֵּה בְּנֵי בִנְיָמִן
Benjamin sons-of and-from-tribe-of Simeon sons-of and-from-tribe-of Judah

אֵת הֶעָרִים הָאֵלֶּה אֲשֶׁר־ יִקְרְאוּ אֶתְהֶם בְּשֵׁמוֹת׃
by-names them they-called which the-these the-towns ***

וּמִמִּשְׁפְּחוֹת בְּנֵי קְהָת וַיְהִי עָרֵי גְבוּלָם
territory-of-them towns-of and-he-was Kohath sons-of and-from-clans-of (51[66])

מִמַּטֵּה אֶפְרָיִם׃ וַיִּתְּנוּ לָהֶם אֶת־ עָרֵי הַמִּקְלָט
the-refuge cities-of *** to-them and-they-gave (52[67]) Ephraim from-tribe-of

Aaron were given Hebron
(a city of refuge), and Libnah,[a] Jattir, Eshtemoa,
58Hilen, Debir, 59Ashan, Juttah[b] and Beth Shemesh, together with their pasturelands. 60And from the tribe
of Benjamin they were giv-
en Gibeon,[c] Geba, Alemeth
and Anathoth, together
with their pasturelands.

These towns, which were
distributed among the Ko-
hathite clans, were thirteen
in all.

61The rest of Kohath's descendants were allotted ten
towns from the clans of half
the tribe of Manasseh.

62The descendants of Ger-
shon, clan by clan, were allotted thirteen towns from the
tribes of Issachar, Asher and
Naphtali, and from the part of
the tribe of Manasseh that is
in Bashan.

63The descendants of Merari,
clan by clan, were allotted
twelve towns from the tribes
of Reuben, Gad and Zebulun.

64So the Israelites gave the
Levites these towns and their
pasturelands. 65From the tribes
of Judah, Simeon and Benjamin they allotted the previ-
ously named towns.

66Some of the Kohathite
clans were given as their territory towns from the tribe of
Ephraim.

67In the hill country of
Ephraim they were given
Shechem (a city of refuge),

[a]57 See Joshua 21:13; Hebrew *given the cities of refuge: Hebron, Libnah.*
[b]59 Syriac (see also Septuagint and Joshua 21:16); Hebrew does not have *Juttah.*
[c]60 See Joshua 21:17; Hebrew does not have *Gibeon.*

*See the note on page 15.

אֶת־שְׁכֶם וְאֶת־מִגְרָשֶׁהָ בְּהַר אֶפְרָיִם וְאֶת־גֶּזֶר וְאֶת־
and Gezer and Ephraim in-hill-country-of pastures-of-her and Shechem ***

מִגְרָשֶׁהָ׃ וְאֶת־יָקְמְעָם וְאֶת־מִגְרָשֶׁהָ וְאֶת־בֵּית חוֹרוֹן
Horon Beth and pastures-of-her and Jokmeam and (53[68]) pastures-of-her

וְאֶת־מִגְרָשֶׁהָ׃ וְאֶת־אַיָּלוֹן וְאֶת־מִגְרָשֶׁהָ וְאֶת־גַּת־רִמּוֹן
Rimmon Gath and pastures-of-her and Aijalon and (54[69]) pastures-of-her and

וְאֶת־מִגְרָשֶׁהָ׃ וּמִמַּחֲצִית מַטֵּה מְנַשֶּׁה אֶת־עָנֵר
Aner *** Manasseh tribe-of and-from-half-of (55[70]) pastures-of-her and

וְאֶת־מִגְרָשֶׁהָ וְאֶת־בִּלְעָם וְאֶת־מִגְרָשֶׁהָ לְמִשְׁפַּחַת לִבְנֵי־
of-sons-of to-clan pastures-of-her and Bileam and pastures-of-her and

קְהָת הַנּוֹתָרִים׃ לִבְנֵי גֵּרְשׁוֹם מִמִּשְׁפַּחַת חֲצִי
half-of from-clan-of Gershom to-sons-of (56[71]) the-ones-being-left Kohath

מַטֵּה מְנַשֶּׁה אֶת־גּוֹלָן בַּבָּשָׁן וְאֶת־מִגְרָשֶׁהָ וְאֶת־עַשְׁתָּרוֹת
Ashtaroth and pastures-of-her and in-the-Bashan Golan *** Manasseh tribe-of

וְאֶת־מִגְרָשֶׁיהָ׃ וּמִמַּטֵּה יִשָּׂשכָר אֶת־קֶדֶשׁ וְאֶת־
and Kedesh *** Issachar and-from-tribe-of (57[72]) pastures-of-her and

מִגְרָשֶׁהָ אֶת־דָּבְרַת וְאֶת־מִגְרָשֶׁהָ׃ וְאֶת־רָאמוֹת וְאֶת־
and Ramoth and (58[73]) pastures-of-her and Daberath *** pastures-of-her

מִגְרָשֶׁהָ וְאֶת־עָנֵם וְאֶת־מִגְרָשֶׁהָ׃ וּמִמַּטֵּה
and-from-tribe-of (59[74]) pastures-of-her and Anem and pastures-of-her

אָשֵׁר אֶת־מָשָׁל וְאֶת־מִגְרָשֶׁהָ וְאֶת־עַבְדּוֹן וְאֶת־מִגְרָשֶׁהָ׃
pastures-of-her and Abdon and pastures-of-her and Mashal *** Asher

וְאֶת־חוּקֹק וְאֶת־מִגְרָשֶׁהָ וְאֶת־רְחֹב וְאֶת־מִגְרָשֶׁהָ׃
pastures-of-her and Rehob and pastures-of-her and Hukok and (60[75])

וּמִמַּטֵּה נַפְתָּלִי אֶת־קֶדֶשׁ בַּגָּלִיל וְאֶת־
and in-the-Galilee Kedesh *** Naphtali and-from-tribe-of (61[76])

מִגְרָשֶׁהָ וְאֶת־חַמּוֹן וְאֶת־מִגְרָשֶׁהָ וְאֶת־קִרְיָתַיִם וְאֶת־
and Kiriathaim and pastures-of-her and Hammon and pastures-of-her

מִגְרָשֶׁהָ׃ לִבְנֵי מְרָרִי הַנּוֹתָרִים מִמַּטֵּה
from-tribe-of the-ones-being-left Merari to-sons-of (62[77]) pastures-of-her

זְבוּלֻן אֶת־רִמּוֹנוֹ וְאֶת־מִגְרָשֶׁהָ אֶת־תָּבוֹר וְאֶת־מִגְרָשֶׁהָ׃
pastures-of-her and Tabor *** pastures-of-her and Rimmono *** Zebulun

וּמֵעֵבֶר לְיַרְדֵּן יְרֵחוֹ לְמִזְרַח הַיַּרְדֵּן
the-Jordan at-east-of Jericho of-Jordan and-from-across (63[78])

מִמַּטֵּה רְאוּבֵן אֶת־בֶּצֶר בַּמִּדְבָּר וְאֶת־מִגְרָשֶׁהָ וְאֶת־יַהְצָה
Jahzah and pastures-of-her and in-the-desert Bezer *** Reuben from-tribe-of

וְאֶת־מִגְרָשֶׁהָ׃ וְאֶת־קְדֵמוֹת וְאֶת־מִגְרָשֶׁהָ וְאֶת־מֵיפַעַת
Mephaath and pastures-of-her and Kedemoth and (64[79]) pastures-of-her and

and Gezer,[d] [68]Jokmeam, Beth Horon, [69]Aijalon and Gath Rimmon, together with their pasturelands.

[70]And from half the tribe of Manasseh the Israelites gave Aner and Bileam, together with their pasturelands, to the rest of the Kohathite clans.

[71]The Gershonites received the following:
From the clan of the half-tribe of Manasseh
they received Golan in Bashan and also Ashtaroth, together with their pasturelands;
[72]from the tribe of Issachar
they received Kedesh, Daberath, [73]Ramoth and Anem, together with their pasturelands;
[74]from the tribe of Asher
they received Mashal, Abdon, [75]Hukok and Rehob, together with their pasturelands;
[76]and from the tribe of Naphtali
they received Kedesh in Galilee, Hammon and Kiriathaim, together with their pasturelands.

[77]The Merarites (the rest of the Levites) received the following:
From the tribe of Zebulun
they received Jokneam, Kartah,[e] Rimmono and Tabor, together with their pasturelands;
[78]from the tribe of Reuben across the Jordan east of Jericho
they received Bezer in the desert, Jahzah, [79]Kedemoth and Mephaath, together with their pasturelands;

[d]67 See Joshua 21:21; Hebrew *given the cities of refuge: Shechem, Gezer.*
[e]77 See Septuagint and Joshua 21:34; Hebrew does not have *Jokneam, Kartah.*

*See the note on page 15.

וְאֶת־ מִגְרָשֶׁיהָ׃ וּמִמַּטֵּה־ גָד אֶת־ רָאמוֹת בַּגִּלְעָד
in-the-Gilead Ramoth *** Gad and-from-tribe-of (65[80]) pastures-of-her and

וְאֶת־ מִגְרָשֶׁיהָ וְאֶת־ מַחֲנַיִם וְאֶת־ מִגְרָשֶׁיהָ׃ וְאֶת־ חֶשְׁבּוֹן
Heshbon and (66[81]) pastures-of-her and Mahanaim and pastures-of-her and

וְאֶת־ מִגְרָשֶׁיהָ וְאֶת־ יַעְזֵיר וְאֶת־ מִגְרָשֶׁיהָ׃ וְלִבְנֵי
and-to-sons-of (7:1) pastures-of-her and Jazer and pastures-of-her and

יִשָּׂשכָר תּוֹלָע וּפוּאָה יָשִׁיב וְשִׁמְרוֹן אַרְבָּעָה׃ וּבְנֵי תוֹלָע עֻזִּי
Uzzi Tola and-sons-of (2) four and-Shimron Jashub and-Puah Tola Issachar

וּרְפָיָה וִירִיאֵל וְיַחְמַי וְיִבְשָׂם וּשְׁמוּאֵל רָאשִׁים לְבֵית־
of-family-of heads and-Samuel and-Ibsam and-Jahmai and-Jeriel and-Rephaiah

אֲבוֹתָם לְתוֹלָע גִּבּוֹרֵי חַיִל לְתֹלְדוֹתָם מִסְפָּרָם
number-of-them in-genealogies-of-them fight men-of of-Tola fathers-of-them

בִּימֵי דָוִיד עֶשְׂרִים־ וּשְׁנַיִם אֶלֶף וְשֵׁשׁ מֵאוֹת׃ וּבְנֵי
and-sons-of (3) hundreds and-six thousand and-two twenty David in-days-of

עֻזִּי יִזְרַחְיָה וּבְנֵי יִזְרַחְיָה מִיכָאֵל וְעֹבַדְיָה וְיוֹאֵל יִשִּׁיָּה
Isshiah and-Joel and-Obadiah Michael Izrahiah and-sons-of Izrahiah Uzzi

חֲמִשָּׁה רָאשִׁים כֻּלָּם׃ וַעֲלֵיהֶם לְתֹלְדוֹתָם לְבֵית
by-family-of by-genealogies-of-them and-with-them (4) all-of-them chiefs five

אֲבוֹתָם גְּדוּדֵי צְבָא מִלְחָמָה שְׁלֹשִׁים וְשִׁשָּׁה אֶלֶף כִּי־
for thousand and-six thirty battle army-of men-of fathers-of-them

הִרְבּוּ נָשִׁים וּבָנִים׃ וַאֲחֵיהֶם לְכֹל
of-all-of and-relatives-of-them (5) and-children wives they-had-many

מִשְׁפְּחוֹת יִשָּׂשכָר גִּבּוֹרֵי חֲיָלִים שְׁמוֹנִים וְשִׁבְעָה אֶלֶף הִתְיַחְשָׂם
to-be-listed-them thousand and-seven eighty fights men-of Issachar clans-of

לַכֹּל׃ בִּנְיָמִן בֶּלַע וָבֶכֶר וִידִיעֲאֵל שְׁלֹשָׁה׃ וּבְנֵי
and-sons-of (7) three and-Jediael and-Beker Bela Benjamin (6) as-the-total

בֶּלַע אֶצְבּוֹן וְעֻזִּי וְעֻזִּיאֵל וִירִימוֹת וְעִירִי חֲמִשָּׁה רָאשֵׁי
heads-of five and-Iri and-Jerimoth and-Uzziel and-Uzzi Ezbon Bela

בֵּית אָבוֹת גִּבּוֹרֵי חֲיָלִים וְהִתְיַחְשָׂם עֶשְׂרִים וּשְׁנַיִם
and-two twenty and-to-be-listed-them fights men-of fathers family-of

אֶלֶף וּשְׁלֹשִׁים וְאַרְבָּעָה׃ וּבְנֵי בֶכֶר זְמִירָה וְיוֹעָשׁ
and-Joash Zemirah Beker and-sons-of (8) and-four and-thirty thousand

וֶאֱלִיעֶזֶר וְאֶלְיוֹעֵינַי וְעָמְרִי וִירֵמוֹת וַאֲבִיָּה וַעֲנָתוֹת
and-Anathoth and-Abijah and-Jeremoth and-Omri and-Elioenai and-Eliezer

וְעָלָמֶת כָּל־ אֵלֶּה בְּנֵי־ בָכֶר׃ וְהִתְיַחְשָׂם
and-to-be-listed-them (9) Beker sons-of these all-of and-Alemeth

לְתֹלְדוֹתָם רָאשֵׁי בֵּית אֲבוֹתָם גִּבּוֹרֵי חָיִל
fight men-of fathers-of-them family-of heads-of in-genealogies-of-them

---

[80]and from the tribe of Gad they received Ramoth in Gilead, Mahanaim, [81]Heshbon and Jazer, together with their pasturelands.

Issachar

7 The sons of Issachar: Tola, Puah, Jashub and Shimron—four in all.
[2]The sons of Tola:
Uzzi, Rephaiah, Jeriel, Jahmai, Ibsam and Samuel—heads of their families. During the reign of David, the descendants of Tola listed as fighting men in their genealogy numbered 22,600.
[3]The son of Uzzi:
Izrahiah.
The sons of Izrahiah:
Michael, Obadiah, Joel and Isshiah. All five of them were chiefs. [4]According to their family genealogy, they had 36,000 men ready for battle, for they had many wives and children.
[5]The relatives who were fighting men belonging to all the clans of Issachar, as listed in their genealogy, were 87,000 in all.

Benjamin

[6]Three sons of Benjamin:
Bela, Beker and Jediael.
[7]The sons of Bela:
Ezbon, Uzzi, Uzziel, Jerimoth and Iri, heads of families—five in all. Their genealogical record listed 22,034 fighting men.
[8]The sons of Beker:
Zemirah, Joash, Eliezer, Elioenai, Omri, Jeremoth, Abijah, Anathoth and Alemeth. All these were the sons of Beker. [9]Their genealogical record listed the heads of families and 20,200 fighting men.

*See the note on page 15.

°1 ק ישוב

עֶשְׂרִים אֶלֶף וּמָאתָיִם׃ (10) וּבְנֵי יְדִיעֲאֵל בִּלְהָן וּבְנֵי

and-sons-of Bilhan Jediael and-sons-of (10) and-two-hundreds thousand twenty

בִלְהָן יְעִישׁ וּבִנְיָמִן וְאֵהוּד וּכְנַעֲנָה וְזֵיתָן וְתַרְשִׁישׁ

and-Tarshish and-Zethan and-Kenaanah and-Ehud and-Benjamin Jeush Bilhan

וַאֲחִישָׁחַר׃ (11) כָּל־ אֵלֶּה בְּנֵי יְדִיעֲאֵל לְרָאשֵׁי הָאָבוֹת

the-fathers of-heads-of Jediael sons-of these all-of (11) and-Ahishahar

גִּבּוֹרֵי חֲיָלִים שִׁבְעָה־עָשָׂר אֶלֶף וּמָאתַיִם יֹצְאֵי צָבָא

army ones-going-out-of and-two-hundreds thousand ten seven fights men-of

לַמִּלְחָמָה׃ (12) וְשֻׁפִּם וְחֻפִּם בְּנֵי עִיר חֻשִׁם

Hushites Ir descendants-of and-Huppites and-Shuppites (12) to-the-war

בְּנֵי אַחֵר׃ (13) בְּנֵי נַפְתָּלִי יַחֲצִיאֵל וְגוּנִי וְיֵצֶר

and-Jezer and-Guni Jahziel Naphtali sons-of (13) Aher descendants-of

וְשַׁלּוּם בְּנֵי בִלְהָה׃ (14) בְּנֵי מְנַשֶּׁה אַשְׂרִיאֵל אֲשֶׁר יָלָדָה

she-bore whom Asriel Manasseh descendants-of (14) Bilhah sons-of and-Shallum

פִּילַגְשׁוֹ הָאֲרַמִּיָּה יָלְדָה אֶת־ מָכִיר אֲבִי גִלְעָד׃

Gilead father-of Makir *** she-bore the-Aramean concubine-of-him

(15) וּמָכִיר לָקַח אִשָּׁה לְחֻפִּים וּלְשֻׁפִּים וְשֵׁם

and-name-of and-from-Shuppites from-Huppites wife he-took and-Makir (15)

אֲחֹתוֹ מַעֲכָה וְשֵׁם הַשֵּׁנִי צְלָפְחָד וַתִּהְיֶנָה

and-they-were Zelophehad the-second and-name-of Maacah sister-of-him

לִצְלָפְחָד בָּנוֹת׃ (16) וַתֵּלֶד מַעֲכָה אֵשֶׁת־ מָכִיר בֵּן

son Makir wife-of Maacah and-she-bore (16) daughters to-Zelophehad

וַתִּקְרָא שְׁמוֹ פֶּרֶשׁ וְשֵׁם אָחִיו שָׁרֶשׁ

Sheresh brother-of-him and-name-of Peresh name-of-him and-she-called

וּבָנָיו אוּלָם וָרָקֶם׃ (17) וּבְנֵי אוּלָם בְּדָן אֵלֶּה בְּנֵי

sons-of these Bedan Ulam and-sons-of (17) and-Rakem Ulam and-sons-of-him

גִלְעָד בֶּן־ מָכִיר בֶּן־ מְנַשֶּׁה׃ (18) וַאֲחֹתוֹ הַמֹּלֶכֶת

Hammoleketh and-sister-of-him (18) Manasseh son-of Makir son-of Gilead

יָלְדָה אֶת־ אִישְׁהוֹד וְאֶת־ אֲבִיעֶזֶר וְאֶת־ מַחְלָה׃ (19) וַיִּהְיוּ בְּנֵי

sons-of and-they-were (19) Mahlah and Abiezer and Ishhod *** she-bore

שְׁמִידָע אַחְיָן וָשֶׁכֶם וְלִקְחִי וַאֲנִיעָם׃ (20) וּבְנֵי

and-descendants-of (20) and-Aniam and-Likhi and-Shechem Ahian Shemida

אֶפְרַיִם שׁוּתֶלַח וּבֶרֶד בְּנוֹ וְתַחַת בְּנוֹ וְאֶלְעָדָה

and-Eleadah son-of-him and-Tahath son-of-him and-Bered Shuthelah Ephraim

בְנוֹ וְתַחַת בְּנוֹ׃ (21) וְזָבָד בְּנוֹ וְשׁוּתֶלַח

and-Shuthelah son-of-him and-Zabad (21) son-of-him and-Tahath son-of-him

בְּנוֹ וְעֵזֶר וְאֶלְעָד וַהֲרָגוּם אַנְשֵׁי־ גַת

Gath men-of now-they-killed-them and-Elead now-Ezer son-of-him

[10]The son of Jediael:
Bilhan.
The sons of Bilhan:
Jeush, Benjamin, Ehud,
Kenaanah, Zethan, Tar-
shish and Ahishahar.
[11]All these sons of Jediael
were heads of families.
There were 17,200
fighting men ready to go
out to war.
[12]The Shuppites and Huppites were the descend-
ants of Ir, and the Hush-
ites the descendants of
Aher.

Naphtali

[13]The sons of Naphtali:
Jahziel, Guni, Jezer and
Shillem[f]—his sons by
Bilhah.

Manasseh

[14]The descendants of Manasseh:
Asriel was his descend-
ant through his Aramean
concubine. She gave birth
to Makir the father of Gilead. [15]Makir took a wife
from among the Huppites
and Shuppites. His sister's
name was Maacah.
Another descendant was
named Zelophehad, who
had only daughters.
[16]Makir's wife Maacah
gave birth to a son and
named him Peresh. His
brother was named She-
resh, and his sons were
Ulam and Rakem.
[17]The son of Ulam:
Bedan.
These were the sons of Gilead son of Makir, the son
of Manasseh. [18]His sister
Hammoleketh gave birth
to Ishhod, Abiezer and
Mahlah.
[19]The sons of Shemida were:
Ahian, Shechem, Likhi
and Aniam.

Ephraim

[20]The descendants of
Ephraim:
Shuthelah, Bered his son,
Tahath his son, Eleadah
his son,
Tahath his son, [21]Zabad
his son
and Shuthelah his son.
Ezer and Elead were
killed by the native-born
men of Gath, when they

[f]13 Some Hebrew and Septuagint manuscripts (see also Gen. 46:24 and Num. 26:49); most Hebrew manuscripts *Shallum*

°10 ק יעוש

הַנּוֹלָדִים בָּאָרֶץ כִּי יָרְדוּ לָקַחַת אֶת־
*** to-seize they-went-down when in-the-land the-ones-being-born

מִקְנֵיהֶם׃ וַיִּתְאַבֵּל אֶפְרַיִם אֲבִיהֶם יָמִים רַבִּים
many days father-of-them Ephraim and-he-mourned (22) livestocks-of-them

וַיָּבֹאוּ אֶחָיו לְנַחֲמוֹ׃ וַיָּבֹא אֶל־
into then-he-went (23) to-comfort-him relatives-of-him and-they-came

אִשְׁתּוֹ וַתַּהַר וַתֵּלֶד בֵּן וַיִּקְרָא אֶת־
*** and-he-called son and-she-bore and-she-became-pregnant wife-of-him

שְׁמוֹ בְּרִיעָה כִּי בְרָעָה הָיְתָה בְּבֵיתוֹ׃
in-family-of-him she-was in-misfortune because Beriah name-of-him

וּבִתּוֹ שֶׁאֱרָה וַתִּבֶן אֶת־ בֵּית־ חוֹרוֹן הַתַּחְתּוֹן
the-Lower Horon Beth *** and-she-built Sheerah and-daughter-of-him (24)

וְאֶת־ הָעֶלְיוֹן וְאֵת אֻזֵּן שֶׁאֱרָה׃ וְרֶפַח בְּנוֹ וְרֶשֶׁף
and-Resheph son-of-him and-Rephah (25) Sheerah Uzzen and the-Upper and

וְתֶלַח בְּנוֹ וְתַחַן בְּנוֹ׃ לַעְדָּן בְּנוֹ עַמִּיהוּד
Ammihud son-of-him Ladan (26) son-of-him and-Tahan son-of-him and-Telah

בְּנוֹ אֱלִישָׁמָע בְּנוֹ׃ נוֹן בְּנוֹ יְהוֹשֻׁעַ בְּנוֹ׃
son-of-him Joshua son-of-him Nun (27) son-of-him Elishama son-of-him

וַאֲחֻזָּתָם וּמֹשְׁבוֹתָם בֵּית־ אֵל וּבְנֹתֶיהָ
and-villages-of-her El Beth and-settlements-of-them and-land-of-them (28)

וְלַמִּזְרָח נַעֲרָן וְלַמַּעֲרָב גֶּזֶר וּבְנֹתֶיהָ וּשְׁכֶם
and-Shechem and-villages-of-her Gezer and-to-the-west Naaran and-to-the-east

וּבְנֹתֶיהָ עַד־ עַיָּה וּבְנֹתֶיהָ׃ וְעַל־ יְדֵי
borders-of and-along (29) and-villages-of-her Ayyah to and-villages-of-her

בְנֵי־ מְנַשֶּׁה בֵּית־ שְׁאָן וּבְנֹתֶיהָ תַּעְנַךְ וּבְנֹתֶיהָ
and-villages-of-her Taanach and-villages-of-her Shan Beth Manasseh sons-of

מְגִדּוֹ וּבְנוֹתֶיהָ דּוֹר וּבְנוֹתֶיהָ בְּאֵלֶּה יָשְׁבוּ
they-lived in-these and-villages-of-her Dor and-villages-of-her Megiddo

בְּנֵי יוֹסֵף בֶּן־ יִשְׂרָאֵל׃ בְּנֵי אָשֵׁר יִמְנָה וְיִשְׁוָה
and-Ishvah Imnah Asher sons-of (30) Israel son-of Joseph descendants-of

וְיִשְׁוִי וּבְרִיעָה וְשֶׂרַח אֲחוֹתָם׃ וּבְנֵי בְרִיעָה
Beriah and-sons-of (31) sister-of-them and-Serah and-Beriah and-Ishvi

חֶבֶר וּמַלְכִּיאֵל הוּא אֲבִי בִרְזָוִת׃ וְחֶבֶר הוֹלִיד אֶת־
*** he-fathered and-Heber (32) Birzaith father-of he and-Malkiel Heber

יַפְלֵט וְאֶת־ שׁוֹמֵר וְאֶת־ חוֹתָם וְאֵת שׁוּעָא אֲחוֹתָם׃ וּבְנֵי
and-sons-of (33) sister-of-them Shua and Hotham and Shomer and Japhlet

יַפְלֵט פָּסַךְ וּבִמְהָל וְעַשְׁוָת אֵלֶּה בְּנֵי יַפְלֵט׃
Japhlet sons-of these and-Ashvath and-Bimhal Pasach Japhlet

°31 ק ברזית

went down to seize their livestock. [22]Their father Ephraim mourned for them many days, and his relatives came to comfort him. [23]Then he lay with his wife again, and she became pregnant and gave birth to a son. He named him Beriah,[g] because there had been misfortune in his family. [24]His daughter was Sheerah, who built Lower and Upper Beth Horon as well as Uzzen Sheerah.

[25]Rephah was his son, Resheph his son,
Telah his son, Tahan his son,
[26]Ladan his son, Ammihud his son,
Elishama his son, [27]Nun his son
and Joshua his son.

[28]Their lands and settlements included Bethel and its surrounding villages, Naaran to the east, Gezer and its villages to the west, and Shechem and its villages all the way to Ayyah and its villages. [29]Along the borders of Manasseh were Beth Shan, Taanach, Megiddo and Dor, together with their villages. The descendants of Joseph son of Israel lived in these towns.

Asher

[30]The sons of Asher:
Imnah, Ishvah, Ishvi and Beriah. Their sister was Serah.
[31]The sons of Beriah:
Heber and Malkiel, who was the father of Birzaith.
[32]Heber was the father of Japhlet, Shomer and Hotham and of their sister Shua.
[33]The sons of Japhlet:
Pasach, Bimhal and Ashvath.
These were Japhlet's sons.

g23 *Beriah* sounds like the Hebrew for *misfortune*.

ובני שמר אחי ורוהגה יחבה וארם׃ ובן־
and-son-of (35) and-Aram and-Hubbah and-Rohgah Ahi Shomer and-sons-of (34)

הלם אחיו צופח וימנע ושלש ועמל׃ בני
sons-of (36) and-Amal and-Shelesh and-Imna Zophah brother-of-him Helem

צופח סוח וחרנפר ושועל ובירי וימרה׃ בצר והוד
and-Hod Bezer (37) and-Imrah and-Beri and-Shual and-Harnepher Suah Zophah

ושמא ושלשה ויתרן ובארא׃ ובני יתר
Jether and-sons-of (38) and-Beera and-Ithran and-Shilshah and-Shamma

יפנה ופספה וארא׃ ובני עלא ארח וחניאל
and-Hanniel Arah Ulla and-sons-of (39) and-Ara and-Pispah Jephunneh

ורציא׃ כל־ אלה בני־ אשר ראשי בית־
family-of heads-of Asher descendants-of these all-of (40) and-Rizia

האבות ברורים גבורי חילים ראשי
outstanding-ones-of brave-ones warriors-of ones-being-choice the-fathers

הנשיאים והתיחשם בצבא במלחמה מספרם
number-of-them for-the-battle in-the-army and-to-be-listed-them the-leaders

אנשים עשרים וששה אלף׃ ובנימן הוליד את־בלע
Bela *** he-fathered and-Benjamin (8:1) thousand and-six twenty men

בכרו אשבל השני ואחרח השלישי׃ נוחה הרביעי
the-fourth Nohah (2) the-third and-Aharah the-second Ashbel firstborn-of-him

ורפא החמישי׃ ויהיו בנים לבלע אדר וגרא ואביהוד׃
and-Abihud and-Gera Addar of-Bela sons and-they-were (3) the-fifth and-Rapha

ואבישוע ונעמן ואחוח׃ וגרא ושפופן וחורם׃
and-Huram and-Shephuphan and-Gera (5) and-Ahoah and-Naaman and-Abishua (4)

ואלה בני אחוד אלה הם ראשי אבות
fathers heads-of they these Ehud descendants-of and-these (6)

ליושבי גבע ויגלום אל־ מנחת׃ ונעמן
and-Naaman (7) Manahath to and-they-deported-them Geba of-ones-living-of

ואחיה וגרא הוא הגלם והוליד את־עזא ואת־אחיחד׃
Ahihud and Uzza *** and-he-fathered he-deported-them he and-Gera and-Ahijah

ושחרים הוליד בשדה מואב מן־ שלחו אתם
them to-divorce-him after Moab in-country-of he-fathered and-Shaharaim (8)

חושים ואת־בערא נשיו׃ ויולד מן־ חדש אשתו
wife-of-him Hodesh by and-he-fathered (9) wives-of-him Baara and Hushim

את־יובב ואת־צביא ואת־מישא ואת־מלכם׃ ואת־יעוץ ואת־שכיה ואת־
and Sakia and Jeuz and (10) Malcam and Mesha and Zibia and Jobab ***

מרמה אלה בניו ראשי אבות׃ ומחשים הוליד
he-fathered and-by-Hushim (11) fathers heads-of sons-of-him these Mirmah

34 The sons of Shomer:
Ahi, Rohgah,[h] Hubbah
and Aram.
35 The sons of his brother
Helem:
Zophah, Imna, Shelesh
and Amal.
36 The sons of Zophah:
Suah, Harnepher, Shual,
Beri, Imrah, 37 Bezer, Hod,
Shamma, Shilshah, Ith-
ran[i] and Beera.
38 The sons of Jether:
Jephunneh, Pispah and
Ara.
39 The sons of Ulla:
Arah, Hanniel and Rizia.
40 All these were descendants
of Asher—heads of families,
choice men, brave warriors
and outstanding leaders. The
number of men ready for battle, as listed in their genealogy, was 26,000.

The Genealogy of Saul the Benjamite

8 Benjamin was the father
of Bela his firstborn,
Ashbel the second son,
Aharah the third,
2 Nohah the fourth and
Rapha the fifth.
3 The sons of Bela were:
Addar, Gera, Abihud,[j]
4 Abishua, Naaman,
Ahoah, 5 Gera, Shephu-
phan and Huram.
6 These were the descend-
ants of Ehud, who were
heads of families of those
living in Geba and were
deported to Manahath:
7 Naaman, Ahijah, and
Gera, who deported them
and who was the father
of Uzza and Ahihud.
8 Sons were born to Shaha-
raim in Moab after he
had divorced his wives
Hushim and Baara. 9 By
his wife Hodesh he had
Jobab, Zibia, Mesha,
Malcam, 10 Jeuz, Sakia and
Mirmah. These were his
sons, heads of families.

[h] 34 Or *of his brother Shomer: Rohgah*
[i] 37 Possibly a variant of *Jether*
[j] 3 Or *Gera the father of Ehud*

°34a ק ורהגה
°34b ק וחבה

אֶת־אֲבִיטוּב וְאֶת־אֶלְפָּעַל׃ וּבְנֵי אֶלְפַּעַל עֵבֶר וּמִשְׁעָם וָשָׁמֶד
*** Abitub and Elpaal (12) and-sons-of Elpaal Eber and-Misham and-Shemed

הוּא בָּנָה אֶת־אוֹנוֹ וְאֶת־לֹד וּבְנֹתֶיהָ׃ וּבְרִעָה וָשֶׁמַע
he he-built *** Ono and Lod and-villages-of-her (13) and-Beriah and-Shema

הֵמָּה רָאשֵׁי הָאָבוֹת לְיוֹשְׁבֵי אַיָּלוֹן הֵמָּה הִבְרִיחוּ אֶת־
they heads-of the-fathers of-ones-living-of Aijalon they they-drove-out ***

יוֹשְׁבֵי גַת׃ וְאַחְיוֹ שָׁשַׁק וִירֵמוֹת׃ וּזְבַדְיָה
ones-inhabiting-of Gath (14) and-Ahio Shashak and-Jeremoth (15) and-Zebadiah

וַעֲרָד וָעָדֶר׃ וּמִיכָאֵל וְיִשְׁפָּה וְיוֹחָא בְּנֵי בְרִיעָה׃
and-Arad and-Eder (16) and-Michael and-Ishpah and-Joha sons-of Beriah

וּזְבַדְיָה וּמְשֻׁלָּם וְחִזְקִי וָחָבֶר׃ וְיִשְׁמְרַי
(17) and-Zebadiah and-Meshullam and-Hizki and-Heber (18) and-Ishmerai

וְיִזְלִיאָה וְיוֹבָב בְּנֵי אֶלְפָּעַל׃ וְיָקִים וְזִכְרִי וְזַבְדִּי׃
and-Izliah and-Jobab sons-of Elpaal (19) and-Jakim and-Zicri and-Zabdi

וֶאֱלִיעֵנַי וְצִלְּתַי וֶאֱלִיאֵל׃ וַעֲדָיָה וּבְרָאיָה
(20) and-Elienai and-Zillethai and-Eliel (21) and-Adaiah and-Beraiah

וְשִׁמְרָת בְּנֵי שִׁמְעִי׃ וְיִשְׁפָּן וָעֵבֶר וֶאֱלִיאֵל׃
and-Shimrath sons-of Shimei (22) and-Ishpan and-Eber and-Eliel

וְעַבְדּוֹן וְזִכְרִי וְחָנָן׃ וַחֲנַנְיָה וְעֵילָם וְעַנְתֹתִיָּה׃
(23) and-Abdon and-Zicri and-Hanan (24) and-Hananiah and-Elam and-Anthothijah

וְיִפְדְיָה וּפְנִיאֵל° בְּנֵי שָׁשָׁק׃ וְשַׁמְשְׁרַי
(25) and-Iphdeiah and-Penuel sons-of Shashak (26) and-Shamsherai

וּשְׁחַרְיָה וַעֲתַלְיָה׃ וְיַעֲרֶשְׁיָה וְאֵלִיָּה וְזִכְרִי בְּנֵי
and-Shehariah and-Athaliah (27) and-Jaareshiah and-Elijah and-Zicri sons-of

יְרֹחָם׃ אֵלֶּה רָאשֵׁי אָבוֹת לְתֹלְדוֹתָם רָאשִׁים אֵלֶּה
Jeroham (28) these heads-of fathers in-genealogies-of-them chiefs these

יָשְׁבוּ בִּירוּשָׁלָםִ׃ וּבְגִבְעוֹן יָשְׁבוּ אֲבִי גִבְעוֹן
they-lived in-Jerusalem (29) and-in-Gibeon they-lived father-of Gibeon

וְשֵׁם אִשְׁתּוֹ מַעֲכָה׃ וּבְנוֹ הַבְּכוֹר עַבְדּוֹן
and-name-of wife-of-him Maacah (30) and-son-of-him the-firstborn Abdon

וְצוּר וְקִישׁ וּבַעַל וְנָדָב׃ וּגְדוֹר וְאַחְיוֹ וָזָכֶר׃
and-Zur and-Kish and-Baal and-Nadab (31) and-Gedor and-Ahio and-Zeker

וּמִקְלוֹת הוֹלִיד אֶת־שִׁמְאָה וְאַף־הֵמָּה נֶגֶד אֲחֵיהֶם
(32) and-Mikloth he-fathered *** Shimeah and-also they near relatives-of-them

יָשְׁבוּ בִּירוּשָׁלַםִ עִם־אֲחֵיהֶם׃ וְנֵר הוֹלִיד אֶת־
they-lived in-Jerusalem with relatives-of-them (33) and-Ner he-fathered ***

קִישׁ וְקִישׁ הוֹלִיד אֶת־שָׁאוּל וְשָׁאוּל הוֹלִיד אֶת־יְהוֹנָתָן וְאֶת־
Kish and-Kish he-fathered *** Saul and-Saul he-fathered *** Jonathan and

11By Hushim he had Abi-
tub and Elpaal.
12The sons of Elpaal:
Eber, Misham, Shemed
(who built Ono and Lod
with its surrounding vil-
lages), 13and Beriah and
Shema, who were heads
of families of those living
in Aijalon and who
drove out the inhabitants
of Gath.
14Ahio, Shashak, Jeremoth,
15Zebadiah, Arad, Eder,
16Michael, Ishpah and
Joha were the sons of Be-
riah.
17Zebadiah, Meshullam, Hiz-
ki, Heber, 18Ishmerai,
Izliah and Jobab were the
sons of Elpaal.
19Jakim, Zicri, Zabdi, 20Elie-
nai, Zillethai, Eliel,
21Adaiah, Beraiah and
Shimrath were the sons
of Shimei.
22Ishpan, Eber, Eliel, 23Ab-
don, Zicri, Hanan,
24Hananiah, Elam, An-
thothijah, 25Iphdeiah and
Penuel were the sons of
Shashak.
26Shamsherai, Shehariah,
Athaliah, 27Jaareshiah,
Elijah and Zicri were the
sons of Jeroham.
28All these were heads of
families, chiefs as listed in
their genealogy, and they
lived in Jerusalem.

29Jeiel[k] the father[l] of Gibeon
lived in Gibeon.
His wife's name was
Maacah, 30and his
firstborn son was Abdon,
followed by Zur, Kish,
Baal, Ner,[m] Nadab, 31Ge-
dor, Ahio, Zeker 32and
Mikloth, who was the fa-
ther of Shimeah. They
too lived near their relatives in Jerusalem.
33Ner was the father of Kish,
Kish the father of Saul,
and Saul the father of
Jonathan, Malki-Shua,

[k] 29 Some Septuagint manuscripts (see also 1 Chron. 9:35); Hebrew does not have *Jeiel.*
[l] 29 *Father* may mean *civic leader* or *military leader.*
[m] 30 Some Septuagint manuscripts (see also 1 Chron. 9:36); Hebrew does not have *Ner.*

°25 ק ופנואל

מַלְכִּי־שׁוּעַ וְאֶת־אֲבִינָדָב וְאֶת־אֶשְׁבָּעַל׃ וּבֶן־ יְהוֹנָתָן מְרִיב בָּעַל
Baal Merib Jonathan and-son-of (34) Esh-Baal and Abinadab and Shua Malki

וּמְרִיב בַּעַל הוֹלִיד אֶת־מִיכָה׃ וּבְנֵי מִיכָה פִּיתוֹן וָמֶלֶךְ
and-Melech Pithon Micah and-sons-of (35) Micah *** he-fathered Baal and-Merib

וְתַאְרֵעַ וְאָחָז׃ וְאָחָז הוֹלִיד אֶת־ יְהוֹעַדָּה וִיהוֹעַדָּה
and-Jehoaddah Jehoaddah *** he-fathered and-Ahaz (36) and-Ahaz and-Tarea

הוֹלִיד אֶת־ עָלֶמֶת וְאֶת־ עַזְמָוֶת וְאֶת־ זִמְרִי וְזִמְרִי הוֹלִיד אֶת־
*** he-fathered and-Zimri Zimri and Azmaveth and Alemeth *** he-fathered

מוֹצָא׃ וּמוֹצָא הוֹלִיד אֶת־ בִּנְעָא רָפָה בְנוֹ אֶלְעָשָׂה
Eleasah son-of-him Raphah Binea *** he-fathered and-Moza (37) Moza

בְנוֹ אָצֵל בְּנוֹ׃ וּלְאָצֵל שִׁשָּׁה בָנִים וְאֵלֶּה שְׁמוֹתָם
names-of-them and-these sons six and-to-Azel (38) son-of-him Azel son-of-him

עַזְרִיקָם ׀ בֹּכְרוּ וְיִשְׁמָעֵאל וּשְׁעַרְיָה וְעֹבַדְיָה וְחָנָן כָּל־ אֵלֶּה
these all-of and-Hanan and-Obadiah and-Sheariah and-Ishmael Bokeru Azrikam

בְּנֵי אָצֵל׃ וּבְנֵי עֵשֶׁק אָחִיו אוּלָם בְּכֹרוֹ
firstborn-of-him Ulam brother-of-him Eshek and-sons-of (39) Azel sons-of

יְעוּשׁ הַשֵּׁנִי וֶאֱלִיפֶלֶט הַשְּׁלִשִׁי׃ וַיִּהְיוּ בְנֵי־ אוּלָם
Ulam sons-of and-they-were (40) the-third and-Eliphelet the-second Jeush

אֲנָשִׁים גִּבֹּרֵי־ חַיִל דֹּרְכֵי קֶשֶׁת וּמַרְבִּים בָּנִים
sons and-ones-having-many bow ones-handling-of bravery warriors-of men

וּבְנֵי בָנִים מֵאָה וַחֲמִשִּׁים כָּל־ אֵלֶּה מִבְּנֵי בִנְיָמִן׃
Benjamin from-descendants-of these all-of and-fifty hundred sons and-sons-of

וְכָל־ יִשְׂרָאֵל הִתְיַחְשׂוּ וְהִנָּם כְּתוּבִים
ones-being-recorded and-see-they! they-were-listed Israel and-all-of (9:1)

עַל־ סֵפֶר מַלְכֵי יִשְׂרָאֵל וִיהוּדָה הָגְלוּ לְבָבֶל
to-Babylon they-were-taken-captive and-Judah Israel kings-of book-of in

בְּמַעֲלָם׃ וְהַיּוֹשְׁבִים הָרִאשֹׁנִים אֲשֶׁר
who the-first-ones now-the-ones-resettling (2) for-unfaithfulness-of-them

בַּאֲחֻזָּתָם בְּעָרֵיהֶם יִשְׂרָאֵל הַכֹּהֲנִים הַלְוִיִּם
the-Levites the-priests Israel in-towns-of-them on-property-of-them

וְהַנְּתִינִים׃ וּבִירוּשָׁלַםִ יָשְׁבוּ מִן־ בְּנֵי יְהוּדָה
Judah sons-of from they-lived and-in-Jerusalem (3) and-the-temple-servants

וּמִן־ בְּנֵי בִנְיָמִן וּמִן־ בְּנֵי אֶפְרַיִם וּמְנַשֶּׁה׃ עוּתַי
Uthai (4) and-Manasseh Ephraim sons-of and-from Benjamin sons-of and-from

בֶּן־ עַמִּיהוּד בֶּן־ עָמְרִי בֶּן־ אִמְרִי בֶּן־ בָּנִימִן־ בְּנֵי־
descendants-of from Bani son-of Imri son-of Omri son-of Ammihud son-of

פֶּרֶץ בֶּן־ יְהוּדָה׃ וּמִן־ הַשִּׁילוֹנִי עֲשָׂיָה הַבְּכוֹר
the-firstborn Asaiah the-Shilonite and-from (5) Judah son-of Perez

Abinadab and Esh-Baal.[o]
[34]The son of Jonathan:
Merib-Baal,[p] who was
the father of Micah.
[35]The sons of Micah:
Pithon, Melech, Tarea
and Ahaz.
[36]Ahaz was the father of Jehoaddah, Jehoaddah was
the father of Alemeth,
Azmaveth and Zimri,
and Zimri was the father
of Moza. [37]Moza was the
father of Binea; Raphah
was his son, Eleasah his
son and Azel his son.
[38]Azel had six sons, and these
were their names:
Azrikam, Bokeru, Ishma-
el, Sheariah, Obadiah
and Hanan. All these
were the sons of Azel.
[39]The sons of his brother
Eshek:
Ulam his firstborn, Jeush
the second son and
Eliphelet the third. [40]The
sons of Ulam were brave
warriors who could han-
dle the bow. They had
many sons and grand-
sons—150 in all.
All these were the descendants of Benjamin.

9 All Israel was listed in the genealogies recorded in the book of the kings of Israel.

The People in Jerusalem

The people of Judah were taken captive to Babylon because of their unfaithfulness.
[2]Now the first to resettle on their own property in their own towns were some Israelites, priests, Levites and temple servants.
[3]Those from Judah, from Benjamin, and from Ephraim and Manasseh who lived in Jerusalem were:
[4]Uthai son of Ammihud, the
son of Omri, the son of
Imri, the son of Bani, a
descendant of Perez son
of Judah.
[5]Of the Shilonites:
Asaiah the firstborn and

[o]33 Also known as *Ish-Bosheth*
[p]34 Also known as *Mephibosheth*

°4 ק בני מן־

וּבָנָיו׃ וּמִן־ בְּנֵי־ זֶרַח יְעוּאֵל וַאֲחֵיהֶם
and-brothers-of-them Jeuel Zerah sons-of and-from (6) and-sons-of-him

שֵׁשׁ־ מֵאוֹת וְתִשְׁעִים׃ וּמִן־ בְּנֵי בִּנְיָמִן סַלּוּא בֶּן־ מְשֻׁלָּם
Meshullam son-of Sallu Benjamin sons-of and-from (7) and-ninety hundreds six

בֶּן־ הוֹדַוְיָה בֶּן־ הַסְּנֻאָה׃ וְיִבְנְיָה בֶּן־ יְרֹחָם וְאֵלָה
and-Elah Jeroham son-of and-Ibneiah (8) Hassenuah son-of Hodaviah son-of

בֶּן־ עֻזִּי בֶּן־ מִכְרִי וּמְשֻׁלָּם בֶּן־ שְׁפַטְיָה בֶּן־ רְעוּאֵל
Reuel son-of Shephatiah son-of and-Meshullam Micri son-of Uzzi son-of

בֶּן־ יִבְנִיָּה׃ וַאֲחֵיהֶם לְתֹלְדוֹתָם תְּשַׁע
nine-of in-genealogies-of-them and-brothers-of-them (9) Ibnijah son-of

מֵאוֹת וַחֲמִשִּׁים וְשִׁשָּׁה כָּל־ אֵלֶּה אֲנָשִׁים רָאשֵׁי אָבוֹת לְבֵית
of-family-of fathers heads-of men these all-of and-six and-fifty hundreds

אֲבֹתֵיהֶם׃ וּמִן־ הַכֹּהֲנִים יְדַעְיָה וִיהוֹיָרִיב וְיָכִין׃
and-Jakin and-Jehoiarib Jedaiah the-priests and-from (10) fathers-of-them

וַעֲזַרְיָה בֶּן־ חִלְקִיָּה בֶּן־ מְשֻׁלָּם בֶּן־ צָדוֹק בֶּן־
son-of Zadok son-of Meshullam son-of Hilkiah son-of and-Azariah (11)

מְרָיוֹת בֶּן־ אֲחִיטוּב נְגִיד בֵּית הָאֱלֹהִים׃ וַעֲדָיָה בֶּן־
son-of and-Adaiah (12) the-God house-of official-of Ahitub son-of Meraioth

יְרֹחָם בֶּן־ פַּשְׁחוּר בֶּן־ מַלְכִּיָּה וּמַעְשַׂי בֶּן־ עֲדִיאֵל בֶּן־
son-of Adiel son-of and-Maasai Malkijah son-of Pashhur son-of Jeroham

יַחְזֵרָה בֶּן־ מְשֻׁלָּם בֶּן־ מְשִׁלֵּמִית בֶּן־ אִמֵּר׃
Immer son-of Meshillemith son-of Meshullam son-of Jahzerah

וַאֲחֵיהֶם רָאשִׁים לְבֵית אֲבוֹתָם אֶלֶף
thousand fathers-of-them of-family-of heads and-brothers-of-them (13)

וּשְׁבַע מֵאוֹת וְשִׁשִּׁים גִּבּוֹרֵי חֵיל מְלֶאכֶת עֲבוֹדַת
ministry-of responsible-of ability men-of and-sixty hundreds and-seven-of

בֵּית־ הָאֱלֹהִים׃ וּמִן־ הַלְוִיִּם שְׁמַעְיָה בֶן־ חַשּׁוּב בֶּן־
son-of Hasshub son-of Shemaiah the-Levites and-from (14) the-God house-of

עַזְרִיקָם בֶּן־ חֲשַׁבְיָה מִן־ בְּנֵי מְרָרִי׃ וּבַקְבַּקַּר חֶרֶשׁ
Heresh and-Bakbakkar (15) Merari sons-of from Hashabiah son-of Azrikam

וְגָלָל וּמַתַּנְיָה בֶּן־ מִיכָא בֶּן־ זִכְרִי בֶּן־ אָסָף׃
Asaph son-of Zicri son-of Mica son-of and-Mattaniah and-Galal

וְעֹבַדְיָה בֶּן־ שְׁמַעְיָה בֶּן־ גָּלָל בֶּן־ יְדוּתוּן וּבֶרֶכְיָה
and-Berekiah Jeduthun son-of Galal son-of Shemaiah son-of and-Obadiah (16)

בֶּן־ אָסָא בֶּן־ אֶלְקָנָה הַיּוֹשֵׁב בְּחַצְרֵי נְטוֹפָתִי׃
Netophathite in-villages-of the-one-living Elkanah son-of Asa son-of

וְהַשֹּׁעֲרִים שַׁלּוּם וְעַקּוּב וְטַלְמֹן וַאֲחִימָן
and-Ahiman and-Talmon and-Akkub Shallum and-the-gatekeepers (17)

his sons.
6 Of the Zerahites:
Jeuel.
The people from Judah
numbered 690.
7 Of the Benjamites:
Sallu son of Meshullam,
the son of Hodaviah, the
son of Hassenuah;
8 Ibneiah son of Jeroham;
Elah son of Uzzi, the son
of Micri; and Meshullam
son of Shephatiah, the
son of Reuel, the son of
Ibnijah.
9 The people from Benja-
min, as listed in their
genealogy, numbered
956. All these men were
heads of their families.
10 Of the priests:
Jedaiah; Jehoiarib; Jakin;
11 Azariah son of Hilkiah,
the son of Meshullam,
the son of Zadok, the son
of Meraioth, the son of
Ahitub, the official in
charge of the house of
God;
12 Adaiah son of Jeroham,
the son of Pashhur, the
son of Malkijah; and
Maasai son of Adiel, the
son of Jahzerah, the son
of Meshullam, the son of
Meshillemith, the son of
Immer.
13 The priests, who were
heads of families, num-
bered 1,760. They were
able men, responsible for
ministering in the house
of God.
14 Of the Levites:
Shemaiah son of Has-
shub, the son of Az-
rikam, the son of Hasha-
biah, a Merarite; 15 Bak-
bakkar, Heresh, Galal
and Mattaniah son of
Mica, the son of Zicri, the
son of Asaph; 16 Obadiah
son of Shemaiah, the son
of Galal, the son of Jeduthun; and Berekiah son
of Asa, the son of Elka-
nah, who lived in the villages of the Netopha-
thites.
17 The gatekeepers:
Shallum, Akkub, Tal-
mon, Ahiman and their

וַאֲחִיהֶם שַׁלּוּם הָרֹאשׁ׃ וְעַד־ הֵנָּה בְּשַׁעַר הַמֶּלֶךְ
the-King at-Gate-of now and-to (18) the-chief Shallum and-brother-of-them

מִזְרָחָה הֵמָּה הַשֹּׁעֲרִים לְמַחֲנוֹת בְּנֵי לֵוִי׃ וְשַׁלּוּם
and-Shallum (19) Levi sons-of of-camps-of the-gatekeepers they on-east

בֶּן־ קוֹרֵא בֶּן־ אֶבְיָסָף בֶּן־ קֹרַח וְאֶחָיו לְבֵית־
from-family-of and-fellows-of-him Korah son-of Ebiasaph son-of Kore son-of

אָבִיו הַקָּרְחִים עַל מְלֶאכֶת הָעֲבוֹדָה שֹׁמְרֵי
ones-guarding-of the-service responsibility-of over the-Korahites father-of-him

הַסִּפִּים לָאֹהֶל וַאֲבֹתֵיהֶם עַל־ מַחֲנֵה יְהוָה
Yahweh dwelling-of over and-fathers-of-them of-the-tent the-thresholds

שֹׁמְרֵי הַמָּבוֹא׃ וּפִינְחָס בֶּן־ אֶלְעָזָר נָגִיד
leader Eleazar son-of and-Phinehas (20) the-entrance ones-guarding-of

הָיָה עֲלֵיהֶם לְפָנִים יְהוָה ׀ עִמּוֹ׃ זְכַרְיָה בֶּן מְשֶׁלֶמְיָה
Meshelemiah son-of Zechariah (21) with-him Yahweh earlier over-them he-was

שֹׁעֵר פֶּתַח לְאֹהֶל מוֹעֵד׃ כֻּלָּם
all-of-them (22) Meeting of-Tent-of entrance gatekeeper-of

הַבְּרוּרִים לְשֹׁעֲרִים בַּסִּפִּים מָאתַיִם וּשְׁנֵים
and-two two-hundreds at-the-thresholds as-gatekeepers the-ones-being-chosen

עָשָׂר הֵמָּה בְחַצְרֵיהֶם הִתְיַחְשָׂם הֵמָּה יִסַּד דָּוִיד
David he-assigned them to-be-registered-them in-villages-of-them they ten

וּשְׁמוּאֵל הָרֹאֶה בֶּאֱמוּנָתָם׃ וְהֵם וּבְנֵיהֶם
and-descendants-of-them and-they (23) to-trust-of-them the-seer and-Samuel

עַל־ הַשְּׁעָרִים לְבֵית־ יְהוָה לְבֵית־ הָאֹהֶל לְמִשְׁמָרוֹת׃
as-guards the-Tent of-house-of Yahweh of-house-of the-gates over

לְאַרְבַּע רוּחוֹת יִהְיוּ הַשֹּׁעֲרִים מִזְרָח יָמָּה צָפוֹנָה
at-north at-west east the-gatekeepers they-were sides at-four-of (24)

וָנֶגְבָּה׃ וַאֲחֵיהֶם בְּחַצְרֵיהֶם לָבוֹא
to-come in-villages-of-them and-brothers-of-them (25) and-at-south

לְשִׁבְעַת הַיָּמִים מֵעֵת אֶל־ עֵת עִם־ אֵלֶּה׃ כִּי בֶאֱמוּנָה הֵמָּה
they in-trust but (26) these with time to from-time the-days for-seven-of

אַרְבַּעַת גִּבֹּרֵי הַשֹּׁעֲרִים הֵם הַלְוִיִּם וְהָיוּ עַל־
over and-they-were the-Levites they the-gatekeepers principal-ones-of four-of

הַלְּשָׁכוֹת וְעַל הָאֹצְרוֹת בֵּית הָאֱלֹהִים׃ וּסְבִיבוֹת
and-ones-around-of (27) the-God house-of the-treasuries and-over the-rooms

בֵּית־ הָאֱלֹהִים יָלִינוּ כִּי־ עֲלֵיהֶם מִשְׁמֶרֶת וְהֵם
and-they guard-duty upon-them because they-spent-night the-God house-of

עַל־ הַמַּפְתֵּחַ וְלַבֹּקֶר לַבֹּקֶר׃ וּמֵהֶם עַל־
over and-from-them (28) for-the-morning also-for-the-morning the-key over

brothers, Shallum their
chief [18]being stationed at
the King's Gate on the
east, up to the present
time. These were the
gatekeepers belonging to
the camp of the Levites.
[19]Shallum son of Kore,
the son of Ebiasaph, the
son of Korah, and his fellow gatekeepers from his
family (the Korahites)
were responsible for
guarding the thresholds
of the tent[q] just as their
fathers had been respon-
sible for guarding the entrance to the dwelling of
the LORD. [20]In earlier
times Phinehas son of
Eleazar was in charge of
the gatekeepers, and the
LORD was with him.
[21]Zechariah son of Me-
shelemiah was the gate-
keeper at the entrance to
the Tent of Meeting.
[22]Altogether, those chosen to
be gatekeepers at the thresholds numbered 212. They were
registered by genealogy in
their villages. The gatekeepers
had been assigned to their positions of trust by David and
Samuel the seer. [23]They and
their descendants were in
charge of guarding the gates of
the house of the LORD—the
house called the Tent. [24]The
gatekeepers were on the four
sides: east, west, north and
south. [25]Their brothers in their
villages had to come from time
to time and share their duties
for seven-day periods. [26]But
the four principal gatekeepers,
who were Levites, were entrusted with the responsibility
for the rooms and treasuries in
the house of God. [27]They
would spend the night stationed around the house of
God, because they had to
guard it; and they had charge
of the key for opening it each
morning.
[28]Some of them were in

q19 That is, the temple; also in verse 21

כְּלֵי הָעֲבוֹדָה כִּי־ בְמִסְפָּר יְבִיאוּם
they-brought-in-them according-to-count indeed the-service articles-of

וּבְמִסְפָּר יוֹצִיאוּם׃ (29) וּמֵהֶם מְמֻנִּים
ones-being-assigned and-from-them (29) they-took-out-them and-according-to-count

עַל־ הַכֵּלִים וְעַל כָּל־ כְּלֵי הַקֹּדֶשׁ וְעַל־
and-over the-sanctuary articles-of all-of and-over the-furnishings over

הַסֹּלֶת וְהַיַּיִן וְהַשֶּׁמֶן וְהַלְּבוֹנָה וְהַבְּשָׂמִים׃
and-the-spices and-the-incense and-the-oil and-the-wine the-flour

(30) וּמִן־ בְּנֵי הַכֹּהֲנִים רֹקְחֵי הַמִּרְקַחַת לַבְּשָׂמִים׃
of-the-spices the-mixture ones-mixing-of the-priests sons-of but-from (30)

(31) וּמַתִּתְיָה מִן־ הַלְוִיִּם הוּא הַבְּכוֹר לְשַׁלֻּם הַקָּרְחִי
the-Korahite of-Shallum the-firstborn he the-Levites from and-Mattithiah (31)

בֶּאֱמוּנָה עַל מַעֲשֵׂה הַחֲבִתִּים׃ (32) וּמִן־ בְּנֵי
sons-of and-from (32) the-offering-bread baking-of over with-trust

הַקְּהָתִי מִן־ אֲחֵיהֶם עַל־ לֶחֶם הַמַּעֲרָכֶת לְהָכִין
to-prepare the-setting-out bread-of over brothers-of-them from the-Kohathite

שַׁבַּת שַׁבָּת׃ (33) וְאֵלֶּה הַמְשֹׁרְרִים רָאשֵׁי אָבוֹת
fathers heads-of the-ones-making-music and-those (33) Sabbath Sabbath-of

לַלְוִיִּם בַּלְּשָׁכֹת פְּטוּרִים כִּי־ יוֹמָם וָלַיְלָה
and-night by-day because ones-being-exempt in-the-rooms of-the-Levites

עֲלֵיהֶם בַּמְּלָאכָה׃ (34) אֵלֶּה רָאשֵׁי הָאָבוֹת לַלְוִיִּם
of-the-Levites the-fathers heads-of these (34) for-the-work upon-them

לְתֹלְדוֹתָם רָאשִׁים אֵלֶּה יָשְׁבוּ בִירוּשָׁלָםִ׃ (35) וּבְגִבְעוֹן
and-in-Gibeon (35) in-Jerusalem they-lived these chiefs by-genealogies-of-them

יָשְׁבוּ אֲבִי־ גִבְעוֹן יְעוּאֵל וְשֵׁם אִשְׁתּוֹ מַעֲכָה׃
Maacah wife-of-him and-name-of Jeiel Gibeon father-of they-lived

(36) וּבְנוֹ הַבְּכוֹר עַבְדּוֹן וְצוּר וְקִישׁ וּבַעַל וְנֵר
and-Ner and-Baal and-Kish and-Zur Abdon the-firstborn and-son-of-him (36)

וְנָדָב׃ (37) וּגְדוֹר וְאַחְיוֹ וּזְכַרְיָה וּמִקְלוֹת׃ (38) וּמִקְלוֹת
and-Mikloth (38) and-Mikloth and-Zechariah and-Ahio and-Gedor (37) and-Nadab

הוֹלִיד אֶת־ שִׁמְאָם וְאַף־ הֵם נֶגֶד אֲחֵיהֶם יָשְׁבוּ
they-lived relatives-of-them near they and-also Shimeam *** he-fathered

בִירוּשָׁלַםִ עִם־ אֲחֵיהֶם׃ (39) וְנֵר הוֹלִיד אֶת־ קִישׁ
Kish *** he-fathered and-Ner (39) relatives-of-them with in-Jerusalem

וְקִישׁ הוֹלִיד אֶת־ שָׁאוּל וְשָׁאוּל הוֹלִיד אֶת־ יְהוֹנָתָן וְאֶת־
and Jonathan *** he-fathered and-Saul Saul *** he-fathered and-Kish

מַלְכִּי־ שׁוּעַ וְאֶת־ אֲבִינָדָב וְאֶת־ אֶשְׁבָּעַל׃ (40) וּבֶן־ יְהוֹנָתָן מְרִיב בָּעַל
Baal Merib Jonathan and-son-of (40) Esh-Baal and Abinadab and Shua Malki

charge of the articles used in the temple service; they counted them when they were brought in and when they were taken out. 29 Others were assigned to take care of the furnishings and all the other articles of the sanctuary, as well as the flour and wine, and the oil, incense and spices. 30 But some of the priests took care of mixing the spices. 31 A Levite named Mattithiah, the firstborn son of Shallum the Korahite, was entrusted with the responsibility for baking the offering bread. 32 Some of their Kohathite brothers were in charge of preparing for every Sabbath the bread set out on the table.

33 Those who were musicians, heads of Levite families, stayed in the rooms of the temple and were exempt from other duties because they were responsible for the work day and night.

34 All these were heads of Levite families, chiefs as listed in their genealogy, and they lived in Jerusalem.

The Genealogy of Saul

35 Jeiel the father[r] of Gibeon lived in Gibeon.
His wife's name was Maacah, 36 and his firstborn son was Abdon, followed by Zur, Kish, Baal, Ner, Nadab, 37 Gedor, Ahio, Zechariah and Mikloth. 38 Mikloth was the father of Shimeam. They too lived near their relatives in Jerusalem.
39 Ner was the father of Kish, Kish the father of Saul, and Saul the father of Jonathan, Malki-Shua, Abinadab and Esh-Baal.[s]
40 The son of Jonathan:
Merib-Baal,[t] who was

[r]35 *Father* may mean *civic leader* or *military leader.*
[s]39 Also known as *Ish-Bosheth*
[t]40 Also known as *Mephibosheth*

°33 ק פטורים
°35 ק יעיאל

וּמְרִי־ בָעַל הוֹלִיד אֶת־ מִיכָה׃ וּבְנֵי מִיכָה פִּיתֹון
Pithon Micah and-sons-of (41) Micah *** he-fathered Baal and-Merib

וָמֶלֶךְ וְתַחְרֵעַ׃ וְאָחָז הוֹלִיד אֶת־ יַעְרָה וְיַעְרָה
and-Jarah Jarah *** he-fathered and-Ahaz (42) and-Tahrea and-Melech

הוֹלִיד אֶת־ עָלֶמֶת וְאֶת־ עַזְמָוֶת וְאֶת־ זִמְרִי וְזִמְרִי הוֹלִיד אֶת־
*** he-fathered and-Zimri Zimri and Azmaveth and Alemeth *** he-fathered

מוֹצָא׃ וּמוֹצָא הוֹלִיד אֶת־ בִּנְעָא וּרְפָיָה בְנוֹ אֶלְעָשָׂה
Eleasah son-of-him and-Rephaiah Binea *** he-fathered and-Moza (43) Moza

בְנוֹ אָצֵל בְּנוֹ׃ וּלְאָצֵל שִׁשָּׁה בָנִים וְאֵלֶּה שְׁמוֹתָם
names-of-them and-these sons six and-to-Azel (44) son-of-him Azel son-of-him

עַזְרִיקָם ׀ בֹּכְרוּ וְיִשְׁמָעֵאל וּשְׁעַרְיָה וְעֹבַדְיָה וְחָנָן אֵלֶּה בְּנֵי
sons-of these and-Hanan and-Obadiah and-Sheariah and-Ishmael Bokeru Azrikam

אָצֵל׃ וּפְלִשְׁתִּים נִלְחֲמוּ בְיִשְׂרָאֵל וַיָּנָס אִישׁ־
man-of and-he-fled against-Israel they-fought now-Philistines (10:1) Azel

יִשְׂרָאֵל מִפְּנֵי פְלִשְׁתִּים וַיִּפְּלוּ חֲלָלִים בְּהַר גִּלְבֹּעַ׃
Gilboa on-Mount-of ones-slain and-they-fell Philistines from-before Israel

וַיַּדְבְּקוּ פְלִשְׁתִּים אַחֲרֵי שָׁאוּל וְאַחֲרֵי בָנָיו
sons-of-him and-after Saul after Philistines and-they-pressed-hard (2)

וַיַּכּוּ פְלִשְׁתִּים אֶת־ יוֹנָתָן וְאֶת־ אֲבִינָדָב וְאֶת־ מַלְכִּי־ שׁוּעַ
Shua Malki and Abinadab and Jonathan *** Philistines and-they-killed

בְּנֵי שָׁאוּל׃ וַתִּכְבַּד הַמִּלְחָמָה עַל־ שָׁאוּל
Saul around the-fighting and-she-grew-fierce (3) Saul sons-of

וַיִּמְצָאֻהוּ הַמּוֹרִים בַּקָּשֶׁת וַיָּחֶל
and-he-was-wounded with-the-bow the-ones-shooting and-they-overtook-him

מִן־ הַיּוֹרִים׃ וַיֹּאמֶר שָׁאוּל אֶל־ נֹשֵׂא כֵלָיו
armors-of-him one-bearing-of to Saul and-he-said (4) the-ones-shooting by

שְׁלֹף חַרְבְּךָ ׀ וְדָקְרֵנִי בָהּ פֶּן־ יָבֹאוּ
they-will-come or with-her and-run-through-me! sword-of-you draw!

הָעֲרֵלִים הָאֵלֶּה וְהִתְעַלְּלוּ־ בִי וְלֹא
but-not against-me and-they-will-abuse the-these the-uncircumcised-ones

אָבָה נֹשֵׂא כֵלָיו כִּי יָרֵא מְאֹד וַיִּקַּח
so-he-took very he-was-terrified for armors-of-him one-bearing-of he-would

שָׁאוּל אֶת־ הַחֶרֶב וַיִּפֹּל עָלֶיהָ׃ וַיַּרְא נֹשֵׂא־
one-bearing-of when-he-saw (5) on-her and-he-fell the-sword *** Saul

כֵלָיו כִּי מֵת שָׁאוּל וַיִּפֹּל גַּם־ הוּא עַל־ הַחֶרֶב
the-sword on he also then-he-fell Saul he-was-dead that armors-of-him

וַיָּמֹת׃ וַיָּמָת שָׁאוּל וּשְׁלֹשֶׁת בָּנָיו וְכָל־
and-all-of sons-of-him and-three-of Saul so-he-died (6) and-he-died

the father of Micah.
41 The sons of Micah:
Pithon, Melech, Tahrea and Ahaz.[u]
42 Ahaz was the father of Jadah, Jadah[v] was the father of Alemeth, Azmaveth and Zimri, and Zimri was the father of
Moza. 43 Moza was the father of Binea; Rephaiah was his son, Eleasah his son and Azel his son.
44 Azel had six sons, and these were their names: Azrikam, Bokeru, Ishmael, Sheariah, Obadiah and Hanan. These were the sons of Azel.

Saul Takes His Life

10 Now the Philistines fought against Israel; the Israelites fled before them, and many fell slain on Mount
Gilboa. 2 The Philistines pressed hard after Saul and his sons, and they killed his sons Jonathan, Abinadab and
Malki-Shua. 3 The fighting grew fierce around Saul, and when the archers overtook him, they wounded him.
4 Saul said to his armor-bearer, "Draw your sword and run me through, or these uncircumcised fellows will come and abuse me."
But his armor-bearer was terrified and would not do it; so Saul took his own sword and fell on it.
5 When the armor-bearer saw that Saul was dead, he too fell on his sword and died.
6 So Saul and three of his sons died, and all his

[u] 41 Vulgate and Syriac (see also Septuagint and 1 Chron. 8:35); Hebrew does not have *and Ahaz.*
[v] 42 Some Hebrew manuscripts and Septuagint (see also 1 Chron. 8:36); most Hebrew manuscripts *Jarah, Jarah*

בֵּיתוֹ יַחְדָּו מֵתוּ׃ (7) וַיִּרְאוּ כָּל־ אִישׁ יִשְׂרָאֵל אֲשֶׁר־
who Israel man-of all-of when-they-saw (7) they-died together house-of-him

בָּעֵמֶק כִּי נָסוּ וְכִי־ מֵתוּ שָׁאוּל וּבָנָיו
and-sons-of-him Saul they-were-dead and-that they-fled that in-the-valley

וַיַּעַזְבוּ עָרֵיהֶם וַיָּנֻסוּ וַיָּבֹאוּ פְלִשְׁתִּים
Philistines and-they-came and-they-fled towns-of-them then-they-abandoned

וַיֵּשְׁבוּ בָּהֶם׃ (8) וַיְהִי מִמָּחֳרָת וַיָּבֹאוּ
when-they-came on-next-day and-he-was (8) in-them and-they-occupied

פְלִשְׁתִּים לְפַשֵּׁט אֶת־ הַחֲלָלִים וַיִּמְצְאוּ אֶת־ שָׁאוּל וְאֶת־
and Saul *** then-they-found the-dead-ones *** to-strip Philistines

בָּנָיו נֹפְלִים בְּהַר גִּלְבֹּעַ׃ (9) וַיַּפְשִׁיטֻהוּ
and-they-stripped-him (9) Gilboa on-Mount-of ones-having-fallen sons-of-him

וַיִּשְׂאוּ אֶת־ רֹאשׁוֹ וְאֶת־ כֵּלָיו וַיְשַׁלְּחוּ בְאֶרֶץ־
through-land-of and-they-sent armors-of-him and head-of-him *** and-they-took

פְלִשְׁתִּים* סָבִיב לְבַשֵּׂר אֶת־ עֲצַבֵּיהֶם וְאֶת־ הָעָם׃
the-people and-among idols-of-them among to-proclaim-news around Philistines

(10) וַיָּשִׂימוּ אֶת־ כֵּלָיו בֵּית אֱלֹהֵיהֶם וְאֶת־ גֻּלְגָּלְתּוֹ
head-of-him and gods-of-them temple-of armors-of-him *** and-they-put (10)

תָקְעוּ בֵּית דָּגוֹן׃ (11) וַיִּשְׁמְעוּ כֹּל יָבֵישׁ גִּלְעָד אֵת
*** Gilead Jabesh all-of when-they-heard (11) Dagon temple-of they-hung-up

כָּל־ אֲשֶׁר־ עָשׂוּ פְלִשְׁתִּים לְשָׁאוּל׃ (12) וַיָּקוּמוּ כָּל־ אִישׁ
man-of every-of then-they-went (12) to-Saul Philistines they-did that all

חַיִל וַיִּשְׂאוּ אֶת־ גּוּפַת שָׁאוּל וְאֵת גּוּפֹת בָּנָיו
sons-of-him bodies-of and Saul body-of *** and-they-took valor

וַיְבִיאוּם יָבֵישָׁה וַיִּקְבְּרוּ אֶת־ עַצְמוֹתֵיהֶם תַּחַת
under bones-of-them *** then-they-buried to-Jabesh and-they-brought-them

הָאֵלָה בְּיָבֵשׁ וַיָּצוּמוּ שִׁבְעַת יָמִים׃ (13) וַיָּמָת שָׁאוּל
Saul and-he-died (13) days seven-of and-they-fasted in-Jabesh the-great-tree

בְּמַעֲלוֹ אֲשֶׁר מָעַל בַּיהוָה עַל־ דְּבַר
word-of against to-Yahweh he-was-unfaithful when for-unfaithfulness-of-him

יְהוָה אֲשֶׁר לֹא־ שָׁמָר וְגַם־ לִשְׁאוֹל בָּאוֹב לִדְרוֹשׁ׃
to-seek-guidance with-medium to-consult and-even he-kept not which Yahweh

(14) וְלֹא־ דָרַשׁ בַּיהוָה וַיְמִיתֵהוּ וַיַּסֵּב אֶת־
*** and-he-turned-over so-he-killed-him of-Yahweh he-inquired and-not (14)

הַמְּלוּכָה לְדָוִיד בֶּן־ יִשָׁי׃ (11:1) וַיִּקָּבְצוּ כָל־
all-of and-they-came-together (11:1) Jesse son-of to-David the-kingdom

יִשְׂרָאֵל אֶל־ דָּוִיד חֶבְרוֹנָה לֵאמֹר הִנֵּה עַצְמְךָ וּבְשָׂרְךָ אֲנָחְנוּ׃
we and-flesh-of-you bone-of-you see! to-say at-Hebron David to Israel

house died together.
7When all the Israelites in
the valley saw that the army
had fled and that Saul and his
sons had died, they abandoned their towns and fled.
And the Philistines came and
occupied them.
8The next day, when the
Philistines came to strip the
dead, they found Saul and his
sons fallen on Mount Gilboa.
9They stripped him and took
his head and his armor, and
sent messengers throughout
the land of the Philistines to
proclaim the news among
their idols and their people.
10They put his armor in the
temple of their gods and hung
up his head in the temple of
Dagon.
11When all the inhabitants
of Jabesh Gilead heard of
everything the Philistines had
done to Saul, 12all their valiant
men went and took the bodies
of Saul and his sons and
brought them to Jabesh. Then
they buried their bones under
the great tree in Jabesh, and
they fasted seven days.
13Saul died because he was
unfaithful to the LORD; he did
not keep the word of the LORD
and even consulted a medium
for guidance, 14and did not inquire of the LORD. So the LORD
put him to death and turned
the kingdom over to David
son of Jesse.

David Becomes King Over Israel

11 All Israel came together
to David at Hebron
and said, "We are your own
flesh and blood. 2In the past,

*9 Most mss have *dagesh* in the *pe* (פּ׳).

גַּם־ תְּמוֹל גַּם־ שִׁלְשׁוֹם גַּם בִּהְיוֹת שָׁאוּל מֶלֶךְ אַתָּה
you king Saul while-to-be even before even yesterday even (2)

הַמּוֹצִיא וְהַמֵּבִיא אֶת־ יִשְׂרָאֵל וַיֹּאמֶר יְהוָה
Yahweh and-he-said Israel *** and-the-one-leading-in the-one-leading-out

אֱלֹהֶיךָ לְךָ אַתָּה תִרְעֶה אֶת־ עַמִּי אֶת־יִשְׂרָאֵל וְאַתָּה
and-you Israel *** people-of-me *** you-will-shepherd you to-you God-of-you

תִּהְיֶה נָגִיד עַל עַמִּי יִשְׂרָאֵל׃ וַיָּבֹאוּ כָּל־
all-of when-they-came (3) Israel people-of-me over ruler you-will-become

זִקְנֵי יִשְׂרָאֵל אֶל־ הַמֶּלֶךְ חֶבְרוֹנָה וַיִּכְרֹת לָהֶם דָּוִיד בְּרִית
compact David with-them then-he-made at-Hebron the-king to Israel elders-of

בְּחֶבְרוֹן לִפְנֵי יְהוָה וַיִּמְשְׁחוּ אֶת־ דָּוִיד לְמֶלֶךְ עַל־ יִשְׂרָאֵל
Israel over as-king David *** and-they-anointed Yahweh before at-Hebron

כִּדְבַר יְהוָה בְּיַד־ שְׁמוּאֵל׃ וַיֵּלֶךְ דָּוִיד וְכָל־
and-all-of David then-he-marched (4) Samuel by-hand-of Yahweh as-promise-of

יִשְׂרָאֵל יְרוּשָׁלִַם הִיא יְבוּס וְשָׁם הַיְבוּסִי יֹשְׁבֵי הָאָרֶץ׃
the-land ones-living-of the-Jebusite and-there Jebus that Jerusalem Israel

וַיֹּאמְרוּ יֹשְׁבֵי יְבוּס לְדָוִיד לֹא תָבוֹא הֵנָּה
to-here you-will-get-in not to-David Jebus ones-living-of and-they-said (5)

וַיִּלְכֹּד דָּוִיד אֶת־ מְצֻדַת צִיּוֹן הִיא עִיר דָּוִיד׃ וַיֹּאמֶר
and-he-said (6) David City-of that Zion fortress-of *** David but-he-captured

דָּוִיד כָּל־ מַכֵּה יְבוּסִי בָּרִאשֹׁנָה יִהְיֶה לְרֹאשׁ
as-commander he-will-become at-the-first Jebusite one-attacking any-of David

וּלְשָׂר וַיַּעַל בָּרִאשׁוֹנָה יוֹאָב בֶּן־ צְרוּיָה וַיְהִי
so-he-became Zeruiah son-of Joab at-the-first and-he-went-up and-as-chief

לְרֹאשׁ׃ וַיֵּשֶׁב דָּוִיד בַּמְצָד עַל־ כֵּן קָרְאוּ־
they-called this for in-the-fortress David then-he-resided (7) as-commander

לוֹ עִיר דָּוִיד׃ וַיִּבֶן הָעִיר מִסָּבִיב מִן־ הַמִּלּוֹא
the-terrace from at-around the-city and-he-built-up (8) David City-of to-him

וְעַד־ הַסָּבִיב וְיוֹאָב יְחַיֶּה אֶת־ שְׁאָר הָעִיר
the-city rest-of *** he-restored while-Joab the-one-surrounding and-to

וַיֵּלֶךְ דָּוִיד הָלוֹךְ וְגָדוֹל וַיהוָה
and-Yahweh-of and-to-become-powerful to-continue David and-he-continued (9)

צְבָאוֹת עִמּוֹ׃ וְאֵלֶּה רָאשֵׁי הַגִּבּוֹרִים אֲשֶׁר לְדָוִיד
of-David who the-mighty-men chiefs-of and-these (10) with-him Hosts

הַמִּתְחַזְּקִים עִמּוֹ בְמַלְכוּתוֹ עִם־ כָּל־ יִשְׂרָאֵל
Israel all-of with in-kingship-of-him to-him the-ones-giving-support

לְהַמְלִיכוֹ כִּדְבַר יְהוָה עַל־ יִשְׂרָאֵל׃ וְאֵלֶּה מִסְפַּר
list-of and-these (11) Israel over Yahweh as-promise-of to-make-king-him

even while Saul was king, you
were the one who led Israel on
their military campaigns. And
the LORD your God said to you,
'You will shepherd my people
Israel, and you will become
their ruler.' "
3When all the elders of Israel
had come to King David at
Hebron, he made a compact
with them at Hebron before
the LORD, and they anointed
David king over Israel, as the
LORD had promised through
Samuel.

David Conquers Jerusalem

4David and all the Israelites
marched to Jerusalem, that is,
Jebus. The Jebusites who lived
there 5said to David, "You will
not get in here." Nevertheless,
David captured the fortress of
Zion, the City of David.
6David had said, "Whoever
leads the attack on the Jebusites will become commander-
in-chief." Joab son of Zeruiah
went up first, and so he received the command.
7David then took up resi-
dence in the fortress, and so it
was called the City of David.
8He built up the city around it,
from the supporting terraces[w]
to the surrounding wall, while
Joab restored the rest of the
city. 9And David became more
and more powerful, because
the LORD Almighty was with
him.

David's Mighty Men

10These were the chiefs of
David's mighty men—they,
together with all Israel, gave
his kingship strong support to
extend it over the whole land,
as the LORD had promised—

[w]8 Or *the Millo*

הַגִּבֹּרִים אֲשֶׁר לְדָוִיד יָשָׁבְעָם בֶּן־ חַכְמוֹנִי רֹאשׁ הַשָּׁלוֹשִׁים
the-Thirty chief-of Hacmoni son-of Jashobeam of-David who the-mighty-men

הוּא־ עוֹרֵר אֶת־ חֲנִיתוֹ עַל־ שְׁלֹשׁ־ מֵאוֹת חָלָל
killed hundreds three-of against spear-of-him *** one-raising he

בְּפַעַם אֶחָת׃ וְאַחֲרָיו אֶלְעָזָר בֶּן־ דּוֹדוֹ הָאֲחוֹחִי הוּא
he the-Ahohite Dodai son-of Eleazar and-next-to-him (12) one in-encounter

בִּשְׁלוֹשָׁה הַגִּבֹּרִים׃ הוּא־ הָיָה עִם־ דָּוִיד בַּפַּס דַּמִּים
Dammim at-the-Pas David with he-was he (13) the-mighty-men of-three

וְהַפְּלִשְׁתִּים נֶאֶסְפוּ־ שָׁם לַמִּלְחָמָה וַתְּהִי
and-she-was for-the-battle there they-gathered when-the-Philistines

חֶלְקַת הַשָּׂדֶה מְלֵאָה שְׂעוֹרִים וְהָעָם נָסוּ מִפְּנֵי
from-before they-fled and-the-troop barleys full the-field place-of

פְלִשְׁתִּים׃ וַיִּתְיַצְּבוּ בְתוֹךְ־ הַחֶלְקָה
the-field in-middle-of but-they-took-stand (14) Philistines

וַיַּצִּילוּהָ וַיַּכּוּ אֶת־ פְּלִשְׁתִּים
Philistines *** and-they-struck-down and-they-defended-her

וַיּוֹשַׁע יְהוָה תְּשׁוּעָה גְדוֹלָה׃ וַיֵּרְדוּ שְׁלוֹשָׁה
three and-they-came-down (15) great victory Yahweh and-he-brought-victory

מִן־ הַשְּׁלוֹשִׁים רֹאשׁ עַל־ הַצֻּר אֶל־ דָּוִיד אֶל־ מְעָרַת עֲדֻלָּם וּמַחֲנֵה
and-band-of Adullam cave-of at David to the-rock to chief the-thirty from

פְלִשְׁתִּים חֹנָה בְּעֵמֶק רְפָאִים׃ וְדָוִיד אָז בַּמְּצוּדָה
in-the-stronghold then and-David (16) Rephaim in-Valley-of camping Philistines

וּנְצִיב פְּלִשְׁתִּים אָז בְּבֵית לָחֶם׃ וַיִּתְאָו דָּוִיד
David and-he-longed (17) Lehem at-Beth then Philistines and-garrison-of

וַיֹּאמַר מִי יַשְׁקֵנִי מַיִם מִבּוֹר בֵּית־ לֶחֶם אֲשֶׁר
that Lehem Beth from-well-of waters he-will-draw-for-me who? and-he-said

בַּשָּׁעַר׃ וַיִּבְקְעוּ הַשְּׁלֹשָׁה בְּמַחֲנֵה פְלִשְׁתִּים
Philistines through-line-of the-Three and-they-broke (18) near-the-gate

וַיִּשְׁאֲבוּ־ מַיִם מִבּוֹר בֵּית־ לֶחֶם אֲשֶׁר בַּשַּׁעַר
near-the-gate that Lehem Beth from-well-of waters and-they-drew

וַיִּשְׂאוּ וַיָּבִאוּ אֶל־ דָּוִיד וְלֹא־ אָבָה דָוִיד
David he-would but-not David to and-they-brought and-they-carried

לִשְׁתּוֹתָם וַיְנַסֵּךְ אֹתָם לַיהוָה׃ וַיֹּאמֶר
and-he-said (19) before-Yahweh them and-he-poured-out to-drink-them

חָלִילָה לִּי מֵאֱלֹהַי מֵעֲשׂוֹת זֹאת הֲדַם הָאֲנָשִׁים
the-men blood-of? this from-to-do from-God-of-me from-me far-be-it!

הָאֵלֶּה אֶשְׁתֶּה בְנַפְשׁוֹתָם כִּי בְנַפְשׁוֹתָם
at-lives-of-them because at-lives-of-them should-I-drink the-these

°11 ק השלישים
°17 ק ויתאיו

[11]this is the list of David's mighty men:
Jashobeam,[x] a Hacmonite, was chief of the officers[y]; he raised his spear against three hundred men, whom he killed in one encounter.
[12]Next to him was Eleazar son of Dodai the Ahohite, one of the three mighty men. [13]He was with David at Pas Dammim when the Philistines gathered there for battle. At a place where there was a field full of barley, the troops fled from the Philistines. [14]But they took their stand in the middle of the field. They defended it and struck the Philistines down, and the LORD brought about a great victory.
[15]Three of the thirty chiefs came down to David to the rock at the cave of Adullam, while a band of Philistines was encamped in the Valley of Rephaim. [16]At that time David was in the stronghold, and the Philistine garrison was at Bethlehem. [17]David longed for water and said, "Oh, that someone would get me a drink of water from the well near the gate of Bethlehem!" [18]So the Three broke through the Philistine lines, drew water from the well near the gate of Bethlehem and carried it back to David. But he refused to drink it; instead, he poured it out before the LORD. [19]"God forbid that I should do this!" he said. "Should I drink the blood of these men who went at the risk of their lives?" Because they risked their lives to bring

x11 Possibly a variant of *Jashob-Baal*
y11 Or *Thirty;* some Septuagint manuscripts *Three* (see also 2 Samuel 23:8)

הֱבִיאוּם וְלֹא אָבָה לִשְׁתּוֹתָם אֵלֶּה עָשׂוּ שְׁלֹשֶׁת
three-of they-did these to-drink-them he-would then-not they-brought-them

הַגִּבּוֹרִים׃ וְאַבְשַׁי אֲחִי־יוֹאָב הוּא הָיָה רֹאשׁ הַשְּׁלוֹשָׁה
the-Three chief-of he-was he Joab brother-of and-Abishai (20) the-mighty-men

וְהוּא עוֹרֵר אֶת־חֲנִיתוֹ עַל־שְׁלֹשׁ מֵאוֹת חָלָל
one-killed hundreds three-of against spear-of-him *** one-raising and-he

וְלֹא־שֵׁם בַּשְּׁלוֹשָׁה׃ מִן־הַשְּׁלוֹשָׁה בַשְּׁנַיִם
by-the-two-times the-Three above (21) among-the-Three name so-to-him

נִכְבָּד וַיְהִי לָהֶם לְשָׂר וְעַד־הַשְּׁלוֹשָׁה לֹא־
not the-Three though-among as-commander to-them and-he-became being-honored

בָא׃ בְּנָיָה בֶן־יְהוֹיָדָע בֶּן־אִישׁ־חַיִל רַב־
great-of valor man-of son-of Jehoiada son-of Benaiah (22) he-entered

פְּעָלִים מִן־קַבְצְאֵל הוּא הִכָּה אֵת שְׁנֵי אֲרִיאֵל מוֹאָב וְהוּא
and-he Moab best-man-of two-of *** he-struck-down he Kabzeel from exploits

יָרַד וְהִכָּה אֶת־הָאֲרִי בְּתוֹךְ הַבּוֹר בְּיוֹם הַשָּׁלֶג׃
the-snow on-day-of the-pit inside-of the-lion *** and-he-killed he-went-down

וְהוּא־הִכָּה אֶת־הָאִישׁ הַמִּצְרִי אִישׁ מִדָּה ׀ חָמֵשׁ
five size man-of the-Egyptian the-man *** he-struck-down and-he (23)

בָּאַמָּה וּבְיַד הַמִּצְרִי חֲנִית כִּמְנוֹר אֹרְגִים
ones-weaving like-rod-of spear the-Egyptian though-in-hand-of by-the-cubit

וַיֵּרֶד אֵלָיו בַּשָּׁבֶט וַיִּגְזֹל אֶת־הַחֲנִית
the-spear *** and-he-snatched with-the-club against-him and-he-went

מִיַּד הַמִּצְרִי וַיַּהַרְגֵהוּ בַּחֲנִיתוֹ׃ אֵלֶּה
these (24) with-spear-of-him and-he-killed-him the-Egyptian from-hand-of

עָשָׂה בְּנָיָהוּ בֶּן־יְהוֹיָדָע וְלוֹ־שֵׁם בִּשְׁלוֹשָׁה הַגִּבֹּרִים׃
the-mighty-men among-three name and-to-him Jehoiada son-of Benaiah he-did

מִן־הַשְּׁלוֹשִׁים הִנּוֹ נִכְבָּד הוּא וְאֶל־הַשְּׁלוֹשָׁה לֹא־
not the-Three but-among he being-honored see-he! the-Thirty more-than (25)

בָא וַיְשִׂימֵהוּ דָוִיד עַל־מִשְׁמַעְתּוֹ׃
bodyguard-of-him over David and-he-put-in-charge-him he-entered

וְגִבּוֹרֵי הַחֲיָלִים עֲשָׂה־אֵל אֲחִי יוֹאָב אֶלְחָנָן
Elhanan Joab brother-of El Asah the-valiant-ones and-mighty-men-of (26)

בֶּן־דּוֹדוֹ מִבֵּית לָחֶם׃ שַׁמּוֹת הַהֲרוֹרִי חֶלֶץ הַפְּלוֹנִי׃
the-Pelonite Helez the-Harorite Shammoth (27) Lehem from-Beth Dodo son-of

עִירָא בֶּן־עִקֵּשׁ הַתְּקוֹעִי אֲבִיעֶזֶר הָעַנְּתוֹתִי׃ סִבְּכַי
Sibbecai (29) the-Anathothite Abiezer the-Tekoaite Ikkesh son-of Ira (28)

הַחֻשָׁתִי עִילַי הָאֲחוֹחִי׃ מַהְרַי הַנְּטֹפָתִי חֵלֶד בֶּן־
son-of Heled the-Netophathite Maharai (30) the-Ahohite Ilai the-Hushathite

°20 ק ולו

it back, David would not drink it.

Such were the exploits of the three mighty men.

20Abishai the brother of Joab was chief of the Three. He raised his spear against three hundred men, whom he killed, and so he became as famous as the Three. 21He was doubly honored above the Three and became their commander, even though he was not included among them.

22Benaiah son of Jehoiada was a valiant fighter from Kabzeel, who performed great exploits. He struck down two of Moab's best men. He also went down into a pit on a snowy day and killed a lion. 23And he struck down an Egyptian who was seven and a half feet[z] tall. Although the Egyptian had a spear like a weaver's rod in his hand, Benaiah went against him with a club. He snatched the spear from the Egyptian's hand and killed him with his own spear. 24Such were the exploits of Benaiah son of Jehoiada; he too was as famous as the three mighty men. 25He was held in greater honor than any of the Thirty, but he was not included among the Three. And David put him in charge of his bodyguard.

26The mighty men were:
Asahel the brother of Joab,
Elhanan son of Dodo from Bethlehem,
27Shammoth the Harorite,
Helez the Pelonite,
28Ira son of Ikkesh from Tekoa,
Abiezer from Anathoth,
29Sibbecai the Hushathite,
Ilai the Ahohite,
30Maharai the Netophathite,
Heled son of Baanah the

z23 Hebrew *five cubits* (about 2.3 meters)

בַּעֲנָה הַנְּטוֹפָתִי׃ אִיתַי בֶּן־ רִיבַי מִגִּבְעַת בְּנֵי
sons-of from-Gibeah-of Ribai son-of Ithai (31) the-Netophathite Baanah

בִּנְיָמִן בְּנָיָה הַפִּרְעָתֹנִי׃ חוּרַי מִנַּחֲלֵי גָעַשׁ אֲבִיאֵל
Abiel Gaash from-ravines-of Hurai (32) the-Pirathonite Benaiah Benjamin

הָעַרְבָתִי׃ עַזְמָוֶת הַבַּחֲרוּמִי אֶלְיַחְבָּא הַשַּׁעַלְבֹנִי׃
the-Shaalbonite Eliahba the-Baharumite Azmaveth (33) the-Arbathite

בְּנֵי הָשֵׁם הַגִּזוֹנִי יוֹנָתָן בֶּן־ שָׁגֵה הַהֲרָרִי׃
the-Hararite Shagee son-of Jonathan the-Gizonite Hashem sons-of (34)

אֲחִיאָם בֶּן־ שָׂכָר הַהֲרָרִי אֱלִיפַל בֶּן־ אוּר׃ חֵפֶר
Hepher (36) Ur son-of Eliphal the-Hararite Sacar son-of Ahiam (35)

הַמְּכֵרָתִי אֲחִיָּה הַפְּלֹנִי׃ חֶצְרוֹ הַכַּרְמְלִי נַעֲרַי בֶּן־
son-of Naarai the-Carmelite Hezro (37) the-Pelonite Ahijah the-Mekerathite

אֶזְבָּי׃ יוֹאֵל אֲחִי נָתָן מִבְחָר בֶּן־ הַגְרִי׃ צֶלֶק
Zelek (39) Hagri son-of Mibhar Nathan brother-of Joel (38) Ezbai

הָעַמּוֹנִי נַחְרַי הַבֵּרֹתִי נֹשֵׂא כְּלֵי יוֹאָב בֶּן־
son-of Joab armors-of one-bearing-of the-Berothite Naharai the-Ammonite

צְרוּיָה׃ עִירָא הַיִּתְרִי גָּרֵב הַיִּתְרִי׃ אוּרִיָּה הַחִתִּי
the-Hittite Uriah (41) the-Ithrite Gareb the-Ithrite Ira (40) Zeruiah

זָבָד בֶּן־ אַחְלָי׃ עֲדִינָא בֶּן־ שִׁיזָא הָרְאוּבֵנִי רֹאשׁ
chief the-Reubenite Shiza son-of Adina (42) Ahlai son-of Zabad

לָרְאוּבֵנִי וְעָלָיו שְׁלוֹשִׁים׃ חָנָן בֶּן־ מַעֲכָה וְיוֹשָׁפָט
and-Joshaphat Maacah son-of Hanan (43) thirty and-with-him of-the-Reubenite

הַמִּתְנִי׃ עֻזִּיָּא הָעַשְׁתְּרָתִי שָׁמָע וִיעוּאֵל בְּנֵי חוֹתָם
Hotham sons-of and-Jeiel Shama the-Ashterathite Uzzia (44) the-Mithnite

הָעֲרֹעֵרִי׃ יְדִיעֲאֵל בֶּן־ שִׁמְרִי וְיֹחָא אָחִיו הַתִּיצִי׃
the-Tizite brother-of-him and-Joha Shimri son-of Jediael (45) the-Aroerite

אֱלִיאֵל הַמַּחֲוִים וִירִיבַי וְיוֹשַׁוְיָה בְּנֵי אֶלְנָעַם וְיִתְמָה
and-Ithmah Elnaam sons-of and-Joshaviah and-Jeribai the-Mahavite Eliel (46)

הַמּוֹאָבִי׃ אֱלִיאֵל וְעוֹבֵד וְיַעֲשִׂיאֵל הַמְּצֹבָיָה׃ וְאֵלֶּה
and-these (12:1) the-Mezobaite and-Jaasiel and-Obed Eliel (47) the-Moabite

הַבָּאִים אֶל־ דָּוִיד לְצִיקְלַג עוֹד עָצוּר מִפְּנֵי
from-presences-of being-banished while at-Ziklag David to the-ones-coming

שָׁאוּל בֶּן־ קִישׁ וְהֵמָּה בַּגִּבּוֹרִים עֹזְרֵי הַמִּלְחָמָה׃
the-battle ones-helping-of among-the-warriors and-they Kish son-of Saul

נֹשְׁקֵי קֶשֶׁת מַיְמִינִים וּמַשְׂמְאִלִים
and-ones-using-left-hand ones-using-right-hand bow ones-being-armed-of (2)

בָּאֲבָנִים וּבַחִצִּים בַּקֶּשֶׁת מֵאֲחֵי שָׁאוּל
Saul from-kinsmen-of with-the-bow and-with-the-arrows with-the-stones

Netophathite,
31 Ithai son of Ribai from
Gibeah of Benjamin,
Benaiah the Pirathonite,
32 Hurai from the ravines of
Gaash,
Abiel the Arbathite,
33 Azmaveth the Baharu-
mite,
Eliahba the Shaalbonite,
34 the sons of Hashem the
Gizonite,
Jonathan son of Shagee
the Hararite,
35 Ahiam son of Sacar the
Hararite,
Eliphal son of Ur,
36 Hepher the Mekerathite,
Ahijah the Pelonite,
37 Hezro the Carmelite,
Naarai son of Ezbai,
38 Joel the brother of Nathan,
Mibhar son of Hagri,
39 Zelek the Ammonite,
Naharai the Berothite,
the armor-bearer of Joab
son of Zeruiah,
40 Ira the Ithrite,
Gareb the Ithrite,
41 Uriah the Hittite,
Zabad son of Ahlai,
42 Adina son of Shiza the
Reubenite, who was
chief of the Reubenites,
and the thirty with him,
43 Hanan son of Maacah,
Joshaphat the Mithnite,
44 Uzzia the Ashterathite,
Shama and Jeiel the sons
of Hotham the Aroerite,
45 Jediael son of Shimri,
his brother Joha the Ti-
zite,
46 Eliel the Mahavite,
Jeribai and Joshaviah the
sons of Elnaam,
Ithmah the Moabite,
47 Eliel, Obed and Jaasiel
the Mezobaite.

Warriors Join David

12 These were the men who came to David at Ziklag, while he was banished from the presence of Saul son of Kish (they were among the warriors who helped him in battle; 2 they were armed with bows and were able to shoot arrows or to sling stones right-handed or left-handed; they were kinsmen of Saul from the

°44 ק ויעיאל

מִבִּנְיָמִן׃ (3) הָרֹאשׁ אֲחִיעֶזֶר וְיוֹאָשׁ בְּנֵי הַשְּׁמָעָה
the-Shemaah sons-of and-Joash Ahiezer the-chief (3) from-Benjamin

הַגִּבְעָתִי וִיזוּאֵל וָפֶלֶט בְּנֵי עַזְמָוֶת וּבְרָכָה וְיֵהוּא
and-Jehu and-Beracah Azmaveth sons-of and-Pelet and-Jeziel the-Gibeathite

הָעֲנְּתֹתִי׃ (4) וְיִשְׁמַעְיָה הַגִּבְעוֹנִי גִּבּוֹר בַּשְּׁלֹשִׁים
among-the-Thirty mighty-man the-Gibeonite and-Ishmaiah (4) the-Anathothite

וְעַל־ הַשְּׁלֹשִׁים׃ *(5) וְיִרְמְיָה וְיַחֲזִיאֵל וְיוֹחָנָן וְיוֹזָבָד
and-Jozabad and-Johanan and-Jahaziel and-Jeremiah *(5) the-Thirty and-over

הַגְּדֵרָתִי׃ (6) אֶלְעוּזַי וִירִימוֹת וּבְעַלְיָה וּשְׁמַרְיָהוּ
and-Shemariah and-Bealiah and-Jerimoth Eluzai (6) the-Gederathite

וּשְׁפַטְיָהוּ הַחֲרִיפִי׃ (7) אֶלְקָנָה וְיִשִּׁיָּהוּ וַעֲזַרְאֵל וְיוֹעֶזֶר
and-Joezer and-Azarel and-Isshiah Elkanah (7) the-Haruphite and-Shephatiah

וְיָשָׁבְעָם הַקָּרְחִים׃ (8) וְיוֹעֵאלָה וּזְבַדְיָה בְּנֵי יְרֹחָם
Jeroham sons-of and-Zebadiah and-Joelah (8) the-Korahites and-Jashobeam

מִן־ הַגְּדוֹר׃ (9) וּמִן־ הַגָּדִי נִבְדְּלוּ אֶל־ דָּוִיד
David to they-defected the-Gadite and-from (9) the-Gedor from

לַמְצַד מִדְבָּרָה גִּבֹּרֵי הַחַיִל אַנְשֵׁי צָבָא
army men-of the-bravery warriors-of in-desert at-the-stronghold

לַמִּלְחָמָה עֹרְכֵי צִנָּה וָרֹמַח וּפְנֵי אַרְיֵה
lion and-faces-of and-spear shield ones-handling-of for-the-battle

פְּנֵיהֶם וְכִצְבָאיִם עַל־ הֶהָרִים לְמַהֵר׃ (10) עֵזֶר
Ezer (10) to-be-swift the-mountains in and-as-gazelles faces-of-them

הָרֹאשׁ עֹבַדְיָה הַשֵּׁנִי אֱלִיאָב הַשְּׁלִשִׁי׃ (11) מִשְׁמַנָּה הָרְבִיעִי
the-fourth Mishmannah (11) the-third Eliab the-second Obadiah the-chief

יִרְמְיָה הַחֲמִשִׁי׃ (12) עַתַּי הַשִּׁשִּׁי אֱלִיאֵל הַשְּׁבִעִי׃ (13) יוֹחָנָן
Johanan (13) the-seventh Eliel the-sixth Attai (12) the-fifth Jeremiah

הַשְּׁמִינִי אֶלְזָבָד הַתְּשִׁיעִי׃ (14) יִרְמְיָהוּ הָעֲשִׂירִי מַכְבַּנַּי עַשְׁתֵּי עָשָׂר׃
ten one-of Macbannai the-tenth Jeremiah (14) the-ninth Elzabad the-eighth

(15) אֵלֶּה מִבְּנֵי־ גָד רָאשֵׁי הַצָּבָא אֶחָד לְמֵאָה הַקָּטָן
the-least for-hundred one the-army commanders-of Gad from-sons-of these (15)

וְהַגָּדוֹל לְאָלֶף׃ (16) אֵלֶּה הֵם אֲשֶׁר עָבְרוּ אֶת־
*** they-crossed who they these (16) for-thousand and-the-greatest

הַיַּרְדֵּן בַּחֹדֶשׁ הָרִאשׁוֹן וְהוּא מְמַלֵּא עַל־ כָּל־
all-of over overflowing when-he the-first in-the-month the-Jordan

גְּדִיֹתָיו וַיַּבְרִיחוּ אֶת־ כָּל־ הָעֲמָקִים לַמִּזְרָח
to-the-east the-valleys all-of *** and-they-put-to-flight banks-of-him

וְלַמַּעֲרָב׃ (17) וַיָּבֹאוּ מִן־ בְּנֵי בִנְיָמִן וִיהוּדָה עַד־
to and-Judah Benjamin sons-of from and-they-came (17) and-to-the-west

tribe of Benjamin):
3Ahiezer their chief and
Joash the sons of Shemaah
the Gibeathite; Jeziel and
Pelet the sons of Azmaveth;
Beracah, Jehu the Ana-
thothite, 4and Ishmaiah the
Gibeonite, a mighty man
among the Thirty, who was
a leader of the Thirty; Jeremiah, Jahaziel, Johanan,
Jozabad the Gederathite,
5Eluzai, Jerimoth, Bealiah,
Shemariah and Shephatiah
the Haruphite; 6Elkanah,
Isshiah, Azarel, Joezer and
Jashobeam the Korahites;
7and Joelah and Zebadiah
the sons of Jeroham from
Gedor.

8Some Gadites defected to
David at his stronghold in the
desert. They were brave warriors, ready for battle and able to
handle the shield and spear.
Their faces were the faces of
lions, and they were as swift
as gazelles in the mountains.
9Ezer was the chief,
Obadiah the second in
command, Eliab the
third,
10Mishmannah the fourth,
Jeremiah the fifth,
11Attai the sixth, Eliel the
seventh,
12Johanan the eighth, El-
zabad the ninth,
13Jeremiah the tenth and
Macbannai the eleventh.
14These Gadites were army
commanders; the least was a
match for a hundred, and the
greatest for a thousand. 15It
was they who crossed the Jordan in the first month when it
was overflowing all its banks,
and they put to flight everyone living in the valleys, to the
east and to the west.
16Other Benjamites and
some men from Judah also

*5 Verse 5 in Hebrew is equivalent to the second half of verse 4 in English; thus, there is a one-verse discrepancy through the rest of the chapter.

°3 ק ויזיאל
°6 ק החרופי
°16 ק גדותיו

לְמָצֵד֙ לְדָוִ֔יד׃ (18) וַיֵּצֵ֣א דָוִ֗יד לִפְנֵיהֶם֒
to-the-stronghold   to-David   (18)   and-he-went-out   David   before-them

וַיַּ֣עַן וַיֹּ֣אמֶר לָהֶ֗ם אִם־לְשָׁל֞וֹם בָּאתֶ֤ם אֵלַי֙ לְעָזְרֵ֔נִי
and-he-replied   and-he-said   to-them   if   in-peace   you-came   to-me   to-help-me

יִהְיֶה־לִּ֧י עֲלֵיכֶ֛ם לֵבָ֥ב לְיָ֖חַד וְאִם־לְרַמּוֹתַ֣נִי לְצָרַ֗י
he-will-be   of-me   with-you   heart   as-one   but-if   to-betray-me   to-enemies-of-me

בְּלֹ֤א חָמָס֙ בְּכַפַּ֔י יֵ֛רֶא אֱלֹהֵ֥י אֲבוֹתֵ֖ינוּ
when-not   violence   in-hands-of-me   may-he-see   God-of   fathers-of-us

וְיוֹכַֽח׃ (19) וְר֣וּחַ לָבְשָׁ֗ה אֶת־עֲמָשַׂ֣י רֹ֣אשׁ
and-may-he-judge   (19)   then-Spirit   she-came-upon   ***   Amasai   chief-of

הַשָּׁלוֹשִׁים֒ לְךָ֤ דָוִיד֙ וְעִמְּךָ֣ בֶן־יִשַׁ֔י שָׁל֧וֹם שָׁל֣וֹם לְךָ֗
the-Thirty   to-you   David   and-with-you   son-of   Jesse   success   success   to-you

וְשָׁל֣וֹם לְעֹזְרֶ֗ךָ כִּ֥י עֲזָרְךָ֖ אֱלֹהֶ֑ךָ
and-success   to-one-helping-you   for   he-will-help-you   God-of-you

וַיְקַבְּלֵ֣ם דָּוִ֔יד וַֽיִּתְּנֵ֖ם בְּרָאשֵׁ֥י הַגְּדֽוּד׃
so-he-received-them   David   and-he-made-them   as-leaders-of   the-raiding-band

(20) וּמִֽמְּנַשֶּׁ֗ה נָפְל֤וּ עַל־דָּוִיד֙ בְּבֹא֣וֹ עִם־
(20)   and-from-Manasseh   they-defected   to   David   when-to-go-him   with

פְּלִשְׁתִּ֧ים עַל־שָׁא֛וּל לַמִּלְחָמָ֖ה וְלֹ֣א עֲזָרֻ֑ם כִּ֣י
Philistines   against   Saul   to-the-fight   but-not   they-helped-them   because

בְעֵצָ֗ה שִׁלְּחֻ֛הוּ סַרְנֵ֥י פְלִשְׁתִּ֖ים לֵאמֹ֑ר
after-consultation   they-sent-away-him   rulers-of   Philistines   to-say

בְּרָאשֵׁ֣ינוּ יִפּ֗וֹל אֶל־אֲדֹנָ֖יו שָׁאֽוּל׃ (21) בְּלֶכְתּ֣וֹ אֶל־
at-heads-of-us   if-he-deserts   to   masters-of-him   Saul   (21)   when-to-go-him   to

צִֽיקְלַג֒ נָפְל֣וּ עָלָ֣יו ׀ מִֽמְּנַשֶּׁ֗ה עַדְנַ֤ח וְיוֹזָבָד֙ וִֽידִֽיעֲאֵ֔ל
Ziklag   they-defected   to-him   from-Manasseh   Adnah   and-Jozabad   and-Jediael

וּמִיכָאֵ֣ל וְיוֹזָבָ֔ד וֶֽאֱלִיה֖וּא וְצִלְּתָ֑י רָאשֵׁ֥י הָאֲלָפִ֖ים
and-Michael   and-Jozabad   and-Elihu   and-Zillethai   leaders-of   the-thousands

אֲשֶׁ֥ר לִמְנַשֶּֽׁה׃ (22) וְהֵ֗מָּה עָזְר֤וּ עִם־דָּוִיד֙ עַל־הַגְּד֔וּד
who   in-Manasseh   (22)   and-they   they-helped   to   David   against   the-raiding-band

כִּֽי־גִבּ֥וֹרֵי חַ֖יִל כֻּלָּ֑ם וַיִּהְי֥וּ שָׂרִ֖ים בַּצָּבָֽא׃
for   warriors-of   bravery   all-of-them   and-they-were   commanders   in-the-army

(23) כִּ֚י לְעֶת־י֣וֹם בְּי֔וֹם יָבֹ֥אוּ עַל־דָּוִ֖יד לְעָזְר֑וֹ עַד־
(23)   indeed   at-time-of   day   after-day   they-came   to   David   to-help-him   until

לְמַחֲנֶ֥ה גָד֖וֹל כְּמַחֲנֵ֥ה אֱלֹהִֽים׃ (24) וְאֵ֗לֶּה מִסְפְּרֵ֛י רָאשֵׁ֥י
to-army   great   like-army-of   mighty-ones   (24)   and-these   numbers-of   heads-of

הֶֽחָלוּץ֙ לַצָּבָ֔א בָּ֥אוּ עַל־דָּוִ֖יד חֶבְר֑וֹנָה לְהָסֵ֛ב
the-one-being-armed   for-the-battle   they-came   to   David   at-Hebron   to-turn-over

came to David in his stronghold. [17]David went out to meet them and said to them, "If you have come to me in peace, to help me, I am ready to have you unite with me. But if you have come to betray me to my enemies when my hands are free from violence, may the God of our fathers see it and judge you."

[18]Then the Spirit came upon Amasai, chief of the Thirty, and he said:

"We are yours, O David!
  We are with you, O son
    of Jesse!
Success, success to you,
  and success to those who
    help you,
for your God will help
  you."

So David received them and made them leaders of his raiding bands.

[19]Some of the men of Manasseh defected to David when he went with the Philistines to fight against Saul. (He and his men did not help the Philistines because, after consultation, their rulers sent him away. They said, "It will cost us our heads if he deserts to his master Saul.") [20]When David went to Ziklag, these were the men of Manasseh who defected to him: Adnah, Jozabad, Jediael, Michael, Jozabad, Elihu and Zillethai, leaders of units of a thousand in Manasseh. [21]They helped David against raiding bands, for all of them were brave warriors, and they were commanders in his army. [22]Day after day men came to help David, until he had a great and mighty army.

Others Join David at Hebron

[23]These are the numbers of the men armed for battle who came to David at Hebron to

*See the note on page 36.
ק הַשָּׁלוֹשִׁים °19

מַלְכוּת שָׁאוּל אֵלָיו כְּפִי יְהוָה׃ בְּנֵי יְהוּדָה נֹשְׂאֵי
ones-carrying-of Judah men-of (25) Yahweh as-saying-of to-him Saul kingdom-of

צִנָּה וָרֹמַח שֵׁשֶׁת אֲלָפִים וּשְׁמוֹנֶה מֵאוֹת חֲלוּצֵי
ones-being-armed-of hundreds and-eight thousands six-of and-spear shield

צָבָא׃ מִן־ בְּנֵי שִׁמְעוֹן גִּבּוֹרֵי חַיִל לַצָּבָא שִׁבְעַת
seven-of for-the-battle bravery warriors-of Simeon men-of from (26) battle

אֲלָפִים וּמֵאָה׃ מִן־ בְּנֵי הַלֵּוִי אַרְבַּעַת אֲלָפִים וְשֵׁשׁ
and-six thousands four-of the-Levite men-of from (27) and-hundred thousands

מֵאוֹת׃ וִיהוֹיָדָע הַנָּגִיד לְאַהֲרֹן וְעִמּוֹ שְׁלֹשֶׁת
three-of and-with-him of-Aaron the-leader and-Jehoiada (28) hundreds

אֲלָפִים וּשְׁבַע מֵאוֹת׃ וְצָדוֹק נַעַר גִּבּוֹר חָיִל
bravery warrior-of young and-Zadok (29) hundreds and-seven-of thousands

וּבֵית־ אָבִיו שָׂרִים עֶשְׂרִים וּשְׁנָיִם׃ וּמִן־ בְּנֵי
men-of and-from (30) and-two twenty officers father-of-him and-family-of

בִנְיָמִן אֲחֵי שָׁאוּל שְׁלֹשֶׁת אֲלָפִים וְעַד־ הֵנָּה מַרְבִּיתָם
most-of-them to-then and-until thousands three-of Saul kinsmen-of Benjamin

שֹׁמְרִים מִשְׁמֶרֶת בֵּית שָׁאוּל׃ וּמִן־ בְּנֵי אֶפְרַיִם
Ephraim men-of and-from (31) Saul house-of loyalty-of ones-being-loyal

עֶשְׂרִים אֶלֶף וּשְׁמוֹנֶה מֵאוֹת גִּבּוֹרֵי חַיִל אַנְשֵׁי שֵׁמוֹת
names men-of bravery warriors-of hundreds and-eight thousand twenty

לְבֵית אֲבוֹתָם׃ וּמֵחֲצִי מַטֵּה מְנַשֶּׁה שְׁמוֹנָה
eight Manasseh tribe-of and-from-half-of (32) fathers-of-them in-family-of

עָשָׂר אֶלֶף אֲשֶׁר נִקְּבוּ בְּשֵׁמוֹת לָבוֹא לְהַמְלִיךְ אֶת־
*** and-to-make-king to-come by-names they-were-designated who thousand ten

דָּוִיד׃ וּמִבְּנֵי יִשָּׂשכָר יוֹדְעֵי בִינָה לַעִתִּים
of-the-times understanding ones-knowing-of Issachar and-from-men-of (33) David

לָדַעַת מַה־ יַּעֲשֶׂה יִשְׂרָאֵל רָאשֵׁיהֶם מָאתַיִם וְכָל־
and-all-of two-hundreds chiefs-of-them Israel he-should-do what to-know

אֲחֵיהֶם עַל־ פִּיהֶם׃ מִזְּבֻלוּן יוֹצְאֵי
ones-going-out-of from-Zebulun (34) command-of-them under relatives-of-them

צָבָא עֹרְכֵי מִלְחָמָה בְּכָל־ כְּלֵי מִלְחָמָה חֲמִשִּׁים
fifty battle weapons-of with-all-of battle ones-being-prepared-of army

אֶלֶף וְלַעֲדֹר בְּלֹא־ לֵב וָלֵב׃ וּמִנַּפְתָּלִי שָׂרִים
officers and-from-Naphtali (35) and-heart heart with-not and-to-help thousand

אָלֶף וְעִמָּהֶם בְּצִנָּה וַחֲנִית שְׁלֹשִׁים וְשִׁבְעָה אָלֶף׃
thousand and-seven thirty and-spear with-shield and-with-them thousand

וּמִן־ הַדָּנִי עֹרְכֵי מִלְחָמָה עֶשְׂרִים־ וּשְׁמוֹנָה אֶלֶף
thousand and-eight twenty battle ones-being-ready-of the-Danite and-from (36)

turn Saul's kingdom over to him, as the LORD had said:

24men of Judah, carrying shield and spear—6,800 armed for battle;

25men of Simeon, warriors ready for battle—7,100;

26men of Levi—4,600, 27including Jehoiada, leader of the family of Aaron, with 3,700 men, 28and Zadok, a brave young warrior, with 22 officers from his family;

29men of Benjamin, Saul's kinsmen—3,000, most of whom had remained loyal to Saul's house until then;

30men of Ephraim, brave warriors, famous in their own clans—20,800;

31men of half the tribe of Manasseh, designated by name to come and make David king—18,000;

32men of Issachar, who understood the times and knew what Israel should do—200 chiefs, with all their relatives under their command;

33men of Zebulun, experienced soldiers prepared for battle with every type of weapon, to help David with undivided loyalty—50,000;

34men of Naphtali—1,000 officers, together with 37,000 men carrying shields and spears;

35men of Dan, ready for battle—28,600;

*See the note on page 36.

וְשֵׁשׁ מֵאוֹת׃ וּמֵאָשֵׁר יוֹצְאֵי צָבָא לַעֲרֹךְ

to-be-prepared army ones-going-out-of and-from-Asher (37) hundreds and-six

מִלְחָמָה אַרְבָּעִים אָלֶף׃ וּמֵעֵבֶר לַיַּרְדֵּן מִן־ הָרְאוּבֵנִי

the-Reubenite from of-the-Jordan and-from-east (38) thousand forty battle

וְהַגָּדִי וַחֲצִי ׀ שֵׁבֶט מְנַשֶּׁה בְּכֹל כְּלֵי צְבָא

army-of weapons-of with-all-of Manasseh tribe-of and-half-of and-the-Gadite

מִלְחָמָה מֵאָה וְעֶשְׂרִים אָלֶף׃ כָּל־ אֵלֶּה אַנְשֵׁי מִלְחָמָה

fight men-of these all-of (39) thousand and-twenty hundred war

עֹדְרֵי מַעֲרָכָה בְּלֵבָב שָׁלֵם בָּאוּ חֶבְרוֹנָה לְהַמְלִיךְ אֶת־

*** to-make-king to-Hebron they-came whole with-heart rank ones-serving-of

דָּוִיד עַל־ כָּל־ יִשְׂרָאֵל וְגַם כָּל־ שֵׁרִית יִשְׂרָאֵל לֵב אֶחָד

one mind Israel rest-of all-of and-also Israel all-of over David

לְהַמְלִיךְ אֶת־ דָּוִיד׃ וַיִּהְיוּ־ שָׁם עִם־ דָּוִיד יָמִים שְׁלוֹשָׁה

three days David with there and-they-were (40) David *** to-make-king

אֹכְלִים וְשׁוֹתִים כִּי־ הֵכִינוּ לָהֶם אֲחֵיהֶם׃

families-of-them for-them they-supplied for and-ones-drinking ones-eating

וְגַם הַקְּרוֹבִים־ אֲלֵיהֶם עַד־ יִשָּׂשכָר וּזְבֻלוּן

and-Zebulun Issachar as-far-as to-them the-neighbors and-also (41)

וְנַפְתָּלִי מְבִיאִים לֶחֶם בַּחֲמוֹרִים וּבַגְּמַלִּים

and-on-the-camels on-the-donkeys food ones-bringing and-Naphtali

וּבַפְּרָדִים ׀ וּבַבָּקָר מַאֲכָל קֶמַח דְּבֵלִים וְצִמּוּקִים

and-raisin-cakes fig-cakes flour supply and-on-the-ox and-on-the-mules

וְיַיִן־ וְשֶׁמֶן וּבָקָר וְצֹאן לָרֹב כִּי שִׂמְחָה בְּיִשְׂרָאֵל׃

in-Israel joy for to-plenty and-sheep and-cattle and-oil and-wine

וַיִּוָּעַץ דָּוִיד עִם־ שָׂרֵי הָאֲלָפִים

the-thousands commanders-of with David and-he-conferred (13:1)

וְהַמֵּאוֹת לְכָל־ נָגִיד׃ וַיֹּאמֶר דָּוִיד לְכֹל ׀

to-whole-of David then-he-said (2) officer with-each-of and-the-hundreds

קְהַל יִשְׂרָאֵל אִם־עֲלֵיכֶם טוֹב וּמִן־ יְהוָה אֱלֹהֵינוּ נִפְרְצָה

let-us-spread-out God-of-us Yahweh and-from good to-you if Israel assembly-of

נִשְׁלְחָה עַל־ אַחֵינוּ הַנִּשְׁאָרִים בְּכֹל

through-all-of the-ones-being-left brothers-of-us to let-us-send

אַרְצוֹת יִשְׂרָאֵל וְעִמָּהֶם הַכֹּהֲנִים וְהַלְוִיִּם בְּעָרֵי

in-towns-of and-the-Levites the-priests and-with-them Israel territories-of

מִגְרְשֵׁיהֶם וְיִקָּבְצוּ אֵלֵינוּ׃ וְנָסֵבָּה אֶת־

*** and-let-us-bring-back (3) with-us and-let-them-join pastures-of-them

אֲרוֹן אֱלֹהֵינוּ אֵלֵינוּ כִּי־ לֹא דְרַשְׁנֻהוּ בִּימֵי שָׁאוּל׃

Saul in-days-of we-inquired-of-him not for to-us God-of-us ark-of

36 men of Asher, experienced soldiers prepared for battle—40,000;
37 and from east of the Jordan, men of Reuben, Gad and the half-tribe of Manasseh, armed with every type of weapon—120,000.
38 All these were fighting men who volunteered to serve in the ranks. They came to Hebron fully determined to make David king over all Israel. All the rest of the Israelites were also of one mind to make David king.
39 The men spent three days there with David, eating and drinking, for their families had supplied provisions for them.
40 Also, their neighbors from as far away as Issachar, Zebulun and Naphtali came bringing food on donkeys, camels, mules and oxen. There were plentiful supplies of flour, fig cakes, raisin cakes, wine, oil, cattle and sheep, for there was joy in Israel.

Bringing Back the Ark

13 David conferred with each of his officers, the commanders of thousands and commanders of hundreds.
2 He then said to the whole assembly of Israel, "If it seems good to you and if it is the will of the LORD our God, let us send word far and wide to the rest of our brothers throughout the territories of Israel, and also to the priests and Levites who are with them in their towns and pasturelands, to come and join us.
3 Let us bring the ark of our God back to us, for we did not inquire of[a] it[b] during the reign of

[a] 3 Or *we neglected* [b] 3 Or *him*

*See the note on page 36.

וַיֹּאמְרוּ כָל־ הַקָּהָל לַעֲשׂוֹת כֵּן כִּי־ יָשַׁר
he-was-right because this to-do the-assembly whole-of and-they-said (4)

הַדָּבָר בְּעֵינֵי כָל־ הָעָם׃ וַיַּקְהֵל דָּוִיד אֶת־ כָּל־
all-of *** David so-he-assembled (5) the-people all-of in-eyes-of the-thing

יִשְׂרָאֵל מִן־ שִׁיחוֹר מִצְרַיִם וְעַד־ לְבוֹא חֲמָת לְהָבִיא אֶת־ אֲרוֹן
ark-of *** to-bring Hamath Lebo and-to Egypt Shihor-of from Israel

הָאֱלֹהִים מִקִּרְיַת יְעָרִים׃ וַיַּעַל דָּוִיד וְכָל־ יִשְׂרָאֵל
Israel and-all-of David and-he-went (6) Jearim from-Kiriath the-God

בַּעֲלָתָה אֶל־ קִרְיַת יְעָרִים אֲשֶׁר לִיהוּדָה לְהַעֲלוֹת מִשָּׁם אֵת אֲרוֹן
ark-of *** from-there to-bring-up in-Judah that Jearim Kiriath to to-Baalah

הָאֱלֹהִים ׀ יְהוָה יוֹשֵׁב הַכְּרוּבִים אֲשֶׁר־ נִקְרָא שֵׁם׃
Name he-is-called that the-cherubim being-enthroned-of Yahweh the-God

וַיַּרְכִּיבוּ אֶת־אֲרוֹן הָאֱלֹהִים עַל־עֲגָלָה חֲדָשָׁה מִבֵּית אֲבִינָדָב
Abinadab from-house-of new cart on the-God ark-of *** and-they-moved (7)

וְעֻזָּא וְאַחְיוֹ נֹהֲגִים בָּעֲגָלָה׃ וְדָוִיד וְכָל־ יִשְׂרָאֵל
Israel and-all-of and-David (8) to-the-cart ones-guiding and-Ahio and-Uzzah

מְשַׂחֲקִים לִפְנֵי הָאֱלֹהִים בְּכָל־ עֹז וּבְשִׁירִים
and-with-songs might with-all-of the-God before ones-celebrating

וּבְכִנֹּרוֹת וּבִנְבָלִים וּבְתֻפִּים וּבִמְצִלְתַּיִם
and-with-cymbals and-with-tambourines and-with-lyres and-with-harps

וּבַחֲצֹצְרוֹת׃ וַיָּבֹאוּ עַד־ גֹּרֶן כִּידֹן
Kidon threshing-floor-of to when-they-came (9) and-with-trumpets

וַיִּשְׁלַח עֻזָּא אֶת־ יָדוֹ לֶאֱחֹז אֶת־ הָאָרוֹן כִּי
because the-ark *** to-steady hand-of-him *** Uzzah then-he-reached

שָׁמְטוּ הַבָּקָר׃ וַיִּחַר־ אַף יְהוָה בְּעֻזָּא
against-Uzzah Yahweh anger-of and-he-burned (10) the-ox they-stumbled

וַיַּכֵּהוּ עַל אֲשֶׁר־ שָׁלַח יָדוֹ עַל־ הָאָרוֹן וַיָּמָת
so-he-died the-ark on hand-of-him he-put that because and-he-struck-down-him

שָׁם לִפְנֵי אֱלֹהִים׃ וַיִּחַר לְדָוִיד כִּי־ פָרַץ יְהוָה
Yahweh he-broke-out because to-David then-he-angered (11) God before there

פֶּרֶץ בְּעֻזָּא וַיִּקְרָא לַמָּקוֹם הַהוּא פֶּרֶץ עֻזָּא
Uzzah Perez the-that to-the-place and-he-called against-Uzzah breaking-out

עַד הַיּוֹם הַזֶּה׃ וַיִּרָא דָוִיד אֶת־הָאֱלֹהִים בַּיּוֹם
on-the-day the-God *** David and-he-was-afraid (12) the-this the-day to

הַהוּא לֵאמֹר הֵיךְ אָבִיא אֵלַי אֵת אֲרוֹן הָאֱלֹהִים׃ וְלֹא־
and-not (13) the-God ark-of *** to-me can-I-bring how? to-ask the-that

הֵסִיר דָּוִיד אֶת־ הָאָרוֹן אֵלָיו אֶל־ עִיר דָּוִיד וַיַּטֵּהוּ
but-he-took-aside-him David City-of to with-him the-ark *** David he-took

Saul." 4The whole assembly
agreed to do this, because it
seemed right to all the people.
5So David assembled all the
Israelites, from the Shihor
River in Egypt to Lebo[c]
Hamath, to bring the ark of
God from Kiriath Jearim. 6Da-
vid and all the Israelites with
him went to Baalah of Judah
(Kiriath Jearim) to bring up
from there the ark of God the
LORD, who is enthroned between the cherubim—the ark
that is called by the Name.
7They moved the ark of God
from Abinadab's house on a
new cart, with Uzzah and
Ahio guiding it. 8David and all
the Israelites were celebrating
with all their might before
God, with songs and with
harps, lyres, tambourines,
cymbals and trumpets.
9When they came to the
threshing floor of Kidon, Uzzah reached out his hand to
steady the ark, because the
oxen stumbled. 10The LORD's
anger burned against Uzzah,
and he struck him down because he had put his hand on
the ark. So he died there before God.
11Then David was angry because the LORD's wrath had
broken out against Uzzah, and
to this day that place is called
Perez Uzzah.[d]
12David was afraid of God
that day and asked, "How can
I ever bring the ark of God to
me?" 13He did not take the ark
to be with him in the City of
David. Instead, he took it

[c]5 Or *to the entrance to*
[d]11 *Perez Uzzah* means *outbreak against Uzzah.*

אֶל־ בֵּית עֹבֵד־ אֱדֹם הַגִּתִּי׃ וַיֵּשֶׁב אֲרוֹן הָאֱלֹהִים עִם־
with the-God ark-of and-he-remained (14) the-Gittite Edom Obed house-of to

בֵּית עֹבֵד אֱדֹם בְּבֵיתוֹ שְׁלֹשָׁה חֳדָשִׁים וַיְבָרֶךְ יְהוָה אֶת־
*** Yahweh and-he-blessed months three in-house-of-him Edom Obed family-of

בֵּית עֹבֵד־אֱדֹם וְאֶת־כָּל־אֲשֶׁר־לוֹ׃ וַיִּשְׁלַח חִירָם° מֶלֶךְ־
king-of Hiram now-he-sent (14:1) to-him that all and Edom Obed household-of

צֹר מַלְאָכִים אֶל־ דָּוִיד וַעֲצֵי אֲרָזִים וְחָרָשֵׁי קִיר
wall and-stonemasons-of cedars and-logs-of David to messengers Tyre

וְחָרָשֵׁי עֵצִים לִבְנוֹת לוֹ בָּיִת׃ וַיֵּדַע דָּוִיד כִּי־
that David and-he-knew (2) palace for-him to-build woods and-craftsmen-of

הֱכִינוֹ יְהוָה לְמֶלֶךְ עַל־ יִשְׂרָאֵל כִּי־ נִשֵּׂאת לְמַעְלָה
to-above being-exalted that Israel over as-king Yahweh he-established-him

מַלְכוּתוֹ בַּעֲבוּר עַמּוֹ יִשְׂרָאֵל׃ וַיִּקַּח דָּוִיד עוֹד
more David and-he-took (3) Israel people-of-him for-sake-of kingdom-of-him

נָשִׁים בִּירוּשָׁלִָם וַיּוֹלֶד דָּוִיד עוֹד בָּנִים וּבָנוֹת׃
and-daughters sons more David and-he-fathered in-Jerusalem wives

וְאֵלֶּה שְׁמוֹת הַיְלוּדִים אֲשֶׁר הָיוּ־ לוֹ בִּירוּשָׁלִָם
in-Jerusalem to-him they-were who the-ones-being-born names-of and-these (4)

שַׁמּוּעַ וְשׁוֹבָב נָתָן וּשְׁלֹמֹה׃ וְיִבְחָר וֶאֱלִישׁוּעַ וְאֶלְפָּלֶט׃
and-Elpelet and-Elishua and-Ibhar (5) and-Solomon Nathan and-Shobab Shammua

וְנֹגַהּ וְנֶפֶג וְיָפִיעַ׃ וֶאֱלִישָׁמָע וּבְעֶלְיָדָע
and-Beeliada and-Elishama (7) and-Japhia and-Nepheg and-Nogah (6)

וֶאֱלִיפָלֶט׃ וַיִּשְׁמְעוּ פְלִשְׁתִּים כִּי־ נִמְשַׁח דָּוִיד
David he-was-anointed that Philistines when-they-heard (8) and-Eliphelet

לְמֶלֶךְ עַל־ כָּל־ יִשְׂרָאֵל וַיַּעֲלוּ כָל־ פְּלִשְׁתִּים לְבַקֵּשׁ
to-search Philistines all-of then-they-went-up Israel all-of over as-king

אֶת־ דָּוִיד וַיִּשְׁמַע דָּוִיד וַיֵּצֵא לִפְנֵיהֶם׃ וּפְלִשְׁתִּים
now-Philistines (9) against-them and-he-went-out David but-he-heard David ***

בָּאוּ וַיִּפְשְׁטוּ בְּעֵמֶק רְפָאִים׃ וַיִּשְׁאַל דָּוִיד
David so-he-inquired (10) Rephaim in-Valley-of and-they-raided they-came

בֵּאלֹהִים לֵאמֹר הַאֶעֱלֶה עַל־ פְּלִשְׁתִּיִּים° וּנְתַתָּם
and-will-you-give-them Philistines against shall-I-go? to-say of-God

בְּיָדִי וַיֹּאמֶר לוֹ יְהוָה עֲלֵה וּנְתַתִּים
and-I-will-give-them go! Yahweh to-him and-he-answered into-hand-of-me

בְּיָדֶךָ׃ וַיַּעֲלוּ בְּבַעַל־ פְּרָצִים וַיַּכֵּם
and-he-defeated-them Perazim to-Baal so-they-went-up (11) into-hand-of-you

שָׁם דָּוִיד וַיֹּאמֶר דָּוִיד פָּרַץ הָאֱלֹהִים אֶת־ אוֹיְבַי
being-enemies-of-me against the-God he-broke-out David and-he-said David there

aside to the house of Obed-
Edom the Gittite. [14]The ark of
God remained with the family
of Obed-Edom in his house
for three months, and the
LORD blessed his household
and everything he had.

David's House and Family

14 Now Hiram king of
Tyre sent messengers
to David, along with cedar
logs, stonemasons and carpenters to build a palace for
him. [2]And David knew that
the LORD had established him
as king over Israel and that his
kingdom had been highly exalted for the sake of his people
Israel.

[3]In Jerusalem David took
more wives and became the
father of more sons and
daughters. [4]These are the
names of the children born to
him there: Shammua, Shobab,
Nathan, Solomon, [5]Ibhar, Elishua, Elpelet, [6]Nogah, Nepheg, Japhia, [7]Elishama,
Beeliada[e] and Eliphelet.

David Defeats the Philistines

[8]When the Philistines heard
that David had been anointed
king over all Israel, they went
up in full force to search for
him, but David heard about it
and went out to meet them.
[9]Now the Philistines had come
and raided the Valley of Rephaim; [10]so David inquired of
God: "Shall I go and attack the
Philistines? Will you hand
them over to me?"

The LORD answered him,
"Go, I will hand them over to
you."

[11]So David and his men
went up to Baal Perazim, and
there he defeated them. He
said, "As waters break out,
God has broken out against
my enemies by my hand." So

[e]7 A variant of *Eliada*

°*1* ק חורם
°*10* ק פלשתים

בְּיָדִי כְּפֶרֶץ מָיִם עַל־ כֵּן קָרְאוּ שֵׁם־
name-of they-called this for waters as-breaking-out-of by-hand-of-me

הַמָּקוֹם הַהוּא בַּעַל פְּרָצִים׃ וַיַּעַזְבוּ־ שָׁם אֶת־ אֱלֹהֵיהֶם
gods-of-them *** there and-they-abandoned (12) Perazim Baal the-that the-place

וַיֹּאמֶר דָּוִיד וַיִּשָּׂרְפוּ בָּאֵשׁ׃ וַיֹּסִיפוּ
and-they-repeated (13) in-the-fire and-they-were-burned David and-he-ordered

עוֹד פְּלִשְׁתִּים וַיִּפְשְׁטוּ בָּעֵמֶק׃ וַיִּשְׁאַל עוֹד
again so-he-inquired (14) in-the-valley and-they-raided Philistines again

דָּוִיד בֵּאלֹהִים וַיֹּאמֶר לוֹ הָאֱלֹהִים לֹא תַעֲלֶה אַחֲרֵיהֶם
after-them you-go-up not the-God to-him and-he-answered of-God David

הָסֵב מֵעֲלֵיהֶם וּבָאתָ לָהֶם מִמּוּל הַבְּכָאִים׃
the-balsams at-front-of to-them and-you-attack from-upon-them circle-around!

וִיהִי כְּשָׁמְעֲךָ אֶת־ קוֹל הַצְּעָדָה בְּרָאשֵׁי
in-tops-of the-marching sound-of *** as-to-hear-you and-he-will-be (15)

הַבְּכָאִים אָז תֵּצֵא בַמִּלְחָמָה כִּי־ יָצָא הָאֱלֹהִים
the-God he-went-out because to-the-battle you-move-out then the-balsams

לְפָנֶיךָ לְהַכּוֹת אֶת־ מַחֲנֵה פְּלִשְׁתִּים׃ וַיַּעַשׂ דָּוִיד כַּאֲשֶׁר
just-as David so-he-did (16) Philistines army-of *** to-strike before-you

צִוָּהוּ הָאֱלֹהִים וַיַּכּוּ אֶת־ מַחֲנֵה פְּלִשְׁתִּים
Philistines army-of *** and-they-struck-down the-God he-commanded-him

מִגִּבְעוֹן וְעַד־ גָּזְרָה׃ וַיֵּצֵא שֵׁם־ דָּוִיד
David name-of so-he-spread-out (17) to-Gezer even-to from-Gibeon

בְּכָל־ הָאֲרָצוֹת וַיהוָה נָתַן אֶת־ פַּחְדּוֹ עַל־ כָּל־
all-of on fear-of-him *** he-put and-Yahweh the-lands through-all-of

הַגּוֹיִם׃ וַיַּעַשׂ־ לוֹ בָתִּים בְּעִיר דָּוִיד
David in-City-of buildings for-him and-he-constructed (15:1) the-nations

וַיָּכֶן מָקוֹם לַאֲרוֹן הָאֱלֹהִים וַיֶּט־ לוֹ אֹהֶל׃
tent for-him and-he-pitched the-God for-ark-of place and-he-prepared

אָז אָמַר דָּוִיד לֹא לָשֵׂאת אֶת־ אֲרוֹן הָאֱלֹהִים כִּי אִם־
only except the-God ark-of *** to-carry not David he-said then (2)

הַלְוִיִּם כִּי־ בָם ׀ בָּחַר יְהוָה לָשֵׂאת אֶת־ אֲרוֹן יְהוָה
Yahweh ark-of *** to-carry Yahweh he-chose to-them because the-Levites

וּלְשָׁרְתוֹ עַד־ עוֹלָם׃ וַיַּקְהֵל דָּוִיד אֶת־ כָּל־
all-of *** David and-he-assembled (3) forever to and-to-minister-to-him

יִשְׂרָאֵל אֶל־ יְרוּשָׁלִַם לְהַעֲלוֹת אֶת־ אֲרוֹן יְהוָה אֶל־ מְקוֹמוֹ אֲשֶׁר־
that place-of-him to Yahweh ark-of *** to-bring-up Jerusalem to Israel

הֵכִין לוֹ׃ וַיֶּאֱסֹף דָּוִיד אֶת־ בְּנֵי
descendants-of *** David and-he-called-together (4) for-him he-prepared

that place was called Baal Perazim.[f] [12]The Philistines had
abandoned their gods there,
and David gave orders to burn
them in the fire.

[13]Once more the Philistines
raided the valley; [14]so David
inquired of God again, and
God answered him, "Do not
go straight up, but circle
around them and attack them
in front of the balsam trees.
[15]As soon as you hear the
sound of marching in the tops
of the balsam trees, move out
to battle, because that will
mean God has gone out in
front of you to strike the Philistine army." [16]So David did as
God commanded him, and
they struck down the Philistine army, all the way from
Gibeon to Gezer.

[17]So David's fame spread
throughout every land, and
the LORD made all the nations
fear him.

The Ark Brought to Jerusalem

15 After David had con-
structed buildings for
himself in the City of David,
he prepared a place for the ark
of God and pitched a tent for
it. [2]Then David said, "No one
but the Levites may carry the
ark of God, because the LORD
chose them to carry the ark of
the LORD and to minister before him forever."

[3]David assembled all Israel
in Jerusalem to bring up the
ark of the LORD to the place he
had prepared for it. [4]He called
together the descendants of

[f]11 Baal Perazim means *the lord who breaks out.*

אַהֲרֹן וְאֶת־הַלְוִיִּם׃ לִבְנֵי קְהָת אוּרִיאֵל הַשָּׂר
the-leader Uriel Kohath from-descendants-of (5) the-Levites and Aaron

וְאֶחָיו מֵאָה וְעֶשְׂרִים׃ לִבְנֵי מְרָרִי
Merari from-descendants-of (6) and-twenty hundred and-relatives-of-him

עֲשָׂיָה הַשָּׂר וְאֶחָיו מָאתַיִם וְעֶשְׂרִים׃
and-twenty two-hundreds and-relatives-of-him the-leader Asaiah

לִבְנֵי גֵּרְשׁוֹם יוֹאֵל הַשָּׂר וְאֶחָיו מֵאָה
hundred and-relatives-of-him the-leader Joel Gershom from-descendants-of (7)

וּשְׁלֹשִׁים׃ לִבְנֵי אֱלִיצָפָן שְׁמַעְיָה הַשָּׂר
the-leader Shemaiah Elizaphan from-descendants-of (8) and-thirty

וְאֶחָיו מָאתָיִם׃ לִבְנֵי חֶבְרוֹן אֱלִיאֵל
Eliel Hebron from-descendants-of (9) two-hundreds and-relatives-of-him

הַשָּׂר וְאֶחָיו שְׁמוֹנִים׃ לִבְנֵי עֻזִּיאֵל
Uzziel from-descendants-of (10) eighty and-relatives-of-him the-leader

עַמִּינָדָב הַשָּׂר וְאֶחָיו מֵאָה וּשְׁנַיִם עָשָׂר׃
ten and-two hundred and-relatives-of-him the-leader Amminadab

וַיִּקְרָא דָוִיד לְצָדוֹק וּלְאֶבְיָתָר הַכֹּהֲנִים
the-priests and-to-Abiathar to-Zadok David then-he-summoned (11)

וְלַלְוִיִּם לְאוּרִיאֵל עֲשָׂיָה וְיוֹאֵל שְׁמַעְיָה וֶאֱלִיאֵל
and-Eliel Shemaiah and-Joel Asaiah and-to-Uriel and-to-the-Levites

וְעַמִּינָדָב׃ וַיֹּאמֶר לָהֶם אַתֶּם רָאשֵׁי הָאָבוֹת
the-fathers heads-of you to-them and-he-said (12) and-Amminadab

לַלְוִיִּם הִתְקַדְּשׁוּ אַתֶּם וַאֲחֵיכֶם וְהַעֲלִיתֶם
and-you-bring-up and-fellows-of-you you consecrate-yourselves! of-the-Levites

אֵת אֲרוֹן יְהוָה אֱלֹהֵי יִשְׂרָאֵל אֶל־הֲכִינוֹתִי לוֹ׃ כִּי
because (13) for-him I-prepared to Israel God-of Yahweh ark-of ***

לְמַבָּרִאשׁוֹנָה לֹא אַתֶּם פָּרַץ יְהוָה אֱלֹהֵינוּ בָּנוּ כִּי־לֹא
not for against-us God-of-us Yahweh he-broke-out you not for-what-the-first

דְרַשְׁנֻהוּ כַּמִּשְׁפָּט׃ וַיִּתְקַדְּשׁוּ
so-they-consecrated-themselves (14) in-the-prescribed-way we-inquired-of-him

הַכֹּהֲנִים וְהַלְוִיִּם לְהַעֲלוֹת אֶת־אֲרוֹן יְהוָה אֱלֹהֵי יִשְׂרָאֵל׃
Israel God-of Yahweh ark-of *** to-bring-up and-the-Levites the-priests

וַיִּשְׂאוּ בְנֵי־הַלְוִיִּם אֵת אֲרוֹן הָאֱלֹהִים כַּאֲשֶׁר
just-as the-God ark-of *** the-Levites sons-of and-they-carried (15)

צִוָּה מֹשֶׁה כִּדְבַר יְהוָה בִּכְתֵפָם בַּמֹּטוֹת
with-the-poles on-shoulder-of-them Yahweh as-word-of Moses he-commanded

עֲלֵיהֶם׃ וַיֹּאמֶר דָּוִיד לְשָׂרֵי הַלְוִיִּם לְהַעֲמִיד אֶת־
*** to-appoint the-Levites to-leaders-of David and-he-told (16) on-them

Aaron and the Levites:
5From the descendants of
Kohath,
Uriel the leader and 120
relatives;
6from the descendants of
Merari,
Asaiah the leader and
220 relatives;
7from the descendants of
Gershon,[g]
Joel the leader and 130
relatives;
8from the descendants of Elizaphan,
Shemaiah the leader and
200 relatives;
9from the descendants of
Hebron,
Eliel the leader and 80
relatives;
10from the descendants of
Uzziel,
Amminadab the leader
and 112 relatives.
11Then David summoned
Zadok and Abiathar the
priests, and Uriel, Asaiah, Joel,
Shemaiah, Eliel and Am-
minadab the Levites. 12He said
to them, "You are the heads of
the Levitical families; you and
your fellow Levites are to
consecrate yourselves and
bring up the ark of the LORD,
the God of Israel, to the place
I have prepared for it. 13It was
because you, the Levites, did
not bring it up the first time
that the LORD our God broke
out in anger against us. We
did not inquire of him about
how to do it in the prescribed
way." 14So the priests and Levites consecrated themselves
in order to bring up the ark of
the LORD, the God of Israel.
15And the Levites carried the
ark of God with the poles on
their shoulders, as Moses had
commanded in accordance
with the word of the LORD.
16David told the leaders of
the Levites to appoint their

[g]7 Hebrew *Gershom*, a variant of *Gershon*

אֲחֵיהֶם הַמְשֹׁרְרִים בִּכְלֵי־ שִׁיר נְבָלִים וְכִנֹּרוֹת
and-harps lyres music with-instruments-of the-ones-singing brothers-of-them

וּמְצִלְתָּיִם מַשְׁמִיעִים לְהָרִים־ בְּקוֹל לְשִׂמְחָה׃
of-joy with-sound to-raise-high ones-making-sound and-cymbals

(17) וַיַּעֲמִידוּ הַלְוִיִּם אֶת הֵימָן בֶּן־ יוֹאֵל וּמִן־
and-from Joel son-of Heman *** the-Levites so-they-appointed (17)

אֶחָיו אָסָף בֶּן־ בֶּרֶכְיָהוּ וּמִן־ בְּנֵי מְרָרִי אֲחֵיהֶם
brothers-of-them Merari sons-of and-from Berekiah son-of Asaph brothers-of-him

אֵיתָן בֶּן־ קוּשָׁיָהוּ׃ (18) וְעִמָּהֶם אֲחֵיהֶם הַמִּשְׁנִים
the-next-ones brothers-of-them and-with-them (18) Kushaiah son-of Ethan

זְכַרְיָהוּ בֵּן וְיַעֲזִיאֵל וּשְׁמִירָמוֹת וִיחִיאֵל ׀ וְעֻנִּי אֱלִיאָב
Eliab and-Unni and-Jehiel and-Shemiramoth and-Jaaziel son Zechariah

וּבְנָיָהוּ וּמַעֲשֵׂיָהוּ וּמַתִּתְיָהוּ וֶאֱלִיפְלֵהוּ וּמִקְנֵיָהוּ
and-Mikneiah and-Eliphelehu and-Mattithiah and-Maaseiah and-Benaiah

וְעֹבֵד אֱדֹם וִיעִיאֵל הַשֹּׁעֲרִים׃ (19) וְהַמְשֹׁרְרִים
and-the-ones-making-music (19) the-gatekeepers and-Jeiel Edom and-Obed

הֵימָן אָסָף וְאֵיתָן בִּמְצִלְתַּיִם נְחֹשֶׁת לְהַשְׁמִיעַ׃ (20) וּזְכַרְיָה
and-Zechariah (20) to-make-sound bronze with-cymbals and-Ethan Asaph Heman

וַעֲזִיאֵל וּשְׁמִירָמוֹת וִיחִיאֵל וְעֻנִּי וֶאֱלִיאָב וּמַעֲשֵׂיָהוּ
and-Maaseiah and-Eliab and-Unni and-Jehiel and-Shemiramoth and-Aziel

וּבְנָיָהוּ בִּנְבָלִים עַל־ עֲלָמוֹת׃ (21) וּמַתִּתְיָהוּ
and-Mattithiah (21) alamoth according-to with-lyres and-Benaiah

וֶאֱלִיפְלֵהוּ וּמִקְנֵיָהוּ וְעֹבֵד אֱדֹם וִיעִיאֵל וַעֲזַזְיָהוּ בְּכִנֹּרוֹת
with-harps and-Azaziah and-Jeiel Edom and-Obed and-Mikneiah and-Eliphelehu

עַל־ הַשְּׁמִינִית לְנַצֵּחַ׃ (22) וּכְנַנְיָהוּ שַׂר־ הַלְוִיִּם
the-Levites head-of and-Kenaniah (22) to-direct the-sheminith according-to

בְּמַשָּׂא יָסֹר בַּמַּשָּׂא כִּי מֵבִין הוּא׃
he being-skillful because of-the-singing to-be-in-charge of-singing

(23) וּבֶרֶכְיָה וְאֶלְקָנָה שֹׁעֲרִים לָאָרוֹן׃ (24) וּשְׁבַנְיָהוּ
and-Shebaniah (24) for-the-ark doorkeepers and-Elkanah and-Berekiah (23)

וְיוֹשָׁפָט וּנְתַנְאֵל וַעֲמָשַׂי וּזְכַרְיָהוּ וּבְנָיָהוּ וֶאֱלִיעֶזֶר
and-Eliezer and-Benaiah and-Zechariah and-Amasai and-Nethanel and-Joshaphat

הַכֹּהֲנִים מַחְצְצְרִים° בַּחֲצֹצְרוֹת לִפְנֵי אֲרוֹן הָאֱלֹהִים וְעֹבֵד אֱדֹם
Edom and-Obed the-God ark-of before on-the-trumpets ones-blowing the-priests

וִיחִיָּה שֹׁעֲרִים לָאָרוֹן׃ (25) וַיְהִי דָוִיד וְזִקְנֵי יִשְׂרָאֵל
Israel and-elders-of David so-he-was (25) for-the-ark doorkeepers and-Jehiah

וְשָׂרֵי הָאֲלָפִים הַהֹלְכִים לְהַעֲלוֹת אֶת־ אֲרוֹן
ark-of *** to-bring-up the-ones-going the-thousands and-commanders-of

brothers as singers to sing joyful songs, accompanied by
musical instruments: lyres,
harps and cymbals.
17So the Levites appointed
Heman son of Joel; from his
brothers, Asaph son of Berekiah; and from their brothers
the Merarites, Ethan son of
Kushaiah; 18and with them
their brothers next in rank:
Zechariah,[h] Jaaziel, Shemiramoth, Jehiel, Unni, Eliab, Benaiah, Maaseiah, Mattithiah,
Eliphelehu, Mikneiah, Obed-
Edom and Jeiel,[i] the gatekeepers.
19The musicians Heman,
Asaph and Ethan were to
sound the bronze cymbals;
20Zechariah, Aziel, Shemiramoth, Jehiel, Unni, Eliab,
Maaseiah and Benaiah were to
play the lyres according to
alamoth,[j] 21and Mattithiah,
Eliphelehu, Mikneiah, Obed-
Edom, Jeiel and Azaziah were
to play the harps, directing according to *sheminith.*[j] 22Kena-
niah the head Levite was in
charge of the singing; that was
his responsibility because he
was skillful at it.
23Berekiah and Elkanah
were to be doorkeepers for the
ark. 24Shebaniah, Joshaphat,
Nethanel, Amasai, Zechariah,
Benaiah and Eliezer the
priests were to blow trumpets
before the ark of God. Obed-
Edom and Jehiah were also to
be doorkeepers for the ark.
25So David and the elders of
Israel and the commanders of
units of a thousand went to

[h] *18* Three Hebrew manuscripts and Septuagint (see also verse 20 and 1 Chron. 16:5); most Hebrew manuscripts *Zechariah son and* or *Zechariah, Ben and*

[i] *18* Hebrew; Septuagint (see also verse 21) *Jeiel and Azaziah*

[j] *20,21* Probably a musical term

°*24* ק מחצרים

בְּרִית־ יְהוָה מִן־ בֵּית עֹבֵד־ אֱדֹם בְּשִׂמְחָה׃ וַיְהִי
and-he-was (26) with-rejoicing Edom Obed house-of from Yahweh covenant-of

בְּעְזֹר הָאֱלֹהִים אֶת־ הַלְוִיִּם נֹשְׂאֵי אֲרוֹן בְּרִית־
covenant-of ark-of ones-carrying-of the-Levites *** the-God because-to-help

יְהוָה וַיִּזְבְּחוּ שִׁבְעָה־ פָרִים וְשִׁבְעָה אֵילִים׃ וְדָוִיד
now-David (27) rams and-seven bulls seven then-they-sacrificed Yahweh

מְכֻרְבָּל ׀ בִּמְעִיל בּוּץ וְכָל־ הַלְוִיִּם הַנֹּשְׂאִים
the-ones-carrying the-Levites and-all-of fine-linen in-robe-of being-clothed

אֶת־ הָאָרוֹן וְהַמְשֹׁרְרִים וּכְנַנְיָה הַשַּׂר הַמַּשָּׂא
the-song the-leader and-Kenaniah and-the-ones-singing the-ark ***

הַמְשֹׁרְרִים וְעַל־ דָּוִיד אֵפוֹד בָּד׃ וְכָל־ יִשְׂרָאֵל
Israel so-all-of (28) linen ephod-of David and-on the-ones-singing

מַעֲלִים אֶת־ אֲרוֹן בְּרִית־ יְהוָה בִּתְרוּעָה וּבְקוֹל
and-with-sound-of with-shout Yahweh covenant-of ark-of *** ones-bringing-up

שׁוֹפָר וּבַחֲצֹצְרוֹת וּבִמְצִלְתָּיִם מַשְׁמִעִים בִּנְבָלִים
on-lyres ones-making-sound and-with-cymbals and-with-trumpets horn-of-ram

וְכִנֹּרוֹת׃ וַיְהִי אֲרוֹן בְּרִית יְהוָה בָּא עַד־ עִיר
City-of into entering Yahweh covenant-of ark-of and-he-was (29) and-harps

דָּוִיד וּמִיכַל בַּת־ שָׁאוּל נִשְׁקְפָה ׀ בְּעַד הַחַלּוֹן וַתֵּרֶא
when-she-saw the-window from she-watched Saul daughter-of and-Michal David

אֶת־ הַמֶּלֶךְ דָּוִיד מְרַקֵּד וּמְשַׂחֵק וַתִּבֶז לוֹ
against-him then-she-despised and-celebrating dancing David the-king ***

בְּלִבָּהּ׃ וַיָּבִיאוּ אֶת־ אֲרוֹן הָאֱלֹהִים וַיַּצִּיגוּ
and-they-set the-God ark-of *** and-they-brought (16:1) in-heart-of-her

אֹתוֹ בְּתוֹךְ הָאֹהֶל אֲשֶׁר נָטָה־ לוֹ דָּוִיד וַיַּקְרִיבוּ
and-they-presented David for-him he-pitched that the-tent inside-of him

עֹלוֹת וּשְׁלָמִים לִפְנֵי הָאֱלֹהִים׃ וַיְכַל
when-he-finished (2) the-God before and-fellowship-offerings burnt-offerings

דָּוִיד מֵהַעֲלוֹת הָעֹלָה וְהַשְּׁלָמִים
and-the-fellowship-offerings the-burnt-offerings from-to-sacrifice David

וַיְבָרֶךְ אֶת־ הָעָם בְּשֵׁם יְהוָה׃ וַיְחַלֵּק לְכָל־
to-each-of then-he-gave (3) Yahweh in-name-of the-people *** then-he-blessed

אִישׁ יִשְׂרָאֵל מֵאִישׁ וְעַד־ אִשָּׁה לְאִישׁ כִּכַּר־ לֶחֶם וְאֶשְׁפָּר
and-date-cake bread loaf-of to-each woman even-to from-man Israel person-of

וַאֲשִׁישָׁה׃ וַיִּתֵּן לִפְנֵי אֲרוֹן יְהוָה מִן־ הַלְוִיִּם
the-Levites from Yahweh ark-of before and-he-appointed (4) and-raisin-cake

מְשָׁרְתִים וּלְהַזְכִּיר וּלְהוֹדוֹת וּלְהַלֵּל לַיהוָה
to-Yahweh and-to-praise and-to-give-thanks and-to-petition ones-ministering

bring up the ark of the covenant of the LORD from the
house of Obed-Edom, with rejoicing. 26Because God had
helped the Levites who were
carrying the ark of the covenant of the LORD, seven bulls
and seven rams were sac-
rificed. 27Now David was
clothed in a robe of fine linen,
as were all the Levites who
were carrying the ark, and as
were the singers, and Kenaniah, who was in charge of the
singing of the choirs. David
also wore a linen ephod. 28So
all Israel brought up the ark of
the covenant of the LORD with
shouts, with the sounding of
rams' horns and trumpets,
and of cymbals, and the playing of lyres and harps.
29As the ark of the covenant
of the LORD was entering the
City of David, Michal daughter of Saul watched from a
window. And when she saw
King David dancing and celebrating, she despised him in
her heart.

16 They brought the ark of
God and set it inside
the tent that David had
pitched for it, and they
presented burnt offerings and
fellowship offerings[k] before
God. 2After David had
finished sacrificing the burnt
offerings and fellowship
offerings, he blessed the
people in the name of the
LORD. 3Then he gave a loaf of
bread, a cake of dates and a
cake of raisins to each Israelite
man and woman.
4He appointed some of the
Levites to minister before the
ark of the LORD, to make petition, to give thanks, and to

[k]1 Traditionally *peace offerings;* also in verse 2

אֱלֹהֵי יִשְׂרָאֵל׃ (5) אָסָף הָרֹאשׁ וּמִשְׁנֵהוּ זְכַרְיָה יְעִיאֵל
Jeiel Zechariah and-second-of-him the-chief Asaph (5) Israel God-of

וּשְׁמִירָמוֹת וִיחִיאֵל וּמַתִּתְיָה וֶאֱלִיאָב וּבְנָיָהוּ וְעֹבֵד אֱדֹם
Edom and-Obed and-Benaiah and-Eliab and-Mattithiah and-Jehiel and-Shemiramoth

וִיעִיאֵל בִּכְלֵי נְבָלִים וּבְכִנֹּרוֹת וְאָסָף בַּמְצִלְתַּיִם
with-the-cymbals and-Asaph and-with-harps lyres with-instruments-of and-Jeiel

מַשְׁמִיעַ׃ (6) וּבְנָיָהוּ וְיַחֲזִיאֵל הַכֹּהֲנִים בַּחֲצֹצְרוֹת
with-trumpets the-priests and-Jahaziel and-Benaiah (6) ones-making-sound

תָּמִיד לִפְנֵי אֲרוֹן בְּרִית־הָאֱלֹהִים׃ (7) בַּיּוֹם הַהוּא אָז
then the-that on-the-day (7) the-God covenant-of ark-of before regularly

נָתַן דָּוִיד בָּרֹאשׁ לְהֹדוֹת לַיהוָה בְּיַד־אָסָף
Asaph into-hand-of to-Yahweh to-give-thanks at-the-first David he-committed

וְאֶחָיו׃ (8) הוֹדוּ לַיהוָה קִרְאוּ בִשְׁמוֹ
on-name-of-him call! to-Yahweh give-thanks! (8) and-associates-of-him

הוֹדִיעוּ בָעַמִּים עֲלִילֹתָיו׃ (9) שִׁירוּ לוֹ זַמְּרוּ־
sing-praise! to-him sing! (9) deeds-of-him among-the-nations make-known!

לוֹ שִׂיחוּ בְּכָל־נִפְלְאֹתָיו׃ (10) הִתְהַלְלוּ בְּשֵׁם
in-name-of glory! (10) acts-being-wonders-of-him of-all-of tell! to-him

קָדְשׁוֹ יִשְׂמַח לֵב מְבַקְשֵׁי יְהוָה׃ (11) דִּרְשׁוּ
look-to! (11) Yahweh ones-seeking-of heart-of let-him-rejoice holiness-of-him

יְהוָה וְעֻזּוֹ בַּקְּשׁוּ פָנָיו תָּמִיד׃ (12) זִכְרוּ
remember! (12) always faces-of-him seek! and-strength-of-him Yahweh

נִפְלְאֹתָיו אֲשֶׁר עָשָׂה מֹפְתָיו וּמִשְׁפְּטֵי־
and-judgments-of miracles-of-him he-did that acts-being-wonders-of-him

פִיהוּ׃ (13) זֶרַע יִשְׂרָאֵל עַבְדּוֹ בְּנֵי יַעֲקֹב
Jacob sons-of servant-of-him Israel descendant-of (13) mouth-of-him

בְּחִירָיו׃ (14) הוּא יְהוָה אֱלֹהֵינוּ בְּכָל־הָאָרֶץ
the-earth in-all-of God-of-us Yahweh he (14) chosen-ones-of-him

מִשְׁפָּטָיו׃ (15) זִכְרוּ לְעוֹלָם בְּרִיתוֹ דָּבָר צִוָּה
he-commanded word covenant-of-him to-forever remember! (15) judgments-of-him

לְאֶלֶף דּוֹר׃ (16) אֲשֶׁר כָּרַת אֶת־אַבְרָהָם וּשְׁבוּעָתוֹ
and-oath-of-him Abraham with he-made which (16) generation for-thousand-of

לְיִצְחָק׃ (17) וַיַּעֲמִידֶהָ לְיַעֲקֹב לְחֹק לְיִשְׂרָאֵל בְּרִית
covenant-of to-Israel as-decree to-Jacob and-he-confirmed-her (17) to-Isaac

עוֹלָם׃ (18) לֵאמֹר לְךָ אֶתֵּן אֶרֶץ־כְּנָעַן חֶבֶל
portion-of Canaan land-of I-will-give to-you to-say (18) everlasting

נַחֲלַתְכֶם׃ (19) בִּהְיוֹתְכֶם מְתֵי מִסְפָּר כִּמְעַט
as-few number people-of when-to-be-you (19) inheritance-of-you

praise the LORD, the God of Israel: [5]Asaph was the chief, Zechariah second, then Jeiel, Shemiramoth, Jehiel, Mattithiah, Eliab, Benaiah, Obed-Edom and Jeiel. They were to play the lyres and harps, Asaph was to sound the cymbals, [6]and Benaiah and Jahaziel the priests were to blow the trumpets regularly before the ark of the covenant of God.

David's Psalm of Thanks

[7]That day David first committed to Asaph and his associates this psalm of thanks to the LORD:

[8]Give thanks to the LORD, call on his name;
make known among the nations what he has done.
[9]Sing to him, sing praise to him;
tell of all his wonderful acts.
[10]Glory in his holy name;
let the hearts of those who seek the LORD rejoice.
[11]Look to the LORD and his strength;
seek his face always.
[12]Remember the wonders he has done,
his miracles, and the judgments he pronounced,
[13]O descendants of Israel his servant,
O sons of Jacob, his chosen ones.

[14]He is the LORD our God;
his judgments are in all the earth.
[15]He remembers[l] his covenant forever,
the word he commanded, for a thousand generations,
[16]the covenant he made with Abraham,
the oath he swore to Isaac.
[17]He confirmed it to Jacob as a decree,
to Israel as an everlasting covenant:
[18]"To you I will give the land of Canaan
as the portion you will inherit."

[19]When they were but few in number,

[l]15 Some Septuagint manuscripts (see also Psalm 105:8); Hebrew *Remember*

וְגָרִים בָּהּ׃ (20) וַיִּתְהַלְּכוּ מִגּוֹי אֶל־ גּוֹי
nation to from-nation and-they-wandered (20) in-her and-ones-being-strangers

וּמִמַּמְלָכָה אֶל־ עַם אַחֵר׃ (21) לֹא־ הִנִּיחַ לְאִישׁ
to-man he-allowed not (21) another people to and-from-kingdom

לְעָשְׁקָם וַיּוֹכַח עֲלֵיהֶם מְלָכִים׃ (22) אַל־ תִּגְּעוּ
you-touch not (22) kings for-them and-he-rebuked to-oppress-them

בִּמְשִׁיחָי וּבִנְבִיאַי אַל־ תָּרֵעוּ׃ (23) שִׁירוּ
sing! (23) you-do-harm not and-to-prophets-of-me on-anointed-ones-of-me

לַיהוָה כָּל־ הָאָרֶץ בַּשְּׂרוּ מִיּוֹם־ אֶל־ יוֹם יְשׁוּעָתוֹ׃
salvation-of-him day to from-day proclaim! the-earth all-of to-Yahweh

(24) סַפְּרוּ בַגּוֹיִם אֶת־ כְּבוֹדוֹ בְּכָל־ הָעַמִּים
the-peoples among-all-of glory-of-him *** among-the-nations declare! (24)

נִפְלְאֹתָיו׃ (25) כִּי גָדוֹל יְהוָה וּמְהֻלָּל מְאֹד
greatly and-being-praised Yahweh great for (25) deeds-being-marvelous-of-him

וְנוֹרָא הוּא עַל־ כָּל־ אֱלֹהִים׃ (26) כִּי כָּל־ אֱלֹהֵי הָעַמִּים
the-nations gods-of all-of for (26) gods all-of above he and-being-feared

אֱלִילִים וַיהוָה שָׁמַיִם עָשָׂה׃ (27) הוֹד וְהָדָר לְפָנָיו
before-him and-majesty splendor (27) he-made heavens but-Yahweh idols

עֹז וְחֶדְוָה בִּמְקֹמוֹ׃ (28) הָבוּ לַיהוָה מִשְׁפְּחוֹת
families-of to-Yahweh ascribe! (28) in-dwelling-of-him and-joy strength

עַמִּים הָבוּ לַיהוָה כָּבוֹד וָעֹז׃ (29) הָבוּ לַיהוָה
to-Yahweh ascribe! (29) and-strength glory to-Yahweh ascribe! nations

כְּבוֹד שְׁמוֹ שְׂאוּ מִנְחָה וּבֹאוּ לְפָנָיו הִשְׁתַּחֲווּ לַיהוָה
to-Yahweh worship! before-him and-come! offering bring! name-of-him glory-of

בְּהַדְרַת־ קֹדֶשׁ׃ (30) חִילוּ מִלְּפָנָיו כָּל־ הָאָרֶץ
the-earth all-of at-before-him tremble! (30) holiness in-splendor-of

אַף־ תִּכּוֹן תֵּבֵל בַּל־ תִּמּוֹט׃ (31) יִשְׂמְחוּ
let-them-rejoice (31) she-can-be-moved not world she-is-established indeed

הַשָּׁמַיִם וְתָגֵל הָאָרֶץ וְיֹאמְרוּ בַגּוֹיִם
among-the-nations and-let-them-say the-earth and-let-her-be-glad the-heavens

יְהוָה מָלָךְ׃ (32) יִרְעַם הַיָּם וּמְלוֹאוֹ
and-fullness-of-him the-sea let-him-resound (32) he-reigns Yahweh

יַעֲלֹץ הַשָּׂדֶה וְכָל־ אֲשֶׁר־ בּוֹ׃ (33) אָז יְרַנְּנוּ
they-will-sing then (33) in-him that and-all the-field let-him-be-jubilant

עֲצֵי הַיָּעַר מִלִּפְנֵי יְהוָה כִּי־ בָא לִשְׁפּוֹט אֶת־ הָאָרֶץ׃
the-earth *** to-judge he-comes for Yahweh at-before the-forest trees-of

(34) הוֹדוּ לַיהוָה כִּי טוֹב כִּי לְעוֹלָם חַסְדּוֹ׃
love-of-him to-forever for good for to-Yahweh give-thanks! (34)

few indeed, and
strangers in it,
20 they[m] wandered from
nation to nation,
from one kingdom to
another.
21 He allowed no man to
oppress them;
for their sake he rebuked
kings:
22 "Do not touch my anointed
ones;
do my prophets no
harm."

23 Sing to the LORD, all the
earth;
proclaim his salvation
day after day.
24 Declare his glory among
the nations,
his marvelous deeds
among all peoples.
25 For great is the LORD and
most worthy of praise;
he is to be feared above
all gods.
26 For all the gods of the
nations are idols,
but the LORD made the
heavens.
27 Splendor and majesty are
before him;
strength and joy in his
dwelling place.
28 Ascribe to the LORD, O
families of nations,
ascribe to the LORD glory
and strength,
29 ascribe to the LORD the
glory due his name.
Bring an offering and come
before him;
worship the LORD in the
splendor of his[n]
holiness.
30 Tremble before him, all the
earth!
The world is firmly
established; it cannot
be moved.
31 Let the heavens rejoice, let
the earth be glad;
let them say among the
nations, "The LORD
reigns!"
32 Let the sea resound, and all
that is in it;
let the fields be jubilant,
and everything in
them!
33 Then the trees of the forest
will sing,
they will sing for joy
before the LORD,
for he comes to judge the
earth.

34 Give thanks to the LORD,
for he is good;
his love endures forever.

[m] 18-20 One Hebrew manuscript, Septuagint and Vulgate (see also Psalm 105:12); most Hebrew manuscripts *inherit,* / [19] *though you are but few in number, / few indeed, and strangers in it."* / [20] *They*

[n] 29 Or *LORD with the splendor of*

וְאִמְרוּ הוֹשִׁיעֵנוּ אֱלֹהֵי יִשְׁעֵנוּ וְקַבְּצֵנוּ
and-gather-us! salvation-of-us God-of save-us! and-cry-out! (35)

וְהַצִּילֵנוּ מִן־ הַגּוֹיִם לְהֹדוֹת לְשֵׁם קָדְשֶׁךָ
holiness-of-you to-name-of to-give-thanks the-nations from and-deliver-us!

לְהִשְׁתַּבֵּחַ בִּתְהִלָּתֶךָ׃ בָּרוּךְ יְהוָֹה אֱלֹהֵי יִשְׂרָאֵל מִן־
from Israel God-of Yahweh being-praised (36) in-praise-of-you to-glory

הָעוֹלָם וְעַד הָעֹלָם וַיֹּאמְרוּ כָל־ הָעָם אָמֵן
amen the-people all-of and-they-said the-everlasting and-to the-everlasting

וְהַלֵּל לַיהוָֹה׃ וַיַּעֲזָב־ שָׁם לִפְנֵי אֲרוֹן בְּרִית־
covenant-of ark-of before there and-he-left (37) to-Yahweh and-praise!

יְהוָֹה לְאָסָף וּלְאֶחָיו לְשָׁרֵת לִפְנֵי הָאָרוֹן תָּמִיד
regularly the-ark before to-minister and-to-associates-of-him to-Asaph Yahweh

לִדְבַר־ יוֹם בְּיוֹמוֹ׃ וְעֹבֵד אֱדֹם וַאֲחֵיהֶם
and-associates-of-them Edom and-Obed (38) in-day-of-him day as-requirement-of

שִׁשִּׁים וּשְׁמוֹנָה וְעֹבֵד אֱדֹם בֶּן־ יְדִיתוּן וְחֹסָה לְשֹׁעֲרִים׃
as-gatekeepers and-Hosah Jeduthun son-of Edom and-Obed and-eight sixty

וְאֵת ׀ צָדוֹק הַכֹּהֵן וְאֶחָיו הַכֹּהֲנִים לִפְנֵי מִשְׁכַּן
tabernacle-of before the-priests and-fellows-of-him the-priest Zadok and (39)

יְהוָֹה בַּבָּמָה אֲשֶׁר בְּגִבְעוֹן׃ לְהַעֲלוֹת עֹלוֹת
burnt-offerings to-present (40) in-Gibeon that at-the-high-place Yahweh

לַיהוָֹה עַל־ מִזְבַּח הָעֹלָה תָּמִיד לַבֹּקֶר
in-the-morning regularly the-burnt-offering altar-of on to-Yahweh

וְלָעֶרֶב וּלְכָל־ הַכָּתוּב בְּתוֹרַת יְהוָֹה
Yahweh in-Law-of the-thing-being-written and-as-all-of and-in-the-evening

אֲשֶׁר צִוָּה עַל־יִשְׂרָאֵל׃ וְעִמָּהֶם הֵימָן וִידוּתוּן וּשְׁאָר
and-rest-of and-Jeduthun Heman and-with-them (41) Israel to he-gave which

הַבְּרוּרִים אֲשֶׁר נִקְּבוּ בְּשֵׁמוֹת לְהֹדוֹת
to-give-thanks by-names they-were-designated who the-ones-being-chosen

לַיהוָֹה כִּי לְעוֹלָם חַסְדּוֹ׃ וְעִמָּהֶם הֵימָן וִידוּתוּן
and-Jeduthun Heman and-with-them (42) love-of-him to-forever for to-Yahweh

חֲצֹצְרוֹת וּמְצִלְתַּיִם לְמַשְׁמִיעִים וּכְלֵי שִׁיר
song-of and-instruments-of for-ones-making-sound and-cymbals trumpets

הָאֱלֹהִים וּבְנֵי יְדוּתוּן לַשָּׁעַר׃ וַיֵּלְכוּ כָל־
all-of then-they-left (43) at-the-gate Jeduthun and-sons-of the-God

הָעָם אִישׁ לְבֵיתוֹ וַיִּסֹּב דָּוִיד לְבָרֵךְ אֶת־
*** to-bless David and-he-returned for-house-of-him each the-people

בֵּיתוֹ׃ וַיְהִי כַּאֲשֶׁר יָשַׁב דָּוִיד בְּבֵיתוֹ
in-palace-of-him David he-settled just-as and-he-was (17:1) family-of-him

35 Cry out, "Save us, O God
our Savior;
gather us and deliver us
from the nations,
that we may give thanks to
your holy name,
that we may glory in
your praise."
36 Praise be to the LORD, the
God of Israel,
from everlasting to
everlasting.

Then all the people said
"Amen" and "Praise the
LORD."

37 David left Asaph and his
associates before the ark of the
covenant of the LORD to minister there regularly, according
to each day's requirements.
38 He also left Obed-Edom and
his sixty-eight associates to
minister with them. Obed-
Edom son of Jeduthun, and
also Hosah, were gatekeepers.
39 David left Zadok the priest
and his fellow priests before
the tabernacle of the LORD at
the high place in Gibeon 40 to
present burnt offerings to the
LORD on the altar of burnt
offering regularly, morning
and evening, in accordance
with everything written in the
Law of the LORD, which he had
given Israel. 41 With them were
Heman and Jeduthun and the
rest of those chosen and designated by name to give thanks
to the LORD, "for his love endures forever." 42 Heman and
Jeduthun were responsible for
the sounding of the trumpets
and cymbals and for the playing of the other instruments
for sacred song. The sons of
Jeduthun were stationed at the
gate.
43 Then all the people left,
each for his own home, and
David returned home to bless
his family.

God's Promise to David

17 After David was settled
in his palace, he said to

וַיֹּאמֶר דָּוִיד אֶל־ נָתָן הַנָּבִיא הִנֵּה אָנֹכִי יוֹשֵׁב בְּבֵית
in-palace-of living I see! the-prophet Nathan to David then-he-said

הָאֲרָזִים וַאֲרוֹן בְּרִית־ יְהוָה תַּחַת יְרִיעוֹת׃
tent-curtains under Yahweh covenant-of while-ark-of the-cedars

(2) וַיֹּאמֶר נָתָן אֶל־ דָּוִיד כֹּל אֲשֶׁר בִּלְבָבְךָ עֲשֵׂה כִּי
for do! in-mind-of-you that all David to Nathan and-he-replied (2)

הָאֱלֹהִים עִמָּךְ׃ (3) וַיְהִי בַּלַּיְלָה הַהוּא וַיְהִי דְבַר־
word-of and-he-came the-that in-the-night and-he-was (3) with-you the-God

אֱלֹהִים אֶל־נָתָן לֵאמֹר׃ (4) לֵךְ וְאָמַרְתָּ אֶל־ דָּוִיד עַבְדִּי כֹּה
this servant-of-me David to and-you-tell go! (4) to-say Nathan to God

אָמַר יְהוָה לֹא אַתָּה תִּבְנֶה־ לִּי הַבַּיִת לָשָׁבֶת׃ (5) כִּי לֹא
not for (5) to-dwell the-house for-me you-will-build you not Yahweh he-says

יָשַׁבְתִּי בְּבַיִת מִן־ הַיּוֹם אֲשֶׁר הֶעֱלֵיתִי אֶת־ יִשְׂרָאֵל עַד הַיּוֹם
the-day to Israel *** I-brought-up when the-day from in-house I-dwelt

הַזֶּה וָאֶהְיֶה מֵאֹהֶל אֶל־ אֹהֶל וּמִמִּשְׁכָּן׃ (6) בְּכֹל אֲשֶׁר־
where in-all (6) and-from-dwelling tent to from-tent but-I-moved the-this

הִתְהַלַּכְתִּי בְּכָל־ יִשְׂרָאֵל הֲדָבָר דִּבַּרְתִּי אֶת־ אַחַד שֹׁפְטֵי
ones-leading-of one-of to I-said statement? Israel with-all-of I-moved

יִשְׂרָאֵל אֲשֶׁר צִוִּיתִי לִרְעוֹת אֶת־ עַמִּי לֵאמֹר לָמָּה לֹא־
not why? to-say people-of-me *** to-shepherd I-commanded whom Israel

בְנִיתֶם לִי בֵּית אֲרָזִים׃ (7) וְעַתָּה כֹּה־ תֹאמַר לְעַבְדִּי
to-servant-of-me you-tell this then-now (7) cedars house-of for-me you-built

לְדָוִיד כֹּה אָמַר יְהוָה צְבָאוֹת אֲנִי לְקַחְתִּיךָ מִן־ הַנָּוֶה מִן־
from the-pasture from I-took-you I Hosts Yahweh-of he-says this to-David

אַחֲרֵי הַצֹּאן לִהְיוֹת נָגִיד עַל עַמִּי יִשְׂרָאֵל׃ (8) וָאֶהְיֶה עִמְּךָ
with-you and-I-was (8) Israel people-of-me over ruler to-be the-flock after

בְּכֹל אֲשֶׁר הָלַכְתָּ וָאַכְרִית אֶת־ כָּל־ אוֹיְבֶיךָ
ones-being-enemies-of-you all-of *** and-I-cut-off you-went where in-all

מִפָּנֶיךָ וְעָשִׂיתִי לְךָ שֵׁם כְּשֵׁם הַגְּדוֹלִים
the-great-men like-name-of name for-you and-I-will-make from-before-you

אֲשֶׁר בָּאָרֶץ׃ (9) וְשַׂמְתִּי מָקוֹם לְעַמִּי יִשְׂרָאֵל
Israel for-people-of-me place and-I-will-provide (9) of-the-earth who

וּנְטַעְתִּיהוּ וְשָׁכַן תַּחְתָּיו וְלֹא יִרְגַּז
he-will-be-disturbed and-not in-him so-he-can-make-home and-I-will-plant-him

עוֹד וְלֹא־ יוֹסִיפוּ בְנֵי־ עַוְלָה לְבַלֹּתוֹ כַּאֲשֶׁר
just-as to-oppress-him wickedness sons-of they-will-repeat and-not again

בָּרִאשׁוֹנָה׃ (10) וּלְמִיָּמִים אֲשֶׁר צִוִּיתִי שֹׁפְטִים עַל־
over ones-leading I-appointed when and-at-from-days (10) at-the-beginning

Nathan the prophet, "Here I
am, living in a palace of cedar,
while the ark of the covenant
of the LORD is under a tent."
[2]Nathan replied to David,
"Whatever you have in mind,
do it, for God is with you."
[3]That night the word of God
came to Nathan, saying:

[4]"Go and tell my servant
David, 'This is what the
LORD says: You are not the
one to build me a house to
dwell in. [5]I have not dwelt
in a house from the day I
brought Israel up out of
Egypt to this day. I have
moved from one tent site to
another, from one dwelling
place to another. [6]Wherever
I have moved with all the
Israelites, did I ever say to
any of their leaders[o] whom
I commanded to shepherd
my people, "Why have you
not built me a house of cedar?"'
[7]"Now then, tell my servant David, 'This is what
the LORD Almighty says: I
took you from the pasture
and from following the
flock, to be ruler over my
people Israel. [8]I have been
with you wherever you
have gone, and I have cut
off all your enemies from
before you. Now I will
make your name like the
names of the greatest men
of the earth. [9]And I will
provide a place for my
people Israel and will plant
them so that they can have
a home of their own and no
longer be disturbed.
Wicked people will not oppress them anymore, as
they did at the beginning
[10]and have done ever since
the time I appointed leaders over my people Israel. I

[o]6 Traditionally *judges;* also in verse 10

עַמִּי יִשְׂרָאֵל וְהִכְנַעְתִּי אֶת־ כָּל־ אוֹיְבֶיךָ
ones-being-enemies-of-you all-of *** and-I-will-subdue Israel people-of-me

וָאַגִּד לָךְ וּבַיִת יִבְנֶה־ לְּךָ יְהוָה׃
Yahweh for-you he-will-build also-house to-you now-I-declare

וְהָיָה כִּי־ מָלְאוּ יָמֶיךָ לָלֶכֶת עִם־ אֲבֹתֶיךָ
fathers-of-you with to-go days-of-you they-are-over when and-he-will-be (11)

וַהֲקִימוֹתִי אֶת־ זַרְעֲךָ אַחֲרֶיךָ אֲשֶׁר יִהְיֶה
he-will-be who after-you offspring-of-you *** then-I-will-raise-up

מִבָּנֶיךָ וַהֲכִינוֹתִי אֶת־ מַלְכוּתוֹ׃ הוּא יִבְנֶה־
he-will-build he (12) kingdom-of-him *** and-I-will-establish from-sons-of-you

לִּי בָּיִת וְכֹנַנְתִּי אֶת־ כִּסְאוֹ עַד־ עוֹלָם׃ אֲנִי
I (13) forever to throne-of-him *** and-I-will-establish house for-me

אֶהְיֶה־ לּוֹ לְאָב וְהוּא יִהְיֶה־ לִּי לְבֵן וְחַסְדִּי
and-love-of-me as-son to-me he-will-be and-he as-father to-him I-will-be

לֹא־ אָסִיר מֵעִמּוֹ כַּאֲשֶׁר הֲסִירוֹתִי מֵאֲשֶׁר הָיָה לְפָנֶיךָ׃
before-you he-was from-whom I-took just-as from-with-him I-will-take never

וְהַעֲמַדְתִּיהוּ בְּבֵיתִי וּבְמַלְכוּתִי עַד־
to and-over-kingdom-of-me over-house-of-me and-I-will-set-him (14)

הָעוֹלָם וְכִסְאוֹ יִהְיֶה נָכוֹן עַד־ עוֹלָם׃
forever to being-established he-will-be and-throne-of-him the-forever

כְּכֹל הַדְּבָרִים הָאֵלֶּה וּכְכֹל הֶחָזוֹן הַזֶּה
the-this the-revelation and-as-all-of the-these the-words as-all-of (15)

כֵּן דִּבֶּר נָתָן אֶל־ דָּוִיד׃ וַיָּבֹא הַמֶּלֶךְ דָּוִיד וַיֵּשֶׁב
and-he-sat David the-king then-he-went (16) David to Nathan he-reported so

לִפְנֵי יְהוָה וַיֹּאמֶר מִי־ אֲנִי יְהוָה אֱלֹהִים וּמִי בֵיתִי כִּי
that family-of-me and-what? God Yahweh I who? and-he-said Yahweh before

הֲבִיאֹתַנִי עַד־ הֲלֹם׃ וַתִּקְטַן זֹאת בְּעֵינֶיךָ אֱלֹהִים
God in-eyes-of-you this and-she-is-not-enough (17) here to you-brought-me

וַתְּדַבֵּר עַל־ בֵּית־ עַבְדְּךָ לְמֵרָחוֹק וּרְאִיתַנִי
and-you-saw-me about-at-future servant-of-you house-of about and-you-spoke

כְּתוֹר הָאָדָם הַמַּעֲלָה יְהוָה אֱלֹהִים׃ מַה־ יּוֹסִיף עוֹד דָּוִיד
David more can-he-add what? (18) God Yahweh the-exalted the-man as-rank-of

אֵלֶיךָ לְכָבוֹד אֶת־ עַבְדֶּךָ וְאַתָּה אֶת־ עַבְדְּךָ יָדָעְתָּ׃
you-know servant-of-you *** for-you servant-of-you *** for-honor to-you

יְהוָה בַּעֲבוּר עַבְדְּךָ וּכְלִבְּךָ עָשִׂיתָ אֵת
*** you-did and-as-will-of-you servant-of-you for-sake-of Yahweh (19)

כָּל־ הַגְּדוּלָּה הַזֹּאת לְהֹדִיעַ אֶת־ כָּל־ הַגְּדֻלּוֹת׃
the-great-things all-of *** to-make-known the-this the-greatness all-of

will also subdue all your enemies.

" 'I declare to you that the LORD will build a house for you: 11When your days are over and you go to be with your fathers, I will raise up your offspring to succeed you, one of your own sons, and I will establish his kingdom. 12He is the one who will build a house for me, and I will establish his throne forever. 13I will be his father, and he will be my son. I will never take my love away from him, as I took it away from your predecessor. 14I will set him over my house and my kingdom forever; his throne will be established forever.' "

15Nathan reported to David all the words of this entire revelation.

David's Prayer

16Then King David went in and sat before the LORD, and he said:

"Who am I, O LORD God, and what is my family, that you have brought me this far? 17And as if this were not enough in your sight, O God, you have spoken about the future of the house of your servant. You have looked on me as though I were the most exalted of men, O LORD God.

18"What more can David say to you for honoring your servant? For you know your servant, 19O LORD. For the sake of your servant and according to your will, you have done this great thing and made known all these great promises.

יְהוָה אֵין כָּמוֹךָ וְאֵין אֱלֹהִים זוּלָתֶךָ בְּכֹל אֲשֶׁר־
that as-all but-you God and-there-is-no like-you there-is-none Yahweh (20)

שָׁמַעְנוּ בְּאָזְנֵינוּ׃ וּמִי כְּעַמְּךָ יִשְׂרָאֵל גּוֹי אֶחָד
one nation Israel like-people-of-you and-who? (21) with-ears-of-us we-heard

בָּאָרֶץ אֲשֶׁר הָלַךְ הָאֱלֹהִים לִפְדּוֹת לוֹ עָם לָשׂוּם
to-make people for-him to-redeem the-God he-went-out who on-the-earth

לְךָ שֵׁם גְּדֻלּוֹת וְנֹרָאוֹת לְגָרֵשׁ מִפְּנֵי
from-before to-drive-out and-wonders-being-awesome great-things name for-you

עַמְּךָ אֲשֶׁר־ פָּדִיתָ מִמִּצְרַיִם גּוֹיִם׃ וַתִּתֵּן אֶת־
*** and-you-made (22) nations from-Egypt you-redeemed whom people-of-you

עַמְּךָ יִשְׂרָאֵל ׀ לְךָ לְעָם עַד־ עוֹלָם וְאַתָּה יְהוָה הָיִיתָ
you-became Yahweh and-you forever to as-people for-you Israel people-of-you

לָהֶם לֵאלֹהִים׃ וְעַתָּה יְהוָה הַדָּבָר אֲשֶׁר דִּבַּרְתָּ עַל־
concerning you-promised that the-promise Yahweh and-now (23) as-God for-them

עַבְדְּךָ וְעַל־ בֵּיתוֹ יֵאָמֵן עַד־ עוֹלָם
forever to let-him-be-established house-of-him and-concerning servant-of-you

וַעֲשֵׂה כַּאֲשֶׁר דִּבַּרְתָּ׃ וְיֵאָמֵן
so-he-will-be-established (24) you-promised just-as and-do!

וְיִגְדַּל שִׁמְךָ עַד־ עוֹלָם לֵאמֹר יְהוָה צְבָאוֹת אֱלֹהֵי
God-of Hosts Yahweh-of to-say forever to name-of-you and-he-will-be-great

יִשְׂרָאֵל אֱלֹהִים לְיִשְׂרָאֵל וּבֵית־ דָּוִיד עַבְדְּךָ נָכוֹן
being-established servant-of-you David and-house-of of-Israel God Israel

לְפָנֶיךָ׃ כִּי ׀ אַתָּה אֱלֹהַי גָּלִיתָ אֶת־ אֹזֶן עַבְדְּךָ
servant-of-you ear-of *** you-uncovered God-of-me you indeed (25) before-you

לִבְנוֹת לוֹ בַּיִת עַל־ כֵּן מָצָא עַבְדְּךָ לְהִתְפַּלֵּל לְפָנֶיךָ׃
before-you to-pray servant-of-you he-found this for house for-him to-build

וְעַתָּה יְהוָה אַתָּה־הוּא הָאֱלֹהִים וַתְּדַבֵּר עַל־ עַבְדְּךָ
servant-of-you to and-you-promised the-God he you Yahweh and-now (26)

הַטּוֹבָה הַזֹּאת׃ וְעַתָּה הוֹאַלְתָּ לְבָרֵךְ אֶת־ בֵּית
house-of *** to-bless you-are-pleased and-now (27) the-this the-good

עַבְדְּךָ לִהְיוֹת לְעוֹלָם לְפָנֶיךָ כִּי־ אַתָּה יְהוָה בֵּרַכְתָּ
you-blessed Yahweh you for before-you to-forever to-be servant-of-you

וּמְבֹרָךְ לְעוֹלָם׃ וַיְהִי אַחֲרֵי־ כֵן וַיַּךְ
then-he-defeated this after and-he-was (18:1) to-forever and-being-blessed

דָּוִיד אֶת־ פְּלִשְׁתִּים וַיַּכְנִיעֵם וַיִּקַּח אֶת־ גַּת
Gath *** and-he-took and-he-subdued-them Philistines *** David

וּבְנֹתֶיהָ מִיַּד פְּלִשְׁתִּים׃ וַיַּךְ אֶת־ מוֹאָב
Moab *** also-he-defeated (2) Philistines from-control-of and-villages-of-her

[20]"There is no one like
you, O LORD, and there is
no God but you, as we have
heard with our own ears.
[21]And who is like your
people Israel—the one na-
tion on earth whose God
went out to redeem a
people for himself, and to
make a name for yourself,
and to perform great and
awesome wonders by driv-
ing out nations from before
your people, whom you re-
deemed from Egypt? [22]You
made your people Israel
your very own forever, and
you, O LORD, have become
their God.

[23]"And now, LORD, let the
promise you have made
concerning your servant
and his house be estab-
lished forever. Do as you
promised, [24]so that it will be
established and that your
name will be great forever.
Then men will say, 'The
LORD Almighty, the God
over Israel, is Israel's God!'
And the house of your servant David will be estab-
lished before you.

[25]"You, my God, have revealed to your servant that
you will build a house for
him. So your servant has
found courage to pray to
you. [26]O LORD, you are God!
You have given this good
promise to your servant.
[27]Now you have been
pleased to bless the house
of your servant, that it may
continue forever in your
sight; for you, O LORD, have
blessed it, and it will be
blessed forever."

David's Victories

18 In the course of time,
David defeated the
Philistines and subdued them,
and he took Gath and its surrounding villages from the
control of the Philistines.

וַיִּהְיוּ מוֹאָב עֲבָדִים לְדָוִיד נֹשְׂאֵי מִנְחָה׃
tribute ones-bringing-of to-David subjects Moab and-they-became

וַיַּךְ דָּוִיד אֶת־הֲדַדְעֶזֶר מֶלֶךְ־צוֹבָה חֲמָתָה בְּלֶכְתּוֹ
when-to-go-him to-Hamath Zobah king-of Hadadezer *** David and-he-fought (3)

לְהַצִּיב יָדוֹ בִּנְהַר־פְּרָת׃ וַיִּלְכֹּד
and-he-captured (4) Euphrates along-River-of control-of-him to-establish

דָּוִיד מִמֶּנּוּ אֶלֶף רֶכֶב וְשִׁבְעַת אֲלָפִים פָּרָשִׁים
charioteers thousands and-seven-of chariot thousand from-him David

וְעֶשְׂרִים אֶלֶף אִישׁ רַגְלִי וַיְעַקֵּר דָּוִיד אֶת־כָּל־
all-of *** David and-he-hamstrung foot-soldier man thousand and-twenty

הָרֶכֶב וַיּוֹתֵר מִמֶּנּוּ מֵאָה רָכֶב׃ וַיָּבֹא
when-he-came (5) chariot-horse hundred from-him but-he-left the-chariot-horse

אֲרַם דַּרְמֶשֶׂק לַעְזוֹר לַהֲדַדְעֶזֶר מֶלֶךְ צוֹבָה וַיַּךְ
then-he-struck-down Zobah king-of to-Hadadezer to-help Damascus Aram-of

דָּוִיד בַּאֲרָם עֶשְׂרִים־וּשְׁנַיִם אֶלֶף אִישׁ׃ וַיָּשֶׂם דָּוִיד
David and-he-put-garrison (6) man thousand and-two twenty of-Aram David

בַּאֲרַם דַּרְמֶשֶׂק וַיְהִי אֲרָם לְדָוִיד עֲבָדִים נֹשְׂאֵי
ones-bearing-of subjects to-David Aram and-he-became Damascus in-Aram-of

מִנְחָה וַיּוֹשַׁע יְהוָה לְדָוִיד בְּכֹל אֲשֶׁר הָלָךְ׃
he-went where in-all to-David Yahweh and-he-gave-victory tribute

וַיִּקַּח דָּוִיד אֵת שִׁלְטֵי הַזָּהָב אֲשֶׁר הָיוּ עַל עַבְדֵי
officers-of on they-were that the-gold shields-of *** David and-he-took (7)

הֲדַדְעָזֶר וַיְבִיאֵם יְרוּשָׁלָםִ׃ וּמִטִּבְחַת וּמִכּוּן
and-from-Cun and-from-Tibhath (8) Jerusalem and-he-brought-them Hadadezer

עָרֵי הֲדַדְעֶזֶר לָקַח דָּוִיד נְחֹשֶׁת רַבָּה מְאֹד בָּהּ׀ עָשָׂה שְׁלֹמֹה
Solomon he-made with-her very much bronze David he-took Hadadezer towns-of

אֶת־יָם הַנְּחֹשֶׁת וְאֶת־הָעַמּוּדִים וְאֵת כְּלֵי הַנְּחֹשֶׁת׃
the-bronze articles-of and the-pillars and the-bronze Sea-of ***

וַיִּשְׁמַע תֹּעוּ מֶלֶךְ חֲמָת כִּי הִכָּה דָּוִיד אֶת־כָּל־
entire-of *** David he-defeated that Hamath king-of Tou when-he-heard (9)

חֵיל הֲדַדְעֶזֶר מֶלֶךְ־צוֹבָה׃ וַיִּשְׁלַח אֶת־הֲדוֹרָם־בְּנוֹ אֶל־
to son-of-him Hadoram *** then-he-sent (10) Zobah king-of Hadadezer army-of

הַמֶּלֶךְ־דָּוִיד לִשְׁאָול°־לוֹ לְשָׁלוֹם וּלְבָרְכוֹ עַל אֲשֶׁר
when on and-to-congratulate-him about-peace to-him to-greet David the-king

נִלְחַם בַּהֲדַדְעֶזֶר וַיַּכֵּהוּ כִּי־אִישׁ מִלְחֲמוֹת תֹּעוּ
Tou wars-of man-of for and-he-defeated-him against-Hadadezer he-fought

הָיָה הֲדַדְעָזֶר וְכֹל כְּלֵי זָהָב וָכֶסֶף וּנְחֹשֶׁת׃
and-bronze and-silver gold articles-of and-all-of Hadadezer he-was

[2]David also defeated the Moabites, and they became subject to him and brought tribute.
[3]Moreover, David fought
Hadadezer king of Zobah, as
far as Hamath, when he went
to establish his control along
the Euphrates River. [4]David
captured a thousand of his
chariots, seven thousand
charioteers and twenty thousand foot soldiers. He ham-
strung all but a hundred of the
chariot horses.
[5]When the Arameans of
Damascus came to help Hadadezer king of Zobah, David
struck down twenty-two
thousand of them. [6]He put garrisons in the Aramean kingdom of Damascus, and the
Arameans became subject to
him and brought tribute. The
LORD gave David victory
everywhere he went.
[7]David took the gold shields
carried by the officers of Hadadezer and brought them to
Jerusalem. [8]From Tebah[p] and
Cun, towns that belonged to
Hadadezer, David took a great
quantity of bronze, which
Solomon used to make the
bronze Sea, the pillars and
various bronze articles.
[9]When Tou king of Hamath
heard that David had defeated
the entire army of Hadadezer
king of Zobah, [10]he sent his
son Hadoram to King David to
greet him and congratulate
him on his victory in battle
over Hadadezer, who had
been at war with Tou. Ha-
doram brought all kinds of articles of gold and silver and
bronze.

[p] 8 Hebrew *Tibhath*, a variant of *Tebah*

°10 ק לשאל

(11) גַּם־ אֹתָם הִקְדִּישׁ הַמֶּלֶךְ דָּוִיד לַיהוָה עִם־ הַכֶּסֶף
the-silver with to-Yahweh David the-king he-dedicated them also (11)

וְהַזָּהָב אֲשֶׁר נָשָׂא מִכָּל־ הַגּוֹיִם מֵאֱדוֹם וּמִמּוֹאָב
and-from-Moab from-Edom the-nations from-all-of he-took that and-the-gold

וּמִבְּנֵי עַמּוֹן וּמִפְּלִשְׁתִּים וּמֵעֲמָלֵק׃ (12) וְאַבְשַׁי
and-Abishai (12) and-from-Amalek and-from-Philistines Ammon and-from-sons-of

בֶּן־ צְרוּיָה הִכָּה אֶת־ אֱדוֹם בְּגֵיא הַמֶּלַח שְׁמוֹנָה עָשָׂר
ten eight the-Salt in-Valley-of Edom *** he-struck-down Zeruiah son-of

אָלֶף׃ (13) וַיָּשֶׂם בֶּאֱדוֹם נְצִיבִים וַיִּהְיוּ כָל־ אֱדוֹם
Edom all-of and-they-became garrisons in-Edom and-he-put (13) thousand

עֲבָדִים לְדָוִיד וַיּוֹשַׁע יְהוָה אֶת־ דָּוִיד בְּכֹל אֲשֶׁר הָלָךְ׃
he-went where in-all David *** Yahweh and-he-gave-victory to-David subjects

(14) וַיִּמְלֹךְ דָּוִיד עַל־ כָּל־ יִשְׂרָאֵל וַיְהִי עֹשֶׂה מִשְׁפָּט
justice doing and-he-was Israel all-of over David and-he-reigned (14)

וּצְדָקָה לְכָל־ עַמּוֹ׃ (15) וְיוֹאָב בֶּן־ צְרוּיָה עַל־
over Zeruiah son-of and-Joab (15) people-of-him for-all-of and-righteousness

הַצָּבָא וִיהוֹשָׁפָט בֶּן־ אֲחִילוּד מַזְכִּיר׃ (16) וְצָדוֹק בֶּן־
son-of and-Zadok (16) one-recording Ahilud son-of and-Jehoshaphat the-army

אֲחִיטוּב וַאֲבִימֶלֶךְ בֶּן־ אֶבְיָתָר כֹּהֲנִים וְשַׁוְשָׁא סוֹפֵר׃
secretary and-Shavsha priests Abiathar son-of and-Abimelech Ahitub

(17) וּבְנָיָהוּ בֶּן־ יְהוֹיָדָע עַל־ הַכְּרֵתִי וְהַפְּלֵתִי
and-the-Pelethite the-Kerethite over Jehoiada son-of and-Benaiah (17)

וּבְנֵי־ דָוִיד הָרִאשֹׁנִים לְיַד הַמֶּלֶךְ׃ (19:1) וַיְהִי
and-he-was (19:1) the-king at-side-of the-chief-officials David and-sons-of

אַחֲרֵי־ כֵן וַיָּמָת נָחָשׁ מֶלֶךְ בְּנֵי־ עַמּוֹן וַיִּמְלֹךְ
and-he-became-king Ammon sons-of king-of Nahash then-he-died this after

בְּנוֹ תַּחְתָּיו׃ (2) וַיֹּאמֶר דָּוִיד אֶעֱשֶׂה־ חֶסֶד ׀
kindness I-will-show David and-he-thought (2) in-place-of-him son-of-him

עִם־ חָנוּן בֶּן־ נָחָשׁ כִּי־ עָשָׂה אָבִיו עִמִּי חֶסֶד
kindness to-me father-of-him he-showed because Nahash son-of Hanun to

וַיִּשְׁלַח דָּוִיד מַלְאָכִים לְנַחֲמוֹ עַל־ אָבִיו
father-of-him about to-express-sympathy-to-him delegates David so-he-sent

וַיָּבֹאוּ עַבְדֵי דָוִיד אֶל־ אֶרֶץ בְּנֵי־ עַמּוֹן אֶל־ חָנוּן
Hanun to Ammon sons-of land-of to David men-of when-they-came

לְנַחֲמוֹ׃ (3) וַיֹּאמְרוּ שָׂרֵי בְנֵי־ עַמּוֹן
Ammon sons-of nobles-of and-they-said (3) to-express-sympathy-to-him

לְחָנוּן הַמְכַבֵּד דָּוִיד אֶת־ אָבִיךָ בְּעֵינֶיךָ כִּי־ שָׁלַח
he-sent because in-eyes-of-you father-of-you *** David honoring? to-Hanun

11 King David dedicated
these articles to the LORD, as he
had done with the silver and
gold he had taken from all
these nations: Edom and
Moab, the Ammonites and the
Philistines, and Amalek.
12 Abishai son of Zeruiah
struck down eighteen thousand Edomites in the Valley of
Salt. 13 He put garrisons in
Edom, and all the Edomites
became subject to David. The
LORD gave David victory
everywhere he went.

David's Officials

14 David reigned over all
Israel, doing what was just
and right for all his people.
15 Joab son of Zeruiah was
over the army; Jehoshaphat
son of Ahilud was recorder;
16 Zadok son of Ahitub and
Ahimelech[b] son of Abiathar
were priests; Shavsha was
secretary; 17 Benaiah son of
Jehoiada was over the Kere-
thites and Pelethites; and David's sons were chief officials
at the king's side.

The Battle Against the Ammonites

19 In the course of time,
Nahash king of the
Ammonites died, and his son
succeeded him as king. 2 David
thought, "I will show kindness to Hanun son of Nahash,
because his father showed
kindness to me." So David
sent a delegation to express his
sympathy to Hanun con-
cerning his father.
When David's men came to
Hanun in the land of the Ammonites to express sympathy
to him, 3 the Ammonite nobles
said to Hanun, "Do you think
David is honoring your father

[b]16 Some Hebrew manuscripts, Vulgate and Syriac (see also 2 Samuel 8:17); most Hebrew manuscripts *Abimelech*

לְךָ מְנַחֲמִים הֲלֹא בַּעֲבוּר לַחְקֹר וְלַהֲפֹךְ

and-to-overthrow to-explore in-order-to not? ones-sympathizing to-you

וּלְרַגֵּל הָאָרֶץ בָּאוּ עֲבָדָיו אֵלֶיךָ׃ (4) וַיִּקַּח חָנוּן

Hanun so-he-seized (4) to-you men-of-him they-came the-country and-to-spy-out

אֶת־ עַבְדֵי דָוִיד וַיְגַלְּחֵם וַיִּכְרֹת אֶת־ מַדְוֵיהֶם

garments-of-them *** and-he-cut-off and-he-shaved-them David men-of ***

בַּחֵצִי עַד־ הַמִּפְשָׂעָה וַיְשַׁלְּחֵם׃ (5) וַיֵּלְכוּ

when-they-came (5) and-he-sent-away-them the-buttocks at in-the-middle

וַיַּגִּידוּ לְדָוִיד עַל־ הָאֲנָשִׁים וַיִּשְׁלַח לִקְרָאתָם כִּי־ הָיוּ

they-were for to-meet-them then-he-sent the-men about to-David and-they-told

הָאֲנָשִׁים נִכְלָמִים מְאֹד וַיֹּאמֶר הַמֶּלֶךְ שְׁבוּ בִירֵחוֹ

at-Jericho stay! the-king and-he-said greatly ones-being-humiliated the-men

עַד אֲשֶׁר־ יְצַמַּח זְקַנְכֶם וְשַׁבְתֶּם׃ (6) וַיִּרְאוּ

when-they-realized (6) then-you-come-back beard-of-you he-grows when till

בְּנֵי עַמּוֹן כִּי הִתְבָּאֲשׁוּ עִם־ דָּוִיד וַיִּשְׁלַח חָנוּן

Hanun then-he-sent David to they-became-stench that Ammon sons-of

וּבְנֵי עַמּוֹן אֶלֶף כִּכַּר־ כֶּסֶף לִשְׂכֹּר לָהֶם מִן־ אֲרַם

Aram-of from for-them to-hire silver talent-of thousand Ammon and-sons-of

נַהֲרַיִם וּמִן־ אֲרַם מַעֲכָה וּמִצּוֹבָה רֶכֶב וּפָרָשִׁים׃

and-charioteers chariot and-from-Zobah Maacah Aram-of and-from Naharaim

(7) וַיִּשְׂכְּרוּ לָהֶם שְׁנַיִם וּשְׁלֹשִׁים אֶלֶף רֶכֶב וְאֶת־ מֶלֶךְ

king-of and chariot thousand and-thirty two for-them and-they-hired (7)

מַעֲכָה וְאֶת־ עַמּוֹ וַיָּבֹאוּ וַיַּחֲנוּ לִפְנֵי מֵידְבָא וּבְנֵי

and-sons-of Medeba near and-they-camped and-they-came troop-of-him and Maacah

עַמּוֹן נֶאֶסְפוּ מֵעָרֵיהֶם וַיָּבֹאוּ לַמִּלְחָמָה׃

for-the-battle and-they-moved-out from-towns-of-them they-were-mustered Ammon

(8) וַיִּשְׁמַע דָּוִיד וַיִּשְׁלַח אֶת־ יוֹאָב וְאֵת כָּל־ צָבָא

army entire-of and Joab *** then-he-sent-out David when-he-heard (8)

הַגִּבּוֹרִים׃ (9) וַיֵּצְאוּ בְּנֵי עַמּוֹן וַיַּעַרְכוּ

and-they-drew-up Ammon sons-of and-they-came-out (9) the-fighting-men

מִלְחָמָה פֶּתַח הָעִיר וְהַמְּלָכִים אֲשֶׁר־ בָּאוּ לְבַדָּם

by-themselves they-came who and-the-kings the-city entrance-of battle

בַּשָּׂדֶה׃ (10) וַיַּרְא יוֹאָב כִּי־ הָיְתָה פְנֵי־ הַמִּלְחָמָה

the-battle lines-of she-was that Joab and-he-saw (10) in-the-open-country

אֵלָיו פָּנִים וְאָחוֹר וַיִּבְחַר מִכָּל־ בָּחוּר בְּיִשְׂרָאֵל

in-Israel being-best from-all-of so-he-selected and-behind fronts to-him

וַיַּעֲרֹךְ לִקְרַאת אֲרָם׃ (11) וְאֵת יֶתֶר הָעָם נָתַן בְּיַד

under-hand-of he-put the-people rest-of and (11) Aram to-meet and-he-deployed

by sending men to you to express sympathy? Haven't his
men come to you to explore
and spy out the country and
overthrow it?" 4So Hanun
seized David's men, shaved
them, cut off their garments in
the middle at the buttocks,
and sent them away.
5When someone came and
told David about the men, he
sent messengers to meet them,
for they were greatly humili-
ated. The king said, "Stay at
Jericho till your beards have
grown, and then come back."
6When the Ammonites real-
ized that they had become a
stench in David's nostrils,
Hanun and the Ammonites
sent a thousand talents[r] of silver to hire chariots and charioteers from Aram Naharaim,[s]
Aram Maacah and Zobah.
7They hired thirty-two thousand chariots and charioteers,
as well as the king of Maacah
with his troops, who came
and camped near Medeba,
while the Ammonites were
mustered from their towns
and moved out for battle.
8On hearing this, David sent
Joab out with the entire army
of fighting men. 9The Am-
monites came out and drew up
in battle formation at the entrance to their city, while the
kings who had come were by
themselves in the open country.
10Joab saw that there were
battle lines in front of him and
behind him; so he selected
some of the best troops in Israel and deployed them against
the Arameans. 11He put the
rest of the men under the command of Abishai his brother,

[r]6 That is, about 37 tons (about 34 metric tons)

[s]6 That is, Northwest Mesopotamia

אַבְשַׁי אָחִיו וַיַּעַרְכוּ לִקְרַאת בְּנֵי עַמּוֹן׃
Ammon sons-of to-meet and-they-deployed brother-of-him Abishai

(12) וַיֹּאמֶר אִם־ תֶּחֱזַק מִמֶּנִּי אֲרָם וְהָיִיתָ לִּי
to-me then-you-be Aram more-than-me she-is-strong if and-he-said (12)

לִתְשׁוּעָה וְאִם־ בְּנֵי עַמּוֹן יֶחֶזְקוּ מִמְּךָ
more-than-you they-are-strong Ammon sons-of but-if for-rescue

וְהוֹשַׁעְתִּיךָ׃ (13) חֲזַק וְנִתְחַזְּקָה בְּעַד־
for and-let-us-fight-bravely! be-strong! (13) then-I-will-rescue-you

עַמֵּנוּ וּבְעַד עָרֵי אֱלֹהֵינוּ וַיהוָה הַטּוֹב בְּעֵינָיו
in-eyes-of-him the-good and-Yahweh God-of-us cities-of and-for people-of-us

יַעֲשֶׂה׃ (14) וַיִּגַּשׁ יוֹאָב וְהָעָם אֲשֶׁר־ עִמּוֹ לִפְנֵי
against with-him who and-the-troop Joab then-he-advanced (14) he-will-do

אֲרָם לַמִּלְחָמָה וַיָּנוּסוּ מִפָּנָיו׃ (15) וּבְנֵי עַמּוֹן
Ammon when-sons-of (15) from-before-him and-they-fled to-the-fight Aram

רָאוּ כִּי־ נָס אֲרָם וַיָּנוּסוּ גַם־ הֵם מִפְּנֵי אַבְשַׁי
Abishai from-before they also then-they-fled Aram fleeing that they-saw

אָחִיו וַיָּבֹאוּ הָעִירָה וַיָּבֹא יוֹאָב יְרוּשָׁלִָם׃
Jerusalem Joab so-he-went-back into-the-city and-they-went brother-of-him

(16) וַיַּרְא אֲרָם כִּי נִגְּפוּ לִפְנֵי יִשְׂרָאֵל וַיִּשְׁלְחוּ
then-they-sent Israel before they-were-routed that Aram after-he-saw (16)

מַלְאָכִים וַיּוֹצִיאוּ אֶת־ אֲרָם אֲשֶׁר מֵעֵבֶר הַנָּהָר וְשׁוֹפַךְ
and-Shophach the-River from-beyond who Aram *** and-they-brought messengers

שַׂר־ צְבָא הֲדַדְעֶזֶר לִפְנֵיהֶם׃ (17) וַיֻּגַּד לְדָוִיד
to-David when-he-was-told (17) before-them Hadadezer army-of commander-of

וַיֶּאֱסֹף אֶת־ כָּל־ יִשְׂרָאֵל וַיַּעֲבֹר הַיַּרְדֵּן וַיָּבֹא
and-he-advanced the-Jordan and-he-crossed Israel all-of *** then-he-gathered

אֲלֵהֶם וַיַּעֲרֹךְ אֲלֵהֶם וַיַּעֲרֹךְ דָּוִיד לִקְרַאת אֲרָם
Aram to-meet David and-he-formed opposite-them and-he-formed against-them

מִלְחָמָה וַיִּלָּחֲמוּ עִמּוֹ׃ (18) וַיָּנָס אֲרָם מִלִּפְנֵי יִשְׂרָאֵל
Israel from-before Aram but-he-fled (18) against-him and-they-fought battle

וַיַּהֲרֹג דָּוִיד מֵאֲרָם שִׁבְעַת אֲלָפִים רֶכֶב וְאַרְבָּעִים
and-forty charioteer thousands seven-of from-Aram David and-he-killed

אֶלֶף אִישׁ רַגְלִי וְאֵת שׁוֹפַךְ שַׂר־ הַצָּבָא הֵמִית׃
he-killed the-army commander-of Shophach and foot-soldier man thousand

(19) וַיִּרְאוּ עַבְדֵי הֲדַדְעֶזֶר כִּי נִגְּפוּ לִפְנֵי
before they-were-defeated that Hadadezer vassals-of when-they-saw (19)

יִשְׂרָאֵל וַיַּשְׁלִימוּ עִם־ דָּוִיד וַיַּעַבְדֻהוּ
and-they-became-subject-to-him David with then-they-made-peace Israel

and they were deployed
against the Ammonites. 12Joab
said, "If the Arameans are too
strong for me, then you are to
rescue me; but if the Ammonites are too strong for you,
then I will rescue you. 13Be
strong and let us fight bravely
for our people and the cities of
our God. The LORD will do
what is good in his sight."
14Then Joab and the troops
with him advanced to fight
the Arameans, and they fled
before him. 15When the Ammonites saw that the Ara-
means were fleeing, they too
fled before his brother Abishai
and went inside the city. So
Joab went back to Jerusalem.
16After the Arameans saw
that they had been routed by
Israel, they sent messengers
and had Arameans brought
from beyond the River,[t] with
Shophach the commander of
Hadadezer's army leading
them.
17When David was told of
this, he gathered all Israel and
crossed the Jordan; he advanced against them and
formed his battle lines opposite them. David formed his
lines to meet the Arameans in
battle, and they fought against
him. 18But they fled before Israel, and David killed seven
thousand of their charioteers
and forty thousand of their
foot soldiers. He also killed
Shophach the commander of
their army.
19When the vassals of Hadadezer saw that they had been
defeated by Israel, they made
peace with David and became
subject to him.

[t] 16 That is, the Euphrates

וְלֹא־ אָבָה אֲרָם לְהוֹשִׁיעַ אֶת־ בְּנֵי־ עַמּוֹן עוֹד׃ וַיְהִי
and-he-was (20:1) again Ammon sons-of *** to-help Aram he-was-willing so-not

לְעֵת תְּשׁוּבַת הַשָּׁנָה לְעֵת ׀ צֵאת הַמְּלָכִים וַיִּנְהַג
then-he-led-out the-kings to-go-off at-time-of the-year return-of at-time-of

יוֹאָב אֶת־ חֵיל הַצָּבָא וַיַּשְׁחֵת ׀ אֶת־ אֶרֶץ בְּנֵי־ עַמּוֹן
Ammon sons-of land-of *** and-he-laid-waste the-army force-of *** Joab

וַיָּבֹא וַיָּצַר אֶת־ רַבָּה וְדָוִיד יֹשֵׁב בִּירוּשָׁלִָם
in-Jerusalem remaining but-David Rabbah *** and-he-besieged and-he-went

וַיַּךְ יוֹאָב אֶת־ רַבָּה וַיֶּהֶרְסֶהָ׃ וַיִּקַּח דָּוִיד אֶת־
*** David and-he-took (2) and-he-ruined-her Rabbah *** Joab and-he-attacked

עֲטֶרֶת־ מַלְכָּם מֵעַל רֹאשׁוֹ וַיִּמְצָאָהּ ׀ מִשְׁקַל
weight-of and-he-found-her head-of-him from-upon king-of-them crown-of

כִּכַּר־ זָהָב וּבָהּ אֶבֶן יְקָרָה וַתְּהִי עַל־ רֹאשׁ דָּוִיד
David head-of on and-she-was precious stone and-in-her gold talent-of

וּשְׁלַל הָעִיר הוֹצִיא הַרְבֵּה מְאֹד׃ וְאֶת־ הָעָם אֲשֶׁר־
who the-people and (3) very to-be-great he-took the-city and-plunder-of

בָּהּ הוֹצִיא וַיָּשַׂר בַּמְּגֵרָה וּבַחֲרִיצֵי הַבַּרְזֶל
the-iron and-to-picks-of to-the-saw and-he-consigned he-brought-out in-her

וּבַמְּגֵרוֹת וְכֵן יַעֲשֶׂה דָוִיד לְכֹל עָרֵי בְנֵי־ עַמּוֹן
Ammon sons-of towns-of to-all-of David he-did and-this and-to-the-axes

וַיָּשָׁב דָּוִיד וְכָל־ הָעָם יְרוּשָׁלִָם׃ וַיְהִי
and-he-was (4) Jerusalem the-army and-entire-of David then-he-returned

אַחֲרֵיכֵן וַתַּעֲמֹד מִלְחָמָה בְּגֶזֶר עִם־ פְּלִשְׁתִּים אָז הִכָּה
he-killed then Philistines with at-Gezer war then-she-broke-out after-this

סִבְּכַי הַחֻשָׁתִי אֶת־ סִפַּי מִילִדֵי הָרְפָאִים
the-Rephaites from-descendants-of Sippai *** the-Hushathite Sibbecai

וַיִּכָּנֵעוּ׃ וַתְּהִי־ עוֹד מִלְחָמָה אֶת־ פְּלִשְׁתִּים
Philistines with battle another and-she-was (5) and-they-were-subjugated

וַיַּךְ אֶלְחָנָן בֶּן־ יָעוֹר אֶת־ לַחְמִי אֲחִי גָּלְיָת הַגִּתִּי
the-Gittite Goliath brother-of Lahmi *** Jair son-of Elhanan and-he-killed

וְעֵץ חֲנִיתוֹ כִּמְנוֹר אֹרְגִים׃ וַתְּהִי־ עוֹד
another and-she-was (6) ones-weaving like-rod-of spear-of-him and-shaft-of

מִלְחָמָה בְּגַת וַיְהִי ׀ אִישׁ מִדָּה וְאֶצְבְּעֹתָיו שֵׁשׁ־ וָשֵׁשׁ
and-six six and-fingers-of-him size man-of and-he-was at-Gath battle

עֶשְׂרִים וְאַרְבַּע וְגַם־ הוּא נוֹלַד לְהָרָפָא׃
from-the-Rapha he-was-descended he and-also and-four twenty

וַיְחָרֵף אֶת־יִשְׂרָאֵל וַיַּכֵּהוּ יְהוֹנָתָן בֶּן־ שִׁמְעָא
Shimea son-of Jonathan then-he-killed-him Israel *** when-he-taunted (7)

So the Arameans were not willing to help the Ammonites anymore.

The Capture of Rabbah

20 In the spring, at the time when kings go off to war, Joab led out the armed forces. He laid waste the land of the Ammonites and went to Rabbah and besieged it, but David remained in Jerusalem. Joab attacked Rabbah and left it in ruins. [2]David took the crown from the head of their king[u]—its weight was found to be a talent[v] of gold, and it was set with precious stones—and it was placed on David's head. He took a great quantity of plunder from the city [3]and brought out the people who were there, consigning them to labor with saws and with iron picks and axes. David did this to all the Ammonite towns. Then David and his entire army returned to Jerusalem.

War With the Philistines

[4]In the course of time, war broke out with the Philistines, at Gezer. At that time Sibbecai the Hushathite killed Sippai, one of the descendants of the Rephaites, and the Philistines were subjugated.

[5]In another battle with the Philistines, Elhanan son of Jair killed Lahmi the brother of Goliath the Gittite, who had a spear with a shaft like a weaver's rod.

[6]In still another battle, which took place at Gath, there was a huge man with six fingers on each hand and six toes on each foot—twenty-four in all. He also was descended from Rapha. [7]When he taunted Israel, Jonathan

[u]2 Or *of Milcom,* that is, Molech
[v]2 That is, about 75 pounds (about 34 kilograms)

°5 ק יעיר

אֲחִי דָוִיד׃ אֵל נוּלְּדוּ לְהָרָפָא בְּגַת
in-Gath from-the-Rapha they-were-descended these (8) David brother-of

וַיִּפְּלוּ בְיַד־ דָּוִיד וּבְיַד־ עֲבָדָיו׃ וַיַּעֲמֹד
and-he-rose (21:1) men-of-him and-at-hand-of David at-hand-of and-they-fell

שָׂטָן עַל־ יִשְׂרָאֵל וַיָּסֶת אֶת־ דָּוִיד לִמְנוֹת אֶת־ יִשְׂרָאֵל׃
Israel *** to-take-census David *** and-he-incited Israel against Satan

וַיֹּאמֶר דָּוִיד אֶל־ יוֹאָב וְאֶל־ שָׂרֵי הָעָם לְכוּ סִפְרוּ
and-count! go! the-troop commanders-of and-to Joab to David so-he-said (2)

אֶת־ יִשְׂרָאֵל מִבְּאֵר שֶׁבַע וְעַד־ דָּן וְהָבִיאוּ אֵלַי וְאֵדְעָה
so-I-may-know to-me and-report-back! Dan even-to Sheba from-Beer Israel ***

אֶת־ מִסְפָּרָם׃ וַיֹּאמֶר יוֹאָב יוֹסֵף יְהוָה עַל־
to Yahweh may-he-multiply Joab but-he-replied (3) number-of-them ***

עַמּוֹ ׀ כָּהֵם מֵאָה פְעָמִים הֲלֹא אֲדֹנִי הַמֶּלֶךְ כֻּלָּם
all-of-them the-king lord-of-me not? times hundred as-they troop-of-him

לַאדֹנִי לַעֲבָדִים לָמָּה יְבַקֵּשׁ זֹאת אֲדֹנִי לָמָּה יִהְיֶה
should-he-be why? lord-of-me this he-wants why? as-subjects to-lord-of-me

לְאַשְׁמָה לְיִשְׂרָאֵל׃ וּדְבַר־ הַמֶּלֶךְ חָזַק עַל־ יוֹאָב וַיֵּצֵא
so-he-left Joab over he-prevailed the-king but-word-of (4) on-Israel for-guilt

יוֹאָב וַיִּתְהַלֵּךְ בְּכָל־ יִשְׂרָאֵל וַיָּבֹא יְרוּשָׁלִָם׃
Jerusalem then-he-came-back Israel through-all-of and-he-went Joab

וַיִּתֵּן יוֹאָב אֶת־ מִסְפַּר מִפְקַד־ הָעָם אֶל־ דָּוִיד
David to the-people group-of number-of *** Joab and-he-reported (5)

וַיְהִי כָל־ יִשְׂרָאֵל אֶלֶף אֲלָפִים וּמֵאָה אֶלֶף אִישׁ
man thousand and-hundred thousands thousand-of Israel all-of and-he-was

שֹׁלֵף חֶרֶב וִיהוּדָה אַרְבַּע מֵאוֹת וְשִׁבְעִים אֶלֶף אִישׁ
man thousand and-seventy hundreds four-of and-Judah sword handling-of

שֹׁלֵף חָרֶב׃ וְלֵוִי וּבִנְיָמִן לֹא פָקַד בְּתוֹכָם
in-among-them he-included not and-Benjamin but-Levi (6) sword handling-of

כִּי־ נִתְעַב דְּבַר־ הַמֶּלֶךְ אֶת־ יוֹאָב׃ וַיֵּרַע
and-he-was-evil (7) Joab *** the-king command-of he-was-repulsive because

בְּעֵינֵי הָאֱלֹהִים עַל־ הַדָּבָר הַזֶּה וַיַּךְ אֶת־ יִשְׂרָאֵל׃
Israel *** so-he-punished the-this the-command concerning the-God in-eyes-of

וַיֹּאמֶר דָּוִיד אֶל־ הָאֱלֹהִים חָטָאתִי מְאֹד אֲשֶׁר עָשִׂיתִי אֶת־ הַדָּבָר
the-thing *** I-did that greatly I-sinned the-God to David then-he-said (8)

הַזֶּה וְעַתָּה הַעֲבֶר־ נָא אֶת־ עֲוֹן עַבְדְּךָ כִּי
for servant-of-you guilt-of *** now! take-away! and-now the-this

נִסְכַּלְתִּי מְאֹד׃ וַיְדַבֵּר יְהוָה אֶל־ גָּד חֹזֵה דָוִיד לֵאמֹר׃
to-say David seer-of Gad to Yahweh and-he-said (9) very I-acted-foolishly

son of Shimea, David's brother, killed him.
[8]These were descendants of
Rapha in Gath, and they fell at
the hands of David and his
men.

David Numbers the Fighting Men

21 Satan rose up against
Israel and incited Da-
vid to take a census of Israel.
[2]So David said to Joab and the
commanders of the troops,
"Go and count the Israelites
from Beersheba to Dan. Then
report back to me so that I may
know how many there are."
[3]But Joab replied, "May the
LORD multiply his troops a
hundred times over. My lord
the king, are they not all my
lord's subjects? Why does my
lord want to do this? Why
should he bring guilt on Israel?"
[4]The king's word, however,
overruled Joab; so Joab left and
went throughout Israel and
then came back to Jerusalem.
[5]Joab reported the number of
the fighting men to David: In
all Israel there were one million one hundred thousand
men who could handle a
sword, including four hundred and seventy thousand in
Judah.
[6]But Joab did not include
Levi and Benjamin in the
numbering, because the
king's command was repul-
sive to him. [7]This command
was also evil in the sight of
God; so he punished Israel.
[8]Then David said to God, "I
have sinned greatly by doing
this. Now, I beg you, take
away the guilt of your servant.
I have done a very foolish
thing."

לֵךְ וְדִבַּרְתָּ אֶל־דָּוִיד לֵאמֹר כֹּה אָמַר יְהוָה שָׁלוֹשׁ אֲנִי נֹטֶה

giving I three Yahweh he-says this to-say David to and-you-tell go! (10)

עָלֶיךָ בְּחַר־ לְךָ אַחַת מֵהֵנָּה וְאֶעֱשֶׂה־ לָּךְ׃

against-you and-I-will-carry-out of-them one for-you choose! to-you

וַיָּבֹא גָד אֶל־דָּוִיד וַיֹּאמֶר לוֹ כֹּה־ אָמַר יְהוָה קַבֶּל־

choose! Yahweh he-says this to-him and-he-said David to Gad so-he-went (11)

לָךְ׃ אִם־ שָׁלוֹשׁ שָׁנִים רָעָב וְאִם־ שְׁלֹשָׁה חֳדָשִׁים

months three or-whether famine years three whether (12) for-you

נִסְפֶּה מִפְּנֵי־ צָרֶיךָ וְחֶרֶב אוֹיְבֶיךָ |

being-enemies-of-you and-sword-of enemies-of-you from-before being-swept-away

לְמַשֶּׂגֶת וְאִם־ שְׁלֹשֶׁת יָמִים חֶרֶב יְהוָה וְדֶבֶר בָּאָרֶץ

in-the-land and-plague Yahweh sword-of days three-of or-whether as-overtaking

וּמַלְאַךְ יְהוָה מַשְׁחִית בְּכָל־ גְּבוּל יִשְׂרָאֵל וְעַתָּה רְאֵה

decide! then-now Israel part-of in-every-of ravaging Yahweh and-angel-of

מָה־ אָשִׁיב אֶת־ שֹׁלְחִי דָּבָר׃ וַיֹּאמֶר דָּוִיד אֶל־ גָּד

Gad to David and-he-said (13) answer one-sending-me *** I-should-give how

צַר־ לִי מְאֹד אֶפְּלָה־ נָּא בְיַד־ יְהוָה כִּי־ רַבִּים

great-ones for Yahweh into-hand-of now! let-me-fall deeply to-me distress

רַחֲמָיו מְאֹד וּבְיַד־ אָדָם אַל־ אֶפֹּל׃ וַיִּתֵּן

so-he-sent (14) let-me-fall not man but-into-hand-of very mercies-of-him

יְהוָה דֶּבֶר בְּיִשְׂרָאֵל וַיִּפֹּל מִיִּשְׂרָאֵל שִׁבְעִים אֶלֶף אִישׁ׃

man thousand seventy of-Israel and-he-fell on-Israel plague Yahweh

וַיִּשְׁלַח הָאֱלֹהִים | מַלְאָךְ | לִירוּשָׁלַםִ לְהַשְׁחִיתָהּ וּכְהַשְׁחִית

but-as-to-destroy to-destroy-her to-Jerusalem angel the-God and-he-sent (15)

רָאָה יְהוָה וַיִּנָּחֶם עַל־ הָרָעָה וַיֹּאמֶר

and-he-said the-calamity because-of and-he-was-grieved Yahweh he-saw

לַמַּלְאָךְ הַמַּשְׁחִית רַב עַתָּה הֶרֶף יָדֶךָ וּמַלְאַךְ

now-angel-of hand-of-you withdraw! now enough the-one-destroying to-the-angel

יְהוָה עֹמֵד עִם־ גֹּרֶן אָרְנָן הַיְבוּסִי׃ וַיִּשָּׂא

and-he-raised (16) the-Jebusite Ornan threshing-floor-of at standing Yahweh

דָּוִיד אֶת־ עֵינָיו וַיַּרְא אֶת־ מַלְאַךְ יְהוָה עֹמֵד בֵּין

between standing Yahweh angel-of *** and-he-saw eyes-of-him *** David

הָאָרֶץ וּבֵין הַשָּׁמַיִם וְחַרְבּוֹ שְׁלוּפָה בְּיָדוֹ

in-hand-of-him being-drawn and-sword-of-him the-heavens and-between the-earth

נְטוּיָה עַל־ יְרוּשָׁלָםִ וַיִּפֹּל דָּוִיד וְהַזְּקֵנִים

and-the-elders David then-he-fell Jerusalem over being-extended

מְכֻסִּים בַּשַּׂקִּים עַל־ פְּנֵיהֶם׃ וַיֹּאמֶר דָּוִיד

David and-he-said (17) faces-of-them on in-the-sackcloths ones-being-clothed

9The LORD said to Gad, David's seer, 10"Go and tell David, 'This is what the LORD
says: I am giving you three op-
tions. Choose one of them for
me to carry out against you.' "
11So Gad went to David and
said to him, "This is what the
LORD says: 'Take your choice:
12three years of famine, three
months of being swept away[w]
before your enemies, with
their swords overtaking you,
or three days of the sword of
the LORD—days of plague in
the land, with the angel of the
LORD ravaging every part of Israel.' Now then, decide how I
should answer the one who
sent me."
13David said to Gad, "I am in
deep distress. Let me fall into
the hands of the LORD, for his
mercy is very great; but do not
let me fall into the hands of
men."
14So the LORD sent a plague
on Israel, and seventy thousand men of Israel fell dead.
15And God sent an angel to destroy Jerusalem. But as the angel was doing so, the LORD saw
it and was grieved because of
the calamity and said to the
angel who was destroying the
people, "Enough! Withdraw
your hand." The angel of the
LORD was then standing at the
threshing floor of Araunah[x]
the Jebusite.
16David looked up and saw
the angel of the LORD standing
between heaven and earth,
with a drawn sword in his
hand extended over Jerusalem. Then David and the elders, clothed in sackcloth, fell
facedown.
17David said to God, "Was it

[w]12 Hebrew; Septuagint and Vulgate (see also 2 Samuel 24:13) *of fleeing*

[x]15 Hebrew *Ornan*, a variant of *Araunah*; also in verses 18-28

אֶל־הָאֱלֹהִים הֲלֹא אֲנִי אָמַרְתִּי לִמְנוֹת בָּעָם וַאֲנִי־הוּא אֲשֶׁר־חָטָאתִי

I-sinned who he and-I of-the-people to-count I-ordered I not? the-God to

וְהָרֵעַ הֲרֵעוֹתִי וְאֵלֶּה הַצֹּאן מֶה עָשׂוּ יְהוָה אֱלֹהַי

God-of-me Yahweh they-did what? the-sheep and-these I-did-wrong and-to-do-wrong

תְּהִי נָא יָדְךָ בִּי וּבְבֵית אָבִי

father-of-me and-upon-family-of upon-me hand-of-you now! let-her-fall

וּבְעַמְּךָ לֹא לְמַגֵּפָה׃ וּמַלְאַךְ יְהוָה אָמַר

he-ordered Yahweh then-angel-of (18) with-plague not but-on-people-of-you

אֶל־גָּד לֵאמֹר לְדָוִיד כִּי יַעֲלֶה דָוִיד לְהָקִים מִזְבֵּחַ לַיהוָה

to-Yahweh altar to-build David he-go-up that to-David to-tell Gad to

בְּגֹרֶן אָרְנָן הַיְבֻסִי׃ וַיַּעַל דָּוִיד בִּדְבַר־

at-word-of David so-he-went-up (19) the-Jebusite Ornan on-threshing-floor-of

גָּד אֲשֶׁר דִּבֶּר בְּשֵׁם יְהוָה׃ וַיָּשָׁב אָרְנָן וַיַּרְא אֶת־

*** and-he-saw Ornan and-he-turned (20) Yahweh in-name-of he-spoke that Gad

הַמַּלְאָךְ וְאַרְבַּעַת בָּנָיו עִמּוֹ מִתְחַבְּאִים וְאָרְנָן דָּשׁ

threshing now-Ornan ones-hiding with-him sons-of-him and-four-of the-angel

חִטִּים׃ וַיָּבֹא דָוִיד עַד־אָרְנָן וַיַּבֵּט אָרְנָן וַיַּרְא

and-he-saw Ornan when-he-looked Ornan to David then-he-approached (21) wheats

אֶת־דָּוִיד וַיֵּצֵא מִן־הַגֹּרֶן וַיִּשְׁתַּחוּ לְדָוִיד

before-David and-he-bowed the-threshing-floor from then-he-left David ***

אַפַּיִם אָרְצָה׃ וַיֹּאמֶר דָּוִיד אֶל־אָרְנָן תְּנָה־לִּי מְקוֹם

site-of to-me sell! Ornan to David and-he-said (22) to-ground faces

הַגֹּרֶן וְאֶבְנֶה־בּוֹ מִזְבֵּחַ לַיהוָה בְּכֶסֶף מָלֵא

full at-price to-Yahweh altar on-him so-I-can-build the-threshing-floor

תְּנֵהוּ לִי וְתֵעָצַר הַמַּגֵּפָה מֵעַל הָעָם׃

the-people from-on the-plague so-she-may-be-stopped to-me sell-him!

וַיֹּאמֶר אָרְנָן אֶל־דָּוִיד קַח־לָךְ וְיַעַשׂ אֲדֹנִי

lord-of-me and-let-him-do for-you take! David to Ornan and-he-said (23)

הַמֶּלֶךְ הַטּוֹב בְּעֵינָיו רְאֵה נָתַתִּי הַבָּקָר לָעֹלוֹת

for-the-offerings the-ox I-will-give look! in-eyes-of-him the-good the-king

וְהַמּוֹרִגִּים לָעֵצִים וְהַחִטִּים לַמִּנְחָה

for-the-grain-offering and-the-wheats for-the-woods and-the-threshing-sledges

הַכֹּל נָתָתִּי׃ וַיֹּאמֶר הַמֶּלֶךְ דָּוִיד לְאָרְנָן לֹא כִּי־

for no to-Ornan David the-king but-he-replied (24) I-will-give the-whole

קָנֹה אֶקְנֶה בְּכֶסֶף מָלֵא כִּי לֹא־אֶשָּׂא אֲשֶׁר־לְךָ לַיהוָה

for-Yahweh to-you what I-will-take not for full at-price I-will-pay to-pay

וְהַעֲלוֹת עוֹלָה חִנָּם׃ וַיִּתֵּן דָּוִיד לְאָרְנָן

to-Ornan David so-he-paid (25) without-cost burnt-offering or-to-sacrifice

not I who ordered the fighting
men to be counted? I am the
one who has sinned and done
wrong. These are but sheep.
What have they done? O LORD
my God, let your hand fall
upon me and my family, but
do not let this plague remain
on your people."
18Then the angel of the LORD
ordered Gad to tell David to go
up and build an altar to the
LORD on the threshing floor of
Araunah the Jebusite. 19So David went up in obedience to
the word that Gad had spoken
in the name of the LORD.
20While Araunah was
threshing wheat, he turned
and saw the angel; his four
sons who were with him hid
themselves. 21Then David approached, and when Araunah
looked and saw him, he left
the threshing floor and bowed
down before David with his
face to the ground.
22David said to him, "Let me
have the site of your threshing
floor so I can build an altar to
the LORD, that the plague on
the people may be stopped.
Sell it to me at the full price."
23Araunah said to David,
"Take it! Let my lord the king
do whatever pleases him.
Look, I will give the oxen for
the burnt offerings, the
threshing sledges for the
wood, and the wheat for the
grain offering. I will give all
this."
24But King David replied to
Araunah, "No, I insist on pay-
ing the full price. I will not
take for the LORD what is
yours, or sacrifice a burnt
offering that costs me nothing."
25So David paid Araunah six

בַּמָּקוֹם שִׁקְלֵי זָהָב מִשְׁקַל שֵׁשׁ מֵאוֹת׃ וַיִּבֶן
and-he-built (26) hundreds six-of weight gold shekels-of for-the-site

שָׁם דָּוִיד מִזְבֵּחַ לַיהוָה וַיַּעַל עֹלוֹת
burnt-offerings and-he-sacrificed to-Yahweh altar David there

וּשְׁלָמִים וַיִּקְרָא אֶל־ יְהוָה וַיַּעֲנֵהוּ
and-he-answerered-him Yahweh on and-he-called and-fellowship-offerings

בָּאֵשׁ מִן־ הַשָּׁמַיִם עַל מִזְבַּח הָעֹלָה׃ וַיֹּאמֶר
then-he-spoke (27) the-burnt-offering altar-of on the-heavens from with-fire

יְהוָה לַמַּלְאָךְ וַיָּשֶׁב חַרְבּוֹ אֶל־ נְדָנָהּ׃
sheath-of-her into sword-of-him and-he-put-back to-the-angel Yahweh

בָּעֵת הַהִיא בִּרְאוֹת דָּוִיד כִּי־ עָנָהוּ יְהוָה
Yahweh he-answered-him that David when-to-see the-that at-the-time (28)

בְּגֹרֶן אָרְנָן הַיְבוּסִי וַיִּזְבַּח שָׁם׃
there then-he-sacrificed the-Jebusite Ornan on-threshing-floor-of

וּמִשְׁכַּן יְהוָה אֲשֶׁר־ עָשָׂה מֹשֶׁה בַמִּדְבָּר וּמִזְבַּח
and-altar-of in-the-desert Moses he-made which Yahweh now-tabernacle-of (29)

הָעוֹלָה בָּעֵת הַהִיא בַּבָּמָה בְּגִבְעוֹן׃
at-Gibeon on-the-high-place the-that at-the-time the-burnt-offering

וְלֹא־ יָכֹל דָּוִיד לָלֶכֶת לְפָנָיו לִדְרֹשׁ אֱלֹהִים כִּי
because God to-inquire before-him to-go David he-could but-not (30)

נִבְעַת מִפְּנֵי חֶרֶב מַלְאַךְ יְהוָה׃ וַיֹּאמֶר דָּוִיד
David then-he-said (22:1) Yahweh angel-of sword-of because-of he-was-afraid

זֶה הוּא בֵּית יְהוָה הָאֱלֹהִים וְזֶה־ מִזְבֵּחַ לְעֹלָה לְיִשְׂרָאֵל׃
for-Israel of-burnt-offering altar and-here the-God Yahweh house-of he here

וַיֹּאמֶר דָּוִיד לִכְנוֹס אֶת־ הַגֵּרִים אֲשֶׁר בְּאֶרֶץ יִשְׂרָאֵל
Israel in-land-of who the-aliens *** to-assemble David so-he-ordered (2)

וַיַּעֲמֵד חֹצְבִים לַחְצוֹב אַבְנֵי גָזִית לִבְנוֹת בֵּית
house-of to-build dressed stones-of to-prepare ones-cutting and-he-appointed

הָאֱלֹהִים׃ וּבַרְזֶל ׀ לָרֹב לַמִּסְמְרִים לְדַלְתוֹת הַשְּׁעָרִים
the-gateways for-doors-of for-the-nails for-much and-iron (3) the-God

וְלַמְחַבְּרוֹת הֵכִין דָּוִיד וּנְחֹשֶׁת לָרֹב אֵין
there-was-no for-much and-bronze David he-provided and-for-the-fittings

מִשְׁקָל׃ וַעֲצֵי אֲרָזִים לְאֵין מִסְפָּר כִּי הֵבִיאוּ
they-brought for count as-there-was-no cedars and-logs-of (4) weight

הַצִּידֹנִים וְהַצֹּרִים עֲצֵי אֲרָזִים לָרֹב לְדָוִיד׃ וַיֹּאמֶר
and-he-said (5) to-David for-much cedars logs-of and-the-Tyrians the-Sidonians

דָּוִיד שְׁלֹמֹה בְּנִי נַעַר וָרָךְ וְהַבַּיִת לִבְנוֹת
to-build and-the-house and-inexperienced young son-of-me Solomon David

hundred shekels[y] of gold for
the site. 26 David built an altar
to the LORD there and sacrificed burnt offerings and fellowship offerings.[z] He called
on the LORD, and the LORD answered him with fire from
heaven on the altar of burnt
offering.
27 Then the LORD spoke to the
angel, and he put his sword
back into its sheath. 28 At that
time, when David saw that
the LORD had answered him
on the threshing floor of Araunah the Jebusite, he offered
sacrifices there. 29 The tabernacle of the LORD, which
Moses had made in the desert,
and the altar of burnt offering
were at that time on the high
place at Gibeon. 30 But David
could not go before it to inquire of God, because he was
afraid of the sword of the angel of the LORD.
22 Then David said, "The
house of the LORD God
is to be here, and also the altar
of burnt offering for Israel."

Preparations for the Temple

2 So David gave orders to assemble the aliens living in Israel, and from among them he
appointed stonecutters to prepare dressed stone for building the house of God. 3 He provided a large amount of iron to
make nails for the doors of the
gateways and for the fittings,
and more bronze than could
be weighed. 4 He also provided
more cedar logs than could be
counted, for the Sidonians
and Tyrians had brought large
numbers of them to David.
5 David said, "My son Solomon is young and inex-
perienced, and the house to be

[y]25 That is, about 15 pounds (about 7 kilograms)
[z]26 Traditionally *peace offerings*

לַיהוָה לְהַגְדִּיל ׀ לְמַעְלָה לְשֵׁם וּלְתִפְאֶרֶת לְכָל־
before-all-of and-of-splendor of-name of-magnificence to-make-great for-Yahweh

הָאֲרָצוֹת אָכִינָה נָּא לוֹ וַיָּכֶן דָּוִיד לָרֹב לִפְנֵי
before for-much David so-he-prepared for-him now! I-will-prepare the-nations

מוֹתוֹ׃ וַיִּקְרָא לִשְׁלֹמֹה בְנוֹ וַיְצַוֵּהוּ
and-he-charged-him son-of-him for-Solomon then-he-called (6) death-of-him

לִבְנוֹת בַּיִת לַיהוָה אֱלֹהֵי יִשְׂרָאֵל׃ וַיֹּאמֶר דָּוִיד לִשְׁלֹמֹה
to-Solomon David and-he-said (7) Israel God-of for-Yahweh house to-build

בְּנוֹ אֲנִי הָיָה עִם־ לְבָבִי לִבְנוֹת בַּיִת לְשֵׁם יְהוָה
Yahweh for-Name-of house to-build heart-of-me in he-was I son-of-me

אֱלֹהָי׃ וַיְהִי עָלַי דְּבַר־ יְהוָה לֵאמֹר דָּם לָרֹב
for-much blood to-say Yahweh word-of to-me but-he-came (8) God-of-me

שָׁפַכְתָּ וּמִלְחָמוֹת גְּדֹלוֹת עָשִׂיתָ לֹא־ תִבְנֶה בַיִת
house you-shall-build not you-fought many-ones and-wars you-shed

לִשְׁמִי כִּי דָּמִים רַבִּים שָׁפַכְתָּ אַרְצָה לְפָנָי׃
before-faces-of-me on-earth you-shed many-ones bloods because for-Name-of-me

הִנֵּה־ בֵן נוֹלָד לָךְ הוּא יִהְיֶה אִישׁ מְנוּחָה וַהֲנִחוֹתִי
and-I-will-give-rest rest man-of he-will-be he to-you being-born son see! (9)

לוֹ מִכָּל־ אוֹיְבָיו מִסָּבִיב כִּי שְׁלֹמֹה יִהְיֶה
he-will-be Solomon indeed at-around being-enemies-of-him from-all-of to-him

שְׁמוֹ וְשָׁלוֹם וָשֶׁקֶט אֶתֵּן עַל־ יִשְׂרָאֵל בְּיָמָיו׃
during-days-of-him Israel to I-will-grant and-quiet and-peace name-of-him

הוּא־ יִבְנֶה בַיִת לִשְׁמִי וְהוּא יִהְיֶה־ לִּי לְבֵן
as-son to-me he-will-be and-he for-Name-of-me house he-will-build he (10)

וַאֲנִי־ לוֹ לְאָב וַהֲכִינוֹתִי כִּסֵּא מַלְכוּתוֹ עַל־
over kingdom-of-him throne-of and-I-will-establish as-father to-him and-I

יִשְׂרָאֵל עַד־ עוֹלָם׃ עַתָּה בְנִי יְהִי יְהוָה עִמָּךְ
with-you Yahweh may-he-be son-of-me now (11) forever to Israel

וְהִצְלַחְתָּ וּבָנִיתָ בֵּית יְהוָה אֱלֹהֶיךָ כַּאֲשֶׁר
just-as God-of-you Yahweh house-of and-may-you-build and-may-you-succeed

דִּבֶּר עָלֶיךָ׃ אַךְ יִתֶּן־ לְךָ יְהוָה שֶׂכֶל
discretion Yahweh to-you may-he-give also (12) about-you he-said

וּבִינָה וִיצַוְּךָ עַל־ יִשְׂרָאֵל וְלִשְׁמוֹר אֶת־
*** and-to-keep Israel over when-he-puts-in-command-you and-understanding

תּוֹרַת יְהוָה אֱלֹהֶיךָ׃ אָז תַּצְלִיחַ אִם־ תִּשְׁמוֹר
you-are-careful if you-will-succeed then (13) God-of-you Yahweh law-of

לַעֲשׂוֹת אֶת־ הַחֻקִּים וְאֶת־ הַמִּשְׁפָּטִים אֲשֶׁר צִוָּה יְהוָה אֶת־ מֹשֶׁה עַל־
for Moses *** Yahweh he-gave that the-laws and the-decrees *** to-observe

°7 ק בני

built for the LORD should be of great magnificence and fame and splendor in the sight of all the nations. Therefore I will make preparations for it." So David made extensive preparations before his death.
6Then he called for his son Solomon and charged him to build a house for the LORD, the God of Israel.
7David said to Solomon: "My son, I had it in my heart to build a house for the Name of the LORD my God.
8But this word of the LORD came to me: 'You have shed much blood and have fought many wars. You are not to build a house for my Name, because you have shed much blood on the earth in my sight.
9But you will have a son who will be a man of peace and rest, and I will give him rest from all his enemies on every side. His name will be Solomon,[a] and I will grant Israel peace and quiet during his
reign. 10He is the one who will build a house for my Name. He will be my son, and I will be his father. And I will establish the throne of his kingdom over Israel forever.'
11"Now, my son, the LORD be with you, and may you have success and build the house of the LORD your God, as he said
you would. 12May the LORD give you discretion and understanding when he puts you in command over Israel, so that you may keep the law of the LORD your God.
13Then you will have success if you are careful to observe the decrees and laws that the LORD gave Moses for Israel. Be

[a]9 *Solomon* sounds like and may be derived from the Hebrew for *peace*.

יִשְׂרָאֵל חֲזַק וֶאֱמָץ אַל־ תִּירָא וְאַל־
and-not you-be-afraid not and-be-courageous! be-strong! Israel

תֵּחָת׃ (14) וְהִנֵּה בְעָנְיִי הֲכִינוֹתִי לְבֵית־
for-temple-of I-provided in-pain-of-me now-see! (14) you-be-discouraged

יְהוָה זָהָב כִּכָּרִים מֵאָה־ אֶלֶף וְכֶסֶף אֶלֶף אֲלָפִים
thousands thousand-of and-silver thousand hundred talents gold Yahweh

כִּכָּרִים וְלַנְּחֹשֶׁת וְלַבַּרְזֶל אֵין מִשְׁקָל כִּי לָרֹב
as-much for weight there-is-no and-of-the-iron and-of-the-bronze talents

הָיָה וְעֵצִים וַאֲבָנִים הֲכִינוֹתִי וַעֲלֵיהֶם תּוֹסִיף׃
you-may-add and-to-them I-provided and-stones and-woods he-is

(15) וְעִמְּךָ לָרֹב עֹשֵׂי מְלָאכָה חֹצְבִים וְחָרָשֵׁי
and-carvers-of ones-cutting work ones-doing-of as-many now-with-you (15)

אֶבֶן וָעֵץ וְכָל־ חָכָם בְּכָל־ מְלָאכָה׃ (16) לַזָּהָב
in-the-gold (16) work in-every-of one-skilled and-every-of and-wood stone

לַכֶּסֶף וְלַנְּחֹשֶׁת וְלַבַּרְזֶל אֵין מִסְפָּר קוּם
begin! number there-no-is and-in-the-iron and-in-the-bronze in-the-silver

וַעֲשֵׂה וִיהִי יְהוָה עִמָּךְ׃ (17) וַיְצַו דָּוִיד
David then-he-ordered (17) with-you Yahweh and-may-he-be and-do-work!

לְכָל־ שָׂרֵי יִשְׂרָאֵל לַעְזֹר לִשְׁלֹמֹה בְנוֹ׃ (18) הֲלֹא יְהוָה
Yahweh not? (18) son-of-him to-Solomon to-help Israel leaders-of to-all-of

אֱלֹהֵיכֶם עִמָּכֶם וְהֵנִיחַ לָכֶם מִסָּבִיב כִּי ׀ נָתַן
he-gave for at-around to-you and-he-granted-rest with-you God-of-you

בְּיָדִי אֵת יֹשְׁבֵי הָאָרֶץ וְנִכְבְּשָׁה הָאָרֶץ
the-land and-she-is-subject the-land ones-inhabiting-of *** into-hand-of-me

לִפְנֵי יְהוָה וְלִפְנֵי עַמּוֹ׃ (19) עַתָּה תְּנוּ לְבַבְכֶם
heart-of-you devote! now (19) people-of-him and-before Yahweh before

וְנַפְשְׁכֶם לִדְרוֹשׁ לַיהוָה אֱלֹהֵיכֶם וְקוּמוּ וּבְנוּ אֶת־
*** and-build! and-begin! God-of-you to-Yahweh to-seek and-soul-of-you

מִקְדַּשׁ יְהוָה הָאֱלֹהִים לְהָבִיא אֶת־ אֲרוֹן בְּרִית־ יְהוָה
Yahweh covenant-of ark-of *** to-bring the-God Yahweh sanctuary-of

וּכְלֵי קֹדֶשׁ הָאֱלֹהִים לַבַּיִת הַנִּבְנֶה
the-one-being-built into-the-temple the-God sacredness-of and-articles-of

לְשֵׁם־ יְהוָה׃ (23:1) וְדָוִיד זָקֵן וְשָׂבַע יָמִים
days and-he-was-full he-was-old when-David (23:1) Yahweh for-Name-of

וַיַּמְלֵךְ אֶת־ שְׁלֹמֹה בְנוֹ עַל־ יִשְׂרָאֵל׃ (2) וַיֶּאֱסֹף
and-he-gathered (2) Israel over son-of-him Solomon *** then-he-made-king

אֶת־ כָּל־ שָׂרֵי יִשְׂרָאֵל וְהַכֹּהֲנִים וְהַלְוִיִּם׃
and-the-Levites and-the-priests Israel leaders-of all-of ***

strong and courageous. Do not be afraid or discouraged.
14"I have taken great pains to provide for the temple of the LORD a hundred thousand talents[b] of gold, a million talents[c] of silver, quantities of bronze and iron too great to be weighed, and wood and stone. And you may add to them.
15You have many workmen: stonecutters, masons and carpenters, as well as men skilled in every kind of work
16in gold and silver, bronze and iron—craftsmen beyond number. Now begin the work, and the LORD be with you."
17Then David ordered all the leaders of Israel to help his son Solomon.
18He said to them, "Is not the LORD your God with you? And has he not granted you rest on every side? For he has handed the inhabitants of the land over to me, and the land is subject to the LORD and to his people.
19Now devote your heart and soul to seeking the LORD your God. Begin to build the sanctuary of the LORD God, so that you may bring the ark of the covenant of the LORD and the sacred articles belonging to God into the temple that will be built for the Name of the LORD."

The Levites

23 When David was old and full of years, he made his son Solomon king over Israel.
2He also gathered together all the leaders of Israel, as well as the priests and Levites.
3The

[b]14 That is, about 3,750 tons (about 3,450 metric tons)
[c]14 That is, about 37,500 tons (about 34,500 metric tons)

וַיִּסָּפְרוּ הַלְוִיִּם מִבֶּן שְׁלֹשִׁים שָׁנָה וָמָעְלָה
and-upward year thirty from-son-of the-Levites and-they-were-counted (3)

וַיְהִי מִסְפָּרָם לְגֻלְגְּלֹתָם לִגְבָרִים שְׁלֹשִׁים וּשְׁמוֹנָה אָלֶף׃
thousand and-eight thirty of-men by-totals-of-them number-of-them and-he-was

מֵאֵלֶּה לְנַצֵּחַ עַל־מְלֶאכֶת בֵּית־ יְהוָה עֶשְׂרִים וְאַרְבָּעָה
and-four twenty Yahweh temple-of work-of over to-supervise and-of-these (4)

אָלֶף וְשֹׁטְרִים וְשֹׁפְטִים שֵׁשֶׁת אֲלָפִים׃ וְאַרְבַּעַת
and-four-of (5) thousands six-of and-ones-being-judges and-officials thousand

אֲלָפִים שֹׁעֲרִים וְאַרְבַּעַת אֲלָפִים מְהַלְלִים לַיהוָה
to-Yahweh ones-praising thousands and-four-of gatekeepers thousands

בַּכֵּלִים אֲשֶׁר עָשִׂיתִי לְהַלֵּל׃ וַיֶּחָלְקֵם דָּוִיד
David and-he-divided-them (6) to-praise I-provided that with-the-instruments

מַחְלְקוֹת לִבְנֵי לֵוִי לְגֵרְשׁוֹן קְהָת וּמְרָרִי׃ לַגֵּרְשֻׁנִּי
of-the-Gershonite (7) and-Merari Kohath of-Gershon Levi of-sons-of groups

לַעְדָּן וְשִׁמְעִי׃ בְּנֵי לַעְדָּן הָרֹאשׁ יְחִיאֵל וְזֵתָם וְיוֹאֵל
and-Joel and-Zetham Jehiel the-first Ladan sons-of (8) and-Shimei Ladan

שְׁלֹשָׁה׃ בְּנֵי שִׁמְעִי שְׁלֹמוֹת° וַחֲזִיאֵל וְהָרָן שְׁלֹשָׁה אֵלֶּה רָאשֵׁי
heads-of these three and-Haran and-Haziel Shelomoth Shimei sons-of (9) three

הָאָבוֹת לְלַעְדָּן׃ וּבְנֵי שִׁמְעִי יַחַת זִינָא וִיעוּשׁ
and-Jeush Zina Jahath Shimei and-sons-of (10) of-Ladan the-fathers

וּבְרִיעָה אֵלֶּה בְּנֵי־ שִׁמְעִי אַרְבָּעָה׃ וַיְהִי־ יַחַת הָרֹאשׁ
the-first Jahath and-he-was (11) four Shimei sons-of these and-Beriah

וְזִיזָה הַשֵּׁנִי וִיעוּשׁ וּבְרִיעָה לֹא־ הִרְבּוּ בָנִים וַיִּהְיוּ
so-they-were sons they-had-many not and-Beriah but-Jeush the-second and-Ziza

לְבֵית אָב לִפְקֻדָּה אֶחָת׃ בְּנֵי קְהָת עַמְרָם יִצְהָר
Izhar Amram Kohath sons-of (12) one as-assignment father as-family-of

חֶבְרוֹן וְעֻזִּיאֵל אַרְבָּעָה׃ בְּנֵי עַמְרָם אַהֲרֹן וּמֹשֶׁה וַיִּבָּדֵל
and-he-was-set-apart and-Moses Aaron Amram sons-of (13) four and-Uzziel Hebron

אַהֲרֹן לְהַקְדִּישׁוֹ קֹדֶשׁ קָדָשִׁים הוּא־ וּבָנָיו
and-descendants-of-him he holy-things most-holy-of to-consecrate-him Aaron

עַד־ עוֹלָם לְהַקְטִיר לִפְנֵי יְהוָה לְשָׁרְתוֹ וּלְבָרֵךְ
and-to-bless to-minister-to-him Yahweh before to-sacrifice forever to

בִּשְׁמוֹ עַד־ עוֹלָם׃ וּמֹשֶׁה אִישׁ הָאֱלֹהִים בָּנָיו
sons-of-him the-God man-of and-Moses (14) forever to in-name-of-him

יִקָּרְאוּ עַל־ שֵׁבֶט הַלֵּוִי׃ בְּנֵי מֹשֶׁה גֵּרְשֹׁם
Gershom Moses sons-of (15) the-Levi tribe-of as they-were-counted

וֶאֱלִיעֶזֶר׃ בְּנֵי גֵּרְשׁוֹם שְׁבוּאֵל הָרֹאשׁ׃ וַיִּהְיוּ
and-they-were (17) the-first Shubael Gershom descendants-of (16) and-Eliezer

Levites thirty years old or more were counted, and the total number of men was thirty-eight thousand. [4]David said, "Of these, twenty-four thousand are to supervise the work of the temple of the LORD and six thousand are to be officials and judges. [5]Four thousand are to be gatekeepers and four thousand are to praise the LORD with the musical instruments I have provided for that purpose."

[6]David divided the Levites into groups corresponding to the sons of Levi: Gershon, Kohath and Merari.

Gershonites

[7]Belonging to the Gershonites:
Ladan and Shimei.
[8]The sons of Ladan:
Jehiel the first, Zetham and Joel—three in all.
[9]The sons of Shimei:
Shelomoth, Haziel and Haran—three in all.
These were the heads of the families of Ladan.
[10]And the sons of Shimei:
Jahath, Ziza,[d] Jeush and Beriah.
These were the sons of Shimei—four in all.
[11]Jahath was the first and Ziza the second, but Jeush and Beriah did not have many sons; so they were counted as one family with one assignment.

Kohathites

[12]The sons of Kohath:
Amram, Izhar, Hebron and Uzziel—four in all.
[13]The sons of Amram:
Aaron and Moses.
Aaron was set apart, he and his descendants forever, to consecrate the most holy things, to offer sacrifices before the LORD, to minister before him and to pronounce blessings in his name forever. [14]The sons of Moses the man of God were counted as part of the tribe of Levi.
[15]The sons of Moses:
Gershom and Eliezer.
[16]The descendants of Gershom:
Shubael was the first.

[d] *10* One Hebrew manuscript, Septuagint and Vulgate (see also verse 11); most Hebrew manuscripts *Zina*

°9 ק שלומית

בְנֵי־ אֱלִיעֶזֶר רְחַבְיָה הָרֹאשׁ וְלֹא־ הָיָה לֶאֱלִיעֶזֶר בָּנִים
sons to-Eliezer he-was but-not the-first Rehabiah Eliezer descendants-of

אֲחֵרִים וּבְנֵי רְחַבְיָה רָבוּ לְמָעְלָה׃ (18) בְּנֵי
sons-of (18) to-above they-were-numerous Rehabiah but-sons-of other-ones

יִצְהָר שְׁלֹמִית הָרֹאשׁ׃ (19) בְּנֵי חֶבְרוֹן יְרִיָּהוּ הָרֹאשׁ אֲמַרְיָה
Amariah the-first Jeriah Hebron sons-of (19) the-first Shelomith Izhar

הַשֵּׁנִי יַחֲזִיאֵל הַשְּׁלִישִׁי וִיקַמְעָם הָרְבִיעִי׃ (20) בְּנֵי עֻזִּיאֵל
Uzziel sons-of (20) the-fourth and-Jekameam the-third Jahaziel the-second

מִיכָה הָרֹאשׁ וְיִשִּׁיָּה הַשֵּׁנִי׃ (21) בְּנֵי מְרָרִי מַחְלִי וּמוּשִׁי
and-Mushi Mahli Merari sons-of (21) the-second and-Isshiah the-first Micah

בְּנֵי מַחְלִי אֶלְעָזָר וְקִישׁ׃ (22) וַיָּמָת אֶלְעָזָר וְלֹא־ הָיוּ
they-were and-not Eleazar and-he-died (22) and-Kish Eleazar Mahli sons-of

לוֹ בָּנִים כִּי אִם־ בָּנוֹת וַיִּשָּׂאוּם בְּנֵי־ קִישׁ
Kish sons-of and-they-married-them daughters only but sons to-him

אֲחֵיהֶם׃ (23) בְּנֵי מוּשִׁי מַחְלִי וְעֵדֶר וִירֵמוֹת שְׁלֹשָׁה׃
three and-Jeremoth and-Eder Mahli Mushi sons-of (23) cousins-of-them

(24) אֵלֶּה בְנֵי־ לֵוִי לְבֵית אֲבֹתֵיהֶם רָאשֵׁי
heads-of fathers-of-them by-family-of Levi descendants-of these (24)

הָאָבוֹת לִפְקוּדֵיהֶם בְּמִסְפַּר שֵׁמוֹת לְגֻלְגְּלֹתָם
by-heads-of-them names by-count-of as-ones-being-registered-of-them the-fathers

עֹשֵׂה הַמְּלָאכָה לַעֲבֹדַת בֵּית יְהוָה מִבֶּן עֶשְׂרִים שָׁנָה
year twenty from-son-of Yahweh temple-of for-service-of the-work one-doing

וָמָעְלָה׃ (25) כִּי אָמַר דָּוִיד הֵנִיחַ יְהוָה אֱלֹהֵי־ יִשְׂרָאֵל
Israel God-of Yahweh he-granted-rest David he-said for (25) and-upward

לְעַמּוֹ וַיִּשְׁכֹּן בִּירוּשָׁלִַם עַד־ לְעוֹלָם׃
to-forever to in-Jerusalem and-he-came-to-dwell to-people-of-him

(26) וְגַם לַלְוִיִּם אֵין־ לָשֵׂאת אֶת־ הַמִּשְׁכָּן וְאֶת־
or the-tabernacle *** to-carry there-is-not to-the-Levites and-also (26)

כָּל־ כֵּלָיו לַעֲבֹדָתוֹ׃ (27) כִּי בְדִבְרֵי
at-instructions-of indeed (27) for-service-of-him articles-of-him any-of

דָוִיד הָאַחֲרֹנִים הֵמָּה מִסְפַּר בְּנֵי־ לֵוִי מִבֶּן עֶשְׂרִים שָׁנָה
year twenty from-son-of Levi sons-of count-of they the-last-ones David

וּלְמָעְלָה׃ (28) כִּי מַעֲמָדָם לְיַד־ בְּנֵי אַהֲרֹן
Aaron descendants-of at-hand-of duty-of-them indeed (28) and-to-upward

לַעֲבֹדַת בֵּית יְהוָה עַל־ הַחֲצֵרוֹת וְעַל־ הַלְּשָׁכוֹת
the-side-rooms and-over the-courtyards over Yahweh temple-of in-service-of

וְעַל־ טָהֳרַת לְכָל־ קֹדֶשׁ וּמַעֲשֵׂה עֲבֹדַת
duty-of and-performance-of sacred-thing of-all-of purification-of and-over

17 The descendants of Eliezer:
Rehabiah was the first.
Eliezer had no other
sons, but the sons of
Rehabiah were very numerous.
18 The sons of Izhar:
Shelomith was the first.
19 The sons of Hebron:
Jeriah the first, Amariah
the second, Jahaziel the
third and Jekameam the
fourth.
20 The sons of Uzziel:
Micah the first and Isshiah the second.

Merarites

21 The sons of Merari:
Mahli and Mushi.
The sons of Mahli:
Eleazar and Kish.
22 Eleazar died without
having sons: he had only
daughters. Their cousins,
the sons of Kish, married
them.
23 The sons of Mushi:
Mahli, Eder and Jeremoth—three in all.

24 These were the descendants of Levi by their families—
the heads of families as they
were registered under their
names and counted individually, that is, the workers
twenty years old or more who
served in the temple of the
LORD. 25 For David had said,
"Since the LORD, the God of Israel, has granted rest to his
people and has come to dwell
in Jerusalem forever, 26 the Levites no longer need to carry
the tabernacle or any of the articles used in its service." 27 According to the last instructions
of David, the Levites were
counted from those twenty
years old or more.
28 The duty of the Levites was
to help Aaron's descendants
in the service of the temple of
the LORD: to be in charge of the
courtyards, the side rooms, the
purification of all sacred
things and the performance of

בֵּית הָאֱלֹהִים׃ וּלְלֶחֶם הַמַּעֲרֶכֶת וּלְסֹלֶת
and-over-flour the-one-set-out and-over-bread-of (29) the-God house-of

לְמִנְחָה וְלִרְקִיקֵי הַמַּצּוֹת וְלַמַּחֲבַת
and-over-the-baking the-unleavened-ones and-over-wafers-of for-grain-offering

וְלַמֻּרְבֶּכֶת וּלְכָל־ מְשׂוּרָה וּמִדָּה׃ וְלַעֲמֹד
and-to-stand (30) and-size measurement and-over-all-of and-over-the-mixing

בַּבֹּקֶר בַּבֹּקֶר לְהֹדוֹת וּלְהַלֵּל לַיהוָה וְכֵן
and-same to-Yahweh and-to-praise to-thank in-the-morning in-the-morning

לָעָרֶב׃ וּלְכֹל הַעֲלוֹת עֹלוֹת לַיהוָה
to-Yahweh burnt-offerings to-present and-over-all-of (31) in-the-evening

לַשַּׁבָּתוֹת לֶחֳדָשִׁים וְלַמֹּעֲדִים בְּמִסְפָּר כְּמִשְׁפָּט
and-as-way in-number and-at-the-feasts at-the-New-Moons on-the-Sabbaths

עֲלֵיהֶם תָּמִיד לִפְנֵי יְהוָה׃ וְשָׁמְרוּ אֶת־
*** so-they-carried-out (32) Yahweh before regularly upon-them

מִשְׁמֶרֶת אֹהֶל־ מוֹעֵד וְאֵת מִשְׁמֶרֶת הַקֹּדֶשׁ
the-Holy-Place responsibility-of and Meeting Tent-of responsibility-of

וּמִשְׁמֶרֶת בְּנֵי אַהֲרֹן אֲחֵיהֶם לַעֲבֹדַת
for-service-of brothers-of-them Aaron descendants-of and-responsibility-of

בֵּית יְהוָה׃ וְלִבְנֵי אַהֲרֹן מַחְלְקוֹתָם בְּנֵי אַהֲרֹן
Aaron sons-of divisions-of-them Aaron and-of-sons-of (24:1) Yahweh temple-of

נָדָב וַאֲבִיהוּא אֶלְעָזָר וְאִיתָמָר׃ וַיָּמָת נָדָב וַאֲבִיהוּא לִפְנֵי
before and-Abihu Nadab but-he-died (2) and-Ithamar Eleazar and-Abihu Nadab

אֲבִיהֶם וּבָנִים לֹא־ הָיוּ לָהֶם וַיְכַהֲנוּ אֶלְעָזָר
Eleazar so-they-became-priests to-them they-were not and-sons father-of-them

וְאִיתָמָר׃ וַיֶּחָלְקֵם דָּוִיד וְצָדוֹק מִן־ בְּנֵי
descendants-of from and-Zadok David and-he-divided-them (3) and-Ithamar

אֶלְעָזָר וַאֲחִימֶלֶךְ מִן־ בְּנֵי אִיתָמָר לִפְקֻדָּתָם
for-order-of-them Ithamar descendants-of from and-Ahimelech Eleazar

בַּעֲבֹדָתָם׃ וַיִּמָּצְאוּ בְנֵי־ אֶלְעָזָר רַבִּים
many Eleazar descendants-of and-they-were-found (4) for-ministry-of-them

לְרָאשֵׁי הַגְּבָרִים מִן־ בְּנֵי אִיתָמָר וַיַּחְלְקוּם
and-they-divided-them Ithamar descendants-of more-than the-men of-leaders-of

לִבְנֵי אֶלְעָזָר רָאשִׁים לְבֵית־ אָבוֹת שִׁשָּׁה עָשָׂר
ten six fathers of-family-of heads Eleazar from-descendants-of

וְלִבְנֵי אִיתָמָר לְבֵית אֲבוֹתָם שְׁמוֹנָה׃
eight fathers-of-them of-family-of Ithamar and-from-descendants-of

וַיַּחְלְקוּם בְּגוֹרָלוֹת אֵלֶּה עִם־ אֵלֶּה כִּי־ הָיוּ שָׂרֵי־
officials-of they-were for these with these by-lots and-they-divided-them (5)

other duties at the house of
God. 29They were in charge of
the bread set out on the table,
the flour for the grain
offerings, the unleavened waf-
ers, the baking and the mixing, and all measurements of
quantity and size. 30They were
also to stand every morning to
thank and praise the LORD.
They were to do the same in
the evening 31and whenever
burnt offerings were pre-
sented to the LORD on Sabbaths and at New Moon festivals and at appointed feasts.
They were to serve before the
LORD regularly in the proper
number and in the way prescribed for them.
32And so the Levites carried
out their responsibilities for
the Tent of Meeting, for the
Holy Place and, under their
brothers the descendants of
Aaron, for the service of the
temple of the LORD.

The Divisions of Priests

24 These were the divi-
sions of the sons of
Aaron:
The sons of Aaron were
Nadab, Abihu, Eleazar and
Ithamar. 2But Nadab and
Abihu died before their father
did, and they had no sons; so
Eleazar and Ithamar served as
the priests. 3With the help of
Zadok a descendant of Eleazar
and Ahimelech a descendant
of Ithamar, David separated
them into divisions for their
appointed order of ministering. 4A larger number of leaders were found among Eleazar's descendants than among
Ithamar's, and they were divided accordingly: sixteen
heads of families from Eleazar's descendants and eight
heads of families from Ithamar's descendants. 5They divided them impartially by
drawing lots, for there were

קֹדֶשׁ וְשָׂרֵי הָאֱלֹהִים מִבְּנֵי אֶלְעָזָר
Eleazar among-descendants-of the-God and-officials-of sanctuary

וּבִבְנֵי אִיתָמָר׃ וַיִּכְתְּבֵם שְׁמַעְיָה בֶן־
son-of Shemaiah and-he-recorded-them (6) Ithamar and-among-descendants-of

נְתַנְאֵל הַסּוֹפֵר מִן־ הַלֵּוִי לִפְנֵי הַמֶּלֶךְ וְהַשָּׂרִים
and-the-officials the-king in-presences-of the-Levite from the-scribe Nethanel

וְצָדוֹק הַכֹּהֵן וַאֲחִימֶלֶךְ בֶּן־ אֶבְיָתָר וְרָאשֵׁי הָאָבוֹת
the-fathers and-heads-of Abiathar son-of and-Ahimelech the-priest and-Zadok

לַכֹּהֲנִים וְלַלְוִיִּם בֵּית־ אָב אֶחָד אָחֻז
being-taken one father family-of and-of-the-Levites of-the-priests

לְאֶלְעָזָר וְאָחֻז ׀ אָחֻז לְאִיתָמָר׃ וַיֵּצֵא
and-he-fell (7) from-Ithamar being-taken and-being-taken from-Eleazar

הַגּוֹרָל הָרִאשׁוֹן לִיהוֹיָרִיב לִידַעְיָה הַשֵּׁנִי׃ לְחָרִם הַשְּׁלִשִׁי
the-third to-Harim (8) the-second to-Jedaiah to-Jehoiarib the-first the-lot

לִשְׂעֹרִים הָרְבִעִי׃ לְמַלְכִּיָּה הַחֲמִישִׁי לְמִיָּמִן הַשִּׁשִּׁי׃
the-sixth to-Mijamin the-fifth to-Malkijah (9) the-fourth to-Seorim

לְהַקּוֹץ הַשְּׁבִעִי לַאֲבִיָּה הַשְּׁמִינִי׃ לְיֵשׁוּעַ הַתְּשִׁעִי
the-ninth to-Jeshua (11) the-eighth to-Abijah the-seventh to-Hakkoz (10)

לִשְׁכַנְיָהוּ הָעֲשִׂרִי׃ לְאֶלְיָשִׁיב עַשְׁתֵּי עָשָׂר לְיָקִים שְׁנַיִם עָשָׂר׃
ten two to-Jakim ten one to-Eliashib (12) the-tenth to-Shecaniah

לְחֻפָּה שְׁלֹשָׁה עָשָׂר לְיֶשֶׁבְאָב אַרְבָּעָה עָשָׂר׃ לְבִלְגָּה חֲמִשָּׁה עָשָׂר
ten five to-Bilgah (14) ten four to-Jeshebeab ten three to-Huppah (13)

לְאִמֵּר שִׁשָּׁה עָשָׂר׃ לְחֵזִיר שִׁבְעָה עָשָׂר לְהַפִּצֵּץ שְׁמוֹנָה עָשָׂר׃
ten eight to-Happizzez ten seven to-Hezir (15) ten six to-Immer

לִפְתַחְיָה תִּשְׁעָה עָשָׂר לִיחֶזְקֵאל הָעֶשְׂרִים׃ לְיָכִין אֶחָד
one to-Jakin (17) the-twenty to-Jehezkel ten nine to-Pethahiah (16)

וְעֶשְׂרִים לְגָמוּל שְׁנַיִם וְעֶשְׂרִים׃ לִדְלָיָהוּ שְׁלֹשָׁה וְעֶשְׂרִים
and-twenty three to-Delaiah (18) and-twenty two to-Gamul and-twenty

לְמַעַזְיָהוּ אַרְבָּעָה וְעֶשְׂרִים׃ אֵלֶּה פְקֻדָּתָם לַעֲבֹדָתָם
for-ministry-of-them order-of-them these (19) and-twenty four to-Maaziah

לָבוֹא לְבֵית־ יְהוָה כְּמִשְׁפָּטָם בְּיַד אַהֲרֹן
Aaron by-hand-of as-regulation-of-them Yahweh into-temple-of to-enter

אֲבִיהֶם כַּאֲשֶׁר צִוָּהוּ יְהוָה אֱלֹהֵי יִשְׂרָאֵל׃
Israel God-of Yahweh he-commanded-him just-as father-of-them

וְלִבְנֵי לֵוִי הַנּוֹתָרִים לִבְנֵי עַמְרָם
Amram from-sons-of the-ones-being-left Levi and-for-descendants-of (20)

שׁוּבָאֵל לִבְנֵי שׁוּבָאֵל יֶחְדְּיָהוּ׃ לִרְחַבְיָהוּ לִבְנֵי
from-sons-of for-Rehabiah (21) Jehdeiah Shubael from-sons-of Shubael

officials of the sanctuary and officials of God among the descendants of both Eleazar and Ithamar.

[6]The scribe Shemaiah son of Nethanel, a Levite, recorded their names in the presence of the king and of the officials: Zadok the priest, Ahimelech son of Abiathar and the heads of families of the priests and of the Levites—one family being taken from Eleazar and then one from Ithamar.

[7]The first lot fell to Jehoiarib,
the second to Jedaiah,
[8]the third to Harim,
the fourth to Seorim,
[9]the fifth to Malkijah,
the sixth to Mijamin,
[10]the seventh to Hakkoz,
the eighth to Abijah,
[11]the ninth to Jeshua,
the tenth to Shecaniah,
[12]the eleventh to Eliashib,
the twelfth to Jakim,
[13]the thirteenth to Huppah,
the fourteenth to Jeshebeab,
[14]the fifteenth to Bilgah,
the sixteenth to Immer,
[15]the seventeenth to Hezir,
the eighteenth to Happizzez,
[16]the nineteenth to Pethahiah,
the twentieth to Jehezkel,
[17]the twenty-first to Jakin,
the twenty-second to Gamul,
[18]the twenty-third to Delaiah
and the twenty-fourth to Maaziah.

[19]This was their appointed order of ministering when they entered the temple of the LORD, according to the regulations prescribed for them by their forefather Aaron, as the LORD, the God of Israel, had commanded him.

The Rest of the Levites

[20]As for the rest of the descendants of Levi:
from the sons of Amram: Shubael;
from the sons of Shubael: Jehdeiah.
[21]As for Rehabiah, from his sons:

רְחַבְיָהוּ הָרֹאשׁ יִשִּׁיָּה׃ לַיִּצְהָרִי שְׁלֹמוֹת לִבְנֵי
from-sons-of Shelomoth from-the-Izharite (22) Isshiah the-first Rehabiah

שְׁלֹמוֹת יָחַת׃ וּבְנַי יְרִיָּהוּ אֲמַרְיָהוּ הַשֵּׁנִי יַחֲזִיאֵל
Jahaziel the-second Amariah Jeriah and-sons-of (23) Jahath Shelomoth

הַשְּׁלִישִׁי יְקַמְעָם הָרְבִיעִי׃ בְּנֵי עֻזִּיאֵל מִיכָה לִבְנֵי מִיכָה
Micah from-sons-of Micah Uzziel sons-of (24) the-fourth Jekameam the-third

שָׁמִור׃ אֲחִי מִיכָה יִשִּׁיָּה לִבְנֵי יִשִּׁיָּה זְכַרְיָהוּ׃
Zechariah Isshiah from-sons-of Isshiah Micah brother-of (25) Shamir

בְּנֵי מְרָרִי מַחְלִי וּמוּשִׁי בְּנֵי יַעֲזִיָּהוּ בְנוֹ׃ בְּנֵי
sons-of (27) Beno Jaaziah sons-of and-Mushi Mahli Merari sons-of (26)

מְרָרִי לְיַעֲזִיָּהוּ בְּנוֹ וְשֹׁהַם וְזַכּוּר וְעִבְרִי׃ לְמַחְלִי
from-Mahli (28) and-Ibri and-Zaccur and-Shoham Beno from-Jaaziah Merari

אֶלְעָזָר וְלֹא־ הָיָה לוֹ בָּנִים׃ לְקִישׁ בְּנֵי־ קִישׁ יְרַחְמְאֵל׃
Jerahmeel Kish sons-of from-Kish (29) sons to-him he-was now-not Eleazar

וּבְנֵי מוּשִׁי מַחְלִי וְעֵדֶר וִירִימוֹת אֵלֶּה בְּנֵי הַלְוִיִּם
the-Levites sons-of these and-Jerimoth and-Eder Mahli Mushi and-sons-of (30)

לְבֵית אֲבֹתֵיהֶם׃ וַיַּפִּילוּ גַם־ הֵם גּוֹרָלוֹת לְעֻמַּת
just-as lots they also and-they-cast (31) fathers-of-them by-family-of

אֲחֵיהֶם בְּנֵי־ אַהֲרֹן לִפְנֵי דָּוִיד הַמֶּלֶךְ
the-king David in-presences-of Aaron descendants-of brothers-of-them

וְצָדוֹק וַאֲחִימֶלֶךְ וְרָאשֵׁי הָאָבוֹת לַכֹּהֲנִים
of-the-priests the-fathers and-heads-of and-Ahimelech and-Zadok

וְלַלְוִיִּם אָבוֹת הָרֹאשׁ לְעֻמַּת אָחִיו הַקָּטָן׃
the-young brother-of-him same-as the-head fathers and-of-the-Levites

וַיַּבְדֵּל דָּוִיד וְשָׂרֵי הַצָּבָא לַעֲבֹדָה
for-the-ministry the-army and-commanders-of David and-he-set-apart (25:1)

לִבְנֵי אָסָף וְהֵימָן וִידוּתוּן הַנְּבִיאִים בְּכִנֹּרוֹת
with-harps the-ones-prophesying and-Jeduthun and-Heman Asaph from-sons-of

בִּנְבָלִים וּבִמְצִלְתָּיִם וַיְהִי מִסְפָּרָם אַנְשֵׁי מְלָאכָה
work men-of list-of-them and-he-was and-with-cymbals with-lyres

לַעֲבֹדָתָם׃ לִבְנֵי אָסָף זַכּוּר וְיוֹסֵף וּנְתַנְיָה
and-Nethaniah and-Joseph Zaccur Asaph from-sons-of (2) of-service-of-them

וַאֲשַׂרְאֵלָה בְּנֵי אָסָף עַל יַד־ אָסָף הַנִּבָּא עַל־
under the-one-prophesying Asaph hand-of under Asaph sons-of and-Asarelah

יְדֵי הַמֶּלֶךְ׃ לִידוּתוּן בְּנֵי יְדוּתוּן גְּדַלְיָהוּ וּצְרִי
and-Zeri Gedaliah Jeduthun sons-of for-Jeduthun (3) the-king hands-of

וִישַׁעְיָהוּ חֲשַׁבְיָהוּ וּמַתִּתְיָהוּ שִׁשָּׁה עַל יְדֵי אֲבִיהֶם
father-of-them hands-of under six and-Mattithiah Hashabiah and-Jeshaiah

Isshiah was the first.
22 From the Izharites: Shelomoth;
from the sons of Shelomoth: Jahath.
23 The sons of Hebron: Jeriah the first,[e] Amariah the second, Jahaziel the third and Jekameam the fourth.
24 The son of Uzziel: Micah;
from the sons of Micah: Shamir.
25 The brother of Micah: Isshiah;
from the sons of Isshiah: Zechariah.
26 The sons of Merari: Mahli and Mushi.
The son of Jaaziah: Beno.
27 The sons of Merari:
from Jaaziah: Beno, Shoham, Zaccur and Ibri.
28 From Mahli: Eleazar, who had no sons.
29 From Kish: the son of Kish: Jerahmeel.
30 And the sons of Mushi: Mahli, Eder and Jerimoth.

These were the Levites, according to their families.
31 They also cast lots, just as their brothers the descendants of Aaron did, in the presence of King David and of Zadok, Ahimelech, and the heads of families of the priests and of the Levites. The families of the oldest brother were treated the same as those of the youngest.

The Singers

25 David, together with the commanders of the army, set apart some of the sons of Asaph, Heman and Jeduthun for the ministry of prophesying, accompanied by harps, lyres and cymbals. Here is the list of the men who performed this service:

2 From the sons of Asaph:
Zaccur, Joseph, Nethaniah and Asarelah. The sons of Asaph were under the supervision of Asaph, who prophesied under the king's supervision.
3 As for Jeduthun, from his sons:
Gedaliah, Zeri, Jeshaiah, Shimei,[f] Hashabiah and Mattithiah, six in all, under

[e] 23 Two Hebrew manuscripts and some Septuagint manuscripts (see also 1 Chron. 23:19); most Hebrew manuscripts *The sons of Jeriah:*

[f] 3 One Hebrew manuscript and some Septuagint manuscripts (see also verse 17); most Hebrew manuscripts do not have *Shimei.*

°24 ק שמיר

°1 ק הנבאים

יְדוּתוּן בַּכִּנּוֹר הַנִּבָּא עַל־ הֹדוֹת וְהַלֵּל
and-to-praise to-thank in the-one-prophesying with-the-harp Jeduthun

לַיהוָה׃ (4) לְהֵימָן בְּנֵי הֵימָן בֻּקִּיָּהוּ מַתַּנְיָהוּ עֻזִּיאֵל שְׁבוּאֵל
Shubael Uzziel Mattaniah Bukkiah Heman sons-of for-Heman (4) to-Yahweh

וִירִימוֹת חֲנַנְיָה חֲנָנִי אֱלִיאָתָה גִדַּלְתִּי וְרֹמַמְתִּי עֶזֶר יָשְׁבְּקָשָׁה
Joshbekashah Ezer and-Romamti Giddalti Eliathah Hanani Hananiah and-Jerimoth

מַלּוֹתִי הוֹתִיר מַחֲזִיאוֹת׃ (5) כָּל־ אֵלֶּה בָנִים לְהֵימָן חֹזֵה הַמֶּלֶךְ
the-king seer-of of-Heman sons these all-of (5) Mahazioth Hothir Mallothi

בְּדִבְרֵי הָאֱלֹהִים לְהָרִים קָרֶן וַיִּתֵּן הָאֱלֹהִים לְהֵימָן
to-Heman the-God and-he-gave horn to-exalt the-God through-promises-of

בָּנִים אַרְבָּעָה עָשָׂר וּבָנוֹת שָׁלוֹשׁ׃ (6) כָּל־ אֵלֶּה עַל־ יְדֵי
hands-of under these all-of (6) three and-daughters ten four sons

אֲבִיהֶם בַּשִּׁיר בֵּית יְהוָה בִּמְצִלְתַּיִם נְבָלִים וְכִנֹּרוֹת
and-harps lyres with-cymbals Yahweh temple-of for-the-music father-of-them

לַעֲבֹדַת בֵּית הָאֱלֹהִים עַל יְדֵי הַמֶּלֶךְ אָסָף וִידוּתוּן
and-Jeduthun Asaph the-king hands-of under the-God house-of for-ministry-of

וְהֵימָן׃ (7) וַיְהִי מִסְפָּרָם עִם־ אֲחֵיהֶם
relatives-of-them with number-of-them and-he-was (7) and-Heman

מְלֻמְּדֵי־ שִׁיר לַיהוָה כָּל־ הַמֵּבִין
the-one-being-skilled all-of for-Yahweh music ones-being-trained-of

מָאתַיִם שְׁמוֹנִים וּשְׁמוֹנָה׃ (8) וַיַּפִּילוּ גּוֹרָלוֹת מִשְׁמֶרֶת לְעֻמַּת
just-as duty lots-of and-they-cast (8) and-eight eighty two-hundreds

כַּקָּטֹן כַּגָּדוֹל מֵבִין עִם־ תַּלְמִיד׃ (9) וַיֵּצֵא הַגּוֹרָל
the-lot and-he-fell (9) student as one-teaching so-the-old as-the-young

הָרִאשׁוֹן לְאָסָף לְיוֹסֵף גְּדַלְיָהוּ הַשֵּׁנִי הוּא־ וְאֶחָיו
and-relatives-of-him he the-second Gedaliah to-Joseph for-Asaph the-first

וּבָנָיו שְׁנֵים עָשָׂר׃ (10) הַשְּׁלִשִׁי זַכּוּר בָּנָיו וְאֶחָיו
and-relatives-of-him sons-of-him Zaccur the-third (10) ten two and-sons-of-him

שְׁנֵים עָשָׂר׃ (11) הָרְבִיעִי לַיִּצְרִי בָּנָיו וְאֶחָיו
and-relatives-of-him sons-of-him to-the-Izrite the-fourth (11) ten two

שְׁנֵים עָשָׂר׃ (12) הַחֲמִישִׁי נְתַנְיָהוּ בָּנָיו וְאֶחָיו שְׁנֵים עָשָׂר׃
ten two and-relatives-of-him sons-of-him Nethaniah the-fifth (12) ten two

(13) הַשִּׁשִּׁי בֻּקִּיָּהוּ בָּנָיו וְאֶחָיו שְׁנֵים עָשָׂר׃
ten two and-relatives-of-him sons-of-him Bukkiah the-sixth (13)

(14) הַשְּׁבִיעִי יְשַׂרְאֵלָה בָּנָיו וְאֶחָיו שְׁנֵים עָשָׂר׃
ten two and-relatives-of-him sons-of-him Jesarelah the-seventh (14)

(15) הַשְּׁמִינִי יְשַׁעְיָהוּ בָּנָיו וְאֶחָיו שְׁנֵים עָשָׂר׃
ten two and-relatives-of-him sons-of-him Jeshaiah the-eighth (15)

the supervision of their father Jeduthun, who proph-
esied, using the harp in
thanking and praising the
LORD.
4 As for Heman, from his sons:
Bukkiah, Mattaniah, Uzzi-
el, Shubael and Jerimoth;
Hananiah, Hanani, Elia-
thah, Giddalti and Romam-
ti-Ezer; Joshbekashah, Mallothi, Hothir and Maha-
zioth. 5 All these were sons
of Heman the king's seer.
They were given him
through the promises of
God to exalt him.[g] God gave
Heman fourteen sons and
three daughters.

6 All these men were under
the supervision of their fathers for the music of the temple of the LORD, with cymbals,
lyres and harps, for the ministry at the house of God. Asaph,
Jeduthun and Heman were
under the supervision of the
king. 7 Along with their relatives—all of them trained and
skilled in music for the LORD—
they numbered 288. 8 Young
and old alike, teacher as well
as student, cast lots for their
duties.

9 The first lot, which was
for Asaph, fell to
Joseph,
his sons and
relatives,[h] 12[i]
the second to Gedaliah,
he and his relatives
and sons, 12
10 the third to Zaccur,
his sons and relatives, 12
11 the fourth to Izri,[j]
his sons and relatives, 12
12 the fifth to Nethaniah,
his sons and relatives, 12
13 the sixth to Bukkiah,
his sons and relatives, 12
14 the seventh to Jesarelah,[k]
his sons and relatives, 12
15 the eighth to Jeshaiah,
his sons and relatives, 12

g5 Hebrew *exalt the horn*
h9 See Septuagint; Hebrew does not have *his sons and relatives.*
i9 See the total in verse 7; Hebrew does not have *twelve.*
j11 A variant of *Zeri*
k14 A variant of *Asarelah*

הַתְּשִׁיעִי מַתַּנְיָהוּ בָּנָיו וְאֶחָיו שְׁנֵים עָשָׂר׃
ten two and-relatives-of-him sons-of-him Mattaniah the-ninth (16)

הָעֲשִׂירִי שִׁמְעִי בָּנָיו וְאֶחָיו שְׁנֵים עָשָׂר׃
ten two and-relatives-of-him sons-of-him Shimei the-tenth (17)

עַשְׁתֵּי־עָשָׂר עֲזַרְאֵל בָּנָיו וְאֶחָיו שְׁנֵים עָשָׂר׃
ten two and-relatives-of-him sons-of-him Azarel ten one (18)

הַשְּׁנַיִם עָשָׂר לַחֲשַׁבְיָה בָּנָיו וְאֶחָיו שְׁנֵים עָשָׂר׃
ten two and-relatives-of-him sons-of-him to-Hashabiah ten the-two (19)

לִשְׁלֹשָׁה עָשָׂר שׁוּבָאֵל בָּנָיו וְאֶחָיו שְׁנֵים עָשָׂר׃
ten two and-relatives-of-him sons-of-him Shubael ten to-three (20)

לְאַרְבָּעָה עָשָׂר מַתִּתְיָהוּ בָּנָיו וְאֶחָיו שְׁנֵים עָשָׂר׃
ten two and-relatives-of-him sons-of-him Mattithiah ten to-four (21)

לַחֲמִשָּׁה עָשָׂר לִירֵמוֹת בָּנָיו וְאֶחָיו שְׁנֵים עָשָׂר׃
ten two and-relatives-of-him sons-of-him to-Jerimoth ten to-five (22)

לְשִׁשָּׁה עָשָׂר לַחֲנַנְיָהוּ בָּנָיו וְאֶחָיו שְׁנֵים עָשָׂר׃
ten two and-relatives-of-him sons-of-him to-Hananiah ten to-six (23)

לְשִׁבְעָה עָשָׂר לְיָשְׁבְּקָשָׁה בָּנָיו וְאֶחָיו שְׁנֵים עָשָׂר׃
ten two and-relatives-of-him sons-of-him to-Joshbekashah ten to-seven (24)

לִשְׁמוֹנָה עָשָׂר לַחֲנָנִי בָּנָיו וְאֶחָיו שְׁנֵים עָשָׂר׃
ten two and-relatives-of-him sons-of-him to-Hanani ten to-eight (25)

לְתִשְׁעָה עָשָׂר לְמַלּוֹתִי בָּנָיו וְאֶחָיו שְׁנֵים עָשָׂר׃
ten two and-relatives-of-him sons-of-him to-Mallothi ten to-nine (26)

לְעֶשְׂרִים לְאֱלִיָּתָה בָּנָיו וְאֶחָיו שְׁנֵים עָשָׂר׃
ten two and-relatives-of-him sons-of-him to-Eliathah to-twenty (27)

לְאֶחָד וְעֶשְׂרִים לְהוֹתִיר בָּנָיו וְאֶחָיו שְׁנֵים עָשָׂר׃
ten two and-relatives-of-him sons-of-him to-Hothir and-twenty to-one (28)

לִשְׁנַיִם וְעֶשְׂרִים לְגִדַּלְתִּי בָּנָיו וְאֶחָיו שְׁנֵים עָשָׂר׃
ten two and-relatives-of-him sons-of-him to-Giddalti and-twenty to-two (29)

לִשְׁלֹשָׁה וְעֶשְׂרִים לְמַחֲזִיאוֹת בָּנָיו וְאֶחָיו שְׁנֵים
two and-relatives-of-him sons-of-him to-Mahazioth and-twenty to-three (30)

עָשָׂר׃ לְאַרְבָּעָה וְעֶשְׂרִים לְרוֹמַמְתִּי עֶזֶר בָּנָיו וְאֶחָיו
and-relatives-of-him sons-of-him Ezer to-Romamti and-twenty to-four (31) ten

שְׁנֵים עָשָׂר׃ לְמַחְלְקוֹת לְשֹׁעֲרִים לַקָּרְחִים מְשֶׁלֶמְיָהוּ
Meshelemiah from-the-Korahites of-gatekeepers of-divisions (26:1) ten two

בֶּן־קֹרֵא מִן־בְּנֵי אָסָף׃ וְלִמְשֶׁלֶמְיָהוּ בָּנִים זְכַרְיָהוּ
Zechariah sons and-to-Meshelemiah (2) Asaph sons-of from Kore son-of

הַבְּכוֹר יְדִיעֲאֵל הַשֵּׁנִי זְבַדְיָהוּ הַשְּׁלִישִׁי יַתְנִיאֵל הָרְבִיעִי׃
the-fourth Jathniel the-third Zebadiah the-second Jediael the-firstborn

16the ninth to Mattaniah,
his sons and relatives,
12
17the tenth to Shimei,
his sons and relatives,
12
18the eleventh to Azarel,[l]
his sons and relatives,
12
19the twelfth to
Hashabiah,
his sons and relatives,
12
20the thirteenth to
Shubael,
his sons and relatives,
12
21the fourteenth to
Mattithiah,
his sons and relatives,
12
22the fifteenth to Jerimoth,
his sons and relatives,
12
23the sixteenth to
Hananiah,
his sons and relatives,
12
24the seventeenth to
Joshbekashah,
his sons and relatives,
12
25the eighteenth to
Hanani,
his sons and relatives,
12
26the nineteenth to
Mallothi,
his sons and relatives,
12
27the twentieth to
Eliathah,
his sons and relatives,
12
28the twenty-first to
Hothir,
his sons and relatives,
12
29the twenty-second to
Giddalti,
his sons and relatives,
12
30the twenty-third to
Mahazioth,
his sons and relatives,
12
31the twenty-fourth to
Romamti-Ezer,
his sons and relatives,
12

The Gatekeepers

26 The divisions of the gatekeepers:

From the Korahites: Meshelemiah son of Kore, one of the sons of Asaph.
2Meshelemiah had sons:
Zechariah the firstborn,
Jediael the second,
Zebadiah the third,
Jathniel the fourth,

[l]18 A variant of *Uzziel*

עֵילָם הַחֲמִישִׁי יְהוֹחָנָן הַשִּׁשִּׁי אֶלְיְהוֹעֵינַי הַשְּׁבִיעִי׃ וּלְעֹבֵד
and-to-Obed (4) the-seventh Eliehoenai the-sixth Jehohanan the-fifth Elam (3)

אֱדֹם בָּנִים שְׁמַעְיָה הַבְּכוֹר יְהוֹזָבָד הַשֵּׁנִי יוֹאָח הַשְּׁלִשִׁי
the-third Joah the-second Jehozabad the-firstborn Shemaiah sons Edom

וְשָׂכָר הָרְבִיעִי וּנְתַנְאֵל הַחֲמִישִׁי׃ עַמִּיאֵל הַשִּׁשִּׁי יִשָּׂשכָר
Issachar the-sixth Ammiel (5) the-fifth and-Nethanel the-fourth and-Sacar

הַשְּׁבִיעִי פְּעֻלְּתַי הַשְּׁמִינִי כִּי בֵרֲכוֹ אֱלֹהִים׃ וְלִשְׁמַעְיָה
and-to-Shemaiah (6) God he-blessed-him for the-eighth Peullethai the-seventh

בְנוֹ נוֹלַד בָּנִים הַמִּמְשָׁלִים לְבֵית אֲבִיהֶם כִּי־
because father-of-them in-family-of the-leaders sons he-was-born son-of-him

גִבּוֹרֵי חַיִל הֵמָּה׃ בְּנֵי שְׁמַעְיָה עָתְנִי וּרְפָאֵל וְעוֹבֵד
and-Obed and-Rephael Othni Shemaiah sons-of (7) they capability men-of

אֶלְזָבָד אֶחָיו בְּנֵי־ חָיִל אֱלִיהוּ וּסְמַכְיָהוּ׃ כָּל־ אֵלֶּה
these all-of (8) and-Semakiah Elihu ability men-of relatives-of-him Elzabad

מִבְּנֵי ׀ עֹבֵד אֱדֹם הֵמָּה וּבְנֵיהֶם וַאֲחֵיהֶם
and-relatives-of-them and-sons-of-them they Edom Obed from-descendants-of

אִישׁ־ חַיִל בַּכֹּחַ לַעֲבֹדָה שִׁשִּׁים וּשְׁנַיִם לְעֹבֵד אֱדֹם׃
Edom of-Obed and-two sixty for-the-work with-the-strength capability man-of

וְלִמְשֶׁלֶמְיָהוּ בָּנִים וְאַחִים בְּנֵי־ חַיִל שְׁמוֹנָה עָשָׂר׃
ten eight ability men-of and-relatives sons and-to-Meshelemiah (9)

וּלְחֹסָה מִן־ בְּנֵי־ מְרָרִי בָּנִים שִׁמְרִי הָרֹאשׁ כִּי לֹא־
not although the-first Shimri sons Merari sons-of from and-to-Hosah (10)

הָיָה בְכוֹר וַיְשִׂימֵהוּ אָבִיהוּ לְרֹאשׁ׃ חִלְקִיָּהוּ
Hilkiah (11) as-first father-of-him but-he-appointed-him firstborn he-was

הַשֵּׁנִי טְבַלְיָהוּ הַשְּׁלִשִׁי זְכַרְיָהוּ הָרְבִעִי כָּל־ בָּנִים וְאַחִים
and-relatives sons all-of the-fourth Zechariah the-third Tabaliah the-second

לְחֹסָה שְׁלֹשָׁה עָשָׂר׃ לְאֵלֶּה מַחְלְקוֹת הַשֹּׁעֲרִים לְרָאשֵׁי
through-chiefs-of the-gatekeepers divisions-of to-these (12) ten three of-Hosah

הַגְּבָרִים מִשְׁמָרוֹת לְעֻמַּת אֲחֵיהֶם לְשָׁרֵת בְּבֵית יְהוָה׃
Yahweh in-temple-of to-minister relatives-of-them just-as duties the-men

וַיַּפִּילוּ גוֹרָלוֹת כַּקָּטֹן כַּגָּדוֹל לְבֵית אֲבוֹתָם
fathers-of-them by-family-of so-the-old as-the-young lots and-they-cast (13)

לְשַׁעַר וָשָׁעַר׃ וַיִּפֹּל הַגּוֹרָל מִזְרָחָה לְשֶׁלֶמְיָהוּ
for-Shelemiah to-East the-lot and-he-fell (14) and-gate for-gate

וּזְכַרְיָהוּ בְנוֹ יוֹעֵץ ׀ בְּשֶׂכֶל הִפִּילוּ גּוֹרָלוֹת
lots they-cast with-wisdom one-counseling son-of-him then-Zechariah

וַיֵּצֵא גוֹרָלוֹ צָפוֹנָה׃ לְעֹבֵד אֱדֹם נֶגְבָּה וּלְבָנָיו
and-to-sons-of-him to-South Edom to-Obed (15) to-North lot-of-him and-he-fell

3Elam the fifth,
Jehohanan the sixth
and Eliehoenai the seventh.
4Obed-Edom also had sons:
Shemaiah the firstborn,
Jehozabad the second,
Joah the third,
Sacar the fourth,
Nethanel the fifth,
5Ammiel the sixth,
Issachar the seventh
and Peullethai the eighth.
(For God had blessed Obed-Edom.)

6His son Shemaiah also had
sons, who were leaders
in their father's family
because they were very
capable men. 7The sons
of Shemaiah: Othni, Rephael,
Obed and Elzabad; his relatives Elihu
and Semakiah were also
able men. 8All these were
descendants of Obed-Edom;
they and their
sons and their relatives
were capable men with
the strength to do the
work—descendants of
Obed-Edom, 62 in all.
9Meshelemiah had sons and
relatives, who were able
men—18 in all.

10Hosah the Merarite had
sons: Shimri the first (although
he was not the
firstborn, his father had
appointed him the first),
11Hilkiah the second,
Tabaliah the third and
Zechariah the fourth.
The sons and relatives of
Hosah were 13 in all.
12These divisions of the gatekeepers,
through their chief
men, had duties for ministering
in the temple of the LORD,
just as their relatives had.
13Lots were cast for each gate,
according to their families,
young and old alike.
14The lot for the East Gate fell
to Shelemiah.[m] Then lots were
cast for his son Zechariah, a
wise counselor, and the lot for
the North Gate fell to him.
15The lot for the South Gate fell
to Obed-Edom, and the lot for
the storehouse fell to his sons.

[m]14 A variant of *Meshelemiah*

בֵּית הָאֲסֻפִּים׃ לְשֻׁפִּים וּלְחֹסָה לַמַּעֲרָב עִם שַׁעַר

Gate-of with for-the-West and-to-Hosah to-Shuppim (16) the-stores house-of

שַׁלֶּכֶת בַּמְסִלָּה הָעוֹלָה מִשְׁמָר לְעֻמַּת מִשְׁמָר׃

guard alongside-of guard the-one-going-up on-the-road Shalleketh

לַמִּזְרָח הַלְוִיִּם שִׁשָּׁה לַצָּפוֹנָה לַיּוֹם אַרְבָּעָה לַנֶּגְבָּה

on-the-south four for-the-day on-the-north six the-Levites on-the-east (17)

לַיּוֹם אַרְבָּעָה וְלָאֲסֻפִּים שְׁנַיִם שְׁנָיִם׃ לַפַּרְבָּר לַמַּעֲרָב

to-the-west for-the-court (18) two two and-at-the-storehouses four for-the-day

אַרְבָּעָה לַמְסִלָּה שְׁנַיִם לַפַּרְבָּר׃ אֵלֶּה מַחְלְקוֹת הַשֹּׁעֲרִים

the-gatekeepers divisions-of these (19) at-the-court two at-the-road four

לִבְנֵי הַקָּרְחִי וְלִבְנֵי מְרָרִי׃ וְהַלְוִיִּם

and-the-Levites (20) Merari and-of-descendants-of the-Korahite of-descendants-of

אֲחִיָּה עַל־ אוֹצְרוֹת בֵּית הָאֱלֹהִים וּלְאֹצְרוֹת

and-of-treasuries-of the-God house-of treasuries-of over Ahijah

הַקֳּדָשִׁים׃ בְּנֵי לַעְדָּן בְּנֵי הַגֵּרְשֻׁנִּי

the-Gershonite sons-of Ladan descendants-of (21) the-dedicated-things

לְלַעְדָּן רָאשֵׁי הָאָבוֹת לְלַעְדָּן הַגֵּרְשֻׁנִּי יְחִיאֵלִי׃

Jehieli the-Gershonite of-Ladan the-fathers heads-of through-Ladan

בְּנֵי יְחִיאֵלִי זֵתָם וְיוֹאֵל אָחִיו עַל־ אֹצְרוֹת

treasuries-of over brother-of-him and-Joel Zetham Jehieli sons-of (22)

בֵּית יְהוָה׃ לַעַמְרָמִי לַיִּצְהָרִי לַחֶבְרוֹנִי

from-the-Hebronite from-the-Izharite from-the-Amramite (23) Yahweh temple-of

לָעָזִּיאֵלִי׃ וּשְׁבֻאֵל בֶּן־ גֵּרְשׁוֹם בֶּן־ מֹשֶׁה

Moses son-of Gershom descendant-of and-Shubael (24) from-the-Uzzielite

נָגִיד עַל־ הָאֹצָרוֹת׃ וְאֶחָיו לֶאֱלִיעֶזֶר

through-Eliezer and-relatives-of-him (25) the-treasuries over officer

רְחַבְיָהוּ בְּנוֹ וִישַׁעְיָהוּ בְּנוֹ וְיֹרָם בְּנוֹ וְזִכְרִי

and-Zicri son-of-him and-Joram son-of-him and-Jeshaiah son-of-him Rehabiah

בְּנוֹ וּשְׁלֹמוֹת בְּנוֹ׃ הוּא שְׁלֹמוֹת וְאֶחָיו

and-relatives-of-him Shelomith he (26) son-of-him and-Shelomith son-of-him

עַל כָּל־ אֹצְרוֹת הַקֳּדָשִׁים אֲשֶׁר הִקְדִּישׁ דָּוִיד

David he-dedicated that the-dedicated-things treasuries-of all-of over

הַמֶּלֶךְ וְרָאשֵׁי הָאָבוֹת לְשָׂרֵי־ הָאֲלָפִים

the-thousands of-commanders-of the-fathers and-heads-of the-king

וְהַמֵּאוֹת וְשָׂרֵי הַצָּבָא׃ מִן־ הַמִּלְחָמוֹת וּמִן־

and-from the-battles from (27) the-army and-commanders-of and-the-hundreds

הַשָּׁלָל הִקְדִּישׁוּ לְחַזֵּק לְבֵית יְהוָה׃ וְכֹל

and-all-of (28) Yahweh to-temple-of to-repair they-dedicated the-plunder

16The lots for the West Gate
and the Shalleketh Gate on the
upper road fell to Shuppim
and Hosah.
Guard was alongside of
guard: 17There were six Levites
a day on the east, four a day on
the north, four a day on the
south and two at a time at the
storehouse. 18As for the court
to the west, there were four at
the road and two at the court
itself.
19These were the divisions of
the gatekeepers who were descendants of Korah and
Merari.

The Treasurers and Other Officials

20Their fellow Levites were[n]
in charge of the treasuries of
the house of God and the
treasuries for the dedicated
things.
21The descendants of Ladan,
who were Gershonites
through Ladan and who were
heads of families belonging to
Ladan the Gershonite, were
Jehieli, 22the sons of Jehieli,
Zetham and his brother Joel.
They were in charge of the
treasuries of the temple of the
LORD.
23From the Amramites, the
Izharites, the Hebronites and
the Uzzielites:
24Shubael, a descendant of
Gershom son of Moses,
was the officer in charge
of the treasuries. 25His
relatives through Eliezer:
Rehabiah his son, Je-
shaiah his son, Joram his
son, Zicri his son and
Shelomith his son.
26Shelomith and his rela-
tives were in charge of all
the treasuries for the
things dedicated by King
David, by the heads of
families who were the
commanders of thou-
sands and commanders
of hundreds, and by the
other army commanders.
27Some of the plunder
taken in battle they dedicated for the repair of the
temple of the LORD. 28And

n20 Septuagint; Hebrew *As for the Levites, Ahijah was*

°25 ק ושלמית

הַהִקְדִּישׁ שְׁמוּאֵל הָרֹאֶה וְשָׁאוּל בֶּן־ קִישׁ וְאַבְנֵר בֶּן־ נֵר
Ner son-of and-Abner Kish son-of and-Saul the-seer Samuel what-he-dedicated

וְיוֹאָב בֶּן־ צְרוּיָה כֹּל הַמַּקְדִּישׁ עַל יַד־
hand-of in the-thing-being-dedicated all-of Zeruiah son-of and-Joab

שְׁלֹמִית וְאֶחָיו׃ לַיִּצְהָרִי כְּנַנְיָהוּ וּבָנָיו
and-sons-of-him Kenaniah from-the-Izharite (29) and-relatives-of-him Shelomith

לַמְּלָאכָה הַחִיצוֹנָה עַל־ יִשְׂרָאֵל לְשֹׁטְרִים וּלְשֹׁפְטִים׃
and-as-ones-being-judges as-officials Israel over at-the-outside for-the-duty

לַחֶבְרוֹנִי חֲשַׁבְיָהוּ וְאֶחָיו בְּנֵי־ חַיִל
ability men-of and-relatives-of-him Hashabiah from-the-Hebronite (30)

אֶלֶף וּשְׁבַע־ מֵאוֹת עַל פְּקֻדַּת יִשְׂרָאֵל מֵעֵבֶר
at-near Israel responsibility-of over hundreds and-seven-of thousand

לַיַּרְדֵּן מַעְרָבָה לְכֹל מְלֶאכֶת יְהוָה וְלַעֲבֹדַת הַמֶּלֶךְ׃
the-king and-for-service-of Yahweh work-of for-all-of at-west to-the-Jordan

לַחֶבְרוֹנִי יְרִיָּה הָרֹאשׁ לַחֶבְרוֹנִי לְתֹלְדֹתָיו
by-records-of-him of-the-Hebronite the-chief Jeriah for-the-Hebronite (31)

לְאָבוֹת בִּשְׁנַת הָאַרְבָּעִים לְמַלְכוּת דָּוִיד נִדְרָשׁוּ
they-were-searched David of-reign-of the-forty in-year-of of-fathers

וַיִּמָּצֵא בָהֶם גִּבּוֹרֵי חַיִל בְּיַעְזֵיר גִּלְעָד׃
Gilead at-Jazer-of capability men-of among-them and-he-was-found

וְאֶחָיו בְּנֵי־ חַיִל אַלְפַּיִם וּשְׁבַע מֵאוֹת
hundreds and-seven-of two-thousands ability men-of and-relatives-of-him (32)

רָאשֵׁי הָאָבוֹת וַיַּפְקִידֵם דָּוִיד הַמֶּלֶךְ עַל־
over the-king David and-he-put-in-charge-them the-fathers heads-of

הָראוּבֵנִי וְהַגָּדִי וַחֲצִי שֵׁבֶט הַמְנַשִּׁי לְכָל־
for-every-of the-Manassite tribe-of and-half-of and-the-Gadite the-Reubenite

דְּבַר הָאֱלֹהִים וּדְבַר הַמֶּלֶךְ׃ וּבְנֵי יִשְׂרָאֵל
Israel and-sons-of (27:1) the-king and-affair-of the-God matter-of

לְמִסְפָּרָם רָאשֵׁי הָאָבוֹת וְשָׂרֵי הָאֲלָפִים
the-thousands and-commanders-of the-fathers heads-of by-list-of-them

וְהַמֵּאוֹת וְשֹׁטְרֵיהֶם הַמְשָׁרְתִים אֶת־ הַמֶּלֶךְ
the-king *** the-ones-serving and-officers-of-them and-the-hundreds

לְכֹל דְּבַר הַמַּחְלְקוֹת הַבָּאָה וְהַיֹּצֵאת
and-the-one-going-out the-one-coming-in the-divisions concern-of in-every-of

חֹדֶשׁ בְּחֹדֶשׁ לְכֹל חָדְשֵׁי הַשָּׁנָה הַמַּחֲלֹקֶת הָאַחַת
the-each the-division the-year months-of through-all-of by-month month

עֶשְׂרִים וְאַרְבָּעָה אָלֶף׃ עַל הַמַּחֲלֹקֶת הָרִאשׁוֹנָה לַחֹדֶשׁ
for-the-month the-first the-division over (2) thousand and-four twenty

everything dedicated by Samuel the seer and by Saul son of Kish, Abner son of Ner and Joab son of Zeruiah, and all the other dedicated things were in the care of Shelomith and his relatives.
29 From the Izharites: Kenaniah and his sons were assigned duties away from the temple, as officials and judges over Israel.
30 From the Hebronites: Hashabiah and his relatives—seventeen hundred able men—were responsible in Israel west of the Jordan for all the work of the LORD and for
the king's service. 31 As for the Hebronites, Jeriah was their chief according to the genealogical records of their families. In the fortieth year of David's reign a search was made in the records, and capable men among the Hebronites were found at Jazer in Gilead.
32 Jeriah had twenty-seven hundred relatives, who were able men and heads of families, and King David put them in charge of the Reubenites, the Gadites and the half-tribe of Manasseh for every matter pertaining to God and for the affairs of the king.

Army Divisions

27 This is the list of the Israelites—heads of families, commanders of thousands and commanders of hundreds, and their officers, who served the king in all that concerned the army divisions that were on duty month by month throughout the year. Each division consisted of 24,000 men.

2 In charge of the first division, for the first month,

הָרִאשׁוֹן יָשָׁבְעָם בֶּן־ זַבְדִּיאֵל וְעַל מַחֲלֻקְתּוֹ עֶשְׂרִים וְאַרְבָּעָה
and-four twenty division-of-him and-in Zabdiel son-of Jashobeam the-first

אָלֶף׃ מִן־ בְּנֵי־ פֶרֶץ הָרֹאשׁ לְכָל־ שָׂרֵי
officers-of of-all-of the-chief Perez descendants-of from (3) thousand

הַצְּבָאוֹת לַחֹדֶשׁ הָרִאשׁוֹן׃ וְעַל מַחֲלֹקֶת ׀ הַחֹדֶשׁ
the-month division-of and-over (4) the-first for-the-month the-armies

הַשֵּׁנִי דּוֹדַי הָאֲחוֹחִי וּמַחֲלֻקְתּוֹ וּמִקְלוֹת הַנָּגִיד
the-leader and-Mikloth and-division-of-him the-Ahohite Dodai the-second

וְעַל מַחֲלֻקְתּוֹ עֶשְׂרִים וְאַרְבָּעָה אָלֶף׃ שַׂר הַצָּבָא
the-army commander-of (5) thousand and-four twenty division-of-him and-in

הַשְּׁלִישִׁי לַחֹדֶשׁ הַשְּׁלִישִׁי בְּנָיָהוּ בֶן־ יְהוֹיָדָע הַכֹּהֵן רֹאשׁ
chief the-priest Jehoiada son-of Benaiah the-third for-the-month the-third

וְעַל מַחֲלֻקְתּוֹ עֶשְׂרִים וְאַרְבָּעָה אָלֶף׃ הוּא בְנָיָהוּ גִּבּוֹר
mighty-man-of Benaiah this (6) thousand and-four twenty division-of-him and-in

הַשְּׁלֹשִׁים וְעַל־ הַשְּׁלֹשִׁים וּמַחֲלֻקְתּוֹ עַמִּיזָבָד בְּנוֹ׃
son-of-him Ammizabad and-division-of-him the-Thirty and-over the-Thirty

הָרְבִיעִי לַחֹדֶשׁ הָרְבִיעִי עֲשָׂה־אֵל אֲחִי יוֹאָב וּזְבַדְיָה
and-Zebadiah Joab brother-of El Asah the-fourth for-the-month the-fourth* (7)

בְנוֹ אַחֲרָיו וְעַל מַחֲלֻקְתּוֹ עֶשְׂרִים וְאַרְבָּעָה אָלֶף׃
thousand and-four twenty division-of-him and-in after-him son-of-him

הַחֲמִישִׁי לַחֹדֶשׁ הַחֲמִישִׁי הַשַּׂר שַׁמְהוּת הַיִּזְרָח
the-Izrahite Shamhuth the-commander the-fifth for-the-month the-fifth (8)

וְעַל מַחֲלֻקְתּוֹ עֶשְׂרִים וְאַרְבָּעָה אָלֶף׃ הַשִּׁשִּׁי לַחֹדֶשׁ
for-the-month the-sixth (9) thousand and-four twenty division-of-him and-in

הַשִּׁשִּׁי עִירָא בֶן־ עִקֵּשׁ הַתְּקוֹעִי וְעַל מַחֲלֻקְתּוֹ עֶשְׂרִים
twenty division-of-him and-in the-Tekoite Ikkesh son-of Ira the-sixth

וְאַרְבָּעָה אָלֶף׃ הַשְּׁבִיעִי לַחֹדֶשׁ הַשְּׁבִיעִי חֶלֶץ
Helez the-seventh for-the-month the-seventh (10) thousand and-four

הַפְּלוֹנִי מִן־ בְּנֵי אֶפְרָיִם וְעַל מַחֲלֻקְתּוֹ עֶשְׂרִים וְאַרְבָּעָה
and-four twenty division-of-him and-in Ephraim sons-of from the-Pelonite

אָלֶף׃ הַשְּׁמִינִי לַחֹדֶשׁ הַשְּׁמִינִי סִבְּכַי הַחֻשָׁתִי
the-Hushathite Sibbecai the-eighth for-the-month the-eighth (11) thousand

לַזַּרְחִי וְעַל מַחֲלֻקְתּוֹ עֶשְׂרִים וְאַרְבָּעָה אָלֶף׃
thousand and-four twenty division-of-him and-in of-the-Zerahite

הַתְּשִׁיעִי לַחֹדֶשׁ הַתְּשִׁיעִי אֲבִיעֶזֶר הָעַנְּתֹתִי
the-Anathothite Abiezer the-ninth for-the-month the-ninth (12)

לַבֵּנְוֹמִינִי וְעַל מַחֲלֻקְתּוֹ עֶשְׂרִים וְאַרְבָּעָה אָלֶף׃
thousand and-four twenty division-of-him and-in of-the-Benjamite

was Jashobeam son of
Zabdiel. There were 24,-
000 men in his division.
[3]He was a descendant of
Perez and chief of all the
army officers for the first
month.
[4]In charge of the division for
the second month was
Dodai the Ahohite; Mik-
loth was the leader of his
division. There were 24,-
000 men in his division.
[5]The third army commander,
for the third month, was
Benaiah son of Jehoiada
the priest. He was chief
and there were 24,000
men in his division. [6]This
was the Benaiah who was
a mighty man among the
Thirty and was over the
Thirty. His son Am-
mizabad was in charge of
his division.
[7]The fourth, for the fourth
month, was Asahel the
brother of Joab; his son
Zebadiah was his succes-
sor. There were 24,000
men in his division.
[8]The fifth, for the fifth month,
was the commander
Shamhuth the Izrahite.
There were 24,000 men in
his division.
[9]The sixth, for the sixth
month, was Ira the son of
Ikkesh the Tekoite. There
were 24,000 men in his
division.
[10]The seventh, for the seventh
month, was Helez the
Pelonite, an Ephraimite.
There were 24,000 men in
his division.
[11]The eighth, for the eighth
month, was Sibbecai the
Hushathite, a Zerahite.
There were 24,000 men in
his division.
[12]The ninth, for the ninth
month, was Abiezer the
Anathothite, a Benjamite.
There were 24,000 men in
his division.

*8 Most mss have *hateph pathah* under the *beth* (הַחֲ).

°12 ק לבן ימיני

הָעֲשִׂירִי לַחֹדֶשׁ הָעֲשִׂירִי מַהְרַי הַנְּטוֹפָתִי
the-Netophathite Maharai the-tenth for-the-month the-tenth (13)

לַזַּרְחִי וְעַל מַחֲלֻקְתּוֹ עֶשְׂרִים וְאַרְבָּעָה אָלֶף׃ עַשְׁתֵּי־
one (14) thousand and-four twenty division-of-him and-in of-the-Zerahite

עָשָׂר לְעַשְׁתֵּי־עָשָׂר הַחֹדֶשׁ בְּנָיָה הַפִּרְעָתוֹנִי מִן־ בְּנֵי אֶפְרָיִם
Ephraim sons-of from the-Pirathonite Benaiah the-month ten for-one ten

וְעַל מַחֲלֻקְתּוֹ עֶשְׂרִים וְאַרְבָּעָה אָלֶף׃ הַשְּׁנֵים עָשָׂר לִשְׁנֵים
for-two ten the-two (15) thousand and-four twenty division-of-him and-in

עָשָׂר הַחֹדֶשׁ חֶלְדַּי הַנְּטוֹפָתִי לְעָתְנִיאֵל וְעַל מַחֲלֻקְתּוֹ
division-of-him and-in of-Othniel the-Netophathite Heldai the-month ten

עֶשְׂרִים וְאַרְבָּעָה אָלֶף׃ וְעַל שִׁבְטֵי יִשְׂרָאֵל לָרְאוּבֵנִי
over-the-Reubenite Israel tribes-of and-over (16) thousand and-four twenty

נָגִיד אֱלִיעֶזֶר בֶּן־ זִכְרִי לַשִּׁמְעוֹנִי שְׁפַטְיָהוּ בֶּן־ מַעֲכָה׃
Maacah son-of Shephatiah over-the-Simeonite Zicri son-of Eliezer officer

לְלֵוִי חֲשַׁבְיָה בֶן־ קְמוּאֵל לְאַהֲרֹן צָדוֹק׃ לִיהוּדָה
over-Judah (18) Zadok over-Aaron Kemuel son-of Hashabiah over-Levi (17)

אֱלִיהוּ מֵאֲחֵי דָוִיד לְיִשָּׂשכָר עָמְרִי בֶּן־ מִיכָאֵל׃
Michael son-of Omri over-Issachar David from-brothers-of Elihu

לִזְבוּלֻן יִשְׁמַעְיָהוּ בֶּן־ עֹבַדְיָהוּ לְנַפְתָּלִי יְרִימוֹת בֶּן־
son-of Jerimoth over-Naphtali Obadiah son-of Ishmaiah over-Zebulun (19)

עַזְרִיאֵל׃ לִבְנֵי אֶפְרַיִם הוֹשֵׁעַ בֶּן־ עֲזַזְיָהוּ לַחֲצִי שֵׁבֶט
tribe-of over-half-of Azaziah son-of Hoshea Ephraim over-sons-of (20) Azriel

מְנַשֶּׁה יוֹאֵל בֶּן־ פְּדָיָהוּ׃ לַחֲצִי הַמְנַשֶּׁה גִּלְעָדָה יִדּוֹ
Iddo in-Gilead the-Manasseh over-half-of (21) Pedaiah son-of Joel Manasseh

בֶּן־ זְכַרְיָהוּ לְבִנְיָמִן יַעֲשִׂיאֵל בֶּן־ אַבְנֵר׃ לְדָן עֲזַרְאֵל
Azarel over-Dan (22) Abner son-of Jaasiel over-Benjamin Zechariah son-of

בֶּן־ יְרֹחָם אֵלֶּה שָׂרֵי שִׁבְטֵי יִשְׂרָאֵל׃ וְלֹא־ נָשָׂא
he-took and-not (23) Israel tribes-of officers-of these Jeroham son-of

דָוִיד מִסְפָּרָם לְמִבֶּן עֶשְׂרִים שָׁנָה וּלְמָטָּה כִּי
because or-of-less year twenty of-from-son-of from-number-of-them David

אָמַר יְהוָה לְהַרְבּוֹת אֶת־ יִשְׂרָאֵל כְּכוֹכְבֵי הַשָּׁמָיִם׃
the-skies as-stars-of Israel *** to-make-numerous Yahweh he-promised

יוֹאָב בֶּן־ צְרוּיָה הֵחֵל לִמְנוֹת וְלֹא כִלָּה וַיְהִי
and-he-came he-finished but-not to-count he-began Zeruiah son-of Joab (24)

בָזֹאת קֶצֶף עַל־ יִשְׂרָאֵל וְלֹא עָלָה הַמִּסְפָּר בְּמִסְפַּר
in-number-of the-number he-entered and-not Israel on wrath on-account-of-this

דִּבְרֵי־ הַיָּמִים לַמֶּלֶךְ דָּוִיד׃ וְעַל אֹצְרוֹת הַמֶּלֶךְ
the-king storehouses-of and-over (25) David of-the-king the-days annals-of

13 The tenth, for the tenth month, was Maharai the Netophathite, a Zerahite. There were 24,000 men in his division.
14 The eleventh, for the eleventh month, was Benaiah the Pirathonite, an Ephraimite. There were 24,000 men in his division.
15 The twelfth, for the twelfth month, was Heldai the Netophathite, from the family of Othniel. There were 24,000 men in his division.

Officers of the Tribes

16 The officers over the tribes of Israel:

over the Reubenites: Eliezer son of Zicri;
over the Simeonites: Shephatiah son of Maacah;
17 over Levi: Hashabiah son of Kemuel;
over Aaron: Zadok;
18 over Judah: Elihu, a brother of David;
over Issachar: Omri son of Michael;
19 over Zebulun: Ishmaiah son of Obadiah;
over Naphtali: Jerimoth son of Azriel;
20 over the Ephraimites: Hoshea son of Azaziah;
over half the tribe of Manasseh: Joel son of Pedaiah;
21 over the half-tribe of Manasseh in Gilead: Iddo son of Zechariah;
over Benjamin: Jaasiel son of Abner;
22 over Dan: Azarel son of Jeroham.
These were the officers over the tribes of Israel.

23 David did not take the
number of the men twenty
years old or less, because the
LORD had promised to make
Israel as numerous as the stars
in the sky. 24 Joab son of Zeruiah began to count the men
but did not finish. Wrath came
on Israel on account of this
numbering, and the number
was not entered in the book[o]
of the annals of King David.

The King's Overseers

25 Azmaveth son of Adiel was in charge of the royal storehouses.

[o] 24 Septuagint; Hebrew *number*

עַזְמָוֶת בֶּן־ עֲדִיאֵל וְעַל הָאֹצָרוֹת בַּשָּׂדֶה בֶּעָרִים
in-the-towns in-the-field the-storehouses and-over Adiel son-of Azmaveth

וּבַכְּפָרִים וּבַמִּגְדָּלוֹת יְהוֹנָתָן בֶּן־ עֻזִּיָּהוּ׃
Uzziah son-of Jonathan and-in-the-watchtowers and-in-the-villages

וְעַל עֹשֵׂי מְלֶאכֶת הַשָּׂדֶה לַעֲבֹדַת הָאֲדָמָה עֶזְרִי בֶּן־
son-of Ezri the-land to-farm the-field work-of ones-doing-of and-over (26)

כְּלוּב׃ וְעַל־ הַכְּרָמִים שִׁמְעִי הָרָמָתִי וְעַל
and-over the-Ramathite Shimei the-vineyards and-over (27) Kelub

שֶׁבַּכְּרָמִים לְאֹצְרוֹת הַיַּיִן זַבְדִּי הַשִּׁפְמִי׃
the-Shiphmite Zabdi the-wine for-vats-of what-from-the-vineyards

וְעַל־ הַזֵּיתִים וְהַשִּׁקְמִים אֲשֶׁר בַּשְּׁפֵלָה
in-the-foothill that and-the-sycamore-trees the-olive-trees and-over (28)

בַּעַל חָנָן הַגְּדֵרִי וְעַל־ אֹצְרוֹת הַשֶּׁמֶן יוֹעָשׁ׃
Joash the-olive-oil supplies-of and-over the-Gederite Hanan Baal

וְעַל־ הַבָּקָר הָרֹעִים בַּשָּׁרוֹן שִׁטְרַי הַשָּׁרוֹנִי
the-Sharonite Shitrai in-the-Sharon the-ones-grazing the-herd and-over (29)

וְעַל־ הַבָּקָר בָּעֲמָקִים שָׁפָט בֶּן־ עַדְלָי׃ וְעַל־
and-over (30) Adlai son-of Shaphat in-the-valleys the-herd and-over

הַגְּמַלִּים אוֹבִיל הַיִּשְׁמְעֵלִי וְעַל־ הָאֲתֹנוֹת יֶחְדְּיָהוּ הַמֵּרֹנֹתִי׃
the-Meronothite Jehdeiah the-donkeys and-over the-Ishmaelite Obil the-camels

וְעַל־ הַצֹּאן יָזִיז הַהַגְרִי כָּל־ אֵלֶּה שָׂרֵי
officials-of these all-of the-Hagrite Jaziz the-flock and-over (31)

הָרְכוּשׁ אֲשֶׁר לַמֶּלֶךְ דָּוִיד׃ וִיהוֹנָתָן דּוֹד־ דָּוִיד
David uncle-of and-Jonathan (32) David to-the-king that the-property

יוֹעֵץ אִישׁ־ מֵבִין וְסוֹפֵר הוּא וִיחִיאֵל בֶּן־ חַכְמוֹנִי
Hacmoni son-of and-Jehiel he and-scribe having-insight man-of one-counseling

עִם־ בְּנֵי הַמֶּלֶךְ׃ וַאֲחִיתֹפֶל יוֹעֵץ לַמֶּלֶךְ
to-the-king one-counseling and-Ahithophel (33) the-king sons-of with

וְחוּשַׁי הָאַרְכִּי רֵעַ הַמֶּלֶךְ׃ וְאַחֲרֵי אֲחִיתֹפֶל יְהוֹיָדָע
Jehoiada Ahithophel and-after (34) the-king friend-of the-Arkite and-Hushai

בֶּן־ בְּנָיָהוּ וְאֶבְיָתָר וְשַׂר־ צָבָא לַמֶּלֶךְ יוֹאָב׃
Joab of-the-king army and-commander-of and-Abiathar Benaiah son-of

וַיַּקְהֵל דָּוִיד אֶת־ כָּל־ שָׂרֵי יִשְׂרָאֵל שָׂרֵי
officers-of Israel officials-of all-of *** David and-he-summoned (28:1)

הַשְּׁבָטִים וְשָׂרֵי הַמַּחְלְקוֹת הַמְשָׁרְתִים אֶת־ הַמֶּלֶךְ
the-king *** the-ones-serving the-divisions and-commanders-of the-tribes

וְשָׂרֵי הָאֲלָפִים וְשָׂרֵי הַמֵּאוֹת וְשָׂרֵי
and-officials-of the-hundreds and-commanders-of the-thousands and-commanders-of

Jonathan son of Uzziah was
in charge of the storehouses in
the outlying districts, in the
towns, the villages and the
watchtowers.
[26]Ezri son of Kelub was in
charge of the field workers
who farmed the land.
[27]Shimei the Ramathite was
in charge of the vineyards.
Zabdi the Shiphmite was in
charge of the produce of the
vineyards for the wine vats.
[28]Baal-Hanan the Gederite
was in charge of the olive and
sycamore-fig trees in the west-
ern foothills.
Joash was in charge of the
supplies of olive oil.
[29]Shitrai the Sharonite was
in charge of the herds grazing
in Sharon.
Shaphat son of Adlai was in
charge of the herds in the valleys.
[30]Obil the Ishmaelite was in
charge of the camels.
Jehdeiah the Meronothite
was in charge of the donkeys.
[31]Jaziz the Hagrite was in
charge of the flocks.
All these were the officials in
charge of King David's property.

[32]Jonathan, David's uncle,
was a counselor, a man of insight and a scribe. Jehiel son of
Hacmoni took care of the
king's sons.
[33]Ahithophel was the king's
counselor.
Hushai the Arkite was the
king's friend. [34]Ahithophel
was succeeded by Jehoiada
son of Benaiah and by Abiathar.
Joab was the commander of
the royal army.

David's Plans for the Temple

28 David summoned all
the officials of Israel to
assemble at Jerusalem: the
officers over the tribes, the
commanders of the divisions
in the service of the king, the
commanders of thousands
and commanders of hundreds,
and the officials in charge of

°29 ק שרטי

כָל־ רְכוּשׁ־ וּמִקְנֶה ׀ לַמֶּלֶךְ וּלְבָנָיו עִם־
with and-of-sons-of-him of-the-king and-livestock property all-of

הַסָּרִיסִים וְהַגִּבּוֹרִים וּלְכָל־ גִּבּוֹר חָיִל
bravery warrior-of and-to-all-of and-the-mighty-men the-palace-officials

אֶל־ יְרוּשָׁלִָם׃ וַיָּקָם דָּוִיד הַמֶּלֶךְ עַל־ רַגְלָיו וַיֹּאמֶר
and-he-said feet-of-him to the-king David and-he-rose (2) Jerusalem to

שְׁמָעוּנִי אַחַי וְעַמִּי אֲנִי עִם־ לְבָבִי לִבְנוֹת
to-build heart-of-me in I and-people-of-me brothers-of-me listen-to-me!

בֵּית מְנוּחָה לַאֲרוֹן בְּרִית־ יְהוָה וְלַהֲדֹם רַגְלֵי
feet-of even-for-footstool-of Yahweh covenant-of for-ark-of rest house-of

אֱלֹהֵינוּ וַהֲכִינוֹתִי לִבְנוֹת׃ וְהָאֱלֹהִים אָמַר לִי לֹא־
not to-me he-said but-the-God (3) to-build and-I-made-plans God-of-us

תִבְנֶה בַיִת לִשְׁמִי כִּי אִישׁ מִלְחָמוֹת אַתָּה וְדָמִים
and-bloods you wars man-of because for-Name-of-me house you-will-build

שָׁפָכְתָּ׃ וַיִּבְחַר יְהוָה אֱלֹהֵי יִשְׂרָאֵל בִּי מִכֹּל בֵּית־
family-of from-whole-of to-me Israel God-of Yahweh yet-he-chose (4) you-shed

אָבִי לִהְיוֹת לְמֶלֶךְ עַל־ יִשְׂרָאֵל לְעוֹלָם כִּי בִיהוּדָה בָּחַר
he-chose to-Judah indeed to-forever Israel over as-king to-be father-of-me

לְנָגִיד וּבְבֵית יְהוּדָה בֵּית אָבִי וּבִבְנֵי
and-from-sons-of father-of-me family-of Judah and-from-house-of as-leader

אָבִי בִּי רָצָה לְהַמְלִיךְ עַל־ כָּל־יִשְׂרָאֵל׃
Israel all-of over to-make-king he-was-pleased with-me father-of-me

וּמִכָּל־ בָּנַי כִּי רַבִּים בָּנִים נָתַן לִי יְהוָה
Yahweh to-me he-gave sons many indeed sons-of-me and-of-all-of (5)

וַיִּבְחַר בִּשְׁלֹמֹה בְנִי לָשֶׁבֶת עַל־ כִּסֵּא מַלְכוּת יְהוָה
Yahweh kingdom-of throne-of on to-sit son-of-me to-Solomon now-he-chose

עַל־ יִשְׂרָאֵל׃ וַיֹּאמֶר לִי שְׁלֹמֹה בִנְךָ הוּא־ יִבְנֶה
he-will-build he son-of-you Solomon to-me and-he-said (6) Israel over

בֵיתִי וַחֲצֵרוֹתָי כִּי־ בָחַרְתִּי בוֹ לִי לְבֵן וַאֲנִי
and-I as-son for-me to-him I-chose for and-courts-of-me house-of-me

אֶהְיֶה־ לּוֹ לְאָב׃ וַהֲכִינוֹתִי אֶת־ מַלְכוּתוֹ עַד־
to kingdom-of-him *** and-I-will-establish (7) as-father to-him I-will-be

לְעוֹלָם אִם־ יֶחֱזַק לַעֲשׂוֹת מִצְוֺתַי וּמִשְׁפָּטַי
and-laws-of-me commands-of-me to-carry-out he-will-be-unswerving if to-forever

כַּיּוֹם הַזֶּה׃ וְעַתָּה לְעֵינֵי כָל־ יִשְׂרָאֵל קְהַל־ יְהוָה
Yahweh assembly-of Israel all-of in-eyes-of so-now (8) the-this as-the-day

וּבְאָזְנֵי אֱלֹהֵינוּ שִׁמְרוּ וְדִרְשׁוּ כָּל־ מִצְוֺת יְהוָה
Yahweh commands-of all-of and-follow! be-careful! God-of-us and-in-ears-of

all the property and livestock
belonging to the king and his
sons, together with the palace
officials, the mighty men and
all the brave warriors.
2King David rose to his feet
and said: "Listen to me, my
brothers and my people. I had
it in my heart to build a house
as a place of rest for the ark of
the covenant of the LORD, for
the footstool of our God, and I
made plans to build it. 3But
God said to me, 'You are not to
build a house for my Name,
because you are a warrior and
have shed blood.'
4"Yet the LORD, the God of
Israel, chose me from my
whole family to be king over
Israel forever. He chose Judah
as leader, and from the house
of Judah he chose my family,
and from my father's sons he
was pleased to make me king
over all Israel. 5Of all my
sons—and the LORD has given
me many—he has chosen my
son Solomon to sit on the
throne of the kingdom of the
LORD over Israel. 6He said to
me: 'Solomon your son is the
one who will build my house
and my courts, for I have chosen him to be my son, and I
will be his father. 7I will establish his kingdom forever if he
is unswerving in carrying out
my commands and laws, as is
being done at this time.'
8"So now I charge you in the
sight of all Israel and of the
assembly of the LORD, and in
the hearing of our God: Be
careful to follow all the commands of the LORD your God,

אֱלֹהֵיכֶם לְמַעַן תִּירְשׁוּ אֶת־ הָאָרֶץ הַטּוֹבָה וְהִנְחַלְתֶּם
and-you-may-pass-on the-good the-land *** you-may-possess so-that God-of-you

לִבְנֵיכֶם אַחֲרֵיכֶם עַד־ עוֹלָם׃ וְאַתָּה שְׁלֹמֹה־ בְנִי
son-of-me Solomon and-you (9) forever to after-you to-descendants-of-you

דַּע אֶת־ אֱלֹהֵי אָבִיךָ וְעָבְדֵהוּ בְּלֵב שָׁלֵם
whole with-heart and-serve-him! father-of-you God-of *** acknowledge!

וּבְנֶפֶשׁ חֲפֵצָה כִּי כָל־ לְבָבוֹת דּוֹרֵשׁ יְהוָה וְכָל־
and-every-of Yahweh searching hearts all-of for willing and-with-mind

יֵצֶר מַחֲשָׁבוֹת מֵבִין אִם־ תִּדְרְשֶׁנּוּ יִמָּצֵא לָךְ
by-you he-will-be-found you-seek-him if understanding thoughts motive-of

וְאִם־ תַּעַזְבֶנּוּ יַזְנִיחֲךָ לָעַד׃ רְאֵה׀ עַתָּה כִּי־
for now consider! (10) for-ever he-will-reject-you you-forsake-him but-if

יְהוָה בָּחַר בְּךָ לִבְנוֹת־ בַּיִת לַמִּקְדָּשׁ חֲזַק
be-strong! as-the-sanctuary temple to-build to-you he-chose Yahweh

וַעֲשֵׂה׃ וַיִּתֵּן דָּוִיד לִשְׁלֹמֹה בְנוֹ אֶת־ תַּבְנִית
plan-of *** son-of-him to-Solomon David then-he-gave (11) and-do-work!

הָאוּלָם וְאֶת־ בָּתָּיו וְגַנְזַכָּיו וַעֲלִיֹּתָיו
and-upper-parts-of-him and-storerooms-of-him buildings-of-him and the-portico

וַחֲדָרָיו הַפְּנִימִים וּבֵית הַכַּפֹּרֶת׃ וְתַבְנִית
and-plan-of (12) the-atonement and-place-of the-inner-ones and-rooms-of-him

כֹּל אֲשֶׁר הָיָה בָרוּחַ עִמּוֹ לְחַצְרוֹת בֵּית־ יְהוָה
Yahweh temple-of for-courts-of in-him by-the-Spirit he-was that all

וּלְכָל־ הַלְּשָׁכוֹת סָבִיב לְאֹצְרוֹת בֵּית הָאֱלֹהִים
the-God temple-of for-treasuries-of surrounding the-rooms and-for-all-of

וּלְאֹצְרוֹת הַקֳּדָשִׁים׃ וּלְמַחְלְקוֹת
and-for-divisions-of (13) the-dedicated-things and-for-treasuries-of

הַכֹּהֲנִים וְהַלְוִיִּם וּלְכָל־ מְלֶאכֶת עֲבוֹדַת בֵּית־
temple-of service-of work-of and-for-all-of and-the-Levites the-priests

יְהוָה וּלְכָל־ כְּלֵי עֲבוֹדַת בֵּית־ יְהוָה׃
Yahweh temple-of service-of articles-of and-for-all-of Yahweh

לַזָּהָב בַּמִּשְׁקָל לַזָּהָב לְכָל־ כְּלֵי עֲבוֹדָה
service articles-of for-all-of for-the-gold by-the-weight for-the-gold (14)

וַעֲבוֹדָה לְכֹל כְּלֵי הַכֶּסֶף בְּמִשְׁקָל לְכָל־
for-all-of by-weight the-silver articles-of for-all-of and-service

כְּלֵי עֲבוֹדָה וַעֲבוֹדָה׃ וּמִשְׁקָל לִמְנֹרוֹת הַזָּהָב
the-gold for-lampstands-of and-weight (15) and-service service articles-of

וְנֵרֹתֵיהֶם זָהָב בְּמִשְׁקַל־ מְנוֹרָה וּמְנוֹרָה
and-lampstand lampstand with-weight-of gold and-lamps-of-them

that you may possess this
good land and pass it on as an
inheritance to your descendants forever.
9"And you, my son Solo-
mon, acknowledge the God of
your father, and serve him
with wholehearted devotion
and with a willing mind, for
the LORD searches every heart
and understands every motive
behind the thoughts. If you
seek him, he will be found by
you; but if you forsake him, he
will reject you forever. 10Con-
sider now, for the LORD has
chosen you to build a temple
as a sanctuary. Be strong and
do the work."
11Then David gave his son
Solomon the plans for the portico of the temple, its buildings, its storerooms, its upper
parts, its inner rooms and the
place of atonement. 12He gave
him the plans of all that the
Spirit had put in his mind for
the courts of the temple of the
LORD and all the surrounding
rooms, for the treasuries of the
temple of God and for the
treasuries for the dedicated
things. 13He gave him instructions for the divisions of the
priests and Levites, and for all
the work of serving in the
temple of the LORD, as well as
for all the articles to be used in
its service. 14He designated the
weight of gold for all the gold
articles to be used in various
kinds of service, and the
weight of silver for all the silver articles to be used in various kinds of service: 15the
weight of gold for the gold
lampstands and their lamps,
with the weight for each

וְנֵרֹתֶיהָ וְלִמְנֹרוֹת הַכֶּסֶף בְּמִשְׁקָל לִמְנוֹרָה
of-lampstand with-weight the-silver and-for-lampstands-of and-lamps-of-her

וְנֵרֹתֶיהָ כַּעֲבוֹדַת מְנוֹרָה וּמְנוֹרָה׃ (16) וְאֶת־ הַזָּהָב מִשְׁקָל
weight the-gold and (16) and-lampstand lampstand as-use-of and-lamps-of-her

לְשֻׁלְחֲנוֹת הַמַּעֲרֶכֶת לְשֻׁלְחָן וְשֻׁלְחָן וְכֶסֶף
and-silver and-table for-table the-consecrated-bread for-tables-of

לְשֻׁלְחֲנוֹת הַכָּסֶף׃ (17) וְהַמִּזְלָגוֹת וְהַמִּזְרָקוֹת
and-the-sprinkling-bowls and-the-forks (17) the-silver for-tables-of

וְהַקְּשָׂוֹת זָהָב טָהוֹר וְלִכְפוֹרֵי הַזָּהָב בְּמִשְׁקָל לִכְפוֹר
for-dish by-weight the-gold and-for-dishes-of pure gold and-the-pitchers

וּכְפוֹר וְלִכְפוֹרֵי הַכֶּסֶף בְּמִשְׁקָל לִכְפוֹר וּכְפוֹר׃
and-dish for-dish by-weight the-silver and-for-dishes-of and-dish

וּלְמִזְבַּח הַקְּטֹרֶת זָהָב מְזֻקָּק בַּמִּשְׁקָל
by-the-weight being-refined gold the-incense and-for-altar-of (18)

וּלְתַבְנִית הַמֶּרְכָּבָה הַכְּרֻבִים זָהָב לְפֹרְשִׂים
for-ones-spreading gold the-cherubim the-chariot and-for-plan-of

וְסֹכְכִים עַל־ אֲרוֹן בְּרִית־ יְהוָה׃ הַכֹּל בִּכְתָב
in-writing the-whole (19) Yahweh covenant-of ark-of over and-ones-sheltering

מִיַּד יְהוָה עָלַי הִשְׂכִּיל כֹּל מַלְאֲכוֹת הַתַּבְנִית׃
the-plan details-of all-of he-gave-understanding on-me Yahweh because-hand-of

וַיֹּאמֶר דָּוִיד לִשְׁלֹמֹה בְּנוֹ חֲזַק וֶאֱמָץ
and-be-courageous! be-strong! son-of-him to-Solomon David and-he-said (20)

וַעֲשֵׂה אַל־ תִּירָא וְאַל־ תֵּחָת כִּי יְהוָה אֱלֹהִים
God Yahweh for you-be-discouraged and-not you-be-afraid not and-do-work!

אֱלֹהַי עִמָּךְ לֹא יַרְפְּךָ וְלֹא יַעַזְבֶךָּ עַד־
until he-will-forsake-you and-not he-will-fail-you not with-you God-of-me

לִכְלוֹת כָּל־ מְלֶאכֶת עֲבוֹדַת בֵּית־ יְהוָה׃ וְהִנֵּה
now-see! (21) Yahweh temple-of service-of work-of all-of to-be-finished

מַחְלְקוֹת הַכֹּהֲנִים וְהַלְוִיִּם לְכָל־ עֲבוֹדַת בֵּית
temple-of work-of for-all-of and-the-Levites the-priests divisions-of

הָאֱלֹהִים וְעִמְּךָ בְכָל־ מְלָאכָה לְכָל־ נָדִיב בַּחָכְמָה
with-the-skill one-willing from-every-of work in-all-of and-with-you the-God

לְכָל־ עֲבוֹדָה וְהַשָּׂרִים וְכָל־ הָעָם לְכָל־
in-all-of the-people and-all-of and-the-officials craft in-any-of

דְּבָרֶיךָ׃ וַיֹּאמֶר דָּוִיד הַמֶּלֶךְ לְכָל־ הַקָּהָל
the-assembly to-whole-of the-king David then-he-said (29:1) commands-of-you

שְׁלֹמֹה בְנִי אֶחָד בָּחַר־ בּוֹ אֱלֹהִים נַעַר וָרָךְ
and-inexperienced young God to-him he-chose one son-of-me Solomon

lampstand and its lamps; and the weight of silver for each silver lampstand and its lamps, according to the use of each lampstand; [16]the weight of gold for each table for consecrated bread; the weight of silver for the silver tables; [17]the weight of pure gold for the forks, sprinkling bowls and pitchers; the weight of gold for each gold dish; the weight of silver for each silver dish; [18]and the weight of the refined gold for the altar of incense. He also gave him the plan for the chariot, that is, the cherubim of gold that spread their wings and shelter the ark of the covenant of the LORD.

[19]"All this is in writing," David said, "because the hand of the LORD was upon me, and he gave me understanding in all the details of the plan."

[20]David also said to Solomon his son, "Be strong and courageous, and do the work. Do not be afraid or discouraged, for the LORD God, my God, is with you. He will not fail you or forsake you until all the work for the service of the temple of the LORD is finished. [21]The divisions of the priests and Levites are ready for all the work on the temple of God, and every willing man skilled in any craft will help you in all the work. The officials and all the people will obey your every command."

Gifts for Building the Temple

29 Then King David said to the whole assembly: "My son Solomon, the one whom God has chosen, is young and inexperienced. The

*16 Most mss have *qamets* under the *beth* (חָן־).

וְהַמְּלָאכָה גְדוֹלָה כִּי לֹא לְאָדָם הַבִּירָה כִּי לַיהוָה אֱלֹהִים׃

God for-Yahweh but the-palace for-man not for great and-the-task

(2) וּבְכָל־ כֹּחִי הֲכִינוֹתִי לְבֵית־ אֱלֹהַי

God-of-me for-temple-of I-provided resource-of-me and-with-all-of (2)

הַזָּהָב ׀ לַזָּהָב וְהַכֶּסֶף לַכֶּסֶף וְהַנְּחֹשֶׁת

and-the-bronze for-the-silver and-the-silver for-the-gold the-gold

לַנְּחֹשֶׁת הַבַּרְזֶל לַבַּרְזֶל וְהָעֵצִים לָעֵצִים אַבְנֵי־

stones-of for-the-woods and-the-woods for-the-iron the-iron for-the-bronze

שֹׁהַם וּמִלּוּאִים אַבְנֵי־ פוּךְ[a] וְרִקְמָה וְכֹל אֶבֶן

stone and-every-of and-colored-stone turquoise stones-of and-settings onyx

יְקָרָה וְאַבְנֵי־ שַׁיִשׁ לָרֹב׃ (3) וְעוֹד בִּרְצוֹתִי

in-to-devote-me and-besides (3) as-many marble and-stones-of fine

בְּבֵית אֱלֹהַי יֶשׁ־ לִי סְגֻלָּה זָהָב וָכָסֶף נָתַתִּי

I-give and-silver gold treasure of-me there-is God-of-me to-temple-of

לְבֵית־ אֱלֹהַי לְמַעְלָה מִכָּל־ הֲכִינוֹתִי לְבֵית הַקֹּדֶשׁ׃

the-holiness for-temple-of I-provided over-all to-above God-of-me for-temple-of

(4) שְׁלֹשֶׁת אֲלָפִים כִּכְּרֵי זָהָב מִזְּהַב אוֹפִיר וְשִׁבְעַת

and-seven-of Ophir of-gold-of gold talents-of thousands three-of (4)

אֲלָפִים כִּכַּר־ כֶּסֶף מְזֻקָּק לָטוּחַ קִירוֹת הַבָּתִּים׃

the-buildings walls-of to-overlay being-refined silver talent-of thousands

(5) לַזָּהָב לַזָּהָב וְלַכֶּסֶף לַכֶּסֶף וּלְכָל־

and-for-all-of for-the-silver and-for-the-silver for-the-gold for-the-gold (5)

מְלָאכָה בְּיַד חָרָשִׁים וּמִי מִתְנַדֵּב לְמַלֹּאות יָדוֹ

hand-of-him to-consecrate one-willing now-who? craftsmen by-hand-of work

הַיּוֹם לַיהוָה׃ (6) וַיִּתְנַדְּבוּ שָׂרֵי הָאָבוֹת

the-fathers leaders-of then-they-gave-willingly (6) to-Yahweh the-day

וְשָׂרֵי ׀ שִׁבְטֵי יִשְׂרָאֵל וְשָׂרֵי הָאֲלָפִים

the-thousands and-commanders-of Israel tribes-of and-officers-of

וְהַמֵּאוֹת וּלְשָׂרֵי מְלֶאכֶת הַמֶּלֶךְ׃ (7) וַיִּתְּנוּ

and-they-gave (7) the-king work-of and-of-officials-of and-the-hundreds

לַעֲבוֹדַת בֵּית־ הָאֱלֹהִים זָהָב כִּכָּרִים חֲמֵשֶׁת־ אֲלָפִים וַאֲדַרְכֹנִים*

and-darics thousands five-of talents gold the-God temple-of to-work-of

רִבּוֹ וְכֶסֶף כִּכָּרִים עֲשֶׂרֶת אֲלָפִים וּנְחֹשֶׁת רִבּוֹ

ten-thousand and-bronze thousands ten-of talents and-silver ten-thousand

וּשְׁמוֹנַת אֲלָפִים כִּכָּרִים וּבַרְזֶל מֵאָה־ אֶלֶף כִּכָּרִים׃

talents thousand hundred and-iron talents thousands and-eight-of

(8) וְהַנִּמְצָא אִתּוֹ אֲבָנִים נָתְנוּ לְאוֹצַר

to-treasury-of they-gave stones with-him and-the-one-being-found (8)

task is great, because this palatial structure is not for man
but for the LORD God. [2]With all
my resources I have provided
for the temple of my God—
gold for the gold work, silver
for the silver, bronze for the
bronze, iron for the iron and
wood for the wood, as well as
onyx for the settings, turquoise, stones of various col-
ors, and all kinds of fine stone
and marble—all of these in
large quantities. [3]Besides, in
my devotion to the temple of
my God I now give my per-
sonal treasures of gold and silver for the temple of my God,
over and above everything I
have provided for this holy
temple: [4]three thousand talents[p] of gold (gold of Ophir)
and seven thousand talents[q]
of refined silver, for the over-
laying of the walls of the
buildings, [5]for the gold work
and the silver work, and for all
the work to be done by the
craftsmen. Now, who is willing to consecrate himself today to the LORD?"
[6]Then the leaders of families, the officers of the tribes of
Israel, the commanders of
thousands and commanders
of hundreds, and the officials
in charge of the king's work
gave willingly. [7]They gave
toward the work on the temple
of God five thousand talents[r]
and ten thousand darics[s] of
gold, ten thousand talents[t] of
silver, eighteen thousand talents[u] of bronze and a hundred
thousand talents[v] of iron.
[8]Any who had precious stones
gave them to the treasury of

[p]4 That is, about 110 tons (about 100 metric tons)
[q]4 That is, about 260 tons (about 240 metric tons)
[r]7 That is, about 190 tons (about 170 metric tons)
[s]7 That is, about 185 pounds (about 84 kilograms)
[t]7 That is, about 375 tons (about 345 metric tons)
[u]7 That is, about 675 tons (about 610 metric tons)
[v]7 That is, about 3,750 tons (about 3,450 metric tons)

*7 Most mss have *dagesh* in the *kaph* (כֹּנִים—).

בֵּית־ יְהוָה עַל יַד־ יְחִיאֵל הַגֵּרְשֻׁנִּי׃ וַיִּשְׂמְחוּ
and-they-rejoiced (9) the-Gershonite Jehiel hand-of into Yahweh temple-of

הָעָם עַל־ הִֽתְנַדְּבָם כִּי בְּלֵב שָׁלֵם הִֽתְנַדְּבוּ
they-gave-freely whole with-heart for to-be-willing-them at the-people

לַיהוָה וְגַם דָּוִיד הַמֶּלֶךְ שָׂמַח שִׂמְחָה גְדוֹלָה׃ וַיְבָרֶךְ
and-he-praised (10) great joy he-rejoiced the-king David and-also to-Yahweh

דָּוִיד אֶת־ יְהוָה לְעֵינֵי כָּל־ הַקָּהָל וַיֹּאמֶר דָּוִיד
David and-he-said the-assembly whole-of in-eyes-of Yahweh *** David

בָּרוּךְ אַתָּה יְהוָה אֱלֹהֵי יִשְׂרָאֵל אָבִינוּ מֵעוֹלָם וְעַד־
and-to from-everlasting father-of-us Israel God-of Yahweh you being-praised

עוֹלָם׃ לְךָ יְהוָה הַגְּדֻלָּה וְהַגְּבוּרָה וְהַתִּפְאֶרֶת
and-the-glory and-the-power the-greatness Yahweh to-you (11) everlasting

וְהַנֵּצַח וְהַהוֹד כִּי־ כֹל בַּשָּׁמַיִם וּבָאָרֶץ
and-in-the-earth in-the-heavens all for and-the-splendor and-the-majesty

לְךָ יְהוָה הַמַּמְלָכָה וְהַמִּתְנַשֵּׂא לְכֹל ׀ לְרֹאשׁ׃
as-head over-all and-the-one-being-exalted the-kingdom Yahweh to-you

וְהָעֹשֶׁר וְהַכָּבוֹד מִלְּפָנֶיךָ וְאַתָּה מוֹשֵׁל
one-ruling and-you from-before-you and-the-honor and-the-wealth (12)

בַּכֹּל וּבְיָדְךָ כֹּחַ וּגְבוּרָה וּבְיָדְךָ
and-in-hand-of-you and-power strength and-in-hand-of-you over-the-all

לְגַדֵּל וּלְחַזֵּק לַכֹּל׃ וְעַתָּה אֱלֹהֵינוּ
God-of-us and-now (13) to-the-all and-to-give-strength to-exalt

מוֹדִים אֲנַחְנוּ לָךְ וּמְהַלְלִים לְשֵׁם תִּפְאַרְתֶּךָ׃
glory-of-you to-name-of and-ones-praising to-you we ones-giving-thanks

וְכִי מִי אֲנִי וּמִי עַמִּי כִּי־ נַעְצֹר כֹּחַ
ability we-should-have that people-of-me and-who? I who? but-indeed (14)

לְהִתְנַדֵּב כָּזֹאת כִּי־ מִמְּךָ הַכֹּל וּמִיָּדְךָ נָתַנּוּ
we-gave and-from-hand-of-you the-all from-you for as-this to-give-generously

לָךְ׃ כִּי־ גֵרִים אֲנַחְנוּ לְפָנֶיךָ וְתוֹשָׁבִים כְּכָל־ אֲבֹתֵינוּ
fathers-of-us as-all-of and-strangers before-you we aliens for (15) to-you

כַּצֵּל ׀ יָמֵינוּ עַל־ הָאָרֶץ וְאֵין מִקְוֶה׃ יְהוָה
Yahweh (16) hope and-there-is-no the-earth on days-of-us like-the-shadow

אֱלֹהֵינוּ כֹל* הֶהָמוֹן הַזֶּה אֲשֶׁר הֲכִינֹנוּ לִבְנוֹת־ לְךָ
for-you to-build we-provided that the-this the-abundance all-of God-of-us

בַיִת לְשֵׁם קָדְשֶׁךָ מִיָּדְךָ הִיא° וּלְךָ הַכֹּל׃
the-all and-to-you he from-hand-of-you Holiness-of-you for-Name-of temple

וְיָדַעְתִּי אֱלֹהַי כִּי אַתָּה בֹּחֵן לֵבָב וּמֵישָׁרִים תִּרְצֶה
you-enjoy and-integrities heart one-testing you that God-of-me and-I-know (17)

the temple of the LORD in the
custody of Jehiel the Gershonite. 9The people rejoiced
at the willing response of
their leaders, for they had
given freely and wholeheartedly to the LORD. David the
king also rejoiced greatly.

David's Prayer

10David praised the LORD in
the presence of the whole assembly, saying,

"Praise be to you, O LORD,
God of our father Israel,
from everlasting to
everlasting.
11Yours, O LORD, is the
greatness and the
power
and the glory and the
majesty and the
splendor,
for everything in heaven
and earth is yours.
Yours, O LORD, is the
kingdom;
you are exalted as head
over all.
12Wealth and honor come
from you;
you are the ruler of all
things.
In your hands are strength
and power
to exalt and give strength
to all.
13Now, our God, we give you
thanks,
and praise your glorious
name.

14"But who am I, and who
are my people, that we should
be able to give as generously
as this? Everything comes
from you, and we have given
you only what comes from
your hand. 15We are aliens and
strangers in your sight, as
were all our forefathers. Our
days on earth are like a shadow, without hope. 16O LORD
our God, as for all this abundance that we have provided
for building you a temple for
your Holy Name, it comes
from your hand, and all of it
belongs to you. 17I know, my
God, that you test the heart
and are pleased with integrity.

*16 Most mss have *dagesh* in the *kaph* (כֹּל).

°16 ק הוא

אֲנִי בְּיֹשֶׁר לְבָבִי הִתְנַדַּבְתִּי כָל־ אֵלֶּה וְעַתָּה
and-now these all-of I-gave-willingly intent-of-me in-honesty-of I

עַמְּךָ הַנִּמְצְאוּ־ פֹה רָאִיתִי בְשִׂמְחָה לְהִתְנַדֶּב־ לָךְ׃
to-you to-give-willingly with-joy I-saw here who-they-are-found people-of-you

יְהוָה אֱלֹהֵי אַבְרָהָם יִצְחָק וְיִשְׂרָאֵל אֲבֹתֵינוּ שָׁמְרָה־זֹּאת
this keep! fathers-of-us and-Israel Isaac Abraham God-of Yahweh (18)

לְעוֹלָם לְיֵצֶר מַחְשְׁבוֹת לְבַב עַמֶּךָ וְהָכֵן
and-keep-loyal! people-of-you heart-of thoughts-of as-desire-of to-forever

לְבָבָם אֵלֶיךָ׃ וְלִשְׁלֹמֹה בְנִי תֵּן לֵבָב שָׁלֵם לִשְׁמוֹר
to-keep whole heart give! son-of-me and-to-Solomon (19) to-you heart-of-them

מִצְוֺתֶיךָ עֵדְוֺתֶיךָ וְחֻקֶּיךָ וְלַעֲשׂוֹת הַכֹּל
the-everything and-to-do and-decrees-of-you requirements-of-you commands-of-you

וְלִבְנוֹת הַבִּירָה אֲשֶׁר־ הֲכִינוֹתִי׃ וַיֹּאמֶר דָּוִיד לְכָל־
to-whole-of David then-he-said (20) I-provided which the-palace and-to-build

הַקָּהָל בָּרְכוּ־ נָא אֶת־ יְהוָה אֱלֹהֵיכֶם וַיְבָרְכוּ כָל־
whole-of so-they-praised God-of-you Yahweh *** now! praise! the-assembly

הַקָּהָל לַיהוָה אֱלֹהֵי אֲבֹתֵיהֶם וַיִּקְּדוּ
and-they-bowed-low fathers-of-them God-of to-Yahweh the-assembly

וַיִּשְׁתַּחֲווּ לַיהוָה וְלַמֶּלֶךְ׃
and-before-the-king before-Yahweh and-they-fell-prostrate

וַיִּזְבְּחוּ לַיהוָה ׀ זְבָחִים וַיַּעֲלוּ עֹלוֹת
burnt-offerings and-they-presented sacrifices to-Yahweh and-they-sacrificed (21)

לַיהוָה לְמָחֳרַת הַיּוֹם הַהוּא פָּרִים אֶלֶף אֵילִים אֶלֶף
thousand rams thousand bulls the-that the-day on-next-day-of to-Yahweh

כְּבָשִׂים אֶלֶף וְנִסְכֵּיהֶם וּזְבָחִים לָרֹב
in-abundance and-sacrifices and-drink-offerings-of-them thousand male-lambs

לְכָל־ יִשְׂרָאֵל׃ וַיֹּאכְלוּ וַיִּשְׁתּוּ לִפְנֵי יְהוָה
Yahweh in-presences-of and-they-drank and-they-ate (22) Israel for-all-of

בַּיּוֹם הַהוּא בְּשִׂמְחָה גְדוֹלָה וַיַּמְלִיכוּ שֵׁנִית
second-time then-they-acknowledged-as-king great with-joy the-that on-the-day

לִשְׁלֹמֹה בֶן־ דָּוִיד וַיִּמְשְׁחוּ לַיהוָה לְנָגִיד
as-ruler before-Yahweh and-they-anointed David son-of to-Solomon

וּלְצָדוֹק לְכֹהֵן׃ וַיֵּשֶׁב שְׁלֹמֹה עַל־ כִּסֵּא יְהוָה ׀ לְמֶלֶךְ
as-king Yahweh throne-of on Solomon so-he-sat (23) as-priest and-to-Zadok

תַּחַת־ דָּוִיד אָבִיו וַיַּצְלַח וַיִּשְׁמְעוּ אֵלָיו
to-him and-they-obeyed and-he-prospered father-of-him David in-place-of

כָּל־ יִשְׂרָאֵל׃ וְכָל־ הַשָּׂרִים וְהַגִּבֹּרִים וְגַם
and-also and-the-mighty-men the-officers and-all-of (24) Israel all-of

All these things have I given
willingly and with honest intent. And now I have seen
with joy how willingly your
people who are here have giv-
en to you.
[18]O LORD, God of our
fathers Abraham, Isaac and Israel, keep this desire in the
hearts of your people forever,
and keep their hearts loyal to
you.
[19]And give my son Solo-
mon the wholehearted devotion to keep your commands,
requirements and decrees and
to do everything to build the
palatial structure for which I
have provided."
[20]Then David said to the
whole assembly, "Praise the
LORD your God." So they all
praised the LORD, the God of
their fathers; they bowed low
and fell prostrate before the
LORD and the king.

Solomon Acknowledged as King

[21]The next day they made
sacrifices to the LORD and
presented burnt offerings to
him: a thousand bulls, a thousand rams and a thousand
male lambs, together with
their drink offerings, and other sacrifices in abundance for
all Israel.
[22]They ate and drank
with great joy in the presence
of the LORD that day.
Then they acknowledged
Solomon son of David as king
a second time, anointing him
before the LORD to be ruler and
Zadok to be priest.
[23]So Solo-
mon sat on the throne of the
LORD as king in place of his
father David. He prospered
and all Israel obeyed him.
[24]All
the officers and mighty men,

כָּל־ בְּנֵי הַמֶּלֶךְ דָּוִיד נָתְנוּ יָד תַּחַת שְׁלֹמֹה הַמֶּלֶךְ׃
the-king Solomon under hand they-put David the-king sons-of all-of

וַיְגַדֵּל יְהוָה אֶת־ שְׁלֹמֹה לְמַעְלָה לְעֵינֵי כָּל־ יִשְׂרָאֵל
Israel all-of in-eyes-of to-upward Solomon *** Yahweh and-he-exalted (25)

וַיִּתֵּן עָלָיו הוֹד מַלְכוּת אֲשֶׁר לֹא־ הָיָה עַל־ כָּל־ מֶלֶךְ
king any-of on he-was not that royalty splendor-of on-him and-he-bestowed

לְפָנָיו עַל־יִשְׂרָאֵל׃ וְדָוִיד בֶּן־ יִשָׁי מָלַךְ עַל־ כָּל־
all-of over he-was-king Jesse son-of and-David (26) Israel over before-him

יִשְׂרָאֵל׃ וְהַיָּמִים אֲשֶׁר מָלַךְ עַל־יִשְׂרָאֵל אַרְבָּעִים שָׁנָה בְּחֶבְרוֹן
in-Hebron year forty Israel over he-ruled which and-the-days (27) Israel

מָלַךְ שֶׁבַע שָׁנִים וּבִירוּשָׁלַםִ מָלַךְ שְׁלֹשִׁים וְשָׁלוֹשׁ׃
and-three thirty he-ruled and-in-Jerusalem years seven he-ruled

וַיָּמָת בְּשֵׂיבָה טוֹבָה שְׂבַע יָמִים עֹשֶׁר וְכָבוֹד
and-honor wealth days full-of good at-old-age and-he-died (28)

וַיִּמְלֹךְ שְׁלֹמֹה בְנוֹ תַּחְתָּיו׃ וְדִבְרֵי
and-events-of (29) in-place-of-him son-of-him Solomon and-he-became-king

דָּוִיד הַמֶּלֶךְ הָרִאשֹׁנִים וְהָאֲחֲרֹנִים* הִנָּם כְּתוּבִים
ones-being-written see-they! and-the-ends the-beginnings the-king David

עַל־ דִּבְרֵי שְׁמוּאֵל הָרֹאֶה וְעַל־ דִּבְרֵי נָתָן הַנָּבִיא
the-prophet Nathan records-of and-in the-seer Samuel records-of in

וְעַל־ דִּבְרֵי גָּד הַחֹזֶה׃ עִם כָּל־ מַלְכוּתוֹ
reign-of-him all-of with (30) the-seer Gad records-of and-in

וּגְבוּרָתוֹ וְהָעִתִּים אֲשֶׁר עָבְרוּ עָלָיו
around-him they-surrounded that and-the-circumstances and-power-of-him

וְעַל־ יִשְׂרָאֵל וְעַל כָּל־ מַמְלְכוֹת הָאֲרָצוֹת׃
the-lands kingdoms-of all-of and-around Israel and-around

as well as all of King David's
sons, pledged their submis-
sion to King Solomon.
25The LORD highly exalted
Solomon in the sight of all Israel and bestowed on him royal splendor such as no king
over Israel ever had before.

The Death of David

26David son of Jesse was
king over all Israel. 27He ruled
over Israel forty years—seven
in Hebron and thirty-three in
Jerusalem. 28He died at a good
old age, having enjoyed long
life, wealth and honor. His
son Solomon succeeded him
as king.
29As for the events of King
David's reign, from beginning
to end, they are written in the
records of Samuel the seer, the
records of Nathan the prophet
and the records of Gad the
seer, 30together with the details of his reign and power,
and the circumstances that
surrounded him and Israel
and the kingdoms of all the
other lands.

*29 Most mss have *pathah* under the *aleph* and *hateph pathah* under the *beth* (אַחֲ־).

וַיִּתְחַזֵּק שְׁלֹמֹה בֶן־ דָּוִיד עַל־ מַלְכוּתוֹ
kingdom-of-him over David son-of Solomon and-he-established-himself (1:1)

וַיהוָה אֱלֹהָיו עִמּוֹ וַיְגַדְּלֵהוּ לְמָעְלָה׃
to-upward and-he-made-great-him with-him God-of-him for-Yahweh

וַיֹּאמֶר שְׁלֹמֹה לְכָל־ יִשְׂרָאֵל לְשָׂרֵי הָאֲלָפִים
the-thousands to-commanders-of Israel to-all-of Solomon then-he-spoke (2)

וְהַמֵּאוֹת וְלַשֹּׁפְטִים וּלְכֹל נָשִׂיא לְכָל־
in-all-of leader and-to-all-of and-to-the-ones-being-judges and-the-hundreds

יִשְׂרָאֵל רָאשֵׁי הָאָבוֹת׃ וַיֵּלְכוּ שְׁלֹמֹה וְכָל־ הַקָּהָל
the-assembly and-all-of Solomon and-they-went (3) the-fathers heads-of Israel

עִמּוֹ לַבָּמָה אֲשֶׁר בְּגִבְעוֹן כִּי־ שָׁם הָיָה אֹהֶל
Tent-of he-was there for at-Gibeon that to-the-high-place with-him

מוֹעֵד הָאֱלֹהִים אֲשֶׁר עָשָׂה מֹשֶׁה עֶבֶד־ יְהוָה בַּמִּדְבָּר׃
in-the-desert Yahweh servant-of Moses he-made which the-God Meeting-of

אֲבָל אֲרוֹן הָאֱלֹהִים הֶעֱלָה דָוִיד מִקִּרְיַת יְעָרִים
Jearim from-Kiriath David he-brought-up the-God ark-of now (4)

בַּהֵכִין לוֹ דָּוִיד כִּי נָטָה־ לוֹ אֹהֶל
tent for-him he-pitched because David for-him to-what-he-prepared

בִּירוּשָׁלִָם׃ וּמִזְבַּח הַנְּחֹשֶׁת אֲשֶׁר עָשָׂה בְּצַלְאֵל בֶּן־ אוּרִי
Uri son-of Bezalel he-made that the-bronze but-altar-of (5) in-Jerusalem

בֶן־ חוּר שָׂם* לִפְנֵי מִשְׁכַּן יְהוָה וַיִּדְרְשֵׁהוּ
and-he-inquired-of-him Yahweh tabernacle-of in-front-of he-put Hur son-of

שְׁלֹמֹה וְהַקָּהָל׃ וַיַּעַל שְׁלֹמֹה שָׁם עַל־ מִזְבַּח
altar-of to there Solomon and-he-went-up (6) and-the-assembly Solomon

הַנְּחֹשֶׁת לִפְנֵי יְהוָה אֲשֶׁר לְאֹהֶל מוֹעֵד וַיַּעַל עָלָיו
on-him and-he-offered Meeting in-Tent-of that Yahweh before the-bronze

עֹלוֹת אָלֶף׃ בַּלַּיְלָה הַהוּא נִרְאָה אֱלֹהִים
God he-appeared the-that in-the-night (7) thousand burnt-offerings

לִשְׁלֹמֹה וַיֹּאמֶר לוֹ שְׁאַל מָה אֶתֶּן־ לָךְ׃
to-you I-should-give whatever ask! to-him and-he-said to-Solomon

וַיֹּאמֶר שְׁלֹמֹה לֵאלֹהִים אַתָּה עָשִׂיתָ עִם־ דָּוִיד אָבִי
father-of-me David to you-showed you to-God Solomon and-he-answered (8)

חֶסֶד גָּדוֹל וְהִמְלַכְתַּנִי תַּחְתָּיו׃ עַתָּה יְהוָה אֱלֹהִים
God Yahweh now (9) in-place-of-him and-you-made-king-me great kindness

יֵאָמֵן דְּבָרְךָ עִם דָּוִיד אָבִי כִּי אַתָּה
you for father-of-me David to promise-of-you let-him-be-confirmed

הִמְלַכְתַּנִי עַל־ עַם רַב כַּעֲפַר הָאָרֶץ׃ עַתָּה חָכְמָה
wisdom now (10) the-earth as-dust-of numerous people over you-made-king-me

Solomon Asks for Wisdom

1 Solomon son of David
established himself firmly
over his kingdom, for the
LORD his God was with him
and made him exceedingly
great.
[2]Then Solomon spoke to all
Israel—to the commanders of
thousands and commanders
of hundreds, to the judges and
to all the leaders in Israel, the
heads of families— [3]and Solomon and the whole assembly
went to the high place at Gibeon, for God's Tent of Meeting
was there, which Moses the
LORD's servant had made in
the desert. [4]Now David had
brought up the ark of God
from Kiriath Jearim to the
place he had prepared for it,
because he had pitched a tent
for it in Jerusalem. [5]But the
bronze altar that Bezalel son of
Uri, the son of Hur, had made
was in Gibeon in front of the
tabernacle of the LORD; so
Solomon and the assembly inquired of him there. [6]Solomon
went up to the bronze altar before the LORD in the Tent of
Meeting and offered a thousand burnt offerings on it.
[7]That night God appeared to
Solomon and said to him,
"Ask for whatever you want
me to give you."
[8]Solomon answered God,
"You have shown great kindness to David my father and
have made me king in his
place. [9]Now, LORD God, let
your promise to my father David be confirmed, for you have
made me king over a people
who are as numerous as the
dust of the earth. [10]Give me

*5 The NIV reads this word as שָׁם, *there.*

וּמַדָּע תֶּן־ לִי וְאֵצְאָה לִפְנֵי הָעָם־ הַזֶּה
the-this the-people before that-I-may-go-out to-me give! and-knowledge

וְאָבוֹאָה כִּי־ מִי יִשְׁפֹּט אֶת־ עַמְּךָ הַזֶּה
the-this people-of-you *** he-can-govern who? for and-I-may-come-in

הַגָּדוֹל׃ (11) וַיֹּאמֶר־ אֱלֹהִים ׀ לִשְׁלֹמֹה יַעַן אֲשֶׁר הָיְתָה זֹאת עִם־
in this she-was that since to-Solomon God and-he-said (11) the-great

לְבָבֶךָ וְלֹא־ שָׁאַלְתָּ עֹשֶׁר נְכָסִים וְכָבוֹד וְאֵת נֶפֶשׁ
life-of nor or-honor riches wealth you-asked and-not heart-of-you

שֹׂנְאֶיךָ וְגַם־ יָמִים רַבִּים לֹא שָׁאָלְתָּ וַתִּשְׁאַל־
but-you-asked you-asked not many days and-also ones-being-enemies-of-you

לְךָ חָכְמָה וּמַדָּע אֲשֶׁר תִּשְׁפּוֹט אֶת־ עַמִּי אֲשֶׁר
whom people-of-me *** you-will-govern which and-knowledge wisdom for-you

הִמְלַכְתִּיךָ עָלָיו׃ (12) הַחָכְמָה וְהַמַּדָּע נָתוּן
being-given and-the-knowledge the-wisdom (12) over-him I-made-king-you

לָךְ וְעֹשֶׁר וּנְכָסִים וְכָבוֹד אֶתֶּן־ לָךְ אֲשֶׁר ׀ לֹא־ הָיָה
he-was not that to-you I-will-give and-honor and-riches also-wealth to-you

כֵן לַמְּלָכִים אֲשֶׁר לְפָנֶיךָ וְאַחֲרֶיךָ לֹא יִהְיֶה־ כֵּן׃
such he-will-be not and-after-you before-you who to-the-kings such

(13) וַיָּבֹא שְׁלֹמֹה לַבָּמָה אֲשֶׁר־ בְּגִבְעוֹן יְרוּשָׁלַםִ
Jerusalem in-Gibeon that from-the-high-place Solomon then-he-went (13)

מִלִּפְנֵי אֹהֶל מוֹעֵד וַיִּמְלֹךְ עַל־ יִשְׂרָאֵל׃ (14) וַיֶּאֱסֹף
and-he-accumulated (14) Israel over and-he-reigned Meeting Tent-of from-before

שְׁלֹמֹה רֶכֶב וּפָרָשִׁים וַיְהִי־ לוֹ אֶלֶף וְאַרְבַּע־ מֵאוֹת
hundreds and-four-of thousand to-him and-he-was and-horses chariot Solomon

רֶכֶב וּשְׁנֵים־ עָשָׂר אֶלֶף פָּרָשִׁים וַיַּנִּיחֵם בְּעָרֵי הָרֶכֶב
the-chariot in-cities-of and-he-kept-them horses thousand ten and-two chariot

וְעִם־ הַמֶּלֶךְ בִּירוּשָׁלִָם׃ (15) וַיִּתֵּן הַמֶּלֶךְ אֶת־ הַכֶּסֶף
the-silver *** the-king and-he-made (15) in-Jerusalem the-king and-with

וְאֶת־ הַזָּהָב בִּירוּשָׁלִַם כָּאֲבָנִים וְאֵת הָאֲרָזִים נָתַן
he-made the-cedars and like-the-stones in-Jerusalem the-gold and

כַּשִּׁקְמִים אֲשֶׁר־ בַּשְּׁפֵלָה לָרֹב׃
as-plentiful in-the-foothill that like-the-sycamore-fig-trees

(16) וּמוֹצָא הַסּוּסִים אֲשֶׁר לִשְׁלֹמֹה מִמִּצְרָיִם וּמִקְוֵא
and-from-Kue from-Egypt of-Solomon that the-horses and-import-of (16)

סֹחֲרֵי הַמֶּלֶךְ מִקְוֵא יִקְחוּ בִּמְחִיר׃
by-purchase they-acquired from-Kue the-king ones-being-merchants-of

(17) וַיַּעֲלוּ וַיּוֹצִיאוּ מִמִּצְרַיִם מֶרְכָּבָה בְּשֵׁשׁ
for-six-of chariot from-Egypt and-they-brought-out and-they-brought-up (17)

wisdom and knowledge, that I
may lead this people, for who
is able to govern this great
people of yours?"
11God said to Solomon,
"Since this is your heart's desire and you have not asked
for wealth, riches or honor,
nor for the death of your enemies, and since you have not
asked for a long life but for
wisdom and knowledge to
govern my people over whom
I have made you king, 12there-
fore wisdom and knowledge
will be given you. And I will
also give you wealth, riches
and honor, such as no king
who was before you ever had
and none after you will have."
13Then Solomon went to
Jerusalem from the high place
at Gibeon, from before the
Tent of Meeting. And he
reigned over Israel.
14Solomon accumulated
chariots and horses; he had
fourteen hundred chariots and
twelve thousand horses,[a]
which he kept in the chariot
cities and also with him in
Jerusalem. 15The king made
silver and gold as common in
Jerusalem as stones, and cedar
as plentiful as sycamore-fig
trees in the foothills. 16Solo-
mon's horses were imported
from Egypt[b] and from
Kue[c]—the royal merchants
purchased them from Kue.
17They imported a chariot
from Egypt for six hundred

[a]14 Or *charioteers*
[b]16 Or possibly *Muzur*, a region in Cilicia; also in verse 17
[c]16 Probably Cilicia

מֵאוֹת כֶּסֶף וְסוּס בַּחֲמִשִּׁים וּמֵאָה וְכֵן לְכָל־
to-all-of and-same and-hundred for-fifty and-horse silver hundreds

מַלְכֵי הַחִתִּים וּמַלְכֵי אֲרָם בְּיָדָם יוֹצִיאוּ׃
they-exported by-hand-of-them Aram and-kings-of the-Hittites kings-of

וַיֹּאמֶר שְׁלֹמֹה לִבְנוֹת בַּיִת לְשֵׁם יְהוָה וּבַיִת
and-palace Yahweh for-Name-of temple to-build Solomon and-he-ordered *(18)

לְמַלְכוּתוֹ׃ וַיִּסְפֹּר שְׁלֹמֹה שִׁבְעִים אֶלֶף אִישׁ
man thousand seventy Solomon and-he-conscripted (2:1) for-royalty-of-him

סַבָּל וּשְׁמוֹנִים אֶלֶף אִישׁ חֹצֵב בָּהָר וּמְנַצְּחִים
and-ones-being-foremen in-the-hill cutting man thousand and-eighty carrier

עֲלֵיהֶם שְׁלֹשֶׁת אֲלָפִים וְשֵׁשׁ מֵאוֹת׃ וַיִּשְׁלַח שְׁלֹמֹה
Solomon and-he-sent (2) hundreds and-six-of thousands three-of over-them

אֶל־חוּרָם מֶלֶךְ־צֹר לֵאמֹר כַּאֲשֶׁר עָשִׂיתָ עִם־דָּוִיד אָבִי
father-of-me David for you-did just-as to-say Tyre king-of Huram to

וַתִּשְׁלַח־לוֹ אֲרָזִים לִבְנוֹת־לוֹ בַיִת לָשֶׁבֶת בּוֹ׃ הִנֵּה
see! (3) in-him to-live palace for-him to-build cedars to-him when-you-sent

אֲנִי בוֹנֶה־בַיִת לְשֵׁם ׀ יְהוָה אֱלֹהָי לְהַקְדִּישׁ לוֹ לְהַקְטִיר
to-burn to-him to-dedicate God-of-me Yahweh for-Name-of temple building I

לְפָנָיו קְטֹרֶת־סַמִּים וּמַעֲרֶכֶת תָּמִיד
regularly and-consecrated-bread fragrances incense-of before-him

וְעֹלוֹת לַבֹּקֶר וְלָעֶרֶב לַשַּׁבָּתוֹת
on-the-Sabbaths and-for-the-evening for-the-morning and-burnt-offerings

וְלֶחֳדָשִׁים וּלְמוֹעֲדֵי יְהוָה אֱלֹהֵינוּ לְעוֹלָם
to-forever God-of-us Yahweh and-at-appointed-feasts-of and-on-the-New-Moons

זֹאת עַל־יִשְׂרָאֵל׃ וְהַבַּיִת אֲשֶׁר־אֲנִי בוֹנֶה גָּדוֹל כִּי־גָדוֹל
great because great building I that and-the-temple (4) Israel over this

אֱלֹהֵינוּ מִכָּל־הָאֱלֹהִים׃ וּמִי יַעֲצָר־כֹּחַ לִבְנוֹת־
to-build ability he-has but-who? (5) the-gods more-than-all-of God-of-us

לוֹ בַיִת כִּי הַשָּׁמַיִם וּשְׁמֵי הַשָּׁמַיִם לֹא
not the-heavens even-heavens-of the-heavens since temple for-him

יְכַלְכְּלֻהוּ וּמִי אֲנִי אֲשֶׁר אֶבְנֶה־לוֹ בַיִת כִּי
except temple for-him I-should-build that I then-who? they-can-contain-him

אִם־לְהַקְטִיר לְפָנָיו׃ וְעַתָּה שְׁלַח־לִי אִישׁ־חָכָם
skilled man to-me send! so-now (6) before-him to-burn-sacrifice only

לַעֲשׂוֹת בַּזָּהָב וּבַכֶּסֶף וּבַנְּחֹשֶׁת וּבַבַּרְזֶל
and-in-the-iron and-in-the-bronze and-in-the-silver in-the-gold to-work

וּבָאַרְגְּוָן וְכַרְמִיל וּתְכֵלֶת וְיֹדֵעַ לְפַתֵּחַ
to-engrave and-being-experienced and-blue-yarn and-crimson and-in-the-purple

shekels[d] of silver, and a horse
for a hundred and fifty.[e] They
also exported them to all the
kings of the Hittites and of the
Arameans.

Preparations for Building the Temple

2 Solomon gave orders to
build a temple for the
Name of the LORD and a royal
palace for himself. ²He conscripted seventy thousand
men as carriers and eighty
thousand as stonecutters in
the hills and thirty-six hundred as foremen over them.
³Solomon sent this message
to Hiram[f] king of Tyre:

"Send me cedar logs as
you did for my father Da-
vid when you sent him ce-
dar to build a palace to live
in. ⁴Now I am about to
build a temple for the
Name of the LORD my God
and to dedicate it to him for
burning fragrant incense
before him, for setting out
the consecrated bread regularly, and for making burnt
offerings every morning
and evening and on Sab-
baths and New Moons and
at the appointed feasts of
the LORD our God. This is a
lasting ordinance for Israel.
⁵"The temple I am going
to build will be great, because our God is greater
than all other gods. ⁶But
who is able to build a temple for him, since the heavens, even the highest heavens, cannot contain him?
Who then am I to build a
temple for him, except as a
place to burn sacrifices before him?
⁷"Send me, therefore, a
man skilled to work in gold
and silver, bronze and iron,
and in purple, crimson and
blue yarn, and experienced

[d]17 That is, about 15 pounds (about 7 kilograms)
[e]17 That is, about 3 3/4 pounds (about 1.7 kilograms)
[f]3 Hebrew *Huram*, a variant of *Hiram*; also in verses 11 and 12

**18* The Hebrew numeration of chapter 2 begins with verse 2 in the English; thus, there is a one-verse discrepancy throughout the chapter.

פִּתּוּחִים עִם־ הַחֲכָמִים אֲשֶׁר עִמִּי בִּיהוּדָה וּבִירוּשָׁלִַם
and-in-Jerusalem in-Judah with-me who the-skilled-craftsmen with engravings

אֲשֶׁר הֵכִין דָּוִיד אָבִי׃ וּשְׁלַח־ לִי עֲצֵי אֲרָזִים
cedars logs-of to-me and-send! (7) father-of-me David he-provided whom

בְּרוֹשִׁים וְאַלְגּוּמִּים מֵהַלְּבָנוֹן כִּי אֲנִי יָדַעְתִּי אֲשֶׁר עֲבָדֶיךָ
men-of-you that I-know I for from-the-Lebanon and-algums pines

יוֹדְעִים לִכְרוֹת עֲצֵי לְבָנוֹן וְהִנֵּה עֲבָדַי עִם־
with men-of-me and-see! Lebanon timbers-of to-cut ones-being-skilled

עֲבָדֶיךָ׃ וּלְהָכִין לִי עֵצִים לָרֹב כִּי הַבַּיִת
the-temple because as-plenty lumbers to-me and-to-provide (8) men-of-you

אֲשֶׁר־ אֲנִי בוֹנֶה גָּדוֹל וְהַפְלֵא׃ וְהִנֵּה
and-see! (9) and-to-be-magnificent large building I that

לַחֹטְבִים ׀ לְכֹרְתֵי ׀ הָעֵצִים נָתַתִּי חִטִּים ׀
wheats I-will-give the-timbers to-ones-cutting-of to-the-ones-being-woodsmen

מַכּוֹת לַעֲבָדֶיךָ כֹּרִים עֶשְׂרִים אֶלֶף וּשְׂעֹרִים כֹּרִים עֶשְׂרִים
twenty cors and-barleys thousand twenty cors to-servants-of-you ones-ground

אֶלֶף וְיַיִן בַּתִּים עֶשְׂרִים אֶלֶף וְשֶׁמֶן בַּתִּים עֶשְׂרִים אָלֶף׃
thousand twenty baths and-olive-oil thousand twenty baths and-wine thousand

וַיֹּאמֶר חוּרָם מֶלֶךְ־ צֹר בִּכְתָב וַיִּשְׁלַח אֶל־ שְׁלֹמֹה
Solomon to and-he-sent by-letter Tyre king-of Huram and-he-replied (10)

בְּאַהֲבַת יְהוָה אֶת־ עַמּוֹ נְתָנְךָ עֲלֵיהֶם מֶלֶךְ׃
king over-them he-made-you people-of-him *** Yahweh because-to-love

וַיֹּאמֶר חוּרָם בָּרוּךְ יְהוָה אֱלֹהֵי יִשְׂרָאֵל אֲשֶׁר עָשָׂה אֶת־
*** he-made who Israel God-of Yahweh being-praised Huram and-he-said (11)

הַשָּׁמַיִם וְאֶת־ הָאָרֶץ אֲשֶׁר נָתַן לְדָוִיד הַמֶּלֶךְ בֵּן חָכָם יוֹדֵעַ
knowing-of wise son the-king to-David he-gave who the-earth and the-heavens

שֵׂכֶל וּבִינָה אֲשֶׁר יִבְנֶה־ בַיִת לַיהוָה וּבַיִת
and-palace for-Yahweh temple he-will-build who and-discernment intelligence

לְמַלְכוּתוֹ׃ וְעַתָּה שָׁלַחְתִּי אִישׁ־ חָכָם יוֹדֵעַ בִּינָה
discernment knowing-of skilled man I-send and-now (12) for-kingdom-of-him

לְחוּרָם אָבִי׃ בֶּן־ אִשָּׁה מִן־ בְּנוֹת דָּן וְאָבִיו
and-father-of-him Dan daughters-of from woman son-of (13) Abi namely-Huram

אִישׁ־ צֹרִי יוֹדֵעַ לַעֲשׂוֹת בַּזָּהָב־ וּבַכֶּסֶף בַּנְּחֹשֶׁת
in-the-bronze and-in-the-silver in-the-gold to-work being-trained Tyrian man

בַּבַּרְזֶל בָּאֲבָנִים וּבָעֵצִים בָּאַרְגָּמָן בַּתְּכֵלֶת
with-the-blue-yarn with-the-purple and-in-the-woods in-the-stones in-the-iron

וּבַבּוּץ וּבַכַּרְמִיל וּלְפַתֵּחַ כָּל־ פִּתּוּחַ
engraving every-of and-to-engrave and-with-the-crimson and-with-the-fine-linen

in the art of engraving, to work in Judah and Jerusalem with my skilled craftsmen, whom my father David provided.

8"Send me also cedar, pine and algum[g] logs from Lebanon, for I know that your men are skilled in cutting timber there. My men will work with yours 9to provide me with plenty of lumber, because the temple I build must be large and magnificent. 10I will give your servants, the woodsmen who cut the timber, twenty thousand cors[h] of ground wheat, twenty thousand cors of barley, twenty thousand baths[i] of wine and twenty thousand baths of olive oil."

11Hiram king of Tyre replied by letter to Solomon:

"Because the LORD loves his people, he has made you their king."

12And Hiram added:

"Praise be to the LORD, the God of Israel, who made heaven and earth! He has given King David a wise son, endowed with intelligence and discernment, who will build a temple for the LORD and a palace for himself.

13"I am sending you Huram-Abi, a man of great skill, 14whose mother was from Dan and whose father was from Tyre. He is trained to work in gold and silver, bronze and iron, stone and wood, and with purple and blue and crimson yarn and fine linen. He is experienced in all kinds

g8 Probably a variant of *almug;* possibly juniper

h10 That is, probably about 125,000 bushels (about 4,400 kiloliters)

i10 That is, probably about 115,000 gallons (about 440 kiloliters)

*See the note on page 85.

וְלַחְשֹׁב כָּל־ מַחֲשֶׁבֶת אֲשֶׁר יִנָּתֶן־ לוֹ עִם־ חֲכָמֶיךָ
craftsmen-of-you with to-him he-is-given that design any-of and-to-execute

וְחַכְמֵי אֲדֹנִי דָּוִיד אָבִיךָ׃ (14) וְעַתָּה הַחִטִּים
the-wheats and-now (14) father-of-you David lord-of-me and-craftsmen-of

וְהַשְּׂעֹרִים הַשֶּׁמֶן וְהַיַּיִן אֲשֶׁר אָמַר אֲדֹנִי
lord-of-me he-promised that and-the-wine the-olive-oil and-the-barleys

יִשְׁלַח לַעֲבָדָיו׃ (15) וַאֲנַחְנוּ נִכְרֹת עֵצִים מִן־
from logs we-will-cut and-we (15) to-servants-of-him let-him-send

הַלְּבָנוֹן כְּכָל־ צָרְכֶּךָ וּנְבִיאֵם לְךָ רַפְסֹדוֹת עַל־יָם
sea by rafts to-you and-we-will-send-them need-of-you as-all-of the-Lebanon

יָפוֹ וְאַתָּה תַּעֲלֶה אֹתָם יְרוּשָׁלָםִ׃ (16) וַיִּסְפֹּר
then-he-took-census (16) Jerusalem them you-can-take-up then-you Joppa

שְׁלֹמֹה כָּל־ הָאֲנָשִׁים הַגֵּירִים אֲשֶׁר בְּאֶרֶץ יִשְׂרָאֵל אַחֲרֵי הַסְּפָר
the-census after Israel in-land-of who the-aliens the-men all-of Solomon

אֲשֶׁר סְפָרָם דָּוִיד אָבִיו וַיִּמָּצְאוּ מֵאָה
hundred and-they-were-found father-of-him David he-took-census-of-them that

וַחֲמִשִּׁים אֶלֶף וּשְׁלֹשֶׁת אֲלָפִים וְשֵׁשׁ מֵאוֹת׃
hundreds and-six-of thousands and-three-of thousand and-fifty

(17) וַיַּעַשׂ מֵהֶם שִׁבְעִים אֶלֶף סַבָּל וּשְׁמֹנִים אֶלֶף
thousand and-eighty carrier thousand seventy of-them and-he-assigned (17)

חֹצֵב בָּהָר וּשְׁלֹשֶׁת אֲלָפִים וְשֵׁשׁ מֵאוֹת
hundreds and-six-of thousands and-three-of in-the-hill cutting

מְנַצְּחִים לְהַעֲבִיד אֶת־ הָעָם׃ (3:1) וַיָּחֶל שְׁלֹמֹה
Solomon then-he-began (3:1) the-people *** to-make-work ones-being-foremen

לִבְנוֹת אֶת־ בֵּית־ יְהוָה בִּירוּשָׁלַםִ בְּהַר הַמּוֹרִיָּה אֲשֶׁר
where the-Moriah on-Mount-of in-Jerusalem Yahweh temple-of *** to-build

נִרְאָה לְדָוִיד אָבִיהוּ אֲשֶׁר הֵכִין בִּמְקוֹם דָּוִיד
David on-place-of he-provided which father-of-him to-David he-appeared

בְּגֹרֶן אָרְנָן הַיְבוּסִי׃ (2) וַיָּחֶל לִבְנוֹת
to-build and-he-began (2) the-Jebusite Ornan on-threshing-floor-of

בַּחֹדֶשׁ הַשֵּׁנִי בַּשֵּׁנִי בִּשְׁנַת אַרְבַּע לְמַלְכוּתוֹ׃
of-reign-of-him four in-year-of on-the-second the-second in-the-month

(3) וְאֵלֶּה הוּסַד שְׁלֹמֹה לִבְנוֹת אֶת־ בֵּית הָאֱלֹהִים
the-God temple-of *** to-build Solomon to-be-founded and-these (3)

הָאֹרֶךְ אַמּוֹת בַּמִּדָּה הָרִאשׁוֹנָה אַמּוֹת שִׁשִּׁים וְרֹחַב אַמּוֹת
cubits and-width sixty cubits the-old by-the-standard cubits the-length

עֶשְׂרִים׃ (4) וְהָאוּלָם אֲשֶׁר עַל־ פְּנֵי הָאֹרֶךְ עַל־ פְּנֵי רֹחַב־
width-of fronts-of at the-length fronts-of at that and-the-portico (4) twenty

of engraving and can execute any design given to him. He will work with your craftsmen and with those of my lord, David your father.

15"Now let my lord send his servants the wheat and barley and the olive oil and wine he promised,
16and we will cut all the logs from Lebanon that you need and will float them in rafts by sea down to Joppa. You can then take them up to Jerusalem."

17Solomon took a census of all the aliens who were in Israel, after the census his father David had taken; and they were found to be 153,600.
18He assigned 70,000 of them to be carriers and 80,000 to be stonecutters in the hills, with 3,600 foremen over them to keep the people working.

Solomon Builds the Temple

3 Then Solomon began to build the temple of the LORD in Jerusalem on Mount Moriah, where the LORD had appeared to his father David. It was on the threshing floor of Araunah[j] the Jebusite, the place provided by David.
2He began building on the second day of the second month in the fourth year of his reign.
3The foundation Solomon laid for building the temple of God was sixty cubits long and twenty cubits wide[k] (using the cubit of the old standard).
4The

[j]1 Hebrew *Ornan*, a variant of *Araunah*
[k]3 That is, about 90 feet (about 27 meters) long and 30 feet (about 9 meters) wide

*See the note on page 85.

הַבַּיִת אַמּוֹת עֶשְׂרִים וְהַגֹּבַהּ מֵאָה וְעֶשְׂרִים וַיְצַפֵּהוּ
and-he-overlaid-him and-twenty hundred and-the-height twenty cubits the-temple

מִפְּנִימָה זָהָב טָהוֹר׃ וְאֵת׀ הַבַּיִת הַגָּדוֹל חִפָּה עֵץ בְּרוֹשִׁים
pines wood-of he-paneled the-main the-hall and (5) pure gold on-inside

וַיְחַפֵּהוּ זָהָב טוֹב וַיַּעַל עָלָיו תִּמֹּרִים וְשַׁרְשְׁרוֹת׃
and-chains palm-trees on-him and-he-decorated fine gold and-he-covered-him

וַיְצַף אֶת־ הַבַּיִת אֶבֶן יְקָרָה לְתִפְאָרֶת וְהַזָּהָב
and-the-gold for-beauty precious stone the-temple *** and-he-adorned (6)

זְהַב פַּרְוָיִם׃ וַיְחַף אֶת־ הַבַּיִת הַקֹּרוֹת
the-ceiling-beams the-temple *** and-he-overlaid (7) Parvaim gold-of

הַסִּפִּים וְקִירוֹתָיו וְדַלְתוֹתָיו זָהָב וּפִתַּח כְּרוּבִים
cherubim and-he-carved gold and-doors-of-him and-walls-of-him the-doorframes

עַל־ הַקִּירוֹת׃ וַיַּעַשׂ אֶת־ בֵּית־ קֹדֶשׁ הַקֳּדָשִׁים
the-Holy-Ones Most-Holy-of Place-of *** and-he-built (8) the-walls on

אָרְכּוֹ עַל־ פְּנֵי רֹחַב־ הַבַּיִת אַמּוֹת עֶשְׂרִים
twenty cubits the-temple width-of dimensions-of as length-of-him

וְרָחְבּוֹ אַמּוֹת עֶשְׂרִים וַיְחַפֵּהוּ זָהָב טוֹב לְכִכָּרִים
with-talents fine gold and-he-overlaid-him twenty cubits and-width-of-him

שֵׁשׁ מֵאוֹת׃ וּמִשְׁקָל לְמִסְמְרוֹת לִשְׁקָלִים חֲמִשִּׁים זָהָב
gold fifty in-shekels of-nails and-weight (9) hundreds six-of

וְהָעֲלִיּוֹת חִפָּה זָהָב׃ וַיַּעַשׂ בְּבֵית־
in-Place-of and-he-made (10) gold he-overlaid and-the-upper-parts

קֹדֶשׁ הַקֳּדָשִׁים כְּרוּבִים שְׁנַיִם מַעֲשֵׂה צַעֲצֻעִים וַיְצַפּוּ
and-they-overlaid sculptures work-of pair cherubim the-Holy-Ones Most-Holy-of

אֹתָם זָהָב׃ וְכַנְפֵי הַכְּרוּבִים אָרְכָּם אַמּוֹת עֶשְׂרִים כְּנַף
wing-of twenty cubits span-of-them the-cherubim and-wings-of (11) gold them

הָאֶחָד לְאַמּוֹת חָמֵשׁ מַגַּעַת לְקִיר הַבַּיִת וְהַכָּנָף הָאַחֶרֶת
the-other and-the-wing the-temple on-wall-of touching five in-cubits the-one

אַמּוֹת חָמֵשׁ מַגִּיעַ לִכְנַף הַכְּרוּב הָאַחֵר׃ וּכְנַף
and-wing-of (12) the-other the-cherub on-wing-of touching five cubits

הַכְּרוּב הָאֶחָד* אַמּוֹת חָמֵשׁ מַגִּיעַ לְקִיר הַבַּיִת וְהַכָּנָף
and-the-wing the-temple on-wall-of touching five cubits *the-one the-cherub

הָאַחֶרֶת אַמּוֹת חָמֵשׁ דְּבֵקָה לִכְנַף הַכְּרוּב הָאַחֵר׃ כַּנְפֵי
wings-of (13) the-other the-cherub on-wing-of touching five cubits the-other

הַכְּרוּבִים הָאֵלֶּה פֹּרְשִׂים אַמּוֹת עֶשְׂרִים וְהֵם עֹמְדִים
ones-standing and-they twenty cubits ones-extending the-these the-cherubim

עַל־ רַגְלֵיהֶם וּפְנֵיהֶם לַבָּיִת׃ וַיַּעַשׂ אֶת־
*** and-he-made (14) toward-the-hall and-faces-of-them feet-of-them on

portico at the front of the temple was twenty cubits[l] long
across the width of the building and twenty cubits[m] high.
He overlaid the inside with
pure gold. 5 He paneled the
main hall with pine and
covered it with fine gold and
decorated it with palm tree
and chain designs. 6 He
adorned the temple with precious stones. And the gold he
used was gold of Parvaim. 7 He
overlaid the ceiling beams,
doorframes, walls and doors of
the temple with gold, and he
carved cherubim on the walls.
8 He built the Most Holy
Place, its length corresponding to the width of the temple—twenty cubits long and
twenty cubits wide. He overlaid the inside with six hundred talents[n] of fine gold. 9 The
gold nails weighed fifty
shekels.[o] He also overlaid the
upper parts with gold.
10 In the Most Holy Place he
made a pair of sculptured
cherubim and overlaid them
with gold. 11 The total wing-
span of the cherubim was
twenty cubits. One wing of
the first cherub was five cubits[p] long and touched the
temple wall, while its other
wing, also five cubits long,
touched the wing of the other
cherub. 12 Similarly one wing
of the second cherub was five
cubits long and touched the
other temple wall, and its other wing, also five cubits long,
touched the wing of the first
cherub. 13 The wings of these
cherubim extended twenty cubits. They stood on their feet,
facing the main hall.[q]
14 He made the curtain of

[l]4 That is, about 30 feet (about 9 meters); also in verses 8, 11 and 13
[m]4 Some Septuagint and Syriac manuscripts; Hebrew *a hundred and twenty*
[n]8 That is, about 23 tons (about 21 metric tons)
[o]9 That is, about 1 1/4 pounds (about 0.6 kilogram)
[p]11 That is, about 7 1/2 feet (about 2.3 meters); also in verse 15
[q]13 Or *facing inward*

*12 The NIV reads this word as the last (and vice versa), assuming the confusion of similar final letters.

הַפָּרֹכֶת תְּכֵלֶת וְאַרְגָּמָן וְכַרְמִיל וּבוּץ וַיַּעַל
and-he-worked and-fine-linen and-crimson and-purple blue-yarn the-curtain

עָלָיו כְּרוּבִים׃ (15) וַיַּעַשׂ לִפְנֵי הַבַּיִת עַמּוּדִים שְׁנַיִם
two pillars the-temple in-front-of and-he-made (15) cherubim into-him

אַמּוֹת שְׁלֹשִׁים וְחָמֵשׁ אֹרֶךְ וְהַצֶּפֶת אֲשֶׁר־עַל־רֹאשׁוֹ אַמּוֹת חָמֵשׁ׃
five cubits top-of-him on that and-the-capital length and-five thirty cubits

(16) וַיַּעַשׂ שַׁרְשְׁרוֹת בַּדְּבִיר* וַיִּתֵּן עַל־רֹאשׁ
top-of on and-he-put *in-the-inner-sanctuary chains and-he-made (16)

הָעַמֻּדִים וַיַּעַשׂ רִמּוֹנִים מֵאָה וַיִּתֵּן בַּשַּׁרְשְׁרוֹת׃
to-the-chains and-he-attached hundred pomegranates and-he-made the-pillars

(17) וַיָּקֶם אֶת־הָעַמּוּדִים עַל־פְּנֵי הַהֵיכָל אֶחָד מִיָּמִין
to-south one the-temple front-of in the-pillars *** and-he-erected (17)

וְאֶחָד מֵהַשְּׂמֹאול וַיִּקְרָא שֵׁם־הַיְמָנִי° יָכִין וְשֵׁם
and-name-of Jakin the-southern name-of and-he-called to-the-north and-one

הַשְּׂמָאלִי בֹּעַז׃ (4:1) וַיַּעַשׂ מִזְבַּח נְחֹשֶׁת עֶשְׂרִים אַמָּה אָרְכּוֹ
length-of-him cubit twenty bronze altar-of and-he-made (4:1) Boaz the-northern

וְעֶשְׂרִים אַמָּה רָחְבּוֹ וְעֶשֶׂר אַמּוֹת קוֹמָתוֹ׃ (2) וַיַּעַשׂ
and-he-made (2) height-of-him cubits and-ten width-of-him cubit and-twenty

אֶת־הַיָּם מוּצָק עֶשֶׂר בָּאַמָּה מִשְּׂפָתוֹ אֶל־שְׂפָתוֹ
rim-of-him to from-rim-of-him by-the-cubit ten being-cast the-Sea ***

עָגוֹל ׀ סָבִיב וְחָמֵשׁ בָּאַמָּה קוֹמָתוֹ וְקָו שְׁלֹשִׁים
thirty and-line height-of-him by-the-cubit and-five around circular

בָּאַמָּה יָסֹב אֹתוֹ סָבִיב׃ (3) וּדְמוּת בְּקָרִים תַּחַת
below bulls and-figure-of (3) around him he-measured-around by-the-cubit

לוֹ סָבִיב ׀ סָבִיב סוֹבְבִים אֹתוֹ עֶשֶׂר בָּאַמָּה מַקִּיפִים
ones-encircling to-the-cubit ten him ones-encircling around around to-him

אֶת־הַיָּם סָבִיב שְׁנַיִם טוּרִים הַבָּקָר יְצוּקִים בְּמֻצַקְתּוֹ׃
with-casting-of-him ones-being-cast the-bull rows two around the-Sea ***

(4) עוֹמֵד עַל־שְׁנֵים עָשָׂר בָּקָר שְׁלֹשָׁה פֹנִים ׀ צָפוֹנָה וּשְׁלוֹשָׁה
and-three to-north ones-facing three bull ten two on standing (4)

פֹנִים ׀ יָמָּה וּשְׁלֹשָׁה ׀ פֹּנִים נֶגְבָּה וּשְׁלֹשָׁה פֹּנִים
ones-facing and-three to-south ones-facing and-three to-west ones-facing

מִזְרָחָה וְהַיָּם עֲלֵיהֶם מִלְמָעְלָה וְכָל־אֲחֹרֵיהֶם
hindquarters-of-them and-all-of on-top on-them and-the-Sea to-east

בָּיְתָה׃ (5) וְעָבְיוֹ טֶפַח וּשְׂפָתוֹ כְּמַעֲשֵׂה
like-work-of and-rim-of-him handbreadth and-thickness-of-him (5) toward-center

שְׂפַת־כּוֹס פֶּרַח שׁוֹשַׁנָּה מַחֲזִיק בַּתִּים שְׁלֹשֶׁת אֲלָפִים יָכִיל׃
he-contained thousands three-of baths holding lily blossom-of cup rim-of

blue, purple and crimson yarn and fine linen, with cherubim worked into it.

15In the front of the temple
he made two pillars, which
together were thirty-five cubits[r] long, each with a capital
on top measuring five cubits.
16He made interwoven chains[s] and put them on top of the pillars. He also made a hundred pomegranates and attached them to the chains.
17He erected the pillars in the front of the temple, one to the south and one to the north. The one to the south he named Jakin[t] and the one to the north Boaz.[u]

The Temple's Furnishings

4 He made a bronze altar twenty cubits long, twenty cubits wide and ten cubits high.[v]
2He made the Sea of cast metal, circular in shape, measuring ten cubits from rim to rim and five cubits[w] high. It took a line of thirty cubits[x] to measure around it.
3Below the rim, figures of bulls encircled it—ten to a cubit.[y] The bulls were cast in two rows in one piece with the Sea.
4The Sea stood on twelve bulls, three facing north, three facing west, three facing south and three facing east. The Sea rested on top of them, and their hindquarters were toward the center.
5It was a handbreadth in thickness, and its rim was like the rim of a cup, like a lily blossom. It held three thousand baths.[z]

r15 That is, about 52 feet (about 16 meters)
s16 Or possibly *made chains in the inner sanctuary*; the meaning of the Hebrew for this phrase is uncertain.
t17 *Jakin* probably means *he establishes.*
u17 *Boaz* probably means *in him is strength.*
v1 That is, about 30 feet (about 9 meters) long and wide, and about 15 feet (about 4.5 meters) high
w2 That is, about 7 1/2 feet (about 2.3 meters)
x2 That is, about 45 feet (about 13.5 meters)
y3 That is, about 1 1/2 feet (about 0.5 meter)
z5 That is, about 17,500 gallons (about 66 kiloliters)

*16 Or possibly (כְּרָבִיד), *like-a-necklace* or *-weaving.*

°17 ק הימיני

וַיַּעַשׂ כִּיּוֹרִים עֲשָׂרָה וַיִּתֵּן חֲמִשָּׁה מִיָּמִין וַחֲמִשָּׁה מִשְּׂמֹאול
on-north and-five on-south five and-he-placed ten basins then-he-made (6)

לְרָחְצָה בָּהֶם אֶת־ מַעֲשֵׂה הָעוֹלָה יָדִיחוּ בָם
in-them they-rinsed the-burnt-offering thing-of *** in-them to-wash

וְהַיָּם לְרָחְצָה לַכֹּהֲנִים בּוֹ׃ וַיַּעַשׂ אֶת־ מְנֹרוֹת
lampstands-of *** and-he-made (7) in-him by-the-priests to-wash but-the-Sea

הַזָּהָב עֶשֶׂר כְּמִשְׁפָּטָם וַיִּתֵּן בַּהֵיכָל חָמֵשׁ
five in-the-temple and-he-placed as-specification-of-them ten the-gold

מִיָּמִין וְחָמֵשׁ מִשְּׂמֹאול׃ וַיַּעַשׂ שֻׁלְחָנוֹת עֲשָׂרָה וַיַּנַּח
and-he-placed ten tables and-he-made (8) on-north and-five on-south

בַּהֵיכָל חֲמִשָּׁה מִיָּמִין וַחֲמִשָּׁה מִשְּׂמֹאול וַיַּעַשׂ מִזְרְקֵי
sprinkling-bowls-of and-he-made on-north and-five on-south five in-the-temple

זָהָב מֵאָה׃ וַיַּעַשׂ חֲצַר הַכֹּהֲנִים וְהָעֲזָרָה הַגְּדוֹלָה
the-large and-the-court the-priests courtyard-of and-he-made (9) hundred gold

וּדְלָתוֹת לָעֲזָרָה וְדַלְתוֹתֵיהֶם צִפָּה נְחֹשֶׁת׃ וְאֶת־
and (10) bronze he-overlaid and-doors-of-them for-the-court and-doors

הַיָּם נָתַן מִכֶּתֶף הַיְמָנִית קֵדְמָה מִמּוּל נֶגְבָּה׃
to-south in-front-of to-east the-south on-side-of he-placed the-Sea

וַיַּעַשׂ חוּרָם אֶת־הַסִּירוֹת וְאֶת־ הַיָּעִים וְאֶת־ הַמִּזְרָקוֹת
the-sprinkling-bowls and the-shovels and the-pots *** Huram and-he-made (11)

וַיְכַל חִירָם לַעֲשׂוֹת אֶת־ הַמְּלָאכָה אֲשֶׁר עָשָׂה לַמֶּלֶךְ
for-the-king he-undertook that the-work *** to-do Huram so-he-finished

שְׁלֹמֹה בְּבֵית הָאֱלֹהִים׃ עַמּוּדִים שְׁנַיִם וְהַגֻּלּוֹת
and-the-bowl-shapes two pillars (12) the-God in-temple-of Solomon

וְהַכֹּתָרוֹת עַל־ רֹאשׁ הָעַמּוּדִים שְׁתָּיִם וְהַשְּׂבָכוֹת שְׁתַּיִם לְכַסּוֹת
to-decorate two and-the-networks two the-pillars top-of on and-the-capitals

אֶת־ שְׁתֵּי גֻּלּוֹת הַכֹּתָרוֹת אֲשֶׁר עַל־ רֹאשׁ הָעַמּוּדִים׃ וְאֶת־
and (13) the-pillars top-of on that the-capitals bowl-shapes-of two-of ***

הָרִמּוֹנִים אַרְבַּע מֵאוֹת לִשְׁתֵּי הַשְּׂבָכוֹת שְׁנַיִם טוּרִים
rows two the-networks for-two-of hundreds four-of the-pomegranates

רִמּוֹנִים לַשְּׂבָכָה הָאֶחָת לְכַסּוֹת אֶת־ שְׁתֵּי גֻּלּוֹת
bowl-shapes-of two-of *** to-decorate the-each for-the-network pomegranates

הַכֹּתָרוֹת אֲשֶׁר עַל־ פְּנֵי הָעַמּוּדִים׃ וְאֶת־ הַמְּכֹנוֹת עָשָׂה וְאֶת־
and he-made the-stands and (14) the-pillars tops-of on that the-capitals

הַכִּיֹּרוֹת עָשָׂה עַל־ הַמְּכֹנוֹת׃ אֶת־הַיָּם אֶחָד וְאֶת־ הַבָּקָר שְׁנֵים־עָשָׂר
ten two the-bull and one the-Sea *** (15) the-stands on he-made the-basins

תַּחְתָּיו׃ וְאֶת־הַסִּירוֹת וְאֶת־ הַיָּעִים וְאֶת־ הַמִּזְלָגוֹת וְאֶת־ כָּל־
all-of and the-meat-forks and the-shovels and the-pots and (16) under-him

°11 ק חורם

6 He then made ten basins for washing and placed five on the south side and five on the north. In them the things to be used for the burnt offerings were rinsed, but the Sea was to be used by the priests for washing.

7 He made ten gold lampstands according to the specifications for them and placed them in the temple, five on the south side and five on the north.

8 He made ten tables and placed them in the temple, five on the south side and five on the north. He also made a hundred gold sprinkling bowls.

9 He made the courtyard of the priests, and the large court and the doors for the court, and overlaid the doors with bronze. 10 He placed the Sea on the south side, at the southeast corner.

11 He also made the pots and shovels and sprinkling bowls.

So Huram finished the work he had undertaken for King Solomon in the temple of God:

12 the two pillars;
the two bowl-shaped capitals on top of the pillars;
the two sets of network decorating the two bowl-shaped capitals on top of the pillars;
13 the four hundred pomegranates for the two sets of network (two rows of pomegranates for each network, decorating the bowl-shaped capitals on top of the pillars);
14 the stands with their basins;
15 the Sea and the twelve bulls under it;
16 the pots, shovels, meat

כְּלֵיהֶם עָשָׂה חוּרָם אָבִיו לַמֶּלֶךְ שְׁלֹמֹה
Solomon for-the-king Abi Huram he-made articles-of-them

לְבֵית יְהוָה נְחֹשֶׁת מָרוּק׃ (17) בְּכִכַּר הַיַּרְדֵּן
the-Jordan in-plain-of (17) being-polished bronze Yahweh for-temple-of

יְצָקָם הַמֶּלֶךְ בַּעֲבִי הָאֲדָמָה בֵּין סֻכּוֹת וּבֵין
and-between Succoth between the-clay in-mold-of the-king he-cast-them

צְרֵדָתָה׃ (18) וַיַּעַשׂ שְׁלֹמֹה כָּל־ הַכֵּלִים הָאֵלֶּה לָרֹב מְאֹד
very to-much the-these the-things all-of Solomon and-he-made (18) Zeredatha

כִּי לֹא נֶחְקַר מִשְׁקַל הַנְּחֹשֶׁת׃ (19) וַיַּעַשׂ שְׁלֹמֹה אֵת
*** Solomon and-he-made (19) the-bronze weight-of he-was-determined not that

כָּל־ הַכֵּלִים אֲשֶׁר בֵּית הָאֱלֹהִים וְאֵת מִזְבַּח הַזָּהָב וְאֶת־
and the-gold altar-of and the-God house-of that the-furnishings all-of

הַשֻּׁלְחָנוֹת וַעֲלֵיהֶם לֶחֶם הַפָּנִים׃ (20) וְאֶת־ הַמְּנֹרוֹת
the-lampstands and (20) the-Presences bread-of and-on-them the-tables

וְנֵרֹתֵיהֶם לְבַעֲרָם כַּמִּשְׁפָּט לִפְנֵי
in-front-of as-the-prescription to-burn-them and-lamps-of-them

הַדְּבִיר זָהָב סָגוּר׃ (21) וְהַפֶּרַח וְהַנֵּרוֹת
and-the-lamps and-the-floral-work (21) pure gold the-inner-sanctuary

וְהַמֶּלְקָחַיִם* זָהָב הוּא מִכְלוֹת זָהָב׃ (22) וְהַמְזַמְּרוֹת
and-the-wick-trimmers (22) gold ones-solid-of this gold and-the-tongs

וְהַמִּזְרָקוֹת וְהַכַּפּוֹת וְהַמַּחְתּוֹת זָהָב סָגוּר וּפֶתַח
and-door-of pure gold and-the-censers and-the-ladles and-the-sprinkling-bowls

הַבַּיִת דַּלְתוֹתָיו הַפְּנִימִיּוֹת לְקֹדֶשׁ הַקֳּדָשִׁים
the-Holy-Places to-Most-Holy-of the-inner-ones doors-of-him the-temple

וְדַלְתֵי הַבַּיִת לְהֵיכָל זָהָב׃ (5:1) וַתִּשְׁלַם
when-she-was-finished (5:1) gold of-the-temple the-main-hall and-doors-of

כָּל־ הַמְּלָאכָה אֲשֶׁר־ עָשָׂה שְׁלֹמֹה לְבֵית יְהוָה וַיָּבֵא
and-he-brought Yahweh for-temple-of Solomon he-did that the-work all-of

שְׁלֹמֹה אֶת־ קָדְשֵׁי ׀ דָּוִיד אָבִיו וְאֶת־ הַכֶּסֶף וְאֶת־
and the-silver and father-of-him David dedicated-things-of *** Solomon

הַזָּהָב וְאֶת־ כָּל־ הַכֵּלִים נָתַן בְּאֹצְרוֹת בֵּית
temple-of in-treasuries-of he-placed the-furnishings all-of and the-gold

הָאֱלֹהִים׃ (2) אָז יַקְהֵיל שְׁלֹמֹה אֶת־ זִקְנֵי יִשְׂרָאֵל וְאֶת־ כָּל־
all-of and Israel elders-of *** Solomon he-summoned then (2) the-God

רָאשֵׁי הַמַּטּוֹת נְשִׂיאֵי הָאָבוֹת לִבְנֵי יִשְׂרָאֵל אֶל־ יְרוּשָׁלִָם
Jerusalem to Israel of-sons-of the-fathers chiefs-of the-tribes heads-of

לְהַעֲלוֹת אֶת־ אֲרוֹן בְּרִית־ יְהוָה מֵעִיר דָּוִיד הִיא צִיּוֹן׃
Zion that David from-City-of Yahweh covenant-of ark-of *** to-bring-up

*21 Most mss have *qamets* under the *qoph* (קָחִים–).

forks and all related articles.

All the objects that Huram-Abi made for King Solomon for the temple of the LORD were of polished bronze.
17The king had them cast in clay molds in the plain of the Jordan between Succoth and Zarethan.[a]
18All these things that Solomon made amounted to so much that the weight of the bronze was not determined.
19Solomon also made all the furnishings that were in God's temple:

the golden altar;
the tables on which was the bread of the Presence;
20the lampstands of pure gold with their lamps, to burn in front of the inner sanctuary as prescribed;
21the gold floral work and lamps and tongs (they were solid gold);
22the pure gold wick trimmers, sprinkling bowls, ladles and censers; and the gold doors of the temple: the inner doors to the Most Holy Place and the doors of the main hall.

5 When all the work Solomon had done for the temple of the LORD was finished, he brought in the things his father David had dedicated—the silver and gold and all the furnishings—and he placed them in the treasuries of God's temple.

The Ark Brought to the Temple

2Then Solomon summoned to Jerusalem the elders of Israel, all the heads of the tribes and the chiefs of the Israelite families, to bring up the ark of the LORD's covenant from Zion, the City of David.
3And

[a]17 Hebrew *Zeredatha*, a variant of *Zarethan*

וַיִּקָּהֲל֞וּ אֶל־הַמֶּ֣לֶךְ כָּל־אִ֣ישׁ יִשְׂרָאֵ֗ל בֶּחָ֛ג
(3) and-they-came-together   to   the-king   all-of   man-of   Israel   at-the-festival

ה֥וּא הַחֹ֖דֶשׁ הַשְּׁבִעִֽי׃ וַיָּבֹ֕אוּ כֹּ֖ל זִקְנֵ֣י יִשְׂרָאֵ֑ל
that   the-month   the-seventh   (4) when-they-arrived   all-of   elders-of   Israel

וַיִּשְׂא֥וּ הַלְוִיִּ֖ם אֶת־הָאָרֽוֹן׃ וַיַּעֲל֣וּ אֶת־
then-they-took-up   the-Levites   ***   the-ark   (5) and-they-brought-up   ***

הָאָר֗וֹן וְאֶת־אֹ֤הֶל מוֹעֵד֙ וְאֶת־כָּל־כְּלֵ֣י הַקֹּ֔דֶשׁ אֲשֶׁ֖ר
the-ark   and   Tent-of   Meeting   and   all-of   furnishings-of   the-sacred   that

בָּאֹ֑הֶל הֶעֱל֣וּ אֹתָ֔ם הַכֹּהֲנִ֖ים הַלְוִיִּֽם׃ וְהַמֶּ֣לֶךְ
in-the-Tent   they-carried-up   them   the-priests   (6) the-Levites   and-the-king

שְׁלֹמֹ֗ה וְכָל־עֲדַ֤ת יִשְׂרָאֵל֙ הַנּוֹעָדִ֣ים עָלָ֔יו
Solomon   and-entire-of   assembly-of   Israel   the-ones-having-gathered   about-him

לִפְנֵ֖י הָאָר֑וֹן מְזַבְּחִים֙ צֹ֣אן וּבָקָ֔ר אֲשֶׁ֛ר לֹֽא־יִסָּפְר֥וּ
before   the-ark   ones-sacrificing   sheep   and-cattle   that   not   they-were-recorded

וְלֹ֥א יִמָּנ֖וּ מֵרֹֽב׃ וַיָּבִ֣יאוּ הַכֹּהֲנִ֗ים
and-not   they-were-numbered   for-greatness   (7) then-they-brought   the-priests

אֶת־אֲר֧וֹן בְּרִית־יְהוָ֛ה אֶל־מְקוֹמ֖וֹ אֶל־דְּבִ֣יר
***   ark-of   covenant-of   Yahweh   to   place-of-him   in   inner-sanctuary-of

הַבַּ֑יִת אֶל־קֹ֥דֶשׁ הַקֳּדָשִׁ֖ים אֶל־תַּ֣חַת כַּנְפֵ֥י הַכְּרוּבִֽים׃
the-temple   in   Most-Holy-of   the-Holy-Places   at   beneath   wings-of   the-cherubim

וַיִּהְי֤וּ הַכְּרוּבִים֙ פֹּרְשִׂ֣ים כְּנָפַ֔יִם עַל־מְק֖וֹם הָאָר֑וֹן
and-they-were   the-cherubim   ones-spreading   wings   over   place-of   the-ark

וַיְכַסּ֧וּ הַכְּרוּבִ֛ים עַל־הָאָר֖וֹן וְעַל־בַּדָּ֥יו מִלְמָֽעְלָה׃
and-they-covered   the-cherubim   over   the-ark   and-over   poles-of-him   at-above

וַֽיַּאֲרִ֖יכוּ הַבַּדִּים֒ וַיֵּרָאוּ֩ רָאשֵׁ֨י הַבַּדִּ֜ים מִן־
and-they-were-long   the-poles   so-they-were-seen   ends-of   the-poles   from

הָאָר֗וֹן עַל־פְּנֵ֣י הַדְּבִ֔יר וְלֹ֥א יֵרָא֖וּ הַחֽוּצָה
the-ark   in   front-of   the-inner-sanctuary   but-not   they-were-seen   at-the-outside

וַֽיְהִי־שָׁ֔ם עַ֖ד הַיּ֥וֹם הַזֶּֽה׃ אֵ֣ין בָּאָר֔וֹן רַ֚ק
and-he-is   there   to   the-day   the-this   (10) there-was-nothing   in-the-ark   except

שְׁנֵ֣י הַלֻּח֔וֹת אֲשֶׁר־נָתַ֥ן מֹשֶׁ֖ה בְּחֹרֵ֑ב אֲשֶׁ֨ר כָּרַ֤ת
two-of   the-tablets   that   he-placed   Moses   at-Horeb   where   he-made-covenant

יְהוָה֙ עִם־בְּנֵ֣י יִשְׂרָאֵ֔ל בְּצֵאתָ֖ם מִמִּצְרָֽיִם׃ וַיְהִ֕י
Yahweh   with   sons-of   Israel   after-to-come-them   from-Egypt   (11) then-he-was

בְּצֵ֥את הַכֹּהֲנִ֖ים מִן־הַקֹּ֑דֶשׁ כִּ֤י כָּל־הַכֹּהֲנִ֣ים
when-to-withdraw   the-priests   from   the-Holy-Place   for   all-of   the-priests

הַנִּמְצְאִים֙ הִתְקַדָּ֔שׁוּ אֵ֖ין לִשְׁמ֥וֹר לְמַחְלְקֽוֹת׃
the-ones-being-found   they-consecrated-themselves   not   to-regard   for-divisions

all the men of Israel came together to the king at the time of the festival in the seventh month.

⁴When all the elders of Israel had arrived, the Levites took up the ark, ⁵and they brought up the ark and the Tent of Meeting and all the sacred furnishings in it. The priests, who were Levites, carried them up; ⁶and King Solomon and the entire assembly of Israel that had gathered about him were before the ark, sacrificing so many sheep and cattle that they could not be recorded or counted.

⁷The priests then brought the ark of the LORD's covenant to its place in the inner sanctuary of the temple, the Most Holy Place, and put it beneath the wings of the cherubim. ⁸The cherubim spread their wings over the place of the ark and covered the ark and its carrying poles. ⁹These poles were so long that their ends, extending from the ark, could be seen from in front of the inner sanctuary, but not from outside the Holy Place; and they are still there today. ¹⁰There was nothing in the ark except the two tablets that Moses had placed in it at Horeb, where the LORD made a covenant with the Israelites after they came out of Egypt.

¹¹The priests then withdrew from the Holy Place. All the priests who were there had consecrated themselves, regardless of their divisions.

*7 Most mss have *hateph qamets* under the *qoph* (הַקֳּ).

לְאָסָף	לְכֻלָּם	הַמְשֹׁרְרִים	וְהַלְוִיִּם	
indeed-Asaph	indeed-all-of-them	the-ones-making-music	and-the-Levites	(12)

וְלַאֲחֵיהֶם	וְלִבְנֵיהֶם	לִידֻתוּן	לְהֵימָן
and-indeed-relatives-of-them	and-indeed-sons-of-them	indeed-Jeduthun	indeed-Heman

וְכִנֹּרוֹת	וּבִנְבָלִים	בִּמְצִלְתַּיִם	בּוּץ	מְלֻבָּשִׁים
and-lyres	and-with-harps	with-cymbals	fine-linen	ones-being-dressed

לְמֵאָה	כֹּהֲנִים	וְעִמָּהֶם	לַמִּזְבֵּחַ	מִזְרָח	עֹמְדִים
indeed-hundred	priests	and-with-them	of-the-altar	east	ones-standing

כְּאֶחָד	וַיְהִי		בַּחֲצֹצְרוֹת׃	מַחְצְרִים°	וְעֶשְׂרִים
as-one	and-he-was	(13)	on-the-trumpets	ones-sounding	and-twenty

לְהַשְׁמִיעַ	וְלַמְשֹׁרְרִים	לַמְחַצְּצְרִים°
to-make-heard	and-indeed-the-ones-singing	indeed-the-ones-sounding-trumpets

קוֹל	וּכְהָרִים	לַיהוָה	וּלְהֹדוֹת	לְהַלֵּל	אֶחָד	קוֹל־
voice	and-as-to-raise	to-Yahweh	and-to-thank	to-praise	one	voice

הַשִּׁיר	וּבִכְלֵי	וּבִמְצִלְתַּיִם	בַּחֲצֹצְרוֹת
the-music	and-with-instruments-of	and-with-the-cymbals	with-the-trumpets

חַסְדּוֹ	לְעוֹלָם	כִּי	טוֹב	כִּי	לַיהוָה	וּבְהַלֵּל
love-of-him	to-forever	indeed	good	that	to-Yahweh	and-when-to-praise

יָכְלוּ	וְלֹא־		יְהוָה׃	בֵּית	עָנָן	מָלֵא	וְהַבַּיִת
they-could	and-not	(14)	Yahweh	temple-of	cloud	he-was-filled	then-the-temple

מָלֵא	כִּי־	הֶעָנָן	מִפְּנֵי	לְשָׁרֵת	לַעֲמוֹד	הַכֹּהֲנִים
he-filled	for	the-cloud	because-of	to-perform	to-continue	the-priests

יְהוָה	שְׁלֹמֹה	אָמַר	אָז		הָאֱלֹהִים׃	בֵּית	אֶת־	יְהוָה	כְבוֹד־
Yahweh	Solomon	he-said	then	(6:1)	the-God	temple-of	***	Yahweh	glory-of

זְבֻל	בֵית־	בָּנִיתִי	וַאֲנִי		בָּעֲרָפֶל׃	לִשְׁכּוֹן	אָמַר
magnificence	temple-of	I-built	and-I	(2)	in-the-dark-cloud	to-dwell	he-said

אֶת־	הַמֶּלֶךְ	וַיַּסֵּב		עוֹלָמִים׃	לְשִׁבְתְּךָ	וּמָכוֹן	לָךְ
***	the-king	and-he-turned	(3)	forevers	to-dwell-you	even-place	for-you

וְכָל־	יִשְׂרָאֵל	קְהַל	כָּל־	אֵת	וַיְבָרֶךְ	פָּנָיו
while-whole-of	Israel	assembly-of	whole-of	***	and-he-blessed	faces-of-him

אֱלֹהֵי	יְהוָה	בָּרוּךְ	וַיֹּאמֶר		עוֹמֵד׃	יִשְׂרָאֵל	קְהַל
God-of	Yahweh	being-praised	then-he-said	(4)	standing	Israel	assembly-of

אָבִי	דָּוִיד	אֵת	בְּפִיו	דִּבֶּר	אֲשֶׁר	יִשְׂרָאֵל
father-of-me	David	***	with-mouth-of-him	he-promised	who	Israel

הוֹצֵאתִי	אֲשֶׁר	הַיּוֹם	מִן־		לֵאמֹר׃	מִלֵּא	וּבְיָדָיו
I-brought	when	the-day	since	(5)	to-say	he-fulfilled	and-with-hands-of-him

מִכֹּל	בְּעִיר	בָחַרְתִּי	לֹא־	מִצְרַיִם	מֵאֶרֶץ	עַמִּי	אֶת־
from-any-of	to-city	I-chose	not	Egypt	from-land-of	people-of-me	***

°12 ק מחצרים
°13 ק למחצרים

[12]All the Levites who were musicians—Asaph, Heman, Jeduthun and their sons and relatives—stood on the east side of the altar, dressed in fine linen and playing cymbals, harps and lyres. They were accompanied by 120 priests sounding trumpets.
[13]The trumpeters and singers joined in unison, as with one voice, to give praise and thanks to the LORD. Accompanied by trumpets, cymbals and other instruments, they raised their voices in praise to the LORD and sang:

"He is good;
his love endures
forever."

Then the temple of the LORD was filled with a cloud, [14]and
the priests could not perform their service because of the cloud, for the glory of the LORD filled the temple of God.

6 Then Solomon said, "The LORD has said that he would dwell in a dark cloud; [2]I
have built a magnificent temple for you, a place for you to dwell forever."
[3]While the whole assembly of Israel was standing there, the king turned around and blessed them. [4]Then he said:

"Praise be to the LORD, the God of Israel, who with his hands has fulfilled what he promised with his mouth to my father David. For he said, [5]'Since the day I brought my people out of Egypt, I have not chosen a city in any tribe of Israel to

שִׁבְטֵי יִשְׂרָאֵל לִבְנוֹת בַּיִת לִהְיוֹת שְׁמִי שָׁם וְלֹא־ בָחַרְתִּי
I-chose and-not there Name-of-me to-be temple to-build Israel tribes-of

בְאִישׁ לִהְיוֹת נָגִיד עַל־ עַמִּי יִשְׂרָאֵל׃ (6) וָאֶבְחַר בִּירוּשָׁלַםִ
to-Jerusalem but-I-chose (6) Israel people-of-me over leader to-be to-anyone

לִהְיוֹת שְׁמִי שָׁם וָאֶבְחַר בְּדָוִיד לִהְיוֹת עַל־ עַמִּי יִשְׂרָאֵל׃
Israel people-of-me over to-be to-David and-I-chose there Name-of-me to-be

(7) וַיְהִי עִם־ לְבַב דָּוִיד אָבִי לִבְנוֹת בַּיִת לְשֵׁם
for-Name-of temple to-build father-of-me David heart-of in and-he-was (7)

יְהוָה אֱלֹהֵי יִשְׂרָאֵל׃ (8) וַיֹּאמֶר יְהוָה אֶל־ דָּוִיד אָבִי יַעַן
because father-of-me David to Yahweh but-he-said (8) Israel God-of Yahweh

אֲשֶׁר הָיָה עִם־ לְבָבְךָ לִבְנוֹת בַּיִת לִשְׁמִי הֱטִיבוֹתָ
you-did-well for-Name-of-me temple to-build heart-of-you in he-was that

כִּי הָיָה עִם־ לְבָבֶךָ׃ (9) רַק אַתָּה לֹא תִבְנֶה
you-will-build not you nevertheless (9) heart-of-you in he-was because

הַבָּיִת כִּי בִנְךָ הַיּוֹצֵא מֵחֲלָצֶיךָ הוּא־ יִבְנֶה
he-will-build he from-loins-of-you the-one-coming son-of-you but the-temple

הַבַּיִת לִשְׁמִי׃ (10) וַיָּקֶם יְהוָה אֶת־ דְּבָרוֹ אֲשֶׁר
that promise-of-him *** Yahweh and-he-kept (10) for-Name-of-me the-temple

דִּבֵּר וָאָקוּם תַּחַת דָּוִיד אָבִי וָאֵשֵׁב ׀ עַל־ כִּסֵּא
throne-of on and-I-sit father-of-me David after and-I-succeeded he-promised

יִשְׂרָאֵל כַּאֲשֶׁר דִּבֶּר יְהוָה וָאֶבְנֶה הַבַּיִת לְשֵׁם יְהוָה
Yahweh for-Name-of the-temple and-I-built Yahweh he-promised just-as Israel

אֱלֹהֵי יִשְׂרָאֵל׃ (11) וָאָשִׂים שָׁם אֶת־ הָאָרוֹן אֲשֶׁר־ שָׁם בְּרִית
covenant-of there which the-ark *** there and-I-placed (11) Israel God-of

יְהוָה אֲשֶׁר כָּרַת עִם־ בְּנֵי יִשְׂרָאֵל׃ (12) וַיַּעֲמֹד לִפְנֵי מִזְבַּח
altar-of before then-he-stood (12) Israel people-of with he-made that Yahweh

יְהוָה נֶגֶד כָּל־ קְהַל יִשְׂרָאֵל וַיִּפְרֹשׂ כַּפָּיו׃
hands-of-him and-he-spread Israel assembly-of whole-of in-front-of Yahweh

(13) כִּי־ עָשָׂה שְׁלֹמֹה כִּיּוֹר נְחֹשֶׁת וַיִּתְּנֵהוּ בְּתוֹךְ
in-center-of and-he-placed-him bronze platform-of Solomon he-made now (13)

הָעֲזָרָה חָמֵשׁ אַמּוֹת אָרְכּוֹ וְחָמֵשׁ אַמּוֹת רָחְבּוֹ
width-of-him cubits and-five length-of-him cubits five the-outer-court

וְאַמּוֹת שָׁלוֹשׁ קוֹמָתוֹ וַיַּעֲמֹד עָלָיו וַיִּבְרַךְ עַל־
on then-he-knelt on-him and-he-stood height-of-him three and-cubits

בִּרְכָּיו נֶגֶד כָּל־ קְהַל יִשְׂרָאֵל וַיִּפְרֹשׂ כַּפָּיו
hands-of-him and-he-spread Israel assembly-of whole-of before knees-of-him

הַשָּׁמָיְמָה׃ (14) וַיֹּאמַר יְהוָה אֱלֹהֵי יִשְׂרָאֵל אֵין־
there-is-no Israel God-of Yahweh and-he-said (14) toward-the-heavens

have a temple built for my
Name to be there, nor have
I chosen anyone to be the
leader over my people Israel. [6]But now I have chosen
Jerusalem for my Name to
be there, and I have chosen
David to rule my people Israel.'
[7]"My father David had it
in his heart to build a temple for the Name of the
LORD, the God of Israel. [8]But
the LORD said to my father
David, 'Because it was in
your heart to build a temple
for my Name, you did well
to have this in your heart.
[9]Nevertheless, you are not
the one to build the temple,
but your son, who is your
own flesh and blood—he is
the one who will build the
temple for my Name.'
[10]"The LORD has kept the
promise he made. I have
succeeded David my father
and now I sit on the throne
of Israel, just as the LORD
promised, and I have built
the temple for the Name of
the LORD, the God of Israel.
[11]There I have placed the
ark, in which is the cov-
enant of the LORD that he
made with the people of Israel."

Solomon's Prayer of Dedication

[12]Then Solomon stood before the altar of the LORD in
front of the whole assembly of
Israel and spread out his
hands. [13]Now he had made a
bronze platform, five cubits[b]
long, five cubits wide and
three cubits[c] high, and had
placed it in the center of the
outer court. He stood on the
platform and then knelt down
before the whole assembly of
Israel and spread out his
hands toward heaven. [14]He
said:

"O LORD, God of Israel,

[b]13 That is, about 7 1/2 feet (about 2.3 meters)
[c]13 That is, about 4 1/2 feet (about 1.3 meters)

כָּמוֹךָ אֱלֹהִים בַּשָּׁמַיִם וּבָאָרֶץ שֹׁמֵר הַבְּרִית וְהַחֶסֶד
and-the-love the-covenant keeping or-on-the-earth in-the-heavens God like-you

לַעֲבָדֶיךָ הַהֹלְכִים לְפָנֶיךָ בְּכָל־
with-whole-of before-you the-ones-continuing with-servants-of-you

לִבָּם׃ (15) אֲשֶׁר שָׁמַרְתָּ לְעַבְדְּךָ דָּוִיד אָבִי אֵת
*** father-of-me David to-servant-of-you you-kept who (15) heart-of-them

אֲשֶׁר־ דִּבַּרְתָּ לוֹ וַתְּדַבֵּר בְּפִיךָ
with-mouth-of-you and-you-promised to-him you-promised what

וּבְיָדְךָ מִלֵּאתָ כַּיּוֹם הַזֶּה׃ (16) וְעַתָּה יְהוָה ׀
Yahweh and-now (16) the-this as-the-day you-fulfilled and-with-hand-of-you

אֱלֹהֵי יִשְׂרָאֵל שְׁמֹר לְעַבְדְּךָ דָוִיד אָבִי אֵת אֲשֶׁר
what *** father-of-me David for-servant-of-you keep! Israel God-of

דִּבַּרְתָּ לוֹ לֵאמֹר לֹא־ יִכָּרֵת לְךָ אִישׁ מִלְּפָנַי
from-before-me man of-you he-shall-be-cut-off not to-say to-him you-promised

יוֹשֵׁב עַל־ כִּסֵּא יִשְׂרָאֵל רַק אִם־ יִשְׁמְרוּ בָנֶיךָ אֶת־
*** sons-of-you they-are-careful if only Israel throne-of on sitting

דַּרְכָּם לָלֶכֶת בְּתוֹרָתִי כַּאֲשֶׁר הָלַכְתָּ לְפָנָי׃
before-me you-walked just-as according-to-law-of-me to-walk way-of-them

(17) וְעַתָּה יְהוָה אֱלֹהֵי יִשְׂרָאֵל יֵאָמֵן דְּבָרְךָ אֲשֶׁר
that word-of-you let-him-come-true Israel God-of Yahweh and-now (17)

דִּבַּרְתָּ לְעַבְדְּךָ לְדָוִיד׃ (18) כִּי הַאֻמְנָם יֵשֵׁב אֱלֹהִים
God will-he-dwell really? but (18) to-David to-servant-of-you you-promised

אֶת־ הָאָדָם עַל־ הָאָרֶץ הִנֵּה שָׁמַיִם וּשְׁמֵי הַשָּׁמַיִם לֹא
not the-heavens even-heavens-of heavens see! the-earth on the-man with

יְכַלְכְּלוּךָ אַף כִּי־ הַבַּיִת הַזֶּה אֲשֶׁר בָּנִיתִי׃
I-built that the-this the-temple indeed how-much-less they-can-contain-you

(19) וּפָנִיתָ אֶל־ תְּפִלַּת עַבְדְּךָ וְאֶל־
and-to servant-of-you prayer-of to yet-you-give-attention (19)

תְּחִנָּתוֹ יְהוָה אֱלֹהָי לִשְׁמֹעַ אֶל־ הָרִנָּה וְאֶל־ הַתְּפִלָּה
the-prayer and-to the-cry to to-hear God-of-me Yahweh mercy-plea-of-him

אֲשֶׁר עַבְדְּךָ מִתְפַּלֵּל לְפָנֶיךָ׃ (20) לִהְיוֹת עֵינֶיךָ
eyes-of-you to-be (20) in-presences-of-you praying servant-of-you that

פְתֻחוֹת אֶל־ הַבַּיִת הַזֶּה יוֹמָם וָלַיְלָה אֶל־ הַמָּקוֹם
the-place toward and-night by-day the-this the-temple toward ones-being-open

אֲשֶׁר אָמַרְתָּ לָשׂוּם שִׁמְךָ שָׁם לִשְׁמוֹעַ אֶל־ הַתְּפִלָּה אֲשֶׁר יִתְפַּלֵּל
he-prays that the-prayer to to-hear there Name-of-you to-put you-said which

עַבְדְּךָ אֶל־ הַמָּקוֹם הַזֶּה׃ (21) וְשָׁמַעְתָּ אֶל־ תַּחֲנוּנֵי
supplications-of to and-you-hear (21) the-this the-place toward servant-of-you

there is no God like you in
heaven or on earth—you
who keep your covenant of
love with your servants
who continue wholeheart-
edly in your way. [15]You
have kept your promise to
your servant David my fa-
ther; with your mouth you
have promised and with
your hand you have
fulfilled it—as it is today.
[16]"Now LORD, God of Is-
rael, keep for your servant
David my father the prom-
ises you made to him when
you said, 'You shall never
fail to have a man to sit before me on the throne of Israel, if only your sons are
careful in all they do to
walk before me according
to my law, as you have
done.' [17]And now, O LORD,
God of Israel, let your word
that you promised your servant David come true.
[18]"But will God really
dwell on earth with men?
The heavens, even the
highest heavens, cannot
contain you. How much
less this temple I have built!
[19]Yet give attention to your
servant's prayer and his
plea for mercy, O LORD my
God. Hear the cry and the
prayer that your servant is
praying in your presence.
[20]May your eyes be open
toward this temple day and
night, this place of which
you said you would put
your Name there. May you
hear the prayer your ser-
vant prays toward this
place. [21]Hear the supplica-
tions of your servant and of

עַבְדְּךָ וְעַמְּךָ יִשְׂרָאֵל אֲשֶׁר יִתְפַּלְלוּ אֶל־ הַמָּקוֹם
servant-of-you and-people-of-you Israel when they-pray toward the-place

הַזֶּה וְאַתָּה תִּשְׁמַע מִמְּקוֹם שִׁבְתְּךָ מִן־ הַשָּׁמַיִם
the-this and-you you-hear from-place-of to-dwell-you from the-heavens

וְשָׁמַעְתָּ וְסָלָחְתָּ׃ (22) אִם־ יֶחֱטָא אִישׁ לְרֵעֵהוּ
when-you-hear then-you-forgive (22) when he-wrongs man to-neighbor-of-him

וְנָשָׁא־ בוֹ אָלָה לְהַאֲלֹתוֹ וּבָא אָלָה לִפְנֵי
and-he-takes on-him oath to-take-oath-him and-he-comes he-swears-oath before

מִזְבַּחֲךָ בַּבַּיִת הַזֶּה׃ (23) וְאַתָּה תִּשְׁמַע מִן־ הַשָּׁמַיִם
altar-of-you in-the-temple the-this (23) then-you you-hear from the-heavens

וְעָשִׂיתָ וְשָׁפַטְתָּ אֶת־ עֲבָדֶיךָ לְהָשִׁיב לְרָשָׁע לָתֵת
and-you-act and-you-judge *** servants-of-you to-repay to-guilty to-bring

דַּרְכּוֹ בְּרֹאשׁוֹ וּלְהַצְדִּיק צַדִּיק לָתֶת לוֹ
way-of-him on-head-of-him and-to-declare-innocent innocent to-establish for-him

כְּצִדְקָתוֹ׃ (24) וְאִם־ יִנָּגֵף עַמְּךָ יִשְׂרָאֵל לִפְנֵי
as-innocence-of-him (24) and-when he-is-defeated people-of-you Israel before

אוֹיֵב כִּי יֶחֶטְאוּ־ לָךְ וְשָׁבוּ
one-being-enemy because they-sinned against-you when-they-turn-back

וְהוֹדוּ אֶת־ שְׁמֶךָ וְהִתְפַּלְלוּ וְהִתְחַנְּנוּ
and-they-confess *** name-of-you and-they-pray and-they-make-supplication

לְפָנֶיךָ בַּבַּיִת הַזֶּה׃ (25) וְאַתָּה תִּשְׁמַע מִן־ הַשָּׁמַיִם
before-you in-the-temple the-this (25) then-you you-hear from the-heavens

וְסָלַחְתָּ לְחַטַּאת עַמְּךָ יִשְׂרָאֵל וַהֲשֵׁיבוֹתָם אֶל־
and-you-forgive to-sin-of people-of-you Israel and-you-bring-back-them to

הָאֲדָמָה אֲשֶׁר־ נָתַתָּה לָהֶם וְלַאֲבֹתֵיהֶם׃ (26) בְּהֵעָצֵר
the-land that you-gave to-them and-to-fathers-of-them (26) when-to-be-shut-up

הַשָּׁמַיִם וְלֹא־ יִהְיֶה מָטָר כִּי יֶחֶטְאוּ־ לָךְ וְהִתְפַּלְלוּ
the-heavens and-not he-is rain because they-sinned against-you when-they-pray

אֶל־ הַמָּקוֹם הַזֶּה וְהוֹדוּ אֶת־ שְׁמֶךָ מֵחַטָּאתָם
toward the-place the-this and-they-confess *** name-of-you from-sin-of-them

יְשׁוּבוּן כִּי תַעֲנֵם׃ (27) וְאַתָּה תִּשְׁמַע הַשָּׁמַיִם
they-turn because you-afflicted-them (27) then-you you-hear the-heavens

וְסָלַחְתָּ לְחַטַּאת עֲבָדֶיךָ וְעַמְּךָ יִשְׂרָאֵל כִּי
and-you-forgive to-sin-of servants-of-you and-people-of-you Israel indeed

תוֹרֵם אֶל־ הַדֶּרֶךְ הַטּוֹבָה אֲשֶׁר יֵלְכוּ־ בָהּ
you-teach-them about the-way the-right that they-should-walk in-her

וְנָתַתָּה מָטָר עַל־ אַרְצְךָ אֲשֶׁר־ נָתַתָּה לְעַמְּךָ
and-you-send rain on land-of-you that you-gave to-people-of-you

your people Israel when
they pray toward this place.
Hear from heaven, your
dwelling place; and when
you hear, forgive.
22"When a man wrongs
his neighbor and is re-
quired to take an oath and
he comes and swears the
oath before your altar in
this temple, 23then hear
from heaven and act. Judge
between your servants,
repaying the guilty by
bringing down on his own
head what he has done. Declare the innocent not
guilty and so establish his
innocence.
24"When your people Is-
rael have been defeated by
an enemy because they
have sinned against you
and when they turn back
and confess your name,
praying and making sup-
plication before you in this
temple, 25then hear from
heaven and forgive the sin
of your people Israel and
bring them back to the land
you gave to them and their
fathers.
26"When the heavens are
shut up and there is no rain
because your people have
sinned against you, and
when they pray toward this
place and confess your
name and turn from their
sin because you have
afflicted them, 27then hear
from heaven and forgive
the sin of your servants,
your people Israel. Teach
them the right way to live,
and send rain on the land
you gave your people for an

לְנַחֲלָה׃ רָעָב כִּי־ יִהְיֶה בָאָרֶץ דֶּבֶר כִּי־ יִהְיֶה
he-comes when plague to-the-land he-comes when famine (28) for-inheritance

שִׁדָּפוֹן וְיֵרָקוֹן אַרְבֶּה וְחָסִיל כִּי יִהְיֶה כִּי יָצַר־
he-besieges when he-comes when or-grasshopper locust or-mildew blight

לוֹ אוֹיְבָיו בְּאֶרֶץ שְׁעָרָיו כָּל־ נֶגַע
disaster any-of gates-of-him in-land-of ones-being-enemies-of-him against-him

וְכָל־ מַחֲלָה׃ כָּל־ תְּפִלָּה כָל־ תְּחִנָּה אֲשֶׁר יִהְיֶה לְכָל־
from-any-of he-comes that plea any-of prayer any-of (29) disease or-any-of

הָאָדָם וּלְכֹל עַמְּךָ יִשְׂרָאֵל אֲשֶׁר יֵדְעוּ אִישׁ
each they-are-aware who Israel people-of-you indeed-from-any-of the-person

נִגְעוֹ וּמַכְאֹבוֹ וּפָרַשׂ כַּפָּיו אֶל־
toward hands-of-him and-he-spreads-out and-pain-of-him affliction-of-him

הַבַּיִת הַזֶּה׃ וְאַתָּה תִּשְׁמַע מִן־ הַשָּׁמַיִם מְכוֹן
place-of the-heavens from you-hear then-you (30) the-this the-temple

שִׁבְתְּךָ וְסָלַחְתָּ וְנָתַתָּה לָאִישׁ כְּכָל־ דְּרָכָיו
ways-of-him as-all-of with-the-each and-you-deal and-you-forgive to-dwell-you

אֲשֶׁר תֵּדַע אֶת־ לְבָבוֹ כִּי אַתָּה לְבַדְּךָ יָדַעְתָּ אֶת־ לְבַב
heart-of *** you-know by-yourself you for heart-of-him *** you-know since

בְּנֵי הָאָדָם׃ לְמַעַן יִירָאוּךָ לָלֶכֶת בִּדְרָכֶיךָ
in-ways-of-you to-walk they-will-fear-you so-that (31) the-man sons-of

כָּל־ הַיָּמִים אֲשֶׁר־ הֵם חַיִּים עַל־ פְּנֵי הָאֲדָמָה אֲשֶׁר נָתַתָּה
you-gave that the-land faces-of on ones-alive they that the-days all-of

לַאֲבֹתֵינוּ׃ וְגַם אֶל־ הַנָּכְרִי אֲשֶׁר לֹא מֵעַמְּךָ
from-people-of-you not who the-foreigner for and-also (32) to-fathers-of-us

יִשְׂרָאֵל הוּא וּבָא ׀ מֵאֶרֶץ רְחוֹקָה לְמַעַן שִׁמְךָ הַגָּדוֹל
the-great name-of-you because-of distant from-land but-he-came he Israel

וְיָדְךָ הַחֲזָקָה וּזְרוֹעֲךָ הַנְּטוּיָה
the-one-being-outstretched and-arm-of-you the-mighty and-hand-of-you

וּבָאוּ וְהִתְפַּלְלוּ אֶל־ הַבַּיִת הַזֶּה׃ וְאַתָּה
then-you (33) the-this the-temple toward and-they-pray when-they-come

תִּשְׁמַע מִן־ הַשָּׁמַיִם מִמְּכוֹן שִׁבְתְּךָ וְעָשִׂיתָ כְּכֹל אֲשֶׁר־
that as-all and-you-do to-dwell-you from-place-of the-heavens from you-hear

יִקְרָא אֵלֶיךָ הַנָּכְרִי לְמַעַן יֵדְעוּ כָל־ עַמֵּי
peoples-of all-of they-may-know so-that the-foreigner of-you he-asks

הָאָרֶץ אֶת־ שְׁמֶךָ וּלְיִרְאָה אֹתְךָ כְּעַמְּךָ יִשְׂרָאֵל
Israel as-people-of-you you and-to-fear name-of-you *** the-earth

וְלָדַעַת כִּי־ שִׁמְךָ נִקְרָא עַל־ הַבַּיִת הַזֶּה אֲשֶׁר בָּנִיתִי׃
I-built that the-this the-house to he-is-called Name-of-you that and-to-know

inheritance.
28“When famine or
plague comes to the land, or
blight or mildew, locusts or
grasshoppers, or when enemies besiege them in any
of their cities, whatever
disaster or disease may
come, 29and when a prayer
or plea is made by any of
your people Israel—each
one aware of his afflictions
and pains, and spreading
out his hands toward this
temple— 30then hear from
heaven, your dwelling
place. Forgive, and deal
with each man according to
all he does, since you know
his heart (for you alone
know the hearts of men),
31so that they will fear you
and walk in your ways all
the time they live in the
land you gave our fathers.
32“As for the foreigner
who does not belong to
your people Israel but has
come from a distant land
because of your great name
and your mighty hand and
your outstretched arm—
when he comes and prays
toward this temple, 33then
hear from heaven, your
dwelling place, and do
whatever the foreigner asks
of you, so that all the peoples of the earth may know
your name and fear you, as
do your own people Israel,
and may know that this
house I have built bears
your Name.

כִּי־ יֵצֵא עַמְּךָ לַמִּלְחָמָה עַל־ אוֹיְבָיו
being-enemies-of-him against to-the-war people-of-you he-goes-out when (34)

בַּדֶּרֶךְ אֲשֶׁר תִּשְׁלָחֵם וְהִתְפַּלְלוּ אֵלֶיךָ דֶּרֶךְ הָעִיר
the-city direction-of to-you and-they-pray you-send-them that in-the-way

הַזֹּאת אֲשֶׁר בָּחַרְתָּ בָּהּ וְהַבַּיִת אֲשֶׁר־ בָּנִיתִי לִשְׁמֶךָ׃
for-Name-of-you I-built that and-the-temple to-her you-chose that the-this

וְשָׁמַעְתָּ מִן־ הַשָּׁמַיִם אֶת־ תְּפִלָּתָם וְאֶת־ תְּחִנָּתָם
plea-of-them and prayer-of-them *** the-heavens from then-you-hear (35)

וְעָשִׂיתָ מִשְׁפָּטָם׃ כִּי יֶחֶטְאוּ־ לָךְ כִּי אֵין אָדָם
person no for against-you they-sin when (36) cause-of-them and-you-uphold

אֲשֶׁר לֹא־ יֶחֱטָא וְאָנַפְתָּ בָם וּנְתַתָּם לִפְנֵי
over-to and-you-give-them with-them and-you-become-angry he-sins not who

אוֹיֵב וְשָׁבוּם שׁוֹבֵיהֶם אֶל־אֶרֶץ
land to ones-being-captive-of-them and-they-take-captive-them one-being-enemy

רְחוֹקָה אוֹ קְרוֹבָה׃ וְהֵשִׁיבוּ אֶל־ לְבָבָם בָּאָרֶץ אֲשֶׁר
where in-the-land heart-of-them in and-they-change (37) near or far

נִשְׁבּוּ־ שָׁם וְשָׁבוּ ׀ וְהִתְחַנְּנוּ אֵלֶיךָ
with-you and-they-plead and-they-repent there they-are-held-captive

בְּאֶרֶץ שִׁבְיָם לֵאמֹר חָטָאנוּ הֶעֱוִינוּ וְרָשָׁעְנוּ׃
and-we-acted-wickedly we-did-wrong we-sinned to-say captivity-of-them in-land-of

וְשָׁבוּ אֵלֶיךָ בְּכָל־ לִבָּם וּבְכָל־
and-with-all-of heart-of-them with-all-of to-you and-they-turn (38)

נַפְשָׁם בְּאֶרֶץ שִׁבְיָם אֲשֶׁר־ שָׁבוּ אֹתָם
them they-took-captive where captivity-of-them in-land-of soul-of-them

וְהִתְפַּלְלוּ דֶּרֶךְ אַרְצָם אֲשֶׁר נָתַתָּה לַאֲבוֹתָם
to-fathers-of-them you-gave that land-of-them direction-of and-they-pray

וְהָעִיר אֲשֶׁר בָּחַרְתָּ וְלַבַּיִת אֲשֶׁר־ בָּנִיתִי
I-built that and-toward-the-temple you-chose that and-the-city

לִשְׁמֶךָ׃ וְשָׁמַעְתָּ מִן־ הַשָּׁמַיִם מִמְּכוֹן
from-place-of the-heavens from then-you-hear (39) for-Name-of-you

שִׁבְתְּךָ אֶת־ תְּפִלָּתָם וְאֶת־ תְּחִנֹּתֵיהֶם וְעָשִׂיתָ
and-you-uphold pleas-of-them and prayer-of-them *** to-dwell-you

מִשְׁפָּטָם וְסָלַחְתָּ לְעַמְּךָ אֲשֶׁר חָטְאוּ־ לָךְ׃
against-you they-sinned who to-people-of-you and-you-forgive cause-of-them

עַתָּה אֱלֹהַי יִהְיוּ־ נָא עֵינֶיךָ פְּתֻחוֹת
ones-being-open eyes-of-you now! may-they-be God-of-me now (40)

וְאָזְנֶיךָ קַשֻּׁבוֹת לִתְפִלַּת הַמָּקוֹם הַזֶּה׃ וְעַתָּה
and-now (41) the-this the-place to-prayer-of ones-attentive and-ears-of-you

34"When your people go to war against their enemies, wherever you send them, and when they pray to you toward this city you have chosen and the temple I have built for your Name, 35then hear from heaven their prayer and their plea, and uphold their cause.

36"When they sin against you—for there is no one who does not sin—and you become angry with them and give them over to the enemy, who takes them captive to a land far away or near; 37and if they have a change of heart in the land where they are held captive, and repent and plead with you in the land of their captivity and say, 'We have sinned, we have done wrong and acted wickedly'; 38and if they turn back to you with all their heart and soul in the land of their captivity where they were taken, and pray toward the land you gave their fathers, toward the city you have chosen and toward the temple I have built for your Name; 39then from heaven, your dwelling place, hear their prayer and their pleas, and uphold their cause. And forgive your people, who have sinned against you.

40"Now, my God, may your eyes be open and your ears attentive to the prayers offered in this place.

קוּמָה יְהוָה אֱלֹהִים לְנוּחֶךָ אַתָּה וַאֲרוֹן עֻזֶּךָ
might-of-you and-ark-of you to-resting-place-of-you God Yahweh arise!

כֹּהֲנֶיךָ יְהוָה אֱלֹהִים יִלְבְּשׁוּ תְשׁוּעָה וַחֲסִידֶיךָ
and-saints-of-you salvation may-they-be-clothed God Yahweh priests-of-you

יִשְׂמְחוּ בַטּוֹב׃ (42) יְהוָה אֱלֹהִים אַל־ תָּשֵׁב פְּנֵי
faces-of you-reject not God Yahweh (42) in-the-goodness may-they-rejoice

מְשִׁיחֶךָ* זָכְרָה לְחַסְדֵי דָּוִיד עַבְדֶּךָ׃
servant-of-you David to-kindnesses-of remember! *anointed-ones-of-you

(7:1) וּכְכַלּוֹת שְׁלֹמֹה לְהִתְפַּלֵּל וְהָאֵשׁ יָרְדָה
she-came-down then-the-fire to-pray Solomon and-when-to-finish (7:1)

מֵהַשָּׁמַיִם וַתֹּאכַל הָעֹלָה וְהַזְּבָחִים
and-the-sacrifices the-burnt-offering and-she-consumed from-the-heavens

וּכְבוֹד יְהוָה מָלֵא אֶת־ הַבָּיִת׃ (2) וְלֹא יָכְלוּ
they-could and-not (2) the-temple *** he-filled Yahweh and-glory-of

הַכֹּהֲנִים לָבוֹא אֶל־ בֵּית יְהוָה כִּי־ מָלֵא כְבוֹד־ יְהוָה
Yahweh glory-of he-filled because Yahweh temple-of into to-enter the-priests

אֶת־ בֵּית יְהוָה׃ (3) וְכֹל ׀ בְּנֵי יִשְׂרָאֵל רֹאִים
ones-seeing Israel sons-of when-all-of (3) Yahweh temple-of ***

בְּרֶדֶת הָאֵשׁ וּכְבוֹד יְהוָה עַל־ הַבָּיִת
the-temple above Yahweh and-glory-of the-fire when-to-come-down

וַיִּכְרְעוּ אַפַּיִם אַרְצָה עַל־ הָרִצְפָה וַיִּשְׁתַּחֲווּ
and-they-worshiped the-pavement on to-ground faces then-they-knelt

וְהוֹדוֹת לַיהוָה כִּי טוֹב כִּי לְעוֹלָם חַסְדּוֹ׃
love-of-him to-forever indeed good that to-Yahweh and-to-give-thanks

(4) וְהַמֶּלֶךְ וְכָל־ הָעָם זֹבְחִים זֶבַח לִפְנֵי יְהוָה׃
Yahweh before sacrifice ones-offering the-people and-all-of then-the-king (4)

(5) וַיִּזְבַּח הַמֶּלֶךְ שְׁלֹמֹה אֶת־ זֶבַח הַבָּקָר עֶשְׂרִים וּשְׁנַיִם
and-two twenty the-cattle sacrifice-of *** Solomon the-king and-he-offered (5)

אֶלֶף וְצֹאן מֵאָה וְעֶשְׂרִים אָלֶף וַיַּחְנְכוּ אֶת־
*** so-they-dedicated thousand and-twenty hundred and-sheep thousand

בֵּית הָאֱלֹהִים הַמֶּלֶךְ וְכָל־ הָעָם׃ (6) וְהַכֹּהֲנִים עַל־
at and-the-priests (6) the-people and-all-of the-king the-God temple-of

מִשְׁמְרוֹתָם עֹמְדִים וְהַלְוִיִּם בִּכְלֵי־ שִׁיר
music-of with-instruments-of and-the-Levites ones-standing positions-of-them

יְהוָה אֲשֶׁר עָשָׂה דָּוִיד הַמֶּלֶךְ לְהֹדוֹת לַיהוָה כִּי־ לְעוֹלָם
to-forever indeed to-Yahweh to-give-thanks the-king David he-made which Yahweh

חַסְדּוֹ בְּהַלֵּל דָּוִיד בְּיָדָם וְהַכֹּהֲנִים
and-the-priests by-hand-of-them David when-to-praise love-of-him

41"Now arise, O LORD
God, and come to
your resting place,
you and the ark of
your might.
May your priests, O
LORD God, be
clothed with
salvation,
may your saints
rejoice in your
goodness.
42O LORD God, do not
reject your anointed
one.
Remember the
kindnesses
promised to David
your servant."

The Dedication of the Temple

7 When Solomon finished
praying, fire came down
from heaven and consumed
the burnt offering and the sacrifices, and the glory of the
LORD filled the temple.
2The
priests could not enter the
temple of the LORD because the
glory of the LORD filled it.
3When all the Israelites saw
the fire coming down and the
glory of the LORD above the
temple, they knelt on the
pavement with their faces to
the ground, and they wor-
shiped and gave thanks to the
LORD, saying,

"He is good;
his love endures
forever."

4Then the king and all the
people offered sacrifices before
the LORD.
5And King Solomon
offered a sacrifice of twenty-
two thousand head of cattle
and a hundred and twenty
thousand sheep and goats. So
the king and all the people
dedicated the temple of God.
6The priests took their positions, as did the Levites with
the LORD's musical instruments, which King David had
made for praising the LORD
and which were used when he
gave thanks, saying, "His love
endures forever." Opposite
the Levites, the priests blew

*42 Many mss (and Ps. 132:10) have this word in the singular (חֶךָ—).

מַחְצְצְרִים נֶגְדָּם וְכָל־ יִשְׂרָאֵל עֹמְדִים׃
ones-standing Israel and-all-of opposite-them ones-blowing-trumpets

וַיְקַדֵּשׁ שְׁלֹמֹה אֶת־ תּוֹךְ הֶחָצֵר אֲשֶׁר לִפְנֵי
in-front-of that the-courtyard middle-of *** Solomon and-he-consecrated (7)

בֵית־ יְהוָה כִּי־ עָשָׂה שָׁם הָעֹלוֹת וְאֵת חֶלְבֵי
fat-parts-of and the-burnt-offerings here he-offered for Yahweh temple-of

הַשְּׁלָמִים כִּי־ מִזְבַּח הַנְּחֹשֶׁת אֲשֶׁר עָשָׂה שְׁלֹמֹה
Solomon he-made that the-bronze altar-of because the-fellowship-offerings

לֹא יָכוֹל לְהָכִיל אֶת־ הָעֹלָה וְאֶת־ הַמִּנְחָה וְאֶת־
and the-grain-offering and the-burnt-offering *** to-hold he-could not

הַחֲלָבִים׃ וַיַּעַשׂ שְׁלֹמֹה אֶת־ הֶחָג בָּעֵת
at-the-time the-festival *** Solomon so-he-observed (8) the-fat-portions

הַהִיא שִׁבְעַת יָמִים וְכָל־ יִשְׂרָאֵל עִמּוֹ קָהָל גָּדוֹל מְאֹד
very vast assembly with-him Israel and-all-of days seven-of the-that

מִלְּבוֹא חֲמָת עַד־ נַחַל מִצְרָיִם׃ וַיַּעֲשׂוּ בַּיּוֹם הַשְּׁמִינִי
the-eighth on-the-day and-they-held (9) Egypt Wadi-of to Hamath from-Lebo

עֲצָרֶת כִּי ׀ חֲנֻכַּת הַמִּזְבֵּחַ עָשׂוּ שִׁבְעַת יָמִים
days seven-of they-celebrated the-altar dedication-of for assembly

וְהֶחָג שִׁבְעַת יָמִים׃ וּבְיוֹם עֶשְׂרִים וּשְׁלֹשָׁה
and-three twenty and-on-day-of (10) days seven-of and-the-festival

לַחֹדֶשׁ הַשְּׁבִיעִי שִׁלַּח אֶת־ הָעָם לְאָהֳלֵיהֶם שְׂמֵחִים
ones-joyful to-homes-of-them the-people *** he-sent the-seventh of-the-month

וְטוֹבֵי לֵב עַל־ הַטּוֹבָה אֲשֶׁר עָשָׂה יְהוָה לְדָוִיד
for-David Yahweh he-did that the-good for heart and-ones-glad-of

וְלִשְׁלֹמֹה וּלְיִשְׂרָאֵל עַמּוֹ׃ וַיְכַל שְׁלֹמֹה
Solomon when-he-finished (11) people-of-him and-for-Israel and-for-Solomon

אֶת־ בֵּית יְהוָה וְאֶת־ בֵּית הַמֶּלֶךְ וְאֵת כָּל־ הַבָּא עַל־
into the-thing-coming all-of and the-king palace-of and Yahweh temple-of ***

לֵב שְׁלֹמֹה לַעֲשׂוֹת בְּבֵית־ יְהוָה וּבְבֵיתוֹ
and-in-palace-of-him Yahweh in-temple-of to-do Solomon mind-of

הִצְלִיחַ׃ וַיֵּרָא יְהוָה אֶל־ שְׁלֹמֹה בַּלָּיְלָה
in-the-night Solomon to Yahweh then-he-appeared (12) he-carried-out

וַיֹּאמֶר לוֹ שָׁמַעְתִּי אֶת־ תְּפִלָּתֶךָ וּבָחַרְתִּי בַּמָּקוֹם
to-the-place and-I-chose prayer-of-you *** I-heard to-him and-he-said

הַזֶּה לִי לְבֵית זָבַח׃ הֵן אֶעֱצֹר הַשָּׁמַיִם
the-heavens I-shut-up when (13) sacrifice as-temple-of for-me the-this

וְלֹא־ יִהְיֶה מָטָר וְהֵן־ אֲצַוֶּה עַל־ חָגָב לֶאֱכוֹל הָאָרֶץ וְאִם־
or-when the-land to-devour locust to I-command or-when rain he-is so-not

their trumpets, and all the Israelites were standing.
7Solomon consecrated the
middle part of the courtyard in
front of the temple of the
LORD, and there he offered
burnt offerings and the fat of
the fellowship offerings,[d] because the bronze altar he had
made could not hold the burnt
offerings, the grain offerings
and the fat portions.
8So Solomon observed the
festival at that time for seven
days, and all Israel with him—
a vast assembly, people from
Lebo[e] Hamath to the Wadi of
Egypt. 9On the eighth day
they held an assembly, for
they had celebrated the dedication of the altar for seven
days and the festival for seven
days more. 10On the twenty-third day of the seventh
month he sent the people to
their homes, joyful and glad in
heart for the good things the
LORD had done for David and
Solomon and for his people Israel.

The LORD Appears to Solomon

11When Solomon had
finished the temple of the
LORD and the royal palace, and
had succeeded in carrying out
all he had in mind to do in the
temple of the LORD and in his
own palace, 12the LORD appeared to him at night and
said:

"I have heard your
prayer and have chosen
this place for myself as a
temple for sacrifices.
13"When I shut up the
heavens so that there is no
rain, or command locusts to
devour the land or send a

[d]7 Traditionally *peace offerings*
[e]8 Or *from the entrance to*

°6 ק מחצרים

אֲשַׁלַּח דֶּבֶר בְּעַמִּי׃ וְיִכָּנְעוּ עַמִּי
people-of-me if-they-humble-themselves (14) among-people-of-me plague I-send

אֲשֶׁר נִקְרָא־ שְׁמִי עֲלֵיהֶם וְיִתְפַּלְלוּ וִיבַקְשׁוּ פָנַי
faces-of-me and-they-seek and-they-pray on-them name-of-me he-is-called who

וְיָשֻׁבוּ מִדַּרְכֵיהֶם הָרָעִים וַאֲנִי אֶשְׁמַע מִן־
from I-will-hear then-I the-wicked-ones from-ways-of-them and-they-turn

הַשָּׁמַיִם וְאֶסְלַח לְחַטָּאתָם וְאֶרְפָּא אֶת־ אַרְצָם׃
land-of-them *** and-I-will-heal to-sin-of-them and-I-will-forgive the-heavens

עַתָּה עֵינַי יִהְיוּ פְתֻחוֹת וְאָזְנַי קַשֻּׁבוֹת
ones-attentive and-ears-of-me ones-being-open they-will-be eyes-of-me now (15)

לִתְפִלַּת הַמָּקוֹם הַזֶּה׃ וְעַתָּה בָּחַרְתִּי וְהִקְדַּשְׁתִּי אֶת־
*** and-I-consecrated I-chose and-now (16) the-this the-place to-prayer-of

הַבַּיִת הַזֶּה לִהְיוֹת־ שְׁמִי שָׁם עַד־ עוֹלָם וְהָיוּ
and-they-will-be forever to there Name-of-me to-be the-this the-temple

עֵינַי וְלִבִּי שָׁם כָּל־ הַיָּמִים׃ וְאַתָּה אִם־ תֵּלֵךְ
you-walk if and-you (17) the-days all-of there and-heart-of-me eyes-of-me

לְפָנַי כַּאֲשֶׁר הָלַךְ דָּוִיד אָבִיךָ וְלַעֲשׂוֹת כְּכֹל אֲשֶׁר
that as-all and-to-do father-of-you David he-walked just-as before-me

צִוִּיתִיךָ וְחֻקַּי וּמִשְׁפָּטַי תִּשְׁמוֹר׃
you-observe and-laws-of-me and-decrees-of-me I-command-you

וַהֲקִימוֹתִי אֵת כִּסֵּא מַלְכוּתֶךָ כַּאֲשֶׁר כָּרַתִּי
I-covenanted just-as kingdom-of-you throne-of *** then-I-will-establish (18)

לְדָוִיד אָבִיךָ לֵאמֹר לֹא־ יִכָּרֵת לְךָ אִישׁ מוֹשֵׁל
ruling man of-you he-shall-be-cut-off not to-say father-of-you with-David

בְּיִשְׂרָאֵל׃ וְאִם־ תְּשׁוּבוּן אַתֶּם וַעֲזַבְתֶּם חֻקּוֹתַי
decrees-of-me and-you-forsake you you-turn but-if (19) over-Israel

וּמִצְוֺתַי אֲשֶׁר נָתַתִּי לִפְנֵיכֶם וַהֲלַכְתֶּם וַעֲבַדְתֶּם אֱלֹהִים
gods and-you-serve and-you-go before-you I-gave that and-commands-of-me

אֲחֵרִים וְהִשְׁתַּחֲוִיתֶם לָהֶם׃ וּנְתַשְׁתִּים מֵעַל
from-on then-I-will-uproot-them (20) to-them and-you-worship other-ones

אַדְמָתִי אֲשֶׁר נָתַתִּי לָהֶם וְאֶת־ הַבַּיִת הַזֶּה אֲשֶׁר הִקְדַּשְׁתִּי
I-consecrated that the-this the-temple and to-them I-gave which land-of-me

לִשְׁמִי אַשְׁלִיךְ מֵעַל פָּנָי וְאֶתְּנֶנּוּ
and-I-will-make-him faces-of-me from-before I-will-reject for-Name-of-me

לְמָשָׁל וְלִשְׁנִינָה בְּכָל־ הָעַמִּים׃
the-peoples among-all-of and-as-object-of-ridicule as-byword

וְהַבַּיִת הַזֶּה אֲשֶׁר הָיָה עֶלְיוֹן לְכָל־ עֹבֵר
one-passing to-every-of imposing he-is that the-this though-the-temple (21)

plague among my people,
[14]if my people, who are
called by my name, will
humble themselves and
pray and seek my face and
turn from their wicked
ways, then will I hear from
heaven and will forgive
their sin and will heal their
land. [15]Now my eyes will be
open and my ears attentive
to the prayers offered in
this place. [16]I have chosen
and consecrated this tem-
ple so that my Name may
be there forever. My eyes
and my heart will always
be there.
[17]"As for you, if you walk
before me as David your father did, and do all I command, and observe my de-
crees and laws, [18]I will
establish your royal throne,
as I covenanted with David
your father when I said,
'You shall never fail to have
a man to rule over Israel.'
[19]"But if you[f] turn away
and forsake the decrees and
commands I have given
you[f] and go off to serve
other gods and worship
them, [20]then I will uproot
Israel from my land, which
I have given them, and will
reject this temple I have
consecrated for my Name. I
will make it a byword and
an object of ridicule among
all peoples. [21]And though
this temple is now so im-
posing, all who pass by will

[f]19 The Hebrew is plural.

עָלָיו יִשֹּׁם וְאָמַר בַּמֶּה עָשָׂה יְהוָה כָּכָה
such Yahweh he-did for-the-why? and-he-will-say he-will-be-appalled by-him

לָאָרֶץ הַזֹּאת וְלַבַּיִת הַזֶּה׃ וְאָמְרוּ
and-they-will-answer (22) the-this and-to-the-temple the-this to-the-land

עַל אֲשֶׁר עָזְבוּ אֶת־ יְהוָה׀ אֱלֹהֵי אֲבֹתֵיהֶם אֲשֶׁר
who fathers-of-them God-of Yahweh *** they-forsook that because

הוֹצִיאָם מֵאֶרֶץ מִצְרַיִם וַיַּחֲזִיקוּ בֵּאלֹהִים אֲחֵרִים
other-ones on-gods and-they-embraced Egypt from-land-of he-brought-them

וַיִּשְׁתַּחֲווּ לָהֶם וַיַּעַבְדוּם עַל־ כֵּן הֵבִיא עֲלֵיהֶם
on-them he-brought this for and-they-served-them to-them and-they-worshiped

אֵת כָּל־ הָרָעָה הַזֹּאת׃ וַיְהִי מִקֵּץ׀ עֶשְׂרִים שָׁנָה אֲשֶׁר
when year twenty at-end-of and-he-was (8:1) the-this the-disaster all-of ***

בָּנָה שְׁלֹמֹה אֶת־ בֵּית יְהוָה וְאֶת־ בֵּיתוֹ׃ וְהֶעָרִים
and-the-villages (2) palace-of-him and Yahweh temple-of *** Solomon he-built

אֲשֶׁר נָתַן חוּרָם לִשְׁלֹמֹה בָּנָה שְׁלֹמֹה אֹתָם וַיּוֹשֶׁב שָׁם
there and-he-settled them Solomon he-rebuilt to-Solomon Huram he-gave that

אֶת־ בְּנֵי יִשְׂרָאֵל׃ וַיֵּלֶךְ שְׁלֹמֹה חֲמָת צוֹבָה וַיֶּחֱזַק
and-he-captured Zobah Hamath Solomon then-he-went (3) Israel sons-of ***

עָלֶיהָ׃ וַיִּבֶן אֶת־ תַּדְמֹר בַּמִּדְבָּר וְאֵת כָּל־ עָרֵי
cities-of all-of and in-the-desert Tadmor *** and-he-built-up (4) to-her

הַמִּסְכְּנוֹת אֲשֶׁר בָּנָה בַּחֲמָת׃ וַיִּבֶן אֶת־ בֵּית חוֹרוֹן
Horon Beth *** and-he-rebuilt (5) in-Hamath he-built that the-stores

הָעֶלְיוֹן וְאֶת־ בֵּית חוֹרוֹן הַתַּחְתּוֹן עָרֵי מָצוֹר חוֹמוֹת דְּלָתַיִם
gates walls fortification cities-of the-Lower Horon Beth and the-Upper

וּבְרִיחַ׃ וְאֶת־ בַּעֲלָת וְאֵת כָּל־ עָרֵי הַמִּסְכְּנוֹת אֲשֶׁר הָיוּ
they-were that the-stores cities-of all-of and Baalath and (6) and-bar

לִשְׁלֹמֹה וְאֵת כָּל־ עָרֵי הָרֶכֶב וְאֵת עָרֵי הַפָּרָשִׁים וְאֵת׀
and the-horses cities-of and the-chariot cities-of all-of and to-Solomon

כָּל־ חֵשֶׁק שְׁלֹמֹה אֲשֶׁר חָשַׁק לִבְנוֹת בִּירוּשָׁלַםִ
in-Jerusalem to-build he-desired that Solomon desire-of every-of

וּבַלְּבָנוֹן וּבְכֹל אֶרֶץ מֶמְשַׁלְתּוֹ׃ כָּל־
all-of (7) rule-of-him territory-of and-through-all-of and-in-the-Lebanon

הָעָם הַנּוֹתָר מִן־ הַחִתִּי וְהָאֱמֹרִי
and-the-Amorite the-Hittite from the-one-being-left the-people

וְהַפְּרִזִּי וְהַחִוִּי וְהַיְבוּסִי אֲשֶׁר לֹא מִיִּשְׂרָאֵל הֵמָּה׃
they from-Israel not who and-the-Jebusite and-the-Hivite and-the-Perizzite

מִן־ בְּנֵיהֶם אֲשֶׁר נוֹתְרוּ אַחֲרֵיהֶם בָּאָרֶץ אֲשֶׁר
who in-the-land after-them they-remained who descendants-of-them from (8)

be appalled and say, 'Why has the LORD done such a thing to this land and to this temple?'
22 People will answer, 'Because they have forsaken the LORD, the God of their fathers, who brought them out of Egypt, and have embraced other gods, worshiping and serving them—that is why he brought all this disaster on them.' "

Solomon's Other Activities

8 At the end of twenty years, during which Solomon built the temple of the LORD and his own palace,
2 Solomon rebuilt the villages that Hiram[g] had given him, and settled Israelites in them.
3 Solomon then went to Hamath Zobah and captured it.
4 He also built up Tadmor in the desert and all the store cities he had built in Hamath.
5 He rebuilt Upper Beth Horon and Lower Beth Horon as fortified cities, with walls and with gates and bars,
6 as well as Baalath and all his store cities, and all the cities for his chariots and for his horses[h]—whatever he desired to build in Jerusalem, in Lebanon and throughout all the territory he ruled.
7 All the people left from the Hittites, Amorites, Perizzites, Hivites and Jebusites (these peoples were not Israelites),
8 that is, their descendants remaining in the land, whom

[g]2 Hebrew *Huram*, a variant of *Hiram*; also in verse 18
[h]6 Or *charioteers*

לֹא־ כִלּוּם בְּנֵי יִשְׂרָאֵל וַיַּעֲלֵם שְׁלֹמֹה
Solomon now-he-conscripted-them Israel sons-of they-destroyed-them not

לְמַס עַד הַיּוֹם הַזֶּה׃ וּמִן־ בְּנֵי יִשְׂרָאֵל אֲשֶׁר לֹא־
not who Israel sons-of but-from (9) the-this the-day to for-slave-labor

נָתַן שְׁלֹמֹה לַעֲבָדִים לִמְלַאכְתּוֹ כִּי־ הֵמָּה אַנְשֵׁי מִלְחָמָה
fight men-of they for for-work-of-him as-slaves Solomon he-made

וְשָׂרֵי שָׁלִישָׁיו וְשָׂרֵי רִכְבּוֹ
chariot-of-him and-commanders-of captains-of-him and-commanders-of

וּפָרָשָׁיו׃ וְאֵלֶּה שָׂרֵי הַנִּצִּיבִים°
the-ones-being-officials chiefs-of and-these (10) and-charioteers-of-him

אֲשֶׁר־ לַמֶּלֶךְ שְׁלֹמֹה חֲמִשִּׁים וּמָאתַיִם הָרֹדִים
the-ones-supervising and-two-hundreds fifty Solomon of-the-king who

בָּעָם׃ וְאֶת־ בַּת־ פַּרְעֹה הֶעֱלָה שְׁלֹמֹה
Solomon he-brought-up Pharaoh daughter-of and (11) over-the-people

מֵעִיר דָּוִיד לַבַּיִת אֲשֶׁר בָּנָה־ לָהּ כִּי אָמַר לֹא־
not he-said for for-her he-built that to-the-palace David from-City-of

תֵשֵׁב אִשָּׁה לִי בְּבֵית דָּוִיד מֶלֶךְ־ יִשְׂרָאֵל כִּי־ קֹדֶשׁ
holy because Israel king-of David in-palace-of of-me wife she-must-live

הֵמָּה אֲשֶׁר־ בָּאָה אֲלֵיהֶם אֲרוֹן יְהוָה׃ אָז הֶעֱלָה
he-sacrificed then (12) Yahweh ark-of into-them she-entered where they

שְׁלֹמֹה עֹלוֹת לַיהוָה עַל מִזְבַּח יְהוָה אֲשֶׁר בָּנָה לִפְנֵי
in-front-of he-built that Yahweh altar-of on to-Yahweh burnt-offerings Solomon

הָאוּלָם׃ וּבִדְבַר־ יוֹם בְּיוֹם לְהַעֲלוֹת
to-offer by-day day and-for-requirement-of (13) the-portico

כְּמִצְוַת מֹשֶׁה לַשַּׁבָּתוֹת וְלֶחֳדָשִׁים וְלַמּוֹעֲדוֹת
and-for-the-feasts and-for-the-New-Moons for-the-Sabbaths Moses as-command-of

שָׁלוֹשׁ פְּעָמִים בַּשָּׁנָה בְּחַג הַמַּצּוֹת
the-Unleavened-Breads for-Feast-of during-the-year times three

וּבְחַג הַשָּׁבֻעוֹת וּבְחַג הַסֻּכּוֹת׃
the-Tabernacles and-for-Feast-of the-Weeks and-for-Feast-of

וַיַּעֲמֵד כְּמִשְׁפַּט דָּוִיד־ אָבִיו אֶת־ מַחְלְקוֹת
divisions-of *** father-of-him David as-ordinance-of and-he-appointed (14)

הַכֹּהֲנִים עַל־ עֲבֹדָתָם וְהַלְוִיִּם עַל־ מִשְׁמְרוֹתָם
leaderships-of-them for and-the-Levites duty-of-them for the-priests

לְהַלֵּל וּלְשָׁרֵת נֶגֶד הַכֹּהֲנִים לִדְבַר־ יוֹם
day for-requirement-of the-priests before and-to-assist to-praise

בְּיוֹמוֹ וְהַשּׁוֹעֲרִים בְּמַחְלְקוֹתָם לְשַׁעַר וָשָׁעַר
and-gate for-gate by-divisions-of-them and-the-gatekeepers by-day-of-him

the Israelites had not destroyed—these Solomon conscripted for his slave labor
force, as it is to this day. [9]But
Solomon did not make slaves of the Israelites for his work; they were his fighting men, commanders of his captains, and commanders of his chariots and charioteers. [10]They
were also King Solomon's chief officials—two hundred and fifty officials supervising the men.
[11]Solomon brought Pharaoh's daughter up from the City of David to the palace he had built for her, for he said, "My wife must not live in the palace of David king of Israel, because the places the ark of the LORD has entered are holy."
[12]On the altar of the LORD
that he had built in front of the portico, Solomon sacrificed burnt offerings to the
LORD, [13]according to the daily
requirement for offerings commanded by Moses for Sabbaths, New Moons and the three annual feasts—the Feast of Unleavened Bread, the Feast of Weeks and the Feast
of Tabernacles. [14]Following
the ordinance of his father David, he appointed the divisions of the priests for their duties, and the Levites to lead the praise and to assist the priests according to each day's requirement. He also appointed the gatekeepers by divisions for the various gates, because this was what David the

°10 ק הנצבים

כִּי כֵן מִצְוַת דָּוִיד אִישׁ־ הָאֱלֹהִים׃ וְלֹא סָרוּ
they-deviated and-not (15) the-God man-of David order-of this because

מִצְוַת הַמֶּלֶךְ עַל־ הַכֹּהֲנִים וְהַלְוִיִּם לְכָל־ דָּבָר
matter in-any-of and-the-Levites the-priests to the-king command-of

וְלָאֹצָרוֹת׃ וַתִּכֹּן כָּל־ מְלֶאכֶת שְׁלֹמֹה
Solomon work-of all-of and-she-was-carried-out (16) even-about-the-treasuries

עַד־ הַיּוֹם מוּסַד בֵּית־ יְהוָה וְעַד־ כְּלֹתוֹ
to-be-completed-him and-to Yahweh temple-of foundation-of the-day from

שָׁלֵם בֵּית יְהוָה׃ אָז הָלַךְ שְׁלֹמֹה לְעֶצְיוֹן־ גֶּבֶר וְאֶל־
and-to Geber to-Ezion Solomon he-went then (17) Yahweh temple-of finished

אֵילוֹת עַל־ שְׂפַת הַיָּם בְּאֶרֶץ אֱדוֹם׃ וַיִּשְׁלַח־ לוֹ חוּרָם
Huram to-him and-he-sent (18) Edom in-land-of the-sea coast-of on Elath

בְּיַד־ עֲבָדָיו אֳנִיּוֹת° וַעֲבָדִים יוֹדְעֵי יָם וַיָּבֹאוּ
and-they-sailed sea ones-knowing-of and-men ships officers-of-him by-hand-of

עִם־ עַבְדֵי שְׁלֹמֹה אוֹפִירָה וַיִּקְחוּ מִשָּׁם אַרְבַּע־ מֵאוֹת
hundreds four from-there and-they-brought to-Ophir Solomon men-of with

וַחֲמִשִּׁים כִּכַּר זָהָב וַיָּבִיאוּ אֶל־ הַמֶּלֶךְ שְׁלֹמֹה׃
Solomon the-king to and-they-delivered gold talent-of and-fifty

וּמַלְכַּת־ שְׁבָא שָׁמְעָה אֶת־ שֵׁמַע שְׁלֹמֹה וַתָּבוֹא
then-she-came Solomon fame-of *** she-heard Sheba when-queen-of (9:1)

לְנַסּוֹת אֶת־ שְׁלֹמֹה בְחִידוֹת בִּירוּשָׁלִַם בְּחַיִל כָּבֵד מְאֹד
very great with-caravan to-Jerusalem with-hard-questions Solomon *** to-test

וּגְמַלִּים נֹשְׂאִים בְּשָׂמִים וְזָהָב לָרֹב וְאֶבֶן יְקָרָה
precious and-stone in-quantity and-gold spices ones-carrying and-camels

וַתָּבוֹא אֶל־ שְׁלֹמֹה וַתְּדַבֵּר עִמּוֹ אֵת כָּל־ אֲשֶׁר הָיָה עִם־
on he-was that all *** with-him and-she-talked Solomon to and-she-came

לְבָבָהּ׃ וַיַּגֶּד־ לָהּ שְׁלֹמֹה אֶת־ כָּל־ דְּבָרֶיהָ
questions-of-her all-of *** Solomon to-her and-he-answered (2) mind-of-her

וְלֹא־ נֶעְלַם דָּבָר מִשְּׁלֹמֹה אֲשֶׁר לֹא הִגִּיד לָהּ׃
to-her he-explained not that for-Solomon question he-was-too-hard and-not

וַתֵּרֶא מַלְכַּת־ שְׁבָא אֵת חָכְמַת שְׁלֹמֹה וְהַבַּיִת אֲשֶׁר
that and-the-palace Solomon wisdom-of *** Sheba queen-of when-she-saw (3)

בָּנָה׃ וּמַאֲכַל שֻׁלְחָנוֹ וּמוֹשַׁב עֲבָדָיו
officials-of-him and-seating-of table-of-him and-food-of (4) he-built

וּמַעֲמַד מְשָׁרְתָיו וּמַלְבּוּשֵׁיהֶם וּמַשְׁקָיו
and-cupbearers-of-him and-robes-of-them ones-attending-him and-station-of

וּמַלְבּוּשֵׁיהֶם וַעֲלִיָּתוֹ* אֲשֶׁר יַעֲלֶה בֵּית יְהוָה
Yahweh temple-of he-went-up which *and-ascent-of-him and-robes-of-them

man of God had ordered.
[15]They did not deviate from
the king's commands to the
priests or to the Levites in any
matter, including that of the
treasuries.
[16]All Solomon's work was
carried out, from the day the
foundation of the temple of
the LORD was laid until its
completion. So the temple of
the LORD was finished.
[17]Then Solomon went to
Ezion Geber and Elath on the
seacoast of Edom. [18]And
Hiram sent him ships com-
manded by his own officers,
men who knew the sea. These,
with Solomon's men, sailed to
Ophir and brought back four
hundred and fifty talents[i] of
gold, which they delivered to
King Solomon.

The Queen of Sheba Visits Solomon

9 When the queen of Sheba
heard of Solomon's fame,
she came to Jerusalem to test
him with hard questions. Arriving with a very great cara-
van—with camels carrying
spices, large quantities of gold,
and precious stones—she
came to Solomon and talked
with him about all she had on
her mind. [2]Solomon answered
all her questions; nothing was
too hard for him to explain to
her. [3]When the queen of
Sheba saw the wisdom of
Solomon, as well as the palace
he had built, [4]the food on his
table, the seating of his
officials, the attending servants in their robes, the cup-
bearers in their robes and the
burnt offerings he made at[j]
the temple of the LORD, she

[i]18 That is, about 17 tons (about 16 metric tons)

[j]4 Or *the ascent by which he went up to*

*4 The NIV reads this word as in 1 Kings 10:5 (וְעֹלָתוֹ), *and-burnt-offering-of-him.*

°18 ק אניות

וְלֹא־ הָיָה עוֹד בָּהּ רֽוּחַ׃ וַתֹּאמֶר אֶל־ הַמֶּלֶךְ אֱמֶת
true the-king to and-she-said (5) breath in-her longer he-was then-not

הַדָּבָר אֲשֶׁר שָׁמַעְתִּי בְּאַרְצִי עַל־ דְּבָרֶיךָ וְעַל־
and-about achievements-of-you about in-country-of-me I-heard that the-report

חָכְמָתֶךָ׃ וְלֹא־ הֶאֱמַנְתִּי לְדִבְרֵיהֶם עַד אֲשֶׁר־ בָּאתִי
I-came when until in-sayings-of-them I-believed but-not (6) wisdom-of-you

וַתִּרְאֶינָה עֵינַי וְהִנֵּה לֹא הֻגַּד־ לִי חֲצִי מַרְבִּית
greatness-of half-of to-me he-was-told not and-see! eyes-of-me and-they-saw

חָכְמָתֶךָ יָסַפְתָּ עַל־ הַשְּׁמוּעָה אֲשֶׁר שָׁמָעְתִּי׃ אַשְׁרֵי
happinesses-of (7) I-heard that the-report over you-exceeded wisdom-of-you

אֲנָשֶׁיךָ וְאַשְׁרֵי עֲבָדֶיךָ אֵלֶּה הָעֹמְדִים
the-ones-standing these officials-of-you and-happinesses-of men-of-you

לְפָנֶיךָ תָּמִיד וְשֹׁמְעִים אֶת־ חָכְמָתֶךָ׃ יְהִי
may-he-be (8) wisdom-of-you *** and-ones-hearing continually before-you

יְהוָה אֱלֹהֶיךָ בָּרוּךְ אֲשֶׁר | חָפֵץ בְּךָ לְתִתְּךָ עַל־
on to-place-you in-you he-delighted who being-praised God-of-you Yahweh

כִּסְאוֹ לְמֶלֶךְ לַיהוָה אֱלֹהֶיךָ בְּאַהֲבַת אֱלֹהֶיךָ אֶת־
*** God-of-you because-to-love God-of-you for-Yahweh as-king throne-of-him

יִשְׂרָאֵל לְהַעֲמִידוֹ לְעוֹלָם וַיִּתֶּנְךָ עֲלֵיהֶם לְמֶלֶךְ לַעֲשׂוֹת
to-maintain as-king over-them then-he-made-you to-forever to-uphold-him Israel

מִשְׁפָּט וּצְדָקָה׃ וַתִּתֵּן לַמֶּלֶךְ מֵאָה וְעֶשְׂרִים |
and-twenty hundred to-the-king then-she-gave (9) and-righteousness justice

כִּכַּר זָהָב וּבְשָׂמִים לָרֹב מְאֹד וְאֶבֶן יְקָרָה וְלֹא
and-never precious and-stone large in-quantity and-spices gold talent-of

הָיָה כַּבֹּשֶׂם הַהוּא אֲשֶׁר־ נָתְנָה מַלְכַּת־ שְׁבָא לַמֶּלֶךְ
to-the-king Sheba queen-of she-gave that the-this like-the-spice he-was

שְׁלֹמֹה׃ וְגַם־ עַבְדֵי חירָם° וְעַבְדֵי שְׁלֹמֹה אֲשֶׁר־ הֵבִיאוּ זָהָב
gold they-brought who Solomon and-men-of Hiram men-of and-also (10) Solomon

מֵאוֹפִיר הֵבִיאוּ עֲצֵי אַלְגּוּמִּים וְאֶבֶן יְקָרָה׃ וַיַּעַשׂ
and-he-made (11) precious and-stone algums woods-of they-brought from-Ophir

הַמֶּלֶךְ אֶת־ עֲצֵי הָאַלְגּוּמִּים מְסִלּוֹת לְבֵית־ יְהוָה וּלְבֵית
and-for-palace-of Yahweh for-temple-of steps the-algums woods-of *** the-king

הַמֶּלֶךְ וְכִנֹּרוֹת וּנְבָלִים לַשָּׁרִים וְלֹא־
and-never for-the-ones-making-music and-lyres and-harps the-king

נִרְאוּ כָהֵם לְפָנִים בְּאֶרֶץ יְהוּדָה׃ וְהַמֶּלֶךְ שְׁלֹמֹה
Solomon and-the-king (12) Judah in-land-of before like-them they-were-seen

נָתַן לְמַלְכַּת־ שְׁבָא אֶת־ כָּל־ חֶפְצָהּ אֲשֶׁר שָׁאָלָה
she-asked-for that desire-of-her all-of *** Sheba to-queen-of he-gave

°10 ק חורם

was overwhelmed.
[5]She said to the king, "The
report I heard in my own
country about your achieve-
ments and your wisdom is
true. [6]But I did not believe
what they said until I came
and saw with my own eyes.
Indeed, not even half the
greatness of your wisdom was
told me; you have far exceeded
the report I heard. [7]How happy your men must be! How
happy your officials, who continually stand before you and
hear your wisdom! [8]Praise be
to the LORD your God, who has
delighted in you and placed
you on his throne as king to
rule for the LORD your God. Because of the love of your God
for Israel and his desire to
uphold them forever, he has
made you king over them, to
maintain justice and righteousness."
[9]Then she gave the king 120
talents[k] of gold, large quantities of spices, and precious
stones. There had never been
such spices as those the queen
of Sheba gave to King Solomon.
[10](The men of Hiram and the
men of Solomon brought gold
from Ophir; they also brought
algumwood[l] and precious
stones. [11]The king used the algumwood to make steps for
the temple of the LORD and for
the royal palace, and to make
harps and lyres for the musicians. Nothing like them had
ever been seen in Judah.)
[12]King Solomon gave the
queen of Sheba all she desired
and asked for; he gave her

[k]9 That is, about 4 1/2 tons (about 4 metric tons)
[l]10 Probably a variant of *almugwood*

מִלְּבַד אֲשֶׁר־הֵבִיאָה אֶל־הַמֶּלֶךְ וַתַּהֲפֹךְ וַתֵּלֶךְ
and-she-returned then-she-left the-king to she-brought what more-than

לְאַרְצָהּ הִיא וַעֲבָדֶיהָ׃ (13) וַיְהִי מִשְׁקַל הַזָּהָב
the-gold weight-of and-he-was (13) and-servants-of-her she to-country-of-her

אֲשֶׁר־בָּא לִשְׁלֹמֹה בְּשָׁנָה אֶחָת שֵׁשׁ מֵאוֹת וְשִׁשִּׁים וָשֵׁשׁ
and-six and-sixty hundreds six each in-year to-Solomon he-came that

כִּכְּרֵי זָהָב׃ (14) לְבַד מֵאַנְשֵׁי הַתָּרִים
the-ones-being-merchants from-men-of besides (14) gold talents-of

וְהַסֹּחֲרִים מְבִיאִים וְכָל־מַלְכֵי עֲרַב
Arabia kings-of and-all-of ones-bringing and-the-ones-trading

וּפַחוֹת הָאָרֶץ מְבִיאִים זָהָב וָכֶסֶף לִשְׁלֹמֹה׃
to-Solomon and-silver gold ones-bringing the-land and-governors-of

(15) וַיַּעַשׂ הַמֶּלֶךְ שְׁלֹמֹה מָאתַיִם צִנָּה זָהָב שָׁחוּט
being-hammered gold shield two-hundreds Solomon the-king and-he-made (15)

שֵׁשׁ מֵאוֹת זָהָב שָׁחוּט יַעֲלֶה עַל־הַצִּנָּה הָאֶחָת׃
the-each the-shield into he-went being-hammered gold hundreds six

(16) וּשְׁלֹשׁ־מֵאוֹת מָגִנִּים זָהָב שָׁחוּט שְׁלֹשׁ
three-of being-hammered gold small-shields hundreds and-three-of (16)

מֵאוֹת זָהָב יַעֲלֶה עַל־הַמָּגֵן הָאֶחָת וַיִּתְּנֵם הַמֶּלֶךְ
the-king and-he-put-them the-each the-shield into he-went gold hundreds

בְּבֵית יַעַר הַלְּבָנוֹן׃ (17) וַיַּעַשׂ הַמֶּלֶךְ כִּסֵּא־
throne-of the-king then-he-made (17) the-Lebanon Forest-of in-Palace-of

שֵׁן גָּדוֹל וַיְצַפֵּהוּ זָהָב טָהוֹר׃ (18) וְשֵׁשׁ מַעֲלוֹת לַכִּסֵּא
to-the-throne steps and-six-of (18) pure gold and-he-overlaid-him great ivory

וְכֶבֶשׁ בַּזָּהָב לַכִּסֵּא מָאֳחָזִים וְיָדוֹת
and-armrests ones-being-attached to-the-throne of-the-gold and-footstool

מִזֶּה וּמִזֶּה עַל־מְקוֹם הַשָּׁבֶת וּשְׁנַיִם אֲרָיוֹת
lions and-two the-seat place-of at and-on-that-side on-this-side

עֹמְדִים אֵצֶל הַיָּדוֹת׃ (19) וּשְׁנֵים עָשָׂר אֲרָיוֹת עֹמְדִים שָׁם
there ones-standing lions ten and-two (19) the-armrests beside ones-standing

עַל־שֵׁשׁ הַמַּעֲלוֹת מִזֶּה וּמִזֶּה לֹא־נַעֲשָׂה כֵן
like he-was-made not and-on-that-end on-this-end the-steps six-of on

לְכָל־מַמְלָכָה׃ (20) וְכֹל כְּלֵי מַשְׁקֵה הַמֶּלֶךְ שְׁלֹמֹה
Solomon the-king drinking-of goblets-of and-all-of (20) kingdom for-any-of

זָהָב וְכֹל כְּלֵי בֵית־יַעַר הַלְּבָנוֹן זָהָב סָגוּר
pure gold the-Lebanon Forest-of Palace-of articles-of and-all-of gold

אֵין כֶּסֶף נֶחְשָׁב בִּימֵי שְׁלֹמֹה לִמְאוּמָה׃ (21) כִּי־
indeed (21) as-anything Solomon in-days-of being-considered silver nothing-of

more than she had brought to
him. Then she left and returned with her retinue to her
own country.

Solomon's Splendor

13 The weight of the gold that
Solomon received yearly was
666 talents,[m] 14 not including
the revenues brought in by
merchants and traders. Also
all the kings of Arabia and the
governors of the land brought
gold and silver to Solomon.

15 King Solomon made two
hundred large shields of hammered gold; six hundred
bekas[n] of hammered gold
went into each shield. 16 He
also made three hundred small
shields of hammered gold,
with three hundred bekas[o] of
gold in each shield. The king
put them in the Palace of the
Forest of Lebanon.

17 Then the king made a great
throne inlaid with ivory and
overlaid with pure gold. 18 The
throne had six steps, and a
footstool of gold was attached
to it. On both sides of the seat
were armrests, with a lion
standing beside each of them.
19 Twelve lions stood on the six
steps, one at either end of each
step. Nothing like it had ever
been made for any other kingdom. 20 All King Solomon's
goblets were gold, and all the
household articles in the Palace of the Forest of Lebanon
were pure gold. Nothing was
made of silver, because silver
was considered of little value
in Solomon's day. 21 The king

[m] *13* That is, about 25 tons (about 23 metric tons)

[n] *15* That is, about 7 1/2 pounds (about 3.5 kilograms)

[o] *16* That is, about 3 3/4 pounds (about 1.7 kilograms)

אֳנִיּוֹת לַמֶּלֶךְ הֹלְכוֹת תַּרְשִׁישׁ עִם עַבְדֵי חוּרָם אַחַת לְשָׁלוֹשׁ שָׁנִים
years in-three once Huram men-of with Tarshish ones-going to-the-king ships

תָּבוֹאנָה׀ אֳנִיּוֹת תַּרְשִׁישׁ נֹשְׂאוֹת זָהָב וָכֶסֶף שֶׁנְהַבִּים וְקוֹפִים
and-apes ivories and-silver gold ones-carrying Tarshish ships-of they-returned

וְתוּכִּיִּים׃ (22) וַיִּגְדַּל הַמֶּלֶךְ שְׁלֹמֹה מִכֹּל מַלְכֵי
kings-of more-than-all-of Solomon the-king and-he-was-great (22) and-baboons

הָאָרֶץ לְעֹשֶׁר וְחָכְמָה׃ (23) וְכֹל מַלְכֵי הָאָרֶץ
the-earth kings-of and-all-of (23) and-wisdom in-wealth the-earth

מְבַקְשִׁים אֶת־ פְּנֵי שְׁלֹמֹה לִשְׁמֹעַ אֶת־ חָכְמָתוֹ אֲשֶׁר־ נָתַן
he-put that wisdom-of-him *** to-hear Solomon faces-of *** ones-seeking

הָאֱלֹהִים בְּלִבּוֹ׃ (24) וְהֵם מְבִיאִים אִישׁ מִנְחָתוֹ
gift-of-him each ones-bringing and-they (24) in-heart-of-him the-God

כְּלֵי כֶסֶף וּכְלֵי זָהָב וּשְׂלָמוֹת נֵשֶׁק וּבְשָׂמִים סוּסִים
horses and-spices weapon and-robes gold and-articles-of silver articles-of

וּפְרָדִים דְּבַר־ שָׁנָה בְּשָׁנָה׃ (25) וַיְהִי לִשְׁלֹמֹה אַרְבַּעַת
four-of to-Solomon and-he-was (25) after-year year event-of and-mules

אֲלָפִים אֻרְיוֹת סוּסִים וּמַרְכָּבוֹת וּשְׁנֵים־ עָשָׂר אֶלֶף פָּרָשִׁים
horses thousand ten and-two and-chariots horses stalls-of thousands

וַיַּנִּיחֵם בְּעָרֵי הָרֶכֶב וְעִם־ הַמֶּלֶךְ בִּירוּשָׁלִָם׃
in-Jerusalem the-king and-with the-chariot in-cities-of and-he-kept-them

(26) וַיְהִי מוֹשֵׁל בְּכָל־ הַמְּלָכִים מִן־ הַנָּהָר וְעַד־ אֶרֶץ
land-of even-to the-River from the-kings over-all-of ruling and-he-was (26)

פְּלִשְׁתִּים וְעַד גְּבוּל מִצְרָיִם׃ (27) וַיִּתֵּן הַמֶּלֶךְ אֶת־ הַכֶּסֶף
the-silver *** the-king and-he-made (27) Egypt border-of and-to Philistines

בִּירוּשָׁלִַם כָּאֲבָנִים וְאֵת הָאֲרָזִים נָתַן כַּשִּׁקְמִים
as-the-sycamore-trees he-made the-cedars and as-the-stones in-Jerusalem

אֲשֶׁר־ בַּשְּׁפֵלָה לָרֹב׃ (28) וּמוֹצִיאִים סוּסִים מִמִּצְרַיִם
from-Egypt horses and-ones-importing (28) in-number in-the-foothill that

לִשְׁלֹמֹה וּמִכָּל־ הָאֲרָצוֹת׃ (29) וּשְׁאָר דִּבְרֵי שְׁלֹמֹה
Solomon events-of and-other-of (29) the-countries and-from-all-of to-Solomon

הָרִאשֹׁנִים וְהָאַחֲרוֹנִים* הֲלֹא־ הֵם כְּתוּבִים עַל־ דִּבְרֵי
records-of in ones-being-written they not? and-the-ends the-beginnings

נָתָן הַנָּבִיא וְעַל־ נְבוּאַת אֲחִיָּה הַשִּׁילוֹנִי וּבַחֲזוֹת
and-in-visions-of the-Shilonite Ahijah prophecy-of and-in the-prophet Nathan

יֶעְדִּי° הַחֹזֶה עַל־ יָרָבְעָם בֶּן־ נְבָט׃ (30) וַיִּמְלֹךְ שְׁלֹמֹה
Solomon and-he-reigned (30) Nebat son-of Jeroboam concerning the-seer Iddo

בִירוּשָׁלִַם עַל־ כָּל־ יִשְׂרָאֵל אַרְבָּעִים שָׁנָה׃ (31) וַיִּשְׁכַּב שְׁלֹמֹה עִם־
with Solomon then-he-rested (31) year forty Israel all-of over in-Jerusalem

had a fleet of trading ships[p]
manned by Hiram's[q] men.
Once every three years it returned, carrying gold, silver
and ivory, and apes and ba-
boons.
[22]King Solomon was greater
in riches and wisdom than all
the other kings of the earth.
[23]All the kings of the earth
sought audience with Solomon to hear the wisdom God
had put in his heart. [24]Year after year, everyone who came
brought a gift—articles of silver and gold, and robes, weapons and spices, and horses
and mules.
[25]Solomon had four thousand stalls for horses and
chariots, and twelve thousand
horses,[r] which he kept in the
chariot cities and also with
him in Jerusalem. [26]He ruled
over all the kings from the
River[s] to the land of the Philistines, as far as the border of
Egypt. [27]The king made silver
as common in Jerusalem as
stones, and cedar as plentiful
as sycamore-fig trees in the
foothills. [28]Solomon's horses
were imported from Egypt[t]
and from all other countries.

Solomon's Death

[29]As for the other events of
Solomon's reign, from beginning to end, are they not written in the records of Nathan
the prophet, in the prophecy
of Ahijah the Shilonite and in
the visions of Iddo the seer
concerning Jeroboam son of
Nebat? [30]Solomon reigned in
Jerusalem over all Israel forty
years. [31]Then he rested with

p21 Hebrew *of ships that could go to Tarshish*
q21 Hebrew *Huram*, a variant of *Hiram*
r25 Or *charioteers*
s26 That is, the Euphrates
t28 Or possibly *Muzur*, a region in Cilicia

*29 Most mss have *pathah* under the *aleph* (וְהָאַחֲ).

°29 ק יעדו

אֲבֹתָיו וַיִּקְבְּרֻהוּ בְּעִיר דָּוִיד אָבִיו
father-of-him David in-city-of and-they-buried-him fathers-of-him

וַיִּמְלֹךְ רְחַבְעָם בְּנוֹ תַּחְתָּיו׃ וַיֵּלֶךְ
and-he-went (10:1) in-place-of-him son-of-him Rehoboam and-he-became-king

רְחַבְעָם שְׁכֶמָה כִּי שְׁכֶם בָּאוּ כָל־יִשְׂרָאֵל לְהַמְלִיךְ אֹתוֹ׃
him to-make-king Israel all-of they-went Shechem for to-Shechem Rehoboam

וַיְהִי כִּשְׁמֹעַ יָרָבְעָם בֶּן־ נְבָט וְהוּא בְמִצְרַיִם אֲשֶׁר
where in-Egypt now-he Nebat son-of Jeroboam when-to-hear and-he-was (2)

בָּרַח מִפְּנֵי שְׁלֹמֹה הַמֶּלֶךְ וַיָּשָׁב יָרָבְעָם מִמִּצְרָיִם׃
from-Egypt Jeroboam then-he-returned the-king Solomon from-before he-fled

וַיִּשְׁלְחוּ וַיִּקְרְאוּ־ לוֹ וַיָּבֹא יָרָבְעָם וְכָל־
and-all-of Jeroboam and-he-went for-him and-they-called so-they-sent (3)

יִשְׂרָאֵל וַיְדַבְּרוּ אֶל־ רְחַבְעָם לֵאמֹר׃ אָבִיךָ הִקְשָׁה אֶת־
*** he-made-heavy father-of-you (4) to-say Rehoboam to and-they-said Israel

עֻלֵּנוּ וְעַתָּה הָקֵל מֵעֲבֹדַת אָבִיךָ הַקָּשָׁה
the-harsh father-of-you from-labor-of lighten! but-now yoke-of-us

וּמֵעֻלּוֹ הַכָּבֵד אֲשֶׁר־ נָתַן עָלֵינוּ וְנַעַבְדֶךָּ׃
and-we-will-serve-you on-us he-put that the-heavy and-from-yoke-of-him

וַיֹּאמֶר אֲלֵהֶם עוֹד שְׁלֹשֶׁת יָמִים וְשׁוּבוּ אֵלָי
to-me then-come-back! days three-of still to-them and-he-answered (5)

וַיֵּלֶךְ הָעָם׃ וַיִּוָּעַץ הַמֶּלֶךְ רְחַבְעָם אֶת־
with Rehoboam the-king then-he-consulted (6) the-people so-he-went-away

הַזְּקֵנִים אֲשֶׁר־ הָיוּ עֹמְדִים לִפְנֵי שְׁלֹמֹה אָבִיו
father-of-him Solomon before ones-serving they-were who the-elders

בִּהְיֹתוֹ חַי לֵאמֹר אֵיךְ אַתֶּם נוֹעָצִים לְהָשִׁיב לָעָם־
to-the-people to-return ones-advising you how? to-ask alive while-to-be-him

הַזֶּה דָּבָר׃ וַיְדַבְּרוּ אֵלָיו לֵאמֹר אִם - תִּהְיֶה לְטוֹב
as-kind you-will-be if to-say to-him and-they-replied (7) answer the-this

לְהָעָם הַזֶּה וּרְצִיתָם וְדִבַּרְתָּ אֲלֵהֶם דְּבָרִים
answers to-them and-you-give and-you-please-them the-this to-the-people

טוֹבִים וְהָיוּ לְךָ עֲבָדִים כָּל־ הַיָּמִים׃
the-days all-of servants to-you and-they-will-be favorable-ones

וַיַּעֲזֹב אֶת־ עֲצַת הַזְּקֵנִים אֲשֶׁר יְעָצֻהוּ
they-gave-him that the-elders advice-of with but-he-rejected (8)

וַיִּוָּעַץ אֶת־ הַיְלָדִים אֲשֶׁר גָּדְלוּ אִתּוֹ הָעֹמְדִים
the-ones-serving with-him they-grew-up who the-young-men *** and-he-consulted

לְפָנָיו׃ וַיֹּאמֶר אֲלֵהֶם מָה אַתֶּם נוֹעָצִים וְנָשִׁיב
that-we-should-give ones-advising you what? to-them and-he-asked (9) before-him

his fathers and was buried in the city of David his father. And Rehoboam his son succeeded him as king.

Israel Rebels Against Rehoboam

10 Rehoboam went to Shechem, for all the Israelites had gone there to make him king.
2When Jeroboam son of Nebat heard this (he was in Egypt, where he had fled from King Solomon), he returned from Egypt.
3So they sent for Jeroboam, and he and all Israel went to Rehoboam and said to him:
4"Your father put a heavy yoke on us, but now lighten the harsh labor and the heavy yoke he put on us, and we will serve you."
5Rehoboam answered, "Come back to me in three days." So the people went away.
6Then King Rehoboam consulted the elders who had served his father Solomon during his lifetime. "How would you advise me to answer these people?" he asked.
7They replied, "If you will be kind to these people and please them and give them a favorable answer, they will always be your servants."
8But Rehoboam rejected the advice the elders gave him and consulted the young men who had grown up with him and were serving him.
9He asked them, "What is your advice? How should we answer

דָּבָר אֶת־ הָעָם הַזֶּה אֲשֶׁר דִּבְּרוּ אֵלַי לֵאמֹר הָקֵל מִן־
from lighten! to-say to-me they-say who the-this the-people *** answer

הָעֹל אֲשֶׁר־ נָתַן אָבִיךָ עָלֵינוּ׃ וַיְדַבְּרוּ אִתּוֹ
to-him and-they-replied (10) on-us father-of-you he-put that the-yoke

הַיְלָדִים אֲשֶׁר גָּדְלוּ אִתּוֹ לֵאמֹר כֹּה־ תֹאמַר לָעָם
to-the-people you-tell this to-say with-him they-grew-up who the-young-men

אֲשֶׁר־ דִּבְּרוּ אֵלֶיךָ לֵאמֹר אָבִיךָ הִכְבִּיד אֶת־ עֻלֵּנוּ
yoke-of-us *** he-made-heavy father-of-you to-say to-you they-said who

וְאַתָּה הָקֵל מֵעָלֵינוּ כֹּה תֹאמַר אֲלֵהֶם קָטָנִּי
little-one-of-me to-them you-tell this from-on-us you-make-light but-you

עָבָה מִמָּתְנֵי אָבִי׃ וְעַתָּה אָבִי
father-of-me and-now (11) father-of-me more-than-waists-of he-is-thick

הֶעְמִיס עֲלֵיכֶם עֹל כָּבֵד וַאֲנִי אֹסִיף עַל־ עֻלְּכֶם אָבִי
father-of-me yoke-of-you to I-will-add but-I heavy yoke on-you he-laid

יִסַּר אֶתְכֶם בַּשּׁוֹטִים וַאֲנִי בָּעַקְרַבִּים׃* וַיָּבֹא
and-he-returned (12) with-the-scorpions but-I with-the-whips you he-scourged

יָרָבְעָם וְכָל־ הָעָם אֶל־ רְחַבְעָם בַּיּוֹם הַשְּׁלִשִׁי כַּאֲשֶׁר
just-as the-third on-the-day Rehoboam to the-people and-all-of Jeroboam

דִּבֶּר הַמֶּלֶךְ לֵאמֹר שׁוּבוּ אֵלַי בַּיּוֹם הַשְּׁלִשִׁי׃
the-third on-the-day to-me come-back! to-say the-king he-said

וַיַּעֲנֵם הַמֶּלֶךְ קָשָׁה וַיַּעֲזֹב הַמֶּלֶךְ רְחַבְעָם
Rehoboam the-king and-he-rejected harshly the-king and-he-answered-them (13)

אֵת עֲצַת הַזְּקֵנִים׃ וַיְדַבֵּר אֲלֵהֶם כַּעֲצַת הַיְלָדִים
the-young-men as-advice-of to-them and-he-spoke (14) the-elders advice-of ***

לֵאמֹר אַכְבִּיד† אֶת־ עֻלְּכֶם וַאֲנִי אֹסִיף עָלָיו אָבִי
father-of-me to-him I-will-add but-I yoke-of-you *** †I-made-heavy to-say

יִסַּר אֶתְכֶם בַּשּׁוֹטִים וַאֲנִי בָּעַקְרַבִּים׃* וְלֹא־
so-not (15) with-the-scorpions but-I with-the-whips you he-scourged

שָׁמַע הַמֶּלֶךְ אֶל־ הָעָם כִּי־ הָיְתָה נְסִבָּה מֵעִם
from-with turn-of-events she-was for the-people to the-king he-listened

הָאֱלֹהִים לְמַעַן הָקִים יְהוָה אֶת־ דְּבָרוֹ אֲשֶׁר דִּבֶּר
he-spoke that word-of-him *** Yahweh to-fulfill in-order-to the-God

בְּיַד אֲחִיָּהוּ הַשִּׁלוֹנִי אֶל־ יָרָבְעָם בֶּן־ נְבָט׃ וְכָל־
when-all-of (16) Nebat son-of Jeroboam to the-Shilonite Ahijah by-hand-of

יִשְׂרָאֵל כִּי לֹא־ שָׁמַע הַמֶּלֶךְ לָהֶם וַיָּשִׁבוּ הָעָם
the-people then-they-answered to-them the-king he-listened not that Israel

אֶת־הַמֶּלֶךְ ׀ לֵאמֹר מַה־ לָּנוּ חֵלֶק בְּדָוִיד וְלֹא־ נַחֲלָה בְּבֶן־ יִשַׁי
Jesse in-son-of part and-not in-David share to-us what? to-say the-king ***

these people who say to me, 'Lighten the yoke your father put on us'?"

10 The young men who had grown up with him replied, "Tell the people who have said to you, 'Your father put a heavy yoke on us, but make our yoke lighter'—tell them, 'My little finger is thicker than my father's waist. 11 My father laid on you a heavy yoke; I will make it even heavier. My father scourged you with whips; I will scourge you with scorpions.'"

12 Three days later Jeroboam and all the people returned to Rehoboam, as the king had said, "Come back to me in three days." 13 The king answered them harshly. Rejecting the advice of the elders, 14 he followed the advice of the young men and said, "My father made your yoke heavy; I will make it even heavier. My father scourged you with whips; I will scourge you with scorpions." 15 So the king did not listen to the people, for this turn of events was from God, to fulfill the word the LORD had spoken to Jeroboam son of Nebat through Ahijah the Shilonite.

16 When all Israel saw that the king refused to listen to them, they answered the king:

"What share do we have in David,
what part in Jesse's son?

*11, 14 Most mss have *pathah* under the *ayin* (בַּעְ).

†14 Many mss read אָבִי הִכְבִּיד, *he-made-heavy father-of-me*

אִישׁ לְאֹהָלֶיךָ יִשְׂרָאֵל עַתָּה רְאֵה בֵיתְךָ דָּוִיד וַיֵּלֶךְ
so-he-went David house-of-you look-after! now Israel to-tents-of-you each

כָּל־ יִשְׂרָאֵל לְאֹהָלָיו׃ וּבְנֵי יִשְׂרָאֵל הַיֹּשְׁבִים
the-ones-living Israel but-sons-of (17) to-homes-of-him Israel all-of

בְּעָרֵי יְהוּדָה וַיִּמְלֹךְ עֲלֵיהֶם רְחַבְעָם׃ וַיִּשְׁלַח
and-he-sent-out (18) Rehoboam over-them and-he-ruled Judah in-towns-of

הַמֶּלֶךְ רְחַבְעָם אֶת־ הֲדֹרָם אֲשֶׁר עַל־ הַמַּס וַיִּרְגְּמוּ־
but-they-stoned the-forced-labor over who Hadoram *** Rehoboam the-king

בוֹ בְנֵי־ יִשְׂרָאֵל אֶבֶן וַיָּמֹת וְהַמֶּלֶךְ רְחַבְעָם הִתְאַמֵּץ
he-managed Rehoboam but-the-king and-he-died stone Israel sons-of on-him

לַעֲלוֹת בַּמֶּרְכָּבָה לָנוּס יְרוּשָׁלִָם׃ וַיִּפְשְׁעוּ יִשְׂרָאֵל
Israel so-they-rebelled (19) Jerusalem to-escape into-the-chariot to-get-up

בְּבֵית דָּוִיד עַד הַיּוֹם הַזֶּה׃ וַיָּבֹא רְחַבְעָם
Rehoboam when-he-arrived (11:1) the-this the-day to David against-house-of

יְרוּשָׁלִַם וַיַּקְהֵל אֶת־ בֵּית יְהוּדָה וּבִנְיָמִן מֵאָה וּשְׁמוֹנִים
and-eighty hundred and-Benjamin Judah house-of *** then-he-mustered Jerusalem

אֶלֶף בָּחוּר עֹשֵׂה מִלְחָמָה לְהִלָּחֵם עִם־ יִשְׂרָאֵל לְהָשִׁיב אֶת־
*** to-regain Israel against to-make-war fight doing being-chosen thousand

הַמַּמְלָכָה לִרְחַבְעָם׃ וַיְהִי דְּבַר־ יְהוָה אֶל־שְׁמַעְיָהוּ אִישׁ־
man-of Shemaiah to Yahweh word-of but-he-came (2) for-Rehoboam the-kingdom

הָאֱלֹהִים לֵאמֹר׃ אֱמֹר אֶל־ רְחַבְעָם בֶּן־ שְׁלֹמֹה מֶלֶךְ יְהוּדָה וְאֶל
and-to Judah king-of Solomon son-of Rehoboam to say! (3) to-say the-God

כָּל־ יִשְׂרָאֵל בִּיהוּדָה וּבִנְיָמִן לֵאמֹר׃ כֹּה אָמַר יְהוָה לֹא־
not Yahweh he-says this (4) to-say and-Benjamin in-Judah Israel all-of

תַעֲלוּ וְלֹא־ תִלָּחֲמוּ עִם־ אֲחֵיכֶם שׁוּבוּ אִישׁ
each go-back! brothers-of-you against you-fight and-not you-go-up

לְבֵיתוֹ כִּי מֵאִתִּי נִהְיָה הַדָּבָר הַזֶּה וַיִּשְׁמְעוּ
so-they-obeyed the-this the-thing he-is-done from-with-me for to-home-of-him

אֶת־ דִּבְרֵי יְהוָה וַיָּשֻׁבוּ מִלֶּכֶת אֶל־ יָרָבְעָם׃
Jeroboam against from-to-march and-they-turned-back Yahweh words-of ***

וַיֵּשֶׁב רְחַבְעָם בִּירוּשָׁלִָם וַיִּבֶן עָרִים לְמָצוֹר
for-defense towns and-he-built-up in-Jerusalem Rehoboam and-he-lived (5)

בִּיהוּדָה׃ וַיִּבֶן אֶת־ בֵּית־ לֶחֶם וְאֶת־ עֵיטָם וְאֶת־ תְּקוֹעַ׃ וְאֶת־
and (7) Tekoa and Etam and Lehem Beth *** and-he-built-up (6) in-Judah

בֵּית־צוּר וְאֶת־שׂוֹכוֹ וְאֶת־ עֲדֻלָּם׃ וְאֶת־ גַּת וְאֶת־ מָרֵשָׁה וְאֶת־ זִיף׃ וְאֶת־
and (9) Ziph and Mareshah and Gath and (8) Adullam and Soco and Zur Beth

אֲדוֹרַיִם וְאֶת־ לָכִישׁ וְאֶת־ עֲזֵקָה׃ וְאֶת־צָרְעָה וְאֶת־אַיָּלוֹן וְאֶת־חֶבְרוֹן אֲשֶׁר
that Hebron and Aijalon and Zorah and (10) Azekah and Lachish and Adoraim

To your tents, O Israel!
Look after your own
house, O David!"

So all the Israelites went
home. 17 But as for the Israelites
who were living in the towns
of Judah, Rehoboam still ruled
over them.
18 King Rehoboam sent out
Adoniram,[u] who was in
charge of forced labor, but the
Israelites stoned him to death.
King Rehoboam, however,
managed to get into his chariot
and escape to Jerusalem.
19 So Israel has been in rebellion
against the house of David
to this day.

11 When Rehoboam arrived in Jerusalem, he
mustered the house of Judah
and Benjamin—a hundred
and eighty thousand fighting
men—to make war against Israel
and to regain the kingdom
for Rehoboam.
2 But this word of the LORD
came to Shemaiah the man of
God: 3 "Say to Rehoboam son
of Solomon king of Judah and
to all the Israelites in Judah
and Benjamin, 4 'This is what
the LORD says: Do not go up to
fight against your brothers. Go
home, every one of you, for
this is my doing.' " So they
obeyed the words of the LORD
and turned back from marching
against Jeroboam.

Rehoboam Fortifies Judah

5 Rehoboam lived in Jerusalem
and built up towns for defense
in Judah: 6 Bethlehem,
Etam, Tekoa, 7 Beth Zur, Soco,
Adullam, 8 Gath, Mareshah,
Ziph, 9 Adoraim, Lachish, Azekah,
10 Zorah, Aijalon and Hebron.
These were fortified cities
in Judah and Benjamin.

[u] 18 Hebrew *Hadoram*, a variant of *Adoniram*

בִּיהוּדָה וּבְבִנְיָמִן עָרֵי מְצֻרוֹת׃ וַיְחַזֵּק אֶת־

*** and-he-strengthened (11) fortifications cities-of and-in-Benjamin in-Judah

הַמְּצֻרוֹת וַיִּתֵּן בָּהֶם נְגִידִים וְאֹצְרוֹת מַאֲכָל וְשֶׁמֶן

and-olive-oil food and-supplies-of commanders in-them and-he-put the-defenses

וָיָיִן׃ וּבְכָל־ עִיר וָעִיר צִנּוֹת וּרְמָחִים וַיְחַזְּקֵם

and-he-made-strong-them and-spears shields and-city city and-in-all-of (12) and-wine

לְהַרְבֵּה מְאֹד וַיְהִי־ לוֹ יְהוּדָה וּבִנְיָמִן׃ וְהַכֹּהֲנִים

and-the-priests (13) and-Benjamin Judah to-him so-he-was very to-be-great

וְהַלְוִיִּם אֲשֶׁר בְּכָל־ יִשְׂרָאֵל הִתְיַצְּבוּ עָלָיו מִכָּל־

from-all-of with-him they-sided Israel in-all-of who and-the-Levites

גְּבוּלָם׃ כִּי־ עָזְבוּ הַלְוִיִּם אֶת־ מִגְרְשֵׁיהֶם

pastures-of-them *** the-Levites they-abandoned indeed (14) district-of-them

וַאֲחֻזָּתָם וַיֵּלְכוּ לִיהוּדָה וְלִירוּשָׁלִָם כִּי־

because and-to-Jerusalem to-Judah and-they-came and-property-of-them

הִזְנִיחָם יָרָבְעָם וּבָנָיו מִכַּהֵן לַיהוָה׃

of-Yahweh from-to-be-priest and-sons-of-him Jeroboam he-rejected-them

וַיַּעֲמֶד־ לוֹ כֹּהֲנִים לַבָּמוֹת וְלַשְּׂעִירִים

and-for-the-goat-idols for-the-high-places priests for-him and-he-appointed (15)

וְלָעֲגָלִים אֲשֶׁר עָשָׂה׃ וְאַחֲרֵיהֶם מִכֹּל שִׁבְטֵי

tribes-of from-all-of and-after-them (16) he-made that and-for-the-calf-idols

יִשְׂרָאֵל הַנֹּתְנִים אֶת־ לְבָבָם לְבַקֵּשׁ אֶת־ יְהוָה אֱלֹהֵי יִשְׂרָאֵל

Israel God-of Yahweh *** to-seek heart-of-them *** the-ones-setting Israel

בָּאוּ יְרוּשָׁלִַם לִזְבּוֹחַ לַיהוָה אֱלֹהֵי אֲבוֹתֵיהֶם׃

fathers-of-them God-of to-Yahweh to-sacrifice Jerusalem they-followed

וַיְחַזְּקוּ אֶת־ מַלְכוּת יְהוּדָה וַיְאַמְּצוּ אֶת־

*** and-they-supported Judah kingdom-of *** and-they-strengthened (17)

רְחַבְעָם בֶּן־ שְׁלֹמֹה לְשָׁנִים שָׁלוֹשׁ כִּי הָלְכוּ בְּדֶרֶךְ דָּוִיד

David in-way-of they-walked indeed three for-years Solomon son-of Rehoboam

וּשְׁלֹמֹה לְשָׁנִים שָׁלוֹשׁ׃ וַיִּקַּח־ לוֹ רְחַבְעָם אִשָּׁה אֶת־

*** wife Rehoboam for-him and-he-married (18) three for-years and-Solomon

מָחֲלַת בַּן ־ יְרִימוֹת בֶּן־ דָּוִיד אֲבִיהַיִל בַּת־ אֱלִיאָב בֶּן־

son-of Eliab daughter-of Abihail David son-of Jerimoth daughter-of Mahalath

יִשָׁי׃ וַתֵּלֶד לוֹ בָּנִים אֶת־ יְעוּשׁ וְאֶת־ שְׁמַרְיָה וְאֶת־ זָהַם׃

Zaham and Shemariah and Jeush *** sons to-him and-she-bore (19) Jesse

וְאַחֲרֶיהָ לָקַח אֶת־ מַעֲכָה בַּת־ אַבְשָׁלוֹם וַתֵּלֶד

and-she-bore Absalom daughter-of Maacah *** he-married then-after-her (20)

לוֹ אֶת־ אֲבִיָּה וְאֶת־ עַתַּי וְאֶת־ זִיזָא וְאֶת־ שְׁלֹמִית׃ וַיֶּאֱהַב

and-he-loved (21) Shelomith and Ziza and Attai and Abijah *** to-him

[11]He strengthened their defenses and put commanders in them, with supplies of food, olive oil and wine. [12]He put shields and spears in all the cities, and made them very strong. So Judah and Benjamin were his.

[13]The priests and Levites from all their districts sided with him. [14]The Levites even abandoned their pasturelands and property, and came to Judah and Jerusalem because Jeroboam and his sons had rejected them as priests of the LORD. [15]And he appointed his own priests for the high places and for the goat and calf idols he had made. [16]Those from every tribe of Israel who set their hearts on seeking the LORD, the God of Israel, followed the Levites to Jerusalem to offer sacrifices to the LORD, the God of their fathers. [17]They strengthened the kingdom of Judah and supported Rehoboam son of Solomon three years, walking in the ways of David and Solomon during this time.

Rehoboam's Family

[18]Rehoboam married Mahalath, who was the daughter of David's son Jerimoth and of Abihail, the daughter of Jesse's son Eliab. [19]She bore him sons: Jeush, Shemariah and Zaham. [20]Then he married Maacah daughter of Absalom, who bore him Abijah, Attai, Ziza and Shelomith. [21]Rehoboam loved Maacah daughter

°18 ק בת

רְחַבְעָם אֶת־ מַעֲכָה בַּת־ אַבְשָׁלוֹם מִכָּל־ נָשָׁיו
wives-of-him more-than-any-of Absalom daughter-of Maacah *** Rehoboam

וּפִילַגְשָׁיו כִּי נָשִׁים שְׁמוֹנֶה־עֶשְׂרֵה נָשָׂא וּפִילַגְשִׁים שִׁשִּׁים
sixty and-concubines he-took ten eight wives indeed and-concubines-of-him

וַיּוֹלֶד עֶשְׂרִים וּשְׁמוֹנָה בָּנִים וְשִׁשִּׁים בָּנוֹת׃ וַיַּעֲמֵד
and-he-appointed (22) daughters and-sixty sons and-eight twenty and-he-fathered

לָרֹאשׁ רְחַבְעָם אֶת־ אֲבִיָּה בֶן־ מַעֲכָה לְנָגִיד בְּאֶחָיו
among-brothers-of-him as-prince Maacah son-of Abijah *** Rehoboam as-chief

כִּי לְהַמְלִיכוֹ׃ וַיָּבֶן וַיִּפְרֹץ
and-he-dispersed and-he-acted-wisely (23) to-make-king-him in-order-to

מִכָּל־ בָּנָיו לְכָל־ אַרְצוֹת יְהוּדָה וּבִנְיָמִן
and-Benjamin Judah districts-of through-all-of sons-of-him from-all-of

לְכֹל עָרֵי הַמְּצֻרוֹת וַיִּתֵּן לָהֶם הַמָּזוֹן
the-provision to-them and-he-gave the-fortifications cities-of to-all-of

לָרֹב וַיִּשְׁאַל הֲמוֹן נָשִׁים׃ וַיְהִי כְּהָכִין
as-to-establish and-he-was (12:1) wives many-of and-he-took in-abundance

מַלְכוּת רְחַבְעָם וּכְחֶזְקָתוֹ עָזַב אֶת־ תּוֹרַת
law-of *** he-abandoned and-as-to-become-strong-him Rehoboam kingdom-of

יְהוָה וְכָל־ יִשְׂרָאֵל עִמּוֹ׃ וַיְהִי בַּשָּׁנָה הַחֲמִישִׁית
the-fifth in-the-year and-he-was (2) with-him Israel and-all-of Yahweh

לַמֶּלֶךְ רְחַבְעָם עָלָה שִׁישַׁק מֶלֶךְ־ מִצְרַיִם עַל־ יְרוּשָׁלִָם
Jerusalem against Egypt king-of Shishak he-attacked Rehoboam of-the-king

כִּי מָעֲלוּ בַּיהוָה׃ בְּאֶלֶף וּמָאתַיִם
and-two-hundreds with-thousand (3) to-Yahweh they-were-unfaithful because

רֶכֶב וּבְשִׁשִּׁים אֶלֶף פָּרָשִׁים וְאֵין מִסְפָּר לָעָם אֲשֶׁר־
that of-the-troop number and-not horsemen thousand and-with-sixty chariot

בָּאוּ עִמּוֹ מִמִּצְרַיִם לוּבִים סֻכִּיִּים וְכוּשִׁים׃ וַיִּלְכֹּד
and-he-captured (4) and-Cushites Sukkites Libyans from-Egypt with-him they-came

אֶת־ עָרֵי הַמְּצֻרוֹת אֲשֶׁר לִיהוּדָה וַיָּבֹא עַד־ יְרוּשָׁלִָם׃
Jerusalem as-far-as and-he-came in-Judah that the-fortifications cities-of ***

וּשְׁמַעְיָה הַנָּבִיא בָּא אֶל־ רְחַבְעָם וְשָׂרֵי יְהוּדָה אֲשֶׁר־
who Judah and-leaders-of Rehoboam to he-came the-prophet then-Shemaiah (5)

נֶאֶסְפוּ אֶל־ יְרוּשָׁלִָם מִפְּנֵי שִׁישָׁק וַיֹּאמֶר לָהֶם כֹּה־
this to-them and-he-said Shishak because-of Jerusalem in they-assembled

אָמַר יְהוָה אַתֶּם עֲזַבְתֶּם אֹתִי וְאַף־ אֲנִי עָזַבְתִּי אֶתְכֶם בְּיַד־
to-hand-of you I-abandon I now-therefore me you-abandoned you Yahweh he-says

שִׁישָׁק׃ וַיִּכָּנְעוּ שָׂרֵי־ יִשְׂרָאֵל וְהַמֶּלֶךְ
and-the-king Israel leaders-of and-they-humbled-themselves (6) Shishak

of Absalom more than any of his other wives and concubines. In all, he had eighteen wives and sixty concubines, twenty-eight sons and sixty daughters.
[22]Rehoboam appointed Abijah son of Maacah to be the chief prince among his brothers, in order to make him king.
[23]He acted wisely, dispersing some of his sons throughout the districts of Judah and Benjamin, and to all the fortified cities. He gave them abundant provisions and took many wives for them.

Shishak Attacks Jerusalem

12 After Rehoboam's position as king was established and he had become strong, he and all Israel[v] with him abandoned the law of the LORD.
[2]Because they had been unfaithful to the LORD, Shishak king of Egypt attacked Jerusalem in the fifth year of King Rehoboam.
[3]With twelve hundred chariots and sixty thousand horsemen and the innumerable troops of Libyans, Sukkites and Cushites[w] that came with him from Egypt,
[4]he captured the fortified cities of Judah and came as far as Jerusalem.
[5]Then the prophet Shemaiah came to Rehoboam and to the leaders of Judah who had assembled in Jerusalem for fear of Shishak, and he said to them, "This is what the LORD says, 'You have abandoned me; therefore, I now abandon you to Shishak.' "
[6]The leaders of Israel and the king humbled themselves and

[v]1 That is, Judah, as frequently in 2 Chronicles
[w]3 That is, people from the upper Nile region

וַיֹּאמְרוּ צַדִּיק | יְהוָה׃ וּבִרְאוֹת יְהוָה כִּי
that Yahweh and-when-to-see (7) Yahweh just and-they-said

נִכְנָעוּ הָיָה דְבַר־ יְהוָה אֶל־ שְׁמַעְיָה | לֵאמֹר
to-say Shemaiah to Yahweh word-of he-came they-humbled-themselves

נִכְנְעוּ לֹא אַשְׁחִיתֵם וְנָתַתִּי לָהֶם
to-them but-I-will-give I-will-destroy-them not they-humbled-themselves

כִּמְעַט לִפְלֵיטָה וְלֹא־ תִתַּךְ חֲמָתִי
wrath-of-me she-will-be-poured-out and-not for-deliverance as-soon

בִּירוּשָׁלִַם בְּיַד־ שִׁישָׁק׃ כִּי יִהְיוּ־ לוֹ לַעֲבָדִים
as-subjects to-him they-will-be however (8) Shishak by-hand-of on-Jerusalem

וְיֵדְעוּ עֲבוֹדָתִי וַעֲבוֹדַת מַמְלְכוֹת הָאֲרָצוֹת׃
the-lands kingdoms-of and-service-of service-of-me so-they-may-learn

וַיַּעַל שִׁישַׁק מֶלֶךְ־ מִצְרַיִם עַל־ יְרוּשָׁלִַם
Jerusalem against Egypt king-of Shishak when-he-attacked (9)

וַיִּקַּח אֶת־ אֹצְרוֹת בֵּית־ יְהוָה וְאֶת־ אֹצְרוֹת
treasures-of and Yahweh temple-of treasures-of *** then-he-carried-off

בֵּית הַמֶּלֶךְ אֶת־ הַכֹּל לָקָח וַיִּקַּח אֶת־ מָגִנֵּי הַזָּהָב
the-gold shields-of *** and-he-took he-took the-whole *** the-king palace-of

אֲשֶׁר עָשָׂה שְׁלֹמֹה׃ וַיַּעַשׂ הַמֶּלֶךְ רְחַבְעָם תַּחְתֵּיהֶם
in-place-of-them Rehoboam the-king so-he-made (10) Solomon he-made that

מָגִנֵּי נְחֹשֶׁת וְהִפְקִיד עַל־ יַד שָׂרֵי
commanders-of hand-of under and-he-assigned bronze shields-of

הָרָצִים הַשֹּׁמְרִים פֶּתַח בֵּית הַמֶּלֶךְ׃
the-king palace-of entrance-of the-ones-being-on-duty the-ones-guarding

וַיְהִי מִדֵּי־ בוֹא הַמֶּלֶךְ בֵּית יְהוָה בָּאוּ
they-went Yahweh temple-of the-king to-go as-often-as and-he-was (11)

הָרָצִים וּנְשָׂאוּם וֶהֱשִׁבוּם אֶל־ תָּא
room-of to then-they-returned-them and-they-bore-them the-ones-guarding

הָרָצִים׃ וּבְהִכָּנְעוֹ שָׁב מִמֶּנּוּ
from-him he-turned and-because-to-be-humbled-him (12) the-ones-guarding

אַף־ יְהוָה וְלֹא לְהַשְׁחִית לְכָלָה וְגַם בִּיהוּדָה הָיָה
he-was in-Judah indeed-also to-totality to-destroy and-not Yahweh anger-of

דְּבָרִים טוֹבִים׃ וַיִּתְחַזֵּק הַמֶּלֶךְ רְחַבְעָם
Rehoboam the-king and-he-established-himself (13) good-ones things

בִּירוּשָׁלִַם וַיִּמְלֹךְ כִּי בֶן־ אַרְבָּעִים וְאַחַת שָׁנָה רְחַבְעָם
Rehoboam year and-one forty son-of indeed and-he-was-king in-Jerusalem

בְמָלְכוֹ וּשְׁבַע עֶשְׂרֵה שָׁנָה | מָלַךְ בִּירוּשָׁלִַם
in-Jerusalem he-reigned year ten and-seven-of when-to-become-king-him

said, "The LORD is just."
[7]When the LORD saw that
they humbled themselves, this
word of the LORD came to
Shemaiah: "Since they have
humbled themselves, I will
not destroy them but will soon
give them deliverance. My
wrath will not be poured out
on Jerusalem through Shishak.
[8]They will, however, become
subject to him, so that they
may learn the difference between serving me and serving
the kings of other lands."
[9]When Shishak king of
Egypt attacked Jerusalem, he
carried off the treasures of the
temple of the LORD and the
treasures of the royal palace.
He took everything, including
the gold shields Solomon had
made. [10]So King Rehoboam
made bronze shields to replace
them and assigned these to
the commanders of the guard
on duty at the entrance to the
royal palace. [11]Whenever the
king went to the LORD's temple, the guards went with him,
bearing the shields, and afterward they returned them to
the guardroom.
[12]Because Rehoboam hum-
bled himself, the LORD's anger
turned from him, and he was
not totally destroyed. Indeed,
there was some good in Judah.
[13]King Rehoboam estab-
lished himself firmly in
Jerusalem and continued as
king. He was forty-one years
old when he became king, and
he reigned seventeen years in

הָעִיר אֲשֶׁר־ בָּחַר יְהוָה לָשׂוּם אֶת־ שְׁמוֹ שָׁם מִכֹּל
from-all-of there Name-of-him *** to-put Yahweh he-chose that the-city

שִׁבְטֵי יִשְׂרָאֵל וְשֵׁם אִמּוֹ נַעֲמָה הָעַמֹּנִית׃
the-Ammonite Naamah mother-of-him and-name-of Israel tribes-of

וַיַּעַשׂ הָרָע כִּי לֹא הֵכִין לִבּוֹ לִדְרוֹשׁ אֶת־ יְהוָה׃
Yahweh *** to-seek heart-of-him he-set not because the-evil and-he-did (14)

וְדִבְרֵי רְחַבְעָם הָרִאשֹׁנִים וְהָאַחֲרוֹנִים* הֲלֹא־ הֵם
they not? and-the-ends the-beginnings Rehoboam and-events-of (15)

כְּתוּבִים בְּדִבְרֵי שְׁמַעְיָה הַנָּבִיא וְעִדּוֹ הַחֹזֶה
the-seer and-Iddo the-prophet Shemaiah in-records-of ones-being-written

לְהִתְיַחֵשׂ וּמִלְחֲמוֹת רְחַבְעָם וְיָרָבְעָם כָּל־ הַיָּמִים׃
the-days all-of and-Jeroboam Rehoboam and-wars-of to-be-recorded

וַיִּשְׁכַּב רְחַבְעָם עִם־ אֲבֹתָיו וַיִּקָּבֵר בְּעִיר
in-City-of and-he-was-buried fathers-of-him with Rehoboam and-he-rested (16)

דָּוִיד וַיִּמְלֹךְ אֲבִיָּה בְנוֹ תַּחְתָּיו׃ בִּשְׁנַת
in-year-of (13:1) in-place-of-him son-of-him Abijah and-he-became-king David

שְׁמוֹנֶה עֶשְׂרֵה לַמֶּלֶךְ יָרָבְעָם וַיִּמְלֹךְ אֲבִיָּה עַל־ יְהוּדָה׃
Judah over Abijah then-he-became-king Jeroboam of-the-king ten eight

שָׁלוֹשׁ שָׁנִים מָלַךְ בִּירוּשָׁלִָם וְשֵׁם אִמּוֹ מִיכָיָהוּ
Micaiah mother-of-him and-name-of in-Jerusalem he-reigned years three (2)

בַּת־ אוּרִיאֵל מִן־ גִּבְעָה וּמִלְחָמָה הָיְתָה בֵּין אֲבִיָּה וּבֵין
and-between Abijah between she-was and-war Gibeah from Uriel daughter-of

יָרָבְעָם׃ וַיֶּאְסֹר אֲבִיָּה אֶת־ הַמִּלְחָמָה בְּחַיִל גִּבּוֹרֵי מִלְחָמָה
fight men-of with-force the-battle *** Abijah and-he-went-into (3) Jeroboam

אַרְבַּע־ מֵאוֹת אֶלֶף אִישׁ בָּחוּר וְיָרָבְעָם עָרַךְ עִמּוֹ
against-him he-drew and-Jeroboam being-able man thousand hundreds four-of

מִלְחָמָה בִּשְׁמוֹנֶה מֵאוֹת אֶלֶף אִישׁ בָּחוּר גִּבּוֹר חָיִל׃
valiant troop-of being-able man thousand hundreds with-eight battle-line

וַיָּקָם אֲבִיָּה מֵעַל לְהַר צְמָרַיִם אֲשֶׁר בְּהַר
in-hill-country-of that Zemaraim on-Mount-of at-upon Abijah and-he-stood (4)

אֶפְרָיִם וַיֹּאמֶר שְׁמָעוּנִי יָרָבְעָם וְכָל־ יִשְׂרָאֵל׃ הֲלֹא
not? (5) Israel and-all-of Jeroboam listen-to-me! and-he-said Ephraim

לָכֶם לָדַעַת כִּי יְהוָה ׀ אֱלֹהֵי יִשְׂרָאֵל נָתַן מַמְלָכָה לְדָוִיד עַל־
over to-David kingship he-gave Israel God-of Yahweh that to-know to-you

יִשְׂרָאֵל לְעוֹלָם לוֹ וּלְבָנָיו בְּרִית מֶלַח׃
salt covenant-of and-to-descendants-of-him to-him to-forever Israel

וַיָּקָם יָרָבְעָם בֶּן־ נְבָט עֶבֶד שְׁלֹמֹה בֶן־ דָּוִיד
David son-of Solomon official-of Nebat son-of Jeroboam yet-he-rose (6)

Jerusalem, the city the LORD
had chosen out of all the tribes
of Israel in which to put his
Name. His mother's name was
Naamah; she was an Ammon-
ite. [14]He did evil because he
had not set his heart on seeking the LORD.
[15]As for the events of Rehoboam's reign, from beginning
to end, are they not written in
the records of Shemaiah the
prophet and of Iddo the seer
that deal with genealogies?
There was continual warfare
between Rehoboam and Jeroboam. [16]Rehoboam rested
with his fathers and was buried in the City of David. And
Abijah his son succeeded him
as king.

Abijah King of Judah

13 In the eighteenth year
of the reign of Jero-
boam, Abijah became king of
Judah, [2]and he reigned in
Jerusalem three years. His
mother's name was Maacah,[x]
a daughter[y] of Uriel of Gibeah.
There was war between
Abijah and Jeroboam. [3]Abijah
went into battle with a force of
four hundred thousand able
fighting men, and Jeroboam
drew up a battle line against
him with eight hundred thousand able troops.
[4]Abijah stood on Mount
Zemaraim, in the hill country
of Ephraim, and said, "Jeroboam and all Israel, listen to
me! [5]Don't you know that the
LORD, the God of Israel, has
given the kingship of Israel to
David and his descendants
forever by a covenant of salt?
[6]Yet Jeroboam son of Nebat,
an official of Solomon son of

[x]2 Septuagint and Syriac (see also 2 Chron. 11:20 and 1 Kings 15:2); Hebrew *Micaiah*
[y]2 Or *granddaughter*

*15 Most mss have *hateph pathah* under the *beth* and *pathah* under the *aleph* (וְהָאַחֲ).

וַיִּמְרֹד עַל־ אֲדֹנָיו׃ וַיִּקָּבְצוּ עָלָיו

around-him and-they-gathered (7) masters-of-him against and-he-rebelled

אֲנָשִׁים רֵקִים בְּנֵי בְלִיַּעַל וַיִּתְאַמְּצוּ עַל־ רְחַבְעָם

Rehoboam against and-they-opposed scoundrel sons-of worthless-ones men

בֶּן־ שְׁלֹמֹה וּרְחַבְעָם הָיָה נַעַר וְרַךְ־ לֵבָב וְלֹא

and-not heart and-indecisive-of young he-was when-Rehoboam Solomon son-of

הִתְחַזַּק לִפְנֵיהֶם׃ וְעַתָּה ׀ אַתֶּם אֹמְרִים לְהִתְחַזֵּק לִפְנֵי

against to-resist ones-planning you and-now (8) against-them he-was-strong

מַמְלֶכֶת יְהוָה בְּיַד בְּנֵי דָוִיד וְאַתֶּם הָמוֹן רָב

vast army and-you David descendants-of in-hand-of Yahweh kingdom-of

וְעִמָּכֶם עֶגְלֵי זָהָב אֲשֶׁר עָשָׂה לָכֶם יָרָבְעָם לֵאלֹהִים׃ הֲלֹא

not? (9) as-gods Jeroboam for-you he-made that gold calves-of and-with-you

הִדַּחְתֶּם אֶת־ כֹּהֲנֵי יְהוָה אֶת־ בְּנֵי אַהֲרֹן וְהַלְוִיִּם

and-the-Levites Aaron sons-of *** Yahweh priests-of *** you-drove-out

וַתַּעֲשׂוּ לָכֶם כֹּהֲנִים כְּעַמֵּי הָאֲרָצוֹת כָּל־ הַבָּא

the-one-coming any-of the-lands as-peoples-of priests of-you and-you-made

לְמַלֵּא יָדוֹ בְּפַר בֶּן־ בָּקָר וְאֵילִם שִׁבְעָה

seven and-rams cattle son-of with-bull hand-of-him to-consecrate

וְהָיָה כֹהֵן לְלֹא אֱלֹהִים׃ וַאֲנַחְנוּ יְהוָה אֱלֹהֵינוּ וְלֹא

and-not God-of-us Yahweh and-we (10) gods of-not priest and-he-may-become

עֲזַבְנֻהוּ וְכֹהֲנִים מְשָׁרְתִים לַיהוָה בְּנֵי אַהֲרֹן

Aaron sons-of to-Yahweh ones-serving and-priests we-forsook-him

וְהַלְוִיִּם בִּמְלָאכֶת׃ וּמַקְטִרִים לַיהוָה עֹלוֹת

burnt-offerings to-Yahweh and-ones-presenting (11) in-the-work and-the-Levites

בַּבֹּקֶר־ בַּבֹּקֶר וּבָעֶרֶב־ בָּעֶרֶב וּקְטֹרֶת־

and-incense-of in-the-evening and-in-the-evening in-the-morning in-the-morning

סַמִּים וּמַעֲרֶכֶת לֶחֶם עַל־ הַשֻּׁלְחָן הַטָּהוֹר וּמְנֹרַת

and-lampstand-of the-clean the-table on bread and-setting-of fragrances

הַזָּהָב וְנֵרֹתֶיהָ לְבָעֵר בָּעֶרֶב בָּעֶרֶב כִּי־

indeed in-the-evening in-the-evening to-light and-lamps-of-her the-gold

שֹׁמְרִים אֲנַחְנוּ אֶת־ מִשְׁמֶרֶת יְהוָה אֱלֹהֵינוּ וְאַתֶּם עֲזַבְתֶּם

you-forsook but-you God-of-us Yahweh requirement-of *** we ones-observing

אֹתוֹ׃ וְהִנֵּה עִמָּנוּ בָרֹאשׁ הָאֱלֹהִים ׀ וְכֹהֲנָיו

and-priests-of-him the-God as-the-leader with-us and-see! (12) him

וַחֲצֹצְרוֹת הַתְּרוּעָה לְהָרִיעַ עֲלֵיכֶם בְּנֵי יִשְׂרָאֵל אַל־

not Israel men-of against-you to-sound the-battle-cry and-trumpets

תִּלָּחֲמוּ עִם־ יְהוָה אֱלֹהֵי־ אֲבֹתֵיכֶם כִּי־ לֹא תַצְלִיחוּ׃

you-will-succeed not for fathers-of-you God-of Yahweh against you-fight

David, rebelled against his
master. 7 Some worthless
scoundrels gathered around
him and opposed Rehoboam
son of Solomon when he was
young and indecisive and not
strong enough to resist them.
8 "And now you plan to resist the kingdom of the LORD,
which is in the hands of David's descendants. You are indeed a vast army and have
with you the golden calves
that Jeroboam made to be your
gods. 9 But didn't you drive out
the priests of the LORD, the
sons of Aaron, and the Levites, and make priests of your
own as the peoples of other
lands do? Whoever comes to
consecrate himself with a
young bull and seven rams
may become a priest of what
are not gods.
10 "As for us, the LORD is our
God, and we have not forsak-
en him. The priests who serve
the LORD are sons of Aaron,
and the Levites assist them.
11 Every morning and evening
they present burnt offerings
and fragrant incense to the
LORD. They set out the bread
on the ceremonially clean table and light the lamps on the
gold lampstand every eve-
ning. We are observing the requirements of the LORD our
God. But you have forsaken
him. 12 God is with us; he is our
leader. His priests with their
trumpets will sound the battle
cry against you. Men of Israel,
do not fight against the LORD,
the God of your fathers, for
you will not succeed."

וְיָרָבְעָם הֵסֵב אֶת־ הַמַּאְרָב לָבוֹא מֵאַחֲרֵיהֶם
to-rear-of-them to-go the-troop *** he-sent-around now-Jeroboam (13)

וַיִּהְיוּ לִפְנֵי יְהוּדָה וְהַמַּאְרָב מֵאַחֲרֵיהֶם׃
at-behind-them and-the-ambush Judah in-front-of so-they-were

וַיִּפְנוּ יְהוּדָה וְהִנֵּה לָהֶם הַמִּלְחָמָה פָּנִים וְאָחוֹר
and-rear fronts the-attack against-them and-see! Judah and-they-turned (14)

וַיִּצְעֲקוּ לַיהוָה וְהַכֹּהֲנִים מַחְצְצְרִים בַּחֲצֹצְרוֹת׃
on-the-trumpets ones-blowing and-the-priests to-Yahweh then-they-cried

וַיָּרִיעוּ אִישׁ יְהוּדָה וַיְהִי בְּהָרִיעַ אִישׁ
man-of when-to-raise-cry and-he-was Judah man-of and-they-raised-cry (15)

יְהוּדָה וְהָאֱלֹהִים נָגַף אֶת־ יָרָבְעָם וְכָל־ יִשְׂרָאֵל לִפְנֵי אֲבִיָּה
Abijah before Israel and-all-of Jeroboam *** he-routed then-the-God Judah

וִיהוּדָה׃ וַיָּנוּסוּ בְנֵי־ יִשְׂרָאֵל מִפְּנֵי יְהוּדָה
Judah from-before Israel sons-of and-they-fled (16) and-Judah

וַיִּתְּנֵם אֱלֹהִים בְּיָדָם׃ וַיַּכּוּ בָהֶם
on-them and-he-inflicted (17) into-hand-of-them God and-he-delivered-them

אֲבִיָּה וְעַמּוֹ מַכָּה רַבָּה וַיִּפְּלוּ חֲלָלִים מִיִּשְׂרָאֵל
from-Israel casualties so-they-fell heavy loss and-people-of-him Abijah

חֲמֵשׁ־ מֵאוֹת אֶלֶף אִישׁ בָּחוּר׃ וַיִּכָּנְעוּ בְנֵי־
men-of and-they-were-subdued (18) being-able man thousand hundreds five-of

יִשְׂרָאֵל בָּעֵת הַהִיא וַיֶּאֶמְצוּ בְּנֵי יְהוּדָה כִּי
because Judah men-of and-they-were-victorious the-that on-the-occasion Israel

נִשְׁעֲנוּ עַל־ יְהוָה אֱלֹהֵי אֲבוֹתֵיהֶם׃ וַיִּרְדֹּף אֲבִיָּה
Abijah and-he-pursued (19) fathers-of-them God-of Yahweh on they-relied

אַחֲרֵי יָרָבְעָם וַיִּלְכֹּד מִמֶּנּוּ עָרִים אֶת־ בֵּית־אֵל וְאֶת־ בְּנוֹתֶיהָ
villages-of-her and El Beth *** towns from-him and-he-took Jeroboam after

וְאֶת־ יְשָׁנָה וְאֶת־ בְּנוֹתֶיהָ וְאֶת־ עֶפְרוֹן וּבְנֹתֶיהָ׃ וְלֹא־
and-not (20) and-villages-of-her Ephron and villages-of-her and Jeshanah and

עָצַר כֹּחַ־ יָרָבְעָם עוֹד בִּימֵי אֲבִיָּהוּ וַיִּגְּפֵהוּ
and-he-struck-down-him Abijah in-days-of again Jeroboam power he-regained

יְהוָה וַיָּמֹת׃ וַיִּתְחַזֵּק אֲבִיָּהוּ וַיִּשָּׂא־ לוֹ
to-him and-he-married Abijah but-he-gained-strength (21) and-he-died Yahweh

נָשִׁים אַרְבַּע עֶשְׂרֵה וַיּוֹלֶד עֶשְׂרִים וּשְׁנַיִם בָּנִים וְשֵׁשׁ עֶשְׂרֵה בָּנוֹת׃
daughters ten and-six sons and-two twenty and-he-fathered ten four wives

וְיֶתֶר דִּבְרֵי אֲבִיָּה וּדְרָכָיו וּדְבָרָיו
and-words-of-him and-deeds-of-him Abijah events-of and-other-of (22)

כְּתוּבִים בְּמִדְרַשׁ הַנָּבִיא עִדּוֹ׃ וַיִּשְׁכַּב
and-he-rested *(23) Iddo the-prophet in-annotation-of ones-being-written

[13]Now Jeroboam had sent troops around to the rear, so that while he was in front of Judah the ambush was behind them. [14]Judah turned and saw that they were being attacked at both front and rear. Then they cried out to the LORD. The priests blew their trumpets [15]and the men of Judah raised the battle cry. At the sound of their battle cry, God routed Jeroboam and all Israel before Abijah and Judah. [16]The Israelites fled before Judah, and God delivered them into their hands. [17]Abijah and his men inflicted heavy losses on them, so that there were five hundred thousand casualties among Israel's able men. [18]The men of Israel were subdued on that occasion, and the men of Judah were victorious because they relied on the LORD, the God of their fathers.

[19]Abijah pursued Jeroboam and took from him the towns of Bethel, Jeshanah and Ephron, with their surrounding villages. [20]Jeroboam did not regain power during the time of Abijah. And the LORD struck him down and he died.

[21]But Abijah grew in strength. He married fourteen wives and had twenty-two sons and sixteen daughters.

[22]The other events of Abijah's reign, what he did and what he said, are written in the annotations of the prophet Iddo.

*23 The Hebrew numeration of chapter 14 begins with verse 2 of the English; thus, there is a one-verse discrepancy throughout the chapter.

°14 ק מחצרים

°19 ק עפרין

אֲבִיָּה עִם־ אֲבֹתָיו וַיִּקְבְּרוּ אֹתוֹ בְּעִיר דָּוִיד
David in-City-of him and-they-buried fathers-of-him with Abijah

וַיִּמְלֹךְ אָסָא בְנוֹ תַּחְתָּיו בְּיָמָיו
in-days-of-him in-place-of-him son-of-him Asa and-he-became-king

שָׁקְטָה הָאָרֶץ עֶשֶׂר שָׁנִים׃ וַיַּעַשׂ אָסָא הַטּוֹב
the-good Asa and-he-did (14:1) years ten the-country she-was-at-peace

וְהַיָּשָׁר בְּעֵינֵי יְהוָה אֱלֹהָיו׃ וַיָּסַר אֶת־ מִזְבְּחוֹת
altars-of *** and-he-removed (2) God-of-him Yahweh in-eyes-of and-the-right

הַנֵּכָר וְהַבָּמוֹת וַיְשַׁבֵּר אֶת־ הַמַּצֵּבוֹת
the-sacred-stones *** and-he-smashed and-the-high-places the-foreign

וַיְגַדַּע אֶת־ הָאֲשֵׁרִים׃ וַיֹּאמֶר לִיהוּדָה לִדְרוֹשׁ
to-seek to-Judah and-he-commanded (3) the-Asherah-poles *** and-he-cut-down

אֶת־ יְהוָה אֱלֹהֵי אֲבוֹתֵיהֶם וְלַעֲשׂוֹת הַתּוֹרָה וְהַמִּצְוָה׃
and-the-command the-law and-to-obey fathers-of-them God-of Yahweh ***

וַיָּסַר מִכָּל־ עָרֵי יְהוּדָה אֶת־ הַבָּמוֹת וְאֶת־
and the-high-places *** Judah towns-of from-all-of and-he-removed (4)

הַחַמָּנִים וַתִּשְׁקֹט הַמַּמְלָכָה לְפָנָיו׃
under-him the-kingdom and-she-was-at-peace the-incense-altars

וַיִּבֶן עָרֵי מְצוּרָה בִּיהוּדָה כִּי־ שָׁקְטָה
she-was-at-peace since in-Judah fortification cities-of and-he-built-up (5)

הָאָרֶץ וְאֵין־ עִמּוֹ מִלְחָמָה בַּשָּׁנִים הָאֵלֶּה כִּי־ הֵנִיחַ
he-gave-rest for the-those during-the-years war with-him and-no-one the-land

יְהוָה לוֹ׃ וַיֹּאמֶר לִיהוּדָה נִבְנֶה ׀ אֶת־ הֶעָרִים
the-towns *** let-us-build-up to-Judah and-he-said (6) to-him Yahweh

הָאֵלֶּה וְנָסֵב חוֹמָה וּמִגְדָּלִים דְּלָתַיִם וּבְרִיחִים עוֹדֶנּוּ
still-he and-bars gates and-towers wall and-let-us-put-around the-these

הָאָרֶץ לְפָנֵינוּ כִּי דָרַשְׁנוּ אֶת־ יְהוָה אֱלֹהֵינוּ דָּרַשְׁנוּ
we-sought God-of-us Yahweh *** we-sought because before-us the-land

וַיָּנַח לָנוּ מִסָּבִיב וַיִּבְנוּ וַיַּצְלִיחוּ׃
and-they-prospered so-they-built at-around to-us and-he-gave-rest

וַיְהִי לְאָסָא חַיִל נֹשֵׂא צִנָּה וָרֹמַח מִיהוּדָה
from-Judah and-spear large-shield carrying army to-Asa and-he-was (7)

שְׁלֹשׁ מֵאוֹת אֶלֶף וּמִבִּנְיָמִן נֹשְׂאֵי מָגֵן
small-shield ones-carrying-of and-from-Benjamin thousand hundreds three-of

וְדֹרְכֵי קֶשֶׁת מָאתַיִם וּשְׁמוֹנִים אֶלֶף כָּל־ אֵלֶּה
these all-of thousand and-eighty two-hundreds bow and-ones-drawing-of

גִּבּוֹרֵי חָיִל׃ וַיֵּצֵא אֲלֵיהֶם זֶרַח הַכּוּשִׁי
the-Cushite Zerah against-them and-he-marched-out (8) bravery fighting-men-of

14 And Abijah rested with his fathers and was buried in the City of David. Asa his son succeeded him as king, and in his days the country was at peace for ten years.

Asa King of Judah

2 Asa did what was good and right in the eyes of the LORD his God. 3 He removed the foreign altars and the high places, smashed the sacred stones and cut down the Asherah poles.[z] 4 He commanded Judah to seek the LORD, the God of their fathers, and to obey his laws and commands. 5 He removed the high places and incense altars in every town in Judah, and the kingdom was at peace under him. 6 He built up the fortified cities of Judah, since the land was at peace. No one was at war with him during those years, for the LORD gave him rest.

7 "Let us build up these towns," he said to Judah, "and put walls around them, with towers, gates and bars. The land is still ours, because we have sought the LORD our God; we sought him and he has given us rest on every side." So they built and prospered.

8 Asa had an army of three hundred thousand men from Judah, equipped with large shields and with spears, and two hundred and eighty thousand from Benjamin, armed with small shields and with bows. All these were brave fighting men.

9 Zerah the Cushite marched

z3 That is, symbols of the goddess Asherah; here and elsewhere in 2 Chronicles

*See the note on page 116.

בְּחַיִל אֶלֶף אֲלָפִים וּמַרְכָּבוֹת שְׁלֹשׁ מֵאוֹת וַיָּבֹא
and-he-came hundreds three-of and-chariots thousands thousand-of with-army

עַד־ מָרֵשָׁה׃ וַיֵּצֵא אָסָא לְפָנָיו וַיַּעַרְכוּ
and-they-took-up before-him Asa and-he-went-out (9) Mareshah as-far-as

מִלְחָמָה בְּגֵיא צְפַתָה לְמָרֵשָׁה׃ וַיִּקְרָא אָסָא
Asa then-he-called (10) near-Mareshah Zephathah in-Valley-of battle-position

אֶל־ יְהוָה אֱלֹהָיו וַיֹּאמַר יְהוָה אֵין־ עִמְּךָ לַעְזוֹר
to-help like-you there-is-no-one Yahweh and-he-said God-of-him Yahweh to

בֵּין רַב לְאֵין כֹּחַ עָזְרֵנוּ יְהוָה אֱלֹהֵינוּ כִּי־ עָלֶיךָ
on-you for God-of-us Yahweh help-us! power to-one-without mighty against

נִשְׁעַנּוּ וּבְשִׁמְךָ בָאנוּ עַל־ הֶהָמוֹן הַזֶּה יְהוָה
Yahweh the-this the-vast-army against we-came and-in-name-of-you we-rely

אֱלֹהֵינוּ אַתָּה אַל־ יַעְצֹר עִמְּךָ אֱנוֹשׁ׃ וַיִּגֹּף
and-he-struck-down (11) men against-you let-him-prevail not you God-of-us

יְהוָה אֶת־ הַכּוּשִׁים לִפְנֵי אָסָא וְלִפְנֵי יְהוּדָה וַיָּנֻסוּ הַכּוּשִׁים׃
the-Cushites and-they-fled Judah and-before Asa before the-Cushites *** Yahweh

וַיִּרְדְּפֵם אָסָא וְהָעָם אֲשֶׁר־ עִמּוֹ עַד־ לִגְרָר
to-Gerar as-far-as with-him who and-the-army Asa and-he-pursued-them (12)

וַיִּפֹּל מִכּוּשִׁים לְאֵין לָהֶם מִחְיָה כִּי־ נִשְׁבְּרוּ
they-were-crushed that recovery to-them so-not from-Cushites and-he-fell

לִפְנֵי־ יְהוָה וְלִפְנֵי מַחֲנֵהוּ וַיִּשְׂאוּ שָׁלָל
plunder and-they-carried-off force-of-him and-before Yahweh before

הַרְבֵּה מְאֹד׃ וַיַּכּוּ אֵת כָּל־ הֶעָרִים סְבִיבוֹת
ones-around the-villages all-of *** and-they-destroyed (13) very to-be-large

גְּרָר כִּי־ הָיָה פַחַד־ יְהוָה עֲלֵיהֶם וַיָּבֹזּוּ אֶת־ כָּל־
all-of *** and-they-plundered upon-them Yahweh terror-of he-fell for Gerar

הֶעָרִים כִּי־ בִזָּה רַבָּה הָיְתָה בָהֶם׃ וְגַם־ אָהֳלֵי
camps-of and-also (14) in-them she-was much booty since the-villages

מִקְנֶה הִכּוּ וַיִּשְׁבּוּ צֹאן לָרֹב וּגְמַלִּים
and-camels in-quantity flock and-they-carried-off they-attacked herdsman

וַיָּשֻׁבוּ יְרוּשָׁלָםִ׃ וַעֲזַרְיָהוּ בֶּן־ עוֹדֵד הָיְתָה עָלָיו
upon-him she-came Oded son-of and-Azariah (15:1) Jerusalem then-they-returned

רוּחַ אֱלֹהִים׃ וַיֵּצֵא לִפְנֵי אָסָא וַיֹּאמֶר לוֹ שְׁמָעוּנִי
listen-to-me! to-him and-he-said Asa before and-he-went-out (2) God Spirit-of

אָסָא וְכָל־ יְהוּדָה וּבִנְיָמִן יְהוָה עִמָּכֶם בִּהְיוֹתְכֶם עִמּוֹ
with-him when-to-be-you with-you Yahweh and-Benjamin Judah and-all-of Asa

וְאִם־ תִּדְרְשֻׁהוּ יִמָּצֵא לָכֶם וְאִם־ תַּעַזְבֻהוּ
you-forsake-him but-if by-you he-will-be-found you-seek-him and-if

out against them with a vast
army[a] and three hundred
chariots, and came as far as
Mareshah. [10]Asa went out to
meet him, and they took up
battle positions in the Valley
of Zephathah near Mareshah.
[11]Then Asa called to the LORD
his God and said, "LORD, there
is no one like you to help the
powerless against the mighty.
Help us, O LORD our God, for
we rely on you, and in your
name we have come against
this vast army. O LORD, you
are our God; do not let man
prevail against you."
[12]The LORD struck down the
Cushites before Asa and
Judah. The Cushites fled, [13]and
Asa and his army pursued
them as far as Gerar. Such a
great number of Cushites fell
that they could not recover;
they were crushed before the
LORD and his forces. The men
of Judah carried off a large
amount of plunder. [14]They destroyed all the villages around
Gerar, for the terror of the
LORD had fallen upon them.
They plundered all these villages, since there was much
booty there. [15]They also attacked the camps of the herdsmen and carried off droves of
sheep and goats and camels.
Then they returned to Jerusalem.

Asa's Reform

15 The Spirit of God came
upon Azariah son of
Oded. [2]He went out to meet
Asa and said to him, "Listen
to me, Asa and all Judah and
Benjamin. The LORD is with
you when you are with him. If
you seek him, he will be found
by you, but if you forsake him,

[a]9 Hebrew *with an army of a thousand thousands* or *with an army of thousands upon thousands*

*See the note on page 116.

יַעֲזֹב אֶתְכֶם׃ וְיָמִים רַבִּים לְיִשְׂרָאֵל לְלֹא ׀ אֱלֹהֵי אֱמֶת
truth God-of that-not in-Israel many and-days (3) you he-will-forsake

וּלְלֹא כֹּהֵן מוֹרֶה וּלְלֹא תוֹרָה׃ וַיָּשָׁב
but-he-turned (4) law and-that-not teaching priest and-that-not

בַּצַּר־ לוֹ עַל־ יְהוָה אֱלֹהֵי יִשְׂרָאֵל וַיְבַקְשֻׁהוּ
and-they-sought-him Israel God-of Yahweh to of-him in-the-distress

וַיִּמָּצֵא לָהֶם׃ וּבָעִתִּים הָהֵם אֵין שָׁלוֹם
safe not the-those and-in-the-days (5) by-them and-he-was-found

לַיּוֹצֵא וְלַבָּא כִּי מְהוּמֹת רַבּוֹת עַל כָּל־
all-of to great-ones turmoils for and-for-the-one-coming for-the-one-going

יוֹשְׁבֵי הָאֲרָצוֹת׃ וְכֻתְּתוּ גוֹי־ בְּגוֹי
by-nation nation and-they-were-crushed (6) the-lands ones-inhabiting-of

וְעִיר בְּעִיר כִּי־ אֱלֹהִים הֲמָמָם בְּכָל־ צָרָה׃
distress with-every-of he-troubled-them God because by-city and-city

וְאַתֶּם חִזְקוּ וְאַל־ יִרְפּוּ יְדֵיכֶם כִּי יֵשׁ
there-is for hands-of-you let-them-give-up and-not be-strong! but-you (7)

שָׂכָר לִפְעֻלַּתְכֶם׃ וְכִשְׁמֹעַ אָסָא הַדְּבָרִים הָאֵלֶּה
the-these the-words Asa and-when-to-hear (8) for-work-of-you reward

וְהַנְּבוּאָה עֹדֵד הַנָּבִיא הִתְחַזַּק וַיַּעֲבֵר
and-he-removed he-took-courage the-prophet Oded and-the-prophecy

הַשִּׁקּוּצִים מִכָּל־ אֶרֶץ יְהוּדָה וּבִנְיָמִן וּמִן־
and-from and-Benjamin Judah land-of from-whole-of the-detestable-things

הֶעָרִים אֲשֶׁר לָכַד מֵהַר אֶפְרָיִם וַיְחַדֵּשׁ אֶת־ מִזְבַּח
altar-of *** and-he-repaired Ephraim in-hill-of he-captured that the-towns

יְהוָה אֲשֶׁר לִפְנֵי אוּלָם יְהוָה׃ וַיִּקְבֹּץ אֶת־ כָּל־
all-of *** then-he-assembled (9) Yahweh portico-of in-front-of that Yahweh

יְהוּדָה וּבִנְיָמִן וְהַגָּרִים עִמָּהֶם מֵאֶפְרַיִם וּמְנַשֶּׁה
and-Manasseh from-Ephraim among-them and-the-ones-settling and-Benjamin Judah

וּמִשִּׁמְעוֹן כִּי־ נָפְלוּ עָלָיו מִיִּשְׂרָאֵל לָרֹב
in-number from-Israel to-him they-came-over for and-from-Simeon

בִּרְאֹתָם כִּי־ יְהוָה אֱלֹהָיו עִמּוֹ׃ וַיִּקָּבְצוּ
and-they-assembled (10) with-him God-of-him Yahweh that when-to-see-them

יְרוּשָׁלַםִ בַּחֹדֶשׁ הַשְּׁלִישִׁי לִשְׁנַת חֲמֵשׁ־ עֶשְׂרֵה לְמַלְכוּת אָסָא׃
Asa of-reign-of ten five-of of-year-of the-third in-the-month Jerusalem

וַיִּזְבְּחוּ לַיהוָה בַּיּוֹם הַהוּא מִן־ הַשָּׁלָל
the-plunder from the-that on-the-day to-Yahweh and-they-sacrificed (11)

הֵבִיאוּ בָּקָר שְׁבַע מֵאוֹת וְצֹאן שִׁבְעַת אֲלָפִים׃
thousands seven-of and-flock hundreds seven-of cattle they-brought-back

he will forsake you. 3For a long
time Israel was without the
true God, without a priest to
teach and without the law.
4But in their distress they
turned to the LORD, the God of
Israel, and sought him, and he
was found by them. 5In those
days it was not safe to travel
about, for all the inhabitants
of the lands were in great turmoil. 6One nation was being
crushed by another and one
city by another, because God
was troubling them with
every kind of distress. 7But as
for you, be strong and do not
give up, for your work will be
rewarded."
8When Asa heard these
words and the prophecy of
Azariah son of[b] Oded the
prophet, he took courage. He
removed the detestable idols
from the whole land of Judah
and Benjamin and from the
towns he had captured in the
hills of Ephraim. He repaired
the altar of the LORD that was
in front of the portico of the
LORD's temple.
9Then he assembled all
Judah and Benjamin and the
people from Ephraim, Manasseh and Simeon who had settled among them, for large
numbers had come over to
him from Israel when they
saw that the LORD his God was
with him.
10They assembled at Jerusalem in the third month of the
fifteenth year of Asa's reign.
11At that time they sacrificed
to the LORD seven hundred
head of cattle and seven thousand sheep and goats from the
plunder they had brought

[b]8 Vulgate and Syriac (see also Septuagint and verse 1); Hebrew does not have *Azariah son of*.

וַיָּבֹאוּ בַבְּרִית לִדְרוֹשׁ אֶת־ יְהוָה אֱלֹהֵי
God-of Yahweh *** to-seek into-the-covenant and-they-entered (12)

אֲבוֹתֵיהֶם בְּכָל־ לְבָבָם וּבְכָל־ נַפְשָׁם׃
soul-of-them and-with-all-of heart-of-them with-all-of fathers-of-them

וְכֹל אֲשֶׁר לֹא־ יִדְרֹשׁ לַיהוָה אֱלֹהֵי־יִשְׂרָאֵל יוּמָת
he-was-killed Israel God-of to-Yahweh he-would-seek not who and-all (13)

לְמִן־ קָטֹן וְעַד־ גָּדוֹל לְמֵאִישׁ וְעַד־ אִשָּׁה׃
woman or-to whether-from-man great or-to small whether-from

וַיִּשָּׁבְעוּ לַיהוָה בְּקוֹל גָּדוֹל וּבִתְרוּעָה
and-with-shouting loud with-acclamation to-Yahweh and-they-took-oath (14)

וּבַחֲצֹצְרוֹת וּבְשׁוֹפָרוֹת׃ וַיִּשְׂמְחוּ כָל־ יְהוּדָה עַל־
about Judah all-of and-they-rejoiced (15) and-with-horns and-with-trumpets

הַשְּׁבוּעָה כִּי בְכָל־ לְבָבָם נִשְׁבָּעוּ וּבְכָל־
and-with-all-of they-swore heart-of-them with-whole-of because the-oath

רְצוֹנָם בִּקְשֻׁהוּ וַיִּמָּצֵא לָהֶם וַיָּנַח
so-he-gave-rest by-them and-he-was-found they-sought-him eagerness-of-them

יְהוָה לָהֶם מִסָּבִיב׃ וְגַם־ מַעֲכָה אֵם ׀ אָסָא הַמֶּלֶךְ
the-king Asa grandmother-of Maacah and-also (16) at-around to-them Yahweh

הֱסִירָהּ מִגְּבִירָה אֲשֶׁר־ עָשְׂתָה לַאֲשֵׁרָה מִפְלָצֶת
repulsive-pole to-Asherah she-made because from-queen-mother he-deposed-her

וַיִּכְרֹת אָסָא אֶת־ מִפְלַצְתָּהּ וַיָּדֶק וַיִּשְׂרֹף
and-he-burned and-he-broke-up repulsive-pole-of-her *** Asa and-he-cut-down

בְּנַחַל קִדְרוֹן׃ וְהַבָּמוֹת לֹא־ סָרוּ מִיִּשְׂרָאֵל
from-Israel they-removed not but-the-high-places (17) Kidron in-Valley-of

רַק לְבַב־ אָסָא הָיָה שָׁלֵם כָּל־ יָמָיו׃
days-of-him all-of fully-committed he-was Asa heart-of however

וַיָּבֵא אֶת־ קָדְשֵׁי אָבִיו
father-of-him dedicated-things-of *** and-he-brought (18)

וְקָדָשָׁיו בֵּית הָאֱלֹהִים כֶּסֶף וְזָהָב וְכֵלִים׃
and-articles and-gold silver the-God temple-of and-dedicated-things-of-him

וּמִלְחָמָה לֹא הָיָתָה עַד שְׁנַת־ שְׁלֹשִׁים וְחָמֵשׁ לְמַלְכוּת אָסָא׃
Asa of-reign-of and-five thirty year-of until she-was not and-war (19)

בִּשְׁנַת שְׁלֹשִׁים וָשֵׁשׁ לְמַלְכוּת אָסָא עָלָה בַּעְשָׁא מֶלֶךְ־
king-of Baasha he-went-up Asa of-reign-of and-six thirty in-year-of (16:1)

יִשְׂרָאֵל עַל־ יְהוּדָה וַיִּבֶן אֶת־ הָרָמָה לְבִלְתִּי תֵּת יוֹצֵא
one-leaving to-allow not the-Ramah *** and-he-fortified Judah against Israel

וָבָא לְאָסָא מֶלֶךְ יְהוּדָה׃ וַיֹּצֵא אָסָא כֶּסֶף וְזָהָב
and-gold silver Asa then-he-took (2) Judah king-of to-Asa or-one-entering

back. 12They entered into a
covenant to seek the LORD, the
God of their fathers, with all
their heart and soul. 13All who
would not seek the LORD, the
God of Israel, were to be put to
death, whether small or great,
man or woman. 14They took
an oath to the LORD with loud
acclamation, with shouting
and with trumpets and horns.
15All Judah rejoiced about the
oath because they had sworn
it wholeheartedly. They
sought God eagerly, and he
was found by them. So the
LORD gave them rest on every
side.

16King Asa also deposed his
grandmother Maacah from
her position as queen mother,
because she had made a repulsive Asherah pole. Asa cut the
pole down, broke it up and
burned it in the Kidron Valley. 17Although he did not
remove the high places from
Israel, Asa's heart was fully
committed ⌊to the LORD⌋ all his
life. 18He brought into the temple of God the silver and gold
and the articles that he and his
father had dedicated.

19There was no more war
until the thirty-fifth year of
Asa's reign.

Asa's Last Years

16 In the thirty-sixth year
of Asa's reign Baasha
king of Israel went up against
Judah and fortified Ramah to
prevent anyone from leaving
or entering the territory of Asa
king of Judah.

2Asa then took the silver and

מֵאֹצְרוֹת בֵּית יְהוָה וּבֵית הַמֶּלֶךְ וַיִּשְׁלַח אֶל־
to and-he-sent the-king and-palace-of Yahweh temple-of from-treasuries-of

בֶּן־ הֲדַד מֶלֶךְ אֲרָם הַיּוֹשֵׁב בְּדַרְמֶשֶׂק לֵאמֹר׃ בְּרִית
treaty (3) to-say in-Damascus the-one-ruling Aram king-of Hadad Ben

בֵּינִי וּבֵינֶךָ וּבֵין אָבִי וּבֵין אָבִיךָ
father-of-you and-between father-of-me and-between and-between-you between-me

הִנֵּה שָׁלַחְתִּי לְךָ כֶּסֶף וְזָהָב לֵךְ הָפֵר בְּרִיתְךָ אֶת־ בַּעְשָׁא
Baasha with treaty-of-you break! come! and-gold silver to-you I-send see!

מֶלֶךְ יִשְׂרָאֵל וְיַעֲלֶה מֵעָלָי׃ וַיִּשְׁמַע
and-he-agreed (4) from-against-me so-he-will-withdraw Israel king-of

*בֶּן הֲדַד אֶל־ הַמֶּלֶךְ אָסָא וַיִּשְׁלַח אֶת־ שָׂרֵי הַחֲיָלִים אֲשֶׁר־
that the-forces commanders-of *** and-he-sent Asa the-king with Hadad Ben

לוֹ אֶל־ עָרֵי יִשְׂרָאֵל וַיַּכּוּ אֶת־ עִיּוֹן וְאֶת־ דָּן וְאֵת
and Dan and Ijon *** and-they-conquered Israel towns-of against to-him

אָבֵל מַיִם וְאֵת כָּל־ מִסְכְּנוֹת עָרֵי נַפְתָּלִי׃ וַיְהִי כִּשְׁמֹעַ
when-to-hear and-he-was (5) Naphtali cities-of stores-of all-of and Maim Abel

בַּעְשָׁא וַיֶּחְדַּל מִבְּנוֹת אֶת־ הָרָמָה וַיַּשְׁבֵּת אֶת־
*** and-he-abandoned the-Ramah *** from-to-build then-he-stopped Baasha

מְלַאכְתּוֹ׃ וְאָסָא הַמֶּלֶךְ לָקַח אֶת־ כָּל־ יְהוּדָה
Judah all-of *** he-brought the-king then-Asa (6) work-of-him

וַיִּשְׂאוּ אֶת־ אַבְנֵי הָרָמָה וְאֶת־ עֵצֶיהָ אֲשֶׁר
that timbers-of-her and the-Ramah stones-of *** and-they-carried-away

בָּנָה בַּעְשָׁא וַיִּבֶן בָּהֶם אֶת־ גֶּבַע וְאֶת־ הַמִּצְפָּה׃
the-Mizpah and Geba *** with-them and-he-built-up Baasha he-used

וּבָעֵת הַהִיא בָּא חֲנָנִי הָרֹאֶה אֶל־אָסָא מֶלֶךְ יְהוּדָה
Judah king-of Asa to the-seer Hanani he-came the-that and-at-the-time (7)

וַיֹּאמֶר אֵלָיו בְּהִשָּׁעֶנְךָ עַל־ מֶלֶךְ אֲרָם וְלֹא נִשְׁעַנְתָּ
you-relied and-not Aram king-of on because-to-rely-you to-him and-he-said

עַל־יְהוָה אֱלֹהֶיךָ עַל־ כֵּן נִמְלַט חֵיל מֶלֶךְ־ אֲרָם מִיָּדֶךָ׃
from-hand-of-you Aram king-of army-of he-escaped this for God-of-you Yahweh on

הֲלֹא הַכּוּשִׁים וְהַלּוּבִים הָיוּ לְחַיִל ׀ לָרֹב
in-greatness as-army they-were and-the-Libyans the-Cushites not? (8)

לְרֶכֶב וּלְפָרָשִׁים לְהַרְבֵּה מְאֹד וּבְהִשָּׁעֶנְךָ עַל־
on yet-when-to-rely-you very to-be-great and-with-horsemen with-chariot

יְהוָה נְתָנָם בְּיָדֶךָ׃ כִּי יְהוָה עֵינָיו
eyes-of-him Yahweh for (9) into-hand-of-you he-delivered-them Yahweh

מְשֹׁטְטוֹת בְּכָל־ הָאָרֶץ לְהִתְחַזֵּק עִם־ לְבָבָם
heart-of-them to to-strengthen the-earth through-all-of ones-ranging

gold out of the treasuries of the
LORD's temple and of his own
palace and sent it to Ben-
Hadad king of Aram, who was
ruling in Damascus. 3"Let
there be a treaty between me
and you," he said, "as there
was between my father and
your father. See, I am sending
you silver and gold. Now
break your treaty with Baasha
king of Israel so he will withdraw from me."
4Ben-Hadad agreed with
King Asa and sent the commanders of his forces against
the towns of Israel. They conquered Ijon, Dan, Abel Maim[c]
and all the store cities of
Naphtali. 5When Baasha
heard this, he stopped building Ramah and abandoned
his work. 6Then King Asa
brought all the men of Judah,
and they carried away from
Ramah the stones and timber
Baasha had been using. With
them he built up Geba and
Mizpah.
7At that time Hanani the
seer came to Asa king of Judah
and said to him: "Because you
relied on the king of Aram and
not on the LORD your God, the
army of the king of Aram has
escaped from your hand.
8Were not the Cushites[d] and
Libyans a mighty army with
great numbers of chariots and
horsemen[e]? Yet when you relied on the LORD, he delivered
them into your hand. 9For the
eyes of the LORD range
throughout the earth to
strengthen those whose hearts

[c]4 Also known as *Abel Beth Maacah*
[d]8 That is, people from the upper Nile region
[e]8 Or *charioteers*

*4 Most mss connect these two words with *maqqeph* (בן־הדד).

שָׁלֵם אֵלָיו נִסְכַּלְתָּ עַל־זֹאת כִּי מֵעַתָּה יֵשׁ
there-is from-now indeed this in you-acted-foolishly to-him fully-committed

עִמְּךָ מִלְחָמוֹת׃ וַיִּכְעַס אָסָא אֶל־הָרֹאֶה וַיִּתְּנֵהוּ
and-he-put-him the-seer with Asa and-he-was-angry (10) wars against-you

בֵּית הַמַּהְפֶּכֶת כִּי־בְזַעַף עִמּוֹ עַל־זֹאת וַיְרַצֵּץ
and-he-oppressed this for against-him of-rage because the-prisons house-of

אָסָא מִן־הָעָם בָּעֵת הַהִיא׃ וְהִנֵּה דִּבְרֵי אָסָא
Asa events-of and-see! (11) the-that at-the-time the-people from Asa

הָרִאשׁוֹנִים וְהָאַחֲרוֹנִים הִנָּם כְּתוּבִים עַל־סֵפֶר הַמְּלָכִים
the-kings book-of in ones-being-written see-they! and-the-ends the-beginnings

לִיהוּדָה וְיִשְׂרָאֵל׃ וַיֶּחֱלֵא אָסָא בִּשְׁנַת שְׁלוֹשִׁים
thirty in-year-of Asa and-he-became-diseased (12) and-Israel of-Judah

וָתֵשַׁע לְמַלְכוּתוֹ בְּרַגְלָיו עַד־לְמַעְלָה חָלְיוֹ
disease-of-him to-severity to in-feet-of-him of-reign-of-him and-nine

וְגַם־בְּחָלְיוֹ לֹא־דָרַשׁ אֶת־יְהוָה כִּי
only Yahweh *** he-sought not in-illness-of-him yet-even

בָּרֹפְאִים׃ וַיִּשְׁכַּב אָסָא עִם־אֲבֹתָיו
fathers-of-him with Asa then-he-rested (13) to-the-ones-being-physicians

וַיָּמָת בִּשְׁנַת אַרְבָּעִים וְאַחַת לְמָלְכוֹ׃ וַיִּקְבְּרֻהוּ
and-they-buried-him (14) of-reign-of-him and-one forty in-year-of and-he-died

בְקִבְרֹתָיו אֲשֶׁר כָּרָה־לוֹ בְּעִיר דָּוִיד וַיַּשְׁכִּיבֻהוּ
and-they-laid-him David in-City-of for-him he-cut-out that in-tombs-of-him

בַּמִּשְׁכָּב אֲשֶׁר מִלֵּא בְּשָׂמִים וּזְנִים מְרֻקָּחִים
ones-being-blended and-various-kinds spices he-was-covered that on-the-bier

בְּמִרְקַחַת מַעֲשֶׂה וַיִּשְׂרְפוּ־לוֹ שְׂרֵפָה גְּדוֹלָה עַד־לִמְאֹד׃
to-very to huge fire for-him and-they-burned mixture with-perfume-of

וַיִּמְלֹךְ יְהוֹשָׁפָט בְּנוֹ תַּחְתָּיו
in-place-of-him son-of-him Jehoshaphat and-he-became-king (17:1)

וַיִּתְחַזֵּק עַל־יִשְׂרָאֵל׃ וַיִּתֶּן־חַיִל
troop and-he-stationed (2) Israel against and-he-strengthened-himself

בְּכָל־עָרֵי יְהוּדָה הַבְּצֻרוֹת וַיִּתֵּן נְצִיבִים
garrisons and-he-put the-ones-being-fortified Judah cities-of in-all-of

בְּאֶרֶץ יְהוּדָה וּבְעָרֵי אֶפְרַיִם אֲשֶׁר לָכַד אָסָא אָבִיו׃
father-of-him Asa he-captured that Ephraim and-in-towns-of Judah in-land-of

וַיְהִי יְהוָה עִם־יְהוֹשָׁפָט כִּי הָלַךְ בְּדַרְכֵי דָּוִיד
David in-ways-of he-walked because Jehoshaphat with Yahweh and-he-was (3)

אָבִיו הָרִאשֹׁנִים וְלֹא דָרַשׁ לַבְּעָלִים׃ כִּי
but (4) to-the-Baals he-consulted and-not the-early-ones father-of-him

are fully committed to him. You have done a foolish thing, and from now on you will be at war."

10 Asa was angry with the seer because of this; he was so enraged that he put him in prison. At the same time Asa brutally oppressed some of the people.

11 The events of Asa's reign, from beginning to end, are written in the book of the kings of Judah and Israel. 12 In the thirty-ninth year of his reign Asa was afflicted with a disease in his feet. Though his disease was severe, even in his illness he did not seek help from the LORD, but only from the physicians. 13 Then in the forty-first year of his reign Asa died and rested with his fathers. 14 They buried him in the tomb that he had cut out for himself in the City of David. They laid him on a bier covered with spices and various blended perfumes, and they made a huge fire in his honor.

Jehoshaphat King of Judah

17 Jehoshaphat his son succeeded him as king and strengthened himself against Israel. 2 He stationed troops in all the fortified cities of Judah and put garrisons in Judah and in the towns of Ephraim that his father Asa had captured.

3 The LORD was with Jehoshaphat because in his early years he walked in the ways his father David had followed. He did not consult the Baals

לֵאלֹהֵי אָבִיו דָּרָשׁ וּבְמִצְוֹתָיו הָלָךְ וְלֹא
and-not he-followed and-to-commands-of-him he-sought father-of-him to-God-of

כְּמַעֲשֵׂה יִשְׂרָאֵל׃ וַיָּכֶן יְהוָה אֶת־ הַמַּמְלָכָה
the-kingdom *** Yahweh and-he-established (5) Israel as-practice-of

בְּיָדוֹ וַיִּתְּנוּ כָל־ יְהוּדָה מִנְחָה לִיהוֹשָׁפָט
to-Jehoshaphat gift Judah all-of and-they-brought under-hand-of-him

וַיְהִי־ לוֹ עֹשֶׁר־ וְכָבוֹד לָרֹב׃ וַיִּגְבַּהּ
and-he-was-devoted (6) in-greatness and-honor wealth to-him so-he-was

לִבּוֹ בְּדַרְכֵי יְהוָה וְעוֹד הֵסִיר אֶת־ הַבָּמוֹת
the-high-places *** he-removed and-furthermore Yahweh to-ways-of heart-of-him

וְאֶת־ הָאֲשֵׁרִים מִיהוּדָה׃ וּבִשְׁנַת שָׁלוֹשׁ לְמָלְכוֹ שָׁלַח
he-sent to-reign-him three in-year-of (7) from-Judah the-Asherah-poles and

לְשָׂרָיו לְבֶן־ חַיִל וּלְעֹבַדְיָה וְלִזְכַרְיָה
and-namely-Zechariah and-namely-Obadiah Hail namely-Ben of-officials-of-him

וְלִנְתַנְאֵל וּלְמִיכָיָהוּ לְלַמֵּד בְּעָרֵי יְהוּדָה׃
Judah in-cities-of to-teach and-namely-Micaiah and-namely-Nethanel

וְעִמָּהֶם הַלְוִיִּם שְׁמַעְיָהוּ וּנְתַנְיָהוּ וּזְבַדְיָהוּ וַעֲשָׂהאֵל
and-Asahel and-Zebadiah and-Nethaniah Shemaiah the-Levites and-with-them (8)

וּשְׁמְרִימוֹת וִיהוֹנָתָן וַאֲדֹנִיָּהוּ וְטוֹבִיָּהוּ וְטוֹב אֲדוֹנִיָּה
Adonijah and-Tob and-Tobijah and-Adonijah and-Jehonathan and-Shemiramoth

הַלְוִיִּם וְעִמָּהֶם אֱלִישָׁמָע וִיהוֹרָם הַכֹּהֲנִים׃ וַיְלַמְּדוּ
and-they-taught (9) the-priests and-Jehoram Elishama and-with-them the-Levites

בִּיהוּדָה וְעִמָּהֶם סֵפֶר תּוֹרַת יְהוָה וַיָּסֹבּוּ
and-they-went-around Yahweh Law-of Book-of and-with-them throughout-Judah

בְּכָל־ עָרֵי יְהוּדָה וַיְלַמְּדוּ בָּעָם׃ וַיְהִי ׀
and-he-fell (10) to-the-people and-they-taught Judah towns-of to-all-of

פַּחַד יְהוָה עַל כָּל־ מַמְלְכוֹת הָאֲרָצוֹת אֲשֶׁר סְבִיבוֹת יְהוּדָה
Judah ones-surrounding that the-lands kingdoms-of all-of on Yahweh fear-of

וְלֹא נִלְחֲמוּ עִם־ יְהוֹשָׁפָט׃ וּמִן־ פְּלִשְׁתִּים מְבִיאִים
ones-bringing Philistines and-from (11) Jehoshaphat with they-made-war so-not

לִיהוֹשָׁפָט מִנְחָה וְכֶסֶף מַשָּׂא גַּם הָעַרְבִיאִים מְבִיאִים לוֹ
to-him ones-bringing the-Arabs and tribute and-silver-of gift to-Jehoshaphat

צֹאן אֵילִים שִׁבְעַת אֲלָפִים וּשְׁבַע מֵאוֹת וּתְיָשִׁים שִׁבְעַת
seven-of and-goats hundreds and-seven-of thousands seven-of rams flock

אֲלָפִים וּשְׁבַע מֵאוֹת׃ וַיְהִי יְהוֹשָׁפָט הֹלֵךְ
growing Jehoshaphat and-he-was (12) hundreds and-seven-of thousands

וְגָדֵל עַד־ לְמָעְלָה וַיִּבֶן בִּיהוּדָה בִּירָנִיּוֹת וְעָרֵי
and-cities-of forts in-Judah and-he-built to-more to and-he-became-powerful

°8 ק ושמירמות

4but sought the God of his father and followed his commands rather than the practices of Israel. 5The LORD established the kingdom under his
control; and all Judah brought
gifts to Jehoshaphat, so that he
had great wealth and honor.
6His heart was devoted to the
ways of the LORD; furthermore, he removed the high
places and the Asherah poles
from Judah.
7In the third year of his
reign he sent his officials Ben-
Hail, Obadiah, Zechariah, Nethanel and Micaiah to teach in
the towns of Judah. 8With
them were certain Levites—
Shemaiah, Nethaniah, Zebadiah, Asahel, Shemiramoth,
Jehonathan, Adonijah, Tobi-
jah and Tob-Adonijah—and
the priests Elishama and Jehoram. 9They taught throughout Judah, taking with them
the Book of the Law of the
LORD; they went around to all
the towns of Judah and taught
the people.
10The fear of the LORD fell on
all the kingdoms of the lands
surrounding Judah, so that
they did not make war with
Jehoshaphat. 11Some Philistines brought Jehoshaphat
gifts and silver as tribute, and
the Arabs brought him flocks:
seven thousand seven hun-
dred rams and seven thousand
seven hundred goats.
12Jehoshaphat became more
and more powerful; he built
forts and store cities in Judah

מִסְכְּנוֹת׃ וּמְלָאכָה רַבָּה הָיָה לוֹ בְּעָרֵי יְהוּדָה וְאַנְשֵׁי
and-men-of Judah in-towns-of to-him he-was large and-supply (13) stores

מִלְחָמָה גִּבּוֹרֵי חַיִל בִּירוּשָׁלָםִ׃ וְאֵלֶּה פְקֻדָּתָם
enrollment-of-them and-these (14) in-Jerusalem valor warriors-of fight

לְבֵית אֲבוֹתֵיהֶם לִיהוּדָה שָׂרֵי אֲלָפִים עַדְנָה
Adnah thousands commanders-of from-Judah fathers-of-them by-family-of

הַשָּׂר וְעִמּוֹ גִּבּוֹרֵי חַיִל שְׁלֹשׁ מֵאוֹת אָלֶף׃
thousand hundreds three-of fight men-of and-with-him the-commander

וְעַל־ יָדוֹ יְהוֹחָנָן הַשָּׂר וְעִמּוֹ מָאתַיִם
two-hundreds and-with-him the-commander Jehohanan hand-of-him and-at (15)

וּשְׁמוֹנִים אָלֶף׃ וְעַל־ יָדוֹ עֲמַסְיָה בֶן־ זִכְרִי
Zicri son-of Amasiah hand-of-him and-at (16) thousand and-eighty

הַמִּתְנַדֵּב לַיהוָה וְעִמּוֹ מָאתַיִם אֶלֶף
thousand two-hundreds and-with-him to-Yahweh the-one-volunteering-himself

גִּבּוֹר חָיִל׃ וּמִן־ בִּנְיָמִן גִּבּוֹר חַיִל אֶלְיָדָע וְעִמּוֹ
and-with-him Eliada valor soldier-of Benjamin and-from (17) fight man-of

נֹשְׁקֵי־ קֶשֶׁת וּמָגֵן מָאתַיִם אָלֶף׃ וְעַל־
and-at (18) thousand two-hundreds and-shield bow ones-being-armed-of

יָדוֹ יְהוֹזָבָד וְעִמּוֹ מֵאָה־ וּשְׁמוֹנִים אֶלֶף
thousand and-eighty hundred and-with-him Jehozabad hand-of-him

חֲלוּצֵי צָבָא׃ אֵלֶּה הַמְשָׁרְתִים אֶת־ הַמֶּלֶךְ מִלְּבַד
besides the-king *** the-ones-serving these (19) battle ones-being-armed-of

אֲשֶׁר־ נָתַן הַמֶּלֶךְ בְּעָרֵי הַמִּבְצָר בְּכָל־
through-all-of the-fortification in-cities-of the-king he-stationed whom

יְהוּדָה׃ וַיְהִי לִיהוֹשָׁפָט עֹשֶׁר וְכָבוֹד לָרֹב
in-greatness and-honor wealth to-Jehoshaphat now-he-was (18:1) Judah

וַיִּתְחַתֵּן לְאַחְאָב׃ וַיֵּרֶד לְקֵץ שָׁנִים אֶל־אַחְאָב
Ahab to years at-end-of and-he-went-down (2) with-Ahab and-he-allied-himself

לְשֹׁמְרוֹן וַיִּזְבַּח־ לוֹ אַחְאָב צֹאן וּבָקָר לָרֹב
in-quantity and-cattle sheep Ahab for-him and-he-slaughtered in-Samaria

וְלָעָם אֲשֶׁר עִמּוֹ וַיְסִיתֵהוּ לַעֲלוֹת אֶל־ רָמוֹת גִּלְעָד׃
Gilead Ramoth *** to-attack and-he-urged-him with-him who and-for-the-people

וַיֹּאמֶר אַחְאָב מֶלֶךְ־ יִשְׂרָאֵל אֶל־ יְהוֹשָׁפָט מֶלֶךְ יְהוּדָה
Judah king-of Jehoshaphat to Israel king-of Ahab and-he-asked (3)

הֲתֵלֵךְ עִמִּי רָמֹת גִּלְעָד וַיֹּאמֶר לוֹ כָּמוֹנִי כָמוֹךָ
as-you so-me to-him and-he-replied Gilead Ramoth with-me will-you-go?

וּכְעַמְּךָ עַמִּי וְעִמְּךָ בַּמִּלְחָמָה׃ וַיֹּאמֶר
but-he-said (4) in-the-war and-with-you people-of-me and-as-people-of-you

[13]and had large supplies in the towns of Judah. He also kept experienced fighting men in Jerusalem. [14]Their enrollment by families was as follows:

From Judah, commanders of units of 1,000:
Adnah the commander, with 300,000 fighting men;
[15]next, Jehohanan the commander, with 280,000;
[16]next, Amasiah son of Zicri, who volunteered himself for the service of the LORD, with 200,000.
[17]From Benjamin:
Eliada, a valiant soldier, with 200,000 men armed with bows and shields;
[18]next, Jehozabad, with 180,000 men armed for battle.

[19]These were the men who served the king, besides those he stationed in the fortified cities throughout Judah.

Micaiah Prophesies Against Ahab

18 Now Jehoshaphat had great wealth and honor, and he allied himself with Ahab by marriage. [2]Some years later he went down to visit Ahab in Samaria. Ahab slaughtered many sheep and cattle for him and the people with him and urged him to attack Ramoth Gilead. [3]Ahab king of Israel asked Jehoshaphat king of Judah, "Will you go with me against Ramoth Gilead?"

Jehoshaphat replied, "I am as you are, and my people as your people; we will join you in the war." [4]But Jehoshaphat

יְהוֹשָׁפָט֙ אֶל־ מֶ֣לֶךְ יִשְׂרָאֵ֔ל דְּרָשׁ־ נָ֥א כַיּ֖וֹם אֶת־ דְּבַ֥ר יְהוָֽה׃
Yahweh counsel-of *** as-the-day now! seek! Israel king-of to Jehoshaphat

וַיִּקְבֹּ֤ץ מֶֽלֶךְ־יִשְׂרָאֵ֜ל אֶֽת־ הַנְּבִאִ֗ים אַרְבַּ֤ע מֵא֣וֹת אִ֔ישׁ
man hundreds four the-prophets *** Israel king-of so-he-brought-together (5)

וַיֹּ֤אמֶר אֲלֵהֶם֙ הֲנֵלֵ֞ךְ אֶל־ רָמֹ֥ת גִּלְעָ֛ד לַמִּלְחָמָ֖ה אִם־
or to-the-war Gilead Ramoth against shall-we-go? to-them and-he-asked

אֶחְדָּ֑ל וַיֹּאמְר֣וּ עֲלֵ֔ה וְיִתֵּ֥ן הָאֱלֹהִ֖ים בְּיַ֥ד
into-hand-of the-God for-he-will-give go! and-they-answered shall-I-refrain

הַמֶּֽלֶךְ׃ וַיֹּ֙אמֶר֙ יְה֣וֹשָׁפָ֔ט הַאֵ֨ין פֹּ֥ה נָבִ֛יא לַיהוָ֖ה ע֑וֹד
still of-Yahweh prophet here not? Jehoshaphat but-he-asked (6) the-king

וְנִדְרְשָׁ֖ה מֵאֹתֽוֹ׃ וַיֹּ֣אמֶר מֶֽלֶךְ־יִשְׂרָאֵ֣ל ׀ אֶל־יְהוֹשָׁפָ֗ט
Jehoshaphat to Israel king-of and-he-answered (7) of-him that-we-can-inquire

ע֣וֹד אִישׁ־אֶחָ֡ד לִדְר֣וֹשׁ אֶת־יְהוָה֩ מֵאֹת֨וֹ וַאֲנִ֤י שְׂנֵאתִ֙יהוּ֙ כִּֽי־
because I-hate-him but-I through-him Yahweh *** to-inquire one man still

אֵ֠ינֶנּוּ מִתְנַבֵּ֨א עָלַ֤י לְטוֹבָה֙ כִּ֤י כָל־ יָמָ֔יו לְרָעָ֖ה ה֑וּא
he for-bad days-of-him all-of but for-good about-me prophesying never-he

מִיכָ֣יְהוּ בֶן־ יִמְלָ֑א וַיֹּ֙אמֶר֙ יְה֣וֹשָׁפָ֔ט אַל־ יֹאמַ֖ר הַמֶּֽלֶךְ׃
the-king he-should-say not Jehoshaphat and-he-replied Imlah son-of Micaiah

כֵּ֑ן וַיִּקְרָא֙ מֶ֣לֶךְ יִשְׂרָאֵ֔ל אֶל־ סָרִ֖יס אֶחָ֑ד וַיֹּ֕אמֶר
and-he-said one official to Israel king-of so-he-called (8) that

מַהֵ֖ר מִיכָ֥יְהוּ בֶן־ יִמְלָֽא׃ וּמֶ֣לֶךְ יִשְׂרָאֵ֡ל וִֽיהוֹשָׁפָ֣ט
and-Jehoshaphat Israel and-king-of (9) Imlah son-of Micaiah bring-at-once!

מֶֽלֶךְ־ יְהוּדָ֡ה יוֹשְׁבִים֩ אִ֨ישׁ עַל־ כִּסְא֜וֹ מְלֻבָּשִׁ֤ים בְּגָדִים֙
robes ones-being-dressed throne-of-him on each ones-sitting Judah king-of

וְיֹשְׁבִ֣ים בְּגֹ֔רֶן פֶּ֖תַח שַׁ֣עַר שֹׁמְר֑וֹן וְכָל־
and-all-of Samaria gate-of entrance-of at-threshing-floor and-ones-sitting

הַנְּבִיאִ֔ים מִֽתְנַבְּאִ֖ים לִפְנֵיהֶֽם׃ וַיַּ֥עַשׂ ל֛וֹ צִדְקִיָּ֥הוּ
Zedekiah for-him now-he-made (10) before-them ones-prophesying the-prophets

בֶן־ כְּנַעֲנָ֖ה קַרְנֵ֣י בַרְזֶ֑ל וַיֹּ֙אמֶר֙ כֹּֽה־ אָמַ֣ר יְהוָ֔ה בְּאֵ֖לֶּה
with-these Yahweh he-says this and-he-declared iron horns-of Kenaanah son-of

תְּנַגַּ֥ח אֶת־ אֲרָ֖ם עַד־ כַּלּוֹתָֽם׃ וְכָל־ הַנְּבִאִ֗ים
the-prophets and-all-of (11) to-destroy-them until Aram *** you-will-gore

נִבְּאִ֥ים כֵּ֖ן לֵאמֹ֑ר עֲלֵ֞ה רָמֹ֤ת גִּלְעָד֙ וְהַצְלַ֔ח
and-be-victorious! Gilead Ramoth attack! to-say same ones-prophesying

וְנָתַ֥ן יְהוָ֖ה בְּיַ֥ד הַמֶּֽלֶךְ׃ וְהַמַּלְאָ֞ךְ אֲשֶׁר־
who and-the-messenger (12) the-king into-hand-of Yahweh for-he-will-give

הָלַךְ֮ לִקְרֹ֣א לְמִיכָ֒יְהוּ֒ דִּבֶּ֤ר אֵלָיו֙ לֵאמֹ֔ר הִנֵּ֖ה דִּבְרֵ֥י
words-of look! to-say to-him he-said to-Micaiah to-summon he-went

8 ק מִיכָיְהוּ

also said to the king of Israel, "First seek the counsel of the LORD."

[5]So the king of Israel brought together the prophets—four hundred men—and asked them, "Shall we go to war against Ramoth Gilead, or shall I refrain?"

"Go," they answered, "for God will give it into the king's hand."

[6]But Jehoshaphat asked, "Is there not a prophet of the LORD here whom we can inquire of?"

[7]The king of Israel answered Jehoshaphat, "There is still one man through whom we can inquire of the LORD, but I hate him because he never prophesies anything good about me, but always bad. He is Micaiah son of Imlah."

"The king should not say that," Jehoshaphat replied.

[8]So the king of Israel called one of his officials and said, "Bring Micaiah son of Imlah at once."

[9]Dressed in their royal robes, the king of Israel and Jehoshaphat king of Judah were sitting on their thrones at the threshing floor by the entrance to the gate of Samaria, with all the prophets prophesying before them. [10]Now Zedekiah son of Kenaanah had made iron horns, and he declared, "This is what the LORD says: 'With these you will gore the Arameans until they are destroyed.'"

[11]All the other prophets were prophesying the same thing. "Attack Ramoth Gilead and be victorious," they said, "for the LORD will give it into the king's hand."

[12]The messenger who had gone to summon Micaiah said to him, "Look, as one man the

הַנְּבִאִים פֶּה־אֶחָד טוֹב אֶל־הַמֶּלֶךְ וִיהִי־נָא דְבָרְךָ
word-of-you now! so-let-him-be the-king for success one mouth the-prophets

כְּאַחַד מֵהֶם וְדִבַּרְתָּ טּוֹב׃ וַיֹּאמֶר מִיכָיְהוּ חַי־
life-of Micaiah but-he-said (13) favorably and-you-speak with-them as-one

יְהוָה כִּי אֶת־אֲשֶׁר־יֹאמַר אֱלֹהַי אֹתוֹ אֲדַבֵּר׃ וַיָּבֹא
when-he-arrived (14) I-can-tell him God-of-me he-says what *** only Yahweh

אֶל־הַמֶּלֶךְ וַיֹּאמֶר הַמֶּלֶךְ אֵלָיו מִיכָה הֲנֵלֵךְ אֶל־רָמֹת
Ramoth against shall-we-go? Micaiah to-him the-king then-he-asked the-king at

גִּלְעָד לַמִּלְחָמָה אִם־אֶחְדָּל וַיֹּאמֶר עֲלוּ
attack! and-he-answered shall-I-refrain or to-the-war Gilead

וְהַצְלִיחוּ וְיִנָּתְנוּ בְּיֶדְכֶם׃ וַיֹּאמֶר
but-he-said (15) into-hand-of-you for-they-will-be-given and-be-victorious!

אֵלָיו הַמֶּלֶךְ עַד־כַּמֶּה פְעָמִים אֲנִי מַשְׁבִּיעֶךָ אֲשֶׁר לֹא־
not that making-swear-you I times as-the-how-many? to the-king to-him

תְדַבֵּר אֵלַי רַק־אֱמֶת בְּשֵׁם יְהוָה׃ וַיֹּאמֶר רָאִיתִי אֶת־
*** I-saw then-he-answered (16) Yahweh in-name-of truth only to-me you-tell

כָּל־יִשְׂרָאֵל נְפוֹצִים עַל־הֶהָרִים כַּצֹּאן אֲשֶׁר אֵין־
not that like-the-sheep the-hills on ones-being-scattered Israel all-of

לָהֶן רֹעֶה וַיֹּאמֶר יְהוָה לֹא־אֲדֹנִים לָאֵלֶּה יָשׁוּבוּ
let-them-go to-these masters not Yahweh and-he-said one-shepherding to-them

אִישׁ־לְבֵיתוֹ בְּשָׁלוֹם׃ וַיֹּאמֶר מֶלֶךְ־יִשְׂרָאֵל אֶל־יְהוֹשָׁפָט
Jehoshaphat to Israel king-of and-he-said (17) in-peace to-home-of-him each

הֲלֹא אָמַרְתִּי אֵלֶיךָ לֹא־יִתְנַבֵּא עָלַי טוֹב כִּי אִם־לְרָע׃
for-bad only but good about-me he-prophesies not to-you I-told not?

וַיֹּאמֶר לָכֵן שִׁמְעוּ דְבַר־יְהוָה רָאִיתִי אֶת־יְהוָה יוֹשֵׁב
sitting Yahweh *** I-saw Yahweh word-of hear! therefore and-he-said (18)

עַל־כִּסְאוֹ וְכָל־צְבָא הַשָּׁמַיִם עֹמְדִים עַל־יְמִינוֹ
right-of-him on ones-standing the-heavens host-of and-all-of throne-of-him on

וּשְׂמֹאלוֹ׃ וַיֹּאמֶר יְהוָה מִי יְפַתֶּה אֶת־אַחְאָב מֶלֶךְ־
king-of Ahab *** he-will-lure who? Yahweh and-he-said (19) and-left-of-him

יִשְׂרָאֵל וְיַעַל וְיִפֹּל בְּרָמוֹת גִּלְעָד וַיֹּאמֶר זֶה
this and-he-said Gilead at-Ramoth and-he-falls so-he-attacks Israel

אֹמֵר כָּכָה וְזֶה אֹמֵר כָּכָה׃ וַיֵּצֵא הָרוּחַ
the-spirit and-he-came-forward (20) such suggesting and-that such suggesting

וַיַּעֲמֹד לִפְנֵי יְהוָה וַיֹּאמֶר אֲנִי אֲפַתֶּנּוּ וַיֹּאמֶר יְהוָה
Yahweh and-he-asked I-will-lure-him I and-he-said Yahweh before and-he-stood

אֵלָיו בַּמָּה׃ וַיֹּאמֶר אֵצֵא וְהָיִיתִי לְרוּחַ שֶׁקֶר
lying as-spirit and-I-will-be I-will-go and-he-said (21) by-the-how? to-him

other prophets are predicting
success for the king. Let your
word agree with theirs, and
speak favorably."
13But Micaiah said, "As surely as the LORD lives, I can tell
him only what my God says."
14When he arrived, the king
asked him, "Micaiah, shall we
go to war against Ramoth Gilead, or shall I refrain?"
"Attack and be victorious,"
he answered, "for they will be
given into your hand."
15The king said to him,
"How many times must I
make you swear to tell me
nothing but the truth in the
name of the LORD?"
16Then Micaiah answered,
"I saw all Israel scattered on
the hills like sheep without a
shepherd, and the LORD said,
'These people have no master.
Let each one go home in
peace.' "
17The king of Israel said to
Jehoshaphat, "Didn't I tell you
that he never prophesies anything good about me, but only
bad?"
18Micaiah continued,
"Therefore hear the word of
the LORD: I saw the LORD sitting on his throne with all the
host of heaven standing on
his right and on his left. 19And
the LORD said, 'Who will lure
Ahab king of Israel into attacking Ramoth Gilead and
going to his death there?'
"One suggested this, and
another that. 20Finally, a spirit
came forward, stood before
the LORD and said, 'I will lure
him.'
" 'By what means?' the LORD
asked.
21" 'I will go and be a lying

בְּפִי כָּל־ נְבִיאָיו וַיֹּאמֶר תְּפַתֶּה וְגַם־
and-also you-will-lure and-he-said prophets-of-him all-of in-mouth-of

תּוּכָל צֵא וַעֲשֵׂה־ כֵן׃ (22) וְעַתָּה הִנֵּה נָתַן יְהוָה רוּחַ
spirit Yahweh he-put see! so-now (22) this and-do! go! you-will-succeed

שֶׁקֶר בְּפִי נְבִיאֶיךָ אֵלֶּה וַיהוָה דִּבֶּר עָלֶיךָ רָעָה׃
disaster for-you he-decreed and-Yahweh these prophets-of-you in-mouth-of lying

(23) וַיִּגַּשׁ צִדְקִיָּהוּ בֶן־ כְּנַעֲנָה וַיַּךְ אֶת־ מִיכָיְהוּ
Micaiah *** and-he-slapped Kenaanah son-of Zedekiah then-he-went-up (23)

עַל־ הַלֶּחִי וַיֹּאמֶר אֵי זֶה הַדֶּרֶךְ עָבַר רוּחַ־ יְהוָה
Yahweh spirit-of he-went the-way this where? and-he-asked the-cheek on

מֵאִתִּי לְדַבֵּר אֹתָךְ׃ (24) וַיֹּאמֶר מִיכָיְהוּ הִנְּךָ רֹאֶה
finding-out see-you? Micaiah and-he-replied (24) to-you to-speak from-with-me

בַּיּוֹם הַהוּא אֲשֶׁר תָּבוֹא חֶדֶר בְּחֶדֶר לְהֵחָבֵא׃ (25) וַיֹּאמֶר
then-he-ordered (25) to-hide in-room room you-go when the-that on-the-day

מֶלֶךְ יִשְׂרָאֵל קְחוּ אֶת־ מִיכָיְהוּ וַהֲשִׁיבֻהוּ אֶל־ אָמוֹן שַׂר־
ruler-of Amon to and-send-back-him! Micaiah *** take! Israel king-of

הָעִיר וְאֶל־ יוֹאָשׁ בֶּן־ הַמֶּלֶךְ׃ (26) וַאֲמַרְתֶּם כֹּה אָמַר הַמֶּלֶךְ
the-king he-says this and-you-say (26) the-king son-of Joash and-to the-city

שִׂימוּ זֶה בֵּית הַכֶּלֶא וְהַאֲכִלֻהוּ לֶחֶם לַחַץ
scanty bread and-give-to-eat-him! the-prison house-of this-one put!

וּמַיִם לַחַץ עַד שׁוּבִי בְשָׁלוֹם׃ (27) וַיֹּאמֶר מִיכָיְהוּ
Micaiah and-he-declared (27) in-safety to-return-me until scanty and-waters

אִם־ שׁוֹב תָּשׁוּב בְּשָׁלוֹם לֹא־ דִבֶּר יְהוָה בִּי וַיֹּאמֶר
then-he-said through-me Yahweh he-spoke not in-safety you-return to-return if

שִׁמְעוּ עַמִּים כֻּלָּם׃ (28) וַיַּעַל מֶלֶךְ־ יִשְׂרָאֵל
Israel king-of so-he-went-up (28) all-of-them peoples mark-words!

וִיהוֹשָׁפָט מֶלֶךְ־ יְהוּדָה אֶל־ רָמֹת גִּלְעָד׃ (29) וַיֹּאמֶר מֶלֶךְ
king-of and-he-said (29) Gilead Ramoth to Judah king-of and-Jehoshaphat

יִשְׂרָאֵל אֶל־ יְהוֹשָׁפָט הִתְחַפֵּשׂ וָבוֹא בַּמִּלְחָמָה
into-the-battle and-to-enter to-disguise-himself Jehoshaphat to Israel

וְאַתָּה לְבַשׁ בְּגָדֶיךָ וַיִּתְחַפֵּשׂ מֶלֶךְ יִשְׂרָאֵל וַיָּבֹאוּ
and-he-went Israel king-of so-he-disguised-himself robes-of-you wear! but-you

בַּמִּלְחָמָה׃ (30) וּמֶלֶךְ אֲרָם צִוָּה אֶת־ שָׂרֵי הָרֶכֶב
the-chariot commanders-of *** he-ordered Aram now-king-of (30) into-the-battle

אֲשֶׁר־ לוֹ לֵאמֹר לֹא תִּלָּחֲמוּ אֶת־ הַקָּטֹן אֶת־ הַגָּדוֹל כִּי אִם־
only except the-great *** the-small *** you-fight not to-say to-him that

אֶת־ מֶלֶךְ יִשְׂרָאֵל לְבַדּוֹ׃ (31) וַיְהִי כִּרְאוֹת שָׂרֵי
commanders-of when-to-see and-he-was (31) by-himself Israel king-of ***

spirit in the mouths of all his
prophets,' he said.
" 'You will succeed in luring
him,' said the LORD. 'Go and
do it.'
22"So now the LORD has put a
lying spirit in the mouths of
these prophets of yours. The
LORD has decreed disaster for
you."
23Then Zedekiah son of
Kenaanah went up and
slapped Micaiah in the face.
"Which way did the spirit
from[f] the LORD go when he
went from me to speak to
you?" he asked.
24Micaiah replied, "You will
find out on the day you go to
hide in an inner room."
25The king of Israel then ordered, "Take Micaiah and
send him back to Amon the
ruler of the city and to Joash
the king's son, 26and say, 'This
is what the king says: Put this
fellow in prison and give him
nothing but bread and water
until I return safely.' "
27Micaiah declared, "If you
ever return safely, the LORD
has not spoken through me."
Then he added, "Mark my
words, all you people!"

Ahab Killed at Ramoth Gilead

28So the king of Israel and Jehoshaphat king of Judah went
up to Ramoth Gilead. 29The
king of Israel said to Jehoshaphat, "I will enter the battle in
disguise, but you wear your
royal robes." So the king of Israel disguised himself and
went into battle.
30Now the king of Aram had
ordered his chariot commanders, "Do not fight with anyone, small or great, except the
king of Israel." 31When the

[f]23 Or *Spirit of*

הָֽרֶכֶב אֶת־ יְהוֹשָׁפָט וְהֵמָּה אָמְרוּ מֶלֶךְ יִשְׂרָאֵל הוּא
this Israel king-of they-thought then-they Jehoshaphat *** the-chariot

וַיָּסֹבּוּ עָלָיו לְהִלָּחֵם וַיִּזְעַק יְהוֹשָׁפָט וַיהוָה
and-Yahweh Jehoshaphat but-he-cried-out to-attack against-him so-they-turned

עֲזָרוֹ וַיְסִיתֵם אֱלֹהִים מִמֶּנּוּ׃ וַיְהִי כִּרְאוֹת
when-to-see for-he-was (32) from-him God and-he-drew-away-them he-helped-him

שָׂרֵי הָרֶכֶב כִּי לֹא־ הָיָה מֶלֶךְ יִשְׂרָאֵל וַיָּשֻׁבוּ
then-they-turned Israel king-of he-was not that the-chariot commanders-of

מֵאַחֲרָיו׃ וְאִישׁ מָשַׁךְ בַּקֶּשֶׁת לְתֻמּוֹ וַיַּךְ
and-he-hit at-random-of-him on-the-bow he-drew but-someone (33) from-after-him

אֶת־ מֶלֶךְ יִשְׂרָאֵל בֵּין הַדְּבָקִים וּבֵין הַשִּׁרְיָן וַיֹּאמֶר
and-he-told the-armor and-between the-sections between Israel king-of ***

לָרַכָּב הֲפֹךְ יָדֶיךָ° וְהוֹצֵאתַנִי מִן־ הַמַּחֲנֶה
the-fight from and-get-out-me! hand-of-you turn-around! to-the-chariot-driver

כִּי הָחֳלֵיתִי׃ וַתַּעַל הַמִּלְחָמָה בַּיּוֹם הַהוּא
the-that through-the-day the-battle and-she-raged (34) I-am-wounded for

וּמֶלֶךְ יִשְׂרָאֵל הָיָה מַעֲמִיד בַּמֶּרְכָּבָה נֹכַח אֲרָם עַד־
until Aram facing in-the-chariot being-propped-up he-was Israel and-king-of

הָעָרֶב וַיָּמָת לְעֵת בּוֹא הַשָּׁמֶשׁ׃ וַיָּשָׁב
when-he-returned (19:1) the-sun to-set at-time-of then-he-died the-evening

יְהוֹשָׁפָט מֶלֶךְ־ יְהוּדָה אֶל־ בֵּיתוֹ בְּשָׁלוֹם לִירוּשָׁלִָם׃
in-Jerusalem in-safety palace-of-him to Judah king-of Jehoshaphat

וַיֵּצֵא אֶל־ פָּנָיו יֵהוּא בֶן־ חֲנָנִי הַחֹזֶה וַיֹּאמֶר
and-he-said the-seer Hanani son-of Jehu faces-of-him to then-he-went-out (2)

אֶל־ הַמֶּלֶךְ יְהוֹשָׁפָט הֲלָרָשָׁע לַעְזֹר וּלְשֹׂנְאֵי יְהוָה
Yahweh and-to-ones-hating-of to-help to-the-wicked? Jehoshaphat the-king to

תֶּאֱהָב וּבָזֹאת עָלֶיךָ קֶּצֶף מִלִּפְנֵי יְהוָה׃ אֲבָל
however (3) Yahweh from-before wrath upon-you and-because-of-this you-love

דְּבָרִים טוֹבִים נִמְצְאוּ עִמָּךְ כִּי־ בִעַרְתָּ הָאֲשֵׁרוֹת
the-Asherah-poles you-got-rid for in-you they-are-found good-ones things

מִן־ הָאָרֶץ וַהֲכִינוֹתָ לְבָבְךָ לִדְרֹשׁ הָאֱלֹהִים׃ וַיֵּשֶׁב
and-he-lived (4) the-God to-seek heart-of-you and-you-set the-land from

יְהוֹשָׁפָט בִּירוּשָׁלִָם וַיָּשָׁב וַיֵּצֵא בָעָם
among-the-people and-he-went-out and-he-returned in-Jerusalem Jehoshaphat

מִבְּאֵר שֶׁבַע עַד־ הַר אֶפְרַיִם וַיְשִׁיבֵם אֶל־ יְהוָה
Yahweh to and-he-turned-back-them Ephraim hill-country-of to Sheba from-Beer

אֱלֹהֵי אֲבוֹתֵיהֶם׃ וַיַּעֲמֵד שֹׁפְטִים בָּאָרֶץ
in-the-land ones-judging and-he-appointed (5) fathers-of-them God-of

chariot commanders saw Jehoshaphat, they thought,
"This is the king of Israel." So
they turned to attack him, but
Jehoshaphat cried out, and the
LORD helped him. God drew
them away from him, [32]for
when the chariot commanders
saw that he was not the king
of Israel, they stopped pursuing him.
[33]But someone drew his bow
at random and hit the king of
Israel between the sections of
his armor. The king told the
chariot driver, "Wheel around
and get me out of the fighting.
I've been wounded." [34]All day
long the battle raged, and the
king of Israel propped himself
up in his chariot facing the
Arameans until evening.
Then at sunset he died.

19 When Jehoshaphat
king of Judah returned
safely to his palace in Jerusalem, [2]Jehu the seer, the son of
Hanani, went out to meet him
and said to the king, "Should
you help the wicked and love[g]
those who hate the LORD? Because of this, the wrath of the
LORD is upon you. [3]There is,
however, some good in you,
for you have rid the land of
the Asherah poles and have
set your heart on seeking
God."

Jehoshaphat Appoints Judges

[4]Jehoshaphat lived in
Jerusalem, and he went out
again among the people from
Beersheba to the hill country
of Ephraim and turned them
back to the LORD, the God of
their fathers. [5]He appointed
judges in the land, in each of

g2 Or *and make alliances with*

°33 ק ידך

בְּכָל־ עָרֵי יְהוּדָה הַבְּצֻרוֹת לְעִיר וָעִיר׃
and-city in-city the-ones-being-fortified Judah cities-of in-each-of

וַיֹּאמֶר אֶל־ הַשֹּׁפְטִים רְאוּ מָה־ אַתֶּם עֹשִׂים כִּי
because ones-doing you what consider! the-ones-judging to and-he-told (6)

לֹא לְאָדָם תִּשְׁפְּטוּ כִּי לַיהוָה וְעִמָּכֶם בִּדְבַר מִשְׁפָּט׃
verdict in-word-of and-with-you for-Yahweh but you-judge for-man not

וְעַתָּה יְהִי־ פַחַד־ יְהוָה עֲלֵיכֶם שִׁמְרוּ וַעֲשׂוּ כִּי־ אֵין
there-is-no for and-do! judge! upon-you Yahweh fear-of let-him-be and-now (7)

עִם־ יְהוָה אֱלֹהֵינוּ עַוְלָה וּמַשֹּׂא פָנִים וּמִקַּח־ שֹׁחַד׃
bribe or-taking-of faces or-lifting-of injustice God-of-us Yahweh with

וְגַם בִּירוּשָׁלִַם הֶעֱמִיד יְהוֹשָׁפָט מִן־ הַלְוִיִּם
the-Levites from Jehoshaphat he-appointed in-Jerusalem and-also (8)

וְהַכֹּהֲנִים וּמֵרָאשֵׁי הָאָבוֹת לְיִשְׂרָאֵל לְמִשְׁפַּט יְהוָה
Yahweh for-law-of of-Israel the-fathers and-from-heads-of and-the-priests

וְלָרִיב וַיָּשֻׁבוּ יְרוּשָׁלִָם׃ וַיְצַו עֲלֵיהֶם לֵאמֹר
to-say to-them and-he-ordered (9) Jerusalem and-they-lived and-for-dispute

כֹּה תַעֲשׂוּן בְּיִרְאַת יְהוָה בֶּאֱמוּנָה וּבְלֵבָב שָׁלֵם׃
whole and-with-heart in-faith Yahweh in-fear-of you-must-serve thus

וְכָל־ רִיב אֲשֶׁר־ יָבוֹא עֲלֵיכֶם מֵאֲחֵיכֶם ׀
from-fellows-of-you before-you he-comes that case and-every-of (10)

הַיֹּשְׁבִים בְּעָרֵיהֶם בֵּין־ דָּם ׀ לְדָם בֵּין־ תּוֹרָה
law between to-blood blood between in-cities-of-them the-ones-living

לְמִצְוָה לְחֻקִּים וּלְמִשְׁפָּטִים וְהִזְהַרְתֶּם אֹתָם וְלֹא
so-not them and-you-must-warn or-to-ordinances to-decrees to-command

יֶאְשְׁמוּ לַיהוָה וְהָיָה־ קֶצֶף עֲלֵיכֶם וְעַל־ אֲחֵיכֶם כֹּה
this brothers-of-you and-on on-you wrath or-he-will-come against-Yahweh they-sin

תַעֲשׂוּן וְלֹא תֶאְשָׁמוּ׃ וְהִנֵּה אֲמַרְיָהוּ כֹהֵן הָרֹאשׁ עֲלֵיכֶם
over-you the-chief priest Amariah and-see! (11) you-will-sin and-not you-do

לְכֹל דְּבַר־ יְהוָה וּזְבַדְיָהוּ בֶן־ יִשְׁמָעֵאל הַנָּגִיד לְבֵית־
of-tribe-of the-leader Ishmael son-of and-Zebadiah Yahweh matter-of in-any-of

יְהוּדָה לְכֹל דְּבַר־ הַמֶּלֶךְ וְשֹׁטְרִים הַלְוִיִּם לִפְנֵיכֶם
before-you the-Levites and-officials the-king matter-of in-any-of Judah

חִזְקוּ וַעֲשׂוּ וִיהִי יְהוָה עִם־ הַטּוֹב׃ וַיְהִי
and-he-was (20:1) the-good with Yahweh and-may-he-be and-act! be-courageous!

אַחֲרֵיכֵן בָּאוּ בְנֵי־ מוֹאָב וּבְנֵי עַמּוֹן וְעִמָּהֶם ׀
and-with-them Ammon and-sons-of Moab sons-of they-came after-this

מֵהָעַמּוֹנִים עַל־ יְהוֹשָׁפָט לַמִּלְחָמָה׃ וַיָּבֹאוּ
and-they-came (2) to-the-war Jehoshaphat against from-the-Ammonites

the fortified cities of Judah.
6He told them, "Consider carefully what you do, because you
are not judging for man but
for the LORD, who is with you
whenever you give a verdict.
7Now let the fear of the LORD
be upon you. Judge carefully,
for with the LORD our God
there is no injustice or partiality or bribery."
8In Jerusalem also, Jehoshaphat appointed some of the
Levites, priests and heads of
Israelite families to administer
the law of the LORD and to settle disputes. And they lived in
Jerusalem. 9He gave them
these orders: "You must serve
faithfully and wholeheartedly
in the fear of the LORD. 10In
every case that comes before
you from your fellow countrymen who live in the cities—
whether bloodshed or other
concerns of the law, com-
mands, decrees or ordi-
nances—you are to warn them
not to sin against the LORD;
otherwise his wrath will come
on you and your brothers. Do
this, and you will not sin.
11"Amariah the chief priest
will be over you in any matter
concerning the LORD, and
Zebadiah son of Ishmael, the
leader of the tribe of Judah,
will be over you in any matter
concerning the king, and the
Levites will serve as officials
before you. Act with courage,
and may the LORD be with
those who do well."

Jehoshaphat Defeats Moab and Ammon

20 After this, the Moab-
ites and Ammonites
with some of the Meunites[h]
came to make war on Jehoshaphat.

[h]1 Some Septuagint manuscripts; Hebrew *Ammonites*

וַיַּגִּידוּ לִיהוֹשָׁפָט לֵאמֹר בָּא עָלֶיךָ הָמוֹן רָב
vast army against-you he-comes to-say to-Jehoshaphat and-they-told

מֵעֵבֶר לַיָּם מֵאֲרָם וְהִנָּם בְּחַצְצוֹן תָּמָר הִיא
that Tamar in-Hazazon and-see-they! from-Aram of-the-Sea from-other-side

עֵין גֶּדִי׃ וַיִּרָא וַיִּתֵּן יְהוֹשָׁפָט אֶת־ פָּנָיו
faces-of-him *** Jehoshaphat and-he-set and-he-was-alarmed (3) Gedi En

לִדְרוֹשׁ לַיהוָה וַיִּקְרָא־ צוֹם עַל־ כָּל־ יְהוּדָה׃
Judah all-of for fast and-he-proclaimed of-Yahweh to-inquire

וַיִּקָּבְצוּ יְהוּדָה לְבַקֵּשׁ מִיְהוָה גַּם מִכָּל־
from-all-of indeed from-Yahweh to-seek-help Judah and-they-came-together (4)

עָרֵי יְהוּדָה בָּאוּ לְבַקֵּשׁ אֶת־ יְהוָה׃ וַיַּעֲמֹד יְהוֹשָׁפָט
Jehoshaphat then-he-stood-up (5) Yahweh *** to-seek they-came Judah towns-of

בִּקְהַל יְהוּדָה וִירוּשָׁלִַם בְּבֵית יְהוָה לִפְנֵי
in-front-of Yahweh at-temple-of and-Jerusalem Judah in-assembly-of

הֶחָצֵר הַחֲדָשָׁה׃ וַיֹּאמַר יְהוָה אֱלֹהֵי אֲבֹתֵינוּ הֲלֹא אַתָּה־
you not? fathers-of-us God-of Yahweh and-he-said (6) the-new the-courtyard

הוּא אֱלֹהִים בַּשָּׁמַיִם וְאַתָּה מוֹשֵׁל בְּכֹל מַמְלְכוֹת הַגּוֹיִם
the-nations kingdoms-of over-all-of ruling and-you in-the-heavens God he

וּבְיָדְךָ כֹּחַ וּגְבוּרָה וְאֵין עִמְּךָ לְהִתְיַצֵּב׃
to-withstand against-you and-no-one and-might power and-in-hand-of-you

הֲלֹא ׀ אַתָּה אֱלֹהֵינוּ הוֹרַשְׁתָּ אֶת־ יֹשְׁבֵי הָאָרֶץ הַזֹּאת
the-this the-land ones-inhabiting-of *** you-drove-out God-of-us you not? (7)

מִלִּפְנֵי עַמְּךָ יִשְׂרָאֵל וַתִּתְּנָהּ לְזֶרַע אַבְרָהָם
Abraham to-descendant-of and-you-gave-her Israel people-of-you from-before

אֹהַבְךָ לְעוֹלָם׃ וַיֵּשְׁבוּ־ בָהּ וַיִּבְנוּ לְךָ ׀
for-you and-they-built in-her and-they-lived (8) to-forever friend-of-you

בָּהּ מִקְדָּשׁ לְשִׁמְךָ לֵאמֹר׃ אִם־ תָּבוֹא עָלֵינוּ רָעָה
calamity upon-us she-comes if (9) to-say for-Name-of-you sanctuary in-her

חֶרֶב שְׁפוֹט וָדֶבֶר וְרָעָב נַעַמְדָה לִפְנֵי הַבַּיִת
the-temple before we-will-stand or-famine or-plague judgment sword-of

הַזֶּה וּלְפָנֶיךָ כִּי שִׁמְךָ בַּבַּיִת הַזֶּה
the-this in-the-temple Name-of-you that and-in-presences-of-you the-this

וְנִזְעַק אֵלֶיךָ מִצָּרָתֵנוּ וְתִשְׁמַע וְתוֹשִׁיעַ׃
and-you-will-save and-you-will-hear in-distress-of-us to-you and-we-will-cry-out

וְעַתָּה הִנֵּה בְנֵי־ עַמּוֹן וּמוֹאָב וְהַר־ שֵׂעִיר אֲשֶׁר לֹא־
not who Seir and-Mount-of and-Moab Ammon men-of see! but-now (10)

נָתַתָּה לְיִשְׂרָאֵל לָבוֹא בָהֶם בְּבֹאָם מֵאֶרֶץ
from-land-of when-to-come-them into-them to-invade to-Israel you-would-allow

2Some men came and told Jehoshaphat, "A vast army is
coming against you from
Edom,[i] from the other side of
the Sea.[j] It is already in Haza-
zon Tamar" (that is, En Gedi).
3Alarmed, Jehoshaphat re-
solved to inquire of the LORD,
and he proclaimed a fast for all
Judah. 4The people of Judah
came together to seek help
from the LORD; indeed, they
came from every town in
Judah to seek him.
5Then Jehoshaphat stood up
in the assembly of Judah and
Jerusalem at the temple of the
LORD in the front of the new
courtyard 6and said:

"O LORD, God of our fa-
thers, are you not the God
who is in heaven? You rule
over all the kingdoms of the
nations. Power and might
are in your hand, and no
one can withstand you. 7O
our God, did you not drive
out the inhabitants of this
land before your people Israel and give it forever to
the descendants of Abra-
ham your friend? 8They
have lived in it and have
built in it a sanctuary for
your Name, saying, 9'If
calamity comes upon us,
whether the sword of judgment, or plague or famine,
we will stand in your presence before this temple that
bears your Name and will
cry out to you in our distress, and you will hear us
and save us.'
10"But now here are men
from Ammon, Moab and
Mount Seir, whose terri-
tory you would not allow
Israel to invade when they

[i]2 One Hebrew manuscript; most Hebrew manuscripts, Septuagint and Vulgate *Aram*
[j]2 That is, the Dead Sea

מִצְרָיִם כִּי סָרוּ מֵעֲלֵיהֶם וְלֹא הִשְׁמִידוּם׃
they-destroyed-them and-not from-against-them they-turned so Egypt

וְהִנֵּה־ הֵם גֹּמְלִים עָלֵינוּ לָבוֹא לְגָרְשֵׁנוּ
to-drive-out-us to-come to-us ones-repaying they now-see! (11)

מִיְּרֻשָּׁתְךָ אֲשֶׁר הוֹרַשְׁתָּנוּ׃ אֱלֹהֵינוּ הֲלֹא תִשְׁפָּט־
will-you-judge not? God-of-us (12) you-gave-us that from-possession-of-you

בָּם כִּי אֵין בָּנוּ כֹּחַ לִפְנֵי הֶהָמוֹן הָרָב הַזֶּה
the-this the-vast the-army before power to-us not for against-them

הַבָּא עָלֵינוּ וַאֲנַחְנוּ לֹא נֵדַע מַה־ נַּעֲשֶׂה כִּי
but we-should-do what we-know not and-we against-us the-one-attacking

עָלֶיךָ עֵינֵינוּ׃ וְכָל־ יְהוּדָה עֹמְדִים לִפְנֵי יְהוָה גַּם־
also Yahweh before ones-standing Judah and-all-of (13) eyes-of-us upon-you

טַפָּם נְשֵׁיהֶם וּבְנֵיהֶם׃ וְיַחֲזִיאֵל בֶּן־
son-of then-Jahaziel (14) and-little-ones-of-them wives-of-them child-of-them

זְכַרְיָהוּ בֶּן־ בְּנָיָה בֶּן־ יְעִיאֵל בֶּן־ מַתַּנְיָה הַלֵּוִי מִן־
from the-Levite Mattaniah son-of Jeiel son-of Benaiah son-of Zechariah

בְּנֵי אָסָף הָיְתָה עָלָיו רוּחַ יְהוָה בְּתוֹךְ הַקָּהָל׃
the-assembly in-midst-of Yahweh Spirit-of upon-him she-came Asaph sons-of

וַיֹּאמֶר הַקְשִׁיבוּ כָל־ יְהוּדָה וְיֹשְׁבֵי יְרוּשָׁלִַם
Jerusalem and-ones-living-of Judah all-of listen! and-he-said (15)

וְהַמֶּלֶךְ יְהוֹשָׁפָט כֹּה־ אָמַר יְהוָה לָכֶם אַתֶּם אַל־ תִּירְאוּ
you-be-afraid not you to-you Yahweh he-says this Jehoshaphat and-the-king

וְאַל־ תֵּחַתּוּ מִפְּנֵי הֶהָמוֹן הָרָב הַזֶּה כִּי לֹא
not for the-this the-vast the-army because-of you-be-discouraged and-not

לָכֶם הַמִּלְחָמָה כִּי לֵאלֹהִים׃ מָחָר רְדוּ עֲלֵיהֶם
against-them march-down! tomorrow (16) to-God but the-battle to-you

הִנָּם עֹלִים בְּמַעֲלֵה הַצִּיץ וּמְצָאתֶם אֹתָם
them and-you-will-find the-Ziz by-Pass-of ones-climbing-up see-they!

בְּסוֹף הַנַּחַל פְּנֵי מִדְבַּר יְרוּאֵל׃ לֹא לָכֶם לְהִלָּחֵם בָּזֹאת
in-this to-fight to-you not (17) Jeruel Desert-of facing the-gorge at-end-of

הִתְיַצְּבוּ עִמְדוּ וּרְאוּ אֶת־ יְשׁוּעַת יְהוָה עִמָּכֶם יְהוּדָה
Judah with-you Yahweh deliverance-of *** and-see! stand-firm! take-positions!

וִירוּשָׁלִַם אַל־ תִּירְאוּ וְאַל־ תֵּחַתּוּ מָחָר צְאוּ
go-out! tomorrow you-be-discouraged and-not you-be-afraid not and-Jerusalem

לִפְנֵיהֶם וַיהוָה עִמָּכֶם׃ וַיִּקֹּד יְהוֹשָׁפָט אַפַּיִם
faces Jehoshaphat and-he-bowed (18) with-you and-Yahweh to-faces-of-them

אַרְצָה וְכָל־ יְהוּדָה וְיֹשְׁבֵי יְרוּשָׁלִַם נָפְלוּ
they-fell-down Jerusalem and-ones-living-of Judah and-all-of to-ground

came from Egypt; so they
turned away from them
and did not destroy them.
11See how they are repaying
us by coming to drive us
out of the possession you
gave us as an inheritance.
12O our God, will you not
judge them? For we have
no power to face this vast
army that is attacking us.
We do not know what to
do, but our eyes are upon
you."

13All the men of Judah, with
their wives and children and
little ones, stood there before
the LORD.

14Then the Spirit of the LORD
came upon Jahaziel son of
Zechariah, the son of Benaiah,
the son of Jeiel, the son of Mattaniah,
a Levite and descendant of Asaph,
as he stood in the assembly.

15He said: "Listen, King Jehoshaphat
and all who live in
Judah and Jerusalem! This is
what the LORD says to you: 'Do
not be afraid or discouraged
because of this vast army. For
the battle is not yours, but
God's.
16Tomorrow march
down against them. They will
be climbing up by the Pass of
Ziz, and you will find them at
the end of the gorge in the
Desert of Jeruel.
17You will not
have to fight this battle. Take
up your positions; stand firm
and see the deliverance the
LORD will give you, O Judah
and Jerusalem. Do not be
afraid; do not be discouraged.
Go out to face them tomorrow,
and the LORD will be with
you.' "

18Jehoshaphat bowed with
his face to the ground, and all
the people of Judah and

לִפְנֵי יְהוָה לְהִשְׁתַּחֲוֺת לַיהוָה׃ וַיָּקֻמוּ הַלְוִיִּם מִן־
from the-Levites then-they-stood-up (19) to-Yahweh to-worship Yahweh before

בְּנֵי הַקְּהָתִים וּמִן־ בְּנֵי הַקָּרְחִים לְהַלֵּל לַיהוָה אֱלֹהֵי
God-of to-Yahweh to-praise the-Korahites sons-of and-from the-Kohathites sons-of

יִשְׂרָאֵל בְּקוֹל גָּדוֹל לְמָעְלָה׃ וַיַּשְׁכִּימוּ בַבֹּקֶר וַיֵּצְאוּ
and-they-left in-the-morning and-they-rose (20) to-upward loud with-voice Israel

לְמִדְבַּר תְּקוֹעַ וּבְצֵאתָם עָמַד יְהוֹשָׁפָט וַיֹּאמֶר
and-he-said Jehoshaphat he-stood and-as-to-set-out-them Tekoa for-Desert-of

שְׁמָעוּנִי יְהוּדָה וְיֹשְׁבֵי יְרוּשָׁלִַם הַאֲמִינוּ בַּיהוָה
in-Yahweh have-faith! Jerusalem and-ones-living-of Judah listen-to-me!

אֱלֹהֵיכֶם וְתֵאָמֵנוּ הַאֲמִינוּ בִנְבִיאָיו וְהַצְלִיחוּ׃
and-succeed! in-prophets-of-him have-faith! and-you-will-be-upheld God-of-you

וַיִּוָּעַץ אֶל־ הָעָם וַיַּעֲמֵד מְשֹׁרְרִים
ones-singing then-he-appointed the-people with after-he-consulted (21)

לַיהוָה וּמְהַלְלִים לְהַדְרַת־ קֹדֶשׁ בְּצֵאת לִפְנֵי
before as-to-go-out holiness to-splendor-of and-ones-praising to-Yahweh

הֶחָלוּץ וְאֹמְרִים הוֹדוּ לַיהוָה כִּי לְעוֹלָם
to-forever for to-Yahweh give-thanks! and-ones-saying the-one-being-in-army

חַסְדּוֹ׃ וּבְעֵת הֵחֵלּוּ בְרִנָּה וּתְהִלָּה נָתַן יְהוָה ׀
Yahweh he-set and-praise with-song they-began and-at-time-of (22) love-of-him

מְאָרְבִים עַל־ בְּנֵי עַמּוֹן מוֹאָב וְהַר־ שֵׂעִיר
Seir and-Mount-of Moab Ammon men-of against ones-being-ambushes

הַבָּאִים לִיהוּדָה וַיִּנָּגֵפוּ׃ וַיַּעַמְדוּ
and-they-rose-up (23) and-they-were-defeated into-Judah the-ones-invading

בְּנֵי עַמּוֹן וּמוֹאָב עַל־ יֹשְׁבֵי הַר־ שֵׂעִיר לְהַחֲרִים
to-destroy Seir Mount-of ones-living-of against and-Moab Ammon men-of

וּלְהַשְׁמִיד וּכְכַלּוֹתָם בְּיוֹשְׁבֵי שֵׂעִיר
Seir with-ones-living-of and-after-to-finish-them and-to-annihilate

עָזְרוּ אִישׁ־ בְּרֵעֵהוּ לְמַשְׁחִית׃ וִיהוּדָה בָּא עַל־
to he-came when-Judah (24) to-destroy to-other-of-him each they-helped

הַמִּצְפֶּה לַמִּדְבָּר וַיִּפְנוּ אֶל־ הֶהָמוֹן
the-vast-army toward and-they-looked in-the-desert the-watchtower

וְהִנָּם פְּגָרִים נֹפְלִים אַרְצָה וְאֵין פְּלֵיטָה׃
escapee and-no-one on-ground ones-lying dead-bodies then-see-they!

וַיָּבֹא יְהוֹשָׁפָט וְעַמּוֹ לָבֹז אֶת־ שְׁלָלָם
plunder-of-them *** to-carry-off and-people-of-him Jehoshaphat so-he-went (25)

וַיִּמְצְאוּ בָהֶם לָרֹב וּרְכוּשׁ וּפְגָרִים
and-corpses both-equipment in-quantity among-them and-they-found

Jerusalem fell down in worship before the LORD. 19Then
some Levites from the Kohathites and Korahites stood up and praised the LORD, the God of Israel, with very loud voice.

20Early in the morning they left for the Desert of Tekoa. As they set out, Jehoshaphat stood and said, "Listen to me, Judah and people of Jerusalem! Have faith in the LORD your God and you will be upheld; have faith in his prophets and
you will be successful." 21After
consulting the people, Jehoshaphat appointed men to sing to the LORD and to praise him for the splendor of his[k] holiness as they went out at the head of the army, saying:

"Give thanks to the LORD,
for his love endures
forever."

22As they began to sing and praise, the LORD set ambushes against the men of Ammon and Moab and Mount Seir who were invading Judah,
and they were defeated. 23The
men of Ammon and Moab rose up against the men from Mount Seir to destroy and annihilate them. After they finished slaughtering the men from Seir, they helped to destroy one another.

24When the men of Judah came to the place that overlooks the desert and looked toward the vast army, they saw only dead bodies lying on the ground; no one had escaped. 25So Jehoshaphat and
his men went to carry off their plunder, and they found among them a great amount of equipment and clothing[l] and

[k]21 Or *him with the splendor of*
[l]25 Some Hebrew manuscripts and Vulgate; most Hebrew manuscripts *corpses*

וּכְלֵי חֲמֻדוֹת וַיְנַצְּלוּ לָהֶם לְאֵין מַשָּׂא
taking-away to-not for-them and-they-stripped values and-articles-of

וַיִּהְיוּ יָמִים שְׁלוֹשָׁה בֹּזְזִים אֶת־ הַשָּׁלָל כִּי רַב־הוּא׃
he much for the-plunder *** ones-collecting three days and-they-were

(26) וּבַיּוֹם הָרְבִעִי נִקְהֲלוּ לְעֵמֶק בְּרָכָה כִּי־
for Beracah in-Valley-of they-assembled the-fourth and-on-the-day (26)

שָׁם בֵּרְכוּ אֶת־ יְהוָה עַל־ כֵּן קָרְאוּ אֶת־ שֵׁם הַמָּקוֹם
the-place name-of *** they-call this for Yahweh *** they-praised there

הַהוּא עֵמֶק בְּרָכָה עַד־ הַיּוֹם׃ (27) וַיָּשֻׁבוּ כָּל־ אִישׁ
man-of all-of then-they-returned (27) the-day to Beracah Valley-of the-that

יְהוּדָה וִירוּשָׁלִַם וִיהוֹשָׁפָט בְּרֹאשָׁם לָשׁוּב אֶל־ יְרוּשָׁלִַם
Jerusalem to to-return at-head-of-them and-Jehoshaphat and-Jerusalem Judah

בְּשִׂמְחָה כִּי־ שִׂמְּחָם יְהוָה מֵאוֹיְבֵיהֶם׃
over-ones-being-enemies-of-them Yahweh he-made-rejoice-them for with-joy

(28) וַיָּבֹאוּ יְרוּשָׁלִַם בִּנְבָלִים וּבְכִנֹּרוֹת וּבַחֲצֹצְרוֹת
and-with-trumpets and-with-lutes with-harps Jerusalem and-they-entered (28)

אֶל־ בֵּית יְהוָה׃ (29) וַיְהִי פַּחַד אֱלֹהִים עַל כָּל־ מַמְלְכוֹת
kingdoms-of all-of upon God fear-of and-he-came (29) Yahweh temple-of to

הָאֲרָצוֹת בְּשָׁמְעָם כִּי נִלְחַם יְהוָה עִם
against Yahweh he-fought how when-to-hear-them the-countries

אוֹיְבֵי יִשְׂרָאֵל׃ (30) וַתִּשְׁקֹט מַלְכוּת יְהוֹשָׁפָט
Jehoshaphat kingdom-of and-she-was-at-peace (30) Israel ones-being-enemies-of

וַיָּנַח לוֹ אֱלֹהָיו מִסָּבִיב׃ (31) וַיִּמְלֹךְ יְהוֹשָׁפָט עַל־יְהוּדָה
Judah over Jehoshaphat so-he-reigned (31) at-around God-of-him to-him for-he-gave-rest

בֶּן־ שְׁלֹשִׁים וְחָמֵשׁ שָׁנָה בְּמָלְכוֹ וְעֶשְׂרִים וְחָמֵשׁ
and-five and-twenty when-to-become-king-him year and-five thirty son-of

שָׁנָה מָלַךְ בִּירוּשָׁלִַם וְשֵׁם אִמּוֹ עֲזוּבָה בַּת־
daughter-of Azubah mother-of-him and-name-of in-Jerusalem he-reigned year

שִׁלְחִי׃ (32) וַיֵּלֶךְ בְּדֶרֶךְ אָבִיו אָסָא וְלֹא־ סָר
he-strayed and-not Asa father-of-him in-way-of and-he-walked (32) Shilhi

מִמֶּנָּה לַעֲשׂוֹת הַיָּשָׁר בְּעֵינֵי יְהוָה׃ (33) אַךְ הַבָּמוֹת לֹא־
not the-high-places however (33) Yahweh in-eyes-of the-right to-do from-her

סָרוּ וְעוֹד הָעָם לֹא־ הֵכִינוּ לְבָבָם לֵאלֹהֵי
to-God-of heart-of-them they-set not the-people and-still they-removed

אֲבֹתֵיהֶם׃ (34) וְיֶתֶר דִּבְרֵי יְהוֹשָׁפָט הָרִאשֹׁנִים
the-beginnings Jehoshaphat events-of and-other-of (34) fathers-of-them

וְהָאַחֲרֹנִים הִנָּם כְּתוּבִים בְּדִבְרֵי יֵהוּא בֶּן־ חֲנָנִי
Hanani son-of Jehu in-annals-of ones-being-written see-they! and-the-ends

also articles of value—more
than they could take away.
There was so much plunder
that it took three days to collect it. 26On the fourth day
they assembled in the Valley
of Beracah, where they
praised the LORD. This is why
it is called the Valley of Beracah[m] to this day.
27Then, led by Jehoshaphat,
all the men of Judah and
Jerusalem returned joyfully to
Jerusalem, for the LORD had
given them cause to rejoice
over their enemies. 28They entered Jerusalem and went to
the temple of the LORD with
harps and lutes and trumpets.
29The fear of God came upon
all the kingdoms of the countries when they heard how the
LORD had fought against the
enemies of Israel. 30And the
kingdom of Jehoshaphat was
at peace, for his God had given
him rest on every side.

The End of Jehoshaphat's Reign

31So Jehoshaphat reigned
over Judah. He was thirty-five
years old when he became
king of Judah, and he reigned
in Jerusalem twenty-five
years. His mother's name was
Azubah daughter of Shilhi.
32He walked in the ways of his
father Asa and did not stray
from them; he did what was
right in the eyes of the LORD.
33The high places, however,
were not removed, and the
people still had not set their
hearts on the God of their fathers.
34The other events of Jehoshaphat's reign, from beginning
to end, are written in the annals of Jehu son of Hanani,

[m]26 *Beracah* means *praise.*

אֲשֶׁר הֹעֲלָה עַל־ סֵפֶר מַלְכֵי יִשְׂרָאֵל׃ וְאַחֲרֵיכֵן
and-after-this (35) Israel kings-of book-of in he-is-recorded which

אֶתְחַבַּר יְהוֹשָׁפָט מֶלֶךְ־ יְהוּדָה עִם אֲחַזְיָה מֶלֶךְ־יִשְׂרָאֵל הוּא
he Israel king-of Ahaziah with Judah king-of Jehoshaphat he-made-alliance

הִרְשִׁיעַ לַעֲשׂוֹת׃ וַיְחַבְּרֵהוּ עִמּוֹ לַעֲשׂוֹת
to-construct with-him and-he-agreed-with-him (36) to-practice he-was-wicked

אֳנִיּוֹת לָלֶכֶת תַּרְשִׁישׁ וַיַּעֲשׂוּ אֳנִיּוֹת בְּעֶצְיוֹן גָּבֶר׃ וַיִּתְנַבֵּא
and-he-prophesied (37) Geber at-Ezion ships and-they-built Tarshish to-go ships

אֱלִיעֶזֶר בֶּן־ דֹּדָוָהוּ מִמָּרֵשָׁה עַל־ יְהוֹשָׁפָט לֵאמֹר
to-say Jehoshaphat against from-Mareshah Dodavahu son-of Eliezer

כְּהִתְחַבֶּרְךָ עִם־ אֲחַזְיָהוּ פָּרַץ יְהוָה אֶת־
*** Yahweh he-will-destroy Ahaziah with because-to-make-alliance-you

מַעֲשֶׂיךָ וַיִּשָּׁבְרוּ אֳנִיּוֹת וְלֹא עָצְרוּ לָלֶכֶת
to-sail they-were-able and-not ships and-they-were-wrecked works-of-you

אֶל־ תַּרְשִׁישׁ׃ וַיִּשְׁכַּב יְהוֹשָׁפָט עִם־ אֲבֹתָיו
fathers-of-him with Jehoshaphat then-he-rested (21:1) Tarshish to

וַיִּקָּבֵר עִם־ אֲבֹתָיו בְּעִיר דָּוִיד וַיִּמְלֹךְ
and-he-became-king David in-City-of fathers-of-him with and-he-was-buried

יְהוֹרָם בְּנוֹ תַּחְתָּיו׃ וְלוֹ־ אַחִים בְּנֵי
sons-of brothers and-to-him (2) in-place-of-him son-of-him Jehoram

יְהוֹשָׁפָט עֲזַרְיָה וִיחִיאֵל וּזְכַרְיָהוּ וַעֲזַרְיָהוּ וּמִיכָאֵל
and-Michael and-Azariahu and-Zechariah and-Jehiel Azariah Jehoshaphat

וּשְׁפַטְיָהוּ כָּל־ אֵלֶּה בְּנֵי יְהוֹשָׁפָט מֶלֶךְ־ יִשְׂרָאֵל׃ וַיִּתֵּן
and-he-gave (3) Israel king-of Jehoshaphat sons-of these all-of and-Shephatiah

לָהֶם ׀ אֲבִיהֶם מַתָּנוֹת רַבּוֹת לְכֶסֶף וּלְזָהָב
and-of-gold of-silver many-ones gifts father-of-them to-them

וּלְמִגְדָּנוֹת עִם־ עָרֵי מְצֻרוֹת בִּיהוּדָה וְאֶת־
but in-Judah fortifications cities-of as-well-as and-of-articles-of-value

הַמַּמְלָכָה נָתַן לִיהוֹרָם כִּי־ הוּא הַבְּכוֹר׃
the-firstborn he because to-Jehoram he-gave the-kingdom

וַיָּקָם יְהוֹרָם עַל־ מַמְלֶכֶת* אָבִיו
father-of-him kingdom-of over Jehoram when-he-was-established (4)

וַיִּתְחַזַּק וַיַּהֲרֹג אֶת־ כָּל־ אֶחָיו בֶּחָרֶב
with-the-sword brothers-of-him all-of *** then-he-killed and-he-was-firm

וְגַם מִשָּׂרֵי יִשְׂרָאֵל׃ בֶּן־ שְׁלֹשִׁים וּשְׁתַּיִם שָׁנָה יְהוֹרָם
Jehoram year and-two thirty son-of (5) Israel from-princes-of and-also

בְּמָלְכוֹ וּשְׁמוֹנֶה שָׁנִים מָלַךְ בִּירוּשָׁלִָם׃
in-Jerusalem he-reigned years and-eight when-to-become-king-him

which are recorded in the
book of the kings of Israel.
[35]Later, Jehoshaphat king of
Judah made an alliance with
Ahaziah king of Israel, who
was guilty of wickedness. [36]He
agreed with him to construct a
fleet of trading ships.[n] After
these were built at Ezion Geber,
[37]Eliezer son of Dodavahu
of Mareshah prophesied
against Jehoshaphat, saying,
"Because you have made an
alliance with Ahaziah, the
LORD will destroy what you
have made." The ships were
wrecked and were not able to
set sail to trade.[o]

21 Then Jehoshaphat rested with his fathers and
was buried with them in the
City of David. And Jehoram
his son succeeded him as king.
[2]Jehoram's brothers, the sons
of Jehoshaphat, were Azariah,
Jehiel, Zechariah, Azariahu,
Michael and Shephatiah. All
these were sons of Jehoshaphat king of Israel.[p] [3]Their father had given them many
gifts of silver and gold and articles of value, as well as fortified cities in Judah, but he
had given the kingdom to Jehoram because he was his
firstborn son.

Jehoram King of Judah

[4]When Jehoram established
himself firmly over his father's kingdom, he put all his
brothers to the sword along
with some of the princes of Israel. [5]Jehoram was thirty-two
years old when he became
king, and he reigned in
Jerusalem eight years. [6]He

[n]36 Hebrew *of ships that could go to Tarshish*
[o]37 Hebrew *sail for Tarshish*
[p]2 That is, Judah, as frequently in 2 Chronicles

*4 Most mss have *segol* under the *kaph* (כֶת־).

וַיֵּ֜לֶךְ בְּדֶ֣רֶךְ ׀ מַלְכֵ֣י יִשְׂרָאֵ֗ל כַּאֲשֶׁ֤ר עָשׂוּ֙ בֵּ֣ית אַחְאָ֔ב
Ahab house-of they-did just-as Israel kings-of in-way-of and-he-walked (6)

כִּ֚י בַּת־אַחְאָ֔ב הָיְתָה־לּ֖וֹ אִשָּׁ֑ה וַיַּ֥עַשׂ הָרַ֖ע בְּעֵינֵ֥י
in-eyes-of the-evil and-he-did wife to-him she-was Ahab daughter-of for

יְהוָֽה׃ וְלֹא־אָבָ֣ה יְהוָ֗ה לְהַשְׁחִית֙ אֶת־בֵּ֣ית דָּוִ֔יד
David house-of *** to-destroy Yahweh he-was-willing but-not (7) Yahweh

לְמַ֣עַן הַבְּרִ֗ית אֲשֶׁ֤ר כָּרַת֙ לְדָוִ֔יד וְכַאֲשֶׁ֣ר אָמַ֔ר
he-promised and-just-as with-David he-made that the-covenant because-of

לָתֵ֥ת ל֛וֹ נִ֥יר וּלְבָנָ֖יו כָּל־הַיָּמִֽים׃
the-days all-of and-for-sons-of-him lamp for-him to-maintain

בְּיָמָיו֙ פָּשַׁ֣ע אֱד֔וֹם מִתַּ֖חַת יַד־יְהוּדָ֑ה וַיַּמְלִ֖יכוּ
and-they-set-king Judah hand-of from-under Edom he-rebelled in-days-of-him (8)

עֲלֵיהֶ֖ם מֶֽלֶךְ׃ וַיַּֽעֲבֹ֤ר יְהוֹרָם֙ עִם־שָׂרָ֔יו וְכָל־
and-all-of officers-of-him with Jehoram so-he-went (9) king over-them

הָרֶ֖כֶב עִמּ֑וֹ וַיְהִ֞י קָ֣ם לַ֗יְלָה וַיַּ֨ךְ אֶת־
*** and-he-broke-through night he-rose and-he-was with-him the-chariot

אֱדוֹם֙ הַסּוֹבֵ֣ב אֵלָ֔יו וְאֵ֖ת שָׂרֵ֥י הָרָֽכֶב׃
the-chariot commanders-of and around-him the-one-surrounding Edom

וַיִּפְשַׁ֨ע אֱד֜וֹם מִתַּ֣חַת יַד־יְהוּדָ֗ה עַ֚ד הַיּ֣וֹם הַזֶּ֔ה אָ֣ז
then the-this the-day to Judah hand-of from-under Edom and-he-rebels (10)

תִּפְשַׁ֤ע לִבְנָה֙ בָּעֵ֣ת הַהִ֔יא מִתַּ֖חַת יָד֑וֹ כִּֽי
because hand-of-him from-under the-same at-the-time Libnah she-revolted

עָזַ֕ב אֶת־יְהוָ֖ה אֱלֹהֵ֣י אֲבֹתָ֑יו גַּם־ה֞וּא עָשָׂ֤ה בָמוֹת֙
high-places he-built he also (11) fathers-of-him God-of Yahweh *** he-forsook

בְּהָרֵ֣י יְהוּדָ֔ה וַיֶּ֛זֶן אֶת־יֹשְׁבֵ֥י יְרוּשָׁלַ֖͏ִם
Jerusalem ones-living-of *** and-he-led-to-prostitution Judah on-hills-of

וַיַּדַּ֖ח אֶת־יְהוּדָֽה׃ וַיָּבֹ֤א אֵלָיו֙ מִכְתָּ֔ב מֵאֵלִיָּ֥הוּ
from-Elijah letter to-him and-he-came (12) Judah *** and-he-led-astray

הַנָּבִ֖יא לֵאמֹ֑ר כֹּ֣ה ׀ אָמַ֣ר יְהוָ֗ה אֱלֹהֵי֙ דָּוִ֣יד אָבִ֔יךָ תַּ֗חַת
because father-of-you David God-of Yahweh he-says this to-say the-prophet

אֲשֶׁ֤ר לֹֽא־הָלַ֙כְתָּ֙ בְּדַרְכֵ֣י יְהוֹשָׁפָ֣ט אָבִ֔יךָ וּבְדַרְכֵ֖י אָסָ֥א
Asa or-in-ways-of father-of-you Jehoshaphat in-ways-of you-walked not that

מֶֽלֶךְ־יְהוּדָֽה׃ וַתֵּ֗לֶךְ בְּדֶ֙רֶךְ֙ מַלְכֵ֣י יִשְׂרָאֵ֔ל
Israel kings-of in-way-of but-you-walked (13) Judah king-of

וַתַּזְנֶ֤ה אֶת־יְהוּדָה֙ וְאֶת־יֹשְׁבֵ֣י יְרֽוּשָׁלַ֔͏ִם
Jerusalem ones-living-of and Judah *** and-you-led-to-prostitution

כְּהַזְנ֖וֹת בֵּ֣ית אַחְאָ֑ב וְגַ֨ם אֶת־אַחֶ֧יךָ בֵית־
house-of brothers-of-you *** and-also Ahab house-of as-to-be-prostitutes

walked in the ways of the kings of Israel, as the house of Ahab had done, for he married a daughter of Ahab. He did evil in the eyes of the LORD. [7]Nevertheless, because of the covenant the LORD had made with him, the LORD was not willing to destroy the house of David. He had promised to maintain a lamp for David and his descendants forever.

[8]In the time of Jehoram, Edom rebelled against Judah and set up its own king. [9]So Jehoram went there with his officers and all his chariots. The Edomites surrounded him and his chariot commanders, but he rose up and broke through by night. [10]To this day Edom has been in rebellion against Judah.

Libnah revolted at the same time, because Jehoram had forsaken the LORD, the God of his fathers. [11]He had also built high places on the hills of Judah and had caused the people of Jerusalem to prostitute themselves and had led Judah astray.

[12]Jehoram received a letter from Elijah the prophet, which said:

"This is what the LORD, the God of your father David, says: 'You have not walked in the ways of your father Jehoshaphat or Asa king of Judah. [13]But you have walked in the ways of the kings of Israel, and you have led Judah and the people of Jerusalem to prostitute themselves, just as the house of Ahab did. You have also murdered your own brothers, members of

אָבִיךָ הַטּוֹבִים מִמְּךָ הָרָגְתָּ׃ הִנֵּה יְהוָה
Yahweh see! (14) you-murdered than-you the-ones-better father-of-you

נֹגֵף מַגֵּפָה גְדוֹלָה בְּעַמֶּךָ וּבְבָנֶיךָ וּבְנָשֶׁיךָ
and-on-wives-of-you and-on-sons-of-you on-people-of-you heavy blow striking

וּבְכָל־ רְכוּשֶׁךָ׃ וְאַתָּה בָּחֳלָיִים רַבִּים
great-ones with-illnesses and-you (15) possession-of-you and-on-all-of

בְּמַחֲלֵה מֵעֶיךָ עַד־ יֵצְאוּ מֵעֶיךָ מִן־
from bowels-of-you they-come-out until bowels-of-you with-disease-of

הַחֹלִי יָמִים עַל־ יָמִים׃ וַיָּעַר יְהוָה עַל־ יְהוֹרָם אֵת
*** Jehoram against Yahweh and-he-aroused (16) days after days the-disease

רוּחַ הַפְּלִשְׁתִּים וְהָעַרְבִים אֲשֶׁר עַל־ יַד כּוּשִׁים׃
Cushites hand-of at who and-the-Arabs the-Philistines hostility-of

וַיַּעֲלוּ בִיהוּדָה וַיְבַקְעוּהָ וַיִּשְׁבּוּ
and-they-carried-off and-they-invaded-her against-Judah and-they-attacked (17)

אֵת כָּל־ הָרְכוּשׁ הַנִּמְצָא לְבֵית־ הַמֶּלֶךְ וְגַם־
and-also the-king in-palace-of the-one-being-found the-possession all-of ***

בָּנָיו וְנָשָׁיו וְלֹא נִשְׁאַר־ לוֹ בֵּן כִּי אִם־
only except son to-him he-was-left and-not and-wives-of-him sons-of-him

יְהוֹאָחָז קְטַן בָּנָיו׃ וְאַחֲרֵי כָּל־ זֹאת נְגָפוֹ
he-afflicted-him this all-of and-after (18) sons-of-him youngest-of Jehoahaz

יְהוָה ׀ בְּמֵעָיו לָחֳלִי לְאֵין מַרְפֵּא׃ וַיְהִי לְיָמִים ׀
in-days and-he-was (19) curing of-no with-disease in-bowels-of-him Yahweh

מִיָּמִים וּכְעֵת צֵאת הַקֵּץ לְיָמִים שְׁנַיִם יָצְאוּ
they-came-out two of-days the-end to-come and-about-time-of after-days

מֵעָיו עִם־ חָלְיוֹ וַיָּמָת בְּתַחֲלֻאִים רָעִים
severe-ones in-pains and-he-died disease-of-him because-of bowels-of-him

וְלֹא־ עָשׂוּ לוֹ עַמּוֹ שְׂרֵפָה כִּשְׂרֵפַת אֲבֹתָיו׃
fathers-of-him as-fire-of fire people-of-him for-him they-made but-not

בֶּן־ שְׁלֹשִׁים וּשְׁתַּיִם הָיָה בְמָלְכוֹ וּשְׁמוֹנֶה שָׁנִים
years and-eight when-to-become-king-him he-was and-two thirty son-of (20)

מָלַךְ בִּירוּשָׁלִָם וַיֵּלֶךְ בְּלֹא חֶמְדָּה וַיִּקְבְּרֻהוּ
and-they-buried-him regret with-no and-he-passed-away in-Jerusalem he-reigned

בְּעִיר דָּוִיד וְלֹא בְּקִבְרוֹת הַמְּלָכִים׃ וַיַּמְלִיכוּ
and-they-made-king (22:1) the-kings in-tombs-of but-not David in-City-of

יוֹשְׁבֵי יְרוּשָׁלִַם אֶת־ אֲחַזְיָהוּ בְנוֹ הַקָּטֹן תַּחְתָּיו
in-place-of-him the-young son-of-him Ahaziah *** Jerusalem ones-living-of

כִּי כָּל־ הָרִאשֹׁנִים הָרַג הַגְּדוּד הַבָּא בָעַרְבִים
with-the-Arabs the-one-coming the-raider he-killed the-older-ones all-of since

your father's house, men
who were better than you.
14So now the LORD is about
to strike your people, your
sons, your wives and
everything that is yours,
with a heavy blow. 15You
yourself will be very ill
with a lingering disease of
the bowels, until the disease causes your bowels to
come out.' "

16The LORD aroused against
Jehoram the hostility of the
Philistines and of the Arabs
who lived near the Cushites.
17They attacked Judah, invaded it and carried off all the
goods found in the king's palace, together with his sons
and wives. Not a son was left
to him except Ahaziah,[q] the
youngest.
18After all this, the LORD
afflicted Jehoram with an incurable disease of the bowels.
19In the course of time, at the
end of the second year, his
bowels came out because of
the disease, and he died in
great pain. His people made
no fire in his honor, as they
had for his fathers.
20Jehoram was thirty-two
years old when he became
king, and he reigned in
Jerusalem eight years. He
passed away, to no one's regret, and was buried in the
City of David, but not in the
tombs of the kings.

Ahaziah King of Judah

22 The people of Jerusa-
lem made Ahaziah, Je-
horam's youngest son, king in
his place, since the raiders,
who came with the Arabs into
the camp, had killed all the

q17 Hebrew *Jehoahaz*, a variant of *Ahaziah*

לַמַּחֲנֶה וַיִּמְלֹךְ אֲחַזְיָהוּ בֶן־ יְהוֹרָם מֶלֶךְ יְהוּדָה׃ בֶּן־
son-of (2) Judah king-of Jehoram son-of Ahaziah so-he-reigned into-the-camp

אַרְבָּעִים וּשְׁתַּיִם שָׁנָה אֲחַזְיָהוּ בְמָלְכוֹ וְשָׁנָה אַחַת מָלַךְ
he-reigned one and-year when-to-become-king-him Ahaziah year and-two forty

בִּירוּשָׁלִָם וְשֵׁם אִמּוֹ עֲתַלְיָהוּ בַּת־ עָמְרִי׃ גַּם־
also (3) Omri daughter-of Athaliah mother-of-him and-name-of in-Jerusalem

הוּא הָלַךְ בְּדַרְכֵי בֵּית אַחְאָב כִּי אִמּוֹ הָיְתָה
she-was mother-of-him for Ahab house-of in-ways-of he-walked he

יוֹעַצְתּוֹ לְהַרְשִׁיעַ׃ וַיַּעַשׂ הָרַע בְּעֵינֵי יְהוָה
Yahweh in-eyes-of the-evil and-he-did (4) to-do-wrong encouraging-him

כְּבֵית אַחְאָב כִּי־ הֵמָּה הָיוּ־ לוֹ יוֹעֲצִים אַחֲרֵי מוֹת
death-of after ones-advising to-him they-became they for Ahab as-house-of

אָבִיו לְמַשְׁחִית לוֹ׃ גַּם בַּעֲצָתָם הָלַךְ
he-followed to-advice-of-them also (5) of-him to-undoing father-of-him

וַיֵּלֶךְ אֶת־ יְהוֹרָם בֶּן־ אַחְאָב מֶלֶךְ יִשְׂרָאֵל לַמִּלְחָמָה עַל־
against to-the-war Israel king-of Ahab son-of Jehoram with when-he-went

חֲזָאֵל מֶלֶךְ־ אֲרָם בְּרָמוֹת גִּלְעָד וַיַּכּוּ הָרַמִּים אֶת־
*** the-Arameans and-they-wounded Gilead at-Ramoth Aram king-of Hazael

יוֹרָם׃ וַיָּשָׁב לְהִתְרַפֵּא בְיִזְרְעֶאל כִּי הַמַּכִּים אֲשֶׁר
that the-wounds from to-Jezreel to-recover so-he-returned (6) Joram

הִכֻּהוּ בָרָמָה בְּהִלָּחֲמוֹ אֶת־חֲזָהאֵל מֶלֶךְ אֲרָם
Aram king-of Hazael *** when-to-fight-him at-the-Ramah they-inflicted-on-him

וַעֲזַרְיָהוּ בֶן־ יְהוֹרָם מֶלֶךְ יְהוּדָה יָרַד לִרְאוֹת אֶת־ יְהוֹרָם
Jehoram *** to-see he-went-down Judah king-of Jehoram son-of then-Azariah

בֶּן־ אַחְאָב בְּיִזְרְעֶאל כִּי־ חֹלֶה הוּא׃ וּמֵאֱלֹהִים הָיְתָה
she-was and-from-God (7) he being-wounded for to-Jezreel Ahab son-of

תְּבוּסַת אֲחַזְיָהוּ לָבוֹא אֶל־ יוֹרָם וּבְבוֹאוֹ יָצָא
he-went-out now-when-to-arrive-him Joram to to-visit Ahaziah downfall-of

עִם־ יְהוֹרָם אֶל־יֵהוּא בֶן־ נִמְשִׁי אֲשֶׁר מְשָׁחוֹ יְהוָה לְהַכְרִית
to-destroy Yahweh he-anointed-him whom Nimshi son-of Jehu to Jehoram with

אֶת־ בֵּית אַחְאָב׃ וַיְהִי כְּהִשָּׁפֵט יֵהוּא עִם־ בֵּית אַחְאָב
Ahab house-of against Jehu while-to-judge and-he-was (8) Ahab house-of ***

וַיִּמְצָא אֶת־ שָׂרֵי יְהוּדָה וּבְנֵי אֲחֵי אֲחַזְיָהוּ
Ahaziah relatives-of and-sons-of Judah princes-of *** then-he-found

מְשָׁרְתִים לַאֲחַזְיָהוּ וַיַּהַרְגֵם׃ וַיְבַקֵּשׁ אֶת־
*** then-he-searched (9) and-he-killed-them to-Ahaziah ones-attending

אֲחַזְיָהוּ וַיִּלְכְּדֻהוּ וְהוּא מִתְחַבֵּא בְשֹׁמְרוֹן וַיְבִאֻהוּ
and-they-brought-him in-Samaria hiding while-he and-they-captured-him Ahaziah

older sons. So Ahaziah son of
Jehoram king of Judah began
to reign.
2 Ahaziah was twenty-two[r]
years old when he became
king, and he reigned in
Jerusalem one year. His
mother's name was Athaliah,
a granddaughter of Omri.
3 He too walked in the ways
of the house of Ahab, for his
mother encouraged him in doing wrong.
4 He did evil in the
eyes of the LORD, as the house
of Ahab had done, for after his
father's death they became his
advisers, to his undoing.
5 He
also followed their counsel
when he went with Joram[s]
son of Ahab king of Israel to
war against Hazael king of
Aram at Ramoth Gilead. The
Arameans wounded Joram;
6 so he returned to Jezreel to
recover from the wounds they
had inflicted on him at
Ramoth[t] in his battle with
Hazael king of Aram.
Then Ahaziah[u] son of Jehoram king of Judah went
down to Jezreel to see Joram
son of Ahab because he had
been wounded.
7 Through Ahaziah's visit to
Joram, God brought about
Ahaziah's downfall. When
Ahaziah arrived, he went out
with Joram to meet Jehu son of
Nimshi, whom the LORD had
anointed to destroy the house
of Ahab.
8 While Jehu was ex-
ecuting judgment on the
house of Ahab, he found the
princes of Judah and the sons
of Ahaziah's relatives, who
had been attending Ahaziah,
and he killed them.
9 He then
went in search of Ahaziah,
and his men captured him
while he was hiding in Samaria. He was brought to Jehu

[r]2 Some Septuagint manuscripts and Syriac (see also 2 Kings 8:26); Hebrew *forty-two*
[s]5 Hebrew *Jehoram,* a variant of *Joram;* also in verses 6 and 7
[t]6 Hebrew *Ramah,* a variant of *Ramoth*
[u]6 Some Hebrew manuscripts, Septuagint, Vulgate and Syriac (see also 2 Kings 8:29); most Hebrew manuscripts *Azariah*

אֶל־יֵהוּא וַיְמִתֻהוּ וַיִּקְבְּרֻהוּ כִּי אָמְרוּ בֶּן־

son-of they-said for and-they-buried-him and-they-killed-him Jehu to

יְהוֹשָׁפָט הוּא אֲשֶׁר־דָּרַשׁ אֶת־יְהוָה בְּכָל־לְבָבוֹ וְאֵין

so-no-one heart-of-him with-all-of Yahweh *** he-sought who he Jehoshaphat

לְבֵית אֲחַזְיָהוּ לַעְצֹר כֹּחַ לְמַמְלָכָה׃ וַעֲתַלְיָהוּ אֵם

mother-of when-Athaliah (10) for-kingdom power to-have Ahaziah of-house-of

אֲחַזְיָהוּ רָאֲתָה כִּי מֵת בְּנָהּ וַתָּקָם

then-she-proceeded son-of-her he-was-dead that she-saw Ahaziah

וַתְּדַבֵּר אֶת־כָּל־זֶרַע הַמַּמְלָכָה לְבֵית יְהוּדָה׃

Judah of-house-of the-royal family-of whole-of *** and-she-destroyed

וַתִּקַּח יְהוֹשַׁבְעַת בַּת־הַמֶּלֶךְ אֶת־יוֹאָשׁ בֶּן־אֲחַזְיָהוּ

Ahaziah son-of Joash *** the-king daughter-of Jehoshabeath but-she-took (11)

וַתִּגְנֹב אֹתוֹ מִתּוֹךְ בְּנֵי־הַמֶּלֶךְ הַמּוּמָתִים

the-ones-being-murdered the-king sons-of from-among him and-she-stole-away

וַתִּתֵּן אֹתוֹ וְאֶת־מֵינִקְתּוֹ בַּחֲדַר הַמִּטּוֹת וַתַּסְתִּירֵהוּ

and-she-hid-him the-beds in-room-of one-nursing-him and him and-she-put

יְהוֹשַׁבְעַת בַּת־הַמֶּלֶךְ יְהוֹרָם אֵשֶׁת יְהוֹיָדָע הַכֹּהֵן

the-priest Jehoiada wife-of Jehoram the-king daughter-of Jehoshabeath

כִּי הִיא הָיְתָה אֲחוֹת אֲחַזְיָהוּ מִפְּנֵי עֲתַלְיָהוּ וְלֹא

so-not Athaliah from-before Ahaziah sister-of she-was she because

הֱמִיתָתְהוּ׃ וַיְהִי אִתָּם בְּבֵית הָאֱלֹהִים מִתְחַבֵּא

being-hidden the-God at-temple-of with-them and-he-was (12) she-killed-him

שֵׁשׁ שָׁנִים וַעֲתַלְיָה מֹלֶכֶת עַל־הָאָרֶץ׃ וּבַשָּׁנָה

and-in-the-year (23:1) the-land over ruling while-Athaliah years six

הַשְּׁבִעִית הִתְחַזַּק יְהוֹיָדָע וַיִּקַּח אֶת־שָׂרֵי

commanders-of with and-he-made Jehoiada he-showed-strength the-seventh

הַמֵּאוֹת לַעֲזַרְיָהוּ בֶן־יְרֹחָם וּלְיִשְׁמָעֵאל בֶּן־יְהוֹחָנָן

Jehohanan son-of and-with-Ishmael Jeroham son-of with-Azariah the-hundreds

וְלַעֲזַרְיָהוּ בֶן־עוֹבֵד וְאֶת־מַעֲשֵׂיָהוּ בֶן־עֲדָיָהוּ וְאֶת־

and-with Adaiah son-of Maaseiah and-with Obed son-of and-with-Azariah

אֱלִישָׁפָט בֶּן־זִכְרִי עִמּוֹ בַבְּרִית׃ וַיָּסֹבּוּ

and-they-went (2) in-the-covenant with-him Zicri son-of Elishaphat

בִּיהוּדָה וַיִּקְבְּצוּ אֶת־הַלְוִיִּם מִכָּל־עָרֵי

towns-of from-all-of the-Levites *** and-they-gathered throughout-Judah

יְהוּדָה וְרָאשֵׁי הָאָבוֹת לְיִשְׂרָאֵל וַיָּבֹאוּ אֶל־יְרוּשָׁלִָם׃

Jerusalem to when-they-came of-Israel the-fathers and-heads-of Judah

וַיִּכְרֹת כָּל־הַקָּהָל בְּרִית בְּבֵית הָאֱלֹהִים

the-God at-temple-of covenant the-assembly whole-of then-they-made (3)

and put to death. They buried him, for they said, "He was a son of Jehoshaphat, who sought the LORD with all his heart." So there was no one in the house of Ahaziah powerful enough to retain the kingdom.

Athaliah and Joash

10When Athaliah the mother of Ahaziah saw that her son was dead, she proceeded to destroy the whole royal family of the house of Judah. 11But Jehosheba,[v] the daughter of King Jehoram, took Joash son of Ahaziah and stole him away from among the royal princes who were about to be murdered and put him and his nurse in a bedroom. Because Jehosheba,[v] the daughter of King Jehoram and wife of the priest Jehoiada, was Ahaziah's sister, she hid the child from Athaliah so she could not kill him. 12He remained hidden with them at the temple of God for six years while Athaliah ruled the land.

23 In the seventh year Jehoiada showed his strength. He made a covenant with the commanders of units of a hundred: Azariah son of Jeroham, Ishmael son of Jehohanan, Azariah son of Obed, Maaseiah son of Adaiah, and Elishaphat son of Zicri. 2They went throughout Judah and gathered the Levites and the heads of Israelite families from all the towns. When they came to Jerusalem, 3the whole assembly made a covenant with the king at the temple of God.

[v]*11* Hebrew *Jehoshabeath,* a variant of *Jehosheba*

עִם־ הַמֶּלֶךְ וַיֹּאמֶר לָהֶם הִנֵּה בֶן־ הַמֶּלֶךְ יִמְלֹךְ
he-shall-reign the-king son-of see! to-them and-he-said the-king with

כַּאֲשֶׁר דִּבֶּר יְהוָה עַל־ בְּנֵי דָוִיד׃ זֶה הַדָּבָר
the-thing this (4) David descendants-of concerning Yahweh he-promised just-as

אֲשֶׁר תַּעֲשׂוּ הַשְּׁלִשִׁית מִכֶּם בָּאֵי הַשַּׁבָּת
the-Sabbath ones-going-on-duty-of of-you the-third you-must-do that

לַכֹּהֲנִים וְלַלְוִיִּם לְשֹׁעֲרֵי הַסִּפִּים׃ וְהַשְּׁלִשִׁית
and-the-third (5) the-doors as-watchers-of and-of-the-Levites of-the-priests

בְּבֵית הַמֶּלֶךְ וְהַשְּׁלִשִׁית בְּשַׁעַר הַיְסוֹד וְכָל־
and-all-of the-Foundation at-Gate-of and-the-third the-king at-palace-of

הָעָם בְּחַצְרוֹת בֵּית יְהוָה׃ וְאַל־ יָבוֹא
he-may-enter and-not (6) Yahweh temple-of in-courtyards-of the-people

בֵּית־ יְהוָה כִּי אִם־ הַכֹּהֲנִים וְהַמְשָׁרְתִים
and-the-ones-being-on-duty the-priests only except Yahweh temple-of

לַלְוִיִּם הֵמָּה יָבֹאוּ כִּי־ קֹדֶשׁ הֵמָּה וְכָל־
but-all-of they consecrated because they-may-enter they of-the-Levites

הָעָם יִשְׁמְרוּ מִשְׁמֶרֶת יְהוָה׃ וְהִקִּיפוּ
and-they-must-station-selves (7) Yahweh assignment-of they-must-guard the-people

הַלְוִיִּם אֶת־ הַמֶּלֶךְ סָבִיב אִישׁ וְכֵלָיו בְּיָדוֹ
in-hand-of-him with-weapons-of-him each around the-king *** the-Levites

וְהַבָּא אֶל־ הַבַּיִת יוּמָת וִהְיוּ אֶת־
with and-stay! he-must-be-killed the-temple into and-the-one-entering

הַמֶּלֶךְ בְּבֹאוֹ וּבְצֵאתוֹ׃ וַיַּעֲשׂוּ הַלְוִיִּם
the-Levites and-they-did (8) and-when-to-come-him when-to-go-him the-king

וְכָל־ יְהוּדָה כְּכֹל אֲשֶׁר־ צִוָּה יְהוֹיָדָע הַכֹּהֵן וַיִּקְחוּ
and-they-took the-priest Jehoiada he-ordered that as-all Judah and-all-of

אִישׁ אֶת־ אֲנָשָׁיו בָּאֵי הַשַּׁבָּת עִם
with the-Sabbath ones-going-on-duty-of men-of-him *** each

יוֹצְאֵי הַשַּׁבָּת כִּי לֹא פָטַר יְהוֹיָדָע הַכֹּהֵן
the-priest Jehoiada he-released not for the-Sabbath ones-going-off-duty-of

אֶת־ הַמַּחְלְקוֹת׃ וַיִּתֵּן יְהוֹיָדָע הַכֹּהֵן לְשָׂרֵי
to-commanders-of the-priest Jehoiada then-he-gave (9) the-divisions ***

הַמֵּאוֹת אֶת־ הַחֲנִיתִים וְאֶת־ הַמָּגִנּוֹת וְאֶת־ הַשְּׁלָטִים אֲשֶׁר
that the-small-shields and the-large-shields and the-spears *** the-hundreds

לַמֶּלֶךְ דָּוִיד אֲשֶׁר בֵּית הָאֱלֹהִים׃ וַיַּעֲמֵד אֶת־ כָּל־
all-of *** and-he-stationed (10) the-God temple-of that David to-the-king

הָעָם וְאִישׁ ׀ שִׁלְחוֹ בְּיָדוֹ מִכֶּתֶף הַבַּיִת
the-temple from-side-of in-hand-of-him weapon-of-him and-each the-people

Jehoiada said to them, "The
king's son shall reign, as the
LORD promised concerning the
descendants of David. [4]Now
this is what you are to do: A
third of you priests and Levites who are going on duty
on the Sabbath are to keep
watch at the doors, [5]a third of
you at the royal palace and a
third at the Foundation Gate,
and all the other men are to be
in the courtyards of the temple
of the LORD. [6]No one is to enter
the temple of the LORD except
the priests and Levites on
duty; they may enter because
they are consecrated, but all
the other men are to guard
what the LORD has assigned to
them.[w] [7]The Levites are to sta-
tion themselves around the
king, each man with his
weapons in his hand. Anyone
who enters the temple must be
put to death. Stay close to the
king wherever he goes."

[8]The Levites and all the men
of Judah did just as Jehoiada
the priest ordered. Each one
took his men—those who were
going on duty on the Sabbath
and those who were going off
duty—for Jehoiada the priest
had not released any of the
divisions. [9]Then he gave the
commanders of units of a hundred the spears and the large
and small shields that had belonged to King David and that
were in the temple of God.
[10]He stationed all the men,
each with his weapon in his

[w]6 *Or to observe the LORD's command* ⌞*not to enter*⌟

הַיְמָנִית עַד־כֶּתֶף הַבַּיִת הַשְּׂמָאלִית לַמִּזְבֵּחַ וְלַבָּיִת
and-near-the-temple near-the-altar the-north the-temple side-of to the-south

עַל־הַמֶּלֶךְ סָבִיב׃ וַיּוֹצִיאוּ אֶת־בֶּן־הַמֶּלֶךְ וַיִּתְּנוּ
and-they-put the-king son-of *** and-they-brought-out (11) around the-king by

עָלָיו אֶת־הַנֵּזֶר וְאֶת־הָעֵדוּת וַיַּמְלִיכוּ אֹתוֹ
him and-they-proclaimed-king the-covenant and the-crown *** on-him

וַיִּמְשָׁחֻהוּ יְהוֹיָדָע וּבָנָיו וַיֹּאמְרוּ יְחִי
may-he-live and-they-shouted and-sons-of-him Jehoiada and-they-anointed-him

הַמֶּלֶךְ׃ וַתִּשְׁמַע עֲתַלְיָהוּ אֶת־קוֹל הָעָם
the-people noise-of *** Athaliah when-she-heard (12) the-king

הָרָצִים וְהַמְהַלְלִים אֶת־הַמֶּלֶךְ וַתָּבוֹא אֶל־
to then-she-went the-king *** and-the-ones-cheering the-ones-running

הָעָם בֵּית יְהוָה׃ וַתֵּרֶא וְהִנֵּה הַמֶּלֶךְ עוֹמֵד
standing the-king and-see! and-she-looked (13) Yahweh temple-of the-people

עַל־עַמּוּדוֹ בַּמָּבוֹא וְהַשָּׂרִים וְהַחֲצֹצְרוֹת עַל־
beside and-the-trumpeters and-the-officers at-the-entrance pillar-of-him by

הַמֶּלֶךְ וְכָל־עַם הָאָרֶץ שָׂמֵחַ וְתוֹקֵעַ בַּחֲצֹצְרוֹת
on-the-trumpets and-blowing rejoicing the-land people-of and-all-of the-king

וְהַמְשׁוֹרְרִים בִּכְלֵי הַשִּׁיר וּמוֹדִיעִים לְהַלֵּל
to-praise and-ones-leading the-music with-instruments-of and-the-ones-singing

וַתִּקְרַע עֲתַלְיָהוּ אֶת־בְּגָדֶיהָ וַתֹּאמֶר קֶשֶׁר קָשֶׁר׃
treason treason and-she-shouted robes-of-her *** Athaliah then-she-tore

וַיּוֹצֵא יְהוֹיָדָע הַכֹּהֵן אֶת־שָׂרֵי הַמֵּאוֹת ׀
the-hundreds commanders-of *** the-priest Jehoiada and-he-sent-out (14)

פְּקוּדֵי הַחַיִל וַיֹּאמֶר אֲלֵהֶם הוֹצִיאוּהָ אֶל־
to bring-out-her! to-them and-he-said the-troop ones-being-in-charge-of

מִבֵּית הַשְּׂדֵרוֹת וְהַבָּא אַחֲרֶיהָ יוּמַת
he-must-be-killed after-her and-the-one-following the-ranks outside-of

בֶּחָרֶב כִּי אָמַר הַכֹּהֵן לֹא תְמִיתוּהָ בֵּית יְהוָה׃
Yahweh temple-of you-kill-her not the-priest he-said for with-the-sword

וַיָּשִׂימוּ לָהּ יָדַיִם וַתָּבוֹא אֶל־מְבוֹא שַׁעַר־
Gate-of entrance-of to as-she-reached hands on-her so-they-laid (15)

הַסּוּסִים בֵּית הַמֶּלֶךְ וַיְמִיתוּהָ שָׁם׃ וַיִּכְרֹת
then-he-made (16) there and-they-killed-her the-king palace-of the-Horses

יְהוֹיָדָע בְּרִית בֵּינוֹ וּבֵין כָּל־הָעָם וּבֵין
and-between the-people all-of and-between between-him covenant Jehoiada

הַמֶּלֶךְ לִהְיוֹת לְעָם לַיהוָה׃ וַיָּבֹאוּ כָל־הָעָם
the-people all-of and-they-went (17) of-Yahweh as-people to-be the-king

hand, around the king—near
the altar and the temple, from
the south side to the north side
of the temple.
11Jehoiada and his sons
brought out the king's son and
put the crown on him; they
presented him with a copy of
the covenant and proclaimed
him king. They anointed him
and shouted, "Long live the
king!"
12When Athaliah heard the
noise of the people running
and cheering the king, she
went to them at the temple of
the LORD. 13She looked, and
there was the king, standing
by his pillar at the entrance.
The officers and the trumpeters were beside the king, and
all the people of the land were
rejoicing and blowing trumpets, and singers with musical
instruments were leading the
praises. Then Athaliah tore
her robes and shouted, "Treason! Treason!"
14Jehoiada the priest sent out
the commanders of units of a
hundred, who were in charge
of the troops, and said to
them: "Bring her out between
the ranks[x] and put to the
sword anyone who follows
her." For the priest had said,
"Do not put her to death at the
temple of the LORD." 15So they
seized her as she reached the
entrance of the Horse Gate on
the palace grounds, and there
they put her to death.
16Jehoiada then made a covenant that he and the people
and the king[y] would be the
LORD's people. 17All the people

[x]14 *Or out from the precincts*

[y]16 *Or covenant between* ⌊*the* LORD,⌋ *and the people and the king that they* (see 2 Kings 11:17)

בֵּית־ הַבַּעַל֙ וַיִּתְּצֻ֔הוּ וְאֶת־ מִזְבְּחֹתָ֥יו וְאֶת־ צְלָמָ֖יו
temple-of the-Baal and-they-tore-down-him and altars-of-him and idols-of-him

שִׁבֵּ֑רוּ וְאֵ֨ת מַתָּ֜ן כֹּהֵ֤ן הַבַּ֙עַל֙ הָרְג֔וּ לִפְנֵ֖י הַֽמִּזְבְּחֽוֹת׃
they-smashed and Mattan priest-of the-Baal they-killed in-front-of the-altars

וַיָּ֨שֶׂם֙ יְהוֹיָדָ֔ע פְּקֻדֹּ֖ת בֵּ֣ית יְהוָ֑ה בְּיַ֣ד
(18) then-he-placed Jehoiada oversights-of temple-of Yahweh in-hand-of

הַכֹּהֲנִ֣ים הַלְוִיִּ֗ם אֲשֶׁ֨ר חָלַ֤ק דָּוִיד֙ עַל־ בֵּ֣ית יְהוָ֔ה לְהַעֲל֞וֹת
the-priests the-Levites whom he-assigned David in temple-of Yahweh to-present

עֹל֤וֹת יְהוָה֙ כַּכָּת֖וּב בְּתוֹרַ֣ת מֹשֶׁ֑ה בְּשִׂמְחָ֖ה
offerings-of Yahweh as-the-thing-being-written in-Law-of Moses with-rejoicing

וּבְשִׁ֗יר עַ֚ל יְדֵ֣י דָוִֽיד׃ וַֽיַּעֲמֵד֙ הַשּׁוֹעֲרִ֔ים עַֽל־
and-with-song as orders-of David (19) and-he-stationed the-doorkeepers at

שַׁעֲרֵ֖י בֵּ֣ית יְהוָ֑ה וְלֹֽא־ יָבֹ֥א טָמֵ֖א לְכָל־ דָּבָֽר׃
gates-of temple-of Yahweh so-not he-might-enter unclean in-any-of way

וַיִּקַּ֣ח אֶת־ שָׂרֵ֣י הַמֵּא֗וֹת וְאֶת־ הָֽאַדִּירִ֤ים וְאֶת־
(20) and-he-took *** commanders-of the-hundreds and the-nobles and

הַמּֽוֹשְׁלִים֙ בָּעָ֔ם וְאֵ֣ת ׀ כָּל־ עַ֣ם הָאָ֔רֶץ וַיּ֤וֹרֶד
the-ones-ruling of-the-people and all-of people-of the-land and-he-brought-down

אֶת־ הַמֶּ֙לֶךְ֙ מִבֵּ֣ית יְהוָ֔ה וַיָּבֹ֛אוּ בְּתֽוֹךְ־ שַׁ֥עַר הָֽעֶלְי֖וֹן
*** the-king from-temple-of Yahweh and-they-went through Gate-of the-Upper

בֵּ֣ית הַמֶּ֑לֶךְ וַיּוֹשִׁ֙יבוּ֙ אֶת־ הַמֶּ֔לֶךְ עַ֖ל כִּסֵּ֥א הַמַּמְלָכָֽה׃
palace-of the-king and-they-seated *** the-king on throne-of the-royalty

וַיִּשְׂמְח֥וּ כָל־ עַם־ הָאָ֖רֶץ וְהָעִ֣יר שָׁקָ֑טָה
(21) and-they-rejoiced all-of people-of the-land and-the-city she-was-quiet

וְאֶת־ עֲתַלְיָ֖הוּ הֵמִ֥יתוּ בֶחָֽרֶב׃ (24:1) בֶּן־ שֶׁ֤בַע שָׁנִים֙ יֹאָ֔שׁ
and Athaliah they-killed with-the-sword son-of seven years Joash

בְּמָלְכ֔וֹ וְאַרְבָּעִ֣ים שָׁנָ֔ה מָלַ֖ךְ בִּירוּשָׁלָ֑͏ִם וְשֵׁ֣ם
when-to-become-king-him and-forty year he-reigned in-Jerusalem and-name-of

אִמּ֔וֹ צִבְיָ֖ה מִבְּאֵ֥ר שָֽׁבַע׃ (2) וַיַּ֧עַשׂ יוֹאָ֛שׁ הַיָּשָׁ֖ר
mother-of-him Zibiah from-Beer Sheba and-he-did Joash the-right

בְּעֵינֵ֣י יְהוָ֑ה כָּל־ יְמֵ֖י יְהוֹיָדָ֥ע הַכֹּהֵֽן׃ (3) וַיִּשָּׂא־ ל֤וֹ
in-eyes-of Yahweh all-of days-of Jehoiada the-priest and-he-chose for-him

יְהוֹיָדָע֙ נָשִׁ֣ים שְׁתָּ֔יִם וַיּ֖וֹלֶד בָּנִ֥ים וּבָנֽוֹת׃ (4) וַיְהִ֕י
Jehoiada wives two and-he-fathered sons and-daughters (4) and-he-was

אַחֲרֵי־ כֵ֗ן הָיָה֙ עִם־ לֵ֣ב יוֹאָ֔שׁ לְחַדֵּ֖שׁ אֶת־ בֵּ֣ית יְהוָֽה׃
after-this he-was in heart-of Joash to-restore *** temple-of Yahweh

וַיִּקְבֹּץ֙ אֶת־ הַכֹּ֣הֲנִ֔ים וְהַלְוִיִּם֒ וַיֹּ֣אמֶר
(5) and-he-called-together *** the-priests and-the-Levites and-he-said

went to the temple of Baal and tore it down. They smashed the altars and idols and killed Mattan the priest of Baal in front of the altars. [18]Then Jehoiada placed the oversight of the temple of the LORD in the hands of the priests, who were Levites, to whom David had made assignments in the temple, to present the burnt offerings of the LORD as written in the Law of Moses, with rejoicing and singing, as David had ordered. [19]He also stationed doorkeepers at the gates of the LORD's temple so that no one who was in any way unclean might enter.

[20]He took with him the commanders of hundreds, the nobles, the rulers of the people and all the people of the land and brought the king down from the temple of the LORD. They went into the palace through the Upper Gate and seated the king on the royal throne, [21]and all the people of the land rejoiced. And the city was quiet, because Athaliah had been slain with the sword.

Joash Repairs the Temple

24 Joash was seven years old when he became king, and he reigned in Jerusalem forty years. His mother's name was Zibiah; she was from Beersheba. [2]Joash did what was right in the eyes of the LORD all the years of Jehoiada the priest. [3]Jehoiada chose two wives for him, and he had sons and daughters.

[4]Some time later Joash decided to restore the temple of the LORD. [5]He called together the priests and Levites and

לָהֶם צְאוּ לְעָרֵי יְהוּדָה וְקִבְצוּ מִכָּל־ יִשְׂרָאֵל כֶּסֶף

money Israel from-all-of and-collect! Judah to-towns-of go! to-them

לְחַזֵּק ׀ אֶת־ בֵּית אֱלֹהֵיכֶם מִדֵּי שָׁנָה בְּשָׁנָה וְאַתֶּם

and-you by-year year from-dues-of God-of-you temple-of *** to-repair

תְּמַהֲרוּ לַדָּבָר וְלֹא מִהֲרוּ הַלְוִיִּם׃

the-Levites they-acted-at-once but-not in-the-matter you-act-now

וַיִּקְרָא הַמֶּלֶךְ לִיהוֹיָדָע הָרֹאשׁ וַיֹּאמֶר לוֹ מַדּוּעַ

why? to-him and-he-said the-chief for-Jehoiada the-king so-he-summoned (6)

לֹא־ דָרַשְׁתָּ עַל־ הַלְוִיִּם לְהָבִיא מִיהוּדָה וּמִירוּשָׁלִַם

and-from-Jerusalem from-Judah to-bring-in the-Levites from you-required not

אֶת־ מַשְׂאַת מֹשֶׁה עֶבֶד־ יְהוָה וְהַקָּהָל לְיִשְׂרָאֵל לְאֹהֶל

for-Tent-of of-Israel and-the-assembly Yahweh servant-of Moses tax-of ***

הָעֵדוּת׃ כִּי עֲתַלְיָהוּ הַמִּרְשַׁעַת בָּנֶיהָ פָרְצוּ אֶת־

*** they-broke-into sons-of-her the-wicked Athaliah now (7) the-Testimony

בֵּית הָאֱלֹהִים וְגַם כָּל־ קָדְשֵׁי בֵית־ יְהוָה

Yahweh temple-of sacred-objects-of all-of and-even the-God temple-of

עָשׂוּ לַבְּעָלִים׃ וַיֹּאמֶר הַמֶּלֶךְ וַיַּעֲשׂוּ אֲרוֹן

chest and-they-made the-king and-he-commanded (8) for-the-Baals they-used

אֶחָד וַיִּתְּנֻהוּ בְּשַׁעַר בֵּית־ יְהוָה חוּצָה׃

at-outside Yahweh temple-of at-gate-of and-they-placed-him one

וַיִּתְּנוּ־ קוֹל בִּיהוּדָה וּבִירוּשָׁלִַם לְהָבִיא

to-bring and-in-Jerusalem in-Judah proclamation and-they-issued (9)

לַיהוָה מַשְׂאַת מֹשֶׁה עֶבֶד־ הָאֱלֹהִים עַל־ יִשְׂרָאֵל בַּמִּדְבָּר׃

in-the-desert Israel from the-God servant-of Moses tax-of to-Yahweh

וַיִּשְׂמְחוּ כָל־ הַשָּׂרִים וְכָל־ הָעָם

the-people and-all-of the-officials all-of and-they-were-glad (10)

וַיָּבִיאוּ וַיַּשְׁלִיכוּ לָאָרוֹן עַד־ לְכַלֵּה׃

to-fill until into-the-chest and-they-dropped and-they-brought

וַיְהִי בְּעֵת יָבִיא אֶת־ הָאָרוֹן אֶל־ פְּקֻדַּת הַמֶּלֶךְ

the-king official-of to the-chest *** he-brought-in at-time-of and-he-was (11)

בְּיַד הַלְוִיִּם וְכִרְאוֹתָם כִּי־ רַב הַכֶּסֶף

the-money large-amount that and-when-to-see-them the-Levites by-hand-of

וּבָא סוֹפֵר הַמֶּלֶךְ וּפְקִיד כֹּהֵן הָרֹאשׁ

the-chief priest and-officer-of the-king secretary-of then-he-came

וִיעָרוּ אֶת־ הָאָרוֹן וְיִשָּׂאֻהוּ וִישִׁבֻהוּ אֶל־

to and-they-returned-him and-they-carried-him the-chest *** and-they-emptied

מְקֹמוֹ כֹּה עָשׂוּ לְיוֹם ׀ בְּיוֹם וַיַּאַסְפוּ־ כֶסֶף

money and-they-collected after-day for-day they-did this place-of-him

said to them, "Go to the towns of Judah and collect the money due annually from all Israel, to repair the temple of your God. Do it now." But the Levites did not act at once.

[6]Therefore the king summoned Jehoiada the chief priest and said to him, "Why haven't you required the Levites to bring in from Judah and Jerusalem the tax imposed by Moses the servant of the LORD and by the assembly of Israel for the Tent of the Testimony?"

[7]Now the sons of that wicked woman Athaliah had broken into the temple of God and had used even its sacred objects for the Baals.

[8]At the king's command, a chest was made and placed outside, at the gate of the temple of the LORD. [9]A proclamation was then issued in Judah and Jerusalem that they should bring to the LORD the tax that Moses the servant of God had required of Israel in the desert. [10]All the officials and all the people brought their contributions gladly, dropping them into the chest until it was full. [11]Whenever the chest was brought in by the Levites to the king's officials and they saw that there was a large amount of money, the royal secretary and the officer of the chief priest would come and empty the chest and carry it back to its place. They did this regularly and collected a great

לָרֹב׃ וַיִּתְּנֵהוּ הַמֶּלֶךְ וִיהוֹיָדָע אֶל־ עוֹשֵׂה
one-doing-of to and-Jehoiada the-king and-he-gave-him (12) in-great-amount

מְלֶאכֶת עֲבוֹדַת בֵּית־ יְהוָה וַיִּהְיוּ שֹׂכְרִים
ones-hiring and-they-were Yahweh temple-of requirement-of work-of

חֹצְבִים וְחָרָשִׁים לְחַדֵּשׁ בֵּית יְהוָה וְגַם
and-also Yahweh temple-of to-restore and-carpenters ones-being-masons

לְחָרָשֵׁי בַרְזֶל וּנְחֹשֶׁת לְחַזֵּק אֶת־ בֵּית יְהוָה׃
Yahweh temple-of *** to-repair and-bronze iron to-workers-of

וַיַּעֲשׂוּ עֹשֵׂי הַמְּלָאכָה וַתַּעַל
and-she-progressed the-work ones-being-in-charge-of and-they-were-diligent (13)

אֲרוּכָה לַמְּלָאכָה בְּיָדָם וַיַּעֲמִידוּ אֶת־ בֵּית הָאֱלֹהִים
the-God temple-of *** and-they-rebuilt under-hand-of-them of-the-work repair

עַל־ מַתְכֻּנְתּוֹ וַיְאַמְּצֻהוּ׃ וּכְכַלּוֹתָם
and-when-to-finish-them (14) and-they-reinforced-him design-of-him according-to

הֵבִיאוּ לִפְנֵי הַמֶּלֶךְ וִיהוֹיָדָע אֶת־ שְׁאָר הַכֶּסֶף וַיַּעֲשֵׂהוּ
and-he-made-him the-money rest-of *** and-Jehoiada the-king to they-brought

כֵלִים לְבֵית־ יְהוָה כְּלֵי שָׁרֵת וְהַעֲלוֹת
and-the-burnt-offerings service articles-of Yahweh for-temple-of articles

וְכַפּוֹת וּכְלֵי זָהָב וָכָסֶף וַיִּהְיוּ מַעֲלִים
ones-presenting and-they-were and-silver gold and-objects-of and-ladles

עֹלוֹת בְּבֵית־ יְהוָה תָּמִיד כֹּל יְמֵי יְהוֹיָדָע׃
Jehoiada days-of all-of continually Yahweh in-temple-of burnt-offerings

וַיִּזְקַן יְהוֹיָדָע וַיִּשְׂבַּע יָמִים וַיָּמֹת בֶּן־ מֵאָה
hundred son-of and-he-died days and-he-was-full Jehoiada now-he-was-old (15)

וּשְׁלֹשִׁים שָׁנָה בְּמוֹתוֹ׃ וַיִּקְבְּרֻהוּ בְעִיר־ דָּוִיד
David in-City-of and-they-buried-him (16) in-death-of-him year and-thirty

עִם־ הַמְּלָכִים כִּי־ עָשָׂה טוֹבָה בְּיִשְׂרָאֵל וְעִם הָאֱלֹהִים וּבֵיתוֹ׃
and-temple-of-him the-God and-for in-Israel good he-did because the-kings with

וְאַחֲרֵי מוֹת יְהוֹיָדָע בָּאוּ שָׂרֵי יְהוּדָה
Judah officials-of they-came Jehoiada death-of and-after (17)

וַיִּשְׁתַּחֲווּ לַמֶּלֶךְ אָז שָׁמַע הַמֶּלֶךְ אֲלֵיהֶם׃
to-them the-king he-listened then to-the-king and-they-paid-homage

וַיַּעַזְבוּ אֶת־ בֵּית יְהוָה אֱלֹהֵי אֲבוֹתֵיהֶם
fathers-of-them God-of Yahweh temple-of *** and-they-abandoned (18)

וַיַּעַבְדוּ אֶת־ הָאֲשֵׁרִים וְאֶת־ הָעֲצַבִּים וַיְהִי־ קֶצֶף
anger and-he-came the-idols and the-Asherah-poles *** and-they-worshiped

עַל־ יְהוּדָה וִירוּשָׁלִַם בְּאַשְׁמָתָם זֹאת׃ וַיִּשְׁלַח
althought-he-sent (19) this because-of-guilt-of-them and-Jerusalem Judah upon

amount of money. 12 The king
and Jehoiada gave it to the
men who carried out the work
required for the temple of the
LORD. They hired masons and
carpenters to restore the
LORD's temple, and also workers in iron and bronze to repair the temple.
13 The men in charge of the
work were diligent, and the
repairs progressed under
them. They rebuilt the temple
of God according to its original design and reinforced it.
14 When they had finished,
they brought the rest of the
money to the king and Jehoiada, and with it were made articles for the LORD's temple: articles for the service and for
the burnt offerings, and also
ladles and other objects of gold
and silver. As long as Jehoiada
lived, burnt offerings were
presented continually in the
temple of the LORD.
15 Now Jehoiada was old and
full of years, and he died at the
age of a hundred and thirty.
16 He was buried with the
kings in the City of David, because of the good he had done
in Israel for God and his temple.

The Wickedness of Joash

17 After the death of Jehoiada,
the officials of Judah came and
paid homage to the king, and
he listened to them. 18 They
abandoned the temple of the
LORD, the God of their fathers,
and worshiped Asherah poles
and idols. Because of their
guilt, God's anger came upon
Judah and Jerusalem. 19 Although the LORD sent prophets

בָּהֶם נְבִאִים לַהֲשִׁיבָם אֶל־ יְהוָה וַיָּעִידוּ בָם
against-them and-they-testified Yahweh to to-bring-back-them prophets to-them

וְלֹא הֶאֱזִינוּ׃ (20) וְרוּחַ אֱלֹהִים לָבְשָׁה אֶת־ זְכַרְיָה
Zechariah *** she-came-upon God then-Spirit-of (20) they-listened but-not

בֶּן־ יְהוֹיָדָע הַכֹּהֵן וַיַּעֲמֹד מֵעַל לָעָם וַיֹּאמֶר
and-he-said to-the-people at-before and-he-stood the-priest Jehoiada son-of

לָהֶם כֹּה ׀ אָמַר הָאֱלֹהִים לָמָה אַתֶּם עֹבְרִים אֶת־ מִצְוֹת יְהוָה
Yahweh commands-of *** ones-disobeying you why? the-God he-says this to-them

וְלֹא תַצְלִיחוּ כִּי־ עֲזַבְתֶּם אֶת־ יְהוָה וַיַּעֲזֹב אֶתְכֶם׃
you then-he-forsook Yahweh *** you-forsook because you-will-prosper now-not

(21) וַיִּקְשְׁרוּ עָלָיו וַיִּרְגְּמֻהוּ אֶבֶן בְּמִצְוַת
by-order-of stone and-they-stoned-him against-him but-they-plotted (21)

הַמֶּלֶךְ בַּחֲצַר בֵּית יְהוָה׃ (22) וְלֹא־ זָכַר יוֹאָשׁ
Joash he-remembered and-not (22) Yahweh temple-of in-courtyard-of the-king

הַמֶּלֶךְ הַחֶסֶד אֲשֶׁר עָשָׂה יְהוֹיָדָע אָבִיו עִמּוֹ
to-him father-of-him Jehoiada he-showed that the-kindness the-king

וַיַּהֲרֹג אֶת־ בְּנוֹ וּכְמוֹתוֹ אָמַר יֵרֶא יְהוָה
Yahweh may-he-see he-said and-as-to-die-him son-of-him *** but-he-killed

וְיִדְרֹשׁ׃ (23) וַיְהִי ׀ לִתְקוּפַת הַשָּׁנָה עָלָה
he-marched the-year at-turn-of and-he-was (23) and-may-he-call-to-account

עָלָיו חֵיל אֲרָם וַיָּבֹאוּ אֶל־ יְהוּדָה וִירוּשָׁלִַם
and-Jerusalem Judah into and-they-invaded Aram army-of against-him

וַיַּשְׁחִיתוּ אֶת־ כָּל־ שָׂרֵי הָעָם מֵעָם וְכָל־
and-all-of from-people the-people leaders-of all-of *** and-they-killed

שְׁלָלָם שִׁלְּחוּ לְמֶלֶךְ דַּרְמָשֶׂק׃ (24) כִּי בְמִצְעַר אֲנָשִׁים
men with-few-of although (24) Damascus to-king-of they-sent plunder-of-them

בָּאוּ ׀ חֵיל אֲרָם וַיהוָה נָתַן בְּיָדָם חַיִל
army into-hand-of-them he-delivered but-Yahweh Aram army-of they-came

לָרֹב מְאֹד כִּי עָזְבוּ אֶת־ יְהוָה אֱלֹהֵי אֲבוֹתֵיהֶם וְאֶת־
and fathers-of-them God-of Yahweh *** they-forsook because very as-large

יוֹאָשׁ עָשׂוּ שְׁפָטִים׃ (25) וּבְלֶכְתָּם מִמֶּנּוּ כִּי־
then from-him and-when-to-withdraw-them (25) judgments they-executed Joash

עָזְבוּ אֹתוֹ בְּמַחֲלְיִים רַבִּים הִתְקַשְּׁרוּ עָלָיו
against-him and-they-conspired severe-ones with-wounds him they-left

עֲבָדָיו בִּדְמֵי בְּנֵי יְהוֹיָדָע הַכֹּהֵן וַיַּהַרְגֻהוּ
and-they-killed-him the-priest Jehoiada sons-of for-bloods-of officials-of-him

עַל־ מִטָּתוֹ וַיָּמֹת וַיִּקְבְּרֻהוּ בְּעִיר דָּוִיד וְלֹא
but-not David in-City-of and-they-buried-him so-he-died bed-of-him in

to the people to bring them
back to him, and though they
testified against them, they
would not listen.
20Then the Spirit of God
came upon Zechariah son of
Jehoiada the priest. He stood
before the people and said,
"This is what God says: 'Why
do you disobey the LORD's
commands? You will not prosper. Because you have forsak-
en the LORD, he has forsaken
you.' "
21But they plotted against
him, and by order of the king
they stoned him to death in
the courtyard of the LORD's
temple. 22King Joash did not
remember the kindness Zechariah's father Jehoiada had
shown him but killed his son,
who said as he lay dying,
"May the LORD see this and
call you to account."
23At the turn of the year,[z] the
army of Aram marched
against Joash; it invaded
Judah and Jerusalem and
killed all the leaders of the
people. They sent all the plunder to their king in Damascus.
24Although the Aramean army
had come with only a few
men, the LORD delivered into
their hands a much larger
army. Because Judah had forsaken the LORD, the God of
their fathers, judgment was
executed on Joash. 25When the
Arameans withdrew, they left
Joash severely wounded. His
officials conspired against him
for murdering the son of Jehoiada the priest, and they
killed him in his bed. So he
died and was buried in the
City of David, but not in the

z23 That is, in the spring

°25 ק במחלוים

קָבְרֻהוּ בְּקִבְרוֹת הַמְּלָכִים׃ וְאֵלֶּה הַמִּתְקַשְּׁרִים
the-ones-conspiring and-these (26) the-kings in-tombs-of they-buried-him

עָלָיו זָבָד בֶּן־ שִׁמְעָת הָעַמּוֹנִית וִיהוֹזָבָד בֶּן־
son-of and-Jehozabad the-Ammonite-woman Shimeath son-of Zabad against-him

שִׁמְרִית הַמּוֹאָבִית׃ וּבָנָיו וְרֹב[c] הַמַּשָּׂא
the-prophecy he-was-many and-sons-of-him (27) the-Moabite-woman Shimrith

עָלָיו וִיסוֹד בֵּית הָאֱלֹהִים הִנָּם כְּתוּבִים
ones-being-written see-they! the-God temple-of and-restoration-of about-him

עַל־ מִדְרַשׁ סֵפֶר הַמְּלָכִים וַיִּמְלֹךְ אֲמַצְיָהוּ בְנוֹ
son-of-him Amaziah and-he-became-king the-kings book-of annotation-of in

תַּחְתָּיו׃ בֶּן־ עֶשְׂרִים וְחָמֵשׁ שָׁנָה מָלַךְ אֲמַצְיָהוּ
Amaziah he-became-king year and-five twenty son-of (25:1) in-place-of-him

וְעֶשְׂרִים וָתֵשַׁע שָׁנָה מָלַךְ בִּירוּשָׁלָםִ וְשֵׁם אִמּוֹ
mother-of-him and-name-of in-Jerusalem he-reigned year and-nine and-twenty

יְהוֹעַדָּן מִירוּשָׁלָםִ׃ וַיַּעַשׂ הַיָּשָׁר בְּעֵינֵי יְהוָה רַק לֹא
not but Yahweh in-eyes-of the-right and-he-did (2) from-Jerusalem Jehoaddan

בְּלֵבָב שָׁלֵם׃ וַיְהִי כַּאֲשֶׁר חָזְקָה הַמַּמְלָכָה עָלָיו
under-him the-kingdom she-was-firm just-as and-he-was (3) whole with-heart

וַיַּהֲרֹג אֶת־ עֲבָדָיו הַמַּכִּים אֶת־ הַמֶּלֶךְ
the-king *** the-ones-murdering officials-of-him *** then-he-executed

אָבִיו׃ וְאֶת־ בְּנֵיהֶם לֹא הֵמִית כִּי כַכָּתוּב
as-the-one-being-written but he-killed not sons-of-them yet (4) father-of-him

בַּתּוֹרָה בְּסֵפֶר מֹשֶׁה אֲשֶׁר־ צִוָּה יְהוָה לֵאמֹר לֹא־
not to-say Yahweh he-commanded where Moses in-Book-of in-the-Law

יָמוּתוּ אָבוֹת עַל־ בָּנִים וּבָנִים לֹא־ יָמוּתוּ
they-shall-be-killed not and-children children for fathers they-shall-be-killed

עַל־ אָבוֹת כִּי אִישׁ בְּחֶטְאוֹ יָמוּתוּ׃ וַיִּקְבֹּץ
and-he-called-together (5) they-must-die for-sin-of-him each but fathers for

אֲמַצְיָהוּ אֶת־יְהוּדָה וַיַּעֲמִידֵם לְבֵית־ אָבוֹת לְשָׂרֵי
by-commanders-of fathers by-family-of and-he-assigned-them Judah *** Amaziah

הָאֲלָפִים וּלְשָׂרֵי הַמֵּאוֹת לְכָל־ יְהוּדָה וּבִנְיָמִן
and-Benjamin Judah for-all-of the-hundreds and-by-commanders-of the-thousands

וַיִּפְקְדֵם לְמִבֶּן עֶשְׂרִים שָׁנָה וָמַעְלָה וַיִּמְצָאֵם
and-he-found-them and-upward year twenty to-from-son-of then-he-mustered-them

שְׁלֹשׁ־ מֵאוֹת אֶלֶף בָּחוּר יוֹצֵא צָבָא אֹחֵז
handling-of military serving-of being-ready thousand hundreds three-of

רֹמַח וְצִנָּה׃ וַיִּשְׂכֹּר מִיִּשְׂרָאֵל מֵאָה אֶלֶף גִּבּוֹר חָיִל
fight men-of thousand hundred from-Israel and-he-hired (6) and-shield spear

tombs of the kings.
26Those who conspired
against him were Zabad,[a] son
of Shimeath an Ammonite
woman, and Jehozabad, son of
Shimrith[b] a Moabite woman.
27The account of his sons, the
many prophecies about him,
and the record of the restora-
tion of the temple of God are
written in the annotations on
the book of the kings. And
Amaziah his son succeeded
him as king.

Amaziah King of Judah

25 Amaziah was twenty-
five years old when he
became king, and he reigned
in Jerusalem twenty-nine
years. His mother's name was
Jehoaddin[c]; she was from
Jerusalem. 2He did what was
right in the eyes of the LORD,
but not wholeheartedly. 3After
the kingdom was firmly in his
control, he executed the
officials who had murdered
his father the king. 4Yet he did
not put their sons to death, but
acted in accordance with what
is written in the Law, in the
Book of Moses, where the
LORD commanded: "Fathers
shall not be put to death for
their children, nor children
put to death for their fathers;
each is to die for his own
sins."[d]
5Amaziah called the people
of Judah together and as-
signed them according to their
families to commanders of
thousands and commanders
of hundreds for all Judah and
Benjamin. He then mustered
those twenty years old or more
and found that there were
three hundred thousand men
ready for military service, able
to handle the spear and shield.
6He also hired a hundred thousand fighting men from Israel

[a]26 A variant of *Jozabad*
[b]26 A variant of *Shomer*
[c]1 Hebrew *Jehoaddan*, a variant of *Jehoaddin*
[d]4 Deut. 24:16

c27 ק ירב

בְּמֵאָה כִכַּר־ כָּסֶף׃ וְאִישׁ הָאֱלֹהִים בָּא אֵלָיו לֵאמֹר
to-say to-him he-came the-God but-man-of (7) silver talent-of with-hundred

הַמֶּלֶךְ אַל־ יָבֹא עִמְּךָ צְבָא יִשְׂרָאֵל כִּי אֵין יְהוָה עִם־
with Yahweh not for Israel troop-of with-you he-must-march not the-king

יִשְׂרָאֵל כֹּל בְּנֵי אֶפְרָיִם׃ כִּי אִם־ בֹּא אַתָּה עֲשֵׂה
fight! you go! if even (8) Ephraim people-of any-of Israel

חֲזַק לַמִּלְחָמָה יַכְשִׁילְךָ הָאֱלֹהִים לִפְנֵי
before the-God he-will-overthrow-you in-the-battle be-courageous!

אוֹיֵב כִּי יֶשׁ־ כֹּחַ בֵּאלֹהִים לַעְזוֹר וּלְהַכְשִׁיל׃
or-to-overthrow to-help to-God power there-is for one-being-enemy

וַיֹּאמֶר אֲמַצְיָהוּ לְאִישׁ הָאֱלֹהִים וּמַה־ לַּעֲשׂוֹת לִמְאַת
with-hundred-of to-do but-what? the-God to-man-of Amaziah and-he-asked (9)

הַכִּכָּר אֲשֶׁר נָתַתִּי לִגְדוּד יִשְׂרָאֵל וַיֹּאמֶר אִישׁ הָאֱלֹהִים
the-God man-of and-he-replied Israel for-troop-of I-paid that the-talent

יֵשׁ לַיהוָה לָתֵת לְךָ הַרְבֵּה מִזֶּה׃ וַיַּבְדִּילֵם
so-he-dismissed-them (10) than-that to-be-more to-you to-give to-Yahweh there-is

אֲמַצְיָהוּ לְהַגְּדוּד אֲשֶׁר־ בָּא אֵלָיו מֵאֶפְרַיִם לָלֶכֶת לִמְקוֹמָם
to-home-of-them to-go from-Ephraim to-him he-came who to-the-troop Amaziah

וַיִּחַר אַפָּם מְאֹד בִּיהוּדָה וַיָּשׁוּבוּ לִמְקוֹמָם
for-home-of-them and-they-left with-Judah very rage-of-them and-he-was-furious

בָּחֳרִי־ אָף׃ וַאֲמַצְיָהוּ הִתְחַזַּק וַיִּנְהַג אֶת־
*** and-he-led he-marshaled-strength then-Amaziah (11) rage in-heat-of

עַמּוֹ וַיֵּלֶךְ גֵּיא הַמֶּלַח וַיַּךְ אֶת־ בְּנֵי־ שֵׂעִיר
Seir men-of *** and-he-killed the-Salt Valley-of and-he-went army-of-him

עֲשֶׂרֶת אֲלָפִים׃ וַעֲשֶׂרֶת אֲלָפִים חַיִּים שָׁבוּ בְּנֵי
men-of they-captured ones-alive thousands and-ten-of (12) thousands ten-of

יְהוּדָה וַיְבִיאוּם לְרֹאשׁ הַסָּלַע וַיַּשְׁלִיכוּם מֵרֹאשׁ־
from-top-of and-they-threw-them the-cliff to-top-of and-they-took-them Judah

הַסֶּלַע וְכֻלָּם נִבְקָעוּ׃ וּבְנֵי הַגְּדוּד
the-troop and-men-of (13) they-were-dashed-to-pieces so-all-of-them the-cliff

אֲשֶׁר הֵשִׁיב אֲמַצְיָהוּ מִלֶּכֶת עִמּוֹ לַמִּלְחָמָה וַיִּפְשְׁטוּ
and-they-raided in-the-war with-him from-to-take-part Amaziah he-sent-back that

בְּעָרֵי יְהוּדָה מִשֹּׁמְרוֹן וְעַד־ בֵּית חוֹרוֹן וַיַּכּוּ מֵהֶם
from-them and-they-killed Horon Beth even-to from-Samaria Judah in-towns-of

שְׁלֹשֶׁת אֲלָפִים וַיָּבֹזּוּ בִּזָּה רַבָּה׃ וַיְהִי אַחֲרֵי
after and-he-was (14) great plunder and-they-carried-off thousands three-of

בוֹא אֲמַצְיָהוּ מֵהַכּוֹת אֶת־ אֲדוֹמִים וַיָּבֵא אֶת־
*** then-he-brought-back Edomites *** from-to-slaughter Amaziah to-return

for a hundred talents[e] of silver.
7But a man of God came to
him and said, "O king, these
troops from Israel must not
march with you, for the LORD
is not with Israel—not with
any of the people of Ephraim.
8Even if you go and fight
courageously in battle, God
will overthrow you before the
enemy, for God has the power
to help or to overthrow."
9Amaziah asked the man of
God, "But what about the
hundred talents I paid for
these Israelite troops?"
The man of God replied,
"The LORD can give you much
more than that."
10So Amaziah dismissed the
troops who had come to him
from Ephraim and sent them
home. They were furious with
Judah and left for home in a
great rage.
11Amaziah then marshaled
his strength and led his army
to the Valley of Salt, where he
killed ten thousand men of
Seir. 12The army of Judah also
captured ten thousand men
alive, took them to the top of a
cliff and threw them down so
that all were dashed to pieces.
13Meanwhile the troops that
Amaziah had sent back and
had not allowed to take part in
the war raided Judean towns
from Samaria to Beth Horon.
They killed three thousand
people and carried off great
quantities of plunder.
14When Amaziah returned
from slaughtering the Edomites, he brought back the gods

[e]6 That is, about 3 3/4 tons (about 3.4 metric tons); also in verse 9

אֱלֹהֵי בְּנֵי שֵׂעִיר וַיַּעֲמִידֵם לוֹ לֵאלֹהִים וְלִפְנֵיהֶם
and-before-them as-gods for-him and-he-set-up-them Seir people-of gods-of

יִשְׁתַּחֲוֶה וְלָהֶם יְקַטֵּר׃ וַיִּחַר־ אַף יְהוָה
Yahweh anger-of and-he-burned (15) he-burned-sacrifice and-to-them he-bowed

בַּאֲמַצְיָהוּ וַיִּשְׁלַח אֵלָיו נָבִיא וַיֹּאמֶר לוֹ לָמָּה
why? to-him and-he-said prophet to-him and-he-sent against-Amaziah

דָרַשְׁתָּ אֶת־ אֱלֹהֵי הָעָם אֲשֶׁר לֹא־ הִצִּילוּ אֶת־
*** they-could-save not which the-people gods-of *** you-consult

עַמָּם מִיָּדֶךָ׃ וַיְהִי ׀ בְּדַבְּרוֹ אֵלָיו
to-him while-to-speak-him and-he-was (16) from-hand-of-you people-of-them

וַיֹּאמֶר לוֹ הַלְיוֹעֵץ לַמֶּלֶךְ נְתַנּוּךָ חֲדַל־
stop! we-appointed-you to-the-king as-one-advising? to-him then-he-said

לְךָ לָמָּה יַכּוּךָ וַיֶּחְדַּל הַנָּבִיא וַיֹּאמֶר
but-he-said the-prophet so-he-stopped they-should-strike-down-you why? for-you

יָדַעְתִּי כִּי־ יָעַץ אֱלֹהִים לְהַשְׁחִיתֶךָ כִּי־ עָשִׂיתָ זֹּאת וְלֹא
and-not this you-did because to-destroy-you God he-determined that I-know

שָׁמַעְתָּ לַעֲצָתִי׃ וַיִּוָּעַץ אֲמַצְיָהוּ מֶלֶךְ יְהוּדָה
Judah king-of Amaziah after-he-consulted (17) to-counsel-of-me you-listened

וַיִּשְׁלַח אֶל־ יוֹאָשׁ בֶּן־ יְהוֹאָחָז בֶּן־ יֵהוּא מֶלֶךְ יִשְׂרָאֵל לֵאמֹר
to-say Israel king-of Jehu son-of Jehoahaz son-of Joash to then-he-sent

לְךָ נִתְרָאֶה פָנִים׃ וַיִּשְׁלַח יוֹאָשׁ מֶלֶךְ־יִשְׂרָאֵל אֶל־אֲמַצְיָהוּ
Amaziah to Israel king-of Joash but-he-replied (18) faces let-us-meet come!

מֶלֶךְ־ יְהוּדָה לֵאמֹר הַחוֹחַ אֲשֶׁר בַּלְּבָנוֹן שָׁלַח אֶל־ הָאֶרֶז
the-cedar to he-sent in-the-Lebanon that the-thistle to-say Judah king-of

אֲשֶׁר בַּלְּבָנוֹן לֵאמֹר תְּנָה־ אֶת־ בִּתְּךָ לִבְנִי לְאִשָּׁה
as-wife to-son-of-me daughter-of-you *** give! to-say in-the-Lebanon that

וַתַּעֲבֹר חַיַּת הַשָּׂדֶה אֲשֶׁר בַּלְּבָנוֹן וַתִּרְמֹס
and-she-trampled in-the-Lebanon that the-field beast-of then-she-came-along

אֶת־ הַחוֹחַ׃ אָמַרְתָּ הִנֵּה הִכִּיתָ אֶת־ אֱדוֹם וּנְשָׂאֲךָ
and-he-lifted-you Edom *** you-defeated see! you-say (19) the-thistle ***

לִבְּךָ לְהַכְבִּיד עַתָּה שְׁבָה בְּבֵיתֶךָ לָמָּה תִתְגָּרֶה בְּרָעָה
for-trouble you-ask why? at-home-of-you stay! now to-be-proud heart-of-you

וְנָפַלְתָּ אַתָּה וִיהוּדָה עִמָּךְ׃ וְלֹא־ שָׁמַע אֲמַצְיָהוּ כִּי
for Amaziah he-listened but-not (20) with-you and-Judah you so-you-fall

מֵהָאֱלֹהִים הִיא לְמַעַן תִּתָּם בְּיָד כִּי דָרְשׁוּ אֵת
*** they-sought because into-hand to-give-them so-that this from-the-God

אֱלֹהֵי אֱדוֹם׃ וַיַּעַל יוֹאָשׁ מֶלֶךְ־ יִשְׂרָאֵל וַיִּתְרָאוּ פָנִים
faces and-they-met Israel king-of Joash so-he-attacked (21) Edom gods-of

of the people of Seir. He set
them up as his own gods,
bowed down to them and
burned sacrifices to them.
15The anger of the LORD
burned against Amaziah, and
he sent a prophet to him, who
said, "Why do you consult this
people's gods, which could not
save their own people from
your hand?"
16While he was still
speaking, the king said to him,
"Have we appointed you an
adviser to the king? Stop! Why
be struck down?"
So the prophet stopped but
said, "I know that God has determined to destroy you, because you have done this and
have not listened to my counsel."
17After Amaziah king of
Judah consulted his advisers,
he sent this challenge to Jehoash[f] son of Jehoahaz, the
son of Jehu, king of Israel:
"Come, meet me face to face."
18But Jehoash king of Israel
replied to Amaziah king of
Judah: "A thistle in Lebanon
sent a message to a cedar in
Lebanon, 'Give your daughter
to my son in marriage.' Then a
wild beast in Lebanon came
along and trampled the thistle
underfoot. 19You say to yourself that you have defeated
Edom, and now you are arrogant and proud. But stay at
home! Why ask for trouble and
cause your own downfall and
that of Judah also?"
20Amaziah, however, would
not listen, for God so worked
that he might hand them over
to ⌊Jehoash⌋, because they
sought the gods of Edom. 21So
Jehoash king of Israel attacked. He and Amaziah king

f17 Hebrew *Joash*, a variant of *Jehoash*; also in verses 18, 21, 23 and 25

°17 ק לבה

הוּא וַאֲמַצְיָהוּ מֶלֶךְ־יְהוּדָה בְּבֵית שֶׁמֶשׁ אֲשֶׁר לִיהוּדָה׃
in-Judah that Shemesh at-Beth Judah king-of and-Amaziah he

וַיִּנָּגֶף יְהוּדָה לִפְנֵי יִשְׂרָאֵל וַיָּנֻסוּ אִישׁ לְאֹהָלָיו׃
to-homes-of-him each and-they-fled Israel before Judah and-he-was-routed (22)

וְאֵת אֲמַצְיָהוּ מֶלֶךְ־יְהוּדָה בֶּן־יוֹאָשׁ בֶּן־יְהוֹאָחָז תָּפַשׂ
he-captured Jehoahaz son-of Joash son-of Judah king-of Amaziah and (23)

יוֹאָשׁ מֶלֶךְ־יִשְׂרָאֵל בְּבֵית שָׁמֶשׁ וַיְבִיאֵהוּ יְרוּשָׁלִָם
Jerusalem then-he-brought-him Shemesh at-Beth Israel king-of Joash

וַיִּפְרֹץ בְּחוֹמַת יְרוּשָׁלִַם מִשַּׁעַר אֶפְרַיִם עַד־שַׁעַר
Gate-of to Ephraim from-Gate-of Jerusalem through-wall-of and-he-broke

הַפּוֹנֶה אַרְבַּע מֵאוֹת אַמָּה׃ וְכָל־הַזָּהָב וְהַכֶּסֶף וְאֵת
and and-the-silver the-gold and-all-of (24) cubit hundreds four the-Corner

כָּל־הַכֵּלִים הַנִּמְצְאִים בְּבֵית־הָאֱלֹהִים עִם־עֹבֵד אֱדוֹם
Edom Obed with the-God in-temple-of the-ones-being-found the-articles all-of

וְאֶת־אֹצְרוֹת בֵּית הַמֶּלֶךְ וְאֵת בְּנֵי הַתַּעֲרֻבוֹת וַיָּשָׁב
and-he-returned the-hostages sons-of and the-king palace-of treasuries-of and

שֹׁמְרוֹן׃ וַיְחִי אֲמַצְיָהוּ בֶן־יוֹאָשׁ מֶלֶךְ יְהוּדָה אַחֲרֵי מוֹת
death-of after Judah king-of Joash son-of Amaziah and-he-lived (25) Samaria

יוֹאָשׁ בֶּן־יְהוֹאָחָז מֶלֶךְ יִשְׂרָאֵל חֲמֵשׁ עֶשְׂרֵה שָׁנָה׃ וְיֶתֶר
and-other-of (26) year ten five-of Israel king-of Jehoahaz son-of Joash

דִּבְרֵי אֲמַצְיָהוּ הָרִאשֹׁנִים וְהָאַחֲרוֹנִים הֲלֹא הִנָּם
see-they! not? and-the-ends the-beginnings Amaziah events-of

כְּתוּבִים עַל־סֵפֶר מַלְכֵי־יְהוּדָה וְיִשְׂרָאֵל׃ וּמֵעֵת אֲשֶׁר־
that and-from-time (27) and-Israel Judah kings-of book-of in ones-being-written

סָר אֲמַצְיָהוּ מֵאַחֲרֵי יְהוָה וַיִּקְשְׁרוּ עָלָיו קֶשֶׁר
conspiracy against-him then-they-conspired Yahweh from-after Amaziah he-turned

בִּירוּשָׁלִַם וַיָּנָס לָכִישָׁה וַיִּשְׁלְחוּ אַחֲרָיו לָכִישָׁה
to-Lachish after-him but-they-sent to-Lachish and-he-fled in-Jerusalem

וַיְמִיתֻהוּ שָׁם׃ וַיִּשָּׂאֻהוּ עַל־הַסּוּסִים
the-horses by and-they-brought-back-him (28) there and-they-killed-him

וַיִּקְבְּרוּ אֹתוֹ עִם־אֲבֹתָיו בְּעִיר יְהוּדָה׃ וַיִּקְחוּ
then-they-took (26:1) Judah in-City-of fathers-of-him with him and-they-buried

כָּל־עַם יְהוּדָה אֶת־עֻזִּיָּהוּ וְהוּא בֶּן־שֵׁשׁ עֶשְׂרֵה שָׁנָה
year ten six-of son-of now-he Uzziah *** Judah people-of all-of

וַיַּמְלִיכוּ אֹתוֹ תַּחַת אָבִיו אֲמַצְיָהוּ׃ הוּא בָּנָה
he-rebuilt he (2) Amaziah father-of-him in-place-of him and-they-made-king

אֶת־אֵילוֹת וַיְשִׁיבֶהָ לִיהוּדָה אַחֲרֵי שְׁכַב־הַמֶּלֶךְ עִם־
with the-king to-rest after to-Judah and-he-restored-her Elath ***

of Judah faced each other at Beth Shemesh in Judah. [22]Judah was routed by Israel, and every man fled to his home. [23]Jehoash king of Israel captured Amaziah king of Judah, the son of Joash, the son of Ahaziah,[g] at Beth Shemesh. Then Jehoash brought him to Jerusalem and broke down the wall of Jerusalem from the Ephraim Gate to the Corner Gate—a section about six hundred feet[h] long. [24]He took all the gold and silver and all the articles found in the temple of God that had been in the care of Obed-Edom, together with the palace treasures and the hostages, and returned to Samaria.

[25]Amaziah son of Joash king of Judah lived for fifteen years after the death of Jehoash son of Jehoahaz king of Israel. [26]As for the other events of Amaziah's reign, from beginning to end, are they not written in the book of the kings of Judah and Israel? [27]From the time that Amaziah turned away from following the LORD, they conspired against him in Jerusalem and he fled to Lachish, but they sent men after him to Lachish and killed him there. [28]He was brought back by horse and was buried with his fathers in the City of Judah.

Uzziah King of Judah

26 Then all the people of Judah took Uzziah,[i] who was sixteen years old, and made him king in place of his father Amaziah. [2]He was the one who rebuilt Elath and restored it to Judah after Amaziah rested with his fathers.

[g]23 Hebrew *Jehoahaz*, a variant of *Ahaziah*
[h]23 Hebrew *four hundred cubits* (about 180 meters)
[i]1 Also called *Azariah*

אֲבֹתָיו׃ בֶּן־ שֵׁשׁ עֶשְׂרֵה שָׁנָה עֻזִּיָּהוּ בְמָלְכוֹ
when-to-become-king-him Uzziah year ten six-of son-of (3) fathers-of-him

וַחֲמִשִּׁים וּשְׁתַּיִם שָׁנָה מָלַךְ בִּירוּשָׁלָ͏ִם וְשֵׁם אִמּוֹ
mother-of-him and-name-of in-Jerusalem he-reigned year and-two and-fifty

יְכִילְיָה מִן־ יְרוּשָׁלָ͏ִם׃ וַיַּעַשׂ הַיָּשָׁר בְּעֵינֵי יְהוָה כְּכֹל
as-all Yahweh in-eyes-of the-right and-he-did (4) Jerusalem from Jecoliah

אֲשֶׁר־עָשָׂה אֲמַצְיָהוּ אָבִיו׃ וַיְהִי לִדְרֹשׁ אֱלֹהִים בִּימֵי
during-days-of God to-seek and-he-was (5) father-of-him Amaziah he-did that

זְכַרְיָהוּ הַמֵּבִין בִּרְאֹת* הָאֱלֹהִים וּבִימֵי
and-in-days-of the-God *to-have-vision the-one-instructing Zechariah

דָּרְשׁוֹ אֶת־ יְהוָה הִצְלִיחוֹ הָאֱלֹהִים׃ וַיֵּצֵא
and-he-went-out (6) the-God he-gave-success-him Yahweh *** to-seek-him

וַיִּלָּחֶם בַּפְּלִשְׁתִּים וַיִּפְרֹץ אֶת־ חוֹמַת גַּת וְאֵת
and Gath wall-of *** and-he-broke-down against-the-Philistines and-he-warred

חוֹמַת יַבְנֵה וְאֵת חוֹמַת אַשְׁדּוֹד וַיִּבְנֶה עָרִים בְּאַשְׁדּוֹד
near-Ashdod towns then-he-rebuilt Ashdod wall-of and Jabneh wall-of

וּבַפְּלִשְׁתִּים׃ וַיַּעְזְרֵהוּ הָאֱלֹהִים עַל־ פְּלִשְׁתִּים
Philistines against the-God and-he-helped-him (7) and-among-the-Philistines

וְעַל־ הָעַרְבִיִּים הַיֹּשְׁבִים בְּגוּר־ בָּעַל וְהַמְּעוּנִים׃
and-the-Meunites Baal in-Gur the-ones-living the-Arabs and-against

וַיִּתְּנוּ הָעַמּוֹנִים מִנְחָה לְעֻזִּיָּהוּ וַיֵּלֶךְ שְׁמוֹ
name-of-him and-he-spread to-Uzziah tribute the-Ammonites and-they-brought (8)

עַד־ לְבוֹא מִצְרַיִם כִּי הֶחֱזִיק עַד־ לְמָעְלָה׃
to-upward to he-became-powerful because Egypt to-enter as-far-as

וַיִּבֶן עֻזִּיָּהוּ מִגְדָּלִים בִּירוּשָׁלַ͏ִם עַל־ שַׁעַר הַפִּנָּה וְעַל־
and-at the-Corner Gate-of at in-Jerusalem towers Uzziah and-he-built (9)

שַׁעַר הַגַּיְא וְעַל־ הַמִּקְצוֹעַ וַיְחַזְּקֵם׃
and-he-fortified-them the-angle-of-the-wall and-at the-Valley Gate-of

וַיִּבֶן מִגְדָּלִים בַּמִּדְבָּר וַיַּחְצֹב בֹּרוֹת רַבִּים כִּי מִקְנֶה־
livestock because many cisterns and-he-dug in-the-desert towers and-he-built (10)

רַב† הָיָה לוֹ וּבַשְּׁפֵלָה וּבַמִּישׁוֹר אִכָּרִים
field-workers and-in-the-plain and-in-the-foothill to-him he-was much

וְכֹרְמִים בֶּהָרִים וּבַכַּרְמֶל כִּי־ אֹהֵב
loving for and-in-the-fertile-land in-the-hills and-ones-working-vineyards

אֲדָמָה הָיָה׃ וַיְהִי לְעֻזִּיָּהוּ חַיִל עֹשֵׂה מִלְחָמָה
war being-trained-of army to-Uzziah and-he-was (11) he-was soil

יוֹצְאֵי צָבָא לִגְדוּד בְּמִסְפַּר פְּקֻדָּתָם
mustering-of-them by-number-of by-division battle ones-going-out-of

[3]Uzziah was sixteen years
old when he became king, and
he reigned in Jerusalem fifty-
two years. His mother's name
was Jecoliah; she was from
Jerusalem. [4]He did what was
right in the eyes of the LORD,
just as his father Amaziah had
done. [5]He sought God during
the days of Zechariah, who instructed him in the fear[j] of
God. As long as he sought the
LORD, God gave him success.
[6]He went to war against the
Philistines and broke down
the walls of Gath, Jabneh and
Ashdod. He then rebuilt
towns near Ashdod and
elsewhere among the Philistines. [7]God helped him against
the Philistines and against the
Arabs who lived in Gur Baal
and against the Meunites.
[8]The Ammonites brought tribute to Uzziah, and his fame
spread as far as the border of
Egypt, because he had become
very powerful.
[9]Uzziah built towers in
Jerusalem at the Corner Gate,
at the Valley Gate and at the
angle of the wall, and he fortified them. [10]He also built
towers in the desert and dug
many cisterns, because he had
much livestock in the foothills
and in the plain. He had
people working his fields and
vineyards in the hills and in
the fertile lands, for he loved
the soil.
[11]Uzziah had a well-trained
army, ready to go out by divisions according to their numbers as mustered by Jeiel the

[j]5 Many Hebrew manuscripts, Septuagint and Syriac; other Hebrew manuscripts *vision*

*5 Many mss have (בִּירְאַת), *to-fears;* the versions read (בְּיִרְאַת), *in-fear-of*

†10 Most mss have no *dagesh* in the *resh* (רַב).

°3 ק יכליה

°7 ק הערבים

בְּיַד יְעוּאֵל הַסּוֹפֵר וּמַעֲשֵׂיָהוּ הַשּׁוֹטֵר עַל יַד־
hand-of under the-officer and-Maaseiah the-secretary Jeiel by-hand-of

חֲנַנְיָהוּ מִשָּׂרֵי הַמֶּלֶךְ׃ כֹּל מִסְפַּר רָאשֵׁי
leaders-of number-of total-of (12) the-king from-officials-of Hananiah

הָאָבוֹת לְגִבּוֹרֵי חָיִל אַלְפַּיִם וְשֵׁשׁ מֵאוֹת׃
hundreds and-six-of two-thousands fight over-men-of the-fathers

וְעַל־ יָדָם חֵיל צָבָא שְׁלֹשׁ מֵאוֹת אֶלֶף
thousand hundreds three-of battle army-of hand-of-them and-under (13)

וְשִׁבְעַת אֲלָפִים וַחֲמֵשׁ מֵאוֹת עוֹשֵׂי מִלְחָמָה
war ones-being-trained-of hundreds and-five-of thousands and-seven-of

בְּכֹחַ חָיִל לַעְזֹר לַמֶּלֶךְ עַל־ הָאוֹיֵב׃
the-one-being-enemy against to-the-king to-support force with-power-of

וַיָּכֶן לָהֶם עֻזִּיָּהוּ לְכָל־ הַצָּבָא מָגִנִּים וּרְמָחִים
and-spears shields the-army for-entire-of Uzziah to-them and-he-provided (14)

וְכוֹבָעִים וְשִׁרְיֹנוֹת וּקְשָׁתוֹת וּלְאַבְנֵי קְלָעִים׃ וַיַּעַשׂ ׀
and-he-made (15) slings and-for-stones-of and-bows and-coats-of-armor and-helmets

בִּירוּשָׁלַםִ חִשְּׁבֹנוֹת מַחֲשֶׁבֶת חוֹשֵׁב לִהְיוֹת עַל־ הַמִּגְדָּלִים
the-towers on to-use one-being-skillful design-of machines in-Jerusalem

וְעַל־ הַפִּנּוֹת לִירוֹא בַּחִצִּים וּבָאֲבָנִים גְּדֹלוֹת
large-ones and-with-the-stones with-the-arrows to-shoot the-corners and-on

וַיֵּצֵא שְׁמוֹ עַד־ לְמֵרָחוֹק כִּי־ הִפְלִיא לְהֵעָזֵר
to-be-helped he-was-great for to-at-distance to name-of-him and-he-spread

עַד כִּי־ חָזָק׃ וּכְחֶזְקָתוֹ
but-after-to-become-powerful-him (16) he-became-powerful when until

גָּבַהּ לִבּוֹ עַד־ לְהַשְׁחִית וַיִּמְעַל בַּיהוָה
to-Yahweh and-he-was-unfaithful to-fall-down until heart-of-him he-lifted

אֱלֹהָיו וַיָּבֹא אֶל־ הֵיכַל יְהוָה לְהַקְטִיר עַל־ מִזְבַּח
altar-of on to-burn-incense Yahweh temple-of into and-he-entered God-of-him

הַקְּטֹרֶת׃ וַיָּבֹא אַחֲרָיו עֲזַרְיָהוּ הַכֹּהֵן וְעִמּוֹ
and-with-him the-priest Azariah after-him and-he-followed (17) the-incense

כֹּהֲנִים ׀ לַיהוָה שְׁמוֹנִים בְּנֵי־ חָיִל׃ וַיַּעַמְדוּ עַל־
against and-they-confronted (18) courage men-of eighty of-Yahweh priests

עֻזִּיָּהוּ הַמֶּלֶךְ וַיֹּאמְרוּ לוֹ לֹא־ לְךָ עֻזִּיָּהוּ לְהַקְטִיר
to-burn-incense Uzziah for-you not to-him and-they-said the-king Uzziah

לַיהוָה כִּי לַכֹּהֲנִים בְּנֵי־ אַהֲרֹן הַמְקֻדָּשִׁים
the-ones-being-consecrated Aaron descendants-of for-the-priests but to-Yahweh

לְהַקְטִיר צֵא מִן־ הַמִּקְדָּשׁ כִּי מָעַלְתָּ וְלֹא־
and-not you-were-unfaithful for the-sanctuary from leave! to-burn-incense

secretary and Maaseiah the officer under the direction of Hananiah, one of the royal officials. [12]The total number of family leaders over the fighting men was 2,600. [13]Under their command was an army of 307,500 men trained for war, a powerful force to support the king against his enemies. [14]Uzziah provided shields, spears, helmets, coats of armor, bows and slingstones for the entire army. [15]In Jerusalem he made machines designed by skillful men for use on the towers and on the corner defenses to shoot arrows and hurl large stones. His fame spread far and wide, for he was greatly helped until he became powerful.

[16]But after Uzziah became powerful, his pride led to his downfall. He was unfaithful to the LORD his God, and entered the temple of the LORD to burn incense on the altar of incense. [17]Azariah the priest with eighty other courageous priests of the LORD followed him in. [18]They confronted him and said, "It is not right for you, Uzziah, to burn incense to the LORD. That is for the priests, the descendants of Aaron, who have been consecrated to burn incense. Leave the sanctuary, for you have been unfaithful; and you will

11 °ק יעיאל

לְךָ לְכָבוֹד מֵיְהוָה אֱלֹהִים׃ וַיִּזְעַף עֻזִּיָּהוּ
Uzziah and-he-became-angry (19) God by-Yahweh for-honor to-you

וּבְיָדוֹ מִקְטֶרֶת לְהַקְטִיר וּבְזַעְפּוֹ עִם־ הַכֹּהֲנִים
the-priests at and-while-to-rage-him to-burn-incense censer and-in-hand-of-him

וְהַצָּרַעַת זָרְחָה בְמִצְחוֹ לִפְנֵי הַכֹּהֲנִים
the-priests in-presences-of on-forehead-of-him she-broke-out then-the-leprosy

בְּבֵית יְהוָה מֵעַל לְמִזְבַּח הַקְּטֹרֶת׃ וַיִּפֶן
when-he-looked (20) the-incense to-altar-of at-before Yahweh in-temple-of

אֵלָיו עֲזַרְיָהוּ כֹהֵן הָרֹאשׁ וְכָל־ הַכֹּהֲנִים וְהִנֵּה־ הוּא
he then-see! the-priests and-all-of the-chief priest Azariah at-him

מְצֹרָע בְּמִצְחוֹ וַיַּבְהִלוּהוּ מִשָּׁם וְגַם־
and-indeed from-there so-they-hurried-him on-forehead-of-him being-leprous

הוּא נִדְחַף לָצֵאת כִּי נִגְּעוֹ יְהוָה׃ וַיְהִי
and-he-was (21) Yahweh he-afflicted-him because to-leave he-was-eager he

עֻזִּיָּהוּ הַמֶּלֶךְ מְצֹרָע ׀ עַד־ יוֹם מוֹתוֹ וַיֵּשֶׁב
and-he-lived death-of-him day-of until being-leprous the-king Uzziah

בֵּית הַחָפְשׁוּת° מְצֹרָע כִּי נִגְזַר מִבֵּית
from-temple-of he-was-excluded indeed being-leprous the-separate house-of

יְהוָה וְיוֹתָם בְּנוֹ עַל־ בֵּית הַמֶּלֶךְ שׁוֹפֵט אֶת־ עַם
people-of *** governing the-king palace-of over son-of-him and-Jotham Yahweh

הָאָרֶץ׃ וְיֶתֶר דִּבְרֵי עֻזִּיָּהוּ הָרִאשֹׁנִים וְהָאֲחֲרֹנִים*
and-the-ends the-beginnings Uzziah events-of and-other-of (22) the-land

כָּתַב יְשַׁעְיָהוּ בֶן־ אָמוֹץ הַנָּבִיא׃ וַיִּשְׁכַּב עֻזִּיָּהוּ עִם־
with Uzziah and-he-rested (23) the-prophet Amoz son-of Isaiah he-recorded

אֲבֹתָיו וַיִּקְבְּרוּ אֹתוֹ עִם־ אֲבֹתָיו בִּשְׂדֵה הַקְּבוּרָה
the-burial in-field-of fathers-of-him with him and-they-buried fathers-of-him

אֲשֶׁר לַמְּלָכִים כִּי אָמְרוּ מְצוֹרָע הוּא וַיִּמְלֹךְ יוֹתָם
Jotham and-he-became-king he having-leprosy they-said for to-the-kings that

בְּנוֹ תַּחְתָּיו׃ בֶּן־ עֶשְׂרִים וְחָמֵשׁ שָׁנָה יוֹתָם
Jotham year and-five twenty son-of (27:1) in-place-of-him son-of-him

בְּמָלְכוֹ וְשֵׁשׁ־ עֶשְׂרֵה שָׁנָה מָלַךְ בִּירוּשָׁלִָם
in-Jerusalem he-reigned year ten and-six-of when-to-become-king-him

וְשֵׁם אִמּוֹ יְרוּשָׁה בַּת־ צָדוֹק׃ וַיַּעַשׂ הַיָּשָׁר
the-right and-he-did (2) Zadok daughter-of Jerusha mother-of-him and-name-of

בְּעֵינֵי יְהוָה כְּכֹל אֲשֶׁר־ עָשָׂה עֻזִּיָּהוּ אָבִיו רַק לֹא־ בָא
he-entered not but father-of-him Uzziah he-did that as-all Yahweh in-eyes-of

אֶל־ הֵיכַל יְהוָה וְעוֹד הָעָם מַשְׁחִיתִים׃ הוּא
he (3) ones-being-corrupt the-people but-still Yahweh temple-of into

not be honored by the LORD
God."
19 Uzziah, who had a censer
in his hand ready to burn incense, became angry. While
he was raging at the priests in
their presence before the incense altar in the LORD's temple, leprosy[k] broke out on his
forehead. 20 When Azariah the
chief priest and all the other
priests looked at him, they
saw that he had leprosy on his
forehead, so they hurried him
out. Indeed, he himself was
eager to leave, because the
LORD had afflicted him.
21 King Uzziah had leprosy
until the day he died. He lived
in a separate house[l] —leprous,
and excluded from the temple
of the LORD. Jotham his son
had charge of the palace and
governed the people of the
land.
22 The other events of Uzziah's reign, from beginning
to end, are recorded by the
prophet Isaiah son of Amoz.
23 Uzziah rested with his fathers and was buried near
them in a field for burial that
belonged to the kings, for
people said, "He had leprosy."
And Jotham his son succeeded
him as king.

Jotham King of Judah

27 Jotham was twenty-
five years old when he
became king, and he reigned
in Jerusalem sixteen years. His
mother's name was Jerusha
daughter of Zadok. 2 He did
what was right in the eyes of
the LORD, just as his father Uzziah had done, but unlike him
he did not enter the temple of
the LORD. The people, however, continued their corrupt

k19 The Hebrew word was used for various diseases affecting the skin—not necessarily leprosy; also in verses 20, 21 and 23.

l21 Or *in a house where he was relieved of responsibilities*

*22 Most mss have *pathah* under the *aleph* (וְהָאַחֲ).

°21 ק החפשית

בָּנָה אֶת־ שַׁעַר בֵּית־ יְהוָה הָעֶלְיוֹן וּבְחוֹמַת הָעֹפֶל
the-Ophel and-on-wall-of the-Upper Yahweh temple-of Gate-of *** he-rebuilt

בָּנָה לָרֹב׃ וְעָרִים בָּנָה בְּהַר־ יְהוּדָה וּבֶחֳרָשִׁים
and-in-the-woods Judah in-hill-of he-built and-towns (4) to-extent he-worked

בָּנָה בִּירָנִיּוֹת וּמִגְדָּלִים׃ וְהוּא נִלְחַם עִם־ מֶלֶךְ בְּנֵי־ עַמּוֹן
Ammon sons-of king-of on he-made-war and-he (5) and-towers forts he-built

וַיֶּחֱזַק עֲלֵיהֶם וַיִּתְּנוּ־ לוֹ בְנֵי־ עַמּוֹן בַּשָּׁנָה
in-the-year Ammon sons-of to-him and-they-paid against-them and-he-conquered

הַהִיא מֵאָה כִּכַּר־ כֶּסֶף וַעֲשֶׂרֶת אֲלָפִים כֹּרִים חִטִּים
wheats cors thousands and-ten-of silver talent-of hundred the-that

וּשְׂעוֹרִים עֲשֶׂרֶת אֲלָפִים זֹאת הֵשִׁיבוּ לוֹ בְּנֵי עַמּוֹן
Ammon sons-of to-him they-brought same thousands ten-of and-barleys

וּבַשָּׁנָה הַשֵּׁנִית וְהַשְּׁלִשִׁית׃ וַיִּתְחַזֵּק יוֹתָם
Jotham and-he-grew-powerful (6) and-the-third the-second also-in-the-year

כִּי הֵכִין דְּרָכָיו לִפְנֵי יְהוָה אֱלֹהָיו׃
God-of-him Yahweh before ways-of-him he-made-steadfast because

וְיֶתֶר דִּבְרֵי יוֹתָם וְכָל־ מִלְחֲמֹתָיו וּדְרָכָיו
and-ways-of-him wars-of-him and-all-of Jotham events-of and-other-of (7)

הִנָּם כְּתוּבִים עַל־ סֵפֶר מַלְכֵי־ יִשְׂרָאֵל וִיהוּדָה׃ בֶּן־
son-of (8) and-Judah Israel kings-of book-of in ones-being-written see-they!

עֶשְׂרִים וְחָמֵשׁ שָׁנָה הָיָה בְמָלְכוֹ וְשֵׁשׁ־ עֶשְׂרֵה שָׁנָה
year ten and-six-of when-to-become-king-him he-was year and-five twenty

מָלַךְ בִּירוּשָׁלִָם׃ וַיִּשְׁכַּב יוֹתָם עִם־ אֲבֹתָיו
fathers-of-him with Jotham and-he-rested (9) in-Jerusalem he-reigned

וַיִּקְבְּרוּ אֹתוֹ בְּעִיר דָּוִיד וַיִּמְלֹךְ אָחָז בְּנוֹ
son-of-him Ahaz and-he-became-king David in-City-of him and-they-buried

תַּחְתָּיו׃ בֶּן־ עֶשְׂרִים שָׁנָה אָחָז בְּמָלְכוֹ
when-to-become-king-him Ahaz year twenty son-of (28:1) in-place-of-him

וְשֵׁשׁ־ עֶשְׂרֵה שָׁנָה מָלַךְ בִּירוּשָׁלִָם וְלֹא־ עָשָׂה הַיָּשָׁר
the-right he-did but-not in-Jerusalem he-reigned year ten and-six-of

בְּעֵינֵי יְהוָה כְּדָוִיד אָבִיו׃ וַיֵּלֶךְ בְּדַרְכֵי
in-ways-of and-he-walked (2) father-of-him like-David Yahweh in-eyes-of

מַלְכֵי יִשְׂרָאֵל וְגַם מַסֵּכוֹת עָשָׂה לַבְּעָלִים׃ וְהוּא
and-he (3) for-the-Baals he-made cast-idols and-also Israel kings-of

הִקְטִיר בְּגֵיא בֶן־ הִנֹּם וַיַּבְעֵר אֶת־ בָּנָיו
sons-of-him *** and-he-sacrificed Hinnom Ben in-Valley-of he-burned-sacrifice

בָּאֵשׁ כְּתֹעֲבוֹת הַגּוֹיִם אֲשֶׁר הֹרִישׁ יְהוָה
Yahweh he-drove-out that the-nations as-detestable-ways-of in-the-fire

practices. [3]Jotham rebuilt the
Upper Gate of the temple of
the LORD and did extensive
work on the wall at the hill of
Ophel. [4]He built towns in the
Judean hills and forts and towers in the wooded areas.
[5]Jotham made war on the
king of the Ammonites and
conquered them. That year the
Ammonites paid him a hun-
dred talents[m] of silver, ten
thousand cors[n] of wheat and
ten thousand cors of barley.
The Ammonites brought him
the same amount also in the
second and third years.
[6]Jotham grew powerful because he walked steadfastly
before the LORD his God.
[7]The other events in Jotham's reign, including all his
wars and the other things he
did, are written in the book of
the kings of Israel and Judah.
[8]He was twenty-five years old
when he became king, and he
reigned in Jerusalem sixteen
years. [9]Jotham rested with his
fathers and was buried in the
City of David. And Ahaz his
son succeeded him as king.

Ahaz King of Judah

28 Ahaz was twenty years
old when he became
king, and he reigned in
Jerusalem sixteen years. Unlike David his father, he did
not do what was right in the
eyes of the LORD. [2]He walked
in the ways of the kings of Israel and also made cast idols
for worshiping the Baals. [3]He
burned sacrifices in the Valley
of Ben Hinnom and sacrificed
his sons in the fire, following
the detestable ways of the nations the LORD had driven out

[m]5 That is, about 3 3/4 tons (about 3.4 metric tons)
[n]5 That is, probably about 62,000 bushels (about 2,200 kiloliters)

מִפְּנֵי	בְּנֵי	יִשְׂרָאֵל׃		וַיְזַבֵּחַ	וַיְקַטֵּר
from-before	sons-of	Israel	(4)	and-he-sacrificed	and-he-burned-incense

בַּבָּמוֹת	וְעַל־	הַגְּבָעוֹת	וְתַחַת	כָּל־	עֵץ	רַעֲנָן׃
at-the-high-places	and-on	the-hilltops	and-under	every-of	tree-of	spreading

	וַיִּתְּנֵהוּ	יְהוָה	אֱלֹהָיו	בְּיַד	מֶלֶךְ	אֲרָם
(5)	so-he-gave-him	Yahweh	God-of-him	into-hand-of	king-of	Aram

וַיַּכּוּ־	בוֹ	וַיִּשְׁבּוּ	מִמֶּנּוּ	שִׁבְיָה	גְדוֹלָה
and-they-defeated	against-him	and-they-took-prisoner	from-him	prisoner	many

וַיָּבִיאוּ	דַּרְמָשֶׂק	וְגַם	בְּיַד־	מֶלֶךְ	יִשְׂרָאֵל	נִתָּן
and-they-brought	Damascus	and-also	into-hand-of	king-of	Israel	he-was-given

וַיַּךְ־	בּוֹ	מַכָּה	גְדוֹלָה׃		וַיַּהֲרֹג	פֶּקַח	בֶּן־
and-he-inflicted	on-him	casualty	heavy	(6)	and-he-killed	Pekah	son-of

רְמַלְיָהוּ	בִּיהוּדָה	מֵאָה	וְעֶשְׂרִים	אֶלֶף	בְּיוֹם	אֶחָד	הַכֹּל	בְּנֵי־
Remaliah	in-Judah	hundred	and-twenty	thousand	in-day	one	the-whole	soldiers-of

חָיִל	בְּעָזְבָם	אֶת־	יְהוָה	אֱלֹהֵי	אֲבוֹתָם׃
army	because-to-forsake-them	***	Yahweh	God-of	fathers-of-them

	וַיַּהֲרֹג	זִכְרִי ׀	גִּבּוֹר	אֶפְרַיִם	אֶת־	מַעֲשֵׂיָהוּ	בֶּן־	הַמֶּלֶךְ
(7)	and-he-killed	Zicri	warrior-of	Ephraim	***	Maaseiah	son-of	the-king

וְאֶת־	עַזְרִיקָם	נְגִיד	הַבָּיִת	וְאֶת־	אֶלְקָנָה	מִשְׁנֵה	הַמֶּלֶךְ׃
and	Azrikam	officer-of	the-palace	and	Elkanah	second-of	the-king

	וַיִּשְׁבּוּ	בְנֵי־	יִשְׂרָאֵל	מֵאֲחֵיהֶם	מָאתַיִם
(8)	and-they-took-captive	sons-of	Israel	from-kinsmen-of-them	two-hundreds

אֶלֶף	נָשִׁים	בָּנִים	וּבָנוֹת	וְגַם־	שָׁלָל	רָב	בָּזְזוּ	מֵהֶם
thousand	wives	sons	and-daughters	and-also	plunder	great	they-took	from-them

וַיָּבִיאוּ	אֶת־	הַשָּׁלָל	לְשֹׁמְרוֹן׃		וְשָׁם	הָיָה
and-they-carried-back	***	the-plunder	to-Samaria	(9)	but-there	he-was

נָבִיא	לַיהוָה	עֹדֵד	שְׁמוֹ	וַיֵּצֵא	לִפְנֵי	הַצָּבָא
prophet	of-Yahweh	Oded	name-of-him	and-he-went-out	to-faces-of	the-army

הַבָּא	לְשֹׁמְרוֹן	וַיֹּאמֶר	לָהֶם	הִנֵּה	בַּחֲמַת
the-one-returning	to-Samaria	and-he-said	to-them	see!	because-of-anger-of

יְהוָה	אֱלֹהֵי־	אֲבוֹתֵיכֶם	עַל־	יְהוּדָה	נְתָנָם	בְּיֶדְכֶם
Yahweh	God-of	fathers-of-you	with	Judah	he-gave-them	into-hand-of-you

וַתַּהַרְגוּ־	בָם	בְזַעַף*	עַד	לַשָּׁמַיִם	הִגִּיעַ׃		וְעַתָּה
but-you-slaughtered	of-them	in-rage	to	to-the-heavens	he-reaches	(10)	and-now

בְּנֵי־	יְהוּדָה	וִירוּשָׁלִַם	אַתֶּם	אֹמְרִים	לִכְבֹּשׁ	לַעֲבָדִים
people-of	Judah	and-Jerusalem	you	intending	to-make	as-male-slaves

וְלִשְׁפָחוֹת	לָכֶם	הֲלֹא	רַק־	אַתֶּם	עִמָּכֶם	אֲשָׁמוֹת	לַיהוָה
and-as-female-slaves	for-you	not?	also	you	with-you	sins	against-Yahweh

before the Israelites. [4]He
offered sacrifices and burned
incense at the high places, on
the hilltops and under every
spreading tree.
[5]Therefore the LORD his God
handed him over to the king
of Aram. The Arameans de-
feated him and took many of
his people as prisoners and
brought them to Damascus.
He was also given into the
hands of the king of Israel,
who inflicted heavy casualties
on him. [6]In one day Pekah son
of Remaliah killed a hundred
and twenty thousand soldiers
in Judah—because Judah had
forsaken the LORD, the God of
their fathers. [7]Zicri, an Ephraimite warrior, killed Maaseiah
the king's son, Azrikam the
officer in charge of the palace,
and Elkanah, second to the
king. [8]The Israelites took captive from their kinsmen two
hundred thousand wives,
sons and daughters. They also
took a great deal of plunder,
which they carried back to Samaria.
[9]But a prophet of the LORD
named Oded was there, and
he went out to meet the army
when it returned to Samaria.
He said to them, "Because the
LORD, the God of your fathers,
was angry with Judah, he gave
them into your hand. But you
have slaughtered them in a
rage that reaches to heaven.
[10]And now you intend to make
the men and women of Judah
and Jerusalem your slaves. But
aren't you also guilty of sins
against the LORD your God?

*9 Most mss have *dagesh* in the *beth* (בְּ).

אֱלֹהֵיכֶם׃ (11) וְעַתָּה שְׁמָעוּנִי וְהָשִׁיבוּ הַשִּׁבְיָה אֲשֶׁר
whom the-prisoner and-send-back! listen-to-me! and-now (11) God-of-you

שְׁבִיתֶם מֵאֲחֵיכֶם כִּי חֲרוֹן אַף־ יְהוָה
Yahweh anger-of fierceness-of for from-countrymen-of-you you-took-prisoner

עֲלֵיכֶם׃ (12) וַיָּקֻמוּ אֲנָשִׁים מֵרָאשֵׁי בְנֵי־ אֶפְרַיִם עֲזַרְיָהוּ
Azariah Ephraim sons-of from-leaders-of men then-they-confronted (12) on-you

בֶן־ יְהוֹחָנָן בֶּרֶכְיָהוּ בֶן־ מְשִׁלֵּמוֹת וִיחִזְקִיָּהוּ בֶן־ שַׁלֻּם
Shallum son-of and-Jehizkiah Meshillemoth son-of Berekiah Jehohanan son-of

וַעֲמָשָׂא בֶּן־ חַדְלָי עַל־ הַבָּאִים מִן־ הַצָּבָא׃ (13) וַיֹּאמְרוּ
and-they-said (13) the-war from the-ones-arriving to Hadlai son-of and-Amasa

לָהֶם לֹא־ תָבִיאוּ אֶת־ הַשִּׁבְיָה הֵנָּה כִּי לְאַשְׁמַת יְהוָה
Yahweh as-guilt-of or to-here the-prisoner *** you-must-bring not to-them

עָלֵינוּ אַתֶּם אֹמְרִים לְהֹסִיף עַל־ חַטֹּאתֵינוּ וְעַל־ אַשְׁמָתֵינוּ כִּי־ רַבָּה
great for guilts-of-us and-to sins-of-us to to-add intending you to-us

אַשְׁמָה לָנוּ וַחֲרוֹן אָף עַל־ יִשְׂרָאֵל׃ (14) וַיַּעֲזֹב
so-he-gave-up (14) Israel on anger and-fierceness-of of-us guilt

הֶחָלוּץ אֶת־ הַשִּׁבְיָה וְאֶת־ הַבִּזָּה לִפְנֵי
in-presences-of the-plunder and the-prisoner *** the-one-being-soldier

הַשָּׂרִים וְכָל־ הַקָּהָל׃ (15) וַיָּקֻמוּ הָאֲנָשִׁים אֲשֶׁר־
who the-men and-they-rose (15) the-assembly and-all-of the-officials

נִקְּבוּ בְשֵׁמוֹת וַיַּחֲזִיקוּ בַשִּׁבְיָה וְכָל־
and-all-of of-the-prisoner and-they-took by-names they-were-designated

מַעֲרֻמֵּיהֶם הִלְבִּישׁוּ מִן־ הַשָּׁלָל וַיַּלְבִּשׁוּם
and-they-gave-clothes-them the-plunder from they-clothed ones-naked-of-them

וַיַּנְעִלוּם וַיַּאֲכִלוּם וַיַּשְׁקוּם
and-they-gave-drink-them and-they-gave-food-them and-they-gave-sandals-them

וַיְסֻכוּם וַיְנַהֲלוּם בַּחֲמֹרִים לְכָל־ כּוֹשֵׁל
being-weak for-all-of on-donkeys and-they-put-them and-they-gave-balm-them

וַיְבִיאוּם יְרֵחוֹ עִיר־ הַתְּמָרִים אֵצֶל אֲחֵיהֶם
countrymen-of-them to the-Palms City-of Jericho so-they-took-back-them

וַיָּשׁוּבוּ שֹׁמְרוֹן׃ (16) בָּעֵת הַהִיא שָׁלַח הַמֶּלֶךְ אָחָז
Ahaz the-king he-sent the-that at-the-time (16) Samaria and-they-returned

עַל־ מַלְכֵי אַשּׁוּר לַעְזֹר לוֹ׃ (17) וְעוֹד אֲדוֹמִים בָּאוּ
they-came Edomites and-again (17) to-him to-help Assyria kings-of to

וַיַּכּוּ בִיהוּדָה וַיִּשְׁבּוּ־ שֶׁבִי׃
prisoner and-they-carried-away against-Judah and-they-attacked

(18) וּפְלִשְׁתִּים פָּשְׁטוּ בְּעָרֵי הַשְּׁפֵלָה וְהַנֶּגֶב
and-the-Negev the-foothill in-towns-of they-raided while-Philistines (18)

[11]Now listen to me! Send back
your fellow countrymen you
have taken as prisoners, for
the LORD's fierce anger rests on
you."
[12]Then some of the leaders in
Ephraim—Azariah son of
Jehohanan, Berekiah son of
Meshillemoth, Jehizkiah son
of Shallum, and Amasa son of
Hadlai—confronted those
who were arriving from the
war. [13]"You must not bring
those prisoners here," they
said, "or we will be guilty before the LORD. Do you intend
to add to our sin and guilt? For
our guilt is already great, and
his fierce anger rests on Israel."
[14]So the soldiers gave up the
prisoners and plunder in the
presence of the officials and all
the assembly. [15]The men
designated by name took the
prisoners, and from the plunder they clothed all who were
naked. They provided them
with clothes and sandals, food
and drink, and healing balm.
All those who were weak they
put on donkeys. So they took
them back to their fellow
countrymen at Jericho, the
City of Palms, and returned to
Samaria.
[16]At that time King Ahaz
sent to the king[o] of Assyria for
help. [17]The Edomites had
again come and attacked
Judah and carried away prisoners, [18]while the Philistines
had raided towns in the foothills and in the Negev of

[o]16 One Hebrew manuscript, Septuagint and Vulgate (see also 2 Kings 16:7); most Hebrew manuscripts *kings*

לִיהוּדָה֒ וַֽיִּלְכְּד֗וּ אֶת־ בֵּֽית־ שֶׁ֡מֶשׁ וְֽאֶת־ אַיָּל֣וֹן וְאֶֽת־ הַגְּדֵר֗וֹת
the-Gederoth and Aijalon and Shemesh Beth *** and-they-captured of-Judah

וְאֶת־שׂוֹכ֣וֹ וּבְנוֹתֶ֡יהָ וְאֶת־ תִּמְנָה֙ וּבְנוֹתֶ֔יהָ וְאֶת־ גִּמְז֖וֹ וְאֶת־
and Gimzo and and-villages-of-her Timnah and and-villages-of-her Soco and

בְּנֹתֶ֑יהָ וַיֵּשְׁב֖וּ שָֽׁם׃ כִּֽי־ הִכְנִ֤יעַ יְהוָה֙ אֶת־
*** Yahweh he-humbled for (19) there and-they-occupied villages-of-her

יְהוּדָ֔ה בַּעֲב֖וּר אָחָ֣ז מֶֽלֶךְ־ יִשְׂרָאֵ֑ל כִּ֤י הִפְרִ֙יעַ֙ בִּֽיהוּדָ֔ה
in-Judah he-promoted-wickedness for Israel king-of Ahaz because-of Judah

וּמָע֥וֹל מַ֖עַל בַּיהוָֽה׃ וַיָּבֹ֣א עָלָ֔יו תִּלְּגַ֥ת
Tilgath to-him and-he-came (20) to-Yahweh unfaithfulness and-to-be-unfaithful

פִּלְנְאֶ֖סֶר מֶ֣לֶךְ אַשּׁ֑וּר וַיָּ֥צַר ל֖וֹ וְלֹ֥א חֲזָקֽוֹ׃
he-helped-him and-not to-him but-he-troubled Assyria king-of Pilneser

כִּֽי־ חָלַ֤ק אָחָז֙ אֶת־ בֵּ֣ית יְהוָ֔ה וְאֶת־ בֵּ֥ית הַמֶּ֖לֶךְ
the-king palace-of and Yahweh temple-of *** Ahaz he-took-from for (21)

וְהַשָּׂרִ֑ים וַיִּתֵּן֙ לְמֶ֣לֶךְ אַשּׁ֔וּר וְלֹ֥א לְעֶזְרָ֖ה לֽוֹ׃
for-him as-help but-not Assyria to-king-of and-he-presented and-the-princes

וּבְעֵת֙ הָצֵ֣ר ל֔וֹ וַיּ֖וֹסֶף לִמְע֣וֹל
to-be-unfaithful then-he-continued to-him to-trouble and-in-time-of (22)

בַּיהוָ֑ה ה֖וּא הַמֶּ֥לֶךְ אָחָֽז׃ וַיִּזְבַּ֗ח לֵאלֹהֵ֤י דַרְמֶ֙שֶׂק֙
Damascus to-gods-of and-he-sacrificed (23) Ahaz the-king he to-Yahweh

הַמַּכִּ֣ים בּ֔וֹ וַיֹּ֗אמֶר כִּ֠י אֱלֹהֵ֨י מַלְכֵֽי־ אֲרָ֜ם
Aram kings-of gods-of since for-he-thought against-him the-ones-defeating

הֵ֚ם מַעְזְרִ֣ים אוֹתָ֔ם לָהֶ֥ם אֲזַבֵּ֖חַ וְיַעְזְר֑וּנִי
so-they-will-help-me I-will-sacrifice to-them them ones-helping they

וְהֵ֛ם הָיוּ־ ל֥וֹ לְהַכְשִׁיל֖וֹ וּלְכָל־ יִשְׂרָאֵֽל׃
Israel and-to-all-of to-cast-down-him to-him they-were but-they

וַיֶּאֱסֹ֨ף אָחָ֜ז אֶת־ כְּלֵ֣י בֵית־ הָאֱלֹהִ֗ים
the-God temple-of furnishings-of *** Ahaz and-he-gathered (24)

וַיְקַצֵּץ֙ אֶת־ כְּלֵ֣י בֵית־ הָאֱלֹהִ֔ים וַיִּסְגֹּ֖ר אֶת־
*** and-he-shut the-God temple-of furnishings-of *** and-he-took-away

דַּלְת֣וֹת בֵּית־ יְהוָ֑ה וַיַּ֧עַשׂ ל֛וֹ מִזְבְּח֖וֹת בְּכָל־ פִּנָּ֥ה
corner at-every-of altars for-him and-he-set-up Yahweh temple-of doors-of

בִּירוּשָׁלָֽםִ׃ וּבְכָל־ עִ֤יר וָעִיר֙ לִֽיהוּדָ֔ה עָשָׂ֣ה בָמ֔וֹת
high-places he-built in-Judah and-town town and-in-every-of (25) in-Jerusalem

לְקַטֵּ֖ר לֵאלֹהִ֣ים אֲחֵרִ֑ים וַיַּכְעֵ֕ס אֶת־ יְהוָ֖ה אֱלֹהֵ֥י
God-of Yahweh *** and-he-provoked other-ones to-gods to-burn-sacrifice

אֲבֹתָֽיו׃ וְיֶ֤תֶר דְּבָרָיו֙ וְכָל־ דְּרָכָ֔יו
ways-of-him and-all-of events-of-him and-other-of (26) fathers-of-him

Judah. They captured and occupied Beth Shemesh, Aijalon
and Gederoth, as well as Soco,
Timnah and Gimzo, with
their surrounding villages.
19The LORD had humbled
Judah because of Ahaz king of
Israel,[p] for he had promoted
wickedness in Judah and had
been most unfaithful to the
LORD. 20Tiglath-Pileser[q] king of
Assyria came to him, but he
gave him trouble instead of
help. 21Ahaz took some of the
things from the temple of the
LORD and from the royal palace and from the princes and
presented them to the king of
Assyria, but that did not help
him.

22In his time of trouble King
Ahaz became even more un-
faithful to the LORD. 23He
offered sacrifices to the gods of
Damascus, who had defeated
him; for he thought, "Since
the gods of the kings of Aram
have helped them, I will sacrifice to them so they will help
me." But they were his downfall and the downfall of all Israel.

24Ahaz gathered together the
furnishings from the temple of
God and took them away.[r] He
shut the doors of the LORD's
temple and set up altars at
every street corner in Jerusalem. 25In every town in Judah
he built high places to burn
sacrifices to other gods and
provoked the LORD, the God of
his fathers, to anger.

26The other events of his
reign and all his ways, from

[p]19 That is, Judah, as frequently in 2 Chronicles
[q]20 Hebrew *Tilgath-Pilneser*, a variant of *Tiglath-Pileser*
[r]24 Or *and cut them up*

הָרִאשֹׁנִים וְהָאַחֲרוֹנִים הִנָּם כְּתוּבִים עַל־ סֵפֶר מַלְכֵי־
kings-of book-of in ones-being-written see-they! and-the-ends the-beginnings

יְהוּדָה וְיִשְׂרָאֵל׃ וַיִּשְׁכַּב אָחָז עִם־ אֲבֹתָיו
fathers-of-him with Ahaz and-he-rested (27) and-Israel Judah

וַיִּקְבְּרֻהוּ בָעִיר בִּירוּשָׁלִַם כִּי לֹא הֱבִיאֻהוּ
they-placed-him not but in-Jerusalem in-the-city and-they-buried-him

לְקִבְרֵי מַלְכֵי יִשְׂרָאֵל וַיִּמְלֹךְ יְחִזְקִיָּהוּ בְנוֹ
son-of-him Hezekiah and-he-became-king Israel kings-of in-tombs-of

תַּחְתָּיו׃ יְחִזְקִיָּהוּ מָלַךְ בֶּן־ עֶשְׂרִים וְחָמֵשׁ שָׁנָה
year and-five twenty son-of he-became-king Hezekiah (29:1) in-place-of-him

וְעֶשְׂרִים וָתֵשַׁע שָׁנָה מָלַךְ בִּירוּשָׁלָיִם וְשֵׁם אִמּוֹ
mother-of-him and-name-of in-Jerusalem he-reigned year and-nine and-twenty

אֲבִיָּה בַּת־ זְכַרְיָהוּ׃ וַיַּעַשׂ הַיָּשָׁר בְּעֵינֵי יְהוָה
Yahweh in-eyes-of the-right and-he-did (2) Zechariah daughter-of Abijah

כְּכֹל אֲשֶׁר־ עָשָׂה דָּוִיד אָבִיו׃ הוּא בַשָּׁנָה הָרִאשׁוֹנָה
the-first in-the-year he (3) father-of-him David he-did that as-all

לְמָלְכוֹ בַּחֹדֶשׁ הָרִאשׁוֹן פָּתַח אֶת־ דַּלְתוֹת בֵּית־ יְהוָה
Yahweh temple-of doors-of *** he-opened the-first in-the-month to-reign-him

וַיְחַזְּקֵם׃ וַיָּבֵא אֶת־ הַכֹּהֲנִים וְאֶת־ הַלְוִיִּם
the-Levites and the-priests *** and-he-brought-in (4) and-he-repaired-them

וַיַּאַסְפֵם לִרְחוֹב הַמִּזְרָח׃ וַיֹּאמֶר לָהֶם
to-them and-he-said (5) the-east in-square-of and-he-assembled-them

שְׁמָעוּנִי הַלְוִיִּם עַתָּה הִתְקַדְּשׁוּ וְקַדְּשׁוּ אֶת־
*** and-consecrate! consecrate-yourselves! now the-Levites listen-to-me!

בֵּית יְהוָה אֱלֹהֵי אֲבֹתֵיכֶם וְהוֹצִיאוּ אֶת־ הַנִּדָּה מִן־
from the-defilement *** and-remove! fathers-of-you God-of Yahweh temple-of

הַקֹּדֶשׁ׃ כִּי־ מָעֲלוּ אֲבֹתֵינוּ וְעָשׂוּ
and-they-did fathers-of-us they-were-unfaithful for (6) the-sanctuary

הָרַע בְּעֵינֵי יְהוָה־ אֱלֹהֵינוּ וַיַּעַזְבֻהוּ וַיַּסֵּבּוּ
and-they-turned-away and-they-forsook-him God-of-us Yahweh in-eyes-of the-evil

פְנֵיהֶם מִמִּשְׁכַּן יְהוָה וַיִּתְּנוּ־ עֹרֶף׃ גַּם סָגְרוּ
they-shut also (7) back and-they-turned Yahweh from-dwelling-of faces-of-them

דַּלְתוֹת הָאוּלָם וַיְכַבּוּ אֶת־ הַנֵּרוֹת וּקְטֹרֶת לֹא
not and-incense the-lamps *** and-they-put-out the-portico doors-of

הִקְטִירוּ וְעֹלָה לֹא־ הֶעֱלוּ בַקֹּדֶשׁ
at-the-sanctuary they-presented not and-burnt-offering they-burned

לֵאלֹהֵי יִשְׂרָאֵל׃ וַיְהִי קֶצֶף יְהוָה עַל־ יְהוּדָה וִירוּשָׁלִָם
and-Jerusalem Judah on Yahweh anger-of so-he-fell (8) Israel to-God-of

beginning to end, are written
in the book of the kings of
Judah and Israel. 27Ahaz rested
with his fathers and was buried in the city of Jerusalem,
but he was not placed in the
tombs of the kings of Israel.
And Hezekiah his son suc-
ceeded him as king.

Hezekiah Purifies the Temple

29 Hezekiah was twenty-
five years old when he
became king, and he reigned
in Jerusalem twenty-nine
years. His mother's name was
Abijah daughter of Zechariah.
2He did what was right in the
eyes of the LORD, just as his
father David had done.
3In the first month of the
first year of his reign, he
opened the doors of the temple
of the LORD and repaired them.
4He brought in the priests and
the Levites, assembled them
in the square on the east side
5and said: "Listen to me, Levites! Consecrate yourselves
now and consecrate the temple of the LORD, the God of
your fathers. Remove all
defilement from the sanctuary. 6Our fathers were unfaithful; they did evil in the
eyes of the LORD our God and
forsook him. They turned
their faces away from the
LORD's dwelling place and
turned their backs on him.
7They also shut the doors of
the portico and put out the
lamps. They did not burn incense or present any burnt
offerings at the sanctuary to
the God of Israel. 8Therefore,
the anger of the LORD has
fallen on Judah and Jerusalem;

וַיִּתְּנֵם לְזַעֲוָה לְשַׁמָּה וְלִשְׁרֵקָה כַּאֲשֶׁר
just-as and-as-object-of-scorn as-horror as-object-of-dread and-he-made-them

אַתֶּם רֹאִים בְּעֵינֵיכֶם׃ וְהִנֵּה נָפְלוּ אֲבוֹתֵינוּ
fathers-of-us they-fell and-see! (9) with-eyes-of-you ones-seeing you

בֶּחָרֶב וּבָנֵינוּ וּבְנוֹתֵינוּ וְנָשֵׁינוּ
and-wives-of-us and-daughters-of-us and-sons-of-us by-the-sword

בַּשְּׁבִי עַל־זֹאת׃ עַתָּה עִם־לְבָבִי לִכְרוֹת בְּרִית לַיהוָה
with-Yahweh covenant to-make heart-of-me in now (10) this for in-the-captivity

אֱלֹהֵי יִשְׂרָאֵל וְיָשֹׁב מִמֶּנּוּ חֲרוֹן אַפּוֹ׃
anger-of-him fierceness-of from-us so-he-will-turn Israel God-of

בָּנַי עַתָּה אַל־תִּשָּׁלוּ כִּי־בָכֶם בָּחַר יְהוָה
Yahweh he-chose to-you for you-be-negligent not now sons-of-me (11)

לַעֲמֹד לְפָנָיו לְשָׁרְתוֹ וְלִהְיוֹת לוֹ מְשָׁרְתִים
ones-ministering before-him and-to-be to-serve-him before-him to-stand

וּמַקְטִרִים׃ וַיָּקֻמוּ הַלְוִיִּם מַחַת בֶּן־
son-of Mahath the-Levites then-they-set-to-work (12) and-ones-burning-incense

עֲמָשַׂי וְיוֹאֵל בֶּן־עֲזַרְיָהוּ מִן־בְּנֵי הַקְּהָתִי וּמִן־בְּנֵי
sons-of and-from the-Kohathite sons-of from Azariah son-of and-Joel Amasai

מְרָרִי קִישׁ בֶּן־עַבְדִּי וַעֲזַרְיָהוּ בֶּן־יְהַלֶּלְאֵל וּמִן־הַגֵּרְשֻׁנִּי
the-Gershonite and-from Jehallelel son-of and-Azariah Abdi son-of Kish Merari

יוֹאָח בֶּן־זִמָּה וְעֵדֶן בֶּן־יוֹאָח׃ וּמִן־בְּנֵי
descendants-of and-from (13) Joah son-of and-Eden Zimmah son-of Joah

אֱלִיצָפָן שִׁמְרִי °וִיעוּאֵל וּמִן־בְּנֵי אָסָף זְכַרְיָהוּ
Zechariah Asaph descendants-of and-from and-Jeiel Shimri Elizaphan

וּמַתַּנְיָהוּ׃ וּמִן־בְּנֵי הֵימָן °יְחוּאֵל וְשִׁמְעִי וּמִן־
and-from and-Shimei Jehiel Heman descendants-of and-from (14) and-Mattaniah

בְּנֵי יְדוּתוּן שְׁמַעְיָה וְעֻזִּיאֵל׃ וַיַּאַסְפוּ אֶת־
*** when-they-assembled (15) and-Uzziel Shemaiah Jeduthun descendants-of

אֲחֵיהֶם וַיִּתְקַדְּשׁוּ וַיָּבֹאוּ כְמִצְוַת־
as-order-of then-they-went-in and-they-consecrated-themselves brothers-of-them

הַמֶּלֶךְ בְּדִבְרֵי יְהוָה לְטַהֵר בֵּית יְהוָה׃ וַיָּבֹאוּ
and-they-went (16) Yahweh temple-of to-purify Yahweh at-words-of the-king

הַכֹּהֲנִים לִפְנִימָה בֵית־יְהוָה לְטַהֵר וַיּוֹצִיאוּ
and-they-brought-out to-purify Yahweh sanctuary-of into-inside the-priests

אֵת כָּל־הַטֻּמְאָה אֲשֶׁר מָצְאוּ בְּהֵיכַל יְהוָה
Yahweh in-temple-of they-found that the-uncleanness all-of ***

לַחֲצַר בֵּית יְהוָה וַיְקַבְּלוּ הַלְוִיִּם לְהוֹצִיא
to-carry-out the-Levites and-they-took Yahweh temple-of to-courtyard-of

he has made them an object of
dread and horror and scorn, as
you can see with your own
eyes. 9This is why our fathers
have fallen by the sword and
why our sons and daughters
and our wives are in captivity.
10Now I intend to make a covenant with the LORD, the God
of Israel, so that his fierce anger will turn away from us.
11My sons, do not be negligent
now, for the LORD has chosen
you to stand before him and
serve him, to minister before
him and to burn incense."
12Then these Levites set to
work:
from the Kohathites,
Mahath son of Amasai
and Joel son of Aza-
riah;
from the Merarites,
Kish son of Abdi and
Azariah son of Je-
hallelel;
from the Gershonites,
Joah son of Zimmah
and Eden son of Joah;
13from the descendants of
Elizaphan,
Shimri and Jeiel;
from the descendants of
Asaph,
Zechariah and Mat-
taniah;
14from the descendants of
Heman,
Jehiel and Shimei;
from the descendants of
Jeduthun,
Shemaiah and Uzziel.
15When they had assembled
their brothers and consecrated
themselves, they went in to
purify the temple of the LORD,
as the king had ordered, following the word of the LORD.
16The priests went into the
sanctuary of the LORD to purify
it. They brought out to the
courtyard of the LORD's temple
everything unclean that they
found in the temple of the
LORD. The Levites took it and

°8 ק לזועה
°13 ק ויעיאל
°14 ק יחיאל

לְנַ֫חַל־ קִדְר֖וֹן ח֑וּצָה
to-Valley-of / Kidron / to-outside

(17) וַיָּחֵ֖לּוּ בְּאֶחָ֥ד לַחֹ֖דֶשׁ
(17) / and-they-began / on-one / of-the-month

הָרִאשׁ֖וֹן לְקַדֵּ֑שׁ וּבְי֥וֹם שְׁמוֹנָ֛ה לַחֹ֖דֶשׁ בָּ֣אוּ
the-first / to-consecrate / and-on-day / eight / of-the-month / they-reached

לְאוּלָ֣ם יְהוָה֒ וַיְקַדְּשׁ֞וּ אֶת־ בֵּית־ יְהוָ֗ה לְיָמִים֙ שְׁמוֹנָ֔ה
to-portico-of / Yahweh / and-they-consecrated / *** / temple-of / Yahweh / for-days / eight

וּבְי֨וֹם שִׁשָּׁ֥ה עָשָׂ֛ר לַחֹ֥דֶשׁ הָרִאשׁ֖וֹן כִּלּֽוּ׃
and-on-day / six / ten / of-the-month / the-first / they-finished

(18) וַיָּב֣וֹאוּ פְנִ֖ימָה אֶל־ חִזְקִיָּ֣הוּ הַמֶּ֑לֶךְ וַיֹּ֣אמְר֔וּ טִהַ֖רְנוּ אֶת־ כָּל־
(18) / then-they-went / inside / to / Hezekiah / the-king / and-they-reported / we-purified / *** / entire-of

בֵּ֣ית יְהוָ֔ה אֶת־ מִזְבַּ֥ח הָעוֹלָ֖ה וְאֶת־ כָּל־ כֵּלָ֑יו
temple-of / Yahweh / *** / altar-of / the-burnt-offering / and / all-of / utensils-of-him

וְאֶת־ שֻׁלְחַ֣ן הַֽמַּעֲרֶ֔כֶת וְאֶת־ כָּל־ כֵּלָֽיו׃ (19) וְאֵ֣ת
and / table-of / the-consecrated-bread / and / all-of / articles-of-him / (19) / and

כָּל־ הַכֵּלִ֗ים אֲשֶׁ֨ר הִזְנִ֜יחַ הַמֶּ֧לֶךְ אָחָ֛ז בְּמַלְכוּת֥וֹ
all-of / the-articles / that / he-removed / the-king / Ahaz / during-reign-of-him

בְּמַעֲל֖וֹ הֵכַ֣נּוּ וְהִקְדָּ֑שְׁנוּ וְהִנָּ֕ם לִפְנֵ֖י
in-unfaithfulness-of-him / we-prepared / and-we-consecrated / now-see-they! / in-front-of

מִזְבַּ֥ח יְהוָֽה׃ (20) וַיַּשְׁכֵּם֙ יְחִזְקִיָּ֣הוּ הַמֶּ֔לֶךְ וַיֶּאֱסֹ֖ף אֵ֣ת
altar-of / Yahweh / (20) / and-he-got-up / Hezekiah / the-king / and-he-gathered / ***

שָׂרֵ֣י הָעִ֑יר וַיַּ֖עַל בֵּ֣ית יְהוָֽה׃ (21) וַיָּבִ֡יאוּ
officials-of / the-city / and-he-went-up / temple-of / Yahweh / (21) / and-they-brought

פָרִים־שִׁבְעָה֩ וְאֵילִ֨ם שִׁבְעָ֜ה וּכְבָשִׂ֣ים שִׁבְעָ֗ה וּצְפִירֵ֤י עִזִּים֙ שִׁבְעָ֔ה
bulls / seven / and-rams / seven / and-lambs / seven / and-male-goats-of / goats / seven

לְחַטָּ֛את עַל־ הַמַּמְלָכָ֥ה וְעַל־ הַמִּקְדָּ֖שׁ וְעַל־ יְהוּדָ֑ה
as-sin-offering / for / the-kingdom / and-for / the-sanctuary / and-for / Judah

וַיֹּ֗אמֶר לִבְנֵ֤י אַהֲרֹן֙ הַכֹּ֣הֲנִ֔ים לְהַעֲל֖וֹת עַל־ מִזְבַּ֥ח
and-he-commanded / to-descendants-of / Aaron / the-priests / to-offer / on / altar-of

יְהוָֽה׃ (22) וַֽיִּשְׁחֲטוּ֙ הַבָּקָ֔ר וַיְקַבְּל֤וּ הַכֹּֽהֲנִים֙ אֶת־
Yahweh / (22) / so-they-slaughtered / the-bull / and-they-took / the-priests / ***

הַדָּ֔ם וַֽיִּזְרְק֖וּ הַמִּזְבֵּ֑חָה וַֽיִּשְׁחֲטוּ֙ הָ֣אֵלִ֔ים
the-blood / and-they-sprinkled / on-the-altar / then-they-slaughtered / the-rams

וַֽיִּזְרְק֥וּ הַדָּ֖ם הַמִּזְבֵּ֑חָה וַֽיִּשְׁחֲטוּ֙ הַכְּבָשִׂ֔ים
and-they-sprinkled / the-blood / on-the-altar / then-they-slaughtered / the-lambs

וַֽיִּזְרְק֥וּ הַדָּ֖ם הַמִּזְבֵּֽחָה׃ (23) וַיַּגִּ֙ישׁוּ֙ אֶת־ שְׂעִירֵ֣י
and-they-sprinkled / the-blood / on-the-altar / (23) / and-they-brought / *** / goats-of

הַֽחַטָּ֔את לִפְנֵ֥י הַמֶּ֖לֶךְ וְהַקָּהָ֑ל וַיִּסְמְכ֥וּ יְדֵיהֶ֖ם
the-sin-offering / before / the-king / and-the-assembly / and-they-laid / hands-of-them

---

carried it out to the Kidron Valley. 17They began the consecration on the first day of the first month, and by the eighth day of the month they reached the portico of the LORD. For eight more days they consecrated the temple of the LORD itself, finishing on the sixteenth day of the first month.

18Then they went in to King Hezekiah and reported: "We have purified the entire temple of the LORD, the altar of burnt offering with all its utensils, and the table for setting out the consecrated bread, with all its articles. 19We have prepared and consecrated all the articles that King Ahaz removed in his unfaithfulness while he was king. They are now in front of the LORD's altar."

20Early the next morning King Hezekiah gathered the city officials together and went up to the temple of the LORD. 21They brought seven bulls, seven rams, seven male lambs and seven male goats as a sin offering for the kingdom, for the sanctuary and for Judah. The king commanded the priests, the descendants of Aaron, to offer these on the altar of the LORD. 22So they slaughtered the bulls, and the priests took the blood and sprinkled it on the altar; next they slaughtered the rams and sprinkled their blood on the altar; then they slaughtered the lambs and sprinkled their blood on the altar. 23The goats for the sin offering were brought before the king and the assembly, and they laid their hands on them. 24The

עֲלֵיהֶם׃ (24) וַיִּשְׁחָטוּם הַכֹּהֲנִים וַיְחַטְּאוּ
on-them (24) then-they-slaughtered-them the-priests and-they-made-sin-offering

אֶת־ דָּמָם הַמִּזְבֵּחָה לְכַפֵּר עַל־ כָּל־ יִשְׂרָאֵל כִּי לְכָל־
*** blood-of-them on-the-altar to-atone for all-of Israel because for-all-of

יִשְׂרָאֵל אָמַר הַמֶּלֶךְ הָעוֹלָה וְהַחַטָּאת׃
Israel he-ordered the-king the-burnt-offering and-the-sin-offering

(25) וַיַּעֲמֵד אֶת־ הַלְוִיִּם בֵּית יְהוָה בִּמְצִלְתַּיִם
(25) and-he-stationed *** the-Levites temple-of Yahweh with-cymbals

בִּנְבָלִים וּבְכִנֹּרוֹת בְּמִצְוַת דָּוִיד וְגָד חֹזֵה־ הַמֶּלֶךְ
with-harps and-with-lyres as-prescription-of David and-Gad seer-of the-king

וְנָתָן הַנָּבִיא כִּי בְיַד־ יְהוָה הַמִּצְוָה בְּיַד־
and-Nathan the-prophet for by-hand-of Yahweh the-command through-hand-of

נְבִיאָיו׃ (26) וַיַּעַמְדוּ הַלְוִיִּם בִּכְלֵי דָוִיד
prophets-of-him (26) so-they-stood the-Levites with-instruments-of David

וְהַכֹּהֲנִים בַּחֲצֹצְרוֹת׃ (27) וַיֹּאמֶר חִזְקִיָּהוּ לְהַעֲלוֹת
and-the-priests with-the-trumpets (27) and-he-ordered Hezekiah to-sacrifice

הָעֹלָה לְהַמִּזְבֵּחַ וּבְעֵת הֵחֵל הָעוֹלָה הֵחֵל
the-burnt-offering on-the-altar and-at-time he-began the-offering he-began

שִׁיר־ יְהוָה וְהַחֲצֹצְרוֹת וְעַל־ יְדֵי כְּלֵי דָּוִיד מֶלֶךְ־
song-of Yahweh and-the-trumpets and-with hands-of instruments-of David king-of

יִשְׂרָאֵל׃ (28) וְכָל־ הַקָּהָל מִשְׁתַּחֲוִים וְהַשִּׁיר מְשׁוֹרֵר
Israel (28) and-whole-of the-asssembly ones-worshiping while-the-song singing

וְהַחֲצֹצְרוֹת מַחְצְצְרִים° הַכֹּל עַד לִכְלוֹת
and-the-trumpets ones-playing the-whole until to-be-completed

הָעֹלָה׃ (29) וּכְכַלּוֹת לְהַעֲלוֹת כָּרְעוּ הַמֶּלֶךְ
the-burnt-offering (29) and-when-to-be-finished to-offer they-knelt the-king

וְכָל־ הַנִּמְצְאִים אִתּוֹ וַיִּשְׁתַּחֲווּ׃ (30) וַיֹּאמֶר
and-all-of the-ones-being-found with-him and-they-worshiped (30) and-he-ordered

יְחִזְקִיָּהוּ הַמֶּלֶךְ וְהַשָּׂרִים לַלְוִיִּם לְהַלֵּל לַיהוָה
Hezekiah the-king and-the-officials to-the-Levites to-praise to-Yahweh

בְּדִבְרֵי דָּוִיד וְאָסָף הַחֹזֶה וַיְהַלְלוּ עַד־ לְשִׂמְחָה
with-words-of David and-Asaph the-seer so-they-sang-praises to with-gladness

וַיִּקְּדוּ וַיִּשְׁתַּחֲווּ׃ (31) וַיַּעַן יְחִזְקִיָּהוּ
and-they-bowed-heads and-they-worshiped (31) then-he-answered Hezekiah

וַיֹּאמֶר עַתָּה מִלֵּאתֶם יֶדְכֶם לַיהוָה גֹּשׁוּ וְהָבִיאוּ
and-he-said now you-dedicated hand-of-you to-Yahweh come! and-bring!

זְבָחִים וְתוֹדוֹת לְבֵית יְהוָה וַיָּבִיאוּ
sacrifices and-thank-offerings to-temple-of Yahweh so-they-brought

priests then slaughtered the
goats and presented their
blood on the altar for a sin
offering to atone for all Israel,
because the king had ordered
the burnt offering and the sin
offering for all Israel.
25He stationed the Levites in
the temple of the LORD with
cymbals, harps and lyres in
the way prescribed by David
and Gad the king's seer and
Nathan the prophet; this was
commanded by the LORD
through his prophets. 26So the
Levites stood ready with David's instruments, and the
priests with their trumpets.
27Hezekiah gave the order to
sacrifice the burnt offering on
the altar. As the offering began, singing to the LORD began also, accompanied by
trumpets and the instruments
of David king of Israel. 28The
whole assembly bowed in
worship, while the singers
sang and the trumpeters
played. All this continued until the sacrifice of the burnt
offering was completed.
29When the offerings were
finished, the king and everyone present with him knelt
down and worshiped. 30King
Hezekiah and his officials ordered the Levites to praise the
LORD with the words of David
and of Asaph the seer. So they
sang praises with gladness
and bowed their heads and
worshiped.
31Then Hezekiah said, "You
have now dedicated your-
selves to the LORD. Come and
bring sacrifices and thank
offerings to the temple of the
LORD." So the assembly

°28 ק מחצרים

הַקָּהָל זְבָחִים וְתוֹדוֹת וְכָל־ נְדִיב לֵב
heart willing-of and-all-of and-thank-offerings sacrifices the-assembly

עֹלוֹת׃ (32) וַיְהִי מִסְפַּר הָעֹלָה אֲשֶׁר
that the-burnt-offering number-of and-he-was (32) burnt-offerings

הֵבִיאוּ הַקָּהָל בָּקָר שִׁבְעִים אֵילִים מֵאָה כְּבָשִׂים מָאתָיִם
two-hundreds lambs hundred rams seventy bull the-assembly they-brought

לְעֹלָה לַיהוָה כָּל־ אֵלֶּה׃ (33) וְהַקֳּדָשִׁים בָּקָר
bull and-the-ones-consecrated (33) these all-of to-Yahweh for-burnt-offering

שֵׁשׁ מֵאוֹת וְצֹאן שְׁלֹשֶׁת אֲלָפִים׃ (34) רַק הַכֹּהֲנִים
the-priests however (34) thousands three-of and-sheep hundreds six-of

הָיוּ לִמְעָט וְלֹא יָכְלוּ לְהַפְשִׁיט אֶת־ כָּל־ הָעֹלוֹת
the-burnt-offerings all-of *** to-skin they-could and-not as-few they-were

וַיְחַזְּקוּם אֲחֵיהֶם הַלְוִיִּם עַד־ כְּלוֹת הַמְּלָאכָה
the-task to-be-finished until the-Levites kinsmen-of-them so-they-helped-them

וְעַד יִתְקַדְּשׁוּ הַכֹּהֲנִים כִּי הַלְוִיִּם
the-Levites for the-priests they-were-consecrated and-until

יִשְׁרֵי לֵבָב לְהִתְקַדֵּשׁ מֵהַכֹּהֲנִים׃
more-than-the-priests to-consecrate-themselves heart ones-conscientious-of

(35) וְגַם־ עֹלָה לָרֹב בְּחֶלְבֵי הַשְּׁלָמִים
the-fellowship-offerings with-fats-of in-abundance burnt-offering and-also (35)

וּבַנְּסָכִים לָעֹלָה וַתִּכּוֹן
so-she-was-reestablished with-the-burnt-offering and-with-the-drink-offerings

עֲבוֹדַת בֵּית־ יְהוָה׃ (36) וַיִּשְׂמַח יְחִזְקִיָּהוּ וְכָל־
and-all-of Hezekiah and-he-rejoiced (36) Yahweh temple-of service-of

הָעָם עַל הַהֵכִין הָאֱלֹהִים לָעָם כִּי
because for-the-people the-God what-he-brought-about at the-people

בְּפִתְאֹם הָיָה הַדָּבָר׃ (30:1) וַיִּשְׁלַח יְחִזְקִיָּהוּ עַל־ כָּל־ יִשְׂרָאֵל
Israel all-of to Hezekiah and-he-sent (30:1) the-thing he-was in-quickness

וִיהוּדָה וְגַם־ אִגְּרוֹת כָּתַב עַל־ אֶפְרַיִם וּמְנַשֶּׁה לָבוֹא
to-come and-Manasseh Ephraim to he-wrote letters and-also and-Judah

לְבֵית־ יְהוָה בִּירוּשָׁלִַם לַעֲשׂוֹת פֶּסַח לַיהוָה אֱלֹהֵי
God-of to-Yahweh Passover to-celebrate in-Jerusalem Yahweh to-temple-of

יִשְׂרָאֵל׃ (2) וַיִּוָּעַץ הַמֶּלֶךְ וְשָׂרָיו וְכָל־
and-whole-of and-officials-of-him the-king and-he-decided (2) Israel

הַקָּהָל בִּירוּשָׁלִָם לַעֲשׂוֹת הַפֶּסַח בַּחֹדֶשׁ הַשֵּׁנִי׃
the-second in-the-month the-Passover to-celebrate in-Jerusalem the-assembly

(3) כִּי לֹא יָכְלוּ לַעֲשֹׂתוֹ בָּעֵת הַהִיא כִּי
because the-that at-the-time to-celebrate-him they-were-able not for (3)

brought sacrifices and thank
offerings, and all whose hearts
were willing brought burnt
offerings.
32The number of burnt
offerings the assembly
brought was seventy bulls, a
hundred rams and two hun-
dred male lambs—all of them
for burnt offerings to the LORD.
33The animals consecrated as
sacrifices amounted to six
hundred bulls and three thousand sheep and goats. 34The
priests, however, were too few
to skin all the burnt offerings;
so their kinsmen the Levites
helped them until the task was
finished and until other
priests had been consecrated,
for the Levites had been more
conscientious in consecrating
themselves than the priests
had been. 35There were burnt
offerings in abundance, together with the fat of the fellowship offerings[s] and the
drink offerings that accompanied the burnt offerings.
So the service of the temple
of the LORD was reestablished.
36Hezekiah and all the people
rejoiced at what God had
brought about for his people,
because it was done so quickly.

Hezekiah Celebrates the Passover

30 Hezekiah sent word to
all Israel and Judah and
also wrote letters to Ephraim
and Manasseh, inviting them
to come to the temple of the
LORD in Jerusalem and celebrate the Passover to the LORD,
the God of Israel. 2The king
and his officials and the whole
assembly in Jerusalem decided
to celebrate the Passover in the
second month. 3They had not
been able to celebrate it at the
regular time because not

s35 Traditionally *peace offerings*

הַכֹּהֲנִים לֹא־ הִתְקַדְּשׁוּ לְמַדַּי וְהָעָם לֹא־
not and-the-people as-what-enough they-consecrated-themselves not the-priests

נֶאֶסְפוּ לִירוּשָׁלִָם׃ (4) וַיִּשַׁר הַדָּבָר בְּעֵינֵי הַמֶּלֶךְ
the-king in-eyes-of the-plan and-he-was-right (4) in-Jerusalem they-assembled

וּבְעֵינֵי כָּל־ הַקָּהָל׃ (5) וַיַּעֲמִידוּ דָבָר לְהַעֲבִיר
to-send issue and-they-decided (5) the-assembly whole-of and-in-eyes-of

קוֹל בְּכָל־ יִשְׂרָאֵל מִבְּאֵר־ שֶׁבַע וְעַד־ דָּן לָבוֹא
to-come Dan even-to Sheba from-Beer Israel through-all-of proclamation

לַעֲשׂוֹת פֶּסַח לַיהוָה אֱלֹהֵי־ יִשְׂרָאֵל בִּירוּשָׁלִָם כִּי לֹא
not for to-Jerusalem Israel God-of to-Yahweh Passover to-celebrate

לָרֹב עָשׂוּ כַּכָּתוּב׃ (6) וַיֵּלְכוּ
and-they-went (6) as-the-one-being-written they-celebrated in-large-number

הָרָצִים בָּאִגְּרוֹת מִיַּד הַמֶּלֶךְ
the-king from-hand-of with-the-letters the-ones-being-couriers

וְשָׂרָיו בְּכָל־ יִשְׂרָאֵל וִיהוּדָה וּכְמִצְוַת
and-at-command-of and-Judah Israel through-all-of and-officials-of-him

הַמֶּלֶךְ לֵאמֹר בְּנֵי יִשְׂרָאֵל שׁוּבוּ אֶל־ יְהוָה אֱלֹהֵי אַבְרָהָם יִצְחָק
Isaac Abraham God-of Yahweh to return! Israel people-of to-say the-king

וְיִשְׂרָאֵל וְיָשֹׁב אֶל־ הַפְּלֵיטָה הַנִּשְׁאֶרֶת לָכֶם
of-you the-one-being-left the-escapee to that-he-may-return and-Israel

מִכַּף מַלְכֵי אַשּׁוּר׃ (7) וְאַל־ תִּהְיוּ כַּאֲבוֹתֵיכֶם
like-fathers-of-you you-be and-not (7) Assyria kings-of from-hand-of

וְכַאֲחֵיכֶם אֲשֶׁר מָעֲלוּ בַּיהוָה אֱלֹהֵי
God-of to-Yahweh they-were-unfaithful who and-like-brothers-of-you

אֲבוֹתֵיהֶם וַיִּתְּנֵם לְשַׁמָּה כַּאֲשֶׁר אַתֶּם רֹאִים׃
ones-seeing you just-as as-object-of-horror so-he-made-them fathers-of-them

(8) עַתָּה אַל־ תַּקְשׁוּ עָרְפְּכֶם כַּאֲבוֹתֵיכֶם תְּנוּ־ יָד
hand submit! as-fathers-of-you neck-of-you you-make-stiff not now (8)

לַיהוָה וּבֹאוּ לְמִקְדָּשׁוֹ אֲשֶׁר הִקְדִּישׁ לְעוֹלָם
to-forever he-consecrated which to-sanctuary-of-him and-come! to-Yahweh

וְעִבְדוּ אֶת־ יְהוָה אֱלֹהֵיכֶם וְיָשֹׁב מִכֶּם חֲרוֹן
fierceness-of from-you so-he-will-turn God-of-you Yahweh *** and-serve!

אַפּוֹ׃ (9) כִּי בְשׁוּבְכֶם עַל־ יְהוָה אֲחֵיכֶם
brothers-of-you Yahweh to when-to-return-you if (9) anger-of-him

וּבְנֵיכֶם לְרַחֲמִים לִפְנֵי שׁוֹבֵיהֶם וְלָשׁוּב
and-to-come-back ones-capturing-them before to-compassions and-children-of-you

לָאָרֶץ הַזֹּאת כִּי־ חַנּוּן וְרַחוּם יְהוָה אֱלֹהֵיכֶם וְלֹא־
and-not God-of-you Yahweh and-compassionate gracious for the-this to-the-land

enough priests had consecrated themselves and the people
had not assembled in Jerusalem. 4The plan seemed right
both to the king and to the
whole assembly. 5They de-
cided to send a proclamation
throughout Israel, from Beersheba to Dan, calling the
people to come to Jerusalem
and celebrate the Passover to
the LORD, the God of Israel. It
had not been celebrated in
large numbers according to
what was written.
6At the king's command,
couriers went throughout Israel and Judah with letters from
the king and from his officials,
which read:

"People of Israel, return
to the LORD, the God of
Abraham, Isaac and Israel,
that he may return to you
who are left, who have escaped from the hand of the
kings of Assyria. 7Do not be
like your fathers and brothers, who were unfaithful to
the LORD, the God of their
fathers, so that he made
them an object of horror, as
you see. 8Do not be
stiff-necked, as your fathers
were; submit to the LORD.
Come to the sanctuary,
which he has consecrated
forever. Serve the LORD
your God, so that his fierce
anger will turn away from
you. 9If you return to the
LORD, then your brothers
and your children will be
shown compassion by their
captors and will come back
to this land, for the LORD
your God is gracious and
compassionate. He will not

יָסִיר פָּנִים מִכֶּם אִם־ תָּשׁוּבוּ אֵלָיו׃ וַיִּהְיוּ
and-they-were (10) to-him you-return if from-you faces he-will-turn

הָרָצִים עֹבְרִים מֵעִיר ׀ לָעִיר בְּאֶרֶץ־ אֶפְרַיִם
Ephraim in-land-of to-town from-town ones-going the-ones-being-couriers

וּמְנַשֶּׁה וְעַד־ זְבֻלוּן וַיִּהְיוּ מַשְׂחִיקִים עֲלֵיהֶם
against-them ones-scorning but-they-were Zebulun and-as-far-as and-Manasseh

וּמַלְעִגִים בָּם׃ אַךְ־ אֲנָשִׁים מֵאָשֵׁר וּמְנַשֶּׁה
and-Manasseh from-Asher men nevertheless (11) at-them and-ones-ridiculing

וּמִזְּבֻלוּן נִכְנְעוּ וַיָּבֹאוּ לִירוּשָׁלָםִ׃ גַּם
also (12) to-Jerusalem and-they-went they-humbled-themselves and-from-Zebulun

בִּיהוּדָה הָיְתָה יַד הָאֱלֹהִים לָתֵת לָהֶם לֵב אֶחָד לַעֲשׂוֹת
to-carry-out one mind to-them to-give the-God hand-of she-was in-Judah

מִצְוַת הַמֶּלֶךְ וְהַשָּׂרִים בִּדְבַר יְהוָה׃ וַיֵּאָסְפוּ
and-they-assembled (13) Yahweh at-word-of and-the-officials the-king order-of

יְרוּשָׁלַםִ עַם־ רָב לַעֲשׂוֹת אֶת־ חַג הַמַּצּוֹת
the-Unleavened-Breads Feast-of *** to-celebrate large people Jerusalem

בַּחֹדֶשׁ הַשֵּׁנִי קָהָל לָרֹב מְאֹד׃ וַיָּקֻמוּ
and-they-rose (14) very as-large crowd the-second in-the-month

וַיָּסִירוּ אֶת־ הַמִּזְבְּחוֹת אֲשֶׁר בִּירוּשָׁלָםִ וְאֵת כָּל־
all-of and in-Jerusalem that the-altars *** and-they-removed

הַמְקַטְּרוֹת הֵסִירוּ וַיַּשְׁלִיכוּ לְנַחַל קִדְרוֹן׃
Kidron into-Valley-of and-they-threw they-cleared the-incense-altars

וַיִּשְׁחֲטוּ הַפֶּסַח בְּאַרְבָּעָה עָשָׂר לַחֹדֶשׁ
of-the-month ten on-four the-Passover-lamb and-they-slaughtered (15)

הַשֵּׁנִי וְהַכֹּהֲנִים וְהַלְוִיִּם נִכְלְמוּ
they-were-ashamed and-the-Levites and-the-priests the-second

וַיִּתְקַדְּשׁוּ וַיָּבִיאוּ עֹלוֹת בֵּית
temple-of burnt-offerings and-they-brought and-they-consecrated-themselves

יְהוָה׃ וַיַּעַמְדוּ עַל־ עָמְדָם כְּמִשְׁפָּטָם
as-prescription-of-them position-of-them at then-they-took-up (16) Yahweh

כְּתוֹרַת מֹשֶׁה אִישׁ־ הָאֱלֹהִים הַכֹּהֲנִים זֹרְקִים אֶת־ הַדָּם
the-blood *** ones-sprinkling the-priests the-God man-of Moses as-Law-of

מִיַּד הַלְוִיִּם׃ כִּי־ רַבַּת בַּקָּהָל אֲשֶׁר לֹא־
not who in-the-crowd many since (17) the-Levites from-hand-of

הִתְקַדָּשׁוּ וְהַלְוִיִּם עַל־ שְׁחִיטַת הַפְּסָחִים
the-Passover-lambs killing-of for then-the-Levites they-consecrated-themselves

לְכֹל לֹא טָהוֹר לְהַקְדִּישׁ לַיהוָה׃ כִּי מַרְבִּית הָעָם
the-people most-of although (18) to-Yahweh to-consecrate clean not for-all

turn his face from you if
you return to him."

10 The couriers went from
town to town in Ephraim and
Manasseh, as far as Zebulun,
but the people scorned and
ridiculed them. 11 Nevertheless, some men of Asher,
Manasseh and Zebulun hum-
bled themselves and went to
Jerusalem. 12 Also in Judah the
hand of God was on the
people to give them unity of
mind to carry out what the
king and his officials had ordered, following the word of
the LORD.
13 A very large crowd of
people assembled in Jerusalem
to celebrate the Feast of Unleavened Bread in the second
month. 14 They removed the altars in Jerusalem and cleared
away the incense altars and
threw them into the Kidron
Valley.
15 They slaughtered the Passover lamb on the fourteenth
day of the second month. The
priests and the Levites were
ashamed and consecrated
themselves and brought burnt
offerings to the temple of the
LORD. 16 Then they took up
their regular positions as prescribed in the Law of Moses
the man of God. The priests
sprinkled the blood handed to
them by the Levites. 17 Since
many in the crowd had not
consecrated themselves, the
Levites had to kill the Passover
lambs for all those who were
not ceremonially clean and
could not consecrate ⌞their
lambs⌟ to the LORD. 18 Although
most of the many people who

רַבַּת מֵאֶפְרַיִם וּמְנַשֶּׁה יִשָּׂשכָר וּזְבֻלוּן לֹא הִטֶּהָרוּ
they-purified-themselves not and-Zebulun Issachar and-Manasseh from-Ephraim many

כִּי־ אָכְלוּ אֶת־ הַפֶּסַח בְּלֹא כַכָּתוּב כִּי
but to-the-thing-being-written in-contrary the-Passover *** they-ate yet

הִתְפַּלֵּל יְחִזְקִיָּהוּ עֲלֵיהֶם לֵאמֹר יְהוָה הַטּוֹב יְכַפֵּר בְּעַד׃
to may-he-pardon the-good Yahweh to-say for-them Hezekiah he-prayed

כָּל־ לְבָבוֹ הֵכִין לִדְרוֹשׁ הָאֱלֹהִים ׀ יְהוָה אֱלֹהֵי אֲבוֹתָיו
fathers-of-him God-of Yahweh the-God to-seek he-set heart-of-him every-of (19)

וְלֹא כְּטָהֳרַת הַקֹּדֶשׁ׃ וַיִּשְׁמַע יְהוָה אֶל־ יְחִזְקִיָּהוּ
Hezekiah to Yahweh and-he-heard (20) the-sanctuary as-cleanness-of even-not

וַיִּרְפָּא אֶת־ הָעָם׃ וַיַּעֲשׂוּ בְנֵי־ יִשְׂרָאֵל
Israel sons-of and-they-celebrated (21) the-people *** and-he-healed

הַנִּמְצְאִים בִּירוּשָׁלִַם אֶת־ חַג הַמַּצּוֹת שִׁבְעַת
seven-of the-Unleavened-Breads Feast-of *** in-Jerusalem the-ones-being-found

יָמִים בְּשִׂמְחָה גְדוֹלָה וּמְהַלְלִים לַיהוָה יוֹם ׀ בְּיוֹם הַלְוִיִּם
the-Levites by-day day to-Yahweh while-ones-singing great with-rejoicing days

וְהַכֹּהֲנִים בִּכְלֵי־ עֹז לַיהוָה׃ וַיְדַבֵּר
and-he-spoke (22) to-Yahweh praise with-instruments-of and-the-priests

יְחִזְקִיָּהוּ עַל־ לֵב כָּל־ הַלְוִיִּם הַמַּשְׂכִּילִים
the-ones-showing-understanding the-Levites all-of heart-of to Hezekiah

שֵׂכֶל־ טוֹב לַיהוָה וַיֹּאכְלוּ אֶת־ הַמּוֹעֵד שִׁבְעַת
seven-of the-assigned-portion *** and-they-ate of-Yahweh good understanding-of

הַיָּמִים מְזַבְּחִים זִבְחֵי שְׁלָמִים וּמִתְוַדִּים לַיהוָה
to-Yahweh and-ones-praising fellowships offerings-of ones-offering the-days

אֱלֹהֵי אֲבוֹתֵיהֶם׃ וַיִּוָּעֲצוּ כָּל־ הַקָּהָל
the-assembly whole-of then-they-agreed (23) fathers-of-them God-of

לַעֲשׂוֹת שִׁבְעַת יָמִים אֲחֵרִים וַיַּעֲשׂוּ שִׁבְעַת־ יָמִים
days seven-of so-they-celebrated ones-more days seven-of to-celebrate

שִׂמְחָה׃ כִּי חִזְקִיָּהוּ מֶלֶךְ־ יְהוּדָה הֵרִים לַקָּהָל
for-the-assembly he-provided Judah king-of Hezekiah now (24) joyfully

אֶלֶף פָּרִים וְשִׁבְעַת אֲלָפִים צֹאן וְהַשָּׂרִים הֵרִימוּ
they-provided and-the-officials sheep thousands and-seven-of bulls thousand-of

לַקָּהָל פָּרִים אֶלֶף וְצֹאן עֲשֶׂרֶת אֲלָפִים
thousands ten-of and-sheep thousand bulls for-the-assembly

וַיִּתְקַדְּשׁוּ כֹהֲנִים לָרֹב׃ וַיִּשְׂמְחוּ ׀
and-they-rejoiced (25) in-number priests and-they-consecrated-themselves

כָּל־ קְהַל יְהוּדָה וְהַכֹּהֲנִים וְהַלְוִיִּם וְכָל־
and-all-of and-the-Levites and-the-priests Judah assembly-of entire-of

came from Ephraim, Manasseh, Issachar and Zebulun had not purified themselves, yet they ate the Passover, contrary to what was written. But Hezekiah prayed for them, saying, "May the LORD, who is good, pardon everyone
[19]who sets his heart on seeking God—the LORD, the God of his fathers—even if he is not clean according to the rules of the sanctuary."
[20]And the LORD heard Hezekiah and healed the people.
[21]The Israelites who were present in Jerusalem celebrated the Feast of Unleavened Bread for seven days with great rejoicing, while the Levites and priests sang to the LORD every day, accompanied by the LORD's instruments of praise.[t]
[22]Hezekiah spoke encouragingly to all the Levites, who showed good understanding of the service of the LORD. For the seven days they ate their assigned portion and offered fellowship offerings[u] and praised the LORD, the God of their fathers.
[23]The whole assembly then agreed to celebrate the festival seven more days; so for another seven days they celebrated joyfully.
[24]Hezekiah king of Judah provided a thousand bulls and seven thousand sheep and goats for the assembly, and the officials provided them with a thousand bulls and ten thousand sheep and goats. A great number of priests consecrated themselves.
[25]The entire assembly of Judah rejoiced,

[t]21 Or *priests praised the LORD every day with resounding instruments belonging to the LORD*
[u]22 Traditionally *peace offerings*

הַבָּאִים	וְהַגֵּרִים	מִיִּשְׂרָאֵל	הַבָּאִים	הַקָּהָל
the-ones-coming	and-the-aliens	from-Israel	the-ones-coming	the-assembly

וַתְּהִי שִׂמְחָה־		בִּיהוּדָה׃	וְהַיּוֹשְׁבִים	יִשְׂרָאֵל	מֵאֶרֶץ
joy and-she-was	(26)	in-Judah	and-the-ones-living	Israel	from-land-of

יִשְׂרָאֵל	מֶלֶךְ	דָּוִיד	בֶן־	שְׁלֹמֹה	מִימֵי	כִּי	בִּירוּשָׁלִַם	גְדוֹלָה
Israel	king-of	David	son-of	Solomon	since-days-of	for	in-Jerusalem	great

הַלְוִיִּם	הַכֹּהֲנִים	וַיָּקֻמוּ		בִּירוּשָׁלִָם׃	כָזֹאת	לֹא
the-Levites	the-priests	and-they-stood	(27)	in-Jerusalem	like-this	not

בְּקוֹלָם	וַיִּשָּׁמַע	הָעָם	אֶת־	וַיְבָרְכוּ
to-voice-of-them	and-he-was-heard	the-people	***	and-they-blessed

לַשָּׁמָיִם׃	קָדְשׁוֹ	לִמְעוֹן	תְפִלָּתָם	וַתָּבוֹא
to-the-heavens	holy-place-of-him	to-dwelling-of	prayer-of-them	for-she-reached

יִשְׂרָאֵל	כָּל־	יָצְאוּ	זֹאת	כָּל־	וּכְכַלּוֹת	
Israel	all-of	they-went-out	this	all-of	and-when-to-end	(31:1)

הַמַּצֵּבוֹת	וַיְשַׁבְּרוּ	יְהוּדָה	לְעָרֵי	הַנִּמְצְאִים
the-sacred-stones	and-they-smashed	Judah	to-towns-of	the-ones-being-found

הַבָּמוֹת	אֶת־	וַיְנַתְּצוּ	הָאֲשֵׁרִים	וַיְגַדְּעוּ
the-high-places	***	and-they-destroyed	the-Asherah-poles	and-they-cut-down

וּמְנַשֶּׁה	וּבְאֶפְרַיִם	וּבִנְיָמִן	יְהוּדָה	מִכָּל־	הַמִּזְבְּחֹת	וְאֶת־
and-Manasseh	and-in-Ephraim	and-Benjamin	Judah	through-all-of	the-altars	and

אִישׁ	יִשְׂרָאֵל	בְּנֵי	כָּל־	וַיָּשׁוּבוּ	לְכַלֵּה	עַד־
each	Israel	sons-of	all-of	then-they-returned	to-finish	until

אֶת־	יְחִזְקִיָּהוּ	וַיַּעֲמֵד		לְעָרֵיהֶם׃	לַאֲחֻזָּתוֹ
***	Hezekiah	and-he-assigned	(2)	to-towns-of-them	to-property-of-him

אִישׁ ׀	מַחְלְקוֹתָם	עַל־	וְהַלְוִיִּם	הַכֹּהֲנִים	מַחְלְקוֹת
each	divisions-of-them	by	and-the-Levites	the-priests	divisions-of

לְעֹלָה	וְלַלְוִיִּם	לַכֹּהֲנִים	עֲבֹדָתוֹ	כְּפִי
for-burnt-offering	and-as-the-Levites	as-the-priests	duty-of-him	according-to

וּלְהַלֵּל	וּלְהֹדוֹת	לְשָׁרֵת	וְלִשְׁלָמִים
and-to-praise	and-to-give-thanks	to-minister	and-for-fellowship-offerings

מִן־	הַמֶּלֶךְ	וּמְנָת		יְהוָה׃	מַחֲנוֹת	בְּשַׁעֲרֵי
from	the-king	and-contribution-of	(3)	Yahweh	dwellings-of	at-gates-of

הַבֹּקֶר	לְעֹלוֹת	לָעֹלוֹת	רְכוּשׁוֹ
the-morning	for-burnt-offerings-of	for-the-burnt-offerings	possession-of-him

וְלֶחֳדָשִׁים	לַשַּׁבָּתוֹת	וְהָעֹלוֹת	וְהָעֶרֶב
and-on-the-New-Moons	on-the-Sabbaths	and-the-burnt-offerings	and-the-evening

יְהוָה׃	בְּתוֹרַת	כַּכָּתוּב	וְלַמֹּעֲדִים
Yahweh	in-Law-of	as-the-thing-being-written	and-on-the-appointed-feasts

along with the priests and Levites and all who had assembled from Israel, including the aliens who had come from Israel and those who lived in Judah. [26]There was great joy in Jerusalem, for since the days of Solomon son of David king of Israel there had been nothing like this in Jerusalem. [27]The priests and the Levites stood to bless the people, and God heard them, for their prayer reached heaven, his holy dwelling place.

31 When all this had ended, the Israelites who were there went out to the towns of Judah, smashed the sacred stones and cut down the Asherah poles. They destroyed the high places and the altars throughout Judah and Benjamin and in Ephraim and Manasseh. After they had destroyed all of them, the Israelites returned to their own towns and to their own property.

Contributions for Worship

[2]Hezekiah assigned the priests and Levites to divisions—each of them according to their duties as priests or Levites—to offer burnt offerings and fellowship offerings,[v] to minister, to give thanks and to sing praises at the gates of the LORD's dwelling. [3]The king contributed from his own possessions for the morning and evening burnt offerings and for the burnt offerings on the Sabbaths, New Moons and appointed feasts as written in

[v]2 Traditionally *peace offerings*

וַיֹּאמֶר לָעָם לְיוֹשְׁבֵי יְרוּשָׁלַ͏ִם לָתֵת
to-give Jerusalem to-ones-living-of to-the-people and-he-ordered (4)

מְנָת הַכֹּהֲנִים וְהַלְוִיִּם לְמַעַן יֶחֶזְקוּ
they-could-devote-themselves so-that and-the-Levites the-priests portion-of

בְּתוֹרַת יְהוָה׃ וְכִפְרֹץ הַדָּבָר הִרְבּוּ בְנֵי־
sons-of they-gave-generously the-order and-as-to-go-out (5) Yahweh to-Law-of

יִשְׂרָאֵל רֵאשִׁית דָּגָן תִּירוֹשׁ וְיִצְהָר וּדְבַשׁ וְכֹל תְּבוּאַת
produce-of and-all-of and-honey and-oil new-wine grain firstfruit-of Israel

שָׂדֶה וּמַעְשַׂר הַכֹּל לָרֹב הֵבִיאוּ׃ וּבְנֵי
and-men-of (6) they-brought as-great-amount the-whole and-tithe-of field

יִשְׂרָאֵל וִיהוּדָה הַיּוֹשְׁבִים בְּעָרֵי יְהוּדָה גַּם־ הֵם מַעְשַׂר בָּקָר
herd tithe-of they also Judah in-towns-of the-ones-living and-Judah Israel

וָצֹאן וּמַעְשַׂר קֳדָשִׁים הַמְקֻדָּשִׁים לַיהוָה
to-Yahweh the-ones-being-dedicated holy-things and-tithe-of and-flock

אֱלֹהֵיהֶם הֵבִיאוּ וַיִּתְּנוּ עֲרֵמוֹת עֲרֵמוֹת׃ בַּחֹדֶשׁ
in-the-month (7) heaps heaps and-they-piled they-brought God-of-them

הַשְּׁלִשִׁי הֵחֵלּוּ הָעֲרֵמוֹת לִיסּוֹד וּבַחֹדֶשׁ הַשְּׁבִיעִי
the-seventh and-in-the-month to-pile the-heaps they-began the-third

כִּלּוּ׃ וַיָּבֹאוּ יְחִזְקִיָּהוּ וְהַשָּׂרִים וַיִּרְאוּ
and-they-saw and-the-officials Hezekiah when-they-came (8) they-finished

אֶת־ הָעֲרֵמוֹת וַיְבָרְכוּ אֶת־ יְהוָה וְאֵת עַמּוֹ יִשְׂרָאֵל׃
Israel people-of-him and Yahweh *** then-they-blessed the-heaps ***

וַיִּדְרֹשׁ יְחִזְקִיָּהוּ עַל־ הַכֹּהֲנִים וְהַלְוִיִּם עַל־ הָעֲרֵמוֹת׃
the-heaps about and-the-Levites the-priests to Hezekiah and-he-asked (9)

וַיֹּאמֶר אֵלָיו עֲזַרְיָהוּ הַכֹּהֵן הָרֹאשׁ לְבֵית
from-family-of the-chief the-priest Azariah to-him and-he-answered (10)

צָדוֹק וַיֹּאמֶר מֵהָחֵל הַתְּרוּמָה לָבִיא בֵית־ יְהוָה
Yahweh temple-of to-bring the-contribution since-to-begin and-he-said Zadok

אָכוֹל וְשָׂבוֹעַ וְהוֹתֵר עַד־ לָרוֹב כִּי יְהוָה
Yahweh because as-plenty to and-to-have-spare and-to-have-enough to-eat

בֵּרַךְ אֶת־ עַמּוֹ וְהַנּוֹתָר אֶת־ הֶהָמוֹן
the-great-amount *** and-the-one-being-left-over people-of-him *** he-blessed

הַזֶּה׃ וַיֹּאמֶר יְחִזְקִיָּהוּ לְהָכִין לְשָׁכוֹת בְּבֵית
in-temple-of storerooms to-prepare Hezekiah and-he-ordered (11) the-this

יְהוָה וַיָּכִינוּ׃ וַיָּבִיאוּ אֶת־ הַתְּרוּמָה
the-contribution *** then-they-brought (12) and-they-prepared Yahweh

וְהַמַּעֲשֵׂר וְהַקֳּדָשִׁים בֶּאֱמוּנָה וַעֲלֵיהֶם נָגִיד
leader and-over-them in-faithfulness and-the-dedicated-gifts and-the-tithe

the Law of the LORD. [4]He ordered the people living in
Jerusalem to give the portion
due the priests and Levites so
they could devote themselves
to the Law of the LORD. [5]As
soon as the order went out, the
Israelites generously gave the
firstfruits of their grain, new
wine, oil and honey and all
that the fields produced. They
brought a great amount, a
tithe of everything. [6]The men
of Israel and Judah who lived
in the towns of Judah also
brought a tithe of their herds
and flocks and a tithe of the
holy things dedicated to the
LORD their God, and they piled
them in heaps. [7]They began
doing this in the third month
and finished in the seventh
month. [8]When Hezekiah and
his officials came and saw the
heaps, they praised the LORD
and blessed his people Israel.

[9]Hezekiah asked the priests
and Levites about the heaps;
[10]and Azariah the chief priest,
from the family of Zadok, answered, "Since the people began to bring their contributions to the temple of the
LORD, we have had enough to
eat and plenty to spare, because the LORD has blessed his
people, and this great amount
is left over."

[11]Hezekiah gave orders to
prepare storerooms in the
temple of the LORD, and this
was done. [12]Then they faithfully brought in the contributions, tithes and dedicated

כּוֹנַנְיָהוּ הַלֵּוִי וְשִׁמְעִי אָחִיהוּ מִשְׁנֶה׃ (13) וִיחִיאֵל
Conaniah the-Levite and-Shimei brother-of-him next (13) and-Jehiel

וַעֲזַזְיָהוּ וְנַחַת וַעֲשָׂהאֵל וִירִימוֹת וְיוֹזָבָד וֶאֱלִיאֵל
and-Azaziah and-Nahath and-Asahel and-Jerimoth and-Jozabad and-Eliel

וְיִסְמַכְיָהוּ וּמַחַת וּבְנָיָהוּ פְּקִידִים מִיַּד כּוֹנַנְיָהוּ
and-Ismakiah and-Mahath and-Benaiah supervisors under-hand-of Conaniah

וְשִׁמְעִי אָחִיו בְּמִפְקַד יְחִזְקִיָּהוּ הַמֶּלֶךְ וַעֲזַרְיָהוּ
and-Shimei brother-of-him by-appointment-of Hezekiah the-king and-Azariah

נְגִיד בֵּית־ הָאֱלֹהִים׃ (14) וְקוֹרֵא בֶן־ יִמְנָה הַלֵּוִי
official-of temple-of the-God (14) and-Kore son-of Imnah the-Levite

הַשּׁוֹעֵר לַמִּזְרָחָה עַל נִדְבוֹת הָאֱלֹהִים
the-gatekeeper of-to-the-east over freewill-offerings-of the-God

לָתֵת תְּרוּמַת יְהוָה וְקָדְשֵׁי
to-distribute contribution-of Yahweh and-consecrated-ones-of

הַקֳּדָשִׁים׃ (15) וְעַל־ יָדוֹ עֵדֶן וּמִנְיָמִן וְיֵשׁוּעַ
the-consecrated-gifts (15) and-at hand-of-him Eden and-Miniamin and-Jeshua

וּשְׁמַעְיָהוּ אֲמַרְיָהוּ וּשְׁכַנְיָהוּ בְּעָרֵי הַכֹּהֲנִים בֶּאֱמוּנָה
and-Shemaiah Amariah and-Shecaniah in-towns-of the-priests in-faithfulness

לָתֵת לַאֲחֵיהֶם בְּמַחְלְקוֹת כַּגָּדוֹל כַּקָּטָן׃
to-distribute to-fellows-of-them by-divisions as-the-old so-the-young

(16) מִלְּבַד הִתְיַחְשָׂם לִזְכָרִים מִבֶּן שָׁלוֹשׁ שָׁנִים
(16) in-addition-to to-be-recorded-them to-males from-son-of three years

וּלְמַעְלָה לְכָל־ הַבָּא לְבֵית־ יְהוָה לִדְבַר־
and-to-upward to-all-of the-one-entering into-temple-of Yahweh for-duty-of

יוֹם בְּיוֹמוֹ לַעֲבוֹדָתָם בְּמִשְׁמְרוֹתָם
day in-day-of-him for-task-of-them according-to-responsibilities-of-them

כְּמַחְלְקוֹתֵיהֶם׃ (17) וְאֵת הִתְיַחֵשׂ הַכֹּהֲנִים לְבֵית
by-divisions-of-them (17) and to-be-enrolled the-priests by-family-of

אֲבוֹתֵיהֶם וְהַלְוִיִּם מִבֶּן עֶשְׂרִים שָׁנָה וּלְמָעְלָה
fathers-of-them and-the-Levites from-son-of twenty year and-to-upward

בְּמִשְׁמְרוֹתֵיהֶם בְּמַחְלְקוֹתֵיהֶם׃
according-to-responsibilities-of-them by-divisions-of-them

(18) וּלְהִתְיַחֵשׂ בְּכָל־ טַפָּם נְשֵׁיהֶם
(18) and-to-be-recorded of-all-of little-one-of-them wives-of-them

וּבְנֵיהֶם וּבְנוֹתֵיהֶם לְכָל־ קָהָל כִּי
and-sons-of-them and-daughters-of-them of-whole-of community for

בֶאֱמוּנָתָם יִתְקַדְּשׁוּ־ קֹדֶשׁ׃
in-faithfulness-of-them they-consecrated-themselves consecration

gifts. Conaniah, a Levite, was in charge of these things, and his brother Shimei was next in rank.
13Jehiel, Azaziah, Nahath, Asahel, Jerimoth, Jozabad, Eliel, Ismakiah, Mahath and Benaiah were supervisors under Conaniah and Shimei his brother, by appointment of King Hezekiah and Azariah the official in charge of the temple of God.
14Kore son of Imnah the Levite, keeper of the East Gate, was in charge of the freewill offerings given to God, distributing the contributions made to the LORD and also the consecrated gifts.
15Eden, Miniamin, Jeshua, Shemaiah, Amariah and Shecaniah assisted him faithfully in the towns of the priests, distributing to their fellow priests according to their divisions, old and young alike.
16In addition, they distributed to the males three years old or more whose names were in the genealogical records—all who would enter the temple of the LORD to perform the daily duties of their various tasks, according to their responsibilities and their divisions.
17And they distributed to the priests enrolled by their families in the genealogical records and likewise to the Levites twenty years old or more, according to their responsibilities and their divisions.
18They included all the little ones, the wives, and the sons and daughters of the whole community listed in these genealogical records. For they were faithful in consecrating themselves.

°12 ק כנניהו
°13 ק כנניהו

וְלִבְנֵי אַהֲרֹן הַכֹּהֲנִים בִּשְׂדֵי מִגְרַשׁ עָרֵיהֶם

towns-of-them farm-of in-lands-of the-priests Aaron and-for-descendants-of (19)

בְּכָל־ עִיר וָעִיר אֲנָשִׁים אֲשֶׁר נִקְּבוּ בְּשֵׁמוֹת לָתֵת

to-distribute by-names they-were-designated who men or-town town in-any-of

מָנוֹת לְכָל־ זָכָר בַּכֹּהֲנִים וּלְכָל־ הִתְיַחֵשׂ

to-be-recorded and-to-all-of among-the-priests male to-every-of portions

בַּלְוִיִּם׃ וַיַּעַשׂ כָּזֹאת יְחִזְקִיָּהוּ בְּכָל־ יְהוּדָה

Judah through-all-of Hezekiah as-this and-he-did (20) of-the-Levites

וַיַּעַשׂ הַטּוֹב וְהַיָּשָׁר וְהָאֱמֶת לִפְנֵי יְהוָה אֱלֹהָיו׃

God-of-him Yahweh before and-the-faithful and-the-right the-good and-he-did

וּבְכָל־ מַעֲשֶׂה אֲשֶׁר־ הֵחֵל ׀ בַּעֲבוֹדַת בֵּית־ הָאֱלֹהִים

the-God temple-of in-service-of he-undertook that deed and-in-all-of (21)

וּבַתּוֹרָה וּבַמִּצְוָה לִדְרֹשׁ לֵאלֹהָיו בְּכָל־

with-whole-of to-God-of-him to-seek and-for-the-command and-for-the-law

לְבָבוֹ עָשָׂה וְהִצְלִיחַ׃ אַחֲרֵי הַדְּבָרִים

the-things after (32:1) and-he-prospered he-worked heart-of-him

וְהָאֱמֶת הָאֵלֶּה בָּא סַנְחֵרִיב מֶלֶךְ־ אַשּׁוּר

Assyria king-of Sennacherib he-came the-these and-the-faithfulness

וַיָּבֹא בִיהוּדָה וַיִּחַן עַל־ הֶעָרִים

the-cities to and-he-laid-siege into-Judah and-he-invaded

הַבְּצֻרוֹת וַיֹּאמֶר לְבִקְעָם אֵלָיו׃ וַיַּרְא

when-he-saw (2) for-him to-conquer-them and-he-thought the-ones-being-fortified

יְחִזְקִיָּהוּ כִּי־ בָא סַנְחֵרִיב וּפָנָיו לַמִּלְחָמָה עַל־יְרוּשָׁלִָם׃

Jerusalem on to-the-war and-faces-of-him Sennacherib he-came that Hezekiah

וַיִּוָּעַץ עִם־ שָׂרָיו וְגִבֹּרָיו

and-military-staffs-of-him officials-of-him with then-he-consulted (3)

לִסְתּוֹם אֶת־ מֵימֵי הָעֲיָנוֹת אֲשֶׁר מִחוּץ לָעִיר

to-the-city at-outside-of that the-springs waters-of *** to-block-off

וַיַּעְזְרוּהוּ׃ וַיִּקָּבְצוּ עַם־ רָב וַיִּסְתְּמוּ אֶת־

*** and-they-blocked large force and-they-assembled (4) and-they-helped-him

כָּל־ הַמַּעְיָנוֹת וְאֶת־ הַנַּחַל הַשּׁוֹטֵף בְּתוֹךְ־ הָאָרֶץ לֵאמֹר

to-say the-land through the-one-flowing the-stream and the-springs all-of

לָמָּה יָבוֹאוּ מַלְכֵי אַשּׁוּר וּמָצְאוּ מַיִם רַבִּים׃

ones-plentiful waters and-they-find Assyria kings-of should-they-come why?

וַיִּתְחַזַּק וַיִּבֶן אֶת־ כָּל־ הַחוֹמָה

the-wall all-of *** and-he-repaired then-he-worked-hard (5)

הַפְּרוּצָה וַיַּעַל עַל־ הַמִּגְדָּלוֹת וְלַחוּצָה הַחוֹמָה

the-wall and-to-the-outside the-towers on and-he-built the-one-being-broken

---

19 As for the priests, the descendants of Aaron, who lived on the farm lands around their towns or in any other towns, men were designated by name to distribute portions to every male among them and to all who were recorded in the genealogies of the Levites.

20 This is what Hezekiah did throughout Judah, doing what was good and right and faithful before the LORD his God. 21 In everything that he undertook in the service of God's temple and in obedience to the law and the commands, he sought his God and worked wholeheartedly. And so he prospered.

Sennacherib Threatens Jerusalem

32 After all that Hezekiah had so faithfully done, Sennacherib king of Assyria came and invaded Judah. He laid siege to the fortified cities, thinking to conquer them for himself. 2 When Hezekiah saw that Sennacherib had come and that he intended to make war on Jerusalem, 3 he consulted with his officials and military staff about blocking off the water from the springs outside the city, and they helped him. 4 A large force of men assembled, and they blocked all the springs and the stream that flowed through the land. "Why should the kings[w] of Assyria come and find plenty of water?" they said. 5 Then he worked hard repairing all the broken sections of the wall and building towers on it. He built another wall

[w] 4 Hebrew; Septuagint and Syriac *king*

אַחֶרֶת וַיְחַזֵּק אֶת־ הַמִּלּוֹא עִיר דָּוִיד
David City-of the-supporting-terrace *** and-he-reinforced another

וַיַּעַשׂ שֶׁלַח לָרֹב וּמָגִנִּים׃ וַיִּתֵּן שָׂרֵי
officers-of and-he-appointed (6) and-shields in-number weapon and-he-made

מִלְחָמוֹת עַל־ הָעָם וַיִּקְבְּצֵם אֵלָיו אֶל־ רְחוֹב
square-of in before-him and-he-assembled-them the-people over militaries

שַׁעַר הָעִיר וַיְדַבֵּר עַל־ לְבָבָם לֵאמֹר׃ חִזְקוּ
be-strong! (7) to-say heart-of-them to and-he-spoke the-city gate-of

וְאִמְצוּ אַל־ תִּירְאוּ וְאַל־ תֵּחַתּוּ מִפְּנֵי
because-of you-be-discouraged and-not you-be-afraid not and-be-courageous!

מֶלֶךְ אַשּׁוּר וּמִלִּפְנֵי כָּל־ הֶהָמוֹן אֲשֶׁר־ עִמּוֹ כִּי־
for with-him that the-vast-army all-of and-because-of Assyria king-of

עִמָּנוּ רַב מֵעִמּוֹ׃ עִמּוֹ זְרוֹעַ בָּשָׂר וְעִמָּנוּ
but-with-us flesh arm-of with-him (8) more-than-with-him great-power with-us

יְהוָה אֱלֹהֵינוּ לְעָזְרֵנוּ וּלְהִלָּחֵם מִלְחֲמֹתֵנוּ וַיִּסָּמְכוּ
and-they-gained-confidence battles-of-us and-to-fight to-help-us God-of-us Yahweh

הָעָם עַל־ דִּבְרֵי יְחִזְקִיָּהוּ מֶלֶךְ־ יְהוּדָה׃ אַחַר זֶה שָׁלַח
he-sent this after (9) Judah king-of Hezekiah words-of from the-people

סַנְחֵרִיב מֶלֶךְ־ אַשּׁוּר עֲבָדָיו יְרוּשָׁלַיְמָה וְהוּא עַל־
against when-he to-Jerusalem officers-of-him Assyria king-of Sennacherib

לָכִישׁ וְכָל־ מֶמְשַׁלְתּוֹ עִמּוֹ עַל־ יְחִזְקִיָּהוּ מֶלֶךְ יְהוּדָה וְעַל־
and-to Judah king-of Hezekiah to with-him force-of-him and-all-of Lachish

כָּל־ יְהוּדָה אֲשֶׁר בִּירוּשָׁלִַם לֵאמֹר׃ כֹּה אָמַר סַנְחֵרִיב מֶלֶךְ
king-of Sennacherib he-says this (10) to-say in-Jerusalem who Judah all-of

אַשּׁוּר עַל־ מָה אַתֶּם בֹּטְחִים וְיֹשְׁבִים בְּמָצוֹר
under-siege and-ones-remaining ones-basing-confidence you what? on Assyria

בִּירוּשָׁלִָם׃ הֲלֹא יְחִזְקִיָּהוּ מַסִּית אֶתְכֶם לָתֵת אֶתְכֶם לָמוּת בְּרָעָב
of-hunger to-die you to-let you misleading Hezekiah not? (11) in-Jerusalem

וּבְצָמָא לֵאמֹר יְהוָה אֱלֹהֵינוּ יַצִּילֵנוּ מִכַּף מֶלֶךְ
king-of from-hand-of he-will-save-us God-of-us Yahweh to-say and-of-thirst

אַשּׁוּר׃ הֲלֹא־ הוּא יְחִזְקִיָּהוּ הֵסִיר אֶת־ בָּמֹתָיו וְאֶת־
and high-places-of-him *** he-removed Hezekiah himself not? (12) Assyria

מִזְבְּחֹתָיו וַיֹּאמֶר לִיהוּדָה וְלִירוּשָׁלִַם לֵאמֹר לִפְנֵי מִזְבֵּחַ אֶחָד
one altar before to-say and-to-Jerusalem to-Judah and-he-said altars-of-him

תִּשְׁתַּחֲווּ וְעָלָיו תַּקְטִירוּ׃ הֲלֹא תֵדְעוּ מֶה
what you-know not? (13) you-must-burn-sacrifice and-on-him you-must-worship

עָשִׂיתִי אֲנִי וַאֲבוֹתַי לְכֹל עַמֵּי הָאֲרָצוֹת הֲיָכוֹל
to-be-able? the-lands peoples-of to-all-of and-fathers-of-me I I-did

outside that one and reinforced the supporting terraces[x]
of the City of David. He also
made large numbers of weapons and shields.
6He appointed military
officers over the people and assembled them before him in
the square at the city gate and
encouraged them with these
words: 7"Be strong and courageous. Do not be afraid or discouraged because of the king
of Assyria and the vast army
with him, for there is a greater
power with us than with him.
8With him is only the arm of
flesh, but with us is the LORD
our God to help us and to fight
our battles." And the people
gained confidence from what
Hezekiah the king of Judah
said.
9Later, when Sennacherib
king of Assyria and all his
forces were laying siege to Lachish, he sent his officers to
Jerusalem with this message
for Hezekiah king of Judah
and for all the people of Judah
who were there:

10"This is what Sennacherib king of Assyria says:
On what are you basing
your confidence, that you
remain in Jerusalem under
siege? 11When Hezekiah
says, 'The LORD our God
will save us from the hand
of the king of Assyria,' he is
misleading you, to let you
die of hunger and thirst.
12Did not Hezekiah himself
remove this god's high
places and altars, saying to
Judah and Jerusalem, 'You
must worship before one
altar and burn sacrifices on
it'?
13"Do you not know what
I and my fathers have done
to all the peoples of the other lands? Were the gods of

x5 Or *the Millo*

יָכְלוּ אֱלֹהֵי גּוֹיֵ הָאֲרָצוֹת לְהַצִּיל אֶת־ אַרְצָם
land-of-them *** to-deliver the-lands nations-of gods-of were-they-able

מִיָּדִי׃ מִי בְּכָל־ אֱלֹהֵי הַגּוֹיִם הָאֵלֶּה אֲשֶׁר
that the-these the-nations gods-of of-all-of who? (14) from-hand-of-me

הֶחֱרִימוּ אֲבוֹתַי אֲשֶׁר יָכוֹל לְהַצִּיל אֶת־ עַמּוֹ
people-of-him *** to-save he-was-able who fathers-of-me they-destroyed

מִיָּדִי כִּי יוּכַל אֱלֹהֵיכֶם לְהַצִּיל אֶתְכֶם מִיָּדִי׃
from-hand-of-me you to-deliver God-of-you is-he-able how from-hand-of-me

וְעַתָּה אַל־ יַשִּׁיא אֶתְכֶם חִזְקִיָּהוּ וְאַל־ יַסִּית אֶתְכֶם
you let-him-mislead and-not Hezekiah you let-him-deceive not and-now (15)

כָּזֹאת וְאַל־ תַּאֲמִינוּ לוֹ כִּי־ לֹא יוּכַל כָּל־ אֱלוֹהַ*
god-of any-of he-was-able not for in-him you-believe and-not like-this

כָּל־ גּוֹי וּמַמְלָכָה לְהַצִּיל עַמּוֹ מִיָּדִי
from-hand-of-me people-of-him to-deliver or-kingdom nation any-of

וּמִיַּד אֲבוֹתָי אַף כִּי אֱלֹהֵיכֶם לֹא־
not gods-of-you then how-much-less fathers-of-me or-from-hand-of

יַצִּילוּ אֶתְכֶם מִיָּדִי׃ וְעוֹד דִּבְּרוּ
they-spoke and-further (16) from-hand-of-me you they-will-deliver

עֲבָדָיו עַל־ יְהוָה הָאֱלֹהִים וְעַל יְחִזְקִיָּהוּ עַבְדּוֹ׃
servant-of-him Hezekiah and-against the-God Yahweh against officers-of-him

וּסְפָרִים כָּתַב לְחָרֵף לַיהוָה אֱלֹהֵי יִשְׂרָאֵל וְלֵאמֹר
and-to-say Israel God-of to-Yahweh to-insult he-wrote and-letters (17)

עָלָיו לֵאמֹר כֵּאלֹהֵי גּוֹיֵ הָאֲרָצוֹת אֲשֶׁר לֹא־ הִצִּילוּ
they-rescued not that the-lands peoples-of as-gods-of to-say against-him

עַמָּם מִיָּדִי כֵּן לֹא־ יַצִּיל אֱלֹהֵי יְחִזְקִיָּהוּ
Hezekiah God-of he-will-rescue not so from-hand-of-me people-of-them

עַמּוֹ מִיָּדִי׃ וַיִּקְרְאוּ בְקוֹל־ גָּדוֹל יְהוּדִית
Hebrew loud with-voice then-they-called (18) from-hand-of-me people-of-him

עַל־ עַם יְרוּשָׁלִַם אֲשֶׁר עַל־ הַחוֹמָה לְיָרְאָם וּלְבַהֲלָם
and-to-make-afraid-them to-terrify-them the-wall on who Jerusalem people-of to

לְמַעַן יִלְכְּדוּ אֶת־ הָעִיר׃ וַיְדַבְּרוּ אֶל־ אֱלֹהֵי
God-of about and-they-spoke (19) the-city *** they-could-capture so-that

יְרוּשָׁלִָם כְּעַל אֱלֹהֵי עַמֵּי הָאָרֶץ מַעֲשֵׂה יְדֵי הָאָדָם׃
the-man hands-of work-of the-world peoples-of gods-of as-about Jerusalem

וַיִּתְפַּלֵּל יְחִזְקִיָּהוּ הַמֶּלֶךְ וִישַׁעְיָהוּ בֶן־ אָמוֹץ הַנָּבִיא
the-prophet Amoz son-of and-Isaiah the-king Hezekiah and-he-prayed (20)

עַל־ זֹאת וַיִּזְעֲקוּ הַשָּׁמָיִם׃ וַיִּשְׁלַח יְהוָה מַלְאָךְ
angel Yahweh and-he-sent (21) the-heavens and-they-cried-out this about

those nations ever able to deliver their land from my hand? [14]Who of all the gods of these nations that my fathers destroyed has been able to save his people from me? How then can your god deliver you from my hand? [15]Now do not let Hezekiah deceive you and mislead you like this. Do not believe him, for no god of any nation or kingdom has been able to deliver his people from my hand or the hand of my fathers. How much less will your god deliver you from my hand!"

[16]Sennacherib's officers spoke further against the LORD God and against his servant Hezekiah. [17]The king also wrote letters insulting the LORD, the God of Israel, and saying this against him: "Just as the gods of the peoples of the other lands did not rescue their people from my hand, so the god of Hezekiah will not rescue his people from my hand." [18]Then they called out in Hebrew to the people of Jerusalem who were on the wall, to terrify them and make them afraid in order to capture the city. [19]They spoke about the God of Jerusalem as they did about the gods of the other peoples of the world—the work of men's hands.

[20]King Hezekiah and the prophet Isaiah son of Amoz cried out in prayer to heaven about this. [21]And the LORD

*15 Most mss have *mappiq* in the *he* (הּ).

וַיַּכְחֵד כָּל־ גִּבּוֹר חַיִל וְנָגִיד וְשַׂר בְּמַחֲנֵה
and-he-annihilated all-of men-of fight and-leader and-officer in-camp-of

מֶלֶךְ אַשּׁוּר וַיָּשָׁב בְּבֹשֶׁת פָּנִים לְאַרְצוֹ וַיָּבֹא
king-of Assyria so-he-withdrew in-disgrace-of faces to-land-of-him and-he-went

בֵּית אֱלֹהָיו וּמִיצִיאֵו מֵעָיו שָׁם הִפִּילֻהוּ
temple-of gods-of-him and-from-sons-of loins-of-him there they-cut-down-him

בֶחָרֶב׃ (22) וַיּוֹשַׁע יְהוָה אֶת־ יְחִזְקִיָּהוּ וְאֵת ׀ יֹשְׁבֵי
with-the-sword (22) so-he-saved Yahweh *** Hezekiah and ones-living-of

יְרוּשָׁלִַם מִיַּד סַנְחֵרִיב מֶלֶךְ־ אַשּׁוּר וּמִיַּד־ כֹּל
Jerusalem from-hand-of Sennacherib king-of Assyria and-from-hand-of all

וַיְנַהֲלֵם מִסָּבִיב׃ (23) וְרַבִּים מְבִאִים מִנְחָה
and-he-took-care-of-them at-around (23) and-many ones-bringing offering

לַיהוָה לִירוּשָׁלִַם וּמִגְדָּנוֹת לִיחִזְקִיָּהוּ מֶלֶךְ יְהוּדָה
for-Yahweh to-Jerusalem and-valuable-gifts for-Hezekiah king-of Judah

וַיִּנַּשֵּׂא לְעֵינֵי כָל־ הַגּוֹיִם מֵאַחֲרֵי־ כֵן׃
and-he-was-regarded in-eyes-of all-of the-nations from-after then

(24) בַּיָּמִים הָהֵם חָלָה יְחִזְקִיָּהוּ עַד־ לָמוּת וַיִּתְפַּלֵּל
(24) in-the-days the-those he-became-ill Hezekiah until to-die and-he-prayed

אֶל־ יְהוָה וַיֹּאמֶר לוֹ וּמוֹפֵת נָתַן לוֹ׃
to Yahweh and-he-answered to-him and-miraculous-sign he-gave to-him

(25) וְלֹא־ כִגְמֻל עָלָיו הֵשִׁיב יְחִזְקִיָּהוּ כִּי גָבַהּ
(25) but-not as-kindness to-him he-responded Hezekiah but he-was-proud

לִבּוֹ וַיְהִי עָלָיו קֶצֶף וְעַל־ יְהוּדָה וִירוּשָׁלִָם׃
heart-of-him so-he-was on-him wrath and-on Judah and-Jerusalem

(26) וַיִּכָּנַע יְחִזְקִיָּהוּ בְּגֹבַהּ לִבּוֹ הוּא וְיֹשְׁבֵי
(26) then-he-repented Hezekiah of-pride-of heart-of-him he and-ones-living-of

יְרוּשָׁלִָם וְלֹא־ בָא עֲלֵיהֶם קֶצֶף יְהוָה בִּימֵי יְחִזְקִיָּהוּ׃
Jerusalem so-not he-came upon-them wrath-of Yahweh during-days-of Hezekiah

(27) וַיְהִי לִיחִזְקִיָּהוּ עֹשֶׁר וְכָבוֹד הַרְבֵּה מְאֹד וְאֹצָרוֹת
(27) and-he-was to-Hezekiah wealth and-honor to-be-great very and-treasuries

עָשָׂה־ לוֹ לְכֶסֶף וּלְזָהָב וּלְאֶבֶן יְקָרָה וְלִבְשָׂמִים
he-made for-him for-silver and-for-gold and-for-stone precious and-for-spices

וּלְמָגִנִּים וּלְכֹל כְּלֵי חֶמְדָּה׃ (28) וּמִסְכְּנוֹת
and-for-shields and-for-all-of things-of value (28) and-buildings

לִתְבוּאַת דָּגָן וְתִירוֹשׁ וְיִצְהָר וְאֻרָוֹת לְכָל־ בְּהֵמָה
for-harvest-of grain and-new-wine and-oil and-stalls for-every-of cattle

וּבְהֵמָה וַעֲדָרִים לָאֲוֵרוֹת׃ (29) וְעָרִים עָשָׂה לוֹ
and-cattle and-flocks in-the-pens (29) and-villages he-built for-him

sent an angel, who annihilated all the fighting men and the leaders and officers in the camp of the Assyrian king. So he withdrew to his own land in disgrace. And when he went into the temple of his god, some of his sons cut him down with the sword.

22 So the LORD saved Hezekiah and the people of Jerusalem from the hand of Sennacherib king of Assyria and from the hand of all others. He took care of them[y] on every
side. 23 Many brought offerings to Jerusalem for the LORD and valuable gifts for Hezekiah king of Judah. From then on he was highly regarded by all the nations.

Hezekiah's Pride, Success and Death

24 In those days Hezekiah became ill and was at the point of death. He prayed to the LORD, who answered him and gave him a miraculous
sign. 25 But Hezekiah's heart was proud and he did not respond to the kindness shown him; therefore the LORD's wrath was on him and on
Judah and Jerusalem. 26 Then Hezekiah repented of the pride of his heart, as did the people of Jerusalem; therefore the LORD's wrath did not come upon them during the days of Hezekiah.

27 Hezekiah had very great riches and honor, and he made treasuries for his silver and gold and for his precious stones, spices, shields and all
kinds of valuables. 28 He also made buildings to store the harvest of grain, new wine and oil; and he made stalls for various kinds of cattle, and
pens for the flocks. 29 He built

[y]22 Hebrew; Septuagint and Vulgate *He gave them rest*

°21 ק ומיציאי

וּמִקְנֵה־	צֹאן	וּבָקָר	לָרֹב	כִּי	נָֽתַן־	לוֹ	אֱלֹהִים	רְכ֣וּשׁ
and-acquisition-of	flock	and-herd	in-number	for	he-gave	to-him	God	richness

רָ֥ב מְאֹֽד:	(30)	וְה֣וּא	יְחִזְקִיָּ֗הוּ	סָתַם֙	אֶת־	מוֹצָ֤א	מֵימֵ֣י	גִיחוֹן֙
very great	(30)	now-he	Hezekiah	he-blocked	***	outlet-of	springs-of	Gihon

הָֽעֶלְי֔וֹן	וַֽיַּישְׁרֵם֙	לְמַ֔טָּה	מַעְרָ֖בָה	לְעִ֣יר	דָּוִ֑יד
the-upper	and-he-channeled-them	to-downward	to-west	of-City-of	David

וַיַּצְלַ֥ח	יְחִזְקִיָּ֖הוּ	בְּכָל־	מַֽעֲשֵֽׂהוּ:	(31)	וְכֵ֞ן
and-he-succeeded	Hezekiah	in-all-of	undertaking-of-him	(31)	but-this

בִּמְלִיצֵ֣י	שָׂרֵ֣י	בָּבֶ֗ל	הַֽמְשַׁלְּחִ֤ים	עָלָיו֙
when-ones-being-envoys-of	rulers-of	Babylon	the-ones-sending	to-him

לִדְרֹ֗שׁ	הַמּוֹפֵת֙	אֲשֶׁ֣ר	הָיָ֣ה	בָאָ֔רֶץ	עֲזָב֖וֹ
to-ask-about	the-miraculous-sign	that	he-occurred	in-the-land	he-left-him

הָ֣אֱלֹהִ֑ים	לְנַסּוֹת֔וֹ	לָדַ֖עַת	כָּל־	בִּלְבָבֽוֹ:	(32)	וְיֶ֨תֶר
the-God	to-test-him	to-know	all-of	in-heart-of-him	(32)	and-other-of

דִּבְרֵ֥י	יְחִזְקִיָּ֖הוּ	וַחֲסָדָ֑יו	הִנָּ֣ם	כְּתוּבִ֗ים
events-of	Hezekiah	and-acts-of-devotion-of-him	see-they!	ones-being-written

בַּחֲז֞וֹן	יְשַֽׁעְיָ֤הוּ	בֶן־	אָמוֹץ֙	הַנָּבִ֔יא	עַל־	סֵ֥פֶר	מַלְכֵֽי־	יְהוּדָ֖ה
in-vision-of	Isaiah	son-of	Amoz	the-prophet	in	book-of	kings-of	Judah

וְיִשְׂרָאֵֽל:	(33)	וַיִּשְׁכַּ֨ב	יְחִזְקִיָּ֜הוּ	עִם־	אֲבֹתָ֗יו	וַֽיִּקְבְּרֻ֙הוּ֙
and-Israel	(33)	and-he-rested	Hezekiah	with	fathers-of-him	and-they-buried-him

בְּֽמַעֲלֵה֙	קִבְרֵ֣י	בְנֵי־	דָוִ֔יד	וְכָבוֹד֙	עָֽשׂוּ־	ל֣וֹ
on-hill-of	tombs-of	descendants-of	David	and-honor	they-gave	to-him

בְמוֹת֔וֹ	כָּל־	יְהוּדָ֖ה	וְיֹשְׁבֵ֣י	יְרוּשָׁלָ֑͏ִם	וַיִּמְלֹ֛ךְ
in-death-of-him	all-of	Judah	and-ones-living-of	Jerusalem	and-he-became-king

מְנַשֶּׁ֥ה	בְנ֖וֹ	תַּחְתָּֽיו:	(33:1)	בֶּן־	שְׁתֵּ֧ים	עֶשְׂרֵ֛ה	שָׁנָ֖ה	מְנַשֶּׁ֣ה
Manasseh	son-of-him	in-place-of-him	(33:1)	son-of	two	ten	year	Manasseh

בְמָלְכ֑וֹ	וַחֲמִשִּׁ֤ים	וְחָמֵשׁ֙	שָׁנָ֔ה	מָלַ֖ךְ	בִּירוּשָׁלָֽ͏ִם:
when-to-become-king-him	and-fifty	and-five	year	he-reigned	in-Jerusalem

וַיַּ֥עַשׂ	(2)	הָרַ֖ע	בְּעֵינֵ֣י	יְהוָ֑ה	כְּתֽוֹעֲבוֹת֙
and-he-did	(2)	the-evil	in-eyes-of	Yahweh	as-detestable-practices-of

הַגּוֹיִ֔ם	אֲשֶׁר֙	הוֹרִ֣ישׁ	יְהוָ֔ה	מִפְּנֵ֖י	בְּנֵ֥י	יִשְׂרָאֵֽל:
the-nations	that	he-drove-out	Yahweh	from-before	sons-of	Israel

וַיָּ֗שָׁב	וַיִּ֙בֶן֙	אֶת־	הַבָּמ֔וֹת	אֲשֶׁ֥ר	נִתַּ֖ץ
and-he-returned	and-he-rebuilt	***	the-high-places	that	he-demolished

(3)	יְחִזְקִיָּ֣הוּ	אָבִ֑יו	וַיָּ֨קֶם	מִזְבְּחוֹת֙	לַבְּעָלִ֔ים	וַיַּ֥עַשׂ
(3)	Hezekiah	father-of-him	and-he-erected	altars	to-the-Baals	and-he-made

אֲשֵׁר֔וֹת	וַיִּשְׁתַּ֙חוּ֙	לְכָל־	צְבָ֣א	הַשָּׁמַ֔יִם	וַֽיַּעֲבֹ֖ד	אֹתָֽם:
Asherah-poles	and-he-bowed	to-all-of	host-of	the-heavens	and-he-worshiped	them

villages and acquired great numbers of flocks and herds, for God had given him very great riches. [30]It was Hezekiah who blocked the upper outlet of the Gihon spring and channeled the water down to the west side of the City of David. He succeeded in everything he undertook. [31]But when envoys were sent by the rulers of Babylon to ask him about the miraculous sign that had occurred in the land, God left him to test him and to know everything that was in his heart.

[32]The other events of Hezekiah's reign and his acts of devotion are written in the vision of the prophet Isaiah son of Amoz in the book of the kings of Judah and Israel. [33]Hezekiah rested with his fathers and was buried on the hill where the tombs of David's descendants are. All Judah and the people of Jerusalem honored him when he died. And Manasseh his son succeeded him as king.

Manasseh King of Judah

33 Manasseh was twelve years old when he became king, and he reigned in Jerusalem fifty-five years. [2]He did evil in the eyes of the LORD, following the detestable practices of the nations the LORD had driven out before the Israelites. [3]He rebuilt the high places his father Hezekiah had demolished; he also erected altars to the Baals and made Asherah poles. He bowed down to all the starry hosts and worshiped them.

*30 Most mss have *sheva* under the first *yod* and *pathah* under the second (וַיְיַשֵּׁר) as a *Kethib* form, and omit the first *yod* and *sheva* in the *Qere* (וַיֵּשׁ').

וּבָנָה מִזְבְּחוֹת בְּבֵית יְהוָה אֲשֶׁר אָמַר יְהוָה בִּירוּשָׁלַםִ
in-Jerusalem Yahweh he-said which Yahweh in-temple-of altars and-he-built (4)

יִהְיֶה־ שְׁמִי לְעוֹלָם׃ וַיִּבֶן מִזְבְּחוֹת לְכָל־
to-all-of altars and-he-built (5) to-forever Name-of-me he-will-remain

צְבָא הַשָּׁמָיִם בִּשְׁתֵּי חַצְרוֹת בֵּית־ יְהוָה׃ וְהוּא
and-he (6) Yahweh temple-of courts-of in-both-of the-heavens host-of

הֶעֱבִיר אֶת־ בָּנָיו בָּאֵשׁ בְּגֵי בֶן־ הִנֹּם
Hinnom Ben in-Valley-of through-the-fire sons-of-him *** he-made-pass

וְעוֹנֵן וְנִחֵשׁ וְכִשֵּׁף
and-he-practiced-witchcraft and-he-practiced-divination and-he-practiced-sorcery

וְעָשָׂה אוֹב וְיִדְּעוֹנִי הִרְבָּה לַעֲשׂוֹת הָרַע בְּעֵינֵי
in-eyes-of the-evil to-do he-did-much and-spiritist medium and-he-consulted

יְהוָה לְהַכְעִיסוֹ׃ וַיָּשֶׂם אֶת־ פֶּסֶל הַסֶּמֶל אֲשֶׁר
that the-carving image-of *** and-he-put (7) to-provoke-to-anger-him Yahweh

עָשָׂה בְּבֵית הָאֱלֹהִים אֲשֶׁר אָמַר אֱלֹהִים אֶל־דָּוִיד וְאֶל־ שְׁלֹמֹה
Solomon and-to David to God he-said which the-God in-temple-of he-made

בְנוֹ בַּבַּיִת הַזֶּה וּבִירוּשָׁלַםִ אֲשֶׁר בָּחַרְתִּי מִכֹּל
from-all-of I-chose which and-in-Jerusalem the-this in-the-temple son-of-him

שִׁבְטֵי יִשְׂרָאֵל אָשִׂים אֶת־ שְׁמִי לְעֵילוֹם׃ וְלֹא
and-not (8) to-forever Name-of-me *** I-will-put Israel tribes-of

אוֹסִיף לְהָסִיר אֶת־ רֶגֶל יִשְׂרָאֵל מֵעַל הָאֲדָמָה אֲשֶׁר
that the-land from-on Israel foot-of *** to-make-leave I-will-repeat

הֶעֱמַדְתִּי לַאֲבֹתֵיכֶם רַק ׀ אִם־ יִשְׁמְרוּ לַעֲשׂוֹת אֵת כָּל־ אֲשֶׁר
that all *** to-do they-are-careful if only to-fathers-of-you I-assigned

צִוִּיתִים לְכָל־ הַתּוֹרָה וְהַחֻקִּים וְהַמִּשְׁפָּטִים
and-the-ordinances and-the-decrees the-law about-all-of I-commanded-them

בְּיַד־ מֹשֶׁה׃ וַיֶּתַע מְנַשֶּׁה אֶת־יְהוּדָה וְיֹשְׁבֵי
and-ones-living-of Judah *** Manasseh but-he-led-astray (9) Moses by-hand-of

יְרוּשָׁלָםִ לַעֲשׂוֹת רָע מִן־ הַגּוֹיִם אֲשֶׁר הִשְׁמִיד יְהוָה
Yahweh he-destroyed that the-nations more-than evil to-do Jerusalem

מִפְּנֵי בְּנֵי יִשְׂרָאֵל׃ וַיְדַבֵּר יְהוָה אֶל־ מְנַשֶּׁה וְאֶל־
and-to Manasseh to Yahweh and-he-spoke (10) Israel sons-of from-before

עַמּוֹ וְלֹא הִקְשִׁיבוּ׃ וַיָּבֵא יְהוָה
Yahweh so-he-brought (11) they-paid-attention but-not people-of-him

עֲלֵיהֶם אֶת־ שָׂרֵי הַצָּבָא אֲשֶׁר לְמֶלֶךְ אַשּׁוּר
Assyria of-king-of that the-army commanders-of *** against-them

וַיִּלְכְּדוּ אֶת־ מְנַשֶּׁה בַּחֹחִים וַיַּאַסְרֻהוּ
and-they-bound-him with-the-hooks Manasseh *** and-they-took-prisoner

4He built altars in the temple
of the LORD, of which the LORD
had said, "My Name will remain in Jerusalem forever."
5In both courts of the temple of
the LORD, he built altars to all
the starry hosts. 6He sacrificed
his sons in[z] the fire in the Valley of Ben Hinnom, practiced
sorcery, divination and witch-
craft, and consulted mediums
and spiritists. He did much
evil in the eyes of the LORD,
provoking him to anger.
7He took the carved image
he had made and put it in
God's temple, of which God
had said to David and to his
son Solomon, "In this temple
and in Jerusalem, which I
have chosen out of all the
tribes of Israel, I will put my
Name forever. 8I will not again
make the feet of the Israelites
leave the land I assigned to
your forefathers, if only they
will be careful to do everything I commanded them concerning all the laws, decrees
and ordinances given through
Moses." 9But Manasseh led
Judah and the people of
Jerusalem astray, so that they
did more evil than the nations
the LORD had destroyed before
the Israelites.
10The LORD spoke to Manasseh and his people, but they
paid no attention. 11So the
LORD brought against them
the army commanders of the
king of Assyria, who took
Manasseh prisoner, put a
hook in his nose, bound him

[z]6 Or *He made his sons pass through*

בַּנְחֻשְׁתַּיִם וַיּוֹלִיכֻהוּ בָּבֶלָה׃ וּכְהָצֵר
and-in-to-distress (12) to-Babylon and-they-took-him with-the-bronze-shackles

לוֹ חִלָּה אֶת־ פְּנֵי יְהוָה אֱלֹהָיו וַיִּכָּנַע
and-he-humbled-himself God-of-him Yahweh faces-of *** he-sought to-him

מְאֹד מִלִּפְנֵי אֱלֹהֵי אֲבֹתָיו׃ וַיִּתְפַּלֵּל אֵלָיו
to-him when-he-prayed (13) fathers-of-him God-of at-before greatly

וַיֵּעָתֶר לוֹ וַיִּשְׁמַע תְּחִנָּתוֹ וַיְשִׁיבֵהוּ
so-he-brought-back-him plea-of-him and-he-listened-to by-him then-he-was-moved

יְרוּשָׁלַםִ לְמַלְכוּתוֹ וַיֵּדַע מְנַשֶּׁה כִּי יְהוָה הוּא הָאֱלֹהִים׃
the-God he Yahweh that Manasseh then-he-knew to-kingdom-of-him Jerusalem

וְאַחֲרֵי־ כֵן בָּנָה חוֹמָה חִיצוֹנָה ׀ לְעִיר־ דָּוִיד מַעְרָבָה לְגִיחוֹן
of-Gihon to-west David of-City-of outer wall he-rebuilt this and-after (14)

בַּנַּחַל וְלָבוֹא בְשַׁעַר הַדָּגִים וְסָבַב לָעֹפֶל
to-the-Ophel and-he-encircled the-Fishes to-Gate-of as-to-go in-the-valley

וַיַּגְבִּיהֶהָ מְאֹד וַיָּשֶׂם שָׂרֵי־ חַיִל בְּכָל־
in-all-of military commanders-of and-he-stationed much and-he-made-high-her

הֶעָרִים הַבְּצֻרוֹת בִּיהוּדָה׃ וַיָּסַר אֶת־ אֱלֹהֵי
gods-of *** and-he-got-rid (15) in-Judah the-ones-being-fortified the-cities

הַנֵּכָר וְאֶת־ הַסֶּמֶל מִבֵּית יְהוָה וְכָל־ הַמִּזְבְּחוֹת אֲשֶׁר
that the-altars and-all-of Yahweh from-temple-of the-image and the-foreign

בָּנָה בְּהַר בֵּית־ יְהוָה וּבִירוּשָׁלָםִ וַיַּשְׁלֵךְ חוּצָה
to-outside and-he-threw and-in-Jerusalem Yahweh temple-of on-hill-of he-built

לָעִיר׃ וַיִּכֶן° אֶת־ מִזְבַּח יְהוָה וַיִּזְבַּח
and-he-sacrificed Yahweh altar-of *** then-he-restored (16) of-the-city

עָלָיו זִבְחֵי שְׁלָמִים וְתוֹדָה וַיֹּאמֶר לִיהוּדָה לַעֲבוֹד
to-serve to-Judah and-he-told and-thanksgiving fellowships offerings-of on-him

אֶת־ יְהוָה אֱלֹהֵי יִשְׂרָאֵל׃ אֲבָל עוֹד הָעָם זֹבְחִים
ones-sacrificing the-people still however (17) Israel God-of Yahweh ***

בַּבָּמוֹת רַק לַיהוָה אֱלֹהֵיהֶם׃ וְיֶתֶר דִּבְרֵי
events-of and-other-of (18) God-of-them to-Yahweh but at-the-high-places

מְנַשֶּׁה וּתְפִלָּתוֹ אֶל־ אֱלֹהָיו וְדִבְרֵי הַחֹזִים
the-seers and-words-of God-of-him to and-prayer-of-him Manasseh

הַמְדַבְּרִים אֵלָיו בְּשֵׁם יְהוָה אֱלֹהֵי יִשְׂרָאֵל הִנָּם עַל־
in see-they! Israel God-of Yahweh in-name-of to-him the-ones-speaking

דִּבְרֵי מַלְכֵי יִשְׂרָאֵל׃ וּתְפִלָּתוֹ וְהֵעָתֶר־ לוֹ
by-him and-to-be-moved and-prayer-of-him (19) Israel kings-of annals-of

וְכָל־ חַטָּאתוֹ וּמַעְלוֹ וְהַמְּקֹמוֹת אֲשֶׁר
where and-the-sites and-unfaithfulness-of-him sin-of-him and-all-of

with bronze shackles and took
him to Babylon. 12 In his distress he sought the favor of the
LORD his God and humbled
himself greatly before the God
of his fathers. 13 And when he
prayed to him, the LORD was
moved by his entreaty and listened to his plea; so he
brought him back to Jerusalem
and to his kingdom. Then
Manasseh knew that the LORD
is God.
14 Afterward he rebuilt the
outer wall of the City of David,
west of the Gihon spring in
the valley, as far as the entrance of the Fish Gate and en-
circling the hill of Ophel; he
also made it much higher. He
stationed military commanders in all the fortified cities in
Judah.
15 He got rid of the foreign
gods and removed the image
from the temple of the LORD, as
well as all the altars he had
built on the temple hill and in
Jerusalem; and he threw them
out of the city. 16 Then he restored the altar of the LORD
and sacrificed fellowship[b] and
thank offerings on it, and told
Judah to serve the LORD, the
God of Israel. 17 The people,
however, continued to sacrifice at the high places, but
only to the LORD their God.
18 The other events of Manasseh's reign, including his
prayer to his God and the
words the seers spoke to him
in the name of the LORD, the
God of Israel, are written in
the annals of the kings of Israel.[c] 19 His prayer and how God
was moved by his entreaty, as
well as all his sins and unfaithfulness, and the sites

[b] *16* Traditionally *peace*
[c] *18* That is, Judah, as frequently in 2 Chronicles

°*16* ק ויבן

בָּנָה בָהֶם בָּמוֹת וְהֶעֱמִיד הָאֲשֵׁרִים וְהַפְּסִלִים
and-the-idols the-Asherah-poles and-he-set-up high-places on-them he-built

לִפְנֵי הִכָּנְעוֹ הִנָּם כְּתוּבִים עַל דִּבְרֵי חוֹזָי׃
Hozai records-of in ones-being-written see-they! to-be-humbled-him before

(20) וַיִּשְׁכַּב מְנַשֶּׁה עִם־ אֲבֹתָיו וַיִּקְבְּרֻהוּ
and-they-buried-him fathers-of-him with Manasseh and-he-rested (20)

בֵּיתוֹ וַיִּמְלֹךְ אָמוֹן בְּנוֹ תַּחְתָּיו׃ (21) בֶּן־
son-of (21) in-place-of-him son-of-him Amon and-he-became-king palace-of-him

עֶשְׂרִים וּשְׁתַּיִם שָׁנָה אָמוֹן בְּמָלְכוֹ וּשְׁתַּיִם שָׁנִים מָלַךְ
he-reigned years and-two when-to-become-king-him Amon year and-two twenty

בִּירוּשָׁלִָם׃ (22) וַיַּעַשׂ הָרַע בְּעֵינֵי יְהוָה כַּאֲשֶׁר עָשָׂה
he-did just-as Yahweh in-eyes-of the-evil and-he-did (22) in-Jerusalem

מְנַשֶּׁה אָבִיו וּלְכָל־ הַפְּסִילִים אֲשֶׁר עָשָׂה מְנַשֶּׁה
Manasseh he-made that the-idols and-to-all-of father-of-him Manasseh

אָבִיו זִבַּח אָמוֹן וַיַּעַבְדֵם׃ (23) וְלֹא
but-not (23) and-he-worshiped-them Amon he-sacrificed father-of-him

נִכְנַע מִלִּפְנֵי יְהוָה כְּהִכָּנַע מְנַשֶּׁה
Manasseh like-to-humble-himself Yahweh at-before he-humbled-himself

אָבִיו כִּי הוּא אָמוֹן הִרְבָּה אַשְׁמָה׃ (24) וַיִּקְשְׁרוּ
and-they-conspired (24) guilt he-increased Amon he instead father-of-him

עָלָיו עֲבָדָיו וַיְמִיתֻהוּ בְּבֵיתוֹ׃
in-palace-of-him and-they-assassinated-him officials-of-him against-him

(25) וַיַּכּוּ עַם־ הָאָרֶץ אֵת כָּל־ הַקֹּשְׁרִים עַל־
against the-ones-plotting all-of *** the-land people-of then-they-killed (25)

הַמֶּלֶךְ אָמוֹן וַיַּמְלִיכוּ עַם־ הָאָרֶץ אֶת־ יֹאשִׁיָּהוּ בְנוֹ
son-of-him Josiah *** the-land people-of and-they-made-king Amon the-king

תַּחְתָּיו׃ (34:1) בֶּן־ שְׁמוֹנֶה שָׁנִים יֹאשִׁיָּהוּ בְמָלְכוֹ
when-to-become-king-him Josiah years eight son-of (34:1) in-place-of-him

וּשְׁלֹשִׁים וְאַחַת שָׁנָה מָלַךְ בִּירוּשָׁלִָם׃ (2) וַיַּעַשׂ הַיָּשָׁר
the-right and-he-did (2) in-Jerusalem he-reigned year and-one and-thirty

בְּעֵינֵי יְהוָה וַיֵּלֶךְ בְּדַרְכֵי דָּוִיד אָבִיו וְלֹא־
and-not father-of-him David in-ways-of and-he-walked Yahweh in-eyes-of

סָר יָמִין וּשְׂמֹאול׃ (3) וּבִשְׁמוֹנֶה שָׁנִים לְמָלְכוֹ וְהוּא
while-he to-reign-him years and-in-eight (3) or-left right he-turned

עוֹדֶנּוּ נַעַר הֵחֵל לִדְרוֹשׁ לֵאלֹהֵי דָּוִיד אָבִיו וּבִשְׁתֵּים
and-in-two father-of-him David to-God-of to-seek he-began young still-he

עֶשְׂרֵה שָׁנָה הֵחֵל לְטַהֵר אֶת־ יְהוּדָה וִירוּשָׁלִַם מִן־ הַבָּמוֹת
the-high-places of and-Jerusalem Judah *** to-purge he-began year ten

where he built high places and
set up Asherah poles and idols
before he humbled himself—
all are written in the records of
the seers.[d] 20Manasseh rested
with his fathers and was buried in his palace. And Amon
his son succeeded him as king.

Amon King of Judah

21Amon was twenty-two
years old when he became
king, and he reigned in
Jerusalem two years. 22He did
evil in the eyes of the LORD, as
his father Manasseh had
done. Amon worshiped and
offered sacrifices to all the
idols Manasseh had made.
23But unlike his father Manasseh, he did not humble himself before the LORD; Amon increased his guilt.
24Amon's officials conspired
against him and assassinated
him in his palace. 25Then the
people of the land killed all
who had plotted against King
Amon, and they made Josiah
his son king in his place.

Josiah's Reforms

34 Josiah was eight years
old when he became
king, and he reigned in
Jerusalem thirty-one years.
2He did what was right in the
eyes of the LORD and walked
in the ways of his father David, not turning aside to the
right or to the left.
3In the eighth year of his
reign, while he was still
young, he began to seek the
God of his father David. In his
twelfth year he began to purge
Judah and Jerusalem of high

[d]19 One Hebrew manuscript and Septuagint; most Hebrew manuscripts *of Hozai*

וְהָאֲשֵׁרִים וְהַפְּסִלִים וְהַמַּסֵּכוֹת׃
and-the-cast-images and-the-carved-idols and-the-Asherah-poles

(4) וַיְנַתְּצוּ לְפָנָיו אֵת מִזְבְּחוֹת הַבְּעָלִים וְהַחַמָּנִים
and-the-incense-altars the-Baals altars-of *** before-him and-they-tore-down (4)

אֲשֶׁר־לְמַעְלָה מֵעֲלֵיהֶם גִּדֵּעַ וְהָאֲשֵׁרִים וְהַפְּסִלִים
and-the-idols and-the-Asherah-poles he-cut-to-pieces at-over-them at-above that

וְהַמַּסֵּכוֹת שִׁבַּר וְהֵדַק וַיִּזְרֹק עַל־
over and-he-scattered and-he-broke-to-pieces he-smashed and-the-images

פְּנֵי הַקְּבָרִים הַזֹּבְחִים לָהֶם׃ (5) וְעַצְמוֹת כֹּהֲנִים
priests and-bones-of (5) to-them the-ones-sacrificing the-graves surfaces-of

שָׂרַף עַל־ מִזְבְּחוֹתָים וַיְטַהֵר אֶת־ יְהוּדָה וְאֶת־ יְרוּשָׁלִָם׃
Jerusalem and Judah *** so-he-purged altars-of-them on he-burned

(6) וּבְעָרֵי מְנַשֶּׁה וְאֶפְרַיִם וְשִׁמְעוֹן וְעַד־ נַפְתָּלִי
Naphtali and-as-far-as and-Simeon and-Ephraim Manasseh and-in-towns-of (6)

בְּהַר° בְּתֵיהֶם סָבִיב׃ (7) וַיְנַתֵּץ אֶת־ הַמִּזְבְּחוֹת וְאֶת־
and the-altars *** then-he-tore-down (7) around in-ruins-of-them

הָאֲשֵׁרִים וְהַפְּסִלִים כִּתַּת לְהֵדַק וְכָל־
and-all-of to-be-powder he-crushed and-the-idols the-Asherah-poles

הַחַמָּנִים גִּדַּע בְּכָל־ אֶרֶץ יִשְׂרָאֵל
Israel land-of through-all-of he-cut-to-pieces the-incense-altars

וַיָּשָׁב לִירוּשָׁלִָם׃ (8) וּבִשְׁנַת שְׁמוֹנֶה עֶשְׂרֵה לְמָלְכוֹ
to-reign-him ten eight and-in-year-of (8) to-Jerusalem then-he-went-back

לְטַהֵר הָאָרֶץ וְהַבָּיִת שָׁלַח אֶת־ שָׁפָן בֶּן־ אֲצַלְיָהוּ וְאֶת־
and Azaliah son-of Shaphan *** he-sent and-the-temple the-land to-purify

מַעֲשֵׂיָהוּ שַׂר־ הָעִיר וְאֵת יוֹאָח בֶּן־ יוֹאָחָז הַמַּזְכִּיר
the-one-recording Joahaz son-of Joah with the-city ruler-of Maaseiah

לְחַזֵּק אֶת־ בֵּית יְהוָה אֱלֹהָיו׃ (9) וַיָּבֹאוּ אֶל־חִלְקִיָּהוּ
Hilkiah to and-they-went (9) God-of-him Yahweh temple-of *** to-repair

הַכֹּהֵן הַגָּדוֹל וַיִּתְּנוּ אֶת־ הַכֶּסֶף הַמּוּבָא
the-one-being-brought the-money *** and-they-gave the-high the-priest

בֵּית־ אֱלֹהִים אֲשֶׁר אָסְפוּ־ הַלְוִיִּם שֹׁמְרֵי הַסַּף
the-door ones-keeping-of the-Levites they-collected which God temple-of

מִיַּד מְנַשֶּׁה וְאֶפְרַיִם וּמִכֹּל שְׁאֵרִית יִשְׂרָאֵל
Israel remnant-of and-from-entire-of and-Ephraim Manasseh from-hand-of

וּמִכָּל־ יְהוּדָה וּבִנְיָמִן וַיָּשֻׁבוּ יְרוּשָׁלִָם׃
Jerusalem *and-they-returned and-Benjamin Judah and-from-all-of

(10) וַיִּתְּנוּ עַל־ יַד עֹשֵׂה הַמְּלָאכָה
the-work one-supervising-of hand-of to then-they-entrusted (10)

places, Asherah poles, carved
idols and cast images. [4]Under
his direction the altars of the
Baals were torn down; he cut
to pieces the incense altars
that were above them, and
smashed the Asherah poles,
the idols and the images.
These he broke to pieces and
scattered over the graves of
those who had sacrificed to
them. [5]He burned the bones of
the priests on their altars, and
so he purged Judah and
Jerusalem. [6]In the towns of
Manasseh, Ephraim and
Simeon, as far as Naphtali,
and in the ruins around them,
[7]he tore down the altars and
the Asherah poles and crushed
the idols to powder and cut to
pieces all the incense altars
throughout Israel. Then he
went back to Jerusalem.

[8]In the eighteenth year of Josiah's reign, to purify the land
and the temple, he sent Shaphan son of Azaliah and Maaseiah the ruler of the city, with
Joah son of Joahaz, the
recorder, to repair the temple
of the LORD his God.

[9]They went to Hilkiah the
high priest and gave him the
money that had been brought
into the temple of God, which
the Levites who were the
doorkeepers had collected
from the people of Manasseh,
Ephraim and the entire remnant of Israel and from all the
people of Judah and Benjamin
and the inhabitants of Jerusalem. [10]Then they entrusted it
to the men appointed to supervise the work on the LORD's

*9 The interlinear translation follows the *Qere*; the NIV points the consonants of the *Kethib* as a Qal participle (וְיֹשְׁבֵי), *and-ones-inhabiting-of*.

°5 ק מזבחותם

°6 ק בחרבתיהם

°9 ק וישבו

הַמֻּפְקָדִים בְּבֵית יְהוָה וַיִּתְּנוּ אֹתוֹ עוֹשֵׂי

ones-doing-of him and-they-paid Yahweh to-temple-of the-ones-being-appointed

הַמְּלָאכָה אֲשֶׁר עֹשִׂים בְּבֵית יְהוָה לִבְדּוֹק וּלְחַזֵּק

and-to-restore to-repair Yahweh on-temple-of ones-working who the-work

הַבָּיִת׃ וַיִּתְּנוּ לֶחָרָשִׁים וְלַבֹּנִים

and-to-the-ones-building to-the-carpenters and-they-gave (11) the-temple

לִקְנוֹת אַבְנֵי מַחְצֵב וְעֵצִים לַמְחַבְּרוֹת וּלְקָרוֹת

and-to-furnish-beams for-the-joists and-timbers dressed stones-of to-purchase

אֶת־ הַבָּתִּים אֲשֶׁר הִשְׁחִיתוּ מַלְכֵי יְהוּדָה׃

Judah kings-of they-allowed-to-fall-into-ruin that the-buildings ***

וְהָאֲנָשִׁים עֹשִׂים בֶּאֱמוּנָה בַּמְּלָאכָה וַעֲלֵיהֶם ׀

and-over-them in-the-work in-faith ones-doing and-the-men (12)

מֻפְקָדִים יַחַת וְעֹבַדְיָהוּ הַלְוִיִּם מִן־ בְּנֵי מְרָרִי

Merari descendants-of from the-Levites and-Obadiah Jahath ones-being-appointed

וּזְכַרְיָה וּמְשֻׁלָּם מִן־ בְּנֵי הַקְּהָתִים לְנַצֵּחַ

to-direct the-Kohathites descendants-of from and-Meshullam and-Zechariah

וְהַלְוִיִּם כָּל־ מֵבִין בִּכְלֵי־ שִׁיר׃ וְעַל

and-over (13) music with-instruments-of being-skilled all-of and-the-Levites

הַסַּבָּלִים וּמְנַצְּחִים לְכֹל עֹשֵׂה מְלָאכָה לַעֲבוֹדָה

to-job work one-doing-of over-all-of and-ones-supervising the-laborers

וַעֲבוֹדָה וּמֵהַלְוִיִּם סוֹפְרִים וְשֹׁטְרִים וְשׁוֹעֲרִים׃

and-doorkeepers and-scribes secretaries and-from-the-Levites and-job

וּבְהוֹצִיאָם אֶת־ הַכֶּסֶף הַמּוּבָא בֵּית

temple-of the-one-being-taken the-money *** and-while-to-bring-out-them (14)

יְהוָה מָצָא חִלְקִיָּהוּ הַכֹּהֵן אֶת־ סֵפֶר תּוֹרַת־ יְהוָה בְּיַד־

through-hand-of Yahweh Law-of Book-of *** the-priest Hilkiah he-found Yahweh

מֹשֶׁה׃ וַיַּעַן חִלְקִיָּהוּ וַיֹּאמֶר אֶל־ שָׁפָן הַסּוֹפֵר סֵפֶר

Book-of the-secretary Shaphan to and-he-said Hilkiah and-he-spoke (15) Moses

הַתּוֹרָה מָצָאתִי בְּבֵית יְהוָה וַיִּתֵּן חִלְקִיָּהוּ אֶת־הַסֵּפֶר אֶל־ שָׁפָן׃

Shaphan to the-book *** Hilkiah and-he-gave Yahweh in-temple-of I-found the-Law

וַיָּבֵא שָׁפָן אֶת־ הַסֵּפֶר אֶל־ הַמֶּלֶךְ וַיָּשֶׁב עוֹד אֶת־

*** again and-he-gave the-king to the-book *** Shaphan then-he-took (16)

הַמֶּלֶךְ דָּבָר לֵאמֹר כֹּל אֲשֶׁר־ נִתַּן בְּיַד־ עֲבָדֶיךָ

officials-of-you into-hand-of he-was-committed that all to-say report the-king

הֵם עֹשִׂים׃ וַיַּתִּיכוּ אֶת־ הַכֶּסֶף הַנִּמְצָא

the-one-being-found the-money *** and-they-paid-out (17) ones-doing they

בְּבֵית־ יְהוָה וַיִּתְּנוּהוּ עַל־ יַד הַמֻּפְקָדִים

the-ones-supervising hand-of into and-they-entrusted-him Yahweh in-temple-of

temple. These men paid the workers who repaired and restored the temple. [11]They also gave money to the carpenters and builders to purchase dressed stone, and timber for joists and beams for the buildings that the kings of Judah had allowed to fall into ruin.

[12]The men did the work faithfully. Over them to direct them were Jahath and Obadiah, Levites descended from Merari, and Zechariah and Meshullam, descended from Kohath. The Levites—all who were skilled in playing musical instruments— [13]had charge of the laborers and supervised all the workers from job to job. Some of the Levites were secretaries, scribes and doorkeepers.

The Book of the Law Found

[14]While they were bringing out the money that had been taken into the temple of the LORD, Hilkiah the priest found the Book of the Law of the LORD that had been given through Moses. [15]Hilkiah said to Shaphan the secretary, "I have found the Book of the Law in the temple of the LORD." He gave it to Shaphan.

[16]Then Shaphan took the book to the king and reported to him: "Your officials are doing everything that has been committed to them. [17]They have paid out the money that was in the temple of the LORD and have entrusted it to the

וְעַל־ יַד עוֹשֵׂי הַמְּלָאכָה׃ וַיַּגֵּד שָׁפָן
Shaphan then-he-informed (18) the-work ones-doing-of hand-of and-into

הַסּוֹפֵר לַמֶּלֶךְ לֵאמֹר סֵפֶר נָתַן לִי חִלְקִיָּהוּ הַכֹּהֵן
the-priest Hilkiah to-me he-gave book to-say to-the-king the-secretary

וַיִּקְרָא־ בוֹ שָׁפָן לִפְנֵי הַמֶּלֶךְ׃ וַיְהִי
and-he-was (19) the-king in-presences-of Shaphan from-him and-he-read

כִּשְׁמֹעַ הַמֶּלֶךְ אֵת דִּבְרֵי הַתּוֹרָה וַיִּקְרַע אֶת־ בְּגָדָיו׃
robes-of-him *** then-he-tore the-Law words-of *** the-king when-to-hear

וַיְצַו הַמֶּלֶךְ אֶת־ חִלְקִיָּהוּ וְאֶת־אֲחִיקָם בֶּן־ שָׁפָן וְאֶת־עַבְדּוֹן
Abdon and Shaphan son-of Ahikam and Hilkiah *** the-king and-he-ordered (20)

בֶּן־ מִיכָה וְאֵת ׀ שָׁפָן הַסּוֹפֵר וְאֵת עֲשָׂיָה עֶבֶד־ הַמֶּלֶךְ
the-king attendant-of Asaiah and the-secretary Shaphan and Micah son-of

לֵאמֹר׃ לְכוּ דִרְשׁוּ אֶת־ יְהוָה בַּעֲדִי וּבְעַד הַנִּשְׁאָר בְּיִשְׂרָאֵל
in-Israel the-one-remaining and-for for-me Yahweh *** inquire! go! (21) to-say

וּבִיהוּדָה עַל־ דִּבְרֵי הַסֵּפֶר אֲשֶׁר נִמְצָא כִּי־ גְדוֹלָה חֲמַת־
anger-of great for he-was-found that the-book words-of about and-in-Judah

יְהוָה אֲשֶׁר נִתְּכָה בָנוּ עַל אֲשֶׁר לֹא־ שָׁמְרוּ אֲבוֹתֵינוּ
fathers-of-us they-kept not that because on-us she-is-poured-out that Yahweh

אֶת־ דְּבַר יְהוָה לַעֲשׂוֹת כְּכָל־ הַכָּתוּב עַל־ הַסֵּפֶר
the-book in the-thing-being-written as-all-of to-act Yahweh word-of ***

הַזֶּה׃ וַיֵּלֶךְ חִלְקִיָּהוּ וַאֲשֶׁר הַמֶּלֶךְ אֶל־חֻלְדָּה הַנְּבִיאָה
the-prophetess Huldah to the-king and-who Hilkiah and-he-went (22) the-this

אֵשֶׁת ׀ שַׁלֻּם בֶּן־ תָּוקְהַת בֶּן־ חַסְרָה שׁוֹמֵר הַבְּגָדִים
the-clothes one-keeping-of Hasrah son-of Tokhath son-of Shallum wife-of

וְהִיא יוֹשֶׁבֶת בִּירוּשָׁלִַם בַּמִּשְׁנֶה וַיְדַבְּרוּ אֵלֶיהָ
to-her and-they-spoke in-the-Second-District in-Jerusalem living now-she

כָּזֹאת׃ וַתֹּאמֶר לָהֶם כֹּה־ אָמַר יְהוָה אֱלֹהֵי יִשְׂרָאֵל אִמְרוּ
tell! Israel God-of Yahweh he-says this to-them and-she-said (23) as-this

לָאִישׁ אֲשֶׁר־ שָׁלַח אֶתְכֶם אֵלָי׃ כֹּה אָמַר יְהוָה הִנְנִי מֵבִיא
bringing see-I! Yahweh he-says this (24) to-me you he-sent who to-the-man

רָעָה עַל־ הַמָּקוֹם הַזֶּה וְעַל־ יוֹשְׁבָיו אֵת כָּל־
all-of *** ones-living-of-him and-on the-this the-place on disaster

הָאָלוֹת הַכְּתוּבוֹת עַל־ הַסֵּפֶר אֲשֶׁר קָרְאוּ לִפְנֵי
in-presences-of they-read that the-book in the-ones-being-written the-curses

מֶלֶךְ יְהוּדָה׃ תַּחַת ׀ אֲשֶׁר עֲזָבוּנִי וַיְקַטִּירוּ
and-they-burned-incense they-forsook-me that because (25) Judah king-of

לֵאלֹהִים אֲחֵרִים לְמַעַן הַכְעִיסֵנִי בְּכֹל מַעֲשֵׂי יְדֵיהֶם
hands-of-them works-of by-all-of to-anger-me in-order-to other-ones to-gods

supervisors and workers."
18 Then Shaphan the secretary
informed the king, "Hilkiah
the priest has given me a
book." And Shaphan read
from it in the presence of the
king.
19 When the king heard the
words of the Law, he tore his
robes. 20 He gave these orders
to Hilkiah, Ahikam son of
Shaphan, Abdon son of
Micah,[e] Shaphan the secretary
and Asaiah the king's atten-
dant: 21 "Go and inquire of the
LORD for me and for the remnant in Israel and Judah about
what is written in this book
that has been found. Great is
the LORD's anger that is poured
out on us because our fathers
have not kept the word of the
LORD; they have not acted in
accordance with all that is
written in this book."
22 Hilkiah and those the king
had sent with him[f] went to
speak to the prophetess Huldah, who was the wife of Shallum son of Tokhath,[g] the son
of Hasrah,[h] keeper of the
wardrobe. She lived in Jerusalem, in the Second District.
23 She said to them, "This is
what the LORD, the God of Israel, says: Tell the man who
sent you to me, 24 'This is what
the LORD says: I am going to
bring disaster on this place
and its people—all the curses
written in the book that has
been read in the presence of
the king of Judah. 25 Because
they have forsaken me and
burned incense to other gods
and provoked me to anger by
all that their hands have

[e]20 Also called *Acbor son of Micaiah*
[f]22 One Hebrew manuscript, Vulgate and Syriac; most Hebrew manuscripts do not have *had sent with him.*
[g]22 Also called *Tikvah*
[h]22 Also called *Harhas*

°22 ק תקהת
°25 ק ויקטרו

וְתִתַּךְ חֲמָתִי בַּמָּקוֹם הַזֶּה וְלֹא
and-not the-this on-the-place anger-of-me and-she-will-be-poured-out

תִכְבֶּה׃ וְאֶל־ מֶלֶךְ יְהוּדָה הַשֹּׁלֵחַ אֶתְכֶם לִדְרוֹשׁ
to-inquire you the-one-sending Judah king-of and-to (26) she-will-be-quenched

בַּיהוָה כֹּה תֹאמְרוּ אֵלָיו כֹּה־ אָמַר יְהוָה אֱלֹהֵי יִשְׂרָאֵל הַדְּבָרִים
the-words Israel God-of Yahweh he-says this to-him you-tell this of-Yahweh

אֲשֶׁר שָׁמָעְתָּ׃ יַעַן רַךְ־ לְבָבְךָ וַתִּכָּנַע ׀
and-you-humbled-self heart-of-you he-was-responsive because (27) you-heard that

מִלִּפְנֵי אֱלֹהִים בְּשָׁמְעֲךָ אֶת־ דְּבָרָיו עַל־ הַמָּקוֹם הַזֶּה
the-this the-place against words-of-him *** when-to-hear-you God at-before

וְעַל־ יֹשְׁבָיו וַתִּכָּנַע לְפָנַי וַתִּקְרַע
and-you-tore before-me and-you-humbled-self ones-living-of-him and-against

אֶת־ בְּגָדֶיךָ וַתֵּבְךְּ לְפָנָי וְגַם־ אֲנִי שָׁמַעְתִּי
I-heard I now-indeed in-presences-of-me and-you-wept robes-of-you ***

נְאֻם־ יְהוָה׃ הִנְנִי אֹסִפְךָ אֶל־ אֲבֹתֶיךָ
fathers-of-you to I-will-gather-you see-I! (28) Yahweh declaration-of

וְנֶאֱסַפְתָּ אֶל־ קִבְרֹתֶיךָ בְּשָׁלוֹם וְלֹא־ תִרְאֶינָה
they-will-see and-not in-peace tombs-of-you in and-you-will-be-buried

עֵינֶיךָ בְּכֹל הָרָעָה אֲשֶׁר אֲנִי מֵבִיא עַל־ הַמָּקוֹם הַזֶּה
the-this the-place on bringing I that the-disaster to-all-of eyes-of-you

וְעַל־ יֹשְׁבָיו וַיָּשִׁיבוּ אֶת־ הַמֶּלֶךְ דָּבָר׃
answer the-king *** so-they-took-back ones-living-of-him and-on

וַיִּשְׁלַח הַמֶּלֶךְ וַיֶּאֱסֹף אֶת־ כָּל־ זִקְנֵי יְהוּדָה
Judah elders-of all-of *** and-he-brought-together the-king then-he-called (29)

וִירוּשָׁלָם׃ וַיַּעַל הַמֶּלֶךְ בֵּית־ יְהוָה וְכָל־
and-all-of Yahweh temple-of the-king and-he-went-up (30) and-Jerusalem

אִישׁ יְהוּדָה וְיֹשְׁבֵי יְרוּשָׁלַם וְהַכֹּהֲנִים וְהַלְוִיִּם
and-the-Levites and-the-priests Jerusalem and-ones-living-of Judah man-of

וְכָל־ הָעָם מִגָּדוֹל וְעַד־ קָטָן וַיִּקְרָא בְאָזְנֵיהֶם
in-ears-of-them and-he-read least even-to from-greatest the-people and-all-of

אֶת־ כָּל־ דִּבְרֵי סֵפֶר הַבְּרִית הַנִּמְצָא בֵּית יְהוָה׃
Yahweh temple-of the-one-being-found the-Covenant Book-of words-of all-of ***

וַיַּעֲמֹד הַמֶּלֶךְ עַל־ עָמְדוֹ וַיִּכְרֹת אֶת־ הַבְּרִית
the-covenant *** and-he-renewed pillar-of-him by the-king and-he-stood (31)

לִפְנֵי יְהוָה לָלֶכֶת אַחֲרֵי יְהוָה וְלִשְׁמוֹר אֶת־ מִצְוֹתָיו
commands-of-him *** and-to-keep Yahweh after to-follow Yahweh in-presences-of

וְעֵדְוֹתָיו וְחֻקָּיו בְּכָל־ לְבָבוֹ
heart-of-him with-all-of and-decrees-of-him and-regulations-of-him

made,[i] my anger will be
poured out on this place and
will not be quenched.' [26]Tell
the king of Judah, who sent
you to inquire of the LORD,
'This is what the LORD, the
God of Israel, says concerning
the words you heard: [27]Be-
cause your heart was respon-
sive and you humbled yourself before God when you
heard what he spoke against
this place and its people, and
because you humbled yourself
before me and tore your robes
and wept in my presence, I
have heard you, declares the
LORD. [28]Now I will gather you
to your fathers, and you will
be buried in peace. Your eyes
will not see all the disaster I
am going to bring on this
place and on those who live
here.' "

So they took her answer
back to the king.

[29]Then the king called together all the elders of Judah
and Jerusalem. [30]He went up to
the temple of the LORD with
the men of Judah, the people
of Jerusalem, the priests and
the Levites—all the people
from the least to the greatest.
He read in their hearing all the
words of the Book of the Covenant, which had been found
in the temple of the LORD.
[31]The king stood by his pillar
and renewed the covenant in
the presence of the LORD—to
follow the LORD and keep his
commands, regulations and
decrees with all his heart and

[i]25 Or *by everything they have done*

וּבְכָל־ נַפְשׁוֹ לַעֲשׂוֹת אֶת־ דִּבְרֵי הַבְּרִית
the-covenant words-of *** to-obey soul-of-him and-with-all-of

הַכְּתוּבִים עַל־ הַסֵּפֶר הַזֶּה׃ וַיַּעֲמֵד אֵת
*** and-he-made-pledge (32) the-this the-book in the-ones-being-written

כָּל־ הַנִּמְצָא בִירוּשָׁלַםִ וּבִנְיָמִן וַיַּעֲשׂוּ
and-they-did and-Benjamin in-Jerusalem the-one-being-found all-of

יֹשְׁבֵי יְרוּשָׁלַםִ כִּבְרִית אֱלֹהִים אֱלֹהֵי אֲבוֹתֵיהֶם׃
fathers-of-them God-of God as-covenant-of Jerusalem ones-living-of

וַיָּסַר יֹאשִׁיָּהוּ אֶת־ כָּל־ הַתּוֹעֵבוֹת מִכָּל־
from-all-of the-detestable-idols all-of *** Josiah and-he-removed (33)

הָאֲרָצוֹת אֲשֶׁר לִבְנֵי יִשְׂרָאֵל וַיַּעֲבֵד אֵת כָּל־
all-of *** and-he-had-serve Israel to-sons-of that the-territories

הַנִּמְצָא בְּיִשְׂרָאֵל לַעֲבוֹד אֶת־ יְהוָה אֱלֹהֵיהֶם כָּל־
all-of God-of-them Yahweh *** to-serve in-Israel the-one-being-present

יָמָיו לֹא סָרוּ מֵאַחֲרֵי יְהוָה אֱלֹהֵי אֲבוֹתֵיהֶם׃
fathers-of-them God-of Yahweh from-after they-turned not days-of-him

וַיַּעַשׂ יֹאשִׁיָּהוּ בִירוּשָׁלַםִ פֶּסַח לַיהוָה
to-Yahweh Passover in-Jerusalem Josiah and-he-celebrated (35:1)

וַיִּשְׁחֲטוּ הַפֶּסַח בְּאַרְבָּעָה עָשָׂר לַחֹדֶשׁ הָרִאשׁוֹן׃
the-first of-the-month ten on-four the-Passover-lamb and-they-slaughtered

וַיַּעֲמֵד הַכֹּהֲנִים עַל־ מִשְׁמְרוֹתָם וַיְחַזְּקֵם
and-he-encouraged-them duties-of-them to the-priests and-he-appointed (2)

לַעֲבוֹדַת בֵּית יְהוָה׃ וַיֹּאמֶר לַלְוִיִּם
to-the-Levites and-he-said (3) Yahweh temple-of in-service-of

הַמְּבוֹנִים לְכָל־ יִשְׂרָאֵל הַקְּדוֹשִׁים לַיהוָה תְּנוּ
put! to-Yahweh the-ones-consecrated Israel to-all-of the-ones-instructing

אֶת־ אֲרוֹן־ הַקֹּדֶשׁ בַּבַּיִת אֲשֶׁר בָּנָה שְׁלֹמֹה בֶן־ דָּוִיד
David son-of Solomon he-built that in-the-temple the-sacred ark-of ***

מֶלֶךְ יִשְׂרָאֵל אֵין־ לָכֶם מַשָּׂא בַּכָּתֵף עַתָּה עִבְדוּ אֶת־
*** serve! now on-the-shoulder something-carried to-you not Israel king-of

יְהוָה אֱלֹהֵיכֶם וְאֵת עַמּוֹ יִשְׂרָאֵל׃ וְהָכִונוּ
now-prepare-yourselves! (4) Israel people-of-him and God-of-you Yahweh

לְבֵית־ אֲבוֹתֵיכֶם כְּמַחְלְקוֹתֵיכֶם בִּכְתָב דָּוִיד מֶלֶךְ
king-of David as-writing-of in-divisions-of-you fathers-of-you by-family-of

יִשְׂרָאֵל וּבְמִכְתַּב שְׁלֹמֹה בְנוֹ׃ וְעִמְדוּ בַקֹּדֶשׁ
in-the-holy-place and-stand! (5) son-of-him Solomon and-as-writing-of Israel

לִפְלֻגּוֹת בֵּית הָאָבוֹת לַאֲחֵיכֶם בְּנֵי הָעָם
the-people sons-of of-fellows-of-you the-fathers family-of by-subdivisions-of

all his soul, and to obey the words of the covenant written in this book.
[32]Then he had everyone in Jerusalem and Benjamin pledge themselves to it; the people of Jerusalem did this in accordance with the covenant of God, the God of their fathers.
[33]Josiah removed all the detestable idols from all the territory belonging to the Israelites, and he had all who were present in Israel serve the LORD their God. As long as he lived, they did not fail to follow the LORD, the God of their fathers.

Josiah Celebrates the Passover

35 Josiah celebrated the Passover to the LORD in Jerusalem, and the Passover lamb was slaughtered on the fourteenth day of the first month.
[2]He appointed the priests to their duties and encouraged them in the service of the LORD's temple.
[3]He said to the Levites, who instructed all Israel and who had been consecrated to the LORD: "Put the sacred ark in the temple that Solomon son of David king of Israel built. It is not to be carried about on your shoulders. Now serve the LORD your God and his people Israel.
[4]Prepare yourselves by families in your divisions, according to the directions written by David king of Israel and by his son Solomon.
[5]"Stand in the holy place with a group of Levites for

°3 ק המבינים
°4 ק והכינו

וַחֲלֻקַּת בֵּית־ אָב לַלְוִיִּם׃ (6) וְשַׁחֲטוּ
and-group-of family-of father of-the-Levites (6) and-slaughter!

הַפָּסַח וְהִתְקַדְּשׁוּ וְהָכִינוּ לַאֲחֵיכֶם
the-Passover-lamb and-consecrate-yourselves! and-prepare! for-fellows-of-you

לַעֲשׂוֹת כִּדְבַר־ יְהוָה בְּיַד־ מֹשֶׁה׃ (7) וַיָּרֶם יֹאשִׁיָּהוּ
to-do as-command-of Yahweh by-hand-of Moses (7) and-he-provided Josiah

לִבְנֵי הָעָם צֹאן כְּבָשִׂים וּבְנֵי־ עִזִּים הַכֹּל
for-sons-of the-people flock-of sheeps and-offsprings-of goats the-total

לַפְּסָחִים לְכָל־ הַנִּמְצָא לְמִסְפַּר שְׁלֹשִׁים
for-the-Passover-offerings for-all-of the-one-being-found in-number thirty

אֶלֶף וּבָקָר שְׁלֹשֶׁת אֲלָפִים אֵלֶּה מֵרְכוּשׁ הַמֶּלֶךְ׃
thousand and-cattle three-of thousands these from-possession-of the-king

(8) וְשָׂרָיו לִנְדָבָה לָעָם
(8) and-officials-of-him with-volunteer-contribution to-the-people

לַכֹּהֲנִים וְלַלְוִיִּם הֵרִימוּ חִלְקִיָּה וּזְכַרְיָהוּ
to-the-priests and-to-the-Levites they-gave Hilkiah and-Zechariah

וִיחִיאֵל נְגִידֵי בֵּית הָאֱלֹהִים לַכֹּהֲנִים נָתְנוּ
and-Jehiel administrators-of temple-of the-God to-the-priests they-gave

לַפְּסָחִים אַלְפַּיִם וְשֵׁשׁ מֵאוֹת וּבָקָר
for-the-Passover-offerings two-thousands and-six-of hundreds and-cattle

שְׁלֹשׁ מֵאוֹת׃ (9) °וְכוֹנַנְיָהוּ וּשְׁמַעְיָהוּ וּנְתַנְאֵל אֶחָיו
three-of hundreds (9) also-Conaniah and-Shemaiah and-Nethanel brothers-of-him

וַחֲשַׁבְיָהוּ וִיעִיאֵל וְיוֹזָבָד שָׂרֵי הַלְוִיִּם הֵרִימוּ
and-Hashabiah and-Jeiel and-Jozabad leaders-of the-Levites they-provided

לַלְוִיִּם לַפְּסָחִים חֲמֵשֶׁת אֲלָפִים וּבָקָר
for-the-Levites for-the-Passover-offerings five-of thousands and-cattle

חֲמֵשׁ מֵאוֹת׃ (10) וַתִּכּוֹן הָעֲבוֹדָה וַיַּעַמְדוּ
five-of hundreds (10) and-she-was-arranged the-service and-they-stood

הַכֹּהֲנִים עַל־ עָמְדָם וְהַלְוִיִּם עַל־ מַחְלְקוֹתָם כְּמִצְוַת
the-priests in place-of-them and-the-Levites in divisions-of-them as-order-of

הַמֶּלֶךְ׃ (11) וַיִּשְׁחֲטוּ הַפָּסַח וַיִּזְרְקוּ
the-king (11) and-they-slaughtered the-Passover-lamb and-they-sprinkled

הַכֹּהֲנִים מִיָּדָם וְהַלְוִיִּם מַפְשִׁיטִים׃
the-priests from-hand-of-them while-the-Levites ones-skinning

(12) וַיָּסִירוּ הָעֹלָה לְתִתָּם לְמִפְלַגּוֹת
(12) and-they-set-aside the-burnt-offering to-give-them to-subdivisions

לְבֵית־ אָבוֹת לִבְנֵי הָעָם לְהַקְרִיב לַיהוָה
of-family-of fathers of-sons-of the-people to-offer to-Yahweh

°9 ק וכנניהו

each subdivision of the families of your fellow countrymen, the lay people. 6Slaughter the Passover lambs, consecrate yourselves and prepare ⌊the lambs⌋ for your fellow countrymen, doing what the LORD commanded through Moses."

7Josiah provided for all the lay people who were there a total of thirty thousand sheep and goats for the Passover offerings, and also three thousand cattle—all from the king's own possessions.

8His officials also contributed voluntarily to the people and the priests and Levites. Hilkiah, Zechariah and Jehiel, the administrators of God's temple, gave the priests twenty-six hundred Passover offerings and three hundred cattle. 9Also Conaniah along with Shemaiah and Nethanel, his brothers, and Hashabiah, Jeiel and Jozabad, the leaders of the Levites, provided five thousand Passover offerings and five hundred head of cattle for the Levites.

10The service was arranged and the priests stood in their places with the Levites in their divisions as the king had ordered. 11The Passover lambs were slaughtered, and the priests sprinkled the blood handed to them, while the Levites skinned the animals. 12They set aside the burnt offerings to give them to the subdivisions of the families of the people to offer to the LORD,

כַּכָּתוּב בְּסֵפֶר מֹשֶׁה וְכֵן לַבָּקָר׃
with-the-cattle and-same Moses in-Book-of as-the-thing-being-written

(13) וַיְבַשְּׁלוּ הַפֶּסַח בָּאֵשׁ כַּמִּשְׁפָּט
as-the-prescription over-the-fire the-Passover-animal and-they-roasted (13)

וְהַקֳּדָשִׁים בִּשְּׁלוּ בַּסִּירוֹת וּבַדְּוָדִים֙
and-in-the-caldrons in-the-pots they-boiled and-the-holy-offerings

וּבַצֵּלָחוֹת וַיָּרִיצוּ לְכָל־ בְּנֵי הָעָם׃
the-people sons-of to-all-of and-they-served-quickly and-in-the-pans

(14) וְאַחַר הֵכִינוּ לָהֶם֙ וְלַכֹּהֲנִים כִּי הַכֹּהֲנִים֩
the-priests because and-for-the-priests for-them they-prepared and-after (14)

בְּנֵי אַהֲרֹן בְּהַעֲלוֹת הָעוֹלָה וְהַחֲלָבִים
and-the-fat-portions the-burnt-offering in-to-sacrifice Aaron descendants-of

עַד־ לָיְלָה וְהַלְוִיִּם֙ הֵכִינוּ לָהֶם וְלַכֹּהֲנִים
and-for-the-priests for-them they-prepared so-the-Levites nightfall until

בְּנֵי אַהֲרֹן׃ (15) וְהַמְשֹׁרְרִים בְּנֵי־ אָסָף עַל־
in Asaph descendants-of and-the-ones-making-music (15) Aaron sons-of

מַעֲמָדָם כְּמִצְוַת דָּוִיד וְאָסָף וְהֵימָן וִידֻתוּן֙ חוֹזֵה
seer-of and-Jeduthun and-Heman and-Asaph David as-prescription-of place-of-them

הַמֶּלֶךְ וְהַשֹּׁעֲרִים לְשַׁעַר וָשָׁעַר אֵין לָהֶם לָסוּר֙ מֵעַל
from-at to-leave to-them not and-gate at-gate and-the-gatekeepers the-king

עֲבֹדָתָם כִּי־ אֲחֵיהֶם הַלְוִיִּם הֵכִינוּ לָהֶם׃
for-them they-prepared the-Levites fellows-of-them because post-of-them

(16) וַתִּכּוֹן כָּל־ עֲבוֹדַת יְהוָה בַּיּוֹם הַהוּא֙
the-that on-the-day Yahweh service-of entire-of so-she-was-carried-out (16)

לַעֲשׂוֹת הַפֶּסַח וְהַעֲלוֹת עֹלוֹת עַל מִזְבַּח יְהוָה
Yahweh altar-of on burnt-offerings and-to-offer the-Passover to-celebrate

כְּמִצְוַת הַמֶּלֶךְ יֹאשִׁיָּהוּ׃ (17) וַיַּעֲשׂוּ בְנֵי־ יִשְׂרָאֵל
Israel sons-of and-they-celebrated (17) Josiah the-king as-order-of

הַנִּמְצְאִים אֶת־ הַפֶּסַח בָּעֵת הַהִיא וְאֶת־ חַג
Feast-of and the-that at-the-time the-Passover *** the-ones-being-found

הַמַּצּוֹת שִׁבְעַת יָמִים׃ (18) וְלֹא־ נַעֲשָׂה פֶּסַח
Passover she-was-observed and-not (18) days seven-of the-Unleavened-Breads

כָּמֹהוּ בְּיִשְׂרָאֵל מִימֵי שְׁמוּאֵל הַנָּבִיא וְכָל־ מַלְכֵי
kings-of and-all-of the-prophet Samuel since-days-of in-Israel like-him

יִשְׂרָאֵל ׀ לֹא־ עָשׂוּ כַּפֶּסַח אֲשֶׁר־ עָשָׂה יֹאשִׁיָּהוּ
Josiah he-did that like-the-Passover they-celebrated not Israel

וְהַכֹּהֲנִים וְהַלְוִיִּם וְכָל־ יְהוּדָה֙ וְיִשְׂרָאֵל הַנִּמְצָא
the-one-being-found and-Israel Judah and-all-of and-the-Levites with-the-priests

as is written in the Book of
Moses. They did the same
with the cattle. 13 They roasted
the Passover animals over the
fire as prescribed, and boiled
the holy offerings in pots, cal-
drons and pans and served
them quickly to all the people.
14 After this, they made preparations for themselves and for
the priests, because the
priests, the descendants of
Aaron, were sacrificing the
burnt offerings and the fat
portions until nightfall. So the
Levites made preparations for
themselves and for the
Aaronic priests.
15 The musicians, the de-
scendants of Asaph, were in
the places prescribed by David, Asaph, Heman and Jeduthun the king's seer. The gatekeepers at each gate did not
need to leave their posts, because their fellow Levites
made the preparations for
them.
16 So at that time the entire
service of the LORD was carried
out for the celebration of the
Passover and the offering of
burnt offerings on the altar of
the LORD, as King Josiah had
ordered. 17 The Israelites who
were present celebrated the
Passover at that time and observed the Feast of Unleavened Bread for seven days.
18 The Passover had not been
observed like this in Israel
since the days of the prophet
Samuel; and none of the kings
of Israel had ever celebrated
such a Passover as did Josiah,
with the priests, the Levites
and all Judah and Israel who

וְיוֹשְׁבֵי יְרוּשָׁלִָם׃ בִּשְׁמוֹנֶה עֶשְׂרֵה שָׁנָה לְמַלְכוּת יֹאשִׁיָּהוּ
Josiah of-reign-of year ten in-eight (19) Jerusalem and-ones-living-of

נַעֲשָׂה הַפֶּסַח הַזֶּה׃ אַחֲרֵי כָל־ זֹאת אֲשֶׁר
when this all-of after (20) the-this the-Passover she-was-celebrated

הֵכִין יֹאשִׁיָּהוּ אֶת־ הַבַּיִת עָלָה נְכוֹ מֶלֶךְ־מִצְרַיִם לְהִלָּחֵם
to-fight Egypt king-of Neco he-went-up the-temple *** Josiah he-set-in-order

בְּכַרְכְּמִישׁ עַל־ פְּרָת וַיֵּצֵא לִקְרָאתוֹ יֹאשִׁיָּהוּ׃
Josiah to-meet-him and-he-marched-out Euphrates on at-Carchemish

וַיִּשְׁלַח אֵלָיו מַלְאָכִים ׀ לֵאמֹר ׀ מַה־ לִּי וָלָךְ
and-between-you between-me what? to-say messengers to-him but-he-sent (21)

מֶלֶךְ יְהוּדָה לֹא־ עָלֶיךָ אַתָּה הַיּוֹם כִּי אֶל־ בֵּית מִלְחַמְתִּי
war-of-me house-of against but the-day you against-you not Judah king-of

וֵאלֹהִים אָמַר לְבַהֲלֵנִי חֲדַל־ לְךָ מֵאֱלֹהִים אֲשֶׁר־ עִמִּי וְאַל־
so-not with-me who against-God for-you stop! to-hurry-me he-told and-God

יַשְׁחִיתֶךָ׃ וְלֹא־ הֵסֵב יֹאשִׁיָּהוּ פָנָיו מִמֶּנּוּ
from-him faces-of-him Josiah he-turned-away but-not (22) he-destroys-you

כִּי לְהִלָּחֵם־ בּוֹ הִתְחַפֵּשׂ וְלֹא שָׁמַע אֶל־
to he-listened and-not he-disguised-himself against-him to-battle but

דִּבְרֵי נְכוֹ מִפִּי אֱלֹהִים וַיָּבֹא לְהִלָּחֵם בְּבִקְעַת מְגִדּוֹ׃
Megiddo on-plain-of to-fight but-he-went God at-command-of Neco words-of

וַיֹּרוּ הַיֹּרִים לַמֶּלֶךְ יֹאשִׁיָּהוּ וַיֹּאמֶר
and-he-told Josiah to-the-king the-ones-being-archers but-they-shot (23)

הַמֶּלֶךְ לַעֲבָדָיו הַעֲבִירוּנִי כִּי הָחֳלֵיתִי מְאֹד׃
badly I-am-wounded for take-away-me! to-officers-of-him the-king

וַיַּעֲבִירֻהוּ עֲבָדָיו מִן־ הַמֶּרְכָּבָה וַיַּרְכִּיבֻהוּ עַל
in and-they-put-him the-chariot from officers-of-him so-they-took-him (24)

רֶכֶב הַמִּשְׁנֶה אֲשֶׁר־ לוֹ וַיּוֹלִיכֻהוּ יְרוּשָׁלִַם וַיָּמָת
and-he-died Jerusalem and-they-brought-him to-him that the-other chariot-of

וַיִּקָּבֵר בְּקִבְרוֹת אֲבֹתָיו וְכָל־ יְהוּדָה וִירוּשָׁלִַם
and-Jerusalem Judah and-all-of fathers-of-him in-tombs-of and-he-was-buried

מִתְאַבְּלִים עַל־ יֹאשִׁיָּהוּ׃ וַיְקוֹנֵן יִרְמְיָהוּ עַל־ יֹאשִׁיָּהוּ
Josiah for Jeremiah and-he-composed-lament (25) Josiah for ones-mourning

וַיֹּאמְרוּ כָל־ הַשָּׁרִים ׀ וְהַשָּׁרוֹת
and-the-women-singing the-men-singing all-of and-they-commemorate

בְּקִינוֹתֵיהֶם עַל־ יֹאשִׁיָּהוּ עַד־ הַיּוֹם וַיִּתְּנוּם לְחֹק עַל־
in as-tradition and-they-made-them the-day to Josiah for in-laments-of-them

יִשְׂרָאֵל וְהִנָּם כְּתוּבִים עַל־ הַקִּינוֹת׃ וְיֶתֶר
and-other-of (26) the-Laments in ones-being-written and-see-they! Israel

were there with the people of
Jerusalem. [19]This Passover was
celebrated in the eighteenth
year of Josiah's reign.

The Death of Josiah

[20]After all this, when Josiah
had set the temple in order,
Neco king of Egypt went up to
fight at Carchemish on the Euphrates,
and Josiah marched
out to meet him in battle. [21]But
Neco sent messengers to him,
saying, "What quarrel is there
between you and me, O king
of Judah? It is not you I am
attacking at this time, but the
house with which I am at war.
God has told me to hurry; so
stop opposing God, who is
with me, or he will destroy
you."
[22]Josiah, however, would
not turn away from him, but
disguised himself to engage
him in battle. He would not
listen to what Neco had said at
God's command but went to
fight him on the plain of
Megiddo.
[23]Archers shot King Josiah,
and he told his officers, "Take
me away; I am badly wounded."
[24]So they took him out of
his chariot, put him in the other
chariot he had and brought
him to Jerusalem, where he
died. He was buried in the
tombs of his fathers, and all
Judah and Jerusalem mourned
for him.
[25]Jeremiah composed laments
for Josiah, and to this
day all the men and women
singers commemorate Josiah
in the laments. These became
a tradition in Israel and are
written in the Laments.

דִּבְרֵי יֹאשִׁיָּהוּ וַחֲסָדָיו כַּכָּתוּב
as-the-thing-being-written and-acts-of-devotion-of-him Josiah events-of

בְּתוֹרַת יְהוָה׃ וּדְבָרָיו הָרִאשֹׁנִים וְהָאַחֲרֹנִים הִנָּם
see-they! and-the-ends the-beginnings and-events-of-him (27) Yahweh in-Law-of

כְּתוּבִים עַל־ סֵפֶר מַלְכֵי־ יִשְׂרָאֵל וִיהוּדָה׃ וַיִּקְחוּ
and-they-took (36:1) and-Judah Israel kings-of book-of in ones-being-written

עַם־ הָאָרֶץ אֶת־ יְהוֹאָחָז בֶּן־ יֹאשִׁיָּהוּ וַיַּמְלִיכֻהוּ
and-they-made-king-him Josiah son-of Jehoahaz *** the-land people-of

תַחַת־ אָבִיו בִּירוּשָׁלִָם׃ בֶּן־ שָׁלוֹשׁ וְעֶשְׂרִים שָׁנָה
year and-twenty three son-of (2) in-Jerusalem father-of-him in-place-of

יוֹאָחָז בְּמָלְכוֹ וּשְׁלֹשָׁה חֳדָשִׁים מָלַךְ בִּירוּשָׁלִָם׃
in-Jerusalem he-reigned months and-three when-to-become-king-him Joahaz

וַיְסִירֵהוּ מֶלֶךְ־ מִצְרַיִם בִּירוּשָׁלִָם וַיַּעֲנֹשׁ אֶת־
*** and-he-imposed-levy in-Jerusalem Egypt king-of and-he-dethroned-him (3)

הָאָרֶץ מֵאָה כִכַּר־ כֶּסֶף וְכִכַּר זָהָב׃ וַיַּמְלֵךְ
and-he-made-king (4) gold and-talent-of silver talent-of hundred the-land

מֶלֶךְ־ מִצְרַיִם אֶת־ אֶלְיָקִים אָחִיו עַל־ יְהוּדָה וִירוּשָׁלִַם
and-Jerusalem Judah over brother-of-him Eliakim *** Egypt king-of

וַיַּסֵּב אֶת־ שְׁמוֹ יְהוֹיָקִים וְאֶת־ יוֹאָחָז אָחִיו לָקַח
he-took brother-of-him Joahaz but Jehoiakim name-of-him *** and-he-changed

נְכוֹ וַיְבִיאֵהוּ מִצְרָיְמָה׃ בֶּן־ עֶשְׂרִים וְחָמֵשׁ שָׁנָה
year and-five twenty son-of (5) to-Egypt and-he-carried-off-him Neco

יְהוֹיָקִים בְּמָלְכוֹ וְאַחַת עֶשְׂרֵה שָׁנָה מָלַךְ בִּירוּשָׁלִָם
in-Jerusalem he-reigned year ten and-one-of when-to-become-king-him Jehoiakim

וַיַּעַשׂ הָרַע בְּעֵינֵי יְהוָה אֱלֹהָיו׃ עָלָיו עָלָה
he-attacked against-him (6) God-of-him Yahweh in-eyes-of the-evil and-he-did

נְבוּכַדְנֶאצַּר מֶלֶךְ בָּבֶל וַיַּאַסְרֵהוּ בַּנְחֻשְׁתַּיִם
with-the-bronze-shackles and-he-bound-him Babylon king-of Nebuchadnezzar

לְהֹלִיכוֹ בָּבֶלָה׃ וּמִכְּלֵי בֵּית יְהוָה הֵבִיא
he-took Yahweh temple-of and-from-articles-of (7) to-Babylon to-take-him

נְבוּכַדְנֶאצַּר לְבָבֶל וַיִּתְּנֵם בְּהֵיכָלוֹ בְּבָבֶל׃
in-Babylon in-temple-of-him and-he-put-them to-Babylon Nebuchadnezzar

וְיֶתֶר דִּבְרֵי יְהוֹיָקִים וְתֹעֲבֹתָיו אֲשֶׁר־ עָשָׂה
he-did that and-detestable-things-of-him Jehoiakim events-of and-other-of (8)

וְהַנִּמְצָא עָלָיו הִנָּם כְּתוּבִים עַל־ סֵפֶר
book-of in ones-being-written see-they! against-him and-the-thing-being-found

מַלְכֵי יִשְׂרָאֵל וִיהוּדָה וַיִּמְלֹךְ יְהוֹיָכִין בְּנוֹ
son-of-him Jehoiachin and-he-became-king and-Judah Israel kings-of

[26]The other events of Josiah's reign and his acts of devotion, according to what is
written in the Law of the
LORD— [27]all the events, from
beginning to end, are written
in the book of the kings of Is-
36 rael and Judah. [1]And
the people of the land
took Jehoahaz son of Josiah
and made him king in Jerusalem in place of his father.

Jehoahaz King of Judah

[2]Jehoahaz[j] was twenty-
three years old when he
became king, and he reigned
in Jerusalem three months.
[3]The king of Egypt dethroned
him in Jerusalem and imposed
on Judah a levy of a hundred
talents[k] of silver and a talent[l]
of gold. [4]The king of Egypt
made Eliakim, a brother of
Jehoahaz, king over Judah and
Jerusalem and changed Eliakim's name to Jehoiakim. But
Neco took Eliakim's brother
Jehoahaz and carried him off
to Egypt.

Jehoiakim King of Judah

[5]Jehoiakim was twenty-five
years old when he became
king, and he reigned in
Jerusalem eleven years. He did
evil in the eyes of the LORD his
God. [6]Nebuchadnezzar king of
Babylon attacked him and
bound him with bronze
shackles to take him to Babylon. [7]Nebuchadnezzar also
took to Babylon articles from
the temple of the LORD and put
them in his temple[m] there.
[8]The other events of Jehoiakim's reign, the detestable
things he did and all that was
found against him, are written
in the book of the kings of Israel and Judah. And Jehoiachin his son succeeded him as
king.

j2 Hebrew *Joahaz*, a variant of *Jehoahaz*; also in verse 4
k3 That is, about 3 3/4 tons (about 3.4 metric tons)
l3 That is, about 75 pounds (about 34 kilograms)
m7 Or *palace*

תַּחְתָּיו׃ בֶּן־ שְׁמוֹנֶה שָׁנִים יְהוֹיָכִין בְּמָלְכוֹ
when-to-become-king-him Jehoiachin years eight son-of (9) in-place-of-him

וּשְׁלֹשָׁה חֳדָשִׁים וַעֲשֶׂרֶת יָמִים מָלַךְ בִּירוּשָׁלָ͏ִם וַיַּעַשׂ הָרַע
the-evil and-he-did in-Jerusalem he-reigned days and-ten-of months and-three

בְּעֵינֵי יְהוָה׃ וְלִתְשׁוּבַת הַשָּׁנָה שָׁלַח הַמֶּלֶךְ נְבוּכַדְנֶאצַּר
Nebuchadnezzar the-king he-sent the-year and-at-turn-of (10) Yahweh in-eyes-of

וַיְבִאֵהוּ בָבֶלָה עִם־ כְּלֵי חֶמְדַּת בֵּית־ יְהוָה
Yahweh temple-of value-of articles-of with to-Babylon and-he-brought-him

וַיַּמְלֵךְ אֶת־ צִדְקִיָּהוּ אָחִיו עַל־ יְהוּדָה וִירוּשָׁלָ͏ִם׃
and-Jerusalem Judah over brother-of-him Zedekiah *** and-he-made-king

בֶּן־ עֶשְׂרִים וְאַחַת שָׁנָה צִדְקִיָּהוּ בְמָלְכוֹ וְאַחַת
and-one-of when-to-become-king-him Zedekiah year and-one twenty son-of (11)

עֶשְׂרֵה שָׁנָה מָלַךְ בִּירוּשָׁלָ͏ִם׃ וַיַּעַשׂ הָרַע בְּעֵינֵי יְהוָה
Yahweh in-eyes-of the-evil and-he-did (12) in-Jerusalem he-reigned year ten

אֱלֹהָיו לֹא נִכְנַע מִלִּפְנֵי יִרְמְיָהוּ הַנָּבִיא מִפִּי
at-word-of the-prophet Jeremiah at-before he-humbled-himself not God-of-him

יְהוָה׃ וְגַם בַּמֶּלֶךְ נְבוּכַדְנֶאצַּר מָרָד אֲשֶׁר
who he-rebelled Nebuchadnezzar against-the-king and-also (13) Yahweh

הִשְׁבִּיעוֹ בֵּאלֹהִים וַיֶּקֶשׁ אֶת־ עָרְפּוֹ וַיְאַמֵּץ
and-he-hardened neck-of-him *** and-he-became-stiff by-God he-made-take-oath

אֶת־ לְבָבוֹ מִשּׁוּב אֶל־ יְהוָה אֱלֹהֵי יִשְׂרָאֵל׃ גַּם כָּל־
all-of furthermore (14) Israel God-of Yahweh to from-to-turn heart-of-him ***

שָׂרֵי הַכֹּהֲנִים וְהָעָם הִרְבּוּ לִמְעָוֹל־
to-be-unfaithful they-became-more and-the-people the-priests leaders-of

מַעַל כְּכֹל תֹּעֲבוֹת הַגּוֹיִם וַיְטַמְּאוּ
and-they-defiled the-nations detestable-practices-of as-all-of unfaithfulness

אֶת־ בֵּית יְהוָה אֲשֶׁר הִקְדִּישׁ בִּירוּשָׁלָ͏ִם׃ וַיִּשְׁלַח יְהוָה
Yahweh and-he-sent (15) in-Jerusalem he-consecrated which Yahweh temple-of ***

אֱלֹהֵי אֲבוֹתֵיהֶם עֲלֵיהֶם בְּיַד מַלְאָכָיו הַשְׁכֵּם
to-get-up messengers-of-him by-hand-of to-them fathers-of-them God-of

וְשָׁלוֹחַ כִּי־ חָמַל עַל־ עַמּוֹ וְעַל־ מְעוֹנוֹ׃
dwelling-of-him and-on people-of-him on he-had-pity because and-to-send

וַיִּהְיוּ מַלְעִבִים בְּמַלְאֲכֵי הָאֱלֹהִים וּבוֹזִים
and-ones-despising the-God at-messengers-of ones-mocking but-they-were (16)

דְּבָרָיו וּמִתַּעְתְּעִים בִּנְבִאָיו עַד עֲלוֹת חֲמַת־
wrath-of to-be-aroused until at-prophets-of-him and-ones-scoffing words-of-him

יְהוָה בְּעַמּוֹ עַד־ לְאֵין מַרְפֵּא׃ וַיַּעַל
and-he-brought (17) remedy to-there-was-no until against-people-of-him Yahweh

°14 ק למעל

Jehoiachin King of Judah

9Jehoiachin was eighteen[n]
years old when he became
king, and he reigned in
Jerusalem three months and
ten days. He did evil in the
eyes of the LORD. 10At the turn
of the year,[o] King Nebuchadnezzar sent for him and
brought him to Babylon, together with articles of value
from the temple of the LORD,
and he made Jehoiachin's uncle,[p] Zedekiah, king over
Judah and Jerusalem.

Zedekiah King of Judah

11Zedekiah was twenty-one
years old when he became
king, and he reigned in
Jerusalem eleven years. 12He
did evil in the eyes of the LORD
his God and did not humble
himself before Jeremiah the
prophet, who spoke the word
of the LORD. 13He also rebelled
against King Nebuchadnez-
zar, who had made him take
an oath in God's name. He
became stiff-necked and hard-
ened his heart and would not
turn to the LORD, the God of
Israel. 14Furthermore, all the
leaders of the priests and the
people became more and more
unfaithful, following all the
detestable practices of the nations and defiling the temple
of the LORD, which he had
consecrated in Jerusalem.

The Fall of Jerusalem

15The LORD, the God of their
fathers, sent word to them
through his messengers again
and again, because he had
pity on his people and on his
dwelling place. 16But they
mocked God's messengers, despised his words and scoffed
at his prophets until the wrath
of the LORD was aroused
against his people and there
was no remedy. 17He brought

[n]9 One Hebrew manuscript, some Septuagint manuscripts and Syriac (see also 2 Kings 24:8); most Hebrew manuscripts *eight*
[o]10 That is, in the spring
[p]10 Hebrew *brother*, that is, relative (see 2 Kings 24:17)

עֲלֵיהֶם אֶת־ מֶלֶךְ כַּשְׂדִּיים וַיַּהֲרֹג בַּחוּרֵיהֶם
young-men-of-them and-he-killed Chaldeans king-of *** against-them

בַּחֶרֶב בְּבֵית מִקְדָּשָׁם וְלֹא חָמַל עַל־ בָּחוּר
young-man to he-spared and-not sanctuary-of-them in-house-of with-the-sword

וּבְתוּלָה זָקֵן וְיָשֵׁשׁ הַכֹּל נָתַן בְּיָדוֹ׃
into-hand-of-him he-gave the-whole or-aged old-man or-young-woman

וְכֹל כְּלֵי בֵּית הָאֱלֹהִים הַגְּדֹלִים וְהַקְּטַנִּים
and-the-small-ones the-large-ones the-God temple-of articles-of and-all-of (18)

וְאֹצְרוֹת בֵּית יְהוָה וְאֹצְרוֹת הַמֶּלֶךְ וְשָׂרָיו
and-officials-of-him the-king and-treasures-of Yahweh temple-of and-treasures-of

הַכֹּל הֵבִיא בָבֶל׃ וַיִּשְׂרְפוּ אֶת־ בֵּית הָאֱלֹהִים
the-God temple-of *** and-they-set-fire (19) Babylon he-carried the-whole

וַיְנַתְּצוּ אֵת חוֹמַת יְרוּשָׁלִָם וְכָל־ אַרְמְנוֹתֶיהָ
palaces-of-her and-all-of Jerusalem wall-of *** and-they-broke-down

שָׂרְפוּ בָאֵשׁ וְכָל־ כְּלֵי מַחֲמַדֶּיהָ לְהַשְׁחִית׃
to-destroy valuable-ones-of-her articles-of and-all-of with-fire they-burned

וַיֶּגֶל הַשְּׁאֵרִית מִן־ הַחֶרֶב אֶל־ בָּבֶל וַיִּהְיוּ־
and-they-became Babylon to the-sword from the-remnant and-he-exiled (20)

לוֹ וּלְבָנָיו לַעֲבָדִים עַד־ מְלֹךְ מַלְכוּת פָּרָס׃
Persia kingdom-of to-come-to-power until as-servants and-to-sons-of-him to-him

לְמַלֹּאות דְּבַר־ יְהוָה בְּפִי יִרְמְיָהוּ עַד־ רָצְתָה הָאָרֶץ
the-land she-enjoyed until Jeremiah by-mouth-of Yahweh word-of to-fulfill (21)

אֶת־ שַׁבְּתוֹתֶיהָ כָּל־ יְמֵי הָשַּׁמָּה שָׁבָתָה לְמַלֹּאות
to-complete she-rested to-be-desolate days-of all-of Sabbaths-of-her ***

שִׁבְעִים שָׁנָה׃ וּבִשְׁנַת אַחַת לְכוֹרֶשׁ מֶלֶךְ פָּרַס לִכְלוֹת
to-fulfill Persia king-of of-Cyrus one now-in-year-of (22) year seventy

דְּבַר־ יְהוָה בְּפִי יִרְמְיָהוּ הֵעִיר יְהוָה אֶת־ רוּחַ כּוֹרֶשׁ מֶלֶךְ־
king-of Cyrus heart-of *** Yahweh he-moved Jeremiah by-mouth-of Yahweh word-of

פָּרַס וַיַּעֲבֶר־ קוֹל בְּכָל־ מַלְכוּתוֹ וְגַם־ בְּמִכְתָּב
in-writing and-also realm-of-him through-all-of proclamation so-he-made Persia

לֵאמֹר׃ כֹּה־ אָמַר כּוֹרֶשׁ ׀ מֶלֶךְ פָּרַס כָּל־ מַמְלְכוֹת הָאָרֶץ
the-earth kingdoms-of all-of Persia king-of Cyrus he-says this (23) to-say

נָתַן לִי יְהוָה אֱלֹהֵי הַשָּׁמַיִם וְהוּא־ פָקַד עָלַי לִבְנוֹת־
to-build to-me he-appointed and-he the-heavens God-of Yahweh to-me he-gave

לוֹ בַּיִת בִּירוּשָׁלִַם אֲשֶׁר בִּיהוּדָה מִי־ בָכֶם מִכָּל־
from-all-of among-you anyone in-Judah that at-Jerusalem temple for-him

עַמּוֹ יְהוָה אֱלֹהָיו עִמּוֹ וְיָעַל׃
and-let-him-go-up with-him God-of-him Yahweh people-of-him

up against them the king of
the Babylonians,[q] who killed
their young men with the
sword in the sanctuary, and
spared neither young man nor
young woman, old man or
aged. God handed all of them
over to Nebuchadnezzar. [18]He
carried to Babylon all the articles from the temple of God,
both large and small, and the
treasures of the LORD's temple
and the treasures of the king
and his officials. [19]They set fire
to God's temple and broke
down the wall of Jerusalem;
they burned all the palaces
and destroyed everything of
value there.
[20]He carried into exile to
Babylon the remnant, who escaped from the sword, and
they became servants to him
and his sons until the kingdom of Persia came to power.
[21]The land enjoyed its Sabbath
rests; all the time of its desolation it rested, until the seventy
years were completed in
fulfillment of the word of the
LORD spoken by Jeremiah.
[22]In the first year of Cyrus
king of Persia, in order to
fulfill the word of the LORD
spoken by Jeremiah, the LORD
moved the heart of Cyrus king
of Persia to make a proclamation throughout his realm and
to put it in writing:

[23]"This is what Cyrus king
of Persia says:
"'The LORD, the God of
heaven, has given me all
the kingdoms of the earth
and he has appointed me to
build a temple for him at
Jerusalem in Judah. Any-
one of his people among
you—may the LORD his God
be with him, and let him go
up.'"

q17 Or *Chaldeans*

°17 ק כשדים

וּבִשְׁנַת אַחַת לְכוֹרֶשׁ מֶלֶךְ פָּרַס לִכְלוֹת דְּבַר־ יְהוָה

Yahweh word-of to-fulfill Persia king-of of-Cyrus one now-in-year-of (1:1)

מִפִּי יִרְמְיָה הֵעִיר יְהוָה אֶת־ רוּחַ כֹּרֶשׁ מֶלֶךְ־ פָּרַס

Persia king-of Cyrus heart-of *** Yahweh he-moved Jeremiah by-mouth-of

וַיַּעֲבֶר־ קוֹל בְּכָל־ מַלְכוּתוֹ וְגַם־ בְּמִכְתָּב

in-writing and-also realm-of-him through-all-of proclamation so-he-made

לֵאמֹר׃ כֹּה אָמַר כֹּרֶשׁ מֶלֶךְ פָּרַס כֹּל מַמְלְכוֹת הָאָרֶץ

the-earth kingdoms-of all-of Persia king-of Cyrus he-says this (2) to-say

נָתַן לִי יְהוָה אֱלֹהֵי הַשָּׁמָיִם וְהוּא־ פָקַד עָלַי לִבְנוֹת־

to-build to-me he-appointed and-he the-heavens God-of Yahweh to-me he-gave

לוֹ בַיִת בִּירוּשָׁלַםִ אֲשֶׁר בִּיהוּדָה׃ מִי־ בָכֶם מִכָּל־

from-all-of among-you anyone (3) in-Judah that at-Jerusalem temple for-him

עַמּוֹ יְהִי אֱלֹהָיו עִמּוֹ וְיַעַל לִירוּשָׁלַםִ

to-Jerusalem and-let-him-go-up with-him God-of-him may-he-be people-of-him

אֲשֶׁר בִּיהוּדָה וְיִבֶן אֶת־ בֵּית יְהוָה אֱלֹהֵי יִשְׂרָאֵל הוּא

he Israel God-of Yahweh temple-of *** and-let-him-build in-Judah that

הָאֱלֹהִים אֲשֶׁר בִּירוּשָׁלָםִ׃ וְכָל־ הַנִּשְׁאָר מִכָּל־

from-any-of the-one-surviving and-all-of (4) in-Jerusalem who the-God

הַמְּקֹמוֹת אֲשֶׁר הוּא גָר־ שָׁם יְנַשְּׂאוּהוּ אַנְשֵׁי מְקֹמוֹ

place-of-him people-of let-them-provide-him there living he where the-places

בְּכֶסֶף וּבְזָהָב וּבִרְכוּשׁ וּבִבְהֵמָה עִם־

with and-with-livestock and-with-goods and-with-gold with-silver

הַנְּדָבָה לְבֵית הָאֱלֹהִים אֲשֶׁר בִּירוּשָׁלָםִ׃

in-Jerusalem that the-God for-temple-of the-freewill-offering

וַיָּקוּמוּ רָאשֵׁי הָאָבוֹת לִיהוּדָה וּבִנְיָמִן

and-Benjamin of-Judah the-fathers heads-of then-they-prepared (5)

וְהַכֹּהֲנִים וְהַלְוִיִּם לְכֹל הֵעִיר הָאֱלֹהִים אֶת־ רוּחוֹ

heart-of-him *** the-God he-moved to-everyone and-the-Levites and-the-priests

לַעֲלוֹת לִבְנוֹת אֶת־ בֵּית יְהוָה אֲשֶׁר בִּירוּשָׁלָםִ׃ וְכָל־

and-all-of (6) in-Jerusalem that Yahweh temple-of *** and-to-build to-go-up

סְבִיבֹתֵיהֶם חִזְּקוּ בִידֵיהֶם בִּכְלֵי־ כֶסֶף

silver with-articles-of to-hands-of-them they-assisted neighbors-of-them

בַּזָּהָב בָּרְכוּשׁ וּבַבְּהֵמָה וּבַמִּגְדָּנוֹת

and-with-the-valuable-gifts and-with-the-livestock with-the-goods with-the-gold

לְבַד עַל־ כָּל־ הִתְנַדֵּב׃ וְהַמֶּלֶךְ כּוֹרֶשׁ

Cyrus and-the-king (7) to-be-freely-given all-of to in-addition-to

הוֹצִיא אֶת־ כְּלֵי בֵית־ יְהוָה אֲשֶׁר הוֹצִיא

he-carried-away which Yahweh temple-of articles-of *** he-brought-out

Cyrus Helps the Exiles to Return

1 In the first year of Cyrus
king of Persia, in order to
fulfill the word of the LORD
spoken by Jeremiah, the LORD
moved the heart of Cyrus king
of Persia to make a proclamation throughout his realm and
to put it in writing:

2 "This is what Cyrus king
of Persia says:
" 'The LORD, the God of
heaven, has given me all
the kingdoms of the earth
and he has appointed me to
build a temple for him at
Jerusalem in Judah. 3 Anyone of his people among
you—may his God be with
him, and let him go up to
Jerusalem in Judah and
build the temple of the
LORD, the God of Israel, the
God who is in Jerusalem.
4 And the people of any
place where survivors may
now be living are to pro-
vide him with silver and
gold, with goods and livestock, and with freewill
offerings for the temple of
God in Jerusalem.' "

5 Then the family heads of
Judah and Benjamin, and the
priests and Levites—everyone
whose heart God had moved—
prepared to go up and build
the house of the LORD in
Jerusalem. 6 All their neighbors
assisted them with articles of
silver and gold, with goods
and livestock, and with valuable gifts, in addition to all the
freewill offerings. 7 Moreover,
King Cyrus brought out the
articles belonging to the temple of the LORD, which Nebuchadnezzar had carried away

נְבוּכַדְנֶצַּר מִירוּשָׁלִַם וַיִּתְּנֵם בְּבֵית אֱלֹהָיו׃
gods-of-him in-temple-of and-he-placed-them from-Jerusalem Nebuchadnezzar

(8) וַיּוֹצִיאֵם כּוֹרֶשׁ מֶלֶךְ פָּרַס עַל־ יַד מִתְרְדָת
Mithredath hand-of by Persia king-of Cyrus and-he-had-brought-them (8)

הַגִּזְבָּר וַיִּסְפְּרֵם לְשֵׁשְׁבַּצַּר הַנָּשִׂיא לִיהוּדָה׃
of-Judah the-prince to-Sheshbazzar and-he-counted-them the-treasurer

(9) וְאֵלֶּה מִסְפָּרָם אֲגַרְטְלֵי זָהָב שְׁלֹשִׁים אֲגַרְטְלֵי־ כֶסֶף
silver dishes-of thirty gold dishes-of inventory-of-them and-these (9)

אָלֶף מַחֲלָפִים תִּשְׁעָה וְעֶשְׂרִים׃ (10) כְּפוֹרֵי זָהָב שְׁלֹשִׁים כְּפוֹרֵי כֶסֶף
silver bowls-of thirty gold bowls-of (10) and-twenty nine pans thousand

מִשְׁנִים אַרְבַּע מֵאוֹת וַעֲשָׂרָה כֵּלִים אֲחֵרִים אָלֶף׃
thousand other-ones articles and-ten hundreds four-of matching-ones

(11) כָּל־ כֵּלִים לַזָּהָב וְלַכֶּסֶף חֲמֵשֶׁת אֲלָפִים
thousands five-of and-of-the-silver of-the-gold articles all-of (11)

וְאַרְבַּע מֵאוֹת הַכֹּל הֶעֱלָה שֵׁשְׁבַּצַּר עִם הֵעָלוֹת
to-come-up when Sheshbazzar he-brought-up the-whole hundreds and-four-of

הַגּוֹלָה מִבָּבֶל לִירוּשָׁלִָם׃ (2:1) וְאֵלֶּה ׀ בְּנֵי
people-of now-these (2:1) to-Jerusalem from-Babylon the-exile

הַמְּדִינָה הָעֹלִים מִשְּׁבִי הַגּוֹלָה אֲשֶׁר
whom the-exile from-captivity-of the-ones-coming-up the-province

הֶגְלָה נְבוּכַדְנֶצּוֹר[c] מֶלֶךְ־ בָּבֶל לְבָבֶל וַיָּשׁוּבוּ
and-they-returned to-Babylon Babylon king-of Nebuchadnezzar he-took-captive

לִירוּשָׁלִַם וִיהוּדָה אִישׁ לְעִירוֹ׃ (2) אֲשֶׁר־ בָּאוּ עִם־ זְרֻבָּבֶל
Zerubbabel with they-came who (2) to-town-of-him each and-Judah to-Jerusalem

יֵשׁוּעַ נְחֶמְיָה שְׂרָיָה רְעֵלָיָה מָרְדֳּכַי בִּלְשָׁן מִסְפָּר בִּגְוַי רְחוּם
Rehum Bigvai Mispar Bilshan Mordecai Reelaiah Seraiah Nehemiah Jeshua

בַּעֲנָה מִסְפַּר אַנְשֵׁי עַם יִשְׂרָאֵל׃ (3) בְּנֵי פַרְעֹשׁ
Parosh descendants-of (3) Israel people-of men-of list-of Baanah

אַלְפַּיִם מֵאָה שִׁבְעִים וּשְׁנָיִם׃ (4) בְּנֵי שְׁפַטְיָה שְׁלֹשׁ
three-of Shephatiah descendants-of (4) and-two seventy hundred two-thousands

מֵאוֹת שִׁבְעִים וּשְׁנָיִם׃ (5) בְּנֵי אָרַח שְׁבַע מֵאוֹת חֲמִשָּׁה
five hundreds seven-of Arah descendants-of (5) and-two seventy hundreds

וְשִׁבְעִים׃ (6) בְּנֵי־ פַחַת מוֹאָב לִבְנֵי יֵשׁוּעַ
Jeshua through-descendants-of Moab Pahath descendants-of (6) and-seventy

יוֹאָב אַלְפַּיִם שְׁמֹנֶה מֵאוֹת וּשְׁנֵים עָשָׂר׃ (7) בְּנֵי עֵילָם
Elam descendants-of (7) ten and-two hundreds eight two-thousands Joab

אֶלֶף מָאתַיִם חֲמִשִּׁים וְאַרְבָּעָה׃ (8) בְּנֵי זַתּוּא תְּשַׁע
nine-of Zattu descendants-of (8) and-four fifty two-hundreds thousand

from Jerusalem and had
placed in the temple of his
god.[a] 8Cyrus king of Persia had
them brought by Mithredath
the treasurer, who counted
them out to Sheshbazzar the
prince of Judah.
9This was the inventory:

gold dishes	30
silver dishes	1,000
silver pans[b]	29
10gold bowls	30
matching silver bowls	410
other articles	1,000

11In all, there were 5,400
articles of gold and of silver.
Sheshbazzar brought all these
along when the exiles came
up from Babylon to Jerusalem.

The List of the Exiles Who Returned

2 Now these are the people
of the province who came
up from the captivity of the exiles, whom Nebuchadnezzar
king of Babylon had taken
captive to Babylon (they returned to Jerusalem and
Judah, each to his own town,
2in company with Zerubbabel,
Jeshua, Nehemiah, Seraiah,
Reelaiah, Mordecai, Bilshan,
Mispar, Bigvai, Rehum and
Baanah):

The list of the men of the people of Israel:

3the descendants of Parosh	2,172
4of Shephatiah	372
5of Arah	775
6of Pahath-Moab (through the line of Jeshua and Joab)	2,812
7of Elam	1,254
8of Zattu	945

[a]7 Or *gods*
[b]9 The meaning of the Hebrew for this word is uncertain.

[c]1 ק נבוכדנצר

מֵאוֹת וְאַרְבָּעִים וַחֲמִשָּׁה׃ בְּנֵי זַכָּי שְׁבַע מֵאוֹת
hundreds seven-of Zaccai descendants-of (9) and-five and-forty hundreds

וְשִׁשִּׁים׃ בְּנֵי בָנִי שֵׁשׁ מֵאוֹת אַרְבָּעִים וּשְׁנָיִם׃
and-two forty hundreds six-of Bani descendants-of (10) and-sixty

בְּנֵי בֵבָי שֵׁשׁ מֵאוֹת עֶשְׂרִים וּשְׁלֹשָׁה׃ בְּנֵי
descendants-of (12) and-three twenty hundreds six-of Bebai descendants-of (11)

עַזְגָּד אֶלֶף מָאתַיִם עֶשְׂרִים וּשְׁנָיִם׃ בְּנֵי אֲדֹנִיקָם
Adonikam descendants-of (13) and-two twenty two-hundreds thousand Azgad

שֵׁשׁ מֵאוֹת שִׁשִּׁים וְשִׁשָּׁה׃ בְּנֵי בִגְוָי אַלְפַּיִם חֲמִשִּׁים
fifty two-thousands Bigvai descendants-of (14) and-six sixty hundreds six-of

וְשִׁשָּׁה׃ בְּנֵי עָדִין אַרְבַּע מֵאוֹת חֲמִשִּׁים וְאַרְבָּעָה׃
and-four fifty hundreds four-of Adin descendants-of (15) and-six

בְּנֵי־אָטֵר לִיחִזְקִיָּה תִּשְׁעִים וּשְׁמֹנָה׃ בְּנֵי
descendants-of (17) and-eight ninety through-Hezekiah Ater descendants-of (16)

בֵצָי שְׁלֹשׁ מֵאוֹת עֶשְׂרִים וּשְׁלֹשָׁה׃ בְּנֵי יוֹרָה מֵאָה
hundred Jorah descendants-of (18) and-three twenty hundreds three-of Bezai

וּשְׁנֵים עָשָׂר׃ בְּנֵי חָשֻׁם מָאתַיִם עֶשְׂרִים וּשְׁלֹשָׁה׃
and-three twenty two-hundreds Hashum descendants-of (19) ten and-two

בְּנֵי גִבָּר תִּשְׁעִים וַחֲמִשָּׁה׃ בְּנֵי בֵית־לָחֶם מֵאָה
hundred Lehem Beth men-of (21) and-five ninety Gibbar descendants-of (20)

עֶשְׂרִים וּשְׁלֹשָׁה׃ אַנְשֵׁי נְטֹפָה חֲמִשִּׁים וְשִׁשָּׁה׃ אַנְשֵׁי עֲנָתוֹת
Anathoth men-of (23) and-six fifty Netophah men-of (22) and-three twenty

מֵאָה עֶשְׂרִים וּשְׁמֹנָה׃ בְּנֵי עַזְמָוֶת אַרְבָּעִים וּשְׁנָיִם׃ בְּנֵי
men-of (25) and-two forty Azmaveth men-of (24) and-eight twenty hundred

קִרְיַת עָרִים כְּפִירָה וּבְאֵרוֹת שְׁבַע מֵאוֹת וְאַרְבָּעִים וּשְׁלֹשָׁה׃
and-three and-forty hundreds seven-of and-Beeroth Kephirah Arim Kiriath

בְּנֵי הָרָמָה וָגָבַע שֵׁשׁ מֵאוֹת עֶשְׂרִים וְאֶחָד׃ אַנְשֵׁי
men-of (27) and-one twenty hundreds six-of and-Geba the-Ramah men-of (26)

מִכְמָס מֵאָה עֶשְׂרִים וּשְׁנָיִם׃ אַנְשֵׁי בֵית־אֵל וְהָעָי מָאתָיִם
two-hundreds and-the-Ai El Beth men-of (28) and-two twenty hundred Micmash

עֶשְׂרִים וּשְׁלֹשָׁה׃ בְּנֵי נְבוֹ חֲמִשִּׁים וּשְׁנָיִם׃ בְּנֵי מַגְבִּישׁ מֵאָה
hundred Magbish men-of (30) and-two fifty Nebo men-of (29) and-three twenty

חֲמִשִּׁים וְשִׁשָּׁה׃ בְּנֵי עֵילָם אַחֵר אֶלֶף מָאתַיִם חֲמִשִּׁים וְאַרְבָּעָה׃
and-four fifty two-hundreds thousand other Elam men-of (31) and-six fifty

בְּנֵי חָרִם שְׁלֹשׁ מֵאוֹת וְעֶשְׂרִים׃ בְּנֵי־לֹד חָדִיד וְאוֹנוֹ
and-Ono Hadid Lod men-of (33) and-twenty hundreds three-of Harim men-of (32)

שְׁבַע מֵאוֹת עֶשְׂרִים וַחֲמִשָּׁה׃ בְּנֵי יְרֵחוֹ שְׁלֹשׁ מֵאוֹת
hundreds three-of Jericho men-of (34) and-five twenty hundreds seven-of

9 of Zaccai 760
10 of Bani 642
11 of Bebai 623
12 of Azgad 1,222
13 of Adonikam 666
14 of Bigvai 2,056
15 of Adin 454
16 of Ater (through Hezekiah) 98
17 of Bezai 323
18 of Jorah 112
19 of Hashum 223
20 of Gibbar 95
21 the men of Bethlehem 123
22 of Netophah 56
23 of Anathoth 128
24 of Azmaveth 42
25 of Kiriath Jearim,[c] Kephirah and Beeroth 743
26 of Ramah and Geba 621
27 of Micmash 122
28 of Bethel and Ai 223
29 of Nebo 52
30 of Magbish 156
31 of the other Elam 1,254
32 of Harim 320
33 of Lod, Hadid and Ono 725
34 of Jericho 345

[c] 25 See Septuagint (see also Neh. 7:29); Hebrew *Kiriath Arim*.

אַרְבָּעִים וַחֲמִשָּׁה׃ בְּנֵי סְנָאָה שְׁלֹשֶׁת אֲלָפִים וְשֵׁשׁ מֵאוֹת
hundreds and-six-of thousands three-of Senaah men-of (35) and-five forty

וּשְׁלֹשִׁים׃ הַכֹּהֲנִים בְּנֵי יְדַעְיָה לְבֵית יֵשׁוּעַ
Jeshua through-family-of Jedaiah descendants-of the-priests (36) and-thirty

תְּשַׁע מֵאוֹת שִׁבְעִים וּשְׁלֹשָׁה׃ בְּנֵי אִמֵּר אֶלֶף חֲמִשִּׁים
fifty thousand Immer descendants-of (37) and-three seventy hundreds nine-of

וּשְׁנָיִם׃ בְּנֵי פַּשְׁחוּר אֶלֶף מָאתַיִם אַרְבָּעִים וְשִׁבְעָה׃
and-seven forty two-hundreds thousand Pashhur descendants-of (38) and-two

בְּנֵי חָרִם אֶלֶף וְשִׁבְעָה עָשָׂר׃ הַלְוִיִּם
the-Levites (40) ten and-seven thousand Harim descendants-of (39)

בְּנֵי־יֵשׁוּעַ וְקַדְמִיאֵל לִבְנֵי הוֹדַוְיָה שִׁבְעִים
seventy Hodaviah through-descendants-of and-Kadmiel Jeshua descendants-of

וְאַרְבָּעָה׃ הַמְשֹׁרְרִים בְּנֵי אָסָף מֵאָה עֶשְׂרִים וּשְׁמֹנָה׃
and-eight twenty hundred Asaph descendants-of the-ones-singing (41) and-four

בְּנֵי הַשֹּׁעֲרִים בְּנֵי־שַׁלּוּם בְּנֵי־
descendants-of Shallum descendants-of the-gatekeepers descendants-of (42)

אָטֵר בְּנֵי־טַלְמוֹן בְּנֵי־עַקּוּב בְּנֵי חֲטִיטָא
Hatita descendants-of Akkub descendants-of Talmon descendants-of Ater

בְּנֵי שֹׁבָי הַכֹּל מֵאָה שְׁלֹשִׁים וְתִשְׁעָה׃ הַנְּתִינִים
the-temple-servants (43) and-nine thirty hundred the-total Shobai descendants-of

בְּנֵי־צִיחָא בְנֵי־חֲשׂוּפָא בְּנֵי טַבָּעוֹת׃
Tabbaoth descendants-of Hasupha descendants-of Ziha descendants-of

בְּנֵי־קֵרֹס בְּנֵי־סִיעֲהָא בְּנֵי פָדוֹן׃
Padon descendants-of Siaha descendants-of Keros descendants-of (44)

בְּנֵי־לְבָנָה בְנֵי־חֲגָבָה בְּנֵי עַקּוּב׃
Akkub descendants-of Hagabah descendants-of Lebanah descendants-of (45)

בְּנֵי־חָגָב בְּנֵי־שַׁמְלַי° בְּנֵי חָנָן׃
Hanan descendants-of Shalmai descendants-of Hagab descendants-of (46)

בְּנֵי־גִדֵּל בְּנֵי־גַחַר בְּנֵי רְאָיָה׃
Reaiah descendants-of Gahar descendants-of Giddel descendants-of (47)

בְּנֵי־רְצִין בְּנֵי־נְקוֹדָא בְּנֵי גַזָּם׃
Gazzam descendants-of Nekoda descendants-of Rezin descendants-of (48)

בְּנֵי־עֻזָּא בְנֵי־פָסֵחַ בְּנֵי בֵסָי׃
Besai descendants-of Paseah descendants-of Uzza descendants-of (49)

בְּנֵי־אַסְנָה בְנֵי־מְעִינִים° בְּנֵי נְפִיסִים°׃
Nephussim descendants-of Meunim descendants-of Asnah descendants-of (50)

בְּנֵי־בַקְבּוּק בְּנֵי־חֲקוּפָא בְּנֵי חַרְחוּר׃
Harhur descendants-of Hakupha descendants-of Bakbuk descendants-of (51)

---

35 of Senaah 3,630

36 The priests:

the descendants of Jedaiah (through the family of Jeshua) 973
37 of Immer 1,052
38 of Pashhur 1,247
39 of Harim 1,017

40 The Levites:

the descendants of Jeshua and Kadmiel (through the line of Hodaviah) 74

41 The singers:

the descendants of Asaph 128

42 The gatekeepers of the temple:

the descendants of Shallum, Ater, Talmon, Akkub, Hatita and Shobai 139

43 The temple servants:

the descendants of Ziha, Hasupha, Tabbaoth,
44 Keros, Siaha, Padon,
45 Lebanah, Hagabah, Akkub,
46 Hagab, Shalmai, Hanan,
47 Giddel, Gahar, Reaiah,
48 Rezin, Nekoda, Gazzam,
49 Uzza, Paseah, Besai,
50 Asnah, Meunim, Nephussim,
51 Bakbuk, Hakupha, Harhur,

°46 ק שלמי
°50a ק מעונים
°50b ק נפוסים

(52) בְּנֵי־בַצְלוּת בְּנֵי־מְחִידָא בְּנֵי חַרְשָׁא׃
(52) descendants-of Bazluth descendants-of Mehida descendants-of Harsha

(53) בְּנֵי־בַרְקוֹס בְּנֵי־סִיסְרָא בְּנֵי־תָמַח׃
(53) descendants-of Barkos descendants-of Sisera descendants-of Temah

(54) בְּנֵי נְצִיחַ בְּנֵי חֲטִיפָא׃ (55) בְּנֵי
(54) descendants-of Neziah descendants-of Hatipha (55) descendants-of

עַבְדֵי שְׁלֹמֹה בְּנֵי־סֹטַי בְּנֵי־הַסֹּפֶרֶת
servants-of Solomon descendants-of Sotai descendants-of Hassophereth

בְּנֵי פְרוּדָא׃ (56) בְּנֵי־יַעְלָה בְנֵי־דַרְקוֹן
descendants-of Peruda (56) descendants-of Jaala descendants-of Darkon

בְּנֵי גִדֵּל׃ (57) בְּנֵי שְׁפַטְיָה בְנֵי־חַטִּיל
descendants-of Giddel (57) descendants-of Shephatiah descendants-of Hattil

בְּנֵי פֹּכֶרֶת הַצְּבָיִים בְּנֵי אָמִי׃ (58) כָּל־
descendants-of Pokereth Hazzebaim descendants-of Ami (58) total-of

הַנְּתִינִים וּבְנֵי עַבְדֵי שְׁלֹמֹה שְׁלֹשׁ מֵאוֹת
the-temple-servants and-descendants-of servants-of Solomon three-of hundreds

תִּשְׁעִים וּשְׁנָיִם׃ (59) וְאֵלֶּה הָעֹלִים מִתֵּל מֶלַח תֵּל חַרְשָׁא כְּרוּב
ninety and-two (59) these the-ones-coming from-Tel Melah Tel Harsha Kerub

אַדָּן אִמֵּר וְלֹא יָכְלוּ לְהַגִּיד בֵּית־אֲבוֹתָם
Addon Immer but-not they-could to-show family-of fathers-of-them

וְזַרְעָם אִם מִיִּשְׂרָאֵל הֵם׃ (60) בְּנֵי־דְלָיָה
and-descent-of-them whether from-Israel they (60) descendants-of Delaiah

בְנֵי־טוֹבִיָּה בְּנֵי נְקוֹדָא שֵׁשׁ מֵאוֹת חֲמִשִּׁים וּשְׁנָיִם׃
descendants-of Tobiah descendants-of Nekoda six-of hundreds fifty and-two

(61) וּמִבְּנֵי הַכֹּהֲנִים בְּנֵי חֳבַיָּה
(61) and-from-descendants-of the-priests descendants-of Hobaiah

בְּנֵי הַקּוֹץ בְּנֵי בַרְזִלַּי אֲשֶׁר לָקַח מִבְּנוֹת
descendants-of Hakkoz descendants-of Barzillai who he-married of-daughters-of

בַּרְזִלַּי הַגִּלְעָדִי אִשָּׁה וַיִּקָּרֵא עַל־ שְׁמָם׃ (62) אֵלֶּה
Barzillai the-Gileadite wife and-he-was-called by name-of-them (62) these

בִּקְשׁוּ כְתָבָם הַמִּתְיַחְשִׂים וְלֹא נִמְצָאוּ
they-searched record-of-them the-ones-being-recorded but-not they-could-find

וַיְגֹאֲלוּ מִן־ הַכְּהֻנָּה׃ (63) וַיֹּאמֶר הַתִּרְשָׁתָא
so-they-were-excluded from the-priesthood (63) and-he-ordered the-governor

לָהֶם אֲשֶׁר לֹא־ יֹאכְלוּ מִקֹּדֶשׁ הַקֳּדָשִׁים עַד עֲמֹד
to-them that not they-eat from-most-holy-of the-holy-things until to-minister

כֹּהֵן לְאוּרִים וּלְתֻמִּים׃ (64) כָּל־ הַקָּהָל כְּאֶחָד אַרְבַּע
priest with-Urim and-with-Thummim (64) whole-of the-company as-one four-of

[52]Bazluth, Mehida,
Harsha,
[53]Barkos, Sisera, Temah,
[54]Neziah and Hatipha

[55]The descendants of the servants of Solomon:

the descendants of
Sotai, Hassophereth,
Peruda,
[56]Jaala, Darkon, Giddel,
[57]Shephatiah, Hattil,
Pokereth-Hazzebaim
and Ami

[58]The temple servants and the descendants of the servants of Solomon 392

[59]The following came up from the towns of Tel Melah, Tel Harsha, Kerub, Addon and Immer, but they could not show that their families were descended from Israel:

[60]The descendants of
Delaiah, Tobiah and
Nekoda 652

[61]And from among the priests:

The descendants of
Hobaiah, Hakkoz and
Barzillai (a man who
had married a
daughter of Barzillai
the Gileadite and was
called by that name).
[62]These searched for their family records, but they could not find them and so were excluded from the priesthood as unclean.
[63]The governor ordered them not to eat any of the most sacred food until there was a priest ministering with the Urim and Thummim.

[64]The whole company

רִבּוֹא אַלְפַּיִם שְׁלֹשׁ־ מֵאוֹת שִׁשִּׁים׃ מִלְּבַד
from-besides (65) sixty hundreds three-of two-thousands ten-thousand

עַבְדֵיהֶם וְאַמְהֹתֵיהֶם אֵלֶּה שִׁבְעַת אֲלָפִים
thousands seven-of these and-maidservants-of-them menservants-of-them

שְׁלֹשׁ מֵאוֹת שְׁלֹשִׁים וְשִׁבְעָה וְלָהֶם מְשֹׁרְרִים וּמְשֹׁרְרוֹת
and-women-singing men-singing and-to-them and-seven thirty hundreds three-of

מָאתָיִם׃ סוּסֵיהֶם שְׁבַע מֵאוֹת שְׁלֹשִׁים וְשִׁשָּׁה
and-six thirty hundreds seven-of horses-of-them (66) two-hundreds

פִּרְדֵיהֶם מָאתַיִם אַרְבָּעִים וַחֲמִשָּׁה׃ גְּמַלֵּיהֶם אַרְבַּע
four-of camels-of-them (67) and-five forty two-hundreds mules-of-them

מֵאוֹת שְׁלֹשִׁים וַחֲמִשָּׁה חֲמֹרִים שֵׁשֶׁת אֲלָפִים שְׁבַע מֵאוֹת
hundreds seven-of thousands six-of donkeys and-five thirty hundreds

וְעֶשְׂרִים׃ וּמֵרָאשֵׁי הָאָבוֹת בְּבוֹאָם
when-to-arrive-them the-fathers and-from-heads-of (68) and-twenty

לְבֵית יְהוָה אֲשֶׁר בִּירוּשָׁלִָם הִתְנַדְּבוּ
they-gave-freewill-offerings in-Jerusalem that Yahweh at-house-of

לְבֵית הָאֱלֹהִים לְהַעֲמִידוֹ עַל־ מְכוֹנוֹ׃ כְּכֹחָם
as-ability-of-them (69) site-of-him on to-rebuild-him the-God to-house-of

נָתְנוּ לְאוֹצַר הַמְּלָאכָה זָהָב דַּרְכְּמוֹנִים שֵׁשׁ־ רִבָּאוֹת
ten-thousands six-of drachmas gold the-work to-treasury-of they-gave

וָאֶלֶף וְכֶסֶף מָנִים חֲמֵשֶׁת אֲלָפִים וְכָתְנֹת כֹּהֲנִים
priests and-garments-of thousands five-of minas and-silver and-thousand

מֵאָה׃ וַיֵּשְׁבוּ הַכֹּהֲנִים וְהַלְוִיִּם וּמִן־ הָעָם
the-people and-from and-the-Levites the-priests and-they-settled (70) hundred

וְהַמְשֹׁרְרִים וְהַשּׁוֹעֲרִים וְהַנְּתִינִים
and-the-temple-servants and-the-gatekeepers and-the-ones-singing

בְּעָרֵיהֶם וְכָל־ יִשְׂרָאֵל בְּעָרֵיהֶם׃ וַיִּגַּע
when-he-came (3:1) in-towns-of-them Israel and-all-of in-towns-of-them

הַחֹדֶשׁ הַשְּׁבִיעִי וּבְנֵי יִשְׂרָאֵל בֶּעָרִים וַיֵּאָסְפוּ
then-they-assembled in-the-towns Israel and-sons-of the-seventh the-month

הָעָם כְּאִישׁ אֶחָד אֶל־יְרוּשָׁלִָם׃ וַיָּקָם יֵשׁוּעַ בֶּן־ יוֹצָדָק
Jozadak son-of Jeshua then-he-began (2) Jerusalem in one as-man the-people

וְאֶחָיו הַכֹּהֲנִים וּזְרֻבָּבֶל בֶּן־ שְׁאַלְתִּיאֵל
Shealtiel son-of and-Zerubbabel the-priests and-fellows-of-him

וְאֶחָיו וַיִּבְנוּ אֶת־ מִזְבַּח אֱלֹהֵי יִשְׂרָאֵל לְהַעֲלוֹת
to-sacrifice Israel God-of altar-of *** and-they-built and-associates-of-him

עָלָיו עֹלוֹת כַּכָּתוּב בְּתוֹרַת מֹשֶׁה אִישׁ־הָאֱלֹהִים׃
the-God man-of Moses in-Law-of as-the-thing-written burnt-offerings on-him

numbered 42,360, 65besides
their 7,337 menservants
and maidservants; and
they also had 200 men and
women singers. 66They had
736 horses, 245 mules,
67435 camels and 6,720
donkeys.

68When they arrived at the
house of the LORD in Jerusalem, some of the heads of the
families gave freewill
offerings toward the rebuilding of the house of God on its
site. 69According to their ability they gave to the treasury for
this work 61,000 drachmas[d] of
gold, 5,000 minas[e] of silver
and 100 priestly garments.
70The priests, the Levites, the
singers, the gatekeepers and
the temple servants settled in
their own towns, along with
some of the other people, and
the rest of the Israelites settled
in their towns.

Rebuilding the Altar

3 When the seventh month
came and the Israelites
had settled in their towns, the
people assembled as one man
in Jerusalem. 2Then Jeshua son
of Jozadak and his fellow
priests and Zerubbabel son of
Shealtiel and his associates began to build the altar of the
God of Israel to sacrifice burnt
offerings on it, in accordance
with what is written in the
Law of Moses the man of God.

[d]69 That is, about 1,100 pounds (about 500 kilograms)
[e]69 That is, about 3 tons (about 2.9 metric tons)

וַיָּכִינוּ הַמִּזְבֵּחַ עַל־ מְכוֹנֹתָיו כִּי בְּאֵימָה עֲלֵיהֶם
to-them of-fear despite foundations-of-him on the-altar and-they-built (3)

מֵעַמֵּי הָאֲרָצוֹת וַיַּעַל עָלָיו עֹלוֹת לַיהוָה
to-Yahweh burnt-offerings on-him and-they-sacrificed the-lands from-peoples-of

עֹלוֹת לַבֹּקֶר וְלָעָרֶב׃ וַיַּעֲשׂוּ אֶת־
*** then-they-celebrated (4) and-for-the-evening for-the-morning sacrifices

חַג הַסֻּכּוֹת כַּכָּתוּב וְעֹלַת
and-burnt-offering-of as-the-thing-being-written the-Tabernacles Feast-of

יוֹם בְּיוֹם בְּמִסְפָּר כְּמִשְׁפַּט דְּבַר־ יוֹם בְּיוֹמוֹ׃
for-day-of-him day matter-of as-prescription-of by-number for-day day

וְאַחֲרֵי־כֵן עֹלַת תָּמִיד וְלֶחֳדָשִׁים
and-for-the-New-Moons regular burnt-offering-of and-after-that (5)

וּלְכָל־ מוֹעֲדֵי יְהוָה הַמְקֻדָּשִׁים וּלְכֹל
and-for-all-of the-ones-being-sacred Yahweh appointed-feasts-of and-for-all-of

מִתְנַדֵּב נְדָבָה לַיהוָה׃ מִיּוֹם אֶחָד לַחֹדֶשׁ
of-the-month one on-day (6) to-Yahweh freewill-offering one-being-brought

הַשְּׁבִיעִי הֵחֵלּוּ לְהַעֲלוֹת עֹלוֹת לַיהוָה וְהֵיכַל
though-temple-of to-Yahweh burnt-offerings to-offer they-began the-seventh

יְהוָה לֹא יֻסָּד׃ וַיִּתְּנוּ־ כֶסֶף לַחֹצְבִים
to-the-ones-being-masons money then-they-gave (7) he-was-founded not Yahweh

וְלֶחָרָשִׁים וּמַאֲכָל וּמִשְׁתֶּה וָשֶׁמֶן לַצִּדֹנִים
to-the-Sidonians and-oil and-drink and-food and-to-the-carpenters

וְלַצֹּרִים לְהָבִיא עֲצֵי אֲרָזִים מִן־ הַלְּבָנוֹן אֶל־ יָם יָפוֹא
Joppa sea by the-Lebanon from cedars woods-of to-bring and-to-the-Tyrians

כְּרִשְׁיוֹן כּוֹרֶשׁ מֶלֶךְ־ פָּרַס עֲלֵיהֶם׃ וּבַשָּׁנָה
and-in-the-year (8) to-them Persia king-of Cyrus as-authorization-of

הַשֵּׁנִית לְבוֹאָם אֶל־ בֵּית הָאֱלֹהִים לִירוּשָׁלַםִ בַּחֹדֶשׁ
in-the-month in-Jerusalem the-God house-of at to-arrive-them the-second

הַשֵּׁנִי הֵחֵלּוּ זְרֻבָּבֶל בֶּן־ שְׁאַלְתִּיאֵל וְיֵשׁוּעַ בֶּן־ יוֹצָדָק
Jozadak son-of and-Jeshua Shealtiel son-of Zerubbabel they-began the-second

וּשְׁאָר אֲחֵיהֶם ׀ הַכֹּהֲנִים וְהַלְוִיִּם וְכָל־
and-all-of and-the-Levites the-priests brothers-of-them and-rest-of

הַבָּאִים מֵהַשְּׁבִי יְרוּשָׁלַםִ וַיַּעֲמִידוּ אֶת־
*** and-they-appointed Jerusalem from-the-captivity the-ones-returning

הַלְוִיִּם מִבֶּן עֶשְׂרִים שָׁנָה וָמַעְלָה לְנַצֵּחַ עַל־ מְלֶאכֶת
building-of over to-supervise and-upward year twenty from-son-of the-Levites

בֵּית־ יְהוָה׃ וַיַּעֲמֹד יֵשׁוּעַ בָּנָיו וְאֶחָיו
and-brothers-of-him sons-of-him Jeshua and-he-joined (9) Yahweh house-of

3 Despite their fear of the peoples around them, they built
the altar on its foundation and
sacrificed burnt offerings on it
to the LORD, both the morning
and evening sacrifices. 4 Then
in accordance with what is
written, they celebrated the
Feast of Tabernacles with the
required number of burnt
offerings prescribed for each
day. 5 After that, they
presented the regular burnt
offerings, the New Moon sacrifices and the sacrifices for all
the appointed feasts of the
LORD, as well as those brought
as freewill offerings to the
LORD. 6 On the first day of the
seventh month they began to
offer burnt offerings to the
LORD, though the foundation
of the LORD's temple had not
yet been laid.

Rebuilding the Temple

7 Then they gave money to
the masons and carpenters,
and gave food and drink and
oil to the people of Sidon and
Tyre, so that they would bring
cedar logs by sea from Lebanon to Joppa, as authorized by
Cyrus king of Persia.
8 In the second month of the
second year after their arrival
at the house of God in Jerusalem, Zerubbabel son of Shealtiel, Jeshua son of Jozadak
and the rest of their brothers
(the priests and the Levites
and all who had returned from
the captivity to Jerusalem) began the work, appointing Levites twenty years of age and
older to supervise the building
of the house of the LORD.
9 Jeshua and his sons and
brothers and Kadmiel and his

3 ק ויעלו

קַדְמִיאֵל֙ וּבָנָ֣יו בְּנֵי־ יְהוּדָה֙ כְּאֶחָ֔ד לְנַצֵּ֖חַ עַל־
Kadmiel and-sons-of-him descendants-of Yehudah as-one to-supervise over

עֹשֵׂ֥ה הַמְּלָאכָ֖ה בְּבֵ֣ית הָאֱלֹהִ֑ים בְּנֵ֥י חֵנָדָ֖ד בְּנֵיהֶ֥ם
one-doing-of the-work on-house-of the-God sons-of Henadad sons-of-them

וַאֲחֵיהֶ֖ם הַלְוִיִּֽם׃ וְיַסְּד֥וּ הַבֹּנִ֖ים
and-brothers-of-them the-Levites (10) when-they-laid-foundation the-ones-building

אֶת־ הֵיכַ֣ל יְהוָ֑ה וַיַּעֲמִ֨ידוּ הַכֹּהֲנִ֜ים מְלֻבָּשִׁ֗ים
*** temple-of Yahweh then-they-took-places the-priests ones-being-dressed

בַּחֲצֹֽצְרֹות֙ וְהַלְוִיִּ֣ם בְּנֵֽי־ אָסָ֤ף בַּֽמְצִלְתַּ֨יִם֙ לְהַלֵּ֣ל אֶת־
with-the-trumpets and-the-Levites sons-of Asaph with-the-cymbals to-praise ***

יְהוָ֔ה עַל־ יְדֵ֖י דָּוִ֣יד מֶֽלֶךְ־ יִשְׂרָאֵֽל׃ וַֽיַּעֲנ֡וּ בְּהַלֵּ֣ל
Yahweh at hands-of David king-of Israel (11) and-they-sang when-to-praise

וּבְהֹודֹ֨ת לַֽיהוָ֜ה כִּ֣י טֹ֗וב כִּֽי־ לְעֹולָ֤ם חַסְדֹּו֙
and-when-to-give-thanks to-Yahweh indeed good indeed to-forever love-of-him

עַל־יִשְׂרָאֵ֔ל וְכָל־ הָעָ֡ם הֵרִ֨יעוּ תְרוּעָ֤ה גְדֹולָה֙ בְהַלֵּ֣ל
to Israel and-all-of the-people they-shouted shout great when-to-praise

לַֽיהוָ֔ה עַ֥ל הוּסַ֖ד בֵּית־ יְהוָֽה׃ וְרַבִּ֡ים מֵהַכֹּהֲנִ֣ים
to-Yahweh because he-was-founded house-of Yahweh (12) but-many of-the-priests

וְהַלְוִיִּם֩ וְרָאשֵׁ֨י הָאָבֹ֜ות הַזְּקֵנִ֗ים אֲשֶׁ֨ר רָא֤וּ אֶת־
and-the-Levites and-heads-of the-fathers the-older-ones who they-saw ***

הַבַּ֤יִת הָרִאשֹׁון֙ בְּיָסְדֹ֔ו זֶ֥ה הַבַּ֖יִת
the-temple the-former when-to-lay-foundation-of-him this the-temple

בְּעֵינֵיהֶ֑ם בֹּכִ֖ים בְּקֹ֣ול גָּדֹ֑ול וְרַבִּ֥ים בִּתְרוּעָ֖ה
with-eyes-of-them ones-weeping with-voice loud while-many with-shout

בְּשִׂמְחָ֖ה לְהָרִ֣ים קֹֽול׃ וְאֵ֣ין הָעָ֗ם מַכִּירִים֙
with-joy to-raise voice (13) and-no-one-of the-people ones-distinguishing

קֹ֚ול תְּרוּעַ֣ת הַשִּׂמְחָ֔ה לְקֹ֖ול בְּכִ֣י הָעָ֑ם כִּ֣י הָעָ֗ם
sound-of shout-of the-joy from-sound-of weeping-of the-people because the-people

מְרִיעִים֙ תְּרוּעָ֣ה גְדֹולָ֔ה וְהַקֹּ֥ול נִשְׁמַ֖ע עַד־ לְמֵרָחֹֽוק׃
ones-making-noise noise much and-the-sound he-was-heard to to-at-distance

וַֽיִּשְׁמְע֔וּ צָרֵ֥י יְהוּדָ֖ה וּבִנְיָמִ֑ן כִּֽי־ בְּנֵ֣י
(4:1) when-they-heard enemies-of Judah and-Benjamin that sons-of

הַגֹּולָ֗ה בֹּונִ֤ים הֵיכָל֙ לַֽיהוָ֔ה אֱלֹהֵ֖י יִשְׂרָאֵֽל׃
the-exile ones-building temple for-Yahweh God-of Israel

וַיִּגְּשׁ֨וּ אֶל־ זְרֻבָּבֶ֜ל וְאֶל־ רָאשֵׁ֣י הָֽאָבֹ֗ות וַיֹּאמְר֤וּ
(2) then-they-came to Zerubbabel and-to heads-of the-fathers and-they-said

לָהֶם֙ נִבְנֶ֣ה עִמָּכֶ֔ם כִּ֥י כָכֶ֖ם נִדְרֹ֣ושׁ לֵֽאלֹהֵיכֶ֑ם
to-them let-us-build with-you because like-you we-seek to-God-of-you

---

sons (descendants of Hoda-viah[f]) and the sons of Hena-dad and their sons and broth-ers—all Levites—joined to-gether in supervising those working on the house of God. [10]When the builders laid the foundation of the temple of the LORD, the priests in their vestments and with trumpets, and the Levites (the sons of Asaph) with cymbals, took their places to praise the LORD, as prescribed by David king of Israel. [11]With praise and thanksgiving they sang to the LORD:

"He is good;
his love to Israel endures forever."

And all the people gave a great shout of praise to the LORD, be-cause the foundation of the house of the LORD was laid. [12]But many of the older priests and Levites and family heads, who had seen the former tem-ple, wept aloud when they saw the foundation of this temple being laid, while many others shouted for joy. [13]No one could distinguish the sound of the shouts of joy from the sound of weeping, because the people made so much noise. And the sound was heard far away.

Opposition to the Rebuilding

4 When the enemies of Judah and Benjamin heard that the exiles were building a temple for the LORD, the God of Israel, [2]they came to Zerubbabel and to the heads of the families and said, "Let us help you build because, like you, we seek your God and

f 9 Hebrew Yehudah, probably a variant of Hodaviah

וְלֹא ׀ אֲנַחְנוּ זֹבְחִים מִימֵי אֵסַר חַדֹּן מֶלֶךְ אַשּׁוּר
Assyria king-of Haddon Esar since-days-of ones-sacrificing we and-to-him

הַמַּעֲלֶה אֹתָנוּ פֹּה׃ (3) וַיֹּאמֶר לָהֶם זְרֻבָּבֶל וְיֵשׁוּעַ
and-Jeshua Zerubbabel to-them but-he-answered (3) here us the-one-bringing

וּשְׁאָר רָאשֵׁי הָאָבוֹת לְיִשְׂרָאֵל לֹא־לָכֶם וָלָנוּ לִבְנוֹת
to-build and-to-us to-you not of-Israel the-fathers heads-of and-rest-of

בַּיִת לֵאלֹהֵינוּ כִּי אֲנַחְנוּ יַחַד נִבְנֶה לַיהוָה אֱלֹהֵי יִשְׂרָאֵל
Israel God-of for-Yahweh we-will-build alone we but to-God-of-us temple

כַּאֲשֶׁר צִוָּנוּ הַמֶּלֶךְ כּוֹרֶשׁ מֶלֶךְ־פָּרָס׃ (4) וַיְהִי
then-he-was (4) Persia king-of Cyrus the-king he-commanded-us just-as

עַם־הָאָרֶץ מְרַפִּים יְדֵי עַם־יְהוּדָה
Judah people-of hands-of ones-discouraging the-land people-of

וּמְבַלְּהִים אוֹתָם לִבְנוֹת׃ (5) וְסֹכְרִים עֲלֵיהֶם
against-them and-ones-hiring (5) to-build them and-ones-making-afraid

יוֹעֲצִים לְהָפֵר עֲצָתָם כָּל־יְמֵי כּוֹרֶשׁ מֶלֶךְ פָּרַס
Persia king-of Cyrus days-of all-of plan-of-them to-frustrate ones-counseling

וְעַד־מַלְכוּת דָּרְיָוֶשׁ מֶלֶךְ־פָּרָס׃ (6) וּבְמַלְכוּת אֲחַשְׁוֵרוֹשׁ
Ahasuerus and-in-reign-of (6) Persia king-of Darius reign-of and-to

בִּתְחִלַּת מַלְכוּתוֹ כָּתְבוּ שִׂטְנָה עַל־יֹשְׁבֵי
ones-living-of against accusation they-wrote reign-of-him at-beginning-of

יְהוּדָה וִירוּשָׁלִָם׃ (7) וּבִימֵי אַרְתַּחְשַׁשְׂתָּא כָּתַב בִּשְׁלָם
Bishlam he-wrote Artaxerxes and-in-days-of (7) and-Jerusalem Judah

מִתְרְדָת טָבְאֵל וּשְׁאָר כְּנָוֺתָו עַל־אַרְתַּחְשַׁשְׂתְּא מֶלֶךְ פָּרָס
Persia king-of Artaxerxes to associates-of-him and-rest-of Tabeel Mithredath

וּכְתָב הַנִּשְׁתְּוָן כָּתוּב אֲרָמִית וּמְתֻרְגָּם אֲרָמִית׃
Aramaic and-being-translated Aramaic being-written the-letter and-writing-of

(8) רְחוּם בְּעֵל־טְעֵם וְשִׁמְשַׁי סָפְרָא כְּתַבוּ אִגְּרָה
letter they-wrote the-secretary and-Shimshai command officer-of Rehum (8)

חֲדָה עַל־יְרוּשְׁלֶם לְאַרְתַּחְשַׁשְׂתְּא מַלְכָּא כְּנֵמָא׃ (9) אֱדַיִן רְחוּם
Rehum then (9) as-follows the-king to-Artaxerxes Jerusalem against a

בְּעֵל־טְעֵם וְשִׁמְשַׁי סָפְרָא וּשְׁאָר כְּנָוָתְהוֹן
associates-of-them and-rest-of the-secretary and-Shimshai command officer-of

דִּינָיֵא וַאֲפַרְסַתְכָיֵא טַרְפְּלָיֵא אֲפָרְסָיֵא אַרְכְּוָיֵ
the-Erechites the-Persians the-men-from-Tripolis and-the-officials the-judges

בָבְלָיֵא שׁוּשַׁנְכָיֵא דֶּהָוֵא עֵלְמָיֵא׃ (10) וּשְׁאָר
and-other-of (10) the-Elamites who-that the-Susaites the-Babylonians

אֻמַיָּא דִּי הַגְלִי אָסְנַפַּר רַבָּא וְיַקִּירָא
and-the-honorable the-great Osnapper he-deported whom the-peoples

have been sacrificing to him since the time of Esarhaddon king of Assyria, who brought us here."

[3]But Zerubbabel, Jeshua and the rest of the heads of the families of Israel answered, "You have no part with us in building a temple to our God. We alone will build it for the LORD, the God of Israel, as King Cyrus, the king of Persia, commanded us."

[4]Then the peoples around them set out to discourage the people of Judah and make them afraid to go on building.[g] [5]They hired counselors to work against them and frustrate their plans during the entire reign of Cyrus king of Persia and down to the reign of Darius king of Persia.

Later Opposition Under Artaxerxes

[6]At the beginning of the reign of Xerxes,[h] they lodged an accusation against the people of Judah and Jerusalem.

[7]And in the days of Artaxerxes king of Persia, Bishlam, Mithredath, Tabeel and the rest of his associates wrote a letter to Artaxerxes. The letter was written in Aramaic script and in the Aramaic language.[i, j]

[8]Rehum the commanding officer and Shimshai the secretary wrote a letter against Jerusalem to Artaxerxes the king as follows:

> [9]Rehum the commanding officer and Shimshai the secretary, together with the rest of their associates—the judges and officials over the men from Tripolis, Persia,[k] Erech and Babylon, the Elamites of Susa, [10]and the other people whom the great and honorable Ashurbanipal[l] deported and settled in the city of Samaria

g4 Or *and troubled them as they built*
h6 Hebrew *Ahasuerus,* a variant of Xerxes' name
i7 Or *written in Aramaic and translated*
j7 The text of Ezra 4:8–6:18 is in Aramaic.
k9 Or *officials, magistrates and governors over the men from*
l10 Aramaic *Osnapper,* a variant of *Ashurbanipal*

°2 ק ולו
°4 ק ומבהלים
°7a ק כנותיו
°7b ק שת
°9a ק ארכויא
°9b ק דהיא

וְהוֹתֵב הִמּוֹ בְּקִרְיָה דִּי שָׁמְרָיִן וּשְׁאָר עֲבַר־נַהֲרָה
the-River Beyond-of and-elsewhere-of Samaria of in-city them and-he-settled

וּכְעֶנֶת׃ דְּנָה פַּרְשֶׁגֶן אִגַּרְתָּא דִּי שְׁלַחוּ עֲלוֹהִי עַל־אַרְתַּחְשַׁשְׂתְּא
Artaxerxes to to-him they-sent that the-letter copy-of this (11) and-now

מַלְכָּא עַבְדָיךְ אֱנָשׁ עֲבַר־נַהֲרָה וּכְעֶנֶת׃ יְדִיעַ
being-known (12) and-now the-River Beyond-of man-of servant-of-you the-king

לֶהֱוֵא לְמַלְכָּא דִּי יְהוּדָיֵא דִּי סְלִקוּ מִן־לְוָתָךְ עֲלֶינָא
to-us with-you from they-came-up who the-Jews that to-the-king let-him-be

אֲתוֹ לִירוּשְׁלֶם קִרְיְתָא מָרָדְתָּא וּבִאישְׁתָּא בָּנַיִן
ones-rebuilding and-the-wicked the-rebellious the-city to-Jerusalem they-went

וְשׁוּרַיָּ אשכללו וְאֻשַּׁיָּא יַחִיטוּ׃ כְּעַן
furthermore (13) they-repair and-the-foundations they-restore and-the-walls

יְדִיעַ לֶהֱוֵא לְמַלְכָּא דִּי הֵן קִרְיְתָא דָךְ תִּתְבְּנֵא
she-is-built this the-city if that to-the-king let-him-be being-known

וְשׁוּרַיָּה יִשְׁתַּכְלְלוּן מִנְדָּה־בְלוֹ וַהֲלָךְ לָא יִנְתְּנוּן
they-will-pay not or-duty tribute tax they-are-restored and-the-walls

וְאַפְּתֹם מַלְכִים תְּהַנְזִק׃ כְּעַן כָּל־קֳבֵל דִּי־מְלַח
salt-of that because since now (14) she-will-suffer royalties and-revenue-of

הֵיכְלָא מְלַחְנָא וְעַרְוַת מַלְכָּא לָא אֲרִיךְ לַנָא לְמֶחֱזֵא
to-see for-us proper not the-king and-dishonor-of we-ate-salt the-palace

עַל־דְּנָה שְׁלַחְנָא וְהוֹדַעְנָא לְמַלְכָּא׃ דִּי יְבַקַּר
he-may-search that (15) to-the-king and-we-inform we-send this because-of

בִּסְפַר־דָּכְרָנַיָּא דִּי אֲבָהָתָךְ וּתְהַשְׁכַּח בִּסְפַר
in-record-of and-you-will-find predecessors-of-you of the-archives in-record-of

דָּכְרָנַיָּא וְתִנְדַּע דִּי קִרְיְתָא דָךְ קִרְיָא מָרָדָא
rebellious city this the-city that and-you-will-know the-archives

וּמְהַנְזְקַת מַלְכִין וּמְדִנָן וְאֶשְׁתַּדּוּר עָבְדִין
ones-doing and-rebellion and-provinces kings and-one-troubling-of

בְּגַוַּהּ מִן־יוֹמָת עָלְמָא עַל־דְּנָה קִרְיְתָא דָךְ
this the-city this for the-ancient days-of from in-midst-of-her

הָחָרְבַת׃ מְהוֹדְעִין אֲנַחְנָה לְמַלְכָּא דִּי הֵן קִרְיְתָא דָךְ
this the-city if that to-the-king we ones-informing (16) she-was-destroyed

תִּתְבְּנֵא וְשׁוּרַיָּה יִשְׁתַּכְלְלוּן לָקֳבֵל דְּנָה חֲלָק
portion this because-of they-are-restored and-the-walls she-is-built

בַּעֲבַר נַהֲרָא לָא אִיתַי לָךְ׃ פִּתְגָמָא שְׁלַח מַלְכָּא
the-king he-sent the-reply (17) for-you there-is not the-River in-Beyond-of

עַל־רְחוּם בְּעֵל־טְעֵם וְשִׁמְשַׁי סָפְרָא וּשְׁאָר
and-rest-of the-secretary and-Shimshai command officer-of Rehum to

and elsewhere in Trans-Euphrates.

11(This is a copy of the letter they sent him.)

To King Artaxerxes,

From your servants, the men of Trans-Euphrates:

12The king should know
that the Jews who came up
to us from you have gone to
Jerusalem and are rebuilding
that rebellious and
wicked city. They are restoring
the walls and repairing
the foundations.
13Furthermore, the king
should know that if this
city is built and its walls are
restored, no more taxes,
tribute or duty will be paid,
and the royal revenues will
suffer. 14Now since we are
under obligation to the palace
and it is not proper for
us to see the king dishonored,
we are sending this
message to inform the king,
15so that a search may be
made in the archives of
your predecessors. In these
records you will find that
this city is a rebellious city,
troublesome to kings and
provinces, a place of rebellion
from ancient times.
That is why this city was
destroyed. 16We inform the
king that if this city is built
and its walls are restored,
you will be left with nothing
in Trans-Euphrates.

17The king sent this reply:

To Rehum the commanding
officer, Shimshai the
secretary and the rest of

°11 ק עבדך
°12a ק ובישתא
°12b ק ושוריא
°12c ק שכלילו

כְּנָוָתְהוֹן דִּי יָתְבִין בְּשָׁמְרָיִן וּשְׁאָר עֲבַר־
Beyond-of and-elsewhere-of in-Samaria ones-living who associates-of-them

נַהֲרָה שְׁלָם וּכְעֶת׃ נִשְׁתְּוָנָא דִּי שְׁלַחְתּוּן עֲלֶינָא
to-us you-sent that the-letter (18) and-now greeting the-River

מְפָרַשׁ קֱרִי קָדָמָי׃ וּמִנִּי שִׂים
he-was-issued and-from-me (19) in-presence-of-me he-was-read being-translated

טְעֵם וּבַקַּרוּ וְהַשְׁכַּחוּ דִּי קִרְיְתָא דָךְ מִן־ יוֹמָת
days-of from this the-city that and-they-found and-they-searched order

עָלְמָא עַל־ מַלְכִין מִתְנַשְּׂאָה וּמְרַד וְאֶשְׁתַּדּוּר מִתְעֲבֶד־
happening and-sedition and-rebellion one-revolting kings against the-ancient

בַּהּ׃ וּמַלְכִין תַּקִּיפִין הֲווֹ עַל־ יְרוּשְׁלֶם וְשַׁלִּיטִין
and-rulers Jerusalem over they-were powerful-ones and-kings (20) in-her

בְּכֹל עֲבַר נַהֲרָה וּמִדָּה בְלוֹ וַהֲלָךְ מִתְיְהֵב
being-paid and-duty tribute and-tax the-River Beyond-of over-whole-of

לְהוֹן׃ כְּעַן שִׂימוּ טְעֵם לְבַטָּלָא גֻּבְרַיָּא אִלֵּךְ וְקִרְיְתָא
so-the-city these the-men to-make-stop order issue! now (21) to-them

דָךְ לָא תִתְבְּנֵא עַד־ מִנִּי טַעְמָא יִתְּשָׂם׃
he-is-issued the-order from-me until she-will-be-rebuilt not this

וּזְהִירִין הֱווֹ שָׁלוּ לְמֶעְבַּד עַל־ דְּנָה לְמָה יִשְׂגֵּא
let-him-grow why? this in to-do neglect be! and-ones-being-careful (22)

חֲבָלָא לְהַנְזָקַת מַלְכִין׃ אֱדַיִן מִן־ דִּי פַּרְשֶׁגֶן
copy-of when from as-soon-as (23) royalties to-be-detrimental the-threat

נִשְׁתְּוָנָא דִּי אַרְתַּחְשַׁשְׂתְּא מַלְכָּא קֱרִי קֳדָם־ רְחוּם וְשִׁמְשַׁי
and-Shimshai Rehum to he-was-read the-king Artaxerxes of the-letter

סָפְרָא וּכְנָוָתְהוֹן אֲזַלוּ בִבְהִילוּ לִירוּשְׁלֶם עַל־
to to-Jerusalem in-immediacy they-went and-associates-of-them the-secretary

יְהוּדָיֵא וּבַטִּלוּ הִמּוֹ בְּאֶדְרָע וְחָיִל׃ בֵּאדַיִן
by-thus (24) and-force by-compulsion them and-they-stopped the-Jews

בְּטֵלַת עֲבִידַת בֵּית־ אֱלָהָא דִּי בִּירוּשְׁלֶם וַהֲוָת
and-she-was in-Jerusalem that the-God house-of work-of she-stood-still

בָּטְלָא עַד שְׁנַת תַּרְתֵּין לְמַלְכוּת דָּרְיָוֶשׁ מֶלֶךְ־ פָּרָס׃
Persia king-of Darius of-reign-of two year-of until standing-still

וְהִתְנַבִּי חַגַּי נְבִיָּאה וּזְכַרְיָה בַר־ עִדּוֹא
Iddo descendant-of and-Zechariah prophet Haggai now-he-prophesied (5:1)

נְבִיַּאיָּא עַל־ יְהוּדָיֵא דִּי בִיהוּד וּבִירוּשְׁלֶם בְּשֻׁם אֱלָהּ
God-of in-name-of and-in-Jerusalem in-Judah who the-Jews to the-prophets

יִשְׂרָאֵל עֲלֵיהוֹן׃ בֵּאדַיִן קָמוּ זְרֻבָּבֶל בַּר־שְׁאַלְתִּיאֵל
Shealtiel son-of Zerubbabel they-set-to-work at-then (2) over-them Israel

their associates living in Samaria and elsewhere in Trans-Euphrates:

Greetings.

18The letter you sent us has been read and translated in my presence. 19I issued an order and a search was made, and it was found that this city has a long history of revolt against kings and has been a place of rebellion and sedition. 20Jerusalem has had powerful kings ruling over the whole of Trans-Euphrates, and taxes, tribute and duty were paid to them. 21Now issue an order to these men to stop work, so that this city will not be rebuilt until I so order. 22Be careful not to neglect this matter. Why let this threat grow, to the detriment of the royal interests?

23As soon as the copy of the letter of King Artaxerxes was read to Rehum and Shimshai the secretary and their associates, they went immediately to the Jews in Jerusalem and compelled them by force to stop.

24Thus the work on the house of God in Jerusalem came to a standstill until the second year of the reign of Darius king of Persia.

Tattenai's Letter to Darius

5 Now Haggai the prophet and Zechariah the prophet, a descendant of Iddo, prophesied to the Jews in Judah and Jerusalem in the name of the God of Israel, who was over them. 2Then Zerubbabel son of Shealtiel and

°23 ק ששת
°1a ק נביא
°1b ק נביאיא

וְיֵשׁוּעַ בַּר־יוֹצָדָק וְשָׁרִיו לְמִבְנֵא בֵּית אֱלָהָא דִּי
that the-God house-of to-rebuild and-they-began Jozadak son-of and-Jeshua

בִירוּשְׁלֶם וְעִמְּהוֹן נְבִיַּאיָּא° דִי־אֱלָהָא מְסָעֲדִין לְהוֹן׃
to-them ones-helping the-God of the-prophets and-with-them in-Jerusalem

(3) בֵּהּ־זִמְנָא אֲתָא עֲלֵיהוֹן תַּתְּנַי פַּחַת עֲבַר־נַהֲרָה
the-River Beyond-of governor-of Tattenai to-them he-went the-time at-him (3)

וּשְׁתַר בּוֹזְנַי וּכְנָוָתְהוֹן וְכֵן אָמְרִין לְהֹם
to-them ones-asking and-this and-associates-of-them Bozenai and-Shethar

מַן־שָׂם לְכֹם טְעֵם בַּיְתָא דְנָה לִבְּנֵא וְאֻשַּׁרְנָא
and-the-structure to-rebuild this the-temple authorization to-you he-gave who?

דְנָה לְשַׁכְלָלָה׃ (4) אֱדַיִן כְּנֵמָא אֲמַרְנָא לְּהֹם מַן־אִנּוּן שְׁמָהָת
names-of they what? to-them we-told following also (4) to-restore this

גֻּבְרַיָּא דִּי־דְנָה בִנְיָנָא בָּנַיִן׃ (5) וְעֵין אֱלָהֲהֹם
God-of-them but-eye-of (5) ones-constructing the-building this who the-men

הֲוָת עַל־שָׂבֵי יְהוּדָיֵא וְלָא־בַטִּלוּ הִמּוֹ עַד־
until them they-stopped and-not the-Jews ones-being-elders-of over she-was

טַעְמָא לְדָרְיָוֶשׁ יְהָךְ וֶאֱדַיִן יְתִיבוּן נִשְׁתְּוָנָא
the-written-reply they-could-return and-then he-could-go to-Darius the-report

עַל־דְּנָה׃ (6) פַּרְשֶׁגֶן אִגַּרְתָּא דִּי־שְׁלַח תַּתְּנַי ׀ פַּחַת
governor-of Tattenai he-sent that the-letter copy-of (6) this about

עֲבַר־נַהֲרָה וּשְׁתַר בּוֹזְנַי וּכְנָוָתֵהּ אֲפַרְסְכָיֵא
the-officials and-associates-of-him Bozenai and-Shethar the-River Beyond-of

דִּי בַּעֲבַר נַהֲרָה עַל־דָּרְיָוֶשׁ מַלְכָּא׃ (7) פִּתְגָמָא שְׁלַחוּ עֲלוֹהִי
to-him they-sent the-report (7) the-king Darius to the-River of-Beyond-of who

וְכִדְנָה כְּתִיב בְּגַוֵּהּ לְדָרְיָוֶשׁ מַלְכָּא שְׁלָמָא
the-greeting the-king to-Darius within-him he-was-written and-as-this

כֹלָּא׃ (8) יְדִיעַ ׀ לֶהֱוֵא לְמַלְכָּא דִּי־אֲזַלְנָא לִיהוּד
to-Judah we-went that to-the-king let-him-be being-known (8) the-cordial

מְדִינְתָּא לְבֵית אֱלָהָא רַבָּא וְהוּא מִתְבְּנֵא אֶבֶן גְּלָל
large stone being-built and-he the-great the-God to-temple-of the-district

וְאָע מִתְּשָׂם בְּכֻתְלַיָּא וַעֲבִידְתָּא דָךְ אָסְפַּרְנָא
diligently this and-the-work in-the-walls being-placed and-timber

מִתְעַבְדָא וּמַצְלַח בִּידֵהֹם׃ (9) אֱדַיִן שְׁאֵלְנָא
we-questioned then (9) under-hand-of-them and-making-progress being-carried-on

לְשָׂבַיָּא אִלֵּךְ כְּנֵמָא אֲמַרְנָא לְּהֹם מַן־שָׂם לְכֹם
to-you he-gave who? to-them we-asked this these to-the-ones-being-elders

טְעֵם בַּיְתָא דְנָה לְמִבְנְיָה וְאֻשַּׁרְנָא דְנָה לְשַׁכְלָלָה׃
to-restore this and-the-structure to-rebuild this the-temple authorization

Jeshua son of Jozadak set to work to rebuild the house of God in Jerusalem. And the prophets of God were with them, helping them.

[3]At that time Tattenai, governor of Trans-Euphrates, and Shethar-Bozenai and their associates went to them and asked, "Who authorized you to rebuild this temple and restore this structure?" [4]They also asked, "What are the names of the men constructing this building?"[m] [5]But the eye of their God was watching over the elders of the Jews, and they were not stopped until a report could go to Darius and his written reply be received.

[6]This is a copy of the letter that Tattenai, governor of Trans-Euphrates, and Shethar-Bozenai and their associates, the officials of Trans-Euphrates, sent to King Darius. [7]The report they sent him read as follows:

To King Darius:

Cordial greetings.

[8]The king should know that we went to the district of Judah, to the temple of the great God. The people are building it with large stones and placing the timbers in the walls. The work is being carried on with diligence and is making rapid progress under their direction.

[9]We questioned the elders and asked them, "Who authorized you to rebuild this temple and restore this

[m]4 See Septuagint; Aramaic [4]*We told them the names of the man constructing this building.*

°2 ק נבייא

(10) וְאַף שְׁמָהָתְהֹם שְׁאֵלְנָא לְהֹם לְהוֹדָעוּתָךְ דִּי
that to-inform-you of-them we-asked names-of-them and-also (10)

נִכְתֻּב שֻׁם־ גֻּבְרַיָּא דִּי בְרָאשֵׁיהֹם׃ (11) וּכְנֵמָא
and-this (11) over-heads-of-them who the-men name-of we-could-write-down

פִתְגָמָא הֲתִיבוּנָא לְמֵמַר אֲנַחְנָא הִמּוֹ עַבְדוֹהִי דִי־ אֱלָהּ שְׁמַיָּא
the-heavens God-of who servants-of-him they we to-say they-gave-us the-answer

וְאַרְעָא וּבָנַיִן בַּיְתָא דִּי־ הֲוָא בְנֵה
being-built he-was that the-temple and-ones-rebuilding and-the-earth

מִקַּדְמַת דְּנָה שְׁנִין שַׂגִּיאָן וּמֶלֶךְ לְיִשְׂרָאֵל רַב בְּנָהִי
he-built-him great of-Israel and-king many years this from-before-of

וְשַׁכְלְלֵהּ׃ (12) לָהֵן מִן־ דִּי הַרְגִּזוּ אֲבָהֳתַנָא*
fathers-of-us they-angered that because but (12) and-he-finished-him

לֶאֱלָהּ שְׁמַיָּא יְהַב הִמּוֹ בְּיַד נְבוּכַדְנֶצַּר מֶלֶךְ־
king-of Nebuchadnezzar into-hand-of them he-gave the-heavens to-God-of

בָּבֶל כַּסְדָּיָא° וּבַיְתָה דְנָה סַתְרֵהּ וְעַמָּה
and-the-people he-destroyed-him this and-the-temple the-Chaldean Babylon

הַגְלִי לְבָבֶל׃ (13) בְּרַם בִּשְׁנַת חֲדָה לְכוֹרֶשׁ מַלְכָּא דִּי
of the-king of-Cyrus one in-year-of however (13) to-Babylon he-deported

בָבֶל כּוֹרֶשׁ מַלְכָּא שָׂם טְעֵם בֵּית־ אֱלָהָא דְנָה לִבְּנֵא׃
to-rebuild this the-God house-of decree he-issued the-king Cyrus Babylon

(14) וְאַף מָאנַיָּא דִי־ בֵית־ אֱלָהָא דִּי דַהֲבָה וְכַסְפָּא
and-the-silver the-gold of the-God house-of of the-articles and-even (14)

דִּי נְבוּכַדְנֶצַּר הַנְפֵּק מִן־ הֵיכְלָא דִּי בִירוּשְׁלֶם וְהֵיבֵל
and-he-brought in-Jerusalem that the-temple from he-took Nebuchadnezzar which

הִמּוֹ לְהֵיכְלָא דִּי בָבֶל הַנְפֵּק הִמּוֹ כּוֹרֶשׁ מַלְכָּא מִן־ הֵיכְלָא
the-temple from the-king Cyrus them he-removed Babylon in to-the-temple them

דִּי בָבֶל וִיהִיבוּ לְשֵׁשְׁבַּצַּר שְׁמֵהּ דִּי פֶחָה
governor who name-of-him to-Sheshbazzar then-they-were-given Babylon of

שָׂמֵהּ׃ (15) וַאֲמַר־ לֵהּ° אֵלֶּה מָאנַיָּא שֵׂא אֲזֶל־
go! take! the-articles these to-him and-he-told (15) he-appointed-him

אֲחֵת הִמּוֹ בְּהֵיכְלָא דִּי בִירוּשְׁלֶם וּבֵית אֱלָהָא
the-God and-house-of in-Jerusalem that in-the-temple them deposit!

יִתְבְּנֵא עַל־ אַתְרֵהּ׃ (16) אֱדַיִן שֵׁשְׁבַּצַּר דֵּךְ אֲתָא יְהַב
he-laid he-came this Sheshbazzar so (16) site-of-him on let-him-be-rebuilt

אֻשַּׁיָּא דִּי־ בֵית אֱלָהָא דִּי בִירוּשְׁלֶם וּמִן־ אֱדַיִן וְעַד־
and-to then and-from in-Jerusalem that the-God house-of of the-foundations

כְּעַן מִתְבְּנֵא וְלָא שְׁלִם׃ (17) וּכְעַן הֵן עַל־ מַלְכָּא
the-king to if and-now (17) being-finished but-not being-constructed present

structure?" [10]We also asked them their names, so that we could write down the names of their leaders for your information.

[11]This is the answer they gave us:

"We are the servants of the God of heaven and earth, and we are rebuilding the temple that was built many years ago, one that a great king of Israel built and finished. [12]But because our fathers angered the God of heaven, he handed them over to Nebuchadnezzar the Chaldean, king of Babylon, who destroyed this temple and deported the people to Babylon.

[13]"However, in the first year of Cyrus king of Babylon, King Cyrus issued a decree to rebuild this house of God. [14]He even removed from the temple[n] of Babylon the gold and silver articles of the house of God, which Nebuchadnezzar had taken from the temple in Jerusalem and brought to the temple[n] in Babylon.

"Then King Cyrus gave them to a man named Sheshbazzar, whom he had appointed governor, [15]and he told him, 'Take these articles and go and deposit them in the temple in Jerusalem. And rebuild the house of God on its site.' [16]So this Sheshbazzar came and laid the foundations of the house of God in Jerusalem. From that day to the present it has been under construction but is not yet finished."

[17]Now if it pleases the

n14 Or *palace*

*12 Most mss have *qamets* under the *he* (הָ׳).

°12 ק כסדאה

°15 ק אל

טָב יִתְבַּקַּר בְּבֵית גִּנְזַיָּא דִּי־ מַלְכָּא תַמָּה

there the-king of the-archives in-house-of let-him-be-searched pleasing

דִּי בְּבָבֶל הֵן אִיתַי דִּי־ מִן־ כּוֹרֶשׁ מַלְכָּא שִׂים טְעֵם

decree he-issued the-king Cyrus from of there-is if in-Babylon that

לְמִבְנֵא בֵּית־ אֱלָהָא דֵךְ בִּירוּשְׁלֶם וּרְעוּת מַלְכָּא עַל־

in the-king then-decision-of in-Jerusalem this the-God house-of to-rebuild

דְּנָה יִשְׁלַח עֲלֶינָא׃ בֵּאדַיִן דָּרְיָוֶשׁ מַלְכָּא שָׂם טְעֵם

order he-issued the-king Darius at-then (6:1) to-us let-him-send this

וּבַקַּרוּ בְּבֵית סִפְרַיָּא דִּי גִנְזַיָּא מְהַחֲתִין

ones-storing the-treasuries of the-archives in-house-of and-they-searched

תַּמָּה בְּבָבֶל׃ וְהִשְׁתְּכַח בְּאַחְמְתָא בְּבִירְתָא דִּי

that in-the-citadel in-Ecbatana and-he-was-found (2) at-Babylon there

בְּמָדַי מְדִינְתָּה מְגִלָּה חֲדָה וְכֵן־ כְּתִיב בְּגַוַּהּ

within-her he-was-written and-this a scroll the-province in-Media

דִּכְרוֹנָה׃ בִּשְׁנַת חֲדָה לְכוֹרֶשׁ מַלְכָּא כּוֹרֶשׁ מַלְכָּא שָׂם

he-issued the-king Cyrus the-king of-Cyrus one in-year-of (3) the-memorandum

טְעֵם בֵּית־ אֱלָהָא בִירוּשְׁלֶם בַּיְתָא יִתְבְּנֵא אֲתַר דִּי־

of place let-him-be-rebuilt the-temple in-Jerusalem the-God temple-of decree

דָבְחִין דִּבְחִין וְאֻשּׁוֹהִי מְסוֹבְלִין

ones-being-laid and-foundations-of-him sacrifices ones-presenting

רוּמֵהּ אַמִּין שִׁתִּין פְּתָיֵהּ אַמִּין שִׁתִּין׃ נִדְבָּכִין דִּי־ אֶבֶן

stone of courses (4) sixty cubits width-of-him sixty cubits height-of-him

גְּלָל תְּלָתָא וְנִדְבָּךְ דִּי־ אָע חֲדַת וְנִפְקְתָא מִן־ בֵּית מַלְכָּא

the-king treasury-of from and-the-cost one wood of and-course three large

תִּתְיְהִב׃ וְאַף מָאנֵי בֵית־ אֱלָהָא דִּי דַהֲבָה

the-gold of the-God house-of articles-of and-also (5) let-her-be-paid

וְכַסְפָּא דִּי נְבוּכַדְנֶצַּר הַנְפֵּק מִן־ הֵיכְלָא דִי־ בִירוּשְׁלֶם

in-Jerusalem that the-temple from he-took Nebuchadnezzar which and-the-silver

וְהֵיבֵל לְבָבֶל יַהֲתִיבוּן וִיהָךְ לְהֵיכְלָא דִי־

that to-the-temple and-let-him-go let-them-return to-Babylon and-he-brought

בִירוּשְׁלֶם לְאַתְרֵהּ וְתַחֵת בְּבֵית אֱלָהָא׃ כְּעַן

now (6) the-God in-house-of and-you-deposit to-place-of-him in-Jerusalem

תַּתְּנַי פַּחַת עֲבַר־ נַהֲרָה שְׁתַר בּוֹזְנַי וּכְנָוָתְהוֹן

and-fellows-of-them Bozenai Shethar the-River Beyond-of governor-of Tattenai

אֲפַרְסְכָיֵא דִּי בַּעֲבַר נַהֲרָה רַחִיקִין הֲווֹ מִן־ תַּמָּה׃

there from stay! ones-away the-River of-Beyond-of that the-officials

שְׁבֻקוּ לַעֲבִידַת בֵּית־ אֱלָהָא דֵךְ פַּחַת

governor-of this the-God temple-of with-work-of do-not-interfere! (7)

king, let a search be made in the royal archives of Babylon to see if King Cyrus did in fact issue a decree to rebuild this house of God in Jerusalem. Then let the king send us his decision in this matter.

The Decree of Darius

6 King Darius then issued an order, and they searched in the archives stored in the treasury at Babylon. [2]A scroll was found in the citadel of Ecbatana in the province of Media, and this was written on it:

Memorandum:

[3]In the first year of King Cyrus, the king issued a decree concerning the temple of God in Jerusalem:

Let the temple be rebuilt as a place to present sacrifices, and let its foundations be laid. It is to be ninety feet[o] high and ninety feet wide, [4]with three courses of large stones and one of timbers. The costs are to be paid by the royal treasury. [5]Also, the gold and silver articles of the house of God, which Nebuchadnezzar took from the temple in Jerusalem and brought to Babylon, are to be returned to their places in the temple in Jerusalem; they are to be deposited in the house of God.

[6]Now then, Tattenai, governor of Trans-Euphrates, and Shethar-Bozenai and you, their fellow officials of that province, stay away from there. [7]Do not interfere with the work on this temple of God. Let

[o]3 Aramaic *sixty cubits* (about 27 meters)

יְהוּדָיֵא וּלְשָׂבֵי יְהוּדָיֵא בֵּית־ אֱלָהָא דֵךְ

this the-God house-of the-Jews and-to-ones-being-elders-of the-Jews

יִבְנוֹן עַל־ אַתְרֵהּ׃ וּמִנִּי שִׂים טְעֵם לְמָא

of-what decree he-is-issued and-from-me (8) site-of-him on let-them-rebuild

דִּי־ תַעַבְדוּן עִם־ שָׂבֵי יְהוּדָיֵא אִלֵּךְ לְמִבְנֵא

to-construct these the-Jews ones-being-elders-of for you-must-do that

בֵּית־ אֱלָהָא דֵךְ וּמִנִּכְסֵי מַלְכָּא דִּי מִדַּת

revenue-of from the-king and-from-treasuries-of this the-God house-of

עֲבַר נַהֲרָה אָסְפַּרְנָא נִפְקְתָא תֶּהֱוֵא מִתְיַהֲבָא לְגֻבְרַיָּא

to-the-men being-paid she-must-be the-expense fully the-River Beyond-of

אִלֵּךְ דִּי־ לָא לְבַטָּלָא׃ וּמָה חַשְׁחָן וּבְנֵי

even-young-ones-of things-needed and-whatever (9) to-stop not that these

תוֹרִין וְדִכְרִין וְאִמְּרִין ׀ לַעֲלָוָן ׀ לֶאֱלָהּ שְׁמַיָּא חִנְטִין

wheats the-heavens to-God-of for-burnt-offerings and-lambs and-rams bulls

מְלַח ׀ חֲמַר וּמְשַׁח כְּמֵאמַר כָּהֲנַיָּא דִּי־ בִירוּשְׁלֶם לֶהֱוֵא מִתְיְהֵב

being-given to-be in-Jerusalem who the-priests as-request-of and-oil wine salt

לְהֹם יוֹם ׀ בְּיוֹם דִּי־ לָא שָׁלוּ׃ דִּי־ לֶהֱוֺן מְהַקְרְבִין

ones-sacrificing they-may-be that (10) fail without that by-day day to-them

נִיחוֹחִין לֶאֱלָהּ שְׁמַיָּא וּמְצַלַּיִן לְחַיֵּי מַלְכָּא

the-king for-lives-of and-ones-praying the-heavens to-God-of things-pleasing

וּבְנוֹהִי׃ וּמִנִּי שִׂים טְעֵם דִּי כָל־ אֱנָשׁ דִּי

who person any-of that decree he-is-issued and-from-me (11) and-sons-of-him

יְהַשְׁנֵא פִּתְגָמָא דְנָה יִתְנְסַח אָע מִן־ בַּיְתֵהּ

house-of-him from beam he-must-be-pulled this the-edict he-changes

וּזְקִיף יִתְמְחֵא עֲלֹהִי וּבַיְתֵהּ נְוָלוּ

rubble-pile and-house-of-him on-him he-must-be-impaled and-being-lifted-up

יִתְעֲבֵד עַל־דְּנָה׃ וֶאֱלָהָא דִּי שַׁכִּן שְׁמֵהּ

name-of-him he-caused-to-dwell who and-the-God (12) this for he-must-be-made

תַּמָּה יְמַגַּר כָּל־ מֶלֶךְ וְעַם דִּי ׀ יִשְׁלַח יְדֵהּ

hand-of-him he-lifts who or-people king any-of may-he-overthrow there

לְהַשְׁנָיָה לְחַבָּלָה בֵּית־ אֱלָהָא דֵךְ דִּי בִירוּשְׁלֶם אֲנָה דָרְיָוֶשׁ

Darius I in-Jerusalem that this the-God temple-of to-destroy to-change

שָׂמֶת טְעֵם אָסְפַּרְנָא יִתְעֲבִד׃ אֱדַיִן תַּתְּנַי

Tattenai then (13) let-him-be-carried-out diligently decree I-issued

פַּחַת עֲבַר־ נַהֲרָה שְׁתַר בּוֹזְנַי וּכְנָוָתְהוֹן

and-associates-of-them Bozenai Shethar the-River Beyond-of governor-of

לָקֳבֵל דִּי־ שְׁלַח דָּרְיָוֶשׁ מַלְכָּא כְּנֵמָא אָסְפַּרְנָא עֲבַדוּ׃

they-carried-out diligently this the-king Darius he-sent that because

the governor of the Jews and the Jewish elders rebuild this house of God on its site.

[8]Moreover, I hereby decree what you are to do for these elders of the Jews in the construction of this house of God:

The expenses of these men are to be fully paid out of the royal treasury, from the revenues of Trans-Euphrates, so that the work will not stop. [9]Whatever is needed—young bulls, rams, male lambs for burnt offerings to the God of heaven, and wheat, salt, wine and oil, as requested by the priests in Jerusalem—must be given them daily without fail, [10]so that they may offer sacrifices pleasing to the God of heaven and pray for the well-being of the king and his sons.

[11]Furthermore, I decree that if anyone changes this edict, a beam is to be pulled from his house and he is to be lifted up and impaled on it. And for this crime his house is to be made a pile of rubble. [12]May God, who has caused his Name to dwell there, overthrow any king or people who lifts a hand to change this decree or to destroy this temple in Jerusalem.

I Darius have decreed it. Let it be carried out with diligence.

Completion and Dedication of the Temple

[13]Then, because of the decree King Darius had sent, Tattenai, governor of Trans-Euphrates, and Shethar-Bozenai and their associates carried it out with diligence.

וְשָׂבֵי יְהוּדָיֵא בָּנַיִן וּמַצְלְחִין

and-ones-prospering ones-building the-Jews so-ones-being-elders-of (14)

בִּנְבוּאַת חַגַּי נְבִיָּאה וּזְכַרְיָה בַּר־ עִדּוֹא וּבְנוֹ

and-they-built Iddo son-of and-Zechariah prophet Haggai under-preaching-of

וְשַׁכְלִלוּ מִן־ טַעַם אֱלָהּ יִשְׂרָאֵל וּמִטְּעֵם

and-at-decree-of Israel God-of command-of according-to and-they-finished

כּוֹרֶשׁ וְדָרְיָוֶשׁ וְאַרְתַּחְשַׁשְׂתְּא מֶלֶךְ פָּרָס׃ וְשֵׁיצִיא

and-he-completed (15) Persia king-of and-Artaxerxes and-Darius Cyrus

בַּיְתָה דְנָה עַד יוֹם תְּלָתָה לִירַח אֲדָר דִּי־ הִיא שְׁנַת־ שֵׁת

six year-of this that Adar of-month-of three day-of on this the-temple

לְמַלְכוּת דָּרְיָוֶשׁ מַלְכָּא׃ וַעֲבַדוּ בְנֵי־ יִשְׂרָאֵל

Israel people-of then-they-celebrated (16) the-king Darius of-reign-of

כָּהֲנַיָּא וְלֵוָיֵא וּשְׁאָר בְּנֵי־ גָלוּתָא חֲנֻכַּת

dedication-of the-exile sons-of and-rest-of and-the-Levites the-priests

בֵּית־ אֱלָהָא דְנָה בְּחֶדְוָה׃ וְהַקְרִבוּ לַחֲנֻכַּת

for-dedication-of and-they-offered (17) with-joy this the-God house-of

בֵּית־ אֱלָהָא דְנָה תּוֹרִין מְאָה דִּכְרִין מָאתַיִן אִמְּרִין אַרְבַּע מְאָה

hundred four-of lambs two-hundreds rams hundred bulls this the-God house-of

וּצְפִירֵי עִזִּין לְחַטָּיָא עַל־ כָּל־ יִשְׂרָאֵל תְּרֵי־ עֲשַׂר

ten two-of Israel all-of for as-the-sin-offering goats and-male-goats-of

לְמִנְיָן שִׁבְטֵי יִשְׂרָאֵל׃ וַהֲקִימוּ כָהֲנַיָּא

the-priests and-they-installed (18) Israel tribes-of as-number-of

בִּפְלֻגָּתְהוֹן וְלֵוָיֵא בְּמַחְלְקָתְהוֹן עַל־ עֲבִידַת אֱלָהָא

the-God service-of for in-groups-of-them and-the-Levites in-divisions-of-them

דִּי בִירוּשְׁלֶם כִּכְתָב סְפַר מֹשֶׁה׃ וַיַּעֲשׂוּ

and-they-celebrated (19) Moses Book-of as-writing-of at-Jerusalem who

בְנֵי־ הַגּוֹלָה אֶת־ הַפָּסַח בְּאַרְבָּעָה עָשָׂר לַחֹדֶשׁ הָרִאשׁוֹן׃

the-first of-the-month ten on-four the-Passover *** the-exile sons-of

כִּי הִטַּהֲרוּ הַכֹּהֲנִים וְהַלְוִיִּם כְּאֶחָד

as-one and-the-Levites the-priests they-purified-themselves for (20)

כֻּלָּם טְהוֹרִים וַיִּשְׁחֲטוּ הַפֶּסַח לְכָל־

for-all-of the-Passover-lamb and-they-slaughtered ones-clean all-of-them

בְּנֵי הַגּוֹלָה וְלַאֲחֵיהֶם הַכֹּהֲנִים וְלָהֶם׃

and-for-themselves the-priests and-for-brothers-of-them the-exile sons-of

וַיֹּאכְלוּ בְנֵי־ יִשְׂרָאֵל הַשָּׁבִים מֵהַגּוֹלָה וְכֹל

and-all-of from-the-exile the-ones-returning Israel sons-of so-they-ate (21)

הַנִּבְדָּל מִטֻּמְאַת גּוֹיֵ־ הָאָרֶץ אֲלֵהֶם

around-them the-land Gentiles-of from-uncleanness-of the-one-separating-himself

14 So the elders of the Jews continued to build and prosper
under the preaching of Haggai
the prophet and Zechariah, a
descendant of Iddo. They
finished building the temple
according to the command of
the God of Israel and the decrees of Cyrus, Darius and Artaxerxes, kings of Persia. 15 The
temple was completed on the
third day of the month Adar,
in the sixth year of the reign of
King Darius.
16 Then the people of Israel—
the priests, the Levites and the
rest of the exiles—celebrated
the dedication of the house of
God with joy. 17 For the dedication of this house of God they
offered a hundred bulls, two
hundred rams, four hundred
male lambs and, as a sin
offering for all Israel, twelve
male goats, one for each of the
tribes of Israel. 18 And they installed the priests in their divisions and the Levites in their
groups for the service of God
at Jerusalem, according to
what is written in the Book of
Moses.

The Passover

19 On the fourteenth day of
the first month, the exiles celebrated the Passover. 20 The
priests and Levites had
purified themselves and were
all ceremonially clean. The Levites slaughtered the Passover
lamb for all the exiles, for their
brothers the priests and for
themselves. 21 So the Israelites
who had returned from the exile ate it, together with all who
had separated themselves
from the unclean practices of

°14 ק נביא

°17 ק לחטאה

לִדְרֹשׁ לַיהוָה אֱלֹהֵי יִשְׂרָאֵל׃ וַיַּעֲשׂוּ חַג־
Feast-of and-they-celebrated (22) Israel God-of to-Yahweh to-seek

מַצּוֹת שִׁבְעַת יָמִים בְּשִׂמְחָה כִּי ׀ שִׂמְּחָם
he-filled-with-joy-them because with-joy days seven-of Unleavened-Breads

יְהוָה וְהֵסֵב לֵב מֶלֶךְ־ אַשּׁוּר עֲלֵיהֶם לְחַזֵּק
to-assist for-them Assyria king-of heart-of and-he-changed Yahweh

יְדֵיהֶם בִּמְלֶאכֶת בֵּית־ הָאֱלֹהִים אֱלֹהֵי יִשְׂרָאֵל׃ וְאַחַר
and-after (7:1) Israel God-of the-God house-of in-work-of hands-of-them

הַדְּבָרִים הָאֵלֶּה בְּמַלְכוּת אַרְתַּחְשַׁסְתְּא מֶלֶךְ־ פָּרָס עֶזְרָא בֶּן־
son-of Ezra Persia king-of Artaxerxes during-reign-of the-these the-things

שְׂרָיָה בֶּן־ עֲזַרְיָה בֶּן־ חִלְקִיָּה׃ בֶּן־ שַׁלּוּם בֶּן־ צָדוֹק
Zadok son-of Shallum son-of (2) Hilkiah son-of Azariah son-of Seraiah

בֶּן־ אֲחִיטוּב׃ בֶּן־ אֲמַרְיָה בֶּן־ עֲזַרְיָה בֶּן־ מְרָיוֹת׃ בֶּן־
son-of (4) Meraioth son-of Azariah son-of Amariah son-of (3) Ahitub son-of

זְרַחְיָה בֶן־ עֻזִּי בֶן־ בֻּקִּי׃ בֶּן־ אֲבִישׁוּעַ בֶּן־ פִּינְחָס בֶּן־
son-of Phinehas son-of Abishua son-of (5) Bukki son-of Uzzi son-of Zerahiah

אֶלְעָזָר בֶּן־ אַהֲרֹן הַכֹּהֵן הָרֹאשׁ׃ הוּא עֶזְרָא עָלָה
he-came-up Ezra this (6) the-chief the-priest Aaron son-of Eleazar

מִבָּבֶל וְהוּא־ סֹפֵר מָהִיר בְּתוֹרַת מֹשֶׁה אֲשֶׁר־ נָתַן יְהוָה
Yahweh he-gave which Moses in-Law-of well-versed teacher now-he from-Babylon

אֱלֹהֵי יִשְׂרָאֵל וַיִּתֶּן־ לוֹ הַמֶּלֶךְ כְּיַד־ יְהוָה אֱלֹהָיו
God-of-him Yahweh for-hand-of the-king to-him and-he-granted Israel God-of

עָלָיו כֹּל בַּקָּשָׁתוֹ׃ וַיַּעֲלוּ מִבְּנֵי־ יִשְׂרָאֵל
Israel from-sons-of and-they-came-up (7) request-of-him every-of on-him

וּמִן־ הַכֹּהֲנִים וְהַלְוִיִּם וְהַמְשֹׁרְרִים וְהַשֹּׁעֲרִים
and-the-gatekeepers and-the-ones-singing and-the-Levites the-priests and-from

וְהַנְּתִינִים אֶל־ יְרוּשָׁלָ͏ִם בִּשְׁנַת־ שֶׁבַע לְאַרְתַּחְשַׁסְתְּא הַמֶּלֶךְ׃
the-king of-Artaxerxes seven in-year-of Jerusalem to and-the-temple-servants

וַיָּבֹא יְרוּשָׁלַ͏ִם בַּחֹדֶשׁ הַחֲמִישִׁי הִיא שְׁנַת הַשְּׁבִיעִית
the-seventh year-of this the-fifth in-the-month Jerusalem and-he-arrived (8)

לַמֶּלֶךְ׃ כִּי בְּאֶחָד לַחֹדֶשׁ הָרִאשׁוֹן הוּא יְסֻד*
beginning-of this the-first of-the-month on-one now (9) of-the-king

הַמַּעֲלָה מִבָּבֶל וּבְאֶחָד לַחֹדֶשׁ הַחֲמִישִׁי בָּא אֶל־
in he-arrived the-fifth of-the-month and-on-one from-Babylon the-journey

יְרוּשָׁלָ͏ִם כְּיַד־ אֱלֹהָיו הַטּוֹבָה עָלָיו׃ כִּי עֶזְרָא הֵכִין
he-devoted Ezra for (10) on-him the-good God-of-him for-hand-of Jerusalem

לְבָבוֹ לִדְרוֹשׁ אֶת־ תּוֹרַת יְהוָה וְלַעֲשֹׂת וּלְלַמֵּד
and-to-teach and-to-observe Yahweh Law-of *** to-study heart-of-him

their Gentile neighbors in order to seek the LORD, the God
of Israel. 22For seven days they
celebrated with joy the Feast
of Unleavened Bread, because
the LORD had filled them with
joy by changing the attitude of
the king of Assyria, so that he
assisted them in the work on
the house of God, the God of
Israel.

Ezra Comes to Jerusalem

7 After these things, during
the reign of Artaxerxes
king of Persia, Ezra son of Seraiah, the son of Azariah, the
son of Hilkiah, 2the son of
Shallum, the son of Zadok, the
son of Ahitub, 3the son of
Amariah, the son of Azariah,
the son of Meraioth, 4the son
of Zerahiah, the son of Uzzi,
the son of Bukki, 5the son of
Abishua, the son of Phinehas,
the son of Eleazar, the son of
Aaron the chief priest— 6this
Ezra came up from Babylon.
He was a teacher well versed
in the Law of Moses, which
the LORD, the God of Israel,
had given. The king had
granted him everything he
asked, for the hand of the
LORD his God was on him.
7Some of the Israelites, including priests, Levites, singers,
gatekeepers and temple servants, also came up to Jerusalem in the seventh year of
King Artaxerxes.
8Ezra arrived in Jerusalem in
the fifth month of the seventh
year of the king. 9He had
begun his journey from Babylon on the first day of the first
month, and he arrived in
Jerusalem on the first day of
the fifth month, for the good
hand of his God was on him.
10For Ezra had devoted himself
to the study and observance of
the Law of the LORD, and to

*9 The NIV repoints this word as יָסַד, he-began.

בְּיִשְׂרָאֵל חֹק וּמִשְׁפָּט׃ (11) וְזֶה | פַּרְשֶׁגֶן הַנִּשְׁתְּוָן אֲשֶׁר נָתַן
in-Israel decree and-law (11) now-this copy-of the-letter that he-gave

הַמֶּלֶךְ אַרְתַּחְשַׁסְתְּא לְעֶזְרָא הַכֹּהֵן הַסֹּפֵר סֹפֵר דִּבְרֵי
the-king Artaxerxes to-Ezra the-priest the-teacher teacher-of matters-of

מִצְוֺת־ יְהוָה וְחֻקָּיו עַל־יִשְׂרָאֵל׃ (12) אַרְתַּחְשַׁסְתְּא מֶלֶךְ
commands-of Yahweh and-decrees-of-him for Israel (12) Artaxerxes king-of

מַלְכַיָּא לְעֶזְרָא כָהֲנָא סָפַר דָּתָא דִּי־ אֱלָהּ שְׁמַיָּא
the-kings to-Ezra the-priest teacher-of the-Law of God-of the-heavens

גְּמִיר וּכְעֶנֶת׃ (13) מִנִּי שִׂים טְעֵם דִּי כָל־
being-greeted and-now (13) from-me he-is-issued decree that any-of

מִתְנַדַּב בְּמַלְכוּתִי מִן־ עַמָּה יִשְׂרָאֵל וְכָהֲנוֹהִי
one-wishing in-kingdom-of-me from the-people Israel and-priests-of-him

וְלֵוָיֵא לִמְהָךְ לִירוּשְׁלֶם עִמָּךְ יְהָךְ׃ (14) כָּל־ קֳבֵל דִּי
and-the-Levites to-go to-Jerusalem with-you he-may-go (14) for because that

מִן־ קֳדָם מַלְכָּא וְשִׁבְעַת יָעֲטֹהִי שְׁלִיחַ לְבַקָּרָא עַל־
from before the-king and-seven-of advisers-of-him being-sent to-inquire about

יְהוּד וְלִירוּשְׁלֶם בְּדָת אֱלָהָךְ דִּי בִידָךְ׃
Judah and-about-Jerusalem regarding-Law-of God-of-you which in-hand-of-you

(15) וּלְהֵיבָלָה כְּסַף וּדְהַב דִּי־ מַלְכָּא וְיָעֲטוֹהִי
(15) and-to-take silver and-gold that the-king and-advisers-of-him

הִתְנַדַּבוּ לֶאֱלָהּ יִשְׂרָאֵל דִּי בִירוּשְׁלֶם מִשְׁכְּנֵהּ׃
they-gave-freely to-God-of Israel who in-Jerusalem dwelling-of-him

(16) וְכֹל כְּסַף וּדְהַב דִּי תְהַשְׁכַּח בְּכֹל מְדִינַת
(16) with-all-of silver and-gold that you-may-obtain from-all-of province-of

בָּבֶל עִם הִתְנַדָּבוּת עַמָּא וְכָהֲנַיָּא מִתְנַדְּבִין
Babylon with to-offer-freely the-people and-the-priests ones-offering-freely

לְבֵית אֱלָהֲהֹם דִּי בִירוּשְׁלֶם׃ (17) כָּל־ קֳבֵל דְּנָה
for-temple-of God-of-them that in-Jerusalem (17) for because-of this

אָסְפַּרְנָא תִקְנֵא בְּכַסְפָּא דְנָה תּוֹרִין | דִּכְרִין אִמְּרִין
diligently you-buy with-the-money this bulls rams lambs

וּמִנְחָתְהוֹן וְנִסְכֵּיהוֹן וּתְקָרֵב הִמּוֹ
and-grain-offerings-of-them and-drink-offerings-of-them and-you-sacrifice them

עַל־מַדְבְּחָה דִּי בֵּית אֱלָהֲכֹם דִּי בִירוּשְׁלֶם׃ (18) וּמָה
on the-altar of temple-of God-of-you that in-Jerusalem (18) and-whatever

דִּי עֲלָיךְ וְעַל־ אֶחָיךְ יֵיטַב בִּשְׁאָר כַּסְפָּא
that to-you and-to brother-of-you he-seems-good with-rest-of the-silver

וְדַהֲבָה לְמֶעְבַּד כִּרְעוּת אֱלָהֲכֹם תַּעַבְדוּן׃ (19) וּמָאנַיָּא
and-the-gold to-do as-will-of God-of-you you-may-do (19) and-the-articles

teaching its decrees and laws in Israel.

King Artaxerxes' Letter to Ezra

[11]This is a copy of the letter King Artaxerxes had given to Ezra the priest and teacher, a man learned in matters concerning the commands and decrees of the LORD for Israel:

[12p]Artaxerxes, king of kings,

To Ezra the priest, a teacher of the Law of the God of heaven:

Greetings.

[13]Now I decree that any of the Israelites in my kingdom, including priests and Levites, who wish to go to Jerusalem with you, may go. [14]You are sent by the king and his seven advisers to inquire about Judah and Jerusalem with regard to the Law of your God, which is in your hand. [15]Moreover, you are to take with you the silver and gold that the king and his advisers have freely given to the God of Israel, whose dwelling is in Jerusalem, [16]together with all the silver and gold you may obtain from the province of Babylon, as well as the freewill offerings of the people and priests for the temple of their God in Jerusalem. [17]With this money be sure to buy bulls, rams and male lambs, together with their grain offerings and drink offerings, and sacrifice them on the altar of the temple of your God in Jerusalem.

[18]You and your brother Jews may then do whatever seems best with the rest of the silver and gold, in accordance with the will of your God. [19]Deliver to the

p12 The text of Ezra 7:12-26 is in Aramaic.

°18a ק עלך
°18b ק אחך

דִּי־ מִתְיַהֲבִין לָךְ לְפׇלְחָן בֵּית אֱלָהָךְ
God-of-you temple-of for-worship-of to-you ones-being-entrusted that

הַשְׁלֵם קֳדָם אֱלָהּ יְרוּשְׁלֶם׃ וּשְׁאָר חַשְׁחוּת בֵּית
temple-of the-thing-needed-of and-rest-of (20) Jerusalem God-of to deliver!

אֱלָהָךְ דִּי יִפֶּל־ לָךְ לְמִנְתַּן תִּנְתֵּן מִן־ בֵּית
house-of from you-may-provide to-supply to-you he-may-fall that God-of-you

גִּנְזֵי מַלְכָּא׃ וּמִנִּי אֲנָה אַרְתַּחְשַׁסְתְּא מַלְכָּא שִׂים
he-is-issued the-king Artaxerxes I now-from-me (21) the-king treasuries-of

טְעֵם לְכֹל גִּזַּבְרַיָּא דִּי בַּעֲבַר נַהֲרָה דִּי כׇל־ דִּי
that all that the-River of-Beyond-of who the-treasurers to-all-of order

יִשְׁאֲלֶנְכוֹן עֶזְרָא כָהֲנָה סָפַר דָּתָא דִּי־ אֱלָהּ שְׁמַיָּא
the-heavens God-of of the-Law teacher-of the-priest Ezra he-may-ask-you

אָסְפַּרְנָא יִתְעֲבִד׃ עַד־ כְּסַף כַּכְּרִין מְאָה וְעַד־
and-up-to hundred talents silver up-to (22) let-him-provide diligently

חִנְטִין כֹּרִין מְאָה וְעַד־ חֲמַר בַּתִּין מְאָה וְעַד־ בַּתִּין מְשַׁח
olive-oil baths and-up-to hundred baths wine and-up-to hundred cors wheats

מְאָה וּמְלַח דִּי־ לָא כְתָב׃ כֹּל־ דִּי מִן־ טַעַם
prescription-of from that all (23) limit without that and-salt hundred

אֱלָהּ שְׁמַיָּא יִתְעֲבֵד אַדְרַזְדָּא לְבֵית אֱלָהּ
God-of for-temple-of diligently let-him-be-done the-heavens God-of

שְׁמַיָּא דִּי־ לְמָה לֶהֱוֵא קְצַף עַל־ מַלְכוּת מַלְכָּא
the-king realm-of against wrath should-he-be why? for the-heavens

וּבְנוֹהִי׃ וּלְכֹם מְהוֹדְעִין דִּי כֹל־ כָּהֲנַיָּא
the-priests any-of that ones-making-known and-to-you (24) and-sons-of-him

וְלֵוָיֵא זַמָּרַיָּא תָרָעַיָּא נְתִינַיָּא
the-temple-servants the-gatekeepers the-singers and-the-Levites

וּפָלְחֵי בֵּית אֱלָהָא דְנָה מִנְדָּה בְלוֹ וַהֲלָךְ לָא שַׁלִּיט
authority no or-duty tribute tax this the-God house-of and-ones-working-of

לְמִרְמֵא עֲלֵיהֹם׃ וְאַנְתְּ עֶזְרָא כְּחׇכְמַת אֱלָהָךְ דִּי־
which God-of-you as-wisdom-of Ezra and-you (25) on-them to-impose

בִידָךְ מֶנִּי שָׁפְטִין וְדַיָּנִין דִּי־ לֶהֱוֺן
they-may-be that and-judges ones-being-magistrates appoint! in-hand-of-you

דָּאנִין° לְכׇל־ עַמָּה דִּי בַּעֲבַר נַהֲרָה לְכׇל־
to-all-of the-River of-Beyond-of who the-people to-all-of ones-administering-justice

יָדְעֵי דָּתֵי אֱלָהָךְ וְדִי לָא יָדַע תְּהוֹדְעוּן׃ וְכׇל־
and-any (26) you-teach knowing not and-who God-of-you laws-of ones-knowing-of

דִּי־ לָא לֶהֱוֵא עָבֵד דָּתָא דִּי־ אֱלָהָךְ וְדָתָא דִּי מַלְכָּא
the-king of and-the-law God-of-you of the-law obeying he-is not who

God of Jerusalem all the articles entrusted to you for worship in the temple of your God. [20]And anything else needed for the temple of your God that you may have occasion to supply, you may provide from the royal treasury.

[21]Now I, King Artaxerxes, order all the treasurers of Trans-Euphrates to provide with diligence whatever Ezra the priest, a teacher of the Law of the God of heaven, may ask of you— [22]up to a hundred talents[r] of silver, a hundred cors[s] of wheat, a hundred baths[t] of wine, a hundred baths[t] of olive oil, and salt without limit. [23]Whatever the God of heaven has prescribed, let it be done with diligence for the temple of the God of heaven. Why should there be wrath against the realm of the king and of his sons? [24]You are also to know that you have no authority to impose taxes, tribute or duty on any of the priests, Levites, singers, gatekeepers, temple servants or other workers at this house of God.

[25]And you, Ezra, in accordance with the wisdom of your God, which you possess, appoint magistrates and judges to administer justice to all the people of Trans-Euphrates—all who know the laws of your God. And you are to teach any who do not know them. [26]Whoever does not obey the law of your God and the law of the king

[r]22 That is, about 3 3/4 tons (about 3.4 metric tons)
[s]22 That is, probably about 600 bushels (about 22 kiloliters)
[t]22 That is, probably about 600 gallons (about 2.2 kiloliters)

°25 ק דאינין

אָסְפַּרְנָא דִּינָה לֶהֱוֵא מִתְעֲבֵד מִנֵּהּ הֵן לְמוֹת הֵן
or by-death whether to-him being-done he-must-be the-punishment diligently

לִשְׁרֹשׁוּ הֵן־ לַעֲנָשׁ נִכְסִין וְלֶאֱסוּרִין׃
or-by-imprisonments properties by-confiscation-of or by-banishment

בָּרוּךְ יְהוָה אֱלָהֵי אֲבוֹתֵינוּ אֲשֶׁר נָתַן כָּזֹאת בְּלֵב
in-heart-of as-this he-put who fathers-of-us God-of Yahweh being-blessed (27)

הַמֶּלֶךְ לְפָאֵר אֶת־ בֵּית יְהוָה אֲשֶׁר בִּירוּשָׁלִָם׃ וְעָלַי
and-to-me (28) in-Jerusalem that Yahweh house-of *** to-honor the-king

הִטָּה־ חֶסֶד לִפְנֵי הַמֶּלֶךְ וְיוֹעֲצָיו וּלְכָל־
and-before-all-of and-ones-advising-him the-king before favor he-extended

שָׂרֵי הַמֶּלֶךְ הַגִּבֹּרִים וַאֲנִי הִתְחַזַּקְתִּי כְּיַד־
because-hand-of I-took-courage and-I the-powerful-ones the-king officials-of

יְהוָה אֱלֹהַי עָלַי וָאֶקְבְּצָה מִיִּשְׂרָאֵל רָאשִׁים לַעֲלוֹת
to-go-up leading-men from-Israel and-I-gathered on-me God-of-me Yahweh

עִמִּי׃ וְאֵלֶּה רָאשֵׁי אֲבֹתֵיהֶם וְהִתְיַחְשָׂם
and-to-be-registered-them fathers-of-them heads-of and-these (8:1) with-me

הָעֹלִים עִמִּי בְּמַלְכוּת אַרְתַּחְשַׁסְתְּא הַמֶּלֶךְ מִבָּבֶל׃
from-Babylon the-king Artaxerxes during-reign-of with-me the-ones-coming-up

מִבְּנֵי פִינְחָס גֵּרְשֹׁם מִבְּנֵי אִיתָמָר דָּנִיֵּאל
Daniel Ithamar of-descendants-of Gershom Phinehas of-descendants-of (2)

מִבְּנֵי דָוִיד חַטּוּשׁ׃ מִבְּנֵי שְׁכַנְיָה
Shecaniah of-descendants-of (3) Hattush David of-descendants-of

מִבְּנֵי פַרְעֹשׁ זְכַרְיָה וְעִמּוֹ הִתְיַחֵשׂ לִזְכָרִים
of-men to-be-registered and-with-him Zechariah Parosh of-descendants-of

מֵאָה וַחֲמִשִּׁים׃ מִבְּנֵי פַּחַת מוֹאָב אֶלְיְהוֹעֵינַי בֶּן־
son-of Eliehoenai Moab Pahath of-descendants-of (4) and-fifty hundred

זְרַחְיָה וְעִמּוֹ מָאתַיִם הַזְּכָרִים׃ מִבְּנֵי שְׁכַנְיָה
Shecaniah of-descendants-of (5) the-men two-hundreds and-with-him Zerahiah

בֶּן־ יַחֲזִיאֵל וְעִמּוֹ שְׁלֹשׁ מֵאוֹת הַזְּכָרִים׃ וּמִבְּנֵי
and-of-descendants-of (6) the-men hundreds three-of and-with-him Jahaziel son-of

עָדִין עֶבֶד בֶּן־ יוֹנָתָן וְעִמּוֹ חֲמִשִּׁים הַזְּכָרִים׃ וּמִבְּנֵי
and-of-descendants-of (7) the-men fifty and-with-him Jonathan son-of Ebed Adin

עֵילָם יְשַׁעְיָה בֶּן־ עֲתַלְיָה וְעִמּוֹ שִׁבְעִים הַזְּכָרִים׃
the-men seventy and-with-him Athaliah son-of Jeshaiah Elam

וּמִבְּנֵי שְׁפַטְיָה זְבַדְיָה בֶן־ מִיכָאֵל וְעִמּוֹ
and-with-him Michael son-of Zebadiah Shephatiah and-of-descendants-of (8)

שְׁמֹנִים הַזְּכָרִים׃ מִבְּנֵי יוֹאָב עֹבַדְיָה בֶּן־ יְחִיאֵל וְעִמּוֹ
and-with-him Jehiel son-of Obadiah Joab of-descendants-of (9) the-men eighty

must surely be punished by death, banishment, confiscation of property, or imprisonment.

[27]Praise be to the LORD, the God of our fathers, who has put it into the king's heart to bring honor to the house of the LORD in Jerusalem in this
way [28]and who has extended his good favor to me before the king and his advisers and all the king's powerful officials. Because the hand of the LORD my God was on me, I took courage and gathered leading men from Israel to go up with me.

List of the Family Heads Returning With Ezra

8 These are the family heads and those registered with them who came up with me from Babylon during the reign of King Artaxerxes:

[2]of the descendants of Phinehas, Gershom;
of the descendants of Ithamar, Daniel;
of the descendants of David, Hattush [3]of the descendants of Shecaniah;

of the descendants of Parosh, Zechariah, and with him were registered 150 men;
[4]of the descendants of Pahath-Moab, Eliehoenai son of Zerahiah, and with him 200 men;
[5]of the descendants of Zattu,[u] Shecaniah son of Jahaziel, and with him 300 men;
[6]of the descendants of Adin, Ebed son of Jonathan, and with him 50 men;
[7]of the descendants of Elam, Jeshaiah son of Athaliah, and with him 70 men;
[8]of the descendants of Shephatiah, Zebadiah son of Michael, and with him 80 men;
[9]of the descendants of Joab, Obadiah son of Jehiel,

[u]5 Some Septuagint manuscripts (also 1 Esdras 8:32); Hebrew does not have *Zattu*.

°26 ק לשרשי

מָאתַיִם וּשְׁמֹנָה עָשָׂר הַזְּכָרִים׃ וּמִבְּנֵי שְׁלוֹמִית
Shelomith and-of-descendants-of (10) the-men ten and-eight two-hundreds

בֶּן־ יוֹסִפְיָה וְעִמּוֹ מֵאָה וְשִׁשִּׁים הַזְּכָרִים׃
the-men and-sixty hundred and-with-him Josiphiah son-of

וּמִבְּנֵי בֵּבָי זְכַרְיָה בֶּן־ בֵּבָי וְעִמּוֹ עֶשְׂרִים
twenty and-with-him Bebai son-of Zechariah Bebai and-of-descendants-of (11)

וּשְׁמֹנָה הַזְּכָרִים׃ וּמִבְּנֵי עַזְגָּד יוֹחָנָן בֶּן־ הַקָּטָן
Hakkatan son-of Johanan Azgad and-of-descendants-of (12) the-men and-eight

וְעִמּוֹ מֵאָה וַעֲשָׂרָה הַזְּכָרִים׃ וּמִבְּנֵי אֲדֹנִיקָם
Adonikam and-of-descendants-of (13) the-men and-ten hundred and-with-him

אַחֲרֹנִים וְאֵלֶּה שְׁמוֹתָם אֱלִיפֶלֶט יְעִיאֵל וּשְׁמַעְיָה וְעִמָּהֶם
and-with-them and-Shemaiah Jeuel Eliphelet names-of-them and-these last-ones

שִׁשִּׁים הַזְּכָרִים׃ וּמִבְּנֵי בִּגְוַי עוּתַי וְזַבּוּד° וְעִמּוֹ
and-with-him and-Zaccur Uthai Bigvai and-of-descendants-of (14) the-men sixty

שִׁבְעִים הַזְּכָרִים׃ וָאֶקְבְּצֵם אֶל־ הַנָּהָר הַבָּא
the-one-flowing the-canal at and-I-assembled-them (15) the-men seventy

אֶל־ אַהֲוָא וַנַּחֲנֶה שָׁם יָמִים שְׁלֹשָׁה וָאָבִינָה בָעָם
among-the-people when-I-checked three days there and-we-camped Ahava toward

וּבַכֹּהֲנִים וּמִבְּנֵי לֵוִי לֹא־ מָצָאתִי שָׁם׃
there I-found not Levi then-from-sons-of and-among-the-priests

וָאֶשְׁלְחָה לֶאֱלִיעֶזֶר לַאֲרִיאֵל לִשְׁמַעְיָה וּלְאֶלְנָתָן
and-for-Elnathan for-Shemaiah for-Ariel for-Eliezer so-I-summoned (16)

וּלְיָרִיב וּלְאֶלְנָתָן וּלְנָתָן וְלִזְכַרְיָה
and-for-Zechariah and-for-Nathan and-for-Elnathan and-for-Jarib

וְלִמְשֻׁלָּם רָאשִׁים וּלְיוֹיָרִיב וּלְאֶלְנָתָן מְבִינִים׃
ones-being-learned and-for-Elnathan and-for-Joiarib leaders and-for-Meshullam

וָאוֹצִאָה° אוֹתָם עַל־ אִדּוֹ הָרֹאשׁ בְּכָסִפְיָא הַמָּקוֹם וָאָשִׂימָה
and-I-put the-place in-Casiphia the-leader Iddo to them and-I-sent (17)

בְּפִיהֶם דְּבָרִים לְדַבֵּר אֶל־ אִדּוֹ אָחִיו הַנְּתוּנִים°
the-temple-servants kin-of-him Iddo to to-say words in-mouth-of-them

בְּכָסִפְיָא הַמָּקוֹם לְהָבִיא־ לָנוּ מְשָׁרְתִים לְבֵית אֱלֹהֵינוּ׃
God-of-us for-house-of ones-attending to-us to-bring the-place in-Casiphia

וַיָּבִיאוּ לָנוּ כְּיַד־ אֱלֹהֵינוּ הַטּוֹבָה עָלֵינוּ אִישׁ
man on-us the-good God-of-us because-hand-of to-us and-they-brought (18)

שֶׂכֶל מִבְּנֵי מַחְלִי בֶּן־ לֵוִי בֶּן־ יִשְׂרָאֵל וְשֵׁרֵבְיָה
even-Sherebiah Israel son-of Levi son-of Mahli from-descendants-of capable

וּבָנָיו וְאֶחָיו שְׁמֹנָה עָשָׂר׃ וְאֶת־ חֲשַׁבְיָה וְאִתּוֹ
and-with-him Hashabiah and (19) ten eight and-brothers-of-him and-sons-of-him

and with him 218 men;
[10]of the descendants of Bani,[v] Shelomith son of Josiphiah, and with him 160 men;
[11]of the descendants of Bebai, Zechariah son of Bebai, and with him 28 men;
[12]of the descendants of Azgad, Johanan son of Hakkatan, and with him 110 men;
[13]of the descendants of Adonikam, the last ones, whose names were Eliphelet, Jeuel and Shemaiah, and with them 60 men;
[14]of the descendants of Bigvai, Uthai and Zaccur, and with them 70 men.

The Return to Jerusalem

[15]I assembled them at the canal that flows toward Ahava, and we camped there three days. When I checked among the people and the priests, I found no Levites there. [16]So I summoned Eliezer, Ariel, Shemaiah, Elnathan, Jarib, Elnathan, Nathan, Zechariah and Meshullam, who were leaders, and Joiarib and Elnathan, who were men of learning, [17]and I sent them to Iddo, the leader in Casiphia. I told them what to say to Iddo and his kinsmen, the temple servants in Casiphia, so that they might bring attendants to us for the house of our God. [18]Because the good hand of our God was on us, they brought us Sherebiah, a capable man, from the descendants of Mahli son of Levi, the son of Israel, and Sherebiah's sons and brothers, 18 men; [19]and Hashabiah, together with Jeshaiah

[v]*10* Some Septuagint manuscripts (also 1 Esdras 8:36); Hebrew does not have *Bani.*

°*14* ק וזכור
°*17a* ק ואצוה
°*17b* ק הנתינים

יְשַׁעְיָה מִבְּנֵי מְרָרִי אֶחָיו וּבְנֵיהֶם עֶשְׂרִים׃
twenty and-sons-of-them brothers-of-him Merari from-descendants-of Jeshaiah

(20) וּמִן־ הַנְּתִינִים שֶׁנָּתַן דָּוִיד וְהַשָּׂרִים
and-the-officials David whom-he-established the-temple-servants and-from (20)

לַעֲבֹדַת הַלְוִיִּם נְתִינִים מָאתַיִם וְעֶשְׂרִים
and-twenty two-hundreds temple-servants the-Levites for-assistance-of

כֻּלָּם נִקְּבוּ בְשֵׁמוֹת׃ (21) וָאֶקְרָא שָׁם צוֹם
fast there and-I-proclaimed (21) by-names they-were-registered all-of-them

עַל־ הַנָּהָר אַהֲוָא לְהִתְעַנּוֹת לִפְנֵי אֱלֹהֵינוּ לְבַקֵּשׁ מִמֶּנּוּ דֶּרֶךְ
journey from-him to-ask God-of-us before to-be-humbled Ahava the-Canal by

יְשָׁרָה לָנוּ וּלְטַפֵּנוּ וּלְכָל־ רְכוּשֵׁנוּ׃ (22) כִּי
indeed (22) possession-of-us and-with-all-of and-for-child-of-us for-us safe

בֹשְׁתִּי לִשְׁאוֹל מִן־ הַמֶּלֶךְ חַיִל וּפָרָשִׁים לְעָזְרֵנוּ
to-protect-us and-horsemen soldier the-king from to-ask I-was-ashamed

מֵאוֹיֵב בַּדָּרֶךְ כִּי־ אָמַרְנוּ לַמֶּלֶךְ לֵאמֹר יַד־
hand-of to-say to-the-king we-told because on-the-road from-one-being-enemy

אֱלֹהֵינוּ עַל־ כָּל־ מְבַקְשָׁיו לְטוֹבָה וְעֻזּוֹ
but-greatness-of-him for-good ones-looking-to-him all-of on God-of-us

וְאַפּוֹ עַל כָּל־ עֹזְבָיו׃ (23) וַנָּצוּמָה
so-we-fasted (23) ones-forsaking-him all-of against and-anger-of-him

וַנְּבַקְשָׁה מֵאֱלֹהֵינוּ עַל־ זֹאת וַיֵּעָתֵר לָנוּ׃
to-us and-he-answered this about from-God-of-us and-we-petitioned

(24) וָאַבְדִּילָה מִשָּׂרֵי הַכֹּהֲנִים שְׁנֵים עָשָׂר לְשֵׁרֵבְיָה
with-Sherebiah ten two the-priests from-leaders-of then-I-set-apart (24)

חֲשַׁבְיָה וְעִמָּהֶם מֵאֲחֵיהֶם עֲשָׂרָה׃ (25) וָאֶשְׁקֳולָה
and-I-weighed-out (25) ten from-brothers-of-them and-with-them Hashabiah

לָהֶם אֶת־ הַכֶּסֶף וְאֶת־ הַזָּהָב וְאֶת־ הַכֵּלִים תְּרוּמַת בֵּית־
house-of offering-of the-articles and the-gold and the-silver *** to-them

אֱלֹהֵינוּ הַהֵרִימוּ הַמֶּלֶךְ וְיֹעֲצָיו וְשָׂרָיו
and-officials-of-him and-ones-advising-him the-king that-they-donated God-of-us

וְכָל־ יִשְׂרָאֵל הַנִּמְצָאִים׃ (26) וָאֶשְׁקֲלָה עַל־
to and-I-weighed-out (26) the-ones-being-present Israel and-all-of

יָדָם כֶּסֶף כִּכָּרִים שֵׁשׁ־ מֵאוֹת וַחֲמִשִּׁים וּכְלֵי־ כֶסֶף
silver and-articles-of and-fifty hundreds six-of talents silver hand-of-them

מֵאָה לְכִכָּרִים זָהָב מֵאָה כִכָּר׃ (27) וּכְפֹרֵי זָהָב עֶשְׂרִים
twenty gold and-bowls-of (27) talent hundred gold of-talents hundred

לַאֲדַרְכֹנִים אָלֶף וּכְלֵי נְחֹשֶׁת מֻצְהָב טוֹבָה שְׁנַיִם
two fine being-polished bronze and-articles-of thousand in-darics

from the descendants of
Merari, and his brothers and
nephews, 20 men. [20]They also
brought 220 of the temple servants—a body that David and
the officials had established to
assist the Levites. All were registered by name.
[21]There, by the Ahava Canal,
I proclaimed a fast, so that we
might humble ourselves before our God and ask him for a
safe journey for us and our
children, with all our possessions. [22]I was ashamed to ask
the king for soldiers and
horsemen to protect us from
enemies on the road, because
we had told the king, "The
good hand of our God is on
everyone who looks to him,
but his great anger is against
all who forsake him." [23]So we
fasted and petitioned our God
about this, and he answered
our prayer.
[24]Then I set apart twelve of
the leading priests, together
with Sherebiah, Hashabiah
and ten of their brothers, [25]and
I weighed out to them the
offering of silver and gold and
the articles that the king, his
advisers, his officials and all
Israel present there had donat-
ed for the house of our God. [26]I
weighed out to them 650 talents[w] of silver, silver articles
weighing 100 talents,[x] 100 talents[x] of gold, [27]20 bowls of
gold valued at 1,000 darics,[y]
and two fine articles of polished bronze, as precious as

[w]26 That is, about 25 tons (about 22 metric tons)
[x]26 That is, about 3 3/4 tons (about 3.4 metric tons)
[y]27 That is, about 19 pounds (about 8.5 kilograms)

°25 ק ואשקלה

חֲמֻדוֹת כַּזָּהָב׃ וָאֹמְרָה אֲלֵהֶם אַתֶּם קֹדֶשׁ לַיהוָה
to-Yahweh consecrated you to-them and-I-said (28) as-the-gold ones-precious

וְהַכֵּלִים קֹדֶשׁ וְהַכֶּסֶף וְהַזָּהָב נְדָבָה
freewill-offering and-the-gold and-the-silver consecrated and-the-articles

לַיהוָה אֱלֹהֵי אֲבֹתֵיכֶם׃ שִׁקְדוּ וְשִׁמְרוּ עַד־ תִּשְׁקְלוּ
you-weigh until and-be-careful! guard! (29) fathers-of-you God-of to-Yahweh

לִפְנֵי שָׂרֵי הַכֹּהֲנִים וְהַלְוִיִּם וְשָׂרֵי־ הָאָבוֹת
the-fathers and-heads-of and-the-Levites the-priests leaders-of before

לְיִשְׂרָאֵל בִּירוּשָׁלִָם הַלִּשְׁכוֹת בֵּית יְהוָה׃ וְקִבְּלוּ
then-they-received (30) Yahweh house-of the-chambers in-Jerusalem of-Israel

הַכֹּהֲנִים וְהַלְוִיִּם מִשְׁקַל הַכֶּסֶף וְהַזָּהָב וְהַכֵּלִים
and-the-articles and-the-gold the-silver weight-of and-the-Levites the-priests

לְהָבִיא לִירוּשָׁלִָם לְבֵית אֱלֹהֵינוּ׃ וַנִּסְעָה מִנְּהַר
from-Canal-of and-we-set-out (31) God-of-us to-house-of to-Jerusalem to-take

אַהֲוָא בִּשְׁנֵים עָשָׂר לַחֹדֶשׁ הָרִאשׁוֹן לָלֶכֶת יְרוּשָׁלִָם וְיַד־
and-hand-of Jerusalem to-go the-first of-the-month ten on-two Ahava

אֱלֹהֵינוּ הָיְתָה עָלֵינוּ וַיַּצִּילֵנוּ מִכַּף אוֹיֵב
one-being-enemy from-hand-of and-he-protected-us on-us she-was God-of-us

וְאוֹרֵב עַל־ הַדָּרֶךְ׃ וַנָּבוֹא יְרוּשָׁלִָם וַנֵּשֶׁב
and-we-rested Jerusalem so-we-arrived (32) the-way along and-one-being-bandit

שָׁם יָמִים שְׁלֹשָׁה׃ וּבַיּוֹם הָרְבִיעִי נִשְׁקַל הַכֶּסֶף
the-silver we-weighed-out the-fourth and-on-the-day (33) three days there

וְהַזָּהָב וְהַכֵּלִים בְּבֵית אֱלֹהֵינוּ עַל יַד־ מְרֵמוֹת
Meremoth hand-of into God-of-us in-house-of and-the-articles and-the-gold

בֶּן־ אוּרִיָּה הַכֹּהֵן וְעִמּוֹ אֶלְעָזָר בֶּן־ פִּינְחָס וְעִמָּהֶם
and-with-them Phinehas son-of Eleazar and-with-him the-priest Uriah son-of

יוֹזָבָד בֶּן־ יֵשׁוּעַ וְנוֹעַדְיָה בֶן־ בִּנּוּי הַלְוִיִּם׃ בְּמִסְפָּר
by-number (34) the-Levites Binnui son-of and-Noadiah Jeshua son-of Jozabad

בְּמִשְׁקָל לַכֹּל וַיִּכָּתֵב כָּל־ הַמִּשְׁקָל בָּעֵת
at-the-time the-weight entire-of and-he-was-recorded for-the-whole by-weight

הַהִיא׃ הַבָּאִים מֵהַשְּׁבִי בְנֵי־ הַגּוֹלָה
the-exile sons-of from-the-captivity the-ones-returning (35) the-that

הִקְרִיבוּ עֹלוֹת ׀ לֵאלֹהֵי יִשְׂרָאֵל פָּרִים שְׁנֵים־ עָשָׂר עַל־ כָּל־
all-of for ten two bulls Israel to-God-of burnt-offerings they-sacrificed

יִשְׂרָאֵל אֵילִים ׀ תִּשְׁעִים וְשִׁשָּׁה כְּבָשִׂים שִׁבְעִים וְשִׁבְעָה צְפִירֵי חַטָּאת
sin-offering goats-of and-seven seventy lambs and-six ninety rams Israel

שְׁנֵים עָשָׂר הַכֹּל עוֹלָה לַיהוָה׃ וַיִּתְּנוּ ׀ אֶת־
*** also-they-delivered (36) to-Yahweh burnt-offering the-whole ten two

gold.
28I said to them, "You as well
as these articles are consecrated to the LORD. The silver and
gold are a freewill offering to
the LORD, the God of your fathers. 29Guard them carefully
until you weigh them out in
the chambers of the house of
the LORD in Jerusalem before
the leading priests and the Levites and the family heads of
Israel." 30Then the priests and
Levites received the silver and
gold and sacred articles that
had been weighed out to be
taken to the house of our God
in Jerusalem.
31On the twelfth day of the
first month we set out from the
Ahava Canal to go to Jerusalem. The hand of our God was
on us, and he protected us
from enemies and bandits
along the way. 32So we arrived
in Jerusalem, where we rested
three days.
33On the fourth day, in the
house of our God, we weighed
out the silver and gold and the
sacred articles into the hands
of Meremoth son of Uriah, the
priest. Eleazar son of Phinehas
was with him, and so were the
Levites Jozabad son of Jeshua
and Noadiah son of Binnui.
34Everything was accounted
for by number and weight,
and the entire weight was
recorded at that time.
35Then the exiles who had
returned from captivity sacrificed burnt offerings to the
God of Israel: twelve bulls for
all Israel, ninety-six rams, sev-
enty-seven male lambs, and as
a sin offering, twelve male
goats. All this was a burnt
offering to the LORD. 36They

דָּתֵי הַמֶּלֶךְ לַאֲחַשְׁדַּרְפְּנֵי הַמֶּלֶךְ וּפַחֲוֺת עֵבֶר
Beyond-of and-governors-of the-king to-satraps-of the-king orders-of

הַנָּהָר וְנִשְּׂאוּ אֶת־ הָעָם וְאֶת־ בֵּית־ הָאֱלֹהִים׃
the-God house-of and the-people *** then-they-assisted the-River

(9:1) וּכְכַלּוֹת אֵלֶּה נִגְּשׁוּ אֵלַי הַשָּׂרִים לֵאמֹר לֹא־
not to-say the-leaders to-me they-came these and-after-to-complete (9:1)

נִבְדְּלוּ הָעָם יִשְׂרָאֵל וְהַכֹּהֲנִים וְהַלְוִיִּם
and-the-Levites and-the-priests Israel the-people they-kept-separate

מֵעַמֵּי הָאֲרָצוֹת כְּתוֹעֲבֹתֵיהֶם לַכְּנַעֲנִי
like-the-Canaanite with-detestable-practices-of-them the-lands from-peoples-of

הַחִתִּי הַפְּרִזִּי הַיְבוּסִי הָעַמֹּנִי הַמֹּאָבִי הַמִּצְרִי
the-Egyptian the-Moabite the-Ammonite the-Jebusite the-Perizzite the-Hittite

וְהָאֱמֹרִי׃ (2) כִּי־ נָשְׂאוּ מִבְּנֹתֵיהֶם לָהֶם
for-them from-daughters-of-them they-took indeed (2) and-the-Amorite

וְלִבְנֵיהֶם וְהִתְעָרְבוּ זֶרַע הַקֹּדֶשׁ בְּעַמֵּי
with-peoples-of the-holy race-of and-they-mingled and-for-sons-of-them

הָאֲרָצוֹת וְיַד הַשָּׂרִים וְהַסְּגָנִים הָיְתָה
she-was and-the-officials the-leaders and-hand-of the-lands

בַּמַּעַל הַזֶּה רִאשׁוֹנָה׃ (3) וּכְשָׁמְעִי אֶת־ הַדָּבָר
the-thing *** and-when-to-hear-me (3) leader the-this in-the-unfaithfulness

הַזֶּה קָרַעְתִּי אֶת־ בִּגְדִי וּמְעִילִי וָאֶמְרְטָה מִשְּׂעַר
from-hair-of and-I-pulled and-cloak-of-me tunic-of-me *** I-tore the-this

רֹאשִׁי וּזְקָנִי וָאֵשְׁבָה מְשׁוֹמֵם׃ (4) וְאֵלַי
then-around-me (4) being-appalled and-I-sat-down and-beard-of-me head-of-me

יֵאָסְפוּ כֹּל חָרֵד בְּדִבְרֵי אֱלֹהֵי־ יִשְׂרָאֵל עַל
because-of Israel God-of at-words-of trembler every-of they-gathered

מַעַל הַגּוֹלָה וַאֲנִי יֹשֵׁב מְשׁוֹמֵם עַד
until being-appalled sitting and-I the-exile unfaithfulness-of

לְמִנְחַת הָעָרֶב׃ (5) וּבְמִנְחַת הָעֶרֶב קַמְתִּי
I-rose the-evening then-at-sacrifice-of (5) the-evening at-sacrifice-of

מִתַּעֲנִיתִי וּבְקָרְעִי בִגְדִי וּמְעִילִי וָאֶכְרְעָה
and-I-knelt and-cloak-of-me tunic-of-me and-in-to-tear-me from-abasement-of-me

עַל־ בִּרְכַּי וָאֶפְרְשָׂה כַפַּי אֶל־ יְהוָה אֱלֹהָי׃ (6) וָאֹמְרָה
and-I-prayed (6) God-of-me Yahweh to hands-of-me and-I-spread knees-of-me on

אֱלֹהַי בֹּשְׁתִּי וְנִכְלַמְתִּי לְהָרִים אֱלֹהַי פָּנַי
faces-of-me God-of-me to-lift and-I-am-disgraced I-am-ashamed God-of-me

אֵלֶיךָ כִּי עֲוֺנֹתֵינוּ רָבוּ לְמַעְלָה רֹאשׁ וְאַשְׁמָתֵנוּ
and-guilt-of-us head to-over they-are-high sins-of-us because to-you

also delivered the king's orders to the royal satraps and to
the governors of Trans-Euphrates, who then gave assis-
tance to the people and to the
house of God.

Ezra's Prayer About Intermarriage

9 After these things had
been done, the leaders
came to me and said, "The
people of Israel, including the
priests and the Levites, have
not kept themselves separate
from the neighboring peoples
with their detestable practices,
like those of the Canaanites,
Hittites, Perizzites, Jebusites,
Ammonites, Moabites, Egyptians and Amorites. 2They
have taken some of their
daughters as wives for themselves and their sons, and
have mingled the holy race
with the peoples around them.
And the leaders and officials
have led the way in this unfaithfulness."
3When I heard this, I tore my
tunic and cloak, pulled hair
from my head and beard and
sat down appalled. 4Then
everyone who trembled at the
words of the God of Israel
gathered around me because
of this unfaithfulness of the
exiles. And I sat there appalled
until the evening sacrifice.
5Then, at the evening sacrifice, I rose from my self-
abasement, with my tunic and
cloak torn, and fell on my
knees with my hands spread
out to the LORD my God 6and
prayed:

"O my God, I am too
ashamed and disgraced to
lift up my face to you, my
God, because our sins are
higher than our heads and

גָדְלָה עַד לַשָּׁמָיִם׃ (7) מִימֵי אֲבֹתֵינוּ אֲנַחְנוּ בְּאַשְׁמָה
in-guilt we forefathers-of-us from-days-of (7) to-the-heavens to she-reached

גְדֹלָה עַד הַיּוֹם הַזֶּה וּבַעֲוֹנֹתֵינוּ נִתַּנּוּ אֲנַחְנוּ
we we-were-subjected and-because-of-sins-of-us the-this the-day until great

מְלָכֵינוּ כֹהֲנֵינוּ בְּיַד ׀ מַלְכֵי הָאֲרָצוֹת בַּחֶרֶב
to-the-sword the-lands kings-of at-hand-of priests-of-us kings-of-us

בַּשְּׁבִי וּבַבִּזָּה וּבְבֹשֶׁת פָּנִים כְּהַיּוֹם
as-the-day faces and-to-humiliation-of and-to-the-pillage to-the-captivity

הַזֶּה׃ (8) וְעַתָּה כִּמְעַט־ רֶגַע הָיְתָה תְחִנָּה מֵאֵת ׀ יְהוָה
Yahweh from grace she-was moment for-brief-of but-now (8) the-this

אֱלֹהֵינוּ לְהַשְׁאִיר לָנוּ פְּלֵיטָה וְלָתֶת־ לָנוּ יָתֵד
firm-place to-us and-to-give remnant for-us to-leave-remnant God-of-us

בִּמְקוֹם קָדְשׁוֹ לְהָאִיר עֵינֵינוּ אֱלֹהֵינוּ
God-of-us eyes-of-us to-give-light sanctuary-of-him in-place-of

וּלְתִתֵּנוּ מִחְיָה מְעַט בְּעַבְדֻתֵנוּ׃ (9) כִּי־ עֲבָדִים אֲנַחְנוּ
we slaves though (9) in-bondage-of-us little relief and-to-give-us

וּבְעַבְדֻתֵנוּ לֹא עֲזָבָנוּ אֱלֹהֵינוּ וַיַּט־ עָלֵינוּ
to-us and-he-showed God-of-us he-deserted-us not yet-in-bondage-of-us

חֶסֶד לִפְנֵי מַלְכֵי פָרַס לָתֶת־ לָנוּ מִחְיָה לְרוֹמֵם אֶת־
*** to-rebuild new-life to-us to-grant Persia kings-of in-sights-of kindness

בֵּית אֱלֹהֵינוּ וּלְהַעֲמִיד אֶת־ חָרְבֹתָיו וְלָתֶת־ לָנוּ גָדֵר
wall to-us and-to-give ruins-of-him *** and-to-repair God-of-us house-of

בִּיהוּדָה וּבִירוּשָׁלִָם׃ (10) וְעַתָּה מַה־ נֹּאמַר אֱלֹהֵינוּ אַחֲרֵי־זֹאת
this after God-of-us can-we-say what? but-now (10) and-in-Jerusalem in-Judah

כִּי עָזַבְנוּ מִצְוֺתֶיךָ׃ (11) אֲשֶׁר צִוִּיתָ בְּיַד
through-hand-of you-gave that (11) commands-of-you we-disregarded for

עֲבָדֶיךָ הַנְּבִיאִים לֵאמֹר הָאָרֶץ אֲשֶׁר אַתֶּם בָּאִים
ones-entering you that the-land to-say the-prophets servants-of-you

לְרִשְׁתָּהּ אֶרֶץ נִדָּה הִיא בְּנִדַּת עַמֵּי הָאֲרָצוֹת
the-lands peoples-of by-corruption-of she pollution land-of to-possess-her

בְּתוֹעֲבֹתֵיהֶם אֲשֶׁר מִלְאוּהָ מִפֶּה אֶל־ פֶּה
end to from-end they-filled-her that by-detestable-practices-of-them

בְּטֻמְאָתָם׃ (12) וְעַתָּה בְּנוֹתֵיכֶם אַל־ תִּתְּנוּ לִבְנֵיהֶם
to-sons-of-them you-give not daughters-of-you so-now (12) with-impurity-of-them

וּבְנֹתֵיהֶם אַל־ תִּשְׂאוּ לִבְנֵיכֶם וְלֹא־ תִדְרְשׁוּ
you-further and-not for-sons-of-you you-take not and-daughters-of-them

שְׁלֹמָם וְטוֹבָתָם עַד־ עוֹלָם לְמַעַן תֶּחֶזְקוּ
you-may-be-strong that forever to or-prosperity-of-them welfare-of-them

our guilt has reached to the
heavens. 7From the days of
our forefathers until now,
our guilt has been great. Because of our sins, we and
our kings and our priests
have been subjected to the
sword and captivity, to pil-
lage and humiliation at the
hand of foreign kings, as it
is today.

8"But now, for a brief moment, the LORD our God has
been gracious in leaving us
a remnant and giving us a
firm place in his sanctuary,
and so our God gives light
to our eyes and a little relief
in our bondage. 9Though
we are slaves, our God has
not deserted us in our
bondage. He has shown us
kindness in the sight of the
kings of Persia: He has
granted us new life to rebuild the house of our God
and repair its ruins, and he
has given us a wall of protection in Judah and Jerusalem.

10"But now, O our God,
what can we say after this?
For we have disregarded
the commands 11you gave
through your servants the
prophets when you said:
'The land you are entering
to possess is a land polluted
by the corruption of its peoples. By their detestable
practices they have filled it
with their impurity from
one end to the other.
12Therefore, do not give
your daughters in marriage
to their sons or take their
daughters for your sons. Do
not further their welfare or
prosperity at any time, that
you may be strong and eat

וַאֲכַלְתֶּם אֶת־ טוּב הָאָרֶץ וְהוֹרַשְׁתֶּם לִבְנֵיכֶם
to-children-of-you and-you-may-leave the-land good-of *** and-you-may-eat

עַד־ עוֹלָם׃ וְאַחֲרֵי כָּל־ הַבָּא עָלֵינוּ בְּמַעֲשֵׂינוּ
for-deeds-of-us to-us the-thing-happening all-of and-after (13) everlasting to

הָרָעִים וּבְאַשְׁמָתֵנוּ הַגְּדֹלָה כִּי ׀ אַתָּה אֱלֹהֵינוּ חָשַׂכְתָּ
you-withheld God-of-us you yet the-great and-for-guilt-of-us the-evil-ones

לְמַטָּה מֵעֲוֺנֵנוּ וְנָתַתָּה לָּנוּ פְּלֵיטָה כָּזֹאת׃
like-this remnant to-us and-you-gave than-sin-of-us to-less

הֲנָשׁוּב לְהָפֵר מִצְוֺתֶיךָ וּלְהִתְחַתֵּן
and-to-intermarry commands-of-you to-break shall-we-do-again? (14)

בְּעַמֵּי הַתֹּעֵבוֹת הָאֵלֶּה הֲלוֹא תֶאֱנַף־
would-you-be-angry not? the-these the-detestable-practices with-peoples-of

בָּנוּ עַד־ כַּלֵּה לְאֵין שְׁאֵרִית וּפְלֵיטָה׃ יְהוָה אֱלֹהֵי יִשְׂרָאֵל
Israel God-of Yahweh (15) or-survivor remnant to-no to-destroy to with-us

צַדִּיק אַתָּה כִּי־ נִשְׁאַרְנוּ פְלֵיטָה כְּהַיּוֹם הַזֶּה הִנְנוּ
see-we! the-this as-the-day remnant we-are-left indeed you righteous

לְפָנֶיךָ בְּאַשְׁמָתֵינוּ כִּי אֵין לַעֲמוֹד לְפָנֶיךָ
in-presences-of-you to-stand none though in-guilt-of-us before-you

עַל־ זֹאת׃ וּכְהִתְפַּלֵּל עֶזְרָא וּכְהִתְוַדֹּתוֹ
and-while-to-confess-him Ezra and-while-to-pray (10:1) this because-of

בֹּכֶה וּמִתְנַפֵּל לִפְנֵי בֵּית הָאֱלֹהִים נִקְבְּצוּ אֵלָיו
around-him they-gathered the-God house-of before and-throwing-himself weeping

מִיִּשְׂרָאֵל קָהָל רַב־ מְאֹד אֲנָשִׁים וְנָשִׁים וִילָדִים כִּי־ בָכוּ
they-wept also and-children and-women men very large crowd from-Israel

הָעָם הַרְבֵּה־ בֶכֶה׃ וַיַּעַן שְׁכַנְיָה בֶן־ יְחִיאֵל
Jehiel son-of Shecaniah then-he-spoke (2) weeping to-be-bitter the-people

מִבְּנֵי עוֹלָם° וַיֹּאמֶר לְעֶזְרָא אֲנַחְנוּ מָעַלְנוּ בֵאלֹהֵינוּ
to-God-of-us we-were-unfaithful we to-Ezra and-he-said Elam of-descendants-of

וַנֹּשֶׁב נָשִׁים נָכְרִיּוֹת מֵעַמֵּי הָאָרֶץ וְעַתָּה יֵשׁ־
there-is but-now the-land from-peoples-of foreigners women and-we-married

מִקְוֶה לְיִשְׂרָאֵל עַל־ זֹאת׃ וְעַתָּה נִכְרָת־ בְּרִית
covenant let-us-make and-now (3) this in-spite-of for-Israel hope

לֵאלֹהֵינוּ לְהוֹצִיא כָל־ נָשִׁים וְהַנּוֹלָד מֵהֶם
of-them and-the-one-being-born women all-of to-send-away before-God-of-us

בַּעֲצַת אֲדֹנָי וְהַחֲרֵדִים בְּמִצְוַת אֱלֹהֵינוּ
God-of-us to-command-of and-the-ones-who-fear lords-of-me as-counsel-of

וְכַתּוֹרָה יֵעָשֶׂה׃ קוּם כִּי־ עָלֶיךָ הַדָּבָר וַאֲנַחְנוּ
and-we the-matter to-you for rise-up! (4) let-him-be-done and-as-the-law

°2 ק עילם

the good things of the land
and leave it to your children as an everlasting inheritance.'
13"What has happened to
us is a result of our evil
deeds and our great guilt,
and yet, our God, you have
punished us less than our
sins have deserved and
have given us a remnant
like this. 14Shall we again
break your commands and
intermarry with the peo-
ples who commit such de-
testable practices? Would
you not be angry enough
with us to destroy us, leaving us no remnant or survivor? 15O LORD, God of Israel,
you are righteous! We are
left this day as a remnant.
Here we are before you in
our guilt, though because of
it not one of us can stand in
your presence."

The People's Confession of Sin

10 While Ezra was pray-
ing and confessing,
weeping and throwing him-
self down before the house of
God, a large crowd of Israelites—men, women and chil-
dren—gathered around him.
They too wept bitterly. 2Then
Shecaniah son of Jehiel, one of
the descendants of Elam, said
to Ezra, "We have been unfaithful to our God by marrying foreign women from the
peoples around us. But in spite
of this, there is still hope for
Israel. 3Now let us make a covenant before our God to send
away all these women and
their children, in accordance
with the counsel of my lord
and of those who fear the
commands of our God. Let it
be done according to the Law.
4Rise up; this matter is in your

עִמָּךְ חֲזַק וַעֲשֵׂה׃ וַיָּקָם עֶזְרָא וַיַּשְׁבַּע אֶת־

*** and-he-put-under-oath Ezra so-he-rose (5) and-do! take-courage! with-you

שָׂרֵי הַכֹּהֲנִים הַלְוִיִּם וְכָל־ יִשְׂרָאֵל לַעֲשׂוֹת כַּדָּבָר

as-the-suggestion to-do Israel and-all-of the-Levites the-priests leaders-of

הַזֶּה וַיִּשָּׁבֵעוּ׃ וַיָּקָם עֶזְרָא מִלִּפְנֵי בֵּית

house-of from-before Ezra then-he-withdrew (6) and-they-took-oath the-this

הָאֱלֹהִים וַיֵּלֶךְ אֶל־לִשְׁכַּת יְהוֹחָנָן בֶּן־ אֶלְיָשִׁיב וַיֵּלֶךְ שָׁם

there when-he-went Eliashib son-of Jehohanan room-of to and-he-went the-God

לֶחֶם לֹא־ אָכַל וּמַיִם לֹא־ שָׁתָה כִּי מִתְאַבֵּל עַל־

over mourning because he-drank not and-waters he-ate not food

מַעַל הַגּוֹלָה׃ וַיַּעֲבִירוּ קוֹל בִּיהוּדָה

in-Judah proclamation and-they-issued (7) the-exile unfaithfulness-of

וִירוּשָׁלִַם לְכֹל בְּנֵי הַגּוֹלָה לְהִקָּבֵץ יְרוּשָׁלִָם׃ וְכֹל

and-any (8) Jerusalem to-assemble the-exile sons-of for-all-of and-Jerusalem

אֲשֶׁר לֹא־ יָבוֹא לִשְׁלֹשֶׁת הַיָּמִים כַּעֲצַת הַשָּׂרִים

the-officials as-decision-of the-days in-three-of he-appeared not who

וְהַזְּקֵנִים יָחֳרַם כָּל־ רְכוּשׁוֹ וְהוּא

and-he property-of-him all-of he-would-forfeit and-the-elders

יִבָּדֵל מִקְּהַל הַגּוֹלָה׃ וַיִּקָּבְצוּ כָל־

all-of and-they-gathered (9) the-exile from-assembly-of he-would-be-expelled

אַנְשֵׁי־ יְהוּדָה וּבִנְיָמִן ׀ יְרוּשָׁלִַם לִשְׁלֹשֶׁת הַיָּמִים הוּא חֹדֶשׁ

month-of that the-days in-three-of Jerusalem and-Benjamin Judah men-of

הַתְּשִׁיעִי בְּעֶשְׂרִים בַּחֹדֶשׁ וַיֵּשְׁבוּ כָל־ הָעָם בִּרְחוֹב

in-square-of the-people all-of and-they-sat of-the-month on-twenty the-ninth

בֵּית הָאֱלֹהִים מַרְעִידִים עַל־ הַדָּבָר וּמֵהַגְּשָׁמִים׃

and-by-the-rains the-occasion by ones-being-distressed the-God house-of

וַיָּקָם עֶזְרָא הַכֹּהֵן וַיֹּאמֶר אֲלֵהֶם אַתֶּם

you to-them and-he-said the-priest Ezra then-he-stood-up (10)

מְעַלְתֶּם וַתֹּשִׁיבוּ נָשִׁים נָכְרִיּוֹת לְהוֹסִיף עַל־ אַשְׁמַת

guilt-of to to-add foreign-ones women and-you-married you-were-unfaithful

יִשְׂרָאֵל׃ וְעַתָּה תְּנוּ תוֹדָה לַיהוָה אֱלֹהֵי־ אֲבֹתֵיכֶם וַעֲשׂוּ

and-do! fathers-of-you God-of to-Yahweh confession make! and-now (11) Israel

רְצוֹנוֹ וְהִבָּדְלוּ מֵעַמֵּי הָאָרֶץ וּמִן־

and-from the-land from-peoples-of and-separate-yourselves! will-of-him

הַנָּשִׁים הַנָּכְרִיּוֹת׃ וַיַּעֲנוּ כָל־ הַקָּהָל

the-assembly whole-of and-they-responded (12) the-foreign-ones the-wives

וַיֹּאמְרוּ קוֹל גָּדוֹל כֵּן כִּדְבָרְךָ עָלֵינוּ לַעֲשׂוֹת׃ אֲבָל הָעָם

the-people but (13) to-do to-us as-word-of-you right loud voice and-they-said

°12 ק כדברך

hands. We will support you, so
take courage and do it."
5So Ezra rose up and put the
leading priests and Levites
and all Israel under oath to do
what had been suggested. And
they took the oath. 6Then Ezra
withdrew from before the
house of God and went to the
room of Jehohanan son of Eliashib. While he was there, he
ate no food and drank no
water, because he continued
to mourn over the unfaithfulness of the exiles.
7A proclamation was then
issued throughout Judah and
Jerusalem for all the exiles to
assemble in Jerusalem. 8Any-
one who failed to appear within three days would forfeit all
his property, in accordance
with the decision of the
officials and elders, and would
himself be expelled from the
assembly of the exiles.

9Within the three days, all
the men of Judah and Benjamin had gathered in Jerusalem. And on the twentieth day
of the ninth month, all the
people were sitting in the
square before the house of
God, greatly distressed by the
occasion and because of the
rain. 10Then Ezra the priest
stood up and said to them,
"You have been unfaithful;
you have married foreign
women, adding to Israel's
guilt. 11Now make confession
to the LORD, the God of your
fathers, and do his will. Separate yourselves from the peoples around you and from
your foreign wives."
12The whole assembly re-
sponded with a loud voice:
"You are right! We must do as
you say. 13But there are many

רַ֗ב וְהָעֵ֣ת גְּשָׁמִ֔ים וְאֵ֥ין כֹּ֖חַ לַעֲמ֣וֹד בַּח֑וּץ וְהַמְּלָאכָ֗ה
and-the-matter at-outside to-stand ability so-not rains and-the-season many

לֹֽא־לְי֤וֹם אֶחָד֙ וְלֹ֣א לִשְׁנַ֔יִם כִּֽי־הִרְבִּ֥ינוּ לִפְשֹׁ֖עַ בַּדָּבָ֥ר
in-the-thing to-sin we-made-great because in-two and-not one in-day not

הַזֶּֽה׃ יַעֲמְדוּ־* נָ֨א שָׂרֵ֜ינוּ לְכָל־הַקָּהָ֗ל
the-assembly for-whole-of officials-of-us now! let-them-act (14) the-this

וְכֹ֣ל ׀ אֲשֶׁ֣ר בֶּעָרֵ֗ינוּ הַהֹשִׁ֣יב נָשִׁים֮ נָכְרִיּוֹת֒
foreign-ones women who-he-married in-the-towns-of-us who then-all

יָבֹא֙ לְעִתִּ֣ים מְזֻמָּנִ֔ים וְעִמָּהֶ֛ם זִקְנֵי־עִ֥יר וָעִ֖יר
and-town town elders-of and-with-them ones-being-set at-times let-him-come

וְשֹׁפְטֶ֑יהָ עַ֠ד לְהָשִׁ֞יב חֲר֤וֹן אַף־אֱלֹהֵ֙ינוּ֙
God-of-us anger-of fierceness-of to-turn until and-ones-judging-of-her

מִמֶּ֔נּוּ עַ֖ד לַדָּבָ֥ר הַזֶּֽה׃ אַ֣ךְ יוֹנָתָ֧ן בֶּן־עֲשָׂהאֵ֛ל
Asahel son-of Jonathan only (15) the-this in-the-matter to from-us

וְיַחְזְיָ֥ה בֶן־תִּקְוָ֖ה עָמְד֣וּ עַל־זֹ֑את וּמְשֻׁלָּ֗ם
and-Meshullam this against they-opposed Tikvah son-of and-Jahzeiah

וְשַׁבְּתַ֥י הַלֵּוִ֖י עֲזָרֻֽם׃ וַיַּעֲשׂוּ־כֵן֮ בְּנֵ֣י
sons-of so and-they-did (16) they-supported-them the-Levite and-Shabbethai

הַגּוֹלָה֒ וַיִּבָּדְל֞וּ עֶזְרָ֣א הַכֹּהֵ֗ן אֲנָשִׁ֞ים רָאשֵׁ֧י הָאָב֛וֹת
the-fathers heads-of men the-priest Ezra and-they-were-selected the-exile

לְבֵ֥ית אֲבֹתָ֖ם וְכֻלָּ֣ם בְּשֵׁמ֑וֹת וַיֵּשְׁב֗וּ
and-they-sat-down by-names and-all-of-them fathers-of-them by-family-of

בְּי֥וֹם אֶחָד֙ לַחֹ֣דֶשׁ הָעֲשִׂירִ֔י לְדַרְי֖וֹשׁ הַדָּבָֽר׃
the-matter to-investigate the-tenth of-the-month one on-day

וַיְכַלּ֣וּ בַכֹּ֔ל אֲנָשִׁ֕ים הַהֹשִׁ֖יבוּ נָשִׁ֣ים נָכְרִיּ֑וֹת
foreign-ones women who-they-married men with-the-all and-they-finished (17)

עַ֚ד י֣וֹם אֶחָ֔ד לַחֹ֖דֶשׁ הָרִאשֽׁוֹן׃ וַיִּמָּצֵא֙ מִבְּנֵ֣י
among-descendants-of and-he-was-found (18) the-first of-the-month one day by

הַכֹּהֲנִ֔ים אֲשֶׁ֥ר הֹשִׁ֖יבוּ נָשִׁ֣ים נָכְרִיּ֑וֹת מִבְּנֵ֨י יֵשׁ֤וּעַ
Jeshua from-descendants-of foreign-ones women they-married who the-priests

בֶּן־יֽוֹצָדָק֙ וְאֶחָ֔יו מַעֲשֵׂיָ֣ה וֶאֱלִיעֶ֔זֶר וְיָרִ֖יב וּגְדַלְיָֽה׃
and-Gedaliah and-Jarib and-Eliezer Maaseiah and-brothers-of-him Jozadak son-of

וַיִּתְּנ֥וּ יָדָ֖ם לְהוֹצִ֣יא נְשֵׁיהֶ֑ם וַאֲשֵׁמִ֥ים
and-guilt-offerings wives-of-them to-put-away hand-of-them and-they-gave (19)

אֵֽיל־צֹ֖אן עַל־אַשְׁמָתָֽם׃ וּמִבְּנֵ֣י אִמֵּ֔ר חֲנָנִ֖י
Hanani Immer and-from-descendants-of (20) guilt-of-them for flock ram-of

וּזְבַדְיָֽה׃ וּמִבְּנֵ֖י חָרִ֑ם מַעֲשֵׂיָ֗ה וְאֵֽלִיָּה֙
and-Elijah Maaseiah Harim and-from-descendants-of (21) and-Zebadiah

people here and it is the rainy
season; so we cannot stand
outside. Besides, this matter
cannot be taken care of in a
day or two, because we have
sinned greatly in this thing.
14Let our officials act for the
whole assembly. Then let
everyone in our towns who
has married a foreign woman
come at a set time, along with
the elders and judges of each
town, until the fierce anger of
our God in this matter is
turned away from us." 15Only
Jonathan son of Asahel and
Jahzeiah son of Tikvah, supported by Meshullam and
Shabbethai the Levite, opposed this.
16So the exiles did as was
proposed. Ezra the priest selected men who were family
heads, one from each family
division, and all of them
designated by name. On the
first day of the tenth month
they sat down to investigate
the cases, 17and by the first day
of the first month they
finished dealing with all the
men who had married foreign
women.

Those Guilty of Intermarriage

18Among the descendants of the priests, the following had married foreign women:

From the descendants of Jeshua son of Jozadak, and his brothers: Maaseiah, Eliezer, Jarib and
Gedaliah. 19(They all gave
their hands in pledge to put away their wives, and for their guilt they each presented a ram from the flock as a guilt offering.)
20From the descendants of Immer:
Hanani and Zebadiah.
21From the descendants of Harim:
Maaseiah, Elijah, Shemaiah, Jehiel and Uzziah.
22From the descendants of Pashhur:
Elioenai, Maaseiah, Ishmael, Nethanel, Jozabad

*14 Most mss have *pathah* under the *ayin* (יַעַמְדוּ).

וּשְׁמַעְיָה וִיחִיאֵל וְעֻזִּיָּה׃ וּמִבְּנֵי פַּשְׁחוּר

Pashhur and-from-descendants-of (22) and-Uzziah and-Jehiel and-Shemaiah

אֶלְיוֹעֵינַי מַעֲשֵׂיָה יִשְׁמָעֵאל נְתַנְאֵל יוֹזָבָד וְאֶלְעָשָׂה׃ וּמִן־

and-among (23) and-Elasah Jozabad Nethanel Ishmael Maaseiah Elioenai

הַלְוִיִּם יוֹזָבָד וְשִׁמְעִי וְקֵלָיָה הוּא קְלִיטָא פְּתַחְיָה יְהוּדָה

Judah Pethahiah Kelita that and-Kelaiah and-Shimei Jozabad the-Levites

וֶאֱלִיעֶזֶר׃ וּמִן־ הַמְשֹׁרְרִים אֶלְיָשִׁיב וּמִן־ הַשֹּׁעֲרִים

the-gatekeepers and-from Eliashib the-ones-singing and-from (24) and-Eliezer

שַׁלֻּם וָטֶלֶם וְאוּרִי׃ וּמִיִּשְׂרָאֵל מִבְּנֵי פַרְעֹשׁ

Parosh from-descendants-of and-among-Israel (25) and-Uri and-Telem Shallum

רַמְיָה וְיִזִּיָּה וּמַלְכִּיָּה וּמִיָּמִן וְאֶלְעָזָר וּמַלְכִּיָּה

and-Malkijah and-Eleazar and-Mijamin and-Malkijah and-Izziah Ramiah

וּבְנָיָה׃ וּמִבְּנֵי עֵילָם מַתַּנְיָה זְכַרְיָה וִיחִיאֵל

and-Jehiel Zechariah Mattaniah Elam and-from-descendants-of (26) and-Benaiah

וְעַבְדִּי וִירֵמוֹת וְאֵלִיָּה׃ וּמִבְּנֵי זַתּוּא אֶלְיוֹעֵנַי

Elioenai Zattu and-from-descendants-of (27) and-Elijah and-Jeremoth and-Abdi

אֶלְיָשִׁיב מַתַּנְיָה וִירֵמוֹת וְזָבָד וַעֲזִיזָא׃ וּמִבְּנֵי

and-from-descendants-of (28) and-Aziza and-Zabad and-Jeremoth Mattaniah Eliashib

בֵּבָי יְהוֹחָנָן חֲנַנְיָה זַבַּי עַתְלָי׃ וּמִבְּנֵי בָּנִי

Bani and-from-descendants-of (29) Athlai Zabbai Hananiah Jehohanan Bebai

מְשֻׁלָּם מַלּוּךְ וַעֲדָיָה יָשׁוּב וּשְׁאָל יְרָמוֹת׃

Jeremoth and-Sheal Jashub and-Adaiah Malluch Meshullam

וּמִבְּנֵי פַּחַת מוֹאָב עַדְנָא וּכְלָל בְּנָיָה מַעֲשֵׂיָה

Maaseiah Benaiah and-Kelal Adna Moab Pahath and-from-descendants-of (30)

מַתַּנְיָה בְצַלְאֵל וּבִנּוּי וּמְנַשֶּׁה׃ וּבְנֵי חָרִם

Harim and-descendants-of (31) and-Manasseh and-Binnui Bezalel Mattaniah

אֱלִיעֶזֶר יִשִּׁיָּה מַלְכִּיָּה שְׁמַעְיָה שִׁמְעוֹן׃ בְּנְיָמִן* מַלּוּךְ שְׁמַרְיָה׃

Shemariah Malluch Benjamin (32) Shimeon Shemaiah Malkijah Ishijah Eliezer

מִבְּנֵי חָשֻׁם מַתְּנַי מַתַּתָּה זָבָד אֱלִיפֶלֶט יְרֵמַי

Jeremai Eliphelet Zabad Mattattah Mattenai Hashum from-descendants-of (33)

מְנַשֶּׁה שִׁמְעִי׃ מִבְּנֵי בָנִי מַעֲדַי עַמְרָם וְאוּאֵל׃

and-Uel Amram Maadai Bani from-descendants-of (34) Shimei Manasseh

בְּנָיָה בֵדְיָה כְּלֻהִי׃ וַנְיָה מְרֵמוֹת אֶלְיָשִׁיב׃ מַתַּנְיָה

Mattaniah (37) Eliashib Meremoth Vaniah (36) Keluhi Bedeiah Benaiah (35)

מַתְּנַי וְיַעֲשָׂו׃ וּבָנִי† וּבִנּוּי שִׁמְעִי׃ וְשֶׁלֶמְיָה

and-Shelemiah (39) Shimei and-Binnui †and-Bani (38) and-Jaasu Mattenai

וְנָתָן וַעֲדָיָה׃ מַכְנַדְבַי שָׁשַׁי שָׁרָי׃ עֲזַרְאֵל

Azarel (41) Sharai Shashai Macnadebai (40) and-Adaiah and-Nathan

and Elasah.

[23]Among the Levites:

Jozabad, Shimei, Kelaiah (that is Kelita), Pethahiah, Judah and Eliezer.

[24]From the singers:
Eliashib.

From the gatekeepers:
Shallum, Telem and Uri.

[25]And among the other Israelites:

From the descendants of Parosh:
Ramiah, Izziah, Malkijah, Mijamin, Eleazar, Malkijah and Benaiah.

[26]From the descendants of Elam:
Mattaniah, Zechariah, Jehiel, Abdi, Jeremoth and Elijah.

[27]From the descendants of Zattu:
Elioenai, Eliashib, Mattaniah, Jeremoth, Zabad and Aziza.

[28]From the descendants of Bebai:
Jehohanan, Hananiah, Zabbai and Athlai.

[29]From the descendants of Bani:
Meshullam, Malluch, Adaiah, Jashub, Sheal and Jeremoth.

[30]From the descendants of Pahath-Moab:
Adna, Kelal, Benaiah, Maaseiah, Mattaniah, Bezalel, Binnui and Manasseh.

[31]From the descendants of Harim:
Eliezer, Ishijah, Malkijah, Shemaiah, Shimeon, [32]Benjamin, Malluch and Shemariah.

[33]From the descendants of Hashum:
Mattenai, Mattattah, Zabad, Eliphelet, Jeremai, Manasseh and Shimei.

[34]From the descendants of Bani:
Maadai, Amram and Uel, [35]Benaiah, Bedeiah, Keluhi, [36]Vaniah, Meremoth, Eliashib, [37]Mattaniah, Mattenai and Jaasu.

[38]From the descendants of Binnui:[a]

[a]37,38 See Septuagint (also 1 Esdras 9:34); Hebrew *Jaasu* [38]*and Bani and Binnui,*

*32 Most mss have *hireq* under the *beth* (בִּ).

†38 The NIV, following the Septuagint (note *a* above), repoints this word to וּבְנֵי *and-descendants-of.*

°29 ק ורמות

°35 ק כלוהו

°37 ק ויעשי

וְשֶֽׁלֶמְיָ֖הוּ שְׁמַרְיָֽה׃ (42) שַׁלּ֖וּם אֲמַרְיָ֖ה יוֹסֵֽף׃

Joseph Amariah Shallum (42) Shemariah and-Shelemiah

(43) מִבְּנֵ֖י נְב֑וֹ יְעִיאֵ֡ל מַתִּתְיָה֩ זָבָ֨ד זְבִינָ֜א יַדּ֧וֹ°

Jaddai Zebina Zabad Mattithiah Jeiel Nebo from-descendants-of (43)

וְיוֹאֵ֖ל בְּנָיָֽה׃ (44) כָּל־ אֵ֕לֶּה נָשְׂא֖וּ*° נָשִׁ֣ים נָכְרִיּ֑וֹת

foreign-ones women they-married these all-of (44) Benaiah and-Joel

וְיֵ֣שׁ מֵהֶ֔ם נָשִׁ֖ים וַיָּשִׂ֥ימוּ בָּנִֽים׃

children that-they-had wives from-them and-there-were

Shimei, 39Shelemiah, Na-
than, Adaiah, 40Mac-
nadebai, Shashai, Sharai,
41Azarel, Shelemiah,
Shemariah, 42Shallum,
Amariah and Joseph.
43From the descendants of
Nebo:
Jeiel, Mattithiah, Zabad,
Zebina, Jaddai, Joel and
Benaiah.

44All these had married foreign women, and some of
them had children by these
wives.[b]

[b]44 *Or and they sent them away with their children*

*44 The original text of L reads **נשאי** ; the text was later changed to match the *Qere* form.

°43 ק ידי

°44 ק נשאו

דִּבְרֵי נְחֶמְיָה בֶּן־חֲכַלְיָה וַיְהִי בְחֹדֶשׁ־כִּסְלֵו°
Kislev in-month-of and-he-was Hacaliah son-of Nehemiah words-of (1:1)

שְׁנַת עֶשְׂרִים וַאֲנִי הָיִיתִי בְּשׁוּשַׁן הַבִּירָה׃ וַיָּבֹא חֲנָנִי
Hanani then-he-came (2) the-citadel in-Susa I-was while-I twenty year-of

אֶחָד מֵאַחַי הוּא וַאֲנָשִׁים מִיהוּדָה וָאֶשְׁאָלֵם עַל־
about and-I-questioned-them from-Judah and-men he of-brothers-of-me one

הַיְּהוּדִים הַפְּלֵיטָה אֲשֶׁר־נִשְׁאֲרוּ מִן־הַשֶּׁבִי וְעַל־יְרוּשָׁלִָם׃
Jerusalem and-about the-exile from they-survived that the-remnant the-Jews

וַיֹּאמְרוּ לִי הַנִּשְׁאָרִים אֲשֶׁר־נִשְׁאֲרוּ מִן־הַשְּׁבִי
the-exile from they-survived who the-ones-surviving to-me and-they-said (3)

שָׁם בַּמְּדִינָה בְּרָעָה גְדֹלָה וּבְחֶרְפָּה וְחוֹמַת יְרוּשָׁלִַם
Jerusalem and-wall-of and-in-disgrace great in-trouble in-the-province there

מְפֹרָצֶת וּשְׁעָרֶיהָ נִצְּתוּ בָאֵשׁ׃ וַיְהִי
and-he-was (4) with-fire they-were-burned and-gates-of-her being-broken-down

כְּשָׁמְעִי ׀ אֶת־הַדְּבָרִים הָאֵלֶּה יָשַׁבְתִּי וָאֶבְכֶּה וָאֶתְאַבְּלָה
and-I-mourned and-I-wept I-sat-down the-these the-things *** when-to-hear-me

יָמִים וָאֱהִי צָם וּמִתְפַּלֵּל לִפְנֵי אֱלֹהֵי הַשָּׁמָיִם׃ וָאֹמַר
then-I-said (5) the-heavens God-of before and-praying fasting and-I-was days

אָנָּא יְהוָה אֱלֹהֵי הַשָּׁמַיִם הָאֵל הַגָּדוֹל וְהַנּוֹרָא
and-the-one-being-awesome the-great the-God the-heavens God-of Yahweh O!

שֹׁמֵר הַבְּרִית וָחֶסֶד לְאֹהֲבָיו וּלְשֹׁמְרֵי
and-with-ones-obeying-of with-ones-loving-him and-love the-covenant keeping-of

מִצְוֹתָיו׃ תְּהִי נָא אָזְנְךָ־קַשֶּׁבֶת וְעֵינֶיךָ
and-eyes-of-you attentive ear-of-you now! let-her-be (6) commands-of-him

פְתוּחוֹת* לִשְׁמֹעַ אֶל־תְּפִלַּת עַבְדְּךָ אֲשֶׁר אָנֹכִי מִתְפַּלֵּל
praying I that servant-of-you prayer-of to to-hear ones-being-open

לְפָנֶיךָ הַיּוֹם יוֹמָם וָלַיְלָה עַל־בְּנֵי יִשְׂרָאֵל עֲבָדֶיךָ
servants-of-you Israel people-of for and-night by-day the-day before-you

וּמִתְוַדֶּה עַל־חַטֹּאות בְּנֵי־יִשְׂרָאֵל אֲשֶׁר חָטָאנוּ לָךְ
against-you we-committed-sin that Israel people-of sins-of to and-confessing

וַאֲנִי וּבֵית־אָבִי חָטָאנוּ׃ חֲבֹל
to-act-wickedly (7) we-committed-sin father-of-me and-house-of even-I

חָבַלְנוּ לָךְ וְלֹא־שָׁמַרְנוּ אֶת־הַמִּצְוֹת וְאֶת־
and the-commands *** we-obeyed and-not toward-you we-acted-wickedly

הַחֻקִּים וְאֶת־הַמִּשְׁפָּטִים אֲשֶׁר צִוִּיתָ אֶת־מֹשֶׁה עַבְדֶּךָ׃
servant-of-you Moses *** you-gave that the-laws and the-decrees

זְכָר־נָא אֶת־הַדָּבָר אֲשֶׁר צִוִּיתָ אֶת־מֹשֶׁה עַבְדְּךָ
servant-of-you Moses *** you-gave that the-instruction *** now! remember! (8)

Nehemiah's Prayer

1 The words of Nehemiah son of Hacaliah:

In the month of Kislev in the twentieth year, while I was in the citadel of Susa, [2]Hanani, one of my brothers, came from Judah with some other men, and I questioned them about the Jewish remnant that survived the exile, and also about Jerusalem.

[3]They said to me, "Those who survived the exile and are back in the province are in great trouble and disgrace. The wall of Jerusalem is broken down, and its gates have been burned with fire."

[4]When I heard these things, I sat down and wept. For some days I mourned and fasted and prayed before the God of heaven. [5]Then I said:

"O Lord, God of heaven, the great and awesome God, who keeps his covenant of love with those who love him and obey his commands, [6]let your ear be attentive and your eyes open to hear the prayer your servant is praying before you day and night for your servants, the people of Israel. I confess the sins we Israelites, including myself and my father's house, have committed against you. [7]We have acted very wickedly toward you. We have not obeyed the commands, decrees and laws you gave your servant Moses.

[8]"Remember the instruction you gave your servant

*6 Most mss have no *qibbuts* under the *tav* (פְּתוּ׳).

°1 כסליו ק

לֵאמֹר אַתֶּם תִּמְעָלוּ אֲנִי אָפִיץ אֶתְכֶם בָּעַמִּים׃
among-the-nations you I-will-scatter I you-are-unfaithful you to-say

(9) וְשַׁבְתֶּם אֵלַי וּשְׁמַרְתֶּם מִצְוֹתַי וַעֲשִׂיתֶם אֹתָם אִם־יִהְיֶה
he-is if them and-you-do commands-of-me and-you-obey to-me but-you-return (9)

נִדַּחֲכֶם בִּקְצֵה הַשָּׁמַיִם מִשָּׁם אֲקַבְּצֵם
I-will-gather-them from-there the-heavens at-horizon-of one-being-exiled-of-you

וַהֲבִוֹאתִים° אֶל־הַמָּקוֹם אֲשֶׁר בָּחַרְתִּי לְשַׁכֵּן אֶת־שְׁמִי
Name-of-me *** to-make-dwell I-chose that the-place to and-I-will-bring-them

שָׁם׃ (10) וְהֵם עֲבָדֶיךָ וְעַמְּךָ אֲשֶׁר פָּדִיתָ
you-redeemed whom and-people-of-you servants-of-you and-they (10) there

בְּכֹחֲךָ הַגָּדוֹל וּבְיָדְךָ הַחֲזָקָה׃ (11) אָנָּא אֲדֹנָי
Lord O! (11) the-mighty and-by-hand-of-you the-great by-strength-of-you

תְּהִי נָא אָזְנְךָ־קַשֶּׁבֶת אֶל־תְּפִלַּת עַבְדְּךָ וְאֶל־
and-to servant-of-you prayer-of to attentive ear-of-you now! let-her-be

תְּפִלַּת עֲבָדֶיךָ הַחֲפֵצִים לְיִרְאָה אֶת־שְׁמֶךָ
name-of-you *** to-revere the-ones-who-delight servants-of-you prayer-of

וְהַצְלִיחָה־נָּא לְעַבְדְּךָ הַיּוֹם וּתְנֵהוּ לְרַחֲמִים
with-favors and-grant-him! the-day to-servant-of-you now! and-give-success!

לִפְנֵי הָאִישׁ הַזֶּה וַאֲנִי הָיִיתִי מַשְׁקֶה לַמֶּלֶךְ׃
to-the-king cupbearer I-was now-I the-this the-man in-presences-of

(2:1) וַיְהִי ׀ בְּחֹדֶשׁ נִיסָן שְׁנַת עֶשְׂרִים לְאַרְתַּחְשַׁסְתְּא הַמֶּלֶךְ
the-king of-Artaxerxes twenty year-of Nisan in-month-of and-he-was (2:1)

יַיִן לְפָנָיו וָאֶשָּׂא אֶת־הַיַּיִן וָאֶתְּנָה לַמֶּלֶךְ וְלֹא־הָיִיתִי
I-was now-not to-the-king and-I-gave the-wine *** and-I-took before-him wine

רַע לְפָנָיו׃ (2) וַיֹּאמֶר לִי הַמֶּלֶךְ מַדּוּעַ ׀ פָּנֶיךָ
faces-of-you why? the-king to-me so-he-asked (2) in-presences-of-him sad

רָעִים וְאַתָּה אֵינְךָ חוֹלֶה אֵין זֶה כִּי־אִם רֹעַ לֵב
heart sadness-of only but this nothing being-ill not-you when-you ones-sad

וָאִירָא הַרְבֵּה מְאֹד׃ (3) וָאֹמַר לַמֶּלֶךְ הַמֶּלֶךְ
the-king to-the-king but-I-said (3) very to-be-much and-I-was-afraid

לְעוֹלָם יִחְיֶה מַדּוּעַ לֹא־יֵרְעוּ פָנַי אֲשֶׁר
when faces-of-me they-should-look-sad not why? may-he-live to-forever

הָעִיר בֵּית־קִבְרוֹת אֲבֹתַי חֲרֵבָה וּשְׁעָרֶיהָ
and-gates-of-her she-lies-in-ruin fathers-of-me burials-of house-of the-city

אֻכְּלוּ בָאֵשׁ׃ (4) וַיֹּאמֶר לִי הַמֶּלֶךְ עַל־מַה־זֶּה
this what? to the-king to-me and-he-said (4) by-fire they-were-destroyed

אַתָּה מְבַקֵּשׁ וָאֶתְפַּלֵּל אֶל־אֱלֹהֵי הַשָּׁמָיִם׃ (5) וָאֹמַר לַמֶּלֶךְ
to-the-king and-I-answered (5) the-heavens God-of to then-I-prayed wanting you

Moses, saying, 'If you are
unfaithful, I will scatter you
among the nations, [9]but if
you return to me and obey
my commands, then even
if your exiled people are at
the farthest horizon, I will
gather them from there and
bring them to the place I
have chosen as a dwelling
for my Name.'
[10]"They are your servants
and your people, whom
you redeemed by your
great strength and your
mighty hand. [11]O Lord, let
your ear be attentive to the
prayer of this your servant
and to the prayer of your
servants who delight in
revering your name. Give
your servant success today
by granting him favor in
the presence of this man."

I was cupbearer to the king.

Artaxerxes Sends Nehemiah to Jerusalem

2 In the month of Nisan in
the twentieth year of King
Artaxerxes, when wine was
brought for him, I took the
wine and gave it to the king. I
had not been sad in his presence before; [2]so the king asked
me, "Why does your face look
so sad when you are not ill?
This can be nothing but sad-
ness of heart."
I was very much afraid, [3]but
I said to the king, "May the
king live forever! Why should
my face not look sad when the
city where my fathers are buried lies in ruins, and its gates
have been destroyed by fire?"
[4]The king said to me, "What
is it you want?"
Then I prayed to the God of
heaven, [5]and I answered the

°9 ק והביאותים

אִם־עַל־הַמֶּ֫לֶךְ ט֔וֹב וְאִם־ יִיטַ֥ב עַבְדְּךָ֖ לְפָנֶ֑יךָ
if — to the-king pleasing and-if he-found-favor servant-of-you before-you

אֲשֶׁ֧ר תִּשְׁלָחֵ֣נִי אֶל־יְהוּדָ֗ה אֶל־ עִ֣יר קִבְר֥וֹת אֲבֹתַ֖י
then you-send-me to Judah to city-of burials-of fathers-of-me

וְאֶבְנֶֽנָּה׃ (6) וַיֹּ֩אמֶר֩ לִ֨י הַמֶּ֜לֶךְ וְהַשֵּׁגַ֣ל ׀ יוֹשֶׁ֣בֶת
so-I-can-rebuild-her then-he-asked to-me the-king with-the-queen sitting

אֶצְל֗וֹ עַד־ מָתַ֛י יִהְיֶ֥ה מַֽהֲלָכֲךָ֖ וּמָתַ֣י תָּשׁ֑וּב
beside-him until when? will-he-be journey-of-you and-when? will-you-get-back

וַיִּיטַ֧ב לִפְנֵֽי־הַמֶּ֛לֶךְ וַיִּשְׁלָחֵ֖נִי וָֽאֶתְּנָ֥ה ל֖וֹ זְמָֽן׃ (7) וָאוֹמַר֮
and-he-pleased the-king to and-he-sent-me so-I-set for-him time also-I-said

לַמֶּלֶךְ֒ אִם־ עַל־ הַמֶּ֣לֶךְ ט֔וֹב אִגְּרוֹת֙ יִתְּנוּ־ לִ֔י עַל־
to-the-king if to the-king pleasing letters let-them-give to-me to

פַּחֲווֹת֙ עֵ֣בֶר הַנָּהָ֔ר אֲשֶׁר֙ יַעֲבִיר֔וּנִי
governors-of Beyond-of the-River that they-will-provide-safe-conduct-to-me

עַ֥ד אֲשֶׁר־ אָב֖וֹא אֶל־יְהוּדָֽה׃ (8) וְאִגֶּ֡רֶת אֶל־ אָסָ֣ף שֹׁמֵר֩
until when I-arrive in Judah and-letter to Asaph one-keeping-of

הַפַּרְדֵּ֜ס אֲשֶׁ֣ר לַמֶּ֗לֶךְ אֲשֶׁ֣ר יִתֶּן־ לִ֣י עֵצִ֡ים לְקָר֣וֹת
the-forest that to-the-king that he-will-give to-me timbers to-make-beam

אֶת־ שַׁעֲרֵ֣י הַבִּירָ֣ה אֲשֶׁר־ לַבַּ֙יִת֙ וּלְחוֹמַ֣ת הָעִ֔יר
••• gates-of the-citadel that by-the-temple and-for-wall-of the-city

וְלַבַּ֖יִת אֲשֶׁר־ אָב֣וֹא אֵלָ֑יו וַיִּתֶּן־ לִ֣י הַמֶּ֔לֶךְ
and-for-the-residence that I-will-occupy in-him and-he-granted to-me the-king

כְּיַד־ אֱלֹהַ֖י הַטּוֹבָ֥ה עָלָֽי׃ (9) וָאָב֕וֹא אֶל־ פַּחֲווֹת֙
because-hand-of God-of-me the-gracious upon-me so-I-went to governors-of

עֵ֣בֶר הַנָּהָ֔ר וָאֶתְּנָ֣ה לָהֶ֔ם אֵ֖ת אִגְּר֣וֹת הַמֶּ֑לֶךְ וַיִּשְׁלַ֤ח
Beyond-of the-River and-I-gave to-them ••• letters-of the-king also-he-sent

עִמִּי֙ הַמֶּ֔לֶךְ שָׂ֥רֵי חַ֖יִל וּפָרָשִֽׁים׃ (10) וַיִּשְׁמַ֞ע סַנְבַלַּ֣ט
with-me the-king officers-of army and-cavalrymen when-he-heard Sanballat

הַחֹרֹנִ֗י וְטֽוֹבִיָּה֙ הָעֶ֣בֶד הָֽעַמֹּנִ֔י וַיֵּ֥רַע לָהֶ֖ם
the-Horonite and-Tobiah the-official the-Ammonite and-he-disturbed to-them

רָעָ֣ה גְדֹלָ֑ה אֲשֶׁר־ בָּ֣א אָדָ֔ם לְבַקֵּ֥שׁ טוֹבָ֖ה לִבְנֵ֥י יִשְׂרָאֵֽל׃
disturbance great that he-came someone to-promote welfare of-sons-of Israel

וָאָב֖וֹא אֶל־יְרֽוּשָׁלִָ֑ם וָאֱהִי־ שָׁ֖ם יָמִ֥ים שְׁלֹשָֽׁה׃ (12) וָאָק֣וּם ׀
and-I-went to Jerusalem and-I-stayed there days three and-I-set-out

לַ֗יְלָה אֲנִי֮ וַאֲנָשִׁ֣ים ׀ מְעַט֮ עִמִּי֒ וְלֹא־ הִגַּ֣דְתִּי לְאָדָ֔ם מָ֗ה אֱלֹהַי֙ נֹתֵ֣ן
night I and-men few with-me and-not I-told to-anyone what God-of-me putting

אֶל־ לִבִּ֖י לַעֲשׂ֣וֹת לִירֽוּשָׁלִָ֑ם וּבְהֵמָה֙ אֵ֣ין עִמִּ֔י כִּ֚י
in heart-of-me to-do for-Jerusalem and-mount there-was-no with-me except

---

king, "If it pleases the king and if your servant has found favor in his sight, let him send me to the city in Judah where my fathers are buried so that I can rebuild it."

[6]Then the king, with the queen sitting beside him, asked me, "How long will your journey take, and when will you get back?" It pleased the king to send me; so I set a time.

[7]I also said to him, "If it pleases the king, may I have letters to the governors of Trans-Euphrates, so that they will provide me safe-conduct until I arrive in Judah? [8]And may I have a letter to Asaph, keeper of the king's forest, so he will give me timber to make beams for the gates of the citadel by the temple and for the city wall and for the residence I will occupy?" And because the gracious hand of my God was upon me, the king granted my requests. [9]So I went to the governors of Trans-Euphrates and gave them the king's letters. The king had also sent army officers and cavalry with me. [10]When Sanballat the Horonite and Tobiah the Ammonite official heard about this, they were very much disturbed that someone had come to promote the welfare of the Israelites.

Nehemiah Inspects Jerusalem's Walls

[11]I went to Jerusalem, and after staying there three days [12]I set out during the night with a few men. I had not told anyone what my God had put in my heart to do for Jerusalem. There were no mounts with

אִם־ הַבְּהֵמָה אֲשֶׁר אֲנִי רֹכֵב בָּהּ׃ וָאֵצְאָה בְשַׁעַר־
through-Gate-of and-I-went-out (13) on-her riding I that the-mount only

הַגַּיְא לַיְלָה וְאֶל־ פְּנֵי עֵין הַתַּנִּין וְאֶל־ שַׁעַר
Gate-of and-toward the-Jackal Well-of faces-of and-toward night the-Valley

הָאַשְׁפֹּת וָאֱהִי שֹׂבֵר בְּחוֹמֹת יְרוּשָׁלִַם אֲשֶׁר־
which Jerusalem to-walls-of examining and-I-was the-Dungs

הֵמפְּרוּצִים* וּשְׁעָרֶיהָ אֻכְּלוּ בָאֵשׁ׃
by-fire they-were-destroyed and-gates-of-her *they-ones-being-broken-down

וָאֶעֱבֹר אֶל־ שַׁעַר הָעַיִן וְאֶל־ בְּרֵכַת הַמֶּלֶךְ
the-King Pool-of and-toward the-Fountain Gate-of toward then-I-moved-on (14)

וְאֵין־ מָקוֹם לַבְּהֵמָה לַעֲבֹר תַּחְתָּי׃ וָאֱהִי
so-I-was (15) under-me to-get-through for-the-mount room but-there-was-no

עֹלֶה בַנַּחַל לַיְלָה וָאֱהִי שֹׂבֵר בַּחוֹמָה וָאָשׁוּב
and-I-turned-back to-the-wall examining and-I-was night in-the-valley going-up

וָאָבוֹא בְּשַׁעַר הַגַּיְא וָאָשׁוּב׃
and-I-turned-back the-Valley through-Gate-of and-I-reentered

וְהַסְּגָנִים לֹא יָדְעוּ אָנָה הָלַכְתִּי וּמָה אֲנִי עֹשֶׂה
doing I or-what I-went to-where they-knew not and-the-officials (16)

וְלַיְּהוּדִים וְלַכֹּהֲנִים וְלַחֹרִים וְלַסְּגָנִים
or-to-the-officials or-to-the-nobles or-to-the-priests because-to-the-Jews

וּלְיֶתֶר עֹשֵׂה הַמְּלָאכָה עַד־ כֵּן לֹא הִגַּדְתִּי׃ וָאוֹמַר
then-I-said (17) I-said nothing yet until the-work one-doing-of or-to-other-of

אֲלֵהֶם אַתֶּם רֹאִים הָרָעָה אֲשֶׁר אֲנַחְנוּ בָהּ אֲשֶׁר יְרוּשָׁלִַם
Jerusalem that in-her we that the-trouble ones-seeing you to-them

חֲרֵבָה וּשְׁעָרֶיהָ נִצְּתוּ בָאֵשׁ לְכוּ
come! with-fire they-were-burned and-gates-of-her she-lies-in-ruin

וְנִבְנֶה אֶת־ חוֹמַת יְרוּשָׁלִַם וְלֹא־ נִהְיֶה עוֹד חֶרְפָּה׃
disgrace longer we-will-be and-not Jerusalem wall-of *** and-let-us-rebuild

וָאַגִּיד לָהֶם אֶת־ יַד אֱלֹהַי אֲשֶׁר־הִיא טוֹבָה עָלַי
upon-me gracious she that God-of-me hand-of *** to-them also-I-told (18)

וְאַף־ דִּבְרֵי הַמֶּלֶךְ אֲשֶׁר אָמַר־ לִי וַיֹּאמְרוּ נָקוּם
let-us-start and-they-replied to-me he-said that the-king words-of and-also

וּבָנִינוּ וַיְחַזְּקוּ יְדֵיהֶם לַטּוֹבָה׃ וַיִּשְׁמַע°
when-he-heard (19) in-the-good hands-of-them so-they-began and-let-us-rebuild

סַנְבַלַּט הַחֹרֹנִי וְטֹבִיָּה ׀ הָעֶבֶד הָעַמּוֹנִי וְגֶשֶׁם
and-Geshem the-Ammonite the-official and-Tobiah the-Horonite Sanballat

הָעַרְבִי וַיַּלְעִגוּ לָנוּ וַיִּבְזוּ עָלֵינוּ וַיֹּאמְרוּ
and-they-asked at-us and-they-ridiculed at-us then-they-mocked the-Arab

me except the one I was riding
on.
13By night I went out
through the Valley Gate
toward the Jackal[a] Well and
the Dung Gate, examining the
walls of Jerusalem, which had
been broken down, and its
gates, which had been de-
stroyed by fire. 14Then I moved
on toward the Fountain Gate
and the King's Pool, but there
was not enough room for my
mount to get through; 15so I
went up the valley by night,
examining the wall. Finally, I
turned back and reentered
through the Valley Gate. 16The
officials did not know where I
had gone or what I was doing,
because as yet I had said nothing to the Jews or the priests or
nobles or officials or any
others who would be doing
the work.
17Then I said to them, "You
see the trouble we are in:
Jerusalem lies in ruins, and its
gates have been burned with
fire. Come, let us rebuild the
wall of Jerusalem, and we will
no longer be in disgrace." 18I
also told them about the gracious hand of my God upon
me and what the king had said
to me.
They replied, "Let us start
rebuilding." So they began
this good work.
19But when Sanballat the
Horonite, Tobiah the Am-
monite official and Geshem
the Arab heard about it, they
mocked and ridiculed us.

[a]13 Or *Serpent* or *Fig*

*13 The *Qere* reading separates the *Kethib* form into two words, the pronoun *they* preceding the participle *ones-being-broken-down*.

°13 ק הם | פרוצים

מַה־ הַדָּבָר הַזֶּה אֲשֶׁר אַתֶּם עֹשִׂים הַעַל הַמֶּלֶךְ אַתֶּם
you the-king against? ones-doing you that the-this the-thing what?

מֹרְדִים׃ (20) וָאָשִׁיב אוֹתָם דָּבָר וָאוֹמַר לָהֶם אֱלֹהֵי הַשָּׁמַיִם
the-heavens God-of to-them and-I-said answer them and-I-gave (20) ones-rebelling

הוּא יַצְלִיחַ לָנוּ וַאֲנַחְנוּ עֲבָדָיו נָקוּם
we-will-start servants-of-him and-we to-us he-will-give-success he

וּבָנִינוּ וְלָכֶם אֵין־ חֵלֶק וּצְדָקָה וְזִכָּרוֹן
or-historic-right or-claim share there-is-no but-for-you and-we-will-rebuild

בִּירוּשָׁלָםִ׃ (3:1) וַיָּקָם אֶלְיָשִׁיב הַכֹּהֵן הַגָּדוֹל
the-high the-priest Eliashib so-he-went-to-work (3:1) in-Jerusalem

וְאֶחָיו הַכֹּהֲנִים וַיִּבְנוּ אֶת־ שַׁעַר הַצֹּאן הֵמָּה
they the-Sheep Gate-of *** and-they-rebuilt the-priests and-fellows-of-him

קִדְּשׁוּהוּ וַיַּעֲמִידוּ דַּלְתֹתָיו וְעַד־ מִגְדַּל
Tower-of and-as-far-as doors-of-him and-they-set-in-place they-dedicated-him

הַמֵּאָה קִדְּשׁוּהוּ עַד מִגְדַּל חֲנַנְאֵל׃ (2) וְעַל־
and-at (2) Hananel Tower-of as-far-as they-dedicated-him the-Hundred

יָדוֹ בָנוּ אַנְשֵׁי יְרֵחוֹ וְעַל־ יָדוֹ בָּנָה זַכּוּר
Zaccur he-built side-of-him and-at Jericho men-of they-built side-of-him

בֶּן־ אִמְרִי׃ (3) וְאֵת שַׁעַר הַדָּגִים בָּנוּ בְּנֵי הַסְּנָאָה הֵמָּה
they Hassenaah sons-of they-rebuilt the-Fishes Gate-of and (3) Imri son-of

קֵרוּהוּ וַיַּעֲמִידוּ דַּלְתֹתָיו מַנְעוּלָיו
bolts-of-him doors-of-him and-they-put-in-place they-laid-beams-of-him

וּבְרִיחָיו׃ (4) וְעַל־ יָדָם הֶחֱזִיק מְרֵמוֹת בֶּן־ אוּרִיָּה
Uriah son-of Meremoth he-repaired side-of-them and-at (4) and-bars-of-him

בֶּן־ הַקּוֹץ וְעַל־ יָדָם הֶחֱזִיק מְשֻׁלָּם בֶּן־ בֶּרֶכְיָה
Berekiah son-of Meshullam he-repaired side-of-them and-at Hakkoz son-of

בֶּן־ מְשֵׁיזַבְאֵל וְעַל־ יָדָם הֶחֱזִיק צָדוֹק בֶּן־ בַּעֲנָא׃
Baana son-of Zadok he-repaired side-of-them and-at Meshezabel son-of

(5) וְעַל־ יָדָם הֶחֱזִיקוּ הַתְּקוֹעִים וְאַדִּירֵיהֶם לֹא־
not but-nobles-of-them the-Tekoaites they-repaired side-of-them and-at (5)

הֵבִיאוּ צַוָּרָם בַּעֲבֹדַת אֲדֹנֵיהֶם׃ (6) וְאֵת שַׁעַר
Gate-of and (6) supervisors-of-them to-work-of shoulder-of-them they-put

הַיְשָׁנָה הֶחֱזִיקוּ יוֹיָדָע בֶּן־ פָּסֵחַ וּמְשֻׁלָּם בֶּן־
son-of and-Meshullam Paseah son-of Joiada they-repaired the-Jeshanah

בְּסוֹדְיָה הֵמָּה קֵרוּהוּ וַיַּעֲמִידוּ דַּלְתֹתָיו
doors-of-him and-they-put-in-place they-laid-beams-of-him they Besodeiah

וּמַנְעֻלָיו וּבְרִיחָיו׃ (7) וְעַל־ יָדָם הֶחֱזִיק מְלַטְיָה
Melatiah he-repaired side-of-them and-at (7) and-bars-of-him and-bolts-of-him

"What is this you are doing?"
they asked. "Are you rebelling
against the king?"
[20]I answered them by saying, "The God of heaven will give us success. We his servants will start rebuilding, but as for you, you have no share in Jerusalem or any claim or historic right to it."

Builders of the Wall

3 Eliashib the high priest and his fellow priests went to work and rebuilt the Sheep Gate. They dedicated it and set its doors in place, building as far as the Tower of the Hundred, which they dedicated, and as far as the
Tower of Hananel. [2]The men of Jericho built the adjoining section, and Zaccur son of Imri built next to them.

[3]The Fish Gate was rebuilt by the sons of Hassenaah. They laid its beams and put its doors and bolts and bars in
place. [4]Meremoth son of Uriah, the son of Hakkoz, repaired the next section. Next to him Meshullam son of Berekiah, the son of Meshezabel, made repairs, and next to him Zadok son of Baana also made
repairs. [5]The next section was repaired by the men of Tekoa, but their nobles would not put their shoulders to the work under their supervisors.[b]

[6]The Jeshanah[c] Gate was repaired by Joiada son of Paseah and Meshullam son of Besodeiah. They laid its beams and put its doors and bolts and
bars in place. [7]Next to them, repairs were made by men

[b]5 Or *their Lord* or *the governor*
[c]6 Or *Old*

הַגִּבְעֹנִי וְיָדוֹן הַמֵּרֹנֹתִי אַנְשֵׁי גִבְעוֹן וְהַמִּצְפָּה
and-the-Mizpah Gibeon men-of the-Meronothite and-Jadon the-Gibeonite

לְכִסֵּא פַּחַת עֵבֶר הַנָּהָר׃ (8) עַל־ יָדוֹ
side-of-him at (8) the-River Beyond-of governor-of under-authority-of

הֶחֱזִיק עֻזִּיאֵל בֶּן־ חַרְהֲיָה צוֹרְפִים וְעַל־ יָדוֹ
side-of-him and-at ones-being-goldsmiths Harhaiah son-of Uzziel he-repaired

הֶחֱזִיק חֲנַנְיָה בֶּן־ הָרַקָּחִים וַיַּעַזְבוּ יְרוּשָׁלִַם
Jerusalem and-they-restored the-perfume-makers son-of Hananiah he-repaired

עַד הַחוֹמָה הָרְחָבָה׃ (9) וְעַל־ יָדָם הֶחֱזִיק רְפָיָה
Rephaiah he-repaired side-of-them and-at (9) the-Broad the-Wall as-far-as

בֶּן־ חוּר שַׂר חֲצִי פֶּלֶךְ יְרוּשָׁלִָם׃ (10) וְעַל־ יָדָם
side-of-them and-at (10) Jerusalem district-of half-of ruler-of Hur son-of

הֶחֱזִיק יְדָיָה בֶן־ חֲרוּמַף וְנֶגֶד בֵּיתוֹ וְעַל־
and-at house-of-him and-opposite Harumaph son-of Jedaiah he-repaired

יָדוֹ הֶחֱזִיק חַטּוּשׁ בֶּן־ חֲשַׁבְנְיָה׃ (11) מִדָּה שֵׁנִית
another section (11) Hashabneiah son-of Hattush he-repaired side-of-him

הֶחֱזִיק מַלְכִּיָּה בֶן־ חָרִם וְחַשּׁוּב בֶּן־ פַּחַת מוֹאָב וְאֵת
and Moab Pahath son-of and-Hasshub Harim son-of Malkijah he-repaired

מִגְדַּל הַתַּנּוּרִים׃ (12) וְעַל־ יָדוֹ הֶחֱזִיק שַׁלּוּם בֶּן־
son-of Shallum he-repaired side-of-him and-at (12) the-Ovens Tower-of

הַלּוֹחֵשׁ שַׂר חֲצִי פֶּלֶךְ יְרוּשָׁלִָם הוּא וּבְנוֹתָיו׃
and-daughters-of-him he Jerusalem district-of half-of ruler-of Hallohesh

(13) אֵת שַׁעַר הַגַּיְא הֶחֱזִיק חָנוּן וְיֹשְׁבֵי זָנוֹחַ
Zanoah and-ones-residing-of Hanun he-repaired the-Valley Gate-of *** (13)

הֵמָּה בָנוּהוּ וַיַּעֲמִידוּ דַּלְתֹתָיו מַנְעֻלָיו
bolts-of-him doors-of-him and-they-put-in-place they-rebuilt-him they

וּבְרִיחָיו וְאֶלֶף אַמָּה בַּחוֹמָה עַד שַׁעַר הָשְׁפוֹת׃
the-Dungs Gate-of as-far-as of-the-wall cubit and-thousand-of and-bars-of-him

(14) וְאֵת ׀ שַׁעַר הָאַשְׁפּוֹת הֶחֱזִיק מַלְכִּיָּה בֶן־ רֵכָב שַׂר
ruler-of Recab son-of Malkijah he-repaired the-Dungs Gate-of and (14)

פֶּלֶךְ בֵּית־ הַכֶּרֶם הוּא יִבְנֶנּוּ וְיַעֲמִיד דַּלְתֹתָיו
doors-of-him and-he-put-in-place he-rebuilt-him he Haccerem Beth district-of

מַנְעֻלָיו וּבְרִיחָיו׃ (15) וְאֵת שַׁעַר הָעַיִן הֶחֱזִיק
he-repaired the-Fountain Gate-of and (15) and-bars-of-him bolts-of-him

שַׁלּוּן בֶּן־ כָּל־ חֹזֶה שַׂר פֶּלֶךְ הַמִּצְפָּה הוּא יִבְנֶנּוּ
he-rebuilt-him he the-Mizpah district-of ruler-of Hozeh Col son-of Shallun

וִיטַלְלֶנּוּ וְיַעֲמִידוּ דַּלְתֹתָיו מַנְעֻלָיו
bolts-of-him doors-of-him and-he-put-in-place and-he-roofed-him

from Gibeon and Mizpah—Melatiah of Gibeon and Jadon of Meronoth—places under the authority of the governor of Trans-Euphrates. [8]Uzziel son of Harhaiah, one of the goldsmiths, repaired the next section; and Hananiah, one of the perfume-makers, made repairs next to that. They restored[d] Jerusalem as far as the Broad Wall. [9]Rephaiah son of Hur, ruler of a half-district of Jerusalem, repaired the next section. [10]Adjoining this, Jedaiah son of Harumaph made repairs opposite his house, and Hattush son of Hashabneiah made repairs next to him. [11]Malkijah son of Harim and Hasshub son of Pahath-Moab repaired another section and the Tower of the Ovens. [12]Shallum son of Hallohesh, ruler of a half-district of Jerusalem, repaired the next section with the help of his daughters.

[13]The Valley Gate was repaired by Hanun and the residents of Zanoah. They rebuilt it and put its doors and bolts and bars in place. They also repaired five hundred yards[e] of the wall as far as the Dung Gate.

[14]The Dung Gate was repaired by Malkijah son of Recab, ruler of the district of Beth Haccerem. He rebuilt it and put its doors and bolts and bars in place.

[15]The Fountain Gate was repaired by Shallun son of Col-Hozeh, ruler of the district of Mizpah. He rebuilt it, roofing it over and putting its doors and bolts and bars in place. He

[d]8 Or *They left out part of*
[e]13 Hebrew *a thousand cubits* (about 450 meters)

°15 ק ויעמיד

וּבְרִיחָיו וְאֵת חוֹמַת בְּרֵכַת הַשֶּׁלַח לְגַן־הַמֶּלֶךְ
the-King by-Garden-of the-Shelah Pool-of wall-of also and-bars-of-him

וְעַד־הַמַּעֲלוֹת הַיּוֹרְדוֹת מֵעִיר דָּוִיד׃ אַחֲרָיו
beyond-him (16) David from-City-of the-ones-going-down the-steps and-as-far-as

הֶחֱזִיק נְחֶמְיָה בֶן־עַזְבּוּק שַׂר חֲצִי פֶּלֶךְ בֵּית־צוּר
Zur Beth district-of half-of ruler-of Azbuk son-of Nehemiah he-repaired

עַד־נֶגֶד קִבְרֵי דָוִיד וְעַד־הַבְּרֵכָה הָעֲשׂוּיָה
the-one-being-artificial the-pool and-as-far-as David tombs-of opposite up-to

וְעַד בֵּית הַגִּבֹּרִים׃ אַחֲרָיו הֶחֱזִיקוּ הַלְוִיִּם
the-Levites they-repaired next-to-him (17) the-Heroes House-of and-as-far-as

רְחוּם בֶּן־בָּנִי עַל־יָדוֹ הֶחֱזִיק חֲשַׁבְיָה שַׂר־חֲצִי־
half-of ruler-of Hashabiah he-repaired side-of-him at Bani son-of Rehum

פֶּלֶךְ קְעִילָה לְפִלְכּוֹ׃ אַחֲרָיו הֶחֱזִיקוּ
they-repaired next-to-him (18) for-district-of-him Keilah district-of

אֲחֵיהֶם בַּוַּי בֶּן־חֵנָדָד שַׂר חֲצִי פֶּלֶךְ קְעִילָה׃
Keilah district-of half-of ruler-of Henadad son-of Bavvai countrymen-of-them

וַיְחַזֵּק עַל־יָדוֹ עֵזֶר בֶּן־יֵשׁוּעַ שַׂר הַמִּצְפָּה
the-Mizpah ruler-of Jeshua son-of Ezer side-of-him at and-he-repaired (19)

מִדָּה שֵׁנִית מִנֶּגֶד עֲלֹת הַנֶּשֶׁק הַמִּקְצֹעַ׃ אַחֲרָיו
next-to-him (20) the-angle the-armory to-ascend from-facing another section

הֶחֱרָה הֶחֱזִיק בָּרוּךְ בֶּן־זַבַּי° מִדָּה שֵׁנִית מִן־
from another section Zabbai son-of Baruch he-repaired he-was-zealous

הַמִּקְצוֹעַ עַד־פֶּתַח בֵּית אֶלְיָשִׁיב הַכֹּהֵן הַגָּדוֹל׃
the-high the-priest Eliashib house-of entrance-of to the-angle

אַחֲרָיו הֶחֱזִיק מְרֵמוֹת בֶּן־אוּרִיָּה בֶּן־הַקּוֹץ מִדָּה
section Hakkoz son-of Uriah son-of Meremoth he-repaired next-to-him (21)

שֵׁנִית מִפֶּתַח בֵּית אֶלְיָשִׁיב וְעַד־תַּכְלִית בֵּית אֶלְיָשִׁיב׃
Eliashib house-of end-of and-to Eliashib house-of from-entrance-of another

וְאַחֲרָיו הֶחֱזִיקוּ הַכֹּהֲנִים אַנְשֵׁי הַכִּכָּר׃
the-surrounding-region men-of the-priests they-repaired and-next-to-him (22)

אַחֲרָיו הֶחֱזִיק בִּנְיָמִן וְחַשּׁוּב נֶגֶד בֵּיתָם
house-of-them in-front-of and-Hasshub Benjamin he-repaired beyond-him (23)

אַחֲרָיו הֶחֱזִיק עֲזַרְיָה בֶּן־מַעֲשֵׂיָה בֶּן־עֲנַנְיָה אֵצֶל
beside Ananiah son-of Maaseiah son-of Azariah he-repaired next-to-him

בֵּיתוֹ׃ אַחֲרָיו הֶחֱזִיק בִּנּוּי בֶּן־חֵנָדָד מִדָּה
section Henadad son-of Binnui he-repaired next-to-him (24) house-of-him

שֵׁנִית מִבֵּית עֲזַרְיָה עַד־הַמִּקְצוֹעַ וְעַד־הַפִּנָּה׃ פָּלָל
Palal (25) the-corner and-to the-angle to Azariah from-house-of another

°20 ק זכי

also repaired the wall of the
Pool of Siloam,[f] by the King's
Garden, as far as the steps going down from the City of David. [16]Beyond him, Nehemiah
son of Azbuk, ruler of a half-
district of Beth Zur, made repairs up to a point opposite
the tombs[g] of David, as far as
the artificial pool and the
House of the Heroes.
[17]Next to him, the repairs
were made by the Levites under Rehum son of Bani. Beside
him, Hashabiah, ruler of half
the district of Keilah, carried
out repairs for his district.
[18]Next to him, the repairs were
made by their countrymen
under Binnui[h] son of Henadad, ruler of the other half-district of Keilah. [19]Next to him,
Ezer son of Jeshua, ruler of
Mizpah, repaired another section, from a point facing the
ascent to the armory as far as
the angle. [20]Next to him, Baruch son of Zabbai zealously
repaired another section, from
the angle to the entrance of the
house of Eliashib the high
priest. [21]Next to him, Meremoth son of Uriah, the son of
Hakkoz, repaired another section, from the entrance of Eliashib's house to the end of it.
[22]The repairs next to him
were made by the priests from
the surrounding region.
[23]Beyond them, Benjamin and
Hasshub made repairs in front
of their house; and next to
them, Azariah son of Maa-
seiah, the son of Ananiah,
made repairs beside his house.
[24]Next to him, Binnui son of
Henadad repaired another
section, from Azariah's house
to the angle and the corner,

[f]15 Hebrew *Shelah*, a variant of *Shiloah*, that is, Siloam
[g]16 Hebrew; Septuagint, some Vulgate manuscripts and Syriac *tomb*
[h]18 Two Hebrew manuscripts, some Septuagint manuscripts and Syriac (see also verse 24); most Hebrew manuscripts *Bavvai*

בֶּן־ אוּזַי מִנֶּגֶד הַמִּקְצוֹעַ וְהַמִּגְדָּל הַיּוֹצֵא
the-one-projecting and-the-tower the-angle at-opposite Uzai son-of

מִבֵּית הַמֶּלֶךְ הָעֶלְיוֹן אֲשֶׁר לַחֲצַר הַמַּטָּרָה אַחֲרָיו
next-to-him the-guard near-court-of that the-upper the-king from-palace-of

פְּדָיָה בֶּן־ פַּרְעֹשׁ׃ וְהַנְּתִינִים הָיוּ יֹשְׁבִים
ones-living they-were and-the-temple-servants (26) Parosh son-of Pedaiah

בָּעֹפֶל עַד נֶגֶד שַׁעַר הַמַּיִם לַמִּזְרָח וְהַמִּגְדָּל
and-the-tower toward-the-east the-Waters Gate-of opposite up-to on-the-Ophel

הַיּוֹצֵא׃ אַחֲרָיו הֶחֱזִיקוּ הַתְּקֹעִים מִדָּה
section the-Tekoaites they-repaired next-to-him (27) the-one-projecting

שֵׁנִית מִנֶּגֶד הַמִּגְדָּל הַגָּדוֹל הַיּוֹצֵא וְעַד חוֹמַת
wall-of and-to the-one-projecting the-great the-tower from-before another

הָעֹפֶל׃ מֵעַל | שַׁעַר הַסּוּסִים הֶחֱזִיקוּ הַכֹּהֲנִים אִישׁ
each the-priests they-repaired the-Horses Gate-of at-above (28) the-Ophel

לְנֶגֶד בֵּיתוֹ׃ אַחֲרָיו הֶחֱזִיק צָדוֹק בֶּן־ אִמֵּר
Immer son-of Zadok he-repaired next-to-him (29) house-of-him in-front-of

נֶגֶד בֵּיתוֹ וְאַחֲרָיו הֶחֱזִיק שְׁמַעְיָה בֶן־ שְׁכַנְיָה
Shecaniah son-of Shemaiah he-repaired and-next-to-him house-of-him opposite

שֹׁמֵר שַׁעַר הַמִּזְרָח׃ אַחֲרָי° הֶחֱזִיק חֲנַנְיָה
Hananiah he-repaired next-to-him (30) the-East Gate-of one-guarding-of

בֶן־ שֶׁלֶמְיָה וְחָנוּן בֶּן־ צָלָף הַשִּׁשִּׁי מִדָּה שֵׁנִי
another section the-sixth Zalaph son-of and-Hanun Shelemiah son-of

אַחֲרָיו הֶחֱזִיק מְשֻׁלָּם בֶּן־ בֶּרֶכְיָה נֶגֶד נִשְׁכָּתוֹ׃
living-quarter-of-him opposite Berekiah son-of Meshullam he-repaired next-to-him

אַחֲרָי° הֶחֱזִיק מַלְכִּיָּה בֶּן־ הַצֹּרְפִי עַד־
as-far-as the-goldsmith son-of Malkijah he-repaired next-to-him (31)

בֵּית הַנְּתִינִים וְהָרֹכְלִים נֶגֶד שַׁעַר
Gate-of opposite and-the-ones-being-merchants the-temple-servants house-of

הַמִּפְקָד וְעַד עֲלִיַּת הַפִּנָּה׃ וּבֵין
and-between (32) the-corner room-above-of and-as-far-as the-Inspection

עֲלִיַּת הַפִּנָּה לְשַׁעַר הַצֹּאן הֶחֱזִיקוּ
they-repaired the-Sheep to-Gate-of the-corner room-above-of

הַצֹּרְפִים וְהָרֹכְלִים׃ וַיְהִי
and-he-was *(33[1]) and-the-ones-being-merchants the-ones-being-goldsmiths

כַּאֲשֶׁר שָׁמַע סַנְבַלַּט כִּי־אֲנַחְנוּ בוֹנִים אֶת־הַחוֹמָה וַיִּחַר
then-he-angered the-wall *** ones-rebuilding we that Sanballat he-heard as-when

לוֹ וַיִּכְעַס הַרְבֵּה וַיַּלְעֵג עַל־ הַיְּהוּדִים׃
the-Jews at and-he-ridiculed to-be-great and-he-was-incensed to-him

[25]and Palal son of Uzai worked opposite the angle and the tower projecting from the upper palace near the court of the guard. Next to him, Pedaiah son of Parosh [26]and the temple servants living on the hill of Ophel made repairs up to a point opposite the Water Gate toward the east and the projecting tower. [27]Next to them, the men of Tekoa repaired another section, from the great projecting tower to the wall of Ophel.

[28]Above the Horse Gate, the priests made repairs, each in front of his own house. [29]Next to them, Zadok son of Immer made repairs opposite his house. Next to him, Shemaiah son of Shecaniah, the guard at the East Gate, made repairs. [30]Next to him, Hananiah son of Shelemiah, and Hanun, the sixth son of Zalaph, repaired another section. Next to them, Meshullam son of Berekiah made repairs opposite his living quarters. [31]Next to him, Malkijah, one of the goldsmiths, made repairs as far as the house of the temple servants and the merchants, opposite the Inspection Gate, and as far as the room above the corner; [32]and between the room above the corner and the Sheep Gate the goldsmiths and merchants made repairs.

Opposition to the Rebuilding

4 When Sanballat heard that we were rebuilding the wall, he became angry and was greatly incensed. He ridiculed the Jews, [2]and in the

*33 The Hebrew numeration of chapter 4 begins with verse 7 in the English; the number in brackets indicates the English numeration.

°30 ק אחריו
°31 ק אחריו

(34[2]) וַיֹּאמֶר ׀ לִפְנֵי אֶחָיו וְחֵיל שֹׁמְרוֹן
Samaria and-army-of associates-of-him in-presences-of and-he-said (34[2])

וַיֹּאמֶר מָה הַיְּהוּדִים הָאֲמֵלָלִים עֹשִׂים הֲיַעַזְבוּ
will-they-restore? ones-doing the-feeble-ones the-Jews what? and-he-said

לָהֶם הֲיִזְבָּחוּ הַיְכַלּוּ בַיּוֹם
in-the-day will-they-finish? will-they-offer-sacrifices? for-them

הַיְחַיּוּ אֶת־ הָאֲבָנִים מֵעֲרֵמוֹת הֶעָפָר וְהֵמָּה
for-they the-rubble from-heaps-of the-stones *** can-they-bring-to-life?

שְׂרוּפוֹת׃ (35[3]) וְטוֹבִיָּה הָעַמֹּנִי אֶצְלוֹ וַיֹּאמֶר
and-he-said at-side-of-him the-Ammonite and-Tobiah (35[3]) ones-being-burned

גַּם אֲשֶׁר־ הֵם בּוֹנִים אִם־ יַעֲלֶה שׁוּעָל וּפָרַץ
then-he-would-break-down fox he-climbed-up if ones-building they what indeed

חוֹמַת אַבְנֵיהֶם׃ (36[4]) שְׁמַע אֱלֹהֵינוּ כִּי־ הָיִינוּ בוּזָה וְהָשֵׁב
and-turn! despised we-are for God-of-us hear! (36[4]) stones-of-them wall-of

חֶרְפָּתָם אֶל־ רֹאשָׁם וּתְנֵם לְבִזָּה בְּאֶרֶץ
in-land-of as-plunder and-give-them! head-of-them on insult-of-them

שִׁבְיָה׃ (37[5]) וְאַל־ תְּכַס עַל־ עֲוֺנָם וְחַטָּאתָם
or-sin-of-them guilt-of-them over you-cover and-not (37[5]) captivity

מִלְּפָנֶיךָ אַל־ תִּמָּחֶה כִּי הִכְעִיסוּ לְנֶגֶד
in-face-of they-threw-insults for you-blot-out not from-before-you

הַבּוֹנִים׃ (38[6]) וַנִּבְנֶה אֶת־ הַחוֹמָה וַתִּקָּשֵׁר
and-she-reached-height the-wall *** so-we-rebuilt (38[6]) the-ones-building

כָּל־ הַחוֹמָה עַד־ חֶצְיָהּ וַיְהִי לֵב לָעָם לַעֲשׂוֹת׃
to-work of-the-people heart for-he-was half-of-her to the-wall all-of

(4:1[7]) וַיְהִי כַאֲשֶׁר שָׁמַע סַנְבַלַּט וְטוֹבִיָּה וְהָעַרְבִים
and-the-Arabs and-Tobiah Sanballat he-heard as-when but-he-was (4:1[7])

וְהָעַמֹּנִים וְהָאַשְׁדּוֹדִים כִּי־ עָלְתָה אֲרוּכָה לְחֹמוֹת
of-walls-of repair she-went-ahead that and-the-Ashdodites and-the-Ammonites

יְרוּשָׁלִַם כִּי־ הֵחֵלּוּ הַפְּרֻצִים לְהִסָּתֵם וַיִּחַר
then-he-angered to-be-closed the-ones-being-gaps they-began that Jerusalem

לָהֶם מְאֹד׃ (2[8]) וַיִּקְשְׁרוּ כֻלָּם יַחְדָּו לָבוֹא לְהִלָּחֵם
to-fight to-come together all-of-them and-they-plotted (2[8]) very to-them

בִּירוּשָׁלִָם וְלַעֲשׂוֹת לוֹ תּוֹעָה׃ (3[9]) וַנִּתְפַּלֵּל
but-we-prayed (3[9]) trouble against-him and-to-stir-up against-Jerusalem

אֶל־ אֱלֹהֵינוּ וַנַּעֲמִיד מִשְׁמָר עֲלֵיהֶם יוֹמָם וָלַיְלָה מִפְּנֵיהֶם׃
because-of-them and-night by-day for-them guard and-we-posted God-of-us to

(4[10]) וַיֹּאמֶר יְהוּדָה כָּשַׁל כֹּחַ הַסַּבָּל וְהֶעָפָר
and-the-rubble the-laborer strength-of he-gives-out Judah and-he-said (4[10])

presence of his associates and
the army of Samaria, he said,
"What are those feeble Jews
doing? Will they restore their
wall? Will they offer sacrifices?
Will they finish in a day? Can
they bring the stones back to
life from those heaps of rubble—burned as they are?"
[3]Tobiah the Ammonite, who
was at his side, said, "What
they are building—if even a
fox climbed up on it, he would
break down their wall of
stones!"

[4]Hear us, O our God, for we
are despised. Turn their insults back on their own heads.
Give them over as plunder in
a land of captivity. [5]Do not
cover up their guilt or blot out
their sins from your sight, for
they have thrown insults in
the face of[i] the builders.

[6]So we rebuilt the wall till all
of it reached half its height, for
the people worked with all
their heart.
[7]But when Sanballat, Tobiah, the Arabs, the Ammonites and the men of Ashdod
heard that the repairs to
Jerusalem's walls had gone
ahead and that the gaps were
being closed, they were very
angry. [8]They all plotted together to come and fight
against Jerusalem and stir up
trouble against it. [9]But we
prayed to our God and posted
a guard day and night to meet
this threat.
[10]Meanwhile, the people in
Judah said, "The strength of
the laborers is giving out, and

[i]5 Or *have provoked you to anger before*

*See the note on page 223.

הַרְבֵּה וַאֲנַחְנוּ לֹא נוּכַל לִבְנוֹת בַּחוֹמָה׃ וַיֹּאמְרוּ
also-they-said (5[11]) on-the-wall to-rebuild we-are-able not that-we to-be-much

צָרֵינוּ לֹא יֵדְעוּ וְלֹא יִרְאוּ עַד אֲשֶׁר־נָבוֹא
we-will-be when until they-will-see and-not they-will-know not enemies-of-us

אֶל־תּוֹכָם וַהֲרַגְנוּם וְהִשְׁבַּתְנוּ אֶת־הַמְּלָאכָה׃
the-work *** and-we-will-end and-we-will-kill-them among-them in

וַיְהִי כַּאֲשֶׁר־בָּאוּ הַיְּהוּדִים הַיֹּשְׁבִים אֶצְלָם
near-them the-ones-living the-Jews they-came as-when then-he-was (6[12])

וַיֹּאמְרוּ לָנוּ עֶשֶׂר פְּעָמִים מִכָּל־הַמְּקֹמוֹת אֲשֶׁר־תָּשׁוּבוּ עָלֵינוּ׃
against-us you-turn where the-places at-any-of times ten to-us and-they-told

וָאַעֲמִיד מִתַּחְתִּיּוֹת לַמָּקוֹם מֵאַחֲרֵי לַחוֹמָה
of-the-wall at-behind at-the-point at-lowest-ones so-I-stationed (7[13])

בַּצְּחִחִיים וָאַעֲמִיד אֶת־הָעָם לְמִשְׁפָּחוֹת עִם־
with by-families the-people *** and-I-posted at-the-exposed-places

חַרְבֹתֵיהֶם רָמְחֵיהֶם וְקַשְּׁתֹתֵיהֶם׃ וָאֵרֶא
after-I-looked-over (8[14]) and-bows-of-them spears-of-them swords-of-them

וָאָקוּם וָאֹמַר אֶל־הַחֹרִים וְאֶל־הַסְּגָנִים וְאֶל־יֶתֶר
rest-of and-to the-officials and-to the-nobles to and-I-said then-I-stood-up

הָעָם אַל־תִּירְאוּ מִפְּנֵיהֶם אֶת־אֲדֹנָי הַגָּדוֹל
the-great Lord *** because-of-them you-be-afraid not the-people

וְהַנּוֹרָא זְכֹרוּ וְהִלָּחֲמוּ עַל־אֲחֵיכֶם בְּנֵיכֶם
sons-of-you brothers-of-you for and-fight! remember! and-the-one-being-awesome

וּבְנֹתֵיכֶם נְשֵׁיכֶם וּבָתֵּיכֶם׃ וַיְהִי
and-he-was (9[15]) and-homes-of-you wives-of-you and-daughters-of-you

כַּאֲשֶׁר־שָׁמְעוּ אוֹיְבֵינוּ כִּי־נוֹדַע לָנוּ
to-us he-was-aware that ones-being-enemies-of-us they-heard as-when

וַיָּפֶר הָאֱלֹהִים אֶת־עֲצָתָם וַנָּשָׁוב כֻּלָּנוּ אֶל־
to all-of-us then-we-returned plot-of-them *** the-God and-he-frustrated

הַחוֹמָה אִישׁ אֶל־מְלַאכְתּוֹ׃ וַיְהִי | מִן־הַיּוֹם הַהוּא
the-that the-day from and-he-was (10[16]) work-of-him to each the-wall

חֲצִי נְעָרַי עֹשִׂים בַּמְּלָאכָה וְחֶצְיָם מַחֲזִיקִים
ones-being-equipped while-half-of-them in-the-work ones-doing men-of-me half-of

וְהָרְמָחִים הַמָּגִנִּים וְהַקְּשָׁתוֹת וְהַשִּׁרְיֹנִים וְהַשָּׂרִים
and-the-officers and-the-armors and-the-bows the-shields with-the-spears

אַחֲרֵי כָּל־בֵּית יְהוּדָה׃ הַבּוֹנִים בַּחוֹמָה
on-the-wall the-ones-building (11[17]) Judah house-of all-of behind

וְהַנֹּשְׂאִים בַּסֶּבֶל עֹמְשִׂים בְּאַחַת יָדוֹ
hand-of-him with-one-of ones-loading of-the-material and-the-ones-carrying

there is so much rubble that
we cannot rebuild the wall."
11Also our enemies said,
"Before they know it or see us,
we will be right there among
them and will kill them and
put an end to the work."
12Then the Jews who lived
near them came and told us
ten times over, "Wherever you
turn, they will attack us."
13Therefore I stationed some
of the people behind the lowest points of the wall at the exposed places, posting them by
families, with their swords,
spears and bows. 14After I
looked things over, I stood up
and said to the nobles, the
officials and the rest of the
people, "Don't be afraid of
them. Remember the Lord,
who is great and awesome,
and fight for your brothers,
your sons and your daughters,
your wives and your homes."
15When our enemies heard
that we were aware of their
plot and that God had frustrat-
ed it, we all returned to the
wall, each to his own work.
16From that day on, half of
my men did the work, while
the other half were equipped
with spears, shields, bows and
armor. The officers posted
themselves behind all the
people of Judah 17who were
building the wall. Those who
carried materials did their
work with one hand and held

*See the note on page 223.

°7 ק בצחיחים
°9 ק ונשב

עֹשֶׂה בַמְּלָאכָה וְאַחַת מַחֲזֶקֶת הַשָּׁלַח׃ וְהַבּוֹנִים
and-the-ones-building (12[18]) the-weapon holding and-one in-the-work doing

אִישׁ חַרְבּוֹ אֲסוּרִים עַל־ מָתְנָיו וּבוֹנִים
and-ones-working sides-of-him at ones-being-worn sword-of-him each

וְהַתּוֹקֵעַ בַּשּׁוֹפָר אֶצְלִי׃ וָאֹמַר אֶל־ הַחֹרִים
the-nobles to then-I-said (13[19]) with-me on-the-trumpet but-the-one-sounding

וְאֶל־ הַסְּגָנִים וְאֶל־ יֶתֶר הָעָם הַמְּלָאכָה הַרְבֵּה
to-be-extensive the-work the-people rest-of and-to the-officials and-to

וּרְחָבָה וַאֲנַחְנוּ נִפְרָדִים עַל־ הַחוֹמָה רְחוֹקִים אִישׁ
each ones-distant the-wall along ones-being-separated and-we and-spread-out

מֵאָחִיו׃ בִּמְקוֹם אֲשֶׁר תִּשְׁמְעוּ אֶת־ קוֹל הַשּׁוֹפָר
the-trumpet sound-of *** you-hear where at-place-of (14[20]) from-fellows-of-him

שָׁמָּה תִּקָּבְצוּ אֵלֵינוּ אֱלֹהֵינוּ יִלָּחֶם לָנוּ׃ וַאֲנַחְנוּ
so-we (15[21]) for-us he-will-fight God-of-us with-us you-join at-there

עֹשִׂים בַּמְּלָאכָה וְחֶצְיָם מַחֲזִיקִים בָּרְמָחִים
on-the-spears ones-holding with-half-of-them in-the-work ones-doing

מֵעֲלוֹת הַשַּׁחַר עַד צֵאת הַכּוֹכָבִים׃ גַּם בָּעֵת
at-the-time also (16[22]) the-stars to-come-out till the-dawn from-to-come-up

הַהִיא אָמַרְתִּי לָעָם אִישׁ וְנַעֲרוֹ יָלִינוּ
have-them-spend-night and-helper-of-him man to-the-people I-said the-that

בְּתוֹךְ יְרוּשָׁלִַם וְהָיוּ־ לָנוּ הַלַּיְלָה מִשְׁמָר וְהַיּוֹם
and-the-day guard the-night for-us so-they-can-serve Jerusalem inside-of

מְלָאכָה׃ וְאֵין אֲנִי וְאַחַי וּנְעָרַי וְאַנְשֵׁי
nor-men-of nor-men-of-me nor-brothers-of-me I and-neither (17[23]) workman

הַמִּשְׁמָר אֲשֶׁר אַחֲרַי אֵין־אֲנַחְנוּ פֹשְׁטִים בְּגָדֵינוּ אִישׁ שִׁלְחוֹ
weapon-of-him each clothes-of-us ones-taking-off we not with-me who the-guard

הַמָּיִם׃ וַתְּהִי צַעֲקַת הָעָם וּנְשֵׁיהֶם גְּדוֹלָה
great and-wives-of-them the-people outcry-of now-she-was (5:1) the-waters

אֶל־ אֲחֵיהֶם הַיְּהוּדִים׃ וְיֵשׁ אֲשֶׁר אֹמְרִים
ones-saying who and-there-was (2) the-Jewish-ones brothers-of-them against

בָּנֵינוּ וּבְנֹתֵינוּ אֲנַחְנוּ רַבִּים וְנִקְחָה דָגָן
grain and-we-must-get ones-numerous we and-daughters-of-us sons-of-us

וְנֹאכְלָה וְנִחְיֶה׃ וְיֵשׁ אֲשֶׁר אֹמְרִים שְׂדֹתֵינוּ
fields-of-us ones-saying who and-there-was (3) and-we-may-live so-we-may-eat

וּכְרָמֵינוּ וּבָתֵּינוּ אֲנַחְנוּ עֹרְבִים וְנִקְחָה דָגָן
grain so-we-can-get ones-mortgaging we and-homes-of-us and-vineyards-of-us

בָּרָעָב׃ וְיֵשׁ אֲשֶׁר אֹמְרִים לָוִינוּ כֶסֶף
money we-borrowed ones-saying who and-there-was (4) during-the-famine

a weapon in the other, [18]and each of the builders wore his sword at his side as he worked. But the man who sounded the trumpet stayed with me.

[19]Then I said to the nobles, the officials and the rest of the people, "The work is extensive and spread out, and we are widely separated from each other along the wall. [20]Wherever you hear the sound of the trumpet, join us there. Our God will fight for us!"

[21]So we continued the work with half the men holding spears, from the first light of dawn till the stars came out. [22]At that time I also said to the people, "Have every man and his helper stay inside Jerusalem at night, so they can serve us as guards by night and workmen by day." [23]Neither I nor my brothers nor my men nor the guards with me took off our clothes; each had his weapon, even when he went for water.[j]

Nehemiah Helps the Poor

5 Now the men and their wives raised a great outcry against their Jewish brothers. [2]Some were saying, "We and our sons and daughters are numerous; in order for us to eat and stay alive, we must get grain."

[3]Others were saying, "We are mortgaging our fields, our vineyards and our homes to get grain during the famine."

[4]Still others were saying, "We have had to borrow

j23 The meaning of the Hebrew for this clause is uncertain.

*See the note on page 223.

וְעַתָּה (5) וּכְרָמֵינוּ׃ שְׂדֹתֵינוּ הַמֶּלֶךְ לְמִדַּת
although-now (5) and-vineyards-of-us fields-of-us the-king for-tax-of

וְהִנֵּה בָּנֵינוּ כִּבְנֵיהֶם בְּשָׂרֵנוּ אַחֵינוּ כִּבְשַׂר
yet-see! sons-of-us as-sons-of-them flesh-of-us countrymen-of-us as-flesh-of

אֲנַחְנוּ כֹבְשִׁים אֶת־ בָּנֵינוּ וְאֶת־ בְּנֹתֵינוּ לַעֲבָדִים וְיֵשׁ
and-there-is as-slaves daughters-of-us and sons-of-us *** ones-subjecting we

מִבְּנֹתֵינוּ נִכְבָּשׁוֹת וְאֵין לְאֵל יָדֵנוּ
hand-of-us in-power-of but-not ones-being-enslaved from-daughters-of-us

וּשְׂדֹתֵינוּ וּכְרָמֵינוּ לַאֲחֵרִים׃ (6) וַיִּחַר לִי
to-me and-he-angered (6) to-others and-vineyards-of-us because-fields-of-us

מְאֹד כַּאֲשֶׁר שָׁמַעְתִּי אֶת־ זַעֲקָתָם וְאֵת הַדְּבָרִים הָאֵלֶּה׃
the-these the-charges and outcry-of-them *** I-heard as-when very

(7) וַיִּמָּלֵךְ לִבִּי עָלַי וָאָרִיבָה אֶת־ הַחֹרִים וְאֶת־
and the-nobles *** then-I-accused with-me mind-of-me and-he-pondered (7)

הַסְּגָנִים וָאֹמְרָה לָהֶם מַשָּׁא אִישׁ־ בְּאָחִיו אַתֶּם
you from-countryman-of-him each usury to-them and-I-told the-officials

נֹשִׁאים וָאֶתֵּן עֲלֵיהֶם קְהִלָּה גְדוֹלָה׃ (8) וָאֹמְרָה לָהֶם
to-them and-I-said (8) large meeting against-them so-I-called ones-exacting

אֲנַחְנוּ קָנִינוּ אֶת־ אַחֵינוּ הַיְּהוּדִים הַנִּמְכָּרִים
the-ones-being-sold the-Jewish-ones brothers-of-us *** we-bought-back we

לַגּוֹיִם כְּדֵי בָנוּ וְגַם־ אַתֶּם תִּמְכְּרוּ אֶת־ אֲחֵיכֶם
brothers-of-you *** you-sell you now-indeed to-us as-possible-of to-the-Gentiles

וְנִמְכְּרוּ־ לָנוּ וַיַּחֲרִישׁוּ וְלֹא מָצְאוּ
they-found because-not and-they-kept-quiet to-us but-they-were-sold-back

דָּבָר׃ (9) וַיֹּאמַר לֹא־ טוֹב הַדָּבָר אֲשֶׁר־אַתֶּם עֹשִׂים הֲלוֹא בְּיִרְאַת
in-fear-of not? ones-doing you that the-thing right not so-I-said (9) word

אֱלֹהֵינוּ תֵּלֵכוּ מֵחֶרְפַּת הַגּוֹיִם אוֹיְבֵינוּ׃
being-enemies-of-us the-Gentiles from-reproach-of you-should-walk God-of-us

(10) וְגַם־ אֲנִי אַחַי וּנְעָרַי נֹשִׁים בָּהֶם כֶּסֶף
money to-them ones-lending and-men-of-me brothers-of-me I and-also (10)

וְדָגָן נַעַזְבָה־ נָּא אֶת־ הַמַּשָּׁא הַזֶּה׃ (11) הָשִׁיבוּ נָא
now! give-back! (11) the-this the-usury *** now! let-us-stop and-grain

לָהֶם כְּהַיּוֹם שְׂדֹתֵיהֶם כַּרְמֵיהֶם זֵיתֵיהֶם
olive-groves-of-them vineyards-of-them fields-of-them as-the-day to-them

וּבָתֵּיהֶם וּמְאַת הַכֶּסֶף וְהַדָּגָן הַתִּירוֹשׁ
the-new-wine and-the-grain the-money and-hundredth-of and-houses-of-them

וְהַיִּצְהָר אֲשֶׁר אַתֶּם נֹשִׁים בָּהֶם׃ (12) וַיֹּאמְרוּ נָשִׁיב
we-will-give-back and-they-said (12) to-them ones-charging you that and-the-oil

money to pay the king's tax on
our fields and vineyards. [5]Al-
though we are of the same
flesh and blood as our countrymen and though our sons
are as good as theirs, yet we
have to subject our sons and
daughters to slavery. Some of
our daughters have already
been enslaved, but we are
powerless, because our fields
and our vineyards belong to
others."

[6]When I heard their outcry
and these charges, I was very
angry. [7]I pondered them in my
mind and then accused the
nobles and officials. I told
them, "You are exacting usury
from your own countrymen!"
So I called together a large
meeting to deal with them
[8]and said: "As far as possible,
we have bought back our
Jewish brothers who were sold
to the Gentiles. Now you are
selling your brothers, only for
them to be sold back to us!"
They kept quiet, because they
could find nothing to say.

[9]So I continued, "What you
are doing is not right.
Shouldn't you walk in the fear
of our God to avoid the reproach of our Gentile enemies? [10]I and my brothers and
my men are also lending the
people money and grain. But
let the exacting of usury stop!
[11]Give back to them immediately their fields, vineyards,
olive groves and houses, and
also the usury you are charging them—the hundredth part
of the money, grain, new
wine and oil."

[12]"We will give it back,"

°9 ק ואמר

וּמֵהֶם לֹא נְבַקֵּשׁ כֵּן נַעֲשֶׂה כַּאֲשֶׁר אַתָּה אוֹמֵר
saying you just-as we-will-do same we-will-demand not and-from-them

וָאֶקְרָא אֶת־ הַכֹּהֲנִים וָאַשְׁבִּיעֵם לַעֲשׂוֹת כַּדָּבָר
as-the-promise to-do and-I-made-take-oath-them the-priests *** then-I-summoned

הַזֶּה׃ גַּם־ חָצְנִי נָעַרְתִּי וָאֹמְרָה כָּכָה
this-way and-I-said I-shook-out fold-of-robe-of-me also (13) the-this

יְנַעֵר הָאֱלֹהִים אֶת־ כָּל־ הָאִישׁ אֲשֶׁר לֹא־ יָקִים אֶת־
*** he-keeps not who the-man every-of *** the-God may-he-shake-out

הַדָּבָר הַזֶּה מִבֵּיתוֹ וּמִיגִיעוֹ וְכָכָה
and-so and-from-possession-of-him from-house-of-him the-this the-promise

יִהְיֶה נָעוּר וָרֵק וַיֹּאמְרוּ כָל־ הַקָּהָל
the-assembly whole-of and-they-said and-empty being-shaken-out may-he-be

אָמֵן וַיְהַלְלוּ אֶת־ יְהוָה וַיַּעַשׂ הָעָם כַּדָּבָר
as-the-promise the-people and-he-did Yahweh *** and-they-praised amen

הַזֶּה׃ גַּם מִיּוֹם ׀ אֲשֶׁר־ צִוָּה אֹתִי לִהְיוֹת פֶּחָם
governor-of-them to-be me he-appointed when from-day moreover (14) the-this

בְּאֶרֶץ יְהוּדָה מִשְּׁנַת עֶשְׂרִים וְעַד שְׁנַת שְׁלֹשִׁים וּשְׁתַּיִם
and-two thirty year-of and-until twenty from-year-of Judah in-land-of

לְאַרְתַּחְשַׁסְתְּא הַמֶּלֶךְ שָׁנִים שְׁתֵּים עֶשְׂרֵה אֲנִי וְאַחַי לֶחֶם
food-of and-brothers-of-me I ten two years the-king of-Artaxerxes

הַפֶּחָה לֹא אָכַלְתִּי׃ וְהַפַּחוֹת הָרִאשֹׁנִים אֲשֶׁר־ לְפָנַי
before-me who the-earlier-ones but-the-governors (15) I-ate not the-governor

הִכְבִּידוּ עַל־ הָעָם וַיִּקְחוּ מֵהֶם בְּלֶחֶם
with-food from-them and-they-took the-people on they-placed-heavy-burden

וָיַיִן אַחַר כֶּסֶף־ שְׁקָלִים אַרְבָּעִים גַּם נַעֲרֵיהֶם
assistants-of-them also forty shekels silver-of in-addition-to and-wine

שָׁלְטוּ עַל־ הָעָם וַאֲנִי לֹא־ עָשִׂיתִי כֵן מִפְּנֵי יִרְאַת
reverence-of because-of same I-acted not but-I the-people over they-lorded

אֱלֹהִים׃ וְגַם בִּמְלֶאכֶת הַחוֹמָה הַזֹּאת הֶחֱזַקְתִּי וְשָׂדֶה
and-land I-devoted-myself the-this the-wall to-work-of but-instead (16) God

לֹא קָנִינוּ וְכָל־ נְעָרַי קְבוּצִים שָׁם עַל־
for there ones-being-assembled men-of-me and-all-of we-acquired not

הַמְּלָאכָה׃ וְהַיְּהוּדִים וְהַסְּגָנִים מֵאָה וַחֲמִשִּׁים אִישׁ
man and-fifty hundred and-the-officials furthermore-the-Jews (17) the-work

וְהַבָּאִים אֵלֵינוּ מִן־ הַגּוֹיִם אֲשֶׁר־ סְבִיבֹתֵינוּ עַל־ שֻׁלְחָנִי׃
table-of-me at ones-around-us who the-nations from to-us and-the-ones-coming

וַאֲשֶׁר הָיָה נַעֲשֶׂה לְיוֹם אֶחָד שׁוֹר אֶחָד צֹאן שֵׁשׁ־
six-of sheep one ox each for-day being-prepared he-was and-what (18)

they said. "And we will not
demand anything more from
them. We will do as you say."
Then I summoned the
priests and made the nobles
and officials take an oath to do
what they had promised. [13]I
also shook out the folds of my
robe and said, "In this way
may God shake out of his
house and possessions every
man who does not keep this
promise. So may such a man
be shaken out and emptied!"
At this the whole assembly
said, "Amen," and praised the
LORD. And the people did as
they had promised.
[14]Moreover, from the twentieth year of King Artaxerxes,
when I was appointed to be
their governor in the land of
Judah, until his thirty-second
year—twelve years—neither I
nor my brothers ate the food
allotted to the governor. [15]But
the earlier governors—those
preceding me—placed a heavy
burden on the people and took
forty shekels[k] of silver from
them in addition to food and
wine. Their assistants also
lorded it over the people. But
out of reverence for God I did
not act like that. [16]Instead, I
devoted myself to the work on
this wall. All my men were assembled there for the work;
we[l] did not acquire any land.
[17]Furthermore, a hundred
and fifty Jews and officials ate
at my table, as well as those
who came to us from the surrounding nations. [18]Each day
one ox, six choice sheep and

[k] *15* That is, about 1 pound (about 0.5 kilogram)

[l] *16* Most Hebrew manuscripts; some Hebrew manuscripts, Septuagint, Vulgate and Syriac *I*

בְּרֻרוֹת וְצִפֳּרִים נַעֲשׂוּ־ לִי וּבֵין עֲשֶׂרֶת
ten-of and-between for-me they-were-prepared and-poultry ones-being-chosen

יָמִים בְּכָל־ יַיִן לְהַרְבֵּה וְעִם־ זֶה לֶחֶם
food-of this but-in-spite-of to-be-abundant wine with-all-of days

הַפֶּחָה לֹא בִקַּשְׁתִּי כִּי־ כָבְדָה הָעֲבֹדָה עַל־ הָעָם
the-people on the-demand she-was-heavy because I-demanded never the-governor

הַזֶּה׃ (19) זָכְרָה־ לִּי אֱלֹהַי לְטוֹבָה כֹּל אֲשֶׁר־עָשִׂיתִי עַל־
for I-did that all with-favor God-of-me to-me remember! (19) the-this

הָעָם הַזֶּה׃ (6:1) וַיְהִי כַאֲשֶׁר נִשְׁמַע לְסַנְבַלַּט
by-Sanballat he-was-heard as-when and-he-was (6:1) the-this the-people

וְטוֹבִיָּה וּלְגֶשֶׁם הָעַרְבִי וּלְיֶתֶר אֹיְבֵינוּ
ones-being-enemies-of-us and-by-rest-of the-Arab and-by-Geshem and-Tobiah

כִּי בָנִיתִי אֶת־ הַחוֹמָה וְלֹא־ נוֹתַר בָּהּ פָּרֶץ גַּם עַד־
up-to though gap in-her he-was-left and-not the-wall *** I-rebuilt that

הָעֵת הַהִיא דְּלָתוֹת לֹא־הֶעֱמַדְתִּי בַשְּׁעָרִים׃ (2) וַיִּשְׁלַח סַנְבַלַּט
Sanballat then-he-sent (2) in-the-gates I-set not doors the-that the-time

וְגֶשֶׁם אֵלַי לֵאמֹר לְכָה וְנִוָּעֲדָה יַחְדָּו בַּכְּפִירִים
in-the-villages together and-let-us-meet come! to-say to-me and-Geshem

בְּבִקְעַת אוֹנוֹ וְהֵמָּה חֹשְׁבִים לַעֲשׂוֹת לִי רָעָה׃ (3) וָאֶשְׁלְחָה
so-I-sent (3) harm to-me to-do ones-scheming but-they Ono on-plain-of

עֲלֵיהֶם מַלְאָכִים לֵאמֹר מְלָאכָה גְדוֹלָה אֲנִי עֹשֶׂה וְלֹא אוּכַל
I-can and-not carrying-on I great project to-say messengers to-them

לָרֶדֶת לָמָּה תִשְׁבַּת הַמְּלָאכָה כַּאֲשֶׁר אַרְפֶּהָ וְיָרַדְתִּי
and-I-go-down I-leave-her as-while the-work should-she-stop why? to-go-down

אֲלֵיכֶם׃ (4) וַיִּשְׁלְחוּ אֵלַי כַּדָּבָר הַזֶּה אַרְבַּע פְּעָמִים וָאָשִׁיב
and-I-gave times four the-this as-the-message to-me and-they-sent (4) to-you

אוֹתָם כַּדָּבָר הַזֶּה׃ (5) וַיִּשְׁלַח אֵלַי סַנְבַלַּט כַּדָּבָר
as-the-message Sanballat to-me then-he-sent (5) the-this as-the-answer them

הַזֶּה פַּעַם חֲמִישִׁית אֶת־ נַעֲרוֹ וְאִגֶּרֶת פְּתוּחָה בְּיָדוֹ׃
in-hand-of-him being-unsealed and-letter aide-of-him with fifth time the-this

(6) כָּתוּב בָּהּ בַּגּוֹיִם נִשְׁמָע וְגַשְׁמוּ אֹמֵר
saying and-Gashmu he-is-reported among-the-nations in-her being-written (6)

אַתָּה וְהַיְּהוּדִים חֹשְׁבִים לִמְרוֹד עַל־ כֵּן אַתָּה בוֹנֶה הַחוֹמָה
the-wall building you this for to-revolt ones-plotting and-the-Jews you

וְאַתָּה הֹוֶה לָהֶם לְמֶלֶךְ כַּדְּבָרִים הָאֵלֶּה׃ (7) וְגַם־
and-even (7) the-these as-the-reports as-king to-them becoming moreover-you

נְבִיאִים הֶעֱמַדְתָּ לִקְרֹא עָלֶיךָ בִירוּשָׁלִַם לֵאמֹר מֶלֶךְ
king to-say in-Jerusalem about-you to-proclaim you-appointed prophets

some poultry were prepared for me, and every ten days an abundant supply of wine of all kinds. In spite of all this, I never demanded the food allotted to the governor, because the demands were heavy on these people.

19 Remember me with favor, O my God, for all I have done for these people.

Further Opposition to the Rebuilding

6 When word came to Sanballat, Tobiah, Geshem the Arab and the rest of our enemies that I had rebuilt the wall and not a gap was left in it—though up to that time I had not set the doors in the
gates— 2 Sanballat and Geshem sent me this message: "Come, let us meet together in one of the villages[m] on the plain of Ono."

But they were scheming to harm me;
3 so I sent messengers to them with this reply: "I am carrying on a great project and cannot go down. Why should the work stop while I leave it and go down to you?"
4 Four times they sent me the same message, and each time I gave them the same answer.
5 Then, the fifth time, Sanballat sent his aide to me with the same message, and in his hand was an unsealed letter
6 in which was written:

"It is reported among the nations—and Geshem[n] says it is true—that you and the Jews are plotting to revolt, and therefore you are building the wall. Moreover, according to these reports you are about to become their king
7 and have even appointed prophets to make this proclamation about you in Jerusalem: 'There is a king

[m]2 Or *in Kephirim*
[n]6 Hebrew *Gashmu*, a variant of *Geshem*

בִּיהוּדָה וְעַתָּה יִשָּׁמַע לַמֶּלֶךְ כַּדְּבָרִים הָאֵלֶּה
the-these as-the-reports to-the-king he-will-be-reported and-now in-Judah

וְעַתָּה לְכָה וְנִוָּעֲצָה יַחְדָּו׃ וָאֶשְׁלְחָה אֵלָיו לֵאמֹר לֹא
not to-say to-him and-I-sent (8) together and-let-us-confer come! so-now

נִהְיָה כַּדְּבָרִים הָאֵלֶּה אֲשֶׁר אַתָּה אוֹמֵר כִּי מִלִּבְּךָ
from-mind-of-you but saying you that the-these like-the-things he-happens

אַתָּה בוֹדָאם׃ כִּי כֻלָּם מְיָרְאִים אוֹתָנוּ לֵאמֹר
to-say us ones-frightening all-of-them for (9) making-up-them you

יִרְפּוּ יְדֵיהֶם מִן־הַמְּלָאכָה וְלֹא תֵעָשֶׂה
she-will-be-completed and-not the-work for hands-of-them they-will-get-weak

וְעַתָּה חַזֵּק אֶת־ יָדָי׃ וַאֲנִי־ בָאתִי בֵּית שְׁמַעְיָה
Shemaiah house-of I-went and-I (10) hands-of-me *** strengthen! so-now

בֶּן־ דְּלָיָה בֶּן־ מְהֵיטַבְאֵל וְהוּא עָצוּר וַיֹּאמֶר נִוָּעֵד
let-us-meet and-he-said being-shut-in now-he Mehetabel son-of Delaiah son-of

אֶל־ בֵּית הָאֱלֹהִים אֶל־ תּוֹךְ הַהֵיכָל וְנִסְגְּרָה דַּלְתוֹת
doors-of and-let-us-close the-temple inside-of at the-God house-of in

הַהֵיכָל כִּי בָּאִים לְהָרְגֶךָ וְלַיְלָה בָּאִים לְהָרְגֶךָ׃
to-kill-you men-coming and-night to-kill-you men-coming because the-temple

וָאֹמְרָה הַאִישׁ כָּמוֹנִי יִבְרָח וּמִי כָמוֹנִי אֲשֶׁר־ יָבוֹא
he-should-go who like-me or-who? should-he-run like-me man? but-I-said (11)

אֶל־ הַהֵיכָל וָחָי לֹא אָבוֹא׃ וָאַכִּירָה וְהִנֵּה
that-see! and-I-realized (12) I-will-go not so-he-might-live the-temple into

לֹא־ אֱלֹהִים שְׁלָחוֹ כִּי הַנְּבוּאָה דִּבֶּר עָלַי וְטוֹבִיָּה
because-Tobiah against-me he-spoke the-prophecy but he-sent-him God not

וְסַנְבַלַּט שְׂכָרוֹ׃ לְמַעַן שָׂכוּר הוּא לְמַעַן־
so-that he being-hired so-that (13) he-hired-him and-Sanballat

אִירָא וְאֶעֱשֶׂה־ כֵּן וְחָטָאתִי וְהָיָה
then-he-would-be so-I-would-sin this and-I-would-do I-would-be-intimidated

לָהֶם לְשֵׁם רָע לְמַעַן יְחָרְפוּנִי׃ זָכְרָה אֱלֹהַי
God-of-me remember! (14) they-could-discredit-me so-that bad for-name to-them

לְטוֹבִיָּה וּלְסַנְבַלַּט כְּמַעֲשָׂיו אֵלֶּה וְגַם לְנוֹעַדְיָה
to-Noadiah and-also these as-deeds-of-him and-to-Sanballat to-Tobiah

הַנְּבִיאָה וּלְיֶתֶר הַנְּבִיאִים אֲשֶׁר הָיוּ מְיָרְאִים
ones-intimidating they-were who the-prophets and-to-rest-of the-prophetess

אוֹתִי׃ וַתִּשְׁלַם הַחוֹמָה בְּעֶשְׂרִים וַחֲמִשָּׁה לֶאֱלוּל לַחֲמִשִּׁים
in-fifty of-Elul and-five on-twenty the-wall so-she-was-completed (15) me

וּשְׁנַיִם יוֹם׃ וַיְהִי כַּאֲשֶׁר שָׁמְעוּ כָּל־ אוֹיְבֵינוּ
being-enemies-of-us all-of they-heard as-when and-he-was (16) day and-two

in Judah!' Now this report will get back to the king; so come, let us confer together."

8I sent him this reply:
"Nothing like what you are saying is happening; you are just making it up out of your head."
9They were all trying to
frighten us, thinking, "Their hands will get too weak for the work, and it will not be completed."
⌊But I prayed,⌋ "Now strengthen my hands."
10One day I went to the
house of Shemaiah son of Delaiah, the son of Mehetabel, who was shut in at his home. He said, "Let us meet in the house of God, inside the temple, and let us close the temple doors, because men are coming to kill you—by night they are coming to kill you."
11But I said, "Should a man
like me run away? Or should one like me go into the temple to save his life? I will not go!"
12I realized that God had not
sent him, but that he had prophesied against me because Tobiah and Sanballat had hired him. 13He had been
hired to intimidate me so that I would commit a sin by doing this, and then they would give me a bad name to discredit me.

14Remember Tobiah and
Sanballat, O my God, because of what they have done; remember also the prophetess Noadiah and the rest of the prophets who have been trying to intimidate me.

The Completion of the Wall

15So the wall was completed
on the twenty-fifth of Elul, in fifty-two days. 16When all our
enemies heard about this and

וַיִּרְאוּ כָּל־ הַגּוֹיִם אֲשֶׁר סְבִיבֹתֵינוּ וַיִּפְּלוּ מְאֹד
greatly then-they-fell ones-around-us that the-nations all-of and-they-saw

בְּעֵינֵיהֶם וַיֵּדְעוּ כִּי מֵאֵת אֱלֹהֵינוּ נֶעֶשְׂתָה
she-was-done God-of-us from-with that because-they-realized in-eyes-of-them

הַמְּלָאכָה הַזֹּאת׃ (17) גַּם ׀ בַּיָּמִים הָהֵם מַרְבִּים חֹרֵי
nobles-of ones-sending-many the-those in-the-days also (17) the-this the-work

יְהוּדָה אִגְּרֹתֵיהֶם הוֹלְכוֹת עַל־טוֹבִיָּה וַאֲשֶׁר לְטוֹבִיָּה בָּאוֹת
ones-coming from-Tobiah and-that Tobiah to ones-going letters-of-them Judah

אֲלֵיהֶם׃ (18) כִּי־ רַבִּים בִּיהוּדָה בַּעֲלֵי שְׁבוּעָה לוֹ כִּי־ חָתָן הוּא
he son-in-law since to-him oath masters-of in-Judah many for (18) to-them

לִשְׁכַנְיָה בֶן־ אָרַח וִיהוֹחָנָן בְּנוֹ לָקַח אֶת־ בַּת־
daughter-of *** he-married son-of-him and-Jehohanan Arah son-of to-Shecaniah

מְשֻׁלָּם בֶּן בֶּרֶכְיָה׃ (19) גַּם טוֹבֹתָיו הָיוּ
they-were good-deeds-of-him moreover (19) Berekiah son-of Meshullam

אֹמְרִים לְפָנַי וּדְבָרַי הָיוּ מוֹצִיאִים לוֹ אִגְּרוֹת
letters to-him ones-telling they-were then-words-of-me to-me ones-reporting

שָׁלַח טוֹבִיָּה לְיָרְאֵנִי׃ (7:1) וַיְהִי כַּאֲשֶׁר נִבְנְתָה
she-was-rebuilt as-when and-he-was (7:1) to-intimidate-me Tobiah he-sent

הַחוֹמָה וָאַעֲמִיד הַדְּלָתוֹת וַיִּפָּקְדוּ הַשּׁוֹעֲרִים
the-gatekeepers then-they-were-appointed the-doors and-I-set-in-place the-wall

וְהַמְשֹׁרְרִים וְהַלְוִיִּם׃ (2) וָאֲצַוֶּה אֶת־ חֲנָנִי
Hanani *** and-I-put-in-charge (2) and-the-Levites and-the-ones-singing

אָחִי וְאֶת־ חֲנַנְיָה שַׂר הַבִּירָה עַל־ יְרוּשָׁלִָם כִּי־
because Jerusalem over the-citadel commander-of Hananiah and brother-of-me

הוּא כְּאִישׁ אֱמֶת וְיָרֵא אֶת־ הָאֱלֹהִים מֵרַבִּים׃ (3) וָאֹמַר
and-I-said (3) more-than-most the-God *** and-he-feared integrity as-man-of he

לָהֶם לֹא יִפָּתְחוּ שַׁעֲרֵי יְרוּשָׁלִַם עַד־ חֹם הַשֶּׁמֶשׁ
the-sun to-be-hot until Jerusalem gates-of they-must-be-opened not to-them

וְעַד הֵם עֹמְדִים יָגִיפוּ הַדְּלָתוֹת וֶאֱחֹזוּ
and-bar! the-doors let-them-shut ones-being-on-duty they and-while

וְהַעֲמִיד מִשְׁמְרוֹת יֹשְׁבֵי יְרוּשָׁלִַם אִישׁ בְּמִשְׁמָרוֹ
at-post-of-him one Jerusalem ones-residing-of guards also-appoint!

וְאִישׁ נֶגֶד בֵּיתוֹ׃ (4) וְהָעִיר רַחֲבַת יָדַיִם וּגְדוֹלָה
and-large hands spacious-of now-the-city (4) house-of-him near and-one

וְהָעָם מְעַט בְּתוֹכָהּ וְאֵין בָּתִּים בְּנוּיִם׃
ones-being-rebuilt houses and-not within-her few but-the-people

(5) וַיִּתֵּן אֱלֹהַי אֶל־ לִבִּי וָאֶקְבְּצָה אֶת־ הַחֹרִים וְאֶת־
and the-nobles *** and-I-assembled heart-of-me into God-of-me so-he-put (5)

---

all the surrounding nations saw it, our enemies lost their self-confidence, because they realized that this work had been done with the help of our God.

[17]Also, in those days the nobles of Judah were sending many letters to Tobiah, and replies from Tobiah kept coming to them. [18]For many in Judah were under oath to him, since he was son-in-law to Shecaniah son of Arah, and his son Jehohanan had married the daughter of Meshullam son of Berekiah. [19]Moreover, they kept reporting to me his good deeds and then telling him what I said. And Tobiah sent letters to intimidate me.

7 After the wall had been rebuilt and I had set the doors in place, the gatekeepers and the singers and the Levites were appointed. [2]I put in charge of Jerusalem my brother Hanani, along with° Hananiah the commander of the citadel, because he was a man of integrity and feared God more than most men do. [3]I said to them, "The gates of Jerusalem are not to be opened until the sun is hot. While the gatekeepers are still on duty, have them shut the doors and bar them. Also appoint residents of Jerusalem as guards, some at their posts and some near their own houses."

The List of the Exiles Who Returned

[4]Now the city was large and spacious, but there were few people in it, and the houses had not yet been rebuilt. [5]So my God put it into my heart to assemble the nobles, the

°2 Or *Hanani, that is,*

°3 ק ואמר

הַסְּגָנִים וְאֶת־ הָעָם לְהִתְיַחֵשׂ וָאֶמְצָא סֵפֶר
record-of and-I-found to-be-registered the-people and the-officials

הַיַּחַשׂ הָעוֹלִים בָּרִאשׁוֹנָה וָאֶמְצָא כָּתוּב
being-written and-I-found at-the-first the-ones-returning the-genealogy

בּוֹ׃ (6) אֵלֶּה ׀ בְּנֵי הַמְּדִינָה הָעֹלִים מִשְּׁבִי
from-captivity-of the-ones-coming-up the-province people-of these (6) in-him

הַגּוֹלָה אֲשֶׁר הֶגְלָה נְבוּכַדְנֶצַּר מֶלֶךְ בָּבֶל וַיָּשׁוּבוּ
and-they-returned Babylon king-of Nebuchadnezzar he-took-captive whom the-exile

לִירוּשָׁלִַם וְלִיהוּדָה אִישׁ לְעִירוֹ׃ (7) הַבָּאִים עִם־
with the-ones-coming (7) to-town-of-him each and-to-Judah to-Jerusalem

זְרֻבָּבֶל יֵשׁוּעַ נְחֶמְיָה עֲזַרְיָה רַעַמְיָה נַחֲמָנִי מָרְדֳּכַי בִּלְשָׁן
Bilshan Mordecai Nahamani Raamiah Azariah Nehemiah Jeshua Zerubbabel

מִסְפֶּרֶת בִּגְוַי נְחוּם בַּעֲנָה מִסְפַּר אַנְשֵׁי עַם יִשְׂרָאֵל׃
Israel people-of men-of list-of Baanah Nehum Bigvai Mispereth

(8) בְּנֵי פַרְעֹשׁ אַלְפַּיִם מֵאָה וְשִׁבְעִים וּשְׁנָיִם׃
and-two and-seventy hundred two-thousands Parosh descendants-of (8)

(9) בְּנֵי שְׁפַטְיָה שְׁלֹשׁ מֵאוֹת שִׁבְעִים וּשְׁנָיִם׃
and-two seventy hundreds three-of Shephatiah descendants-of (9)

(10) בְּנֵי אָרַח שֵׁשׁ מֵאוֹת חֲמִשִּׁים וּשְׁנָיִם׃ (11) בְּנֵי־
descendants-of (11) and-two fifty hundreds six-of Arah descendants-of (10)

פַחַת מוֹאָב לִבְנֵי יֵשׁוּעַ וְיוֹאָב אַלְפַּיִם וּשְׁמֹנֶה מֵאוֹת
hundreds and-eight-of two-thousands and-Joab Jeshua through-sons-of Moab Pahath

שְׁמֹנָה עָשָׂר׃ (12) בְּנֵי עֵילָם אֶלֶף מָאתַיִם חֲמִשִּׁים וְאַרְבָּעָה׃
and-four fifty two-hundreds thousand Elam descendants-of (12) ten eight

(13) בְּנֵי זַתּוּא שְׁמֹנֶה מֵאוֹת אַרְבָּעִים וַחֲמִשָּׁה׃ (14) בְּנֵי
descendants-of (14) and-five forty hundreds eight-of Zattu descendants-of (13)

זַכָּי שְׁבַע מֵאוֹת וְשִׁשִּׁים׃ (15) בְּנֵי בִנּוּי שֵׁשׁ מֵאוֹת
hundreds six-of Binnui descendants-of (15) and-sixty hundreds seven-of Zaccai

אַרְבָּעִים וּשְׁמֹנָה׃ (16) בְּנֵי בֵבָי שֵׁשׁ מֵאוֹת עֶשְׂרִים וּשְׁמֹנָה׃
and-eight twenty hundreds six-of Bebai descendants-of (16) and-eight forty

(17) בְּנֵי עַזְגָּד אַלְפַּיִם שְׁלֹשׁ מֵאוֹת עֶשְׂרִים וּשְׁנָיִם׃
and-two twenty hundreds three-of two-thousands Azgad descendants-of (17)

(18) בְּנֵי אֲדֹנִיקָם שֵׁשׁ מֵאוֹת שִׁשִּׁים וְשִׁבְעָה׃
and-seven sixty hundreds six-of Adonikam descendants-of (18)

(19) בְּנֵי בִגְוָי אַלְפַּיִם שִׁשִּׁים וְשִׁבְעָה׃ (20) בְּנֵי
descendants-of (20) and-seven sixty two-thousands Bigvai descendants-of (19)

עָדִין שֵׁשׁ מֵאוֹת חֲמִשִּׁים וַחֲמִשָּׁה׃ (21) בְּנֵי־ אָטֵר לְחִזְקִיָּה
through-Hezekiah Ater descendants-of (21) and-five fifty hundreds six-of Adin

officials and the common people for registration by families. I found the genealogical record of those who had been the first to return. This is what I found written there:

[6]These are the people of the province who came up from the captivity of the exiles whom Nebuchadnezzar king of Babylon had taken captive (they returned to Jerusalem and Judah, each to his own
town, [7]in company with Zerubbabel, Jeshua, Nehemiah, Azariah, Raamiah, Nahamani, Mordecai, Bilshan, Mispereth, Bigvai, Nehum and Baanah):

The list of the men of Israel:

[8]the descendants of Parosh 2,172
[9]of Shephatiah 372
[10]of Arah 652
[11]of Pahath-Moab (through the line of Jeshua and Joab) 2,818
[12]of Elam 1,254
[13]of Zattu 845
[14]of Zaccai 760
[15]of Binnui 648
[16]of Bebai 628
[17]of Azgad 2,322
[18]of Adonikam 667
[19]of Bigvai 2,067
[20]of Adin 655
[21]of Ater (through Hezekiah) 98

תִּשְׁעִים וּשְׁמֹנָה׃ בְּנֵי חָשֻׁם שְׁלֹשׁ מֵאוֹת עֶשְׂרִים
twenty hundreds three-of Hashum descendants-of (22) and-eight ninety

וּשְׁמֹנָה׃ בְּנֵי בֵצָי שְׁלֹשׁ מֵאוֹת עֶשְׂרִים וְאַרְבָּעָה׃
and-four twenty hundreds three-of Bezai descendants-of (23) and-eight

בְּנֵי חָרִיף מֵאָה שְׁנֵים עָשָׂר׃ בְּנֵי גִבְעוֹן
Gibeon descendants-of (25) ten two hundred Hariph descendants-of (24)

תִּשְׁעִים וַחֲמִשָּׁה׃ אַנְשֵׁי בֵית־לֶחֶם וּנְטֹפָה מֵאָה שְׁמֹנִים וּשְׁמֹנָה׃
and-eight eighty hundred and-Netophah Lehem Beth men-of (26) and-five ninety

אַנְשֵׁי עֲנָתוֹת מֵאָה עֶשְׂרִים וּשְׁמֹנָה׃ אַנְשֵׁי בֵית־עַזְמָוֶת
Azmaveth Beth men-of (28) and-eight twenty hundred Anathoth men-of (27)

אַרְבָּעִים וּשְׁנָיִם׃ אַנְשֵׁי קִרְיַת יְעָרִים כְּפִירָה וּבְאֵרוֹת שְׁבַע
seven-of and-Beeroth Kephirah Jearim Kiriath men-of (29) and-two forty

מֵאוֹת אַרְבָּעִים וּשְׁלֹשָׁה׃ אַנְשֵׁי הָרָמָה וָגָבַע שֵׁשׁ מֵאוֹת
hundreds six-of and-Geba the-Ramah men-of (30) and-three forty hundreds

עֶשְׂרִים וְאֶחָד׃ אַנְשֵׁי מִכְמָס מֵאָה וְעֶשְׂרִים וּשְׁנָיִם׃ אַנְשֵׁי
men-of (32) and-two and-twenty hundred Micmash men-of (31) and-one twenty

בֵית־אֵל וְהָעָי מֵאָה עֶשְׂרִים וּשְׁלֹשָׁה׃ אַנְשֵׁי נְבוֹ אַחֵר חֲמִשִּׁים
fifty other Nebo men-of (33) and-three twenty hundred and-the-Ai El Beth

וּשְׁנָיִם׃ בְּנֵי עֵילָם אַחֵר אֶלֶף מָאתַיִם חֲמִשִּׁים וְאַרְבָּעָה׃
and-four fifty two-hundreds thousand other Elam men-of (34) and-two

בְּנֵי חָרִם שְׁלֹשׁ מֵאוֹת וְעֶשְׂרִים׃ בְּנֵי יְרֵחוֹ שְׁלֹשׁ
three-of Jericho men-of (36) and-twenty hundreds three-of Harim men-of (35)

מֵאוֹת אַרְבָּעִים וַחֲמִשָּׁה׃ בְּנֵי־לֹד חָדִיד וְאוֹנוֹ שְׁבַע מֵאוֹת
hundreds seven-of and-Ono Hadid Lod men-of (37) and-five forty hundreds

וְעֶשְׂרִים וְאֶחָד׃ בְּנֵי סְנָאָה שְׁלֹשֶׁת אֲלָפִים תְּשַׁע מֵאוֹת
hundreds nine-of thousands three-of Senaah men-of (38) and-one and-twenty

וּשְׁלֹשִׁים׃ הַכֹּהֲנִים בְּנֵי יְדַעְיָה לְבֵית יֵשׁוּעַ
Jeshua through-family-of Jedaiah descendants-of the-priests (39) and-thirty

תְּשַׁע מֵאוֹת שִׁבְעִים וּשְׁלֹשָׁה׃ בְּנֵי אִמֵּר אֶלֶף
thousand Immer descendants-of (40) and-three seventy hundreds nine-of

חֲמִשִּׁים וּשְׁנָיִם׃ בְּנֵי פַשְׁחוּר אֶלֶף מָאתַיִם אַרְבָּעִים
forty two-hundreds thousand Pashhur descendants-of (41) and-two fifty

וְשִׁבְעָה׃ בְּנֵי חָרִם אֶלֶף שִׁבְעָה עָשָׂר׃ הַלְוִיִּם
the-Levites (43) ten seven thousand Harim descendants-of (42) and-seven

בְּנֵי־יֵשׁוּעַ לְקַדְמִיאֵל לִבְנֵי לְהוֹדְוָה שִׁבְעִים
seventy of-Hodaviah through-sons-of through-Kadmiel Jeshua descendants-of

וְאַרְבָּעָה׃ הַמְשֹׁרְרִים בְּנֵי אָסָף מֵאָה אַרְבָּעִים וּשְׁמֹנָה׃
and-eight forty hundred Asaph descendants-of the-ones-singing (44) and-four

[22]of Hashum 328
[23]of Bezai 324
[24]of Hariph 112
[25]of Gibeon 95

[26]the men of Bethlehem and Netophah 188
[27]of Anathoth 128
[28]of Beth Azmaveth 42
[29]of Kiriath Jearim, Kephirah and Beeroth 743
[30]of Ramah and Geba 621
[31]of Micmash 122
[32]of Bethel and Ai 123
[33]of the other Nebo 52
[34]of the other Elam 1,254
[35]of Harim 320
[36]of Jericho 345
[37]of Lod, Hadid and Ono 721
[38]of Senaah 3,930

[39]The priests:

the descendants of Jedaiah (through the family of Jeshua) 973
[40]of Immer 1,052
[41]of Pashhur 1,247
[42]of Harim 1,017

[43]The Levites:

the descendants of Jeshua (through Kadmiel through the line of Hodaviah) 74

[44]The singers:

the descendants of Asaph 148

הַשֹּׁעֲרִים בְּנֵי־ שַׁלּוּם בְּנֵי־ אָטֵר
Ater descendants-of Shallum descendants-of the-gatekeepers (45)

בְּנֵי־ טַלְמֹן בְּנֵי־ עַקּוּב בְּנֵי חֲטִיטָא
Hatita descendants-of Akkub descendants-of Talmon descendants-of

בְּנֵי שֹׁבָי מֵאָה שְׁלֹשִׁים וּשְׁמֹנָה׃ הַנְּתִינִים
the-temple-servants (46) and-eight thirty hundred Shobai descendants-of

בְּנֵי־ צִחָא בְנֵי־ חֲשֻׂפָא בְנֵי טַבָּעוֹת׃
Tabbaoth descendants-of Hasupha descendants-of Ziha descendants-of

בְּנֵי־ קֵירֹס בְּנֵי־ סִיעָא בְנֵי פָדוֹן׃
Padon descendants-of Sia descendants-of Keros descendants-of (47)

בְּנֵי־ לְבָנָה בְנֵי־ חֲגָבָה בְנֵי שַׁלְמָי׃
Shalmai descendants-of Hagaba descendants-of Lebana descendants-of (48)

בְּנֵי־ חָנָן בְּנֵי־ גִדֵּל בְּנֵי־ גָחַר׃
Gaher descendants-of Giddel descendants-of Hanan descendants-of (49)

בְּנֵי־ רְאָיָה בְנֵי־ רְצִין בְּנֵי נְקוֹדָא׃
Nekoda descendants-of Rezin descendants-of Reaiah descendants-of (50)

בְּנֵי־ גַזָּם בְּנֵי־ עֻזָּא בְּנֵי פָסֵחַ׃
Paseah descendants-of Uzza descendants-of Gazzam descendants-of (51)

בְּנֵי־ בֵסָי בְּנֵי־ מְעוּנִים בְּנֵי °נְפוּשְׁסִים׃
Nephussim descendants-of Meunim descendants-of Besai descendants-of (52)

בְּנֵי־ בַקְבּוּק בְּנֵי־ חֲקוּפָא בְּנֵי חַרְחוּר׃
Harhur descendants-of Hakupha descendants-of Bakbuk descendants-of (53)

בְּנֵי־ בַצְלִית בְּנֵי־ מְחִידָא בְּנֵי חַרְשָׁא׃
Harsha descendants-of Mehida descendants-of Bazluth descendants-of (54)

בְּנֵי־ בַרְקוֹס בְּנֵי־ סִיסְרָא בְּנֵי־ תָמַח׃
Temah descendants-of Sisera descendants-of Barkos descendants-of (55)

בְּנֵי נְצִיחַ בְּנֵי חֲטִיפָא׃ בְּנֵי
descendants-of (57) Hatipha descendants-of Neziah descendants-of (56)

עַבְדֵי שְׁלֹמֹה בְּנֵי־ סוֹטַי בְּנֵי־ סֹפֶרֶת
Sophereth descendants-of Sotai descendants-of Solomon servants-of

בְּנֵי פְרִידָא׃ בְּנֵי־ יַעְלָא בְנֵי־ דַרְקוֹן
Darkon descendants-of Jaala descendants-of (58) Perida descendants-of

בְּנֵי גִדֵּל׃ בְּנֵי שְׁפַטְיָה בְנֵי־ חַטִּיל
Hattil descendants-of Shephatiah descendants-of (59) Giddel descendants-of

בְּנֵי פֹּכֶרֶת הַצְּבָיִים בְּנֵי אָמוֹן׃ כָּל־
total-of (60) Amon descendants-of Hazzebaim Pokereth descendants-of

הַנְּתִינִים וּבְנֵי עַבְדֵי שְׁלֹמֹה שְׁלֹשׁ מֵאוֹת
hundreds three-of Solomon servants-of and-descendants-of the-temple-servants

45 The gatekeepers:

the descendants of
Shallum, Ater,
Talmon, Akkub, Hatita
and Shobai 138

46 The temple servants:

the descendants of
Ziha, Hasupha,
Tabbaoth,
47 Keros, Sia, Padon,
48 Lebana, Hagaba,
Shalmai,
49 Hanan, Giddel, Gaher,
50 Reaiah, Rezin,
Nekoda,
51 Gazzam, Uzza, Paseah,
52 Besai, Meunim,
Nephussim,
53 Bakbuk, Hakupha,
Harhur,
54 Bazluth, Mehida,
Harsha,
55 Barkos, Sisera, Temah,
56 Neziah and Hatipha

57 The descendants of the servants of Solomon:

the descendants of
Sotai, Sophereth,
Perida,
58 Jaala, Darkon, Giddel,
59 Shephatiah, Hattil,
Pokereth-Hazzebaim
and Amon

60 The temple servants and
the descendants of the
servants of Solomon
392

°52 ק נפישסים

תִּשְׁעִים וּשְׁנָיִם׃ וְאֵלֶּה הָעוֹלִים מִתֵּל מֶלַח תֵּל חַרְשָׁא
Harsha Tel Melah from-Tel the-ones-coming-up and-these (61) and-two ninety

כְּרוּב אַדּוֹן וְאִמֵּר וְלֹא יָכְלוּ לְהַגִּיד בֵּית־ אֲבוֹתָם
fathers-of-them family-of to-show they-could but-not and-Immer Addon Kerub

וְזַרְעָם אִם מִיִּשְׂרָאֵל הֵם׃ בְּנֵי־ דְלָיָה
Delaiah descendants-of (62) they from-Israel whether and-descent-of-them

בְנֵי־ טוֹבִיָּה בְּנֵי נְקוֹדָא שֵׁשׁ מֵאוֹת וְאַרְבָּעִים
and-forty hundreds six-of Nekoda descendants-of Tobiah descendants-of

וּשְׁנָיִם׃ וּמִן־ הַכֹּהֲנִים בְּנֵי חֳבַיָּה בְּנֵי
descendants-of Hobaiah descendants-of the-priests and-from (63) and-two

הַקּוֹץ בְּנֵי בַרְזִלַּי אֲשֶׁר לָקַח מִבְּנוֹת בַּרְזִלַּי
Barzillai of-daughters-of he-married who Barzillai descendants-of Hakkoz

הַגִּלְעָדִי אִשָּׁה וַיִּקָּרֵא עַל־ שְׁמָם׃ אֵלֶּה בִּקְשׁוּ
they-searched these (64) name-of-them by and-he-was-called wife the-Gileadite

כְתָבָם הַמִּתְיַחְשִׂים וְלֹא נִמְצָא
he-was-found but-not the-ones-being-enrolled-by-family record-of-them

וַיְגֹאֲלוּ מִן־ הַכְּהֻנָּה׃ וַיֹּאמֶר
so-he-ordered (65) the-priesthood from so-they-were-excluded-as-unclean

הַתִּרְשָׁתָא לָהֶם אֲשֶׁר לֹא־ יֹאכְלוּ מִקֹּדֶשׁ
from-most-sacred-of they-could-eat not that to-them the-governor

הַקֳּדָשִׁים עַד עֲמֹד הַכֹּהֵן לְאוּרִים וְתוּמִּים׃
and-Thummim with-Urim the-priest to-minister until the-sacred-things

כָּל־ הַקָּהָל כְּאֶחָד אַרְבַּע רִבּוֹא אַלְפַּיִם שְׁלֹשׁ־
three-of two-thousands ten-thousand four-of as-one the-company whole-of (66)

מֵאוֹת וְשִׁשִּׁים׃ מִלְּבַד עַבְדֵיהֶם וְאַמְהֹתֵיהֶם
and-maidservants-of-them menservants-of-them from-besides (67) and-sixty hundreds

אֵלֶּה שִׁבְעַת אֲלָפִים שְׁלֹשׁ מֵאוֹת שְׁלֹשִׁים וְשִׁבְעָה וְלָהֶם
also-to-them and-seven thirty hundreds three-of thousands seven-of these

מְשֹׁרְרִים וּמְשֹׁרְרוֹת מָאתַיִם וְאַרְבָּעִים וַחֲמִשָּׁה׃ גְּמַלִּים
camels *(68) and-five and-forty two-hundreds and-women-singing men-singing

אַרְבַּע מֵאוֹת שְׁלֹשִׁים וַחֲמִשָּׁה חֲמֹרִים שֵׁשֶׁת אֲלָפִים שְׁבַע מֵאוֹת
hundreds seven-of thousands six-of donkeys and-five thirty hundreds four-of

וְעֶשְׂרִים׃ וּמִקְצָת רָאשֵׁי הָאָבוֹת נָתְנוּ
they-contributed the-fathers heads-of and-from-end-of (69) and-twenty

לַמְּלָאכָה הַתִּרְשָׁתָא נָתַן לָאוֹצָר זָהָב דַּרְכְּמֹנִים אֶלֶף
thousand drachmas gold to-the-treasury he-gave the-governor to-the-work

מִזְרָקוֹת חֲמִשִּׁים כָּתְנוֹת כֹּהֲנִים שְׁלֹשִׁים וַחֲמֵשׁ מֵאוֹת׃
hundreds and-five-of thirty priests garments-of fifty bowls

61 The following came up
from the towns of Tel
Melah, Tel Harsha, Kerub,
Addon and Immer, but
they could not show that
their families were de-
scended from Israel:

62 the descendants of
Delaiah, Tobiah and
Nekoda 642

63 And from among the
priests:

the descendants of
Hobaiah, Hakkoz and
Barzillai (a man who
had married a
daughter of Barzillai
the Gileadite and was
called by that name).
64 These searched for their
family records, but they
could not find them and so
were excluded from the
priesthood as unclean.
65 The governor, therefore,
ordered them not to eat any
of the most sacred food until there should be a priest
ministering with the Urim
and Thummim.

66 The whole company
numbered 42,360, 67 besides
their 7,337 menservants
and maidservants; and
they also had 245 men and
women singers. 68 There
were 736 horses, 245
mules,[p] 69 435 camels and 6,-
720 donkeys.

70 Some of the heads of the
families contributed to the
work. The governor gave to
the treasury 1,000 drach-
mas[q] of gold, 50 bowls and
530 garments for priests.

p68 Some Hebrew manuscripts (see also Ezra 2:66); most Hebrew manuscripts do not have this verse.
q70 That is, about 19 pounds (about 8.5 kilograms)

*68 Most mss do not have this verse; thus, there is a one-verse discrepancy through the rest of chapter 7.

וּמֵרָאשֵׁי הָאָבוֹת נָתְנוּ לָאוֹצָר הַמְּלָאכָה זָהָב
gold the-work to-treasury-of they-gave the-fathers and-from-heads-of (70)

דַּרְכְּמוֹנִים שְׁתֵּי רִבּוֹת וְכֶסֶף מָנִים אַלְפַּיִם וּמָאתָיִם׃
and-two-hundreds two-thousands minas and-silver ten-thousands two-of drachmas

וַאֲשֶׁר נָתְנוּ שְׁאֵרִית הָעָם זָהָב דַּרְכְּמוֹנִים שְׁתֵּי רִבֹּא
ten-thousand two-of drachmas gold the-people rest-of they-gave and-what (71)

וְכֶסֶף מָנִים אַלְפָּיִם וְכָתְנֹת כֹּהֲנִים שִׁשִּׁים וְשִׁבְעָה׃
and-seven sixty priests and-garments-of two-thousands minas and-silver

וַיֵּשְׁבוּ הַכֹּהֲנִים וְהַלְוִיִּם וְהַשּׁוֹעֲרִים
and-the-gatekeepers and-the-Levites the-priests and-they-settled (72)

וְהַמְשֹׁרְרִים וּמִן־ הָעָם וְהַנְּתִינִים וְכָל־
and-all-of and-the-temple-servants the-people and-from and-the-ones-singing

יִשְׂרָאֵל בְּעָרֵיהֶם וַיִּגַּע הַחֹדֶשׁ הַשְּׁבִיעִי וּבְנֵי
and-sons-of the-seventh the-month when-he-came in-towns-of-them Israel

יִשְׂרָאֵל בְּעָרֵיהֶם׃ וַיֵּאָסְפוּ כָל־ הָעָם כְּאִישׁ
as-man the-people all-of and-they-assembled (8:1) in-towns-of-them Israel

אֶחָד אֶל־ הָרְחוֹב אֲשֶׁר לִפְנֵי שַׁעַר־ הַמָּיִם וַיֹּאמְרוּ לְעֶזְרָא
to-Ezra and-they-told the-Waters Gate-of before that the-square in one

הַסֹּפֵר לְהָבִיא אֶת־ סֵפֶר תּוֹרַת מֹשֶׁה אֲשֶׁר־ צִוָּה יְהוָה
Yahweh he-commanded which Moses Law-of Book-of *** to-bring-out the-scribe

אֶת־יִשְׂרָאֵל׃ וַיָּבִיא עֶזְרָא הַכֹּהֵן אֶת־ הַתּוֹרָה לִפְנֵי הַקָּהָל
the-assembly before the-Law *** the-priest Ezra so-he-brought (2) Israel ***

מֵאִישׁ וְעַד־ אִשָּׁה וְכֹל מֵבִין לִשְׁמֹעַ בְּיוֹם אֶחָד לַחֹדֶשׁ
of-the-month one on-day to-hear understanding and-all-of woman and-to from-man

הַשְּׁבִיעִי׃ וַיִּקְרָא־ בוֹ לִפְנֵי הָרְחוֹב אֲשֶׁר ׀ לִפְנֵי שַׁעַר־
Gate-of before that the-square facing from-him and-he-read (3) the-seventh

הַמַּיִם מִן־ הָאוֹר עַד־ מַחֲצִית הַיּוֹם נֶגֶד הָאֲנָשִׁים
the-men in-presence-of the-day noon-of till the-daybreak from the-Waters

וְהַנָּשִׁים וְהַמְּבִינִים וְאָזְנֵי כָל־ הָעָם אֶל־
to the-people all-of and-ears-of and-the-ones-understanding and-the-women

סֵפֶר הַתּוֹרָה׃ וַיַּעֲמֹד עֶזְרָא הַסֹּפֵר עַל־ מִגְדַּל־ עֵץ
wood high-platform-of on the-scribe Ezra and-he-stood (4) the-Law Book-of

אֲשֶׁר עָשׂוּ לַדָּבָר וַיַּעֲמֹד אֶצְלוֹ מַתִּתְיָה
Mattithiah beside-him and-he-stood for-the-occasion they-built that

וְשֶׁמַע וַעֲנָיָה וְאוּרִיָּה וְחִלְקִיָּה וּמַעֲשֵׂיָה עַל־ יְמִינוֹ
right-of-him on and-Maaseiah and-Hilkiah and-Uriah and-Anaiah and-Shema

וּמִשְּׂמֹאלוֹ פְּדָיָה וּמִישָׁאֵל וּמַלְכִּיָּה וְחָשֻׁם וְחַשְׁבַּדָּנָה
and-Hashbaddanah and-Hashum and-Malkijah and-Mishael Pedaiah and-on-left-of-him

71Some of the heads of the
families gave to the treasury for the work 20,000
drachmas[r] of gold and 2,-
200 minas[s] of silver. 72The
total given by the rest of the
people was 20,000 drach-
mas of gold, 2,000 minas[t]
of silver and 67 garments
for priests.
73The priests, the Levites,
the gatekeepers, the singers
and the temple servants,
along with certain of the
people and the rest of the
Israelites, settled in their
own towns.

Ezra Reads the Law

When the seventh month
came and the Israelites had
8 settled in their towns, 1all
the people assembled as
one man in the square before
the Water Gate. They told Ezra
the scribe to bring out the
Book of the Law of Moses,
which the LORD had com-
manded for Israel.
2So on the first day of the
seventh month Ezra the priest
brought the Law before the assembly, which was made up
of men and women and all
who were able to understand.
3He read it aloud from daybreak till noon as he faced the
square before the Water Gate
in the presence of the men,
women and others who could
understand. And all the
people listened attentively to
the Book of the Law.
4Ezra the scribe stood on a
high wooden platform built
for the occasion. Beside him
on his right stood Mattithiah,
Shema, Anaiah, Uriah, Hilkiah and Maaseiah; and on his
left were Pedaiah, Mishael,

r71 That is, about 375 pounds (about 170 kilograms); also in verse 72
s71 That is, about 1 1/3 tons (about 1.2 metric tons)
t72 That is, about 1 1/4 tons (about 1.1 metric tons)

*See the note on page 235.

זְכַרְיָה מְשֻׁלָּם׃ (5) וַיִּפְתַּח עֶזְרָא הַסֵּפֶר לְעֵינֵי כָל־
all-of before-eyes-of the-book Ezra and-he-opened (5) Meshullam Zechariah

הָעָם כִּי־ מֵעַל כָּל־ הָעָם הָיָה וּכְפִתְחוֹ
and-as-to-open-him he-was the-people all-of at-above because the-people

עָמְדוּ כָל־ הָעָם׃ (6) וַיְבָרֶךְ עֶזְרָא אֶת־ יְהוָה הָאֱלֹהִים
the-God Yahweh *** Ezra and-he-praised (6) the-people all-of they-stood-up

הַגָּדוֹל וַיַּעֲנוּ כָל־ הָעָם אָמֵן | אָמֵן בְּמֹעַל
with-lifting-of amen amen the-people all-of and-they-responded the-great

יְדֵיהֶם וַיִּקְּדוּ וַיִּשְׁתַּחֲוֻּ* לַיהוָה אַפַּיִם אָרְצָה׃
to-ground faces to-Yahweh and-they-worshiped then-they-bowed hands-of-them

(7) וְיֵשׁוּעַ וּבָנִי וְשֵׁרֵבְיָה | יָמִין עַקּוּב שַׁבְּתַי | הוֹדִיָּה מַעֲשֵׂיָה
Maaseiah Hodiah Shabbethai Akkub Jamin and-Sherebiah and-Bani and-Jeshua (7)

קְלִיטָא עֲזַרְיָה יוֹזָבָד חָנָן פְּלָאיָה וְהַלְוִיִּם מְבִינִים אֶת־
*** ones-instructing namely-the-Levites Pelaiah Hanan Jozabad Azariah Kelita

הָעָם לַתּוֹרָה וְהָעָם עַל־ עָמְדָם׃
standing-place-of-them at while-the-people in-the-Law the-people

(8) וַיִּקְרְאוּ בַסֵּפֶר בְּתוֹרַת הָאֱלֹהִים מְפֹרָשׁ וְשׂוֹם
and-to-give making-clear the-God of-Law-of from-the-Book and-they-read (8)

שֶׂכֶל וַיָּבִינוּ בַּמִּקְרָא׃ (9) וַיֹּאמֶר נְחֶמְיָה
Nehemiah then-he-said (9) to-the-reading so-they-could-understand meaning

הוּא הַתִּרְשָׁתָא וְעֶזְרָא הַכֹּהֵן | הַסֹּפֵר וְהַלְוִיִּם
and-the-Levites the-scribe the-priest and-Ezra the-governor he

הַמְּבִינִים אֶת־ הָעָם לְכָל־ הָעָם הַיּוֹם קָדֹשׁ־הוּא
this sacred the-day the-people to-all-of the-people *** the-ones-instructing

לַיהוָה אֱלֹהֵיכֶם אַל־ תִּתְאַבְּלוּ וְאַל־ תִּבְכּוּ כִּי בוֹכִים כָּל־
all-of ones-weeping for you-weep and-not you-mourn not God-of-you to-Yahweh

הָעָם כְּשָׁמְעָם אֶת־ דִּבְרֵי הַתּוֹרָה׃ (10) וַיֹּאמֶר לָהֶם
to-them and-he-said (10) the-Law words-of *** as-to-listen-them the-people

לְכוּ אִכְלוּ מַשְׁמַנִּים וּשְׁתוּ מַמְתַקִּים וְשִׁלְחוּ מָנוֹת לְאֵין
to-nothing portions and-send! sweet-things and-drink! choice-foods eat! go!

נָכוֹן לוֹ כִּי־ קָדוֹשׁ הַיּוֹם לַאֲדֹנֵינוּ וְאַל־ תֵּעָצֵבוּ
you-grieve and-not to-Lord-of-us the-day sacred for for-him being-prepared

כִּי־ חֶדְוַת יְהוָה הִיא מָעֻזְּכֶם׃ (11) וְהַלְוִיִּם מַחְשִׁים
ones-calming and-the-Levites (11) strength-of-you she Yahweh joy-of for

לְכָל־ הָעָם לֵאמֹר הַסּוּ כִּי הַיּוֹם קָדֹשׁ וְאַל־ תֵּעָצֵבוּ׃
you-grieve and-not sacred the-day for be-still! to-say the-people to-all-of

(12) וַיֵּלְכוּ כָל־ הָעָם לֶאֱכֹל וְלִשְׁתּוֹת וּלְשַׁלַּח
and-to-send and-to-drink to-eat the-people all-of then-they-went-away (12)

Malkijah, Hashum, Hashbaddanah, Zechariah and Meshullam.

[5]Ezra opened the book. All the people could see him because he was standing above them; and as he opened it, the people all stood up. [6]Ezra praised the LORD, the great God; and all the people lifted their hands and responded, "Amen! Amen!" Then they bowed down and worshiped the LORD with their faces to the ground.

[7]The Levites—Jeshua, Bani, Sherebiah, Jamin, Akkub, Shabbethai, Hodiah, Maaseiah, Kelita, Azariah, Jozabad, Hanan and Pelaiah—instructed the people in the Law while the people were standing there. [8]They read from the Book of the Law of God, making it clear[v] and giving the meaning so that the people could understand what was being read.

[9]Then Nehemiah the governor, Ezra the priest and scribe, and the Levites who were instructing the people said to them all, "This day is sacred to the LORD your God. Do not mourn or weep." For all the people had been weeping as they listened to the words of the Law.

[10]Nehemiah said, "Go and enjoy choice food and sweet drinks, and send some to those who have nothing prepared. This day is sacred to our Lord. Do not grieve, for the joy of the LORD is your strength."

[11]The Levites calmed all the people, saying, "Be still, for this is a sacred day. Do not grieve."

[12]Then all the people went away to eat and drink, to send

[v]8 Or *God, translating it*

*6 Most mss have no *dagesh* in the *vav* and *shureq* in place of the *qibbuts* (וּ־).

מָנוֹת וְלַעֲשׂוֹת שִׂמְחָה גְדוֹלָה כִּי הֵבִינוּ בַּדְּבָרִים אֲשֶׁר
that to-the-words they-understood because great joy and-to-celebrate portions

הוֹדִיעוּ לָהֶם׃ וּבַיּוֹם הַשֵּׁנִי נֶאֶסְפוּ רָאשֵׁי
heads-of they-gathered the-second and-on-the-day (13) to-them they-made-known

הָאָבוֹת לְכָל־ הָעָם הַכֹּהֲנִים וְהַלְוִיִּם אֶל־ עֶזְרָא
Ezra around and-the-Levites the-priests the-people of-all-of the-fathers

הַסֹּפֵר וּלְהַשְׂכִּיל אֶל־ דִּבְרֵי הַתּוֹרָה׃ וַיִּמְצְאוּ
and-they-found (14) the-Law words-of to and-to-give-attention the-scribe

כָּתוּב בַּתּוֹרָה אֲשֶׁר צִוָּה יְהוָה בְּיַד־ מֹשֶׁה אֲשֶׁר
that Moses by-hand-of Yahweh he-commanded which in-the-Law being-written

יֵשְׁבוּ בְנֵי־ יִשְׂרָאֵל בַּסֻּכּוֹת בֶּחָג בַּחֹדֶשׁ
of-the-month during-the-feast in-the-booths Israel sons-of they-live

הַשְּׁבִיעִי׃ וַאֲשֶׁר יַשְׁמִיעוּ וְיַעֲבִירוּ קוֹל בְּכָל־
through-all-of word and-they-spread they-proclaim and-that (15) the-seventh

עָרֵיהֶם וּבִירוּשָׁלִַם לֵאמֹר צְאוּ הָהָר וְהָבִיאוּ
and-bring! the-hill-country go-out! to-say and-in-Jerusalem towns-of-them

עֲלֵי־ זַיִת וַעֲלֵי־ עֵץ שֶׁמֶן וַעֲלֵי הֲדַס
myrtle and-branches-of wild-olive tree-of and-branches-of olive branches-of

וַעֲלֵי תְמָרִים וַעֲלֵי עֵץ עָבֹת לַעֲשֹׂת סֻכֹּת
booths to-make shade tree-of and-branches-of palms and-branches-of

כַּכָּתוּב׃ וַיֵּצְאוּ הָעָם וַיָּבִיאוּ
and-they-brought the-people so-they-went-out (16) as-the-thing-being-written

וַיַּעֲשׂוּ לָהֶם סֻכּוֹת אִישׁ עַל־ גַּגּוֹ וּבְחַצְרֹתֵיהֶם
and-in-courtyards-of-them roof-of-him on each booths for-them and-they-built

וּבְחַצְרוֹת בֵּית הָאֱלֹהִים וּבִרְחוֹב שַׁעַר הַמַּיִם
the-Waters Gate-of and-in-square-of the-God house-of and-in-courts-of

וּבִרְחוֹב שַׁעַר אֶפְרָיִם׃ וַיַּעֲשׂוּ כָל־ הַקָּהָל
the-company whole-of and-they-built (17) Ephraim Gate-of and-in-square-of

הַשָּׁבִים מִן־ הַשְּׁבִי ׀ סֻכּוֹת וַיֵּשְׁבוּ בַסֻּכּוֹת כִּי
indeed in-the-booths and-they-lived booths the-exile from the-ones-returning

לֹא־ עָשׂוּ מִימֵי יֵשׁוּעַ בִּן־ נוּן כֵּן בְּנֵי יִשְׂרָאֵל עַד
until Israel sons-of thus Nun son-of Joshua from-days-of they-celebrated not

הַיּוֹם הַהוּא וַתְּהִי שִׂמְחָה גְּדוֹלָה מְאֹד׃ וַיִּקְרָא בְּסֵפֶר
from-Book-of and-he-read (18) very great joy and-she-was the-that the-day

תּוֹרַת הָאֱלֹהִים יוֹם ׀ בְּיוֹם מִן־ הַיּוֹם הָרִאשׁוֹן עַד הַיּוֹם הָאַחֲרוֹן
the-last the-day to the-first the-day from after-day day the-God Law-of

וַיַּעֲשׂוּ־ חָג שִׁבְעַת יָמִים וּבַיּוֹם הַשְּׁמִינִי עֲצֶרֶת
assembly the-eighth and-on-the-day days seven-of feast and-they-celebrated

portions of food and to celebrate with great joy, because
they now understood the
words that had been made
known to them.
13On the second day of the
month, the heads of all the
families, along with the
priests and the Levites, gathered around Ezra the scribe to
give attention to the words of
the Law. 14They found written
in the Law, which the LORD
had commanded through
Moses, that the Israelites were
to live in booths during the
feast of the seventh month
15and that they should proclaim this word and spread it
throughout their towns and in
Jerusalem: "Go out into the
hill country and bring back
branches from olive and wild
olive trees, and from myrtles,
palms and shade trees, to
make booths"—as it is written.[w]
16So the people went out and
brought back branches and
built themselves booths on
their own roofs, in their courtyards, in the courts of the
house of God and in the
square by the Water Gate and
the one by the Gate of
Ephraim. 17The whole com-
pany that had returned from
exile built booths and lived in
them. From the days of Joshua
son of Nun until that day, the
Israelites had not celebrated it
like this. And their joy was
very great.
18Day after day, from the
first day to the last, Ezra read
from the Book of the Law of
God. They celebrated the feast
for seven days, and on the
eighth day, in accordance

w15 See Lev. 23:37-40.

כַּמִּשְׁפָּט׃ וּבְיוֹם עֶשְׂרִים וְאַרְבָּעָה לַחֹדֶשׁ הַזֶּה
the-same of-the-month and-four twenty and-on-day-of (9:1) as-the-regulation

נֶאֶסְפוּ בְנֵי־יִשְׂרָאֵל בְּצוֹם וּבְשַׂקִּים וַאֲדָמָה
and-dust and-with-sackcloths with-fasting Israel sons-of they-gathered

עֲלֵיהֶם׃ וַיִּבָּדְלוּ זֶרַע יִשְׂרָאֵל מִכֹּל
from-all-of Israel descendant-of and-they-separated-themselves (2) on-them

בְּנֵי נֵכָר וַיַּעַמְדוּ וַיִּתְוַדּוּ עַל־חַטֹּאתֵיהֶם
sins-of-them to and-they-confessed and-they-stood foreigner sons-of

וַעֲוֺנוֹת אֲבֹתֵיהֶם׃ וַיָּקוּמוּ עַל־עָמְדָם
place-of-them at and-they-stood (3) fathers-of-them and-wickednesses-of

וַיִּקְרְאוּ בְּסֵפֶר תּוֹרַת יְהוָה אֱלֹהֵיהֶם רְבִעִית הַיּוֹם
the-day fourth-of God-of-them Yahweh Law-of from-Book-of and-they-read

וּרְבִעִית מִתְוַדִּים וּמִשְׁתַּחֲוִים לַיהוָה אֱלֹהֵיהֶם׃
God-of-them to-Yahweh and-ones-worshiping ones-confessing and-fourth

וַיָּקָם עַל־מַעֲלֵה הַלְוִיִּם יֵשׁוּעַ וּבָנִי קַדְמִיאֵל
and-Kadmiel and-Bani Jeshua the-Levites stair-of on and-he-stood (4)

שְׁבַנְיָה בֻּנִּי שֵׁרֵבְיָה בָּנִי כְנָנִי וַיִּזְעֲקוּ בְּקוֹל גָּדוֹל אֶל־
to loud with-voice and-they-called Kenani Bani Sherebiah Bunni Shebaniah

יְהוָה אֱלֹהֵיהֶם׃ וַיֹּאמְרוּ הַלְוִיִּם יֵשׁוּעַ וְקַדְמִיאֵל בָּנִי
Bani and-Kadmiel Jeshua the-Levites and-they-said (5) God-of-them Yahweh

חֲשַׁבְנְיָה שֵׁרֵבְיָה הוֹדִיָּה שְׁבַנְיָה פְתַחְיָה קוּמוּ בָּרְכוּ אֶת־
*** praise! stand-up! Pethahiah Shebaniah Hodiah Sherebiah Hashabneiah

יְהוָה אֱלֹהֵיכֶם מִן־הָעוֹלָם עַד־הָעוֹלָם וִיבָרְכוּ
and-may-they-bless the-everlasting to the-everlasting from God-of-you Yahweh

שֵׁם כְּבוֹדֶךָ וּמְרוֹמַם עַל־כָּל־בְּרָכָה וּתְהִלָּה׃
and-praise blessing all-of above and-being-exalted glory-of-you name-of

אַתָּה־הוּא יְהוָה לְבַדֶּךָ אַתְּ עָשִׂיתָ אֶת־הַשָּׁמַיִם שְׁמֵי
heavens-of the-heavens *** you-made you by-yourself Yahweh he you (6)

הַשָּׁמַיִם וְכָל־צְבָאָם הָאָרֶץ וְכָל־אֲשֶׁר עָלֶיהָ הַיַּמִּים
the-seas on-her that and-all-of the-earth host-of-them and-all-of the-heavens

וְכָל־אֲשֶׁר בָּהֶם וְאַתָּה מְחַיֶּה אֶת־כֻּלָּם וּצְבָא
and-multitude-of all-of-them *** giving-life and-you in-them that and-all-of

הַשָּׁמַיִם לְךָ מִשְׁתַּחֲוִים׃ אַתָּה־הוּא יְהוָה הָאֱלֹהִים אֲשֶׁר בָּחַרְתָּ
you-chose who the-God Yahweh he you (7) ones-worshiping to-you the-heavens

בְּאַבְרָם וְהוֹצֵאתוֹ מֵאוּר כַּשְׂדִּים וְשַׂמְתָּ שְּׁמוֹ
name-of-him and-you-made Chaldeans from-Ur-of and-you-brought-him to-Abram

אַבְרָהָם׃ וּמָצָאתָ אֶת־לְבָבוֹ נֶאֱמָן לְפָנֶיךָ וְכָרוֹת
and-to-make to-you being-faithful heart-of-him *** and-you-found (8) Abraham

with the regulation, there was an assembly.

The Israelites Confess Their Sins

9 On the twenty-fourth day of the same month, the Israelites gathered together, fasting and wearing sackcloth and having dust on their heads. [2]Those of Israelite descent had separated themselves from all foreigners. They stood in their places and confessed their sins and the wickedness of their fathers. [3]They stood where they were and read from the Book of the Law of the LORD their God for a fourth of the day, and spent another fourth in confession and in worshiping the LORD their God. [4]Standing on the stairs were the Levites—Jeshua, Bani, Kadmiel, Shebaniah, Bunni, Sherebiah, Bani and Kenani—who called with loud voices to the LORD their God. [5]And the Levites—Jeshua, Kadmiel, Bani, Hashabneiah, Sherebiah, Hodiah, Shebaniah and Pethahiah—said: "Stand up and praise the LORD your God, who is from everlasting to everlasting.[x]"

"Blessed be your glorious name, and may it be exalted above all blessing and praise. [6]You alone are the LORD. You made the heavens, even the highest heavens, and all their starry host, the earth and all that is on it, the seas and all that is in them. You give life to everything, and the multitudes of heaven worship you.

[7]"You are the LORD God, who chose Abram and brought him out of Ur of the Chaldeans and named him Abraham. [8]You found his heart faithful to you, and you made a covenant

x5 Or *God for ever and ever*

°6 ק אתה

עִמּוֹ הַבְּרִית לָתֵת אֶת־ אֶרֶץ הַכְּנַעֲנִי הַחִתִּי
the-Hittite the-Canaanite land-of *** to-give the-covenant with-him

הָאֱמֹרִי וְהַפְּרִזִּי וְהַיְבוּסִי וְהַגִּרְגָּשִׁי לָתֵת
to-give and-the-Girgashite and-the-Jebusite and-the-Perizzite the-Amorite

לְזַרְעוֹ וַתָּקֶם אֶת־ דְּבָרֶיךָ כִּי צַדִּיק אָתָּה׃
you righteous because promises-of-you *** and-you-kept to-descendant-of-him

(9) וַתֵּרֶא אֶת־ עֳנִי אֲבֹתֵינוּ בְּמִצְרָיִם וְאֶת־ זַעֲקָתָם
cry-of-them and in-Egypt fathers-of-us suffering-of *** and-you-saw (9)

שָׁמַעְתָּ עַל־ יַם־ סוּף׃ (10) וַתִּתֵּן אֹתֹת וּמֹפְתִים בְּפַרְעֹה
against-Pharaoh and-wonders signs and-you-sent (10) Reed Sea-of at you-heard

וּבְכָל־ עֲבָדָיו וּבְכָל־ עַם אַרְצוֹ
land-of-him people-of and-against-all-of officials-of-him and-against-all-of

כִּי יָדַעְתָּ כִּי הֵזִידוּ עֲלֵיהֶם וַתַּעַשׂ־ לְךָ שֵׁם
name for-you and-you-made to-them they-treated-arrogantly how you-knew for

כְּהַיּוֹם הַזֶּה׃ (11) וְהַיָּם בָּקַעְתָּ לִפְנֵיהֶם וַיַּעַבְרוּ
so-they-passed before-them you-divided and-the-sea (11) the-this to-the-day

בְתוֹךְ־ הַיָּם בַּיַּבָּשָׁה וְאֶת־ רֹדְפֵיהֶם הִשְׁלַכְתָּ
you-hurled ones-pursuing-them but on-the-dry-ground the-sea through-midst-of

בִמְצוֹלֹת כְּמוֹ־ אֶבֶן בְּמַיִם עַזִּים׃ (12) וּבְעַמּוּד עָנָן
cloud and-with-pillar-of (12) mighty-ones into-waters stone like into-depths

הִנְחִיתָם יוֹמָם וּבְעַמּוּד אֵשׁ לַיְלָה לְהָאִיר לָהֶם
to-them to-give-light night fire and-with-pillar-of by-day you-led-them

אֶת־הַדֶּרֶךְ אֲשֶׁר יֵלְכוּ־ בָהּ׃ (13) וְעַל הַר־ סִינַי יָרַדְתָּ
you-came-down Sinai Mount-of and-on (13) on-her they-walked which the-way ***

וְדַבֵּר עִמָּהֶם מִשָּׁמָיִם וַתִּתֵּן לָהֶם מִשְׁפָּטִים יְשָׁרִים
just-ones regulations to-them and-you-gave from-heavens to-them and-to-speak

וְתוֹרוֹת אֱמֶת חֻקִּים וּמִצְוֹת טוֹבִים׃ (14) וְאֶת־ שַׁבַּת
Sabbath-of and (14) good-ones and-commands decrees right and-laws-of

קָדְשְׁךָ הוֹדַעְתָּ* לָהֶם וּמִצְווֹת וְחֻקִּים וְתוֹרָה
and-law and-decrees and-commands to-them you-made-known holiness-of-you

צִוִּיתָ לָהֶם בְּיַד מֹשֶׁה עַבְדֶּךָ׃ (15) וְלֶחֶם מִשָּׁמַיִם
from-heavens and-bread (15) servant-of-you Moses by-hand-of to-them you-gave

נָתַתָּה לָהֶם לִרְעָבָם וּמַיִם מִסֶּלַע הוֹצֵאתָ לָהֶם
to-them you-brought from-rock and-waters in-hunger-of-them to-them you-gave

לִצְמָאָם וַתֹּאמֶר לָהֶם לָבוֹא לָרֶשֶׁת אֶת־ הָאָרֶץ אֲשֶׁר־
that the-land *** to-possess to-go-in to-them and-you-told in-thirst-of-them

נָשָׂאתָ אֶת־ יָדְךָ לָתֵת לָהֶם׃ (16) וְהֵם וַאֲבֹתֵינוּ
indeed-fathers-of-us but-they (16) to-them to-give hand-of-you *** you-lifted

with him to give to his descendants the land of the
Canaanites, Hittites, Amorites, Perizzites, Jebusites
and Girgashites. You have
kept your promise because
you are righteous.
9"You saw the suffering
of our forefathers in Egypt;
you heard their cry at the
Red Sea.[a] 10You sent miraculous signs and wonders
against Pharaoh, against all
his officials and all the
people of his land, for you
knew how arrogantly the
Egyptians treated them.
You made a name for your-
self, which remains to this
day. 11You divided the sea
before them, so that they
passed through it on dry
ground, but you hurled
their pursuers into the
depths, like a stone into
mighty waters. 12By day
you led them with a pillar
of cloud, and by night with
a pillar of fire to give them
light on the way they were
to take.
13"You came down on
Mount Sinai; you spoke to
them from heaven. You
gave them regulations and
laws that are just and right,
and decrees and commands
that are good. 14You made
known to them your holy
Sabbath and gave them
commands, decrees and
laws through your servant
Moses. 15In their hunger
you gave them bread from
heaven and in their thirst
you brought them water
from the rock; you told
them to go in and take
possession of the land you
had sworn with uplifted
hand to give them.
16"But they, our forefa-
thers, became arrogant and

[a]9 Hebrew *Yam Suph;* that is, Sea of Reeds

*14 Most mss have *sheva* under the *ayin* and *dagesh* in the *tav* (עְתָּ–).

הֵזִידוּ וַיַּקְשׁוּ אֶת־ עָרְפָּם וְלֹא
and-not neck-of-them *** and-they-made-stiff they-became-arrogant

שָׁמְעוּ אֶל־ מִצְוֺתֶיךָ׃ וַיְמָאֲנוּ לִשְׁמֹעַ וְלֹא־
and-not to-listen and-they-refused (17) commands-of-you to they-obeyed

זָכְרוּ נִפְלְאֹתֶיךָ אֲשֶׁר עָשִׂיתָ עִמָּהֶם
among-them you-performed that ones-being-miracles-of-you they-remembered

וַיַּקְשׁוּ אֶת־ עָרְפָּם וַיִּתְּנוּ־ רֹאשׁ לָשׁוּב
to-return leader and-they-appointed neck-of-them *** and-they-made-stiff

לְעַבְדֻתָם בְּמִרְיָם וְאַתָּה אֱלוֹהַּ סְלִיחוֹת חַנּוּן
gracious forgivings God-of but-you in-rebellion-of-them to-slavery-of-them

וְרַחוּם אֶרֶךְ־ אַפַּיִם וְרַב־ וְחֶסֶד° וְלֹא עֲזַבְתָּם׃
you-deserted-them so-not love and-abundant-of angers slow-of and-compassionate

אַף כִּי־ עָשׂוּ לָהֶם עֵגֶל מַסֵּכָה וַיֹּאמְרוּ זֶה אֱלֹהֶיךָ
god-of-you this and-they-said image calf-of for-them they-cast when even (18)

אֲשֶׁר הֶעֶלְךָ מִמִּצְרָיִם וַיַּעֲשׂוּ נֶאָצוֹת גְּדֹלוֹת׃
awful-ones blasphemies or-they-committed from-Egypt he-brought-up-you who

וְאַתָּה בְּרַחֲמֶיךָ הָרַבִּים לֹא עֲזַבְתָּם
you-abandoned-them not the-great-ones because-of-compassions-of-you and-you (19)

בַּמִּדְבָּר אֶת־ עַמּוּד הֶעָנָן לֹא־ סָר מֵעֲלֵיהֶם
from-before-them he-ceased not the-cloud pillar-of *** in-the-desert

בְּיוֹמָם לְהַנְחֹתָם בְּהַדֶּרֶךְ וְאֶת־ עַמּוּד הָאֵשׁ בְּלַיְלָה לְהָאִיר
to-shine by-night the-fire pillar-of nor on-the-path to-guide-them at-by-day

לָהֶם וְאֶת ־הַדֶּרֶךְ אֲשֶׁר יֵלְכוּ־ בָהּ׃ וְרוּחֲךָ הַטּוֹבָה
the-good and-Spirit-of-you (20) on-her they-walked that the-way and on-them

נָתַתָּ לְהַשְׂכִּילָם וּמַנְךָ לֹא־ מָנַעְתָּ מִפִּיהֶם
from-mouth-of-them you-withheld not and-manna-of-you to-instruct-them you-gave

וּמַיִם נָתַתָּה לָהֶם לִצְמָאָם׃ וְאַרְבָּעִים שָׁנָה
year and-forty (21) for-thirst-of-them to-them you-gave and-waters

כִּלְכַּלְתָּם בַּמִּדְבָּר לֹא חָסֵרוּ שַׂלְמֹתֵיהֶם לֹא
not clothes-of-them they-lacked nothing in-the-desert you-sustained-them

בָלוּ וְרַגְלֵיהֶם לֹא בָצֵקוּ׃ וַתִּתֵּן
and-you-gave (22) they-became-swollen not and-feet-of-them they-wore-out

לָהֶם מַמְלָכוֹת וַעֲמָמִים וַתַּחְלְקֵם לְפֵאָה
for-remote-frontier and-you-allotted-them and-nations kingdoms to-them

וַיִּירְשׁוּ אֶת־ אֶרֶץ סִיחוֹן וְאֶת־ אֶרֶץ מֶלֶךְ חֶשְׁבּוֹן וְאֶת־
and Heshbon king-of country-of namely Sihon country-of *** and-they-took-over

אֶרֶץ עוֹג מֶלֶךְ־ הַבָּשָׁן׃ וּבְנֵיהֶם הִרְבִּיתָ
you-made-numerous and-sons-of-them (23) the-Bashan king-of Og country-of

stiff-necked, and did not
obey your commands.
17They refused to listen and
failed to remember the
miracles you performed
among them. They became
stiff-necked and in their rebellion appointed a leader
in order to return to their
slavery. But you are a forgiving God, gracious and
compassionate, slow to anger and abounding in love.
Therefore you did not
desert them, 18even when
they cast for themselves an
image of a calf and said,
'This is your god, who
brought you up out of
Egypt,' or when they com-
mitted awful blasphemies.
19"Because of your great
compassion you did not
abandon them in the
desert. By day the pillar of
cloud did not cease to guide
them on their path, nor the
pillar of fire by night to
shine on the way they were
to take. 20You gave your
good Spirit to instruct
them. You did not with-
hold your manna from
their mouths, and you gave
them water for their thirst.
21For forty years you sus-
tained them in the desert;
they lacked nothing, their
clothes did not wear out
nor did their feet become
swollen.
22"You gave them king-
doms and nations, allotting
to them even the remotest
frontiers. They took over
the country of Sihon[b] king
of Heshbon and the coun-
try of Og king of Bashan.
23You made their sons as

[b]22 One Hebrew manuscript and Septuagint; most Hebrew manuscripts *Sihon, that is, the country of the*

°17 ק חסד

כְּכֹכְבֵי הַשָּׁמַיִם וַתְּבִיאֵם֙ אֶל־ הָאָרֶץ אֲשֶׁר אָמַרְתָּ
as-stars-of / the-skies / and-you-brought-them / into / the-land / that / you-told

לַאֲבֹתֵיהֶם לָבוֹא לָרֶשֶׁת: (24) וַיָּבֹ֣אוּ הַבָּנִים֙
to-fathers-of-them / to-enter / to-possess / (24) / and-they-went-in / the-sons

וַיִּֽרְשׁ֣וּ אֶת־ הָאָרֶץ וַתַּכְנַ֨ע לִפְנֵיהֶ֜ם אֶת־ יֹשְׁבֵי
and-they-possessed / *** / the-land / and-you-subdued / before-them / *** / ones-living-of

הָאָרֶץ הַכְּנַעֲנִים וַֽתִּתְּנֵם֙ בְּיָדָ֔ם וְאֶת־ מַלְכֵיהֶם֙
the-land / the-Canaanites / and-you-gave-them / into-hand-of-them / and / kings-of-them

וְאֶת־ עַמְמֵי הָאָ֔רֶץ לַעֲשׂ֥וֹת בָּהֶ֖ם כִּרְצוֹנָֽם:
and / peoples-of / the-land / to-deal / with-them / as-pleasure-of-them

(25) וַֽיִּלְכְּד֞וּ עָרִים֙ בְּצֻרוֹת֙ וַאֲדָמָ֣ה שְׁמֵנָ֔ה
(25) / and-they-captured / cities / ones-being-fortified / and-land / fertile

וַיִּֽירְשׁ֣וּ בָּתִּ֣ים מְלֵֽאִים־ כָּל־ ט֠וּב בֹּר֨וֹת חֲצוּבִ֜ים
and-they-possessed / houses / ones-filled / all-of / good / wells / ones-being-dug

כְּרָמִ֧ים וְזֵיתִ֛ים וְעֵ֥ץ מַאֲכָ֖ל לָרֹ֑ב וַיֹּאכְל֣וּ
vineyards / and-olive-groves / and-tree-of / fruit / in-abundance / and-they-ate

וַֽיִּשְׂבְּעוּ֮ וַיַּשְׁמִ֒ינוּ֒ וַיִּֽתְעַדְּנ֖וּ
and-they-were-full / and-they-were-well-nourished / and-they-reveled

בְּטוּבְךָ֣ הַגָּדֽוֹל: (26) וַיַּמְר֞וּ וַיִּמְרְד֣וּ
in-goodness-of-you / the-great / (26) / but-they-were-disobedient / and-they-rebelled

בָ֗ךְ וַיַּשְׁלִ֤כוּ אֶת־ תּוֹרָֽתְךָ֙ אַחֲרֵ֣י גַוָּ֔ם וְאֶת־
against-you / and-they-put / *** / law-of-you / behind / back-of-them / and

נְבִיאֶ֣יךָ הָרָ֔גוּ אֲשֶׁר־ הֵעִ֥ידוּ בָ֖ם לַהֲשִׁיבָ֣ם
prophets-of-you / they-killed / who / they-admonished / to-them / to-turn-back-them

אֵלֶ֑יךָ וַֽיַּעֲשׂ֔וּ נֶאָצ֖וֹת גְּדֹלֹֽת: (27) וַֽתִּתְּנֵם֙
to-you / and-they-committed / blasphemies / awful-ones / (27) / so-you-gave-them

בְּיַ֣ד צָֽרֵיהֶ֔ם וַיָּצֵ֖רוּ לָהֶ֑ם וּבְעֵ֤ת
into-hand-of / enemies-of-them / and-they-oppressed / to-them / but-at-time-of

צָֽרָתָם֙ יִצְעֲק֣וּ אֵלֶ֔יךָ וְאַתָּה֙ מִשָּׁמַ֣יִם תִּשְׁמָ֔ע
oppression-of-them / they-cried-out / to-you / and-you / from-heavens / you-heard

וּֽכְרַחֲמֶ֣יךָ הָֽרַבִּ֔ים תִּתֵּ֥ן לָהֶ֖ם מֽוֹשִׁיעִ֑ים
and-in-compassions-of-you / the-great-ones / you-gave / to-them / ones-delivering

וְי֣וֹשִׁיע֔וּם מִיַּ֖ד צָרֵיהֶֽם: (28) וּכְנ֣וֹחַ
and-they-rescued-them / from-hand-of / enemies-of-them / (28) / but-as-to-be-rest

לָהֶ֔ם יָשׁ֕וּבוּ לַעֲשׂ֥וֹת רַ֖ע לְפָנֶ֑יךָ וַתַּֽעַזְבֵ֞ם
to-them / they-did-again / to-do / evil / before-you / then-you-abandoned-them

בְּיַ֤ד אֹֽיְבֵיהֶם֙ וַיִּרְדּ֣וּ בָהֶ֔ם
into-hand-of / ones-being-enemies-of-them / so-they-ruled / over-them

numerous as the stars in the sky, and you brought them into the land that you told their fathers to enter and possess. [24]Their sons went in and took possession of the land. You subdued before them the Canaanites, who lived in the land; you handed the Canaanites over to them, along with their kings and the peoples of the land, to deal with them as they pleased. [25]They captured fortified cities and fertile land; they took possession of houses filled with all kinds of good things, wells already dug, vineyards, olive groves and fruit trees in abundance. They ate to the full and were well-nourished; they reveled in your great goodness.

[26]"But they were disobedient and rebelled against you; they put your law behind their backs. They killed your prophets, who had admonished them in order to turn them back to you; they committed awful blasphemies. [27]So you handed them over to their enemies, who oppressed them. But when they were oppressed they cried out to you. From heaven you heard them, and in your great compassion you gave them deliverers, who rescued them from the hand of their enemies.

[28]"But as soon as they were at rest, they again did what was evil in your sight. Then you abandoned them to the hand of their enemies so that they ruled over

וַיָּשׁוּבוּ וַיִּזְעָקוּךָ וְאַתָּה מִשָּׁמַיִם תִּשְׁמַע

you-heard from-heavens then-you and-they-cried-out-to-you when-they-did-again

וְתַצִּילֵם כְּרַחֲמֶיךָ רַבּוֹת עִתִּים: וַתָּעַד

and-you-warned (29) times many-of in-compassions-of-you and-you-delivered-them

בָּהֶם לַהֲשִׁיבָם אֶל־ תּוֹרָתֶךָ וְהֵמָּה הֵזִידוּ וְלֹא־

and-not they-became-arrogant but-they law-of-you to to-return-them to-them

שָׁמְעוּ לְמִצְוֹתֶיךָ וּבְמִשְׁפָּטֶיךָ חָטְאוּ־

they-sinned and-against-ordinances-of-you to-commands-of-you they-obeyed

בָם אֲשֶׁר־ יַעֲשֶׂה אָדָם וְחָיָה בָהֶם וַיִּתְּנוּ

and-they-turned by-them then-he-will-live man he-obeys which against-them

כָתֵף סוֹרֶרֶת וְעָרְפָּם הִקְשׁוּ וְלֹא שָׁמֵעוּ:

they-listened and-not they-made-stiff and-neck-of-them being-stubborn back

וַתִּמְשֹׁךְ עֲלֵיהֶם שָׁנִים רַבּוֹת וַתָּעַד בָּם

to-them and-you-admonished many years with-them and-you-were-patient (30)

בְּרוּחֲךָ בְּיַד־ נְבִיאֶיךָ וְלֹא הֶאֱזִינוּ

they-paid-attention yet-not prophets-of-you by-hand-of by-Spirit-of-you

וַתִּתְּנֵם בְּיַד עַמֵּי הָאֲרָצֹת: וּבְרַחֲמֶיךָ

but-in-mercies-of-you (31) the-lands peoples-of into-hand-of so-you-gave-them

הָרַבִּים לֹא־ עֲשִׂיתָם כָּלָה וְלֹא עֲזַבְתָּם כִּי אֵל־

God-of for you-abandoned-them and-not end you-put-them not the-great-ones

חַנּוּן וְרַחוּם אָתָּה: וְעַתָּה אֱלֹהֵינוּ הָאֵל הַגָּדוֹל הַגִּבּוֹר

the-mighty the-great the-God God-of-us so-now (32) you and-mercy grace

וְהַנּוֹרָא שׁוֹמֵר הַבְּרִית וְהַחֶסֶד אַל־

not and-the-love the-covenant keeping and-the-one-being-awesome

יִמְעַט לְפָנֶיךָ אֵת כָּל־ הַתְּלָאָה אֲשֶׁר־

that the-hardship all-of *** before-you let-him-seem-trifling

מְצָאַתְנוּ לִמְלָכֵינוּ לְשָׂרֵינוּ וּלְכֹהֲנֵינוּ

and-upon-priests-of-us upon-leaders-of-us upon-kings-of-us she-came-upon-us

וְלִנְבִיאֵנוּ וְלַאֲבֹתֵינוּ וּלְכָל־ עַמֶּךָ

people-of-you and-upon-all-of and-upon-fathers-of-us and-upon-prophets-of-us

מִימֵי מַלְכֵי אַשּׁוּר עַד הַיּוֹם הַזֶּה: וְאַתָּה צַדִּיק עַל

in just and-you (33) the-this the-day until Assyria kings-of from-days-of

כָּל־ הַבָּא עָלֵינוּ כִּי־ אֱמֶת עָשִׂיתָ וַאֲנַחְנוּ הִרְשָׁעְנוּ:

we-did-wrong while-we you-acted faithfully for to-us the-thing-happening all-of

וְאֶת־ מְלָכֵינוּ שָׂרֵינוּ כֹּהֲנֵינוּ וַאֲבֹתֵינוּ לֹא

not and-fathers-of-us priests-of-us leaders-of-us kings-of-us and (34)

עָשׂוּ תּוֹרָתֶךָ וְלֹא הִקְשִׁיבוּ אֶל־ מִצְוֹתֶיךָ

commands-of-you to they-paid-attention and-not law-of-you they-followed

them. And when they cried
out to you again, you heard
from heaven, and in your
compassion you delivered
them time after time.
29"You warned them to
return to your law, but they
became arrogant and dis-
obeyed your commands.
They sinned against your
ordinances, by which a
man will live if he obeys
them. Stubbornly they
turned their backs on you,
became stiff-necked and
refused to listen. 30For
many years you were pa-
tient with them. By your
Spirit you admonished
them through your proph-
ets. Yet they paid no attention, so you handed them
over to the neighboring
peoples. 31But in your great
mercy you did not put an
end to them or abandon
them, for you are a gracious
and merciful God.
32"Now therefore, O our
God, the great, mighty and
awesome God, who keeps
his covenant of love, do not
let all this hardship seem
trifling in your eyes—the
hardship that has come
upon us, upon our kings
and leaders, upon our
priests and prophets, upon
our fathers and all your
people, from the days of the
kings of Assyria until today. 33In all that has happened to us, you have been
just; you have acted faithfully, while we did wrong.
34Our kings, our leaders,
our priests and our fathers
did not follow your law;
they did not pay attention
to your commands or the

וּלְעֵדְוֹתֶיךָ אֲשֶׁר הַעִידֹתָ בָּהֶם׃ וְהֵם בְּמַלְכוּתָם
in-kingdom-of-them while-they (35) to-them you-gave that or-to-warnings-of-you

וּבְטוּבְךָ הָרָב אֲשֶׁר־ נָתַתָּ לָהֶם וּבְאֶרֶץ
and-in-land-of to-them you-gave that the-great and-in-goodness-of-you

הָרְחָבָה וְהַשְּׁמֵנָה אֲשֶׁר־ נָתַתָּ לִפְנֵיהֶם לֹא עֲבָדוּךָ
they-served-you not to-them you-gave that and-the-fertile the-spacious

וְלֹא־ שָׁבוּ מִמַּעַלְלֵיהֶם הָרָעִים׃ הִנֵּה אֲנַחְנוּ הַיּוֹם
the-day we see! (36) the-evil-ones from-ways-of-them they-turned and-not

עֲבָדִים וְהָאָרֶץ אֲשֶׁר־ נָתַתָּה לַאֲבֹתֵינוּ לֶאֱכֹל אֶת־ פִּרְיָהּ
fruit-of-her *** to-eat to-forefathers-of-us you-gave that and-the-land slaves

וְאֶת־ טוּבָהּ הִנֵּה אֲנַחְנוּ עֲבָדִים עָלֶיהָ׃ וּתְבוּאָתָהּ מַרְבָּה
being-abundant and-harvest-of-her (37) in-her slaves we see! good-of-her and

לַמְּלָכִים אֲשֶׁר־ נָתַתָּה עָלֵינוּ בְּחַטֹּאותֵינוּ וְעַל
and-over because-of-sins-of-us over-us you-placed whom to-the-kings

גְּוִיֹּתֵינוּ מֹשְׁלִים וּבִבְהֶמְתֵּנוּ כִּרְצוֹנָם
as-pleasure-of-them and-over-cattle-of-us ones-ruling bodies-of-us

וּבְצָרָה גְדוֹלָה אֲנָחְנוּ׃ וּבְכָל־ זֹאת אֲנַחְנוּ
we this and-because-of-all-of *(10:1) we great and-in-distress

כֹּרְתִים אֲמָנָה וְכֹתְבִים וְעַל הֶחָתוּם
the-one-being-sealed and-to and-ones-writing binding ones-making-agreement

שָׂרֵינוּ לְוִיֵּנוּ כֹּהֲנֵינוּ׃ וְעַל הַחֲתוּמִים
the-ones-being-sealed and-to (2) priests-of-us Levites-of-us leaders-of-us

נְחֶמְיָה הַתִּרְשָׁתָא בֶּן־ חֲכַלְיָה וְצִדְקִיָּה׃ שְׂרָיָה עֲזַרְיָה
Azariah Seraiah (3) and-Zedekiah Hacaliah son-of the-governor Nehemiah

יִרְמְיָה׃ פַּשְׁחוּר אֲמַרְיָה מַלְכִּיָּה׃ חַטּוּשׁ שְׁבַנְיָה מַלּוּךְ׃
Malluch Shebaniah Hattush (5) Malkijah Amariah Pashhur (4) Jeremiah

חָרִם מְרֵמוֹת עֹבַדְיָה׃ דָּנִיֵּאל גִּנְּתוֹן בָּרוּךְ׃ מְשֻׁלָּם אֲבִיָּה
Abijah Meshullam (8) Baruch Ginnethon Daniel (7) Obadiah Meremoth Harim (6)

מִיָּמִן׃ מַעַזְיָה בִלְגַּי שְׁמַעְיָה אֵלֶּה הַכֹּהֲנִים׃ וְהַלְוִיִּם
and-the-Levites (10) the-priests these Shemaiah Bilgai Maaziah (9) Mijamin

וְיֵשׁוּעַ בֶּן־ אֲזַנְיָה בִּנּוּי מִבְּנֵי חֵנָדָד קַדְמִיאֵל׃
Kadmiel Henadad of-sons-of Binnui Azaniah son-of and-Jeshua

וַאֲחֵיהֶם שְׁבַנְיָה הוֹדִיָּה קְלִיטָא פְּלָאיָה חָנָן׃ מִיכָא
Mica (12) Hanan Pelaiah Kelita Hodiah Shebaniah and-associates-of-them (11)

רְחוֹב חֲשַׁבְיָה׃ זַכּוּר שֵׁרֵבְיָה שְׁבַנְיָה׃ הוֹדִיָּה בָנִי בְּנִינוּ׃
Beninu Bani Hodiah (14) Shebaniah Sherebiah Zaccur (13) Hashabiah Rehob

רָאשֵׁי הָעָם פַּרְעֹשׁ פַּחַת מוֹאָב עֵילָם זַתּוּא בָּנִי׃ בֻּנִּי
Bunni (16) Bani Zattu Elam Moab Pahath Parosh the-people leaders-of (15)

warnings you gave them.
35 Even while they were in
their kingdom, enjoying
your great goodness to
them in the spacious and
fertile land you gave them,
they did not serve you or
turn from their evil ways.
36 "But see, we are slaves
today, slaves in the land
you gave our forefathers so
they could eat its fruit and
the other good things it
produces. 37 Because of our
sins, its abundant harvest
goes to the kings you have
placed over us. They rule
over our bodies and our
cattle as they please. We are
in great distress.

The Agreement of the People

38 "In view of all this, we are making a binding agreement, putting it in writing, and our leaders, our Levites and our priests are affixing their seals to it."

10 Those who sealed it were:

Nehemiah the governor, the son of Hacaliah.

Zedekiah, 2 Seraiah, Azariah, Jeremiah,
3 Pashhur, Amariah, Malkijah,
4 Hattush, Shebaniah, Malluch,
5 Harim, Meremoth, Obadiah,
6 Daniel, Ginnethon, Baruch,
7 Meshullam, Abijah, Mijamin,
8 Maaziah, Bilgai and Shemaiah.
These were the priests.

9 The Levites:

Jeshua son of Azaniah, Binnui of the sons of Henadad, Kadmiel,
10 and their associates: Shebaniah,
Hodiah, Kelita, Pelaiah, Hanan,
11 Mica, Rehob, Hashabiah,
12 Zaccur, Sherebiah, Shebaniah,
13 Hodiah, Bani and Beninu.

14 The leaders of the people:

Parosh, Pahath-Moab, Elam, Zattu, Bani,

*1 The Hebrew numeration of chapter 10 begins with verse 38 of chapter 9 in English; thus, there is a one-verse discrepancy throughout chapter 10.

עַזְגָּד בֵּבָי׃ אֲדֹנִיָּה בִגְוַי עָדִין׃ אָטֵר חִזְקִיָּה עַזּוּר׃ הוֹדִיָּה

Hodiah (19) Azzur Hezekiah Ater (18) Adin Bigvai Adonijah (17) Bebai Azgad

חָשֻׁם בֵּצָי׃ חָרִיף עֲנָתוֹת נוֹבָי׃° מַגְפִּיעָשׁ מְשֻׁלָּם חֵזִיר׃

Hezir Meshullam Magpiash (21) Nebai Anathoth Hariph (20) Bezai Hashum

מְשֵׁיזַבְאֵל צָדוֹק יַדּוּעַ׃ פְּלַטְיָה חָנָן עֲנָיָה׃ הוֹשֵׁעַ

Hoshea (24) Anaiah Hanan Pelatiah (23) Jaddua Zadok Meshezabel (22)

חֲנַנְיָה חַשּׁוּב׃ הַלּוֹחֵשׁ פִּלְחָא שׁוֹבֵק׃ רְחוּם חֲשַׁבְנָה מַעֲשֵׂיָה׃

Maaseiah Hashabnah Rehum (26) Shobek Pilha Hallohesh (25) Hasshub Hananiah

וַאֲחִיָּה חָנָן עָנָן׃ מַלּוּךְ חָרִם בַּעֲנָה׃ וּשְׁאָר

and-rest-of (29) Baanah Harim Malluch (28) Anan Hanan and-Ahiah (27)

הָעָם הַכֹּהֲנִים הַלְוִיִּם הַשּׁוֹעֲרִים הַמְשֹׁרְרִים

the-ones-singing the-gatekeepers the-Levites the-priests the-people

הַנְּתִינִים וְכָל־ הַנִּבְדָּל מֵעַמֵּי

from-peoples-of the-one-separating-himself and-all-of the-temple-servants

הָאֲרָצוֹת אֶל־ תּוֹרַת הָאֱלֹהִים נְשֵׁיהֶם בְּנֵיהֶם וּבְנֹתֵיהֶם

and-daughters-of-them sons-of-them wives-of-them the-God Law-of for the-lands

כֹּל יוֹדֵעַ מֵבִין׃ מַחֲזִיקִים עַל־ אֲחֵיהֶם

brothers-of-them with ones-joining (30) one-understanding one-knowing all-of

אַדִּירֵיהֶם וּבָאִים בְּאָלָה וּבִשְׁבוּעָה לָלֶכֶת בְּתוֹרַת

to-Law-of to-follow and-with-oath with-curse and-ones-binding nobles-of-them

הָאֱלֹהִים אֲשֶׁר נִתְּנָה בְּיַד מֹשֶׁה עֶבֶד־ הָאֱלֹהִים

the-God servant-of Moses by-hand-of she-was-given that the-God

וְלִשְׁמוֹר וְלַעֲשׂוֹת אֶת־ כָּל־ מִצְוֹת יְהוָה אֲדֹנֵינוּ

Lord-of-us Yahweh commands-of all-of *** and-to-obey and-to-be-careful

וּמִשְׁפָּטָיו וְחֻקָּיו׃ וַאֲשֶׁר לֹא־ נִתֵּן

we-will-give not and-that (31) and-decrees-of-him and-regulations-of-him

בְּנֹתֵינוּ לְעַמֵּי הָאָרֶץ וְאֶת־ בְּנֹתֵיהֶם לֹא נִקַּח

we-will-take not daughters-of-them and the-land to-peoples-of daughters-of-us

לְבָנֵינוּ׃ וְעַמֵּי הָאָרֶץ הַמְבִיאִים אֶת־

*** the-ones-bringing the-land when-peoples-of (32) for-sons-of-us

הַמַּקָּחוֹת וְכָל־ שֶׁבֶר בְּיוֹם הַשַּׁבָּת לִמְכּוֹר לֹא־

not to-sell the-Sabbath on-day-of grain or-any-of the-merchandises

נִקַּח מֵהֶם בַּשַּׁבָּת וּבְיוֹם קֹדֶשׁ וְנִטֹּשׁ

and-we-will-forgo holy or-on-day-of on-the-Sabbath from-them we-will-buy

אֶת־ הַשָּׁנָה הַשְּׁבִיעִית וּמַשָּׁא כָל־ יָד׃ וְהֶעֱמַדְנוּ

and-we-will-assume (33) hand all-of and-debt-of the-seventh the-year ***

עָלֵינוּ מִצְוֹת לָתֵת עָלֵינוּ שְׁלִשִׁית הַשֶּׁקֶל בַּשָּׁנָה לַעֲבֹדַת

for-service-of in-the-year the-shekel third-of of-us to-give commands on-us

---

[15]Bunni, Azgad, Bebai,
[16]Adonijah, Bigvai, Adin,
[17]Ater, Hezekiah, Azzur,
[18]Hodiah, Hashum, Bezai,
[19]Hariph, Anathoth, Nebai,
[20]Magpiash, Meshullam, Hezir,
[21]Meshezabel, Zadok, Jaddua,
[22]Pelatiah, Hanan, Anaiah,
[23]Hoshea, Hananiah, Hasshub,
[24]Hallohesh, Pilha, Shobek,
[25]Rehum, Hashabnah, Maaseiah,
[26]Ahiah, Hanan, Anan,
[27]Malluch, Harim and Baanah.

[28]"The rest of the people—priests, Levites, gatekeepers, singers, temple servants and all who separated themselves from the neighboring peoples for the sake of the Law of God, together with their wives and all their sons and daughters who are able to understand— [29]all these now join their brothers the nobles, and bind themselves with a curse and an oath to follow the Law of God given through Moses the servant of God and to obey carefully all the commands, regulations and decrees of the LORD our God.

[30]"We promise not to give our daughters in marriage to the peoples around us or take their daughters for our sons.

[31]"When the neighboring peoples bring merchandise or grain to sell on the Sabbath, we will not buy from them on the Sabbath or on any holy day. Every seventh year we will forgo working the land and will cancel all debts.

[32]"We assume the responsibility for carrying out the commands to give a third of a shekel[c] each year for the service of the house of

[c]32 That is, about 1/8 ounce (about 4 grams)

*See the note on page 244.

°20 ק נֵיבָי

בֵּית אֱלֹהֵינוּ׃ לְלֶחֶם הַמַּעֲרֶכֶת וּמִנְחַת
house-of God-of-us (34) for-bread-of the-one-set-out and-grain-offering-of

הַתָּמִיד וּלְעוֹלַת הַתָּמִיד הַשַּׁבָּתוֹת הֶחֳדָשִׁים
the-regular and-for-burnt-offering-of the-regular the-Sabbaths the-New-Moons

לַמּוֹעֲדִים וְלַקֳּדָשִׁים וְלַחַטָּאוֹת
for-the-appointed-feasts and-for-the-holy-offerings and-for-the-sin-offerings

לְכַפֵּר עַל־יִשְׂרָאֵל וְכֹל מְלֶאכֶת בֵּית־אֱלֹהֵינוּ׃ וְהַגּוֹרָלוֹת
to-atone for Israel and-all-of duty-of house-of God-of-us (35) and-the-lots

הִפַּלְנוּ עַל־קֻרְבַּן הָעֵצִים הַכֹּהֲנִים הַלְוִיִּם וְהָעָם
we-cast for contribution-of the-woods the-priests the-Levites and-the-people

לְהָבִיא לְבֵית אֱלֹהֵינוּ לְבֵית־אֲבֹתֵינוּ לְעִתִּים
to-bring to-house-of God-of-us by-family-of fathers-of-us at-times

מְזֻמָּנִים שָׁנָה בְשָׁנָה לְבַעֵר עַל־מִזְבַּח יְהוָה אֱלֹהֵינוּ
ones-being-set year by-year to-burn on altar-of Yahweh God-of-us

כַּכָּתוּב בַּתּוֹרָה׃ וּלְהָבִיא אֶת־בִּכּוּרֵי
as-the-thing-being-written in-the-Law (36) and-to-bring *** firstfruits-of

אַדְמָתֵנוּ וּבִכּוּרֵי כָּל־פְּרִי כָּל־עֵץ שָׁנָה בְשָׁנָה
land-of-us and-firstfruits-of every-of fruit-of every-of tree year by-year

לְבֵית יְהוָה׃ וְאֶת־בְּכֹרוֹת בָּנֵינוּ וּבְהֶמְתֵּינוּ
to-house-of Yahweh (37) and ones-firstborn-of sons-of-us and-cattles-of-us

כַּכָּתוּב בַּתּוֹרָה וְאֶת־בְּכוֹרֵי בְקָרֵינוּ
as-the-thing-being-written in-the-Law and ones-firstborn-of herds-of-us

וְצֹאנֵינוּ לְהָבִיא לְבֵית אֱלֹהֵינוּ לַכֹּהֲנִים
and-flocks-of-us to-bring to-house-of God-of-us to-the-priests

הַמְשָׁרְתִים בְּבֵית אֱלֹהֵינוּ׃ וְאֶת־רֵאשִׁית
the-ones-ministering at-house-of God-of-us (38) moreover first-of

עֲרִיסֹתֵינוּ וּתְרוּמֹתֵינוּ וּפְרִי כָּל־עֵץ תִּירוֹשׁ
ground-meals-of-us and-offerings-of-us and-fruit-of all-of tree new-wine

וְיִצְהָר נָבִיא לַכֹּהֲנִים אֶל־לִשְׁכוֹת בֵּית־אֱלֹהֵינוּ
and-oil we-will-bring to-the-priests to storerooms-of house-of God-of-us

וּמַעְשַׂר אַדְמָתֵנוּ לַלְוִיִּם וְהֵם הַלְוִיִּם
and-tithe-of land-of-us to-the-Levites for-they the-Levites

הַמְעַשְּׂרִים בְּכֹל עָרֵי עֲבֹדָתֵנוּ׃ וְהָיָה
the-ones-collecting-tithes in-all-of towns-of work-of-us (39) and-he-must-be

הַכֹּהֵן בֶּן־אַהֲרֹן עִם־הַלְוִיִּם בַּעְשֵׂר
the-priest descendant-of Aaron with the-Levites when-to-receive-tithe

הַלְוִיִּם וְהַלְוִיִּם יַעֲלוּ אֶת־מַעֲשַׂר הַמַּעֲשֵׂר
the-Levites and-the-Levites they-must-bring-up *** tenth-of the-tithe

our God: 33for the bread set
out on the table; for the regular grain offerings and
burnt offerings; for the
offerings on the Sabbaths,
New Moon festivals and
appointed feasts; for the
holy offerings; for sin
offerings to make atone-
ment for Israel; and for all
the duties of the house of
our God.
34"We—the priests, the
Levites and the people—
have cast lots to determine
when each of our families
is to bring to the house of
our God at set times each
year a contribution of
wood to burn on the altar of
the LORD our God, as it is
written in the Law.
35"We also assume
responsibility for bringing
to the house of the LORD
each year the firstfruits of
our crops and of every fruit
tree.
36"As it is also written in
the Law, we will bring the
firstborn of our sons and of
our cattle, of our herds and
of our flocks to the house of
our God, to the priests ministering there.
37"Moreover, we will
bring to the storerooms of
the house of our God, to the
priests, the first of our
ground meal, of our ⌞grain⌟
offerings, of the fruit of all
our trees and of our new
wine and oil. And we will
bring a tithe of our crops to
the Levites, for it is the Levites who collect the tithes
in all the towns where we
work. 38A priest descended
from Aaron is to accom-
pany the Levites when they
receive the tithes, and the
Levites are to bring a tenth
of the tithes up to the house

*See the note on page 244.

לְבֵית אֱלֹהֵינוּ אֶל־הַלְּשָׁכוֹת לְבֵית הָאוֹצָר׃ כִּי

for (40) the-treasury of-house-of the-storerooms to God-of-us to-house-of

אֶל־הַלְּשָׁכוֹת יָבִיאוּ בְנֵי־יִשְׂרָאֵל וּבְנֵי הַלֵּוִי

the-Levite and-people-of Israel people-of they-must-bring the-storerooms to

אֶת־תְּרוּמַת הַדָּגָן הַתִּירוֹשׁ וְהַיִּצְהָר וְשָׁם כְּלֵי

articles-of and-there and-the-oil the-new-wine the-grain contribution-of ***

הַמִּקְדָּשׁ וְהַכֹּהֲנִים הַמְשָׁרְתִים וְהַשּׁוֹעֲרִים

and-the-gatekeepers the-ones-ministering and-the-priests the-sanctuary

וְהַמְשֹׁרְרִים וְלֹא נַעֲזֹב אֶת־בֵּית אֱלֹהֵינוּ׃

God-of-us house-of *** we-will-neglect and-not and-the-ones-singing

וַיֵּשְׁבוּ שָׂרֵי־הָעָם בִּירוּשָׁלִָם וּשְׁאָר

and-rest-of in-Jerusalem the-people leaders-of now-they-settled (11:1)

הָעָם הִפִּילוּ גוֹרָלוֹת לְהָבִיא ׀ אֶחָד מִן־הָעֲשָׂרָה לָשֶׁבֶת בִּירוּשָׁלִַם

in-Jerusalem to-live the-ten of one to-bring lots they-cast the-people

עִיר הַקֹּדֶשׁ וְתֵשַׁע הַיָּדוֹת בֶּעָרִים׃ וַיְבָרְכוּ

and-they-commended (2) in-the-towns the-others and-nine the-holy city-of

הָעָם לְכֹל הָאֲנָשִׁים הַמִּתְנַדְּבִים לָשֶׁבֶת בִּירוּשָׁלִָם׃

in-Jerusalem to-live the-ones-volunteering the-men to-all-of the-people

וְאֵלֶּה רָאשֵׁי הַמְּדִינָה אֲשֶׁר יָשְׁבוּ בִּירוּשָׁלִָם

in-Jerusalem they-settled who the-province leaders-of and-these (3)

וּבְעָרֵי יְהוּדָה יָשְׁבוּ אִישׁ בַּאֲחֻזָּתוֹ בְּעָרֵיהֶם

in-towns-of-them on-property-of-him each they-lived Judah now-in-towns-of

יִשְׂרָאֵל הַכֹּהֲנִים וְהַלְוִיִּם וְהַנְּתִינִים וּבְנֵי

and-descendants-of and-the-temple-servants and-the-Levites the-priests Israel

עַבְדֵי שְׁלֹמֹה׃ וּבִירוּשָׁלִַם יָשְׁבוּ מִבְּנֵי יְהוּדָה

Judah from-people-of they-lived while-in-Jerusalem (4) Solomon servants-of

וּמִבְּנֵי בִנְיָמִן מִבְּנֵי יְהוּדָה עֲתָיָה בֶן־עֻזִּיָּה

Uzziah son-of Athaiah Judah from-descendants-of Benjamin and-from-people-of

בֶּן־זְכַרְיָה בֶן־אֲמַרְיָה בֶן־שְׁפַטְיָה בֶן־מַהֲלַלְאֵל

Mahalalel son-of Shephatiah son-of Amariah son-of Zechariah son-of

מִבְּנֵי־פָרֶץ׃ וּמַעֲשֵׂיָה בֶן־בָּרוּךְ בֶּן־כָּל־חֹזֶה בֶּן־

son-of Hozeh Col son-of Baruch son-of and-Maaseiah (5) Perez from-descendants-of

חֲזָיָה בֶן־עֲדָיָה בֶן־יוֹיָרִיב בֶּן־זְכַרְיָה בֶּן־הַשִּׁלֹנִי׃

the-Shilonite descendant-of Zechariah son-of Joiarib son-of Adaiah son-of Hazaiah

כָּל־בְּנֵי־פֶרֶץ הַיֹּשְׁבִים בִּירוּשָׁלִָם אַרְבַּע

four-of in-Jerusalem the-ones-living Perez descendants-of total-of (6)

מֵאוֹת שִׁשִּׁים וּשְׁמֹנָה אַנְשֵׁי־חָיִל׃ וְאֵלֶּה בְּנֵי בִנְיָמִן

Benjamin descendants-of and-these (7) bravery men-of and-eight sixty hundreds

of our God, to the storerooms of the treasury. [39]The people of Israel, including the Levites, are to bring their contributions of grain, new wine and oil to the storerooms where the articles for the sanctuary are kept and where the ministering priests, the gatekeepers and the singers stay.

"We will not neglect the house of our God."

The New Residents of Jerusalem

11 Now the leaders of the people settled in Jerusalem, and the rest of the people cast lots to bring one out of every ten to live in Jerusalem, the holy city, while the remaining nine were to stay in their own towns. [2]The people commended all the men who volunteered to live in Jerusalem.

[3]These are the provincial leaders who settled in Jerusalem (now some Israelites, priests, Levites, temple servants and descendants of Solomon's servants lived in the towns of Judah, each on his own property in the various towns, [4]while other people from both Judah and Benjamin lived in Jerusalem):

From the descendants of Judah:

Athaiah son of Uzziah, the son of Zechariah, the son of Amariah, the son of Shephatiah, the son of Mahalalel, a descendant of Perez; [5]and Maaseiah son of Baruch, the son of Col-Hozeh, the son of Hazaiah, the son of Adaiah, the son of Joiarib, the son of Zechariah, a descendant of Shelah. [6]The descendants of Perez who lived in Jerusalem totaled 468 brave men.

[7]From the descendants of Benjamin:

*See the note on page 244.

סַלֻּא בֶּן־ מְשֻׁלָּם בֶּן־ יוֹעֵד בֶּן־ פְּדָיָה בֶּן־ קוֹלָיָה בֶּן־

son-of Kolaiah son-of Pedaiah son-of Joed son-of Meshullam son-of Sallu

מַעֲשֵׂיָה בֶּן־ אִיתִיאֵל בֶּן־ יְשַׁעְיָה׃ וְאַחֲרָיו גַּבַּי סַלָּי

Sallai Gabbai and-after-him (8) Jeshaiah son-of Ithiel son-of Maaseiah

תְּשַׁע מֵאוֹת עֶשְׂרִים וּשְׁמֹנָה׃ וְיוֹאֵל בֶּן־ זִכְרִי פָּקִיד

chief-officer Zicri son-of and-Joel (9) and-eight twenty hundreds nine-of

עֲלֵיהֶם וִיהוּדָה בֶן־ הַסְּנוּאָה עַל־ הָעִיר מִשְׁנֶה׃ מִן־

from (10) Second-District the-city over Hassenuah son-of and-Judah over-them

הַכֹּהֲנִים יְדַעְיָה בֶן־ יוֹיָרִיב יָכִין׃ שְׂרָיָה בֶן־ חִלְקִיָּה בֶּן־

son-of Hilkiah son-of Seraiah (11) Jakin Joiarib son-of Jedaiah the-priests

מְשֻׁלָּם בֶּן־ צָדוֹק בֶּן־ מְרָיוֹת בֶּן־ אֲחִיטוּב נְגִד בֵּית

house-of supervisor-of Ahitub son-of Meraioth son-of Zadok son-of Meshullam

הָאֱלֹהִים׃ וַאֲחֵיהֶם עֹשֵׂי הַמְּלָאכָה

the-work ones-carrying-on-of and-associates-of-them (12) the-God

לַבַּיִת שְׁמֹנֶה מֵאוֹת עֶשְׂרִים וּשְׁנָיִם וַעֲדָיָה בֶּן־ יְרֹחָם

Jeroham son-of and-Adaiah and-two twenty hundreds eight-of for-the-temple

בֶּן־ פְּלַלְיָה בֶּן־ אַמְצִי בֶן־ זְכַרְיָה בֶן־ פַּשְׁחוּר בֶּן־ מַלְכִּיָּה׃

Malkijah son-of Pashhur son-of Zechariah son-of Amzi son-of Pelaliah son-of

וְאֶחָיו רָאשִׁים לְאָבוֹת מָאתַיִם אַרְבָּעִים וּשְׁנָיִם

and-two forty two-hundreds of-fathers heads and-associates-of-him (13)

וַעֲמַשְׁסַי בֶן־ עֲזַרְאֵל בֶּן־ אַחְזַי בֶּן־ מְשִׁלֵּמוֹת בֶּן־ אִמֵּר׃

Immer son-of Meshillemoth son-of Ahzai son-of Azarel son-of and-Amashsai

וַאֲחֵיהֶם גִּבֹּרֵי חַיִל מֵאָה עֶשְׂרִים וּשְׁמֹנָה

and-eight twenty hundred bravery warriors-of and-associates-of-them (14)

וּפָקִיד עֲלֵיהֶם זַבְדִּיאֵל בֶּן־ הַגְּדוֹלִים׃ וּמִן־

and-from (15) Haggedolim son-of Zabdiel over-them and-chief-officer

הַלְוִיִּם שְׁמַעְיָה בֶן־ חַשּׁוּב בֶּן־ עַזְרִיקָם בֶּן־ חֲשַׁבְיָה בֶּן־

son-of Hashabiah son-of Azrikam son-of Hasshub son-of Shemaiah the-Levites

בּוּנִּי׃ וְשַׁבְּתַי וְיוֹזָבָד עַל־ הַמְּלָאכָה הַחִיצֹנָה לְבֵית

of-house-of the-outside the-work over and-Jozabad and-Shabbethai (16) Bunni

הָאֱלֹהִים מֵרָאשֵׁי הַלְוִיִּם׃ וּמַתַּנְיָה בֶן־ מִיכָה בֶּן־ זַבְדִּי

Zabdi son-of Mica son-of and-Mattaniah (17) the-Levites from-heads-of the-God

בֶן־ אָסָף רֹאשׁ הַתְּחִלָּה יְהוֹדֶה לַתְּפִלָּה וּבַקְבֻּקְיָה

and-Bakbukiah to-the-prayer he-led the-thanksgiving director-of Asaph son-of

מִשְׁנֶה מֵאֶחָיו וְעַבְדָּא בֶּן־ שַׁמּוּעַ בֶּן־ גָּלָל בֶּן־

son-of Galal son-of Shammua son-of and-Abda among-associates-of-him second

יְדִיתוּן׃ כָּל־ הַלְוִיִּם בְּעִיר הַקֹּדֶשׁ מָאתַיִם שְׁמֹנִים

eighty two-hundreds the-holy in-city-of the-Levites total-of (18) Jeduthun

Sallu son of Meshullam, the son of Joed, the son of Pedaiah, the son of Kolaiah, the son of Maaseiah, the son of Ithiel, the son of Jeshaiah, [8]and his followers, Gabbai and Sallai—928 men. [9]Joel son of Zicri was their chief officer, and Judah son of Hassenuah was over the Second District of the city.

[10]From the priests:

Jedaiah; the son[d] of Joiarib; Jakin; [11]Seraiah son of Hilkiah, the son of Meshullam, the son of Zadok, the son of Meraioth, the son of Ahitub, supervisor in the house of God, [12]and their associates, who carried on work for the temple—822 men; Adaiah son of Jeroham, the son of Pelaliah, the son of Amzi, the son of Zechariah, the son of Pashhur, the son of Malkijah, [13]and his associates, who were heads of families—242 men; Amashsai son of Azarel, the son of Ahzai, the son of Meshillemoth, the son of Immer, [14]and his[e] associates, who were brave warriors—128 men. Their chief officer was Zabdiel son of Haggedolim.

[15]From the Levites:

Shemaiah son of Hasshub, the son of Azrikam, the son of Hashabiah, the son of Bunni; [16]Shabbethai and Jozabad, two of the heads of the Levites, who had charge of the outside work of the house of God; [17]Mattaniah son of Mica, the son of Zabdi, the son of Asaph, the director who led in thanksgiving and prayer; Bakbukiah, second among his associates; and Abda son of Shammua, the son of Galal, the son of Jeduthun. [18]The Levites in the holy city totaled 284.

[d]10 Or *Jedaiah*
[e]14 Most Septuagint manuscripts; Hebrew *their*

°17 ק ידותון

וְאַרְבָּעָה: וְהַשּׁוֹעֲרִים֙ עַקּוּב טַלְמ֤וֹן וַאֲחֵיהֶ֖ם
and-associates-of-them — Talmon — Akkub — and-the-gatekeepers — (19) — and-four

הַשֹּׁמְרִים֙ בַּשְּׁעָרִ֔ים מֵאָ֖ה שִׁבְעִ֣ים וּשְׁנָ֑יִם: וּשְׁאָ֣ר
and-rest-of — (20) — and-two — seventy — hundred — at-the-gates — the-ones-watching

יִשְׂרָאֵ֤ל הַכֹּֽהֲנִים֙ הַלְוִיִּ֔ם בְּכָל־ עָרֵ֖י יְהוּדָ֑ה אִ֕ישׁ
each — Judah — towns-of — in-all-of — the-Levites — the-priests — Israel

בְּנַחֲלָת֑וֹ: וְהַנְּתִינִ֗ים יֹֽשְׁבִ֖ים בָּעֹ֑פֶל
on-the-Ophel — ones-living — and-the-temple-servants — (21) — on-property-of-him

וְצִיחָ֥א וְגִשְׁפָּ֖א עַל־ הַנְּתִינִ֑ים: וּפְקִ֣יד
and-chief-officer-of — (22) — the-temple-servants — over — and-Gishpa — and-Ziha

הַלְוִיִּם֙ בִּירוּשָׁלִַ֔ם עֻזִּ֤י בֶן־ בָּנִ֣י בֶן־ חֲשַׁבְיָ֔ה בֶּן־ מַתַּנְיָ֖ה
Mattaniah — son-of — Hashabiah — son-of — Bani — son-of — Uzzi — in-Jerusalem — the-Levites

בֶּן־ מִיכָ֑א מִבְּנֵ֤י אָסָף֙ הַמְשֹׁרְרִ֔ים לְנֶ֖גֶד מְלֶ֣אכֶת
service-of — in-front-of — the-ones-singing — Asaph — from-descendants-of — Mica — son-of

בֵּית־ הָאֱלֹהִ֑ים: כִּֽי־ מִצְוַ֤ת הַמֶּ֙לֶךְ֙ עֲלֵיהֶ֔ם וַאֲמָנָ֛ה
and-regulation — over-them — the-king — order-of — indeed — (23) — the-God — house-of

עַל־ הַמְשֹׁרְרִ֖ים דְּבַר־ יֹ֣ום בְּיֹומֹ֑ו: וּפְתַֽחְיָ֨ה בֶן־
son-of — and-Pethahiah — (24) — in-day-of-him — day — activity-of — the-ones-singing — for

מְשֵׁיזַבְאֵ֜ל מִבְּנֵי־ זֶ֣רַח בֶּן־ יְהוּדָ֗ה לְיַ֤ד הַמֶּ֙לֶךְ֙ לְכָל־
in-all-of — the-king — at-hand-of — Judah — son-of — Zerah — of-descendants-of — Meshezabel

דְּבַ֖ר לָעָֽם: וְאֶל־ הַחֲצֵרִ֖ים בִּשְׂדֹתָ֑ם
with-fields-of-them — the-villages — and-for — (25) — of-the-people — affair

מִבְּנֵ֣י יְהוּדָ֗ה יָֽשְׁבוּ֙ בְּקִרְיַ֣ת הָֽאַרְבַּ֔ע וּבְנֹתֶ֖יהָ
and-settlements-of-her — the-Arba — in-Kiriath — they-lived — Judah — from-people-of

וּבְדִיבֹן֙ וּבְנֹתֶ֔יהָ וּבִֽיקַבְצְאֵ֖ל וַחֲצֵרֶֽיהָ:
and-villages-of-her — and-in-Jekabzeel — and-settlements-of-her — and-in-Dibon

וּבְיֵשׁ֥וּעַ וּבְמוֹלָדָ֖ה וּבְבֵ֣ית פָּ֑לֶט וּבַחֲצַ֥ר שׁוּעָ֖ל
Shual — and-in-Hazar — (27) — Pelet — and-in-Beth — and-in-Moladah — and-in-Jeshua — (26)

וּבִבְאֵ֥ר שֶׁ֖בַע וּבְנֹתֶֽיהָ: וּבְצִֽקְלַ֖ג וּבִמְכֹנָ֥ה
and-in-Meconah — and-in-Ziklag — (28) — and-settlements-of-her — Sheba — and-in-Beer

וּבְנֹתֶֽיהָ: וּבְעֵ֥ין רִמֹּ֖ון וּבְצָרְעָ֖ה וּבְיַרְמֽוּת:
and-in-Jarmuth — and-in-Zorah — Rimmon — and-in-En — (29) — and-in-settlements-of-her

זָנֹ֤חַ עֲדֻלָּם֙ וְחַצְרֵיהֶ֔ם לָכִ֖ישׁ וּשְׂדֹתֶ֑יהָ עֲזֵקָ֖ה
Azekah — and-fields-of-her — Lachish — and-villages-of-them — Adullam — Zanoah — (30)

וּבְנֹתֶ֑יהָ וַיַּחֲנ֥וּ מִבְּאֵֽר־ שֶׁ֖בַע עַד־ גֵּֽיא־ הִנֹּֽם:
Hinnom — Valley-of — to — Sheba — from-Beer — so-they-lived — and-settlements-of-her

וּבְנֵ֥י בִנְיָמִ֖ן מִגֶּ֑בַע מִכְמָ֥שׂ וְעַיָּ֖ה וּבֵֽית־ אֵ֑ל
El — and-Beth — and-Aija — Micmash — from-Geba — Benjamin — and-descendants-of — (31)

[19]The gatekeepers:

Akkub, Talmon and their associates, who kept watch at the gates—172 men.

[20]The rest of the Israelites, with the priests and Levites, were in all the towns of Judah, each on his ancestral property. [21]The temple servants lived on the hill of Ophel, and Ziha and Gishpa were in charge of them.

[22]The chief officer of the Levites in Jerusalem was Uzzi son of Bani, the son of Hashabiah, the son of Mattaniah, the son of Mica. Uzzi was one of Asaph's descendants, who were the singers responsible for the service of the house of God. [23]The singers were under the king's orders, which regulated their daily activity.

[24]Pethahiah son of Meshezabel, one of the descendants of Zerah son of Judah, was the king's agent in all affairs relating to the people.

[25]As for the villages with their fields, some of the people of Judah lived in Kiriath Arba and its surrounding settlements, in Dibon and its settlements, in Jekabzeel and its villages, [26]in Jeshua, in Moladah, in Beth Pelet, [27]in Hazar Shual, in Beersheba and its settlements, [28]in Ziklag, in Meconah and its settlements, [29]in En Rimmon, in Zorah, in Jarmuth, [30]Zanoah, Adullam and their villages, in Lachish and its fields, and in Azekah and its settlements. So they were living all the way from Beersheba to the Valley of Hinnom.

[31]The descendants of the Benjamites from Geba lived in Micmash, Aija, Bethel and its

וּבְנֹתֶיהָ׃ עֲנָתוֹת נֹב עֲנָנְיָה׃ חָצוֹר ׀ רָמָה גִּתָּיִם׃
Gittaim Ramah Hazor (33) Ananiah Nob Anathoth (32) and-settlements-of-her

חָדִיד צְבֹעִים נְבַלָּט׃ לֹד וְאוֹנוֹ גֵּי הַחֲרָשִׁים׃
the-Craftsmen Valley-of and-Ono Lod (35) Neballat Zeboim Hadid (34)

וּמִן־ הַלְוִיִּם מַחְלְקוֹת יְהוּדָה לְבִנְיָמִין׃ וְאֵלֶּה
and-these (12:1) in-Benjamin Judah divisions-of the-Levites and-of (36)

הַכֹּהֲנִים וְהַלְוִיִּם אֲשֶׁר עָלוּ עִם־ זְרֻבָּבֶל בֶּן־
son-of Zerubbabel with they-returned who and-the-Levites the-priests

שְׁאַלְתִּיאֵל וְיֵשׁוּעַ שְׂרָיָה יִרְמְיָה עֶזְרָא׃ אֲמַרְיָה מַלּוּךְ חַטּוּשׁ׃
Hattush Malluch Amariah (2) Ezra Jeremiah Seraiah and-Jeshua Shealtiel

שְׁכַנְיָה רְחֻם מְרֵמֹת׃ עִדּוֹא גִנְּתוֹי אֲבִיָּה׃ מִיָּמִין מַעַדְיָה
Maadiah Mijamin (5) Abijah Ginnethoi Iddo (4) Meremoth Rehum Shecaniah (3)

בִּלְגָּה׃ שְׁמַעְיָה וְיוֹיָרִיב יְדַעְיָה׃ סַלּוּ עָמוֹק חִלְקִיָּה יְדַעְיָה
Jedaiah Hilkiah Amok Sallu (7) Jedaiah and-Joiarib Shemaiah (6) Bilgah

אֵלֶּה רָאשֵׁי הַכֹּהֲנִים וַאֲחֵיהֶם בִּימֵי יֵשׁוּעַ׃
Jeshua in-days-of and-associates-of-them the-priests leaders-of these

וְהַלְוִיִּם יֵשׁוּעַ בִּנּוּי קַדְמִיאֵל שֵׁרֵבְיָה יְהוּדָה מַתַּנְיָה עַל־
over Mattaniah Judah Sherebiah Kadmiel Binnui Jeshua and-the-Levites (8)

הֻיְּדוֹת הוּא וְאֶחָיו׃ וּבַקְבֻּקְיָה וְעֻנּוֹ
and-Unni and-Bakbukiah (9) and-associates-of-him he songs-of-thanksgiving

אֲחֵיהֶם לְנֶגְדָּם לְמִשְׁמָרוֹת׃ וְיֵשׁוּעַ הוֹלִיד
he-fathered and-Jeshua (10) in-services at-opposite-them associates-of-them

אֶת־ יוֹיָקִים וְיוֹיָקִים הוֹלִיד אֶת־ אֶלְיָשִׁיב וְאֶלְיָשִׁיב אֶת־יוֹיָדָע׃
Joiada *** and-Eliashib Eliashib *** he-fathered and-Joiakim Joiakim ***

וְיוֹיָדָע הוֹלִיד אֶת־ יוֹנָתָן וְיוֹנָתָן הוֹלִיד אֶת־ יַדּוּעַ׃
Jaddua *** he-fathered and-Jonathan Jonathan *** he-fathered and-Joiada (11)

וּבִימֵי יוֹיָקִים הָיוּ כֹהֲנִים רָאשֵׁי הָאָבוֹת לִשְׂרָיָה
of-Seraiah the-fathers heads-of priests they-were Joiakim and-in-days-of (12)

מְרָיָה לְיִרְמְיָה חֲנַנְיָה׃ לְעֶזְרָא מְשֻׁלָּם לַאֲמַרְיָה יְהוֹחָנָן׃
Jehohanan of-Amariah Meshullam of-Ezra (13) Hananiah of-Jeremiah Meraiah

לִמְלוּכִי יוֹנָתָן לִשְׁבַנְיָה יוֹסֵף׃ לְחָרִם עַדְנָא לִמְרָיוֹת
of-Meraioth Adna of-Harim (15) Joseph of-Shebaniah Jonathan of-Malluch (14)

חֶלְקָי׃ לְעִדְּיא זְכַרְיָה לְגִנְּתוֹן מְשֻׁלָּם׃ לַאֲבִיָּה זִכְרִי
Zicri of-Abijah (17) Meshullam of-Ginnethon Zechariah of-Iddo (16) Helkai

לְמִנְיָמִין לְמוֹעַדְיָה פִּלְטָי׃ לְבִלְגָּה שַׁמּוּעַ לִשְׁמַעְיָה יְהוֹנָתָן׃
Jehonathan of-Shemaiah Shammua of-Bilgah (18) Piltai of-Maadiah of-Miniamin

וּלְיוֹיָרִיב מַתְּנַי לִידַעְיָה עֻזִּי׃ לְסַלַּי קַלָּי לְעָמוֹק
of-Amok Kallai of-Sallu (20) Uzzi of-Jedaiah Mattenai and-of-Joiarib (19)

settlements, 32 in Anathoth,
Nob and Ananiah, 33 in Hazor,
Ramah and Gittaim, 34 in Hadid, Zeboim and Neballat, 35 in
Lod and Ono, and in the Valley of the Craftsmen.
36 Some of the divisions of
the Levites of Judah settled in
Benjamin.

Priests and Levites

12 These were the priests
and Levites who re-
turned with Zerubbabel son of
Shealtiel and with Jeshua:
Seraiah, Jeremiah, Ezra,
2 Amariah, Malluch, Hat-
tush,
3 Shecaniah, Rehum, Mere-
moth,
4 Iddo, Ginnethon,[f] Abijah,
5 Mijamin, Maadiah, Bilgah,
6 Shemaiah, Joiarib, Jedaiah,
7 Sallu, Amok, Hilkiah and
Jedaiah.
These were the leaders of the
priests and their associates in
the days of Jeshua.
8 The Levites were Jeshua,
Binnui, Kadmiel, Sherebiah,
Judah, and also Mattaniah,
who, together with his associates, was in charge of the
songs of thanksgiving. 9 Bakbukiah and Unni, their associates, stood opposite them in
the services.
10 Jeshua was the father of
Joiakim, Joiakim the father of
Eliashib, Eliashib the father of
Joiada, 11 Joiada the father of
Jonathan, and Jonathan the
father of Jaddua.
12 In the days of Joiakim,
these were the heads of the
priestly families:
of Seraiah's family, Me-
raiah;
of Jeremiah's, Hananiah;
13 of Ezra's, Meshullam;
of Amariah's, Jehohanan;
14 of Malluch's, Jonathan;
of Shecaniah's,[g] Joseph;
15 of Harim's, Adna;
of Meremoth's,[h] Helkai;
16 of Iddo's, Zechariah;
of Ginnethon's, Meshul-
lam;
17 of Abijah's, Zicri;
of Miniamin's and of Maa-
diah's, Piltai;
18 of Bilgah's, Shammua;
of Shemaiah's, Jehonathan;
19 of Joiarib's, Mattenai;
of Jedaiah's, Uzzi;
20 of Sallu's, Kallai;

[f] 4 Many Hebrew manuscripts and Vulgate (see also Neh. 12:16); most Hebrew manuscripts *Ginnethoi*
[g] 14 Very many Hebrew manuscripts, some Septuagint manuscripts and Syriac (see also Neh. 12:3); most Hebrew manuscripts *Shebaniah's*
[h] 15 Some Septuagint manuscripts (see also Neh. 12:3); Hebrew *Meraioth's*

°9 ק ועני , °14 ק למליכו
°16 ק לעדוא

עֵבֶר׃ לְחִלְקִיָּה חֲשַׁבְיָה לִידַעְיָה נְתַנְאֵל׃ הַלְוִיִּם

the-Levites (22) Nethanel of-Jedaiah Hashabiah of-Hilkiah (21) Eber

בִּימֵי אֶלְיָשִׁיב יוֹיָדָע וְיוֹחָנָן וְיַדּוּעַ כְּתוּבִים

ones-being-recorded and-Jaddua and-Johanan Joiada Eliashib in-days-of

רָאשֵׁי אָבוֹת וְהַכֹּהֲנִים עַל־מַלְכוּת דָּרְיָוֶשׁ הַפָּרְסִי׃

the-Persian Darius reign-of in and-the-priests fathers heads-of

בְּנֵי לֵוִי רָאשֵׁי הָאָבוֹת כְּתוּבִים עַל־סֵפֶר

book-of in ones-being-recorded the-fathers heads-of Levi descendants-of (23)

דִּבְרֵי הַיָּמִים וְעַד־יְמֵי יוֹחָנָן בֶּן־אֶלְיָשִׁיב׃

Eliashib son-of Johanan days-of and-up-to the-days annals-of

וְרָאשֵׁי הַלְוִיִּם חֲשַׁבְיָה שֵׁרֵבְיָה וְיֵשׁוּעַ בֶּן־קַדְמִיאֵל

Kadmiel son-of and-Jeshua Sherebiah Hashabiah the-Levites and-leaders-of (24)

וַאֲחֵיהֶם לְנֶגְדָּם לְהַלֵּל לְהוֹדוֹת

to-give-thanks to-give-praise at-opposite-them and-associates-of-them

בְּמִצְוַת דָּוִיד אִישׁ־הָאֱלֹהִים מִשְׁמָר לְעֻמַּת מִשְׁמָר׃

section responding-to section the-God man-of David as-prescription-of

מַתַּנְיָה וּבַקְבֻּקְיָה עֹבַדְיָה מְשֻׁלָּם טַלְמוֹן עַקּוּב שֹׁמְרִים

ones-guarding Akkub Talmon Meshullam Obadiah and-Bakbukiah Mattaniah (25)

שׁוֹעֲרִים מִשְׁמָר בַּאֲסֻפֵּי הַשְּׁעָרִים׃ אֵלֶּה בִּימֵי יוֹיָקִים

Joiakim in-days-of these (26) the-gates over-storerooms-of guard gatekeepers

בֶּן־יֵשׁוּעַ בֶּן־יוֹצָדָק וּבִימֵי נְחֶמְיָה הַפֶּחָה וְעֶזְרָא

and-Ezra the-governor Nehemiah and-in-days-of Jozadak son-of Jeshua son-of

הַכֹּהֵן הַסּוֹפֵר׃ וּבַחֲנֻכַּת חוֹמַת יְרוּשָׁלַםִ בִּקְשׁוּ

they-sought Jerusalem wall-of and-at-dedication-of (27) the-scribe the-priest

אֶת־הַלְוִיִּם מִכָּל־מְקוֹמֹתָם לַהֲבִיאָם לִירוּשָׁלָםִ

to-Jerusalem to-bring-them dwellings-of-them from-all-of the-Levites ***

לַעֲשֹׂת חֲנֻכָּה וְשִׂמְחָה וּבְתוֹדוֹת וּבְשִׁיר

and-with-music and-with-songs-of-thanksgiving and-joy dedication to-celebrate

מְצִלְתַּיִם נְבָלִים וּבְכִנֹּרוֹת׃ וַיֵּאָסְפוּ בְּנֵי

sons-of and-they-were-brought-together (28) and-with-lyres harps cymbals

הַמְשֹׁרְרִים וּמִן־הַכִּכָּר סְבִיבוֹת יְרוּשָׁלִַם וּמִן־

and-from Jerusalem ones-around-of the-region and-from the-ones-singing

חַצְרֵי נְטֹפָתִי׃ וּמִבֵּית הַגִּלְגָּל וּמִשְּׂדוֹת

and-from-areas-of the-Gilgal and-from-Beth (29) Netophathite villages-of

גֶּבַע וְעַזְמָוֶת כִּי חֲצֵרִים בָּנוּ לָהֶם הַמְשֹׁרְרִים

the-ones-singing for-them they-built villages for and-Azmaveth Geba

סְבִיבוֹת יְרוּשָׁלִָם׃ וַיִּטַּהֲרוּ הַכֹּהֲנִים

the-priests when-they-purified-themselves (30) Jerusalem ones-around-of

of Amok's, Eber;
21 of Hilkiah's, Hashabiah;
of Jedaiah's, Nethanel.
22 The family heads of the Levites in the days of Eliashib,
Joiada, Johanan and Jaddua,
as well as those of the priests,
were recorded in the reign of
Darius the Persian. 23 The
family heads among the descendants of Levi up to the
time of Johanan son of Eliashib were recorded in the
book of the annals. 24 And the
leaders of the Levites were
Hashabiah, Sherebiah, Jeshua
son of Kadmiel, and their associates, who stood opposite
them to give praise and
thanksgiving, one section re-
sponding to the other, as prescribed by David the man of
God.
25 Mattaniah, Bakbukiah,
Obadiah, Meshullam, Talmon
and Akkub were gatekeepers
who guarded the storerooms
at the gates. 26 They served in
the days of Joiakim son of
Jeshua, the son of Jozadak,
and in the days of Nehemiah
the governor and of Ezra the
priest and scribe.

Dedication of the Wall of Jerusalem

27 At the dedication of the
wall of Jerusalem, the Levites
were sought out from where
they lived and were brought to
Jerusalem to celebrate joyfully
the dedication with songs of
thanksgiving and with the
music of cymbals, harps and
lyres. 28 The singers also were
brought together from the region around Jerusalem—from
the villages of the Netophathites, 29 from Beth Gilgal, and
from the area of Geba and Azmaveth, for the singers had
built villages for themselves
around Jerusalem. 30 When the
priests and Levites had

וְהַלְוִיִּם וַיְטַהֲרוּ אֶת־ הָעָם וְאֶת־ הַשְּׁעָרִים וְאֶת־
and the-gates and the-people *** then-they-purified and-the-Levites

הַחוֹמָה׃ וָאַעֲלֶה אֶת־ שָׂרֵי יְהוּדָה מֵעַל לַחוֹמָה
of-the-wall on-top Judah leaders-of *** and-I-made-go-up (31) the-wall

וָאַעֲמִידָה שְׁתֵּי תוֹדֹת גְּדוֹלֹת וְתַהֲלֻכֹת לַיָּמִין מֵעַל
on-top to-the-right and-processions large-ones choirs two-of also-I-assigned

לַחוֹמָה לְשַׁעַר הָאַשְׁפֹּת׃ וַיֵּלֶךְ אַחֲרֵיהֶם הוֹשַׁעְיָה
Hoshaiah after-them and-he-followed (32) the-Dungs toward-Gate-of of-the-wall

וַחֲצִי שָׂרֵי יְהוּדָה׃ וַעֲזַרְיָה עֶזְרָא וּמְשֻׁלָּם׃ יְהוּדָה
Judah (34) and-Meshullam Ezra with-Azariah (33) Judah leaders-of and-half-of

וּבִנְיָמִן וּשְׁמַעְיָה וְיִרְמְיָה׃ וּמִבְּנֵי הַכֹּהֲנִים
the-priests and-from-sons-of (35) and-Jeremiah and-Shemaiah and-Benjamin

בַּחֲצֹצְרוֹת זְכַרְיָה בֶן־ יוֹנָתָן בֶּן־ שְׁמַעְיָה בֶּן־ מַתַּנְיָה
Mattaniah son-of Shemaiah son-of Jonathan son-of Zechariah with-trumpets

בֶּן־ מִיכָיָה בֶּן־ זַכּוּר בֶּן־ אָסָף׃ וְאֶחָיו שְׁמַעְיָה
Shemaiah and-associates-of-him (36) Asaph son-of Zaccur son-of Micaiah son-of

וַעֲזַרְאֵל מִלֲלַי גִּלֲלַי מָעַי נְתַנְאֵל וִיהוּדָה חֲנָנִי בִּכְלֵי־
with-instruments-of Hanani and-Judah Nethanel Maai Gilalai Milalai and-Azarel

שִׁיר דָּוִיד אִישׁ הָאֱלֹהִים וְעֶזְרָא הַסּוֹפֵר לִפְנֵיהֶם׃ וְעַל
and-at (37) before-them the-scribe and-Ezra the-God man-of David music-of

שַׁעַר הָעַיִן וְנֶגְדָּם עָלוּ עַל־ מַעֲלוֹת עִיר דָּוִיד
David City-of steps-of on they-went-up and-before-them the-Fountain Gate-of

בַּמַּעֲלֶה לַחוֹמָה מֵעַל לְבֵית דָּוִיד וְעַד שַׁעַר
Gate-of and-to David of-house-of at-above to-the-wall on-the-ascent

הַמַּיִם מִזְרָח׃ וְהַתּוֹדָה הַשֵּׁנִית הַהוֹלֶכֶת לְמוֹאל
in-opposite the-one-proceeding the-second and-the-choir (38) east the-Waters

וַאֲנִי אַחֲרֶיהָ וַחֲצִי הָעָם מֵעַל לְהַחוֹמָה מֵעַל
to-past of-the-wall on-top the-people with-half-of after-her and-I

לְמִגְדַּל הַתַּנּוּרִים וְעַד הַחוֹמָה הָרְחָבָה׃ וּמֵעַל לְשַׁעַר־
to-Gate-of and-to-over (39) the-Broad the-Wall and-to the-Ovens to-Tower-of

אֶפְרַיִם וְעַל־ שַׁעַר הַיְשָׁנָה וְעַל־ שַׁעַר הַדָּגִים וּמִגְדַּל
and-Tower-of the-Fishes Gate-of and-over the-Jeshanah Gate-of and-over Ephraim

חֲנַנְאֵל וּמִגְדַּל הַמֵּאָה וְעַד שַׁעַר הַצֹּאן
the-Sheep Gate-of and-as-far-as the-Hundred and-Tower-of Hananel

וְעָמְדוּ בְּשַׁעַר הַמַּטָּרָה׃ וַתַּעֲמֹדְנָה שְׁתֵּי
two-of then-they-took-places (40) the-Guard at-Gate-of and-they-stopped

הַתּוֹדֹת בְּבֵית הָאֱלֹהִים וַאֲנִי וַחֲצִי הַסְּגָנִים עִמִּי׃
with-me the-officials and-half-of and-I the-God in-house-of the-choirs

purified themselves ceremonially, they purified the people,
the gates and the wall.
31I had the leaders of Judah
go up on top[i] of the wall. I also
assigned two large choirs to
give thanks. One was to proceed on top[j] of the wall to the
right, toward the Dung Gate.
32Hoshaiah and half the leaders of Judah followed them,
33along with Azariah, Ezra,
Meshullam, 34Judah, Benjamin, Shemaiah, Jeremiah, as
well 35as some priests with
trumpets, and also Zechariah
son of Jonathan, the son of
Shemaiah, the son of Mat-
taniah, the son of Micaiah, the
son of Zaccur, the son of
Asaph, 36and his associates—
Shemaiah, Azarel, Milalai,
Gilalai, Maai, Nethanel, Judah
and Hanani—with musical instruments ⌊prescribed by⌋ David the man of God. Ezra the
scribe led the procession. 37At
the Fountain Gate they continued directly up the steps of
the City of David on the ascent to the wall and passed
above the house of David to
the Water Gate on the east.
38The second choir proceeded in the opposite direction. I
followed them on top[k] of the
wall, together with half the
people—past the Tower of the
Ovens to the Broad Wall,
39over the Gate of Ephraim,
the Jeshanah[l] Gate, the Fish
Gate, the Tower of Hananel
and the Tower of the Hun-
dred, as far as the Sheep Gate.
At the Gate of the Guard they
stopped.
40The two choirs that gave
thanks then took their places
in the house of God; so did I,
together with half the officials,

[i]31 Or *go alongside*
[j]31 Or *proceed alongside*
[k]38 Or *them alongside*
[l]39 Or *Old*

וְהַכֹּהֲנִים אֶלְיָקִים מַעֲשֵׂיָה מִנְיָמִין מִיכָיָה אֶלְיוֹעֵינַי זְכַרְיָה
Zechariah Elioenai Micaiah Mijamin Maaseiah Eliakim and-the-priests (41)

חֲנַנְיָה בַּחֲצֹצְרוֹת׃ וּמַעֲשֵׂיָה וּשְׁמַעְיָה וְאֶלְעָזָר וְעֻזִּי
and-Uzzi and-Eleazar and-Shemaiah also-Maaseiah (42) with-trumpets Hananiah

וִיהוֹחָנָן וּמַלְכִּיָּה וְעֵילָם וָעָזֶר וַיַּשְׁמִיעוּ הַמְשֹׁרְרִים
the-ones-singing and-they-sang and-Ezer and-Elam and-Malkijah and-Jehohanan

וְיִזְרַחְיָה הַפָּקִיד׃ וַיִּזְבְּחוּ בַיּוֹם־ הַהוּא
the-that on-the-day and-they-offered (43) the-director and-Jezrahiah

זְבָחִים גְּדוֹלִים וַיִּשְׂמָחוּ כִּי הָאֱלֹהִים שִׂמְּחָם
he-gave-joy-to-them the-God because and-they-rejoiced great-ones sacrifices

שִׂמְחָה גְדוֹלָה וְגַם הַנָּשִׁים וְהַיְלָדִים שָׂמֵחוּ וַתִּשָּׁמַע
and-she-was-heard they-rejoiced and-the-children the-women and-also great joy

שִׂמְחַת יְרוּשָׁלִַם מֵרָחוֹק׃ וַיִּפָּקְדוּ בַיּוֹם
at-the-time and-they-were-appointed (44) at-far Jerusalem rejoicing-of

הַהוּא אֲנָשִׁים עַל־ הַנְּשָׁכוֹת לָאוֹצָרוֹת לַתְּרוּמוֹת
for-the-contributions of-the-treasuries the-storerooms over men the-that

לָרֵאשִׁית וְלַמַּעַשְׂרוֹת לִכְנוֹס בָּהֶם לִשְׂדֵי
from-fields-of into-them to-bring and-for-the-tithes for-the-firstfruit

הֶעָרִים מְנָאוֹת הַתּוֹרָה לַכֹּהֲנִים וְלַלְוִיִּם כִּי
for and-for-the-Levites for-the-priests the-Law portions-of the-towns

שִׂמְחַת יְהוּדָה עַל־ הַכֹּהֲנִים וְעַל־ הַלְוִיִּם הָעֹמְדִים׃
the-ones-ministering the-Levites and-with the-priests with Judah pleasure-of

וַיִּשְׁמְרוּ מִשְׁמֶרֶת אֱלֹהֵיהֶם וּמִשְׁמֶרֶת הַטָּהֳרָה
the-purification and-service-of God-of-them service-of and-they-performed (45)

וְהַמְשֹׁרְרִים וְהַשֹּׁעֲרִים כְּמִצְוַת דָּוִיד שְׁלֹמֹה
Solomon David as-command-of and-the-gatekeepers also-the-ones-singing

בְנוֹ׃ כִּי־ בִימֵי דָוִיד וְאָסָף מִקֶּדֶם רֹאשׁ
directors-of at-long-ago and-Asaph David in-days-of for (46) son-of-him

הַמְשֹׁרְרִים וְשִׁיר־ תְּהִלָּה וְהֹדוֹת לֵאלֹהִים׃ וְכָל־
so-all-of (47) to-God and-thanksgivings praise and-song-of the-ones-singing

יִשְׂרָאֵל בִּימֵי זְרֻבָּבֶל וּבִימֵי נְחֶמְיָה נֹתְנִים
ones-contributing Nehemiah and-in-days-of Zerubbabel in-days-of Israel

מְנָיוֹת הַמְשֹׁרְרִים וְהַשֹּׁעֲרִים דְּבַר־ יוֹם בְּיוֹמוֹ
in-day-of-him day amount-of and-the-gatekeepers the-ones-singing portions-of

וּמַקְדִּשִׁים לַלְוִיִּם וְהַלְוִיִּם מַקְדִּשִׁים
ones-setting-aside and-the-Levites for-the-Levites and-ones-setting-aside

לִבְנֵי אַהֲרֹן׃ בַּיּוֹם הַהוּא נִקְרָא בְּסֵפֶר
in-Book-of he-was-read the-that on-the-day (13:1) Aaron for-descendants-of

41 as well as the priests—
Eliakim, Maaseiah, Mijamin,
Micaiah, Elioenai, Zechariah
and Hananiah with their
trumpets— 42 and also Maaseiah, Shemaiah, Eleazar,
Uzzi, Jehohanan, Malkijah,
Elam and Ezer. The choirs
sang under the direction of
Jezrahiah. 43 And on that day
they offered great sacrifices,
rejoicing because God had
given them great joy. The
women and children also rejoiced. The sound of rejoicing
in Jerusalem could be heard
far away.
44 At that time men were appointed to be in charge of the
storerooms for the contributions, firstfruits and tithes.
From the fields around the
towns they were to bring into
the storerooms the portions
required by the Law for the
priests and the Levites, for
Judah was pleased with the
ministering priests and Levites. 45 They performed the
service of their God and the
service of purification, as did
also the singers and gatekeepers, according to the commands of David and his son
Solomon. 46 For long ago, in the
days of David and Asaph,
there had been directors for
the singers and for the songs
of praise and thanksgiving to
God. 47 So in the days of Zerubbabel and of Nehemiah, all Israel contributed the daily portions for the singers and gatekeepers. They also set aside
the portion for the other Levites, and the Levites set aside
the portion for the descendants of Aaron.

Nehemiah's Final Reforms

13 On that day the Book
of Moses was read

°46 ק ראשי

מֹשֶׁה בְּאָזְנֵי הָעָם וְנִמְצָא כָּתוּב בּוֹ אֲשֶׁר לֹא־
not that in-him being-written and-he-was-found the-people in-ears-of Moses

יָבוֹא עַמֹּנִי וּמֹאָבִי בִּקְהַל הָאֱלֹהִים עַד־עוֹלָם׃
ever to the-God into-assembly-of or-Moabite Ammonite he-should-enter

כִּי לֹא קִדְּמוּ אֶת־ בְּנֵי יִשְׂרָאֵל בַּלֶּחֶם וּבַמָּיִם
and-with-the-waters with-the-food Israel sons-of *** they-met not because (2)

וַיִּשְׂכֹּר עָלָיו אֶת־ בִּלְעָם לְקַלְלוֹ וַיַּהֲפֹךְ אֱלֹהֵינוּ
God-of-us but-he-turned to-curse-him Balaam *** against-him but-they-hired

הַקְּלָלָה לִבְרָכָה׃ וַיְהִי כְּשָׁמְעָם אֶת־ הַתּוֹרָה
the-law *** when-to-hear-them and-he-was (3) into-blessing the-curse

וַיַּבְדִּילוּ כָל־ עֵרֶב מִיִּשְׂרָאֵל׃ וְלִפְנֵי מִזֶּה
to-this and-before (4) from-Israel foreign-descent all-of then-they-excluded

אֶלְיָשִׁיב הַכֹּהֵן נָתוּן בְּלִשְׁכַּת בֵּית־ אֱלֹהֵינוּ קָרוֹב
close God-of-us house-of over-storeroom-of being-put the-priest Eliashib

לְטוֹבִיָּה׃ וַיַּעַשׂ לוֹ לִשְׁכָּה גְדוֹלָה וְשָׁם הָיוּ
they-were and-there large room to-him and-he-provided (5) to-Tobiah

לְפָנִים נֹתְנִים אֶת־ הַמִּנְחָה הַלְּבוֹנָה וְהַכֵּלִים
and-the-articles the-incense the-grain-offering *** ones-storing formerly

וּמַעְשַׂר הַדָּגָן הַתִּירוֹשׁ וְהַיִּצְהָר מִצְוַת הַלְוִיִּם
the-Levites prescription-of and-the-oil the-new-wine the-grain also-tithe-of

וְהַמְשֹׁרְרִים וְהַשֹּׁעֲרִים וּתְרוּמַת הַכֹּהֲנִים׃
the-priests and-contribution-of and-the-gatekeepers and-the-ones-singing

וּבְכָל־ זֶה לֹא הָיִיתִי בִּירוּשָׁלִָם כִּי בִּשְׁנַת שְׁלֹשִׁים
thirty in-year-of for in-Jerusalem I-was not this but-while-all-of (6)

וּשְׁתַּיִם לְאַרְתַּחְשַׁסְתְּא מֶלֶךְ־ בָּבֶל בָּאתִי אֶל־ הַמֶּלֶךְ וּלְקֵץ
and-at-end-of the-king to I-returned Babylon king-of of-Artaxerxes and-two

יָמִים נִשְׁאַלְתִּי מִן־ הַמֶּלֶךְ׃ וָאָבוֹא לִירוּשָׁלִָם וָאָבִינָה
and-I-learned to-Jerusalem and-I-came-back (7) the-king from I-asked days

בָרָעָה אֲשֶׁר עָשָׂה אֶלְיָשִׁיב לְטוֹבִיָּה לַעֲשׂוֹת לוֹ נִשְׁכָּה
room to-him to-provide to-Tobiah Eliashib he-did that about-the-evil-thing

בְּחַצְרֵי בֵּית הָאֱלֹהִים׃ וַיֵּרַע לִי מְאֹד
greatly to-me and-he-displeased (8) the-God house-of in-courts-of

וָאַשְׁלִיכָה אֶת־ כָּל־ כְּלֵי בֵית־ טוֹבִיָּה הַחוּץ מִן־
from the-outside Tobiah house-of goods-of all-of *** and-I-threw-out

הַלִּשְׁכָּה׃ וָאֹמְרָה וַיְטַהֲרוּ הַלְּשָׁכוֹת וָאָשִׁיבָה
then-I-put-back the-rooms and-they-purified and-I-ordered (9) the-room

שָׁם כְּלֵי בֵּית הָאֱלֹהִים אֶת־ הַמִּנְחָה וְהַלְּבוֹנָה׃
and-the-incense the-grain-offering with the-God house-of equipments-of there

aloud in the hearing of the people and there it was found written that no Ammonite or Moabite should ever be admitted into the assembly of God, 2 because they had not met the Israelites with food and water but had hired Balaam to call a curse down on them. (Our God, however, turned the curse into a blessing.) 3 When the people heard this law, they excluded from Israel all who were of foreign descent.

4 Before this, Eliashib the priest had been put in charge of the storerooms of the house of our God. He was closely associated with Tobiah, and he had 5 provided him with a large room formerly used to store the grain offerings and incense and temple articles, and also the tithes of grain, new wine and oil prescribed for the Levites, singers and gatekeepers, as well as the contributions for the priests.

6 But while all this was going on, I was not in Jerusalem, for in the thirty-second year of Artaxerxes king of Babylon I had returned to the king. Some time later I asked his permission 7 and came back to Jerusalem. Here I learned about the evil thing Eliashib had done in providing Tobiah a room in the courts of the house of God. 8 I was greatly displeased and threw all Tobiah's household goods out of the room. 9 I gave orders to purify the rooms, and then I put back into them the equipment of the house of God, with the grain offerings and the incense.

וָאֵדְעָה כִּי־ מְנָיוֹת הַלְוִיִּם לֹא נִתָּנָה
she-was-given not the-Levites portions-of that also-I-learned (10)

וַיִּבְרְחוּ אִישׁ־ לְשָׂדֵהוּ הַלְוִיִּם וְהַמְשֹׁרְרִים
and-the-ones-singing the-Levites to-field-of-him each and-they-went-back

עֹשֵׂי הַמְּלָאכָה׃ וָאָרִיבָה אֶת־ הַסְּגָנִים
the-officials *** so-I-rebuked (11) the-service ones-being-responsible-of

וָאֹמְרָה מַדּוּעַ נֶעֱזַב בֵּית־ הָאֱלֹהִים וָאֶקְבְּצֵם
then-I-called-together-them the-God house-of he-is-neglected why? and-I-asked

וָאַעֲמִדֵם עַל־ עָמְדָם׃ וְכָל־ יְהוּדָה הֵבִיאוּ
they-brought Judah and-all-of (12) post-of-them at and-I-stationed-them

מַעְשַׂר הַדָּגָן וְהַתִּירוֹשׁ וְהַיִּצְהָר לָאוֹצָרוֹת׃
into-the-storerooms and-the-oil and-the-new-wine the-grain tithe-of

וָאוֹצְרָה עַל־ אוֹצָרוֹת שֶׁלֶמְיָה הַכֹּהֵן וְצָדוֹק הַסּוֹפֵר
the-scribe and-Zadok the-priest Shelemiah storerooms over and-I-put (13)

וּפְדָיָה מִן־ הַלְוִיִּם וְעַל־ יָדָם חָנָן בֶּן־ זַכּוּר בֶּן־
son-of Zaccur son-of Hanan hand-of-them and-at the-Levites from and-Pedaiah

מַתַּנְיָה כִּי נֶאֱמָנִים נֶחְשָׁבוּ וַעֲלֵיהֶם
and-to-them they-were-considered ones-being-trustworthy because Mattaniah

לַחֲלֹק לַאֲחֵיהֶם׃ זָכְרָה־ לִּי אֱלֹהַי עַל־ זֹאת
this for God-of-me to-me remember! (14) to-brothers-of-them to-distribute

וְאַל־ תֶּמַח חֲסָדַי אֲשֶׁר עָשִׂיתִי בְּבֵית אֱלֹהַי
God-of-me for-house-of I-did that faithful-deeds-of-me you-blot-out and-not

וּבְמִשְׁמָרָיו׃ בַּיָּמִים הָהֵמָּה רָאִיתִי בִיהוּדָה ׀
in-Judah I-saw the-those in-the-days (15) and-for-services-of-him

דֹרְכִים־ גִּתּוֹת ׀ בַּשַּׁבָּת וּמְבִיאִים הָעֲרֵמוֹת
the-grains and-ones-bringing-in on-the-Sabbath winepresses men-treading

וְעֹמְסִים עַל־ הַחֲמֹרִים וְאַף־ יַיִן עֲנָבִים וּתְאֵנִים וְכָל־
and-all-of and-figs grapes wine and-also the-donkeys on and-ones-loading

מַשָּׂא וּמְבִיאִים יְרוּשָׁלַםִ בְּיוֹם הַשַּׁבָּת וָאָעִיד בְּיוֹם
on-day so-I-warned the-Sabbath on-day-of Jerusalem and-ones-bringing load

מִכְרָם צָיִד׃ וְהַצֹּרִים יָשְׁבוּ בָהּ מְבִיאִים דָּאג
fish ones-bringing in-her they-lived and-the-Tyrians (16) food to-sell-them

וְכָל־ מֶכֶר וּמֹכְרִים בַּשַּׁבָּת לִבְנֵי יְהוּדָה
Judah to-people-of on-the-Sabbath and-ones-selling merchandise and-all-of

וּבִירוּשָׁלָםִ׃ וָאָרִיבָה אֵת חֹרֵי יְהוּדָה וָאֹמְרָה לָהֶם
to-them and-I-said Judah nobles-of *** and-I-rebuked (17) and-in-Jerusalem

מָה־ הַדָּבָר הָרָע הַזֶּה אֲשֶׁר אַתֶּם עֹשִׂים וּמְחַלְּלִים
and-ones-desecrating ones-doing you that the-this the-wicked the-thing what?

10 I also learned that the portions assigned to the Levites
had not been given to them,
and that all the Levites and
singers responsible for the service had gone back to their
own fields. 11 So I rebuked the
officials and asked them,
"Why is the house of God neglected?" Then I called them
together and stationed them at
their posts.
12 All Judah brought the
tithes of grain, new wine and
oil into the storerooms. 13 I put
Shelemiah the priest, Zadok
the scribe, and a Levite named
Pedaiah in charge of the storerooms and made Hanan son of
Zaccur, the son of Mattaniah,
their assistant, because these
men were considered trustworthy. They were made responsible for distributing the
supplies to their brothers.

14 Remember me for this, O
my God, and do not blot out
what I have so faithfully done
for the house of my God and
its services.

15 In those days I saw men in
Judah treading winepresses
on the Sabbath and bringing
in grain and loading it on
donkeys, together with wine,
grapes, figs and all other kinds
of loads. And they were bringing all this into Jerusalem on
the Sabbath. Therefore I
warned them against selling
food on that day. 16 Men from
Tyre who lived in Jerusalem
were bringing in fish and all
kinds of merchandise and selling them in Jerusalem on the
Sabbath to the people of
Judah. 17 I rebuked the nobles
of Judah and said to them,
"What is this wicked thing
you are doing—desecrating

אֶת־יוֹם הַשַּׁבָּת׃ הֲלוֹא כֹה עָשׂוּ אֲבֹתֵיכֶם וַיָּבֵא
so-he-brought forefathers-of-you they-did same not? (18) the-Sabbath day-of ***

אֱלֹהֵינוּ עָלֵינוּ אֵת כָּל־הָרָעָה הַזֹּאת וְעַל הָעִיר הַזֹּאת
the-this the-city and-upon the-this the-calamity all-of *** upon-us God-of-us

וְאַתֶּם מוֹסִיפִים חָרוֹן עַל־יִשְׂרָאֵל לְחַלֵּל אֶת־הַשַּׁבָּת׃
the-Sabbath *** to-desecrate Israel against wrath ones-stirring-up-more now-you

וַיְהִי כַּאֲשֶׁר צָלֲלוּ שַׁעֲרֵי יְרוּשָׁלַם לִפְנֵי
before Jerusalem gates-of they-became-shadowed as-when and-he-was (19)

הַשַּׁבָּת וָאֹמְרָה וַיִּסָּגְרוּ הַדְּלָתוֹת וָאֹמְרָה אֲשֶׁר לֹא
not that and-I-ordered the-doors and-they-were-shut then-I-ordered the-Sabbath

יִפְתָּחוּם עַד אַחַר הַשַּׁבָּת וּמִנְּעָרַי הֶעֱמַדְתִּי עַל־
at I-stationed and-from-men-of-me the-Sabbath after until they-open-them

הַשְּׁעָרִים לֹא־יָבוֹא מַשָּׂא בְּיוֹם הַשַּׁבָּת׃
the-Sabbath on-day-of load they-could-bring-in not the-gates

וַיָּלִינוּ הָרֹכְלִים וּמֹכְרֵי כָל־
all-of and-ones-selling-of the-ones-being-merchants and-they-spent-night (20)

מִמְכָּר מִחוּץ לִירוּשָׁלָם פַּעַם וּשְׁתָּיִם׃ וָאָעִידָה בָהֶם
to-them but-I-warned (21) or-twice once of-Jerusalem at-outside good

וָאֹמְרָה אֲלֵיהֶם מַדּוּעַ אַתֶּם לֵנִים נֶגֶד הַחוֹמָה אִם־תִּשְׁנוּ
you-do-again if the-wall by ones-spending-night you why? to-them and-I-said

יָד אֶשְׁלַח בָּכֶם מִן־הָעֵת הַהִיא לֹא־בָאוּ בַּשַּׁבָּת׃
on-the-Sabbath they-came not the-that the-time from on-you I-will-lay hand

וָאֹמְרָה לַלְוִיִּם אֲשֶׁר יִהְיוּ מִטַּהֲרִים
ones-purifying-themselves they-must-be that to-the-Levites then-I-commanded (22)

וּבָאִים שֹׁמְרִים הַשְּׁעָרִים לְקַדֵּשׁ אֶת־יוֹם
day-of *** to-keep-holy the-gates and-ones-guarding and-ones-going

הַשַּׁבָּת גַּם־זֹאת זָכְרָה־לִּי אֱלֹהַי וְחוּסָה עָלַי
to-me and-show-mercy! God-of-me to-me remember! this also the-Sabbath

כְּרֹב חַסְדֶּךָ׃ גַּם ׀ בַּיָּמִים הָהֵם רָאִיתִי אֶת־
*** I-saw the-those in-the-days moreover (23) love-of-you as-greatness-of

הַיְּהוּדִים הֹשִׁיבוּ נָשִׁים אַשְׁדֳּודִיּוֹת עַמֳּנִיּוֹת מוֹאֲבִיּוֹת׃
Moabites Ammonites Ashdodites women they-married the-Judahites

וּבְנֵיהֶם חֲצִי מְדַבֵּר אַשְׁדּוֹדִית וְאֵינָם
and-not-they Ashdodite one-speaking half-of and-children-of-them (24)

מַכִּירִים לְדַבֵּר יְהוּדִית וְכִלְשׁוֹן עַם וָעָם׃
or-people people or-as-language-of Judahite to-speak ones-knowing

וָאָרִיב עִמָּם וָאֲקַלְלֵם וָאַכֶּה מֵהֶם אֲנָשִׁים
men of-them and-I-beat and-I-cursed-them to-them and-I-rebuked (25)

the Sabbath day? 18Didn't your
forefathers do the same
things, so that our God
brought all this calamity upon
us and upon this city? Now
you are stirring up more wrath
against Israel by desecrating
the Sabbath."
19When evening shadows
fell on the gates of Jerusalem
before the Sabbath, I ordered
the doors to be shut and not
opened until the Sabbath was
over. I stationed some of my
own men at the gates so that
no load could be brought in on
the Sabbath day. 20Once or
twice the merchants and sell-
ers of all kinds of goods spent
the night outside Jerusalem.
21But I warned them and said,
"Why do you spend the night
by the wall? If you do this
again, I will lay hands on
you." From that time on they
no longer came on the Sabbath. 22Then I commanded the
Levites to purify themselves
and go and guard the gates in
order to keep the Sabbath day
holy.

Remember me for this also,
O my God, and show mercy to
me according to your great
love.

23Moreover, in those days I
saw men of Judah who had
married women from Ashdod,
Ammon and Moab. 24Half of
their children spoke the language of Ashdod or the language of one of the other peoples, and did not know how to
speak the language of Judah.
25I rebuked them and called
curses down on them. I beat
some of the men and pulled

°23a ק אשדדיות
°23b ק עמניות

וָאֶמְרְטֵם וָאַשְׁבִּיעֵם בֵּאלֹהִים אִם־
not by-God and-I-made-take-oath-them and-I-pulled-out-hair-of-them

תִּתְּנוּ בְנֹתֵיכֶם לִבְנֵיהֶם וְאִם־ תִּשְׂאוּ
you-shall-take and-not to-sons-of-them daughters-of-you you-shall-give

מִבְּנֹתֵיהֶם לִבְנֵיכֶם וְלָכֶם׃ הֲלוֹא עַל־ אֵלֶּה
these because-of not? (26) or-for-you for-sons-of-you from-daughters-of-them

חָטָא־ שְׁלֹמֹה מֶלֶךְ יִשְׂרָאֵל וּבַגּוֹיִם הָרַבִּים לֹא־ הָיָה
he-was not the-many and-among-the-nations Israel king-of Solomon he-sinned

מֶלֶךְ כָּמֹהוּ וְאָהוּב לֵאלֹהָיו הָיָה וַיִּתְּנֵהוּ אֱלֹהִים
God and-he-made-him he-was by-God-of-him and-being-loved like-him king

מֶלֶךְ עַל־ כָּל־ יִשְׂרָאֵל גַּם־ אוֹתוֹ הֶחֱטִיאוּ הַנָּשִׁים הַנָּכְרִיּוֹת׃
the-foreigners the-women they-led-to-sin him even Israel all-of over king

וְלָכֶם הֲנִשְׁמַע לַעֲשֹׂת אֵת כָּל־ הָרָעָה
the-wickedness all-of *** to-do must-we-hear? now-about-you (27)

הַגְּדוֹלָה הַזֹּאת לִמְעֹל בֵּאלֹהֵינוּ לְהֹשִׁיב נָשִׁים
women to-marry to-God-of-us to-be-unfaithful the-this the-terrible

נָכְרִיּוֹת׃ וּמִבְּנֵי יוֹיָדָע בֶּן־ אֶלְיָשִׁיב הַכֹּהֵן הַגָּדוֹל
the-high the-priest Eliashib son-of Joiada and-from-sons-of (28) foreigners

חָתָן לְסַנְבַלַּט הַחֹרֹנִי וָאַבְרִיחֵהוּ מֵעָלָי׃
from-with-me and-I-drove-away-him the-Horonite of-Sanballat son-in-law

זָכְרָה לָהֶם אֱלֹהָי עַל גָּאֳלֵי הַכְּהֻנָּה
the-priesthood defilements-of because-of God-of-me to-them remember! (29)

וּבְרִית הַכְּהֻנָּה וְהַלְוִיִּם׃ וְטִהַרְתִּים
so-I-purified-them (30) and-the-Levites the-priesthood and-covenant-of

מִכָּל־ נֵכָר וָאַעֲמִידָה מִשְׁמָרוֹת לַכֹּהֲנִים
to-the-priests duties and-I-assigned foreign from-every-of

וְלַלְוִיִּם אִישׁ בִּמְלַאכְתּוֹ׃ וּלְקֻרְבַּן
and-for-contribution-of (31) to-task-of-him each and-to-the-Levites

הָעֵצִים בְּעִתִּים מְזֻמָּנוֹת וְלַבִּכּוּרִים
and-for-the-firstfruits ones-being-designated at-times the-woods

זָכְרָה־ לִּי אֱלֹהַי לְטוֹבָה׃
with-favor God-of-me to-me remember!

out their hair. I made them
take an oath in God's name
and said: "You are not to give
your daughters in marriage to
their sons, nor are you to take
their daughters in marriage
for your sons or for yourselves.
26 Was it not because of mar-
riages like these that Solomon
king of Israel sinned? Among
the many nations there was
no king like him. He was
loved by his God, and God
made him king over all Israel,
but even he was led into sin
by foreign women. 27 Must we
hear now that you too are doing all this terrible wickedness
and are being unfaithful to our
God by marrying foreign
women?"

28 One of the sons of Joiada
son of Eliashib the high priest
was son-in-law to Sanballat
the Horonite. And I drove him
away from me.

29 Remember them, O my
God, because they defiled the
priestly office and the covenant of the priesthood and of
the Levites.

30 So I purified the priests
and the Levites of everything
foreign, and assigned them
duties, each to his own task. 31 I
also made provision for contributions of wood at designated times, and for the
firstfruits.

Remember me with favor, O
my God.

וַיְהִי בִּימֵי אֲחַשְׁוֵרוֹשׁ הוּא אֲחַשְׁוֵרוֹשׁ הַמֹּלֵךְ מֵהֹדּוּ
from-India the-one-ruling Ahasuerus he Ahasuerus in-days-of and-he-was (1:1)

וְעַד־ כּוּשׁ שֶׁבַע וְעֶשְׂרִים וּמֵאָה מְדִינָה׃ בַּיָּמִים הָהֵם
the-those in-the-days (2) province and-hundred and-twenty seven Cush even-to

כְּשֶׁבֶת ׀ הַמֶּלֶךְ אֲחַשְׁוֵרוֹשׁ עַל כִּסֵּא מַלְכוּתוֹ אֲשֶׁר בְּשׁוּשַׁן
in-Susa that royalty-of-him throne-of from Ahasuerus the-king as-to-reign

הַבִּירָה׃ בִּשְׁנַת שָׁלוֹשׁ לְמָלְכוֹ עָשָׂה מִשְׁתֶּה לְכָל־
for-all-of banquet he-gave to-reign-him three in-year-of (3) the-citadel

שָׂרָיו וַעֲבָדָיו חֵיל ׀ פָּרַס וּמָדַי
and-Media Persia military-leader-of and-officials-of-him nobles-of-him

הַפַּרְתְּמִים וְשָׂרֵי הַמְּדִינוֹת לְפָנָיו׃ בְּהַרְאֹתוֹ אֶת־
*** when-to-display-him (4) before-him the-provinces and-nobles-of the-princes

עֹשֶׁר כְּבוֹד מַלְכוּתוֹ וְאֶת־ יְקָר תִּפְאֶרֶת גְּדוּלָּתוֹ
majesty-of-him glory-of splendor-of and kingdom-of-him vastness-of wealth-of

יָמִים רַבִּים שְׁמוֹנִים וּמְאַת יוֹם׃ וּבִמְלוֹאת ׀ הַיָּמִים
the-days and-when-to-be-over (5) day and-hundred-of eighty many days

הָאֵלֶּה עָשָׂה הַמֶּלֶךְ לְכָל־ הָעָם הַנִּמְצְאִים בְּשׁוּשַׁן
in-Susa the-ones-being-found the-people for-all-of the-king he-gave the-these

הַבִּירָה לְמִגָּדוֹל וְעַד־ קָטָן מִשְׁתֶּה שִׁבְעַת יָמִים
days seven-of banquet least even-to for-from-greatest the-citadel

בַּחֲצַר גִּנַּת בִּיתַן הַמֶּלֶךְ׃ חוּר ׀ כַּרְפַּס וּתְכֵלֶת
and-blue linen white (6) the-king palace-of garden-of in-enclosure-of

אָחוּז בְּחַבְלֵי־ בוּץ וְאַרְגָּמָן עַל־ גְּלִילֵי כֶסֶף
silver rings-of to and-purple white-linen with-cords-of being-fastened

וְעַמּוּדֵי שֵׁשׁ מִטּוֹת ׀ זָהָב וָכֶסֶף עַל רִצְפַת בַּהַט־
porphyry pavement-of on and-silver gold couches-of marble and-pillars-of

וָשֵׁשׁ וְדַר וְסֹחָרֶת׃ וְהַשְׁקוֹת
and-to-serve-wine (7) and-costly-stone and-mother-of-pearl and-marble

בִּכְלֵי זָהָב וְכֵלִים מִכֵּלִים שׁוֹנִים וְיֵין
and-wine-of ones-differing from-goblets and-goblets gold in-goblets-of

מַלְכוּת רָב כְּיַד הַמֶּלֶךְ׃ וְהַשְּׁתִיָּה כַדָּת
by-the-command and-the-drinking (8) the-king as-hand-of abundant royalty

אֵין אֹנֵס כִּי־ כֵן ׀ יִסַּד הַמֶּלֶךְ עַל כָּל־ רַב
wine-steward-of all-of to the-king he-instructed so for compelling no

בֵּיתוֹ לַעֲשׂוֹת כִּרְצוֹן אִישׁ־ וָאִישׁ׃ גַּם וַשְׁתִּי הַמַּלְכָּה
the-queen Vashti also (9) and-man man as-wish-of to-serve palace-of-him

עָשְׂתָה מִשְׁתֵּה נָשִׁים בֵּית הַמַּלְכוּת אֲשֶׁר לַמֶּלֶךְ אֲחַשְׁוֵרוֹשׁ׃
Ahasuerus of-the-king that the-royalty palace-of women banquet-of she-gave

Queen Vashti Deposed

1 This is what happened during the time of Xerxes,[a] the Xerxes who ruled over 127 provinces stretching from India to Cush[b]:
[2]At that time King Xerxes reigned from his royal throne in the citadel of Susa,
[3]and in the third year of his reign he gave a banquet for all his nobles and officials. The military leaders of Persia and Media, the princes, and the nobles of the provinces were present.
[4]For a full 180 days he displayed the vast wealth of his kingdom and the splendor and glory of his majesty.
[5]When these days were over, the king gave a banquet, lasting seven days, in the enclosed garden of the king's palace, for all the people from the least to the greatest, who were in the citadel of Susa.
[6]The garden had hangings of white and blue linen, fastened with cords of white linen and purple material to silver rings on marble pillars. There were couches of gold and silver on a mosaic pavement of porphyry, marble, mother-of-pearl and other costly stones.
[7]Wine was served in goblets of gold, each one different from the other, and the royal wine was abundant, in keeping with the king's liberality.
[8]By the king's command each guest was allowed to drink in his own way, for the king instructed all the wine stewards to serve each man what he wished.
[9]Queen Vashti also gave a banquet for the women in the royal palace of King Xerxes.

[a]1 Hebrew *Ahasuerus,* a variant of Xerxes' name; here and throughout Esther
[b]1 That is, the upper Nile region

בַּיּוֹם֙	הַשְּׁבִיעִ֔י	כְּט֥וֹב	לֵב־	הַמֶּ֖לֶךְ	בַּיָּ֑יִן
on-the-day (10)	the-seventh	when-high	spirit-of	the-king	from-the-wine

אָמַ֡ר	לִ֠מְהוּמָן	בִּזְּתָ֨א	חַרְבוֹנָ֜א	בִּגְתָ֤א	וַאֲבַגְתָא֙	זֵתַ֣ר	וְכַרְכַּ֔ס
he-commanded	to-Mehuman	Biztha	Harbona	Bigtha	and-Abagtha	Zethar	and-Carcas

שִׁבְעַת֙	הַסָּ֣רִיסִ֔ים	הַמְשָׁ֣רְתִ֔ים	אֶת־	פְּנֵ֖י	הַמֶּ֥לֶךְ	אֲחַשְׁוֵרֽוֹשׁ׃
seven-of	the-eunuchs	the-ones-serving	***	before	the-king	Ahasuerus

לְ֠הָבִיא	אֶת־	וַשְׁתִּ֧י	הַמַּלְכָּ֛ה	לִפְנֵ֥י	הַמֶּ֖לֶךְ	בְּכֶ֣תֶר	מַלְכ֑וּת
to-bring (11)	***	Vashti	the-queen	before	the-king	with-crown-of	royalty

לְהַרְא֨וֹת	הָֽעַמִּ֤ים	וְהַשָּׂרִים֙	אֶת־	יָפְיָ֔הּ	כִּי־	טוֹבַ֥ת
to-display	the-peoples	and-the-nobles	***	beauty-of-her	for	lovely-of

מַרְאֶ֖ה	הִֽיא׃	וַתְּמָאֵ֞ן	הַמַּלְכָּ֣ה	וַשְׁתִּ֗י	לָב֞וֹא	בִּדְבַ֤ר
appearance	she	but-she-refused (12)	the-queen	Vashti	to-come	at-command-of

הַמֶּ֙לֶךְ֙	אֲשֶׁ֣ר	בְּיַ֣ד	הַסָּרִיסִ֔ים	וַיִּקְצֹ֥ף	הַמֶּ֖לֶךְ	מְאֹ֑ד
that	the-king	by-hand-of	the-attendants	then-he-became-furious	the-king	very

וַחֲמָת֖וֹ	בָּעֲרָ֥ה	בֽוֹ׃	וַיֹּ֣אמֶר	הַמֶּ֔לֶךְ	לַחֲכָמִ֖ים
and-anger-of-him	she-burned	in-him (13)	and-he-spoke	the-king	with-wise-men

יֹדְעֵ֣י	הָֽעִתִּ֑ים	כִּי־	כֵ֣ן	דְּבַ֤ר	הַמֶּ֙לֶךְ֙	לִפְנֵ֔י	כָּל־
ones-understanding-of	the-times	since	so	custom-of	the-king	before	all-of

יֹדְעֵ֖י	דָּ֥ת	וָדִֽין׃	וְהַקָּרֹ֣ב	אֵלָ֗יו	כַּרְשְׁנָ֤א
ones-being-expert-of	law	and-justice (14)	and-the-one-close	to-him	Carshena

שֵׁתָר֙	אַדְמָ֣תָא	תַרְשִׁ֔ישׁ	מֶ֥רֶס	מַרְסְנָ֖א	מְמוּכָ֑ן	שִׁבְעַ֞ת	שָׂרֵ֣י	פָּרַ֣ס ׀
Shethar	Admatha	Tarshish	Meres	Marsena	Memucan	seven-of	nobles-of	Persia

וּמָדַ֗י	רֹאֵי֙	פְּנֵ֣י	הַמֶּ֔לֶךְ	הַיֹּשְׁבִ֥ים	רִאשֹׁנָ֖ה
and-Media	ones-seeing-of	faces-of	the-king	the-ones-being	highest

בַּמַּלְכֽוּת׃	כְּדָת֙	מַֽה־	לַעֲשׂ֔וֹת	בַּמַּלְכָּ֖ה	וַשְׁתִּ֑י	עַ֣ל ׀
in-the-kingdom	according-to-law (15)	what?	to-do	to-the-queen	Vashti	because

אֲשֶׁ֣ר	לֹֽא־	עָשְׂתָ֗ה	אֶֽת־	מַאֲמַר֙	הַמֶּ֣לֶךְ	אֲחַשְׁוֵר֔וֹשׁ	בְּיַ֖ד	הַסָּרִיסִֽים׃
that	not	she-obeyed	***	command-of	the-king	Ahasuerus	by-hand-of	the-eunuchs

וַיֹּ֣אמֶר	מְמוּכָ֗ן	לִפְנֵ֤י	הַמֶּ֙לֶךְ֙	וְהַשָּׂרִ֔ים	לֹ֤א
then-he-replied (16)	Memucan	in-presences-of	the-king	and-the-nobles	not

עַל־	הַמֶּ֙לֶךְ֙	לְבַדּ֔וֹ	עָוְתָ֖ה	וַשְׁתִּ֣י	הַמַּלְכָּ֑ה	כִּ֤י	עַל־
against	the-king	by-himself	she-did-wrong	Vashti	the-queen	but	against

כָּל־	הַשָּׂרִ֔ים	וְעַל־	כָּל־	הָ֣עַמִּ֔ים	אֲשֶׁ֕ר	בְּכָל־	מְדִינ֖וֹת
all-of	the-nobles	and-against	all-of	the-peoples	who	in-all-of	provinces-of

הַמֶּ֥לֶךְ	אֲחַשְׁוֵרֽוֹשׁ׃	כִּֽי־	יֵצֵ֤א	דְבַר־	הַמַּלְכָּה֙	עַ֣ל־	כָּל־
the-king	Ahasuerus (17)	for	he-will-go-out	conduct-of	the-queen	to	all-of

הַנָּשִׁ֔ים	לְהַבְז֥וֹת	בַּעְלֵיהֶ֖ן	בְּעֵינֵיהֶ֑ן	בְּאָמְרָ֗ם
the-women	to-despise	husbands-of-them	in-eyes-of-them	when-to-say-them

[10]On the seventh day, when King Xerxes was in high spirits from wine, he commanded the seven eunuchs who served him—Mehuman, Biztha, Harbona, Bigtha, Abagtha, Zethar and Carcas— [11]to bring before him Queen Vashti, wearing her royal crown, in order to display her beauty to the people and nobles, for she was lovely to look at. [12]But when the attendants delivered the king's command, Queen Vashti refused to come. Then the king became furious and burned with anger.

[13]Since it was customary for the king to consult experts in matters of law and justice, he spoke with the wise men who understood the laws [14]and were closest to the king—Carshena, Shethar, Admatha, Tarshish, Meres, Marsena and Memucan, the seven nobles of Persia and Media who had special access to the king and were highest in the kingdom.

[15]"According to law, what must be done to Queen Vashti?" he asked. "She has not obeyed the command of King Xerxes that the eunuchs have taken to her."

[16]Then Memucan replied in the presence of the king and the nobles, "Queen Vashti has done wrong, not only against the king but also against all the nobles and the peoples of all the provinces of King Xerxes. [17]For the queen's conduct will become known to all the women, and so they will despise their husbands and

ק מְמוּכָן ° 16

הַמֶּלֶךְ אֲחַשְׁוֵרוֹשׁ אָמַר לְהָבִיא אֶת־וַשְׁתִּי הַמַּלְכָּה לְפָנָיו
before-him the-queen Vashti *** to-bring he-commanded Ahasuerus the-king

וְלֹא־בָאָה׃ וְהַיּוֹם הַזֶּה תֹּאמַרְנָה ׀ שָׂרוֹת
noble-women-of they-will-respond the-this and-the-day (18) she-came but-not

פָּרַס־וּמָדַי אֲשֶׁר שָׁמְעוּ אֶת־דְּבַר הַמַּלְכָּה לְכֹל שָׂרֵי
nobles-of of-all-of the-queen conduct-of *** they-heard who and-Media Persia

הַמֶּלֶךְ וּכְדַי בִּזָּיוֹן וָקָצֶף׃ אִם־עַל־הַמֶּלֶךְ טוֹב
pleasing the-king to if (19) and-discord disrespect and-as-no-end-of the-king

יֵצֵא דְבַר־מַלְכוּת מִלְּפָנָיו וְיִכָּתֵב
and-let-him-be-written from-before-him royalty decree-of let-him-issue

בְּדָתֵי פָרַס־וּמָדַי וְלֹא יַעֲבוֹר אֲשֶׁר לֹא־תָבוֹא
she-may-enter never that he-can-be-repealed that-not and-Media Persia in-laws-of

וַשְׁתִּי לִפְנֵי הַמֶּלֶךְ אֲחַשְׁוֵרוֹשׁ וּמַלְכוּתָהּ יִתֵּן
let-him-give also-royal-position-of-her Ahasuerus the-king presences-of Vashti

הַמֶּלֶךְ לִרְעוּתָהּ הַטּוֹבָה מִמֶּנָּה׃ וְנִשְׁמַע
when-he-is-heard (20) than-her the-one-better to-contemporary-of-her the-king

פִּתְגָם הַמֶּלֶךְ אֲשֶׁר־יַעֲשֶׂה בְּכָל־מַלְכוּתוֹ כִּי
indeed realm-of-him through-all-of he-proclaims that the-king edict-of

רַבָּה הִיא וְכָל־הַנָּשִׁים יִתְּנוּ יְקָר לְבַעְלֵיהֶן
to-husbands-of-them respect they-will-give the-women and-all-of she vast

לְמִגָּדוֹל וְעַד־קָטָן׃ וַיִּיטַב הַדָּבָר בְּעֵינֵי
in-eyes-of the-advice and-he-was-pleasing (21) least even-to to-from-greatest

הַמֶּלֶךְ וְהַשָּׂרִים וַיַּעַשׂ הַמֶּלֶךְ כִּדְבַר מְמוּכָן׃
Memucan as-proposal-of the-king so-he-did and-the-nobles the-king

וַיִּשְׁלַח סְפָרִים אֶל־כָּל־מְדִינוֹת הַמֶּלֶךְ אֶל־מְדִינָה
province to the-king provinces-of all-of to dispatches and-he-sent (22)

וּמְדִינָה כִּכְתָבָהּ וְאֶל־עַם וָעָם כִּלְשׁוֹנוֹ
in-language-of-him and-people people and-to in-script-of-her and-province

לִהְיוֹת כָּל־אִישׁ שֹׂרֵר בְּבֵיתוֹ וּמְדַבֵּר כִּלְשׁוֹן
in-tongue-of and-proclaiming over-household-of-him ruling man every-of to-be

עַמּוֹ׃ אַחַר הַדְּבָרִים הָאֵלֶּה כְּשֹׁךְ חֲמַת
anger-of when-to-subside the-these the-things after (2:1) people-of-him

הַמֶּלֶךְ אֲחַשְׁוֵרוֹשׁ זָכַר אֶת־וַשְׁתִּי וְאֵת אֲשֶׁר־עָשָׂתָה וְאֵת אֲשֶׁר־
what and she-did what and Vashti *** he-remembered Ahasuerus the-king

נִגְזַר עָלֶיהָ׃ וַיֹּאמְרוּ נַעֲרֵי־הַמֶּלֶךְ
the-king attendants-of then-they-proposed (2) about-her he-was-decreed

מְשָׁרְתָיו יְבַקְשׁוּ לַמֶּלֶךְ נְעָרוֹת בְּתוּלוֹת
virgins young-women for-the-king let-them-search ones-serving-him

say, 'King Xerxes commanded
Queen Vashti to be brought
before him, but she would not
come.' 18This very day the Persian and Median women of
the nobility who have heard
about the queen's conduct will
respond to all the king's nobles in the same way. There
will be no end of disrespect
and discord.
19"Therefore, if it pleases the
king, let him issue a royal decree and let it be written in the
laws of Persia and Media,
which cannot be repealed,
that Vashti is never again to
enter the presence of King
Xerxes. Also let the king give
her royal position to someone
else who is better than she.
20Then when the king's edict
is proclaimed throughout all
his vast realm, all the women
will respect their husbands,
from the least to the greatest."
21The king and his nobles
were pleased with this advice,
so the king did as Memucan
proposed. 22He sent dispatches
to all parts of the kingdom, to
each province in its own script
and to each people in its own
language, proclaiming in each
people's tongue that every
man should be ruler over his
own household.

Esther Made Queen

2 Later when the anger of
King Xerxes had subsided,
he remembered Vashti and
what she had done and what
he had decreed about her.
2Then the king's personal attendants proposed, "Let a
search be made for beautiful
young virgins for the king.

טוֹבוֹת מַרְאֶה׃ וְיַפְקֵד הַמֶּלֶךְ פְּקִידִים

commissioners the-king and-let-him-appoint (3) appearance ones-beautiful-of

בְּכָל־ מְדִינוֹת מַלְכוּתוֹ וְיִקְבְּצוּ אֶת־ כָּל־ נַעֲרָה־

girl all-of *** and-let-them-bring realm-of-him provinces-of in-all-of

בְתוּלָה טוֹבַת מַרְאֶה אֶל־שׁוּשַׁן הַבִּירָה אֶל־ בֵּית הַנָּשִׁים

the-women harem-of into the-citadel Susa to appearance beautiful-of virgin

אֶל־ יַד הֵגֶא סְרִיס הַמֶּלֶךְ שֹׁמֵר הַנָּשִׁים

the-women one-having-charge-of the-king eunuch-of Hegai hand-of under

וְנָתוֹן תַּמְרוּקֵיהֶן׃ וְהַנַּעֲרָה אֲשֶׁר תִּיטַב

she-is-pleasing who then-the-girl (4) beauty-treatments-of-them and-to-give

בְּעֵינֵי הַמֶּלֶךְ תִּמְלֹךְ תַּחַת וַשְׁתִּי וַיִּיטַב

and-he-was-appealing Vashti instead-of let-her-be-queen the-king in-eyes-of

הַדָּבָר בְּעֵינֵי הַמֶּלֶךְ וַיַּעַשׂ כֵּן׃ אִישׁ יְהוּדִי הָיָה בְּשׁוּשַׁן

in-Susa he-was Jew man (5) this and-he-did the-king in-eyes-of the-advice

הַבִּירָה וּשְׁמוֹ מָרְדֳּכַי בֶּן יָאִיר בֶּן־ שִׁמְעִי בֶּן־ קִישׁ

Kish son-of Shimei son-of Jair son-of Mordecai and-name-of-him the-citadel

אִישׁ יְמִינִי׃ אֲשֶׁר הָגְלָה מִירוּשָׁלַיִם עִם־ הַגֹּלָה אֲשֶׁר

who the-captive among from-Jerusalem he-was-exiled who (6) Benjamite man

הָגְלְתָה עִם יְכָנְיָה מֶלֶךְ־ יְהוּדָה אֲשֶׁר הֶגְלָה נְבוּכַדְנֶאצַּר

Nebuchadnezzar he-captured whom Judah king-of Jeconiah with she-was-captured

מֶלֶךְ בָּבֶל׃ וַיְהִי אֹמֵן אֶת־ הֲדַסָּה הִיא אֶסְתֵּר בַּת־

daughter-of Esther she Hadassah *** bringing-up and-he-was (7) Babylon king-of

דֹּדוֹ כִּי אֵין לָהּ אָב וָאֵם וְהַנַּעֲרָה יְפַת־ תֹּאַר

form lovely-of and-the-girl or-mother father to-her not because uncle-of-him

וְטוֹבַת מַרְאֶה וּבְמוֹת אָבִיהָ וְאִמָּהּ

and-mother-of-her father-of-her and-at-death-of feature and-fine-of

לְקָחָהּ מָרְדֳּכַי לוֹ לְבַת׃ וַיְהִי בְּהִשָּׁמַע

when-to-be-heard and-he-was (8) as-daughter to-him Mordecai he-took-her

דְּבַר־ הַמֶּלֶךְ וְדָתוֹ וּבְהִקָּבֵץ נְעָרוֹת רַבּוֹת אֶל־

to many girls and-when-to-be-brought and-edict-of-him the-king order-of

שׁוּשַׁן הַבִּירָה אֶל־ יַד הֵגָי וַתִּלָּקַח אֶסְתֵּר אֶל־ בֵּית

palace-of to Esther also-she-was-taken Hegai hand-of under the-citadel Susa

הַמֶּלֶךְ אֶל־ יַד הֵגַי שֹׁמֵר הַנָּשִׁים׃ וַתִּיטַב

and-she-was-pleasing (9) the-women one-having-charge-of Hegai hand-of to the-king

הַנַּעֲרָה בְעֵינָיו וַתִּשָּׂא חֶסֶד לְפָנָיו וַיְבַהֵל אֶת־

*** and-he-was-immediate before-him favor and-she-won in-eyes-of-him the-girl

תַּמְרוּקֶיהָ וְאֶת־ מָנוֹתֶהָ לָתֵת לָהּ וְאֵת שֶׁבַע

seven-of and to-her to-provide foods-of-her and beauty-treatments-of-her

[3]Let the king appoint commissioners in every province of
his realm to bring all these
beautiful girls into the harem
at the citadel of Susa. Let them
be placed under the care of
Hegai, the king's eunuch, who
is in charge of the women; and
let beauty treatments be given
to them. [4]Then let the girl who
pleases the king be queen instead of Vashti." This advice
appealed to the king, and he
followed it.

[5]Now there was in the citadel of Susa a Jew of the tribe of
Benjamin, named Mordecai
son of Jair, the son of Shimei,
the son of Kish, [6]who had
been carried into exile from
Jerusalem by Nebuchadnezzar
king of Babylon, among those
taken captive with Jehoiachin[c] king of Judah. [7]Mordecai
had a cousin named Hadas-
sah, whom he had brought up
because she had neither father
nor mother. This girl, who was
also known as Esther, was
lovely in form and features,
and Mordecai had taken her as
his own daughter when her
father and mother died.

[8]When the king's order and
edict had been proclaimed,
many girls were brought to the
citadel of Susa and put under
the care of Hegai. Esther also
was taken to the king's palace
and entrusted to Hegai, who
had charge of the harem. [9]The
girl pleased him and won his
favor. Immediately he provided her with her beauty
treatments and special food.

[c]6 Hebrew *Jeconiah*, a variant of *Jehoiachin*

הַנְּעָרוֹת הָרְאֻיוֹת לָתֶת־ לָהּ מִבֵּית הַמֶּלֶךְ
the-king from-palace-of to-her to-assign the-ones-being-selected the-maids

וַיְשַׁנֶּהָ וְאֶת־ נַעֲרוֹתֶיהָ לְטוֹב בֵּית הַנָּשִׁים׃ לֹא־
not (10) the-women harem-of to-best-of maids-of-her and and-he-moved-her

הִגִּידָה אֶסְתֵּר אֶת־ עַמָּהּ וְאֶת־ מוֹלַדְתָּהּ כִּי מָרְדֳּכַי
Mordecai because family-of-her and nationality-of-her *** Esther she-revealed

צִוָּה עָלֶיהָ אֲשֶׁר לֹא־ תַגִּיד׃ וּבְכָל־ יוֹם
day and-on-every-of (11) she-should-reveal not that to-her he-commanded

וָיוֹם מָרְדֳּכַי מִתְהַלֵּךְ לִפְנֵי חֲצַר בֵּית־ הַנָּשִׁים לָדַעַת
to-find-out the-women harem-of courtyard-of near walking Mordecai and-day

אֶת־ שְׁלוֹם אֶסְתֵּר וּמַה־ יֵּעָשֶׂה בָּהּ׃ וּבְהַגִּיעַ
and-before-to-come (12) to-her he-happened and-what Esther welfare-of ***

תֹּר נַעֲרָה וְנַעֲרָה לָבוֹא ׀ אֶל־ הַמֶּלֶךְ אֲחַשְׁוֵרוֹשׁ מִקֵּץ הֱיוֹת
to-be when-completion Ahasuerus the-king to to-go-in and-girl girl turn-of

לָהּ כְּדָת הַנָּשִׁים שְׁנֵים עָשָׂר חֹדֶשׁ כִּי כֵּן יִמְלְאוּ
they-were-completed so for month ten two the-women as-prescription-of to-her

יְמֵי מְרוּקֵיהֶן שִׁשָּׁה חֳדָשִׁים בְּשֶׁמֶן הַמֹּר וְשִׁשָּׁה
and-six the-myrrh with-oil-of months six beauty-treatments-of-her days-of

חֳדָשִׁים בַּבְּשָׂמִים וּבְתַמְרוּקֵי הַנָּשִׁים׃ וּבָזֶה
and-as-this (13) the-women and-with-cosmetics-of with-the-perfumes months

הַנַּעֲרָה בָּאָה אֶל־ הַמֶּלֶךְ אֵת כָּל־ אֲשֶׁר תֹּאמַר יִנָּתֵן לָהּ
to-her he-was-given she-wanted that anything *** the-king to going the-girl

לָבוֹא עִמָּהּ מִבֵּית הַנָּשִׁים עַד־ בֵּית הַמֶּלֶךְ׃
the-king palace-of to the-women from-harem-of with-her to-take

בָּעֶרֶב ׀ הִיא בָאָה וּבַבֹּקֶר הִיא שָׁבָה אֶל־ בֵּית
harem-of to returning she and-in-the-morning going she in-the-evening (14)

הַנָּשִׁים שֵׁנִי אֶל־ יַד שַׁעַשְׁגַז סְרִיס הַמֶּלֶךְ
the-king eunuch-of Shaashgaz hand-of to another-part the-women

שֹׁמֵר הַפִּילַגְשִׁים לֹא־ תָבוֹא עוֹד אֶל־ הַמֶּלֶךְ
the-king to again she-returned not the-concubines one-being-in-charge-of

כִּי אִם־ חָפֵץ בָּהּ הַמֶּלֶךְ וְנִקְרְאָה בְשֵׁם׃
by-name and-she-was-summoned the-king with-her he-was-pleased if unless

וּבְהַגִּיעַ תֹּר־ אֶסְתֵּר בַּת־ אֲבִיחַיִל דֹּד מָרְדֳּכַי
Mordecai uncle-of Abihail daughter-of Esther turn-of and-when-to-come (15)

אֲשֶׁר לָקַח־ לוֹ לְבַת לָבוֹא אֶל־ הַמֶּלֶךְ לֹא בִקְשָׁה
she-asked-for not the-king to to-go as-daughter for-him he-adopted whom

דָּבָר כִּי אִם אֶת־ אֲשֶׁר יֹאמַר הֵגַי סְרִיס־ הַמֶּלֶךְ
the-king eunuch-of Hegai he-suggested what *** than other anything

He assigned to her seven
maids selected from the king's
palace and moved her and her
maids into the best place in
the harem.
10 Esther had not revealed
her nationality and family
background, because Mor-
decai had forbidden her to do
so. 11 Every day he walked back
and forth near the courtyard
of the harem to find out how
Esther was and what was happening to her.
12 Before a girl's turn came to
go in to King Xerxes, she had
to complete twelve months of
beauty treatments prescribed
for the women, six months
with oil of myrrh and six with
perfumes and cosmetics.
13 And this is how she would
go to the king: Anything she
wanted was given her to take
with her from the harem to the
king's palace. 14 In the evening
she would go there and in the
morning return to another
part of the harem to the care of
Shaashgaz, the king's eunuch
who was in charge of the concubines. She would not return
to the king unless he was
pleased with her and sum-
moned her by name.
15 When the turn came for Esther (the girl Mordecai had
adopted, the daughter of his
uncle Abihail) to go to the
king, she asked for nothing
other than what Hegai, the
king's eunuch who was in

שֹׁמֵר הַנָּשִׁים וַתְּהִי אֶסְתֵּר נֹשֵׂאת חֵן בְּעֵינֵי

in-eyes-of favor winning Esther and-she-was the-women one-being-in-charge-of

כָּל־ רֹאֶיהָ׃ וַתִּלָּקַח אֶסְתֵּר אֶל־ הַמֶּלֶךְ אֲחַשְׁוֵרוֹשׁ

Ahasuerus the-king to Esther and-she-was-taken (16) ones-seeing-her all-of

אֶל־ בֵּית מַלְכוּתוֹ בַּחֹדֶשׁ הָעֲשִׂירִי הוּא־ חֹדֶשׁ טֵבֵת

Tebeth month-of that the-tenth in-the-month royalty-of-him residence-of in

בִּשְׁנַת־ שֶׁבַע לְמַלְכוּתוֹ׃ וַיֶּאֱהַב הַמֶּלֶךְ אֶת־

*** the-king now-he-was-attracted (17) of-reign-of-him seven in-year-of

אֶסְתֵּר מִכָּל־ הַנָּשִׁים וַתִּשָּׂא־ חֵן וָחֶסֶד לְפָנָיו

before-him and-approval favor and-she-won the-women more-than-any-of Esther

מִכָּל־ הַבְּתוּלֹת וַיָּשֶׂם כֶּתֶר־ מַלְכוּת בְּרֹאשָׁהּ

on-head-of-her royalty crown-of so-he-set the-virgins more-than-any-of

וַיַּמְלִיכֶהָ תַּחַת וַשְׁתִּי׃ וַיַּעַשׂ הַמֶּלֶךְ מִשְׁתֶּה

banquet the-king and-he-gave (18) Vashti instead-of and-he-made-queen-her

גָדוֹל לְכָל־ שָׂרָיו וַעֲבָדָיו אֵת מִשְׁתֵּה אֶסְתֵּר

Esther banquet-of *** and-officials-of-him nobles-of-him for-all-of great

וַהֲנָחָה לַמְּדִינוֹת עָשָׂה וַיִּתֵּן מַשְׂאֵת

gift and-he-distributed he-proclaimed throughout-the-provinces and-holiday

כְּיַד הַמֶּלֶךְ׃ וּבְהִקָּבֵץ בְּתוּלוֹת שֵׁנִית

second-time virgins and-when-to-be-assembled (19) the-king as-hand-of

וּמָרְדֳּכַי יֹשֵׁב בְּשַׁעַר־ הַמֶּלֶךְ׃ אֵין אֶסְתֵּר מַגֶּדֶת

revealing Esther not (20) the-king at-gate-of sitting then-Mordecai

מוֹלַדְתָּהּ וְאֶת־ עַמָּהּ כַּאֲשֶׁר צִוָּה עָלֶיהָ מָרְדֳּכָי וְאֶת־

and Mordecai to-her he-told just-as nationality-of-her or family-of-her

מַאֲמַר מָרְדֳּכַי אֶסְתֵּר עֹשָׂה כַּאֲשֶׁר הָיְתָה בְאָמְנָה

when-bringing-up she-did just-as following Esther Mordecai instruction-of

אִתּוֹ׃ בַּיָּמִים הָהֵם וּמָרְדֳּכַי יֹשֵׁב בְּשַׁעַר־

at-gate-of sitting when-Mordecai the-those during-the-days (21) with-him

הַמֶּלֶךְ קָצַף בִּגְתָן וָתֶרֶשׁ שְׁנֵי־ סָרִיסֵי הַמֶּלֶךְ

the-king officers-of two-of and-Teresh Bigthan he-became-angry the-king

מִשֹּׁמְרֵי הַסַּף וַיְבַקְשׁוּ לִשְׁלֹחַ יָד

hand to-send and-they-conspired the-doorway from-ones-guarding-of

בַּמֶּלֶךְ אֲחַשְׁוֵרֹשׁ׃ וַיִּוָּדַע הַדָּבָר לְמָרְדֳּכַי

by-Mordecai the-plot but-he-was-found-out (22) Ahasuerus against-the-king

וַיַּגֵּד לְאֶסְתֵּר הַמַּלְכָּה וַתֹּאמֶר אֶסְתֵּר לַמֶּלֶךְ בְּשֵׁם

in-name-of to-the-king Esther and-she-reported the-queen to-Esther and-he-told

מָרְדֳּכָי׃ וַיְבֻקַּשׁ הַדָּבָר וַיִּמָּצֵא

and-he-was-found the-report when-he-was-investigated (23) Mordecai

charge of the harem, suggested. And Esther won the favor of everyone who saw her.
16 She was taken to King Xerxes
in the royal residence in the tenth month, the month of Tebeth, in the seventh year of his reign.
17 Now the king was attracted to Esther more than to any of the other women, and she won his favor and approval more than any of the other virgins. So he set a royal crown on her head and made her queen instead of Vashti.
18 And the king gave a great banquet, Esther's banquet, for all his nobles and officials. He proclaimed a holiday throughout the provinces and distributed gifts with royal liberality.

Mordecai Uncovers a Conspiracy

19 When the virgins were assembled a second time, Mordecai was sitting at the king's
gate. 20 But Esther had kept secret her family background and nationality just as Mordecai had told her to do, for she continued to follow Mordecai's instructions as she had done when he was bringing her up.
21 During the time Mordecai was sitting at the king's gate, Bigthana[d] and Teresh, two of the king's officers who guarded the doorway, became angry and conspired to assassinate King Xerxes.
22 But Mordecai found out about the plot and told Queen Esther, who in turn reported it to the king, giving credit to Mordecai.
23 And when the report was investigated and found to be

[d] 21 Hebrew *Bigthan*, a variant of *Bigthana*

וַיִּתָּלוּ שְׁנֵיהֶם עַל־ עֵץ וַיִּכָּתֵב בְּסֵפֶר
in-book-of and-he-was-recorded gallows on two-of-them then-they-were-hanged

דִּבְרֵי הַיָּמִים לִפְנֵי הַמֶּלֶךְ׃ אַחַר ׀ הַדְּבָרִים הָאֵלֶּה
the-these the-events after (3:1) the-king in-presences-of the-days annals-of

גִּדַּל הַמֶּלֶךְ אֲחַשְׁוֵרוֹשׁ אֶת־ הָמָן בֶּן־ הַמְּדָתָא הָאֲגָגִי
the-Agagite Hammedatha son-of Haman *** Ahasuerus the-king he-honored

וַיְנַשְּׂאֵהוּ וַיָּשֶׂם אֶת־ כִּסְאוֹ מֵעַל כָּל־ הַשָּׂרִים
the-nobles all-of at-above seat-of-him *** and-he-gave and-he-elevated-him

אֲשֶׁר אִתּוֹ׃ וְכָל־ עַבְדֵי הַמֶּלֶךְ אֲשֶׁר־ בְּשַׁעַר הַמֶּלֶךְ
the-king at-gate-of who the-king officials-of and-all-of (2) with-him who

כֹּרְעִים וּמִשְׁתַּחֲוִים לְהָמָן כִּי־ כֵן צִוָּה־ לוֹ
about-him he-commanded this for to-Haman and-ones-paying-honor ones-kneeling

הַמֶּלֶךְ וּמָרְדֳּכַי לֹא יִכְרַע וְלֹא יִשְׁתַּחֲוֶה׃ וַיֹּאמְרוּ
then-they-asked (3) he-paid-honor and-not he-knelt not but-Mordecai the-king

עַבְדֵי הַמֶּלֶךְ אֲשֶׁר־ בְּשַׁעַר הַמֶּלֶךְ לְמָרְדֳּכָי מַדּוּעַ אַתָּה
you why? to-Mordecai the-king at-gate-of who the-king officials-of

עוֹבֵר אֵת מִצְוַת הַמֶּלֶךְ׃ וַיְהִי בְּאָמְרָם° אֵלָיו
to-him when-to-speak-them and-he-was (4) the-king command-of *** disobeying

יוֹם וָיוֹם וְלֹא שָׁמַע אֲלֵיהֶם וַיַּגִּידוּ לְהָמָן לִרְאוֹת
to-see to-Haman so-they-told with-them he-complied but-not after-day day

הֲיַעַמְדוּ דִּבְרֵי מָרְדֳּכַי כִּי־ הִגִּיד לָהֶם אֲשֶׁר־
that to-them he-told for Mordecai behaviors-of whether-they-would-be-tolerated

הוּא יְהוּדִי׃ וַיַּרְא הָמָן כִּי־ אֵין מָרְדֳּכַי כֹּרֵעַ וּמִשְׁתַּחֲוֶה
or-paying-honor kneeling Mordecai not that Haman when-he-saw (5) Jew he

לוֹ וַיִּמָּלֵא הָמָן חֵמָה׃ וַיִּבֶז בְּעֵינָיו
in-eyes-of-him yet-he-scorned (6) rage Haman then-he-was-filled to-him

לִשְׁלָח* יָד בְּמָרְדֳּכַי לְבַדּוֹ כִּי־ הִגִּידוּ לוֹ אֶת־ עַם
people-of *** to-him they-told for by-himself against-Mordecai hand to-send

מָרְדֳּכָי וַיְבַקֵּשׁ הָמָן לְהַשְׁמִיד אֶת־ כָּל־ הַיְּהוּדִים אֲשֶׁר בְּכָל־
in-whole-of who the-Jews all-of *** to-destroy Haman so-he-looked Mordecai

מַלְכוּת אֲחַשְׁוֵרוֹשׁ עַם מָרְדֳּכָי׃ בַּחֹדֶשׁ הָרִאשׁוֹן הוּא־
that the-first in-the-month (7) Mordecai people-of Ahasuerus kingdom-of

חֹדֶשׁ נִיסָן בִּשְׁנַת שְׁתֵּים עֶשְׂרֵה לַמֶּלֶךְ אֲחַשְׁוֵרוֹשׁ הִפִּיל פּוּר הוּא
that pur he-cast Ahasuerus of-the-king ten two in-year-of Nisan month-of

הַגּוֹרָל לִפְנֵי הָמָן מִיּוֹם ׀ לְיוֹם וּמֵחֹדֶשׁ לְחֹדֶשׁ שְׁנֵים־
two to-month and-from-month to-day from-day Haman in-presences-of the-lot

עָשָׂר הוּא־ חֹדֶשׁ אֲדָר׃ וַיֹּאמֶר הָמָן לַמֶּלֶךְ אֲחַשְׁוֵרוֹשׁ
Ahasuerus to-the-king Haman then-he-said (8) Adar month-of that ten

true, the two officials were hanged on a gallows.[e] All this was recorded in the book of the annals in the presence of the king.

Haman's Plot to Destroy the Jews

3 After these events, King Xerxes honored Haman son of Hammedatha, the Agagite, elevating him and giving him a seat of honor higher than that of all the other nobles. 2All the royal officials at the king's gate knelt down and paid honor to Haman, for the king had commanded this concerning him. But Mordecai would not kneel down or pay him honor.

3Then the royal officials at the king's gate asked Mordecai, "Why do you disobey the king's command?" 4Day after day they spoke to him but he refused to comply. Therefore they told Haman about it to see whether Mordecai's behavior would be tolerated, for he had told them he was a Jew.

5When Haman saw that Mordecai would not kneel down or pay him honor, he was enraged. 6Yet having learned who Mordecai's people were, he scorned the idea of killing only Mordecai. Instead Haman looked for a way to destroy all Mordecai's people, the Jews, throughout the whole kingdom of Xerxes.

7In the twelfth year of King Xerxes, in the first month, the month of Nisan, they cast the *pur* (that is, the lot) in the presence of Haman to select a day and month. And the lot fell on[f] the twelfth month, the month of Adar.

8Then Haman said to King

[e]23 Or *were hung on a post;* here and elsewhere in Esther

[f]7 Septuagint; Hebrew does not have *And the lot fell on.*

*6 Most mss have *pathah* under the *beth* (לַחַ–).

°4 קְ כאמרם

יֶשְׁנוֹ עַם־ אֶחָד מְפֻזָּר וּמְפֹרָד בֵּין
among and-being-scattered being-dispersed certain people there-is-he

הָעַמִּים בְּכֹל מְדִינוֹת מַלְכוּתֶךָ וְדָתֵיהֶם
and-customs-of-them kingdom-of-you provinces-of in-all-of the-peoples

שֹׁנוֹת מִכָּל־ עָם וְאֶת־ דָּתֵי הַמֶּלֶךְ אֵינָם עֹשִׂים
ones-obeying not-they the-king laws-of and people from-all-of ones-differing

וְלַמֶּלֶךְ אֵין־ שֹׁוֶה לְהַנִּיחָם׃ אִם־עַל־ הַמֶּלֶךְ
the-king to if (9) to-tolerate-them being-in-best-interest not and-to-the-king

טוֹב יִכָּתֵב לְאַבְּדָם וַעֲשֶׂרֶת אֲלָפִים כִּכַּר־
talent-of thousands and-ten-of to-destroy-them let-him-be-decreed pleasing

כֶּסֶף אֶשְׁקוֹל עַל־ יְדֵי עֹשֵׂי הַמְּלָאכָה לְהָבִיא אֶל־
into to-put the-business ones-carrying-out-of hands-of in I-will-put silver

גִּנְזֵי הַמֶּלֶךְ׃ וַיָּסַר הַמֶּלֶךְ אֶת־ טַבַּעְתּוֹ
signet-ring-of-him *** the-king so-he-took-off (10) the-king treasuries-of

מֵעַל יָדוֹ וַיִּתְּנָהּ לְהָמָן בֶּן־ הַמְּדָתָא הָאֲגָגִי
the-Agagite Hammedatha son-of to-Haman and-he-gave-her hand-of-him from-on

צֹרֵר הַיְּהוּדִים׃ וַיֹּאמֶר הַמֶּלֶךְ לְהָמָן הַכֶּסֶף
the-money to-Haman the-king and-he-said (11) the-Jews being-enemy-of

נָתוּן לָךְ וְהָעָם לַעֲשׂוֹת בּוֹ כַּטּוֹב בְּעֵינֶיךָ׃
in-eyes-of-you as-the-pleasing with-him to-do and-the-people by-you being-kept

וַיִּקָּרְאוּ סֹפְרֵי הַמֶּלֶךְ בַּחֹדֶשׁ הָרִאשׁוֹן
the-first in-the-month the-king secretaries-of then-they-were-summoned (12)

בִּשְׁלוֹשָׁה עָשָׂר יוֹם בּוֹ וַיִּכָּתֵב כְּכָל־אֲשֶׁר־ צִוָּה הָמָן אֶל
to Haman he-ordered that as-all and-he-was-written of-him day ten on-three

אֲחַשְׁדַּרְפְּנֵי־הַמֶּלֶךְ וְאֶל־ הַפַּחוֹת אֲשֶׁר ׀ עַל־ מְדִינָה וּמְדִינָה
and-province province over who the-governors and-to the-king satraps-of

וְאֶל־ שָׂרֵי עַם וָעָם מְדִינָה וּמְדִינָה כִּכְתָבָהּ
in-script-of-her and-province province and-people people nobles-of and-to

וְעַם וָעָם כִּלְשׁוֹנוֹ בְּשֵׁם הַמֶּלֶךְ אֲחַשְׁוֵרֹשׁ
Ahasuerus the-king in-name-of in-language-of-him and-people and-people

נִכְתָּב וְנֶחְתָּם בְּטַבַּעַת הַמֶּלֶךְ׃ וְנִשְׁלוֹחַ
and-to-be-sent (13) the-king with-signet-ring-of and-being-sealed being-written

סְפָרִים בְּיַד הָרָצִים אֶל־ כָּל־ מְדִינוֹת הַמֶּלֶךְ
the-king provinces-of all-of to the-ones-being-couriers by-hand-of dispatches

לְהַשְׁמִיד לַהֲרֹג וּלְאַבֵּד אֶת־ כָּל־ הַיְּהוּדִים מִנַּעַר וְעַד־
and-to from-young the-Jews all-of *** and-to-annihilate to-kill to-destroy

זָקֵן טַף וְנָשִׁים בְּיוֹם אֶחָד בִּשְׁלוֹשָׁה עָשָׂר לְחֹדֶשׁ שְׁנֵים־עָשָׂר
ten two of-month-of ten on-three single on-day and-women little-child old

Xerxes, "There is a certain
people dispersed and scattered
among the peoples in all the
provinces of your kingdom
who keep themselves sepa-
rate. Their customs are
different from those of all other people, and they do not
obey the king's laws; it is not
in the king's best interest to
tolerate them. 9If it pleases the
king, let a decree be issued to
destroy them, and I will put
ten thousand talents[g] of silver
into the royal treasury for the
men who carry out this
business."
10So the king took the signet
ring off his finger and gave it
to Haman son of Hammeda-
tha, the Agagite, the enemy of
the Jews. 11"Keep the money,"
the king said to Haman, "and
do with the people as you
please."
12Then on the thirteenth day
of the first month the royal
secretaries were summoned.
They wrote out in the script of
each province and in the language of each people all Haman's orders to the king's satraps, the governors of the
various provinces and the nobles of the various peoples.
These were written in the
name of King Xerxes himself
and sealed with his own ring.
13Dispatches were sent by
couriers to all the king's provinces with the order to destroy, kill and annihilate all
the Jews—young and old,
women and little children—on
a single day, the thirteenth
day of the twelfth month, the

g9 That is, about 375 tons (about 345 metric tons)

הוּא־ חֹדֶשׁ אֲדָר וּשְׁלָלָם לָבוֹז׃ פַּתְשֶׁגֶן הַכְּתָב
the-edict copy-of (14) to-plunder and-good-of-them Adar month-of that

לְהִנָּתֵן דָּת בְּכָל־ מְדִינָה וּמְדִינָה גָּלוּי
being-made-known and-province province in-every-of law to-be-issued

לְכָל־ הָעַמִּים לִהְיוֹת עֲתִדִים לַיּוֹם הַזֶּה׃
the-that for-the-day ones-ready to-be the-peoples to-every-of

הָרָצִים יָצְאוּ דְחוּפִים
ones-being-spurred-on they-went-out the-ones-being-couriers (15)

בִּדְבַר הַמֶּלֶךְ וְהַדָּת נִתְּנָה בְּשׁוּשַׁן הַבִּירָה
the-citadel in-Susa she-was-issued and-the-edict the-king by-command-of

וְהַמֶּלֶךְ וְהָמָן יָשְׁבוּ לִשְׁתּוֹת וְהָעִיר שׁוּשָׁן נָבוֹכָה׃
she-was-bewildered Susa but-the-city to-drink they-sat and-Haman and-the-king

וּמָרְדֳּכַי יָדַע אֶת־ כָּל־ אֲשֶׁר נַעֲשָׂה וַיִּקְרַע מָרְדֳּכַי
Mordecai then-he-tore being-done that all *** he-learned when-Mordecai (4:1)

אֶת־ בְּגָדָיו וַיִּלְבַּשׁ שַׂק וָאֵפֶר וַיֵּצֵא בְּתוֹךְ
in-midst-of and-he-went-out and-ash sackcloth and-he-put-on clothes-of-him ***

הָעִיר וַיִּזְעַק זְעָקָה גְדֹלָה וּמָרָה׃ וַיָּבוֹא עַד
as-far-as but-he-went (2) and-bitter loud wailing and-he-wailed the-city

לִפְנֵי שַׁעַר־ הַמֶּלֶךְ כִּי אֵין לָבוֹא אֶל־ שַׁעַר הַמֶּלֶךְ
the-king gate-of into to-enter no-one because the-king gate-of before

בִּלְבוּשׁ שָׂק׃ וּבְכָל־ מְדִינָה וּמְדִינָה מְקוֹם
place-of and-province province and-in-every-of (3) sackcloth in-clothing-of

אֲשֶׁר דְּבַר־ הַמֶּלֶךְ וְדָתוֹ מַגִּיעַ אֵבֶל גָּדוֹל לַיְּהוּדִים
among-the-Jews great mourning coming and-order-of-him the-king edict-of which

וְצוֹם וּבְכִי וּמִסְפֵּד שַׂק וָאֵפֶר יֻצַּע
he-was-laid-on and-ash sackcloth and-wailing and-weeping with-fasting

לָרַבִּים׃ °וַתָּבוֹאינָה נַעֲרוֹת אֶסְתֵּר וְסָרִיסֶיהָ
and-eunuchs-of-her Esther maids-of when-they-came (4) by-the-many

וַיַּגִּידוּ לָהּ וַתִּתְחַלְחַל הַמַּלְכָּה מְאֹד וַתִּשְׁלַח
and-she-sent great the-queen then-she-was-in-distress to-her and-they-told

בְּגָדִים לְהַלְבִּישׁ אֶת־ מָרְדֳּכַי וּלְהָסִיר שַׂקּוֹ מֵעָלָיו
from-on-him sackcloth-of-him and-to-take-off Mordecai *** to-put-on clothes

וְלֹא קִבֵּל׃ וַתִּקְרָא° אֶסְתֵּר לַהֲתָךְ מִסָּרִיסֵי
from-eunuchs-of to-Hathach Esther then-she-summoned (5) he-accepted but-not

הַמֶּלֶךְ אֲשֶׁר הֶעֱמִיד לְפָנֶיהָ וַתְּצַוֵּהוּ עַל־ מָרְדֳּכַי
Mordecai about and-she-ordered-him to-her he-assigned whom the-king

לָדַעַת מַה־ זֶּה וְעַל־ מַה־ זֶּה׃ וַיֵּצֵא הֲתָךְ אֶל־
to Hathach so-he-went-out (6) this what? and-for this what? to-find-out

month of Adar, and to plunder their goods. [14]A copy of the text of the edict was to be issued as law in every province and made known to the people of every nationality so they would be ready for that day.

[15]Spurred on by the king's command, the couriers went out, and the edict was issued in the citadel of Susa. The king and Haman sat down to drink, but the city of Susa was bewildered.

Mordecai Persuades Esther to Help

4 When Mordecai learned of all that had been done, he tore his clothes, put on sackcloth and ashes, and went out into the city, wailing loudly and bitterly. [2]But he went only as far as the king's gate, because no one clothed in sackcloth was allowed to enter it. [3]In every province to which the edict and order of the king came, there was great mourning among the Jews, with fasting, weeping and wailing. Many lay on sackcloth and ashes.

[4]When Esther's maids and eunuchs came and told her about Mordecai, she was in great distress. She sent clothes for him to put on instead of his sackcloth, but he would not accept them. [5]Then Esther summoned Hathach, one of the king's eunuchs assigned to attend her, and ordered him to find out what was troubling Mordecai and why.

[6]So Hathach went out to

°4 ק ותבואנה

מָרְדֳּכַי אֶל־ רְחוֹב הָעִיר אֲשֶׁר לִפְנֵי שַׁעַר־ הַמֶּלֶךְ׃

the-king gate-of in-front-of that the-city open-square-of in Mordecai

(7) וַיַּגֶּד־ לוֹ מָרְדֳּכַי אֵת כָּל־ אֲשֶׁר קָרָהוּ וְאֵת ׀

and he-happened-to-him that everything *** Mordecai to-him and-he-told (7)

פָּרָשַׁת הַכֶּסֶף אֲשֶׁר אָמַר הָמָן לִשְׁקוֹל עַל־ גִּנְזֵי

treasuries-of into to-pay Haman he-promised that the-money exact-amount-of

הַמֶּלֶךְ בַּיְּהוּדִיים לְאַבְּדָם׃ (8) וְאֶת־ פַּתְשֶׁגֶן כְּתָב־ הַדָּת

the-edict text-of copy-of also (8) to-destroy-them for-the-Jews the-king

אֲשֶׁר־ נִתַּן בְּשׁוּשָׁן לְהַשְׁמִידָם נָתַן לוֹ לְהַרְאוֹת

to-show to-him he-gave to-annihilate-them in-Susa he-was-published which

אֶת־ אֶסְתֵּר וּלְהַגִּיד לָהּ וּלְצַוּוֹת עָלֶיהָ לָבוֹא אֶל־ הַמֶּלֶךְ

the-king to to-go to-her and-to-urge to-her and-to-explain Esther ***

לְהִתְחַנֶּן־ לוֹ וּלְבַקֵּשׁ מִלְּפָנָיו עַל־ עַמָּהּ׃

people-of-her for from-before-him and-to-plead with-him to-beg-for-mercy

(9) וַיָּבוֹא הֲתָךְ וַיַּגֵּד לְאֶסְתֵּר אֵת דִּבְרֵי מָרְדֳּכָי׃

Mordecai words-of *** to-Esther and-he-reported Hathach then-he-went-back (9)

(10) וַתֹּאמֶר אֶסְתֵּר לַהֲתָךְ וַתְּצַוֵּהוּ אֶל־ מָרְדֳּכָי׃

Mordecai to and-she-instructed-him to-Hathach Esther then-she-said (10)

(11) כָּל־ עַבְדֵי הַמֶּלֶךְ וְעַם־ מְדִינוֹת הַמֶּלֶךְ

the-king provinces-of and-people-of the-king officials-of all-of (11)

יֹדְעִים אֲשֶׁר כָּל־ אִישׁ וְאִשָּׁה אֲשֶׁר יָבוֹא־ אֶל־הַמֶּלֶךְ אֶל־

in the-king to he-approaches who or-woman man any-of that ones-knowing

הֶחָצֵר הַפְּנִימִית אֲשֶׁר לֹא־ יִקָּרֵא אַחַת דָּתוֹ לְהָמִית לְבַד

except to-kill law-of-him one he-was-summoned not who the-inner the-court

מֵאֲשֶׁר יוֹשִׁיט־ לוֹ הַמֶּלֶךְ אֶת־ שַׁרְבִיט הַזָּהָב וְחָיָה

and-he-lives the-gold scepter-of *** the-king to-him he-extends from-whom

וַאֲנִי לֹא נִקְרֵאתִי לָבוֹא אֶל־ הַמֶּלֶךְ זֶה שְׁלוֹשִׁים יוֹם׃ (12) וַיַּגִּידוּ

when-they-reported (12) day thirty this the-king to to-go I-was-called not but-I

לְמָרְדֳּכָי אֵת דִּבְרֵי אֶסְתֵּר׃ (13) וַיֹּאמֶר מָרְדֳּכַי לְהָשִׁיב

to-send-back Mordecai and-he-answered (13) Esther words-of *** to-Mordecai

אֶל־אֶסְתֵּר אַל־ תְּדַמִּי בְנַפְשֵׁךְ לְהִמָּלֵט בֵּית־ הַמֶּלֶךְ מִכָּל־

of-all-of the-king house-of to-escape in-self-of-you you-think not Esther to

הַיְּהוּדִים׃ (14) כִּי אִם־ הַחֲרֵשׁ תַּחֲרִישִׁי בָּעֵת הַזֹּאת

the-this at-the-time you-remain-silent to-remain-silent if for (14) the-Jews

רֶוַח וְהַצָּלָה יַעֲמוֹד לַיְּהוּדִים מִמָּקוֹם אַחֵר

another from-place for-the-Jews he-will-arise and-deliverance relief

וְאַתְּ וּבֵית־ אָבִיךְ תֹּאבֵדוּ וּמִי יוֹדֵעַ אִם־

but knowing and-who? you-will-perish father-of-you and-family-of but-you

Mordecai in the open square
of the city in front of the
king's gate. [7]Mordecai told
him everything that had happened to him, including the
exact amount of money Ha-
man had promised to pay into
the royal treasury for the destruction of the Jews. [8]He also
gave him a copy of the text of
the edict for their annihilation, which had been pub-
lished in Susa, to show to Esther and explain it to her, and
he told him to urge her to go
into the king's presence to beg
for mercy and plead with him
for her people.
[9]Hathach went back and reported to Esther what Mordecai had said. [10]Then she instructed him to say to Mordecai, [11]"All the king's officials
and the people of the royal
provinces know that for any
man or woman who ap-
proaches the king in the inner
court without being sum-
moned the king has but one
law: that he be put to death.
The only exception to this is
for the king to extend the gold
scepter to him and spare his
life. But thirty days have
passed since I was called to go
to the king."
[12]When Esther's words were
reported to Mordecai, [13]he sent
back this answer: "Do not
think that because you are in
the king's house you alone of
all the Jews will escape. [14]For if
you remain silent at this time,
relief and deliverance for the
Jews will arise from another
place, but you and your father's family will perish. And

°7 ק ביהודים

לָעֵת כָּזֹאת הִגַּעַתְּ לַמַּלְכוּת׃ וַתֹּאמֶר אֶסְתֵּר לְהָשִׁיב אֶל־
to to-send Esther then-she-replied (15) to-the-royalty you-came as-this for-time

מָרְדֳּכָי׃ לֵךְ כְּנוֹס אֶת־ כָּל־ הַיְּהוּדִים הַנִּמְצְאִים
the-ones-being-found the-Jews all-of *** gather-together! go! (16) Mordecai

בְּשׁוּשָׁן וְצוּמוּ עָלַי וְאַל־ תֹּאכְלוּ וְאַל־ תִּשְׁתּוּ שְׁלֹשֶׁת יָמִים
days three-of you-drink and-not you-eat and-not for-me and-fast! in-Susa

לַיְלָה וָיוֹם גַּם־אֲנִי וְנַעֲרֹתַי אָצוּם כֵּן וּבְכֵן אָבוֹא
I-will-go and-when-so same I-will-fast and-maids-of-me I and or-day night

אֶל־ הַמֶּלֶךְ אֲשֶׁר לֹא־ כַדָּת וְכַאֲשֶׁר אָבַדְתִּי אָבָדְתִּי׃
I-perish I-perish and-as-if according-to-the-law not though the-king to

וַיַּעֲבֹר מָרְדֳּכָי וַיַּעַשׂ כְּכֹל אֲשֶׁר־ צִוְּתָה
she-instructed that as-all and-he-carried-out Mordecai so-he-went-away (17)

עָלָיו אֶסְתֵּר׃ וַיְהִי׀ בַּיּוֹם הַשְּׁלִישִׁי וַתִּלְבַּשׁ אֶסְתֵּר
Esther then-she-put-on the-third on-the-day and-he-was (5:1) Esther to-him

מַלְכוּת וַתַּעֲמֹד בַּחֲצַר בֵּית־ הַמֶּלֶךְ הַפְּנִימִית נֹכַח
in-front-of the-inner the-king palace-of in-court-of and-she-stood royalty

בֵּית הַמֶּלֶךְ וְהַמֶּלֶךְ יוֹשֵׁב עַל־ כִּסֵּא מַלְכוּתוֹ בְּבֵית
in-hall-of royalty-of-him throne-of on sitting and-the-king the-king hall-of

הַמַּלְכוּת נֹכַח פֶּתַח הַבָּיִת׃ וַיְהִי כִרְאוֹת הַמֶּלֶךְ
the-king when-to-see and-he-was (2) the-hall entrance-of facing the-royalty

אֶת־אֶסְתֵּר הַמַּלְכָּה עֹמֶדֶת בֶּחָצֵר נָשְׂאָה חֵן בְּעֵינָיו
in-eyes-of-him pleasure she-found in-the-court standing the-queen Esther ***

וַיּוֹשֶׁט הַמֶּלֶךְ לְאֶסְתֵּר אֶת־ שַׁרְבִיט הַזָּהָב אֲשֶׁר
that the-gold scepter-of *** to-Esther the-king and-he-held-out

בְּיָדוֹ וַתִּקְרַב אֶסְתֵּר וַתִּגַּע בְּרֹאשׁ הַשַּׁרְבִיט׃
the-scepter on-tip-of and-she-touched Esther so-she-approached in-hand-of-him

וַיֹּאמֶר לָהּ הַמֶּלֶךְ מַה־ לָּךְ אֶסְתֵּר הַמַּלְכָּה וּמַה־
and-what? the-queen Esther to-you what? the-king to-her then-he-asked (3)

בַּקָּשָׁתֵךְ עַד־ חֲצִי הַמַּלְכוּת וְיִנָּתֵן לָךְ׃
to-you and-he-will-be-given the-kingdom half-of up-to request-of-you

וַתֹּאמֶר אֶסְתֵּר אִם־ עַל־ הַמֶּלֶךְ טוֹב יָבוֹא הַמֶּלֶךְ
the-king let-him-come pleasing the-king to if Esther and-she-replied (4)

וְהָמָן הַיּוֹם אֶל־ הַמִּשְׁתֶּה אֲשֶׁר־ עָשִׂיתִי לוֹ׃ וַיֹּאמֶר
and-he-said (5) for-him I-prepared that the-banquet to the-day with-Haman

הַמֶּלֶךְ מַהֲרוּ אֶת־ הָמָן לַעֲשׂוֹת אֶת־ דְּבַר אֶסְתֵּר וַיָּבֹא
so-he-went Esther request-of *** to-do Haman *** bring-at-once! the-king

הַמֶּלֶךְ וְהָמָן אֶל־ הַמִּשְׁתֶּה אֲשֶׁר־ עָשְׂתָה אֶסְתֵּר׃ וַיֹּאמֶר
and-he-asked (6) Esther she-prepared that the-banquet to and-Haman the-king

who knows but that you have
come to royal position for such
a time as this?"
[15]Then Esther sent this reply
to Mordecai: [16]"Go, gather together all the Jews who are in
Susa, and fast for me. Do not
eat or drink for three days,
night or day. I and my maids
will fast as you do. When this
is done, I will go to the king,
even though it is against the
law. And if I perish, I perish."
[17]So Mordecai went away
and carried out all of Esther's
instructions.

Esther's Request to the King

5 On the third day Esther
put on her royal robes and
stood in the inner court of the
palace, in front of the king's
hall. The king was sitting on
his royal throne in the hall,
facing the entrance. [2]When he
saw Queen Esther standing in
the court, he was pleased with
her and held out to her the
gold scepter that was in his
hand. So Esther approached
and touched the tip of the
scepter.
[3]Then the king asked, "What
is it, Queen Esther? What is
your request? Even up to half
the kingdom, it will be given
you."
[4]"If it pleases the king," replied Esther, "let the king, together with Haman, come today to a banquet I have prepared for him."
[5]"Bring Haman at once," the
king said, "so that we may do
what Esther asks."
So the king and Haman
went to the banquet Esther
had prepared. [6]As they were

הַמֶּלֶךְ לְאֶסְתֵּר בְּמִשְׁתֵּה הַיַּיִן מַה־ שְּׁאֵלָתֵךְ
petition-of-you what? the-wine as-drinking-of to-Esther the-king

וְיִנָּתֵן לָךְ וּמַה־ בַּקָּשָׁתֵךְ עַד־ חֲצִי
half-of up-to request-of-you and-what? to-you and-he-will-be-given

הַמַּלְכוּת וְתֵעָשׂ׃ וַתַּעַן אֶסְתֵּר וַתֹּאמַר
and-she-said Esther and-she-replied (7) and-she-will-be-granted the-kingdom

שְׁאֵלָתִי וּבַקָּשָׁתִי׃ אִם־מָצָאתִי חֵן בְּעֵינֵי הַמֶּלֶךְ
the-king in-eyes-of favor I-find if (8) and-request-of-me petition-of-me

וְאִם־ עַל־ הַמֶּלֶךְ טוֹב לָתֵת אֶת־ שְׁאֵלָתִי וְלַעֲשׂוֹת אֶת־
*** and-to-fulfill petition-of-me *** to-grant pleasing the-king to and-if

בַּקָּשָׁתִי יָבוֹא הַמֶּלֶךְ וְהָמָן אֶל־ הַמִּשְׁתֶּה אֲשֶׁר
that the-banquet to and-Haman the-king let-him-come request-of-me

אֶעֱשֶׂה לָהֶם וּמָחָר אֶעֱשֶׂה כִּדְבַר הַמֶּלֶךְ׃
the-king as-question-of I-will-answer then-tomorrow for-them I-will-prepare

וַיֵּצֵא הָמָן בַּיּוֹם הַהוּא שָׂמֵחַ וְטוֹב לֵב
spirit and-high-of happy the-that on-the-day Haman and-he-went-out (9)

וְכִרְאוֹת הָמָן אֶת־ מָרְדֳּכַי בְּשַׁעַר הַמֶּלֶךְ וְלֹא־ קָם
he-rose and-not the-king at-gate-of Mordecai *** Haman but-when-to-see

וְלֹא־ זָע מִמֶּנּוּ וַיִּמָּלֵא הָמָן עַל־ מָרְדֳּכַי חֵמָה׃
rage Mordecai against Haman then-he-was-filled of-him he-showed-fear and-not

וַיִּתְאַפַּק הָמָן וַיָּבוֹא אֶל־ בֵּיתוֹ וַיִּשְׁלַח
and-he-called home-of-him to and-he-went Haman but-he-restrained-himself (10)

וַיָּבֵא אֶת־ אֹהֲבָיו וְאֶת־ זֶרֶשׁ אִשְׁתּוֹ׃
wife-of-him Zeresh and ones-being-friends-of-him *** and-he-brought

וַיְסַפֵּר לָהֶם הָמָן אֶת־ כְּבוֹד עָשְׁרוֹ וְרֹב
and-many-of wealth-of-him vastness-of *** Haman to-them and-he-boasted (11)

בָּנָיו וְאֵת כָּל־ אֲשֶׁר גִּדְּלוֹ הַמֶּלֶךְ וְאֵת אֲשֶׁר נִשְּׂאוֹ
he-elevated-him how and the-king he-honored-him that all and sons-of-him

עַל־ הַשָּׂרִים וְעַבְדֵי הַמֶּלֶךְ׃ וַיֹּאמֶר הָמָן אַף לֹא־
not also Haman and-he-said (12) the-king and-officials-of the-nobles above

הֵבִיאָה אֶסְתֵּר הַמַּלְכָּה עִם־ הַמֶּלֶךְ אֶל־ הַמִּשְׁתֶּה אֲשֶׁר־ עָשָׂתָה כִּי
but she-gave that the-banquet to the-king with the-queen Esther she-invited

אִם־ אוֹתִי וְגַם־ לְמָחָר אֲנִי קָרוּא־ לָהּ עִם־ הַמֶּלֶךְ׃
the-king with by-her being-invited I for-tomorrow and-also me only

וְכָל־ זֶה אֵינֶנּוּ שֹׁוֶה לִי בְּכָל־ עֵת אֲשֶׁר אֲנִי
I that time at-every-of to-me satisfying not-he this but-all-of (13)

רֹאֶה אֶת־ מָרְדֳּכַי הַיְּהוּדִי יוֹשֵׁב בְּשַׁעַר הַמֶּלֶךְ׃ וַתֹּאמֶר
and-she-said (14) the-king at-gate-of sitting the-Jew Mordecai *** seeing

drinking wine, the king again asked Esther, "Now what is your petition? It will be given you. And what is your request? Even up to half the kingdom, it will be granted."

7 Esther replied, "My petition and my request is this: 8 If the king regards me with favor and if it pleases the king to grant my petition and fulfill my request, let the king and Haman come tomorrow to the banquet I will prepare for them. Then I will answer the king's question."

Haman's Rage Against Mordecai

9 Haman went out that day happy and in high spirits. But when he saw Mordecai at the king's gate and observed that he neither rose nor showed fear in his presence, he was filled with rage against Mordecai. 10 Nevertheless, Haman restrained himself and went home.

Calling together his friends and Zeresh, his wife, 11 Haman boasted to them about his vast wealth, his many sons, and all the ways the king had honored him and how he had elevated him above the other nobles and officials. 12 "And that's not all," Haman added. "I'm the only person Queen Esther invited to accompany the king to the banquet she gave. And she has invited me along with the king tomorrow. 13 But all this gives me no satisfaction as long as I see that Jew Mordecai sitting at the king's gate."

לוֹ זֶרֶשׁ אִשְׁתּוֹ וְכָל־ אֹהֲבָיו יַעֲשׂוּ־
let-them-build ones-being-friends-of-him and-all-of wife-of-him Zeresh to-him

עֵץ גָּבֹהַּ חֲמִשִּׁים אַמָּה וּבַבֹּקֶר | אֱמֹר לַמֶּלֶךְ
to-the-king ask! and-in-the-morning cubit fifty height gallows

וְיִתְלוּ אֶת־ מָרְדֳּכַי עָלָיו וּבֹא־ עִם־ הַמֶּלֶךְ אֶל־ הַמִּשְׁתֶּה
the-dinner to the-king with then-go! on-him Mordecai *** and-let-them-hang

שָׂמֵחַ וַיִּיטַב הַדָּבָר לִפְנֵי הָמָן וַיַּעַשׂ הָעֵץ׃
the-gallows and-he-built Haman before the-suggestion and-he-was-delightful happy

(6:1) בַּלַּיְלָה הַהוּא נָדְדָה שְׁנַת הַמֶּלֶךְ וַיֹּאמֶר
so-he-ordered the-king sleep-of she-fled the-that in-the-night (6:1)

לְהָבִיא אֶת־ סֵפֶר הַזִּכְרֹנוֹת דִּבְרֵי הַיָּמִים וַיִּהְיוּ
and-they-were the-days records-of the-chronicles book-of *** to-bring

נִקְרָאִים לִפְנֵי הַמֶּלֶךְ׃ (2) וַיִּמָּצֵא כָתוּב אֲשֶׁר
that being-recorded and-he-was-found (2) the-king before ones-being-read

הִגִּיד מָרְדֳּכַי עַל־ בִּגְתָנָא וָתֶרֶשׁ שְׁנֵי סָרִיסֵי הַמֶּלֶךְ
the-king officers-of two-of and-Teresh Bigthana about Mordecai he-exposed

מִשֹּׁמְרֵי הַסַּף אֲשֶׁר בִּקְשׁוּ לִשְׁלֹחַ יָד
hand to-send they-conspired who the-doorway from-ones-guarding-of

בַּמֶּלֶךְ אֲחַשְׁוֵרוֹשׁ׃ (3) וַיֹּאמֶר הַמֶּלֶךְ מַה־ נַּעֲשָׂה
he-was-done what? the-king and-he-asked (3) Ahasuerus against-the-king

יְקָר וּגְדוּלָּה לְמָרְדֳּכַי עַל־ זֶה וַיֹּאמְרוּ נַעֲרֵי הַמֶּלֶךְ
the-king men-of and-they-answered this for for-Mordecai and-recognition honor

מְשָׁרְתָיו לֹא־ נַעֲשָׂה עִמּוֹ דָּבָר׃ (4) וַיֹּאמֶר הַמֶּלֶךְ
the-king and-he-said (4) anything for-him he-was-done not ones-attending-him

מִי בֶחָצֵר וְהָמָן בָּא לַחֲצַר בֵּית־ הַמֶּלֶךְ
the-king palace-of into-court-of he-entered now-Haman in-the-court who?

הַחִיצוֹנָה לֵאמֹר לַמֶּלֶךְ לִתְלוֹת אֶת־ מָרְדֳּכַי עַל־ הָעֵץ אֲשֶׁר־
that the-gallows on Mordecai *** to-hang to-the-king to-speak the-outer

הֵכִין לוֹ׃ (5) וַיֹּאמְרוּ נַעֲרֵי הַמֶּלֶךְ אֵלָיו הִנֵּה
see! to-him the-king attendants-of and-they-answered (5) for-him he-erected

הָמָן עֹמֵד בֶּחָצֵר וַיֹּאמֶר הַמֶּלֶךְ יָבוֹא׃
let-him-come-in the-king and-he-ordered in-the-court standing Haman

(6) וַיָּבוֹא הָמָן וַיֹּאמֶר לוֹ הַמֶּלֶךְ מַה־לַּעֲשׂוֹת
to-do what? the-king to-him then-he-asked Haman when-he-entered (6)

בָּאִישׁ אֲשֶׁר הַמֶּלֶךְ חָפֵץ בִּיקָרוֹ וַיֹּאמֶר הָמָן
Haman now-he-thought in-honor-of-him he-delights the-king whom for-the-man

בְּלִבּוֹ לְמִי יַחְפֹּץ הַמֶּלֶךְ לַעֲשׂוֹת יְקָר יוֹתֵר מִמֶּנִּי׃
than-me other honor to-do the-king he-would-rather to-whom? to-self-of-him

14His wife Zeresh and all his
friends said to him, "Have a
gallows built, seventy-five
feet[h] high, and ask the king in
the morning to have Mordecai
hanged on it.[i] Then go with
the king to the dinner and be
happy." This suggestion delighted Haman, and he had
the gallows built.

Mordecai Honored

6 That night the king could
not sleep; so he ordered
the book of the chronicles, the
record of his reign, to be
brought in and read to him. 2It
was found recorded there that
Mordecai had exposed Big-
thana and Teresh, two of the
king's officers, who guarded
the doorway and who had
conspired to assassinate King
Xerxes.
3"What honor and recogni-
tion has Mordecai received for
this?" the king asked.
"Nothing has been done for
him," his attendants an-
swered.
4The king said, "Who is in
the court?" Now Haman had
just entered the outer court of
the palace to speak to the king
about hanging Mordecai on
the gallows he had erected for
him.
5His attendants answered,
"Haman is standing in the
court."
"Bring him in," the king ordered.
6When Haman entered, the
king asked him, "What should
be done for the man the king
delights to honor?"
Now Haman thought to
himself, "Who is there that
the king would rather honor

[h]14 Hebrew *fifty cubits* (about 23 meters)
[i]14 Or *Have poles erected ... Mordecai hung on it*

*6 Most mss have *dagesh* in the *lamed* (לִּ).

וַיֹּאמֶר הָמָן אֶל־הַמֶּלֶךְ אִישׁ אֲשֶׁר הַמֶּלֶךְ חָפֵץ
he-delights the-king whom man the-king to Haman so-he-answered (7)

בִּיקָרוֹ׃ יָבִיאוּ לְבוּשׁ מַלְכוּת אֲשֶׁר לָבַשׁ־ בּוֹ
on-him he-wore that royalty robe-of have-them-bring (8) in-honor-of-him

הַמֶּלֶךְ וְסוּס אֲשֶׁר רָכַב עָלָיו הַמֶּלֶךְ וַאֲשֶׁר נִתַּן
he-was-placed and-that the-king on-him he-rode that and-horse the-king

כֶּתֶר מַלְכוּת בְּרֹאשׁוֹ׃ וְנָתוֹן הַלְּבוּשׁ וְהַסּוּס
and-the-horse the-robe and-to-entrust (9) on-head-of-him royalty crest-of

עַל־ יַד־ אִישׁ מִשָּׂרֵי הַמֶּלֶךְ הַפַּרְתְּמִים וְהִלְבִּישׁוּ אֶת־
*** and-let-them-robe the-nobles the-king from-princes-of man hand-of to

הָאִישׁ אֲשֶׁר הַמֶּלֶךְ חָפֵץ בִּיקָרוֹ וְהִרְכִּיבֻהוּ עַל־
on and-let-them-lead-him in-honor-of-him he-delights the-king whom the-man

הַסּוּס בִּרְחוֹב הָעִיר וְקָרְאוּ לְפָנָיו כָּכָה
this before-him and-let-them-proclaim the-city through-street-of the-horse

יֵעָשֶׂה לָאִישׁ אֲשֶׁר הַמֶּלֶךְ חָפֵץ בִּיקָרוֹ׃
in-honor-of-him he-delights the-king whom for-the-man he-is-done

וַיֹּאמֶר הַמֶּלֶךְ לְהָמָן מַהֵר קַח אֶת־הַלְּבוּשׁ וְאֶת־
and the-robe *** get! go-at-once! to-Haman the-king and-he-commanded (10)

הַסּוּס כַּאֲשֶׁר דִּבַּרְתָּ וַעֲשֵׂה־ כֵן לְמָרְדֳּכַי הַיְּהוּדִי
the-Jew for-Mordecai this and-do! you-suggested just-as the-horse

הַיּוֹשֵׁב בְּשַׁעַר הַמֶּלֶךְ אַל־ תַּפֵּל דָּבָר מִכֹּל אֲשֶׁר
that of-all anything you-neglect not the-king at-gate-of the-one-sitting

דִּבַּרְתָּ׃ וַיִּקַּח הָמָן אֶת־ הַלְּבוּשׁ וְאֶת־ הַסּוּס וַיַּלְבֵּשׁ
and-he-robed the-horse and the-robe *** Haman so-he-got (11) you-recommended

אֶת־ מָרְדֳּכָי וַיַּרְכִּיבֵהוּ בִּרְחוֹב הָעִיר
the-city through-street-of and-he-led-on-horse-him Mordecai ***

וַיִּקְרָא לְפָנָיו כָּכָה יֵעָשֶׂה לָאִישׁ אֲשֶׁר חָפֵץ
the-king whom for-the-man he-is-done this before-him and-he-proclaimed

הַמֶּלֶךְ בִּיקָרוֹ׃ וַיָּשָׁב מָרְדֳּכַי אֶל־ שַׁעַר
gate-of to Mordecai then-he-returned (12) in-honor-of-him he-delights

הַמֶּלֶךְ וְהָמָן נִדְחַף אֶל־ בֵּיתוֹ אָבֵל וַחֲפוּי רֹאשׁ׃
head and-being-covered-of grief home-of-him to he-rushed but-Haman the-king

וַיְסַפֵּר הָמָן לְזֶרֶשׁ אִשְׁתּוֹ וּלְכָל־
and-to-all-of wife-of-him to-Zeresh Haman and-he-told (13)

אֹהֲבָיו אֵת כָּל־אֲשֶׁר קָרָהוּ וַיֹּאמְרוּ לוֹ
to-him and-they-said he-happened-to-him that all *** ones-being-friends-of-him

חֲכָמָיו וְזֶרֶשׁ אִשְׁתּוֹ אִם מִזֶּרַע הַיְּהוּדִים
the-Jews from-descendant-of since wife-of-him and-Zeresh advisers-of-him

than me?" 7So he answered the king, "For the man the king delights to honor, 8have them bring a royal robe the king has worn and a horse the king has ridden, one with a royal crest placed on its head. 9Then let the robe and horse be entrusted to one of the king's most noble princes. Let them robe the man the king delights to honor, and lead him on the horse through the city streets, proclaiming before him, 'This is what is done for the man the king delights to honor!' "

10"Go at once," the king commanded Haman. "Get the robe and the horse and do just as you have suggested for Mordecai the Jew, who sits at the king's gate. Do not neglect anything you have recommended."

11So Haman got the robe and the horse. He robed Mordecai, and led him on horseback through the city streets, proclaiming before him, "This is what is done for the man the king delights to honor!"

12Afterward Mordecai returned to the king's gate. But Haman rushed home, with his head covered in grief, 13and told Zeresh his wife and all his friends everything that had happened to him.

His advisers and his wife Zeresh said to him, "Since

מָרְדֳּכַי אֲשֶׁר הַחִלּוֹתָ לִנְפֹּל לְפָנָיו לֹא־ תוּכַל לוֹ כִּי־

surely against-him you-can-stand not before-him to-fall you-began whom Mordecai

נָפוֹל תִּפּוֹל לְפָנָיו׃ עוֹדָם מְדַבְּרִים

ones-talking still-they (14) before-him you-will-come-to-ruin to-come-to-ruin

עִמּוֹ וְסָרִיסֵי הַמֶּלֶךְ הִגִּיעוּ וַיַּבְהִלוּ לְהָבִיא אֶת־

*** to-take and-they-hurried they-arrived the-king and-eunuchs-of with-him

הָמָן אֶל־ הַמִּשְׁתֶּה אֲשֶׁר־ עָשְׂתָה אֶסְתֵּר׃ וַיָּבֹא הַמֶּלֶךְ

the-king so-he-went (7:1) Esther she-prepared that the-banquet to Haman

וְהָמָן לִשְׁתּוֹת עִם־ אֶסְתֵּר הַמַּלְכָּה׃ וַיֹּאמֶר הַמֶּלֶךְ לְאֶסְתֵּר

to-Esther the-king and-he-asked (2) the-queen Esther with to-dine and-Haman

גַּם בַּיּוֹם הַשֵּׁנִי בְּמִשְׁתֵּה הַיַּיִן מַה־ שְּׁאֵלָתֵךְ

petition-of-you what? the-wine as-drinking-of the-second on-the-day again

אֶסְתֵּר הַמַּלְכָּה וְתִנָּתֵן לָךְ וּמַה־ בַּקָּשָׁתֵךְ

request-of-you and-what? to-you and-she-will-be-given the-queen Esther

עַד־ חֲצִי הַמַּלְכוּת וְתֵעָשׂ׃ וַתַּעַן אֶסְתֵּר

Esther then-she-answered (3) and-she-will-be-granted the-kingdom half-of up-to

הַמַּלְכָּה וַתֹּאמַר אִם־מָצָאתִי חֵן בְּעֵינֶיךָ הַמֶּלֶךְ וְאִם־עַל־

to and-if the-king in-eyes-of-you favor I-found if and-she-said the-queen

הַמֶּלֶךְ טוֹב תִּנָּתֶן־ לִי נַפְשִׁי בִּשְׁאֵלָתִי

as-petition-of-me life-of-me to-me let-her-be-granted pleasing the-king

וְעַמִּי בְּבַקָּשָׁתִי׃ כִּי נִמְכַּרְנוּ אֲנִי וְעַמִּי

and-people-of-me I we-were-sold for (4) as-request-of-me and-people-of-me

לְהַשְׁמִיד לַהֲרוֹג וּלְאַבֵּד וְאִלּוּ לַעֲבָדִים

as-male-slaves and-if and-to-annihilate and-to-slaughter to-destroy

וְלִשְׁפָחוֹת נִמְכַּרְנוּ הֶחֱרַשְׁתִּי כִּי אֵין הַצָּר

the-distress not because I-would-keep-quiet we-were-sold and-as-female-slaves

שֹׁוֶה בְּנֵזֶק הַמֶּלֶךְ׃ וַיֹּאמֶר הַמֶּלֶךְ אֲחַשְׁוֵרוֹשׁ

Ahasuerus the-king and-he-asked (5) the-king for-disturbance-of justifying

וַיֹּאמֶר לְאֶסְתֵּר הַמַּלְכָּה מִי הוּא זֶה וְאֵי־ זֶה הוּא אֲשֶׁר־

who he this and-where? this he who? the-queen to-Esther and-he-said

מְלָאוֹ לִבּוֹ לַעֲשׂוֹת כֵּן׃ וַתֹּאמֶר־* אֶסְתֵּר אִישׁ צַר

adversary man Esther and-she-said (6) such to-do heart-of-him he-filled-him

וְאוֹיֵב הָמָן הָרָע הַזֶּה וְהָמָן נִבְעַת

he-was-terrified then-Haman the-this the-vile Haman and-being-enemy

מִלִּפְנֵי הַמֶּלֶךְ וְהַמַּלְכָּה׃ וְהַמֶּלֶךְ קָם בַּחֲמָתוֹ

in-rage-of-him he-got-up and-the-king (7) and-the-queen the-king from-before

מִמִּשְׁתֵּה הַיַּיִן אֶל־ גִּנַּת הַבִּיתָן וְהָמָן עָמַד

he-stayed but-Haman the-palace garden-of into the-wine from-drinking-of

Mordecai, before whom your downfall has started, is of Jewish origin, you cannot stand against him—you will surely come to ruin!" [14]While they were still talking with him, the king's eunuchs arrived and hurried Haman away to the banquet Esther had prepared.

Haman Hanged

7 So the king and Haman went to dine with Queen Esther, [2]and as they were drinking wine on that second day, the king again asked, "Queen Esther, what is your petition? It will be given you. What is your request? Even up to half the kingdom, it will be granted."

[3]Then Queen Esther answered, "If I have found favor with you, O king, and if it pleases your majesty, grant me my life—this is my petition. And spare my people—this is my request. [4]For I and my people have been sold for destruction and slaughter and annihilation. If we had merely been sold as male and female slaves, I would have kept quiet, because no such distress would justify disturbing the king.[j]"

[5]King Xerxes asked Queen Esther, "Who is he? Where is the man who has dared to do such a thing?"

[6]Esther said, "The adversary and enemy is this vile Haman."

Then Haman was terrified before the king and queen. [7]The king got up in a rage, left his wine and went out into the palace garden. But Haman,

j4 Or *quiet, but the compensation our adversary offers cannot be compared with the loss the king would suffer*

*6 Most mss have no *maqqeph* after this word (וַתֹּאמֶר).

לְבַקֵּשׁ עַל־ נַפְשׁוֹ מֵאֶסְתֵּר הַמַּלְכָּה כִּי רָאָה כִּי־
that he-realized for the-queen from-Esther life-of-him for to-beg

כָלְתָה אֵלָיו הָרָעָה מֵאֵת הַמֶּלֶךְ׃ וְהַמֶּלֶךְ
and-the-king (8) the-king from-with the-fate about-him she-was-decided

שָׁב מִגִּנַּת הַבִּיתָן אֶל־ בֵּית ׀ מִשְׁתֵּה הַיַּיִן וְהָמָן
and-Haman the-wine banquet-of hall-of to the-palace from-garden-of returning

נֹפֵל עַל־ הַמִּטָּה אֲשֶׁר אֶסְתֵּר עָלֶיהָ וַיֹּאמֶר הַמֶּלֶךְ הֲגַם
even? the-king and-he-exclaimed on-her Esther where the-couch on falling

לִכְבּוֹשׁ אֶת־ הַמַּלְכָּה עִמִּי בַּבָּיִת הַדָּבָר יָצָא מִפִּי
from-mouth-of he-left the-word in-the-house with-me the-queen *** to-molest

הַמֶּלֶךְ וּפְנֵי הָמָן חָפוּ׃ וַיֹּאמֶר חַרְבוֹנָה אֶחָד מִן־
from one Harbona then-he-said (9) they-covered Haman and-faces-of the-king

הַסָּרִיסִים לִפְנֵי הַמֶּלֶךְ גַּם הִנֵּה־ הָעֵץ אֲשֶׁר־ עָשָׂה הָמָן
Haman he-made that the-gallows see! also the-king before the-eunuchs

לְמָרְדֳּכַי אֲשֶׁר דִּבֶּר־ טוֹב עַל־ הַמֶּלֶךְ עֹמֵד בְּבֵית הָמָן
Haman by-house-of standing the-king for help he-spoke-up who for-Mordecai

גָּבֹהַּ חֲמִשִּׁים אַמָּה וַיֹּאמֶר הַמֶּלֶךְ תְּלֻהוּ עָלָיו׃ וַיִּתְלוּ
so-they-hanged (10) on-him hang-him! the-king and-he-said cubit fifty height

אֶת־ הָמָן עַל־ הָעֵץ אֲשֶׁר־ הֵכִין לְמָרְדֳּכָי וַחֲמַת הַמֶּלֶךְ
the-king then-fury-of for-Mordecai he-prepared that the-gallows on Haman ***

שָׁכָכָה׃ בַּיּוֹם הַהוּא נָתַן הַמֶּלֶךְ אֲחַשְׁוֵרוֹשׁ לְאֶסְתֵּר
to-Esther Ahasuerus the-king he-gave the-same on-the-day (8:1) she-subsided

הַמַּלְכָּה אֶת־ בֵּית הָמָן צֹרֵר הַיְּהוּדִיים וּמָרְדֳּכַי
and-Mordecai the-Jews one-being-enemy-of Haman estate-of *** the-queen

בָּא לִפְנֵי הַמֶּלֶךְ כִּי־ הִגִּידָה אֶסְתֵּר מַה הוּא־ לָהּ׃
to-her he how Esther she-told for the-king into-presences-of he-came

וַיָּסַר הַמֶּלֶךְ אֶת־ טַבַּעְתּוֹ אֲשֶׁר הֶעֱבִיר
he-reclaimed which signet-ring-of-him *** the-king and-he-took-off (2)

מֵהָמָן וַיִּתְּנָהּ לְמָרְדֳּכָי וַתָּשֶׂם אֶסְתֵּר אֶת־
*** Esther and-she-appointed to-Mordecai and-he-presented-her from-Haman

מָרְדֳּכַי עַל־ בֵּית הָמָן׃ וַתּוֹסֶף אֶסְתֵּר וַתְּדַבֵּר
and-she-pleaded Esther and-she-did-again (3) Haman estate-of over Mordecai

לִפְנֵי הַמֶּלֶךְ וַתִּפֹּל לִפְנֵי רַגְלָיו וַתֵּבְךְּ וַתִּתְחַנֶּן־
and-she-begged and-she-wept feet-of-him before and-she-fell the-king before

לוֹ לְהַעֲבִיר אֶת־ רָעַת הָמָן הָאֲגָגִי וְאֵת מַחֲשַׁבְתּוֹ אֲשֶׁר
which plan-of-him and the-Agagite Haman evil-of *** to-put-end to-him

חָשַׁב עַל־ הַיְּהוּדִים׃ וַיּוֹשֶׁט הַמֶּלֶךְ לְאֶסְתֵּר אֵת
*** to-Esther the-king then-he-extended (4) the-Jews against he-devised

°1 ק היהודים

realizing that the king had already decided his fate, stayed behind to beg Queen Esther for his life.
[8]Just as the king returned from the palace garden to the banquet hall, Haman was falling on the couch where Esther was reclining.
The king exclaimed, "Will he even molest the queen while she is with me in the house?"
As soon as the word left the king's mouth, they covered Haman's face.
[9]Then Harbona, one of the eunuchs attending the king, said, "A gallows seventy-five feet[k] high stands by Haman's house. He had it made for Mordecai, who spoke up to help the king."
The king said, "Hang him on it!"
[10]So they hanged Haman on the gallows he had prepared for Mordecai. Then the king's fury subsided.

The King's Edict in Behalf of the Jews

8 That same day King Xerxes gave Queen Esther the estate of Haman, the enemy of the Jews. And Mordecai came into the presence of the king, for Esther had told how he was related to her.
[2]The king took off his signet ring, which he had reclaimed from Haman, and presented it to Mordecai. And Esther appointed him over Haman's estate.
[3]Esther again pleaded with the king, falling at his feet and weeping. She begged him to put an end to the evil plan of Haman the Agagite, which he had devised against the Jews.
[4]Then the king extended the

[k]9 Hebrew *fifty cubits* (about 23 meters)

שַׁרְבִט הַזָּהָב וַתָּקָם אֶסְתֵּר וַתַּעֲמֹד לִפְנֵי הַמֶּלֶךְ׃
the-king before and-she-stood Esther and-she-arose the-gold scepter-of

וַתֹּאמֶר אִם־עַל־הַמֶּלֶךְ טוֹב וְאִם־מָצָאתִי חֵן לְפָנָיו
before-him favor I-find and-if pleasing the-king to if and-she-said (5)

וְכָשֵׁר הַדָּבָר לִפְנֵי הַמֶּלֶךְ וְטוֹבָה אֲנִי בְּעֵינָיו
in-eyes-of-him I and-pleasing the-king before the-thing and-he-is-right

יִכָּתֵב לְהָשִׁיב אֶת־הַסְּפָרִים מַחֲשֶׁבֶת הָמָן בֶּן־
son-of Haman device-of the-dispatches *** to-overrule let-him-be-written

הַמְּדָתָא הָאֲגָגִי אֲשֶׁר כָּתַב לְאַבֵּד אֶת־הַיְּהוּדִים אֲשֶׁר בְּכָל־
in-all-of who the-Jews *** to-destroy he-wrote that the-Agagite Hammedatha

מְדִינוֹת הַמֶּלֶךְ׃ כִּי אֵיכָכָה אוּכַל וְרָאִיתִי בָּרָעָה אֲשֶׁר־
that to-the-disaster and-I-see can-I-bear how? for (6) the-king provinces-of

יִמְצָא אֶת־עַמִּי וְאֵיכָכָה אוּכַל וְרָאִיתִי בְּאָבְדַן
to-destruction-of and-I-see can-I-bear and-how? people-of-me *** he-will-fall-on

מוֹלַדְתִּי׃ וַיֹּאמֶר הַמֶּלֶךְ אֲחַשְׁוֵרֹשׁ לְאֶסְתֵּר הַמַּלְכָּה
the-queen to-Esther Ahasuerus the-king and-he-replied (7) family-of-me

וּלְמָרְדֳּכַי הַיְּהוּדִי הִנֵּה בֵית־הָמָן נָתַתִּי לְאֶסְתֵּר וְאֹתוֹ
and-him to-Esther I-gave Haman estate-of see! the-Jew and-to-Mordecai

תָּלוּ עַל־הָעֵץ עַל אֲשֶׁר־שָׁלַח יָדוֹ בַּיְּהוּדִיים°׃
against-the-Jews hand-of-him he-sent that because the-gallows on they-hanged

וְאַתֶּם כִּתְבוּ עַל־הַיְּהוּדִים כַּטּוֹב בְּעֵינֵיכֶם
in-eyes-of-you as-the-best the-Jews in-behalf-of write! now-you (8)

בְּשֵׁם הַמֶּלֶךְ וְחִתְמוּ בְּטַבַּעַת הַמֶּלֶךְ כִּי־כְתָב
document for the-king with-signet-ring-of and-seal! the-king in-name-of

אֲשֶׁר־נִכְתָּב בְּשֵׁם־הַמֶּלֶךְ וְנַחְתּוֹם בְּטַבַּעַת
with-signet-ring-of and-to-be-sealed the-king in-name-of being-written which

הַמֶּלֶךְ אֵין לְהָשִׁיב׃ וַיִּקָּרְאוּ סֹפְרֵי־הַמֶּלֶךְ
the-king secretaries-of and-they-were-summoned (9) to-revoke not the-king

בָּעֵת־הַהִיא בַּחֹדֶשׁ הַשְּׁלִישִׁי הוּא־חֹדֶשׁ סִיוָן בִּשְׁלוֹשָׁה
on-three Sivan month-of that the-third in-the-month the-that at-the-time

וְעֶשְׂרִים בּוֹ וַיִּכָּתֵב כְּכָל־אֲשֶׁר־צִוָּה מָרְדֳּכַי אֶל־
to Mordecai he-ordered that as-all and-he-was-written of-him and-twenty

הַיְּהוּדִים וְאֶל הָאֲחַשְׁדַּרְפְּנִים־וְהַפַּחוֹת וְשָׂרֵי הַמְּדִינוֹת
the-provinces and-nobles-of and-the-governors the-satraps and-to the-Jews

אֲשֶׁר ׀ מֵהֹדּוּ וְעַד־כּוּשׁ שֶׁבַע וְעֶשְׂרִים וּמֵאָה מְדִינָה מְדִינָה
province province and-hundred and-twenty seven Cush and-to from-India that

וּמְדִינָה כִּכְתָבָהּ וְעַם וָעָם כִּלְשֹׁנוֹ וְאֶל־
and-to in-language-of-him and-people and-people in-script-of-her and-province

gold scepter to Esther and she
arose and stood before him.
5"If it pleases the king," she
said, "and if he regards me
with favor and thinks it the
right thing to do, and if he is
pleased with me, let an order
be written overruling the dispatches that Haman son of
Hammedatha, the Agagite,
devised and wrote to destroy
the Jews in all the king's provinces. 6For how can I bear to
see disaster fall on my people?
How can I bear to see the destruction of my family?"
7King Xerxes replied to
Queen Esther and to Mordecai
the Jew, "Because Haman attacked the Jews, I have given
his estate to Esther, and they
have hanged him on the gallows.[l] 8Now write another decree in the king's name in behalf of the Jews as seems best
to you, and seal it with the
king's signet ring—for no
document written in the
king's name and sealed with
his ring can be revoked."
9At once the royal secretaries
were summoned—on the
twenty-third day of the third
month, the month of Sivan.
They wrote out all Mordecai's
orders to the Jews, and to the
satraps, governors and nobles
of the 127 provinces stretching from India to Cush.[m] These
orders were written in the
script of each province and the
language of each people and

[l]7 Or *have hung him on a pole*
[m]9 That is, the upper Nile region

°7 ק׳ ביהודים

היהודים כִּכְתָבָם וְכִלְשׁוֹנָם׃ (10) וַיִּכְתֹּב
and-he-wrote (10) and-in-language-of-them in-script-of-them the-Jews

בְּשֵׁם הַמֶּלֶךְ אֲחַשְׁוֵרֹשׁ וַיַּחְתֹּם בְּטַבַּעַת הַמֶּלֶךְ
the-king with-signet-ring-of and-he-sealed Ahasuerus the-king in-name-of

וַיִּשְׁלַח סְפָרִים בְּיַד הָרָצִים בַּסּוּסִים
on-the-mounts the-ones-being-couriers by-hand-of dispatches and-he-sent

רֹכְבֵי הָרֶכֶשׁ הָאֲחַשְׁתְּרָנִים בְּנֵי הָרַמָּכִים׃
the-studs ones-bred-of the-royal-ones the-fast-horse ones-riding-of

(11) אֲשֶׁר נָתַן הַמֶּלֶךְ לַיְּהוּדִים ׀ אֲשֶׁר בְּכָל־ עִיר־ וָעִיר
and-city city in-every-of who to-the-Jews the-king he-granted that (11)

לְהִקָּהֵל וְלַעֲמֹד עַל־ נַפְשָׁם לְהַשְׁמִיד וְלַהֲרֹג
and-to-kill to-destroy self-of-them to and-to-protect to-assemble

וּלְאַבֵּד אֶת־ כָּל־ חֵיל עַם וּמְדִינָה
or-province nation armed-force-of any-of *** and-to-annihilate

הַצָּרִים אֹתָם טַף וְנָשִׁים וּשְׁלָלָם לָבוֹז׃
to-plunder and-property-of-them and-women child them the-ones-attacking

(12) בְּיוֹם אֶחָד בְּכָל־ מְדִינוֹת הַמֶּלֶךְ אֲחַשְׁוֵרוֹשׁ בִּשְׁלוֹשָׁה עָשָׂר
ten on-three Ahasuerus the-king provinces-of in-all-of one on-day (12)

לְחֹדֶשׁ שְׁנֵים־עָשָׂר הוּא־ חֹדֶשׁ אֲדָר׃ (13) פַּתְשֶׁגֶן הַכְּתָב לְהִנָּתֵן
to-be-issued the-text copy-of (13) Adar month-of that ten two of-month-of

דָּת בְּכָל־ מְדִינָה וּמְדִינָה גָּלוּי לְכָל־ הָעַמִּים
the-peoples to-all-of being-made-known and-province province in-every-of law

וְלִהְיוֹת הַיְּהוּדִיים עֲתוּדִים לַיּוֹם הַזֶּה לְהִנָּקֵם
to-avenge-self the-this on-the-day ones-ready the-Jews so-to-be

מֵאֹיְבֵיהֶם׃ (14) הָרָצִים רֹכְבֵי
ones-riding-of the-ones-being-couriers (14) on-ones-being-enemies-of-them

הָרֶכֶשׁ הָאֲחַשְׁתְּרָנִים יָצְאוּ מְבֹהָלִים וּדְחוּפִים
and-ones-being-spurred-on ones-racing they-went-out the-royal-ones the-horse

בִּדְבַר הַמֶּלֶךְ וְהַדָּת נִתְּנָה בְּשׁוּשַׁן הַבִּירָה׃
the-citadel in-Susa she-was-issued and-the-edict the-king by-command-of

(15) וּמָרְדֳּכַי יָצָא ׀ מִלִּפְנֵי הַמֶּלֶךְ בִּלְבוּשׁ מַלְכוּת
royalty in-garment-of the-king from-presences-of he-left and-Mordecai (15)

תְּכֵלֶת וָחוּר וַעֲטֶרֶת זָהָב גְּדוֹלָה וְתַכְרִיךְ בּוּץ וְאַרְגָּמָן
and-purple fine-linen and-robe-of large gold and-crown-of and-white blue

וְהָעִיר שׁוּשָׁן צָהֲלָה וְשָׂמֵחָה׃ (16) לַיְּהוּדִים הָיְתָה
she-was for-the-Jews (16) and-she-rejoiced she-celebrated Susa and-the-city

אוֹרָה וְשִׂמְחָה וְשָׂשֹׂן וִיקָר׃ (17) וּבְכָל־ מְדִינָה
province and-in-every-of (17) and-honor and-gladness and-joy happiness

also to the Jews in their own script and language. [10]Mordecai wrote in the name of King Xerxes, sealed the dispatches with the king's signet ring, and sent them by mounted couriers, who rode fast horses especially bred for the king.

[11]The king's edict granted the Jews in every city the right to assemble and protect themselves; to destroy, kill and annihilate any armed force of any nationality or province that might attack them and their women and children; and to plunder the property of their enemies. [12]The day appointed for the Jews to do this in all the provinces of King Xerxes was the thirteenth day of the twelfth month, the month of Adar. [13]A copy of the text of the edict was to be issued as law in every province and made known to the people of every nationality so that the Jews would be ready on that day to avenge themselves on their enemies.

[14]The couriers, riding the royal horses, raced out, spurred on by the king's command. And the edict was also issued in the citadel of Susa.

[15]Mordecai left the king's presence wearing royal garments of blue and white, a large crown of gold and a purple robe of fine linen. And the city of Susa held a joyous celebration. [16]For the Jews it was a time of happiness and joy, gladness and honor. [17]In every

°13a ק היהודים
°13b ק עתידים

וּמְדִינָה וּבְכָל־ עִיר וָעִיר מְקוֹם אֲשֶׁר דְּבַר־ הַמֶּלֶךְ
the-king command-of where place-of and-city city and-in-every-of and-province

וְדָתוֹ מַגִּיעַ שִׂמְחָה וְשָׂשׂוֹן לַיְּהוּדִים מִשְׁתֶּה וְיוֹם
and-day-of feast among-the-Jews and-gladness joy going and-edict-of-him

טוֹב וְרַבִּים מֵעַמֵּי הָאָרֶץ מִתְיַהֲדִים כִּי־
because ones-becoming-Jews the-nation from-peoples-of and-many celebration

נָפַל פַּחַד־ הַיְּהוּדִים עֲלֵיהֶם׃ וּבִשְׁנֵים עָשָׂר חֹדֶשׁ הוּא־ חֹדֶשׁ
month-of that month ten and-in-two (9:1) to-them the-Jews fear-of he-seized

אֲדָר בִּשְׁלוֹשָׁה עָשָׂר יוֹם בּוֹ אֲשֶׁר הִגִּיעַ דְּבַר־ הַמֶּלֶךְ וְדָתוֹ
and-command-of-him the-king edict-of he-came when of-him day ten on-three Adar

לְהֵעָשׂוֹת בַּיּוֹם אֲשֶׁר שִׂבְּרוּ אֹיְבֵי הַיְּהוּדִים
the-Jews ones-being-enemies-of they-hoped when on-the-day to-be-carried-out

לִשְׁלוֹט בָּהֶם וְנַהֲפוֹךְ הוּא אֲשֶׁר יִשְׁלְטוּ
they-got-upper-hand for this but-to-be-overturned over-them to-overpower

הַיְּהוּדִים הֵמָּה בְּשֹׂנְאֵיהֶם׃ נִקְהֲלוּ הַיְּהוּדִים
the-Jews and-they-assembled (2) over-ones-hating-them they the-Jews

בְּעָרֵיהֶם בְּכָל־ מְדִינוֹת הַמֶּלֶךְ אֲחַשְׁוֵרוֹשׁ* לִשְׁלֹחַ יָד
hand to-send Ahasuerus the-king provinces-of in-all-of in-cities-of-them

בִּמְבַקְשֵׁי רָעָתָם וְאִישׁ לֹא־ עָמַד
he-could-stand not and-man destruction-of-them against-ones-seeking-of

לִפְנֵיהֶם כִּי־ נָפַל פַּחְדָּם עַל־ כָּל־ הָעַמִּים׃
the-peoples all-of on fear-of-them he-fell because against-them

וְכָל־ שָׂרֵי הַמְּדִינוֹת וְהָאֲחַשְׁדַּרְפְּנִים וְהַפַּחוֹת
and-the-governors and-the-satraps the-provinces nobles-of and-all-of (3)

וְעֹשֵׂי הַמְּלָאכָה אֲשֶׁר לַמֶּלֶךְ מְנַשְּׂאִים אֶת־הַיְּהוּדִים
the-Jews *** ones-helping of-the-king who the-work and-ones-administering-of

כִּי־ נָפַל פַּחַד־ מָרְדֳּכַי עֲלֵיהֶם׃ כִּי־ גָדוֹל מָרְדֳּכַי
Mordecai prominent for (4) to-them Mordecai fear-of he-seized because

בְּבֵית הַמֶּלֶךְ וְשָׁמְעוֹ הוֹלֵךְ בְּכָל־
through-all-of spreading and-reputation-of-him the-king in-palace-of

הַמְּדִינוֹת כִּי־ הָאִישׁ מָרְדֳּכַי הוֹלֵךְ וְגָדוֹל׃
and-powerful becoming-more Mordecai the-man for the-provinces

וַיַּכּוּ הַיְּהוּדִים בְּכָל־ אֹיְבֵיהֶם
ones-being-enemies-of-them to-all-of the-Jews and-they-struck-down (5)

מַכַּת־ חֶרֶב וְהֶרֶג וְאַבְדָן וַיַּעֲשׂוּ בְשֹׂנְאֵיהֶם
to-ones-hating-them and-they-did and-destruction and-killing sword striking-of

כִּרְצוֹנָם׃ וּבְשׁוּשַׁן הַבִּירָה הָרְגוּ הַיְּהוּדִים
the-Jews they-killed the-citadel and-in-Susa (6) as-pleasure-of-them

province and in every city, wherever the edict of the king went, there was joy and gladness among the Jews, with feasting and celebrating. And many people of other nationalities became Jews because fear of the Jews had seized them.

Triumph of the Jews

9 On the thirteenth day of the twelfth month, the month of Adar, the edict commanded by the king was to be carried out. On this day the enemies of the Jews had hoped to overpower them, but now the tables were turned and the Jews got the upper hand over those who hated them. 2The Jews assembled in their cities in all the provinces of King Xerxes to attack those seeking their destruction. No one could stand against them, because the people of all the other nationalities were afraid of them. 3And all the nobles of the provinces, the satraps, the governors and the king's administrators helped the Jews, because fear of Mordecai had seized them. 4Mordecai was prominent in the palace; his reputation spread throughout the provinces, and he became more and more powerful.

5The Jews struck down all their enemies with the sword, killing and destroying them, and they did what they pleased to those who hated them. 6In the citadel of Susa, the Jews killed and destroyed

*2 Most mss have *hateph pathah* under the *aleph* (אֲ).

וְאַבֵּד חֲמֵשׁ מֵאוֹת אִישׁ׃ וְאֵת ׀ פַּרְשַׁנְדָּתָא וְאֵת ׀ דַּלְפוֹן וְאֵת ׀
and Dalphon and Parshandatha also (7) man hundreds five-of and-to-destroy

אַסְפָּתָא׃ וְאֵת ׀ פּוֹרָתָא וְאֵת ׀ אֲדַלְיָא וְאֵת ׀ אֲרִידָתָא׃ וְאֵת ׀ פַּרְמַשְׁתָּא וְאֵת ׀ אֲרִיסַי
Arisai and Parmashta and (9) Aridatha and Adalia and Poratha and (8) Aspatha

וְאֵת ׀ אֲרִדַי וְאֵת ׀ וַיְזָתָא׃ עֲשֶׂרֶת בְּנֵי הָמָן בֶּן־ הַמְּדָתָא
Hammedatha son-of Haman sons-of ten-of (10) Vaizatha and Aridai and

צֹרֵר הַיְּהוּדִים הָרָגוּ וּבַבִּזָּה לֹא שָׁלְחוּ אֶת־
*** they-laid not but-on-the-plunder they-killed the-Jews one-being-enemy-of

יָדָם׃ בַּיּוֹם הַהוּא בָּא מִסְפַּר הַהֲרוּגִים
the-ones-being-slain number-of he-came the-same on-the-day (11) hand-of-them

בְּשׁוּשַׁן הַבִּירָה לִפְנֵי הַמֶּלֶךְ׃ וַיֹּאמֶר הַמֶּלֶךְ לְאֶסְתֵּר
to-Esther the-king and-he-said (12) the-king before the-citadel in-Susa

הַמַּלְכָּה בְּשׁוּשַׁן הַבִּירָה הָרְגוּ הַיְּהוּדִים וְאַבֵּד חֲמֵשׁ
five-of and-to-destroy the-Jews they-killed the-citadel in-Susa the-queen

מֵאוֹת אִישׁ וְאֵת עֲשֶׂרֶת בְּנֵי־ הָמָן בִּשְׁאָר מְדִינוֹת הַמֶּלֶךְ
the-king provinces-of in-rest-of Haman sons-of ten-of and man hundreds

מֶה עָשׂוּ וּמַה־ שְּׁאֵלָתֵךְ וְיִנָּתֵן לָךְ
to-you and-he-will-be-given petition-of-you now-what? they-did what?

וּמַה־ בַּקָּשָׁתֵךְ עוֹד וְתֵעָשׂ׃ וַתֹּאמֶר
and-she-answered (13) and-she-will-be-granted also request-of-you and-what?

אֶסְתֵּר אִם־עַל־ הַמֶּלֶךְ טוֹב יִנָּתֵן גַּם־ מָחָר לַיְּהוּדִים
to-the-Jews tomorrow also let-him-be-given pleasing the-king to if Esther

אֲשֶׁר בְּשׁוּשָׁן לַעֲשׂוֹת כְּדָת הַיּוֹם וְאֵת עֲשֶׂרֶת בְּנֵי־ הָמָן
Haman sons-of ten-of and the-day as-edict-of to-carry-out in-Susa who

יִתְלוּ עַל־ הָעֵץ׃ וַיֹּאמֶר הַמֶּלֶךְ לְהֵעָשׂוֹת כֵּן
this to-be-done the-king so-he-commanded (14) the-gallows on let-them-hang

וַתִּנָּתֵן דָּת בְּשׁוּשָׁן וְאֵת עֲשֶׂרֶת בְּנֵי־ הָמָן תָּלוּ׃
they-hanged Haman sons-of ten-of and in-Susa edict and-she-was-issued

וַיִּקָּהֲלוּ הַיְּהוּדִיים אֲשֶׁר־ בְּשׁוּשָׁן גַּם בְּיוֹם אַרְבָּעָה עָשָׂר
ten four on-day-of also in-Susa who the-Jews and-they-came-together (15)

לְחֹדֶשׁ אֲדָר וַיַּהַרְגוּ בְשׁוּשָׁן שְׁלֹשׁ מֵאוֹת אִישׁ
man hundreds three-of in-Susa and-they-killed Adar of-month-of

וּבַבִּזָּה לֹא שָׁלְחוּ אֶת־ יָדָם׃ וּשְׁאָר
and-remainder-of (16) hand-of-them *** they-laid not but-on-the-plunder

הַיְּהוּדִים אֲשֶׁר בִּמְדִינוֹת הַמֶּלֶךְ נִקְהֲלוּ ׀ וְעָמֹד עַל־
to and-to-protect they-assembled the-king in-provinces-of who the-Jews

נַפְשָׁם וְנוֹחַ מֵאֹיְבֵיהֶם וְהָרֹג
and-to-kill from-ones-being-enemies-of-them and-to-get-relief self-of-them

°15 ק היהודים

five hundred men. [7]They also killed Parshandatha, Dalphon, Aspatha, [8]Poratha, Adalia, Aridatha, [9]Parmashta, Arisai, Aridai and Vaizatha, [10]the ten sons of Haman son of Hammedatha, the enemy of the Jews. But they did not lay their hands on the plunder.

[11]The number of those slain in the citadel of Susa was reported to the king that same day. [12]The king said to Queen Esther, "The Jews have killed five hundred men and the ten sons of Haman in the citadel of Susa. What have they done in the rest of the king's provinces? Now what is your petition? It will be given you. What is your request? It will also be granted."

[13]"If it pleases the king," Esther answered, "give the Jews in Susa permission to carry out this day's edict tomorrow also, and let Haman's ten sons be hanged on gallows.[n]"

[14]So the king commanded that this be done. An edict was issued in Susa, and they hanged[o] the ten sons of Haman. [15]The Jews in Susa came together on the fourteenth day of the month of Adar, and they put to death in Susa three hundred men, but they did not lay their hands on the plunder.

[16]Meanwhile, the remainder of the Jews who were in the king's provinces also assembled to protect themselves and get relief from their enemies.

[n]13 Or *be hung on poles;* also in verse 25
[o]14 Or *hung*

בְּשֹׂנְאֵיהֶם חֲמִשָּׁה וְשִׁבְעִים אָלֶף וּבַבִּזָּה לֹא
not but-on-the-plunder thousand and-seventy five of-ones-hating-them

שָׁלְחוּ אֶת־ יָדָם׃ בְּיוֹם־שְׁלוֹשָׁה עָשָׂר לְחֹדֶשׁ אֲדָר וְנוֹחַ
and-to-rest Adar of-month-of ten three on-day-of (17) hand-of-them *** they-laid

בְּאַרְבָּעָה עָשָׂר בּוֹ וְעָשֹׂה אֹתוֹ יוֹם מִשְׁתֶּה וְשִׂמְחָה׃ וְהַיְּהוּדִיים°
but-the-Jews (18) and-joy feasting day-of him and-to-make of-him ten on-four

אֲשֶׁר־ בְּשׁוּשָׁן נִקְהֲלוּ בִּשְׁלוֹשָׁה עָשָׂר בּוֹ וּבְאַרְבָּעָה עָשָׂר בּוֹ
of-him ten and-on-four of-him ten on-three they-assembled in-Susa who

וְנוֹחַ בַּחֲמִשָּׁה עָשָׂר בּוֹ וְעָשֹׂה אֹתוֹ יוֹם מִשְׁתֶּה וְשִׂמְחָה׃
and-joy feasting day-of him and-to-make of-him ten on-five and-to-rest

עַל־ כֵּן הַיְּהוּדִים הַפְּרָוזִים° הַיֹּשְׁבִים בְּעָרֵי
in-villages-of the-ones-living the-rural-ones the-Jews this for (19)

הַפְּרָזוֹת עֹשִׂים אֵת יוֹם אַרְבָּעָה עָשָׂר לְחֹדֶשׁ אֲדָר שִׂמְחָה
joy Adar of-month-of ten four day-of *** ones-observing the-rural-areas

וּמִשְׁתֶּה וְיוֹם טוֹב וּמִשְׁלוֹחַ מָנוֹת אִישׁ לְרֵעֵהוּ׃
to-fellow-of-him each presents and-giving good and-day-of and-feasting

וַיִּכְתֹּב מָרְדֳּכַי אֶת־ הַדְּבָרִים הָאֵלֶּה וַיִּשְׁלַח סְפָרִים
letters and-he-sent the-these the-events *** Mordecai and-he-recorded (20)

אֶל־ כָּל־ הַיְּהוּדִים אֲשֶׁר בְּכָל־ מְדִינוֹת הַמֶּלֶךְ אֲחַשְׁוֵרוֹשׁ
Ahasuerus the-king provinces-of in-all-of who the-Jews all-of to

הַקְּרוֹבִים וְהָרְחוֹקִים׃ לְקַיֵּם עֲלֵיהֶם לִהְיוֹת
to-be on-them to-impose (21) and-the-ones-far the-ones-near

עֹשִׂים אֵת יוֹם אַרְבָּעָה עָשָׂר לְחֹדֶשׁ אֲדָר וְאֵת יוֹם־חֲמִשָּׁה עָשָׂר
ten five day-of and Adar of-month-of ten four day-of *** ones-celebrating

בּוֹ בְּכָל־ שָׁנָה וְשָׁנָה׃ כַּיָּמִים אֲשֶׁר־ נָחוּ
they-got-relief when as-the-days (22) and-year year in-every-of of-him

בָהֶם הַיְּהוּדִים מֵאוֹיְבֵיהֶם וְהַחֹדֶשׁ אֲשֶׁר
when and-the-month from-ones-being-enemies-of-them the-Jews for-them

נֶהְפַּךְ לָהֶם מִיָּגוֹן לְשִׂמְחָה וּמֵאֵבֶל לְיוֹם
to-day-of and-from-mourning to-joy from-sorrow for-them he-was-turned

טוֹב לַעֲשׂוֹת אוֹתָם יְמֵי מִשְׁתֶּה וְשִׂמְחָה וּמִשְׁלוֹחַ מָנוֹת
food-presents and-giving and-joy feasting days-of them to-observe celebration

אִישׁ לְרֵעֵהוּ וּמַתָּנוֹת לָאֶבְיוֹנִים׃ וְקִבֵּל הַיְּהוּדִים
the-Jews so-he-agreed (23) to-the-poor-ones and-gifts to-fellow-of-him one

אֵת אֲשֶׁר־ הֵחֵלּוּ לַעֲשׂוֹת וְאֵת אֲשֶׁר־ כָּתַב מָרְדֳּכַי אֲלֵיהֶם׃ כִּי
for (24) to-them Mordecai he-wrote what and to-celebrate they-began what ***

הָמָן בֶּן־ הַמְּדָתָא הָאֲגָגִי צֹרֵר כָּל־ הַיְּהוּדִים חָשַׁב
he-plotted the-Jews all-of being-enemy-of the-Agagite Hammedatha son-of Haman

They killed seventy-five thousand of them but did not lay
their hands on the plunder.
17This happened on the thirteenth day of the month of
Adar, and on the fourteenth
they rested and made it a day
of feasting and joy.

Purim Celebrated

18The Jews in Susa, however,
had assembled on the thirteenth and fourteenth, and
then on the fifteenth they rested and made it a day of feasting and joy.
19That is why rural Jews—
those living in villages—
observe the fourteenth of the
month of Adar as a day of joy
and feasting, a day for giving
presents to each other.
20Mordecai recorded these
events, and he sent letters to
all the Jews throughout the
provinces of King Xerxes, near
and far, 21to have them celebrate annually the fourteenth
and fifteenth days of the
month of Adar 22as the time
when the Jews got relief from
their enemies, and as the
month when their sorrow was
turned into joy and their
mourning into a day of celebration. He wrote them to observe the days as days of feasting and joy and giving
presents of food to one another and gifts to the poor.
23So the Jews agreed to continue the celebration they had
begun, doing what Mordecai
had written to them. 24For Haman son of Hammedatha, the
Agagite, the enemy of all the
Jews, had plotted against the

°*18* ק והיהודים
°*19* ק הפרזים

עַל־הַיְּהוּדִים לְאַבְּדָם וְהִפִּל פּוּר הוּא הַגּוֹרָל לְהֻמָּם
to-ruin-them the-lot that pur and-he-cast to-destroy-them the-Jews against

וּלְאַבְּדָם׃ (25) וּבְבֹאָהּ לִפְנֵי הַמֶּלֶךְ אָמַר
he-ordered the-king before but-when-to-come-her (25) and-to-destroy-them

עִם־הַסֵּפֶר יָשׁוּב מַחֲשַׁבְתּוֹ הָרָעָה אֲשֶׁר־חָשַׁב
he-devised that the-evil scheme-of-him he-should-come-back the-writing with

עַל־הַיְּהוּדִים עַל־רֹאשׁוֹ וְתָלוּ אֹתוֹ וְאֶת־בָּנָיו עַל־
on sons-of-him and him and-they-should-hang head-of-him on the-Jews against

הָעֵץ׃ (26) עַל־כֵּן קָרְאוּ לַיָּמִים הָאֵלֶּה פוּרִים עַל־שֵׁם
name-of from Purim the-these to-the-days they-called this for (26) the-gallows

הַפּוּר עַל־כֵּן עַל־כָּל־דִּבְרֵי הָאִגֶּרֶת הַזֹּאת וּמָה־
and-what the-this the-letter words-of all-of because-of this for the-pur

רָאוּ עַל־כָּכָה וּמָה הִגִּיעַ אֲלֵיהֶם׃ (27) קִיְּמוּ
they-established (27) to-them he-happened and-what this because-of they-saw

וְקִבְּל° הַיְּהוּדִים עֲלֵיהֶם ׀ וְעַל־זַרְעָם וְעַל כָּל־
all-of and-upon descendant-of-them and-upon upon-them the-Jews and-they-took

הַנִּלְוִים עֲלֵיהֶם וְלֹא יַעֲבוֹר לִהְיוֹת עֹשִׂים אֵת
*** ones-observing to-be they-should-fail so-not with-them the-ones-joining

שְׁנֵי הַיָּמִים הָאֵלֶּה כִּכְתָבָם וְכִזְמַנָּם
and-as-appointed-time-of-them as-prescription-of-them the-these the-days two-of

בְּכָל־שָׁנָה וְשָׁנָה׃ (28) וְהַיָּמִים הָאֵלֶּה נִזְכָּרִים
ones-being-remembered the-these and-the-days (28) and-year year in-every-of

וְנַעֲשִׂים בְּכָל־דּוֹר וָדוֹר מִשְׁפָּחָה
family and-generation generation in-every-of and-ones-being-observed

וּמִשְׁפָּחָה מְדִינָה וּמְדִינָה וְעִיר וָעִיר וִימֵי הַפּוּרִים
the-Purim and-days-of and-city and-city and-province province and-family

הָאֵלֶּה לֹא יַעַבְרוּ מִתּוֹךְ הַיְּהוּדִים וְזִכְרָם
and-memory-of-them the-Jews from-among they-should-cease never the-these

לֹא־יָסוּף מִזַּרְעָם׃ (29) וַתִּכְתֹּב
so-she-wrote (29) among-descendant-of-them he-should-die-out not

אֶסְתֵּר הַמַּלְכָּה בַת־אֲבִיחַיִל וּמָרְדֳּכַי הַיְּהוּדִי אֶת־כָּל־
full-of with the-Jew and-Mordecai Abihail daughter-of the-queen Esther

תֹּקֶף לְקַיֵּם אֵת אִגֶּרֶת הַפֻּרִים הַזֹּאת הַשֵּׁנִית׃
the-second the-this the-Purim letter-of *** to-confirm authority

(30) וַיִּשְׁלַח סְפָרִים אֶל־כָּל־הַיְּהוּדִים אֶל־שֶׁבַע וְעֶשְׂרִים וּמֵאָה
and-hundred and-twenty seven in the-Jews all-of to letters and-he-sent (30)

מְדִינָה מַלְכוּת אֲחַשְׁוֵרוֹשׁ דִּבְרֵי שָׁלוֹם וֶאֱמֶת׃
and-assurance good-will words-of Ahasuerus kingdom-of province

Jews to destroy them and had
cast the *pur* (that is, the lot) for
their ruin and destruction.
25But when the plot came to
the king's attention,[p] he issued written orders that the
evil scheme Haman had de-
vised against the Jews should
come back onto his own head,
and that he and his sons
should be hanged on the gallows. 26(Therefore these days
were called Purim, from the
word *pur*.) Because of everything written in this letter and
because of what they had seen
and what had happened to
them, 27the Jews took it upon
themselves to establish the
custom that they and their descendants and all who join
them should without fail observe these two days every
year, in the way prescribed
and at the time appointed.
28These days should be
remembered and observed in
every generation by every
family, and in every province
and in every city. And these
days of Purim should never
cease to be celebrated by the
Jews, nor should the memory
of them die out among their
descendants.
29So Queen Esther, daughter
of Abihail, along with Mordecai the Jew, wrote with full
authority to confirm this second letter concerning Purim.
30And Mordecai sent letters to
all the Jews in the 127 provinces of the kingdom of
Xerxes—words of good will
and assurance— 31to establish

[p]25 Or *when Esther came before the king*

°27 ק וקבלו

(31) לְקַיֵּם אֶת־* יְמֵי הַפֻּרִים הָאֵלֶּה בִּזְמַנֵּיהֶם
at-designated-times-of-them the-these the-Purim days-of *** to-establish (31)

כַּאֲשֶׁר קִיַּם עֲלֵיהֶם מָרְדֳּכַי הַיְּהוּדִי וְאֶסְתֵּר הַמַּלְכָּה
the-queen and-Esther the-Jew Mordecai for-them he-decreed just-as

וְכַאֲשֶׁר קִיְּמוּ עַל־ נַפְשָׁם וְעַל־ זַרְעָם
descendant-of-them and-for self-of-them for they-established and-just-as

דִּבְרֵי הַצֹּמוֹת וְזַעֲקָתָם׃ (32) וּמַאֲמַר אֶסְתֵּר
Esther and-decree-of (32) and-lamentation-of-them the-fastings times-of

קִיַּם דִּבְרֵי הַפֻּרִים הָאֵלֶּה וְנִכְתָּב
and-being-written the-these the-Purim regulations-of he-confirmed

בַּסֵּפֶר׃ (10:1) וַיָּשֶׂם הַמֶּלֶךְ אֲחַשְׁרֵשׁ° ׀ מַס עַל־
throughout tribute Ahasuerus the-king and-he-imposed (10:1) in-the-record

הָאָרֶץ וְאִיֵּי הַיָּם׃ (2) וְכָל־ מַעֲשֵׂה תָקְפּוֹ
power-of-him act-of and-all-of (2) the-sea and-shores-of the-empire

וּגְבוּרָתוֹ וּפָרָשַׁת גְּדֻלַּת מָרְדֳּכַי אֲשֶׁר
which Mordecai greatness-of with-full-account-of and-might-of-him

גִּדְּלוֹ הַמֶּלֶךְ הֲלוֹא־ הֵם כְּתוּבִים עַל־ סֵפֶר דִּבְרֵי
annals-of book-of in ones-being-written they not? the-king he-raised-him

הַיָּמִים לְמַלְכֵי מָדַי וּפָרָס׃ (3) כִּי ׀ מָרְדֳּכַי הַיְּהוּדִי מִשְׁנֶה
second the-Jew Mordecai indeed (3) and-Persia Media of-kings-of the-days

לַמֶּלֶךְ אֲחַשְׁוֵרוֹשׁ וְגָדוֹל לַיְּהוּדִים וְרָצוּי
and-being-esteemed among-the-Jews and-preeminent Ahasuerus to-the-king

לְרֹב אֶחָיו דֹּרֵשׁ טוֹב לְעַמּוֹ
of-people-of-him good working-for fellows-of-him by-many-of

וְדֹבֵר שָׁלוֹם לְכָל־ זַרְעוֹ׃
relative-of-him of-all-of welfare and-speaking-up

these days of Purim at their designated times, as Mordecai the Jew and Queen Esther had decreed for them, and as they had established for themselves and their descendants in regard to their times of fasting and lamentation.
[32]Esther's decree confirmed these regulations about Purim, and it was written down in the records.

The Greatness of Mordecai

10 King Xerxes imposed tribute throughout the empire, to its distant shores.
[2]And all his acts of power and might, together with a full account of the greatness of Mordecai to which the king had raised him, are they not written in the book of the annals of the kings of Media and Persia?
[3]Mordecai the Jew was second in rank to King Xerxes, preeminent among the Jews, and held in high esteem by his many fellow Jews, because he worked for the good of his people and spoke up for the welfare of all the Jews.

*31 Most mss have *segol* under the *aleph* (אֶת).

°1 ק אחשורוש

אִישׁ הָיָה בְאֶרֶץ־עוּץ אִיּוֹב שְׁמוֹ וְהָיָה ׀ הָאִישׁ הַהוּא

the-this the-man and-he-was name-of-him Job Uz in-land-of he-lived man (1:1)

תָּם וְיָשָׁר וִירֵא אֱלֹהִים וְסָר מֵרָע׃

from-evil and-shunning God and-fearing-of and-upright blameless

וַיִּוָּלְדוּ לוֹ שִׁבְעָה בָנִים וְשָׁלוֹשׁ בָּנוֹת׃ וַיְהִי

and-he-was (3) daughters and-three sons seven to-him and-they-were-born (2)

מִקְנֵהוּ שִׁבְעַת אַלְפֵי־צֹאן וּשְׁלֹשֶׁת אַלְפֵי

thousands-of and-three-of sheep thousands-of seven-of possession-of-him

גְמַלִּים וַחֲמֵשׁ מֵאוֹת צֶמֶד־בָּקָר וַחֲמֵשׁ מֵאוֹת אֲתוֹנוֹת

donkeys hundreds and-five-of oxen yoke-of hundreds and-five-of camels

וַעֲבֻדָּה רַבָּה מְאֹד וַיְהִי הָאִישׁ הַהוּא גָּדוֹל

great the-this the-man and-he-was very large-number and-servant

מִכָּל־ בְּנֵי־ קֶדֶם׃ וְהָלְכוּ בָנָיו

sons-of-him and-they-took-turns (4) East peoples-of more-than-all-of

וְעָשׂוּ מִשְׁתֶּה בֵּית אִישׁ יוֹמוֹ וְשָׁלְחוּ וְקָרְאוּ

and-they-invited and-they-sent day-of-him each home-of feast and-they-held

לִשְׁלֹשֶׁת אַחְיֹתֵיהֶם לֶאֱכֹל וְלִשְׁתּוֹת עִמָּהֶם׃ וַיְהִי

and-he-was (5) with-them and-to-drink to-eat sisters-of-them to-three-of

כִּי הִקִּיפוּ יְמֵי הַמִּשְׁתֶּה וַיִּשְׁלַח אִיּוֹב וַיְקַדְּשֵׁם

and-he-purified-them Job then-he-sent the-feast days-of they-ran-course when

וְהִשְׁכִּים בַּבֹּקֶר וְהֶעֱלָה עֹלוֹת מִסְפַּר

number-of burnt-offerings and-he-sacrificed in-the-morning then-he-got-up

כֻּלָּם כִּי אָמַר אִיּוֹב אוּלַי חָטְאוּ בָנַי

children-of-me they-sinned perhaps Job he-thought for each-of-them

וּבֵרְכוּ אֱלֹהִים בִּלְבָבָם כָּכָה יַעֲשֶׂה אִיּוֹב כָּל־ הַיָּמִים׃

the-days all-of Job he-did this in-heart-of-them God and-they-cursed

וַיְהִי הַיּוֹם וַיָּבֹאוּ בְּנֵי הָאֱלֹהִים לְהִתְיַצֵּב עַל־

before to-present-self the-God sons-of that-they-came the-day and-he-was (6)

יְהוָה וַיָּבוֹא גַם־ הַשָּׂטָן בְּתוֹכָם׃ וַיֹּאמֶר יְהוָה אֶל־

to Yahweh and-he-said (7) in-among-them the-Satan also and-he-came Yahweh

הַשָּׂטָן מֵאַיִן תָּבֹא וַיַּעַן הַשָּׂטָן אֶת־ יְהוָה

Yahweh *** the-Satan and-he-answered you-came from-where? the-Satan

וַיֹּאמַר מִשּׁוּט בָּאָרֶץ וּמֵהִתְהַלֵּךְ בָּהּ׃ וַיֹּאמֶר

then-he-said (8) in-her and-from-to-go through-the-earth from-to-roam and-he-said

יְהוָה אֶל־ הַשָּׂטָן הֲשַׂמְתָּ לִבְּךָ עַל־ עַבְדִּי אִיּוֹב

Job servant-of-me to heart-of-you have-you-considered? the-Satan to Yahweh

כִּי אֵין כָּמֹהוּ בָּאָרֶץ אִישׁ תָּם וְיָשָׁר יְרֵא

fearing-of and-upright blameless man on-the-earth like-him there-is-no-one for

Prologue

1 In the land of Uz there lived a
man whose name was Job.
This man was blameless and upright; he feared God and shunned
evil. 2 He had seven sons and three
daughters, 3 and he owned seven
thousand sheep, three thousand
camels, five hundred yoke of oxen
and five hundred donkeys, and
had a large number of servants.
He was the greatest man among
all the people of the East.
4 His sons used to take turns
holding feasts in their homes, and
they would invite their three sisters to eat and drink with them.
5 When a period of feasting had
run its course, Job would send and
have them purified. Early in the
morning he would sacrifice a
burnt offering for each of them,
thinking, "Perhaps my children
have sinned and cursed God in
their hearts." This was Job's regular custom.

Job's First Test

6 One day the angels[a] came to
present themselves before the
LORD, and Satan[b] also came with
them. 7 The LORD said to Satan,
"Where have you come from?"
Satan answered the LORD,
"From roaming through the earth
and going back and forth in it."
8 Then the LORD said to Satan,
"Have you considered my servant
Job? There is no one on earth like
him; he is blameless and upright,

[a]6 Hebrew *the sons of God*
[b]6 *Satan* means *accuser.*

°4 ק אחיותיהם

אֱלֹהִים וְסָר מֵרָע׃ וַיַּעַן הַשָּׂטָן אֶת־יְהוָה
Yahweh *** the-Satan and-he-replied (9) from-evil and-shunning God

וַיֹּאמַר הַחִנָּם יָרֵא אִיּוֹב אֱלֹהִים׃ הֲלֹא־אַתְּ שַׂכְתָּ
you-put-hedge you not? (10) God Job fearing for-nothing? and-he-said

בַעֲדוֹ וּבְעַד־בֵּיתוֹ וּבְעַד כָּל־אֲשֶׁר־לוֹ מִסָּבִיב
at-around to-him that all and-around household-of-him and-around around-him

מַעֲשֵׂה יָדָיו בֵּרַכְתָּ וּמִקְנֵהוּ פָּרַץ בָּאָרֶץ׃
through-the-land he-spreads so-flock-of-him you-blessed hands-of-him work-of

(11) וְאוּלָם שְׁלַח־נָא יָדְךָ וְגַע בְּכָל־אֲשֶׁר־לוֹ
to-him that against-all and-strike! hand-of-you now! stretch! now-but (11)

אִם־לֹא עַל־פָּנֶיךָ יְבָרְכֶךָּ׃ וַיֹּאמֶר יְהוָה אֶל־
to Yahweh and-he-said (12) he-will-curse-you faces-of-you to surely indeed

הַשָּׂטָן הִנֵּה כָל־אֲשֶׁר־לוֹ בְּיָדֶךָ רַק אֵלָיו אַל־תִּשְׁלַח
you-lay not on-him but in-hand-of-you to-him that all see! the-Satan

יָדֶךָ וַיֵּצֵא הַשָּׂטָן מֵעִם פְּנֵי יְהוָה׃
Yahweh presences-of from-in the-Satan then-he-went-out hand-of-you

(13) וַיְהִי הַיּוֹם וּבָנָיו וּבְנֹתָיו אֹכְלִים
ones-feasting and-daughters-of-him when-sons-of-him the-day and-he-was (13)

וְשֹׁתִים יַיִן בְּבֵית אֲחִיהֶם הַבְּכוֹר׃ וּמַלְאָךְ
then-messenger (14) the-oldest brother-of-them at-house-of wine and-ones-drinking

בָּא אֶל־אִיּוֹב וַיֹּאמַר הַבָּקָר הָיוּ חֹרְשׁוֹת וְהָאֲתֹנוֹת
and-the-donkeys ones-plowing they-were the-oxen and-he-said Job to he-came

רֹעוֹת עַל־יְדֵיהֶם׃ וַתִּפֹּל שְׁבָא וַתִּקָּחֵם
and-she-carried-away-them Sabean and-she-attacked (15) hands-of-them at ones-grazing

וְאֶת־הַנְּעָרִים הִכּוּ לְפִי־חָרֶב וָאִמָּלְטָה רַק־אֲנִי לְבַדִּי
by-myself I only and-I-escaped sword with-edge-of they-killed the-servants and

לְהַגִּיד לָךְ׃ עוֹד ׀ זֶה מְדַבֵּר וְזֶה בָּא וַיֹּאמַר אֵשׁ
fire-of and-he-said he-came then-this speaking this while (16) to-you to-tell

אֱלֹהִים נָפְלָה מִן־הַשָּׁמַיִם וַתִּבְעַר בַּצֹּאן וּבַנְּעָרִים
and-to-the-servants to-the-sheep and-she-burned the-skies from she-fell God

וַתֹּאכְלֵם וָאִמָּלְטָה רַק־אֲנִי לְבַדִּי לְהַגִּיד לָךְ׃
to-you to-tell by-myself I only and-I-escaped and-she-consumed-them

(17) עוֹד ׀ זֶה מְדַבֵּר וְזֶה בָּא וַיֹּאמַר כַּשְׂדִּים שָׂמוּ ׀
they-formed Chaldeans and-he-said he-came then-this speaking this while (17)

שְׁלֹשָׁה רָאשִׁים וַיִּפְשְׁטוּ עַל־הַגְּמַלִּים וַיִּקָּחוּם
and-she-carried-off-them the-camels on and-they-swept-down raiding-parties three

וְאֶת־הַנְּעָרִים הִכּוּ לְפִי־חָרֶב וָאִמָּלְטָה רַק־אֲנִי
I only and-I-escaped sword with-edge-of they-killed the-servants and

°10 ק אתה

a man who fears God and shuns evil."

[9]"Does Job fear God for nothing?" Satan replied. [10]"Have you not put a hedge around him and his household and everything he has? You have blessed the work of his hands, so that his flocks and herds are spread throughout the land. [11]But stretch out your hand and strike everything he has, and he will surely curse you to your face."

[12]The LORD said to Satan, "Very well, then, everything he has is in your hands, but on the man himself do not lay a finger."

Then Satan went out from the presence of the LORD.

[13]One day when Job's sons and daughters were feasting and drinking wine at the oldest brother's house, [14]a messenger came to Job and said, "The oxen were plowing and the donkeys were grazing nearby, [15]and the Sabeans attacked and carried them off. They put the servants to the sword, and I am the only one who has escaped to tell you!"

[16]While he was still speaking, another messenger came and said, "The fire of God fell from the sky and burned up the sheep and the servants, and I am the only one who has escaped to tell you!"

[17]While he was still speaking, another messenger came and said, "The Chaldeans formed three raiding parties and swept down on your camels and carried them off. They put the servants to the sword, and I am the only one who

לְבַדִּי לְהַגִּיד לָךְ׃ עַד זֶה מְדַבֵּר וְזֶה בָּא
he-came then-this speaking this while (18) to-you to-tell by-myself

וַיֹּאמַר בָּנֶיךָ וּבְנוֹתֶיךָ אֹכְלִים וְשֹׁתִים
and-ones-drinking ones-feasting and-daughters-of-you sons-of-you and-he-said

יַיִן בְּבֵית אֲחִיהֶם הַבְּכוֹר׃ וְהִנֵּה רוּחַ גְּדוֹלָה
mighty wind when-see! (19) the-oldest brother-of-them at-house-of wine

בָּאָה מֵעֵבֶר הַמִּדְבָּר וַיִּגַּע בְּאַרְבַּע פִּנּוֹת
corners-of on-four-of and-he-struck the-desert from-across-of she-swept-in

הַבַּיִת וַיִּפֹּל עַל־הַנְּעָרִים וַיָּמוּתוּ וָאִמָּלְטָה
and-I-escaped and-they-are-dead the-youths on and-he-collapsed the-house

רַק־אֲנִי לְבַדִּי לְהַגִּיד לָךְ׃ וַיָּקָם אִיּוֹב וַיִּקְרַע אֶת־
*** and-he-tore Job and-he-got-up (20) to-you to-tell by-myself I only

מְעִלוֹ וַיָּגָז אֶת־רֹאשׁוֹ וַיִּפֹּל אַרְצָה
to-ground then-he-fell head-of-him *** and-he-shaved robe-of-him

וַיִּשְׁתָּחוּ׃ וַיֹּאמֶר עָרֹם יָצָתִי° מִבֶּטֶן אִמִּי
mother-of-me from-womb-of I-came naked and-he-said (21) and-he-worshiped

וְעָרֹם אָשׁוּב שָׁמָּה* יְהוָה נָתַן וַיהוָה לָקָח
he-took-away and-Yahweh he-gave Yahweh to-there I-will-depart and-naked

יְהִי שֵׁם יְהוָה מְבֹרָךְ׃ בְּכָל־זֹאת לֹא־חָטָא
he-sinned not this in-all-of (22) being-praised Yahweh name-of may-he-be

אִיּוֹב וְלֹא־נָתַן תִּפְלָה לֵאלֹהִים׃ וַיְהִי הַיּוֹם
the-day and-he-was (2:1) to-God wrongdoing he-charged for-not Job

וַיָּבֹאוּ בְּנֵי הָאֱלֹהִים לְהִתְיַצֵּב עַל־יְהוָה וַיָּבוֹא
and-he-came Yahweh before to-present-self the-God sons-of then-they-came

גַם־הַשָּׂטָן בְּתֹכָם לְהִתְיַצֵּב עַל־יְהוָה׃ וַיֹּאמֶר
and-he-said (2) Yahweh before to-present-self in-among-them the-Satan also

יְהוָה אֶל־הַשָּׂטָן אֵי מִזֶּה תָּבֹא וַיַּעַן הַשָּׂטָן
the-Satan and-he-answered you-came from-there where? the-Satan to Yahweh

אֶת־יְהוָה וַיֹּאמַר מִשֻּׁט בָּאָרֶץ וּמֵהִתְהַלֵּךְ בָּהּ׃
in-her and-from-to-go through-the-earth from-to-roam and-he-said Yahweh ***

וַיֹּאמֶר יְהוָה אֶל־הַשָּׂטָן הֲשַׂמְתָּ לִבְּךָ אֶל־
to heart-of-you have-you-considered? the-Satan to Yahweh then-he-said (3)

עַבְדִּי אִיּוֹב כִּי אֵין כָּמֹהוּ בָּאָרֶץ אִישׁ תָּם
blameless man on-the-earth like-him there-is-no-one for Job servant-of-me

וְיָשָׁר יְרֵא אֱלֹהִים וְסָר מֵרָע וְעֹדֶנּוּ מַחֲזִיק
maintaining and-still-he from-evil and-shunning God fearing-of and-upright

בְּתֻמָּתוֹ וַתְּסִיתֵנִי בוֹ לְבַלְּעוֹ חִנָּם׃
without-reason to-ruin-him against-him though-you-incited-me to-integrity-of-him

has escaped to tell you!"
18 While he was still speaking, yet another messenger came and said, "Your sons and daughters were feasting and drinking wine at the oldest brother's house,
19 when suddenly a mighty wind swept in from the desert and struck the four corners of the house. It collapsed on them and they are dead, and I am the only one who has escaped to tell you!"
20 At this, Job got up and tore his robe and shaved his head. Then he fell to the ground in worship
21 and said:

"Naked I came from my
mother's womb,
and naked I will depart.[c]
The LORD gave and the LORD
has taken away;
may the name of the LORD
be praised."

22 In all this, Job did not sin by charging God with wrongdoing.

Job's Second Test

2 On another day the angels[d] came to present themselves before the LORD, and Satan also came with them to present himself before him.
2 And the LORD said to Satan, "Where have you come from?"
Satan answered the LORD, "From roaming through the earth and going back and forth in it."
3 Then the LORD said to Satan, "Have you considered my servant Job? There is no one on earth like him; he is blameless and upright, a man who fears God and shuns evil. And he still maintains his integrity, though you incited me against him to ruin him without any reason."

[c] 21 Or *will return there*
[d] 1 Hebrew *the sons of God*

*21 Most mss have *dagesh* in the *mem* (שָׁמָּה).

°21 ק יצאתי

וַיַּעַן הַשָּׂטָן אֶת־ יְהוָה וַיֹּאמַר עוֹר בְּעַד־ עוֹר וְכֹל

and-all skin for skin and-he-said Yahweh *** the-Satan and-he-replied (4)

אֲשֶׁר לָאִישׁ יִתֵּן בְּעַד נַפְשׁוֹ׃ אוּלָם שְׁלַח־ נָא יָדְךָ

hand-of-you now! stretch! but (5) life-of-him for he-will-give to-man that

וְגַע אֶל־ עַצְמוֹ וְאֶל־ בְּשָׂרוֹ אִם־ לֹא אֶל־ פָּנֶיךָ

faces-of-you to surely indeed flesh-of-him and-to bone-of-him to and-strike!

יְבָרְכֶךָּ׃ וַיֹּאמֶר יְהוָה אֶל־ הַשָּׂטָן הִנּוֹ בְיָדֶךָ

in-hand-of-you see-he! the-Satan to Yahweh and-he-said (6) he-will-curse-you

אַךְ אֶת־ נַפְשׁוֹ שְׁמֹר׃ וַיֵּצֵא הַשָּׂטָן מֵאֵת פְּנֵי

presences-of from the-Satan so-he-went-out (7) spare! life-of-him *** but

יְהוָה וַיַּךְ אֶת־אִיּוֹב בִּשְׁחִין רָע מִכַּף רַגְלוֹ

foot-of-him from-sole-of painful with-sore Job *** and-he-afflicted Yahweh

°עַד קָדְקֳדוֹ׃ וַיִּקַּח־ לוֹ חֶרֶשׂ לְהִתְגָּרֵד

to-scrape-himself broken-pottery for-him then-he-took (8) head-of-him and-to

בּוֹ וְהוּא יֹשֵׁב בְּתוֹךְ־ הָאֵפֶר׃ וַתֹּאמֶר לוֹ אִשְׁתּוֹ

wife-of-him to-him and-she-said (9) the-ash in-among sitting as-he with-him

עֹדְךָ מַחֲזִיק בְּתֻמָּתֶךָ בָּרֵךְ אֱלֹהִים וָמֻת׃ וַיֹּאמֶר

and-he-replied (10) and-die! God curse! to-integrity-of-you holding still-you

אֵלֶיהָ כְּדַבֵּר אַחַת הַנְּבָלוֹת תְּדַבֵּרִי גַּם אֶת־ הַטּוֹב

the-good *** indeed you-talk the-foolish-women one-of like-to-talk to-her

נְקַבֵּל מֵאֵת הָאֱלֹהִים וְאֶת־ הָרָע לֹא נְקַבֵּל בְּכָל־

in-all-of we-shall-accept not the-trouble and the-God from we-shall-accept

זֹאת לֹא־ חָטָא אִיּוֹב בִּשְׂפָתָיו׃ וַיִּשְׁמְעוּ שְׁלֹשֶׁת ׀

three-of when-they-heard (11) with-sayings-of-him Job he-sinned not this

רֵעֵי אִיּוֹב אֵת כָּל־ הָרָעָה הַזֹּאת הַבָּאָה עָלָיו

upon-him that-she-came the-this the-trouble all-of *** Job friends-of

וַיָּבֹאוּ אִישׁ מִמְּקֹמוֹ אֱלִיפַז הַתֵּימָנִי וּבִלְדַּד

and-Bildad the-Temanite Eliphaz from-home-of-him each then-they-set-out

הַשּׁוּחִי וְצוֹפַר הַנַּעֲמָתִי וַיִּוָּעֲדוּ יַחְדָּו לָבוֹא

to-go together and-they-met the-Naamathite and-Zophar the-Shuhite

לָנוּד־ לוֹ וּלְנַחֲמוֹ׃ וַיִּשְׂאוּ אֶת־

*** when-they-raised (12) and-to-comfort-him with-him to-sympathize

עֵינֵיהֶם מֵרָחוֹק וְלֹא הִכִּירֻהוּ וַיִּשְׂאוּ

and-they-raised they-recognized-him then-not from-distance eyes-of-them

קוֹלָם וַיִּבְכּוּ וַיִּקְרְעוּ אִישׁ מְעִלוֹ וַיִּזְרְקוּ

and-they-sprinkled robe-of-him each and-they-tore and-they-wept voice-of-them

עָפָר עַל־ רָאשֵׁיהֶם הַשָּׁמָיְמָה׃ וַיֵּשְׁבוּ אִתּוֹ לָאָרֶץ

on-the-ground with-him then-they-sat (13) to-the-skies heads-of-them on dust

°7 ק ועד

4“Skin for skin!” Satan replied. “A man will give all he has for his own life. 5But stretch out your hand and strike his flesh and bones, and he will surely curse you to your face.”

6The LORD said to Satan, “Very well, then, he is in your hands; but you must spare his life.”

7So Satan went out from the presence of the LORD and afflicted Job with painful sores from the soles of his feet to the top of his head. 8Then Job took a piece of broken pottery and scraped himself with it as he sat among the ashes.

9His wife said to him, “Are you still holding on to your integrity? Curse God and die!”

10He replied, “You are talking like a foolish[c] woman. Shall we accept good from God, and not trouble?”

In all this, Job did not sin in what he said.

Job's Three Friends

11When Job's three friends, Eliphaz the Temanite, Bildad the Shuhite and Zophar the Naamathite, heard about all the troubles that had come upon him, they set out from their homes and met together by agreement to go and sympathize with him and comfort him. 12When they saw him from a distance, they could hardly recognize him; they began to weep aloud, and they tore their robes and sprinkled dust on their heads. 13Then they sat on the ground

[c]10 The Hebrew word rendered *foolish* denotes moral deficiency.

שִׁבְעַת יָמִים וְשִׁבְעַת לֵילוֹת וְאֵין־ דֹּבֵר אֵלָיו דָּבָר כִּי
because word to-him saying and-no-one nights and-seven-of days seven-of

רָאוּ כִּי־ גָדַל הַכְּאֵב מְאֹד׃ אַחֲרֵי־ כֵן פָּתַח
he-opened this after (3:1) very the-suffering he-was-great how they-saw

אִיּוֹב אֶת־ פִּיהוּ וַיְקַלֵּל אֶת־ יוֹמוֹ׃ וַיַּעַן אִיּוֹב
Job and-he-spoke (2) day-of-him *** and-he-cursed mouth-of-him *** Job

וַיֹּאמַר׃ יֹאבַד יוֹם אִוָּלֶד בּוֹ וְהַלַּיְלָה אָמַר
he-said and-the-night on-him I-was-born day may-he-perish (3) and-he-said

הֹרָה גָבֶר׃ הַיּוֹם הַהוּא יְהִי חֹשֶׁךְ אַל־ יִדְרְשֵׁהוּ
may-he-care-for-him not dark may-he-turn the-that the-day (4) boy he-is-born

אֱלוֹהַּ מִמָּעַל וְאַל־ תּוֹפַע עָלָיו נְהָרָה׃ יִגְאָלֻהוּ
may-they-claim-him (5) light upon-him may-she-shine and-not at-above God

חֹשֶׁךְ וְצַלְמָוֶת תִּשְׁכָּן־ עָלָיו עֲנָנָה יְבַעֲתֻהוּ
may-they-overwhelm-him cloud over-him may-she-settle and-deep-shadow darkness

כִּמְרִירֵי יוֹם׃ הַלַּיְלָה הַהוּא יִקָּחֵהוּ אֹפֶל
thick-darkness may-he-seize-him the-that the-night (6) day as-blacknesses-of

אַל־ יִחַדְּ בִּימֵי שָׁנָה בְּמִסְפַּר יְרָחִים אַל־ יָבֹא׃
may-he-enter not months in-number-of year among-days-of may-he-be-included not

הִנֵּה הַלַּיְלָה הַהוּא יְהִי גַלְמוּד אַל־ תָּבֹא רְנָנָה
shout-of-joy may-she-come not barren may-he-be the-that the-night see! (7)

בוֹ׃ יִקְּבֻהוּ אֹרְרֵי־ יוֹם הָעֲתִידִים עֹרֵר
to-rouse the-ones-ready day ones-cursing-of may-they-curse-him (8) into-him

לִוְיָתָן׃ יֶחְשְׁכוּ כּוֹכְבֵי נִשְׁפּוֹ יְקַו־
may-he-wait morning-of-him stars-of may-they-become-dark (9) Leviathan

לְאוֹר וָאַיִן וְאַל־ יִרְאֶה בְּעַפְעַפֵּי־ שָׁחַר׃
dawn to-first-rays-of may-he-see and-not but-there-is-not for-daylight

כִּי לֹא סָגַר דַּלְתֵי בִטְנִי וַיַּסְתֵּר עָמָל מֵעֵינָי׃
from-eyes-of-me trouble nor-he-hid womb-of-me doors-of he-shut not for (10)

לָמָּה לֹּא מֵרֶחֶם אָמוּת מִבֶּטֶן יָצָאתִי וְאֶגְוָע׃ מַדּוּעַ
why? (12) and-I-died I-came from-womb did-I-perish at-birth not why? (11)

קִדְּמוּנִי בִרְכָּיִם וּמַה־ שָּׁדַיִם כִּי אִינָק׃ כִּי־ עַתָּה
now for (13) I-was-nursed that breasts and-why? knees they-received-me

שָׁכַבְתִּי וְאֶשְׁקוֹט יָשַׁנְתִּי אָז יָנוּחַ
he-would-be-rest then I-would-sleep and-I-would-be-at-peace I-would-lie

לִי׃ עִם־ מְלָכִים וְיֹעֲצֵי אָרֶץ הַבֹּנִים
the-ones-building earth and-ones-counseling-of kings with (14) to-me

חֳרָבוֹת לָמוֹ׃ אוֹ עִם־ שָׂרִים זָהָב לָהֶם הַמְמַלְאִים בָּתֵּיהֶם
houses-of-them the-ones-filling to-them gold rulers with or (15) for-them ruins

---

with him for seven days and seven nights. No one said a word to him, because they saw how great his suffering was.

Job Speaks

3 After this, Job opened his mouth and cursed the day of his birth. 2He said:

3“May the day of my birth perish,
and the night it was said, ‘A boy is born!’
4That day—may it turn to darkness;
may God above not care about it;
may no light shine upon it.
5May darkness and deep shadow[f] claim it once more;
may a cloud settle over it;
may blackness overwhelm its light.
6That night—may thick darkness seize it;
may it not be included among the days of the year
nor be entered in any of the months.
7May that night be barren;
may no shout of joy be heard in it.
8May those who curse days[g] curse that day,
those who are ready to rouse Leviathan.
9May its morning stars become dark;
may it wait for daylight in vain
and not see the first rays of dawn,
10for it did not shut the doors of the womb on me
to hide trouble from my eyes.

11“Why did I not perish at birth,
and die as I came from the womb?
12Why were there knees to receive me
and breasts that I might be nursed?
13For now I would be lying down in peace;
I would be asleep and at rest
14with kings and counselors of the earth,
who built for themselves places now lying in ruins,
15with rulers who had gold,
who filled their houses with

f5 Or *and the shadow of death*
g8 Or *the sea*

כָּֽסֶף׃ (16) אוֹ כְנֵפֶל טָמוּן לֹא אֶהְיֶה כְּעֹלְלִים
like-infants I-was not being-hidden like-stillborn-child or (16) silver

לֹא־רָאוּ אוֹר׃ (17) שָׁם רְשָׁעִים חָדְלוּ רֹגֶז וְשָׁם
and-there turmoil they-cease wicked-ones there (17) light they-saw never

יָנוּחוּ יְגִיעֵי כֹחַ׃ (18) יַחַד אֲסִירִים שַׁאֲנָנוּ לֹא
not they-enjoy-ease captives together (18) strength ones-weary-of they-rest

שָׁמְעוּ קוֹל נֹגֵשׂ׃ (19) קָטֹן וְגָדוֹל שָׁם הוּא וְעֶבֶד חָפְשִׁי
free and-slave he there and-great small (19) one-driving shout-of they-hear

מֵאֲדֹנָיו׃ (20) לָמָּה יִתֵּן לְעָמֵל אוֹר וְחַיִּים
and-lives light to-miserable he-gives why? (20) from-masters-of-him

לְמָרֵי נָפֶשׁ׃ (21) הַֽמְחַכִּים לַמָּוֶת וְאֵינֶנּוּ
and-not-he for-the-death the-ones-longing (21) soul to-ones-bitter-of

וַֽיַּחְפְּרֻהוּ מִמַּטְמוֹנִים׃ (22) הַשְּׂמֵחִים אֱלֵי־
to the-ones-joyful (22) more-than-hidden-treasures and-they-search-for-him

גִיל יָשִׂישׂוּ כִּי יִמְצְאוּ־קָבֶר׃ (23) לְגֶבֶר אֲשֶׁר־דַּרְכּוֹ
way-of-him who to-man (23) grave they-reach when they-rejoice gladness

נִסְתָּרָה וַיָּסֶךְ אֱלוֹהַּ בַּעֲדוֹ׃ (24) כִּי־לִפְנֵי לַחְמִי
food-of-me instead-of for (24) around-him God and-he-hedged-in she-is-hidden

אַנְחָתִי תָבֹא וַיִּתְּכוּ כַמַּיִם שַׁאֲגֹתָי׃
groans-of-me like-waters and-they-pour-out she-comes sighing-of-me

(25) כִּי פַחַד פָּחַדְתִּי וַיֶּאֱתָיֵנִי וַאֲשֶׁר יָגֹרְתִּי יָבֹא
he-happened I-dreaded and-what and-he-came-upon-me I-feared fear for (25)

לִי׃ (26) לֹא שָׁלַוְתִּי ׀ וְלֹא שָׁקַטְתִּי וְלֹא־נָחְתִּי
I-have-rest and-not I-have-quiet and-not I-have-peace not (26) to-me

וַיָּבֹא רֹגֶז׃ (4:1) וַיַּעַן אֱלִיפַז הַתֵּימָנִי וַיֹּאמַר׃
and-he-said the-Temanite Eliphaz then-he-replied (4:1) turmoil but-he-came

(2) הֲנִסָּה דָבָר אֵלֶיךָ תִּלְאֶה וַעְצֹר בְּמִלִּין
from-words but-to-keep will-you-be-impatient with-you word he-ventures? (2)

מִי יוּכָל׃ (3) הִנֵּה יִסַּרְתָּ רַבִּים וְיָדַיִם רָפוֹת
feeble-ones and-hands many you-instructed see! (3) he-can who?

תְּחַזֵּק׃ (4) כּוֹשֵׁל יְקִימוּן מִלֶּיךָ וּבִרְכַּיִם
and-knees words-of-you they-supported one-stumbling (4) you-strengthened

כֹּרְעוֹת תְּאַמֵּץ׃ (5) כִּי עַתָּה ׀ תָּבוֹא אֵלֶיךָ
to-you she-comes now but (5) you-strengthened ones-faltering

וַתֵּלֶא תִּגַּע עָדֶיךָ וַתִּבָּהֵל׃ (6) הֲלֹא
not? (6) and-you-are-dismayed against-you she-strikes and-you-are-discouraged

יִרְאָתְךָ כִּסְלָתֶךָ תִּקְוָתְךָ וְתֹם דְּרָכֶיךָ׃
ways-of-you and-blamelessness-of hope-of-you confidence-of-you piety-of-you

silver.
16 Or why was I not hidden in the ground like a stillborn child,
like an infant who never saw the light of day?
17 There the wicked cease from turmoil,
and there the weary are at rest.
18 Captives also enjoy their ease;
they no longer hear the slave driver's shout.
19 The small and the great are there,
and the slave is freed from his master.

20 "Why is light given to those in misery,
and life to the bitter of soul,
21 to those who long for death that does not come,
who search for it more than for hidden treasure,
22 who are filled with gladness
and rejoice when they reach the grave?
23 Why is life given to a man
whose way is hidden,
whom God has hedged in?
24 For sighing comes to me instead of food;
my groans pour out like water.
25 What I feared has come upon me;
what I dreaded has happened to me.
26 I have no peace, no quietness;
I have no rest, but only turmoil."

Eliphaz

4 Then Eliphaz the Temanite replied:

2 "If someone ventures a word with you, will you be impatient?
But who can keep from speaking?
3 Think how you have instructed many,
how you have strengthened feeble hands.
4 Your words have supported those who stumbled;
you have strengthened faltering knees.
5 But now trouble comes to you, and you are discouraged;
it strikes you, and you are dismayed.
6 Should not your piety be your confidence
and your blameless ways your hope?

(7) זְכָר־ נָא מִי הוּא נָקִי אָבָד וְאֵיפֹה יְשָׁרִים
(7) consider! now! who? he innocent he-perished and-where? upright-ones

נִכְחָדוּ׃ (8) כַּאֲשֶׁר רָאִיתִי חֹרְשֵׁי אָוֶן
they-were-destroyed (8) just-as I-observed ones-plowing-of evil

וְזֹרְעֵי עָמָל יִקְצְרֻהוּ׃ (9) מִנִּשְׁמַת אֱלוֹהַּ
and-ones-sowing-of trouble they-reap-him (9) at-breath-of God

יֹאבֵדוּ וּמֵרוּחַ אַפּוֹ יִכְלוּ׃ (10) שַׁאֲגַת
they-are-destroyed and-at-blast-of anger-of-him they-perish (10) roar-of

אַרְיֵה וְקוֹל שָׁחַל וְשִׁנֵּי כְפִירִים נִתָּעוּ׃ (11) לַיִשׁ
lion and-growl-of lion yet-teeth-of lions they-are-broken (11) lion

אֹבֵד מִבְּלִי־ טָרֶף וּבְנֵי לָבִיא יִתְפָּרָדוּ׃
perishing from-lack-of prey and-cubs-of lioness they-are-scattered

(12) וְאֵלַי דָּבָר יְגֻנָּב וַתִּקַּח אָזְנִי שֵׁמֶץ
(12) now-to-me word he-was-secretly-brought and-she-caught ear-of-me whisper

מֶנְהוּ׃ (13) בִּשְׂעִפִּים מֵחֶזְיֹנוֹת לָיְלָה בִּנְפֹל תַּרְדֵּמָה
of-him (13) amid-disquieting-ones of-dreams-of night when-to-fall deep-sleep

עַל־ אֲנָשִׁים׃ (14) פַּחַד קְרָאַנִי וּרְעָדָה וְרֹב עַצְמוֹתַי
on men (14) fear he-seized-me and-trembling and-all-of bones-of-me

הִפְחִיד׃ (15) וְרוּחַ עַל־ פָּנַי יַחֲלֹף תְּסַמֵּר
he-made-shake (15) and-spirit by faces-of-me he-glided she-stood-on-end

שַׂעֲרַת בְּשָׂרִי׃ (16) יַעֲמֹד וְלֹא־ אַכִּיר מַרְאֵהוּ
hair-of body-of-me (16) he-stopped but-not I-could-tell appearance-of-him

תְּמוּנָה לְנֶגֶד עֵינָי דְּמָמָה וָקוֹל אֶשְׁמָע׃ (17) הַאֱנוֹשׁ
form at-before eyes-of-me hushed and-voice I-heard (17) mortal?

מֵאֱלוֹהַּ יִצְדָּק אִם מֵעֹשֵׂהוּ יִטְהַר־ גָּבֶר׃
more-than-God is-he-righteous or more-than-one-making-him is-he-pure man

(18) הֵן בַּעֲבָדָיו לֹא יַאֲמִין וּבְמַלְאָכָיו
(18) if in-servants-of-him not he-places-trust and-to-angels-of-him

יָשִׂים תָּהֳלָה׃ (19) אַף שֹׁכְנֵי בָתֵּי־ חֹמֶר אֲשֶׁר־
he-charges error (19) how-much-more ones-living-of houses-of clay which

בֶּעָפָר יְסוֹדָם יְדַכְּאוּם לִפְנֵי־ עָשׁ׃ (20) מִבֹּקֶר
in-the-dust foundation-of-them they-crush-them before moth (20) from-dawn

לָעֶרֶב יֻכַּתּוּ מִבְּלִי מֵשִׂים לָנֶצַח יֹאבֵדוּ׃
to-the-dusk they-are-broken from-not being-noticed to-forever they-perish

(21) הֲלֹא־ נִסַּע יִתְרָם בָּם יָמוּתוּ וְלֹא
(21) not? he-is-pulled-up tent-cord-of-them from-them they-die and-not

בְּחָכְמָה׃ (5:1) קְרָא־ נָא הֲיֵשׁ עוֹנֶךָּ וְאֶל־ מִי
with-wisdom (5:1) call! now! is-there? one-answering-you and-to which?

7 "Consider now: Who, being
innocent, has ever
perished?
Where were the upright ever
destroyed?
8 As I have observed, those who
plow evil
and those who sow trouble
reap it.
9 At the breath of God they are
destroyed;
at the blast of his anger they
perish.
10 The lions may roar and growl,
yet the teeth of the great
lions are broken.
11 The lion perishes for lack of
prey,
and the cubs of the lioness
are scattered.

12 "A word was secretly brought
to me,
my ears caught a whisper of
it.
13 Amid disquieting dreams in
the night,
when deep sleep falls on
men,
14 fear and trembling seized me
and made all my bones
shake.
15 A spirit glided past my face,
and the hair on my body
stood on end.
16 It stopped,
but I could not tell what it
was.
A form stood before my eyes,
and I heard a hushed voice:
17 'Can a mortal be more
righteous than God?
Can a man be more pure
than his Maker?
18 If God places no trust in his
servants,
if he charges his angels with
error,
19 how much more those who
live in houses of clay,
whose foundations are in
the dust,
who are crushed more
readily than a moth!
20 Between dawn and dusk they
are broken to pieces;
unnoticed, they perish
forever.
21 Are not the cords of their tent
pulled up,
so that they die without
wisdom?'

5 "Call if you will, but who
will answer you?

מִקְּדֹשִׁים תִּפְנֶה׃ כִּי־לֶאֱוִיל יַהֲרָג־כַּעַשׂ
resentment he-kills to-fool for (2) will-you-turn of-holy-ones

וּפֹתֶה תָּמִית קִנְאָה׃ אֲנִי־רָאִיתִי אֱוִיל מַשְׁרִישׁ וָאֶקּוֹב
but-I-cursed taking-root fool I-saw I (3) envy she-slays and-one-being-simple

נָוֵהוּ פִתְאֹם׃ יִרְחֲקוּ בָנָיו מִיֶּשַׁע
from-safety children-of-him they-are-far (4) suddenly house-of-him

וְיִדַּכְּאוּ בַשַּׁעַר וְאֵין מַצִּיל׃ אֲשֶׁר קְצִירוֹ ׀
harvest-of-him who (5) one-defending and-no in-the-court and-they-are-crushed

רָעֵב יֹאכֵל וְאֶל־מִצִּנִּים יִקָּחֵהוּ וְשָׁאַף צַמִּים
ones-thirsty and-he-pants he-takes-him from-thorns even-to he-consumes hungry

חֵילָם׃ כִּי ׀ לֹא־יֵצֵא מֵעָפָר אָוֶן וּמֵאֲדָמָה לֹא־
not or-from-ground hardship from-soil he-springs not for (6) wealth-of-them

יִצְמַח עָמָל׃ כִּי־אָדָם לְעָמָל יוּלָּד וּבְנֵי־רֶשֶׁף
flame as-sons-of he-is-born to-trouble man yet (7) trouble he-sprouts

יַגְבִּיהוּ עוּף׃ אוּלָם אֲנִי אֶדְרֹשׁ אֶל־אֵל וְאֶל־אֱלֹהִים
God and-before God to I-would-appeal I but-if (8) to-fly they-go-upward

אָשִׂים דִּבְרָתִי׃ עֹשֶׂה גְדֹלוֹת וְאֵין חֵקֶר
fathomable and-not wonders performing (9) cause-of-me I-would-lay

נִפְלָאוֹת עַד־אֵין מִסְפָּר׃ הַנֹּתֵן מָטָר עַל־
on rain the-one-bestowing (10) count no to things-being-miraculous

פְּנֵי־אָרֶץ וְשֹׁלֵחַ מַיִם* עַל־פְּנֵי חוּצוֹת׃
countrysides surfaces-of on waters and-sending earth surfaces-of

לָשׂוּם שְׁפָלִים לְמָרוֹם וְקֹדְרִים שָׂגְבוּ יֶשַׁע׃
safety they-are-lifted and-ones-mourning on-high lowly-ones to-set (11)

מֵפֵר מַחְשְׁבוֹת עֲרוּמִים וְלֹא־תַעֲשֶׂינָה יְדֵיהֶם תּוּשִׁיָּה׃
success hands-of-them they-achieve so-not crafty-ones plans-of thwarting (12)

לֹכֵד חֲכָמִים בְּעָרְמָם וַעֲצַת נִפְתָּלִים
ones-being-wily and-scheme-of in-craftiness-of-them wise-ones catching (13)

נִמְהָרָה׃ יוֹמָם יְפַגְּשׁוּ־חֹשֶׁךְ וְכַלַּיְלָה
and-as-the-night darkness they-are-overcome by-day (14) she-is-swept-away

יְמַשְׁשׁוּ בַצָּהֳרָיִם׃ וַיֹּשַׁע מֵחֶרֶב מִפִּיהֶם
in-mouth-of-them from-sword and-he-saves (15) at-the-noon they-grope

וּמִיַּד חָזָק אֶבְיוֹן׃ וַתְּהִי לַדַּל תִּקְוָה
hope to-the-poor so-she-is (16) needy powerful and-from-clutch-of

וְעֹלָתָה קָפְצָה פִּיהָ׃ הִנֵּה אַשְׁרֵי אֱנוֹשׁ
man blessings-of see! (17) mouth-of-her she-shuts and-injustice

יוֹכִחֶנּוּ אֱלוֹהַּ וּמוּסַר שַׁדַּי אַל־תִּמְאָס׃ כִּי הוּא
he for (18) you-despise not Almighty so-discipline-of God he-corrects-him

To which of the holy ones
will you turn?
2 Resentment kills a fool,
and envy slays the simple.
3 I myself have seen a fool
taking root,
but suddenly his house was
cursed.
4 His children are far from
safety,
crushed in court without a
defender.
5 The hungry consume his
harvest,
taking it even from among
thorns,
and the thirsty pant after
his wealth.
6 For hardship does not spring
from the soil,
nor does trouble sprout from
the ground.
7 Yet man is born to trouble
as surely as sparks fly
upward.
8 "But if it were I, I would
appeal to God;
I would lay my cause before
him.
9 He performs wonders that
cannot be fathomed,
miracles that cannot be
counted.
10 He bestows rain on the earth;
he sends water upon the
countryside.
11 The lowly he sets on high,
and those who mourn are
lifted to safety.
12 He thwarts the plans of the
crafty,
so that their hands achieve
no success.
13 He catches the wise in their
craftiness,
and the schemes of the wily
are swept away.
14 Darkness comes upon them in
the daytime;
at noon they grope as in the
night.
15 He saves the needy from the
sword in their mouth;
he saves them from the
clutches of the powerful.
16 So the poor have hope,
and injustice shuts its
mouth.

17 "Blessed is the man whom
God corrects;
so do not despise the
discipline of the
Almighty.[h]

[h]17 Hebrew *Shaddai*; here and throughout Job

*10 Most mss have the accent *rebia mugrash* (ֶ׳).

יַכְאִיב וְיֶחְבָּשׁ יִמְחַץ וְיָדָו° תִּרְפֶּינָה׃
they-heal but-hands-of-him he-injures but-he-binds-up he-wounds

(19) בְּשֵׁשׁ צָרוֹת יַצִּילֶךָּ וּבְשֶׁבַע ׀ לֹא־ יִגַּע
he-will-befall not and-in-seven he-will-rescue-you calamities from-six-of (19)

בְּךָ רָע׃ (20) בְּרָעָב פָּדְךָ מִמָּוֶת וּבְמִלְחָמָה
and-in-battle from-death he-will-ransom-you in-famine (20) harm on-you

מִידֵי חָרֶב׃ (21) בְּשׁוֹט לָשׁוֹן תֵּחָבֵא וְלֹא־
and-not you-will-be-protected tongue from-lash-of (21) sword from-strokes-of

תִירָא מִשֹּׁד כִּי יָבוֹא׃ (22) לְשֹׁד וּלְכָפָן
and-at-famine at-destruction (22) he-comes when of-destruction you-will-fear

תִּשְׂחָק וּמֵחַיַּת הָאָרֶץ אַל־ תִּירָא׃ (23) כִּי עִם־
with for (23) you-will-fear not the-earth and-of-beast-of you-will-laugh

אַבְנֵי הַשָּׂדֶה בְרִיתֶךָ וְחַיַּת הַשָּׂדֶה הָשְׁלְמָה־
she-will-be-at-peace the-wild and-animal-of covenant-of-you the-field stones-of

לָךְ׃ (24) וְיָדַעְתָּ כִּי־ שָׁלוֹם אָהֳלֶךָ וּפָקַדְתָּ
and-you-will-take-stock tent-of-you secure that and-you-will-know (24) with-you

נָוְךָ וְלֹא תֶחֱטָא׃ (25) וְיָדַעְתָּ כִּי־ רַב
many that and-you-will-know (25) you-will-miss and-nothing property-of-you

זַרְעֶךָ וְצֶאֱצָאֶיךָ כְּעֵשֶׂב הָאָרֶץ׃ (26) תָּבוֹא
you-will-come (26) the-earth like-grass-of and-descendants-of-you child-of-you

בְכֶלַח אֱלֵי־ קָבֶר כַּעֲלוֹת גָּדִישׁ בְּעִתּוֹ׃ (27) הִנֵּה־ זֹאת
this see! (27) in-season-of-him sheaf like-to-gather grave to in-vigor

חֲקַרְנוּהָ כֶּן־ הִיא שְׁמָעֶנָּה וְאַתָּה דַע־ לָךְ׃ (6:1) וַיַּעַן
then-he-replied (6:1) to-you apply! and-you hear-her! she true we-examined-her

אִיּוֹב וַיֹּאמַר׃ (2) לוּ שָׁקוֹל יִשָּׁקֵל כַּעְשִׂי
anguish-of-me he-was-weighed to-be-weighed if-only (2) and-he-said Job

וְהַיָּתִי° בְּמֹאזְנַיִם יִשְׂאוּ־ יָחַד׃ (3) כִּי־ עַתָּה
now surely (3) together they-placed on-scales and-misery-of-me

מֵחוֹל יַמִּים יִכְבָּד עַל־ כֵּן דְּבָרַי לָעוּ׃
they-were-impetuous words-of-me this for he-would-weigh seas more-than-sand-of

(4) כִּי חִצֵּי שַׁדַּי עִמָּדִי אֲשֶׁר חֲמָתָם שֹׁתָה רוּחִי
spirit-of-me drinking poison-of-them that in-me Almighty arrows-of indeed (4)

בִּעוּתֵי אֱלוֹהַּ יַעַרְכוּנִי׃ (5) הֲיִנְהַק־ פֶּרֶא עֲלֵי־
over wild-donkey does-he-bray? (5) they-are-marshaled-against-me God terrors-of

דֶשֶׁא אִם יִגְעֶה־ שּׁוֹר עַל־ בְּלִילוֹ׃ (6) הֲיֵאָכֵל תָּפֵל
tasteless-food is-he-eaten? (6) fodder-of-him over ox does-he-bellow or grass

מִבְּלִי־ מֶלַח אִם־ יֶשׁ־ טַעַם בְּרִיר חַלָּמוּת׃ (7) מֵאֲנָה
she-refuses (7) egg-white in-slime-of flavor is-there or salt without

18For he wounds, but he also
binds up;
he injures, but his hands
also heal.
19From six calamities he will
rescue you;
in seven no harm will befall
you.
20In famine he will ransom you
from death,
and in battle from the stroke
of the sword.
21You will be protected from the
lash of the tongue,
and need not fear when
destruction comes.
22You will laugh at destruction
and famine
and need not fear the beasts
of the earth.
23For you will have a covenant
with the stones of the
field,
and the wild animals will be
at peace with you.
24You will know that your tent
is secure;
you will take stock of your
property and find
nothing missing.
25You will know that your
children will be many,
and your descendants like
the grass of the earth.
26You will come to the grave in
full vigor,
like sheaves gathered in
season.

27"We have examined this, and
it is true.
So hear it and apply it to
yourself."

Job

6 Then Job replied:
2"If only my anguish could
be weighed
and all my misery be placed
on the scales!
3It would surely outweigh the
sand of the seas—
no wonder my words have
been impetuous.
4The arrows of the Almighty
are in me,
my spirit drinks in their
poison;
God's terrors are marshaled
against me.
5Does a wild donkey bray
when it has grass,
or an ox bellow when it has
fodder?
6Is tasteless food eaten without
salt,
or is there flavor in the
white of an egg[i]?

[i]6 The meaning of the Hebrew for this phrase is uncertain.

°18 ק וידיו
°2 ק והותי

לִנְגּוֹעַ נַפְשִׁי הֵמָּה כִּדְוֵי לַחְמִי׃ מִי־ יִתֵּן
he-will-grant who? (8) food-of-me illnessess-of they self-of-me to-touch

תָּבוֹא שֶׁאֱלָתִי וְתִקְוָתִי יִתֵּן אֱלוֹהַּ׃
God he-would-grant and-hope-of-me request-of-me she-will-come

וְיֹאֵל אֱלוֹהַּ וִידַכְּאֵנִי יַתֵּר
he-would-let-loose and-he-would-crush-me God and-he-was-willing (9)

יָדוֹ וִיבַצְּעֵנִי׃ וּתְהִי* עוֹד*
still then-she-would-be (10) and-he-would-cut-off-me hand-of-him

נֶחָמָתִי וַאֲסַלְּדָה בְחִילָה לֹא יַחְמוֹל כִּי־ לֹא
not that he-would-relent not in-pain and-I-would-rejoice consolation-of-me

כִחַדְתִּי אִמְרֵי קָדוֹשׁ׃ מַה־ כֹּחִי כִי־ אֲיַחֵל
I-should-hope that strength-of-me what? (11) Holy-One words-of I-denied

וּמַה־ קִּצִּי כִּי־ אַאֲרִיךְ נַפְשִׁי׃ אִם־
indeed (12) soul-of-me I-should-make-patient that prospect-of-me and-what?

כֹּחַ אֲבָנִים כֹּחִי אִם־ בְּשָׂרִי נָחוּשׁ׃ הַאִם אֵין
no indeed? (13) bronze flesh-of-me or strength-of-me stones strength-of

עֶזְרָתִי בִי וְתֻשִׁיָּה נִדְּחָה מִמֶּנִּי׃ לַמָּס
for-the-desperate (14) from-me she-was-driven now-success for-me help-of-me

מֵרֵעֵהוּ חָסֶד וְיִרְאַת שַׁדַּי יַעֲזוֹב׃
he-forsakes Almighty though-fear-of devotion from-friends-of-him

אַחַי בָּגְדוּ כְמוֹ־ נָחַל
intermittent-stream as they-are-undependable brothers-of-me (15)

כַּאֲפִיק נְחָלִים יַעֲבֹרוּ׃ הַקֹּדְרִים מִנִּי־קָרַח עָלֵימוֹ
with-them ice by the-ones-being-dark (16) they-overflow streams as-channel-of

יִתְעַלֶּם־ שָׁלֶג׃ בְּעֵת יְזֹרְבוּ נִצְמָתוּ
they-cease-to-flow they-are-dry by-season (17) snow he-is-swollen

בְּחֻמּוֹ נִדְעֲכוּ מִמְּקוֹמָם׃ יִלָּפְתוּ
they-turn-aside (18) from-channel-of-them they-vanish when-to-be-hot-him

אָרְחוֹת דַּרְכָּם יַעֲלוּ בַתֹּהוּ וְיֹאבֵדוּ׃
and-they-perish into-the-wasteland they-go-up route-of-them caravans

הִבִּיטוּ אָרְחוֹת תֵּמָא הֲלִיכֹת שְׁבָא קִוּוּ־
they-hope Sheba traveling-merchants-of Tema caravans-of they-look (19)

לָמוֹ׃ בֹּשׁוּ כִּי־ בָטָח בָּאוּ עָדֶיהָ
at-her they-arrive he-was-confident because they-are-distressed (20) for-them

וַיֶּחְפָּרוּ׃ כִּי־ עַתָּה הֱיִיתֶם לֹא° תִּרְאוּ חֲתַת
dreadful you-see nothing you-were you too (21) but-they-are-disappointed

וַתִּירָאוּ׃ הֲכִי־ אָמַרְתִּי הָבוּ לִי וּמִכֹּחֲכֶם
and-from-wealth-of-you to-me give! I-said ever? (22) and-you-are-afraid

7 I refuse to touch it;
such food makes me ill.
8 "Oh, that I might have my
request,
that God would grant what I
hope for,
9 that God would be willing to
crush me,
to let loose his hand and cut
me off!
10 Then I would still have this
consolation—
my joy in unrelenting
pain—
that I had not denied the
words of the Holy One.

11 "What strength do I have, that
I should still hope?
What prospects, that I
should be patient?
12 Do I have the strength of
stone?
Is my flesh bronze?
13 Do I have any power to help
myself,
now that success has been
driven from me?

14 "A despairing man should
have the devotion of his
friends,
even though he forsakes the
fear of the Almighty.
15 But my brothers are as
undependable as
intermittent streams,
as the streams that overflow
16 when darkened by thawing ice
and swollen with melting
snow,
17 but that cease to flow in the
dry season,
and in the heat vanish from
their channels.
18 Caravans turn aside from their
routes;
they go up into the
wasteland and perish.
19 The caravans of Tema look for
water,
the traveling merchants of
Sheba look in hope.
20 They are distressed, because
they had been confident;
they arrive there, only to be
disappointed.
21 Now you too have proved to
be of no help;
you see something dreadful
and are afraid.
22 Have I ever said, 'Give
something on my behalf,

*10 Most mss connect these two words with *maqqeph* (ותהי־עוד).

°21 ק לו

שַׁחֲדוּ בַּעֲדִי׃ וּמַלְּטוּנִי מִיַּד־ צָר וּמִיַּד

and-from-clutch-of enemy from-hand-of and-deliver-me! (23) for-me pay-ransom!

עָרִיצִים תִּפְדּוּנִי׃ הוֹרוּנִי וַאֲנִי אַחֲרִישׁ וּמַה־

and-what I-will-be-quiet and-I teach-me! (24) you-ransom-me ruthless-ones

שָׁגִיתִי הָבִינוּ לִי׃ מַה־ נִּמְרְצוּ אִמְרֵי־ יֹשֶׁר וּמַה־

but-what? honesty words-of they-are-painful how! (25) to-me show! I-did-wrong

יוֹכִיחַ הוֹכֵחַ מִכֶּם׃ הַלְהוֹכַח מִלִּים תַּחְשֹׁבוּ וּלְרוּחַ

and-as-wind do-you-mean sayings to-correct? (26) from-you to-prove he-proves

אִמְרֵי נֹאָשׁ׃ אַף־ עַל־ יָתוֹם תַּפִּילוּ

you-would-cast-lot fatherless for even (27) despairing-man words-of

וְתִכְרוּ עַל־ רֵיעֲכֶם׃ וְעַתָּה הוֹאִילוּ פְנוּ־ בִי

at-me look! be-kind! but-now (28) friend-of-you over and-you-would-barter

וְעַל־ פְּנֵיכֶם אִם־ אֲכַזֵּב׃ שֻׁבוּ־ נָא אַל־ תְּהִי עַוְלָה

unjust you-be not now! relent! (29) would-I-lie indeed faces-of-you and-to

וְשֻׁבִי עוֹד צִדְקִי־ בָהּ׃ הֲיֵשׁ־ בִּלְשׁוֹנִי

on-lip-of-me is-there? (30) in-her integrity-of-me again and-consider!

עַוְלָה אִם־ חִכִּי לֹא־ יָבִין הַוּוֹת׃ הֲלֹא־

not? (7:1) malice he-can-discern not mouth-of-me indeed wickedness

צָבָא לֶאֱנוֹשׁ עֲלֵי־ אֶרֶץ וְכִימֵי שָׂכִיר יָמָיו׃

days-of-him hired-man and-like-days-of earth on to-man hard-service

כְּעֶבֶד יִשְׁאַף־ צֵל וּכְשָׂכִיר יְקַוֶּה פָעֳלוֹ׃

wage-of-him he-waits-for or-like-hired-man shadow he-longs-for like-slave (2)

כֵּן הָנְחַלְתִּי לִי יַרְחֵי־ שָׁוְא וְלֵילוֹת עָמָל

misery and-nights-of futility months-of to-me I-was-allotted so (3)

מִנּוּ־ לִי׃ אִם־ שָׁכַבְתִּי וְאָמַרְתִּי מָתַי

how-long? then-I-think I-lie-down when (4) to-me they-assigned

אָקוּם וּמִדַּד־ עָרֶב וְשָׂבַעְתִּי נְדֻדִים עֲדֵי־ נָשֶׁף׃

dawn till tossings and-I-am-full night now-he-drags-on will-I-get-up

לָבַשׁ בְּשָׂרִי רִמָּה וְגִישׁ עָפָר עוֹרִי רָגַע

he-is-broken skin-of-me dust and-scab-of worm body-of-me he-is-clothed (5)

וַיִּמָּאֵס׃ יָמַי קַלּוּ מִנִּי־ אָרֶג

shuttle-of-weaver more-than they-are-swift days-of-me (6) and-he-festers

וַיִּכְלוּ בְּאֶפֶס תִּקְוָה׃ זְכֹר כִּי־ רוּחַ חַיָּי לֹא־

never lives-of-me breath that remember! (7) hope with-no and-they-end

תָשׁוּב עֵינִי לִרְאוֹת טוֹב׃ לֹא־ תְשׁוּרֵנִי עֵין

eye-of she-will-see-me not (8) happiness to-see eye-of-me she-will-do-again

רֹאִי עֵינֶיךָ בִּי וְאֵינֶנִּי׃ כָּלָה עָנָן וַיֵּלַךְ

and-he-goes cloud he-vanishes (9) but-no-more-I to-me eyes-of-you seeing-me

---

pay a ransom for me from
your wealth,
23 deliver me from the hand of
the enemy,
ransom me from the
clutches of the ruthless'?

24 "Teach me, and I will be quiet;
show me where I have been
wrong.
25 How painful are honest words!
But what do your arguments
prove?
26 Do you mean to correct what I
say,
and treat the words of a
despairing man as wind?
27 You would even cast lots for
the fatherless
and barter away your friend.

28 "But now be so kind as to look
at me.
Would I lie to your face?
29 Relent, do not be unjust;
reconsider, for my integrity
is at stake.[l]
30 Is there any wickedness on my
lips?
Can my mouth not discern
malice?

7 "Does not man have hard
service on earth?
Are not his days like those
of a hired man?
2 Like a slave longing for the
evening shadows,
or a hired man waiting
eagerly for his wages,
3 so I have been allotted months
of futility,
and nights of misery have
been assigned to me.
4 When I lie down I think,
'How long before I get
up?'
The night drags on, and I
toss till dawn.
5 My body is clothed with
worms and scabs,
my skin is broken and
festering.

6 "My days are swifter than a
weaver's shuttle,
and they come to an end
without hope.
7 Remember, O God, that my
life is but a breath;
my eyes will never see
happiness again.
8 The eye that now sees me will
see me no longer;
you will look for me, but I
will be no more.
9 As a cloud vanishes and is
gone,

l29 Or *my righteousness still stands*

°29 ק ושבו
°1 ק עלי
°5 ק וגוש

כֵּן יוֹרֵד שְׁאוֹל לֹא יַעֲלֶה׃ לֹא־ יָשׁוּב עוֹד

again he-will-come never (10) he-returns not Sheol one-going-down so

לְבֵיתוֹ וְלֹא־ יַכִּירֶנּוּ עוֹד מְקֹמוֹ׃ גַּם־ אֲנִי

I therefore (11) place-of-him more he-will-know-him and-not to-house-of-him

לֹא אֶחֱשָׂךְ פִּי אֲדַבְּרָה בְּצַר רוּחִי

spirit-of-me in-anguish-of I-will-speak-out mouth-of-me I-will-keep-silent not

אָשִׂיחָה בְּמַר נַפְשִׁי׃ הֲיָם־אָנִי אִם־ תַּנִּין

monster-of-the-deep or I sea? (12) soul-of-me in-bitterness-of I-will-complain

כִּי־ תָשִׂים עָלַי מִשְׁמָר׃ כִּי־ אָמַרְתִּי תְּנַחֲמֵנִי עַרְשִׂי

bed-of-me she-will-comfort-me I-think when (13) guard over-me you-put that

יִשָּׂא בְשִׂיחִי מִשְׁכָּבִי׃ וְחִתַּתַּנִי

then-you-frighten-me (14) couch-of-me to-complaint-of-me he-will-ease

בַחֲלֹמוֹת וּמֵחֶזְיֹנוֹת תְּבַעֲתַנִּי׃ וַתִּבְחַר מַחֲנָק

strangling so-she-prefers (15) you-terrify-me and-with-visions with-dreams

נַפְשִׁי מָוֶת מֵעַצְמוֹתָי׃ מָאַסְתִּי לֹא־ לְעֹלָם

to-forever not I-despise (16) rather-than-bodies-of-me death life-of-me

אֶחְיֶה חֲדַל מִמֶּנִּי כִּי־ הֶבֶל יָמָי׃ מָה־ אֱנוֹשׁ

man what? (17) days-of-me meaningless for from-me let-alone! I-would-live

כִּי תְגַדְּלֶנּוּ וְכִי־ תָשִׁית אֵלָיו לִבֶּךָ׃

heart-of-you to-him you-give-attention and-that you-make-much-of-him that

וַתִּפְקְדֶנּוּ לִבְקָרִים לִרְגָעִים תִּבְחָנֶנּוּ׃

you-test-him in-moments in-mornings that-you-examine-him (18)

כַּמָּה לֹא־ תִשְׁעֶה מִמֶּנִּי לֹא־ תַרְפֵּנִי

you-will-let-alone-me not from-me you-will-look-away not as-the-when? (19)

עַד־ בִּלְעִי רֻקִּי׃ חָטָאתִי מָה אֶפְעַל ׀ לָךְ

to-you I-did what? I-sinned (20) spittle-of-me to-swallow-me even

נֹצֵר הָאָדָם לָמָה שַׂמְתַּנִי לְמִפְגָּע לָךְ וָאֶהְיֶה עָלַי

to-me and-I-became of-you as-target you-made-me why? the-man one-watching

לְמַשָּׂא׃ וּמֶה ׀ לֹא־ תִשָּׂא פִשְׁעִי וְתַעֲבִיר אֶת־

*** and-you-forgive offense-of-me you-pardon not and-why? (21) as-burden

עֲוֹנִי כִּי־ עַתָּה לֶעָפָר אֶשְׁכָּב וְשִׁחַרְתַּנִי*

and-you-will-search-for-me I-will-lie-down in-the-dust soon for sin-of-me

וְאֵינֶנִּי׃ וַיַּעַן בִּלְדַּד הַשּׁוּחִי וַיֹּאמַר†׃ עַד־

until (2) and-he-said the-Shuhite Bildad then-he-replied (8:1) but-no-more-I

אָן תְּמַלֶּל־ אֵלֶּה וְרוּחַ כַּבִּיר אִמְרֵי־ פִיךָ׃

mouth-of-you words-of blustering now-wind these-things will-you-say when?

הַאֵל יְעַוֵּת מִשְׁפָּט וְאִם־ שַׁדַּי יְעַוֵּת־ צֶדֶק׃ אִם־

when (4) right he-perverts Almighty or-indeed justice he-perverts God? (3)

so he who goes down to the
grave[k] does not return.
10He will never come to his
house again;
his place will know him no
more.

11"Therefore I will not keep
silent;
I will speak out in the
anguish of my spirit,
I will complain in the
bitterness of my soul.
12Am I the sea, or the monster
of the deep,
that you put me under
guard?
13When I think my bed will
comfort me
and my couch will ease my
complaint,
14even then you frighten me
with dreams
and terrify me with visions,
15so that I prefer strangling and
death,
rather than this body of
mine.
16I despise my life; I would not
live forever.
Let me alone; my days have
no meaning.

17"What is man that you make
so much of him,
that you give him so much
attention,
18that you examine him every
morning
and test him every moment?
19Will you never look away from
me,
or let me alone even for an
instant?
20If I have sinned, what have I
done to you,
O watcher of men?
Why have you made me your
target?
Have I become a burden to
you?[l]
21Why do you not pardon my
offenses
and forgive my sins?
For I will soon lie down in the
dust;
you will search for me, but I
will be no more."

Bildad

8 Then Bildad the Shuhite replied:

2"How long will you say such
things?
Your words are a blustering
wind.
3Does God pervert justice?
Does the Almighty pervert
what is right?

[k]9 Hebrew *Sheol*

[l]20 A few manuscripts of the Masoretic Text, an ancient Hebrew scribal tradition and Septuagint; most manuscripts of the Masoretic Text *I have become a burden to myself.*

*21 Most mss have *pathah* under the *beth* (וְשִׁחַרְ).

†1 Most mss have *dagesh* in the *yod* (יּ).

בָּנֶיךָ חָֽטְאוּ־ לוֹ וַֽיְשַׁלְּחֵם בְּיַד־

into-hand-of then-he-gave-over-them against-him they-sinned children-of-you

פִּשְׁעָם׃ אִם־אַתָּה תְּשַׁחֵר אֶל־אֵל וְאֶל־ שַׁדַּי תִּתְחַנָּן׃

you-will-plead Almighty and-with God to you-will-look you if (5) sin-of-them

אִם־זַךְ וְיָשָׁר אָתָּה כִּי־ עַתָּה יָעִיר עָלֶיךָ

on-behalf-of-you he-will-rouse-himself now even you and-upright pure if (6)

וְשִׁלַּם נְוַת צִדְקֶךָ׃ וְהָיָה רֵאשִׁיתְךָ

beginning-of-you and-he-will-be (7) right-of-you place-of and-he-will-restore

מִצְעָר וְאַחֲרִיתְךָ יִשְׂגֶּה מְאֹד׃ כִּי־ שְׁאַל־ נָא

now! ask! indeed (8) greatly he-will-prosper and-future-of-you humble

לְדֹר רִישׁוֹן וְכוֹנֵן לְחֵקֶר אֲבוֹתָם׃

fathers-of-them about-learning-of and-find-out! former to-generation

כִּי־ תְמוֹל אֲנַחְנוּ וְלֹא נֵדָע כִּי צֵל יָמֵינוּ עֲלֵי־אָרֶץ׃

earth on days-of-us shadow for we-know and-nothing we yesterday for (9)

הֲלֹא־ הֵם יוֹרוּךָ יֹאמְרוּ לָךְ

to-you they-will-tell they-will-instruct-you they not? (10)

וּמִלִּבָּם יוֹצִאוּ מִלִּים׃ הֲיִגְאֶה־

can-he-grow? (11) words they-will-bring-forth and-from-understanding-of-them

גֹּמֶא בְּלֹא בִצָּה יִשְׂגֶּה־ אָחוּ בְלִי־ מָיִם׃ עֹדֶנּוּ

still-he (12) waters without reed can-he-thrive marsh with-no papyrus

בְאִבּוֹ לֹא יִקָּטֵף וְלִפְנֵי כָל־ חָצִיר יִיבָשׁ׃ כֵּן

such (13) he-withers grass all-of yet-before he-was-cut not in-growth-of-him

אָרְחוֹת כָּל־ שֹׁכְחֵי אֵל וְתִקְוַת חָנֵף תֹּאבֵד׃

she-perishes godless so-hope-of God ones-forgetting-of all-of destinies-of

אֲשֶׁר־ יָקוֹט כִּסְלוֹ וּבֵית עַכָּבִישׁ מִבְטַחוֹ׃

reliance-of-him spider and-web-of trust-of-him he-is-fragile what (14)

יִשָּׁעֵן עַל־ בֵּיתוֹ וְלֹא יַעֲמֹד יַחֲזִיק בּוֹ וְלֹא

but-not to-him he-clings he-stands but-not web-of-him on he-leans (15)

יָקוּם׃ רָטֹב הוּא לִפְנֵי־ שָׁמֶשׁ וְעַל־ גַּנָּתוֹ

garden-of-him and-over sunshine in he watered-plant (16) he-holds

יֹנַקְתּוֹ תֵצֵא׃ עַל־ גַּל שָׁרָשָׁיו יְסֻבָּכוּ

they-entwine roots-of-him rock-pile around (17) she-spreads shoot-of-him

בֵּית אֲבָנִים יֶחֱזֶה׃ אִם־ יְבַלְּעֶנּוּ מִמְּקוֹמוֹ

from-spot-of-him he-tears-him when (18) he-looks-for stones place-of

וְכִחֶשׁ בּוֹ לֹא רְאִיתִיךָ׃ הֶן־ הוּא מְשׂוֹשׂ דַּרְכּוֹ

way-of-him joy-of this surely (19) I-saw-you never to-him then-he-disowns

וּמֵעָפָר אַחֵר יִצְמָחוּ׃ הֶן־ אֵל לֹא יִמְאַס־ תָּם

blameless-man he-rejects not God surely (20) they-grow other and-from-soil

4 When your children sinned
against him,
he gave them over to the
penalty of their sin.
5 But if you will look to God
and plead with the
Almighty,
6 if you are pure and upright,
even now he will rouse
himself on your behalf
and restore you to your
rightful place.
7 Your beginnings will seem
humble,
so prosperous will your
future be.

8 "Ask the former generations
and find out what their
fathers learned,
9 for we were born only
yesterday and know
nothing,
and our days on earth are
but a shadow.
10 Will they not instruct you and
tell you?
Will they not bring forth
words from their
understanding?
11 Can papyrus grow tall where
there is no marsh?
Can reeds thrive without
water?
12 While still growing and uncut,
they wither more quickly
than grass.
13 Such is the destiny of all who
forget God;
so perishes the hope of the
godless.
14 What he trusts in is fragile[m];
what he relies on is a
spider's web.
15 He leans on his web, but it
gives way;
he clings to it, but it does
not hold.
16 He is like a well-watered plant
in the sunshine,
spreading its shoots over the
garden;
17 it entwines its roots around a
pile of rocks
and looks for a place among
the stones.
18 But when it is torn from its
spot,
that place disowns it and
says, 'I never saw you.'
19 Surely its life withers away,
and[n] from the soil other
plants grow.

20 "Surely God does not reject a
blameless man

[m]14 The meaning of the Hebrew for this word is uncertain.
[n]19 Or *Surely all the joy it has / is that*

וְלֹא־ יַחֲזִיק בְּיַד־ מְרֵעִים׃ עַד־ יְמַלֵּה

he-will-fill yet (21) ones-doing-evil to-hand-of he-strengthens and-not

שְׂחוֹק פִּיךָ וּשְׂפָתֶיךָ תְרוּעָה׃ שֹׂנְאֶיךָ

ones-hating-you (22) shout-of-joy and-lips-of-you mouth-of-you laughter

יִלְבְּשׁוּ־ בֹשֶׁת וְאֹהֶל רְשָׁעִים אֵינֶנּוּ׃

no-more-he wicked-ones and-tent-of shame they-will-be-clothed

וַיַּעַן אִיּוֹב וַיֹּאמַר׃ אָמְנָם יָדַעְתִּי כִי־ כֵן וּמַה־

but-how? true that I-know indeed (2) and-he-said Job then-he-replied (9:1)

יִּצְדַּק אֱנוֹשׁ עִם־ אֵל׃ אִם־ יַחְפֹּץ לָרִיב

to-dispute he-wished though (3) God before mortal can-he-be-righteous

עִמּוֹ לֹא־ יַעֲנֶנּוּ אַחַת מִנִּי־ אָלֶף׃ חֲכַם לֵבָב

heart wise-of (4) thousand out-of one he-could-answer-him not with-him

וְאַמִּיץ כֹּחַ מִי־ הִקְשָׁה אֵלָיו וַיִּשְׁלָם׃

and-he-was-unscathed against-him he-resisted who? power and-vast-of

הַמַּעְתִּיק הָרִים וְלֹא יָדָעוּ אֲשֶׁר הֲפָכָם

he-overturns-them who they-know so-not mountains the-one-moving (5)

בְּאַפּוֹ׃ הַמַּרְגִּיז אֶרֶץ מִמְּקוֹמָהּ וְעַמּוּדֶיהָ

and-pillars-of-her from-place-of-her earth the-one-shaking (6) in-anger-of-him

יִתְפַלָּצוּן׃ הָאֹמֵר לַחֶרֶס וְלֹא יִזְרָח וּבְעַד

and-behind he-shines and-not to-the-sun the-one-speaking (7) they-tremble

כּוֹכָבִים יַחְתֹּם׃ נֹטֶה שָׁמַיִם לְבַדּוֹ וְדוֹרֵךְ

and-one-treading by-himself heavens one-stretching-out (8) he-seals-off stars

עַל־ בָּמֳתֵי יָם׃ עֹשֶׂה־ עָשׁ כְּסִיל וְכִימָה וְחַדְרֵי

and-constellations-of and-Pleiades Orion Bear One-Making (9) sea waves-of on

תֵמָן׃ עֹשֶׂה גְדֹלוֹת עַד־אֵין חֵקֶר וְנִפְלָאוֹת

and-things-being-miracles fathomable not to wonders one-performing (10) south

עַד־אֵין מִסְפָּר׃ הֵן יַעֲבֹר עָלַי וְלֹא אֶרְאֶה וְיַחֲלֹף וְלֹא־

and-not and-he-goes-by I-see and-not by-me he-passes see! (11) number no to

אָבִין לוֹ׃ הֵן יַחְתֹּף מִי יְשִׁיבֶנּוּ מִי־

who? he-can-stop-him who? he-snatches-away if (12) to-him I-perceive

יֹאמַר אֵלָיו מַה־ תַּעֲשֶׂה׃ אֱלוֹהַּ לֹא־ יָשִׁיב אַפּוֹ

anger-of-him he-restrains not God (13) you-do what? to-him he-can-say

תַּחְתָּו° שָׁחֲחוּ עֹזְרֵי רָהַב׃ אַף כִּי־אָנֹכִי

I then how (14) Rahab ones-being-cohorts-of they-cower under-him

אֶעֱנֶנּוּ אֶבְחֲרָה דְבָרַי עִמּוֹ׃ אֲשֶׁר אִם־

though that (15) with-him words-of-me can-I-find I-can-dispute-with-him

צָדַקְתִּי לֹא אֶעֱנֶה לִמְשֹׁפְטִי אֶתְחַנָּן׃

I-could-plead-for-mercy to-one-judging-me I-could-answer not I-were-innocent

or strengthen the hands of evildoers.
21 He will yet fill your mouth with laughter
and your lips with shouts of joy.
22 Your enemies will be clothed in shame,
and the tents of the wicked will be no more."

Job

9 Then Job replied:
2 "Indeed, I know that this is true.
But how can a mortal be righteous before God?
3 Though one wished to dispute with him,
he could not answer him one time out of a thousand.
4 His wisdom is profound, his power is vast.
Who has resisted him and come out unscathed?
5 He moves mountains without their knowing it
and overturns them in his anger.
6 He shakes the earth from its place
and makes its pillars tremble.
7 He speaks to the sun and it does not shine;
he seals off the light of the stars.
8 He alone stretches out the heavens
and treads on the waves of the sea.
9 He is the Maker of the Bear and Orion,
the Pleiades and the constellations of the south.
10 He performs wonders that cannot be fathomed,
miracles that cannot be numbered.
11 When he passes me, I cannot see him;
when he goes by, I cannot perceive him.
12 If he snatches away, who can stop him?
Who can say to him, 'What are you doing?'
13 God does not restrain his anger;
even the cohorts of Rahab cowered at his feet.

14 "How then can I dispute with him?
How can I find words to argue with him?
15 Though I were innocent, I could not answer him;
I could only plead with my Judge for mercy.

°13 ק תחתיו

אִם־ קָרָאתִי וַיַּעֲנֵנִי לֹא־ אַאֲמִין כִּי־ יַאֲזִין
he-would-hear that I-believe not and-he-responded-to-me I-summoned if (16)

קוֹלִי׃ אֲשֶׁר־ בִּשְׂעָרָה יְשׁוּפֵנִי וְהִרְבָּה
and-he-would-multiply he-would-crush-me with-storm who (17) voice-of-me

פְּצָעַי חִנָּם׃ לֹא־ יִתְּנֵנִי הָשֵׁב רוּחִי כִּי
but breath-of-me to-regain he-would-let-me not (18) no-reason wounds-of-me

יַשְׂבִּעַנִי מַמְּרֹרִים׃ אִם־ לְכֹחַ אַמִּיץ הִנֵּה וְאִם־
and-if see! mighty of-strength if (19) miseries he-would-overwhelm-me

לְמִשְׁפָּט מִי יוֹעִידֵנִי׃ אִם־ אֶצְדָּק פִּי
mouth-of-me I-were-innocent if (20) he-will-summon-me who? of-justice

יַרְשִׁיעֵנִי תָּם־ אָנִי וַיַּעְקְשֵׁנִי׃ תָּם־
blameless (21) then-he-would-pronounce-guilty-me I blameless he-would-condemn-me

אָנִי לֹא־ אֵדַע נַפְשִׁי אֶמְאַס חַיָּי׃ אַחַת הִיא עַל־
for she same (22) lives-of-me I-despise self-of-me I-am-concerned not I

כֵּן אָמַרְתִּי תָּם וְרָשָׁע הוּא מְכַלֶּה׃ אִם־ שׁוֹט
scourge when (23) destroying he and-wicked blameless I-say this

יָמִית פִּתְאֹם לְמַסַּת נְקִיִּם יִלְעָג׃ אֶרֶץ ׀
land (24) he-mocks innocent-ones at-despair-of sudden he-brings-death

נִתְּנָה בְיַד־ רָשָׁע פְּנֵי־ שֹׁפְטֶיהָ יְכַסֶּה אִם־
if he-blindfolds ones-judging-her faces-of wicked into-hand-of she-falls

לֹא אֵפוֹא מִי־ הוּא׃ וְיָמַי קַלּוּ מִנִּי־ רָץ
one-running more-than they-are-swift and-days-of-me (25) he who? then not

בָּרְחוּ לֹא־ רָאוּ טוֹבָה׃ חָלְפוּ עִם־ אֳנִיּוֹת אֵבֶה
papyrus boats-of like they-skim-past (26) joy they-glimpse not they-fly-away

כְּנֶשֶׁר יָטוּשׂ עֲלֵי־ אֹכֶל׃ אִם־ אָמְרִי אֶשְׁכְּחָה
I-will-forget to-say-me if (27) prey on he-swoops-down like-eagle

שִׂיחִי אֶעֶזְבָה פָנַי וְאַבְלִיגָה׃ יָגֹרְתִּי
I-dread (28) and-I-will-smile expressions-of-me I-will-change complaint-of-me

כָל־ עַצְּבֹתָי יָדַעְתִּי כִּי־ לֹא תְנַקֵּנִי׃ אָנֹכִי
I (29) you-will-hold-innocent-me not that I-know sufferings-of-me all-of

אֶרְשָׁע לָמָּה־ זֶּה הֶבֶל אִיגָע׃ אִם־ הִתְרָחַצְתִּי
I-washed-myself if (30) I-should-struggle in-vain this why? I-am-guilty

בְמוֹ־ שָׁלֶג וַהֲזִכּוֹתִי בְּבֹר כַּפָּי׃ אָז
then (31) hands-of-me with-washing-soda and-I-washed soap *with

בַּשַּׁחַת תִּטְבְּלֵנִי וְתִעֲבוּנִי שַׂלְמוֹתָי׃
clothes-of-me so-they-would-detest-me you-would-plunge-me in-the-slime-pit

כִּי־ לֹא־ אִישׁ כָּמֹנִי אֶעֱנֶנּוּ נָבוֹא יַחְדָּו
together we-might-come I-might-answer-him like-me man not for (32)

16 Even if I summoned him and
he responded,
I do not believe he would
give me a hearing.
17 He would crush me with a
storm
and multiply my wounds for
no reason.
18 He would not let me regain
my breath
but would overwhelm me
with misery.
19 If it is a matter of strength, he
is mighty!
And if it is a matter of
justice, who will summon
him[o]?
20 Even if I were innocent, my
mouth would condemn
me;
if I were blameless, it would
pronounce me guilty.

21 "Although I am blameless,
I have no concern for
myself;
I despise my own life.
22 It is all the same; that is why I
say,
'He destroys both the
blameless and the
wicked.'
23 When a scourge brings sudden
death,
he mocks the despair of the
innocent.
24 When a land falls into the
hands of the wicked,
he blindfolds its judges.
If it is not he, then who is
it?

25 "My days are swifter than a
runner;
they fly away without a
glimpse of joy.
26 They skim past like boats of
papyrus,
like eagles swooping down
on their prey.
27 If I say, 'I will forget my
complaint,
I will change my expression,
and smile,'
28 I still dread all my sufferings,
for I know you will not hold
me innocent.
29 Since I am already found
guilty,
why should I struggle in
vain?
30 Even if I washed myself with
soap[p]
and my hands with
washing soda,
31 you would plunge me into a
slime pit
so that even my clothes
would detest me.

32 "He is not a man like me that
I might answer him,
that we might confront each

o19 See Septuagint; Hebrew *me.*
p30 Or *snow*

*30 The *Qere* reads *with-waters-of.*

°30 ק במי

בַּמִּשְׁפָּט׃ לֹא* יֵשׁ־ בֵּינֵינוּ מוֹכִיחַ יָשֵׁת
he-may-lay one-arbitrating between-us there-is *not (33) in-the-court

יָדוֹ עַל־ שְׁנֵינוּ׃ יָסֵר מֵעָלַי שִׁבְטוֹ
rod-of-him from-against-me he-might-remove (34) both-of-us on hand-of-him

וְאֵמָתוֹ אַל־ תְּבַעֲתַנִּי׃ אֲדַבְּרָה† וְלֹא
and-not I-would-speak-up (35) she-would-frighten-me not so-terror-of-him

אִירָאֶנּוּ כִּי לֹא־ כֵן אָנֹכִי עִמָּדִי׃ נָקְטָה נַפְשִׁי
soul-of-me she-loathes (10:1) with-me I so not but I-would-fear-him

בְּחַיָּי אֶעֶזְבָה עָלַי שִׂיחִי אֲדַבְּרָה††
I-will-speak-out complaint-of-me to-me I-will-give-free-rein to-lives-of-me

בְּמַר נַפְשִׁי׃ אֹמַר אֶל־ אֱלוֹהַּ אַל־ תַּרְשִׁיעֵנִי
you-condemn-me not God to I-will-say (2) soul-of-me in-bitterness-of

הוֹדִיעֵנִי עַל מַה־ תְּרִיבֵנִי׃ הֲטוֹב לְךָ׀ כִּי־ תַעֲשֹׁק
you-oppress that to-you pleasing? (3) you-charge-me what about tell-me!

כִּי־ תִמְאַס יְגִיעַ כַּפֶּיךָ וְעַל־ עֲצַת רְשָׁעִים הוֹפָעְתָּ׃
you-smile wicked-ones scheme-of while-on hands-of-you work-of you-spurn that

הַעֵינֵי בָשָׂר לָךְ אִם־ כִּרְאוֹת אֱנוֹשׁ תִּרְאֶה׃ הֲכִימֵי
like-days-of? (5) you-see mortal as-to-see indeed to-you flesh eyes-of? (4)

אֱנוֹשׁ יָמֶיךָ אִם־ שְׁנוֹתֶיךָ כִּימֵי גָבֶר׃ כִּי־ תְבַקֵּשׁ
you-must-search that (6) man like-days-of years-of-you or days-of-you mortal

לַעֲוֺנִי וּלְחַטָּאתִי תִדְרוֹשׁ׃ עַל־ דַּעְתְּךָ
knowledge-of-you though (7) you-must-probe and-after-sin-of-me to-fault-of-me

כִּי־ לֹא אֶרְשָׁע וְאֵין מִיָּדְךָ מַצִּיל׃ יָדֶיךָ
hands-of-you (8) rescuing from-hand-of-you and-no-one I-am-guilty not that

עִצְּבוּנִי וַיַּעֲשׂוּנִי יַחַד סָבִיב וַתְּבַלְּעֵנִי׃
and-you-will-swallow-me around altogether and-they-made-me they-shaped-me

זְכָר־ נָא כִּי־ כַחֹמֶר עֲשִׂיתָנִי וְאֶל־ עָפָר
dust now-to you-molded-me like-the-clay that now! remember! (9)

תְּשִׁיבֵנִי׃ הֲלֹא כֶחָלָב תַּתִּיכֵנִי וְכַגְּבִנָּה
and-like-the-cheese you-poured-out-me like-the-milk not? (10) will-you-turn-me

תַּקְפִּיאֵנִי׃ עוֹר וּבָשָׂר תַּלְבִּישֵׁנִי וּבַעֲצָמוֹת וְגִידִים
and-sinews and-with-bones you-clothed-me and-flesh skin (11) you-curdled-me

תְּסֹכְכֵנִי׃ חַיִּים וָחֶסֶד עָשִׂיתָ עִמָּדִי
to-me you-gave and-kindness lives (12) you-knit-together-me

וּפְקֻדָּתְךָ שָׁמְרָה רוּחִי׃ וְאֵלֶּה
but-these (13) spirit-of-me she-watched-over and-providence-of-you

צָפַנְתָּ בִלְבָבֶךָ יָדַעְתִּי כִּי־ זֹאת עִמָּךְ׃ אִם־ חָטָאתִי
I-sinned if (14) in-you this that I-know in-heart-of-you you-concealed

other in court.
33If only there were someone to
arbitrate between us,
to lay his hand upon us
both,
34someone to remove God's rod
from me,
so that his terror would
frighten me no more.
35Then I would speak up
without fear of him,
but as it now stands with
me, I cannot.

10 "I loathe my very life;
therefore I will give free
rein to my complaint
and speak out in the
bitterness of my soul.
2I will say to God: Do not
condemn me,
but tell me what charges
you have against me.
3Does it please you to oppress
me,
to spurn the work of your
hands,
while you smile on the
schemes of the wicked?
4Do you have eyes of flesh?
Do you see as a mortal sees?
5Are your days like those of a
mortal
or your years like those of a
man,
6that you must search out my
faults
and probe after my sin—
7though you know that I am
not guilty
and that no one can rescue
me from your hand?

8"Your hands shaped me and
made me.
Will you now turn and
destroy me?
9Remember that you molded
me like clay.
Will you now turn me to
dust again?
10Did you not pour me out like
milk
and curdle me like cheese,
11clothe me with skin and flesh
and knit me together with
bones and sinews?
12You gave me life and showed
me kindness,
and in your providence
watched over my spirit.

13"But this is what you
concealed in your heart,
and I know that this was in
your mind:
14If I sinned, you would be
watching me

*33 The NIV reads לֻא, *if-only*, with the Septuagint and Syriac versions.

†35 Most mss have *hateph pathah* under the *aleph* (אֲ).

††1 Most mss have the accent over the *resh* (רָה—).

וּשְׁמַרְתָּנִי וּמֵעֲוֺנִי לֹא תְנַקֵּנִי׃
you-would-let-go-unpunished-me not and-from-offense-of-me then-you-would-watch-me

(15) אִם־ רָשַׁעְתִּי אַלְלַי לִי וְצָדַקְתִּי לֹא־ אֶשָּׂא רֹאשִׁי
head-of-me I-can-lift not if-I-am-innocent to-me woe! I-am-guilty if (15)

שְׂבַע קָלוֹן וּרְאֵה* עָנְיִי׃ (16) וְיִגְאֶה כַּשַּׁחַל
like-the-lion if-he-is-high (16) affliction-of-me *and-aware-of shame full-of

תְּצוּדֵנִי וְתָשֹׁב תִּתְפַּלָּא־ בִי׃
against-me you-display-awesome-power and-you-do-again you-stalk-me

(17) תְּחַדֵּשׁ עֵדֶיךָ ׀ נֶגְדִּי וְתֶרֶב כַּעַשְׂךָ
anger-of-you and-you-increase against-me witnesses-of-you you-make-new (17)

עִמָּדִי חֲלִיפוֹת וְצָבָא עִמִּי׃ (18) וְלָמָּה מֵרֶחֶם הֹצֵאתָנִי
you-brought-me from-womb then-why? (18) against-me and-force waves toward-me

אֶגְוַע וְעַיִן לֹא־ תִרְאֵנִי׃ (19) כַּאֲשֶׁר לֹא־ הָיִיתִי
I-came-to-be never if-only (19) she-saw-me never and-eye I-should-have-died

אֶהְיֶה מִבֶּטֶן לַקֶּבֶר אוּבָל׃ (20) הֲלֹא־ מְעַט יָמַי
days-of-me few-of not? (20) I-was-carried to-the-grave from-womb I-came-to-be

יֶחְדָּל° יָשִׁית° מִמֶּנִּי וְאַבְלִיגָה מְּעָט׃ (21) בְּטֶרֶם
at-before (21) momentary so-I-can-have-joy from-me now-turn-away! he-is-over

אֵלֵךְ וְלֹא אָשׁוּב אֶל־ אֶרֶץ חֹשֶׁךְ וְצַלְמָוֶת׃ (22) אֶרֶץ עֵיפָתָה ׀
darkness land-of (22) and-deep-shadow gloom land-of to I-return and-not I-go

כְּמוֹ אֹפֶל צַלְמָוֶת וְלֹא סְדָרִים וַתֹּפַע כְּמוֹ־ אֹפֶל׃
darkness like and-she-is-light orders and-no deep-shadow night like

(11:1) וַיַּעַן צֹפַר הַנַּעֲמָתִי וַיֹּאמַר׃ (2) הֲרֹב דְּבָרִים
words all-of? (2) and-he-said the-Naamathite Zophar then-he-replied (11:1)

לֹא יֵעָנֶה וְאִם־ אִישׁ שְׂפָתַיִם יִצְדָּק׃
is-he-vindicated speeches man-of and-indeed he-is-answered not

(3) בַּדֶּיךָ מְתִים יַחֲרִישׁוּ וַתִּלְעַג וְאֵין מַכְלִם׃
rebuking then-no-one when-you-mock will-they-silence men idle-talks-of-you (3)

(4) וַתֹּאמֶר זַךְ לִקְחִי וּבַר הָיִיתִי בְעֵינֶיךָ׃ (5) וְאוּלָם
if-only (5) in-eyes-of-you I-am and-pure belief-of-me flawless and-you-say (4)

מִי־ יִתֵּן אֱלוֹהַּ דַּבֵּר וְיִפְתַּח שְׂפָתָיו עִמָּךְ׃
against-you lips-of-him and-he-would-open to-speak God he-would-give someone

(6) וְיַגֶּד־ לְךָ ׀ תַּעֲלֻמוֹת חָכְמָה כִּי־ כִפְלַיִם לְתוּשִׁיָּה
to-true-wisdom two-sides for wisdom secrets-of to-you and-he-would-disclose (6)

וְדַע כִּי־ יַשֶּׁה לְךָ אֱלוֹהַּ† מֵעֲוֺנֶךָ׃ (7) הַחֵקֶר אֱלוֹהַּ†
God mystery-of? (7) from-sin-of-you God of-you he-forgot that and-know!

תִּמְצָא אִם עַד־ תַּכְלִית שַׁדַּי תִּמְצָא׃ (8) גָּבְהֵי
ones-higher-of (8) can-you-probe Almighty limit-of to or can-you-fathom

and would not let my
offense go unpunished.
15 If I am guilty—woe to me!
Even if I am innocent, I
cannot lift my head,
for I am full of shame
and drowned in[q] my
affliction.
16 If I hold my head high, you
stalk me like a lion
and again display your
awesome power against
me.
17 You bring new witnesses
against me
and increase your anger
toward me;
your forces come against me
wave upon wave.

18 "Why then did you bring me
out of the womb?
I wish I had died before any
eye saw me.
19 If only I had never come into
being,
or had been carried straight
from the womb to the
grave!
20 Are not my few days almost
over?
Turn away from me so I can
have a moment's joy
21 before I go to the place of no
return,
to the land of gloom and
deep shadow,[r]
22 to the land of deepest night,
of deep shadow and
disorder,
where even the light is like
darkness."

Zophar

11 Then Zophar the Naamathite replied:

2 "Are all these words to go
unanswered?
Is this talker to be
vindicated?
3 Will your idle talk reduce men
to silence?
Will no one rebuke you
when you mock?
4 You say to God, 'My beliefs
are flawless
and I am pure in your
sight.'
5 Oh, how I wish that God
would speak,
that he would open his lips
against you
6 and disclose to you the secrets
of wisdom,
for true wisdom has two
sides.
Know this: God has even
forgotten some of your
sin.

7 "Can you fathom the
mysteries of God?
Can you probe the limits of
the Almighty?

q15 Or *and aware of*
r21 Or *and the shadow of death*; also in verse 22

**15* The NIV reads וּרְוֵה , *and-drowned-of*.

†6, 7 Most mss have *mappiq* in the *he* (הּ־).

°20a ק וחדל
°20b ק ושית

שָׁמַיִם מַה־ תִּפְעָל עֲמֻקָּה מִשְּׁאוֹל מַה־ תֵּדָע׃ אֲרֻכָּה
long (9) can-you-know what? more-than-Sheol deep can-you-do what? heavens

מֵאֶרֶץ מִדָּהּ וּרְחָבָה מִנִּי־ יָם׃ אִם־ יַחֲלֹף
he-comes-along if (10) sea more-than and-wide measure more-than-earth

וְיַסְגִּיר וְיַקְהִיל וּמִי יְשִׁיבֶנּוּ׃ כִּי־
surely (11) he-can-oppose-him then-who? and-he-convenes-court and-he-confines

הוּא יָדַע מְתֵי־ שָׁוְא וַיַּרְא־ אָוֶן וְלֹא יִתְבּוֹנָן׃
does-he-take-note then-not evil when-he-sees deceit men-of he-recognizes he

וְאִישׁ נָבוּב יִלָּבֵב וְעַיִר פֶּרֶא אָדָם
man wild-donkey if-colt he-can-become-wise being-witless but-man (12)

יִוָּלֵד׃ אִם־אַתָּה הֲכִינוֹתָ לִבֶּךָ וּפָרַשְׂתָּ אֵלָיו
to-him and-you-stretch-out heart-of-you you-devote you if (13) he-can-be-born

כַּפֶּךָ׃ אִם־אָוֶן בְּיָדְךָ הַרְחִיקֵהוּ וְאַל־ תַּשְׁכֵּן
you-let-dwell and-not put-away-him! in-hand-of-you sin if (14) hand-of-you

בְּאֹהָלֶיךָ עַוְלָה׃ כִּי־ אָז׀ תִּשָּׂא פָנֶיךָ מִמּוּם
without-shame faces-of-you you-will-lift then surely (15) evil in-tents-of-you

וְהָיִיתָ מֻצָק וְלֹא תִירָא׃ כִּי־ אַתָּה עָמָל
trouble you surely (16) you-will-fear and-not standing-firm and-you-will-be

תִּשְׁכָּח כְּמַיִם עָבְרוּ תִזְכֹּר׃ וּמִצָּהֳרַיִם
and-more-than-noonday (17) you-will-recall they-go-by as-waters you-will-forget

יָקוּם חָלֶד תָּעֻפָה כַּבֹּקֶר תִּהְיֶה׃
she-will-become like-the-morning darkness life he-will-be-bright

וּבָטַחְתָּ כִּי־ יֵשׁ תִּקְוָה וְחָפַרְתָּ
and-you-will-look-around hope there-is because and-you-will-be-secure (18)

לָבֶטַח תִּשְׁכָּב׃ וְרָבַצְתָּ וְאֵין מַחֲרִיד
making-afraid with-no-one and-you-will-lie-down (19) you-will-rest in-safety

וְחִלּוּ פָנֶיךָ רַבִּים׃ וְעֵינֵי רְשָׁעִים
wicked-ones but-eyes-of (20) many faces-of-you and-they-will-court-favor

תִּכְלֶינָה וּמָנוֹס אָבַד מִנְהֶם וְתִקְוָתָם מַפַּח־
gasp-of and-hope-of-them from-them he-will-elude and-escape they-will-fail

נָפֶשׁ׃ וַיַּעַן אִיּוֹב וַיֹּאמַר׃ אָמְנָם כִּי אַתֶּם־ עָם
people you that doubtless (2) and-he-said Job then-he-replied (12:1) life

וְעִמָּכֶם תָּמוּת חָכְמָה׃ גַּם־ לִי לֵבָב׀ כְּמוֹכֶם לֹא־
not as-well-as-you mind to-me but (3) wisdom she-will-die and-with-you

נֹפֵל אָנֹכִי מִכֶּם וְאֶת־ מִי־ אֵין כְּמוֹ־ אֵלֶּה׃ שְׂחֹק
laughingstock (4) these-things like not whom? and-with to-you I being-inferior

לְרֵעֵהוּ׀ אֶהְיֶה קֹרֵא לֶאֱלוֹהַּ וַיַּעֲנֵהוּ שְׂחוֹק
laughingstock and-he-answered-him to-God calling I-became to-friends-of-him

8They are higher than the heavens—what can you do?
They are deeper than the depths of the grave[s]—what can you know?
9Their measure is longer than the earth
and wider than the sea.

10"If he comes along and confines you in prison
and convenes a court, who can oppose him?
11Surely he recognizes deceitful men;
and when he sees evil, does he not take note?
12But a witless man can no more become wise
than a wild donkey's colt can be born a man.[t]

13"Yet if you devote your heart to him
and stretch out your hands to him,
14if you put away the sin that is in your hand
and allow no evil to dwell in your tent,
15then you will lift up your face without shame;
you will stand firm and without fear.
16You will surely forget your trouble,
recalling it only as waters gone by.
17Life will be brighter than noonday,
and darkness will become like morning.
18You will be secure, because there is hope;
you will look about you and take your rest in safety.
19You will lie down, with no one to make you afraid,
and many will court your favor.
20But the eyes of the wicked will fail,
and escape will elude them;
their hope will become a dying gasp."

Job

12 Then Job replied:
2"Doubtless you are the people,
and wisdom will die with you!
3But I have a mind as well as you;
I am not inferior to you.
Who does not know all these things?

4"I have become a laughingstock to my friends,
though I called upon God and he answered—
a mere laughingstock,

s8 Hebrew *than Sheol*
t12 Or *wild donkey can be born tame*

צַדִּיק תָּמִים׃ (5) לַפִּיד בּוּז לְעַשְׁתּוּת
in-thinking-of contempt for-the-misfortune (5) blameless righteous

שַׁאֲנָן נָכוֹן לְמוֹעֲדֵי רָגֶל׃ (6) יִשְׁלָיוּ אֹהָלִים ׀
tents they-are-undisturbed (6) foot of-ones-slipping-of fate man-at-ease

לְשֹׁדְדִים וּבַטֻּחוֹת לְמַרְגִּיזֵי אֵל לַאֲשֶׁר
to-whom God to-ones-provoking-of and-securities of-ones-marauding

הֵבִיא אֱלוֹהַּ בְּיָדוֹ׃ (7) וְאוּלָם שְׁאַל־ נָא בְהֵמוֹת
animals now! ask! but-however (7) in-hand-of-him god he-carries

וְתֹרֶךָּ וְעוֹף הַשָּׁמַיִם וְיַגֶּד־ לָךְ׃ (8) אוֹ
or (8) to-you and-he-will-tell the-airs or-bird-of and-she-will-teach-you

שִׂיחַ לָאָרֶץ וְתֹרֶךָּ וִיסַפְּרוּ לְךָ דְּגֵי
fishes-of to-you or-let-them-inform and-she-will-teach-you to-the-earth speak!

הַיָּם׃ (9) מִי לֹא־ יָדַע בְּכָל־ אֵלֶּה כִּי יַד־ יְהוָה עָשְׂתָה
she-did Yahweh hand-of that these of-all-of he-knows not which? (9) the-sea

זֹּאת׃ (10) אֲשֶׁר בְּיָדוֹ נֶפֶשׁ כָּל־ חָי וְרוּחַ כָּל־
all-of and-breath-of creature every-of life-of in-hand-of-him that (10) this

בְּשַׂר־ אִישׁ׃ (11) הֲלֹא־ אֹזֶן מִלִּין תִּבְחָן וְחֵךְ אֹכֶל יִטְעַם־
he-tastes food as-tongue she-tests words ear not? (11) mankind flesh-of

לוֹ׃ (12) בִּישִׁישִׁים חָכְמָה וְאֹרֶךְ יָמִים תְּבוּנָה׃
understanding days and-length-of wisdom among-aged-ones (12) for-him

(13) עִמּוֹ חָכְמָה וּגְבוּרָה לוֹ עֵצָה וּתְבוּנָה׃ (14) הֵן
see! (14) and-understanding counsel to-him and-power wisdom to-him (13)

יַהֲרוֹס וְלֹא יִבָּנֶה יִסְגֹּר עַל־ אִישׁ וְלֹא
and-not man to he-imprisons he-can-be-rebuilt and-not he-tears-down

יִפָּתֵחַ׃ (15) הֵן יַעְצֹר בַּמַּיִם וְיִבָשׁוּ
and-they-have-drought to-the-waters he-holds-back see! (15) he-can-be-released

וִישַׁלְּחֵם וְיַהַפְכוּ אָרֶץ׃ (16) עִמּוֹ עֹז
strength to-him (16) land then-they-devastate if-he-lets-loose-them

וְתוּשִׁיָּה לוֹ שֹׁגֵג וּמַשְׁגֶּה׃ (17) מוֹלִיךְ
leading-away (17) and-one-deceiving one-being-deceived to-him and-victory

יוֹעֲצִים שׁוֹלָל וְשֹׁפְטִים יְהוֹלֵל׃ (18) מוּסַר מְלָכִים
kings shackle-of (18) he-makes-fool and-ones-judging stripped ones-counseling

פִּתֵּחַ וַיֶּאְסֹר אֵזוֹר בְּמָתְנֵיהֶם׃ (19) מוֹלִיךְ
leading-away (19) around-waists-of-them loincloth and-he-ties he-takes-off

כֹּהֲנִים שׁוֹלָל וְאֵתָנִים יְסַלֵּף׃ (20) מֵסִיר שָׂפָה
lip silencing (20) he-overthrows and-established-men stripped priests

לְנֶאֱמָנִים וְטַעַם זְקֵנִים יִקָּח׃ (21) שׁוֹפֵךְ
pouring (21) he-takes-away elders and-discernment-of of-ones-being-trusted

though righteous and
blameless!
5 Men at ease have contempt for
misfortune
as the fate of those whose
feet are slipping.
6 The tents of marauders are
undisturbed,
and those who provoke God
are secure—
those who carry their god in
their hands.[u]

7 "But ask the animals, and they
will teach you,
or the birds of the air, and
they will tell you;
8 or speak to the earth, and it
will teach you,
or let the fish of the sea
inform you.
9 Which of all these does not
know
that the hand of the LORD
has done this?
10 In his hand is the life of every
creature
and the breath of all
mankind.
11 Does not the ear test words
as the tongue tastes food?
12 Is not wisdom found among
the aged?
Does not long life bring
understanding?

13 "To God belong wisdom and
power;
counsel and understanding
are his.
14 What he tears down cannot be
rebuilt;
the man he imprisons
cannot be released.
15 If he holds back the waters,
there is drought;
if he lets them loose, they
devastate the land.
16 To him belong strength and
victory;
both deceived and deceiver
are his.
17 He leads counselors away
stripped
and makes fools of judges.
18 He takes off the shackles put
on by kings
and ties a loincloth[v] around
their waist.
19 He leads priests away stripped
and overthrows men long
established.
20 He silences the lips of trusted
advisers
and takes away the
discernment of elders.

[u] 6 Or *secure / in what God's hand brings them*
[v] 18 Or *shackles of kings / and ties a belt*

בּוּז עַל־נְדִיבִים וּמְזִיחַ אֲפִיקִים רִפָּה׃ מְגַלֶּה
revealing (22) he-disarms mighty-ones and-belt-of nobles on contempt

עֲמֻקוֹת מִנִּי־חֹשֶׁךְ וַיֹּצֵא לָאוֹר צַלְמָוֶת׃ מַשְׂגִּיא
making-great (23) deep-shadow to-light and-he-brings darkness from deep-things

לַגּוֹיִם וַיְאַבְּדֵם שֹׁטֵחַ לַגּוֹיִם
to-the-nations enlarging and-he-destroys-them to-the-nations

וַיַּנְחֵם׃ מֵסִיר לֵב רָאשֵׁי עַם־הָאָרֶץ
the-earth people-of leaders-of reason-of depriving (24) and-he-disperses-them

וַיַּתְעֵם בְּתֹהוּ לֹא־דָרֶךְ׃ יְמַשְׁשׁוּ־חֹשֶׁךְ וְלֹא־
with-no darkness they-grope (25) track no through-waste and-he-sends-them

אוֹר וַיַּתְעֵם כַּשִּׁכּוֹר׃ הֶן־כֹּל רָאֲתָה
she-saw all see! (13:1) like-the-drunkard and-he-makes-stagger-them light

עֵינִי שָׁמְעָה אָזְנִי וַתָּבֶן לָהּ׃ כְּדַעְתְּכֶם
as-knowledge-of-you (2) to-her and-she-understood ear-of-me she-heard eye-of-me

יָדַעְתִּי גַם־אָנִי לֹא־נֹפֵל אָנֹכִי מִכֶּם׃ אוּלָם אֲנִי אֶל־שַׁדַּי
Almighty to I but (3) to-you I being-inferior not I also I-know

אֲדַבֵּר וְהוֹכֵחַ אֶל־אֵל אֶחְפָּץ׃ וְאוּלָם אַתֶּם
you but-however (4) I-desire God with and-to-argue-case I-would-speak

טֹפְלֵי־שָׁקֶר רֹפְאֵי אֱלִל כֻּלְּכֶם׃ מִי־
who? (5) all-of-you worthlessness ones-being-physicians-of lie ones-smearing-of

יִתֵּן הַחֲרֵשׁ תַּחֲרִישׁוּן וּתְהִי לָכֶם
for-you and-she-would-be you-would-be-silent to-be-silent he-would-make

לְחָכְמָה׃ שִׁמְעוּ־נָא תוֹכַחְתִּי וְרִבוֹת שְׂפָתַי הַקְשִׁיבוּ׃
listen! lips-of-me and-pleas-of argument-of-me now! hear! (6) as-wisdom

הַלְאֵל תְּדַבְּרוּ עַוְלָה וְלוֹ תְּדַבְּרוּ
will-you-speak and-for-him wickedly will-you-speak on-behalf-of-God? (7)

רְמִיָּה׃ הֲפָנָיו תִּשָּׂאוּן אִם־לָאֵל
for-God or will-you-show-partiality faces-of-him? (8) deceitfully

תְּרִיבוּן׃ הֲטוֹב כִּי־יַחְקֹר אֶתְכֶם אִם־כְּהָתֵל בֶּאֱנוֹשׁ
to-man as-to-deceive or you he-examined if well? (9) will-you-argue-case

תְּהָתֵלּוּ בוֹ׃ הוֹכֵחַ יוֹכִיחַ אֶתְכֶם אִם־בַּסֵּתֶר
in-the-secret if you he-would-rebuke to-rebuke (10) to-him could-you-deceive

פָּנִים תִּשָּׂאוּן׃ הֲלֹא שְׂאֵתוֹ תְּבַעֵת אֶתְכֶם
you she-would-terrify splendor-of-him not? (11) you-showed-partiality faces

וּפַחְדּוֹ יִפֹּל עֲלֵיכֶם׃ זִכְרֹנֵיכֶם מִשְׁלֵי־אֵפֶר
ash proverbs-of maxims-of-you (12) on-you he-would-fall and-dread-of-him

לְגַבֵּי־חֹמֶר גַּבֵּיכֶם׃ הַחֲרִישׁוּ מִמֶּנִּי
from-me keep-silent! (13) defenses-of-you clay as-defenses-of

[21]He pours contempt on nobles
and disarms the mighty.
[22]He reveals the deep things of
darkness
and brings deep shadows
into the light.
[23]He makes nations great, and
destroys them;
he enlarges nations, and
disperses them.
[24]He deprives the leaders of the
earth of their reason;
he sends them wandering
through a trackless waste.
[25]They grope in darkness with
no light;
he makes them stagger like
drunkards.

13 "My eyes have seen all
this,
my ears have heard and
understood it.
[2]What you know, I also know;
I am not inferior to you.
[3]But I desire to speak to the
Almighty
and to argue my case with
God.
[4]You, however, smear me with
lies;
you are worthless
physicians, all of you!
[5]If only you would be
altogether silent!
For you, that would be
wisdom.
[6]Hear now my argument;
listen to the plea of my lips.
[7]Will you speak wickedly on
God's behalf?
Will you speak deceitfully
for him?
[8]Will you show him partiality?
Will you argue the case for
God?
[9]Would it turn out well if he
examined you?
Could you deceive him as
you might deceive men?
[10]He would surely rebuke you
if you secretly showed
partiality.
[11]Would not his splendor terrify
you?
Would not the dread of him
fall on you?
[12]Your maxims are proverbs of
ashes;
your defenses are defenses
of clay.
[13]"Keep silent and let me speak;

וַאֲדַבְּרָה־ אָנִי וְיַעֲבֹר עָלַי מָה: עַל־ מָה | אֶשָּׂא
I-put why? for (14) whatever to-me then-let-him-come I and-let-me-speak

בְשָׂרִי בְשִׁנָּי וְנַפְשִׁי אָשִׂים בְּכַפִּי: הֵן
though (15) in-hands-of-me I-take and-life-of-me in-teeth-of-me flesh-of-me

יִקְטְלֵנִי לֹא° אֲיַחֵל אַךְ־ דְּרָכַי אֶל־ פָּנָיו אוֹכִיחַ:
I-will-defend faces-of-him to ways-of-me surely I-will-hope in-him he-slay-me

גַּם־ הוּא־ לִי לִישׁוּעָה כִּי־ לֹא לְפָנָיו חָנֵף
godless-man before-him not for for-deliverance to-me this indeed (16)

יָבוֹא: שִׁמְעוּ שָׁמוֹעַ מִלָּתִי וְאַחֲוָתִי
and-saying-of-me word-of-me to-listen listen! (17) he-would-come

בְּאָזְנֵיכֶם: הִנֵּה־ נָא עָרַכְתִּי מִשְׁפָּט יָדַעְתִּי כִּי־ אֲנִי
I that I-know case I-prepared now! see! (18) in-ears-of-you

אֶצְדָּק: מִי־ הוּא יָרִיב עִמָּדִי כִּי־ עַתָּה
now if-so against-me can-he-bring-charges he who? (19) I-will-be-vindicated

אַחֲרִישׁ וְאֶגְוָע: אַךְ־ שְׁתַּיִם אַל־* תַּעַשׂ עִמָּדִי אָז
then to-me you-do *not two only (20) and-I-will-die I-will-be-silent

מִפָּנֶיךָ לֹא אֶסָּתֵר: כַּפְּךָ מֵעָלַי הַרְחַק
withdraw-far! from-upon-me hand-of-you (21) I-will-hide not from-before-you

וְאֵמָתְךָ אַל־ תְּבַעֲתַנִּי: וּקְרָא וְאָנֹכִי אֶעֱנֶה
I-will-answer and-I then-summon! (22) you-frighten-me not and-terror-of-you

אוֹ־ אֲדַבֵּר וַהֲשִׁיבֵנִי: כַּמָּה לִי עֲוֹנוֹת וְחַטָּאוֹת
and-sins wrongs to-me as-the-how-many? (23) and-reply-to-me! let-me-speak or

פִּשְׁעִי וְחַטָּאתִי הֹדִיעֵנִי: לָמָּה־ פָנֶיךָ תַסְתִּיר
you-hide faces-of-you why? (24) show-me! and-sin-of-me offense-of-me

וְתַחְשְׁבֵנִי לְאוֹיֵב לָךְ: הֶעָלֶה נִדָּף
being-wind-blown leaf? (25) to-you as-being-enemy and-you-consider-me

תַּעֲרוֹץ וְאֶת־ קַשׁ יָבֵשׁ תִּרְדֹּף: כִּי־ תִכְתֹּב
you-write-down for (26) will-you-chase dry chaff and will-you-torment

עָלַי מְרֹרוֹת וְתוֹרִישֵׁנִי עֲוֹנוֹת נְעוּרָי:
youths-of-me sins-of and-you-make-inherit-me bitter-things against-me

וְתָשֵׂם בַּסַּד | רַגְלַי וְתִשְׁמוֹר כָּל־
all-of and-you-watch feet-of-me in-the-shackle and-you-fasten (27)

אָרְחֹתַי עַל־ שָׁרְשֵׁי רַגְלַי תִּתְחַקֶּה: וְהוּא כְּרָקָב
like-rotten-thing so-he (28) you-put-mark feet-of-me soles-of on paths-of-me

יִבְלֶה כְּבֶגֶד אֲכָלוֹ עָשׁ: אָדָם יְלוּד אִשָּׁה
woman being-born-of man (14:1) moth he-eats-him like-garment he-wastes-away

קְצַר יָמִים וּשְׂבַע־ רֹגֶז: כְּצִיץ יָצָא וַיִּמָּל
and-he-withers he-springs-up like-flower (2) trouble and-full-of days few-of

then let come to me what
may.
14 Why do I put myself in
jeopardy
and take my life in my
hands?
15 Though he slay me, yet will I
hope in him;
I will surely[w] defend my
ways to his face.
16 Indeed, this might turn out for
my deliverance,
for no godless man would
dare come before him!
17 Listen carefully to my words;
let your ears take in what I
say.
18 Now that I have prepared my
case,
I know I will be vindicated.
19 Can anyone bring charges
against me?
If so, I will be silent and
die.
20 "Only grant me these two
things, O God,
and then I will not hide
from you:
21 Withdraw your hand far from
me,
and stop frightening me
with your terrors.
22 Then summon me and I will
answer,
or let me speak, and you
reply.
23 How many wrongs and sins
have I committed?
Show me my offense and
my sin.
24 Why do you hide your face
and consider me your
enemy?
25 Will you torment a
wind-blown leaf?
Will you chase after dry
chaff?
26 For you write down bitter
things against me
and make me inherit the
sins of my youth.
27 You fasten my feet in shackles;
you keep close watch on all
my paths
by putting marks on the
soles of my feet.

28 "So man wastes away like
something rotten,
like a garment eaten by
moths.

14 "Man born of woman
is of few days and full of
trouble.
2 He springs up like a flower
and withers away;

w15 Or *He will surely slay me; I have no hope — / yet I will*

*20 The NIV repoints this word as אֵל־, *God.*

°15 ק לו

וַיִּבְרַח כַּצֵּל וְלֹא יַעֲמוֹד׃ אַף־עַל־זֶה פָּקַחְתָּ
do-you-fix this on indeed (3) he-endures and-not like-the-shadow and-he-flees

עֵינֶךָ וְאֹתִי תָבִיא בְמִשְׁפָּט עִמָּךְ׃ מִי־יִתֵּן
he-can-bring who? (4) before-you for-judgment will-you-bring and-me eye-of-you

טָהוֹר מִטָּמֵא לֹא אֶחָד׃ אִם חֲרוּצִים ׀ יָמָיו
days-of-him ones-being-determined indeed (5) one no from-impure pure

מִסְפַּר־חֳדָשָׁיו אִתָּךְ חֻקָּו עָשִׂיתָ וְלֹא יַעֲבוֹר׃
he-can-exceed and-not you-set limits-of-him with-you months-of-him number-of

שְׁעֵה מֵעָלָיו וְיֶחְדָּל עַד־יִרְצֶה כְּשָׂכִיר
like-hired-man he-enjoys till and-let-him-be-alone away-from-him look! (6)

יוֹמוֹ׃ כִּי יֵשׁ לָעֵץ תִּקְוָה אִם־יִכָּרֵת
he-is-cut-down if hope for-tree there-is at-least (7) time-of-him

וְעוֹד יַחֲלִיף וְיֹנַקְתּוֹ לֹא תֶחְדָּל׃ אִם־
if (8) she-will-fail not and-new-shoot-of-him he-will-sprout then-again

יַזְקִין בָּאָרֶץ שָׁרְשׁוֹ וּבֶעָפָר יָמוּת גִּזְעוֹ׃
stump-of-him he-dies and-in-the-soil root-of-him in-the-ground he-grows-old

מֵרֵיחַ מַיִם יַפְרִחַ וְעָשָׂה קָצִיר כְּמוֹ־נָטַע׃
plant like shoot and-he-will-put-forth he-will-bud waters at-scent-of (9)

וְגֶבֶר יָמוּת וַיֶּחֱלָשׁ וַיִּגְוַע אָדָם וְאַיּוֹ׃
and-no-more-he man and-he-breathes-last and-he-is-laid-low he-dies but-man (10)

אָזְלוּ־מַיִם מִנִּי־יָם וְנָהָר יֶחֱרַב
he-becomes-parched or-riverbed sea from waters they-disappear (11)

וְיָבֵשׁ׃ וְאִישׁ שָׁכַב וְלֹא־יָקוּם עַד־בִּלְתִּי
no-longer till he-rises and-not he-lies-down so-man (12) and-he-becomes-dry

שָׁמַיִם לֹא יָקִיצוּ וְלֹא־יֵעֹרוּ מִשְּׁנָתָם׃
from-sleep-of-them they-will-be-roused and-not they-will-awake not heavens

מִי יִתֵּן ׀ בִּשְׁאוֹל תַּצְפִּנֵנִי תַּסְתִּירֵנִי
you-would-conceal-me you-would-hide-me in-Sheol he-would-grant who? (13)

עַד־שׁוּב אַפֶּךָ תָּשִׁית לִי חֹק וְתִזְכְּרֵנִי׃
then-you-would-remember-me time for-me you-would-set anger-of-you to-pass till

אִם־יָמוּת גֶּבֶר הֲיִחְיֶה כָּל־יְמֵי צְבָאִי
hard-service-of-me days-of all-of will-he-live-again? man he-dies if (14)

אֲיַחֵל עַד־בּוֹא חֲלִיפָתִי׃ תִּקְרָא וְאָנֹכִי
and-I you-will-call (15) renewal-of-me to-come until I-will-wait

אֶעֱנֶךָּ לְמַעֲשֵׂה יָדֶיךָ תִכְסֹף׃ כִּי־
surely (16) you-will-long hands-of-you for-creature-of I-will-answer-you

עַתָּה צְעָדַי תִּסְפּוֹר לֹא־תִשְׁמוֹר עַל־חַטָּאתִי׃
sin-of-me of you-will-keep-track not you-will-count steps-of-me then

like a fleeting shadow, he does not endure.
3 Do you fix your eye on such a one?
Will you bring him[x] before you for judgment?
4 Who can bring what is pure from the impure?
No one!
5 Man's days are determined;
you have decreed the number of his months
and have set limits he cannot exceed.
6 So look away from him and let him alone,
till he has put in his time like a hired man.

7 "At least there is hope for a tree:
If it is cut down, it will sprout again,
and its new shoots will not fail.
8 Its roots may grow old in the ground
and its stump die in the soil,
9 yet at the scent of water it will bud
and put forth shoots like a plant.
10 But man dies and is laid low;
he breathes his last and is no more.
11 As water disappears from the sea
or a riverbed becomes parched and dry,
12 so man lies down and does not rise;
till the heavens are no more, men will not awake
or be roused from their sleep.

13 "If only you would hide me in the grave[y]
and conceal me till your anger has passed!
If only you would set me a time
and then remember me!
14 If a man dies, will he live again?
All the days of my hard service
I will wait for my renewal[z] to come.
15 You will call and I will answer you;
you will long for the creature your hands have made.
16 Surely then you will count my steps
but not keep track of my sin.

x3 Septuagint, Vulgate and Syriac; Hebrew *me*
y13 Hebrew *Sheol* z14 Or *release*

5 ק חקיו

חָתֻם בִּצְרוֹר פִּשְׁעִי וַתִּטְפֹּל עַל־ עֲוֹנִי׃

sin-of-me over and-you-will-cover offense-of-me in-bag being-sealed (17)

וְאוּלָם הַר־ נוֹפֵל יִבּוֹל וְצוּר יֶעְתַּק

he-moves and-rock he-crumbles eroding mountain but-however (18)

מִמְּקֹמוֹ׃ אֲבָנִים ׀ שָׁחֲקוּ מַיִם תִּשְׁטֹף־

she-washes-away waters they-wear-away stones (19) from-place-of-him

סְפִיחֶיהָ עֲפַר־ אֶרֶץ וְתִקְוַת אֱנוֹשׁ הֶאֱבַדְתָּ׃ תִּתְקְפֵהוּ

you-overpower-him (20) you-destroy man so-hope-of land soil-of torrents-of-her

לָנֶצַח וַיַּהֲלֹךְ מְשַׁנֶּה פָנָיו וַתְּשַׁלְּחֵהוּ׃

and-you-send-away-him countenances-of-him changing and-he-is-gone for-ever

יִכְבְּדוּ בָנָיו וְלֹא יֵדָע וְיִצְעֲרוּ

if-they-are-brought-low he-knows but-not sons-of-him they-are-honored (21)

וְלֹא־ יָבִין לָמוֹ׃ אַךְ־ בְּשָׂרוֹ עָלָיו יִכְאָב

he-feels-pain to-him body-of-him only (22) to-them he-sees then-not

וְנַפְשׁוֹ עָלָיו תֶּאֱבָל׃ וַיַּעַן אֱלִיפַז הַתֵּימָנִי

the-Temanite Eliphaz then-he-replied (15:1) she-mourns for-him and-self-of-him

וַיֹּאמַר׃ הֶחָכָם יַעֲנֶה דַעַת־ רוּחַ וִימַלֵּא

or-would-he-fill empty notion-of would-he-answer wise-man? (2) and-he-said

קָדִים בִּטְנוֹ׃ הוֹכֵחַ בְּדָבָר לֹא יִסְכּוֹן

he-would-be-useful not with-word to-argue (3) belly-of-him hot-east-wind

וּמִלִּים לֹא־ יוֹעִיל בָּם׃ אַף־ אַתָּה תָּפֵר

you-undermine you but (4) with-them he-would-have-value not and-speeches

יִרְאָה וְתִגְרַע שִׂיחָה לִפְנֵי־ אֵל׃ כִּי יְאַלֵּף עֲוֹנְךָ

sin-of-you he-prompts for (5) God to devotion and-you-hinder piety

פִיךָ וְתִבְחַר לְשׁוֹן עֲרוּמִים׃ יַרְשִׁיעֲךָ

he-condemns-you (6) crafty-ones tongue-of and-you-adopt mouth-of-you

פִיךָ וְלֹא־ אָנִי וּשְׂפָתֶיךָ יַעֲנוּ־ בָךְ׃ הֲרִאישׁוֹן

first? (7) against-you they-testify and-lips-of-you I and-not mouth-of-you

אָדָם תִּוָּלֵד וְלִפְנֵי גְבָעוֹת חוֹלָלְתָּ׃ הַבְסוֹד

on-council-of? (8) you-were-brought-forth hills and-before you-were-born man

אֱלוֹהַ* תִּשְׁמָע וְתִגְרַע אֵלֶיךָ חָכְמָה׃ מַה־ יָּדַעְתָּ וְלֹא

that-not you-know what? (9) wisdom to-you and-you-limit you-listen God

נֵדָע תָּבִין וְלֹא־ עִמָּנוּ הוּא׃ גַּם־ שָׂב גַּם־

also gray-haired also (10) he with-us that-not you-have-insight we-know

יָשִׁישׁ בָּנוּ כַּבִּיר מֵאָבִיךָ יָמִים׃ הַמְעַט מִמְּךָ

for-you not-enough? (11) days more-than-father-of-you great with-us aged

תַּנְחֻמוֹת אֵל וְדָבָר לָאַט עִמָּךְ׃ מַה־ יִּקָּחֲךָ

he-carried-away-you why? (12) to-you in-gentleness and-word God consolations-of

17 My offenses will be sealed up
in a bag;
you will cover over my sin.

18 "But as a mountain erodes and
crumbles
and as a rock is moved from
its place,
19 as water wears away stones
and torrents wash away the
soil,
so you destroy man's hope.
20 You overpower him once for
all, and he is gone;
you change his countenance
and send him away.
21 If his sons are honored, he
does not know it;
if they are brought low, he
does not see it.
22 He feels but the pain of his
own body
and mourns only for
himself."

Eliphaz

15 Then Eliphaz the Temanite
replied:

2 "Would a wise man answer
with empty notions
or fill his belly with the hot
east wind?
3 Would he argue with useless
words,
with speeches that have no
value?
4 But you even undermine piety
and hinder devotion to God.
5 Your sin prompts your mouth;
you adopt the tongue of the
crafty.
6 Your own mouth condemns
you, not mine;
your own lips testify against
you.

7 "Are you the first man ever
born?
Were you brought forth
before the hills?
8 Do you listen in on God's
council?
Do you limit wisdom to
yourself?
9 What do you know that we do
not know?
What insights do you have
that we do not have?
10 The gray-haired and the aged
are on our side,
men even older than your
father.
11 Are God's consolations not
enough for you,
words spoken gently to you?
12 Why has your heart carried
you away,

*8 Most mss have *mappiq* in the *he* (הּ).

לִבֶּךָ וּמַה־ יִּרְזְמוּן עֵינֶיךָ׃ כִּי־ תָשִׁיב אֶל־
against you-vent that (13) eyes-of-you they-flash and-why? heart-of-you

אֵל רוּחֶךָ וְהֹצֵאתָ מִפִּיךָ מִלִּין׃ מָה־ אֱנוֹשׁ
man what? (14) words from-mouth-of-you and-you-pour-out rage-of-you God

כִּי־ יִזְכֶּה וְכִי־ יִצְדַּק יְלוּד אִשָּׁה׃
woman one-being-born-of he-could-be-righteous or-that he-could-be-pure that

הֵן בִּקְדֹשָׁו לֹא יַאֲמִין וְשָׁמַיִם לֹא־ זַכּוּ
they-are-pure not if-heavens he-places-trust not in-holy-ones-of-him if (15)

בְעֵינָיו׃ אַף כִּי־ נִתְעָב וְנֶאֱלָח
and-one-being-corrupt one-being-vile indeed how-much-less (16) in-eyes-of-him

אִישׁ־ שֹׁתֶה כַמַּיִם עַוְלָה׃ אֲחַוְךָ שְׁמַע־ לִי
to-me listen! I-will-explain-to-you (17) evil like-the-waters drinking-up man

וְזֶה־ חָזִיתִי וַאֲסַפֵּרָה׃ אֲשֶׁר־ חֲכָמִים יַגִּידוּ וְלֹא
and-nothing they-declared wise-men what (18) so-let-me-tell I-saw and-this

כִחֲדוּ מֵאֲבוֹתָם׃ לָהֶם לְבַדָּם נִתְּנָה
she-was-given by-themselves to-them (19) from-fathers-of-them they-hid

הָאָרֶץ וְלֹא־ עָבַר זָר בְּתוֹכָם׃ כָּל־ יְמֵי
days-of all-of (20) among-them one-being-alien he-passed when-not the-land

רָשָׁע הוּא מִתְחוֹלֵל וּמִסְפַּר שָׁנִים נִצְפְּנוּ
they-are-stored-up years and-number-of suffering-torment he wicked-man

לֶעָרִיץ׃ קוֹל־ פְּחָדִים בְּאָזְנָיו בַּשָּׁלוֹם
during-the-peace in-ears-of-him terrifying-things sound-of (21) for-the-ruthless

שׁוֹדֵד יְבוֹאֶנּוּ׃ לֹא־ יַאֲמִין שׁוּב מִנִּי־ חֹשֶׁךְ
darkness from to-escape he-trusts not (22) he-attacks-him one-marauding

וְצָפוּ הוּא אֱלֵי־חָרֶב׃ נֹדֵד הוּא לַלֶּחֶם אַיֵּה יֹדֵעַ ׀
he-knows *where? for-the-food he wandering (23) sword for he and-being-marked

כִּי־ נָכוֹן בְּיָדוֹ יוֹם־ חֹשֶׁךְ׃ יְבַעֲתֻהוּ צַר
distress they-terrify-him (24) darkness day-of at-hand-of-him he-is-set that

וּמְצוּקָה תִּתְקְפֵהוּ כְּמֶלֶךְ ׀ עָתִיד לַכִּידוֹר׃ כִּי־
because (25) for-the-attack poised like-king she-overwhelms-him and-anguish

נָטָה אֶל־ אֵל יָדוֹ וְאֶל־ שַׁדַּי יִתְגַּבָּר׃
he-vaunts-himself Almighty and-against fist-of-him God at he-shakes

יָרוּץ אֵלָיו בְּצַוָּאר בַּעֲבִי גַּבֵּי
backs-of with-thickness-of in-defiance against-him he-charges (26)

מָגִנָּיו׃ כִּי־ כִסָּה פָנָיו בְחֶלְבּוֹ
with-fat-of-him faces-of-him he-covers though (27) shields-of-him

וַיַּעַשׂ פִּימָה עֲלֵי־כָסֶל׃ וַיִּשְׁכּוֹן ׀ עָרִים נִכְחָדוֹת
ones-being-ruined towns yet-he-will-inhabit (28) waist at bulge and-he-makes

and why do your eyes flash,
13so that you vent your rage
against God
and pour out such words
from your mouth?

14"What is man, that he could
be pure,
or one born of woman, that
he could be righteous?
15If God places no trust in his
holy ones,
if even the heavens are not
pure in his eyes,
16how much less man, who is
vile and corrupt,
who drinks up evil like
water!

17"Listen to me and I will
explain to you;
let me tell you what I have
seen,
18what wise men have declared,
hiding nothing received
from their fathers
19(to whom alone the land was
given
when no alien passed
among them):
20All his days the wicked man
suffers torment,
the ruthless through all the
years stored up for him.
21Terrifying sounds fill his ears;
when all seems well,
marauders attack him.
22He despairs of escaping the
darkness;
he is marked for the sword.
23He wanders about—food for
vultures[a];
he knows the day of
darkness is at hand.
24Distress and anguish fill him
with terror;
they overwhelm him, like a
king poised to attack,
25because he shakes his fist at
God
and vaunts himself against
the Almighty,
26defiantly charging against him
with a thick, strong shield.

27"Though his face is covered
with fat
and his waist bulges with
flesh,
28he will inhabit ruined towns

[a]23 Or *about, looking for food*

*23 The NIV repoints this word as אַיָּה, *vulture.*

°15 ק בקדשיו

°22 ק וצפוי

בָּתִּים לֹא־ יֵשְׁבוּ לָמוֹ אֲשֶׁר הִתְעַתְּדוּ לְגַלִּים׃ לֹא־
not (29) to-rubbles they-crumble that in-them they-live not houses

יֶעְשַׁר וְלֹא־ יָקוּם חֵילוֹ וְלֹא־ יִטֶּה
he-will-spread and-not wealth-of-him he-will-endure and-not he-will-be-rich

לָאָרֶץ מִנְלָם׃ לֹא־ יָסוּר ׀ מִנִּי־ חֹשֶׁךְ
darkness from he-will-escape not (30) possession-of-them over-the-land

יֹנַקְתּוֹ תְּיַבֵּשׁ שַׁלְהָבֶת וְיָסוּר בְּרוּחַ
by-breath-of and-he-will-be-carried-away flame she-will-wither shoot-of-him

פִּיו׃ אַל־ יַאֲמֵן בַּשָּׁו נִתְעָה כִּי־
for deceiving-himself in-the-worthless let-him-trust not (31) mouth-of-him

שָׁוְא תִּהְיֶה תְמוּרָתוֹ׃ בְּלֹא־ יוֹמוֹ תִּמָּלֵא
she-will-be-paid day-of-him when-not (32) return-of-him she-will-be nothing

וְכִפָּתוֹ לֹא רַעֲנָנָה׃ יַחְמֹס כַּגֶּפֶן
like-the-vine he-will-be-stripped (33) she-will-flourish not and-branch-of-him

בִּסְרוֹ וְיַשְׁלֵךְ כַּזַּיִת נִצָּתוֹ׃
blossom-of-him like-the-olive-tree and-he-will-shed unripe-grape-of-him

כִּי־ עֲדַת חָנֵף גַּלְמוּד וְאֵשׁ אָכְלָה אָהֳלֵי־
tents-of she-will-consume and-fire barren godless company-of for (34)

שֹׁחַד׃ הָרֹה עָמָל וְיָלֹד אָוֶן וּבִטְנָם
and-womb-of-them evil and-to-bear trouble to-conceive (35) bribe

תָּכִין מִרְמָה׃ וַיַּעַן אִיּוֹב וַיֹּאמַר׃ שָׁמַעְתִּי
I-heard (2) and-he-said Job then-he-replied (16:1) deceit she-fashions

כָאֵלֶּה רַבּוֹת מְנַחֲמֵי עָמָל כֻּלְּכֶם׃ הֲקֵץ
end? (3) all-of-you misery ones-comforting-of many-things like-these

לְדִבְרֵי־ רוּחַ אוֹ מַה־ יַּמְרִיצְךָ כִּי תַעֲנֶה׃ גַּם ׀ אָנֹכִי כָּכֶם
like-you I also (4) you-argue that he-ails-you what? or wind of-speeches-of

אֲדַבֵּרָה לוּ־ יֵשׁ נַפְשְׁכֶם תַּחַת נַפְשִׁי אַחְבִּירָה
I-could-make-fine self-of-me in-place-of self-of-you there-was if I-could-speak

עֲלֵיכֶם בְּמִלִּים וְאָנִיעָה עֲלֵיכֶם בְּמוֹ רֹאשִׁי׃
head-of-me with at-you and-I-could-shake with-speeches against-you

אֲאַמִּצְכֶם בְּמוֹ־ פִי וְנִיד שְׂפָתַי
lips-of-me and-comfort-of mouth-of-me with I-would-encourage-you (5)

יַחְשֹׂךְ׃ אִם־ אֲדַבְּרָה לֹא־ יֵחָשֵׂךְ כְּאֵבִי
pain-of-me he-is-relieved not I-speak if (6) he-would-bring-relief

וְאַחְדְּלָה מַה־ מִנִּי* יַהֲלֹךְ׃ אַךְ־ עַתָּה הֶלְאָנִי
he-wore-out-me now surely (7) he-goes-away from-me what? if-I-refrain

הֲשִׁמּוֹתָ כָּל־ עֲדָתִי׃ וַתִּקְמְטֵנִי לְעֵד
as-witness and-you-bound-me (8) household-of-me entire-of you-devastated

and houses where no one
lives,
houses crumbling to rubble.
29He will no longer be rich and
his wealth will not
endure,
nor will his possessions
spread over the land.
30He will not escape the
darkness;
a flame will wither his
shoots,
and the breath of God's
mouth will carry him
away.
31Let him not deceive himself by
trusting what is
worthless,
for he will get nothing in
return.
32Before his time he will be paid
in full,
and his branches will not
flourish.
33He will be like a vine stripped
of its unripe grapes,
like an olive tree shedding
its blossoms.
34For the company of the
godless will be barren,
and fire will consume the
tents of those who love
bribes.
35They conceive trouble and give
birth to evil;
their womb fashions
deceit."

Job

16 Then Job replied:
2"I have heard many
things like these;
miserable comforters are you
all!
3Will your long-winded
speeches never end?
What ails you that you keep
on arguing?
4I also could speak like you,
if you were in my place;
I could make fine speeches
against you
and shake my head at you.
5But my mouth would
encourage you;
comfort from my lips would
bring you relief.

6"Yet if I speak, my pain is not
relieved;
and if I refrain, it does not
go away.
7Surely, O God, you have worn
me out;
you have devastated my
entire household.
8You have bound me—and it
has become a witness;

*6 Most mss have *dagesh* in the *mem* (מּ).

°31 ק בשיו

הָיָה וַיָּקָם בִּי כַחֲשִׁי בְּפָנַי
he-became and-he-rises against-me gauntness-of-me against-faces-of-me

יַעֲנֶה׃ (9) אַפּוֹ טָרַף׀ וַיִּשְׂטְמֵנִי חָרַק עָלַי
he-testifies (9) anger-of-him he-tears and-he-assails-me he-gnashes at-me

בְּשִׁנָּיו צָרִי׀ יִלְטוֹשׁ עֵינָיו לִי׃ (10) פָּעֲרוּ
with-teeth-of-him opponent-of-me he-pierces eyes-of-him on-me (10) they-open

עָלַי׀ בְּפִיהֶם בְּחֶרְפָּה הִכּוּ לְחָיָי יַחַד
against-me with-mouth-of-them in-scorn they-strike cheeks-of-me together

עָלַי יִתְמַלָּאוּן׃ (11) יַסְגִּירֵנִי אֵל אֶל עֲוִיל וְעַל־
against-me they-unite (11) he-turned-over-me God to evil-man and-into

יְדֵי רְשָׁעִים יִרְטֵנִי׃ (12) שָׁלֵו הָיִיתִי׀ וַיְפַרְפְּרֵנִי
clutches-of wicked-ones he-threw-me (12) well I-was but-he-shattered-me

וְאָחַז בְּעָרְפִּי וַיְפַצְפְּצֵנִי וַיְקִימֵנִי לוֹ
and-he-seized by-neck-of-me and-he-crushed-me and-he-made-me for-him

לְמַטָּרָה׃ (13) יָסֹבּוּ עָלַי׀ רַבָּיו יְפַלַּח
as-target (13) they-surround around-me archers-of-him he-pierces

כִּלְיוֹתַי וְלֹא יַחְמוֹל יִשְׁפֹּךְ לָאָרֶץ מְרֵרָתִי׃
kidneys-of-me and-not he-pities he-spills on-the-ground gall-of-me

(14) יִפְרְצֵנִי פֶרֶץ עַל־ פְּנֵי־ פָרֶץ יָרֻץ עָלַי כְּגִבּוֹר׃
(14) he-bursts-upon-me burst upon faces-of burst he-rushes at-me like-warrior

(15) שַׂק תָּפַרְתִּי עֲלֵי גִלְדִּי וְעֹלַלְתִּי בֶעָפָר קַרְנִי׃
(15) sackcloth I-sewed over skin-of-me and-I-buried in-the-dust brow-of-me

(16) פָּנַי °חֳמַרְמְרָה מִנִּי־ בֶכִי וְעַל עַפְעַפַּי צַלְמָוֶת׃
(16) faces-of-me they-are-red with weeping and-around eyes-of-me deep-shadow

(17) עַל לֹא־ חָמָס בְּכַפָּי וּתְפִלָּתִי זַכָּה׃ (18) אֶרֶץ אַל־
(17) yet not violence in-hands-of-me and-prayer-of-me pure (18) earth not

תְּכַסִּי דָמִי וְאַל־ יְהִי מָקוֹם לְזַעֲקָתִי׃ (19) גַּם־
you-cover blood-of-me and-not may-he-be place-of-rest to-cry-of-me (19) even

עַתָּה הִנֵּה־ בַשָּׁמַיִם עֵדִי וְשָׂהֲדִי בַּמְּרוֹמִים׃
now see! in-the-heavens witness-of-me and-advocate-of-me in-the-high-places

(20) *מְלִיצַי רֵעָי* אֶל־ אֱלוֹהַ† דָּלְפָה עֵינִי׃
(20) ones-scorning-me* *friends-of-me to God she-pours-tears eye-of-me

(21) וְיוֹכַח לְגֶבֶר עִם־ אֱלוֹהַּ וּבֶן־ אָדָם לְרֵעֵהוּ׃
(21) and-he-pleads on-behalf-of-man with God and-son-of man for-friend-of-him

(22) כִּי־ שְׁנוֹת מִסְפָּר יֶאֱתָיוּ וְאֹרַח לֹא־ אָשׁוּב אֶהֱלֹךְ׃
(22) for years-of few they-will-pass and-journey not I-will-return I-will-go

(17:1) רוּחִי חֻבָּלָה יָמַי נִזְעָכוּ קְבָרִים לִי׃
(17:1) spirit-of-me she-is-broken days-of-me they-are-cut-short graves for-me

---

my gauntness rises up and
testifies against me.
9 God assails me and tears me
in his anger
and gnashes his teeth at me;
my opponent fastens on me
his piercing eyes.
10 Men open their mouths to jeer
at me;
they strike my cheek in
scorn
and unite together against
me.
11 God has turned me over to evil
men
and thrown me into the
clutches of the wicked.
12 All was well with me, but he
shattered me;
he seized me by the neck
and crushed me.
He has made me his target;
13 his archers surround me.
Without pity, he pierces my
kidneys
and spills my gall on the
ground.
14 Again and again he bursts
upon me;
he rushes at me like a
warrior.

15 "I have sewed sackcloth over
my skin
and buried my brow in the
dust.
16 My face is red with weeping,
deep shadows ring my eyes;
17 yet my hands have been free
of violence
and my prayer is pure.

18 "O earth, do not cover my
blood;
may my cry never be laid to
rest!
19 Even now my witness is in
heaven;
my advocate is on high.
20 My intercessor is my friend[b]
as my eyes pour out tears to
God;
21 on behalf of a man he pleads
with God
as a man pleads for his
friend.

22 "Only a few years will pass
before I go on the journey
of no return.

17 My spirit is broken,
my days are cut short,
the grave awaits me.

[b] 20 Or *My friends treat me with scorn*

*20 With singular forms (as in the versions, to stand in concord with vss. 19 and 21), מְלִיצִי רֵעִי—, *one-interceding-for-me friend-of-me.*

†20 Most mss have *mappiq* in the *he* (הּ).

°16 ק חמרמרו

אִם־ לֹא הֲתֻלִים עִמָּדִי וּבְהַמְּרוֹתָם תָּלַן
she-must-dwell and-on-to-be-hostile-them around-me mockers surely indeed (2)

עֵינִי׃ שִׂימָה־ נָּא עָרְבֵנִי עִמָּךְ מִי הוּא* לְיָדִי
into-hand-of-me he who? for-you pledge-of-me now! give! (3) eye-of-me

יִתָּקֵעַ׃ כִּי־ לִבָּם צָפַנְתָּ מִשָּׂכֶל עַל־
for to-understanding you-closed mind-of-them for (4) he-will-put-security

כֵּן לֹא תְרֹמֵם׃ לְחֵלֶק יַגִּיד רֵעִים וְעֵינֵי
and-eyes-of friends he-denounces for-reward (5) you-will-let-triumph not this

בָנָיו תִּכְלֶנָה׃ וְהִצִּגַנִי לִמְשֹׁל עַמִּים
peoples to-be-byword and-he-made-me (6) they-will-fail children-of-him

וְתֹפֶת לְפָנִים אֶהְיֶה׃ וַתֵּכַהּ מִכַּעַשׂ עֵינִי
eye-of-me with-grief and-she-grew-dim (7) I-am in-faces and-one-spitting

וִיצֻרַי כַּצֵּל כֻּלָּם׃ יָשֹׁמּוּ
they-are-appalled (8) all-of-them like-the-shadow and-frames-of-me

יְשָׁרִים עַל־ זֹאת וְנָקִי עַל־ חָנֵף יִתְעֹרָר׃
he-is-aroused ungodly against and-innocent this at upright-men

וְיֹאחֵז צַדִּיק דַּרְכּוֹ וּטֳהָר־ יָדַיִם יֹסִיף
he-will-grow hands and-clean-of way-of-him righteous but-he-will-hold (9)

אֹמֶץ׃ וְאוּלָם כֻּלָּם תָּשֻׁבוּ וּבֹאוּ נָא וְלֹא־
and-not now! and-come! you-do-again all-of-them but-now (10) strong

אֶמְצָא בָכֶם חָכָם׃ יָמַי עָבְרוּ זִמֹּתַי
plans-of-me they-passed days-of-me (11) wise-man among-you I-will-find

נִתְּקוּ מוֹרָשֵׁי לְבָבִי׃ לַיְלָה לְיוֹם יָשִׂימוּ
they-turn into-day night (12) heart-of-me desires-of they-are-shattered

אוֹר קָרוֹב מִפְּנֵי־ חֹשֶׁךְ׃ אִם־ אֲקַוֶּה שְׁאוֹל בֵּיתִי
home-of-me Sheol I-hope if (13) darkness in-faces-of near light

בַּחֹשֶׁךְ רִפַּדְתִּי יְצוּעָי׃ לַשַּׁחַת קָרָאתִי אָבִי
father-of-me I-say to-the-corruption (14) beds-of-me I-spread in-the-darkness

אָתָּה אִמִּי וַאֲחֹתִי לָרִמָּה׃ וְאַיֵּה אֵפוֹ תִקְוָתִי
hope-of-me then and-where? (15) to-the-worm sister-of-me mother-of-me you

וְתִקְוָתִי מִי יְשׁוּרֶנָּה׃ בַּדֵּי שְׁאֹל תֵּרַדְנָה
will-they-go-down Sheol gates-of (16) he-can-see-her who? and-hope-of-me

אִם־ יַחַד עַל־ עָפָר נָחַת׃ וַיַּעַן בִּלְדַּד
Bildad then-he-replied (18:1) will-we-descend dust into together or

הַשֻּׁחִי וַיֹּאמַר׃ עַד־ אָנָה תְּשִׂימוּן קִנְצֵי לְמִלִּין
of-speeches ends-of will-you-make when? until (2) and-he-said the-Shuhite

תָּבִינוּ וְאַחַר נְדַבֵּר׃ מַדּוּעַ נֶחְשַׁבְנוּ כַבְּהֵמָה
as-the-cattle are-we-regarded why? (3) we-can-talk and-then be-sensible!

2 Surely mockers surround me;
my eyes must dwell on their hostility.
3 "Give me, O God, the pledge you demand.
Who else will put up security for me?
4 You have closed their minds to understanding;
therefore you will not let them triumph.
5 If a man denounces his friends for reward,
the eyes of his children will fail.

6 "God has made me a byword to everyone,
a man in whose face people spit.
7 My eyes have grown dim with grief;
my whole frame is but a shadow.
8 Upright men are appalled at this;
the innocent are aroused against the ungodly.
9 Nevertheless, the righteous will hold to their ways,
and those with clean hands will grow stronger.

10 "But come on, all of you, try again!
I will not find a wise man among you.
11 My days have passed, my plans are shattered,
and so are the desires of my heart.
12 These men turn night into day;
in the face of darkness they say, 'Light is near.'
13 If the only home I hope for is the grave,[c]
if I spread out my bed in darkness,
14 if I say to corruption, 'You are my father,'
and to the worm, 'My mother' or 'My sister,'
15 where then is my hope?
Who can see any hope for me?
16 Will it go down to the gates of death[c]?
Will we descend together into the dust?"

Bildad

18 Then Bildad the Shuhite replied:

2 "When will you end these speeches?
Be sensible, and then we can talk.
3 Why are we regarded as cattle

[c] *13,16* Hebrew *Sheol*

*3 Most mss connect these two words with *maqqeph* מִי־הוּא.

נִטְמִינוּ בְּעֵינֵיכֶם׃ (4) טֹרֵף נַפְשׁוֹ בְּאַפּוֹ
we-are-stupid in-eyes-of-you (4) tearing self-of-him in-anger-of-him

הַלְמַעַנְךָ תֵּעָזַב אָרֶץ וְיֶעְתַּק־ צוּר מִמְּקֹמוֹ׃
for-sake-of-you? she-is-abandoned earth or-he-is-moved rock from-place-of-him

(5) גַּם אוֹר רְשָׁעִים יִדְעָךְ וְלֹא־ יִגַּהּ שְׁבִיב
(5) indeed lamp-of wicked-ones he-is-snuffed-out and-not he-burns flame-of

אִשּׁוֹ׃ (6) אוֹר חָשַׁךְ בְּאָהֳלוֹ וְנֵרוֹ
fire-of-him (6) light he-becomes-dark in-tent-of-him and-lamp-of-him

עָלָיו יִדְעָךְ׃ (7) יֵצְרוּ צַעֲדֵי אוֹנוֹ
beside-him he-goes-out (7) they-are-weakened steps-of vigor-of-him

וְתַשְׁלִיכֵהוּ עֲצָתוֹ׃ (8) כִּי־ שֻׁלַּח בְרֶשֶׁת
and-she-throws-down-him scheme-of-him (8) indeed he-was-thrust into-net

בְּרַגְלָיו וְעַל־ שְׂבָכָה יִתְהַלָּךְ׃ (9) יֹאחֵז בְּעָקֵב פָּח
by-feet-of-him and-into mesh he-wanders (9) he-seizes by-heel trap

יַחֲזֵק עָלָיו צַמִּים׃ (10) טָמוּן בָּאָרֶץ חַבְלוֹ
he-holds-fast to-him snare (10) being-hidden on-the-ground noose-of-him

וּמַלְכֻּדְתּוֹ עֲלֵי נָתִיב׃ (11) סָבִיב בִּעֲתֻהוּ בַלָּהוֹת
and-trap-of-him in path (11) every-side they-startle-him terrors

וֶהֱפִיצֻהוּ לְרַגְלָיו׃ (12) יְהִי־ רָעֵב אֹנוֹ
and-they-dog-him at-steps-of-him (12) he-is hungry calamity-of-him

וְאֵיד נָכוֹן לְצַלְעוֹ׃ (13) יֹאכַל בַּדֵּי
and-disaster he-is-ready for-fall-of-him (13) he-eats-away parts-of

עוֹרוֹ יֹאכַל בַּדָּיו בְּכוֹר מָוֶת׃ (14) יִנָּתֵק
skin-of-him he-devours limbs-of-him firstborn-of death (14) he-is-torn

מֵאָהֳלוֹ מִבְטַחוֹ וְתַצְעִדֵהוּ לְמֶלֶךְ בַּלָּהוֹת׃
from-tent-of-him security-of-him and-she-marches-him to-king-of terrors

(15) תִּשְׁכּוֹן בְּאָהֳלוֹ מִבְּלִי־ לוֹ יְזֹרֶה עַל־
(15) she-resides in-tent-of-him from-nothing to-him he-is-scattered over

נָוֵהוּ גָפְרִית׃ (16) מִתַּחַת שָׁרָשָׁיו יִבָשׁוּ
dwelling-of-him burning-sulfur (16) at-below roots-of-him they-dry-up

וּמִמַּעַל יִמַּל קְצִירוֹ׃ (17) זִכְרוֹ־ אָבַד מִנִּי־
and-at-above he-withers branch-of-him (17) memory-of-him he-perishes from

אֶרֶץ וְלֹא־ שֵׁם לוֹ עַל־ פְּנֵי־ חוּץ׃ (18) יֶהְדְּפֻהוּ מֵאוֹר
earth and-no name for-him in surfaces-of land (18) they-drive-him from-light

אֶל־ חֹשֶׁךְ וּמִתֵּבֵל יְנִדֻּהוּ׃ (19) לֹא נִין לוֹ וְלֹא־
into darkness and-from-world they-banish-him (19) no offspring to-him and-no

נֶכֶד בְּעַמּוֹ וְאֵין שָׂרִיד בִּמְגוּרָיו׃
descendant among-people-of-him and-no survivor in-living-places-of-him

and considered stupid in
your sight?
4You who tear yourself to
pieces in your anger,
is the earth to be abandoned
for your sake?
Or must the rocks be moved
from their place?

5"The lamp of the wicked is
snuffed out;
the flame of his fire stops
burning.
6The light in his tent becomes
dark;
the lamp beside him goes
out.
7The vigor of his step is
weakened;
his own schemes throw him
down.
8His feet thrust him into a net
and he wanders into its
mesh.
9A trap seizes him by the heel;
a snare holds him fast.
10A noose is hidden for him on
the ground;
a trap lies in his path.
11Terrors startle him on every
side
and dog his every step.
12Calamity is hungry for him;
disaster is ready for him
when he falls.
13It eats away parts of his skin;
death's firstborn devours his
limbs.
14He is torn from the security of
his tent
and marched off to the king
of terrors.
15Fire resides[d] in his tent;
burning sulfur is scattered
over his dwelling.
16His roots dry up below
and his branches wither
above.
17The memory of him perishes
from the earth;
he has no name in the land.
18He is driven from light into
darkness
and is banished from the
world.
19He has no offspring or
descendants among his
people,
no survivor where once he
lived.

[d]15 Or *Nothing he had remains*

עַל־ יוֹמוֹ נָשַׁמּוּ אַחֲרֹנִים וְקַדְמֹנִים אָחֲזוּ
they-seize and-men-of-east men-of-west they-are-appalled day-of-him at (20)

שָׂעַר׃ אַךְ־ אֵלֶּה מִשְׁכְּנוֹת עַוָּל וְזֶה מְקוֹם לֹא־
not place-of and-this evil-man dwellings-of these surely (21) horror

יָדַע־ אֵל׃ וַיַּעַן אִיּוֹב וַיֹּאמַר׃ עַד־ אָנָה
when? until (2) and-he-said Job then-he-replied (19:1) God he-knows

תּוֹגְיוּן נַפְשִׁי וּתְדַכְּאוּנַנִי בְמִלִּים׃ זֶה
this (3) with-words and-you-will-crush-me self-of-me you-will-torment

עֶשֶׂר פְּעָמִים תַּכְלִימוּנִי לֹא־ תֵבֹשׁוּ תַּהְכְּרוּ־ לִי׃
against-me you-attack you-are-ashamed not you-reproached-me times ten-of

וְאַף־ אָמְנָם שָׁגִיתִי אִתִּי תָּלִין מְשׁוּגָתִי׃ אִם־
if (5) error-of-me she-remains with-me I-went-astray true if-indeed (4)

אָמְנָם עָלַי תַּגְדִּילוּ וְתוֹכִיחוּ עָלַי
against-me and-you-would-use you-would-exalt-yourselves above-me indeed

חֶרְפָּתִי׃ דְּעוּ־ אֵפוֹ כִּי־ אֱלוֹהַּ עִוְּתָנִי וּמְצוּדוֹ
and-net-of-him he-wronged-me God that then know! (6) humiliation-of-me

עָלַי הִקִּיף׃ הֵן אֶצְעַק חָמָס וְלֹא אֵעָנֶה
I-get-response then-not wrong I-cry though (7) he-drew-around around-me

אֲשַׁוַּע וְאֵין מִשְׁפָּט׃ אָרְחִי גָדַר וְלֹא
so-not he-blocked way-of-me (8) justice but-there-is-no I-call-for-help

אֶעֱבוֹר וְעַל נְתִיבוֹתַי חֹשֶׁךְ יָשִׂים׃ כְּבוֹדִי
honor-of-me (9) he-shrouded darkness paths-of-me and-over I-can-pass

מֵעָלַי הִפְשִׁיט וַיָּסַר עֲטֶרֶת רֹאשִׁי׃ יִתְּצֵנִי
he-tears-down-me (10) head-of-me crown-of and-he-removed he-stripped from-on-me

סָבִיב וָאֵלַךְ וַיַּסַּע כָּעֵץ תִּקְוָתִי׃ וַיַּחַר
and-he-burns (11) hope-of-me like-tree and-he-uproots till-I-am-gone on-every-side

עָלַי אַפּוֹ וַיַּחְשְׁבֵנִי לוֹ כְצָרָיו׃
among-enemies-of-him to-him and-he-counts-me anger-of-him against-me

יַחַד ׀ יָבֹאוּ גְדוּדָיו וַיָּסֹלּוּ עָלַי
against-me and-they-build troops-of-him they-advance in-force (12)

דַּרְכָּם וַיַּחֲנוּ סָבִיב לְאָהֳלִי׃ אַחַי
brothers-of-me (13) at-tent-of-me around and-they-encamp siege-ramp-of-them

מֵעָלַי הִרְחִיק וְיֹדְעַי אַךְ־
also and-ones-being-acquainted-with-me he-alienated from-with-me

זָרוּ מִמֶּנִּי׃ חָדְלוּ קְרוֹבָי
kinsmen-of-me they-went-away (14) from-me they-are-estranged

וּמְיֻדָּעַי שְׁכֵחוּנִי׃ גָּרֵי בֵיתִי
house-of-me ones-being-guests-of (15) they-forgot-me and-ones-being-friends-of-me

20 Men of the west are appalled
at his fate;
men of the east are seized
with horror.
21 Surely such is the dwelling of
an evil man;
such is the place of one who
knows not God."

Job

19 Then Job replied:
2 "How long will you
torment me
and crush me with words?
3 Ten times now you have
reproached me;
shamelessly you attack me.
4 If it is true that I have gone
astray,
my error remains my
concern alone.
5 If indeed you would exalt
yourselves above me
and use my humiliation
against me,
6 then know that God has
wronged me
and drawn his net around
me.

7 "Though I cry, 'I've been
wronged!' I get no
response;
though I call for help, there
is no justice.
8 He has blocked my way so I
cannot pass;
he has shrouded my paths
in darkness.
9 He has stripped me of my
honor
and removed the crown
from my head.
10 He tears me down on every
side till I am gone;
he uproots my hope like a
tree.
11 His anger burns against me;
he counts me among his
enemies.
12 His troops advance in force;
they build a siege ramp
against me
and encamp around my
tent.

13 "He has alienated my brothers
from me;
my acquaintances are
completely estranged from
me.
14 My kinsmen have gone away;
my friends have forgotten
me.
15 My guests and my

*5 Most mss have no *dagesh* in the *tav* (תִי־).

וְאַמְהֹתַי לְזָר תַּחְשְׁבֻנִי נָכְרִי הָיִיתִי

I-am alien they-count-me as-being-stranger and-maidservants-of-me

בְעֵינֵיהֶם׃ לְעַבְדִּי קָרָאתִי וְלֹא יַעֲנֶה בְּמוֹ־

with he-answers but-not I-summon to-servant-of-me (16) in-eyes-of-them

פִי אֶתְחַנֶּן־ לוֹ׃ רוּחִי זָרָה לְאִשְׁתִּי

to-wife-of-me she-is-offensive breath-of-me (17) with-him I-beg mouth-of-me

וְחַנֹּתִי לִבְנֵי בִטְנִי׃ גַּם־ עֲוִילִים מָאֲסוּ

they-scorn little-boys even (18) womb-of-me to-sons-of and-I-am-loathsome

בִי אָקוּמָה וַיְדַבְּרוּ־ בִי׃ תִּעֲבוּנִי

they-detest-me (19) against-me and-they-ridicule I-appear against-me

כָּל־ מְתֵי סוֹדִי וְזֶה־ אָהַבְתִּי נֶהְפְּכוּ־ בִי׃

against-me they-turned I-love and-this intimacy-of-me friends-of all-of

בְּעוֹרִי וּבִבְשָׂרִי דָּבְקָה עַצְמִי וָאֶתְמַלְּטָה

and-I-escaped bone-of-me she-sticks and-to-flesh-of-me to-skin-of-me (20)

בְּעוֹר שִׁנָּי׃ חָנֻּנִי חָנֻּנִי אַתֶּם רֵעָי כִּי

for friends-of-me you pity-me! pity-me! (21) teeth-of-me with-skin-of

יַד־ אֱלוֹהַּ נָגְעָה בִּי׃ לָמָּה תִּרְדְּפֻנִי כְמוֹ־ אֵל

God as you-pursue-me why? (22) against-me she-struck God hand-of

וּמִבְּשָׂרִי לֹא תִשְׂבָּעוּ׃ מִי־ יִתֵּן אֵפוֹ

then he-would-give who? (23) you-get-enough never and-of-flesh-of-me

וְיִכָּתְבוּן מִלָּי מִי־ יִתֵּן בַּסֵּפֶר

on-the-scroll he-would-give who? words-of-me that-they-were-recorded

וְיֻחָקוּ׃ בְּעֶט־ בַּרְזֶל וְעֹפֶרֶת לָעַד בַּצּוּר

in-the-rock to-forever and-lead iron with-tool-of (24) that-they-were-written

יֵחָצְבוּן׃ וַאֲנִי יָדַעְתִּי גֹּאֲלִי חָי וְאַחֲרוֹן עַל־

upon and-end alive One-Redeeming-me I-know and-I (25) they-were-engraved

עָפָר יָקוּם׃ וְאַחַר עוֹרִי נִקְּפוּ־ זֹאת

this they-destroy skin-of-me and-after (26) he-will-stand earth

וּמִבְּשָׂרִי אֶחֱזֶה אֱלוֹהַּ׃ אֲשֶׁר אֲנִי | אֶחֱזֶה־ לִּי

indeed-I I-will-see I that (27) God I-will-see yet-in-flesh-of-me

וְעֵינַי רָאוּ וְלֹא־ זָר כָּלוּ כִלְיֹתַי

hearts-of-me they-yearn one-being-other and-not they-will-see and-eyes-of-me

בְּחֵקִי׃ כִּי תֹאמְרוּ מַה־ נִּרְדָּף־ לוֹ וְשֹׁרֶשׁ

since-root-of after-him we-will-hound how? you-say if (28) in-breast-of-me

דָּבָר נִמְצָא־ בִי׃ גּוּרוּ לָכֶם | מִפְּנֵי־ חֶרֶב כִּי־ חֵמָה

wrath for sword because-of for-you fear! (29) in-me he-lies trouble

עֲוֺנוֹת חֶרֶב לְמַעַן תֵּדְעוּן שַׁדִּין׃ וַיַּעַן

then-he-replied (20:1) that-judgment you-will-know that sword punishments-of

maidservants count me a stranger;
they look upon me as an alien.
[16]I summon my servant, but he does not answer,
though I beg him with my own mouth.
[17]My breath is offensive to my wife;
I am loathsome to my own brothers.
[18]Even the little boys scorn me;
when I appear, they ridicule me.
[19]All my intimate friends detest me;
those I love have turned against me.
[20]I am nothing but skin and bones;
I have escaped with only the skin of my teeth.[e]

[21]"Have pity on me, my friends, have pity,
for the hand of God has struck me.
[22]Why do you pursue me as God does?
Will you never get enough of my flesh?

[23]"Oh, that my words were recorded,
that they were written on a scroll,
[24]that they were inscribed with an iron tool on[f] lead,
or engraved in rock forever!
[25]I know that my Redeemer[g] lives,
and that in the end he will stand upon the earth.[h]
[26]And after my skin has been destroyed,
yet[i] in[j] my flesh I will see God;
[27]I myself will see him
with my own eyes—I, and not another.
How my heart yearns within me!

[28]"If you say, 'How we will hound him,
since the root of the trouble lies in him,'
[29]you should fear the sword yourselves;
for wrath will bring punishment by the sword,
and then you will know that there is judgment.[k]"

[e]20 Or *only my gums* [f]24 Or *and*
[g]25 Or *defender* [h]25 Or *upon my grave*
[i]26 Or *And after I awake, / though this ⌞body⌟ has been destroyed, / then*
[j]26 Or */ apart from*
[k]29 Or */ that you may come to know the Almighty*

°29 ק שדון

צֹפַר הַנַּעֲמָתִי וַיֹּאמַר׃ (2) לָכֵן שְׂעִפַּי

troubled-thoughts-of-me therefore (2) and-he-said the-Naamathite Zophar

יְשִׁיבוּנִי וּבַעֲבוּר חוּשִׁי בִי׃ (3) מוּסַר

rebuke-of (3) in-me disturbance-of-me and-because-of they-prompt-me

כְּלִמָּתִי אֶשְׁמָע וְרוּחַ מִבִּינָתִי יַעֲנֵנִי׃

he-makes-reply-me from-understanding-of-me and-spirit I-hear dishonor-of-me

(4) הֲזֹאת יָדַעְתָּ מִנִּי־ עַד מִנִּי שִׂים אָדָם עֲלֵי־אָרֶץ׃ (5) כִּי

that (5) earth on man to-place since of-old from you-know this? (4)

רִנְנַת רְשָׁעִים מִקָּרוֹב וְשִׂמְחַת חָנֵף עֲדֵי־ רָגַע׃ (6) אִם־

though (6) moment to godless and-joy-of at-near wicked-ones mirth-of

יַעֲלֶה לַשָּׁמַיִם שִׂיאוֹ וְרֹאשׁוֹ לָעָב

to-the-cloud and-head-of-him pride-of-him to-the-heavens he-reaches

יַגִּיעַ׃ (7) כְּגֶלֲלוֹ לָנֶצַח יֹאבֵד רֹאָיו

ones-seeing-him he-will-perish to-forever like-dung-of-him (7) he-touches

יֹאמְרוּ אַיּוֹ׃ (8) כַּחֲלוֹם יָעוּף וְלֹא יִמְצָאֻהוּ

they-find-him and-not he-flies-away like-dream (8) where-he? they-will-say

וְיֻדַּד כְּחֶזְיוֹן לָיְלָה׃ (9) עַיִן שְׁזָפַתּוּ וְלֹא

then-not she-sees-him eye (9) night like-vision-of and-he-is-banished

תוֹסִיף וְלֹא־ עוֹד תְּשׁוּרֶנּוּ מְקוֹמוֹ׃

place-of-him she-will-look-on-him more and-no she-will-do-again

(10) בָּנָיו יְרַצּוּ דַלִּים וְיָדָיו

and-hands-of-him poor-ones they-must-make-amends children-of-him (10)

תָּשֵׁבְנָה אוֹנוֹ׃ (11) עַצְמוֹתָיו מָלְאוּ

they-are-filled bones-of-him (11) wealth-of-him they-must-give-back

עֲלוּמָו וְעִמּוֹ עַל־ עָפָר תִּשְׁכָּב׃ (12) אִם־

though (12) she-will-lie dust in and-with-him youthful-vigors-of-him

תַּמְתִּיק בְּפִיו רָעָה יַכְחִידֶנָּה תַּחַת לְשׁוֹנוֹ׃

tongue-of-him under he-hides-her evil in-mouth-of-him she-is-sweet

(13) יַחְמֹל עָלֶיהָ וְלֹא יַעַזְבֶנָּה וְיִמְנָעֶנָּה בְּתוֹךְ חִכּוֹ׃

mouth-of-him in and-he-keeps-her he-lets-go-her and-not to-her he-spares (13)

(14) לַחְמוֹ בְּמֵעָיו נֶהְפָּךְ מְרוֹרַת פְּתָנִים

serpents venom-of he-will-turn-sour in-stomachs-of-him food-of-him (14)

בְּקִרְבּוֹ׃ (15) חַיִל בָּלַע וַיְקִאֶנּוּ

then-he-will-spit-out-him he-swallowed richness (15) in-inside-of-him

מִבִּטְנוֹ יֹרִשֶׁנּוּ אֵל׃ (16) רֹאשׁ־ פְּתָנִים

serpents poison-of (16) God he-will-make-vomit-him from-stomach-of-him

יִינָק תַּהַרְגֵהוּ לְשׁוֹן אֶפְעֶה׃ (17) אַל־ יֵרֶא

he-will-enjoy not (17) adder fang-of she-will-kill-him he-will-suck

Zophar

20 Then Zophar the Naamathite replied:

2 "My troubled thoughts prompt
me to answer
because I am greatly
disturbed.
3 I hear a rebuke that dishonors
me,
and my understanding
inspires me to reply.

4 "Surely you know how it has
been from of old,
ever since man[l] was placed
on the earth,
5 that the mirth of the wicked is
brief,
the joy of the godless lasts
but a moment.
6 Though his pride reaches to
the heavens
and his head touches the
clouds,
7 he will perish forever, like his
own dung;
those who have seen him
will say, 'Where is he?'
8 Like a dream he flies away, no
more to be found,
banished like a vision of the
night.
9 The eye that saw him will not
see him again;
his place will look on him
no more.
10 His children must make
amends to the poor;
his own hands must give
back his wealth.
11 The youthful vigor that fills
his bones
will lie with him in the
dust.

12 "Though evil is sweet in his
mouth
and he hides it under his
tongue,
13 though he cannot bear to let it
go
and keeps it in his mouth,
14 yet his food will turn sour in
his stomach;
it will become the venom of
serpents within him.
15 He will spit out the riches he
swallowed;
God will make his stomach
vomit them up.
16 He will suck the poison of
serpents;
the fangs of an adder will
kill him.
17 He will not enjoy the streams,

l4 Or *Adam*

°11 ק עלומיו

בִּפְלַגּוֹת נַהֲרֵי נַחֲלֵי דְּבַשׁ וְחֶמְאָה׃ מֵשִׁיב יָגָע
to-streams rivers-of flows-of honey and-cream (18) giving-back produce-of-toil

וְלֹא יִבְלָע כְּחֵיל תְּמוּרָתוֹ וְלֹא יַעֲלֹס׃ כִּי־
and-not he-ate as-profit-of trade-of-him and-not he-will-enjoy (19) for

רִצַּץ עָזַב דַּלִּים בַּיִת גָּזַל וְלֹא
he-oppressed he-left-destitute poor-ones house he-seized that-not

יִבְנֵהוּ׃ כִּי לֹא־ יָדַע שָׁלֵו בְּבִטְנוֹ
he-built-him (20) surely not he-will-know respite from-craving-of-him

בַּחֲמוּדוֹ לֹא יְמַלֵּט׃ אֵין־ שָׂרִיד
by-one-being-treasured-of-him not he-can-save-himself (21) nothing left

לְאָכְלוֹ עַל־ כֵּן לֹא־ יָחִיל טוּבוֹ׃
to-devour-him for this not he-will-endure prosperity-of-him

בִּמְלֹאות שִׂפְקוֹ יֵצֶר לוֹ כָּל־ יַד
(22) in-to-be-full plenty-of-him he-will-be-in-distress to-him full-of force-of

עָמֵל תְּבוֹאֶנּוּ׃ יְהִי לְמַלֵּא בִטְנוֹ יְשַׁלַּח־
misery she-will-come-upon-him (23) he-is to-fill belly-of-him he-will-vent

בּוֹ חֲרוֹן אַפּוֹ וְיַמְטֵר עָלֵימוֹ
against-him burning-of anger-of-him and-he-will-rain-down upon-him

בִּלְחוּמוֹ׃ יִבְרַח מִנֶּשֶׁק בַּרְזֶל תַּחְלְפֵהוּ קֶשֶׁת
with-blow-of-him (24) he-flees from-weapon-of iron she-pierces-him arrow-of

נְחוּשָׁה׃ שָׁלַף וַיֵּצֵא מִגֵּוָה וּבָרָק
bronze (25) he-pulls-out and-he-comes-out from-back and-gleaming-point

מִמְּרֹרָתוֹ יַהֲלֹךְ עָלָיו אֵמִים׃ כָּל־ חֹשֶׁךְ
from-liver-of-him he-will-come over-him terrors (26) total-of darkness

טָמוּן לִצְפּוּנָיו תְּאָכְלֵהוּ אֵשׁ לֹא־
lying-in-wait for-ones-being-treasured-of-him she-will-consume-him fire not

נֻפָּח יֵרַע שָׂרִיד בְּאָהֳלוֹ׃ יְגַלּוּ
he-was-fanned he-will-devour left in-tent-of-him (27) they-will-expose

שָׁמַיִם עֲוֹנוֹ וְאֶרֶץ מִתְקוֹמָמָה לוֹ׃ יִגֶל
heavens guilt-of-him and-earth rising-up against-him (28) he-will-carry-off

יְבוּל בֵּיתוֹ נִגָּרוֹת בְּיוֹם אַפּוֹ׃ זֶה
possession-of house-of-him ones-rushing on-day-of wrath-of-him (29) such

חֵלֶק־ אָדָם רָשָׁע מֵאֱלֹהִים וְנַחֲלַת אִמְרוֹ מֵאֵל׃
fate-of man wicked from-God and-heritage-of appointment-of-him by-God

וַיַּעַן אִיּוֹב וַיֹּאמַר׃ שִׁמְעוּ שָׁמוֹעַ מִלָּתִי
(21:1) then-he-replied Job and-he-said (2) listen! to-listen word-of-me

וּתְהִי־ זֹאת תַּנְחוּמֹתֵיכֶם׃ שָׂאוּנִי וְאָנֹכִי אֲדַבֵּר
and-let-her-be this consolations-of-you (3) bear-with-me! while-I I-speak

the rivers flowing with
honey and cream.
18 What he toiled for he must
give back uneaten;
he will not enjoy the profit
from his trading.
19 For he has oppressed the poor
and left them destitute;
he has seized houses he did
not build.

20 "Surely he will have no respite
from his craving;
he cannot save himself by
his treasure.
21 Nothing is left for him to
devour;
his prosperity will not
endure.
22 In the midst of his plenty,
distress will overtake him;
the full force of misery will
come upon him.
23 When he has filled his belly,
God will vent his burning
anger against him
and rain down his blows
upon him.
24 Though he flees from an iron
weapon,
a bronze-tipped arrow
pierces him.
25 He pulls it out of his back,
the gleaming point out of
his liver.
Terrors will come over him;
26 total darkness lies in wait
for his treasures.
A fire unfanned will consume
him
and devour what is left in
his tent.
27 The heavens will expose his
guilt;
the earth will rise up against
him.
28 A flood will carry off his
house,
rushing waters[m] on the day
of God's wrath.
29 Such is the fate God allots the
wicked,
the heritage appointed for
them by God."

Job

21 Then Job replied:
2 "Listen carefully to my
words;
let this be the consolation
you give me.
3 Bear with me while I speak,

m28 Or *The possessions in his house will be carried off, / washed away*

וְאַחַר	and-after
דַּבְּרִי	to-speak-me
תַלְעִיג׃	you-mock-on
(4)	
הֶאָנֹכִי	I?
לְאָדָם	to-man
שִׂיחִי	complaint-of-me
וְאִם־מַדּוּעַ	why? and-if
לֹא	not
תִקְצַר	she-should-be-impatient
רוּחִי׃	spirit-of-me
(5)	
פְּנוּ	look!
אֵלַי	at-me
וְהָשַׁמּוּ	and-be-astonished!
וְשִׂימוּ	and-clap!
יַד	hand
עַל־	over
פֶּה׃	mouth
(6)	
וְאִם־	and-when
זָכַרְתִּי	I-think
וְנִבְהָלְתִּי	then-I-am-terrified
וְאָחַז	and-he-seizes
בְּשָׂרִי	body-of-me
פַּלָּצוּת׃	trembling
(7)	
מַדּוּעַ	why?
רְשָׁעִים	wicked-ones
יִחְיוּ	they-live-on
עָתְקוּ	they-grow-old
גַּם־	and
גָּבְרוּ	they-increase
חָיִל׃	power
(8)	
זַרְעָם	child-of-them
נָכוֹן	he-is-established
לִפְנֵיהֶם	before-them
עִמָּם	around-them
וְצֶאֱצָאֵיהֶם	and-offsprings-of-them
לְעֵינֵיהֶם׃	before-eyes-of-them
(9)	
בָּתֵּיהֶם	homes-of-them
שָׁלוֹם	safe
מִפָּחַד	from-fear
וְלֹא	and-not
שֵׁבֶט	rod-of
אֱלוֹהַּ	God
עֲלֵיהֶם׃	upon-them
(10)	
שׁוֹרוֹ	bull-of-him
עִבַּר	he-breeds
וְלֹא	and-never
יַגְעִל	he-fails
תְּפַלֵּט	she-calves
פָּרָתוֹ	cow-of-him
וְלֹא	and-not
תְשַׁכֵּל׃	she-miscarries
(11)	
יְשַׁלְּחוּ	they-send-forth
כַצֹּאן	as-the-flock
עֲוִילֵיהֶם	children-of-them
וְיַלְדֵיהֶם	and-little-ones-of-them
יְרַקֵּדוּן׃	they-dance-about
(12)	
יִשְׂאוּ	they-sing
כְּתֹף	with-tambourine
וְכִנּוֹר	and-harp
וְיִשְׂמְחוּ	and-they-make-merry
לְקוֹל	to-sound-of
עוּגָב׃	flute
(13)	
יְכַלּוּ	they-spend
בַטּוֹב	in-the-prosperity
יְמֵיהֶם	days-of-them
וּבְרֶגַע	and-in-instant
שְׁאוֹל	Sheol
יֵחָתּוּ׃	they-go-down
(14)	
וַיֹּאמְרוּ	yet-they-say
לָאֵל	to-God
סוּר	leave-alone!
מִמֶּנּוּ	from-us
וְדַעַת	and-to-know
דְּרָכֶיךָ	ways-of-you
לֹא	not
חָפָצְנוּ׃	we-desire
(15)	
מַה־	who?
שַׁדַּי*	Almighty
כִּי	that
נַעַבְדֶנּוּ	we-should-serve-him
וּמַה־	and-what?
נוֹעִיל	would-we-gain
כִּי	that
נִפְגַּע־	we-should-pray
בּוֹ׃	to-him
(16)	
הֵן	see!
לֹא	not
בְיָדָם	in-hand-of-them
טוּבָם	prosperity-of-them
עֲצַת	counsel-of
רְשָׁעִים	wicked-ones
רָחֲקָה	she-is-distant
מֶנִּי׃	from-me
(17)	
כַּמָּה	as-the-how-often?
נֵר	lamp-of
רְשָׁעִים	wicked-ones
יִדְעָךְ	he-is-snuffed-out
וְיָבֹא	and-he-comes
עָלֵימוֹ	upon-them
אֵידָם	calamity-of-them
חֲבָלִים	fates
יְחַלֵּק	he-allots
בְּאַפּוֹ׃	in-anger-of-him
(18)	
יִהְיוּ	they-are
כְּתֶבֶן	like-straw
לִפְנֵי־	before
רוּחַ	wind
וּכְמֹץ	and-like-chaff
גְּנָבַתּוּ	she-sweeps-away-him
סוּפָה׃	gale
(19)	
אֱלוֹהַּ	God
יִצְפֹּן	he-stores-up
לְבָנָיו	for-sons-of-him
אוֹנוֹ	punishment-of-him

and after I have spoken,
mock on.

4"Is my complaint directed to man?
Why should I not be impatient?

5Look at me and be astonished;
clap your hand over your mouth.

6When I think about this, I am terrified;
trembling seizes my body.

7Why do the wicked live on,
growing old and increasing in power?

8They see their children established around them,
their offspring before their eyes.

9Their homes are safe and free from fear;
the rod of God is not upon them.

10Their bulls never fail to breed;
their cows calve and do not miscarry.

11They send forth their children as a flock;
their little ones dance about.

12They sing to the music of tambourine and harp;
they make merry to the sound of the flute.

13They spend their years in prosperity
and go down to the grave° in peace.°

14Yet they say to God, 'Leave us alone!
We have no desire to know your ways.

15Who is the Almighty, that we should serve him?
What would we gain by praying to him?'

16But their prosperity is not in their own hands,
so I stand aloof from the counsel of the wicked.

17"Yet how often is the lamp of the wicked snuffed out?
How often does calamity come upon them,
the fate God allots in his anger?

18How often are they like straw before the wind,
like chaff swept away by a gale?

19It is said,ᵖ 'God stores up a man's punishment for his sons.'"

n13 Hebrew Sheol   o13 Or in an instant
p17-20 Verses 17 and 18 may be taken as exclamations and 19 and 20 as declarations.

*15 Most mss have dagesh in the shin (שׁ).

ק13 יכלו

יְשַׁלֵּם אֵלָיו וְיֵדָע׃ (20) יִרְאוּ עֵינָו
let-him-repay to-him so-he-will-know (20) let-them-see eyes-of-him

כִּידוֹ וּמֵחֲמַת שַׁדַּי יִשְׁתֶּה׃ (21) כִּי מַה־
destruction-of-him and-of-wrath-of Almighty let-him-drink (21) for what?

חֶפְצוֹ בְּבֵיתוֹ אַחֲרָיו וּמִסְפַּר חֳדָשָׁיו
care-of-him about-family-of-him behind-him when-allotment-of months-of-him

חֻצָּצוּ׃ (22) הַלְאֵל יְלַמֶּד־ דָּעַת וְהוּא רָמִים
they-end (22) to-God? can-he-teach knowledge since-he ones-being-high

יִשְׁפּוֹט׃ (23) זֶה יָמוּת בְּעֶצֶם תֻּמּוֹ כֻּלּוֹ
he-judges (23) this-one he-dies in-vigor-of fullness-of-him whole-of-him

שַׁלְאֲנַן וְשָׁלֵיו׃ (24) עֲטִינָיו מָלְאוּ חָלָב
secure and-at-ease (24) bodies-of-him they-are-full nourishment

וּמֹחַ עַצְמוֹתָיו יְשֻׁקֶּה׃ (25) וְזֶה יָמוּת בְּנֶפֶשׁ
and-marrow-of bones-of-him he-is-rich (25) and-another he-dies in-soul

מָרָה וְלֹא־ אָכַל בַּטּוֹבָה׃ (26) יַחַד עַל־ עָפָר יִשְׁכָּבוּ
bitter but-never he-enjoyed of-the-good (26) together in dust they-lie

וְרִמָּה תְּכַסֶּה עֲלֵיהֶם׃ (27) הֵן יָדַעְתִּי מַחְשְׁבוֹתֵיכֶם וּמְזִמּוֹת
and-worm she-covers over-them (27) see! I-know thoughts-of-you and-schemes

עָלַי תַּחְמֹסוּ׃ (28) כִּי תֹאמְרוּ אַיֵּה בֵית־ נָדִיב
against-me you-would-do-wrong (28) for you-say where? house-of great-man

וְאַיֵּה אֹהֶל | מִשְׁכְּנוֹת רְשָׁעִים׃ (29) הֲלֹא שְׁאֶלְתֶּם
and-where? tent-of living-places-of wicked-men (29) never? you-questioned

עוֹבְרֵי דֶרֶךְ וְאֹתֹתָם לֹא תְנַכֵּרוּ׃ (30) כִּי
ones-traveling-of way and-accounts-of-them not you-regarded (30) that

לְיוֹם אֵיד יֵחָשֶׂךְ רָע לְיוֹם עֲבָרוֹת
from-day-of calamity he-is-spared evil-man from-day-of wraths

יוּבָלוּ׃ (31) מִי־ יַגִּיד עַל־ פָּנָיו דַּרְכּוֹ
they-are-delivered (31) who? he-denounces to faces-of-him conduct-of-him

וְהוּא־ עָשָׂה מִי יְשַׁלֶּם־ לוֹ׃ (32) וְהוּא לִקְבָרוֹת יוּבָל
and-he he-did who? he-repays to-him (32) and-he to-graves he-is-carried

וְעַל־ גָּדִישׁ יִשְׁקוֹד׃ (33) מָתְקוּ־ לוֹ רִגְבֵי נָחַל
and-over tomb he-watches (33) they-are-sweet to-him soils-of valley

וְאַחֲרָיו כָּל־ אָדָם יִמְשׁוֹךְ וּלְפָנָיו אֵין מִסְפָּר׃
and-after-him all-of man he-follows and-before-him there-is-no count

(34) וְאֵיךְ תְּנַחֲמוּנִי הָבֶל וּתְשׁוּבֹתֵיכֶם נִשְׁאַר־
(34) so-how? can-you-console-me nonsense and-answers-of-you he-is-left

מָעַל׃ (22:1) וַיַּעַן אֱלִיפַז הַתֵּמָנִי וַיֹּאמַר׃
falsehood (22:1) then-he-replied Eliphaz the-Temanite and-he-said

Let him repay the man himself, so that he will know it!
20 Let his own eyes see his destruction;
let him drink of the wrath of the Almighty.[p]
21 For what does he care about the family he leaves behind
when his allotted months come to an end?

22 "Can anyone teach knowledge to God,
since he judges even the highest?
23 One man dies in full vigor,
completely secure and at ease,
24 his body[q] well nourished,
his bones rich with marrow.
25 Another man dies in bitterness of soul,
never having enjoyed anything good.
26 Side by side they lie in the dust,
and worms cover them both.

27 "I know full well what you are thinking,
the schemes by which you would wrong me.
28 You say, 'Where now is the great man's house,
the tents where wicked men lived?'
29 Have you never questioned those who travel?
Have you paid no regard to their accounts—
30 that the evil man is spared from the day of calamity,
that he is delivered from[r] the day of wrath?
31 Who denounces his conduct to his face?
Who repays him for what he has done?
32 He is carried to the grave,
and watch is kept over his tomb.
33 The soil in the valley is sweet to him;
all men follow after him,
and a countless throng goes[s] before him.

34 "So how can you console me with your nonsense?
Nothing is left of your answers but falsehood!"

Eliphaz

22 Then Eliphaz the Temanite replied:

[q]24 The meaning of the Hebrew for this word is uncertain.
[r]30 *Or man is reserved for the day of calamity, / that he is brought forth to*
[s]33 Or / *as a countless throng went*

°20 ק עיניו

הַלְאֵל יִסְכָּן־ גָּבֶר כִּי־ יִסְכֹּן עָלֵימוֹ מַשְׂכִּיל׃
one-being-wise to-him can-he-benefit even man can-he-be-of-benefit to-God? (2)

הַחֵפֶץ לְשַׁדַּי כִּי תִצְדָּק וְאִם־ בֶּצַע כִּי־
if gain and-if you-were-righteous if to-Almighty pleasure? (3)

תַתֵּם דְּרָכֶיךָ׃ הֲמִיִּרְאָתְךָ יֹכִיחֶךָ יָבוֹא
he-brings he-rebukes-you for-piety-of-you? (4) ways-of-you she-was-blameless

עִמְּךָ בַּמִּשְׁפָּט׃ הֲלֹא רָעָתְךָ רַבָּה וְאֵין־ קֵץ
end and-not great wickedness-of-you not? (5) with-the-charge against-you

לַעֲוֺנֹתֶיךָ׃ כִּי־ תַחְבֹּל אַחֶיךָ חִנָּם
for-no-reason brothers-of-you you-demanded-security for (6) to-sins-of-you

וּבִגְדֵי עֲרוּמִּים תַּפְשִׁיט׃ לֹא־ מַיִם עָיֵף תַּשְׁקֶה
you-gave-drink weary waters no (7) you-stripped naked-ones and-clothings-of

וּמֵרָעֵב תִּמְנַע־ לָחֶם׃ וְאִישׁ זְרוֹעַ לוֹ הָאָרֶץ
the-land to-him power though-man-of (8) food you-withheld and-from-hungry

וּנְשׂוּא פָנִים יֵשֶׁב בָּהּ׃ אַלְמָנוֹת שִׁלַּחְתָּ
you-sent-away widows (9) on-her he-lived faces and-being-honored-of

רֵיקָם וּזְרֹעוֹת יְתֹמִים יְדֻכָּא׃ עַל־ כֵּן
this for (10) he-was-broken fatherless-ones and-strengths-of empty-handed

סְבִיבוֹתֶיךָ פַחִים וִיבַהֶלְךָ פַּחַד פִּתְאֹם׃ אוֹ־ חֹשֶׁךְ לֹא־
not dark or (11) sudden peril and-he-terrifies-you snares ones-around-you

תִרְאֶה וְשִׁפְעַת־ מַיִם תְּכַסֶּךָּ׃ הֲלֹא־אֱלוֹהַּ גֹּבַהּ שָׁמָיִם
heavens height-of God not? (12) she-covers-you waters and-flood-of you-see

וּרְאֵה רֹאשׁ כּוֹכָבִים כִּי־ רָמּוּ׃ וְאָמַרְתָּ מַה־ יָּדַע
he-knows what? yet-you-say (13) they-are-lofty how! stars height-of and-see!

אֵל הַבְעַד עֲרָפֶל יִשְׁפּוֹט׃ עָבִים סֵתֶר־ לוֹ וְלֹא יִרְאֶה
he-sees so-not to-him veil thick-clouds (14) he-judges darkness through? God

וְחוּג שָׁמַיִם יִתְהַלָּךְ׃ הַאֹרַח עוֹלָם תִּשְׁמֹר אֲשֶׁר
that will-you-keep old path-of? (15) he-goes-about heavens and-vault-of

דָּרְכוּ מְתֵי־ אָוֶן׃ אֲשֶׁר־ קֻמְּטוּ וְלֹא־ עֵת נָהָר
flood time and-no they-were-carried-off that (16) evil men-of they-trod

יוּצַק יְסוֹדָם׃ הָאֹמְרִים לָאֵל סוּר
leave-alone! to-God the-ones-saying (17) foundation-of-them he-was-washed-away

מִמֶּנּוּ וּמַה־ יִּפְעַל שַׁדַּי לָמוֹ׃ וְהוּא מִלֵּא
he-filled yet-he (18) to-us Almighty can-he-do and-what? from-us

בָתֵּיהֶם טוֹב וַעֲצַת רְשָׁעִים רָחֲקָה מֶנִּי׃
from-me she-is-distant wicked-ones and-counsel-of good houses-of-them

יִרְאוּ צַדִּיקִים וְיִשְׂמָחוּ וְנָקִי יִלְעַג־ לָמוֹ׃
at-them he-mocks and-innocent and-they-rejoice righteous-ones they-see (19)

---

2 “Can a man be of benefit to God?
Can even a wise man benefit him?
3 What pleasure would it give the Almighty if you were righteous?
What would he gain if your ways were blameless?

4 “Is it for your piety that he rebukes you
and brings charges against you?
5 Is not your wickedness great?
Are not your sins endless?
6 You demanded security from your brothers for no reason;
you stripped men of their clothing, leaving them naked.
7 You gave no water to the weary
and you withheld food from the hungry,
8 though you were a powerful man, owning land—
an honored man, living on it.
9 And you sent widows away empty-handed
and broke the strength of the fatherless.
10 That is why snares are all around you,
why sudden peril terrifies you,
11 why it is so dark you cannot see,
and why a flood of water covers you.

12 “Is not God in the heights of heaven?
And see how lofty are the highest stars!
13 Yet you say, ‘What does God know?
Does he judge through such darkness?
14 Thick clouds veil him, so he does not see us
as he goes about in the vaulted heavens.’
15 Will you keep to the old path
that evil men have trod?
16 They were carried off before their time,
their foundations washed away by a flood.
17 They said to God, ‘Leave us alone!
What can the Almighty do to us?’
18 Yet it was he who filled their houses with good things,
so I stand aloof from the counsel of the wicked.

19 “The righteous see their ruin and rejoice;
the innocent mock them, saying,

אִם־ לֹא נִכְחַד קִימָנוּ וְיִתְרָם אָכְלָה
she-devours and-wealth-of-them foe-of-us he-is-destroyed indeed surely (20)

אֵשׁ׃ הַסְכֶּן־ נָא עִמּוֹ וּשְׁלם* בָּהֶם תְּבוֹאַתְךָ
she-will-come-to-you in-them and-be-at-peace! with-him now! submit! (21) fire

טוֹבָה׃ קַח־ נָא מִפִּיו תּוֹרָה וְשִׂים
and-lay-up! instruction from-mouth-of-him now! accept! (22) prosperity

אֲמָרָיו בִּלְבָבֶךָ׃ אִם־ תָּשׁוּב עַד־ שַׁדַּי תִּבָּנֶה
you-will-be-restored Almighty to you-return if (23) in-heart-of-you words-of-him

תַּרְחִיק עַוְלָה מֵאָהֳלֶךָ׃ וְשִׁית־ עַל־ עָפָר בָּצֶר
nugget dust to and-assign! (24) from-tent-of-you wickedness you-remove-far

וּבְצוּר נְחָלִים אוֹפִיר׃ וְהָיָה שַׁדַּי בְּצָרֶיךָ
golds-of-you Almighty then-he-will-be (25) Ophir ravines and-to-rock-of

וְכֶסֶף תּוֹעָפוֹת לָךְ׃ כִּי־ אָז עַל־ שַׁדַּי
Almighty in then surely (26) for-you choicest-ones and-silver-of

תִּתְעַנָּג וְתִשָּׂא אֶל־אֱלוֹהַּ פָּנֶיךָ׃ תַּעְתִּיר
you-will-pray (27) faces-of-you God to and-you-will-lift-up you-will-delight

אֵלָיו וְיִשְׁמָעֶךָּ וּנְדָרֶיךָ תְשַׁלֵּם׃
you-will-fulfill and-vows-of-you and-he-will-hear-you to-him

וְתִגְזַר־ אוֹמֶר וְיָקָם לָךְ וְעַל־ דְּרָכֶיךָ
ways-of-you and-on for-you then-he-will-be-done matter when-you-decide (28)

נָגַהּ אוֹר׃ כִּי־ הִשְׁפִּילוּ וַתֹּאמֶר גֵּוָה
lifting-up and-you-say they-bring-low when (29) light he-will-shine

וְשַׁח עֵינַיִם יוֹשִׁעַ׃ יְמַלֵּט אִי־ נָקִי
innocent not he-will-deliver (30) he-will-save eyes then-downcast-of

וְנִמְלַט בְּבֹר כַּפֶּיךָ׃ וַיַּעַן
then-he-replied (23:1) hands-of-you through-cleanness-of and-he-will-be-delivered

אִיּוֹב וַיֹּאמַר׃ גַּם־ הַיּוֹם מְרִי שִׂחִי יָדִי כָּבְדָה
she-is-heavy hand-of-me complaint-of-me bitter the-day even (2) and-he-said Job

עַל־ אַנְחָתִי׃ מִי־ יִתֵּן יָדַעְתִּי וְאֶמְצָאֵהוּ
so-I-could-find-him I-knew he-would-allow who? (3) groaning-of-me in

אָבוֹא עַד־ תְּכוּנָתוֹ׃ אֶעֶרְכָה לְפָנָיו מִשְׁפָּט וּפִי
and-mouth-of-me case before-him I-would-state (4) dwelling-of-him to I-could-go

אֲמַלֵּא תוֹכָחוֹת׃ אֵדְעָה מִלִּים יַעֲנֵנִי
he-would-answer-me words I-would-find-out (5) arguments I-would-fill

וְאָבִינָה מַה־ יֹּאמַר לִי׃ הַבְּרָב־ כֹּחַ
power with-greatness-of? (6) to-me he-would-say what and-I-would-consider

יָרִיב עִמָּדִי לֹא אַךְ־ הוּא יָשִׂם בִּי׃
against-me he-would-press-charges he indeed no against-me would-he-oppose

[20]'Surely our foes are destroyed,
and fire devours their wealth.'
[21]"Submit to God and be at peace with him;
in this way prosperity will come to you.
[22]Accept instruction from his mouth
and lay up his words in your heart.
[23]If you return to the Almighty, you will be restored:
If you remove wickedness far from your tent
[24]and assign your nuggets to the dust,
your gold of Ophir to the rocks in the ravines,
[25]then the Almighty will be your gold,
the choicest silver for you.
[26]Surely then you will find delight in the Almighty
and will lift up your face to God.
[27]You will pray to him, and he will hear you,
and you will fulfill your vows.
[28]What you decide on will be done,
and light will shine on your ways.
[29]When men are brought low and you say, 'Lift them up!'
then he will save the downcast.
[30]He will deliver even one who is not innocent,
who will be delivered through the cleanness of your hands."

Job

23 Then Job replied:
[2]"Even today my complaint is bitter;
his hand[t] is heavy in spite of[u] my groaning.
[3]If only I knew where to find him;
if only I could go to his dwelling!
[4]I would state my case before him
and fill my mouth with arguments.
[5]I would find out what he would answer me,
and consider what he would say.
[6]Would he oppose me with great power?
No, he would not press charges against me.

[t]2 Septuagint and Syriac; Hebrew *I the hand on me*
[u]2 Or *heavy on me in*

*21 Most mss have *qamets* and *atnah* under the *lamed* (וּשְׁלָם).

שָׁם יָשָׁר נוֹכָח עִמּוֹ וַאֲפַלְּטָה
and-I-would-be-delivered before-him he-could-present-case upright-man there (7)

לָנֶצַח מִשֹּׁפְטִי׃ הֵן קֶדֶם אֶהֱלֹךְ וְאֵינֶנּוּ וְאָחוֹר וְלֹא־
then-not if-west then-not-he I-go east if (8) from-one-judging-me to-forever

אָבִין לוֹ׃ שְׂמֹאול בַּעֲשֹׂתוֹ וְלֹא־ אָחַז יַעְטֹף יָמִין
south he-turns I-see then-not when-to-work-him north (9) to-him I-find

וְלֹא אֶרְאֶה׃ כִּי־ יָדַע דֶּרֶךְ עִמָּדִי בְּחָנַנִי כַּזָּהָב
as-the-gold he-tests-me with-me way he-knows but (10) I-glimpse and-not

אֵצֵא׃ בַּאֲשֻׁרוֹ אָחֲזָה רַגְלִי דַּרְכּוֹ
way-of-him foot-of-me she-follows at-step-of-him (11) I-will-come-forth

שָׁמַרְתִּי וְלֹא־ אָט׃ מִצְוַת שְׂפָתָיו וְלֹא אָמִישׁ
I-departed and-not lips-of-him command-of (12) I-turned-aside and-not I-kept

מֵחֻקִּי צָפַנְתִּי אִמְרֵי־ פִיו׃ וְהוּא
but-he (13) mouth-of-him words-of I-treasured more-than-daily-bread-of-me

בְאֶחָד וּמִי יְשִׁיבֶנּוּ וְנַפְשׁוֹ אִוְּתָה וַיָּעַשׂ׃
and-he-does she-pleases and-self-of-him he-can-oppose-him and-who? as-alone

כִּי יַשְׁלִים חֻקִּי וְכָהֵנָּה רַבּוֹת עִמּוֹ׃
with-him many and-like-them decree-of-me he-carries-out indeed (14)

עַל־ כֵּן מִפָּנָיו אֶבָּהֵל אֶתְבּוֹנֵן וְאֶפְחַד מִמֶּנּוּ׃
from-him and-I-fear I-think I-am-terrified from-before-him this for (15)

וְאֵל הֵרַךְ לִבִּי וְשַׁדַּי הִבְהִילָנִי׃ כִּי־
yet (17) he-terrified-me and-Almighty heart-of-me he-made-faint and-God (16)

לֹא נִצְמַתִּי מִפְּנֵי־ חֹשֶׁךְ וּמִפָּנַי כִּסָּה־
she-covers and-over-faces-of-me darkness by-presences-of I-am-silenced not

אֹפֶל׃ מַדּוּעַ מִשַּׁדַּי לֹא־ נִצְפְּנוּ עִתִּים
times they-are-set not from-Almighty why? (24:1) thick-darkness

וידעו° לֹא־ חָזוּ יָמָיו׃ גְּבֻלוֹת יַשִּׂיגוּ
they-move boundary-stones (2) days-of-him they-see not and-ones-knowing-him

עֵדֶר גָּזְלוּ וַיִּרְעוּ׃ חֲמוֹר יְתוֹמִים יִנְהָגוּ
they-drive-away orphans donkey-of (3) and-they-pasture they-stole flock

יַחְבְּלוּ שׁוֹר אַלְמָנָה׃ יַטּוּ אֶבְיוֹנִים מִדָּרֶךְ
from-path needy-ones they-thrust (4) widow ox-of they-take-in-pledge

יַחַד חֻבְּאוּ עֲנִיֵּי־ אָרֶץ׃ הֵן פְּרָאִים ׀
wild-donkeys see! (5) land poor-ones-of they-are-forced-to-hide together

בַּמִּדְבָּר יָצְאוּ בְּפָעֳלָם מְשַׁחֲרֵי לַטָּרֶף
for-the-food ones-foraging-of in-labor-of-them they-go-about in-the-desert

עֲרָבָה לוֹ לֶחֶם לַנְּעָרִים׃ בַּשָּׂדֶה בְּלִילוֹ
fodder-of-him in-the-field (6) for-the-children food for-him wasteland

7There an upright man could
present his case before
him,
and I would be delivered
forever from my judge.
8"But if I go to the east, he is
not there;
if I go to the west, I do not
find him.
9When he is at work in the
north, I do not see him;
when he turns to the south,
I catch no glimpse of
him.
10But he knows the way that I
take;
when he has tested me, I
will come forth as gold.
11My feet have closely followed
his steps;
I have kept to his way
without turning aside.
12I have not departed from the
commands of his lips;
I have treasured the words
of his mouth more than
my daily bread.
13"But he stands alone, and who
can oppose him?
He does whatever he
pleases.
14He carries out his decree
against me,
and many such plans he still
has in store.
15That is why I am terrified
before him;
when I think of all this, I
fear him.
16God has made my heart faint;
the Almighty has terrified
me.
17Yet I am not silenced by the
darkness,
by the thick darkness that
covers my face.

24 "Why does the Almighty
not set times for
judgment?
Why must those who know
him look in vain for such
days?
2Men move boundary stones;
they pasture flocks they
have stolen.
3They drive away the orphan's
donkey
and take the widow's ox in
pledge.
4They thrust the needy from
the path
and force all the poor of the
land into hiding.
5Like wild donkeys in the
desert,
the poor go about their labor
of foraging food;
the wasteland provides food
for their children.
6They gather fodder in the
fields

°1 ק וידעיו

יִקְצ֑וֹרוּ וְכֶ֥רֶם רָ֝שָׁ֗ע יְלַקֵּֽשׁוּ׃ עָר֣וֹם יָ֭לִינוּ
they-spend-night naked (7) they-glean wicked and-vineyard-of they-gather

מִבְּלִ֣י לְב֑וּשׁ וְאֵ֥ין כְּ֝ס֗וּת בַּקָּרָֽה׃ מִזֶּ֣רֶם
from-rain-of (8) in-the-cold covering and-nothing clothing from-lack-of

הָרִ֣ים יִרְטָ֑בוּ וּֽמִבְּלִ֥י מַ֝חְסֶ֗ה חִבְּקוּ־ צֽוּר׃
rock they-hug shelter and-from-lack-of they-are-drenched mountains

(9) יִ֭גְזְלוּ מִשֹּׁ֣ד יָת֑וֹם וְֽעַל־* עָנִ֥י
poor *and-infant-of fatherless-child from-breast they-snatch (9)

יַחְבֹּֽלוּ׃ עָר֣וֹם הִ֭לְּכוּ בְּלִ֣י לְב֑וּשׁ וּ֝רְעֵבִ֗ים
and-hungry-ones clothing lacking-of they-go-about naked (10) they-seize-for-debt

נָ֣שְׂאוּ עֹֽמֶר׃ בֵּין־ שׁוּרֹתָ֥ם יַצְהִ֑ירוּ יְקָבִ֥ים
winepresses they-crush-olives terraces-of-them among (11) sheaf they-carry

דָּ֝רְכ֗וּ וַיִּצְמָֽאוּ׃ מֵ֘עִ֤יר מְתִ֨ים׀ יִנְאָ֗קוּ וְנֶֽפֶשׁ־
and-soul-of they-groan †men from-city (12) yet-they-thirst they-tread

חֲלָלִ֥ים תְּשַׁוֵּ֑עַ וֶ֝אֱל֗וֹהַּ לֹא־ יָשִׂ֥ים תִּפְלָֽה׃ הֵ֤מָּה׀
those (13) wrongdoing he-charges not but-God she-cries-for-help wounded-ones

הָיוּ֮ בְּֽמֹרְדֵ֫י־ א֥וֹר לֹֽא־ הִכִּ֥ירוּ דְרָכָ֑יו וְלֹ֥א
and-not ways-of-him they-know not light among-ones-rebelling-of they-are

יָ֝שְׁב֗וּ בִּנְתִיבֹתָֽיו׃ לָא֡וֹר יָ֤קוּם רוֹצֵ֗חַ
one-murdering he-rises-up after-daylight (14) in-paths-of-him they-stay

יִֽקְטָל־ עָנִ֥י וְאֶבְי֑וֹן וּ֝בַלַּ֗יְלָה יְהִ֣י כַגַּנָּֽב׃ וְעֵ֤ין
and-eye-of (15) like-the-thief he-is and-in-the-night and-needy poor he-kills

נֹאֵ֨ף׀ שָׁ֤מְרָֽה נֶ֥שֶׁף לֵ֭אמֹר לֹא־ תְשׁוּרֵ֣נִי עָ֑יִן
eye she-will-see-me not to-think dusk she-watches one-commiting-adultery

וְסֵ֖תֶר פָּנִ֣ים יָשִֽׂים׃ חָ֚תַר בַּחֹ֗שֶׁךְ בָּ֫תִּ֥ים
houses in-the-dark they-break-into (16) he-keeps faces and-concealing-of

יוֹמָ֥ם חִתְּמוּ־ לָ֗מוֹ לֹא־ יָ֥דְעוּ אֽוֹר׃ כִּ֤י יַחְדָּ֨ו׀ בֹּ֣קֶר
morning together for (17) light they-know not for-them they-shut-in by-day

לָ֣מוֹ צַלְמָ֑וֶת כִּֽי־ יַ֝כִּ֗יר בַּלְה֥וֹת צַלְמָֽוֶת׃ קַל־הֽוּא׀
he foam (18) darkness terrors-of he-befriends for deep-darkness to-them

עַל־ פְּנֵי־ מַ֗יִם תְּקֻלַּ֣ל חֶלְקָתָ֣ם בָּאָ֑רֶץ לֹֽא־
no-one in-the-land portion-of-them she-is-cursed waters surfaces-of on

יִ֝פְנֶ֗ה דֶּ֣רֶךְ כְּרָמִֽים׃ צִיָּ֣ה גַם־ חֹ֭ם יִגְזְל֣וּ מֵֽימֵי־
waters-of they-snatch-away heat and drought (19) vineyards way-of he-goes

שֶׁ֑לֶג שְׁא֣וֹל חָטָֽאוּ׃ יִשְׁכָּחֵ֬הוּ רֶ֙חֶם׀ מְתָק֣וֹ רִ֭מָּה ע֣וֹד
longer worm he-feasts-on-him womb he-forgets-him (20) they-sinned Sheol snow

לֹֽא־ יִזָּכֵ֑ר וַתִּשָּׁבֵ֖ר כָּעֵ֣ץ עַוְלָֽה׃ רֹעֶ֣ה עֲ֭קָרָה
barren preying-of (21) evil like-tree but-she-is-broken he-is-remembered not

and glean in the vineyards
of the wicked.
7 Lacking clothes, they spend
the night naked;
they have nothing to cover
themselves in the cold.
8 They are drenched by
mountain rains
and hug the rocks for lack of
shelter.
9 The fatherless child is
snatched from the breast;
the infant of the poor is
seized for a debt.
10 Lacking clothes, they go about
naked;
they carry the sheaves, but
still go hungry.
11 They crush olives among the
terraces[v];
they tread the winepresses,
yet suffer thirst.
12 The groans of the dying rise
from the city,
and the souls of the
wounded cry out for help.
But God charges no one
with wrongdoing.

13 "There are those who rebel
against the light,
who do not know its ways
or stay in its paths.
14 When daylight is gone, the
murderer rises up
and kills the poor and
needy;
in the night he steals forth
like a thief.
15 The eye of the adulterer
watches for dusk;
he thinks, 'No eye will see
me,'
and he keeps his face
concealed.
16 In the dark, men break into
houses,
but by day they shut
themselves in;
they want nothing to do
with the light.
17 For all of them, deep darkness
is their morning[w];
they make friends with the
terrors of darkness.[x]

18 "Yet they are foam on the
surface of the water;
their portion of the land is
cursed,
so that no one goes to the
vineyards.
19 As heat and drought snatch
away the melted snow,
so the grave[y] snatches away
those who have sinned.
20 The womb forgets them,
the worm feasts on them;
evil men are no longer
remembered
but are broken like a tree.
21 They prey on the barren and

[v] 11 Or *olives between the millstones;* the meaning of the Hebrew for this word is uncertain.
[w] 17 Or *them, their morning is like the shadow of death*
[x] 17 Or *of the shadow of death*
[y] 19 Hebrew *Sheol*

*9 The NIV repoints this word as וְעַל; the text as pointed reads *and-over.*

†12 The NIV repoints this word with *tsere* under the *mem* מֵ, *dying-ones.*

°6 ק יקצורו

לֹא תֵלֵד וְאַלְמָנָה לֹא יְיֵטִיב׃ וּמָשַׁךְ

but-he-drags-away (22) he-shows-kindness not and-widow she-bore-child not

אַבִּירִים בְּכֹחוֹ יָקוּם וְלֹא־ יַאֲמִין

he-has-assurance but-not he-becomes-established by-power-of-him mighty-ones

בַּחַיִּין׃ יִתֶּן־ לוֹ לָבֶטַח וְיִשָּׁעֵן וְעֵינֵיהוּ

but-eyes-of-him and-may-he-rest in-security to-him he-may-let (23) of-the-lives

עַל־ דַּרְכֵיהֶם׃ רוֹמּוּ מְּעַט ׀ וְאֵינֶנּוּ

then-not-he little-while they-are-exalted (24) ways-of-them on

וְהֻמְּכוּ כַּכֹּל יִקָּפְצוּן וּכְרֹאשׁ

and-like-head-of they-are-gathered-up like-the-all and-they-are-brought-low

שִׁבֹּלֶת יִמָּלוּ׃ וְאִם־ לֹא אֵפוֹ מִי יַכְזִיבֵנִי

he-can-prove-false-me who? then not and-if (25) they-are-cut-off grain

וְיָשֵׂם לְאַל מִלָּתִי׃ וַיַּעַן בִּלְדַּד

Bildad then-he-replied (25:1) word-of-me to-nothing and-he-can-reduce

הַשֻּׁחִי וַיֹּאמַר׃ הַמְשֵׁל וָפַחַד עִמּוֹ עֹשֶׂה

establishing to-him and-awe to-have-dominion (2) and-he-said the-Shuhite

שָׁלוֹם בִּמְרוֹמָיו׃ הֲיֵשׁ מִסְפָּר לִגְדוּדָיו וְעַל־ מִי

whom? and-upon to-forces-of-him number is-there? (3) in-heights-of-him order

לֹא־ יָקוּם אוֹרֵהוּ׃ וּמַה־ יִּצְדַּק אֱנוֹשׁ עִם־ אֵל

God before man can-he-be-righteous then-how? (4) light-of-him he-rises not

וּמַה־ יִּזְכֶּה יְלוּד אִשָּׁה׃ הֵן עַד־ יָרֵחַ וְלֹא

and-not moon even if (5) woman one-being-born-of can-he-be-pure and-how?

יַאֲהִיל וְכוֹכָבִים לֹא־ זַכּוּ בְעֵינָיו׃ אַף

how-much-less (6) in-eyes-of-him they-are-pure not and-stars he-is-bright

כִּי־ אֱנוֹשׁ רִמָּה וּבֶן־ אָדָם תּוֹלֵעָה׃ וַיַּעַן אִיּוֹב וַיֹּאמַר׃

and-he-said Job then-he-replied (26:1) worm man and-son-of maggot man then

מֶה־ עָזַרְתָּ לְלֹא־ כֹחַ הוֹשַׁעְתָּ זְרוֹעַ לֹא־ עֹז׃ מַה־

what! (3) strength no arm you-saved power to-no you-helped how! (2)

יָּעַצְתָּ לְלֹא חָכְמָה וְתוּשִׁיָּה לָרֹב הוֹדָעְתָּ׃ אֶת־

with (4) you-displayed in-greatness and-insight wisdom to-no you-advised

מִי הִגַּדְתָּ מִלִּין וְנִשְׁמַת־ מִי יָצְאָה מִמֶּךָּ׃

from-you she-came-out who? and-spirit-of words you-uttered whom?

הָרְפָאִים יְחוֹלָלוּ מִתַּחַת מַיִם וְשֹׁכְנֵיהֶם׃

and-ones-living-of-them waters at-beneath they-are-in-anguish the-dead-ones (5)

עָרוֹם שְׁאוֹל נֶגְדּוֹ וְאֵין כְּסוּת לָאֲבַדּוֹן׃ נֹטֶה צָפוֹן

north spreading-out (7) to-Abaddon cover and-no before-him Sheol naked (6)

עַל־ תֹּהוּ תֹּלֶה אֶרֶץ עַל־ בְּלִי־ מָה׃ צֹרֵר־ מַיִם

waters wrapping-up (8) what not over earth suspending empty-space over

---

childless woman,
and to the widow show no kindness.
22 But God drags away the mighty by his power;
though they become established, they have no assurance of life.
23 He may let them rest in a feeling of security,
but his eyes are on their ways.
24 For a little while they are exalted, and then they are gone;
they are brought low and gathered up like all others;
they are cut off like heads of grain.

25 "If this is not so, who can prove me false
and reduce my words to nothing?"

Bildad

25 Then Bildad the Shuhite replied:

2 "Dominion and awe belong to God;
he establishes order in the heights of heaven.
3 Can his forces be numbered?
Upon whom does his light not rise?
4 How then can a man be righteous before God?
How can one born of woman be pure?
5 If even the moon is not bright
and the stars are not pure in his eyes,
6 how much less man, who is but a maggot—
a son of man, who is only a worm!"

Job

26 Then Job replied:

2 "How you have helped the powerless!
How you have saved the arm that is feeble!
3 What advice you have offered to one without wisdom!
And what great insight you have displayed!
4 Who has helped you utter these words?
And whose spirit spoke from your mouth?

5 "The dead are in deep anguish,
those beneath the waters and all that live in them.
6 Death[z] is naked before God;
Destruction[a] lies uncovered.
7 He spreads out the northern ⌊skies⌋ over empty space;
he suspends the earth over nothing.
8 He wraps up the waters in his

z6 Hebrew *Sheol* a6 Hebrew *Abaddon*

*6 Most mss have *pathah* under the *lamed* (לַ).

בְּעָבָיו וְלֹא־ נִבְקַע עָנָן תַּחְתָּם׃ מְאַחֵז פְּנֵי־
faces-of covering (9) under-them cloud he-bursts yet-not in-clouds-of-him

כִּסֵּה* פַּרְשֵׁז עָלָיו עֲנָנוֹ׃ חֹק־ חָג עַל־
on he-marks-out horizon (10) cloud-of-him over-him to-spread *full-moon

פְּנֵי־ מָיִם עַד־ תַּכְלִית אוֹר עִם־ חֹשֶׁךְ׃ עַמּוּדֵי
pillars-of (11) darkness between light boundary-of for waters faces-of

שָׁמַיִם יְרוֹפָפוּ וְיִתְמְהוּ מִגַּעֲרָתוֹ׃ בְּכֹחוֹ
by-power-of-him (12) at-rebuke-of-him and-they-are-aghast they-quake heavens

רָגַע הַיָּם וּבתוּבָנָתוֹ° מָחַץ רָהַב׃
Rahab he-cut-to-pieces and-by-wisdom-of-him the-sea he-churned-up

בְּרוּחוֹ שָׁמַיִם שִׁפְרָה חֹלֲלָה יָדוֹ נָחָשׁ בָּרִיחַ׃
gliding serpent hand-of-him piercing fair skies by-breath-of-him (13)

הֶן־ אֵלֶּה קְצוֹת דְּרָכוֹ° וּמַה־ שֵּׁמֶץ דָּבָר
whisper faint-of and-how! ways-of-him outer-fringes-of these see! (14)

נִשְׁמַע־ בּוֹ וְרַעַם גְּבוּרֹתוֹ° מִי יִתְבּוֹנָן׃
he-can-understand who? powers-of-him then-thunder-of of-him we-hear

וַיֹּסֶף אִיּוֹב שְׂאֵת מְשָׁלוֹ וַיֹּאמַר׃
and-he-said discourse-of-him to-take-up Job and-he-continued (27:1)

חַי־ אֵל הֵסִיר מִשְׁפָּטִי וְשַׁדַּי הֵמַר
he-made-bitter and-Almighty justice-of-me he-denied God life-of (2)

נַפְשִׁי׃ כִּי־ כָל־ עוֹד נִשְׁמָתִי בִי וְרוּחַ אֱלוֹהַּ
God and-breath-of in-me life-of-me length-of all-of for (3) soul-of-me

בְּאַפִּי׃ אִם־ תְּדַבֵּרְנָה שְׂפָתַי עַוְלָה וּלְשׁוֹנִי
and-tongue-of-me wickedness lips-of-me she-will-speak not (4) in-nostril-of-me

אִם־ יֶהְגֶּה רְמִיָּה׃ חָלִילָה לִּי אִם־ אַצְדִּיק
I-will-declare-right never from-me far-be-it! (5) deceit he-will-utter not

אֶתְכֶם עַד־אֶגְוָע לֹא־אָסִיר תֻּמָּתִי מִמֶּנִּי׃ בְּצִדְקָתִי
to-righteousness-of-me (6) from-me integrity-of-me I-will-deny not I-die till you

הֶחֱזַקְתִּי וְלֹא אַרְפֶּהָ לֹא־ יֶחֱרַף
he-will-reproach not I-will-let-go-of-her and-never I-will-maintain

לְבָבִי מִיָּמָי׃ יְהִי כְרָשָׁע אֹיְבִי
being-enemy-of-me like-wicked may-he-be (7) from-days-of-me conscience-of-me

וּמִתְקוֹמְמִי כְעַוָּל׃ כִּי מַה־ תִּקְוַת חָנֵף כִּי
when godless hope-of what? for (8) like-unjust and-one-being-adversary-of-me

יִבְצָע כִּי יֵשֶׁל אֱלוֹהַּ נַפְשׁוֹ׃ הֲצַעֲקָתוֹ יִשְׁמַע ׀
he-listens cry-of-him? (9) life-of-him God he-takes-away when he-is-cut-off

אֵל כִּי־ תָבוֹא עָלָיו צָרָה׃ אִם־עַל־ שַׁדַּי יִתְעַנָּג
will-he-delight Almighty in or (10) distress upon-him she-comes when God

clouds,
yet the clouds do not burst
under their weight.
9 He covers the face of the full
moon,
spreading his clouds over it.
10 He marks out the horizon on
the face of the waters
for a boundary between
light and darkness.
11 The pillars of the heavens
quake,
aghast at his rebuke.
12 By his power he churned up
the sea;
by his wisdom he cut Rahab
to pieces.
13 By his breath the skies became
fair;
his hand pierced the gliding
serpent.
14 And these are but the outer
fringe of his works;
how faint the whisper we
hear of him!
Who then can understand
the thunder of his
power?"

27 And Job continued his discourse:

2 "As surely as God lives, who
has denied me justice,
the Almighty, who has
made me taste bitterness
of soul,
3 as long as I have life within
me,
the breath of God in my
nostrils,
4 my lips will not speak
wickedness,
and my tongue will utter no
deceit.
5 I will never admit you are in
the right;
till I die, I will not deny my
integrity.
6 I will maintain my
righteousness and never
let go of it;
my conscience will not
reproach me as long as I
live.

7 "May my enemies be like the
wicked,
my adversaries like the
unjust!
8 For what hope has the godless
when he is cut off,
when God takes away his
life?
9 Does God listen to his cry
when distress comes upon
him?
10 Will he find delight in the
Almighty?

*9 The NIV repoints this word as כֶּסֶה; the text as pointed reads *throne*.

°12 ק ובתבונתו
°14a ק דרכיו
°14b ק גבורתיו

יִקְרָא אֱלוֹהַּ בְּכָל־עֵת׃ אוֹרֶה אֶתְכֶם בְּיַד־אֵל
God about-power-of you I-will-teach (11) time at-all-of God will-he-call-upon

אֲשֶׁר עִם־שַׁדַּי לֹא אֲכַחֵד׃ הֵן־אַתֶּם כֻּלְּכֶם חֲזִיתֶם
you-saw all-of-you you see! (12) I-will-conceal not Almighty with what

וְלָמָּה־זֶּה הֶבֶל תֶּהְבָּלוּ׃ זֶה ׀ חֵלֶק־אָדָם
man allotment-of this (13) you-talk-meaninglessly meaningless this then-why?

רָשָׁע ׀ עִם־אֵל וְנַחֲלַת עָרִיצִים מִשַּׁדַּי יִקָּחוּ׃
they-receive from-Almighty ruthless-ones and-heritage-of God from wicked

אִם־יִרְבּוּ בָנָיו לְמוֹ־חָרֶב וְצֶאֱצָאָיו
and-offsprings-of-him sword to children-of-him they-are-many if (14)

לֹא יִשְׂבְּעוּ־לָחֶם׃ שְׂרִידָו° בַּמָּוֶת
by-the-plague survivors-of-him (15) food they-will-have-enough never

יִקָּבֵרוּ וְאַלְמְנֹתָיו לֹא תִבְכֶּינָה׃ אִם־
though (16) they-will-weep not and-widows-of-him they-will-be-buried

יִצְבֹּר כֶּעָפָר כָּסֶף וְכַחֹמֶר יָכִין מַלְבּוּשׁ׃
clothing he-piles and-like-the-clay silver like-the-dust he-heaps-up

יָכִין וְצַדִּיק יִלְבָּשׁ וְכֶסֶף נָקִי יַחֲלֹק׃
he-will-divide innocent and-silver he-will-wear but-righteous he-lays-up (17)

בָּנָה כָעָשׁ בֵּיתוֹ וּכְסֻכָּה עָשָׂה נֹצֵר׃
man-watching he-made and-like-hut house-of-him like-the-moth he-builds (18)

עָשִׁיר יִשְׁכַּב וְלֹא יֵאָסֵף עֵינָיו פָּקַח
he-opens eyes-of-him he-will-do-again but-not he-lies-down wealthy (19)

וְאֵינֶנּוּ׃ תַּשִּׂיגֵהוּ כַמַּיִם בַּלָּהוֹת לַיְלָה
night terrors like-the-floods she-overtakes-him (20) and-not-he

גְּנָבַתּוּ סוּפָה׃ יִשָּׂאֵהוּ קָדִים וְיֵלַךְ
and-he-is-gone east-wind he-carries-off-him (21) tempest she-snatches-him

וִישָׂעֲרֵהוּ מִמְּקֹמוֹ׃ וְיַשְׁלֵךְ עָלָיו וְלֹא
and-not against-him and-he-hurls (22) from-place-of-him and-he-sweeps-him

יַחְמֹל מִיָּדוֹ בָּרוֹחַ יִבְרָח׃ יִשְׂפֹּק עָלֵימוֹ
against-him he-claps (23) he-flees to-flee from-power-of-him he-shows-mercy

כַפֵּימוֹ וְיִשְׁרֹק עָלָיו מִמְּקֹמוֹ׃ כִּי
indeed (28:1) from-place-of-him against-him and-he-hisses hands-of-him

יֵשׁ לַכֶּסֶף מוֹצָא וּמָקוֹם לַזָּהָב יָזֹקּוּ׃ בַּרְזֶל
iron (2) they-refine for-the-gold and-place mine for-the-silver there-is

מֵעָפָר יֻקָּח וְאֶבֶן יָצוּק נְחוּשָׁה׃ קֵץ ׀ שָׂם לַחֹשֶׁךְ
to-the-darkness he-puts end (3) copper being-smelted and-ore he-is-taken from-earth

וּלְכָל־תַּכְלִית הוּא חוֹקֵר אֶבֶן אֹפֶל וְצַלְמָוֶת׃ פָּרַץ
he-cuts (4) and-darkness blackness ore searching he recess and-to-every-of

Will he call upon God at all
times?
11"I will teach you about the
power of God;
the ways of the Almighty I
will not conceal.
12You have all seen this
yourselves.
Why then this meaningless
talk?
13"Here is the fate God allots to
the wicked,
the heritage a ruthless man
receives from the
Almighty:
14However many his children,
their fate is the sword;
his offspring will never
have enough to eat.
15The plague will bury those
who survive him,
and their widows will not
weep for them.
16Though he heaps up silver like
dust
and clothes like piles of clay,
17what he lays up the righteous
will wear,
and the innocent will divide
his silver.
18The house he builds is like a
moth's cocoon,
like a hut made by a
watchman.
19He lies down wealthy, but will
do so no more;
when he opens his eyes, all
is gone.
20Terrors overtake him like a
flood;
a tempest snatches him
away in the night.
21The east wind carries him off,
and he is gone;
it sweeps him out of his
place.
22It hurls itself against him
without mercy
as he flees headlong from its
power.
23It claps its hands in derision
and hisses him out of his
place.

28 "There is a mine for silver
and a place where gold is
refined.
2Iron is taken from the earth,
and copper is smelted from
ore.
3Man puts an end to the
darkness;
he searches the farthest
recesses
for ore in the blackest
darkness.

°15 ק שרידיו

נַחַל | מֵעִם־ גָּר הַנִּשְׁכָּחִים מִנִּי־ רָגֶל דַּלּוּ
they-dangle foot by the-ones-being-forgotten one-dwelling from-with shaft

מֵאֱנוֹשׁ נָעוּ׃ אֶרֶץ מִמֶּנָּה יֵצֵא־ לָחֶם וְתַחְתֶּיהָ
and-below-her food he-comes from-her earth (5) they-sway from-man

נֶהְפַּךְ כְּמוֹ־ אֵשׁ׃ מְקוֹם־ סַפִּיר אֲבָנֶיהָ וְעַפְרֹת
and-dusts-of rocks-of-her sapphire place-of (6) fire as he-is-transformed

זָהָב לוֹ׃ נָתִיב לֹא־ יְדָעוֹ עָיִט וְלֹא
and-not bird-of-prey he-knows-him not hidden-path (7) to-him gold

שְׁזָפַתּוּ עֵין אַיָּה׃ לֹא־ הִדְרִיכֻהוּ בְנֵי־ שָׁחַץ לֹא־
not pride sons-of they-set-foot-on-him not (8) falcon eye-of she-saw-him

עָדָה עָלָיו שָׁחַל׃ בַּחַלָּמִישׁ שָׁלַח יָדוֹ
hand-of-him he-assaults against-the-flinty-rock (9) lion on-him he-prowls

הָפַךְ מִשֹּׁרֶשׁ הָרִים׃ בַּצּוּרוֹת יְאֹרִים בִּקֵּעַ
he-digs tunnels through-the-rocks (10) mountains from-root-of he-lays-bare

וְכָל־ יְקָר רָאֲתָה עֵינוֹ׃ מִבְּכִי* נְהָרוֹת חִבֵּשׁ
he-searches rivers *sources-of (11) eye-of-him she-sees treasure and-all-of

וְתַעֲלֻמָהּ יֹצִא אוֹר׃ וְהַחָכְמָה מֵאַיִן
at-where? but-the-wisdom (12) light he-brings and-hidden-thing-of-her

תִּמָּצֵא וְאֵי זֶה מְקוֹם בִּינָה׃ לֹא־
not (13) understanding dwelling-of this and-where? can-she-be-found

יָדַע אֱנוֹשׁ עֶרְכָּהּ וְלֹא תִמָּצֵא בְּאֶרֶץ
in-land-of she-can-be-found and-not worth-of-her man he-comprehends

הַחַיִּים׃ תְּהוֹם אָמַר לֹא בִי־ הִיא וְיָם אָמַר אֵין עִמָּדִי׃
with-me not he-says and-sea she in-me not he-says deep (14) the-living-ones

לֹא־ יֻתַּן סְגוֹר תַּחְתֶּיהָ וְלֹא יִשָּׁקֵל
he-can-be-weighed and-not with-her fine-gold he-can-be-bought not (15)

כֶּסֶף מְחִירָהּ׃ לֹא־ תְסֻלֶּה בְּכֶתֶם אוֹפִיר בְּשֹׁהַם
with-onyx Ophir with-gold-of she-can-be-bought not (16) price-of-her silver

יָקָר וְסַפִּיר׃ לֹא־ יַעַרְכֶנָּה זָהָב וּזְכוֹכִית
or-crystal gold he-can-compare-with-her not (17) or-sapphire precious

וּתְמוּרָתָהּ כְּלִי־ פָז׃ רָאמוֹת וְגָבִישׁ לֹא יִזָּכֵר
he-is-mentioned not and-jasper corals (18) gold jewel-of or-having-of-her

וּמֶשֶׁךְ חָכְמָה מִפְּנִינִים׃ לֹא־ יַעַרְכֶנָּה פִּטְדַת־
topaz-of he-can-compare-with-her not (19) beyond-rubies wisdom and-price-of

כּוּשׁ בְּכֶתֶם טָהוֹר לֹא תְסֻלֶּה׃ וְהַחָכְמָה מֵאַיִן
from-where? and-the-wisdom (20) she-can-be-bought not pure with-gold Cush

תָּבוֹא וְאֵי זֶה מְקוֹם בִּינָה׃ וְנֶעֶלְמָה
and-she-is-hidden (21) understanding dwelling-of this and-where? she-comes

[4]Far from where people dwell
he cuts a shaft,
in places forgotten by the
foot of man;
far from men he dangles
and sways.
[5]The earth, from which food
comes,
is transformed below as by
fire;
[6]sapphires[b] come from its rocks,
and its dust contains
nuggets of gold.
[7]No bird of prey knows that
hidden path,
no falcon's eye has seen it.
[8]Proud beasts do not set foot on
it,
and no lion prowls there.
[9]Man's hand assaults the flinty
rock
and lays bare the roots of
the mountains.
[10]He tunnels through the rock;
his eyes see all its treasures.
[11]He searches[c] the sources of the
rivers
and brings hidden things to
light.

[12]"But where can wisdom be
found?
Where does understanding
dwell?
[13]Man does not comprehend its
worth;
it cannot be found in the
land of the living.
[14]The deep says, 'It is not in
me';
the sea says, 'It is not with
me.'
[15]It cannot be bought with the
finest gold,
nor can its price be weighed
in silver.
[16]It cannot be bought with the
gold of Ophir,
with precious onyx or
sapphires.
[17]Neither gold nor crystal can
compare with it,
nor can it be had for jewels
of gold.
[18]Coral and jasper are not
worthy of mention;
the price of wisdom is
beyond rubies.
[19]The topaz of Cush cannot
compare with it;
it cannot be bought with
pure gold.

[20]"Where then does wisdom
come from?
Where does understanding
dwell?
[21]It is hidden from the eyes of

[b]6 Or *lapis lazuli*; also in verse 16
[c]11 Septuagint, Aquila and Vulgate; Hebrew *He dams up*

**11* The NIV repoints this word as מַבְּכֵי; the text as pointed reads *from-weeping-of*.

מֵעֵינֵי כָל־ חָי וּמֵעוֹף הַשָּׁמַיִם נִסְתָּרָה׃
she-is-concealed the-airs and-from-bird-of living-thing every-of from-eyes-of

אֲבַדּוֹן וָמָוֶת אָמְרוּ בְּאָזְנֵינוּ שָׁמַעְנוּ שִׁמְעָהּ׃
rumor-of-her we-heard with-ears-of-us they-say and-Death Abaddon (22)

אֱלֹהִים הֵבִין דַּרְכָּהּ וְהוּא יָדַע אֶת־ מְקוֹמָהּ׃
dwelling-of-her *** he-knows and-he way-of-her he-understands God (23)

כִּי־ הוּא לִקְצוֹת־ הָאָרֶץ יַבִּיט תַּחַת כָּל־ הַשָּׁמַיִם יִרְאֶה׃
he-sees the-heavens all-of under he-views the-earth to-ends-of he for (24)

לַעֲשׂוֹת לָרוּחַ מִשְׁקָל וּמַיִם תִּכֵּן בְּמִדָּה׃
by-measure he-measured and-waters force of-the-wind to-establish (25)

בַּעֲשֹׂתוֹ לַמָּטָר חֹק וְדֶרֶךְ לַחֲזִיז קֹלוֹת׃
thunders for-storm-of and-path decree for-the-rain when-to-make-him (26)

אָז רָאָהּ וַיְסַפְּרָהּ הֱכִינָהּ וְגַם־
and-also he-confirmed-her and-he-appraised-her he-looked-at-her then (27)

חֲקָרָהּ׃ וַיֹּאמֶר ׀ לָאָדָם הֵן יִרְאַת אֲדֹנָי הִיא חָכְמָה
wisdom that Lord fear-of see! to-the-man and-he-said (28) he-tested-her

וְסוּר מֵרָע בִּינָה׃ וַיֹּסֶף אִיּוֹב שְׂאֵת
to-take-up Job and-he-continued (29:1) understanding from-evil and-to-shun

מְשָׁלוֹ וַיֹּאמַר׃ מִי־ יִתְּנֵנִי כְיַרְחֵי־ קֶדֶם
gone-by as-months-of he-would-grant-me who? (2) and-he-said discourse-of-him

כִּימֵי אֱלוֹהַּ יִשְׁמְרֵנִי׃ בְּהִלּוֹ נֵרוֹ עֲלֵי
upon lamp-of-him when-to-shine-him (3) he-watched-over-me God as-days-of

רֹאשִׁי לְאוֹרוֹ אֵלֶךְ חֹשֶׁךְ׃ כַּאֲשֶׁר הָיִיתִי בִּימֵי
in-days-of I-was as-when (4) darkness I-walked by-light-of-him head-of-me

חָרְפִּי בְּסוֹד אֱלוֹהַּ עֲלֵי אָהֳלִי׃ בְּעוֹד שַׁדַּי
Almighty when-still (5) house-of-me on God when-friendship-of prime-of-me

עִמָּדִי סְבִיבוֹתַי נְעָרָי׃ בִּרְחֹץ הֲלִיכַי
paths-of-me when-to-be-drenched (6) children-of-me ones-around-me with-me

בְּחֵמָה וְצוּר יָצוּק עִמָּדִי פַּלְגֵי־ שָׁמֶן׃ בְּצֵאתִי
when-to-go-me (7) olive-oil streams-of for-me being-poured-out and-rock with-cream

שַׁעַר עֲלֵי־ קָרֶת בָּרְחוֹב אָכִין מוֹשָׁבִי׃ רָאוּנִי נְעָרִים
young-men they-saw-me (8) seat-of-me I-took in-the-public-square city of gate

וְנֶחְבָּאוּ וִישִׁישִׁים קָמוּ עָמָדוּ׃ שָׂרִים
chief-men (9) they-stood they-rose and-old-men and-they-stepped-aside

עָצְרוּ בְמִלִּים וְכַף יָשִׂימוּ לְפִיהֶם׃ קוֹל־
voice-of (10) over-mouth-of-them they-covered and-hand from-speeches they-refrained

נְגִידִים נֶחְבָּאוּ וּלְשׁוֹנָם לְחִכָּם דָּבֵקָה׃
she-stuck to-roof-of-mouth-of-them and-tongue-of-them they-were-hushed nobles

every living thing,
concealed even from the birds of the air.
22 Destruction[d] and Death say,
'Only a rumor of it has reached our ears.'
23 God understands the way to it
and he alone knows where it dwells,
24 for he views the ends of the earth
and sees everything under the heavens.
25 When he established the force of the wind
and measured out the waters,
26 when he made a decree for the rain
and a path for the thunderstorm,
27 then he looked at wisdom and appraised it;
he confirmed it and tested it.
28 And he said to man,
'The fear of the Lord—that is wisdom,
and to shun evil is understanding.' "

29 Job continued his discourse:

2 "How I long for the months gone by,
for the days when God watched over me,
3 when his lamp shone upon my head
and by his light I walked through darkness!
4 Oh, for the days when I was in my prime,
when God's intimate friendship blessed my house,
5 when the Almighty was still with me
and my children were around me,
6 when my path was drenched with cream
and the rock poured out for me streams of olive oil.

7 "When I went to the gate of the city
and took my seat in the public square,
8 the young men saw me and stepped aside
and the old men rose to their feet;
9 the chief men refrained from speaking
and covered their mouths with their hands;
10 the voices of the nobles were hushed,
and their tongues stuck to the roof of their mouths.

d22 Hebrew *Abaddon*

כִּי אֹזֶן שָׁמְעָה וַתְּאַשְּׁרֵנִי וְעַיִן רָאֲתָה
she-saw and-eye then-she-spoke-well-of-me she-heard ear when (11)

וַתְּעִידֵנִי׃ כִּי־אֲמַלֵּט עָנִי מְשַׁוֵּעַ וְיָתוֹם
and-fatherless crying-out poor I-rescued because (12) then-she-commended-me

וְלֹא־עֹזֵר לוֹ׃ בִּרְכַּת אֹבֵד עָלַי תָּבֹא
she-came on-me man-dying blessing-of (13) to-him one-assisting and-not

וְלֵב אַלְמָנָה אַרְנִן׃ צֶדֶק לָבַשְׁתִּי וַיִּלְבָּשֵׁנִי
and-he-clothed-me I-put-on righteousness (14) I-made-sing widow and-heart-of

כִּמְעִיל וְצָנִיף מִשְׁפָּטִי׃ עֵינַיִם הָיִיתִי לַעִוֵּר וְרַגְלַיִם
and-feet to-the-blind I-was eyes (15) justice-of-me and-turban as-robe

לַפִּסֵּחַ אָנִי׃ אָב אָנֹכִי לָאֶבְיוֹנִים וְרִב לֹא־יָדַעְתִּי
I-knew not and-case to-the-needy-ones I father (16) I to-the-lame

אֶחְקְרֵהוּ׃ וָאֲשַׁבְּרָה מְתַלְּעוֹת עַוָּל וּמִשִּׁנָּיו
and-from-teeth-of-him wicked fangs-of and-I-broke (17) I-took-up-him

אַשְׁלִיךְ טָרֶף׃ וָאֹמַר עִם־קִנִּי אֶגְוָע
I-will-die house-of-me in and-I-thought (18) victim I-snatched

וְכַחוֹל אַרְבֶּה יָמִים׃ שָׁרְשִׁי פָתוּחַ אֱלֵי־מָיִם וְטַל
and-dew waters to reaching root-of-me (19) days I-number and-as-the-sand

יָלִין בִּקְצִירִי׃ כְּבוֹדִי חָדָשׁ עִמָּדִי
with-me fresh glory-of-me (20) on-branch-of-me he-will-spend-night

וְקַשְׁתִּי בְּיָדִי תַחֲלִיף׃ לִי־שָׁמְעוּ
they-listened to-me (21) she-will-be-new in-hand-of-me and-bow-of-me

וְיִחֵלּוּ וְיִדְּמוּ לְמוֹ עֲצָתִי׃
counsel-of-me for and-they-waited-in-silence and-they-were-expectant

אַחֲרֵי דְבָרִי לֹא יִשְׁנוּ וְעָלֵימוֹ תִּטֹּף מִלָּתִי׃
word-of-me she-fell and-on-them they-spoke-more not speech-of-me after (22)

וְיִחֲלוּ כְמָטָר לִי וּפִיהֶם פָּעֲרוּ
they-drank and-mouth-of-them for-me as-the-shower and-they-waited (23)

לְמַלְקוֹשׁ׃ אֶשְׂחַק אֲלֵהֶם לֹא יַאֲמִינוּ וְאוֹר
and-light-of they-believed not at-them I-smiled (24) as-spring-rain

פָּנַי לֹא יַפִּילוּן׃ אֶבְחַר דַּרְכָּם וְאֵשֵׁב רֹאשׁ
chief and-I-sat way-of-them I-chose (25) they-rejected not faces-of-me

וְאֶשְׁכּוֹן כְּמֶלֶךְ בַּגְּדוּד כַּאֲשֶׁר אֲבֵלִים יְנַחֵם׃ וְעַתָּה ׀
but-now (30:1) he-comforts mourners as-like among-the-troop as-king and-I-dwelt

שָׂחֲקוּ עָלַי צְעִירִים מִמֶּנִּי לְיָמִים אֲשֶׁר־מָאַסְתִּי
I-would-have-disdained whom in-days more-than-me men-young at-me they-mock

אֲבוֹתָם לָשִׁית עִם־כַּלְבֵי צֹאנִי׃ גַּם־כֹּחַ
strength-of also (2) sheep-of-me dogs-of with to-put fathers-of-them

11Whoever heard me spoke well
of me,
and those who saw me
commended me,
12because I rescued the poor
who cried for help,
and the fatherless who had
none to assist him.
13The man who was dying
blessed me;
I made the widow's heart
sing.
14I put on righteousness as my
clothing;
justice was my robe and my
turban.
15I was eyes to the blind
and feet to the lame.
16I was a father to the needy;
I took up the case of the
stranger.
17I broke the fangs of the
wicked
and snatched the victims
from their teeth.

18"I thought, 'I will die in my
own house,
my days as numerous as the
grains of sand.
19My roots will reach to the
water,
and the dew will lie all
night on my branches.
20My glory will remain fresh in
me,
the bow ever new in my
hand.'

21"Men listened to me
expectantly,
waiting in silence for my
counsel.
22After I had spoken, they spoke
no more;
my words fell gently on
their ears.
23They waited for me as for
showers
and drank in my words as
the spring rain.
24When I smiled at them, they
scarcely believed it;
the light of my face was
precious to them.[e]
25I chose the way for them and
sat as their chief;
I dwelt as a king among his
troops;
I was like one who comforts
mourners.

30 "But now they mock me,
men younger than I,
whose fathers I would have
disdained
to put with my sheep dogs.
2Of what use was the strength

[e]24 The meaning of the Hebrew for this clause is uncertain.

*11 Most mss have *ḥireq* under the *yod* (יִ־).

יְדֵיהֶם לָמָּה לִּי עָלֵימוֹ אָבַד כָּלַח׃ בְּחֶסֶר
from-want (3) vigor he-went from-them to-me what? hands-of-them

וּבְכָפָן גַּלְמוּד הַעֹרְקִים צִיָּה אֶמֶשׁ שׁוֹאָה
desolation night parched-land the-ones-roaming haggard and-from-hunger

וּמְשֹׁאָה׃ הַקֹּטְפִים מַלּוּחַ עֲלֵי־שִׂיחַ וְשֹׁרֶשׁ
and-root-of brush in salt-herb the-ones-gathering (4) and-wasteland

רְתָמִים לַחְמָם׃ מִן־גֵּו יְגֹרָשׁוּ יָרִיעוּ
they-shouted they-were-banished fellowship from (5) food-of-them broom-trees

עָלֵימוֹ כַּגַּנָּב׃ בַּעֲרוּץ נְחָלִים לִשְׁכֹּן חֹרֵי עָפָר
ground holes-of to-live stream-beds in-dryness-of (6) as-the-thief at-them

וְכֵפִים׃ בֵּין־שִׂיחִים יִנְהָקוּ תַּחַת חָרוּל יְסֻפָּחוּ׃
they-huddled underbrush under they-brayed bushes among (7) and-rocks

בְּנֵי־נָבָל גַּם־בְּנֵי בְלִי־שֵׁם נִכְּאוּ מִן־
from they-were-driven name without broods-of and baseness broods-of (8)

הָאָרֶץ׃ וְעַתָּה נְגִינָתָם הָיִיתִי וָאֱהִי לָהֶם
among-them and-I-became I-am mocking-song-of-them and-now (9) the-land

לְמִלָּה׃ תִּעֲבוּנִי רָחֲקוּ מֶנִּי וּמִפָּנַי
and-in-faces-of-me from-me they-keep-distance they-detest-me (10) as-byword

לֹא־חָשְׂכוּ רֹק׃ כִּי־יִתְרוֹ פִּתַּח וַיְעַנֵּנִי
and-he-afflicted-me he-unstrung bow-of-me now (11) spit they-hesitate not

וְרֶסֶן מִפָּנַי שִׁלֵּחוּ׃ עַל־יָמִין פִּרְחַח
tribe right on (12) they-throw-off in-presences-of-me and-restraint

יָקוּמוּ רַגְלַי שִׁלֵּחוּ וַיָּסֹלּוּ עָלַי אָרְחוֹת
ramps-of against-me and-they-build they-lay-snare feet-of-me they-attack

אֵידָם׃ נָתְסוּ נְתִיבָתִי לְהַוָּתִי־ יֹעִילוּ
they-succeed in-destruction-of-me road-of-me they-break-up (13) siege-of-them

לֹא עֹזֵר לָמוֹ׃ כְּפֶרֶץ רָחָב יֶאֱתָיוּ תַּחַת שֹׁאָה
ruin amid they-advance gaping as-breach (14) to-them one-helping not

הִתְגַּלְגָּלוּ׃ הָהְפַּךְ עָלַי בַּלָּהוֹת תִּרְדֹּף כָּרוּחַ
like-the-wind she-drives-away terrors over-me he-is-overwhelmed (15) they-roll-in

נְדִבָתִי וּכְעָב עָבְרָה יְשֻׁעָתִי׃ וְעַתָּה עָלַי
from-me and-now (16) safety-of-me she-vanishes and-like-cloud dignity-of-me

תִּשְׁתַּפֵּךְ נַפְשִׁי יֹאחֲזוּנִי יְמֵי־עֹנִי׃ לַיְלָה
night (17) suffering-of-me days-of they-grip-me life-of-me she-ebbs-away

עֲצָמַי נִקַּר מֵעָלָי וְעֹרְקַי לֹא יִשְׁכָּבוּן׃
they-rest never and-ones-gnawing-me from-upon-me he-pierces bones-of-me

בְּרָב־כֹּחַ יִתְחַפֵּשׂ לְבוּשִׁי כְּפִי
like-neck-of clothing-of-me he-becomes-like power in-greatness-of (18)

°11 ק יתרי

of their hands to me,
since their vigor had gone
from them?
3 Haggard from want and
hunger,
they roamed[f] the parched
land
in desolate wastelands at
night.
4 In the brush they gathered salt
herbs,
and their food[g] was the root
of the broom tree.
5 They were banished from their
fellow men,
shouted at as if they were
thieves.
6 They were forced to live in the
dry stream beds,
among the rocks and in
holes in the ground.
7 They brayed among the
bushes
and huddled in the
underbrush.
8 A base and nameless brood,
they were driven out of the
land.

9 "And now their sons mock me
in song;
I have become a byword
among them.
10 They detest me and keep their
distance;
they do not hesitate to spit
in my face.
11 Now that God has unstrung
my bow and afflicted me,
they throw off restraint in
my presence.
12 On my right the tribe[h] attacks;
they lay snares for my feet,
they build their siege ramps
against me.
13 They break up my road;
they succeed in destroying
me—
without anyone's helping
them.[i]
14 They advance as through a
gaping breach;
amid the ruins they come
rolling in.
15 Terrors overwhelm me;
my dignity is driven away
as by the wind,
my safety vanishes like a
cloud.

16 "And now my life ebbs away;
days of suffering grip me.
17 Night pierces my bones;
my gnawing pains never
rest.
18 In his great power ⌊God⌋
becomes like clothing to
me[j];

f3 Or *gnawed* g4 Or *fuel*
h12 The meaning of the Hebrew for this word is uncertain.
i13 Or *me. / 'No one can help him,' ⌊they say⌋.*
j18 Hebrew; Septuagint *⌊God⌋ grasps my clothing*

כְּתָנְתִּי יַאַזְרֵנִי׃ הֹרָנִי לַחֹמֶר וָאֶתְמַשֵּׁל
and-I-am-reduced into-the-mud he-throws-me (19) he-binds-me garment-of-me

כֶּעָפָר וָאֵפֶר׃ אֲשַׁוַּע אֵלֶיךָ וְלֹא תַעֲנֵנִי עָמַדְתִּי
I-stand-up you-answer-me but-not to-you I-cry-out (20) and-ash to-the-dust

וַתִּתְבֹּנֶן בִּי׃ תֵּהָפֵךְ לְאַכְזָר לִי בְּעֹצֶם
with-might-of on-me with-ruthlessness you-turn (21) at-me but-you-look

יָדְךָ תִשְׂטְמֵנִי׃ תִּשָּׂאֵנִי אֶל־ רוּחַ תַּרְכִּיבֵנִי
you-drive-me wind before you-snatch-up-me (22) you-attack-me hand-of-you

וּתְמֹגְגֵנִי תְּשֻׁוָּה׃ כִּי־ יָדַעְתִּי מָוֶת תְּשִׁיבֵנִי
you-will-bring-down-me death I-know for (23) storm and-you-toss-about-me

וּבֵית מוֹעֵד לְכָל־ חָי׃ אַךְ לֹא־ בְעִי
on-broken-man no-one surely (24) living for-all-of appointed and-place-of

יִשְׁלַח־ יָד אִם־ בְּפִידוֹ לָהֶן שׁוּעַ׃ אִם־ לֹא
not indeed (25) cry-for-help to-them in-distress-of-him when hand he-lays

בָכִיתִי לִקְשֵׁה־ יוֹם עָגְמָה נַפְשִׁי לָאֶבְיוֹן׃ כִּי
when (26) for-the-poor soul-of-me she-grieved day for-troubled-of I-wept

טוֹב קִוִּיתִי וַיָּבֹא רָע וַאֲיַחֲלָה לְאוֹר וַיָּבֹא
then-he-came for-light when-I-looked evil then-he-came I-hoped-for good

אֹפֶל׃ מֵעַי רֻתְּחוּ וְלֹא־ דָמּוּ קִדְּמֻנִי
they-confront-me they-stop and-never they-churn insides-of-me (27) darkness

יְמֵי־ עֹנִי׃ קֹדֵר הִלַּכְתִּי בְּלֹא חַמָּה קַמְתִּי
I-stand-up sun by-not I-go-about being-blackened (28) suffering-of-me days-of

בַקָּהָל אֲשַׁוֵּעַ׃ אָח הָיִיתִי לְתַנִּים וְרֵעַ
and-companion of-jackals I-became brother (29) I-cry-for-help in-the-assembly

לִבְנוֹת יַעֲנָה׃ עוֹרִי שָׁחַר מֵעָלָי וְעַצְמִי־
and-body-of-me from-on-me she-grows-black skin-of-me (30) owl to-daughters-of

חָרָה מִנִּי־ חֹרֶב׃ וַיְהִי לְאֵבֶל כִּנֹּרִי וְעֻגָבִי
and-flute-of-me harp-of-me to-mourning and-he-is (31) fever with she-burns

לְקוֹל בֹּכִים׃ בְּרִית כָּרַתִּי לְעֵינָי וּמָה
so-how? with-eyes-of-me I-made covenant (31:1) ones-wailing to-sound-of

אֶתְבּוֹנֵן עַל־ בְּתוּלָה׃ וּמֶה׀ חֵלֶק אֱלוֹהַּ מִמַּעַל וְנַחֲלַת
and-heritage-of from-above God lot-of for-what? (2) girl at can-I-look

שַׁדַּי מִמְּרֹמִים׃ הֲלֹא־ אֵיד לְעַוָּל וְנֵכֶר לְפֹעֲלֵי
for-ones-doing-of and-disaster for-wicked ruin not? (3) from-heights Almighty

אָוֶן׃ הֲלֹא־ הוּא יִרְאֶה דְרָכָי וְכָל־ צְעָדַי יִסְפּוֹר׃
he-counts steps-of-me and-every-of ways-of-me he-sees he not? (4) wrong

אִם־ הָלַכְתִּי עִם־ שָׁוְא וַתַּחַשׁ עַל־ מִרְמָה רַגְלִי׃
foot-of-me deceit after or-she-hurried falsehood in I-walked if (5)

he binds me like the neck of
my garment.
19He throws me into the mud,
and I am reduced to dust
and ashes.

20"I cry out to you, O God, but
you do not answer;
I stand up, but you merely
look at me.
21You turn on me ruthlessly;
with the might of your hand
you attack me.
22You snatch me up and drive
me before the wind;
you toss me about in the
storm.
23I know you will bring me
down to death,
to the place appointed for all
the living.

24"Surely no one lays a hand on
a broken man
when he cries for help in
his distress.
25Have I not wept for those in
trouble?
Has not my soul grieved for
the poor?
26Yet when I hoped for good,
evil came;
when I looked for light,
then came darkness.
27The churning inside me never
stops;
days of suffering confront
me.
28I go about blackened, but not
by the sun;
I stand up in the assembly
and cry for help.
29I have become a brother of
jackals,
a companion of owls.
30My skin grows black and
peels;
my body burns with fever.
31My harp is tuned to mourning,
and my flute to the sound of
wailing.

31 "I made a covenant with
my eyes
not to look lustfully at a girl.
2For what is man's lot from
God above,
his heritage from the
Almighty on high?
3Is it not ruin for the wicked,
disaster for those who do
wrong?
4Does he not see my ways
and count my every step?

5"If I have walked in falsehood
or my foot has hurried after
deceit—

°22 ק תושיה

יִשְׁקְלֵנִי בְמֹאזְנֵי־ צֶדֶק וְיֵדַע אֱלוֹהַּ
God and-he-will-know honesty in-scales-of let-him-weigh-me (6)

תֻּמָּתִי׃ אִם תִּטֶּה אַשֻּׁרִי מִנִּי הַדָּרֶךְ וְאַחַר
if-after the-path from step-of-me she-turned if (7) blamelessness-of-me

עֵינַי הָלַךְ לִבִּי וּבְכַפַּי דָּבַק מֻאוּם׃*
defilement he-clings if-to-hands-of-me heart-of-me he-followed eyes-of-me

אֶזְרְעָה וְאַחֵר יֹאכֵל וְצֶאֱצָאַי יְשֹׁרָשׁוּ׃ אִם־
if (9) may-they-be-uprooted and-crops-of-me may-he-eat but-other I-sow (8)

נִפְתָּה לִבִּי עַל־ אִשָּׁה וְעַל־ פֶּתַח רֵעִי אָרָבְתִּי׃
I-lurked neighbor-of-me door-of or-at woman by heart-of-me he-was-enticed

תִּטְחַן לְאַחֵר אִשְׁתִּי וְעָלֶיהָ יִכְרְעוּן אֲחֵרִין׃
others may-they-sleep and-with-her wife-of-me for-another may-she-grind (10)

כִּי־הִוא זִמָּה וְהִיא עָוֹן פְּלִילִים׃ כִּי אֵשׁ הִיא עַד־אֲבַדּוֹן
Abaddon to she fire for (12) judgments sin and-that shameful that for (11)

תֹּאכֵל וּבְכָל־ תְּבוּאָתִי תְשָׁרֵשׁ׃ אִם־ אֶמְאַס
I-denied if (13) she-would-uproot harvest-of-me and-to-all-of she-burns

מִשְׁפַּט עַבְדִּי וַאֲמָתִי בְּרִבָם
when-grievance-of-them and-maidservant-of-me manservant-of-me justice-of

עִמָּדִי׃ וּמָה אֶעֱשֶׂה כִּי־ יָקוּם אֵל וְכִי־ יִפְקֹד
he-calls and-when God he-confronts when will-I-do then-what? (14) against-me

מָה אֲשִׁיבֶנּוּ׃ הֲלֹא־ בַבֶּטֶן עֹשֵׂנִי עָשָׂהוּ
he-made-him one-making-me in-the-womb not? (15) will-I-answer-him what?

וַיְכֻנֶנּוּ בָּרֶחֶם אֶחָד׃ אִם־ אֶמְנַע מֵחֵפֶץ דַּלִּים
poor-ones from-desire-of I-denied if (16) same in-the-womb and-he-formed-us

וְעֵינֵי אַלְמָנָה אֲכַלֶּה׃ וְאֹכַל פִּתִּי לְבַדִּי וְלֹא־
and-not by-myself bread-of-me if-I-ate (17) I-let-grow-weary widow or-eyes-of

אָכַל יָתוֹם מִמֶּנָּה׃ כִּי מִנְּעוּרַי גְּדֵלַנִי כְאָב
as-father he-was-reared-by-me from-youths-of-me but (18) of-her fatherless he-ate

וּמִבֶּטֶן אִמִּי אַנְחֶנָּה׃ אִם־אֶרְאֶה אוֹבֵד
one-perishing I-saw if (19) I-guided-her mother-of-me and-from-womb-of

מִבְּלִי לְבוּשׁ וְאֵין כְּסוּת לָאֶבְיוֹן׃ אִם־ לֹא
not if (20) to-the-needy-man garment or-no clothing from-lack-of

בֵרְכוּנִי חֲלָצָו וּמִגֵּז כְּבָשַׂי יִתְחַמָּם׃
he-was-warmed sheeps-of-me or-with-fleece-of hearts-of-him they-blessed-me

אִם־הֲנִיפוֹתִי עַל־ יָתוֹם יָדִי כִּי־ אֶרְאֶה בַשַּׁעַר
in-the-court I-knew when hand-of-me fatherless against I-raised if (21)

עֶזְרָתִי׃ כְּתֵפִי מִשִּׁכְמָה תִפּוֹל וְאֶזְרֹעִי
and-arm-of-me let-her-fall from-shoulder arm-of-me (22) influence-of-me

6 let God weigh me in honest scales
and he will know that I am blameless—
7 if my steps have turned from the path,
if my heart has been led by my eyes,
or if my hands have been defiled,
8 then may others eat what I have sown,
and may my crops be uprooted.

9 "If my heart has been enticed by a woman,
or if I have lurked at my neighbor's door,
10 then may my wife grind another man's grain,
and may other men sleep with her.
11 For that would have been shameful,
a sin to be judged.
12 It is a fire that burns to Destruction[k];
it would have uprooted my harvest.

13 "If I have denied justice to my menservants and maidservants
when they had a grievance against me,
14 what will I do when God confronts me?
What will I answer when called to account?
15 Did not he who made me in the womb make them?
Did not the same one form us both within our mothers?

16 "If I have denied the desires of the poor
or let the eyes of the widow grow weary,
17 if I have kept my bread to myself,
not sharing it with the fatherless—
18 but from my youth I reared him as would a father,
and from my birth I guided the widow—
19 if I have seen anyone perishing for lack of clothing,
or a needy man without a garment,
20 and his heart did not bless me
for warming him with the fleece from my sheep,
21 if I have raised my hand against the fatherless,
knowing that I had influence in court,
22 then let my arm fall from the shoulder,

k 12 Hebrew *Abaddon*

*7 Most mss have no *qibbuts* under the *mem* (מְאוּם)

° 11a ק היא
° 11b ק והוא
° 20 ק חלציו

מִקָּנָה תִשָּׁבֵר׃ (23) כִּי פַחַד אֵלַי אֵיד אֵל
God destruction-of to-me dread for (23) let-her-be-broken-off at-joint

וּמִשְּׂאֵתוֹ לֹא אוּכָל׃ (24) אִם־שַׂמְתִּי זָהָב כִּסְלִי
trust-of-me gold I-put if (24) I-could-do not and-because-of-splendor-of-him

וְלַכֶּתֶם אָמַרְתִּי מִבְטַחִי׃ (25) אִם־אֶשְׂמַח כִּי־רַב
great that I-rejoiced if (25) security-of-me I-said or-to-the-pure-gold

חֵילִי וְכִי־כַבִּיר מָצְאָה יָדִי׃ (26) אִם־אֶרְאֶה אוֹר
sun I-regarded if (26) hand-of-me she-gained fortune and-that wealth-of-me

כִּי יָהֵל וְיָרֵחַ יָקָר הֹלֵךְ׃ (27) וַיִּפְתְּ
so-he-was-enticed (27) moving splendor or-moon he-was-radiant that

בַּסֵּתֶר לִבִּי וַתִּשַּׁק יָדִי לְפִי׃
to-mouth-of-me hand-of-me and-she-kissed heart-of-me in-the-secret

(28) גַּם־הוּא עָוֺן פְּלִילִי כִּי־כִחַשְׁתִּי לָאֵל מִמָּעַל׃
on-high to-God I-would-be-unfaithful for judgment sin this also (28)

(29) אִם־אֶשְׂמַח בְּפִיד מְשַׂנְאִי וְהִתְעֹרַרְתִּי כִּי־
that or-I-gloated one-being-enemy-of-me at-misfortune-of I-rejoiced if (29)

מְצָאוֹ רָע׃ (30) וְלֹא־נָתַתִּי לַחֲטֹא חִכִּי לִשְׁאֹל
to-invoke mouth-of-me to-sin I-allowed now-not (30) trouble he-came-to-him

בְּאָלָה נַפְשׁוֹ׃ (31) אִם־לֹא אָמְרוּ מְתֵי אָהֳלִי מִי־
who? house-of-me men-of they-said never if (31) life-of-him to-curse

יִתֵּן מִבְּשָׂרוֹ לֹא נִשְׂבָּע׃ (32) בַּחוּץ לֹא־
not in-the-street (32) he-had-fill not from-meat-of-him he-would-give

יָלִין גֵּר דְּלָתַי לָאֹרַח* אֶפְתָּח׃ (33) אִם־כִּסִּיתִי
I-concealed if (33) I-opened *to-the-road doors-of-me stranger he-spent-night

כְאָדָם פְּשָׁעָי לִטְמוֹן בְּחֻבִּי עֲוֺנִי׃ (34) כִּי אֶעֱרוֹץ ׀
I-feared because (34) guilt-of-me in-heart-of-me to-hide sins-of-me as-man

הָמוֹן רַבָּה וּבוּז־מִשְׁפָּחוֹת יְחִתֵּנִי וָאֶדֹּם לֹא־
not that-I-kept-silent he-made-dread-me clans and-contempt-of greatly crowd

אֵצֵא פָתַח׃ (35) מִי יִתֶּן־לִי ׀ שֹׁמֵעַ לִי הֶן־
see! to-me one-hearing to-me he-would-give who? (35) door I-went-out

תָּוִי שַׁדַּי יַעֲנֵנִי וְסֵפֶר כָּתַב
let-him-write and-indictment let-him-answer-me Almighty signature-of-me

אִישׁ רִיבִי׃ (36) אִם־לֹא עַל־שִׁכְמִי אֶשָּׂאֶנּוּ
I-would-wear-him shoulder-of-me on surely indeed (36) accusation-of-me man-of

אֶעֶנְדֶנּוּ עֲטָרוֹת לִי׃ (37) מִסְפַּר צְעָדַי אַגִּידֶנּוּ
I-would-give-him steps-of-me account-of (37) on-me crowns I-would-put-on-him

כְּמוֹ־נָגִיד אֲקָרְבֶנּוּ׃ (38) אִם־עָלַי אַדְמָתִי תִזְעָק
she-cries-out land-of-me against-me if (38) I-would-approach-him prince like

let it be broken off at the
joint.
23For I dreaded destruction from
God,
and for fear of his splendor
I could not do such
things.

24"If I have put my trust in gold
or said to pure gold, 'You
are my security,'
25if I have rejoiced over my
great wealth,
the fortune my hands had
gained,
26if I have regarded the sun in
its radiance
or the moon moving in
splendor,
27so that my heart was secretly
enticed
and my hand offered them a
kiss of homage,
28then these also would be sins
to be judged,
for I would have been
unfaithful to God on
high.

29"If I have rejoiced at my
enemy's misfortune
or gloated over the trouble
that came to him—
30I have not allowed my mouth
to sin
by invoking a curse against
his life—
31if the men of my household
have never said,
'Who has not had his fill of
Job's meat?'—
32but no stranger had to spend
the night in the street,
for my door was always
open to the traveler—
33if I have concealed my sin as
men do,[l]
by hiding my guilt in my
heart
34because I so feared the crowd
and so dreaded the
contempt of the clans
that I kept silent and would
not go outside

35("Oh, that I had someone to
hear me!
I sign now my defense—let
the Almighty answer me;
let my accuser put his
indictment in writing.
36Surely I would wear it on my
shoulder,
I would put it on like a
crown.
37I would give him an account
of my every step;
like a prince I would
approach him.)—

38"if my land cries out against
me

l33 Or *as Adam did*

*32 The NIV repoints the word as רֵחַ–, *to-the-one-traveling*.

וְיַחַד תְּלָמֶיהָ יִבְכָּיוּן׃ אִם־ כֹּחָהּ אָכַלְתִּי
I-devoured yield-of-her if (39) they-weep furrows-of-her and-together

בְלִי־ כָסֶף וְנֶפֶשׁ בְּעָלֶיהָ הִפָּחְתִּי׃ תַּחַת חִטָּה ׀
wheat instead-of (40) I-broke tenants-of-her or-spirit-of payment without

יֵצֵא חוֹחַ וְתַחַת־ שְׂעֹרָה בָאְשָׁה תַּמּוּ דִּבְרֵי אִיּוֹב׃
Job words-of they-are-ended weed barley and-instead-of brier let-him-come-up

וַיִּשְׁבְּתוּ שְׁלֹשֶׁת הָאֲנָשִׁים הָאֵלֶּה מֵעֲנוֹת אֶת־אִיּוֹב
Job *** from-to-answer the-these the-men three-of so-they-stopped (32:1)

כִּי הוּא צַדִּיק בְּעֵינָיו׃ וַיִּחַר אַף ׀ אֱלִיהוּא
Elihu anger-of but-he-burned (2) in-eyes-of-him righteous he because

בֶן־ בַּרַכְאֵל הַבּוּזִי מִמִּשְׁפַּחַת רָם בְּאִיּוֹב חָרָה אַפּוֹ
anger-of-him he-burned against-Job Ram of-family-of the-Buzite Barakel son-of

עַל־ צַדְּקוֹ נַפְשׁוֹ מֵאֱלֹהִים׃ וּבִשְׁלֹשֶׁת
also-against-three-of (93) rather-than-God self-of-him to-justify-him because

רֵעָיו חָרָה אַפּוֹ עַל אֲשֶׁר לֹא־ מָצְאוּ מַעֲנֶה
refutation they-found not that because anger-of-him he-burned friends-of-him

וַיַּרְשִׁיעוּ אֶת־אִיּוֹב׃ וֶאֱלִיהוּ חִכָּה אֶת־אִיּוֹב בִּדְבָרִים
with-speeches Job *** he-waited now-Elihu (4) Job *** yet-they-condemned

כִּי זְקֵנִים־ הֵמָּה מִמֶּנּוּ לְיָמִים׃ וַיַּרְא אֱלִיהוּא כִּי אֵין
no that Elihu when-he-saw (5) in-days more-than-he they ones-old because

מַעֲנֶה בְּפִי שְׁלֹשֶׁת הָאֲנָשִׁים וַיִּחַר אַפּוֹ׃
anger-of-him then-he-was-aroused the-men three-of in-mouth-of saying

וַיַּעַן ׀ אֱלִיהוּא בֶן־ בַּרַכְאֵל הַבּוּזִי וַיֹּאמַר צָעִיר אֲנִי
I young and-he-said the-Buzite Barakel son-of Elihu so-he-responded (6)

לְיָמִים וְאַתֶּם יְשִׁישִׁים עַל־ כֵּן זָחַלְתִּי וָאִירָא ׀ מֵחַוֺּת
from-to-tell and-I-feared I-was-afraid this for old-ones and-you in-days

דֵּעִי אֶתְכֶם׃ אָמַרְתִּי יָמִים יְדַבֵּרוּ וְרֹב שָׁנִים
years and-many-of they-should-speak days I-thought (7) you knowledge-of-me

יֹדִיעוּ חָכְמָה׃ אָכֵן רוּחַ־ הִיא בֶאֱנוֹשׁ וְנִשְׁמַת שַׁדַּי
Almighty even-breath-of in-man she spirit but (8) wisdom they-should-teach

תְּבִינֵם׃ לֹא־ רַבִּים יֶחְכָּמוּ וּזְקֵנִים
nor-aged-ones they-are-wise many not (9) she-gives-understanding-to-them

יָבִינוּ מִשְׁפָּט׃ לָכֵן אָמַרְתִּי שִׁמְעָה־ לִּי אֲחַוֶּה
I-will-tell to-me listen! I-say therefore (10) right they-understand

דֵעִי אַף־אָנִי׃ הֵן הוֹחַלְתִּי ׀ לְדִבְרֵיכֶם אָזִין
I-listened through-speeches-of-you I-waited see! (11) I also knowledge-of-me

עַד־ תְּבוּנֹתֵיכֶם עַד־ תַּחְקְרוּן מִלִּין׃ וְעָדֵיכֶם
and-to-you (12) words you-searched-for while reasonings-of-you to

and all its furrows are wet
with tears,
39 if I have devoured its yield
without payment
or broken the spirit of its
tenants,
40 then let briers come up instead
of wheat
and weeds instead of
barley."

The words of Job are ended.

Elihu

32 So these three men stopped
answering Job, because he
was righteous in his own eyes.
2 But Elihu son of Barakel the Bu-
zite, of the family of Ram, became
very angry with Job for justifying
himself rather than God. 3 He was
also angry with the three friends,
because they had found no way to
refute Job, and yet had condemned him.[m] 4 Now Elihu had
waited before speaking to Job because they were older than he.
5 But when he saw that the three
men had nothing more to say, his
anger was aroused.
6 So Elihu son of Barakel the Bu-
zite said:

"I am young in years,
and you are old;
that is why I was fearful,
not daring to tell you what I
know.
7 I thought, 'Age should speak;
advanced years should teach
wisdom.'
8 But it is the spirit[n] in a man,
the breath of the Almighty,
that gives him
understanding.
9 It is not only the old[o] who are
wise,
not only the aged who
understand what is right.

10 "Therefore I say: Listen to me;
I too will tell you what I
know.
11 I waited while you spoke,
I listened to your reasoning;
while you were searching for
words,

[m]3 Masoretic Text; an ancient Hebrew scribal tradition *Job, and so had condemned God*

[n]8 Or *Spirit*; also in verse 18

[o]9 Or *many*; or *great*

אֶתְבּוֹנָן וְהִנֵּה אֵין לְאִיּוֹב מוֹכִיחַ עוֹנֶה
answering proving-wrong to-Job no-one but-see! I-gave-attention

אֲמָרָיו מִכֶּם׃ פֶּן־ תֹּאמְרוּ מָצָאנוּ חָכְמָה אֵל
God wisdom we-found you-say not (13) of-you arguments-of-him

יִדְּפֶנּוּ לֹא־ אִישׁ׃ וְלֹא־ עָרַךְ אֵלַי מִלִּין
words against-me he-marshaled but-not (14) man not let-him-refute-him

וּבְאִמְרֵיכֶם לֹא אֲשִׁיבֶנּוּ׃ חַתּוּ לֹא־
not they-are-dismayed (15) I-will-answer-him not and-with-arguments-of-you

עָנוּ עוֹד הֶעְתִּיקוּ מֵהֶם מִלִּים׃ וְהוֹחַלְתִּי כִּי־ לֹא
not because now-must-I-wait (16) words from-them they-failed more they-say

יְדַבֵּרוּ כִּי עָמְדוּ לֹא־ עָנוּ עוֹד׃ אַעֲנֶה אַף־אֲנִי
I also I-will-say (17) more they-reply not they-stand because they-speak

חֶלְקִי אֲחַוֶּה דֵעִי אַף־אָנִי׃ כִּי מָלֵתִי מִלִּים
words I-am-full for (18) I also knowledge-of-me I-will-tell portion-of-me

הֱצִיקַתְנִי רוּחַ בִּטְנִי׃ הִנֵּה־ בִטְנִי כְּיַיִן לֹא־
not like-wine inside-of-me see! (19) inside-of-me spirit-of she-compels-me

יִפָּתֵחַ כְּאֹבוֹת חֲדָשִׁים יִבָּקֵעַ׃ אֲדַבְּרָה
I-must-speak (20) he-bursts new-ones like-wineskins he-is-open

וְיִרְוַח־ לִי אֶפְתַּח שְׂפָתַי וְאֶעֱנֶה׃ אַל־
not (21) and-I-must-reply lips-of-me I-must-open to-me and-he-will-relieve

נָא אֶשָּׂא פְנֵי־ אִישׁ וְאֶל־ אָדָם לֹא אֲכַנֶּה׃
I-will-flatter not man or-to man faces-of I-will-show-partiality now!

כִּי לֹא יָדַעְתִּי אֲכַנֶּה כִּמְעַט יִשָּׂאֵנִי
he-would-take-away-me as-soon I-can-flatter I-am-skilled not for (22)

עֹשֵׂנִי׃ וְאוּלָם שְׁמַע־ נָא אִיּוֹב מִלָּי וְכָל־
and-all-of words-of-me Job now! listen! but-now (33:1) One-Making-me

דְּבָרַי הַאֲזִינָה׃ הִנֵּה־ נָא פָּתַחְתִּי פִי דִּבְּרָה
she-speaks mouth-of-me I-open now! see! (2) pay-attention! sayings-of-me

לְשׁוֹנִי בְחִכִּי׃ יֹשֶׁר־ לִבִּי אֲמָרָי
words-of-me heart-of-me uprightness-of (3) in-mouth-of-me tongue-of-me

וְדַעַת שְׂפָתַי בָּרוּר מִלֵּלוּ׃ רוּחַ־ אֵל
God Spirit-of (4) they-speak being-sincere lips-of-me and-knowledge-of

עָשָׂתְנִי וְנִשְׁמַת שַׁדַּי תְּחַיֵּנִי׃ אִם־ תּוּכַל
you-can if (5) she-gives-life-to-me Almighty and-breath-of she-made-me

הֲשִׁיבֵנִי עֶרְכָה לְפָנַי הִתְיַצָּבָה׃ הֵן־אֲנִי כְפִיךָ
like-mouth-of-you I see! (6) prepare-yourself! before-me confront! answer-me!

לָאֵל מֵחֹמֶר קֹרַצְתִּי גַם־ אָנִי׃ הִנֵּה אֵמָתִי לֹא
not fear-of-me see! (7) I also I-was-taken from-clay before-God

12 I gave you my full attention.
But not one of you has proved
Job wrong;
none of you has answered
his arguments.
13 Do not say, 'We have found
wisdom;
let God refute him, not
man.'
14 But Job has not marshaled his
words against me,
and I will not answer him
with your arguments.

15 "They are dismayed and have
no more to say;
words have failed them.
16 Must I wait, now that they are
silent,
now that they stand there
with no reply?
17 I too will have my say;
I too will tell what I know.
18 For I am full of words,
and the spirit within me
compels me;
19 inside I am like bottled-up
wine,
like new wineskins ready to
burst.
20 I must speak and find relief;
I must open my lips and
reply.
21 I will show partiality to no
one,
nor will I flatter any man;
22 for if I were skilled in flattery,
my Maker would soon take
me away.

33 "But now, Job, listen to
my words;
pay attention to everything
I say.
2 I am about to open my mouth;
my words are on the tip of
my tongue.
3 My words come from an
upright heart;
my lips sincerely speak what
I know.
4 The Spirit of God has made
me;
the breath of the Almighty
gives me life.
5 Answer me then, if you can;
prepare yourself and
confront me.
6 I am just like you before God;
I too have been taken from
clay.
7 No fear of me should alarm
you,

תְבַעֲתֶךָ וְאַכְפִּי עָלֶיךָ לֹא־ יִכְבָּד׃
he-should-be-heavy not upon-you or-hand-of-me she-should-alarm-you

אַךְ אָמַרְתָּ בְאָזְנָי וְקוֹל מִלִּין אֶשְׁמָע׃ זַךְ אֲנִי
I pure (9) I-heard words and-sound-of in-ears-of-me you-said but (8)

בְּלִי פָשַׁע חַף אָנֹכִי וְלֹא עָוֺן לִי׃ הֵן תְּנוּאוֹת עָלַי יִמְצָא
he-found with-me faults yet (10) to-me guilt and-not I clean sin without

יַחְשְׁבֵנִי לְאוֹיֵב לוֹ׃ יָשֵׂם בַּסַּד רַגְלָי
feet-of-me in-the-shackle he-fastens (11) of-him as-being-enemy he-considers-me

יִשְׁמֹר כָּל־ אָרְחֹתָי׃ הֶן־ זֹאת לֹא־ צָדַקְתָּ אֶעֱנֶךָּ
I-tell-you you-are-right not this but (12) paths-of-me all-of he-watches

כִּי־ יִרְבֶּה אֱלוֹהַּ* מֵאֱנוֹשׁ׃ מַדּוּעַ אֵלָיו רִיבוֹתָ כִּי כָל־
any-of that you-complain to-him why? (13) more-than-man God he-is-great for

דְּבָרָיו לֹא־ יַעֲנֶה׃ כִּי־ בְאַחַת יְדַבֶּר־ אֵל וּבִשְׁתַּיִם לֹא
not now-in-two God he-speaks in-one for (14) he-answers not words-of-him

יְשׁוּרֶנָּה׃ בַּחֲלוֹם ׀ חֶזְיוֹן לַיְלָה בִּנְפֹל תַּרְדֵּמָה עַל־
on deep-sleep when-to-fall night vision-of in-dream (15) he-perceives-her

אֲנָשִׁים בִּתְנוּמוֹת עֲלֵי מִשְׁכָּב׃ אָז יִגְלֶה אֹזֶן אֲנָשִׁים וּבְמֹסָרָם
and-with-warning-of-them men ear-of he-may-open then (16) bed in in-slumbers men

יַחְתֹּם†׃ לְהָסִיר אָדָם מַעֲשֶׂה וְגֵוָה מִגֶּבֶר יְכַסֶּה׃
he-keeps from-man and-pride deed man to-turn (17) †he-may-seal

יַחְשֹׂךְ נַפְשׁוֹ מִנִּי־ שָׁחַת וְחַיָּתוֹ מֵעֲבֹר
from-to-perish and-life-of-him pit from soul-of-him he-preserves (18)

בַּשָּׁלַח׃ וְהוּכַח בְמַכְאוֹב עַל־ מִשְׁכָּבוֹ וְרִיב
with-distress-of bed-of-him on by-pain or-he-is-chastened (19) by-the-sword

עֲצָמָיו אֵתָן׃ וְזִהֲמַתּוּ חַיָּתוֹ לָחֶם
food being-of-him so-she-finds-repulsive-him (20) constant bones-of-him

וְנַפְשׁוֹ מַאֲכַל תַּאֲוָה׃ יִכֶל בְּשָׂרוֹ מֵרֹאִי
from-sight flesh-of-him he-wastes-away (21) choice meal-of and-soul-of-him

וְשֻׁפִּי עַצְמוֹתָיו לֹא רֻאּוּ׃ וַתִּקְרַב
and-she-draws-near (22) they-were-seen not bones-of-him now-they-stick-out

לַשַּׁחַת נַפְשׁוֹ וְחַיָּתוֹ לַמְמִתִים׃ אִם־
if (23) to-the-ones-bringing-death and-life-of-him soul-of-him to-the-pit

יֵשׁ עָלָיו ׀ מַלְאָךְ מֵלִיץ אֶחָד מִנִּי־ אָלֶף לְהַגִּיד לְאָדָם
to-man to-tell thousand from one one-mediating angel beside-him there-is

יָשְׁרוֹ׃ וַיְחֻנֶּנּוּ וַיֹּאמֶר
and-he-should-say then-he-should-be-gracious-to-him (24) right-of-him

פְּדָעֵהוּ מֵרֶדֶת שַׁחַת מָצָאתִי כֹפֶר׃ רֻטֲפַשׁ
he-is-renewed (25) ransom I-found pit from-to-go-down spare-him!

nor should my hand be
heavy upon you.
[8]"But you have said in my
hearing—
I heard the very words—
[9]'I am pure and without sin;
I am clean and free from
guilt.
[10]Yet God has found fault with
me;
he considers me his enemy.
[11]He fastens my feet in shackles;
he keeps close watch on all
my paths.'
[12]"But I tell you, in this you are
not right,
for God is greater than man.
[13]Why do you complain to him
that he answers none of
man's words[p]?
[14]For God does speak—now one
way, now another—
though man may not
perceive it.
[15]In a dream, in a vision of the
night,
when deep sleep falls on
men
as they slumber in their
beds,
[16]he may speak in their ears
and terrify them with
warnings,
[17]to turn man from wrongdoing
and keep him from pride,
[18]to preserve his soul from the
pit,[q]
his life from perishing by
the sword.[r]
[19]Or a man may be chastened
on a bed of pain
with constant distress in his
bones,
[20]so that his very being finds
food repulsive
and his soul loathes the
choicest meal.
[21]His flesh wastes away to
nothing,
and his bones, once hidden,
now stick out.
[22]His soul draws near to the
pit,[s]
and his life to the
messengers of death.[t]
[23]"Yet if there is an angel on his
side
as a mediator, one out of a
thousand,
to tell a man what is right
for him,
[24]to be gracious to him and say,
'Spare him from going
down to the pit[u];
I have found a ransom for
him'—
[25]then his flesh is renewed like

[p]13 *Or that he does not answer for any of his actions*
[q]18 *Or preserve him from the grave*
[r]18 *Or from crossing the River*
[s]22 *Or He draws near to the grave*
[t]22 *Or to the dead* [u]24 *Or grave*

*12 Most mss have *mappiq* in the *he* (הּ־).

†16 The NIV repoints this word as יְחִתֵּם, *be-may-terrify-them*.

°19 ק וְרוֹב

°21 ק וְשֻׁפוּ

בְּשָׂרוֹ מִנֹּעַר יָשׁוּב לִימֵי עֲלוּמָיו׃
youths-of-him to-days-of he-is-restored like-child flesh-of-him

(26) יֶעְתַּר אֶל־אֱלוֹהַּ ׀ וַיִּרְצֵהוּ וַיַּרְא פָּנָיו
faces-of-him and-he-sees and-he-finds-favor-with-him God to he-prays (26)

בִּתְרוּעָה וַיָּשֶׁב לֶאֱנוֹשׁ צִדְקָתוֹ׃ (27) יָשֹׁר ׀
he-comes (27) righteous-state-of-him to-man and-he-restores with-shout-of-joy

עַל־אֲנָשִׁים וַיֹּאמֶר חָטָאתִי וְיָשָׁר הֶעֱוֵיתִי וְלֹא־ שָׁוָה
he-gave-desert but-not I-perverted and-right I-sinned and-he-says men to

לִי׃ (28) פָּדָה נַפְשִׁי מֵעֲבֹר בַּשָּׁחַת וְחַיָּתִי
and-life-of-me to-the-pit from-to-go-down soul-of-me he-redeemed (28) to-me

בָּאוֹר תִּרְאֶה׃ (29) הֶן־ כָּל־ אֵלֶּה יִפְעַל־ אֵל פַּעֲמַיִם שָׁלוֹשׁ
thrice twice God he-does these all-of see! (29) she-will-see to-the-light

עִם־גָּבֶר׃ (30) לְהָשִׁיב נַפְשׁוֹ מִנִּי־ שָׁחַת לֵאוֹר בְּאוֹר
by-light-of to-be-shined-on pit from soul-of-him to-turn-back (30) man to

הַחַיִּים׃ (31) הַקְשֵׁב אִיּוֹב שְׁמַע־ לִי הַחֲרֵשׁ וְאָנֹכִי אֲדַבֵּר׃
I-will-speak and-I be-silent! to-me listen! Job pay-attention! (31) the-lives

(32) אִם־ יֵשׁ־ מִלִּין הֲשִׁיבֵנִי דַּבֵּר כִּי־ חָפַצְתִּי צַדְּקֶךָּ׃
to-clear-you I-want for speak-up! answer-me! words there-are if (32)

(33) אִם־ אַיִן אַתָּה שְׁמַע־ לִי הַחֲרֵשׁ וַאֲאַלֶּפְךָ חָכְמָה׃
wisdom and-I-will-teach-you be-silent! to-me listen! you not if (33)

(34:1) וַיַּעַן אֱלִיהוּא וַיֹּאמַר׃ (2) שִׁמְעוּ חֲכָמִים מִלָּי
words-of-me wise-men hear! (2) and-he-said Elihu then-he-spoke (34:1)

וְיֹדְעִים הַאֲזִינוּ לִי׃ (3) כִּי־ אֹזֶן מִלִּין תִּבְחָן וְחֵךְ
and-tongue she-tests words ear for (3) to-me listen! and-ones-learning

יִטְעַם לֶאֱכֹל׃ (4) מִשְׁפָּט נִבְחֲרָה־ לָּנוּ נֵדְעָה בֵינֵינוּ מַה־
what among-us let-us-learn for-us let-us-discern right (4) to-eat he-tastes

טּוֹב׃ (5) כִּי־ אָמַר אִיּוֹב צָדַקְתִּי וְאֵל הֵסִיר מִשְׁפָּטִי׃
justice-of-me he-denies but-God I-am-innocent Job he-says for (5) good

(6) עַל־ מִשְׁפָּטִי אֲכַזֵּב אָנוּשׁ חִצִּי בְלִי־ פָשַׁע׃
guilt without arrow-of-me being-incurable I-lie right-of-me although (6)

(7) מִי־ גֶבֶר כְּאִיּוֹב יִשְׁתֶּה־ לַּעַג כַּמָּיִם׃ (8) וְאָרַח
and-he-keeps (8) like-the-waters scorn he-drinks like-Job man what? (7)

לְחֶבְרָה עִם־ פֹּעֲלֵי אָוֶן וְלָלֶכֶת עִם־ אַנְשֵׁי־ רֶשַׁע׃
wickedness men-of with and-to-associate evil ones-doing-of with in-company

(9) כִּי־ אָמַר לֹא יִסְכָּן־ גָּבֶר בִּרְצֹתוֹ עִם־אֱלֹהִים׃ (10) לָכֵן ׀
so (10) God to when-to-please-him man he-profits nothing he-says for (9)

אַנְשֵׁי לֵבָב שִׁמְעוּ לִי חָלִלָה לָאֵל מֵרֶשַׁע וְשַׁדַּי
and-Almighty from-evil from-God far-be-it! to-me listen! understanding men-of

a child's;
it is restored as in the days
of his youth.
26 He prays to God and finds
favor with him,
he sees God's face and
shouts for joy;
he is restored by God to his
righteous state.
27 Then he comes to men and
says,
'I sinned, and perverted
what was right,
but I did not get what I
deserved.
28 He redeemed my soul from
going down to the pit,[v]
and I will live to enjoy the
light.'

29 "God does all these things to a
man—
twice, even three times—
30 to turn back his soul from the
pit,[w]
that the light of life may
shine on him.

31 "Pay attention, Job, and listen
to me;
be silent, and I will speak.
32 If you have anything to say,
answer me;
speak up, for I want you to
be cleared.
33 But if not, then listen to me;
be silent, and I will teach
you wisdom."

34 Then Elihu said:
2 "Hear my words, you
wise men;
listen to me, you men of
learning.
3 For the ear tests words
as the tongue tastes food.
4 Let us discern for ourselves
what is right;
let us learn together what is
good.

5 "Job says, 'I am innocent,
but God denies me justice.
6 Although I am right,
I am considered a liar;
although I am guiltless,
his arrow inflicts an
incurable wound.'
7 What man is like Job,
who drinks scorn like water?
8 He keeps company with
evildoers;
he associates with wicked
men.
9 For he says, 'It profits a man
nothing
when he tries to please
God.'
10 "So listen to me, you men of
understanding.
Far be it from God to do
evil,
from the Almighty to do

[v]28 *Or redeemed me from going down to the grave*
[w]30 *Or turn him back from the grave*

*30 Most mss have the accent on the final syllable (הַחַיִּים).

°28a ק נפשו
°28b ק וחיתו

מֵעָוֶל׃ כִּי פֹּעַל אָדָם יְשַׁלֶּם־ לוֹ וּכְאֹרַח אִישׁ

man and-as-conduct-of to-him he-repays man deed-of for (11) from-wrong

יַמְצִאֶנּוּ׃ אַף־ אָמְנָם אֵל לֹא־ יַרְשִׁיעַ וְשַׁדַּי לֹא־

not and-Almighty he-does-wrong not God indeed surely (12) he-brings-upon-him

יְעַוֵּת מִשְׁפָּט׃ מִי־ פָקַד עָלָיו אָרְצָה וּמִי

and-who? over-earth to-him he-appointed who? (13) justice he-perverts

שָׂם תֵּבֵל כֻּלָּהּ׃ אִם־ יָשִׂים אֵלָיו לִבּוֹ

heart-of-him to-him he-intended if (14) whole-of-her world he-put-in-charge

רוּחוֹ וְנִשְׁמָתוֹ אֵלָיו יֶאֱסֹף׃ יִגְוַע

he-would-perish (15) he-withdrew to-him and-breath-of-him spirit-of-him

כָּל־ בָּשָׂר יַחַד וְאָדָם עַל־ עָפָר יָשׁוּב׃ וְאִם־

and-if (16) he-would-return dust to and-man together mankind all-of

בִּינָה שִׁמְעָה־ זֹּאת הַאֲזִינָה לְקוֹל מִלָּי׃ הַאַף

indeed? (17) sayings-of-me to-sound-of listen! this hear! understanding

שׂוֹנֵא מִשְׁפָּט יַחֲבוֹשׁ וְאִם־ צַדִּיק כַּבִּיר תַּרְשִׁיעַ׃

will-you-condemn Mighty-One Just-One or-indeed can-he-govern justice one-hating

הַאֲמֹר לְמֶלֶךְ בְּלִיָּעַל רָשָׁע אֶל־ נְדִיבִים׃ אֲשֶׁר לֹא־

not who (19) nobles to wicked worthless to-king to-say? (18)

נָשָׂא׀ פְּנֵי שָׂרִים וְלֹא נִכַּר־ שׁוֹעַ לִפְנֵי־ דָל כִּי־

for poor over rich he-favors and-not princes faces-of he-shows-partiality

מַעֲשֵׂה יָדָיו כֻּלָּם׃ רֶגַע׀ יָמֻתוּ וַחֲצוֹת לָיְלָה

night and-middle-of they-die instant (20) all-of-them hands-of-him work-of

יְגֹעֲשׁוּ עָם וְיַעֲבֹרוּ וְיָסִירוּ אַבִּיר לֹא בְיָד׃

by-hand not mighty and-they-remove and-they-pass-away people they-are-shaken

כִּי־ עֵינָיו עַל־ דַּרְכֵי־ אִישׁ וְכָל־ צְעָדָיו יִרְאֶה׃

he-sees steps-of-him and-every-of man ways-of on eyes-of-him for (21)

אֵין־ חֹשֶׁךְ וְאֵין צַלְמָוֶת לְהִסָּתֶר שָׁם

there to-be-hidden deep-shadow and-there-is-no dark-place there-is-no (22)

פֹּעֲלֵי אָוֶן׃ כִּי לֹא עַל־אִישׁ יָשִׂים עוֹד לַהֲלֹךְ אֶל־

before to-come further he-examines man to not for (23) evil ones-doing-of

אֵל בַּמִּשְׁפָּט׃ יָרֹעַ כַּבִּירִים לֹא־ חֵקֶר

inquiry without mighty-ones he-shatters (24) for-the-judgment God

וַיַּעֲמֵד אֲחֵרִים תַּחְתָּם׃ לָכֵן יַכִּיר מַעְבָּדֵיהֶם

deeds-of-them he-notes because (25) in-place-of-them others and-he-sets-up

וְהָפַךְ לַיְלָה וְיִדַּכָּאוּ׃ תַּחַת־ רְשָׁעִים

wickednesses for (26) and-they-are-crushed night then-he-overthrows

סְפָקָם בִּמְקוֹם רֹאִים׃ אֲשֶׁר עַל־ כֵּן סָרוּ

they-turned that because for (27) ones-seeing in-place-of he-punishes-them

wrong.
11 He repays a man for what he
has done;
he brings upon him what
his conduct deserves.
12 It is unthinkable that God
would do wrong,
that the Almighty would
pervert justice.
13 Who appointed him over the
earth?
Who put him in charge of
the whole world?
14 If it were his intention
and he withdrew his spirit[x]
and breath,
15 all mankind would perish
together
and man would return to
the dust.

16 "If you have understanding,
hear this;
listen to what I say.
17 Can he who hates justice
govern?
Will you condemn the just
and mighty One?
18 Is he not the One who says to
kings, 'You are worthless,'
and to nobles, 'You are
wicked,'
19 who shows no partiality to
princes
and does not favor the rich
over the poor,
for they are all the work of
his hands?
20 They die in an instant, in the
middle of the night;
the people are shaken and
they pass away;
the mighty are removed
without human hand.

21 "His eyes are on the ways of
men;
he sees their every step.
22 There is no dark place, no
deep shadow,
where evildoers can hide.
23 God has no need to examine
men further,
that they should come
before him for judgment.
24 Without inquiry he shatters
the mighty
and sets up others in their
place.
25 Because he takes note of their
deeds,
he overthrows them in the
night and they are
crushed.
26 He punishes them for their
wickedness
where everyone can see
them,
27 because they turned from

[x]14 Or *Spirit*

מֵאַחֲרָיו וְכָל־ דְּרָכָיו לֹא הִשְׂכִּילוּ׃ לְהָבִיא
to-make-come (28) they-regarded not ways-of-him and-any-of from-after-him

עָלָיו צַעֲקַת־ דָּל וְצַעֲקַת עֲנִיִּים יִשְׁמָע׃ וְהוּא
but-he (29) he-heard needy-ones so-cry-of poor cry-of before-him

יַשְׁקִט | וּמִי יַרְשִׁעַ וְיַסְתֵּר פָּנִים וּמִי
then-who? faces if-he-hides he-can-condemn then-who? he-remains-silent

יְשׁוּרֶנּוּ וְעַל־ גּוֹי וְעַל־ אָדָם יָחַד׃ מִמְּלֹךְ אָדָם
man from-to-rule (30) alike man and-over nation yet-over he-can-see-him

חָנֵף מִמֹּקְשֵׁי עָם׃ כִּי־ אֶל־ אֵל הֶאָמַר נָשָׂאתִי
I-am-guilty he-says? God to suppose (31) people from-snares-of godless

לֹא אֶחְבֹּל׃ בִּלְעֲדֵי אֶחֱזֶה אַתָּה הֹרֵנִי אִם־ עָוֶל פָּעַלְתִּי
I-did wrong if teach-me! you I-see what-not (32) I-will-offend no-more

לֹא אֹסִיף׃ הֲמֵעִמְּךָ יְשַׁלְמֶנָּה* כִּי־ מָאַסְתָּ
you-refuse when should-he-reward-her from-with-you? (33) I-will-do-again not

כִּי־ אַתָּה תִבְחַר וְלֹא־ אָנִי וּמַה־ יָדַעְתָּ† דַבֵּר׃ אַנְשֵׁי
men-of (34) tell! you-know so-what I and-not you-decide you for

לֵבָב יֹאמְרוּ לִי וְגֶבֶר חָכָם שֹׁמֵעַ לִי׃ אִיּוֹב לֹא־
not Job (35) to-me hearing wise and-man to-me they-declare understanding

בְדַעַת יְדַבֵּר וּדְבָרָיו לֹא בְהַשְׂכֵּיל׃ אָבִי
oh! (36) with-to-have-insight not and-words-of-him he-speaks with-knowledge

יִבָּחֵן אִיּוֹב עַד־ נֶצַח עַל־ תְּשֻׁבֹת בְּאַנְשֵׁי־ אָוֶן׃ כִּי
for (37) wickedness of-men-of answers for utmost to Job he-might-be-tested

יֹסִיף עַל־ חַטָּאתוֹ פֶשַׁע בֵּינֵינוּ יִסְפּוֹק וְיֶרֶב
and-he-multiplies he-claps among-us rebellion sin-of-him to he-adds

אֲמָרָיו לָאֵל׃ וַיַּעַן אֱלִיהוּ וַיֹּאמַר׃ הֲזֹאת
this? (2) and-he-said Elihu then-he-spoke (35:1) against-God words-of-him

חָשַׁבְתָּ לְמִשְׁפָּט אָמַרְתָּ צִדְקִי מֵאֵל׃ כִּי־ תֹאמַר מַה־
what? you-ask yet (3) by-God clearing-of-me you-say as-just you-think

יִסְכָּן־ לָךְ מָה־ אֹעִיל מֵחַטָּאתִי׃ אֲנִי אֲשִׁיבְךָ
I-would-reply-to-you I (4) from-sin-of-me I-gain what? to-you he-profits

מִלִּין וְאֶת־ רֵעֶיךָ עִמָּךְ׃ הַבֵּט שָׁמַיִם וּרְאֵה וְשׁוּר
and-gaze! and-see! heavens look! (5) with-you friends-of-you and words

שְׁחָקִים גָּבְהוּ מִמֶּךָּ׃ אִם־ חָטָאתָ מַה־ תִּפְעָל־ בּוֹ
to-him she-affects how? you-sin if (6) above-you they-are-high clouds

וְרַבּוּ פְּשָׁעֶיךָ מַה־ תַּעֲשֶׂה־ לּוֹ׃ אִם־ צָדַקְתָּ
you-are-righteous if (7) to-him she-does what? sins-of-you if-they-are-many

מַה־ תִּתֶּן־ לוֹ אוֹ מַה־ מִיָּדְךָ יִקָּח׃ לְאִישׁ־
to-man (8) he-receives from-hand-of-you what? or to-him you-give what?

following him
and had no regard for any of his ways.
28 They caused the cry of the poor to come before him,
so that he heard the cry of the needy.
29 But if he remains silent, who can condemn him?
If he hides his face, who can see him?
Yet he is over man and nation alike,
30 to keep a godless man from ruling,
from laying snares for the people.

31 "Suppose a man says to God,
'I am guilty but will offend no more.
32 Teach me what I cannot see;
if I have done wrong, I will not do so again.'
33 Should God then reward you on your terms,
when you refuse to repent?
You must decide, not I;
so tell me what you know.

34 "Men of understanding declare,
wise men who hear me say to me,
35 'Job speaks without knowledge;
his words lack insight.'
36 Oh, that Job might be tested to the utmost
for answering like a wicked man!
37 To his sin he adds rebellion;
scornfully he claps his hands among us
and multiplies his words against God."

35 Then Elihu said:
2 "Do you think this is just?
You say, 'I will be cleared by God.[y]'
3 Yet you ask him, 'What profit is it to me,[z]
and what do I gain by not sinning?'

4 "I would like to reply to you
and to your friends with you.
5 Look up at the heavens and see;
gaze at the clouds so high above you.
6 If you sin, how does that affect him?
If your sins are many, what does that do to him?
7 If you are righteous, what do you give to him,
or what does he receive from your hand?

y2 Or *My righteousness is more than God's*
z3 Or *you*

*33a Most mss have *dagesh* in the lamed (יְשַׁלְּ).
†33b Most mss have dagesh in the *yod* (יּ).

כָמוֹךָ רִשְׁעֶךָ וּלְבֶן־ אָדָם צִדְקָתֶךָ׃
righteousness-of-you man and-to-son-of wickedness-of-you like-you

מֵרֹב עֲשׁוּקִים יַזְעִיקוּ יְשַׁוְּעוּ מִזְּרוֹעַ
from-arm-of they-plead-for-relief they-cry-out oppressions under-load-of (9)

רַבִּים׃ וְלֹא־ אָמַר אַיֵּה אֱלוֹהַּ עֹשָׂי נֹתֵן זְמִרוֹת
songs giving Ones-Making-me God where? he-says but-no-one (10) powerful-ones

בַּלָּיְלָה׃ מַלְּפֵנוּ מִבַּהֲמוֹת אָרֶץ וּמֵעוֹף
and-more-than-bird-of earth more-than-beasts-of teaching-us (11) in-the-night

הַשָּׁמַיִם יְחַכְּמֵנוּ׃ שָׁם יִצְעֲקוּ וְלֹא יַעֲנֶה
he-answers then-not they-cry-out when (12) he-makes-wise-us the-airs

מִפְּנֵי גְּאוֹן רָעִים׃ אַךְ־ שָׁוְא לֹא־ יִשְׁמַע ׀ אֵל
God he-listens not emptiness indeed (13) wicked-ones arrogance-of because-of

וְשַׁדַּי לֹא יְשׁוּרֶנָּה׃ אַף כִּי־ תֹאמַר
you-say when how-much-less (14) he-pays-attention-to-her not and-Almighty

לֹא תְשׁוּרֶנּוּ דִּין לְפָנָיו וּתְחוֹלֵל לוֹ׃ וְעַתָּה
and-further (15) for-him and-you-must-wait before-him case you-see-him not

כִּי־ אַיִן פָּקַד אַפּוֹ וְלֹא־ יָדַע בַּפַּשׁ
to-the-wickedness he-notices and-not anger-of-him he-punishes never that

מְאֹד׃ וְאִיּוֹב הֶבֶל יִפְצֶה־ פִּיהוּ בִּבְלִי־ דַעַת מִלִּין
words knowledge with-no mouth-of-him he-opens emptiness so-Job (16) least

יַכְבִּר׃ וַיֹּסֶף אֱלִיהוּא וַיֹּאמַר׃ כַּתַּר־ לִי
with-me bear! (2) and-he-said Elihu and-he-continued (36:1) he-multiplies

זְעֵיר וַאֲחַוֶּךָּ כִּי עוֹד לֶאֱלוֹהַּ מִלִּים׃
sayings in-behalf-of-God more that and-I-will-show-you little-longer

אֶשָּׂא דֵעִי לְמֵרָחוֹק וּלְפֹעֲלִי אֶתֵּן־
I-ascribe and-to-One-Making-me at-from-afar knowledge-of-me I-get (3)

צֶדֶק׃ כִּי־ אָמְנָם לֹא־ שֶׁקֶר מִלָּי תְּמִים דֵּעוֹת
knowledges perfect-of words-of-me false not assuredly for (4) justice

עִמָּךְ׃ הֶן־ אֵל כַּבִּיר וְלֹא יִמְאָס כַּבִּיר כֹּחַ לֵב׃
purpose firm-of mighty he-despises but-not mighty God see! (5) with-you

לֹא־ יְחַיֶּה רָשָׁע וּמִשְׁפַּט עֲנִיִּים יִתֵּן׃ לֹא־
not (7) he-gives afflicted-ones but-right-of wicked he-keeps-alive not (6)

יִגְרַע מִצַּדִּיק עֵינָיו וְאֶת־ מְלָכִים לַכִּסֵּא
on-the-throne kings and-with eyes-of-him from-righteous he-takes

וַיֹּשִׁיבֵם לָנֶצַח וַיִּגְבָּהוּ׃ וְאִם־
but-if (8) and-they-are-exalted to-forever and-he-enthrones-them

אֲסוּרִים בַּזִּקִּים יִלָּכְדוּן בְּחַבְלֵי־ עֹנִי׃
affliction by-cords-of and-they-are-held-fast in-the-chains ones-being-bound

8 Your wickedness affects only a
man like yourself,
and your righteousness only
the sons of men.
9 "Men cry out under a load of
oppression;
they plead for relief from
the arm of the powerful.
10 But no one says, 'Where is
God my Maker,
who gives songs in the
night,
11 who teaches more to us than
to[a] the beasts of the earth
and makes us wiser than[b]
the birds of the air?'
12 He does not answer when
men cry out
because of the arrogance of
the wicked.
13 Indeed, God does not listen to
their empty plea;
the Almighty pays no
attention to it.
14 How much less, then, will he
listen
when you say that you do
not see him,
that your case is before him
and you must wait for him,
15 and further, that his anger
never punishes
and he does not take the
least notice of
wickedness.[c]
16 So Job opens his mouth with
empty talk;
without knowledge he
multiplies words."

36 Elihu continued:
2 "Bear with me a little
longer and I will show
you
that there is more to be said
in God's behalf.
3 I get my knowledge from afar;
I will ascribe justice to my
Maker.
4 Be assured that my words are
not false;
one perfect in knowledge is
with you.

5 "God is mighty, but does not
despise men;
he is mighty, and firm in
his purpose.
6 He does not keep the wicked
alive
but gives the afflicted their
rights.
7 He does not take his eyes off
the righteous;
he enthrones them with
kings
and exalts them forever.
8 But if men are bound in
chains,
held fast by cords of
affliction,

[a] 11 Or *teaches us by*
[b] 11 Or *us wise by*
[c] 15 Symmachus, Theodotion and Vulgate; the meaning of the Hebrew for this word is uncertain.

וַיַּגֵּד לָהֶם פָּעֳלָם וּפִשְׁעֵיהֶם כִּי יִתְגַּבָּרוּ׃
they-did-arrogantly that and-sins-of-them deed-of-them to-them then-he-tells (9)

וַיִּגֶל אָזְנָם לַמּוּסָר וַיֹּאמֶר כִּי־יְשֻׁבוּן
they-repent that and-he-commands to-the-correction ear-of-them and-he-opens (10)

מֵאָוֶן׃ אִם־יִשְׁמְעוּ וְיַעַבְדוּ יְכַלּוּ יְמֵיהֶם
days-of-them they-will-finish and-they-serve they-obey if (11) of-evil

בַּטּוֹב וּשְׁנֵיהֶם בַּנְּעִימִים׃ וְאִם־לֹא
not but-if (12) in-the-contentments and-years-of-them in-the-prosperity

יִשְׁמְעוּ בְּשֶׁלַח יַעֲבֹרוּ וְיִגְוְעוּ כִּבְלִי־* דָעַת׃
knowledge as-without and-they-will-die they-will-perish by-sword they-listen

וְחַנְפֵי־לֵב יָשִׂימוּ אָף לֹא יְשַׁוְּעוּ
they-cry-for-help not resentment they-harbor heart and-ones-godless-of (13)

כִּי אֲסָרָם׃ תָּמֹת בַּנֹּעַר נַפְשָׁם וְחַיָּתָם
and-life-of-them soul-of-them in-the-youth she-dies (14) he-fetters-them when

בַּקְּדֵשִׁים׃ יְחַלֵּץ עָנִי בְעָנְיוֹ
in-suffering-of-him sufferer he-delivers (15) among-the-male-prostitutes

וְיִגֶל בַּלַּחַץ אָזְנָם׃ וְאַף הֲסִיתְךָ
he-woos-you and-also (16) ear-of-them in-the-affliction and-he-opens

מִפִּי־צָר רַחַב לֹא־מוּצָק תַּחְתֶּיהָ וְנַחַת
and-comfort-of to-her restriction no spacious-place distress from-jaw-of

שֻׁלְחָנְךָ מָלֵא דָשֶׁן׃ וְדִין־רָשָׁע
wicked but-judgment-of (17) choice-food he-is-laden table-of-you

מָלֵאתָ דִּין וּמִשְׁפָּט יִתְמֹכוּ׃ כִּי־חֵמָה† פֶּן־
not †wrath for (18) they-took-hold and-justice judgment you-are-laden

יְסִיתְךָ בְסָפֶק וְרָב־כֹּפֶר אַל־יַטֶּךָּ׃
let-him-turn-you not bribe and-largeness-of by-richness he-should-entice-you

הֲיַעֲרֹךְ שׁוּעֲךָ לֹא בְצָר וְכֹל מַאֲמַצֵּי־
efforts-of or-all-of in-distress not wealth-of-you would-he-sustain? (19)

כֹחַ׃ אַל־תִּשְׁאַף הַלָּיְלָה לַעֲלוֹת עַמִּים תַּחְתָּם׃
place-of-them peoples to-drag-away the-night you-long-for not (20) might

הִשָּׁמֶר אַל־תֵּפֶן אֶל־אָוֶן כִּי־עַל־זֶה בָּחַרְתָּ מֵעֹנִי׃
to-affliction you-prefer this to for evil to you-turn not beware! (21)

הֶן־אֵל יַשְׂגִּיב בְּכֹחוֹ מִי כָמֹהוּ מוֹרֶה׃
teacher like-him who? in-power-of-him he-is-exalted God see! (22)

מִי־פָקַד עָלָיו דַּרְכּוֹ וּמִי־אָמַר פָּעַלְתָּ עַוְלָה׃
wrong you-did he-said or-who? way-of-him for-him he-prescribed who? (23)

זְכֹר כִּי־תַשְׂגִּיא פָעֳלוֹ אֲשֶׁר שֹׁרְרוּ אֲנָשִׁים׃
men they-praised which work-of-him you-must-extol that remember! (24)

9 he tells them what they have
done—
that they have sinned
arrogantly.
10 He makes them listen to
correction
and commands them to
repent of their evil.
11 If they obey and serve him,
they will spend the rest of
their days in prosperity
and their years in
contentment.
12 But if they do not listen,
they will perish by the
sword[d]
and die without knowledge.

13 "The godless in heart harbor
resentment;
even when he fetters them,
they do not cry for help.
14 They die in their youth,
among male prostitutes of
the shrines.
15 But those who suffer he
delivers in their suffering;
he speaks to them in their
affliction.

16 "He is wooing you from the
jaws of distress
to a spacious place free from
restriction,
to the comfort of your table
laden with choice food.
17 But now you are laden with
the judgment due the
wicked;
judgment and justice have
taken hold of you.
18 Be careful that no one entices
you by riches;
do not let a large bribe turn
you aside.
19 Would your wealth
or even all your mighty
efforts
sustain you so you would
not be in distress?
20 Do not long for the night
to drag people away from
their homes.[e]
21 Beware of turning to evil,
which you seem to prefer to
affliction.

22 "God is exalted in his power.
Who is a teacher like him?
23 Who has prescribed his ways
for him,
or said to him, 'You have
done wrong'?
24 Remember to extol his work,
which men have praised in
song.

[d] 12 Or *will cross the River*
[e] 20 The meaning of the Hebrew for verses 18-20 is uncertain.

*12 Many mss have *beth* instead of *kaph* (בִּבְ׳).

†18 The NIV repoints this word as חֲמֵה, *be-careful!*

(25) כָּל־ אָדָם חָזוּ־ בוֹ אֱנוֹשׁ יַבִּיט מֵרָחוֹק׃ (26) הֶן־ אֵל

(25) all-of mankind they-saw to-him man he-gazes from-afar (26) see! God

שַׂגִּיא וְלֹא נֵדָע מִסְפַּר שָׁנָיו וְלֹא־ חֵקֶר׃

great and-not we-comprehend number-of years-of-him and-no finding-out

(27) כִּי יְגָרַע נִטְפֵי־ מָיִם יָזֹקּוּ מָטָר לְאֵדוֹ׃

(27) for he-draws-up drops-of waters they-distill rain to-stream-of-him

(28) אֲשֶׁר־ יִזְּלוּ שְׁחָקִים יִרְעֲפוּ עֲלֵי ׀ אָדָם רָב׃

(28) that they-pour-moisture clouds they-shower on mankind abundance

(29) אַף אִם־ יָבִין מִפְרְשֵׂי־ עָב תְּשֻׁאוֹת

(29) indeed if he-understands spreadings-out-of cloud thunders-of

סֻכָּתוֹ׃ (30) הֶן־ פָּרַשׂ עָלָיו אוֹרוֹ וְשָׁרְשֵׁי

pavilion-of-him (30) see! he-scatters about-him lightning-of-him and-depths-of

הַיָּם כִּסָּה׃ (31) כִּי־ בָם יָדִין עַמִּים יִתֶּן־ אֹכֶל

the-sea he-bathes (31) for by-them he-governs nations he-provides food

לְמַכְבִּיר׃ (32) עַל־ כַּפַּיִם כִּסָּה־ אוֹר וַיְצַו עָלֶיהָ

to-be-abundant (32) in hands he-fills lightning and-he-commands to-her

בְמַפְגִּיעַ׃ (33) יַגִּיד עָלָיו רֵעוֹ מִקְנֶה אַף עַל־

to-one-striking (33) he-announces about-him thunder-of-him cattle even about

עוֹלֶה׃ (37:1) אַף־ לְזֹאת יֶחֱרַד לִבִּי וְיִתַּר

approaching (37:1) indeed at-this he-pounds heart-of-me and-he-leaps

מִמְּקוֹמוֹ׃ (2) שִׁמְעוּ שָׁמוֹעַ בְּרֹגֶז קֹלוֹ וְהֶגֶה

from-place-of-him (2) listen! to-listen to-roar-of voice-of-him and-rumbling

מִפִּיו יֵצֵא׃ (3) תַּחַת־ כָּל־ הַשָּׁמַיִם יִשְׁרֵהוּ

from-mouth-of-him he-comes (3) beneath whole-of the-heavens he-unleashes-him

וְאוֹרוֹ עַל־ כַּנְפוֹת הָאָרֶץ׃ (4) אַחֲרָיו ׀ יִשְׁאַג־ קוֹל

and-lightning-of-him to ends-of the-earth (4) after-him he-roars sound

יַרְעֵם בְּקוֹל גְּאוֹנוֹ וְלֹא יְעַקְּבֵם

he-thunders with-voice-of majesty-of-him and-nothing he-holds-back-them

כִּי־ יִשָּׁמַע קוֹלוֹ׃ (5) יַרְעֵם אֵל בְּקוֹלוֹ

when he-is-heard voice-of-him (5) he-thunders God with-voice-of-him

נִפְלָאוֹת עֹשֶׂה גְדֹלוֹת וְלֹא נֵדָע׃ (6) כִּי

ways-being-marvelous doing great-things and-not we-understand (6) for

לַשֶּׁלַג ׀ יֹאמַר הֱוֵא אָרֶץ וְגֶשֶׁם מָטָר וְגֶשֶׁם מִטְרוֹת

to-the-snow he-says fall! earth and-shower-of rain and-downpour-of rains

עֻזּוֹ׃† (7) בְּיַד־ כָּל־ אָדָם יַחְתּוֹם לָדַעַת כָּל־ אַנְשֵׁי

†might-of-him (7) to-labor-of every-of man he-stops to-know all-of men-of

מַעֲשֵׂהוּ׃ (8) וַתָּבֹא חַיָּה בְמוֹ־ אָרֶב וּבִמְעוֹנֹתֶיהָ תִשְׁכֹּן׃

work-of-him (8) and-she-goes animal into cover and-in-dens-of-her she-remains

25 All mankind has seen it;
men gaze on it from afar.
26 How great is God—beyond our
understanding!
The number of his years is
past finding out.
27 "He draws up the drops of
water,
which distill as rain to the
streams[f];
28 the clouds pour down their
moisture
and abundant showers fall
on mankind.
29 Who can understand how he
spreads out the clouds,
how he thunders from his
pavilion?
30 See how he scatters his
lightning about him,
bathing the depths of the
sea.
31 This is the way he governs[g]
the nations
and provides food in
abundance.
32 He fills his hands with
lightning
and commands it to strike
its mark.
33 His thunder announces the
coming storm;
even the cattle make known
its approach.[h]

37 "At this my heart pounds
and leaps from its place.
2 Listen! Listen to the roar of his
voice,
to the rumbling that comes
from his mouth.
3 He unleashes his lightning
beneath the whole
heaven
and sends it to the ends of
the earth.
4 After that comes the sound of
his roar;
he thunders with his
majestic voice.
When his voice resounds,
he holds nothing back.
5 God's voice thunders in
marvelous ways;
he does great things beyond
our understanding.
6 He says to the snow, 'Fall on
the earth,'
and to the rain shower, 'Be
a mighty downpour.'
7 So that all men he has made
may know his work,
he stops every man from his
labor.[i]
8 The animals take cover;
they remain in their dens.

f27 Or *distill from the mist as rain*
g31 Or *nourishes*
h33 Or *announces his coming— / the One zealous against evil*
i7 Or / *he fills all men with fear by his power*

*6a Most mss have *segol* under the *lamed* (לֶג־).

†6b The NIV repoints this word as עֹז, *be-mighty!*

מִן־ הַחֶדֶר תָּבוֹא סוּפָה וּמִמְּזָרִים קָרָה׃
cold and-from-ones-driving tempest she-comes the-chamber from (9)

מִנִּשְׁמַת־ אֵל יִתֶּן־ קָרַח וְרֹחַב מַיִם בְּמוּצָק׃
in-frozenness waters and-breadth-of ice he-produces God from-breath-of (10)

אַף־ בְּרִי יַטְרִיחַ עָב יָפִיץ עֲנַן אוֹרוֹ׃
lightning-of-him cloud-of he-scatters cloud he-loads with-moisture also (11)

וְהוּא מְסִבּוֹת ׀ מִתְהַפֵּךְ בְּתַחְבּוּלֹתָו לְפָעֳלָם כֹּל אֲשֶׁר
that all to-do-them at-directions-of-him swirling ones-around and-he (12)

יְצַוֵּם ׀ עַל־ פְּנֵי תֵבֵל אָרְצָה׃ אִם־ לְשֵׁבֶט אִם־
or as-rod whether (13) to-earth world-of faces-of over he-commands-them

לְאַרְצוֹ אִם־ לְחֶסֶד יַמְצִאֵהוּ׃ הַאֲזִינָה זֹּאת אִיּוֹב עֲמֹד
stop! Job this listen! (14) he-brings-him for-love or for-earth-of-him

וְהִתְבּוֹנֵן ׀ נִפְלְאוֹת אֵל׃ הֲתֵדַע בְּשׂוּם־
how-to-control do-you-know? (15) God things-being-wonders-of and-consider!

אֱלוֹהַּ עֲלֵיהֶם וְהוֹפִיעַ אוֹר עֲנָנוֹ׃ הֲתֵדַע
do-you-know? (16) cloud-of-him lightning-of and-he-makes-flash over-them God

עַל־ מִפְלְשֵׂי־ עָב מִפְלְאוֹת תְּמִים דֵּעִים׃ אֲשֶׁר־
who (17) knowledges one-perfect-of wonders-of cloud hangings-of how

בְּגָדֶיךָ חַמִּים בְּהַשְׁקִט אֶרֶץ מִדָּרוֹם׃
under-south-wind land when-to-lie-hushed ones-sweltering clothes-of-you

תַּרְקִיעַ עִמּוֹ לִשְׁחָקִים חֲזָקִים כִּרְאִי מוּצָק׃
being-cast as-mirror-of ones-hard to-skies with-him can-you-spread-out (18)

הוֹדִיעֵנוּ מַה־ נֹּאמַר לוֹ לֹא־ נַעֲרֹךְ מִפְּנֵי־
because-of we-can-draw-up-case not to-him we-should-say what tell-us! (19)

חֹשֶׁךְ׃ הַיְסֻפַּר־ לוֹ כִּי אֲדַבֵּר אִם־ אָמַר
would-he-ask or I-would-speak that to-him should-he-be-told? (20) darkness

אִישׁ כִּי יְבֻלָּע׃ וְעַתָּה ׀ לֹא רָאוּ אוֹר בָּהִיר הוּא
he bright sun they-look-at not and-now (21) he-be-swallowed-up that man

בַּשְּׁחָקִים וְרוּחַ עָבְרָה וַתְּטַהֲרֵם׃ מִצָּפוֹן זָהָב
gold from-north (22) and-she-cleans-them she-sweeps after-wind in-the-skies

יֶאֱתֶה עַל־אֱלוֹהַּ נוֹרָא הוֹד׃ שַׁדַּי לֹא־ מְצָאנֻהוּ
we-can-reach-him not Almighty (23) majesty being-awesome-of God to he-comes

שַׂגִּיא־ כֹחַ וּמִשְׁפָּט וְרֹב־ צְדָקָה לֹא יְעַנֶּה׃
he-oppresses not righteousness and-greatness-of and-justice power exalted-of

לָכֵן יְרֵאוּהוּ אֲנָשִׁים לֹא־ יִרְאֶה כָּל־ חַכְמֵי־ לֵב׃
heart ones-wise-of all-of he-regards not men they-revere-him therefore (24)

וַיַּעַן־ יְהוָה אֶת־אִיּוֹב מִנ ׀ הַסְּעָרָה וַיֹּאמַר׃ מִי
who? (2) and-he-said the-storm from Job *** Yahweh then-he-answered (38:1)

9The tempest comes out from
its chamber,
the cold from the driving
winds.
10The breath of God produces
ice,
and the broad waters
become frozen.
11He loads the clouds with
moisture;
he scatters his lightning
through them.
12At his direction they swirl
around
over the face of the whole
earth
to do whatever he
commands them.
13He brings the clouds to punish
men,
or to water his earth[i] and
show his love.

14"Listen to this, Job;
stop and consider God's
wonders.
15Do you know how God
controls the clouds
and makes his lightning
flash?
16Do you know how the clouds
hang poised,
those wonders of him who
is perfect in knowledge?
17You who swelter in your
clothes
when the land lies hushed
under the south wind,
18can you join him in spreading
out the skies,
hard as a mirror of cast
bronze?

19"Tell us what we should say to
him;
we cannot draw up our case
because of our darkness.
20Should he be told that I want
to speak?
Would any man ask to be
swallowed up?
21Now no one can look at the
sun,
bright as it is in the skies
after the wind has swept
them clean.
22Out of the north he comes in
golden splendor;
God comes in awesome
majesty.
23The Almighty is beyond our
reach and exalted in
power;
in his justice and great
righteousness, he does
not oppress.
24Therefore, men revere him,
for does he not have regard
for all the wise in
heart?[k]"

The Lord *Speaks*

38 Then the Lord answered
Job out of the storm.
He said:

i 13 Or *to favor them*
k 24 Or *for he does not have regard for any who think they are wise*

°12 ק בתחבולתיו
°1 ק מן הסערה

זֶה׀ מַחְשִׁיךְ עֵצָה בְמִלִּין בְּלִי־ דָעַת׃ אֱזָר־ נָא
now! brace-yourself! (3) knowledge without with-words counsel darkening this

כְגֶבֶר חֲלָצֶיךָ וְאֶשְׁאָלְךָ וְהוֹדִיעֵנִי׃ אֵיפֹה
where? (4) then-answer-me! and-I-will-question-you loins-of-you like-man

הָיִיתָ בְּיָסְדִי־ אָרֶץ הַגֵּד אִם־ יָדַעְתָּ בִינָה׃ מִי־
who? (5) understanding you-know if tell! earth when-to-found-me were-you

שָׂם מְמַדֶּיהָ כִּי תֵדָע אוֹ מִי־ נָטָה
he-stretched who? or you-know surely dimensions-of-her he-marked-off

עָלֶיהָ קָו׃ עַל־ מָה אֲדָנֶיהָ הָטְבָּעוּ אוֹ
or they-were-set footings-of-her what? on (6) measuring-line across-her

מִי־ יָרָה אֶבֶן פִּנָּתָהּ׃ בְּרָן־ יַחַד כּוֹכְבֵי
stars-of together while-to-sing (7) corner-of-her stone-of he-laid who?

בֹקֶר וַיָּרִיעוּ כָּל־ בְּנֵי אֱלֹהִים׃ וַיָּסֶךְ
and-he-shut-up (8) God sons-of all-of and-they-shouted-for-joy morning

בִּדְלָתַיִם יָם בְּגִיחוֹ מֵרֶחֶם יֵצֵא׃ בְּשׂוּמִי
when-to-make-me (9) he-came-forth from-womb when-to-burst-him sea behind-doors

עָנָן לְבֻשׁוֹ וַעֲרָפֶל חֲתֻלָּתוֹ׃ וָאֶשְׁבֹּר
when-I-fixed (10) wrapping-of-him and-thick-darkness garment-of-him cloud

עָלָיו חֻקִּי וָאָשִׂים בְּרִיחַ וּדְלָתָיִם׃ וָאֹמַר עַד־ פֹּה
here to when-I-said (11) and-doors bar and-I-set-in-place limit-of-me for-him

תָבוֹא וְלֹא תֹסִיף וּפֹא־ יָשִׁית בִּגְאוֹן גַּלֶּיךָ׃
waves-of-you to-pride-of he-halts and-here you-go-farther and-not you-may-come

הֲמִיָּמֶיךָ* צִוִּיתָ בֹּקֶר יִדַּעְתָּה° שַׁחַר מְקֹמוֹ׃
place-of-him the-dawn you-showed morning you-ordered in-days-of-you? (12)

לֶאֱחֹז בְּכַנְפוֹת הָאָרֶץ וְיִנָּעֲרוּ רְשָׁעִים מִמֶּנָּה׃
from-her wicked-ones that-they-be-shaken the-earth by-edges-of to-take (13)

תִּתְהַפֵּךְ כְּחֹמֶר חוֹתָם וְיִתְיַצְּבוּ כְּמוֹ לְבוּשׁ׃
garment like and-they-stand-out seal like-clay-of she-takes-shape (14)

וְיִמָּנַע מֵרְשָׁעִים אוֹרָם וּזְרוֹעַ רָמָה
being-upraised and-arm light-of-them from-wicked-ones and-he-is-denied (15)

תִּשָּׁבֵר׃ הֲבָאתָ עַד־ נִבְכֵי־ יָם וּבְחֵקֶר תְּהוֹם
deep or-in-recess-of sea springs-of to you-journeyed? (16) she-is-broken

הִתְהַלָּכְתָּ׃ הֲנִגְלוּ לְךָ שַׁעֲרֵי־ מָוֶת וְשַׁעֲרֵי
or-gates-of death gates-of to-you were-they-shown? (17) you-walked

צַלְמָוֶת תִּרְאֶה׃ הִתְבֹּנַנְתָּ עַד־ רַחֲבֵי־ אֶרֶץ הַגֵּד
tell! earth vast-expanses-of to you-comprehended (18) you-saw deep-shadow

אִם־יָדַעְתָּ כֻלָּהּ׃ אֵי־ זֶה הַדֶּרֶךְ יִשְׁכָּן־ אוֹר וְחֹשֶׁךְ
and-darkness light he-abides the-way this what? (19) all-of-her you-know if

2 "Who is this that darkens my counsel
with words without knowledge?
3 Brace yourself like a man;
I will question you,
and you shall answer me.

4 "Where were you when I laid the earth's foundation?
Tell me, if you understand.
5 Who marked off its dimensions? Surely you know!
Who stretched a measuring line across it?
6 On what were its footings set,
or who laid its cornerstone—
7 while the morning stars sang together
and all the angels[l] shouted for joy?

8 "Who shut up the sea behind doors
when it burst forth from the womb,
9 when I made the clouds its garment
and wrapped it in thick darkness,
10 when I fixed limits for it
and set its doors and bars in place,
11 when I said, 'This far you may come and no farther;
here is where your proud waves halt'?

12 "Have you ever given orders to the morning,
or shown the dawn its place,
13 that it might take the earth by the edges
and shake the wicked out of it?
14 The earth takes shape like clay under a seal;
its features stand out like those of a garment.
15 The wicked are denied their light,
and their upraised arm is broken.

16 "Have you journeyed to the springs of the sea
or walked in the recesses of the deep?
17 Have the gates of death been shown to you?
Have you seen the gates of the shadow of death[m]?
18 Have you comprehended the vast expanses of the earth?
Tell me, if you know all this.
19 "What is the way to the abode of light?

[l]7 Hebrew *the sons of God*
[m]17 Or *gates of deep shadows*

*12 Most mss have *hateph pathah* under the *he* (הֲ).

°12 ק ידעת השחר

אֵי־ זֶה מְקֹמֽוֹ׃ כִּי תִֽקָּחֶנּוּ אֶל־ גְּבוּלוֹ

place-of-him to can-you-take-him indeed (20) residence-of-him this where?

וְכִי תָבִין נְתִיבוֹת בֵּיתֽוֹ׃ יָדַעְתָּ כִּי־ אָז

then surely you-know (21) dwelling-of-him paths-of do-you-know and-indeed

תִּוָּלֵד וּמִסְפַּר יָמֶיךָ רַבִּֽים׃ הֲבָאתָ אֶל־

into you-entered? (22) many days-of-you and-number-of you-were-born

אֹצְרוֹת שָׁלֶג וְאֹצְרוֹת בָּרָד תִּרְאֶֽה׃ אֲשֶׁר־ חָשַׂכְתִּי

I-reserve which (23) you-saw hail or-storehouses-of snow storehouses-of

לְעֶת־ צָר לְיוֹם קְרָב וּמִלְחָמָֽה׃ אֵי־ זֶה הַדֶּרֶךְ

the-way this what? (24) and-battle war for-day-of trouble for-time-of

יֵחָלֶק אוֹר יָפֵץ קָדִים עֲלֵי־ אָֽרֶץ׃ מִֽי־ פִלַּג

he-cuts who? (25) earth over east-wind he-scatters lightning he-is-dispersed

לַשֶּׁטֶף תְּעָלָה וְדֶרֶךְ לַחֲזִיז קֹלֽוֹת׃ לְהַמְטִיר

to-water (26) thunders for-storm-of and-path channel for-the-rain-torrent

עַל־אֶרֶץ לֹא־ אִישׁ מִדְבָּר לֹא־אָדָם בּֽוֹ׃ לְהַשְׂבִּיעַ שֹׁאָה

desolation to-satisfy (27) in-him one no desert man without land on

וּמְשֹׁאָה וּלְהַצְמִיחַ מֹצָא דֶֽשֶׁא׃ הֲיֵשׁ־ לַמָּטָר

to-the-rain is-there? (28) grass shoot-of and-to-make-sprout and-wasteland

אָב אוֹ מִֽי־ הוֹלִיד אֶגְלֵי־ טָֽל׃ מִבֶּטֶן מִי יָצָא

he-comes whom? from-womb-of (29) dew drops-of he-fathers who? or father

הַקָּרַח וּכְפֹר שָׁמַיִם מִי יְלָדֽוֹ׃ כָּאֶבֶן מַיִם

waters as-the-stone (30) he-bears-him who? heavens and-frost-of the-ice

יִתְחַבָּאוּ וּפְנֵי תְהוֹם יִתְלַכָּֽדוּ׃ הַתְקַשֵּׁר

can-you-bind? (31) they-freeze deep when-surfaces-of they-become-hard

מַעֲדַנּוֹת כִּימָה אוֹ־ מֹשְׁכוֹת כְּסִיל תְּפַתֵּֽחַ׃ הֲתֹצִיא

can-you-bring-forth? (32) can-you-loose Orion cords-of or Pleiades beauties-of

מַזָּרוֹת בְּעִתּוֹ וְעַיִשׁ עַל־ בָּנֶיהָ תַנְחֵֽם׃

can-you-lead-out-them cubs-of-her with or-Bear in-season-of-him constellations

הֲיָדַעְתָּ חֻקּוֹת שָׁמָיִם אִם־ תָּשִׂים מִשְׁטָרוֹ

dominion-of-him can-you-set-up or heavens laws-of do-you-know? (33)

בָאָֽרֶץ׃ הֲתָרִים לָעָב קוֹלֶךָ וְשִׁפְעַת־

and-flood-of voice-of-you to-the-cloud can-you-raise? (34) over-the-earth

מַיִם תְּכַסֶּֽךָּ׃ הַֽתְשַׁלַּח בְּרָקִים וְיֵלֵכוּ

so-they-go lightning-bolts do-you-send? (35) can-you-cover-yourself waters

וְיֹאמְרוּ לְךָ הִנֵּֽנוּ׃ מִי־ שָׁת בַּטֻּחוֹת חָכְמָה

wisdom to-the-hearts he-endowed who? (36) here-we! to-you and-do-they-report

אוֹ מִֽי־ נָתַן לַשֶּׂכְוִי בִינָֽה׃ מִֽי־ יְסַפֵּר שְׁחָקִים

clouds he-counts who? (37) understanding to-the-mind he-gave who? or

---

And where does darkness reside?
20 Can you take them to their places?
Do you know the paths to their dwellings?
21 Surely you know, for you were already born!
You have lived so many years!

22 "Have you entered the storehouses of the snow
or seen the storehouses of the hail,
23 which I reserve for times of trouble,
for days of war and battle?
24 What is the way to the place where the lightning is dispersed,
or the place where the east winds are scattered over the earth?
25 Who cuts a channel for the torrents of rain,
and a path for the thunderstorm,
26 to water a land where no man lives,
a desert with no one in it,
27 to satisfy a desolate wasteland
and make it sprout with grass?
28 Does the rain have a father?
Who fathers the drops of dew?
29 From whose womb comes the ice?
Who gives birth to the frost from the heavens
30 when the waters become hard as stone,
when the surface of the deep is frozen?

31 "Can you bind the beautiful[n] Pleiades?
Can you loose the cords of Orion?
32 Can you bring forth the constellations in their seasons[o]
or lead out the Bear[p] with its cubs?
33 Do you know the laws of the heavens?
Can you set up ⌊God's[q]⌋ dominion over the earth?

34 "Can you raise your voice to the clouds
and cover yourself with a flood of water?
35 Do you send the lightning bolts on their way?
Do they report to you, 'Here we are'?
36 Who endowed the heart[r] with wisdom
or gave understanding to the mind[r]?
37 Who has the wisdom to count the clouds?

n31 Or *the twinkling;* or *the chains of the*
o32 Or *the morning star in its season*
p32 Or *out Leo* q33 Or *his;* or *their*
r36 The meaning of the Hebrew for this word is uncertain.

בְּחָכְמָה וְנִבְלֵי שָׁמַיִם מִי יַשְׁכִּיב׃ בְּצֶקֶת עָפָר
dust when-to-harden (38) he-can-tip-over who? heavens or-jars-of in-wisdom

לַמּוּצָק וּרְגָבִים יְדֻבָּקוּ׃ הֲתָצוּד
do-you-hunt? (39) they-stick-together and-clods-of-earth into-the-hard-thing

לְלָבִיא טָרֶף וְחַיַּת כְּפִירִים תְּמַלֵּא׃ כִּי־ יָשֹׁחוּ
they-crouch when (40) you-satisfy lions and-hunger-of prey for-lioness

בַמְּעוֹנוֹת יֵשְׁבוּ בַסֻּכָּה לְמוֹ־ אָרֶב׃ מִי יָכִין
he-provides who? (41) wait in in-the-thicket they-lie in-the-dens

לָעֹרֵב צֵידוֹ כִּי־ יְלָדָו אֶל־ אֵל יְשַׁוֵּעוּ
they-cry-out God to young-ones-of-him when food-of-him for-the-raven

יִתְעוּ לִבְלִי־ אֹכֶל׃ הֲיָדַעְתָּ עֵת לֶדֶת יַעֲלֵי־
goats-of to-give-birth time-of do-you-know? (39:1) food for-lack-of they-wander

סָלַע חֹלֵל אַיָּלוֹת תִּשְׁמֹר׃ תִּסְפֹּר יְרָחִים תְּמַלֶּאנָה
they-complete-term months do-you-count (2) do-you-watch fawns to-bear mountain

וְיָדַעְתָּ עֵת לִדְתָּנָה׃ תִּכְרַעְנָה יַלְדֵיהֶן
young-ones-of-them they-crouch-down (3) to-give-birth-them time-of and-do-you-know

תְּפַלַּחְנָה חֶבְלֵיהֶם תְּשַׁלַּחְנָה׃ יַחְלְמוּ בְנֵיהֶם
young-ones-of-them they-thrive (4) they-end labor-pains-of-them they-bring-forth

יִרְבּוּ בַבָּר יָצְאוּ וְלֹא־ שָׁבוּ לָמוֹ׃ מִי־
who? (5) to-them they-return and-not they-leave in-the-wild they-grow-strong

שִׁלַּח פֶּרֶא חָפְשִׁי וּמֹסְרוֹת עָרוֹד מִי פִתֵּחַ׃ אֲשֶׁר־
that (6) he-untied who? donkey and-ropes-of free wild-donkey he-let-go

שַׂמְתִּי עֲרָבָה בֵיתוֹ וּמִשְׁכְּנוֹתָיו מְלֵחָה׃ יִשְׂחַק
he-laughs (7) salt-flat and-habitats-of-him home-of-him wasteland I-gave

לַהֲמוֹן קִרְיָה תְּשֻׁאוֹת נוֹגֵשׂ לֹא יִשְׁמָע׃ יְתוּר הָרִים
hills he-ranges (8) he-hears not one-driving shouts-of town at-commotion-of

מִרְעֵהוּ וְאַחַר כָּל־ יָרוֹק יִדְרוֹשׁ׃ הֲיֹאבֶה
will-he-consent? (9) he-searches green-thing any-of and-for pasture-of-him

רֵים עָבְדֶךָ אִם־ יָלִין עַל־ אֲבוּסֶךָ׃ הֲתִקְשָׁר־
can-you-hold? (10) manger-of-you by will-he-stay-night or to-serve-you wild-ox

רֵים בְּתֶלֶם עֲבֹתוֹ אִם־ יְשַׂדֵּד עֲמָקִים אַחֲרֶיךָ׃
behind-you valleys will-he-till or harness-of-him to-furrow-of wild-ox

הֲתִבְטַח־ בּוֹ כִּי־ רַב כֹּחוֹ וְתַעֲזֹב
and-will-you-leave strength-of-him greatness-of for on-him will-you-rely? (11)

אֵלָיו יְגִיעֶךָ׃ הֲתַאֲמִין בּוֹ כִּי־ יָשׁוּב
he-will-bring-in that in-him can-you-trust? (12) heavy-work-of-you to-him

זַרְעֶךָ וְגָרְנְךָ יֶאֱסֹף׃ כְּנַף־ רְנָנִים
ostriches wing-of (13) he-will-gather and-threshing-floor-of-you grain-of-you

Who can tip over the water
jars of the heavens
38 when the dust becomes hard
and the clods of earth stick
together?

39 "Do you hunt the prey for the
lioness
and satisfy the hunger of
the lions
40 when they crouch in their
dens
or lie in wait in a thicket?
41 Who provides food for the
raven
when its young cry out to
God
and wander about for lack
of food?

39 "Do you know when the
mountain goats give
birth?
Do you watch when the doe
bears her fawn?
2 Do you count the months till
they bear?
Do you know the time they
give birth?
3 They crouch down and bring
forth their young;
their labor pains are ended.
4 Their young thrive and grow
strong in the wilds;
they leave and do not
return.

5 "Who let the wild donkey go
free?
Who untied his ropes?
6 I gave him the wasteland as
his home,
the salt flats as his habitat.
7 He laughs at the commotion in
the town;
he does not hear a driver's
shout.
8 He ranges the hills for his
pasture
and searches for any green
thing.

9 "Will the wild ox consent to
serve you?
Will he stay by your manger
at night?
10 Can you hold him to the
furrow with a harness?
Will he till the valleys
behind you?
11 Will you rely on him for his
great strength?
Will you leave your heavy
work to him?
12 Can you trust him to bring in
your grain
and gather it to your
threshing floor?

13 "The wings of the ostrich flap

°41 ק ילדיו
°12 ק ישיב

נֶעֱלָסָה אִם־אֶבְרָה חֲסִידָה וְנֹצָה׃ (14) כִּי־תַעֲזֹב
she-flaps-joyfully not pinion stork and-feather (14) indeed she-lays

לָאָרֶץ בֵּצֶיהָ וְעַל־עָפָר תְּחַמֵּם׃ (15) וַתִּשְׁכַּח
on-the-ground eggs-of-her and-in sand she-warms-them (15) and-she-is-unmindful

כִּי־רֶגֶל תְּזוּרֶהָ וְחַיַּת הַשָּׂדֶה תְּדוּשֶׁהָ׃
that foot she-may-crush-her or-animal-of the-wild she-may-trample-her

(16) הִקְשִׁיחַ בָּנֶיהָ לְּלֹא־לָהּ לְרִיק יְגִיעָהּ
(16) he-treats-harshly young-ones-of-her as-not to-her in-vain labor-of-her

בְּלִי־פָחַד׃ (17) כִּי־הִשָּׁהּ אֱלוֹהַּ חָכְמָה וְלֹא־חָלַק
without care (17) for he-did-not-endow-her God wisdom and-not he-gave-share

לָהּ בַּבִּינָה׃ (18) כָּעֵת בַּמָּרוֹם תַּמְרִיא
to-her of-the-good-sense (18) yet-the-time to-the-height she-spreads-feathers

תִּשְׂחַק לַסּוּס וּלְרֹכְבוֹ׃ (19) הֲתִתֵּן לַסּוּס
she-laughs at-the-horse and-at-one-riding-him (19) do-you-give? to-the-horse

גְּבוּרָה הֲתַלְבִּישׁ צַוָּארוֹ רַעְמָה׃ (20) הְתַרְעִישֶׁנּוּ*
strength do-you-clothe? neck-of-him flowing-mane (20) do-you-make-leap-him?

כָּאַרְבֶּה הוֹד נַחְרוֹ אֵימָה׃ (21) יַחְפְּרוּ
like-the-locust pride-of snorting-of-him terror (21) they-paw

בָעֵמֶק וְיָשִׂישׂ בְּכֹחַ יֵצֵא לִקְרַאת־נָשֶׁק׃
with-the-fierceness and-he-rejoices in-strength he-charges to-meet fray

(22) יִשְׂחַק לְפַחַד וְלֹא יֵחָת וְלֹא־יָשׁוּב מִפְּנֵי־
(22) he-laughs at-fear and-nothing he-fears and-not he-shys-away from-edges-of

חָרֶב׃ (23) עָלָיו תִּרְנֶה אַשְׁפָּה לַהַב חֲנִית וְכִידוֹן׃
sword (23) beside-him she-rattles quiver flash-of spear and-lance

(24) בְּרַעַשׁ וְרֹגֶז יְגַמֶּא־אָרֶץ וְלֹא־יַאֲמִין כִּי־
(24) in-frenzy and-excitement he-eats-up ground and-not he-stands-still when

קוֹל שׁוֹפָר׃ (25) בְּדֵי שֹׁפָר ׀ יֹאמַר הֶאָח וּמֵרָחוֹק
sound-of trumpet (25) as-often-as trumpet he-snorts aha! and-from-afar

יָרִיחַ מִלְחָמָה רַעַם שָׂרִים וּתְרוּעָה׃
he-catches-scent battle shout-of commanders and-battle-cry

(26) הֲמִבִּינָתְךָ יַאֲבֶר־נֵץ יִפְרֹשׂ כְּנָפָו°
(26) by-wisdom-of-you? he-takes-flight hawk he-spreads wings-of-him

לְתֵימָן׃ (27) אִם־עַל־פִּיךָ יַגְבִּיהַּ נָשֶׁר וְכִי יָרִים
toward-south (27) or at command-of-you he-soars eagle and-indeed he-builds-high

קִנּוֹ׃ (28) סֶלַע יִשְׁכֹּן וְיִתְלֹנָן עַל־שֶׁן־סֶלַע
nest-of-him (28) cliff he-dwells and-he-stays-night on crag-of rock

וּמְצוּדָה׃ (29) מִשָּׁם חָפַר־אֹכֶל לְמֵרָחוֹק עֵינָיו
and-stronghold (29) from-there he-seeks-out food at-from-afar eyes-of-him

joyfully,
but they cannot compare
with the pinions and
feathers of the stork.
14 She lays her eggs on the
ground
and lets them warm in the
sand,
15 unmindful that a foot may
crush them,
that some wild animal may
trample them.
16 She treats her young harshly,
as if they were not hers;
she cares not that her labor
was in vain,
17 for God did not endow her
with wisdom
or give her a share of good
sense.
18 Yet when she spreads her
feathers to run,
she laughs at horse and
rider.

19 "Do you give the horse his
strength
or clothe his neck with a
flowing mane?
20 Do you make him leap like a
locust,
striking terror with his
proud snorting?
21 He paws fiercely, rejoicing in
his strength,
and charges into the fray.
22 He laughs at fear, afraid of
nothing;
he does not shy away from
the sword.
23 The quiver rattles against his
side,
along with the flashing
spear and lance.
24 In frenzied excitement he eats
up the ground;
he cannot stand still when
the trumpet sounds.
25 At the blast of the trumpet he
snorts, 'Aha!'
He catches the scent of
battle from afar,
the shout of commanders
and the battle cry.

26 "Does the hawk take flight by
your wisdom
and spread his wings
toward the south?
27 Does the eagle soar at your
command
and build his nest on high?
28 He dwells on a cliff and stays
there at night;
a rocky crag is his
stronghold.
29 From there he seeks out his
food;

*20 Most mss have *hateph pathah* under the *he* (הֲ).

°26 ק כנפיו

יַבִּיטוּ׃ וְאֶפְרֹחָו יְעַלְעוּ־ דָם וּבַאֲשֶׁר חֲלָלִים

slain-ones and-at-where blood they-feast and-young-ones-of-him (30) they-detect

שָׁם הוּא׃ וַיַּעַן יְהוָה אֶת־אִיּוֹב וַיֹּאמַר׃ הֲרֹב

to-contend? (2) and-he-said Job *** Yahweh and-he-spoke (40:1) he there

עִם־ שַׁדַּי יִסּוֹר מוֹכִיחַ אֱלוֹהַּ יַעֲנֶנָּה׃

let-him-answer-her God one-accusing will-he-correct Almighty with

וַיַּעַן אִיּוֹב אֶת־ יְהוָה וַיֹּאמַר׃ הֵן קַלֹּתִי מָה

how? I-am-unworthy see! (4) and-he-said Yahweh *** Job then-he-answered (3)

אֲשִׁיבֶךָּ יָדִי שַׂמְתִּי לְמוֹ־ פִי׃ אַחַת דִּבַּרְתִּי וְלֹא

but-not I-spoke once (5) mouth-of-me over I-put hand-of-me can-I-reply-to-you

אֶעֱנֶה וּשְׁתַּיִם וְלֹא אוֹסִיף׃ וַיַּעַן־ יְהוָה אֶת־אִיּוֹב

Job *** Yahweh then-he-spoke (6) I-will-say-more but-not and-twice I-answer

מִן ׀ סְעָרָה וַיֹּאמַר׃ אֱזָר־ נָא כְגֶבֶר חֲלָצֶיךָ

loins-of-you like-man now! brace-yourself! (7) and-he-said storm from

אֶשְׁאָלְךָ וְהוֹדִיעֵנִי׃ הַאַף תָּפֵר מִשְׁפָּטִי

justice-of-me would-you-discredit indeed? (8) and-answer-me! I-will-question-you

תַּרְשִׁיעֵנִי לְמַעַן תִּצְדָּק׃ וְאִם־ זְרוֹעַ

arm now-indeed (9) you-would-justify-yourself so-that would-you-condemn-me

כָּאֵל ׀ לָךְ וּבְקוֹל כָּמֹהוּ תַרְעֵם׃ עֲדֵה

adorn-yourself! (10) can-you-thunder like-his and-with-voice to-you like-God

נָא גָאוֹן וָגֹבַהּ וְהוֹד וְהָדָר תִּלְבָּשׁ׃

you-clothe-yourself and-majesty and-honor and-splendor glory now!

הָפֵץ עֶבְרוֹת אַפֶּךָ וּרְאֵה כָל־ גֵּאֶה

proud-man every-of and-look! wrath-of-you furies-of unleash! (11)

וְהַשְׁפִּילֵהוּ׃ רְאֵה כָל־ גֵּאֶה הַכְנִיעֵהוּ וַהֲדֹךְ

and-crush! humble-him! proud-man every-of look! (12) and-bring-low-him!

רְשָׁעִים תַּחְתָּם׃ טָמְנֵם בֶּעָפָר יָחַד פְּנֵיהֶם

faces-of-them together in-the-dust bury-them! (13) in-place-of-them wicked-ones

חֲבֹשׁ בַּטָּמוּן׃ וְגַם־ אֲנִי אוֹדֶךָּ כִּי־ תוֹשִׁעַ

she-can-save that I-will-admit-to-you I then-also (14) in-the-grave shroud!

לְךָ יְמִינֶךָ׃ הִנֵּה־ נָא בְהֵמוֹת אֲשֶׁר־ עָשִׂיתִי עִמָּךְ חָצִיר

grass with-you I-made which behemoth now! see! (15) right-hand-of-you to-you

כַּבָּקָר יֹאכֵל׃ הִנֵּה־ נָא כֹחוֹ בְמָתְנָיו

in-loins-of-him strength-of-him now! see! (16) he-feeds-on like-the-ox

וְאֹנוֹ בִּשְׁרִירֵי בִטְנוֹ׃ יַחְפֹּץ זְנָבוֹ כְמוֹ־

like tail-of-him he-sways (17) belly-of-him in-muscles-of and-power-of-him

אֶרֶז גִּידֵי פַחֲדָו יְשֹׂרָגוּ׃ עֲצָמָיו אֲפִיקֵי

tubes-of bones-of-him (18) they-are-close-knit thighs-of-him sinews-of cedar

his eyes detect it from afar.
30 His young ones feast on blood,
and where the slain are,
there is he."

40 The LORD said to Job:
2 "Will the one who
contends with the
Almighty correct him?
Let him who accuses God
answer him!"
3 Then Job answered the LORD:
4 "I am unworthy—how can I
reply to you?
I put my hand over my
mouth.
5 I spoke once, but I have no
answer—
twice, but I will say no
more."
6 Then the LORD spoke to Job out
of the storm:
7 "Brace yourself like a man;
I will question you,
and you shall answer me.
8 "Would you discredit my
justice?
Would you condemn me to
justify yourself?
9 Do you have an arm like
God's,
and can your voice thunder
like his?
10 Then adorn yourself with glory
and splendor,
and clothe yourself in honor
and majesty.
11 Unleash the fury of your
wrath,
look at every proud man
and bring him low,
12 look at every proud man and
humble him,
crush the wicked where they
stand.
13 Bury them all in the dust
together;
shroud their faces in the
grave.
14 Then I myself will admit to
you
that your own right hand
can save you.
15 "Look at the behemoth,[s]
which I made along with
you
and which feeds on grass
like an ox.
16 What strength he has in his
loins,
what power in the muscles
of his belly!
17 His tail[t] sways like a cedar;
the sinews of his thighs are
close-knit.
18 His bones are tubes of bronze,

[s] 15 Possibly the hippopotamus or the elephant
[t] 17 Possibly trunk

°30 ק ואפרחיו
°6 ק מן סערה
°17 ק פחדיו

נְחוּשָׁה גְּרָמָיו כִּמְטִיל בַּרְזֶל׃ הוּא רֵאשִׁית דַּרְכֵי־אֵל

God works-of first-of he (19) iron like-rod-of limbs-of-him bronze

הָעֹשׂוֹ יַגֵּשׁ חַרְבּוֹ׃ כִּי־בוּל הָרִים

hills produce-of indeed (20) sword-of-him he-can-approach the-One-Making-him

יִשְׂאוּ־לוֹ וְכָל־חַיַּת הַשָּׂדֶה יְשַׂחֲקוּ־שָׁם׃ תַּחַת־

under (21) nearby they-play the-wild animal-of and-all-of to-him they-bring

צֶאֱלִים יִשְׁכָּב בְּסֵתֶר קָנֶה וּבִצָּה׃ יְסֻכֻּהוּ

they-conceal-him (22) and-marsh reed in-hiding-of he-lies lotus-plants

צֶאֱלִים צִלֲלוֹ יְסֻבּוּהוּ עַרְבֵי־נָחַל׃ הֵן יַעֲשֹׁק

he-rages see! (23) stream poplars-of they-surround-him shadow-of-him lotuses

נָהָר לֹא יַחְפּוֹז יִבְטַח ׀ כִּי־יָגִיחַ יַרְדֵּן אֶל־

against Jordan he-should-surge though he-is-secure he-is-alarmed not river

פִּיהוּ׃ בְּעֵינָיו יִקָּחֶנּוּ בְּמוֹקְשִׁים יִנְקָב־

can-he-pierce with-traps can-he-capture-him by-eyes-of-him (24) mouth-of-him

אָף׃ תִּמְשֹׁךְ לִוְיָתָן בְּחַכָּה וּבְחֶבֶל

or-with-rope with-fishhook leviathan can-you-pull-in *(25[1]) nose

תַּשְׁקִיעַ לְשֹׁנוֹ׃ הֲתָשִׂים אַגְמֹן בְּאַפּוֹ

through-nose-of-him cord can-you-put? (26[2]) tongue-of-him can-you-tie-down

וּבְחוֹחַ תִּקֹּב לֶחֱיוֹ׃† הֲיַרְבֶּה אֵלֶיךָ

to-you will-he-continue? (27[3]) jaw-of-him can-you-pierce or-with-hook

תַּחֲנוּנִים אִם־יְדַבֵּר אֵלֶיךָ רַכּוֹת׃ הֲיִכְרֹת

will-he-make? (28[4]) gentle-words to-you will-he-speak or beggings-for-mercy

בְּרִית עִמָּךְ תִּקָּחֶנּוּ לְעֶבֶד עוֹלָם׃ הַתְשַׂחֶק־

can-you-make-pet? (29[5]) for-life as-slave will-you-take-him with-you agreement

בּוֹ כַּצִּפּוֹר וְתִקְשְׁרֶנּוּ לְנַעֲרוֹתֶיךָ׃

for-girls-of-you or-will-you-put-leash-on-him like-the-bird of-him

יִכְרוּ עָלָיו חַבָּרִים יֶחֱצוּהוּ בֵּין כְּנַעֲנִים׃

merchants among will-they-divide-him traders for-him will-they-barter (30[6])

הַתְמַלֵּא בְשֻׂכּוֹת עוֹרוֹ וּבְצִלְצַל דָּגִים

fishes or-with-spear-of hide-of-him with-harpoons can-you-fill? (31[7])

רֹאשׁוֹ׃ שִׂים־עָלָיו כַּפֶּךָ זְכֹר מִלְחָמָה אַל־

never struggle remember! hand-of-you on-him lay! (32[8]) head-of-him

תּוֹסַף׃ הֵן־תֹּחַלְתּוֹ נִכְזָבָה הֲגַם אֶל־

at indeed? she-is-false hope-of-him see! (41:1[9]) you-will-do-again

מַרְאָיו יֻטָל׃ לֹא־אַכְזָר כִּי יְעוּרֶנּוּ

he-can-rouse-him that fierce no-one (2[10]) he-is-overpowered sights-of-him

וּמִי הוּא לְפָנַי יִתְיַצָּב׃ מִי הִקְדִּימַנִי

he-has-claim-against-me who? (3[11]) he-can-stand against-me he then-who?

his limbs like rods of iron.
19 He ranks first among the
works of God,
yet his Maker can approach
him with his sword.
20 The hills bring him their
produce,
and all the wild animals
play nearby.
21 Under the lotus plants he lies,
hidden among the reeds in
the marsh.
22 The lotuses conceal him in
their shadow;
the poplars by the stream
surround him.
23 When the river rages, he is not
alarmed;
he is secure, though the
Jordan should surge
against his mouth.
24 Can anyone capture him by
the eyes,[u]
or trap him and pierce his
nose?

41 "Can you pull in the
leviathan[v] with a
fishhook
or tie down his tongue with
a rope?
2 Can you put a cord through
his nose
or pierce his jaw with a
hook?
3 Will he keep begging you for
mercy?
Will he speak to you with
gentle words?
4 Will he make an agreement
with you
for you to take him as your
slave for life?
5 Can you make a pet of him
like a bird
or put him on a leash for
your girls?
6 Will traders barter for him?
Will they divide him up
among the merchants?
7 Can you fill his hide with
harpoons
or his head with fishing
spears?
8 If you lay a hand on him,
you will remember the
struggle and never do it
again!
9 Any hope of subduing him is
false;
the mere sight of him is
overpowering.
10 No one is fierce enough to
rouse him.
Who then is able to stand
against me?
11 Who has a claim against me

[u]24 Or *by a water hole*
[v]1 Possibly the crocodile

*25 The Hebrew numeration of chapter 41 begins with verse 9 in English; the number in brackets indicates the English numeration.

†26 Most mss have the accent on the final syllable (יוֹ—).

וַאֲשַׁלֵּם תַּחַת כָּל־ הַשָּׁמַיִם לִי־ הוּא׃ לֹא־ אַחֲרִישׁ
I-will-not-speak not (4[12]) he to-me the-heavens all-of under that-I-must-pay

בַּדָּיו וּדְבַר־ גְּבוּרוֹת וְחִין עֶרְכּוֹ׃ מִי־
who? (5[13]) form-of-him and-grace-of strengths or-account-of limbs-of-him

גִּלָּה פְּנֵי לְבוּשׁוֹ בְּכֶפֶל רִסְנוֹ
bridle-of-him with-double-of coat-of-him outer-parts-of he-can-strip-off

מִי יָבוֹא׃ דַּלְתֵי פָנָיו מִי פִתֵּחַ
he-would-open who? mouths-of-him doors-of (6[14]) he-would-approach who?

סְבִיבוֹת שִׁנָּיו אֵימָה׃ גַּאֲוָה† אֲפִיקֵי מָגִנִּים
shields rows-of †pride (7[15]) fearsome teeth-of-him ones-ringed-about-of

סָגוּר חוֹתָם צָר׃ אֶחָד בְּאֶחָד יִגַּשׁוּ וְרוּחַ לֹא־
not that-air they-are-close to-next each (8[16]) tight seal being-closed

יָבוֹא בֵינֵיהֶם׃ אִישׁ־ בְּאָחִיהוּ יְדֻבָּקוּ
they-are-joined-fast to-other-of-him one (9[17]) between-them he-passes

יִתְלַכְּדוּ וְלֹא יִתְפָּרָדוּ׃ עֲטִישֹׁתָיו
sneezings-of-him (10[18]) they-can-be-parted and-not they-cling-together

תָּהֶל אוֹר וְעֵינָיו כְּעַפְעַפֵּי־ שָׁחַר׃ מִפִּיו
from-mouth-of-him (11[19]) dawn like-rays-of and-eyes-of-him light she-flashes

לַפִּידִים יַהֲלֹכוּ כִּידוֹדֵי אֵשׁ יִתְמַלָּטוּ׃
they-shoot-out fire sparks-of they-stream firebrands

מִנְּחִירָיו יֵצֵא עָשָׁן כְּדוּד נָפוּחַ וְאַגְמֹן׃
and-reed boiling as-pot smoke he-pours from-nostrils-of-him (12[20])

נַפְשׁוֹ גֶּחָלִים תְּלַהֵט וְלַהַב מִפִּיו
mouth-of-him and-flame-of she-sets-ablaze coals breath-of-him (13[21])

יֵצֵא׃ בְּצַוָּארוֹ יָלִין עֹז וּלְפָנָיו
and-before-him strength he-resides in-neck-of-him (14[22]) he-darts-out

תָּדוּץ דְּאָבָה׃ מַפְּלֵי בְשָׂרוֹ דָבֵקוּ
they-are-tightly-joined flesh-of-him folds-of (15[23]) dismay she-goes

יָצוּק עָלָיו בַּל־ יִמּוֹט׃ לִבּוֹ יָצוּק כְּמוֹ־אָבֶן
rock as being-hard chest-of-him (16[24]) he-is-moved not on-him being-firm

וְיָצוּק כְּפֶלַח תַּחְתִּית׃ מִשֵּׂתוֹ יָגוּרוּ
they-are-terrified when-to-rise-him (17[25]) lower as-millstone and-being-hard

אֵלִים מִשְּׁבָרִים יִתְחַטָּאוּ׃ מַשִּׂיגֵהוּ חֶרֶב
sword one-reaching-him (18[26]) they-retreat from-thrashings mighty-ones

בְּלִי תָקוּם חֲנִית מַסָּע וְשִׁרְיָה׃ יַחְשֹׁב לְתֶבֶן בַּרְזֶל
iron like-straw he-treats (19[27]) or-javelin dart spear she-has-effect not

לְעֵץ רִקָּבוֹן נְחוּשָׁה׃ לֹא־ יַבְרִיחֶנּוּ בֶן־ קָשֶׁת לְקַשׁ
like-chaff bow son-of he-makes-flee-him not (20[28]) bronze rottenness like-wood-of

that I must pay?
Everything under heaven
belongs to me.
12 "I will not fail to speak of his
limbs,
his strength and his graceful
form.
13 Who can strip off his outer
coat?
Who would approach him
with a bridle?
14 Who dares open the doors of
his mouth,
ringed about with his
fearsome teeth?
15 His back has[w] rows of shields
tightly sealed together;
16 each is so close to the next
that no air can pass
between.
17 They are joined fast to one
another;
they cling together and
cannot be parted.
18 His sneezing throws out
flashes of light;
his eyes are like the rays of
dawn.
19 Firebrands stream from his
mouth;
sparks of fire shoot out.
20 Smoke pours from his nostrils
as from a boiling pot over a
fire of reeds.
21 His breath sets coals ablaze,
and flames dart from his
mouth.
22 Strength resides in his neck;
dismay goes before him.
23 The folds of his flesh are
tightly joined;
they are firm and
immovable.
24 His chest is hard as rock,
hard as a lower millstone.
25 When he rises up, the mighty
are terrified;
they retreat before his
thrashing.
26 The sword that reaches him
has no effect,
nor does the spear or the
dart or the javelin.
27 Iron he treats like straw
and bronze like rotten wood.
28 Arrows do not make him flee;

w15 *Or His pride is his*

*See the note on page 344.

†7 The NIV reads this word as גֵּוֹה, *back-of-him*.

°4 ק לו

נֶהְפְּכוּ־ לוֹ אַבְנֵי־ קָלַע׃ כְּקַשׁ נֶחְשְׁבוּ תוֹתָח
club they-seem like-straw (21[29]) sling stones-of to-him they-are-turned

וְיִשְׂחַק לְרַעַשׁ כִּידוֹן׃ תַּחְתָּיו חַדּוּדֵי
jagged-pieces-of undersides-of-him (22[30]) lance at-rattling-of and-he-laughs

חָרֶשׂ יִרְפַּד חָרוּץ עֲלֵי־ טִיט׃ יַרְתִּיחַ
he-makes-churn (23[31]) mud in threshing-sledge he-leaves-trail potsherd

כַּסִּיר מְצוּלָה יָם יָשִׂים כַּמֶּרְקָחָה׃ אַחֲרָיו
behind-him (24[32]) like-the-ointment-pot he-stirs sea depth like-the-caldron

יָאִיר נָתִיב יַחְשֹׁב תְּהוֹם לְשֵׂיבָה׃ אֵין־עַל־
on nothing (25[33]) as-white-haired deep he-would-think wake he-makes-glisten

עָפָר מָשְׁלוֹ הֶעָשׂוּ לִבְלִי־ חָת׃ אֵת־ כָּל־
all-of *** (26[34]) fear without the-one-being-created equal-of-him earth

גָּבֹהַּ יִרְאֶה הוּא מֶלֶךְ עַל־ כָּל־ בְּנֵי־ שָׁחַץ׃ וַיַּעַן
then-he-replied (42:1) pride sons-of all-of over king he he-looks haughty

אִיּוֹב אֶת־ יְהוָה וַיֹּאמַר׃ יָדַעְתְּ כִּי־ כֹל תּוּכָל וְלֹא־
and-not you-can-do all that I-know (2) and-he-said Yahweh *** Job

יִבָּצֵר מִמְּךָ מְזִמָּה׃ מִי זֶה ׀ מַעְלִים עֵצָה בְּלִי
without counsel obscuring this who? (3) plan of-you he-can-be-thwarted

דָעַת לָכֵן הִגַּדְתִּי וְלֹא אָבִין נִפְלָאוֹת
things-being-wonderful I-understood and-not I-spoke surely knowledge

מִמֶּנִּי וְלֹא אֵדָע׃ שְׁמַע־ נָא וְאָנֹכִי אֲדַבֵּר
I-will-speak and-I now! listen! (4) I-knew and-not more-than-me

אֶשְׁאָלְךָ וְהוֹדִיעֵנִי׃ לְשֵׁמַע־ אֹזֶן שְׁמַעְתִּיךָ
I-heard-of-you ear with-hearing-of (5) and-answer-me! I-will-question-you

וְעַתָּה עֵינִי רָאָתְךָ׃ עַל־ כֵּן אֶמְאַס וְנִחַמְתִּי עַל־
in and-I-repent I-despise-myself this for (6) she-saw-you eye-of-me but-now

עָפָר וָאֵפֶר׃ וַיְהִי אַחַר דִּבֶּר יְהוָה אֶת־ הַדְּבָרִים הָאֵלֶּה
the-these the-things *** Yahweh he-said after and-he-was (7) and-ash dust

אֶל־אִיּוֹב וַיֹּאמֶר יְהוָה אֶל־ אֱלִיפַז הַתֵּימָנִי חָרָה אַפִּי
anger-of-me he-burns the-Temanite Eliphaz to Yahweh then-he-said Job to

בְךָ וּבִשְׁנֵי רֵעֶיךָ כִּי לֹא דִבַּרְתֶּם אֵלַי
of-me you-spoke not because friends-of-you and-against-two-of against-you

נְכוֹנָה כְּעַבְדִּי אִיּוֹב׃ וְעַתָּה קְחוּ־ לָכֶם שִׁבְעָה־פָרִים
bulls seven for-you take! so-now (8) Job as-servant-of-me being-right

וְשִׁבְעָה אֵילִים וּלְכוּ ׀ אֶל־ עַבְדִּי אִיּוֹב וְהַעֲלִיתֶם עוֹלָה
burnt-offering and-you-sacrifice Job servant-of-me to and-go! rams and-seven

בַּעַדְכֶם וְאִיּוֹב עַבְדִּי יִתְפַּלֵּל עֲלֵיכֶם כִּי אִם־ פָּנָיו
faces-of-him surely indeed for-you he-will-pray servant-of-me and-Job for-you

---

slingstones are like chaff to him.
29 A club seems to him but a piece of straw;
he laughs at the rattling of the lance.
30 His undersides are jagged potsherds,
leaving a trail in the mud like a threshing sledge.
31 He makes the depths churn like a boiling caldron
and stirs up the sea like a pot of ointment.
32 Behind him he leaves a glistening wake;
one would think the deep had white hair.
33 Nothing on earth is his equal—
a creature without fear.
34 He looks down on all that are haughty;
he is king over all that are proud."

Job

42 Then Job replied to the LORD:

2 "I know that you can do all things;
no plan of yours can be thwarted.
3 ⌊You asked,⌋ 'Who is this that obscures my counsel without knowledge?'
Surely I spoke of things I did not understand,
things too wonderful for me to know.

4 ⌊"You said,⌋ 'Listen now, and I will speak;
I will question you,
and you shall answer me.'
5 My ears had heard of you
but now my eyes have seen you.
6 Therefore I despise myself
and repent in dust and ashes."

Epilogue

7 After the LORD had said these
things to Job, he said to Eliphaz
the Temanite, "I am angry with
you and your two friends, because
you have not spoken of me what is
right, as my servant Job has. 8 So
now take seven bulls and seven
rams and go to my servant Job and
sacrifice a burnt offering for yourselves. My servant Job will pray
for you, and I will accept his

*See the note on page 344.

°2 ק ידעתי

אֶשָּׂא לְבִלְתִּי עֲשׂוֹת עִמָּכֶם נְבָלָה כִּי לֹא דִבַּרְתֶּם אֵלַי נְכוֹנָה
being-right of-me you-spoke not for folly with-you to-deal not I-will-accept

כְּעַבְדִּי אִיּוֹב׃ וַיֵּלְכוּ אֱלִיפַז הַתֵּימָנִי וּבִלְדַּד
and-Bildad the-Temanite Eliphaz so-they-went (9) Job as-servant-of-me

הַשּׁוּחִי צֹפַר הַנַּעֲמָתִי וַיַּעֲשׂוּ כַּאֲשֶׁר דִּבֶּר אֲלֵיהֶם יְהוָה
Yahweh to-them he-told as-what and-they-did the-Naamathite Zophar the-Shuhite

וַיִּשָּׂא יְהוָה אֶת־ פְּנֵי אִיּוֹב׃ וַיהוָה שָׁב אֶת־
*** he-returned then-Yahweh (10) Job faces-of *** Yahweh and-he-accepted

שְׁבִית אִיּוֹב בְּהִתְפַּלְלוֹ בְּעַד רֵעֵהוּ וַיֹּסֶף יְהוָה
Yahweh and-he-increased friends-of-him for after-to-pray-him Job prosperity-of

אֶת־כָּל־אֲשֶׁר לְאִיּוֹב לְמִשְׁנֶה׃ וַיָּבֹאוּ אֵלָיו כָּל־ אֶחָיו
brothers-of-him all-of to-him and-they-came (11) by-twice to-Job that all ***

וְכָל־ אַחְיֹתָיו וְכָל־ יֹדְעָיו לְפָנִים וַיֹּאכְלוּ
and-they-ate before ones-knowing-him and-all-of sisters-of-him and-all-of

עִמּוֹ לֶחֶם בְּבֵיתוֹ וַיָּנֻדוּ לוֹ וַיְנַחֲמוּ אֹתוֹ
him and-they-consoled to-him and-they-comforted in-house-of-him food with-him

עַל כָּל־ הָרָעָה אֲשֶׁר־ הֵבִיא יְהוָה עָלָיו וַיִּתְּנוּ־ לוֹ
to-him and-they-gave upon-him Yahweh he-brought that the-trouble all-of over

אִישׁ קְשִׂיטָה אֶחָת וְאִישׁ נֶזֶם זָהָב אֶחָד׃ וַיהוָה בֵּרַךְ אֶת־
*** he-blessed and-Yahweh (12) one gold ring-of and-each one kesitah each

אַחֲרִית אִיּוֹב מֵרֵאשִׁתוֹ וַיְהִי־ לוֹ אַרְבָּעָה עָשָׂר אֶלֶף
thousand ten four to-him and-he-was more-than-first-of-him Job latter-part-of

צֹאן וְשֵׁשֶׁת אֲלָפִים גְּמַלִּים וְאֶלֶף־ צֶמֶד בָּקָר וְאֶלֶף אֲתוֹנוֹת׃
donkeys and-thousand ox yoke-of and-thousand camels thousands and-six-of sheep

וַיְהִי־ לוֹ שִׁבְעָנָה בָנִים וְשָׁלוֹשׁ בָּנוֹת׃ וַיִּקְרָא
and-he-called (14) daughters and-three sons seven to-him also-he-was (13)

שֵׁם־ הָאַחַת יְמִימָה וְשֵׁם הַשֵּׁנִית קְצִיעָה וְשֵׁם הַשְּׁלִישִׁית
the-third and-name-of Keziah the-second and-name-of Jemimah the-first name-of

קֶרֶן הַפּוּךְ׃ וְלֹא נִמְצָא נָשִׁים יָפוֹת כִּבְנוֹת
as-daughters-of beautiful-ones women he-was-found and-not (15) Happuch Keren

אִיּוֹב בְּכָל־ הָאָרֶץ וַיִּתֵּן לָהֶם אֲבִיהֶם נַחֲלָה בְּתוֹךְ
with inheritance father-of-them to-them and-he-granted the-land in-all-of Job

אֲחֵיהֶם׃ וַיְחִי אִיּוֹב אַחֲרֵי־ זֹאת מֵאָה וְאַרְבָּעִים שָׁנָה
year and-forty hundred this after Job and-he-lived (16) brothers-of-them

וַיַּרְא אֶת־ בָּנָיו וְאֶת־ בְּנֵי בָנָיו אַרְבָּעָה
four children-of-him children-of and children-of-him *** and-he-saw

דֹּרוֹת׃ וַיָּמָת אִיּוֹב זָקֵן וּשְׂבַע יָמִים׃
days and-full-of old Job so-he-died (17) generations

prayer and not deal with you according to your folly. You have
not spoken of me what is right, as
my servant Job has." 9 So Eliphaz
the Temanite, Bildad the Shuhite
and Zophar the Naamathite did
what the LORD told them; and the
LORD accepted Job's prayer.
10 After Job had prayed for his
friends, the LORD made him prosperous again and gave him twice
as much as he had before. 11 All his
brothers and sisters and everyone
who had known him before came
and ate with him in his house.
They comforted and consoled him
over all the trouble the LORD had
brought upon him, and each one
gave him a piece of silver[x] and a
gold ring.
12 The LORD blessed the latter part
of Job's life more than the first. He
had fourteen thousand sheep, six
thousand camels, a thousand yoke
of oxen and a thousand donkeys.
13 And he also had seven sons and
three daughters. 14 The first daughter he named Jemimah, the second
Keziah and the third Keren-Hap-
puch. 15 Nowhere in all the land
were there found women as
beautiful as Job's daughters, and
their father granted them an inheritance along with their brothers.
16 After this, Job lived a hundred
and forty years; he saw his children and their children to the
fourth generation. 17 And so he
died, old and full of years.

[x] 11 Hebrew *him a kesitah;* a kesitah was a unit of money of unknown weight and value.

°10 ק שבות
°11 ק אחיותיו
°16 ק ויראה

אַשְׁרֵי הָאִישׁ אֲשֶׁר ׀ לֹא הָלַךְ בַּעֲצַת רְשָׁעִים
wicked-ones in-counsel-of he-walks not who the-man blessednesses-of (1:1)

וּבְדֶרֶךְ חַטָּאִים לֹא עָמָד וּבְמוֹשַׁב לֵצִים לֹא יָשָׁב׃
he-sits not ones-mocking or-in-seat-of he-stands not sinners or-in-way-of

כִּי אִם בְּתוֹרַת יְהוָה חֶפְצוֹ וּבְתוֹרָתוֹ יֶהְגֶּה
he-meditates and-on-law-of-him delight-of-him Yahweh in-law-of rather but (2)

יוֹמָם וָלָיְלָה׃ וְהָיָה כְּעֵץ שָׁתוּל עַל־ פַּלְגֵי מָיִם
waters streams-of by being-planted like-tree and-he-is (3) and-night by-day

אֲשֶׁר פִּרְיוֹ ׀ יִתֵּן בְּעִתּוֹ וְעָלֵהוּ לֹא־ יִבּוֹל
he-withers not and-leaf-of-him in-season-of-him he-yields fruit-of-him which

וְכֹל אֲשֶׁר־ יַעֲשֶׂה יַצְלִיחַ׃ לֹא־ כֵן הָרְשָׁעִים כִּי אִם־
rather but the-wicked-ones so not (4) he-prospers he-does that and-all

כַּמֹּץ אֲשֶׁר־ תִּדְּפֶנּוּ רוּחַ׃ עַל־ כֵּן ׀ לֹא־ יָקֻמוּ
they-will-stand not this for (5) wind she-blows-away-him that like-the-chaff

רְשָׁעִים בַּמִּשְׁפָּט וְחַטָּאִים בַּעֲדַת צַדִּיקִים׃ כִּי־
for (6) righteous-ones in-assembly-of or-sinners in-the-judgment wicked-ones

יוֹדֵעַ יְהוָה דֶּרֶךְ צַדִּיקִים וְדֶרֶךְ רְשָׁעִים
wicked-ones but-way-of righteous-ones way-of Yahweh watching-over

תֹּאבֵד׃ לָמָּה רָגְשׁוּ גוֹיִם וּלְאֻמִּים יֶהְגּוּ־ רִיק׃
vanity they-plot and-peoples nations they-rage why? (2:1) she-will-perish

יִתְיַצְּבוּ ׀ מַלְכֵי־ אֶרֶץ וְרוֹזְנִים נוֹסְדוּ־ יָחַד
together they-gather and-ones-ruling earth kings-of they-take-stand (2)

עַל־ יְהוָה* וְעַל־ מְשִׁיחוֹ׃ נְנַתְּקָה אֶת־
*** let-us-break (3) anointed-one-of-him and-against Yahweh against

מוֹסְרוֹתֵימוֹ וְנַשְׁלִיכָה מִמֶּנּוּ עֲבֹתֵימוֹ׃
fetters-of-them from-us and-let-us-throw-off chains-of-them

יוֹשֵׁב בַּשָּׁמַיִם יִשְׂחָק אֲדֹנָי יִלְעַג־ לָמוֹ׃
at-them he-scoffs Lord he-laughs in-the-heavens One-being-enthroned (4)

אָז יְדַבֵּר אֵלֵימוֹ בְאַפּוֹ וּבַחֲרוֹנוֹ
and-in-wrath-of-him in-anger-of-him against-them he-rebukes then (5)

יְבַהֲלֵמוֹ׃ וַאֲנִי נָסַכְתִּי מַלְכִּי עַל־ צִיּוֹן הַר־
hill-of Zion on king-of-me I-installed indeed-I (6) he-terrifies-them

קָדְשִׁי׃ אֲסַפְּרָה אֶל חֹק יְהוָה אָמַר אֵלַי
to-me he-said Yahweh decree-of to I-will-proclaim (7) holiness-of-me

בְּנִי אַתָּה אֲנִי הַיּוֹם יְלִדְתִּיךָ׃ שְׁאַל מִמֶּנִּי
of-me ask! (8) I-became-father-of-you the-day I you son-of-me

וְאֶתְּנָה גוֹיִם נַחֲלָתֶךָ וַאֲחֻזָּתְךָ אַפְסֵי־ אָרֶץ׃
earth ends-of and-possession-of-you inheritance-of-you nations and-I-will-make

BOOK I

Psalms 1-41

Psalm 1

1 Blessed is the man
who does not walk in the counsel of the wicked
or stand in the way of sinners
or sit in the seat of mockers.
2 But his delight is in the law of the LORD,
and on his law he meditates day and night.
3 He is like a tree planted by streams of water,
which yields its fruit in season
and whose leaf does not wither.
Whatever he does prospers.

4 Not so the wicked!
They are like chaff
that the wind blows away.
5 Therefore the wicked will not stand in the judgment,
nor sinners in the assembly of the righteous.

6 For the LORD watches over the way of the righteous,
but the way of the wicked will perish.

Psalm 2

1 Why do the nations rage
and the peoples plot in vain?
2 The kings of the earth take their stand
and the rulers gather together
against the LORD
and against his Anointed One.[a]
3 "Let us break their chains," they say,
"and throw off their fetters."

4 The One enthroned in heaven laughs;
the Lord scoffs at them.
5 Then he rebukes them in his anger
and terrifies them in his wrath, saying,
6 "I have installed my King[b]
on Zion, my holy hill."

7 I will proclaim the decree of the LORD:

He said to me, "You are my Son[c];
today I have become your Father.[d]
8 Ask of me,
and I will make the nations your inheritance,
the ends of the earth your possession.

[a]2 Or *anointed one*
[b]6 Or *king* [c]7 Or *son*; also in verse 12
[d]7 Or *have begotten you*

*2 Most mss have the accent *rebia mugrash* (·′).

תְּרֹעֵם בְּשֵׁבֶט בַּרְזֶל כִּכְלִי יוֹצֵר
one-making-pottery like-article-of iron with-scepter-of you-will-rule-them (9)

תְּנַפְּצֵם׃ וְעַתָּה מְלָכִים הַשְׂכִּילוּ הִוָּסְרוּ
be-warned! be-wise! kings therefore-now (10) you-will-dash-to-pieces-them

שֹׁפְטֵי אָרֶץ׃ עִבְדוּ אֶת־ יְהוָה בְּיִרְאָה וְגִילוּ בִּרְעָדָה׃
with-trembling and-rejoice! with-fear Yahweh *** serve! (11) earth ones-ruling-of

נַשְּׁקוּ־ בַר פֶּן־ יֶאֱנַף ׀ וְתֹאבְדוּ דֶרֶךְ כִּי־ יִבְעַר
he-can-flare-up for way and-you-be-destroyed he-be-angry lest son kiss! (12)

כִּמְעַט אַפּוֹ אַשְׁרֵי כָּל־ חוֹסֵי בוֹ׃
in-him ones-taking-refuge-of all-of blessednesses-of wrath-of-him in-moment

מִזְמוֹר לְדָוִד בְּבָרְחוֹ מִפְּנֵי ׀ אַבְשָׁלוֹם בְּנוֹ׃
son-of-him Absalom from-faces-of when-to-flee-him of-David psalm *(3:1)

יְהוָה מָה־ רַבּוּ צָרָי רַבִּים קָמִים עָלָי׃
against-me ones-rising-up many foes-of-me they-are-many how! Yahweh (2)

רַבִּים אֹמְרִים לְנַפְשִׁי אֵין יְשׁוּעָתָה לּוֹ בֵאלֹהִים סֶלָה׃
selah by-God for-him deliverance no of-self-of-me ones-saying many (3)

וְאַתָּה יְהוָה מָגֵן בַּעֲדִי כְּבוֹדִי וּמֵרִים
and-one-lifting Glorious-One-of-me around-me shield Yahweh but-you (4)

רֹאשִׁי׃ קוֹלִי אֶל־ יְהוָה אֶקְרָא וַיַּעֲנֵנִי מֵהַר
from-hill-of and-he-answers-me I-cry Yahweh to voice-of-me (5) head-of-me

קָדְשׁוֹ סֶלָה׃ אֲנִי שָׁכַבְתִּי וָאִישָׁנָה הֱקִיצוֹתִי כִּי יְהוָה
Yahweh because I-wake and-I-sleep I-lie-down I (6) selah holiness-of-him

יִסְמְכֵנִי׃ לֹא־ אִירָא מֵרִבְבוֹת עָם אֲשֶׁר
who people of-tens-of-thousands-of I-will-fear not (7) he-sustains-me

סָבִיב שָׁתוּ עָלָי׃ קוּמָה יְהוָה ׀ הוֹשִׁיעֵנִי אֱלֹהַי
God-of-me deliver-me! Yahweh arise! (8) against-me they-are-drawn-up every-side

כִּי־ הִכִּיתָ אֶת־ כָּל־ אֹיְבַי לֶחִי שִׁנֵּי רְשָׁעִים
wicked-ones teeth-of jaw ones-being-enemies-of-me all-of *** you-struck for

שִׁבַּרְתָּ׃ לַיהוָה הַיְשׁוּעָה עַל־ עַמְּךָ בִרְכָתֶךָ
blessing-of-you people-of-you on the-deliverance from-Yahweh (9) you-broke

סֶלָה׃ לַמְנַצֵּחַ בִּנְגִינוֹת מִזְמוֹר לְדָוִד׃
of-David psalm with-stringed-instruments for-the-one-directing *(4:1) selah

בְּקָרְאִי עֲנֵנִי ׀ אֱלֹהֵי צִדְקִי בַּצָּר
from-the-distress righteousness-of-me God-of answer-me! when-to-call-me (2)

הִרְחַבְתָּ לִּי חָנֵּנִי וּשְׁמַע תְּפִלָּתִי׃ בְּנֵי
sons-of (3) prayer-of-me and-hear! be-merciful-to-me! to-me you-give-relief

אִישׁ עַד־ מֶה כְבוֹדִי לִכְלִמָּה תֶּאֱהָבוּן רִיק תְּבַקְשׁוּ
will-you-seek delusion will-you-love into-shame glory-of-me when? until man

9 You will rule them with an
iron scepter[e];
you will dash them to pieces
like pottery."
10 Therefore, you kings, be wise;
be warned, you rulers of the
earth.
11 Serve the LORD with fear
and rejoice with trembling.
12 Kiss the Son, lest he be angry
and you be destroyed in
your way,
for his wrath can flare up in a
moment.
Blessed are all who take
refuge in him.

Psalm 3

A psalm of David. When he fled from his son Absalom.

1 O LORD, how many are my
foes!
How many rise up against
me!
2 Many are saying of me,
"God will not deliver him."
Selah[f]
3 But you are a shield around
me, O LORD,
my Glorious One, who lifts
up my head.
4 To the LORD I cry aloud,
and he answers me from his
holy hill. *Selah*
5 I lie down and sleep;
I wake again, because the
LORD sustains me.
6 I will not fear the tens of
thousands
drawn up against me on
every side.
7 Arise, O LORD!
Deliver me, O my God!
For you have struck all my
enemies on the jaw;
you have broken the teeth
of the wicked.
8 From the LORD comes
deliverance.
May your blessing be on
your people. *Selah*

Psalm 4

For the director of music. With stringed instruments. A psalm of David.

1 Answer me when I call to you,
O my righteous God.
Give me relief from my
distress;
be merciful to me and hear
my prayer.
2 How long, O men, will you
turn my glory into
shame[g]?
How long will you love
delusions and seek false

e9 Or *will break them with a rod of iron*
f2 A word of uncertain meaning, occurring frequently in the Psalms; possibly a musical term
g2 Or *you dishonor my Glorious One*

***1 The Hebrew numeration of this psalm begins with the "superscription" of the English translation; thus there is a one-verse discrepancy throughout the psalm.**

כָזָב סֶלָה׃ וּדְעוּ כִּי־הִפְלָה יְהוָה חָסִיד לוֹ יְהוָה
Yahweh for-him godly Yahweh he-set-apart that and-know! (4) selah lie

יִשְׁמַע בְּקָרְאִי אֵלָיו׃ רִגְזוּ וְאַל־תֶּחֱטָאוּ אִמְרוּ
search! you-sin and-not be-angry! (5) to-him when-to-call-me he-will-hear

בִלְבַבְכֶם עַל־מִשְׁכַּבְכֶם וְדֹמּוּ סֶלָה׃ זִבְחוּ זִבְחֵי־
sacrifices-of offer! (6) selah and-be-silent! bed-of-you on in-heart-of-you

צֶדֶק וּבִטְחוּ אֶל־יְהוָה׃ רַבִּים אֹמְרִים מִי־יַרְאֵנוּ טוֹב
good he-can-show-us who? ones-asking many (7) Yahweh in and-trust! right

נְסָה־עָלֵינוּ אוֹר פָּנֶיךָ יְהוָה׃ נָתַתָּה שִׂמְחָה
joy you-put (8) Yahweh faces-of-you light-of upon-us let-shine!

בְלִבִּי מֵעֵת דְּגָנָם וְתִירוֹשָׁם
and-new-wine-of-them grain-of-them more-than-time-of in-heart-of-me

רָבּוּ׃ בְּשָׁלוֹם יַחְדָּו אֶשְׁכְּבָה וְאִישָׁן כִּי־אַתָּה
you for and-I-will-sleep I-will-lie-down together in-peace (9) they-abound

יְהוָה לְבָדָד לָבֶטַח תּוֹשִׁיבֵנִי׃ לַמְנַצֵּחַ אֶל־
for for-the-one-directing *(5:1) you-make-dwell-me in-safety alone Yahweh

הַנְּחִילוֹת מִזְמוֹר לְדָוִד׃ אֲמָרַי הַאֲזִינָה ׀ יְהוָה בִּינָה
consider! Yahweh give-ear! words-of-me (2) of-David psalm the-flutes

הֲגִיגִי׃ הַקְשִׁיבָה ׀ לְקוֹל שַׁוְעִי מַלְכִּי
King-of-me cry-for-help-of-me to-sound-of listen! (3) sighing-of-me

וֵאלֹהָי כִּי־אֵלֶיךָ אֶתְפַּלָּל׃ יְהוָה בֹּקֶר תִּשְׁמַע קוֹלִי
voice-of-me you-hear morning Yahweh (4) I-pray to-you for and-God-of-me

בֹּקֶר אֶעֱרָךְ־לְךָ וַאֲצַפֶּה׃ כִּי ׀ לֹא אֵל־חָפֵץ
pleased-in God-of not for (5) and-I-wait before-you I-lay-request morning

רֶשַׁע ׀ אָתָּה לֹא יְגֻרְךָ רָע׃ לֹא־יִתְיַצְּבוּ
they-can-stand not (6) wicked he-can-dwell-with-you not you evil

הוֹלְלִים לְנֶגֶד עֵינֶיךָ שָׂנֵאתָ כָּל־פֹּעֲלֵי אָוֶן׃
wrong ones-doing-of all-of you-hate eyes-of-you at-before ones-being-arrogant

תְּאַבֵּד דֹּבְרֵי כָזָב אִישׁ־דָּמִים וּמִרְמָה יְתָעֵב ׀
he-abhors and-deceit bloods man-of lie ones-telling-of you-destroy (7)

יְהוָה׃ וַאֲנִי בְּרֹב חַסְדְּךָ אָבוֹא בֵיתֶךָ
house-of-you I-will-come-into mercy-of-you by-greatness-of but-I (8) Yahweh

אֶשְׁתַּחֲוֶה אֶל־הֵיכַל־קָדְשְׁךָ בְּיִרְאָתֶךָ׃ יְהוָה ׀
Yahweh (9) in-reverence-of-you holiness-of-you temple-of toward I-will-bow

נְחֵנִי בְצִדְקָתֶךָ לְמַעַן שׁוֹרְרָי
ones-being-enemies-of-me because-of in-righteousness-of-you lead-me!

הַוְשַׁר לְפָנַי דַּרְכֶּךָ׃ כִּי אֵין בְּפִיהוּ נְכוֹנָה
being-trusted from-mouth-of-him not for (10) way-of-you before-me make-straight!

gods[h]? *Selah*
3 Know that the LORD has set
apart the godly for
himself;
the LORD will hear when I
call to him.

4 In your anger do not sin;
when you are on your beds,
search your hearts and be
silent. *Selah*
5 Offer right sacrifices
and trust in the LORD.

6 Many are asking, "Who can
show us any good?"
Let the light of your face
shine upon us, O LORD.
7 You have filled my heart with
greater joy
than when their grain and
new wine abound.
8 I will lie down and sleep in
peace,
for you alone, O LORD,
make me dwell in safety.

Psalm 5

For the director of music. For flutes. A psalm of David.

1 Give ear to my words, O LORD,
consider my sighing.
2 Listen to my cry for help,
my King and my God,
for to you I pray.
3 Morning by morning, O LORD,
you hear my voice;
morning by morning I lay
my requests before you
and wait in expectation.

4 You are not a God who takes
pleasure in evil;
with you the wicked cannot
dwell.
5 The arrogant cannot stand in
your presence;
you hate all who do wrong.
6 You destroy those who tell lies;
bloodthirsty and deceitful
men
the LORD abhors.

7 But I, by your great mercy,
will come into your house;
in reverence will I bow down
toward your holy temple.
8 Lead me, O LORD, in your
righteousness
because of my enemies—
make straight your way
before me.

9 Not a word from their mouth
can be trusted;

h2 Hebrew *seek lies*

*Heading, *1* See the note on page 349.

°9 ק הישר

קִרְבָּם הַוּוֹת קֶבֶר־ פָּתוּחַ גְּרוֹנָם לְשׁוֹנָם
tongue-of-them throat-of-them being-open grave destructions heart-of-them

יַחֲלִיקוּן׃ הַאֲשִׁימֵם ׀ אֱלֹהִים יִפְּלוּ
let-them-fall God declare-guilty-them! (11) they-speak-deceit

מִמֹּעֲצוֹתֵיהֶם בְּרֹב פִּשְׁעֵיהֶם הַדִּיחֵמוֹ כִּי־ מָרוּ
they-rebelled for banish-them! sins-of-them for-many-of by-intrigues-of-them

בָךְ׃ וְיִשְׂמְחוּ כָל־ חוֹסֵי בָךְ
in-you ones-taking-refuge-of all-of but-let-them-be-glad (12) against-you

לְעוֹלָם יְרַנֵּנוּ וְתָסֵךְ עָלֵימוֹ
over-them and-you-spread-protection let-them-sing-for-joy for-ever

וְיַעְלְצוּ בְךָ אֹהֲבֵי שְׁמֶךָ׃ כִּי־ אַתָּה
you for (13) name-of-you ones-loving-of in-you that-they-may-rejoice

תְּבָרֵךְ צַדִּיק יְהוָה כַּצִּנָּה רָצוֹן תַּעְטְרֶנּוּ׃
you-surround-him favor as-the-shield Yahweh righteous you-bless

לַמְנַצֵּחַ בִּנְגִינוֹת עַל־ הַשְּׁמִינִית
the-sheminith according-to with-stringed-instruments for-the-one-directing *(6:1)

מִזְמוֹר לְדָוִד׃ יְהוָה אַל־ בְּאַפְּךָ תוֹכִיחֵנִי וְאַל־
or-not you-rebuke-me in-anger-of-you not Yahweh (2) of-David psalm

בַּחֲמָתְךָ תְיַסְּרֵנִי׃ חָנֵּנִי יְהוָה כִּי אֻמְלַל
faint for Yahweh be-merciful-to-me! (3) you-discipline-me in-wrath-of-you

אָנִי רְפָאֵנִי יְהוָה כִּי נִבְהֲלוּ עֲצָמָי׃ וְנַפְשִׁי
and-soul-of-me (4) bones-of-me they-are-in-agony for Yahweh heal-me! I

נִבְהֲלָה מְאֹד וְאַתָּ יְהוָה עַד־ מָתָי׃ שׁוּבָה יְהוָה חַלְּצָה
deliver! Yahweh turn! (5) when? until Yahweh but-you great she-is-in-anguish

נַפְשִׁי הוֹשִׁיעֵנִי לְמַעַן חַסְדֶּךָ׃ כִּי אֵין בַּמָּוֶת
in-the-death not for (6) unfailing-love-of-you because-of save-me! soul-of-me

זִכְרֶךָ בִּשְׁאוֹל מִי יוֹדֶה־ לָּךְ׃ יָגַעְתִּי ׀
I-am-worn-out (7) to-you he-praises who? from-Sheol remembrance-of-you

בְּאַנְחָתִי אַשְׂחֶה בְכָל־ לַיְלָה מִטָּתִי בְּדִמְעָתִי
with-tear-of-me bed-of-me night through-all-of I-flood from-groaning-of-me

עַרְשִׂי אַמְסֶה׃ עָשְׁשָׁה מִכַּעַס עֵינִי עָתְקָה
she-fails eye-of-me with-sorrow she-grows-weak (8) I-drench couch-of-me

בְּכָל־ צוֹרְרָי׃ סוּרוּ מִמֶּנִּי כָּל־ פֹּעֲלֵי
ones-doing-of all-of from-me away! (9) ones-being-foes-of-me because-of-all-of

אָוֶן כִּי־ שָׁמַע יְהוָה קוֹל בִּכְיִי׃ שָׁמַע יְהוָה
Yahweh he-heard (10) weeping-of-me sound-of Yahweh he-heard for evil

תְּחִנָּתִי יְהוָה תְּפִלָּתִי יִקָּח׃ יֵבֹשׁוּ ׀
may-they-be-ashamed (11) he-accepts prayer-of-me Yahweh cry-for-mercy-of-me

their heart is filled with destruction.
Their throat is an open grave;
with their tongue they speak deceit.
10 Declare them guilty, O God!
Let their intrigues be their downfall.
Banish them for their many sins,
for they have rebelled against you.
11 But let all who take refuge in you be glad;
let them ever sing for joy.
Spread your protection over them,
that those who love your name may rejoice in you.
12 For surely, O LORD, you bless the righteous;
you surround them with your favor as with a shield.

Psalm 6

For the director of music. With stringed instruments. According to *sheminith*.[t] A psalm of David.

1 O LORD, do not rebuke me in your anger
or discipline me in your wrath.
2 Be merciful to me, LORD, for I am faint;
O LORD, heal me, for my bones are in agony.
3 My soul is in anguish.
How long, O LORD, how long?

4 Turn, O LORD, and deliver me;
save me because of your unfailing love.
5 No one remembers you when he is dead.
Who praises you from the grave[j]?

6 I am worn out from groaning;
all night long I flood my bed with weeping
and drench my couch with tears.
7 My eyes grow weak with sorrow;
they fail because of all my foes.

8 Away from me, all you who do evil,
for the LORD has heard my weeping.
9 The LORD has heard my cry for mercy;
the LORD accepts my prayer.

tTitle: Probably a musical term
j5 Hebrew *Sheol*

*Heading, *1* See the note on page 349.
†*10* Most mss have the accent on the final syllable.
°*4* ק ואתה

וְיִבָּהֲלוּ מְאֹד כָּל־אֹיְבָי
and-may-they-be-dismayed greatly all-of ones-being-enemies-of-me

יָשֻׁבוּ יֵבֹשׁוּ רָגַע׃ שִׁגָּיוֹן לְדָוִד
may-they-turn-back may-they-be-disgraced suddenly *(7:1) shiggaion of-David

אֲשֶׁר־שָׁר לַיהוָה עַל־דִּבְרֵי־כוּשׁ בֶּן־יְמִינִי׃ יְהוָה
which he-sang to-Yahweh concerning matters-of Cush Benjamite (2) Yahweh

אֱלֹהַי בְּךָ חָסִיתִי הוֹשִׁיעֵנִי מִכָּל־רֹדְפַי
God-of-me in-you I-take-refuge save-me! from-all-of ones-pursuing-me

וְהַצִּילֵנִי׃ פֶּן־יִטְרֹף כְּאַרְיֵה נַפְשִׁי פֹּרֵק
and-deliver-me! (3) or he-will-tear like-lion self-of-me ripping-to-pieces

וְאֵין מַצִּיל׃ יְהוָה אֱלֹהַי אִם־עָשִׂיתִי זֹאת אִם־יֶשׁ־עָוֶל
and-no-one rescuing (4) Yahweh God-of-me if I-did this if there-is guilt

בְּכַפָּי׃ אִם־גָּמַלְתִּי שׁוֹלְמִי רָע וָאֲחַלְּצָה
on-hands-of-me (5) if I-did one-being-at-peace-with-me evil or-I-robbed

צוֹרְרִי רֵיקָם׃ יִרַדֹּף אוֹיֵב ׀
one-being-foe-of-me without-cause (6) let-him-pursue one-being-enemy

נַפְשִׁי וְיַשֵּׂג וְיִרְמֹס לָאָרֶץ חַיָּי
self-of-me and-let-him-overtake and-let-him-trample to-the-ground lives-of-me

וּכְבוֹדִי ׀ לֶעָפָר יַשְׁכֵּן סֶלָה׃ קוּמָה יְהוָה ׀
and-honor-of-me in-the-dust let-him-make-sleep selah (7) arise! Yahweh

בְּאַפֶּךָ הִנָּשֵׂא בְּעַבְרוֹת צוֹרְרָי וְעוּרָה
in-anger-of-you rise-up! against-rages-of ones-being-enemies-of-me and-awake!

אֵלַי מִשְׁפָּט צִוִּיתָ׃ וַעֲדַת לְאֻמִּים תְּסוֹבְבֶךָּ
God-of-me justice you-decree (8) and-assembly-of peoples let-her-surround-you

וְעָלֶיהָ לַמָּרוֹם שׁוּבָה׃ יְהוָה יָדִין עַמִּים
and-over-her from-the-height rule! (9) Yahweh let-him-judge peoples

שָׁפְטֵנִי יְהוָה כְּצִדְקִי וּכְתֻמִּי עָלָי׃
judge-me! Yahweh as-righteousness-of-me and-as-integrity-of-me Most-High

יִגְמָר־נָא רַע ׀ רְשָׁעִים וּתְכוֹנֵן צַדִּיק
(10) may-he-end now! violence-of wicked-ones and-you-make-secure righteous

וּבֹחֵן לִבּוֹת וּכְלָיוֹת אֱלֹהִים צַדִּיק׃ מָגִנִּי עַל־אֱלֹהִים
and-searching minds and-hearts God righteous (11) shield-of-me Most-High God

מוֹשִׁיעַ יִשְׁרֵי־לֵב׃ אֱלֹהִים שׁוֹפֵט צַדִּיק וְאֵל
saving ones-upright-of heart (12) God judging righteous and-God

זֹעֵם בְּכָל־יוֹם׃ אִם־לֹא יָשׁוּב חַרְבּוֹ
expressing-wrath in-every-of day (13) if not he-relents sword-of-him

יִלְטוֹשׁ קַשְׁתּוֹ דָרַךְ וַיְכוֹנְנֶהָ׃
he-will-sharpen bow-of-him he-will-bend and-he-will-string-her

*Heading, 1 See the note on page 349.

10 May all my enemies be
ashamed and dismayed;
may they turn back in
sudden disgrace.

Psalm 7

A *shiggaion*[k] of David, which he sang to the LORD concerning Cush, a Benjamite.

1 O LORD my God, I take refuge
in you;
save and deliver me from all
who pursue me,
2 or they will tear me like a lion
and rip me to pieces with
no one to rescue me.

3 O LORD my God, if I have
done this
and there is guilt on my
hands—
4 if I have done evil to him who
is at peace with me
or without cause have
robbed my foe—
5 then let my enemy pursue and
overtake me;
let him trample my life to
the ground
and make me sleep in the
dust. *Selah*

6 Arise, O LORD, in your anger;
rise up against the rage of
my enemies.
Awake, my God; decree
justice.
7 Let the assembled peoples
gather around you.
Rule over them from on
high;
8 let the LORD judge the
peoples.
Judge me, O LORD, according
to my righteousness,
according to my integrity, O
Most High.
9 O righteous God,
who searches minds and
hearts,
bring to an end the violence of
the wicked
and make the righteous
secure.

10 My shield[l] is God Most High,
who saves the upright in
heart.
11 God is a righteous judge,
a God who expresses his
wrath every day.
12 If he does not relent,
he[m] will sharpen his sword;
he will bend and string his
bow.

[k] Title: Probably a literary or musical term
[l] 10 Or *sovereign*
[m] 12 Or *If a man does not repent, / God*

וְלוֹ הֵכִין כְּלֵי־ מָוֶת חִצָּיו לְדֹלְקִים
of-ones-flaming arrows-of-him death weapons-of he-prepared and-for-him (14)

יִפְעָל׃ הִנֵּה יְחַבֶּל־ אָוֶן וְהָרָה עָמָל
trouble and-he-conceives evil he-is-pregnant see! (15) he-makes-ready

וְיָלַד שָׁקֶר׃ בּוֹר כָּרָה וַיַּחְפְּרֵהוּ
and-he-scoops-out-him he-digs hole (16) disillusionment then-he-gives-birth

וַיִּפֹּל בְּשַׁחַת יִפְעָל׃ יָשׁוּב עֲמָלוֹ בְרֹאשׁוֹ
on-head-of-him trouble-of-him he-recoils (17) he-made into-pit but-he-falls

וְעַל קָדְקֳדוֹ חֲמָסוֹ יֵרֵד׃ אוֹדֶה יְהוָה
Yahweh I-will-thank (18) he-comes-down violence-of-him head-of-him and-on

כְּצִדְקוֹ וַאֲזַמְּרָה שֵׁם־ יְהוָה עֶלְיוֹן׃
Most-High Yahweh name-of and-I-will-sing-praise because-of-righteousness-of-him

לַמְנַצֵּחַ עַל־ הַגִּתִּית מִזְמוֹר לְדָוִד׃
of-David psalm the-gittith according-to for-the-one-directing *(8:1)

יְהוָה אֲדֹנֵינוּ מָה־ אַדִּיר שִׁמְךָ בְּכָל־ הָאָרֶץ אֲשֶׁר
who the-earth in-all-of name-of-you majestic how! Lord-of-us Yahweh (2)

תְּנָה הוֹדְךָ עַל־ הַשָּׁמָיִם׃ מִפִּי עוֹלְלִים ׀
children from-lip-of (3) the-heavens above glory-of-you set!

וְיֹנְקִים יִסַּדְתָּ עֹז לְמַעַן צוֹרְרֶיךָ
ones-being-enemies-of-you because-of strength you-ordained and-ones-being-infants

לְהַשְׁבִּית אוֹיֵב וּמִתְנַקֵּם׃ כִּי־ אֶרְאֶה שָׁמֶיךָ
heavens-of-you I-consider when (4) and-one-avenging one-being-foe to-silence

מַעֲשֵׂי אֶצְבְּעֹתֶיךָ יָרֵחַ וְכוֹכָבִים אֲשֶׁר כּוֹנָנְתָּה׃ מָה־
what? (5) you-set-in-place which and-stars moon fingers-of-you works-of

אֱנוֹשׁ כִּי־ תִזְכְּרֶנּוּ וּבֶן־ אָדָם כִּי תִפְקְדֶנּוּ׃
you-care-for-him that man and-son-of you-are-mindful-of-him that man

וַתְּחַסְּרֵהוּ מְּעַט מֵאֱלֹהִים וְכָבוֹד וְהָדָר תְּעַטְּרֵהוּ׃
you-crowned-him and-honor and-glory than-God little and-you-made-lower-him (6)

תַּמְשִׁילֵהוּ בְּמַעֲשֵׂי יָדֶיךָ כֹּל שַׁתָּה תַחַת־
under you-put everything hands-of-you over-works-of you-made-ruler-him (7)

רַגְלָיו׃ צֹנֶה וַאֲלָפִים כֻּלָּם וְגַם בַּהֲמוֹת שָׂדָי׃
field beasts-of and-also all-of-them and-herds flock (8) feet-of-him

צִפּוֹר שָׁמַיִם וּדְגֵי הַיָּם עֹבֵר אָרְחוֹת יַמִּים׃
seas paths-of swimming-through the-sea and-fishes-of airs bird-of (9)

יְהוָה אֲדֹנֵינוּ מָה־ אַדִּיר שִׁמְךָ בְּכָל־ הָאָרֶץ׃
the-earth in-all-of name-of-you majestic how! Lord-of-us Yahweh (10)

לַמְנַצֵּחַ עַלְמוּת לַבֵּן מִזְמוֹר לְדָוִד׃
of-David psalm of-the-son to-death-of for-the-one-directing *(9:1)

13 He has prepared his deadly weapons;
he makes ready his flaming arrows.
14 He who is pregnant with evil
and conceives trouble gives birth to disillusionment.
15 He who digs a hole and scoops it out
falls into the pit he has made.
16 The trouble he causes recoils on himself;
his violence comes down on his own head.

17 I will give thanks to the LORD because of his righteousness
and will sing praise to the name of the LORD Most High.

Psalm 8

For the director of music. According to *gittith.*[n] A psalm of David.

1 O LORD, our Lord,
how majestic is your name in all the earth!

You have set your glory
above the heavens.
2 From the lips of children and infants
you have ordained praise[o]
because of your enemies,
to silence the foe and the avenger.

3 When I consider your heavens,
the work of your fingers,
the moon and the stars,
which you have set in place,
4 what is man that you are mindful of him,
the son of man that you care for him?
5 You made him a little lower than the heavenly beings[p]
and crowned him with glory and honor.

6 You made him ruler over the works of your hands;
you put everything under his feet:
7 all flocks and herds,
and the beasts of the field,
8 the birds of the air,
and the fish of the sea,
all that swim the paths of the seas.

9 O LORD, our Lord,
how majestic is your name in all the earth!

Psalm 9[q]

For the director of music. To the tune of "The Death of the Son." A psalm of David.

[n]Title: Probably a musical term
[o]2 Or *strength*
[p]5 Or *than God*
[q]Psalms 9 and 10 may have been originally a single acrostic poem, the stanzas of which begin with the successive letters of the Hebrew alphabet. In the Septuagint they constitute one psalm.

*Heading, *1* See the note on page 349.

(2) אוֹדֶה יְהוָה בְּכָל־ לִבִּי אֲסַפְּרָה כָּל־
(2) I-will-praise Yahweh with-all-of heart-of-me I-will-tell all-of

נִפְלְאוֹתֶיךָ׃ (3) אֶשְׂמְחָה וְאֶעֶלְצָה בָךְ
things-being-wonders-of-you (3) I-will-be-glad and-I-will-rejoice in-you

אֲזַמְּרָה שִׁמְךָ עֶלְיוֹן׃ (4) בְּשׁוּב־ אוֹיְבַי
I-will-sing-praise name-of-you Most-High (4) when-to-turn being-enemies-of-me

אָחוֹר יִכָּשְׁלוּ וְיֹאבְדוּ מִפָּנֶיךָ׃ (5) כִּי־ עָשִׂיתָ מִשְׁפָּטִי
back they-stumble and-they-perish at-before-you (5) for you-upheld right-of-me

וְדִינִי יָשַׁבְתָּ לְכִסֵּא שׁוֹפֵט צֶדֶק׃ (6) גָּעַרְתָּ גוֹיִם
and-cause-of-me you-sat on-throne judging righteous (6) you-rebuked nations

אִבַּדְתָּ רָשָׁע שְׁמָם מָחִיתָ לְעוֹלָם וָעֶד׃
you-destroyed wicked name-of-them you-blotted-out to-forever and-ever

(7) הָאוֹיֵב ׀ תַּמּוּ חֳרָבוֹת לָנֶצַח וְעָרִים
(7) the-one-being-enemy they-are-overtaken ruins to-endless and-cities

נָתַשְׁתָּ אָבַד זִכְרָם הֵמָּה׃ (8) וַיהוָה לְעוֹלָם
you-uprooted he-perished memory-of-them they (8) and-Yahweh to-forever

יֵשֵׁב כּוֹנֵן לַמִּשְׁפָּט כִּסְאוֹ׃ (9) וְהוּא
he-reigns he-established for-the-judgment throne-of-him (9) and-he

יִשְׁפֹּט־ תֵּבֵל בְּצֶדֶק יָדִין לְאֻמִּים בְּמֵישָׁרִים׃
he-will-judge world in-righteousness he-will-govern peoples with-justices

(10) וִיהִי יְהוָה מִשְׂגָּב לַדָּךְ מִשְׂגָּב לְעִתּוֹת
(10) and-he-is Yahweh refuge for-the-oppressed stronghold in-times

בַּצָּרָה׃ (11) וְיִבְטְחוּ בְךָ יוֹדְעֵי שְׁמֶךָ כִּי
of-the-trouble (11) and-they-will-trust in-you ones-knowing-of name-of-you for

לֹא־ עָזַבְתָּ דֹרְשֶׁיךָ יְהוָה׃ (12) זַמְּרוּ לַיהוָה
never you-forsook ones-seeking-of-you Yahweh (12) sing-praises! to-Yahweh

יֹשֵׁב צִיּוֹן הַגִּידוּ בָעַמִּים עֲלִילוֹתָיו׃ (13) כִּי־
one-being-enthroned-of Zion proclaim! among-the-nations deeds-of-him (13) for

דֹרֵשׁ דָּמִים אוֹתָם זָכָר לֹא־ שָׁכַח צַעֲקַת עֲנִיִּים׃
one-avenging bloods them he-remembers not he-ignores cry-of afflicted-ones

(14) חָנְנֵנִי יְהוָה רְאֵה עָנְיִי מִשֹּׂנְאָי
(14) have-mercy-on-me! Yahweh see! persecution-of-me by-ones-being-enemies-of-me

מְרוֹמְמִי מִשַּׁעֲרֵי מָוֶת׃ (15) לְמַעַן אֲסַפְּרָה כָּל־
lifting-up-me from-gates-of death (15) that I-may-declare all-of

תְּהִלָּתֶיךָ בְּשַׁעֲרֵי בַת־ צִיּוֹן אָגִילָה בִּישׁוּעָתֶךָ׃
praises-of-you in-gates-of daughter-of Zion I-will-rejoice in-salvation-of-you

(16) טָבְעוּ גוֹיִם בְּשַׁחַת עָשׂוּ בְּרֶשֶׁת־ זוּ טָמָנוּ נִלְכְּדָה
(16) they-fell nations into-pit they-dug in-net that they-hid she-is-caught

[1] I will praise you, O LORD, with
all my heart;
I will tell of all your
wonders.
[2] I will be glad and rejoice in
you;
I will sing praise to your
name, O Most High.

[3] My enemies turn back;
they stumble and perish
before you.
[4] For you have upheld my right
and my cause;
you have sat on your
throne, judging
righteously.
[5] You have rebuked the nations
and destroyed the wicked;
you have blotted out their
name for ever and ever.
[6] Endless ruin has overtaken the
enemy,
you have uprooted their
cities;
even the memory of them
has perished.

[7] The LORD reigns forever;
he has established his
throne for judgment.
[8] He will judge the world in
righteousness;
he will govern the peoples
with justice.
[9] The LORD is a refuge for the
oppressed,
a stronghold in times of
trouble.
[10] Those who know your name
will trust in you,
for you, LORD, have never
forsaken those who seek
you.

[11] Sing praises to the LORD,
enthroned in Zion;
proclaim among the nations
what he has done.
[12] For he who avenges blood
remembers;
he does not ignore the cry
of the afflicted.

[13] O LORD, see how my enemies
persecute me!
Have mercy and lift me up
from the gates of death,
[14] that I may declare your praises
in the gates of the Daughter
of Zion
and there rejoice in your
salvation.
[15] The nations have fallen into
the pit they have dug;
their feet are caught in the
net they have hidden.

*See the note on page 349.

°13 ק ענוים

רַגְלָם׃ נוֹדַע ׀ יְהוָה מִשְׁפָּט עָשָׂה בְּפֹעַל כַּפָּיו
hands-of-him by-work-of he-does justice Yahweh he-is-known (17) foot-of-them

נוֹקֵשׁ רָשָׁע הִגָּיוֹן סֶלָה׃ יָשׁוּבוּ רְשָׁעִים לִשְׁאֹלָה
to-Sheol wicked-ones they-return (18) selah higgaion wicked being-ensnared

כָּל־ גּוֹיִם שְׁכֵחֵי אֱלֹהִים׃ כִּי לֹא לָנֶצַח
to-always not but (19) God ones-forgetful-of nations all-of

יִשָּׁכַח אֶבְיוֹן תִּקְוַת עֲנָוִים° תֹּאבַד לָעַד׃
to-ever she-will-perish afflicted-ones hope-of needy he-will-be-forgotten

קוּמָה יְהוָה אַל־ יָעֹז אֱנוֹשׁ יִשָּׁפְטוּ גוֹיִם עַל־
in nations let-them-be-judged man let-him-triumph not Yahweh arise! (20)

פָּנֶיךָ׃ שִׁיתָה יְהוָה ׀ מוֹרָה לָהֶם יֵדְעוּ גוֹיִם
nations let-them-know to-them terror Yahweh strike! (21) presences-of-you

אֱנוֹשׁ הֵמָּה סֶלָה׃ לָמָה יְהוָה תַּעֲמֹד בְּרָחוֹק תַּעְלִים לְעִתּוֹת
in-times you-hide at-far-off you-stand Yahweh why? (10:1) selah they man

בַּצָּרָה׃ בְּגַאֲוַת רָשָׁע יִדְלַק עָנִי יִתָּפְשׂוּ ׀
they-are-caught weak he-hunts wicked in-arrogance-of (2) of-the-trouble

בִּמְזִמּוֹת זוּ חָשָׁבוּ׃ כִּי־ הִלֵּל רָשָׁע עַל־ תַּאֲוַת
craving-of about wicked he-boasts for (3) they-devise that in-schemes

נַפְשׁוֹ וּבֹצֵעַ בֵּרֵךְ נִאֵץ ׀ יְהוָה׃ רָשָׁע
wicked (4) Yahweh he-reviles he-blesses and-one-being-greedy heart-of-him

כְּגֹבַהּ אַפּוֹ בַּל־ יִדְרֹשׁ אֵין אֱלֹהִים כָּל־ מְזִמּוֹתָיו׃
thoughts-of-him all-of God not he-seeks not nose-of-him in-pride-of

יָחִילוּ דְרָכָו° ׀ בְּכָל־ עֵת מָרוֹם מִשְׁפָּטֶיךָ מִנֶּגְדּוֹ
from-near-him laws-of-you haughty time at-all-of ways-of-him they-prosper (5)

כָּל־ צוֹרְרָיו יָפִיחַ בָּהֶם׃ אָמַר בְּלִבּוֹ
to-self-of-him he-says (6) at-them he-sneers ones-being-enemies-of-him all-of

בַּל־ אֶמּוֹט לְדֹר וָדֹר אֲשֶׁר לֹא־ בְרָע׃
in-trouble not happy and-generation to-generation I-will-be-shaken not

אָלָה פִּיהוּ מָלֵא וּמִרְמוֹת וָתֹךְ תַּחַת לְשׁוֹנוֹ
tongue-of-him under and-threat and-lies he-is-full mouth-of-him curse (7)

עָמָל וָאָוֶן׃ יֵשֵׁב ׀ בְּמַאְרַב חֲצֵרִים בַּמִּסְתָּרִים יַהֲרֹג
he-murders from-the-ambushes villages in-wait-of he-lies (8) and-evil trouble

נָקִי עֵינָיו לְחֵלְכָה יִצְפֹּנוּ׃ יֶאֱרֹב
he-lies-in-wait (9) they-are-secret for-victim eyes-of-him innocent

בַּמִּסְתָּר ׀ כְּאַרְיֵה בְסֻכֹּה יֶאֱרֹב לַחֲטוֹף עָנִי
helpless to-catch he-lies-in-wait in-cover-of-him like-lion in-the-ambush

יַחְטֹף עָנִי בְּמָשְׁכוֹ בְרִשְׁתּוֹ׃ וְדָכֶה°
he-is-crushed (10) in-net-of-him when-to-drag-off-him helpless he-catches

[16]The LORD is known by his justice;
the wicked are ensnared by the work of their hands.
Higgaion.[r] *Selah*
[17]The wicked return to the grave,[s]
all the nations that forget God.
[18]But the needy will not always be forgotten,
nor the hope of the afflicted ever perish.

[19]Arise, O LORD, let not man triumph;
let the nations be judged in your presence.
[20]Strike them with terror, O LORD;
let the nations know they are but men. *Selah*

Psalm 10[t]

[1]Why, O LORD, do you stand far off?
Why do you hide yourself in times of trouble?

[2]In his arrogance the wicked man hunts down the weak,
who are caught in the schemes he devises.
[3]He boasts of the cravings of his heart;
he blesses the greedy and reviles the LORD.
[4]In his pride the wicked does not seek him;
in all his thoughts there is no room for God.
[5]His ways are always prosperous;
he is haughty and your laws are far from him;
he sneers at all his enemies.
[6]He says to himself, "Nothing will shake me;
I'll always be happy and never have trouble."
[7]His mouth is full of curses and lies and threats;
trouble and evil are under his tongue.
[8]He lies in wait near the villages;
from ambush he murders the innocent,
watching in secret for his victims.
[9]He lies in wait like a lion in cover;
he lies in wait to catch the helpless;
he catches the helpless and drags them off in his net.

[r]16 Or *Meditation;* possibly a musical notation
[s]17 Hebrew *Sheol*
[t]Psalms 9 and 10 may have been originally a single acrostic poem, the stanzas of which begin with the successive letters of the Hebrew alphabet. In the Septuagint they constitute one psalm.

*See the note on page 349.

°*19* ק עניים
°*5* ק דרכיו
°*10* ק ידכה

יָשֹׁחַ וְנָפַל בַּעֲצוּמָיו חֵלְכָּאִים׃ אָמַר
he-says (11) *victims under-strengths-of-him and-he-falls he-collapses

בְּלִבּוֹ שָׁכַח אֵל הִסְתִּיר פָּנָיו בַּל־ רָאָה לָנֶצַח׃
to-ever he-sees not faces-of-him he-covers God he-forgot to-self-of-him

(12) קוּמָה יְהוָה אֵל נְשָׂא יָדֶךָ אַל־ תִּשְׁכַּח עֲנָיִים׃
helpless-ones you-forget not hand-of-you lift-up! God Yahweh arise! (12)

(13) עַל־ מֶה׀ נִאֵץ רָשָׁע׀ אֱלֹהִים אָמַר בְּלִבּוֹ לֹא
not to-self-of-him he-says God wicked he-reviles why? for (13)

תִּדְרֹשׁ׃ (14) רָאִתָה כִּי־ אַתָּה׀ עָמָל וָכַעַס׀ תַּבִּיט
you-consider and-grief trouble you but you-see (14) you-will-call-account

לָתֵת בְּיָדֶךָ עָלֶיךָ יַעֲזֹב חֵלֶכָה יָתוֹם אַתָּה׀ הָיִיתָ
you-are you fatherless victim he-commits to-you into-hand-of-you to-take

עוֹזֵר׃ (15) שְׁבֹר זְרוֹעַ רָשָׁע וָרָע תִּדְרוֹשׁ־ רִשְׁעוֹ
wickedness-of-him you-call-account and-evil wicked arm-of break! (15) one-helping

בַל־ תִּמְצָא׃ (16) יְהוָה מֶלֶךְ עוֹלָם וָעֶד אָבְדוּ
they-will-perish and-ever forever King Yahweh (16) she-would-be-found-out not

גוֹיִם מֵאַרְצוֹ׃ (17) תַּאֲוַת עֲנָוִים שָׁמַעְתָּ יְהוָה
Yahweh you-hear afflicted-ones desire-of (17) from-land-of-him nations

תָּכִין לִבָּם תַּקְשִׁיב אָזְנֶךָ׃ (18) לִשְׁפֹּט
to-defend (18) ear-of-you you-make-listen heart-of-them you-encourage

יָתוֹם וָדָךְ בַּל־ יוֹסִיף עוֹד לַעֲרֹץ אֱנוֹשׁ מִן־ הָאָרֶץ׃
the-earth from man to-terrify more he-may-repeat not and-oppressed fatherless

(11:1) לַמְנַצֵּחַ לְדָוִד בַּיהוָה׀ חָסִיתִי אֵיךְ תֹּאמְרוּ
can-you-say how? I-take-refuge in-Yahweh of-David for-the-one-directing (11:1)

לְנַפְשִׁי נוּדוּ הַרְכֶם צִפּוֹר׃ (2) כִּי הִנֵּה הָרְשָׁעִים
the-wicked-ones look! for (2) bird mountain-of-you flee! to-self-of-me

יִדְרְכוּן קֶשֶׁת כּוֹנְנוּ חִצָּם עַל־ יֶתֶר לִירוֹת בְּמוֹ־ אֹפֶל
shadow from to-shoot string against arrow-of-them they-set bow they-bend

לְיִשְׁרֵי־ לֵב׃ (3) כִּי הַשָּׁתוֹת יֵהָרֵסוּן צַדִּיק
righteous they-are-destroyed the-foundations when (3) heart at-ones-upright-of

מַה־ פָּעָל׃ (4) יְהוָה׀ בְּהֵיכַל קָדְשׁוֹ יְהוָה בַּשָּׁמַיִם
in-the-heavens Yahweh holiness-of-him in-temple-of Yahweh (4) can-he-do what?

כִּסְאוֹ עֵינָיו יֶחֱזוּ עַפְעַפָּיו יִבְחֲנוּ בְּנֵי
sons-of they-examine eyes-of-him they-observe eyes-of-him throne-of-him

אָדָם׃ (5) יְהוָה צַדִּיק יִבְחָן וְרָשָׁע וְאֹהֵב חָמָס
violence and-one-loving but-wicked he-examines righteous Yahweh (5) man

שָׂנְאָה נַפְשׁוֹ׃ (6) יַמְטֵר עַל־ רְשָׁעִים פַּחִים אֵשׁ וְגָפְרִית
and-sulfur fire coal-of wicked-ones on he-will-rain (6) soul-of-him she-hates

10 His victims are crushed, they
collapse;
they fall under his strength.
11 He says to himself, "God has
forgotten;
he covers his face and never
sees."
12 Arise, LORD! Lift up your hand,
O God.
Do not forget the helpless.
13 Why does the wicked man
revile God?
Why does he say to himself,
"He won't call me to
account"?
14 But you, O God, do see trouble
and grief;
you consider it to take it in
hand.
The victim commits himself to
you;
you are the helper of the
fatherless.
15 Break the arm of the wicked
and evil man;
call him to account for his
wickedness
that would not be found out.
16 The LORD is King for ever and
ever;
the nations will perish from
his land.
17 You hear, O LORD, the desire
of the afflicted;
you encourage them, and
you listen to their cry,
18 defending the fatherless and
the oppressed,
in order that man, who is of
the earth, may terrify no
more.

Psalm 11

For the director of music. Of David.

1 In the LORD I take refuge.
How then can you say to
me:
"Flee like a bird to your
mountain.
2 For look, the wicked bend
their bows;
they set their arrows against
the strings
to shoot from the shadows
at the upright in heart.
3 When the foundations are
being destroyed,
what can the righteous
do[u]?"
4 The LORD is in his holy
temple;
the LORD is on his heavenly
throne.
He observes the sons of men;
his eyes examine them.
5 The LORD examines the
righteous,
but the wicked[v] and those
who love violence
his soul hates.
6 On the wicked he will rain
fiery coals and burning
sulfur;

[u]3 Or *what is the Righteous One doing*
[v]5 Or *The LORD, the Righteous One, examines the wicked, /*

*10 The *Qere* reads *host-of afflicted-ones.*

°10 ק חיל כאים °12 ק ענוים
°1 ק נודי

וְר֣וּחַ זִלְעָפ֔וֹת מְנָ֣ת כּוֹסָֽם׃ כִּֽי־ צַדִּ֣יק יְ֭הוָה צְדָק֣וֹת
justices Yahweh righteous for (7) cup-of-them lot-of scorchings and-wind-of

אָהֵ֑ב יָ֝שָׁ֗ר יֶחֱז֥וּ פָנֵֽימוֹ׃ לַמְנַצֵּ֥חַ
for-the-one-directing *(12:1) faces-of-him they-will-see upright he-loves

עַֽל־ הַשְּׁמִינִ֗ית מִזְמ֥וֹר לְדָוִֽד׃ הוֹשִׁ֣יעָה יְ֭הוָה כִּי־ גָ֣מַר
he-is-no-more for Yahweh help! (2) of-David psalm the-sheminith according-to

חָסִ֑יד כִּֽי־ פַ֥סּוּ אֱ֝מוּנִ֗ים מִבְּנֵ֥י אָדָֽם׃ שָׁ֤וְא ׀
lie (3) man from-sons-of ones-being-faithful they-vanished for godly

יְדַבְּרוּ֮ אִ֤ישׁ אֶת־ רֵ֫עֵ֥הוּ שְׂפַ֥ת חֲלָק֑וֹת בְּלֵ֖ב וָלֵ֣ב
and-heart with-heart flatterings lip-of neighbor-of-him *** each they-speak

יְדַבֵּֽרוּ׃ יַכְרֵ֣ת יְ֭הוָה כָּל־ שִׂפְתֵ֣י חֲלָק֑וֹת לָ֝שׁ֗וֹן
tongue flatterings lips-of all-of Yahweh may-he-cut-off (4) they-speak

מְדַבֶּ֥רֶת גְּדֹלֽוֹת׃ אֲשֶׁ֤ר אָֽמְר֨וּ ׀ לִֽלְשֹׁנֵ֣נוּ נַגְבִּ֗יר
we-will-triumph with-tongue-of-us they-say that (5) boasts speaking

שְׂפָתֵ֣ינוּ אִתָּ֑נוּ מִ֖י אָד֣וֹן לָֽנוּ׃ מִשֹּׁ֥ד עֲנִיִּים֮
weak-ones because-of-oppression-of (6) of-us master who? with-us lips-of-us

מֵאַנְקַ֪ת אֶבְי֫וֹנִ֥ים עַתָּ֣ה אָ֭קוּם יֹאמַ֣ר יְהוָ֑ה אָשִׁ֥ית
I-will-put Yahweh he-says I-will-arise now needy-ones because-of-groaning-of

בְּ֝יֵ֗שַׁע יָפִ֥יחַ לֽוֹ׃ אִֽמֲר֣וֹת יְהוָה֮ אֲמָר֪וֹת טְהֹ֫ר֥וֹת
flawless-ones words Yahweh words-of (7) against-him he-maligns in-protection

כֶּ֣סֶף צָ֭רוּף בַּעֲלִ֣יל לָאָ֑רֶץ מְ֝זֻקָּ֗ק שִׁבְעָתָֽיִם׃
seven-times being-purified of-the-clay in-furnace being-refined silver

אַתָּֽה־ יְהוָ֥ה תִּשְׁמְרֵ֑ם תִּצְּרֶ֓נּוּ ׀ מִן־ הַדּ֖וֹר
the-people from you-will-protect-us you-will-keep-safe-them Yahweh you (8)

ז֣וּ לְעוֹלָֽם׃ סָבִ֗יב רְשָׁעִ֥ים יִתְהַלָּכ֑וּן כְּרֻ֥ם זֻ֝לּ֗וּת
vileness when-to-be-honored they-strut wicked-ones about (9) to-forever such

לִבְנֵ֥י אָדָֽם׃ לַמְנַצֵּ֗חַ מִזְמ֥וֹר לְדָוִֽד׃ עַד־
until (2) of-David psalm for-the-one-directing *(13:1) man among-sons-of

אָ֣נָה יְ֭הוָה תִּשְׁכָּחֵ֣נִי נֶ֑צַח עַד־ אָ֓נָה ׀ תַּסְתִּ֖יר אֶת־
*** will-you-hide when? until forever will-you-forget-me Yahweh when?

פָּנֶ֣יךָ מִמֶּֽנִּי׃ עַד־ אָ֨נָה אָשִׁ֪ית עֵצ֡וֹת בְּנַפְשִׁ֗י
of-soul-of-me thoughts must-I-wrestle when? until (3) from-me faces-of-you

יָג֣וֹן בִּלְבָבִ֣י יוֹמָ֑ם עַד־ אָ֓נָה ׀ יָר֖וּם אֹיְבִ֣י
one-being-enemy-of-me will-he-triumph when? until by-day in-heart-of-me sorrow

עָלָֽי׃ הַבִּ֣יטָה עֲ֭נֵנִי יְהוָ֣ה אֱלֹהָ֑י הָאִ֥ירָה עֵ֝ינַ֗י פֶּן־
or eyes-of-me give-light! God-of-me Yahweh answer-me! look! (4) over-me

אִישַׁ֥ן הַמָּֽוֶת׃ פֶּן־ יֹאמַ֣ר אֹיְבִ֣י יְכָלְתִּ֑יו
I-overcame-him one-being-enemy-of-me he-will-say or (5) the-death I-will-sleep

a scorching wind will be
their lot.

7For the LORD is righteous,
he loves justice;
upright men will see his
face.

Psalm 12

For the director of music. According to *sheminith*.[w] A psalm of David.

1Help, LORD, for the godly are
no more;
the faithful have vanished
from among men.
2Everyone lies to his neighbor;
their flattering lips speak
with deception.

3May the LORD cut off all
flattering lips
and every boastful tongue
4that says, "We will triumph
with our tongues;
we own our lips[x]—who is
our master?"

5"Because of the oppression of
the weak
and the groaning of the
needy,
I will now arise," says the
LORD.
"I will protect them from
those who malign them."
6And the words of the LORD are
flawless,
like silver refined in a
furnace of clay,
purified seven times.

7O LORD, you will keep us safe
and protect us from such
people forever.
8The wicked freely strut about
when what is vile is
honored among men.

Psalm 13

For the director of music. A psalm of David.

1How long, O LORD? Will you
forget me forever?
How long will you hide
your face from me?
2How long must I wrestle with
my thoughts
and every day have sorrow
in my heart?
How long will my enemy
triumph over me?

3Look on me and answer, O
LORD my God.
Give light to my eyes, or I
will sleep in death;
4my enemy will say, "I have
overcome him,"

[w]Title: Probably a musical term
[x]4 Or / *our lips are our plowshares*

*Heading, *1* See the note on page 349.

צָרַי יָגִילוּ כִּי אֶמּוֹט׃ וַאֲנִי ׀ בְּחַסְדְּךָ
in-unfailing-love-of-you but-I (6) I-fall when they-will-rejoice foes-of-me

בָּטַחְתִּי יָגֵל לִבִּי בִּישׁוּעָתֶךָ אָשִׁירָה לַיהוָה
to-Yahweh I-will-sing in-salvation-of-you heart-of-me he-rejoices I-trust

כִּי גָמַל עָלָי׃ לַמְנַצֵּחַ לְדָוִד אָמַר נָבָל
fool he-says of-David for-the-one-directing (14:1) to-me he-was-good for

בְּלִבּוֹ אֵין אֱלֹהִים הִשְׁחִיתוּ הִתְעִיבוּ עֲלִילָה
deed they-are-vile they-are-corrupt God there-is-no in-heart-of-him

אֵין עֹשֵׂה־ טוֹב׃ יְהוָה מִשָּׁמַיִם הִשְׁקִיף עַל־ בְּנֵי־
sons-of on he-looks-down from-heavens Yahweh (2) good one-doing-of there-is-no

אָדָם לִרְאוֹת הֲיֵשׁ מַשְׂכִּיל דֹּרֵשׁ אֶת־אֱלֹהִים׃ הַכֹּל
the-all (3) God *** one-seeking one-understanding if-there-is to-see man

סָר יַחְדָּו נֶאֱלָחוּ אֵין עֹשֵׂה־ טוֹב אֵין
not good one-doing-of there-is-no they-became-corrupt together he-turned-aside

גַּם־ אֶחָד׃ הֲלֹא יָדְעוּ כָּל־ פֹּעֲלֵי אָוֶן אֹכְלֵי
ones-devouring-of evil ones-doing-of all-of will-they-learn never? (4) one even

עַמִּי אָכְלוּ לֶחֶם יְהוָה לֹא קָרָאוּ׃ שָׁם ׀ פָּחֲדוּ
they-dread there (5) they-call-on not Yahweh bread they-eat people-of-me

פָחַד כִּי־אֱלֹהִים בְּדוֹר צַדִּיק׃ עֲצַת־ עָנִי תָבִישׁוּ כִּי
but you-frustrate poor plan-of (6) righteous in-company-of God for dread

יְהוָה מַחְסֵהוּ׃ מִי יִתֵּן מִצִּיּוֹן יְשׁוּעַת יִשְׂרָאֵל
Israel salvation-of from-Zion he-would-bring who? (7) refuge-of-him Yahweh

בְּשׁוּב יְהוָה שְׁבוּת עַמּוֹ יָגֵל יַעֲקֹב
Jacob let-him-rejoice people-of-him fortune-of Yahweh when-to-restore

יִשְׂמַח יִשְׂרָאֵל׃ מִזְמוֹר לְדָוִד יְהוָה מִי־ יָגוּר
he-may-dwell who? Yahweh of-David psalm (15:1) Israel let-him-be-glad

בְּאָהֳלֶךָ מִי־ יִשְׁכֹּן בְּהַר קָדְשֶׁךָ׃
holiness-of-you on-hill-of he-may-live who? in-sanctuary-of-you

הוֹלֵךְ תָּמִים וּפֹעֵל צֶדֶק וְדֹבֵר אֱמֶת
truth and-one-speaking righteousness and-one-doing blamelessly one-walking (2)

בִּלְבָבוֹ׃ לֹא־ רָגַל ׀ עַל־ לְשֹׁנוֹ לֹא־ עָשָׂה
he-does not tongue-of-him with he-slanders not (3) from-heart-of-him

לְרֵעֵהוּ רָעָה וְחֶרְפָּה לֹא־ נָשָׂא עַל־ קְרֹבוֹ׃
fellow-man-of-him on he-casts not and-slur wrong to-neighbor-of-him

נִבְזֶה ׀ בְּעֵינָיו נִמְאָס וְאֶת־ יִרְאֵי יְהוָה
Yahweh ones-fearing-of but man-being-vile in-eyes-of-him he-is-despised (4)

יְכַבֵּד נִשְׁבַּע לְהָרַע וְלֹא יָמִר׃ כַּסְפּוֹ ׀ לֹא־
not money-of-him (5) he-changes and-not to-hurt he-swears-oath he-honors

and my foes will rejoice
when I fall.

[5]But I trust in your unfailing
love;
my heart rejoices in your
salvation.
[6]I will sing to the LORD,
for he has been good to me.

Psalm 14

For the director of music. Of David.

[1]The fool[v] says in his heart,
"There is no God."
They are corrupt, their deeds
are vile;
there is no one who does
good.
[2]The LORD looks down from
heaven
on the sons of men
to see if there are any who
understand,
any who seek God.
[3]All have turned aside,
they have together become
corrupt;
there is no one who does
good,
not even one.
[4]Will evildoers never learn—
those who devour my
people as men eat bread
and who do not call on the
LORD?
[5]There they are, overwhelmed
with dread,
for God is present in the
company of the righteous.
[6]You evildoers frustrate the
plans of the poor,
but the LORD is their refuge.
[7]Oh, that salvation for Israel
would come out of Zion!
When the LORD restores the
fortunes of his people,
let Jacob rejoice and Israel
be glad!

Psalm 15

A psalm of David.

[1]LORD, who may dwell in your
sanctuary?
Who may live on your holy
hill?
[2]He whose walk is blameless
and who does what is
righteous,
who speaks the truth from his
heart
[3] and has no slander on his
tongue,
who does his neighbor no
wrong
and casts no slur on his
fellow man,
[4]who despises a vile man
but honors those who fear
the LORD,
who keeps his oath
even when it hurts,
[5]who lends his money without

v1 The Hebrew words rendered *fool* in Psalms denote one who is morally deficient.

*See the note on page 349.

נֹתַן בְּנֶשֶׁךְ וְשֹׁחַד עַל־ נָקִי לֹא לָקָח עֹשֵׂה־
one-doing-of he-accepts not innocent against and-bribe with-usury he-lends

אֵלֶּה לֹא יִמּוֹט לְעוֹלָם׃ מִכְתָּם לְדָוִד שָׁמְרֵנִי
keep-safe-me! of-David miktam (16:1) to-forever he-will-be-shaken not these

אֵל כִּי־ חָסִיתִי בָךְ׃ אָמַרְתְּ* לַיהוָה אֲדֹנָי אַתָּה טוֹבָתִי
good-of-me you Lord-of-me to-Yahweh *I-said (2) in-you I-take-refuge for God

בַּל־ עָלֶיךָ׃ לִקְדוֹשִׁים אֲשֶׁר־ בָּאָרֶץ הֵמָּה וְאַדִּירֵי
even-glorious-ones-of they in-the-land who as-for-saints (3) apart-from-you not

כָּל־ חֶפְצִי־ בָם׃ יִרְבּוּ עַצְּבוֹתָם אַחֵר
other sorrows-of-them they-will-increase (4) in-them delight-of-me all-of

מָהָרוּ בַּל־ אַסִּיךְ נִסְכֵּיהֶם מִדָּם וּבַל־
and-not of-blood libations-of-them I-will-pour-out not they-run-after

אֶשָּׂא אֶת־ שְׁמוֹתָם עַל־ שְׂפָתָי׃ יְהוָה מְנָת־
assignment-of Yahweh (5) lips-of-me on names-of-them *** I-will-take-up

חֶלְקִי וְכוֹסִי אַתָּה תּוֹמִיךְ גּוֹרָלִי׃ חֲבָלִים
boundary-lines (6) lot-of-me you-made-secure you and-cup-of-me portion-of-me

נָפְלוּ־ לִי בַּנְּעִמִים אַף־ נַחֲלָת שָׁפְרָה
she-is-delightful inheritance surely in-the-pleasant-places for-me they-fell

עָלָי׃ אֲבָרֵךְ אֶת־ יְהוָה אֲשֶׁר יְעָצָנִי אַף־ לֵילוֹת
nights even he-counsels-me who Yahweh *** I-will-praise (7) to-me

יִסְּרוּנִי כִלְיוֹתָי׃ שִׁוִּיתִי יְהוָה לְנֶגְדִּי תָמִיד כִּי
because always at-before-me Yahweh I-set (8) hearts-of-me they-instruct-me

מִימִינִי בַּל־ אֶמּוֹט׃ לָכֵן שָׂמַח לִבִּי
heart-of-me he-is-glad therefore (9) I-will-be-shaken not at-right-hand-of-me

וַיָּגֶל כְּבוֹדִי אַף־ בְּשָׂרִי יִשְׁכֹּן לָבֶטַח׃
in-security he-will-rest body-of-me also tongue-of-me and-he-rejoices

כִּי לֹא־ תַעֲזֹב נַפְשִׁי לִשְׁאוֹל לֹא־ תִתֵּן
you-will-let not to-Sheol self-of-me you-will-abandon not because (10)

חֲסִידְךָ לִרְאוֹת שָׁחַת׃ תּוֹדִיעֵנִי אֹרַח חַיִּים
lives path-of you-will-make-known-to-me (11) decay to-see holy-one-of-you

שֹׂבַע שְׂמָחוֹת אֶת־ פָּנֶיךָ נְעִמוֹת בִּימִינְךָ נֶצַח׃
eternally at-right-hand-of-you pleasures presences-of-you in joys fullness-of

תְּפִלָּה לְדָוִד שִׁמְעָה יְהוָה צֶדֶק הַקְשִׁיבָה רִנָּתִי
cry-of-me listen! righteous-plea Yahweh hear! of-David prayer (17:1)

הַאֲזִינָה תְפִלָּתִי בְּלֹא שִׂפְתֵי מִרְמָה׃ מִלְּפָנֶיךָ
from-before-you (2) deceit lips-of from-not prayer-of-me give-ear!

מִשְׁפָּטִי יֵצֵא עֵינֶיךָ תֶּחֱזֶינָה מֵישָׁרִים׃
right-ones may-they-see eyes-of-you may-he-come vindication-of-me

---

usury
and does not accept a bribe
against the innocent.

He who does these things
will never be shaken.

Psalm 16

A *miktam*[z] of David.

1 Keep me safe, O God,
for in you I take refuge.

2 I said to the LORD, "You are my Lord;
apart from you I have no good thing."
3 As for the saints who are in the land,
they are the glorious ones in whom is all my delight.[a]
4 The sorrows of those will increase
who run after other gods.
I will not pour out their libations of blood
or take up their names on my lips.

5 LORD, you have assigned me my portion and my cup;
you have made my lot secure.
6 The boundary lines have fallen for me in pleasant places;
surely I have a delightful inheritance.

7 I will praise the LORD, who counsels me;
even at night my heart instructs me.
8 I have set the LORD always before me.
Because he is at my right hand,
I will not be shaken.

9 Therefore my heart is glad and my tongue rejoices;
my body also will rest secure,
10 because you will not abandon me to the grave,[b]
nor will you let your Holy One[c] see decay.
11 You have made[d] known to me the path of life;
you will fill me with joy in your presence,
with eternal pleasures at your right hand.

Psalm 17

A prayer of David.

1 Hear, O LORD, my righteous plea;
listen to my cry.
Give ear to my prayer—
it does not rise from deceitful lips.
2 May my vindication come from you;
may your eyes see what is right.

[z]Title: Probably a literary or musical term
[a]3 Or *As for the pagan priests who are in the land / and the nobles in whom all delight, I said:*
[b]10 Hebrew *Sheol*
[c]10 Or *your faithful one*
[d]11 Or *You will make*

*2 Most mss have *hireq yod* with the *tav* (תִּי־).

בָּחַנְתָּ לִבִּי ׀ פָּקַדְתָּ לַּיְלָה צְרַפְתַּנִי בַל־ תִּמְצָא
you-will-find not you-test-me night you-examine heart-of-me you-probe (3)

זַמֹּתִי בַּל־ יַעֲבָר־ פִּי׃ לִפְעֻלּוֹת אָדָם בִּדְבַר
by-word-of man for-deeds-of (4) mouth-of-me he-will-sin not I-resolved

שְׂפָתֶיךָ אֲנִי שָׁמַרְתִּי אָרְחוֹת פָּרִיץ׃ תָּמֹךְ אֲשֻׁרַי
steps-of-me to-hold (5) violent ways-of I-kept I lips-of-you

בְּמַעְגְּלוֹתֶיךָ בַּל־ נָמוֹטּוּ פְעָמָי׃ אֲנִי־ קְרָאתִיךָ כִי־
for I-call-on-you I (6) feet-of-me they-slipped not to-paths-of-you

תַעֲנֵנִי אֵל הַט־ אָזְנְךָ לִי שְׁמַע אִמְרָתִי׃
prayer-of-me hear! to-me ear-of-you give! God you-will-answer-me

הַפְלֵה חֲסָדֶיךָ מוֹשִׁיעַ חוֹסִים
ones-taking-refuge one-saving great-loves-of-you show-wonder! (7)

מִמִּתְקוֹמְמִים בִּימִינֶךָ׃ שָׁמְרֵנִי כְּאִישׁוֹן בַּת־
daughter-of as-apple-of keep-me! (8) by-right-hand-of-you from-ones-being-foes

עָיִן בְּצֵל כְּנָפֶיךָ תַּסְתִּירֵנִי׃ מִפְּנֵי רְשָׁעִים זוּ
who wicked-ones from-before (9) you-hide-me wings-of-you in-shadow-of eye

שַׁדּוּנִי אֹיְבַי בְּנֶפֶשׁ יַקִּיפוּ עָלָי׃
around-me they-surround of-life ones-being-enemies-of-me they-assail-me

חֶלְבָּמוֹ סָּגְרוּ פִּימוֹ דִּבְּרוּ בְגֵאוּת׃
with-arrogance they-speak mouth-of-them they-close callous-heart-of-them (10)

אַשֻּׁרֵינוּ עַתָּה סְבָבוּנִי עֵינֵיהֶם יָשִׁיתוּ לִנְטוֹת
to-throw they-are-alert eyes-of-them they-surround-us now tracks-of-us (11)

בָּאָרֶץ׃ דִּמְיֹנוֹ כְּאַרְיֵה יִכְסוֹף לִטְרוֹף
to-tear-prey he-is-hungry like-lion likeness-of-him (12) to-the-ground

וְכִכְפִיר יֹשֵׁב בְּמִסְתָּרִים׃ קוּמָה יְהוָה קַדְּמָה
confront! Yahweh rise-up! (13) in-covers crouching and-like-great-lion

פָנָיו הַכְרִיעֵהוּ פַּלְּטָה נַפְשִׁי מֵרָשָׁע חַרְבֶּךָ׃
sword-of-you from-wicked self-of-me rescue! bring-down-him! before-him

מִמְתִים יָדְךָ ׀ יְהוָה מִמְתִים מֵחֶלֶד חֶלְקָם
reward-of-them from-world from-men Yahweh hand-of-you from-men (14)

בַּחַיִּים וּצְפִינְךָ תְּמַלֵּא בִטְנָם
belly-of-them you-fill and-one-being-cherished-of-you in-the-lives

יִשְׂבְּעוּ בָנִים וְהִנִּיחוּ יִתְרָם לְעוֹלְלֵיהֶם׃
for-children-of-them wealth-of-them and-they-store-up sons they-have-plenty

אֲנִי בְּצֶדֶק אֶחֱזֶה פָנֶיךָ אֶשְׂבְּעָה בְהָקִיץ
when-to-wake I-will-be-satisfied faces-of-you I-will-see in-righteousness I (15)

תְּמוּנָתֶךָ׃ לַמְנַצֵּחַ ׀ לְעֶבֶד יְהוָה לְדָוִד
of-David Yahweh of-servant-of for-the-one-directing *(18:1) likeness-of-you

3 Though you probe my heart
and examine me at night,
though you test me, you will
find nothing;
I have resolved that my
mouth will not sin.
4 As for the deeds of men—
by the word of your lips
I have kept myself
from the ways of the
violent.
5 My steps have held to your
paths;
my feet have not slipped.

6 I call on you, O God, for you
will answer me;
give ear to me and hear my
prayer.
7 Show the wonder of your great
love,
you who save by your right
hand
those who take refuge in
you from their foes.
8 Keep me as the apple of your
eye;
hide me in the shadow of
your wings
9 from the wicked who assail
me,
from my mortal enemies
who surround me.

10 They close up their callous
hearts,
and their mouths speak with
arrogance.
11 They have tracked me down,
they now surround me,
with eyes alert, to throw me
to the ground.
12 They are like a lion hungry for
prey,
like a great lion crouching
in cover.

13 Rise up, O LORD, confront
them, bring them down;
rescue me from the wicked
by your sword.
14 O LORD, by your hand save me
from such men,
from men of this world
whose reward is in this
life.

You still the hunger of those
you cherish;
their sons have plenty,
and they store up wealth for
their children.
15 And I—in righteousness I will
see your face;
when I awake, I will be
satisfied with seeing your
likeness.

Psalm 18

For the director of music. Of David
the servant of the LORD. He sang to

*Heading, *1* See the note on page 349.

°*11* ק סבבונו

°*14* ק וצפונך

אֲשֶׁר דִּבֶּר׀ לַיהוָה אֶת־ דִּבְרֵי הַשִּׁירָה הַזֹּאת בְּיוֹם הִצִּיל־
he-delivered on-day the-this the-song words-of *** to-Yahweh he-sang who

יְהוָה אוֹתוֹ מִכַּף כָּל־ אֹיְבָיו וּמִיַּד
and-from-hand-of ones-being-enemies-of-him all-of from-hand-of him Yahweh

שָׁאוּל׃ וַיֹּאמַר אֶרְחָמְךָ יְהוָה חִזְקִי׃ יְהוָה׀ סַלְעִי
rock-of-me Yahweh (3) strength-of-me Yahweh I-love-you and-he-said (2) Saul

וּמְצוּדָתִי וּמְפַלְטִי אֵלִי צוּרִי אֶחֱסֶה־
I-take-refuge rock-of-me God-of-me and-one-delivering-me and-fortress-of-me

בּוֹ מָגִנִּי וְקֶרֶן־ יִשְׁעִי מִשְׂגַּבִּי׃
stronghold-of-me salvation-of-me and-horn-of shield-of-me in-him

מְהֻלָּל אֶקְרָא יְהוָה וּמִן־ אֹיְבַי
ones-being-enemies-of-me and-from Yahweh I-call one-being-praised (4)

אִוָּשֵׁעַ׃ אֲפָפוּנִי חֶבְלֵי־ מָוֶת וְנַחֲלֵי בְלִיַּעַל
destruction and-torrents-of death cords-of they-entangled-me (5) I-am-saved

יְבַעֲתוּנִי׃ חֶבְלֵי שְׁאוֹל סְבָבוּנִי קִדְּמוּנִי
they-confronted-me they-coiled-around-me Sheol cords-of (6) they-overwhelmed-me

מוֹקְשֵׁי מָוֶת׃ בַּצַּר־ לִי׀ אֶקְרָא יְהוָה וְאֶל־ אֱלֹהַי
God-of-me and-to Yahweh I-called of-me in-the-distress (7) death snares-of

אֲשַׁוֵּעַ יִשְׁמַע מֵהֵיכָלוֹ קוֹלִי וְשַׁוְעָתִי
and-cry-of-me voice-of-me from-temple-of-him he-heard I-cried-for-help

לְפָנָיו׀ תָּבוֹא בְאָזְנָיו׃ וַתִּגְעַשׁ וַתִּרְעַשׁ׀
and-she-quaked and-she-trembled (8) into-ears-of-him she-came before-him

הָאָרֶץ וּמוֹסְדֵי הָרִים יִרְגָּזוּ וַיִּתְגָּעֲשׁוּ כִּי־
because and-they-trembled they-shook mountains and-foundations-of the-earth

חָרָה לוֹ׃ עָלָה עָשָׁן׀ בְּאַפּוֹ וְאֵשׁ־
and-fire from-nostril-of-him smoke he-rose (9) to-him he-was-angry

מִפִּיו תֹּאכֵל גֶּחָלִים בָּעֲרוּ מִמֶּנּוּ׃ וַיֵּט
and-he-parted (10) from-him they-blazed coals she-consumed from-mouth-of-him

שָׁמַיִם וַיֵּרַד וַעֲרָפֶל תַּחַת רַגְלָיו׃ וַיִּרְכַּב
and-he-mounted (11) feet-of-him under and-dark-cloud and-he-came-down heavens

עַל־כְּרוּב וַיָּעֹף וַיֵּדֶא עַל־ כַּנְפֵי־ רוּחַ׃ יָשֶׁת חֹשֶׁךְ׀
darkness he-made (12) wind wings-of on and-he-soared and-he-flew cherub on

סִתְרוֹ סְבִיבוֹתָיו סֻכָּתוֹ חֶשְׁכַת־ מַיִם עָבֵי
clouds-of waters darkness-of canopy-of-him ones-around-him covering-of-him

שְׁחָקִים׃ מִנֹּגַהּ נֶגְדּוֹ עָבָיו עָבְרוּ
they-advanced clouds-of-him presence-of-him from-brightness-of (13) skies

בָּרָד וְגַחֲלֵי־ אֵשׁ׃ וַיַּרְעֵם בַּשָּׁמַיִם׀
from-the-heavens and-he-thundered (14) lightning and-bolts-of hailstone

the LORD the words of this song when the LORD delivered him from the hand of all his enemies and from the hand of Saul. He said:

1 I love you, O LORD, my
strength.

2 The LORD is my rock, my
fortress and my deliverer;
my God is my rock, in
whom I take refuge.
He is my shield and the
horn[e] of my salvation,
my stronghold.
3 I call to the LORD, who is
worthy of praise,
and I am saved from my
enemies.

4 The cords of death entangled
me;
the torrents of destruction
overwhelmed me.
5 The cords of the grave[f] coiled
around me;
the snares of death
confronted me.
6 In my distress I called to the
LORD;
I cried to my God for help.
From his temple he heard my
voice;
my cry came before him,
into his ears.

7 The earth trembled and
quaked,
and the foundations of the
mountains shook;
they trembled because he
was angry.
8 Smoke rose from his nostrils;
consuming fire came from
his mouth,
burning coals blazed out of
it.
9 He parted the heavens and
came down;
dark clouds were under his
feet.
10 He mounted the cherubim and
flew;
he soared on the wings of
the wind.
11 He made darkness his
covering, his canopy
around him—
the dark rain clouds of the
sky.
12 Out of the brightness of his
presence clouds advanced,
with hailstones and bolts of
lightning.
13 The LORD thundered from
heaven;

e2 *Horn* here symbolizes strength.
f5 Hebrew *Sheol*

*See the note on page 349.

יהוה ועליון יתן קלו ברד וגחלי־ אש :
lightning and-bolts-of hailstone voice-of-him he-resounded and-Most-High Yahweh

(15) וישלח חציו ויפיצם וברקים
and-lightning-bolts and-he-scattered-them arrows-of-him and-he-shot (15)

רב ויהמם : (16) ויראו אפיקי מים
waters valleys-of and-they-were-exposed (16) and-he-routed-them great

ויגלו מוסדות תבל מגערתך יהוה
Yahweh at-rebuke-of-you earth foundations-of and-they-were-laid-bare

מנשמת רוח אפך : (17) ישלח ממרום
from-on-high he-reached (17) nostril-of-you breath-of at-blast-of

יקחני ימשני ממים רבים : (18) יצילני
he-rescued-me (18) deep-ones from-waters he-drew-out-me he-took-hold-of-me

מאיבי עז ומשנאי כי־
for and-from-ones-being-foes-of-me powerful from-one-being-enemy-of-me

אמצו ממני : (19) יקדמוני ביום־ אידי
disaster-of-me in-day-of they-confronted-me (19) for-me they-were-too-strong

ויהי־ יהוה למשען לי : (20) ויוציאני
and-he-brought-out-me (20) to-me as-support Yahweh but-he-was

למרחב יחלצני כי חפץ בי :
in-me he-delighted because he-rescued-me to-the-spacious-place

(21) יגמלני יהוה כצדקי כבר ידי
hands-of-me as-cleanness-of as-righteousness-of-me Yahweh he-dealt-with-me (21)

ישיב לי : (22) כי־ שמרתי דרכי יהוה ולא־ רשעתי
I-did-evil and-not Yahweh ways-of I-kept for (22) to-me he-rewarded

מאלהי : (23) כי כל־ משפטיו לנגדי וחקתיו
and-decrees-of-him at-before-me laws-of-him all-of indeed (23) from-God-of-me

לא־ אסיר מני : (24) ואהי תמים עמו ואשתמר
and-I-kept-myself before-him blameless and-I-was (24) from-me I-turned not

מעוני : (25) וישב־ יהוה לי כצדקי
as-righteousness-of-me to-me Yahweh and-he-rewarded (25) from-sin-of-me

כבר ידי לנגד עיניו : (26) עם־ חסיד
faithful to (26) eyes-of-him at-before hands-of-me as-cleanness-of

תתחסד עם־ גבר תמים תתמם :
you-show-yourself-blameless blameless man-of to you-show-yourself-faithful

(27) עם־ נבר תתברר ועם־ עקש תתפתל :
you-show-yourself-shrewd crooked but-to you-show-yourself-pure one-being-pure to (27)

(28) כי־ אתה עם־ עני תושיע ועינים רמות
ones-being-haughty but-eyes you-save humble people you for (28)

the voice of the Most High
resounded.[g]
14He shot his arrows and
scattered ⌊the enemies⌋,
great bolts of lightning and
routed them.
15The valleys of the sea were
exposed
and the foundations of the
earth laid bare
at your rebuke, O LORD,
at the blast of breath from
your nostrils.

16He reached down from on
high and took hold of me;
he drew me out of deep
waters.
17He rescued me from my
powerful enemy,
from my foes, who were too
strong for me.
18They confronted me in the day
of my disaster,
but the LORD was my
support.
19He brought me out into a
spacious place;
he rescued me because he
delighted in me.

20The LORD has dealt with me
according to my
righteousness;
according to the cleanness of
my hands he has
rewarded me.
21For I have kept the ways of
the LORD;
I have not done evil by
turning from my God.
22All his laws are before me;
I have not turned away
from his decrees.
23I have been blameless before
him
and have kept myself from
sin.
24The LORD has rewarded me
according to my
righteousness,
according to the cleanness of
my hands in his sight.

25To the faithful you show
yourself faithful,
to the blameless you show
yourself blameless,
26to the pure you show yourself
pure,
but to the crooked you show
yourself shrewd.
27You save the humble
but bring low those whose
eyes are haughty.

g13 Some Hebrew manuscripts and Septuagint (see also 2 Samuel 22:14); most Hebrew manuscripts *resounded, / amid hailstones and bolts of lightning*

*See the note on page 349.

תַּשְׁפִּיל׃ כִּי־ אַתָּה תָּאִיר נֵרִי יְהוָה אֱלֹהַי

God-of-me Yahweh lamp-of-me you-make-burn you indeed (29) you-bring-low

יַגִּיהַּ חָשְׁכִּי׃ כִּי־ בְךָ אָרֻץ גְּדוּד

troop I-can-advance with-you indeed (30) darkness-of-me he-makes-light

וּבֵאלֹהַי אֲדַלֶּג־ שׁוּר׃ הָאֵל תָּמִים דַּרְכּוֹ אִמְרַת־

word-of way-of-him perfect the-God (31) wall I-can-scale and-with-God-of-me

יְהוָה צְרוּפָה מָגֵן הוּא לְכֹל ׀ הַחֹסִים בּוֹ׃

in-him the-ones-taking-refuge to-all-of he shield being-flawless Yahweh

כִּי מִי אֱלוֹהַּ מִבַּלְעֲדֵי יְהוָה וּמִי צוּר זוּלָתִי אֱלֹהֵינוּ׃ הָאֵל

the-God (33) God-of-us except Rock and-who? Yahweh besides God who? for (32)

הַמְאַזְּרֵנִי חָיִל וַיִּתֵּן תָּמִים דַּרְכִּי׃ מְשַׁוֶּה

one-making (34) way-of-me perfect and-he-makes strength the-one-arming-me

רַגְלַי כָּאַיָּלוֹת וְעַל בָּמֹתַי יַעֲמִידֵנִי׃ מְלַמֵּד

training (35) he-makes-stand-me heights-of-me and-on like-the-deer feet-of-me

יָדַי לַמִּלְחָמָה וְנִחֲתָה קֶשֶׁת־ נְחוּשָׁה זְרוֹעֹתָי׃

arms-of-me bronze bow-of and-she-can-bend for-the-battle hands-of-me

וַתִּתֶּן־ לִי מָגֵן יִשְׁעֶךָ וִימִינְךָ

and-right-hand-of-you victory-of-you shield-of to-me and-you-give (36)

תִסְעָדֵנִי וְעַנְוַתְךָ תַרְבֵּנִי׃ תַּרְחִיב

you-broaden (37) you-make-great-me and-stooping-of-you she-sustains-me

צַעֲדִי תַחְתָּי וְלֹא מָעֲדוּ קַרְסֻלָּי׃ אֶרְדּוֹף

I-pursued (38) ankles-of-me they-turn so-not beneath-me path-of-me

אוֹיְבַי וְאַשִּׂיגֵם וְלֹא־ אָשׁוּב עַד־

till I-turned-back and-not and-I-overtook-them ones-being-enemies-of-me

כַּלּוֹתָם׃ אֶמְחָצֵם וְלֹא־ יֻכְלוּ קוּם יִפְּלוּ

they-fell to-rise they-could so-not I-crushed-them (39) to-destroy-them

תַּחַת רַגְלָי׃ וַתְּאַזְּרֵנִי חַיִל לַמִּלְחָמָה תַּכְרִיעַ

you-made-bow for-the-battle strength and-you-armed-me (40) feet-of-me beneath

קָמַי תַּחְתָּי׃ וְאֹיְבַי נָתַתָּה

you-turned and-ones-being-enemies-of-me (41) beneath-me adversaries-of-me

לִּי עֹרֶף וּמְשַׂנְאַי אַצְמִיתֵם׃ יְשַׁוְּעוּ

they-cried-for-help (42) I-destroyed-them and-ones-being-foes-of-me back to-me

וְאֵין־ מוֹשִׁיעַ עַל־ יְהוָה וְלֹא עָנָם׃ וְאֶשְׁחָקֵם

and-I-beat-them (43) he-answered-them but-not Yahweh to saving but-no-one

כְּעָפָר עַל־ פְּנֵי־ רוּחַ כְּטִיט חוּצוֹת אֲרִיקֵם׃

I-poured-out-them streets like-mud-of wind surfaces-of on as-dust

תְּפַלְּטֵנִי מֵרִיבֵי עָם תְּשִׂימֵנִי לְרֹאשׁ גּוֹיִם

nations as-head-of you-made-me people from-attacks-of you-delivered-me (44)

28You, O LORD, keep my lamp
burning;
my God turns my darkness
into light.
29With your help I can advance
against a troop[h];
with my God I can scale a
wall.

30As for God, his way is perfect;
the word of the LORD is
flawless.
He is a shield
for all who take refuge in
him.
31For who is God besides the
LORD?
And who is the Rock except
our God?
32It is God who arms me with
strength
and makes my way perfect.
33He makes my feet like the feet
of a deer;
he enables me to stand on
the heights.
34He trains my hands for battle;
my arms can bend a bow of
bronze.
35You give me your shield of
victory,
and your right hand
sustains me;
you stoop down to make me
great.
36You broaden the path beneath
me,
so that my ankles do not
turn.

37I pursued my enemies and
overtook them;
I did not turn back till they
were destroyed.
38I crushed them so that they
could not rise;
they fell beneath my feet.
39You armed me with strength
for battle;
you made my adversaries
bow at my feet.
40You made my enemies turn
their backs in flight,
and I destroyed my foes.
41They cried for help, but there
was no one to save
them—
to the LORD, but he did not
answer.
42I beat them as fine as dust
borne on the wind;
I poured them out like mud
in the streets.

43You have delivered me from
the attacks of the people;
you have made me the head
of nations;

[h]29 Or *can run through a barricade*

*See the note on page 349.

עָם לֹא־יָדַעְתִּי יַעַבְדוּנִי׃ (45) לְשֵׁמַע אֹזֶן יִשָּׁמְעוּ לִי
people not I-knew they-are-subject-to-me (45) in-hearing-of ear they-obey to-me

בְּנֵי־נֵכָר יְכַחֲשׁוּ־לִי׃ (46) בְּנֵי־נֵכָר יִבֹּלוּ
sons-of foreigner they-cringe before-me (46) sons-of foreigner they-lose-heart

וְיַחְרְגוּ מִמִּסְגְּרוֹתֵיהֶם׃ (47) חַי־יְהוָה וּבָרוּךְ
and-they-tremble from-strongholds-of-them (47) alive Yahweh and-being-praised

צוּרִי וְיָרוּם אֱלוֹהֵי יִשְׁעִי׃ (48) הָאֵל
Rock-of-me and-may-he-be-exalted God-of salvation-of-me (48) the-God

הַנּוֹתֵן נְקָמוֹת לִי וַיַּדְבֵּר עַמִּים תַּחְתָּי׃
the-one-giving vengeances to-me and-he-subdues nations under-me

(49) מְפַלְּטִי מֵאֹיְבָי אַף מִן־קָמַי תְּרוֹמְמֵנִי
(49) one-saving-me from-being-enemies-of-me also above foes-of-me you-exalted-me

מֵאִישׁ חָמָס תַּצִּילֵנִי׃ (50) עַל־כֵּן | אוֹדְךָ
from-man-of violence you-rescued-me (50) for this I-will-praise-you

בַגּוֹיִם | יְהוָה וּלְשִׁמְךָ אֲזַמֵּרָה׃
among-the-nations Yahweh and-to-name-of-you I-will-sing-praise

(51) מַגְדִּל יְשׁוּעוֹת מַלְכּוֹ וְעֹשֶׂה חֶסֶד |
(51) making-great victories-of king-of-him and-showing unfailing-kindness

לִמְשִׁיחוֹ לְדָוִד וּלְזַרְעוֹ עַד־עוֹלָם׃
to-anointed-of-him to-David and-to-descendant-of-him to forever

*(19:1) לַמְנַצֵּחַ מִזְמוֹר לְדָוִד׃ (2) הַשָּׁמַיִם מְסַפְּרִים
*(19:1) for-the-one-directing psalm of-David (2) the-heavens ones-declaring

כְּבוֹד־אֵל וּמַעֲשֵׂה יָדָיו מַגִּיד הָרָקִיעַ׃ (3) יוֹם לְיוֹם
glory-of God and-work-of hands-of-him proclaiming the-sky (3) day after-day

יַבִּיעַ אֹמֶר וְלַיְלָה לְּלַיְלָה יְחַוֶּה־דָּעַת׃
he-pours-forth speech and-night after-night he-displays knowledge

(4) אֵין־אֹמֶר וְאֵין דְּבָרִים בְּלִי נִשְׁמָע קוֹלָם׃
(4) there-is-no speech and-there-are-no languages not he-is-heard sound-of-them

(5) בְּכָל־הָאָרֶץ | יָצָא קַוָּם וּבִקְצֵה תֵבֵל
(5) into-all-of the-earth he-goes-out line-of-them and-to-end-of world

מִלֵּיהֶם לַשֶּׁמֶשׁ שָׂם־אֹהֶל בָּהֶם׃ (6) וְהוּא כְּחָתָן
words-of-them for-the-sun he-pitched tent in-them (6) and-he like-bridegroom

יֹצֵא מֵחֻפָּתוֹ יָשִׂישׂ כְּגִבּוֹר לָרוּץ אֹרַח׃
coming-forth from-pavilion-of-him he-rejoices like-champion to-run course

(7) מִקְצֵה הַשָּׁמַיִם | מוֹצָאוֹ וּתְקוּפָתוֹ עַל־קְצוֹתָם
(7) at-end-of the-heavens rise-of-him and-circuit-of-him to ends-of-them

וְאֵין נִסְתָּר מֵחַמָּתוֹ׃ (8) תּוֹרַת יְהוָה תְּמִימָה
and-nothing being-hidden from-heat-of-him (8) law-of Yahweh perfect

---

people I did not know are
subject to me.
44 As soon as they hear me, they
obey me;
foreigners cringe before me.
45 They all lose heart;
they come trembling from
their strongholds.

46 The LORD lives! Praise be to my
Rock!
Exalted be God my Savior!
47 He is the God who avenges
me,
who subdues nations under
me,
48 who saves me from my
enemies.
You exalted me above my foes;
from violent men you
rescued me.
49 Therefore I will praise you
among the nations, O
LORD;
I will sing praises to your
name.
50 He gives his king great
victories;
he shows unfailing kindness
to his anointed,
to David and his
descendants forever.

Psalm 19

For the director of music. A psalm of David.

1 The heavens declare the glory
of God;
the skies proclaim the work
of his hands.
2 Day after day they pour forth
speech;
night after night they
display knowledge.
3 There is no speech or language
where their voice is not
heard.[i]
4 Their voice[j] goes out into all
the earth,
their words to the ends of
the world.

In the heavens he has pitched
a tent for the sun,
5 which is like a bridegroom
coming forth from his
pavilion,
like a champion rejoicing to
run his course.
6 It rises at one end of the
heavens
and makes its circuit to the
other;
nothing is hidden from its
heat.

7 The law of the LORD is perfect,

i3 Or *They have no speech, there are no words; / no sound is heard from them*
j4 Septuagint, Jerome and Syriac; Hebrew *line*

*Heading, *1* See the note on page 349.

°51 ק מגדיל

מְשִׁיבַת נָפֶשׁ עֵדוּת יְהוָה נֶאֱמָנָה מַחְכִּימַת פֶּתִי׃
simple making-wise-of being-trustworthy Yahweh statute-of soul reviving-of

פִּקּוּדֵי יְהוָה יְשָׁרִים מְשַׂמְּחֵי־ לֵב מִצְוַת יְהוָה
Yahweh command-of heart ones-giving-joy-of right-ones Yahweh precepts-of (9)

בָּרָה מְאִירַת עֵינָיִם׃ יִרְאַת יְהוָה ׀ טְהוֹרָה עוֹמֶדֶת לָעַד
to-forever enduring pure Yahweh fear-of (10) eyes giving-light-of radiant

מִשְׁפְּטֵי־ יְהוָה אֱמֶת צָדְקוּ יַחְדָּו׃
altogether they-are-righteous sure Yahweh ordinances-of

הַנֶּחֱמָדִים מִזָּהָב וּמִפַּז רָב
much and-more-than-pure-gold more-than-gold the-ones-being-precious (11)

וּמְתוּקִים מִדְּבַשׁ וְנֹפֶת צוּפִים׃ גַּם־
also (12) honeycombs and-honey-of more-than-honey and-ones-sweet

עַבְדְּךָ נִזְהָר בָּהֶם בְּשָׁמְרָם עֵקֶב רָב׃ שְׁגִיאוֹת
errors (13) great reward in-to-keep-them by-them being-warned servant-of-you

מִי־ יָבִין מִנִּסְתָּרוֹת נַקֵּנִי׃ גַּם
also (14) forgive-me! from-ones-being-hidden he-can-discern who?

מִזֵּדִים ׀ חֲשֹׂךְ עַבְדֶּךָ אַל־ יִמְשְׁלוּ־ בִי אָז
then over-me may-they-rule not servant-of-you keep! from-willful-sins

אֵיתָם וְנִקֵּיתִי מִפֶּשַׁע רָב׃
great of-transgression and-I-will-be-innocent I-will-be-blameless

יִהְיוּ לְרָצוֹן ׀ אִמְרֵי־ פִי וְהֶגְיוֹן
and-meditation-of mouth-of-me words-of as-pleasing may-they-be (15)

לִבִּי לְפָנֶיךָ יְהוָה צוּרִי וְגֹאֲלִי׃
and-One-Redeeming-me Rock-of-me Yahweh before-you heart-of-me

לַמְנַצֵּחַ מִזְמוֹר לְדָוִד׃ יַעַנְךָ יְהוָה
Yahweh may-he-answer-you (2) of-David psalm for-the-one-directing *(20:1)

בְּיוֹם צָרָה יְשַׂגֶּבְךָ שֵׁם ׀ אֱלֹהֵי יַעֲקֹב׃ יִשְׁלַח־
may-he-send (3) Jacob God-of name-of may-he-protect-you distress on-day-of

עֶזְרְךָ מִקֹּדֶשׁ וּמִצִּיּוֹן יִסְעָדֶךָּ׃ יִזְכֹּר
may-he-remember (4) may-he-support-you and-from-Zion from-sanctuary help-of-you

כָּל־ מִנְחֹתֶךָ וְעוֹלָתְךָ יְדַשְּׁנֶה סֶלָה׃
selah may-he-accept and-burnt-offering-of-you sacrifices-of-you all-of

יִתֶּן־ לְךָ כִלְבָבֶךָ וְכָל־ עֲצָתְךָ
plan-of-you and-all-of as-heart-of-you to-you may-he-give (5)

יְמַלֵּא׃ נְרַנְּנָה ׀ בִּישׁוּעָתֶךָ וּבְשֵׁם־
and-in-name-of at-victory-of-you we-will-shout-for-joy (6) may-he-make-succeed

אֱלֹהֵינוּ נִדְגֹּל יְמַלֵּא יְהוָה כָּל־ מִשְׁאֲלוֹתֶיךָ׃
requests-of-you all-of Yahweh may-he-grant we-will-lift-banner God-of-us

reviving the soul.
The statutes of the LORD are
trustworthy,
making wise the simple.
8 The precepts of the LORD are
right,
giving joy to the heart.
The commands of the LORD are
radiant,
giving light to the eyes.
9 The fear of the LORD is pure,
enduring forever.
The ordinances of the LORD are
sure
and altogether righteous.
10 They are more precious than
gold,
than much pure gold;
they are sweeter than honey,
than honey from the comb.
11 By them is your servant
warned;
in keeping them there is
great reward.

12 Who can discern his errors?
Forgive my hidden faults.
13 Keep your servant also from
willful sins;
may they not rule over me.
Then will I be blameless,
innocent of great
transgression.

14 May the words of my mouth
and the meditation of my
heart
be pleasing in your sight,
O LORD, my Rock and my
Redeemer.

Psalm 20

For the director of music. A psalm of David.

1 May the LORD answer you
when you are in distress;
may the name of the God of
Jacob protect you.
2 May he send you help from
the sanctuary
and grant you support from
Zion.
3 May he remember all your
sacrifices
and accept your burnt
offerings. *Selah*
4 May he give you the desire of
your heart
and make all your plans
succeed.
5 We will shout for joy when
you are victorious
and will lift up our banners
in the name of our God.
May the LORD grant all your
requests.

*Heading, *1* See the note on page 349.

עַתָּה יָדַעְתִּי כִּי הוֹשִׁיעַ ׀ יְהוָה מְשִׁיחוֹ יַעֲנֵהוּ
he-answers-him anointed-of-him Yahweh he-saves that I-know now (7)

מִשְּׁמֵי קָדְשׁוֹ בִּגְבֻרוֹת יֵשַׁע יְמִינוֹ :
right-hand-of-him salvation-of with-powers-of holiness-of-him from-heavens-of

אֵלֶּה בָרֶכֶב וְאֵלֶּה בַסּוּסִים וַאֲנַחְנוּ ׀ בְּשֵׁם־ יְהוָה
Yahweh in-name-of but-we in-the-horses and-these in-the-chariot these (8)

אֱלֹהֵינוּ נַזְכִּיר : הֵמָּה כָּרְעוּ וְנָפָלוּ וַאֲנַחְנוּ קַּמְנוּ†
we-rise-up but-we and-they-fall they-kneel they (9) we-trust God-of-us

וַנִּתְעוֹדָד : יְהוָה הוֹשִׁיעָה הַמֶּלֶךְ יַעֲנֵנוּ בְיוֹם־
on-day-of may-he-answer-us the-king save! Yahweh (10) and-we-stand-firm

קָרְאֵנוּ : לַמְנַצֵּחַ מִזְמוֹר לְדָוִד : יְהוָה
Yahweh (2) of-David psalm for-the-one-directing *(21:1) to-call-us

בְּעָזְּךָ יִשְׂמַח־ מֶלֶךְ וּבִישׁוּעָתְךָ מַה־ יָּגֶיל
he-has-joy how! and-in-victory-of-you king he-rejoices in-strength-of-you

מְאֹד : תַּאֲוַת לִבּוֹ נָתַתָּה לּוֹ וַאֲרֶשֶׁת שְׂפָתָיו
lips-of-him and-request-of to-him you-granted heart-of-him desire-of (3) great

בַּל־ מָנַעְתָּ סֶּלָה : כִּי־ תְקַדְּמֶנּוּ בִּרְכוֹת טוֹב תָּשִׁית
you-placed richness blessings-of you-welcomed-him indeed (4) selah you-withheld not

לְרֹאשׁוֹ עֲטֶרֶת פָּז : חַיִּים ׀ שָׁאַל מִמְּךָ נָתַתָּה לּוֹ
to-him you-gave from-you he-asked lives (5) pure-gold crown-of on-head-of-him

אֹרֶךְ יָמִים עוֹלָם וָעֶד : גָּדוֹל כְּבוֹדוֹ בִּישׁוּעָתֶךָ
through-victory-of-you glory-of-him great (6) and-ever forever days length-of

הוֹד וְהָדָר תְּשַׁוֶּה עָלָיו : כִּי־ תְשִׁיתֵהוּ
you-granted-him surely (7) on-him you-bestowed and-majesty splendor

בְרָכוֹת לָעַד תְּחַדֵּהוּ בְשִׂמְחָה אֶת־ פָּנֶיךָ :
presences-of-you in with-joy you-made-glad-him for-eternity blessings

כִּי־ הַמֶּלֶךְ בֹּטֵחַ בַּיהוָה וּבְחֶסֶד עֶלְיוֹן
Most-High and-through-unfailing-love-of in-Yahweh trusting the-king for (8)

בַּל־ יִמּוֹט : תִּמְצָא יָדְךָ לְכָל־
on-all-of hand-of-you she-will-lay-hold (9) he-will-be-shaken not

אֹיְבֶיךָ יְמִינְךָ תִּמְצָא שֹׂנְאֶיךָ :
ones-being-foes-of-you she-will-seize right-hand-of-you ones-being-enemies-of-you

תְּשִׁיתֵמוֹ ׀ כְּתַנּוּר אֵשׁ לְעֵת פָּנֶיךָ
appearances-of-you at-time-of fire like-furnace-of you-will-make-them (10)

יְהוָה בְּאַפּוֹ יְבַלְּעֵם וְתֹאכְלֵם אֵשׁ :
fire and-she-will-consume-them he-will-swallow-them in-wrath-of-him Yahweh

פִּרְיָמוֹ מֵאֶרֶץ תְּאַבֵּד וְזַרְעָם
and-posterity-of-them you-will-destroy from-earth descendant-of-them (11)

6 Now I know that the LORD saves his anointed;
he answers him from his holy heaven
with the saving power of his right hand.
7 Some trust in chariots and some in horses,
but we trust in the name of the LORD our God.
8 They are brought to their knees and fall,
but we rise up and stand firm.

9 O LORD, save the king!
Answer[k] us when we call!

Psalm 21

For the director of music. A psalm of David.

1 O LORD, the king rejoices in your strength.
How great is his joy in the victories you give!
2 You have granted him the desire of his heart
and have not withheld the request of his lips. *Selah*
3 You welcomed him with rich blessings
and placed a crown of pure gold on his head.
4 He asked you for life, and you gave it to him—
length of days, for ever and ever.
5 Through the victories you gave, his glory is great;
you have bestowed on him splendor and majesty.
6 Surely you have granted him eternal blessings
and made him glad with the joy of your presence.
7 For the king trusts in the LORD;
through the unfailing love of the Most High
he will not be shaken.

8 Your hand will lay hold on all your enemies;
your right hand will seize your foes.
9 At the time of your appearing
you will make them like a fiery furnace.
In his wrath the LORD will swallow them up,
and his fire will consume them.
10 You will destroy their descendants from the earth,
their posterity from

k9 Or *save! / O King, answer*

*Heading, *1* See the note on page 349.

†9 Most mss have no *dagesh* in the *qoph* (ק).

מִבְּנֵי אָדָם׃ כִּי־ נָטוּ עָלֶיךָ רָעָה חָשְׁבוּ
they-devise evil against-you they-plot though (12) mankind from-sons-of

מְזִמָּה בַּל־ יוּכָלוּ׃ כִּי תְּשִׁיתֵמוֹ שֶׁכֶם
back you-will-make-turn-them for (13) they-can-succeed not scheme

בְּמֵיתָרֶיךָ תְּכוֹנֵן עַל־ פְּנֵיהֶם׃ רוּמָה יְהוָה
Yahweh be-exalted! (14) faces-of-them at you-aim when-bowstrings-of-you

בְעֻזֶּךָ נָשִׁירָה וּנְזַמְּרָה גְּבוּרָתֶךָ׃
might-of-you and-we-will-praise we-will-sing in-strength-of-you

לַמְנַצֵּחַ עַל־ אַיֶּלֶת הַשַּׁחַר מִזְמוֹר לְדָוִד׃
of-David psalm the-morning doe-of to for-the-one-directing *(22:1)

אֵלִי אֵלִי לָמָה עֲזַבְתָּנִי רָחוֹק מִישׁוּעָתִי דִּבְרֵי
words-of from-salvation-of-me far you-forsook-me why? God-of-me God-of-me (2)

שַׁאֲגָתִי׃ אֱלֹהַי אֶקְרָא יוֹמָם וְלֹא תַעֲנֶה וְלַיְלָה
and-night you-answer but-not by-day I-cry-out God-of-me (3) groan-of-me

וְלֹא־ דוּמִיָּה לִי׃ וְאַתָּה קָדוֹשׁ יוֹשֵׁב תְּהִלּוֹת יִשְׂרָאֵל׃
Israel praises-of being-enthroned Holy-One yet-you (4) to-me silence and-not

בְּךָ בָּטְחוּ אֲבֹתֵינוּ בָּטְחוּ וַתְּפַלְּטֵמוֹ׃
and-you-delivered-them they-trusted fathers-of-us they-trusted in-you (5)

אֵלֶיךָ זָעֲקוּ וְנִמְלָטוּ בְּךָ בָטְחוּ וְלֹא־
and-not they-trusted in-you and-they-were-saved they-cried to-you (6)

בוֹשׁוּ׃ וְאָנֹכִי תוֹלַעַת וְלֹא־ אִישׁ חֶרְפַּת אָדָם
man scorn-of man and-not worm but-I (7) they-were-disappointed

וּבְזוּי עָם׃ כָּל־ רֹאַי יַלְעִגוּ לִי
at-me they-mock ones-seeing-me all-of (8) people and-being-despised-of

יַפְטִירוּ בְשָׂפָה יָנִיעוּ רֹאשׁ׃ גֹּל† אֶל־ יְהוָה יְפַלְּטֵהוּ
let-him-rescue-him Yahweh in trust! (9) head they-shake with-lip they-insult

יַצִּילֵהוּ כִּי חָפֵץ בּוֹ׃ כִּי־ אַתָּה גֹחִי
one-bringing-out-me you yet (10) in-him he-delights since let-him-deliver-him

מִבָּטֶן מַבְטִיחִי עַל־ שְׁדֵי אִמִּי׃ עָלֶיךָ
upon-you (11) mother-of-me breasts-of at one-making-trust-me from-womb

הָשְׁלַכְתִּי מֵרָחֶם מִבֶּטֶן אִמִּי אֵלִי אָתָּה׃ אַל־
not (12) you God-of-me mother-of-me from-womb-of from-womb I-was-cast

תִּרְחַק מִמֶּנִּי כִּי־ צָרָה קְרוֹבָה כִּי־ אֵין עוֹזֵר׃
one-helping there-is-not for near trouble for from-me you-be-far

סְבָבוּנִי פָּרִים רַבִּים אַבִּירֵי בָשָׁן כִּתְּרוּנִי׃
they-encircle-me Bashan strong-ones-of many bulls they-surround-me (13)

פָּצוּ עָלַי פִּיהֶם אַרְיֵה טֹרֵף וְשֹׁאֵג׃
and-roaring tearing-prey lion mouth-of-them against-me they-open-wide (14)

mankind.
[11]Though they plot evil against
you
and devise wicked schemes,
they cannot succeed;
[12]for you will make them turn
their backs
when you aim at them with
drawn bow.

[13]Be exalted, O LORD, in your
strength;
we will sing and praise your
might.

Psalm 22

For the director of music. To the tune of "The Doe of the Morning." A psalm of David.

[1]My God, my God, why have
you forsaken me?
Why are you so far from
saving me,
so far from the words of my
groaning?
[2]O my God, I cry out by day,
but you do not answer,
by night, and am not silent.

[3]Yet you are enthroned as the
Holy One;
you are the praise of Israel.[l]
[4]In you our fathers put their
trust;
they trusted and you
delivered them.
[5]They cried to you and were
saved;
in you they trusted and
were not disappointed.

[6]But I am a worm and not a
man,
scorned by men and
despised by the people.
[7]All who see me mock me;
they hurl insults, shaking
their heads:
[8]"He trusts in the LORD;
let the LORD rescue him.
Let him deliver him,
since he delights in him."

[9]Yet you brought me out of the
womb;
you made me trust in you
even at my mother's breast.
[10]From birth I was cast upon
you;
from my mother's womb
you have been my God.
[11]Do not be far from me,
for trouble is near
and there is no one to help.

[12]Many bulls surround me;
strong bulls of Bashan
encircle me.
[13]Roaring lions tearing their
prey
open their mouths wide
against me.

l3 Or *Yet you are holy, / enthroned on the praises of Israel*

*Heading, *1* See the note on page 349.
†9 The NIV repoints as גַּל, *be-trusts.*

כַּמַּיִם נִשְׁפַּכְתִּי וְהִתְפָּרְדוּ כָּל־
(15) like-the-waters I-am-poured-out and-they-are-out-of-joint all-of

עַצְמוֹתָי הָיָה לִבִּי כַּדּוֹנָג נָמֵס בְּתוֹךְ
bones-of-me he-is heart-of-me like-the-wax he-melted-away within

מֵעָי׃ יָבֵשׁ כַּחֶרֶשׂ ׀ כֹּחִי
insides-of-me (16) he-is-dried-up like-the-potsherd strength-of-me

וּלְשׁוֹנִי מֻדְבָּק מַלְקוֹחָי וְלַעֲפַר־ מָוֶת תִּשְׁפְּתֵנִי׃
and-tongue-of-me being-stuck roofs-of-mouth-of-me and-in-dust-of death you-lay-me

כִּי סְבָבוּנִי כְּלָבִים עֲדַת מְרֵעִים הִקִּיפוּנִי
(17) indeed they-surrounded-me dogs band-of men-being-evil they-encircled-me

†כָּאֲרִי יָדַי וְרַגְלָי׃ אֲסַפֵּר כָּל־ עַצְמוֹתָי
†like-the-lion hands-of-me and-feet-of-me (18) I-can-count all-of bones-of-me

הֵמָּה יַבִּיטוּ יִרְאוּ־ בִי׃ יְחַלְּקוּ בְגָדַי לָהֶם
they they-stare they-gloat over-me (19) they-divide garments-of-me among-them

וְעַל־ לְבוּשִׁי יַפִּילוּ גוֹרָל׃ וְאַתָּה יְהוָה אַל־ תִּרְחָק
and-for clothing-of-me they-cast lot (20) but-you Yahweh not you-be-far-off

אֱיָלוּתִי לְעֶזְרָתִי חוּשָׁה׃ הַצִּילָה מֵחֶרֶב
Strength-of-me as-help-of-me come-quickly! (21) deliver! from-sword

נַפְשִׁי מִיַּד־ כֶּלֶב יְחִידָתִי׃ הוֹשִׁיעֵנִי מִפִּי
life-of-me from-power-of dog precious-one-of-me (22) rescue-me! from-mouth-of

אַרְיֵה וּמִקַּרְנֵי רֵמִים עֲנִיתָנִי׃ אֲסַפְּרָה שִׁמְךָ
lion and-from-horns-of wild-oxen you-heard-me (23) I-will-declare name-of-you

לְאֶחָי בְּתוֹךְ קָהָל אֲהַלְלֶךָּ׃ יִרְאֵי
to-brothers-of-me within congregation I-will-praise-you (24) ones-fearing-of

יְהוָה ׀ הַלְלוּהוּ כָּל־ זֶרַע יַעֲקֹב כַּבְּדוּהוּ וְגוּרוּ
Yahweh praise-him! all-of descendant-of Jacob honor-him! and-revere!

מִמֶּנּוּ כָּל־ זֶרַע יִשְׂרָאֵל׃ כִּי לֹא־ בָזָה וְלֹא
before-him all-of descendant-of Israel (25) for not he-despised and-not

שִׁקַּץ עֱנוּת עָנִי וְלֹא־ הִסְתִּיר פָּנָיו מִמֶּנּוּ
he-disdained suffering-of afflicted and-not he-hid faces-of-him from-him

וּבְשַׁוְּעוֹ אֵלָיו שָׁמֵעַ׃ מֵאִתְּךָ תְּהִלָּתִי
but-when-to-cry-for-help-him to-him he-heard (26) from-with-you praise-of-me

בְּקָהָל רָב נְדָרַי אֲשַׁלֵּם נֶגֶד יְרֵאָיו׃
in-assembly great vows-of-me I-will-fulfill before ones-fearing-him

יֹאכְלוּ עֲנָוִים ׀ וְיִשְׂבָּעוּ יְהַלְלוּ יְהוָה
(27) they-will-eat poor-ones and-they-will-be-satisfied they-will-praise Yahweh

דֹּרְשָׁיו יְחִי לְבַבְכֶם לָעַד׃ יִזְכְּרוּ ׀
ones-seeking-him may-he-live heart-of-you to-forever (28) they-will-remember

14 I am poured out like water,
and all my bones are out of joint.
My heart has turned to wax;
it has melted away within me.
15 My strength is dried up like a potsherd,
and my tongue sticks to the roof of my mouth;
you lay me[m] in the dust of death.
16 Dogs have surrounded me;
a band of evil men has encircled me,
they have pierced[n] my hands and my feet.
17 I can count all my bones;
people stare and gloat over me.
18 They divide my garments among them
and cast lots for my clothing.

19 But you, O LORD, be not far off;
O my Strength, come quickly to help me.
20 Deliver my life from the sword,
my precious life from the power of the dogs.
21 Rescue me from the mouth of the lions;
save[o] me from the horns of the wild oxen.

22 I will declare your name to my brothers;
in the congregation I will praise you.
23 You who fear the LORD, praise him!
All you descendants of Jacob, honor him!
Revere him, all you descendants of Israel!
24 For he has not despised or disdained
the suffering of the afflicted one;
he has not hidden his face from him
but has listened to his cry for help.

25 From you comes my praise in the great assembly;
before those who fear you[p] will I fulfill my vows.
26 The poor will eat and be satisfied;
they who seek the LORD will praise him—
may your hearts live forever!

m15 Or */ I am laid*
n16 Some Hebrew manuscripts, Septuagint and Syriac; most Hebrew manuscripts */ like the lion,*
o21 Or *lions; / you have heard*
p25 Hebrew *him*

*See the note on page 349.

†17 The NIV reads with some mss כָּרוּ or כארו, *they-pierced.*

וְיָשֻׁבוּ אֶל־יְהוָה כָּל־אַפְסֵי־אָרֶץ וְיִשְׁתַּחֲווּ
and-they-will-bow-down earth ends-of all-of Yahweh to and-they-will-turn

לְפָנֶיךָ כָּל־מִשְׁפְּחוֹת גּוֹיִם׃ כִּי לַיהוָה הַמְּלוּכָה
the-dominion to-Yahweh for (29) nations families-of all-of before-you

וּמֹשֵׁל בַּגּוֹיִם׃ אָכְלוּ וַיִּשְׁתַּחֲווּ ׀
and-they-will-worship they-will-feast (30) over-the-nations and-ruling

כָּל־דִּשְׁנֵי־אֶרֶץ לְפָנָיו יִכְרְעוּ כָּל־יוֹרְדֵי
ones-going-down-of all-of they-will-kneel before-him earth rich-ones-of all-of

עָפָר וְנַפְשׁוֹ לֹא חִיָּה׃ זֶרַע יַעַבְדֶנּוּ
he-will-serve-him posterity (31) he-keeps-alive not and-self-of-him dust

יְסֻפַּר לַאדֹנָי לַדּוֹר׃ יָבֹאוּ
they-will-come (32) to-the-generation about-Lord he-will-be-told

וְיַגִּידוּ צִדְקָתוֹ לְעַם נוֹלָד כִּי עָשָׂה׃
he-did for being-born to-people righteousness-of-him and-they-will-proclaim

מִזְמוֹר לְדָוִד יְהוָה רֹעִי לֹא אֶחְסָר׃
I-shall-lack nothing one-being-shepherd-of-me Yahweh of-David psalm (23:1)

בִּנְאוֹת דֶּשֶׁא יַרְבִּיצֵנִי עַל־מֵי מְנֻחוֹת
quiet-ones waters-of beside he-makes-lie-down-me greenness in-pastures-of (2)

יְנַהֲלֵנִי׃ נַפְשִׁי יְשׁוֹבֵב יַנְחֵנִי בְמַעְגְּלֵי־צֶדֶק
righteousness in-paths-of he-guides-me he-restores soul-of-me (3) he-leads-me

לְמַעַן שְׁמוֹ׃ גַּם כִּי־אֵלֵךְ בְּגֵיא צַלְמָוֶת
deep-darkness in-valley-of I-walk though even (4) name-of-him for-sake-of

לֹא־אִירָא רָע כִּי־אַתָּה עִמָּדִי שִׁבְטְךָ וּמִשְׁעַנְתֶּךָ הֵמָּה
they and-staff-of-you rod-of-you with-me you for evil I-will-fear not

יְנַחֲמֻנִי׃ תַּעֲרֹךְ לְפָנַי ׀ שֻׁלְחָן נֶגֶד
in-presence-of table before-me you-prepare (5) they-comfort-me

צֹרְרָי דִּשַּׁנְתָּ בַשֶּׁמֶן רֹאשִׁי כּוֹסִי
cup-of-me head-of-me with-the-oil you-anoint ones-being-enemies-of-me

רְוָיָה׃ אַךְ ׀ טוֹב וָחֶסֶד יִרְדְּפוּנִי כָּל־יְמֵי
days-of all-of they-will-follow-me and-love goodness surely (6) overflow

חַיָּי וְשַׁבְתִּי בְּבֵית־יְהוָה לְאֹרֶךְ יָמִים׃
days for-length-of Yahweh in-house-of and-I-will-dwell lives-of-me

לְדָוִד מִזְמוֹר לַיהוָה הָאָרֶץ וּמְלוֹאָהּ תֵּבֵל
world and-everything-in-her the-earth to-Yahweh psalm of-David (24:1)

וְיֹשְׁבֵי בָהּ׃ כִּי־הוּא עַל־יַמִּים יְסָדָהּ וְעַל־
and-upon he-founded-her seas upon he for (2) in-her and-ones-living-of

נְהָרוֹת יְכוֹנְנֶהָ׃ מִי־יַעֲלֶה בְהַר־יְהוָה וּמִי־
and-who? Yahweh to-hill-of he-may-ascend who? (3) he-established-her waters

27 All the ends of the earth
will remember and turn to
the LORD,
and all the families of the
nations
will bow down before him,
28 for dominion belongs to the
LORD
and he rules over the
nations.

29 All the rich of the earth will
feast and worship;
all who go down to the dust
will kneel before him—
those who cannot keep
themselves alive.
30 Posterity will serve him;
future generations will be
told about the Lord.
31 They will proclaim his
righteousness
to a people yet unborn—
for he has done it.

Psalm 23

A psalm of David.

1 The LORD is my shepherd, I
shall lack nothing.
2 He makes me lie down in
green pastures,
he leads me beside quiet
waters,
3 he restores my soul.
He guides me in paths of
righteousness
for his name's sake.
4 Even though I walk
through the valley of the
shadow of death,[a]
I will fear no evil,
for you are with me;
your rod and your staff,
they comfort me.

5 You prepare a table before me
in the presence of my
enemies.
You anoint my head with oil;
my cup overflows.
6 Surely goodness and love will
follow me
all the days of my life,
and I will dwell in the house
of the LORD
forever.

Psalm 24

Of David. A psalm.

1 The earth is the LORD's, and
everything in it,
the world, and all who live
in it;
2 for he founded it upon the
seas
and established it upon the
waters.

3 Who may ascend the hill of
the LORD?

a4 Or *through the darkest valley*

*See the note on page 349.

יָקוּם בִּמְקוֹם קָדְשׁוֹ׃ (4) נְקִי כַפַּיִם וּבַר־
and-pure-of hands clean-of (4) holiness-of-him in-place-of he-may-stand

לֵבָב אֲשֶׁר ׀ לֹא־ נָשָׂא לַשָּׁוְא נַפְשִׁי וְלֹא נִשְׁבַּע
he-swears and-not soul-of-me to-the-idol he-lifts-up not who heart

לְמִרְמָה׃ (5) יִשָּׂא בְרָכָה מֵאֵת יְהוָה וּצְדָקָה
and-vindication Yahweh from-with blessing he-will-receive (5) by-falsehood

מֵאֱלֹהֵי יִשְׁעוֹ׃ (6) זֶה דּוֹר דֹּרְשָׁו
ones-seeking-him generation-of such (6) salvation-of-him from-God-of

מְבַקְשֵׁי פָנֶיךָ יַעֲקֹב סֶלָה׃ (7) שְׂאוּ שְׁעָרִים ׀ רָאשֵׁיכֶם
heads-of-you gates lift-up! (7) selah Jacob faces-of-you ones-seeking-of

וְהִנָּשְׂאוּ פִּתְחֵי עוֹלָם וְיָבוֹא מֶלֶךְ הַכָּבוֹד׃
the-glory King-of that-he-may-come-in ancient doors-of and-be-lifted-up!

(8) מִי זֶה מֶלֶךְ הַכָּבוֹד יְהוָה עִזּוּז וְגִבּוֹר יְהוָה גִּבּוֹר
mighty-of Yahweh and-mighty strong Yahweh the-glory King-of this who? (8)

מִלְחָמָה׃ (9) שְׂאוּ שְׁעָרִים ׀ רָאשֵׁיכֶם וּשְׂאוּ פִּתְחֵי עוֹלָם
ancient doors-of and-lift-up! heads-of-you gates lift-up! (9) battle

וְיָבֹא מֶלֶךְ הַכָּבוֹד׃ (10) מִי הוּא זֶה מֶלֶךְ הַכָּבוֹד
the-glory King-of this he who? (10) the-glory King-of that-he-may-come-in

יְהוָה צְבָאוֹת הוּא מֶלֶךְ הַכָּבוֹד סֶלָה׃ (25:1) לְדָוִד אֵלֶיךָ יְהוָה
Yahweh to-you of-David (25:1) selah the-glory King-of he Hosts Yahweh-of

נַפְשִׁי אֶשָּׂא׃ (2) אֱלֹהַי בְּךָ בָטַחְתִּי אַל־ אֵבוֹשָׁה אַל־
not let-me-be-shamed not I-trust in-you God-of-me (2) I-lift-up soul-of-me

יַעַלְצוּ אֹיְבַי לִי׃ (3) גַּם כָּל־
all-of indeed (3) over-me ones-being-enemies-of-me let-them-triumph

קֹוֶיךָ לֹא יֵבֹשׁוּ יֵבֹשׁוּ
they-will-be-shamed they-will-be-shamed not ones-hoping-in-you

הַבּוֹגְדִים רֵיקָם׃ (4) דְּרָכֶיךָ יְהוָה הוֹדִיעֵנִי
show-me! Yahweh ways-of-you (4) without-excuse the-ones-being-treacherous

אֹרְחוֹתֶיךָ לַמְּדֵנִי׃ (5) הַדְרִיכֵנִי בַאֲמִתֶּךָ ׀ וְלַמְּדֵנִי כִּי־ אַתָּה
you for and-teach-me! in-truth-of-you guide-me! (5) teach-me! paths-of-you

אֱלֹהֵי יִשְׁעִי אוֹתְךָ קִוִּיתִי כָּל־ הַיּוֹם׃ (6) זְכֹר־ רַחֲמֶיךָ
mercies-of-you remember! (6) the-day all-of I-hope-in you salvation-of-me God-of

יְהוָה וַחֲסָדֶיךָ כִּי מֵעוֹלָם הֵמָּה׃ (7) חַטֹּאות נְעוּרַי ׀
youths-of-me sins-of (7) they from-of-old for and-loves-of-you Yahweh

וּפְשָׁעַי אַל־ תִּזְכֹּר כְּחַסְדְּךָ זְכָר־ לִי־
to-me remember! as-love-of-you you-remember not and-rebellious-ways-of-me

אַתָּה לְמַעַן טוּבְךָ יְהוָה׃ (8) טוֹב־ וְיָשָׁר יְהוָה עַל־ כֵּן
this for Yahweh and-upright good (8) Yahweh goodness-of-you for you

---

Who may stand in his holy
place?
4He who has clean hands and a
pure heart,
who does not lift up his soul
to an idol
or swear by what is false.
5He will receive blessing from
the LORD
and vindication from God
his Savior.
6Such is the generation of those
who seek him,
who seek your face, O God
of Jacob.[r] *Selah*

7Lift up your heads, O you
gates;
be lifted up, you ancient
doors,
that the King of glory may
come in.
8Who is this King of glory?
The LORD strong and
mighty,
the LORD mighty in battle.
9Lift up your heads, O you
gates;
lift them up, you ancient
doors,
that the King of glory may
come in.
10Who is he, this King of glory?
The LORD Almighty—
he is the King of glory. *Selah*

Psalm 25[s]

Of David.

1To you, O LORD, I lift up my
soul;
2 in you I trust, O my God.
Do not let me be put to shame,
nor let my enemies triumph
over me.
3No one whose hope is in you
will ever be put to shame,
but they will be put to shame
who are treacherous without
excuse.

4Show me your ways, O LORD,
teach me your paths;
5guide me in your truth and
teach me,
for you are God my Savior,
and my hope is in you all
day long.
6Remember, O LORD, your great
mercy and love,
for they are from of old.
7Remember not the sins of my
youth
and my rebellious ways;
according to your love
remember me,
for you are good, O LORD.

8Good and upright is the LORD;

[r]6 Two Hebrew manuscripts and Syriac (see also Septuagint); most Hebrew manuscripts *face, Jacob*
[s]This psalm is an acrostic poem, the verses of which begin with the successive letters of the Hebrew alphabet.

°6 ק דרשיו

יוֹרֶה חַטָּאִים בַּדָּרֶךְ׃ (9) יַדְרֵךְ עֲנָוִים בַּמִּשְׁפָּט
in-the-right humble-ones he-guides (9) in-the-way sinners he-instructs

וִילַמֵּד עֲנָוִים דַּרְכּוֹ׃ (10) כָּל־ אָרְחוֹת יְהוָה חֶסֶד
loving Yahweh ways-of all-of (10) way-of-him humble-ones and-he-teaches

וֶאֱמֶת לְנֹצְרֵי בְרִיתוֹ וְעֵדֹתָיו׃
and-demands-of-him covenant-of-him for-ones-keeping-of and-faithful

(11) לְמַעַן־ שִׁמְךָ יְהוָה וְסָלַחְתָּ לַעֲוֹנִי כִּי
though to-iniquity-of-me now-you-forgive Yahweh name-of-you for-sake-of (11)

רַב־ הוּא׃ (12) מִי־ זֶה הָאִישׁ יְרֵא יְהוָה יוֹרֶנּוּ
he-will-instruct-him Yahweh fearing-of the-man this who? (12) he great

בְּדֶרֶךְ יִבְחָר׃ (13) נַפְשׁוֹ בְּטוֹב תָּלִין
she-will-spend-days in-prosperity life-of-him (13) he-chooses in-way

וְזַרְעוֹ יִירַשׁ אָרֶץ׃ (14) סוֹד יְהוָה
Yahweh confidence-of (14) land he-will-inherit and-descendant-of-him

לִירֵאָיו וּבְרִיתוֹ לְהוֹדִיעָם׃ (15) עֵינַי
eyes-of-me (15) to-make-known-to-them and-covenant-of-him in-ones-fearing-him

תָּמִיד אֶל־ יְהוָה כִּי הוּא־ יוֹצִיא מֵרֶשֶׁת רַגְלָי׃ (16) פְּנֵה־
turn! (16) feet-of-me from-snare he-will-release he for Yahweh on ever

אֵלַי וְחָנֵּנִי כִּי־ יָחִיד וְעָנִי אָנִי׃ (17) צָרוֹת
troubles-of (17) I and-afflicted lonely for and-be-gracious-to-me! to-me

לְבָבִי הִרְחִיבוּ מִמְּצוּקוֹתַי הוֹצִיאֵנִי׃ (18) רְאֵה
look-upon! (18) free-me! from-anguishes-of-me they-multiplied heart-of-me

עָנְיִי וַעֲמָלִי וְשָׂא לְכָל־ חַטֹּאותָי׃
sins-of-me to-all-of and-take-away! and-distress-of-me affliction-of-me

(19) רְאֵה־ אוֹיְבַי כִּי־ רָבּוּ וְשִׂנְאַת חָמָס
fierceness and-hate-of they-increased how! ones-being-enemies-of-me see! (19)

שְׂנֵאוּנִי׃ (20) שָׁמְרָה נַפְשִׁי וְהַצִּילֵנִי אַל־ אֵבוֹשׁ כִּי־
for let-me-be-shamed not and-rescue-me! life-of-me guard! (20) they-hate-me

חָסִיתִי בָךְ׃ (21) תֹּם־ וָיֹשֶׁר יִצְּרוּנִי כִּי
because may-they-protect-me and-uprightness integrity (21) in-you I-take-refuge

קִוִּיתִיךָ׃ (22) פְּדֵה אֱלֹהִים אֶת־ יִשְׂרָאֵל מִכֹּל צָרוֹתָיו׃
troubles-of-him from-all-of Israel *** God redeem! (22) I-hope-in-you

(26:1) לְדָוִד ׀ שָׁפְטֵנִי יְהוָה כִּי־ אֲנִי בְּתֻמִּי הָלַכְתִּי
I-walked in-blameless-life-of-me I for Yahweh vindicate-me! of-David (26:1)

וּבַיהוָה בָּטַחְתִּי לֹא אֶמְעָד׃ (2) בְּחָנֵנִי יְהוָה וְנַסֵּנִי
and-try-me! Yahweh test-me! (2) I-wavered not I-trusted and-in-Yahweh

צְרוֹפָה כִלְיוֹתַי וְלִבִּי׃ (3) כִּי־ חַסְדְּךָ לְנֶגֶד עֵינָי
eyes-of-me at-before love-of-you for (3) and-mind-of-me hearts-of-me examine!

°2 ק צרפה

therefore he instructs
sinners in his ways.
9He guides the humble in what
is right
and teaches them his way.
10All the ways of the LORD are
loving and faithful
for those who keep the
demands of his covenant.
11For the sake of your name, O
LORD,
forgive my iniquity, though
it is great.
12Who, then, is the man that
fears the LORD?
He will instruct him in the
way chosen for him.
13He will spend his days in
prosperity,
and his descendants will
inherit the land.
14The LORD confides in those
who fear him;
he makes his covenant
known to them.
15My eyes are ever on the LORD,
for only he will release my
feet from the snare.

16Turn to me and be gracious to
me,
for I am lonely and afflicted.
17The troubles of my heart have
multiplied;
free me from my anguish.
18Look upon my affliction and
my distress
and take away all my sins.
19See how my enemies have
increased
and how fiercely they hate
me!
20Guard my life and rescue me;
let me not be put to shame,
for I take refuge in you.
21May integrity and uprightness
protect me,
because my hope is in you.

22Redeem Israel, O God,
from all their troubles!

Psalm 26

Of David.

1Vindicate me, O LORD,
for I have led a blameless
life;
I have trusted in the LORD
without wavering.
2Test me, O LORD, and try me,
examine my heart and my
mind;
3for your love is ever before
me,

וְהִתְהַלַּכְתִּי בַּאֲמִתֶּךָ׃ לֹא־יָשַׁבְתִּי עִם־מְתֵי־שָׁוְא וְעִם

or-with deceit men-of with I-sit not (4) in-truth-of-you and-I-walk

נַעֲלָמִים לֹא אָבוֹא׃ שָׂנֵאתִי קְהַל מְרֵעִים

ones-doing-evil assembly-of I-abhor (5) I-consort not ones-being-hypocrites

וְעִם־רְשָׁעִים לֹא אֵשֵׁב׃ אֶרְחַץ בְּנִקָּיוֹן כַּפָּי

hands-of-me in-innocence I-wash (6) I-sit not wicked-ones and-with

וַאֲסֹבְבָה אֶת־מִזְבַּחֲךָ יְהוָה׃ לַשְׁמִעַ בְּקוֹל תּוֹדָה

praise with-voice-of to-proclaim (7) Yahweh altar-of-you *** and-I-go-about

וּלְסַפֵּר כָּל־נִפְלְאוֹתֶיךָ׃ יְהוָה אָהַבְתִּי

I-love Yahweh (8) deeds-being-wonderful-of-you all-of and-to-tell

מְעוֹן בֵּיתֶךָ וּמְקוֹם מִשְׁכַּן כְּבוֹדֶךָ׃ אַל־

not (9) glory-of-you dwelling-of and-place-of house-of-you living-place-of

תֶּאֱסֹף עִם־חַטָּאִים נַפְשִׁי וְעִם־אַנְשֵׁי דָמִים חַיָּי׃

lives-of-me bloods men-of or-with soul-of-me sinners with you-take-away

אֲשֶׁר־בִּידֵיהֶם זִמָּה וִימִינָם מָלְאָה שֹּׁחַד׃

bribe she-is-full and-right-hand-of-them scheme in-hands-of-them who (10)

וַאֲנִי בְּתֻמִּי אֵלֵךְ פְּדֵנִי וְחָנֵּנִי׃

and-be-merciful-to-me! redeem-me! I-walk in-blameless-life-of-me but-I (11)

רַגְלִי עָמְדָה בְמִישׁוֹר בְּמַקְהֵלִים אֲבָרֵךְ

I-will-praise in-great-assemblies on-level-ground she-stands foot-of-me (12)

יְהוָה׃ לְדָוִד | יְהוָה | אוֹרִי וְיִשְׁעִי מִמִּי

of-whom? and-salvation-of-me light-of-me Yahweh of-David (27:1) Yahweh

אִירָא יְהוָה מָעוֹז־חַיַּי מִמִּי אֶפְחָד׃

shall-I-be-afraid of-whom? lives-of-me stronghold-of Yahweh shall-I-fear

בִּקְרֹב עָלַי | מְרֵעִים לֶאֱכֹל אֶת־בְּשָׂרִי

flesh-of-me *** to-devour men-being-evil against-me when-to-advance (2)

צָרַי וְאֹיְבַי לִי הֵמָּה כָשְׁלוּ

they-will-stumble they against-me and-ones-being-foes-of-me enemies-of-me

וְנָפָלוּ׃ אִם־תַּחֲנֶה עָלַי | מַחֲנֶה לֹא־יִירָא

he-will-fear not army against-me she-besiege though (3) and-they-will-fall

לִבִּי אִם־תָּקוּם עָלַי מִלְחָמָה בְּזֹאת אֲנִי בוֹטֵחַ׃

being-confident I in-this war against-me she-break-out though heart-of-me

אַחַת | שָׁאַלְתִּי מֵאֵת־יְהוָה אוֹתָהּ אֲבַקֵּשׁ שִׁבְתִּי בְּבֵית־יְהוָה

Yahweh in-house-of to-dwell-me I-seek her Yahweh from-with I-ask one (4)

כָּל־יְמֵי חַיַּי לַחֲזוֹת בְּנֹעַם־יְהוָה וּלְבַקֵּר

and-to-seek Yahweh upon-beauty-of to-gaze lives-of-me days-of all-of

בְּהֵיכָלוֹ׃ כִּי יִצְפְּנֵנִי | בְּסֻכֹּה בְּיוֹם

in-day-of in-dwelling-of-him he-will-keep-safe-me for (5) in-temple-of-him

and I walk continually in
your truth.
4 I do not sit with deceitful
men,
nor do I consort with
hypocrites;
5 I abhor the assembly of
evildoers
and refuse to sit with the
wicked.
6 I wash my hands in
innocence,
and go about your altar, O
LORD,
7 proclaiming aloud your praise
and telling of all your
wonderful deeds.
8 I love the house where you
live, O LORD,
the place where your glory
dwells.

9 Do not take away my soul
along with sinners
or my life with bloodthirsty
men,
10 in whose hands are wicked
schemes,
whose right hands are full
of bribes.
11 But I lead a blameless life;
redeem me and be merciful
to me.
12 My feet stand on level ground;
in the great assembly I will
praise the LORD.

Psalm 27

Of David.

1 The LORD is my light and my
salvation—
whom shall I fear?
The LORD is the stronghold of
my life—
of whom shall I be afraid?
2 When evil men advance
against me
to devour my flesh,[2]
when my enemies and my
foes attack me,
they will stumble and fall.
3 Though an army besiege me,
my heart will not fear;
though war break out against
me,
even then will I be
confident.

4 One thing I ask of the LORD,
this is what I seek:
that I may dwell in the house
of the LORD
all the days of my life,
to gaze upon the beauty of the
LORD
and to seek him in his
temple.
5 For in the day of trouble
he will keep me safe in his
dwelling;

[2] 2 Or *to slander me*

רָעָה יַסְתִּרֵנִי בְּסֵתֶר אָהֳלוֹ בְּצוּר
upon-rock tabernacle-of-him in-shelter-of he-will-hide-me trouble

יְרוֹמְמֵנִי׃ (6) וְעַתָּה יָרוּם רֹאשִׁי עַל
above head-of-me he-will-be-exalted and-then (6) he-will-set-high-me

אֹיְבַי סְבִיבוֹתַי וְאֶזְבְּחָה בְאָהֳלוֹ
at-tabernacle-of-him and-I-will-sacrifice ones-around-me ones-being-enemies-of-me

זִבְחֵי תְרוּעָה אָשִׁירָה וַאֲזַמְּרָה לַיהוָה׃
to-Yahweh and-I-will-make-music I-will-sing shout-of-joy sacrifices-of

(7) שְׁמַע־ יְהוָה קוֹלִי אֶקְרָא וְחָנֵּנִי וַעֲנֵנִי׃
and-answer-me! and-be-merciful-to-me! I-call voice-of-me Yahweh hear! (7)

(8) לְךָ ׀ אָמַר לִבִּי בַּקְּשׁוּ פָנָי אֶת־ פָּנֶיךָ יְהוָה
Yahweh faces-of-you *** faces-of-me seek! heart-of-me he-says of-you (8)

אֲבַקֵּשׁ׃ (9) אַל־ תַּסְתֵּר פָּנֶיךָ ׀ מִמֶּנִּי אַל־ תַּט־ בְּאַף
in-anger you-turn-away not from-me faces-of-you you-hide not (9) I-will-seek

עַבְדֶּךָ עֶזְרָתִי הָיִיתָ אַל־ תִּטְּשֵׁנִי וְאַל־ תַּעַזְבֵנִי
you-forsake-me and-not you-reject-me not you-are help-of-me servant-of-you

אֱלֹהֵי יִשְׁעִי׃ (10) כִּי־ אָבִי וְאִמִּי עֲזָבוּנִי
they-forsake-me and-mother-of-me father-of-me though (10) salvation-of-me God-of

וַיהוָה יַאַסְפֵנִי׃ (11) הוֹרֵנִי יְהוָה דַּרְכֶּךָ וּנְחֵנִי
and-lead-me! way-of-you Yahweh teach-me! (11) he-will-receive-me yet-Yahweh

בְּאֹרַח מִישׁוֹר לְמַעַן שׁוֹרְרָי׃ (12) אַל־ תִּתְּנֵנִי
you-turn-over-me not (12) oppressors-of-me because-of straight in-path-of

בְּנֶפֶשׁ צָרָי כִּי קָמוּ־ בִי עֵדֵי־ שֶׁקֶר
falsehood witnesses-of against-me they-rise-up for foes-of-me to-desire-of

וִיפֵחַ חָמָס׃ (13) לוּלֵא הֶאֱמַנְתִּי לִרְאוֹת בְּטוּב־
on-goodness-of to-see I-am-confident still (13) violence and-breather-of

יְהוָה בְּאֶרֶץ חַיִּים׃ (14) קַוֵּה אֶל־ יְהוָה חֲזַק וְיַאֲמֵץ
and-strengthen! be-strong! Yahweh for wait! (14) live-ones in-land-of Yahweh

לִבֶּךָ וְקַוֵּה אֶל־ יְהוָה׃ (28:1) לְדָוִד אֵלֶיךָ יְהוָה ׀ אֶקְרָא
I-call Yahweh to-you of-David (28:1) Yahweh for and-wait! heart-of-you

צוּרִי אַל־ תֶּחֱרַשׁ מִמֶּנִּי פֶּן־ תֶּחֱשֶׁה מִמֶּנִּי
from-me you-remain-silent for-if to-me you-turn-deaf-ear not Rock-of-me

וְנִמְשַׁלְתִּי עִם־ יוֹרְדֵי בוֹר׃ (2) שְׁמַע קוֹל
sound-of hear! (2) pit ones-going-down-of with then-I-will-be-like

תַּחֲנוּנַי בְּשַׁוְּעִי אֵלֶיךָ בְּנָשְׂאִי יָדַי
hands-of-me as-to-lift-me to-you as-to-call-for-help-me cries-for-mercy-of-me

אֶל־ דְּבִיר קָדְשֶׁךָ׃ (3) אַל־ תִּמְשְׁכֵנִי עִם־ רְשָׁעִים
wicked-ones with you-drag-away-me not (3) Holiness-of-you Holy-Place-of toward

he will hide me in the shelter
of his tabernacle
and set me high upon a
rock.
6 Then my head will be exalted
above the enemies who
surround me;
at his tabernacle will I sacrifice
with shouts of joy;
I will sing and make music
to the LORD.

7 Hear my voice when I call, O
LORD;
be merciful to me and
answer me.
8 My heart says of you, "Seek
his[u] face!"
Your face, LORD, I will seek.
9 Do not hide your face from
me,
do not turn your servant
away in anger;
you have been my helper.
Do not reject me or forsake
me,
O God my Savior.
10 Though my father and mother
forsake me,
the LORD will receive me.
11 Teach me your way, O LORD;
lead me in a straight path
because of my oppressors.
12 Do not turn me over to the
desire of my foes,
for false witnesses rise up
against me,
breathing out violence.

13 I am still confident of this:
I will see the goodness of
the LORD
in the land of the living.
14 Wait for the LORD;
be strong and take heart
and wait for the LORD.

Psalm 28

Of David.

1 To you I call, O LORD my
Rock;
do not turn a deaf ear to me.
For if you remain silent,
I will be like those who
have gone down to the
pit.
2 Hear my cry for mercy
as I call to you for help,
as I lift up my hands
toward your Most Holy
Place.

3 Do not drag me away with the
wicked,

[u]8 Or *To you, O my heart, he has said, "Seek my*

וְעִם־ פֹּעֲלֵי אָוֶן דֹּבְרֵי שָׁלוֹם עִם־ רֵעֵיהֶם
even-with ones-doing-of evil ones-speaking-of cordiality with neighbors-of-them

וְרָעָה בִּלְבָבָם׃ (4) תֶּן־ לָהֶם כְּפָעֳלָם וּכְרֹעַ
but-malice in-heart-of-them (4) repay! to-them as-deed-of-them and-as-evil-of

מַעַלְלֵיהֶם כְּמַעֲשֵׂה יְדֵיהֶם תֵּן לָהֶם הָשֵׁב
works-of-them as-deed-of hands-of-them repay! to-them bring-back!

גְּמוּלָם לָהֶם׃ (5) כִּי לֹא יָבִינוּ אֶל־ פְּעֻלֹּת יְהוָה
desert-of-them upon-them (5) since not they-show-regard for works-of Yahweh

וְאֶל־ מַעֲשֵׂה יָדָיו יֶהֶרְסֵם וְלֹא יִבְנֵם׃
and-for deed-of hands-of-him he-will-tear-down-them and-never he-will-rebuild-them

(6) בָּרוּךְ יְהוָה כִּי־ שָׁמַע קוֹל תַּחֲנוּנָי׃
(6) being-praised Yahweh for he-heard sound-of cries-for-mercy-of-me

(7) יְהוָה׀ עֻזִּי וּמָגִנִּי בּוֹ בָטַח לִבִּי
(7) Yahweh strength-of-me and-shield-of-me in-him he-trusts heart-of-me

וְנֶעֱזָרְתִּי וַיַּעֲלֹז לִבִּי וּמִשִּׁירִי
and-I-am-helped and-he-leaps-for-joy heart-of-me and-in-song-of-me

אֲהוֹדֶנּוּ׃ (8) יְהוָה עֹז־ לָמוֹ וּמָעוֹז יְשׁוּעוֹת
I-will-thank-him (8) Yahweh strength of-them and-fortress-of salvations-of

מְשִׁיחוֹ הוּא׃ (9) הוֹשִׁיעָה׀ אֶת־ עַמֶּךָ וּבָרֵךְ אֶת־
anointed-of-him he (9) save! *** people-of-you and-bless! ***

נַחֲלָתֶךָ וּרְעֵם וְנַשְּׂאֵם עַד־ הָעוֹלָם׃
inheritance-of-you and-be-shepherd-of-them! and-carry-them! to the-forever

(29:1) מִזְמוֹר לְדָוִד הָבוּ לַיהוָה בְּנֵי אֵלִים הָבוּ
(29:1) psalm of-David ascribe! to-Yahweh sons-of mighty-ones ascribe!

לַיהוָה כָּבוֹד וָעֹז׃ (2) הָבוּ לַיהוָה כְּבוֹד שְׁמוֹ
to-Yahweh glory and-strength (2) ascribe! to-Yahweh glory-of name-of-him

הִשְׁתַּחֲווּ לַיהוָה בְּהַדְרַת־ קֹדֶשׁ׃ (3) קוֹל יְהוָה עַל־
worship! to-Yahweh in-splendor-of holiness (3) voice-of Yahweh over

הַמָּיִם אֵל־ הַכָּבוֹד הִרְעִים יְהוָה עַל־ מַיִם רַבִּים׃
the-waters God-of the-glory he-thunders Yahweh over waters mighty-ones

(4) קוֹל־ יְהוָה בַּכֹּחַ קוֹל יְהוָה בֶּהָדָר׃ (5) קוֹל
(4) voice-of Yahweh in-the-power voice-of Yahweh in-the-majesty (5) voice-of

יְהוָה שֹׁבֵר אֲרָזִים וַיְשַׁבֵּר יְהוָה אֶת־ אַרְזֵי הַלְּבָנוֹן׃
Yahweh breaking cedars and-he-breaks Yahweh *** cedars-of the-Lebanon

(6) וַיַּרְקִידֵם כְּמוֹ־ עֵגֶל לְבָנוֹן וְשִׂרְיֹן כְּמוֹ בֶן־ רְאֵמִים׃
(6) and-he-makes-skip like calf Lebanon and-Sirion like son-of wild-oxen

(7) קוֹל־ יְהוָה חֹצֵב לַהֲבוֹת אֵשׁ׃ (8) קוֹל יְהוָה
(7) voice-of Yahweh striking flashes-of lightning (8) voice-of Yahweh

with those who do evil,
who speak cordially with their neighbors
but harbor malice in their hearts.
4 Repay them for their deeds
and for their evil work;
repay them for what their hands have done
and bring back upon them what they deserve.
5 Since they show no regard for the works of the LORD
and what his hands have done,
he will tear them down
and never build them up again.

6 Praise be to the LORD,
for he has heard my cry for mercy.
7 The LORD is my strength and my shield;
my heart trusts in him, and I am helped.
My heart leaps for joy
and I will give thanks to him in song.

8 The LORD is the strength of his people,
a fortress of salvation for his anointed one.
9 Save your people and bless your inheritance;
be their shepherd and carry them forever.

Psalm 29

A psalm of David.

1 Ascribe to the LORD, O mighty ones,
ascribe to the LORD glory and strength.
2 Ascribe to the LORD the glory due his name;
worship the LORD in the splendor of his[v] holiness.

3 The voice of the LORD is over the waters;
the God of glory thunders,
the LORD thunders over the mighty waters.
4 The voice of the LORD is powerful;
the voice of the LORD is majestic.
5 The voice of the LORD breaks the cedars;
the LORD breaks in pieces the cedars of Lebanon.
6 He makes Lebanon skip like a calf,
Sirion[w] like a young wild ox.
7 The voice of the LORD strikes
with flashes of lightning.
8 The voice of the LORD shakes

[v] 2 Or *LORD with the splendor of*
[w] 6 That is, Mount Hermon

*6 Most mss have the accent *rebia mugrash* (ׂ֗).

יָחִיל מִדְבָּר יָחִיל יְהוָה מִדְבַּר קָדֵשׁ׃ קוֹל יְהוָה ׀
he-shakes desert he-shakes Yahweh Desert-of Kadesh (9) voice-of Yahweh

יְחוֹלֵל אַיָּלוֹת† וַיֶּחֱשֹׂף־ יְעָרוֹת וּבְהֵיכָלוֹ
he-makes-give-birth† †deers and-he-strips-bare forests and-temple-of-him

כֻּלּוֹ אֹמֵר כָּבוֹד׃ יְהוָה לַמַּבּוּל יָשָׁב וַיֵּשֶׁב
all-of-him crying glory (10) Yahweh over-the-flood he-sits and-he-is-enthroned

יְהוָה מֶלֶךְ לְעוֹלָם׃ יְהוָה עֹז לְעַמּוֹ יִתֵּן יְהוָה ׀
Yahweh King to-forever (11) Yahweh strength to-people-of-him he-gives Yahweh

יְבָרֵךְ אֶת־ עַמּוֹ בַשָּׁלוֹם׃ מִזְמוֹר שִׁיר־ חֲנֻכַּת
he-blesses *** people-of-him with-the-peace *(30:1) psalm song-of dedication-of

הַבַּיִת לְדָוִד׃ אֲרוֹמִמְךָ יְהוָה כִּי דִלִּיתָנִי וְלֹא־
the-temple of-David (2) I-will-exalt-you Yahweh for you-lifted-me and-not

שִׂמַּחְתָּ אֹיְבַי לִי׃ יְהוָה אֱלֹהָי
you-let-gloat ones-being-enemies-of-me over-me (3) Yahweh God-of-me

שִׁוַּעְתִּי אֵלֶיךָ וַתִּרְפָּאֵנִי׃ יְהוָה הֶעֱלִיתָ מִן־
I-cried-for-help to-you and-you-healed-me (4) Yahweh you-brought-up from

שְׁאוֹל נַפְשִׁי חִיִּיתַנִי מִיָּורְדִי־° בוֹר׃ זַמְּרוּ לַיהוָה
Sheol self-of-me you-spared-me from-to-go-down-me pit (5) sing! to-Yahweh

חֲסִידָיו וְהוֹדוּ לְזֵכֶר קָדְשׁוֹ׃ כִּי רֶגַע ׀
saints-of-him and-praise! to-name-of holiness-of-him (6) for moment

בְּאַפּוֹ חַיִּים בִּרְצוֹנוֹ בָּעֶרֶב יָלִין בֶּכִי
in-anger-of-him lifetimes in-favor-of-him in-the-night he-remains weeping

וְלַבֹּקֶר רִנָּה׃ וַאֲנִי אָמַרְתִּי בְשַׁלְוִי בַּל־
but-in-the-morning rejoicing (7) when-I I-said in-security-of-me not

אֶמּוֹט לְעוֹלָם׃ יְהוָה בִּרְצוֹנְךָ הֶעֱמַדְתָּה
I-will-be-shaken to-forever (8) Yahweh in-favor-of-you you-made-stand

לְהַרְרִי עֹז הִסְתַּרְתָּ פָנֶיךָ הָיִיתִי נִבְהָל׃ אֵלֶיךָ
to-mountain-of-me firm you-hid faces-of-you I-was being-dismayed (9) to-you

יְהוָה אֶקְרָא וְאֶל־ אֲדֹנָי אֶתְחַנָּן׃ מַה־ בֶּצַע בְּדָמִי
Yahweh I-called and-to Lord I-cried-for-mercy (10) what? gain in-destruction-of-me

בְּרִדְתִּי אֶל־ שָׁחַת הֲיוֹדְךָ עָפָר הֲיַגִּיד
in-to-go-down-me into pit will-he-praise-you? dust will-he-proclaim?

אֲמִתֶּךָ׃ שְׁמַע־ יְהוָה וְחָנֵּנִי יְהוָה הֱיֵה־
faithfulness-of-you (11) hear! Yahweh and-be-merciful-to-me! Yahweh be!

עֹזֵר לִי׃ הָפַכְתָּ מִסְפְּדִי לְמָחוֹל לִי
one-helping to-me (12) you-turned wailing-of-me into-dancing for-me

פִּתַּחְתָּ שַׂקִּי וַתְּאַזְּרֵנִי שִׂמְחָה׃ לְמַעַן ׀
you-removed sackcloth-of-me and-you-clothed-me joy (13) so-that

the desert;
the LORD shakes the Desert
of Kadesh.
9The voice of the LORD twists
the oaks[x]
and strips the forests bare.
And in his temple all cry,
"Glory!"

10The LORD sits[y] enthroned over
the flood;
the LORD is enthroned as
King forever.
11The LORD gives strength to his
people;
the LORD blesses his people
with peace.

Psalm 30

A psalm. A song. For the dedication of the temple.[z] Of David.

1I will exalt you, O LORD,
for you lifted me out of the
depths
and did not let my enemies
gloat over me.
2O LORD my God, I called to
you for help
and you healed me.
3O LORD, you brought me up
from the grave[a];
you spared me from going
down into the pit.

4Sing to the LORD, you saints of
his;
praise his holy name.
5For his anger lasts only a
moment,
but his favor lasts a lifetime;
weeping may remain for a
night,
but rejoicing comes in the
morning.

6When I felt secure, I said,
"I will never be shaken."
7O LORD, when you favored me,
you made my mountain[b]
stand firm;
but when you hid your face,
I was dismayed.

8To you, O LORD, I called;
to the Lord I cried for
mercy:
9"What gain is there in my
destruction,[c]
in my going down into the
pit?
Will the dust praise you?
Will it proclaim your
faithfulness?
10Hear, O LORD, and be merciful
to me;
O LORD, be my help."

11You turned my wailing into
dancing;
you removed my sackcloth
and clothed me with joy,

x9 Or *LORD makes the deer give birth*
y10 Or *sat* zTitle: Or *palace*
a3 Hebrew *Sheol* b7 Or *hill country*
c9 Or *there if I am silenced*

*Heading, *1* See the note on page 349.

†9 The NIV reads the second word as אֵילוֹת, and translates the phrase *he-twists oaks.*

°4 ק מירדי

יְזַמֶּרְךָ כָבוֹד וְלֹא יִדֹּם יְהוָה אֱלֹהַי לְעוֹלָם
to-forever God-of-me Yahweh he-may-be-silent and-not heart he-may-sing-to-you

אוֹדֶךָּ׃ *(31:1) לַמְנַצֵּחַ מִזְמוֹר לְדָוִד׃ (2) בְּךָ
in-you (2) of-David psalm for-the-one-directing *(31:1) I-will-thank-you

יְהוָה חָסִיתִי אַל־אֵבוֹשָׁה לְעוֹלָם בְּצִדְקָתְךָ
in-righteousness-of-you to-forever let-me-be-shamed not I-took-refuge Yahweh

פַלְּטֵנִי׃ (3) הַטֵּה אֵלַי ׀ אָזְנְךָ מְהֵרָה הַצִּילֵנִי הֱיֵה לִי ׀
for-me be! rescue-me! quickly ear-of-you to-me turn! (3) deliver-me!

לְצוּר־מָעוֹז לְבֵית מְצוּדוֹת לְהוֹשִׁיעֵנִי׃ (4) כִּי־סַלְעִי
rock-of-me since (4) to-save-me fortresses as-house-of refuge as-rock-of

וּמְצוּדָתִי אָתָּה וּלְמַעַן שִׁמְךָ תַּנְחֵנִי וּתְנַהֲלֵנִי׃
and-you-guide-me you-lead-me name-of-you and-for-sake-of you and-fortress-of-me

(5) תּוֹצִיאֵנִי מֵרֶשֶׁת זוּ טָמְנוּ לִי כִּי־אַתָּה מָעוּזִּי׃
refuge-of-me you for for-me they-set that from-trap you-free-me (5)

(6) בְּיָדְךָ אַפְקִיד רוּחִי פָּדִיתָה אוֹתִי יְהוָה אֵל אֱמֶת׃
truth God-of Yahweh me you-redeem spirit-of-me I-commit into-hand-of-you (6)

(7) שָׂנֵאתִי הַשֹּׁמְרִים הַבְלֵי־שָׁוְא וַאֲנִי אֶל־יְהוָה בָּטָחְתִּי׃
I-trust Yahweh in and-I worthlessness idols-of the-ones-clinging-to I-hate (7)

(8) אָגִילָה וְאֶשְׂמְחָה בְּחַסְדֶּךָ אֲשֶׁר רָאִיתָ אֶת־
*** you-saw for in-love-of-you and-I-will-rejoice I-will-be-glad (8)

עָנְיִי יָדַעְתָּ בְּצָרוֹת נַפְשִׁי׃ (9) וְלֹא הִסְגַּרְתַּנִי
you-put-me and-not (9) soul-of-me to-anguishes-of you-knew affliction-of-me

בְּיַד־אוֹיֵב הֶעֱמַדְתָּ בַמֶּרְחָב רַגְלָי׃
feet-of-me in-the-spacious-place you-set one-being-enemy into-hand-of

(10) חָנֵּנִי יְהוָה כִּי צַר־לִי עָשְׁשָׁה בְכַעַס
with-sorrow she-grows-weak to-me distress for Yahweh be-merciful-to-me! (10)

עֵינִי נַפְשִׁי וּבִטְנִי׃ (11) כִּי כָלוּ בְיָגוֹן
by-anguish they-are-consumed for (11) and-body-of-me soul-of-me eye-of-me

חַיַּי וּשְׁנוֹתַי בַּאֲנָחָה כָּשַׁל בַּעֲוֹנִי†
†because-of-guilt-of-me he-fails by-groaning and-years-of-me lives-of-me

כֹּחִי וַעֲצָמַי עָשֵׁשׁוּ׃ (12) מִכָּל־
because-of-all-of (12) they-grow-weak and-bones-of-me strength-of-me

צֹרְרַי הָיִיתִי חֶרְפָּה וְלִשְׁכֵנַי ׀ מְאֹד
utterly even-of-neighbors-of-me contempt I-am ones-being-enemies-of-me

וּפַחַד לִמְיֻדָּעָי רֹאַי בַּחוּץ נָדְדוּ
they-flee on-the-street ones-seeing-me to-ones-being-friends-of-me and-dread

מִמֶּנִּי׃ (13) נִשְׁכַּחְתִּי כְּמֵת מִלֵּב הָיִיתִי כִּכְלִי
like-pottery I-became from-heart as-dead I-am-forgotten (13) from-me

12that my heart may sing to you
and not be silent.
O LORD my God, I will give
you thanks forever.

Psalm 31

For the director of music. A psalm of David.

1In you, O LORD, I have taken
refuge;
let me never be put to
shame;
deliver me in your
righteousness.
2Turn your ear to me,
come quickly to my rescue;
be my rock of refuge,
a strong fortress to save me.
3Since you are my rock and my
fortress,
for the sake of your name
lead and guide me.
4Free me from the trap that is
set for me,
for you are my refuge.
5Into your hands I commit my
spirit;
redeem me, O LORD, the
God of truth.

6I hate those who cling to
worthless idols;
I trust in the LORD.
7I will be glad and rejoice in
your love,
for you saw my affliction
and knew the anguish of
my soul.
8You have not handed me over
to the enemy
but have set my feet in a
spacious place.

9Be merciful to me, O LORD, for
I am in distress;
my eyes grow weak with
sorrow,
my soul and my body with
grief.
10My life is consumed by
anguish
and my years by groaning;
my strength fails because of
my affliction,[d]
and my bones grow weak.
11Because of all my enemies,
I am the utter contempt of
my neighbors;
I am a dread to my friends—
those who see me on the
street flee from me.
12I am forgotten by them as
though I were dead;
I have become like broken
pottery.

[d]10 Or *guilt*

*Heading, *1* See the note on page 349.

†*11* The NIV reads this word as בְּעָנְיִי, *from-affliction-of-me.*

אֹבֵד׃ (14) כִּי שָׁמַעְתִּי דִּבַּת רַבִּים מָגוֹר מִסָּבִיב
on-every-side terror many slander-of I-hear for (14) being-broken

בְּהִוָּסְדָם יַחַד עָלַי לָקַחַת נַפְשִׁי זָמָמוּ׃
they-plot life-of-me to-take against-me together when-to-conspire-them

(15) וַאֲנִי עָלֶיךָ בָטַחְתִּי יְהוָה אָמַרְתִּי אֱלֹהַי אָתָּה׃ (16) בְּיָדְךָ
in-hand-of-you (16) you God-of-me I-say Yahweh I-trust in-you but-I (15)

עִתֹּתָי הַצִּילֵנִי מִיַּד־ אוֹיְבַי
ones-being-enemies-of-me from-hand-of deliver-me! times-of-me

וּמֵרֹדְפָי׃ (17) הָאִירָה פָנֶיךָ עַל־ עַבְדֶּךָ הוֹשִׁיעֵנִי
save-me! servant-of-you on faces-of-you shine! (17) and-from-ones-pursuing-me

בְחַסְדֶּךָ׃ (18) יְהוָה אַל־ אֵבוֹשָׁה כִּי קְרָאתִיךָ
I-cried-to-you for let-me-be-shamed not Yahweh (18) in-unfailing-love-of-you

יֵבֹשׁוּ רְשָׁעִים יִדְּמוּ לִשְׁאוֹל׃
in-Sheol let-them-lie-silent wicked-ones let-them-be-shamed

(19) תֵּאָלַמְנָה שִׂפְתֵי שָׁקֶר הַדֹּבְרוֹת עַל־ צַדִּיק
righteous against the-ones-speaking lying lips-of let-them-be-silenced (19)

עָתָק בְּגַאֲוָה וָבוּז׃ (20) מָה רַב־ טוּבְךָ אֲשֶׁר־
which goodness-of-you great how! (20) and-contempt with-pride arrogance

צָפַנְתָּ לִּירֵאֶיךָ פָּעַלְתָּ לַחֹסִים
on-the-ones-taking-refuge you-bestow for-ones-fearing-you you-stored-up

בָּךְ נֶגֶד בְּנֵי אָדָם׃ (21) תַּסְתִּירֵם בְּסֵתֶר פָּנֶיךָ
presences-of-you in-shelter-of you-hide-them (21) man sons-of in-sight-of in-you

מֵרֻכְסֵי אִישׁ תִּצְפְּנֵם בְּסֻכָּה מֵרִיב לְשֹׁנוֹת׃
tongues from-strife-of in-dwelling you-keep-safe-them man from-intrigues-of

(22) בָּרוּךְ יְהוָה כִּי הִפְלִיא חַסְדּוֹ לִי בְּעִיר
in-city-of to-me love-of-him he-showed-wonderful for Yahweh being-praised (22)

מָצוֹר׃ (23) וַאֲנִי אָמַרְתִּי בְחָפְזִי נִגְרַזְתִּי מִנֶּגֶד
from-before I-am-cut-off when-to-be-alarmed-me I-said and-I (23) siege

עֵינֶיךָ אָכֵן שָׁמַעְתָּ קוֹל תַּחֲנוּנַי בְּשַׁוְּעִי
when-to-call-for-help-me cries-for-mercy-of-me sound-of you-heard yet eyes-of-you

אֵלֶיךָ׃ (24) אֶהֱבוּ אֶת־ יְהוָה כָּל־ חֲסִידָיו אֱמוּנִים
ones-being-faithful saints-of-him all-of Yahweh *** love! (24) to-you

נֹצֵר יְהוָה וּמְשַׁלֵּם עַל־ יֶתֶר עֹשֵׂה גַאֲוָה׃
pride one-acting-of full in but-one-paying-back Yahweh one-preserving

(25) חִזְקוּ וְיַאֲמֵץ לְבַבְכֶם כָּל־ הַמְיַחֲלִים לַיהוָה׃
in-Yahweh the-ones-hoping all-of heart-of-you and-strengthen! be-strong! (25)

(32:1) לְדָוִד מַשְׂכִּיל אַשְׁרֵי נְשׂוּי־ פֶּשַׁע
transgression one-being-forgiven-of blessednesses-of maskil of-David (32:1)

13 For I hear the slander of
many;
there is terror on every side;
they conspire against me
and plot to take my life.

14 But I trust in you, O LORD;
I say, "You are my God."
15 My times are in your hands;
deliver me from my enemies
and from those who pursue
me.
16 Let your face shine on your
servant;
save me in your unfailing
love.
17 Let me not be put to shame, O
LORD,
for I have cried out to you;
but let the wicked be put to
shame
and lie silent in the grave.[e]
18 Let their lying lips be silenced,
for with pride and contempt
they speak arrogantly
against the righteous.

19 How great is your goodness,
which you have stored up
for those who fear you,
which you bestow in the sight
of men
on those who take refuge in
you.
20 In the shelter of your presence
you hide them
from the intrigues of men;
in your dwelling you keep
them safe
from the strife of tongues.

21 Praise be to the LORD,
for he showed his wonderful
love to me
when I was in a besieged
city.
22 In my alarm I said,
"I am cut off from your
sight!"
Yet you heard my cry for
mercy
when I called to you for
help.

23 Love the LORD, all his saints!
The LORD preserves the
faithful,
but the proud he pays back
in full.
24 Be strong and take heart,
all you who hope in the
LORD.

Psalm 32

Of David. A *maskil*.[f]

1 Blessed is he
whose transgressions are
forgiven,

[e]17 Hebrew *Sheol*
[f]Title: Probably a literary or musical term

*See the note on page 349.

כְּסוּי חֲטָאָה׃ אַשְׁרֵי אָדָם לֹא יַחְשֹׁב יְהוָה
one-being-covered-of sin (2) blessednesses-of man not he-counts Yahweh

לוֹ עָוֺן וְאֵין בְּרוּחוֹ רְמִיָּה׃ כִּי־
against-him sin and-there-is-not in-spirit-of-him deceit (3) when

הֶחֱרַשְׁתִּי בָּלוּ עֲצָמָי בְּשַׁאֲגָתִי כָּל־
I-kept-silent they-wasted-away bones-of-me through-groaning-of-me all-of

הַיּוֹם׃ כִּי ׀ יוֹמָם וָלַיְלָה תִּכְבַּד עָלַי יָדֶךָ
the-day (4) for by-day and-night she-was-heavy upon-me hand-of-you

נֶהְפַּךְ לְשַׁדִּי בְּחַרְבֹנֵי קַיִץ סֶלָה׃ חַטָּאתִי
he-was-sapped strength-of-me in-heats-of summer selah (5) sin-of-me

אוֹדִיעֲךָ וַעֲוֺנִי לֹא־כִסִּיתִי אָמַרְתִּי אוֹדֶה
I-acknowledged-to-you and-iniquity-of-me not I-covered-up I-said I-will-confess

עֲלֵי פְשָׁעַי לַיהוָה וְאַתָּה נָשָׂאתָ עֲוֺן חַטָּאתִי
to transgressions-of-me to-Yahweh and-you you-forgave guilt-of sin-of-me

סֶלָה׃ עַל־זֹאת יִתְפַּלֵּל כָּל־חָסִיד ׀ אֵלֶיךָ לְעֵת מְצֹא
selah (6) for this let-him-pray every-of godly-one to-you at-time-of to-find

רַק לְשֵׁטֶף מַיִם רַבִּים אֵלָיו לֹא יַגִּיעוּ׃ אַתָּה ׀
surely at-rising-of waters mighty-ones to-him not they-will-reach (7) you

סֵתֶר לִי מִצַּר תִּצְּרֵנִי רָנֵּי פַלֵּט
hiding-place for-me from-trouble you-will-protect-me songs-of to-deliver

תְּסוֹבְבֵנִי סֶלָה׃ אַשְׂכִּילְךָ ׀ וְאוֹרְךָ
you-will-surround-me selah (8) I-will-instruct-you and-I-will-teach-you

בְּדֶרֶךְ־זוּ תֵלֵךְ אִיעֲצָה עָלֶיךָ עֵינִי׃ אַל־תִּהְיוּ ׀
in-way that you-should-go I-will-counsel over-you eye-of-me (9) not you-be

כְּסוּס כְּפֶרֶד אֵין הָבִין בְּמֶתֶג־וָרֶסֶן עֶדְיוֹ
like-horse like-mule not to-understand by-bit and-bridle harness-of-him

לִבְלוֹם בַּל קְרֹב אֵלֶיךָ׃ רַבִּים מַכְאוֹבִים לָרָשָׁע
to-control not to-come to-you (10) many woes of-the-wicked

וְהַבּוֹטֵחַ בַּיהוָה חֶסֶד יְסוֹבְבֶנּוּ׃ שִׂמְחוּ
but-the-one-trusting in-Yahweh unfailing-love he-surrounds-him (11) rejoice!

בַּיהוָה וְגִילוּ צַדִּיקִים וְהַרְנִינוּ כָּל־יִשְׁרֵי־לֵב׃
in-Yahweh and-be-glad! righteous-ones and-sing! all-of ones-upright-of heart

רַנְּנוּ צַדִּיקִים בַּיהוָה לַיְשָׁרִים נָאוָה
(33:1) sing-joyfully! righteous-ones to-Yahweh for-the-upright-ones fitting

תְהִלָּה׃ הוֹדוּ לַיהוָה בְּכִנּוֹר בְּנֵבֶל עָשׂוֹר זַמְּרוּ־לוֹ׃
praise (2) praise! to-Yahweh with-harp on-lyre-of ten make-music! to-him

שִׁירוּ־לוֹ שִׁיר חָדָשׁ הֵיטִיבוּ נַגֵּן בִּתְרוּעָה׃
(3) sing! to-him song new be-skillful! to-play with-shout-of-joy

---

whose sins are covered.
2 Blessed is the man
whose sin the LORD does not count against him
and in whose spirit is no deceit.

3 When I kept silent,
my bones wasted away
through my groaning all day long.
4 For day and night
your hand was heavy upon me;
my strength was sapped
as in the heat of summer. *Selah*
5 Then I acknowledged my sin to you
and did not cover up my iniquity.
I said, "I will confess
my transgressions to the LORD"—
and you forgave
the guilt of my sin. *Selah*

6 Therefore let everyone who is godly pray to you
while you may be found;
surely when the mighty waters rise,
they will not reach him.
7 You are my hiding place;
you will protect me from trouble
and surround me with songs of deliverance. *Selah*

8 I will instruct you and teach you in the way you should go;
I will counsel you and watch over you.
9 Do not be like the horse or the mule,
which have no understanding
but must be controlled by bit and bridle
or they will not come to you.
10 Many are the woes of the wicked,
but the LORD's unfailing love
surrounds the man who trusts in him.

11 Rejoice in the LORD and be glad, you righteous;
sing, all you who are upright in heart!

Psalm 33

1 Sing joyfully to the LORD, you righteous;
it is fitting for the upright to praise him.
2 Praise the LORD with the harp;
make music to him on the ten-stringed lyre.
3 Sing to him a new song;
play skillfully, and shout for joy.

(4) כִּֽי־יָשָׁר דְּבַר־יְהוָה וְכָל־מַעֲשֵׂהוּ בֶּאֱמוּנָה׃ (5) אֹהֵב

(4) for right word-of Yahweh and-all-of deed-of-him in-faithfulness (5) one-loving

צְדָקָה וּמִשְׁפָּט חֶסֶד יְהוָה מָלְאָה הָאָֽרֶץ׃

righteousness and-justice unfailing-love-of Yahweh she-is-full the-earth

(6) בִּדְבַר יְהוָה שָׁמַיִם נַעֲשׂוּ וּבְרוּחַ פִּיו

(6) by-word-of Yahweh heavens they-were-made and-by-breath-of mouth-of-him

כָּל־צְבָאָם׃ (7) כֹּנֵס *כַּנֵּד מֵי הַיָּם

all-of host-of-them (7) one-gathering *as-the-heap waters-of the-sea

נֹתֵן בְּאֹצָרוֹת תְּהוֹמוֹת׃ (8) יִֽירְאוּ מֵיְהוָה כָּל־

one-putting into-storehouses deeps (8) let-them-fear of-Yahweh all-of

הָאָרֶץ מִמֶּנּוּ יָגוּרוּ כָּל־יֹשְׁבֵי תֵבֵל׃ (9) כִּי הוּא

the-earth of-him let-them-revere all-of ones-living-of world (9) for he

אָמַר וַיֶּהִי הֽוּא־צִוָּה וַֽיַּעֲמֹד׃ (10) יְהוָה

he-spoke and-he-came-to-be he he-commanded and-he-stood-firm (10) Yahweh

הֵפִיר עֲצַת־גּוֹיִם הֵנִיא מַחְשְׁבוֹת עַמִּים׃ (11) עֲצַת יְהוָה

he-foils plan-of nations he-thwarts purposes-of peoples (11) plan-of Yahweh

לְעוֹלָם תַּעֲמֹד מַחְשְׁבוֹת לִבּוֹ לְדֹר

to-forever she-stands-firm purposes-of heart-of-him to-generation

וָדֹר׃ (12) אַשְׁרֵי הַגּוֹי אֲשֶׁר־יְהוָה אֱלֹהָיו

and-generation (12) blessednesses-of the-nation who Yahweh God-of-him

הָעָם ׀ בָּחַר לְנַחֲלָה לוֹ׃ (13) מִשָּׁמַיִם הִבִּיט

the-people he-chose for-inheritance of-him (13) from-heavens he-looks-down

יְהוָה רָאָה אֶת־כָּל־בְּנֵי הָאָדָם׃ (14) מִמְּכוֹן־שִׁבְתּוֹ

Yahweh he-sees *** all-of sons-of the-mankind (14) from-place-of to-dwell-him

הִשְׁגִּיחַ אֶל כָּל־יֹשְׁבֵי הָאָרֶץ׃ (15) הַיֹּצֵר יַחַד

he-watches on all-of ones-living-of the-earth (15) the-one-forming together

לִבָּם הַמֵּבִין אֶל־כָּל־מַעֲשֵׂיהֶם׃ (16) אֵין־

heart-of-them the-one-considering to all-of deeds-of-them (16) there-is-no

הַמֶּלֶךְ נוֹשָׁע בְּרָב־חָיִל גִּבּוֹר לֹא־יִנָּצֵל בְּרָב־

the-king being-saved by-size-of army warrior not he-escapes by-greatness-of

כֹּחַ׃ (17) שֶׁקֶר הַסּוּס לִתְשׁוּעָה וּבְרֹב

strength (17) vain-hope the-horse for-deliverance and-despite-greatness-of

חֵילוֹ לֹא יְמַלֵּט׃ (18) הִנֵּה עֵין יְהוָה אֶל־יְרֵאָיו

strength-of-him not he-can-save (18) see! eye-of Yahweh on ones-fearing-him

לַמְיַחֲלִים לְחַסְדּוֹ׃ (19) לְהַצִּיל מִמָּוֶת נַפְשָׁם

on-ones-hoping in-unfailing-love-of-him (19) to-deliver from-death self-of-them

וּלְחַיּוֹתָם בָּרָעָב׃ (20) נַפְשֵׁנוּ חִכְּתָה לַיהוָה

and-to-keep-alive-them in-the-famine (20) self-of-us she-waits for-Yahweh

4For the word of the LORD is
right and true;
he is faithful in all he does.
5The LORD loves righteousness
and justice;
the earth is full of his
unfailing love.

6By the word of the LORD were
the heavens made,
their starry host by the
breath of his mouth.
7He gathers the waters of the
sea into jars[g];
he puts the deep into
storehouses.
8Let all the earth fear the LORD;
let all the people of the
world revere him.
9For he spoke, and it came to
be;
he commanded, and it stood
firm.
10The LORD foils the plans of the
nations;
he thwarts the purposes of
the peoples.
11But the plans of the LORD
stand firm forever,
the purposes of his heart
through all generations.

12Blessed is the nation whose
God is the LORD,
the people he chose for his
inheritance.
13From heaven the LORD looks
down
and sees all mankind;
14from his dwelling place he
watches
all who live on earth—
15he who forms the hearts of all,
who considers everything
they do.
16No king is saved by the size of
his army;
no warrior escapes by his
great strength.
17A horse is a vain hope for
deliverance;
despite all its great strength
it cannot save.
18But the eyes of the LORD are
on those who fear him,
on those whose hope is in
his unfailing love,
19to deliver from death
and keep them alive in
famine.

20We wait in hope for the LORD;

g7 Or *sea as into a heap*

*7 The NIV reads כְּנֹ(א)ד, *into-jar.*

עֶזְרֵנוּ וּמָגִנֵּנוּ הוּא׃ כִּי־ בוֹ יִשְׂמַח לִבֵּנוּ כִּי
for heart-of-us he-rejoices in-him for (21) he and-shield-of-us help-of-us

בְשֵׁם קָדְשׁוֹ בָטָחְנוּ׃ יְהִי־ חַסְדְּךָ
unfailing-love-of-you may-he-rest (22) we-trust holiness-of-him in-name-of

יְהוָה עָלֵינוּ כַּאֲשֶׁר יִחַלְנוּ לָךְ׃ לְדָוִד בְּשַׁנּוֹתוֹ
when-to-feign-him of-David *(34:1) in-you we-hope even-as upon-us Yahweh

אֶת־ טַעְמוֹ לִפְנֵי אֲבִימֶלֶךְ וַיְגָרְשֵׁהוּ וַיֵּלַךְ׃
and-he-left and-he-drove-away-him Abimelech before insanity-of-him ***

אֲבָרֲכָה אֶת־ יְהוָה בְּכָל־ עֵת תָּמִיד תְּהִלָּתוֹ בְּפִי׃
on-lip-of-me praise-of-him always time at-all-of Yahweh *** I-will-extol (2)

בַּיהוָה תִּתְהַלֵּל נַפְשִׁי יִשְׁמְעוּ עֲנָוִים
afflicted-ones let-them-hear soul-of-me she-will-boast in-Yahweh (3)

וְיִשְׂמָחוּ׃ גַּדְּלוּ לַיהוָה אִתִּי וּנְרוֹמְמָה
and-let-us-exalt with-me to-Yahweh glorify! (4) and-let-them-rejoice

שְׁמוֹ יַחְדָּו׃ דָּרַשְׁתִּי אֶת־ יְהוָה וְעָנָנִי
and-he-answered-me Yahweh *** I-sought (5) together name-of-him

וּמִכָּל־ מְגוּרוֹתַי הִצִּילָנִי׃ הִבִּיטוּ אֵלָיו
to-him they-look (6) he-delivered-me fears-of-me and-from-all-of

וְנָהָרוּ וּפְנֵיהֶם אַל־ יֶחְפָּרוּ׃ זֶה
this (7) they-are-covered-with-shame never and-faces-of-them and-they-are-radiant

עָנִי קָרָא וַיהוָה שָׁמֵעַ וּמִכָּל־ צָרוֹתָיו
troubles-of-him and-from-all-of he-heard and-Yahweh he-called poor-man

הוֹשִׁיעוֹ׃ חֹנֶה מַלְאַךְ־ יְהוָה סָבִיב לִירֵאָיו
about-ones-fearing-him around Yahweh angel-of one-encamping (8) he-saved-him

וַיְחַלְּצֵם׃ טַעֲמוּ וּרְאוּ כִּי־ טוֹב יְהוָה אַשְׁרֵי
blessednesses-of Yahweh good that and-see! taste! (9) and-he-delivers-them

הַגֶּבֶר יֶחֱסֶה־ בּוֹ׃ יְראוּ אֶת־ יְהוָה קְדֹשָׁיו כִּי־
for saints-of-him Yahweh *** fear! (10) in-him he-takes-refuge the-man

אֵין מַחְסוֹר לִירֵאָיו׃ כְּפִירִים רָשׁוּ
they-may-grow-weak lions (11) for-ones-fearing-him lack there-is-no

וְרָעֵבוּ וְדֹרְשֵׁי יְהוָה לֹא־ יַחְסְרוּ כָל־
any-of they-lack not Yahweh but-ones-seeking-of and-they-may-grow-hungry

טוֹב׃ לְכוּ־ בָנִים שִׁמְעוּ־ לִי יִרְאַת יְהוָה אֲלַמֶּדְכֶם׃
I-will-teach-you Yahweh fear-of to-me listen! children come! (12) good

מִי־ הָאִישׁ הֶחָפֵץ חַיִּים אֹהֵב יָמִים לִרְאוֹת טוֹב׃
good to-see days one-desiring lives the-one-loving the-man who? (13)

נְצֹר לְשׁוֹנְךָ מֵרָע וּשְׂפָתֶיךָ מִדַּבֵּר מִרְמָה׃
lie from-to-speak and-lips-of-you from-evil tongue-of-you keep! (14)

he is our help and our
shield.
21 In him our hearts rejoice,
for we trust in his holy
name.
22 May your unfailing love rest
upon us, O LORD,
even as we put our hope in
you.

Psalm 34[h]

Of David. When he feigned insanity before Abimelech, who drove him away, and he left.

1 I will extol the LORD at all
times;
his praise will always be on
my lips.
2 My soul will boast in the
LORD;
let the afflicted hear and
rejoice.
3 Glorify the LORD with me;
let us exalt his name
together.

4 I sought the LORD, and he
answered me;
he delivered me from all my
fears.
5 Those who look to him are
radiant;
their faces are never covered
with shame.
6 This poor man called, and the
LORD heard him;
he saved him out of all his
troubles.
7 The angel of the LORD encamps
around those who fear
him,
and he delivers them.

8 Taste and see that the LORD is
good;
blessed is the man who
takes refuge in him.
9 Fear the LORD, you his saints,
for those who fear him lack
nothing.
10 The lions may grow weak and
hungry,
but those who seek the LORD
lack no good thing.

11 Come, my children, listen to
me;
I will teach you the fear of
the LORD.
12 Whoever of you loves life
and desires to see many
good days,
13 keep your tongue from evil
and your lips from speaking
lies.

[h] This psalm is an acrostic poem, the verses of which begin with the successive letters of the Hebrew alphabet.

*Heading, *1* See the note on page 349.

סוּר מֵרָע וַעֲשֵׂה־טוֹב בַּקֵּשׁ שָׁלוֹם וְרָדְפֵהוּ׃ עֵינֵי
eyes-of (16) and-pursue-him! peace seek! good and-do! from-evil turn! (15)

יְהוָה אֶל־צַדִּיקִים וְאָזְנָיו אֶל־שַׁוְעָתָם׃ פְּנֵי יְהוָה
Yahweh faces-of (17) cry-of-them to and-ears-of-him righteous-ones on Yahweh

בְּעֹשֵׂי רָע לְהַכְרִית מֵאֶרֶץ זִכְרָם׃ צָעֲקוּ
they-cry (18) memory-of-them from-earth to-cut-off evil against-ones-doing-of

וַיהוָה שָׁמֵעַ וּמִכָּל־צָרוֹתָם הִצִּילָם׃
he-delivers-them troubles-of-them and-from-all-of he-hears and-Yahweh

קָרוֹב יְהוָה לְנִשְׁבְּרֵי־לֵב וְאֶת־דַּכְּאֵי־
ones-crushed-of and heart to-ones-being-broken-of Yahweh close (19)

רוּחַ יוֹשִׁיעַ׃ רַבּוֹת רָעוֹת צַדִּיק וּמִכֻּלָּם
but-from-all-of-them righteous troubles-of many (20) he-saves spirit

יַצִּילֶנּוּ יְהוָה׃ שֹׁמֵר כָּל־עַצְמוֹתָיו אַחַת מֵהֵנָּה
of-them one bones-of-him all-of one-protecting (21) Yahweh he-delivers-him

לֹא נִשְׁבָּרָה׃ תְּמוֹתֵת רָשָׁע רָעָה וְשֹׂנְאֵי
and-ones-being-foes-of evil wicked she-will-slay (22) she-will-be-broken not

צַדִּיק יֶאְשָׁמוּ׃ פּוֹדֶה יְהוָה נֶפֶשׁ
life-of Yahweh one-redeeming (23) they-will-be-condemned righteous

עֲבָדָיו וְלֹא יֶאְשְׁמוּ כָּל־הַחֹסִים
the-ones-taking-refuge any-of they-will-be-condemned and-not servants-of-him

בּוֹ׃ לְדָוִד | רִיבָה יְהוָה אֶת־יְרִיבַי לְחַם אֶת־
against fight! contenders-of-me with Yahweh contend! of-David (35:1) in-him

לֹחֲמָי׃ הַחֲזֵק מָגֵן וְצִנָּה וְקוּמָה
and-arise! and-buckler shield take-up! (2) ones-fighting-against-me

בְּעֶזְרָתִי׃ וְהָרֵק חֲנִית וּסְגֹר לִקְרַאת רֹדְפָי
ones-pursuing-me to-encounter †and-block! spear and-brandish! (3) to-aid-of-me

אֱמֹר לְנַפְשִׁי יְשֻׁעָתֵךְ אָנִי׃ יֵבֹשׁוּ
may-they-be-disgraced (4) I salvation-of-you to-soul-of-me say!

וְיִכָּלְמוּ מְבַקְשֵׁי נַפְשִׁי יִסֹּגוּ
may-they-be-turned life-of-me ones-seeking-of and-may-they-be-put-to-shame

אָחוֹר וְיַחְפְּרוּ חֹשְׁבֵי רָעָתִי׃ יִהְיוּ
may-they-be (5) ruin-of-me ones-plotting-of and-may-they-be-dismayed back

כְּמֹץ לִפְנֵי־רוּחַ וּמַלְאַךְ יְהוָה דּוֹחֶה׃ יְהִי־
may-he-be (6) driving-away Yahweh with-angel-of wind before like-chaff

דַרְכָּם חֹשֶׁךְ וַחֲלַקְלַקּוֹת וּמַלְאַךְ יְהוָה רֹדְפָם׃
pursuing-them Yahweh with-angel-of and-slippery-ones dark way-of-them

כִּי־חִנָּם טָמְנוּ־לִי שַׁחַת רִשְׁתָּם חִנָּם
without-cause net-of-them pit for-me they-hid without-cause since (7)

14Turn from evil and do good;
seek peace and pursue it.
15The eyes of the LORD are on
the righteous
and his ears are attentive to
their cry;
16the face of the LORD is against
those who do evil,
to cut off the memory of
them from the earth.
17The righteous cry out, and the
LORD hears them;
he delivers them from all
their troubles.
18The LORD is close to the
brokenhearted
and saves those who are
crushed in spirit.
19A righteous man may have
many troubles,
but the LORD delivers him
from them all;
20he protects all his bones,
not one of them will be
broken.
21Evil will slay the wicked;
the foes of the righteous will
be condemned.
22The LORD redeems his
servants;
no one who takes refuge in
him will be condemned.

Psalm 35

Of David.

1Contend, O LORD, with those
who contend with me;
fight against those who
fight against me.
2Take up shield and buckler;
arise and come to my aid.
3Brandish spear and javelin[t]
against those who pursue
me.
Say to my soul,
"I am your salvation."
4May those who seek my life
be disgraced and put to
shame;
may those who plot my ruin
be turned back in dismay.
5May they be like chaff before
the wind,
with the angel of the LORD
driving them away;
6may their path be dark and
slippery,
with the angel of the LORD
pursuing them.
7Since they hid their net for me
without cause

t3 Or *and block the way*

*See the note on page 349.

†3 The NIV repoints this word as סְגֹר or וְסֶגֶר, *and-javelin*.

חפרו לנפשי: (8) תבואהו שואה לא־ידע
they-dug for-self-of-me (8) may-she-overtake-him ruin not he-knows

ורשתו אשר־טמן תלכדו בשואה יפל־בה:
and-net-of-him that he-hid may-she-entangle-him to-ruin may-he-fall into-her

(9) ונפשי תגיל ביהוה תשיש
(9) then-soul-of-me she-will-rejoice in-Yahweh she-will-delight

בישועתו: (10) כל עצמותי | תאמרנה יהוה מי
in-salvation-of-him (10) all-of bones-of-me they-will-exclaim Yahweh who?

כמוך מציל עני מחזק ממנו ועני ואביון
like-you one-rescuing poor from-one-strong more-than-him even-poor and-needy

מגזלו: (11) יקומון עדי חמס אשר
from-one-robbing-him (11) they-come-forward witnesses-of ruthlessness which

לא־ידעתי ישאלוני: (12) ישלמוני רעה תחת טובה שכול
not I-know they-question-me (12) they-repay-me evil for good forlornness

לנפשי: (13) ואני | בחלותם לבושי שק
of-soul-of-me (13) yet-I when-to-be-ill-them clothing-of-me sackcloth

עניתי בצום נפשי ותפלתי על־חיקי
I-humbled with-the-fasting self-of-me when-prayer-of-me to breast-of-me

תשוב: (14) כרע־כאח לי התהלכתי כאבל־
she-returned (14) as-friend as-brother of-me I-went-about like-weeping-of

אם קדר שחותי: (15) ובצלעי שמחו
mother grieving I-bowed (15) but-at-stumbling-of-me they-were-gleeful

ונאספו נאספו עלי נכים ולא ידעתי
and-they-gathered they-gathered against-me attackers when-not I-was-aware

קרעו ולא־דמו: (16) בחנפי לעגי מעוג
they-slandered and-not they-ceased (16) like-ungodly-ones-of mockers-of circle

חרק עלי שנימו: (17) אדני כמה תראה
to-gnash against-me teeth-of-them (17) Lord until-the-when? will-you-look-on

השיבה נפשי משאיהם מכפירים יחידתי:
rescue! life-of-me from-ravages-of-them from-lions precious-one-of-me

(18) אודך בקהל רב בעם עצום
(18) I-will-give-thanks-to-you in-assembly great among-people thronging

אהללך: (19) אל־ישמחו־לי איבי
I-will-praise-you (19) not let-them-gloat over-me ones-being-enemies-of-me

שקר שנאי חנם יקרצו־עין: (20) כי לא
without-cause ones-hating-me without-reason let-them-wink eye (20) for not

שלום ידברו ועל רגעי־ארץ דברי מרמות
peaceably they-speak but-against quiet-ones-of land accusations-of false-ones

and without cause dug a pit for me,
8may ruin overtake them by surprise—
may the net they hid entangle them,
may they fall into the pit, to their ruin.
9Then my soul will rejoice in the LORD
and delight in his salvation.
10My whole being will exclaim,
"Who is like you, O LORD?
You rescue the poor from those too strong for them,
the poor and needy from those who rob them."

11Ruthless witnesses come forward;
they question me on things I know nothing about.
12They repay me evil for good
and leave my soul forlorn.
13Yet when they were ill, I put on sackcloth
and humbled myself with fasting.
When my prayers returned to me unanswered,
14I went about mourning
as though for my friend or brother.
I bowed my head in grief
as though weeping for my mother.
15But when I stumbled, they gathered in glee;
attackers gathered against me when I was unaware.
They slandered me without ceasing.
16Like the ungodly they maliciously mocked[j];
they gnashed their teeth at me.

17O LORD, how long will you look on?
Rescue my life from their ravages,
my precious life from these lions.
18I will give you thanks in the great assembly;
among throngs of people I will praise you.
19Let not those gloat over me who are my enemies without cause;
let not those who hate me without reason maliciously wink the eye.
20They do not speak peaceably,
but devise false accusations against those who live quietly in the land.

j16 Septuagint; Hebrew may mean *ungodly circle of mockers.*

יַחֲשֹׁבוּן׃ וַיַּרְחִיבוּ עָלַי פִּיהֶם אָמְרוּ הֶאָח ׀ הֶאָח

aha! aha! they-say mouth-of-them at-me and-they-open-wide (21) they-devise

רָאֲתָה עֵינֵינוּ׃ רָאִיתָה יְהוָה אַל־ תֶּחֱרַשׁ אֲדֹנָי אַל־ תִּרְחַק

you-be-far not Lord you-be-silent not Yahweh you-saw (22) eyes-of-us she-saw

מִמֶּנִּי׃ הָעִירָה וְהָקִיצָה לְמִשְׁפָּטִי אֱלֹהַי וַאדֹנָי

and-Lord God-of-me to-defense-of-me and-rise! awake! (23) from-me

לְרִיבִי׃ שָׁפְטֵנִי כְצִדְקְךָ יְהוָה אֱלֹהָי

God-of-me Yahweh in-righteousness-of-you vindicate-me! (24) to-contention-of-me

וְאַל־ יִשְׂמְחוּ־ לִי׃ אַל־ יֹאמְרוּ בְלִבָּם הֶאָח

aha! in-heart-of-them let-them-think not (25) over-me let-them-gloat and-not

נַפְשֵׁנוּ אַל־ יֹאמְרוּ בִּלַּעֲנוּהוּ׃ יֵבֹשׁוּ

may-they-be-put-to-shame (26) we-swallowed-him let-them-say not want-of-us

וְיַחְפְּרוּ ׀ יַחְדָּו שְׂמֵחֵי רָעָתִי יִלְבְּשׁוּ־

may-they-be-clothed distress-of-me gloaters-of together and-may-they-be-confused

בֹשֶׁת וּכְלִמָּה הַמַּגְדִּילִים עָלָי׃ יָרֹנּוּ

may-they-shout (27) over-me the-ones-exalting-themselves and-disgrace shame

וְיִשְׂמְחוּ חֲפֵצֵי צִדְקִי וְיֹאמְרוּ תָמִיד

always and-may-they-say vindication-of-me delighters-of and-may-they-be-glad

יִגְדַּל יְהוָה הֶחָפֵץ שְׁלוֹם עַבְדּוֹ׃

servant-of-him well-being-of the-one-delighting Yahweh may-he-be-exalted

וּלְשׁוֹנִי תֶּהְגֶּה צִדְקֶךָ כָּל־ הַיּוֹם

the-day all-of righteousness-of-you she-will-speak and-tongue-of-me (28)

תְּהִלָּתֶךָ׃ לַמְנַצֵּחַ ׀ לְעֶבֶד־ יְהוָה לְדָוִד׃

of-David Yahweh of-servant-of for-the-one-directing *(36:1) praise-of-you

נְאֻם־ פֶּשַׁע לָרָשָׁע בְּקֶרֶב לִבִּי אֵין־

there-is-no heart-of-me in-midst-of of-the-wicked sinfulness oracle-of (2)

פַּחַד אֱלֹהִים לְנֶגֶד עֵינָיו׃ כִּי־ הֶחֱלִיק אֵלָיו בְּעֵינָיו

in-eyes-of-him to-him he-flatters for (3) eyes-of-him at-before God fear-of

לִמְצֹא עֲוֺנוֹ לִשְׂנֹא׃ דִּבְרֵי־ פִיו אָוֶן וּמִרְמָה

and-deceitful wicked mouth-of-him words-of (4) to-hate sin-of-him to-detect

חָדַל לְהַשְׂכִּיל לְהֵיטִיב׃ אָוֶן ׀ יַחְשֹׁב עַל־ מִשְׁכָּבוֹ

bed-of-him on he-plots evil (5) to-do-good to-be-wise he-ceased

יִתְיַצֵּב עַל־ דֶּרֶךְ לֹא־ טוֹב רָע לֹא יִמְאָס׃ יְהוָה

Yahweh (6) he-rejects not wrong good not course to he-commits-himself

בְּהַשָּׁמַיִם חַסְדֶּךָ אֱמוּנָתְךָ עַד־ שְׁחָקִים׃

skies to faithfulness-of-you love-of-you to-the-heavens

צִדְקָתְךָ ׀ כְּהַרְרֵי־ אֵל מִשְׁפָּטֶךָ תְּהוֹם רַבָּה

great deep justice-of-you might like-mountains-of righteousness-of-you (7)

21 They gape at me and say,
"Aha! Aha!
With our own eyes we have seen it."
22 O LORD, you have seen this; be not silent.
Do not be far from me, O Lord.
23 Awake, and rise to my defense!
Contend for me, my God and Lord.
24 Vindicate me in your righteousness, O LORD my God;
do not let them gloat over me.
25 Do not let them think, "Aha, just what we wanted!"
or say, "We have swallowed him up."

26 May all who gloat over my distress
be put to shame and confusion;
may all who exalt themselves over me
be clothed with shame and disgrace.
27 May those who delight in my vindication
shout for joy and gladness;
may they always say, "The LORD be exalted,
who delights in the well-being of his servant."
28 My tongue will speak of your righteousness
and of your praises all day long.

Psalm 36

For the director of music. Of David the servant of the LORD.

1 An oracle is within my heart
concerning the sinfulness of the wicked:[k]
There is no fear of God
before his eyes.
2 For in his own eyes he flatters himself
too much to detect or hate his sin.
3 The words of his mouth are wicked and deceitful;
he has ceased to be wise and to do good.
4 Even on his bed he plots evil;
he commits himself to a sinful course
and does not reject what is wrong.

5 Your love, O LORD, reaches to the heavens,
your faithfulness to the skies.
6 Your righteousness is like the mighty mountains,
your justice like the great deep.

k 1 Or *heart: / Sin proceeds from the wicked.*

*Heading, *1* See the note on page 349.

†*22* Most mss have *pathah* under the *aleph* (אַל).

אָדָם־וּבְהֵמָה תוֹשִׁיעַ יְהוָה׃ מַה־יָּקָר חַסְדְּךָ
unfailing-love-of-you priceless how! (8) Yahweh you-preserve and-beast man

אֱלֹהִים וּבְנֵי אָדָם בְּצֵל כְּנָפֶיךָ יֶחֱסָיוּן׃
they-find-refuge wings-of-you in-shadow-of man and-sons-of high-ones

יִרְוְיֻן מִדֶּשֶׁן בֵּיתֶךָ וְנַחַל עֲדָנֶיךָ
delights-of-you and-river-of house-of-you on-abundance-of they-feast (9)

תַשְׁקֵם׃ כִּי־עִמְּךָ מְקוֹר חַיִּים בְּאוֹרְךָ
in-light-of-you lives fountain-of with-you for (10) you-give-drink-them

נִרְאֶה־אוֹר׃ מְשֹׁךְ חַסְדְּךָ לְיֹדְעֶיךָ
to-ones-knowing-you love-of-you continue! (11) light we-see

וְצִדְקָתְךָ לְיִשְׁרֵי־לֵב׃ אַל־תְּבוֹאֵנִי
let-her-come-to-me not (12) heart to-ones-upright-of and-righteousness-of-you

רֶגֶל גַּאֲוָה וְיַד־רְשָׁעִים אַל־תְּנִדֵנִי׃ שָׁם
see! (13) let-her-drive-away-me not wicked-ones or-hand-of pride foot-of

נָפְלוּ פֹּעֲלֵי אָוֶן דֹּחוּ וְלֹא־יָכְלוּ
they-are-able and-not they-are-thrown-down evil ones-doing-of they-lie-fallen

קוּם׃ לְדָוִד ׀ אַל־תִּתְחַר בַּמְּרֵעִים אַל־
not because-of-the-men-being-evil you-fret not of-David (37:1) to-rise

תְּקַנֵּא בְּעֹשֵׂי עַוְלָה׃ כִּי כֶחָצִיר מְהֵרָה
soon like-the-grass for (2) wrong of-ones-doing-of you-be-envious

יִמָּלוּ וּכְיֶרֶק דֶּשֶׁא יִבּוֹלוּן׃ בְּטַח
trust! (3) they-will-die-away plant and-like-green-of they-will-wither

בַּיהוָה וַעֲשֵׂה־טוֹב שְׁכָן־אֶרֶץ וּרְעֵה אֱמוּנָה׃ וְהִתְעַנַּג
and-delight! (4) safe and-enjoy-pasture! land dwell! good and-do! in-Yahweh

עַל־יְהוָה וְיִתֶּן־לְךָ מִשְׁאֲלֹת לִבֶּךָ׃ גּוֹל עַל־
to commit! (5) heart-of-you desires-of to-you and-he-will-give Yahweh in

יְהוָה דַּרְכֶּךָ וּבְטַח עָלָיו וְהוּא יַעֲשֶׂה׃ וְהוֹצִיא
and-he-will-make-shine (6) he-will-do and-he in-him and-trust! way-of-you Yahweh

כָאוֹר צִדְקֶךָ וּמִשְׁפָּטֶךָ כַּצָּהֳרָיִם׃
like-the-noonday-sun and-justice-of-you righteousness-of-you like-the-dawn

דּוֹם ׀ לַיהוָה וְהִתְחוֹלֵל לוֹ אַל־תִּתְחַר
you-fret not for-him and-wait-patiently! before-Yahweh be-still! (7)

בְּמַצְלִיחַ דַּרְכּוֹ בְּאִישׁ עֹשֶׂה מְזִמּוֹת׃ הֶרֶף
refrain! (8) schemes carrying-out over-man way-of-him over-one-making-succeed

מֵאַף וַעֲזֹב חֵמָה אַל־תִּתְחַר אַךְ־לְהָרֵעַ׃ כִּי־
for (9) to-bring-evil only you-fret not wrath and-turn-from! from-anger

מְרֵעִים יִכָּרֵתוּן וְקֹוֵי יְהוָה הֵמָּה
they Yahweh but-ones-hoping-of they-will-be-cut-off men-being-evil

O LORD, you preserve both
man and beast.
7 How priceless is your
unfailing love!
Both high and low among
men
find[l] refuge in the shadow
of your wings.
8 They feast on the abundance
of your house;
you give them drink from
your river of delights.
9 For with you is the fountain of
life;
in your light we see light.

10 Continue your love to those
who know you,
your righteousness to the
upright in heart.
11 May the foot of the proud not
come against me,
nor the hand of the wicked
drive me away.
12 See how the evildoers lie
fallen—
thrown down, not able to
rise!

Psalm 37[m]

Of David.

1 Do not fret because of evil
men
or be envious of those who
do wrong;
2 for like the grass they will
soon wither,
like green plants they will
soon die away.

3 Trust in the LORD and do good;
dwell in the land and enjoy
safe pasture.
4 Delight yourself in the LORD
and he will give you the
desires of your heart.

5 Commit your way to the LORD;
trust in him and he will do
this:
6 He will make your
righteousness shine like
the dawn,
the justice of your cause like
the noonday sun.

7 Be still before the LORD and
wait patiently for him;
do not fret when men
succeed in their ways,
when they carry out their
wicked schemes.

8 Refrain from anger and turn
from wrath;
do not fret—it leads only to
evil.
9 For evil men will be cut off,
but those who hope in the

[l] 7 Or *love, O God! / Men find;* or *love! / Both heavenly beings and men / find*
[m] This psalm is an acrostic poem, the stanzas of which begin with the successive letters of the Hebrew alphabet.

*See the note on page 349.

יִֽירְשׁוּ־ אָֽרֶץ׃ וְעוֹד מְעַט וְאֵין רָשָׁע

wicked and-there-is-no little and-while (10) land they-will-inherit

וְהִתְבּוֹנַנְתָּ עַל־ מְקוֹמוֹ וְאֵינֶֽנּוּ׃ וַעֲנָוִים

but-meek-ones (11) then-not-he place-of-him for though-you-look

יִֽירְשׁוּ־ אָרֶץ וְהִֽתְעַנְּגוּ עַל־ רֹב שָׁלֽוֹם׃ זֹמֵם

plotting (12) peace greatness-of to and-they-will-enjoy land they-will-inherit

רָשָׁע לַצַּדִּיק וְחֹרֵק עָלָיו שִׁנָּֽיו׃ אֲדֹנָי

Lord (13) teeth-of-him at-him and-gnashing against-the-righteous wicked

יִשְׂחַק־ לוֹ כִּֽי־ רָאָה כִּֽי־ יָבֹא יוֹמֽוֹ׃ חֶרֶב ׀ פָּתְחוּ

they-draw sword (14) day-of-him he-comes that he-knows for at-him he-laughs

רְשָׁעִים וְדָרְכוּ קַשְׁתָּם לְהַפִּיל עָנִי וְאֶבְיוֹן לִטְבוֹחַ

to-slay and-needy poor to-bring-down bow-of-them and-they-bend wicked-ones

יִשְׁרֵי־ דָֽרֶךְ׃ חַרְבָּם תָּבוֹא בְלִבָּם

into-heart-of-them she-will-pierce sword-of-them (15) way ones-upright-of

וְקַשְּׁתוֹתָם תִּשָּׁבַֽרְנָה׃ טוֹב־ מְעַט לַצַּדִּיק

of-the-righteous little better (16) they-will-be-broken and-bows-of-them

מֵהֲמוֹן רְשָׁעִים רַבִּֽים׃ כִּי זְרוֹעוֹת רְשָׁעִים

wicked-ones powers-of for (17) many wicked-ones than-wealth-of

תִּשָּׁבַרְנָה וְסוֹמֵךְ צַדִּיקִים יְהוָֽה׃ יוֹדֵעַ

one-knowing (18) Yahweh righteous-ones but-one-upholding they-will-be-broken

יְהוָה יְמֵי תְמִימִם וְנַחֲלָתָם לְעוֹלָם תִּהְיֶֽה׃

she-will-endure to-forever and-inheritance-of-them blameless-ones days-of Yahweh

לֹֽא־ יֵבֹשׁוּ בְּעֵת רָעָה וּבִימֵי רְעָבוֹן

famine and-in-days-of disaster in-time-of they-will-wither not (19)

יִשְׂבָּֽעוּ׃ כִּי רְשָׁעִים ׀ יֹאבֵדוּ

they-will-perish wicked-ones but (20) they-will-enjoy-plenty

וְאֹיְבֵי יְהוָה כִּיקַר כָּרִים כָּלוּ

they-will-vanish fields like-beauty-of Yahweh and-ones-being-enemies-of

בֶעָשָׁן כָּֽלוּ׃ לֹוֶה רָשָׁע וְלֹא יְשַׁלֵּם

he-repays and-not wicked borrowing (21) they-will-vanish like-the-smoke

וְצַדִּיק חוֹנֵן וְנוֹתֵֽן׃ כִּי מְבֹרָכָיו

ones-being-blessed-of-him indeed (22) and-giving being-generous but-righteous

יִירְשׁוּ אָרֶץ וּמְקֻלָּלָיו יִכָּרֵֽתוּ׃

they-will-be-cut-off but-ones-being-cursed-of-him land they-will-inherit

מֵיְהוָה מִֽצְעֲדֵי־ גֶבֶר כּוֹנָנוּ וְדַרְכּוֹ יֶחְפָּֽץ׃

he-delights-in and-way-of-him they-are-made-firm man steps-of by-Yahweh (23)

כִּֽי־ יִפֹּל לֹֽא־ יוּטָל כִּֽי־ יְהוָה סוֹמֵךְ יָדֽוֹ׃

hand-of-him one-upholding Yahweh for he-will-fall not he-stumble though (24)

LORD will inherit the
land.

10 A little while, and the wicked
will be no more;
though you look for them,
they will not be found.

11 But the meek will inherit the
land
and enjoy great peace.

12 The wicked plot against the
righteous
and gnash their teeth at
them;

13 but the Lord laughs at the
wicked,
for he knows their day is
coming.

14 The wicked draw the sword
and bend the bow
to bring down the poor and
needy,
to slay those whose ways
are upright.

15 But their swords will pierce
their own hearts,
and their bows will be
broken.

16 Better the little that the
righteous have
than the wealth of many
wicked;

17 for the power of the wicked
will be broken,
but the LORD upholds the
righteous.

18 The days of the blameless are
known to the LORD,
and their inheritance will
endure forever.

19 In times of disaster they will
not wither;
in days of famine they will
enjoy plenty.

20 But the wicked will perish:
The LORD's enemies will be
like the beauty of the
fields,
they will vanish—vanish
like smoke.

21 The wicked borrow and do not
repay,
but the righteous give
generously;

22 those the LORD blesses will
inherit the land,
but those he curses will be
cut off.

23 The LORD delights in the way
of the man
whose steps he has made
firm;

24 though he stumble, he will not
fall,
for the LORD upholds him
with his hand.

נַעַר | הָיִיתִי גַּם־זָקַנְתִּי וְלֹא־רָאִיתִי צַדִּיק נֶעֱזָב
being-forsaken righteous I-saw yet-never I-am-old now I-was young (25)

וְזַרְעוֹ מְבַקֶּשׁ־לָחֶם׃ כָּל־הַיּוֹם חוֹנֵן וּמַלְוֶה
and-lending being-generous the-day all-of (26) bread begging or-child-of-him

וְזַרְעוֹ לִבְרָכָה׃ סוּר מֵרָע וַעֲשֵׂה־טוֹב וּשְׁכֹן
then-live! good and-do! from-evil turn! (27) for-blessing and-child-of-him

לְעוֹלָם׃ כִּי יְהוָה | אֹהֵב מִשְׁפָּט וְלֹא־יַעֲזֹב אֶת־
*** he-will-forsake and-not just one-loving Yahweh for (28) to-always

חֲסִידָיו לְעוֹלָם נִשְׁמָרוּ וְזֶרַע
but-offspring-of they-will-be-protected to-forever faithful-ones-of-him

רְשָׁעִים נִכְרָת׃ צַדִּיקִים יִירְשׁוּ־אָרֶץ
land they-will-inherit righteous-ones (29) he-will-be-cut-off wicked-ones

וְיִשְׁכְּנוּ לָעַד עָלֶיהָ׃ פִּי־צַדִּיק יֶהְגֶּה
he-utters righteous mouth-of (30) in-her to-forever and-they-will-dwell

חָכְמָה וּלְשׁוֹנוֹ תְּדַבֵּר מִשְׁפָּט׃ תּוֹרַת אֱלֹהָיו
God-of-him law-of (31) justice she-speaks and-tongue-of-him wisdom

בְּלִבּוֹ לֹא תִמְעַד אֲשֻׁרָיו׃ צוֹפֶה רָשָׁע
wicked one-lying-in-wait (32) feet-of-him she-slips not in-heart-of-him

לַצַּדִּיק וּמְבַקֵּשׁ לַהֲמִיתוֹ׃ יְהוָה לֹא־יַעַזְבֶנּוּ
he-will-leave-him not Yahweh (33) to-kill-him and-one-seeking for-the-righteous

בְיָדוֹ וְלֹא יַרְשִׁיעֶנּוּ בְּהִשָּׁפְטוֹ׃ קַוֵּה
wait! (34) when-to-be-on-trial-him he-will-condemn-him or-not in-power-of-him

אֶל־יְהוָה | וּשְׁמֹר דַּרְכּוֹ וִירוֹמִמְךָ לָרֶשֶׁת אָרֶץ
land to-possess and-he-will-exalt-you way-of-him and-keep! Yahweh for

בְּהִכָּרֵת רְשָׁעִים תִּרְאֶה׃ רָאִיתִי רָשָׁע עָרִיץ
ruthless-man wicked-man I-saw (35) you-will-see wicked-ones when-to-be-cut-off

וּמִתְעָרֶה כְּאֶזְרָח רַעֲנָן׃ וַיַּעֲבֹר וְהִנֵּה
and-see! but-he-passed-away (36) green-tree like-native and-flourishing

אֵינֶנּוּ וָאֲבַקְשֵׁהוּ וְלֹא נִמְצָא׃ שְׁמָר־
consider! (37) he-was-found then-not though-I-looked-for-him no-more-he

תָּם וּרְאֵה יָשָׁר כִּי־אַחֲרִית לְאִישׁ שָׁלוֹם׃
peace for-man-of future for upright and-observe! blameless

וּפֹשְׁעִים נִשְׁמְדוּ יַחְדָּו אַחֲרִית רְשָׁעִים
wicked-ones future-of together they-will-be-destroyed but-ones-sinning (38)

נִכְרָתָה׃ וּתְשׁוּעַת צַדִּיקִים מֵיְהוָה
from-Yahweh righteous-ones and-salvation-of (39) she-will-be-cut-off

מָעוּזָּם בְּעֵת צָרָה׃ וַיַּעְזְרֵם יְהוָה
Yahweh and-he-helps-them (40) trouble in-time-of stronghold-of-them

25 I was young and now I am old,
yet I have never seen the righteous forsaken
or their children begging bread.
26 They are always generous and lend freely;
their children will be blessed.

27 Turn from evil and do good;
then you will always live securely.
28 For the LORD loves the just
and will not forsake his faithful ones.

They will be protected forever,
but the offspring of the wicked will be cut off;
29 the righteous will inherit the land
and dwell in it forever.

30 The mouth of the righteous man utters wisdom,
and his tongue speaks what is just.
31 The law of his God is in his heart;
his feet do not slip.

32 The wicked lie in wait for the righteous,
seeking their very lives;
33 but the LORD will not leave them in their power
or let them be condemned when brought to trial.

34 Wait for the LORD
and keep his way.
He will exalt you to possess the land;
when the wicked are cut off, you will see it.

35 I have seen a wicked and ruthless man
flourishing like a green tree in its native soil,
36 but he soon passed away and was no more;
though I looked for him, he could not be found.

37 Consider the blameless, observe the upright;
there is a future[n] for the man of peace.
38 But all sinners will be destroyed;
the future[o] of the wicked will be cut off.

39 The salvation of the righteous comes from the LORD;
he is their stronghold in time of trouble.
40 The LORD helps them and

[n]37 *Or there will be posterity*
[o]38 *Or posterity*

וַֽיְפַלְּטֵם יְפַלְּטֵם מֵֽרְשָׁעִים וְיוֹשִׁיעֵם

and-he-saves-them from-wicked-ones he-delivers-them and-he-delivers-them

כִּֽי־ חָסוּ בֽוֹ׃ מִזְמוֹר לְדָוִד לְהַזְכִּיר׃

to-make-petition of-David psalm *(38:1) in-him they-take-refuge because

(2) יְהוָה אַל־ בְּקֶצְפְּךָ תוֹכִיחֵנִי וּבַחֲמָתְךָ תְיַסְּרֵנִי׃

you-discipline-me or-in-wrath-of-you you-rebuke-me in-anger-of-you not Yahweh (2)

(3) כִּֽי־ חִצֶּיךָ נִחֲתוּ בִי וַתִּנְחַת עָלַי

upon-me and-she-came-down into-me they-pierced arrows-of-you for (3)

יָדֶֽךָ׃ (4) אֵין־ מְתֹם בִּבְשָׂרִי מִפְּנֵי זַעְמֶךָ

wrath-of-you because-of in-body-of-me health there-is-no (4) hand-of-you

אֵין־ שָׁלוֹם בַּעֲצָמַי מִפְּנֵי חַטָּאתִֽי׃ (5) כִּי

indeed (5) sin-of-me because-of in-bones-of-me soundness there-is-no

עֲוֺנֹתַי עָבְרוּ רֹאשִׁי כְּמַשָּׂא כָבֵד יִכְבְּדוּ

they-are-too-heavy heavy like-burden head-of-me they-overwhelmed guilts-of-me

מִמֶּֽנִּי׃ (6) הִבְאִישׁוּ נָמַקּוּ חַבּוּרֹתָי מִפְּנֵי

because-of wounds-of-me they-fester they-are-loathsome (6) for-me

אִוַּלְתִּֽי׃ (7) נַעֲוֵיתִי שַׁחֹתִי עַד־ מְאֹד כָּל־

all-of very-much to I-am-brought-low I-am-bowed-down (7) sinful-folly-of-me

הַיּוֹם קֹדֵר הִלָּֽכְתִּי׃ (8) כִּֽי־ כְסָלַי מָלְאוּ נִקְלֶה

one-searing they-are-filled backs-of-me indeed (8) I-go-about mourning the-day

וְאֵין מְתֹם בִּבְשָׂרִֽי׃ (9) נְפוּגוֹתִי וְנִדְכֵּיתִי עַד־

to and-I-am-crushed I-am-feeble (9) in-body-of-me health and-there-is-no

מְאֹד שָׁאַגְתִּי מִנַּהֲמַת לִבִּֽי׃ (10) אֲדֹנָי† נֶגְדְּךָ כָל־

all-of before-you Lord (10) heart-of-me in-anguish-of I-groan utterly

תַּאֲוָתִי וְאַנְחָתִי מִמְּךָ לֹא־ נִסְתָּֽרָה׃ (11) לִבִּי

heart-of-me (11) she-is-hidden not from-you and-sighing-of-me longing-of-me

סְחַרְחַר עֲזָבַנִי כֹחִי וְאוֹר־ עֵינַי גַּם־ הֵם

they even eyes-of-me and-light-of strength-of-me he-fails-me he-pounds

אֵין אִתִּֽי׃ (12) אֹהֲבַי ׀ וְרֵעַי מִנֶּגֶד

from-before and-companions-of-me ones-being-friends-of-me (12) with-me not

נִגְעִי יַעֲמֹדוּ וּקְרוֹבַי מֵרָחֹק עָמָֽדוּ׃

they-stay at-far-away and-neighbors-of-me they-avoid wound-of-me

(13) וַיְנַקְשׁוּ ׀ מְבַקְשֵׁי נַפְשִׁי וְדֹרְשֵׁי

and-ones-wanting-of life-of-me ones-seeking-of and-they-set-traps (13)

רָעָתִי דִּבְּרוּ הַוּוֹת וּמִרְמוֹת כָּל־ הַיּוֹם יֶהְגּֽוּ׃

they-plot the-day all-of and-deceptions ruins they-talk-of harm-of-me

(14) וַאֲנִי כְחֵרֵשׁ לֹא אֶשְׁמָע וּכְאִלֵּם לֹא יִפְתַּח־

he-can-open not and-like-mute I-can-hear not like-deaf-man and-I (14)

delivers them;
he delivers them from the wicked and saves them,
because they take refuge in him.

Psalm 38

A psalm of David. A petition.

1 O LORD, do not rebuke me in your anger
or discipline me in your wrath.
2 For your arrows have pierced me,
and your hand has come down upon me.
3 Because of your wrath there is no health in my body;
my bones have no soundness because of my sin.
4 My guilt has overwhelmed me
like a burden too heavy to bear.

5 My wounds fester and are loathsome
because of my sinful folly.
6 I am bowed down and brought very low;
all day long I go about mourning.
7 My back is filled with searing pain;
there is no health in my body.
8 I am feeble and utterly crushed;
I groan in anguish of heart.

9 All my longings lie open before you, O Lord;
my sighing is not hidden from you.
10 My heart pounds, my strength fails me;
even the light has gone from my eyes.
11 My friends and companions avoid me because of my wounds;
my neighbors stay far away.
12 Those who seek my life set their traps,
those who would harm me talk of my ruin;
all day long they plot deception.

13 I am like a deaf man, who cannot hear,
like a mute, who cannot open his mouth;

*Heading, *1* See the note on page 349.

†*10* Most mss have the accent *rebia* (נִ֗י–).

פִּיו׃ וָאֱהִי כְּאִישׁ אֲשֶׁר לֹא־ שֹׁמֵעַ וְאֵין
and-there-are-not one-hearing not who like-man and-I-became (15) mouth-of-him

בְּפִיו תּוֹכָחוֹת׃ כִּי־ לְךָ יְהוָה הוֹחָלְתִּי אַתָּה תַעֲנֶה
you-will-answer you I-wait Yahweh for-you indeed (16) replies in-mouth-of-him

אֲדֹנָי אֱלֹהָי׃ כִּי־ אָמַרְתִּי פֶּן־ יִשְׂמְחוּ־ לִי בְּמוֹט
when-to-slip over-me let-them-gloat not I-said for (17) God-of-me Lord

רַגְלִי עָלַי הִגְדִּילוּ׃ כִּי־ אֲנִי לְצֶלַע נָכוֹן
being-ready for-fall I for (18) let-them-exalt-themselves over-me foot-of-me

וּמַכְאוֹבִי נֶגְדִּי תָמִיד׃ כִּי־ עֲוֹנִי אַגִּיד אֶדְאַג
I-am-troubled I-confess iniquity-of-me indeed (19) ever with-me and-pain-of-me

מֵחַטָּאתִי׃ וְאֹיְבַי חַיִּים עָצֵמוּ
they-are-many vigorous-ones and-ones-being-enemies-of-me (20) by-sin-of-me

וְרַבּוּ שֹׂנְאַי שָׁקֶר׃ וּמְשַׁלְּמֵי
and-ones-repaying-of (21) without-reason ones-hating-me and-they-are-numerous

רָעָה תַּחַת טוֹבָה יִשְׂטְנוּנִי תַּחַת רָדְופִי־ טוֹב׃ אַל־ תַּעַזְבֵנִי
you-forsake-me not (22) good to-seek-me when they-slander-me good for evil

יְהוָה אֱלֹהַי אַל־ תִּרְחַק מִמֶּנִּי׃ חוּשָׁה לְעֶזְרָתִי
to-help-of-me come-quickly! (23) from-me you-be-far not God-of-me Yahweh

אֲדֹנָי תְּשׁוּעָתִי׃ לַמְנַצֵּחַ לִידִיתוּן מִזְמוֹר לְדָוִד׃
of-David psalm for-Jeduthun for-the-one-directing *(39:1) salvation-of-me Lord

אָמַרְתִּי אֶשְׁמְרָה דְרָכַי מֵחֲטוֹא בִלְשׁוֹנִי אֶשְׁמְרָה
I-will-put with-tongue-of-me from-to-sin ways-of-me I-will-watch I-said (2)

לְפִי מַחְסוֹם בְּעֹד רָשָׁע לְנֶגְדִּי׃ נֶאֱלַמְתִּי
I-was-silent (3) in-presence-of-me wicked as-long-as muzzle on-mouth-of-me

דוּמִיָּה הֶחֱשֵׁיתִי מִטּוֹב וּכְאֵבִי נֶעְכָּר׃ חַם־
he-grew-hot (4) he-increased and-anguish-of-me of-good I-said-nothing still

לִבִּי ׀ בְּקִרְבִּי בַּהֲגִיגִי תִבְעַר־ אֵשׁ דִּבַּרְתִּי
I-spoke fire she-burned in-meditation-of-me in-inside-of-me heart-of-me

בִּלְשׁוֹנִי׃ הוֹדִיעֵנִי יְהוָה ׀ קִצִּי וּמִדַּת יָמַי
days-of-me and-number-of end-of-me Yahweh show-me! (5) with-tongue-of-me

מַה־ הִיא אֵדְעָה מֶה־ חָדֵל אָנִי׃ הִנֵּה טְפָחוֹת ׀ נָתַתָּה
you-made handbreadths see! (6) I fleeting how let-me-know she what?

יָמַי וְחֶלְדִּי כְאַיִן נֶגְדֶּךָ אַךְ כָּל־ הֶבֶל
breath all-of indeed before-you as-nothing and-span-of-me days-of-me

כָּל־ אָדָם נִצָּב סֶלָה׃ אַךְ־ בְּצֶלֶם ׀ יִתְהַלֶּךְ־ אִישׁ אַךְ־
indeed man he-goes-about as-phantom indeed (7) selah he-stands man each-of

הֶבֶל יֶהֱמָיוּן יִצְבֹּר וְלֹא־ יֵדַע מִי־
who? he-knows but-not he-heaps-up-wealth they-bustle-about vainly

14 I have become like a man who does not hear,
whose mouth can offer no reply.
15 I wait for you, O LORD;
you will answer, O Lord my God.
16 For I said, "Do not let them gloat
or exalt themselves over me when my foot slips."
17 For I am about to fall,
and my pain is ever with me.
18 I confess my iniquity;
I am troubled by my sin.
19 Many are those who are my vigorous enemies;
those who hate me without reason are numerous.
20 Those who repay my good with evil
slander me when I seek what is good.
21 O LORD, do not forsake me;
be not far from me, O my God.
22 Come quickly to help me,
O Lord my Savior.

Psalm 39

For the director of music. For Jeduthun. A psalm of David.

1 I said, "I will watch my ways
and keep my tongue from sin;
I will put a muzzle on my mouth
as long as the wicked are in my presence."
2 But when I was silent and still,
not even saying anything good,
my anguish increased.
3 My heart grew hot within me,
and as I meditated, the fire burned;
then I spoke with my tongue:
4 "Show me, O LORD, my life's end
and the number of my days;
let me know how fleeting is my life.
5 You have made my days a mere handbreadth;
the span of my years is as nothing before you.
Each man's life is but a breath. *Selah*
6 Man is a mere phantom as he goes to and fro:
He bustles about, but only in vain;
he heaps up wealth, not knowing who will get it.

*Heading, *1* See the note on page 349.

°*21* ק רדפי

°*1* ק לידותון

אֹסְפָם׃ וְעַתָּה מַה־ קִּוִּיתִי אֲדֹנָי תּוֹחַלְתִּי לְךָ הִיא׃
she in-you hope-of-me Lord do-I-look-for what? but-now (8) one-getting-them

מִכָּל־ פְּשָׁעַי הַצִּילֵנִי חֶרְפַּת נָבָל אַל־ תְּשִׂימֵנִי׃
you-make-me not fool scorn-of save-me! transgressions-of-me from-all-of (9)

נֶאֱלַמְתִּי לֹא אֶפְתַּח־ פִּי כִּי אַתָּה עָשִׂיתָ׃ הָסֵר
remove! (11) you-did you for mouth-of-me I-opened not I-was-silent (10)

מֵעָלַי נִגְעֶךָ מִתִּגְרַת יָדְךָ אֲנִי כָלִיתִי׃
I-am-overcome I hand-of-you from-blow-of scourge-of-you from-upon-me

בְּתוֹכָחוֹת עַל־ עָוֺן ׀ יִסַּרְתָּ אִישׁ וַתֶּמֶס כָּעָשׁ
like-the-moth and-you-consume man you-discipline sin for with-rebukes (12)

חֲמוּדוֹ אַךְ הֶבֶל כָּל־ אָדָם סֶלָה׃ שִׁמְעָה־ תְפִלָּתִי ׀
prayer-of-me hear! (13) selah man each-of breath indeed wealth-of-him

יְהוָה וְשַׁוְעָתִי ׀ הַאֲזִינָה אֶל־ דִּמְעָתִי אַל־ תֶּחֱרַשׁ כִּי
for you-be-deaf not weeping-of-me to listen! and-cry-for-help-of-me Yahweh

גֵר אָנֹכִי עִמָּךְ תּוֹשָׁב כְּכָל־ אֲבוֹתָי׃ הָשַׁע מִמֶּנִּי
away-from-me look! (14) fathers-of-me as-all-of stranger with-you I alien

וְאַבְלִיגָה בְּטֶרֶם אֵלֵךְ וְאֵינֶנִּי׃ לַמְנַצֵּחַ
for-the-one-directing *(40:1) and-no-more-I I-depart at-before that-I-may-rejoice

לְדָוִד מִזְמוֹר׃ קַוֹּה קִוִּיתִי יְהוָה וַיֵּט אֵלַי
to-me and-he-turned Yahweh I-waited-for to-wait-for (2) psalm of-David

וַיִּשְׁמַע שַׁוְעָתִי׃ וַיַּעֲלֵנִי ׀ מִבּוֹר שָׁאוֹן מִטִּיט
from-mud-of slime from-pit-of and-he-lifted-me (3) cry-of-me and-he-heard

הַיָּוֵן וַיָּקֶם עַל־ סֶלַע רַגְלָי כּוֹנֵן אֲשֻׁרָי׃
standing-places-of-me making-firm feet-of-me rock on and-he-set the-mire

וַיִּתֵּן בְּפִי ׀ שִׁיר חָדָשׁ תְּהִלָּה לֵאלֹהֵינוּ
to-God-of-us hymn-of-praise new song in-mouth-of-me and-he-put (4)

יִרְאוּ רַבִּים וְיִירָאוּ וְיִבְטְחוּ בַּיהוָה׃
in-Yahweh and-they-will-trust and-they-will-fear many they-will-see

אַשְׁרֵי הַגֶּבֶר אֲשֶׁר־ שָׂם יְהוָה מִבְטַחוֹ וְלֹא־
and-not trust-of-him Yahweh he-makes who the-man blessednesses-of (5)

פָנָה אֶל־ רְהָבִים וְשָׂטֵי כָזָב׃ רַבּוֹת עָשִׂיתָ ׀ אַתָּה ׀
you you-did many (6) false-god and-ones-turning-of proud-ones to he-looks

יְהוָה אֱלֹהַי נִפְלְאֹתֶיךָ וּמַחְשְׁבֹתֶיךָ אֵלֵינוּ אֵין ׀
no-one for-us and-plans-of-you things-being-wonders-of-you God-of-me Yahweh

עֲרֹךְ אֵלֶיךָ אַגִּידָה וַאֲדַבֵּרָה עָצְמוּ
they-would-be-too-many and-should-I-tell should-I-speak to-you to-recount

מִסַּפֵּר׃ זֶבַח וּמִנְחָה ׀ לֹא־ חָפַצְתָּ אָזְנַיִם כָּרִיתָ
you-pierced ears you-desired not and-offering sacrifice (7) than-to-declare

7"But now, Lord, what do I look for?
My hope is in you.
8Save me from all my transgressions;
do not make me the scorn of fools.
9I was silent; I would not open my mouth,
for you are the one who has done this.
10Remove your scourge from me;
I am overcome by the blow of your hand.
11You rebuke and discipline men for their sin;
you consume their wealth like a moth—
each man is but a breath.
Selah

12"Hear my prayer, O LORD,
listen to my cry for help;
be not deaf to my weeping.
For I dwell with you as an alien,
a stranger, as all my fathers were.
13Look away from me, that I may rejoice again
before I depart and am no more."

Psalm 40

For the director of music. Of David. A psalm.

1I waited patiently for the LORD;
he turned to me and heard my cry.
2He lifted me out of the slimy pit,
out of the mud and mire;
he set my feet on a rock
and gave me a firm place to stand.
3He put a new song in my mouth,
a hymn of praise to our God.
Many will see and fear
and put their trust in the LORD.

4Blessed is the man
who makes the LORD his trust,
who does not look to the proud,
to those who turn aside to false gods.[p]
5Many, O LORD my God,
are the wonders you have done.
The things you planned for us
no one can recount to you;
were I to speak and tell of them,
they would be too many to declare.

6Sacrifice and offering you did not desire,
but my ears you have pierced[q,r];

p4 Or *to falsehood*
q6 Hebrew; Septuagint *but a body you have prepared for me* (see also Symmachus and Theodotion)
r6 Or *opened*

*Heading, *1* See the note on page 349.

אָמַרְתִּי	אָז		שָׁאָלְתָּ׃	לֹא	וַחֲטָאָה	עוֹלָה	לִי
I-said	then	(8)	you-required	not	and-sin-offering	burnt-offering	for-me

רְצוֹנְךָ	לַעֲשׂוֹת־		עָלָי׃	כָּתוּב	סֵפֶר	בִמְגִלַּת־	בָאתִי	הִנֵּה־
will-of-you	to-do	(9)	about-me	one-being-written	book	in-scroll-of	I-came	here!

בִּשַּׂרְתִּי		מֵעָי׃	בְּתוֹךְ	וְתוֹרָתְךָ	חָפָצְתִּי	אֱלֹהַי
I-proclaim	(10)	hearts-of-me	within	and-law-of-you	I-desire	God-of-me

אַתָּה	יְהוָה	אֶכְלָא	לֹא	שְׂפָתַי	הִנֵּה	רָב	בְּקָהָל	צֶדֶק
you	Yahweh	I-seal	not	lips-of-me	see!	great	in-assembly	righteousness

לִבִּי	בְּתוֹךְ	כִסִּיתִי	לֹא־	צִדְקָתְךָ		יָדָעְתָּ׃
heart-of-me	within	I-hide	not	righteousness-of-you	(11)	you-know

חַסְדְּךָ	כִחַדְתִּי	לֹא־	אָמָרְתִּי	וּתְשׁוּעָתְךָ	אֱמוּנָתְךָ
love-of-you	I-conceal	not	I-speak	and-salvation-of-you	faithfulness-of-you

תִכְלָא	לֹא־	יְהוָה	אַתָּה		רָב׃	לְקָהָל	וַאֲמִתְּךָ
you-withhold	not	Yahweh	you	(12)	great	from-assembly	and-truth-of-you

יִצְּרוּנִי׃	תָּמִיד	וַאֲמִתְּךָ	חַסְדְּךָ	מִמֶּנִּי	רַחֲמֶיךָ
may-they-protect-me	always	and-truth-of-you	love-of-you	from-me	mercies-of-you

מִסְפָּר	אֵין	עַד־	רָעוֹת	עָלַי	אָפְפוּ־	כִּי	
number	there-is-no	to	troubles	around-me	they-surround	for	(13)

מִשַּׂעֲרוֹת	עָצְמוּ	לִרְאוֹת	יָכֹלְתִּי	וְלֹא־	עֲוֺנֹתַי	הִשִּׂיגוּנִי
than-hairs-of	they-are-more	to-see	I-can	and-not	sins-of-me	they-overtook-me

לְהַצִּילֵנִי	יְהוָה	רְצֵה		עֲזָבָנִי׃	וְלִבִּי	רֹאשִׁי
to-save-me	Yahweh	be-pleased!	(14)	he-fails-me	and-heart-of-me	head-of-me

יֵבֹשׁוּ		חוּשָׁה׃	לְעֶזְרָתִי	יְהוָה
may-they-be-shamed	(15)	come-quickly!	to-help-of-me	Yahweh

לִסְפּוֹתָהּ	נַפְשִׁי	מְבַקְשֵׁי	יַחַד	וְיַחְפְּרוּ
to-take-her	life-of-me	ones-seeking-of	together	and-may-they-be-confused

רָעָתִי׃	חֲפֵצֵי	וְיִכָּלְמוּ	אָחוֹר	יִסֹּגוּ
ruin-of-me	desirers-of	and-may-they-be-disgraced	back	may-they-be-turned

לִי	הָאֹמְרִים	בָּשְׁתָּם	עֵקֶב	עַל־	יָשֹׁמּוּ	
to-me	the-ones-saying	shame-of-them	cause-of	for	may-they-be-appalled	(16)

כָּל־	בְּךָ	וְיִשְׂמְחוּ	יָשִׂישׂוּ		הֶאָח׃	הֶאָח
all-of	in-you	and-may-they-be-glad	may-they-rejoice	(17)	aha!	aha!

אֹהֲבֵי	יְהוָה	יִגְדַּל	תָּמִיד	יֹאמְרוּ	מְבַקְשֶׁיךָ
ones-loving-of	Yahweh	may-he-be-exalted	always	may-they-say	ones-seeking-you

לִי	יַחֲשָׁב	אֲדֹנָי	וְאֶבְיוֹן	עָנִי	וַאֲנִי		תְּשׁוּעָתֶךָ׃
of-me	may-he-think	Lord	and-needy	poor	yet-I	(18)	salvation-of-you

תְּאַחַר׃	אַל־	אֱלֹהַי	אַתָּה	וּמְפַלְטִי	עֶזְרָתִי
you-delay	not	God-of-me	you	and-one-delivering-me	help-of-me

burnt offerings and sin
offerings
you did not require.
7 Then I said, "Here I am, I
have come—
it is written about me in the
scroll.[s]
8 I desire to do your will, O my
God;
your law is within my
heart."

9 I proclaim righteousness in the
great assembly;
I do not seal my lips,
as you know, O LORD.
10 I do not hide your
righteousness in my
heart;
I speak of your faithfulness
and salvation.
I do not conceal your love and
your truth
from the great assembly.

11 Do not withhold your mercy
from me, O LORD;
may your love and your
truth always protect me.
12 For troubles without number
surround me;
my sins have overtaken me,
and I cannot see.
They are more than the hairs
of my head,
and my heart fails within
me.

13 Be pleased, O LORD, to save
me;
O LORD, come quickly to
help me.
14 May all who seek to take my
life
be put to shame and
confusion;
may all who desire my ruin
be turned back in disgrace.
15 May those who say to me,
"Aha! Aha!"
be appalled at their own
shame.
16 But may all who seek you
rejoice and be glad in you;
may those who love your
salvation always say,
"The LORD be exalted!"

17 Yet I am poor and needy;
may the Lord think of me.
You are my help and my
deliverer;
O my God, do not delay.

[s]7 Or *come / with the scroll written for me*

*See the note on page 349.

לַמְנַצֵּחַ מִזְמוֹר לְדָוִד׃ אַשְׁרֵי מַשְׂכִּיל

one-regarding blessednesses-of (2) of-David psalm for-the-one-directing *(41:1)

אֶל־דָּל בְּיוֹם רָעָה יְמַלְּטֵהוּ יְהוָה׃ יְהוָה ׀

Yahweh (3) Yahweh he-delivers-him trouble in-time-of weak to

יִשְׁמְרֵהוּ וִיחַיֵּהוּ יְאֻשַּׁר°

and-he-is-blessed and-he-will-preserve-life-of-him he-will-protect-him

בָּאָרֶץ וְאַל־תִּתְּנֵהוּ בְּנֶפֶשׁ אֹיְבָיו׃

ones-being-foes-of-him to-desire-of he-will-surrender-him and-not in-the-land

יְהוָה יִסְעָדֶנּוּ עַל־עֶרֶשׂ דְּוָי כָּל־מִשְׁכָּבוֹ

bed-of-him all-of sickness bed-of on he-will-sustain-him Yahweh (4)

הָפַכְתָּ בְחָלְיוֹ׃ אֲנִי־אָמַרְתִּי יְהוָה חָנֵּנִי

have-mercy-on-me! Yahweh I-said I (5) from-illness-of-him you-will-restore

רְפָאָה נַפְשִׁי כִּי־חָטָאתִי לָךְ׃ אוֹיְבַי

ones-being-enemies-of-me (6) against-you I-sinned for self-of-me heal!

יֹאמְרוּ רַע לִי מָתַי יָמוּת וְאָבַד שְׁמוֹ׃

name-of-him and-will-he-perish will-he-die when? of-me malice they-say

וְאִם־בָּא לִרְאוֹת ׀ שָׁוְא יְדַבֵּר לִבּוֹ יִקְבָּץ־

he-gathers heart-of-him he-speaks falsely to-see he-comes when-ever (7)

אָוֶן לוֹ יֵצֵא לַחוּץ יְדַבֵּר׃ יַחַד

together (8) he-speaks to-the-outside he-goes-out for-him slander

עָלַי יִתְלַחֲשׁוּ כָּל־שֹׂנְאָי עָלַי ׀ יַחְשְׁבוּ

they-imagine for-me ones-being-enemies-of-me all-of they-whisper against-me

רָעָה לִי׃ דְּבַר־בְּלִיַּעַל יָצוּק בּוֹ וַאֲשֶׁר שָׁכַב לֹא־

not he-lies and-where upon-him being-set vileness disease-of (9) for-me worst

יוֹסִיף לָקוּם׃ גַּם־אִישׁ שְׁלוֹמִי ׀ אֲשֶׁר־בָּטַחְתִּי

I-trusted whom close-friend-of-me man even (10) to-get-up he-will-do-again

בוֹ אוֹכֵל לַחְמִי הִגְדִּיל עָלַי עָקֵב׃ וְאַתָּה יְהוָה

Yahweh but-you (11) heel against-me he-lifted bread-of-me one-eating in-him

חָנֵּנִי וַהֲקִימֵנִי וַאֲשַׁלְּמָה לָהֶם׃ בְּזֹאת

in-this (12) to-them that-I-may-repay and-raise-up-me! have-mercy-on-me!

יָדַעְתִּי כִּי־חָפַצְתָּ בִּי כִּי לֹא־יָרִיעַ אֹיְבִי

one-being-enemy-of-me he-triumphs not for with-me you-are-pleased that I-know

עָלָי׃ וַאֲנִי בְּתֻמִּי תָּמַכְתָּ בִּי וַתַּצִּיבֵנִי

and-you-set-me to-me you-uphold in-integrity-of-me and-I (13) over-me

לְפָנֶיךָ לְעוֹלָם׃ בָּרוּךְ יְהוָה ׀ אֱלֹהֵי יִשְׂרָאֵל

Israel God-of Yahweh being-praised (14) to-forever in-presences-of-you

מֵהָעוֹלָם וְעַד הָעוֹלָם אָמֵן ׀ וְאָמֵן׃

and-amen amen the-everlasting and-to from-the-everlasting

Psalm 41

For the director of music. A psalm of David.

1 Blessed is he who has regard for the weak;
the LORD delivers him in times of trouble.
2 The LORD will protect him and preserve his life;
he will bless him in the land
and not surrender him to the desire of his foes.
3 The LORD will sustain him on his sickbed
and restore him from his bed of illness.

4 I said, "O LORD, have mercy on me;
heal me, for I have sinned against you."
5 My enemies say of me in malice,
"When will he die and his name perish?"
6 Whenever one comes to see me,
he speaks falsely, while his heart gathers slander;
then he goes out and spreads it abroad.

7 All my enemies whisper together against me;
they imagine the worst for me, saying,
8 "A vile disease has beset him;
he will never get up from the place where he lies."
9 Even my close friend, whom I trusted,
he who shared my bread,
has lifted up his heel against me.

10 But you, O LORD, have mercy on me;
raise me up, that I may repay them.
11 I know that you are pleased with me,
for my enemy does not triumph over me.
12 In my integrity you uphold me
and set me in your presence forever.

13 Praise be to the LORD, the God of Israel,
from everlasting to everlasting.
Amen and Amen.

*Heading, *1* See the note on page 349.

°3 ק ואשר

לַמְנַצֵּחַ מַשְׂכִּיל לִבְנֵי־ קֹרַח׃ כְּאַיָּל תַּעֲרֹג
she-pants as-deer (2) Korah of-sons-of maskil for-the-one-directing *(42:1)

עַל־ אֲפִיקֵי־ מָיִם כֵּן נַפְשִׁי תַעֲרֹג אֵלֶיךָ אֱלֹהִים׃ צָמְאָה
she-thirsts (3) God for-you she-pants soul-of-me so waters streams-of for

נַפְשִׁי ׀ לֵאלֹהִים לְאֵל חָי מָתַי אָבוֹא וְאֵרָאֶה פְּנֵי
faces-of and-can-I-be-met can-I-go when? living for-God for-God soul-of-me

אֱלֹהִים׃ הָיְתָה־ לִּי דִמְעָתִי לֶחֶם יוֹמָם וָלַיְלָה בֶּאֱמֹר אֵלַי
to-me while-to-say and-night by-day food tear-of-me for-me she-was (4) God

כָּל־ הַיּוֹם אַיֵּה אֱלֹהֶיךָ׃ אֵלֶּה אֶזְכְּרָה ׀ וְאֶשְׁפְּכָה עָלַי ׀
before-me as-I-pour-out I-remember these (5) God-of-you where? the-day all-of

נַפְשִׁי כִּי אֶעֱבֹר ׀ בַּסָּךְ אֶדַּדֵּם עַד־ בֵּית
house-of to I-would-lead-them with-the-multitude I-would-go how! soul-of-me

אֱלֹהִים בְּקוֹל־ רִנָּה וְתוֹדָה הָמוֹן חוֹגֵג׃
being-festive throng and-thanksgiving shout-of-joy with-sound-of God

מַה־ תִּשְׁתּוֹחֲחִי ׀ נַפְשִׁי וַתֶּהֱמִי עָלָי
within-me and-are-you-disturbed soul-of-me are-you-downcast why? (6)

הוֹחִילִי לֵאלֹהִים כִּי־ עוֹד אוֹדֶנּוּ יְשׁוּעוֹת †פָּנָיו׃
presences-of-him† saving-helps-of I-will-praise-him yet for in-God put-hope!

אֱלֹהַי† עָלַי נַפְשִׁי תִשְׁתּוֹחָח עַל־ כֵּן אֶזְכָּרְךָ
I-will-remember-you this for she-is-downcast soul-of-me within-me †God-of-me (7)

מֵאֶרֶץ יַרְדֵּן וְחֶרְמוֹנִים מֵהַר מִצְעָר׃ תְּהוֹם־אֶל־
to deep (8) Mizar from-Mount-of and-heights-of-Hermon Jordan from-land-of

תְּהוֹם קוֹרֵא לְקוֹל צִנּוֹרֶיךָ כָּל־ מִשְׁבָּרֶיךָ
waves-of-you all-of waterfalls-of-you in-roar-of one-calling deep

וְגַלֶּיךָ עָלַי עָבָרוּ׃ יוֹמָם ׀ יְצַוֶּה יְהוָה ׀
Yahweh he-directs by-day (9) they-swept over-me and-breakers-of-you

חַסְדּוֹ וּבַלַּיְלָה שִׁירֹה° עִמִּי תְּפִלָּה לְאֵל
to-God-of prayer with-me song-of-him and-at-the-night love-of-him

חַיָּי׃ אוֹמְרָה ׀ לְאֵל סַלְעִי לָמָה שְׁכַחְתָּנִי לָמָּה־ קֹדֵר
mourning why? you-forgot-me why? Rock-of-me to-God I-say (10) lives-of-me

אֵלֵךְ בְּלַחַץ אוֹיֵב׃ בְּרֶצַח ׀
with-mortal-agony (11) one-being-enemy in-oppression-of I-must-go-about

בְּעַצְמוֹתַי חֵרְפוּנִי צוֹרְרָי בְּאָמְרָם אֵלַי
to-me as-to-say-them ones-being-foes-of-me they-taunt-me in-bones-of-me

כָּל־ הַיּוֹם אַיֵּה אֱלֹהֶיךָ׃ מַה־ תִּשְׁתּוֹחֲחִי ׀ נַפְשִׁי
soul-of-me are-you-downcast why? (12) God-of-you where? the-day all-of

וּמַה־ תֶּהֱמִי עָלַי הוֹחִילִי לֵאלֹהִים כִּי־עוֹד אוֹדֶנּוּ
I-will-praise-him yet for in-God put-hope! within-me are-you-disturbed and-why?

BOOK II

Psalms 42-72

Psalm 42[a]

For the director of music. A *maskil*[b] of the Sons of Korah.

1 As the deer pants for streams
of water,
so my soul pants for you, O
God.
2 My soul thirsts for God, for the
living God.
When can I go and meet
with God?
3 My tears have been my food
day and night,
while men say to me all day
long,
"Where is your God?"
4 These things I remember
as I pour out my soul:
how I used to go with the
multitude,
leading the procession to the
house of God,
with shouts of joy and
thanksgiving
among the festive throng.

5 Why are you downcast, O my
soul?
Why so disturbed within
me?
Put your hope in God,
for I will yet praise him,
my Savior and 6 my God.

My[c] soul is downcast within
me;
therefore I will remember
you
from the land of the Jordan,
the heights of
Hermon—from Mount
Mizar.
7 Deep calls to deep
in the roar of your
waterfalls;
all your waves and breakers
have swept over me.

8 By day the LORD directs his
love,
at night his song is with
me—
a prayer to the God of my
life.

9 I say to God my Rock,
"Why have you forgotten
me?
Why must I go about
mourning,
oppressed by the enemy?"
10 My bones suffer mortal agony
as my foes taunt me,
saying to me all day long,
"Where is your God?"

11 Why are you downcast, O my

[a] In many Hebrew manuscripts Psalms 42 and 43 constitute one psalm.
[b] Title: Probably a literary or musical term
[c] 5,6 A few Hebrew manuscripts, Septuagint and Syriac; most Hebrew manuscripts *praise him for his saving help. / 6O my God, my*

*Heading, *1* See the note on page 349.

†6,7 The NIV reads with some mss and versions פָּנַי וֵאלֹהָי׃ *and-God-of-me faces-of-me* as in verse 12.

°9 ק שִׁירוֹ

יְשׁוּעֹת פָּנַי וֵאלֹהָי׃ שָׁפְטֵנִי אֱלֹהִים׀
God vindicate-me! (43:1) and-God-of-me faces-of-me saving-helps-of

וְרִיבָה רִיבִי מִגּוֹי לֹא־חָסִיד מֵאִישׁ־מִרְמָה
deceit from-man-of godly not against-nation cause-of-me and-plead!

וְעַוְלָה תְפַלְּטֵנִי׃ כִּי־אַתָּה׀ אֱלֹהֵי מָעוּזִּי לָמָה
why? stronghold-of-me God-of you indeed (2) you-rescue-me and-wickedness

זְנַחְתָּנִי לָמָּה־קֹדֵר אֶתְהַלֵּךְ בְּלַחַץ אוֹיֵב׃
one-being-enemy in-oppression-of must-I-go-about mourning why? you-rejected-me

שְׁלַח־אוֹרְךָ וַאֲמִתְּךָ הֵמָּה יַנְחוּנִי
let-them-guide-me they and-truth-of-you light-of-you send-forth! (3)

יְבִיאוּנִי אֶל־הַר־קָדְשְׁךָ וְאֶל־מִשְׁכְּנוֹתֶיךָ׃
dwellings-of-you and-to holiness-of-you mountain-of to let-them-bring-me

וְאָבוֹאָה׀ אֶל־מִזְבַּח אֱלֹהִים אֶל־אֵל שִׂמְחַת גִּילִי
delight-of-me joy-of God to God altar-of to then-I-will-go (4)

וְאוֹדְךָ בְכִנּוֹר אֱלֹהִים אֱלֹהָי׃ מַה־תִּשְׁתּוֹחֲחִי׀
are-you-downcast why? (5) God-of-me God with-harp and-I-will-praise-you

נַפְשִׁי וּמַה־תֶּהֱמִי עָלָי הוֹחִילִי לֵאלֹהִים כִּי־עוֹד
yet for in-God put-hope! within-me are-you-disturbed and-why? soul-of-me

אוֹדֶנּוּ יְשׁוּעֹת פָּנַי וֵאלֹהָי׃
and-God-of-me faces-of-me saving-helps-of I-will-praise-him

לַמְנַצֵּחַ לִבְנֵי־קֹרַח מַשְׂכִּיל׃ אֱלֹהִים׀ בְּאָזְנֵינוּ
with-ears-of-us God (2) maskil Korah of-sons-of for-the-one-directing *(44:1)

שָׁמַעְנוּ אֲבוֹתֵינוּ סִפְּרוּ־לָנוּ פֹּעַל פָּעַלְתָּ בִימֵיהֶם
in-days-of-them you-did deed to-us they-told fathers-of-us we-heard

בִּימֵי קֶדֶם׃ אַתָּה׀ יָדְךָ גּוֹיִם הוֹרַשְׁתָּ
you-drove-out nations hand-of-you you (3) long-ago in-days-of

וַתִּטָּעֵם תָּרַע לְאֻמִּים וַתְּשַׁלְּחֵם׃
and-you-made-flourish-them to-peoples you-crushed and-you-planted-them

כִּי לֹא בְחַרְבָּם יָרְשׁוּ אָרֶץ וּזְרוֹעָם לֹא־
not and-arm-of-them land they-won by-sword-of-them not for (4)

הוֹשִׁיעָה לָּמוֹ כִּי־יְמִינְךָ וּזְרוֹעֲךָ וְאוֹר
and-light-of and-arm-of-you right-hand-of-you but to-them she-brought-victory

פָּנֶיךָ כִּי רְצִיתָם׃ אַתָּה־הוּא מַלְכִּי אֱלֹהִים צַוֵּה
decree! God King-of-me he you (5) you-loved-them for faces-of-you

יְשׁוּעוֹת יַעֲקֹב׃ בְּךָ צָרֵינוּ נְנַגֵּחַ
we-push-back enemies-of-us through-you (6) Jacob victories-of

בְּשִׁמְךָ נָבוּס קָמֵינוּ׃ כִּי לֹא
not indeed (7) ones-being-foes-of-us we-trample through-name-of-you

soul?
Why so disturbed within me?
Put your hope in God,
for I will yet praise him,
my Savior and my God.

Psalm 43[w]

1 Vindicate me, O God,
and plead my cause against an ungodly nation;
rescue me from deceitful and wicked men.
2 You are God my stronghold.
Why have you rejected me?
Why must I go about mourning,
oppressed by the enemy?
3 Send forth your light and your truth,
let them guide me;
let them bring me to your holy mountain,
to the place where you dwell.
4 Then will I go to the altar of God,
to God, my joy and my delight.
I will praise you with the harp,
O God, my God.

5 Why are you downcast, O my soul?
Why so disturbed within me?
Put your hope in God,
for I will yet praise him,
my Savior and my God.

Psalm 44

For the director of music. Of the Sons of Korah. A *maskil.*[x]

1 We have heard with our ears, O God;
our fathers have told us
what you did in their days,
in days long ago.
2 With your hand you drove out the nations
and planted our fathers;
you crushed the peoples
and made our fathers flourish.
3 It was not by their sword that they won the land,
nor did their arm bring them victory;
it was your right hand, your arm,
and the light of your face,
for you loved them.

4 You are my King and my God,
who decrees[y] victories for Jacob.
5 Through you we push back our enemies;
through your name we trample our foes.

[w] In many Hebrew manuscripts Psalms 42 and 43 constitute one psalm.
[x] Title: Probably a literary or musical term
[y] 4 Septuagint, Aquila and Syriac; Hebrew *King, O God; / command*

*Heading, *1* See the note on page 349.

בְקַשְׁתִּי אֶבְטָח וְחַרְבִּי לֹא תוֹשִׁיעֵנִי׃ כִּי

in-bow-of-me I-trust and-sword-of-me not she-brings-victory-to-me (8) but

הוֹשַׁעְתָּנוּ מִצָּרֵינוּ וּמְשַׂנְאֵינוּ

you-give-victory-to-us over-enemies-of-us and-ones-being-adversaries-of-us

הֱבִישׁוֹתָ׃ בֵּאלֹהִים הִלַּלְנוּ כָל־ הַיּוֹם וְשִׁמְךָ ׀ לְעוֹלָם

you-shame (9) in-God we-boast all-of the-day and-name-of-you to-forever

נוֹדֶה סֶלָה׃ אַף־ זָנַחְתָּ וַתַּכְלִימֵנוּ וְלֹא־

we-will-praise selah (10) but you-rejected and-you-humbled-us and-not

תֵצֵא בְּצִבְאוֹתֵינוּ׃ תְּשִׁיבֵנוּ אָחוֹר מִנִּי־ צָר

you-go-out with-armies-of-us (11) you-turned-us back before enemy

וּמְשַׂנְאֵינוּ שָׁסוּ לָמוֹ׃ תִּתְּנֵנוּ

and-ones-being-adversaries-of-us they-plundered from-us (12) you-gave-up-us

כְּצֹאן מַאֲכָל וּבַגּוֹיִם זֵרִיתָנוּ׃ תִּמְכֹּר־

like-sheep-of devouring and-among-the-nations you-scattered-us (13) you-sold

עַמְּךָ בְלֹא־ הוֹן וְלֹא־ רִבִּיתָ בִּמְחִירֵיהֶם׃

people-of-you for-no great-price and-nothing you-gained from-sales-of-them

תְּשִׂימֵנוּ חֶרְפָּה לִשְׁכֵנֵינוּ לַעַג וָקֶלֶס

(14) you-made-us reproach to-neighbors-of-us scorn and-derision

לִסְבִיבוֹתֵינוּ׃ תְּשִׂימֵנוּ מָשָׁל בַּגּוֹיִם מְנוֹד־ רֹאשׁ

to-ones-around-us (15) you-made-us byword among-the-nations shaking-of head

†בַּל־אֻמִּים׃ כָּל־ הַיּוֹם כְּלִמָּתִי נֶגְדִּי וּבֹשֶׁת

†among-the-peoples (16) all-of the-day disgrace-of-me before-me and-shame-of

פָּנַי כִּסָּתְנִי׃ מִקּוֹל מְחָרֵף וּמְגַדֵּף

faces-of-me she-covers-me (17) at-taunt-of one-reproaching and-one-reviling

מִפְּנֵי אוֹיֵב וּמִתְנַקֵּם׃ כָּל־ זֹאת

because-of one-being-enemy even-one-avenging (18) all-of this

בָּאַתְנוּ וְלֹא שְׁכַחֲנוּךָ וְלֹא־ שִׁקַּרְנוּ

she-happened-to-us though-not we-forgot-you and-not we-were-false

בִּבְרִיתֶךָ׃ לֹא־ נָסוֹג אָחוֹר לִבֵּנוּ וַתֵּט

to-covenant-of-you (19) not he-turned back heart-of-us or-she-strayed

אֲשֻׁרֵינוּ מִנִּי אָרְחֶךָ׃ כִּי דִכִּיתָנוּ בִּמְקוֹם תַּנִּים

feet-of-us from path-of-you (20) but you-crushed-us into-haunt-of jackals

וַתְּכַס עָלֵינוּ בְצַלְמָוֶת׃ אִם־ שָׁכַחְנוּ שֵׁם

and-you-covered over-us with-deep-darkness (21) if we-forgot name-of

אֱלֹהֵינוּ וַנִּפְרֹשׂ כַּפֵּינוּ לְאֵל זָר׃ הֲלֹא

God-of-us or-we-spread-out hands-of-us to-god being-foreign (22) not?

אֱלֹהִים יַחֲקָר־ זֹאת כִּי־ הוּא יֹדֵעַ תַּעֲלֻמוֹת לֵב׃

God would-he-have-discovered this since he one-knowing secrets-of heart

6 I do not trust in my bow,
my sword does not bring
me victory;
7 but you give us victory over
our enemies,
you put our adversaries to
shame.
8 In God we make our boast all
day long,
and we will praise your
name forever. *Selah*

9 But now you have rejected and
humbled us;
you no longer go out with
our armies.
10 You made us retreat before the
enemy,
and our adversaries have
plundered us.
11 You gave us up to be devoured
like sheep
and have scattered us
among the nations.
12 You sold your people for a
pittance,
gaining nothing from their
sale.

13 You have made us a reproach
to our neighbors,
the scorn and derision of
those around us.
14 You have made us a byword
among the nations;
the peoples shake their
heads at us.
15 My disgrace is before me all
day long,
and my face is covered with
shame
16 at the taunts of those who
reproach and revile me,
because of the enemy, who
is bent on revenge.

17 All this happened to us,
though we had not forgotten
you
or been false to your
covenant.
18 Our hearts had not turned
back;
our feet had not strayed
from your path.
19 But you crushed us and made
us a haunt for jackals
and covered us over with
deep darkness.

20 If we had forgotten the name
of our God
or spread out our hands to a
foreign god,
21 would not God have
discovered it,
since he knows the secrets
of the heart?

*See the note on page 349.

†*15* Most mss read these two words as one with *sheva* under the *lamed* (בלא׳).

כִּֽי־עָ֭לֶיךָ הֹרַ֣גְנוּ כָל־הַיּ֑וֹם נֶ֝חְשַׁ֗בְנוּ כְּצֹ֣אן
as-sheep-of we-are-considered the-day all-of we-face-death for-you yet (23)

טִבְחָֽה׃ ע֤וּרָה׀ לָ֖מָּה תִישַׁ֥ן׀ אֲדֹנָ֑י הָ֝קִ֗יצָה אַל־תִּזְנַ֥ח
you-reject not rouse-yourself! Lord you-sleep why? awake! (24) slaughter

לָנֶֽצַח׃ לָֽמָּה־פָנֶ֥יךָ תַסְתִּ֑יר תִּשְׁכַּ֖ח עָנְיֵ֣נוּ
misery-of-us you-forget you-hide faces-of-you why? (25) to-forever

וְֽלַחֲצֵֽנוּ׃ כִּ֤י שָׁ֣חָה לֶעָפָ֣ר נַפְשֵׁ֑נוּ
self-of-us to-the-dust she-is-brought-down indeed (26) and-oppression-of-us

דָּבְקָ֖ה לָאָ֣רֶץ בִּטְנֵֽנוּ׃ ק֭וּמָה עֶזְרָ֣תָה לָּ֑נוּ
to-us as-help rise-up! (27) body-of-us to-the-ground she-clings

וּ֝פְדֵ֗נוּ לְמַ֣עַן חַסְדֶּֽךָ׃ לַמְנַצֵּ֥חַ
for-the-one-directing *(45:1) unfailing-love-of-you because-of and-redeem-us!

עַל־שֹׁשַׁנִּ֗ים לִבְנֵי־קֹ֑רַח מַ֝שְׂכִּ֗יל שִׁ֣יר יְדִידֹֽת׃ רָ֘חַ֤שׁ
he-is-stirred (2) weddings song-of maskil Korah of-sons-of lilies to

לִבִּ֨י׀ דָּ֘בָ֤ר ט֗וֹב אֹמֵ֣ר אָ֭נִי מַעֲשַׂ֣י לְמֶ֑לֶךְ לְ֝שׁוֹנִ֗י
tongue-of-me for-king verses-of-me I one-reciting noble theme heart-of-me

עֵ֤ט׀ סוֹפֵ֬ר מָהִֽיר׃ יָפְיָפִ֡יתָ מִבְּנֵ֬י אָדָ֗ם
man more-than-sons-of you-are-excellent (3) skillful writer pen-of

ה֣וּצַק חֵ֭ן בְּשְׂפְתוֹתֶ֑יךָ† עַל־כֵּ֤ן בֵּרַכְךָ֖ אֱלֹהִ֣ים לְעוֹלָֽם׃
to-forever God he-blessed-you this for on-lips-of-you grace he-was-anointed

חֲגוֹר־חַרְבְּךָ֣ עַל־יָרֵ֣ךְ גִּבּ֑וֹר ה֝וֹדְךָ֗ וַהֲדָרֶֽךָ׃
and-majesty-of-you splendor-of-you mighty-one side upon sword-of-you gird! (4)

וַהֲדָרְךָ֙׀ צְלַ֬ח רְכַ֗ב עַֽל־דְּבַר־אֱ֭מֶת
truth behalf-of in ride-forth! be-victorious! and-majesty-of-you (5)

וְעַנְוָה־צֶ֑דֶק וְתוֹרְךָ֖ נוֹרָא֣וֹת
deeds-being-awesome and-let-her-display-you righteousness and-humility

יְמִינֶֽךָ׃ חִצֶּ֗יךָ שְׁנוּנִ֥ים עַ֭מִּים תַּחְתֶּ֣יךָ
beneath-you nations ones-being-sharp arrows-of-you (6) right-hand-of-you

יִפְּל֑וּ בְּ֝לֵ֗ב אוֹיְבֵ֥י הַמֶּֽלֶךְ׃ כִּסְאֲךָ֣
throne-of-you (7) the-king ones-being-enemies-of into-heart-of let-them-fall

אֱ֭לֹהִים עוֹלָ֣ם וָעֶ֑ד שֵׁ֥בֶט מִ֝ישֹׁ֗ר שֵׁ֣בֶט מַלְכוּתֶֽךָ׃
kingdom-of-you scepter-of justice scepter-of and-ever forever God

אָהַ֣בְתָּ צֶּדֶק֮ וַתִּשְׂנָ֫א רֶ֥שַׁע עַל־כֵּ֤ן׀ מְשָׁחֲךָ֡
he-anointed-you this for wickedness and-you-hate righteousness you-love (8)

אֱלֹהִ֣ים אֱ֭לֹהֶיךָ שֶׁ֥מֶן שָׂשׂ֗וֹן מֵֽחֲבֵרֶֽיךָ׃ מֹר־וַאֲהָל֣וֹת
and-aloes myrrh (9) above-companions-of-you joy oil-of God-of-you God

קְ֭צִיעוֹת כָּל־בִּגְדֹתֶ֑יךָ מִֽן־הֵ֥יכְלֵי שֵׁ֝֗ן מִנִּ֥י שִׂמְּחֽוּךָ׃
they-made-glad-you strings ivory palaces-of from robes-of-you all-of cassias

22 Yet for your sake we face death all day long;
we are considered as sheep to be slaughtered.
23 Awake, O Lord! Why do you sleep?
Rouse yourself! Do not reject us forever.
24 Why do you hide your face
and forget our misery and oppression?
25 We are brought down to the dust;
our bodies cling to the ground.
26 Rise up and help us;
redeem us because of your unfailing love.

Psalm 45

For the director of music. To the tune of "Lilies." Of the Sons of Korah. A *maskil*.[z] A wedding song.

1 My heart is stirred by a noble theme
as I recite my verses for the king;
my tongue is the pen of a skillful writer.
2 You are the most excellent of men
and your lips have been anointed with grace,
since God has blessed you forever.
3 Gird your sword upon your side, O mighty one;
clothe yourself with splendor and majesty.
4 In your majesty ride forth victoriously
in behalf of truth, humility and righteousness;
let your right hand display awesome deeds.
5 Let your sharp arrows pierce the hearts of the king's enemies;
let the nations fall beneath your feet.
6 Your throne, O God, will last for ever and ever;
a scepter of justice will be the scepter of your kingdom.
7 You love righteousness and hate wickedness;
therefore God, your God, has set you above your companions
by anointing you with the oil of joy.
8 All your robes are fragrant with myrrh and aloes and cassia;
from palaces adorned with ivory
the music of the strings makes you glad.

z Title: Probably a literary or musical term

*Heading, *1* See the note on page 349.

†*3* Most mss have *hireq* under the *sin* (בִּשְׂפְ׳).

בְּנוֹת מְלָכִים בְּיִקְּרוֹתֶיךָ נִצְּבָה שֵׁגַל
royal-bride she-stands among-honored-women-of-you kings daughters-of (10)

לִימִינְךָ בְּכֶתֶם אוֹפִיר׃ שִׁמְעִי־ בַת וּרְאִי
and-consider! daughter listen! (11) Ophir in-gold-of at-right-hand-of-you

וְהַטִּי אָזְנֵךְ וְשִׁכְחִי עַמֵּךְ וּבֵית אָבִיךְ׃
father-of-you and-house-of people-of-you and-forget! ear-of-you and-give!

וְיִתְאָו הַמֶּלֶךְ יָפְיֵךְ כִּי־ הוּא אֲדֹנַיִךְ
lords-of-you he for beauty-of-you the-king and-he-is-enthralled (12)

וְהִשְׁתַּחֲוִי־ לוֹ׃ וּבַת־ צֹר בְּמִנְחָה פָּנַיִךְ יְחַלּוּ
they-will-seek faces-of-you with-gift Tyre and-Daughter-of (13) to-him so-honor!

עֲשִׁירֵי עָם׃ כָּל־ כְּבוּדָּה בַת־ מֶלֶךְ פְּנִימָה
at-within king daughter-of glorious all-of (14) people wealthy-men-of

מִמִּשְׁבְּצוֹת זָהָב לְבוּשָׁהּ׃ לִרְקָמוֹת תּוּבַל
she-is-led in-embroidered-garments (15) gown-of-her gold with-interweavings-of

לַמֶּלֶךְ בְּתוּלוֹת אַחֲרֶיהָ רֵעוֹתֶיהָ מוּבָאוֹת לָךְ׃
to-you ones-being-brought companions-of-her following-her virgins to-the-king

תּוּבַלְנָה בִּשְׂמָחֹת וָגִיל תְּבֹאֶינָה בְּהֵיכַל מֶלֶךְ׃
king into-palace-of they-enter and-gladness with-joy they-are-led-in (16)

תַּחַת אֲבֹתֶיךָ יִהְיוּ בָנֶיךָ תְּשִׁיתֵמוֹ
you-will-make-them sons-of-you they-will-be fathers-of-you in-place-of (17)

לְשָׂרִים בְּכָל־ הָאָרֶץ׃ אַזְכִּירָה שִׁמְךָ
name-of-you I-will-perpetuate-memory (18) the-land through-all-of as-princes

בְּכָל־ דֹּר וָדֹר עַל־ כֵּן עַמִּים יְהוֹדֻךָ
they-will-praise-you nations this for and-generation generation through-all-of

לְעֹלָם וָעֶד׃ לַמְנַצֵּחַ לִבְנֵי־ קֹרַח
Korah of-sons-of for-the-one-directing *(46:1) and-ever to-forever

עַל־ עֲלָמוֹת שִׁיר׃ אֱלֹהִים לָנוּ מַחֲסֶה וָעֹז עֶזְרָה בְצָרוֹת
in-troubles help and-strength refuge to-us God (2) song alamoth according-to

נִמְצָא מְאֹד׃ עַל־ כֵּן לֹא־ נִירָא בְּהָמִיר אָרֶץ
earth through-to-give-way we-will-fear not this for (3) ever one-being-present

וּבְמוֹט הָרִים בְּלֵב יַמִּים׃ יֶהֱמוּ יֶחְמְרוּ
they-foam they-roar (4) seas into-heart-of mountains and-though-to-fall

מֵימָיו יִרְעֲשׁוּ־ הָרִים בְּגַאֲוָתוֹ סֶלָה׃ נָהָר
river (5) selah with-surging-of-him mountains they-quake waters-of-him

פְּלָגָיו יְשַׂמְּחוּ עִיר־אֱלֹהִים קְדֹשׁ מִשְׁכְּנֵי עֶלְיוֹן׃
Most-High dwellings-of holy-place-of God city-of they-make-glad streams-of-him

אֱלֹהִים בְּקִרְבָּהּ בַּל־ תִּמּוֹט יַעְזְרֶהָ אֱלֹהִים לִפְנוֹת
to-come God he-will-help-her she-will-fall not in-inside-of-her God (6)

9Daughters of kings are among
your honored women;
at your right hand is the
royal bride in gold of
Ophir.
10Listen, O daughter, consider
and give ear:
Forget your people and your
father's house.
11The king is enthralled by your
beauty;
honor him, for he is your
lord.
12The Daughter of Tyre will
come with a gift,[a]
men of wealth will seek
your favor.
13All glorious is the princess
within ⌞her chamber⌟;
her gown is interwoven
with gold.
14In embroidered garments she
is led to the king;
her virgin companions
follow her
and are brought to you.
15They are led in with joy and
gladness;
they enter the palace of the
king.
16Your sons will take the place
of your fathers;
you will make them princes
throughout the land.
17I will perpetuate your memory
through all generations;
therefore the nations will
praise you for ever and
ever.

Psalm 46

For the director of music. Of the Sons of Korah. According to *alamoth*.[b] A song.

1God is our refuge and
strength,
an ever present help in
trouble.
2Therefore we will not fear,
though the earth give
way
and the mountains fall into
the heart of the sea,
3though its waters roar and
foam
and the mountains quake
with their surging. *Selah*
4There is a river whose streams
make glad the city of
God,
the holy place where the
Most High dwells.
5God is within her, she will not
fall;
God will help her at break
of day.

[a]12 Or *A Tyrian robe is among the gifts*
[b]Title: Probably a musical term

*Heading, *1* See the note on page 349.

בֹּקֶר׃ הָמוּ גוֹיִם מָטוּ מַמְלָכוֹת נָתַן
he-lifts kingdoms they-fall nations they-are-in-uproar (7) daybreak

בְּקוֹלוֹ תָּמוּג אָרֶץ׃ יְהוָה צְבָאוֹת עִמָּנוּ מִשְׂגָּב־לָנוּ
to-us fortress with-us Hosts Yahweh-of (8) earth she-melts to-voice-of-him

אֱלֹהֵי יַעֲקֹב סֶלָה׃ לְכוּ־חֲזוּ מִפְעֲלוֹת יְהוָה אֲשֶׁר־שָׂם שַׁמּוֹת
desolations he-brought that Yahweh works-of see! come! (9) selah Jacob God-of

בָּאָרֶץ׃ מַשְׁבִּית מִלְחָמוֹת עַד־קְצֵה הָאָרֶץ קֶשֶׁת יְשַׁבֵּר
he-breaks bow the-earth end-of to wars one-making-cease (10) on-the-earth

וְקִצֵּץ חֲנִית עֲגָלוֹת† יִשְׂרֹף בָּאֵשׁ׃ הַרְפּוּ וּדְעוּ
and-know! be-still! (11) with-fire he-burns †chariots spear and-he-shatters

כִּי־אָנֹכִי אֱלֹהִים אָרוּם בַּגּוֹיִם אָרוּם בָּאָרֶץ׃
in-the-earth I-will-be-exalted among-the-nations I-will-be-exalted God I that

יְהוָה צְבָאוֹת עִמָּנוּ מִשְׂגָּב־לָנוּ אֱלֹהֵי יַעֲקֹב סֶלָה׃
selah Jacob God-of to-us fortress with-us Hosts Yahweh-of (12)

לַמְנַצֵּחַ ׀ לִבְנֵי־קֹרַח מִזְמוֹר׃ כָּל־הָעַמִּים
the-nations all-of (2) psalm Korah of-sons-of for-the-one-directing *(47:1)

תִּקְעוּ־כָף הָרִיעוּ לֵאלֹהִים בְּקוֹל רִנָּה׃ כִּי־יְהוָה עֶלְיוֹן
Most-High Yahweh how! (3) joy with-cry-of to-God shout! hand clap!

נוֹרָא מֶלֶךְ גָּדוֹל עַל־כָּל־הָאָרֶץ׃ יַדְבֵּר עַמִּים
nations he-subdued (4) the-earth all-of over great King one-being-awesome

תַּחְתֵּינוּ וּלְאֻמִּים תַּחַת רַגְלֵינוּ׃ יִבְחַר־לָנוּ אֶת־נַחֲלָתֵנוּ
inheritance-of-us *** for-us he-chose (5) feet-of-us under and-peoples under-us

אֶת גְּאוֹן יַעֲקֹב אֲשֶׁר־אָהֵב סֶלָה׃ עָלָה אֱלֹהִים בִּתְרוּעָה
with-shout-of-joy God he-ascended (6) selah he-loved whom Jacob pride-of ***

יְהוָה בְּקוֹל שׁוֹפָר׃ זַמְּרוּ אֱלֹהִים זַמֵּרוּ
sing-praises! God sing-praises! (7) trumpet amid-sound-of Yahweh

זַמְּרוּ לְמַלְכֵּנוּ זַמֵּרוּ׃ כִּי מֶלֶךְ כָּל־הָאָרֶץ
the-earth all-of King-of for (8) sing-praises! to-King-of-us sing-praises!

אֱלֹהִים זַמְּרוּ מַשְׂכִּיל׃ מָלַךְ אֱלֹהִים עַל־גּוֹיִם אֱלֹהִים יָשַׁב ׀
he-sits God nations over God he-reigns (9) maskil sing-praise! God

עַל־כִּסֵּא קָדְשׁוֹ׃ נְדִיבֵי עַמִּים ׀ נֶאֱסָפוּ עַם
people-of they-assemble nations nobles-of (10) holiness-of-him throne-of on

אֱלֹהֵי אַבְרָהָם כִּי לֵאלֹהִים מָגִנֵּי־אֶרֶץ מְאֹד נַעֲלָה׃
he-is-exalted greatly earth shields-of to-God for Abraham God-of

שִׁיר מִזְמוֹר לִבְנֵי־קֹרַח׃ גָּדוֹל יְהוָה וּמְהֻלָּל
and-one-being-praised Yahweh great (2) Korah of-sons-of psalm song *(48:1)

מְאֹד בְּעִיר אֱלֹהֵינוּ הַר־קָדְשׁוֹ׃ יְפֵה
beautiful-of (3) holiness-of-him mountain-of God-of-us in-city-of greatly

---

6 Nations are in uproar,
kingdoms fall;
he lifts his voice, the earth
melts.

7 The LORD Almighty is with us;
the God of Jacob is our
fortress. *Selah*

8 Come and see the works of the
LORD,
the desolations he has
brought on the earth.
9 He makes wars cease to the
ends of the earth;
he breaks the bow and
shatters the spear,
he burns the shields[c] with
fire.
10 "Be still, and know that I am
God;
I will be exalted among the
nations,
I will be exalted in the
earth."

11 The LORD Almighty is with us;
the God of Jacob is our
fortress. *Selah*

Psalm 47

For the director of music. Of the Sons of Korah. A psalm.

1 Clap your hands, all you
nations;
shout to God with cries of
joy.
2 How awesome is the LORD
Most High,
the great King over all the
earth!
3 He subdued nations under us,
peoples under our feet.
4 He chose our inheritance for
us,
the pride of Jacob, whom he
loved. *Selah*

5 God has ascended amid shouts
of joy,
the LORD amid the sounding
of trumpets.
6 Sing praises to God, sing
praises;
sing praises to our King,
sing praises.

7 For God is the King of all the
earth;
sing to him a psalm[d] of
praise.
8 God reigns over the nations;
God is seated on his holy
throne.
9 The nobles of the nations
assemble
as the people of the God of
Abraham,
for the kings[e] of the earth
belong to God;
he is greatly exalted.

Psalm 48

A song. A psalm of the Sons of Korah.

1 Great is the LORD, and most

[c]9 Or *chariots*
[d]7 Or *a maskil* (probably a literary or musical term)
[e]9 Or *shields*

***Heading, *1* See the note on page 349.**

†*10* The NIV repoints this word as וַעֲגָלוֹת, *and-shields.*

נוֹף מְשׂוֹשׂ כָּל־ הָאָרֶץ הַר־ צִיּוֹן יַרְכְּתֵי צָפוֹן

Zaphon utmost-heights-of Zion Mount-of the-earth whole-of joy-of loftiness

קִרְיַת מֶלֶךְ רָב׃ אֱלֹהִים בְּאַרְמְנוֹתֶיהָ נוֹדַע לְמִשְׂגָּב׃

as-fortress he-showed-himself in-citadels-of-her God (4) Great King city-of

כִּי־ הִנֵּה הַמְּלָכִים נוֹעֲדוּ עָבְרוּ יַחְדָּו׃

together they-advanced they-joined-forces the-kings see! when (5)

הֵמָּה רָאוּ כֵּן תָּמָהוּ נִבְהֲלוּ נֶחְפָּזוּ׃

they-fled they-were-terrified they-were-astounded thus they-saw they (6)

רְעָדָה אֲחָזָתַם שָׁם חִיל כַּיּוֹלֵדָה׃

like-the-woman-being-in-labor pain there she-seized-them trembling (7)

בְּרוּחַ קָדִים תְּשַׁבֵּר אֳנִיּוֹת תַּרְשִׁישׁ׃ כַּאֲשֶׁר שָׁמַעְנוּ ׀

we-heard just-as (9) Tarshish ships-of you-destroyed east by-wind-of (8)

כֵּן רָאִינוּ בְּעִיר־ יְהוָה צְבָאוֹת בְּעִיר אֱלֹהֵינוּ אֱלֹהִים

God God-of-us in-city-of Hosts Yahweh-of in-city-of we-saw so

יְכוֹנְנֶהָ עַד־ עוֹלָם סֶלָה׃ דִּמִּינוּ אֱלֹהִים חַסְדֶּךָ

unfailing-love-of-you God we-meditate (10) selah forever to he-makes-secure-her

בְּקֶרֶב הֵיכָלֶךָ׃ כְּשִׁמְךָ אֱלֹהִים כֵּן תְּהִלָּתְךָ עַל־

to praise-of-you so God like-name-of-you (11) temple-of-you at-within

קַצְוֵי־ אֶרֶץ צֶדֶק מָלְאָה יְמִינֶךָ׃ יִשְׂמַח ׀

he-rejoices (12) right-hand-of-you she-is-filled righteousness earth ends-of

הַר־ צִיּוֹן תָּגֵלְנָה בְּנוֹת יְהוּדָה לְמַעַן מִשְׁפָּטֶיךָ׃

judgments-of-you because-of Judah villages-of they-are-glad Zion Mount-of

סֹבּוּ צִיּוֹן וְהַקִּיפוּהָ סִפְרוּ מִגְדָּלֶיהָ׃ שִׁיתוּ

consider! (14) towers-of-her count! and-go-around-her! Zion walk-about! (13)

לִבְּכֶם ׀ לְחֵילָה פַּסְּגוּ אַרְמְנוֹתֶיהָ לְמַעַן תְּסַפְּרוּ

you-may-tell so-that citadels-of-her view! to-rampart-of-her heart-of-you

לְדוֹר אַחֲרוֹן׃ כִּי זֶה ׀ אֱלֹהִים אֱלֹהֵינוּ עוֹלָם וָעֶד הוּא

he and-ever forever God-of-us God this for (15) next to-generation

יְנַהֲגֵנוּ עַל־ מוּת׃ לַמְנַצֵּחַ ׀ לִבְנֵי־ קֹרַח

Korah of-sons-of for-the-one-directing *(49:1) to-die to he-will-guide-us

מִזְמוֹר׃ שִׁמְעוּ־ זֹאת כָּל־ הָעַמִּים הַאֲזִינוּ כָּל־ יֹשְׁבֵי חָלֶד׃

world ones-living-of all-of listen! the-peoples all-of this hear! (2) psalm

גַּם־ בְּנֵי אָדָם גַּם־ בְּנֵי־ אִישׁ יַחַד עָשִׁיר וְאֶבְיוֹן׃ פִּי

mouth-of-me (4) and-poor rich alike man sons-of both mankind sons-of both (3)

יְדַבֵּר חָכְמוֹת וְהָגוּת לִבִּי תְבוּנוֹת׃

understanding-things heart-of-me and-utterance-of words-of-wisdom he-will-speak

אַטֶּה לְמָשָׁל אָזְנִי אֶפְתַּח בְּכִנּוֹר חִידָתִי׃

riddle-of-me with-harp I-will-expound ear-of-me to-proverb I-will-turn (5)

worthy of praise,
in the city of our God, his
holy mountain.
2 It is beautiful in its loftiness,
the joy of the whole earth.
Like the utmost heights of
Zaphon[f] is Mount Zion,
the[g] city of the Great King.
3 God is in her citadels;
he has shown himself to be
her fortress.

4 When the kings joined forces,
when they advanced
together,
5 they saw ⌞her⌟ and were
astounded;
they fled in terror.
6 Trembling seized them there,
pain like that of a woman
in labor.
7 You destroyed them like ships
of Tarshish
shattered by an east wind.

8 As we have heard,
so have we seen
in the city of the LORD
Almighty,
in the city of our God:
God makes her secure
forever. *Selah*

9 Within your temple, O God,
we meditate on your
unfailing love.
10 Like your name, O God,
your praise reaches to the
ends of the earth;
your right hand is filled
with righteousness.
11 Mount Zion rejoices,
the villages of Judah are glad
because of your judgments.

12 Walk about Zion, go around
her,
count her towers,
13 consider well her ramparts,
view her citadels,
that you may tell of them to
the next generation.
14 For this God is our God for
ever and ever;
he will be our guide even to
the end.

Psalm 49

For the director of music. Of the Sons of Korah. A psalm.

1 Hear this, all you peoples;
listen, all who live in this
world,
2 both low and high,
rich and poor alike:
3 My mouth will speak words of
wisdom;
the utterance from my heart
will give understanding.
4 I will turn my ear to a
proverb;
with the harp I will
expound my riddle:

f2 *Zaphon* can refer to a sacred mountain or the direction north.
g2 Or *earth,* / *Mount Zion, on the northern side* / *of the*

*Heading, *1* See the note on page 349.

לָמָּה אִירָא בִּימֵי רָע עֲוֺן עֲקֵבַי

deceivers-of-me wickedness-of evil in-days-of should-I-fear why? (6)

יְסוּבֵּנִי׃ הַבֹּטְחִים עַל־ חֵילָם וּבְרֹב

and-in-greatness-of wealth-of-them in the-ones-trusting (7) he-surrounds-me

עָשְׁרָם יִתְהַלָּלוּ׃ אָח לֹא־ פָדֹה יִפְדֶּה אִישׁ

man he-can-redeem to-redeem not another (8) they-boast richness-of-them

לֹא־ יִתֵּן לֵאלֹהִים כָּפְרוֹ׃ וְיֵקַר פִּדְיוֹן

ransom-of for-he-is-costly (9) ransom-of-him to-God he-can-give not

נַפְשָׁם וְחָדַל לְעוֹלָם׃ וִיחִי־ עוֹד

on that-he-should-live (10) to-forever and-he-is-not-enough life-of-them

לָנֶצַח לֹא יִרְאֶה הַשָּׁחַת׃ כִּי יִרְאֶה ׀ חֲכָמִים יָמוּתוּ

they-die wise-men he-sees for (11) the-decay he-should-see not to-forever

יַחַד כְּסִיל וָבַעַר יֹאבֵדוּ וְעָזְבוּ לַאֲחֵרִים

to-others and-they-leave they-perish and-senseless foolish alike

חֵילָם׃ קִרְבָּם† בָּתֵּימוֹ ׀ לְעוֹלָם מִשְׁכְּנֹתָם

dwellings-of-them to-forever houses-of-them †thought-of-them (12) wealth-of-them

לְדֹר וָדֹר קָרְאוּ בִשְׁמוֹתָם עֲלֵי אֲדָמוֹת׃

lands to by-names-of-them they-called and-generation for-generation

וְאָדָם בִּיקָר בַּל־ יָלִין נִמְשַׁל כַּבְּהֵמוֹת

like-the-beasts he-is-like he-endures not despite-richness but-man (13)

נִדְמוּ׃ זֶה דַרְכָּם כֶּסֶל לָמוֹ וְאַחֲרֵיהֶם ׀

and-follower-of-them in-themselves trust fate-of-them this (14) they-perish

בְּפִיהֶם יִרְצוּ סֶלָה׃ כַּצֹּאן ׀ לִשְׁאוֹל

for-Sheol like-the-sheep (15) selah they-approve to-saying-of-them

שַׁתּוּ מָוֶת יִרְעֵם וַיִּרְדּוּ בָם

over-them and-they-will-rule he-will-feed-on-them death they-are-destined

יְשָׁרִים ׀ לַבֹּקֶר וְצִירָם° לְבַלּוֹת שְׁאוֹל מִזְּבֻל

from-mansion Sheol to-decay and-form-of-them in-the-morning upright-ones

לוֹ׃ אַךְ־אֱלֹהִים יִפְדֶּה נַפְשִׁי מִיַּד־ שְׁאוֹל כִּי

surely Sheol from-hand-of soul-of-me he-will-redeem God but (16) of-him

יִקָּחֵנִי סֶלָה׃ אַל־ תִּירָא כִּי־ יַעֲשִׁר אִישׁ כִּי־

when man he-grows-rich when you-be-overawed not (17) selah he-will-take-me

יִרְבֶּה כְּבוֹד בֵּיתוֹ׃ כִּי לֹא בְמוֹתוֹ

in-death-of-him not for (18) house-of-him splendor-of he-increases

יִקַּח הַכֹּל לֹא־ יֵרֵד אַחֲרָיו כְּבוֹדוֹ׃

splendor-of-him with-him he-will-descend not the-whole he-will-take

כִּי־ נַפְשׁוֹ בְּחַיָּיו יְבָרֵךְ וְיוֹדֻךָ

and-they-praise-you he-blessed during-lives-of-him self-of-him though (19)

5 Why should I fear when evil
days come,
when wicked deceivers
surround me—
6 those who trust in their wealth
and boast of their great
riches?
7 No man can redeem the life of
another
or give to God a ransom for
him—
8 the ransom for a life is costly,
no payment is ever
enough—
9 that he should live on forever
and not see decay.

10 For all can see that wise men
die;
the foolish and the senseless
alike perish
and leave their wealth to
others.
11 Their tombs will remain their
houses[h] forever,
their dwellings for endless
generations,
though they had[i] named
lands after themselves.

12 But man, despite his riches,
does not endure;
he is[j] like the beasts that
perish.

13 This is the fate of those who
trust in themselves,
and of their followers, who
approve their sayings.
Selah
14 Like sheep they are destined
for the grave,[k]
and death will feed on
them.
The upright will rule over
them in the morning;
their forms will decay in the
grave,[k]
far from their princely
mansions.
15 But God will redeem my soul[l]
from the grave;
he will surely take me to
himself. *Selah*

16 Do not be overawed when a
man grows rich,
when the splendor of his
house increases;
17 for he will take nothing with
him when he dies,
his splendor will not
descend with him.
18 Though while he lived he
counted himself blessed—
and men praise you when

[h] 11 Septuagint and Syriac; Hebrew *In their thoughts their houses will remain*
[i] 11 Or / *for they have*
[j] 12 Hebrew; Septuagint and Syriac *But a man who has riches without understanding / is*
[k] 14 Hebrew *Sheol;* also in verse 15
[l] 15 Or *redeem me*

*See the note on page 349.

†12 The NIV reads with some versions קִבְרָם, *tomb-of-them.*

°15 ק וצורם

כִּי־ תֵיטִיב לָךְ׃ תָּבוֹא עַד־ דּוֹר אֲבוֹתָיו
fathers-of-him generation-of to she-will-go (20) to-you you-prosper when

עַד־נֵצַח לֹא יִרְאוּ־ אוֹר׃ אָדָם בִּיקָר וְלֹא יָבִין
he-understands but-not with-richness man (21) light they-see not forever to

נִמְשַׁל כַּבְּהֵמוֹת נִדְמוּ׃ מִזְמוֹר לְאָסָף אֵל ׀ אֱלֹהִים
God Mighty-One of-Asaph psalm (50:1) they-perish like-the-beasts he-is-like

יְהוָה דִּבֶּר וַיִּקְרָא־ אָרֶץ מִמִּזְרַח־ שֶׁמֶשׁ עַד־ מְבֹאוֹ׃
setting-of-him to sun from-rising-of earth and-he-summons he-speaks Yahweh

מִצִּיּוֹן מִכְלַל־ יֹפִי אֱלֹהִים הוֹפִיעַ׃ יָבֹא אֱלֹהֵינוּ
God-of-us he-comes (3) he-shines-forth God beauty perfect-of from-Zion (2)

וְאַל־ יֶחֱרַשׁ אֵשׁ־ לְפָנָיו תֹּאכֵל וּסְבִיבָיו
and-ones-around-him she-devours before-him fire he-will-be-silent and-not

נִשְׂעֲרָה מְאֹד׃ יִקְרָא אֶל־ הַשָּׁמַיִם מֵעָל וְאֶל־ הָאָרֶץ
the-earth and-to at-above the-heavens to he-summons (4) greatly she-storms

לָדִין עַמּוֹ׃ אִסְפוּ־ לִי חֲסִידָי כֹּרְתֵי
ones-making-of consecrated-ones-of-me to-me gather! (5) people-of-him to-judge

בְרִיתִי עֲלֵי־ זָבַח׃ וַיַּגִּידוּ שָׁמַיִם צִדְקוֹ
righteousness-of-him heavens and-they-proclaim (6) sacrifice by covenant-of-me

כִּי־ אֱלֹהִים ׀ שֹׁפֵט הוּא סֶלָה׃ שִׁמְעָה עַמִּי ׀ וַאֲדַבֵּרָה יִשְׂרָאֵל
Israel and-I-will-speak people-of-me hear! (7) selah he one-judging God for

וְאָעִידָה בָּךְ אֱלֹהִים אֱלֹהֶיךָ אָנֹכִי׃ לֹא עַל־ זְבָחֶיךָ
sacrifices-of-you for not (8) I God-of-you God against-you and-I-will-testify

אוֹכִיחֶךָ וְעוֹלֹתֶיךָ לְנֶגְדִּי תָמִיד׃ לֹא־ אֶקַּח
I-need not (9) ever at-before-me or-burnt-offerings-of-you I-rebuke-you

מִבֵּיתְךָ פָר מִמִּכְלְאֹתֶיךָ עַתּוּדִים׃ כִּי־ לִי כָל־
every-of to-me for (10) goats from-pens-of-you bull from-stall-of-you

חַיְתוֹ־ יָעַר בְּהֵמוֹת בְּהַרְרֵי־ אָלֶף׃ יָדַעְתִּי כָּל־ עוֹף
bird-of every-of I-know (11) thousand on-hills-of cattles forest animal-of

הָרִים וְזִיז שָׂדַי עִמָּדִי׃ אִם־ אֶרְעַב לֹא־ אֹמַר
I-would-tell not I-were-hungry if (12) to-me field and-creature-of mountains

לָךְ כִּי־ לִי תֵּבֵל וּמְלֹאָהּ׃ הַאוֹכַל בְּשַׂר אַבִּירִים
bulls flesh-of do-I-eat? (13) and-all-in-her world to-me for to-you

וְדַם עַתּוּדִים אֶשְׁתֶּה׃ זְבַח לֵאלֹהִים תּוֹדָה
thank-offering to-God sacrifice! (14) do-I-drink goats or-blood-of

וְשַׁלֵּם לְעֶלְיוֹן נְדָרֶיךָ׃ וּקְרָאֵנִי בְּיוֹם צָרָה
trouble in-day-of and-call-upon-me! (15) vows-of-you to-Most-High and-fulfill!

אֲחַלֶּצְךָ וּתְכַבְּדֵנִי׃ וְלָרָשָׁע ׀ אָמַר
he-says but-to-the-wicked (16) and-you-will-honor-me I-will-deliver-you

you prosper—
19 he will join the generation of his fathers,
who will never see the light ⌊of life⌋.
20 A man who has riches without understanding
is like the beasts that perish.

Psalm 50

A psalm of Asaph.

1 The Mighty One, God, the LORD,
speaks and summons the earth
from the rising of the sun to the place where it sets.
2 From Zion, perfect in beauty,
God shines forth.
3 Our God comes and will not be silent;
a fire devours before him,
and around him a tempest rages.
4 He summons the heavens above,
and the earth, that he may judge his people:
5 "Gather to me my consecrated ones,
who made a covenant with me by sacrifice."
6 And the heavens proclaim his righteousness,
for God himself is judge.
Selah

7 "Hear, O my people, and I will speak,
O Israel, and I will testify against you:
I am God, your God.
8 I do not rebuke you for your sacrifices
or your burnt offerings,
which are ever before me.
9 I have no need of a bull from your stall
or of goats from your pens,
10 for every animal of the forest is mine,
and the cattle on a thousand hills.
11 I know every bird in the mountains,
and the creatures of the field are mine.
12 If I were hungry I would not tell you,
for the world is mine, and all that is in it.
13 Do I eat the flesh of bulls
or drink the blood of goats?
14 Sacrifice thank offerings to God,
fulfill your vows to the Most High,
15 and call upon me in the day of trouble;
I will deliver you, and you will honor me."
16 But to the wicked, God says:

*See the note on page 349.

אֱלֹהִים מַה־ לְּךָ לְסַפֵּר חֻקָּי וַתִּשָּׂא בְרִיתִי עֲלֵי־
on covenant-of-me or-you-take laws-of-me to-recite to-you what? God

פִיךָ׃ (17) וְאַתָּה שָׂנֵאתָ מוּסָר וַתַּשְׁלֵךְ דְּבָרַי
words-of-me and-you-cast instruction you-hate for-you (17) lip-of-you

אַחֲרֶיךָ׃ (18) אִם־ רָאִיתָ גַנָּב וַתִּרֶץ עִמּוֹ וְעִם
and-with with-him then-you-join thief you-see when (18) behind-you

מְנָאֲפִים חֶלְקֶךָ׃ (19) פִּיךָ שָׁלַחְתָּ בְרָעָה
for-evil you-use mouth-of-you (19) lot-of-you ones-committing-adultery

וּלְשׁוֹנְךָ תַּצְמִיד מִרְמָה׃ (20) תֵּשֵׁב בְּאָחִיךָ
against-brother-of-you you-sit (20) deceit you-harness-to and-tongue-of-you

תְּדַבֵּר בְּבֶן־ אִמְּךָ תִּתֶּן־ דֹּפִי׃ (21) אֵלֶּה עָשִׂיתָ
you-did these (21) slander you-give mother-of-you against-son-of you-speak

וְהֶחֱרַשְׁתִּי דִּמִּיתָ הֱיוֹת־ אֶהְיֶה כָמוֹךָ אוֹכִיחֲךָ
I-will-rebuke-you like-you I-was to-be you-thought and-I-kept-silent

וְאֶעֶרְכָה לְעֵינֶיךָ׃ (22) בִּינוּ־ נָא זֹאת
this now! consider! (22) before-eyes-of-you and-I-will-accuse

שֹׁכְחֵי אֱלוֹהַּ פֶּן־ אֶטְרֹף וְאֵין מַצִּיל׃
one-rescuing and-there-is-not I-will-tear-to-pieces or God ones-forgetting-of

(23) זֹבֵחַ תּוֹדָה יְכַבְּדָנְנִי וְשָׂם דֶּרֶךְ
way and-he-prepares he-honors-me thank-offering one-sacrificing (23)

אַרְאֶנּוּ בְּיֵשַׁע אֱלֹהִים׃ *(51:1) לַמְנַצֵּחַ מִזְמוֹר
psalm for-the-one-directing *(51:1) God to-salvation-of I-will-show-him

לְדָוִד׃ (2) בְּבוֹא־ אֵלָיו נָתָן הַנָּבִיא כַּאֲשֶׁר־ בָּא אֶל־
into he-went after-when the-prophet Nathan to-him when-to-come (2) of-David

בַּת־ שָׁבַע׃ (3) חָנֵּנִי אֱלֹהִים כְּחַסְדֶּךָ
according-to-unfailing-love-of-you God have-mercy-on-me! (3) Sheba Bath

כְּרֹב רַחֲמֶיךָ מְחֵה פְשָׁעָי׃
transgressions-of-me blot-out! compassions-of-you according-to-greatness-of

(4) הֶרֶבה° כַּבְּסֵנִי מֵעֲוֹנִי וּמֵחַטָּאתִי טַהֲרֵנִי׃
cleanse-me! and-from-sin-of-me of-iniquity-of-me wash-me! †make-many! (4)

(5) כִּי־ פְשָׁעַי אֲנִי אֵדָע וְחַטָּאתִי נֶגְדִּי תָמִיד׃
always before-me and-sin-of-me I-know I transgressions-of-me for (5)

(6) לְךָ לְבַדְּךָ חָטָאתִי וְהָרַע בְּעֵינֶיךָ עָשִׂיתִי
I-did in-eyes-of-you and-the-evil I-sinned by-yourself against-you (6)

לְמַעַן תִּצְדַּק בְּדָבְרֶךָ תִּזְכֶּה
you-are-justified when-to-speak-you you-are-proved-right so-that

בְשָׁפְטֶךָ׃ (7) הֵן־ בְּעָווֹן חוֹלָלְתִּי וּבְחֵטְא יֶחֱמַתְנִי
she-conceived-me and-in-sin I-was-born in-sin surely (7) when-to-judge-you

"What right have you to recite my laws
or take my covenant on your lips?
17 You hate my instruction
and cast my words behind you.
18 When you see a thief, you join with him;
you throw in your lot with adulterers.
19 You use your mouth for evil
and harness your tongue to deceit.
20 You speak continually against your brother
and slander your own mother's son.
21 These things you have done and I kept silent;
you thought I was altogether[m] like you.
But I will rebuke you
and accuse you to your face.

22 "Consider this, you who forget God,
or I will tear you to pieces, with none to rescue:
23 He who sacrifices thank offerings honors me,
and he prepares the way
so that I may show him[n] the salvation of God."

Psalm 51

For the director of music. A psalm of David. When the prophet Nathan came to him after David had committed adultery with Bathsheba.

1 Have mercy on me, O God,
according to your unfailing love;
according to your great compassion
blot out my transgressions.
2 Wash away all my iniquity
and cleanse me from my sin.

3 For I know my transgressions,
and my sin is always before me.
4 Against you, you only, have I sinned
and done what is evil in your sight,
so that you are proved right when you speak
and justified when you judge.
5 Surely I have been a sinner from birth,

m21 Or *thought the 'I AM' was*
n23 Or *and to him who considers his way / I will show*

***Heading, *1* The Hebrew numeration of this psalm begins with the "superscription" in English; thus there is a two-verse discrepancy throughout the psalm.**

†4 The Kethib form (הַרְבֵּה) is an infinitive, *to-be-many*.

°4 ק הרב

אִמִּי׃ (8) הֵן־ אֱמֶת חָפַצְתָּ בַטֻּחוֹת
in-the-inner-parts you-desire truth surely (8) mother-of-me

וּבְסָתֻם חָכְמָה תוֹדִיעֵנִי׃ (9) תְּחַטְּאֵנִי בְאֵזוֹב
with-hyssop you-cleanse-me (9) you-teach-me wisdom and-in-place-being-inmost

וְאֶטְהָר תְּכַבְּסֵנִי וּמִשֶּׁלֶג אַלְבִּין׃
I-will-be-white and-more-than-snow you-wash-me and-I-will-be-clean

(10) תַּשְׁמִיעֵנִי שָׂשׂוֹן וְשִׂמְחָה תָּגֵלְנָה עֲצָמוֹת דִּכִּיתָ׃
you-crushed bones let-them-rejoice and-gladness joy you-let-hear-me (10)

(11) הַסְתֵּר פָּנֶיךָ מֵחֲטָאָי וְכָל־ עֲוֺנֹתַי מְחֵה׃
blot-out! iniquities-of-me and-all-of from-sins-of-me faces-of-you hide! (11)

(12) לֵב טָהוֹר בְּרָא־ לִי אֱלֹהִים וְרוּחַ נָכוֹן חַדֵּשׁ
renew! being-steadfast and-spirit God in-me create! pure heart (12)

בְּקִרְבִּי׃ (13) אַל־ תַּשְׁלִיכֵנִי מִלְּפָנֶיךָ וְרוּחַ
or-Spirit-of from-in-presences-of-you you-cast-me not (13) in-inside-of-me

קָדְשְׁךָ אַל־ תִּקַּח מִמֶּנִּי׃ (14) הָשִׁיבָה לִּי שְׂשׂוֹן
joy-of to-me restore! (14) from-me you-take not Holiness-of-you

יִשְׁעֶךָ וְרוּחַ נְדִיבָה תִסְמְכֵנִי׃
you-sustain-me willing and-spirit salvation-of-you

(15) אֲלַמְּדָה פֹשְׁעִים דְּרָכֶיךָ וְחַטָּאִים אֵלֶיךָ
to-you and-sinners ways-of-you ones-transgressing I-will-teach (15)

יָשׁוּבוּ׃ (16) הַצִּילֵנִי מִדָּמִים ׀ אֱלֹהִים אֱלֹהֵי תְּשׁוּעָתִי
salvation-of-me God-of God from-bloodguilts save-me! (16) they-will-turn-back

תְּרַנֵּן לְשׁוֹנִי צִדְקָתֶךָ׃ (17) אֲדֹנָי שְׂפָתַי תִּפְתָּח
you-open lips-of-me Lord (17) righteousness-of-you tongue-of-me she-will-sing

וּפִי יַגִּיד תְּהִלָּתֶךָ׃ (18) כִּי ׀ לֹא־ תַחְפֹּץ
you-delight-in not for (18) praise-of-you he-will-declare and-mouth-of-me

זֶבַח וְאֶתֵּנָה עוֹלָה לֹא תִרְצֶה׃
you-take-pleasure-in not burnt-offering or-I-would-bring sacrifice

(19) זִבְחֵי אֱלֹהִים רוּחַ נִשְׁבָּרָה לֵב־ נִשְׁבָּר וְנִדְכֶּה
and-being-contrite being-broken heart being-broken spirit God sacrifices-of (19)

אֱלֹהִים לֹא תִבְזֶה׃ (20) הֵיטִיבָה בִרְצוֹנְךָ אֶת־ צִיּוֹן
Zion *** in-pleasure-of-you make-prosper! (20) you-will-despise not God

תִּבְנֶה חוֹמוֹת יְרוּשָׁלָםִ׃ (21) אָז תַּחְפֹּץ זִבְחֵי־
sacrifices-of you-will-delight-in then (21) Jerusalem walls-of you-build-up

צֶדֶק עוֹלָה וְכָלִיל אָז יַעֲלוּ עַל־
on they-will-offer then and-whole-offering burnt-offering righteous

מִזְבַּחֲךָ פָרִים׃ *(52:1) לַמְנַצֵּחַ מַשְׂכִּיל לְדָוִד׃ (2) בְּבוֹא ׀
when-to-go (2) of-David maskil for-the-one-directing *(52:1) bulls altar-of-you

sinful from the time my
mother conceived me.
6Surely you desire truth in the
inner parts[o];
you teach[p] me wisdom in
the inmost place.

7Cleanse me with hyssop, and I
will be clean;
wash me, and I will be
whiter than snow.
8Let me hear joy and gladness;
let the bones you have
crushed rejoice.
9Hide your face from my sins
and blot out all my iniquity.

10Create in me a pure heart, O
God,
and renew a steadfast spirit
within me.
11Do not cast me from your
presence
or take your Holy Spirit
from me.
12Restore to me the joy of your
salvation
and grant me a willing
spirit, to sustain me.

13Then I will teach transgressors
your ways,
and sinners will turn back
to you.
14Save me from bloodguilt, O
God,
the God who saves me,
and my tongue will sing of
your righteousness.
15O Lord, open my lips,
and my mouth will declare
your praise.
16You do not delight in sacrifice,
or I would bring it;
you do not take pleasure in
burnt offerings.
17The sacrifices of God are[q] a
broken spirit;
a broken and contrite heart,
O God, you will not despise.

18In your good pleasure make
Zion prosper;
build up the walls of
Jerusalem.
19Then there will be righteous
sacrifices,
whole burnt offerings to
delight you;
then bulls will be offered on
your altar.

Psalm 52

For the director of music. A *maskil*[r] of

[o]6 The meaning of the Hebrew for this phrase is uncertain.
[p]6 Or *you desired ... ; / you taught*
[q]17 Or *My sacrifice, O God, is*
[r]Title: Probably a literary or musical term

*Heading, *1* See the note on page 401.

דּוֹאֵג הָאֲדֹמִי וַיַּגֵּד לְשָׁאוּל וַיֹּאמֶר לוֹ בָּא דָוִד
David he-went to-him and-he-said to-Saul and-he-told the-Edomite Doeg

אֶל־ בֵּית אֲחִימֶלֶךְ׃ מַה־ תִּתְהַלֵּל בְּרָעָה הַגִּבּוֹר חֶסֶד
disgrace-of the-mighty-man of-evil you-boast why? (3) Ahimelech house-of to

אֵל כָּל־ הַיּוֹם׃ הַוּוֹת תַּחְשֹׁב לְשׁוֹנֶךָ כְּתַעַר
like-razor tongue-of-you she-plots destructions (4) the-day all-of God

מְלֻטָּשׁ עֹשֵׂה רְמִיָּה׃ אָהַבְתָּ רָּע מִטּוֹב
rather-than-good evil you-love (5) deceit one-practicing-of being-sharpened

שֶׁקֶר ׀ מִדַּבֵּר צֶדֶק סֶלָה׃ אָהַבְתָּ כָל־ דִּבְרֵי־
words-of all-of you-love (6) selah truth rather-than-to-speak falsehood

בָלַע לְשׁוֹן מִרְמָה׃ גַּם־ אֵל יִתָּצְךָ לָנֶצַח
to-everlasting he-will-bring-down-you God surely (7) deceit tongue-of harmful

יַחְתְּךָ וְיִסָּחֲךָ מֵאֹהֶל וְשֵׁרֶשְׁךָ
and-he-will-uproot-you from-tent and-he-will-tear-you he-will-snatch-up-you

מֵאֶרֶץ חַיִּים סֶלָה׃ וְיִרְאוּ צַדִּיקִים
righteous-ones then-they-will-see (8) selah living-ones from-land-of

וְיִירָאוּ וְעָלָיו יִשְׂחָקוּ׃ הִנֵּה הַגֶּבֶר לֹא יָשִׂים
he-made not the-man see! (9) they-will-laugh and-at-him and-they-will-fear

אֱלֹהִים מָעוּזּוֹ וַיִּבְטַח בְּרֹב עָשְׁרוֹ
wealth-of-him in-greatness-of but-he-trusted stronghold-of-him God

יָעֹז בְּהַוָּתוֹ׃ וַאֲנִי ׀ כְּזַיִת רַעֲנָן
flourishing like-olive-tree but-I (10) by-destruction-of-him he-grew-strong

בְּבֵית אֱלֹהִים בָּטַחְתִּי בְחֶסֶד־ אֱלֹהִים עוֹלָם וָעֶד׃
and-ever forever God in-unfailing-love-of I-trust God in-house-of

אוֹדְךָ לְעוֹלָם כִּי עָשִׂיתָ וַאֲקַוֶּה שִׁמְךָ
name-of-you and-I-will-hope-in you-did for to-forever I-will-praise-you (11)

כִּי־ טוֹב נֶגֶד חֲסִידֶיךָ׃ לַמְנַצֵּחַ
for-the-one-directing †(53:1) saints-of-you in-presence-of good for

עַל־ מָחֲלַת מַשְׂכִּיל לְדָוִד׃ אָמַר נָבָל בְּלִבּוֹ
in-heart-of-him fool he-says (2) of-David maskil mahalath according-to

אֵין אֱלֹהִים הִשְׁחִיתוּ וְהִתְעִיבוּ עָוֶל אֵין
there-is-no evil-way and-they-are-vile they-are-corrupt God there-is-no

עֹשֵׂה־ טוֹב׃ אֱלֹהִים מִשָּׁמַיִם הִשְׁקִיף עַל־ בְּנֵי אָדָם לִרְאוֹת
to-see man sons-of on he-looks from-heavens God (3) good one-doing-of

הֲיֵשׁ מַשְׂכִּיל דֹּרֵשׁ אֶת־ אֱלֹהִים׃ כֻּלּוֹ
all-of-him (4) God *** one-seeking one-understanding if-there-is

סָג יַחְדָּו נֶאֱלָחוּ אֵין עֹשֵׂה־ טוֹב
good one-doing-of there-is-no they-became-corrupt together he-turned-away

David. When Doeg the Edomite had gone to Saul and told him: "David has gone to the house of Ahimelech."

1Why do you boast of evil, you
mighty man?
Why do you boast all day
long,
you who are a disgrace in
the eyes of God?
2Your tongue plots destruction;
it is like a sharpened razor,
you who practice deceit.
3You love evil rather than good,
falsehood rather than
speaking the truth. *Selah*
4You love every harmful word,
O you deceitful tongue!

5Surely God will bring you
down to everlasting ruin:
He will snatch you up and
tear you from your tent;
he will uproot you from the
land of the living. *Selah*
6The righteous will see and
fear;
they will laugh at him,
saying,
7"Here now is the man
who did not make God his
stronghold
but trusted in his great wealth
and grew strong by
destroying others!"

8But I am like an olive tree
flourishing in the house of
God;
I trust in God's unfailing love
for ever and ever.
9I will praise you forever for
what you have done;
in your name I will hope,
for your name is good.
I will praise you in the
presence of your saints.

Psalm 53

For the director of music. According to *mahalath*.[s] A *maskil*[t] of David.

1The fool says in his heart,
"There is no God."
They are corrupt, and their
ways are vile;
there is no one who does
good.

2God looks down from heaven
on the sons of men
to see if there are any who
understand,
any who seek God.
3Everyone has turned away,
they have together become
corrupt;
there is no one who does
good,

[s]Title: Probably a musical term
[t]Title: Probably a literary or musical term

*See the note on page 401.
†Heading, *1* See the note on page 349.

אֵין גַּם־אֶחָד׃ הֲלֹא יָדְעוּ פֹּעֲלֵי אָוֶן אֹכְלֵי

ones-devouring-of evil ones-doing-of will-they-learn never? (5) one even not

עַמִּי אָכְלוּ לֶחֶם אֱלֹהִים לֹא קָרָאוּ׃ שָׁם׀ פָּחֲדוּ־

they-dreaded there (6) they-call-on not God bread they-eat people-of-me

פַחַד לֹא־הָיָה פָחַד כִּי־אֱלֹהִים פִּזַּר עַצְמוֹת חֹנָךְ

one-attacking-you bones-of he-scattered God for dread he-was not dread

הֱבִשֹׁתָה כִּי־אֱלֹהִים מְאָסָם׃ מִי יִתֵּן מִצִּיּוֹן

from-Zion he-would-bring who? (7) he-despised-them God for you-put-to-shame

יְשֻׁעוֹת יִשְׂרָאֵל בְּשׁוּב אֱלֹהִים שְׁבוּת עַמּוֹ

people-of-him fortune-of God when-to-restore Israel salvations-of

יָגֵל יַעֲקֹב יִשְׂמַח יִשְׂרָאֵל׃ לַמְנַצֵּחַ

for-the-one-directing †(54:1) Israel let-him-be-glad Jacob let-him-rejoice

בִּנְגִינֹת מַשְׂכִּיל לְדָוִד׃ בְּבוֹא הַזִּיפִים

the-Ziphites when-to-go (2) of-David maskil with-stringed-instruments

וַיֹּאמְרוּ לְשָׁאוּל הֲלֹא דָוִד מִסְתַּתֵּר עִמָּנוּ׃ אֱלֹהִים בְּשִׁמְךָ

by-name-of-you God (3) among-us hiding David not? to-Saul and-they-said

הוֹשִׁיעֵנִי וּבִגְבוּרָתְךָ תְדִינֵנִי׃ אֱלֹהִים שְׁמַע תְּפִלָּתִי

prayer-of-me hear! God (4) you-vindicate-me and-by-might-of-you save-me!

הַאֲזִינָה לְאִמְרֵי־ פִי׃ כִּי זָרִים׀ קָמוּ

they-attack ones-being-strangers for (5) mouth-of-me to-words-of listen!

עָלַי וְעָרִיצִים בִּקְשׁוּ נַפְשִׁי לֹא שָׂמוּ אֱלֹהִים

God they-regard not life-of-me they-seek and-ruthless-men against-me

לְנֶגְדָּם סֶלָה׃ הִנֵּה אֱלֹהִים עֹזֵר לִי אֲדֹנָי בְּסֹמְכֵי

among-ones-sustaining-of Lord to-me one-helping God see! (6) selah at-before-them

נַפְשִׁי׃ יָשׁוֹב° הָרַע לְשֹׁרְרָי בַּאֲמִתְּךָ

in-faithfulness-of-you on-slanderers-of-me the-evil let-him-recoil (7) self-of-me

הַצְמִיתֵם׃ בִּנְדָבָה אֶזְבְּחָה־ לָּךְ אוֹדֶה

I-will-praise to-you I-will-sacrifice with-freewill-offering (8) destroy-them!

שִׁמְךָ יְהוָה כִּי־ טוֹב׃ כִּי מִכָּל־ צָרָה הִצִּילָנִי

he-delivered-me trouble from-all-of for (9) good for Yahweh name-of-you

וּבְאֹיְבַי רָאֲתָה עֵינִי׃ לַמְנַצֵּחַ

for-the-one-directing *(55:1) eye-of-me she-looked and-on-ones-being-foes-of-me

בִּנְגִינֹת מַשְׂכִּיל לְדָוִד׃ הַאֲזִינָה אֱלֹהִים תְּפִלָּתִי

prayer-of-me God listen! (2) of-David maskil with-stringed-instruments

וְאַל־ תִּתְעַלַּם מִתְּחִנָּתִי׃ הַקְשִׁיבָה לִּי וַעֲנֵנִי אָרִיד

I-am-troubled and-answer-me! to-me hear! (3) to-plea-of-me you-ignore and-not

בְּשִׂיחִי וְאָהִימָה׃ מִקּוֹל אוֹיֵב

one-being-enemy at-voice-of (4) and-I-am-distraught by-thought-of-me

---

not even one.

[4]Will the evildoers never learn—
those who devour my people as men eat bread
and who do not call on God?

[5]There they were, overwhelmed with dread,
where there was nothing to dread.
God scattered the bones of those who attacked you;
you put them to shame, for God despised them.

[6]Oh, that salvation for Israel would come out of Zion!
When God restores the fortunes of his people,
let Jacob rejoice and Israel be glad!

Psalm 54

For the director of music. With stringed instruments. A *maskil*[a] of David. When the Ziphites had gone to Saul and said, "Is not David hiding among us?"

[1]Save me, O God, by your name;
vindicate me by your might.

[2]Hear my prayer, O God;
listen to the words of my mouth.

[3]Strangers are attacking me;
ruthless men seek my life—
men without regard for God. *Selah*

[4]Surely God is my help;
the Lord is the one who sustains me.

[5]Let evil recoil on those who slander me;
in your faithfulness destroy them.

[6]I will sacrifice a freewill offering to you;
I will praise your name, O LORD,
for it is good.

[7]For he has delivered me from all my troubles,
and my eyes have looked in triumph on my foes.

Psalm 55

For the director of music. With stringed instruments. A *maskil*[a] of David.

[1]Listen to my prayer, O God,
do not ignore my plea;

[2] hear me and answer me.
My thoughts trouble me and I am distraught

[3] at the voice of the enemy,

[a]Title: Probably a literary or musical term

*Heading, *1* See the note on page 349.

†*1* See the note on page 401.

°7 ק ישיב

מִפְּנֵי עָקַת רָשָׁע כִּי־ יָמִיטוּ עָלַי אָוֶן וּבְאַף
and-in-anger suffering upon-me they-bring-down for wicked stare-of at-faces-of

יִשְׂטְמוּנִי׃ לִבִּי יָחִיל בְּקִרְבִּי וְאֵימוֹת
and-terrors-of at-within-me he-is-in-anguish heart-of-me (5) they-revile-me

מָוֶת נָפְלוּ עָלָי׃ יִרְאָה וָרַעַד יָבֹא בִי
against-me he-beset and-trembling fear (6) on-me they-assail death

וַתְּכַסֵּנִי פַּלָּצוּת׃ וָאֹמַר מִי־ יִתֶּן־ לִּי
to-me he-would-allow who? and-I-said (7) horror and-she-overwhelmed-me

אֵבֶר כַּיּוֹנָה אָעוּפָה וְאֶשְׁכֹּנָה׃ הִנֵּה אַרְחִיק
I-would-be-far see! (8) and-I-would-rest I-would-fly-away like-the-dove wing

נְדֹד אָלִין בַּמִּדְבָּר סֶלָה׃ אָחִישָׁה מִפְלָט
place-of-shelter I-would-hurry (9) selah in-the-desert I-would-stay to-flee

לִי מֵרוּחַ סֹעָה מִסָּעַר׃ בַּלַּע אֲדֹנָי פַּלַּג
confound! Lord confuse! (10) from-storm being-tempestuous from-wind to-me

לְשׁוֹנָם כִּי־ רָאִיתִי חָמָס וְרִיב בָּעִיר׃ יוֹמָם
by-day (11) in-the-city and-strife violence I-see for speech-of-them

וָלַיְלָה יְסוֹבְבֻהָ עַל־ חוֹמֹתֶיהָ וְאָוֶן וְעָמָל
and-abuse and-malice walls-of-her on they-prowl-about-her and-night

בְּקִרְבָּהּ׃ הַוּוֹת בְּקִרְבָּהּ וְלֹא־ יָמִישׁ
he-leaves and-never at-within-her destructive-forces (12) at-within-her

מֵרְחֹבָהּ תֹּךְ וּמִרְמָה׃ כִּי לֹא־ אוֹיֵב יְחָרְפֵנִי
he-insults-me one-being-enemy †not for (13) and-lie threat from-street-of-her

וְאֶשָּׂא לֹא־ מְשַׂנְאִי עָלַי הִגְדִּיל וְאֶסָּתֵר מִמֶּנּוּ׃
from-him and-I-hide he-raises against-me one-being-foe-of-me †not and-I-endure

וְאַתָּה אֱנוֹשׁ כְּעֶרְכִּי אַלּוּפִי וּמְיֻדָּעִי׃
and-one-being-friend-of-me companion-of-me as-order-of-me man but-you (14)

אֲשֶׁר יַחְדָּו נַמְתִּיק סוֹד בְּבֵית אֱלֹהִים נְהַלֵּךְ
we-walked God at-house-of fellowship we-made-sweet together who (15)

בְּרָגֶשׁ׃ יַשִּׁי°מָוֶת ׀ עָלֵימוֹ יֵרְדוּ שְׁאוֹל חַיִּים
alive-ones Sheol let-them-go-down to-them death let-him-take (16) with-throng

כִּי־רָעוֹת בִּמְגוּרָם בְּקִרְבָּם׃ אֲנִי אֶל־אֱלֹהִים אֶקְרָא וַיהוָה
and-Yahweh I-call God to I (17) in-among-them in-lodging-of-them evils for

יוֹשִׁיעֵנִי׃ עֶרֶב וָבֹקֶר וְצָהֳרַיִם אָשִׂיחָה וְאֶהֱמֶה
and-I-tell-distress I-cry-out and-noon and-morning evening (18) he-saves-me

וַיִּשְׁמַע קוֹלִי׃ פָּדָה בְשָׁלוֹם נַפְשִׁי מִקְּרָב־
from-battle self-of-me in-wholeness he-ransoms (19) voice-of-me and-he-hears

לִי כִּי־ בְרַבִּים הָיוּ עִמָּדִי׃ יִשְׁמַע ׀ אֵל ׀
God he-will-hear (20) opposite-me they-are among-many though against-me

at the stares of the wicked;
for they bring down suffering upon me
and revile me in their anger.

4 My heart is in anguish within me;
the terrors of death assail me.
5 Fear and trembling have beset me;
horror has overwhelmed me.
6 I said, "Oh, that I had the wings of a dove!
I would fly away and be at rest—
7 I would flee far away
and stay in the desert; *Selah*
8 I would hurry to my place of shelter,
far from the tempest and storm."

9 Confuse the wicked, O Lord,
confound their speech,
for I see violence and strife in the city.
10 Day and night they prowl about on its walls;
malice and abuse are within it.
11 Destructive forces are at work in the city;
threats and lies never leave its streets.

12 If an enemy were insulting me,
I could endure it;
if a foe were raising himself against me,
I could hide from him.
13 But it is you, a man like myself,
my companion, my close friend,
14 with whom I once enjoyed sweet fellowship
as we walked with the throng at the house of God.

15 Let death take my enemies by surprise;
let them go down alive to the grave,[v]
for evil finds lodging among them.

16 But I call to God,
and the LORD saves me.
17 Evening, morning and noon
I cry out in distress,
and he hears my voice.
18 He ransoms me unharmed
from the battle waged against me,
even though many oppose me.

[v]15 Hebrew *Sheol*

*See the note on page 349.

†13 The NIV points this word as לֹ֫א, *if.*

°16 ק ישי מות

וְיַעֲנֵם וְיֹשֵׁב קֶדֶם סֶלָה אֲשֶׁר אֵין
never who selah forever even-one-being-enthroned and-he-will-afflict-them

חֲלִיפוֹת לָמוֹ וְלֹא יָרְאוּ אֱלֹהִים׃ שָׁלַח יָדָיו
hands-of-him he-sends (21) God they-fear and-not to-them changes

בִּשְׁלֹמָיו חִלֵּל בְּרִיתוֹ׃ חָלְקוּ ׀
they-are-smooth (22) covenant-of-him he-violates against-friends-of-him

מַחְמָאֹת פִּיו וּקְרָב־ לִבּוֹ רַכּוּ
they-are-soothing heart-of-him yet-war-of mouth-of-him butters-of

דְבָרָיו מִשֶּׁמֶן וְהֵמָּה פְתִחוֹת׃ הַשְׁלֵךְ עַל־ יְהוָה ׀
Yahweh on cast! (23) drawn-swords yet-they more-than-oil words-of-him

יְהָבְךָ וְהוּא יְכַלְכְּלֶךָ לֹא־ יִתֵּן לְעוֹלָם מוֹט
fall to-forever he-will-let not he-will-sustain-you and-he care-of-you

לַצַּדִּיק׃ וְאַתָּה אֱלֹהִים ׀ תּוֹרִדֵם ׀ לִבְאֵר
into-pit-of you-will-bring-down-them God but-you (24) of-the-righteous

שַׁחַת אַנְשֵׁי דָמִים וּמִרְמָה לֹא־ יֶחֱצוּ יְמֵיהֶם
days-of-them they-will-live-half not and-deceit bloods men-of corruption

וַאֲנִי אֶבְטַח־ בָּךְ׃ לַמְנַצֵּחַ ׀ עַל־ יוֹנַת אֵלֶם†
†silence-of dove-of to for-the-one-directing *(56:1) in-you I-will-trust but-I

רְחֹקִים לְדָוִד מִכְתָּם בֶּאֱחֹז אֹתוֹ פְלִשְׁתִּים בְּגַת׃
in-Gath Philistines him when-to-seize miktam of-David distant-ones

חָנֵּנִי אֱלֹהִים כִּי־ שְׁאָפַנִי אֱנוֹשׁ כָּל־ הַיּוֹם לֹחֵם
one-attacking the-day all-of man he-pursues-me for God be-merciful-to-me! (2)

יִלְחָצֵנִי׃ שָׁאֲפוּ שׁוֹרְרַי כָּל־ הַיּוֹם כִּי־ רַבִּים
many indeed the-day all-of ones-slandering-me they-pursue (3) he-oppresses-me

לֹחֲמִים לִי מָרוֹם׃ יוֹם אִירָא אֲנִי אֵלֶיךָ אֶבְטָח׃
I-trust in-you I I-am-afraid day (4) pride against-me ones-attacking

בֵּאלֹהִים אֲהַלֵּל דְּבָרוֹ בֵּאלֹהִים בָּטַחְתִּי לֹא אִירָא מַה־
what? I-will-be-afraid not I-trust in-God word-of-him I-praise in-God (5)

יַּעֲשֶׂה בָשָׂר לִי׃ כָּל־ הַיּוֹם דְּבָרַי יְעַצֵּבוּ עָלַי
against-me they-twist words-of-me the-day all-of (6) to-me mortal can-he-do

כָּל־ מַחְשְׁבֹתָם לָרָע׃ יָגוּרוּ ׀ יִצְפִּינוּ הֵמָּה עֲקֵבַי
steps-of-me they they-lurk they-conspire (7) for-harm plots-of-them all-of

יִשְׁמֹרוּ כַּאֲשֶׁר קִוּוּ נַפְשִׁי׃ עַל־ אָוֶן
no-account on (8) life-of-me they-are-eager-for as-that they-watch

פַּלֶּט־ לָמוֹ בְּאַף עַמִּים ׀ הוֹרֵד אֱלֹהִים׃ נֹדִי
lament-of-me (9) God bring-down! nations in-anger to-them let-escape!

סָפַרְתָּה אָתָּה שִׂימָה דִמְעָתִי בְנֹאדֶךָ הֲלֹא בְּסִפְרָתֶךָ׃
in-record-of-you not? in-wineskin-of-you tear-of-me put! you you-record

19 God, who is enthroned
forever,
will hear them and afflict
them— *Selah*
men who never change their
ways
and have no fear of God.

20 My companion attacks his
friends;
he violates his covenant.
21 His speech is smooth as butter,
yet war is in his heart;
his words are more soothing
than oil,
yet they are drawn swords.

22 Cast your cares on the LORD
and he will sustain you;
he will never let the
righteous fall.
23 But you, O God, will bring
down the wicked
into the pit of corruption;
bloodthirsty and deceitful men
will not live out half their
days.

But as for me, I trust in you.

Psalm 56

For the director of music. To the tune of "A Dove on Distant Oaks." Of David. A *miktam*.[w] When the Philistines had seized him in Gath.

1 Be merciful to me, O God, for
men hotly pursue me;
all day long they press their
attack.
2 My slanderers pursue me all
day long;
many are attacking me in
their pride.

3 When I am afraid,
I will trust in you.
4 In God, whose word I praise,
in God I trust; I will not be
afraid.
What can mortal man do to
me?

5 All day long they twist my
words;
they are always plotting to
harm me.
6 They conspire, they lurk,
they watch my steps,
eager to take my life.
7 On no account let them
escape;
in your anger, O God, bring
down the nations.
8 Record my lament;
list my tears on your
scroll[x]—
are they not in your record?

w Title: Probably a literary or musical term
x 8 Or / *put my tears in your wineskin*

*Heading, *1* See the note on page 349.
†*1* The NIV repoints this word as אֵלִם, *oaks*.
°7 ק יצפונו

(10) אָז יָשׁוּבוּ אוֹיְבַי אָחוֹר בְּיוֹם אֶקְרָא זֶה־

this I-call on-day back ones-being-enemies-of-me they-will-turn then (10)

יָדַעְתִּי כִּי־אֱלֹהִים לִי׃ (1) בֵּאלֹהִים אֲהַלֵּל דָּבָר בַּיהוָה אֲהַלֵּל

I-praise in-Yahweh word I-praise in-God (1) for-me God that I-will-know

דָּבָר׃ (12) בֵּאלֹהִים בָּטַחְתִּי לֹא אִירָא מַה־ יַּעֲשֶׂה אָדָם לִי׃

to-me man can-he-do what? I-will-be-afraid not I-trust in-God (12) word

(13) עָלַי אֱלֹהִים נְדָרֶיךָ אֲשַׁלֵּם תּוֹדֹת לָךְ׃

to-you thank-offerings I-will-present vows-of-you God upon-me (13)

(14) כִּי הִצַּלְתָּ נַפְשִׁי מִמָּוֶת הֲלֹא רַגְלַי מִדֶּחִי

from-stumbling feet-of-me not? from-death soul-of-me you-delivered for (14)

לְהִתְהַלֵּךְ לִפְנֵי אֱלֹהִים בְּאוֹר הַחַיִּים׃ *(57:1) לַמְנַצֵּחַ אַל־

not for-the-one-directing *(57:1) the-lives in-light-of God before to-walk

תַּשְׁחֵת לְדָוִד מִכְתָּם בְּבָרְחוֹ מִפְּנֵי־ שָׁאוּל בַּמְּעָרָה׃

into-the-cave Saul from-before when-to-flee-him miktam of-David you-destroy

(2) חָנֵּנִי אֱלֹהִים ׀ חָנֵּנִי כִּי בְךָ חָסָיָה

she-takes-refuge in-you for have-mercy-on-me! God have-mercy-on-me! (2)

נַפְשִׁי וּבְצֵל־ כְּנָפֶיךָ אֶחְסֶה עַד יַעֲבֹר

he-passed until I-will-take-refuge wings-of-you and-in-shadow-of soul-of-me

הַוּוֹת׃ (3) אֶקְרָא לֵאלֹהִים עֶלְיוֹן לָאֵל גֹּמֵר עָלָי׃

for-me one-fulfilling to-God Most-High to-God I-cry-out (3) disasters

(4) יִשְׁלַח מִשָּׁמַיִם ׀ וְיוֹשִׁיעֵנִי חֵרֵף שֹׁאֲפִי סֶלָה

selah one-pursuing-me he-rebukes and-he-saves-me from-heavens he-sends (4)

יִשְׁלַח אֱלֹהִים חַסְדּוֹ וַאֲמִתּוֹ׃ (5) נַפְשִׁי ׀ בְּתוֹךְ

in-midst-of self-of-me (5) and-faithfulness-of-him love-of-him God he-sends

לְבָאִם אֶשְׁכְּבָה לֹהֲטִים בְּנֵי־ אָדָם שִׁנֵּיהֶם חֲנִית וְחִצִּים

and-arrows spear teeth-of-them man sons-of ones-being-ravenous I-lie lions

וּלְשׁוֹנָם חֶרֶב חַדָּה׃ (6) רוּמָה עַל־ הַשָּׁמַיִם אֱלֹהִים עַל

over God the-heavens above be-exalted! (6) sharp sword and-tongue-of-them

כָּל־ הָאָרֶץ כְּבוֹדֶךָ׃ (7) רֶשֶׁת ׀ הֵכִינוּ לִפְעָמַי כָּפַף

he-was-bowed for-feet-of-me they-spread net (7) glory-of-you the-earth all-of

נַפְשִׁי כָּרוּ לְפָנַי שִׁיחָה נָפְלוּ בְתוֹכָהּ סֶלָה׃

selah into-inside-of-her they-fell pit before-me they-dug self-of-me

(8) נָכוֹן לִבִּי אֱלֹהִים נָכוֹן לִבִּי אָשִׁירָה

I-will-sing heart-of-me he-is-steadfast God heart-of-me he-is-steadfast (8)

וַאֲזַמֵּרָה׃ (9) עוּרָה כְבוֹדִי עוּרָה הַנֵּבֶל וְכִנּוֹר

and-lyre the-harp awake! soul-of-me awake! (9) and-I-will-make-music

אָעִירָה שָּׁחַר׃ (10) אוֹדְךָ בָעַמִּים ׀ אֲדֹנָי

Lord among-the-nations I-will-praise-you (10) dawn I-will-awaken

9 Then my enemies will turn
back
when I call for help.
By this I will know that God
is for me.
10 In God, whose word I praise,
in the LORD, whose word I
praise—
11 in God I trust; I will not be
afraid.
What can man do to me?

12 I am under vows to you, O
God;
I will present my thank
offerings to you.
13 For you have delivered my
soul from death
and my feet from stumbling,
that I may walk before God
in the light of life.[y]

Psalm 57

For the director of music. ⌊To the tune of⌋ "Do Not Destroy." Of David. A *miktam*.[z] When he had fled from Saul into the cave.

1 Have mercy on me, O God,
have mercy on me,
for in you my soul takes
refuge.
I will take refuge in the
shadow of your wings
until the disaster has passed.

2 I cry out to God Most High,
to God, who fulfills ⌊his
purpose⌋ for me.
3 He sends from heaven and
saves me,
rebuking those who hotly
pursue me; *Selah*
God sends his love and his
faithfulness.

4 I am in the midst of lions;
I lie among ravenous
beasts—
men whose teeth are spears
and arrows,
whose tongues are sharp
swords.

5 Be exalted, O God, above the
heavens;
let your glory be over all the
earth.

6 They spread a net for my
feet—
I was bowed down in
distress.
They dug a pit in my path—
but they have fallen into it
themselves. *Selah*

7 My heart is steadfast, O God,
my heart is steadfast;
I will sing and make music.
8 Awake, my soul!
Awake, harp and lyre!
I will awaken the dawn.

9 I will praise you, O Lord,
among the nations;

[y]13 Or *the land of the living*
[z]Title: Probably a literary or musical term

*Heading, *1* See the note on page 349.

אֲזַמֶּרְךָ בַּל־אֻמִּים׃† כִּי־ גָדֹל עַד־ שָׁמַיִם חַסְדֶּךָ
love-of-you heavens to great for (11) †among-the-peoples I-will-sing-of-you

וְעַד־ שְׁחָקִים אֲמִתֶּךָ׃ רוּמָה עַל־ שָׁמַיִם אֱלֹהִים עַל
over God heavens above be-exalted! (12) faithfulness-of-you skies and-to

כָּל־ הָאָרֶץ כְּבוֹדֶךָ׃ לַמְנַצֵּחַ אַל־ תַּשְׁחֵת
you-destroy not for-the-one-directing *(58:1) glory-of-you the-earth all-of

לְדָוִד מִכְתָּם׃ הַאֻמְנָם אֵלֶם†† צֶדֶק תְּדַבֵּרוּן מֵישָׁרִים תִּשְׁפְּטוּ
you-judge ones-upright you-speak justly ††silence indeed? (2) miktam of-David

בְּנֵי אָדָם׃ אַף־ בְּלֵב עוֹלֹת תִּפְעָלוּן בָּאָרֶץ חֲמַס
violence-of on-the-earth you-devise injustices in-heart no (3) man sons-of

יְדֵיכֶם תְּפַלֵּסוּן׃ זֹרוּ רְשָׁעִים מֵרָחֶם
from-birth wicked-ones they-go-astray (4) you-mete-out hands-of-you

תָּעוּ מִבֶּטֶן דֹּבְרֵי כָזָב׃ חֲמַת־ לָמוֹ
of-them venom-of (5) lie ones-speaking-of from-womb they-are-wayward

כִּדְמוּת חֲמַת־ נָחָשׁ כְּמוֹ־ פֶתֶן חֵרֵשׁ יַאְטֵם אָזְנוֹ׃
ear-of-him he-stopped deaf cobra like snake venom-of as-likeness-of

אֲשֶׁר לֹא־ יִשְׁמַע לְקוֹל מְלַחֲשִׁים חוֹבֵר חֲבָרִים
enchantments one-enchanting ones-charming to-tune-of he-heeds not that (6)

מְחֻכָּם׃ אֱלֹהִים הֲרָס־ שִׁנֵּימוֹ בְּפִימוֹ מַלְתְּעוֹת כְּפִירִים
lions fangs-of in-mouth-of-them teeth-of-them break! God (7) being-skillful

נְתֹץ ׀ יְהוָה׃ יִמָּאֲסוּ כְמוֹ־ מַיִם יִתְהַלְּכוּ־ לָמוֹ
of-themselves they-flow-away waters like let-them-vanish (8) Yahweh tear-out!

יִדְרֹךְ חִצָּו כְּמוֹ יִתְמֹלָלוּ׃ כְּמוֹ שַׁבְּלוּל תֶּמֶס
melting-away slug like (9) let-them-be-blunted so arrows-of-him he-draws-bow

יַהֲלֹךְ נֵפֶל אֵשֶׁת בַּל־ חָזוּ שָׁמֶשׁ׃ בְּטֶרֶם
at-before (10) sun may-they-see not woman-of stillborn-child-of he-moves-along

יָבִינוּ סִּירֹתֵיכֶם אָטָד כְּמוֹ־ חַי כְּמוֹ־ חָרוֹן יִשְׂעָרֶנּוּ׃
he-will-sweep-away-him dry whether green whether thorn pots-of-you they-feel

יִשְׂמַח צַדִּיק כִּי־ חָזָה נָקָם פְּעָמָיו יִרְחַץ
he-bathes feet-of-him vengeance he-sees when righteous he-will-be-glad (11)

בְּדַם הָרָשָׁע׃ וְיֹאמַר אָדָם אַךְ־ פְּרִי לַצַּדִּיק
for-the-righteous reward surely man then-he-will-say (12) the-wicked in-blood-of

אַךְ יֵשׁ־ אֱלֹהִים שֹׁפְטִים בָּאָרֶץ׃ לַמְנַצֵּחַ
for-the-one-directing *(59:1) over-the-earth ones-judging God there-is surely

אַל־ תַּשְׁחֵת לְדָוִד מִכְתָּם בִּשְׁלֹחַ שָׁאוּל וַיִּשְׁמְרוּ אֶת־
*** and-they-watched Saul when-to-send miktam of-David you-destroy not

הַבַּיִת לַהֲמִיתוֹ׃ הַצִּילֵנִי מֵאֹיְבַי ׀ אֱלֹהָי
God-of-me from-ones-being-enemies-of-me deliver-me! (2) to-kill-him the-house

I will sing of you among the
peoples.
[10]For great is your love, reaching
to the heavens;
your faithfulness reaches to
the skies.
[11]Be exalted, O God, above the
heavens;
let your glory be over all the
earth.

Psalm 58

For the director of music. ⌊To the tune of⌋ "Do Not Destroy." Of David. A *miktam*.[a]

[1]Do you rulers indeed speak
justly?
Do you judge uprightly
among men?
[2]No, in your heart you devise
injustice,
and your hands mete out
violence on the earth.
[3]Even from birth the wicked go
astray;
from the womb they are
wayward and speak lies.
[4]Their venom is like the venom
of a snake,
like that of a cobra that has
stopped its ears,
[5]that will not heed the tune of
the charmer,
however skillful the
enchanter may be.

[6]Break the teeth in their
mouths, O God;
tear out, O LORD, the fangs
of the lions!
[7]Let them vanish like water
that flows away;
when they draw the bow,
let their arrows be
blunted.
[8]Like a slug melting away as it
moves along,
like a stillborn child, may
they not see the sun.

[9]Before your pots can feel ⌊the
heat of⌋ the thorns—
whether they be green or
dry—the wicked will be
swept away.[b]
[10]The righteous will be glad
when they are avenged,
when they bathe their feet
in the blood of the
wicked.
[11]Then men will say,
"Surely the righteous still
are rewarded;
surely there is a God who
judges the earth."

Psalm 59

For the director of music. ⌊To the tune of⌋ "Do Not Destroy." Of David. A *miktam*.[c] When Saul had sent men to watch David's house in order to kill him.

[a]Title: Probably a literary or musical term
[b]9 The meaning of the Hebrew for this verse is uncertain.
[c]Title: Probably a literary or musical term

*Heading, *1* See the note on page 349.

†*10* Most mss read these two words as one (בְלַא).

††*2* The NIV reads this word as אֵלִם, *rams = leaders*.

°*8* ק חציו

מִמִּתְקוֹמְמַי† תְּשַׂגְּבֵנִי׃ הַצִּילֵנִי מִפֹּעֲלֵי

from-ones-doing-of deliver-me! (3) you-protect-me from-ones-rising-up-against-me

אָוֶן וּמֵאַנְשֵׁי דָמִים הוֹשִׁיעֵנִי׃ כִּי הִנֵּה אָרְבוּ

they-lie-in-wait see! for (4) save-me! bloods and-from-men-of evil

לְנַפְשִׁי יָגוּרוּ עָלַי עַזִּים†† לֹא־ פִשְׁעִי וְלֹא־

and-no offense-of-me no fierce-men against-me they-conspire for-self-of-me

חַטָּאתִי יְהוָה׃ בְּלִי־ עָוֹן יְרוּצוּן וְיִכּוֹנָנוּ עוּרָה לִקְרָאתִי

to-help-me arise! and-they-are-ready they-attack wrong no (5) Yahweh sin-of-me

וּרְאֵה׃ וְאַתָּה יְהוָה־אֱלֹהִים צְבָאוֹת אֱלֹהֵי יִשְׂרָאֵל הָקִיצָה

rouse-yourself! Israel God-of Hosts God Yahweh and-you (6) and-look!

לִפְקֹד כָּל־ הַגּוֹיִם אַל־ תָּחֹן כָּל־ בֹּגְדֵי

ones-being-traitors-of all-of you-show-mercy not the-nations all-of to-punish

אָוֶן סֶלָה׃ יָשׁוּבוּ לָעֶרֶב יֶהֱמוּ כַכָּלֶב

like-the-dog they-snarl at-the-evening they-return (7) selah wickedness

וִיסוֹבְבוּ עִיר׃ הִנֵּה׀ יַבִּיעוּן בְּפִיהֶם חֲרָבוֹת

swords from-mouth-of-them they-spew see! (8) city and-they-prowl-about

בְּשִׂפְתוֹתֵיהֶם כִּי־ מִי שֹׁמֵעַ׃ וְאַתָּה יְהוָה תִּשְׂחַק־

you-laugh Yahweh but-you (9) one-hearing who? that from-lips-of-them

לָמוֹ תִּלְעַג לְכָל־ גּוֹיִם׃ עֻזּוֹ אֵלֶיךָ אֶשְׁמֹרָה

I-watch for-you Strength-of-him (10) nations at-all-of you-scoff at-them

כִּי־אֱלֹהִים מִשְׂגַּבִּי׃ אֱלֹהֵי חַסְדּוֹ° יְקַדְּמֵנִי אֱלֹהִים

God he-will-go-before-me love-of-me God-of (11) fortress-of-me God for

יַרְאֵנִי בְשֹׁרְרָי׃ אַל־ תַּהַרְגֵם׀ פֶּן־

or you-kill-them not (12) over-ones-slandering-me he-will-let-gloat-me

יִשְׁכְּחוּ עַמִּי הֲנִיעֵמוֹ בְחֵילְךָ

in-might-of-you make-wander-them! people-of-me they-will-forget

וְהוֹרִידֵמוֹ מָגִנֵּנוּ אֲדֹנָי׃ חַטַּאת־ פִּימוֹ דְּבַר־

word-of mouth-of-them sin-of (13) Lord shield-of-us and-bring-down-them!

שְׂפָתֵימוֹ וְיִלָּכְדוּ בִגְאוֹנָם וּמֵאָלָה וּמִכַּחַשׁ

and-for-lie and-for-curse in-pride-of-them and-let-them-be-caught lips-of-them

יְסַפֵּרוּ׃ כַּלֵּה בְחֵמָה כַּלֵּה וְאֵינֵמוֹ וְיֵדְעוּ

then-they-will-know and-no-more-they consume! in-wrath consume! (14) they-utter

כִּי־אֱלֹהִים מֹשֵׁל בְּיַעֲקֹב לְאַפְסֵי הָאָרֶץ סֶלָה׃ וְיָשׁוּבוּ

now-they-return (15) selah the-earth to-ends-of over-Jacob ruling God that

לָעֶרֶב יֶהֱמוּ כַכָּלֶב וִיסוֹבְבוּ עִיר׃ הֵמָּה

they (16) city and-they-prowl-about like-the-dog they-snarl at-the-evening

יְנוּעוּן° לֶאֱכֹל אִם־ לֹא יִשְׂבְּעוּ וַיָּלִינוּ׃

then-they-howl they-are-satisfied not if to-eat they-wander-about

[1]Deliver me from my enemies, O God;
protect me from those who rise up against me.
[2]Deliver me from evildoers
and save me from bloodthirsty men.

[3]See how they lie in wait for me!
Fierce men conspire against me
for no offense or sin of mine, O LORD.
[4]I have done no wrong, yet they are ready to attack me.
Arise to help me; look on my plight!
[5]O LORD God Almighty, the God of Israel,
rouse yourself to punish all the nations;
show no mercy to wicked traitors. *Selah*

[6]They return at evening,
snarling like dogs,
and prowl about the city.
[7]See what they spew from their mouths—
they spew out swords from their lips,
and they say, "Who can hear us?"
[8]But you, O LORD, laugh at them;
you scoff at all those nations.

[9]O my Strength, I watch for you;
you, O God, are my fortress,
[10]my loving God.

God will go before me
and will let me gloat over those who slander me.
[11]But do not kill them, O Lord our shield,[d]
or my people will forget.
In your might make them wander about,
and bring them down.
[12]For the sins of their mouths,
for the words of their lips,
let them be caught in their pride.
For the curses and lies they utter,
13 consume them in wrath,
consume them till they are no more.
Then it will be known to the ends of the earth
that God rules over Jacob. *Selah*

[14]They return at evening,
snarling like dogs,
and prowl about the city.
[15]They wander about for food
and howl if not satisfied.

[d]*11 Or sovereign*

*See the note on page 349.

†2 Most mss have *dagesh* in the second *mem* (מִמְּ).

††4 Most mss have *dagesh* in the *zayin* (עזּים).

°*11* ק חסדי

°*16* ק יניעון

וַאֲנִי | אָשִׁיר עֻזֶּךָ וַאֲרַנֵּן לַבֹּקֶר
in-the-morning and-I-will-sing strength-of-you I-will-sing but-I (17)

חַסְדֶּךָ כִּי־ הָיִיתָ מִשְׂגָּב לִי וּמָנוֹס בְּיוֹם צַר־ לִי׃
to-me trouble in-time-of and-refuge of-me fortress you-are for love-of-you

עֻזִּי אֵלֶיךָ אֲזַמֵּרָה כִּי־אֱלֹהִים מִשְׂגַּבִּי אֱלֹהֵי
God-of fortress-of-me God for I-sing-praise to-you Strength-of-me (18)

חַסְדִּי׃ לַמְנַצֵּחַ עַל־ שׁוּשַׁן עֵדוּת מִכְתָּם לְדָוִד
of-David miktam covenant lily-of to for-the-one-directing †(60:1) love-of-me

לְלַמֵּד׃ בְּהַצּוֹתוֹ | אֶת אֲרַם נַהֲרַיִם וְאֶת־ אֲרַם צוֹבָה
Zobah Aram-of and Naharaim Aram-of *** when-to-fight-him (2) to-teach

וַיָּשָׁב יוֹאָב וַיַּךְ אֶת־ אֱדוֹם בְּגֵיא־ מֶלַח שְׁנֵים
two Salt in-Valley-of Edom *** and-he-struck-down Joab when-he-returned

עָשָׂר אָלֶף׃ אֱלֹהִים זְנַחְתָּנוּ פְרַצְתָּנוּ אָנַפְתָּ
you-were-angry you-burst-forth-upon-us you-rejected-us God (3) thousand ten

תְּשׁוֹבֵב לָנוּ׃ הִרְעַשְׁתָּה אֶרֶץ פְּצַמְתָּהּ רְפָה שְׁבָרֶיהָ
fractures-of-her mend! you-tore-open-her land you-shook (4) to-us you-restore

כִי־ מָטָה׃ הִרְאִיתָה עַמְּךָ קָשָׁה הִשְׁקִיתָנוּ
you-made-drink-us desperate-time people-of-you you-showed (5) she-quakes for

יַיִן תַּרְעֵלָה׃ נָתַתָּה לִּירֵאֶיךָ נֵּס לְהִתְנוֹסֵס
to-be-unfurled banner for-ones-fearing-you you-raised (6) staggering wine

מִפְּנֵי קֹשֶׁט סֶלָה׃ לְמַעַן יֵחָלְצוּן יְדִידֶיךָ הוֹשִׁיעָה
save! loved-ones-of-you they-may-be-delivered so-that (7) selah bow against

יְמִינְךָ וַעֲנֵנוּ׃ אֱלֹהִים | דִּבֶּר בְּקָדְשׁוֹ
from-sanctuary-of-him he-spoke God (8) and-help-us! right-hand-of-you

אֶעְלֹזָה אֲחַלְּקָה שְׁכֶם וְעֵמֶק סֻכּוֹת אֲמַדֵּד׃
I-will-measure Succoth and-Valley-of Shechem I-will-parcel-out I-will-triumph

לִי גִלְעָד | וְלִי מְנַשֶּׁה וְאֶפְרַיִם מָעוֹז רֹאשִׁי יְהוּדָה
Judah head-of-me helmet-of and-Ephraim Manasseh and-to-me Gilead to-me (9)

מְחֹקְקִי׃ מוֹאָב | סִיר רַחְצִי עַל־אֱדוֹם אַשְׁלִיךְ
I-toss Edom upon washing-of-me basin-of Moab (10) one-being-scepter-of-me

נַעֲלִי עָלַי פְּלֶשֶׁת הִתְרֹעָעִי׃ מִי יֹבִלֵנִי
he-will-bring-in-me who? (11) I-shout-in-triumph Philistia over sandal-of-me

עִיר מָצוֹר מִי נָחַנִי עַד־אֱדוֹם׃ הֲלֹא־אַתָּה אֱלֹהִים
God you not? (12) Edom to he-will-lead-me who? fortification city-of

זְנַחְתָּנוּ וְלֹא־ תֵצֵא אֱלֹהִים בְּצִבְאוֹתֵינוּ׃ הָבָה־ לָּנוּ
to-us give! (13) with-armies-of-us God you-go-out and-not you-rejected-us

עֶזְרָת מִצָּר וְשָׁוְא תְּשׁוּעַת אָדָם׃ בֵּאלֹהִים נַעֲשֶׂה־
we-will-gain with-God (14) man help-of for-worthless against-enemy aid

[16]But I will sing of your
strength,
in the morning I will sing
of your love;
for you are my fortress,
my refuge in times of
trouble.
[17]O my Strength, I sing praise to
you;
you, O God, are my fortress,
my loving God.

Psalm 60

For the director of music. To the tune of, "The Lily of the Covenant." A *miktam*[e] of David. For teaching. When he fought Aram Naharaim[f] and Aram Zobah,[g] and when Joab returned and struck down twelve thousand Edomites in the Valley of Salt.

[1]You have rejected us, O God,
and burst forth upon us;
you have been angry—now
restore us!
[2]You have shaken the land and
torn it open;
mend its fractures, for it is
quaking.
[3]You have shown your people
desperate times;
you have given us wine that
makes us stagger.
[4]But for those who fear you,
you have raised a banner
to be unfurled against the
bow. *Selah*
[5]Save us and help us with your
right hand,
that those you love may be
delivered.
[6]God has spoken from his
sanctuary:
"In triumph I will parcel out
Shechem
and measure off the Valley
of Succoth.
[7]Gilead is mine, and Manasseh
is mine;
Ephraim is my helmet,
Judah my scepter.
[8]Moab is my washbasin,
upon Edom I toss my
sandal;
over Philistia I shout in
triumph."
[9]Who will bring me to the
fortified city?
Who will lead me to Edom?
[10]Is it not you, O God, you who
have rejected us
and no longer go out with
our armies?
[11]Give us aid against the enemy,
for the help of man is
worthless.
[12]With God we will gain the

[e]Title: Probably a literary or musical term
[f]Title: That is, Arameans of Northwest Mesopotamia
[g]Title: That is, Arameans of central Syria

*See the note on page 349.

| Heading, *1* See the note on page 401.

°7 ק ועננִי

חַיִל וְהוּא יָבוּס צָרֵינוּ׃ לַמְנַצֵּחַ ׀
for-the-one-directing †(61:1) enemies-of-us he-will-trample and-he victory

עַל־ נְגִינַת לְדָוִד׃ שִׁמְעָה אֱלֹהִים רִנָּתִי הַקְשִׁיבָה
listen-to! cry-of-me God hear! (2) of-David stringed-instrument with

תְּפִלָּתִי׃ מִקְצֵה הָאָרֶץ ׀ אֵלֶיךָ אֶקְרָא בַּעֲטֹף
as-to-grow-faint I-call to-you the-earth from-end-of (3) prayer-of-me

לִבִּי בְּצוּר־ יָרוּם מִמֶּנִּי תַנְחֵנִי׃ כִּי־ הָיִיתָ
you-are for (4) you-lead-me more-than-me he-is-high to-rock heart-of-me

מַחְסֶה לִי מִגְדַּל־ עֹז מִפְּנֵי אוֹיֵב׃ אָגוּרָה
I-would-dwell (5) one-being-foe at-against strength tower-of to-me refuge

בְאָהָלְךָ עוֹלָמִים אֶחֱסֶה בְסֵתֶר כְּנָפֶיךָ סֶּלָה׃
selah wings-of-you in-shelter-of I-would-take-refuge forevers in-tent-of-you

כִּי־אַתָּה אֱלֹהִים שָׁמַעְתָּ לִנְדָרָי נָתַתָּ יְרֻשַּׁת יִרְאֵי
ones-fearing-of inheritance-of you-gave to-vows-of-me you-heard God you for (6)

שְׁמֶךָ׃ יָמִים עַל־ יְמֵי־ מֶלֶךְ תּוֹסִיף שְׁנוֹתָיו כְּמוֹ־
for years-of-him you-increase king days-of upon days (7) name-of-you

דֹר וָדֹר׃ יֵשֵׁב עוֹלָם לִפְנֵי
in-presences-of forever may-he-be-enthroned (8) and-generation generation

אֱלֹהִים חֶסֶד וֶאֱמֶת מַן יִנְצְרֻהוּ׃ כֵּן
then (9) they-will-protect-him appoint! and-faithfulness love God

אֲזַמְּרָה שִׁמְךָ לָעַד לְשַׁלְּמִי נְדָרַי יוֹם ׀ יוֹם׃
day day vows-of-me to-fulfill-me for-ever name-of-you I-will-sing-praise

לַמְנַצֵּחַ עַל־ יְדוּתוּן מִזְמוֹר לְדָוִד׃ אַךְ אֶל־אֱלֹהִים
God in alone (2) of-David psalm Jeduthun to for-the-one-directing †(62:1)

דּוּמִיָּה נַפְשִׁי מִמֶּנּוּ יְשׁוּעָתִי׃ אַךְ־ הוּא צוּרִי
rock-of-me he alone (3) salvation-of-me from-him soul-of-me rest

וִישׁוּעָתִי מִשְׂגַּבִּי לֹא־ אֶמּוֹט רַבָּה׃ עַד־
until (4) greatly I-will-be-shaken never fortress-of-me and-salvation-of-me

אָנָה ׀ תְּהוֹתְתוּ עַל אִישׁ תְּרָצְּחוּ כֻלְּכֶם כְּקִיר
like-wall all-of-you you-would-throw-down man on you-will-assault to-when?

נָטוּי גָּדֵר הַדְּחוּיָה׃ אַךְ מִשְּׂאֵתוֹ ׀
from-lofty-place-of-him fully (5) the-one-tottering fence one-leaning

יָעֲצוּ לְהַדִּיחַ יִרְצוּ כָזָב בְּפִיו יְבָרֵכוּ
they-bless with-mouth-of-him lie they-delight-in to-topple they-intend

וּבְקִרְבָּם יְקַלְלוּ־ סֶלָה׃ אַךְ לֵאלֹהִים דּוֹמִּי נַפְשִׁי
soul-of-me find-rest! in-God alone (6) selah they-curse but-in-heart-of-them

כִּי־ מִמֶּנּוּ תִּקְוָתִי׃ אַךְ־ הוּא צוּרִי וִישׁוּעָתִי
and-salvation-of-me rock-of-me he alone (7) hope-of-me from-him for

victory,
and he will trample down
our enemies.

Psalm 61

For the director of music. With stringed instruments. Of David.

1 Hear my cry, O God;
listen to my prayer.
2 From the ends of the earth I
call to you,
I call as my heart grows
faint;
lead me to the rock that is
higher than I.
3 For you have been my refuge,
a strong tower against the
foe.
4 I long to dwell in your tent
forever
and take refuge in the
shelter of your wings.
Selah
5 For you have heard my vows,
O God;
you have given me the
heritage of those who fear
your name.
6 Increase the days of the king's
life,
his years for many
generations.
7 May he be enthroned in God's
presence forever;
appoint your love and
faithfulness to protect
him.
8 Then will I ever sing praise to
your name
and fulfill my vows day
after day.

Psalm 62

For the director of music. To Jeduthun. A psalm of David.

1 My soul finds rest in God
alone;
my salvation comes from
him.
2 He alone is my rock and my
salvation;
he is my fortress, I will
never be shaken.
3 How long will you assault a
man?
Would all of you throw him
down—
this leaning wall, this
tottering fence?
4 They fully intend to topple
him
from his lofty place;
they take delight in lies.
With their mouths they bless,
but in their hearts they
curse. *Selah*
5 Find rest, O my soul, in God
alone;
my hope comes from him.
6 He alone is my rock and my
salvation;

*See the note on page 401.

†Heading, *1* See the note on page 349.

מִשְׂגַּבִּי לֹא אֶמּוֹט׃ (8) עַל־אֱלֹהִים יִשְׁעִי וּכְבוֹדִי
and-honor-of-me salvation-of-me God on (8) I-will-be-shaken not fortress-of-me

צוּר־עֻזִּי מַחְסִי בֵּאלֹהִים׃ (9) בִּטְחוּ בוֹ בְכָל־עֵת ׀
time at-all-of in-him trust! (9) in-God refuge-of-me might-of-me rock-of

עָם שִׁפְכוּ־לְפָנָיו לְבַבְכֶם אֱלֹהִים מַחֲסֶה־לָּנוּ סֶלָה׃ (10) אַךְ ׀ הֶבֶל
breath but (10) selah to-us refuge God heart-of-you to-him pour-out! people

בְּנֵי־אָדָם כָּזָב בְּנֵי אִישׁ בְּמֹאזְנַיִם לַעֲלוֹת הֵמָּה מֵהֶבֶל יָחַד׃
together only-breath they to-go-up on-balances man sons-of lie mankind sons-of

(11) אַל־תִּבְטְחוּ בְעֹשֶׁק וּבְגָזֵל אַל־תֶּהְבָּלוּ
you-take-pride not or-in-stolen-thing in-extortion you-trust not (11)

חַיִל ׀ כִּי־יָנוּב אַל־תָּשִׁיתוּ לֵב׃ (12) אַחַת ׀ דִּבֶּר אֱלֹהִים
God he-spoke one-thing (12) heart you-set not he-increases though richness

שְׁתַּיִם־זוּ שָׁמָעְתִּי כִּי עֹז לֵאלֹהִים׃ (13) וּלְךָ־אֲדֹנָי חָסֶד
love Lord and-to-you (13) to-God strength that I-heard which two-things

כִּי־אַתָּה תְשַׁלֵּם לְאִישׁ כְּמַעֲשֵׂהוּ׃ *(63:1) מִזְמוֹר לְדָוִד
of-David psalm *(63:1) as-deed-of-him to-each you-will-reward you surely

בִּהְיוֹתוֹ בְּמִדְבַּר יְהוּדָה׃ (2) אֱלֹהִים ׀ אֵלִי אַתָּה אֲשַׁחֲרֶךָּ
I-earnestly-seek-you you God-of-me God (2) Judah in-desert-of when-to-be-him

צָמְאָה לְךָ ׀ נַפְשִׁי כָּמַהּ לְךָ בְשָׂרִי בְּאֶרֶץ־צִיָּה
dry in-land body-of-me for-you he-longs soul-of-me for-you she-thirsts

וְעָיֵף בְּלִי־מָיִם׃ (3) כֵּן בַּקֹּדֶשׁ חֲזִיתִיךָ לִרְאוֹת עֻזְּךָ
power-of-you to-behold I-saw-you in-the-sanctuary so (3) waters no and-weary

וּכְבוֹדֶךָ׃ (4) כִּי־טוֹב חַסְדְּךָ מֵחַיִּים שְׂפָתַי
lips-of-me than-lives love-of-you better because (4) and-glory-of-you

יְשַׁבְּחוּנְךָ׃ (5) כֵּן אֲבָרֶכְךָ בְחַיָּי בְּשִׁמְךָ
in-name-of-you in-lives-of-me I-will-praise-you so (5) they-will-glorify-you

אֶשָּׂא כַפָּי׃ (6) כְּמוֹ חֵלֶב וָדֶשֶׁן תִּשְׂבַּע
she-will-be-satisfied and-richness fatness as (6) hands-of-me I-will-lift-up

נַפְשִׁי וְשִׂפְתֵי רְנָנוֹת יְהַלֶּל־פִּי׃ (7) אִם־
when (7) mouth-of-me he-will-praise singings and-lips-of soul-of-me

זְכַרְתִּיךָ עַל־יְצוּעָי בְּאַשְׁמֻרוֹת אֶהְגֶּה־בָּךְ׃ (8) כִּי־
because (8) of-you I-think through-night-watches beds-of-me on I-remember-you

הָיִיתָ עֶזְרָתָה לִּי וּבְצֵל כְּנָפֶיךָ אֲרַנֵּן׃ (9) דָּבְקָה
she-stays (9) I-sing wings-of-you then-in-shadow-of to-me help you-are

נַפְשִׁי אַחֲרֶיךָ בִּי תָּמְכָה יְמִינֶךָ׃ (10) וְהֵמָּה
and-they (10) right-hand-of-you she-upholds to-me close-to-you self-of-me

לְשׁוֹאָה יְבַקְשׁוּ נַפְשִׁי יָבֹאוּ בְּתַחְתִּיּוֹת הָאָרֶץ׃
the-earth to-depths-of they-will-go life-of-me they-seek for-destruction

he is my fortress, I will not
be shaken.
7 My salvation and my honor
depend on God[h];
he is my mighty rock, my
refuge.
8 Trust in him at all times, O
people;
pour out your hearts to him,
for God is our refuge. *Selah*
9 Lowborn men are but a
breath,
the highborn are but a lie;
if weighed on a balance, they
are nothing;
together they are only a
breath.
10 Do not trust in extortion
or take pride in stolen
goods;
though your riches increase,
do not set your heart on
them.
11 One thing God has spoken,
two things have I heard:
that you, O God, are strong,
12 and that you, O Lord, are
loving.
Surely you will reward each
person
according to what he has
done.

Psalm 63

A psalm of David. When he was in the desert of Judah.

1 O God, you are my God,
earnestly I seek you;
my soul thirsts for you,
my body longs for you,
in a dry and weary land
where there is no water.
2 I have seen you in the
sanctuary
and beheld your power and
your glory.
3 Because your love is better
than life,
my lips will glorify you.
4 I will praise you as long as I
live,
and in your name I will lift
up my hands.
5 My soul will be satisfied as
with the richest of foods;
with singing lips my mouth
will praise you.
6 On my bed I remember you;
I think of you through the
watches of the night.
7 Because you are my help,
I sing in the shadow of your
wings.
8 I stay close to you;
your right hand upholds me.
9 They who seek my life will be
destroyed;
they will go down to the
depths of the earth.

h7 Or *I God Most High is my salvation and my honor*

*Heading, *1* See the note on page 349.

יַגִּירֻהוּ עַל־ יְדֵי־ חָרֶב מְנָת שֻׁעָלִים יִהְיוּ׃

they-will-become jackals food-of sword hands-of to they-will-give-him (11)

וְהַמֶּלֶךְ יִשְׂמַח בֵּאלֹהִים יִתְהַלֵּל כָּל־ הַנִּשְׁבָּע

the-one-swearing all-of he-will-praise in-God he-will-rejoice but-the-king (12)

בּוֹ כִּי יִסָּכֵר פִּי דוֹבְרֵי־ שָׁקֶר׃

lie ones-speaking-of mouth-of he-will-be-silenced while by-him

לַמְנַצֵּחַ מִזְמוֹר לְדָוִד׃ שְׁמַע־אֱלֹהִים קוֹלִי

voice-of-me God hear! (2) of-David psalm for-the-one-directing *(64:1)

בְשִׂיחִי מִפַּחַד אוֹיֵב תִּצֹּר חַיָּי׃

lives-of-me you-protect one-being-enemy from-threat-of in-complaint-of-me

תַּסְתִּירֵנִי מִסּוֹד מְרֵעִים מֵרִגְשַׁת

from-noisy-crowd-of ones-being-wicked from-conspiracy-of you-hide-me (3)

פֹּעֲלֵי אָוֶן׃ אֲשֶׁר שָׁנְנוּ כַחֶרֶב לְשׁוֹנָם

tongue-of-them like-the-sword they-sharpen who (4) evil ones-doing-of

דָּרְכוּ חִצָּם דָּבָר מָר׃ לִירוֹת בַּמִּסְתָּרִים תָּם

innocent-man from-the-ambushes to-shoot (5) deadly word arrow-of-them they-aim

פִּתְאֹם יֹרֻהוּ וְלֹא יִירָאוּ׃ יְחַזְּקוּ־ לָמוֹ ׀ דָּבָר

plan to-them they-encourage (6) they-fear and-not they-shoot-him suddenly

רָע יְסַפְּרוּ לִטְמוֹן מוֹקְשִׁים אָמְרוּ מִי יִרְאֶה־ לָמוֹ׃ יַחְפְּשׂוּ־

they-plot (7) to-them he-will-see who? they-say snares to-hide they-talk evil

עוֹלֹת תַּמְנוּ חֵפֶשׂ מְחֻפָּשׂ וְקֶרֶב אִישׁ

man surely-mind-of one-being-planned plan we-made-perfect injustices

וְלֵב עָמֹק׃ וַיֹּרֵם אֱלֹהִים חֵץ פִּתְאוֹם הָיוּ

they-will-be suddenly arrow God but-he-will-shoot-them (8) cunning and-heart

מַכּוֹתָם׃ וַיַּכְשִׁילוּהוּ עָלֵימוֹ לְשׁוֹנָם

tongue-of-them against-them and-they-will-ruin-him (9) strikings-down-of-them

יִתְנֹדְדוּ כָּל־ רֹאֵה בָם׃ וַיִּירְאוּ

and-they-will-fear (10) to-them one-seeing-of all-of they-will-shake-head

כָּל־ אָדָם וַיַּגִּידוּ פֹּעַל אֱלֹהִים וּמַעֲשֵׂהוּ

and-deed-of-him God work-of and-they-will-proclaim mankind all-of

הִשְׂכִּילוּ׃ יִשְׂמַח צַדִּיק בַּיהוָה וְחָסָה

and-let-him-take-refuge in-Yahweh righteous let-him-rejoice (11) they-will-ponder

בוֹ וְיִתְהַלְלוּ כָּל־ יִשְׁרֵי־ לֵב׃

heart ones-upright-of all-of and-let-them-praise in-him

לַמְנַצֵּחַ מִזְמוֹר לְדָוִד שִׁיר׃ לְךָ דֻמִיָּה תְהִלָּה

praise silence for-you (2) song of-David psalm for-the-one-directing *(65:1)

אֱלֹהִים בְּצִיּוֹן וּלְךָ יְשֻׁלַּם־ נֶדֶר׃ שֹׁמֵעַ תְּפִלָּה

prayer one-hearing (3) vow he-will-be-fulfilled and-to-you in-Zion God

10 They will be given over to the sword
and become food for jackals.

11 But the king will rejoice in God;
all who swear by God's name will praise him,
while the mouths of liars will be silenced.

Psalm 64

For the director of music. A psalm of David.

1 Hear me, O God, as I voice my complaint;
protect my life from the threat of the enemy.

2 Hide me from the conspiracy of the wicked,
from that noisy crowd of evildoers,
3 who sharpen their tongues like swords
and aim their words like deadly arrows.
4 They shoot from ambush at the innocent man;
they shoot at him suddenly, without fear.

5 They encourage each other in evil plans,
they talk about hiding their snares;
they say, "Who will see them[i]?"
6 They plot injustice and say,
"We have devised a perfect plan!"
Surely the mind and heart of man are cunning.

7 But God will shoot them with arrows;
suddenly they will be struck down.
8 He will turn their own tongues against them
and bring them to ruin;
all who see them will shake their heads in scorn.
9 All mankind will fear;
they will proclaim the works of God
and ponder what he has done.

10 Let the righteous rejoice in the Lord
and take refuge in him;
let all the upright in heart praise him!

Psalm 65

For the director of music. A psalm of David. A song.

1 Praise awaits[j] you, O God, in Zion;
to you our vows will be fulfilled.
2 O you who hear prayer,

i5 Or *us*
j1 Or *befits;* the meaning of the Hebrew for this word is uncertain.

*Heading, *1* See the note on page 349.

עדיך כל- בשר יבאו׃ דברי עונת גברו מני
to-you all-of man they-will-come (4) matters-of sins they-overwhelmed over-me

פשעינו אתה תכפרם׃ אשרי | תבחר
transgressions-of-us you you-atoned-for-them (5) blessednesses-of you-choose

ותקרב ישכן חצריך נשבעה בטוב
and-you-bring-near he-lives courts-of-you we-are-filled with-goodness-of

ביתך קדש היכלך׃ נוראות |
house-of-you holiness-of temple-of-you (6) deeds-being-awesome

בצדק תעננו אלהי ישענו מבטח כל- קצוי- ארץ
of-righteousness you-answer-us God-of salvation-of-us hope all-of ends-of earth

וים רחקים׃ מכין הרים בכחו נאזר
and-sea-of far-ones (7) one-forming mountains by-power-of-him one-arming-himself

בגבורה׃ משביח | שאון ימים שאון גליהם
with-strength (8) one-stilling roar-of seas roar-of waves-of-them

והמון לאמים׃ וייראו | ישבי קצות
and-turmoil-of nations (9) and-they-fear ones-living-of places-far-away

מאותתיך מוצאי- בקר וערב תרנין׃
of-wonders-of-you dawns-of morning and-evening you-call-forth-songs-of-joy

פקדת הארץ | ותשקקה רבת תעשרנה
(10) you-care-for the-land and-you-water-her abundantly you-enrich-her

פלג אלהים מלא מים תכין דגנם כי- כן
stream-of God filled-of waters you-provide grain-of-them for so

תכינה׃ תלמיה רוה נחת גדודיה
you-ordained-her (11) furrows-of-her to-drench to-level ridges-of-her

ברביבים תמגגנה צמחה תברך׃ עטרת שנת
with-showers you-soften-her crop-of-her you-bless (12) you-crown year-of

טובתך ומעגליך ירעפון דשן׃ ירעפו
bounty-of-you and-carts-of-you they-overflow abundance (13) they-overflow

נאות מדבר וגיל גבעות תחגרנה׃ לבשו
grasslands-of desert and-gladness hills they-are-clothed (14) they-are-covered

כרים | הצאן ועמקים יעטפו- בר יתרועעו
meadows the-flock and-valleys they-are-mantled grain they-shout-for-joy

אף- ישירו׃ למנצח שיר מזמור הריעו לאלהים
also they-sing (66:1) for-the-one-directing song psalm shout! to-God

כל- הארץ׃ זמרו כבוד- שמו שימו כבוד תהלתו׃
all-of the-earth (2) sing! glory-of name-of-him offer! glory praise-of-him

אמרו לאלהים מה- נורא מעשיך ברב
(3) say! to-God how! one-being-awesome deeds-of-you in-greatness-of

to you all men will come.
3 When we were overwhelmed
by sins,
you atoned for our
transgressions.
4 Blessed is the man you choose
and bring near to live in
your courts!
We are filled with the good
things of your house,
of your holy temple.

5 You answer us with awesome
deeds of righteousness,
O God our Savior,
the hope of all the ends of the
earth
and of the farthest seas,
6 who formed the mountains by
your power,
having armed yourself with
strength,
7 who stilled the roaring of the
seas,
the roaring of their waves,
and the turmoil of the
nations.
8 Those living far away fear
your wonders;
where morning dawns and
evening fades
you call forth songs of joy.

9 You care for the land and
water it;
you enrich it abundantly.
The streams of God are filled
with water
to provide the people with
grain,
for so you have ordained it.[k]
10 You drench its furrows
and level its ridges;
you soften it with showers
and bless its crops.
11 You crown the year with your
bounty,
and your carts overflow
with abundance.
12 The grasslands of the desert
overflow;
the hills are clothed with
gladness.
13 The meadows are covered with
flocks
and the valleys are mantled
with grain;
they shout for joy and sing.

Psalm 66

For the director of music. A song. A psalm.

1 Shout with joy to God, all the
earth!
2 Sing to the glory of his
name;
offer him glory and praise!
3 Say to God, "How awesome
are your deeds!

[k]9 Or *for that is how you prepare the land*

*See the note on page 349.

עֻזְּךָ יְכַחֲשׁוּ לְךָ אֹיְבֶיךָ׃ כָּל־
all-of (4) ones-being-enemies-of-you before-you they-cringe power-of-you

הָאָרֶץ ׀ יִשְׁתַּחֲווּ לְךָ וִיזַמְּרוּ־ לָךְ יְזַמְּרוּ
they-sing-praise to-you and-they-sing-praise to-you they-bow-down the-earth

שִׁמְךָ סֶלָה׃ לְכוּ וּרְאוּ מִפְעֲלוֹת אֱלֹהִים נוֹרָא עֲלִילָה
work one-being-awesome God deeds-of and-see! come! (5) selah name-of-you

עַל־ בְּנֵי אָדָם׃ הָפַךְ יָם ׀ לְיַבָּשָׁה בַּנָּהָר
through-the-river into-dry-land sea he-turned (6) man sons-of in-behalf-of

יַעַבְרוּ בְרָגֶל שָׁם נִשְׂמְחָה־ בּוֹ׃ מֹשֵׁל בִּגְבוּרָתוֹ ׀
by-power-of-him one-ruling (7) in-him let-us-rejoice there on-foot they-passed

עוֹלָם עֵינָיו בַּגּוֹיִם תִּצְפֶּינָה הַסּוֹרְרִים ׀ אַל־
not the-ones-rebelling they-watch on-the-nations eyes-of-him forever

יָרִימוּ° לָמוֹ סֶלָה׃ בָּרְכוּ עַמִּים ׀ אֱלֹהֵינוּ
God-of-us peoples praise! (8) selah against-him let-them-rise-up

וְהַשְׁמִיעוּ קוֹל תְּהִלָּתוֹ׃ הַשָּׂם נַפְשֵׁנוּ
life-of-us the-one-preserving (9) praise-of-him sound-of and-make-heard!

בַּחַיִּים וְלֹא־ נָתַן לַמּוֹט רַגְלֵנוּ׃
foot-of-us for-the-slipping he-allowed and-not among-the-living-ones

כִּי־ בְחַנְתָּנוּ אֱלֹהִים צְרַפְתָּנוּ כִּצְרָף־ כָּסֶף׃
silver like-to-refine you-refined-us God you-tested-us for (10)

הֲבֵאתָנוּ בַמְּצוּדָה שַׂמְתָּ מוּעָקָה בְמָתְנֵינוּ׃
on-backs-of-us burden you-laid into-the-prison you-brought-us (11)

הִרְכַּבְתָּ אֱנוֹשׁ לְרֹאשֵׁנוּ בָּאנוּ־ בָאֵשׁ
through-the-fire we-went over-head-of-us man you-let-ride (12)

וּבַמַּיִם וַתּוֹצִיאֵנוּ לָרְוָיָה׃
to-the-place-of-abundance and-you-brought-us and-through-the-waters

אָבוֹא בֵיתְךָ בְעוֹלוֹת אֲשַׁלֵּם לְךָ
to-you I-will-fulfill with-burnt-offerings temple-of-you I-will-come (13)

נְדָרָי׃ אֲשֶׁר־ פָּצוּ שְׂפָתָי וְדִבֶּר־ פִּי
mouth-of-me and-he-spoke lips-of-me they-promised which (14) vows-of-me

בַּצַּר־ לִי׃ עֹלוֹת מֵחִים אַעֲלֶה־ לָּךְ
to-you I-will-sacrifice fat-animals sacrifices-of (15) of-me in-the-trouble

עִם־ קְטֹרֶת אֵילִים אֶעֱשֶׂה בָקָר עִם־עַתּוּדִים סֶלָה׃ לְכוּ־ שִׁמְעוּ
listen! come! (16) selah goats with bull I-will-offer rams offering-of with

וַאֲסַפְּרָה כָּל־ יִרְאֵי אֱלֹהִים אֲשֶׁר עָשָׂה לְנַפְשִׁי׃
for-self-of-me he-did what God ones-fearing-of all-of and-let-me-tell

אֵלָיו פִּי־ קָרָאתִי וְרוֹמַם תַּחַת לְשׁוֹנִי׃ אָוֶן אִם־
if sin (18) tongue-of-me on and-praise I-cried-out mouth-of-me to-him (17)

So great is your power
that your enemies cringe
before you.
4All the earth bows down to
you;
they sing praise to you,
they sing praise to your
name." *Selah*

5Come and see what God has
done,
how awesome his works in
man's behalf!
6He turned the sea into dry
land,
they passed through the
river on foot—
come, let us rejoice in him.
7He rules forever by his power,
his eyes watch the nations—
let not the rebellious rise up
against him. *Selah*

8Praise our God, O peoples,
let the sound of his praise
be heard;
9he has preserved our lives
and kept our feet from
slipping.
10For you, O God, tested us;
you refined us like silver.
11You brought us into prison
and laid burdens on our
backs.
12You let men ride over our
heads;
we went through fire and
water,
but you brought us to a
place of abundance.

13I will come to your temple
with burnt offerings
and fulfill my vows to you—
14vows my lips promised and
my mouth spoke
when I was in trouble.
15I will sacrifice fat animals to
you
and an offering of rams;
I will offer bulls and goats.
Selah

16Come and listen, all you who
fear God;
let me tell you what he has
done for me.
17I cried out to him with my
mouth;
his praise was on my
tongue.

°7 ק ירומו

רָאִיתִי בְלִבִּי לֹא יִשְׁמַע ׀ אֲדֹנָי׃ אָכֵן
surely (19) Lord he-would-have-listened not in-heart-of-me I-cherished

שָׁמַע אֱלֹהִים הִקְשִׁיב בְּקוֹל תְּפִלָּתִי׃ בָּרוּךְ אֱלֹהִים
God being-praised (20) prayer-of-me to-voice-of he-heard God he-listened

אֲשֶׁר לֹא־הֵסִיר תְּפִלָּתִי וְחַסְדּוֹ מֵאִתִּי׃
from-with-me or-love-of-him prayer-of-me he-rejected not who

לַמְנַצֵּחַ† בִּנְגִינֹת מִזְמוֹר שִׁיר׃ אֱלֹהִים
God (2) song psalm with-stringed-instruments for-the-one-directing *(67:1)

יְחָנֵּנוּ וִיבָרְכֵנוּ יָאֵר פָּנָיו
faces-of-him may-he-make-shine and-may-he-bless-us may-he-be-gracious-to-us

אִתָּנוּ סֶלָה׃ לָדַעַת בָּאָרֶץ דַּרְכֶּךָ בְּכָל־גּוֹיִם
nations among-all-of way-of-you on-the-earth to-know (3) selah upon-us

יְשׁוּעָתֶךָ׃ יוֹדוּךָ עַמִּים ׀ אֱלֹהִים יוֹדוּךָ
may-they-praise-you God peoples may-they-praise-you (4) salvation-of-you

עַמִּים כֻּלָּם׃ יִשְׂמְחוּ וִירַנְּנוּ לְאֻמִּים
nations and-may-they-sing-for-joy may-they-be-glad (5) all-of-them peoples

כִּי־תִשְׁפֹּט עַמִּים מִישׁוֹר וּלְאֻמִּים ׀ בָּאָרֶץ תַּנְחֵם סֶלָה׃
selah you-guide-them of-the-earth and-nations justly peoples you-rule for

יוֹדוּךָ עַמִּים ׀ אֱלֹהִים יוֹדוּךָ עַמִּים כֻּלָּם׃
all-of-them peoples may-they-praise-you God peoples may-they-praise-you (6)

אֶרֶץ נָתְנָה יְבוּלָהּ יְבָרְכֵנוּ אֱלֹהִים אֱלֹהֵינוּ׃
God-of-us God he-will-bless-us harvest-of-her she-will-yield land (7)

יְבָרְכֵנוּ אֱלֹהִים וְיִירְאוּ אֹתוֹ כָּל־אַפְסֵי־אָרֶץ׃
earth ends-of all-of him and-they-will-fear God he-will-bless-us (8)

לַמְנַצֵּחַ לְדָוִד מִזְמוֹר שִׁיר׃ יָקוּם אֱלֹהִים
God may-he-arise (2) song psalm of-David for-the-one-directing *(68:1)

יָפוּצוּ אוֹיְבָיו וְיָנוּסוּ
and-may-they-flee ones-being-enemies-of-him may-they-be-scattered

מְשַׂנְאָיו מִפָּנָיו׃ כְּהִנְדֹּף עָשָׁן תִּנְדֹּף
may-you-blow smoke as-to-be-blown (3) from-before-him ones-being-foes-of-him

כְּהִמֵּס דּוֹנַג מִפְּנֵי־אֵשׁ יֹאבְדוּ רְשָׁעִים מִפְּנֵי אֱלֹהִים׃
God from-before wicked-ones may-they-perish fire at-before wax as-to-melt

וְצַדִּיקִים יִשְׂמְחוּ יַעַלְצוּ לִפְנֵי אֱלֹהִים
God before may-they-rejoice may-they-be-glad but-righteous-ones (4)

וְיָשִׂישׂוּ בְשִׂמְחָה׃ שִׁירוּ ׀ לֵאלֹהִים זַמְּרוּ שְׁמוֹ
name-of-him sing-praise! to-God sing! (5) with-joy and-may-they-be-happy

סֹלּוּ לָרֹכֵב בָּעֲרָבוֹת בְּיָהּ שְׁמוֹ וְעִלְזוּ
and-rejoice! name-of-him to-Yahweh on-the-clouds to-the-one-riding extol!

18 If I had cherished sin in my heart,
the Lord would not have listened;
19 but God has surely listened
and heard my voice in prayer.
20 Praise be to God,
who has not rejected my prayer
or withheld his love from me!

Psalm 67

For the director of music. With stringed instruments. A psalm. A song.

1 May God be gracious to us and bless us
and make his face shine upon us; *Selah*
2 may your ways be known on earth,
your salvation among all nations.

3 May the peoples praise you, O God;
may all the peoples praise you.
4 May the nations be glad and sing for joy,
for you rule the peoples justly
and guide the nations of the earth. *Selah*
5 May the peoples praise you, O God;
may all the peoples praise you.

6 Then the land will yield its harvest,
and God, our God, will bless us.
7 God will bless us,
and all the ends of the earth will fear him.

Psalm 68

For the director of music. Of David. A psalm. A song.

1 May God arise, may his enemies be scattered;
may his foes flee before him.
2 As smoke is blown away by the wind,
may you blow them away;
as wax melts before the fire,
may the wicked perish before God.
3 But may the righteous be glad
and rejoice before God;
may they be happy and joyful.

4 Sing to God, sing praise to his name,
extol him who rides on the clouds[l] –
his name is the LORD–
and rejoice before him.

[l] 4 Or *I prepare the way for him who rides through the deserts*

*Heading, *1* See the note on page 349.
†*1* Most mss have *pathah* under the *beth* (צַח–).

לְפָנָיו׃ אֲבִי יְתוֹמִים וְדַיַּן אַלְמָנוֹת אֱלֹהִים

God widows and-defender-of fatherless-ones father-of (6) before-him

בִּמְעוֹן קָדְשׁוֹ׃ אֱלֹהִים ׀ מוֹשִׁיב יְחִידִים ׀ בַּיְתָה

in-family lonely-ones one-setting God (7) holiness-of-him in-dwelling-of

מוֹצִיא אֲסִירִים בַּכּוֹשָׁרוֹת אַךְ סוֹרְרִים שָׁכְנוּ

they-live ones-rebelling but with-the-songs prisoners one-leading-forth

צְחִיחָה׃ אֱלֹהִים בְּצֵאתְךָ לִפְנֵי עַמֶּךָ

people-of-you before when-to-go-out-you God (8) sun-scorched-land

בְּצַעְדְּךָ בִישִׁימוֹן סֶלָה׃ אֶרֶץ רָעָשָׁה ׀ אַף־ שָׁמַיִם

heavens also she-shook earth (9) selah through-wasteland when-to-march-you

נָטְפוּ מִפְּנֵי אֱלֹהִים זֶה סִינַי מִפְּנֵי אֱלֹהִים אֱלֹהֵי יִשְׂרָאֵל׃

Israel God-of God at-before Sinai One-of God at-before they-poured-rain

גֶּשֶׁם נְדָבוֹת תָּנִיף אֱלֹהִים נַחֲלָתְךָ וְנִלְאָה

even-one-being-weary inheritance-of-you God you-gave abundances shower-of (10)

אַתָּה כוֹנַנְתָּהּ׃ חַיָּתְךָ יָשְׁבוּ־ בָהּ תָּכִין

you-provided in-her they-settled people-of-you (11) you-refreshed-her you

בְּטוֹבָתְךָ לֶעָנִי אֱלֹהִים׃ אֲדֹנָי יִתֶּן־ אֹמֶר

word he-announced Lord (12) God for-the-poor from-bounty-of-you

הַמְבַשְּׂרוֹת צָבָא רָב׃ מַלְכֵי צְבָאוֹת יִדֹּדוּן יִדֹּדוּן

they-flee they-flee armies kings-of (13) great company the-ones-proclaiming

וּנְוַת בַּיִת תְּחַלֵּק שָׁלָל׃ אִם־ תִּשְׁכְּבוּן בֵּין

among you-sleep while (14) plunder she-divides residence and-camp-of

שְׁפַתָּיִם כַּנְפֵי יוֹנָה נֶחְפָּה בַכֶּסֶף וְאֶבְרוֹתֶיהָ

and-feathers-of-her with-the-silver being-sheathed dove wings-of campfires

בִּירַקְרַק חָרוּץ׃ בְּפָרֵשׂ שַׁדַּי מְלָכִים בָּהּ תַּשְׁלֵג

she-snowed in-her kings Almighty when-to-scatter (15) gold with-shine-of

בְּצַלְמוֹן׃ הַר־ אֱלֹהִים הַר־ בָּשָׁן הַר

mountain-of Bashan mountain-of majesties mountain-of (16) on-Zalmon

גַּבְנֻנִּים הַר־ בָּשָׁן׃ לָמָּה ׀ תְּרַצְּדוּן הָרִים

mountains you-gaze-in-envy why? (17) Bashan mountain-of rugged-ones

גַּבְנֻנִּים הָהָר חָמַד אֱלֹהִים לְשִׁבְתּוֹ אַף־ יְהוָה

Yahweh indeed to-reign-him God he-chooses the-mountain rugged-ones

יִשְׁכֹּן לָנֶצַח׃ רֶכֶב אֱלֹהִים רִבֹּתַיִם אַלְפֵי

thousands-of tens-of-thousands God chariot-of (18) to-forever he-will-dwell

שִׁנְאָן אֲדֹנָי בָם סִינַי בַּקֹּדֶשׁ׃ עָלִיתָ לַמָּרוֹם ׀

to-the-height you-ascended (19) into-the-sanctuary Sinai †in-them Lord multitude

שָׁבִיתָ שֶּׁבִי לָקַחְתָּ מַתָּנוֹת בָּאָדָם וְאַף סוֹרְרִים

ones-rebelling even-also from-the-man gifts you-received captive you-led

5 A father to the fatherless, a
defender of widows,
is God in his holy dwelling.
6 God sets the lonely in
families,[m]
he leads forth the prisoners
with singing;
but the rebellious live in a
sun-scorched land.

7 When you went out before
your people, O God,
when you marched through
the wasteland, *Selah*
8 the earth shook,
the heavens poured down
rain,
before God, the One of Sinai,
before God, the God of
Israel.
9 You gave abundant showers,
O God;
you refreshed your weary
inheritance.
10 Your people settled in it,
and from your bounty, O
God, you provided for the
poor.

11 The Lord announced the word,
and great was the company
of those who proclaimed
it:
12 "Kings and armies flee in
haste;
in the camps men divide the
plunder.
13 Even while you sleep among
the campfires,[n]
the wings of ⌊my⌋ dove are
sheathed with silver,
its feathers with shining
gold."
14 When the Almighty[o] scattered
the kings in the land,
it was like snow fallen on
Zalmon.

15 The mountains of Bashan are
majestic mountains;
rugged are the mountains of
Bashan.
16 Why gaze in envy, O rugged
mountains,
at the mountain where God
chooses to reign,
where the LORD himself will
dwell forever?
17 The chariots of God are tens of
thousands
and thousands of thousands;
the Lord ⌊has come⌋ from
Sinai into his sanctuary.
18 When you ascended on high,
you led captives in your
train;
you received gifts from men,
even from[p] the rebellious—

[m] 6 Or *the desolate in a homeland*
[n] 13 Or *saddlebags*
[o] 14 Hebrew *Shaddai*
[p] 18 Or *gifts for men, / even*

*See the note on page 349.

†*18* The NIV repoints this word as (בָּם(ו, *from.*

לִשְׁכֹּן ׀ יָהּ אֱלֹהִים׃ בָּרוּךְ אֲדֹנָי יוֹם ׀ יוֹם יַעֲמָס־ לָנוּ

for-us he-bears-burden day day Lord being-praised (20) God Yahweh to-dwell

הָאֵל יְשׁוּעָתֵנוּ סֶלָה׃ הָאֵל ׀ לָנוּ אֵל לְמוֹשָׁעוֹת וְלֵיהוִה

and-from-Yahweh of-salvations God of-us the-God (21) selah salvation-of-us the-God

אֲדֹנָי לַמָּוֶת תּוֹצָאוֹת׃ אַךְ־ אֱלֹהִים יִמְחַץ רֹאשׁ

head-of he-will-crush God surely (22) escapes from-the-death Lord

אֹיְבָיו קָדְקֹד שֵׂעָר מִתְהַלֵּךְ בַּאֲשָׁמָיו׃

in-sins-of-him one-going-on hair crown-of ones-being-enemies-of-him

אָמַר אֲדֹנָי מִבָּשָׁן אָשִׁיב אָשִׁיב מִמְּצֻלוֹת יָם׃

sea from-depths-of I-will-bring I-will-bring from-Bashan Lord he-says (23)

לְמַעַן ׀ תִּמְחַץ† רַגְלְךָ בְּדָם לְשׁוֹן כְּלָבֶיךָ

dogs-of-you tongue-of in-blood foot-of-you †you-may-shatter so-that (24)

מֵאֹיְבִים מִנֵּהוּ׃ רָאוּ הֲלִיכוֹתֶיךָ אֱלֹהִים

God processions-of-you they-view (25) share-of-him from-ones-being-foes

הֲלִיכוֹת אֵלִי מַלְכִּי בַקֹּדֶשׁ׃ קִדְּמוּ

they-are-in-front (26) into-the-sanctuary King-of-me God-of-me processions-of

שָׁרִים אַחַר נֹגְנִים בְּתוֹךְ עֲלָמוֹת תּוֹפֵפוֹת׃

ones-playing-tambourines maidens in-among ones-playing-music after ones-singing

בְּמַקְהֵלוֹת בָּרְכוּ אֱלֹהִים יְהוָה מִמְּקוֹר יִשְׂרָאֵל׃

Israel in-assembly-of Yahweh God praise! in-great-congregations (27)

שָׁם בִּנְיָמִן ׀ צָעִיר רֹדֵם שָׂרֵי יְהוּדָה רִגְמָתָם

throng-of-them Judah princes-of one-leading-them little Benjamin there (28)

שָׂרֵי זְבֻלוּן שָׂרֵי נַפְתָּלִי׃ צִוָּה אֱלֹהֶיךָ

God-of-you he-summoned (29) Naphtali princes-of Zebulun princes-of

עֻזֶּךָ עוּזָּה אֱלֹהִים זוּ פָּעַלְתָּ לָּנוּ׃ מֵהֵיכָלֶךָ

because-of-temple-of-you (30) for-us you-did as God show-strength! power-of-you

עַל־יְרוּשָׁלָםִ לְךָ יוֹבִילוּ מְלָכִים שָׁי׃ גְּעַר חַיַּת קָנֶה

reed beast-of rebuke! (31) gift kings they-will-bring to-you Jerusalem at

עֲדַת אַבִּירִים ׀ בְּעֶגְלֵי עַמִּים מִתְרַפֵּס בְּרַצֵּי־ כָסֶף

silver with-bars-of one-being-humbled nations among-calves-of bulls herd-of

בִּזַּר עַמִּים קְרָבוֹת יֶחְפָּצוּ׃ יֶאֱתָיוּ חַשְׁמַנִּים מִנִּי

from envoys they-will-come (32) they-delight-in wars nations he-scatters

מִצְרָיִם כּוּשׁ תָּרִיץ יָדָיו לֵאלֹהִים׃ מַמְלְכוֹת הָאָרֶץ

the-earth kingdoms-of (33) to-God hands-of-him she-will-submit Cush Egypt

שִׁירוּ לֵאלֹהִים זַמְּרוּ אֲדֹנָי סֶלָה׃ לָרֹכֵב בִּשְׁמֵי

in-skies-of to-the-one-riding (34) selah Lord sing-praise! to-God sing!

שְׁמֵי־ קֶדֶם הֵן יִתֵּן בְּקוֹלוֹ קוֹל עֹז׃

might voice-of with-voice-of-him he-thunders see! ancient skies-of

that you,[q] O LORD God,
might dwell there.

19 Praise be to the Lord, to God
our Savior,
who daily bears our
burdens. *Selah*
20 Our God is a God who saves;
from the Sovereign LORD
comes escape from death.

21 Surely God will crush the
heads of his enemies,
the hairy crowns of those
who go on in their sins.
22 The Lord says, "I will bring
you from Bashan;
I will bring you from the
depths of the sea,
23 that you may plunge your feet
in the blood of your foes,
while the tongues of your
dogs have their share."

24 Your procession has come into
view, O God,
the procession of my God
and King into the
sanctuary.
25 In front are the singers, after
them the musicians;
with them are the maidens
playing tambourines.
26 Praise God in the great
congregation;
praise the LORD in the
assembly of Israel.
27 There is the little tribe of
Benjamin, leading them,
there the great throng of
Judah's princes,
and there the princes of
Zebulun and of Naphtali.

28 Summon your power, O God[r];
show us your strength, O
God, as you have done
before.
29 Because of your temple at
Jerusalem
kings will bring you gifts.
30 Rebuke the beast among the
reeds,
the herd of bulls among the
calves of the nations.
Humbled, may it bring bars of
silver.
Scatter the nations who
delight in war.
31 Envoys will come from Egypt;
Cush[s] will submit herself to
God.

32 Sing to God, O kingdoms of
the earth,
sing praise to the Lord, *Selah*
33 to him who rides the ancient
skies above,
who thunders with mighty
voice.

q18 Or *they*
r28 Many Hebrew manuscripts, Septuagint and Syriac; most Hebrew manuscripts *Your God has summoned power for you*
s31 That is, the upper Nile region

*See the note on page 349.

†24 The NIV reads this word as תִּרְחַץ, *you-may-wash.*

תְּנוּ עֹז לֵאלֹהִים עַל־יִשְׂרָאֵל גַּאֲוָתוֹ וְעֻזּוֹ
and-power-of-him majesty-of-him Israel over of-God power proclaim! (35)

בַּשְּׁחָקִים׃ נוֹרָא אֱלֹהִים מִמִּקְדָּשֶׁיךָ אֵל יִשְׂרָאֵל
Israel God-of in-sanctuaries-of-you God one-being-awesome (36) in-the-skies

הוּא נֹתֵן עֹז וְתַעֲצֻמוֹת לָעָם בָּרוּךְ אֱלֹהִים׃
God being-praised to-the-people and-strengths power one-giving he

לַמְנַצֵּחַ עַל־שׁוֹשַׁנִּים לְדָוִד׃ הוֹשִׁיעֵנִי אֱלֹהִים כִּי
for God save-me! (2) of-David lilies to for-the-one-directing *(69:1)

בָאוּ מַיִם עַד־נָפֶשׁ׃ טָבַעְתִּי בִּיוֵן מְצוּלָה וְאֵין
and-there-is-no depth into-mire-of I-sink (3) neck to waters they-came

מָעֳמָד בָּאתִי בְמַעֲמַקֵּי־מַיִם וְשִׁבֹּלֶת שְׁטָפָתְנִי׃
she-engulfs-me and-flood waters into-depths-of I-came foothold

יָגַעְתִּי בְקָרְאִי נִחַר גְּרוֹנִי כָּלוּ
they-fail throat-of-me he-is-parched from-to-call-out-me I-am-worn-out (4)

עֵינַי מְיַחֵל לֵאלֹהָי׃ רַבּוּ מִשַּׂעֲרוֹת
more-than-hairs-of they-are-numerous (5) for-God-of-me one-looking eyes-of-me

רֹאשִׁי שֹׂנְאַי חִנָּם עָצְמוּ מַצְמִיתַי
ones-destroying-me they-are-many without-reason ones-hating-me head-of-me

אֹיְבַי שֶׁקֶר אֲשֶׁר לֹא־גָזַלְתִּי אָז אָשִׁיב׃
I-must-restore then I-stole not what without-cause ones-being-enemies-of-me

אֱלֹהִים אַתָּה יָדַעְתָּ לְאִוַּלְתִּי וְאַשְׁמוֹתַי מִמְּךָ לֹא־
not from-you and-guilts-of-me to-folly-of-me you-know you God (6)

נִכְחָדוּ׃ אַל־יֵבֹשׁוּ בִי קֹוֶיךָ
ones-hoping-of-you because-of-me may-they-be-disgraced not (7) they-are-hidden

אֲדֹנָי יְהוִה צְבָאוֹת אַל־יִכָּלְמוּ בִי מְבַקְשֶׁיךָ
ones-seeking-you because-of-me may-they-be-shamed not Hosts Yahweh-of Lord

אֱלֹהֵי יִשְׂרָאֵל׃ כִּי־עָלֶיךָ נָשָׂאתִי חֶרְפָּה כִּסְּתָה כְלִמָּה
shame she-covers scorn I-endure for-sake-of-you for (8) Israel God-of

פָנָי׃ מוּזָר הָיִיתִי לְאֶחָי וְנָכְרִי לִבְנֵי
to-sons-of and-alien to-brothers-of-me I-am one-being-stranger (9) faces-of-me

אִמִּי׃ כִּי־קִנְאַת בֵּיתְךָ אֲכָלָתְנִי וְחֶרְפּוֹת
and-insults-of she-consumes-me house-of-you zeal-of for (10) mother-of-me

חוֹרְפֶיךָ נָפְלוּ עָלָי׃ וָאֶבְכֶּה בַצּוֹם נַפְשִׁי
self-of-me in-the-fast when-I-weep (11) on-me they-fall ones-insulting-you

וַתְּהִי לַחֲרָפוֹת לִי׃ וָאֶתְּנָה לְבוּשִׁי שָׂק
sackcloth clothing-of-me when-I-put-on (12) to-me of-scorns then-she-is

וָאֱהִי לָהֶם לְמָשָׁל׃ יָשִׂיחוּ בִי יֹשְׁבֵי שַׁעַר
gate ones-sitting-of at-me they-mock (13) as-sport to-them then-I-am

34 Proclaim the power of God,
whose majesty is over Israel,
whose power is in the skies.
35 You are awesome, O God, in
your sanctuary;
the God of Israel gives
power and strength to his
people.

Praise be to God!

Psalm 69

For the director of music. To the tune of "Lilies." Of David.

1 Save me, O God,
for the waters have come up
to my neck.
2 I sink in the miry depths,
where there is no foothold.
I have come into the deep
waters;
the floods engulf me.
3 I am worn out calling for help;
my throat is parched.
My eyes fail,
looking for my God.
4 Those who hate me without
reason
outnumber the hairs of my
head;
many are my enemies without
cause,
those who seek to destroy
me.
I am forced to restore
what I did not steal.

5 You know my folly, O God;
my guilt is not hidden from
you.

6 May those who hope in you
not be disgraced because of
me,
O Lord, the LORD Almighty;
may those who seek you
not be put to shame because
of me,
O God of Israel.
7 For I endure scorn for your
sake,
and shame covers my face.
8 I am a stranger to my brothers,
an alien to my own
mother's sons;
9 for zeal for your house
consumes me,
and the insults of those who
insult you fall on me.
10 When I weep and fast,
I must endure scorn;
11 when I put on sackcloth,
people make sport of me.
12 Those who sit at the gate mock
me,

*Heading, *1* See the note on page 349.

וּנְגִינוֹת שׁוֹתֵי שֵׁכָר׃ וַאֲנִי תְפִלָּתִי־
prayer-of-me but-I (14) strong-drink ones-drinking-of and-songs-of

לְךָ ׀ יְהוָה עֵת רָצוֹן אֱלֹהִים בְּרָב־ חַסְדֶּךָ עֲנֵנִי
answer-me! love-of-you in-greatness-of God favor time-of Yahweh to-you

בֶּאֱמֶת יִשְׁעֶךָ׃ הַצִּילֵנִי מִטִּיט וְאַל־ אֶטְבָּעָה
let-me-sink and-not from-mire rescue-me! (15) salvation-of-you with-sureness-of

אִנָּצְלָה מִשֹּׂנְאַי וּמִמַּעֲמַקֵּי־ מָיִם׃ אַל־
not (16) waters and-from-depths-of from-ones-hating-me let-me-be-delivered

תִּשְׁטְפֵנִי ׀ שִׁבֹּלֶת מַיִם וְאַל־ תִּבְלָעֵנִי מְצוּלָה וְאַל־
and-not depth let-her-swallow-me and-not waters flood-of let-her-engulf-me

תֶּאְטַר־ עָלַי בְּאֵר פִּיהָ׃ עֲנֵנִי יְהוָה כִּי־ טוֹב
good for Yahweh answer-me! (17) mouth-of-her pit over-me let-her-close

חַסְדֶּךָ כְּרֹב רַחֲמֶיךָ פְּנֵה אֵלָי׃ וְאַל־ תַּסְתֵּר
you-hide and-not (18) to-me turn! mercies-of-you in-greatness-of love-of-you

פָּנֶיךָ מֵעַבְדֶּךָ כִּי־ צַר־ לִי מַהֵר עֲנֵנִי׃
answer-me! be-quick! to-me trouble for from-servant-of-you faces-of-you

קָרְבָה אֶל־ נַפְשִׁי גְאָלָהּ לְמַעַן אֹיְבַי
ones-being-foes-of-me because-of rescue-her! self-of-me to come-near! (19)

פְּדֵנִי׃ אַתָּה יָדַעְתָּ חֶרְפָּתִי וּבָשְׁתִּי וּכְלִמָּתִי
and-shame-of-me and-disgrace-of-me scorn-of-me you-know you (20) redeem-me!

נֶגְדְּךָ כָּל־ צוֹרְרָי׃ חֶרְפָּה ׀ שָׁבְרָה לִבִּי
heart-of-me she-broke scorn (21) ones-being-enemies-of-me all-of before-you

וָאָנוּשָׁה וָאֲקַוֶּה לָנוּד וָאַיִן
but-there-was-none to-have-sympathy and-I-looked and-I-became-helpless

וְלַמְנַחֲמִים וְלֹא מָצָאתִי׃ וַיִּתְּנוּ בְּבָרוּתִי
in-food-of-me and-they-put (22) I-found but-none and-for-ones-comforting

רֹאשׁ וְלִצְמָאִי יַשְׁקוּנִי חֹמֶץ׃ יְהִי־
may-he-become (23) vinegar they-gave-drink-me and-for-thirst-of-me gall

שֻׁלְחָנָם לִפְנֵיהֶם לְפָח וְלִשְׁלוֹמִים לְמוֹקֵשׁ׃
as-trap and-as-retributions as-snare before-them table-of-them

תֶּחְשַׁכְנָה עֵינֵיהֶם מֵרְאוֹת וּמָתְנֵיהֶם תָּמִיד
forever and-backs-of-them from-to-see eyes-of-them may-they-be-darkened (24)

הַמְעַד׃ שְׁפָךְ־ עֲלֵיהֶם זַעְמֶךָ וַחֲרוֹן אַפְּךָ
anger-of-you and-fierceness-of wrath-of-you on-them pour-out! (25) bend!

יַשִּׂיגֵם׃ תְּהִי־ טִירָתָם נְשַׁמָּה
one-being-deserted place-of-them may-she-be (26) let-him-overtake-them

בְּאָהֳלֵיהֶם אַל־ יְהִי יֹשֵׁב׃ כִּי־ אַתָּה אֲשֶׁר־ הִכִּיתָ
you-wound whom you for (27) one-dwelling let-him-be not in-tents-of-them

and I am the song of the
drunkards.
13But I pray to you, O LORD,
in the time of your favor;
in your great love, O God,
answer me with your sure
salvation.
14Rescue me from the mire,
do not let me sink;
deliver me from those who
hate me,
from the deep waters.
15Do not let the floodwaters
engulf me
or the depths swallow me
up
or the pit close its mouth
over me.
16Answer me, O LORD, out of the
goodness of your love;
in your great mercy turn to
me.
17Do not hide your face from
your servant;
answer me quickly, for I am
in trouble.
18Come near and rescue me;
redeem me because of my
foes.
19You know how I am scorned,
disgraced and shamed;
all my enemies are before
you.
20Scorn has broken my heart
and has left me helpless;
I looked for sympathy, but
there was none,
for comforters, but I found
none.
21They put gall in my food
and gave me vinegar for my
thirst.
22May the table set before them
become a snare;
may it become retribution
and[f] a trap.
23May their eyes be darkened so
they cannot see,
and their backs be bent
forever.
24Pour out your wrath on them;
let your fierce anger
overtake them.
25May their place be deserted;
let there be no one to dwell
in their tents.
26For they persecute those you
wound

[f]22 Or *snare / and their fellowship become*

*See the note on page 349.

רדפו ואל־ מכאוב חלליך יספרו׃ תנה־
charge! (28) they-talk ones-hurt-of-you pain-of and-about they-persecute

עון על־ עונם ואל־ יבאו בצדקתך׃
in-salvation-of-you let-them-share and-not crime-of-them upon crime

ימחו מספר חיים ועם צדיקים אל־
not righteous-ones and-with lives of-book-of may-they-be-blotted-out (29)

יכתבו׃ ואני עני וכואב ישועתך אלהים
God salvation-of-you and-one-suffering pain and-I (30) may-they-be-listed

תשגבני׃ אהללה שם־ אלהים בשיר ואגדלנו
and-I-will-glorify-him in-song God name-of I-will-praise (31) may-she-protect-me

בתודה׃ ותיטב ליהוה משור פר
bull more-than-ox to-Yahweh and-she-will-please (32) with-thanksgiving

מקרן מפריס׃ ראו ענוים ישמחו
they-will-be-glad poor-ones they-will-see (33) one-having-hoof one-having-horn

דרשי אלהים ויחי לבבכם׃ כי־ שמע אל־
to one-hearing for (34) heart-of-you now-may-he-live God ones-seeking-of

אביונים יהוה ואת־ אסיריו לא בזה׃ יהללוהו
let-them-praise-him (35) he-despises not captives-of-him and Yahweh needy-ones

שמים וארץ ימים וכל־ רמש בם׃ כי אלהים
God for (36) in-them one-moving and-all-of seas and-earth heavens

יושיע ציון ויבנה ערי יהודה וישבו
then-they-will-settle Judah cities-of and-he-will-rebuild Zion he-will-save

שם וירשוה׃ וזרע עבדיו
servants-of-him and-child-of (37) and-they-will-possess-her there

ינחלוה ואהבי שמו ישכנו־ בה׃
in-her they-will-dwell name-of-him and-ones-loving-of they-will-inherit-her

למנצח לדוד להזכיר׃ אלהים להצילני
to-save-me God (2) to-make-petition of-David for-the-one-directing *(70:1)

יהוה לעזרתי חושה׃ יבשו ויחפרו
and-may-they-be-confused may-they-be-shamed (3) hasten! to-help-of-me Yahweh

מבקשי נפשי יסגו אחור ויכלמו
and-may-they-be-disgraced back may-they-be-turned life-of-me ones-seeking-of

חפצי רעתי׃ ישובו על־ עקב בשתם
shame-of-them cause-of at may-they-turn-back (4) ruin-of-me ones-desirous-of

האמרים האח׀ האח׃ ישישו וישמחו׀ בך
in-you and-may-they-be-glad may-they-rejoice (5) aha! aha! the-ones-saying

כל־ מבקשיך ויאמרו תמיד יגדל אלהים
God let-him-be-exalted always and-may-they-say ones-seeking-you all-of

and talk about the pain of those you hurt.
27 Charge them with crime upon crime;
do not let them share in your salvation.
28 May they be blotted out of the book of life
and not be listed with the righteous.

29 I am in pain and distress;
may your salvation, O God, protect me.

30 I will praise God's name in song
and glorify him with thanksgiving.
31 This will please the LORD more than an ox,
more than a bull with its horns and hoofs.
32 The poor will see and be glad—
you who seek God, may your hearts live!
33 The LORD hears the needy
and does not despise his captive people.

34 Let heaven and earth praise him,
the seas and all that move in them,
35 for God will save Zion
and rebuild the cities of Judah.
Then people will settle there and possess it;
36 the children of his servants will inherit it,
and those who love his name will dwell there.

Psalm 70

For the director of music. Of David. A petition.

1 Hasten, O God, to save me;
O LORD, come quickly to help me.
2 May those who seek my life
be put to shame and confusion;
may all who desire my ruin
be turned back in disgrace.
3 May those who say to me, "Aha! Aha!"
turn back because of their shame.
4 But may all who seek you
rejoice and be glad in you;
may those who love your salvation always say,
"Let God be exalted!"

*Heading, 1 See the note on page 349.

אֹהֲבֵי יְשׁוּעָתֶךָ׃ וַאֲנִי ׀ עָנִי וְאֶבְיוֹן אֱלֹהִים חוּשָׁה־

come-quickly! God and-needy poor yet-I (6) salvation-of-you ones-loving-of

לִּי עֶזְרִי וּמְפַלְטִי אַתָּה יְהוָה אַל־ תְּאַחַר׃ בְּךָ־

in-you (71:1) you-delay not Yahweh you and-one-delivering-me help-of-me to-me

יְהוָה חָסִיתִי אַל־ אֵבוֹשָׁה לְעוֹלָם׃ בְּצִדְקָתְךָ

in-righteousness-of-you (2) to-forever let-me-be-shamed not I-took-refuge Yahweh

תַּצִּילֵנִי וּתְפַלְּטֵנִי הַטֵּה־ אֵלַי אָזְנְךָ וְהוֹשִׁיעֵנִי׃ הֱיֵה

be! (3) and-save-me! ear-of-you to-me turn! and-you-deliver-me you-rescue-me

לִי ׀ לְצוּר מָעוֹן לָבוֹא תָּמִיד צִוִּיתָ לְהוֹשִׁיעֵנִי כִּי־ סַלְעִי

rock-of-me for to-save-me you-command always to-go refuge as-rock-of to-me

וּמְצוּדָתִי אָתָּה׃ אֱלֹהַי פַּלְּטֵנִי מִיַּד רָשָׁע

wicked from-hand-of deliver-me! God-of-me (4) you and-fortress-of-me

מִכַּף מְעַוֵּל וְחוֹמֵץ׃ כִּי־ אַתָּה תִקְוָתִי אֲדֹנָי

Lord hope-of-me you for (5) and-one-being-cruel one-being-evil from-grasp-of

יְהוִה מִבְטַחִי מִנְּעוּרָי׃ עָלֶיךָ ׀ נִסְמַכְתִּי מִבֶּטֶן

from-birth I-relied on-you (6) since-youths-of-me confidence-of-me Yahweh

מִמְּעֵי אִמִּי אַתָּה גוֹזִי בְּךָ תְהִלָּתִי

praise-of-me to-you one-bringing-forth-me you mother-of-me from-wombs-of

תָמִיד׃ כְּמוֹפֵת הָיִיתִי לְרַבִּים וְאַתָּה מַחֲסִי־ עֹז׃

strong refuge-of-me but-you to-many I-became like-portent (7) ever

יִמָּלֵא פִי תְּהִלָּתֶךָ כָּל־ הַיּוֹם תִּפְאַרְתֶּךָ׃

splendor-of-you the-day all-of praise-of-you mouth-of-me he-is-filled (8)

אַל־ תַּשְׁלִיכֵנִי לְעֵת זִקְנָה כִּכְלוֹת כֹּחִי

strength-of-me when-to-be-gone old-age at-time-of you-cast-away-me not (9)

אַל־ תַּעַזְבֵנִי׃ כִּי־ אָמְרוּ אוֹיְבַי לִי

against-me ones-being-enemies-of-me they-speak for (10) you-forsake-me not

וְשֹׁמְרֵי נַפְשִׁי נוֹעֲצוּ יַחְדָּו׃ לֵאמֹר אֱלֹהִים

God to-say (11) together they-conspire life-of-me and-ones-waiting-of

עֲזָבוֹ רִדְפוּ וְתִפְשׂוּהוּ כִּי־ אֵין מַצִּיל׃

one-rescuing there-is-not for and-seize-him! pursue! he-forsook-him

אֱלֹהִים אַל־ תִּרְחַק מִמֶּנִּי אֱלֹהַי לְעֶזְרָתִי חִישָׁה°׃

come-quickly! to-help-of-me God-of-me from-me you-be-far not God (12)

יֵבֹשׁוּ יִכְלוּ שֹׂטְנֵי נַפְשִׁי

self-of-me ones-accusing-of may-they-perish may-they-be-shamed (13)

יַעֲטוּ חֶרְפָּה וּכְלִמָּה מְבַקְשֵׁי רָעָתִי׃ וַאֲנִי

but-I (14) harm-of-me ones-wanting-of and-disgrace scorn may-they-be-covered

תָּמִיד אֲיַחֵל וְהוֹסַפְתִּי עַל־ כָּל־ תְּהִלָּתֶךָ׃ פִּי ׀

mouth-of-me (15) praise-of-you all-of to and-I-will-add I-will-hope always

5Yet I am poor and needy;
come quickly to me, O God.
You are my help and my deliverer;
O LORD, do not delay.

Psalm 71

1In you, O LORD, I have taken refuge;
let me never be put to shame.
2Rescue me and deliver me in your righteousness;
turn your ear to me and save me.
3Be my rock of refuge,
to which I can always go;
give the command to save me,
for you are my rock and my fortress.
4Deliver me, O my God, from the hand of the wicked,
from the grasp of evil and cruel men.

5For you have been my hope, O Sovereign LORD,
my confidence since my youth.
6From birth I have relied on you;
you brought me forth from my mother's womb.
I will ever praise you.
7I have become like a portent to many,
but you are my strong refuge.
8My mouth is filled with your praise,
declaring your splendor all day long.

9Do not cast me away when I am old;
do not forsake me when my strength is gone.
10For my enemies speak against me;
those who wait to kill me conspire together.
11They say, "God has forsaken him;
pursue him and seize him,
for no one will rescue him."
12Be not far from me, O God;
come quickly, O my God, to help me.
13May my accusers perish in shame;
may those who want to harm me
be covered with scorn and disgrace.

14But as for me, I will always have hope;
I will praise you more and more.

*See the note on page 349.

°12 ק חושה

יְסַפֵּר צִדְקָתֶךָ כָּל־הַיּוֹם תְּשׁוּעָתֶךָ כִּי לֹא

not though salvation-of-you the-day all-of righteousness-of-you he-will-tell

יָדַעְתִּי סְפֹרוֹת׃ אָבוֹא בִּגְבֻרוֹת אֲדֹנָי יְהוִה אַזְכִּיר

I-will-proclaim Yahweh Lord in-mighty-acts-of I-will-come (16) measures I-know

צִדְקָתְךָ לְבַדֶּךָ׃ אֱלֹהִים לִמַּדְתַּנִי מִנְּעוּרָי

since-youths-of-me you-taught-me God (17) by-yourself righteousness-of-you

וְעַד־הֵנָּה אַגִּיד נִפְלְאוֹתֶיךָ׃ וְגַם עַד־זִקְנָה ׀

old-age in and-even (18) deeds-being-marvelous-of-you I-declare to-now and-to

וְשֵׂיבָה אֱלֹהִים אַל־תַּעַזְבֵנִי עַד־אַגִּיד זְרוֹעֲךָ

power-of-you I-declare till you-forsake-me not God and-gray-hair

לְדוֹר לְכָל־יָבוֹא גְּבוּרָתֶךָ׃ וְצִדְקָתְךָ

and-righteousness-of-you (19) might-of-you he-will-come to-all-of to-generation

אֱלֹהִים עַד־מָרוֹם אֲשֶׁר־עָשִׂיתָ גְדֹלוֹת אֱלֹהִים מִי כָמוֹךָ׃ אֲשֶׁר

though (20) like-you who? God great-things you-did who sky to God

הִרְאִיתַנוּ ׀ צָרוֹת רַבּוֹת וְרָעוֹת תָּשׁוּב

you-will-do-again and-bitter-ones many troubles you-made-see-me

תְּחַיֵּינוּ וּמִתְּהֹמוֹת הָאָרֶץ תָּשׁוּב

you-will-do-again the-earth and-from-depths-of you-will-let-live-me

תַּעֲלֵנִי׃ תֶּרֶב ׀ גְּדֻלָּתִי וְתִסֹּב

and-you-will-do-again honor-of-me you-will-increase (21) you-will-bring-up-me

תְּנַחֲמֵנִי׃ גַּם־אֲנִי ׀ אוֹדְךָ בִכְלִי־נֶבֶל

harp with-instrument-of I-will-praise-you I also (22) you-will-comfort-me

אֲמִתְּךָ אֱלֹהָי אֲזַמְּרָה לְךָ בְכִנּוֹר קְדוֹשׁ

Holy-One-of with-lyre to-you I-will-sing-praise God-of-me faithfulness-of-you

יִשְׂרָאֵל׃ תְּרַנֵּנָּה שְׂפָתַי כִּי אֲזַמְּרָה־לָּךְ

to-you I-sing-praise when lips-of-me they-will-shout-for-joy (23) Israel

וְנַפְשִׁי אֲשֶׁר פָּדִיתָ׃ גַּם־לְשׁוֹנִי כָּל־הַיּוֹם

the-day all-of tongue-of-me also (24) you-redeemed whom even-self-of-me

תֶּהְגֶּה צִדְקָתֶךָ כִּי־בֹשׁוּ כִּי־

for they-have-been-shamed for righteousness-of-you she-will-tell

חָפְרוּ מְבַקְשֵׁי רָעָתִי׃ לִשְׁלֹמֹה ׀ אֱלֹהִים

God of-Solomon (72:1) harm-of-me ones-wanting-of they-have-been-confused

מִשְׁפָּטֶיךָ לְמֶלֶךְ תֵּן וְצִדְקָתְךָ לְבֶן־מֶלֶךְ׃

royalty to-son-of and-righteousness-of-you endow! to-king justices-of-you

יָדִין עַמְּךָ בְצֶדֶק וַעֲנִיֶּיךָ

and-afflicted-ones-of-you in-righteousness people-of-you he-will-judge (2)

בְמִשְׁפָּט׃ יִשְׂאוּ הָרִים שָׁלוֹם לָעָם וּגְבָעוֹת

and-hills to-the-people prosperity mountains they-will-bring (3) with-justice

15My mouth will tell of your
righteousness,
of your salvation all day
long,
though I know not its
measure.
16I will come and proclaim your
mighty acts, O Sovereign
LORD;
I will proclaim your
righteousness, yours
alone.
17Since my youth, O God, you
have taught me,
and to this day I declare
your marvelous deeds.
18Even when I am old and gray,
do not forsake me, O God,
till I declare your power to the
next generation,
your might to all who are to
come.

19Your righteousness reaches to
the skies, O God,
you who have done great
things.
Who, O God, is like you?
20Though you have made me see
troubles, many and bitter,
you will restore my life
again;
from the depths of the earth
you will again bring me up.
21You will increase my honor
and comfort me once again.

22I will praise you with the harp
for your faithfulness, O my
God;
I will sing praise to you with
the lyre,
O Holy One of Israel.
23My lips will shout for joy
when I sing praise to you—
I, whom you have
redeemed.
24My tongue will tell of your
righteous acts
all day long,
for those who wanted to harm
me
have been put to shame and
confusion.

Psalm 72

Of Solomon.

1Endow the king with your
justice, O God,
the royal son with your
righteousness.
2He will[a] judge your people in
righteousness,
your afflicted ones with
justice.
3The mountains will bring
prosperity to the people,

[a]2 Or *May he;* similarly in verses 3-11 and 17

°20a ק הראיתני
°20b ק תחייני

בִּצְדָקָה׃ יִשְׁפֹּט | עֲנִיֵּי־ עָם יוֹשִׁיעַ

he-will-save people afflicted-ones-of he-will-defend (4) in-righteousness

לִבְנֵי אֶבְיוֹן וִידַכֵּא עוֹשֵׁק׃ יִירָאוּךָ

they-will-fear-you (5) one-oppressing and-he-will-crush needy to-children-of

עִם־ שֶׁמֶשׁ וְלִפְנֵי יָרֵחַ דּוֹר דּוֹרִים׃ יֵרֵד

he-will-fall (6) generations generation-of moon and-as-long-as sun as-long-as

כְּמָטָר עַל־ גֵּז כִּרְבִיבִים זַרְזִיף אָרֶץ׃ יִפְרַח־

he-will-flourish (7) earth watering-of like-showers mown-field on like-rain

בְּיָמָיו צַדִּיק וְרֹב שָׁלוֹם עַד־ בְּלִי יָרֵחַ׃

moon no-more till prosperity and-abundance-of righteous in-days-of-him

וְיֵרְדְּ מִיָּם עַד־ יָם וּמִנָּהָר עַד־ אַפְסֵי־ אָרֶץ׃

earth ends-of to and-from-River sea to from-sea and-he-will-rule (8)

לְפָנָיו יִכְרְעוּ צִיִּים וְאֹיְבָיו

and-ones-being-enemies-of-him desert-tribes they-will-bow before-him (9)

עָפָר יְלַחֵכוּ׃ מַלְכֵי תַרְשִׁישׁ וְאִיִּים מִנְחָה

tribute and-distant-shores Tarshish kings-of (10) they-will-lick dust

יָשִׁיבוּ מַלְכֵי שְׁבָא וּסְבָא אֶשְׁכָּר יַקְרִיבוּ׃

they-will-present gift and-Seba Sheba kings-of they-will-bring

וְיִשְׁתַּחֲווּ־ לוֹ כָל־ מְלָכִים כָּל־ גּוֹיִם יַעַבְדוּהוּ׃

they-will-serve-him nations all-of kings all-of to-him and-they-will-bow (11)

כִּי־ יַצִּיל אֶבְיוֹן מְשַׁוֵּעַ וְעָנִי וְאֵין־

when-there-is-not and-afflicted one-crying-out needy he-will-deliver for (12)

עֹזֵר לוֹ׃ יָחֹס עַל־ דַּל וְאֶבְיוֹן וְנַפְשׁוֹת

and-lives-of and-needy weak on he-will-take-pity (13) to-him one-helping

אֶבְיוֹנִים יוֹשִׁיעַ׃ מִתּוֹךְ וּמֵחָמָס יִגְאַל

he-will-rescue and-from-violence from-oppression (14) he-will-save needy-ones

נַפְשָׁם וְיֵיקַר דָּמָם בְּעֵינָיו׃

in-eyes-of-him blood-of-them for-he-is-precious life-of-them

וִיחִי וְיִתֶּן־ לוֹ מִזְּהַב שְׁבָא וְיִתְפַּלֵּל

and-may-he-pray Sheba from-gold-of to-him and-may-he-give and-may-he-live (15)

בַּעֲדוֹ תָמִיד כָּל־ הַיּוֹם יְבָרְכֶנְהוּ׃ יְהִי פִסַּת־

abundance-of let-him-be (16) may-he-bless-him the-day all-of ever for-him

בַר | בָּאָרֶץ בְּרֹאשׁ הָרִים יִרְעַשׁ כַּלְּבָנוֹן

like-the-Lebanon let-him-sway hills on-top-of throughout-the-land grain

פִּרְיוֹ וְיָצִיצוּ מֵעִיר כְּעֵשֶׂב הָאָרֶץ׃

the-field like-grass-of one-thriving and-let-them-flourish fruit-of-him

יְהִי שְׁמוֹ לְעוֹלָם לִפְנֵי־ שֶׁמֶשׁ יִנּוֹן

may-he-continue sun as-long-as to-forever name-of-him may-he-endure (17)

the hills the fruit of
righteousness.
4 He will defend the afflicted
among the people
and save the children of the
needy;
he will crush the oppressor.

5 He will endure[v] as long as the
sun,
as long as the moon,
through all generations.
6 He will be like rain falling on
a mown field,
like showers watering the
earth.
7 In his days the righteous will
flourish;
prosperity will abound till
the moon is no more.

8 He will rule from sea to sea
and from the River[w] to the
ends of the earth.[x]
9 The desert tribes will bow
before him
and his enemies will lick the
dust.
10 The kings of Tarshish and of
distant shores
will bring tribute to him;
the kings of Sheba and Seba
will present him gifts.
11 All kings will bow down to
him
and all nations will serve
him.

12 For he will deliver the needy
who cry out,
the afflicted who have no
one to help.
13 He will take pity on the weak
and the needy
and save the needy from
death.
14 He will rescue them from
oppression and violence,
for precious is their blood in
his sight.

15 Long may he live!
May gold from Sheba be
given him.
May people ever pray for him
and bless him all day long.
16 Let grain abound throughout
the land;
on the tops of the hills may
it sway.
Let its fruit flourish like
Lebanon;
let it thrive like the grass of
the field.
17 May his name endure forever;
may it continue as long as
the sun.

v5 Septuagint; Hebrew / *You will be feared*
w8 That is, the Euphrates
x8 Or *the end of the land*

°17 ק ינון

שְׁמוֹ וְיִתְבָּרְכוּ בוֹ כָּל־ גּוֹיִם
nations all-of through-him and-they-will-be-blessed name-of-him

יְאַשְּׁרוּהוּ׃ בָּרוּךְ ׀ יְהוָה אֱלֹהִים אֱלֹהֵי יִשְׂרָאֵל
Israel God-of God Yahweh being-praised (18) they-will-call-blessed-him

עֹשֵׂה נִפְלָאוֹת לְבַדּוֹ׃ וּבָרוּךְ ׀ שֵׁם
name-of and-being-praised (19) by-himself deeds-being-marvelous one-doing-of

כְּבוֹדוֹ לְעוֹלָם וְיִמָּלֵא כְבוֹדוֹ אֶת־ כֹּל
whole-of *** glory-of-him and-may-he-be-filled to-forever glory-of-him

הָאָרֶץ אָמֵן ׀ וְאָמֵן׃ כָּלּוּ תְפִלּוֹת דָּוִד בֶּן־ יִשָׁי׃
Jesse son-of David prayers-of they-are-concluded (20) and-amen amen the-earth

מִזְמוֹר לְאָסָף אַךְ טוֹב לְיִשְׂרָאֵל אֱלֹהִים לְבָרֵי לֵבָב׃
heart to-ones-pure-of God to-Israel good surely of-Asaph psalm (73:1)

וַאֲנִי כִּמְעַט נָטָיוּ רַגְלָי כְּאַיִן שֻׁפְּכָה
they-were-lost as-nearly feet-of-me they-slipped as-almost but-I (2)

אֲשֻׁרָי׃ כִּי־ קִנֵּאתִי בַּהוֹלְלִים שְׁלוֹם
prosperity-of to-the-ones-being-arrogant I-envied for (3) footholds-of-me

רְשָׁעִים אֶרְאֶה׃ כִּי אֵין חַרְצֻבּוֹת לְמוֹתָם וּבָרִיא
and-healthy at-death-of-them struggles no for (4) I-saw wicked-ones

אוּלָם׃ בַּעֲמַל אֱנוֹשׁ אֵינֵמוֹ וְעִם־ אָדָם לֹא
not human and-by not-of-them man from-burden-of (5) body-of-them

יְנֻגָּעוּ׃ לָכֵן עֲנָקַתְמוֹ גַאֲוָה יַעֲטָף־
he-wraps pride she-is-a-necklace-to-them therefore (6) they-are-plagued

שִׁית חָמָס לָמוֹ׃ יָצָא מֵחֵלֶב עֵינֵמוֹ עָבְרוּ
they-pass-limits eye-of-them with-fat he-bulges (7) on-them violence clothing

מַשְׂכִּיּוֹת לֵבָב׃ יָמִיקוּ ׀ וִידַבְּרוּ בְרָע עֹשֶׁק
oppression with-malice and-they-speak they-scoff (8) mind conceits-of

מִמָּרוֹם יְדַבֵּרוּ׃ שַׁתּוּ בַשָּׁמַיִם פִּיהֶם
mouth-of-them to-the-heavens they-lay-claim (9) they-threaten in-arrogance

וּלְשׁוֹנָם תִּהֲלַךְ בָּאָרֶץ׃ לָכֵן ׀ יָשִׁיב
he-turns therefore (10) to-the-earth she-possesses and-tongue-of-them

עַמּוֹ הֲלֹם וּמֵי מָלֵא יִמָּצוּ לָמוֹ׃
for-them they-drink-up abundance and-waters-of to-here people-of-him

וְאָמְרוּ אֵיכָה יָדַע־ אֵל וְיֵשׁ דֵּעָה בְעֶלְיוֹן׃
to-Most-High knowledge and-is-there God he-knows how? and-they-say (11)

הִנֵּה־ אֵלֶּה רְשָׁעִים וְשַׁלְוֵי עוֹלָם הִשְׂגּוּ־ חָיִל׃
wealth they-increase always even-ones-carefree-of wicked-ones these see! (12)

אַךְ־ רִיק זִכִּיתִי לְבָבִי וָאֶרְחַץ בְּנִקָּיוֹן
in-innocence and-I-washed heart-of-me I-kept-pure in-vain surely (13)

All nations will be blessed
through him,
and they will call him
blessed.

[18]Praise be to the LORD God, the
God of Israel,
who alone does marvelous
deeds.
[19]Praise be to his glorious name
forever;
may the whole earth be
filled with his glory.
Amen and Amen.

[20]This concludes the prayers of
David son of Jesse.

BOOK III

Psalms 73-89

Psalm 73

A psalm of Asaph.

[1]Surely God is good to Israel,
to those who are pure in
heart.
[2]But as for me, my feet had
almost slipped;
I had nearly lost my
foothold.
[3]For I envied the arrogant
when I saw the prosperity
of the wicked.
[4]They have no struggles;
their bodies are healthy and
strong.[y]
[5]They are free from the burdens
common to man;
they are not plagued by
human ills.
[6]Therefore pride is their
necklace;
they clothe themselves with
violence.
[7]From their callous hearts
comes iniquity[z];
the evil conceits of their
minds know no limits.
[8]They scoff, and speak with
malice;
in their arrogance they
threaten oppression.
[9]Their mouths lay claim to
heaven,
and their tongues take
possession of the earth.
[10]Therefore their people turn to
them
and drink up waters in
abundance.[a]
[11]They say, "How can God
know?
Does the Most High have
knowledge?"
[12]This is what the wicked are
like—
always carefree, they
increase in wealth.
[13]Surely in vain have I kept my

y4 With a different word division of the Hebrew; Masoretic Text *struggles at their death; / their bodies are healthy*
z7 Syriac (see also Septuagint); Hebrew *Their eyes bulge with fat*
a10 The meaning of the Hebrew for this verse is uncertain.

°2a ק נטיו
°2b ק שפכו
°10 ק ישוב

כַּפָּי׃ hands-of-me (14) וָאֱהִי but-I-am נָגוּעַ being-plagued כָּל־ all-of הַיּוֹם the-day וְתוֹכַחְתִּי and-punishment-of-me

לַבְּקָרִים׃ in-the-mornings (15) אִם־ if אָמַרְתִּי I-said אֲסַפְּרָה I-will-speak כְמוֹ thus הִנֵּה see! דוֹר generation-of

בָּנֶיךָ children-of-you בָגַדְתִּי׃ I-would-have-betrayed (16) וָאֲחַשְּׁבָה when-I-tried לָדַעַת to-understand זֹאת this

עָמָל oppressive הִיא° he בְעֵינָי׃ to-eyes-of-me (17) עַד־ till אָבוֹא I-entered אֶל־ into מִקְדְּשֵׁי־ sanctuaries-of אֵל God

אָבִינָה I-understood לְאַחֲרִיתָם׃ about-final-destiny-of-them (18) אַךְ surely בַּחֲלָקוֹת on-slippery-grounds

תָּשִׁית you-place לָמוֹ to-them הִפַּלְתָּם you-cast-down-them לְמַשּׁוּאוֹת׃ to-ruins (19) אֵיךְ how! הָיוּ they-are

לְשַׁמָּה for-destruction כְרָגַע in-suddenness סָפוּ they-are-swept-away תַּמּוּ they-are-completed מִן־ by

בַּלָּהוֹת׃ terrors (20) כַּחֲלוֹם as-dream מֵהָקִיץ when-to-awaken אֲדֹנָי Lord בָּעִיר ׀ when-to-arise צַלְמָם fantasy-of-them

תִּבְזֶה׃ you-will-despise (21) כִּי when יִתְחַמֵּץ he-was-grieved לְבָבִי heart-of-me וְכִלְיוֹתַי and-spirits-of-me

אֶשְׁתּוֹנָן׃ I-was-embittered (22) וַאֲנִי־ and-I בַעַר senseless וְלֹא and-not אֵדָע I-knew בְּהֵמוֹת brute-beasts הָיִיתִי I-was

עִמָּךְ׃ before-you (23) וַאֲנִי yet-I תָמִיד always עִמָּךְ with-you אָחַזְתָּ you-hold בְּיַד־ by-hand-of יְמִינִי׃ right-of-me

(24) בַּעֲצָתְךָ with-counsel-of-you תַנְחֵנִי you-guide-me וְאַחַר and-afterward כָּבוֹד glory תִּקָּחֵנִי׃ you-will-take-me

(25) מִי־ who? לִי to-me בַשָּׁמָיִם in-the-heavens וְעִמְּךָ and-with-you לֹא־ nothing חָפַצְתִּי I-desire בָאָרֶץ׃ on-the-earth

(26) כָּלָה he-may-fail שְׁאֵרִי flesh-of-me וּלְבָבִי and-heart-of-me צוּר־ strength-of לְבָבִי heart-of-me

וְחֶלְקִי and-portion-of-me אֱלֹהִים God לְעוֹלָם׃ to-forever (27) כִּי־ for הִנֵּה see! רְחֵקֶיךָ ones-far-from-you

יֹאבֵדוּ they-will-perish הִצְמַתָּה you-destroy כָּל־ all-of זוֹנֶה one-being-unfaithful מִמֶּךָּ׃ to-you (28) וַאֲנִי ׀ but-I

קִרֲבַת nearness-of אֱלֹהִים God לִי־ to-me טוֹב good שַׁתִּי ׀ I-made בַּאדֹנָי to-Lord יְהוִה Yahweh מַחְסִי refuge-of-me לְסַפֵּר to-tell

כָּל־ all-of מַלְאֲכוֹתֶיךָ׃ deeds-of-you (74:1) מַשְׂכִּיל maskil לְאָסָף of-Asaph לָמָה why? אֱלֹהִים God זָנַחְתָּ you-rejected לָנֶצַח to-forever

יֶעְשַׁן he-smolders אַפְּךָ anger-of-you בְּצֹאן against-sheep-of מַרְעִיתֶךָ׃ pasture-of-you (2) זְכֹר remember!

heart pure;
in vain have I washed my hands in innocence.
14 All day long I have been plagued;
I have been punished every morning.

15 If I had said, "I will speak thus,"
I would have betrayed this generation of your children.
16 When I tried to understand all this,
it was oppressive to me
17 till I entered the sanctuary of God;
then I understood their final destiny.

18 Surely you place them on slippery ground;
you cast them down to ruin.
19 How suddenly are they destroyed,
completely swept away by terrors!
20 As a dream when one awakes,
so when you arise, O Lord,
you will despise them as fantasies.

21 When my heart was grieved
and my spirit embittered,
22 I was senseless and ignorant;
I was a brute beast before you.

23 Yet I am always with you;
you hold me by my right hand.
24 You guide me with your counsel,
and afterward you will take me into glory.
25 Whom have I in heaven but you?
And being with you, I desire nothing on earth.
26 My flesh and my heart may fail,
but God is the strength of my heart
and my portion forever.

27 Those who are far from you will perish;
you destroy all who are unfaithful to you.
28 But as for me, it is good to be near God.
I have made the Sovereign LORD my refuge;
I will tell of all your deeds.

Psalm 74

A *maskil*[b] of Asaph.

1 Why have you rejected us forever, O God?
Why does your anger smolder against the sheep of your pasture?

[b] Title: Probably a literary or musical term

°16 ק הוא

עֲדָתְךָ ׀ קָּנִיתָ קֶּדֶם גָּאַלְתָּ שֵׁבֶט נַחֲלָתֶךָ

inheritance-of-you tribe-of you-redeemed of-old you-purchased people-of-you

הַר־ צִיּוֹן זֶה ׀ שָׁכַנְתָּ בּוֹ׃ הָרִימָה פְעָמֶיךָ

steps-of-you lift-high! (3) in-him you-dwelt where Zion Mount-of

לְמַשֻּׁאוֹת נֶצַח כָּל־ הֵרַע אוֹיֵב בַּקֹּדֶשׁ׃

to-the-sanctuary one-being-enemy to-destroy all-of everlasting through-ruins-of

שָׁאֲגוּ צֹרְרֶיךָ בְּקֶרֶב מוֹעֲדֶךָ שָׂמוּ

they-set-up meeting-of-you in-place-of ones-being-foes-of-you they-roared (4)

אוֹתֹתָם אֹתוֹת׃ יִוָּדַע כְּמֵבִיא לְמָעְלָה

at-above like-one-wielding he-behaved (5) signs standards-of-them

בִּסֲבָךְ־ עֵץ קַרְדֻּמּוֹת׃ וְעַתְּ פִּתּוּחֶיהָ יָּחַד

together carved-panels-of-her and-now (6) axes tree through-thicket-of

בְּכַשִּׁיל וְכֵילַפֹּת יַהֲלֹמוּן׃ שִׁלְחוּ בָאֵשׁ

with-fire they-sent-down (7) they-smashed and-hatchets with-axe

מִקְדָּשֶׁךָ לָאָרֶץ חִלְּלוּ מִשְׁכַּן־ שְׁמֶךָ׃

Name-of-you dwelling-place-of they-defiled to-the-ground sanctuary-of-you

אָמְרוּ בְלִבָּם נִינָם יָחַד שָׂרְפוּ

they-burned completely we-will-crush-them in-heart-of-them they-said (8)

כָל־ מוֹעֲדֵי־ אֵל בָּאָרֶץ׃ אוֹתֹתֵינוּ לֹא רָאִינוּ

we-see not miraculous-signs-of-us (9) in-the-land God worship-places-of all-of

אֵין־ עוֹד נָבִיא וְלֹא־ אִתָּנוּ יֹדֵעַ עַד־ מָה׃

when? until one-knowing among-us and-not prophet longer there-is-no

עַד־ מָתַי אֱלֹהִים יְחָרֶף צָר יְנָאֵץ אוֹיֵב

one-being-foe will-he-revile enemy will-he-mock God when? until (10)

שִׁמְךָ לָנֶצַח׃ לָמָּה תָשִׁיב יָדְךָ

hand-of-you you-hold-back why? (11) to-forever name-of-you

וִימִינֶךָ מִקֶּרֶב חוקך כַלֵּה׃ וֵאלֹהִים

but-God (12) destroy! bosom-of-you from-fold-of even-right-hand-of-you

מַלְכִּי מִקֶּדֶם פֹּעֵל יְשׁוּעוֹת בְּקֶרֶב הָאָרֶץ׃

the-earth upon-midst-of salvations one-bringing from-of-old king-of-me

אַתָּה פוֹרַרְתָּ בְעָזְּךָ יָם שִׁבַּרְתָּ רָאשֵׁי תַנִּינִים עַל־

in monsters heads-of you-broke sea by-power-of-you you-split-open you (13)

הַמָּיִם׃ אַתָּה רִצַּצְתָּ רָאשֵׁי לִוְיָתָן תִּתְּנֶנּוּ מַאֲכָל

food you-gave-him Leviathan heads-of you-crushed you (14) the-waters

לְעָם לְצִיִּים׃ אַתָּה בָקַעְתָּ מַעְיָן וָנָחַל אַתָּה

you and-stream spring you-opened-up you (15) to-desert-creatures to-people

הוֹבַשְׁתָּ נַהֲרוֹת אֵיתָן׃ לְךָ יוֹם אַף־ לְךָ לָיְלָה

night to-you also day to-you (16) ever-flowing rivers-of you-dried-up

---

2 Remember the people you purchased of old,
the tribe you redeemed as your inheritance—
Mount Zion, where you dwelt.
3 Pick your way through these everlasting ruins,
all this destruction the enemy has brought on the sanctuary.
4 Your foes roared in the place where you met with us;
they set up their standards as signs.
5 They behaved like men wielding axes
to cut through a thicket of trees.
6 They smashed all the carved paneling
with their axes and hatchets.
7 They burned your sanctuary to the ground;
they defiled the dwelling place of your Name.
8 They said in their hearts, "We will crush them completely!"
They burned every place where God was worshiped in the land.
9 We are given no miraculous signs;
no prophets are left,
and none of us knows how long this will be.
10 How long will the enemy mock you, O God?
Will the foe revile your name forever?
11 Why do you hold back your hand, your right hand?
Take it from the folds of your garment and destroy them!
12 But you, O God, are my king from of old;
you bring salvation upon the earth.
13 It was you who split open the sea by your power;
you broke the heads of the monster in the waters.
14 It was you who crushed the heads of Leviathan
and gave him as food to the creatures of the desert.
15 It was you who opened up springs and streams;
you dried up the ever flowing rivers.
16 The day is yours, and yours also the night;

°6 ק ועתה
°11 ק חיקך

אַתָּה הֲכִינוֹתָ מָאוֹר וָשָׁמֶשׁ׃ אַתָּה הִצַּבְתָּ כָּל־ גְּבוּלוֹת אָרֶץ
earth boundaries-of all-of you-set you (17) and-sun moon you-established you

קַיִץ וָחֹרֶף אַתָּה יְצַרְתָּם׃ זְכָר־ זֹאת אוֹיֵב
one-being-enemy this remember! (18) you-made-them you and-winter summer

חֵרֵף ׀ יְהוָה וְעַם נָבָל נִאֲצוּ שְׁמֶךָ׃ אַל־
not (19) name-of-you they-reviled foolish and-people Yahweh he-mocked

תִּתֵּן לְחַיַּת נֶפֶשׁ תּוֹרֶךָ חַיַּת עֲנִיֶּיךָ
afflicted-ones-of-you life-of dove-of-you life-of to-wild-beast you-hand-over

אַל־ תִּשְׁכַּח לָנֶצַח׃ הַבֵּט לַבְּרִית כִּי מָלְאוּ
they-fill because for-the-covenant have-regard! (20) to-forever you-forget not

מַחֲשַׁכֵּי־ אֶרֶץ נְאוֹת חָמָס׃ אַל־ יָשֹׁב דַּךְ
oppressed let-him-retreat not (21) violence haunts-of land dark-places-of

נִכְלָם עָנִי וְאֶבְיוֹן יְהַלְלוּ שְׁמֶךָ׃ קוּמָה
rise-up! (22) name-of-you may-they-praise and-needy poor one-being-disgraced

אֱלֹהִים רִיבָה רִיבֶךָ זְכֹר חֶרְפָּתְךָ מִנִּי־נָבָל כָּל־ הַיּוֹם׃
the-day all-of fool by mocking-of-you remember! cause-of-you defend! God

אַל־ תִּשְׁכַּח קוֹל צֹרְרֶיךָ שְׁאוֹן
uproar-of ones-being-adversaries-of-you clamor-of you-ignore not (23)

קָמֶיךָ עֹלֶה תָמִיד׃ לַמְנַצֵּחַ
for-the-one-directing *(75:1) continually one-rising ones-being-enemies-of-you

אַל־ תַּשְׁחֵת מִזְמוֹר לְאָסָף שִׁיר׃ הוֹדִינוּ לְּךָ ׀ אֱלֹהִים
God to-you we-give-thanks (2) song of-Asaph psalm you-destroy not

הוֹדִינוּ וְקָרוֹב שְׁמֶךָ סִפְּרוּ נִפְלְאוֹתֶיךָ׃
deeds-being-wonderful-of-you they-tell Name-of-you for-near we-give-thanks

כִּי אֶקַּח מוֹעֵד אֲנִי מֵישָׁרִים אֶשְׁפֹּט׃ נְמֹגִים
ones-quaking (4) I-judge upright-ones I appointed-time I-choose that (3)

אֶרֶץ וְכָל־ יֹשְׁבֶיהָ אָנֹכִי תִכַּנְתִּי עַמּוּדֶיהָ סֶּלָה׃
selah pillars-of-her I-hold-firm I ones-being-people-of-her and-all-of earth

אָמַרְתִּי לַהוֹלְלִים אַל־ תָּהֹלּוּ וְלָרְשָׁעִים
and-to-the-wicked-ones you-boast not to-the-ones-being-arrogant I-say (5)

אַל־ תָּרִימוּ קָרֶן׃ אַל־ תָּרִימוּ לַמָּרוֹם קַרְנְכֶם
horn-of-you against-the-heaven you-lift not (6) horn you-lift-up not

תְּדַבְּרוּ בְצַוָּאר עָתָק׃ כִּי לֹא מִמּוֹצָא וּמִמַּעֲרָב
or-from-west from-east no-one for (7) outstretched with-neck you-speak

וְלֹא מִמִּדְבַּר הָרִים׃ כִּי־ אֱלֹהִים שֹׁפֵט זֶה
this-one one-judging God but (8) to-exalt from-desert and-no-one

יַשְׁפִּיל וְזֶה יָרִים׃ כִּי כוֹס בְּיַד־ יְהוָה וְיַיִן
and-wine Yahweh in-hand-of cup for (9) he-exalts and-this-one he-brings-down

you established the sun and moon.
17 It was you who set all the boundaries of the earth;
you made both summer and winter.

18 Remember how the enemy has mocked you, O LORD,
how foolish people have reviled your name.
19 Do not hand over the life of your dove to wild beasts;
do not forget the lives of your afflicted people forever.
20 Have regard for your covenant,
because haunts of violence fill the dark places of the land.
21 Do not let the oppressed retreat in disgrace;
may the poor and needy praise your name.

22 Rise up, O God, and defend your cause;
remember how fools mock you all day long.
23 Do not ignore the clamor of your adversaries,
the uproar of your enemies, which rises continually.

Psalm 75

For the director of music. ⌞To the tune of,⌟ "Do Not Destroy." A psalm of Asaph. A song.

1 We give thanks to you, O God,
we give thanks, for your Name is near;
men tell of your wonderful deeds.

2 You say, "I choose the appointed time;
it is I who judge uprightly.
3 When the earth and all its people quake,
it is I who hold its pillars firm. *Selah*
4 To the arrogant I say, 'Boast no more,'
and to the wicked, 'Do not lift up your horns.
5 Do not lift your horns against heaven;
do not speak with outstretched neck.' "

6 No one from the east or the west
or from the desert can exalt a man.
7 But it is God who judges:
He brings one down, he exalts another.
8 In the hand of the LORD is a cup

*Heading, *1* See the note on page 349.

חָמַר ׀ מָלֵא מֶסֶךְ וַיַּגֵּר מִזֶּה אַךְ־ שְׁמָרֶיהָ
dregs-of-her indeed from-this and-he-pours-out mixed-spice he-is-full he-foams

יִמְצוּ יִשְׁתּוּ כֹּל רִשְׁעֵי־ אָרֶץ׃ וַאֲנִי אַגִּיד
I-will-declare and-I (10) earth wicked-ones-of all-of they-drink they-drink

לְעֹלָם אֲזַמְּרָה לֵאלֹהֵי יַעֲקֹב׃ וְכָל־ קַרְנֵי
horns-of and-all-of (11) Jacob to-God-of I-will-sing-praise to-forever

רְשָׁעִים אֲגַדֵּעַ תְּרוֹמַמְנָה קַרְנוֹת צַדִּיק׃
righteous horns-of they-will-be-lifted-up I-will-cut-off wicked-ones

לַמְנַצֵּחַ בִּנְגִינֹת מִזְמוֹר לְאָסָף שִׁיר׃
song of-Asaph psalm with-stringed-instruments for-the-one-directing *(76:1)

נוֹדָע בִּיהוּדָה אֱלֹהִים בְּיִשְׂרָאֵל גָּדוֹל שְׁמוֹ׃ וַיְהִי
and-he-is (3) name-of-him great in-Israel God in-Judah one-being-known (2)

בְשָׁלֵם סֻכּוֹ וּמְעוֹנָתוֹ בְצִיּוֹן׃ שָׁמָּה שִׁבַּר
he-broke at-there (4) in-Zion and-dwelling-place-of-him tent-of-him in-Salem

רִשְׁפֵי־ קָשֶׁת מָגֵן וְחֶרֶב וּמִלְחָמָה סֶלָה׃ נָאוֹר
one-giving-light (5) selah and-weapon-of-war and-sword shield arrow flashes-of

אַתָּה אַדִּיר מֵהַרְרֵי־ טָרֶף׃ אֶשְׁתּוֹלְלוּ ׀ אַבִּירֵי
men-valiant-of they-lie-plundered (6) game more-than-mountains-of majestic you

לֵב נָמוּ שְׁנָתָם וְלֹא־ מָצְאוּ כָל־ אַנְשֵׁי־ חַיִל
war men-of any-of they-can-lift and-not sleep-of-them they-sleep heart

יְדֵיהֶם׃ מִגַּעֲרָתְךָ אֱלֹהֵי יַעֲקֹב נִרְדָּם וְרֶכֶב
both-chariot one-lying-still Jacob God-of at-rebuke-of-you (7) hands-of-them

וָסוּס׃ אַתָּה ׀ נוֹרָא אַתָּה וּמִי־ יַעֲמֹד לְפָנֶיךָ
before-you he-can-stand and-who? you one-being-feared you (8) and-horse

מֵאָז אַפֶּךָ׃ מִשָּׁמַיִם הִשְׁמַעְתָּ דִּין אֶרֶץ יָרְאָה
she-feared land judgment you-pronounced from-heavens (9) anger-of-you at-when

וְשָׁקָטָה׃ בְּקוּם־ לַמִּשְׁפָּט אֱלֹהִים לְהוֹשִׁיעַ כָּל־
all-of to-save God for-the-judgment when-to-rise (10) and-she-was-quiet

עַנְוֵי־ אֶרֶץ סֶלָה׃ כִּי־ חֲמַת אָדָם תּוֹדֶךָּ
she-praises-you man wrath-of surely (11) selah land afflicted-ones-of

שְׁאֵרִית חֵמֹת תַּחְגֹּר׃ נִדְרוּ וְשַׁלְּמוּ לַיהוָה
to-Yahweh and-fulfill! make-vows! (12) you-restrain wraths survivor-of

אֱלֹהֵיכֶם כָּל־ סְבִיבָיו יוֹבִילוּ שַׁי לַמּוֹרָא׃
to-the-One-being-feared gift let-them-bring neighbors-of-him all-of God-of-you

יִבְצֹר רוּחַ נְגִידִים נוֹרָא לְמַלְכֵי־ אָרֶץ׃
earth by-kings-of one-being-feared rulers spirit-of he-breaks (13)

לַמְנַצֵּחַ עַל־ יְדִיתוּן° לְאָסָף מִזְמוֹר׃ קוֹלִי
cry-of-me (2) psalm of-Asaph Jeduthun to for-the-one-directing *(77:1)

full of foaming wine mixed
with spices;
he pours it out, and all the
wicked of the earth
drink it down to its very
dregs.

9 As for me, I will declare this
forever;
I will sing praise to the God
of Jacob.
10 I will cut off the horns of all
the wicked,
but the horns of the
righteous will be lifted
up.

Psalm 76

For the director of music. With stringed instruments. A psalm of Asaph. A song.

1 In Judah God is known;
his name is great in Israel.
2 His tent is in Salem,
his dwelling place in Zion.
3 There he broke the flashing
arrows,
the shields and the swords,
the weapons of war. *Selah*

4 You are resplendent with light,
more majestic than
mountains rich with
game.
5 Valiant men lie plundered,
they sleep their last sleep;
not one of the warriors
can lift his hands.
6 At your rebuke, O God of
Jacob,
both horse and chariot lie
still.
7 You alone are to be feared.
Who can stand before you
when you are angry?
8 From heaven you pronounced
judgment,
and the land feared and was
quiet—
9 when you, O God, rose up to
judge,
to save all the afflicted of
the land. *Selah*
10 Surely your wrath against men
brings you praise,
and the survivors of your
wrath are restrained.[c]

11 Make vows to the LORD your
God and fulfill them;
let all the neighboring lands
bring gifts to the One to be
feared.
12 He breaks the spirit of rulers;
he is feared by the kings of
the earth.

Psalm 77

For the director of music. To Jeduthun. Of Asaph. A psalm.

[c]10 Or *Surely the wrath of men brings you praise, / and with the remainder of wrath you arm yourself*

*Heading, *1* See the note on page 349.

° *1* ק ידותון

אֶל־אֱלֹהִים וְאֶצְעָקָה קוֹלִי אֶל־אֱלֹהִים וְהַאֲזִין אֵלָי׃

to-me and-to-hear God to cry-of-me indeed-I-cried-for-help God to

בְּיוֹם צָרָתִי אֲדֹנָי דָּרָשְׁתִּי יָדִי ׀ לַיְלָה נִגְּרָה

she-was-stretched night hand-of-me I-sought Lord distress-of-me in-day-of (3)

וְלֹא תָפוּג מֵאֲנָה הִנָּחֵם נַפְשִׁי׃ אֶזְכְּרָה

I-remembered (4) soul-of-me to-be-comforted she-refused she-became-tired and-not

אֱלֹהִים וְאֶהֱמָיָה אָשִׂיחָה ׀ וְתִתְעַטֵּף רוּחִי סֶלָה׃ אָחַזְתָּ

you-kept (5) selah spirit-of-me and-she-grew-faint I-mused and-I-groaned God

שְׁמֻרוֹת עֵינָי נִפְעַמְתִּי וְלֹא אֲדַבֵּר׃ חִשַּׁבְתִּי יָמִים

days I-thought-of (6) I-could-speak and-not I-was-troubled eyes-of-me lids-of

מִקֶּדֶם שְׁנוֹת עוֹלָמִים׃ אֶזְכְּרָה נְגִינָתִי בַּלָּיְלָה

in-the-night song-of-me I-remembered (7) ones-long-ago years-of at-formerly

עִם־לְבָבִי אָשִׂיחָה וַיְחַפֵּשׂ רוּחִי׃ הַלְעוֹלָמִים

to-forevers? (8) spirit-of-me and-he-inquired I-mused heart-of-me in

יִזְנַח ׀ אֲדֹנָי וְלֹא־יֹסִיף לִרְצוֹת עוֹד׃

again to-show-favor he-will-do-again and-never Lord will-he-reject

הֶאָפֵס לָנֶצַח חַסְדּוֹ גָּמַר אֹמֶר

promise he-failed unfailing-love-of-him to-forever he-vanished? (9)

לְדֹר וָדֹר׃ הֲשָׁכַח חַנּוֹת אֵל אִם־

or God to-be-merciful he-forgot? (10) and-generation for-generation

קָפַץ בְּאַף רַחֲמָיו סֶלָה׃ וָאֹמַר

then-I-thought (11) selah compassions-of-him in-anger he-withheld

חַלּוֹתִי הִיא שְׁנוֹת יְמִין עֶלְיוֹן׃ אֶזְכִּיר

I-will-remember (12) Most-High right-hand-of years-of this to-appeal-me

מַעַלְלֵי־יָהּ כִּי־אֶזְכְּרָה מִקֶּדֶם פִּלְאֶךָ׃

miracle-of-you of-long-ago I-will-remember yes Yahweh deeds-of

וְהָגִיתִי בְכָל־פָּעֳלֶךָ וּבַעֲלִילוֹתֶיךָ

and-to-mighty-deeds-of-you work-of-you on-all-of and-I-will-meditate (13)

אָשִׂיחָה׃ אֱלֹהִים בַּקֹּדֶשׁ דַּרְכֶּךָ מִי־אֵל גָּדוֹל

great god what? way-of-you in-the-holiness God (14) I-will-consider

כֵּאלֹהִים׃ אַתָּה הָאֵל עֹשֵׂה פֶלֶא הוֹדַעְתָּ בָעַמִּים

among-the-peoples you-display miracle one-performing-of the-God you (15) as-God

עֻזֶּךָ׃ גָּאַלְתָּ בִּזְרוֹעַ עַמֶּךָ בְּנֵי־יַעֲקֹב

Jacob descendants-of people-of-you with-arm you-redeemed (16) power-of-you

וְיוֹסֵף סֶלָה׃ רָאוּךָ מַּיִם ׀ אֱלֹהִים רָאוּךָ מַּיִם יָחִילוּ

they-writhed waters they-saw-you God waters they-saw-you (17) selah and-Joseph

אַף יִרְגְּזוּ תְהֹמוֹת׃ זֹרְמוּ מַיִם ׀ עָבוֹת

clouds waters they-poured-down (18) depths they-were-convulsed indeed

1 I cried out to God for help;
I cried out to God to hear me.
2 When I was in distress, I sought the Lord;
at night I stretched out untiring hands
and my soul refused to be comforted.

3 I remembered you, O God, and I groaned;
I mused, and my spirit grew faint. *Selah*
4 You kept my eyes from closing;
I was too troubled to speak.
5 I thought about the former days,
the years of long ago;
6 I remembered my songs in the night.
My heart mused and my spirit inquired:

7 "Will the Lord reject us forever?
Will he never show his favor again?
8 Has his unfailing love vanished forever?
Has his promise failed for all time?
9 Has God forgotten to be merciful?
Has he in anger withheld his compassion?" *Selah*

10 Then I thought, "To this I will appeal:
the years of the right hand of the Most High."
11 I will remember the deeds of the LORD;
yes, I will remember your miracles of long ago.
12 I will meditate on all your works
and consider all your mighty deeds.

13 Your ways, O God, are holy.
What god is so great as our God?
14 You are the God who performs miracles;
you display your power among the peoples.
15 With your mighty arm you redeemed your people,
the descendants of Jacob and Joseph. *Selah*

16 The waters saw you, O God,
the waters saw you and writhed;
the very depths were convulsed.
17 The clouds poured down water,

*See the note on page 349.

°12 ק אזכור

קוֹל נָתְנוּ שְׁחָקִים אַף־ חֲצָצֶיךָ יִתְהַלָּכוּ׃

they-flashed-around arrows-of-you also skies they-resounded thunder

(19) קוֹל רַעַמְךָ ׀ בַּגַּלְגַּל הֵאִירוּ בְרָקִים תֵּבֵל

world lightnings they-lit-up in-the-whirlwind thunder-of-you sound-of (19)

רָגְזָה וַתִּרְעַשׁ הָאָרֶץ׃ (20) בַּיָּם דַּרְכֶּךָ

path-of-you through-the-sea (20) the-earth and-she-quaked she-trembled

וּשְׁבִילְיךָ בְּמַיִם רַבִּים וְעִקְּבוֹתֶיךָ לֹא

not though-footprints-of-you mighty-ones through-waters and-way-of-you

נֹדָעוּ׃ (21) נָחִיתָ כַצֹּאן עַמֶּךָ בְּיַד־ מֹשֶׁה

Moses by-hand-of people-of-you like-the-flock you-led (21) they-were-seen

וְאַהֲרֹן׃ (78:1) מַשְׂכִּיל לְאָסָף הַאֲזִינָה עַמִּי תּוֹרָתִי הַטּוּ

turn! teaching-of-me people-of-me hear! of-Asaph maskil (78:1) and-Aaron

אָזְנְכֶם לְאִמְרֵי־ פִי׃ (2) אֶפְתְּחָה בְמָשָׁל פִּי

mouth-of-me in-parable I-will-open (2) mouth-of-me to-words-of ear-of-you

אַבִּיעָה חִידוֹת מִנִּי־ קֶדֶם׃ (3) אֲשֶׁר שָׁמַעְנוּ וַנֵּדָעֵם

and-we-knew-them we-heard that (3) of-old from things-hidden I-will-utter

וַאֲבוֹתֵינוּ סִפְּרוּ־ לָנוּ׃ (4) לֹא נְכַחֵד ׀ מִבְּנֵיהֶם

from-children-of-them we-will-hide not (4) to-us they-told and-fathers-of-us

לְדוֹר אַחֲרוֹן מְסַפְּרִים תְּהִלּוֹת יְהוָה וֶעֱזוּזוֹ

and-power-of-him Yahweh praiseworthy-deeds-of ones-telling next to-generation

וְנִפְלְאוֹתָיו אֲשֶׁר עָשָׂה׃ (5) וַיָּקֶם עֵדוּת ׀

statute and-he-decreed (5) he-did that and-deeds-being-wonders-of-him

בְּיַעֲקֹב וְתוֹרָה שָׂם בְּיִשְׂרָאֵל אֲשֶׁר צִוָּה אֶת־

*** he-commanded which in-Israel he-established and-law for-Jacob

אֲבוֹתֵינוּ לְהוֹדִיעָם לִבְנֵיהֶם׃ (6) לְמַעַן יֵדְעוּ ׀

they-would-know so-that (6) to-children-of-them to-teach-them forefathers-of-us

דּוֹר אַחֲרוֹן בָּנִים יִוָּלֵדוּ יָקֻמוּ וִיסַפְּרוּ

and-they-will-tell they-will-rise they-will-be-born children next generation

לִבְנֵיהֶם׃ (7) וְיָשִׂימוּ בֵאלֹהִים כִּסְלָם וְלֹא

and-not trust-of-them in-God then-they-would-put (7) to-children-of-them

יִשְׁכְּחוּ מַעַלְלֵי־ אֵל וּמִצְוֹתָיו יִנְצֹרוּ׃ (8) וְלֹא

and-not (8) they-would-keep but-commands-of-him God deeds-of they-would-forget

יִהְיוּ ׀ כַּאֲבוֹתָם דּוֹר סוֹרֵר

one-being-stubborn generation like-forefathers-of-them they-would-be

וּמֹרֶה דּוֹר לֹא־ הֵכִין לִבּוֹ וְלֹא־

and-not heart-of-him he-was-loyal not generation and-one-rebelling

נֶאֶמְנָה אֶת־ אֵל רוּחוֹ׃ (9) בְּנֵי־ אֶפְרַיִם נוֹשְׁקֵי

ones-being-armed-of Ephraim men-of (9) spirit-of-him God to she-was-faithful

---

the skies resounded with
thunder;
your arrows flashed back
and forth.
18Your thunder was heard in the
whirlwind,
your lightning lit up the
world;
the earth trembled and
quaked.
19Your path led through the sea,
your way through the
mighty waters,
though your footprints were
not seen.
20You led your people like a
flock
by the hand of Moses and
Aaron.

Psalm 78

A *maskil*[d] of Asaph.

1O my people, hear my
teaching;
listen to the words of my
mouth.
2I will open my mouth in
parables,
I will utter things hidden
from of old—
3things we have heard and
known,
things our fathers have told
us.
4We will not hide them from
their children;
we will tell the next
generation
the praiseworthy deeds of the
LORD,
his power, and the wonders
he has done.
5He decreed statutes for Jacob
and established the law in
Israel,
which he commanded our
forefathers
to teach their children,
6so the next generation would
know them,
even the children yet to be
born,
and they in turn would tell
their children.
7Then they would put their
trust in God
and would not forget his
deeds
but would keep his
commands.
8They would not be like their
forefathers—
a stubborn and rebellious
generation,
whose hearts were not loyal to
God,
whose spirits were not
faithful to him.
9The men of Ephraim, though
armed with bows,

[d] Title: Probably a literary or musical term

*See the note on page 349.

°20 ק ושבילך

רוֹמֵי־ קָשֶׁת הָפְכוּ בְּיוֹם קְרָב׃ לֹא שָׁמְרוּ
they-kept not (10) battle on-day-of they-turned-back bow ones-shooting-of

בְּרִית אֱלֹהִים וּבְתוֹרָתוֹ מֵאֲנוּ לָלֶכֶת׃ וַיִּשְׁכְּחוּ
and-they-forgot (11) to-live they-refused and-by-law-of-him God covenant-of

עֲלִילוֹתָיו וְנִפְלְאוֹתָיו אֲשֶׁר הֶרְאָם׃
he-showed-them which and-deeds-being-wonders-of-him deeds-of-him

נֶגֶד אֲבוֹתָם עָשָׂה פֶלֶא בְּאֶרֶץ מִצְרַיִם שְׂדֵה־
region-of Egypt in-land-of miracle he-did fathers-of-them in-sight-of (12)

צֹעַן׃ בָּקַע יָם וַיַּעֲבִירֵם וַיַּצֶּב־ מַיִם
waters and-he-made-stand and-he-led-through-them sea he-divided (13) Zoan

כְּמוֹ־ נֵד׃ וַיַּנְחֵם בֶּעָנָן יוֹמָם וְכָל־ הַלַּיְלָה
the-night and-all-of by-day with-the-cloud and-he-guided-them (14) wall like

בְּאוֹר אֵשׁ׃ יְבַקַּע צֻרִים בַּמִּדְבָּר וַיַּשְׁק
and-he-gave-water in-the-desert rocks he-split (15) fire with-light-of

כִּתְהֹמוֹת רַבָּה׃ וַיּוֹצִא נוֹזְלִים מִסָּלַע
from-rocky-crag ones-streaming and-he-brought-out (16) abundant as-seas

וַיּוֹרֶד כַּנְּהָרוֹת מָיִם׃ וַיּוֹסִיפוּ עוֹד
again but-they-continued (17) waters like-the-rivers and-he-made-flow-down

לַחֲטֹא־ לוֹ לַמְרוֹת עֶלְיוֹן בַּצִּיָּה׃ וַיְנַסּוּ־
and-they-tested (18) in-the-desert Most-High to-rebel-against against-him to-sin

אֵל בִּלְבָבָם לִשְׁאָל־ אֹכֶל לְנַפְשָׁם׃ וַיְדַבְּרוּ
and-they-spoke (19) for-craving-of-them food to-demand by-will-of-them God

בֵּאלֹהִים אָמְרוּ הֲיוּכַל אֵל לַעֲרֹךְ שֻׁלְחָן בַּמִּדְבָּר׃ הֵן
see! (20) in-the-desert table to-spread God can-he? they-said against-God

הִכָּה־ צוּר | וַיָּזוּבוּ מַיִם וּנְחָלִים יִשְׁטֹפוּ הֲגַם־
also? they-flowed and-streams waters and-they-gushed-out rock he-struck

לֶחֶם יוּכַל תֵּת אִם־ יָכִין שְׁאֵר לְעַמּוֹ׃ לָכֵן
when (21) for-people-of-him meat can-he-supply or to-give can-he food

שָׁמַע | יְהוָה וַיִּתְעַבָּר וְאֵשׁ נִשְּׂקָה בְיַעֲקֹב
against-Jacob she-broke-out and-fire then-he-was-angry Yahweh he-heard

וְגַם־ אַף עָלָה בְיִשְׂרָאֵל׃ כִּי לֹא הֶאֱמִינוּ בֵּאלֹהִים
in-God they-believed not for (22) against-Israel he-rose wrath and-also

וְלֹא בָטְחוּ בִּישׁוּעָתוֹ׃ וַיְצַו שְׁחָקִים
skies yet-he-commanded (23) in-deliverance-of-him they-trusted and-not

מִמָּעַל וְדַלְתֵי שָׁמַיִם פָּתָח׃ וַיַּמְטֵר עֲלֵיהֶם
for-them and-he-rained-down (24) he-opened heavens and-doors-of at-above

מָן לֶאֱכֹל וּדְגַן־ שָׁמַיִם נָתַן לָמוֹ׃ לֶחֶם אַבִּירִים
angels bread-of (25) to-them he-gave heavens and-grain-of to-eat manna

turned back on the day of
battle;
10 they did not keep God's
covenant
and refused to live by his
law.
11 They forgot what he had done,
the wonders he had shown
them.
12 He did miracles in the sight of
their fathers
in the land of Egypt, in the
region of Zoan.
13 He divided the sea and led
them through;
he made the water stand
firm like a wall.
14 He guided them with the
cloud by day
and with light from the fire
all night.
15 He split the rocks in the desert
and gave them water as
abundant as the seas;
16 he brought streams out of a
rocky crag
and made water flow down
like rivers.

17 But they continued to sin
against him,
rebelling in the desert
against the Most High.
18 They willfully put God to the
test
by demanding the food they
craved.
19 They spoke against God,
saying,
"Can God spread a table in
the desert?
20 When he struck the rock,
water gushed out,
and streams flowed
abundantly.
But can he also give us food?
Can he supply meat for his
people?"
21 When the LORD heard them,
he was very angry;
his fire broke out against
Jacob,
and his wrath rose against
Israel,
22 for they did not believe in God
or trust in his deliverance.
23 Yet he gave a command to the
skies above
and opened the doors of the
heavens;
24 he rained down manna for the
people to eat,
he gave them the grain of
heaven.
25 Men ate the bread of angels;

אָכַל אִישׁ צֵידָה שָׁלַח לָהֶם לָשֹׂבַע׃ יַסַּע קָדִים
east-wind he-let-loose (26) in-abundance to-them he-sent food man he-ate

בַּשָּׁמָיִם וַיְנַהֵג בְּעֻזּוֹ תֵימָן׃
south-wind by-power-of-him and-he-led-forth from-the-heavens

וַיַּמְטֵר עֲלֵיהֶם כֶּעָפָר שְׁאֵר וּכְחוֹל יַמִּים
seas and-like-sand-of meat like-the-dust on-them and-he-rained-down (27)

עוֹף כָּנָף׃ וַיַּפֵּל בְּקֶרֶב מַחֲנֵהוּ סָבִיב
around camp-of-him to-inside-of and-he-made-come-down (28) flight bird-of

לְמִשְׁכְּנֹתָיו׃ וַיֹּאכְלוּ וַיִּשְׂבְּעוּ מְאֹד וְתַאֲוָתָם
for-craving-of-them more and-they-had-enough and-they-ate (29) about-tents-of-him

יָבִא לָהֶם׃ לֹא־ זָרוּ מִתַּאֲוָתָם עוֹד אָכְלָם
food-of-them still from-craving-of-them they-turned not (30) to-them he-gave

בְּפִיהֶם׃ וְאַף אֱלֹהִים ׀ עָלָה בָהֶם וַיַּהֲרֹג
and-he-killed against-them he-rose God and-anger-of (31) in-mouth-of-them

בְּמִשְׁמַנֵּיהֶם וּבַחוּרֵי יִשְׂרָאֵל הִכְרִיעַ׃ בְּכָל־
in-all-of (32) he-cut-down Israel and-men-being-young-of to-sturdy-ones-of-them

זֹאת חָטְאוּ־ עוֹד וְלֹא־ הֶאֱמִינוּ בְּנִפְלְאוֹתָיו׃
in-deeds-being-wonders-of-him they-believed and-not still they-sinned this

וַיְכַל־ בַּהֶבֶל יְמֵיהֶם וּשְׁנוֹתָם בַּבֶּהָלָה׃
in-the-terror and-years-of-them days-of-them in-the-futility so-he-ended (33)

אִם־ הֲרָגָם וּדְרָשׁוּהוּ וְשָׁבוּ
and-they-turned then-they-would-seek-him he-slew-them whenever (34)

וְשִׁחֲרוּ־ אֵל׃ וַיִּזְכְּרוּ כִּי־אֱלֹהִים צוּרָם
Rock-of-them God that and-they-remembered (35) God and-they-were-eager-for

וְאֵל עֶלְיוֹן גֹּאֲלָם׃ וַיְפַתּוּהוּ
but-they-would-flatter-him (36) One-Redeeming-them Most-High and-God

בְּפִיהֶם וּבִלְשׁוֹנָם יְכַזְּבוּ־ לוֹ׃
to-him they-lied and-with-tongue-of-them with-mouth-of-them

וְלִבָּם לֹא־ נָכוֹן עִמּוֹ וְלֹא נֶאֶמְנוּ
they-were-faithful and-not to-him he-was-loyal not and-heart-of-them (37)

בִּבְרִיתוֹ׃ וְהוּא רַחוּם ׀ יְכַפֵּר עָוֹן וְלֹא־
and-not iniquity he-atoned-for merciful yet-he (38) to-covenant-of-him

יַשְׁחִית וְהִרְבָּה לְהָשִׁיב אַפּוֹ וְלֹא־ יָעִיר
he-stirred-up and-not anger-of-him to-restrain and-he-did-often he-destroyed

כָּל־ חֲמָתוֹ׃ וַיִּזְכֹּר כִּי־ בָשָׂר הֵמָּה רוּחַ הוֹלֵךְ
passing breeze they flesh that and-he-remembered (39) wrath-of-him fullness-of

וְלֹא יָשׁוּב׃ כַּמָּה יַמְרוּהוּ בַמִּדְבָּר
in-the-desert they-rebelled-against-him as-the-how! (40) he-returns and-not

he sent them all the food
they could eat.
26 He let loose the east wind
from the heavens
and led forth the south
wind by his power.
27 He rained meat down on them
like dust,
flying birds like sand on the
seashore.
28 He made them come down
inside their camp,
all around their tents.
29 They ate till they had more
than enough,
for he had given them what
they craved.
30 But before they turned from
the food they craved,
even while it was still in
their mouths,
31 God's anger rose against them;
he put to death the sturdiest
among them,
cutting down the young
men of Israel.
32 In spite of all this, they kept
on sinning;
in spite of his wonders, they
did not believe.
33 So he ended their days in
futility
and their years in terror.
34 Whenever God slew them,
they would seek him;
they eagerly turned to him
again.
35 They remembered that God
was their Rock,
that God Most High was
their Redeemer.
36 But then they would flatter
him with their mouths,
lying to him with their
tongues;
37 their hearts were not loyal to
him,
they were not faithful to his
covenant.
38 Yet he was merciful;
he atoned for their
iniquities
and did not destroy them.
Time after time he restrained
his anger
and did not stir up his full
wrath.
39 He remembered that they were
but flesh,
a passing breeze that does
not return.
40 How often they rebelled
against him in the desert

יַעֲצִיבוּהוּ בִּישִׁימוֹן׃ (41) וַיָּשׁוּבוּ וַיְנַסּוּ אֵל
God and-they-tested and-they-did-again (41) in-wasteland they-grieved-him

וּקְדוֹשׁ יִשְׂרָאֵל הִתְווּ׃ (42) לֹא־ זָכְרוּ אֶת־ יָדוֹ
power-of-him *** they-remembered not (42) they-vexed Israel and-Holy-One-of

יוֹם אֲשֶׁר־ פָּדָם מִנִּי־ צָר׃ (43) אֲשֶׁר־ שָׂם בְּמִצְרַיִם
in-Egypt he-displayed when (43) oppressor from he-redeemed-them that day

אֹתוֹתָיו וּמוֹפְתָיו בִּשְׂדֵה־ צֹעַן׃ (44) וַיַּהֲפֹךְ
and-he-turned (44) Zoan in-region-of and-wonders-of-him miraculous-signs-of-him

לְדָם יְאֹרֵיהֶם וְנֹזְלֵיהֶם בַּל־ יִשְׁתָּיוּן׃
they-could-drink not and-ones-streaming-of-them rivers-of-them to-blood

(45) יְשַׁלַּח בָּהֶם עָרֹב וַיֹּאכְלֵם וּצְפַרְדֵּעַ וַתַּשְׁחִיתֵם׃
and-he-devastated-them and-frog and-he-devoured-them swarm to-them he-sent (45)

(46) וַיִּתֵּן לֶחָסִיל יְבוּלָם וִיגִיעָם
and-produce-of-them crop-of-them to-the-grasshopper and-he-gave (46)

לָאַרְבֶּה׃ (47) יַהֲרֹג בַּבָּרָד גַּפְנָם
vine-of-them with-the-hail he-destroyed (47) to-the-locust

וְשִׁקְמוֹתָם בַּחֲנָמַל׃ (48) וַיַּסְגֵּר לַבָּרָד
to-the-hail and-he-gave-over (48) with-the-sleet and-sycamore-figs-of-them

בְּעִירָם וּמִקְנֵיהֶם לָרְשָׁפִים׃ (49) יְשַׁלַּח־
he-unleashed (49) to-the-lightning-bolts and-livestocks-of-them cattle-of-them

בָּם ׀ חֲרוֹן אַפּוֹ עֶבְרָה וָזַעַם וְצָרָה מִשְׁלַחַת
band-of and-hostility and-indignation wrath anger-of-him heat-of against-them

מַלְאֲכֵי רָעִים׃ (50) יְפַלֵּס נָתִיב לְאַפּוֹ לֹא־ חָשַׂךְ
he-spared not for-anger-of-him path he-prepared (50) destructions angels-of

מִמָּוֶת נַפְשָׁם וְחַיָּתָם לַדֶּבֶר הִסְגִּיר׃
he-gave-over to-the-plague but-life-of-them self-of-them from-death

(51) וַיַּךְ כָּל־ בְּכוֹר בְּמִצְרָיִם רֵאשִׁית אוֹנִים
manhoods firstfruit-of of-Egypt firstborn all-of and-he-struck-down (51)

בְּאָהֳלֵי־ חָם׃ (52) וַיַּסַּע כַּצֹּאן עַמּוֹ
people-of-him like-the-flock but-he-brought-out (52) Ham in-tents-of

וַיְנַהֲגֵם כַּעֵדֶר בַּמִּדְבָּר׃ (53) וַיַּנְחֵם
and-he-guided-them (53) through-the-desert like-the-sheep and-he-led-them

לָבֶטַח וְלֹא פָחָדוּ וְאֶת־ אוֹיְבֵיהֶם כִּסָּה
he-engulfed ones-being-enemies-of-them but they-were-afraid so-not in-safety

הַיָּם׃ (54) וַיְבִיאֵם אֶל־ גְּבוּל קָדְשׁוֹ הַר־
hill-country holiness-of-him border-of to thus-he-brought-them (54) the-sea

זֶה קָנְתָה יְמִינוֹ׃ (55) וַיְגָרֶשׁ מִפְּנֵיהֶם ׀ גּוֹיִם
nations from-before-them and-he-drove-out (55) right-hand-of-him she-took this

and grieved him in the
wasteland!
41 Again and again they put God
to the test;
they vexed the Holy One of
Israel.
42 They did not remember his
power—
the day he redeemed them
from the oppressor,
43 the day he displayed his
miraculous signs in
Egypt,
his wonders in the region of
Zoan.
44 He turned their rivers to
blood;
they could not drink from
their streams.
45 He sent swarms of flies that
devoured them
and frogs that devastated
them.
46 He gave their crops to the
grasshopper,
their produce to the locust.
47 He destroyed their vines with
hail
and their sycamore-figs with
sleet.
48 He gave over their cattle to the
hail,
their livestock to bolts of
lightning.
49 He unleashed against them his
hot anger,
his wrath, indignation and
hostility—
a band of destroying angels.
50 He prepared a path for his
anger;
he did not spare them from
death
but gave them over to the
plague.
51 He struck down all the
firstborn of Egypt,
the firstfruits of manhood in
the tents of Ham.
52 But he brought his people out
like a flock;
he led them like sheep
through the desert.
53 He guided them safely, so they
were unafraid;
but the sea engulfed their
enemies.
54 Thus he brought them to the
border of his holy land,
to the hill country his right
hand had taken.
55 He drove out nations before
them

וַיַּפִּילֵם בְּחֶבֶל נַחֲלָה וַיַּשְׁכֵּן בְּאָהֳלֵיהֶם
in-homes-of-them and-he-settled inheritance from-land and-he-allotted-them

שִׁבְטֵי יִשְׂרָאֵל׃ וַיְנַסּוּ וַיַּמְרוּ אֶת־אֱלֹהִים
God *** and-they-rebelled-against but-they-tested (56) Israel tribes-of

עֶלְיוֹן וְעֵדוֹתָיו לֹא שָׁמָרוּ׃ וַיִּסֹּגוּ
and-they-were-disloyal (57) they-kept not and-statutes-of-him Most-High

וַיִּבְגְּדוּ כַּאֲבוֹתָם נֶהְפְּכוּ כְּקֶשֶׁת רְמִיָּה׃
faultiness as-bow-of they-were-unreliable like-fathers-of-them and-they-were-faithless

וַיַּכְעִיסוּהוּ בְּבָמוֹתָם וּבִפְסִילֵיהֶם
and-with-idols-of-them with-high-places-of-them and-they-angered-him (58)

יַקְנִיאוּהוּ׃ שָׁמַע אֱלֹהִים וַיִּתְעַבָּר וַיִּמְאַס
and-he-rejected and-he-was-angry God he-heard (59) they-made-jealous-him

מְאֹד בְּיִשְׂרָאֵל׃ וַיִּטֹּשׁ מִשְׁכַּן שִׁלוֹ אֹהֶל
tent Shiloh tabernacle-of and-he-abandoned (60) to-Israel completely

שִׁכֵּן בָּאָדָם׃ וַיִּתֵּן לַשְּׁבִי עֻזּוֹ
might-of-him into-the-captivity and-he-sent (61) among-the-man he-set-up

וְתִפְאַרְתּוֹ בְיַד־ צָר׃ וַיַּסְגֵּר לַחֶרֶב
to-the-sword and-he-gave-over (62) enemy into-hand-of and-splendor-of-him

עַמּוֹ וּבְנַחֲלָתוֹ הִתְעַבָּר׃ בַּחוּרָיו
and-young-men-of-him (63) he-was-angry and-with-inheritance-of-him people-of-him

אָכְלָה־ אֵשׁ וּבְתוּלֹתָיו לֹא הוּלָּלוּ׃
they-were-sung-about not and-maidens-of-him fire she-consumed

כֹּהֲנָיו בַּחֶרֶב נָפָלוּ וְאַלְמְנֹתָיו לֹא
not and-widows-of-him they-fell by-the-sword priests-of-him (64)

תִבְכֶּינָה׃ וַיִּקַץ כְּיָשֵׁן ׀ אֲדֹנָי כְּגִבּוֹר מִתְרוֹנֵן
one-being-in-stupor as-man Lord as-sleep then-he-awoke (65) they-could-weep

מִיָּיִן׃ וַיַּךְ־ צָרָיו אָחוֹר חֶרְפַּת עוֹלָם
everlasting shame-of back enemies-of-him and-he-beat (66) from-wine

נָתַן לָמוֹ׃ וַיִּמְאַס בְּאֹהֶל יוֹסֵף וּבְשֵׁבֶט
and-to-tribe-of Joseph to-tent-of then-he-rejected (67) to-them he-put

אֶפְרַיִם לֹא בָחָר׃ וַיִּבְחַר אֶת־ שֵׁבֶט יְהוּדָה אֶת־ הַר צִיּוֹן
Zion Mount-of *** Judah tribe-of *** but-he-chose (68) he-chose not Ephraim

אֲשֶׁר אָהֵב׃ וַיִּבֶן כְּמוֹ־ רָמִים מִקְדָּשׁוֹ
sanctuary-of-him ones-being-high like and-he-built (69) he-loved which

כְּאֶרֶץ יְסָדָהּ לְעוֹלָם׃ וַיִּבְחַר בְּדָוִד
to-David and-he-chose (70) to-forever he-established-her like-earth

עַבְדּוֹ וַיִּקָּחֵהוּ מִמִּכְלְאֹת צֹאן׃ מֵאַחַר עָלוֹת
to-tend from-after (71) sheep from-pens-of and-he-took-him servant-of-him

and allotted their lands to
them as an inheritance;
he settled the tribes of Israel
in their homes.
56But they put God to the test
and rebelled against the
Most High;
they did not keep his
statutes.
57Like their fathers they were
disloyal and faithless,
as unreliable as a faulty
bow.
58They angered him with their
high places;
they aroused his jealousy
with their idols.
59When God heard them, he was
very angry;
he rejected Israel completely.
60He abandoned the tabernacle
of Shiloh,
the tent he had set up
among men.
61He sent ⌊the ark of⌋ his might
into captivity,
his splendor into the hands
of the enemy.
62He gave his people over to the
sword;
he was very angry with his
inheritance.
63Fire consumed their young
men,
and their maidens had no
wedding songs;
64their priests were put to the
sword,
and their widows could not
weep.

65Then the Lord awoke as from
sleep,
as a man wakes from the
stupor of wine.
66He beat back his enemies;
he put them to everlasting
shame.
67Then he rejected the tents of
Joseph,
he did not choose the tribe
of Ephraim;
68but he chose the tribe of
Judah,
Mount Zion, which he
loved.
69He built his sanctuary like the
high mountains,
like the earth that he
established forever.
70He chose David his servant
and took him from the
sheep pens;
71from tending the sheep he

הֱבִיאוֹ לִרְעוֹת בְּיַעֲקֹב עַמּוֹ וּבְיִשְׂרָאֵל
even-to-Israel people-of-him to-Jacob to-shepherd he-brought-him

נַחֲלָתוֹ׃ וַיִּרְעֵם כְּתֹם לְבָבוֹ
heart-of-him with-integrity-of and-he-shepherded-them (72) inheritance-of-him

וּבִתְבוּנוֹת כַּפָּיו יַנְחֵם׃ מִזְמוֹר לְאָסָף אֱלֹהִים
God of-Asaph psalm (79:1) he-led-them hands-of-him and-with-skills-of

בָּאוּ גוֹיִם ׀ בְּנַחֲלָתֶךָ טִמְּאוּ אֶת־ הֵיכַל
temple-of *** they-defiled into-inheritance-of-you nations they-invaded

קָדְשֶׁךָ שָׂמוּ אֶת־ יְרוּשָׁלִַם לְעִיִּים׃ נָתְנוּ אֶת־
*** they-gave (2) to-rubbles Jerusalem *** they-reduced holiness-of-you

נִבְלַת עֲבָדֶיךָ מַאֲכָל לְעוֹף הַשָּׁמָיִם בְּשַׂר חֲסִידֶיךָ
saints-of-you flesh-of the-airs to-bird-of food servants-of-you body-of

לְחַיְתוֹ־ אָרֶץ׃ שָׁפְכוּ דָמָם ׀ כַּמַּיִם
like-the-waters blood-of-them they-poured-out (3) earth to-beast-of

סְבִיבוֹת יְרוּשָׁלִָם וְאֵין קוֹבֵר׃ הָיִינוּ חֶרְפָּה
reproach we-are (4) one-burying and-there-is-not Jerusalem ones-around-of

לִשְׁכֵנֵינוּ לַעַג וָקֶלֶס לִסְבִיבוֹתֵינוּ׃ עַד־ מָה
when? until (5) to-ones-around-us and-derision scorn to-neighbors-of-us

יְהוָה תֶּאֱנַף לָנֶצַח תִּבְעַר כְּמוֹ־ אֵשׁ קִנְאָתֶךָ׃
jealousy-of-you fire like will-she-burn to-forever will-you-be-angry Yahweh

שְׁפֹךְ חֲמָתְךָ אֶל־ הַגּוֹיִם אֲשֶׁר לֹא־ יְדָעוּךָ
they-acknowledge-you not that the-nations on wrath-of-you pour-out! (6)

וְעַל מַמְלָכוֹת אֲשֶׁר בְּשִׁמְךָ לֹא קָרָאוּ׃ כִּי אָכַל אֶת־
*** he-devoured for (7) they-call not on-name-of-you that kingdoms and-on

יַעֲקֹב וְאֶת־ נָוֵהוּ הֵשַׁמּוּ׃ אַל־ תִּזְכָּר־ לָנוּ עֲוֺנֹת
sins-of against-us you-hold not (8) they-destroyed homeland-of-him and Jacob

רִאשֹׁנִים מַהֵר יְקַדְּמוּנוּ רַחֲמֶיךָ כִּי דַלּוֹנוּ
we-are-in-need for mercies-of-you may-they-meet-us to-be-quick fathers

מְאֹד׃ עָזְרֵנוּ ׀ אֱלֹהֵי יִשְׁעֵנוּ עַל־ דְּבַר כְּבוֹד־
glory-of account-of for salvation-of-us God-of help-us! (9) desperately

שְׁמֶךָ וְהַצִּילֵנוּ וְכַפֵּר עַל־ חַטֹּאתֵינוּ לְמַעַן שְׁמֶךָ׃
name-of-you for-sake-of sins-of-us for and-atone! and-deliver-us! name-of-you

לָמָּה ׀ יֹאמְרוּ הַגּוֹיִם אַיֵּה אֱלֹהֵיהֶם יִוָּדַע
let-him-be-known God-of-them where? the-nations should-they-say why? (10)

בַגּיִּים° לְעֵינֵינוּ נִקְמַת דַּם־ עֲבָדֶיךָ
servants-of-you blood-of vengeance-of before-eyes-of-us among-the-nations

הַשָּׁפוּךְ׃ תָּבוֹא לְפָנֶיךָ אֶנְקַת אָסִיר
prisoner groan-of before-you may-she-come (11) the-one-being-poured-out

°10 ק בגוים

brought him
to be the shepherd of his
people Jacob,
of Israel his inheritance.
72And David shepherded them
with integrity of heart;
with skillful hands he led
them.

Psalm 79

A psalm of Asaph.

1O God, the nations have
invaded your inheritance;
they have defiled your holy
temple,
they have reduced Jerusalem
to rubble.
2They have given the dead
bodies of your servants
as food to the birds of the
air,
the flesh of your saints to
the beasts of the earth.
3They have poured out blood
like water
all around Jerusalem,
and there is no one to bury
the dead.
4We are objects of reproach to
our neighbors,
of scorn and derision to
those around us.

5How long, O LORD? Will you
be angry forever?
How long will your jealousy
burn like fire?
6Pour out your wrath on the
nations
that do not acknowledge
you,
on the kingdoms
that do not call on your
name;
7for they have devoured Jacob
and destroyed his homeland.
8Do not hold against us the
sins of the fathers;
may your mercy come
quickly to meet us,
for we are in desperate
need.

9Help us, O God our Savior,
for the glory of your name;
deliver us and atone for our
sins
for your name's sake.
10Why should the nations say,
"Where is their God?"
Before our eyes, make known
among the nations
that you avenge the
outpoured blood of your
servants.
11May the groans of the
prisoners come before
you;

כְּגֹדֶל זְרוֹעֲךָ הוֹתֵר בְּנֵי תְמוּתָה׃ וְהָשֵׁב

and-pay-back! (12) death men-of preserve! arm-of-you by-strength-of

לִשְׁכֵנֵינוּ שִׁבְעָתַיִם אֶל־ חֵיקָם חֶרְפָּתָם אֲשֶׁר

that reproach-of-them lap-of-them into seven-times to-neighbors-of-us

חֵרְפוּךָ אֲדֹנָי׃ וַאֲנַחְנוּ עַמְּךָ׀ וְצֹאן

and-sheep-of people-of-you then-we (13) Lord they-reproached-you

מַרְעִיתֶךָ נוֹדֶה לְּךָ לְעוֹלָם לְדֹר וָדֹר

and-generation to-generation to-forever to-you we-will-praise pasture-of-you

נְסַפֵּר תְּהִלָּתֶךָ׃ לַמְנַצֵּחַ אֶל־שֹׁשַׁנִּים עֵדוּת

covenant lilies to for-the-one-directing *(80:1) praise-of-you we-will-recount

לְאָסָף מִזְמוֹר׃ רֹעֵה יִשְׂרָאֵל׀ הַאֲזִינָה נֹהֵג כַּצֹּאן

like-the-flock one-leading hear! Israel One-Shepherding-of (2) psalm of-Asaph

יוֹסֵף יֹשֵׁב הַכְּרוּבִים הוֹפִיעָה׃ לִפְנֵי אֶפְרַיִם׀

Ephraim before (3) shine-forth! the-cherubim one-being-enthroned-of Joseph

וּבִנְיָמִן וּמְנַשֶּׁה עוֹרְרָה אֶת־ גְּבוּרָתֶךָ וּלְכָה לִישֻׁעָתָה

to-salvation and-come! might-of-you *** awaken! and-Manasseh and-Benjamin

לָּנוּ׃ אֱלֹהִים הֲשִׁיבֵנוּ וְהָאֵר פָּנֶיךָ וְנִוָּשֵׁעָה׃

that-we-may-be-saved faces-of-you and-make-shine! restore-us! God (4) of-us

יְהוָה אֱלֹהִים צְבָאוֹת עַד־ מָתַי עָשַׁנְתָּ בִּתְפִלַּת

against-prayer-of will-you-smolder when? until Hosts God Yahweh (5)

עַמֶּךָ׃ הֶאֱכַלְתָּם לֶחֶם דִּמְעָה וַתַּשְׁקֵמוֹ

and-you-made-drink-them tear bread-of you-fed-them (6) people-of-you

בִּדְמָעוֹת שָׁלִישׁ׃ תְּשִׂימֵנוּ מָדוֹן לִשְׁכֵנֵינוּ

to-neighbors-of-us contention you-made-us (7) bowlful of-tears-of

וְאֹיְבֵינוּ יִלְעֲגוּ־ לָמוֹ׃ אֱלֹהִים צְבָאוֹת הֲשִׁיבֵנוּ

restore-us! Hosts God (8) at-us they-mock and-ones-being-enemies-of-us

וְהָאֵר פָּנֶיךָ וְנִוָּשֵׁעָה׃ גֶּפֶן מִמִּצְרַיִם

from-Egypt vine (9) that-we-may-be-saved faces-of-you and-make-shine!

תַּסִּיעַ תְּגָרֵשׁ גּוֹיִם וַתִּטָּעֶהָ׃ פִּנִּיתָ

you-cleared (10) and-you-planted-her nations you-drove-out you-brought

לְפָנֶיהָ וַתַּשְׁרֵשׁ שָׁרָשֶׁיהָ וַתְּמַלֵּא־ אָרֶץ׃

land and-she-filled roots-of-her and-she-took-root before-her

כָּסּוּ הָרִים צִלָּהּ וַעֲנָפֶיהָ אַרְזֵי־

cedars-of and-branches-of-her shade-of-her mountains they-were-covered (11)

אֵל׃ תְּשַׁלַּח קְצִירֶהָ עַד־ יָם וְאֶל־ נָהָר יוֹנְקוֹתֶיהָ׃

shoots-of-her River and-as-far-as Sea to bough-of-her she-sent-out (12) mighty

לָמָּה פָּרַצְתָּ גְדֵרֶיהָ וְאָרוּהָ כָּל־ עֹבְרֵי

ones-passing-of all-of so-they-pick-her walls-of-her you-broke-down why? (13)

---

by the strength of your arm
preserve those condemned
to die.

[12]Pay back into the laps of our
neighbors seven times
the reproach they have
hurled at you, O Lord.
[13]Then we your people, the
sheep of your pasture,
will praise you forever;
from generation to generation
we will recount your praise.

Psalm 80

For the director of music. To the tune of "The Lilies of the Covenant." Of Asaph. A psalm.

[1]Hear us, O Shepherd of Israel,
you who lead Joseph like a
flock;
you who sit enthroned
between the cherubim,
shine forth
[2] before Ephraim, Benjamin
and Manasseh.
Awaken your might;
come and save us.

[3]Restore us, O God;
make your face shine upon
us,
that we may be saved.

[4]O LORD God Almighty,
how long will your anger
smolder
against the prayers of your
people?
[5]You have fed them with the
bread of tears;
you have made them drink
tears by the bowlful.
[6]You have made us a source of
contention to our
neighbors,
and our enemies mock us.

[7]Restore us, O God Almighty;
make your face shine upon
us,
that we may be saved.

[8]You brought a vine out of
Egypt;
you drove out the nations
and planted it.
[9]You cleared the ground for it,
and it took root and filled
the land.
[10]The mountains were covered
with its shade,
the mighty cedars with its
branches.
[11]It sent out its boughs to the
Sea,[e]
its shoots as far as the
River.[f]

[12]Why have you broken down
its walls
so that all who pass by pick
its grapes?

[e]11 Probably the Mediterranean
[f]11 That is, the Euphrates

*Heading, 1 See the note on page 349.

דָּרֶךְ׃ יְכַרְסְמֶנָּה חֲזִיר מִיָּעַר וְזִיז שָׂדַי
field and-creature-of from-forest boar and-he-ravages-her (14) way

יִרְעֶנָּה׃ אֱלֹהִים צְבָאוֹת שׁוּב־ נָא הַבֵּט מִשָּׁמַיִם וּרְאֵה
and-see! from-heavens look-down! now! return! Hosts God (15) he-feeds-on-her

וּפְקֹד גֶּפֶן זֹאת׃ וְכַנָּה אֲשֶׁר־ נָטְעָה יְמִינֶךָ
right-hand-of-you she-planted that and-root (16) this vine and-watch-over!

וְעַל־ בֵּן אִמַּצְתָּה לָּךְ׃ שְׂרֻפָה בָאֵשׁ
with-fire one-being-burned (17) for-you you-raised-up son and-over

כְּסוּחָה מִגַּעֲרַת פָּנֶיךָ יֹאבֵדוּ׃ תְּהִי־
let-her-be (18) they-perish faces-of-you at-rebuke-of one-being-cut-down

יָדְךָ עַל־ אִישׁ יְמִינֶךָ עַל־ בֶּן־ אָדָם אִמַּצְתָּ לָּךְ׃
for-you you-raised-up man son-of on right-hand-of-you man-of on hand-of-you

וְלֹא־ נָסוֹג מִמֶּךָּ תְּחַיֵּנוּ וּבְשִׁמְךָ
and-on-name-of-you you-revive-us from-you we-will-turn-away then-not (19)

נִקְרָא׃ יְהוָה אֱלֹהִים צְבָאוֹת הֲשִׁיבֵנוּ הָאֵר פָּנֶיךָ
faces-of-you make-shine! restore-us! Hosts God Yahweh (20) we-will-call

וְנִוָּשֵׁעָה׃ לַמְנַצֵּחַ עַל־ הַגִּתִּית
the-gittith according-to for-the-one-directing *(81:1) that-we-may-be-saved

לְאָסָף׃ הַרְנִינוּ לֵאלֹהִים עוּזֵּנוּ הָרִיעוּ לֵאלֹהֵי יַעֲקֹב׃
Jacob to-God-of shout! strength-of-us to-God sing-for-joy! (2) of-Asaph

שְׂאוּ־ זִמְרָה וּתְנוּ־ תֹף כִּנּוֹר נָעִים עִם־ נָבֶל׃ תִּקְעוּ
sound! (4) lyre and melodious harp tambourine and-strike! music begin! (3)

בַחֹדֶשׁ שׁוֹפָר בַּכֵּסֶה לְיוֹם חַגֵּנוּ׃ כִּי
for (5) Feast-of-us on-day-of at-the-full-moon horn-of-ram at-the-New-Moon

חֹק לְיִשְׂרָאֵל הוּא מִשְׁפָּט לֵאלֹהֵי יַעֲקֹב׃ עֵדוּת בִּיהוֹסֵף
for-Joseph statute (6) Jacob of-God-of ordinance this for-Israel decree

שָׂמוֹ בְּצֵאתוֹ עַל־ אֶרֶץ מִצְרָיִם שְׂפַת לֹא־
not language-of Egypt land-of against when-to-go-out-him he-established-him

יָדַעְתִּי אֶשְׁמָע׃ הֲסִירוֹתִי מִסֵּבֶל שִׁכְמוֹ כַּפָּיו
hands-of-him shoulder-of-him from-burden I-removed (7) I-heard I-understood

מִדּוּד תַּעֲבֹרְנָה׃ בַּצָּרָה קָרָאתָ וָאֲחַלְּצֶךָּ
and-I-rescued-you you-called in-the-distress (8) they-were-freed from-basket

אֶעֶנְךָ בְּסֵתֶר רַעַם אֶבְחָנְךָ עַל־ מֵי מְרִיבָה סֶלָה׃
selah Meribah waters-of at I-tested-you thunder from-cloud-of I-answered-you

שְׁמַע עַמִּי וְאָעִידָה בָּךְ יִשְׂרָאֵל אִם־ תִּשְׁמַע־
you-would-listen if Israel to-you and-I-will-warn people-of-me hear! (9)

לִי׃ לֹא־ יִהְיֶה בְךָ אֵל זָר וְלֹא תִשְׁתַּחֲוֶה
you-shall-bow and-not being-foreign god among-you he-shall-be not (10) to-me

13 Boars from the forest ravage it
and the creatures of the field feed on it.
14 Return to us, O God Almighty!
Look down from heaven and see!
Watch over this vine,
15 the root your right hand has planted,
the son[g] you have raised up for yourself.

16 Your vine is cut down, it is burned with fire;
at your rebuke your people perish.
17 Let your hand rest on the man at your right hand,
the son of man you have raised up for yourself.
18 Then we will not turn away from you;
revive us, and we will call on your name.

19 Restore us, O LORD God Almighty;
make your face shine upon us,
that we may be saved.

Psalm 81

For the director of music. According to *gittith*.[h] Of Asaph.

1 Sing for joy to God our strength;
shout aloud to the God of Jacob!
2 Begin the music, strike the tambourine,
play the melodious harp and lyre.

3 Sound the ram's horn at the New Moon,
and when the moon is full, on the day of our Feast;
4 this is a decree for Israel,
an ordinance of the God of Jacob.
5 He established it as a statute for Joseph
when he went out against Egypt,
where we heard a language we did not understand.[i]

6 He says, "I removed the burden from their shoulders;
their hands were set free from the basket.
7 In your distress you called and I rescued you,
I answered you out of a thundercloud;
I tested you at the waters of Meribah. *Selah*

8 "Hear, O my people, and I will warn you—
if you would but listen to me, O Israel!
9 You shall have no foreign god among you;
you shall not bow down to

g15 Or branch
*h*Title: Probably a musical term
i5 Or / and we heard a voice we had not known

*Heading, *1* See the note on page 349.

לְאֵל נֵכָר׃ אָנֹכִי ׀ יְהוָה אֱלֹהֶיךָ הַמַּעַלְךָ מֵאֶרֶץ

from-land-of the-one-bringing-up-you God-of-you Yahweh I (11) alien to-god

מִצְרָיִם הַרְחֶב־ פִּיךָ וַאֲמַלְאֵהוּ׃ וְלֹא־ שָׁמַע

he-listened but-not (12) and-I-will-fill-him mouth-of-you open-wide! Egypt

עַמִּי לְקוֹלִי וְיִשְׂרָאֵל לֹא־ אָבָה לִי׃ וָאֲשַׁלְּחֵהוּ

so-I-gave-him (13) to-me he-submitted not and-Israel to-voice-of-me people-of-me

בִּשְׁרִירוּת לִבָּם יֵלְכוּ בְּמוֹעֲצוֹתֵיהֶם׃ לוּ

if (14) to-devices-of-them they-followed heart-of-them to-stubbornness-of

עַמִּי שֹׁמֵעַ לִי יִשְׂרָאֵל בִּדְרָכַי יְהַלֵּכוּ׃

they-would-follow to-ways-of-me Israel to-me one-listening people-of-me

כִּמְעַט אוֹיְבֵיהֶם אַכְנִיעַ וְעַל

and-against I-would-subdue ones-being-enemies-of-them as-quickly (15)

צָרֵיהֶם אָשִׁיב יָדִי׃ מְשַׂנְאֵי יְהוָה

Yahweh ones-hating-of (16) hand-of-me I-would-turn foes-of-them

יְכַחֲשׁוּ־ לוֹ וִיהִי עִתָּם לְעוֹלָם׃

to-forever punishment-of-them and-he-would-last before-him they-would-cringe

וַיַּאֲכִילֵהוּ מֵחֵלֶב חִטָּה וּמִצּוּר דְּבַשׁ

honey and-from-rock wheat with-finest-of but-he-would-feed-him (17)

אַשְׂבִּיעֶךָ׃ מִזְמוֹר לְאָסָף אֱלֹהִים נִצָּב בַּעֲדַת־

in-assembly-of one-presiding God of-Asaph psalm (82:1) I-would-satisfy-you

אֵל בְּקֶרֶב אֱלֹהִים יִשְׁפֹּט׃ עַד־ מָתַי תִּשְׁפְּטוּ־ עָוֶל

unjust will-you-defend when? until (2) he-gives-judgment gods in-among great

וּפְנֵי רְשָׁעִים תִּשְׂאוּ־ סֶלָה׃ שִׁפְטוּ־ דַל

weak defend! (3) selah you-will-show-partiality wicked-ones and-faces-of

וְיָתוֹם עָנִי וָרָשׁ הַצְדִּיקוּ׃ פַּלְּטוּ־

rescue! (4) maintain-rights! and-one-being-oppressed poor and-fatherless

דַל וְאֶבְיוֹן מִיַּד רְשָׁעִים הַצִּילוּ׃ לֹא יָדְעוּ

they-know nothing (5) deliver! wicked-ones from-hand-of and-needy weak

וְלֹא יָבִינוּ בַּחֲשֵׁכָה יִתְהַלָּכוּ יִמּוֹטוּ כָּל־

all-of they-are-shaken they-walk in-darkness they-understand and-nothing

מוֹסְדֵי אָרֶץ׃ אֲנִי־אָמַרְתִּי אֱלֹהִים אַתֶּם וּבְנֵי עֶלְיוֹן כֻּלְּכֶם׃

all-of-you Most-High and-sons-of you gods I-said I (6) earth foundations-of

אָכֵן כְּאָדָם תְּמוּתוּן וּכְאַחַד הַשָּׂרִים תִּפֹּלוּ׃

you-will-fall the-rulers and-like-other-of you-will-die like-man but (7)

קוּמָה אֱלֹהִים שָׁפְטָה הָאָרֶץ כִּי־ אַתָּה תִנְחַל בְּכָל־ הַגּוֹיִם׃

the-nations of-all-of you-inherit you for the-earth judge! God rise-up! (8)

שִׁיר מִזְמוֹר לְאָסָף׃ אֱלֹהִים אַל־ דֳּמִי־ לָךְ אַל־ תֶּחֱרָשׁ

you-be-quiet not to-you silence not God (2) of-Asaph psalm song *(83:1)

---

an alien god.
10I am the LORD your God,
who brought you up out of
Egypt.
Open wide your mouth and
I will fill it.
11"But my people would not
listen to me;
Israel would not submit to
me.
12So I gave them over to their
stubborn hearts
to follow their own devices.
13"If my people would but listen
to me,
if Israel would follow my
ways,
14how quickly would I subdue
their enemies
and turn my hand against
their foes!
15Those who hate the LORD
would cringe before him,
and their punishment would
last forever.
16But you would be fed with the
finest of wheat;
with honey from the rock I
would satisfy you."

Psalm 82

A psalm of Asaph.

1God presides in the great
assembly;
he gives judgment among
the "gods":
2"How long will you[i] defend
the unjust
and show partiality to the
wicked? *Selah*
3Defend the cause of the weak
and fatherless;
maintain the rights of the
poor and oppressed.
4Rescue the weak and needy;
deliver them from the hand
of the wicked.
5"They know nothing, they
understand nothing.
They walk about in
darkness;
all the foundations of the
earth are shaken.
6"I said, 'You are "gods";
you are all sons of the Most
High.'
7But you will die like mere
men;
you will fall like every other
ruler."
8Rise up, O God, judge the
earth,
for all the nations are your
inheritance.

Psalm 83

A song. A psalm of Asaph.

1O God, do not keep silent;

i2 The Hebrew is plural.

*Heading, 1 See the note on page 349.

וְאַל־ תִּשְׁקֹט אֵל׃ כִּי־ הִנֵּה אוֹיְבֶיךָ יֶהֱמָיוּן
they-are-astir ones-being-enemies-of-you see! for (3) God you-be-still and-not

וּמְשַׂנְאֶיךָ נָשְׂאוּ רֹאשׁ׃ עַל־ עַמְּךָ
people-of-you against (4) head they-rear and-ones-being-foes-of-you

יַעֲרִימוּ סוֹד וְיִתְיָעֲצוּ עַל־ צְפוּנֶיךָ׃
ones-being-cherished-of-you against and-they-plot conspiracy they-make-cunning

אָמְרוּ לְכוּ וְנַכְחִידֵם מִגּוֹי וְלֹא־
that-not as-nation and-let-us-destroy-them come! they-say (5)

יִזָּכֵר שֵׁם־ יִשְׂרָאֵל עוֹד׃ כִּי נוֹעֲצוּ לֵב יַחְדָּו
together mind they-plot for (6) more Israel name-of he-will-be-remembered

עָלֶיךָ בְּרִית יִכְרֹתוּ׃ אָהֳלֵי אֱדוֹם וְיִשְׁמְעֵאלִים מוֹאָב
Moab and-Ishmaelites Edom tents-of (7) they-form alliance against-you

וְהַגְרִים׃ גְּבָל וְעַמּוֹן וַעֲמָלֵק פְּלֶשֶׁת עִם־ יֹשְׁבֵי
ones-living-of with Philistia and-Amalek and-Ammon Gebal (8) and-Hagrites

צוֹר׃ גַּם־ אַשּׁוּר נִלְוָה עִמָּם הָיוּ זְרוֹעַ לִבְנֵי־
to-descendants-of strength they-are with-them he-joined Assyria even (9) Tyre

לוֹט סֶלָה׃ עֲשֵׂה־ לָהֶם כְּמִדְיָן כְּסִיסְרָא כְיָבִין בְּנַחַל קִישׁוֹן׃
Kishon at-river-of as-Jabin as-Sisera as-Midian to-them do! (10) selah Lot

נִשְׁמְדוּ בְעֵין־ דֹּאר הָיוּ דֹּמֶן לָאֲדָמָה׃ שִׁיתֵמוֹ
make-them! (12) on-the-ground refuse they-became Dor at-En they-perished (11)

נְדִיבֵמוֹ כְּעֹרֵב וְכִזְאֵב וּכְזֶבַח וּכְצַלְמֻנָּע
and-like-Zalmunna and-like-Zebah and-like-Zeeb like-Oreb nobles-of-them

כָּל־ נְסִיכֵמוֹ׃ אֲשֶׁר אָמְרוּ נִירְשָׁה לָּנוּ אֵת
*** for-us let-us-take-possession they-said who (13) princes-of-them all-of

נְאוֹת אֱלֹהִים׃ אֱלֹהַי שִׁיתֵמוֹ כַגַּלְגַּל כְּקַשׁ
like-chaff like-the-tumbleweed make-them! God-of-me (14) God pasturelands-of

לִפְנֵי־ רוּחַ׃ כְּאֵשׁ תִּבְעַר־ יַעַר וּכְלֶהָבָה תְּלַהֵט
she-sets-ablaze or-as-flame forest she-consumes as-fire (15) wind before

הָרִים׃ כֵּן תִּרְדְּפֵם בְּסַעֲרֶךָ וּבְסוּפָתְךָ
and-with-storm-of-you with-tempest-of-you you-pursue-them so (16) mountains

תְּבַהֲלֵם׃ מַלֵּא פְנֵיהֶם קָלוֹן וִיבַקְשׁוּ
so-they-will-seek shame faces-of-them cover! (17) you-terrify-them

שִׁמְךָ יְהוָה׃ יֵבֹשׁוּ וְיִבָּהֲלוּ עֲדֵי־
to and-may-they-be-dismayed may-they-be-ashamed (18) Yahweh name-of-you

עַד וְיַחְפְּרוּ וְיֹאבֵדוּ׃ וְיֵדְעוּ
and-let-them-know (19) and-may-they-perish and-may-they-be-disgraced ever

כִּי־ אַתָּה שִׁמְךָ יְהוָה לְבַדֶּךָ עֶלְיוֹן עַל־ כָּל־ הָאָרֶץ׃
the-earth all-of over Most-High by-yourself Yahweh name-of-you you that

be not quiet, O God, be not still.
2 See how your enemies are astir,
how your foes rear their heads.
3 With cunning they conspire against your people;
they plot against those you cherish.
4 "Come," they say, "let us destroy them as a nation,
that the name of Israel be remembered no more."

5 With one mind they plot together;
they form an alliance against you—
6 the tents of Edom and the Ishmaelites,
of Moab and the descendants of Hagar,
7 Gebal,[k] Ammon and Amalek,
Philistia, with the people of Tyre.
8 Even Assyria has joined them
to lend strength to the descendants of Lot. *Selah*

9 Do to them as you did to Midian,
as you did to Sisera and Jabin at the river Kishon,
10 who perished at Endor
and became like refuse on the ground.
11 Make their nobles like Oreb and Zeeb,
all their princes like Zebah and Zalmunna,
12 who said, "Let us take possession
of the pasturelands of God."

13 Make them like tumbleweed, O my God,
like chaff before the wind.
14 As fire consumes the forest
or a flame sets the mountains ablaze,
15 so pursue them with your tempest
and terrify them with your storm.
16 Cover their faces with shame
so that men will seek your name, O LORD.

17 May they ever be ashamed and dismayed;
may they perish in disgrace.
18 Let them know that you, whose name is the LORD—
that you alone are the Most High over all the earth.

[k]7 That is, Byblos

*See the note on page 349.

לַמְנַצֵּחַ עַל־ הַגִּתִּית לִבְנֵי־ קֹרַח מִזְמוֹר׃
psalm Korah of-Sons-of the-gittith according-to for-the-one-directing *(84:1)

מַה־ יְּדִידוֹת מִשְׁכְּנוֹתֶיךָ יְהוָה צְבָאוֹת׃ נִכְסְפָה וְגַם־
and-even she-yearns (3) Hosts Yahweh-of dwellings-of-you lovely-ones how! (2)

כָּלְתָה ׀ נַפְשִׁי לְחַצְרוֹת יְהוָה לִבִּי וּבְשָׂרִי
and-flesh-of-me heart-of-me Yahweh for-courts-of soul-of-me she-faints

יְרַנְּנוּ אֶל אֵל־ חָי׃ גַּם־ צִפּוֹר ׀ מָצְאָה בַיִת וּדְרוֹר ׀ קֵן
nest and-swallow home she-found sparrow even (4) living God for they-cry-out

לָהּ אֲשֶׁר־ שָׁתָה אֶפְרֹחֶיהָ אֶת־ מִזְבְּחוֹתֶיךָ יְהוָה
Yahweh-of altars-of-you near young-ones-of-her she-may-have where for-her

צְבָאוֹת מַלְכִּי וֵאלֹהָי׃ אַשְׁרֵי יוֹשְׁבֵי
ones-dwelling-of blessednesses-of (5) and-God-of-me King-of-me Hosts

בֵיתֶךָ עוֹד יְהַלְלוּךָ סֶּלָה׃ אַשְׁרֵי אָדָם עוֹז־
strength man blessednesses-of (6) selah they-praise-you ever house-of-you

לוֹ בָךְ מְסִלּוֹת בִּלְבָבָם׃ עֹבְרֵי ׀ בְּעֵמֶק
through-Valley-of ones-passing-of (7) in-heart-of-them pilgrimages in-you of-him

הַבָּכָא מַעְיָן יְשִׁיתוּהוּ גַּם־בְּרָכוֹת יַעְטֶה מוֹרֶה׃ יֵלְכוּ
they-go (8) autumn-rain he-covers pools also they-make-him spring the-Baca

מֵחַיִל אֶל־ חָיִל יֵרָאֶה אֶל־אֱלֹהִים בְּצִיּוֹן׃ יְהוָה אֱלֹהִים
God Yahweh (9) in-Zion God before he-appears strength to from-strength

צְבָאוֹת שִׁמְעָה תְפִלָּתִי הַאֲזִינָה אֱלֹהֵי יַעֲקֹב סֶלָה׃ מָגִנֵּנוּ רְאֵה
look! shield-of-us (10) selah Jacob God-of listen! prayer-of-me hear! Hosts

אֱלֹהִים וְהַבֵּט פְּנֵי מְשִׁיחֶךָ׃ כִּי טוֹב־ יוֹם בַּחֲצֵרֶיךָ
in-courts-of-you day better for (11) anointed-one-of-you faces-of and-look! God

מֵאָלֶף בָּחַרְתִּי הִסְתּוֹפֵף בְּבֵית אֱלֹהַי
God-of-me in-house-of to-be-doorkeeper I-would-rather than-thousand

מִדּוּר בְּאָהֳלֵי־ רֶשַׁע׃ כִּי שֶׁמֶשׁ ׀ וּמָגֵן יְהוָה אֱלֹהִים חֵן
favor God Yahweh and-shield sun for (12) wicked in-tents-of than-to-dwell

וְכָבוֹד יִתֵּן יְהוָה לֹא יִמְנַע־ טוֹב לַהֹלְכִים
from-ones-walking good-thing he-withholds not Yahweh he-bestows and-honor

בְּתָמִים׃ יְהוָה צְבָאוֹת אַשְׁרֵי אָדָם בֹּטֵחַ בָּךְ׃
in-you one-trusting man blessednesses-of Hosts Yahweh-of (13) in-blamelessness

לַמְנַצֵּחַ ׀ לִבְנֵי־ קֹרַח מִזְמוֹר׃ רָצִיתָ
you-showed-favor (2) psalm Korah of-Sons-of for-the-one-directing *(85:1)

יְהוָה אַרְצֶךָ שַׁבְתָּ שְׁבוּת° יַעֲקֹב׃ נָשָׂאתָ עֲוֺן
iniquity-of you-forgave (3) Jacob fortune-of you-restored land-of-you Yahweh

עַמֶּךָ כִּסִּיתָ כָל־ חַטָּאתָם סֶלָה׃ אָסַפְתָּ כָל־
all-of you-set-aside (4) selah sin-of-them all-of you-covered people-of-you

Psalm 84

For the director of music. According to *gittith*.[l] Of the Sons of Korah. A psalm.

1 How lovely is your dwelling place,
O LORD Almighty!
2 My soul yearns, even faints
for the courts of the LORD;
my heart and my flesh cry out
for the living God.

3 Even the sparrow has found a home,
and the swallow a nest for herself,
where she may have her young—
a place near your altar,
O LORD Almighty, my King and my God.
4 Blessed are those who dwell in your house;
they are ever praising you.
Selah

5 Blessed are those whose strength is in you,
who have set their hearts on pilgrimage.
6 As they pass through the Valley of Baca,
they make it a place of springs;
the autumn rains also cover it with pools.[m]
7 They go from strength to strength
till each appears before God in Zion.

8 Hear my prayer, O LORD God Almighty;
listen to me, O God of Jacob. *Selah*
9 Look upon our shield,[n] O God;
look with favor on your anointed one.

10 Better is one day in your courts
than a thousand elsewhere;
I would rather be a doorkeeper
in the house of my God
than dwell in the tents of the wicked.
11 For the LORD God is a sun and shield;
the LORD bestows favor and honor;
no good thing does he withhold
from those whose walk is blameless.

12 O LORD Almighty,
blessed is the man who trusts in you.

Psalm 85

For the director of music. Of the Sons of Korah. A psalm.

1 You showed favor to your land, O LORD;
you restored the fortunes of Jacob.
2 You forgave the iniquity of

[l] Title: Probably a musical term
[m] 6 Or *blessings*
[n] 9 Or *sovereign*

*Heading, *1* See the note on page 349.

°2 ק שבית

עֶבְרָתֶךָ הֱשִׁיבוֹתָ מֵחֲרוֹן אַפֶּךָ׃ שׁוּבֵנוּ
restore-us! (5) anger-of-you from-fierceness-of you-turned wrath-of-you

אֱלֹהֵי יִשְׁעֵנוּ וְהָפֵר כַּעַסְךָ עִמָּנוּ׃ הַלְעוֹלָם
to-forever? (6) toward-us displeasure-of-you and-put-away! salvation-of-us God-of

תֶּאֱנַף־ בָּנוּ תִּמְשֹׁךְ אַפְּךָ לְדֹר
to-generation anger-of-you will-you-prolong with-us will-you-be-angry

וָדֹר׃ הֲלֹא־ אַתָּה תָּשׁוּב תְּחַיֵּנוּ
will-you-revive-us will-you-do-again you not? (7) and-generation

וְעַמְּךָ יִשְׂמְחוּ־ בָךְ׃ הַרְאֵנוּ יְהוָה
Yahweh show-us! (8) in-you they-may-rejoice that-people-of-you

חַסְדֶּךָ וְיֶשְׁעֲךָ תִּתֶּן־ לָנוּ׃ אֶשְׁמְעָה
I-will-listen (9) to-us you-grant and-salvation-of-you unfailing-love-of-you

מַה־ יְדַבֵּר הָאֵל | יְהוָה כִּי | יְדַבֵּר שָׁלוֹם אֶל־ עַמּוֹ
people-of-him to peace he-promises for Yahweh the-God he-will-say what

וְאֶל־ חֲסִידָיו וְאַל־ יָשׁוּבוּ לְכִסְלָה׃ אַךְ | קָרוֹב
near surely (10) to-folly let-them-return but-not saints-of-him even-to

לִירֵאָיו יִשְׁעוֹ לִשְׁכֹּן כָּבוֹד בְּאַרְצֵנוּ׃ חֶסֶד־
love (11) in-land-of-us glory to-dwell salvation-of-him to-ones-fearing-him

וֶאֱמֶת נִפְגָּשׁוּ צֶדֶק וְשָׁלוֹם נָשָׁקוּ׃ אֱמֶת
faithfulness (12) they-kiss and-peace righteousness they-meet and-faithfulness

מֵאֶרֶץ תִּצְמָח וְצֶדֶק מִשָּׁמַיִם נִשְׁקָף׃
he-looks-down from-heavens and-righteousness she-springs-forth from-earth

גַּם־ יְהוָה יִתֵּן הַטּוֹב וְאַרְצֵנוּ תִּתֵּן
she-will-yield and-land-of-us the-good he-will-give Yahweh indeed (13)

יְבוּלָהּ׃ צֶדֶק לְפָנָיו יְהַלֵּךְ וְיָשֵׂם לְדֶרֶךְ
for-way and-he-prepares he-goes before-him righteousness (14) harvest-of-her

פְּעָמָיו׃ תְּפִלָּה לְדָוִד הַטֵּה־ יְהוָה אָזְנְךָ עֲנֵנִי
answer-me! ear-of-you Yahweh hear! of-David prayer (86:1) steps-of-him

כִּי־ עָנִי וְאֶבְיוֹן אָנִי׃ שָׁמְרָה נַפְשִׁי כִּי־ חָסִיד אָנִי הוֹשַׁע
save! I devoted for life-of-me guard! (2) I and-needy poor for

עַבְדְּךָ אַתָּה אֱלֹהַי הַבּוֹטֵחַ אֵלֶיךָ׃ חָנֵּנִי
have-mercy-on-me! (3) in-you the-one-trusting God-of-me you servant-of-you

אֲדֹנָי כִּי אֵלֶיךָ אֶקְרָא כָּל־ הַיּוֹם׃ שַׂמֵּחַ נֶפֶשׁ עַבְדֶּךָ
servant-of-you self-of bring-joy! (4) the-day all-of I-call to-you for Lord

כִּי אֵלֶיךָ אֲדֹנָי נַפְשִׁי אֶשָּׂא׃ כִּי־ אַתָּה אֲדֹנָי טוֹב וְסַלָּח
and-forgiving kind Lord you indeed (5) I-lift-up soul-of-me Lord to-you for

וְרַב־ חֶסֶד לְכָל־ קֹרְאֶיךָ׃ הַאֲזִינָה יְהוָה
Yahweh hear! (6) ones-calling-to-you to-all-of love and-abundant-of

your people
and covered all their sins.
Selah
3 You set aside all your wrath
and turned from your fierce anger.

4 Restore us again, O God our Savior,
and put away your displeasure toward us.
5 Will you be angry with us forever?
Will you prolong your anger through all generations?
6 Will you not revive us again,
that your people may rejoice in you?
7 Show us your unfailing love, O LORD,
and grant us your salvation.

8 I will listen to what God the LORD will say;
he promises peace to his people, his saints—
but let them not return to folly.
9 Surely his salvation is near those who fear him,
that his glory may dwell in our land.

10 Love and faithfulness meet together;
righteousness and peace kiss each other.
11 Faithfulness springs forth from the earth,
and righteousness looks down from heaven.
12 The LORD will indeed give what is good,
and our land will yield its harvest.
13 Righteousness goes before him
and prepares the way for his steps.

Psalm 86

A prayer of David.

1 Hear, O LORD, and answer me,
for I am poor and needy.
2 Guard my life, for I am devoted to you.
You are my God; save your servant
who trusts in you.
3 Have mercy on me, O Lord,
for I call to you all day long.
4 Bring joy to your servant,
for to you, O Lord,
I lift up my soul.

5 You are kind and forgiving, O Lord,
abounding in love to all who call to you.
6 Hear my prayer, O LORD;

*See the note on page 349.

תְּפִלָּתִי וְהַקְשִׁיבָה בְּקוֹל תַּחֲנוּנוֹתָי׃ בְּיוֹם
in-day-of (7) cries-for-mercy-of-me to-sound-of and-listen! prayer-of-me

צָרָתִי אֶקְרָאֶךָּ כִּי תַעֲנֵנִי׃ אֵין־
there-is-none (8) you-will-answer-me for I-will-call-to-you trouble-of-me

כָּמוֹךָ בָאֱלֹהִים ׀ אֲדֹנָי וְאֵין כְּמַעֲשֶׂיךָ׃ כָּל־
all-of (9) like-deeds-of-you and-there-is-not Lord among-the-gods like-you

גּוֹיִם ׀ אֲשֶׁר עָשִׂיתָ יָבוֹאוּ ׀ וְיִשְׁתַּחֲווּ לְפָנֶיךָ אֲדֹנָי
Lord before-you and-they-will-worship they-will-come you-made that nations

וִיכַבְּדוּ לִשְׁמֶךָ׃ כִּי־ גָדוֹל אַתָּה וְעֹשֵׂה
and-one-doing-of you great for (10) to-name-of-you and-they-will-bring-glory

נִפְלָאוֹת אַתָּה אֱלֹהִים לְבַדֶּךָ׃ הוֹרֵנִי יְהוָה ׀ דַּרְכֶּךָ
way-of-you Yahweh teach-me! (11) by-yourself God you deeds-being-marvelous

אֲהַלֵּךְ בַּאֲמִתֶּךָ יַחֵד לְבָבִי לְיִרְאָה שְׁמֶךָ׃
name-of-you to-fear heart-of-me make-undivided! in-truth-of-you I-will-walk

אוֹדְךָ ׀ אֲדֹנָי אֱלֹהַי בְּכָל־ לְבָבִי וַאֲכַבְּדָה
and-I-will-glorify heart-of-me with-all-of God-of-me Lord I-will-praise-you (12)

שִׁמְךָ לְעוֹלָם׃ כִּי־ חַסְדְּךָ גָּדוֹל עָלָי וְהִצַּלְתָּ
and-you-delivered toward-me great love-of-you for (13) to-forever name-of-you

נַפְשִׁי מִשְּׁאוֹל תַּחְתִּיָּה׃ אֱלֹהִים ׀ זֵדִים קָמוּ־ עָלַי
against-me they-attack arrogant-ones God (14) depth from-Sheol soul-of-me

וַעֲדַת עָרִיצִים בִּקְשׁוּ נַפְשִׁי וְלֹא שָׂמוּךָ
they-regard-you and-not life-of-me they-seek ruthless-men and-band-of

לְנֶגְדָּם׃ וְאַתָּה אֲדֹנָי אֵל־ רַחוּם וְחַנּוּן אֶרֶךְ
slow-of and-gracious compassionate God Lord but-you (15) at-before-them

אַפַּיִם וְרַב־ חֶסֶד וֶאֱמֶת׃ פְּנֵה אֵלַי
to-me turn! (16) and-faithfulness love and-abundant-of angers

וְחָנֵּנִי תְּנָה־ עֻזְּךָ לְעַבְדֶּךָ וְהוֹשִׁיעָה
and-save! to-servant-of-you strength-of-you grant! and-have-mercy-on-me!

לְבֶן־ אֲמָתֶךָ׃ עֲשֵׂה־ עִמִּי אוֹת לְטוֹבָה וְיִרְאוּ
that-they-may-see of-goodness sign to-me give! (17) maidservant-of-you to-son-of

שֹׂנְאַי וְיֵבֹשׁוּ כִּי־אַתָּה יְהוָה עֲזַרְתַּנִי
you-helped-me Yahweh you for and-they-may-be-shamed ones-being-enemies-of-me

וְנִחַמְתָּנִי׃ לִבְנֵי־ קֹרַח מִזְמוֹר שִׁיר יְסוּדָתוֹ
foundation-of-him song psalm Korah of-Sons-of (87:1) and-you-comforted-me

בְּהַרְרֵי־ קֹדֶשׁ׃ אֹהֵב יְהוָה שַׁעֲרֵי צִיּוֹן מִכֹּל
more-than-all-of Zion gates-of Yahweh one-loving (2) holiness on-mountains-of

מִשְׁכְּנוֹת יַעֲקֹב׃ נִכְבָּדוֹת מְדֻבָּר בָּךְ עִיר
city-of of-you one-being-said things-being-glorious (3) Jacob dwellings-of

listen to my cry for mercy.
7In the day of my trouble I will
call to you,
for you will answer me.

8Among the gods there is none
like you, O Lord;
no deeds can compare with
yours.
9All the nations you have made
will come and worship
before you, O Lord;
they will bring glory to your
name.
10For you are great and do
marvelous deeds;
you alone are God.

11Teach me your way, O Lord,
and I will walk in your
truth;
give me an undivided heart,
that I may fear your name.
12I will praise you, O Lord my
God, with all my heart;
I will glorify your name
forever.
13For great is your love toward
me;
you have delivered my soul
from the depths of the
grave.[o]

14The arrogant are attacking me,
O God;
a band of ruthless men
seeks my life—
men without regard for you.
15But you, O Lord, are a
compassionate and
gracious God,
slow to anger, abounding in
love and faithfulness.
16Turn to me and have mercy on
me;
grant your strength to your
servant
and save the son of your
maidservant.[p]
17Give me a sign of your
goodness,
that my enemies may see it
and be put to shame,
for you, O Lord, have
helped me and comforted
me.

Psalm 87

Of the Sons of Korah. A psalm. A song.

1He has set his foundation on
the holy mountain;
2 the Lord loves the gates of
Zion
more than all the dwellings
of Jacob.
3Glorious things are said of
you,

[o]13 Hebrew *Sheol*
[p]16 Or *save your faithful son*

הָאֱלֹהִים סֶלָה׃ אַזְכִּיר ׀ רַהַב וּבָבֶל לְיֹדְעָי
among-ones-acknowledging-me and-Babylon Rahab I-will-record (4) selah the-God

הִנֵּה פְלֶשֶׁת וְצוֹר עִם־כּוּשׁ זֶה יֻלַּד־שָׁם׃ וּֽלְצִיּוֹן ׀
indeed-of-Zion (5) there he-was-born this-one Cush with and-Tyre Philistia see!

יֵאָמַר אִישׁ וְאִישׁ יֻלַּד־בָּהּ וְהוּא יְכוֹנְנֶהָ
he-will-establish-her and-he in-her he-was-born and-one one he-will-be-said

עֶלְיוֹן׃ יְהוָה יִסְפֹּר בִּכְתוֹב עַמִּים זֶה
this-one peoples when-to-register he-will-write Yahweh (6) Most-High

יֻלַּד־שָׁם סֶלָה׃ וְשָׁרִים כְּחֹלְלִים כָּל־
all-of as-ones-making-music and-ones-singing (7) selah there he-was-born

מַעְיָנַי בָּךְ׃ שִׁיר מִזְמוֹר לִבְנֵי קֹרַח לַמְנַצֵּחַ
for-the-one-directing Korah of-Sons-of psalm song *(88:1) in-you fountains-of-me

עַל־מָחֲלַת לְעַנּוֹת מַשְׂכִּיל לְהֵימָן הָאֶזְרָחִי׃ יְהוָה
Yahweh (2) the-Ezrahite of-Heman maskil leannoth mahalath according-to

אֱלֹהֵי יְשׁוּעָתִי יוֹם־צָעַקְתִּי בַלַּיְלָה נֶגְדֶּךָ׃ תָּבוֹא
may-she-come (3) before-you in-the-night I-cry-out day salvation-of-me God-of

לְפָנֶיךָ תְּפִלָּתִי הַטֵּה־אָזְנְךָ לְרִנָּתִי׃ כִּי־שָׂבְעָה
she-is-full for (4) to-cry-of-me ear-of-you turn! prayer-of-me before-you

בְרָעוֹת נַפְשִׁי וְחַיַּי לִשְׁאוֹל הִגִּיעוּ׃ נֶחְשַׁבְתִּי
I-am-counted (5) they-draw-near to-Sheol and-lives-of-me soul-of-me of-troubles

עִם־יוֹרְדֵי בוֹר הָיִיתִי כְּגֶבֶר אֵין־אֱיָל׃
strength without like-man I-am pit ones-going-down-of among

בַּמֵּתִים חָפְשִׁי כְּמוֹ חֲלָלִים ׀ שֹׁכְבֵי קֶבֶר אֲשֶׁר
whom grave ones-lying-of slain-ones like set-apart with-the-dead-ones (6)

לֹא זְכַרְתָּם עוֹד וְהֵמָּה מִיָּדְךָ נִגְזָרוּ׃
they-are-cut-off from-care-of-you and-they more you-remember-them not

שַׁתַּנִי בְּבוֹר תַּחְתִּיּוֹת בְּמַחֲשַׁכִּים בִּמְצֹלוֹת׃ עָלַי
upon-me (8) in-depths in-darkest-ones lowest-ones in-pit-of you-put-me (7)

סָמְכָה חֲמָתֶךָ וְכָל־מִשְׁבָּרֶיךָ עִנִּיתָ סֶּלָה׃
selah you-overwhelmed waves-of-you and-all-of wrath-of-you she-lies-heavily

הִרְחַקְתָּ מְיֻדָּעַי מִמֶּנִּי שַׁתַּנִי תוֹעֵבוֹת
repulsive-ones you-made-me from-me ones-being-friends-of-me you-took-away (9)

לָמוֹ כָּלֻא וְלֹא אֵצֵא׃ עֵינִי דָאֲבָה
she-is-dim eye-of-me (10) I-can-escape and-not one-being-confined to-them

מִנִּי עֹנִי קְרָאתִיךָ יְהוָה בְּכָל־יוֹם שִׁטַּחְתִּי אֵלֶיךָ
to-you I-spread-out day in-every-of Yahweh I-call-to-you grief from

כַפָּי׃ הֲלַמֵּתִים תַּעֲשֶׂה־פֶּלֶא אִם־רְפָאִים יָקוּמוּ ׀
they-rise-up dead-ones or wonder you-show to-the-dead-ones? (11) hands-of-me

O city of God: *Selah*
4"I will record Rahab[q] and
Babylon
among those who
acknowledge me—
Philistia too, and Tyre, along
with Cush[r]—
and will say, 'This[s] one was
born in Zion.' "
5Indeed, of Zion it will be said,
"This one and that one were
born in her,
and the Most High himself
will establish her."
6The LORD will write in the
register of the peoples:
"This one was born in
Zion." *Selah*
7As they make music they will
sing,
"All my fountains are in
you."

Psalm 88

A song. A psalm of the Sons of Korah. For the director of music. According to *mahalath leannoth*.[t] A *maskil*[u] of Heman the Ezrahite.

1O LORD, the God who saves
me,
day and night I cry out
before you.
2May my prayer come before
you;
turn your ear to my cry.
3For my soul is full of trouble
and my life draws near the
grave.[v]
4I am counted among those
who go down to the pit;
I am like a man without
strength.
5I am set apart with the dead,
like the slain who lie in the
grave,
whom you remember no more,
who are cut off from your
care.
6You have put me in the lowest
pit,
in the darkest depths.
7Your wrath lies heavily upon
me;
you have overwhelmed me
with all your waves. *Selah*
8You have taken from me my
closest friends
and have made me repulsive
to them.
I am confined and cannot
escape;
9 my eyes are dim with grief.
I call to you, O LORD, every
day;
I spread out my hands to
you.
10Do you show your wonders to
the dead?
Do those who are dead rise

q4 A poetic name for Egypt
r4 That is, the upper Nile region
s4 Or *"O Rahab and Babylon, / Philistia, Tyre and Cush, / I will record concerning those who acknowledge me: / 'This*
tTitle: Possibly a tune, "The Suffering of Affliction"
uTitle: Probably a literary or musical term
v3 Hebrew *Sheol*

*Heading, *1* See the note on page 349.

יוֹדוּךָ סֶלָה׃ (12) הַיְסֻפַּר בַּקֶּבֶר חַסְדֶּךָ
they-praise-you selah (12) is-he-declared? in-the-grave love-of-you

אֱמוּנָתְךָ בָּאֲבַדּוֹן׃ (13) הֲיִוָּדַע בַּחֹשֶׁךְ פִּלְאֶךָ
faithfulness-of-you in-Abaddon (13) is-he-known? in-the-darkness wonder-of-you

וְצִדְקָתְךָ בְּאֶרֶץ נְשִׁיָּה׃ (14) וַאֲנִי ׀ אֵלֶיךָ יְהוָה
or-righteous-deed-of-you in-land-of oblivion (14) but-I to-you Yahweh

שִׁוַּעְתִּי וּבַבֹּקֶר תְּפִלָּתִי תְקַדְּמֶךָּ׃ (15) לָמָה
I-cry-for-help and-in-the-morning prayer-of-me she-comes-before-you (15) why?

יְהוָה תִּזְנַח נַפְשִׁי תַּסְתִּיר פָּנֶיךָ מִמֶּנִּי׃ (16) עָנִי
Yahweh you-reject self-of-me you-hide faces-of-you from-me (16) afflicted

אֲנִי וְגֹוֵעַ מִנֹּעַר נָשָׂאתִי אֵמֶיךָ
I and-one-being-close-to-death from-youth I-suffered terrors-of-you

אָפוּנָה׃ (17) עָלַי עָבְרוּ חֲרוֹנֶיךָ בִּעוּתֶיךָ
and-I-am-in-despair (17) over-me they-swept wraths-of-you terrors-of-you

צִמְּתוּתֻנִי׃ (18) סַבּוּנִי כַמַּיִם כָּל־ הַיּוֹם
they-destroyed-me (18) they-surround-me like-the-floods all-of the-day

הִקִּיפוּ עָלַי יָחַד׃ (19) הִרְחַקְתָּ מִמֶּנִּי אֹהֵב
they-engulfed over-me completely (19) you-took-far from-me one-loving

וָרֵעַ מְיֻדָּעַי מַחְשָׁךְ׃ *(89:1) מַשְׂכִּיל לְאֵיתָן
and-companion ones-being-friends-of-me darkness *(89:1) maskil of-Ethan

הָאֶזְרָחִי׃ (2) חַסְדֵי יְהוָה עוֹלָם אָשִׁירָה לְדֹר
the-Ezrahite (2) great-loves-of Yahweh forever I-will-sing to-generation

וָדֹר ׀ אוֹדִיעַ אֱמוּנָתְךָ בְּפִי׃
and-generation I-will-make-known faithfulness-of-you with-mouth-of-me

(3) כִּי־ אָמַרְתִּי עוֹלָם חֶסֶד יִבָּנֶה שָׁמַיִם ׀ תָּכִן
(3) indeed I-will-declare forever love he-stands-firm heavens you-established

אֱמוּנָתְךָ בָהֶם׃ (4) כָּרַתִּי בְרִית לִבְחִירִי
faithfulness-of-you in-them (4) I-made covenant with-chosen-one-of-me

נִשְׁבַּעְתִּי לְדָוִד עַבְדִּי׃ (5) עַד־ עוֹלָם אָכִין זַרְעֶךָ
I-swore to-David servant-of-me (5) to forever I-will-establish line-of-you

וּבָנִיתִי לְדֹר־ וָדוֹר כִּסְאֲךָ סֶלָה׃
and-I-will-make-firm to-generation and-generation throne-of-you selah

(6) וְיוֹדוּ שָׁמַיִם פִּלְאֲךָ יְהוָה אַף־ אֱמוּנָתְךָ
(6) and-they-praise heavens wonder-of-you Yahweh also faithfulness-of-you

בִּקְהַל קְדֹשִׁים׃ (7) כִּי מִי בַשַּׁחַק יַעֲרֹךְ לַיהוָה
in-assembly-of holy-ones (7) for who? in-the-sky he-can-compare to-Yahweh

יִדְמֶה לַיהוָה בִּבְנֵי אֵלִים׃ (8) אֵל נַעֲרָץ
he-is-like to-Yahweh among-sons-of heavenly-beings (8) God one-being-feared

---

up and praise you? *Selah*
11 Is your love declared in the grave,
your faithfulness in Destruction[w]?
12 Are your wonders known in the place of darkness,
or your righteous deeds in the land of oblivion?

13 But I cry to you for help, O LORD;
in the morning my prayer comes before you.
14 Why, O LORD, do you reject me
and hide your face from me?

15 From my youth I have been afflicted and close to death;
I have suffered your terrors and am in despair.
16 Your wrath has swept over me;
your terrors have destroyed me.
17 All day long they surround me like a flood;
they have completely engulfed me.
18 You have taken my companions and loved ones from me;
the darkness is my closest friend.

Psalm 89

A *maskil*[x] of Ethan the Ezrahite.

1 I will sing of the LORD's great love forever;
with my mouth I will make your faithfulness known through all generations.
2 I will declare that your love stands firm forever,
that you established your faithfulness in heaven itself.

3 You said, "I have made a covenant with my chosen one,
I have sworn to David my servant,
4 'I will establish your line forever
and make your throne firm through all generations.' "
Selah

5 The heavens praise your wonders, O LORD,
your faithfulness too, in the assembly of the holy ones.
6 For who in the skies above can compare with the LORD?
Who is like the LORD among the heavenly beings?

w11 Hebrew *Abaddon*
x Title: Probably a literary or musical term

*Heading, *1* See the note on page 349.

בְּסוֹד־ קְדֹשִׁים רַבָּה וְנוֹרָא עַל־ כָּל־
all-of over and-one-being-awesome greatly holy-ones in-council-of

סְבִיבָיו׃ (9) יְהוָה ׀ אֱלֹהֵי צְבָאוֹת מִי־ כָמוֹךָ חֲסִין ׀ יָהּ
Yahweh mighty like-you who? Hosts God-of Yahweh (9) ones-surrounding-him

וֶאֱמוּנָתְךָ סְבִיבוֹתֶיךָ׃ (10) אַתָּה מוֹשֵׁל בְּגֵאוּת
over-surging-of one-ruling you (10) ones-around-you and-faithfulness-of-you

הַיָּם בְּשׂוֹא גַלָּיו אַתָּה תְשַׁבְּחֵם׃ (11) אַתָּה
you (11) you-still-them you waves-of-him when-to-mount-up the-sea

דִכִּאתָ כֶחָלָל רָהַב בִּזְרוֹעַ עֻזְּךָ פִּזַּרְתָּ
you-scattered strength-of-you with-arm-of Rahab like-the-slain you-crushed

אוֹיְבֶיךָ׃ (12) לְךָ שָׁמַיִם אַף־ לְךָ אֶרֶץ תֵּבֵל
world earth to-you also heavens to-you (12) ones-being-enemies-of-you

וּמְלֹאָהּ אַתָּה יְסַדְתָּם׃ (13) צָפוֹן וְיָמִין אַתָּה
you and-south north (13) you-founded-them you and-fullness-of-her

בְרָאתָם תָּבוֹר וְחֶרְמוֹן בְּשִׁמְךָ יְרַנֵּנוּ׃ (14) לְךָ
to-you (14) they-sing-for-joy at-name-of-you and-Hermon Tabor you-created-them

זְרוֹעַ עִם־ גְּבוּרָה תָּעֹז יָדְךָ תָּרוּם יְמִינֶךָ׃
right-hand-of-you she-is-exalted hand-of-you she-is-strong power with arm

(15) צֶדֶק וּמִשְׁפָּט מְכוֹן כִּסְאֶךָ חֶסֶד וֶאֱמֶת
and-faithfulness love throne-of-you foundation-of and-justice righteousness (15)

יְקַדְּמוּ פָנֶיךָ׃ (16) אַשְׁרֵי הָעָם יוֹדְעֵי
ones-learning-of the-people blessednesses-of (16) faces-of-you they-go-before

תְרוּעָה יְהוָה בְּאוֹר־ פָּנֶיךָ יְהַלֵּכוּן׃ (17) בְּשִׁמְךָ
in-name-of-you (17) they-walk presences-of-you in-light-of Yahweh acclamation

יְגִילוּן כָּל־ הַיּוֹם וּבְצִדְקָתְךָ יָרוּמוּ׃ (18) כִּי־
for (18) they-exult and-in-righteousness-of-you the-day all-of they-rejoice

תִפְאֶרֶת עֻזָּמוֹ אָתָּה וּבִרְצֹנְךָ תָּרִים קַרְנֵנוּ׃
horn-of-us you-exalt and-by-favor-of-you you strength-of-them glory-of

(19) כִּי לַיהוָה מָגִנֵּנוּ וְלִקְדוֹשׁ יִשְׂרָאֵל מַלְכֵּנוּ׃
king-of-us Israel and-to-Holy-One-of shield-of-us to-Yahweh indeed (19)

(20) אָז דִּבַּרְתָּ־ בְחָזוֹן לַחֲסִידֶיךָ וַתֹּאמֶר שִׁוִּיתִי
I-bestowed and-you-said to-faithful-ones-of-you in-vision you-spoke once (20)

עֵזֶר עַל־ גִּבּוֹר הֲרִימוֹתִי בָחוּר מֵעָם׃ (21) מָצָאתִי דָּוִד
David I-found (21) from-people man-being-young I-exalted warrior on strength

עַבְדִּי בְּשֶׁמֶן קָדְשִׁי מְשַׁחְתִּיו׃ (22) אֲשֶׁר יָדִי
hand-of-me that (22) I-anointed-him sacredness-of-me with-oil-of servant-of-me

תִּכּוֹן עִמּוֹ אַף־ זְרוֹעִי תְאַמְּצֶנּוּ׃ (23) לֹא־
not (23) she-will-strengthen-him arm-of-me surely to-him she-will-sustain

7 In the council of the holy ones
God is greatly feared;
he is more awesome than all
who surround him.
8 O LORD God Almighty, who is
like you?
You are mighty, O LORD,
and your faithfulness
surrounds you.

9 You rule over the surging sea;
when its waves mount up,
you still them.
10 You crushed Rahab like one of
the slain;
with your strong arm you
scattered your enemies.
11 The heavens are yours, and
yours also the earth;
you founded the world and
all that is in it.
12 You created the north and the
south;
Tabor and Hermon sing for
joy at your name.
13 Your arm is endued with
power;
your hand is strong, your
right hand exalted.

14 Righteousness and justice are
the foundation of your
throne;
love and faithfulness go
before you.
15 Blessed are those who have
learned to acclaim you,
who walk in the light of
your presence, O LORD.
16 They rejoice in your name all
day long;
they exult in your
righteousness.
17 For you are their glory and
strength,
and by your favor you exalt
our horn.[y]
18 Indeed, our shield[z] belongs to
the LORD,
our king to the Holy One of
Israel.

19 Once you spoke in a vision,
to your faithful people you
said:
"I have bestowed strength on
a warrior;
I have exalted a young man
from among the people.
20 I have found David my
servant;
with my sacred oil I have
anointed him.
21 My hand will sustain him;
surely my arm will
strengthen him.

y17 *Horn* here symbolizes strong one.
z18 Or *sovereign*

*See the note on page 349.

°18 ק תרום

לֹא	עַוְלָה	וּבֶן־	בּוֹ	אוֹיֵב	יַשִּׁא
not	wickedness	and-man-of	to-him	one-being-enemy	he-will-subject-to-tribute

צָרָיו	מִפָּנָיו	וְכַתּוֹתִי		יְעַנֶּנּוּ׃
foes-of-him	at-before-him	and-I-will-crush	(24)	he-will-oppress-him

וֶאֱמוּנָתִי†		אֶגּוֹף׃	וּמְשַׂנְאָיו
and-faithfulness-of-me	(25)	I-will-strike-down	and-ones-being-adversaries-of-him

קַרְנוֹ׃	תָּרוּם	וּבִשְׁמִי	עִמּוֹ	וְחַסְדִּי
horn-of-him	she-will-be-exalted	and-through-name-of-me	with-him	and-love-of-me

וּבַנְּהָרוֹת	יָדוֹ	בַיָּם	וְשַׂמְתִּי	
and-over-the-rivers	hand-of-him	over-the-sea	and-I-will-set	(26)

אֵלִי	אָתָּה	אָבִי	יִקְרָאֵנִי	הוּא		יְמִינוֹ׃
God-of-me	you	Father-of-me	he-will-call-out-to-me	he	(27)	right-hand-of-him

עֶלְיוֹן	אֶתְּנֵהוּ	בְּכוֹר	אָנִי	אַף־		יְשׁוּעָתִי׃	וְצוּר
most-exalted	I-will-appoint-him	firstborn	I	also	(28)	salvation-of-me	and-Rock-of

חַסְדִּי	לוֹ	אֶשְׁמוֹר־°	לְעוֹלָם		אָרֶץ׃	לְמַלְכֵי־
love-of-me	to-him	I-will-maintain	to-forever	(29)	earth	of-kings-of

וְשַׂמְתִּי		לוֹ׃	נֶאֱמֶנֶת	וּבְרִיתִי
and-I-will-establish	(30)	with-him	one-unfailing	and-covenant-of-me

אִם־		שָׁמָיִם׃	כִּימֵי	וְכִסְאוֹ	זַרְעוֹ	לָעַד
if	(31)	heavens	as-days-of	and-throne-of-him	line-of-him	to-forever

יֵלֵכוּן׃	לֹא	וּבְמִשְׁפָּטַי	תּוֹרָתִי	בָנָיו	יַעַזְבוּ
they-follow	not	and-to-statutes-of-me	law-of-me	sons-of-him	they-forsake

יִשְׁמֹרוּ׃	לֹא	וּמִצְוֹתַי	יְחַלֵּלוּ	חֻקֹּתַי	אִם־	
they-keep	not	and-commands-of-me	they-violate	decrees-of-me	if	(32)

וּבִנְגָעִים	פִּשְׁעָם	בְשֵׁבֶט	וּפָקַדְתִּי	
and-with-floggings	sin-of-them	with-rod	then-I-will-punish	(33)

וְלֹא־	מֵעִמּוֹ	אָפִיר	לֹא־	וְחַסְדִּי		עֲוֹנָם׃
and-never	from-with-him	I-will-take	not	but-love-of-me	(34)	iniquity-of-them

בְּרִיתִי	אֲחַלֵּל	לֹא־		בֶּאֱמוּנָתִי׃	אֲשַׁקֵּר
covenant-of-me	I-will-violate	not	(35)	to-faithfulness-of-me	I-will-betray

בְקָדְשִׁי	נִשְׁבַּעְתִּי	אַחַת		אֲשַׁנֶּה׃	לֹא	שְׂפָתַי	וּמוֹצָא
by-holiness-of-me	I-swore	once	(36)	I-will-alter	not	lips-of-me	or-utterance-of

יִהְיֶה	לְעוֹלָם	זַרְעוֹ		אֲכַזֵּב׃	לְדָוִד	אִם־
he-will-continue	to-forever	line-of-him	(37)	I-will-lie	to-David	not

יִכּוֹן	כְּיָרֵחַ		נֶגְדִּי׃	כַשֶּׁמֶשׁ	וְכִסְאוֹ
he-will-be-established	like-moon	(38)	before-me	like-the-sun	and-throne-of-him

וְאַתָּה		סֶלָה׃	נֶאֱמָן	בַּשַּׁחַק	וְעֵד	עוֹלָם
but-you	(39)	selah	one-being-faithful	in-the-sky	and-witness	forever

22No enemy will subject him to
tribute;
no wicked man will oppress
him.
23I will crush his foes before
him
and strike down his
adversaries.
24My faithful love will be with
him,
and through my name his
horn[a] will be exalted.
25I will set his hand over the
sea,
his right hand over the
rivers.
26He will call out to me, 'You are
my Father,
my God, the Rock my
Savior.'
27I will also appoint him my
firstborn,
the most exalted of the kings
of the earth.
28I will maintain my love to him
forever,
and my covenant with him
will never fail.
29I will establish his line forever,
his throne as long as the
heavens endure.

30"If his sons forsake my law
and do not follow my
statutes,
31if they violate my decrees
and fail to keep my
commands,
32I will punish their sin with
the rod,
their iniquity with flogging;
33but I will not take my love
from him,
nor will I ever betray my
faithfulness.
34I will not violate my covenant
or alter what my lips have
uttered.
35Once for all, I have sworn by
my holiness—
and I will not lie to David—
36that his line will continue
forever
and his throne endure
before me like the sun;
37it will be established forever
like the moon,
the faithful witness in the
sky." *Selah*

a24 *Horn* here symbolizes strength.

*See the note on page 349.

†25 Most mss have *hateph segol* under the *aleph* (וֶאֱ).

°29 ק אשמר

זָנַחְתָּ וַתִּמְאָס הִתְעַבַּרְתָּ עִם־ מְשִׁיחֶךָ׃
anointed-one-of-you with you-were-angry and-you-spurned you-rejected

(40) נֵאַרְתָּה בְּרִית עַבְדֶּךָ חִלַּלְתָּ לָאָרֶץ
in-the-dust you-defiled servant-of-you covenant-of you-renounced (40)

נִזְרוֹ׃ (41) פָּרַצְתָּ כָל־ גְּדֵרֹתָיו שַׂמְתָּ
you-reduced walls-of-him all-of you-broke-through (41) crown-of-him

מִבְצָרָיו מְחִתָּה׃ (42) שַׁסֻּהוּ כָּל־ עֹבְרֵי דָרֶךְ
way ones-passing-of all-of they-plundered-him (42) ruin strongholds-of-him

הָיָה חֶרְפָּה לִשְׁכֵנָיו׃ (43) הֲרִימוֹתָ יְמִין צָרָיו
foes-of-him right-hand-of you-exalted (43) of-neighbors-of-him scorn he-became

הִשְׂמַחְתָּ כָּל־ אוֹיְבָיו׃ (44) אַף־ תָּשִׁיב
you-turned-back also (44) ones-being-enemies-of-him all-of you-made-rejoice

צוּר חַרְבּוֹ וְלֹא הֲקֵימֹתוֹ בַּמִּלְחָמָה׃ (45) הִשְׁבַּתָּ
you-ended (45) in-the-battle you-supported-him and-not sword-of-him edge-of

מִטְּהָרוֹ וְכִסְאוֹ לָאָרֶץ מִגַּרְתָּה׃ (46) הִקְצַרְתָּ
you-cut-short (46) you-cast to-the-ground and-throne-of-him to-splendor-of-him

יְמֵי עֲלוּמָיו הֶעֱטִיתָ עָלָיו בּוּשָׁה סֶלָה׃ (47) עַד־ מָה
when? until (47) selah shame over-him you-covered youths-of-him days-of

יְהוָה תִּסָּתֵר לָנֶצַח תִּבְעַר כְּמוֹ־ אֵשׁ חֲמָתֶךָ׃
wrath-of-you fire like will-she-burn to-forever will-you-hide-yourself Yahweh

(48) זְכָר־ אֲנִי מֶה־ חָלֶד עַל־ מַה־ שָּׁוְא בָּרָאתָ כָל־ בְּנֵי־
sons-of all-of you-created futility what for fleeting how I remember! (48)

אָדָם׃ (49) מִי גֶבֶר יִחְיֶה וְלֹא יִרְאֶה־ מָּוֶת יְמַלֵּט
he-can-save death he-can-see and-not he-can-live man what? (49) man

נַפְשׁוֹ מִיַּד־ שְׁאוֹל סֶלָה׃ (50) אַיֵּה ׀ חֲסָדֶיךָ
great-loves-of-you where? (50) selah Sheol from-power-of self-of-him

הָרִאשֹׁנִים ׀ אֲדֹנָי נִשְׁבַּעְתָּ לְדָוִד בֶּאֱמוּנָתֶךָ׃ (51) זְכֹר
remember! (51) in-faithfulness-of-you to-David you-swore Lord the-former-ones

אֲדֹנָי חֶרְפַּת עֲבָדֶיךָ שְׂאֵתִי בְחֵיקִי כָּל־ רַבִּים ׀ עַמִּים׃
nations †many all-of in-heart-of-me to-bear-me servants-of-you mocking-of Lord

(52) אֲשֶׁר חֵרְפוּ אוֹיְבֶיךָ ׀ יְהוָה אֲשֶׁר חֵרְפוּ
they-mocked which Yahweh ones-being-enemies-of-you they-mocked which (52)

עִקְּבוֹת מְשִׁיחֶךָ׃ (53) בָּרוּךְ יְהוָה לְעוֹלָם אָמֵן ׀
amen to-forever Yahweh one-being-praised (53) anointed-one-of-you steps-of

וְאָמֵן׃ (90:1) תְּפִלָּה לְמֹשֶׁה אִישׁ־ הָאֱלֹהִים אֲדֹנָי מָעוֹן אַתָּה
you dwelling-place Lord the-God man-of of-Moses prayer (90:1) and-amen

הָיִיתָ לָּנוּ בְּדֹר וָדֹר׃ (2) בְּטֶרֶם ׀ הָרִים
mountains at-before (2) and-generation through-generation to-us you-are

38 But you have rejected, you have spurned,
you have been very angry with your anointed one.
39 You have renounced the covenant with your servant
and have defiled his crown in the dust.
40 You have broken through all his walls
and reduced his strongholds to ruins.
41 All who pass by have plundered him;
he has become the scorn of his neighbors.
42 You have exalted the right hand of his foes;
you have made all his enemies rejoice.
43 You have turned back the edge of his sword
and have not supported him in battle.
44 You have put an end to his splendor
and cast his throne to the ground.
45 You have cut short the days of his youth;
you have covered him with a mantle of shame. *Selah*
46 How long, O LORD? Will you hide yourself forever?
How long will your wrath burn like fire?
47 Remember how fleeting is my life.
For what futility you have created all men!
48 What man can live and not see death,
or save himself from the power of the grave[b]? *Selah*
49 O Lord, where is your former great love,
which in your faithfulness you swore to David?
50 Remember, Lord, how your servant has[c] been mocked,
how I bear in my heart the taunts of all the nations,
51 the taunts with which your enemies have mocked, O LORD,
with which they have mocked every step of your anointed one.

52 Praise be to the LORD forever!
Amen and Amen.

BOOK IV

Psalms 90-106

Psalm 90

A prayer of Moses the man of God.

1 Lord, you have been our dwelling place
throughout all generations.
2 Before the mountains were

[b] 48 Hebrew *Sheol*
[c] 50 Or *your servants have*

*See the note on page 349.

†51 The NIV reads this word as (רִבִים), *taunts-of.*

יֻלָּדוּ וַתְּחוֹלֵל אֶרֶץ וְתֵבֵל וּמֵעוֹלָם עַד־
to and-from-everlasting and-world earth or-you-brought-forth they-were-born

עוֹלָם אַתָּה אֵל׃ תָּשֵׁב אֱנוֹשׁ עַד־דַּכָּא וַתֹּאמֶר שׁוּבוּ
return! and-you-say dust to man you-turn-back (3) God you everlasting

בְנֵי־אָדָם׃ כִּי אֶלֶף שָׁנִים בְּעֵינֶיךָ כְּיוֹם אֶתְמוֹל כִּי
that yesterday like-day-of in-eyes-of-you years thousand-of for (4) man sons-of

יַעֲבֹר וְאַשְׁמוּרָה בַלָּיְלָה׃ זְרַמְתָּם שֵׁנָה יִהְיוּ
they-are sleep you-sweep-away-them (5) in-the-night or-watch he-went-by

בַּבֹּקֶר כֶּחָצִיר יַחֲלֹף׃ בַּבֹּקֶר יָצִיץ
he-springs-up in-the-morning (6) he-sprouts like-the-new-grass in-the-morning

וְחָלָף לָעֶרֶב יְמוֹלֵל וְיָבֵשׁ׃ כִּי־
indeed (7) and-he-is-dry he-is-withered by-the-evening and-he-sprouts

כָלִינוּ בְאַפֶּךָ וּבַחֲמָתְךָ נִבְהָלְנוּ׃
we-are-terrified and-by-indignation-of-you by-anger-of-you we-are-consumed

שַׁתָּ עֲוֹנֹתֵינוּ לְנֶגְדֶּךָ עֲלֻמֵנוּ לִמְאוֹר
in-light-of one-being-secret-of-us at-before-you iniquities-of-us you-set (8)

פָּנֶיךָ׃ כִּי כָל־יָמֵינוּ פָּנוּ בְעֶבְרָתֶךָ
under-wrath-of-you they-pass-away days-of-us all-of indeed (9) presences-of-you

כִּלִּינוּ שָׁנֵינוּ כְמוֹ־הֶגֶה׃ יְמֵי־שְׁנוֹתֵינוּ בָהֶם שִׁבְעִים
seventy of-them years-of-us days-of (10) moan with years-of-us we-finish

שָׁנָה וְאִם בִּגְבוּרֹת ׀ שְׁמוֹנִים שָׁנָה וְרָהְבָּם* עָמָל וָאָוֶן
and-sorrow trouble *yet-best-of-them year eighty in-strengths or-if year

כִּי־גָז חִישׁ וַנָּעֻפָה׃ מִי־יוֹדֵעַ עֹז
power-of one-knowing who? (11) and-we-fly-away quickly he-passes for

אַפֶּךָ וּכְיִרְאָתְךָ עֶבְרָתֶךָ׃ לִמְנוֹת יָמֵינוּ כֵּן
aright days-of-us to-number (12) wrath-of-you for-as-fear-of-you anger-of-you

הוֹדַע וְנָבִא לְבַב חָכְמָה׃ שׁוּבָה יְהוָה עַד־מָתָי
when? until Yahweh relent! (13) wisdom heart-of that-we-may-gain teach!

וְהִנָּחֵם עַל־עֲבָדֶיךָ׃ שַׂבְּעֵנוּ בַבֹּקֶר
in-the-morning satisfy-us! (14) servants-of-you on and-have-compassion!

חַסְדֶּךָ וּנְרַנְּנָה וְנִשְׂמְחָה בְּכָל־
for-all-of and-we-may-be-glad that-we-may-sing-for-joy unfailing-love-of-you

יָמֵינוּ׃ שַׂמְּחֵנוּ כִּימוֹת עִנִּיתָנוּ שְׁנוֹת רָאִינוּ
we-saw years-of you-afflicted-us as-days-of make-glad-us! (15) days-of-us

רָעָה׃ יֵרָאֶה אֶל־עֲבָדֶיךָ פָעֳלֶךָ וַהֲדָרְךָ
and-splendor-of-you deed-of-you servants-of-you to may-he-be-shown (16) trouble

עַל־בְּנֵיהֶם׃ וִיהִי ׀ נֹעַם אֲדֹנָי אֱלֹהֵינוּ עָלֵינוּ
upon-us God-of-us Lord favor-of and-may-he-rest (17) children-of-them to

born
or you brought forth the earth and the world,
from everlasting to everlasting you are God.

3 You turn men back to dust,
saying, "Return to dust, O sons of men."
4 For a thousand years in your sight
are like a day that has just gone by,
or like a watch in the night.
5 You sweep men away in the sleep of death;
they are like the new grass of the morning—
6 though in the morning it springs up new,
by evening it is dry and withered.

7 We are consumed by your anger
and terrified by your indignation.
8 You have set our iniquities before you,
our secret sins in the light of your presence.
9 All our days pass away under your wrath;
we finish our years with a moan.
10 The length of our days is seventy years—
or eighty, if we have the strength;
yet their span[d] is but trouble and sorrow,
for they quickly pass, and we fly away.

11 Who knows the power of your anger?
For your wrath is as great as the fear that is due you.
12 Teach us to number our days aright,
that we may gain a heart of wisdom.

13 Relent, O LORD! How long will it be?
Have compassion on your servants.
14 Satisfy us in the morning with your unfailing love,
that we may sing for joy and be glad all our days.
15 Make us glad for as many days as you have afflicted us,
for as many years as we have seen trouble.
16 May your deeds be shown to your servants,
your splendor to their children.

17 May the favor[e] of the Lord our God rest upon us;

[d] 10 Or *yet the best of them* [e] 17 Or *beauty*

*10 The NIV reads this word as וְרָחְבָּם, *yet-span-of-them*.

°8 ק שתה

וּמַעֲשֵׂה יָדֵינוּ כּוֹנְנָה עָלֵינוּ וּמַעֲשֵׂה יָדֵינוּ
and-work-of hands-of-us establish! for-us yes-work-of hands-of-us

כּוֹנְנֵהוּ׃ (91:1) יֹשֵׁב בְּסֵתֶר עֶלְיוֹן בְּצֵל
establish-him! (91:1) one-dwelling in-shelter-of Most-High in-shadow-of

שַׁדַּי יִתְלוֹנָן׃ (2) אֹמַר לַיהוָה מַחְסִי וּמְצוּדָתִי
Almighty he-will-rest (2) I-will-say of-Yahweh refuge-of-me and-fortress-of-me

אֱלֹהַי אֶבְטַח־ בּוֹ׃ (3) כִּי הוּא יַצִּילְךָ מִפַּח
God-of-me I-trust in-him (3) surely he he-will-save-you from-snare-of

יָקוּשׁ מִדֶּבֶר הַוּוֹת׃ (4) בְּאֶבְרָתוֹ ׀ יָסֶךְ
fowler from-pestilence-of deadly-ones (4) with-feather-of-him he-will-cover

לָךְ וְתַחַת־ כְּנָפָיו תֶּחְסֶה צִנָּה וְסֹחֵרָה
over-you and-under wings-of-him you-will-find-refuge shield and-rampart

אֲמִתּוֹ׃ (5) לֹא־ תִירָא מִפַּחַד לָיְלָה מֵחֵץ
faithfulness-of-him (5) not you-will-fear of-terror-of night of-arrow

יָעוּף יוֹמָם׃ (6) מִדֶּבֶר בָּאֹפֶל יַהֲלֹךְ מִקֶּטֶב
he-flies by-day (6) of-pestilence in-the-darkness he-stalks of-plague

יָשׁוּד צָהֳרָיִם׃ (7) יִפֹּל מִצִּדְּךָ ׀ אֶלֶף וּרְבָבָה
he-destroys midday (7) he-may-fall at-side-of-you thousand and-ten-thousand

מִימִינֶךָ אֵלֶיךָ לֹא יִגָּשׁ׃ (8) רַק בְּעֵינֶיךָ
at-right-hand-of-you to-you not he-will-come-near (8) only with-eyes-of-you

תַבִּיט וְשִׁלֻּמַת רְשָׁעִים תִּרְאֶה׃ (9) כִּי־ אַתָּה
you-will-observe and-punishment-of wicked-ones you-will-see (9) if you

יְהוָה מַחְסִי עֶלְיוֹן שַׂמְתָּ מְעוֹנֶךָ׃ (10) לֹא־ תְאֻנֶּה
Yahweh refuge-of-me Most-High you-make dwelling-of-you (10) not she-will-befall

אֵלֶיךָ רָעָה וְנֶגַע לֹא־ יִקְרַב בְּאָהֳלֶךָ׃ (11) כִּי
to-you harm and-disaster not he-will-come-near to-tent-of-you (11) for

מַלְאָכָיו יְצַוֶּה־ לָּךְ לִשְׁמָרְךָ בְּכָל־ דְּרָכֶיךָ׃
angels-of-him he-will-command concerning-you to-guard-you in-all-of ways-of-you

(12) עַל־ כַּפַּיִם יִשָּׂאוּנְךָ פֶּן־ תִּגֹּף בָּאֶבֶן
(12) in hands they-will-lift-up-you so-not you-will-strike against-the-stone

רַגְלֶךָ׃ (13) עַל־ שַׁחַל וָפֶתֶן תִּדְרֹךְ תִּרְמֹס
foot-of-you (13) upon lion and-cobra you-will-tread you-will-trample

כְּפִיר וְתַנִּין׃ (14) כִּי בִי חָשַׁק וַאֲפַלְּטֵהוּ
great-lion and-serpent (14) because to-me he-loves then-I-will-rescue-him

אֲשַׂגְּבֵהוּ כִּי־ יָדַע שְׁמִי׃ (15) יִקְרָאֵנִי ׀
I-will-protect-him for he-acknowledges name-of-me (15) he-will-call-upon-me

וְאֶעֱנֵהוּ עִמּוֹ־ אָנֹכִי בְּצָרָה אֲחַלְּצֵהוּ
and-I-will-answer-him with-him I in-trouble I-will-deliver-him

establish the work of our
hands for us—
yes, establish the work of
our hands.

Psalm 91

[1]He who dwells in the shelter
of the Most High
will rest in the shadow of
the Almighty.[f]
[2]I will say of the LORD, "He is
my refuge and my
fortress,
my God, in whom I trust."

[3]Surely he will save you from
the fowler's snare
and from the deadly
pestilence.
[4]He will cover you with his
feathers,
and under his wings you
will find refuge;
his faithfulness will be your
shield and rampart.
[5]You will not fear the terror of
night,
nor the arrow that flies by
day,
[6]nor the pestilence that stalks
in the darkness,
nor the plague that destroys
at midday.
[7]A thousand may fall at your
side,
ten thousand at your right
hand,
but it will not come near
you.
[8]You will only observe with
your eyes
and see the punishment of
the wicked.

[9]If you make the Most High
your dwelling—
even the LORD, who is my
refuge—
[10]then no harm will befall you,
no disaster will come near
your tent.
[11]For he will command his
angels concerning you
to guard you in all your
ways;
[12]they will lift you up in their
hands,
so that you will not strike
your foot against a stone.
[13]You will tread upon the lion
and the cobra;
you will trample the great
lion and the serpent.

[14]"Because he loves me," says
the LORD, "I will rescue
him;
I will protect him, for he
acknowledges my name.
[15]He will call upon me, and I
will answer him;
I will be with him in
trouble,

f1 Hebrew *Shaddai*

וַֽאֲכַבְּדֵֽהוּ׃ אֹ֣רֶךְ יָ֭מִים אַשְׂבִּיעֵ֑הוּ וְ֝אַרְאֵ֗הוּ
and-I-will-show-him I-will-satisfy-him days length-of (16) and-I-will-honor-him

בִּישׁוּעָתִֽי׃ מִזְמ֥וֹר שִׁ֗יר לְי֣וֹם הַשַּׁבָּֽת׃ ט֗וֹב
good (2) the-Sabbath for-day-of song psalm *(92:1) to-salvation-of-me

לְהֹד֥וֹת לַיהוָ֑ה וּלְזַמֵּ֖ר לְשִׁמְךָ֣ עֶלְיֽוֹן׃ לְהַגִּ֣יד
to-proclaim (3) Most-High to-name-of-you and-to-make-music to-Yahweh to-praise

בַּבֹּ֣קֶר חַסְדֶּ֑ךָ וֶ֝אֱמ֥וּנָתְךָ֗ בַּלֵּילֽוֹת׃ עֲלֵי־
to (4) at-the-nights and-faithfulness-of-you love-of-you in-the-morning

עָ֭שׂוֹר וַעֲלֵי־נָ֑בֶל עֲלֵ֖י הִגָּי֣וֹן בְּכִנּֽוֹר׃ כִּ֤י שִׂמַּחְתַּ֣נִי יְהוָ֣ה
Yahweh you-make-glad-me for (5) of-harp melody to lyre and-to ten-stringed

בְּפָעֳלֶ֑ךָ בְּמַעֲשֵׂ֖י יָדֶ֣יךָ אֲרַנֵּֽן׃ מַה־ גָּדְל֣וּ
they-are-great how (6) I-sing-for-joy hands-of-you at-works-of by-deed-of-you

מַעֲשֶׂ֣יךָ יְהוָ֑ה מְ֝אֹ֗ד עָמְק֥וּ מַחְשְׁבֹתֶֽיךָ׃ אִֽישׁ־ בַּ֭עַר
senseless man (7) thoughts-of-you they-are-profound very Yahweh works-of-you

לֹ֣א יֵדָ֑ע וּ֝כְסִ֗יל לֹא־ יָבִ֥ין אֶת־ זֹֽאת׃ בִּפְרֹ֤חַ
though-to-spring-up (8) this *** he-understands not and-fool he-knows not

רְשָׁעִ֨ים ׀ כְּמ֥וֹ עֵ֗שֶׂב וַ֭יָּצִיצוּ כָּל־ פֹּ֣עֲלֵי אָ֑וֶן
evil ones-doing-of all-of and-they-flourish grass like wicked-ones

לְהִשָּֽׁמְדָ֥ם עֲדֵי־ עַֽד׃ וְאַתָּ֥ה מָר֗וֹם לְעֹלָ֥ם יְהוָֽה׃
Yahweh to-forever exalted but-you (9) forever to to-be-destroyed-them

כִּ֤י הִנֵּ֪ה אֹיְבֶ֡יךָ ׀ יְֽהוָ֗ה כִּֽי־ הִנֵּ֣ה
surely! for Yahweh ones-being-enemies-of-you surely! for (10)

אֹיְבֶ֣יךָ יֹאבֵ֑דוּ יִ֝תְפָּרְד֗וּ כָּל־
all-of they-will-be-scattered they-will-perish ones-being-enemies-of-you

פֹּ֣עֲלֵי אָֽוֶן׃ וַתָּ֣רֶם כִּרְאֵ֣ים קַרְנִ֑י בַּ֝לֹּתִ֗י
I-was-anointed horn-of-me like-wild-ox for-you-exalted (11) evil ones-doing-of

בְּשֶׁ֣מֶן רַעֲנָֽן׃ וַתַּבֵּ֥ט עֵינִ֗י בְּשׁ֫וּרָ֥י
†to-walls-of-me eye-of-me and-she-saw (12) fineness with-oil-of

בַּקָּמִ֣ים עָלַ֣י מְ֭רֵעִים תִּשְׁמַ֣עְנָה אָזְנָֽי׃
ears-of-me they-heard ones-being-wicked against-me on-the-ones-being-foes

צַ֭דִּיק כַּתָּמָ֣ר יִפְרָ֑ח כְּאֶ֖רֶז בַּלְּבָנ֣וֹן
of-the-Lebanon like-cedar he-will-flourish like-the-palm-tree righteous (13)

יִשְׂגֶּֽה׃ שְׁ֭תוּלִים בְּבֵ֣ית יְהוָ֑ה בְּחַצְר֖וֹת אֱלֹהֵ֣ינוּ
God-of-us in-courts-of Yahweh in-house-of ones-being-planted (14) he-will-grow

יַפְרִֽיחוּ׃ ע֭וֹד יְנוּב֣וּן בְּשֵׂיבָ֑ה דְּשֵׁנִ֖ים
fresh-ones in-old-age they-will-bear-fruit still (15) they-will-flourish

וְרַעֲנַנִּ֣ים יִהְיֽוּ׃ לְ֭הַגִּיד כִּֽי־ יָשָׁ֣ר יְהוָ֑ה צ֝וּרִ֗י
Rock-of-me Yahweh upright that to-proclaim (16) they-will-stay and-green-ones

I will deliver him and honor
him.
16 With long life will I satisfy
him
and show him my
salvation."

Psalm 92

A psalm. A song. For the Sabbath
day.

1 It is good to praise the LORD
and make music to your
name, O Most High,
2 to proclaim your love in the
morning
and your faithfulness at
night,
3 to the music of the
ten-stringed lyre
and the melody of the harp.

4 For you make me glad by your
deeds, O LORD;
I sing for joy at the works of
your hands.
5 How great are your works, O
LORD,
how profound your
thoughts!
6 The senseless man does not
know,
fools do not understand,
7 that though the wicked spring
up like grass
and all evildoers flourish,
they will be forever destroyed.

8 But you, O LORD, are exalted
forever.

9 For surely your enemies, O
LORD,
surely your enemies will
perish;
all evildoers will be
scattered.
10 You have exalted my horn[g]
like that of a wild ox;
fine oils have been poured
upon me.
11 My eyes have seen the defeat
of my adversaries;
my ears have heard the rout
of my wicked foes.

12 The righteous will flourish like
a palm tree,
they will grow like a cedar
of Lebanon;
13 planted in the house of the
LORD,
they will flourish in the
courts of our God.
14 They will still bear fruit in old
age,
they will stay fresh and
green,
15 proclaiming, "The LORD is
upright;
he is my Rock, and there is

g10 Horn here symbolizes strength.

*Heading, *1* See the note on page 349.

†*12* The NIV reads this word as בְּשׁוֹרָ֑י, *on-adversaries-of-me.*

וְלֹא־עַלְתָה בּוֹ׃ יְהוָה מָלָךְ גֵּאוּת לָבֵשׁ לָבֵשׁ
he-is-robed he-is-robed majesty he-reigns Yahweh (93:1) in-him wickedness and-no

יְהוָה עֹז הִתְאַזָּר אַף־תִּכּוֹן תֵּבֵל בַּל־תִּמּוֹט׃
she-can-be-moved not world she-is-established firmly he-is-armed strength Yahweh

נָכוֹן כִּסְאֲךָ מֵאָז מֵעוֹלָם אָתָּה׃
you from-eternity from-long-ago throne-of-you he-was-established (2)

נָשְׂאוּ נְהָרוֹת ׀ יְהוָה נָשְׂאוּ נְהָרוֹת קוֹלָם יִשְׂאוּ
they-lifted-up voice-of-them seas they-lifted-up Yahweh seas they-lifted-up (3)

נְהָרוֹת דָּכְיָם׃ מִקֹּלוֹת ׀ מַיִם רַבִּים אַדִּירִים
mighty-ones great-ones waters more-than-thunders-of (4) pounding-of-them seas

מִשְׁבְּרֵי־יָם אַדִּיר בַּמָּרוֹם יְהוָה׃ עֵדֹתֶיךָ ׀ נֶאֶמְנוּ
they-stand-firm statutes-of-you (5) Yahweh in-the-height mighty sea breakers-of

מְאֹד לְבֵיתְךָ נַאֲוָה־קֹדֶשׁ יְהוָה לְאֹרֶךְ יָמִים׃
days for-length-of Yahweh holiness adornment to-house-of-you very

אֵל־נְקָמוֹת יְהוָה אֵל נְקָמוֹת הוֹפִיעַ׃ הִנָּשֵׂא
rise-up! (2) shine-forth! vengeances God-of Yahweh vengeances God-of (94:1)

שֹׁפֵט הָאָרֶץ הָשֵׁב גְּמוּל עַל־גֵּאִים׃ עַד־מָתַי
when? until (3) proud-ones to desert pay-back! the-earth One-Judging

רְשָׁעִים ׀ יְהוָה עַד־מָתַי רְשָׁעִים יַעֲלֹזוּ׃
will-they-be-jubilant wicked-ones when? until Yahweh wicked-ones

יַבִּיעוּ יְדַבְּרוּ עָתָק יִתְאַמְּרוּ כָּל־פֹּעֲלֵי אָוֶן׃
evil ones-doing-of all-of they-boast arrogance they-speak they-pour-out (4)

עַמְּךָ יְהוָה יְדַכְּאוּ וְנַחֲלָתְךָ יְעַנּוּ׃
they-oppress and-inheritance-of-you they-crush Yahweh people-of-you (5)

אַלְמָנָה וְגֵר יַהֲרֹגוּ וִיתוֹמִים יְרַצֵּחוּ׃ וַיֹּאמְרוּ
and-they-say (7) they-murder and-fatherless-ones they-slay and-alien widow (6)

לֹא יִרְאֶה־יָּהּ וְלֹא־יָבִין אֱלֹהֵי יַעֲקֹב׃ בִּינוּ
take-heed! (8) Jacob God-of he-heeds and-not Yahweh he-sees not

בֹּעֲרִים בָּעָם וּכְסִילִים מָתַי תַּשְׂכִּילוּ׃
will-you-become-wise when? and-fools among-the-people ones-being-senseless

הֲנֹטַע אֹזֶן הֲלֹא יִשְׁמָע אִם־יֹצֵר עַיִן הֲלֹא יַבִּיט׃
he-sees not? eye one-forming or he-hears not? ear one-implanting? (9)

הֲיֹסֵר גּוֹיִם הֲלֹא יוֹכִיחַ הַמְלַמֵּד אָדָם דָּעַת׃
knowledge man one-teaching? will-he-punish not? nations one-disciplining (10)

יְהוָה יֹדֵעַ מַחְשְׁבוֹת אָדָם כִּי־הֵמָּה הָבֶל׃ אַשְׁרֵי ׀
blessednesses-of (12) futile they that man thoughts-of knowing Yahweh (11)

הַגֶּבֶר אֲשֶׁר־תְּיַסְּרֶנּוּ יָּהּ וּמִתּוֹרָתְךָ תְלַמְּדֶנּוּ׃
you-teach-him and-from-law-of-you Yahweh you-discipline-him whom the-man

no wickedness in him."

Psalm 93

1 The LORD reigns, he is robed in majesty;
the LORD is robed in majesty and is armed with strength.
The world is firmly established;
it cannot be moved.
2 Your throne was established long ago;
you are from all eternity.

3 The seas have lifted up, O LORD,
the seas have lifted up their voice;
the seas have lifted up their pounding waves.
4 Mightier than the thunder of the great waters,
mightier than the breakers of the sea—
the LORD on high is mighty.

5 Your statutes stand firm;
holiness adorns your house
for endless days, O LORD.

Psalm 94

1 O LORD, the God who avenges,
O God who avenges, shine forth.
2 Rise up, O Judge of the earth;
pay back to the proud what they deserve.
3 How long will the wicked, O LORD,
how long will the wicked be jubilant?

4 They pour out arrogant words;
all the evildoers are full of boasting.
5 They crush your people, O LORD;
they oppress your inheritance.
6 They slay the widow and the alien;
they murder the fatherless.
7 They say, "The LORD does not see;
the God of Jacob pays no heed."

8 Take heed, you senseless ones among the people;
you fools, when will you become wise?
9 Does he who implanted the ear not hear?
Does he who formed the eye not see?
10 Does he who disciplines nations not punish?
Does he who teaches man lack knowledge?
11 The LORD knows the thoughts of man;
he knows that they are futile.

12 Blessed is the man you discipline, O LORD,
the man you teach from your law;

*See the note on page 349.

°16 ק עולתה

לְהַשְׁקִיט לוֹ מִימֵי רָע עַד יִכָּרֶה

he-is-dug till trouble from-days-of to-him to-grant-relief (13)

לָרָשָׁע שָׁחַת׃ כִּי ׀ לֹא־יִטֹּשׁ יְהוָה עַמּוֹ

people-of-him Yahweh he-will-reject not for (14) pit for-the-wicked

וְנַחֲלָתוֹ לֹא יַעֲזֹב׃ כִּי־עַד־צֶדֶק

righteousness on for (15) he-will-forsake never and-inheritance-of-him

יָשׁוּב מִשְׁפָּט וְאַחֲרָיו כָּל־יִשְׁרֵי־לֵב׃ מִי־

who? (16) heart ones-upright-of all-of and-after-him judgment he-will-be-again

יָקוּם לִי עִם־מְרֵעִים מִי־יִתְיַצֵּב

he-will-take-stand who? ones-being-wicked against for-me he-will-rise-up

לִי עִם־פֹּעֲלֵי אָוֶן׃ לוּלֵי יְהוָה עֶזְרָתָה לִּי כִּמְעַט ׀

as-soon to-me help Yahweh unless (17) evil ones-doing-of against for-me

שָׁכְנָה דוּמָה נַפְשִׁי׃ אִם־אָמַרְתִּי מָטָה רַגְלִי

foot-of-me she-slips I-said when (18) self-of-me silence she-would-have-dwelt

חַסְדְּךָ יְהוָה יִסְעָדֵנִי׃ בְּרֹב שַׂרְעַפַּי

anxieties-of-me when-to-be-great (19) he-supported-me Yahweh love-of-you

בְּקִרְבִּי תַּנְחוּמֶיךָ יְשַׁעַשְׁעוּ נַפְשִׁי׃

soul-of-me they-brought-joy consolations-of-you at-inside-of-me

הַיְחָבְרְךָ כִּסֵּא הַוּוֹת יֹצֵר עָמָל

misery one-bringing-on corruptions throne-of can-he-be-allied-with-you? (20)

עֲלֵי־חֹק׃ יָגוֹדּוּ עַל־נֶפֶשׁ צַדִּיק וְדָם

and-blood righteous life-of against they-band-together (21) decree by

נָקִי יַרְשִׁיעוּ׃ וַיְהִי יְהוָה לִי לְמִשְׂגָּב וֵאלֹהַי

and-God-of-me as-fortress to-me Yahweh but-he-became (22) they-condemn innocent

לְצוּר מַחְסִי׃ וַיָּשֶׁב עֲלֵיהֶם ׀ אֶת־אוֹנָם

sin-of-them *** to-them and-he-will-repay (23) refuge-of-me as-rock-of

וּבְרָעָתָם יַצְמִיתֵם יַצְמִיתֵם יְהוָה

Yahweh he-will-destroy-them he-will-destroy-them and-for-wickedness-of-them

אֱלֹהֵינוּ׃ לְכוּ נְרַנְּנָה לַיהוָה נָרִיעָה לְצוּר

to-Rock-of let-us-shout to-Yahweh let-us-sing come! (95:1) God-of-us

יִשְׁעֵנוּ׃ נְקַדְּמָה פָנָיו בְּתוֹדָה

with-thanksgiving faces-of-him let-us-come-before (2) salvation-of-us

בִּזְמִרוֹת נָרִיעַ לוֹ׃ כִּי אֵל גָּדוֹל יְהוָה וּמֶלֶךְ גָּדוֹל

great and-King Yahweh great God for (3) to-him let-us-extol with-songs

עַל־כָּל־אֱלֹהִים׃ אֲשֶׁר בְּיָדוֹ מֶחְקְרֵי־אָרֶץ וְתוֹעֲפוֹת

and-peaks-of earth depths-of in-hand-of-him who (4) gods all-of above

הָרִים לוֹ׃ אֲשֶׁר־לוֹ הַיָּם וְהוּא עָשָׂהוּ וְיַבֶּשֶׁת

and-dry-land he-made-him for-he the-sea to-him who (5) to-him mountains

13 you grant him relief from days of trouble,
till a pit is dug for the wicked.
14 For the LORD will not reject his people;
he will never forsake his inheritance.
15 Judgment will again be founded on righteousness,
and all the upright in heart will follow it.

16 Who will rise up for me against the wicked?
Who will take a stand for me against evildoers?
17 Unless the LORD had given me help,
I would soon have dwelt in the silence of death.
18 When I said, "My foot is slipping,"
your love, O LORD, supported me.
19 When anxiety was great within me,
your consolation brought joy to my soul.

20 Can a corrupt throne be allied with you—
one that brings on misery by its decrees?
21 They band together against the righteous
and condemn the innocent to death.
22 But the LORD has become my fortress,
and my God the rock in whom I take refuge.
23 He will repay them for their sins
and destroy them for their wickedness;
the LORD our God will destroy them.

Psalm 95

1 Come, let us sing for joy to the LORD;
let us shout aloud to the Rock of our salvation.
2 Let us come before him with thanksgiving
and extol him with music and song.

3 For the LORD is the great God,
the great King above all gods.
4 In his hand are the depths of the earth,
and the mountain peaks belong to him.
5 The sea is his, for he made it,

יָדָיו יָצָרוּ׃ בֹּאוּ נִשְׁתַּחֲוֶה וְנִכְרָעָה נִבְרְכָה

let-us-kneel and-let-us-bow let-us-worship come! (6) they-formed hands-of-him

לִפְנֵי־ יְהוָה עֹשֵׂנוּ׃ כִּי הוּא אֱלֹהֵינוּ וַאֲנַחְנוּ עַם

people-of and-we God-of-us he for (7) One-Making-us Yahweh before

מַרְעִיתוֹ וְצֹאן יָדוֹ הַיּוֹם אִם־ בְּקֹלוֹ תִשְׁמָעוּ׃

you-hear to-voice-of-him if the-day care-of-him and-flock-of pasture-of-him

אַל־ תַּקְשׁוּ לְבַבְכֶם כִּמְרִיבָה כְּיוֹם מַסָּה בַּמִּדְבָּר׃

in-the-desert Massah as-day-of as-Meribah heart-of-you you-harden not (8)

אֲשֶׁר נִסּוּנִי אֲבוֹתֵיכֶם בְּחָנוּנִי גַּם־ רָאוּ

they-saw though they-tried-me fathers-of-you they-tested-me where (9)

פָעֳלִי׃ אַרְבָּעִים שָׁנָה ׀ אָקוּט בְּדוֹר וָאֹמַר עַם

people and-I-said with-generation I-was-angry year forty (10) deed-of-me

תֹּעֵי לֵבָב הֵם וְהֵם לֹא־ יָדְעוּ דְרָכָי׃ אֲשֶׁר־

so (11) ways-of-me they-knew not and-they they heart ones-straying-of

נִשְׁבַּעְתִּי בְאַפִּי אִם־ יְבֹאוּן אֶל־ מְנוּחָתִי׃

rest-of-me into they-shall-enter never in-anger-of-me I-declared-on-oath

שִׁירוּ לַיהוָה שִׁיר חָדָשׁ שִׁירוּ לַיהוָה כָּל־ הָאָרֶץ׃ שִׁירוּ

sing! (2) the-earth all-of to-Yahweh sing! new song to-Yahweh sing! (96:1)

לַיהוָה בָּרְכוּ שְׁמוֹ בַּשְּׂרוּ מִיּוֹם־ לְיוֹם יְשׁוּעָתוֹ׃

salvation-of-him to-day from-day proclaim! name-of-him praise! to-Yahweh

סַפְּרוּ בַגּוֹיִם כְּבוֹדוֹ בְּכָל־ הָעַמִּים

the-peoples among-all-of glory-of-him among-the-nations declare! (3)

נִפְלְאוֹתָיו׃ כִּי גָדוֹל יְהוָה וּמְהֻלָּל מְאֹד

greatly and-one-being-praised Yahweh great for (4) deeds-being-marvelous-of-him

נוֹרָא הוּא עַל־ כָּל־ אֱלֹהִים׃ כִּי ׀ כָּל־ אֱלֹהֵי הָעַמִּים

the-nations gods-of all-of for (5) gods all-of above he one-being-feared

אֱלִילִים וַיהוָה שָׁמַיִם עָשָׂה׃ הוֹד־ וְהָדָר לְפָנָיו עֹז

strength before-him and-majesty splendor (6) he-made heavens but-Yahweh idols

וְתִפְאֶרֶת בְּמִקְדָּשׁוֹ׃ הָבוּ לַיהוָה מִשְׁפְּחוֹת עַמִּים

nations families-of to-Yahweh ascribe! (7) in-sanctuary-of-him and-glory

הָבוּ לַיהוָה כָּבוֹד וָעֹז׃ הָבוּ לַיהוָה כְּבוֹד

glory-of to-Yahweh ascribe! (8) and-strength glory to-Yahweh ascribe!

שְׁמוֹ שְׂאוּ־ מִנְחָה וּבֹאוּ לְחַצְרוֹתָיו׃ הִשְׁתַּחֲווּ

worship! (9) into-courts-of-him and-come! offering bring! name-of-him

לַיהוָה בְּהַדְרַת־ קֹדֶשׁ חִילוּ מִפָּנָיו כָּל־ הָאָרֶץ׃

the-earth all-of at-before-him tremble! holiness in-splendor-of to-Yahweh

אִמְרוּ בַגּוֹיִם ׀ יְהוָה מָלָךְ אַף־ תִּכּוֹן תֵּבֵל

world she-is-established firmly he-reigns Yahweh among-the-nations say! (10)

and his hands formed the
dry land.

6Come, let us bow down in
worship,
let us kneel before the LORD
our Maker;
7for he is our God
and we are the people of his
pasture,
the flock under his care.

Today, if you hear his voice,
8 do not harden your hearts as
you did at Meribah,[h]
as you did that day at
Massah[i] in the desert,
9where your fathers tested and
tried me,
though they had seen what
I did.
10For forty years I was angry
with that generation;
I said, "They are a people
whose hearts go astray,
and they have not known
my ways."
11So I declared on oath in my
anger,
"They shall never enter my
rest."

Psalm 96

1Sing to the LORD a new song;
sing to the LORD, all the
earth.
2Sing to the LORD, praise his
name;
proclaim his salvation day
after day.
3Declare his glory among the
nations,
his marvelous deeds among
all peoples.

4For great is the LORD and most
worthy of praise;
he is to be feared above all
gods.
5For all the gods of the nations
are idols,
but the LORD made the
heavens.
6Splendor and majesty are
before him;
strength and glory are in his
sanctuary.

7Ascribe to the LORD, O families
of nations,
ascribe to the LORD glory
and strength.
8Ascribe to the LORD the glory
due his name;
bring an offering and come
into his courts.
9Worship the LORD in the
splendor of his[j] holiness;
tremble before him, all the
earth.

10Say among the nations, "The
LORD reigns."
The world is firmly

h8 *Meribah* means *quarreling*.
i8 *Massah* means *testing*.
j9 Or *LORD with the splendor of*

בַּל־ תִּמּוֹט יָדִין עַמִּים בְּמֵישָׁרִים׃ יִשְׂמְחוּ
let-them-rejoice (11) with-equities peoples he-will-judge she-can-be-moved not

הַשָּׁמַיִם וְתָגֵל הָאָרֶץ יִרְעַם הַיָּם
the-sea let-him-resound the-earth and-let-her-be-glad the-heavens

וּמְלֹאוֹ׃ יַעֲלֹז שָׂדַי וְכָל־ אֲשֶׁר־ בּוֹ
in-him that and-all field let-him-be-jubilant (12) and-fullness-of-him

אָז יְרַנְּנוּ כָּל־ עֲצֵי־ יָעַר׃ לִפְנֵי יְהוָה כִּי
for Yahweh before (13) forest trees-of all-of they-will-sing-for-joy then

בָּא כִּי בָא לִשְׁפֹּט הָאָרֶץ יִשְׁפֹּט־ תֵּבֵל בְּצֶדֶק
in-righteousness world he-will-judge the-earth to-judge he-comes for he-comes

וְעַמִּים בֶּאֱמוּנָתוֹ׃ יְהוָה מָלָךְ תָּגֵל הָאָרֶץ
the-earth let-her-be-glad he-reigns Yahweh (97:1) in-truth-of-him and-peoples

יִשְׂמְחוּ אִיִּים רַבִּים׃ עָנָן וַעֲרָפֶל
and-thick-darkness cloud (2) distant-ones shores let-them-rejoice

סְבִיבָיו צֶדֶק וּמִשְׁפָּט מְכוֹן כִּסְאוֹ׃
throne-of-him foundation-of and-justice righteousness ones-around-him

אֵשׁ לְפָנָיו תֵּלֵךְ וּתְלַהֵט סָבִיב צָרָיו׃
foes-of-him on-every-side and-she-consumes she-goes before-him fire (3)

הֵאִירוּ בְרָקָיו תֵּבֵל רָאֲתָה וַתָּחֵל הָאָרֶץ׃
the-earth and-she-trembles she-sees world lightnings-of-him they-light-up (4)

הָרִים כַּדּוֹנַג נָמַסּוּ מִלִּפְנֵי יְהוָה מִלִּפְנֵי אֲדוֹן
Lord-of at-before Yahweh at-before they-melt like-the-wax mountains (5)

כָּל־ הָאָרֶץ׃ הִגִּידוּ הַשָּׁמַיִם צִדְקוֹ וְרָאוּ
and-they-see righteousness-of-him the-heavens they-proclaim (6) the-earth all-of

כָל־ הָעַמִּים כְּבוֹדוֹ׃ יֵבֹשׁוּ כָּל־ עֹבְדֵי
ones-worshiping-of all-of let-them-be-shamed (7) glory-of-him the-peoples all-of

פֶסֶל הַמִּתְהַלְלִים בָּאֱלִילִים הִשְׁתַּחֲווּ־ לוֹ כָּל־ אֱלֹהִים׃ שָׁמְעָה
she-hears (8) gods all-of to-him worship! in-the-idols the-ones-boasting image

וַתִּשְׂמַח צִיּוֹן וַתָּגֵלְנָה בְּנוֹת יְהוּדָה לְמַעַן
because-of Judah villages-of and-they-are-glad Zion and-she-rejoices

מִשְׁפָּטֶיךָ יְהוָה׃ כִּי־אַתָּה יְהוָה עֶלְיוֹן עַל־ כָּל־ הָאָרֶץ
the-earth all-of over Most-High Yahweh you for (9) Yahweh judgments-of-you

מְאֹד נַעֲלֵיתָ עַל־ כָּל־ אֱלֹהִים׃ אֹהֲבֵי יְהוָה שִׂנְאוּ
hate! Yahweh ones-loving-of (10) gods all-of above you-are-exalted far

רָע שֹׁמֵר נַפְשׁוֹת חֲסִידָיו מִיַּד רְשָׁעִים
wicked-ones from-hand-of faithful-ones-of-him lives-of one-guarding evil

יַצִּילֵם׃ אוֹר זָרֻעַ לַצַּדִּיק וּלְיִשְׁרֵי־
and-on-ones-upright-of upon-the-righteous being-shed light (11) he-delivers-them

established, it cannot be
moved;
he will judge the peoples
with equity.
11 Let the heavens rejoice, let the
earth be glad;
let the sea resound, and all
that is in it;
12 let the fields be jubilant, and
everything in them.
Then all the trees of the forest
will sing for joy;
13 they will sing before the
LORD, for he comes,
he comes to judge the earth.
He will judge the world in
righteousness
and the peoples in his truth.

Psalm 97

1 The LORD reigns, let the earth
be glad;
let the distant shores rejoice.
2 Clouds and thick darkness
surround him;
righteousness and justice are
the foundation of his
throne.
3 Fire goes before him
and consumes his foes on
every side.
4 His lightning lights up the
world;
the earth sees and trembles.
5 The mountains melt like wax
before the LORD,
before the Lord of all the
earth.
6 The heavens proclaim his
righteousness,
and all the peoples see his
glory.
7 All who worship images are
put to shame,
those who boast in idols—
worship him, all you gods!
8 Zion hears and rejoices
and the villages of Judah are
glad
because of your judgments,
O LORD.
9 For you, O LORD, are the Most
High over all the earth;
you are exalted far above all
gods.
10 Let those who love the LORD
hate evil,
for he guards the lives of his
faithful ones
and delivers them from the
hand of the wicked.
11 Light is shed upon the
righteous
and joy on the upright in

לֵב שִׂמְחָה׃ שִׂמְחוּ צַדִּיקִים בַּיהוָה וְהוֹדוּ לְזֵכֶר
to-name-of and-praise! in-Yahweh righteous-ones rejoice! (12) joy heart

קָדְשׁוֹ׃ מִזְמוֹר שִׁירוּ לַיהוָה ׀ שִׁיר חָדָשׁ כִּי־ נִפְלָאוֹת
things-being-marvelous for new song to-Yahweh sing! psalm (98:1) holiness-of-him

עָשָׂה הוֹשִׁיעָה־ לּוֹ יְמִינוֹ וּזְרוֹעַ
and-arm-of right-hand-of-him for-him she-worked-salvation he-did

קָדְשׁוֹ׃ הוֹדִיעַ יְהוָה יְשׁוּעָתוֹ לְעֵינֵי
before-eyes-of salvation-of-him Yahweh he-made-known (2) holiness-of-him

הַגּוֹיִם גִּלָּה צִדְקָתוֹ׃ זָכַר חַסְדּוֹ ׀
love-of-him he-remembered (3) righteousness-of-him he-revealed the-nations

וֶאֱמוּנָתוֹ לְבֵית יִשְׂרָאֵל רָאוּ כָל־ אַפְסֵי־ אָרֶץ
earth ends-of all-of they-saw Israel to-house-of and-faithfulness-of-him

אֵת יְשׁוּעַת אֱלֹהֵינוּ׃ הָרִיעוּ לַיהוָה כָּל־ הָאָרֶץ
the-earth all-of to-Yahweh shout-for-joy! (4) God-of-us salvation-of ***

פִּצְחוּ וְרַנְּנוּ וְזַמֵּרוּ׃ זַמְּרוּ לַיהוָה בְּכִנּוֹר
with-harp to-Yahweh make-music! (5) and-make-music! and-sing! burst-forth!

בְּכִנּוֹר וְקוֹל זִמְרָה׃ בַּחֲצֹצְרוֹת וְקוֹל שׁוֹפָר
horn-of-ram and-blast-of with-trumpets (6) singing and-sound-of with-harp

הָרִיעוּ לִפְנֵי ׀ הַמֶּלֶךְ יְהוָה׃ יִרְעַם הַיָּם
the-sea let-him-resound (7) Yahweh the-King before shout-for-joy!

וּמְלֹאוֹ תֵּבֵל וְיֹשְׁבֵי בָהּ׃ נְהָרוֹת יִמְחֲאוּ־
let-them-clap rivers (8) in-her and-ones-living-of world and-fullness-of-him

כָף יַחַד הָרִים יְרַנֵּנוּ׃ לִפְנֵי־ יְהוָה כִּי בָא
he-comes for Yahweh before (9) let-them-sing-for-joy mountains together hand

לִשְׁפֹּט הָאָרֶץ יִשְׁפֹּט־ תֵּבֵל בְּצֶדֶק וְעַמִּים
and-peoples in-righteousness world he-will-judge the-earth to-judge

בְּמֵישָׁרִים׃ יְהוָה מָלָךְ יִרְגְּזוּ עַמִּים
nations let-them-tremble he-reigns Yahweh (99:1) with-equities

יֹשֵׁב כְּרוּבִים תָּנוּט הָאָרֶץ׃ יְהוָה בְּצִיּוֹן
in-Zion Yahweh (2) the-earth let-her-shake cherubim one-sitting-enthroned-of

גָּדוֹל וְרָם הוּא עַל־ כָּל־ הָעַמִּים׃ יוֹדוּ
let-them-praise (3) the-nations all-of over he and-one-being-exalted great

שִׁמְךָ גָּדוֹל וְנוֹרָא קָדוֹשׁ הוּא׃ וְעֹז מֶלֶךְ מִשְׁפָּט
justice King and-mighty (4) he holy and-one-being-awesome great name-of-you

אָהֵב אַתָּה כּוֹנַנְתָּ מֵישָׁרִים מִשְׁפָּט וּצְדָקָה בְּיַעֲקֹב ׀ אַתָּה עָשִׂיתָ׃
you-did you in-Jacob and-right just equities you-established you he-loves

רוֹמְמוּ יְהוָה אֱלֹהֵינוּ וְהִשְׁתַּחֲווּ לַהֲדֹם רַגְלָיו קָדוֹשׁ הוּא׃
he holy feet-of-him at-footstool-of and-worship! God-of-us Yahweh exalt! (5)

heart.
12 Rejoice in the LORD, you who are righteous,
and praise his holy name.

Psalm 98

A psalm.

1 Sing to the LORD a new song,
for he has done marvelous things;
his right hand and his holy arm
have worked salvation for him.
2 The LORD has made his salvation known
and revealed his righteousness to the nations.
3 He has remembered his love
and his faithfulness to the house of Israel;
all the ends of the earth have seen
the salvation of our God.

4 Shout for joy to the LORD, all the earth,
burst into jubilant song with music;
5 make music to the LORD with the harp,
with the harp and the sound of singing,
6 with trumpets and the blast of the ram's horn—
shout for joy before the LORD, the King.

7 Let the sea resound, and everything in it,
the world, and all who live in it.
8 Let the rivers clap their hands,
let the mountains sing together for joy;
9 let them sing before the LORD,
for he comes to judge the earth.
He will judge the world in righteousness
and the peoples with equity.

Psalm 99

1 The LORD reigns,
let the nations tremble;
he sits enthroned between the cherubim,
let the earth shake.
2 Great is the LORD in Zion;
he is exalted over all the nations.
3 Let them praise your great and awesome name—
he is holy.

4 The King is mighty, he loves justice—
you have established equity;
in Jacob you have done what is just and right.
5 Exalt the LORD our God
and worship at his footstool;
he is holy.

מֹשֶׁה וְאַהֲרֹן ׀ בְּכֹהֲנָיו וּשְׁמוּאֵל בְּקֹרְאֵי
among-ones-calling-of and-Samuel among-priests-of-him and-Aaron Moses (6)

שְׁמוֹ קֹרְאִים אֶל־ יְהוָה וְהוּא יַעֲנֵם׃ בְּעַמּוּד
from-pillar-of (7) he-answered-them and-he Yahweh on ones-calling name-of-him

עָנָן יְדַבֵּר אֲלֵיהֶם שָׁמְרוּ עֵדֹתָיו וְחֹק נָתַן־
he-gave and-decree statutes-of-him they-kept to-them he-spoke cloud

לָמוֹ׃ יְהוָה אֱלֹהֵינוּ אַתָּה עֲנִיתָם אֵל נֹשֵׂא הָיִיתָ
you-were one-forgiving God you-answered-them you God-of-us Yahweh (8) to-them

לָהֶם וְנֹקֵם עַל־ עֲלִילוֹתָם׃ רוֹמְמוּ יְהוָה אֱלֹהֵינוּ
God-of-us Yahweh exalt! (9) misdeeds-of-them to though-one-punishing to-them

וְהִשְׁתַּחֲווּ לְהַר קָדְשׁוֹ כִּי־ קָדוֹשׁ יְהוָה אֱלֹהֵינוּ׃
God-of-us Yahweh holy for holiness-of-him at-mountain-of and-worship!

מִזְמוֹר לְתוֹדָה הָרִיעוּ לַיהוָה כָּל־ הָאָרֶץ׃
the-earth all-of to-Yahweh shout-for-joy! for-thanksgiving psalm (100:1)

עִבְדוּ אֶת־ יְהוָה בְּשִׂמְחָה בֹּאוּ לְפָנָיו בִּרְנָנָה׃
with-joyful-song before-him come! with-gladness Yahweh *** serve! (2)

דְּעוּ כִּי־ יְהוָה הוּא אֱלֹהִים הוּא־ עָשָׂנוּ וְלֹא אֲנַחְנוּ עַמּוֹ
people-of-him we and-to-him he-made-us he God he Yahweh that know! (3)

וְצֹאן מַרְעִיתוֹ׃ בֹּאוּ שְׁעָרָיו ׀ בְּתוֹדָה
with-thanksgiving gates-of-him enter! (4) pasture-of-him and-sheep-of

חֲצֵרֹתָיו בִּתְהִלָּה הוֹדוּ־ לוֹ בָּרֲכוּ שְׁמוֹ׃ כִּי־
for (5) name-of-him praise! to-him give-thanks! with-praise courts-of-him

טוֹב יְהוָה לְעוֹלָם חַסְדּוֹ וְעַד־ דֹּר וָדֹר
and-generation generation and-through love-of-him to-forever Yahweh good

אֱמוּנָתוֹ׃ לְדָוִד מִזְמוֹר חֶסֶד־ וּמִשְׁפָּט אָשִׁירָה
I-will-sing and-justice love psalm of-David (101:1) faithfulness-of-him

לְךָ יְהוָה אֲזַמֵּרָה׃ אַשְׂכִּילָה ׀ בְּדֶרֶךְ תָּמִים מָתַי
when? blameless in-life I-will-be-careful (2) I-will-sing-praise Yahweh to-you

תָּבוֹא אֵלָי אֶתְהַלֵּךְ בְּתָם־ לְבָבִי בְּקֶרֶב
in-midst-of heart-of-me with-blamelessness-of I-will-walk to-me will-you-come

בֵּיתִי׃ לֹא־ אָשִׁית ׀ לְנֶגֶד עֵינַי דְּבַר־ בְּלִיָּעַל עֲשֹׂה־
to-do vileness thing-of eyes-of-me at-before I-will-set not (3) house-of-me

סֵטִים שָׂנֵאתִי לֹא יִדְבַּק בִּי׃ לֵבָב עִקֵּשׁ
perverse heart (4) to-me he-will-cling not I-hate faithless-men

יָסוּר מִמֶּנִּי רָע לֹא אֵדָע׃ מְלָושְׁנִי בַסֵּתֶר ׀
in-the-secret one-slandering (5) I-know not evil from-me he-shall-be-far

רֵעֵהוּ אוֹתוֹ אַצְמִית גְּבַהּ־ עֵינַיִם וּרְחַב לֵבָב אֹתוֹ
him heart and-proud-of eyes haughty-of I-will-silence him neighbor-of-him

6 Moses and Aaron were among
his priests,
Samuel was among those
who called on his name;
they called on the LORD
and he answered them.
7 He spoke to them from the
pillar of cloud;
they kept his statutes and
the decrees he gave them.
8 O LORD our God,
you answered them;
you were to Israel[k] a forgiving
God,
though you punished their
misdeeds.[l]
9 Exalt the LORD our God
and worship at his holy
mountain,
for the LORD our God is
holy.

Psalm 100

A psalm. For giving thanks.

1 Shout for joy to the LORD, all
the earth.
2 Serve the LORD with
gladness;
come before him with joyful
songs.
3 Know that the LORD is God.
It is he who made us, and
we are his[m];
we are his people, the sheep
of his pasture.
4 Enter his gates with
thanksgiving
and his courts with praise;
give thanks to him and
praise his name.
5 For the LORD is good and his
love endures forever;
his faithfulness continues
through all generations.

Psalm 101

Of David. A psalm.

1 I will sing of your love and
justice;
to you, O LORD, I will sing
praise.
2 I will be careful to lead a
blameless life—
when will you come to me?
I will walk in my house
with blameless heart.
3 I will set before my eyes
no vile thing.
The deeds of faithless men I
hate;
they will not cling to me.
4 Men of perverse heart shall be
far from me;
I will have nothing to do
with evil.
5 Whoever slanders his neighbor
in secret,
him will I put to silence;
whoever has haughty eyes and
a proud heart,

[k] 8 Hebrew *them*
[l] 8 Or *I an avenger of the wrongs done to them*
[m] 3 Or *and not we ourselves*

°3 ק ולו
°5 ק מלשני

לֹא אוּכָל׃ עֵינַי ׀ בְּנֶאֶמְנֵי־ אֶרֶץ לָשֶׁבֶת
to-dwell land on-ones-being-faithful-of eyes-of-me (6) I-will-endure not

עִמָּדִי הֹלֵךְ בְּדֶרֶךְ תָּמִים הוּא יְשָׁרְתֵנִי׃ לֹא־
not (7) he-will-minister-to-me he blameless in-way one-walking with-me

יֵשֵׁב ׀ בְּקֶרֶב בֵּיתִי עֹשֵׂה רְמִיָּה דֹּבֵר
one-speaking deceit one-practicing-of house-of-me in-midst-of he-will-dwell

שְׁקָרִים לֹא־ יִכּוֹן לְנֶגֶד עֵינָי׃ לַבְּקָרִים
in-the-mornings (8) eyes-of-me at-before he-will-stand not falsehoods

אַצְמִית כָּל־ רִשְׁעֵי־ אָרֶץ לְהַכְרִית מֵעִיר־ יְהוָה
Yahweh from-city-of to-cut-off land wicked-ones-of all-of I-will-silence

כָּל־ פֹּעֲלֵי אָוֶן׃ תְּפִלָּה לְעָנִי כִי־ יַעֲטֹף
he-is-faint when of-afflicted-man prayer *(102:1) evil ones-doing-of all-of

וְלִפְנֵי יְהוָה יִשְׁפֹּךְ שִׂיחוֹ׃ יְהוָה שִׁמְעָה תְפִלָּתִי
prayer-of-me hear! Yahweh (2) lament-of-him he-pours-out Yahweh and-before

וְשַׁוְעָתִי אֵלֶיךָ תָבוֹא׃ אַל־ תַּסְתֵּר פָּנֶיךָ ׀
faces-of-you you-hide not (3) let-her-come to-you and-cry-for-help-of-me

מִמֶּנִּי בְּיוֹם צַר לִי הַטֵּה־ אֵלַי אָזְנֶךָ בְּיוֹם אֶקְרָא
I-call on-day ear-of-you to-me turn! of-me distress on-day-of from-me

מַהֵר עֲנֵנִי׃ כִּי־ כָלוּ בְעָשָׁן יָמָי וְעַצְמוֹתַי
and-bones-of-me days-of-me like-smoke they-vanish for (4) answer-me! quickly

כְּמוֹ־קֵד‡ נִחָרוּ׃ הוּכָּה־ כָעֵשֶׂב
like-the-grass he-is-blighted (5) they-burn like-glowing-ember

וַיִּבַשׁ לִבִּי כִּי־ שָׁכַחְתִּי מֵאֲכֹל לַחְמִי׃
food-of-me from-to-eat I-forget that heart-of-me and-he-is-withered

מִקּוֹל אַנְחָתִי דָּבְקָה עַצְמִי לִבְשָׂרִי׃
to-skin-of-me bone-of-me she-clings groaning-of-me because-of-loudness-of (6)

דָּמִיתִי לִקְאַת מִדְבָּר הָיִיתִי כְּכוֹס חֳרָבוֹת׃ שָׁקַדְתִּי
I-lie-awake (8) ruins like-owl-of I-am desert to-owl-of I-am-like (7)

וָאֶהְיֶה כְּצִפּוֹר בּוֹדֵד עַל־ גָּג׃ כָּל־ הַיּוֹם
the-day all-of (9) housetop on one-being-alone like-bird and-I-became

חֵרְפוּנִי אוֹיְבָי מְהוֹלָלַי בִּי
by-me ones-railing-against-me ones-being-enemies-of-me they-taunt-me

נִשְׁבָּעוּ׃ כִּי־ אֵפֶר כַּלֶּחֶם אָכָלְתִּי וְשִׁקֻּוַי בִּבְכִי
with-tear and-drinks-of-me I-eat as-the-food ash for (10) they-curse

מָסָכְתִּי׃ מִפְּנֵי־ זַעַמְךָ וְקִצְפֶּךָ כִּי נְשָׂאתַנִי
you-took-up-me for and-wrath-of-you anger-of-you because-of (11) I-mingle

וַתַּשְׁלִיכֵנִי׃ יָמַי כְּצֵל נָטוּי וַאֲנִי
and-I one-being-long like-shadow days-of-me (12) and-you-threw-aside-me

him will I not endure.

6 My eyes will be on the faithful
in the land,
that they may dwell with
me;
he whose walk is blameless
will minister to me.

7 No one who practices deceit
will dwell in my house;
no one who speaks falsely
will stand in my presence.

8 Every morning I will put to
silence
all the wicked in the land;
I will cut off every evildoer
from the city of the LORD.

Psalm 102

A prayer of an afflicted man. When he is faint and pours out his lament before the LORD.

1 Hear my prayer, O LORD;
let my cry for help come to
you.
2 Do not hide your face from me
when I am in distress.
Turn your ear to me;
when I call, answer me
quickly.

3 For my days vanish like
smoke;
my bones burn like glowing
embers.
4 My heart is blighted and
withered like grass;
I forget to eat my food.
5 Because of my loud groaning
I am reduced to skin and
bones.
6 I am like a desert owl,
like an owl among the ruins.
7 I lie awake; I have become
like a bird alone on a
housetop.
8 All day long my enemies taunt
me;
those who rail against me
use my name as a curse.
9 For I eat ashes as my food
and mingle my drink with
tears
10 because of your great wrath,
for you have taken me up
and thrown me aside.
11 My days are like the evening
shadow;

*Heading, 1 See the note on page 349.

‡4 Most mss treat these two words as one (כמוקד).

כְּעֵשֶׂב אִיבָשׁ׃ וְאַתָּה יְהוָה לְעוֹלָם תֵּשֵׁב

you-sit-enthroned to-forever Yahweh but-you (13) I-wither-away like-the-grass

וְזִכְרְךָ לְדֹר וָדֹר׃ אַתָּה תָקוּם

you-will-arise you (14) and-generation to-generation and-renown-of-you

תְּרַחֵם צִיּוֹן כִּי־ עֵת לְחֶנְנָהּ כִּי־ בָא

he-came for to-show-favor-to-her time for Zion you-will-have-compassion-on

מוֹעֵד׃ כִּי־ רָצוּ עֲבָדֶיךָ אֶת־ אֲבָנֶיהָ וְאֶת־

and stones-of-her *** servants-of-you they-are-dear for (15) appointed-time

עֲפָרָהּ יְחֹנֵנוּ׃ וְיִירְאוּ גוֹיִם אֶת־ שֵׁם

name-of *** nations and-they-will-fear (16) they-move-to-pity dust-of-her

יְהוָה וְכָל־ מַלְכֵי הָאָרֶץ אֶת־ כְּבוֹדֶךָ׃ כִּי־ בָנָה

he-will-rebuild for (17) glory-of-you *** the-earth kings-of and-all-of Yahweh

יְהוָה צִיּוֹן נִרְאָה בִּכְבוֹדוֹ׃ פָּנָה אֶל־ תְּפִלַּת

prayer-of to he-will-respond (18) in-glory-of-him he-will-appear Zion Yahweh

הָעַרְעָר וְלֹא־ בָזָה אֶת־ תְּפִלָּתָם׃ תִּכָּתֶב

let-her-be-written (19) plea-of-them *** he-will-despise and-not the-destitute

זֹאת לְדוֹר אַחֲרוֹן וְעַם נִבְרָא יְהַלֶּל־

he-may-praise one-being-created that-people future for-generation this

יָהּ׃ כִּי־ הִשְׁקִיף מִמְּרוֹם קָדְשׁוֹ יְהוָה

Yahweh sanctuary-of-him from-high-place-of he-looked-down that (20) Yahweh

מִשָּׁמַיִם ׀ אֶל־ אֶרֶץ הִבִּיט׃ לִשְׁמֹעַ אֶנְקַת אָסִיר לְפַתֵּחַ

to-release prisoner groan-of to-hear (21) he-viewed earth to from-heavens

בְּנֵי תְמוּתָה׃ לְסַפֵּר בְּצִיּוֹן שֵׁם יְהוָה וּתְהִלָּתוֹ

and-praise-of-him Yahweh name-of in-Zion to-declare (22) death men-of

בִּירוּשָׁלִָם׃ בְּהִקָּבֵץ עַמִּים יַחְדָּו וּמַמְלָכוֹת לַעֲבֹד

to-worship and-kingdoms together peoples when-to-assemble (23) in-Jerusalem

אֶת־ יְהוָה׃ עִנָּה בַדֶּרֶךְ כֹּחוֹ° קִצַּר יָמָי׃

days-of-me he-cut-short strength-of-me in-the-course he-broke (24) Yahweh ***

אֹמַר אֵלִי אַל־ תַּעֲלֵנִי בַּחֲצִי יָמָי

days-of-me in-midst-of you-take-away-me not God-of-me I-said (25)

בְּדוֹר דּוֹרִים שְׁנוֹתֶיךָ׃ לְפָנִים הָאָרֶץ

the-earth in-beginning (26) years-of-you generations through-generation-of

יָסַדְתָּ וּמַעֲשֵׂה יָדֶיךָ שָׁמָיִם׃ הֵמָּה ׀ יֹאבֵדוּ

they-will-perish they (27) heavens hands-of-you and-work-of you-founded

וְאַתָּה תַּעֲמֹד וְכֻלָּם כַּבֶּגֶד יִבְלוּ

they-will-wear-out like-the-garment and-all-of-them you-remain but-you

כַּלְּבוּשׁ תַּחֲלִיפֵם וְיַחֲלֹפוּ׃ וְאַתָּה־

but-you (28) and-they-will-be-discarded you-will-change-them like-the-clothing

I wither away like grass.
12 But you, O LORD, sit enthroned
forever;
your renown endures
through all generations.
13 You will arise and have
compassion on Zion,
for it is time to show favor
to her;
the appointed time has
come.
14 For her stones are dear to your
servants;
her very dust moves them to
pity.
15 The nations will fear the name
of the LORD,
all the kings of the earth
will revere your glory.
16 For the LORD will rebuild Zion
and appear in his glory.
17 He will respond to the prayer
of the destitute;
he will not despise their
plea.

18 Let this be written for a future
generation,
that a people not yet created
may praise the LORD:
19 "The LORD looked down from
his sanctuary on high,
from heaven he viewed the
earth,
20 to hear the groans of the
prisoners
and release those
condemned to death."
21 So the name of the LORD will
be declared in Zion
and his praise in Jerusalem
22 when the peoples and the
kingdoms
assemble to worship the
LORD.

23 In the course of my life[n] he
broke my strength;
he cut short my days.
24 So I said:
"Do not take me away, O
my God, in the midst of
my days;
your years go on through all
generations.
25 In the beginning you laid the
foundations of the earth,
and the heavens are the
work of your hands.
26 They will perish, but you
remain;
they will all wear out like a
garment.
Like clothing you will change
them
and they will be discarded.

[n]23 Or *By his power*

*See the note on page 349.

°24 ק כחי

הוּא וּשְׁנוֹתֶיךָ לֹא יִתָּמּוּ׃ בְּנֵי־ עֲבָדֶיךָ
servants-of-you children-of (29) they-end never and-years-of-you same

יִשְׁכּוֹנוּ וְזַרְעָם לְפָנֶיךָ יִכּוֹן׃
he-will-be-established before-you and-descendant-of-them they-will-live

לְדָוִד ׀ בָּרְכִי נַפְשִׁי אֶת־ יְהוָה וְכָל־ קְרָבַי
inmost-beings-of-me and-all-of Yahweh *** soul-of-me praise! of-David (103:1)

אֶת־ שֵׁם קָדְשׁוֹ׃ בָּרְכִי נַפְשִׁי אֶת־ יְהוָה וְאַל־
and-not Yahweh *** soul-of-me praise! (2) holiness-of-him name-of ***

תִּשְׁכְּחִי כָּל־ גְּמוּלָיו׃ הַסֹּלֵחַ לְכָל־ עֲוֺנֵכִי
sin-of-you to-all-of the-one-forgiving (3) benefits-of-him all-of you-forget

הָרֹפֵא לְכָל־ תַּחֲלֻאָיְכִי׃ הַגּוֹאֵל מִשַּׁחַת
from-pit the-one-redeeming (4) diseases-of-you to-all-of the-one-healing

חַיָּיְכִי הַמְעַטְּרֵכִי חֶסֶד וְרַחֲמִים׃ הַמַּשְׂבִּיעַ
the-one-satisfying (5) and-compassions love the-one-crowning-you lives-of-you

בַּטּוֹב עֶדְיֵךְ תִּתְחַדֵּשׁ כַּנֶּשֶׁר נְעוּרָיְכִי׃
youths-of-you like-the-eagle she-is-renewed desire-of-you with-the-good

עֹשֵׂה צְדָקוֹת יְהוָה וּמִשְׁפָּטִים לְכָל־
for-all-of and-justices Yahweh righteousnesses one-working-of (6)

עֲשׁוּקִים׃ יוֹדִיעַ דְּרָכָיו לְמֹשֶׁה לִבְנֵי
to-peoples-of to-Moses ways-of-him he-made-known (7) ones-being-oppressed

יִשְׂרָאֵל עֲלִילוֹתָיו׃ רַחוּם וְחַנּוּן יְהוָה אֶרֶךְ אַפַּיִם
angers slow-of Yahweh and-gracious compassionate (8) deeds-of-him Israel

וְרַב־ חָסֶד׃ לֹא־ לָנֶצַח יָרִיב וְלֹא לְעוֹלָם
to-forever and-not he-will-accuse to-always not (9) love and-abundant-of

יִטּוֹר׃ לֹא כַחֲטָאֵינוּ עָשָׂה לָנוּ וְלֹא
and-not to-us he-treats as-sins-of-us not (10) he-will-harbor-anger

כַעֲוֺנֹתֵינוּ גָּמַל עָלֵינוּ׃ כִּי כִגְבֹהַּ שָׁמַיִם עַל־
above heavens as-to-be-high for (11) to-us he-repays as-iniquities-of-us

הָאָרֶץ גָּבַר חַסְדּוֹ עַל־ יְרֵאָיו׃ כִּרְחֹק
as-to-be-far (12) ones-fearing-him for love-of-him he-is-great the-earth

מִזְרָח מִמַּעֲרָב הִרְחִיק מִמֶּנּוּ אֶת־ פְּשָׁעֵינוּ׃
transgressions-of-us *** from-us he-removed-far from-west east

כְּרַחֵם אָב עַל־ בָּנִים רִחַם יְהוָה עַל־
on Yahweh he-has-compassion children on father as-to-have-compassion (13)

יְרֵאָיו׃ כִּי־ הוּא יָדַע יִצְרֵנוּ זָכוּר כִּי־
that one-being-reminded form-of-us he-knows he for (14) ones-fearing-him

עָפָר אֲנָחְנוּ׃ אֱנוֹשׁ כֶּחָצִיר יָמָיו כְּצִיץ הַשָּׂדֶה כֵּן
so the-field like-flower-of days-of-him like-the-grass man (15) we dust

27 But you remain the same,
and your years will never end.
28 The children of your servants will live in your presence;
their descendants will be established before you."

Psalm 103

Of David.

1 Praise the LORD, O my soul;
all my inmost being, praise his holy name.
2 Praise the LORD, O my soul,
and forget not all his benefits.

3 He forgives all my[o] sins
and heals all my diseases;
4 he redeems my life from the pit
and crowns me with love and compassion.
5 He satisfies my desires with good things,
so that my youth is renewed like the eagle's.
6 The LORD works righteousness
and justice for all the oppressed.
7 He made known his ways to Moses,
his deeds to the people of Israel:
8 The LORD is compassionate and gracious,
slow to anger, abounding in love.
9 He will not always accuse,
nor will he harbor his anger forever;
10 he does not treat us as our sins deserve
or repay us according to our iniquities.
11 For as high as the heavens are above the earth,
so great is his love for those who fear him;
12 as far as the east is from the west,
so far has he removed our transgressions from us.
13 As a father has compassion on his children,
so the LORD has compassion on those who fear him;
14 for he knows how we are formed,
he remembers that we are dust.
15 As for man, his days are like grass,
he flourishes like a flower of the field;

o3 Hebrew *your* (referring to *my soul*); also in verses 3b-5

*See the note on page 349.

יָצִיץ׃ כִּי רוּחַ עָבְרָה־ בּוֹ וְאֵינֶנּוּ וְלֹא־
and-not and-not-he over-him she-blows wind for (16) he-flourishes

יַכִּירֶנּוּ עוֹד מְקוֹמוֹ׃ וְחֶסֶד יְהוָה מֵעוֹלָם
from-everlasting Yahweh but-love-of (17) place-of-him more he-remembers-him

וְעַד־ עוֹלָם עַל־ יְרֵאָיו וְצִדְקָתוֹ
and-righteousness-of-him ones-fearing-him with everlasting and-to

לִבְנֵי בָנִים׃ לְשֹׁמְרֵי בְרִיתוֹ
covenant-of-him with-ones-keeping-of (18) children with-children-of

וּלְזֹכְרֵי פִקֻּדָיו לַעֲשׂוֹתָם׃ יְהוָה
Yahweh (19) to-obey-them precepts-of-him and-with-ones-remembering-of

בַּשָּׁמַיִם הֵכִין כִּסְאוֹ וּמַלְכוּתוֹ בַּכֹּל
over-the-all and-kingdom-of-him throne-of-him he-established in-the-heavens

מָשָׁלָה׃ בָּרְכוּ יְהוָה מַלְאָכָיו גִּבֹּרֵי כֹחַ
strength mighty-ones-of angels-of-him Yahweh praise! (20) she-rules

עֹשֵׂי דְבָרוֹ לִשְׁמֹעַ בְּקוֹל דְּבָרוֹ׃ בָּרְכוּ
praise! (21) word-of-him to-voice-of to-obey bidding-of-him ones-doing-of

יְהוָה כָּל־ צְבָאָיו מְשָׁרְתָיו עֹשֵׂי רְצוֹנוֹ׃
will-of-him ones-doing-of ones-serving-him hosts-of-him all-of Yahweh

בָּרְכוּ יְהוָה כָּל־ מַעֲשָׂיו בְּכָל־ מְקֹמוֹת מֶמְשַׁלְתּוֹ
dominion-of-him places-of in-all-of works-of-him all-of Yahweh praise! (22)

בָּרְכִי נַפְשִׁי אֶת־ יְהוָה׃ בָּרְכִי נַפְשִׁי אֶת־ יְהוָה יְהוָה
Yahweh Yahweh *** soul-of-me praise! (104:1) Yahweh *** soul-of-me praise!

אֱלֹהַי גָּדַלְתָּ מְּאֹד הוֹד וְהָדָר לָבָשְׁתָּ׃
you-are-clothed and-majesty splendor very you-are-great God-of-me

עֹטֶה־ אוֹר כַּשַּׂלְמָה נוֹטֶה שָׁמַיִם
heavens one-stretching-out as-the-garment light one-wrapping-himself (2)

כַּיְרִיעָה׃ הַמְקָרֶה בַמַּיִם עֲלִיּוֹתָיו
upper-chambers-of-him on-the-waters the-one-laying-beams (3) like-the-tent

הַשָּׂם־ עָבִים רְכוּבוֹ הַמְהַלֵּךְ עַל־ כַּנְפֵי־ רוּחַ׃
wind wings-of on the-one-riding chariot-of-him clouds the-one-making

עֹשֶׂה מַלְאָכָיו רוּחוֹת מְשָׁרְתָיו אֵשׁ לֹהֵט׃
flaming fire ones-serving-him winds messengers-of-him one-making (4)

יָסַד־ אֶרֶץ עַל־ מְכוֹנֶיהָ בַּל־ תִּמּוֹט עוֹלָם וָעֶד׃
and-ever for-ever she-can-be-moved not foundations-of-her on earth he-set (5)

תְּהוֹם כַּלְּבוּשׁ כִּסִּיתוֹ עַל־ הָרִים יַעַמְדוּ־ מָיִם׃
waters they-stood mountains above you-covered-him as-the-garment deep (6)

מִן־ גַּעֲרָתְךָ יְנוּסוּן מִן־ קוֹל רַעַמְךָ יֵחָפֵזוּן׃
they-took-to-flight thunder-of-you sound-of at they-fled rebuke-of-you at (7)

16 the wind blows over it and it
is gone,
and its place remembers it
no more.
17 But from everlasting to
everlasting
the LORD's love is with those
who fear him,
and his righteousness with
their children's children—
18 with those who keep his
covenant
and remember to obey his
precepts.

19 The LORD has established his
throne in heaven,
and his kingdom rules over
all.

20 Praise the LORD, you his
angels,
you mighty ones who do his
bidding,
who obey his word.
21 Praise the LORD, all his
heavenly hosts,
you his servants who do his
will.
22 Praise the LORD, all his works
everywhere in his
dominion.

Praise the LORD, O my soul.

Psalm 104

1 Praise the LORD, O my soul.

O LORD my God, you are very
great;
you are clothed with
splendor and majesty.
2 He wraps himself in light as
with a garment;
he stretches out the heavens
like a tent
3 and lays the beams of his
upper chambers on their
waters.
He makes the clouds his
chariot
and rides on the wings of
the wind.
4 He makes winds his
messengers,[p]
flames of fire his servants.

5 He set the earth on its
foundations;
it can never be moved.
6 You covered it with the deep
as with a garment;
the waters stood above the
mountains.
7 But at your rebuke the waters
fled,
at the sound of your
thunder they took to
flight;

[p]4 Or *angels*

יַעֲלוּ הָרִים יֵרְדוּ בְקָעוֹת אֶל־מְקוֹם זֶה ׀
which place-of to valleys they-went-down mountains they-flowed-over (8)

יָסַדְתָּ לָהֶם׃ גְּבוּל־ שַׂמְתָּ בַּל־ יַעֲבֹרוּן בַּל־
never they-can-cross not you-set boundary (9) for-them you-assigned

יְשׁוּבוּן לְכַסּוֹת הָאָרֶץ׃ הַמְשַׁלֵּחַ מַעְיָנִים
springs the-one-making-pour (10) the-earth to-cover they-will-come-again

בַּנְּחָלִים בֵּין הָרִים יְהַלֵּכוּן׃ יַשְׁקוּ כָּל־
all-of they-give-water (11) they-flow mountains between into-the-ravines

חַיְתוֹ שָׂדָי יִשְׁבְּרוּ פְרָאִים צְמָאָם׃ עֲלֵיהֶם עוֹף־
bird-of by-them (12) thirst-of-them donkeys they-quench field beast-of

הַשָּׁמַיִם יִשְׁכּוֹן מִבֵּין עֳפָאיִם יִתְּנוּ־ קוֹל׃ מַשְׁקֶה
one-watering (13) song they-give branches in-among they-nest the-airs

הָרִים מֵעֲלִיּוֹתָיו מִפְּרִי מַעֲשֶׂיךָ תִּשְׂבַּע
she-is-satisfied works-of-you by-fruit-of from-upper-chambers-of-him mountains

הָאָרֶץ׃ מַצְמִיחַ חָצִיר ׀ לַבְּהֵמָה וְעֵשֶׂב לַעֲבֹדַת
for-cultivation-of and-plant for-the-cattle grass one-making-grow (14) the-earth

הָאָדָם לְהוֹצִיא לֶחֶם מִן־ הָאָרֶץ׃ וְיַיִן ׀ יְשַׂמַּח
he-makes-glad and-wine (15) the-earth from food to-bring-forth the-man

לְבַב־ אֱנוֹשׁ לְהַצְהִיל פָּנִים מִשָּׁמֶן וְלֶחֶם לְבַב־ אֱנוֹשׁ יִסְעָד׃
he-sustains man heart-of and-bread with-oil faces to-make-shine man heart-of

יִשְׂבְּעוּ עֲצֵי יְהוָה אַרְזֵי לְבָנוֹן אֲשֶׁר נָטָע׃
he-planted that Lebanon cedars-of Yahweh trees-of they-are-well-watered (16)

אֲשֶׁר־ שָׁם צִפֳּרִים יְקַנֵּנוּ חֲסִידָה בְּרוֹשִׁים בֵּיתָהּ׃
home-of-her pine-trees stork they-make-nests birds there where (17)

הָרִים הַגְּבֹהִים לַיְּעֵלִים סְלָעִים מַחְסֶה לַשְׁפַנִּים׃
for-the-coneys refuge crags to-the-wild-goats the-high-ones mountains (18)

עָשָׂה יָרֵחַ לְמוֹעֲדִים שֶׁמֶשׁ יָדַע מְבוֹאוֹ׃
going-down-of-him he-knows sun to-seasons moon he-marks-off (19)

תָּשֶׁת־ חֹשֶׁךְ וִיהִי לָיְלָה בּוֹ־ תִרְמֹשׂ כָּל־
all-of she-prowls in-him night and-he-becomes darkness you-bring (20)

חַיְתוֹ־ יָעַר׃ הַכְּפִירִים שֹׁאֲגִים לַטָּרֶף וּלְבַקֵּשׁ מֵאֵל
from-God and-to-seek for-the-prey ones-roaring the-lions (21) forest beast-of

אָכְלָם׃ תִּזְרַח הַשֶּׁמֶשׁ יֵאָסֵפוּן וְאֶל־ מְעוֹנֹתָם
dens-of-them and-into they-steal-away the-sun she-rises (22) food-of-them

יִרְבָּצוּן׃ יֵצֵא אָדָם לְפָעֳלוֹ וְלַעֲבֹדָתוֹ עֲדֵי־
until and-to-labor-of-him to-work-of-him man he-goes-out (23) they-lie-down

עָרֶב׃ מָה־ רַבּוּ מַעֲשֶׂיךָ ׀ יְהוָה כֻּלָּם בְּחָכְמָה
in-wisdom all-of-them Yahweh works-of-you they-are-many how! (24) evening

8 they flowed over the mountains,
they went down into the valleys,
to the place you assigned for them.
9 You set a boundary they cannot cross;
never again will they cover the earth.

10 He makes springs pour water into the ravines;
it flows between the mountains.
11 They give water to all the beasts of the field;
the wild donkeys quench their thirst.
12 The birds of the air nest by the waters;
they sing among the branches.
13 He waters the mountains from his upper chambers;
the earth is satisfied by the fruit of his work.
14 He makes grass grow for the cattle,
and plants for man to cultivate—
bringing forth food from the earth:
15 wine that gladdens the heart of man,
oil to make his face shine,
and bread that sustains his heart.
16 The trees of the LORD are well watered,
the cedars of Lebanon that he planted.
17 There the birds make their nests;
the stork has its home in the pine trees.
18 The high mountains belong to the wild goats;
the crags are a refuge for the coneys.[q]

19 The moon marks off the seasons,
and the sun knows when to go down.
20 You bring darkness, it becomes night,
and all the beasts of the forest prowl.
21 The lions roar for their prey
and seek their food from God.
22 The sun rises, and they steal away;
they return and lie down in their dens.
23 Then man goes out to his work,
to his labor until evening.

24 How many are your works, O LORD!
In wisdom you made them all;

q18 That is, the hyrax or rock badger

עָשִׂיתָ מָלְאָה הָאָרֶץ קִנְיָנֶךָ׃ זֶה ׀ הַיָּם גָּדוֹל

vast the-sea there (25) creature-of-you the-earth she-is-full you-made

וּרְחַב יָדָיִם שָׁם־ רֶמֶשׂ וְאֵין מִסְפָּר חַיּוֹת קְטַנּוֹת

small-ones living-things number and-no creature there hands and-spacious-of

עִם־ גְּדֹלוֹת׃ שָׁם אֳנִיּוֹת יְהַלֵּכוּן לִוְיָתָן זֶה־ יָצַרְתָּ

you-formed which leviathan they-go-about ships there (26) large-ones and

לְשַׂחֶק־ בּוֹ׃ כֻּלָּם אֵלֶיךָ יְשַׂבֵּרוּן לָתֵת אָכְלָם

food-of-them to-give they-look to-you all-of-them (27) in-him to-frolic

בְּעִתּוֹ׃ תִּתֵּן לָהֶם יִלְקֹטוּן תִּפְתַּח יָדְךָ

hand-of-you you-open they-gather to-them you-give (28) at-time-of-him

יִשְׂבְּעוּן טוֹב׃ תַּסְתִּיר פָּנֶיךָ יִבָּהֵלוּן

they-are-terrified faces-of-you you-hide (29) good they-are-satisfied

תֹּסֵף רוּחָם יִגְוָעוּן וְאֶל־ עֲפָרָם יְשׁוּבוּן׃

they-return dust-of-them and-to they-die breath-of-them you-take-away

תְּשַׁלַּח רוּחֲךָ יִבָּרֵאוּן וּתְחַדֵּשׁ פְּנֵי אֲדָמָה׃

earth faces-of and-you-renew they-are-created Spirit-of-you you-send (30)

יְהִי כְבוֹד יְהוָה לְעוֹלָם יִשְׂמַח יְהוָה

Yahweh may-he-rejoice to-forever Yahweh glory-of may-he-endure (31)

בְּמַעֲשָׂיו׃ הַמַּבִּיט לָאָרֶץ וַתִּרְעָד יִגַּע

he-touches and-she-trembles at-the-earth the-one-looking (32) in-works-of-him

בֶּהָרִים וְיֶעֱשָׁנוּ׃ אָשִׁירָה לַיהוָה בְּחַיָּי

during-lives-of-me to-Yahweh I-will-sing (33) and-they-smoke on-the-mountains

אֲזַמְּרָה לֵאלֹהַי בְּעוֹדִי׃ יֶעֱרַב עָלָיו

to-him may-he-be-pleasing (34) while-still-I to-God-of-me I-will-sing-praise

שִׂיחִי אָנֹכִי אֶשְׂמַח בַּיהוָה׃ יִתַּמּוּ חַטָּאִים ׀

sinners may-they-vanish (35) in-Yahweh I-rejoice I meditation-of-me

מִן־ הָאָרֶץ וּרְשָׁעִים ׀ עוֹד אֵינָם בָּרְכִי נַפְשִׁי אֶת־ יְהוָה

Yahweh *** soul-of-me praise! not-they more and-wicked-ones the-earth from

הַלְלוּ־ יָהּ׃ הוֹדוּ לַיהוָה קִרְאוּ בִּשְׁמוֹ

on-name-of-him call! to-Yahweh give-thanks! (105:1) Yahweh praise!

הוֹדִיעוּ בָעַמִּים עֲלִילוֹתָיו׃ שִׁירוּ־ לוֹ זַמְּרוּ־

sing-praise! to-him sing! (2) deeds-of-him among-the-nations make-known!

לוֹ שִׂיחוּ בְּכָל־ נִפְלְאוֹתָיו׃ הִתְהַלְלוּ בְּשֵׁם

in-name-of glory! (3) acts-being-wonderful-of-him of-all-of tell! to-him

קָדְשׁוֹ יִשְׂמַח לֵב ׀ מְבַקְשֵׁי יְהוָה׃ דִּרְשׁוּ

look-to! (4) Yahweh ones-seeking-of heart-of let-him-rejoice holiness-of-him

יְהוָה וְעֻזּוֹ בַּקְּשׁוּ פָנָיו תָּמִיד׃ זִכְרוּ

remember! (5) always faces-of-him seek! and-strength-of-him Yahweh

---

the earth is full of your
creatures.
25 There is the sea, vast and
spacious,
teeming with creatures
beyond number—
living things both large and
small.
26 There the ships go to and fro,
and the leviathan, which
you formed to frolic there.

27 These all look to you
to give them their food at
the proper time.
28 When you give it to them,
they gather it up;
when you open your hand,
they are satisfied with good
things.
29 When you hide your face,
they are terrified;
when you take away their
breath,
they die and return to the
dust.
30 When you send your Spirit,
they are created,
and you renew the face of
the earth.

31 May the glory of the LORD
endure forever;
may the LORD rejoice in his
works.
32 He looks at the earth, and it
trembles;
he touches the mountains,
and they smoke.

33 I will sing to the LORD all my
life;
I will sing praise to my God
as long as I live.
34 May my meditation be
pleasing to him,
as I rejoice in the LORD.
35 But may sinners vanish from
the earth
and the wicked be no more.

Praise the LORD, O my soul.

Praise the LORD.[r]

Psalm 105

1 Give thanks to the LORD, call
on his name;
make known among the
nations what he has
done.
2 Sing to him, sing praise to
him;
tell of all his wonderful acts.
3 Glory in his holy name;
let the hearts of those who
seek the LORD rejoice.
4 Look to the LORD and his
strength;
seek his face always.

r35 Hebrew *Hallelu Yah*

נִפְלְאוֹתָיו אֲשֶׁר־ עָשָׂה מֹפְתָיו וּמִשְׁפְּטֵי־
and-judgments-of miracles-of-him he-did that deeds-being-wonders-of-him

פִיו׃ זֶרַע אַבְרָהָם עַבְדּוֹ בְּנֵי יַעֲקֹב
Jacob sons-of servant-of-him Abraham descendant-of (6) mouth-of-him

בְּחִירָיו׃ הוּא יְהוָה אֱלֹהֵינוּ בְּכָל־ הָאָרֶץ מִשְׁפָּטָיו׃
judgments-of-him the-earth in-all-of God-of-us Yahweh he (7) chosen-ones-of-him

זָכַר לְעוֹלָם בְּרִיתוֹ דָּבָר צִוָּה לְאֶלֶף
for-thousand-of he-commanded word covenant-of-him to-forever he-remembers (8)

דּוֹר׃ אֲשֶׁר כָּרַת אֶת־ אַבְרָהָם וּשְׁבוּעָתוֹ לְיִשְׂחָק׃
to-Isaac and-oath-of-him Abraham with he-made that (9) generation

וַיַּעֲמִידֶהָ לְיַעֲקֹב לְחֹק לְיִשְׂרָאֵל בְּרִית עוֹלָם׃
everlasting covenant-of to-Israel as-decree to-Jacob and-he-confirmed-her (10)

לֵאמֹר לְךָ אֶתֵּן אֶת־ אֶרֶץ־ כְּנָעַן חֶבֶל נַחֲלַתְכֶם׃
inheritance-of-you portion-of Canaan land-of *** I-will-give to-you to-say (11)

בִּהְיוֹתָם מְתֵי מִסְפָּר כִּמְעַט וְגָרִים בָּהּ׃
in-her and-ones-being-strangers as-few number ones-few-of when-to-be-them (12)

וַיִּתְהַלְּכוּ מִגּוֹי אֶל־ גּוֹי מִמַּמְלָכָה אֶל־ עַם אַחֵר׃
another people to from-kingdom nation to from-nation then-they-wandered (13)

לֹא־ הִנִּיחַ אָדָם לְעָשְׁקָם וַיּוֹכַח עֲלֵיהֶם
for-sake-of-them and-he-rebuked to-oppress-them anyone he-allowed not (14)

מְלָכִים׃ אַל־ תִּגְּעוּ בִמְשִׁיחָי וְלִנְבִיאַי אַל־
not or-to-prophets-of-me on-anointed-ones-of-me you-touch not (15) kings

תָּרֵעוּ׃ וַיִּקְרָא רָעָב עַל־ הָאָרֶץ כָּל־ מַטֵּה־ לֶחֶם
food supply-of all-of the-land on famine and-he-called (16) you-harm

שָׁבָר׃ שָׁלַח לִפְנֵיהֶם אִישׁ לְעֶבֶד נִמְכַּר יוֹסֵף׃
Joseph he-was-sold as-slave man before-them he-sent (17) he-destroyed

עִנּוּ בַכֶּבֶל רַגְלָיו בַּרְזֶל בָּאָה נַפְשׁוֹ׃
neck-of-him she-entered iron foot-of-him with-the-shackle they-bruised (18)

עַד־ עֵת בֹּא־ דְבָרוֹ אִמְרַת יְהוָה
Yahweh word-of foretelling-of-him to-come-to-pass time-of till (19)

צְרָפָתְהוּ׃ שָׁלַח מֶלֶךְ וַיַּתִּירֵהוּ מֹשֵׁל עַמִּים
peoples one-ruling and-he-released-him king he-sent (20) she-proved-true-him

וַיְפַתְּחֵהוּ׃ שָׂמוֹ אָדוֹן לְבֵיתוֹ וּמֹשֵׁל
and-one-ruling of-household-of-him master he-made-him (21) and-he-set-free-him

בְּכָל־ קִנְיָנוֹ׃ לֶאְסֹר שָׂרָיו
princes-of-him to-discipline (22) possession-of-him over-all-of

בְּנַפְשׁוֹ וּזְקֵנָיו יְחַכֵּם׃ וַיָּבֹא
then-he-entered (23) he-taught-wisdom and-elders-of-him as-pleasure-of-him

5 Remember the wonders he has
done,
his miracles, and the
judgments he
pronounced,
6 O descendants of Abraham his
servant,
O sons of Jacob, his chosen
ones.
7 He is the LORD our God;
his judgments are in all the
earth.
8 He remembers his covenant
forever,
the word he commanded,
for a thousand
generations,
9 the covenant he made with
Abraham,
the oath he swore to Isaac.
10 He confirmed it to Jacob as a
decree,
to Israel as an everlasting
covenant:
11 "To you I will give the land of
Canaan
as the portion you will
inherit."

12 When they were but few in
number,
few indeed, and strangers in
it,
13 they wandered from nation to
nation,
from one kingdom to
another.
14 He allowed no one to oppress
them;
for their sake he rebuked
kings:
15 "Do not touch my anointed
ones;
do my prophets no harm."

16 He called down famine on the
land
and destroyed all their
supplies of food;
17 and he sent a man before
them—
Joseph, sold as a slave.
18 They bruised his feet with
shackles,
his neck was put in irons,
19 till what he foretold came to
pass,
till the word of the LORD
proved him true.
20 The king sent and released
him,
the ruler of peoples set him
free.
21 He made him master of his
household,
ruler over all he possessed,
22 to discipline his princes as he
pleased
and teach his elders
wisdom.

°18 ק רגלו

יִשְׂרָאֵל מִצְרָיִם וְיַעֲקֹב גָּר בְּאֶרֶץ־ חָם׃ וַיֶּפֶר
and-he-made-fruitful (24) Ham in-land-of he-lived-as-alien and-Jacob Egypt Israel

אֶת־ עַמּוֹ מְאֹד וַיַּעֲצִמֵהוּ מִצָּרָיו׃
more-than-foes-of-him and-he-made-numerous-him very people-of-him ***

הָפַךְ לִבָּם לִשְׂנֹא עַמּוֹ לְהִתְנַכֵּל
to-conspire people-of-him to-hate heart-of-them he-turned (25)

בַּעֲבָדָיו׃ שָׁלַח מֹשֶׁה עַבְדּוֹ אַהֲרֹן אֲשֶׁר בָּחַר־
he-chose whom Aaron servant-of-him Moses he-sent (26) against-servants-of-him

בּוֹ׃ שָׂמוּ־ בָם דִּבְרֵי אֹתוֹתָיו וּמֹפְתִים
and-wonders signs-of-him deeds-of among-them they-performed (27) to-him

בְּאֶרֶץ חָם׃ שָׁלַח חֹשֶׁךְ וַיַּחְשִׁךְ וְלֹא־ מָרוּ
they-rebelled for-not and-he-made-dark darkness he-sent (28) Ham in-land-of

אֶת־ °דְּבָרוֹו׃ הָפַךְ אֶת־ מֵימֵיהֶם לְדָם
into-blood waters-of-them *** he-turned (29) *word-of-him against

וַיָּמֶת אֶת־ דְּגָתָם׃ שָׁרַץ אַרְצָם צְפַרְדְּעִים
frogs land-of-them he-teemed (30) fish-of-them *** and-he-caused-to-die

בְּחַדְרֵי מַלְכֵיהֶם׃ אָמַר וַיָּבֹא עָרֹב כִּנִּים
gnats swarm-of-flies and-he-came he-spoke (31) rulers-of-them into-bedrooms-of

בְּכָל־ גְּבוּלָם׃ נָתַן גִּשְׁמֵיהֶם בָּרָד אֵשׁ
flame-of hail rains-of-them he-turned (32) country-of-them through-all-of

לֶהָבוֹת בְּאַרְצָם׃ וַיַּךְ גַּפְנָם
vine-of-them and-he-struck-down (33) through-land-of-them lightnings

וּתְאֵנָתָם וַיְשַׁבֵּר עֵץ גְּבוּלָם׃ אָמַר
he-spoke (34) country-of-them tree-of and-he-shattered and-fig-tree-of-them

וַיָּבֹא אַרְבֶּה וְיֶלֶק וְאֵין מִסְפָּר׃ וַיֹּאכַל כָּל־
every-of and-he-ate-up (35) number with-no and-grasshopper locust and-he-came

עֵשֶׂב בְּאַרְצָם וַיֹּאכַל פְּרִי אַדְמָתָם׃
soil-of-them produce-of and-he-ate-up in-land-of-them green-thing

וַיַּךְ כָּל־ בְּכוֹר בְּאַרְצָם רֵאשִׁית לְכָל־
of-all-of firstfruit in-land-of-them firstborn all-of then-he-struck-down (36)

אוֹנָם׃ וַיּוֹצִיאֵם בְּכֶסֶף וְזָהָב וְאֵין
and-no-one and-gold with-silver and-he-brought-out-them (37) manhood-of-them

בִּשְׁבָטָיו כּוֹשֵׁל׃ שָׂמַח מִצְרַיִם בְּצֵאתָם
when-to-leave-them Egypt he-was-glad (38) faltering among-tribes-of-him

כִּי־ נָפַל פַּחְדָּם עֲלֵיהֶם׃ פָּרַשׂ עָנָן לְמָסָךְ
as-covering cloud he-spread-out (39) on-them dread-of-them he-fell because

וְאֵשׁ לְהָאִיר לָיְלָה׃ שָׁאַל וַיָּבֵא שְׂלָו וְלֶחֶם
and-bread-of quail and-he-brought he-asked (40) night to-give-light and-fire

[23]Then Israel entered Egypt;
Jacob lived as an alien in
the land of Ham.
[24]The LORD made his people
very fruitful;
he made them too numerous
for their foes,
[25]whose hearts he turned to hate
his people,
to conspire against his
servants.
[26]He sent Moses his servant,
and Aaron, whom he had
chosen.
[27]They performed his miraculous
signs among them,
his wonders in the land of
Ham.
[28]He sent darkness and made
the land dark—
for had they not rebelled
against his words?
[29]He turned their waters into
blood,
causing their fish to die.
[30]Their land teemed with frogs,
which went up into the
bedrooms of their rulers.
[31]He spoke, and there came
swarms of flies,
and gnats throughout their
country.
[32]He turned their rain into hail,
with lightning throughout
their land;
[33]he struck down their vines
and fig trees
and shattered the trees of
their country.
[34]He spoke, and the locusts
came,
grasshoppers without
number;
[35]they ate up every green thing
in their land,
ate up the produce of their
soil.
[36]Then he struck down all the
firstborn in their land,
the firstfruits of all their
manhood.

[37]He brought out Israel, laden
with silver and gold,
and from among their tribes
no one faltered.
[38]Egypt was glad when they left,
because dread of Israel had
fallen on them.
[39]He spread out a cloud as a
covering,
and a fire to give light at
night.
[40]They asked, and he brought
them quail

*28 Many mss point the *Kethib* form as a plural (ָ־יו).

°28 ק דברו

שָׁמַיִם יַשְׂבִּיעֵם׃ (41) פָּתַח צוּר וַיָּזוּבוּ מָיִם

waters and-they-gushed-out rock he-opened (41) he-satisfied-them heavens

הָלְכוּ בַּצִּיּוֹת נָהָר׃ (42) כִּי־ זָכַר אֶת־ דְּבַר

promise-of *** he-remembered for (42) river in-the-deserts they-flowed

קָדְשׁוֹ אֶת־ אַבְרָהָם עַבְדּוֹ׃ (43) וַיּוֹצִא

and-he-brought-out (43) servant-of-him Abraham with holiness-of-him

עַמּוֹ בְשָׂשׂוֹן בְּרִנָּה אֶת־ בְּחִירָיו׃

chosen-ones-of-him *** with-shout-of-joy with-rejoicing people-of-him

(44) וַיִּתֵּן לָהֶם אַרְצוֹת גּוֹיִם וַעֲמַל לְאֻמִּים יִירָשׁוּ׃

they-inherited peoples and-toil-of nations lands-of to-them and-he-gave (44)

(45) בַּעֲבוּר ׀ יִשְׁמְרוּ חֻקָּיו וְתוֹרֹתָיו יִנְצֹרוּ

they-might-observe and-laws-of-him precepts-of-him they-might-keep so-that (45)

הַלְלוּ־ יָהּ׃ (106:1) הַלְלוּיָהּ ׀ הוֹדוּ לַיהוָה כִּי־ טוֹב כִּי

for good for to-Yahweh give-thanks! praise-Yahweh! (106:1) Yahweh praise!

לְעוֹלָם חַסְדּוֹ׃ (2) מִי יְמַלֵּל גְּבוּרוֹת יְהוָה

Yahweh mighty-acts-of he-can-proclaim who? (2) love-of-him to-forever

יַשְׁמִיעַ כָּל־ תְּהִלָּתוֹ׃ (3) אַשְׁרֵי

blessednesses-of (3) praise-of-him fullness-of he-can-declare

שֹׁמְרֵי מִשְׁפָּט עֹשֵׂה צְדָקָה בְכָל־ עֵת׃ (4) זָכְרֵנִי

remember-me! (4) time at-all-of right one-doing-of justice ones-maintaining-of

יְהוָה בִּרְצוֹן עַמֶּךָ פָּקְדֵנִי בִּישׁוּעָתֶךָ׃

in-salvation-of-you come-to-aid-of-me! people-of-you in-favor-of Yahweh

(5) לִרְאוֹת ׀ בְּטוֹבַת בְּחִירֶיךָ לִשְׂמֹחַ בְּשִׂמְחַת

in-joy-of to-have-joy chosen-ones-of-you to-prosperity-of to-enjoy (5)

גּוֹיֶךָ לְהִתְהַלֵּל עִם־ נַחֲלָתֶךָ׃ (6) חָטָאנוּ עִם־

with we-sinned (6) inheritance-of-you with to-give-praise nation-of-you

אֲבוֹתֵינוּ הֶעֱוִינוּ הִרְשָׁעְנוּ׃ (7) אֲבוֹתֵינוּ בְמִצְרַיִם ׀ לֹא־

not in-Egypt fathers-of-us (7) we-acted-wickedly we-did-wrong fathers-of-us

הִשְׂכִּילוּ נִפְלְאוֹתֶיךָ לֹא זָכְרוּ אֶת־ רֹב

many-of *** they-remembered not deeds-being-miracles-of-you they-gave-thought

חֲסָדֶיךָ וַיַּמְרוּ עַל־ יָם בְּיַם־ סוּף׃ (8) וַיּוֹשִׁיעֵם

yet-he-saved-them (8) Reed by-Sea-of sea by and-they-rebelled kindnesses-of-you

לְמַעַן שְׁמוֹ לְהוֹדִיעַ אֶת־ גְּבוּרָתוֹ׃ (9) וַיִּגְעַר

and-he-rebuked (9) power-of-him *** to-make-known name-of-him for-sake-of

בְּיַם־ סוּף וַיֶּחֱרָב וַיּוֹלִיכֵם בַּתְּהֹמוֹת

through-the-depths and-he-led-them and-he-dried-up Reed to-Sea-of

כַּמִּדְבָּר׃ (10) וַיּוֹשִׁיעֵם מִיַּד שׂוֹנֵא

one-being-foe from-hand-of and-he-saved-them (10) as-the-desert

and satisfied them with the bread of heaven.
41 He opened the rock, and water gushed out;
like a river it flowed in the desert.
42 For he remembered his holy promise
given to his servant Abraham.
43 He brought out his people with rejoicing,
his chosen ones with shouts of joy;
44 he gave them the lands of the nations,
and they fell heir to what others had toiled for—
45 that they might keep his precepts
and observe his laws.

Praise the LORD.[s]

Psalm 106

1 Praise the LORD.[t]

Give thanks to the LORD, for he is good;
his love endures forever.
2 Who can proclaim the mighty acts of the LORD
or fully declare his praise?
3 Blessed are they who maintain justice,
who constantly do what is right.
4 Remember me, O LORD, when you show favor to your people,
come to my aid when you save them,
5 that I may enjoy the prosperity of your chosen ones,
that I may share in the joy of your nation
and join your inheritance in giving praise.

6 We have sinned, even as our fathers did;
we have done wrong and acted wickedly.
7 When our fathers were in Egypt,
they gave no thought to your miracles;
they did not remember your many kindnesses,
and they rebelled by the sea, the Red Sea.[u]
8 Yet he saved them for his name's sake,
to make his mighty power known.
9 He rebuked the Red Sea, and it dried up;
he led them through the depths as through a desert.
10 He saved them from the hand of the foe;

[s] 45 Hebrew *Hallelu Yah*
[t] 1 Hebrew *Hallelu Yah;* also in verse 48
[u] 7 Hebrew *Yam Suph;* that is, Sea of Reeds; also in verses 9 and 22

וַיִּגְאָלֵם מִיַּד אוֹיֵב׃ וַיְכַסּוּ־
and-they-covered (11) one-being-enemy from-hand-of and-he-redeemed-them

מַיִם צָרֵיהֶם אֶחָד מֵהֶם לֹא נוֹתָר׃ וַיַּאֲמִינוּ
then-they-believed (12) he-survived not of-them one adversaries-of-them waters

בִדְבָרָיו יָשִׁירוּ תְּהִלָּתוֹ׃ מִהֲרוּ שָׁכְחוּ
they-forgot they-did-soon (13) praise-of-him they-sang in-promises-of-him

מַעֲשָׂיו לֹא־חִכּוּ לַעֲצָתוֹ׃ וַיִּתְאַוּוּ תַאֲוָה
craving and-they-craved (14) for-counsel-of-him they-waited not deeds-of-him

בַּמִּדְבָּר וַיְנַסּוּ־אֵל בִּישִׁימוֹן׃ וַיִּתֵּן לָהֶם
to-them so-he-gave (15) in-wasteland God and-they-tested in-the-desert

שֶׁאֱלָתָם וַיְשַׁלַּח רָזוֹן בְּנַפְשָׁם׃
upon-life-of-them wasting-disease but-he-sent request-of-them

וַיְקַנְאוּ לְמֹשֶׁה בַּמַּחֲנֶה לְאַהֲרֹן קְדוֹשׁ יְהוָה׃
Yahweh consecrated-of to-Aaron in-the-camp to-Moses and-they-envied (16)

תִּפְתַּח־אֶרֶץ וַתִּבְלַע דָּתָן וַתְּכַס עַל־
over and-she-buried Dathan and-she-swallowed earth she-opened-up (17)

עֲדַת אֲבִירָם׃ וַתִּבְעַר־אֵשׁ בַּעֲדָתָם לֶהָבָה
flame among-follower-of-them fire and-she-blazed (18) Abiram company-of

תְּלַהֵט רְשָׁעִים׃ יַעֲשׂוּ־עֵגֶל בְּחֹרֵב וַיִּשְׁתַּחֲווּ
and-they-worshiped at-Horeb calf they-made (19) wicked-ones she-consumed

לְמַסֵּכָה׃ וַיָּמִירוּ אֶת־כְּבוֹדָם בְּתַבְנִית שׁוֹר
bull for-image-of Glory-of-them *** and-they-exchanged (20) to-cast-idol

אֹכֵל עֵשֶׂב׃ שָׁכְחוּ אֵל מוֹשִׁיעָם עֹשֶׂה גְדֹלוֹת
great-things one-doing one-saving-them God they-forgot (21) grass one-eating

בְּמִצְרָיִם׃ נִפְלָאוֹת בְּאֶרֶץ חָם נוֹרָאוֹת עַל־
by deeds-being-awesome Ham in-land-of deeds-being-miracles (22) in-Egypt

יַם־סוּף׃ וַיֹּאמֶר לְהַשְׁמִידָם לוּלֵי מֹשֶׁה בְחִירוֹ
chosen-one-of-him Moses if-not to-destroy-them so-he-said (23) Reed Sea-of

עָמַד בַּפֶּרֶץ לְפָנָיו לְהָשִׁיב חֲמָתוֹ מֵהַשְׁחִית׃
from-to-destroy wrath-of-him to-keep before-him in-the-breach he-stood

וַיִּמְאֲסוּ בְּאֶרֶץ חֶמְדָּה לֹא־הֶאֱמִינוּ לִדְבָרוֹ׃
to-promise-of-him they-believed not pleasantness to-land-of then-they-despised (24)

וַיֵּרָגְנוּ בְאָהֳלֵיהֶם לֹא שָׁמְעוּ בְּקוֹל יְהוָה׃
Yahweh to-voice-of they-obeyed not in-tents-of-them and-they-grumbled (25)

וַיִּשָּׂא יָדוֹ לָהֶם לְהַפִּיל אוֹתָם בַּמִּדְבָּר׃
in-the-desert them to-make-fall to-them hand-of-him so-he-lifted (26)

וּלְהַפִּיל זַרְעָם בַּגּוֹיִם וּלְזָרוֹתָם
and-to-scatter-them among-the-nations descendant-of-them and-to-make-fall (27)

from the hand of the enemy
he redeemed them.
11 The waters covered their
adversaries;
not one of them survived.
12 Then they believed his
promises
and sang his praise.

13 But they soon forgot what he
had done
and did not wait for his
counsel.
14 In the desert they gave in to
their craving;
in the wasteland they put
God to the test.
15 So he gave them what they
asked for,
but sent a wasting disease
upon them.

16 In the camp they grew envious
of Moses
and of Aaron, who was
consecrated to the LORD.
17 The earth opened up and
swallowed Dathan;
it buried the company of
Abiram.
18 Fire blazed among their
followers;
a flame consumed the
wicked.
19 At Horeb they made a calf
and worshiped an idol cast
from metal.
20 They exchanged their Glory
for an image of a bull,
which eats grass.
21 They forgot the God who
saved them,
who had done great things
in Egypt,
22 miracles in the land of Ham
and awesome deeds by the
Red Sea.
23 So he said he would destroy
them—
had not Moses, his chosen
one,
stood in the breach before him
to keep his wrath from
destroying them.

24 Then they despised the
pleasant land;
they did not believe his
promise.
25 They grumbled in their tents
and did not obey the LORD.
26 So he swore to them with
uplifted hand
that he would make them
fall in the desert,
27 make their descendants fall
among the nations
and scatter them throughout

בָּאֲרָצוֹת׃ וַיִּצָּמְדוּ לְבַעַל פְּעוֹר וַיֹּאכְלוּ
and-they-ate Peor to-Baal-of and-they-yoked-themselves (28) through-the-lands

זִבְחֵי מֵתִים׃ וַיַּכְעִיסוּ בְּמַעַלְלֵיהֶם
by-deeds-of-them and-they-provoked-anger (29) lifeless-ones sacrifices-of

וַתִּפְרָץ־ בָּם מַגֵּפָה׃ וַיַּעֲמֹד פִּינְחָס
Phinehas but-he-stood-up (30) plague among-them and-she-broke-out

וַיְפַלֵּל וַתֵּעָצַר הַמַּגֵּפָה׃ וַתֵּחָשֶׁב
and-she-was-credited (31) the-plague and-she-was-checked and-he-intervened

לוֹ לִצְדָקָה לְדֹר וָדֹר עַד־ עוֹלָם׃
forever to and-generation for-generation as-righteousness to-him

וַיַּקְצִיפוּ עַל־ מֵי מְרִיבָה וַיֵּרַע לְמֹשֶׁה
to-Moses and-he-was-trouble Meribah waters-of by and-they-angered (32)

בַּעֲבוּרָם׃ כִּי־ הִמְרוּ אֶת־ רוּחוֹ וַיְבַטֵּא
and-he-spoke-rashly Spirit-of-him against they-rebelled for (33) because-of-them

בִּשְׂפָתָיו׃ לֹא־ הִשְׁמִידוּ אֶת־ הָעַמִּים אֲשֶׁר אָמַר
he-commanded as the-peoples *** they-destroyed not (34) with-lips-of-him

יְהוָה לָהֶם׃ וַיִּתְעָרְבוּ בַגּוֹיִם וַיִּלְמְדוּ
and-they-adopted with-the-nations but-they-mingled (35) to-them Yahweh

מַעֲשֵׂיהֶם׃ וַיַּעַבְדוּ אֶת־ עֲצַבֵּיהֶם וַיִּהְיוּ
and-they-became idols-of-them *** and-they-worshiped (36) customs-of-them

לָהֶם לְמוֹקֵשׁ׃ וַיִּזְבְּחוּ אֶת־ בְּנֵיהֶם וְאֶת־ בְּנוֹתֵיהֶם
daughters-of-them and sons-of-them *** and-they-sacrificed (37) as-snare to-them

לַשֵּׁדִים׃ וַיִּשְׁפְּכוּ דָם נָקִי דַּם־ בְּנֵיהֶם
sons-of-them blood-of innocent blood and-they-shed (38) to-the-demons

וּבְנוֹתֵיהֶם אֲשֶׁר זִבְּחוּ לַעֲצַבֵּי כְנָעַן
Canaan to-idols-of they-sacrificed whom and-daughters-of-them

וַתֶּחֱנַף הָאָרֶץ בַּדָּמִים׃ וַיִּטְמְאוּ
and-they-defiled-themselves (39) by-the-bloods the-land and-she-was-desecrated

בְמַעֲשֵׂיהֶם וַיִּזְנוּ בְּמַעַלְלֵיהֶם׃
by-deeds-of-them and-they-prostituted-themselves by-deeds-of-them

וַיִּחַר־ אַף יְהוָה בְּעַמּוֹ וַיְתָעֵב אֶת־
*** and-he-abhorred against-people-of-him Yahweh anger-of so-he-burned (40)

נַחֲלָתוֹ׃ וַיִּתְּנֵם בְּיַד־ גּוֹיִם וַיִּמְשְׁלוּ
and-they-ruled nations into-hand-of and-he-gave-them (41) inheritance-of-him

בָהֶם שֹׂנְאֵיהֶם׃ וַיִּלְחָצוּם
and-they-oppressed-them (42) ones-being-foes-of-them over-them

אוֹיְבֵיהֶם וַיִּכָּנְעוּ תַּחַת יָדָם׃ פְּעָמִים
times (43) power-of-them to and-they-were-subjected ones-being-enemies-of-them

the lands.
28 They yoked themselves to the
Baal of Peor
and ate sacrifices offered to
lifeless gods;
29 they provoked the LORD to
anger by their wicked
deeds,
and a plague broke out
among them.
30 But Phinehas stood up and
intervened,
and the plague was checked.
31 This was credited to him as
righteousness
for endless generations to
come.

32 By the waters of Meribah they
angered the LORD,
and trouble came to Moses
because of them;
33 for they rebelled against the
Spirit of God,
and rash words came from
Moses' lips.[v]

34 They did not destroy the
peoples
as the LORD had commanded
them,
35 but they mingled with the
nations
and adopted their customs.
36 They worshiped their idols,
which became a snare to
them.
37 They sacrificed their sons
and their daughters to
demons.
38 They shed innocent blood,
the blood of their sons and
daughters,
whom they sacrificed to the
idols of Canaan,
and the land was desecrated
by their blood.
39 They defiled themselves by
what they did;
by their deeds they
prostituted themselves.

40 Therefore the LORD was angry
with his people
and abhorred his
inheritance.
41 He handed them over to the
nations,
and their foes ruled over
them.
42 Their enemies oppressed them
and subjected them to their
power.

[v]33 Or *against his spirit, / and rash words came from his lips*

רַבּוֹת יַצִּילֵם וְהֵמָּה יַמְרוּ בַעֲצָתָם
as-decision-of-them they-rebelled but-they he-delivered-them many

וַיָּמֹכּוּ בַּעֲוֹנָם׃ וַיַּרְא בַּצַּר
of-the-distress but-he-took-note (44) in-sin-of-them and-they-wasted-away

לָהֶם בְּשָׁמְעוֹ אֶת־ רִנָּתָם׃ וַיִּזְכֹּר לָהֶם
for-them and-he-remembered (45) cry-of-them *** when-to-hear-him of-them

בְּרִיתוֹ וַיִּנָּחֵם כְּרֹב חֲסָדָו׃ וַיִּתֵּן
and-he-made (46) loves-of-him as-greatness-of and-he-relented covenant-of-him

אוֹתָם לְרַחֲמִים לִפְנֵי כָּל־ שׁוֹבֵיהֶם׃ הוֹשִׁיעֵנוּ ׀
save-us! (47) ones-capturing-them all-of by to-pities them

יְהוָה אֱלֹהֵינוּ וְקַבְּצֵנוּ מִן־ הַגּוֹיִם לְהֹדוֹת לְשֵׁם
to-name-of to-give-thanks the-nations from and-gather-us! God-of-us Yahweh

קָדְשֶׁךָ לְהִשְׁתַּבֵּחַ בִּתְהִלָּתֶךָ׃ בָּרוּךְ־ יְהוָה אֱלֹהֵי
God-of Yahweh being-praised (48) in-praise-of-you to-glory holiness-of-you

יִשְׂרָאֵל מִן־ הָעוֹלָם ׀ וְעַד הָעוֹלָם וְאָמַר כָּל־
all-of and-let-him-say the-everlasting and-to the-everlasting from Israel

הָעָם אָמֵן הַלְלוּ־ יָהּ׃ הֹדוּ לַיהוָה כִּי־ טוֹב
good for to-Yahweh give-thanks! (107:1) Yahweh praise! amen the-people

כִּי לְעוֹלָם חַסְדּוֹ׃ יֹאמְרוּ גְּאוּלֵי יְהוָה
Yahweh ones-being-redeemed-of let-them-say (2) love-of-him to-forever for

אֲשֶׁר גְּאָלָם מִיַּד־ צָר׃ וּמֵאֲרָצוֹת קִבְּצָם
he-gathered-them and-from-lands (3) foe from-hand-of he-redeemed-them whom

מִמִּזְרָח וּמִמַּעֲרָב מִצָּפוֹן וּמִיָּם׃ תָּעוּ בַמִּדְבָּר
in-the-desert they-wandered (4) and-from-sea from-north and-from-west from-east

בִּישִׁימוֹן דֶּרֶךְ עִיר מוֹשָׁב לֹא מָצָאוּ׃ רְעֵבִים גַּם־
and ones-hungry (5) they-found not settlement city-of way in-wasteland

צְמֵאִים נַפְשָׁם בָּהֶם תִּתְעַטָּף׃ וַיִּצְעֲקוּ
then-they-cried-out (6) she-ebbed-away in-them life-of-them ones-thirsty

אֶל־ יְהוָה בַּצַּר לָהֶם מִמְּצוּקוֹתֵיהֶם יַצִּילֵם׃
he-delivered-them from-distresses-of-them of-them in-the-trouble Yahweh to

וַיַּדְרִיכֵם בְּדֶרֶךְ יְשָׁרָה לָלֶכֶת אֶל־ עִיר מוֹשָׁב׃
settlement city-of to to-go straight by-way and-he-led-them (7)

יוֹדוּ לַיהוָה חַסְדּוֹ
unfailing-love-of-him to-Yahweh let-them-give-thanks (8)

וְנִפְלְאוֹתָיו לִבְנֵי אָדָם׃ כִּי־ הִשְׂבִּיעַ נֶפֶשׁ
throat he-satisfies for (9) man for-sons-of and-deeds-being-wonderful-of-him

שֹׁקֵקָה וְנֶפֶשׁ רְעֵבָה מִלֵּא־ טוֹב׃ יֹשְׁבֵי חֹשֶׁךְ
darkness ones-sitting-of (10) good he-fills hungry and-throat one-thirsting

43 Many times he delivered them,
but they were bent on rebellion
and they wasted away in their sin.

44 But he took note of their distress
when he heard their cry;
45 for their sake he remembered his covenant
and out of his great love he relented.
46 He caused them to be pitied
by all who held them captive.

47 Save us, O LORD our God,
and gather us from the nations,
that we may give thanks to your holy name
and glory in your praise.

48 Praise be to the LORD, the God of Israel,
from everlasting to everlasting.
Let all the people say, "Amen!"
Praise the LORD.

BOOK V

Psalms 107-150

Psalm 107

1 Give thanks to the LORD, for he is good;
his love endures forever.
2 Let the redeemed of the LORD say this—
those he redeemed from the hand of the foe,
3 those he gathered from the lands,
from east and west, from north and south.[w]

4 Some wandered in desert wastelands,
finding no way to a city where they could settle.
5 They were hungry and thirsty,
and their lives ebbed away.
6 Then they cried out to the LORD in their trouble,
and he delivered them from their distress.
7 He led them by a straight way
to a city where they could settle.
8 Let them give thanks to the LORD for his unfailing love
and his wonderful deeds for men,
9 for he satisfies the thirsty
and fills the hungry with good things.

10 Some sat in darkness and the

[w] 3 Hebrew *north and the sea*

°45 ק חסדיו

וְצַלְמָוֶת אֲסִירֵי עֳנִי וּבַרְזֶל׃ כִּי־ הִמְרוּ
they-rebelled-against for (11) and-iron suffering prisoners-of and-deepest-gloom

אִמְרֵי־ אֵל וַעֲצַת עֶלְיוֹן נָאָצוּ׃ וַיַּכְנַע
so-he-subjected (12) they-despised Most-High and-counsel-of God words-of

בֶּעָמָל לִבָּם כָּשְׁלוּ וְאֵין עֹזֵר׃
helping and-there-was-no-one they-stumbled heart-of-them to-the-bitter-labor

וַיִּזְעֲקוּ אֶל־ יְהוָה בַּצַּר לָהֶם מִמְּצֻקוֹתֵיהֶם
from-distresses-of-them of-them in-the-trouble Yahweh to then-they-cried (13)

יוֹשִׁיעֵם׃ יוֹצִיאֵם מֵחֹשֶׁךְ וְצַלְמָוֶת
and-deepest-gloom from-darkness he-brought-out-them (14) he-saved-them

וּמוֹסְרוֹתֵיהֶם יְנַתֵּק׃ יוֹדוּ לַיהוָה
to-Yahweh let-them-give-thanks (15) he-broke-away and-chains-of-them

חַסְדּוֹ וְנִפְלְאוֹתָיו לִבְנֵי אָדָם׃
man for-sons-of and-deeds-being-wonderful-of-him unfailing-love-of-him

כִּי־ שִׁבַּר דַּלְתוֹת נְחֹשֶׁת וּבְרִיחֵי בַרְזֶל גִּדֵּעַ׃
he-cuts-through iron and-bars-of bronze gates-of he-breaks-down for (16)

אֱוִלִים מִדֶּרֶךְ פִּשְׁעָם וּמֵעֲוֺנֹתֵיהֶם
and-because-of-iniquities-of-them rebellion-of-them through-way-of fools (17)

יִתְעַנּוּ׃ כָּל־ אֹכֶל תְּתַעֵב נַפְשָׁם וַיַּגִּיעוּ
and-they-drew-near self-of-them she-loathed food all-of (18) they-were-afflicted

עַד־ שַׁעֲרֵי מָוֶת׃ וַיִּזְעֲקוּ אֶל־ יְהוָה בַּצַּר לָהֶם
of-them in-the-trouble Yahweh to then-they-cried (19) death gates-of to

מִמְּצֻקוֹתֵיהֶם יוֹשִׁיעֵם׃ יִשְׁלַח דְּבָרוֹ
word-of-him he-sent-forth (20) he-saved-them from-distresses-of-them

וְיִרְפָּאֵם וִימַלֵּט מִשְּׁחִיתוֹתָם׃ יוֹדוּ
let-them-give-thanks (21) from-graves-of-them and-he-rescued and-he-healed-them

לַיהוָה חַסְדּוֹ וְנִפְלְאוֹתָיו לִבְנֵי
for-sons-of and-deeds-being-wonders-of-him unfailing-love-of-him to-Yahweh

אָדָם׃ וְיִזְבְּחוּ זִבְחֵי תוֹדָה וִיסַפְּרוּ
and-let-them-tell thanksgiving offerings-of and-let-them-sacrifice (22) man

מַעֲשָׂיו בְּרִנָּה׃ יוֹרְדֵי הַיָּם בָּאֳנִיּוֹת
in-the-ships the-sea ones-going-down-of (23) with-song-of-joy works-of-him

עֹשֵׂי מְלָאכָה בְּמַיִם רַבִּים׃ הֵמָּה רָאוּ מַעֲשֵׂי יְהוָה
Yahweh works-of they-saw they (24) mighty-ones on-waters trade ones-doing-of

וְנִפְלְאוֹתָיו בִּמְצוּלָה׃ וַיֹּאמֶר וַיַּעֲמֵד
and-he-stirred-up for-he-spoke (25) in-deep and-deeds-being-wonderful-of-him

רוּחַ סְעָרָה וַתְּרוֹמֵם גַּלָּיו׃ יַעֲלוּ שָׁמַיִם
heavens they-mounted-up (26) waves-of-him and-she-lifted tempest wind

deepest gloom,
prisoners suffering in iron chains,
11 for they had rebelled against the words of God
and despised the counsel of the Most High.
12 So he subjected them to bitter labor;
they stumbled, and there was no one to help.
13 Then they cried to the LORD in their trouble,
and he saved them from their distress.
14 He brought them out of darkness and the deepest gloom
and broke away their chains.
15 Let them give thanks to the LORD for his unfailing love
and his wonderful deeds for men,
16 for he breaks down gates of bronze
and cuts through bars of iron.

17 Some became fools through their rebellious ways
and suffered affliction because of their iniquities.
18 They loathed all food
and drew near the gates of death.
19 Then they cried to the LORD in their trouble,
and he saved them from their distress.
20 He sent forth his word and healed them;
he rescued them from the grave.
21 Let them give thanks to the LORD for his unfailing love
and his wonderful deeds for men.
22 Let them sacrifice thank offerings
and tell of his works with songs of joy.

23 Others went out on the sea in ships;
they were merchants on the mighty waters.
24 They saw the works of the LORD,
his wonderful deeds in the deep.
25 For he spoke and stirred up a tempest
that lifted high the waves.
26 They mounted up to the

יֵרְדוּ תְהוֹמוֹת נַפְשָׁם בְּרָעָה תִתְמוֹגָג׃ יָחוֹגּוּ

they-reeled (27) she-melted-away in-peril courage-of-them depths they-went-down

וְיָנוּעוּ כַּשִּׁכּוֹר וְכָל־ חָכְמָתָם תִּתְבַּלָּע׃

she-ended wit-of-them and-all-of like-the-drunkard and-they-staggered

וַיִּצְעֲקוּ אֶל־ יְהוָה בַּצַּר לָהֶם וּמִמְּצוּקֹתֵיהֶם

and-from-distresses-of-them of-them in-the-trouble Yahweh to then-they-cried (28)

יוֹצִיאֵם׃ יָקֵם סְעָרָה לִדְמָמָה וַיֶּחֱשׁוּ

and-they-were-hushed to-whisper storm he-stilled (29) he-brought-out-them

גַּלֵּיהֶם׃ וַיִּשְׂמְחוּ כִי־ יִשְׁתֹּקוּ וַיַּנְחֵם

and-he-guided-them they-grew-calm when and-they-were-glad (30) waves-of-them

אֶל־ מְחוֹז חֶפְצָם׃ יוֹדוּ לַיהוָה

to-Yahweh let-them-give-thanks (31) desire-of-them haven-of to

חַסְדּוֹ וְנִפְלְאוֹתָיו לִבְנֵי אָדָם׃

man for-sons-of and-deeds-being-wonderful-of-him unfailing-love-of-him

וִירֹמְמוּהוּ בִּקְהַל־ עָם וּבְמוֹשַׁב זְקֵנִים

elders and-in-council-of people in-assembly-of and-let-them-exalt-him (32)

יְהַלְלוּהוּ׃ יָשֵׂם נְהָרוֹת לְמִדְבָּר וּמֹצָאֵי מַיִם

waters and-springs-of into-desert rivers he-turned (33) let-them-praise-him

לְצִמָּאוֹן׃ אֶרֶץ פְּרִי לִמְלֵחָה מֵרָעַת

because-of-wickedness-of into-salt-waste fruit land-of (34) into-thirsty-ground

יֹשְׁבֵי בָהּ׃ יָשֵׂם מִדְבָּר לַאֲגַם־ מַיִם וְאֶרֶץ

and-ground-of waters into-pool-of desert he-turned (35) in-her ones-living-of

צִיָּה לְמֹצָאֵי מָיִם׃ וַיּוֹשֶׁב שָׁם רְעֵבִים

hungry-ones there and-he-brought-to-live (36) waters into-springs-of parched

וַיְכוֹנְנוּ עִיר מוֹשָׁב׃ וַיִּזְרְעוּ שָׂדוֹת וַיִּטְּעוּ

and-they-planted fields and-they-sowed (37) settlement city-of and-they-founded

כְרָמִים וַיַּעֲשׂוּ פְּרִי תְבוּאָה׃ וַיְבָרְכֵם

and-he-blessed-them (38) harvest fruit-of and-they-yielded vineyards

וַיִּרְבּוּ מְאֹד וּבְהֶמְתָּם לֹא יַמְעִיט׃

he-let-diminish not and-herd-of-them greatly and-they-increased

וַיִּמְעֲטוּ וַיָּשֹׁחוּ מֵעֹצֶר רָעָה וְיָגוֹן׃

and-sorrow calamity by-oppression and-they-were-humbled then-they-decreased (39)

שֹׁפֵךְ בּוּז עַל־ נְדִיבִים וַיַּתְעֵם בְּתֹהוּ

in-waste and-he-made-wander-them nobles on contempt one-pouring (40)

לֹא־ דָרֶךְ׃ וַיְשַׂגֵּב אֶבְיוֹן מֵעוֹנִי וַיָּשֶׂם

and-he-increased from-affliction needy but-he-lifted (41) track without

כַּצֹּאן מִשְׁפָּחוֹת׃ יִרְאוּ יְשָׁרִים וְיִשְׂמָחוּ וְכָל־

but-all-of and-they-rejoice upright-ones they-see (42) families like-the-flock

heavens and went down
to the depths;
in their peril their courage
melted away.
27They reeled and staggered like
drunken men;
they were at their wits' end.
28Then they cried out to the
LORD in their trouble,
and he brought them out of
their distress.
29He stilled the storm to a
whisper;
the waves of the sea were
hushed.
30They were glad when it grew
calm,
and he guided them to their
desired haven.
31Let them give thanks to the
LORD for his unfailing
love
and his wonderful deeds for
men.
32Let them exalt him in the
assembly of the people
and praise him in the
council of the elders.

33He turned rivers into a desert,
flowing springs into thirsty
ground,
34and fruitful land into a salt
waste,
because of the wickedness of
those who lived there.
35He turned the desert into pools
of water
and the parched ground into
flowing springs;
36there he brought the hungry to
live,
and they founded a city
where they could settle.
37They sowed fields and planted
vineyards
that yielded a fruitful
harvest;
38he blessed them, and their
numbers greatly
increased,
and he did not let their
herds diminish.

39Then their numbers decreased,
and they were humbled
by oppression, calamity and
sorrow;
40he who pours contempt on
nobles
made them wander in a
trackless waste.
41But he lifted the needy out of
their affliction
and increased their families
like flocks.
42The upright see and rejoice,

עֹ֭וְלָה קָ֣פְצָה פִּֽיהָ׃ מִי־חָכָ֥ם וְיִשְׁמָר־אֵ֑לֶּה
these then-let-him-heed wise whoever (43) mouth-of-her she-shuts wicked

וְ֝יִתְבּֽוֹנְנ֗וּ חַֽסְדֵ֥י יְהוָֽה׃ שִׁ֖יר מִזְמ֣וֹר לְדָוִֽד׃
of-David psalm song *(108:1) Yahweh great-loves-of and-let-them-consider

נָכ֣וֹן לִבִּ֣י אֱלֹהִ֑ים אָשִׁ֥ירָה וַ֝אֲזַמְּרָ֗ה אַף־
even and-I-will-make-music I-will-sing God heart-of-me he-is-steadfast (2)

כְּבוֹדִֽי׃ ע֭וּרָה הַנֵּ֣בֶל וְכִנּ֑וֹר אָעִ֥ירָה שָּֽׁחַר׃
dawn I-will-awaken and-lyre the-harp awake! (3) soul-of-me

אוֹדְךָ֖ בָעַמִּ֥ים׀ יְהוָ֑ה וַ֝אֲזַמֶּרְךָ֗
and-I-will-sing-of-you Yahweh among-the-nations I-will-praise-you (4)

בַּל־אֻמִּֽים׃† כִּֽי־גָד֣וֹל מֵֽעַל־שָׁמַ֣יִם חַסְדֶּ֑ךָ וְֽעַד־שְׁחָקִ֥ים
skies and-to love-of-you heavens than-above greater for (5) †among-the-peoples

אֲמִתֶּֽךָ׃ ר֣וּמָה עַל־שָׁמַ֣יִם אֱלֹהִ֑ים וְעַ֖ל כָּל־הָאָ֣רֶץ
the-earth all-of and-over God heavens above be-exalted! (6) faithfulness-of-you

כְּבוֹדֶֽךָ׃ לְ֭מַעַן יֵחָלְצ֣וּן יְדִידֶ֑יךָ הוֹשִׁ֖יעָה
save! loved-ones-of-you they-may-be-delivered so-that (7) glory-of-you

יְמִֽינְךָ֣ וַעֲנֵֽנִי׃ אֱלֹהִ֤ים׀ דִּבֶּ֥ר בְּקָדְשׁ֗וֹ
from-sanctuary-of-him he-spoke God (8) and-help-me! right-hand-of-you

אֶעְלֹ֗זָה אֲחַלְּקָ֥ה שְׁכֶ֑ם וְעֵ֖מֶק סֻכּ֣וֹת אֲמַדֵּֽד׃
I-will-measure Succoth and-Valley-of Shechem I-will-parcel-out I-will-triumph

לִ֤י גִלְעָ֨ד׀ לִ֬י מְנַשֶּׁ֗ה וְ֭אֶפְרַיִם מָע֣וֹז רֹאשִׁ֑י יְ֝הוּדָ֗ה
Judah head-of-me helmet-of and-Ephraim Manasseh to-me Gilead to-me (9)

מְחֹקְקִֽי׃ מוֹאָ֤ב׀ סִ֬יר רַחְצִ֗י עַל־אֱ֭דוֹם אַשְׁלִ֣יךְ
I-toss Edom upon washing-of-me basin-of Moab (10) one-being-scepter-of-me

נַעֲלִ֑י עֲלֵי־פְ֝לֶ֗שֶׁת אֶתְרוֹעָֽע׃ מִ֣י יֹ֭בִלֵנִי
he-will-bring-me who? (11) I-shout-in-triumph Philistia over sandal-of-me

עִ֣יר מִבְצָ֑ר מִ֖י נָחַ֣נִי עַד־אֱדֽוֹם׃ הֲלֹֽא־אֱלֹהִ֥ים
God not? (12) Edom to he-will-lead-me who? fortification city-of

זְנַחְתָּ֑נוּ וְֽלֹא־תֵצֵ֥א אֱ֝לֹהִ֗ים בְּצִבְאֹתֵֽינוּ׃ הָֽבָה־לָּ֣נוּ
to-us give! (13) with-armies-of-us God you-go-out and-not you-rejected-us

עֶזְרָ֣ת מִצָּ֑ר וְ֝שָׁ֗וְא תְּשׁוּעַ֥ת אָדָֽם׃ בֵּֽאלֹהִ֥ים נַעֲשֶׂה־
we-will-gain with-God (14) man help-of for-worthless against-enemy aid

חָ֑יִל וְ֝ה֗וּא יָב֥וּס צָרֵֽינוּ׃ לַמְנַצֵּ֗חַ
for-the-one-directing (109:1) enemies-of-us he-will-trample and-he victory

לְדָוִ֥ד מִזְמ֑וֹר אֱלֹהֵ֥י תְ֝הִלָּתִ֗י אַֽל־תֶּחֱרַֽשׁ׃ כִּ֤י פִ֪י
mouth-of for (2) you-remain-silent not praise-of-me God-of psalm of-David

רָשָׁ֡ע וּֽפִי־מִ֭רְמָה עָלַ֣י פָּתָ֑חוּ דִּבְּר֥וּ אִ֝תִּ֗י
against-me they-spoke they-opened against-me deceit and-mouth-of wicked

---

but all the wicked shut their
mouths.
43 Whoever is wise, let him heed
these things
and consider the great love
of the LORD.

Psalm 108

A song. A psalm of David.

1 My heart is steadfast, O God;
I will sing and make music
with all my soul.
2 Awake, harp and lyre!
I will awaken the dawn.
3 I will praise you, O LORD,
among the nations;
I will sing of you among the
peoples.
4 For great is your love, higher
than the heavens;
your faithfulness reaches to
the skies.
5 Be exalted, O God, above the
heavens,
and let your glory be over
all the earth.

6 Save us and help us with your
right hand,
that those you love may be
delivered.
7 God has spoken from his
sanctuary:
"In triumph I will parcel out
Shechem
and measure off the Valley
of Succoth.
8 Gilead is mine, Manasseh is
mine;
Ephraim is my helmet,
Judah my scepter.
9 Moab is my washbasin,
upon Edom I toss my
sandal;
over Philistia I shout in
triumph."

10 Who will bring me to the
fortified city?
Who will lead me to Edom?
11 Is it not you, O God, you who
have rejected us
and no longer go out with
our armies?
12 Give us aid against the enemy,
for the help of man is
worthless.
13 With God we will gain the
victory,
and he will trample down
our enemies.

Psalm 109

For the director of music. Of David. A psalm.

1 O God, whom I praise,
do not remain silent,
2 for wicked and deceitful men
have opened their mouths
against me;
they have spoken against

*1 See the note on page 349.

†4 Most mss read these two words as one (בַּל־).

לְשׁוֹן שָׁקֶר׃ וְדִבְרֵי שִׂנְאָה סְבָבוּנִי וַיִּלָּחֲמוּנִי
and-they-attack-me they-surround-me hatred and-words-of (3) lie tongue-of

חִנָּם׃ תַּחַת־ אַהֲבָתִי יִשְׂטְנוּנִי וַאֲנִי תְפִלָּה׃
prayer but-I they-accuse-me friendship-of-me in-return-for (4) without-cause

וַיָּשִׂימוּ עָלַי רָעָה תַּחַת טוֹבָה וְשִׂנְאָה תַּחַת אַהֲבָתִי׃
friendship-of-me for and-hatred good for evil to-me and-they-repay (5)

הַפְקֵד עָלָיו רָשָׁע וְשָׂטָן יַעֲמֹד עַל־ יְמִינוֹ׃
right-hand-of-him at let-him-stand and-accuser evil against-him appoint! (6)

בְּהִשָּׁפְטוֹ יֵצֵא רָשָׁע וּתְפִלָּתוֹ תִּהְיֶה
may-she-be and-prayer-of-him guilty let-him-be-found when-to-be-tried-him (7)

לַחֲטָאָה׃ יִהְיוּ־ יָמָיו מְעַטִּים פְּקֻדָּתוֹ
leadership-of-him few-ones days-of-him may-they-be (8) as-condemnation

יִקַּח אַחֵר׃ יִהְיוּ־ בָנָיו יְתוֹמִים
fatherless-ones children-of-him may-they-be (9) another may-he-take

וְאִשְׁתּוֹ אַלְמָנָה׃ וְנוֹעַ יָנוּעוּ בָנָיו
children-of-him may-they-wander and-to-wander (10) widow and-wife-of-him

וְשִׁאֵלוּ וְדָרְשׁוּ מֵחָרְבוֹתֵיהֶם׃ יְנַקֵּשׁ
may-he-seize (11) from-ruins-of-them and-may-they-be-sought and-may-they-beg

נוֹשֶׁה לְכָל־ אֲשֶׁר־ לוֹ וְיָבֹזּוּ זָרִים
ones-being-strangers and-may-they-plunder to-him that to-all one-being-creditor

יְגִיעוֹ׃ אַל־ יְהִי־ לוֹ מֹשֵׁךְ חָסֶד וְאַל־
and-not kindness one-extending to-him may-he-be not (12) labor-of-him

יְהִי חוֹנֵן לִיתוֹמָיו׃ יְהִי־
may-he-be (13) on-fatherless-ones-of-him one-taking-pity may-he-be

אַחֲרִיתוֹ לְהַכְרִית בְּדוֹר אַחֵר יִמַּח
may-he-be-blotted-out next from-generation to-cut-off descendant-of-him

שְׁמָם׃ יִזָּכֵר ׀ עֲוֺן אֲבֹתָיו אֶל־
before fathers-of-him iniquity-of may-he-be-remembered (14) name-of-them

יְהוָה וְחַטַּאת אִמּוֹ אַל־ תִּמָּח׃ יִהְיוּ
may-they-be (15) may-she-be-blotted-out never mother-of-him and-sin-of Yahweh

נֶגֶד־ יְהוָה תָּמִיד וְיַכְרֵת מֵאֶרֶץ זִכְרָם׃
memory-of-them from-earth that-he-may-cut-off always Yahweh before

יַעַן אֲשֶׁר ׀ לֹא זָכַר עֲשׂוֹת חָסֶד וַיִּרְדֹּף אִישׁ־ עָנִי
poor man but-he-hounded kindness to-do he-thought never that for (16)

וְאֶבְיוֹן וְנִכְאֵה לֵבָב לְמוֹתֵת׃ וַיֶּאֱהַב קְלָלָה
curse and-he-loved (17) to-kill heart and-one-being-broken-of and-needy

וַתְּבוֹאֵהוּ וְלֹא־ חָפֵץ בִּבְרָכָה וַתִּרְחַק
so-may-she-be-far in-blessing he-found-pleasure and-not so-may-she-come-on-him

me with lying tongues.
3With words of hatred they
surround me;
they attack me without
cause.
4In return for my friendship
they accuse me,
but I am a man of prayer.
5They repay me evil for good,
and hatred for my
friendship.

6Appoint[x] an evil man[y] to
oppose him;
let an accuser[z] stand at his
right hand.
7When he is tried, let him be
found guilty,
and may his prayers
condemn him.
8May his days be few;
may another take his place
of leadership.
9May his children be fatherless
and his wife a widow.
10May his children be
wandering beggars;
may they be driven[a] from
their ruined homes.
11May a creditor seize all he has;
may strangers plunder the
fruits of his labor.
12May no one extend kindness
to him
or take pity on his fatherless
children.
13May his descendants be cut
off,
their names blotted out from
the next generation.
14May the iniquity of his fathers
be remembered before the
LORD;
may the sin of his mother
never be blotted out.
15May their sins always remain
before the LORD,
that he may cut off the
memory of them from the
earth.

16For he never thought of doing
a kindness,
but hounded to death the
poor
and the needy and the
brokenhearted.
17He loved to pronounce a
curse—
may it[b] come on him;
he found no pleasure in
blessing—
may it be[c] far from him.

x6 Or *They say:* "*Appoint* (with quotation marks at the end of verse 19)
y6 Or *the Evil One* z6 Or *let Satan*
a10 Septuagint; Hebrew *sought*
b17 Or *curse,* / *and it has*
c17 Or *blessing,* / *and it is*

מִמֶּנּוּ׃ וַיִּלְבַּשׁ קְלָלָה כְּמַדּוֹ וַתָּבֹא
and-she-entered as-garment-of-him cursing and-he-wore (18) from-him

כַמַּיִם בְּקִרְבּוֹ וְכַשֶּׁמֶן בְּעַצְמוֹתָיו׃
into-bones-of-him and-like-the-oil into-body-of-him as-the-waters

תְּהִי־ לוֹ כְּבֶגֶד יַעְטֶה וּלְמֵזַח תָּמִיד
forever and-like-belt he-wraps like-cloak about-him may-she-be (19)

יַחְגְּרֶהָ׃ זֹאת פְּעֻלַּת שֹׂטְנַי מֵאֵת יְהוָה
Yahweh from-with ones-accusing-me payment-of this (20) he-ties-her

וְהַדֹּבְרִים רָע עַל־ נַפְשִׁי׃ וְאַתָּה ׀ יְהוִה אֲדֹנָי
Lord Yahweh but-you (21) self-of-me against evil and-the-ones-speaking

עֲשֵׂה־ אִתִּי לְמַעַן שְׁמֶךָ כִּי־ טוֹב חַסְדְּךָ
love-of-you goodness-of out-of name-of-you for-sake-of with-me deal!

הַצִּילֵנִי׃ כִּי־ עָנִי וְאֶבְיוֹן אָנֹכִי וְלִבִּי חָלַל
he-is-wounded and-heart-of-me I and-needy poor for (22) deliver-me!

בְּקִרְבִּי׃ כְּצֵל־ כִּנְטוֹתוֹ נֶהֱלָכְתִּי
I-fade-away when-to-stretch-him like-shadow-of (23) at-within-me

נִנְעַרְתִּי כָּאַרְבֶּה׃ בִּרְכַּי כָּשְׁלוּ מִצּוֹם
from-fasting they-give-way knees-of-me (24) like-the-locust I-am-shaken-off

וּבְשָׂרִי כָּחַשׁ מִשָּׁמֶן׃ וַאֲנִי ׀ הָיִיתִי חֶרְפָּה לָהֶם יִרְאוּנִי
they-see-me to-them scorn I-am and-I (25) from-fat he-is-thin and-body-of-me

יְנִיעוּן רֹאשָׁם׃ עָזְרֵנִי יְהוָה אֱלֹהָי הוֹשִׁיעֵנִי
save-me! God-of-me Yahweh help-me! (26) head-of-them they-shake

כְחַסְדֶּךָ׃ וְיֵדְעוּ כִּי־ יָדְךָ זֹּאת אַתָּה יְהוָה
Yahweh you this hand-of-you that and-let-them-know (27) as-love-of-you

עֲשִׂיתָהּ׃ יְקַלְלוּ־ הֵמָּה וְאַתָּה תְבָרֵךְ קָמוּ ׀
they-may-attack you-will-bless but-you they they-may-curse (28) you-did-her

וַיֵּבֹשׁוּ וְעַבְדְּךָ יִשְׂמָח׃
he-will-rejoice and-servant-of-you but-they-will-be-shamed

יִלְבְּשׁוּ שׂוֹטְנַי כְּלִמָּה וְיַעֲטוּ
and-they-will-be-wrapped disgrace ones-accusing-me they-will-be-clothed (29)

כַמְעִיל בָּשְׁתָּם׃ אוֹדֶה יְהוָה מְאֹד בְּפִי
with-mouth-of-me greatly Yahweh I-will-extol (30) shame-of-them as-the-cloak

וּבְתוֹךְ רַבִּים אֲהַלְלֶנּוּ׃ כִּי־ יַעֲמֹד
he-stands for (31) I-will-praise-him great-throngs and-in-midst-of

לִימִין אֶבְיוֹן לְהוֹשִׁיעַ מִשֹּׁפְטֵי נַפְשׁוֹ׃
life-of-him from-ones-condemning-of to-save needy at-right-hand-of

לְדָוִד מִזְמוֹר נְאֻם יְהוָה ׀ לַאדֹנִי שֵׁב לִימִינִי
at-right-hand-of-me sit! to-Lord-of-me Yahweh saying-of psalm of-David (110:1)

18He wore cursing as his
garment;
it entered into his body like
water,
into his bones like oil.
19May it be like a cloak wrapped
about him,
like a belt tied forever
around him.
20May this be the LORD's
payment to my accusers,
to those who speak evil of
me.
21But you, O Sovereign LORD,
deal well with me for your
name's sake;
out of the goodness of your
love, deliver me.
22For I am poor and needy,
and my heart is wounded
within me.
23I fade away like an evening
shadow;
I am shaken off like a locust.
24My knees give way from
fasting;
my body is thin and gaunt.
25I am an object of scorn to my
accusers;
when they see me, they
shake their heads.
26Help me, O LORD my God;
save me in accordance with
your love.
27Let them know that it is your
hand,
that you, O LORD, have done
it.
28They may curse, but you will
bless;
when they attack they will
be put to shame,
but your servant will rejoice.
29My accusers will be clothed
with disgrace
and wrapped in shame as in
a cloak.
30With my mouth I will greatly
extol the LORD;
in the great throng I will
praise him.
31For he stands at the right
hand of the needy one,
to save his life from those
who condemn him.

Psalm 110

Of David. A psalm.

1The LORD says to my Lord:
"Sit at my right hand

עַד־ אָשִׁית אֹיְבֶיךָ הֲדֹם לְרַגְלֶיךָ׃
for-feet-of-you footstool ones-being-enemies-of-you I-make until

מַטֵּה־ עֻזְּךָ יִשְׁלַח יְהוָה מִצִּיּוֹן רְדֵה בְּקֶרֶב
in-midst-of rule! from-Zion Yahweh he-will-extend might-of-you scepter-of (2)

אֹיְבֶיךָ׃ עַמְּךָ נְדָבֹת בְּיוֹם חֵילֶךָ
battle-of-you on-day-of willing-ones troop-of-you (3) ones-being-enemies-of-you

בְּהַדְרֵי־ קֹדֶשׁ מֵרֶחֶם מִשְׁחָר לְךָ טַל יַלְדֻתֶיךָ׃
youths-of-you dew-of to-you dawn from-womb-of holiness in-majesties-of

נִשְׁבַּע יְהוָה׀ וְלֹא יִנָּחֵם אַתָּה־ כֹהֵן לְעוֹלָם עַל־
in to-forever priest you he-will-change-mind and-not Yahweh he-swore (4)

דִּבְרָתִי מַלְכִּי־ צֶדֶק׃ אֲדֹנָי עַל־ יְמִינְךָ מָחַץ בְּיוֹם־
on-day-of he-will-crush right-hand-of-you at Lord (5) Zedek Melchi order-of

אַפּוֹ מְלָכִים׃ יָדִין בַּגּוֹיִם מָלֵא גְוִיּוֹת
dead-ones he-will-heap-up to-the-nations he-will-judge (6) kings wrath-of-him

מָחַץ רֹאשׁ עַל־ אֶרֶץ רַבָּה׃ מִנַּחַל בַּדֶּרֶךְ יִשְׁתֶּה
he-will-drink beside-the-way from-brook (7) whole earth of ruler he-will-crush

עַל־ כֵּן יָרִים רֹאשׁ׃ הַלְלוּ יָהּ׀ אוֹדֶה
I-will-extol Yahweh praise! (111:1) head he-will-lift-up this because-of

יְהוָה בְּכָל־ לֵבָב בְּסוֹד יְשָׁרִים וְעֵדָה׃ גְּדֹלִים
great-ones (2) and-assembly upright-ones in-council-of heart with-all-of Yahweh

מַעֲשֵׂי יְהוָה דְּרוּשִׁים לְכָל־ חֶפְצֵיהֶם׃ הוֹד־
glorious (3) delighters-of-them by-all-of ones-being-pondered Yahweh works-of

וְהָדָר פָּעֳלוֹ וְצִדְקָתוֹ עֹמֶדֶת לָעַד׃
to-forever one-enduring and-righteousness-of-him deed-of-him and-majestic

זֵכֶר עָשָׂה לְנִפְלְאוֹתָיו חַנּוּן
gracious for-deeds-being-wonders-of-him he-caused remembrance (4)

וְרַחוּם יְהוָה׃ טֶרֶף נָתַן לִירֵאָיו יִזְכֹּר
he-remembers for-ones-fearing-him he-provides food (5) Yahweh and-compassionate

לְעוֹלָם בְּרִיתוֹ׃ כֹּחַ מַעֲשָׂיו הִגִּיד לְעַמּוֹ
to-people-of-him he-showed works-of-him power-of (6) covenant-of-him to-forever

לָתֵת לָהֶם נַחֲלַת גּוֹיִם׃ מַעֲשֵׂי יָדָיו אֱמֶת וּמִשְׁפָּט
and-just faithful hands-of-him works-of (7) nations land-of to-them to-give

נֶאֱמָנִים כָּל־ פִּקּוּדָיו׃ סְמוּכִים
ones-being-steadfast (8) precepts-of-him all-of ones-being-trustworthy

לָעַד לְעוֹלָם עֲשׂוּיִם בֶּאֱמֶת וְיָשָׁר׃
and-uprightness in-faithfulness ones-being-done to-forever for-ever

פְּדוּת׀ שָׁלַח לְעַמּוֹ צִוָּה־ לְעוֹלָם
to-forever he-ordained for-people-of-him he-provided redemption (9)

until I make your enemies
a footstool for your feet."

2 The LORD will extend your
mighty scepter from Zion;
you will rule in the midst of
your enemies.

3 Your troops will be willing
on your day of battle.
Arrayed in holy majesty,
from the womb of the dawn
you will receive the dew of
your youth.[d]

4 The LORD has sworn
and will not change his
mind:
"You are a priest forever,
in the order of
Melchizedek."

5 The Lord is at your right hand;
he will crush kings on the
day of his wrath.

6 He will judge the nations,
heaping up the dead
and crushing the rulers of
the whole earth.

7 He will drink from a brook
beside the way[e];
therefore he will lift up his
head.

Psalm 111[f]

1 Praise the LORD.[g]

I will extol the LORD with all
my heart
in the council of the upright
and in the assembly.

2 Great are the works of the
LORD;
they are pondered by all
who delight in them.

3 Glorious and majestic are his
deeds,
and his righteousness
endures forever.

4 He has caused his wonders to
be remembered;
the LORD is gracious and
compassionate.

5 He provides food for those
who fear him;
he remembers his covenant
forever.

6 He has shown his people the
power of his works,
giving them the lands of
other nations.

7 The works of his hands are
faithful and just;
all his precepts are
trustworthy.

8 They are steadfast for ever and
ever,
done in faithfulness and
uprightness.

9 He provided redemption for
his people;
he ordained his covenant
forever—

[d]3 Or / *your young men will come to you like the dew*
[e]7 Or / *The One who grants succession will set him in authority*
[f]This psalm is an acrostic poem, the lines of which begin with the successive letters of the Hebrew alphabet.
[g]1 Hebrew *Hallelu Yah*

בְּרִיתוֹ קָדוֹשׁ וְנוֹרָא שְׁמוֹ׃ (10) רֵאשִׁית חָכְמָה ׀
wisdom beginning-of (10) name-of-him and-being-awesome holy covenant-of-him

יִרְאַת יְהוָה שֵׂכֶל טוֹב לְכָל־ עֹשֵׂיהֶם תְּהִלָּתוֹ
praise-of-him ones-following-them to-all-of good understanding Yahweh fear-of

עֹמֶדֶת לָעַד׃ (112:1) הַלְלוּ יָהּ ׀ אַשְׁרֵי־ אִישׁ יָרֵא
he-fears man blessednesses-of Yahweh praise! (112:1) to-eternity one-enduring

אֶת־ יְהוָה בְּמִצְוֹתָיו חָפֵץ מְאֹד׃ (2) גִּבּוֹר בָּאָרֶץ
in-the-land mighty (2) greatly he-delights in-commands-of-him Yahweh ***

יִהְיֶה זַרְעוֹ דּוֹר יְשָׁרִים יְבֹרָךְ׃
he-will-be-blessed upright-ones generation-of child-of-him he-will-be

(3) הוֹן־ וָעֹשֶׁר בְּבֵיתוֹ וְצִדְקָתוֹ עֹמֶדֶת
one-enduring and-righteousness-of-him in-house-of-him and-richness wealth (3)

לָעַד׃ (4) זָרַח בַּחֹשֶׁךְ אוֹר לַיְשָׁרִים חַנּוּן
gracious for-the-upright-ones light in-the-darkness he-dawns (4) to-forever

וְרַחוּם וְצַדִּיק׃ (5) טוֹב־ אִישׁ חוֹנֵן וּמַלְוֶה
and-lending being-generous man good-of (5) and-righteous and-compassionate

יְכַלְכֵּל דְּבָרָיו בְּמִשְׁפָּט׃ (6) כִּי־ לְעוֹלָם לֹא־
not to-forever surely (6) with-justice affairs-of-him he-conducts

יִמּוֹט לְזֵכֶר עוֹלָם יִהְיֶה צַדִּיק׃
righteous he-will-be forever for-remembrance-of he-will-be-shaken

(7) מִשְּׁמוּעָה רָעָה לֹא יִירָא נָכוֹן לִבּוֹ בָּטֻחַ
one-trusting heart-of-him one-being-steadfast he-will-fear not bad of-news (7)

בַּיהוָה׃ (8) סָמוּךְ לִבּוֹ לֹא יִירָא עַד אֲשֶׁר־
when end he-will-fear not heart-of-him one-being-secure (8) in-Yahweh

יִרְאֶה בְצָרָיו׃ (9) פִּזַּר ׀ נָתַן לָאֶבְיוֹנִים
to-the-poor-ones he-gave he-scattered (9) on-foes-of-him he-will-look

צִדְקָתוֹ עֹמֶדֶת לָעַד קַרְנוֹ תָּרוּם
she-will-be-lifted horn-of-him to-forever one-enduring righteousness-of-him

בְּכָבוֹד׃ (10) רָשָׁע יִרְאֶה ׀ וְכָעָס שִׁנָּיו
teeth-of-him and-he-will-be-vexed he-will-see wicked (10) in-honor

יַחֲרֹק וְנָמָס תַּאֲוַת רְשָׁעִים תֹּאבֵד׃
she-comes-to-nothing wicked-ones longing-of and-he-will-waste-away he-will-gnash

(113:1) הַלְלוּ יָהּ ׀ הַלְלוּ עַבְדֵי יְהוָה הַלְלוּ אֶת־ שֵׁם יְהוָה׃
Yahweh name-of *** praise! Yahweh servants-of praise! Yahweh praise! (113:1)

(2) יְהִי שֵׁם יְהוָה מְבֹרָךְ מֵעַתָּה וְעַד־ עוֹלָם׃
forevermore and-to from-now one-being-praised Yahweh name-of let-him-be (2)

(3) מִמִּזְרַח־ שֶׁמֶשׁ עַד־ מְבוֹאוֹ מְהֻלָּל שֵׁם יְהוָה׃
Yahweh name-of being-praised setting-of-him to sun from-rising-of (3)

holy and awesome is his
name.
10 The fear of the LORD is the
beginning of wisdom;
all who follow his precepts
have good understanding.
To him belongs eternal
praise.

Psalm 112[h]

1 Praise the LORD.[i]

Blessed is the man who fears
the LORD,
who finds great delight in
his commands.

2 His children will be mighty in
the land;
each generation of the
upright will be blessed.
3 Wealth and riches are in his
house,
and his righteousness
endures forever.
4 Even in darkness light dawns
for the upright,
for the gracious and
compassionate and
righteous man.[j]
5 Good will come to him who is
generous and lends freely,
who conducts his affairs
with justice.
6 Surely he will never be
shaken;
a righteous man will be
remembered forever.
7 He will have no fear of bad
news;
his heart is steadfast,
trusting in the LORD.
8 His heart is secure, he will
have no fear;
in the end he will look in
triumph on his foes.
9 He has scattered abroad his
gifts to the poor,
his righteousness endures
forever;
his horn[k] will be lifted high
in honor.

10 The wicked man will see and
be vexed,
he will gnash his teeth and
waste away;
the longings of the wicked
will come to nothing.

Psalm 113

1 Praise the LORD.[l]

Praise, O servants of the LORD,
praise the name of the LORD.
2 Let the name of the LORD be
praised,
both now and forevermore.
3 From the rising of the sun to
the place where it sets
the name of the LORD is to
be praised.

[h]This psalm is an acrostic poem, the lines of which begin with the successive letters of the Hebrew alphabet.
[i]1 Hebrew *Hallelu Yah*
[j]4 Or / *for* ⌊*the* LORD⌋ *is gracious and compassionate and righteous*
[k]9 *Horn* here symbolizes dignity.
[l]1 Hebrew *Hallelu Yah*; also in verse 9

רָם עַל־כָּל־גּוֹיִם ׀ יְהוָה עַל הַשָּׁמַיִם כְּבוֹדוֹ׃
glory-of-him the-heavens above Yahweh nations all-of over he-is-exalted (4)

מִי כַּיהוָה אֱלֹהֵינוּ הַמַּגְבִּיהִי לָשָׁבֶת׃
to-sit-enthroned the-one-being-on-high God-of-us like-Yahweh who? (5)

הַמַּשְׁפִּילִי לִרְאוֹת בַּשָּׁמַיִם וּבָאָרֶץ׃
and-on-the-earth on-the-heavens to-look the-one-stooping-down (6)

מְקִימִי מֵעָפָר דָּל מֵאַשְׁפֹּת יָרִים אֶבְיוֹן׃ לְהוֹשִׁיבִי
to-seat (8) needy he-lifts from-ash-heaps poor from-dust one-raising (7)

עִם־נְדִיבִים עִם נְדִיבֵי עַמּוֹ׃ מוֹשִׁיבִי ׀
one-settling (9) people-of-him princes-of with princes with

עֲקֶרֶת הַבַּיִת אֵם־הַבָּנִים שְׂמֵחָה הַלְלוּ־יָהּ׃
Yahweh praise! happy the-children mother-of the-home barren-woman-of

בְּצֵאת יִשְׂרָאֵל מִמִּצְרָיִם בֵּית יַעֲקֹב מֵעַם
from-people Jacob house-of from-Egypt Israel when-to-come-out (114:1)

לֹעֵז׃ הָיְתָה יְהוּדָה לְקָדְשׁוֹ יִשְׂרָאֵל
Israel as-sanctuary-of-him Judah she-became (2) one-having-foreign-tongue

מַמְשְׁלוֹתָיו׃ הַיָּם רָאָה וַיָּנֹס הַיַּרְדֵּן יִסֹּב
he-turned the-Jordan and-he-fled he-looked the-sea (3) dominions-of-him

לְאָחוֹר׃ הֶהָרִים רָקְדוּ כְאֵילִים גְּבָעוֹת כִּבְנֵי־צֹאן׃
flock like-lambs-of hills like-rams they-skipped the-mountains (4) to-back

מַה־לְּךָ הַיָּם כִּי תָנוּס הַיַּרְדֵּן תִּסֹּב לְאָחוֹר׃
to-back you-turned the-Jordan you-fled that the-sea to-you what? (5)

הֶהָרִים תִּרְקְדוּ כְאֵילִים גְּבָעוֹת כִּבְנֵי־צֹאן׃
flock like-lambs-of hills like-rams you-skipped the-mountains (6)

מִלִּפְנֵי אָדוֹן חוּלִי אָרֶץ מִלִּפְנֵי אֱלוֹהַּ יַעֲקֹב׃
Jacob God-of at-presences-of earth tremble! Lord at-presences-of (7)

הַהֹפְכִי הַצּוּר אֲגַם־מָיִם חַלָּמִישׁ לְמַעְיְנוֹ־מָיִם׃
waters into-spring-of hard-rock waters pool-of the-rock the-one-turning (8)

לֹא לָנוּ יְהוָה לֹא לָנוּ כִּי־לְשִׁמְךָ תֵּן כָּבוֹד עַל־
because-of glory give! to-name-of-you but to-us not Yahweh to-us not (115:1)

חַסְדְּךָ עַל־אֲמִתֶּךָ׃ לָמָּה יֹאמְרוּ הַגּוֹיִם
the-nations they-say why? (2) faithfulness-of-you because-of love-of-you

אַיֵּה־נָא אֱלֹהֵיהֶם׃ וֵאלֹהֵינוּ בַשָּׁמָיִם כֹּל אֲשֶׁר־חָפֵץ
he-pleases that all in-the-heavens now-God-of-us (3) God-of-them now! where?

עָשָׂה׃ עֲצַבֵּיהֶם כֶּסֶף וְזָהָב מַעֲשֵׂה יְדֵי אָדָם׃ פֶּה־
mouth (5) man hands-of making-of and-gold silver idols-of-them (4) he-does

לָהֶם וְלֹא יְדַבֵּרוּ עֵינַיִם לָהֶם וְלֹא יִרְאוּ׃
they-can-see but-not to-them eyes they-can-speak but-not to-them

4 The LORD is exalted over all the nations,
his glory above the heavens.
5 Who is like the LORD our God,
the One who sits enthroned on high,
6 who stoops down to look
on the heavens and the earth?

7 He raises the poor from the dust
and lifts the needy from the ash heap;
8 he seats them with princes,
with the princes of their people.
9 He settles the barren woman in her home
as a happy mother of children.

Praise the LORD.

Psalm 114

1 When Israel came out of Egypt,
the house of Jacob from a people of foreign tongue,
2 Judah became God's sanctuary,
Israel his dominion.

3 The sea looked and fled,
the Jordan turned back;
4 the mountains skipped like rams,
the hills like lambs.

5 Why was it, O sea, that you fled,
O Jordan, that you turned back,
6 you mountains, that you skipped like rams,
you hills, like lambs?

7 Tremble, O earth, at the presence of the Lord,
at the presence of the God of Jacob,
8 who turned the rock into a pool,
the hard rock into springs of water.

Psalm 115

1 Not to us, O LORD, not to us
but to your name be the glory,
because of your love and faithfulness.

2 Why do the nations say,
"Where is their God?"
3 Our God is in heaven;
he does whatever pleases him.
4 But their idols are silver and gold,
made by the hands of men.
5 They have mouths, but cannot speak,
eyes, but they cannot see;

אָזְנַיִם לָהֶם וְלֹא יִשְׁמָעוּ אַף לָהֶם וְלֹא יְרִיחוּן׃
they-can-smell but-not to-them nose they-can-hear but-not to-them ears (6)

יְדֵיהֶם ׀ וְלֹא יְמִישׁוּן רַגְלֵיהֶם וְלֹא יְהַלֵּכוּ
they-can-walk but-not feet-of-them they-can-feel but-not hands-of-them (7)

לֹא־ יֶהְגּוּ בִּגְרוֹנָם׃ כְּמוֹהֶם יִהְיוּ
they-will-be like-them (8) with-throat-of-them they-can-utter-sound not

עֹשֵׂיהֶם כֹּל אֲשֶׁר־ בֹּטֵחַ בָּהֶם׃ יִשְׂרָאֵל בְּטַח בַּיהוָה
in-Yahweh trust! Israel (9) in-them one-trusting who all ones-making-them

עֶזְרָם וּמָגִנָּם הוּא׃ בֵּית אַהֲרֹן בִּטְחוּ בַיהוָה
in-Yahweh trust! Aaron house-of (10) he and-shield-of-them help-of-them

עֶזְרָם וּמָגִנָּם הוּא׃ יִרְאֵי יְהוָה בִּטְחוּ
trust! Yahweh ones-fearing-of (11) he and-shield-of-them help-of-them

בַיהוָה עֶזְרָם וּמָגִנָּם הוּא׃ יְהוָה זְכָרָנוּ
he-remembers-us Yahweh (12) he and-shield-of-them help-of-them in-Yahweh

יְבָרֵךְ יְבָרֵךְ אֶת־ בֵּית יִשְׂרָאֵל יְבָרֵךְ אֶת־ בֵּית
house-of *** he-will-bless Israel house-of *** he-will-bless he-will-bless

אַהֲרֹן׃ יְבָרֵךְ יִרְאֵי יְהוָה הַקְּטַנִּים עִם־
with the-small-ones Yahweh ones-fearing-of he-will-bless (13) Aaron

הַגְּדֹלִים׃ יֹסֵף יְהוָה עֲלֵיכֶם עֲלֵיכֶם וְעַל־
and-to to-you to-you Yahweh may-he-make-increase (14) the-great-ones

בְּנֵיכֶם׃ בְּרוּכִים אַתֶּם לַיהוָה עֹשֵׂה שָׁמַיִם
heavens One-Making-of by-Yahweh you ones-being-blessed (15) children-of-you

וָאָרֶץ׃ הַשָּׁמַיִם שָׁמַיִם לַיהוָה וְהָאָרֶץ נָתַן
he-gave but-the-earth to-Yahweh heavens the-heavens (16) and-earth

לִבְנֵי־ אָדָם׃ לֹא הַמֵּתִים יְהַלְלוּ־ יָהּ וְלֹא כָּל־
all-of and-not Yahweh they-praise the-dead-ones not (17) man to-sons-of

יֹרְדֵי דוּמָה׃ וַאֲנַחְנוּ ׀ נְבָרֵךְ יָהּ מֵעַתָּה וְעַד־
and-to from-now Yahweh we-extol but-we (18) silence ones-going-down-of

עוֹלָם הַלְלוּ־ יָהּ׃ אָהַבְתִּי כִּי־ יִשְׁמַע ׀ יְהוָה אֶת־
*** Yahweh he-heard because I-love (116:1) Yahweh praise! forevermore

קוֹלִי תַּחֲנוּנָי׃ כִּי־ הִטָּה אָזְנוֹ לִי
to-me ear-of-him he-turned because (2) cries-for-mercy-of-me voice-of-me

וּבְיָמַי אֶקְרָא׃ אֲפָפוּנִי ׀ חֶבְלֵי־ מָוֶת
death cords-of they-entangled-me (3) I-will-call then-during-days-of-me

וּמְצָרֵי שְׁאוֹל מְצָאוּנִי צָרָה וְיָגוֹן אֶמְצָא׃
I-was-overcome and-sorrow trouble they-came-upon-me Sheol and-anguishes-of

וּבְשֵׁם־ יְהוָה אֶקְרָא אָנָּה יְהוָה מַלְּטָה נַפְשִׁי׃ חַנּוּן
gracious (5) self-of-me save! Yahweh oh! I-called Yahweh then-on-name-of (4)

6 they have ears, but cannot hear,
noses, but they cannot smell;
7 they have hands, but cannot feel,
feet, but they cannot walk;
nor can they utter a sound with their throats.
8 Those who make them will be like them,
and so will all who trust in them.

9 O house of Israel, trust in the LORD—
he is their help and shield.
10 O house of Aaron, trust in the LORD—
he is their help and shield.
11 You who fear him, trust in the LORD—
he is their help and shield.

12 The LORD remembers us and will bless us:
He will bless the house of Israel,
he will bless the house of Aaron,
13 he will bless those who fear the LORD—
small and great alike.

14 May the LORD make you increase,
both you and your children.
15 May you be blessed by the LORD,
the Maker of heaven and earth.

16 The highest heavens belong to the LORD,
but the earth he has given to man.
17 It is not the dead who praise the LORD,
those who go down to silence;
18 it is we who extol the LORD,
both now and forevermore.

Praise the LORD.[m]

Psalm 116

1 I love the LORD, for he heard my voice;
he heard my cry for mercy.
2 Because he turned his ear to me,
I will call on him as long as I live.

3 The cords of death entangled me,
the anguish of the grave[n] came upon me;
I was overcome by trouble and sorrow.
4 Then I called on the name of the LORD:
"O LORD, save me!"

[m] 18 Hebrew *Hallelu Yah*
[n] 3 Hebrew *Sheol*

יְהוָה וְצַדִּיק וֵאלֹהֵינוּ מְרַחֵם׃ שֹׁמֵר
one-protecting (6) one-being-compassionate and-God-of-us and-righteous Yahweh

פְּתָאיִם* יְהוָה דַּלֹּתִי וְלִי יְהוֹשִׁיעַ׃ שׁוּבִי
return! (7) he-saved and-to-me I-was-in-need Yahweh simplehearted-ones

נַפְשִׁי לִמְנוּחָיְכִי כִּי־ יְהוָה גָּמַל עָלָיְכִי׃ כִּי חִלַּצְתָּ
you-delivered for (8) to-you he-was-good Yahweh for to-rests-of-you soul-of-me

נַפְשִׁי מִמָּוֶת אֶת־ עֵינִי מִן־דִּמְעָה אֶת־ רַגְלִי מִדֶּחִי׃
from-stumbling foot-of-me *** tear from eye-of-me *** from-death soul-of-me

אֶתְהַלֵּךְ לִפְנֵי יְהוָה בְּאַרְצוֹת הַחַיִּים׃ הֶאֱמַנְתִּי
I-believed (10) the-living-ones in-lands-of Yahweh before I-may-walk (9)

כִּי אֲדַבֵּר אֲנִי עָנִיתִי מְאֹד׃ אֲנִי אָמַרְתִּי בְחָפְזִי
when-to-be-dismayed-me I-said I (11) greatly I-am-afflicted I I-said therefore

כָּל־ הָאָדָם כֹּזֵב׃ מָה־ אָשִׁיב לַיהוָה כָּל־ תַּגְמוּלוֹהִי
goodness-of-him all-of to-Yahweh can-I-repay how? (12) one-lying the-man all-of

עָלָי׃ כּוֹס־ יְשׁוּעוֹת אֶשָּׂא וּבְשֵׁם יְהוָה אֶקְרָא׃
I-will-call Yahweh and-on-name-of I-will-lift salvations cup-of (13) to-me

נְדָרַי לַיהוָה אֲשַׁלֵּם נֶגְדָה־ נָּא לְכָל־
of-all-of now! in-presence I-will-fulfill to-Yahweh vows-of-me (14)

עַמּוֹ׃ יָקָר בְּעֵינֵי יְהוָה הַמָּוְתָה לַחֲסִידָיו׃
of-saints-of-him to-the-death Yahweh in-eyes-of precious (15) people-of-him

אָנָּה יְהוָה כִּי־ אֲנִי עַבְדֶּךָ אֲנִי־ עַבְדְּךָ בֶּן־
son-of servant-of-you I servant-of-you I truly Yahweh oh! (16)

אֲמָתֶךָ פִּתַּחְתָּ לְמוֹסֵרָי׃ לְךָ־ אֶזְבַּח
I-will-sacrifice to-you (17) from-chains-of-me you-freed maidservant-of-you

זֶבַח תּוֹדָה וּבְשֵׁם יְהוָה אֶקְרָא׃ נְדָרַי
vows-of-me (18) I-will-call Yahweh and-on-name-of thanksgiving offering-of

לַיהוָה אֲשַׁלֵּם נֶגְדָה־ נָּא לְכָל־ עַמּוֹ׃
people-of-him of-all-of now! in-presence I-will-fulfill to-Yahweh

בְּחַצְרוֹת׀ בֵּית יְהוָה בְּתוֹכֵכִי יְרוּשָׁלָםִ הַלְלוּ־ יָהּ׃
Yahweh praise! Jerusalem in-midst-of-you Yahweh house-of in-courts-of (19)

הַלְלוּ אֶת־ יְהוָה כָּל־ גּוֹיִם שַׁבְּחוּהוּ כָּל־ הָאֻמִּים׃
the-peoples all-of extol-him! nations all-of Yahweh *** praise! (117:1)

כִּי גָבַר עָלֵינוּ׀ חַסְדּוֹ וֶאֱמֶת־ יְהוָה
Yahweh and-faithfulness-of love-of-him toward-us he-is-great for (2)

לְעוֹלָם הַלְלוּ־ יָהּ׃ הוֹדוּ לַיהוָה כִּי־ טוֹב כִּי
for good for to-Yahweh give-thanks! (118:1) Yahweh praise! to-forever

לְעוֹלָם חַסְדּוֹ׃ יֹאמַר־ נָא יִשְׂרָאֵל כִּי לְעוֹלָם חַסְדּוֹ׃
love-of-him to-forever that Israel now! let-him-say (2) love-of-him to-forever

[5]The LORD is gracious and
righteous;
our God is full of
compassion.
[6]The LORD protects the
simplehearted;
when I was in great need,
he saved me.

[7]Be at rest once more, O my
soul,
for the LORD has been good
to you.

[8]For you, O LORD, have
delivered my soul from
death,
my eyes from tears,
my feet from stumbling,
[9]that I may walk before the
LORD
in the land of the living.
[10]I believed; therefore[o] I said,
"I am greatly afflicted."
[11]And in my dismay I said,
"All men are liars."

[12]How can I repay the LORD
for all his goodness to me?
[13]I will lift up the cup of
salvation
and call on the name of the
LORD.
[14]I will fulfill my vows to the
LORD
in the presence of all his
people.

[15]Precious in the sight of the
LORD
is the death of his saints.
[16]O LORD, truly I am your
servant;
I am your servant, the son
of your maidservant[p];
you have freed me from my
chains.

[17]I will sacrifice a thank offering
to you
and call on the name of the
LORD.
[18]I will fulfill my vows to the
LORD
in the presence of all his
people,
[19]in the courts of the house of
the LORD—
in your midst, O Jerusalem.

Praise the LORD.[q]

Psalm 117

[1]Praise the LORD, all you
nations;
extol him, all you peoples.
[2]For great is his love toward us,
and the faithfulness of the
LORD endures forever.

Praise the LORD.[r]

Psalm 118

[1]Give thanks to the LORD, for
he is good;
his love endures forever.

[2]Let Israel say:
"His love endures forever."

[o]10 Or *believed even when*
[p]16 Or *servant, your faithful son*
[q]19 Hebrew *Hallelu Yah*
[r]2 Hebrew *Hallelu Yah*

*6 Most mss have *hireq* under the *aleph* (אִים–).

יֹאמְרוּ־ נָא בֵית־ אַהֲרֹן כִּי לְעוֹלָם חַסְדּוֹ׃
love-of-him to-forever that Aaron house-of now! let-them-say (3)

יֹאמְרוּ־ נָא יִרְאֵי יְהוָה כִּי לְעוֹלָם חַסְדּוֹ׃
love-of-him to-forever that Yahweh ones-fearing-of now! let-them-say (4)

מִן־ הַמֵּצַר קָרָאתִי יָּהּ עָנָנִי בַמֶּרְחָב יָהּ׃
Yahweh with-the-freedom he-answered-me Yahweh I-cried-to the-anguish in (5)

יְהוָה לִי לֹא אִירָא מַה־ יַּעֲשֶׂה לִי אָדָם׃ יְהוָה
Yahweh (7) man to-me can-he-do what? I-will-be-afraid not with-me Yahweh (6)

לִי בְּעֹזְרָי וַאֲנִי אֶרְאֶה בְשֹׂנְאָי׃
on-ones-being-enemies-of-me I-will-look and-I as-ones-helping-me with-me

טוֹב לַחֲסוֹת בַּיהוָה מִבְּטֹחַ בָּאָדָם׃ טוֹב
better (9) in-the-man than-to-trust in-Yahweh to-take-refuge better (8)

לַחֲסוֹת בַּיהוָה מִבְּטֹחַ בִּנְדִיבִים׃ כָּל־ גּוֹיִם
nations all-of (10) in-princes than-to-trust in-Yahweh to-take-refuge

סְבָבוּנִי בְּשֵׁם יְהוָה כִּי אֲמִילַם׃
I-cut-off-them indeed Yahweh in-name-of they-surrounded-me

סַבּוּנִי גַם־ סְבָבוּנִי בְּשֵׁם יְהוָה כִּי
indeed Yahweh in-name-of they-surrounded-me indeed they-surrounded-me (11)

אֲמִילַם׃ סַבּוּנִי כִדְבוֹרִים דֹּעֲכוּ כְּאֵשׁ
like-fire-of they-died-out like-bees they-swarmed-around-me (12) I-cut-off-them

קוֹצִים בְּשֵׁם יְהוָה כִּי אֲמִילַם׃ דַּחֹה
to-push-back (13) I-cut-off-them indeed Yahweh in-name-of thorns

דְחִיתַנִי לִנְפֹּל וַיהוָה עֲזָרָנִי׃ עָזִּי
strength-of-me (14) he-helped-me but-Yahweh to-fall you-pushed-back-me

וְזִמְרָת יָהּ וַיְהִי־ לִי לִישׁוּעָה׃ קוֹל ׀ רִנָּה וִישׁוּעָה
and-victory joy shout-of (15) as-salvation to-me and-he-became Yahweh and-song

בְּאָהֳלֵי צַדִּיקִים יְמִין יְהוָה עֹשָׂה חָיִל׃
mighty-thing one-doing Yahweh right-hand-of righteous-ones in-tents-of

יְמִין יְהוָה רוֹמֵמָה יְמִין יְהוָה עֹשָׂה
one-doing Yahweh right-hand-of one-being-lifted-high Yahweh right-hand-of (16)

חָיִל׃ לֹא אָמוּת כִּי־ אֶחְיֶה וַאֲסַפֵּר מַעֲשֵׂי
deeds-of and-I-will-proclaim I-will-live but I-will-die not (17) mighty-thing

יָהּ׃ יַסֹּר יִסְּרַנִּי יָּהּ וְלַמָּוֶת לֹא נְתָנָנִי׃
he-gave-me not but-to-the-death Yahweh he-chastened-me to-chasten (18) Yahweh

פִּתְחוּ־ לִי שַׁעֲרֵי־ צֶדֶק אָבֹא־ בָם
through-them I-will-enter righteousness gates-of for-me open! (19)

אוֹדֶה יָהּ׃ זֶה־ הַשַּׁעַר לַיהוָה צַדִּיקִים
righteous-ones of-Yahweh the-gate this (20) Yahweh I-will-give-thanks

3 Let the house of Aaron say:
"His love endures forever."
4 Let those who fear the LORD
say:
"His love endures forever."

5 In my anguish I cried to the
LORD,
and he answered by setting
me free.
6 The LORD is with me; I will
not be afraid.
What can man do to me?
7 The LORD is with me; he is my
helper.
I will look in triumph on
my enemies.

8 It is better to take refuge in
the LORD
than to trust in man.
9 It is better to take refuge in
the LORD
than to trust in princes.

10 All the nations surrounded me,
but in the name of the LORD
I cut them off.
11 They surrounded me on every
side,
but in the name of the LORD
I cut them off.
12 They swarmed around me like
bees,
but they died out as quickly
as burning thorns;
in the name of the LORD I
cut them off.

13 I was pushed back and about
to fall,
but the LORD helped me.
14 The LORD is my strength and
my song;
he has become my salvation.

15 Shouts of joy and victory
resound in the tents of the
righteous:
"The LORD's right hand has
done mighty things!
16 The LORD's right hand is
lifted high;
the LORD's right hand has
done mighty things!"

17 I will not die but live,
and will proclaim what the
LORD has done.
18 The LORD has chastened me
severely,
but he has not given me
over to death.

19 Open for me the gates of
righteousness;
I will enter and give thanks
to the LORD.
20 This is the gate of the LORD
through which the righteous

יָבֹאוּ בוֹ׃ אוֹדְךָ כִּי עֲנִיתָנִי
you-answered-me for I-will-give-thanks-to-you (21) through-him they-may-enter

וַתְּהִי־ לִי לִישׁוּעָה׃ אֶבֶן מָאֲסוּ הַבּוֹנִים
the-ones-building they-rejected stone (22) as-salvation to-me and-you-became

הָיְתָה לְרֹאשׁ פִּנָּה׃ מֵאֵת יְהוָה הָיְתָה זֹּאת הִיא
she this she-happened Yahweh from-with (23) corner as-capstone-of she-became

נִפְלָאת בְּעֵינֵינוּ׃ זֶה־ הַיּוֹם עָשָׂה יְהוָה
Yahweh he-made the-day this (24) in-eyes-of-us one-being-marvelous

נָגִילָה וְנִשְׂמְחָה בוֹ׃ אָנָּא יְהוָה הוֹשִׁיעָה נָּא אָנָּא יְהוָה
Yahweh oh! now! save! Yahweh oh! (25) in-him and-let-us-be-glad let-us-rejoice

הַצְלִיחָה נָּא׃ בָּרוּךְ הַבָּא בְּשֵׁם יְהוָה
Yahweh in-name-of the-one-coming being-blessed (26) now! grant-success!

בֵּרַכְנוּכֶם מִבֵּית יְהוָה׃ אֵל ׀ יְהוָה וַיָּאֶר לָנוּ
on-us and-he-shined-light Yahweh God (27) Yahweh from-house-of we-bless-you

אִסְרוּ־ חַג בַּעֲבֹתִים עַד־ קַרְנוֹת הַמִּזְבֵּחַ׃ אֵלִי
God-of-me (28) the-altar horns-of up-to with-boughs festal-procession join!

אַתָּה וְאוֹדֶךָּ אֱלֹהַי אֲרוֹמְמֶךָּ׃
and-I-will-exalt-you God-of-me and-I-will-give-thanks-to-you you

הוֹדוּ לַיהוָה כִּי־ טוֹב כִּי לְעוֹלָם חַסְדּוֹ׃
love-of-him to-forever for good for to-Yahweh give-thanks! (29)

אַשְׁרֵי תְמִימֵי־ דָרֶךְ הַהֹלְכִים בְּתוֹרַת
by-law-of the-ones-walking way ones-blameless-of blessednesses-of (119:1)

יְהוָה׃ אַשְׁרֵי נֹצְרֵי עֵדֹתָיו בְּכָל־ לֵב
heart with-all-of statutes-of-him ones-keeping-of blessednesses-of (2) Yahweh

יִדְרְשׁוּהוּ׃ אַף לֹא־ פָעֲלוּ עַוְלָה בִּדְרָכָיו הָלָכוּ׃ אַתָּה
you (4) they-walk in-ways-of-him wrong they-do nothing also (3) they-seek-him

צִוִּיתָה פִקֻּדֶיךָ לִשְׁמֹר מְאֹד׃ אַחֲלַי יִכֹּנוּ
they-were-steadfast oh-that! (5) fully to-obey precepts-of-you you-laid-down

דְרָכָי לִשְׁמֹר חֻקֶּיךָ׃ אָז לֹא־ אֵבוֹשׁ
I-would-be-shamed not then (6) decrees-of-you to-obey ways-of-me

בְּהַבִּיטִי אֶל־ כָּל־ מִצְוֺתֶיךָ׃ אוֹדְךָ
I-will-praise-you (7) commands-of-you all-of to when-to-consider-me

בְּיֹשֶׁר לֵבָב בְּלָמְדִי מִשְׁפְּטֵי צִדְקֶךָ׃
righteousness-of-you laws-of as-to-learn-me heart with-uprightness-of

אֶת־ חֻקֶּיךָ אֶשְׁמֹר אַל־ תַּעַזְבֵנִי עַד־ מְאֹד׃ בַּמֶּה
by-the-how? (9) utterly to you-forsake-me not I-will-obey decrees-of-you *** (8)

יְזַכֶּה־ נַּעַר אֶת־ אָרְחוֹ לִשְׁמֹר כִּדְבָרֶךָ׃
as-word-of-you to-live way-of-him *** young-man he-can-keep-pure

may enter.
21 I will give you thanks, for you
answered me;
you have become my
salvation.

22 The stone the builders rejected
has become the capstone;
23 the LORD has done this,
and it is marvelous in our
eyes.
24 This is the day the LORD has
made;
let us rejoice and be glad in
it.

25 O LORD, save us;
O LORD, grant us success.
26 Blessed is he who comes in
the name of the LORD.
From the house of the LORD
we bless you.[s]
27 The LORD is God,
and he has made his light
shine upon us.
With boughs in hand, join in
the festal procession
up[t] to the horns of the altar.

28 You are my God, and I will
give you thanks;
you are my God, and I will
exalt you.

29 Give thanks to the LORD, for
he is good;
his love endures forever.

Psalm 119[u]

א Aleph

1 Blessed are they whose ways
are blameless,
who walk according to the
law of the LORD.
2 Blessed are they who keep his
statutes
and seek him with all their
heart.
3 They do nothing wrong;
they walk in his ways.
4 You have laid down precepts
that are to be fully obeyed.
5 Oh, that my ways were
steadfast
in obeying your decrees!
6 Then I would not be put to
shame
when I consider all your
commands.
7 I will praise you with an
upright heart
as I learn your righteous
laws.
8 I will obey your decrees;
do not utterly forsake me.

ב Beth

9 How can a young man keep
his way pure?
By living according to your
word.

[s] 26 The Hebrew is plural.
[t] 27 Or *Bind the festal sacrifice with ropes / and take it*
[u] This psalm is an acrostic poem; the verses of each stanza begin with the same letter of the Hebrew alphabet.

תַּשְׁגֵּנִי	אַל־	דְרַשְׁתִּיךָ	לִבִּי	בְּכָל־	
you-let-stray-me	not	I-seek-you	heart-of-me	with-all-of	(10)

לֹא	לְמַעַן	אִמְרָתֶךָ	צָפַנְתִּי	בְּלִבִּי		מִמִּצְוֺתֶיךָ׃
not	so-that	word-of-you	I-hid	in-heart-of-me	(11)	from-commands-of-you

חֻקֶּיךָ׃	לַמְּדֵנִי	יְהוָה	אַתָּה	בָּרוּךְ		לָךְ׃	אֶחֱטָא־
decrees-of-you	teach-me!	Yahweh	you	being-praised	(12)	against-you	I-might-sin

בְּדֶרֶךְ		פִיךָ׃	מִשְׁפְּטֵי־	כֹּל	סִפַּרְתִּי	בִּשְׂפָתַי	
in-way-of	(14)	mouth-of-you	laws-of	all-of	I-recount	with-lips-of-me	(13)

בְּפִקֻּדֶיךָ		הוֹן׃	כָּל־	כְּעַל	שַׂשְׂתִּי	עֵדְוֺתֶיךָ
on-precepts-of-you	(15)	richness	greatness-of	as-in	I-rejoice	statutes-of-you

לֹא	אֶשְׁתַּעֲשָׁע	בְּחֻקֹּתֶיךָ		אֹרְחֹתֶיךָ׃	וְאַבִּיטָה	אָשִׂיחָה
not	I-delight	in-decrees-of-you	(16)	ways-of-you	and-I-consider	I-meditate

אֶחְיֶה	עַבְדְּךָ	עַל־	גְּמֹל		דְּבָרֶךָ׃	אֶשְׁכַּח
I-will-live	servant-of-you	to	do-good!	(17)	word-of-you	and-I-will-neglect

וְאַבִּיטָה	עֵינַי	גַּל־		דְבָרֶךָ׃	וְאֶשְׁמְרָה
that-I-may-see	eyes-of-me	open!	(18)	word-of-you	and-I-will-obey

תַּסְתֵּר	אַל־	בָאָרֶץ	אָנֹכִי	גֵּר		מִתּוֹרָתֶךָ׃	נִפְלָאוֹת
you-hide	not	on-the-earth	I	stranger	(19)	in-law-of-you	things-being-wonderful

אֶל־	לְתַאֲבָה	נַפְשִׁי	גָּרְסָה		מִצְוֺתֶיךָ׃	מִמֶּנִּי
for	with-longing	soul-of-me	she-is-consumed	(20)	commands-of-you	from-me

אֲרוּרִים	זֵדִים	גָּעַרְתָּ		עֵת׃	בְכָל־	מִשְׁפָּטֶיךָ
ones-being-cursed	arrogant-ones	you-rebuke	(21)	time	at-all-of	laws-of-you

חֶרְפָּה	מֵעָלַי	גַּל		מִמִּצְוֺתֶיךָ׃	הַשֹּׁגִים
scorn	from-upon-me	remove!	(22)	from-commands-of-you	the-ones-straying

בִּי	שָׂרִים	יָשְׁבוּ	גַּם		נָצָרְתִּי׃	עֵדֹתֶיךָ	כִּי	וָבוּז
against-me	princes	they-sit	though	(23)	I-keep	statutes-of-you	for	and-contempt

גַּם־		בְּחֻקֶּיךָ׃	יָשִׂיחַ	עַבְדְּךָ	נִדְבָּרוּ
indeed	(24)	on-decrees-of-you	he-will-meditate	servant-of-you	they-slander

דָּבְקָה		עֲצָתִי׃	אַנְשֵׁי	שַׁעֲשֻׁעָי	עֵדֹתֶיךָ
she-is-laid-low	(25)	counsel-of-me	men-of	delights-of-me	statutes-of-you

דְּרָכַי		כִּדְבָרֶךָ׃	חַיֵּנִי	נַפְשִׁי	לֶעָפָר
ways-of-me	(26)	as-word-of-you	make-alive-me!	self-of-me	in-the-dust

דֶּרֶךְ־		חֻקֶּיךָ׃	לַמְּדֵנִי	וַתַּעֲנֵנִי	סִפַּרְתִּי
teaching-of	(27)	decrees-of-you	teach-me!	and-you-answered-me	I-recounted

בְּנִפְלְאוֹתֶיךָ׃	וְאָשִׂיחָה	הֲבִינֵנִי	פִּקּוּדֶיךָ
on-ones-being-wonders-of-you	then-I-will-meditate	let-understand-me!	precepts-of-you

כִּדְבָרֶךָ׃	קַיְּמֵנִי	מִתּוּגָה	נַפְשִׁי	דָּלְפָה	
as-word-of-you	strengthen-me!	with-sorrow	soul-of-me	she-is-weary	(28)

10 I seek you with all my heart;
do not let me stray from your commands.
11 I have hidden your word in my heart
that I might not sin against you.
12 Praise be to you, O LORD;
teach me your decrees.
13 With my lips I recount
all the laws that come from your mouth.
14 I rejoice in following your statutes
as one rejoices in great riches.
15 I meditate on your precepts
and consider your ways.
16 I delight in your decrees;
I will not neglect your word.

ג Gimel

17 Do good to your servant, and I will live;
I will obey your word.
18 Open my eyes that I may see
wonderful things in your law.
19 I am a stranger on earth;
do not hide your commands from me.
20 My soul is consumed with longing
for your laws at all times.
21 You rebuke the arrogant, who are cursed
and who stray from your commands.
22 Remove from me scorn and contempt,
for I keep your statutes.
23 Though princes sit together and slander me,
your servant will meditate on your decrees.
24 Your statutes are my delight;
they are my counselors.

ד Daleth

25 I am laid low in the dust;
renew my life according to your word.
26 I recounted my ways and you answered me;
teach me your decrees.
27 Let me understand the teaching of your precepts;
then I will meditate on your wonders.
28 My soul is weary with sorrow;
strengthen me according to your word.

דֶּרֶךְ־שֶׁקֶר הָסֵר מִמֶּנִּי וְתוֹרָתְךָ חָנֵּנִי׃ דֶּרֶךְ־
way-of (30) be-gracious-to-me! and-law-of-you from-me keep! deceit way-of (29)

אֱמוּנָה בָחָרְתִּי מִשְׁפָּטֶיךָ שִׁוִּיתִי׃ דָּבַקְתִּי בְעֵדְוֺתֶיךָ
to-statutes-of-you I-hold-fast (31) I-set-heart laws-of-you I-chose truth

יְהוָה אַל־תְּבִישֵׁנִי׃ דֶּרֶךְ־מִצְוֺתֶיךָ אָרוּץ כִּי
for I-run commands-of-you path-of (32) you-let-be-shamed-me not Yahweh

תַרְחִיב לִבִּי׃ הוֹרֵנִי יְהוָה דֶּרֶךְ חֻקֶּיךָ
decrees-of-you way-of Yahweh teach-me! (33) heart-of-me you-set-free

וְאֶצְּרֶנָּה עֵקֶב׃ הֲבִינֵנִי וְאֶצְּרָה תוֹרָתֶךָ
law-of-you and-I-will-keep make-understand-me! (34) end then-I-will-keep-her

וְאֶשְׁמְרֶנָּה בְכָל־לֵב׃ הַדְרִיכֵנִי בִּנְתִיב
in-path-of direct-me! (35) heart with-all-of and-I-will-obey-her

מִצְוֺתֶיךָ כִּי־בוֹ חָפָצְתִּי׃ הַט־לִבִּי אֶל־עֵדְוֺתֶיךָ
statutes-of-you to heart-of-me turn! (36) I-delight in-him for commands-of-you

וְאַל אֶל־בָּצַע׃ הַעֲבֵר עֵינַי מֵרְאוֹת שָׁוְא
worthless-thing from-to-see eyes-of-me turn! (37) selfish-gain toward and-not

בִּדְרָכֶךָ חַיֵּנִי׃ הָקֵם לְעַבְדְּךָ אִמְרָתֶךָ
promise-of-you to-servant-of-you fulfill! (38) make-alive-me! in-way-of-you

אֲשֶׁר לְיִרְאָתֶךָ׃ הַעֲבֵר חֶרְפָּתִי אֲשֶׁר יָגֹרְתִּי כִּי מִשְׁפָּטֶיךָ
laws-of-you for I-dread that disgrace-of-me take-away! (39) to-fear-you that

טוֹבִים׃ הִנֵּה תָּאַבְתִּי לְפִקֻּדֶיךָ בְּצִדְקָתְךָ
in-righteousness-of-you for-precepts-of-you I-long see! (40) good-ones

חַיֵּנִי׃ וִיבֹאֻנִי חֲסָדֶךָ יְהוָה
Yahweh unfailing-loves-of-you and-may-they-come-to-me (41) make-alive-me!

תְּשׁוּעָתְךָ כְּאִמְרָתֶךָ׃ וְאֶעֱנֶה חֹרְפִי
one-taunting-me then-I-will-answer (42) as-promise-of-you salvation-of-you

דָבָר כִּי־בָטַחְתִּי בִּדְבָרֶךָ׃ וְאַל־תַּצֵּל מִפִּי
from-mouth-of-me you-snatch and-not (43) in-word-of-you I-trust for word

דְבַר־אֱמֶת עַד־מְאֹד כִּי לְמִשְׁפָּטֶךָ יִחָלְתִּי׃ וְאֶשְׁמְרָה
and-I-will-obey (44) I-put-hope in-laws-of-you for indeed to truth word-of

תוֹרָתְךָ תָמִיד לְעוֹלָם וָעֶד׃ וְאֶתְהַלְּכָה בָרְחָבָה כִּי
for in-the-freedom and-I-will-walk (45) and-ever to-forever always law-of-you

פִקֻּדֶיךָ דָרָשְׁתִּי׃ וַאֲדַבְּרָה בְעֵדֹתֶיךָ נֶגֶד
before of-statutes-of-you and-I-will-speak (46) I-sought-out precepts-of-you

מְלָכִים וְלֹא אֵבוֹשׁ׃ וְאֶשְׁתַּעֲשַׁע בְּמִצְוֺתֶיךָ אֲשֶׁר
because in-commands-of-you for-I-delight (47) I-will-be-shamed and-not kings

אָהָבְתִּי׃ וְאֶשָּׂא־כַפַּי אֶל־מִצְוֺתֶיךָ אֲשֶׁר אָהָבְתִּי
I-love which commands-of-you for hands-of-me and-I-reach-out (48) I-love

[29]Keep me from deceitful ways;
be gracious to me through your law.
[30]I have chosen the way of truth;
I have set my heart on your laws.
[31]I hold fast to your statutes, O LORD;
do not let me be put to shame.
[32]I run in the path of your commands,
for you have set my heart free.

ה He

[33]Teach me, O LORD, to follow your decrees;
then I will keep them to the end.
[34]Give me understanding, and I will keep your law
and obey it with all my heart.
[35]Direct me in the path of your commands,
for there I find delight.
[36]Turn my heart toward your statutes
and not toward selfish gain.
[37]Turn my eyes away from worthless things;
renew my life according to your word.[v]
[38]Fulfill your promise to your servant,
so that you may be feared.
[39]Take away the disgrace I dread,
for your laws are good.
[40]How I long for your precepts!
Renew my life in your righteousness.

ו Waw

[41]May your unfailing love come to me, O LORD,
your salvation according to your promise;
[42]then I will answer the one who taunts me,
for I trust in your word.
[43]Do not snatch the word of truth from my mouth,
for I have put my hope in your laws.
[44]I will always obey your law,
for ever and ever.
[45]I will walk about in freedom,
for I have sought out your precepts.
[46]I will speak of your statutes before kings
and will not be put to shame,
[47]for I delight in your commandments
because I love them.
[48]I reach out my hands for your commandments, which I love,

[v]37 Two manuscripts of the Masoretic Text and Dead Sea Scrolls; most manuscripts of the Masoretic Text *life in your way*

וְאָשִׂיחָה בְחֻקֶּיךָ׃ זְכֹר־ דָּבָר לְעַבְדֶּךָ עַל
for to-servant-of-you word remember! (49) on-decrees-of-you and-I-meditate

אֲשֶׁר יִחַלְתָּנִי׃ זֹאת נֶחָמָתִי בְעָנְיִי כִּי
that in-suffering-of-me comfort-of-me this (50) you-gave-hope-to-me that

אִמְרָתְךָ חִיָּתְנִי׃ זֵדִים הֱלִיצֻנִי עַד־ מְאֹד
excess to they-mock-me arrogant-ones (51) she-makes-alive-me promise-of-you

מִתּוֹרָתְךָ לֹא נָטִיתִי׃ זָכַרְתִּי מִשְׁפָּטֶיךָ מֵעוֹלָם ׀ יְהוָה
Yahweh from-ancient laws-of-you I-remember (52) I-turn not from-law-of-you

וָאֶתְנֶחָם׃ זַלְעָפָה אֲחָזַתְנִי מֵרְשָׁעִים
because-of-wicked-ones she-grips-me indignation (53) and-I-find-comfort

עֹזְבֵי תּוֹרָתֶךָ׃ זְמִרוֹת הָיוּ־ לִי חֻקֶּיךָ
decrees-of-you to-me they-are songs (54) law-of-you ones-forsaking-of

בְּבֵית מְגוּרָי׃ זָכַרְתִּי בַלַּיְלָה שִׁמְךָ יְהוָה
Yahweh name-of-you in-the-night I-remember (55) lodgings-of-me in-house-of

וָאֶשְׁמְרָה תּוֹרָתֶךָ׃ זֹאת הָיְתָה־ לִּי כִּי פִקֻּדֶיךָ נָצָרְתִּי׃
I-obey precepts-of-you that to-me she-is this (56) law-of-you and-I-will-keep

חֶלְקִי יְהוָה אָמַרְתִּי לִשְׁמֹר דְּבָרֶיךָ׃ חִלִּיתִי
I-sought (58) words-of-you to-obey I-promised Yahweh portion-of-me (57)

פָנֶיךָ בְכָל־ לֵב חָנֵּנִי כְּאִמְרָתֶךָ׃
as-promise-of-you be-gracious-to-me! heart with-all-of faces-of-you

חִשַּׁבְתִּי דְרָכָי וָאָשִׁיבָה רַגְלַי אֶל־ עֵדֹתֶיךָ׃
statutes-of-you to steps-of-me and-I-turned ways-of-me I-considered (59)

חַשְׁתִּי וְלֹא הִתְמַהְמָהְתִּי לִשְׁמֹר מִצְוֹתֶיךָ׃ חֶבְלֵי
ropes-of (61) commands-of-you to-obey I-will-delay and-not I-will-hasten (60)

רְשָׁעִים עִוְּדֻנִי תּוֹרָתְךָ לֹא שָׁכָחְתִּי׃ חֲצוֹת־
middles-of (62) I-will-forget not law-of-you they-bind-me wicked-ones

לַיְלָה אָקוּם לְהוֹדוֹת לָךְ עַל מִשְׁפְּטֵי צִדְקֶךָ׃
righteousness-of-you laws-of for to-you to-give-thanks I-rise night

חָבֵר אָנִי לְכָל־ אֲשֶׁר יְרֵאוּךָ וּלְשֹׁמְרֵי פִּקּוּדֶיךָ׃
precepts-of-you and-to-ones-following-of they-fear-you who to-all I friend (63)

חַסְדְּךָ יְהוָה מָלְאָה הָאָרֶץ חֻקֶּיךָ לַמְּדֵנִי׃
teach-me! decrees-of-you the-earth she-is-filled Yahweh love-of-you (64)

טוֹב עָשִׂיתָ עִם־ עַבְדְּךָ יְהוָה כִּדְבָרֶךָ׃ טוּב
goodness-of (66) as-word-of-you Yahweh servant-of-you to you-do good (65)

טַעַם וָדַעַת לַמְּדֵנִי כִּי בְמִצְוֹתֶיךָ הֶאֱמָנְתִּי׃ טֶרֶם
before (67) I-believe in-commands-of-you for teach-me! and-knowledge judgment

אֶעֱנֶה אֲנִי שֹׁגֵג וְעַתָּה אִמְרָתְךָ שָׁמָרְתִּי׃ טוֹב־אַתָּה
you good (68) I-obey word-of-you but-now one-going-astray I I-was-afflicted

and I meditate on your
decrees.

ז Zayin

49 Remember your word to your
servant,
for you have given me hope.
50 My comfort in my suffering is
this:
Your promise renews my
life.
51 The arrogant mock me without
restraint,
but I do not turn from your
law.
52 I remember your ancient laws,
O LORD,
and I find comfort in them.
53 Indignation grips me because
of the wicked,
who have forsaken your
law.
54 Your decrees are the theme of
my song
wherever I lodge.
55 In the night I remember your
name, O LORD,
and I will keep your law.
56 This has been my practice:
I obey your precepts.

ח Heth

57 You are my portion, O LORD;
I have promised to obey
your words.
58 I have sought your face with
all my heart;
be gracious to me according
to your promise.
59 I have considered my ways
and have turned my steps to
your statutes.
60 I will hasten and not delay
to obey your commands.
61 Though the wicked bind me
with ropes,
I will not forget your law.
62 At midnight I rise to give you
thanks
for your righteous laws.
63 I am a friend to all who fear
you,
to all who follow your
precepts.
64 The earth is filled with your
love, O LORD;
teach me your decrees.

ט Teth

65 Do good to your servant
according to your word, O
LORD.
66 Teach me knowledge and good
judgment,
for I believe in your
commands.
67 Before I was afflicted I went
astray,
but now I obey your word.
68 You are good, and what you

וּמֵטִיב לַמְּדֵנִי חֻקֶּיךָ׃ טָפְלוּ עָלַי שֶׁקֶר
lie upon-me they-smeared (69) decrees-of-you teach-me! and-one-doing-good

זֵדִים אֲנִי בְּכָל־ לֵב׀ אֱצֹּר* פִּקּוּדֶיךָ׃
precepts-of-you I-keep heart with-all-of I arrogant-ones

טָפַשׁ כַּחֵלֶב לִבָּם אֲנִי תּוֹרָתְךָ שִׁעֲשָׁעְתִּי׃
I-delight-in law-of-you I heart-of-them as-the-fat he-is-callous (70)

טוֹב־ לִי כִי־ עֻנֵּיתִי לְמַעַן אֶלְמַד חֻקֶּיךָ׃
decrees-of-you I-might-learn so-that I-was-afflicted that to-me good (71)

טוֹב־ לִי תוֹרַת־ פִּיךָ מֵאַלְפֵי זָהָב וָכָסֶף׃
and-silver gold more-than-thousands-of mouth-of-you law-of to-me precious (72)

יָדֶיךָ עָשׂוּנִי וַיְכוֹנְנוּנִי הֲבִינֵנִי
make-understand-me! and-they-formed-me they-made-me hands-of-you (73)

וְאֶלְמְדָה מִצְוֹתֶיךָ׃ יְרֵאֶיךָ יִרְאוּנִי
they-see-me ones-fearing-you (74) commands-of-you that-I-might-learn

וְיִשְׂמָחוּ כִּי לִדְבָרְךָ יִחָלְתִּי׃ יָדַעְתִּי יְהוָה כִּי־
that Yahweh I-know (75) I-hope in-word-of-you for and-they-rejoice

צֶדֶק מִשְׁפָּטֶיךָ וֶאֱמוּנָה עִנִּיתָנִי׃ יְהִי־ נָא
now! may-he-be (76) you-afflicted-me and-faithfulness laws-of-you righteous

חַסְדְּךָ לְנַחֲמֵנִי כְּאִמְרָתְךָ לְעַבְדֶּךָ׃
to-servant-of-you as-promise-of-you to-comfort-me unfailing-love-of-you

יְבֹאוּנִי רַחֲמֶיךָ וְאֶחְיֶה כִּי־ תוֹרָתְךָ
law-of-you for that-I-may-live compassions-of-you let-them-come-to-me (77)

שַׁעֲשֻׁעָי׃ יֵבֹשׁוּ זֵדִים כִּי־ שֶׁקֶר
without-cause for arrogant-ones may-they-be-shamed (78) delights-of-me

עִוְּתוּנִי אֲנִי אָשִׂיחַ בְּפִקּוּדֶיךָ׃ יָשׁוּבוּ
may-they-turn (79) on-precepts-of-you I-will-meditate I they-wronged-me

לִי יְרֵאֶיךָ °וְיֹדְעוּ עֵדֹתֶיךָ׃ יְהִי־
may-he-be (80) statutes-of-you and-ones-understanding-of ones-fearing-you to-me

לִבִּי תָמִים בְּחֻקֶּיךָ לְמַעַן לֹא אֵבוֹשׁ׃
I-may-be-shamed not so-that toward-decrees-of-you blameless heart-of-me

כָּלְתָה לִתְשׁוּעָתְךָ נַפְשִׁי לִדְבָרְךָ יִחָלְתִּי׃
I-put-hope in-word-of-you soul-of-me for-salvation-of-you she-faints (81)

כָּלוּ עֵינַי לְאִמְרָתֶךָ לֵאמֹר מָתַי תְּנַחֲמֵנִי׃
will-you-comfort-me when? to-say for-promise-of-you eyes-of-me they-fail (82)

כִּי־ הָיִיתִי כְּנֹאד בְּקִיטוֹר חֻקֶּיךָ לֹא שָׁכָחְתִּי׃
I-forget not decrees-of-you in-smoke like-wineskin I-am though (83)

כַּמָּה יְמֵי־ עַבְדֶּךָ מָתַי תַּעֲשֶׂה
will-you-execute when? servant-of-you days-of as-the-what? (84)

do is good;
teach me your decrees.
69 Though the arrogant have
smeared me with lies,
I keep your precepts with all
my heart.
70 Their hearts are callous and
unfeeling,
but I delight in your law.
71 It was good for me to be
afflicted
so that I might learn your
decrees.
72 The law from your mouth is
more precious to me
than thousands of pieces of
silver and gold.

י Yodh

73 Your hands made me and
formed me;
give me understanding to
learn your commands.
74 May they who fear you rejoice
when they see me,
for I have put my hope in
your word.
75 I know, O LORD, that your
laws are righteous,
and in faithfulness you have
afflicted me.
76 May your unfailing love be my
comfort,
according to your promise to
your servant.
77 Let your compassion come to
me that I may live,
for your law is my delight.
78 May the arrogant be put to
shame for wronging me
without cause;
but I will meditate on your
precepts.
79 May those who fear you turn
to me,
those who understand your
statutes.
80 May my heart be blameless
toward your decrees,
that I may not be put to
shame.

כ Kaph

81 My soul faints with longing
for your salvation,
but I have put my hope in
your word.
82 My eyes fail, looking for your
promise;
I say, "When will you
comfort me?"
83 Though I am like a wineskin
in the smoke,
I do not forget your decrees.
84 How long must your servant
wait?
When will you punish my

*69 Most mss have *segol* under the *aleph* (אֶ).

°79 ק וידעי

בְרֹדְפַי מִשְׁפָּט׃ כָּרוּ־ לִי זֵדִים שִׁיחוֹת
pitfalls arrogant-ones for-me they-dig (85) punishment on-ones-persecuting-me

אֲשֶׁר לֹא כְתוֹרָתֶךָ׃ כָּל־ מִצְוֹתֶיךָ אֱמוּנָה שֶׁקֶר
without-cause trustworthy commands-of-you all-of (86) as-law-of-you not that

רְדָפוּנִי עָזְרֵנִי׃ כִּמְעַט כִּלּוּנִי בָאָרֶץ וַאֲנִי
but-I from-the-earth they-wiped-me as-almost (87) help-me! they-persecute-me

לֹא־ עָזַבְתִּי פִקֻּדֶיךָ׃ כְּחַסְדְּךָ חַיֵּנִי
preserve-alive-me! as-love-of-you (88) precepts-of-you I-forsook not

וְאֶשְׁמְרָה עֵדוּת פִּיךָ׃ לְעוֹלָם יְהוָה דְּבָרְךָ
word-of-you Yahweh to-eternity (89) mouth-of-you statute-of and-I-will-obey

נִצָּב בַּשָּׁמָיִם׃ לְדֹר וָדֹר
and-generation to-generation (90) in-the-heavens one-standing-firm

אֱמוּנָתֶךָ כּוֹנַנְתָּ אֶרֶץ וַתַּעֲמֹד׃ לְמִשְׁפָּטֶיךָ
as-laws-of-you (91) and-she-endures earth you-established faithfulness-of-you

עָמְדוּ הַיּוֹם כִּי הַכֹּל עֲבָדֶיךָ׃ לוּלֵי תוֹרָתְךָ
law-of-you if-not (92) servants-of-you the-all for the-day they-endure

שַׁעֲשֻׁעָי אָז אָבַדְתִּי בְעָנְיִי׃ לְעוֹלָם
to-forever (93) in-affliction-of-me I-would-have-perished then delights-of-me

לֹא־ אֶשְׁכַּח פִּקּוּדֶיךָ כִּי בָם חִיִּיתָנִי׃ לְךָ־
to-you (94) you-made-alive-me by-them for precepts-of-you I-will-forget not

אֲנִי הוֹשִׁיעֵנִי כִּי פִקּוּדֶיךָ דָרָשְׁתִּי׃ לִי קִוּוּ
they-wait for-me (95) I-sought-out precepts-of-you for save-me! I

רְשָׁעִים לְאַבְּדֵנִי עֵדֹתֶיךָ אֶתְבּוֹנָן׃ לְכָל
to-all-of (96) I-will-ponder statutes-of-you to-destroy-me wicked-ones

תִּכְלָה רָאִיתִי קֵץ רְחָבָה מִצְוָתְךָ מְאֹד׃ מָה־אָהַבְתִּי
I-love how! (97) very command-of-you boundless limit I-see perfection

תוֹרָתֶךָ כָּל־ הַיּוֹם הִיא שִׂיחָתִי׃ מֵאֹיְבַי
than-ones-being-enemies-of-me (98) meditation-of-me she the-day all-of law-of-you

תְּחַכְּמֵנִי מִצְוֹתֶךָ כִּי לְעוֹלָם הִיא־ לִי׃
with-me she to-forever for commands-of-you she-makes-wiser-me

מִכָּל־ מְלַמְּדַי הִשְׂכַּלְתִּי כִּי עֵדְוֹתֶיךָ
statutes-of-you for I-have-insight ones-teaching-me more-than-all-of (99)

שִׂיחָה לִי׃ מִזְּקֵנִים אֶתְבּוֹנָן כִּי פִקּוּדֶיךָ
precepts-of-you for I-understand more-than-elders (100) of-me meditation

נָצָרְתִּי׃ מִכָּל־ אֹרַח רָע כָּלִאתִי רַגְלָי לְמַעַן אֶשְׁמֹר
I-might-obey so-that feet-of-me I-kept evil path from-every-of (101) I-obey

דְּבָרֶךָ׃ מִמִּשְׁפָּטֶיךָ לֹא־ סָרְתִּי כִּי־ אַתָּה הוֹרֵתָנִי׃
you-taught-me you for I-departed not from-laws-of-you (102) word-of-you

persecutors?
85 The arrogant dig pitfalls for me,
contrary to your law.
86 All your commands are trustworthy;
help me, for men persecute me without cause.
87 They almost wiped me from the earth,
but I have not forsaken your precepts.
88 Preserve my life according to your love,
and I will obey the statutes of your mouth.

ל Lamedh

89 Your word, O LORD, is eternal;
it stands firm in the heavens.
90 Your faithfulness continues through all generations;
you established the earth, and it endures.
91 Your laws endure to this day,
for all things serve you.
92 If your law had not been my delight,
I would have perished in my affliction.
93 I will never forget your precepts,
for by them you have renewed my life.
94 Save me, for I am yours;
I have sought out your precepts.
95 The wicked are waiting to destroy me,
but I will ponder your statutes.
96 To all perfection I see a limit;
but your commands are boundless.

מ Mem

97 Oh, how I love your law!
I meditate on it all day long.
98 Your commands make me wiser than my enemies,
for they are ever with me.
99 I have more insight than all my teachers,
for I meditate on your statutes.
100 I have more understanding than the elders,
for I obey your precepts.
101 I have kept my feet from every evil path
so that I might obey your word.
102 I have not departed from your laws,
for you yourself have taught me.

מַה־ נִּמְלְצוּ לְחִכִּי אִמְרָתֶךָ מִדְּבַשׁ

more-than-honey promise-of-you to-taste-of-me they-are-sweet how! (103)

לְפִי׃ מִפִּקּוּדֶיךָ אֶתְבּוֹנָן עַל־ כֵּן

this for I-gain-understanding from-precepts-of-you (104) to-mouth-of-me

שָׂנֵאתִי ׀ כָּל־ אֹרַח שָׁקֶר׃ נֵר־ לְרַגְלִי דְבָרֶךָ וְאוֹר

and-light word-of-you to-foot-of-me lamp (105) wrongness path-of every-of I-hate

לִנְתִיבָתִי׃ נִשְׁבַּעְתִּי וָאֲקַיֵּמָה לִשְׁמֹר מִשְׁפְּטֵי

laws-of to-follow and-I-confirmed I-took-oath (106) for-path-of-me

צִדְקֶךָ׃ נַעֲנֵיתִי עַד־ מְאֹד יְהוָה חַיֵּנִי

make-alive-me! Yahweh much to I-suffered (107) righteousness-of-you

כִדְבָרֶךָ׃ נִדְבוֹת פִּי רְצֵה־ נָא יְהוָה

Yahweh now! accept! mouth-of-me willing-praises-of (108) as-word-of-you

וּמִשְׁפָּטֶיךָ לַמְּדֵנִי׃ נַפְשִׁי בְכַפִּי תָמִיד

constantly in-hand-of-me life-of-me (109) teach-me! and-laws-of-you

וְתוֹרָתְךָ לֹא שָׁכָחְתִּי׃ נָתְנוּ רְשָׁעִים פַּח לִי

for-me snare wicked-ones they-set (110) I-will-forget not but-law-of-you

וּמִפִּקּוּדֶיךָ לֹא תָעִיתִי׃ נָחַלְתִּי עֵדְוֺתֶיךָ

statutes-of-you I-have-heritage (111) I-strayed not but-from-precepts-of-you

לְעוֹלָם כִּי־ שְׂשׂוֹן לִבִּי הֵמָּה׃ נָטִיתִי לִבִּי לַעֲשׂוֹת

to-keep heart-of-me I-set (112) they heart-of-me joy-of indeed to-forever

חֻקֶּיךָ לְעוֹלָם עֵקֶב׃ סֵעֲפִים שָׂנֵאתִי

I-hate double-minded-men (113) very-end to-forever decrees-of-you

וְתוֹרָתְךָ אָהָבְתִּי׃ סִתְרִי וּמָגִנִּי אָתָּה לִדְבָרְךָ

in-word-of-you you and-shield-of-me refuge-of-me (114) I-love but-law-of-you

יִחָלְתִּי׃ סוּרוּ־ מִמֶּנִּי מְרֵעִים וְאֶצְּרָה מִצְוֺת

commands-of that-I-may-keep ones-doing-evil from-me be-away! (115) I-put-hope

אֱלֹהָי׃ סָמְכֵנִי כְאִמְרָתְךָ וְאֶחְיֶה וְאַל־

and-not and-I-will-live as-promise-of-you sustain-me! (116) God-of-me

תְּבִישֵׁנִי מִשִּׂבְרִי׃ סְעָדֵנִי וְאִוָּשֵׁעָה

and-I-will-be-delivered uphold-me! (117) from-hope-of-me you-shame-me

וְאֶשְׁעָה בְחֻקֶּיךָ תָמִיד׃ סָלִיתָ כָּל־

all-of you-reject (118) always for-decrees-of-you and-I-will-have-regard

שׁוֹגִים מֵחֻקֶּיךָ כִּי־ שֶׁקֶר תַּרְמִיתָם׃ סִגִים

drosses (119) deceitfulness-of-them vain for from-decrees-of-you ones-straying

הִשְׁבַּתָּ כָל־ רִשְׁעֵי־ אָרֶץ לָכֵן אָהַבְתִּי עֵדֹתֶיךָ׃

statutes-of-you I-love therefore earth wicked-ones-of all-of you-discard

סָמַר מִפַּחְדְּךָ בְשָׂרִי וּמִמִּשְׁפָּטֶיךָ יָרֵאתִי׃

I-stand-in-awe and-of-laws-of-you flesh-of-me in-fear-of-you he-trembles (120)

103How sweet are your promises
to my taste,
sweeter than honey to my
mouth!
104I gain understanding from
your precepts;
therefore I hate every wrong
path.

נ Nun

105Your word is a lamp to my
feet
and a light for my path.
106I have taken an oath and
confirmed it,
that I will follow your
righteous laws.
107I have suffered much;
renew my life, O LORD,
according to your word.
108Accept, O LORD, the willing
praise of my mouth,
and teach me your laws.
109Though I constantly take my
life in my hands,
I will not forget your law.
110The wicked have set a snare
for me,
but I have not strayed from
your precepts.
111Your statutes are my heritage
forever;
they are the joy of my heart.
112My heart is set on keeping
your decrees
to the very end.

ס Samekh

113I hate double-minded men,
but I love your law.
114You are my refuge and my
shield;
I have put my hope in your
word.
115Away from me, you evildoers,
that I may keep the
commands of my God!
116Sustain me according to your
promise, and I will live;
do not let my hopes be
dashed.
117Uphold me, and I will be
delivered;
I will always have regard for
your decrees.
118You reject all who stray from
your decrees,
for their deceitfulness is in
vain.
119All the wicked of the earth you
discard like dross;
therefore I love your
statutes.
120My flesh trembles in fear of
you;
I stand in awe of your laws.

עָשִׂיתִי מִשְׁפָּט וָצֶדֶק בַּל־ תַּנִּיחֵנִי לְעֹשְׁקָי׃
to-ones-oppressing-me you-leave-me not and-justice righteousness I-did (121)

עֲרֹב עַבְדְּךָ לְטוֹב אַל־ יַעַשְׁקֻנִי
let-them-oppress-me not of-well-being servant-of-you ensure! (122)

זֵדִים׃ עֵינַי כָּלוּ לִישׁוּעָתֶךָ וּלְאִמְרַת
and-for-promise-of for-salvation-of-you they-fail eyes-of-me (123) arrogant-ones

צִדְקֶךָ׃ עֲשֵׂה עִם־ עַבְדְּךָ כְחַסְדֶּךָ
as-love-of-you servant-of-you with deal! (124) righteousness-of-you

וְחֻקֶּיךָ לַמְּדֵנִי׃ עַבְדְּךָ־ אָנִי הֲבִינֵנִי
make-discern-me! I servant-of-you (125) teach-me! and-decrees-of-you

וְאֵדְעָה עֵדֹתֶיךָ׃ עֵת לַעֲשׂוֹת לַיהוָה הֵפֵרוּ
they-break O-Yahweh to-act time (126) statutes-of-you that-I-may-understand

תּוֹרָתֶךָ׃ עַל־ כֵּן אָהַבְתִּי מִצְוֹתֶיךָ מִזָּהָב
more-than-gold commands-of-you I-love this for (127) law-of-you

וּמִפָּז׃ עַל־ כֵּן | כָּל־ פִּקּוּדֵי כֹל יִשָּׁרְתִּי
I-consider-right all precepts-of all-of this for (128) even-more-than-pure-gold

כָּל־ אֹרַח שֶׁקֶר שָׂנֵאתִי׃ פְּלָאוֹת עֵדְוֹתֶיךָ עַל־ כֵּן
this for statutes-of-you wonderful-ones (129) I-hate wrongness path-of every-of

נְצָרָתַם נַפְשִׁי׃ פֵּתַח דְּבָרֶיךָ יָאִיר
he-gives-light words-of-you entrance-of (130) self-of-me she-obeys-them

מֵבִין פְּתָיִים׃ פִּי־ פָעַרְתִּי וָאֶשְׁאָפָה כִּי
for and-I-pant I-open mouth-of-me (131) simple-ones one-giving-understanding

לְמִצְוֹתֶיךָ יָאָבְתִּי׃ פְּנֵה־ אֵלַי וְחָנֵּנִי כְּמִשְׁפָּט
as-custom and-have-mercy-on-me! to-me turn! (132) I-long for-commands-of-you

לְאֹהֲבֵי שְׁמֶךָ׃ פְּעָמַי הָכֵן בְּאִמְרָתֶךָ
as-word-of-you direct! footsteps-of-me (133) name-of-you to-ones-loving-of

וְאַל־ תַּשְׁלֶט־ בִּי כָל־ אָוֶן׃ פְּדֵנִי מֵעֹשֶׁק
from-oppression-of redeem-me! (134) sin any-of over-me you-let-rule and-not

אָדָם וְאֶשְׁמְרָה פִּקּוּדֶיךָ׃ פָּנֶיךָ הָאֵר
make-shine! faces-of-you (135) precepts-of-you that-I-may-obey man

בְּעַבְדֶּךָ וְלַמְּדֵנִי אֶת־ חֻקֶּיךָ׃ פַּלְגֵי־ מַיִם
tears streams-of (136) decrees-of-you *** and-teach-me! upon-servant-of-you

יָרְדוּ עֵינָי עַל לֹא־ שָׁמְרוּ תוֹרָתֶךָ׃ צַדִּיק אַתָּה
you righteous (137) law-of-you they-obey not for eyes-of-me they-flow-down

יְהוָה וְיָשָׁר מִשְׁפָּטֶיךָ׃ צִוִּיתָ צֶדֶק עֵדֹתֶיךָ
statutes-of-you righteous you-laid-down (138) laws-of-you and-right Yahweh

וֶאֱמוּנָה מְאֹד׃ צִמְּתַתְנִי קִנְאָתִי כִּי־ שָׁכְחוּ
they-ignore for zeal-of-me she-wears-out-me (139) fully and-trustworthy

ע Ayin

121 I have done what is righteous
and just;
do not leave me to my
oppressors.
122 Ensure your servant's
well-being;
let not the arrogant oppress
me.
123 My eyes fail, looking for your
salvation,
looking for your righteous
promise.
124 Deal with your servant
according to your love
and teach me your decrees.
125 I am your servant; give me
discernment
that I may understand your
statutes.
126 It is time for you to act, O
LORD;
your law is being broken.
127 Because I love your commands
more than gold, more than
pure gold,
128 and because I consider all your
precepts right,
I hate every wrong path.

פ Pe

129 Your statutes are wonderful;
therefore I obey them.
130 The entrance of your words
gives light;
it gives understanding to
the simple.
131 I open my mouth and pant,
longing for your commands.
132 Turn to me and have mercy on
me,
as you always do to those
who love your name.
133 Direct my footsteps according
to your word;
let no sin rule over me.
134 Redeem me from the
oppression of men,
that I may obey your
precepts.
135 Make your face shine upon
your servant
and teach me your decrees.
136 Streams of tears flow from my
eyes,
for your law is not obeyed.

צ Tsadhe

137 Righteous are you, O LORD,
and your laws are right.
138 The statutes you have laid
down are righteous;
they are fully trustworthy.
139 My zeal wears me out,

דְבָרֶיךָ צָרָי׃ (140) צְרוּפָה אִמְרָתְךָ מְאֹד
thoroughly promise-of-you one-being-tested (140) enemies-of-me words-of-you

וְעַבְדְּךָ אֲהֵבָהּ׃ (141) צָעִיר אָנֹכִי וְנִבְזֶה
and-one-being-despised I lowly (141) he-loves-her and-servant-of-you

פִּקֻּדֶיךָ לֹא שָׁכָחְתִּי׃ (142) צִדְקָתְךָ צֶדֶק לְעוֹלָם
to-everlasting righteousness righteousness-of-you (142) I-forget not precepts-of-you

וְתוֹרָתְךָ אֱמֶת׃ (143) צַר־ וּמָצוֹק מְצָאוּנִי
they-came-upon-me and-distress trouble (143) true and-law-of-you

מִצְוֹתֶיךָ שַׁעֲשֻׁעָי׃ (144) צֶדֶק עֵדְוֺתֶיךָ לְעוֹלָם
to-forever statutes-of-you right (144) delights-of-me commands-of-you

הֲבִינֵנִי וְאֶחְיֶה׃ (145) קָרָאתִי בְכָל־ לֵב עֲנֵנִי
answer-me! heart with-all-of I-call (145) that-I-may-live make-understand-me!

יְהוָה חֻקֶּיךָ אֶצֹּרָה׃ (146) קְרָאתִיךָ הוֹשִׁיעֵנִי וְאֶשְׁמְרָה
and-I-will-keep save-me! I-call-to-you (146) I-will-obey decrees-of-you Yahweh

עֵדֹתֶיךָ׃ (147) קִדַּמְתִּי בַנֶּשֶׁף וָאֲשַׁוֵּעָה לִדְבָרְיךָ°
in-word-of-you and-I-cry-for-help before-the-dawn I-rise (147) statutes-of-you

יִחָלְתִּי׃ (148) קִדְּמוּ עֵינַי אַשְׁמֻרוֹת לָשִׂיחַ
to-meditate night-watches eyes-of-me they-stay-open (148) I-put-hope

בְּאִמְרָתֶךָ׃ (149) קוֹלִי שִׁמְעָה כְחַסְדֶּךָ יְהוָה כְּמִשְׁפָּטֶךָ
as-law-of-you Yahweh as-love-of-you hear! voice-of-me (149) on-promise-of-you

חַיֵּנִי׃ (150) קָרְבוּ רֹדְפֵי זִמָּה מִתּוֹרָתְךָ
from-law-of-you scheme ones-devising-of they-are-near (150) make-alive-me!

רָחָקוּ׃ (151) קָרוֹב אַתָּה יְהוָה וְכָל־ מִצְוֹתֶיךָ אֱמֶת׃
true commands-of-you and-all-of Yahweh you near (151) they-are-far

(152) קֶדֶם יָדַעְתִּי מֵעֵדֹתֶיךָ כִּי לְעוֹלָם
to-forever that from-statutes-of-you I-learned long-ago (152)

יְסַדְתָּם׃ (153) רְאֵה־ עָנְיִי וְחַלְּצֵנִי כִּי־
for and-deliver-me! suffering-of-me look-upon! (153) you-established-them

תוֹרָתְךָ לֹא שָׁכָחְתִּי׃ (154) רִיבָה רִיבִי וּגְאָלֵנִי
and-redeem-me! cause-of-me defend! (154) I-forgot not law-of-you

לְאִמְרָתְךָ חַיֵּנִי׃ (155) רָחוֹק מֵרְשָׁעִים יְשׁוּעָה כִּי־
for salvation from-wicked-ones far (155) make-alive-me! as-promise-of-you

חֻקֶּיךָ לֹא דָרָשׁוּ׃ (156) רַחֲמֶיךָ רַבִּים ׀ יְהוָה
Yahweh great-ones compassions-of-you (156) they-seek-out not decrees-of-you

כְּמִשְׁפָּטֶיךָ חַיֵּנִי׃ (157) רַבִּים רֹדְפַי וְצָרָי
even-foes-of-me ones-persecuting-me many (157) make-alive-me! as-laws-of-you

מֵעֵדְוֺתֶיךָ לֹא נָטִיתִי׃ (158) רָאִיתִי בֹגְדִים
ones-being-faithless I-look-on (158) I-turned not from-statutes-of-you

for my enemies ignore your
words.
140 Your promises have been
thoroughly tested,
and your servant loves
them.
141 Though I am lowly and
despised,
I do not forget your
precepts.
142 Your righteousness is
everlasting
and your law is true.
143 Trouble and distress have
come upon me,
but your commands are my
delight.
144 Your statutes are forever right;
give me understanding that
I may live.

ק Qoph

145 I call with all my heart;
answer me, O LORD,
and I will obey your
decrees.
146 I call out to you; save me
and I will keep your
statutes.
147 I rise before dawn and cry for
help;
I have put my hope in your
word.
148 My eyes stay open through the
watches of the night,
that I may meditate on your
promises.
149 Hear my voice in accordance
with your love;
renew my life, O LORD,
according to your laws.
150 Those who devise wicked
schemes are near,
but they are far from your
law.
151 Yet you are near, O LORD,
and all your commands are
true.
152 Long ago I learned from your
statutes
that you established them to
last forever.

ר Resh

153 Look upon my suffering and
deliver me,
for I have not forgotten your
law.
154 Defend my cause and redeem
me;
renew my life according to
your promise.
155 Salvation is far from the
wicked,
for they do not seek out
your decrees.
156 Your compassion is great, O
LORD;
renew my life according to
your laws.
157 Many are the foes who
persecute me,
but I have not turned from
your statutes.
158 I look on the faithless with

°*147* ק לדברך

וָאֶתְקוֹטָטָה אֲשֶׁר אִמְרָתְךָ לֹא שָׁמָרוּ׃ רְאֵה כִּי־ פִקּוּדֶיךָ
precepts-of-you how see! (159) they-obey not word-of-you for and-I-loathe

אָהַבְתִּי יְהוָה כְּחַסְדְּךָ חַיֵּנִי׃ רֹאשׁ־ דְּבָרְךָ אֱמֶת
true word-of-you all-of (160) keep-alive-me! as-love-of-you Yahweh I-love

וּלְעוֹלָם כָּל־ מִשְׁפַּט צִדְקֶךָ׃ שָׂרִים
rulers (161) righteousness-of-you law-of all-of and-to-eternity

רְדָפוּנִי חִנָּם וּמִדְּבָרְיךָ° פָּחַד לִבִּי׃
heart-of-me he-trembles but-at-word-of-you without-cause they-persecute-me

שָׂשׂ אָנֹכִי עַל־ אִמְרָתֶךָ כְּמוֹצֵא שָׁלָל רָב׃
great spoil like-one-finding promise-of-you in I one-rejoicing (162)

שֶׁקֶר שָׂנֵאתִי וַאֲתַעֵבָה תּוֹרָתְךָ אָהָבְתִּי׃ שֶׁבַע בַּיּוֹם
in-the-day seven (164) I-love law-of-you and-I-abhor I-hate falsehood (163)

הִלַּלְתִּיךָ עַל מִשְׁפְּטֵי צִדְקֶךָ׃ שָׁלוֹם רָב
great peace (165) righteousness-of-you laws-of for I-praise-you

לְאֹהֲבֵי תוֹרָתֶךָ וְאֵין־ לָמוֹ מִכְשׁוֹל׃ שִׂבַּרְתִּי
I-wait (166) stumbling to-them and-nothing law-of-you to-ones-loving-of

לִישׁוּעָתְךָ יְהוָה וּמִצְוֺתֶיךָ עָשִׂיתִי׃ שָׁמְרָה
she-obeys (167) I-follow and-commands-of-you Yahweh for-salvation-of-you

נַפְשִׁי עֵדֹתֶיךָ וָאֹהֲבֵם מְאֹד׃ שָׁמַרְתִּי פִקּוּדֶיךָ
precepts-of-you I-obey (168) greatly for-I-love-them statutes-of-you self-of-me

וְעֵדֹתֶיךָ כִּי כָל־ דְּרָכַי נֶגְדֶּךָ׃ תִּקְרַב
may-she-come (169) before-you ways-of-me all-of for and-statutes-of-you

רִנָּתִי לְפָנֶיךָ יְהוָה כִּדְבָרְךָ הֲבִינֵנִי׃
make-understand-me! as-word-of-you Yahweh before-you cry-of-me

תָּבוֹא תְּחִנָּתִי לְפָנֶיךָ כְּאִמְרָתְךָ הַצִּילֵנִי׃
deliver-me! as-promise-of-you before-you supplication-of-me may-she-come (170)

תַּבַּעְנָה שְׂפָתַי תְּהִלָּה כִּי תְלַמְּדֵנִי חֻקֶּיךָ׃
decrees-of-you you-teach-me for praise lips-of-me may-they-overflow (171)

תַּעַן לְשׁוֹנִי אִמְרָתֶךָ כִּי כָל־ מִצְוֺתֶיךָ
commands-of-you all-of for word-of-you tongue-of-me may-she-sing (172)

צֶדֶק׃ תְּהִי־ יָדְךָ לְעָזְרֵנִי כִּי פִקּוּדֶיךָ בָחָרְתִּי׃
I-chose precepts-of-you for to-help-me hand-of-you may-she-be (173) righteous

תָּאַבְתִּי לִישׁוּעָתְךָ יְהוָה וְתוֹרָתְךָ שַׁעֲשֻׁעָי׃
delights-of-me and-law-of-you Yahweh for-salvation-of-you I-long (174)

תְּחִי־ נַפְשִׁי וּתְהַלְלֶךָּ וּמִשְׁפָּטֶךָ
and-laws-of-you that-she-may-praise-you self-of-me let-her-live (175)

יַעֲזְרֻנִי׃ תָּעִיתִי כְּשֶׂה אֹבֵד בַּקֵּשׁ
seek! one-being-lost like-sheep I-strayed (176) may-they-sustain-me

loathing,
for they do not obey your word.
159 See how I love your precepts;
preserve my life, O LORD, according to your love.
160 All your words are true;
all your righteous laws are eternal.

ש Sin and Shin

161 Rulers persecute me without cause,
but my heart trembles at your word.
162 I rejoice in your promise
like one who finds great spoil.
163 I hate and abhor falsehood
but I love your law.
164 Seven times a day I praise you
for your righteous laws.
165 Great peace have they who love your law,
and nothing can make them stumble.
166 I wait for your salvation, O LORD,
and I follow your commands.
167 I obey your statutes,
for I love them greatly.
168 I obey your precepts and your statutes,
for all my ways are known to you.

ת Taw

169 May my cry come before you, O LORD;
give me understanding according to your word.
170 May my supplication come before you;
deliver me according to your promise.
171 May my lips overflow with praise,
for you teach me your decrees.
172 May my tongue sing of your word,
for all your commands are righteous.
173 May your hand be ready to help me,
for I have chosen your precepts.
174 I long for your salvation, O LORD,
and your law is my delight.
175 Let me live that I may praise you,
and may your laws sustain me.
176 I have strayed like a lost sheep.

°161 ק ומדברך

עַבְדֶּךָ כִּי מִצְוֹתֶיךָ לֹא שָׁכָחְתִּי׃ שִׁיר הַמַּעֲלוֹת
the-ascents song-of (120:1) I-forgot not commands-of-you for servant-of-you

אֶל־יְהוָה בַּצָּרָתָה לִּי קָרָאתִי וַיַּעֲנֵנִי׃ יְהוָה הַצִּילָה
save! Yahweh (2) and-he-answers-me I-call of-me in-the-distress Yahweh on

נַפְשִׁי מִשְּׂפַת־שֶׁקֶר מִלָּשׁוֹן רְמִיָּה׃ מַה־יִּתֵּן לְךָ
to-you will-he-do what? (3) deceitful from-tongue lie from-lip-of self-of-me

וּמַה־יֹּסִיף לָךְ לָשׁוֹן רְמִיָּה׃ חִצֵּי גִבּוֹר
warrior arrows-of (4) deceitful tongue to-you will-he-do-more and-what?

שְׁנוּנִים עִם גַּחֲלֵי רְתָמִים׃ אוֹיָה־לִי כִּי־גַרְתִּי
I-dwell that to-me woe! (5) broom-trees coals-of with ones-being-sharp

מֶשֶׁךְ שָׁכַנְתִּי עִם־אָהֳלֵי קֵדָר׃ רַבַּת שָׁכְנָה־לָּהּ נַפְשִׁי
self-of-me to-her she-lived too-long (6) Kedar tents-of among I-live Meshech

עִם שׂוֹנֵא שָׁלוֹם׃ אֲנִי־שָׁלוֹם וְכִי אֲדַבֵּר הֵמָּה לַמִּלְחָמָה׃
for-the-war they I-speak but-when peaceful I (7) peace one-hating among

שִׁיר לַמַּעֲלוֹת אֶשָּׂא עֵינַי אֶל־הֶהָרִים מֵאַיִן
from-where? the-hills to eyes-of-me I-will-lift-up of-the-ascents song (121:1)

יָבֹא עֶזְרִי׃ עֶזְרִי מֵעִם יְהוָה עֹשֵׂה שָׁמַיִם
heavens One-Making-of Yahweh from-with help-of-me (2) help-of-me he-comes

וָאָרֶץ׃ אַל־יִתֵּן לַמּוֹט רַגְלֶךָ אַל־יָנוּם
he-will-slumber not foot-of-you for-the-slipping he-will-let not (3) and-earth

שֹׁמְרֶךָ׃ הִנֵּה לֹא־יָנוּם וְלֹא יִישָׁן
he-will-sleep and-not he-will-slumber not indeed! (4) one-watching-over-you

שׁוֹמֵר יִשְׂרָאֵל׃ יְהוָה שֹׁמְרֶךָ יְהוָה צִלְּךָ
shade-of-you Yahweh one-watching-over-you Yahweh (5) Israel one-watching-over

עַל־יַד יְמִינֶךָ׃ יוֹמָם הַשֶּׁמֶשׁ לֹא־יַכֶּכָּה וְיָרֵחַ
or-moon he-will-harm-you not the-sun by-day (6) right-of-you hand-of at

בַּלָּיְלָה׃ יְהוָה יִשְׁמָרְךָ מִכָּל־רָע יִשְׁמֹר
he-will-watch-over harm from-all-of he-will-keep-you Yahweh (7) by-the-night

אֶת־נַפְשֶׁךָ׃ יְהוָה יִשְׁמָר־צֵאתְךָ וּבוֹאֶךָ
and-to-come-you to-go-you he-will-watch-over Yahweh (8) life-of-you ***

מֵעַתָּה וְעַד־עוֹלָם׃ שִׁיר הַמַּעֲלוֹת לְדָוִד שָׂמַחְתִּי
I-rejoiced of-David the-ascents song-of (122:1) forevermore and-to from-now

בְּאֹמְרִים לִי בֵּית יְהוָה נֵלֵךְ׃ עֹמְדוֹת הָיוּ
they-are ones-standing (2) let-us-go Yahweh house-of to-me with-ones-saying

רַגְלֵינוּ בִּשְׁעָרַיִךְ יְרוּשָׁלִָם׃ יְרוּשָׁלִַם הַבְּנוּיָה
the-one-being-built Jerusalem (3) Jerusalem in-gates-of-you feet-of-us

כְּעִיר שֶׁחֻבְּרָה־לָּהּ יַחְדָּו׃ שֶׁשָּׁם עָלוּ
they-go-up that-there (4) together to-her that-she-is-compacted like-city

Seek your servant,
for I have not forgotten your commandments.

Psalm 120

A song of ascents.

1 I call on the LORD in my distress,
and he answers me.
2 Save me, O LORD, from lying lips
and from deceitful tongues.

3 What will he do to you,
and what more besides, O deceitful tongue?
4 He will punish you with a warrior's sharp arrows,
with burning coals of the broom tree.

5 Woe to me that I dwell in Meshech,
that I live among the tents of Kedar!
6 Too long have I lived
among those who hate peace.
7 I am a man of peace;
but when I speak, they are for war.

Psalm 121

A song of ascents.

1 I lift up my eyes to the hills—
where does my help come from?
2 My help comes from the LORD,
the Maker of heaven and earth.

3 He will not let your foot slip—
he who watches over you will not slumber;
4 indeed, he who watches over Israel
will neither slumber nor sleep.

5 The LORD watches over you—
the LORD is your shade at your right hand;
6 the sun will not harm you by day,
nor the moon by night.

7 The LORD will keep you from all harm—
he will watch over your life;
8 the LORD will watch over your coming and going
both now and forevermore.

Psalm 122

A song of ascents. Of David.

1 I rejoiced with those who said to me,
"Let us go to the house of the LORD."
2 Our feet are standing
in your gates, O Jerusalem.

3 Jerusalem is built like a city
that is closely compacted together.
4 That is where the tribes go up,

שְׁבָטִים שִׁבְטֵי־ יָהּ עֵדוּת לְיִשְׂרָאֵל לְהֹדוֹת לְשֵׁם יְהוָה׃
Yahweh to-name-of to-praise to-Israel statute Yahweh tribes-of tribes

כִּי שָׁמָּה ׀ יָשְׁבוּ כִסְאוֹת לְמִשְׁפָּט כִּסְאוֹת לְבֵית דָּוִיד׃
David of-house-of thrones for-judgment thrones they-stand at-there for (5)

שַׁאֲלוּ שְׁלוֹם יְרוּשָׁלָ͏ִם יִשְׁלָיוּ אֹהֲבָיִךְ׃ יְהִי־
may-he-be (7) ones-loving-you may-they-be-secure Jerusalem peace-of pray! (6)

שָׁלוֹם בְּחֵילֵךְ שַׁלְוָה בְּאַרְמְנוֹתָיִךְ׃ לְמַעַן
for-sake-of (8) within-citadels-of-you security within-wall-of-you peace

אַחַי וְרֵעָי אֲדַבְּרָה־ נָּא שָׁלוֹם בָּךְ׃
within-you peace now! I-will-say and-friends-of-me brothers-of-me

לְמַעַן בֵּית־ יְהוָה אֱלֹהֵינוּ אֲבַקְשָׁה טוֹב לָךְ׃
of-you prosperity I-will-seek God-of-us Yahweh house-of for-sake-of (9)

שִׁיר הַמַּעֲלוֹת אֵלֶיךָ נָשָׂאתִי אֶת־ עֵינַי הַיֹּשְׁבִי
the-one-sitting eyes-of-me *** I-lift-up to-you the-ascents song-of (123:1)

בַּשָּׁמָיִם׃ הִנֵּה כְעֵינֵי עֲבָדִים אֶל־ יַד אֲדוֹנֵיהֶם
masters-of-them hand-of to slaves as-eyes-of see! (2) in-the-heavens

כְּעֵינֵי שִׁפְחָה אֶל־ יַד גְּבִרְתָּהּ כֵּן עֵינֵינוּ אֶל־ יְהוָה אֱלֹהֵינוּ
God-of-us Yahweh to eyes-of-us so mistress-of-her hand-of to maid as-eyes-of

עַד שֶׁיְּחָנֵּנוּ׃ חָנֵּנוּ יְהוָה חָנֵּנוּ
have-mercy-on-us! Yahweh have-mercy-on-us! (3) when-he-shows-mercy-to-us till

כִּי־ רַב שָׂבַעְנוּ בוּז׃ רַבַּת שָׂבְעָה־ לָּהּ נַפְשֵׁנוּ
self-of-us to-her she-endured much (4) contempt we-endured much for

הַלַּעַג הַשַּׁאֲנַנִּים הַבּוּז לִגְאֵיוֹנִים׃ שִׁיר
song-of (124:1) *of-arrogant-ones the-contempt the-proud-ones the-ridicule

הַמַּעֲלוֹת לְדָוִד לוּלֵי יְהוָה שֶׁהָיָה לָנוּ יֹאמַר־ נָא יִשְׂרָאֵל׃
Israel now! let-him-say for-us who-he-was Yahweh if-not of-David the-ascents

לוּלֵי יְהוָה שֶׁהָיָה לָנוּ בְּקוּם עָלֵינוּ אָדָם׃ אֲזַי
then (3) man against-us when-to-attack for-us who-he-was Yahweh if-not (2)

חַיִּים בְּלָעוּנוּ בַּחֲרוֹת אַפָּם בָּנוּ׃
against-us anger-of-them when-to-flare they-would-have-swallowed-us ones-alive

אֲזַי הַמַּיִם שְׁטָפוּנוּ נַחְלָה עָבַר
he-would-have-swept torrent they-would-have-engulfed-us the-floods then (4)

עַל־ נַפְשֵׁנוּ׃ אֲזַי עָבַר עַל־ נַפְשֵׁנוּ הַמַּיִם
the-waters self-of-us over he-would-have-swept then (5) self-of-us over

הַזֵּידוֹנִים׃ בָּרוּךְ יְהוָה שֶׁלֹּא נְתָנָנוּ טֶרֶף
one-torn he-let-us who-not Yahweh being-praised (6) the-raging-ones

לְשִׁנֵּיהֶם׃ נַפְשֵׁנוּ כְּצִפּוֹר נִמְלְטָה מִפַּח
from-snare-of she-escaped like-bird self-of-us (7) by-teeth-of-them

the tribes of the LORD,
to praise the name of the LORD
according to the statute
given to Israel.
5 There the thrones for
judgment stand,
the thrones of the house of
David.

6 Pray for the peace of
Jerusalem:
"May those who love you be
secure.
7 May there be peace within
your walls
and security within your
citadels."
8 For the sake of my brothers
and friends,
I will say, "Peace be within
you."
9 For the sake of the house of
the LORD our God,
I will seek your prosperity.

Psalm 123

A song of ascents.

1 I lift up my eyes to you,
to you whose throne is in
heaven.
2 As the eyes of slaves look to
the hand of their master,
as the eyes of a maid look to
the hand of her mistress,
so our eyes look to the LORD
our God,
till he shows us his mercy.

3 Have mercy on us, O LORD,
have mercy on us,
for we have endured much
contempt.
4 We have endured much
ridicule from the proud,
much contempt from the
arrogant.

Psalm 124

A song of ascents. Of David.

1 If the LORD had not been on
our side—
let Israel say—
2 if the LORD had not been on
our side
when men attacked us,
3 when their anger flared
against us,
they would have swallowed
us alive;
4 the flood would have engulfed
us,
the torrent would have
swept over us,
5 the raging waters would
have swept us away.

6 Praise be to the LORD,
who has not let us be torn
by their teeth.
7 We have escaped like a bird
out of the fowler's snare;

*4 The *Qere* reads the word as two, *ones-arrogant-of things-being-cruel.*

°4 ק לגאי יונים

יוֹקְשִׁים הַפַּח נִשְׁבָּר וַאֲנַחְנוּ נִמְלָטְנוּ׃
we-escaped and-we one-being-broken the-snare ones-being-fowlers

(8) עֶזְרֵנוּ בְּשֵׁם יְהוָה עֹשֵׂה שָׁמַיִם וָאָרֶץ׃ (125:1) שִׁיר
song-of (125:1) and-earth heavens One-Making-of Yahweh in-name-of help-of-us (8)

הַמַּעֲלוֹת הַבֹּטְחִים בַּיהוָה כְּהַר־ צִיּוֹן לֹא־ יִמּוֹט
he-can-be-shaken not Zion like-Mount-of in-Yahweh the-ones-trusting the-ascents

לְעוֹלָם יֵשֵׁב׃ (2) יְרוּשָׁלַםִ הָרִים סָבִיב לָהּ וַיהוָה
so-Yahweh around-her surrounding mountains Jerusalem (2) he-endures to-forever

סָבִיב לְעַמּוֹ מֵעַתָּה וְעַד־ עוֹלָם׃ (3) כִּי לֹא
not indeed (3) forevermore and-to from-now around-people-of-him surrounding

יָנוּחַ שֵׁבֶט הָרֶשַׁע עַל גּוֹרַל הַצַּדִּיקִים
the-righteous-ones allotment-of over the-wicked scepter-of he-will-remain

לְמַעַן לֹא־ יִשְׁלְחוּ הַצַּדִּיקִים בְּעַוְלָתָה יְדֵיהֶם׃
hands-of-them for-evil the-righteous-ones they-might-use not so-that

(4) הֵיטִיבָה יְהוָה לַטּוֹבִים וְלִישָׁרִים בְּלִבּוֹתָם׃
in-hearts-of-them even-to-ones-upright to-the-good-ones Yahweh do-good! (4)

(5) וְהַמַּטִּים עֲקַלְקַלּוֹתָם יוֹלִיכֵם יְהוָה
Yahweh he-will-banish-them crooked-ways-of-them but-the-ones-turning (5)

אֶת־ פֹּעֲלֵי הָאָוֶן שָׁלוֹם עַל־ יִשְׂרָאֵל׃ (126:1) שִׁיר הַמַּעֲלוֹת
the-ascents song-of (126:1) Israel upon peace the-evil ones-doing-of with

בְּשׁוּב יְהוָה אֶת־ שִׁיבַת צִיּוֹן הָיִינוּ כְּחֹלְמִים׃
like-ones-dreaming we-were Zion captive-of *** Yahweh when-to-bring-back

(2) אָז יִמָּלֵא שְׂחוֹק פִּינוּ וּלְשׁוֹנֵנוּ רִנָּה
song-of-joy and-tongue-of-us mouth-of-us laughter-of he-was-filled then (2)

אָז יֹאמְרוּ בַגּוֹיִם הִגְדִּיל יְהוָה לַעֲשׂוֹת עִם־אֵלֶּה׃
these for to-do Yahweh he-made-great among-the-nations they-said then

(3) הִגְדִּיל יְהוָה לַעֲשׂוֹת עִמָּנוּ הָיִינוּ שְׂמֵחִים׃ (4) שׁוּבָה
restore! (4) ones-being-joyful we-are for-us to-do Yahweh he-made-great (3)

יְהוָה אֶת־ שְׁבוֹתֵנוּ כַּאֲפִיקִים בַּנֶּגֶב׃ (5) הַזֹּרְעִים
the-ones-sowing (5) in-the-Negev like-streams fortune-of-us *** Yahweh

בְּדִמְעָה בְּרִנָּה יִקְצֹרוּ׃ (6) הָלוֹךְ יֵלֵךְ ׀ וּבָכֹה
and-to-weep he-goes-out to-go-out (6) they-will-reap with-song-of-joy in-tear

נֹשֵׂא מֶשֶׁךְ־ הַזָּרַע בֹּא־ יָבוֹא בְרִנָּה נֹשֵׂא
carrying with-song-of-joy he-will-return to-return the-sowing seed-of carrying

אֲלֻמֹּתָיו׃ (127:1) שִׁיר הַמַּעֲלוֹת לִשְׁלֹמֹה אִם־ יְהוָה ׀ לֹא־ יִבְנֶה
he-builds not Yahweh if of-Solomon the-ascents song-of (127:1) sheaves-of-him

בַּיִת שָׁוְא ׀ עָמְלוּ בוֹנָיו בּוֹ אִם־ יְהוָה לֹא־ יִשְׁמָר־
he-watches-over not Yahweh if on-him ones-building-him they-labor vanity house

the snare has been broken,
and we have escaped.
8Our help is in the name of the LORD,
the Maker of heaven and earth.

Psalm 125

A song of ascents.

1Those who trust in the LORD
are like Mount Zion,
which cannot be shaken but endures forever.
2As the mountains surround Jerusalem,
so the LORD surrounds his people
both now and forevermore.
3The scepter of the wicked will not remain
over the land allotted to the righteous,
for then the righteous might use
their hands to do evil.
4Do good, O LORD, to those who are good,
to those who are upright in heart.
5But those who turn to crooked ways
the LORD will banish with the evildoers.
Peace be upon Israel.

Psalm 126

A song of ascents.

1When the LORD brought back the captives to[w] Zion,
we were like men who dreamed.[x]
2Our mouths were filled with laughter,
our tongues with songs of joy.
Then it was said among the nations,
"The LORD has done great things for them."
3The LORD has done great things for us,
and we are filled with joy.
4Restore our fortunes,[y] O LORD,
like streams in the Negev.
5Those who sow in tears
will reap with songs of joy.
6He who goes out weeping,
carrying seed to sow,
will return with songs of joy,
carrying sheaves with him.

Psalm 127

A song of ascents. Of Solomon.

1Unless the LORD builds the house,
its builders labor in vain.
Unless the LORD watches over

w1 Or *LORD restored the fortunes of*
x1 Or *men restored to health*
y4 Or *Bring back our captives*

°4 ק שביתנו

עִיר שָׁוְא ׀ שָׁקַד שׁוֹמֵר׃ שָׁוְא לָכֶם ׀ מַשְׁכִּימֵי
ones-being-early-of to-you vanity (2) one-watching he-stands-guard vanity city

קוּם מְאַחֲרֵי־ שֶׁבֶת אֹכְלֵי לֶחֶם הָעֲצָבִים כֵּן
for the-toils bread-of ones-eating-of to-stay-up ones-being-late-of to-rise

יִתֵּן לִידִידוֹ שֵׁנָא׃ הִנֵּה נַחֲלַת יְהוָה בָּנִים שָׂכָר
reward sons Yahweh heritage-of see! (3) sleep to-loved-one-of-him he-grants

פְּרִי הַבָּטֶן׃ כְּחִצִּים בְּיַד־ גִּבּוֹר כֵּן בְּנֵי הַנְּעוּרִים׃
the-youths sons-of so warrior in-hand-of like-arrows (4) the-womb child-of

אַשְׁרֵי הַגֶּבֶר אֲשֶׁר מִלֵּא אֶת־ אַשְׁפָּתוֹ מֵהֶם
with-them quiver-of-him *** he-is-full who the-man blessednesses-of (5)

לֹא־ יֵבֹשׁוּ כִּי־ יְדַבְּרוּ אֶת־ אוֹיְבִים בַּשָּׁעַר׃
in-the-gate ones-being-enemies with they-contend when they-will-be-shamed not

שִׁיר הַמַּעֲלוֹת אַשְׁרֵי כָּל־ יְרֵא יְהוָה
Yahweh one-fearing-of all-of blessednesses-of the-ascents song-of (128:1)

הַהֹלֵךְ בִּדְרָכָיו׃ יְגִיעַ כַּפֶּיךָ כִּי תֹאכֵל
you-will-eat indeed hands-of-you labor-of (2) in-ways-of-him the-one-walking

אַשְׁרֶיךָ וְטוֹב לָךְ׃ אֶשְׁתְּךָ ׀ כְּגֶפֶן
like-vine wife-of-you (3) to-you and-prosperity blessings-of-you

פֹּרִיָּה בְּיַרְכְּתֵי בֵיתֶךָ בָּנֶיךָ כִּשְׁתִלֵי זֵיתִים
olives like-shoots-of sons-of-you house-of-you at-insides-of one-being-fruitful

סָבִיב לְשֻׁלְחָנֶךָ׃ הִנֵּה כִי־ כֵן יְבֹרַךְ גָּבֶר יְרֵא
one-fearing-of man he-is-blessed thus that see! (4) about-table-of-you around

יְהוָה׃ יְבָרֶכְךָ יְהוָה מִצִּיּוֹן וּרְאֵה בְּטוּב
to-prosperity-of and-see! from-Zion Yahweh may-he-bless-you (5) Yahweh

יְרוּשָׁלָםִ כֹּל יְמֵי חַיֶּיךָ׃ וּרְאֵה־ בָנִים לְבָנֶיךָ
of-children-of-you children and-see! (6) lives-of-you days-of all-of Jerusalem

שָׁלוֹם עַל־ יִשְׂרָאֵל׃ שִׁיר הַמַּעֲלוֹת רַבַּת צְרָרוּנִי
they-oppressed-me greatly the-ascents song-of (129:1) Israel upon peace

מִנְּעוּרָי יֹאמַר־ נָא יִשְׂרָאֵל׃ רַבַּת צְרָרוּנִי
they-oppressed-me greatly (2) Israel now! let-him-say from-youths-of-me

מִנְּעוּרָי גַּם לֹא־ יָכְלוּ לִי׃ עַל־ גַּבִּי
back-of-me on (3) over-me they-gained-victory not but from-youths-of-me

חָרְשׁוּ חֹרְשִׁים הֶאֱרִיכוּ לְמַעֲנוֹתָם׃ יְהוָה צַדִּיק
righteous Yahweh (4) to-furrow-of-them they-made-long ones-plowing they-plowed

קִצֵּץ עֲבוֹת רְשָׁעִים׃ יֵבֹשׁוּ וְיִסֹּגוּ
and-may-they-be-turned may-they-be-shamed (5) wicked-ones cords-of he-cut-free

אָחוֹר כֹּל שֹׂנְאֵי צִיּוֹן׃ יִהְיוּ כַּחֲצִיר גַּגּוֹת
housetops like-grass-of may-they-be (6) Zion ones-hating-of all-of back

ק למעניתם

the city,
the watchmen stand guard
in vain.
2 In vain you rise early
and stay up late,
toiling for food to eat—
for he grants sleep to[a] those
he loves.

3 Sons are a heritage from the
LORD,
children a reward from him.
4 Like arrows in the hands of a
warrior
are sons born in one's
youth.
5 Blessed is the man
whose quiver is full of them.
They will not be put to shame
when they contend with
their enemies in the gate.

Psalm 128

A song of ascents.

1 Blessed are all who fear the
LORD,
who walk in his ways.
2 You will eat the fruit of your
labor;
blessings and prosperity will
be yours.
3 Your wife will be like a fruitful
vine
within your house;
your sons will be like olive
shoots
around your table.
4 Thus is the man blessed
who fears the LORD.

5 May the LORD bless you from
Zion
all the days of your life;
may you see the prosperity of
Jerusalem,
6 and may you live to see
your children's children.

Peace be upon Israel.

Psalm 129

A song of ascents.

1 They have greatly oppressed
me from my youth—
let Israel say—
2 they have greatly oppressed
me from my youth,
but they have not gained
the victory over me.
3 Plowmen have plowed my
back
and made their furrows
long.
4 But the LORD is righteous;
he has cut me free from the
cords of the wicked.

5 May all who hate Zion
be turned back in shame.
6 May they be like grass on the
housetops,

[a]2 Or *eat— / for while they sleep he provides for*

שֶׁקַּדְמַת שָׁלַף יָבֵשׁ׃ (7) שֶׁלֹּא מִלֵּא כַפּוֹ
which-before he-grows he-withers (7) which-not he-can-fill hand-of-him

קוֹצֵר וְחִצְנוֹ מְעַמֵּר׃ (8) וְלֹא אָמְרוּ
one-reaping or-arm-of-him one-gathering (8) and-not may-they-say

הָעֹבְרִים בִּרְכַּת־ יְהוָה אֲלֵיכֶם בֵּרַכְנוּ אֶתְכֶם בְּשֵׁם
the-ones-passing-by blessing-of Yahweh upon-you we-bless you in-name-of

יְהוָה׃ (130:1) שִׁיר הַמַּעֲלוֹת מִמַּעֲמַקִּים קְרָאתִיךָ יְהוָה׃ (2) אֲדֹנָי
Yahweh (130:1) song-of the-ascents from-depths I-cry-to-you Yahweh (2) Lord

שִׁמְעָה בְקוֹלִי תִּהְיֶינָה אָזְנֶיךָ קַשֻּׁבוֹת לְקוֹל
hear! to-voice-of-me let-them-be ears-of-you attentive-ones to-cry-of

תַּחֲנוּנָי׃ (3) אִם־ עֲוֺנוֹת תִּשְׁמָר־ יָהּ אֲדֹנָי מִי יַעֲמֹד׃
cries-for-mercy-of-me (3) if sins you-recorded Yahweh Lord who? he-could-stand

(4) כִּי־ עִמְּךָ הַסְּלִיחָה לְמַעַן תִּוָּרֵא׃ (5) קִוִּיתִי
(4) but with-you the-forgiveness therefore you-are-feared (5) I-wait-for

יְהוָה קִוְּתָה נַפְשִׁי וְלִדְבָרוֹ הוֹחָלְתִּי׃ (6) נַפְשִׁי
Yahweh she-waits soul-of-me and-in-word-of-him I-put-hope (6) soul-of-me

לַאדֹנָי מִשֹּׁמְרִים לַבֹּקֶר שֹׁמְרִים לַבֹּקֶר׃
for-Lord more-than-men-watching for-the-morning men-watching for-the-morning

(7) יַחֵל יִשְׂרָאֵל אֶל־ יְהוָה כִּי־ עִם־ יְהוָה הַחֶסֶד
(7) put-hope! Israel in Yahweh for with Yahweh the-unfailing-love

וְהַרְבֵּה עִמּוֹ פְדוּת׃ (8) וְהוּא יִפְדֶּה אֶת־יִשְׂרָאֵל
and-to-be-full with-him redemption (8) and-he he-will-redeem *** Israel

מִכֹּל עֲוֺנֹתָיו׃ (131:1) שִׁיר הַמַּעֲלוֹת לְדָוִד יְהוָה לֹא־
from-all-of sins-of-him (131:1) song-of the-ascents of-David Yahweh not

גָבַהּ לִבִּי וְלֹא־ רָמוּ עֵינַי וְלֹא־
he-is-proud heart-of-me and-not they-are-haughty eyes-of-me and-not

הִלַּכְתִּי בִּגְדֹלוֹת וּבְנִפְלָאוֹת מִמֶּנִּי׃
I-am-concerned with-great-matters or-with-things-being-wonderful more-than-me

(2) אִם־ לֹא שִׁוִּיתִי וְדוֹמַמְתִּי נַפְשִׁי כְּגָמֻל עֲלֵי
(2) but indeed I-stilled and-I-quieted soul-of-me like-one-being-weaned with

אִמּוֹ כַּגָּמֻל עָלַי נַפְשִׁי׃ (3) יַחֵל יִשְׂרָאֵל
mother-of-him like-the-one-being-weaned in-me soul-of-me (3) put-hope! Israel

אֶל־ יְהוָה מֵעַתָּה וְעַד־ עוֹלָם׃ (132:1) שִׁיר הַמַּעֲלוֹת זְכוֹר־
in Yahweh from-now and-to forevermore (132:1) song-of the-ascents remember!

יְהוָה לְדָוִד אֵת כָּל־ עֻנּוֹתוֹ׃ (2) אֲשֶׁר נִשְׁבַּע
Yahweh to-David *** all-of to-endure-hardship-him (2) that he-swore-oath

לַיהוָה נָדַר לַאֲבִיר יַעֲקֹב׃ (3) אִם־ אָבֹא
to-Yahweh he-made-vow to-Mighty-One-of Jacob (3) not I-will-enter

which withers before it can grow;
7 with it the reaper cannot fill his hands,
nor the one who gathers fill his arms.
8 May those who pass by not say,
"The blessing of the LORD be upon you;
we bless you in the name of the LORD."

Psalm 130

A song of ascents.

1 Out of the depths I cry to you, O LORD;
2 O Lord, hear my voice.
Let your ears be attentive to my cry for mercy.

3 If you, O LORD, kept a record of sins,
O Lord, who could stand?
4 But with you there is forgiveness;
therefore you are feared.

5 I wait for the LORD, my soul waits,
and in his word I put my hope.
6 My soul waits for the Lord
more than watchmen wait for the morning,
more than watchmen wait for the morning.

7 O Israel, put your hope in the LORD,
for with the LORD is unfailing love
and with him is full redemption.
8 He himself will redeem Israel
from all their sins.

Psalm 131

A song of ascents. Of David.

1 My heart is not proud, O LORD,
my eyes are not haughty;
I do not concern myself with great matters
or things too wonderful for me.
2 But I have stilled and quieted my soul;
like a weaned child with its mother,
like a weaned child is my soul within me.

3 O Israel, put your hope in the LORD
both now and forevermore.

Psalm 132

A song of ascents.

1 O LORD, remember David
and all the hardships he endured.

2 He swore an oath to the LORD
and made a vow to the Mighty One of Jacob:
3 "I will not enter my house

בְּאֹהֶל בֵּיתִי אִם־אֶעֱלֶה עַל־עֶרֶשׂ יְצוּעָי׃ אִם־
not (4) beds-of-me mat-of to I-will-go not house-of-me into-structure-of

אֶתֵּן שְׁנַת לְעֵינָי לְעַפְעַפַּי תְּנוּמָה׃ עַד־אֶמְצָא
I-find till (5) slumber to-eyelids-of-me to-eyes-of-me sleep-of I-will-allow

מָקוֹם לַיהוָה מִשְׁכָּנוֹת לַאֲבִיר יַעֲקֹב׃ הִנֵּה־שְׁמַעֲנוּהָ
we-heard-her see! (6) Jacob for-Mighty-One-of dwellings for-Yahweh place

בְאֶפְרָתָה מְצָאנוּהָ בִּשְׂדֵי־יָעַר׃ נָבוֹאָה לְמִשְׁכְּנוֹתָיו
to-dwellings-of-him let-us-go (7) Jaar in-fields-of we-came-upon-her in-Ephrathah

נִשְׁתַּחֲוֶה לַהֲדֹם רַגְלָיו׃ קוּמָה יְהוָה לִמְנוּחָתֶךָ
to-rest-of-you Yahweh arise! (8) feet-of-him at-footstool-of let-us-worship

אַתָּה וַאֲרוֹן עֻזֶּךָ׃ כֹּהֲנֶיךָ יִלְבְּשׁוּ־
may-they-be-clothed priests-of-you (9) might-of-you and-ark-of you

צֶדֶק וַחֲסִידֶיךָ יְרַנֵּנוּ׃ בַּעֲבוּר דָּוִד
David for-sake-of (10) may-they-sing-for-joy and-saints-of-you righteousness

עַבְדֶּךָ אַל־תָּשֵׁב פְּנֵי מְשִׁיחֶךָ׃ נִשְׁבַּע־
he-swore-oath (11) anointed-one-of-you faces-of you-reject not servant-of-you

יְהוָה׀ לְדָוִד אֱמֶת לֹא־יָשׁוּב מִמֶּנָּה מִפְּרִי
from-descendant-of from-her he-will-revoke not sure to-David Yahweh

בִטְנְךָ אָשִׁית לְכִסֵּא־לָךְ׃ אִם־יִשְׁמְרוּ בָנֶיךָ׀
sons-of-you they-keep if (12) of-you on-throne I-will-place body-of-you

בְּרִיתִי וְעֵדֹתִי זוֹ אֲלַמְּדֵם גַּם־בְּנֵיהֶם עֲדֵי־
to sons-of-them then I-teach-them that and-statutes-of-me covenant-of-me

עַד יֵשְׁבוּ לְכִסֵּא־לָךְ׃ כִּי־בָחַר יְהוָה בְּצִיּוֹן
to-Zion Yahweh he-chose for (13) of-you on-throne they-will-sit forever

אִוָּהּ לְמוֹשָׁב לוֹ׃ זֹאת־מְנוּחָתִי עֲדֵי־עַד
forever to resting-place-of-me this (14) for-him for-dwelling he-desired-her

פֹּה־אֵשֵׁב כִּי אִוִּתִיהָ׃ צֵידָהּ בָּרֵךְ אֲבָרֵךְ
I-will-bless to-bless provision-of-her (15) I-desired-her for I-will-sit here

אֶבְיוֹנֶיהָ אַשְׂבִּיעַ לָחֶם׃ וְכֹהֲנֶיהָ אַלְבִּישׁ
I-will-clothe and-priests-of-her (16) food I-will-satisfy poor-ones-of-her

יֶשַׁע וַחֲסִידֶיהָ רַנֵּן יְרַנֵּנוּ׃ שָׁם
here (17) they-will-sing-for-joy to-sing-for-joy and-saints-of-her salvation

אַצְמִיחַ קֶרֶן לְדָוִד עָרַכְתִּי נֵר לִמְשִׁיחִי׃
for-anointed-one-of-me lamp I-will-set-up for-David horn I-will-make-grow

אוֹיְבָיו אַלְבִּישׁ בֹּשֶׁת וְעָלָיו
but-on-him shame I-will-clothe ones-being-enemies-of-him (18)

יָצִיץ נִזְרוֹ׃ שִׁיר הַמַּעֲלוֹת לְדָוִד
of-David the-ascents song-of (133:1) crown-of-him he-will-be-resplendent

or go to my bed—
4 I will allow no sleep to my eyes,
no slumber to my eyelids,
5 till I find a place for the LORD,
a dwelling for the Mighty One of Jacob."

6 We heard it in Ephrathah,
we came upon it in the fields of Jaar[a]:[b]
7 "Let us go to his dwelling place;
let us worship at his footstool—
8 arise, O LORD, and come to your resting place,
you and the ark of your might.
9 May your priests be clothed with righteousness;
may your saints sing for joy."

10 For the sake of David your servant,
do not reject your anointed one.

11 The LORD swore an oath to David,
a sure oath that he will not revoke:
"One of your own descendants
I will place on your throne—
12 if your sons keep my covenant
and the statutes I teach them,
then their sons will sit
on your throne for ever and ever."

13 For the LORD has chosen Zion,
he has desired it for his dwelling:
14 "This is my resting place for ever and ever;
here I will sit enthroned, for I have desired it—
15 I will bless her with abundant provisions;
her poor will I satisfy with food.
16 I will clothe her priests with salvation,
and her saints will ever sing for joy.

17 "Here I will make a horn[c] grow for David
and set up a lamp for my anointed one.
18 I will clothe his enemies with shame,
but the crown on his head will be resplendent."

Psalm 133

A song of ascents. Of David.

[a] 6 That is, Kiriath Jearim
[b] 6 Or *heard of it in Ephrathah, / we found it in the fields of Jaar.* (And no quotes around verses 7-9)
[c] 17 *Horn* here symbolizes strong one, that is, king.

הִנֵּה מַה־ טּוֹב וּמַה־ נָּעִים שֶׁבֶת אַחִים גַּם־ יָחַד׃
together united brothers to-live pleasant and-how! good how! see!

(2) כַּשֶּׁמֶן הַטּוֹב ׀ עַל־ הָרֹאשׁ יֹרֵד עַל־ הַזָּקָן זְקַן־
beard-of the-beard on running-down the-head on the-precious like-the-oil (2)

אַהֲרֹן שֶׁיֹּרֵד עַל־ פִּי מִדּוֹתָיו׃ (3) כְּטַל־ חֶרְמוֹן
Hermon as-dew-of (3) robes-of-him collar-of on that-running-down Aaron

שֶׁיֹּרֵד עַל־ הַרְרֵי צִיּוֹן כִּי שָׁם ׀ צִוָּה יְהוָה אֶת־ הַבְּרָכָה
the-blessing *** Yahweh he-bestows there for Zion Mounts-of on that-falling

חַיִּים עַד־ הָעוֹלָם׃ (134:1) שִׁיר הַמַּעֲלוֹת הִנֵּה ׀ בָּרְכוּ אֶת־ יְהוָה
Yahweh *** praise! see! the-ascents song-of (134:1) the-forever to lives

כָּל־ עַבְדֵי יְהוָה הָעֹמְדִים בְּבֵית־ יְהוָה
Yahweh in-house-of the-ones-ministering Yahweh servants-of all-of

בַּלֵּילוֹת׃ (2) שְׂאוּ־ יְדֵכֶם קֹדֶשׁ וּבָרְכוּ אֶת־ יְהוָה׃
Yahweh *** and-praise! sanctuary hand-of-you lift-up! (2) in-the-nights

(3) יְבָרֶכְךָ יְהוָה מִצִּיּוֹן עֹשֵׂה שָׁמַיִם וָאָרֶץ׃
and-earth heavens One-Making-of from-Zion Yahweh may-he-bless-you (3)

(135:1) הַלְלוּ יָהּ ׀ הַלְלוּ אֶת־ שֵׁם יְהוָה הַלְלוּ עַבְדֵי יְהוָה׃
Yahweh servants-of praise! Yahweh name-of *** praise! Yahweh praise! (135:1)

(2) שֶׁעֹמְדִים בְּבֵית יְהוָה בְּחַצְרוֹת בֵּית אֱלֹהֵינוּ׃
God-of-us house-of in-courts-of Yahweh in-house-of who-ones-ministering (2)

(3) הַלְלוּ־ יָהּ כִּי־ טוֹב יְהוָה זַמְּרוּ לִשְׁמוֹ כִּי נָעִים׃
pleasant for to-name-of-him sing-praise! Yahweh good for Yahweh praise! (3)

(4) כִּי־ יַעֲקֹב בָּחַר לוֹ יָהּ יִשְׂרָאֵל לִסְגֻלָּתוֹ׃ (5) כִּי אֲנִי
I for (5) as-treasure-of-him Israel Yahweh for-him he-chose Jacob for (4)

יָדַעְתִּי כִּי־ גָדוֹל יְהוָה וַאֲדֹנֵינוּ מִכָּל־ אֱלֹהִים׃ (6) כֹּל
all (6) gods greater-than-all-of and-Lord-of-us Yahweh great that I-know

אֲשֶׁר־ חָפֵץ יְהוָה עָשָׂה בַּשָּׁמַיִם וּבָאָרֶץ בַּיַּמִּים
in-the-seas and-on-the-earth in-the-heavens he-does Yahweh he-pleases that

וְכָל־ תְּהוֹמוֹת׃ (7) מַעֲלֶה נְשִׂאִים מִקְצֵה הָאָרֶץ בְּרָקִים
lightnings the-earth from-end-of clouds one-making-rise (7) depths and-all-of

לַמָּטָר עָשָׂה מוֹצֵא־ רוּחַ מֵאוֹצְרוֹתָיו׃
from-storehouses-of-him wind one-bringing-out he-sends with-the-rain

(8) שֶׁהִכָּה בְּכוֹרֵי מִצְרָיִם מֵאָדָם עַד־ בְּהֵמָה׃
animal to from-man Egypt firstborn-ones-of who-he-struck-down (8)

(9) שָׁלַח ׀ אֹתוֹת וּמֹפְתִים בְּתוֹכֵכִי מִצְרָיִם בְּפַרְעֹה
against-Pharaoh Egypt into-midst-of-you and-wonders signs he-sent (9)

וּבְכָל־ עֲבָדָיו׃ (10) שֶׁהִכָּה גּוֹיִם רַבִּים
many nations who-he-struck-down (10) servants-of-him and-against-all-of

1 How good and pleasant it is
when brothers live together
in unity!
2 It is like precious oil poured
on the head,
running down on the beard,
running down on Aaron's
beard,
down upon the collar of his
robes.
3 It is as if the dew of Hermon
were falling on Mount Zion.
For there the LORD bestows his
blessing,
even life forevermore.

Psalm 134

A song of ascents.

1 Praise the LORD, all you
servants of the LORD
who minister by night in
the house of the LORD.
2 Lift up your hands in the
sanctuary
and praise the LORD.
3 May the LORD, the Maker of
heaven and earth,
bless you from Zion.

Psalm 135

1 Praise the LORD.[d]

Praise the name of the LORD;
Praise him, you servants of
the LORD,
2 you who minister in the house
of the LORD,
in the courts of the house of
our God.
3 Praise the LORD, for the LORD
is good;
sing praise to his name, for
that is pleasant.
4 For the LORD has chosen Jacob
to be his own,
Israel to be his treasured
possession.
5 I know that the LORD is great,
that our Lord is greater than
all gods.
6 The LORD does whatever
pleases him,
in the heavens and on the
earth,
in the seas and all their
depths.
7 He makes clouds rise from the
ends of the earth;
he sends lightning with the
rain
and brings out the wind
from his storehouses.
8 He struck down the firstborn
of Egypt,
the firstborn of men and
animals.
9 He sent his signs and wonders
into your midst, O Egypt,
against Pharaoh and all his
servants.
10 He struck down many nations

[d] 1 Hebrew *Hallelu Yah*; also in verses 3 and 21

וְהָרַג מְלָכִים עֲצוּמִים׃ (11) לְסִיחוֹן ׀ מֶלֶךְ הָאֱמֹרִי
the-Amorite king-of namely-Sihon (11) mighty-ones kings and-he-killed

וּלְעוֹג מֶלֶךְ הַבָּשָׁן וּלְכֹל מַמְלְכוֹת כְּנָעַן׃
Canaan kingdoms-of and-namely-all-of the-Bashan king-of and-namely-Og

(12) וְנָתַן אַרְצָם נַחֲלָה נַחֲלָה לְיִשְׂרָאֵל עַמּוֹ׃
people-of-him to-Israel inheritance inheritance land-of-them and-he-gave (12)

(13) יְהוָה שִׁמְךָ לְעוֹלָם יְהוָה זִכְרְךָ לְדֹר־
to-generation renown-of-you Yahweh to-forever name-of-you Yahweh (13)

וָדֹר׃ (14) כִּי־ יָדִין יְהוָה עַמּוֹ וְעַל־
and-on people-of-him Yahweh he-will-vindicate for (14) and-generation

עֲבָדָיו יִתְנֶחָם׃ (15) עֲצַבֵּי הַגּוֹיִם כֶּסֶף
silver the-nations idols-of (15) he-will-have-compassion servants-of-him

וְזָהָב מַעֲשֵׂה יְדֵי אָדָם׃ (16) פֶּה־ לָהֶם וְלֹא יְדַבֵּרוּ
they-can-speak but-not to-them mouth (16) man hands-of making-of and-gold

עֵינַיִם לָהֶם וְלֹא יִרְאוּ׃ (17) אָזְנַיִם לָהֶם וְלֹא יַאֲזִינוּ
they-can-hear but-not to-them ears (17) they-can-see but-not to-them eyes

אַף אֵין־ יֶשׁ־ רוּחַ בְּפִיהֶם׃ (18) כְּמוֹהֶם יִהְיוּ
they-will-be like-them (18) in-mouth-of-them breath there-is not or

עֹשֵׂיהֶם כֹּל אֲשֶׁר־ בֹּטֵחַ בָּהֶם׃ (19) בֵּית יִשְׂרָאֵל בָּרְכוּ אֶת־
*** praise! Israel house-of (19) in-them trusting who all ones-making-them

יְהוָה בֵּית אַהֲרֹן בָּרְכוּ אֶת־ יְהוָה׃ (20) בֵּית הַלֵּוִי בָּרְכוּ אֶת־
*** praise! the-Levite house-of (20) Yahweh *** praise! Aaron house-of Yahweh

יְהוָה יִרְאֵי יְהוָה בָּרְכוּ אֶת־ יְהוָה׃ (21) בָּרוּךְ יְהוָה ׀
Yahweh being-praised (21) Yahweh *** praise! Yahweh ones-fearing-of Yahweh

מִצִּיּוֹן שֹׁכֵן יְרוּשָׁלָ͏ִם הַלְלוּ־ יָהּ׃ (136:1) הוֹדוּ
give-thanks! (136:1) Yahweh praise! Jerusalem one-dwelling-of from-Zion

לַיהוָה כִּי־ טוֹב כִּי לְעוֹלָם חַסְדּוֹ׃ (2) הוֹדוּ לֵאלֹהֵי
to-God-of give-thanks! (2) love-of-him to-forever for good for to-Yahweh

הָאֱלֹהִים כִּי לְעוֹלָם חַסְדּוֹ׃ (3) הוֹדוּ לַאֲדֹנֵי הָאֲדֹנִים
the-lords to-Lord-of give-thanks! (3) love-of-him to-forever for the-gods

כִּי לְעֹלָם חַסְדּוֹ׃ (4) לְעֹשֵׂה נִפְלָאוֹת גְּדֹלוֹת
great-ones things-being-wonders to-one-doing-of (4) love-of-him to-forever for

לְבַדּוֹ כִּי לְעוֹלָם חַסְדּוֹ׃ (5) לְעֹשֵׂה הַשָּׁמַיִם
the-heavens to-one-making-of (5) love-of-him to-forever for by-himself

בִּתְבוּנָה כִּי לְעוֹלָם חַסְדּוֹ׃ (6) לְרֹקַע הָאָרֶץ
the-earth to-one-spreading-out (6) love-of-him to-forever for by-understanding

עַל־ הַמָּיִם כִּי לְעוֹלָם חַסְדּוֹ׃ (7) לְעֹשֵׂה אוֹרִים גְּדֹלִים
great-ones lights to-one-making-of (7) love-of-him to-forever for the-waters upon

---

and killed mighty kings—
11 Sihon king of the Amorites,
Og king of Bashan
and all the kings of
Canaan—
12 and he gave their land as an
inheritance,
an inheritance to his people
Israel.

13 Your name, O LORD, endures
forever,
your renown, O LORD,
through all generations.
14 For the LORD will vindicate his
people
and have compassion on his
servants.

15 The idols of the nations are
silver and gold,
made by the hands of men.
16 They have mouths, but cannot
speak,
eyes, but they cannot see;
17 they have ears, but cannot
hear,
nor is there breath in their
mouths.
18 Those who make them will be
like them,
and so will all who trust in
them.

19 O house of Israel, praise the
LORD;
O house of Aaron, praise
the LORD;
20 O house of Levi, praise the
LORD;
you who fear him, praise
the LORD.
21 Praise be to the LORD from
Zion,
to him who dwells in
Jerusalem.

Praise the LORD.

Psalm 136

1 Give thanks to the LORD, for
he is good.
His love endures forever.
2 Give thanks to the God of
gods.
His love endures forever.
3 Give thanks to the Lord of
lords:
His love endures forever.

4 to him who alone does great
wonders,
His love endures forever.
5 who by his understanding
made the heavens,
His love endures forever.
6 who spread out the earth upon
the waters,
His love endures forever.
7 who made the great lights—

כִּי לְעוֹלָם חַסְדּוֹ׃ אֶת־ הַשֶּׁמֶשׁ לְמֶמְשֶׁלֶת בַּיּוֹם כִּי

for over-the-day as-governor the-sun *** (8) love-of-him to-forever for

לְעוֹלָם חַסְדּוֹ׃ אֶת־ הַיָּרֵחַ וְכוֹכָבִים לְמֶמְשְׁלוֹת

as-governors and-stars the-moon *** (9) love-of-him to-forever

בַּלָּיְלָה כִּי לְעוֹלָם חַסְדּוֹ׃ לְמַכֵּה מִצְרַיִם

Egypt to-one-striking-down (10) love-of-him to-forever for over-the-night

בִּבְכוֹרֵיהֶם כִּי לְעוֹלָם חַסְדּוֹ׃ וַיּוֹצֵא

and-he-brought-out (11) love-of-him to-forever for in-firstborn-ones-of-them

יִשְׂרָאֵל מִתּוֹכָם כִּי לְעוֹלָם חַסְדּוֹ׃ בְּיָד חֲזָקָה

mighty with-hand (12) love-of-him to-forever for from-among-them Israel

וּבִזְרוֹעַ נְטוּיָה כִּי לְעוֹלָם חַסְדּוֹ׃

love-of-him to-forever for one-being-outstretched and-with-arm

לְגֹזֵר יַם־ סוּף לִגְזָרִים כִּי לְעוֹלָם חַסְדּוֹ׃

love-of-him to-forever for into-halves Reed Sea-of to-one-dividing (13)

וְהֶעֱבִיר יִשְׂרָאֵל בְּתוֹכוֹ כִּי לְעוֹלָם חַסְדּוֹ׃

love-of-him to-forever for through-midst-of-him Israel and-he-brought (14)

וְנִעֵר פַּרְעֹה וְחֵילוֹ בְיַם־ סוּף כִּי לְעוֹלָם

to-forever for Reed into-Sea-of and-army-of-him Pharoah but-he-swept (15)

חַסְדּוֹ׃ לְמוֹלִיךְ עַמּוֹ בַּמִּדְבָּר כִּי

for through-the-desert people-of-him to-one-leading (16) love-of-him

לְעוֹלָם חַסְדּוֹ׃ לְמַכֵּה מְלָכִים גְּדֹלִים כִּי

for great-ones kings to-one-striking-down (17) love-of-him to-forever

לְעוֹלָם חַסְדּוֹ׃ וַיַּהֲרֹג מְלָכִים אַדִּירִים כִּי לְעוֹלָם

to-forever for mighty-ones kings and-he-killed (18) love-of-him to-forever

חַסְדּוֹ׃ לְסִיחוֹן מֶלֶךְ הָאֱמֹרִי כִּי לְעוֹלָם חַסְדּוֹ׃

love-of-him to-forever for the-Amorite king-of namely-Sihon (19) love-of-him

וּלְעוֹג מֶלֶךְ הַבָּשָׁן כִּי לְעוֹלָם חַסְדּוֹ׃

love-of-him to-forever for the-Bashan king-of and-namely-Og (20)

וְנָתַן אַרְצָם לְנַחֲלָה כִּי לְעוֹלָם חַסְדּוֹ׃

love-of-him to-forever for as-inheritance land-of-them and-he-gave (21)

נַחֲלָה לְיִשְׂרָאֵל עַבְדּוֹ כִּי לְעוֹלָם חַסְדּוֹ׃

love-of-him to-forever for servant-of-him to-Israel inheritance (22)

שֶׁבְּשִׁפְלֵנוּ זָכַר לָנוּ כִּי לְעוֹלָם חַסְדּוֹ׃

love-of-him to-forever for to-us he-remembered who-in-low-estate-of-us (23)

וַיִּפְרְקֵנוּ מִצָּרֵינוּ כִּי לְעוֹלָם חַסְדּוֹ׃

love-of-him to-forever for from-enemies-of-us and-he-freed-us (24)

נֹתֵן לֶחֶם לְכָל־ בָּשָׂר כִּי לְעוֹלָם חַסְדּוֹ׃

love-of-him to-forever for creature to-every-of food one-giving (25)

His love endures forever.
8 the sun to govern the day,
His love endures forever.
9 the moon and stars to govern the night;
His love endures forever.

10 to him who struck down the firstborn of Egypt
His love endures forever.
11 and brought Israel out from among them
His love endures forever.
12 with a mighty hand and outstretched arm;
His love endures forever.

13 to him who divided the Red Sea[e] asunder
His love endures forever.
14 and brought Israel through the midst of it,
His love endures forever.
15 but swept Pharaoh and his army into the Red Sea;
His love endures forever.

16 to him who led his people through the desert,
His love endures forever.
17 who struck down great kings,
His love endures forever.
18 and killed mighty kings—
His love endures forever.
19 Sihon king of the Amorites
His love endures forever.
20 and Og king of Bashan—
His love endures forever.
21 and gave their land as an inheritance,
His love endures forever.
22 an inheritance to his servant Israel;
His love endures forever.

23 to the One who remembered us in our low estate
His love endures forever.
24 and freed us from our enemies,
His love endures forever.
25 and who gives food to every creature.
His love endures forever.

[e] 13 Hebrew *Yam Suph;* that is, Sea of Reeds; also in verse 15

הוֹדוּ לְאֵל הַשָּׁמָיִם כִּי לְעוֹלָם חַסְדּוֹ׃ עַל
by (137:1) love-of-him to-forever for the-heavens to-God-of give-thanks! (26)

נַהֲרוֹת ׀ בָּבֶל שָׁם יָשַׁבְנוּ גַּם־ בָּכִינוּ בְּזָכְרֵנוּ אֶת־צִיּוֹן׃
Zion *** when-to-remember-us we-wept and we-sat there Babylon rivers-of

עַל־עֲרָבִים בְּתוֹכָהּ תָּלִינוּ כִּנֹּרוֹתֵינוּ׃ כִּי שָׁם שְׁאֵלוּנוּ
they-asked-us there for (3) harps-of-us we-hung in-midst-of-her poplars on (2)

שׁוֹבֵינוּ דִּבְרֵי־ שִׁיר וְתוֹלָלֵינוּ שִׂמְחָה שִׁירוּ לָנוּ
for-us sing! joy and-ones-tormenting-us song words-of ones-capturing-us

מִשִּׁיר צִיּוֹן׃ אֵיךְ נָשִׁיר אֶת־ שִׁיר־ יְהוָה עַל אַדְמַת
land-of in Yahweh song-of *** can-we-sing how? (4) Zion from-song-of

נֵכָר׃ אִם־ אֶשְׁכָּחֵךְ יְרוּשָׁלִָם תִּשְׁכַּח יְמִינִי׃
right-hand-of-me may-she-forget Jerusalem I-forget-you if (5) foreigner

תִּדְבַּק־ לְשׁוֹנִי ׀ לְחִכִּי אִם־ לֹא אֶזְכְּרֵכִי
I-remember-you not if to-roof-of-mouth-of-me tongue-of-me may-she-cling (6)

אִם־לֹא אַעֲלֶה אֶת־ יְרוּשָׁלִַם עַל רֹאשׁ שִׂמְחָתִי׃ זְכֹר יְהוָה ׀
Yahweh remember! (7) joy-of-me height-of at Jerusalem *** I-consider not if

לִבְנֵי אֱדוֹם אֵת יוֹם יְרוּשָׁלִָם הָאֹמְרִים עָרוּ ׀ עָרוּ
tear-down! tear-down! the-ones-crying Jerusalem day-of *** Edom about-sons-of

עַד הַיְסוֹד בָּהּ׃ בַּת־ בָּבֶל הַשְּׁדוּדָה
the-one-being-destroyed Babylon Daughter-of (8) of-her the-foundation to

אַשְׁרֵי שֶׁיְשַׁלֶּם־ לָךְ אֶת־ גְּמוּלֵךְ שֶׁגָּמַלְתְּ לָנוּ׃
to-us that-you-did deed-of-you *** to-you who-he-repays happinesses-of

אַשְׁרֵי ׀ שֶׁיֹּאחֵז וְנִפֵּץ אֶת־ עֹלָלַיִךְ אֶל־
against infants-of-you *** and-he-dashes who-he-seizes happinesses-of (9)

הַסָּלַע׃ לְדָוִד ׀ אוֹדְךָ בְכָל־ לִבִּי נֶגֶד
before heart-of-me with-all-of I-will-praise-you of-David (138:1) the-rock

אֱלֹהִים אֲזַמְּרֶךָּ׃ אֶשְׁתַּחֲוֶה אֶל־ הֵיכַל קָדְשְׁךָ
holiness-of-you temple-of toward I-will-bow (2) I-will-sing-praise-of-you gods

וְאוֹדֶה אֶת־ שְׁמֶךָ עַל־ חַסְדְּךָ וְעַל־ אֲמִתֶּךָ
faithfulness-of-you and-for love-of-you for name-of-you *** and-I-will-praise

כִּי־ הִגְדַּלְתָּ עַל־ כָּל־ שִׁמְךָ אִמְרָתֶךָ׃ בְּיוֹם קָרָאתִי
I-called on-day-of (3) word-of-you name-of-you all-of above you-exalted for

וַתַּעֲנֵנִי תַּרְהִבֵנִי בְנַפְשִׁי עֹז׃
stoutness in-heart-of-me you-made-bold-me then-you-answered-me

יוֹדוּךָ יְהוָה כָּל־ מַלְכֵי־ אָרֶץ כִּי שָׁמְעוּ אִמְרֵי־
words-of they-hear when earth kings-of all-of Yahweh may-they-praise-you (4)

פִיךָ׃ וְיָשִׁירוּ בְּדַרְכֵי יְהוָה כִּי גָדוֹל כְּבוֹד יְהוָה׃
Yahweh glory-of great for Yahweh of-ways-of and-may-they-sing (5) mouth-of-you

26 Give thanks to the God of
heaven.
His love endures forever.

Psalm 137

1 By the rivers of Babylon we
sat and wept
when we remembered Zion.
2 There on the poplars
we hung our harps,
3 for there our captors asked us
for songs,
our tormentors demanded
songs of joy;
they said, "Sing us one of
the songs of Zion!"

4 How can we sing the songs of
the LORD
while in a foreign land?
5 If I forget you, O Jerusalem,
may my right hand forget
⌞its skill⌟.
6 May my tongue cling to the
roof of my mouth
if I do not remember you,
if I do not consider Jerusalem
my highest joy.

7 Remember, O LORD, what the
Edomites did
on the day Jerusalem fell.
"Tear it down," they cried,
"tear it down to its
foundations!"

8 O Daughter of Babylon,
doomed to destruction,
happy is he who repays you
for what you have done to
us—
9 he who seizes your infants
and dashes them against the
rocks.

Psalm 138

Of David.

1 I will praise you, O LORD, with
all my heart;
before the "gods" I will sing
your praise.
2 I will bow down toward your
holy temple
and will praise your name
for your love and your
faithfulness,
for you have exalted above all
things
your name and your word.
3 When I called, you answered
me;
you made me bold and
stouthearted.

4 May all the kings of the earth
praise you, O LORD,
when they hear the words
of your mouth.
5 May they sing of the ways of
the LORD,
for the glory of the LORD is
great.

כִּי־ רָם יְהוָה וְשָׁפָל יִרְאֶה וְגָבֹהַּ מִמֶּרְחָק
from-afar but-proud he-looks-upon yet-lowly Yahweh he-is-on-high though (6)

יְיֵדָע׃ אִם־ אֵלֵךְ ׀ בְּקֶרֶב צָרָה תְּחַיֵּנִי עַל
against you-keep-alive-me trouble in-midst-of I-walk though (7) he-knows

אַף אֹיְבַי תִּשְׁלַח יָדֶךָ וְתוֹשִׁיעֵנִי
and-you-save-me hand-of-you you-stretch-out ones-being-foes-of-me anger-of

יְמִינֶךָ׃ יְהוָה יִגְמֹר בַּעֲדִי יְהוָה חַסְדְּךָ
love-of-you Yahweh for-me he-will-fulfill Yahweh (8) right-hand-of-you

לְעוֹלָם מַעֲשֵׂי יָדֶיךָ אַל־ תֶּרֶף׃ לַמְנַצֵּחַ
for-the-one-directing (139:1) you-abandon not hands-of-you works-of to-forever

לְדָוִד מִזְמוֹר יְהוָה חֲקַרְתַּנִי וַתֵּדָע׃ אַתָּה יָדַעְתָּ שִׁבְתִּי
to-sit-me you-know you (2) and-you-know you-searched-me Yahweh psalm of-David

וְקוּמִי בַּנְתָּה לְרֵעִי מֵרָחוֹק׃ אָרְחִי
to-go-me (3) from-afar to-thought-of-me you-perceive and-to-rise-me

וְרִבְעִי זֵרִיתָ וְכָל־ דְּרָכַי הִסְכַּנְתָּה׃
you-are-familiar-with ways-of-me and-all-of you-discern and-to-lie-down-me

כִּי אֵין מִלָּה בִּלְשׁוֹנִי הֵן יְהוָה יָדַעְתָּ כֻלָּהּ׃ אָחוֹר
behind (5) all-of-her you-know Yahweh see! on-tongue-of-me word not for (4)

וָקֶדֶם צַרְתָּנִי וַתָּשֶׁת עָלַי כַּפֶּכָה׃ פְּלִאָיה
wonderful (6) hand-of-you upon-me and-you-laid you-hem-in-me and-before

דַעַת מִמֶּנִּי נִשְׂגְּבָה לֹא־ אוּכַל לָהּ׃ אָנָה
to-where? (7) to-her I-can-attain not one-being-lofty more-than-me knowledge

אֵלֵךְ מֵרוּחֶךָ וְאָנָה מִפָּנֶיךָ אֶבְרָח׃
can-I-flee from-presences-of-you and-to-where? from-Spirit-of-you can-I-go

אִם־ אֶסַּק שָׁמַיִם שָׁם אָתָּה וְאַצִּיעָה שְּׁאוֹל הִנֶּךָּ׃ אֶשָּׂא
I-rise (9) see-you! Sheol if-I-make-bed you there heavens I-go-up if (8)

כַנְפֵי־ שָׁחַר אֶשְׁכְּנָה בְּאַחֲרִית יָם׃ גַּם־ שָׁם יָדְךָ
hand-of-you there even (10) sea on-far-side-of I-settle dawn wings-of

תַנְחֵנִי וְתֹאחֲזֵנִי יְמִינֶךָ׃ וָאֹמַר
if-I-say (11) right-hand-of-you and-she-will-hold-me she-will-guide-me

אַךְ־ חֹשֶׁךְ יְשׁוּפֵנִי וְלַיְלָה אוֹר בַּעֲדֵנִי׃ גַּם־ חֹשֶׁךְ
darkness even (12) around-me light and-night he-will-hide-me darkness surely

לֹא־ יַחְשִׁיךְ מִמֶּךָ וְלַיְלָה כַּיּוֹם יָאִיר כַּחֲשֵׁיכָה
as-the-darkness he-will-shine as-the-day and-night to-you he-will-be-dark not

כָּאוֹרָה׃ כִּי־ אַתָּה קָנִיתָ כִלְיֹתָי תְּסֻכֵּנִי
you-knit-together-me inmost-beings-of-me you-created you for (13) so-the-light

בְּבֶטֶן אִמִּי׃ אוֹדְךָ עַל כִּי נוֹרָאוֹת
ones-being-fearful that because I-praise-you (14) mother-of-me in-womb-of

6Though the LORD is on high,
he looks upon the lowly,
but the proud he knows
from afar.
7Though I walk in the midst of
trouble,
you preserve my life;
you stretch out your hand
against the anger of my
foes,
with your right hand you
save me.
8The LORD will fulfill ⌊his
purpose⌋ for me;
your love, O LORD, endures
forever—
do not abandon the works
of your hands.

Psalm 139

For the director of music. Of David. A psalm.

1O LORD, you have searched me
and you know me.
2You know when I sit and
when I rise;
you perceive my thoughts
from afar.
3You discern my going out and
my lying down;
you are familiar with all my
ways.
4Before a word is on my tongue
you know it completely, O
LORD.
5You hem me in—behind and
before;
you have laid your hand
upon me.
6Such knowledge is too
wonderful for me,
too lofty for me to attain.
7Where can I go from your
Spirit?
Where can I flee from your
presence?
8If I go up to the heavens, you
are there;
if I make my bed in the
depths,[f] you are there.
9If I rise on the wings of the
dawn,
if I settle on the far side of
the sea,
10even there your hand will
guide me,
your right hand will hold
me fast.
11If I say, "Surely the darkness
will hide me
and the light become night
around me,"
12even the darkness will not be
dark to you;
the night will shine like the
day,
for darkness is as light to
you.
13For you created my inmost
being;
you knit me together in my
mother's womb.
14I praise you because I am
fearfully and wonderfully
made;

f8 Hebrew *Sheol*

°6 ק פליאה

נִפְלֵיתִי נִפְלָאִים מַעֲשֶׂיךָ וְנַפְשִׁי יֹדַעַת
one-knowing and-self-of-me works-of-you ones-being-wonderful I-am-wonderful

מְאֹד׃ לֹא־ נִכְחַד עָצְמִי מִמֶּךָּ אֲשֶׁר־ עֻשֵּׂיתִי
I-was-made when from-you frame-of-me he-was-hidden not (15) well

בַסֵּתֶר רֻקַּמְתִּי בְּתַחְתִּיּוֹת אָרֶץ׃ גָּלְמִי ׀
body-of-me (16) earth in-depths-of I-was-woven-together in-the-secret-place

רָאוּ עֵינֶיךָ וְעַל־ סִפְרְךָ כֻּלָּם יִכָּתֵבוּ יָמִים
days they-were-written all-of-them book-of-you and-in eyes-of-you they-saw

יֻצָּרוּ וְלֹא° אֶחָד בָּהֶם׃ וְלִי מַה־ יָּקְרוּ
they-are-precious how! and-to-me (17) of-them one and-not they-were-ordained

רֵעֶיךָ אֵל מֶה עָצְמוּ רָאשֵׁיהֶם׃ אֶסְפְּרֵם
should-I-count-them (18) sums-of-them they-are-vast how! God thoughts-of-you

מֵחוֹל יִרְבּוּן הֱקִיצֹתִי וְעוֹדִי עִמָּךְ׃ אִם־
if (19) with-you and-still-I I-am-awake they-would-number more-than-sand

תִּקְטֹל אֱלוֹהַּ ׀ רָשָׁע וְאַנְשֵׁי דָמִים סוּרוּ מֶנִּי׃ אֲשֶׁר
who (20) from-me be-away! bloods and-men-of wicked God you-would-slay

יֹאמְרֻךָ לִמְזִמָּה נָשֻׂא† לַשָּׁוְא
for-the-misuse †one-being-used with-evil-intent they-speak-of-you

עָרֶיךָ׃ הֲלוֹא־ מְשַׂנְאֶיךָ יְהוָה ׀ אֶשְׂנָא
I-hate Yahweh ones-hating-you not? (21) adversaries-of-you

וּבִתְקוֹמְמֶיךָ אֶתְקוֹטָט׃ תַּכְלִית שִׂנְאָה שְׂנֵאתִים
I-hate-them hatred completeness-of (22) I-abhor and-to-ones-who-rise-against-you

לְאוֹיְבִים הָיוּ לִי׃ חָקְרֵנִי אֵל וְדַע לְבָבִי
heart-of-me and-know! God search-me! (23) to-me they-are as-ones-being-enemies

בְּחָנֵנִי וְדַע שַׂרְעַפָּי׃ וּרְאֵה אִם־ דֶּרֶךְ־ עֹצֶב
offense way-of if and-see! (24) anxious-thoughts-of-me and-know! test-me!

בִּי וּנְחֵנִי בְּדֶרֶךְ עוֹלָם׃ לַמְנַצֵּחַ מִזְמוֹר
psalm for-the-one-directing *(140:1) everlasting in-way-of and-lead-me! in-me

לְדָוִד׃ חַלְּצֵנִי יְהוָה מֵאָדָם רָע מֵאִישׁ חֲמָסִים
violences from-man-of evil from-man Yahweh rescue-me! (2) of-David

תִּנְצְרֵנִי׃ אֲשֶׁר חָשְׁבוּ רָעוֹת בְּלֵב כָּל־ יוֹם יָגוּרוּ
they-stir-up day every-of in-heart evils they-devise who (3) you-protect-me

מִלְחָמוֹת׃ שָׁנֲנוּ לְשׁוֹנָם כְּמוֹ־ נָחָשׁ חֲמַת עַכְשׁוּב תַּחַת
on viper poison-of serpent as tongue-of-them they-make-sharp (4) wars

שְׂפָתֵימוֹ סֶלָה׃ שָׁמְרֵנִי יְהוָה ׀ מִידֵי רָשָׁע מֵאִישׁ
from-man-of wicked from-hands-of Yahweh keep-me! (5) selah lips-of-them

חֲמָסִים תִּנְצְרֵנִי אֲשֶׁר חָשְׁבוּ לִדְחוֹת פְּעָמָי׃ טָמְנוּ־
they-hid (6) feet-of-me to-trip they-plan who you-protect-me violences

your works are wonderful,
I know that full well.
15 My frame was not hidden
from you
when I was made in the
secret place.
When I was woven together in
the depths of the earth,
16 your eyes saw my unformed
body.
All the days ordained for me
were written in your book
before one of them came to
be.

17 How precious to[g] me are your
thoughts, O God!
How vast is the sum of
them!
18 Were I to count them,
they would outnumber the
grains of sand.
When I awake,
I am still with you.

19 If only you would slay the
wicked, O God!
Away from me, you
bloodthirsty men!
20 They speak of you with evil
intent;
your adversaries misuse
your name.
21 Do I not hate those who hate
you, O LORD,
and abhor those who rise up
against you?
22 I have nothing but hatred for
them;
I count them my enemies.

23 Search me, O God, and know
my heart;
test me and know my
anxious thoughts.
24 See if there is any offensive
way in me,
and lead me in the way
everlasting.

Psalm 140

For the director of music. A psalm of David.

1 Rescue me, O LORD, from evil
men;
protect me from men of
violence,
2 who devise evil plans in their
hearts
and stir up war every day.
3 They make their tongues as
sharp as a serpent's;
the poison of vipers is on
their lips. *Selah*

4 Keep me, O LORD, from the
hands of the wicked;
protect me from men of
violence
who plan to trip my feet.

g17 Or concerning

*Heading, *1* See the note on page 349.

†*20* The NIV repoints this word as נָשְׂאוּ, *they-use.*

°*16* ק ולו

גֵּאִ֨ים ׀ פַּ֥ח לִי֮ וַחֲבָלִ֗ים פָּ֣רְשׂוּ רֶ֭שֶׁת לְיַד־מַעְגָּ֑ל מֹקְשִׁ֖ים
traps path at-side-of net they-spread and-cords for-me snare proud-ones

שָֽׁתוּ־לִ֣י סֶֽלָה׃ אָמַ֣רְתִּי לַ֭יהוָה אֵ֣לִי אָ֑תָּה הַאֲזִ֥ינָה יְ֝הוָ֗ה
Yahweh hear! you God-of-me to-Yahweh I-say (7) selah for-me they-set

ק֣וֹל תַּחֲנוּנָֽי׃ יֱהֹוִ֣ה אֲ֭דֹנָי עֹ֣ז יְשׁוּעָתִ֑י
deliverance-of-me strength-of Lord Yahweh (8) cries-for-mercy-of-me cry-of

סַכֹּ֥תָה לְ֝רֹאשִׁ֗י בְּי֣וֹם נָֽשֶׁק׃ אַל־תִּתֵּ֣ן יְ֭הוָה
Yahweh you-grant not (9) battle in-day-of over-head-of-me you-shield

מַאֲוַיֵּ֣י רָשָׁ֑ע זְמָמ֥וֹ אַל־תָּ֝פֵ֗ק יָר֥וּמוּ סֶֽלָה׃
selah they-will-become-proud you-let-succeed not plan-of-him wicked desires-of

רֹ֥אשׁ מְסִבָּ֑י עֲמַ֖ל שְׂפָתֵ֣ימוֹ °יְכַסּ֥וּמוֹ׃
let-him-cover-them lips-of-them trouble-of ones-surrounding-me head-of (10)

°יָמִ֡יטוּ עֲלֵיהֶ֗ם גֶּֽחָלִ֗ים בָּאֵ֥שׁ יַפִּלֵ֑ם
may-they-throw-them into-the-fire coals upon-them let-them-fall (11)

בְּ֝מַהֲמֹר֗וֹת בַּל־יָקֽוּמוּ׃ אִ֥ישׁ לָשׁ֮וֹן בַּל־יִכּ֪וֹן
may-he-be-established not slander man-of (12) may-they-rise never into-miry-pits

בָּ֫אָ֥רֶץ אִישׁ־חָמָ֥ס רָ֑ע יְ֝צוּדֶ֗נּוּ לְמַדְחֵפֹֽת׃
in-thrusts may-he-hunt-down-him disaster violence man-of in-the-land

°יָדַ֗עְתָּ כִּֽי־יַעֲשֶׂ֣ה יְ֭הוָה דִּ֣ין עָנִ֑י מִ֝שְׁפַּ֗ט אֶבְיֹנִֽים׃
needy-ones cause-of poor justice-of Yahweh he-secures that I-know (13)

אַ֣ךְ צַ֭דִּיקִים יוֹד֣וּ לִשְׁמֶ֑ךָ יֵשְׁב֥וּ
they-will-live to-name-of-you they-will-praise righteous-ones surely (14)

יְ֝שָׁרִ֗ים אֶת־פָּנֶֽיךָ׃ מִזְמ֗וֹר לְדָ֫וִ֥ד יְהוָ֣ה קְ֭רָאתִיךָ
I-call-to-you Yahweh of-David psalm (141:1) faces-of-you before upright-ones

ח֣וּשָׁה לִּ֑י הַאֲזִ֥ינָה ק֝וֹלִ֗י בְּקָרְאִי־לָֽךְ׃ תִּכּ֤וֹן
may-she-be-set (2) to-you when-to-call-me voice-of-me hear! to-me be-quick!

תְּפִלָּתִ֣י קְטֹ֣רֶת לְפָנֶ֑יךָ מַֽשְׂאַ֥ת כַּ֝פַּ֗י מִנְחַת־עָֽרֶב׃
evening sacrifice-of hands-of-me lifting-of before-you incense prayer-of-me

שִׁיתָ֣ה יְ֭הוָה שָׁמְרָ֣ה לְפִ֑י נִ֝צְּרָ֗ה עַל־דַּ֥ל שְׂפָתָֽי׃
lips-of-me door-of over keep-watch! over-mouth-of-me guard Yahweh set! (3)

אַל־תַּט־לִבִּ֨י ׀ לְדָבָ֤ר ׀ רָ֗ע לְהִתְע֬וֹלֵ֨ל עֲלִל֡וֹת ׀
deeds to-take-part evil to-matter heart-of-me you-let-be-drawn not (4)

בְּרֶ֗שַׁע אֶת־אִ֣ישִׁים פֹּֽעֲלֵי־אָ֑וֶן וּבַל־אֶ֝לְחַ֗ם בְּמַנְעַמֵּיהֶֽם׃
of-delicacies-of-them let-me-eat and-not evil ones-doing-of men with of-wickedness

יֶֽהֶלְמֵֽנִי־צַדִּ֨יק ׀ חֶ֡סֶד וְֽיוֹכִיחֵ֗נִי שֶׁ֣מֶן
oil-of and-let-him-rebuke-me kindness righteous-man let-him-strike-me (5)

רֹ֭אשׁ אַל־יָנִ֣י רֹאשִׁ֑י כִּי־ע֥וֹד וּ֝תְפִלָּתִ֗י
also-prayer-of-me ever yet head-of-me he-will-refuse not head

5 Proud men have hidden a
snare for me;
they have spread out the
cords of their net
and have set traps for me
along my path. *Selah*

6 O LORD, I say to you, "You are
my God."
Hear, O LORD, my cry for
mercy.
7 O Sovereign LORD, my strong
deliverer,
who shields my head in the
day of battle—
8 do not grant the wicked their
desires, O LORD;
do not let their plans
succeed,
or they will become proud.
Selah

9 Let the heads of those who
surround me
be covered with the trouble
their lips have caused.
10 Let burning coals fall upon
them;
may they be thrown into
the fire,
into miry pits, never to rise.
11 Let slanderers not be
established in the land;
may disaster hunt down
men of violence.

12 I know that the LORD secures
justice for the poor
and upholds the cause of the
needy.
13 Surely the righteous will praise
your name
and the upright will live
before you.

Psalm 141

A psalm of David.

1 O LORD, I call to you; come
quickly to me.
Hear my voice when I call
to you.
2 May my prayer be set before
you like incense;
may the lifting up of my
hands be like the evening
sacrifice.

3 Set a guard over my mouth, O
LORD;
keep watch over the door of
my lips.
4 Let not my heart be drawn to
what is evil,
to take part in wicked deeds
with men who are evildoers;
let me not eat of their
delicacies.

5 Let a righteous man strike
me—it is a kindness;
let him rebuke me—it is oil
on my head.
My head will not refuse it.

Yet my prayer is ever against

*See the note on page 349.

°10 ק יכסימו
°11 ק ימוטו
°13 ק ידעתי

בְּרָעוֹתֵיהֶם׃ נִשְׁמְטוּ בִידֵי־ סֶלַע
cliff from-edges-of they-will-be-thrown-down (6) against-evil-deeds-of-them

שֹׁפְטֵיהֶם וְשָׁמְעוּ אֲמָרַי כִּי נָעֵמוּ׃
they-were-well-spoken that words-of-me and-they-will-learn ones-ruling-them

כְּמוֹ פֹלֵחַ וּבֹקֵעַ בָּאָרֶץ נִפְזְרוּ
they-were-scattered to-the-earth and-one-breaking-up one-plowing as (7)

עֲצָמֵינוּ לְפִי שְׁאוֹל׃ כִּי אֵלֶיךָ ׀ יְהוִה אֲדֹנָי עֵינָי בְּכָה
in-you eyes-of-me Lord Yahweh on-you but (8) Sheol at-mouth-of bones-of-us

חָסִיתִי אַל־ תְּעַר נַפְשִׁי׃ שָׁמְרֵנִי מִידֵי
from-hands-of keep-me! (9) self-of-me you-give-over-to-death not I-take-refuge

פַּח יָקְשׁוּ לִי וּמֹקְשׁוֹת פֹּעֲלֵי אָוֶן׃ יִפְּלוּ
let-them-fall (10) evil ones-doing-of and-traps-of for-me they-laid snare

בְמַכְמֹרָיו רְשָׁעִים יַחַד אָנֹכִי עַד־ אֶעֱבוֹר׃ מַשְׂכִּיל
maskil *(142:1) I-pass-by while I together wicked-ones into-nets-of-him

לְדָוִד בִּהְיוֹתוֹ בַמְּעָרָה תְפִלָּה׃ קוֹלִי אֶל־ יְהוָה אֶזְעָק
I-cry Yahweh to voice-of-me (2) prayer in-the-cave when-to-be-him of-David

קוֹלִי אֶל־ יְהוָה אֶתְחַנָּן׃ אֶשְׁפֹּךְ לְפָנָיו שִׂיחִי
complaint-of-me before-him I-pour-out (3) I-ask-for-mercy Yahweh to voice-of-me

צָרָתִי לְפָנָיו אַגִּיד׃ בְּהִתְעַטֵּף עָלַי ׀ רוּחִי
spirit-of-me within-me when-to-grow-faint (4) I-tell before-him trouble-of-me

וְאַתָּה יָדַעְתָּ נְתִיבָתִי בְּאֹרַח־ זוּ אֲהַלֵּךְ טָמְנוּ פַח לִי׃
for-me snare they-hid I-walk where in-path way-of-me you-know then-you

הַבֵּיט יָמִין ׀ וּרְאֵה וְאֵין־ לִי מַכִּיר אָבַד
he-fled one-being-concerned for-me that-there-is-not and-see! right look! (5)

מָנוֹס מִמֶּנִּי אֵין דּוֹרֵשׁ לְנַפְשִׁי׃ זָעַקְתִּי אֵלֶיךָ יְהוָה
Yahweh to-you I-cry (6) for-life-of-me one-caring there-is-not from-me refuge

אָמַרְתִּי אַתָּה מַחְסִי חֶלְקִי בְּאֶרֶץ הַחַיִּים׃ הַקְשִׁיבָה ׀ אֶל־
to listen! (7) living-ones in-land-of portion-of-me refuge-of-me you I-say

רִנָּתִי כִּי־ דַלּוֹתִי מְאֹד הַצִּילֵנִי מֵרֹדְפַי כִּי
for from-ones-pursuing-me rescue-me! desperate I-am-in-need for cry-of-me

אָמְצוּ מִמֶּנִּי׃ הוֹצִיאָה מִמַּסְגֵּר ׀ נַפְשִׁי לְהוֹדוֹת
to-praise self-of-me from-prison set-free! (8) more-than-me they-are-strong

אֶת־ שְׁמֶךָ בִּי יַכְתִּרוּ צַדִּיקִים כִּי
because righteous-ones they-will-gather-about to-me name-of-you ***

תִּגְמֹל עָלָי׃ מִזְמוֹר לְדָוִד יְהוָה ׀ שְׁמַע תְּפִלָּתִי
prayer-of-me hear! Yahweh of-David psalm (143:1) to-me you-will-be-good

הַאֲזִינָה אֶל־ תַּחֲנוּנַי בֶּאֱמֻנָתְךָ עֲנֵנִי
relieve-me! in-faithfulness-of-you cries-for-mercy-of-me to listen!

---

the deeds of evildoers;
6 their rulers will be thrown down from the cliffs,
and the wicked will learn that my words were well spoken.
7 ⌞They will say,⌟ "As one plows and breaks up the earth,
so our bones have been scattered at the mouth of the grave.[h]"

8 But my eyes are fixed on you, O Sovereign LORD;
in you I take refuge—do not give me over to death.
9 Keep me from the snares they have laid for me,
from the traps set by evildoers.
10 Let the wicked fall into their own nets,
while I pass by in safety.

Psalm 142

A *maskil*[i] of David. When he was in the cave. A prayer.

1 I cry aloud to the LORD;
I lift up my voice to the LORD for mercy.
2 I pour out my complaint before him;
before him I tell my trouble.

3 When my spirit grows faint within me,
it is you who know my way.
In the path where I walk men have hidden a snare for me.
4 Look to my right and see;
no one is concerned for me.
I have no refuge;
no one cares for my life.

5 I cry to you, O LORD;
I say, "You are my refuge,
my portion in the land of the living."
6 Listen to my cry,
for I am in desperate need;
rescue me from those who pursue me,
for they are too strong for me.
7 Set me free from my prison,
that I may praise your name.

Then the righteous will gather about me
because of your goodness to me.

Psalm 143

A psalm of David.

1 O LORD, hear my prayer,
listen to my cry for mercy;
in your faithfulness and righteousness
come to my relief.

h7 Hebrew *Sheol*
iTitle: Probably a literary or musical term

**1* See the note on page 349.

בְּצִדְקָתֶֽךָ׃ וְאַל־ תָּבוֹא בְמִשְׁפָּט אֶת־ עַבְדֶּךָ

servant-of-you *** into-judgment you-bring and-not (2) in-righteousness-of-you

כִּי לֹא־ יִצְדַּק לְפָנֶיךָ כָל־ חָי׃ כִּי רָדַף

he-pursues indeed (3) one-alive any-of before-you he-is-righteous not for

אוֹיֵב ׀ נַפְשִׁי דִּכָּא לָאָרֶץ חַיָּתִי הוֹשִׁיבַנִי

he-makes-dwell-me life-of-me to-the-ground he-crushes self-of-me one-being-enemy

בְמַחֲשַׁכִּים כְּמֵתֵי עוֹלָם׃ וַתִּתְעַטֵּף עָלַי

within-me so-she-grows-faint (4) long-ago like-dead-ones-of in-dark-places

רוּחִי בְּתוֹכִי יִשְׁתּוֹמֵם לִבִּי׃ זָכַרְתִּי יָמִים ׀

days I-remember (5) heart-of-me he-is-dismayed at-within-me spirit-of-me

מִקֶּדֶם הָגִיתִי בְכָל־ פָּעֳלֶךָ בְּמַעֲשֵׂה יָדֶיךָ

hands-of-you on-deed-of work-of-you on-all-of I-meditate of-long-ago

אֲשׂוֹחֵחַ׃ פֵּרַשְׂתִּי יָדַי אֵלֶיךָ נַפְשִׁי ׀ כְּאֶרֶץ־ עֲיֵפָה

parched like-land soul-of-me to-you hands-of-me I-spread-out (6) I-consider

לְךָ סֶלָה׃ מַהֵר עֲנֵנִי ׀ יְהוָה כָּלְתָה רוּחִי אַל־

not spirit-of-me she-faints Yahweh answer-me! be-quick! (7) selah for-you

תַּסְתֵּר פָּנֶיךָ מִמֶּנִּי וְנִמְשַׁלְתִּי עִם־ יֹרְדֵי בוֹר׃

pit ones-going-down-of with or-I-will-be-like from-me faces-of-you you-hide

הַשְׁמִיעֵנִי בַבֹּקֶר ׀ חַסְדֶּךָ כִּי־ בְךָ

in-you for unfailing-love-of-you in-the-morning bring-word-to-me! (8)

בָטָחְתִּי הוֹדִיעֵנִי דֶּרֶךְ־ זוּ אֵלֵךְ כִּי־ אֵלֶיךָ נָשָׂאתִי נַפְשִׁי׃

soul-of-me I-lift-up to-you for I-should-go that way show-me! I-put-trust

הַצִּילֵנִי מֵאֹיְבַי ׀ יְהוָה אֵלֶיךָ כִסִּתִי׃

I-hide in-you Yahweh from-ones-being-enemies-of-me rescue-me! (9)

לַמְּדֵנִי ׀ לַעֲשׂוֹת רְצוֹנֶךָ כִּי־ אַתָּה אֱלוֹהָי רוּחֲךָ טוֹבָה

good Spirit-of-you God-of-me you for will-of-you to-do teach-me! (10)

תַּנְחֵנִי בְּאֶרֶץ מִישׁוֹר׃ לְמַעַן־ שִׁמְךָ יְהוָה

Yahweh name-of-you for-sake-of (11) levelness on-ground-of may-she-lead-me

תְּחַיֵּנִי בְּצִדְקָתְךָ ׀ תוֹצִיא מִצָּרָה נַפְשִׁי׃

self-of-me from-trouble you-bring-out in-righteousness-of-you you-keep-alive-me

וּבְחַסְדְּךָ תַּצְמִית אֹיְבָי וְהַאֲבַדְתָּ

and-you-destroy ones-being-enemies-of-me you-silence and-in-love-of-you (12)

כָּל־ צֹרֲרֵי נַפְשִׁי כִּי אֲנִי עַבְדֶּךָ׃ לְדָוִד ׀

of-David (144:1) servant-of-you I for self-of-me ones-being-foes-of all-of

בָּרוּךְ יְהוָה ׀ צוּרִי הַמְלַמֵּד יָדַי לַקְרָב

for-the-war hands-of-me the-one-training Rock-of-me Yahweh being-praised

אֶצְבְּעוֹתַי לַמִּלְחָמָה׃ חַסְדִּי וּמְצוּדָתִי מִשְׂגַּבִּי

stronghold-of-me and-fortress-of-me love-of-me (2) for-the-battle fingers-of-me

2 Do not bring your servant into
judgment,
for no one living is
righteous before you.

3 The enemy pursues me,
he crushes me to the
ground;
he makes me dwell in
darkness
like those long dead.
4 So my spirit grows faint
within me;
my heart within me is
dismayed.

5 I remember the days of long
ago;
I meditate on all your works
and consider what your
hands have done.
6 I spread out my hands to you;
my soul thirsts for you like a
parched land. *Selah*

7 Answer me quickly, O LORD;
my spirit faints with
longing.
Do not hide your face from me
or I will be like those who
go down to the pit.
8 Let the morning bring me
word of your unfailing
love,
for I have put my trust in
you.
Show me the way I should go,
for to you I lift up my soul.
9 Rescue me from my enemies,
O LORD,
for I hide myself in you.
10 Teach me to do your will,
for you are my God;
may your good Spirit
lead me on level ground.

11 For your name's sake, O LORD,
preserve my life;
in your righteousness, bring
me out of trouble.
12 In your unfailing love, silence
my enemies;
destroy all my foes,
for I am your servant.

Psalm 144

Of David.

1 Praise be to the LORD, my
Rock,
who trains my hands for
war,
my fingers for battle.
2 He is my loving God and my
fortress,
my stronghold and my

וּמְפַלְטִי לִי מָגִנִּי וּבוֹ חָסִיתִי
I-take-refuge and-in-him shield-of-me to-me and-one-delivering-me

הָרוֹדֵד עַמִּי תַחְתָּי׃ (3) יְהוָה מָה־ אָדָם
man what? Yahweh (3) under-me people-of-me the-one-subduing

וַתֵּדָעֵהוּ בֶּן־ אֱנוֹשׁ וַתְּחַשְּׁבֵהוּ׃ (4) אָדָם לַהֶבֶל
to-the-breath man (4) that-you-think-of-him man son-of that-you-care-for-him

דָּמָה יָמָיו כְּצֵל עוֹבֵר׃ (5) יְהוָה הַט־ שָׁמֶיךָ
heavens-of-you part! Yahweh (5) one-fleeting like-shadow days-of-him he-is-like

וְתֵרֵד גַּע בֶּהָרִים וְיֶעֱשָׁנוּ׃ (6) בְּרוֹק
send-lightning! (6) so-they-smoke to-the-mountains touch! and-you-come-down

בָּרָק וּתְפִיצֵם שְׁלַח חִצֶּיךָ וּתְהֻמֵּם׃
and-you-rout-them arrows-of-you shoot! and-you-scatter-them lightning

(7) שְׁלַח יָדֶיךָ מִמָּרוֹם פְּצֵנִי וְהַצִּילֵנִי מִמַּיִם
from-waters and-rescue-me! deliver-me! from-on-high hands-of-you reach! (7)

רַבִּים מִיַּד בְּנֵי נֵכָר׃ (8) אֲשֶׁר פִּיהֶם דִּבֶּר־ שָׁוְא
lie he-speaks mouth-of-them who (8) foreign men-of from-hand-of mighty-ones

וִימִינָם יְמִין שָׁקֶר׃ (9) אֱלֹהִים שִׁיר חָדָשׁ אָשִׁירָה
I-will-sing new song God (9) deceit right-hand-of and-right-hand-of-them

לָּךְ בְּנֵבֶל עָשׂוֹר אֲזַמְּרָה־ לָּךְ׃ (10) הַנּוֹתֵן תְּשׁוּעָה
victory the-One-giving (10) to-you I-will-make-music ten on-lyre-of to-you

לַמְּלָכִים הַפּוֹצֶה אֶת־ דָּוִד עַבְדּוֹ מֵחֶרֶב רָעָה׃
deadly from-sword servant-of-him David *** the-One-delivering to-the-kings

(11) פְּצֵנִי וְהַצִּילֵנִי מִיַּד בְּנֵי־ נֵכָר אֲשֶׁר פִּיהֶם
mouth-of-them who foreign men-of from-hand-of and-rescue-me! deliver-me! (11)

דִּבֶּר־ שָׁוְא וִימִינָם יְמִין שָׁקֶר׃ (12) אֲשֶׁר בָּנֵינוּ ׀
sons-of-us then (12) deceit right-hand-of and-right-hand-of-them lie he-speaks

כִּנְטִעִים מְגֻדָּלִים בִּנְעוּרֵיהֶם בְּנוֹתֵינוּ
daughters-of-us in-youths-of-them ones-being-well-nurtured like-plants

כְזָוִיֹּת מְחֻטָּבוֹת תַּבְנִית הֵיכָל׃ (13) מְזָוֵינוּ
barns-of-us (13) palace adornment-of ones-being-carved like-pillars

מְלֵאִים מְפִיקִים מִזַּן אֶל־ זַן צֹאונֵנוּ
sheep-of-us kind to from-kind things-being-provided ones-filled

מַאֲלִיפוֹת מְרֻבָּבוֹת בְּחוּצוֹתֵינוּ׃
in-fields-of-us ones-becoming-tens-of-thousands ones-becoming-thousands

(14) אַלּוּפֵינוּ מְסֻבָּלִים אֵין־ פֶּרֶץ וְאֵין יוֹצֵאת וְאֵין
and-no going-away and-no breach no ones-drawing-loads oxen-of-us (14)

צְוָחָה בִּרְחֹבֹתֵינוּ׃ (15) אַשְׁרֵי הָעָם שֶׁכָּכָה
who-true the-people blessednesses-of (15) in-streets-of-us cry-of-distress

---

deliverer,
my shield, in whom I take refuge,
who subdues peoples[j] under me.

3 O LORD, what is man that you care for him,
the son of man that you think of him?
4 Man is like a breath;
his days are like a fleeting shadow.

5 Part your heavens, O LORD, and come down;
touch the mountains, so that they smoke.
6 Send forth lightning and scatter ⌊the enemies⌋;
shoot your arrows and rout them.
7 Reach down your hand from on high;
deliver me and rescue me
from the mighty waters,
from the hands of foreigners
8 whose mouths are full of lies,
whose right hands are deceitful.

9 I will sing a new song to you, O God;
on the ten-stringed lyre I will make music to you,
10 to the One who gives victory to kings,
who delivers his servant David from the deadly sword.

11 Deliver me and rescue me
from the hands of foreigners
whose mouths are full of lies,
whose right hands are deceitful.

12 Then our sons in their youth
will be like well-nurtured plants,
and our daughters will be like pillars
carved to adorn a palace.
13 Our barns will be filled
with every kind of provision.
Our sheep will increase by thousands,
by tens of thousands in our fields;
14 our oxen will draw heavy loads.[k]
There will be no breaching of walls,
no going into captivity,
no cry of distress in our streets.

15 Blessed are the people of whom this is true;

[j]2 Many manuscripts of the Masoretic Text, Dead Sea Scrolls, Aquila, Jerome and Syriac; most manuscripts of the Masoretic Text *subdues my people*

[k]14 Or *our chieftains will be firmly established*

לוֹ אַשְׁרֵי הָעָם שֶׁיְהוָה אֱלֹהָיו׃ תְּהִלָּה
praise-psalm (145:1) God-of-him who-Yahweh the-people blessednesses-of of-him

לְדָוִד אֲרוֹמִמְךָ אֱלוֹהַי הַמֶּלֶךְ וַאֲבָרְכָה שִׁמְךָ
name-of-you and-I-will-praise the-King God-of-me I-will-exalt-you of-David

לְעוֹלָם וָעֶד׃ בְּכָל־ יוֹם אֲבָרְכֶךָּ וַאֲהַלְלָה
and-I-will-extol I-will-praise-you day in-every-of (2) and-ever to-forever

שִׁמְךָ לְעוֹלָם וָעֶד׃ גָּדוֹל יְהוָה וּמְהֻלָּל מְאֹד
greatly and-one-being-praised Yahweh great (3) and-ever to-forever name-of-you

וְלִגְדֻלָּתוֹ אֵין חֵקֶר׃ דּוֹר לְדוֹר
to-generation generation (4) fathoming there-is-no and-to-greatness-of-him

יְשַׁבַּח מַעֲשֶׂיךָ וּגְבוּרֹתֶיךָ יַגִּידוּ׃
they-will-tell and-mighty-acts-of-you works-of-you he-will-commend

הֲדַר כְּבוֹד הוֹדֶךָ וְדִבְרֵי נִפְלְאוֹתֶיךָ
works-being-wonderful-of-you and-deeds-of majesty-of-you glory-of splendor-of (5)

אָשִׂיחָה׃ וֶעֱזוּז נוֹרְאֹתֶיךָ יֹאמֵרוּ
they-will-tell works-being-awesome-of-you and-power-of (6) I-will-meditate

וּגְדוּלֹּתֶיךָ אֲסַפְּרֶנָּה׃ זֵכֶר רַב־ טוּבְךָ
goodness-of-you abundance-of memory-of (7) I-will-proclaim and-great-deed-of-you

יַבִּיעוּ וְצִדְקָתְךָ יְרַנֵּנוּ׃ חַנּוּן
gracious (8) they-will-sing and-righteousness-of-you they-will-celebrate

וְרַחוּם יְהוָה אֶרֶךְ אַפַּיִם וּגְדָל־ חָסֶד׃ טוֹב־ יְהוָה
Yahweh good (9) love and-rich-of angers slow-of Yahweh and-compassionate

לַכֹּל וְרַחֲמָיו עַל־ כָּל־ מַעֲשָׂיו׃
makings-of-him all-of on and-compassions-of-him to-the-all

יוֹדוּךָ יְהוָה כָּל־ מַעֲשֶׂיךָ וַחֲסִידֶיךָ
and-saints-of-you makings-of-you all-of Yahweh they-will-praise-you (10)

יְבָרְכוּכָה׃ כְּבוֹד מַלְכוּתְךָ יֹאמֵרוּ
they-will-tell kingdom-of-you glory-of (11) they-will-extol-you

וּגְבוּרָתְךָ יְדַבֵּרוּ׃ לְהוֹדִיעַ׀ לִבְנֵי הָאָדָם
the-man to-sons-of to-make-known (12) they-will-speak and-might-of-you

גְּבוּרֹתָיו וּכְבוֹד הֲדַר מַלְכוּתוֹ׃ מַלְכוּתְךָ
kingdom-of-you (13) kingdom-of-him splendor-of and-glory-of mighty-acts-of-him

מַלְכוּת כָּל־ עֹלָמִים וּמֶמְשַׁלְתְּךָ בְּכָל־ דּוֹר
generation through-all-of and-dominion-of-you everlastings all-of kingdom-of

וָדוֹר׃ סוֹמֵךְ יְהוָה לְכָל־ הַנֹּפְלִים וְזוֹקֵף
and-lifting the-ones-falling to-all-of Yahweh upholding (14) *and-generation

לְכָל־ הַכְּפוּפִים׃ עֵינֵי־ כֹל אֵלֶיךָ יְשַׂבֵּרוּ וְאַתָּה
and-you they-look to-you all eyes-of (15) the-ones-being-bowed to-all-of

blessed are the people whose
God is the LORD.

Psalm 145[l]

A psalm of praise. Of David.

1 I will exalt you, my God the
King;
I will praise your name for
ever and ever.
2 Every day I will praise you
and extol your name for
ever and ever.

3 Great is the LORD and most
worthy of praise;
his greatness no one can
fathom.
4 One generation will commend
your works to another;
they will tell of your mighty
acts.
5 They will speak of the glorious
splendor of your majesty,
and I will meditate on your
wonderful works.[m]
6 They will tell of the power of
your awesome works,
and I will proclaim your
great deeds.
7 They will celebrate your
abundant goodness
and joyfully sing of your
righteousness.

8 The LORD is gracious and
compassionate,
slow to anger and rich in
love.
9 The LORD is good to all;
he has compassion on all he
has made.
10 All you have made will praise
you, O LORD;
your saints will extol you.
11 They will tell of the glory of
your kingdom
and speak of your might,
12 so that all men may know of
your mighty acts
and the glorious splendor of
your kingdom.
13 Your kingdom is an
everlasting kingdom,
and your dominion endures
through all generations.

The LORD is faithful to all his
promises
and loving toward all he has
made.[n]
14 The LORD upholds all those
who fall
and lifts up all who are
bowed down.

[l] This psalm is an acrostic poem, the verses of which (including verse 13b) begin with the successive letters of the Hebrew alphabet.
[m] 5 Dead Sea Scrolls and Syriac (see also Septuagint); Masoretic Text *On the glorious splendor of your majesty / and on your wonderful works I will meditate*
[n] 13 One manuscript of the Masoretic Text, Dead Sea Scrolls, Septuagint and Syriac; most manuscripts of the Masoretic Text do not have the last two lines of verse 13.

*13 The NIV reads with the mss and versions listed above in footnote *n*:

נֶאֱמָן יהוה בְּכָל־
to-all-of *Yahweh* *one-being-faithful*

דְּבָרָיו וְחָסִיד בְּכָל־
toward-all-of *and-loving* *promises-of-him*

מַעֲשָׂיו
makings-of-him.

°6 ק וגדולתך

נוֹתֵן־ לָהֶם אֶת־ אָכְלָם בְּעִתּוֹ׃ (16) פּוֹתֵחַ אֶת־ יָדֶךָ
hand-of-you *** opening (16) at-time-of-him food-of-them *** to-them giving

וּמַשְׂבִּיעַ לְכָל־ חַי רָצוֹן׃ (17) צַדִּיק יְהוָה
Yahweh righteous (17) desire living-thing to-every-of and-satisfying

בְּכָל־ דְּרָכָיו וְחָסִיד בְּכָל־ מַעֲשָׂיו׃ (18) קָרוֹב
near (18) makings-of-him toward-all-of and-loving ways-of-him in-all-of

יְהוָה לְכָל־ קֹרְאָיו לְכֹל אֲשֶׁר יִקְרָאֻהוּ בֶאֱמֶת׃
in-truth they-call-on-him who to-all ones-calling-on-him to-all-of Yahweh

(19) רְצוֹן־ יְרֵאָיו יַעֲשֶׂה וְאֶת־ שַׁוְעָתָם יִשְׁמַע
he-hears cry-of-them and he-fulfills ones-fearing-him desire-of (19)

וְיוֹשִׁיעֵם׃ (20) שׁוֹמֵר יְהוָה אֶת־ כָּל־ אֹהֲבָיו וְאֵת
but ones-loving-him all-of *** Yahweh watching-over (20) and-he-saves-them

כָּל־ הָרְשָׁעִים יַשְׁמִיד׃ (21) תְּהִלַּת יְהוָה יְדַבֶּר־
he-will-speak Yahweh praise-of (21) he-will-destroy the-wicked-ones all-of

פִּי וִיבָרֵךְ כָּל־ בָּשָׂר שֵׁם קָדְשׁוֹ
holiness-of-him name-of creature every-of and-let-him-praise mouth-of-me

לְעוֹלָם וָעֶד׃ (146:1) הַלְלוּ־ יָהּ הַלְלִי נַפְשִׁי אֶת־ יְהוָה׃
Yahweh *** soul-of-me praise! Yahweh praise! (146:1) and-ever to-forever

(2) אֲהַלְלָה יְהוָה בְּחַיָּי אֲזַמְּרָה לֵאלֹהַי
to-God-of-me I-will-sing-praise during-lives-of-me Yahweh I-will-praise (2)

בְּעוֹדִי׃ (3) אַל־ תִּבְטְחוּ בִנְדִיבִים בְּבֶן־ אָדָם שֶׁאֵין לוֹ
in-him who-not man in-son-of in-princes you-trust not (3) while-still-I

תְשׁוּעָה׃ (4) תֵּצֵא רוּחוֹ יָשֻׁב לְאַדְמָתוֹ בַּיּוֹם
on-the-day to-ground-of-him he-returns spirit-of-him she-departs (4) salvation

הַהוּא אָבְדוּ עֶשְׁתֹּנֹתָיו׃ (5) אַשְׁרֵי שֶׁאֵל
who-God-of blessednesses-of (5) plans-of-him they-come-to-nothing the-that

יַעֲקֹב בְּעֶזְרוֹ שִׂבְרוֹ עַל־ יְהוָה אֱלֹהָיו׃ (6) עֹשֶׂה שָׁמַיִם
heavens One-Making (6) God-of-him Yahweh in hope-of-him as-help-of-him Jacob

וָאָרֶץ אֶת־ הַיָּם וְאֶת־ כָּל־ אֲשֶׁר־ בָּם הַשֹּׁמֵר אֱמֶת
faithful the-one-remaining in-them that all and the-sea *** and-earth

לְעוֹלָם׃ (7) עֹשֶׂה מִשְׁפָּט לָעֲשׁוּקִים נֹתֵן לֶחֶם
food giving of-the-ones-being-oppressed cause upholding (7) to-forever

לָרְעֵבִים יְהוָה מַתִּיר אֲסוּרִים׃ (8) יְהוָה
Yahweh (8) ones-being-prisoners setting-free Yahweh to-the-hungry-ones

פֹּקֵחַ עִוְרִים יְהוָה זֹקֵף כְּפוּפִים יְהוָה אֹהֵב
loving Yahweh ones-being-bowed lifting Yahweh blind-ones giving-sight

צַדִּיקִים׃ (9) יְהוָה שֹׁמֵר אֶת־ גֵּרִים יָתוֹם וְאַלְמָנָה
and-widow fatherless aliens *** watching-over Yahweh (9) righteous-ones

15 The eyes of all look to you,
and you give them their
food at the proper time.
16 You open your hand
and satisfy the desires of
every living thing.
17 The LORD is righteous in all his
ways
and loving toward all he has
made.
18 The LORD is near to all who
call on him,
to all who call on him in
truth.
19 He fulfills the desires of those
who fear him;
he hears their cry and saves
them.
20 The LORD watches over all who
love him,
but all the wicked he will
destroy.
21 My mouth will speak in praise
of the LORD.
Let every creature praise his
holy name
for ever and ever.

Psalm 146

1 Praise the LORD.[a]

Praise the LORD, O my soul.
2 I will praise the LORD all my
life;
I will sing praise to my God
as long as I live.
3 Do not put your trust in
princes,
in mortal men, who cannot
save.
4 When their spirit departs, they
return to the ground;
on that very day their plans
come to nothing.
5 Blessed is he whose help is the
God of Jacob,
whose hope is in the LORD
his God,
6 the Maker of heaven and
earth,
the sea, and everything in
them—
the LORD, who remains
faithful forever.
7 He upholds the cause of the
oppressed
and gives food to the
hungry.
The LORD sets prisoners free,
8 the LORD gives sight to the
blind,
the LORD lifts up those who are
bowed down,
the LORD loves the righteous.
9 The LORD watches over the
alien
and sustains the fatherless
and the widow,

[a] 1 Hebrew *Hallelu Yah*; also in verse 10

יְעוֹדֵד וְדֶרֶךְ רְשָׁעִים יְעַוֵּת׃ יִמְלֹךְ יְהוָה ׀

Yahweh he-reigns (10) he-frustrates wicked-ones but-way-of he-sustains

לְעוֹלָם אֱלֹהַיִךְ צִיּוֹן לְדֹר וָדֹר הַלְלוּ־ יָהּ׃

Yahweh praise! and-generation for-generation Zion God-of-you to-forever

הַלְלוּ יָהּ ׀ כִּי־ טוֹב זַמְּרָה אֱלֹהֵינוּ כִּי־ נָעִים

pleasant how! God-of-us to-sing-praise good how! Yahweh praise! (147:1)

נָאוָה תְהִלָּה׃ בּוֹנֵה יְרוּשָׁלַםִ יְהוָה נִדְחֵי יִשְׂרָאֵל

Israel ones-being-exiled-of Yahweh Jerusalem one-building-of (2) praise fitting

יְכַנֵּס׃ הָרֹפֵא לִשְׁבוּרֵי לֵב וּמְחַבֵּשׁ

and-one-binding heart to-ones-being-broken-of the-one-healing (3) he-gathers

לְעַצְּבוֹתָם׃ מוֹנֶה מִסְפָּר לַכּוֹכָבִים לְכֻלָּם

to-each-of-them of-the-stars number one-determining (4) to-wounds-of-them

שֵׁמוֹת יִקְרָא׃ גָּדוֹל אֲדוֹנֵינוּ וְרַב־ כֹּחַ לִתְבוּנָתוֹ

to-understanding-of-him power and-mighty-of Lord-of-us great (5) he-calls names

אֵין מִסְפָּר׃ מְעוֹדֵד עֲנָוִים יְהוָה מַשְׁפִּיל רְשָׁעִים עֲדֵי־

to wicked-ones one-casting Yahweh humble-ones one-sustaining (6) limit no

אָרֶץ׃ עֱנוּ לַיהוָה בְּתוֹדָה זַמְּרוּ לֵאלֹהֵינוּ בְכִנּוֹר׃

on-harp to-God-of-us make-music! with-thanksgiving to-Yahweh sing! (7) ground

הַמְכַסֶּה שָׁמַיִם ׀ בְּעָבִים הַמֵּכִין לָאָרֶץ מָטָר

rain to-the-earth the-one-supplying with-clouds skies the-one-covering (8)

הַמַּצְמִיחַ הָרִים חָצִיר׃ נוֹתֵן לִבְהֵמָה לַחְמָהּ

food-of-her for-cattle the-one-providing (9) grass hills the-one-making-grow

לִבְנֵי עֹרֵב אֲשֶׁר יִקְרָאוּ׃ לֹא בִגְבוּרַת הַסּוּס

the-horse in-strength-of not (10) they-call when raven for-young-ones-of

יֶחְפָּץ לֹא־ בְשׁוֹקֵי הָאִישׁ יִרְצֶה׃ רוֹצֶה יְהוָה

Yahweh one-delighting (11) he-delights the-man in-legs-of not he-is-pleased

אֶת־ יְרֵאָיו אֶת־ הַמְיַחֲלִים לְחַסְדּוֹ׃ שַׁבְּחִי

extol! (12) in-unfailing-love-of-him the-ones-hoping in ones-fearing-him in

יְרוּשָׁלַםִ אֶת־ יְהוָה הַלְלִי אֱלֹהַיִךְ צִיּוֹן׃ כִּי־ חִזַּק בְּרִיחֵי

bars-of he-strengthens for (13) Zion God-of-you praise! Yahweh *** Jerusalem

שְׁעָרָיִךְ בֵּרַךְ בָּנַיִךְ בְּקִרְבֵּךְ׃ הַשָּׂם־

the-one-granting (14) at-within-you peoples-of-you he-blesses gates-of-you

גְּבוּלֵךְ שָׁלוֹם חֵלֶב חִטִּים יַשְׂבִּיעֵךְ׃ הַשֹּׁלֵחַ

the-one-sending (15) he-satisfies-you wheats finest-of peace border-of-you

אִמְרָתוֹ אָרֶץ עַד־ מְהֵרָה יָרוּץ דְּבָרוֹ׃ הַנֹּתֵן

the-one-spreading (16) word-of-him he-runs swiftness to earth command-of-him

שֶׁלֶג כַּצָּמֶר כְּפוֹר כָּאֵפֶר יְפַזֵּר׃ מַשְׁלִיךְ קַרְחוֹ

hail-of-him one-hurling (17) he-scatters like-the-ash frost like-the-wool snow

---

but he frustrates the ways of
the wicked.

10 The LORD reigns forever,
your God, O Zion, for all
generations.

Praise the LORD.

Psalm 147

1 Praise the LORD.[p]

How good it is to sing praises
to our God,
how pleasant and fitting to
praise him!

2 The LORD builds up Jerusalem;
he gathers the exiles of
Israel.
3 He heals the brokenhearted
and binds up their wounds.

4 He determines the number of
the stars
and calls them each by
name.
5 Great is our Lord and mighty
in power;
his understanding has no
limit.
6 The LORD sustains the humble
but casts the wicked to the
ground.

7 Sing to the LORD with
thanksgiving;
make music to our God on
the harp.
8 He covers the sky with clouds;
he supplies the earth with
rain
and makes grass grow on
the hills.
9 He provides food for the cattle
and for the young ravens
when they call.

10 His pleasure is not in the
strength of the horse,
nor his delight in the legs of
a man;
11 the LORD delights in those who
fear him,
who put their hope in his
unfailing love.

12 Extol the LORD, O Jerusalem;
praise your God, O Zion,
13 for he strengthens the bars of
your gates
and blesses your people
within you.
14 He grants peace to your
borders
and satisfies you with the
finest of wheat.

15 He sends his command to the
earth;
his word runs swiftly.
16 He spreads the snow like wool
and scatters the frost like
ashes.
17 He hurls down his hail like

p1 Hebrew *Hallelu Yah*; also in verse 20

כְּפִתִּים לִפְנֵי קָרָתוֹ מִי יַעֲמֹד׃ יִשְׁלַח דְּבָרוֹ

word-of-him he-sends (18) he-can-stand who? icy-blast-of-him before like-pebbles

וְיַמְסֵם יַשֵּׁב רוּחוֹ יִזְּלוּ־ מָיִם׃ מַגִּיד

revealing (19) waters they-flow breeze-of-him he-stirs-up and-he-melts-them

דְּבָרָו לְיַעֲקֹב חֻקָּיו וּמִשְׁפָּטָיו לְיִשְׂרָאֵל׃ לֹא

not (20) to-Israel and-laws-of-him decrees-of-him to-Jacob words-of-him

עָשָׂה כֵן ׀ לְכָל־ גּוֹי וּמִשְׁפָּטִים בַּל־ יְדָעוּם הַלְלוּ־ יָהּ׃

Yahweh praise! they-know-them not and-laws nation for-any-of this he-did

הַלְלוּ יָהּ ׀ הַלְלוּ אֶת־ יְהוָה מִן־ הַשָּׁמַיִם הַלְלוּהוּ

praise-him! the-heavens from Yahweh *** praise! Yahweh praise! (148:1)

בַּמְּרוֹמִים׃ הַלְלוּהוּ כָל־ מַלְאָכָיו הַלְלוּהוּ כָּל־

all-of praise-him! angels-of-him all-of praise-him! (2) in-the-heights

צְבָאָו׃ הַלְלוּהוּ שֶׁמֶשׁ וְיָרֵחַ הַלְלוּהוּ כָּל־ כּוֹכְבֵי אוֹר׃

shining stars-of all-of praise-him! and-moon sun praise-him! (3) hosts-of-him

הַלְלוּהוּ שְׁמֵי הַשָּׁמָיִם וְהַמַּיִם אֲשֶׁר ׀ מֵעַל הַשָּׁמָיִם׃

the-skies at-above that and-the-waters the-heavens heavens-of praise-him! (4)

יְהַלְלוּ אֶת־ שֵׁם יְהוָה כִּי הוּא צִוָּה וְנִבְרָאוּ׃

and-they-were-created he-commanded he for Yahweh name-of *** let-them-praise (5)

וַיַּעֲמִידֵם לָעַד לְעוֹלָם חָק־ נָתַן וְלֹא

and-not he-gave decree to-forever for-ever and-he-set-in-place-them (6)

יַעֲבוֹר הַלְלוּ אֶת־ יְהוָה מִן־ הָאָרֶץ תַּנִּינִים וְכָל־

and-all-of sea-creatures the-earth from Yahweh *** praise! (7) he-will-pass-away

תְּהֹמוֹת׃ אֵשׁ וּבָרָד שֶׁלֶג וְקִיטוֹר רוּחַ סְעָרָה עֹשָׂה

one-doing storm wind-of and-cloud snow and-hail lightning (8) depths

דְבָרוֹ׃ הֶהָרִים וְכָל־ גְּבָעוֹת עֵץ פְּרִי וְכָל־

and-all-of fruit tree-of hills and-all-of the-mountains (9) bidding-of-him

אֲרָזִים׃ הַחַיָּה וְכָל־ בְּהֵמָה רֶמֶשׂ וְצִפּוֹר כָּנָף׃

flight and-bird-of small-creature cattle and-all-of the-wild-animal (10) cedars

מַלְכֵי־ אֶרֶץ וְכָל־ לְאֻמִּים שָׂרִים וְכָל־ שֹׁפְטֵי אָרֶץ׃

earth ones-ruling-of and-all-of princes nations and-all-of earth kings-of (11)

בַּחוּרִים וְגַם־ בְּתוּלוֹת זְקֵנִים עִם־ נְעָרִים׃ יְהַלְלוּ ׀ אֶת־

*** let-them-praise (13) children and old-men maidens and-also young-men (12)

שֵׁם יְהוָה כִּי־ נִשְׂגָּב שְׁמוֹ לְבַדּוֹ הוֹדוֹ

splendor-of-him by-himself name-of-him one-being-exalted for Yahweh name-of

עַל־ אֶרֶץ וְשָׁמָיִם׃ וַיָּרֶם קֶרֶן ׀ לְעַמּוֹ תְּהִלָּה

praise for-people-of-him horn and-he-raised (14) and-heavens earth above

לְכָל־ חֲסִידָיו לִבְנֵי יִשְׂרָאֵל עַם־ קְרֹבוֹ הַלְלוּ־ יָהּ׃

Yahweh praise! close-to-him people-of Israel of-sons-of saints-of-him of-all-of

pebbles.
Who can withstand his icy
blast?
[18]He sends his word and melts
them;
he stirs up his breezes, and
the waters flow.

[19]He has revealed his word to
Jacob,
his laws and decrees to
Israel.
[20]He has done this for no other
nation;
they do not know his laws.

Praise the LORD.

Psalm 148

[1]Praise the LORD.[q]

Praise the LORD from the
heavens,
praise him in the heights
above.
[2]Praise him, all his angels,
praise him, all his heavenly
hosts.
[3]Praise him, sun and moon,
praise him, all you shining
stars.
[4]Praise him, you highest
heavens
and you waters above the
skies.
[5]Let them praise the name of
the LORD,
for he commanded and they
were created.
[6]He set them in place for ever
and ever;
he gave a decree that will
never pass away.

[7]Praise the LORD from the earth,
you great sea creatures and
all ocean depths,
[8]lightning and hail, snow and
clouds,
stormy winds that do his
bidding,
[9]you mountains and all hills,
fruit trees and all cedars,
[10]wild animals and all cattle,
small creatures and flying
birds,
[11]kings of the earth and all
nations,
you princes and all rulers on
earth,
[12]young men and maidens,
old men and children.

[13]Let them praise the name of
the LORD,
for his name alone is
exalted;
his splendor is above the
earth and the heavens.
[14]He has raised up for his
people a horn,[r]
the praise of all his saints,
of Israel, the people close to
his heart.

Praise the LORD.

[q]1 Hebrew *Hallelu Yah*; also in verse 14
[r]14 *Horn* here symbolizes strong one, that is, king.

°19 ק דבריו
°2 ק צבאיו

הַלְלוּ יָהּ׀ שִׁירוּ לַיהוָה שִׁיר חָדָשׁ תְּהִלָּתוֹ בִּקְהַל
in-assembly-of praise-of-him new song to-Yahweh sing! Yahweh praise! (149:1)

חֲסִידִים׃ יִשְׂמַח יִשְׂרָאֵל בְּעֹשָׂיו בְּנֵי־ צִיּוֹן
Zion peoples-of in-Ones-Making-him Israel let-him-rejoice (2) saints

יָגִילוּ בְמַלְכָּם׃ יְהַלְלוּ שְׁמוֹ בְמָחוֹל
with-dance name-of-him let-them-praise (3) in-King-of-them let-them-be-glad

בְּתֹף וְכִנּוֹר יְזַמְּרוּ־ לוֹ׃ כִּי־ רוֹצֶה יְהוָה
Yahweh delighting for (4) to-him let-them-make-music and-harp with-tambourine

בְּעַמּוֹ יְפָאֵר עֲנָוִים בִּישׁוּעָה׃ יַעְלְזוּ
let-them-rejoice (5) with-salvation humble-ones he-crowns in-people-of-him

חֲסִידִים בְּכָבוֹד יְרַנְּנוּ עַל־ מִשְׁכְּבוֹתָם׃ רוֹמְמוֹת אֵל
God praises-of (6) beds-of-them on let-them-sing-for-joy in-honor saints

בִּגְרוֹנָם וְחֶרֶב פִּיפִיּוֹת בְּיָדָם׃ לַעֲשׂוֹת
to-inflict (7) in-hand-of-them double-edges and-sword-of in-mouth-of-them

נְקָמָה בַּגּוֹיִם תּוֹכֵחֹת בַּל־אֻמִּים*׃ לֶאְסֹר מַלְכֵיהֶם
kings-of-them to-bind (8) *on-the-peoples punishments on-the-nations vengeance

בְּזִקִּים וְנִכְבְּדֵיהֶם בְּכַבְלֵי בַרְזֶל׃ לַעֲשׂוֹת
to-carry-out (9) iron with-shackles-of and-ones-being-nobles-of-them with-fetters

בָּהֶם׀ מִשְׁפָּט כָּתוּב הָדָר הוּא לְכָל־ חֲסִידָיו
saints-of-him of-all-of this glory one-being-written sentence against-them

הַלְלוּ־ יָהּ׃ הַלְלוּ יָהּ׀ הַלְלוּ־ אֵל בְּקָדְשׁוֹ
in-sanctuary-of-him God praise! Yahweh praise! (150:1) Yahweh praise!

הַלְלוּהוּ בִּרְקִיעַ עֻזּוֹ׃ הַלְלוּהוּ בִגְבוּרֹתָיו
for-works-of-power-of-him praise-him! (2) might-of-him in-heaven-of praise-him!

הַלְלוּהוּ כְּרֹב גֻּדְלוֹ׃ הַלְלוּהוּ בְּתֵקַע
with-sounding-of praise-him! (3) greatness-of-him for-surpassing-of praise-him!

שׁוֹפָר הַלְלוּהוּ בְּנֵבֶל וְכִנּוֹר׃ הַלְלוּהוּ בְתֹף
with-tambourine praise-him! (4) and-lyre with-harp praise-him! trumpet

וּמָחוֹל הַלְלוּהוּ בְּמִנִּים וְעוּגָב׃ הַלְלוּהוּ בְצִלְצְלֵי־
with-cymbals-of praise-him! (5) and-flute with-strings praise-him! and-dance

שָׁמַע הַלְלוּהוּ בְּצִלְצְלֵי תְרוּעָה׃ כֹּל הַנְּשָׁמָה
the-breath all-of (6) resounding with-cymbals-of praise-him! clashing

תְּהַלֵּל יָהּ הַלְלוּ־ יָהּ׃
Yahweh praise! Yahweh let-her-praise

Psalm 149

1 Praise the LORD.[s]

Sing to the LORD a new song,
his praise in the assembly of the saints.

2 Let Israel rejoice in their Maker;
let the people of Zion be glad in their King.
3 Let them praise his name with dancing
and make music to him with tambourine and harp.
4 For the LORD takes delight in his people;
he crowns the humble with salvation.
5 Let the saints rejoice in this honor
and sing for joy on their beds.

6 May the praise of God be in their mouths
and a double-edged sword in their hands,
7 to inflict vengeance on the nations
and punishment on the peoples,
8 to bind their kings with fetters,
their nobles with shackles of iron,
9 to carry out the sentence written against them.
This is the glory of all his saints.

Praise the LORD.

Psalm 150

1 Praise the LORD.[t]

Praise God in his sanctuary;
praise him in his mighty heavens.
2 Praise him for his acts of power;
praise him for his surpassing greatness.
3 Praise him with the sounding of the trumpet,
praise him with the harp and lyre,
4 praise him with tambourine and dancing,
praise him with the strings and flute,
5 praise him with the clash of cymbals,
praise him with resounding cymbals.

6 Let everything that has breath praise the LORD.

Praise the LORD.

[s] 1 Hebrew *Hallelu Yah*; also in verse 9
[t] 1 Hebrew *Hallelu Yah*; also in verse 6

**1* Most mss treat these two words as one (בַּלְאֻמִּים).

מִשְׁלֵי שְׁלֹמֹה בֶן־ דָּוִד מֶלֶךְ יִשְׂרָאֵל׃ לָדַעַת חָכְמָה
wisdom to-attain (2) Israel king-of David son-of Solomon proverbs-of (1:1)

וּמוּסָר לְהָבִין אִמְרֵי בִינָה׃ לָקַחַת מוּסַר
discipline-of to-acquire (3) insight words-of to-understand and-discipline

הַשְׂכֵּל צֶדֶק וּמִשְׁפָּט וּמֵשָׁרִים׃ לָתֵת לִפְתָאיִם עָרְמָה
prudence to-simple-ones to-give (4) and-fair-ones and-just right to-be-prudent

לְנַעַר דַּעַת וּמְזִמָּה׃ יִשְׁמַע חָכָם וְיוֹסֶף
and-let-him-add wise let-him-listen (5) and-discretion knowledge to-young

לֶקַח וְנָבוֹן תַּחְבֻּלוֹת יִקְנֶה׃ לְהָבִין מָשָׁל
proverb to-understand (6) let-him-get guidances and-one-discerning learning

וּמְלִיצָה דִּבְרֵי חֲכָמִים וְחִידֹתָם׃ יִרְאַת יְהוָה
Yahweh fear-of (7) and-riddles-of-them wise-ones sayings-of and-parable

רֵאשִׁית דָּעַת חָכְמָה וּמוּסָר אֱוִילִים בָּזוּ׃ שְׁמַע
listen! (8) they-despise fools and-discipline wisdom knowledge beginning-of

בְּנִי מוּסַר אָבִיךָ וְאַל־ תִּטֹּשׁ תּוֹרַת
teaching-of you-forsake and-not father-of-you instruction-of son-of-me

אִמֶּךָ׃ כִּי ׀ לִוְיַת חֵן הֵם לְרֹאשֶׁךָ וַעֲנָקִים
and-chains to-head-of-you they grace garland-of for (9) mother-of-you

לְגַרְגְּרֹתֶךָ׃ בְּנִי אִם־ יְפַתּוּךָ חַטָּאִים אַל־ תֹּבֵא׃
you-give-in not sinners they-entice-you if son-of-me (10) for-necks-of-you

אִם־ יֹאמְרוּ לְכָה אִתָּנוּ נֶאֶרְבָה לְדָם נִצְפְּנָה
let-us-hide for-blood let-us-lie-in-wait with-us come! they-say if (11)

לְנָקִי חִנָּם׃ נִבְלָעֵם כִּשְׁאוֹל חַיִּים
alive-ones like-Sheol let-us-swallow-them (12) without-cause for-harmless-soul

וּתְמִימִים כְּיוֹרְדֵי בוֹר׃ כָּל־ הוֹן יָקָר
value wealth-of all-of (13) pit like-ones-going-down-of and-whole-ones

נִמְצָא נְמַלֵּא בָתֵּינוּ שָׁלָל׃ גּוֹרָלְךָ תַּפִּיל
you-throw lot-of-you (14) plunder houses-of-us we-will-fill we-will-get

בְּתוֹכֵנוּ כִּיס אֶחָד יִהְיֶה לְכֻלָּנוּ׃ בְּנִי אַל־ תֵּלֵךְ
you-go not son-of-me (15) for-all-of-us he-will-be common purse in-among-us

בְּדֶרֶךְ אִתָּם מְנַע רַגְלְךָ מִנְּתִיבָתָם׃ כִּי רַגְלֵיהֶם
feet-of-them for (16) from-path-of-them foot-of-you withhold! with-them in-way

לָרַע יָרוּצוּ וִימַהֲרוּ לִשְׁפָּךְ־ דָּם׃ כִּי־ חִנָּם
useless how! (17) blood to-shed and-they-are-swift they-rush into-sin

מְזֹרָה הָרָשֶׁת בְּעֵינֵי כָּל־ בַּעַל כָּנָף׃ וְהֵם
and-they (18) wing master-of all-of before-eyes-of the-net being-spread

לְדָמָם יֶאֱרֹבוּ יִצְפְּנוּ לְנַפְשֹׁתָם׃ כֵּן
such (19) for-self-of-them they-hide they-lie-in-wait for-blood-of-them

Prologue: Purpose and Theme

1 The proverbs of Solomon son of David, king of Israel:

2 for attaining wisdom and discipline;
for understanding words of insight;
3 for acquiring a disciplined and prudent life,
doing what is right and just and fair;
4 for giving prudence to the simple,
knowledge and discretion to the young—
5 let the wise listen and add to their learning,
and let the discerning get guidance—
6 for understanding proverbs and parables,
the sayings and riddles of the wise.

7 The fear of the LORD is the beginning of knowledge,
but fools[a] despise wisdom and discipline.

Exhortations to Embrace Wisdom

Warning Against Enticement

8 Listen, my son, to your father's instruction
and do not forsake your mother's teaching.
9 They will be a garland to grace your head
and a chain to adorn your neck.

10 My son, if sinners entice you,
do not give in to them.
11 If they say, "Come along with us;
let's lie in wait for someone's blood,
let's waylay some harmless soul;
12 let's swallow them alive, like the grave,[b]
and whole, like those who go down to the pit;
13 we will get all sorts of valuable things
and fill our houses with plunder;
14 throw in your lot with us,
and we will share a common purse"—
15 my son, do not go along with them,
do not set foot on their paths;
16 for their feet rush into sin,
they are swift to shed blood.
17 How useless to spread a net
in full view of all the birds!
18 These men lie in wait for their own blood;
they waylay only themselves!

[a]7 The Hebrew words rendered *fool* in Proverbs, and often elsewhere in the Old Testament, denote one who is morally deficient.
[b]12 Hebrew *Sheol*

אָרְחוֹת כָּל־ בֹּצֵעַ בָּצַע אֶת־ נֶפֶשׁ בְּעָלָיו

owners-of-him life-of *** ill-gotten-gain one-gaining all-of ends-of

יִקָּח׃ חָכְמוֹת בַּחוּץ תָּרֹנָּה בָּרְחֹבוֹת

in-the-public-squares she-calls-aloud in-the-street wisdoms (20) he-takes-away

תִּתֵּן קוֹלָהּ׃ בְּרֹאשׁ הֹמִיּוֹת תִּקְרָא

she-cries-out ones-being-noisy at-head-of (21) voice-of-her she-raises

בְּפִתְחֵי שְׁעָרִים בָּעִיר אֲמָרֶיהָ תֹאמֵר׃ עַד־ מָתַי ׀

when? until (22) she-says speeches-of-her of-the-city gates in-gateways-of

פְּתָיִם תְּאֵהֲבוּ פֶתִי וְלֵצִים לָצוֹן

mockery and-ones-mocking simple-way will-you-love simple-ones

חָמְדוּ לָהֶם וּכְסִילִים יִשְׂנְאוּ־ דָעַת׃

knowledge will-they-hate and-fools for-them will-they-delight

תָּשׁוּבוּ לְתוֹכַחְתִּי הִנֵּה אַבִּיעָה לָכֶם

to-you I-would-have-poured-out see! to-rebuke-of-me had-you-responded (23)

רוּחִי אוֹדִיעָה דְבָרַי אֶתְכֶם׃ יַעַן קָרָאתִי

I-called since (24) to-you thoughts-of-me I-would-have-made-known heart-of-me

וַתְּמָאֵנוּ נָטִיתִי יָדִי וְאֵין מַקְשִׁיב׃

giving-heed and-no-one hand-of-me I-stretched-out and-you-rejected

וַתִּפְרְעוּ כָל־ עֲצָתִי וְתוֹכַחְתִּי לֹא אֲבִיתֶם׃

you-accepted not and-rebuke-of-me advice-of-me all-of and-you-ignored (25)

גַּם־ אֲנִי בְּאֵידְכֶם אֶשְׂחָק אֶלְעַג בְּבֹא

when-to-overtake I-will-mock I-will-laugh at-disaster-of-you I also (26)

פַּחְדְּכֶם׃ בְּבֹא כְשַׁאֲוָה ׀ פַּחְדְּכֶם

calamity-of-you like-storm when-to-overtake (27) calamity-of-you

וְאֵידְכֶם כְּסוּפָה יֶאֱתֶה בְּבֹא עֲלֵיכֶם

over-you when-to-come he-sweeps-over like-whirlwind and-disaster-of-you

צָרָה וְצוּקָה׃ אָז יִקְרָאֻנְנִי וְלֹא אֶעֱנֶה

I-will-answer but-not they-will-call-to-me then (28) and-trouble distress

יְשַׁחֲרֻנְנִי וְלֹא יִמְצָאֻנְנִי׃ תַּחַת כִּי־ שָׂנְאוּ

they-hated that since (29) they-will-find-me but-not they-will-look-for-me

דָעַת וְיִרְאַת יְהוָה לֹא בָחָרוּ׃ לֹא־ אָבוּ

they-would-accept not (30) they-chose not Yahweh and-fear-of knowledge

לַעֲצָתִי נָאֲצוּ כָּל־ תּוֹכַחְתִּי׃ וְיֹאכְלוּ

and-they-will-eat (31) rebuke-of-me all-of they-spurned to-advice-of-me

מִפְּרִי דַרְכָּם וּמִמֹּעֲצֹתֵיהֶם יִשְׂבָּעוּ׃

they-will-be-filled and-from-schemes-of-them way-of-them from-fruit-of

כִּי מְשׁוּבַת פְּתָיִם תַּהַרְגֵם וְשַׁלְוַת

and-complacency-of she-will-kill-them simple-ones waywardness-of for (32)

---

19 Such is the end of all who go
after ill-gotten gain;
it takes away the lives of
those who get it.

Warning Against Rejecting Wisdom

20 Wisdom calls aloud in the
street,
she raises her voice in the
public squares;
21 at the head of the noisy
streets[c] she cries out,
in the gateways of the city
she makes her speech:

22 "How long will you simple
ones[d] love your simple
ways?
How long will mockers
delight in mockery
and fools hate knowledge?
23 If you had responded to my
rebuke,
I would have poured out my
heart to you
and made my thoughts
known to you.
24 But since you rejected me
when I called
and no one gave heed when
I stretched out my hand,
25 since you ignored all my
advice
and would not accept my
rebuke,
26 I in turn will laugh at your
disaster;
I will mock when calamity
overtakes you—
27 when calamity overtakes you
like a storm,
when disaster sweeps over
you like a whirlwind,
when distress and troubles
overwhelm you.

28 "Then they will call to me but
I will not answer;
they will look for me but
will not find me.
29 Since they hated knowledge
and did not choose to fear
the LORD,
30 since they would not accept
my advice
and spurned my rebuke,
31 they will eat the fruit of their
ways
and be filled with the fruit
of their schemes.
32 For the waywardness of the
simple will kill them,
and the complacency of

c21 Hebrew; Septuagint / *on the tops of the walls*
d22 The Hebrew word rendered *simple* in Proverbs generally denotes one without moral direction and inclined to evil.

°27 ק כשואה

כְּסִילִים תְּאַבְּדֵם׃ וְשֹׁמֵעַ לִי יִשְׁכָּן־ בֶּטַח
safety he-will-live to-me but-one-listening (33) she-will-destroy-them fools

וְשַׁאֲנַן מִפַּחַד רָעָה׃ בְּנִי אִם־ תִּקַּח
you-accept if son-of-me (2:1) harm without-fear-of and-he-will-be-at-ease

אֲמָרָי וּמִצְוֺתַי תִּצְפֹּן אִתָּךְ׃ לְהַקְשִׁיב
to-turn (2) within-you you-store-up and-commands-of-me words-of-me

לַחָכְמָה אָזְנֶךָ תַּטֶּה לִבְּךָ לַתְּבוּנָה׃ כִּי
for (3) to-the-understanding heart-of-you you-apply ear-of-you to-the-wisdom

אִם לַבִּינָה תִקְרָא לַתְּבוּנָה תִּתֵּן קוֹלֶךָ׃
voice-of-you you-raise for-the-understanding you-call-out for-the-insight if

אִם־ תְּבַקְשֶׁנָּה כַכָּסֶף וְכַמַּטְמוֹנִים
and-as-the-hidden-treasures as-the-silver you-look-for-her if (4)

תַּחְפְּשֶׂנָּה׃ אָז תָּבִין יִרְאַת יְהוָה וְדַעַת
and-knowledge-of Yahweh fear-of you-will-understand then (5) you-search-for-her

אֱלֹהִים תִּמְצָא׃ כִּי־ יְהוָה יִתֵּן חָכְמָה מִפִּיו דַּעַת
knowledge from-mouth-of-him wisdom he-gives Yahweh for (6) you-will-find God

וּתְבוּנָה׃ °וְצָפַן לַיְשָׁרִים תּוּשִׁיָּה מָגֵן
shield victory for-the-upright-ones and-he-stores (7) and-understanding

לְהֹלְכֵי תֹם׃ לִנְצֹר אָרְחוֹת מִשְׁפָּט וְדֶרֶךְ
and-way-of just courses-of to-guard (8) blamelessness to-ones-walking-of

°חֲסִידָו יִשְׁמֹר׃ אָז תָּבִין צֶדֶק וּמִשְׁפָּט
and-just right you-will-understand then (9) he-protects faithful-ones-of-him

וּמֵישָׁרִים כָּל־ מַעְגַּל־ טוֹב׃ כִּי־ תָבוֹא חָכְמָה
wisdom she-will-enter for (10) good path-of every-of and-fair-ones

בְלִבֶּךָ וְדַעַת לְנַפְשְׁךָ יִנְעָם׃
he-will-be-pleasant to-soul-of-you and-knowledge into-heart-of-you

מְזִמָּה תִּשְׁמֹר עָלֶיךָ תְּבוּנָה תִנְצְרֶכָּה׃
she-will-guard-you understanding to-you she-will-protect discretion (11)

לְהַצִּילְךָ מִדֶּרֶךְ רָע מֵאִישׁ מְדַבֵּר תַּהְפֻּכוֹת׃
perverse-words speaking from-man wicked-man from-way-of to-save-you (12)

הַעֹזְבִים אָרְחוֹת יֹשֶׁר לָלֶכֶת בְּדַרְכֵי־ חֹשֶׁךְ׃
darkness in-ways-of to-walk straightness paths-of the-ones-leaving (13)

הַשְּׂמֵחִים לַעֲשׂוֹת רָע יָגִילוּ בְּתַהְפֻּכוֹת רָע׃
evil in-perversenesses-of they-rejoice wrong to-do the-ones-delighting (14)

אֲשֶׁר אָרְחֹתֵיהֶם עִקְּשִׁים וּנְלוֹזִים בְּמַעְגְּלוֹתָם׃
in-ways-of-them and-ones-being-devious crooked-ones paths-of-them who (15)

לְהַצִּילְךָ מֵאִשָּׁה זָרָה מִנָּכְרִיָּה
from-wayward-woman one-being-adulteress from-woman to-save-you (16)

fools will destroy them;
[33]but whoever listens to me will
live in safety
and be at ease, without fear
of harm."

Moral Benefits of Wisdom

2 My son, if you accept my
words
and store up my commands
within you,
[2]turning your ear to wisdom
and applying your heart to
understanding,
[3]and if you call out for insight
and cry aloud for
understanding,
[4]and if you look for it as for
silver
and search for it as for
hidden treasure,
[5]then you will understand the
fear of the LORD
and find the knowledge of
God.
[6]For the LORD gives wisdom,
and from his mouth come
knowledge and
understanding.
[7]He holds victory in store for
the upright,
he is a shield to those
whose walk is blameless,
[8]for he guards the course of the
just
and protects the way of his
faithful ones.

[9]Then you will understand
what is right and just
and fair—every good path.
[10]For wisdom will enter your
heart,
and knowledge will be
pleasant to your soul.
[11]Discretion will protect you,
and understanding will
guard you.

[12]Wisdom will save you from
the ways of wicked men,
from men whose words are
perverse,
[13]who leave the straight paths
to walk in dark ways,
[14]who delight in doing wrong
and rejoice in the
perverseness of evil,
[15]whose paths are crooked
and who are devious in
their ways.

[16]It will save you also from the
adulteress,
from the wayward wife with

°7 ק יצפן
°8 ק חסידיו

אֲמָרֶיהָ הֶחֱלִיקָה׃ הַעֹזֶבֶת אַלּוּף נְעוּרֶיהָ

youths-of-her partner-of the-one-leaving (17) she-makes-seductive words-of-her

וְאֶת־ בְּרִית אֱלֹהֶיהָ שָׁכֵחָה׃ כִּי שָׁחָה אֶל־ מָוֶת

death to she-leads-down for (18) she-ignored God-of-her covenant-of and

בֵּיתָהּ וְאֶל־ רְפָאִים מַעְגְּלֹתֶיהָ׃ כָּל־ בָּאֶיהָ

ones-going-to-her all-of (19) paths-of-her spirits-of-dead and-to house-of-her

לֹא יְשׁוּבוּן וְלֹא־ יַשִּׂיגוּ אָרְחוֹת חַיִּים׃ לְמַעַן תֵּלֵךְ

you-will-walk so-thus (20) lives paths-of they-attain and-not they-return not

בְּדֶרֶךְ טוֹבִים וְאָרְחוֹת צַדִּיקִים תִּשְׁמֹר׃ כִּי־

for (21) you-will-keep-to righteous-ones and-paths-of good-men in-way-of

יְשָׁרִים יִשְׁכְּנוּ־ אָרֶץ וּתְמִימִים יִוָּתְרוּ בָהּ׃

in-her they-will-remain and-blameless-ones land they-will-live upright-ones

וּרְשָׁעִים מֵאֶרֶץ יִכָּרֵתוּ וּבוֹגְדִים

and-ones-being-unfaithful they-will-be-cut-off from-land but-wicked-ones (22)

יִסְּחוּ מִמֶּנָּה׃ בְּנִי תּוֹרָתִי אַל־ תִּשְׁכָּח

you-forget not teaching-of-me son-of-me (3:1) from-her they-will-be-torn

וּמִצְוֺתַי יִצֹּר לִבֶּךָ׃ כִּי אֹרֶךְ יָמִים

days length-of for (2) heart-of-you let-him-keep but-commands-of-me

וּשְׁנוֹת חַיִּים וְשָׁלוֹם יוֹסִיפוּ לָךְ׃ חֶסֶד

love (3) to-you they-will-bring and-prosperity lives and-years-of

וֶאֱמֶת אַל־ יַעַזְבֻךָ קָשְׁרֵם עַל־ גַּרְגְּרוֹתֶיךָ

necks-of-you around bind-them! let-them-leave-you never and-faithfulness

כָּתְבֵם עַל־ לוּחַ לִבֶּךָ׃ וּמְצָא־ חֵן וְשֵׂכֶל־ טוֹב

good and-name favor then-win! (4) heart-of-you tablet-of on write-them!

בְּעֵינֵי אֱלֹהִים וְאָדָם׃ בְּטַח אֶל־ יְהוָה בְּכָל־ לִבֶּךָ וְאֶל־

and-on heart-of-you with-all-of Yahweh in trust! (5) and-man God in-eyes-of

בִּינָתְךָ אַל־ תִּשָּׁעֵן׃ בְּכָל־ דְּרָכֶיךָ דָעֵהוּ

acknowledge-him! ways-of-you in-all-of (6) you-lean not understanding-of-you

וְהוּא יְיַשֵּׁר אֹרְחֹתֶיךָ׃ אַל־ תְּהִי חָכָם בְּעֵינֶיךָ

in-eyes-of-you wise you-be not (7) paths-of-you he-will-make-straight and-he

יְרָא אֶת־ יְהוָה וְסוּר מֵרָע׃ רִפְאוּת תְּהִי לְשָׁרֶּךָ

to-body-of-you she-will-be health (8) from-evil and-shun! Yahweh *** fear!

וְשִׁקּוּי לְעַצְמוֹתֶיךָ׃ כַּבֵּד אֶת־ יְהוָה מֵהוֹנֶךָ

with-wealth-of-you Yahweh *** honor! (9) to-bones-of-you and-nourishment

וּמֵרֵאשִׁית כָּל־ תְּבוּאָתֶךָ׃ וְיִמָּלְאוּ

then-they-will-be-filled (10) crop-of-you all-of and-with-firstfruit-of

אֲסָמֶיךָ שָׂבָע וְתִירוֹשׁ יְקָבֶיךָ יִפְרֹצוּ׃

they-will-brim-over vats-of-you and-new-wine overflowing barns-of-you

her seductive words,
17who has left the partner of her youth
and ignored the covenant she made before God.[e]
18For her house leads down to death
and her paths to the spirits of the dead.
19None who go to her return
or attain the paths of life.

20Thus you will walk in the ways of good men
and keep to the paths of the righteous.
21For the upright will live in the land,
and the blameless will remain in it;
22but the wicked will be cut off from the land,
and the unfaithful will be torn from it.

Further Benefits of Wisdom

3 My son, do not forget my teaching,
but keep my commands in your heart,
2for they will prolong your life many years
and bring you prosperity.

3Let love and faithfulness never leave you;
bind them around your neck,
write them on the tablet of your heart.
4Then you will win favor and a good name
in the sight of God and man.

5Trust in the LORD with all your heart
and lean not on your own understanding;
6in all your ways acknowledge him,
and he will make your paths straight.[f]

7Do not be wise in your own eyes;
fear the LORD and shun evil.
8This will bring health to your body
and nourishment to your bones.

9Honor the LORD with your wealth,
with the firstfruits of all your crops;
10then your barns will be filled to overflowing,
and your vats will brim over with new wine.

e17 Or *covenant of her God*
f6 Or *will direct your paths*

מוּסַר יְהוָה בְּנִי אַל־ תִּמְאָס וְאַל־ תָּקֹץ
you-resent and-not you-despise not son-of-me Yahweh discipline-of (11)

בְּתוֹכַחְתּוֹ׃ כִּי אֶת אֲשֶׁר יֶאֱהַב יְהוָה יוֹכִיחַ וּכְאָב
and-as-father he-disciplines Yahweh he-loves whom *** for (12) to-rebuke-of-him

אֶת־ בֵּן יִרְצֶה׃ אַשְׁרֵי אָדָם מָצָא חָכְמָה וְאָדָם
and-man wisdom he-finds man blessednesses-of (13) he-delights-in son ***

יָפִיק תְּבוּנָה׃ כִּי טוֹב סַחְרָהּ מִסְּחַר־ כָּסֶף
silver more-than-profit-of profit-of-her good for (14) understanding he-gains

וּמֵחָרוּץ תְּבוּאָתָהּ׃ יְקָרָה הִיא מִפְּנִיִּים
more-than-rubies she precious (15) return-of-her and-more-than-gold

וְכָל־ חֲפָצֶיךָ לֹא יִשְׁווּ־ בָהּ׃ אֹרֶךְ יָמִים
days length-of (16) with-her they-can-compare not desires-of-you and-all-of

בִּימִינָהּ בִּשְׂמֹאולָהּ עֹשֶׁר וְכָבוֹד׃ דְּרָכֶיהָ
ways-of-her (17) and-honor richness and-in-left-hand-of-her in-right-hand-of-her

דַרְכֵי־ נֹעַם וְכָל־ נְתִיבוֹתֶיהָ שָׁלוֹם׃ עֵץ־ חַיִּים הִיא
she lives tree-of (18) peace paths-of-her and-all-of pleasantness ways-of

לַמַּחֲזִיקִים בָּהּ וְתֹמְכֶיהָ מְאֻשָּׁר׃
being-blessed and-ones-laying-hold-of-her to-her to-the-ones-embracing

יְהוָה בְּחָכְמָה יָסַד־ אָרֶץ כּוֹנֵן שָׁמַיִם
heavens he-set-in-place earth he-founded by-wisdom Yahweh (19)

בִּתְבוּנָה׃ בְּדַעְתּוֹ תְּהוֹמוֹת נִבְקָעוּ וּשְׁחָקִים
and-clouds they-were-divided deeps by-knowledge-of-him (20) by-understanding

יִרְעֲפוּ־ טָל׃ בְּנִי אַל־ יָלֻזוּ מֵעֵינֶיךָ
from-eyes-of-you let-them-depart not son-of-me (21) dew they-let-drop

נְצֹר תֻּשִׁיָּה וּמְזִמָּה׃ וְיִהְיוּ חַיִּים
lives and-they-will-be (22) and-discernment sound-judgment preserve!

לְנַפְשֶׁךָ וְחֵן לְגַרְגְּרֹתֶיךָ׃ אָז תֵּלֵךְ לָבֶטַח
in-safety you-will-go then (23) for-necks-of-you and-grace for-self-of-you

דַּרְכֶּךָ וְרַגְלְךָ לֹא תִגּוֹף׃ אִם־ תִּשְׁכַּב לֹא־
not you-lie-down when (24) she-will-stumble not and-foot-of-you way-of-you

תִפְחָד וְשָׁכַבְתָּ וְעָרְבָה שְׁנָתֶךָ׃
sleep-of-you then-she-will-be-sweet when-you-lie-down you-will-be-afraid

אַל־ תִּירָא מִפַּחַד פִּתְאֹם וּמִשֹּׁאַת רְשָׁעִים כִּי
that wicked-ones or-of-ruin-of sudden of-disaster you-fear not (25)

תָבֹא׃ כִּי־ יְהוָה יִהְיֶה בְכִסְלֶךָ וְשָׁמַר
and-he-will-keep as-confidence-of-you he-will-be Yahweh for (26) she-overtakes

רַגְלְךָ מִלָּכֶד׃ אַל־ תִּמְנַע־ טוֹב מִבְּעָלָיו בִּהְיוֹת
when-to-be from-owners-of-him good you-withhold not (27) from-snare foot-of-you

11 My son, do not despise the LORD's discipline
and do not resent his rebuke,
12 because the LORD disciplines those he loves,
as a father[g] the son he delights in.

13 Blessed is the man who finds wisdom,
the man who gains understanding,
14 for she is more profitable than silver
and yields better returns than gold.
15 She is more precious than rubies;
nothing you desire can compare with her.
16 Long life is in her right hand;
in her left hand are riches and honor.
17 Her ways are pleasant ways,
and all her paths are peace.
18 She is a tree of life to those who embrace her;
those who lay hold of her will be blessed.

19 By wisdom the LORD laid the earth's foundations,
by understanding he set the heavens in place;
20 by his knowledge the deeps were divided,
and the clouds let drop the dew.

21 My son, preserve sound judgment and discernment,
do not let them out of your sight;
22 they will be life for you,
an ornament to grace your neck.
23 Then you will go on your way in safety,
and your foot will not stumble;
24 when you lie down, you will not be afraid;
when you lie down, your sleep will be sweet.
25 Have no fear of sudden disaster
or of the ruin that overtakes the wicked,
26 for the LORD will be your confidence
and will keep your foot from being snared.

27 Do not withhold good from those who deserve it,

g12 Hebrew; Septuagint / *and he punishes*

°15 ק מפנינים

לְאֵל יָדֶיךָ לַעֲשׂוֹת׃ אַל־תֹּאמַר לְרֵעֶיךָ | לֵךְ
come! to-neighbor-of-you you-say not (28) to-act hand-of-you in-power-of

וָשׁוּב וּמָחָר אֶתֵּן וְיֵשׁ אִתָּךְ׃ אַל־תַּחֲרֹשׁ
you-plot not (29) with-you when-there-is I-will-give and-tomorrow and-return!

עַל־רֵעֲךָ רָעָה וְהוּא־יוֹשֵׁב לָבֶטַח אִתָּךְ׃ אַל־
not (30) near-you in-trust one-living when-he harm neighbor-of-you against

תָּרוֹב עִם־אָדָם חִנָּם אִם־לֹא גְמָלְךָ רָעָה׃ אַל־תְּקַנֵּא
you-envy not (31) harm he-did-you not when without-reason man to you-accuse

בְּאִישׁ חָמָס וְאַל־תִּבְחַר בְּכָל־דְּרָכָיו׃ כִּי
for (32) ways-of-him to-any-of you-choose and-not violence to-man-of

תּוֹעֲבַת יְהוָה נָלוֹז וְאֶת־יְשָׁרִים סוֹדוֹ׃
confidence-of-him upright-ones but man-being-perverse Yahweh detestable-of

מְאֵרַת יְהוָה בְּבֵית רָשָׁע וּנְוֵה צַדִּיקִים יְבָרֵךְ׃
he-blesses righteous-ones but-home-of wicked on-house-of Yahweh curse-of (33)

אִם־לַלֵּצִים הוּא־יָלִיץ וְלַעֲנָיִים יִתֶּן־
he-gives but-to-the-humble-ones he-mocks he to-the-ones-mocking indeed (34)

חֵן׃ כָּבוֹד חֲכָמִים יִנְחָלוּ וּכְסִילִים מֵרִים קָלוֹן׃
shame one-holding-up but-fools they-inherit wise-ones honor (35) grace

שִׁמְעוּ בָנִים מוּסַר אָב וְהַקְשִׁיבוּ לָדַעַת
to-gain and-pay-attention! father instruction-of sons listen! (4:1)

בִּינָה׃ כִּי לֶקַח טוֹב נָתַתִּי לָכֶם תּוֹרָתִי אַל־
not teaching-of-me to-you I-give sound learning for (2) understanding

תַּעֲזֹבוּ׃ כִּי־בֵן הָיִיתִי לְאָבִי רַךְ וְיָחִיד לִפְנֵי
before and-only-child tender with-father-of-me I-was boy when (3) you-forsake

אִמִּי׃ וַיֹּרֵנִי וַיֹּאמֶר לִי יִתְמָךְ־
let-him-lay-hold to-me and-he-said then-he-taught-me (4) mother-of-me

דְּבָרַי לִבֶּךָ שְׁמֹר מִצְוֹתַי וֶחְיֵה׃ קְנֵה חָכְמָה
wisdom get! (5) and-live! commands-of-me keep! heart-of-you words-of-me

קְנֵה בִינָה אַל־תִּשְׁכַּח וְאַל־תֵּט מֵאִמְרֵי־פִי׃
mouth-of-me from-words-of you-swerve and-not you-forget not understanding get!

אַל־תַּעַזְבֶהָ וְתִשְׁמְרֶךָּ אֱהָבֶהָ וְתִצְּרֶךָּ׃
and-she-will-watch-you love-her! and-she-will-protect-you you-forsake-her not (6)

רֵאשִׁית חָכְמָה קְנֵה חָכְמָה וּבְכָל־קִנְיָנְךָ קְנֵה
get! possession-of-you though-with-all-of wisdom get! wisdom supreme (7)

בִּינָה׃ סַלְסְלֶהָ וּתְרוֹמְמֶךָּ תְּכַבֵּדְךָ כִּי
if she-will-honor-you and-she-will-exalt-you esteem-her! (8) understanding

תְחַבְּקֶנָּה׃ תִּתֵּן לְרֹאשְׁךָ לִוְיַת־חֵן עֲטֶרֶת
crown-of grace garland-of on-head-of-you she-will-set (9) you-embrace-her

when it is in your power to
act.
28 Do not say to your neighbor,
"Come back later; I'll give it
tomorrow"—
when you now have it with
you.
29 Do not plot harm against your
neighbor,
who lives trustfully near
you.
30 Do not accuse a man for no
reason—
when he has done you no
harm.
31 Do not envy a violent man
or choose any of his ways,
32 for the LORD detests a perverse
man
but takes the upright into
his confidence.
33 The LORD's curse is on the
house of the wicked,
but he blesses the home of
the righteous.
34 He mocks proud mockers
but gives grace to the
humble.
35 The wise inherit honor,
but fools he holds up to
shame.

Wisdom Is Supreme

4 Listen, my sons, to a father's
instruction;
pay attention and gain
understanding.
2 I give you sound learning,
so do not forsake my
teaching.
3 When I was a boy in my
father's house,
still tender, and an only
child of my mother,
4 he taught me and said,
"Lay hold of my words with
all your heart;
keep my commands and you
will live.
5 Get wisdom, get
understanding;
do not forget my words or
swerve from them.
6 Do not forsake wisdom, and
she will protect you;
love her, and she will watch
over you.
7 Wisdom is supreme; therefore
get wisdom.
Though it cost all you have,[h]
get understanding.
8 Esteem her, and she will exalt
you;
embrace her, and she will
honor you.
9 She will set a garland of grace
on your head

h7 Or *Whatever else you get*

°27 ק ידך
°28 ק לרעך
°30 ק תריב
°34 ק ולענוים

תִּפְאֶרֶת תְּמַגְּנֶךָּ׃ (10) שְׁמַע בְּנִי וְקַח אֲמָרָי
sayings-of-me and-accept! son-of-me listen! (10) she-will-present-you splendor

וְיִרְבּוּ לְךָ שְׁנוֹת חַיִּים׃ (11) בְּדֶרֶךְ חָכְמָה הֹרֵתִיךָ
I-guide-you wisdom in-way-of (11) lives years-of to-you and-they-will-be-many

הִדְרַכְתִּיךָ בְּמַעְגְּלֵי־ יֹשֶׁר׃ (12) בְּלֶכְתְּךָ לֹא־
not when-to-walk-you (12) straightness along-paths-of I-lead-you

יֵצַר צַעֲדֶךָ וְאִם־ תָּרוּץ לֹא תִכָּשֵׁל׃
you-will-stumble not you-run and-when step-of-you he-will-be-hampered

(13) הַחֲזֵק בַּמּוּסָר אַל־ תֶּרֶף נִצְּרֶהָ כִּי־ הִיא
she for guard-her! you-let-go not to-the-instruction hold-on! (13)

חַיֶּיךָ׃ (14) בְּאֹרַח רְשָׁעִים אַל־ תָּבֹא וְאַל־ תְּאַשֵּׁר בְּדֶרֶךְ
in-way-of you-walk and-not you-go not wicked-ones on-path-of (14) lives-of-you

רָעִים׃ (15) פְּרָעֵהוּ אַל־ תַּעֲבָר־ בּוֹ שְׂטֵה מֵעָלָיו וַעֲבוֹר׃
and-go-on-way! from-on-him turn! on-him you-travel not avoid-him! (15) evil-men

(16) כִּי לֹא יִשְׁנוּ אִם־לֹא יָרֵעוּ וְנִגְזְלָה שְׁנָתָם
slumber-of-them and-she-is-robbed they-do-evil not if they-can-sleep not for (16)

אִם־לֹא יַכְשׁוֹלוּ׃ (17) כִּי לָחֲמוּ לֶחֶם רֶשַׁע וְיֵין
and-wine-of wickedness bread-of they-eat indeed (17) they-make-fall not if

חֲמָסִים יִשְׁתּוּ׃ (18) וְאֹרַח צַדִּיקִים כְּאוֹר נֹגַהּ
dawn like-gleam-of righteous-ones and-path-of (18) they-drink violences

הוֹלֵךְ וָאוֹר עַד־ נְכוֹן הַיּוֹם׃ (19) דֶּרֶךְ רְשָׁעִים
wicked-ones way-of (19) the-day being-full-of till and-to-be-bright continuing

כָּאֲפֵלָה לֹא יָדְעוּ בַּמֶּה יִכָּשֵׁלוּ׃ (20) בְּנִי
son-of-me (20) they-stumble by-the-what they-know not like-the-deep-darkness

לִדְבָרַי הַקְשִׁיבָה לַאֲמָרַי הַט־ אָזְנֶךָ׃ (21) אַל־
not (21) ear-of-you give! to-words-of-me pay-attention! to-sayings-of-me

יַלִּיזוּ מֵעֵינֶיךָ שָׁמְרֵם בְּתוֹךְ לְבָבֶךָ׃ (22) כִּי־ חַיִּים
lives for (22) heart-of-you within keep-them! from-eyes-of-you let-them-go

הֵם לְמֹצְאֵיהֶם וּלְכָל־ בְּשָׂרוֹ מַרְפֵּא׃ (23) מִכָּל־
above-all-of (23) health body-of-him and-to-whole-of to-ones-finding-them they

מִשְׁמָר נְצֹר לִבֶּךָ כִּי־ מִמֶּנּוּ תּוֹצְאוֹת חַיִּים׃ (24) הָסֵר
put-away! (24) lives wellsprings-of from-him for heart-of-you guard! watching

מִמְּךָ עִקְּשׁוּת פֶּה וּלְזוּת שְׂפָתַיִם הַרְחֵק מִמֶּךָּ׃
from-you keep-far! lips and-corruptness-of mouth perversity-of from-you

(25) עֵינֶיךָ לְנֹכַח יַבִּיטוּ וְעַפְעַפֶּיךָ יַיְשִׁרוּ
let-them-be-direct and-gazes-of-you let-them-look to-ahead eyes-of-you (25)

נֶגְדֶּךָ׃ (26) פַּלֵּס מַעְגַּל רַגְלֶךָ וְכָל־ דְּרָכֶיךָ
ways-of-you and-all-of foot-of-you path-of make-level! (26) before-you

and present you with a
crown of splendor."
10 Listen, my son, accept what I
say,
and the years of your life
will be many.
11 I guide you in the way of
wisdom
and lead you along straight
paths.
12 When you walk, your steps
will not be hampered;
when you run, you will not
stumble.
13 Hold on to instruction, do not
let it go;
guard it well, for it is your
life.
14 Do not set foot on the path of
the wicked
or walk in the way of evil
men.
15 Avoid it, do not travel on it;
turn from it and go on your
way.
16 For they cannot sleep till they
do evil;
they are robbed of slumber
till they make someone
fall.
17 They eat the bread of
wickedness
and drink the wine of
violence.

18 The path of the righteous is
like the first gleam of
dawn,
shining ever brighter till the
full light of day.
19 But the way of the wicked is
like deep darkness;
they do not know what
makes them stumble.

20 My son, pay attention to what
I say;
listen closely to my words.
21 Do not let them out of your
sight,
keep them within your
heart;
22 for they are life to those who
find them
and health to a man's whole
body.
23 Above all else, guard your
heart,
for it is the wellspring of
life.
24 Put away perversity from your
mouth;
keep corrupt talk far from
your lips.
25 Let your eyes look straight
ahead,
fix your gaze directly before
you.
26 Make level[1] paths for your feet
and take only ways that are

[1]26 Or *Consider the*

°16 ק יכשילו

יִכֹּנוּ׃ (27) אַל־ תֵּט־ יָמִין וּשְׂמֹאול הָסֵר רַגְלְךָ
let-them-be-firm (27) not you-swerve right or-left keep! foot-of-you

מֵרָע׃ (5:1) בְּנִי לְחָכְמָתִי הַקְשִׁיבָה לִתְבוּנָתִי
from-evil (5:1) son-of-me to-wisdom-of-me pay-attention! to-insight-of-me

הַט־ אָזְנֶךָ׃ (2) לִשְׁמֹר מְזִמּוֹת וְדַעַת שְׂפָתֶיךָ
give! ear-of-you (2) to-maintain discretions and-knowledge lips-of-you

יִנְצֹרוּ׃ (3) כִּי נֹפֶת תִּטֹּפְנָה שִׂפְתֵי זָרָה
they-may-preserve (3) for honey they-drip lips-of one-being-adulteress

וְחָלָק מִשֶּׁמֶן חִכָּהּ׃ (4) וְאַחֲרִיתָהּ מָרָה כַלַּעֲנָה
and-smooth more-than-oil speech-of-her (4) but-end-of-her bitter as-the-gall

חַדָּה כְּחֶרֶב פִּיּוֹת׃ (5) רַגְלֶיהָ יֹרְדוֹת מָוֶת
sharp as-sword-of double-edges (5) feet-of-her ones-going-down-of death

שְׁאוֹל צְעָדֶיהָ יִתְמֹכוּ׃ (6) אֹרַח חַיִּים פֶּן־ תְּפַלֵּס
Sheol steps-of-her they-lead (6) way-of lives not she-gives-thought

נָעוּ מַעְגְּלֹתֶיהָ לֹא תֵדָע׃ (7) וְעַתָּה בָנִים שִׁמְעוּ־ לִי
they-are-crooked paths-of-her not she-knows (7) so-now sons listen! to-me

וְאַל־ תָּסוּרוּ מֵאִמְרֵי־ פִי׃ (8) הַרְחֵק מֵעָלֶיהָ
and-not you-turn from-sayings-of mouth-of-me (8) keep-far! from-by-her

דַרְכֶּךָ וְאַל־ תִּקְרַב אֶל־ פֶּתַח בֵּיתָהּ׃ (9) פֶּן־ תִּתֵּן
path-of-you and-not you-go-near to door-of house-of-her (9) lest you-give

לַאֲחֵרִים הוֹדֶךָ וּשְׁנֹתֶיךָ לְאַכְזָרִי׃ (10) פֶּן־ יִשְׂבְּעוּ
to-others strength-of-you and-years-of-you to-cruel-one (10) lest they-feast

זָרִים כֹּחֶךָ וַעֲצָבֶיךָ בְּבֵית נָכְרִי׃
ones-being-strangers wealth-of-you and-toils-of-you to-house-of another

(11) וְנָהַמְתָּ בְאַחֲרִיתֶךָ בִּכְלוֹת בְּשָׂרְךָ
(11) and-you-will-groan at-end-of-you when-to-be-spent flesh-of-you

וּשְׁאֵרֶךָ׃ (12) וְאָמַרְתָּ אֵיךְ שָׂנֵאתִי מוּסָר וְתוֹכַחַת
and-body-of-you (12) and-you-will-say how! I-hated discipline and-correction

נָאַץ לִבִּי׃ (13) וְלֹא־ שָׁמַעְתִּי בְּקוֹל מוֹרָי
he-spurned heart-of-me (13) and-not I-obeyed to-voice-of teachers-of-me

וְלִמְלַמְּדַי לֹא־ הִטִּיתִי אָזְנִי׃ (14) כִּמְעַט הָיִיתִי
and-to-ones-instructing-me not I-turned ear-of-me (14) at-brink I-was

בְכָל־ רָע בְּתוֹךְ קָהָל וְעֵדָה׃ (15) שְׁתֵה־
of-utterness-of ruin in-midst-of assembly even-congregation (15) drink!

מַיִם מִבּוֹרֶךָ וְנֹזְלִים מִתּוֹךְ בְּאֵרֶךָ׃
waters from-cistern-of-you and-ones-running from-inside-of well-of-you

(16) יָפוּצוּ מַעְיְנֹתֶיךָ חוּצָה בָּרְחֹבוֹת פַּלְגֵי־
(16) should-they-overflow springs-of-you in-street in-the-squares streams-of

firm.
27 Do not swerve to the right or
the left;
keep your foot from evil.

Warning Against Adultery

5 My son, pay attention to my
wisdom,
listen well to my words of
insight,
2 that you may maintain
discretion
and your lips may preserve
knowledge.
3 For the lips of an adulteress
drip honey,
and her speech is smoother
than oil;
4 but in the end she is bitter as
gall,
sharp as a double-edged
sword.
5 Her feet go down to death;
her steps lead straight to the
grave.[f]
6 She gives no thought to the
way of life;
her paths are crooked, but
she knows it not.

7 Now then, my sons, listen to
me;
do not turn aside from what
I say.
8 Keep to a path far from her,
do not go near the door of
her house,
9 lest you give your best
strength to others
and your years to one who
is cruel,
10 lest strangers feast on your
wealth
and your toil enrich another
man's house.
11 At the end of your life you
will groan,
when your flesh and body
are spent.
12 You will say, "How I hated
discipline!
How my heart spurned
correction!
13 I would not obey my teachers
or listen to my instructors.
14 I have come to the brink of
utter ruin
in the midst of the whole
assembly."

15 Drink water from your own
cistern,
running water from your
own well.
16 Should your springs overflow
in the streets,

[f]5 Hebrew *Sheol*

מָיִם׃ יִהְיוּ־ לְךָ לְבַדֶּךָ וְאֵין לְזָרִים
to-ones-being-strangers and-never by-yourself for-you let-them-be (17) waters

אִתָּךְ׃ יְהִי־ מְקוֹרְךָ בָרוּךְ וּשְׂמַח
and-rejoice! one-being-blessed fountain-of-you may-he-be (18) with-you

מֵאֵשֶׁת נְעוּרֶךָ׃ אַיֶּלֶת אֲהָבִים וְיַעֲלַת־ חֵן דַּדֶּיהָ
breasts-of-her grace and-deer-of loves doe-of (19) youths-of-you in-wife-of

יְרַוֻּךָ בְכָל־ עֵת בְּאַהֲבָתָהּ תִּשְׁגֶּה
may-you-be-captivated by-love-of-her time at-all-of may-they-satisfy-you

תָמִיד׃ וְלָמָּה תִשְׁגֶּה בְנִי בְזָרָה
by-one-being-adulteress son-of-me you-be-captivated and-why? (20) ever

וּתְחַבֵּק חֵק נָכְרִיָּה׃ כִּי נֹכַח ׀ עֵינֵי יְהוָה דַּרְכֵי־
ways-of Yahweh eyes-of in-front-of for (21) another bosom-of and-you-embrace

אִישׁ וְכָל־ מַעְגְּלֹתָיו מְפַלֵּס׃ עֲוֹנוֹתָיו*
evil-deeds-of-him (22) one-examining paths-of-him and-all-of man

יִלְכְּדֻנוֹ אֶת־ הָרָשָׁע וּבְחַבְלֵי חַטָּאתוֹ יִתָּמֵךְ׃
he-is-held-fast sin-of-him and-by-cords-of the-wicked *** they-ensnare-him

הוּא יָמוּת בְּאֵין מוּסָר וּבְרֹב אִוַּלְתּוֹ
folly-of-him and-by-greatness-of discipline for-lack-of he-will-die he (23)

יִשְׁגֶּה׃ בְּנִי אִם־ עָרַבְתָּ לְרֵעֶךָ
for-neighbor-of-you you-put-up-security if son-of-me (6:1) he-will-be-led-astray

תָּקַעְתָ† לַזָּר כַּפֶּיךָ׃ נוֹקַשְׁתָּ
you-were-trapped (2) hands-of-you for-the-one-being-other you-struck

בְאִמְרֵי־ פִיךָ נִלְכַּדְתָּ בְּאִמְרֵי־ פִיךָ׃
mouth-of-you by-words-of you-were-ensnared mouth-of-you by-sayings-of

עֲשֵׂה זֹאת אֵפוֹא ׀ בְּנִי וְהִנָּצֵל כִּי בָאתָ בְכַף־
into-hand-of you-fell since and-free-yourself! son-of-me then this do! (3)

רֵעֶךָ לֵךְ הִתְרַפֵּס וּרְהַב רֵעֶיךָ׃ אַל־
not (4) neighbors-of-you and-plead! humble-yourself! go! neighbor-of-you

תִּתֵּן שֵׁנָה לְעֵינֶיךָ וּתְנוּמָה לְעַפְעַפֶּיךָ׃ הִנָּצֵל
free-yourself! (5) to-eyelids-of-you and-slumber to-eyes-of-you sleep you-allow

כִּצְבִי מִיָּד וּכְצִפּוֹר מִיַּד יָקוּשׁ׃ לֵךְ־אֶל־נְמָלָה
ant to go! (6) fowler from-snare-of and-like-bird from-hand like-gazelle

עָצֵל רְאֵה דְרָכֶיהָ וַחֲכָם׃ אֲשֶׁר אֵין־ לָהּ
to-her there-is-not that (7) and-be-wise! ways-of-her consider! sluggard

קָצִין שֹׁטֵר וּמֹשֵׁל׃ תָּכִין בַּקַּיִץ לַחְמָהּ
provision-of-her in-the-summer she-stores (8) or-one-ruling overseer commander

אָגְרָה בַקָּצִיר מַאֲכָלָהּ׃ עַד־ מָתַי עָצֵל ׀ תִּשְׁכָּב
will-you-lie sluggard when? until (9) food-of-her at-the-harvest she-gathers

your streams of water in the public squares?
17 Let them be yours alone,
never to be shared with strangers.
18 May your fountain be blessed,
and may you rejoice in the wife of your youth.
19 A loving doe, a graceful deer—
may her breasts satisfy you always,
may you ever be captivated by her love.
20 Why be captivated, my son, by an adulteress?
Why embrace the bosom of another man's wife?

21 For a man's ways are in full view of the LORD,
and he examines all his paths.
22 The evil deeds of a wicked man ensnare him;
the cords of his sin hold him fast.
23 He will die for lack of discipline,
led astray by his own great folly.

Warnings Against Folly

6 My son, if you have put up security for your neighbor,
if you have struck hands in pledge for another,
2 if you have been trapped by what you said,
ensnared by the words of your mouth,
3 then do this, my son, to free yourself,
since you have fallen into your neighbor's hands:
Go and humble yourself;
press your plea with your neighbor!
4 Allow no sleep to your eyes,
no slumber to your eyelids.
5 Free yourself, like a gazelle from the hand of the hunter,
like a bird from the snare of the fowler.

6 Go to the ant, you sluggard;
consider its ways and be wise!
7 It has no commander,
no overseer or ruler,
8 yet it stores its provisions in summer
and gathers its food at harvest.

9 How long will you lie there, you sluggard?

*22 Most mss have *hateph pathah* under the *ayin* (עֲ).

†1 Most mss have *dagesh* in the *tav* (תָּ—).

מָתַי תָּקוּם מִשְּׁנָתֶךָ׃ מְעַט שֵׁנוֹת מְעַט
little-of sleeps little-of (10) from-sleep-of-you will-you-get-up when?

תְּנוּמוֹת מְעַט ׀ חִבֻּק יָדַיִם לִשְׁכָּב׃ וּבָא־
and-he-will-come (11) to-rest hands folding-of little-of slumbers

כִמְהַלֵּךְ רֵאשֶׁךָ וּמַחְסֹרְךָ כְּאִישׁ מָגֵן׃
armor like-man-of and-scarcity-of-you poverty-of-you like-one-being-bandit

אָדָם בְּלִיַּעַל אִישׁ אָוֶן הוֹלֵךְ עִקְּשׁוּת פֶּה׃
mouth corruptness-of one-going-about villainy man-of scoundrel man (12)

קֹרֵץ בְּעֵינָו מֹלֵל בְּרַגְלָו מֹרֶה
one-motioning with-feet-of-him one-signaling with-eyes-of-him one-winking (13)

בְּאֶצְבְּעֹתָיו׃ תַּהְפֻּכוֹת ׀ בְּלִבּוֹ חֹרֵשׁ רָע בְּכָל־
at-all-of evil one-plotting in-heart-of-him deceits (14) with-fingers-of-him

עֵת מְדָנִים יְשַׁלֵּחַ׃ עַל־ כֵּן פִּתְאֹם יָבוֹא
he-will-overtake instantly this for (15) he-stirs-up dissensions time

אֵידוֹ פֶּתַע יִשָּׁבֵר וְאֵין מַרְפֵּא׃ שֶׁשׁ־ הֵנָּה
they six (16) remedy with-no he-will-be-destroyed suddenly disaster-of-him

שָׂנֵא יְהוָה וְשֶׁבַע תּוֹעֲבֹת נַפְשׁוֹ׃ עֵינַיִם רָמוֹת
ones-being-haughty eyes (17) self-of-him detestable-of and-seven Yahweh he-hates

לְשׁוֹן שָׁקֶר וְיָדַיִם שֹׁפְכוֹת דָּם־ נָקִי׃ לֵב חֹרֵשׁ
one-devising heart (18) innocent blood ones-shedding and-hands lie tongue-of

מַחְשְׁבוֹת אָוֶן רַגְלַיִם מְמַהֲרוֹת לָרוּץ לָרָעָה׃
into-the-evil to-rush ones-being-quick feet wickedness schemes-of

יָפִיחַ כְּזָבִים עֵד שָׁקֶר וּמְשַׁלֵּחַ מְדָנִים בֵּין
among dissensions and-one-stirring-up falsehood witness-of lies he-pours-out (19)

אַחִים׃ נְצֹר בְּנִי מִצְוַת אָבִיךָ וְאַל־ תִּטֹּשׁ
you-forsake and-not father-of-you command-of son-of-me keep! (20) brothers

תּוֹרַת אִמֶּךָ׃ קָשְׁרֵם עַל־ לִבְּךָ תָמִיד
forever heart-of-you upon bind-them! (21) mother-of-you teaching-of

עָנְדֵם עַל־ גַּרְגְּרֹתֶךָ׃ בְּהִתְהַלֶּכְךָ ׀ תַּנְחֶה אֹתָךְ
you she-will-guide when-to-walk-you (22) necks-of-you around fasten-them!

בְּשָׁכְבְּךָ תִּשְׁמֹר עָלֶיךָ וַהֲקִיצוֹתָ הִיא
she when-you-awake over-you she-will-watch when-to-sleep-you

תְשִׂיחֶךָ׃ כִּי נֵר מִצְוָה וְתוֹרָה אוֹר וְדֶרֶךְ
and-way-of light and-teaching command lamp for (23) she-will-speak-to-you

חַיִּים תּוֹכְחוֹת מוּסָר׃ לִשְׁמָרְךָ מֵאֵשֶׁת רָע
immorality from-woman-of to-keep-you (24) discipline corrections-of lives

מֵחֶלְקַת לָשׁוֹן נָכְרִיָּה׃ אַל־ תַּחְמֹד יָפְיָהּ
beauty-of-her you-lust-after not (25) wayward-woman tongue from-smoothness-of

When will you get up from
your sleep?
10 A little sleep, a little slumber,
a little folding of the hands
to rest—
11 and poverty will come on you
like a bandit
and scarcity like an armed
man.[k]

12 A scoundrel and villain,
who goes about with a
corrupt mouth,
13 who winks with his eye,
signals with his feet
and motions with his
fingers,
14 who plots evil with deceit in
his heart—
he always stirs up
dissension.
15 Therefore disaster will overtake
him in an instant;
he will suddenly be
destroyed—without
remedy.

16 There are six things the LORD
hates,
seven that are detestable to
him:
17 haughty eyes,
a lying tongue,
hands that shed innocent
blood,
18 a heart that devises
wicked schemes,
feet that are quick to rush
into evil,
19 a false witness who pours
out lies
and a man who stirs up
dissension among
brothers.

Warning Against Adultery

20 My son, keep your father's
commands
and do not forsake your
mother's teaching.
21 Bind them upon your heart
forever;
fasten them around your
neck.
22 When you walk, they will
guide you;
when you sleep, they will
watch over you;
when you awake, they will
speak to you.
23 For these commands are a
lamp,
this teaching is a light,
and the corrections of
discipline
are the way to life,
24 keeping you from the immoral
woman,
from the smooth tongue of
the wayward wife.
25 Do not lust in your heart after
her beauty

[k] 11 Or *like a vagrant / and scarcity like a beggar*

*18 Most mss have the accent *silluq* on the final syllable (עָה־).

°*13a* ק בעיניו
°*13b* ק ברגליו
°*14* ק מדינים
°*16* ק תועבת

בִּלְבָבֶךָ וְאַל־ תִּקָּחֲךָ בְּעַפְעַפֶּיהָ׃ כִּי
for (26) with-eyes-of-her let-her-captivate-you and-not in-heart-of-you

בְעַד־ אִשָּׁה זוֹנָה עַד־ כִּכַּר לָחֶם וְאֵשֶׁת אִישׁ
man and-wife-of bread loaf-of to one-being-prostitute woman because-of

נֶפֶשׁ יְקָרָה תָצוּד׃ הֲיַחְתֶּה אִישׁ אֵשׁ בְּחֵיקוֹ
into-lap-of-him fire man can-he-scoop? (27) she-preys-upon precious life

וּבְגָדָיו לֹא תִשָּׂרַפְנָה׃ אִם־ יְהַלֵּךְ אִישׁ עַל־הַגֶּחָלִים
the-coals on man can-he-walk or (28) they-are-burned not and-clothes-of-him

וְרַגְלָיו לֹא תִכָּוֶינָה׃ כֵּן הַבָּא אֶל־ אֵשֶׁת
wife-of into the-one-going so (29) they-are-scorched not and-feet-of-him

רֵעֵהוּ לֹא יִנָּקֶה כָּל־ הַנֹּגֵעַ בָּהּ׃
on-her the-one-touching any-of he-will-go-unpunished not neighbor-of-him

לֹא־ יָבוּזוּ לַגַּנָּב כִּי יִגְנוֹב לְמַלֵּא נַפְשׁוֹ
hunger-of-him to-satisfy he-steals if to-the-thief they-despise not (30)

כִּי יִרְעָב׃ וְנִמְצָא יְשַׁלֵּם שִׁבְעָתָיִם אֶת־ כָּל־
all-of *** seven-times he-must-pay if-he-is-caught (31) he-starves when

הוֹן בֵּיתוֹ יִתֵּן׃ נֹאֵף אִשָּׁה
woman one-committing-adultery (32) he-must-give house-of-him wealth-of

חֲסַר־ לֵב מַשְׁחִית נַפְשׁוֹ הוּא יַעֲשֶׂנָּה׃ נֶגַע־
blow (33) he-does-her he self-of-him one-destroying judgment lacking-of

וְקָלוֹן יִמְצָא וְחֶרְפָּתוֹ לֹא תִמָּחֶה׃
he-will-be-wiped-away never and-shame-of-him he-will-find and-disgrace

כִּי־ קִנְאָה חֲמַת־ גָּבֶר וְלֹא־ יַחְמוֹל בְּיוֹם
on-day-of he-will-show-mercy and-not husband fury-of jealousy for (34)

נָקָם׃ לֹא־ יִשָּׂא פְּנֵי כָל־ כֹּפֶר וְלֹא־
and-not compensation any-of presences-of he-will-accept not (35) revenge

יֹאבֶה כִּי תַרְבֶּה־ שֹׁחַד׃ בְּנִי שְׁמֹר אֲמָרָי
words-of-me keep! son-of-me (7:1) bribe she-is-great though he-will-accept

וּמִצְוֹתַי תִּצְפֹּן אִתָּךְ׃ שְׁמֹר מִצְוֹתַי וֶחְיֵה
and-live! commands-of-me keep! (2) within-you you-store-up and-commands-of-me

וְתוֹרָתִי כְּאִישׁוֹן עֵינֶיךָ׃ קָשְׁרֵם עַל־ אֶצְבְּעֹתֶיךָ
fingers-of-you on bind-them! (3) eyes-of-you as-apple-of and-teaching-of-me

כָּתְבֵם עַל־ לוּחַ לִבֶּךָ׃ אֱמֹר לַחָכְמָה אֲחֹתִי אָתְּ
you sister-of-me to-wisdom say! (4) heart-of-you tablet-of on write-them!

וּמֹדָע לַבִּינָה תִקְרָא׃ לִשְׁמָרְךָ מֵאִשָּׁה
from-woman to-keep-you (5) you-call to-the-understanding and-kinsman

זָרָה מִנָּכְרִיָּה אֲמָרֶיהָ הֶחֱלִיקָה׃
she-makes-seductive words-of-her from-wayward-woman one-being-adulteress

or let her captivate you with
her eyes,
26 for the prostitute reduces you
to a loaf of bread,
and the adulteress preys
upon your very life.
27 Can a man scoop fire into his
lap
without his clothes being
burned?
28 Can a man walk on hot coals
without his feet being
scorched?
29 So is he who sleeps with
another man's wife;
no one who touches her will
go unpunished.

30 Men do not despise a thief if
he steals
to satisfy his hunger when
he is starving.
31 Yet if he is caught, he must
pay sevenfold,
though it costs him all the
wealth of his house.
32 But a man who commits
adultery lacks judgment;
whoever does so destroys
himself.
33 Blows and disgrace are his lot,
and his shame will never be
wiped away;
34 for jealousy arouses a
husband's fury,
and he will show no mercy
when he takes revenge.
35 He will not accept any
compensation;
he will refuse the bribe,
however great it is.

Warning Against the Adulteress

7 My son, keep my words
and store up my commands
within you.
2 Keep my commands and you
will live;
guard my teachings as the
apple of your eye.
3 Bind them on your fingers;
write them on the tablet of
your heart.
4 Say to wisdom, "You are my
sister,"
and call understanding your
kinsman;
5 they will keep you from the
adulteress,
from the wayward wife with
her seductive words.

כִּי בְּחַלּוֹן בֵּיתִי בְּעַד אֶשְׁנַבִּי נִשְׁקָפְתִּי׃
I-looked-out lattice-of-me through house-of-me at-window-of for (6)

וָאֵרֶא בַפְּתָאיִם אָבִינָה בַבָּנִים נַעַר
youth among-the-young-men I-noticed among-the-simple-ones and-I-saw (7)

חֲסַר־ לֵב׃ עֹבֵר בַּשּׁוּק אֵצֶל פִּנָּהּ
corner-of-her near down-the-street one-going (8) judgment lacking-of

וְדֶרֶךְ בֵּיתָהּ יִצְעָד׃ בְּנֶשֶׁף־ בְּעֶרֶב יוֹם
day at-evening-of at-twilight (9) he-walked house-of-her and-direction-of

בְּאִישׁוֹן לַיְלָה וַאֲפֵלָה׃ וְהִנֵּה אִשָּׁה לִקְרָאתוֹ שִׁית
dress-of to-meet-him woman then-see! (10) and-darkness night at-middle-of

זוֹנָה וּנְצֻרַת לֵב׃ הֹמִיָּה הִיא
she one-being-loud (11) intent and-one-being-crafty-of one-being-prostitute

וְסֹרָרֶת בְּבֵיתָהּ לֹא־ יִשְׁכְּנוּ רַגְלֶיהָ׃ פַּעַם ׀
now (12) feet-of-her they-stay never at-home-of-her and-one-being-defiant

בַּחוּץ פַּעַם בָּרְחֹבוֹת וְאֵצֶל כָּל־ פִּנָּה תֶאֱרֹב׃
she-lurks corner every-of and-at in-the-squares now in-the-street

וְהֶחֱזִיקָה בּוֹ וְנָשְׁקָה־ לּוֹ הֵעֵזָה
she-made-brazen to-him and-she-kissed of-him and-she-took-hold (13)

פָנֶיהָ וַתֹּאמַר לוֹ׃ זִבְחֵי שְׁלָמִים עָלָי
with-me fellowships offerings-of (14) to-him and-she-said faces-of-her

הַיּוֹם שִׁלַּמְתִּי נְדָרָי׃ עַל־ כֵּן יָצָאתִי לִקְרָאתֶךָ
to-meet-you I-came-out this for (15) vows-of-me I-fulfilled the-day

לְשַׁחֵר פָּנֶיךָ וָאֶמְצָאֶךָּ׃ מַרְבַדִּים רָבַדְתִּי עַרְשִׂי
bed-of-me I-covered coverings (16) and-I-found-you faces-of-you to-look-for

חֲטֻבוֹת אֵטוּן מִצְרָיִם׃ נַפְתִּי מִשְׁכָּבִי מֹר אֲהָלִים וְקִנָּמוֹן׃
and-cinnamon aloes myrrh bed-of-me I-perfumed (17) Egypt linen-of colors-of

לְכָה נִרְוֶה דֹדִים עַד־ הַבֹּקֶר נִתְעַלְּסָה
let-us-enjoy-ourselves the-morning till loves let-us-drink-deep come! (18)

בָּאֳהָבִים׃ כִּי אֵין הָאִישׁ בְּבֵיתוֹ הָלַךְ בְּדֶרֶךְ
on-journey he-went at-home-of-him the-husband not for (19) with-loves

מֵרָחוֹק׃ צְרוֹר־ הַכֶּסֶף לָקַח בְּיָדוֹ לְיוֹם
on-day-of in-hand-of-him he-took the-money purse-of (20) at-distance

הַכֵּסֶא* יָבֹא בֵיתוֹ׃ הִטַּתּוּ בְּרֹב
with-quantity-of she-led-astray-him (21) home-of-him he-will-come the-full-moon

לִקְחָהּ בְּחֵלֶק שְׂפָתֶיהָ תַּדִּיחֶנּוּ׃ הוֹלֵךְ
following (22) she-seduced-him lips-of-her with-smoothness-of persuasion-of-her

אַחֲרֶיהָ פִּתְאֹם כְּשׁוֹר אֶל־ טַבַח† יָבוֹא וּכְעֶכֶס אֶל־ מוּסַר
discipline-of for and-like-noose he-goes slaughter to like-ox at-once after-her

6 At the window of my house
I looked out through the lattice.
7 I saw among the simple,
I noticed among the young men,
a youth who lacked judgment.
8 He was going down the street near her corner,
walking along in the direction of her house
9 at twilight, as the day was fading,
as the dark of night set in.

10 Then out came a woman to meet him,
dressed like a prostitute and with crafty intent.
11 (She is loud and defiant,
her feet never stay at home;
12 now in the street, now in the squares,
at every corner she lurks.)
13 She took hold of him and kissed him
and with a brazen face she said:

14 "I have fellowship offerings[l] at home;
today I fulfilled my vows.
15 So I came out to meet you;
I looked for you and have found you!
16 I have covered my bed
with colored linens from Egypt.
17 I have perfumed my bed
with myrrh, aloes and cinnamon.
18 Come, let's drink deep of love till morning;
let's enjoy ourselves with love!
19 My husband is not at home;
he has gone on a long journey.
20 He took his purse filled with money
and will not be home till full moon."

21 With persuasive words she led him astray;
she seduced him with her smooth talk.
22 All at once he followed her
like an ox going to the slaughter,
like a deer[m] stepping into a noose[n]

[l] 14 Traditionally *peace offerings*
[m] 22 Syriac (see also Septuagint); Hebrew *fool*
[n] 22 The meaning of the Hebrew for this line is uncertain.

*20 Most mss have *segol* under the *kaph* (הַכֶּ).

†22 Most mss have *segol* under the *teth* (טֶ).

אֱוִֽיל׃ עַד יְפַלַּח חֵץ כְּבֵדוֹ כְּמַהֵר צִפּוֹר אֶל־ פָּח
snare into bird like-to-dart liver-of-him arrow he-pierces till (23) fool

וְלֹא־ יָדַע כִּֽי־ בְנַפְשׁוֹ הֽוּא׃ וְעַתָּה בָנִים שִׁמְעוּ־ לִי
to-me listen! sons so-now (24) this for-life-of-him that he-knows and-not

וְהַקְשִׁיבוּ לְאִמְרֵי־ פִֽי׃ אַל־ יֵשְׂטְ אֶל־
to let-him-turn not (25) mouth-of-me to-sayings-of and-pay-attention!

דְּרָכֶיהָ לִבֶּךָ אַל־ תֵּתַע בִּנְתִיבוֹתֶֽיהָ׃ כִּֽי־ רַבִּים
many for (26) into-paths-of-her you-stray not heart-of-you ways-of-her

חֲלָלִים הִפִּילָה וַעֲצֻמִים כָּל־ הֲרֻגֶֽיהָ׃
ones-being-slain-of-her all-of and-mighty-ones she-brought-down victims

דַּרְכֵי שְׁאוֹל בֵּיתָהּ יֹרְדוֹת אֶל־ חַדְרֵי־ מָֽוֶת׃
death chambers-of to ones-leading-down house-of-her Sheol highways-of (27)

הֲלֹא־ חָכְמָה תִקְרָא וּתְבוּנָה תִּתֵּן קוֹלָֽהּ׃
voice-of-her she-raises and-understanding she-calls-out wisdom not? (8:1)

בְּרֹאשׁ־ מְרֹמִים עֲלֵי־ דָרֶךְ בֵּית נְתִיבוֹת נִצָּֽבָה׃
she-takes-stand paths meeting-place-of way along heights on-top-of (2)

לְיַד־ שְׁעָרִים לְפִי־ קָרֶת מְבוֹא פְתָחִים תָּרֹֽנָּה׃
she-cries-aloud doors entrance-of city at-entrance-of gates at-side-of (3)

אֲלֵיכֶם אִישִׁים אֶקְרָא וְקוֹלִי אֶל־ בְּנֵי אָדָֽם׃ הָבִינוּ
gain! (5) mankind sons-of to and-voice-of-me I-call-out men to-you (4)

פְתָאיִם עָרְמָה וּכְסִילִים הָבִינוּ לֵֽב׃ שִׁמְעוּ כִּֽי־
for listen! (6) understanding gain! and-foolish-ones prudence simple-ones

נְגִידִים אֲדַבֵּר וּמִפְתַּח שְׂפָתַי מֵישָׁרִֽים׃ כִּֽי־ אֱמֶת
truth for (7) right-ones lips-of-me and-opening-of I-say worthy-things

יֶהְגֶּה חִכִּי וְתוֹעֲבַת שְׂפָתַי רֶֽשַׁע׃ בְּצֶדֶק
in-justice (8) wickedness lips-of-me and-detestable-of mouth-of-me he-speaks

כָּל־ אִמְרֵי־ פִי אֵין בָּהֶם נִפְתָּל וְעִקֵּֽשׁ׃
or-perverse one-being-crooked of-them none mouth-of-me words-of all-of

כֻּלָּם נְכֹחִים לַמֵּבִין וִישָׁרִים
and-faultless-ones to-the-one-discerning right-ones all-of-them (9)

לְמֹצְאֵי דָֽעַת׃ קְחוּ־ מוּסָרִי וְאַל־ כָּסֶף
silver and-not instruction-of-me choose! (10) knowledge to-ones-having-of

וְדַעַת מֵחָרוּץ נִבְחָֽר׃ כִּֽי־ טוֹבָה חָכְמָה
wisdom precious for (11) one-being-choice rather-than-gold and-knowledge

מִפְּנִינִים וְכָל־ חֲפָצִים לֹא יִשְׁווּ־ בָֽהּ׃ אֲנִֽי־
I (12) with-her they-can-compare not desires and-all-of more-than-rubies

חָכְמָה שָׁכַנְתִּי עָרְמָה וְדַעַת מְזִמּוֹת אֶמְצָֽא׃ יִרְאַת
fear-of (13) I-possess discretions knowledge-of prudence I-dwell wisdom

23 till an arrow pierces his liver,
like a bird darting into a snare,
little knowing it will cost him his life.

24 Now then, my sons, listen to me;
pay attention to what I say.
25 Do not let your heart turn to her ways
or stray into her paths.
26 Many are the victims she has brought down;
her slain are a mighty throng.
27 Her house is a highway to the grave,[o]
leading down to the chambers of death.

Wisdom's Call

8 Does not wisdom call out?
Does not understanding raise her voice?
2 On the heights along the way,
where the paths meet, she takes her stand;
3 beside the gates leading into the city,
at the entrances, she cries aloud:
4 "To you, O men, I call out;
I raise my voice to all mankind.
5 You who are simple, gain prudence;
you who are foolish, gain understanding.
6 Listen, for I have worthy things to say;
I open my lips to speak what is right.
7 My mouth speaks what is true,
for my lips detest wickedness.
8 All the words of my mouth are just;
none of them is crooked or perverse.
9 To the discerning all of them are right;
they are faultless to those who have knowledge.
10 Choose my instruction instead of silver,
knowledge rather than choice gold,
11 for wisdom is more precious than rubies,
and nothing you desire can compare with her.

12 "I, wisdom, dwell together with prudence;
I possess knowledge and discretion.

[o] 27 Hebrew *Sheol*

*25 Most mss have the accent *rebia mugrash* ( ).

יְהוָה שְׂנֹאת רָע גֵּאָה וְגָאוֹן ׀ וְדֶרֶךְ רָע וּפִי

and-speech-of evil and-behavior-of and-arrogance pride evil to-hate Yahweh

תַּהְפֻּכוֹת שָׂנֵאתִי׃ לִי־ עֵצָה וְתוּשִׁיָּה אֲנִי בִינָה

understanding I and-sound-judgment counsel to-me (14) I-hate perversities

לִי גְבוּרָה׃ בִּי מְלָכִים יִמְלֹכוּ וְרוֹזְנִים יְחֹקְקוּ צֶדֶק׃

just they-make-laws and-ones-ruling they-reign kings by-me (15) power to-me

בִּי שָׂרִים יָשֹׂרוּ וּנְדִיבִים כָּל־ שֹׁפְטֵי צֶדֶק׃

righteousness ones-ruling-of all-of and-nobles they-govern princes by-me (16)

אֲנִי אֹהֲבַיה אֵהָב וּמְשַׁחֲרַי יִמְצָאֻנְנִי׃ עֹשֶׁר־

richness (18) they-find-me and-ones-seeking-me I-love ones-loving-me I (17)

וְכָבוֹד אִתִּי הוֹן עָתֵק וּצְדָקָה׃ טוֹב פִּרְיִי

fruit-of-me good (19) and-prosperity enduring wealth-of with-me and-honor

מֵחָרוּץ וּמִפָּז וּתְבוּאָתִי מִכֶּסֶף

more-than-silver and-yield-of-me even-more-than-fine-gold more-than-gold

נִבְחָר׃ בְּאֹרַח־ צְדָקָה אֲהַלֵּךְ בְּתוֹךְ נְתִיבוֹת מִשְׁפָּט׃

justice paths-of at-along I-walk righteousness in-way-of (20) being-choice

לְהַנְחִיל אֹהֲבַי ׀ יֵשׁ וְאֹצְרֹתֵיהֶם אֲמַלֵּא׃ יְהוָה

Yahweh (22) I-fill and-treasuries-of-them wealth ones-loving-me to-bestow (21)

קָנָנִי רֵאשִׁית דַּרְכּוֹ קֶדֶם מִפְעָלָיו מֵאָז׃

from-of-old deeds-of-him before way-of-him beginning-of he-possessed-me

מֵעוֹלָם נִסַּכְתִּי מֵרֹאשׁ מִקַּדְמֵי־ אָרֶץ׃

world from-beginnings-of from-beginning I-was-appointed from-eternity (23)

בְּאֵין־ תְּהֹמוֹת חוֹלָלְתִּי בְּאֵין מַעְיָנוֹת נִכְבַּדֵּי־

ones-abounding-of springs when-no I-was-given-birth oceans when-no (24)

מָיִם׃ בְּטֶרֶם הָרִים הָטְבָּעוּ לִפְנֵי גְבָעוֹת חוֹלָלְתִּי׃

I-was-born hills before they-were-settled mountains at-before (25) waters

עַד־ לֹא עָשָׂה אֶרֶץ וְחוּצוֹת וְרֹאשׁ עַפְרוֹת† תֵּבֵל׃

world dusts-of or-any-of or-fields earth he-made not when (26)

בַּהֲכִינוֹ שָׁמַיִם שָׁם אָנִי בְּחוּקוֹ חוּג

horizon when-to-mark-out-him I there heavens when-to-set-in-place-him (27)

עַל־ פְּנֵי תְהוֹם׃ בְּאַמְּצוֹ שְׁחָקִים מִמָּעַל בַּעֲזוֹז

when-to-secure at-above clouds when-to-establish-him (28) deep faces-of on

עִינוֹת תְּהוֹם׃†† בְּשׂוּמוֹ לַיָּם ׀ חֻקּוֹ וּמַיִם

so-waters boundary-of-him to-the-sea when-to-give-him (29) deep fountains-of

לֹא יַעַבְרוּ־ פִיו בְּחוּקוֹ מוֹסְדֵי

foundations-of when-to-mark-out-him command-of-him they-would-overstep not

אָרֶץ׃ וָאֶהְיֶה אֶצְלוֹ אָמוֹן וָאֶהְיֶה שַׁעֲשֻׁעִים יוֹם ׀ יוֹם

day day delights and-I-was craftsman beside-him then-I-was (30) earth

13 To fear the LORD is to hate
evil;
I hate pride and arrogance,
evil behavior and perverse
speech.
14 Counsel and sound judgment
are mine;
I have understanding and
power.
15 By me kings reign
and rulers make laws that
are just;
16 by me princes govern,
and all nobles who rule on
earth.[p]
17 I love those who love me,
and those who seek me find
me.
18 With me are riches and honor,
enduring wealth and
prosperity.
19 My fruit is better than fine
gold;
what I yield surpasses
choice silver.
20 I walk in the way of
righteousness,
along the paths of justice,
21 bestowing wealth on those
who love me
and making their treasuries
full.

22 "The LORD possessed me[q] at
the beginning of his
work,[r]
before his deeds of old;
23 I was appointed[s] from
eternity,
from the beginning, before
the world began.
24 When there were no oceans, I
was given birth,
when there were no springs
abounding with water;
25 before the mountains were
settled in place,
before the hills, I was given
birth,
26 before he made the earth or its
fields
or any of the dust of the
world.
27 I was there when he set the
heavens in place,
when he marked out the
horizon on the face of the
deep,
28 when he established the clouds
above
and fixed securely the
fountains of the deep,
29 when he gave the sea its
boundary
so the waters would not
overstep his command,
and when he marked out the
foundations of the earth.
30 Then I was the craftsman at
his side.
I was filled with delight day

*p*16 Many Hebrew manuscripts and Septuagint; most Hebrew manuscripts *all righteous rulers*
*q*22 Or *The LORD brought me forth*
*r*22 Or *way;* or *dominion*
*s*23 Or *fashioned*

*20 Most mss have *sheva* in the *kaph* (ךְ—).

†26 Most mss have *pathah* under the *ayin* (עַ).

††28 Most mss have the accent *silluq* on the final syllable (תְהוֹם).

°17 ק אהבי

מְשַׂחֶקֶת לְפָנָיו בְּכָל־ עֵת׃ מְשַׂחֶקֶת בְּתֵבֵל

in-whole-of one-rejoicing (31) time at-all-of in-presences-of-him one-rejoicing

אַרְצוֹ וְשַׁעֲשֻׁעַי אֶת־ בְּנֵי אָדָם׃ וְעַתָּה בָנִים שִׁמְעוּ־

listen! sons so-now (32) mankind sons-of *** and-delights-of-me world-of-him

לִי וְאַשְׁרֵי דְּרָכַי יִשְׁמֹרוּ׃ שִׁמְעוּ מוּסָר

instruction listen! (33) they-keep ways-of-me and-blessednesses-of to-me

וַחֲכָמוּ וְאַל־ תִּפְרָעוּ׃ אַשְׁרֵי אָדָם שֹׁמֵעַ לִי

to-me one-listening man blessednesses-of (34) you-ignore and-not and-be-wise!

לִשְׁקֹד עַל־ דַּלְתֹתַי יוֹם ׀ יוֹם לִשְׁמֹר מְזוּזֹת פְּתָחָי׃ כִּי

for (35) doors-of-me doorways-of to-wait day day doors-of-me at to-watch

מֹצְאִי מָצָאי° חַיִּים וַיָּפֶק רָצוֹן מֵיְהוָה׃

from-Yahweh favor and-he-receives lives he-finds one-finding-me

וְחֹטְאִי חֹמֵס נַפְשׁוֹ כָּל־ מְשַׂנְאַי אָהֲבוּ

they-love ones-hating-me all-of self-of-him harming but-one-missing-me (36)

מָוֶת׃ חָכְמוֹת בָּנְתָה בֵיתָהּ חָצְבָה עַמּוּדֶיהָ שִׁבְעָה׃

seven pillars-of-her she-hewed-out house-of-her she-built wisdoms (9:1) death

טָבְחָה טִבְחָהּ מָסְכָה יֵינָהּ אַף עָרְכָה שֻׁלְחָנָהּ׃

table-of-her she-set also wine-of-her she-mixed meat-of-her she-prepared (2)

שָׁלְחָה נַעֲרֹתֶיהָ תִקְרָא עַל־ גַּפֵּי מְרֹמֵי קָרֶת׃

city high-points-of heights-of from she-calls maids-of-her she-sent-out (3)

מִי־ פֶתִי יָסֻר הֵנָּה חֲסַר־ לֵב אָמְרָה לּוֹ׃

to-him she-says judgment lacking-of to-here let-him-come simple whoever (4)

לְכוּ לַחֲמוּ בְלַחֲמִי וּשְׁתוּ בְּיַיִן מָסָכְתִּי׃ עִזְבוּ

leave! (6) I-mixed of-wine and-drink! of-food-of-me eat! come! (5)

פְתָאיִם וִחְיוּ וְאִשְׁרוּ בְּדֶרֶךְ בִּינָה׃ יֹסֵר ׀

one-correcting (7) understanding in-way-of and-walk! and-live! simple-ways

לֵץ לֹקֵחַ לוֹ קָלוֹן וּמוֹכִיחַ לְרָשָׁע מוּמוֹ׃

abuse-of-him to-wicked-man and-one-rebuking insult to-him inviting one-mocking

אַל־ תּוֹכַח לֵץ פֶּן־ יִשְׂנָאֶךָּ הוֹכַח לְחָכָם

to-wise-man rebuke! he-will-hate-you or one-mocking you-rebuke not (8)

וְיֶאֱהָבֶךָּ׃ תֵּן לְחָכָם וְיֶחְכַּם־ עוֹד

still and-he-will-be-wiser to-wise-man instruct! (9) and-he-will-love-you

הוֹדַע לְצַדִּיק וְיוֹסֶף לֶקַח׃ תְּחִלַּת חָכְמָה

wisdom beginning-of (10) learning and-he-will-add to-righteous-man teach!

יִרְאַת יְהוָה וְדַעַת קְדֹשִׁים בִּינָה׃ כִּי־ בִי

through-me for (11) understanding Holy-Ones and-knowledge-of Yahweh fear-of

יִרְבּוּ יָמֶיךָ וְיוֹסִיפוּ לְּךָ שְׁנוֹת חַיִּים׃

lives years-of to-you and-they-will-add days-of-you they-will-be-many

°35 ק מצא

after day,
rejoicing always in his presence,
31 rejoicing in his whole world
and delighting in mankind.

32 "Now then, my sons, listen to me;
blessed are those who keep my ways.
33 Listen to my instruction and be wise;
do not ignore it.
34 Blessed is the man who listens to me,
watching daily at my doors,
waiting at my doorway.
35 For whoever finds me finds life
and receives favor from the LORD.
36 But whoever fails to find me harms himself;
all who hate me love death."

Invitations of Wisdom and of Folly

9 Wisdom has built her house;
she has hewn out its seven pillars.
2 She has prepared her meat and mixed her wine;
she has also set her table.
3 She has sent out her maids, and she calls
from the highest point of the city.
4 "Let all who are simple come in here!"
she says to those who lack judgment.
5 "Come, eat my food
and drink the wine I have mixed.
6 Leave your simple ways and you will live;
walk in the way of understanding.

7 "Whoever corrects a mocker invites insult;
whoever rebukes a wicked man incurs abuse.
8 Do not rebuke a mocker or he will hate you;
rebuke a wise man and he will love you.
9 Instruct a wise man and he will be wiser still;
teach a righteous man and he will add to his learning.

10 "The fear of the LORD is the beginning of wisdom,
and knowledge of the Holy One is understanding.
11 For through me your days will be many,
and years will be added to your life.

אִם־ חָכַמְתָּ חָכַמְתָּ לָּךְ וְלַצְתָּ לְבַדֶּךָ
by-yourself if-you-mock for-you you-are-wise you-are-wise if (12)

תִּשָּׂא׃ אֵשֶׁת כְּסִילוּת הֹמִיָּה פְּתַיּוּת וּבַל־
and-not undisciplined one-being-loud Folly woman-of (13) you-will-suffer

יָדְעָה מָּה׃ וְיָשְׁבָה לְפֶתַח בֵּיתָהּ עַל־ כִּסֵּא
seat-of on house-of-her at-door-of and-she-sits (14) anything she-knows

מְרֹמֵי קָרֶת׃ לִקְרֹא לְעֹבְרֵי־ דָרֶךְ הַמְיַשְּׁרִים
the-ones-going-straight road to-ones-passing-of to-call (15) city heights-of

אֹרְחוֹתָם׃ מִי־ פֶתִי יָסֻר הֵנָּה וַחֲסַר־ לֵב
judgment and-lacking-of to-here let-him-come simple whoever (16) ways-of-them

וְאָמְרָה לּוֹ׃ מַיִם־ גְּנוּבִים יִמְתָּקוּ וְלֶחֶם
and-food-of they-are-sweet ones-being-stolen waters (17) to-him and-she-says

סְתָרִים יִנְעָם׃ וְלֹא־ יָדַע כִּי־ רְפָאִים שָׁם
there dead-ones that he-knows but-not (18) he-is-delicious secrets

בְּעִמְקֵי שְׁאוֹל קְרֻאֶיהָ׃ מִשְׁלֵי שְׁלֹמֹה בֵּן
son Solomon proverbs-of (10:1) ones-being-guests-of-her Sheol in-depths-of

חָכָם יְשַׂמַּח־ אָב וּבֵן כְּסִיל תּוּגַת אִמּוֹ׃ לֹא־
not (2) mother-of-him grief-of foolish but-son father he-brings-joy wise

יוֹעִילוּ אוֹצְרוֹת רֶשַׁע וּצְדָקָה תַּצִּיל
she-delivers but-righteousness ill-gotten treasures-of they-are-valuable

מִמָּוֶת׃ לֹא־ יַרְעִיב יְהוָה נֶפֶשׁ צַדִּיק וְהַוַּת
but-craving-of righteous life-of Yahweh he-lets-go-hungry not (3) from-death

רְשָׁעִים יֶהְדֹּף׃ רָאשׁ עֹשֶׂה כַף־ רְמִיָּה
laziness hand-of one-making man-being-poor (4) he-thwarts wicked-ones

וְיַד חָרוּצִים תַּעֲשִׁיר׃ אֹגֵר בַּקַּיִץ בֵּן
son in-the-summer one-gathering (5) she-brings-wealth diligent-ones but-hand-of

מַשְׂכִּיל נִרְדָּם בַּקָּצִיר בֵּן מֵבִישׁ׃ בְּרָכוֹת
blessings (6) bringing-disgrace son during-the-harvest one-sleeping being-wise

לְרֹאשׁ צַדִּיק וּפִי רְשָׁעִים יְכַסֶּה חָמָס׃
violence he-overwhelms wicked-ones but-mouth-of righteous on-head-of

זֵכֶר צַדִּיק לִבְרָכָה וְשֵׁם רְשָׁעִים יִרְקָב׃
he-will-rot wicked-ones but-name-of as-blessing righteous memory-of (7)

חֲכַם־ לֵב יִקַּח מִצְוֹת וֶאֱוִיל שְׂפָתַיִם יִלָּבֵט׃
he-comes-to-ruin chatterings but-fool-of commands he-accepts heart wise-of (8)

הוֹלֵךְ בַּתֹּם יֵלֶךְ בֶּטַח וּמְעַקֵּשׁ
but-one-crooked-of security he-walks in-the-integrity one-walking (9)

דְּרָכָיו יִוָּדֵעַ׃ קֹרֵץ עַיִן יִתֵּן עַצָּבֶת
grief he-causes eye one-winking (10) he-will-be-found-out paths-of-him

12 If you are wise, your wisdom
will reward you;
if you are a mocker, you
alone will suffer."

13 The woman Folly is loud;
she is undisciplined and
without knowledge.
14 She sits at the door of her
house,
on a seat at the highest
point of the city,
15 calling out to those who pass
by,
who go straight on their
way.
16 "Let all who are simple come
in here!"
she says to those who lack
judgment.
17 "Stolen water is sweet;
food eaten in secret is
delicious!"
18 But little do they know that
the dead are there,
that her guests are in the
depths of the grave.[t]

Proverbs of Solomon

10 The proverbs of Solomon:
A wise son brings joy to
his father,
but a foolish son grief to his
mother.

2 Ill-gotten treasures are of no
value,
but righteousness delivers
from death.

3 The LORD does not let the
righteous go hungry
but he thwarts the craving
of the wicked.

4 Lazy hands make a man poor,
but diligent hands bring
wealth.

5 He who gathers crops in
summer is a wise son,
but he who sleeps during
harvest is a disgraceful
son.

6 Blessings crown the head of
the righteous,
but violence overwhelms the
mouth of the wicked.[u]

7 The memory of the righteous
will be a blessing,
but the name of the wicked
will rot.

8 The wise in heart accept
commands,
but a chattering fool comes
to ruin.

9 The man of integrity walks
securely,
but he who takes crooked
paths will be found out.

10 He who winks maliciously
causes grief,

t18 Hebrew *Sheol*
u6 Or *but the mouth of the wicked conceals violence;* also in verse 11

וֶאֱוִיל שְׂפָתַיִם יִלָּבֵט׃ מְקוֹר חַיִּים פִּי
mouth-of lives fountain-of (11) he-comes-to-ruin chatterings and-fool-of

צַדִּיק וּפִי רְשָׁעִים יְכַסֶּה חָמָס׃ שִׂנְאָה
hatred (12) violence he-overwhelms wicked-ones but-mouth-of righteous

תְּעוֹרֵר מְדָנִים וְעַל כָּל־פְּשָׁעִים תְּכַסֶּה אַהֲבָה׃ בְּשִׂפְתֵי
on-lips-of (13) love she-covers wrongs all-of but-over dissensions she-stirs-up

נָבוֹן תִּמָּצֵא חָכְמָה וְשֵׁבֶט לְגֵו חֲסַר־לֵב׃
judgment lacking-of for-back-of but-rod wisdom she-is-found discerning

חֲכָמִים יִצְפְּנוּ־דָעַת וּפִי־אֱוִיל מְחִתָּה קְרֹבָה׃
near ruin fool but-mouth-of knowledge they-store-up wise-men (14)

הוֹן עָשִׁיר קִרְיַת עֻזּוֹ מְחִתַּת דַּלִּים
poor-ones ruin-of fortification-of-him city-of rich wealth-of (15)

רֵישָׁם׃ פְּעֻלַּת צַדִּיק לְחַיִּים תְּבוּאַת רָשָׁע לְחַטָּאת׃
as-punishment wicked income-of as-lives righteous wage-of (16) poverty-of-them

אֹרַח לְחַיִּים שׁוֹמֵר מוּסָר וְעוֹזֵב תּוֹכַחַת
correction but-one-ignoring discipline one-heeding to-lives way (17)

מַתְעֶה׃ מְכַסֶּה שִׂנְאָה שִׂפְתֵי־שָׁקֶר וּמוֹצִא
and-one-spreading lie lips-of hatred one-concealing (18) one-leading-astray

דִבָּה הוּא כְסִיל׃ בְּרֹב דְּבָרִים לֹא יֶחְדַּל־פָּשַׁע וְחֹשֵׂךְ
but-one-holding sin he-is-absent not words when-many-of (19) fool he slander

שְׂפָתָיו מַשְׂכִּיל׃ כֶּסֶף נִבְחָר לְשׁוֹן צַדִּיק לֵב
heart-of righteous tongue-of being-choice silver (20) being-wise lips-of-him

רְשָׁעִים כִּמְעָט׃ שִׂפְתֵי צַדִּיק יִרְעוּ רַבִּים וֶאֱוִילִים
but-fools many they-nourish righteous lips-of (21) as-little wicked-ones

בַּחֲסַר־לֵב יָמוּתוּ׃ בִּרְכַּת יְהוָה הִיא תַעֲשִׁיר
she-brings-wealth she Yahweh blessing-of (22) they-die judgment for-lack-of

וְלֹא־יוֹסִף עֶצֶב עִמָּהּ׃ כִּשְׂחוֹק לִכְסִיל עֲשׂוֹת זִמָּה וְחָכְמָה
but-wisdom evil to-do to-fool as-pleasure (23) to-her trouble he-adds and-not

לְאִישׁ תְּבוּנָה׃ מְגוֹרַת רָשָׁע הִיא תְבוֹאֶנּוּ
she-will-overtake-him she wicked dread-of (24) understanding to-man-of

וְתַאֲוַת צַדִּיקִים יִתֵּן׃ כַּעֲבוֹר סוּפָה
storm when-to-sweep-by (25) he-will-grant righteous-ones but-desire-of

וְאֵין רָשָׁע וְצַדִּיק יְסוֹד עוֹלָם׃ כַּחֹמֶץ ׀
as-the-vinegar (26) forever firm but-righteous wicked then-not

לַשִּׁנַּיִם וְכֶעָשָׁן לָעֵינָיִם כֵּן הֶעָצֵל לְשֹׁלְחָיו׃
to-ones-sending-him the-sluggard so to-the-eyes and-as-the-smoke to-the-teeth

יִרְאַת יְהוָה תּוֹסִיף יָמִים וּשְׁנוֹת רְשָׁעִים תִּקְצֹרְנָה׃
they-are-cut-short wicked-ones but-years-of days she-adds Yahweh fear-of (27)

and a chattering fool comes
to ruin.

11 The mouth of the righteous is
a fountain of life,
but violence overwhelms the
mouth of the wicked.

12 Hatred stirs up dissension,
but love covers over all
wrongs.

13 Wisdom is found on the lips
of the discerning,
but a rod is for the back of
him who lacks judgment.

14 Wise men store up knowledge,
but the mouth of a fool
invites ruin.

15 The wealth of the rich is their
fortified city,
but poverty is the ruin of
the poor.

16 The wages of the righteous
bring them life
but the income of the
wicked brings them
punishment.

17 He who heeds discipline
shows the way to life,
but whoever ignores
correction leads others
astray.

18 He who conceals his hatred
has lying lips,
and whoever spreads
slander is a fool.

19 When words are many, sin is
not absent,
but he who holds his tongue
is wise.

20 The tongue of the righteous is
choice silver,
but the heart of the wicked
is of little value.

21 The lips of the righteous
nourish many,
but fools die for lack of
judgment.

22 The blessing of the LORD
brings wealth,
and he adds no trouble to it.

23 A fool finds pleasure in evil
conduct,
but a man of understanding
delights in wisdom.

24 What the wicked dreads will
overtake him;
what the righteous desire
will be granted.

25 When the storm has swept by,
the wicked are gone,
but the righteous stand firm
forever.

26 As vinegar to the teeth and
smoke to the eyes,
so is a sluggard to those
who send him.

27 The fear of the LORD adds
length to life,
but the years of the wicked
are cut short.

(28) תּוֹחֶלֶת צַדִּיקִים שִׂמְחָה וְתִקְוַת רְשָׁעִים תֹּאבֵד׃

she-perishes wicked-ones but-hope-of joy righteous-ones prospect-of (28)

(29) מָעוֹז לַתֹּם דֶּרֶךְ יְהוָה וּמְחִתָּה לְפֹעֲלֵי אָוֶן׃

evil to-ones-doing-of but-ruin Yahweh way-of for-the-righteous refuge (29)

(30) צַדִּיק לְעוֹלָם בַּל־יִמּוֹט וּרְשָׁעִים לֹא

not but-wicked-ones he-will-be-uprooted not to-forever righteous (30)

יִשְׁכְּנוּ־אָרֶץ׃ (31) פִּי־צַדִּיק יָנוּב חָכְמָה

wisdom he-brings-forth righteous mouth-of (31) land they-will-remain

וּלְשׁוֹן תַּהְפֻּכוֹת תִּכָּרֵת׃ (32) שִׂפְתֵי צַדִּיק

righteous lips-of (32) she-will-be-cut-out perversities but-tongue-of

יֵדְעוּן רָצוֹן וּפִי רְשָׁעִים תַּהְפֻּכוֹת׃ (11:1) מֹאזְנֵי

scales-of (11:1) perversities wicked-ones but-mouth-of fitting they-know

מִרְמָה תּוֹעֲבַת יְהוָה וְאֶבֶן שְׁלֵמָה רְצוֹנוֹ׃

delight-of-him accurate but-weight Yahweh abhorrence-of dishonesty

(2) בָּא־זָדוֹן וַיָּבֹא קָלוֹן וְאֶת־צְנוּעִים חָכְמָה׃

wisdom humilities but-with disgrace then-he-comes pride he-comes (2)

(3) תֻּמַּת יְשָׁרִים תַּנְחֵם וְסֶלֶף

but-duplicity-of she-guides-them upright-ones integrity-of (3)

בּוֹגְדִים וְשַׁדָּם׃ (4) לֹא־יוֹעִיל הוֹן בְּיוֹם

in-day-of wealth he-has-worth not (4) he-destroys-them ones-being-unfaithful

עֶבְרָה וּצְדָקָה תַּצִּיל מִמָּוֶת׃ (5) צִדְקַת

righteousness-of (5) from-death she-delivers but-righteousness wrath

תָּמִים תְּיַשֵּׁר דַּרְכּוֹ וּבְרִשְׁעָתוֹ יִפֹּל

he-falls but-by-wickedness-of-him way-of-him he-makes-straight blameless-ones

רָשָׁע׃ (6) צִדְקַת יְשָׁרִים תַּצִּילֵם וּבְהַוַּת

but-by-evil-desire-of she-delivers-them upright-ones righteousness-of (6) wicked

בֹּגְדִים יִלָּכֵדוּ׃ (7) בְּמוֹת אָדָם רָשָׁע תֹּאבַד

she-perishes wicked man in-death-of (7) they-are-trapped ones-being-unfaithful

תִּקְוָה וְתוֹחֶלֶת אוֹנִים אָבָדָה׃ (8) צַדִּיק מִצָּרָה

from-trouble righteous (8) she-comes-to-nothing powers and-expectation-of hope

נֶחֱלָץ וַיָּבֹא רָשָׁע תַּחְתָּיו׃ (9) בְּפֶה חָנֵף

godless with-mouth (9) instead-of-him wicked he-comes-on he-is-rescued

יַשְׁחִת רֵעֵהוּ וּבְדַעַת צַדִּיקִים יֵחָלֵצוּ׃

they-escape righteous-ones but-through-knowledge neighbor-of-him he-destroys

(10) בְּטוּב צַדִּיקִים תַּעֲלֹץ קִרְיָה וּבַאֲבֹד

but-when-to-perish city she-rejoices righteous-ones in-prosperity-of (10)

רְשָׁעִים רִנָּה׃ (11) בְּבִרְכַּת יְשָׁרִים תָּרוּם

she-is-exalted upright-ones through-blessing-of (11) shout-of-joy wicked-ones

°3 ק ישדם

---

28 The prospect of the righteous
is joy,
but the hopes of the wicked
come to nothing.
29 The way of the LORD is a
refuge for the righteous,
but it is the ruin of those
who do evil.
30 The righteous will never be
uprooted,
but the wicked will not
remain in the land.
31 The mouth of the righteous
brings forth wisdom,
but a perverse tongue will
be cut out.
32 The lips of the righteous know
what is fitting,
but the mouth of the wicked
only what is perverse.

11 The LORD abhors
dishonest scales,
but accurate weights are his
delight.
2 When pride comes, then
comes disgrace,
but with humility comes
wisdom.
3 The integrity of the upright
guides them,
but the unfaithful are
destroyed by their
duplicity.
4 Wealth is worthless in the day
of wrath,
but righteousness delivers
from death.
5 The righteousness of the
blameless makes a
straight way for them,
but the wicked are brought
down by their own
wickedness.
6 The righteousness of the
upright delivers them,
but the unfaithful are
trapped by evil desires.
7 When a wicked man dies, his
hope perishes;
all he expected from his
power comes to nothing.
8 The righteous man is rescued
from trouble,
and it comes on the wicked
instead.
9 With his mouth the godless
destroys his neighbor,
but through knowledge the
righteous escape.
10 When the righteous prosper,
the city rejoices;
when the wicked perish,
there are shouts of joy.
11 Through the blessing of the
upright a city is exalted,

קֶרֶת וּבְפִי רְשָׁעִים תֵּהָרֵס׃ בָּז־

he-derides (12) she-is-destroyed wicked-ones but-by-mouth-of city

לְרֵעֵהוּ חֲסַר־ לֵב וְאִישׁ תְּבוּנוֹת יַחֲרִישׁ׃

he-holds-tongue understandings but-man-of judgment lacking-of to-neighbor-of-him

הוֹלֵךְ רָכִיל מְגַלֶּה־ סּוֹד וְנֶאֱמַן־

but-one-being-trustworthy-of confidence one-betraying gossip one-bringing (13)

רוּחַ מְכַסֶּה דָבָר׃ בְּאֵין תַּחְבֻּלוֹת יִפָּל־ עָם

nation he-falls guidances for-lack-of (14) secret one-keeping spirit

וּתְשׁוּעָה בְּרֹב יוֹעֵץ׃ רַע־ יֵרוֹעַ כִּי־

if he-will-suffer suffering (15) one-advising in-many-of but-victory

עָרַב זָר וְשֹׂנֵא תֹקְעִים בּוֹטֵחַ׃

one-being-safe strikings but-one-refusing one-being-other he-puts-up-security

אֵשֶׁת־ חֵן תִּתְמֹךְ כָּבוֹד וְעָרִיצִים יִתְמְכוּ־ עֹשֶׁר׃

wealth they-gain but-ruthless-men respect she-gains kindhearted woman-of (16)

גֹּמֵל נַפְשׁוֹ אִישׁ חָסֶד וְעֹכֵר שְׁאֵרוֹ

self-of-him but-one-harming kindness man-of self-of-him one-benefitting (17)

אַכְזָרִי׃ רָשָׁע עֹשֶׂה פְעֻלַּת־ שָׁקֶר וְזֹרֵעַ צְדָקָה

righteousness but-one-sowing deception wage-of earning wicked (18) cruel-man

שֶׂכֶר אֱמֶת׃ כֵּן־ צְדָקָה לְחַיִּים וּמְרַדֵּף רָעָה

evil but-one-pursuing to-lives righteous truly (19) sure reward-of

לְמוֹתוֹ׃ תּוֹעֲבַת יְהוָה עִקְּשֵׁי־ לֵב

heart men-perverse-of Yahweh detesting-of (20) to-death-of-him

וּרְצוֹנוֹ תְּמִימֵי דָרֶךְ׃ יָד לְיָד לֹא־

not upon-hand hand (21) way · ones-blameless-of but-delight-of-him

יִנָּקֶה רָּע וְזֶרַע צַדִּיקִים נִמְלָט׃

he-will-go-free righteous-ones but-descendant-of wicked he-will-go-unpunished

נֶזֶם זָהָב בְּאַף חֲזִיר אִשָּׁה יָפָה וְסָרַת טָעַם׃

discretion but-turning-away-of beautiful woman pig in-snout-of gold ring-of (22)

תַּאֲוַת צַדִּיקִים אַךְ־ טוֹב תִּקְוַת רְשָׁעִים עֶבְרָה׃

wrath wicked-ones hope-of good only righteous-ones desire-of (23)

יֵשׁ מְפַזֵּר וְנוֹסָף עוֹד וְחוֹשֵׂךְ

and-one-withholding more yet-one-gaining one-giving-freely there-is (24)

מִיֹּשֶׁר אַךְ־ לְמַחְסוֹר׃ נֶפֶשׁ־ בְּרָכָה תְדֻשָּׁן

she-will-prosper generosity person-of (25) to-poverty but without-right

וּמַרְוֶה גַּם־ הוּא יוֹרֶא׃ מֹנֵעַ בָּר

grain one-hoarding (26) he-will-be-refreshed he also and-one-refreshing

יִקְּבֻהוּ לְאוֹם וּבְרָכָה לְרֹאשׁ מַשְׁבִּיר׃ שֹׁחֵר

one-seeking (27) one-selling on-head-of but-blessing people they-curse-him

but by the mouth of the wicked it is destroyed.

12 A man who lacks judgment derides his neighbor, but a man of understanding holds his tongue.

13 A gossip betrays a confidence, but a trustworthy man keeps a secret.

14 For lack of guidance a nation falls, but many advisers make victory sure.

15 He who puts up security for another will surely suffer, but whoever refuses to strike hands in pledge is safe.

16 A kindhearted woman gains respect, but ruthless men gain only wealth.

17 A kind man benefits himself, but a cruel man brings himself harm.

18 The wicked man earns deceptive wages, but he who sows righteousness reaps a sure reward.

19 The truly righteous man attains life, but he who pursues evil goes to his death.

20 The LORD detests men of perverse heart but he delights in those whose ways are blameless.

21 Be sure of this: The wicked will not go unpunished, but those who are righteous will go free.

22 Like a gold ring in a pig's snout is a beautiful woman who shows no discretion.

23 The desire of the righteous ends only in good, but the hope of the wicked only in wrath.

24 One man gives freely, yet gains even more; another withholds unduly, but comes to poverty.

25 A generous man will prosper; he who refreshes others will himself be refreshed.

26 People curse the man who hoards grain, but blessing crowns him who is willing to sell.

טוֹב יְבַקֵּשׁ רָצוֹן וְדֹרֵשׁ רָעָה תְבוֹאֶנּוּ׃

she-will-come-to-him evil but-one-searching-for good-will he-finds good

(28) בּוֹטֵחַ בְּעָשְׁרוֹ הוּא יִפֹּל וְכֶעָלֶה

but-like-the-green-leaf he-will-fall he in-richness-of-him one-trusting (28)

צַדִּיקִים יִפְרָחוּ׃ (29) עוֹכֵר בֵּיתוֹ יִנְחַל־

he-will-inherit family-of-him one-troubling (29) they-will-thrive righteous-ones

רוּחַ וְעֶבֶד אֱוִיל לַחֲכַם־לֵב׃ (30) פְּרִי־צַדִּיק עֵץ חַיִּים

lives tree-of righteous fruit-of (30) heart to-wise-of fool and-servant wind

וְלֹקֵחַ נְפָשׂוֹת* חָכָם׃ (31) הֵן צַדִּיק בָּאָרֶץ יְשֻׁלָּם

he-receives-due on-the-earth righteous if (31) wise souls and-one-winning

אַף כִּי־רָשָׁע וְחוֹטֵא׃ (12:1) אֹהֵב מוּסָר

discipline one-loving (12:1) and-one-sinning ungodly indeed how-much-more

אֹהֵב דָּעַת וְשֹׂנֵא תוֹכַחַת בָּעַר׃ (2) טוֹב יָפִיק

he-obtains good-man (2) stupid correction but-one-hating knowledge one-loving

רָצוֹן מֵיְהוָה וְאִישׁ מְזִמּוֹת יַרְשִׁיעַ׃ (3) לֹא־

not (3) he-condemns craftinesses but-man-of from-Yahweh favor

יִכּוֹן אָדָם בְּרֶשַׁע וְשֹׁרֶשׁ צַדִּיקִים בַּל־

not righteous-ones but-root-of through-wickedness man he-can-be-established

יִמּוֹט׃ (4) אֵשֶׁת־חַיִל עֲטֶרֶת בַּעְלָהּ וּכְרָקָב

but-like-decay husband-of-her crown-of nobility wife-of (4) he-can-be-moved

בְּעַצְמוֹתָיו מְבִישָׁה׃ (5) מַחְשְׁבוֹת צַדִּיקִים מִשְׁפָּט

just righteous-ones plans-of (5) one-bringing-disgrace in-bones-of-him

תַּחְבֻּלוֹת רְשָׁעִים מִרְמָה׃ (6) דִּבְרֵי רְשָׁעִים אֱרָב־

to-lie-in-wait wicked-ones words-of (6) deceitful wicked-ones advices-of

דָּם וּפִי יְשָׁרִים יַצִּילֵם׃ (7) הָפוֹךְ

to-overthrow (7) he-rescues-them upright-ones but-speech-of blood

רְשָׁעִים וְאֵינָם וּבֵית צַדִּיקִים יַעֲמֹד׃

he-stands-firm righteous-ones but-house-of and-no-more-they wicked-ones

(8) לְפִי־שִׂכְלוֹ יְהֻלַּל־אִישׁ וְנַעֲוֵה־

but-one-being-warped-of man he-is-praised wisdom-of-him as-speech-of (8)

לֵב יִהְיֶה לָבוּז׃ (9) טוֹב נִקְלֶה וְעֶבֶד לוֹ

to-him yet-servant one-being-nobody good (9) for-despising he-is mind

מִמְתַּכַּבֵּד† וַחֲסַר־לָחֶם׃ (10) יוֹדֵעַ

one-caring-for (10) food and-lacking-of more-than-one-pretending-greatness

צַדִּיק נֶפֶשׁ בְּהֶמְתּוֹ וְרַחֲמֵי רְשָׁעִים אַכְזָרִי׃

cruel wicked-ones but-kind-acts-of animal-of-him need-of righteous

(11) עֹבֵד אַדְמָתוֹ יִשְׂבַּע־לָחֶם וּמְרַדֵּף

but-one-chasing food he-will-have-abundance land-of-him one-working (11)

27 He who seeks good finds good will,
but evil comes to him who searches for it.

28 Whoever trusts in his riches will fall,
but the righteous will thrive like a green leaf.

29 He who brings trouble on his family will inherit only wind,
and the fool will be servant to the wise.

30 The fruit of the righteous is a tree of life,
and he who wins souls is wise.

31 If the righteous receive their due on earth,
how much more the ungodly and the sinner!

12 Whoever loves discipline loves knowledge,
but he who hates correction is stupid.

2 A good man obtains favor from the LORD,
but the LORD condemns a crafty man.

3 A man cannot be established through wickedness,
but the righteous cannot be uprooted.

4 A wife of noble character is her husband's crown,
but a disgraceful wife is like decay in his bones.

5 The plans of the righteous are just,
but the advice of the wicked is deceitful.

6 The words of the wicked lie in wait for blood,
but the speech of the upright rescues them.

7 Wicked men are overthrown and are no more,
but the house of the righteous stands firm.

8 A man is praised according to his wisdom,
but men with warped minds are despised.

9 Better to be a nobody and yet have a servant
than pretend to be somebody and have no food.

10 A righteous man cares for the needs of his animal,
but the kindest acts of the wicked are cruel.

11 He who works his land will have abundant food,

*30 Most mss have *shin* for *sin* (שׁוֹת—).

†9 Most mss have *hireq* under the *mem* and *sheva* under the *tav* (מִמְתְּ).

רֵיקִים חֲסַר־ לֵב׃ חָמַד רָשָׁע מְצוֹד רָעִים

evil-men plunder-of wicked he-desires (12) judgment lacking-of fantasies

וְשֹׁרֶשׁ צַדִּיקִים יִתֵּן׃ בְּפֶשַׁע שְׂפָתַיִם מוֹקֵשׁ

trap-of lips by-sinfulness-of (13) he-flourishes righteous-ones but-root-of

רָע וַיֵּצֵא מִצָּרָה צַדִּיק׃ מִפְּרִי פִי־

lip-of from-fruit-of (14) righteous-man from-trouble but-he-escapes evil-man

אִישׁ יִשְׂבַּע־ טוֹב וּגְמוּל יְדֵי־ אָדָם יָשׁוֹב לוֹ׃ דֶּרֶךְ

way-of (15) to-him he-rewards man hands-of and-work-of good he-is-filled man

אֱוִיל יָשָׁר בְּעֵינָיו וְשֹׁמֵעַ לְעֵצָה חָכָם׃ אֱוִיל

fool (16) wise-man to-advice but-one-listening in-eyes-of-him right fool

בַּיּוֹם יִוָּדַע כַּעְסוֹ וְכֹסֶה קָלוֹן עָרוּם׃

prudent-man insult but-one-overlooking annoyance-of-him he-shows in-the-day

יָפִיחַ אֱמוּנָה יַגִּיד צֶדֶק וְעֵד שְׁקָרִים מִרְמָה׃

lie fallacies but-witness-of honesty he-testifies truthfulness he-gives (17)

יֵשׁ בּוֹטֶה כְּמַדְקְרוֹת חָרֶב וּלְשׁוֹן

but-tongue-of sword like-piercings-of one-speaking-recklessly there-is (18)

חֲכָמִים מַרְפֵּא׃ שְׂפַת־ אֱמֶת תִּכּוֹן לָעַד וְעַד־

but-while to-forever she-endures truth lip-of (19) healing wise-men

אַרְגִּיעָה לְשׁוֹן שָׁקֶר׃ מִרְמָה בְּלֶב־ חֹרְשֵׁי רָע

evil ones-plotting-of in-heart-of deceit (20) lie tongue-of I-make-momentary

וּלְיֹעֲצֵי שָׁלוֹם שִׂמְחָה׃ לֹא־ יְאֻנֶּה לַצַּדִּיק

to-the-righteous-one he-befalls not (21) joy peace but-to-ones-promoting-of

כָּל־ אָוֶן וּרְשָׁעִים מָלְאוּ רָע׃ תּוֹעֲבַת יְהוָה

Yahweh detesting-of (22) trouble they-are-filled but-wicked-ones harm any-of

שִׂפְתֵי־שָׁקֶר וְעֹשֵׂי אֱמוּנָה רְצוֹנוֹ׃ אָדָם עָרוּם כֹּסֶה

keeping prudent man (23) delight-of-him truth but-ones-doing-of lie lips-of

דָּעַת וְלֵב כְּסִילִים יִקְרָא אִוֶּלֶת׃ יַד־ חָרוּצִים

diligent-ones hand-of (24) folly he-blurts-out fools but-heart-of knowledge

תִּמְשׁוֹל וּרְמִיָּה תִּהְיֶה לָמַס׃ דְּאָגָה בְלֶב־

in-heart-of anxiety (25) in-slave-labor she-ends but-laziness she-will-rule

אִישׁ יַשְׁחֶנָּה וְדָבָר טוֹב יְשַׂמְּחֶנָּה׃ יָתֵר

he-is-cautious (26) he-cheers-her kind but-word he-weighs-down-her man

מֵרֵעֵהוּ צַדִּיק וְדֶרֶךְ רְשָׁעִים תַּתְעֵם׃

she-leads-astray-them wicked-ones but-way-of righteous with-friend-of-him

לֹא־ יַחֲרֹךְ רְמִיָּה צֵידוֹ וְהוֹן־ אָדָם יָקָר חָרוּץ׃

diligent prized man but-possession-of game-of-him lazy-man he-roasts not (27)

בְּאֹרַח־ צְדָקָה חַיִּים וְדֶרֶךְ נְתִיבָה אַל־מָוֶת׃ בֵּן חָכָם

wise son (13:1) death no path and-way-of lives righteousness in-way-of (28)

but he who chases fantasies
lacks judgment.

12 The wicked desire the plunder
of evil men,
but the root of the righteous
flourishes.

13 An evil man is trapped by his
sinful talk,
but a righteous man escapes
trouble.

14 From the fruit of his lips a
man is filled with good
things
as surely as the work of his
hands rewards him.

15 The way of a fool seems right
to him,
but a wise man listens to
advice.

16 A fool shows his annoyance at
once,
but a prudent man overlooks
an insult.

17 A truthful witness gives
honest testimony,
but a false witness tells lies.

18 Reckless words pierce like a
sword,
but the tongue of the wise
brings healing.

19 Truthful lips endure forever,
but a lying tongue lasts only
a moment.

20 There is deceit in the hearts of
those who plot evil,
but joy for those who
promote peace.

21 No harm befalls the righteous,
but the wicked have their
fill of trouble.

22 The LORD detests lying lips,
but he delights in men who
are truthful.

23 A prudent man keeps his
knowledge to himself,
but the heart of fools blurts
out folly.

24 Diligent hands will rule,
but laziness ends in slave
labor.

25 An anxious heart weighs a
man down,
but a kind word cheers him
up.

26 A righteous man is cautious in
friendship,[v]
but the way of the wicked
leads them astray.

27 The lazy man does not roast[w]
his game,
but the diligent man prizes
his possessions.

28 In the way of righteousness
there is life;
along that path is
immortality.

[v]26 Or *man is a guide to his neighbor*
[w]27 The meaning of the Hebrew for this word is uncertain.

°14 ק ישיב

מוּסַר אָב וְלֵץ לֹא־שָׁמַע גְּעָרָה׃ (2) מִפְּרִי
from-fruit-of (2) rebuke he-listens not but-one-mocking father instruction-of

פִּי־אִישׁ יֹאכַל טוֹב וְנֶפֶשׁ בֹּגְדִים חָמָס׃
violence ones-being-unfaithful but-craving-of good he-enjoys man lip-of

(3) נֹצֵר פִּיו שֹׁמֵר נַפְשׁוֹ פֹּשֵׂק
one-opening-wide soul-of-him one-guarding lip-of-him one-guarding (3)

שְׂפָתָיו מְחִתָּה־לוֹ׃ (4) מִתְאַוָּה וָאַיִן נַפְשׁוֹ עָצֵל
sluggard desire-of-him and-nothing one-craving (4) to-him ruin lips-of-him

וְנֶפֶשׁ חָרֻצִים תְּדֻשָּׁן׃ (5) דְּבַר־שֶׁקֶר יִשְׂנָא
he-hates falsehood thing-of (5) she-is-satisfied diligent-ones but-desire-of

צַדִּיק וְרָשָׁע יַבְאִישׁ וְיַחְפִּיר׃ (6) צְדָקָה
righteousness (6) and-he-brings-disgrace he-brings-shame but-wicked righteous

תִּצֹּר תָּם־דָּרֶךְ וְרִשְׁעָה תְּסַלֵּף חַטָּאת׃ (7) יֵשׁ
there-is (7) sinner she-overthrows but-wickedness way integrity-of she-guards

מִתְעַשֵּׁר וְאֵין כֹּל מִתְרוֹשֵׁשׁ וְהוֹן רָב׃
great yet-wealth one-pretending-poverty anything yet-not one-pretending-wealth

(8) כֹּפֶר נֶפֶשׁ־אִישׁ עָשְׁרוֹ וְרָשׁ לֹא־שָׁמַע
he-hears not but-one-being-poor wealth-of-him man life-of ransom-of (8)

גְּעָרָה׃ (9) אוֹר־צַדִּיקִים יִשְׂמָח וְנֵר רְשָׁעִים
wicked-ones but-lamp-of he-shines righteous-ones light-of (9) threat

יִדְעָךְ׃ (10) רַק־בְּזָדוֹן יִתֵּן מַצָּה וְאֶת־
but-in quarrel he-breeds by-pride only (10) he-is-snuffed-out

נוֹעָצִים חָכְמָה׃ (11) הוֹן מֵהֶבֶל יִמְעָט
he-dwindles-away from-dishonesty money (11) wisdom ones-taking-advice

וְקֹבֵץ עַל־יָד יַרְבֶּה׃ (12) תּוֹחֶלֶת מְמֻשָּׁכָה מַחֲלָה־
making-sick being-deferred hope (12) he-makes-grow hand by but-one-gathering

לֵב וְעֵץ חַיִּים תַּאֲוָה בָאָה׃ (13) בָּז לְדָבָר
to-instruction one-scorning (13) being-fulfilled longing lives but-tree-of heart

יֵחָבֶל לוֹ וִירֵא מִצְוָה הוּא יְשֻׁלָּם׃
he-will-be-rewarded he command but-one-respecting-of for-him he-will-pay

(14) תּוֹרַת חָכָם מְקוֹר חַיִּים לָסוּר מִמֹּקְשֵׁי מָוֶת׃
death from-snares-of to-turn lives fountain-of wise teaching-of (14)

(15) שֵׂכֶל־טוֹב יִתֶּן־חֵן וְדֶרֶךְ בֹּגְדִים אֵיתָן׃
hard ones-being-unfaithful but-way-of favor he-wins good understanding (15)

(16) כָּל־עָרוּם יַעֲשֶׂה בְדָעַת וּכְסִיל יִפְרֹשׂ אִוֶּלֶת׃
folly he-exposes but-fool from-knowledge he-acts prudent-man every-of (16)

(17) מַלְאָךְ רָשָׁע יִפֹּל בְּרָע וְצִיר אֱמוּנִים מַרְפֵּא׃
healing trusts but-envoy-of into-trouble he-falls wicked messenger (17)

13 A wise son heeds his
father's instruction,
but a mocker does not listen
to rebuke.

2 From the fruit of his lips a
man enjoys good things,
but the unfaithful have a
craving for violence.

3 He who guards his lips guards
his soul,
but he who speaks rashly
will come to ruin.

4 The sluggard craves and gets
nothing,
but the desires of the
diligent are fully satisfied.

5 The righteous hate what is
false,
but the wicked bring shame
and disgrace.

6 Righteousness guards the man
of integrity,
but wickedness overthrows
the sinner.

7 One man pretends to be rich,
yet has nothing;
another pretends to be poor,
yet has great wealth.

8 A man's riches may ransom
his life,
but a poor man hears no
threat.

9 The light of the righteous
shines brightly,
but the lamp of the wicked
is snuffed out.

10 Pride only breeds quarrels,
but wisdom is found in
those who take advice.

11 Dishonest money dwindles
away,
but he who gathers money
little by little makes it
grow.

12 Hope deferred makes the heart
sick,
but a longing fulfilled is a
tree of life.

13 He who scorns instruction will
pay for it,
but he who respects a
command is rewarded.

14 The teaching of the wise is a
fountain of life,
turning a man from the
snares of death.

15 Good understanding wins
favor,
but the way of the
unfaithful is hard.[x]

16 Every prudent man acts out of
knowledge,
but a fool exposes his folly.

17 A wicked messenger falls into
trouble,
but a trustworthy envoy
brings healing.

x15 Or *unfaithful does not endure*

רֵישׁ וְקָלוֹן פּוֹרֵעַ מוּסָר וְשׁוֹמֵר תּוֹכַחַת

correction but-one-heeding discipline one-ignoring and-shame poverty (18)

יְכֻבָּד׃ תַּאֲוָה נִהְיָה תֶּעֱרַב לְנָפֶשׁ

to-soul she-is-sweet being-fulfilled longing (19) he-is-honored

וְתוֹעֲבַת כְּסִילִים סוּר מֵרָע׃ הָלוֹךְ אֶת־ חֲכָמִים

wise-men with one-walking (20) from-evil to-turn fools but-detesting-of

וְחָכָם וְרֹעֶה כְסִילִים יֵרוֹעַ׃ חַטָּאִים

sinners (21) he-suffers-harm fools but-one-being-companion he-grows-wise

תְּרַדֵּף רָעָה וְאֶת־ צַדִּיקִים יְשַׁלֶּם־ טוֹב׃ טוֹב

good-man (22) prosperity he-rewards righteous-ones but misfortune she-pursues

יַנְחִיל בְּנֵי־ בָנִים וְצָפוּן לַצַּדִּיק

for-the-righteous but-one-being-stored children children-of he-leaves-inheritance

חֵיל חוֹטֵא׃ רָב־ אֹכֶל נִיר רָאשִׁים

men-being-poor field-of food abundance-of (23) one-sinning wealth-of

וְיֵשׁ נִסְפֶּה בְּלֹא מִשְׁפָּט׃ חוֹשֵׂךְ שִׁבְטוֹ

rod-of-him one-sparing (24) justice by-not being-swept-away but-there-is

שׂוֹנֵא בְנוֹ וְאֹהֲבוֹ שִׁחֲרוֹ מוּסָר׃

discipline he-is-careful-about-him but-one-loving-him son-of-him one-hating

צַדִּיק אֹכֵל לְשֹׂבַע נַפְשׁוֹ וּבֶטֶן רְשָׁעִים

wicked-ones but-stomach-of heart-of-him to-contentment-of eating righteous (25)

תֶּחְסָר׃ חַכְמוֹת נָשִׁים בָּנְתָה בֵיתָהּ וְאִוֶּלֶת

but-foolish house-of-her she-builds women wise-ones (14:1) she-goes-hungry

בְּיָדֶיהָ תֶהֶרְסֶנּוּ׃ הוֹלֵךְ בְּיָשְׁרוֹ

in-uprightness-of-him one-walking (2) she-tears-down-him with-hands-of-her

יְרֵא יְהוָה וּנְלוֹז דְּרָכָיו בּוֹזֵהוּ׃

one-despising-him ways-of-him but-one-being-devious-of Yahweh one-fearing-of

בְּפִי־ אֱוִיל חֹטֶר גַּאֲוָה וְשִׂפְתֵי חֲכָמִים תִּשְׁמוּרֵם׃

she-protects-them wise-ones but-lips-of back rod-of fool by-talk-of (3)

בְּאֵין אֲלָפִים אֵבוּס בָּר וְרָב־ תְּבוּאוֹת בְּכֹחַ

from-strength-of harvests but-abundance-of empty manger oxen when-no (4)

שׁוֹר׃ עֵד אֱמוּנִים לֹא יְכַזֵּב וְיָפִיחַ כְּזָבִים עֵד

witness-of lies but-he-pours-out he-deceives not truths witness-of (5) ox

שָׁקֶר׃ בִּקֶּשׁ־ לֵץ חָכְמָה וָאַיִן וְדַעַת

but-knowledge and-there-is-none wisdom one-mocking he-seeks (6) falsehood

לְנָבוֹן נָקָל׃ לֵךְ מִנֶּגֶד לְאִישׁ כְּסִיל

foolish to-man from-near stay-away! (7) he-comes-easily to-one-discerning

וּבַל־ יָדַעְתָּ שִׂפְתֵי־ דָעַת׃ חָכְמַת עָרוּם הָבִין

he-gives-thought prudent wisdom-of (8) knowledge lips-of you-will-find for-not

18 He who ignores discipline comes to poverty and shame,
but whoever heeds correction is honored.

19 A longing fulfilled is sweet to the soul,
but fools detest turning from evil.

20 He who walks with the wise grows wise,
but a companion of fools suffers harm.

21 Misfortune pursues the sinner,
but prosperity is the reward of the righteous.

22 A good man leaves an inheritance for his children's children,
but a sinner's wealth is stored up for the righteous.

23 A poor man's field may produce abundant food,
but injustice sweeps it away.

24 He who spares the rod hates his son,
but he who loves him is careful to discipline him.

25 The righteous eat to their hearts' content,
but the stomach of the wicked goes hungry.

14 The wise woman builds her house,
but with her own hands the foolish one tears hers down.

2 He whose walk is upright fears the LORD,
but he whose ways are devious despises him.

3 A fool's talk brings a rod to his back,
but the lips of the wise protect them.

4 Where there are no oxen, the manger is empty,
but from the strength of an ox comes an abundant harvest.

5 A truthful witness does not deceive,
but a false witness pours out lies.

6 The mocker seeks wisdom and finds none,
but knowledge comes easily to the discerning.

7 Stay away from a foolish man,
for you will not find knowledge on his lips.

8 The wisdom of the prudent is to give thought to their

20a ק הלך
20b ק יחכם

דַּרְכּוֹ וְאִוֶּלֶת כְּסִילִים מִרְמָה׃ (9) אֱוִלִים יָלִיץ אָשָׁם

amends-for-sin he-mocks fools (9) deception fools but-folly-of way-of-him

וּבֵין יְשָׁרִים רָצוֹן׃ (10) לֵב יוֹדֵעַ מָרַּת נַפְשׁוֹ

self-of-him bitterness-of knowing heart (10) good-will upright-ones but-among

וּבְשִׂמְחָתוֹ לֹא־יִתְעָרַב זָר׃ (11) בֵּית

house-of (11) one-being-stranger he-will-share not and-in-joy-of-him

רְשָׁעִים יִשָּׁמֵד וְאֹהֶל יְשָׁרִים יַפְרִיחַ׃

he-will-flourish upright-ones but-tent-of he-will-be-destroyed wicked-ones

(12) יֵשׁ דֶּרֶךְ יָשָׁר לִפְנֵי־אִישׁ וְאַחֲרִיתָהּ* דַּרְכֵי־מָוֶת׃ (13) גַּם־

even (13) death ways-of but-end-of-her man before right way there-is (12)

בִּשְׂחוֹק יִכְאַב־לֵב וְאַחֲרִיתָהּ שִׂמְחָה תוּגָה׃ (14) מִדְּרָכָיו

for-ways-of-him (14) grief joy and-end-of-her heart he-may-ache in-laughter

יִשְׂבַּע סוּג לֵב וּמֵעָלָיו אִישׁ טוֹב׃

good man and-for-with-him heart one-being-faithless-of he-will-be-repaid

(15) פֶּתִי יַאֲמִין לְכָל־דָּבָר וְעָרוּם יָבִין

he-gives-thought but-prudent-man thing to-any-of he-believes simple-man (15)

לַאֲשֻׁרוֹ׃ (16) חָכָם יָרֵא וְסָר מֵרָע וּכְסִיל

but-fool from-evil and-shunning fearing wise-man (16) to-step-of-him

מִתְעַבֵּר וּבוֹטֵחַ׃ (17) קְצַר־אַפַּיִם יַעֲשֶׂה אִוֶּלֶת

folly he-does tempers quickness-of (17) and-being-reckless being-hotheaded

וְאִישׁ מְזִמּוֹת יִשָּׂנֵא׃ (18) נָחֲלוּ פְתָאיִם אִוֶּלֶת

folly simple-ones they-inherit (18) he-is-hated craftinesses and-man-of

וַעֲרוּמִים יַכְתִּרוּ דָעַת׃ (19) שַׁחוּ רָעִים

evil-men they-will-bow (19) knowledge they-crown but-prudent-ones

לִפְנֵי טוֹבִים וּרְשָׁעִים עַל־שַׁעֲרֵי צַדִּיק׃ (20) גַּם־

even (20) righteous gates-of at and-wicked-men good-men in-presences-of

לְרֵעֵהוּ יִשָּׂנֵא רָשׁ וְאֹהֲבֵי

but-ones-being-friends-of one-being-poor he-is-shunned by-neighbor-of-him

עָשִׁיר רַבִּים׃ (21) בָּז־לְרֵעֵהוּ חוֹטֵא וּמְחוֹנֵן

but-one-being-kind sinning to-neighbor-of-him one-despising (21) many rich

עֲנָיִים° אַשְׁרָיו׃ (22) הֲלוֹא־יִתְעוּ חֹרְשֵׁי רָע

evil ones-plotting-of they-go-astray not? (22) blessednesses-of-him needy-ones

וְחֶסֶד וֶאֱמֶת חֹרְשֵׁי טוֹב׃ (23) בְּכָל־עֶצֶב

hard-work by-all-of (23) good ones-planning-of and-faithfulness but-love

יִהְיֶה מוֹתָר וּדְבַר־שְׂפָתַיִם אַךְ־לְמַחְסוֹר׃ (24) עֲטֶרֶת חֲכָמִים

wise-ones crown-of (24) to-poverty only lips but-talk-of profit he-comes

עָשְׁרָם אִוֶּלֶת כְּסִילִים אִוֶּלֶת׃ (25) מַצִּיל נְפָשׁוֹת עֵד אֱמֶת

truth witness-of lives one-saving (25) folly fools folly-of wealth-of-them

ways,
but the folly of fools is
deception.

9 Fools mock at making amends
for sin,
but good will is found
among the upright.

10 Each heart knows its own
bitterness,
and no one else can share
its joy.

11 The house of the wicked will
be destroyed,
but the tent of the upright
will flourish.

12 There is a way that seems
right to a man,
but in the end it leads to
death.

13 Even in laughter the heart
may ache,
and joy may end in grief.

14 The faithless will be fully
repaid for their ways,
and the good man rewarded
for his.

15 A simple man believes
anything,
but a prudent man gives
thought to his steps.

16 A wise man fears the LORD
and shuns evil,
but a fool is hotheaded and
reckless.

17 A quick-tempered man does
foolish things,
and a crafty man is hated.

18 The simple inherit folly,
but the prudent are crowned
with knowledge.

19 Evil men will bow down in
the presence of the good,
and the wicked at the gates
of the righteous.

20 The poor are shunned even by
their neighbors,
but the rich have many
friends.

21 He who despises his neighbor
sins,
but blessed is he who is
kind to the needy.

22 Do not those who plot evil go
astray?
But those who plan what is
good find[y] love and
faithfulness.

23 All hard work brings a profit,
but mere talk leads only to
poverty.

24 The wealth of the wise is their
crown,
but the folly of fools yields
folly.

25 A truthful witness saves lives,

y22 Or *show*

*13 Most mss have the accent *rebia* on the final syllable (תָה–).

°21 ק ענוים

וְיָפִחַ כְּזָבִים מִרְמָה׃ בְּיִרְאַת יְהוָה מִבְטַח־
security-of Yahweh in-fear-of (26) deceitful falsehoods but-he-witnesses

עֹז וּלְבָנָיו יִהְיֶה מַחְסֶה׃ יִרְאַת יְהוָה
Yahweh fear-of (27) refuge he-will-be and-for-children-of-him fortress

מְקוֹר חַיִּים לָסוּר מִמֹּקְשֵׁי מָוֶת׃ בְּרָב־ עָם
population in-largeness-of (28) death from-snares-of to-turn lives fountain-of

הַדְרַת־ מֶלֶךְ וּבְאֶפֶס לְאֹם מְחִתַּת רָזוֹן׃ אֶרֶךְ אַפַּיִם
angers long-of (29) prince ruin-of subject but-in-without king glory-of

רַב־ תְּבוּנָה וּקְצַר־ רוּחַ מֵרִים אִוֶּלֶת׃ חַיֵּי
lives-of (30) folly one-displaying temper but-quick-of understanding great-of

בְשָׂרִים לֵב מַרְפֵּא וּרְקַב עֲצָמוֹת קִנְאָה׃ עֹשֵׁק־ דָּל
poor one-oppressing (31) envy bones but-rot-of peace heart-of bodies

חֵרֵף עֹשֵׂהוּ וּמְכַבְּדוֹ חֹנֵן אֶבְיוֹן׃
needy one-being-kind but-honoring-him One-Making-him he-shows-contempt

בְּרָעָתוֹ יִדָּחֶה רָשָׁע וְחֹסֶה
but-one-having-refuge wicked he-is-brought-down in-calamity-of-him (32)

בְמוֹתוֹ צַדִּיק׃ בְּלֵב נָבוֹן תָּנוּחַ חָכְמָה
wisdom she-reposes one-discerning in-heart-of (33) righteous in-death-of-him

וּבְקֶרֶב כְּסִילִים תִּוָּדֵעַ׃ צְדָקָה תְּרוֹמֵם־
she-exalts righteousness (34) she-lets-herself-be-known fools even-in-among

גּוֹי וְחֶסֶד לְאֻמִּים חַטָּאת׃ רְצוֹן־ מֶלֶךְ לְעֶבֶד מַשְׂכִּיל
being-wise in-servant king delight-of (35) sin peoples but-disgrace-of nation

וְעֶבְרָתוֹ תִּהְיֶה מֵבִישׁ׃ מַעֲנֶה־ רַךְ יָשִׁיב
he-turns-away gentle answer (15:1) one-bringing-shame she-is but-wrath-of-him

חֵמָה וּדְבַר־ עֶצֶב יַעֲלֶה־ אָף׃ לְשׁוֹן חֲכָמִים
wise-ones tongue-of (2) anger he-stirs-up harshness but-word-of wrath

תֵּיטִיב דָּעַת וּפִי כְסִילִים יַבִּיעַ אִוֶּלֶת׃ בְּכָל־
at-every-of (3) folly he-gushes fools but-mouth-of knowledge she-commends

מָקוֹם עֵינֵי יְהוָה צֹפוֹת רָעִים וטוֹבִים*׃ מַרְפֵּא
healing-of (4) and-good-ones wicked-ones ones-watching Yahweh eyes-of place

לָשׁוֹן עֵץ חַיִּים וְסֶלֶף בָּהּ שֶׁבֶר בְּרוּחַ׃ אֱוִיל יִנְאַץ
he-spurns fool (5) to-spirit crushing in-her but-deceit lives tree-of tongue

מוּסַר אָבִיו וְשֹׁמֵר תּוֹכַחַת יַעְרִם׃
he-shows-prudence correction but-one-heeding father-of-him discipline-of

בֵּית צַדִּיק חֹסֶן רָב וּבִתְבוּאַת רָשָׁע
wicked but-in-income-of great treasure righteous house-of (6)

נֶעְכָּרֶת׃ שִׂפְתֵי חֲכָמִים יְזָרוּ דָעַת וְלֵב
but-heart-of knowledge they-spread wise-ones lips-of (7) one-bringing-trouble

but a false witness is
deceitful.

26 He who fears the LORD has a
secure fortress,
and for his children it will
be a refuge.

27 The fear of the LORD is a
fountain of life,
turning a man from the
snares of death.

28 A large population is a king's
glory,
but without subjects a
prince is ruined.

29 A patient man has great
understanding,
but a quick-tempered man
displays folly.

30 A heart at peace gives life to
the body,
but envy rots the bones.

31 He who oppresses the poor
shows contempt for their
Maker,
but whoever is kind to the
needy honors God.

32 When calamity comes, the
wicked are brought down,
but even in death the
righteous have a refuge.

33 Wisdom reposes in the heart
of the discerning
and even among fools she
lets herself be known.[z]

34 Righteousness exalts a nation,
but sin is a disgrace to any
people.

35 A king delights in a wise
servant,
but a shameful servant
incurs his wrath.

15 A gentle answer turns
away wrath,
but a harsh word stirs up
anger.

2 The tongue of the wise
commends knowledge,
but the mouth of the fool
gushes folly.

3 The eyes of the LORD are
everywhere,
keeping watch on the
wicked and the good.

4 The tongue that brings healing
is a tree of life,
but a deceitful tongue
crushes the spirit.

5 A fool spurns his father's
discipline,
but whoever heeds
correction shows
prudence.

6 The house of the righteous
contains great treasure,
but the income of the
wicked brings them
trouble.

7 The lips of the wise spread
knowledge;

z33 Hebrew; Septuagint and Syriac / *but in the heart of fools she is not known*

*3 Most mss have *sheva* under the *vav* (וְט).

כְּסִילִים לֹא־כֵן׃ זֶבַח רְשָׁעִים תּוֹעֲבַת יְהוָה וּתְפִלַּת
but-prayer-of Yahweh detesting-of wicked-ones sacrifice-of (8) so not fools

יְשָׁרִים רְצוֹנוֹ׃ תּוֹעֲבַת יְהוָה דֶּרֶךְ רָשָׁע
wicked way-of Yahweh detesting-of (9) pleasure-of-him upright-ones

וּמְרַדֵּף צְדָקָה יֶאֱהָב׃ מוּסָר רָע לְעֹזֵב
for-one-leaving stern discipline (10) he-loves righteousness but-one-pursuing

אֹרַח שׂוֹנֵא תוֹכַחַת יָמוּת׃ שְׁאוֹל וַאֲבַדּוֹן נֶגֶד יְהוָה
Yahweh before and-Abaddon Sheol (11) he-will-die correction one-hating path

אַף כִּי־לִבּוֹת בְּנֵי־אָדָם׃ לֹא יֶאֱהַב־לֵץ
one-mocking he-loves not (12) man sons-of hearts-of indeed how-much-more

הוֹכֵחַ לוֹ אֶל־חֲכָמִים לֹא יֵלֵךְ׃ לֵב שָׂמֵחַ יֵיטִב
he-cheers happy heart (13) he-will-go not wise-ones to to-him to-correct

פָּנִים וּבְעַצְּבַת־לֵב רוּחַ נְכֵאָה׃ לֵב נָבוֹן יְבַקֶּשׁ־
he-seeks one-discerning heart (14) crushed spirit heart but-in-ache-of faces

דָּעַת וּפְנֵי° כְסִילִים יִרְעֶה אִוֶּלֶת׃ כָּל־יְמֵי עָנִי
oppressed days-of all-of (15) folly he-feeds-on fools but-mouth-of knowledge

רָעִים וְטוֹב־לֵב מִשְׁתֶּה תָמִיד׃ טוֹב־מְעַט
little good (16) continual feast heart but-cheerfulness-of wretched-ones

בְּיִרְאַת יְהוָה מֵאוֹצָר רָב וּמְהוּמָה בוֹ׃ טוֹב
good (17) with-him and-turmoil great more-than-wealth Yahweh with-fear-of

אֲרֻחַת יָרָק וְאַהֲבָה־שָׁם מִשּׁוֹר אָבוּס וְשִׂנְאָה־
and-hatred one-being-fattened more-than-calf there and-love vegetable meal-of

בוֹ׃ אִישׁ חֵמָה יְגָרֶה מָדוֹן וְאֶרֶךְ* אַפַּיִם
angers but-long-of dissension he-stirs-up hot-temper man-of (18) with-him

יַשְׁקִיט רִיב׃ דֶּרֶךְ עָצֵל כִּמְשֻׂכַת חָדֶק וְאֹרַח
but-path-of thorn like-blocking-of sluggard way-of (19) quarrel he-calms

יְשָׁרִים סְלֻלָה׃ בֵּן חָכָם יְשַׂמַּח־אָב וּכְסִיל
but-fool-of father he-brings-joy wise son (20) one-being-highway upright-ones

אָדָם בּוֹזֶה אִמּוֹ׃ אִוֶּלֶת שִׂמְחָה לַחֲסַר־לֵב
judgment to-lacking-of delight folly (21) mother-of-him one-despising man

וְאִישׁ תְּבוּנָה יְיַשֶּׁר־לָכֶת׃ הָפֵר מַחֲשָׁבוֹת
plans he-fails (22) to-go he-keeps-straight understanding but-man-of

בְּאֵין סוֹד וּבְרֹב יוֹעֲצִים תָּקוּם׃ שִׂמְחָה
joy (23) she-succeeds ones-advising but-with-many-of counsel for-lack-of

לָאִישׁ בְּמַעֲנֵה־פִיו וְדָבָר בְּעִתּוֹ מַה־טּוֹב׃
good how! in-time-of-him and-word mouth-of-him with-reply-of to-the-man

אֹרַח חַיִּים לְמַעְלָה לְמַשְׂכִּיל לְמַעַן סוּר מִשְּׁאוֹל
from-Sheol to-keep in-order-to for-one-being-wise to-upward lives path-of (24)

not so the hearts of fools.

8 The LORD detests the sacrifice
of the wicked,
but the prayer of the upright
pleases him.

9 The LORD detests the way of
the wicked
but he loves those who
pursue righteousness.

10 Stern discipline awaits him
who leaves the path;
he who hates correction will
die.

11 Death and Destruction[a] lie
open before the LORD—
how much more the hearts
of men!

12 A mocker resents correction;
he will not consult the wise.

13 A happy heart makes the face
cheerful,
but heartache crushes the
spirit.

14 The discerning heart seeks
knowledge,
but the mouth of a fool
feeds on folly.

15 All the days of the oppressed
are wretched,
but the cheerful heart has a
continual feast.

16 Better a little with the fear of
the LORD
than great wealth with
turmoil.

17 Better a meal of vegetables
where there is love
than a fattened calf with
hatred.

18 A hot-tempered man stirs up
dissension,
but a patient man calms a
quarrel.

19 The way of the sluggard is
blocked with thorns,
but the path of the upright
is a highway.

20 A wise son brings joy to his
father,
but a foolish man despises
his mother.

21 Folly delights a man who lacks
judgment,
but a man of understanding
keeps a straight course.

22 Plans fail for lack of counsel,
but with many advisers they
succeed.

23 A man finds joy in giving an
apt reply—
and how good is a timely
word!

24 The path of life leads upward
for the wise
to keep him from going
down to the grave.[b]

[a] *11* Hebrew *Sheol and Abaddon*
[b] *24* Hebrew *Sheol*

**18* Most mss have *sheva* in the *kaph* (ךְ—).

°*14* ק ופי

מָטָּה׃ בֵּית גֵּאִים יִסַּח ׀ יְהוָה וְיַצֵּב
but-he-keeps-intact Yahweh he-tears-down proud-men house-of (25) downward

גְּבוּל אַלְמָנָה׃ תּוֹעֲבַת יְהוָה מַחְשְׁבוֹת רָע וּטְהֹרִים
but-pure-ones wicked thoughts-of Yahweh detesting-of (26) widow boundary-of

אִמְרֵי־נֹעַם׃ עֹכֵר בֵּיתוֹ בּוֹצֵעַ בָּצַע
greed one-being-greedy family-of-him one-troubling (27) pleasing thoughts-of

וְשׂוֹנֵא מַתָּנֹת יִחְיֶה׃ לֵב צַדִּיק יֶהְגֶּה
he-weighs righteous heart-of (28) he-will-live bribes but-one-hating

לַעֲנוֹת וּפִי רְשָׁעִים יַבִּיעַ רָעוֹת׃ רָחוֹק יְהוָה
Yahweh far (29) evils he-gushes wicked-ones but-mouth-of to-answer

מֵרְשָׁעִים וּתְפִלַּת צַדִּיקִים יִשְׁמָע׃ מְאוֹר־עֵינַיִם
eyes brightness-of (30) he-hears righteous-ones but-prayer-of from-wicked-ones

יְשַׂמַּח־לֵב שְׁמוּעָה טוֹבָה תְּדַשֶּׁן־עָצֶם׃ אֹזֶן שֹׁמַעַת
hearing-of ear (31) bone she-gives-health good news heart he-brings-joy

תּוֹכַחַת חַיִּים בְּקֶרֶב חֲכָמִים תָּלִין׃ פּוֹרֵעַ
one-ignoring (32) she-will-be-at-home wise-ones in-among lives rebuke-of

מוּסָר מוֹאֵס נַפְשׁוֹ וְשׁוֹמֵעַ תּוֹכַחַת קוֹנֶה
gaining correction but-one-heeding self-of-him despising discipline

לֵב׃ יִרְאַת יְהוָה מוּסַר חָכְמָה וְלִפְנֵי כָבוֹד
honor and-before wisdom teaching-of Yahweh fear-of (33) understanding

עֲנָוָה׃ לְאָדָם מַעַרְכֵי־לֵב וּמֵיְהוָה מַעֲנֵה לָשׁוֹן׃
tongue reply-of but-from-Yahweh heart plans-of to-man (16:1) humility

כָּל־דַּרְכֵי־אִישׁ זַךְ בְּעֵינָיו וְתֹכֵן רוּחוֹת
motives but-one-weighing in-eyes-of-him innocent man ways-of all-of (2)

יְהוָה׃ גֹּל אֶל־יְהוָה מַעֲשֶׂיךָ וְיִכֹּנוּ מַחְשְׁבֹתֶיךָ׃
plans-of-you and-they-will-succeed deeds-of-you Yahweh to commit! (3) Yahweh

כֹּל פָּעַל יְהוָה לַמַּעֲנֵהוּ וְגַם־רָשָׁע
wicked and-even for-the-end-of-him Yahweh he-works-out everything (4)

לְיוֹם רָעָה׃ תּוֹעֲבַת יְהוָה כָּל־גְּבַהּ־לֵב יָד
hand heart proud-of all-of Yahweh detesting-of (5) disaster for-day-of

לְיָד לֹא יִנָּקֶה׃ בְּחֶסֶד וֶאֱמֶת
and-faithfulness through-love (6) he-will-go-unpunished not upon-hand

יְכֻפַּר עָוֺן וּבְיִרְאַת יְהוָה סוּר מֵרָע׃
from-evil to-avoid Yahweh and-through-fear-of sin he-is-atoned

בִּרְצוֹת יְהוָה דַּרְכֵי־אִישׁ גַּם־אוֹיְבָיו
ones-being-enemies-of-him even man ways-of Yahweh when-to-please (7)

יַשְׁלִם אִתּוֹ׃ טוֹב־מְעַט בִּצְדָקָה מֵרֹב
more-than-much-of with-righteousness little good (8) with-him he-makes-at-peace

[25]The LORD tears down the proud man's house
but he keeps the widow's boundaries intact.

[26]The LORD detests the thoughts of the wicked,
but those of the pure are pleasing to him.

[27]A greedy man brings trouble to his family,
but he who hates bribes will live.

[28]The heart of the righteous weighs its answers,
but the mouth of the wicked gushes evil.

[29]The LORD is far from the wicked
but he hears the prayer of the righteous.

[30]A cheerful look brings joy to the heart,
and good news gives health to the bones.

[31]He who listens to a life-giving rebuke
will be at home among the wise.

[32]He who ignores discipline despises himself,
but whoever heeds correction gains understanding.

[33]The fear of the LORD teaches a man wisdom,[c]
and humility comes before honor.

16 To man belong the plans of the heart,
but from the LORD comes the reply of the tongue.

[2]All a man's ways seem innocent to him,
but motives are weighed by the LORD.

[3]Commit to the LORD whatever you do,
and your plans will succeed.

[4]The LORD works out everything for his own ends—
even the wicked for a day of disaster.

[5]The LORD detests all the proud of heart.
Be sure of this: They will not go unpunished.

[6]Through love and faithfulness sin is atoned for;
through the fear of the LORD a man avoids evil.

[7]When a man's ways are pleasing to the LORD,
he makes even his enemies live at peace with him.

[8]Better a little with righteousness

[c]33 Or *Wisdom teaches the fear of the LORD*

*31 Most mss have the accent *munah* on the first syllable (אֹ֣).

תְּבוּאוֹת בְּלֹא מִשְׁפָּט׃ לֵב אָדָם יְחַשֵּׁב דַּרְכּוֹ וַיהוָה
but-Yahweh course-of-him he-plans man heart-of (9) justice with-no gains

יָכִין צַעֲדוֹ׃ קֶסֶם ׀ עַל־ שִׂפְתֵי־ מֶלֶךְ בְּמִשְׁפָּט לֹא
not to-justice king lips-of on oracle (10) step-of-him he-determines

יִמְעַל־ פִּיו׃ פֶּלֶס ׀ וּמֹאזְנֵי מִשְׁפָּט לַיהוָה
from-Yahweh honesty and-balances-of scale (11) mouth-of-him he-should-betray

מַעֲשֵׂהוּ כָּל־ אַבְנֵי־ כִיס׃ תּוֹעֲבַת מְלָכִים עֲשׂוֹת רֶשַׁע
wrong to-do kings detesting-of (12) bag weights-of all-of making-of-him

כִּי בִצְדָקָה יִכּוֹן כִּסֵּא׃ רְצוֹן מְלָכִים
kings pleasure-of (13) throne he-is-established through-righteousness for

שִׂפְתֵי־ צֶדֶק וְדֹבֵר יְשָׁרִים יֶאֱהָב׃ חֲמַת־ מֶלֶךְ
king wrath-of (14) he-values truths and-one-speaking honesty lips-of

מַלְאֲכֵי־ מָוֶת וְאִישׁ חָכָם יְכַפְּרֶנָּה׃ בְּאוֹר־
when-to-brighten (15) he-will-appease-her wise but-man death messengers-of

פְּנֵי־ מֶלֶךְ חַיִּים וּרְצוֹנוֹ כְּעָב מַלְקוֹשׁ׃ קְנֹה־
get! (16) spring-rain like-cloud-of and-favor-of-him lives king faces-of

חָכְמָה מַה־ טּוֹב מֵחָרוּץ וּקְנוֹת בִּינָה נִבְחָר
one-being-choice understanding and-to-get more-than-gold good how! wisdom

מִכָּסֶף׃ מְסִלַּת יְשָׁרִים סוּר מֵרָע שֹׁמֵר
guarding from-evil to-avoid upright-ones highway-of (17) more-than-silver

נַפְשׁוֹ נֹצֵר דַּרְכּוֹ׃ לִפְנֵי־ שֶׁבֶר גָּאוֹן וְלִפְנֵי
and-before pride destruction before (18) way-of-him one-guarding soul-of-him

כִשָּׁלוֹן גֹּבַהּ רוּחַ׃ טוֹב שְׁפַל־ רוּחַ אֶת־ עֲנָיִים°
oppressed-ones among spirit lowliness-of good (19) spirit haughtiness-of fall

מֵחַלֵּק שָׁלָל אֶת־ גֵּאִים׃ מַשְׂכִּיל עַל־ דָּבָר
instruction to one-heeding (20) proud-ones with plunder more-than-to-share

יִמְצָא־ טוֹב וּבוֹטֵחַ בַּיהוָה אַשְׁרָיו׃
blessednesses-of-him in-Yahweh and-one-trusting prosperity he-finds

לַחֲכַם־ לֵב יִקָּרֵא נָבוֹן וּמֶתֶק שְׂפָתַיִם
lips and-pleasantness-of one-discerning he-is-called heart to-wise-of (21)

יֹסִיף לֶקַח׃ מְקוֹר חַיִּים שֵׂכֶל בְּעָלָיו
owners-of-him understanding-of lives fountain-of (22) instruction he-promotes

וּמוּסַר אֱוִלִים אִוֶּלֶת׃ לֵב חָכָם יַשְׂכִּיל פִּיהוּ
mouth-of-him he-guides wise-man heart-of (23) folly fools but-punishment-of

וְעַל־ שְׂפָתָיו יֹסִיף לֶקַח׃ צוּף־ דְּבַשׁ אִמְרֵי־
words-of honey honeycomb-of (24) instruction he-promotes lips-of-him and-on

נֹעַם מָתוֹק לַנֶּפֶשׁ וּמַרְפֵּא לָעָצֶם׃ יֵשׁ דֶּרֶךְ
way there-is (25) to-the-bone and-healing to-the-soul sweet pleasantness

than much gain with
injustice.

9 In his heart a man plans his
course,
but the LORD determines his
steps.

10 The lips of a king speak as an
oracle,
and his mouth should not
betray justice.

11 Honest scales and balances are
from the LORD;
all the weights in the bag
are of his making.

12 Kings detest wrongdoing,
for a throne is established
through righteousness.

13 Kings take pleasure in honest
lips;
they value a man who
speaks the truth.

14 A king's wrath is a messenger
of death,
but a wise man will appease
it.

15 When a king's face brightens,
it means life;
his favor is like a rain cloud
in spring.

16 How much better to get
wisdom than gold,
to choose understanding
rather than silver!

17 The highway of the upright
avoids evil;
he who guards his way
guards his soul.

18 Pride goes before destruction,
a haughty spirit before a
fall.

19 Better to be lowly in spirit and
among the oppressed
than to share plunder with
the proud.

20 Whoever gives heed to
instruction prospers,
and blessed is he who trusts
in the LORD.

21 The wise in heart are called
discerning,
and pleasant words promote
instruction.[d]

22 Understanding is a fountain of
life to those who have it,
but folly brings punishment
to fools.

23 A wise man's heart guides his
mouth,
and his lips promote
instruction.[e]

24 Pleasant words are a
honeycomb,
sweet to the soul and
healing to the bones.

25 There is a way that seems

[d] 21 Or *words make a man persuasive*
[e] 23 Or *mouth / and makes his lips persuasive*

°19 ק ענוים

יָשָׁר לִפְנֵי־ אִישׁ וְאַחֲרִיתָהּ דַּרְכֵי־ מָוֶת׃ נֶפֶשׁ עָמֵל

laborer appetite-of (26) death ways-of but-end-of-her man before right

עָמְלָה לּוֹ כִּי־ אָכַף עָלָיו פִּיהוּ׃ אִישׁ בְּלִיַּעַל

scoundrel man (27) hunger-of-him to-him she-drives indeed for-him she-works

כֹּרֶה רָעָה וְעַל־ שְׂפָתָיו כְּאֵשׁ צָרָבֶת׃ אִישׁ

man-of (28) scorching like-fire lip-of-him and-on evil one-plotting

תַּהְפֻּכוֹת יְשַׁלַּח מָדוֹן וְנִרְגָּן מַפְרִיד אַלּוּף׃

friend separating and-one-gossiping dissension he-stirs-up perversities

אִישׁ חָמָס יְפַתֶּה רֵעֵהוּ וְהוֹלִיכוֹ בְּדֶרֶךְ

down-path and-he-leads-him neighbor-of-him he-entices violence man-of (29)

לֹא־ טוֹב׃ עֹצֶה עֵינָיו לַחְשֹׁב תַּהְפֻּכוֹת קֹרֵץ

one-pursing perversities to-plot eyes-of-him one-winking (30) good not

שְׂפָתָיו כִּלָּה רָעָה׃ עֲטֶרֶת תִּפְאֶרֶת שֵׂיבָה בְּדֶרֶךְ

by-life-of gray-hair splendor crown-of (31) evil he-is-bent-on lips-of-him

צְדָקָה תִּמָּצֵא׃ טוֹב אֶרֶךְ אַפַּיִם מִגִּבּוֹר

more-than-warrior angers long-of good (32) she-is-attained righteousness

וּמֹשֵׁל בְּרוּחוֹ מִלֹּכֵד עִיר׃ בַּחֵיק

into-the-lap (33) city more-than-one-taking over-temper-of-him and-one-controlling

יוּטַל אֶת־ הַגּוֹרָל וּמֵיְהוָה כָּל־ מִשְׁפָּטוֹ׃ טוֹב

good (17:1) decision-of-him every-of but-from-Yahweh the-lot *** he-is-cast

פַּת חֲרֵבָה וְשַׁלְוָה־ בָהּ מִבַּיִת מָלֵא זִבְחֵי־ רִיב׃

strife sacrifices-of full more-than-house with-her and-quiet dry crust

עֶבֶד־ מַשְׂכִּיל יִמְשֹׁל בְּבֵן מֵבִישׁ

one-bringing-disgrace over-son he-will-rule one-being-wise servant (2)

וּבְתוֹךְ אַחִים יַחֲלֹק נַחֲלָה׃ מַצְרֵף לַכֶּסֶף

for-the-silver crucible (3) inheritance he-will-share brothers and-in-among

וְכוּר לַזָּהָב וּבֹחֵן לִבּוֹת יְהוָה׃ מֵרַע

man-being-wicked (4) Yahweh hearts but-testing for-the-gold and-furnace

מַקְשִׁיב עַל־ שְׂפַת־ אָוֶן שֶׁקֶר מֵזִין עַל־ לְשׁוֹן הַוֹּת׃

malices tongue-of to paying-attention liar evil lip-of to listening

לֹעֵג לָרָשׁ חֵרֵף עֹשֵׂהוּ

One-Making-him he-shows-contempt to-the-one-being-poor one-mocking (5)

שָׂמֵחַ לְאֵיד לֹא יִנָּקֶה׃ עֲטֶרֶת זְקֵנִים

aged-ones crown-of (6) he-will-go-unpunished not over-disaster gloater

בְּנֵי בָנִים וְתִפְאֶרֶת בָּנִים אֲבוֹתָם׃ לֹא־ נָאוָה

suitable not (7) parents-of-them children and-pride-of children children-of

לְנָבָל שְׂפַת־ יֶתֶר אַף כִּי־ לְנָדִיב שְׂפַת־שָׁקֶר׃ אֶבֶן־

stone-of (8) lie lip-of to-ruler indeed how-much-more arrogance lip-of to-fool

°27 ק שפתו

right to a man
but in the end it leads to death.

26 The laborer's appetite works for him;
his hunger drives him on.

27 A scoundrel plots evil,
and his speech is like a scorching fire.

28 A perverse man stirs up dissension,
and a gossip separates close friends.

29 A violent man entices his neighbor
and leads him down a path that is not good.

30 He who winks with his eye is plotting perversity;
he who purses his lips is bent on evil.

31 Gray hair is a crown of splendor;
it is attained by a righteous life.

32 Better a patient man than a warrior,
a man who controls his temper than one who takes a city.

33 The lot is cast into the lap,
but its every decision is from the LORD.

17 Better a dry crust with peace and quiet
than a house full of feasting,[f] with strife.

2 A wise servant will rule over a disgraceful son,
and will share the inheritance as one of the brothers.

3 The crucible for silver and the furnace for gold,
but the LORD tests the heart.

4 A wicked man listens to evil lips;
a liar pays attention to a malicious tongue.

5 He who mocks the poor shows contempt for their Maker;
whoever gloats over disaster will not go unpunished.

6 Children's children are a crown to the aged,
and parents are the pride of their children.

7 Arrogant[g] lips are unsuited to a fool—
how much worse lying lips to a ruler!

f1 Hebrew *sacrifices*
g7 Or *Eloquent*

חֵן הַשֹּׁחַד בְּעֵינֵי בְעָלָיו אֶל־כָּל־אֲשֶׁר יִפְנֶה
he-turns that everywhere to givers-of-him in-eyes-of the-bribe charm

יַשְׂכִּיל׃ (9) מְכַסֶּה־פֶּשַׁע מְבַקֵּשׁ אַהֲבָה וְשֹׁנֶה
but-one-repeating love promoting offense one-covering (9) he-succeeds

בְדָבָר מַפְרִיד אַלּוּף׃ (10) תֵּחַת גְּעָרָה בְמֵבִין
to-man-discerning rebuke she-impresses (10) friend separating about-matter

מֵהַכּוֹת כְּסִיל מֵאָה׃ (11) אַךְ־מְרִי יְבַקֶּשׁ־רָע
evil-man he-is-bent-on rebellion only (11) hundred fool more-than-to-lash

וּמַלְאָךְ אַכְזָרִי יְשֻׁלַּח־בּוֹ׃ (12) פָּגוֹשׁ דֹּב שַׁכּוּל
one-robbed bear to-meet (12) to-him he-will-be-sent merciless and-official

בְּאִישׁ וְאַל־כְּסִיל בְּאִוַּלְתּוֹ׃ (13) מֵשִׁיב רָעָה תַּחַת טוֹבָה
good for evil one-paying-back (13) in-folly-of-him fool and-not of-cub

לֹא־תָמִישׁ° רָעָה מִבֵּיתוֹ׃ (14) פּוֹטֵר מַיִם רֵאשִׁית
start-of waters breaching-of (14) from-house-of-him evil she-will-leave not

מָדוֹן וְלִפְנֵי הִתְגַּלַּע הָרִיב נְטוֹשׁ׃ (15) מַצְדִּיק רָשָׁע
guilty one-acquitting (15) drop! the-dispute he-breaks-out so-before quarrel

וּמַרְשִׁיעַ צַדִּיק תּוֹעֲבַת יְהוָה גַּם־שְׁנֵיהֶם׃
both-of-them indeed Yahweh detesting-of innocent and-one-condemning

(16) לָמָּה־זֶּה מְחִיר בְּיַד־כְּסִיל לִקְנוֹת חָכְמָה וְלֶב־אָיִן׃
nothing since-desire-of wisdom to-get fool in-hand-of money this what? (16)

(17) בְּכָל־עֵת אֹהֵב הָרֵעַ וְאָח לְצָרָה יִוָּלֵד׃
he-is-born for-adversity and-brother the-friend loving time at-all-of (17)

(18) אָדָם חֲסַר־לֵב תּוֹקֵעַ כָּף עֹרֵב
one-putting-up-security hand one-striking judgment lacking-of man (18)

עֲרֻבָּה לִפְנֵי רֵעֵהוּ׃ (19) אֹהֵב פֶּשַׁע אֹהֵב מַצָּה מַגְבִּיהַּ
one-making-high quarrel one-loving sin loving (19) neighbor-of-him for security

פִּתְחוֹ מְבַקֶּשׁ־שָׁבֶר׃ (20) עִקֶּשׁ־לֵב לֹא יִמְצָא־
he-finds not heart perverse-of (20) destruction inviting gate-of-him

טוֹב וְנֶהְפָּךְ בִּלְשׁוֹנוֹ יִפּוֹל בְּרָעָה׃
into-trouble he-falls in-tongue-of-him and-one-being-deceitful prosperity

(21) יֹלֵד כְּסִיל לְתוּגָה לוֹ וְלֹא־יִשְׂמַח אֲבִי נָבָל׃
fool father-of he-has-joy and-not of-him to-grief fool one-bearing (21)

(22) לֵב שָׂמֵחַ יֵיטִב גֵּהָה וְרוּחַ נְכֵאָה תְּיַבֶּשׁ־
she-dries-up crushed but-spirit medicine he-makes-good cheerful heart (22)

גָּרֶם׃ (23) שֹׁחַד מֵחֵיק רָשָׁע יִקָּח לְהַטּוֹת אָרְחוֹת מִשְׁפָּט׃
justice courses-of to-pervert he-accepts wicked-man in-secret bribe (23) bone

(24) אֶת־פְּנֵי מֵבִין חָכְמָה וְעֵינֵי כְסִיל בִּקְצֵה־אָרֶץ׃
earth to-end-of fool but-eyes-of wisdom one-discerning faces-of *** (24)

8 A bribe is a charm to the one who gives it;
wherever he turns, he succeeds.

9 He who covers over an offense promotes love,
but whoever repeats the matter separates close friends.

10 A rebuke impresses a man of discernment
more than a hundred lashes a fool.

11 An evil man is bent only on rebellion;
a merciless official will be sent against him.

12 Better to meet a bear robbed of her cubs
than a fool in his folly.

13 If a man pays back evil for good,
evil will never leave his house.

14 Starting a quarrel is like breaching a dam;
so drop the matter before a dispute breaks out.

15 Acquitting the guilty and condemning the innocent—
the LORD detests them both.

16 Of what use is money in the hand of a fool,
since he has no desire to get wisdom?

17 A friend loves at all times,
and a brother is born for adversity.

18 A man lacking in judgment strikes hands in pledge
and puts up security for his neighbor.

19 He who loves a quarrel loves sin;
he who builds a high gate invites destruction.

20 A man of perverse heart does not prosper;
he whose tongue is deceitful falls into trouble.

21 To have a fool for a son brings grief;
there is no joy for the father of a fool.

22 A cheerful heart is good medicine,
but a crushed spirit dries up the bones.

23 A wicked man accepts a bribe in secret
to pervert the course of justice.

24 A discerning man keeps wisdom in view,
but a fool's eyes wander to the ends of the earth.

°13 ק תמוש

כַּעַס לְאָבִיו בֵּן כְּסִיל וּמֶמֶר לְיוֹלַדְתּוֹ׃
to-one-bearing-him and-bitterness foolish son to-father-of-him grief (25)

גַּם עֲנוֹשׁ לַצַּדִּיק לֹא־טוֹב לְהַכּוֹת נְדִיבִים עַל־יֹשֶׁר׃
integrity for officials to-flog good not to-the-innocent to-punish also (26)

חוֹשֵׂךְ אֲמָרָיו יוֹדֵעַ דָּעַת וְקַר°־רוּחַ
temper and-even-of knowledge man-knowing words-of-him one-restraining (27)

אִישׁ תְּבוּנָה׃ גַּם אֱוִיל מַחֲרִישׁ חָכָם יֵחָשֵׁב
he-is-thought wise one-keeping-silent fool even (28) understanding man-of

אֹטֵם שְׂפָתָיו נָבוֹן׃ לְתַאֲוָה יְבַקֵּשׁ
he-pursues to-selfishness (18:1) one-discerning lips-of-him one-holding

נִפְרָד בְּכָל־תּוּשִׁיָּה יִתְגַּלָּע׃ לֹא־
not (2) he-defies sound-judgment against-all-of man-being-unfriendly

יַחְפֹּץ כְּסִיל בִּתְבוּנָה כִּי אִם־בְּהִתְגַּלּוֹת לִבּוֹ׃
opinion-of-him in-to-air rather but in-understanding fool he-finds-pleasure

בְּבוֹא־רָשָׁע בָּא גַם־בּוּז וְעִם־קָלוֹן חֶרְפָּה׃
disgrace shame and-with contempt also he-comes wickedness when-to-come (3)

מַיִם עֲמֻקִּים דִּבְרֵי פִי־אִישׁ נַחַל נֹבֵעַ מְקוֹר
fountain-of one-bubbling brook man mouth-of words-of deep-ones waters (4)

חָכְמָה׃ שְׂאֵת פְּנֵי־רָשָׁע לֹא־טוֹב לְהַטּוֹת צַדִּיק
innocent to-deprive good not wicked faces-of to-be-partial (5) wisdom

בַּמִּשְׁפָּט׃ שִׂפְתֵי כְסִיל יָבֹאוּ בְרִיב וּפִיו
and-mouth-of-him into-strife they-come fool lips-of (6) of-the-justice

לְמַהֲלֻמוֹת יִקְרָא׃ פִּי־כְסִיל מְחִתָּה־לוֹ וּשְׂפָתָיו
and-lips-of-him of-him undoing fool mouth-of (7) he-invites to-beatings

מוֹקֵשׁ נַפְשׁוֹ׃ דִּבְרֵי נִרְגָּן כְּמִתְלַהֲמִים
like-morsels-being-choice one-gossiping words-of (8) soul-of-him snare-of

וְהֵם יָרְדוּ חַדְרֵי־בָטֶן׃ גַּם מִתְרַפֶּה
one-being-slack also (9) inmost-part chambers-of they-go-down and-they

בִּמְלַאכְתּוֹ אָח הוּא לְבַעַל מַשְׁחִית׃ מִגְדַּל־עֹז
strength tower-of (10) destruction to-master-of he brother in-work-of-him

שֵׁם יְהוָה בּוֹ־יָרוּץ צַדִּיק וְנִשְׂגָּב׃ הוֹן
wealth-of (11) and-he-is-safe righteous he-runs to-him Yahweh name-of

עָשִׁיר קִרְיַת עֻזּוֹ וּכְחוֹמָה נִשְׂגָּבָה
one-being-unscalable and-like-wall fortification-of-him city-of rich

בְּמַשְׂכִּיתוֹ׃ לִפְנֵי־שֶׁבֶר יִגְבַּהּ לֵב־אִישׁ
man heart-of he-is-proud downfall before (12) in-imagination-of-him

וְלִפְנֵי כָבוֹד עֲנָוָה׃ מֵשִׁיב דָּבָר בְּטֶרֶם יִשְׁמַע אִוֶּלֶת
folly he-listens at-before answer one-giving (13) humility honor but-before

°27 ק יקר

25 A foolish son brings grief to his father
and bitterness to the one who bore him.

26 It is not good to punish an innocent man,
or to flog officials for their integrity.

27 A man of knowledge uses words with restraint,
and a man of understanding is even-tempered.

28 Even a fool is thought wise if he keeps silent,
and discerning if he holds his tongue.

18 An unfriendly man pursues selfish ends;
he defies all sound judgment.

2 A fool finds no pleasure in understanding
but delights in airing his own opinions.

3 When wickedness comes, so does contempt,
and with shame comes disgrace.

4 The words of a man's mouth are deep waters,
but the fountain of wisdom is a bubbling brook.

5 It is not good to be partial to the wicked
or to deprive the innocent of justice.

6 A fool's lips bring him strife,
and his mouth invites a beating.

7 A fool's mouth is his undoing,
and his lips are a snare to his soul.

8 The words of a gossip are like choice morsels;
they go down to a man's inmost parts.

9 One who is slack in his work
is brother to one who destroys.

10 The name of the LORD is a strong tower;
the righteous run to it and are safe.

11 The wealth of the rich is their fortified city;
they imagine it an unscalable wall.

12 Before his downfall a man's heart is proud,
but humility comes before honor.

13 He who answers before listening—

הִיא־ לוֹ וּכְלִמָּה׃ (14) רוּחַ־ אִישׁ יְכַלְכֵּל מַחֲלֵהוּ
that to-him and-shame (14) spirit-of man he-sustains sickness-of-him

וְרוּחַ נְכֵאָה מִי יִשָּׂאֶנָּה׃ (15) לֵב נָבוֹן
but-spirit crushed who? he-can-bear-her (15) heart-of one-discerning

יִקְנֶה־ דָּעַת וְאֹזֶן חֲכָמִים תְּבַקֶּשׁ־ דָּעַת׃
he-acquires knowledge and-ear-of wise-ones she-seeks-out knowledge

(16) מַתָּן אָדָם יַרְחִיב לוֹ וְלִפְנֵי גְדֹלִים
(16) gift-of man he-opens-way for-him and-into-presences-of great-ones

יַנְחֶנּוּ׃ (17) צַדִּיק הָרִאשׁוֹן בְּרִיבוֹ יָבֹא°־
he-ushers-him (17) right the-first with-case-of-him until-he-comes

רֵעֵהוּ וַחֲקָרוֹ׃ (18) מִדְיָנִים יַשְׁבִּית הַגּוֹרָל
another-of-him and-he-questions-him (18) disputes he-settles the-lot

וּבֵין עֲצוּמִים יַפְרִיד׃ (19) אָח נִפְשָׁע
and-between strong-ones he-keeps-apart (19) brother one-being-offended

מִקִּרְיַת־ עֹז וּמִדְוָנִים° כִּבְרִיחַ אַרְמוֹן׃
more-than-city-of fortification and-disputes like-bar-of citadel

(20) מִפְּרִי פִי־ אִישׁ תִּשְׂבַּע בִּטְנוֹ תְּבוּאַת
(20) from-fruit-of mouth-of man he-is-filled stomach-of-him harvest-of

שְׂפָתָיו יִשְׂבָּע׃ (21) מָוֶת וְחַיִּים בְּיַד־ לָשׁוֹן
lips-of-him he-is-satisfied (21) death and-lives in-power-of tongue

וְאֹהֲבֶיהָ יֹאכַל פִּרְיָהּ׃ (22) מָצָא אִשָּׁה מָצָא
and-ones-loving-her he-will-eat fruit-of-her (22) he-finds wife he-finds

טוֹב וַיָּפֶק רָצוֹן מֵיְהוָה׃ (23) תַּחֲנוּנִים יְדַבֶּר־
good and-he-receives favor from-Yahweh (23) pleas-for-mercy he-speaks

רָשׁ וְעָשִׁיר יַעֲנֶה עַזּוֹת׃ (24) אִישׁ רֵעִים
man-being-poor but-rich he-answers harsh-things (24) man-of companions

לְהִתְרֹעֵעַ וְיֵשׁ אֹהֵב דָּבֵק מֵאָח׃
to-be-ruined but-there-is one-being-friend he-sticks-close more-than-brother

(19:1) טוֹב־ רָשׁ הוֹלֵךְ בְּתֻמּוֹ
(19:1) good one-being-poor one-walking in-blamelessness-of-him

מֵעִקֵּשׁ שְׂפָתָיו וְהוּא כְסִיל׃ (2) גַּם בְּלֹא־ דַעַת
more-than-one-perverse-of lips-of-him and-he fool (2) also with-no knowledge

נֶפֶשׁ לֹא־ טוֹב וְאָץ בְּרַגְלַיִם חוֹטֵא׃ (3) אִוֶּלֶת אָדָם
zeal not good or-one-being-hasty with-feet one-missing-way (3) folly-of man

תְּסַלֵּף דַּרְכּוֹ וְעַל־ יְהוָה יִזְעַף לִבּוֹ׃ (4) הוֹן
she-ruins life-of-him yet-against Yahweh he-rages heart-of-him (4) wealth

יֹסִיף רֵעִים רַבִּים וְדָל מֵרֵעהוּ* יִפָּרֵד׃
he-brings friends many but-poor-man by-friend-of-him he-is-deserted

that is his folly and his
shame.

14 A man's spirit sustains him in
sickness,
but a crushed spirit who can
bear?

15 The heart of the discerning
acquires knowledge;
the ears of the wise seek it
out.

16 A gift opens the way for the
giver
and ushers him into the
presence of the great.

17 The first to present his case
seems right,
till another comes forward
and questions him.

18 Casting the lot settles disputes
and keeps strong opponents
apart.

19 An offended brother is more
unyielding than a
fortified city,
and disputes are like the
barred gates of a citadel.

20 From the fruit of his mouth a
man's stomach is filled;
with the harvest from his
lips he is satisfied.

21 The tongue has the power of
life and death,
and those who love it will
eat its fruit.

22 He who finds a wife finds
what is good
and receives favor from the
LORD.

23 A poor man pleads for mercy,
but a rich man answers
harshly.

24 A man of many companions
may come to ruin,
but there is a friend who
sticks closer than a
brother.

19 Better a poor man whose
walk is blameless
than a fool whose lips are
perverse.

2 It is not good to have zeal
without knowledge,
nor to be hasty and miss the
way.

3 A man's own folly ruins his
life,
yet his heart rages against
the LORD.

4 Wealth brings many friends,
but a poor man's friend
deserts him.

*4 Most mss have *sheva* under the *mem* and *tsere* under the *ayin* (מְרֵעֵהוּ).

°17 ק ובא

°19 ק מדינים

עֵד שְׁקָרִים לֹא יִנָּקֶה וְיָפִיחַ כְּזָבִים
lies and-he-pours-out he-will-go-unpunished not falsehoods witness-of (5)

לֹא יִמָּלֵט׃ רַבִּים יְחַלּוּ פְנֵי־נָדִיב וְכָל־
and-all-of ruler faces-of they-curry-favor many (6) he-will-go-free not

הָרֵעַ לְאִישׁ מַתָּן׃ כֹּל אֲחֵי־רָשׁ ׀ שְׂנֵאֻהוּ
they-shun-him man-being-poor relatives-of all-of (7) gift to-man-of the-friend

אַף כִּי מְרֵעֵהוּ רָחֲקוּ מִמֶּנּוּ מְרַדֵּף אֲמָרִים
pleas one-pursuing from-him they-avoid friend-of-him indeed how-much-more

°לֹא־הֵמָּה׃ קֹנֶה־לֵּב אֹהֵב נַפְשׁוֹ שֹׁמֵר תְּבוּנָה
understanding one-cherishing soul-of-him loving wisdom one-getting (8) they not

לִמְצֹא־טוֹב׃ עֵד שְׁקָרִים לֹא יִנָּקֶה
he-will-go-unpunished not falsehoods witness-of (9) prosperity to-find

וְיָפִיחַ כְּזָבִים יֹאבֵד׃ לֹא־נָאוֶה לִכְסִיל תַּעֲנוּג
luxury for-fool fitting not (10) he-will-perish lies and-he-pours-out

אַף כִּי־לְעֶבֶד ׀ מְשֹׁל בְּשָׂרִים׃ שֵׂכֶל אָדָם
man wisdom-of (11) over-princes to-rule for-slave indeed how-much-worse

הֶאֱרִיךְ אַפּוֹ* וְתִפְאַרְתּוֹ עֲבֹר עַל־פָּשַׁע׃
offense by to-overlook and-glory-of-him anger-of-him he-makes-long

נַהַם כַּכְּפִיר זַעַף מֶלֶךְ וּכְטַל עַל־עֵשֶׂב רְצוֹנוֹ׃
favor-of-him grass on but-like-dew king rage-of like-the-lion roar (12)

הַוֺּת לְאָבִיו בֵּן כְּסִיל וְדֶלֶף טֹרֵד
being-constant and-dripping foolish son to-father-of-him ruins (13)

מִדְיְנֵי אִשָּׁה׃ בַּיִת וָהוֹן נַחֲלַת אָבוֹת וּמֵיְהוָה
but-from-Yahweh parents inheritance-of and-wealth house (14) wife quarrels-of

אִשָּׁה מַשְׂכָּלֶת׃ עַצְלָה תַּפִּיל תַּרְדֵּמָה וְנֶפֶשׁ
but-self-of deep-sleep she-brings-on laziness (15) one-being-prudent wife

רְמִיָּה תִרְעָב׃ שֹׁמֵר מִצְוָה שֹׁמֵר נַפְשׁוֹ
soul-of-him guarding instruction one-obeying (16) she-goes-hungry shiftless-man

בּוֹזֵה דְרָכָיו °יוּמָת׃ מַלְוֵה יְהוָה
Yahweh one-lending-of (17) he-will-die ways-of-him one-being-contemptuous-of

חוֹנֵן דָּל וּגְמֻלוֹ יְשַׁלֶּם־לוֹ׃ יַסֵּר
discipline! (18) to-him he-will-reward and-deed-of-him poor one-being-kind

בִּנְךָ כִּי־יֵשׁ תִּקְוָה וְאֶל־הֲמִיתוֹ אַל־תִּשָּׂא נַפְשֶׁךָ׃
will-of-you you-give not to-kill-him and-in hope there-is for son-of-you

°גְּרָל־חֵמָה נֹשֵׂא עֹנֶשׁ כִּי אִם־תַּצִּיל וְעוֹד
then-again you-rescue if indeed penalty one-paying temper great-of (19)

תּוֹסִף׃ שְׁמַע עֵצָה וְקַבֵּל מוּסָר לְמַעַן
so-that instruction and-accept! advice listen! (20) you-must-do-again

[5] A false witness will not go unpunished,
and he who pours out lies will not go free.

[6] Many curry favor with a ruler,
and everyone is the friend of a man who gives gifts.

[7] A poor man is shunned by all his relatives—
how much more do his friends avoid him!
Though he pursues them with pleading,
they are nowhere to be found.[h]

[8] He who gets wisdom loves his own soul;
he who cherishes understanding prospers.

[9] A false witness will not go unpunished,
and he who pours out lies will perish.

[10] It is not fitting for a fool to live in luxury—
how much worse for a slave to rule over princes!

[11] A man's wisdom gives him patience;
it is to his glory to overlook an offense.

[12] A king's rage is like the roar of a lion,
but his favor is like dew on the grass.

[13] A foolish son is his father's ruin,
and a quarrelsome wife is like a constant dripping.

[14] Houses and wealth are inherited from parents,
but a prudent wife is from the LORD.

[15] Laziness brings on deep sleep,
and the shiftless man goes hungry.

[16] He who obeys instructions guards his soul,
but he who is contemptuous of his ways will die.

[17] He who is kind to the poor lends to the LORD,
and he will reward him for what he has done.

[18] Discipline your son, for in that there is hope;
do not be a willing party to his death.

[19] A hot-tempered man must pay the penalty;
if you rescue him, you will have to do it again.

[20] Listen to advice and accept instruction,

[h]7 The meaning of the Hebrew for this sentence is uncertain.

*11 Most mss have *sheva* under the *pe* (פְּ—).

°7 ק לו
°16 ק ימות
°19 ק גדל

תֶּחְכַּם בְּאַחֲרִיתֶךָ׃ רַבּוֹת מַחֲשָׁבוֹת בְּלֶב־ אִישׁ וַעֲצַת
but-purpose-of man in-heart-of plans many (21) in-end-of-you you-will-be-wise

יְהוָה הִיא תָקוּם׃ תַּאֲוַת אָדָם חַסְדּוֹ וְטוֹב־
and-good unfailing-love-of-him man desire-of (22) she-prevails she Yahweh

רָשׁ מֵאִישׁ כָּזָב׃ יִרְאַת יְהוָה לְחַיִּים וְשָׂבֵעַ
then-content to-lives Yahweh fear-of (23) lie more-than-man-of being-poor

יָלִין בַּל־ יִפָּקֶד רָע׃ טָמַן עָצֵל יָדוֹ
hand-of-him sluggard he-buries (24) trouble he-is-touched not he-rests

בַּצַּלָּחַת גַּם־ אֶל־ פִּיהוּ לֹא יְשִׁיבֶנָּה׃ לֵץ
one-mocking (25) he-will-bring-back-her not mouth-of-him to even in-the-dish

תַּכֶּה וּפֶתִי יַעְרִם וְהוֹכִיחַ לְנָבוֹן
to-one-discerning and-rebuke! he-will-learn-prudence and-simple you-flog

יָבִין דָּעַת׃ מְשַׁדֶּד־ אָב יַבְרִיחַ אֵם בֵּן
son mother he-drives-out father one-robbing (26) knowledge he-will-gain

מֵבִישׁ וּמַחְפִּיר׃ חֲדַל־* בְּנִי לִשְׁמֹעַ
to-listen son-of-me stop! (27) and-bringing-disgrace bringing-shame

מוּסָר לִשְׁגּוֹת† מֵאִמְרֵי־ דָעַת׃ עֵד בְּלִיַּעַל
corruptness witness-of (28) knowledge from-words-of to-stray instruction

יָלִיץ מִשְׁפָּט וּפִי רְשָׁעִים יְבַלַּע־ אָוֶן׃
evil he-gulps-down wicked-ones and-mouth-of justice he-mocks

נָכוֹנוּ לַלֵּצִים שְׁפָטִים וּמַהֲלֻמוֹת לְגֵו
for-back-of and-beatings penalties for-the-ones-mocking they-are-prepared (29)

כְּסִילִים׃ לֵץ הַיַּיִן†† הֹמֶה שֵׁכָר וְכָל־
and-every-of beer one-brawling the-wine one-mocking (20:1) fools

שֹׁגֶה בּוֹ לֹא יֶחְכָּם׃ נַהַם כַּכְּפִיר אֵימַת
wrath-of like-the-lion roar (2) he-is-wise not by-him one-being-led-astray

מֶלֶךְ מִתְעַבְּרוֹ חוֹטֵא נַפְשׁוֹ׃ כָּבוֹד לָאִישׁ שֶׁבֶת
avoidance to-man honor (3) life-of-him forfeiting one-angering-him king

מֵרִיב וְכָל־ אֱוִיל יִתְגַּלָּע׃ מֵחֹרֶף עָצֵל לֹא־ יַחֲרֹשׁ
he-plows not sluggard in-season (4) he-quarrels fool but-every-of from-strife

יִשְׁאַל° בַּקָּצִיר וָאָיִן׃ מַיִם עֲמֻקִּים עֵצָה
purpose deep-ones waters (5) but-nothing at-the-harvest so-he-looks

בְלֶב־ אִישׁ וְאִישׁ תְּבוּנָה יִדְלֶנָּה׃ רָב־ אָדָם
man many-of (6) he-draws-out-her understanding but-man-of man of-heart-of

יִקְרָא אִישׁ חַסְדּוֹ וְאִישׁ אֱמוּנִים מִי
who? faithfulnesses but-man-of unfailing-love-of-him man-of he-claims

יִמְצָא׃ מִתְהַלֵּךְ בְּתֻמּוֹ צַדִּיק אַשְׁרֵי
blessednesses-of righteous in-blamelessness-of-him one-walking (7) he-can-find

and in the end you will be wise.

21 Many are the plans in a man's heart,
but it is the LORD's purpose that prevails.

22 What a man desires is unfailing love[i];
better to be poor than a liar.

23 The fear of the LORD leads to life:
Then one rests content, untouched by trouble.

24 The sluggard buries his hand in the dish;
he will not even bring it back to his mouth!

25 Flog a mocker, and the simple will learn prudence;
rebuke a discerning man, and he will gain knowledge.

26 He who robs his father and drives out his mother
is a son who brings shame and disgrace.

27 Stop listening to instruction, my son,
and you will stray from the words of knowledge.

28 A corrupt witness mocks at justice,
and the mouth of the wicked gulps down evil.

29 Penalties are prepared for mockers,
and beatings for the backs of fools.

20 Wine is a mocker and beer a brawler;
whoever is led astray by them is not wise.

2 A king's wrath is like the roar of a lion;
he who angers him forfeits his life.

3 It is to a man's honor to avoid strife,
but every fool is quick to quarrel.

4 A sluggard does not plow in season;
so at harvest time he looks but finds nothing.

5 The purposes of a man's heart are deep waters,
but a man of understanding draws them out.

6 Many a man claims to have unfailing love,
but a faithful man who can find?

7 The righteous man leads a blameless life;

i22 Or *A man's greed is his shame*

*27 Most mss have *hateph pathah* under the *beth* (חֲ).

†27 Most mss have *dagesh* in the *gimel* (גּ—).

††1 Most mss have *hireq* under the second *yod* (יִן—).

°4 ק ושאל

בָּנָיו אַחֲרָיו׃ מֶלֶךְ יוֹשֵׁב עַל־ כִּסֵּא־ דִין
judgment throne-of on sitting king (8) after-him children-of-him

מְזָרֶה בְעֵינָיו כָּל־ רָע׃ מִי־ יֹאמַר
he-can-say who? (9) evil all-of with-eyes-of-him one-winnowing-out

זִכִּיתִי לִבִּי טָהַרְתִּי מֵחַטָּאתִי׃ אֶבֶן וָאֶבֶן
and-weight weight (10) without-sin-of-me I-am-clean heart-of-me I-kept-pure

אֵיפָה וְאֵיפָה תּוֹעֲבַת יְהוָה גַּם־ שְׁנֵיהֶם׃ גַּם
even (11) both-of-them indeed Yahweh detesting-of and-measure measure

בְּמַעֲלָלָיו יִתְנַכֶּר־ נָעַר אִם־ זַךְ וְאִם־ יָשָׁר
right and-whether pure whether child he-is-known by-actions-of-him

פָּעֳלוֹ׃ אֹזֶן שֹׁמַעַת וְעַיִן רֹאָה יְהוָה עָשָׂה גַם־
indeed he-made Yahweh seeing and-eye hearing ear (12) conduct-of-him

שְׁנֵיהֶם׃ אַל־ תֶּאֱהַב שֵׁנָה פֶּן־ תִּוָּרֵשׁ פְּקַח
keep-open! you-will-grow-poor or sleep you-love not (13) both-of-them

עֵינֶיךָ שְׂבַע־ לָחֶם׃ רַע רַע יֹאמַר הַקּוֹנֶה
the-one-buying he-says no-good no-good (14) food have-spare! eyes-of-you

וְאֹזֵל לוֹ אָז יִתְהַלָּל׃ יֵשׁ זָהָב וְרָב־ פְּנִינִים
rubies and-abundance-of gold there-is (15) he-boasts then to-him then-going

וּכְלִי יְקָר שִׂפְתֵי־ דָעַת׃ לְקַח־ בִּגְדוֹ כִּי־
when garment-of-him take! (16) knowledge lips-of rarity but-jewel-of

עָרַב זָר וּבְעַד נָכְרִים חַבְלֵהוּ׃
hold-in-pledge-him! wayward-woman and-for one-being-stranger he-puts-up-security

עָרֵב לָאִישׁ לֶחֶם שָׁקֶר וְאַחַר יִמָּלֵא־ פִיהוּ
mouth-of-him he-is-full but-afterward fraud food-of to-man sweet (17)

חָצָץ׃ מַחֲשָׁבוֹת בְּעֵצָה תִכּוֹן וּבְתַחְבֻּלוֹת עֲשֵׂה מִלְחָמָה׃
war wage! and-by-guidances you-make by-advice plans (18) gravel

גּוֹלֶה־ סּוֹד הוֹלֵךְ רָכִיל וּלְפֹתֶה שְׂפָתָיו
lips-of-him so-with-one-opening gossip one-spreading confidence betraying (19)

לֹא תִתְעָרָב׃ מְקַלֵּל אָבִיו וְאִמּוֹ
or-mother-of-him father-of-him one-cursing (20) you-share not

יִדְעַךְ נֵרוֹ בֶּאֱשׁוּן חֹשֶׁךְ׃ נַחֲלָה
inheritance (21) darkness in-deepest-of lamp-of-him he-will-be-snuffed-out

מְבֻחֶלֶת בָּרִאשֹׁנָה וְאַחֲרִיתָהּ לֹא תְבֹרָךְ׃
she-will-be-blessed not and-end-of-her at-the-beginning being-quickly-gained

אַל־ תֹּאמַר אֲשַׁלְּמָה־ רָע קַוֵּה לַיהוָה וְיֹשַׁע
and-he-will-deliver for-Yahweh wait! wrong I-will-pay-back you-say not (22)

לָךְ׃ תּוֹעֲבַת יְהוָה אֶבֶן וָאֶבֶן וּמֹאזְנֵי מִרְמָה
dishonesty and-scales-of and-weight weight Yahweh detesting-of (23) to-you

blessed are his children after him.

8 When a king sits on his throne to judge,
he winnows out all evil with his eyes.

9 Who can say, "I have kept my heart pure;
I am clean and without sin"?

10 Differing weights and differing measures—
the LORD detests them both.

11 Even a child is known by his actions,
by whether his conduct is pure and right.

12 Ears that hear and eyes that see—
the LORD has made them both.

13 Do not love sleep or you will grow poor;
stay awake and you will have food to spare.

14 "It's no good, it's no good!" says the buyer;
then off he goes and boasts about his purchase.

15 Gold there is, and rubies in abundance,
but lips that speak knowledge are a rare jewel.

16 Take the garment of one who puts up security for a stranger;
hold it in pledge if he does it for a wayward woman.

17 Food gained by fraud tastes sweet to a man,
but he ends up with a mouth full of gravel.

18 Make plans by seeking advice;
if you wage war, obtain guidance.

19 A gossip betrays a confidence;
so avoid a man who talks too much.

20 If a man curses his father or mother,
his lamp will be snuffed out in pitch darkness.

21 An inheritance quickly gained at the beginning
will not be blessed at the end.

22 Do not say, "I'll pay you back for this wrong!"
Wait for the LORD, and he will deliver you.

23 The LORD detests differing weights,
and dishonest scales do not

°16 ק נכריה
°20 ק באשון
°21 ק מבהלת

לֹא־טֽוֹב׃ מֵיְהוָה מִצְעֲדֵי־גָבֶר וְאָדָם מַה־יָּבִין
can-he-understand how? and-anyone man steps-of from-Yahweh (24) pleasing not

דַּרְכּֽוֹ׃ מוֹקֵשׁ אָדָם יָלַע קֹדֶשׁ וְאַחַר נְדָרִים
vows and-later dedication he-makes-rash man trap-of (25) way-of-him

לְבַקֵּֽר׃ מְזָרֶה רְשָׁעִים מֶלֶךְ חָכָם וַיָּשֶׁב
and-he-drives wise king wicked-ones one-winnowing-out (26) to-consider

עֲלֵיהֶם אוֹפָֽן׃ נֵר יְהוָה נִשְׁמַת אָדָם חֹפֵשׂ
one-searching man spirit-of Yahweh lamp-of (27) threshing-wheel over-them

כָּל־חַדְרֵי־בָֽטֶן׃ חֶסֶד וֶאֱמֶת יִצְּרוּ־מֶלֶךְ
king they-keep-safe and-faithfulness love (28) inmost-being parts-of all-of

וְסָעַד בַּחֶסֶד כִּסְאֽוֹ׃ תִּפְאֶרֶת
glory-of (29) throne-of-him through-the-love and-he-is-made-secure

בַּחוּרִים כֹּחָם וַהֲדַר זְקֵנִים שֵׂיבָֽה׃
gray-hair old-men and-splendor-of strength-of-them the-young-men

חַבֻּרוֹת פֶּצַע תַּמְרִיק בְּרָע וּמַכּוֹת חַדְרֵי־בָֽטֶן׃
inmost-being parts-of and-beatings of-evil cleansing wound blows-of (30)

פַּלְגֵי־מַיִם לֶב־מֶלֶךְ בְּיַד־יְהוָה עַל־כָּל־אֲשֶׁר
that everywhere to Yahweh in-hand-of king heart-of waters courses-of (21:1)

יַחְפֹּץ יַטֶּֽנּוּ׃ כָּל־דֶּרֶךְ־אִישׁ יָשָׁר בְּעֵינָיו
in-eyes-of-him right man way-of every-of (2) he-directs-him he-pleases

וְתֹכֵן לִבּוֹת יְהוָֽה׃ עֲשֹׂה צְדָקָה וּמִשְׁפָּט נִבְחָר
being-acceptable and-justice right to-do (3) Yahweh hearts but-one-weighing

לַיהוָה מִזָּֽבַח׃ רוּם־עֵינַיִם וּרְחַב־לֵב
heart and-pride-of eyes haughtiness-of (4) more-than-sacrifice to-Yahweh

נֵר רְשָׁעִים חַטָּֽאת׃ מַחְשְׁבוֹת חָרוּץ אַךְ־לְמוֹתָר וְכָל־
and-all-of to-profit surely diligent plans-of (5) sin wicked-ones lamp-of

אָץ אַךְ־לְמַחְסֽוֹר׃ פֹּעַל אֹצָרוֹת בִּלְשׁוֹן שָׁקֶר
lie by-tongue-of fortunes making-of (6) to-poverty surely one-hastening

הֶבֶל נִדָּף מְבַקְשֵׁי־מָֽוֶת׃ שֹׁד־רְשָׁעִים
wicked-ones violence-of (7) death ones-seeking-of one-fleeting vapor

יְגוֹרֵם כִּי מֵאֲנוּ לַעֲשׂוֹת מִשְׁפָּֽט׃ הֲפַכְפַּךְ דֶּרֶךְ אִישׁ
man way-of devious (8) right to-do they-refuse for he-will-drag-away-them

וָזָר וְזַךְ יָשָׁר פָּעֳלֽוֹ׃ טוֹב לָשֶׁבֶת עַל־פִּנַּת־
corner-of on to-live good (9) conduct-of-him upright but-innocent guilty

גָּג מֵאֵשֶׁת מִדְיָנִים וּבֵית חָֽבֶר׃ נֶפֶשׁ רָשָׁע
wicked self-of (10) sharing and-house-of quarrels more-than-wife-of roof

אִוְּתָה־רָע לֹא־יֻחַן בְּעֵינָיו רֵעֵֽהוּ׃
neighbor-of-him in-eyes-of-him he-gets-mercy not evil she-craves

please him.

24 A man's steps are directed by
the LORD.
How then can anyone
understand his own way?

25 It is a trap for a man to
dedicate something rashly
and only later to consider
his vows.

26 A wise king winnows out the
wicked;
he drives the threshing
wheel over them.

27 The lamp of the LORD searches
the spirit of a man[j];
it searches out his inmost
being.

28 Love and faithfulness keep a
king safe;
through love his throne is
made secure.

29 The glory of young men is
their strength,
gray hair the splendor of the
old.

30 Blows and wounds cleanse
away evil,
and beatings purge the
inmost being.

21 The king's heart is in the
hand of the LORD;
he directs it like a
watercourse wherever he
pleases.

2 All a man's ways seem right to
him,
but the LORD weighs the
heart.

3 To do what is right and just
is more acceptable to the
LORD than sacrifice.

4 Haughty eyes and a proud
heart,
the lamp of the wicked, are
sin!

5 The plans of the diligent lead
to profit
as surely as haste leads to
poverty.

6 A fortune made by a lying
tongue
is a fleeting vapor and a
deadly snare.[k]

7 The violence of the wicked
will drag them away,
for they refuse to do what is
right.

8 The way of the guilty is
devious,
but the conduct of the
innocent is upright.

9 Better to live on a corner of
the roof
than share a house with a
quarrelsome wife.

10 The wicked man craves evil;
his neighbor gets no mercy
from him.

j27 Or *The spirit of man is the LORD's lamp*
k6 Some Hebrew manuscripts, Septuagint and Vulgate; most Hebrew manuscripts *vapor for those who seek death*

°30 ק תמרוק

(11) בַּעְנָשׁ־ לֵץ יֶחְכַּם־ פֶּתִי וּבְהַשְׂכִּיל
and-when-to-instruct simple he-gains-wisdom one-mocking when-to-punish (11)

לְחָכָם יִקַּח־ דָּעַת׃ (12) מַשְׂכִּיל צַדִּיק לְבֵית
of-house-of Righteous-One one-taking-note (12) knowledge he-gets to-wise

רָשָׁע מְסַלֵּף רְשָׁעִים לָרָע׃ (13) אֹטֵם אָזְנוֹ
ear-of-him one-shutting (13) to-ruin wicked-ones one-bringing wicked

מִזַּעֲקַת־ דָּל גַּם־ הוּא יִקְרָא וְלֹא יֵעָנֶה׃ (14) מַתָּן
gift (14) he-will-be-answered and-not he-will-cry-out he also poor to-cry-of

בַּסֵּתֶר יִכְפֶּה־ אָף וְשֹׁחַד בַּחֵק חֵמָה עַזָּה׃ (15) שִׂמְחָה
joy (15) great wrath in-the-cloak and-bribe anger he-soothes in-the-secret

לַצַּדִּיק עֲשׂוֹת מִשְׁפָּט וּמְחִתָּה לְפֹעֲלֵי אָוֶן׃ (16) אָדָם
man (16) evil to-ones-doing-of but-terror justice to-do to-the-righteous

תּוֹעֶה מִדֶּרֶךְ הַשְׂכֵּל בִּקְהַל רְפָאִים יָנוּחַ׃
he-rests dead-ones in-company-of to-understand from-path-of one-straying

(17) אִישׁ מַחְסוֹר אֹהֵב שִׂמְחָה אֹהֵב יַיִן־ וָשֶׁמֶן לֹא
never and-oil wine one-loving pleasure one-loving poverty man-of (17)

יַעֲשִׁיר׃ (18) כֹּפֶר לַצַּדִּיק רָשָׁע וְתַחַת יְשָׁרִים
upright-ones and-for wicked for-the-righteous ransom (18) he-will-be-rich

בּוֹגֵד׃ (19) טוֹב שֶׁבֶת בְּאֶרֶץ־ מִדְבָּר מֵאֵשֶׁת
more-than-wife-of desert in-land-of to-live good (19) one-being-unfaithful

מִדְוָנִים וָכָעַס׃ (20) אוֹצָר | נֶחְמָד וָשֶׁמֶן בִּנְוֵה חָכָם
wise in-house-of and-oil one-being-choice store (20) and-ill-temper quarrels

וּכְסִיל אָדָם יְבַלְּעֶנּוּ׃ (21) רֹדֵף צְדָקָה וָחֶסֶד יִמְצָא
he-finds and-love righteousness one-pursuing (21) he-devours-him man but-fool

חַיִּים צְדָקָה וְכָבוֹד׃ (22) עִיר גִּבֹּרִים עָלָה חָכָם
wise he-attacks mighty-ones city-of (22) and-honor righteousness lives

וַיֹּרֶד עֹז מִבְטֶחָה׃ (23) שֹׁמֵר פִּיו
mouth-of-him one-guarding (23) trust stronghold-of and-he-pulls-down

וּלְשׁוֹנוֹ שֹׁמֵר מִצָּרוֹת נַפְשׁוֹ׃ (24) זֵד
proud (24) self-of-him from-calamities one-keeping and-tongue-of-him

יָהִיר לֵץ שְׁמוֹ עוֹשֶׂה בְּעֶבְרַת זָדוֹן׃
pride with-excess-of one-behaving name-of-him one-mocking arrogant

(25) תַּאֲוַת עָצֵל תְּמִיתֶנּוּ כִּי־ מֵאֲנוּ יָדָיו
hands-of-him they-refuse because she-will-kill-him sluggard craving-of (25)

לַעֲשׂוֹת׃ (26) כָּל־ הַיּוֹם הִתְאַוָּה תַאֲוָה וְצַדִּיק יִתֵּן וְלֹא
and-not he-gives but-righteous craving he-craves the-day all-of (26) to-work

יַחְשֹׂךְ׃ (27) זֶבַח רְשָׁעִים תּוֹעֵבָה אַף כִּי־
when how-much-more detestable wicked-ones sacrifice-of (27) he-spares

[11]When a mocker is punished,
the simple gain wisdom;
when a wise man is
instructed, he gets
knowledge.

[12]The Righteous One[l] takes note
of the house of the
wicked
and brings the wicked to
ruin.

[13]If a man shuts his ears to the
cry of the poor,
he too will cry out and not
be answered.

[14]A gift given in secret soothes
anger,
and a bribe concealed in the
cloak pacifies great wrath.

[15]When justice is done, it brings
joy to the righteous
but terror to evildoers.

[16]A man who strays from the
path of understanding
comes to rest in the
company of the dead.

[17]He who loves pleasure will
become poor;
whoever loves wine and oil
will never be rich.

[18]The wicked become a ransom
for the righteous,
and the unfaithful for the
upright.

[19]Better to live in a desert
than with a quarrelsome
and ill-tempered wife.

[20]In the house of the wise are
stores of choice food and
oil,
but a foolish man devours
all he has.

[21]He who pursues righteousness
and love
finds life, prosperity[m] and
honor.

[22]A wise man attacks the city of
the mighty
and pulls down the
stronghold in which they
trust.

[23]He who guards his mouth and
his tongue
keeps himself from calamity.

[24]The proud and arrogant
man—"Mocker" is his
name;
he behaves with
overweening pride.

[25]The sluggard's craving will be
the death of him,
because his hands refuse to
work.

[26]All day long he craves for
more,
but the righteous give
without sparing.

[27]The sacrifice of the wicked is
detestable—
how much more so when

[l]12 Or *The righteous man*
[m]21 Or *righteousness*

***11 Most mss have *bateph pathah* under the *ayin* (בַּֽעֲ).**

°19 ק מדינים

בְּזִמָּה יְבִיאֶנּוּ׃ עֵד־ כְּזָבִים יֹאבֵד
he-will-perish falsehoods witness-of (28) he-brings-him with-evil-intent

וְאִישׁ שׁוֹמֵעַ לָנֶצַח יְדַבֵּר׃ הֵעֵז אִישׁ רָשָׁע
wicked man he-makes-bold (29) he-will-speak to-forever listening and-man

בְּפָנָיו וְיָשָׁר הוּא ׀ יָכִין דַּרְכָּיו׃ אֵין
there-is-no (30) way-of-him he-gives-thought he but-upright with-fronts-of-him

חָכְמָה וְאֵין תְּבוּנָה וְאֵין עֵצָה לְנֶגֶד יְהוָה׃
Yahweh at-against plan and-there-is-no insight and-there-is-no wisdom

סוּס מוּכָן לְיוֹם מִלְחָמָה וְלַיהוָה הַתְּשׁוּעָה׃
the-victory but-with-Yahweh battle for-day-of being-made-ready horse (31)

נִבְחָר שֵׁם מֵעֹשֶׁר רָב מִכֶּסֶף
more-than-silver great more-than-richness name one-being-desirable (22:1)

וּמִזָּהָב חֵן טוֹב׃ עָשִׁיר וָרָשׁ נִפְגָּשׁוּ
they-have-in-common and-one-being-poor rich (2) good esteem and-more-than-gold

עֹשֵׂה כֻלָּם יְהוָה׃ עָרוּם ׀ רָאָה רָעָה וְיִסְתָּר
and-he-takes-refuge danger he-sees prudent (3) Yahweh all-of-them One-Making-of

וּפְתָיִים עָבְרוּ וְנֶעֱנָשׁוּ׃ עֵקֶב עֲנָוָה יִרְאַת
and-fear-of humility result-of (4) and-they-suffer they-go-on but-simple-ones

יְהוָה עֹשֶׁר וְכָבוֹד וְחַיִּים׃ צִנִּים פַּחִים בְּדֶרֶךְ עִקֵּשׁ
wicked in-path-of snares thorns (5) and-lives and-honor wealth Yahweh

שׁוֹמֵר נַפְשׁוֹ יִרְחַק מֵהֶם׃ חֲנֹךְ לַנַּעַר עַל־
in to-the-child train! (6) from-them he-stays-far soul-of-him one-guarding

פִּי דַרְכּוֹ גַּם כִּי־ יַזְקִין לֹא־ יָסוּר מִמֶּנָּה׃ עָשִׁיר
rich (7) from-him he-will-turn not he-is-old when and way-of-him according-to

בְּרָשִׁים יִמְשׁוֹל וְעֶבֶד לֹוֶה לְאִישׁ מַלְוֶה׃
one-lending of-man one-borrowing and-servant he-rules over-ones-being-poor

זוֹרֵעַ עַוְלָה יִקְצוֹר־ אָוֶן וְשֵׁבֶט עֶבְרָתוֹ
fury-of-him and-rod-of trouble he-reaps wickedness one-sowing (8)

יִכְלֶה׃ טוֹב־ עַיִן הוּא יְבֹרָךְ כִּי־ נָתַן
he-shares for he-will-be-blessed he eye generous-of (9) he-will-be-destroyed

מִלַּחְמוֹ לַדָּל׃ גָּרֵשׁ לֵץ וְיֵצֵא
and-he-goes-out one-mocking drive-out! (10) with-the-poor from-food-of-him

מָדוֹן וְיִשְׁבֹּת דִּין וְקָלוֹן׃ אֹהֵב טְהָור־ לֵב
heart purity-of one-loving (11) and-insult quarrel and-he-ends strife

חֵן שְׂפָתָיו רֵעֵהוּ מֶלֶךְ׃ עֵינֵי יְהוָה נָצְרוּ
they-watch-over Yahweh eyes-of (12) king friend-of-him speeches-of-him grace-of

דַּעַת וַיְסַלֵּף דִּבְרֵי בֹגֵד׃ אָמַר
he-says (13) one-being-unfaithful words-of but-he-frustrates knowledge

brought with evil intent!

[28]A false witness will perish,
and whoever listens to him
will be destroyed forever.[n]

[29]A wicked man puts up a bold
front,
but an upright man gives
thought to his ways.

[30]There is no wisdom, no
insight, no plan
that can succeed against the
LORD.

[31]The horse is made ready for
the day of battle,
but victory rests with the
LORD.

22 A good name is more
desirable than great
riches;
to be esteemed is better than
silver or gold.

[2]Rich and poor have this in
common:
The LORD is the Maker of
them all.

[3]A prudent man sees danger
and takes refuge,
but the simple keep going
and suffer for it.

[4]Humility and the fear of the
LORD
bring wealth and honor and
life.

[5]In the paths of the wicked lie
thorns and snares,
but he who guards his soul
stays far from them.

[6]Train a child in the way he
should go,
and when he is old he will
not turn from it.

[7]The rich rule over the poor,
and the borrower is servant
to the lender.

[8]He who sows wickedness
reaps trouble,
and the rod of his fury will
be destroyed.

[9]A generous man will himself
be blessed,
for he shares his food with
the poor.

[10]Drive out the mocker, and out
goes strife;
quarrels and insults are
ended.

[11]He who loves a pure heart and
whose speech is gracious
will have the king for his
friend.

[12]The eyes of the LORD keep
watch over knowledge,
but he frustrates the words
of the unfaithful.

[n]28 Or / *but the words of an obedient man will live on*

[o]29a ק יבין
[o]29b ק דרכו
[o]3 ק ונסתר
[o]8 ק יקצר
[o]11 ק טהר

עָצֵל אֲרִי בַחוּץ בְּתוֹךְ רְחֹבוֹת אֵרָצֵחַ׃ שׁוּחָה

pit (14) I-will-be-murdered streets in-midst-of at-the-outside lion sluggard

עֲמֻקָּה פִּי זָרוֹת זְעוּם יְהוָה

Yahweh one-being-under-wrath-of ones-being-adulteresses mouth-of deep

יִפָּול־שָׁם׃ אִוֶּלֶת קְשׁוּרָה בְלֶב־נָעַר שֵׁבֶט מוּסָר

discipline rod-of child in-heart-of being-bound folly (15) there he-will-fall

יַרְחִיקֶנָּה מִמֶּנּוּ׃ עֹשֵׁק דָּל לְהַרְבּוֹת לוֹ

for-him to-increase poor one-oppressing (16) from-him he-will-drive-far-her

נֹתֵן לְעָשִׁיר אַךְ־לְמַחְסוֹר׃ הַט אָזְנְךָ וּשְׁמַע

and-listen! ear-of-you pay-attention! (17) to-poverty both to-rich one-giving

דִּבְרֵי חֲכָמִים וְלִבְּךָ תָּשִׁית לְדַעְתִּי׃ כִּי־

for (18) to-teaching-of-me you-apply and-heart-of-you wise-ones sayings-of

נָעִים כִּי־תִשְׁמְרֵם בְּבִטְנֶךָ יִכֹּנוּ יַחְדָּו עַל־

on all they-are-ready in-heart-of-you you-keep-them when pleasing

שְׂפָתֶיךָ׃ לִהְיוֹת בַּיהוָה מִבְטַחֶךָ הוֹדַעְתִּיךָ הַיּוֹם אַף־אָתָּה׃

you even the-day I-teach-you trust-of-you in-Yahweh to-be (19) lips-of-you

הֲלֹא כָתַבְתִּי לְךָ שָׁלִשׁוֹם בְּמֹעֵצוֹת וָדָעַת׃ לְהוֹדִיעֲךָ

to-teach-you (21) and-knowledge of-counsels thirty to-you I-wrote not? (20)

קֹשְׁטְ אִמְרֵי אֱמֶת לְהָשִׁיב אֲמָרִים אֱמֶת לְשֹׁלְחֶיךָ׃ אַל־

not (22) to-ones-sending-you sound answers to-give reliability words-of truth

תִּגְזָל־דָּל כִּי דַל־הוּא וְאַל־תְּדַכֵּא עָנִי בַשָּׁעַר׃

in-the-court needy you-crush and-not he poor because poor you-exploit

כִּי־יְהוָה יָרִיב רִיבָם וְקָבַע אֶת־

*** and-he-will-plunder case-of-them he-will-take-case Yahweh for (23)

קֹבְעֵיהֶם נָפֶשׁ׃ אַל־תִּתְרַע אֶת־בַּעַל אָף וְאֶת־

and-with hot-temper man-of *** you-befriend not (24) life ones-plundering-them

אִישׁ חֵמוֹת לֹא תָבוֹא׃ פֶּן־תֶּאֱלַף אֹרְחֹתָו

ways-of-him you-may-learn or (25) you-associate not angers man-of

וְלָקַחְתָּ מוֹקֵשׁ לְנַפְשֶׁךָ׃ אַל־תְּהִי בְתֹקְעֵי־

among-ones-striking-of you-be not (26) for-self-of-you snare and-you-may-get

כָף בַּעֹרְבִים מַשָּׁאוֹת׃ אִם־אֵין־לְךָ לְשַׁלֵּם

to-pay to-you not if (27) debts among-the-ones-putting-up-security hand

לָמָּה יִקַּח מִשְׁכָּבְךָ מִתַּחְתֶּיךָ׃ אַל־תַּסֵּג

you-move not (28) from-under-you bed-of-you will-he-snatch why?

גְּבוּל עוֹלָם אֲשֶׁר עָשׂוּ אֲבוֹתֶיךָ׃ חָזִיתָ

you-see (29) forefathers-of-you they-set-up that ancient boundary-stone-of

אִישׁ ׀ מָהִיר בִּמְלַאכְתּוֹ לִפְנֵי־מְלָכִים יִתְיַצָּב בַּל־יִתְיַצֵּב

he-will-serve not he-will-serve kings before in-work-of-him skilled man

---

13 The sluggard says, "There is a lion outside!"
or, "I will be murdered in the streets!"

14 The mouth of an adulteress is a deep pit;
he who is under the LORD's wrath will fall into it.

15 Folly is bound up in the heart of a child,
but the rod of discipline will drive it far from him.

16 He who oppresses the poor to increase his wealth
and he who gives gifts to the rich—both come to poverty.

Sayings of the Wise

17 Pay attention and listen to the sayings of the wise;
apply your heart to what I teach,
18 for it is pleasing when you keep them in your heart
and have all of them ready on your lips.
19 So that your trust may be in the LORD,
I teach you today, even you.
20 Have I not written thirty° sayings for you,
sayings of counsel and knowledge,
21 teaching you true and reliable words,
so that you can give sound answers
to him who sent you?

22 Do not exploit the poor because they are poor
and do not crush the needy in court,
23 for the LORD will take up their case
and will plunder those who plunder them.

24 Do not make friends with a hot-tempered man,
do not associate with one easily angered,
25 or you may learn his ways
and get yourself ensnared.

26 Do not be a man who strikes hands in pledge
or puts up security for debts;
27 if you lack the means to pay,
your very bed will be snatched from under you.

28 Do not move an ancient boundary stone
set up by your forefathers.

29 Do you see a man skilled in his work?
He will serve before kings;
he will not serve before

°20 Or *not formerly written;* or *not written excellent*

°15 ק יפל
°20 ק שלישים
°25 ק ארחתיו

לִפְנֵי חֲשֻׁכִּים׃ כִּי־ תֵשֵׁב לִלְחוֹם אֶת־ מוֹשֵׁל בִּין
to-note one-ruling with to-dine you-sit when (23:1) men-being-obscure before

תָּבִין אֶת־ אֲשֶׁר לְפָנֶיךָ׃ וְשַׂמְתָּ שַׂכִּין בְּלֹעֶךָ אִם־
if to-throat-of-you knife and-you-put (2) before-you what *** you-note

בַּעַל נֶפֶשׁ אָתָּה׃ אַל־ תִּתְאָו לְמַטְעַמּוֹתָיו וְהוּא לֶחֶם
food-of for-that to-delicacies-of-him you-crave not (3) you gluttony man-of

כְּזָבִים׃ אַל־ תִּיגַע לְהַעֲשִׁיר מִבִּינָתְךָ
in-wisdom-of-you to-get-rich you-wear-yourself-out not (4) deceits

חֲדָל׃ הֲתָעוּף עֵינֶיךָ בּוֹ וְאֵינֶנּוּ כִּי עָשֹׂה
to-sprout for and-not-he at-him eyes-of-you you-cast? (5) show-restraint!

יַעֲשֶׂה־ לּוֹ כְנָפַיִם כְּנֶשֶׁר וְעָיף הַשָּׁמָיִם׃ אַל־
not (6) the-skies he-will-fly like-eagle wings for-him he-will-sprout

תִּלְחַם אֶת־ לֶחֶם רַע עָיִן וְאַל־ תִּתְאָו לְמַטְעַמֹּתָיו׃
to-delicacies-of-him you-crave and-not eye stingy-of food-of *** you-eat

כִּי ׀ כְּמוֹ־ שָׁעַר בְּנַפְשׁוֹ כֶּן־ הוּא אֱכֹל וּשְׁתֵה יֹאמַר
he-says and-drink! eat! he so about-cost-of-him he-thinks like for (7)

לָךְ וְלִבּוֹ בַּל־ עִמָּךְ׃ פִּתְּךָ־ אָכַלְתָּ
you-ate little-of-you (8) with-you not but-heart-of-him to-you

תְקִיאֶנָּה וְשִׁחַתָּ דְּבָרֶיךָ הַנְּעִימִים׃
the-good-ones words-of-you and-you-will-waste you-will-vomit-up-her

בְּאָזְנֵי כְסִיל אַל־ תְּדַבֵּר כִּי־ יָבוּז לְשֵׂכֶל מִלֶּיךָ׃
words-of-you to-wisdom-of he-will-scorn for you-speak not fool in-ears-of (9)

אַל־ תַּסֵּג גְּבוּל עוֹלָם וּבִשְׂדֵי יְתוֹמִים
fatherless-ones or-into-fields-of ancient boundary-stone-of you-move not (10)

אַל־ תָּבֹא׃ כִּי־ גֹאֲלָם חָזָק הוּא־ יָרִיב
he-will-take-up-case he strong One-Defending-them for (11) you-encroach not

אֶת־ רִיבָם אִתָּךְ׃ הָבִיאָה לַמּוּסָר לִבֶּךָ
heart-of-you to-the-instruction apply! (12) against-you case-of-them ***

וְאָזְנֶךָ לְאִמְרֵי־ דָעַת׃ אַל־ תִּמְנַע מִנַּעַר
from-child you-withhold not (13) knowledge to-words-of and-ear-of-you

מוּסָר כִּי־ תַכֶּנּוּ בַשֵּׁבֶט לֹא יָמוּת׃ אַתָּה
you (14) he-will-die not with-the-rod you-punish-him if discipline

בַּשֵּׁבֶט תַּכֶּנּוּ וְנַפְשׁוֹ מִשְּׁאוֹל תַּצִּיל׃ בְּנִי
son-of-me (15) you-save from-Sheol and-soul-of-him you-punish-him with-the-rod

אִם־ חָכַם לִבֶּךָ יִשְׂמַח לִבִּי גַם־ אָנִי׃
I also heart-of-me he-will-be-glad heart-of-you he-is-wise if

וְתַעְלֹזְנָה כִלְיוֹתָי בְּדַבֵּר שְׂפָתֶיךָ
lips-of-you when-to-speak inmost-beings-of-me and-they-will-rejoice (16)

obscure men.

23 When you sit to dine
with a ruler,
note well what[p] is before
you,
2 and put a knife to your throat
if you are given to gluttony.
3 Do not crave his delicacies,
for that food is deceptive.

4 Do not wear yourself out to get
rich;
have the wisdom to show
restraint.
5 Cast but a glance at riches,
and they are gone,
for they will surely sprout
wings
and fly off to the sky like an
eagle.

6 Do not eat the food of a stingy
man,
do not crave his delicacies;
7 for he is the kind of man
who is always thinking
about the cost.[q]
"Eat and drink," he says to
you,
but his heart is not with
you.
8 You will vomit up the little
you have eaten
and will have wasted your
compliments.

9 Do not speak to a fool,
for he will scorn the wisdom
of your words.

10 Do not move an ancient
boundary stone
or encroach on the fields of
the fatherless,
11 for their Defender is strong;
he will take up their case
against you.

12 Apply your heart to instruction
and your ears to words of
knowledge.

13 Do not withhold discipline
from a child;
if you punish him with the
rod, he will not die.
14 Punish him with the rod
and save his soul from
death.[r]

15 My son, if your heart is wise,
then my heart will be glad;
16 my inmost being will rejoice
when your lips speak what

p1 Or *who*
q7 Or *for as he thinks within himself, / so he is;* or *for as he puts on a feast, / so he is*
r14 Hebrew *Sheol*

°3 ק תתאיו
°5a ק התעיף
°5b ק יעוף
°6 ק תתאיו

מֵישָׁרִים׃ (17) אַל־ יְקַנֵּא לִבְּךָ בַּחַטָּאִים כִּי אִם־

rather but to-the-sinners heart-of-you let-him-envy not (17) right-things

בְּיִרְאַת־ יְהוָה כָּל־ הַיּוֹם׃ (18) כִּי אִם־ יֵשׁ אַחֲרִית

future-hope there-is surely indeed (18) the-day all-of Yahweh for-fear-of

וְתִקְוָתְךָ לֹא תִכָּרֵת׃ (19) שְׁמַע־ אַתָּה בְנִי

son-of-me you listen! (19) she-will-be-cut-off not and-hope-of-you

וַחֲכָם וְאַשֵּׁר בַּדֶּרֶךְ לִבֶּךָ׃ (20) אַל־ תְּהִי

you-be not (20) heart-of-you to-the-path and-keep-right! and-be-wise!

בְסֹבְאֵי־ יָיִן בְּזֹלְלֵי בָשָׂר לָמוֹ׃

for-them meat among-ones-gorging-of wine among-ones-drinking-too-much-of

כִּי־ סֹבֵא וְזוֹלֵל יִוָּרֵשׁ וּקְרָעִים

and-rags he-will-become-poor and-one-being-glutton one-being-drunkard for (21)

תַּלְבִּישׁ נוּמָה׃ (22) שְׁמַע לְאָבִיךָ זֶה יְלָדֶךָ

he-gave-life-you who to-father-of-you listen! (22) drowsiness she-clothes

וְאַל־ תָּבוּז כִּי־ זָקְנָה אִמֶּךָ׃ (23) אֱמֶת קְנֵה וְאַל־

and-not buy! truth (23) mother-of-you she-is-old when you-despise and-not

תִּמְכֹּר חָכְמָה וּמוּסָר וּבִינָה׃ (24) °גּוֹל °יָגוֹל

he-has-joy to-have-joy (24) and-understanding and-discipline wisdom you-sell

אֲבִי צַדִּיק °יוֹלֵד חָכָם °וישמח־ בּוֹ׃

in-him he-delights wise-man and-one-fathering righteous-man father-of

יִשְׂמַח־ אָבִיךָ וְאִמֶּךָ וְתָגֵל

and-may-she-rejoice and-mother-of-you father-of-you may-he-be-glad (25)

יוֹלַדְתֶּךָ׃ (26) תְּנָה־ בְנִי לִבְּךָ לִי וְעֵינֶיךָ

and-eyes-of-you to-me heart-of-you son-of-me give! (26) one-bearing-you

דְּרָכַי °תִּרְצֹנָה׃ (27) כִּי־ שׁוּחָה עֲמֻקָּה זוֹנָה וּבְאֵר

and-well one-being-prostitute deep pit for (27) let-them-keep ways-of-me

צָרָה נָכְרִיָּה׃ (28) אַף־ הִיא כְּחֶתֶף תֶּאֱרֹב

she-lies-in-wait like-bandit she also (28) wayward-wife narrow

וּבוֹגְדִים בְּאָדָם תּוֹסִף׃ (29) לְמִי אוֹי

woe to-whom? (29) she-multiplies among-men and-ones-being-unfaithful

לְמִי אֲבוֹי לְמִי °מִדְוָנִים | לְמִי שִׂיחַ לְמִי פְּצָעִים חִנָּם

needless bruises to-whom? complaint to-whom? strifes to-whom? sorrow to-whom?

לְמִי חַכְלִלוּת עֵינָיִם׃ (30) לַמְאַחֲרִים עַל־ הַיָּיִן

the-wine over to-the-ones-lingering (30) eyes bloodshot-of to-whom?

לַבָּאִים לַחְקֹר מִמְסָךְ׃ (31) אַל־ תֵּרֶא יַיִן כִּי יִתְאַדָּם

he-is-red when wine you-gaze not (31) mixed-wine to-sample to-the-ones-going

כִּי־ יִתֵּן °בַּכִּיס עֵינוֹ יִתְהַלֵּךְ בְּמֵישָׁרִים׃

with-smoothnesses he-goes-down sparkle-of-him in-the-cup he-gives when

is right.

17 Do not let your heart envy
sinners,
but always be zealous for
the fear of the LORD.
18 There is surely a future hope
for you,
and your hope will not be
cut off.

19 Listen, my son, and be wise,
and keep your heart on the
right path.
20 Do not join those who drink
too much wine
or gorge themselves on
meat,
21 for drunkards and gluttons
become poor,
and drowsiness clothes them
in rags.

22 Listen to your father, who
gave you life,
and do not despise your
mother when she is old.
23 Buy the truth and do not sell
it;
get wisdom, discipline and
understanding.
24 The father of a righteous man
has great joy;
he who has a wise son
delights in him.
25 May your father and mother
be glad;
may she who gave you birth
rejoice!

26 My son, give me your heart
and let your eyes keep to
my ways,
27 for a prostitute is a deep pit
and a wayward wife is a
narrow well.
28 Like a bandit she lies in wait,
and multiplies the unfaithful
among men.

29 Who has woe? Who has
sorrow?
Who has strife? Who has
complaints?
Who has needless bruises?
Who has bloodshot eyes?
30 Those who linger over wine,
who go to sample bowls of
mixed wine.
31 Do not gaze at wine when it is
red,
when it sparkles in the cup,
when it goes down
smoothly!

°24a ק גיל, °24b ק יגיל
°24c ק ויולד, °24d ק ישמח
°26 ק תצרנה, °29 ק מדינים
°30 ק בכוס

אַחֲרִיתוֹ כְּנָחָשׁ יִשָּׁךְ וּכְצִפְעֹנִי יַפְרִשׁ׃ עֵינֶיךָ
eyes-of-you (33) he-poisons and-like-viper he-bites like-snake end-of-him (32)

יִרְאוּ זָרוֹת וְלִבְּךָ יְדַבֵּר
he-will-imagine and-mind-of-you things-being-strange they-will-see

תַּהְפֻּכוֹת׃ וְהָיִיתָ כְּשֹׁכֵב בְּלֶב־ יָם
sea on-heart-of like-one-sleeping and-you-will-be (34) confusing-things

וּכְשֹׁכֵב בְּרֹאשׁ חִבֵּל׃ הִכּוּנִי בַל־ חָלִיתִי
I-am-hurt not they-hit-me (35) rigging on-top-of and-like-one-lying

הֲלָמוּנִי בַּל־ יָדָעְתִּי מָתַי אָקִיץ אוֹסִיף אֲבַקְשֶׁנּוּ
I-can-find-him I-can-do-again will-I-wake-up when? I-feel not they-beat-me

עוֹד׃ אַל־ תְּקַנֵּא בְּאַנְשֵׁי רָעָה וְאַל־ תִּתְאָו° לִהְיוֹת
to-be you-desire and-not wickedness to-men-of you-envy not (24:1) another

אִתָּם׃ כִּי־ שֹׁד יֶהְגֶּה לִבָּם וְעָמָל שִׂפְתֵיהֶם
lips-of-them and-trouble heart-of-them he-plots violence for (2) with-them

תְּדַבֵּרְנָה׃ בְּחָכְמָה יִבָּנֶה בָּיִת וּבִתְבוּנָה
and-through-understanding house he-is-built by-wisdom (3) they-talk

יִתְכּוֹנָן׃ וּבְדַעַת חֲדָרִים יִמָּלְאוּ כָּל־
all-of they-are-filled rooms and-through-knowledge (4) he-is-established

הוֹן יָקָר וְנָעִים׃ גֶּבֶר־ חָכָם בַּעוֹז וְאִישׁ־ דַּעַת
knowledge and-man-of in-the-power wise man (5) and-beautiful rare treasure

מְאַמֶּץ־ כֹּחַ׃ כִּי בְתַחְבֻּלוֹת תַּעֲשֶׂה־ לְּךָ מִלְחָמָה וּתְשׁוּעָה
and-victory war for-you you-wage by-guidances for (6) strength increasing

בְּרֹב יוֹעֵץ׃ רָאמוֹת לֶאֱוִיל חָכְמוֹת בַּשַּׁעַר לֹא
not at-the-gate wisdoms for-fool ones-being-high (7) one-advising in-many-of

יִפְתַּח־ פִּיהוּ׃ מְחַשֵּׁב לְהָרֵעַ לוֹ בַּעַל־ מְזִמּוֹת
schemes master-of to-him to-do-evil one-plotting (8) mouth-of-him he-opens

יִקְרָאוּ׃ זִמַּת אִוֶּלֶת חַטָּאת וְתוֹעֲבַת לְאָדָם לֵץ׃
one-mocking to-man and-detesting-of sin folly scheme-of (9) they-will-call

הִתְרַפִּיתָ בְּיוֹם צָרָה צַר כֹּחֶכָה׃ הַצֵּל
rescue! (11) strength-of-you small trouble in-time-of you-falter (10)

לְקֻחִים לַמָּוֶת וּמָטִים לַהֶרֶג אִם־
indeed to-the-slaughter and-ones-staggering to-the-death ones-being-led-away

תַּחְשׂוֹךְ׃ כִּי־ תֹאמַר הֵן לֹא־ יָדַעְנוּ זֶה הֲלֹא־ תֹכֵן לִבּוֹת
hearts one-weighing not? this we-knew not see! you-say if (12) you-hold-back

הוּא־ יָבִין וְנֹצֵר נַפְשְׁךָ הוּא יֵדָע וְהֵשִׁיב
and-he-will-repay he-knows he life-of-you and-one-guarding he-perceives he

לְאָדָם כְּפָעֳלוֹ׃ אֱכָל־ בְּנִי דְבַשׁ כִּי־ טוֹב וְנֹפֶת
and-honey-of-comb good for honey son-of-me eat! (13) as-deed-of-him to-person

32In the end it bites like a snake
and poisons like a viper.
33Your eyes will see strange
sights
and your mind imagine
confusing things.
34You will be like one sleeping
on the high seas,
lying on top of the rigging.
35"They hit me," you will say,
"but I'm not hurt!
They beat me, but I don't
feel it!
When will I wake up
so I can find another
drink?"

24 Do not envy wicked men,
do not desire their
company;
2for their hearts plot violence,
and their lips talk about
making trouble.

3By wisdom a house is built,
and through understanding
it is established;
4through knowledge its rooms
are filled
with rare and beautiful
treasures.

5A wise man has great power,
and a man of knowledge
increases strength;
6for waging war you need
guidance,
and for victory many
advisers.

7Wisdom is too high for a fool;
in the assembly at the gate
he has nothing to say.

8He who plots evil
will be known as a schemer.
9The schemes of folly are sin,
and men detest a mocker.

10If you falter in times of
trouble,
how small is your strength!

11Rescue those being led away
to death;
hold back those staggering
toward slaughter.
12If you say, "But we knew
nothing about this,"
does not he who weighs the
heart perceive it?
Does not he who guards your
life know it?
Will he not repay each
person according to what
he has done?

13Eat honey, my son, for it is
good;
honey from the comb is

°1 ק תתאיו

מָתוֹק עַל־חִכֶּךָ׃ כֵּן ׀ דְּעֶה חָכְמָה לְנַפְשֶׁךָ אִם־מָצָאתָ

you-find if to-soul-of-you wisdom know! also (14) taste-of-you to sweet

וְיֵשׁ אַחֲרִית וְתִקְוָתְךָ לֹא תִכָּרֵת׃ אַל־

not (15) she-will-be-cut-off not and-hope-of-you future-hope then-there-is

תֶּאֱרֹב רָשָׁע לִנְוֵה צַדִּיק אַל־תְּשַׁדֵּד רִבְצוֹ׃

dwelling-of-him you-raid not righteous against-house-of outlaw you-lie-in-wait

כִּי שֶׁבַע ׀ יִפּוֹל צַדִּיק וָקָם וּרְשָׁעִים

but-wicked-ones but-he-rises-again righteous he-falls seven for (16)

יִכָּשְׁלוּ בְרָעָה׃ בִּנְפֹל אוֹיִבְךָ

one-being-enemy-of-you when-to-fall (17) by-calamity they-are-brought-down

אַל־תִּשְׂמָח וּבִכָּשְׁלוֹ אַל־יָגֵל לִבֶּךָ׃

heart-of-you let-him-rejoice not and-when-to-stumble-him you-gloat not

פֶּן־יִרְאֶה יְהוָה וְרַע בְּעֵינָיו

in-eyes-of-him and-he-will-be-disapproved Yahweh he-will-see or (18)

וְהֵשִׁיב מֵעָלָיו אַפּוֹ׃ אַל־תִּתְחַר

you-fret not (19) wrath-of-him from-against-him and-he-will-turn-away

בַּמְּרֵעִים אַל־תְּקַנֵּא בָּרְשָׁעִים׃ כִּי ׀ לֹא־

not for (20) to-the-wicked-ones you-envy not because-of-the-men-being-evil

תִהְיֶה אַחֲרִית לָרָע נֵר רְשָׁעִים יִדְעָךְ׃

he-will-be-snuffed-out wicked-men lamp-of for-the-evil-man future-hope she-is

יְרָא־אֶת־יְהוָה בְּנִי וָמֶלֶךְ עִם־שׁוֹנִים אַל־תִּתְעָרָב׃

you-join not ones-rebelling with and-king son-of-me Yahweh *** fear! (21)

כִּי־פִתְאֹם יָקוּם אֵידָם וּפִיד שְׁנֵיהֶם

two-of-them and-calamity-of destruction-of-them he-will-rise suddenly for (22)

מִי יוֹדֵעַ׃ גַּם־אֵלֶּה לַחֲכָמִים הַכֵּר־פָּנִים

faces to-show-partiality of-wise-men these also (23) knowing who?

בְּמִשְׁפָּט בַּל־טוֹב׃ אֹמֵר ׀ לְרָשָׁע צַדִּיק אָתָּה יִקְּבֻהוּ

they-will-curse-him you innocent to-guilty one-saying (24) good not in-judgment

עַמִּים יִזְעָמוּהוּ לְאֻמִּים׃ וְלַמּוֹכִיחִים

but-to-the-ones-convicting (25) nations they-will-denounce-him peoples

יִנְעָם וַעֲלֵיהֶם תָּבוֹא בִרְכַּת־טוֹב׃ שְׂפָתַיִם

lips (26) richness blessing-of she-will-come and-upon-them he-will-go-well

יִשָּׁק מֵשִׁיב דְּבָרִים נְכֹחִים׃ הָכֵן בַּחוּץ ׀

at-the-outside finish! (27) honest-ones answers one-giving he-kisses

מְלַאכְתֶּךָ וְעַתְּדָהּ בַּשָּׂדֶה לָךְ אַחַר וּבָנִיתָ

then-you-build afterward of-you in-the-field and-get-ready-her! work-of-you

בֵיתֶךָ׃ אַל־תְּהִי עֵד־חִנָּם בְּרֵעֶךָ

against-neighbor-of-you without-cause testifier you-be not (28) house-of-you

sweet to your taste.
14Know also that wisdom is sweet to your soul;
if you find it, there is a future hope for you,
and your hope will not be cut off.

15Do not lie in wait like an outlaw against a righteous man's house,
do not raid his dwelling place;
16for though a righteous man falls seven times, he rises again,
but the wicked are brought down by calamity.

17Do not gloat when your enemy falls;
when he stumbles, do not let your heart rejoice,
18or the LORD will see and disapprove
and turn his wrath away from him.

19Do not fret because of evil men
or be envious of the wicked,
20for the evil man has no future hope,
and the lamp of the wicked will be snuffed out.

21Fear the LORD and the king, my son,
and do not join with the rebellious,
22for those two will send sudden destruction upon them,
and who knows what calamities they can bring?

Further Sayings of the Wise

23These also are sayings of the wise:

To show partiality in judging is not good:
24Whoever says to the guilty, "You are innocent"—
peoples will curse him and nations denounce him.
25But it will go well with those who convict the guilty,
and rich blessing will come upon them.

26An honest answer
is like a kiss on the lips.

27Finish your outdoor work
and get your fields ready;
after that, build your house.

28Do not testify against your neighbor without cause,

°17 ק אויבך

וַהֲפִתִּיתָ בִּשְׂפָתֶיךָ׃ אַל־תֹּאמַר כַּאֲשֶׁר עָשָׂה־לִי כֵּן
so to-me he-did just-as you-say not (29) with-lips-of-you or-you-deceive?

אֶעֱשֶׂה־לּוֹ אָשִׁיב לָאִישׁ כְּפָעֳלוֹ׃ עַל־שְׂדֵה
field-of by (30) as-deed-of-him to-the-man I-will-pay-back to-him I-will-do

אִישׁ־עָצֵל עָבַרְתִּי וְעַל־כֶּרֶם אָדָם חֲסַר־לֵב׃
judgment lacking-of man vineyard-of and-by I-went-past sluggard man

וְהִנֵּה עָלָה כֻלּוֹ ׀ קִמְּשֹׂנִים כָּסּוּ פָנָיו
surfaces-of-him they-covered thorns all-of-him he-came-up and-see! (31)

חֲרֻלִּים וְגֶדֶר אֲבָנָיו נֶהֱרָסָה׃ וָאֶחֱזֶה אָנֹכִי
I and-I-observed (32) she-was-in-ruins stones-of-him and-wall-of weeds

אָשִׁית לִבִּי רָאִיתִי לָקַחְתִּי מוּסָר׃ מְעַט שֵׁנוֹת מְעַט
little-of sleeps little-of (33) lesson I-learned I-saw heart-of-me I-applied

תְּנוּמוֹת מְעַט ׀ חִבֻּק יָדַיִם לִשְׁכָּב׃ וּבָא־
and-he-will-come (34) to-rest hands folding-of little-of slumbers

מִתְהַלֵּךְ רֵישֶׁךָ וּמַחְסֹרֶיךָ כְּאִישׁ מָגֵן׃
armor like-man-of and-scarcities-of-you poverty-of-you one-being-bandit

גַּם־אֵלֶּה מִשְׁלֵי שְׁלֹמֹה אֲשֶׁר הֶעְתִּיקוּ אַנְשֵׁי ׀ חִזְקִיָּה
Hezekiah men-of they-copied that Solomon proverbs-of these also (25:1)

מֶלֶךְ־יְהוּדָה׃ כְּבֹד אֱלֹהִים הַסְתֵּר דָּבָר וּכְבֹד מְלָכִים
kings and-glory-of matter to-conceal God glory-of (2) Judah king-of

חֲקֹר דָּבָר׃ שָׁמַיִם לָרוּם וָאָרֶץ לָעֹמֶק
to-the-depth and-earth to-the-height heavens (3) matter to-search-out

וְלֵב מְלָכִים אֵין חֵקֶר׃ הָגוֹ סִיגִים מִכָּסֶף
from-silver drosses to-remove (4) searching there-is-no kings so-heart-of

וַיֵּצֵא לַצֹּרֵף כֶּלִי׃ הָגוֹ רָשָׁע
wicked to-remove (5) material for-the-one-being-silversmith and-he-comes-out

לִפְנֵי־מֶלֶךְ וְיִכּוֹן בַּצֶּדֶק
through-the-righteousness and-he-will-be-established king from-presences-of

כִּסְאוֹ׃ אַל־תִּתְהַדַּר לִפְנֵי־מֶלֶךְ וּבִמְקוֹם
or-to-place-of king in-presences-of you-exalt-yourself not (6) throne-of-him

גְּדֹלִים אַל־תַּעֲמֹד׃ כִּי טוֹב אֲמָר־לְךָ עֲלֵה הֵנָּה
to-here come-up! to-you to-say good for (7) you-claim not great-men

מֵהַשְׁפִּילְךָ לִפְנֵי נָדִיב אֲשֶׁר רָאוּ עֵינֶיךָ׃ אַל־
not (8) eyes-of-you they-saw what nobleman before more-than-to-humiliate-you

תֵּצֵא לָרִב מַהֵר פֶּן מַה־תַּעֲשֶׂה בְּאַחֲרִיתָהּ בְּהַכְלִים
when-to-shame in-end-of-her will-you-do what? for hastily to-the-court you-bring

אֹתְךָ רֵעֶךָ׃ רִיבְךָ רִיב אֶת־רֵעֶךָ
neighbor-of-you with argue-case! case-of-you (9) neighbor-of-you you

or use your lips to deceive.
29 Do not say, "I'll do to him as
he has done to me;
I'll pay that man back for
what he did."

30 I went past the field of the
sluggard,
past the vineyard of the
man who lacks judgment;
31 thorns had come up
everywhere,
the ground was covered
with weeds,
and the stone wall was in
ruins.
32 I applied my heart to what I
observed
and learned a lesson from
what I saw:
33 A little sleep, a little slumber,
a little folding of the hands
to rest—
34 and poverty will come on you
like a bandit
and scarcity like an armed
man.[s]

More Proverbs of Solomon

25 These are more proverbs of
Solomon, copied by the
men of Hezekiah king of Judah:

2 It is the glory of God to
conceal a matter;
to search out a matter is the
glory of kings.

3 As the heavens are high and
the earth is deep,
so the hearts of kings are
unsearchable.

4 Remove the dross from the
silver,
and out comes material for[t]
the silversmith;
5 remove the wicked from the
king's presence,
and his throne will be
established through
righteousness.

6 Do not exalt yourself in the
king's presence,
and do not claim a place
among great men;
7 it is better for him to say to
you, "Come up here,"
than for him to humiliate
you before a nobleman.

8 What you have seen with your
eyes
do not bring[u] hastily to
court,
for what will you do in the
end
if your neighbor puts you to
shame?

9 If you argue your case with a
neighbor,

[s]34 Or *like a vagrant / and scarcity like a beggar*
[t]4 Or *comes a vessel from*
[u]7,8 Or *nobleman / [8]on whom you had set your eyes. / Do not go*

וְסוֹד אַחֵר אַל־תְּגָל׃ פֶּן־יְחַסֶּדְךָ שֹׁמֵעַ

one-hearing he-may-shame-you or (10) you-betray not another but-confidence-of

וְדִבָּתְךָ לֹא תָשׁוּב׃ תַּפּוּחֵי זָהָב בְּמַשְׂכִּיּוֹת

in-settings-of gold apples-of (11) she-will-go never and-bad-reputation-of-you

כָּסֶף דָּבָר דָּבֻר עַל־אָפְנָיו׃ נֶזֶם זָהָב

gold earring-of (12) aptnesses-of-him in being-spoken word silver

וַחֲלִי־כָתֶם מוֹכִיחַ חָכָם עַל־אֹזֶן שֹׁמָעַת׃

one-listening ear to wise one-rebuking fine-gold or-ornament-of

כְּצִנַּת־שֶׁלֶג ׀ בְּיוֹם קָצִיר צִיר נֶאֱמָן

one-being-trustworthy messenger harvest at-time-of snow like-coolness-of (13)

לְשֹׁלְחָיו וְנֶפֶשׁ אֲדֹנָיו יָשִׁיב׃ נְשִׂיאִים

clouds (14) he-refreshes masters-of-him and-spirit-of to-ones-sending-him

וְרוּחַ וְגֶשֶׁם אָיִן אִישׁ מִתְהַלֵּל בְּמַתַּת־שָׁקֶר׃

deception of-gift-of boasting man there-is-none but-rain and-wind

בְּאֹרֶךְ אַפַּיִם יְפֻתֶּה קָצִין וְלָשׁוֹן רַכָּה

gentle and-tongue ruler he-can-be-persuaded tempers through-length-of (15)

תִּשְׁבָּר־גָּרֶם׃ דְּבַשׁ מָצָאתָ אֱכֹל דַּיֶּךָּ פֶּן־

lest just-enough-of-you eat! you-find honey (16) bone she-can-break

תִּשְׂבָּעֶנּוּ וַהֲקֵאתוֹ׃ הֹקַר רַגְלְךָ

foot-of-you make-seldom! (17) and-you-vomit-out-him you-eat-too-much-of-him

מִבֵּית רֵעֶךָ פֶּן־יִשְׂבָּעֲךָ וּשְׂנֵאֶךָ׃

and-he-hates-you he-have-too-much-of-you lest neighbor-of-you in-house-of

מֵפִיץ וְחֶרֶב וְחֵץ שָׁנוּן אִישׁ* עֹנֶה בְרֵעֵהוּ

against-neighbor-of-him giving man one-being-sharp or-arrow or-sword club (18)

עֵד שָׁקֶר׃ שֵׁן רֹעָה וְרֶגֶל מוּעָדֶת

one-being-lame or-foot one-being-bad tooth (19) falsehood testimony-of

מִבְטָח בּוֹגֵד בְּיוֹם צָרָה׃ מַעֲדֶה

one-taking-away (20) trouble in-time-of one-being-unfaithful reliance

בֶּגֶד ׀ בְּיוֹם קָרָה חֹמֶץ עַל־נָתֶר וְשָׁר בַּשִּׁרִים עַל

to with-the-songs also-one-singing soda on vinegar cold on-day-of garment

לֶב־רָע׃ אִם־רָעֵב שֹׂנַאֲךָ הַאֲכִלֵהוּ

give-to-eat-him! one-being-enemy-of-you hungry if (21) heaviness heart-of

לָחֶם וְאִם־צָמֵא הַשְׁקֵהוּ מָיִם׃ כִּי גֶחָלִים אַתָּה חֹתֶה

heaping you coals for (22) waters give-to-drink-him! thirsty and-if food

עַל־רֹאשׁוֹ וַיהוָה יְשַׁלֶּם־לָךְ׃ רוּחַ צָפוֹן תְּחוֹלֵל

she-brings north wind-of (23) to-you he-will-reward and-Yahweh head-of-him on

גָּשֶׁם וּפָנִים נִזְעָמִים לְשׁוֹן סָתֶר׃ טוֹב שֶׁבֶת עַל־

on to-live good (24) slyness tongue-of ones-being-angry and-looks rain

do not betray another man's confidence,
10 or he who hears it may shame you
and you will never lose your bad reputation.

11 A word aptly spoken
is like apples of gold in settings of silver.

12 Like an earring of gold or an ornament of fine gold
is a wise man's rebuke to a listening ear.

13 Like the coolness of snow at harvest time
is a trustworthy messenger to those who send him;
he refreshes the spirit of his masters.

14 Like clouds and wind without rain
is a man who boasts of gifts he does not give.

15 Through patience a ruler can be persuaded,
and a gentle tongue can break a bone.

16 If you find honey, eat just enough—
too much of it, and you will vomit.
17 Seldom set foot in your neighbor's house—
too much of you, and he will hate you.

18 Like a club or a sword or a sharp arrow
is the man who gives false testimony against his neighbor.

19 Like a bad tooth or a lame foot
is reliance on the unfaithful in times of trouble.

20 Like one who takes away a garment on a cold day,
or like vinegar poured on soda,
is one who sings songs to a heavy heart.

21 If your enemy is hungry, give him food to eat;
if he is thirsty, give him water to drink.
22 In doing this, you will heap burning coals on his head,
and the LORD will reward you.

23 As a north wind brings rain,
so a sly tongue brings angry looks.

24 Better to live on a corner of

*18 Most mss have *maqqeph* (אִישׁ־).

פִּנַּת־ גָּג מֵאֵשֶׁת מִדְוָנִים° וּבֵית חָבֶר׃ מַיִם

waters (25) sharing with-house-of quarrels more-than-wife-of roof corner-of

קָרִים עַל־נֶפֶשׁ עֲיֵפָה וּשְׁמוּעָה טוֹבָה מֵאֶרֶץ מֶרְחָק׃ מַעְיָן

spring (26) distance from-land-of good also-news weary soul to cold-ones

נִרְפָּשׂ וּמָקוֹר מָשְׁחָת צַדִּיק מָט

one-giving-way righteous-man one-being-polluted or-well one-being-muddied

לִפְנֵי־ רָשָׁע׃ אָכֹל דְּבַשׁ הַרְבּוֹת לֹא־ טוֹב וְחֵקֶר

or-seeking-of good not to-be-much honey to-eat (27) wicked before

כְּבֹדָם כָּבוֹד׃ עִיר פְּרוּצָה אֵין חוֹמָה אִישׁ אֲשֶׁר

who man wall no one-being-broken-down city (28) honorable honor-of-them

אֵין מַעְצָר לְרוּחוֹ׃ כַּשֶּׁלֶג ׀ בַּקַּיִץ וְכַמָּטָר

or-like-the-rain in-the-summer like-the-snow (26:1) of-self-of-him control no

בַּקָּצִיר כֵּן לֹא־ נָאוֶה לִכְסִיל כָּבוֹד׃ כַּצִּפּוֹר לָנוּד

to-flutter like-the-sparrow (2) honor for-fool fitting not so in-the-harvest

כַּדְּרוֹר לָעוּף כֵּן קִלְלַת חִנָּם לֹא° תָבֹא׃

she-comes-to-rest not undeserved curse-of so to-dart like-the-swallow

שׁוֹט לַסּוּס מֶתֶג לַחֲמוֹר וְשֵׁבֶט לְגֵו כְּסִילִים׃

fools for-back-of and-rod for-the-donkey halter for-the-horse whip (3)

אַל־ תַּעַן כְּסִיל כְּאִוַּלְתּוֹ פֶּן־ תִּשְׁוֶה־ לּוֹ גַם־אָתָּה׃

you also to-him you-will-be-like or as-folly-of-him fool you-answer not (4)

עֲנֵה כְסִיל כְּאִוַּלְתּוֹ פֶּן־ יִהְיֶה חָכָם בְּעֵינָיו׃

in-eyes-of-him wise he-will-be or as-folly-of-him fool answer! (5)

מְקַצֶּה רַגְלַיִם חָמָס שֹׁתֶה שֹׁלֵחַ דְּבָרִים בְּיַד־ כְּסִיל׃

fool by-hand-of messages one-sending drinking violence feet one-cutting-off (6)

דַּלְיוּ שֹׁקַיִם מִפִּסֵּחַ וּמָשָׁל בְּפִי כְּסִילִים׃

fools in-mouth-of also-proverb of-lame-man legs they-hang-limp (7)

כִּצְרוֹר אֶבֶן בְּמַרְגֵּמָה כֵּן־ נוֹתֵן לִכְסִיל כָּבוֹד׃ חוֹחַ

thornbush (9) honor to-fool giving so in-sling stone like-to-tie (8)

עָלָה בְיַד־ שִׁכּוֹר וּמָשָׁל בְּפִי כְסִילִים׃ רַב

archer (10) fools in-mouth-of also-proverb drunkard into-hand-of he-goes

מְחוֹלֶל־ כֹּל וְשֹׂכֵר כְּסִיל וְשֹׂכֵר עֹבְרִים׃

ones-passing-by or-one-hiring fool also-one-hiring all one-wounding

כְּכֶלֶב שָׁב עַל־ קֵאוֹ כְּסִיל שׁוֹנֶה בְאִוַּלְתּוֹ׃

to-folly-of-him repeating fool vomit-of-him to returning as-dog (11)

רָאִיתָ אִישׁ חָכָם בְּעֵינָיו תִּקְוָה לִכְסִיל מִמֶּנּוּ׃ אָמַר

he-says (13) more-than-him for-fool hope in-eyes-of-him wise man you-see (12)

עָצֵל שַׁחַל בַּדָּרֶךְ אֲרִי בֵּין הָרְחֹבוֹת׃ הַדֶּלֶת

the-door (14) the-streets among fierce-lion in-the-road lion sluggard

the roof
than share a house with a quarrelsome wife.

25 Like cold water to a weary soul
is good news from a distant land.

26 Like a muddied spring or a polluted well
is a righteous man who gives way to the wicked.

27 It is not good to eat too much honey,
nor is it honorable to seek one's own honor.

28 Like a city whose walls are broken down
is a man who lacks self-control.

26 Like snow in summer or rain in harvest,
honor is not fitting for a fool.

2 Like a fluttering sparrow or a darting swallow,
an undeserved curse does not come to rest.

3 A whip for the horse, a halter for the donkey,
and a rod for the backs of fools!

4 Do not answer a fool according to his folly,
or you will be like him yourself.

5 Answer a fool according to his folly,
or he will be wise in his own eyes.

6 Like cutting off one's feet or drinking violence
is the sending of a message by the hand of a fool.

7 Like a lame man's legs that hang limp
is a proverb in the mouth of a fool.

8 Like tying a stone in a sling
is the giving of honor to a fool.

9 Like a thornbush in a drunkard's hand
is a proverb in the mouth of a fool.

10 Like an archer who wounds at random
is he who hires a fool or any passer-by.

11 As a dog returns to its vomit,
so a fool repeats his folly.

12 Do you see a man wise in his own eyes?
There is more hope for a fool than for him.

13 The sluggard says, "There is a lion in the road,
a fierce lion roaming the streets!"

°24 ק מדינים
°2 ק לו

תִּסּוֹב עַל־ צִירָהּ וְעָצֵל עַל־ מִטָּתוֹ׃ טָמַן עָצֵל
sluggard he-buries (15) bed-of-him on also-sluggard hinge-of-her on she-turns

יָדוֹ בַּצַּלָּחַת נִלְאָה לַהֲשִׁיבָהּ אֶל־ פִּיו׃
mouth-of-him to to-bring-back-her he-is-too-lazy in-the-dish hand-of-him

חָכָם עָצֵל בְּעֵינָיו מִשִּׁבְעָה מְשִׁיבֵי טָעַם׃
discretion men-answering-of more-than-seven in-eyes-of-him sluggard wise (16)

מַחֲזִיק בְּאָזְנֵי־ כָלֶב עֹבֵר מִתְעַבֵּר עַל־ רִיב לֹּא־
not quarrel in meddling one-passing-by dog onto-ears-of one-seizing (17)

לוֹ׃ כְּמִתְלַהְלֵהַּ הַיֹּרֶה זִקִּים חִצִּים וָמָוֶת׃
and-death arrows firebrands the-one-shooting like-man-being-mad (18) to-him

כֵּן־ אִישׁ רִמָּה אֶת־ רֵעֵהוּ וְאָמַר הֲלֹא־ מְשַׂחֵק אָנִי׃
I one-joking not? and-he-says neighbor-of-him *** he-deceives man so (19)

בְּאֶפֶס עֵצִים תִּכְבֶּה־ אֵשׁ וּבְאֵין נִרְגָּן
one-gossiping also-when-without fire she-goes-out woods when-without (20)

יִשְׁתֹּק מָדוֹן׃ פֶּחָם לְגֶחָלִים וְעֵצִים לְאֵשׁ וְאִישׁ
also-man-of to-fire and-woods to-embers charcoal (21) quarrel he-dies-down

מִדְוָנִים לְחַרְחַר־ רִיב׃ דִּבְרֵי נִרְגָּן כְּמִתְלַהֲמִים
like-morsels-being-choice one-gossiping words-of (22) strife to-kindle quarrels

וְהֵם יָרְדוּ חַדְרֵי־ בָטֶן׃ *כֶּסֶף סִיגִים*
drosses silver-of (23) inmost-part chambers-of they-go-down and-they

מְצֻפֶּה עַל־ חָרֶשׂ שְׂפָתַיִם דֹּלְקִים וְלֶב־ רָע׃
evil with-heart-of ones-being-fervent lips earthenware over being-coated

בִּשְׂפָתוֹ יִנָּכֵר שׂוֹנֵא וּבְקִרְבּוֹ
but-in-heart-of-him man-being-malicious he-disguises-himself with-lips-of-him (24)

יָשִׁית מִרְמָה׃ כִּי־ יְחַנֵּן קוֹלוֹ אַל־ תַּאֲמֶן־
you-believe not speech-of-him he-is-charming though (25) deceit he-harbors

בּוֹ כִּי שֶׁבַע תּוֹעֵבוֹת בְּלִבּוֹ׃ תִּכַּסֶּה
she-may-be-concealed (26) in-heart-of-him abominations seven for in-him

שִׂנְאָה בְּמַשָּׁאוֹן תִּגָּלֶה רָעָתוֹ בְקָהָל׃
in-assembly wickedness-of-him she-will-be-exposed by-deception malice

כֹּרֶה־ שַׁחַת בָּהּ יִפֹּל וְגֹלֵל אֶבֶן אֵלָיו
on-him stone and-one-rolling he-will-fall into-her pit one-digging (27)

תָּשׁוּב׃ לְשׁוֹן־ שֶׁקֶר יִשְׂנָא דַכָּיו וּפֶה
and-mouth ones-hurt-of-him he-hates lie tongue-of (28) she-will-come-back

חָלָק יַעֲשֶׂה מִדְחֶה׃ אַל־ תִּתְהַלֵּל בְּיוֹם מָחָר כִּי לֹא־
not for tomorrow about-day-of you-boast not (27:1) ruin he-works flattering

תֵדַע מַה־ יֵּלֶד יוֹם׃ יְהַלֶּלְךָ זָר
one-being-other let-him-praise-you (2) day he-may-bring-forth what you-know

14 As a door turns on its hinges,
so a sluggard turns on his bed.

15 The sluggard buries his hand in the dish;
he is too lazy to bring it back to his mouth.

16 The sluggard is wiser in his own eyes
than seven men who answer discreetly.

17 Like one who seizes a dog by the ears
is a passer-by who meddles in a quarrel not his own.

18 Like a madman shooting firebrands or deadly arrows
19 is a man who deceives his neighbor
and says, "I was only joking!"

20 Without wood a fire goes out;
without gossip a quarrel dies down.

21 As charcoal to embers and as wood to fire,
so is a quarrelsome man for kindling strife.

22 The words of a gossip are like choice morsels;
they go down to a man's inmost parts.

23 Like a coating of glaze[v] over earthenware
are fervent lips with an evil heart.

24 A malicious man disguises himself with his lips,
but in his heart he harbors deceit.

25 Though his speech is charming, do not believe him,
for seven abominations fill his heart.

26 His malice may be concealed by deception,
but his wickedness will be exposed in the assembly.

27 If a man digs a pit, he will fall into it;
if a man rolls a stone, it will roll back on him.

28 A lying tongue hates those it hurts,
and a flattering mouth works ruin.

27 Do not boast about tomorrow,
for you do not know what a day may bring forth.

2 Let another praise you, and

[v] 23 With a different word division of the Hebrew; Masoretic Text *of silver dross*

*23 The NIV reads these words as כְּסַפְסָגִים, *like-glazes.*

°21 ק מדינים

°24 ק בשפתיו

וְלֹא־ פִיךָ נָכְרִי וְאַל־ שְׂפָתֶיךָ׃ כֹּבֶד־ אֶבֶן

stone heavy (3) lips-of-you and-not someone-else mouth-of-you and-not

וְנֵטֶל הַחוֹל וְכַעַס אֱוִיל כָּבֵד מִשְּׁנֵיהֶם׃

more-than-both-of-them heavy fool but-provocation-of the-sand and-burden

אַכְזְרִיּוּת חֵמָה וְשֶׁטֶף אָף וּמִי יַעֲמֹד לִפְנֵי קִנְאָה׃

jealousy before he-can-stand but-who? fury and-overwhelming anger cruel (4)

טוֹבָה תּוֹכַחַת מְגֻלָּה מֵאַהֲבָה מְסֻתָּרֶת׃

one-being-hidden more-than-love one-being-open rebuke good (5)

נֶאֱמָנִים פִּצְעֵי אוֹהֵב וְנַעְתָּרוֹת

though-ones-being-profuse one-being-friend wounds-of ones-being-faithful (6)

נְשִׁיקוֹת שׂוֹנֵא׃ נֶפֶשׁ שְׂבֵעָה תָּבוּס נֹפֶת וְנֶפֶשׁ

but-person honey she-loathes full person (7) one-being-enemy kisses-of

רְעֵבָה כָּל־ מַר מָתוֹק׃ כְּצִפּוֹר נוֹדֶדֶת מִן־ קִנָּהּ

nest-of-her from one-straying like-bird (8) sweet bitterness all-of hungry

כֵּן־ אִישׁ נוֹדֵד מִמְּקוֹמוֹ׃ שֶׁמֶן וּקְטֹרֶת יְשַׂמַּח־

he-brings-joy and-incense perfume (9) from-home-of-him one-straying man so

לֵב וּמֶתֶק רֵעֵהוּ מֵעֲצַת־ נָפֶשׁ׃

earnestness from-counsel-of friend-of-him also-pleasantness-of heart

רֵעֲךָ וְרֵעָה אָבִיךָ אַל־ תַּעֲזֹב וּבֵית

and-house-of you-forsake not father-of-you and-friend-of friend-of-you (10)

אָחִיךָ אַל־ תָּבוֹא בְּיוֹם אֵידֶךָ טוֹב שָׁכֵן קָרוֹב

nearby neighbor good disaster-of-you in-day-of you-go not brother-of-you

מֵאָח רָחוֹק׃ חֲכַם בְּנִי וְשַׂמַּח לִבִּי

heart-of-me and-bring-joy! son-of-me be-wise! (11) far more-than-brother

וְאָשִׁיבָה חֹרְפִי דָבָר׃ עָרוּם רָאָה

he-sees prudent (12) answer one-treating-with-contempt-me then-I-can-return

רָעָה נִסְתָּר פְּתָאִים עָבְרוּ נֶעֱנָשׁוּ׃ קַח־

take! (13) they-suffer they-go-on simple-ones he-takes-refuge danger

בִּגְדוֹ כִּי־ עָרַב זָר וּבְעַד

and-for one-being-stranger he-puts-up-security when garment-of-him

נָכְרִיָּה חַבְלֵהוּ׃ מְבָרֵךְ רֵעֵהוּ בְּקוֹל גָּדוֹל

loud with-voice neighbor-of-him one-blessing (14) hold-him! wayward-woman

בַּבֹּקֶר הַשְׁכֵּים קְלָלָה תֵּחָשֶׁב לוֹ׃ דֶּלֶף

dripping (15) by-him she-will-be-taken curse to-be-early in-the-morning

טוֹרֵד בְּיוֹם סַגְרִיר וְאֵשֶׁת מִדְוָנִים נִשְׁתָּוָה׃

she-is-like quarrels also-wife-of rain on-day-of one-being-constant

צֹפְנֶיהָ צָפַן־ רוּחַ וְשֶׁמֶן יְמִינוֹ

right-hand-of-him or-oil-of wind he-restrains ones-restraining-her (16)

not your own mouth;
someone else, and not your own lips.

3Stone is heavy and sand a burden,
but provocation by a fool is heavier than both.

4Anger is cruel and fury overwhelming,
but who can stand before jealousy?

5Better is open rebuke
than hidden love.

6The kisses of an enemy may be profuse,
but faithful are the wounds of a friend.

7He who is full loathes honey,
but to the hungry even what is bitter tastes sweet.

8Like a bird that strays from its nest
is a man who strays from his home.

9Perfume and incense bring joy to the heart,
and the pleasantness of one's friend springs from his earnest counsel.

10Do not forsake your friend and the friend of your father,
and do not go to your brother's house when disaster strikes you—
better a neighbor nearby than a brother far away.

11Be wise, my son, and bring joy to my heart;
then I can answer anyone who treats me with contempt.

12The prudent see danger and take refuge,
but the simple keep going and suffer for it.

13Take the garment of one who puts up security for a stranger;
hold it in pledge if he does it for a wayward woman.

14If a man loudly blesses his neighbor early in the morning,
it will be taken as a curse.

15A quarrelsome wife is like a constant dripping on a rainy day;
16restraining her is like restraining the wind
or grasping oil with the hand.

°10 ק ורע

°15 ק מדינים

יִקְרָא׃ (17) בַּרְזֶל בְּבַרְזֶל יָחַד וְאִישׁ יַחַד פְּנֵי־
faces-of he-sharpens so-man he-sharpens to-iron iron (17) he-grasps

רֵעֵהוּ׃ (18) נֹצֵר תְּאֵנָה יֹאכַל פִּרְיָהּ
fruit-of-her he-will-eat fig-tree one-tending (18) other-of-him

וְשֹׁמֵר אֲדֹנָיו יְכֻבָּד׃ (19) כַּמַּיִם
as-the-waters (19) he-will-be-honored masters-of-him and-one-looking-after

הַפָּנִים לַפָּנִים כֵּן לֵב־ הָאָדָם לָאָדָם׃ (20) שְׁאוֹל וַאֲבַדֹּה°
and-Abaddon Sheol (20) to-the-man the-man heart-of so to-the-faces the-faces

לֹא תִשְׂבַּעְנָה וְעֵינֵי הָאָדָם לֹא תִשְׂבַּעְנָה׃
they-are-satisfied never the-man and-eyes-of they-are-satisfied never

(21) מַצְרֵף לַכֶּסֶף וְכוּר לַזָּהָב וְאִישׁ לְפִי
by-mouth-of but-man for-the-gold and-furnace for-the-silver crucible (21)

מַהֲלָלוֹ׃ (22) אִם תִּכְתּוֹשׁ־ אֶת־ הָאֱוִיל ׀ בַּמַּכְתֵּשׁ בְּתוֹךְ
in-among in-the-mortar the-fool *** you-grind though (22) praise-of-him

הָרִיפוֹת בַּעֱלִי לֹא־ תָסוּר מֵעָלָיו אִוַּלְתּוֹ׃
folly-of-him from-with-him she-will-be-removed not with-the-pestle the-grains

(23) יָדֹעַ תֵּדַע פְּנֵי צֹאנֶךָ שִׁית לִבְּךָ
heart-of-you attend! flock-of-you conditions-of you-know to-know (23)

לַעֲדָרִים׃ (24) כִּי לֹא לְעוֹלָם חֹסֶן וְאִם־ נֵזֶר לְדוֹר
for-generation crown or-even richness to-forever not for (24) to-the-herds

דּוֹר°׃ (25) גָּלָה חָצִיר וְנִרְאָה־ דֶשֶׁא
new-growth and-he-appears hay he-is-removed (25) and-generation

וְנֶאֶסְפוּ עִשְּׂבוֹת הָרִים׃ (26) כְּבָשִׂים לִלְבוּשֶׁךָ
for-clothing-of-you lambs (26) hills grasses-of and-they-are-gathered

וּמְחִיר שָׂדֶה עַתּוּדִים׃ (27) וְדֵי ׀ חֲלֵב עִזִּים לְלַחְמְךָ
for-food-of-you goats milk-of and-plenty-of (27) goats field and-price-of

לְלֶחֶם בֵּיתֶךָ וְחַיִּים לְנַעֲרוֹתֶיךָ׃
to-servant-girls-of-you and-nourishments family-of-you for-food-of

(28:1) נָסוּ וְאֵין־ רֹדֵף רָשָׁע וְצַדִּיקִים כִּכְפִיר
as-lion but-righteous-ones wicked one-pursuing though-not they-flee (28:1)

יִבְטָח׃ (2) בְּפֶשַׁע אֶרֶץ רַבִּים שָׂרֶיהָ וּבְאָדָם
but-by-man rulers-of-her many country in-rebellion-of (2) he-is-bold

מֵבִין יֹדֵעַ כֵּן יַאֲרִיךְ׃ (3) גֶּבֶר רָשׁ
one-being-poor man (3) he-maintains-order so one-knowing one-understanding

וְעֹשֵׁק דַּלִּים מָטָר סֹחֵף וְאֵין לָחֶם׃
crop so-there-is-no driving rain poor-ones also-one-oppressing

(4) עֹזְבֵי תוֹרָה יְהַלְלוּ רָשָׁע וְשֹׁמְרֵי תוֹרָה
law but-ones-keeping-of wicked they-praise law ones-forsaking-of (4)

17 As iron sharpens iron,
so one man sharpens another.
18 He who tends a fig tree will eat its fruit,
and he who looks after his master will be honored.
19 As water reflects a face,
so a man's heart reflects the man.
20 Death and Destruction[w] are never satisfied,
and neither are the eyes of man.
21 The crucible for silver and the furnace for gold,
but man is tested by the praise he receives.
22 Though you grind a fool in a mortar,
grinding him like grain with a pestle,
you will not remove his folly from him.
23 Be sure you know the condition of your flocks,
give careful attention to your herds;
24 for riches do not endure forever,
and a crown is not secure for all generations.
25 When the hay is removed and new growth appears
and the grass from the hills is gathered in,
26 the lambs will provide you with clothing,
and the goats with the price of a field.
27 You will have plenty of goats' milk
to feed you and your family
and to nourish your servant girls.

28 The wicked man flees though no one pursues,
but the righteous are as bold as a lion.
2 When a country is rebellious,
it has many rulers,
but a man of understanding and knowledge maintains order.
3 A ruler[x] who oppresses the poor
is like a driving rain that leaves no crops.
4 Those who forsake the law praise the wicked,
but those who keep the law

w20 Hebrew *Sheol and Abaddon*
x3 Or *A poor man*

°20 ק ואבדו
°24 ק ודור

יִתְגָּרוּ בָם׃ (5) אַנְשֵׁי־רָע לֹא־יָבִינוּ מִשְׁפָּט
justice they-understand not evil men-of (5) against-them they-resist

וּמְבַקְשֵׁי יְהוָה יָבִינוּ כֹל׃ (6) טוֹב־רָשׁ
one-being-poor good (6) fully they-understand Yahweh but-ones-seeking-of

הוֹלֵךְ בְּתֻמּוֹ מֵעִקֵּשׁ דְּרָכַיִם וְהוּא עָשִׁיר׃
rich and-he ways more-than-perverse-of in-blamelessness-of-him walking

(7) נוֹצֵר תּוֹרָה בֵּן מֵבִין וְרֹעֶה
but-one-being-companion-of one-discerning son law one-keeping (7)

זוֹלְלִים יַכְלִים אָבִיו׃ (8) מַרְבֶּה הוֹנוֹ
wealth-of-him one-increasing (8) father-of-him he-disgraces ones-being-gluttons

בְּנֶשֶׁךְ °וּבְתַרְבִּית לְחוֹנֵן דַּלִּים יִקְבְּצֶנּוּ׃
he-amasses-him poor-ones for-one-being-kind and-interest by-interest

(9) מֵסִיר אָזְנוֹ מִשְּׁמֹעַ תּוֹרָה גַּם־תְּפִלָּתוֹ תּוֹעֵבָה׃
detestable prayer-of-him even law from-to-hear ear-of-him one-turning (9)

(10) מַשְׁגֶּה יְשָׁרִים׀ בְּדֶרֶךְ רָע בִּשְׁחוּתוֹ הוּא־יִפּוֹל
he-will-fall he into-trap-of-him evil along-path upright-ones one-leading (10)

וּתְמִימִים יִנְחֲלוּ־טוֹב׃ (11) חָכָם בְּעֵינָיו אִישׁ
man in-eyes-of-him wise (11) good they-will-inherit but-blameless-ones

עָשִׁיר וְדַל מֵבִין יַחְקְרֶנּוּ׃ (12) בַּעֲלֹץ
when-to-triumph (12) he-sees-through-him one-discerning but-poor rich

צַדִּיקִים רַבָּה תִפְאָרֶת וּבְקוּם רְשָׁעִים יְחֻפַּשׂ אָדָם׃
man he-is-hidden wicked-ones but-when-to-rise elation great righteous-ones

(13) מְכַסֶּה פְשָׁעָיו לֹא יַצְלִיחַ וּמוֹדֶה
but-one-confessing he-prospers not sins-of-him one-concealing (13)

וְעֹזֵב יְרֻחָם׃ (14) אַשְׁרֵי אָדָם מְפַחֵד
one-fearing man blessednesses-of (14) he-finds-mercy and-one-renouncing

תָּמִיד וּמַקְשֶׁה לִבּוֹ יִפּוֹל בְּרָעָה׃ (15) אֲרִי־
lion (15) into-trouble he-falls heart-of-him but-one-hardening always

נֹהֵם וְדֹב שׁוֹקֵק מֹשֵׁל רָשָׁע עַל עַם־דָּל׃ (16) נָגִיד
ruler (16) helpless people over wicked ruling charging or-bear roaring

חֲסַר תְּבוּנוֹת וְרַב מַעֲשַׁקּוֹת °שֹׂנֵא בֶצַע
ill-gotten-gain one-hating tyrannies and-great-of judgments lacking-of

יַאֲרִיךְ יָמִים׃ (17) אָדָם עָשֻׁק בְּדַם־נֶפֶשׁ עַד־
till life by-blood-of being-tormented man (17) days he-will-have-long

בּוֹר יָנוּס אַל־יִתְמְכוּ־בוֹ׃ (18) הוֹלֵךְ
one-walking (18) to-him they-will-support not he-will-be-fugitive death

תָּמִים יִוָּשֵׁעַ וְנֶעְקַשׁ דְּרָכַיִם יִפּוֹל
he-will-fall ways but-one-being-perverse-of he-is-kept-safe blamelessly

resist them.

5 Evil men do not understand
justice,
but those who seek the LORD
understand it fully.

6 Better a poor man whose walk
is blameless
than a rich man whose
ways are perverse.

7 He who keeps the law is a
discerning son,
but a companion of gluttons
disgraces his father.

8 He who increases his wealth
by exorbitant interest
amasses it for another, who
will be kind to the poor.

9 If anyone turns a deaf ear to
the law,
even his prayers are
detestable.

10 He who leads the upright
along an evil path
will fall into his own trap,
but the blameless will
receive a good
inheritance.

11 A rich man may be wise in
his own eyes,
but a poor man who has
discernment sees through
him.

12 When the righteous triumph,
there is great elation;
but when the wicked rise to
power, men go into
hiding.

13 He who conceals his sins does
not prosper,
but whoever confesses and
renounces them finds
mercy.

14 Blessed is the man who always
fears the LORD,
but he who hardens his
heart falls into trouble.

15 Like a roaring lion or a
charging bear
is a wicked man ruling over
a helpless people.

16 A tyrannical ruler lacks
judgment,
but he who hates ill-gotten
gain will enjoy a long
life.

17 A man tormented by the guilt
of murder
will be a fugitive till death;
let no one support him.

18 He whose walk is blameless is
kept safe,
but he whose ways are
perverse will suddenly
fall.

°8 ק ותרבית
°16 ק שנא

בְּאֶחָת׃ עֹבֵד אַדְמָתוֹ יִשְׂבַּע־לָחֶם
food he-will-have-abundance land-of-him one-working (19) in-suddenness

וּמְרַדֵּף רֵקִים יִשְׂבַּע־רִישׁ׃ אִישׁ
man-of (20) poverty he-will-have-fill fantasies but-one-chasing

אֱמוּנוֹת רַב־בְּרָכוֹת וְאָץ לְהַעֲשִׁיר לֹא
not to-get-rich but-one-being-eager blessings rich-of faithfulnesses

יִנָּקֶה׃ הַכֵּר־פָּנִים לֹא־טוֹב וְעַל־פַּת־
piece-of yet-for good not faces to-show-partiality (21) he-will-go-unpunished

לֶחֶם יִפְשַׁע־גָּבֶר׃ נִבְהָל לַהוֹן אִישׁ רַע עָיִן
eye stingy-of man for-the-wealth he-is-eager (22) man he-will-do-wrong bread

וְלֹא־יֵדַע כִּי־חֶסֶר יְבֹאֶנּוּ׃ מוֹכִיחַ אָדָם אַחֲרַי
in-end man one-rebuking (23) he-awaits-him poverty that he-is-aware and-not

חֵן יִמְצָא מִמַּחֲלִיק לָשׁוֹן׃ גּוֹזֵל ׀
one-robbing (24) tongue more-than-one-flattering he-will-gain favor

אָבִיו וְאִמּוֹ וְאֹמֵר אֵין־פָּשַׁע חָבֵר הוּא לְאִישׁ
to-man he partner wrong not and-one-saying or-mother-of-him father-of-him

מַשְׁחִית׃ רְחַב־נֶפֶשׁ יְגָרֶה מָדוֹן וּבוֹטֵחַ
but-one-trusting dissension he-stirs-up greed broad-of (25) one-destroying

עַל־יְהוָה יְדֻשָּׁן׃ בּוֹטֵחַ בְּלִבּוֹ הוּא כְסִיל
fool he in-self-of-him one-trusting (26) he-will-prosper Yahweh in

וְהוֹלֵךְ בְּחָכְמָה הוּא יִמָּלֵט׃ נוֹתֵן
one-giving (27) he-is-kept-safe he in-wisdom but-one-walking

לָרָשׁ אֵין מַחְסוֹר וּמַעְלִים עֵינָיו רַב־מְאֵרוֹת׃
curses many-of eyes-of-him but-one-closing lack no to-the-one-being-poor

בְּקוּם רְשָׁעִים יִסָּתֵר אָדָם וּבְאָבְדָם
but-when-to-perish-them person he-is-ridden wicked-ones when-to-rise (28)

יִרְבּוּ צַדִּיקִים׃ אִישׁ תּוֹכָחוֹת מַקְשֶׁה־עֹרֶף פֶּתַע
suddenly neck making-stiff rebukes man-of (29:1) righteous-ones they-thrive

יִשָּׁבֵר וְאֵין מַרְפֵּא׃ בִּרְבוֹת צַדִּיקִים
righteous-ones when-to-thrive (2) remedy with-no he-will-be-destroyed

יִשְׂמַח הָעָם וּבִמְשֹׁל רָשָׁע יֵאָנַח עָם׃ אִישׁ־
man (3) people he-groans wicked but-when-to-rule the-people he-rejoices

אֹהֵב חָכְמָה יְשַׂמַּח אָבִיו וְרֹעֶה
but-one-being-companion-of father-of-him he-brings-joy wisdom loving

זוֹנוֹת יְאַבֶּד־הוֹן׃ מֶלֶךְ בְּמִשְׁפָּט יַעֲמִיד
he-makes-stable by-justice king (4) wealth he-squanders ones-being-prostitutes

אֶרֶץ וְאִישׁ תְּרוּמוֹת יֶהֶרְסֶנָּה׃ גֶּבֶר מַחֲלִיק עַל־
to flattering man (5) he-tears-down-her bribes but-man-of country

19 He who works his land will
have abundant food,
but the one who chases
fantasies will have his fill
of poverty.

20 A faithful man will be richly
blessed,
but one eager to get rich
will not go unpunished.

21 To show partiality is not
good—
yet a man will do wrong for
a piece of bread.

22 A stingy man is eager to get
rich
and is unaware that poverty
awaits him.

23 He who rebukes a man will in
the end gain more favor
than he who has a flattering
tongue.

24 He who robs his father or
mother
and says, "It's not wrong"—
he is partner to him who
destroys.

25 A greedy man stirs up
dissension,
but he who trusts in the
LORD will prosper.

26 He who trusts in himself is a
fool,
but he who walks in
wisdom is kept safe.

27 He who gives to the poor will
lack nothing,
but he who closes his eyes
to them receives many
curses.

28 When the wicked rise to
power, people go into
hiding;
but when the wicked perish,
the righteous thrive.

29 A man who remains
stiff-necked after many
rebukes
will suddenly be
destroyed—without
remedy.

2 When the righteous thrive, the
people rejoice;
when the wicked rule, the
people groan.

3 A man who loves wisdom
brings joy to his father,
but a companion of
prostitutes squanders his
wealth.

4 By justice a king gives a
country stability,
but one who is greedy for
bribes tears it down.

5 Whoever flatters his neighbor

רֵעֵהוּ רֶשֶׁת פּוֹרֵשׂ עַל־ פְּעָמָיו׃ בְּפֶשַׁע אִישׁ רָע מוֹקֵשׁ
snare evil man by-sin (6) feet-of-him for spreading net neighbor-of-him

וְצַדִּיק יָרוּן וְשָׂמֵחַ׃ יֹדֵעַ צַדִּיק
righteous one-caring-about (7) and-he-can-be-glad he-can-sing but-righteous

דִּין דַּלִּים רָשָׁע לֹא־ יָבִין דָּעַת׃ אַנְשֵׁי לָצוֹן
mockery men-of (8) knowledge he-is-concerned not wicked poor-ones justice-of

יָפִיחוּ קִרְיָה וַחֲכָמִים יָשִׁיבוּ אָף׃ אִישׁ־ חָכָם
wise man (9) anger they-turn-away but-wise-men city they-stir-up

נִשְׁפָּט אֶת־ אִישׁ אֱוִיל וְרָגַז וְשָׂחַק וְאֵין נָחַת׃
peace but-no and-he-scoffs and-he-rages fool man with one-going-to-court

אַנְשֵׁי דָמִים יִשְׂנְאוּ־ תָם וִישָׁרִים יְבַקְשׁוּ נַפְשׁוֹ׃
life-of-him they-seek and-upright-ones integrity they-hate bloods men-of (10)

כָּל־ רוּחוֹ יוֹצִיא כְסִיל וְחָכָם בְּאָחוֹר
at-last but-wise fool he-gives anger-of-him fullness-of (11)

יְשַׁבְּחֶנָּה׃ מֹשֵׁל מַקְשִׁיב עַל־ דְּבַר־ שָׁקֶר כָּל־
all-of lie word-of to listening one-ruling (12) he-controls-her

מְשָׁרְתָיו רְשָׁעִים׃ רָשׁ וְאִישׁ
and-man-of man-being-poor (13) wicked-ones ones-being-officials-of-him

תְּכָכִים נִפְגָּשׁוּ מֵאִיר־ עֵינֵי שְׁנֵיהֶם יְהוָה׃
Yahweh both-of-them eyes-of one-giving-sight they-have-in-common oppressions

מֶלֶךְ שׁוֹפֵט בֶּאֱמֶת דַּלִּים כִּסְאוֹ לָעַד
to-always throne-of-him poor-ones with-fairness judging king (14)

יִכּוֹן׃ שֵׁבֶט וְתוֹכַחַת יִתֵּן חָכְמָה וְנַעַר
but-child wisdom he-imparts and-correction rod (15) he-will-be-secure

מְשֻׁלָּח מֵבִישׁ אִמּוֹ׃ בִּרְבוֹת רְשָׁעִים
wicked-ones when-to-thrive (16) mother-of-him disgracing one-being-left

יִרְבֶּה־ פָּשַׁע וְצַדִּיקִים בְּמַפַּלְתָּם יִרְאוּ׃
they-will-see to-downfall-of-them but-righteous-ones sin he-thrives

יַסֵּר בִּנְךָ וִינִיחֶךָ וְיִתֵּן
and-he-will-bring and-he-will-give-peace-you son-of-you discipline! (17)

מַעֲדַנִּים לְנַפְשֶׁךָ׃ בְּאֵין חָזוֹן יִפָּרַע
he-casts-off-restraint revelation where-there-is-no (18) to-soul-of-you delights

עָם וְשֹׁמֵר תּוֹרָה אַשְׁרֵהוּ׃ בִּדְבָרִים לֹא־
not by-words (19) blessedness-of-him law but-one-keeping people

יִוָּסֶר עָבֶד כִּי־ יָבִין וְאֵין מַעֲנֶה׃
response yet-there-is-no he-understands though servant he-can-be-corrected

חָזִיתָ אִישׁ אָץ בִּדְבָרָיו תִּקְוָה לִכְסִיל מִמֶּנּוּ׃
more-than-him for-fool hope with-words-of-him one-being-hasty man you-see (20)

is spreading a net for his feet.

6 An evil man is snared by his own sin,
but a righteous one can sing and be glad.

7 The righteous care about justice for the poor,
but the wicked have no such concern.

8 Mockers stir up a city,
but wise men turn away anger.

9 If a wise man goes to court with a fool,
the fool rages and scoffs, and there is no peace.

10 Bloodthirsty men hate a man of integrity
and seek to kill the upright.

11 A fool gives full vent to his anger,
but a wise man keeps himself under control.

12 If a ruler listens to lies,
all his officials become wicked.

13 The poor man and the oppressor have this in common:
The LORD gives sight to the eyes of both.

14 If a king judges the poor with fairness,
his throne will always be secure.

15 The rod of correction imparts wisdom,
but a child left to itself disgraces his mother.

16 When the wicked thrive, so does sin,
but the righteous will see their downfall.

17 Discipline your son, and he will give you peace;
he will bring delight to your soul.

18 Where there is no revelation, the people cast off restraint;
but blessed is he who keeps the law.

19 A servant cannot be corrected by mere words;
though he understands, he will not respond.

20 Do you see a man who speaks in haste?
There is more hope for a fool than for him.

מְפַנֵּק מִנֹּעַר עַבְדּוֹ וְאַחֲרִיתוֹ יִהְיֶה
he-will-be and-end-of-him servant-of-him from-youth one-pampering (21)

מָנוֹן׃ אִישׁ־ אַף יְגָרֶה מָדוֹן וּבַעַל חֵמָה
hot-temper and-man-of dissension he-stirs-up anger man-of (22) grief

רַב־ פָּשַׁע׃ גַּאֲוַת אָדָם תַּשְׁפִּילֶנּוּ וּשְׁפַל־ רוּחַ
spirit but-lowly-of she-brings-low-him man pride-of (23) sin many-of

יִתְמֹךְ כָּבוֹד׃ חוֹלֵק עִם־ גַּנָּב שׂוֹנֵא נַפְשׁוֹ
self-of-him being-enemy-of thief with one-being-accomplice (24) honor he-gains

אָלָה יִשְׁמַע וְלֹא יַגִּיד׃ חֶרְדַּת אָדָם יִתֵּן
he-will-prove-to-be man fear-of (25) he-dares-testify but-not he-takes oath

מוֹקֵשׁ וּבוֹטֵחַ בַּיהוָה יְשֻׂגָּב׃ רַבִּים מְבַקְשִׁים
ones-seeking many (26) he-is-kept-safe in-Yahweh but-one-trusting snare

פְּנֵי־ מוֹשֵׁל וּמֵיְהוָה מִשְׁפַּט־ אִישׁ׃ תּוֹעֲבַת
detesting-of (27) man justice-of but-from-Yahweh one-ruling faces-of

צַדִּיקִים אִישׁ עָוֶל וְתוֹעֲבַת רָשָׁע יְשַׁר־ דָּרֶךְ׃
way upright-of wicked and-detesting-of dishonesty man-of righteous-ones

דִּבְרֵי ׀ אָגוּר בִּן־ יָקֶה הַמַּשָּׂא נְאֻם הַגֶּבֶר
the-man declaration-of the-oracle Jakeh son-of Agur sayings-of (30:1)

לְאִיתִיאֵל לְאִיתִיאֵל וְאֻכָל׃ כִּי בַעַר אָנֹכִי מֵאִישׁ וְלֹא־
and-not more-than-man I ignorant indeed (2) and-Ucal to-Ithiel to-Ithiel

בִינַת אָדָם לִי׃ וְלֹא־ לָמַדְתִּי חָכְמָה וְדַעַת
or-knowledge-of wisdom I-learned and-not (3) to-me man understanding-of

קְדֹשִׁים אֵדָע׃ מִי עָלָה־ שָׁמַיִם ׀ וַיֵּרַד מִי
who? and-he-came-down heavens he-went-up who? (4) I-know Holy-Ones

אָסַף־ רוּחַ ׀ בְּחָפְנָיו מִי צָרַר־ מַיִם ׀ בַּשִּׂמְלָה
in-the-cloak waters he-wrapped who? in-hollow-of-hands-of-him wind he-gathered

מִי הֵקִים כָּל־ אַפְסֵי־ אָרֶץ מַה־ שְּׁמוֹ וּמַה־ שֶּׁם־
name-of and-what? name-of-him what? earth ends-of all-of he-established who?

בְּנוֹ כִּי תֵדָע׃ כָּל־ אִמְרַת אֱלוֹהַּ צְרוּפָה מָגֵן
shield one-being-flawless God word-of every-of (5) you-know if son-of-him

הוּא לַחֹסִים בּוֹ׃ אַל־ תּוֹסְףְּ עַל־ דְּבָרָיו פֶּן־
or words-of-him to you-add not (6) in-him to-ones-taking-refuge he

יוֹכִיחַ בְּךָ וְנִכְזָבְתָּ׃ שְׁתַּיִם שָׁאַלְתִּי מֵאִתָּךְ
from-with-you I-ask two (7) and-you-will-be-proved-liar to-you he-will-rebuke

אַל־ תִּמְנַע מִמֶּנִּי בְּטֶרֶם אָמוּת׃ שָׁוְא ׀ וּדְבַר־ כָּזָב
lie and-word-of falsehood (8) I-die at-before from-me you-refuse not

הַרְחֵק מִמֶּנִּי רֵאשׁ וָעֹשֶׁר אַל־ תִּתֶּן־ לִי הַטְרִיפֵנִי
give-me! to-me you-give not or-richness poverty from-me keep-far!

21 If a man pampers his servant
from youth,
he will bring grief[y] in the
end.

22 An angry man stirs up
dissension,
and a hot-tempered one
commits many sins.

23 A man's pride brings him low,
but a man of lowly spirit
gains honor.

24 The accomplice of a thief is his
own enemy;
he is put under oath and
dare not testify.

25 Fear of man will prove to be a
snare,
but whoever trusts in the
LORD is kept safe.

26 Many seek an audience with a
ruler,
but it is from the LORD that
man gets justice.

27 The righteous detest the
dishonest;
the wicked detest the
upright.

Sayings of Agur

30 The sayings of Agur son of
Jakeh—an oracle[z]:

This man declared to Ithiel,
to Ithiel and to Ucal:[a]

2 "I am the most ignorant of
men;
I do not have a man's
understanding.
3 I have not learned wisdom,
nor have I knowledge of the
Holy One.
4 Who has gone up to heaven
and come down?
Who has gathered up the
wind in the hollow of his
hands?
Who has wrapped up the
waters in his cloak?
Who has established all the
ends of the earth?
What is his name, and the
name of his son?
Tell me if you know!

5 "Every word of God is
flawless;
he is a shield to those who
take refuge in him.
6 Do not add to his words,
or he will rebuke you and
prove you a liar.

7 "Two things I ask of you, O
LORD;
do not refuse me before I
die:
8 Keep falsehood and lies far
from me;
give me neither poverty nor
riches,

y21 The meaning of the Hebrew for this word is uncertain.
z1 Or *Jakeh of Massa*
a1 Masoretic Text; with a different word division of the Hebrew *declared, "I am weary, O God; / I am weary, O God, and faint.*

לֶחֶם חֻקִּי׃ פֶּן* אֶשְׂבַּע ׀ וְכִחַשְׁתִּי
and-I-may-disown I-may-have-too-much otherwise (9) portion-of-me bread-of

וְאָמַרְתִּי מִי יְהוָה וּפֶן־ אִוָּרֵשׁ וְגָנַבְתִּי
and-I-may-steal I-may-become-poor or-otherwise Yahweh who? and-I-may-say

וְתָפַשְׂתִּי שֵׁם אֱלֹהָי׃ אַל־ תַּלְשֵׁן עֶבֶד אֶל־
to servant you-slander not (10) God-of-me name-of so-I-would-dishonor

אֲדֹנָו° פֶּן־ יְקַלֶּלְךָ וְאָשָׁמְתָּ׃ דּוֹר
generation (11) and-you-will-pay he-will-curse-you or masters-of-him

אָבִיו יְקַלֵּל וְאֶת־ אִמּוֹ לֹא יְבָרֵךְ׃ דּוֹר
generation (12) he-blesses not mother-of-him and he-curses father-of-him

טָהוֹר בְּעֵינָיו וּמִצֹּאָתוֹ לֹא רֻחָץ׃ דּוֹר
generation (13) he-is-cleansed not yet-from-filth-of-him in-eyes-of-him pure

מָה־ רָמוּ עֵינָיו וְעַפְעַפָּיו יִנָּשֵׂאוּ׃
they-are-disdainful and-glances-of-him eyes-of-him they-are-haughty how!

דּוֹר ׀ חֲרָבוֹת שִׁנָּיו וּמַאֲכָלוֹת מְתַלְּעֹתָיו לֶאֱכֹל
to-devour jaws-of-him and-knives teeth-of-him swords generation (14)

עֲנִיִּים מֵאֶרֶץ וְאֶבְיוֹנִים מֵאָדָם׃ לַעֲלוּקָה ׀ שְׁתֵּי
two-of to-leech (15) from-mankind and-needy-ones from-earth poor-ones

בָנוֹת הַב ׀ הַב שָׁלוֹשׁ הֵנָּה לֹא תִשְׂבַּעְנָה אַרְבַּע לֹא־
never four they-are-satisfied never they three give! give! daughters

אָמְרוּ הוֹן׃ שְׁאוֹל וְעֹצֶר רָחַם אֶרֶץ לֹא־ שָׂבְעָה
she-is-satisfied never land womb and-barrenness-of Sheol (16) enough they-say

מַּיִם וְאֵשׁ לֹא־ אָמְרָה הוֹן׃ עַיִן ׀ תִּלְעַג לְאָב
at-father she-mocks eye (17) enough she-says never and-fire waters

וְתָבוּז לִיקֲּהַת־ אֵם יִקְּרוּהָ עֹרְבֵי־
ravens-of they-will-peck-out-her mother at-obedience-of and-she-scorns

נַחַל וְיֹאכְלוּהָ בְנֵי־ נָשֶׁר׃ שְׁלֹשָׁה הֵמָּה
they three (18) vulture young-ones-of and-they-will-eat-her valley

נִפְלְאוּ מִמֶּנִּי וְאַרְבָּעָ° לֹא יְדַעְתִּים׃ דֶּרֶךְ
way-of (19) I-understand-them not and-four more-than-me they-are-amazing

הַנֶּשֶׁר ׀ בַּשָּׁמַיִם דֶּרֶךְ נָחָשׁ עֲלֵי צוּר דֶּרֶךְ־ אֳנִיָּה בְלֶב־ יָם
sea on-heart-of ship way-of rock on snake way-of in-the-skies the-eagle

וְדֶרֶךְ גֶּבֶר בְּעַלְמָה׃ כֵּן ׀ דֶּרֶךְ אִשָּׁה מְנָאָפֶת
one-being-adulteress woman way-of this (20) with-maiden man and-way-of

אָכְלָה וּמָחֲתָה פִיהָ וְאָמְרָה לֹא־פָעַלְתִּי אָוֶן׃ תַּחַת
under (21) wrong I-did not and-she-says mouth-of-her and-she-wipes she-eats

שָׁלוֹשׁ רָגְזָה אֶרֶץ וְתַחַת אַרְבַּע לֹא־ תוּכַל שְׂאֵת׃ תַּחַת־
under (22) to-bear-up she-can not four and-under earth she-trembles three

but give me only my daily
bread.
9 Otherwise, I may have too
much and disown you
and say, 'Who is the LORD?'
Or I may become poor and
steal,
and so dishonor the name
of my God.

10 "Do not slander a servant to
his master,
or he will curse you, and
you will pay for it.

11 "There are those who curse
their fathers
and do not bless their
mothers;
12 those who are pure in their
own eyes
and yet are not cleansed of
their filth;
13 those whose eyes are ever so
haughty,
whose glances are so
disdainful;
14 those whose teeth are swords
and whose jaws are set with
knives
to devour the poor from the
earth,
the needy from among
mankind.

15 "The leech has two daughters.
'Give! Give!' they cry.

"There are three things that
are never satisfied,
four that never say,
'Enough!':
16 the grave,[b] the barren womb,
land, which is never
satisfied with water,
and fire, which never says,
'Enough!'

17 "The eye that mocks a father,
that scorns obedience to a
mother,
will be pecked out by the
ravens of the valley,
will be eaten by the
vultures.

18 "There are three things that
are too amazing for me,
four that I do not
understand:
19 the way of an eagle in the sky,
the way of a snake on a
rock,
the way of a ship on the high
seas,
and the way of a man with
a maiden.

20 "This is the way of an
adulteress:
She eats and wipes her
mouth
and says, 'I've done nothing
wrong.'

21 "Under three things the earth
trembles,
under four it cannot bear
up:

[b] 16 Hebrew *Sheol*

*9 Most mss have *maqqeph* after this word (פֶּן־).

°10 ק אדניו

°18 ק וארבעה

עֶבֶד כִּי יִמְלוֹךְ וְנָבָל כִּי יִשְׂבַּע־לָחֶם׃ תַּחַת
under (23) food he-is-full who and-fool he-becomes-king who servant

שְׂנוּאָה כִּי תִבָּעֵל וְשִׁפְחָה כִּי־תִירַשׁ
she-displaces who and-maidservant she-is-married who woman-being-unloved

גְּבִרְתָּהּ׃ אַרְבָּעָה הֵם קְטַנֵּי־אָרֶץ וְהֵמָּה חֲכָמִים
wise-ones yet-they earth small-ones-of they four (24) mistress-of-her

מְחֻכָּמִים׃ הַנְּמָלִים עַם לֹא־עָז וַיָּכִינוּ
yet-they-store-up strong not creature the-ants (25) ones-being-made-wise

בַקַּיִץ לַחְמָם׃ שְׁפַנִּים עַם לֹא־עָצוּם וַיָּשִׂימוּ
yet-they-make powerful not creature conies (26) food-of-them in-the-summer

בַסֶּלַע בֵּיתָם׃ מֶלֶךְ אֵין לָאַרְבֶּה וַיֵּצֵא
yet-he-advances to-the-locust there-is-no king (27) home-of-them in-the-crag

חֹצֵץ כֻּלּוֹ׃ שְׂמָמִית בְּיָדַיִם תְּתַפֵּשׂ וְהִיא
yet-she you-may-catch in-hands lizard (28) all-of-him one-being-in-ranks

בְּהֵיכְלֵי מֶלֶךְ׃ שְׁלֹשָׁה הֵמָּה מֵיטִיבֵי צָעַד וְאַרְבָּעָה
and-four stride ones-being-stately-of they three (29) king in-palaces-of

מֵיטִבֵי לָכֶת׃ לַיִשׁ גִּבּוֹר בַּבְּהֵמָה וְלֹא־
but-not among-the-beast mighty lion (30) to-move ones-being-stately-of

יָשׁוּב מִפְּנֵי־כֹל׃ זַרְזִיר מָתְנַיִם אוֹ־תָיִשׁ וּמֶלֶךְ
and-king he-goat or loins one-girded-of (31) anything from-before he-retreats

אַלְקוּם עִמּוֹ׃ אִם־נָבַלְתָּ בְהִתְנַשֵּׂא וְאִם־
or-if when-to-exalt-yourself you-played-fool if (32) around-him army

זַמּוֹתָ יָד לְפֶה׃ כִּי מִיץ חָלָב יוֹצִיא
he-produces milk churning-of for (33) over-mouth hand you-planned-evil

חֶמְאָה וּמִיץ־אַף יוֹצִיא דָם וּמִיץ אַפַּיִם
angers so-stirring-up-of blood he-produces nose and-twisting-of butter

יוֹצִיא רִיב׃ דִּבְרֵי לְמוּאֵל מֶלֶךְ מַשָּׂא אֲשֶׁר־יִסְּרַתּוּ
she-taught-him that oracle king Lemuel sayings-of (31:1) strife he-produces

אִמּוֹ׃ מַה־בְּרִי וּמַה־בַּר־בִּטְנִי וּמֶה בַּר־
son-of and-oh! womb-of-me son-of and-oh! son-of-me oh! (2) mother-of-him

נְדָרָי׃ אַל־תִּתֵּן לַנָּשִׁים חֵילֶךָ וּדְרָכֶיךָ
and-vigors-of-you strength-of-you on-the-women you-spend not (3) vows-of-me

לַמְחוֹת מְלָכִין׃ אַל לַמְּלָכִים לְמוֹאֵל אַל לַמְּלָכִים שְׁתוֹ־יָיִן
wine to-drink for-the-kings not Lemuel for-the-kings not (4) kings to-ruin

וּלְרוֹזְנִים אֵו שֵׁכָר׃ פֶּן־יִשְׁתֶּה וְיִשְׁכַּח
and-he-forgets he-drinks lest (5) beer craving-of or-for-ones-ruling

מְחֻקָּק וִישַׁנֶּה דִּין כָּל־בְּנֵי־עֹנִי׃
oppression people-of all-of right-of and-he-deprives one-being-decreed

22 a servant who becomes king,
a fool who is full of food,
23 an unloved woman who is married,
and a maidservant who displaces her mistress.

24 "Four things on earth are small,
yet they are extremely wise:
25 Ants are creatures of little strength,
yet they store up their food in the summer;
26 conies[c] are creatures of little power,
yet they make their home in the crags;
27 locusts have no king,
yet they advance together in ranks;
28 a lizard can be caught with the hand,
yet it is found in kings' palaces.

29 "There are three things that are stately in their stride,
four that move with stately bearing:
30 a lion, mighty among beasts,
who retreats before nothing;
31 a strutting rooster, a he-goat,
and a king with his army around him.[d]

32 "If you have played the fool and exalted yourself,
or if you have planned evil,
clap your hand over your mouth!
33 For as churning the milk produces butter,
and as twisting the nose produces blood,
so stirring up anger produces strife."

Sayings of King Lemuel

31 The sayings of King Lemuel—an oracle[e] his mother taught him:

2 "O my son, O son of my womb,
O son of my vows,[f]
3 do not spend your strength on women,
your vigor on those who ruin kings.

4 "It is not for kings, O Lemuel—
not for kings to drink wine,
not for rulers to crave beer,
5 lest they drink and forget what the law decrees,
and deprive all the oppressed of their rights.

[c] 26 That is, the hyrax or rock badger
[d] 31 *Or king secure against revolt*
[e] 1 *Or of Lemuel king of Massa, which*
[f] 2 *Or / the answer to my prayers*

°4 ק אי

תְּנוּ־ שֵׁכָר לְאוֹבֵד וְיַיִן לְמָרֵי נָפֶשׁ׃
soul to-ones-anguished-of and-wine to-one-perishing beer give! (6)

יִשְׁתֶּה וְיִשְׁכַּח רִישׁוֹ וַעֲמָלוֹ לֹא
not and-misery-of-him poverty-of-him and-let-him-forget let-him-drink (7)

יִזְכָּר־ עוֹד׃ פְּתַח־ פִּיךָ לְאִלֵּם אֶל־ דִּין כָּל־
all-of right-of for for-mute mouth-of-you open! (8) more let-him-remember

בְּנֵי חֲלוֹף׃ פְּתַח־ פִּיךָ שְׁפָט־ צֶדֶק וְדִין
and-defend-right! fairly judge! mouth-of-you open! (9) destitution people-of

עָנִי וְאֶבְיוֹן׃ אֵשֶׁת־ חַיִל מִי יִמְצָא וְרָחֹק מִפְּנִינִים
more-than-rubies and-far he-can-find who? nobility wife-of (10) and-needy poor

מִכְרָהּ׃ בָּטַח בָּהּ לֵב בַּעְלָהּ וְשָׁלָל
and-valuable husband-of-her heart-of in-her confidence (11) worth-of-her

לֹא יֶחְסָר׃ גְּמָלַתְהוּ טוֹב וְלֹא־ רָע כֹּל יְמֵי חַיֶּיהָ*׃
lives-of-her days-of all-of harm and-not good she-brings-him (12) he-lacks not

דָּרְשָׁה צֶמֶר וּפִשְׁתִּים וַתַּעַשׂ בְּחֵפֶץ כַּפֶּיהָ׃
hands-of-her with-eagerness-of and-she-works and-flaxes wool she-selects (13)

הָיְתָה כָּאֳנִיּוֹת סוֹחֵר מִמֶּרְחָק תָּבִיא לַחְמָהּ׃
food-of-her she-brings from-afar one-being-merchant like-ships-of she-is (14)

וַתָּקָם׀ בְּעוֹד לַיְלָה וַתִּתֵּן טֶרֶף לְבֵיתָהּ
for-family-of-her food and-she-provides dark while-still and-she-gets-up (15)

וְחֹק לְנַעֲרֹתֶיהָ׃ זָמְמָה שָׂדֶה וַתִּקָּחֵהוּ
and-she-buys-him field she-considers (16) for-servant-girls-of-her and-portion

מִפְּרִי כַפֶּיהָ נָטְעָ° כָּרֶם׃ חָגְרָה בְעוֹז
with-vigor she-grids (17) vineyard she-plants hands-of-her from-earning-of

מָתְנֶיהָ וַתְּאַמֵּץ זְרוֹעֹתֶיהָ׃ טָעֲמָה כִּי־ טוֹב
profitable that she-sees (18) arms-of-her and-she-strengthens loins-of-her

סַחְרָהּ לֹא־ יִכְבֶּה בַלַּיְל° נֵרָהּ׃ יָדֶיהָ
hands-of-her (19) lamp-of-her at-the-night she-goes-out not trading-of-her

שִׁלְּחָה בַכִּישׁוֹר וְכַפֶּיהָ תָּמְכוּ פָלֶךְ׃
spindle they-grasp and-fingers-of-her onto-the-distaff she-holds

כַּפָּהּ פָּרְשָׂה לֶעָנִי וְיָדֶיהָ שִׁלְּחָה
she-extends and-hands-of-her to-the-poor she-opens arm-of-her (20)

לָאֶבְיוֹן׃ לֹא־ תִירָא לְבֵיתָהּ מִשָּׁלֶג כִּי כָל־
all-of for from-snow for-household-of-her she-fears not (21) to-the-needy

בֵּיתָהּ לָבֻשׁ שָׁנִים׃ מַרְבַדִּים עָשְׂתָה־ לָּהּ
for-her she-makes coverings (22) scarlets one-being-clothed household-of-her

שֵׁשׁ וְאַרְגָּמָן לְבוּשָׁהּ׃ נוֹדָע בַּשְּׁעָרִים
at-the-gates one-being-respected (23) clothing-of-her and-purple fine-linen

6 Give beer to those who are
perishing,
wine to those who are in
anguish;
7 let them drink and forget their
poverty
and remember their misery
no more.
8 "Speak up for those who
cannot speak for
themselves,
for the rights of all who are
destitute.
9 Speak up and judge fairly;
defend the rights of the poor
and needy."

Epilogue: The Wife of Noble Character[g]

10 A wife of noble character
who can find?
She is worth far more than
rubies.
11 Her husband has full
confidence in her
and lacks nothing of value.
12 She brings him good, not
harm,
all the days of her life.
13 She selects wool and flax
and works with eager
hands.
14 She is like the merchant ships,
bringing her food from afar.
15 She gets up while it is still
dark;
she provides food for her
family
and portions for her servant
girls.
16 She considers a field and buys
it;
out of her earnings she
plants a vineyard.
17 She sets about her work
vigorously;
her arms are strong for her
tasks.
18 She sees that her trading is
profitable,
and her lamp does not go
out at night.
19 In her hand she holds the
distaff
and grasps the spindle with
her fingers.
20 She opens her arms to the
poor
and extends her hands to
the needy.
21 When it snows, she has no
fear for her household;
for all of them are clothed in
scarlet.
22 She makes coverings for her
bed;
she is clothed in fine linen
and purple.
23 Her husband is respected at
the city gate,

g *10* Verses 10-31 are an acrostic, each verse beginning with a successive letter of the Hebrew alphabet.

**12* Most mss have *qamets* under the *he* (הָ—).

°*16* ק נטעה

°*18* ק בלילה

סָדִין		אָרֶץ׃	זִקְנֵי־	עִם־	בְּשִׁבְתּוֹ	בַּעְלָהּ
linen-garment	(24)	land	elders-of	among	when-to-sit-him	husband-of-her

עֹז־		לַכְּנַעֲנִי׃	נָתְנָה	וַחֲגוֹר	וַתִּמְכֹּר	עָשְׂתָה
strength	(25)	to-the-merchant	she-supplies	and-sash	and-she-sells	she-makes

פִּיהָ		אַחֲרוֹן׃	לְיוֹם	וַתִּשְׂחַק	לְבוּשָׁהּ	וְהָדָר
mouth-of-her	(26)	coming	at-day	and-she-can-laugh	clothing-of-her	and-dignity

לְשׁוֹנָהּ׃	עַל־	חֶסֶד	וְתוֹרַת־	בְחָכְמָה	פָּתְחָה
tongue-of-her	on	faithfulness	and-instruction-of	with-wisdom	she-opens

עַצְלוּת	וְלֶחֶם	בֵּיתָהּ	הֲלִיכוֹת	צוֹפִיָּה	
idleness	and-bread-of	household-of-her	affairs-of	one-watching-over	(27)

וַיְאַשְּׁרוּהָ	בָנֶיהָ	קָמוּ		תֹאכֵל׃	לֹא
and-they-call-blessed-her	children-of-her	they-arise	(28)	she-eats	not

חָיִל	עָשׂוּ	בָּנוֹת	רַבּוֹת		וַיְהַלְלָהּ׃	בַּעְלָהּ
noble-thing	they-do	women	many	(29)	also-he-praises-her	husband-of-her

וְהֶבֶל	הַחֵן	שֶׁקֶר		כֻּלָּנָה׃	עַל־	עָלִית	וְאַתְּ
and-fleeting	the-charm	deceptive	(30)	all-of-them	over	you-surpass	but-you

לָהּ	תְּנוּ־		תִתְהַלָּל׃	הִיא	יְהוָה	יִרְאַת־	אִשָּׁה	הַיֹּפִי
to-her	give!	(31)	she-is-praised	she	Yahweh	fearer-of	woman	the-beauty

מַעֲשֶׂיהָ׃	בַשְּׁעָרִים	וִיהַלְלוּהָ	יָדֶיהָ	מִפְּרִי
works-of-her	at-the-gates	and-let-them-praise-her	hands-of-her	from-earning-of

where he takes his seat
among the elders of the
land.
24 She makes linen garments and
sells them,
and supplies the merchants
with sashes.
25 She is clothed with strength
and dignity;
she can laugh at the days to
come.
26 She speaks with wisdom,
and faithful instruction is
on her tongue.
27 She watches over the affairs of
her household
and does not eat the bread
of idleness.
28 Her children arise and call her
blessed;
her husband also, and he
praises her:
29 "Many women do noble
things,
but you surpass them all."
30 Charm is deceptive, and
beauty is fleeting;
but a woman who fears the
Lord is to be praised.
31 Give her the reward she has
earned,
and let her works bring her
praise at the city gate.

דִּבְרֵי קֹהֶלֶת בֶּן־ דָּוִד מֶלֶךְ בִּירוּשָׁלָם׃ הֲבֵל
meaninglessness-of (2) in-Jerusalem king David son-of Teacher words-of (1:1)

הֲבָלִים אָמַר קֹהֶלֶת הֲבֵל הֲבָלִים הַכֹּל
the-whole meaninglessnesses meaninglessness-of Teacher he-says meaninglessnesses

הָבֶל׃ מַה־ יִּתְרוֹן לָאָדָם בְּכָל־ עֲמָלוֹ שֶׁיַּעֲמֹל
which-he-toils labor-of-him from-all-of to-the-man gain what? (3) meaningless

תַּחַת הַשָּׁמֶשׁ׃ דּוֹר הֹלֵךְ וְדוֹר בָּא וְהָאָרֶץ
but-the-earth going and-generation coming generation (4) the-sun under

לְעוֹלָם עֹמָדֶת׃ וְזָרַח הַשֶּׁמֶשׁ וּבָא הַשָּׁמֶשׁ וְאֶל־
and-to the-sun and-he-sets the-sun and-he-rises (5) remaining to-forever

מְקוֹמוֹ שׁוֹאֵף זוֹרֵחַ הוּא שָׁם׃ הוֹלֵךְ אֶל־ דָּרוֹם וְסוֹבֵב אֶל־
to and-turning south to blowing (6) there he rising hurrying place-of-him

צָפוֹן סוֹבֵב ׀ סֹבֵב הוֹלֵךְ הָרוּחַ וְעַל־ סְבִיבֹתָיו
courses-of-him and-on the-wind going turning-round turning-round north

שָׁב הָרוּחַ׃ כָּל־ הַנְּחָלִים הֹלְכִים אֶל־ הַיָּם וְהַיָּם
yet-the-sea the-sea to ones-flowing the-streams all-of (7) the-wind returning

אֵינֶנּוּ מָלֵא אֶל־ מְקוֹם שֶׁהַנְּחָלִים הֹלְכִים שָׁם הֵם
they there ones-coming where-the-streams place-of to full never-he

שָׁבִים לָלָכֶת׃ כָּל־ הַדְּבָרִים יְגֵעִים לֹא־ יוּכַל אִישׁ
one he-can not wearisome-ones the-things all-of (8) to-go ones-returning

לְדַבֵּר לֹא־ תִשְׂבַּע עַיִן לִרְאוֹת וְלֹא־ תִמָּלֵא אֹזֶן מִשְּׁמֹעַ׃
from-to-hear ear she-has-fill or-never to-see eye she-has-enough never to-say

מַה־ שֶּׁהָיָה הוּא שֶׁיִּהְיֶה וּמַה־ שֶּׁנַּעֲשָׂה הוּא
he that-he-was-done and-what that-he-will-be he that-he-was what (9)

שֶׁיֵּעָשֶׂה וְאֵין כָּל־ חָדָשׁ תַּחַת הַשָּׁמֶשׁ׃ יֵשׁ
is-there (10) the-sun under new any-of and-there-is-not that-he-will-be-done

דָּבָר שֶׁיֹּאמַר רְאֵה־ זֶה חָדָשׁ הוּא כְּבָר הָיָה לְעֹלָמִים
from-ones-long-ago he-was already he new this look! which-he-can-say anything

אֲשֶׁר הָיָה מִלְּפָנֵנוּ׃ אֵין זִכְרוֹן לָרִאשֹׁנִים
of-the-men-of-old remembrance there-is-no (11) from-before-us he-was that

וְגַם לָאַחֲרֹנִים שֶׁיִּהְיוּ לֹא־ יִהְיֶה לָהֶם
of-them he-will-be not who-they-will-be of-the-coming-ones and-even

זִכָּרוֹן עִם שֶׁיִּהְיוּ לָאַחֲרֹנָה׃ אֲנִי קֹהֶלֶת הָיִיתִי
I-was Teacher I (12) in-the-following-time who-they-will-be by remembrance

מֶלֶךְ עַל־ יִשְׂרָאֵל בִּירוּשָׁלָם׃ וְנָתַתִּי אֶת־ לִבִּי לִדְרוֹשׁ
to-study self-of-me *** and-I-devoted (13) in-Jerusalem Israel over king

וְלָתוּר בַּחָכְמָה עַל כָּל־ אֲשֶׁר נַעֲשָׂה תַּחַת הַשָּׁמַיִם הוּא ׀
this the-heavens under he-is-done that all to by-the-wisdom and-to-explore

Everything Is Meaningless

1 The words of the Teacher,[a] son of David, king in Jerusalem:

2"Meaningless! Meaningless!"
says the Teacher.
"Utterly meaningless!
Everything is meaningless."
3What does man gain from all his labor
at which he toils under the sun?
4Generations come and generations go,
but the earth remains forever.
5The sun rises and the sun sets,
and hurries back to where it rises.
6The wind blows to the south
and turns to the north;
round and round it goes,
ever returning on its course.
7All streams flow into the sea,
yet the sea is never full.
To the place the streams come from,
there they return again.
8All things are wearisome,
more than one can say.
The eye never has enough of seeing,
or the ear its fill of hearing.
9What has been will be again,
what has been done will be done again;
there is nothing new under the sun.
10Is there anything of which one can say,
"Look! This is something new"?
It was here already, long ago;
it was here before our time.
11There is no remembrance of men of old,
and even those who are yet to come
will not be remembered
by those who follow.

Wisdom Is Meaningless

12I, the Teacher, was king over
Israel in Jerusalem. 13I devoted
myself to study and to explore by
wisdom all that is done under

[a]1 *Or leader of the assembly;* also in verses 2 and 12

עִנְיַן רָע נָתַן אֱלֹהִים לִבְנֵי הָאָדָם לַעֲנוֹת בּוֹ׃ רָאִיתִי
I-saw (14) to-him to-afflict the-man on-sons-of God he-laid heaviness burden-of

אֶת־ כָּל־ הַמַּעֲשִׂים שֶׁנַּעֲשׂוּ תַּחַת הַשָּׁמֶשׁ וְהִנֵּה
and-see! the-sun under that-they-are-done the-things-being-done all-of ***

הַכֹּל הֶבֶל וּרְעוּת רוּחַ׃ מְעֻוָּת לֹא־ יוּכַל
he-can not one-being-twisted (15) wind and-chasing-of meaningless the-all

לִתְקֹן וְחֶסְרוֹן לֹא־ יוּכַל לְהִמָּנוֹת׃ דִּבַּרְתִּי אֲנִי עִם־
in I I-thought (16) to-be-counted he-can not and-lack to-be-straightened

לִבִּי לֵאמֹר אֲנִי הִנֵּה הִגְדַּלְתִּי וְהוֹסַפְתִּי חָכְמָה עַל כָּל־ אֲשֶׁר־
who anyone above wisdom and-I-increased I-grew look! I to-say self-of-me

הָיָה לְפָנַי עַל־ יְרוּשָׁלִָם וְלִבִּי רָאָה הַרְבֵּה
to-be-much he-experienced and-heart-of-me Jerusalem over before-me he-was

חָכְמָה וָדָעַת׃ וָאֶתְּנָה לִבִּי לָדַעַת חָכְמָה
wisdom to-understand self-of-me then-I-applied (17) and-knowledge wisdom

וְדַעַת הוֹלֵלוֹת וְשִׂכְלוּת יָדַעְתִּי שֶׁגַּם־ זֶה הוּא רַעְיוֹן
chasing-of he this that-also I-learned and-folly madnesses and-to-understand

רוּחַ׃ כִּי בְּרֹב חָכְמָה רָב־ כָּעַס וְיוֹסִיף
when-he-becomes-more sorrow much-of wisdom with-much-of for (18) wind

דַּעַת יוֹסִיף מַכְאוֹב׃ אָמַרְתִּי אֲנִי בְּלִבִּי
in-heart-of-me I I-thought (2:1) grief then-he-becomes-more knowledge

לְכָה־ נָּא אֲנַסְּכָה* בְשִׂמְחָה וּרְאֵה בְטוֹב וְהִנֵּה
but-see! about-good and-find-out! with-pleasure I-will-test-you now! come!

גַם־ הוּא הָבֶל׃ לִשְׂחוֹק אָמַרְתִּי מְהוֹלָל וּלְשִׂמְחָה
and-with-pleasure being-foolish I-said to-laugh (2) meaningless that also

מַה־ זֹּה עֹשָׂה׃ תַּרְתִּי בְלִבִּי לִמְשׁוֹךְ בַּיַּיִן
with-the-wine to-cheer in-heart-of-me I-tried (3) accomplishing this what?

אֶת־ בְּשָׂרִי וְלִבִּי נֹהֵג בַּחָכְמָה וְלֶאֱחֹז בְּסִכְלוּת
to-folly and-to-embrace with-wisdom one-guiding and-mind-of-me self-of-me ***

עַד אֲשֶׁר־אֶרְאֶה אֵי־ זֶה טוֹב לִבְנֵי הָאָדָם אֲשֶׁר יַעֲשׂוּ
they-do that the-man for-sons-of worthwhile this what I-saw when until

תַּחַת הַשָּׁמַיִם מִסְפַּר יְמֵי חַיֵּיהֶם׃ הִגְדַּלְתִּי מַעֲשָׂי
projects-of-me I-made-great (4) lives-of-them days-of few-of the-heavens under

בָּנִיתִי לִי בָּתִּים נָטַעְתִּי לִי כְּרָמִים׃ עָשִׂיתִי לִי גַּנּוֹת
gardens for-me I-made (5) vineyards for-me I-planted houses for-me I-built

וּפַרְדֵּסִים וְנָטַעְתִּי בָהֶם עֵץ כָּל־ פֶּרִי׃ עָשִׂיתִי לִי
for-me I-made (6) fruit all-of tree-of in-them and-I-planted and-parks

בְּרֵכוֹת מָיִם לְהַשְׁקוֹת מֵהֶם יַעַר צוֹמֵחַ עֵצִים׃
trees one-flourishing-of grove from-them to-water waters reservoirs-of

heaven. What a heavy burden God has laid on men! [14]I have seen all the things that are done under the sun; all of them are meaningless, a chasing after the wind.

[15]What is twisted cannot be
straightened;
what is lacking cannot be
counted.

[16]I thought to myself, "Look, I have grown and increased in wisdom more than anyone who has ruled over Jerusalem before me; I have experienced much of wisdom and knowledge." [17]Then I applied myself to the understanding of wisdom, and also of madness and folly, but I learned that this, too, is a chasing after the wind.

[18]For with much wisdom comes
much sorrow;
the more knowledge, the
more grief.

Pleasures Are Meaningless

2 I thought in my heart, "Come now, I will test you with pleasure to find out what is good." But that also proved to be meaningless. [2]"Laughter," I said, "is foolish. And what does pleasure accomplish?" [3]I tried cheering myself with wine, and embracing folly—my mind still guiding me with wisdom. I wanted to see what was worthwhile for men to do under heaven during the few days of their lives.

[4]I undertook great projects: I built houses for myself and planted vineyards. [5]I made gardens and parks and planted all kinds of fruit trees in them. [6]I made reservoirs to water groves of flourishing trees. [7]I bought male

*1 Most mss have the accent *mereka* (כָה-).

קָנִיתִי עֲבָדִים וּשְׁפָחוֹת וּבְנֵי־ בַיִת הָיָה
he-was house and-ones-born-of and-female-slaves male-slaves I-bought (7)

לִי גַּם מִקְנֶה בָקָר וָצֹאן הַרְבֵּה הָיָה לִי מִכֹּל
more-than-anyone to-me he-was to-be-many and-flock herd cattle also to-me

שֶׁהָיוּ לְפָנַי בִּירוּשָׁלִָם׃ כָּנַסְתִּי לִי גַּם־ כֶּסֶף וְזָהָב
and-gold silver also for-me I-amassed (8) in-Jerusalem before-me who-they-are

וּסְגֻלַּת מְלָכִים וְהַמְּדִינוֹת עָשִׂיתִי לִי שָׁרִים
men-singing for-me I-acquired and-the-provinces kings and-treasure-of

וְשָׁרוֹת וְתַעֲנוּגֹת בְּנֵי הָאָדָם שִׁדָּה וְשִׁדּוֹת׃
and-women woman the-man sons-of and-delights-of and-women-singing

וְגָדַלְתִּי וְהוֹסַפְתִּי מִכֹּל שֶׁהָיָה לְפָנַי
before-me who-he-was more-than-anyone and-I-grew and-I-became-great (9)

בִּירוּשָׁלִָם אַף חָכְמָתִי עָמְדָה לִּי׃ וְכֹל אֲשֶׁר
that and-all (10) with-me she-stayed wisdom-of-me indeed in-Jerusalem

שָׁאֲלוּ עֵינַי לֹא אָצַלְתִּי מֵהֶם לֹא־ מָנַעְתִּי אֶת־ לִבִּי
heart-of-me *** I-refused not from-them I-denied not eyes-of-me they-desired

מִכָּל־ שִׂמְחָה כִּי־ לִבִּי שָׂמֵחַ מִכָּל־ עֲמָלִי
work-of-me in-all-of delighted heart-of-me indeed pleasure from-any-of

וְזֶה־ הָיָה חֶלְקִי מִכָּל־ עֲמָלִי׃ וּפָנִיתִי אֲנִי
I when-I-surveyed (11) labor-of-me for-all-of reward-of-me he-was and-this

בְּכָל־ מַעֲשַׂי שֶׁעָשׂוּ יָדַי וּבֶעָמָל שֶׁעָמַלְתִּי
that-I-toiled and-to-the-toil hands-of-me that-they-did deeds-of-me to-all-of

לַעֲשׂוֹת וְהִנֵּה הַכֹּל הֶבֶל וּרְעוּת רוּחַ וְאֵין יִתְרוֹן
gain and-no wind and-chasing-of meaningless the-all that-see! to-achieve

תַּחַת הַשָּׁמֶשׁ׃ וּפָנִיתִי אֲנִי לִרְאוֹת חָכְמָה וְהוֹלֵלוֹת
also-madnesses wisdom to-consider I then-I-turned (12) the-sun under

וְסִכְלוּת כִּי ׀ מֶה הָאָדָם שֶׁיָּבוֹא אַחֲרֵי הַמֶּלֶךְ אֵת אֲשֶׁר־ כְּבָר
already what *** the-king after who-he-succeeds the-man what? for and-folly

עָשׂוּהוּ׃ וְרָאִיתִי אָנִי שֶׁיֵּשׁ יִתְרוֹן לַחָכְמָה מִן־
more-than to-the-wisdom value that-there-is I and-I-saw (13) they-did-him

הַסִּכְלוּת כִּיתְרוֹן* הָאוֹר מִן־ הַחֹשֶׁךְ׃ הֶחָכָם
the-wise-man (14) the-darkness more-than the-light as-value-of the-folly

עֵינָיו בְּרֹאשׁוֹ וְהַכְּסִיל בַּחֹשֶׁךְ הוֹלֵךְ
walking in-the-darkness while-the-fool in-head-of-him eyes-of-him

וְיָדַעְתִּי גַם־ אָנִי שֶׁמִּקְרֶה אֶחָד יִקְרֶה אֶת־ כֻּלָּם׃
all-of-them *** he-overtakes same that-fate I indeed but-I-realized

וְאָמַרְתִּי אֲנִי בְּלִבִּי כְּמִקְרֵה הַכְּסִיל גַּם־ אֲנִי
I also the-fool as-fate-of in-heart-of-me I then-I-thought (15)

*13 Most mss have *sheva* under the *kaph* and *hireq* under the *yod* (כְּיִ).

and female slaves and had other slaves who were born in my house. I also owned more herds and flocks than anyone in Jerusalem before me. [8]I amassed silver and gold for myself, and the treasure of kings and provinces. I acquired men and women singers, and a harem[b] as well—the delights of the heart of man. [9]I became greater by far than anyone in Jerusalem before me. In all this my wisdom stayed with me.

[10]I denied myself nothing my eyes desired;
I refused my heart no pleasure.
My heart took delight in all my work,
and this was the reward for all my labor.
[11]Yet when I surveyed all that my hands had done
and what I had toiled to achieve,
everything was meaningless, a chasing after the wind;
nothing was gained under the sun.

Wisdom and Folly Are Meaningless

[12]Then I turned my thoughts to consider wisdom,
and also madness and folly.
What more can the king's successor do
than what has already been done?
[13]I saw that wisdom is better than folly,
just as light is better than darkness.
[14]The wise man has eyes in his head,
while the fool walks in the darkness;
but I came to realize
that the same fate overtakes them both.

[15]Then I thought in my heart,
"The fate of the fool will

*b*8 The meaning of the Hebrew for this phrase is uncertain.

יִקְרֵנִי וְלָמָּה חָכַמְתִּי אֲנִי אָז יוֹתֵר וְדִבַּרְתִּי
and-I-said gain then I should-I-be-wise then-why? he-will-overtake-me

בְלִבִּי שֶׁגַּם־ זֶה הָבֶל׃ כִּי אֵין זִכְרוֹן
remembrance-of there-is-no for (16) meaningless this that-also in-heart-of-me

לֶחָכָם עִם־ הַכְּסִיל לְעוֹלָם בְּשֶׁכְּבָר הַיָּמִים
the-days in-that-already to-forever the-fool like for-the-wise-man

הַבָּאִים הַכֹּל נִשְׁכָּח וְאֵיךְ יָמוּת
he-must-die and-indeed! he-will-be-forgotten the-all the-coming-ones

הֶחָכָם עִם־ הַכְּסִיל׃ וְשָׂנֵאתִי אֶת־ הַחַיִּים כִּי רַע
grievous because the-lives *** so-I-hated (17) the-fool like the-wise-man

עָלַי הַמַּעֲשֶׂה שֶׁנַּעֲשָׂה תַּחַת הַשָּׁמֶשׁ כִּי־ הַכֹּל הֶבֶל
meaningless the-all for the-sun under that-he-is-done the-work to-me

וּרְעוּת רוּחַ׃ וְשָׂנֵאתִי אֲנִי אֶת־ כָּל־ עֲמָלִי שֶׁאֲנִי עָמֵל
toiling that-I toil-of-me all-of *** I and-I-hated (18) wind and-chasing-of

תַּחַת הַשָּׁמֶשׁ שֶׁאַנִּיחֶנּוּ לָאָדָם שֶׁיִּהְיֶה אַחֲרָי׃
after-me who-he-comes to-the-one that-I-must-leave-him the-sun under

וּמִי יוֹדֵעַ הֶחָכָם יִהְיֶה אוֹ סָכָל וְיִשְׁלַט
yet-he-will-control fool or he-will-be whether-wise-man knowing and-who? (19)

בְּכָל־ עֲמָלִי שֶׁעָמַלְתִּי וְשֶׁחָכַמְתִּי תַּחַת
under and-which-I-poured-skill which-I-poured-effort work-of-me over-all-of

הַשָּׁמֶשׁ גַּם־ זֶה הָבֶל׃ וְסַבּוֹתִי אֲנִי לְיַאֵשׁ אֶת־ לִבִּי
heart-of-me *** to-despair I so-I-began (20) meaningless this also the-sun

עַל כָּל־ הֶעָמָל שֶׁעָמַלְתִּי תַּחַת הַשָּׁמֶשׁ׃ כִּי־ יֵשׁ אָדָם
man there-is for (21) the-sun under which-I-labored the-toil all-of over

שֶׁעֲמָלוֹ בְּחָכְמָה וּבְדַעַת וּבְכִשְׁרוֹן וּלְאָדָם
then-to-man and-with-skill and-with-knowledge with-wisdom that-work-of-him

שֶׁלֹּא עָמַל־ בּוֹ יִתְּנֶנּוּ חֶלְקוֹ גַּם־ זֶה
this also property-of-him he-must-leave-him for-him he-worked who-not

הֶבֶל וְרָעָה רַבָּה׃ כִּי מֶה־ הֹוֶה לָאָדָם בְּכָל־
for-all-of to-the-man coming what? for (22) great and-misfortune meaningless

עֲמָלוֹ וּבְרַעְיוֹן לִבּוֹ שֶׁהוּא עָמֵל תַּחַת הַשָּׁמֶשׁ׃
the-sun under laboring which-he heart-of-him and-for-striving-of toil-of-him

כִּי כָל־ יָמָיו מַכְאֹבִים וָכַעַס עִנְיָנוֹ גַּם־ בַּלַּיְלָה
at-the-night even work-of-him and-grief-of pains days-of-him all-of for (23)

לֹא־ שָׁכַב לִבּוֹ גַּם־ זֶה הֶבֶל הוּא׃ אֵין־ טוֹב
better nothing (24) he meaningless this also mind-of-him he-rests not

בָּאָדָם שֶׁיֹּאכַל וְשָׁתָה וְהֶרְאָה אֶת־
*** and-he-should-find and-he-should-drink than-he-should-eat for-the-man

overtake me also.
What then do I gain by
being wise?"
I said in my heart,
"This too is meaningless."
16For the wise man, like the
fool, will not be long
remembered;
in days to come both will be
forgotten.
Like the fool, the wise man too
must die!

Toil Is Meaningless

17So I hated life, because the
work that is done under the sun
was grievous to me. All of it is
meaningless, a chasing after the
wind. 18I hated all the things I had
toiled for under the sun, because I
must leave them to the one who
comes after me. 19And who knows
whether he will be a wise man or
a fool? Yet he will have control
over all the work into which I
have poured my effort and skill
under the sun. This too is meaningless. 20So my heart began to despair over all my toilsome labor
under the sun. 21For a man may do
his work with wisdom, knowledge and skill, and then he must
leave all he owns to someone who
has not worked for it. This too is
meaningless and a great misfortune. 22What does a man get for all
the toil and anxious striving with
which he labors under the sun?
23All his days his work is pain and
grief; even at night his mind does
not rest. This too is meaningless.
24A man can do nothing better
than to eat and drink and find

נַפְשׁוֹ טוֹב בַּעֲמָלוֹ גַּם־ זֹה רָאִיתִי אָנִי כִּי מִיַּד
from-hand-of that I I-see this also in-work-of-him satisfaction self-of-him

הָאֱלֹהִים הִיא׃ כִּי מִי יֹאכַל וּמִי יָחוּשׁ חוּץ
without he-can-find-enjoyment and-who? he-can-eat who? for (25) she the-God

מִמֶּנִּי׃ כִּי לְאָדָם שֶׁטּוֹב לְפָנָיו נָתַן חָכְמָה וְדַעַת
and-knowledge wisdom he-gives before-him who-pleasing to-man for (26) from-me

וְשִׂמְחָה וְלַחוֹטֶא נָתַן עִנְיָן לֶאֱסוֹף וְלִכְנוֹס
and-to-store to-gather task he-gives but-to-the-one-sinning and-happiness

לָתֵת לְטוֹב לִפְנֵי הָאֱלֹהִים גַּם־ זֶה הֶבֶל וּרְעוּת
and-chasing-of meaningless this also the-God before to-one-pleasing to-hand

רוּחַ׃ לַכֹּל זְמָן וְעֵת לְכָל־ חֵפֶץ תַּחַת
under activity for-every-of and-season time for-the-everything (3:1) wind

הַשָּׁמָיִם׃ עֵת לָלֶדֶת וְעֵת לָמוּת עֵת לָטַעַת
to-plant time-of to-die and-time-of to-be-born time-of (2) the-heavens

וְעֵת לַעֲקוֹר נָטוּעַ׃ עֵת לַהֲרוֹג וְעֵת
and-time-of to-kill time-of (3) one-being-planted to-uproot and-time-of

לִרְפּוֹא עֵת לִפְרוֹץ וְעֵת לִבְנוֹת׃ עֵת לִבְכּוֹת
to-weep time-of (4) to-build and-time-of to-tear-down time-of to-heal

וְעֵת לִשְׂחוֹק עֵת סְפוֹד וְעֵת רְקוֹד׃ עֵת
time-of (5) to-dance and-time-of to-mourn time-of to-laugh and-time-of

לְהַשְׁלִיךְ אֲבָנִים וְעֵת כְּנוֹס אֲבָנִים עֵת לַחֲבוֹק וְעֵת
and-time-of to-embrace time-of stones to-gather and-time-of stones to-scatter

לִרְחֹק מֵחַבֵּק׃ עֵת לְבַקֵּשׁ וְעֵת לְאַבֵּד
to-give-up and-time-of to-search time-of (6) from-to-embrace to-refrain

עֵת לִשְׁמוֹר וְעֵת לְהַשְׁלִיךְ׃ עֵת לִקְרוֹעַ וְעֵת
and-time-of to-tear time-of (7) to-throw-away and-time-of to-keep time-of

לִתְפּוֹר עֵת לַחֲשׁוֹת וְעֵת לְדַבֵּר׃ עֵת לֶאֱהֹב
to-love time-of (8) to-speak and-time-of to-be-silent time-of to-mend

וְעֵת לִשְׂנֹא עֵת מִלְחָמָה וְעֵת שָׁלוֹם׃ מַה־ יִּתְרוֹן
gain-of what? (9) peace and-time-of war time-of to-hate and-time-of

הָעוֹשֶׂה בַּאֲשֶׁר הוּא עָמֵל׃ רָאִיתִי אֶת־ הָעִנְיָן אֲשֶׁר נָתַן
he-laid that the-burden *** I-saw (10) toiling he from-what the-one-working

אֱלֹהִים לִבְנֵי הָאָדָם לַעֲנוֹת בּוֹ׃ אֶת־ הַכֹּל עָשָׂה יָפֶה
beautiful he-made the-all *** (11) to-him to-afflict the-man on-sons-of God

בְעִתּוֹ גַּם אֶת־ הָעֹלָם נָתַן בְּלִבָּם מִבְּלִי אֲשֶׁר
that yet-not in-heart-of-them he-set the-eternity *** also in-time-of-him

לֹא־ יִמְצָא הָאָדָם אֶת־הַמַּעֲשֶׂה אֲשֶׁר־ עָשָׂה הָאֱלֹהִים מֵרֹאשׁ
from-beginning the-God he-did that the-deed *** the-man he-can-fathom not

satisfaction in his work. This too, I see, is from the hand of God, [25]for without him, who can eat or find enjoyment? [26]To the man who pleases him, God gives wisdom, knowledge and happiness, but to the sinner he gives the task of gathering and storing up wealth to hand it over to the one who pleases God. This too is meaningless, a chasing after the wind.

A Time for Everything

3 There is a time for everything,
and a season for every activity under heaven:

2 a time to be born and a time to die,
a time to plant and a time to uproot,
3 a time to kill and a time to heal,
a time to tear down and a time to build,
4 a time to weep and a time to laugh,
a time to mourn and a time to dance,
5 a time to scatter stones and a time to gather them,
a time to embrace and a time to refrain,
6 a time to search and a time to give up,
a time to keep and a time to throw away,
7 a time to tear and a time to mend,
a time to be silent and a time to speak,
8 a time to love and a time to hate,
a time for war and a time for peace.

[9]What does the worker gain from his toil? [10]I have seen the burden God has laid on men. [11]He has made everything beautiful in its time. He has also set eternity in the hearts of men; yet they cannot fathom what God has done from

וְעַד־ סוֹף׃ יָדַעְתִּי כִּי אֵין טוֹב בָּם כִּי אִם־
if than for-them better there-is-nothing that I-know (12) end and-to

לִשְׂמוֹחַ וְלַעֲשׂוֹת טוֹב בְּחַיָּיו׃ וְגַם כָּל־ הָאָדָם
the-man every-of and-also (13) in-lives-of-him good and-to-do to-be-happy

שֶׁיֹּאכַל וְשָׁתָה וְרָאָה טוֹב בְּכָל־
in-all-of satisfaction and-he-may-find and-he-may-drink that-he-may-eat

עֲמָלוֹ מַתַּת אֱלֹהִים הִיא׃ יָדַעְתִּי כִּי כָּל־אֲשֶׁר יַעֲשֶׂה הָאֱלֹהִים הוּא
he the-God he-does that all that I-know (14) this God gift-of toil-of-him

יִהְיֶה לְעוֹלָם עָלָיו אֵין לְהוֹסִיף וּמִמֶּנּוּ אֵין לִגְרֹעַ
to-take nothing and-from-him to-add nothing to-him to-forever he-will-endure

וְהָאֱלֹהִים עָשָׂה שֶׁיִּרְאוּ מִלְּפָנָיו׃ מַה־
whatever (15) at-before-him who-they-will-revere he-does and-the-God

שֶּׁהָיָה כְּבָר הוּא וַאֲשֶׁר לִהְיוֹת כְּבָר הָיָה וְהָאֱלֹהִים
and-the-God he-was already to-be and-what he already that-he-was

יְבַקֵּשׁ אֶת־ נִרְדָּף׃ וְעוֹד רָאִיתִי תַּחַת הַשָּׁמֶשׁ
the-sun under I-saw and-more (16) one-being-past *** he-calls-to-account

מְקוֹם הַמִּשְׁפָּט שָׁמָּה הָרֶשַׁע וּמְקוֹם הַצֶּדֶק
the-justice and-place-of the-wickedness at-there the-judgment place-of

שָׁמָּה הָרָשַׁע׃ אָמַרְתִּי אֲנִי בְּלִבִּי אֶת־ הַצַּדִּיק
the-righteous *** in-heart-of-me I I-thought (17) the-wickedness at-there

וְאֶת־ הָרָשָׁע יִשְׁפֹּט הָאֱלֹהִים כִּי־ עֵת לְכָל־ חֵפֶץ וְעַל
and-for activity for-every-of time for the-God he-will-judge the-wicked and

כָּל־ הַמַּעֲשֶׂה שָׁם׃ אָמַרְתִּי אֲנִי בְּלִבִּי עַל־ דִּבְרַת בְּנֵי
sons-of matter-of for in-heart-of-me I I-thought (18) there the-deed every-of

הָאָדָם לְבָרָם הָאֱלֹהִים וְלִרְאוֹת שְׁהֶם־ בְּהֵמָה הֵמָּה לָהֶם׃
like-them they animal that-they and-to-see the-God to-test-them the-man

כִּי מִקְרֶה בְנֵי־ הָאָדָם וּמִקְרֶה הַבְּהֵמָה וּמִקְרֶה אֶחָד
same also-fate the-animal and-fate the-man sons-of fate for (19)

לָהֶם כְּמוֹת זֶה כֵּן מוֹת זֶה וְרוּחַ אֶחָד לַכֹּל
to-the-all same and-spirit other death-of so one as-death-of for-them

וּמוֹתַר הָאָדָם מִן־ הַבְּהֵמָה אָיִן כִּי הַכֹּל הָבֶל׃
meaningless the-all for there-is-no the-animal over the-man and-advantage-of

הַכֹּל הוֹלֵךְ אֶל־מָקוֹם אֶחָד הַכֹּל הָיָה מִן־ הֶעָפָר וְהַכֹּל
and-the-all the-dust from he-comes the-all same place to going the-all (20)

שָׁב אֶל־ הֶעָפָר׃ מִי יוֹדֵעַ רוּחַ בְּנֵי הָאָדָם
the-man sons-of spirit-of knowing who? (21) the-dust to he-returns

הָעֹלָה הִיא לְמָעְלָה וְרוּחַ הַבְּהֵמָה הַיֹּרֶדֶת הִיא
she the-one-going-down the-animal and-spirit-of to-upward she the-one-rising

beginning to end. [12]I know that
there is nothing better for men
than to be happy and do good
while they live. [13]That every man
may eat and drink, and find satisfaction in all his toil—this is the
gift of God. [14]I know that everything God does will endure forever; nothing can be added to it
and nothing taken from it. God
does it, so men will revere him.

[15]Whatever is has already been,
and what will be has been before;
and God will call the past to account.[c]

[16]And I saw something else under the sun:

In the place of judgment—wickedness was there,
in the place of justice—wickedness was there.

[17]I thought in my heart,

"God will bring to judgment both the righteous and the wicked,
for there will be a time for every activity,
a time for every deed."

[18]I also thought, "As for men,
God tests them so that they may
see that they are like the animals.
[19]Man's fate is like that of the animals; the same fate awaits them
both: As one dies, so dies the other. All have the same breath[d]; man
has no advantage over the animal.
Everything is meaningless. [20]All
go to the same place; all come from
dust, and to dust all return. [21]Who
knows if the spirit of man rises
upward and if the spirit of the animal goes down into the earth[e]?"

[c]15 Or *God calls back the past*
[d]19 Or *spirit*
[e]21 Or *Who knows the spirit of man, which rises upward, or the spirit of the animal, which goes down into the earth*

לְמַטָּה לָאָרֶץ׃ וְרָאִיתִי כִּי אֵין טוֹב
good there-is-nothing that so-I-saw (22) into-the-earth to-downward

מֵאֲשֶׁר יִשְׂמַח הָאָדָם בְּמַעֲשָׂיו כִּי־ הוּא חֶלְקוֹ כִּי
for lot-of-him that because to-works-of-him the-man he-enjoy more-than-that

מִי יְבִיאֶנּוּ לִרְאוֹת בְּמֶה שֶׁיִּהְיֶה אַחֲרָיו׃
after-him that-he-will-happen to-what to-see he-can-bring-him who?

וְשַׁבְתִּי אֲנִי וָאֶרְאֶה אֶת־ כָּל־ הָעֲשֻׁקִים אֲשֶׁר
that the-ones-being-oppressed all-of *** and-I-saw I then-I-returned (4:1)

נַעֲשִׂים תַּחַת הַשָּׁמֶשׁ וְהִנֵּה׀ דִּמְעַת הָעֲשֻׁקִים
the-ones-being-oppressed tear-of and-see! the-sun under ones-taking-place

וְאֵין לָהֶם מְנַחֵם וּמִיַּד עֹשְׁקֵיהֶם
ones-oppressing-them and-on-side-of one-comforting to-them and-there-was-not

כֹּחַ וְאֵין לָהֶם מְנַחֵם׃ וְשַׁבֵּחַ אֲנִי אֶת־
*** I and-to-declare (2) one-comforting to-them and-there-was-not power

הַמֵּתִים שֶׁכְּבָר מֵתוּ מִן־ הַחַיִּים אֲשֶׁר הֵמָּה
they who the-living-ones more-than they-died who-already the-dead-ones

חַיִּים עֲדֶנָה׃ וְטוֹב מִשְּׁנֵיהֶם אֵת אֲשֶׁר־ עֲדֶן לֹא
not yet who *** more-than-both-of-them but-good (3) still alive-ones

הָיָה אֲשֶׁר לֹא־ רָאָה אֶת־ הַמַּעֲשֶׂה הָרָע אֲשֶׁר נַעֲשָׂה תַּחַת הַשָּׁמֶשׁ׃
the-sun under he-is-done that the-evil the-deed *** he-saw not who he-is

וְרָאִיתִי אֲנִי אֶת־ כָּל־ עָמָל וְאֵת כָּל־ כִּשְׁרוֹן הַמַּעֲשֶׂה כִּי
that the-work achievement-of all-of and labor all-of *** I and-I-saw (4)

הִיא קִנְאַת־ אִישׁ מֵרֵעֵהוּ גַּם־ זֶה הֶבֶל וּרְעוּת רוּחַ׃
wind and-chasing-of meaningless this also of-neighbor-of-him man envy-of she

הַכְּסִיל חֹבֵק אֶת־ יָדָיו וְאֹכֵל אֶת־ בְּשָׂרוֹ׃ טוֹב
good (6) self-of-him *** and-ruining hands-of-him *** folding the-fool (5)

מְלֹא כַף נָחַת מִמְּלֹא חָפְנַיִם עָמָל
toil two-hands more-than-fullness-of tranquility hand fullness-of

וּרְעוּת רוּחַ׃ וְשַׁבְתִּי אֲנִי וָאֶרְאֶה הֶבֶל תַּחַת
under meaninglessness and-I-saw I and-I-did-again (7) wind and-chasing-of

הַשָּׁמֶשׁ׃ יֵשׁ אֶחָד וְאֵין שֵׁנִי גַּם בֵּן וָאָח
or-brother son also other and-there-was-not man there-was (8) the-sun

אֵין־ לוֹ וְאֵין קֵץ לְכָל־ עֲמָלוֹ גַּם־
yet toil-of-him to-all-of end and-there-was-no to-him there-was-not

עֵינָיו לֹא־ תִשְׂבַּע עֹשֶׁר וּלְמִי׀ אֲנִי עָמֵל וּמְחַסֵּר
and-depriving toiling I and-for-whom? wealth she-was-content not eye-of-him

אֶת־ נַפְשִׁי מִטּוֹבָה גַּם־ זֶה הֶבֶל וְעִנְיַן רָע הוּא׃
he misery and-business-of meaningless this also of-enjoyment self-of-me ***

22 So I saw that there is nothing better for a man than to enjoy his work, because that is his lot. For who can bring him to see what will happen after him?

Oppression, Toil, Friendlessness

4 Again I looked and saw all the oppression that was taking place under the sun:

I saw the tears of the oppressed—
and they have no comforter;
power was on the side of their oppressors—
and they have no comforter.
2 And I declared that the dead,
who had already died,
are happier than the living,
who are still alive.
3 But better than both
is he who has not yet been,
who has not seen the evil
that is done under the sun.

4 And I saw that all labor and all achievement spring from man's envy of his neighbor. This too is meaningless, a chasing after the wind.

5 The fool folds his hands
and ruins himself.
6 Better one handful with tranquillity
than two handfuls with toil
and chasing after the wind.

7 Again I saw something meaningless under the sun:

8 There was a man all alone;
he had neither son nor brother.
There was no end to his toil,
yet his eyes were not content with his wealth.
"For whom am I toiling," he asked,
"and why am I depriving myself of enjoyment?"
This too is meaningless—
a miserable business!

°8 ק עינו

טוֹבִים הַשְּׁנַיִם מִן־ הָאֶחָד אֲשֶׁר יֵשׁ־ לָהֶם שָׂכָר טוֹב
good return to-them there-is because the-one more-than the-two good-ones (9)

בַּעֲמָלָם׃ כִּי אִם־ יִפֹּלוּ הָאֶחָד יָקִים אֶת־
*** he-can-help-up the-one they-fall if for (10) for-work-of-them

חֲבֵרוֹ וְאִילוֹ הָאֶחָד שֶׁיִּפּוֹל וְאֵין שֵׁנִי
other and-there-is-no who-he-falls the-one but-pity-to-him! friend-of-him

לַהֲקִימוֹ׃ גַּם אִם־ יִשְׁכְּבוּ שְׁנַיִם וְחַם לָהֶם וּלְאֶחָד
but-to-one to-them then-he-is-warm two they-lie-down if also (11) to-help-up-him

אֵיךְ יֵחָם׃ וְאִם־ יִתְקְפוֹ הָאֶחָד הַשְּׁנַיִם
the-two the-one they-may-overpower and-though (12) can-he-keep-warm how?

יַעַמְדוּ נֶגְדּוֹ וְהַחוּט הַמְשֻׁלָּשׁ לֹא בִמְהֵרָה
in-quickness not the-one-being-tripled and-the-cord before-him they-can-stand

יִנָּתֵק׃ טוֹב יֶלֶד מִסְכֵּן וְחָכָם מִמֶּלֶךְ זָקֵן וּכְסִיל
but-foolish old more-than-king but-wise poor youth good (13) he-is-broken

אֲשֶׁר לֹא־ יָדַע לְהִזָּהֵר עוֹד׃ כִּי־ מִבֵּית
from-house-of indeed (14) longer to-take-warning he-knows not who

הָסוּרִים יָצָא לִמְלֹךְ כִּי גַּם בְּמַלְכוּתוֹ
within-kingdom-of-him rather or to-be-king he-came the-ones-being-imprisoned

נוֹלַד רָשׁ׃ רָאִיתִי אֶת־ כָּל־ הַחַיִּים
the-ones-alive all-of *** I-saw (15) one-being-poor he-was-born

הַמְהַלְּכִים תַּחַת הַשָּׁמֶשׁ עִם הַיֶּלֶד הַשֵּׁנִי אֲשֶׁר יַעֲמֹד
he-succeeded who the-other the-youth with the-sun under the-ones-walking

תַּחְתָּיו׃ אֵין־ קֵץ לְכָל־ הָעָם לְכֹל אֲשֶׁר־ הָיָה
he-was who to-all the-people to-all-of end there-was-no (16) after-him

לִפְנֵיהֶם גַּם הָאַחֲרוֹנִים לֹא יִשְׂמְחוּ־ בוֹ כִּי־ גַם־
also indeed with-him they-were-pleased not the-later-ones but before-them

זֶה הֶבֶל וְרַעְיוֹן רוּחַ׃ שְׁמֹר רַגְלֶיךָ° כַּאֲשֶׁר תֵּלֵךְ
you-go as-when step-of-you guard! *(17) wind and-chasing-of meaningless this

אֶל־ בֵּית הָאֱלֹהִים וְקָרוֹב לִשְׁמֹעַ מִתֵּת הַכְּסִילִים
the-fools rather-than-to-offer to-listen then-to-go-near the-God house-of to

זָבַח כִּי־ אֵינָם יוֹדְעִים לַעֲשׂוֹת רָע׃ אַל־ תְּבַהֵל עַל־
with you-be-quick not (5:1) wrong to-do ones-knowing not-they for sacrifice

פִּיךָ וְלִבְּךָ אַל־ יְמַהֵר לְהוֹצִיא דָבָר לִפְנֵי
before anything to-utter let-him-be-hasty not and-heart-of-you mouth-of-you

הָאֱלֹהִים כִּי הָאֱלֹהִים בַּשָּׁמַיִם וְאַתָּה עַל־ הָאָרֶץ עַל־ כֵּן יִהְיוּ
let-them-be this for the-earth on and-you in-the-heavens the-God for the-God

דְבָרֶיךָ מְעַטִּים׃ כִּי בָּא הַחֲלוֹם בְּרֹב עִנְיָן
care when-many-of the-dream he-comes as (2) few-ones words-of-you

[9]Two are better than one,
because they have a good
return for their work:
[10]If one falls down,
his friend can help him up.
But pity the man who falls
and has no one to help him
up!
[11]Also, if two lie down together,
they will keep warm.
But how can one keep warm
alone?
[12]Though one may be
overpowered,
two can defend themselves.
A cord of three strands is not
quickly broken.

Advancement Is Meaningless

[13]Better a poor but wise youth
than an old but foolish king who
no longer knows how to take
warning. [14]The youth may have
come from prison to the kingship,
or he may have been born in poverty within his kingdom. [15]I saw
that all who lived and walked under the sun followed the youth,
the king's successor. [16]There was
no end to all the people who were
before them. But those who came
later were not pleased with the
successor. This too is meaningless,
a chasing after the wind.

Stand in Awe of God

5 Guard your steps when you go
to the house of God. Go near to
listen rather than to offer the sacrifice of fools, who do not know
that they do wrong.

[2]Do not be quick with your
mouth,
do not be hasty in your
heart
to utter anything before
God.
God is in heaven
and you are on earth,
so let your words be few.
[3]As a dream comes when there
are many cares,

***17 The Hebrew numeration of chapter 5 begins with verse two of the English; thus, there is a one-verse discrepancy throughout the chapter.**

°*17* ק רגלך

וְקוֹל כְּסִיל בְּרֹב דְּבָרִים׃ כַּאֲשֶׁר תִּדֹּר נֶדֶר לֵאלֹהִים

to-God vow you-make-vow as-when (3) words when-many-of fool so-speech-of

אַל־ תְּאַחֵר לְשַׁלְּמוֹ כִּי אֵין חֵפֶץ בַּכְּסִילִים אֵת אֲשֶׁר־

what *** in-the-fools pleasure there-is-no for to-fulfill-him you-delay not

תִּדֹּר שַׁלֵּם׃ טוֹב אֲשֶׁר לֹא־ תִדֹּר מִשֶּׁתִּדּוֹר

more-than-that-you-make-vow you-make-vow not that good (4) fulfill! you-vow

וְלֹא תְשַׁלֵּם׃ אַל־ תִּתֵּן אֶת־ פִּיךָ לַחֲטִיא אֶת־

*** to-lead-into-sin mouth-of-you *** you-let not (5) you-fulfill and-not

בְּשָׂרֶךָ וְאַל־ תֹּאמַר לִפְנֵי הַמַּלְאָךְ כִּי שְׁגָגָה הִיא

she mistake that the-messenger before you-protest and-not self-of-you

לָמָּה יִקְצֹף הָאֱלֹהִים עַל־ קוֹלֶךָ וְחִבֵּל אֶת־ מַעֲשֵׂה

work-of *** and-he-destroy saying-of-you at the-God should-he-be-angry why?

יָדֶיךָ׃ כִּי בְרֹב חֲלֹמוֹת וַהֲבָלִים וּדְבָרִים

and-words also-meaninglessnesses dreams in-much-of for (6) hands-of-you

הַרְבֵּה כִּי אֶת־הָאֱלֹהִים יְרָא׃ אִם־ עֹשֶׁק רָשׁ

one-being-poor oppression-of if (7) fear! the-God *** therefore to-be-many

וְגֵזֶל מִשְׁפָּט וָצֶדֶק תִּרְאֶה בַמְּדִינָה אַל־ תִּתְמַהּ

you-be-surprised not in-the-district you-see and-right justice and-denial-of

עַל־ הַחֵפֶץ כִּי גָבֹהַּ מֵעַל גָּבֹהַּ שֹׁמֵר וּגְבֹהִים

and-officials one-eyeing official at-above official for the-thing at

עֲלֵיהֶם׃ וְיִתְרוֹן אֶרֶץ בַּכֹּל הִיא מֶלֶךְ לְשָׂדֶה נֶעֱבָד׃

he-profits from-field king he to-the-all land and-increase-of (8) over-them

אֹהֵב כֶּסֶף לֹא־ יִשְׂבַּע כֶּסֶף וּמִי־ אֹהֵב

one-loving and-whoever money he-has-enough never money one-loving (9)

בֶּהָמוֹן לֹא תְבוּאָה גַּם־ זֶה הָבֶל׃ בִּרְבוֹת

when-to-increase (10) meaningless this also income never to-the-wealth

הַטּוֹבָה רַבּוּ אוֹכְלֶיהָ וּמַה־ כִּשְׁרוֹן לִבְעָלֶיהָ

to-owners-of-her benefit and-what? ones-consuming-her they-increase the-good

כִּי אִם־ רְאִית עֵינָיו׃ מְתוּקָה שְׁנַת הָעֹבֵד

the-one-laboring sleep-of sweet (11) eyes-of-him feasting-of if except

אִם־ מְעַט וְאִם־ הַרְבֵּה יֹאכֵל וְהַשָּׂבָע לֶעָשִׁיר

of-the-rich but-the-abundance he-eats to-be-much or-whether little whether

אֵינֶנּוּ מַנִּיחַ לוֹ לִישׁוֹן׃ יֵשׁ רָעָה חוֹלָה

one-being-grievous evil there-is (12) to-sleep to-him one-permitting not-he

רָאִיתִי תַּחַת הַשָּׁמֶשׁ עֹשֶׁר שָׁמוּר לִבְעָלָיו לְרָעָתוֹ׃

to-harm-of-him by-owners-of-him being-hoarded wealth the-sun under I-saw

וְאָבַד הָעֹשֶׁר הַהוּא בְּעִנְיַן רָע

misfortune through-event-of the-this the-wealth or-he-is-lost (13)

so the speech of a fool when
there are many words.

[4]When you make a vow to God, do not delay in fulfilling it. He has no pleasure in fools; fulfill your vow. [5]It is better not to vow than to make a vow and not fulfill it. [6]Do not let your mouth lead you into sin. And do not protest to the ⌊temple⌋ messenger, "My vow was a mistake." Why should God be angry at what you say and destroy the work of your hands? [7]Much dreaming and many words are meaningless. Therefore stand in awe of God.

Riches Are Meaningless

[8]If you see the poor oppressed in a district, and justice and rights denied, do not be surprised at such things; for one official is eyed by a higher one, and over them both are others higher still. [9]The increase from the land is taken by all; the king himself profits from the fields.

[10]Whoever loves money never
has money enough;
whoever loves wealth is
never satisfied with his
income.
This too is meaningless.

[11]As goods increase,
so do those who consume
them.
And what benefit are they to
the owner
except to feast his eyes on
them?

[12]The sleep of a laborer is sweet,
whether he eats little or
much,
but the abundance of a rich
man
permits him no sleep.

[13]I have seen a grievous evil under the sun:

wealth hoarded to the harm of
its owner,
14 or wealth lost through some
misfortune,

*See the note on page 576.

°8 ק הוא

°10 ק ראות

וְהוֹלִ֣יד בֵּ֔ן וְאֵ֥ין בְּיָד֖וֹ מְאֽוּמָה׃ כַּאֲשֶׁ֤ר
just-as (14) anything for-hand-of-him and-there-is-not son so-he-fathers

יָצָא֙ מִבֶּ֣טֶן אִמּ֔וֹ עָר֥וֹם יָשׁ֛וּב לָלֶ֖כֶת כְּשֶׁבָּ֑א
as-that-he-comes to-go he-departs naked mother-of-him from-womb-of he-comes

וּמְא֙וּמָה֙ לֹא־יִשָּׂ֣א בַעֲמָל֔וֹ שֶׁיֹּלֵ֖ךְ בְּיָדֽוֹ׃
in-hand-of-him that-he-can-carry from-labor-of-him he-takes not and-anything

(15) וְגַם־זֹה֙ רָעָ֣ה חוֹלָ֔ה כָּל־עֻמַּ֥ת שֶׁבָּ֖א כֵּ֣ן
so that-he-comes as-of all-of being-grievous evil this and-also (15)

יֵלֵ֑ךְ וּמַה־יִּתְר֣וֹן ל֔וֹ שֶׁיַּעֲמֹ֖ל לָרֽוּחַ׃ (16) גַּ֥ם
also (16) for-the-wind since-he-toils for-him gain and-what? he-departs

כָּל־יָמָ֖יו בַּחֹ֣שֶׁךְ יֹאכֵ֑ל וְכָעַ֥ס הַרְבֵּ֖ה
to-be-great and-he-is-frustrated he-eats in-the-darkness days-of-him all-of

וְחָלְי֥וֹ וָקָֽצֶף׃ (17) הִנֵּ֞ה אֲשֶׁר־רָאִ֣יתִי אָ֗נִי ט֣וֹב אֲשֶׁר־
that good I I-realized then see! (17) and-anger and-affliction-of-him

יָפֶ֣ה לֶאֱכוֹל־וְ֠לִשְׁתּוֹת וְלִרְא֨וֹת טוֹבָ֜ה בְּכָל־עֲמָל֣וֹ ׀
labor-of-him in-all-of satisfaction and-to-find and-to-drink to-eat proper

שֶֽׁיַּעֲמֹ֣ל תַּֽחַת־הַשֶּׁ֗מֶשׁ מִסְפַּ֛ר יְמֵי־חַיָּ֛ו אֲשֶׁר־נָֽתַן־ל֥וֹ
to-him he-gave that lives-of-him days-of few-of the-sun under that-he-toils

הָאֱלֹהִ֖ים כִּי־ה֥וּא חֶלְקֽוֹ׃ (18) גַּ֣ם כָּל־הָאָדָ֡ם אֲשֶׁ֣ר נָֽתַן־
he-gives whom the-man any-of moreover (18) lot-of-him this for the-God

ל֣וֹ הָאֱלֹהִים֩ עֹ֨שֶׁר וּנְכָסִ֜ים וְהִשְׁלִיט֨וֹ לֶאֱכֹ֤ל מִמֶּ֙נּוּ֙
from-him to-enjoy and-he-enables-him and-possessions wealth the-God to-him

וְלָשֵׂ֣את אֶת־חֶלְק֔וֹ וְלִשְׂמֹ֖חַ בַּעֲמָל֑וֹ זֹ֕ה מַתַּ֥ת
gift-of this in-work-of-him and-to-be-happy lot-of-him *** and-to-accept

אֱלֹהִ֖ים הִֽיא׃ (19) כִּ֚י לֹ֣א הַרְבֵּ֔ה יִזְכֹּ֖ר אֶת־יְמֵ֣י חַיָּ֑יו
lives-of-him days-of *** he-reflects-on to-be-often not indeed (19) she God

כִּ֧י הָאֱלֹהִ֛ים מַעֲנֶ֖ה בְּשִׂמְחַ֥ת לִבּֽוֹ׃ (6:1) יֵ֣שׁ
there-is (6:1) heart-of-him with-gladness-of one-occupying the-God because

רָעָ֔ה אֲשֶׁ֥ר רָאִ֖יתִי תַּ֣חַת הַשָּׁ֑מֶשׁ וְרַבָּ֥ה הִ֖יא עַל־הָאָדָֽם׃ (2) אִ֣ישׁ אֲשֶׁ֣ר יִתֶּן־
he-gives whom man (2) the-man on she and-heavy the-sun under I-saw that evil

ל֣וֹ הָאֱלֹהִ֗ים עֹ֘שֶׁר֮ וּנְכָסִ֣ים וְכָבוֹד֒ וְאֵינֶ֨נּוּ חָסֵ֥ר לְנַפְשׁ֣וֹ ׀
to-heart-of-him lack so-not-he and-honor and-possessions wealth the-God to-him

מִכֹּ֣ל אֲשֶׁר־יִתְאַוֶּ֗ה וְלֹֽא־יַשְׁלִיטֶ֤נּוּ הָאֱלֹהִים֙ לֶאֱכֹ֣ל מִמֶּ֔נּוּ
from-him to-enjoy the-God he-enables-him but-not he-desires that from-all

כִּ֛י אִ֥ישׁ נָכְרִ֖י יֹאכְלֶ֑נּוּ זֶ֥ה הֶ֛בֶל וָחֳלִ֥י רָ֖ע הֽוּא׃
he grievous and-evil meaningless this he-enjoys-him stranger man but

(3) אִם־יוֹלִ֨יד אִ֜ישׁ מֵאָ֗ה וְשָׁנִ֤ים רַבּוֹת֙ יִֽחְיֶ֔ה וְרַ֣ב ׀
yet-many he-lives many and-years hundred man he-has-children if (3)

so that when he has a son
there is nothing left for him.
15 Naked a man comes from his mother's womb,
and as he comes, so he departs.
He takes nothing from his labor
that he can carry in his hand.

16 This too is a grievous evil:

As a man comes, so he departs,
and what does he gain,
since he toils for the wind?
17 All his days he eats in darkness,
with great frustration, affliction and anger.

18 Then I realized that it is good
and proper for a man to eat and
drink, and to find satisfaction in
his toilsome labor under the sun
during the few days of life God
has given him—for this is his lot.
19 Moreover, when God gives any
man wealth and possessions, and
enables him to enjoy them, to accept his lot and be happy in his
work—this is a gift of God. 20 He
seldom reflects on the days of his
life, because God keeps him occupied with gladness of heart.

6 I have seen another evil under
the sun, and it weighs heavily
on men: 2 God gives a man wealth,
possessions and honor, so that he
lacks nothing his heart desires,
but God does not enable him to
enjoy them, and a stranger enjoys
them instead. This is meaningless, a grievous evil.
3 A man may have a hundred
children and live many years; yet
no matter how long he lives, if he

*See the note on page 576.

†17 Most mss have *hateph segol* under the *aleph* (לֶאֱ).

שֶׁיִּהְיוּ יְמֵי־ שָׁנָיו וְנַפְשׁוֹ לֹא־ תִשְׂבַּע מִן־
from she-enjoys not if-self-of-him years-of-him days-of that-they-are

הַטּוֹבָה וְגַם־ קְבוּרָה לֹא־ הָיְתָה לּוֹ אָמַרְתִּי טוֹב מִמֶּנּוּ
more-than-him good I-say to-him she-is not burial and-also the-prosperity

הַנָּפֶל׃ כִּי־ בַהֶבֶל בָּא וּבַחֹשֶׁךְ
and-in-the-darkness he-comes in-the-meaninglessness indeed (4) the-stillborn-child

יֵלֵךְ וּבַחֹשֶׁךְ שְׁמוֹ יְכֻסֶּה׃ גַּם־ שֶׁמֶשׁ
sun though (5) he-is-shrouded name-of-him and-in-the-darkness he-departs

לֹא־ רָאָה וְלֹא יָדָע נַחַת לָזֶה מִזֶּה׃
more-than-that-one to-this-one rest he-knew and-never he-saw never

וְאִלּוּ חָיָה אֶלֶף שָׁנִים פַּעֲמַיִם וְטוֹבָה לֹא רָאָה
he-enjoys not but-prosperity twice years thousand-of he-lives even-if (6)

הֲלֹא אֶל־ מָקוֹם אֶחָד הַכֹּל הוֹלֵךְ׃ כָּל־ עֲמַל הָאָדָם לְפִיהוּ
for-mouth-of-him the-man effort-of all-of (7) going the-all same place to not?

וְגַם־ הַנֶּפֶשׁ לֹא תִמָּלֵא׃ כִּי מַה־ יּוֹתֵר
advantage what? indeed (8) she-is-satisfied never the-appetite yet-also

לֶחָכָם מִן־ הַכְּסִיל מַה־ לֶּעָנִי יוֹדֵעַ לַהֲלֹךְ
to-conduct-himself knowing to-the-poor-man what? the-fool over to-the-wise

נֶגֶד הַחַיִּים׃ טוֹב מַרְאֵה עֵינַיִם מֵהֲלָךְ־ נָפֶשׁ גַּם־
also appetite more-than-to-rove eyes sight-of good (9) the-others before

זֶה הֶבֶל וּרְעוּת רוּחַ׃ מַה־ שֶּׁהָיָה כְּבָר
already that-he-exists whatever (10) wind and-chasing-of meaningless this

נִקְרָא שְׁמוֹ וְנוֹדָע אֲשֶׁר־ הוּא אָדָם וְלֹא־ יוּכַל
he-can and-not man he what and-being-known name-of-him he-was-called

לָדִין עִם שֶׁהתַּקִּיף מִמֶּנּוּ׃ כִּי יֵשׁ־ דְּבָרִים הַרְבֵּה
to-be-many words there-are for (11) more-than-he who-strong with to-contend

מַרְבִּים הָבֶל מַה־ יֹּתֵר לָאָדָם׃ כִּי מִי־
who? for (12) to-the-man profit what? meaninglessness ones-making-many

יוֹדֵעַ מַה־ טּוֹב לָאָדָם בַּחַיִּים מִסְפַּר יְמֵי־ חַיֵּי
lives-of days-of few-of in-the-lives for-the-man good what? knowing

הֶבְלוֹ וְיַעֲשֵׂם כַּצֵּל אֲשֶׁר מִי־
who? that like-the-shadow and-he-passes-through-them meaninglessness-of-him

יַגִּיד לָאָדָם מַה־ יִּהְיֶה אַחֲרָיו תַּחַת הַשָּׁמֶשׁ׃
the-sun under after-him he-will-happen what? to-the-man he-can-tell

טוֹב שֵׁם מִשֶּׁמֶן טוֹב וְיוֹם הַמָּוֶת מִיּוֹם
more-than-day-of the-death and-day-of fine more-than-perfume name good (7:1)

הִוָּלְדוֹ׃ טוֹב לָלֶכֶת אֶל־ בֵּית־ אֵבֶל מִלֶּכֶת אֶל־
to more-than-to-go mourning house-of to to-go good (2) to-be-born-him

cannot enjoy his prosperity and does not receive proper burial, I say that a stillborn child is better off than he. 4 It comes without meaning, it departs in darkness, and in darkness its name is shrouded. 5 Though it never saw the sun or knew anything, it has more rest than does that man— 6 even if he lives a thousand years twice over but fails to enjoy his prosperity. Do not all go to the same place?

7 All man's efforts are for his
mouth,
yet his appetite is never
satisfied.
8 What advantage has a wise
man
over a fool?
What does a poor man gain
by knowing how to conduct
himself before others?
9 Better what the eye sees
than the roving of the
appetite.
This too is meaningless,
a chasing after the wind.

10 Whatever exists has already
been named,
and what man is has been
known;
no man can contend
with one who is stronger
than he.
11 The more the words,
the less the meaning,
and how does that profit
anyone?

12 For who knows what is good for a man in life, during the few and meaningless days he passes through like a shadow? Who can tell him what will happen under the sun after he is gone?

Wisdom

7 A good name is better than
fine perfume,
and the day of death better
than the day of birth.
2 It is better to go to a house of
mourning

°10 ק שתקיף

בֵּית מִשְׁתֶּה בַּאֲשֶׁר הוּא סוֹף כָּל־הָאָדָם וְהַחַי
and-the-living the-man every-of destiny-of he for-that feasting house-of

יִתֵּן אֶל־לִבּוֹ׃ (3) טוֹב כַּעַס מִשְּׂחֹק כִּי־
because more-than-laughter sorrow good (3) heart-of-him to he-should-take

בְרֹעַ פָּנִים יִיטַב לֵב׃ (4) לֵב חֲכָמִים בְּבֵית
in-house-of wise-men heart-of (4) heart he-is-good faces by-sadness-of

אֵבֶל וְלֵב כְּסִילִים בְּבֵית שִׂמְחָה׃ (5) טוֹב לִשְׁמֹעַ גַּעֲרַת
rebuke-of to-heed good (5) pleasure in-house-of fools but-heart-of mourning

חָכָם מֵאִישׁ שֹׁמֵעַ שִׁיר כְּסִילִים׃ (6) כִּי כְקוֹל
like-crackling-of indeed (6) fools song-of listening more-than-man wise

הַסִּירִים תַּחַת הַסִּיר כֵּן שְׂחֹק הַכְּסִיל וְגַם־זֶה הָבֶל׃
meaningless this and-also the-fool laughter-of so the-pot under the-thorns

(7) כִּי הָעֹשֶׁק יְהוֹלֵל חָכָם וִיאַבֵּד אֶת־לֵב
heart *** and-he-corrupts wise-man he-makes-foolish the-extortion for (7)

מַתָּנָה׃ (8) טוֹב אַחֲרִית דָּבָר מֵרֵאשִׁיתוֹ טוֹב אֶרֶךְ־
patience-of good more-than-beginning-of-him matter end-of good (8) bribe

רוּחַ מִגְּבַהּ־רוּחַ׃ (9) אַל־תְּבַהֵל בְּרוּחֲךָ
in-spirit-of-you you-be-quick not (9) spirit more-than-pride-of spirit

לִכְעוֹס כִּי כַעַס בְּחֵיק כְּסִילִים יָנוּחַ׃ (10) אַל־תֹּאמַר מֶה
why? you-say not (10) he-resides fools in-lap-of anger for to-be-provoked

הָיָה שֶׁהַיָּמִים הָרִאשֹׁנִים הָיוּ טוֹבִים מֵאֵלֶּה כִּי לֹא
not for more-than-these good-ones they-were the-old-ones that-the-days he-was

מֵחָכְמָה שָׁאַלְתָּ עַל־זֶה׃ (11) טוֹבָה חָכְמָה עִם־נַחֲלָה וְיֹתֵר
and-benefit inheritance like wisdom good (11) such about you-ask from-wisdom

לְרֹאֵי הַשָּׁמֶשׁ׃ (12) כִּי בְּצֵל הַחָכְמָה בְּצֵל
in-shelter-of the-wisdom in-shelter-of for (12) the-sun to-ones-seeing-of

הַכָּסֶף וְיִתְרוֹן דַּעַת הַחָכְמָה תְּחַיֶּה
she-keeps-alive the-wisdom knowledge but-advantage-of the-money

בְעָלֶיהָ׃ (13) רְאֵה אֶת־מַעֲשֵׂה הָאֱלֹהִים כִּי מִי יוּכַל
he-can who? for the-God deed-of *** consider! (13) possessors-of-her

לְתַקֵּן אֵת אֲשֶׁר עִוְּתוֹ׃ (14) בְּיוֹם טוֹבָה הֱיֵה
be! good in-time-of (14) he-made-crooked-him what *** to-straighten

בְטוֹב וּבְיוֹם רָעָה רְאֵה גַּם אֶת־זֶה לְעֻמַּת־זֶה
other as-well-as this *** also consider! bad but-in-time-of in-happiness

עָשָׂה הָאֱלֹהִים עַל־דִּבְרַת שֶׁלֹּא יִמְצָא הָאָדָם אַחֲרָיו
after-him the-man he-can-discover that-not account-of on the-God he-made

מְאוּמָה׃ (15) אֶת־הַכֹּל רָאִיתִי בִּימֵי הֶבְלִי יֵשׁ
there-is meaninglessness-of-me in-days-of I-saw the-all *** (15) anything

than to go to a house of
feasting,
for death is the destiny of
every man;
the living should take this to
heart.
3Sorrow is better than laughter,
because a sad face is good
for the heart.
4The heart of the wise is in the
house of mourning,
but the heart of fools is in
the house of pleasure.
5It is better to heed a wise
man's rebuke
than to listen to the song of
fools.
6Like the crackling of thorns
under the pot,
so is the laughter of fools.
This too is meaningless.

7Extortion turns a wise man
into a fool,
and a bribe corrupts the
heart.

8The end of a matter is better
than its beginning,
and patience is better than
pride.
9Do not be quickly provoked in
your spirit,
for anger resides in the lap
of fools.

10Do not say, "Why were the
old days better than
these?"
For it is not wise to ask
such questions.

11Wisdom, like an inheritance,
is a good thing
and benefits those who see
the sun.
12Wisdom is a shelter
as money is a shelter,
but the advantage of
knowledge is this:
that wisdom preserves the
life of its possessor.

13Consider what God has done:

Who can straighten
what he has made crooked?
14When times are good, be
happy;
but when times are bad,
consider:
God has made the one
as well as the other.
Therefore, a man cannot
discover
anything about his future.

15In this meaningless life of
mine I have seen both of these:

צַדִּיק אֹבֵד בְּצִדְקוֹ וְיֵשׁ רָשָׁע
wicked-man and-there-is in-righteousness-of-him perishing righteous-man

מַאֲרִיךְ בְּרָעָתוֹ׃ אַל־ תְּהִי צַדִּיק הַרְבֵּה וְאַל־
and-not to-be-much righteous you-be not (16) in-wickedness-of-him living-long

תִּתְחַכַּם יוֹתֵר לָמָּה תִּשּׁוֹמֵם׃ אַל־ תִּרְשַׁע
you-be-wicked not (17) you-destroy-yourself why? much you-be-overwise

הַרְבֵּה וְאַל־ תְּהִי סָכָל לָמָּה תָמוּת בְּלֹא עִתֶּךָ׃ טוֹב
good (18) time-of-you when-not you-die why? fool you-be and-not to-be-much

אֲשֶׁר תֶּאֱחֹז בָּזֶה וְגַם־ מִזֶּה אַל־ תַּנַּח אֶת־ יָדֶךָ כִּי־
for hand-of-you *** you-let-go not of-other and-also to-one you-grasp that

יְרֵא אֱלֹהִים יֵצֵא אֶת־ כֻּלָּם׃ הַחָכְמָה
the-wisdom (19) all-of-them *** he-will-avoid God one-fearing-of

תָּעֹז לֶחָכָם מֵעֲשָׂרָה שַׁלִּיטִים אֲשֶׁר הָיוּ
they-are who rulers more-than-ten to-the-wise-man she-is-powerful

בָּעִיר׃ כִּי אָדָם אֵין צַדִּיק בָּאָרֶץ אֲשֶׁר יַעֲשֶׂה־
he-does who on-the-earth righteous there-is-not man for (20) in-the-city

טּוֹב וְלֹא יֶחֱטָא׃ גַּם לְכָל־ הַדְּבָרִים אֲשֶׁר יְדַבֵּרוּ אַל־
not they-say that the-words to-all-of also (21) he-sins and-never right

תִּתֵּן לִבֶּךָ אֲשֶׁר לֹא־ תִשְׁמַע אֶת־ עַבְדְּךָ מְקַלְלֶךָ׃
cursing-you servant-of-you *** you-hear not that attention-of-you you-give

כִּי גַּם־פְּעָמִים רַבּוֹת יָדַע לִבֶּךָ אֲשֶׁר גַּם־ אַתְּ קִלַּלְתָּ
you-cursed you also that heart-of-you he-knows many times also for (22)

אֲחֵרִים׃ כָּל־ זֹה נִסִּיתִי בַחָכְמָה אָמַרְתִּי אֶחְכָּמָה וְהִיא
but-this I-will-be-wise I-said by-the-wisdom I-tested this all-of (23) others

רְחוֹקָה מִמֶּנִּי׃ רָחוֹק מַה־ שֶּׁהָיָה וְעָמֹק | עָמֹק
profound and-profound that-he-may-be whatever far-off (24) from-me beyond

מִי יִמְצָאֶנּוּ׃ סַבּוֹתִי אֲנִי וְלִבִּי לָדַעַת
to-understand also-mind-of-me I I-turned (25) he-can-discover-him who?

וְלָתוּר וּבַקֵּשׁ חָכְמָה וְחֶשְׁבּוֹן וְלָדַעַת
and-to-understand and-scheme wisdom and-to-search-out and-to-investigate

רֶשַׁע כֶּסֶל וְהַסִּכְלוּת הוֹלֵלוֹת׃ וּמוֹצֶא אֲנִי מַר
bitter I and-finding (26) madnesses and-the-folly stupidity wickedness-of

מִמָּוֶת אֶת־ הָאִשָּׁה אֲשֶׁר־הִיא מְצוֹדִים וַחֲרָמִים לִבָּהּ אֲסוּרִים
chains heart-of-her and-traps snares she who the-woman *** more-than-death

יָדֶיהָ טוֹב לִפְנֵי הָאֱלֹהִים יִמָּלֵט מִמֶּנָּה
from-her he-will-escape the-God before one-pleasing hands-of-her

וְחוֹטֵא יִלָּכֶד בָּהּ׃ רְאֵה זֶה מָצָאתִי
I-discovered this look! (27) by-her he-will-be-ensnared but-one-sinning

---

a righteous man perishing in
his righteousness,
and a wicked man living
long in his wickedness.
16 Do not be overrighteous,
neither be overwise—
why destroy yourself?
17 Do not be overwicked,
and do not be a fool—
why die before your time?
18 It is good to grasp the one
and not let go of the other.
The man who fears God will
avoid all ⌞extremes⌟.[f]

19 Wisdom makes one wise man
more powerful
than ten rulers in a city.

20 There is not a righteous man
on earth
who does what is right and
never sins.

21 Do not pay attention to every
word people say,
or you may hear your
servant cursing you—
22 for you know in your heart
that many times you
yourself have cursed
others.

23 All this I tested by wisdom and
I said,

"I am determined to be
wise"—
but this was beyond me.
24 Whatever wisdom may be,
it is far off and most
profound—
who can discover it?
25 So I turned my mind to
understand,
to investigate and to search
out wisdom and the
scheme of things
and to understand the
stupidity of wickedness
and the madness of folly.

26 I find more bitter than death
the woman who is a snare,
whose heart is a trap
and whose hands are
chains.
The man who pleases God will
escape her,
but the sinner she will
ensnare.

27 "Look," says the Teacher,[g]
"this is what I have discovered:

f18 Or *will follow them both*
g27 Or *leader of the assembly*

°22 ק אתה

אָמְרָה קֹהֶלֶת אַחַת לְאַחַת לִמְצֹא חֶשְׁבּוֹן׃ אֲשֶׁר עוֹד־
still that (28) scheme to-discover to-another one Teacher she-says

בִּקְשָׁה נַפְשִׁי וְלֹא מָצָאתִי אָדָם אֶחָד מֵאֶלֶף מָצָאתִי
I-found among-thousand one man I-found but-not self-of-me she-searched

וְאִשָּׁה בְכָל־ אֵלֶּה לֹא מָצָאתִי׃ לְבַד רְאֵה־ זֶה מָצָאתִי אֲשֶׁר
that I-found this see! only (29) I-found not these among-all-of but-woman

עָשָׂה הָאֱלֹהִים אֶת־ הָאָדָם יָשָׁר וְהֵמָּה בִקְשׁוּ חִשְּׁבֹנוֹת רַבִּים׃
many schemes they-search-for but-they upright the-mankind *** the-God he-made

מִי כְּהֶחָכָם וּמִי יוֹדֵעַ פֵּשֶׁר דָּבָר חָכְמַת
wisdom-of thing explanation-of knowing and-who? like-the-wise-man who? (8:1)

אָדָם תָּאִיר פָּנָיו וְעֹז פָּנָיו יְשֻׁנֶּא׃
he-is-changed appearances-of-him and-hardness-of faces-of-him she-brightens man

אֲנִי פִּי־ מֶלֶךְ שְׁמוֹר וְעַל דִּבְרַת שְׁבוּעַת אֱלֹהִים׃ אַל־
not (3) God oath-of word-of and-because-of obey! king command-of I (2)

תִּבָּהֵל מִפָּנָיו תֵּלֵךְ אַל־ תַּעֲמֹד בְּדָבָר רָע
bad for-cause you-stand-up not you-leave from-presences-of-him you-hurry

כִּי כָּל־ אֲשֶׁר יַחְפֹּץ יַעֲשֶׂה׃ בַּאֲשֶׁר דְּבַר־ מֶלֶךְ שִׁלְטוֹן
supreme king word-of since-that (4) he-will-do he-pleases that all-of for

וּמִי יֹאמַר־ לוֹ מַה־ תַּעֲשֶׂה׃ שׁוֹמֵר מִצְוָה לֹא
not command one-obeying (5) you-do what? to-him he-can-say then-who?

יֵדַע דָּבָר רָע וְעֵת וּמִשְׁפָּט יֵדַע לֵב
heart he-will-know and-procedure and-time harmful matter he-will-come-to

חָכָם׃ כִּי לְכָל־ חֵפֶץ יֵשׁ עֵת וּמִשְׁפָּט כִּי־
though and-procedure time there-is matter for-every-of for (6) wise

רָעַת הָאָדָם רַבָּה עָלָיו׃ כִּי־ אֵינֶנּוּ יֹדֵעַ מַה־
what knowing not-he since (7) upon-him heavy the-man misery-of

שֶׁיִּהְיֶה כִּי כַּאֲשֶׁר יִהְיֶה מִי יַגִּיד לוֹ׃
to-him he-can-tell who? he-will-come as-what for that-he-will-come

אֵין אָדָם שַׁלִּיט בָּרוּחַ לִכְלוֹא אֶת־ הָרוּחַ וְאֵין שִׁלְטוֹן
powerful so-no-one the-wind *** to-contain over-the-wind powerful man no (8)

בְּיוֹם הַמָּוֶת וְאֵין מִשְׁלַחַת בַּמִּלְחָמָה וְלֹא־ יְמַלֵּט
he-will-release so-not in-the-war discharged and-no-one the-death over-day-of

רֶשַׁע אֶת־ בְּעָלָיו׃ אֶת־ כָּל־ זֶה רָאִיתִי וְנָתוֹן
as-to-apply I-saw this all-of *** (9) practitioners-of-him *** wickedness

אֶת־ לִבִּי לְכָל־ מַעֲשֶׂה אֲשֶׁר נַעֲשָׂה תַּחַת הַשָּׁמֶשׁ עֵת אֲשֶׁר
when time the-sun under he-is-done that deed to-every-of mind-of-me ***

שָׁלַט הָאָדָם בְּאָדָם לְרַע לוֹ׃ וּבְכֵן רָאִיתִי
I-saw and-then-this (10) of-him to-hurt over-other the-man he-lords

"Adding one thing to another
to discover the scheme of things—
28 while I was still searching
but not finding—
I found one ⌞upright⌟ man
among a thousand,
but not one ⌞upright⌟ woman
among them all.
29 This only have I found:
God made mankind upright,
but men have gone in
search of many schemes."

8 Who is like the wise man?
Who knows the explanation
of things?
Wisdom brightens a man's
face
and changes its hard
appearance.

Obey the King

2 Obey the king's command, I
say, because you took an oath before God. 3 Do not be in a hurry to
leave the king's presence. Do not
stand up for a bad cause, for he
will do whatever he pleases. 4 Since
a king's word is supreme, who can
say to him, "What are you doing?"

5 Whoever obeys his command
will come to no harm,
and the wise heart will
know the proper time and
procedure.
6 For there is a proper time and
procedure for every
matter,
though a man's misery
weighs heavily upon him.

7 Since no man knows the
future,
who can tell him what is to
come?
8 No man has power over the
wind to contain it[h];
so no one has power over
the day of his death.
As no one is discharged in
time of war,
so wickedness will not
release those who practice
it.

9 All this I saw, as I applied my
mind to everything done under
the sun. There is a time when a
man lords it over others to his
own[i] hurt. 10 Then too, I saw the

h8 Or *over his spirit to retain it*
i9 Or *to their*

רְשָׁעִים קְבֻרִים וָבָאוּ וּמִמְּקוֹם קָדוֹשׁ
holiness also-from-place-of indeed-they-came ones-being-buried wicked-ones

יְהַלֵּכוּ וְיִשְׁתַּכְּחוּ בָעִיר אֲשֶׁר כֵּן־ עָשׂוּ גַּם־ זֶה
this also they-did this where in-the-city and-they-are-forgotten they-went

הָבֶל׃ אֲשֶׁר אֵין־ נַעֲשָׂה פִתְגָם מַעֲשֵׂה הָרָעָה
the-crime deed-of sentence he-is-carried-out not when (11) meaningless

מְהֵרָה עַל־ כֵּן מָלֵא לֵב בְּנֵי־ הָאָדָם בָּהֶם לַעֲשׂוֹת רָע׃
wrong to-do in-them the-man sons-of heart-of he-is-filled this for quickly

אֲשֶׁר חֹטֶא עֹשֶׂה רָע מְאַת וּמַאֲרִיךְ
and-living-long hundred-of crime committing man-being-wicked although (12)

לוֹ כִּי גַּם־ יוֹדֵעַ אָנִי אֲשֶׁר יִהְיֶה־ טּוֹב לְיִרְאֵי
with-ones-fearing-of better he-will-be that I knowing also indeed to-him

הָאֱלֹהִים אֲשֶׁר יִירְאוּ מִלְּפָנָיו׃ וְטוֹב לֹא־ יִהְיֶה
he-will-be not yet-well (13) at-before-him they-are-reverent who the-God

לָרָשָׁע וְלֹא־ יַאֲרִיךְ יָמִים כַּצֵּל אֲשֶׁר אֵינֶנּוּ
not-he because like-the-shadow days he-will-lengthen and-not with-the-wicked

יָרֵא מִלִּפְנֵי אֱלֹהִים׃ יֶשׁ־ הֶבֶל אֲשֶׁר נַעֲשָׂה עַל־
on he-occurs that meaninglessness there-is (14) God at-before fearing

הָאָרֶץ אֲשֶׁר ׀ יֵשׁ צַדִּיקִים אֲשֶׁר מַגִּיעַ אֲלֵהֶם כְּמַעֲשֵׂה
as-desert-of to-them happening that righteous-men there-are that the-earth

הָרְשָׁעִים וְיֵשׁ רְשָׁעִים שֶׁמַּגִּיעַ אֲלֵהֶם כְּמַעֲשֵׂה
as-desert-of to-them that-happening wicked-men and-there-are the-wicked-men

הַצַּדִּיקִים אָמַרְתִּי שֶׁגַּם־ זֶה הָבֶל׃ וְשִׁבַּחְתִּי אֲנִי אֶת־
*** I so-I-commend (15) meaningless this that-also I-say the-righteous-men

הַשִּׂמְחָה אֲשֶׁר אֵין־ טוֹב לָאָדָם תַּחַת הַשֶּׁמֶשׁ כִּי אִם־
if than the-sun under for-the-man better nothing because the-enjoyment

לֶאֱכוֹל וְלִשְׁתּוֹת וְלִשְׂמוֹחַ וְהוּא יִלְוֶנּוּ
he-will-accompany-him then-he and-to-be-glad and-to-drink to-eat

בַעֲמָלוֹ יְמֵי חַיָּיו אֲשֶׁר־ נָתַן־ לוֹ הָאֱלֹהִים תַּחַת הַשָּׁמֶשׁ׃
the-sun under the-God to-him he-gave that lives-of-him days-of in-work-of-him

כַּאֲשֶׁר נָתַתִּי אֶת־ לִבִּי לָדַעַת חָכְמָה וְלִרְאוֹת אֶת־
*** and-to-observe wisdom to-know mind-of-me *** I-applied as-when (16)

הָעִנְיָן אֲשֶׁר נַעֲשָׂה עַל־ הָאָרֶץ כִּי גַם בַּיּוֹם וּבַלַּיְלָה
or-in-the-night in-the-day also indeed the-earth on he-is-done that the-labor

שֵׁנָה בְּעֵינָיו אֵינֶנּוּ רֹאֶה׃ וְרָאִיתִי אֶת־ כָּל־ מַעֲשֵׂה
deed-of all-of *** then-I-saw (17) seeing not-he with-eyes-of-him sleep

הָאֱלֹהִים כִּי לֹא יוּכַל הָאָדָם לִמְצוֹא אֶת־הַמַּעֲשֶׂה אֲשֶׁר נַעֲשָׂה
he-goes-on that the-deed *** to-comprehend the-man he-can not that the-God

wicked buried—those who used to come and go from the holy place and receive praise[i] in the city where they did this. This too is meaningless.
[11]When the sentence for a crime is not quickly carried out, the hearts of the people are filled with schemes to do wrong. [12]Although a
wicked man commits a hundred crimes and still lives a long time, I know that it will go better with God-fearing men, who are reverent before God. [13]Yet because the
wicked do not fear God, it will not go well with them, and their days will not lengthen like a shadow.
[14]There is something else meaningless that occurs on earth: righteous men who get what the wicked deserve, and wicked men who get what the righteous deserve. This too, I say, is meaningless. [15]So I commend the enjoyment of life, because nothing is better for a man under the sun than to eat and drink and be glad. Then joy will accompany him in his work all the days of the life God has given him under the sun.
[16]When I applied my mind to know wisdom and to observe man's labor on earth—his eyes not seeing sleep day or night— [17]then
I saw all that God has done. No one can comprehend what goes

i10 Some Hebrew manuscripts and Septuagint (Aquila); most Hebrew manuscripts *and are forgotten*

תַּחַת־ הַשֶּׁמֶשׁ בְּשֶׁל אֲשֶׁר יַעֲמֹל הָאָדָם לְבַקֵּשׁ וְלֹא
but-not to-search-out the-man he-tries which in-spite-of the-sun under

יִמְצָא וְגַם אִם־ יֹאמַר הֶחָכָם לָדַעַת לֹא יוּכַל
he-can not to-know the-wise-man he-claims if and-even he-can-discover

לִמְצֹא׃ כִּי אֶת־ כָּל־ זֶה נָתַתִּי אֶל־ לִבִּי וְלָבוּר
and-to-conclude heart-of-me in I-put this all-of *** so (9:1) to-comprehend

אֶת־ כָּל־ זֶה אֲשֶׁר הַצַּדִּיקִים וְהַחֲכָמִים וַעֲבָדֵיהֶם
and-deeds-of-them and-the-wise-men the-righteous-men that this all-of ***

בְּיַד הָאֱלֹהִים גַּם־ אַהֲבָה גַם־שִׂנְאָה אֵין יוֹדֵעַ הָאָדָם הַכֹּל
the-whole the-man knowing not hate or love whether the-God in-hand-of

לִפְנֵיהֶם׃ הַכֹּל כַּאֲשֶׁר לַכֹּל מִקְרֶה אֶחָד לַצַּדִּיק
to-the-righteous common destiny to-the-all just-as the-all (2) awaiting-him

וְלָרָשָׁע לַטּוֹב וְלַטָּהוֹר וְלַטָּמֵא
and-to-the-unclean and-to-the-clean to-the-good and-to-the-wicked

וְלַזֹּבֵחַ וְלַאֲשֶׁר אֵינֶנּוּ זֹבֵחַ כַּטּוֹב
as-the-good-man sacrificing not-he and-to-whom and-to-the-one-sacrificing

כַּחֹטֶא הַנִּשְׁבָּע כַּאֲשֶׁר שְׁבוּעָה יָרֵא׃ זֶה ׀
this (3) one-fearing oath just-as the-one-taking-oath so-the-one-sinning

רָע בְּכֹל אֲשֶׁר־ נַעֲשָׂה תַּחַת הַשֶּׁמֶשׁ כִּי־ מִקְרֶה אֶחָד
same destiny indeed the-sun under he-happens that in-everything evil

לַכֹּל וְגַם לֵב בְּנֵי־ הָאָדָם מָלֵא־ רָע וְהוֹלֵלוֹת
and-madnesses evil he-is-full the-man sons-of heart-of and-also to-the-all

בִּלְבָבָם בְּחַיֵּיהֶם וְאַחֲרָיו אֶל־ הַמֵּתִים׃
the-dead-ones to and-after-him during-lives-of-them in-heart-of-them

כִּי־ מִי אֲשֶׁר יְבֻחַר אֶל כָּל־ הַחַיִּים יֵשׁ בִּטָּחוֹן
hope there-is the-living-ones all-of with he-is-among who anyone indeed (4)

כִּי־ לְכֶלֶב חַי הוּא טוֹב מִן־ הָאַרְיֵה הַמֵּת׃ כִּי הַחַיִּים
the-living-ones for (5) the-dead the-lion more-than good he live to-dog even

יוֹדְעִים שֶׁיָּמֻתוּ וְהַמֵּתִים אֵינָם יוֹדְעִים
ones-knowing not-they but-the-dead-ones that-they-will-die ones-knowing

מְאוּמָה וְאֵין־ עוֹד לָהֶם שָׂכָר כִּי נִשְׁכַּח זִכְרָם׃
memory-of-them he-is-forgotten even reward to-them further and-not anything

גַּם אַהֲבָתָם גַּם־ שִׂנְאָתָם גַּם־ קִנְאָתָם כְּבָר
long-since jealousy-of-them and hate-of-them and love-of-them also (6)

אָבָדָה וְחֵלֶק אֵין־ לָהֶם עוֹד לְעוֹלָם בְּכֹל אֲשֶׁר־ נַעֲשָׂה
he-happens that in-anything to-ever again to-them not and-part she-vanished

תַּחַת הַשָּׁמֶשׁ׃ לֵךְ אֱכֹל בְּשִׂמְחָה לַחְמֶךָ וּשְׁתֵה בְלֶב־
with-heart-of and-drink! food-of-you with-gladness eat! go! (7) the-sun under

on under the sun. Despite all his efforts to search it out, man cannot discover its meaning. Even if a wise man claims he knows, he cannot really comprehend it.

A Common Destiny for All

9 So I reflected on all this and concluded that the righteous and the wise and what they do are in God's hands, but no man knows whether love or hate awaits him. 2 All share a common destiny—the righteous and the wicked, the good and the bad,[k] the clean and the unclean, those who offer sacrifices and those who do not.

As it is with the good man,
so with the sinner;
as it is with those who take oaths,
so with those who are afraid to take them.

3 This is the evil in everything that happens under the sun: The same destiny overtakes all. The hearts of men, moreover, are full of evil and there is madness in their hearts while they live, and afterward they join the dead. 4 Anyone who is among the living has hope[l]—even a live dog is better off than a dead lion!

5 For the living know that they will die,
but the dead know nothing;
they have no further reward,
and even the memory of them is forgotten.
6 Their love, their hate
and their jealousy have long since vanished;
never again will they have a part
in anything that happens under the sun.

7 Go, eat your food with gladness,
and drink your wine with a joyful heart,

[k]2 Septuagint (Aquila), Vulgate and Syriac; Hebrew does not have *and the bad.*
[l]4 Or *What then is to be chosen? With all who live, there is hope*

°4 ק יחבר

טוֹב יֵינֶךָ כִּי כְבָר רָצָה הָאֱלֹהִים אֶת־ מַעֲשֶׂיךָ׃ בְּכָל־
at-all-of (8) deeds-of-you *** the-God he-favors now for wine-of-you joy

עֵת יִהְיוּ בְגָדֶיךָ לְבָנִים וְשֶׁמֶן עַל־ רֹאשְׁךָ אַל־
not head-of-you on and-oil white-ones clothes-of-you let-them-be time

יֶחְסָר׃ רְאֵה חַיִּים עִם־ אִשָּׁה אֲשֶׁר־ אָהַבְתָּ כָּל־ יְמֵי
days-of all-of you-love whom wife with lives enjoy! (9) let-him-be-lacking

חַיֵּי הֶבְלֶךָ אֲשֶׁר נָתַן־ לְךָ תַּחַת הַשֶּׁמֶשׁ כֹּל
all-of the-sun under to-you he-gave that meaninglessness-of-you lives-of

יְמֵי הֶבְלֶךָ כִּי הוּא חֶלְקְךָ בַּחַיִּים
in-the-lives lot-of-you this for meaninglessness-of-you days-of

וּבַעֲמָלְךָ אֲשֶׁר־אַתָּה עָמֵל תַּחַת הַשָּׁמֶשׁ׃ כֹּל אֲשֶׁר תִּמְצָא
she-finds that all (10) the-sun under toiling you that and-in-labor-of-you

יָדְךָ לַעֲשׂוֹת בְּכֹחֲךָ עֲשֵׂה כִּי אֵין מַעֲשֶׂה וְחֶשְׁבּוֹן
or-plan work there-is-no for do! with-might-of-you to-do hand-of-you

וְדַעַת וְחָכְמָה בִּשְׁאוֹל אֲשֶׁר אַתָּה הֹלֵךְ שָׁמָּה׃ שַׁבְתִּי
I-did-again (11) to-there going you where in-Sheol or-wisdom or-knowledge

וְרָאֹה תַחַת־ הַשֶּׁמֶשׁ כִּי לֹא לַקַּלִּים הַמֵּרוֹץ וְלֹא
or-not the-race to-the-swift-ones not that the-sun under and-to-see

לַגִּבּוֹרִים הַמִּלְחָמָה וְגַם לֹא לַחֲכָמִים לֶחֶם וְגַם לֹא
not and-also food to-the-wise-ones not and-also the-battle to-the-strong-ones

לַנְּבֹנִים עֹשֶׁר וְגַם לֹא לַיֹּדְעִים חֵן
favor to-the-ones-being-learned not and-also wealth to-the-ones-being-brilliant

כִּי־ עֵת וָפֶגַע יִקְרֶה אֶת־ כֻּלָּם׃ כִּי גַּם לֹא־
not also moreover (12) all-of-them *** he-happens and-chance time but

יֵדַע הָאָדָם אֶת־ עִתּוֹ כַּדָּגִים שֶׁנֶּאֱחָזִים
that-ones-being-caught as-the-fishes hour-of-him *** the-man he-knows

בִּמְצוֹדָה רָעָה וְכַצִּפֳּרִים הָאֲחֻזוֹת* בַּפָּח כָּהֵם
so-they in-the-snare the-ones-being-taken or-as-the-birds cruel in-net

יוּקָשִׁים בְּנֵי הָאָדָם לְעֵת רָעָה כְּשֶׁתִּפּוֹל עֲלֵיהֶם
upon-them as-that-she-falls evil by-time-of the-man sons-of ones-being-trapped

פִּתְאֹם׃ גַּם־ זֹה רָאִיתִי חָכְמָה תַּחַת הַשָּׁמֶשׁ וּגְדוֹלָה הִיא אֵלָי׃
to-me she and-great the-sun under wisdom I-saw this also (13) unexpectedly

עִיר קְטַנָּה וַאֲנָשִׁים בָּהּ מְעָט וּבָא־ אֵלֶיהָ מֶלֶךְ
king against-her and-he-came few in-her with-peoples small city (14)

גָּדוֹל וְסָבַב אֹתָהּ וּבָנָה עָלֶיהָ מְצוֹדִים גְּדֹלִים׃
huge-ones siegeworks against-her and-he-built her and-he-surrounded powerful

וּמָצָא בָהּ אִישׁ מִסְכֵּן חָכָם וּמִלַּט־ הוּא אֶת־ הָעִיר
the-city *** he and-he-saved wise poor man in-her now-he-found (15)

---

for it is now that God favors
what you do.
[8]Always be clothed in white,
and always anoint your
head with oil.

[9]Enjoy life with your wife, whom you love, all the days of this meaningless life that God has given you under the sun— all your meaningless days. For this is your lot in life and in your toilsome labor under the sun. [10]Whatever your hand finds to do, do it with all your might, for in the grave,[m] where you are going, there is neither working nor planning nor knowledge nor wisdom.

[11]I have seen something else under the sun:

The race is not to the swift
or the battle to the strong,
nor does food come to the
wise
or wealth to the brilliant
or favor to the learned;
but time and chance happen
to them all.

[12]Moreover, no man knows when his hour will come:

As fish are caught in a cruel
net,
or birds are taken in a
snare,
so men are trapped by evil
times
that fall unexpectedly upon
them.

Wisdom Better Than Folly

[13]I also saw under the sun this example of wisdom that greatly impressed me: [14]There was once a small city with only a few people in it. And a powerful king came against it, surrounded it and built huge siegeworks against it. [15]Now there lived in that city a man poor but wise, and he saved the city by

m10 Hebrew *Sheol*

*12 Most mss have *dagesh* in the *zayin* (זּוֹת־).

בְּחָכְמָתוֹ וְאָדָם לֹא זָכַר אֶת־ הָאִישׁ הַמִּסְכֵּן הַהוּא׃
the-that the-poor the-man *** he-remembered not but-man by-wisdom-of-him

וָאָמַרְתִּי אָנִי טוֹבָה חָכְמָה מִגְּבוּרָה וְחָכְמַת הַמִּסְכֵּן
the-poor-man but-wisdom-of more-than-strength wisdom good I so-I-said (16)

בְּזוּיָה וּדְבָרָיו אֵינָם נִשְׁמָעִים׃ דִּבְרֵי
words-of (17) ones-being-heeded not-they and-words-of-him being-despised

חֲכָמִים בְּנַחַת נִשְׁמָעִים מִזַּעֲקַת מוֹשֵׁל
one-ruling more-than-shout-of ones-being-heeded in-quietness wise-ones

בַּכְּסִילִים׃ טוֹבָה חָכְמָה מִכְּלֵי קְרָב וְחוֹטֶא אֶחָד
one but-one-sinning war more-than-weapons-of wisdom good (18) of-the-fools

יְאַבֵּד טוֹבָה הַרְבֵּה׃ זְבוּבֵי מָוֶת יַבְאִישׁ
he-gives-bad-smell death flies-of (10:1) to-be-much good he-destroys

יַבִּיעַ שֶׁמֶן רוֹקֵחַ יָקָר מֵחָכְמָה
more-than-wisdom weighty one-making-perfume oil-of he-makes-reek

מִכָּבוֹד סִכְלוּת מְעָט׃ לֵב חָכָם לִימִינוֹ וְלֵב
but-heart-of to-right-of-him wise heart-of (2) little folly more-than-honor

כְּסִיל לִשְׂמֹאלוֹ׃ וְגַם־ בַּדֶּרֶךְ כְּשֶׁהַסָּכָל הֹלֵךְ לִבּוֹ
sense-of-him walking as-that-fool on-the-road and-even (3) to-left-of-him fool

חָסֵר וְאָמַר לַכֹּל סָכָל הוּא׃ אִם־ רוּחַ הַמּוֹשֵׁל
the-one-ruling anger-of if (4) he stupid to-the-all and-he-shows lacking

תַּעֲלֶה עָלֶיךָ מְקוֹמְךָ אַל־ תַּנַּח כִּי מַרְפֵּא יַנִּיחַ
he-can-lay-to-rest calmness for you-leave not post-of-you against-you she-rises

חֲטָאִים גְּדוֹלִים׃ יֵשׁ רָעָה רָאִיתִי תַּחַת הַשָּׁמֶשׁ כִּשְׁגָגָה
as-error the-sun under I-saw evil there-is (5) great-ones errors

שֶׁיֹּצָא מִלִּפְנֵי הַשַּׁלִּיט׃ נִתַּן הַסֶּכֶל בַּמְּרוֹמִים
in-the-high-positions the-fool he-is-put (6) the-ruler from-before that-arising

רַבִּים וַעֲשִׁירִים בַּשֵּׁפֶל יֵשֵׁבוּ׃ רָאִיתִי עֲבָדִים עַל־סוּסִים
horses on slaves I-saw (7) they-occupy in-the-low-one while-rich-ones many

וְשָׂרִים הֹלְכִים כַּעֲבָדִים עַל־ הָאָרֶץ׃ חֹפֵר גּוּמָּץ
pit one-digging (8) the-ground on like-slaves ones-walking while-princes

בּוֹ יִפּוֹל וּפֹרֵץ גָּדֵר יִשְּׁכֶנּוּ נָחָשׁ׃
snake he-may-bite-him wall and-one-breaking-through he-may-fall into-him

מַסִּיעַ אֲבָנִים יֵעָצֵב בָּהֶם בּוֹקֵעַ עֵצִים
logs one-splitting by-them he-may-be-injured stones one-quarrying (9)

יִסָּכֶן בָּם׃ אִם־ קֵהָה הַבַּרְזֶל וְהוּא לֹא־פָנִים
edges not and-he the-axe he-is-dull if (10) by-them he-may-be-endangered

קִלְקַל וַחֲיָלִים יְגַבֵּר וְיִתְרוֹן הַכְשֵׁיר חָכְמָה׃
skill to-bring but-success he-must-empower then-strengths he-sharpened

°3 ק כשסכל
°10 ק הכשר

his wisdom. But nobody remembered that poor man. [16]So I said,
"Wisdom is better than strength."
But the poor man's wisdom is despised, and his words are no longer heeded.

[17]The quiet words of the wise
are more to be heeded
than the shouts of a ruler of
fools.
[18]Wisdom is better than
weapons of war,
but one sinner destroys
much good.

10 As dead flies give
perfume a bad smell,
so a little folly outweighs
wisdom and honor.
[2]The heart of the wise inclines
to the right,
but the heart of the fool to
the left.
[3]Even as he walks along the
road,
the fool lacks sense
and shows everyone how
stupid he is.
[4]If a ruler's anger rises against
you,
do not leave your post;
calmness can lay great errors
to rest.

[5]There is an evil I have seen
under the sun,
the sort of error that arises
from a ruler:
[6]Fools are put in many high
positions,
while the rich occupy the
low ones.
[7]I have seen slaves on
horseback,
while princes go on foot like
slaves.

[8]Whoever digs a pit may fall
into it;
whoever breaks through a
wall may be bitten by a
snake.
[9]Whoever quarries stones may
be injured by them;
whoever splits logs may be
endangered by them.

[10]If the ax is dull
and its edge unsharpened,
more strength is needed
but skill will bring success.

אִם־ יִשֹּׁךְ הַנָּחָשׁ בְּלוֹא־ לָחַשׁ וְאֵין יִתְרוֹן
profit then-there-is-no charmed when-not the-snake he-bites if (11)

לְבַעַל הַלָּשׁוֹן׃ דִּבְרֵי פִי־ חָכָם חֵן וְשִׂפְתוֹת
but-lips-of gracious wise-man mouth-of words-of (12) the-tongue for-charmer-of

כְּסִיל תְּבַלְּעֶנּוּ׃ תְּחִלַּת דִּבְרֵי־ פִיהוּ סִכְלוּת וְאַחֲרִית
and-end-of folly mouth-of-him words-of beginning-of (13) she-consumes-him fool

פִּיהוּ הוֹלֵלוּת רָעָה׃ וְהַסָּכָל יַרְבֶּה דְבָרִים לֹא־ יֵדַע
he-knows not words he-multiplies and-the-fool (14) wicked madness mouth-of-him

הָאָדָם מַה־ שֶּׁיִּהְיֶה וַאֲשֶׁר יִהְיֶה מֵאַחֲרָיו מִי
who? at-after-him he-will-happen and-what that-he-comes what the-man

יַגִּיד לוֹ׃ עֲמַל הַכְּסִילִים תְּיַגְּעֶנּוּ אֲשֶׁר לֹא־ יָדַע
he-knows not that she-wearies-him the-fools work-of (15) to-him he-can-tell

לָלֶכֶת אֶל־עִיר׃ אִי־ לָךְ אֶרֶץ שֶׁמַּלְכֵּךְ נָעַר וְשָׂרַיִךְ
and-princes-of-you servant that-king-of-you land to-you woe! (16) town to to-go

בַּבֹּקֶר יֹאכֵלוּ׃ אַשְׁרֵיךְ אֶרֶץ שֶׁמַּלְכֵּךְ
that-king-of-you land blessednesses-of-you (17) they-feast in-the-morning

בֶּן־ חוֹרִים וְשָׂרַיִךְ בָּעֵת יֹאכֵלוּ בִּגְבוּרָה
for-strength they-eat at-the-time and-princes-of-you nobilities son-of

וְלֹא בַשְּׁתִי׃ בַּעֲצַלְתַּיִם יִמַּךְ הַמְּקָרֶה
the-rafter he-sags when-lazinesses (18) for-the-drunkenness and-not

וּבְשִׁפְלוּת יָדַיִם יִדְלֹף הַבָּיִת׃ לִשְׂחוֹק עֹשִׂים
ones-making for-laughter (19) the-house he-leaks hands and-when-idleness-of

לֶחֶם וְיַיִן יְשַׂמַּח חַיִּים וְהַכֶּסֶף יַעֲנֶה אֶת־ הַכֹּל׃
the-all *** he-answers but-the-money lives he-makes-merry and-wine feast

גַּם בְּמַדָּעֲךָ מֶלֶךְ אַל־ תְּקַלֵּל וּבְחַדְרֵי מִשְׁכָּבְךָ
bed-of-you or-in-rooms-of you-revile not king in-thought-of-you even (20)

אַל־ תְּקַלֵּל עָשִׁיר כִּי עוֹף הַשָּׁמַיִם יוֹלִיךְ אֶת־ הַקּוֹל
the-word *** he-may-carry the-airs bird-of because rich you-curse not

וּבַעַל הַכְּנָפַיִם יַגֵּיד דָּבָר׃ שַׁלַּח לַחְמְךָ עַל־
on bread-of-you cast! (11:1) saying he-may-report wings and-owner-of

פְּנֵי הַמָּיִם כִּי־ בְרֹב הַיָּמִים תִּמְצָאֶנּוּ׃ תֶּן־
give! (2) you-will-find-him the-days after-many-of for the-waters surfaces-of

חֵלֶק לְשִׁבְעָה וְגַם לִשְׁמוֹנָה כִּי לֹא תֵדַע מַה־ יִּהְיֶה רָעָה
disaster he-may-come what you-know not for to-eight and-also to-seven portion

עַל־ הָאָרֶץ׃ אִם־ יִמָּלְאוּ הֶעָבִים גֶּשֶׁם עַל־ הָאָרֶץ יָרִיקוּ
they-pour the-earth upon rain the-clouds they-are-full if (3) the-land upon

וְאִם־ יִפּוֹל עֵץ בַּדָּרוֹם וְאִם בַּצָּפוֹן מְקוֹם
place-of to-the-north or-whether to-the-south tree he-falls and-whether

11 If a snake bites before it is charmed,
there is no profit for the charmer.
12 Words from a wise man's mouth are gracious,
but a fool is consumed by his own lips.
13 At the beginning his words are folly;
at the end they are wicked madness—
14 and the fool multiplies words.

No one knows what is coming—
who can tell him what will happen after him?

15 A fool's work wearies him;
he does not know the way to town.

16 Woe to you, O land whose king was a servant[n]
and whose princes feast in the morning.
17 Blessed are you, O land whose king is of noble birth
and whose princes eat at a proper time—
for strength and not for drunkenness.

18 If a man is lazy, the rafters sag;
if his hands are idle, the house leaks.

19 A feast is made for laughter,
and wine makes life merry,
but money is the answer for everything.

20 Do not revile the king even in your thoughts,
or curse the rich in your bedroom,
because a bird of the air may carry your words,
and a bird on the wing may report what you say.

Bread Upon the Waters

11 Cast your bread upon the waters,
for after many days you will find it again.
2 Give portions to seven, yes to eight,
for you do not know what disaster may come upon the land.

3 If clouds are full of water,
they pour rain upon the earth.
Whether a tree falls to the south or to the north,

n16 Or *king is a child*

°20 ק כנפים

שֶׁיִּפּוֹל הָעֵץ שָׁם יְהוּא׃ (4) שֹׁמֵר רוּחַ לֹא
not wind one-watching (4) he-will-lie there the-tree that-he-falls

יִזְרָע וְרֹאֶה בֶעָבִים לֹא יִקְצוֹר׃ (5) כַּאֲשֶׁר
just-as (5) he-will-reap not at-the-clouds and-one-looking he-will-plant

אֵינְךָ יוֹדֵעַ מַה־דֶּרֶךְ הָרוּחַ כַּעֲצָמִים בְּבֶטֶן הַמְּלֵאָה כָּכָה
so the-full in-womb-of as-bodies the-wind path-of what knowing not-you

לֹא תֵדַע אֶת־מַעֲשֵׂה הָאֱלֹהִים אֲשֶׁר יַעֲשֶׂה אֶת־הַכֹּל׃
the-all *** he-makes who the-God work-of *** you-can-understand not

(6) בַּבֹּקֶר זְרַע אֶת־זַרְעֶךָ וְלָעֶרֶב אַל־תַּנַּח
you-let-be-idle not and-at-the-evening seed-of-you *** sow! in-the-morning (6)

יָדֶךָ כִּי אֵינְךָ יוֹדֵע* אֵי זֶה יִכְשָׁר† הֲזֶה אוֹ־
or whether-this he-will-succeed this which knowing not-you for hand-of-you

זֶה וְאִם־שְׁנֵיהֶם כְּאֶחָד טוֹבִים׃ (7) וּמָתוֹק הָאוֹר
the-light indeed-sweet (7) ones-well as-equal both-of-them or-whether that

וְטוֹב לַעֵינַיִם לִרְאוֹת אֶת־הַשָּׁמֶשׁ׃ (8) כִּי אִם־שָׁנִים הַרְבֵּה
to-be-many years if however (8) the-sun *** to-see to-the-eyes and-pleasing

יִחְיֶה הָאָדָם בְּכֻלָּם יִשְׂמָח וְיִזְכֹּר אֶת־
*** but-let-him-remember let-him-enjoy to-all-of-them the-man he-may-live

יְמֵי הַחֹשֶׁךְ כִּי־הַרְבֵּה יִהְיוּ כָּל־שֶׁבָּא
what-he-comes all-of they-will-be to-be-many for the-darkness days-of

הָבֶל׃ (9) שְׂמַח בָּחוּר בְּיַלְדוּתֶיךָ וִיטִיבְךָ
and-let-him-give-joy-to-you in-youths-of-you young-man be-happy! (9) meaningless

לִבְּךָ בִּימֵי בְחוּרוֹתֶךָ וְהַלֵּךְ בְּדַרְכֵי לִבְּךָ
heart-of-you after-ways-of and-follow! youths-of-you in-days-of heart-of-you

וּבְמַרְאֵי עֵינֶיךָ וְדָע כִּי עַל־כָּל־אֵלֶּה
these all-of for that but-know! eyes-of-you and-after-sights-of

יְבִיאֲךָ הָאֱלֹהִים בַּמִּשְׁפָּט׃ (10) וְהָסֵר כַּעַס
anxiety so-banish! (10) to-the-judgment the-God he-will-bring-you

מִלִּבֶּךָ וְהַעֲבֵר רָעָה מִבְּשָׂרֶךָ כִּי־הַיַּלְדוּת
the-youth for from-body-of-you trouble and-cast-off! from-heart-of-you

וְהַשַּׁחֲרוּת הָבֶל׃ (12:1) וּזְכֹר אֶת־בּוֹרְאֶיךָ
Ones-Creating-you *** and-remember! (12:1) meaningless and-the-vigor

בִּימֵי בְּחוּרֹתֶיךָ עַד אֲשֶׁר לֹא־יָבֹאוּ יְמֵי הָרָעָה
the-trouble days-of they-come not when before youths-of-you in-days-of

וְהִגִּיעוּ שָׁנִים אֲשֶׁר תֹּאמַר אֵין־לִי בָהֶם חֵפֶץ׃
pleasure in-them to-me there-is-not you-will-say when years and-they-approach

(2) עַד אֲשֶׁר לֹא־תֶחְשַׁךְ הַשֶּׁמֶשׁ וְהָאוֹר וְהַיָּרֵחַ
and-the-moon and-the-light the-sun she-grows-dark not when before (2)

in the place where it falls,
there will it lie.
[4]Whoever watches the wind
will not plant;
whoever looks at the clouds
will not reap.

[5]As you do not know the path
of the wind,
or how the body is formed
in a mother's womb,
so you cannot understand the
work of God,
the Maker of all things.

[6]Sow your seed in the morning,
and at evening let not your
hands be idle,
for you do not know which
will succeed,
whether this or that,
or whether both will do
equally well.

Remember Your Creator While Young

[7]Light is sweet,
and it pleases the eyes to see
the sun.
[8]However many years a man
may live,
let him enjoy them all.
But let him remember the days
of darkness,
for they will be many.
Everything to come is
meaningless.

[9]Be happy, young man, while
you are young,
and let your heart give you
joy in the days of your
youth.
Follow the ways of your heart
and whatever your eyes see,
but know that for all these
things
God will bring you to
judgment.
[10]So then, banish anxiety from
your heart
and cast off the troubles of
your body,
for youth and vigor are
meaningless.

12 Remember your Creator
in the days of your youth,
before the days of trouble
come
and the years approach
when you will say,
"I find no pleasure in
them"–
[2]before the sun and the light
and the moon and the stars
grow dark,

*6 Most mss have *pathah* under the *ayin* (יוֹדֵעַ).

†6 Most mss have *pathah* under the *shin* (יִכְשַׁר).

וְהַכּוֹכָבִים וְשָׁבוּ הֶעָבִים אַחַר הַגָּשֶׁם׃ בַּיּוֹם
on-the-day (3) the-rain after the-clouds and-they-return and-the-stars

שֶׁיָּזֻעוּ שֹׁמְרֵי הַבַּיִת וְהִתְעַוְּתוּ אַנְשֵׁי הֶחָיִל
the-strength men-of and-they-stoop the-house ones-keeping-of that-they-tremble

וּבָטְלוּ הַטֹּחֲנוֹת כִּי מִעֵטוּ וְחָשְׁכוּ
and-they-grow-dim they-are-few because the-ones-grinding when-they-cease

הָרֹאוֹת בָּאֲרֻבּוֹת׃ וְסֻגְּרוּ דְלָתַיִם
doors when-they-are-closed (4) through-the-windows the-ones-looking

בַּשּׁוּק בִּשְׁפַל קוֹל הַטַּחֲנָה וְיָקוּם לְקוֹל
at-sound-of when-he-rises the-grinding sound-of when-to-fade to-the-street

הַצִּפּוֹר וְיִשַּׁחוּ כָּל־ בְּנוֹת הַשִּׁיר׃ גַּם מִגָּבֹהַּ
of-height when (5) the-song daughters-of all-of and-they-grow-faint the-bird

יִרָאוּ וְחַתְחַתִּים בַּדֶּרֶךְ וְיָנֵאץ הַשָּׁקֵד
the-almond-tree when-he-blossoms in-the-street and-dangers they-are-afraid

וְיִסְתַּבֵּל הֶחָגָב וְתָפֵר הָאֲבִיּוֹנָה
the-desire and-she-is-unstirred the-grasshopper and-he-drags-himself-along

כִּי־ הֹלֵךְ הָאָדָם אֶל־ בֵּית עוֹלָמוֹ וְסָבְבוּ בַשּׁוּק
in-the-street and-they-go-about eternity-of-him home-of to the-man going then

הַסֹּפְדִים׃ עַד אֲשֶׁר לֹא־ יֵרָחֵק חֶבֶל הַכֶּסֶף
the-silver cord-of he-is-severed not when before (6) the-ones-mourning

וְתָרֻץ גֻּלַּת הַזָּהָב וְתִשָּׁבֶר כַּד עַל־ הַמַּבּוּעַ
the-spring at pitcher and-she-is-shattered the-gold bowl-of or-she-is-broken

וְנָרֹץ הַגַּלְגַּל אֶל־ הַבּוֹר׃ וְיָשֹׁב הֶעָפָר עַל־
to the-dust and-he-returns (7) the-well at the-wheel or-he-is-broken

הָאָרֶץ כְּשֶׁהָיָה וְהָרוּחַ תָּשׁוּב אֶל־ הָאֱלֹהִים אֲשֶׁר
who the-God to she-returns and-the-spirit as-which-he-came the-ground

נְתָנָהּ׃ הֲבֵל הֲבָלִים אָמַר הַקּוֹהֶלֶת
the-Teacher he-says meaninglessnesses meaninglessness-of (8) he-gave-her

הַכֹּל הָבֶל׃ וְיֹתֵר שֶׁהָיָה קֹהֶלֶת חָכָם עוֹד לִמַּד־
he-imparted also wise Teacher that-he-was and-not-only (9) meaningless the-whole

דַּעַת אֶת־ הָעָם וְאִזֵּן וְחִקֵּר תִּקֵּן
he-set-in-order and-he-searched-out and-he-pondered the-people *** knowledge

מְשָׁלִים הַרְבֵּה׃ בִּקֵּשׁ קֹהֶלֶת לִמְצֹא דִּבְרֵי־ חֵפֶץ
right words-of to-find Teacher he-searched (10) to-be-many proverbs

וְכָתוּב יֹשֶׁר דִּבְרֵי אֱמֶת׃ דִּבְרֵי חֲכָמִים
wise-men words-of (11) truth words-of upright and-one-being-written

כַּדָּרְבֹנוֹת וּכְמַשְׂמְרוֹת נְטוּעִים בַּעֲלֵי אֲסֻפּוֹת
collections masters-of ones-being-embedded and-like-nails like-the-goads

°6 ק ירתק

and the clouds return after
the rain;
3when the keepers of the house
tremble,
and the strong men stoop,
when the grinders cease
because they are few,
and those looking through
the windows grow dim;
4when the doors to the street
are closed
and the sound of grinding
fades;
when men rise up at the
sound of birds,
but all their songs grow
faint;
5when men are afraid of
heights
and of dangers in the
streets;
when the almond tree
blossoms
and the grasshopper drags
himself along
and desire no longer is
stirred.
Then man goes to his eternal
home
and mourners go about the
streets.

6Remember him—before the
silver cord is severed,
or the golden bowl is
broken;
before the pitcher is shattered
at the spring,
or the wheel broken at the
well,
7and the dust returns to the
ground it came from,
and the spirit returns to God
who gave it.

8"Meaningless! Meaningless!"
says the Teacher.[o]
"Everything is
meaningless!"

The Conclusion of the Matter

9Not only was the Teacher wise,
but also he imparted knowledge to
the people. He pondered and
searched out and set in order
many proverbs. 10The Teacher
searched to find just the right
words, and what he wrote was upright and true.
11The words of the wise are like
goads, their collected sayings like
firmly embedded nails—given by

[o]8 Or *the leader of the assembly;* also in verses 9 and 10

מֵהֶמָּה	וְיֹתֵר		אֶחָד׃	מֵרֹעֶה	נִתְּנוּ
to-them	and-addition	(12)	one	by-One-Being-Shepherd	they-are-given

וְלַהַג	קֵץ	אֵין	הַרְבֵּה	סְפָרִים	עֲשׂוֹת	הִזָּהֵר	בְּנִי
and-study	end	there-is-no	to-be-many	books	to-make	be-warned!	son-of-me

נִשְׁמָע	הַכֹּל	דָּבָר	סוֹף		בָּשָׂר׃	יְגִעַת	הַרְבֵּה
he-was-heard	the-all	matter	conclusion-of	(13)	body	weariness-of	to-be-much

כָּל־	זֶה	כִּי־	שְׁמוֹר	מִצְוֺתָיו	וְאֶת־	יְרָא	הָאֱלֹהִים	אֶת־
whole-of	this	for	keep!	commandments-of-him	and	fear!	the-God	***

בְּמִשְׁפָּט	יָבִא	הָאֱלֹהִים	מַעֲשֶׂה	כָּל־	אֶת־	כִּי		הָאָדָם׃
into-judgment	he-will-bring	the-God	deed	every-of	***	for	(14)	the-man

רָע׃	וְאִם־	טוֹב	אִם־	נֶעְלָם	כָּל־	עַל
evil	or-whether	good	whether	thing-being-hidden	every-of	including

one Shepherd. [12]Be warned, my son, of anything in addition to them.

Of making many books there is no end, and much study wearies the body.

[13]Now all has been heard;
here is the conclusion of the matter:
Fear God and keep his commandments,
for this is the whole duty of man.
[14]For God will bring every deed into judgment,
including every hidden thing,
whether it is good or evil.

שיר השירים אשר לשלמה: ישקני מנשיקות

with-kisses-of let-him-kiss-me (2) of-Solomon that the-Songs Song-of (1:1)

פיהו כי־ טובים דדיך מיין: לריח

in-fragrance-of (3) more-than-wine loves-of-you delightful-ones for mouth-of-him

שמניך טובים שמן תורק שמך על־ כן

this for name-of-you she-is-poured-out perfume pleasing-ones perfumes-of-you

עלמות אהבוך: משכני אחריך נרוצה הביאני

he-brought-me let-us-hurry with-you take-away-me! (4) they-love-you maidens

המלך חדריו נגילה ונשמחה בך נזכירה

we-will-praise in-you and-we-delight we-rejoice chambers-of-him the-king

דדיך מיין מישרים אהבוך: שחורה אני ונאוה

yet-lovely I dark (5) they-adore-you right-ones more-than-wine loves-of-you

בנות ירושלם כאהלי קדר כיריעות שלמה:

Solomon like-tent-curtains-of Kedar like-tents-of Jerusalem daughters-of

אל־ תראוני שאני שחרחרת ששזפתני השמש בני

sons-of the-sun because-she-darkened-me dark because-I you-stare-at-me not (6)

אמי נחרו־ בי שמני נטרה את־

*** one-caring-for they-made-me with-me they-were-angry mother-of-me

הכרמים כרמי שלי לא נטרתי: הגידה לי

to-me tell! (7) I-cared-for not that-to-me vineyard-of-me the-vineyards

שאהבה נפשי איכה תרעה איכה תרביץ

you-give-rest where? you-graze-flock where? self-of-me whom-she-loves

בצהרים שלמה אהיה כעטיה על עדרי

flocks-of beside like-one-being-veiled I-should-be that-why? at-the-middays

חבריך: אם־לא תדעי לך היפה בנשים

among-the-women the-beautiful-one to-you you-know not if (8) friends-of-you

צאי־ לך בעקבי הצאן ורעי את־ גדיתיך

young-goats-of-you *** and-graze! the-sheep after-tracks-of to-you follow!

על משכנות הרעים: לססתי ברכבי פרעה

Pharaoh in-chariots-of to-mare-of-me (9) the-ones-being-shepherds tents-of by

דמיתיך רעיתי: נאוו לחייך

cheeks-of-you they-are-beautiful (10) darling-of-me I-liken-you

בתרים צוארך בחרוזים: תורי זהב

gold earrings-of (11) with-the-strings-of-jewels neck-of-you with-the-earrings

נעשה־ לך עם נקדות הכסף: עד־ שהמלך

that-the-king while (12) the-silver studs-of with for-you we-will-make

במסבו נרדי נתן ריחו: צרור

sachet-of (13) fragrance-of-him he-spread perfume-of-me at-table-of-him

---

1 Solomon's Song of Songs.

Beloved[a]

2 Let him kiss me with the
kisses of his mouth—
for your love is more
delightful than wine.
3 Pleasing is the fragrance of
your perfumes;
your name is like perfume
poured out.
No wonder the maidens
love you!
4 Take me away with you—let us
hurry!
The king has brought me
into his chambers.

Friends

We rejoice and delight in you[b];
we will praise your love
more than wine.

Beloved

How right they are to adore
you!
5 Dark am I, yet lovely,
O daughters of Jerusalem,
dark like the tents of Kedar,
like the tent curtains of
Solomon.[c]
6 Do not stare at me because I
am dark,
because I am darkened by
the sun.
My mother's sons were angry
with me
and made me take care of
the vineyards;
my own vineyard I have
neglected.
7 Tell me, you whom I love,
where you graze your
flock
and where you rest your
sheep at midday.
Why should I be like a veiled
woman
beside the flocks of your
friends?

Lover

8 If you do not know, most
beautiful of women,
follow the tracks of the
sheep
and graze your young goats
by the tents of the
shepherds.
9 I liken you, my darling, to a
mare
harnessed to one of the
chariots of Pharaoh.
10 Your cheeks are beautiful with
earrings,
your neck with strings of
jewels.
11 We will make you earrings of
gold,
studded with silver.

Beloved

12 While the king was at his
table,
my perfume spread its
fragrance.

[a] Primarily on the basis of the gender of the Hebrew pronouns used, male and female speakers are indicated in the margins by the captions *Lover* and *Beloved* respectively. The words of others are marked *Friends*. In some instances the divisions and their captions are debatable.
[b] 4 The Hebrew is masculine singular.
[c] 5 Or *Salma*

הַמֹּר ׀ דּוֹדִי לִי בֵּין שָׁדַי יָלִין׃ אֶשְׁכֹּל

cluster-of (14) he-rests breasts-of-me between to-me lover-of-me the-myrrh

הַכֹּפֶר ׀ דּוֹדִי לִי בְּכַרְמֵי עֵין גֶּדִי׃ הִנָּךְ

see-you! (15) Gedi En from-vineyards-of to-me lover-of-me the-henna-blossom

יָפָה רַעְיָתִי הִנָּךְ יָפָה עֵינַיִךְ יוֹנִים׃ הִנְּךָ

see-you! (16) doves eyes-of-you beautiful see-you! darling-of-me beautiful

יָפֶה דוֹדִי אַף נָעִים אַף־ עַרְשֵׂנוּ רַעֲנָנָה׃ קֹרוֹת

beams-of (17) verdant bed-of-us indeed charming how! lover-of-me handsome

בָּתֵּינוּ אֲרָזִים רַחִיטֵנוּ° בְּרוֹתִים׃ אֲנִי חֲבַצֶּלֶת הַשָּׁרוֹן שׁוֹשַׁנַּת

lily-of the-Sharon rose-of I (2:1) firs rafter-of-us cedars houses-of-us

הָעֲמָקִים׃ כְּשׁוֹשַׁנָּה בֵּין הַחוֹחִים כֵּן רַעְיָתִי בֵּין הַבָּנוֹת׃

the-maidens among darling-of-me so the-thorns among like-lily (2) the-valleys

כְּתַפּוּחַ בַּעֲצֵי הַיַּעַר כֵּן דּוֹדִי בֵּין

among lover-of-me so the-forest among-trees-of like-apple-tree (3)

הַבָּנִים בְּצִלּוֹ חִמַּדְתִּי וְיָשַׁבְתִּי וּפִרְיוֹ מָתוֹק

sweet and-fruit-of-him and-I-sit I-delight in-shade-of-him the-young-men

לְחִכִּי׃ הֱבִיאַנִי אֶל־ בֵּית הַיָּיִן וְדִגְלוֹ

and-banner-of-him the-banquet hall-of to he-took-me (4) to-taste-of-me

עָלַי אַהֲבָה׃ סַמְּכוּנִי בָּאֲשִׁישׁוֹת רַפְּדוּנִי בַּתַּפּוּחִים

with-the-apples refresh-me! with-the-raisins strengthen-me! (5) love over-me

כִּי־ חוֹלַת אַהֲבָה אָנִי׃ שְׂמֹאלוֹ תַּחַת לְרֹאשִׁי

to-head-of-me under left-arm-of-him (6) I love being-faint-of for

וִימִינוֹ תְּחַבְּקֵנִי׃ הִשְׁבַּעְתִּי אֶתְכֶם בְּנוֹת יְרוּשָׁלִַם

Jerusalem daughters-of you I-charge (7) she-embraces-me and-right-arm-of-him

בִּצְבָאוֹת אוֹ בְּאַיְלוֹת הַשָּׂדֶה אִם־ תָּעִירוּ ׀ וְאִם־ תְּעוֹרְרוּ אֶת־

*** you-awaken and-not you-arouse not the-field by-does-of and by-gazelles

הָאַהֲבָה עַד שֶׁתֶּחְפָּץ׃ קוֹל דּוֹדִי הִנֵּה־ זֶה בָּא

he-comes there look! lover-of-me sound-of (8) that-she-desires until the-love

מְדַלֵּג עַל־ הֶהָרִים מְקַפֵּץ עַל־ הַגְּבָעוֹת׃ דּוֹמֶה

one-being-like (9) the-hills over bounding the-mountains across leaping

דוֹדִי לִצְבִי אוֹ לְעֹפֶר הָאַיָּלִים הִנֵּה־ זֶה עוֹמֵד

standing here look! the-stags to-young-deer-of or to-gazelle lover-of-me

אַחַר כָּתְלֵנוּ מַשְׁגִּיחַ מִן־ הַחֲלֹּנוֹת* מֵצִיץ מִן־ הַחֲרַכִּים׃

the-lattices through peering the-windows through gazing wall-of-us behind

עָנָה דוֹדִי וְאָמַר לִי קוּמִי לָךְ רַעְיָתִי

darling-of-me to-you arise! to-me and-he-said lover-of-me he-spoke (10)

יָפָתִי וּלְכִי־ לָךְ׃ כִּי־ הִנֵּה הַסְּתָו° עָבָר

he-passed the-winter see! for (11) to-you and-come! beautiful-one-of-me

13 My lover is to me a sachet of
myrrh
resting between my breasts.
14 My lover is to me a cluster of
henna blossoms
from the vineyards of En
Gedi.

Lover

15 How beautiful you are, my
darling!
Oh, how beautiful!
Your eyes are doves.

Beloved

16 How handsome you are, my
lover!
Oh, how charming!
And our bed is verdant.

Lover

17 The beams of our house are
cedars;
our rafters are firs.

Beloved[d]

2 I am a rose[e] of Sharon,
a lily of the valleys.

Lover

2 Like a lily among thorns
is my darling among the
maidens.

Beloved

3 Like an apple tree among the
trees of the forest
is my lover among the
young men.
I delight to sit in his shade,
and his fruit is sweet to my
taste.
4 He has taken me to the
banquet hall,
and his banner over me is
love.
5 Strengthen me with raisins,
refresh me with apples,
for I am faint with love.
6 His left arm is under my head,
and his right arm embraces
me.
7 Daughters of Jerusalem, I
charge you
by the gazelles and by the
does of the field:
Do not arouse or awaken love
until it so desires.

8 Listen! My lover!
Look! Here he comes,
leaping across the mountains,
bounding over the hills.
9 My lover is like a gazelle or a
young stag.
Look! There he stands
behind our wall,
gazing through the windows,
peering through the lattice.
10 My lover spoke and said to
me,
"Arise, my darling,
my beautiful one, and come
with me.
11 See! The winter is past;

[d] 1 Or *Lover*
[e] 1 Possibly a member of the crocus family

*9 Most mss have *pathah* under the *beth* (הַחַלֹּנוֹת).

°17 ק רהיטנו
°11 ק הסתיו

הַגֶּשֶׁם חָלַף הָלַךְ לוֹ׃ הַנִּצָּנִים נִרְאוּ בָאָרֶץ
on-the-earth they-appear the-flowers (12) to-him he-went he-is-over the-rain

עֵת הַזָּמִיר הִגִּיעַ וְקוֹל הַתּוֹר נִשְׁמַע בְּאַרְצֵנוּ׃
in-land-of-us he-is-heard the-dove and-sound-of he-came the-song season-of

הַתְּאֵנָה חָנְטָה פַגֶּיהָ וְהַגְּפָנִים ׀ סְמָדַר
blossom and-the-vines early-fruits-of-her she-forms the-fig-tree (13)

נָתְנוּ רֵיחַ קוּמִי לְכִי רַעְיָתִי יָפָתִי
beautiful-one-of-me darling-of-me come! arise! fragrance they-spread

וּלְכִי־ לָךְ׃ יוֹנָתִי בְּחַגְוֵי הַסֶּלַע בְּסֵתֶר
in-hiding-place-of the-rock in-clefts-of dove-of-me (14) to-you and-come!

הַמַּדְרֵגָה הַרְאִינִי אֶת־ מַרְאַיִךְ הַשְׁמִיעִנִי אֶת־ קוֹלֵךְ כִּי־
for voice-of-you *** let-hear-me! faces-of-you *** show-me! the-mountainside

קוֹלֵךְ עָרֵב וּמַרְאֵיךְ נָאוֶה׃ אֶחֱזוּ־ לָנוּ שׁוּעָלִים שֻׁעָלִים
foxes foxes for-us catch! (15) lovely and-faces-of-you sweet voice-of-you

קְטַנִּים מְחַבְּלִים כְּרָמִים וּכְרָמֵינוּ סְמָדַר׃
bloom indeed-vineyards-of-us vineyards ones-ruining little-ones

דּוֹדִי לִי וַאֲנִי לוֹ הָרֹעֶה בַּשּׁוֹשַׁנִּים׃
among-the-lilies the-one-browsing to-him and-I to-me lover-of-me (16)

עַד שֶׁיָּפוּחַ הַיּוֹם וְנָסוּ הַצְּלָלִים סֹב דְּמֵה־
be-like! turn! the-shadows and-they-flee the-day when-he-breaks until (17)

לְךָ דוֹדִי לִצְבִי אוֹ לְעֹפֶר הָאַיָּלִים עַל־ הָרֵי
hills-of on the-stags to-young-deer-of or to-gazelle lover-of-me to-you

בָתֶר׃ עַל־ מִשְׁכָּבִי בַּלֵּילוֹת בִּקַּשְׁתִּי אֵת שֶׁאָהֲבָה
whom-she-loves *** I-looked-for in-the-nights bed-of-me on (3:1) ruggedness

נַפְשִׁי בִּקַּשְׁתִּיו וְלֹא מְצָאתִיו׃ אָקוּמָה נָּא
now! I-will-get-up (2) I-found-him but-not I-looked-for-him heart-of-me

וַאֲסוֹבְבָה בָעִיר בַּשְּׁוָקִים וּבָרְחֹבוֹת
and-through-the-squares through-the-streets through-the-city and-I-will-go-about

אֲבַקְשָׁה אֵת שֶׁאָהֲבָה נַפְשִׁי בִּקַּשְׁתִּיו וְלֹא
but-not I-looked-for-him heart-of-me whom-she-loves *** I-will-search-for

מְצָאתִיו׃ מְצָאוּנִי הַשֹּׁמְרִים הַסֹּבְבִים
the-ones-going-round the-men-watching they-found-me (3) I-found-him

בָּעִיר אֵת שֶׁאָהֲבָה נַפְשִׁי רְאִיתֶם׃ כִּמְעַט
as-scarcely (4) you-saw heart-of-me whom-she-loves *** in-the-city

שֶׁעָבַרְתִּי מֵהֶם עַד שֶׁמָּצָאתִי אֵת שֶׁאָהֲבָה נַפְשִׁי
heart-of-me whom-she-loves *** that-I-found when from-them that-I-passed

אֲחַזְתִּיו וְלֹא אַרְפֶּנּוּ עַד־ שֶׁהֲבֵיאתִיו אֶל־ בֵּית
house-of to when-I-brought-him till I-would-let-go-him and-not I-held-him

the rains are over and gone.
12 Flowers appear on the earth;
the season of singing has
come,
the cooing of doves
is heard in our land.
13 The fig tree forms its early
fruit;
the blossoming vines spread
their fragrance.
Arise, come, my darling;
my beautiful one, come with
me."

Lover

14 My dove in the clefts of the
rock,
in the hiding places on the
mountainside,
show me your face,
let me hear your voice;
for your voice is sweet,
and your face is lovely.
15 Catch for us the foxes,
the little foxes
that ruin the vineyards,
our vineyards that are in
bloom.

Beloved

16 My lover is mine and I am
his;
he browses among the lilies.
17 Until the day breaks
and the shadows flee,
turn, my lover,
and be like a gazelle
or like a young stag
on the rugged hills.[f]

3 All night long on my bed
I looked for the one my
heart loves;
I looked for him but did not
find him.
2 I will get up now and go about
the city,
through its streets and
squares;
I will search for the one my
heart loves.
So I looked for him but did
not find him.
3 The watchmen found me
as they made their rounds
in the city.
"Have you seen the one my
heart loves?"
4 Scarcely had I passed them
when I found the one my
heart loves.
I held him and would not let
him go
till I had brought him to my
mother's house,

f17 Or *the hills of Bether*

°13 ק לך

אִמִּי וְאֶל־ חֶדֶר הוֹרָתִי׃ הִשְׁבַּעְתִּי אֶתְכֶם בְּנוֹת
daughters-of you I-charge (5) one-conceiving-me room-of and-to mother-of-me

יְרוּשָׁלִַם בִּצְבָאוֹת אוֹ בְּאַיְלוֹת הַשָּׂדֶה אִם־ תָּעִירוּ וְאִם־
and-not you-arouse not the-field by-does-of and by-gazelles Jerusalem

תְּעוֹרְרוּ אֶת־הָאַהֲבָה עַד שֶׁתֶּחְפָּץ׃ מִי זֹאת עֹלָה מִן־
from coming-up this who? (6) that-she-desires until the-love *** you-awaken

הַמִּדְבָּר כְּתִימֲרוֹת עָשָׁן מְקֻטֶּרֶת מוֹר וּלְבוֹנָה
and-incense myrrh being-perfumed-of smoke like-columns-of the-desert

מִכֹּל אַבְקַת רוֹכֵל׃ הִנֵּה מִטָּתוֹ
carriage-of-him look! (7) one-being-merchant spice-of from-all-of

שֶׁלִּשְׁלֹמֹה שִׁשִּׁים גִּבֹּרִים סָבִיב לָהּ מִגִּבֹּרֵי יִשְׂרָאֵל׃
Israel from-noble-ones-of about-her around warriors sixty that-to-Solomon

כֻּלָּם אֲחֻזֵי חֶרֶב מְלֻמְּדֵי מִלְחָמָה אִישׁ
each battle ones-being-experienced-of sword ones-wearing-of all-of-them (8)

חַרְבּוֹ עַל־ יְרֵכוֹ מִפַּחַד בַּלֵּילוֹת׃ אַפִּרְיוֹן עָשָׂה
he-made carriage (9) of-the-nights for-terror side-of-him at sword-of-him

לוֹ הַמֶּלֶךְ שְׁלֹמֹה מֵעֲצֵי הַלְּבָנוֹן׃ עַמּוּדָיו עָשָׂה
he-made posts-of-him (10) the-Lebanon from-woods-of Solomon the-king for-him

כֶּסֶף רְפִידָתוֹ זָהָב מֶרְכָּבוֹ אַרְגָּמָן תּוֹכוֹ רָצוּף
being-inlaid interior-of-him purple seat-of-him gold base-of-him silver

אַהֲבָה מִבְּנוֹת יְרוּשָׁלָםִ׃ צְאֶינָה וּרְאֶינָה בְּנוֹת צִיּוֹן
Zion daughters-of and-look! come-out! (11) Jerusalem by-daughters-of love

בַּמֶּלֶךְ שְׁלֹמֹה בָּעֲטָרָה שֶׁעִטְּרָה־ לּוֹ אִמּוֹ
mother-of-him upon-him which-she-crowned with-the-crown Solomon at-the-king

בְּיוֹם חֲתֻנָּתוֹ וּבְיוֹם שִׂמְחַת לִבּוֹ׃ הִנָּךְ
see-you! (4:1) heart-of-him rejoicing-of on-day-of wedding-of-him on-day-of

יָפָה רַעְיָתִי הִנָּךְ יָפָה עֵינַיִךְ יוֹנִים מִבַּעַד
at-behind doves eyes-of-you beautiful see-you! darling-of-me beautiful

לְצַמָּתֵךְ שַׂעְרֵךְ כְּעֵדֶר הָעִזִּים שֶׁגָּלְשׁוּ
that-they-descend the-goats like-flock-of hair-of-you to-veil-of-you

מֵהַר גִּלְעָד׃ שִׁנַּיִךְ כְּעֵדֶר הַקְּצוּבוֹת
the-ones-being-shorn like-flock-of teeth-of-you (2) Gilead from-Mount-of

שֶׁעָלוּ מִן־ הָרַחְצָה שֶׁכֻּלָּם מַתְאִימוֹת
ones-having-twins that-each-of-them the-washing from that-they-come-up

וְשַׁכֻּלָה אֵין בָּהֶם׃ כְּחוּט הַשָּׁנִי שִׂפְתֹתַיִךְ
lips-of-you the-scarlet like-ribbon-of (3) of-them there-is-not and-alone

וּמִדְבָּרֵיךְ נָאוֶה כְּפֶלַח הָרִמּוֹן רַקָּתֵךְ מִבַּעַד
at-behind temple-of-you the-pomegranate like-half-of lovely and-mouths-of-you

to the room of the one who
conceived me.
5 Daughters of Jerusalem, I
charge you
by the gazelles and by the
does of the field:
Do not arouse or awaken love
until it so desires.

6 Who is this coming up from
the desert
like a column of smoke,
perfumed with myrrh and
incense
made from all the spices of
the merchant?
7 Look! It is Solomon's carriage,
escorted by sixty warriors,
the noblest of Israel,
8 all of them wearing the sword,
all experienced in battle,
each with his sword at his
side,
prepared for the terrors of
the night.
9 King Solomon made for
himself the carriage;
he made it of wood from
Lebanon.
10 Its posts he made of silver,
its base of gold.
Its seat was upholstered with
purple,
its interior lovingly inlaid
by[g] the daughters of
Jerusalem.
11 Come out, you daughters of
Zion,
and look at King Solomon
wearing the crown,
the crown with which his
mother crowned him
on the day of his wedding,
the day his heart rejoiced.

Lover

4 How beautiful you are, my
darling!
Oh, how beautiful!
Your eyes behind your veil
are doves.
Your hair is like a flock of
goats
descending from Mount
Gilead.
2 Your teeth are like a flock of
sheep just shorn,
coming up from the
washing.
Each has its twin;
not one of them is alone.
3 Your lips are like a scarlet
ribbon;
your mouth is lovely.
Your temples behind your veil
are like the halves of a
pomegranate.

g10 Or its inlaid interior a gift of love / from

לְצַמָּתֵךְ׃ (4) כְּמִגְדַּל דָּוִיד צַוָּארֵךְ בָּנוּי
to-veil-of-you (4) like-tower-of David neck-of-you one-being-built

לְתַלְפִּיּוֹת אֶלֶף הַמָּגֵן תָּלוּי עָלָיו כֹּל שִׁלְטֵי
with-elegances thousand-of the-shield being-hung on-him all-of shields-of

הַגִּבּוֹרִים׃ (5) שְׁנֵי שָׁדַיִךְ כִּשְׁנֵי עֳפָרִים תְּאוֹמֵי צְבִיָּה
the-warriors (5) two-of breasts-of-you like-two-of fawns twins-of gazelle

הָרוֹעִים בַּשּׁוֹשַׁנִּים׃ (6) עַד שֶׁיָּפוּחַ הַיּוֹם
the-ones-browsing among-the-lilies (6) until when-he-breaks the-day

וְנָסוּ הַצְּלָלִים אֵלֶךְ לִי אֶל־ הַר הַמּוֹר וְאֶל־
and-they-flee the-shadows I-will-go to-me to mountain-of the-myrrh and-to

גִּבְעַת הַלְּבוֹנָה׃ (7) כֻּלָּךְ יָפָה רַעְיָתִי וּמוּם
hill-of the-incense (7) all-of-you beautiful darling-of-me and-flaw

אֵין בָּךְ׃ (8) אִתִּי מִלְּבָנוֹן כַּלָּה אִתִּי מִלְּבָנוֹן
there-is-not in-you (8) with-me from-Lebanon bride with-me from-Lebanon

תָּבוֹאִי תָּשׁוּרִי ׀ מֵרֹאשׁ אֲמָנָה מֵרֹאשׁ שְׂנִיר וְחֶרְמוֹן
you-come you-descend from-crest-of Amana from-top-of Senir even-Hermon

מִמְּעֹנוֹת אֲרָיוֹת מֵהַרְרֵי נְמֵרִים׃ (9) לִבַּבְתִּנִי
from-dens-of lions from-mountains-of leopards (9) you-stole-heart-of-me

אֲחֹתִי כַלָּה לִבַּבְתִּינִי °בְּאַחַד מֵעֵינַיִךְ
sister-of-me bride you-stole-heart-of-me with-one from-eyes-of-you

בְּאַחַד עֲנָק מִצַּוְּרֹנָיִךְ׃ (10) מַה־ יָּפוּ
with-one-of jewel-of of-necklaces-of-you (10) how! they-are-delightful

דֹדַיִךְ אֲחֹתִי כַלָּה מַה־ טֹּבוּ דֹדַיִךְ
loves-of-you sister-of-me bride how! they-are-pleasing loves-of-you

מִיַּיִן וְרֵיחַ שְׁמָנַיִךְ מִכָּל־ בְּשָׂמִים׃
more-than-wine and-fragrance-of perfumes-of-you more-than-any-of spices

(11) נֹפֶת תִּטֹּפְנָה שִׂפְתוֹתַיִךְ כַּלָּה דְּבַשׁ וְחָלָב תַּחַת לְשׁוֹנֵךְ
(11) honeycomb they-drop lips-of-you bride honey and-milk under tongue-of-you

וְרֵיחַ שַׂלְמֹתַיִךְ כְּרֵיחַ לְבָנוֹן׃ (12) גַּן ׀
and-fragrance-of garments-of-you like-fragrance-of Lebanon (12) garden

נָעוּל אֲחֹתִי כַלָּה גַּל נָעוּל מַעְיָן חָתוּם׃
being-locked sister-of-me bride spring being-enclosed fountain being-sealed

(13) שְׁלָחַיִךְ פַּרְדֵּס רִמּוֹנִים עִם פְּרִי מְגָדִים כְּפָרִים
(13) plants-of-you orchard-of pomegranates with fruit-of choice-ones hennas

עִם־ נְרָדִים׃ (14) נֵרְדְּ ׀ וְכַרְכֹּם קָנֶה וְקִנָּמוֹן עִם כָּל־ עֲצֵי
with nards (14) nard and-saffron calamus and-cinnamon with all-of trees-of

לְבוֹנָה מֹר וַאֲהָלוֹת עִם כָּל־ רָאשֵׁי בְשָׂמִים׃ (15) מַעְיַן
incense myrrh and-aloes and all-of finest-ones-of spices (15) fountain-of

4Your neck is like the tower of David,
built with elegance[h];
on it hang a thousand shields,
all of them shields of warriors.
5Your two breasts are like two fawns,
like twin fawns of a gazelle
that browse among the lilies.
6Until the day breaks
and the shadows flee,
I will go to the mountain of myrrh
and to the hill of incense.
7All beautiful you are, my darling;
there is no flaw in you.

8Come with me from Lebanon, my bride,
come with me from Lebanon.
Descend from the crest of Amana,
from the top of Senir, the summit of Hermon,
from the lions' dens
and the mountain haunts of the leopards.
9You have stolen my heart, my sister, my bride;
you have stolen my heart
with one glance of your eyes,
with one jewel of your necklace.
10How delightful is your love, my sister, my bride!
How much more pleasing is your love than wine,
and the fragrance of your perfume than any spice!
11Your lips drop sweetness as the honeycomb, my bride;
milk and honey are under your tongue.
The fragrance of your garments is like that of Lebanon.
12You are a garden locked up, my sister, my bride;
you are a spring enclosed, a sealed fountain.
13Your plants are an orchard of pomegranates
with choice fruits,
with henna and nard,
14 nard and saffron,
calamus and cinnamon,
with every kind of incense tree,
with myrrh and aloes
and all the finest spices.

h4 The meaning of the Hebrew for this word is uncertain.

°9 ק באחת

גַּנִּים בְּאֵר מַיִם חַיִּים וְנֹזְלִים מִן־ לְבָנוֹן׃
Lebanon from even-ones-streaming-down flowing-ones waters well-of gardens

עוּרִי צָפוֹן וּבוֹאִי תֵימָן הָפִיחִי גַנִּי
garden-of-me blow-on! south-wind and-come! north-wind awake! (16)

יִזְּלוּ בְשָׂמָיו יָבֹא דוֹדִי
lover-of-me let-him-come fragrances-of-him that-they-may-spread

לְגַנּוֹ וְיֹאכַל פְּרִי מְגָדָיו׃ בָּאתִי
I-came (5:1) choice-ones-of-him fruit-of and-let-him-taste into-garden-of-him

לְגַנִּי אֲחֹתִי כַלָּה אָרִיתִי מוֹרִי עִם־ בְּשָׂמִי
spice-of-me with myrrh-of-me I-gathered bride sister-of-me into-garden-of-me

אָכַלְתִּי יַעְרִי עִם־ דִּבְשִׁי שָׁתִיתִי יֵינִי עִם־ חֲלָבִי
milk-of-me and wine-of-me I-drank honey-of-me and honeycomb-of-me I-ate

אִכְלוּ רֵעִים שְׁתוּ וְשִׁכְרוּ דּוֹדִים׃ אֲנִי יְשֵׁנָה וְלִבִּי
but-heart-of-me asleep I (2) lovers and-drink-fill! drink! friends eat!

עֵר קוֹל ׀ דּוֹדִי דוֹפֵק פִּתְחִי־ לִי אֲחֹתִי
sister-of-me to-me open! knocking lover-of-me sound-of being-awake

רַעְיָתִי יוֹנָתִי תַמָּתִי שֶׁרֹּאשִׁי נִמְלָא־
being-drenched for-head-of-me flawless-one-of-me dove-of-me darling-of-me

טָל קְוֻצּוֹתַי* רְסִיסֵי לָיְלָה׃ פָּשַׁטְתִּי אֶת־ כֻּתָּנְתִּי אֵיכָכָה
indeed? robe-of-me *** I-took-off (3) night dampnesses-of hairs-of-me dew

אֶלְבָּשֶׁנָּה רָחַצְתִּי אֶת־ רַגְלַי אֵיכָכָה אֲטַנְּפֵם׃
must-I-soil-them indeed? feet-of-me *** I-washed must-I-put-on-her

דּוֹדִי שָׁלַח יָדוֹ מִן־ הַחֹר וּמֵעַי
and-hearts-of-me the-latch-opening through hand-of-him he-thrust lover-of-me (4)

הָמוּ עָלָיו׃ קַמְתִּי אֲנִי לִפְתֹּחַ לְדוֹדִי וְיָדַי
and-hands-of-me for-lover-of-me to-open I I-arose (5) for-him they-pounded

נָטְפוּ־ מוֹר וְאֶצְבְּעֹתַי מוֹר עֹבֵר עַל כַּפּוֹת הַמַּנְעוּל׃
the-lock handles-of on flowing myrrh and-fingers-of-me myrrh they-dripped

פָּתַחְתִּי אֲנִי לְדוֹדִי וְדוֹדִי חָמַק עָבָר נַפְשִׁי
heart-of-me he-went he-left but-lover-of-me for-lover-of-me I I-opened (6)

יָצְאָה בְדַבְּרוֹ בִּקַּשְׁתִּיהוּ וְלֹא מְצָאתִיהוּ
I-found-him but-not I-looked-for-him when-to-speak-him she-went-out

קְרָאתִיו וְלֹא עָנָנִי׃ מְצָאֻנִי הַשֹּׁמְרִים
the-men-watching they-found-me (7) he-answered-me but-not I-called-him

הַסֹּבְבִים בָּעִיר הִכּוּנִי פְצָעוּנִי נָשְׂאוּ
they-took they-bruised-me they-beat-me in-the-city the-ones-going-around

אֶת־ רְדִידִי מֵעָלַי שֹׁמְרֵי הַחֹמוֹת׃ הִשְׁבַּעְתִּי אֶתְכֶם
you I-charge (8) the-walls ones-watching-of from-on-me cloak-of-me ***

15 You are[l] a garden fountain,
a well of flowing water
streaming down from
Lebanon.

Beloved

16 Awake, north wind,
and come, south wind!
Blow on my garden,
that its fragrance may
spread abroad.
Let my lover come into his
garden
and taste its choice fruits.

Lover

5 I have come into my garden,
my sister, my bride;
I have gathered my myrrh
with my spice.
I have eaten my honeycomb
and my honey;
I have drunk my wine and
my milk.

Friends

Eat, O friends, and drink;
drink your fill, O lovers.

Beloved

2 I slept but my heart was
awake.
Listen! My lover is
knocking:
"Open to me, my sister, my
darling,
my dove, my flawless one.
My head is drenched with
dew,
my hair with the dampness
of the night."
3 I have taken off my robe—
must I put it on again?
I have washed my feet—
must I soil them again?
4 My lover thrust his hand
through the
latch-opening;
my heart began to pound
for him.
5 I arose to open for my lover,
and my hands dripped with
myrrh,
my fingers with flowing
myrrh,
on the handles of the lock.
6 I opened for my lover,
but my lover had left; he
was gone.
My heart had gone out to
him when he spoke.
I looked for him but did not
find him.
I called him but he did not
answer.
7 The watchmen found me
as they made their rounds
in the city.
They beat me, they bruised
me;
they took away my cloak,
those watchmen of the
walls!

[l]15 Or *I am* (spoken by the *Beloved*)

*2 Most mss have no *dagesh* in the *vav* (קְוֻ).

בְּנוֹת יְרוּשָׁלָםִ אִם־תִּמְצְאוּ אֶת־ דּוֹדִי מַה־ תַּגִּידוּ לוֹ
to-him will-you-tell what? lover-of-me *** you-find if Jerusalem daughters-of

שֶׁחוֹלַת אַהֲבָה אָנִי׃ מַה־ דּוֹדֵךְ מִדּוֹד
better-than-beloved beloved-of-you how? (9) I love that-one-being-faint-of

הַיָּפָה בַּנָּשִׁים מַה־ דּוֹדֵךְ מִדּוֹד
better-than-beloved beloved-of-you how? among-the-women the-beautiful-one

שֶׁכָּכָה הִשְׁבַּעְתָּנוּ׃ דּוֹדִי צַח וְאָדוֹם דָּגוּל
being-outstanding and-ruddy radiant lover-of-me (10) you-charge-us that-so

מֵרְבָבָה׃ רֹאשׁוֹ כֶּתֶם פָּז קְוֻצּוֹתָיו* תַּלְתַּלִּים
wavy-ones hairs-of-him purest-gold gold head-of-him (11) among-ten-thousand

שְׁחֹרוֹת כָּעוֹרֵב׃ עֵינָיו כְּיוֹנִים עַל־ אֲפִיקֵי מָיִם
waters streams-of by like-doves eyes-of-him (12) as-the-raven black-ones

רֹחֲצוֹת בֶּחָלָב יֹשְׁבוֹת עַל־מִלֵּאת׃ לְחָיָו
cheeks-of-him (13) jewel like ones-being-mounted in-the-milk ones-being-washed

כַּעֲרוּגַת הַבֹּשֶׂם מִגְדְּלוֹת† מֶרְקָחִים שִׂפְתוֹתָיו שׁוֹשַׁנִּים נֹטְפוֹת
ones-dripping lilies lips-of-him perfumes †towers-of the-spice like-bed-of

מוֹר עֹבֵר׃ יָדָיו גְּלִילֵי זָהָב מְמֻלָּאִים בַּתַּרְשִׁישׁ
with-the-chrysolite ones-being-set gold rods-of arms-of-him (14) flowing myrrh

מֵעָיו עֶשֶׁת שֵׁן מְעֻלֶּפֶת סַפִּירִים׃
sapphires one-being-decorated ivory polished-work-of bodies-of-him

שׁוֹקָיו עַמּוּדֵי שֵׁשׁ מְיֻסָּדִים עַל־ אַדְנֵי־ פָז
pure-gold bases-of on ones-being-set marble pillars-of legs-of-him (15)

מַרְאֵהוּ כַּלְּבָנוֹן בָּחוּר כָּאֲרָזִים׃
as-the-cedars one-being-choice like-the-Lebanon appearance-of-him

חִכּוֹ מַמְתַקִּים וְכֻלּוֹ מַחֲמַדִּים זֶה דוֹדִי
lover-of-me this lovely-ones and-all-of-him sweetnesses mouth-of-him (16)

וְזֶה רֵעִי בְּנוֹת יְרוּשָׁלָםִ׃ אָנָה הָלַךְ
he-went to-where? (6:1) Jerusalem daughters-of friend-of-me and-this

דּוֹדֵךְ הַיָּפָה בַּנָּשִׁים אָנָה פָּנָה דוֹדֵךְ
lover-of-you he-turned to-where? among-the-women the-beautiful-one lover-of-you

וּנְבַקְשֶׁנּוּ עִמָּךְ׃ דּוֹדִי יָרַד לְגַנּוֹ
to-garden-of-him he-went-down lover-of-me (2) with-you that-we-may-look-for-him

לַעֲרוּגוֹת הַבֹּשֶׂם לִרְעוֹת בַּגַּנִּים וְלִלְקֹט שׁוֹשַׁנִּים׃ אֲנִי
I (3) lilies and-to-gather in-the-gardens to-browse the-spice to-beds-of

לְדוֹדִי וְדוֹדִי לִי הָרֹעֶה בַּשּׁוֹשַׁנִּים׃
among-the-lilies the-one-browsing to-me and-lover-of-me to-lover-of-me

יָפָה אַתְּ רַעְיָתִי כְּתִרְצָה נָאוָה כִּירוּשָׁלָםִ אֲיֻמָּה
majestic as-Jerusalem lovely as-Tirzah darling-of-me you beautiful (4)

8 O daughters of Jerusalem, I
charge you—
if you find my lover,
what will you tell him?
Tell him I am faint with
love.

Friends

9 How is your beloved better
than others,
most beautiful of women?
How is your beloved better
than others,
that you charge us so?

Beloved

10 My lover is radiant and ruddy,
outstanding among ten
thousand.
11 His head is purest gold;
his hair is wavy
and black as a raven.
12 His eyes are like doves
by the water streams,
washed in milk,
mounted like jewels.
13 His cheeks are like beds of
spice
yielding perfume.
His lips are like lilies
dripping with myrrh.
14 His arms are rods of gold
set with chrysolite.
His body is like polished ivory
decorated with sapphires.[i]
15 His legs are pillars of marble
set on bases of pure gold.
His appearance is like
Lebanon,
choice as its cedars.
16 His mouth is sweetness itself;
he is altogether lovely.
This is my lover, this my
friend,
O daughters of Jerusalem.

Friends

6 Where has your lover gone,
most beautiful of women?
Which way did your lover
turn,
that we may look for him
with you?

Beloved

2 My lover has gone down to
his garden,
to the beds of spices,
to browse in the gardens
and to gather lilies.
3 I am my lover's and my lover
is mine;
he browses among the lilies.

Lover

4 You are beautiful, my darling,
as Tirzah,
lovely as Jerusalem,

[i]14 Or *lapis lazuli*

*11 Most mss have no *dagesh* in and have *shureq* under the *vav* (קְוֻ).

†13 The NIV repoints this word as (מְגַדְּ), *ones-yielding*.

כַּנִּדְגָּלוֹת׃ הָסֵבִּי עֵינַיִךְ מִנֶּגְדִּי שֶׁהֵם
for-they from-before-me eyes-of-you turn! (5) as-the-ones-having-banners

הִרְהִיבֻנִי שַׂעְרֵךְ כְּעֵדֶר הָעִזִּים שֶׁגָּלְשׁוּ מִן־
from that-they-descend the-goats like-flock-of hair-of-you they-overwhelm-me

הַגִּלְעָד׃ שִׁנַּיִךְ כְּעֵדֶר הָרְחֵלִים שֶׁעָלוּ מִן־
from that-they-come-up the-sheeps like-flock-of teeth-of-you (6) the-Gilead

הָרַחְצָה שֶׁכֻּלָּם מַתְאִימוֹת וְשַׁכֻּלָה אֵין
there-is-not and-alone ones-having-twins that-each-of-them the-washing

בָּהֶם׃ כְּפֶלַח הָרִמּוֹן רַקָּתֵךְ מִבַּעַד
at-behind temple-of-you the-pomegranate like-half-of (7) of-them

לְצַמָּתֵךְ׃ שִׁשִּׁים הֵמָּה מְלָכוֹת† וּשְׁמֹנִים פִּילַגְשִׁים וַעֲלָמוֹת
and-virgins concubines and-eighty queens they sixty (8) to-veil-of-you

אֵין מִסְפָּר׃ אַחַת הִיא יוֹנָתִי תַמָּתִי אַחַת הִיא
she only perfect-one-of-me dove-of-me she unique (9) number there-is-no

לְאִמָּהּ בָּרָה הִיא לְיוֹלַדְתָּהּ רָאוּהָ בָנוֹת
maidens they-saw-her of-one-bearing-her she favorite to-mother-of-her

וַיְאַשְּׁרוּהָ מְלָכוֹת וּפִילַגְשִׁים וַיְהַלְלוּהָ׃
also-they-praised-her and-concubines queens and-they-called-blessed-her

מִי־זֹאת הַנִּשְׁקָפָה כְּמוֹ־שָׁחַר יָפָה כַלְּבָנָה בָּרָה כַּחַמָּה
as-the-sun bright as-the-moon fair dawn like the-one-appearing this who? (10)

אֲיֻמָּה כַּנִּדְגָּלוֹת׃ אֶל־גִּנַּת אֱגוֹז יָרַדְתִּי לִרְאוֹת
to-look I-went-down nut-tree grove-of to (11) as-the-ones-proceeding majestic

בְּאִבֵּי הַנָּחַל לִרְאוֹת הֲפָרְחָה הַגֶּפֶן הֵנֵצוּ
they-bloomed the-vine if-she-budded to-see the-valley at-new-growths-of

הָרִמֹּנִים׃ לֹא יָדַעְתִּי נַפְשִׁי שָׂמַתְנִי מַרְכְּבוֹת
chariots-of she-set-me desire-of-me I-realized not (12) the-pomegranates

עַמִּי־נָדִיב׃ שׁוּבִי שׁוּבִי הַשּׁוּלַמִּית שׁוּבִי
come-back! the-Shulammite come-back! come-back! *(7:1) royal people-of-me

שׁוּבִי וְנֶחֱזֶה־בָּךְ מַה־תֶּחֱזוּ בַּשּׁוּלַמִּית
on-the-Shulammite would-you-gaze why? on-you that-we-may-gaze come-back!

כִּמְחֹלַת הַמַּחֲנָיִם׃ מַה־יָּפוּ פְעָמַיִךְ
feet-of-you they-are-beautiful how! (2) the-Mahanaim as-dance-of

בַּנְּעָלִים בַּת־נָדִיב חַמּוּקֵי יְרֵכַיִךְ כְּמוֹ חֲלָאִים
jewels like legs-of-you graceful-ones-of prince daughter-of in-the-sandals

מַעֲשֵׂה יְדֵי אָמָּן׃ שָׁרְרֵךְ אַגַּן הַסַּהַר אַל־
never the-roundness goblet-of navel-of-you (3) craftsman hands-of work-of

יֶחְסַר הַמָּזֶג בִּטְנֵךְ עֲרֵמַת חִטִּים סוּגָה
being-encircled wheats mound-of waist-of-you the-blended-wine he-lacks

majestic as troops with
banners.
[5]Turn your eyes from me;
they overwhelm me.
Your hair is like a flock of
goats
descending from Gilead.
[6]Your teeth are like a flock of
sheep
coming up from the
washing.
Each has its twin,
not one of them is alone.
[7]Your temples behind your veil
are like the halves of a
pomegranate.
[8]Sixty queens there may be,
and eighty concubines,
and virgins beyond number;
[9]but my dove, my perfect one,
is unique,
the only daughter of her
mother,
the favorite of the one who
bore her.
The maidens saw her and
called her blessed;
the queens and concubines
praised her.

[10]Who is this that appears like
the dawn,
fair as the moon, bright as
the sun,
majestic as the stars in
procession?

[11]I went down to the grove of
nut trees
to look at the new growth in
the valley,
to see if the vines had budded
or the pomegranates were in
bloom.
[12]Before I realized it,
my desire set me among the
royal chariots of my
people.[k]

Friends

[13]Come back, come back, O
Shulammite;
come back, come back, that
we may gaze on you!

Lover

Why would you gaze on the
Shulammite
as on the dance of
Mahanaim?

7 How beautiful your sandaled
feet,
O prince's daughter!
Your graceful legs are like
jewels,
the work of a craftsman's
hands.
[2]Your navel is a rounded goblet
that never lacks blended
wine.
Your waist is a mound of
wheat

[k]12 Or *among the chariots of Amminadab;* or *among the chariots of the people of the prince*

***1 The Hebrew numeration of chapter 7 begins with verse 13 of chapter 6 in English; thus, there is a one-verse discrepancy throughout chapter 7.**

†8 Most mss have no *dagesh* in the *mem* (מָ).

בַּשּׁוֹשַׁנִּים׃ שְׁנֵי שָׁדַיִךְ כִּשְׁנֵי עֳפָרִים תָּאֳמֵי צְבִיָּה׃

gazelle twins-of fawns like-two-of breasts-of-you two-of (4) by-the-lilies

צַוָּארֵךְ כְּמִגְדַּל הַשֵּׁן עֵינַיִךְ בְּרֵכוֹת בְּחֶשְׁבּוֹן עַל־

by of-Heshbon pools eyes-of-you the-ivory like-tower-of neck-of-you (5)

שַׁעַר בַּת־רַבִּים אַפֵּךְ כְּמִגְדַּל הַלְּבָנוֹן צוֹפֶה פְּנֵי

faces-of looking the-Lebanon like-tower-of nose-of-you Rabbim Bath gate-of

דַמָּשֶׂק׃ רֹאשֵׁךְ עָלַיִךְ כַּכַּרְמֶל וְדַלַּת רֹאשֵׁךְ

head-of-you and-hair-of like-the-Carmel upon-you head-of-you (6) Damascus

כָּאַרְגָּמָן מֶלֶךְ אָסוּר בָּרְהָטִים׃ מַה־

how! (7) by-the-tresses being-held-captive king like-the-tapestry

יָּפִית וּמַה־נָּעַמְתְּ אַהֲבָה בַּתַּעֲנוּגִים׃ זֹאת

this (8) with-the-delights love you-are-pleasing and-how! you-are-beautiful

קוֹמָתֵךְ דָּמְתָה לְתָמָר וְשָׁדַיִךְ לְאַשְׁכֹּלוֹת׃

to-clusters-of-fruit and-breasts-of-you to-palm she-is-like stature-of-you

אָמַרְתִּי אֶעֱלֶה בְתָמָר אֹחֲזָה בְּסַנְסִנָּיו

of-fruits-of-him I-will-take-hold on-palm-tree I-will-climb I-said (9)

וְיִהְיוּ־נָא שָׁדַיִךְ כְּאֶשְׁכְּלוֹת הַגֶּפֶן וְרֵיחַ

and-fragrance-of the-vine like-clusters-of breasts-of-you now! and-may-they-be

אַפֵּךְ כַּתַּפּוּחִים׃ וְחִכֵּךְ כְּיֵין הַטּוֹב

the-best like-wine-of and-mouth-of-you (10) like-the-apples breath-of-you

הוֹלֵךְ לְדוֹדִי לְמֵישָׁרִים דּוֹבֵב שִׂפְתֵי יְשֵׁנִים׃ אֲנִי

I (11) sleepers lips-of flowing-gently as-straight-ones to-lover-of-me going

לְדוֹדִי וְעָלַי תְּשׁוּקָתוֹ׃ לְכָה דוֹדִי נֵצֵא

let-us-go lover-of-me come! (12) desire-of-him and-for-me to-lover-of-me

הַשָּׂדֶה נָלִינָה בַּכְּפָרִים׃ נַשְׁכִּימָה

let-us-go-early (13) in-the-villages let-us-spend-night the-countryside

לַכְּרָמִים נִרְאֶה אִם פָּרְחָה הַגֶּפֶן פִּתַּח הַסְּמָדַר

the-blossom he-opened the-vine she-budded if let-us-see to-the-vineyards

הֵנֵצוּ הָרִמּוֹנִים שָׁם אֶתֵּן אֶת־דֹּדַי לָךְ׃

to-you loves-of-me *** I-will-give there the-pomegranates they-bloomed

הַדּוּדָאִים נָתְנוּ־רֵיחַ וְעַל־פְּתָחֵינוּ כָּל־

all-of doors-of-us and-at fragrance they-send-out the-mandrakes (14)

מְגָדִים חֲדָשִׁים גַּם־יְשָׁנִים דּוֹדִי צָפַנְתִּי לָךְ׃ מִי

who? (8:1) for-you I-stored-up lover-of-me old-ones and new-ones delicacies

יִתֶּנְךָ כְּאָח לִי יוֹנֵק שְׁדֵי אִמִּי

mother-of-me breasts-of one-nursing of-me like-brother he-could-make-you

אֶמְצָאֲךָ בַחוּץ אֶשָּׁקְךָ גַּם לֹא־יָבוּזוּ

they-would-despise not then I-would-kiss-you at-the-outside should-I-find-you

encircled by lilies.
3 Your breasts are like two fawns,
twins of a gazelle.
4 Your neck is like an ivory tower.
Your eyes are the pools of Heshbon
by the gate of Bath Rabbim.
Your nose is like the tower of Lebanon
looking toward Damascus.
5 Your head crowns you like Mount Carmel.
Your hair is like royal tapestry;
the king is held captive by its tresses.
6 How beautiful you are and how pleasing,
O love, with your delights!
7 Your stature is like that of the palm,
and your breasts like clusters of fruit.
8 I said, "I will climb the palm tree;
I will take hold of its fruit."
May your breasts be like the clusters of the vine,
the fragrance of your breath like apples,
and your mouth like the best wine.

Beloved

May the wine go straight to my lover,
flowing gently over lips and teeth.[l]
10 I belong to my lover,
and his desire is for me.
11 Come, my lover, let us go to the countryside,
let us spend the night in the villages.[m]
12 Let us go early to the vineyards
to see if the vines have budded,
if their blossoms have opened,
and if the pomegranates are in bloom—
there I will give you my love.
13 The mandrakes send out their fragrance,
and at our door is every delicacy,
both new and old,
that I have stored up for you, my lover.

8 If only you were to me like a brother,
who was nursed at my mother's breasts!
Then, if I found you outside,
I would kiss you,
and no one would despise

[l]9 Septuagint, Aquila, Vulgate and Syriac; Hebrew *lips of sleepers*
[m]11 Or *henna bushes*

*See the note on page 598.

לִי׃ אֶנְהָגְךָ אֲבִיאֲךָ אֶל־ בֵּית אִמִּי
mother-of-me house-of to I-would-bring-you I-would-lead-you (2) to-me

תְּלַמְּדֵנִי אַשְׁקְךָ מִיַּיִן הָרֶקַח מֵעֲסִיס
from-nectar-of the-spice from-wine I-would-give-to-drink-you she-taught-me

רִמֹּנִי׃ שְׂמֹאלוֹ תַּחַת רֹאשִׁי וִימִינוֹ
and-right-arm-of-him head-of-me under left-arm-of-him (3) pomegranate-of-me

תְּחַבְּקֵנִי׃ הִשְׁבַּעְתִּי אֶתְכֶם בְּנוֹת יְרוּשָׁלָםִ מַה־ תָּעִירוּ ׀
you-arouse not Jerusalem daughters-of you I-charge (4) she-embraces-me

וּמַה־ תְּעֹרְרוּ אֶת־ הָאַהֲבָה עַד שֶׁתֶּחְפָּץ׃ מִי זֹאת
this who? (5) that-she-desires until the-love *** you-awaken and-not

עֹלָה מִן־ הַמִּדְבָּר מִתְרַפֶּקֶת עַל־ דּוֹדָהּ תַּחַת הַתַּפּוּחַ
the-apple-tree under lover-of-her on leaning the-desert from coming-up

עוֹרַרְתִּיךָ שָׁמָּה חִבְּלַתְךָ אִמֶּךָ שָׁמָּה
at-there mother-of-you she-conceived-you at-there I-roused-you

חִבְּלָה יְלָדַתְךָ׃ שִׂימֵנִי כַחוֹתָם עַל־ לִבֶּךָ
heart-of-you over like-the-seal place-me! (6) she-bore-you she-was-in-labor

כַּחוֹתָם עַל־ זְרוֹעֶךָ כִּי־ עַזָּה כַמָּוֶת אַהֲבָה קָשָׁה כִשְׁאוֹל
as-Sheol unyielding love as-the-death strong for arm-of-you on like-the-seal

קִנְאָה רְשָׁפֶיהָ רִשְׁפֵּי אֵשׁ שַׁלְהֶבֶתְיָה׃ מַיִם רַבִּים
many-ones waters (7) flame-of-Yahweh fire blazes-of blazes-of-her jealousy

לֹא יוּכְלוּ לְכַבּוֹת אֶת־הָאַהֲבָה וּנְהָרוֹת לֹא יִשְׁטְפוּהָ אִם־
if they-can-wash-away-her not and-rivers the-love *** to-quench they-can not

יִתֵּן אִישׁ אֶת־ כָּל־ הוֹן בֵּיתוֹ בָּאַהֲבָה בּוֹז
to-scorn for-the-love house-of-him wealth-of all-of *** one he-gave

יָבוּזוּ לוֹ׃ אָחוֹת לָנוּ קְטַנָּה וְשָׁדַיִם אֵין לָהּ מַה־
what? to-her not and-breasts young to-us sister (8) at-him they-would-scorn

נַּעֲשֶׂה לַאֲחֹתֵנוּ בַּיּוֹם שֶׁיְּדֻבַּר־ בָּהּ׃ אִם־
if (9) for-her that-he-is-spoken for-the-day for-sister-of-us shall-we-do

חוֹמָה הִיא נִבְנֶה עָלֶיהָ טִירַת כָּסֶף וְאִם־ דֶּלֶת הִיא נָצוּר
we-will-enclose she door and-if silver tower-of on-her we-will-build she wall

עָלֶיהָ לוּחַ אָרֶז׃ אֲנִי חוֹמָה וְשָׁדַי כַּמִּגְדָּלוֹת אָז
thus like-the-towers and-breasts-of-me wall I (10) cedar panel-of to-her

הָיִיתִי בְעֵינָיו כְּמוֹצְאֵת שָׁלוֹם׃ כֶּרֶם הָיָה
he-was vineyard (11) contentment like-one-bringing in-eyes-of-him I-became

לִשְׁלֹמֹה בְּבַעַל הָמוֹן נָתַן אֶת־ הַכֶּרֶם לַנֹּטְרִים
to-the-ones-being-tenants the-vineyard *** he-let-out Hamon in-Baal to-Solomon

אִישׁ יָבִא בְּפִרְיוֹ אֶלֶף כָּסֶף׃ כַּרְמִי
vineyard-of-me (12) silver thousand-of for-fruit-of-him he-would-bring each

me.
2 I would lead you
and bring you to my
mother's house—
she who has taught me.
I would give you spiced wine
to drink,
the nectar of my
pomegranates.
3 His left arm is under my head
and his right arm embraces
me.
4 Daughters of Jerusalem, I
charge you:
Do not arouse or awaken
love
until it so desires.

Friends

5 Who is this coming up from
the desert
leaning on her lover?

Beloved

Under the apple tree I roused
you;
there your mother conceived
you,
there she who was in labor
gave you birth.
6 Place me like a seal over your
heart,
like a seal over your arm;
for love is as strong as death,
its jealousy[n] unyielding as
the grave.[o]
It burns like blazing fire,
like a mighty flame.[p]
7 Many waters cannot quench
love;
rivers cannot wash it away.
If one were to give
all the wealth of his house
for love,
it[q] would be utterly scorned.

Friends

8 We have a young sister,
and her breasts are not yet
grown.
What shall we do for our sister
for the day she is spoken
for?
9 If she is a wall,
we will build towers of
silver on her.
If she is a door,
we will enclose her with
panels of cedar.

Beloved

10 I am a wall,
and my breasts are like
towers.
Thus I have become in his
eyes
like one bringing
contentment.
11 Solomon had a vineyard in
Baal Hamon;
he let out his vineyard to
tenants.
Each was to bring for its fruit
a thousand shekels[r] of
silver.

[n]6 Or *ardor* [o]6 Hebrew *Sheol*
[p]6 Or / *like the very flame of the LORD*
[q]7 Or *he*
[r]11 That is, about 25 pounds (about 11.5 kilograms); also in verse 12

וּמָאתַיִם	שְׁלֹמֹה	לְךָ	הָאֶלֶף	לְפָנָי	שֶׁלִּי
and-two-hundreds	Solomon	for-you	the-thousand	before-me	that-to-me
בַּגַּנִּים	הַיּוֹשֶׁבֶת		פִּרְיוֹ׃	אֶת־	לְנֹטְרִים
in-the-gardens	the-one-dwelling	(13)	fruit-of-him	***	for-ones-tending
בְּרַח ׀		הַשְׁמִיעִנִי׃	לְקוֹלֵךְ	מַקְשִׁיבִים	חֲבֵרִים
come-away!	(14)	let-hear-me!	to-voice-of-you	ones-attending	friends
לְעֹפֶר	אוֹ	לִצְבִי	לְךָ	וּדְמֵה־	דּוֹדִי
to-young-deer-of	or	to-gazelle	to-you	and-be-like!	lover-of-me
בְשָׂמִים׃	הָרֵי		עַל		הָאַיָּלִים
spices	mountains-of		on		the-stags

12 But my own vineyard is mine
to give;
the thousand shekels are for
you, O Solomon,
and two hundred[s] are for
those who tend its fruit.

Lover

13 You who dwell in the gardens
with friends in attendance,
let me hear your voice!

Beloved

14 Come away, my lover,
and be like a gazelle
or like a young stag
on the spice-laden
mountains.

[s] *12* That is, about 5 pounds (about 2.3 kilograms)